OFFICIAL TOURIST BOARD

Self Catering
2007

Contents

VisitBritain

VisitBritain is the organisation created to market Britain to the rest of the world, and England to the British.

Formed by the merger of the British Tourist Authority and the English Tourism Council, its mission is to build the value of tourism by creating world-class destination brands and marketing campaigns.

It will also build partnerships with – and provide insights to – other organisations which have a stake in British and English tourism.

Gaze out over Derwentwater, Cumbria, at dawn

This Enjoy England guide is packed with information from where to stay, to how to get there and what to see and do. **In fact, everything you need to know to Enjoy England.**

The guide that gives you more

endless possibilities for relaxing short breaks and fun-filled holidays

Castles in the sand by St Michael's Mount, Cornwall

Quality accommodation

Choose from a wide range of quality-assessed accommodation to suit all budgets and tastes. This guide contains an exclusive listing of all self-catering properties participating in Enjoy England's Quality Rose assessment scheme, including serviced apartments, boat accommodation and approved caravans. Just look for the Quality Rose – the official marque of Enjoy England quality-assessed accommodation.

Regional information

Every region has its own unique attractions – in each section we highlight a selection of interesting ideas for memorable days out. Regional maps show their location as well as National Trails and sections of the National Cycle Network. For even more ideas go online at enjoyengland.com.

You'll also find contact details for regional tourism organisations together with a list of free and saleable tourism publications.

Useful indexes

Indexes at the back make it easy to find accommodation that matches your requirements – and if you know the name of the establishment you can use the property index.

Tourist information centres

For local information phone or call in to a tourist information centre. Location and contact details can be found at the beginning of each regional section. Alternatively, you can text **TIC LOCATE** to 64118 to find your nearest tourist information centre.

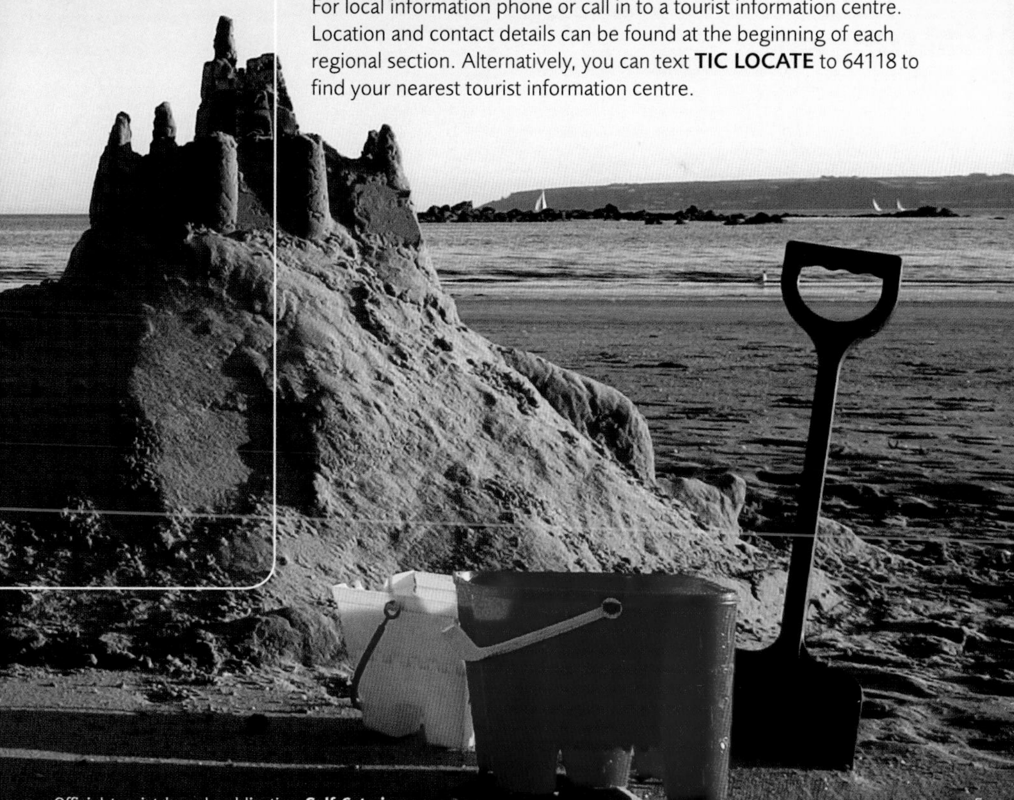

How to use this guide

In this new, fully updated self-catering guide, you'll find a great choice of self-catering properties, serviced apartments, boat accommodation and approved caravan holiday homes.

find over 11,400 places to stay, all quality assessed

Each property has been assessed by Enjoy England's assessors to nationally agreed standards so that you can book with confidence knowing your accommodation has been checked and rated for quality.

Detailed accommodation entries include descriptions, prices and facilities. You'll also find special offers and themed breaks to suit your tastes, interests and budget.

Finding accommodation is easy

Regional entries

The guide is divided into nine regional sections and accommodation is listed alphabetically by place name within each region. (Additionally ALL Enjoy England assessed self-catering holiday homes, which includes those that have not taken a paid entry, are listed at the back of the guide, again by region.)

Colour maps

Use the colour maps, starting on page 18, to pinpoint the location of all accommodation featured in the regional sections. Then refer to the place index at the back of the guide to find the page number. The index also includes tourism areas such as the New Forest and the Cotswolds.

Indexes

The indexes, listed on page 725, will help you find the right accommodation if you have a particular requirement, for example, properties suitable for guests with disabilities or those that have an outdoor pool.

Ratings and awards at a glance

Reliable, rigorous, easy to use – look out for the following ratings and awards to help you choose with confidence:

Ratings made easy

★	Simple, practical, no frills
★★	Well presented and well run
★★★	Good level of quality and comfort
★★★★	Excellent standard throughout
★★★★★	Exceptional with a degree of luxury

For full details of Enjoy England's Quality Rose assessment schemes, go online at **enjoyengland.com/quality**

Some self-catering establishments offer a choice of accommodation units that may have different star ratings. In this case, the entry shows the range available.

rest assured with our official quality ratings

Star ratings

Establishments are awarded a rating of one to five stars based on a combination of quality of facilities and services provided. Put simply, the more stars, the higher the quality and the greater the range of facilities and level of service.

The process to arrive at a star rating is very thorough to ensure that when you book accommodation you can be confident it will meet your expectations. Enjoy England professional assessors visit establishments annually and work to strict criteria to rate the available facilities. They award a quality score for every aspect including the layout and design of the accommodation, the ease of use of all the appliances, the comfort of the beds, the range and quality of the kitchen equipment and, most importantly, the cleanliness. The assessors also score the range and presentation of the visitor information provided. Places that go the extra mile to make every stay a special one will be rewarded with high scores for quality.

From April 2005, all the national assessing bodies (VisitBritain, VisitScotland and Visit Wales) have operated to a common set of standards for rating self-catering accommodation, giving holidaymakers a clear guide on exactly what to expect at each level. An explanation of the standards for each star rating can be found on page 727.

Enjoy England Awards for Excellence

The prestigious and coveted Enjoy England Awards for Excellence showcase the very best in English tourism. Run by VisitBritain in association with England's regions, they include a Self-Catering Holiday of the Year category (see page 17).

National Accessible Scheme

Properities with a National Accessible rating provide access and facilities for guests with special visual, hearing and mobility needs (see page 12).

Walkers and Cyclists Welcome

Participants in these Enjoy England schemes actively encourage walking and cycling. Proprietors go out of their way to make special provision for guests who enjoy these activities to ensure they have a comfortable stay.

Visitor Attraction Quality Assurance

Attractions achieving high standards in all aspects of the visitor experience, from initial telephone enquiry to departure, receive this Enjoy England award and are visited every year by professional assessors.

Self-catering **accommodation** explained

Self-catering holiday homes differ in style and the rating scheme covers a range of accommodation. Every year more than 10,000 different properties in England are assessed. They must all be self-contained and have a kitchen, so there is always the option of eating in.

Holiday cottages, houses and lodges

Choose from cosy country cottages, smart town-centre apartments, seaside villas, grand country houses for large family gatherings, and even quirky conversions of windmills, railway carriages and lighthouses. Most take bookings by the week, generally from a Friday or Saturday, but short breaks are increasingly offered, particularly outside the main season.

Holiday cottage agencies

Our Enjoy England assessors also work with a number of agencies, ranging from small, local organisations that specialise in one particular area, to large Britain-wide operators who can help locate a holiday cottage anywhere in the country. In every case procedures and processes have been checked. Some agencies organise their own assessments, but the majority use Enjoy England quality standards and are gradually bringing all their properties into the star-rating scheme. If you are looking for accommodation during a peak period and for a specific week, it is worth contacting an agency first (see page 436).

Serviced apartments

City-centre serviced apartments are an excellent alternative to hotel accommodation, offering hotel services such as daily cleaning, room service, concierge and business centre services, but with a kitchen and lounge area that allow you to eat in and relax when you choose. A telephone and Internet access tend to be standard. Prices are generally based on the property, so they often represent excellent value for money for families and larger groups. They are also particularly suitable for business travellers who appreciate the extra space, privacy and flexibility. Serviced apartments tend to accept bookings for any length of period, and many are operated by agencies whose in-depth knowledge and choice of properties makes searching easier at busy times.

Boat accommodation

Select from quality-assessed Narrowboats, Cruisers and Hotel Boats. Boat accommodation is explained fully on page 719.

Approved caravan holiday homes

Individual caravans assessed to minimum standards, but without a star rating (see page 724).

Accommodation entries explained

Each accommodation entry contains detailed information to help you decide if it is right for you. This has been provided by proprietors and our aim is to ensure that it is as objective and factual as possible.

1. Listing under town or village with map reference
2. Enjoy England star rating
3. Designator
4. Number of units and how many they sleep
5. Prices per unit per week for low and high season
6. Establishment name, village/town and booking details
7. Indicates when the establishment is open and payment accepted
8. Accommodation details
9. Accessible rating where applicable
10. Walkers/Cyclists Welcome where applicable
11. Travel directions
12. Special promotions
13. At-a-glance facility symbols

A key to symbols can be found on the back-cover flap. Keep it open for easy reference.

National Accessible Scheme

Finding suitable accommodation is not always easy, particularly if you have to seek out ground-floor rooms or specially adapted bathrooms. Use the National Accessible Scheme to help you make your choice.

accessible accommodation for a comfortable stay

Proprietors of accommodation taking part in the National Accessible Scheme have gone out of their way to ensure a comfortable stay for guests with special hearing, visual or mobility needs, and may well have attended a disability awareness course to know what assistance will really be appreciated. These exceptional places are full of extra touches to make everyone's visit trouble-free, from handrails, ramps and step-free entrances (ideal for buggies too) to level-access showers and colour contrast in the bathrooms.

Appropriate National Accessible symbols are included in the guide entries. If you have additional needs or special requirements we strongly recommend that you make sure your chosen accommodation can meet these before you confirm your reservation. The index at the back of the guide gives a full list of establishments that have received a National Accessible rating.

The National Accessible Scheme forms part of the Tourism for All Campaign that is being promoted by VisitBritain and national/regional tourism organisations. Additional help and guidance on finding suitable holiday accommodation for those with special needs can be obtained from:

Tourism for All
c/o Vitalise, Shap Road Industrial Estate, Kendal LA9 6NZ

information helpline 0845 124 9971
reservations 0845 124 9973
(lines open 9-5 Mon-Fri)

f (01539) 735567

e info@tourismforall.org.uk

w tourismforall.org.uk

The criteria VisitBritain and national/regional tourism organisations have adopted do not necessarily conform to British Standards or to Building Regulations. They reflect what the organisations understand to be acceptable to meet the practical needs of guests with mobility or sensory impairments and encourage the industry to increase access to all.

Mobility Symbols

Typically suitable for a person with sufficient mobility to climb a flight of steps but who would benefit from fixtures and fittings to aid balance.

Typically suitable for a person with restricted walking ability and for those who may need to use a wheelchair some of the time and can negotiate a maximum of three steps.

Typically suitable for a person who depends on the use of a wheelchair and transfers unaided to and from the wheelchair in a seated position. This person may be an independent traveller.

Typically suitable for a person who depends on the use of a wheelchair in a seated position.This person also requires personal/mechanical assistance to aid transfer (eg carer, hoist).

Access Exceptional is awarded to establishments that meet the requirements of independent wheelchair users or assisted wheelchair users shown above and also fulfil more demanding requirements with reference to the British Standards BS8300:2001.

Visual Impairment Symbols

Typically provides key additional services and facilities to meet the needs of visually impaired guests.

Typically provides a higher level of additional services and facilities to meet the needs of visually impaired guests.

Hearing Impairment Symbols

Typically provides key additional services and facilities to meet the needs of guests with hearing impairment.

Typically provides a higher level of additional services and facilities to meet the needs of guests with hearing impairment.

take time out, you owe it to yourself

Inspiring ideas for a short break

Want to break out from the daily grind? A short break away is just the tonic. Go with someone special, with the family or a group of friends. Look out for short-stay promotions and weekend deals – offers are highlighted throughout the guide.

Learning curve

Get your hands dirty at **Smallicombe Farm** near Colyton: master the ins and outs of pig keeping from top breeders and enjoy the beautiful, unspoilt countryside. Or gain inspiration at the fascinating Ironbridge Gorge Museums with free tickets offered by **Eleys of Ironbridge** in Shropshire. Feel the breeze on your skin with a spot of sailing at Bewl Water, while staying in nearby **Medway Farm Barn Cottage** in Rotherfield. Try your hand at fishing or simply stroll around the outstanding reservoir and soak up the scenery.

Get the taste

Elms Farm Cottages near Boston is the perfect getaway haven for a distinctly regional retreat. Feel at home straight away with a Tastes of Lincolnshire welcome pack – filled with seasonal local produce such as award-winning plum loaf and locally made jams and marmalades. Or why not explore the pretty Essex beaches and make a beeline for **Spring Hall Cottage** in Little Bentley – where a complimentary bottle of wine awaits every couple's arrival. The stunning views over Nidderdale from **The Barn at Fir Tree Farm** will take your breath away. This luxury barn conversion near Harrogate features beautiful original oak beams and you will be greeted with a superb welcome hamper.

Time to unwind

Treat that special someone to a romantic break and make champagne and roses a feature. At **Hidelow House Cottages** near Malvern they'll sort it all out for you, so you can concentrate on enjoying your weekend. Slip into the hot tub at **Ivyleaf Combe** near Bude and slumber like royalty in a four-poster bed. Relax in the peaceful countryside and visit the sandy beaches nearby. Take a dip in the indoor pool at any time of year at **Mooredge Farm Cottages** near Matlock. Explore the glorious Peak District and enjoy all that Derbyshire has to offer.

Get it together

Get a group together for a special occasion and head to the charming, unspoilt coastal village of Bamburgh. **Point Cottages** sleep up to 17 people and have all you need for that perfect English break – whether you're with family or friends – the stunning views over the Farne Islands and of the nearby castle and golf course will make you want to return. Step back in time and plan a trip en masse to **Knowlton Court** – a cluster of Elizabethan farm cottages near the historic city of Canterbury – where 19 can sleep comfortably. Explore the country's most famous cathedral or tee off at one of the championship golf courses at Sandy Bay and ponder a stroll on the beautiful beach. There's something for everyone at **Ashlack Cottages** near Ulverston – set deep in the heart of the Cumbrian countryside. With accommodation for up to 17 people under one roof, you can keep the whole party together. Not only are fantastic views on offer, but with miles of beach at Duddon Estuary providing an abundance of wildlife, Windermere for watersports, and horse-riding and fishing aplenty, your break away will be action packed.

enjoyEngland™

official tourist board publications

Hotels, including country house and town house hotels, metro and budget hotels in England 2007

£10.99

Guest accommodation, B&Bs, guest houses, farmhouses, inns, restaurants with rooms, campus and hostel accommodation in England 2007

£11.99

Self-catering holiday homes, including serviced apartments and approved caravan holiday homes, boat accommodation and holiday cottage agencies in England 2007

£11.99

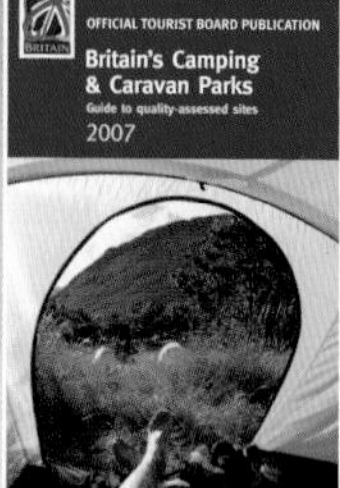

Touring parks, camping parks and holiday parks and villages in Britain 2007

£8.99

informative, easy to use and great value for money

Pet-friendly hotels, B&Bs and self-catering accommodation in England 2007

£9.99

Great ideas for places to visit, eat and stay in England

£12.99

Places to stay and visit in South West England

£9.99

Places to stay and visit in Northern England

£7.99

Accessible places to stay in Britain

£9.99

From good bookshops, online at **visitbritaindirect.com**
or by mail order from:

VisitBritain Fulfilment Centre
t **0870 606 7204** e **fulfilment@visitbritain.org**

Awards for Excellence

Enjoy England Awards for Excellence are all about telling the world what a fantastic place England is to visit, whether it's for a day trip, a weekend break or a fortnight's holiday.

The Awards, now in their 18th year, are run by VisitBritain in association with England's regional tourism organisations. This year there are 13 categories, including Self-Catering Holiday of the Year, Bed & Breakfast of the Year, Tourist Information Centre of the Year and an award for the best tourism website.

Winners of the 2006 Self-Catering Holiday of the Year Award

- GOLD WINNER
  York Luxury Holidays, York, *North Yorkshire*
- SILVER WINNERS
  Combermere Abbey Cottages, Whitchurch, *Shropshire*
  The Northumberland House, Longhoughton, *Northumberland*

Winners of the 2007 awards will receive their trophies at a ceremony in April 2007. The day will celebrate excellence in tourism in England.

For more information about the awards visit enjoyengland.com.

experience the very best of the best

York Luxury Holidays

A

B

1

Location **Maps**

Every place name featured in the regional accommodation sections of this Enjoy England guide has a map reference to help you locate it on the maps which follow. For example, to find Colchester, Essex, which has 'Map ref 3B2', turn to Map 3 and refer to grid square B2.

All place names appearing in the regional sections are shown in black type on the maps. This enables you to find other places in your chosen area which may have suitable accommodation – the place index (at the back of this guide) gives page numbers.

2

3

Tresco Isles of Scilly

St Mary's

Isles of Scilly

Key to regions: South West England

C
D
Weston-super-Mare
Lympsham
Cheddar
Burnham-on-Sea
Highbridge
Lynton
Allerford
Bratton
Ilfracombe
Lee
Berrynarbor
Porlock
Minehead
Blue Anchor
Parracombe
Woolacombe
Simonsbath
Exford
Dunster
EXMOOR
NATIONAL
PARK
Bridgwater
Barnstaple
Brayford
SOMERSET
Burrowbridge
Swimbridge
North Molton
Dulverton
Milverton
Taunton
Bideford
Bampton
Waterrow
Torrington
Stoke sub Hamdon
South Petherton
Otterford
Churchinford
Chulmleigh
Tiverton
DEVON
Willand
Bude
Pancrasweek
Chardstock
Honiton
Whimple
Axminster
Charmouth
Okehampton
Exeter
Exeter International
Uplyme
Colyton
Ashwater
Lyme Regis
Seaton
Drewsteignton
Sidmouth
Morcombelake
St Clether
Moretonhampstead
Bovey Tracey
Launceston
DARTMOOR
NATIONAL
PARK
East Budleigh
Dawlish Warren
Teigngrace
Dawlish
Tavistock
Moorshop
Whitchurch
Ashburton
Dartmeet
Maidencombe
Crapstone
Liskeard
Menheniot
Buckfastleigh
Marldon
Didworthy
Torquay
Lanreath-by-Looe
Plymouth City
Paignton
Stoke Gabriel
Brixham
Plymouth
Churston Ferrers
East Looe
Looe
Polperro
Rame
Modbury
Dartmouth
Mothecombe
Kingsbridge
South Milton
ROSCOFF
SANTANDER
Bigbury-on-Sea
Hope Cove
Salcombe
0
25 Miles
0
40 Km
N

Map 2

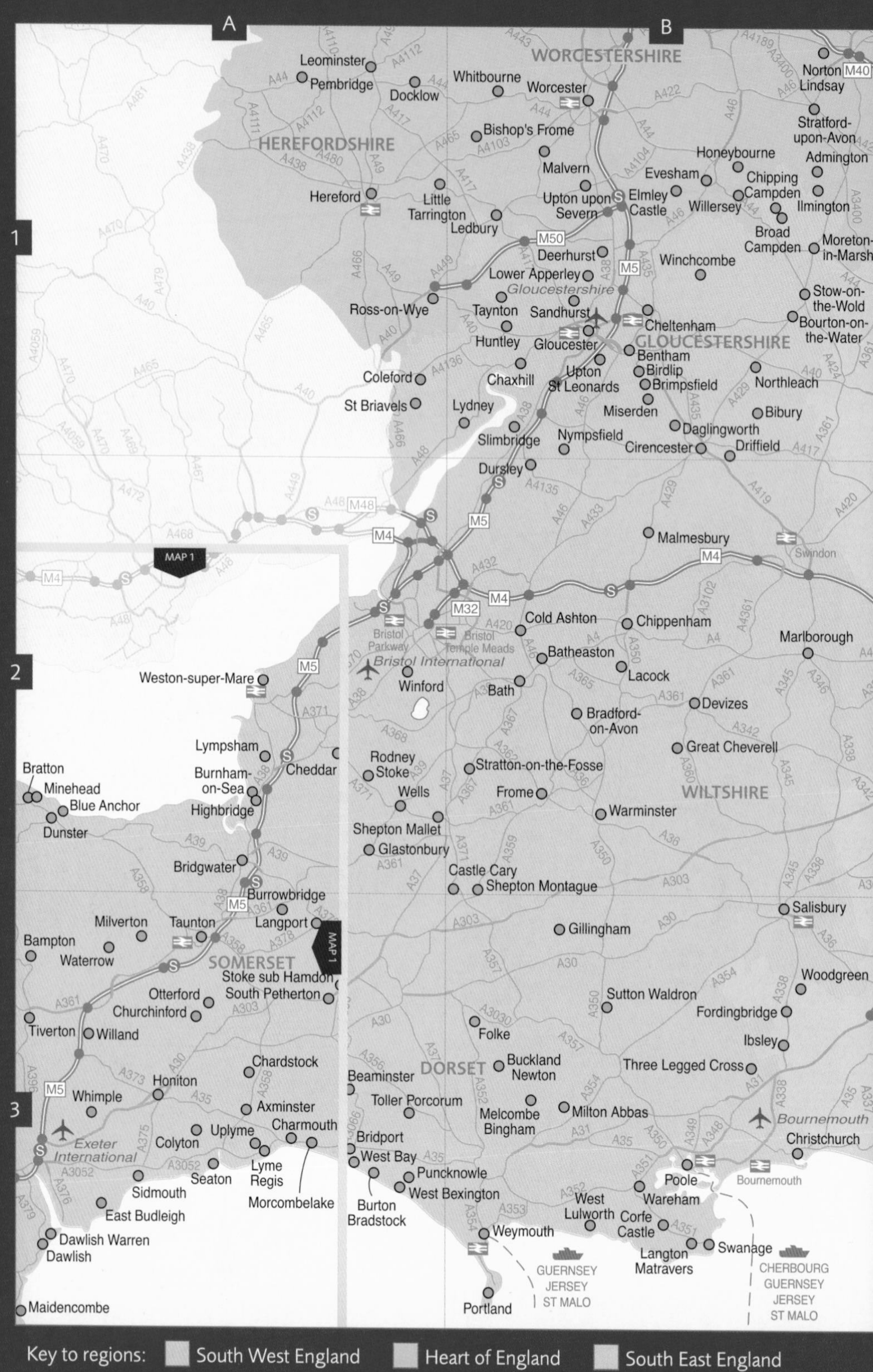

Key to regions: South West England Heart of England South East England

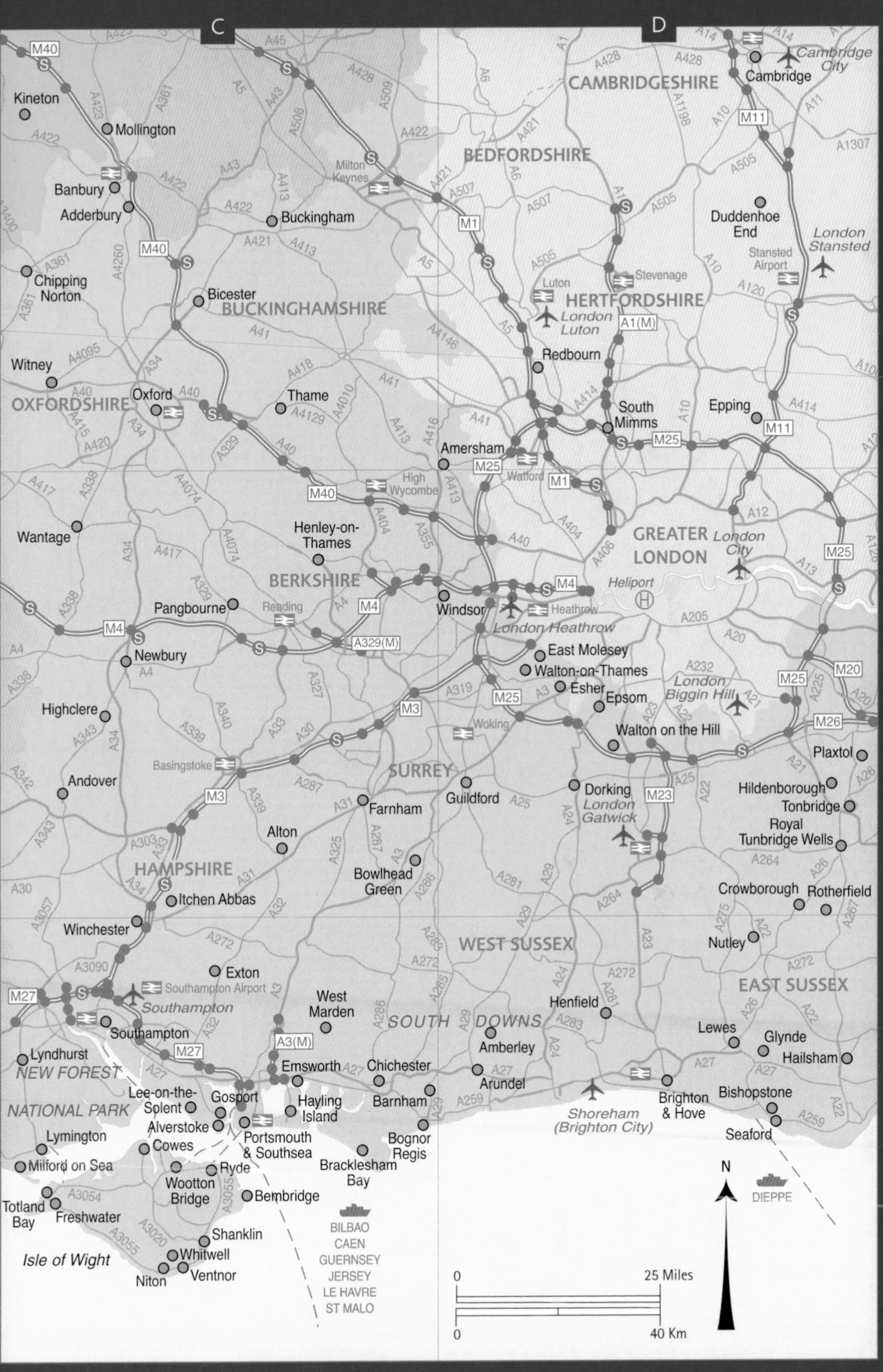

East Midlands East of England London

All place names in black offer accommodation in this guide

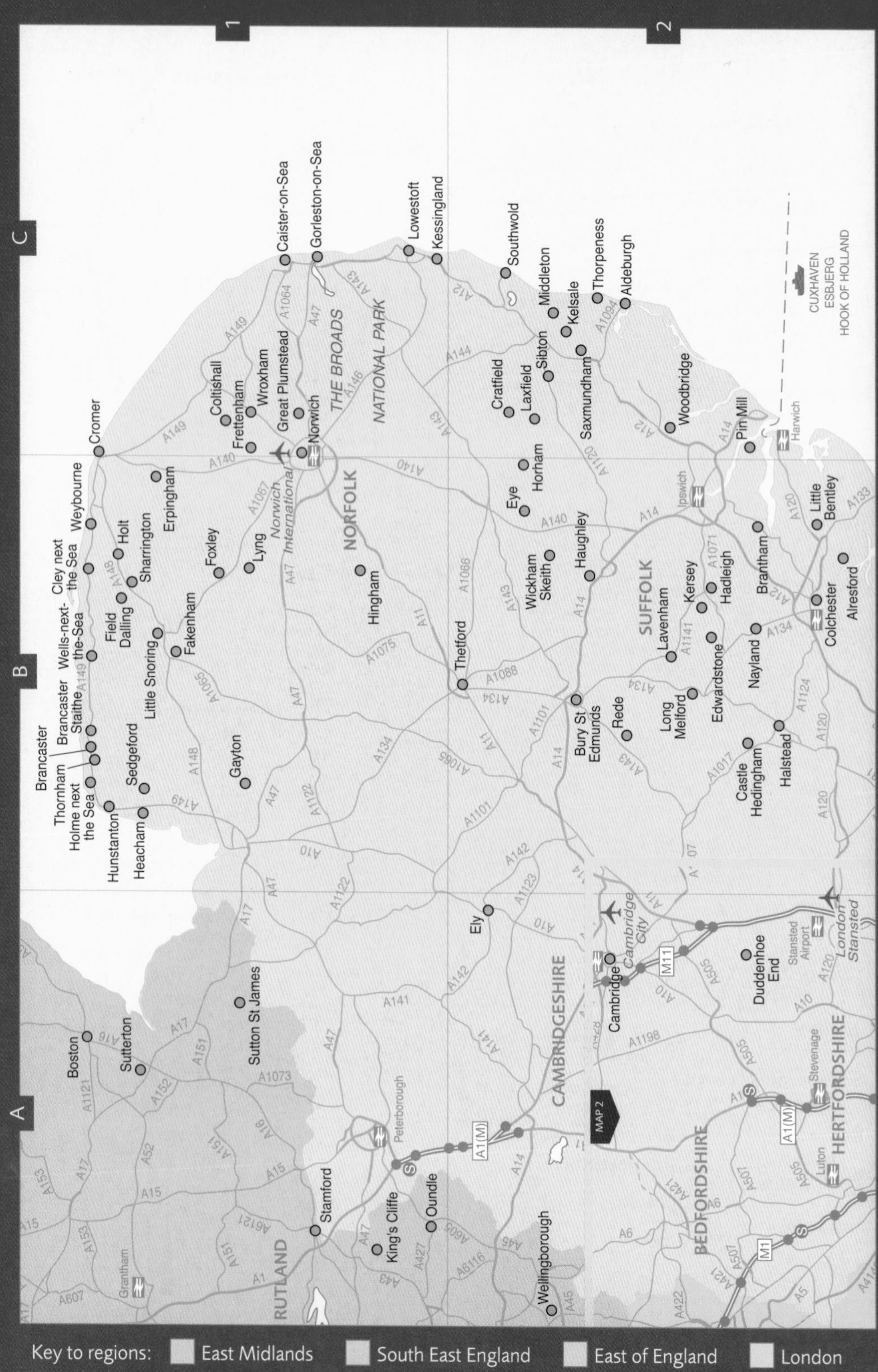

Key to regions: East Midlands South East England East of England London

0 25 Miles
0 40 Km
N
3
4
ESSEX
GREATER LONDON
KENT
SURREY
WEST SUSSEX
EAST SUSSEX
SOUTH DOWNS
Peldon
Billericay
London Southend
Southend-on-Sea
London Luton
Redbourn
South Mimms
Epping
Amersham
Watford
London City
Heliport
Windsor
Heathrow
London Heathrow
East Molesey
Walton-on-Thames
Esher
Epsom
London Biggin Hill
Walton on the Hill
Woking
Plaxtol
Guildford
Dorking
London Gatwick
Hildenborough
Tonbridge
Royal Tunbridge Wells
Bowlhead Green
Crowborough
Rotherfield
MAP 2
Nutley
Henfield
Lewes
Glynde
Hailsham
Amberley
Arundel
Shoreham (Brighton City)
Brighton & Hove
Bishopstone
Seaford
DIEPPE
Rochester
Meopham
Chatham
Faversham
Maidstone
Hollingbourne
Sheldwich
Canterbury
Margate
Broadstairs
Kent International
Ramsgate
OSTEND
Hastingleigh
Ashford
High Halden
Goudhurst
Dover
BOULOGNE
CALAIS
DUNKIRK
Stonegate
Hawkhurst
Tenterden
Ruckinge
Dymchurch
Channel Tunnel
Etchingham
Northiam
Rye
Lydd
Wartling
St Leonards
Eastbourne

Map 4

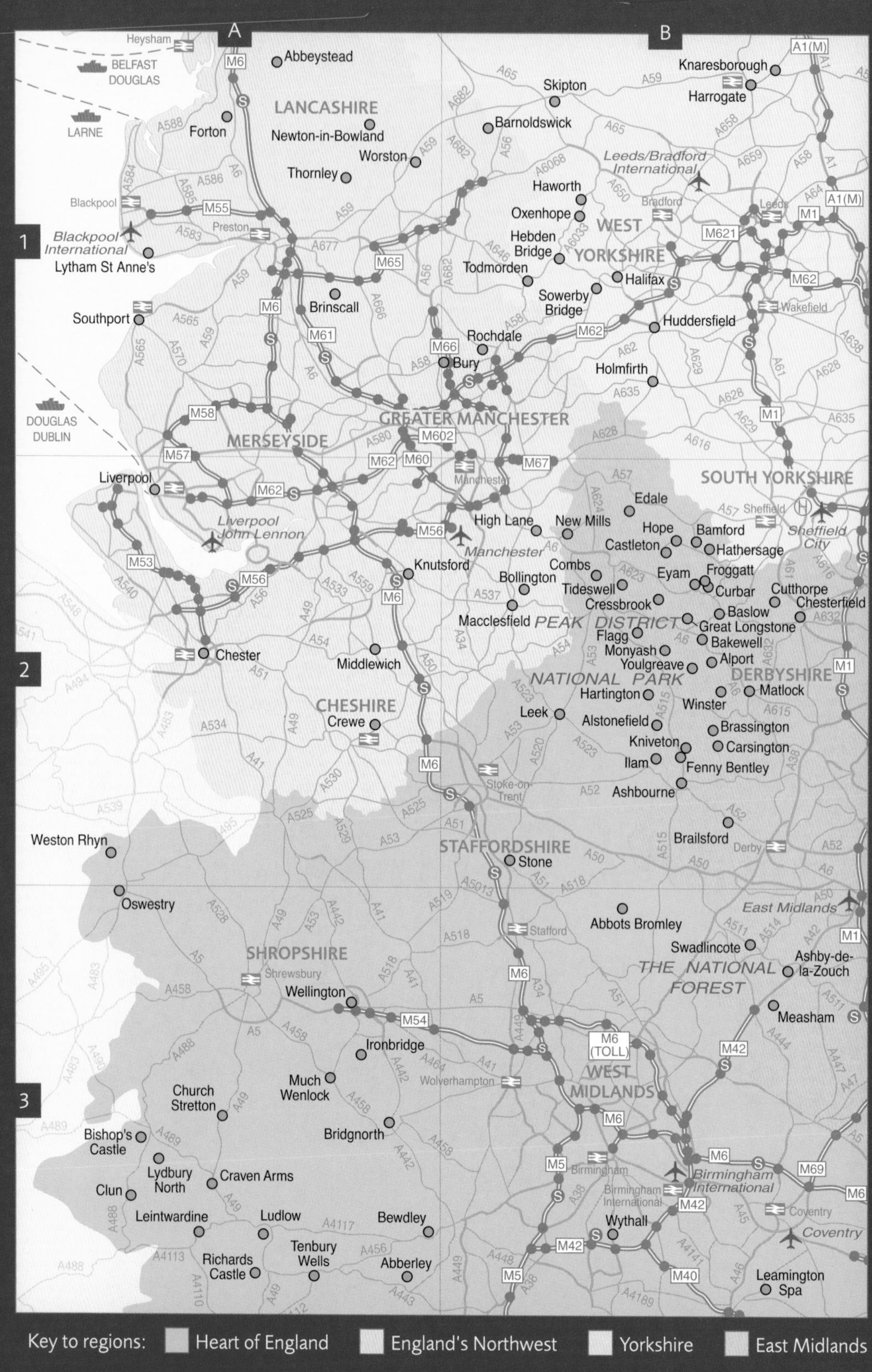

Key to regions: Heart of England | England's Northwest | Yorkshire | East Midlands

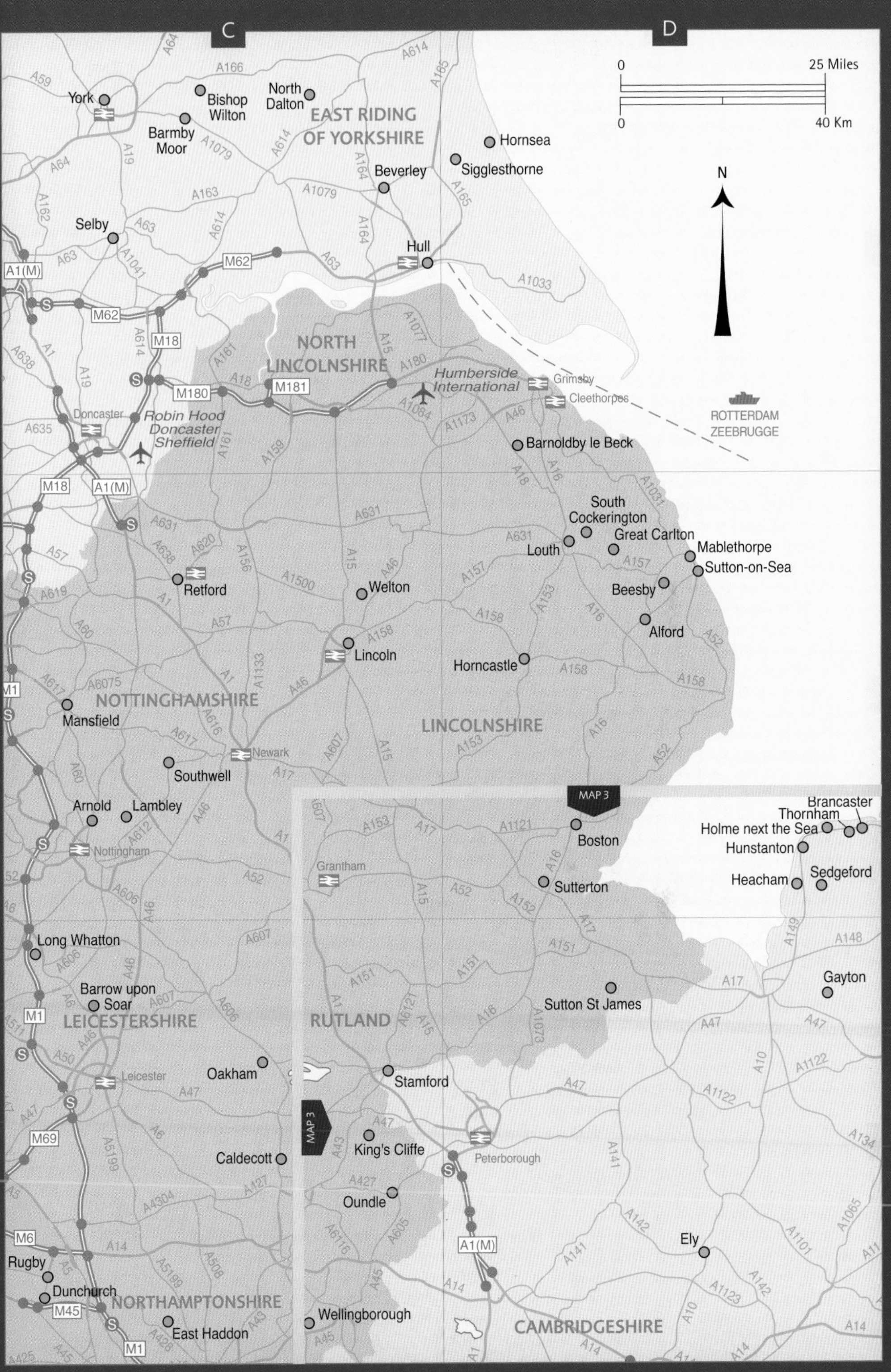

East of England

All place names in black offer accommodation in this guide

Map 5

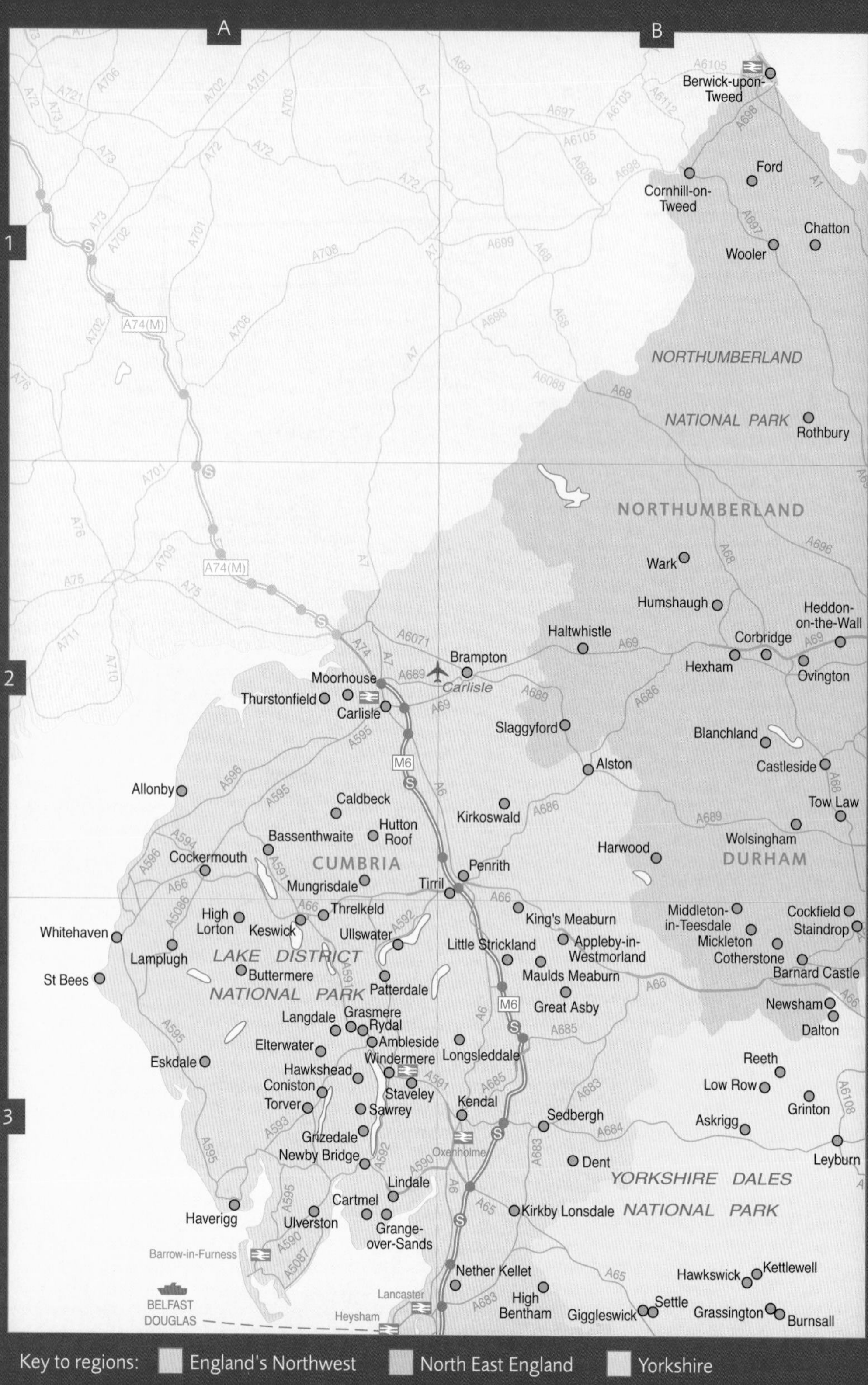

Key to regions: England's Northwest North East England Yorkshire

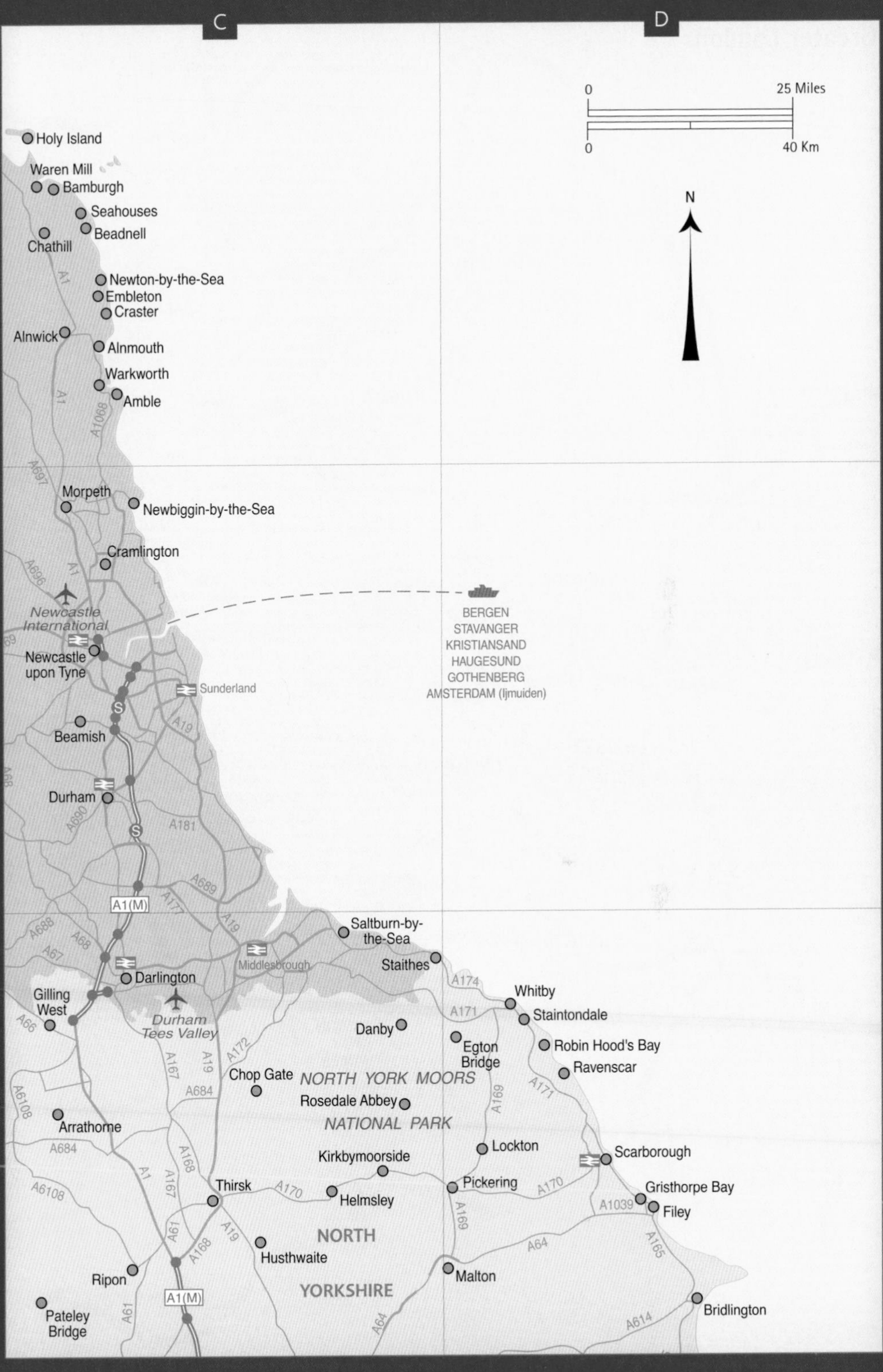

All place names in black offer accommodation in this guide

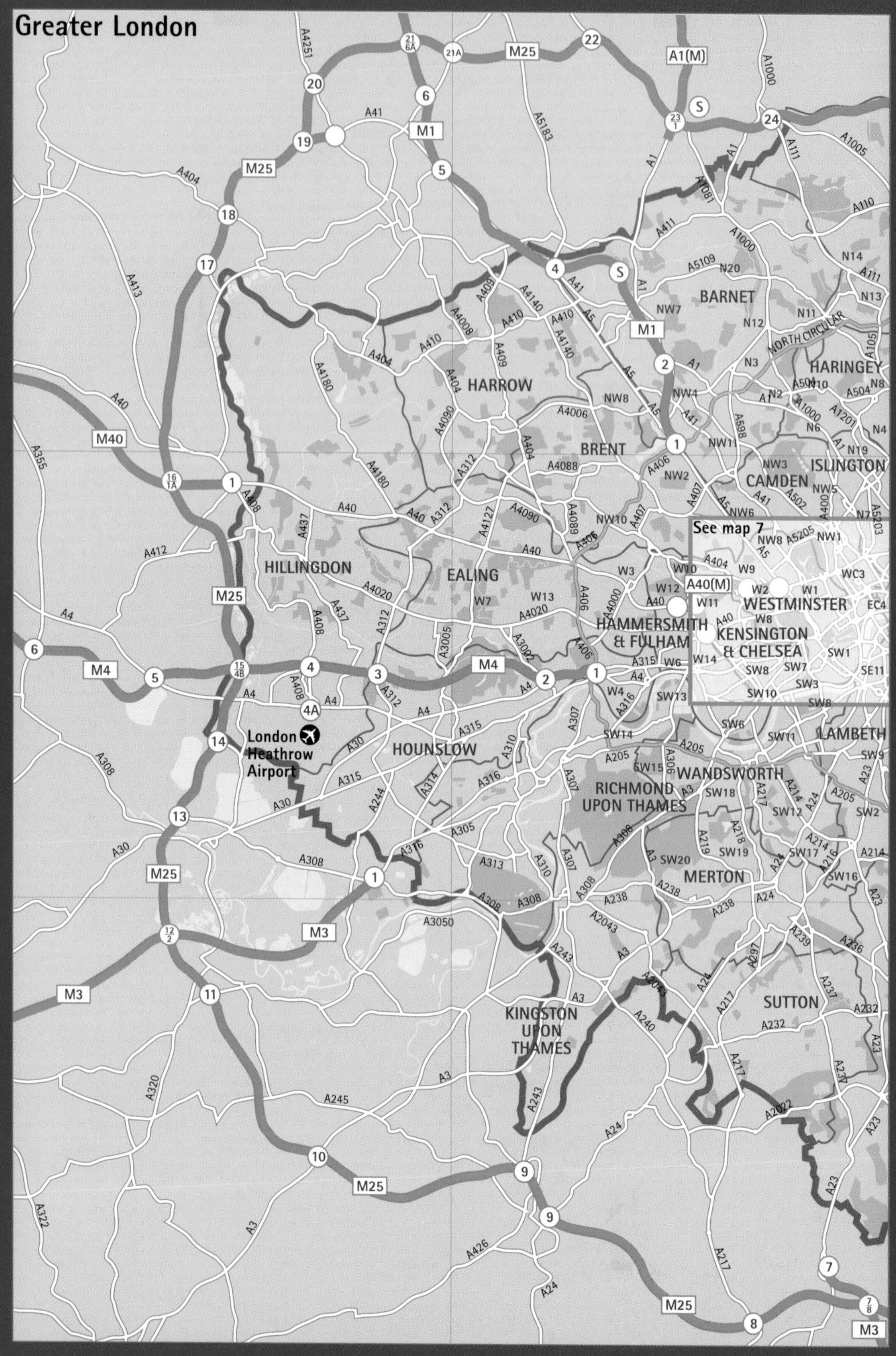
Greater London
M25
A1(M)
M1
M40
M4
M3
A40(M)
BARNET
HARINGEY
HARROW
BRENT
CAMDEN
ISLINGTON
HILLINGDON
EALING
See map 7
WESTMINSTER
HAMMERSMITH
& FULHAM
KENSINGTON
& CHELSEA
HOUNSLOW
London
Heathrow
Airport
LAMBETH
WANDSWORTH
RICHMOND
UPON THAMES
MERTON
SUTTON
KINGSTON
UPON
THAMES
NORTH CIRCULAR

ENFIELD
WALTHAM FOREST
REDBRIDGE
HAVERING
HACKNEY
NEWHAM
BARKING & DAGENHAM
TOWER HAMLETS
CITY
SOUTHWARK
GREENWICH
BEXLEY
LEWISHAM
BROMLEY
CROYDON
M25
M11
M20
M26
M2
A102(M)
SOUTH CIRCULAR
© Arka Cartographics Ltd. 1999

Central London

Finding accommodation
is as easy as 1 2 3 4

Enjoy England official guides to quality accommodation make it quick and easy to find a place to stay. There are several ways to use this guide.

1

PROPERTY INDEX

If you know the name of the establishment you wish to book, turn to the property index at the back where the relevant page number is shown.

2

PLACE INDEX

The place index at the back lists all locations with accommodation featured in the regional sections. A page number is shown where you can find full accommodation and contact details.

3

COLOUR MAPS

All the place names in black on the colour maps at the front have an entry in the regional sections. Refer to the place index for the page number where you will find one or more establishments offering accommodation in your chosen town or village.

4

ALL ASSESSED ACCOMMODATION

Contact details for all Enjoy England assessed accommodation, together with their quality rating, are given in the back section of this guide. Establishments with a full entry in the regional sections are shown in bold. Look in the property index for the page number where their full entry appears.

England's Northwest

Blackpool and Lancashire › Chester and Cheshire
Cumbria – The Lake District › Liverpool and Merseyside › Manchester

Having a ball in Blackpool

England's Northwest
visitenglandsnorthwest.com

Cheshire and Warrington Tourism Board
(01244) 402111
visitchester.com

Cumbria Tourism
(015398) 22222
golakes.co.uk
lakedistrictoutdoors.co.uk

The Lancashire & Blackpool Tourist Board
(01257) 226600
visitlancashire.com

Marketing Manchester
(0161) 237 1010
visitmanchester.com

The Mersey Partnership
(0151) 227 2727
visitliverpool.com

majestic lakes, sunset sands, cutting-edge cities

Main The calming serenity of The Lake District **Left** Amble around Chester and meet the locals; admire great works of art in The Lowry, Manchester; relive childhood memories at The World of Beatrix Potter Attraction, Bowness-on-Windermere; visit the Fab Four's old haunts in Liverpool

Explore Cumbria's soaring peaks or discover the rounded hills and plains of Cheshire. Relax on inland waterways or on Lancashire's sandy beaches. Experience the buzz of Manchester and Liverpool or **the thrill of a rollercoaster ride in Blackpool.**

Explore England's Northwest

Take to the water

Be inspired by the mighty peaks and glorious watery scenes in Cumbria – The Lake District. Take your chances at the Windermere Outdoor Adventure Activities Centre and hop in a canoe, relax in a wayfarer or slice through the waters on a powerboat. Test your climbing skills or swing through the trees in Grizedale Forest on the Go Ape! adventure trail. Alternatively, find your feet on one of the National Trails.

Clear your mind, relax and be mesmerised by the setting sun from Friar's Crag beside Derwentwater. Or take a stroll around Long Meg and Her Daughters near Penrith – one of the largest stone circles in the country – where you can almost hear the spirit of Wordsworth uttering his profound verse.

City culture

Discover the Manchester waterfront at the impressive Quays. Enjoy a play, wander the galleries or dine out in a restaurant at The Lowry, a veritable centre of culture and entertainment. Marvel at the impressive 'B of the Bang' sculpture – the tallest in the UK – and discover how Mancunians lived a hundred or so years ago at the Museum of Science & Industry in Manchester.

Head out of town, roam the Cheshire countryside and admire picturesque black-and-white timbered buildings or listen to the water lapping the edge of your boat on Cheshire's waterways. Amble around Chester Cathedral and find yourself awestruck by the impressive spires and intricate arches.

Take a ferry across the Mersey and visit Liverpool – the European Capital of Culture for 2008. Hop off at Albert Dock, stroll in to the Tate Liverpool and be enthralled by the vast and intriguing array of modern art on display. Do we have lift-off? Head to Spaceport in Merseyside and explore all the universe in this fantastic virtual space adventure.

Thrills and skills

Cruise peacefully through the River Caves at Pleasure Beach, Blackpool, or feel your heart thumping as you plummet down the traditional big dipper (as you feel your stomach flip, imagine one World Record breaker riding it solidly for three months!) Pick out your favourite amongst the sparkling Autumn Illuminations, enjoy high tea in the glitzy Blackpool Tower Ballroom or make your way to one of the nearby beaches and feel the fresh sea breeze fill your lungs.

Learn a new skill and entice a few slimy friends out of the ground at the annual World Worm-Charming Championships near Nantwich in Cheshire. Explore Amazonian life or take a deep breath and swim with the sharks at the Blue Planet Aquarium in Cheshire Oak.

Beauty in many forms

Bask in the Victorian beauty of Port Sunlight Village on Merseyside and catch the scent of the colourful flowers scattered all around. Listen to stories of Liverpool's seafaring heritage at the Merseyside Maritime Museum or follow the remarkable 30-mile Irwell Sculpture Trail that runs from the Salford Quays to the Pennines.

Seek inner peace in the beautiful landscaped gardens or spot roaming fallow deer at Tatton Park in Cheshire. Visit Ness Botanic Gardens – residing in its own microclimate – and delight in the picturesque surroundings awash with dazzling colours and idyllic waterfalls.

Places to **visit**

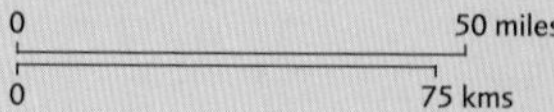

National Park

Area of Outstanding Natural Beauty

Heritage Coast

National Trails
nationaltrail.co.uk

National Trails approved but not yet open

3 Sections of the National Cycle Network
nationalcyclenetwork.org.uk

The Beatles Story
Liverpool, Merseyside
(0151) 709 1963
beatlesstory.com
The history of the Fab Four

Blue Planet Aquarium
Cheshire Oaks, Cheshire
(0151) 357 8800
blueplanetaquarium.com
Take a dip with the sharks

Bowland Wild Boar Park
near Preston, Lancashire
(01995) 61554
wildboarpark.co.uk
Feed animals amid beautiful countryside

Camelot Theme Park
Chorley, Lancashire
(01257) 453044
camelotthemepark.co.uk
Explore King Arthur's magical land

Chester Cathedral
Cheshire
(01244) 324756
chestercathedral.com
Outstanding architecture and famous choir

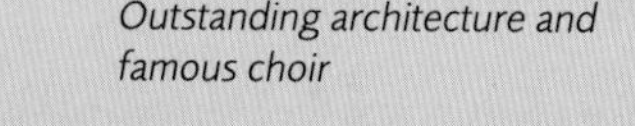

Go Ape! High Ropes Forest Adventure
Grizedale Forest, Cumbria
0870 428 5330
goape.co.uk
Swing through the forest trees

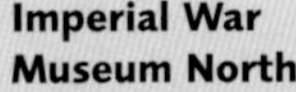

Imperial War Museum North
Manchester
(0161) 836 4000
north.iwm.org.uk
Spectacular and fascinating museum

Long Meg and her Daughters
near Penrith, Cumbria
(015394) 44444
henge.org.uk
Impressive Bronze Age stone circle

The Lowry
Manchester
0870 787 5780
thelowry.com
Centre of culture and entertainment

Merseyside Maritime Museum
Liverpool, Merseyside
(0151) 478 4499
liverpoolmuseums.org.uk
Learn about Liverpool's seafaring heritage

The Museum of Science & Industry in Manchester
(0161) 832 2244
msim.org.uk
Step into Manchester's past

Ness Botanic Gardens
Cheshire
(0151) 353 0123
nessgardens.org.uk
Picturesque colourful gardens and waterfall

Pleasure Beach, Blackpool
Lancashire
0870 444 5566
blackpoolpleasurebeach.com
Breathtaking rides and spectacular shows

South Lakes Wild Animal Park
Dalton-in-Furness, Cumbria
(01229) 466086
wildanimalpark.co.uk
Unique safari and conservation park – meet and handle a variety of animals

Spaceport
Liverpool, Merseyside
(0151) 330 1333
spaceport.org.uk
Fantastic virtual space adventure that's out of this world!

Speke Hall, Gardens and Woodland (NT)
Liverpool, Merseyside
(0151) 427 7231
spekehall.org.uk
Tudor mansion and fine wooded estate

Tate Liverpool
Liverpool, Merseyside
(0151) 702 7400
tate.org.uk/liverpool
Four glorious floors of modern art

Tatton Park (NT)
Knutsford, Cheshire
(01625) 534400
tattonpark.org.uk
Explore the 1,000-acre deer park

Wildfowl and Wetland Trust Martin Mere
near Southport, Lancashire
(01704) 895181
wwt.org.uk
Home to ducks, geese and swans

Windermere Outdoor Adventure Activities Centre
Cumbria
(015394) 47183
southlakelandleisure.org.uk/windermere
A haven of watersports activities

Wythenshawe Hall
Northenden,
Greater Manchester
(0161) 998 2331
manchestergalleries.org
Splendid Tudor house

Tourist information centres 

When you arrive at your destination, visit a tourist information centre for help with accommodation and information about local attractions and events, or email your request before you go.

Accrington	Blackburn Road	(01254) 872595	leisure@hyndburnbc.gov.uk
Alston Moor	Front Street	(01434) 382244	alston.tic@eden.gov.uk
Altrincham	20 Stamford New Road	(0161) 912 5931	tourist.information@trafford.gov.uk
Ambleside	Market Cross	(015394) 32582	amblesidetic@southlakeland.gov.uk
Appleby-in-Westmorland	Boroughgate	(017683) 51177	tic@applebytown.org.uk
Ashton-under-Lyne	Wellington Road	(0161) 343 4343	tourist.information@mail.tameside.gov.uk
Barnoldswick	Fernlea Avenue	(01282) 666704	tourist.info@pendle.gov.uk
Barrow-in-Furness	Duke Street	(01229) 894784	touristinfo@barrowbc.gov.uk
Birkenhead	Woodside Ferry Terminal, Wirral	(0151) 647 6780	touristinfo@wirral.gov.uk
Blackburn	50-54 Church Street	(01254) 53277	visit@blackburn.gov.uk
Blackpool	1 Clifton Street	(01253) 478222	tic@blackpool.gov.uk
Blackpool*	Central Promenade	(01253) 478222	tic@blackpool.gov.uk
Bolton	Le Mans Crescent	(01204) 334321	tourist.info@bolton.gov.uk
Bowness	Glebe Road	(015394) 42895	bownesstic@lake-district.gov.uk
Brampton*	Market Place	(01697) 73433	tourism@carlisle-city.gov.uk
Broughton in Furness	The Square	(01229) 716115	email@broughton-tic.fsnet.co.uk
Burnley	Croft Street	(01282) 664421	tic@burnley.gov.uk
Bury	Market Street	(0161) 253 5111	touristinformation@bury.gov.uk
Carlisle	Greenmarket	(01228) 625600	tourism@carlisle-city.gov.uk
Chester (Town Hall)	Northgate Street	(01244) 402111	tis@chestercc.gov.uk
Chester Visitor Centre	Vicars Lane	(01244) 402111	tis@chestercc.gov.uk
Cleveleys	Victoria Square	(01253) 853378	cleveleystic@wyrebc.gov.uk
Clitheroe	12-14 Market Place	(01200) 425566	tourism@ribblevalley.gov.uk
Cockermouth	Market Street	(01900) 822634	email@cockermouth-tic.fsnet.co.uk
Congleton	High Street	(01260) 271095	tourism@congleton.gov.uk
Coniston	Ruskin Avenue	(015394) 41533	
Egremont	12 Main Street	(01946) 820693	email@egremont-tic.fsnet.co.uk
Ellesmere Port	Kinsey Road	(0151) 356 7879	cheshireoaks-tic@hotmail.co.uk
Fleetwood	The Esplanade	(01253) 773953	fleetwoodtic@wyrebc.gov.uk
Garstang	High Street	(01995) 602125	garstangtic@wyrebc.gov.uk
Grange-over-Sands	Main Street	(015395) 34026	grangetic@southlakeland.gov.uk
Kendal	Highgate	(01539) 725758	kendaltic@southlakeland.gov.uk
Keswick	Market Square	(017687) 72645	keswicktic@lake-district.gov.uk

Kirkby Lonsdale	24 Main Street	(01524) 271437	kltic@southlakeland.gov.uk
Kirkby Stephen	Market Street	(017683) 71199	ks.tic@eden.gov.uk
Knutsford	Toft Road	(01565) 632611	ktic@macclesfield.gov.uk
Lancaster	29 Castle Hill	(01524) 32878	lancastertic@lancaster.gov.uk
Liverpool (Maritime Museum)	Albert Dock	(0151) 233 2008	info@visitliverpool.com
Liverpool	John Lennon Airport	(0151) 907 1057	info@visitliverpool.com
Liverpool 08 Place	Whitechapel	(0151) 233 2008	08place@liverpool.gov.uk
Lytham St Annes	67 St Annes Road West	(01253) 725610	touristinformation@fylde.gov.uk
Macclesfield	Town Hall	(01625) 504114	Informationcentre@macclesfield.gov.uk
Manchester Visitor Information Centre	Lloyd Street	0871 222 8223	touristinformation@ marketing-manchester.co.uk
Maryport	Senhouse Street	(01900) 812101	maryporttic@allerdale.gov.uk
Millom*	Station Road	(01229) 774819	millomtic@copelandbc.gov.uk
Morecambe	Marine Road Central	(01524) 582808	morecambetic@lancaster.gov.uk
Nantwich	Church Walk	(01270) 610983	touristi@crewe-nantwich.gov.uk
Northwich	1 The Arcade	(01606) 353534	tourism@valeroyal.gov.uk
Oldham	12 Albion Street	(0161) 627 1024	ecs.tourist@oldham.gov.uk
Pendle Heritage Centre	Park Hill	(01282) 661701	heritage.centre@pendle.gov.uk
Penrith	Middlegate	(01768) 867466	pen.tic@eden.gov.uk
Preston	Lancaster Road	(01772) 253731	tourism@preston.gov.uk
Rheged		(01768) 860034	tic@rheged.com
Rochdale	The Esplanade	(01706) 864928	tic@rochdale.gov.uk
Saddleworth	High Street, Uppermill	(01457) 870336	ecs.tourist@oldham.gov.uk
Salford	Salford Quays	(0161) 848 8601	tic@salford.gov.uk
Sedbergh	72 Main Street	(015396) 20125	tic@sedbergh.org.uk
Silloth-on-Solway	Liddell Street	(016973) 31944	sillothtic@allerdale.gov.uk
Southport	112 Lord Street	(01704) 533333	info@visitsouthport.com
Southwaite	M6 Service Area	(016974) 73445	southwaitetic@visitscotland.com
St Helens	Chalon Way East	(01744) 755150	info@sthelenstic.com
Stockport	30 Market Place	(0161) 474 4444	tourist.information@stockport.gov.uk
Ullswater	Glenridding	(017684) 82414	ullswatertic@lake-district.gov.uk
Ulverston	County Square	(01229) 587120	ulverstontic@southlakeland.gov.uk
Warrington	Academy Way	(01925) 632571	informationcentre@warrington.gov.uk
Whitehaven	Market Place	(01946) 852939	tic@copelandbc.gov.uk
Wigan	Trencherfield Mill	(01942) 825677	tic@wlct.org
Wilmslow	Rectory Fields	(01625) 522275	i.hillaby@macclesfield.gov.uk
Windermere	Victoria Street	(015394) 46499	windermeretic@southlakeland.gov.uk
Workington	21 Finkle Street	(01900) 606699	workingtontic@allerdale.gov.uk

* *seasonal opening*

Alternatively, you can text **TIC LOCATE** to **64118** to find your nearest tourist information centre

Find out **more**

There are various publications and guides about England's Northwest available from the following Tourist Boards or by logging on to **visitenglandsnorthwest.com** or calling **(01257) 226600**:

Cheshire and Warrington Tourism Board
Grosvenor Park Lodge, Grosvenor Park Road
Chester CH1 1QQ
t (01244) 402111
e info@cwtb.co.uk
w visitchester.com

Cumbria Tourism
Windermere Road, Staveley, Kendal LA8 9PL
t (015398) 22222
e info@cumbriatourism.org
w golakes.co.uk or lakedistrictoutdoors.co.uk

The Lancashire & Blackpool Tourist Board
St George's House, St George's Street
Chorley PR7 2AA
t (01257) 226600 (Brochure request)
e info@visitlancashire.com
w visitlancashire.com

Marketing Manchester – The Tourist Board for Greater Manchester
Churchgate House, 56 Oxford Street
Manchester M1 6EU
t (0161) 237 1010
Brochure request: 0870 609 3013
e touristinformation@marketing-manchester.co.uk
w visitmanchester.com

The Mersey Partnership – The Tourist Board for Liverpool and Merseyside
12 Princes Parade, Liverpool L3 1BG
t (0151) 227 2727
f (0151) 227 2325
Accommodation booking service:
0845 601 1125
e info@visitliverpool.com
w visitliverpool.com

Relax in the beautiful gardens at Tatton Park, Knutsford

Travel **info**

By road:
Motorways intersect within the region which has the best road network in the country. Travelling north or south use the M6, and east or west the M62.

By rail:
Most Northwest coastal resorts are connected to InterCity routes with trains from many parts of the country, and there are through trains to major cities and towns.

By air:
Fly into Liverpool John Lennon, Manchester or Blackpool airports.

where to stay in

England's Northwest

All place names in the blue bands are shown on the maps at the front of this guide.

A complete listing of all Enjoy England assessed accommodation covered by this guide appears at the back.

Accommodation symbols
Symbols give useful information about services and facilities. Inside the back-cover flap you can find a key to these symbols. Keep it open for easy reference.

ALLONBY, Cumbria Map ref 5A2

★★★–★★★★
SELF CATERING

Units **6**
Sleeps **2–6**
Low season per wk
£180.00–£310.00
High season per wk
£290.00–£540.00

Dickinson Place Holiday Cottages, Maryport

contact James Williamson, Dickinson Place Holiday Cottages, Dickinson Place, Allonby CA15 6QE
t (01900) 881440 **f** (01900) 881440 **e** holidays@dickinsonplace.co.uk **w** dickinsonplace.co.uk

Situated in the centre of Allonby on the unspoilt Solway Coast. This Area of Outstanding Natural Beauty offers picturesque scenery and memorable sunsets. Along the grass banks and sandy beach is a variety of wildlife.

open All year
payment Credit/debit cards, cash/cheques

Unit General Leisure Shop < 0.5 miles Pub < 0.5 miles

ALSTON, Cumbria Map ref 5B2

★★★★★
SELF CATERING

Units **1**
Sleeps **5**
Low season per wk
£500.00–£700.00
High season per wk
£600.00–£850.00

Stone Barn Cottage, Alston

contact Mrs Dee Ellis, Stone Barn Cottage, Low Galligill Farm, Nenthead, Alston CA9 3LW
t (01434) 381672 **e** tim@hillfarmer.com **w** hillfarmer.com

payment Cash/cheques

Situated at the heart of a traditional Cumbrian hill farm, our barn conversion offers spacious accommodation, spread over three floors, comprising large kitchen/dining room with Aga, snug with log fire, first-floor sitting area, master bedroom with en suite bathroom, stairs to second-floor bedrooms (one single, one twin).

Located 2.5 miles east of Alston – full directions on request.

Unit General Leisure Shop 2 miles Pub 1 mile

Check it out

Information on accommodation listed in this guide has been supplied by proprietors. As changes may occur you should remember to check all relevant details at the time of booking.

AMBLESIDE, Cumbria Map ref 5A3

★★★
SELF CATERING

Units **1**
Sleeps **2–4**
Low season per wk
Min £200.00
High season per wk
Max £450.00

Birch Cottage, Ambleside

contact Dr Nash, Birch Cottage, c/o 47 Goring Road, Bounds Green, London N11 2BT
t (020) 8888 1252 & 07974 817787 **e** birch@drnash.wanadoo.co.uk
w cottage-lakedistrict.mysite.wanadoo-members.co.uk

Delightful 200-year-old traditional stone cottage in a quiet hamlet with mountain views. Five minutes' walk to Ambleside centre. Comfortably furnished, well equipped. Spectacular hikes without car – you'll love it!

open All year
payment Cash/cheques

Unit General P Leisure Shop 0.5 miles Pub 0.5 miles

AMBLESIDE, Cumbria Map ref 5A3

★★★★
SELF CATERING

Units **3**
Sleeps **4–6**
Low season per wk
Min £250.00
High season per wk
£250.00–£520.00

Chestnuts, Beeches and The Granary, Ambleside

contact Mr Benson, Chestnuts, Beeches and The Granary, c/o High Sett, Sun Hill Lane, Troutbeck Bridge, Windermere LA23 1HJ
t (015394) 42731 **f** (015394) 42731 **e** info@accommodationlakedistrict.com
w accommodationlakedistrict.com

open All year
payment Cash/cheques

Charming cottages and a bungalow converted from a former coach house and tack room, furnished to a high standard. Set in idyllic surroundings overlooking Lake Windermere with panoramic views of the Lakeland mountains. High Wray is a quiet hamlet between Ambleside and Hawkshead, an ideal base for walking/touring.

⊕ *A591 to Ambleside, then A593 to Coniston, after 1 mile take B5286. After 2.5 miles, left to Wray. Cottages are 2 miles along on left in High Wray.*

❤ *3-night stays available low season.*

Unit General P Shop 1.5 miles Pub 1.5 miles

AMBLESIDE, Cumbria Map ref 5A3

★★★
SELF CATERING

Units **1**
Sleeps **5**
Low season per wk
£295.52–£391.38
High season per wk
£447.61–£568.89

Dower House Cottage, Ambleside

contact Mrs Margaret Rigg, The Dower House, Wray Castle, Ambleside LA22 0JA
t (015394) 33211 **f** (015394) 33211

Self-catering cottage with two bedrooms, large kitchen, dining room, large sitting room, bathroom. French windows opening onto terrace and gardens.

open All year
payment Cash/cheques

Unit General Leisure

AMBLESIDE, Cumbria Map ref 5A3

★★★★
SELF CATERING

Units **11**
Sleeps **2–8**
Low season per wk
£275.00–£460.00
High season per wk
£535.00–£860.00

The Lakelands, Ambleside

contact Jackie Kingdom, The Lakelands, Lower Gale, Ambleside LA22 0BD
t (015394) 33777 **f** (015394) 31301 **e** enquiry@the-lakelands.com **w** the-lakelands.com

Self-catering apartments at The Lakelands, set in a unique position overlooking Ambleside with unspoilt views of the surrounding fells. Furnished with quality in mind. Private leisure centre available for use of guests.

open All year
payment Credit/debit cards, cash/cheques

Unit General P Leisure Shop < 0.5 miles Pub < 0.5 miles

Check the maps

Colour maps at the front pinpoint all the places you will find accommodation entries in the regional sections. Pick your location and then refer to the place index at the back to find the page number.

AMBLESIDE, Cumbria Map ref 5A3

★★★
SELF CATERING

Units 1
Sleeps 7
Low season per wk
£250.00–£500.00
High season per wk
£500.00–£1,000.00

Scandale Bridge Cottage, Ambleside

Lakeland Character Cottages, The Kings Head Hotel, Thirlmere CA12 4TN
t 0500 600725 **f** (017687) 72309 **e** stay@lakedistrictinns.co.uk **w** lakedistrictinns.co.uk

open All year
payment Cash/cheques

Located on the outskirts of the bustling market town of Ambleside, this 18thC Lakeland-stone cottage enjoys an idyllic setting in the heart of the National Park, at the foot of Fairfield Horseshoe with Scandale Beck flowing through the perimeter of the grounds.

⊕ *Scandale Bridge Cottage is located on Rydal Road, on the outskirts of Ambleside on the A591.*

❤ *Permanent special offers on last-minute availability.*

Unit General P Leisure Shop 1 mile Pub 1 mile

APPLEBY-IN-WESTMORLAND, Cumbria Map ref 5B3

★★★
SELF CATERING

Units 1
Sleeps 2–4
Low season per wk
£135.00–£185.00
High season per wk
£190.00–£295.00

Wray Cottage, Appleby-in-Westmorland

contact Mrs Cowey, The Hunting House, Great Asby, Appleby-in-Westmorland CA16 6HD
t (01768) 352485

Quiet situation with private garden. Modern, fully equipped bungalow ten minutes' drive from Appleby, within easy reach of the Lakes, the Dales, Howgills and the Pennines. One bedroom plus sofa bed in the lounge.

open All year
payment Cash/cheques

Unit General P S Shop 5 miles Pub < 0.5 miles

BARNOLDSWICK, Lancashire Map ref 4B1

★★★★★
SELF CATERING

Units 1
Sleeps 5
Low season per wk
£275.00–£305.00
High season per wk
£355.00–£465.00

Hill Top Barn, Barnoldswick

contact Mr & Mrs Sharples, Hill Top Farm, Manchester Road, Barnoldswick BB18 5QT
t (01282) 812460 **e** info@hilltopbarn.com **w** hilltopbarn.com

open All year
payment Cash/cheques, euros

Award-winning, mid-18thC split-level barn comprising one double, one twin and one single bedroom, bathroom, through lounge/dining room with underfloor heating, and dining room/kitchen with gas Aga. Fully centrally heated elsewhere, superb panoramic views of Yorkshire Dales/Ribble Valley. Lots of walks and places to visit.

⊕ *Look for Greyhound Inn, Manchester Road (B6251). Two hundred yards on from Greyhound turn left at red post box. Hill Top Barn is 25yds from turning.*

❤ *Permanent special offers on last-minute availability.*

Unit General 2 P S Leisure Shop 0.5 miles Pub < 0.5 miles

BASSENTHWAITE, Cumbria Map ref 5A2

★★★★
SELF CATERING

Units **5**
Sleeps **2–6**
Low season per wk
£325.00–£700.00
High season per wk
£355.00–£730.00

Irton House Farm, Cockermouth

contact Mrs Almond, Irton House Farm, Isel, Cockermouth CA13 9ST
t (01768) 776380 **e** almond@farmersweekly.net **w** irtonhousefarm.com

Immaculate, spacious properties, all furnished to a high specification. Shopping at Keswick and Cockermouth. Superb views, walks and places of interest.

open All year
payment Credit/debit cards, cash/cheques

Unit General Leisure Shop 1 mile Pub 3 miles

BOLLINGTON, Cheshire Map ref 4B2

★★★★★
SELF CATERING

Units **1**
Sleeps **2–8**
Low season per wk
£410.00–£450.00
High season per wk
£490.00–£715.00

Higher Ingersley Barn, Macclesfield

contact Mr Peacock, Higher Ingersley Barn, Higher Ingersley Farm, Oakenbank Lane, Macclesfield SK10 5RP
t (01625) 572245 **e** bw.peacock@ntlword.com **w** higheringerleyfarm.co.uk

Beautiful converted barn on edge of Peak District. Spectacular views. Oak beamed, elegant and comfortable. Sofa bed for two extra. Garden. Superb walking and sightseeing.

open All year
payment Cash/cheques

Unit General Leisure Shop < 0.5 miles
Pub < 0.5 miles

BRAMPTON, Cumbria Map ref 5B2

★★★★★
SELF CATERING

Units **1**
Sleeps **4**
Low season per wk
£350.00–£380.00
High season per wk
£410.00–£490.00

Warren Bank Cottage, Brampton

contact Margie Douglas, Warren Bank Cottage, c/o The Coach House, Halliwell Dene NE46 1HW
t (01434) 607544 **e** margie@warrenbankcottage.com **w** warrenbankcottage.com

open All year
payment Cash/cheques

Your home away from home offering everything you need for a carefree stay. Warren Bank Cottage lies on the edge of Brampton, just ten minutes' walk from the marketplace, in Hadrian's Wall Country. The Lake District, Northumberland and Scottish Borders are easily accessible. Children are welcome and your dog can come too.

⊕ *9 miles from M6 motorway. Directions to the Cottage will be sent to you in advance of your arrival.*

Unit General Leisure
Shop < 0.5 miles Pub < 0.5 miles

Key to symbols

Symbols at the end of each entry help you pick out the services and facilities which are most important for your stay. A key to the symbols can be found inside the back-cover flap. Keep this open for easy reference.

BRINSCALL, Lancashire Map ref 4A1

★★★
SELF CATERING

Units 1
Sleeps 5–8
Low season per wk
£300.00–£350.00
High season per wk
£375.00–£400.00

Moors View Cottage, Chorley

contact Mrs Sheila Smith, Moors View Cottage, Four Seasons Guest House, Thornton FY5 1EP
t (01253) 853537 & 07747 808406

open All year
payment Cash/cheques, euros

Situated amid lovely countryside adjacent to canal, motorways, market towns and coast, this fully equipped cottage comprises two bedrooms and excellent bed-settee, luxury bathroom, separate shower and toilet, large through lounge and dining area, oak kitchen, off-road parking, large rear garden and sun room. Fuel, power and linen included.

⊕ *M61 jct 8, follow signs for Blackburn, A674. Right-hand turn for Brinscall. Or M65 jct 3, follow signs for Wheelton, A674. Left-hand turn for Brinscall.*

♥ *Part- and mid-week bookings accepted.*

Unit General P Leisure Shop < 0.5 miles Pub < 0.5 miles

BURY, Greater Manchester Map ref 4B1

★★★★
SELF CATERING

Units 1
Sleeps 2
Low season per wk
Min £350.00
High season per wk
Min £350.00

Top o' th' Moor Cottage, Bury

contact Mrs Michelle Richardson, Moorbottom Road, Holcombe, Bury BL8 4NR
t 07976 034196 **e** info@topofthemoorcottage.com **w** topofthemoorcottage.com

One-bedroom self-contained cottage, attached to farmhouse, on the edge of the West Pennine Moors.

open All year
payment Cash/cheques

Unit General P Leisure Shop 2 miles Pub 0.5 miles

BUTTERMERE, Cumbria Map ref 5A3

★★★★
SELF CATERING

Units 6
Sleeps 2–6
Low season per wk
Min £240.00
High season per wk
Max £680.00

Bridge Hotel & Self Catering Apartments, Buttermere

contact John McGuire, Bridge Hotel & Self Catering Apartments, Buttermere, Nr Keswick CA13 9UZ
t (01768) 770252 **f** (01768) 770215 **e** enquiries@bridge-hotel.com **w** bridge-hotel.com

open All year
payment Credit/debit cards, cash/cheques, euros

Superbly situated, surrounded by fells in Area of Outstanding Natural Beauty. Each apartment is furnished to a high standard. All modern facilities. Dogs welcome.

Unit General P Leisure

If you have access needs...

Look for the National Accessible Scheme symbols if you have special hearing, visual or mobility needs. An index of all accommodation participating in the scheme can be found at the back of this guide.

BUTTERMERE, Cumbria Map ref 5A3

★★★★
SELF CATERING

Units **1**
Sleeps **2–4**
Low season per wk
Min £290.00
High season per wk
Max £590.00

Lanthwaite Green Farm Cottage, Buttermere

contact John McGuire, Bridge Hotel & Self Catering Apartments, Buttermere, Nr Keswick CA13 9UZ
t (01768) 770252 **f** (01768) 770215 **e** enquiries@bridge-hotel.com **w** bridge-hotel.com

open All year
payment Credit/debit cards, cash/cheques, euros

Situated at the foot of Melbreak on a working farm. Looking towards Crummock Water, luxury, cosy 16thC cottage. Boasts all modern facilities.

Unit General P Leisure Shop 6 miles Pub 3 miles

CALDBECK, Cumbria Map ref 5A2

★★★★
SELF CATERING

Units **1**
Sleeps **1–3**
Low season per wk
Min £170.00
High season per wk
Max £320.00

The Barn, Manor Cottage, Caldbeck

contact Ann Wade, Manor Cottage, Fellside, Caldbeck CA7 8HA
t (01697) 478214 **e** walterwade@tiscali.co.uk

Converted barn nestling in the timelessness of the Caldbeck Fells in unspoilt Northern Lakeland. Comfortable, well-equipped, ideal for walkers or those who just want to relax and unwind.

open All year except Christmas and New Year
payment Cash/cheques

Unit General P Leisure Shop 2 miles Pub 2 miles

CARLISLE, Cumbria Map ref 5A2

★★★★
SELF CATERING

Units **1**
Sleeps **1–4**
Low season per wk
£240.00–£285.00
High season per wk
£330.00–£460.00

West Cottage, Cumwhinton, Carlisle

contact Mrs Allison Stamper, West Cottage, Cringles, Cumwhinton CA4 8DL
t (01228) 561600

A spacious, tastefully furnished and well-equipped cottage adjoining a Georgian listed house in a village location three miles from historic Carlisle city. Shop, post office and pub in village.

open All year
payment Cash/cheques

Unit General P Leisure Shop < 0.5 miles Pub < 0.5 miles

CARTMEL, Cumbria Map ref 5A3

★★★-★★★★
SELF CATERING

Units **8**
Sleeps **1–18**
Low season per wk
£240.00–£350.00
High season per wk
£400.00–£780.00

Longlands at Cartmel, Grange-over-Sands

contact Martin Ainscough, Longlands at Cartmel, Cartmel, Grange-over-Sands LA11 6HG
t (015395) 36475 **f** (015395) 36172 **e** longlands@cartmel.com **w** cartmel.com

open All year
payment Cash/cheques

Extremely well-equipped cottages, furnished to a very high standard, set in a courtyard behind a beautiful Georgian house set in parkland on the side of Hampsfell outside Cartmel. Restored walled garden. Great walks, and superb pubs and restaurants in the village.

⊕ *M6 jct 36, follow signs for Barrow (A590) for 12 miles. Left to Cartmel, left at crossroads, left at T-junction. Longlands set back in fields on left.*

❤ *Short breaks available from Nov-Easter and throughout the year if availability allows.*

Unit General Leisure Shop 1 mile Pub 1 mile

CARTMEL, Cumbria Map ref 5A3

★★★★
SELF CATERING

Units **1**
Sleeps **3**
Low season per wk
£280.00–£300.00
High season per wk
£320.00–£340.00

The Old Vicarage, Field Broughton, Cartmel

contact Mrs Sharphouse, The Old Vicarage Flat, Field Broughton, Cartmel LA11 6HW
t (015395) 36540 **e** theflat@sharphouse.co.uk **w** sharphouse.co.uk/theflat

A lovely 17thC Lakeland house situated in the quiet, unspoilt hamlet of Field Broughton, two miles north of picturesque Cartmel, with its priory and racecourse, and only four miles from Lake Windermere.

open All year
payment Cash/cheques

Unit General 12 P Shop 2.5 miles Pub 2.5 miles

CHESTER, Cheshire Map ref 4A2

★★★
SELF CATERING

Units **1**
Sleeps **1–4**
Low season per wk
£150.00–£200.00
High season per wk
£200.00–£250.00

Kingswood Coach House, Chester

contact Mrs C Perry, Kingswood Coach House, Kingswood, Parkgate Road, Chester CH1 6JS
t (01244) 851204 **f** (01244) 851244 **e** caroline.m.perry@btopenworld.com

Ideal for couples. Large bedroom, fitted kitchen, living room, toilet and shower. Garden and patio, off-road parking. Close to bus route. Near Wales and Wirral.

open All year
payment Cash/cheques

Unit General P Leisure

COCKERMOUTH, Cumbria Map ref 5A2

★★★
SELF CATERING

Units **1**
Sleeps **1–6**
Low season per wk
Max £250.00
High season per wk
Max £350.00

37 Kirkgate, Cockermouth

contact Nelson & Val Chicken, 39 Kirkgate, Cockermouth CA13 9PJ
t (01900) 823236 **e** valandnelson@btopenworld.com **w** 37kirkgate.com

An ideal base for touring Cumbria, this spacious and comfortable three-bedroomed Georgian house overlooks the tree-lined, cobbled area of Kirkgate.

open All year
payment Cash/cheques

Unit General P Leisure

COCKERMOUTH, Cumbria Map ref 5A2

★★★
SELF CATERING

Units **1**
Sleeps **4–6**
Low season per wk
£320.00–£390.00
High season per wk
£450.00–£680.00

The Stables, Dean, Workington

contact Veronica Roper, Sunnyside, Gib Lane, Hoghton PR5 0RS
t (01254) 852027 **e** veronica@vroper.fsnet.co.uk **w** vholidays.moonfruit.com

open All year
payment Cash/cheques, euros

Delightful 18thC, comfortable, well-equipped cottage with inglenooks, exposed beams and log fires – an excellent base at any time of year. Dean is a peaceful village, ideally situated for exploring the Northern Lakes, West Cumbria, Carlisle and the Scottish Borders. Secluded garden – perfect for a peaceful, relaxing holiday. Walking, cycling, golf, fishing. Ospreys nearby.

⊕ *M6 jct 40, Workington. A66, Cockermouth. At roundabout, left (Egremont A5086), 4 miles right Dean, 1 mile right Dean. Pass Royal Yew. Left after barn conversion.*

❤ *3-night breaks available Oct-Mar. 20% discount for 2 people, depending on season.*

Unit General P Leisure Shop 5 miles
Pub < 0.5 miles

COCKERMOUTH, Cumbria Map ref 5A2

★★★★
SELF CATERING

Units 1
Sleeps 2
Low season per wk
£150.00–£260.00
High season per wk
£260.00–£320.00

Stoneygate, Cockermouth

contact Dr & Mrs Pearson, Stoneygate, Pardshaw, Cockermouth CA13 0SP
t (01900) 823595 **e** g.w.pearson@btinternet.com

open All year
payment Cash/cheques

On the fringe of the Lake District National Park, the studio accommodation adjoins the owners' detached cottage and is set in a beautiful one-acre garden with large pond, waterfall, summerhouse and patios. Magnificent views down the Buttermere Valley. Excellent access for fell-walking and Solway coast. Cockermouth four miles, pub one mile.

⊕ *From A66 Cockermouth roundabout take A5086. After 3.5 miles turn left to Pardshaw. At T-junction turn right. Stoneygate is approx 100yds on right.*

❤ *3- or 4-night stays available.*

Unit General P Leisure Shop 4 miles Pub 1 mile

CONISTON, Cumbria Map ref 5A3

★★★★
SELF CATERING

Units 2
Sleeps 6
Low season per wk
Min £325.00
High season per wk
Max £500.00

1 and 2 Ash Gill Cottages, Torver, Coniston

contact Dorothy Cowburn, Lyndene, Pope Lane, Whitestake, Preston PR4 4JR
t (01772) 612832

open All year
payment Cash/cheques

Set amidst the rolling hills surrounding Coniston Water, the houses are equipped to the highest standard. Ample parking, gardens and patios. Central heating throughout for the cooler months. Excellent base for walking, touring, watersports and pony-trekking. Sorry, no pets.

⊕ *M6 jct 36 take A590 and turn right at Greenodd and then right to Torver (A5084). By bus to Ambleside, Coniston and then Torver.*

❤ *Short breaks available.*

Unit General 3 P Leisure Shop 3 miles Pub < 0.5 miles

CONISTON, Cumbria Map ref 5A3

★★★
SELF CATERING

Units 1
Low season per wk
Min £250.00
High season per wk
Max £490.00

Shelt Gill, Coniston

contact Rosalind Dean, Shelt Gill, c/o 9 The Fairway, Sheffield S10 4LX
t 0845 009 3998 **f** 0845 009 3998 **e** holiday@sheltgill.co.uk **w** sheltgill.co.uk

Medieval cottage with a view of Lake Coniston from the timbered living room. There is a stream in the garden and easy access to hill walks.

open All year
payment Cash/cheques, euros

Unit General P Leisure Shop 1 mile Pub < 0.5 miles

Our quality rating schemes

For a detailed explanation of the quality and facilities represented by the stars please refer to the information pages at the back of this guide.

CONISTON, Cumbria Map ref 5A3

★★-★★★★

SELF CATERING

Units **8**
Sleeps **1–6**
Low season per wk
£95.00–£195.00
High season per wk
£160.00–£390.00

Thurston House & Thurston View, Coniston

contact Alan Jefferson, Thurston House & Thurston View, c/o 21 Chale Green, Bolton BL2 3NJ
t (01204) 419261 **e** alan@jefferson99.freeserve.co.uk **w** jefferson99.freeserve.co.uk

open All year
payment Cash/cheques

Thurston House: large Victorian house converted into individual apartments. Quiet location close to village centre. Private parking at rear of property. Thurston View: lovely stone cottage with superb views. Sorry, no pets/smoking in cottage. Short walk to village centre. Parking for one car.

⊕ *In centre of village. Map showing location is sent with brochure.*

❤ *Short breaks may be available – please phone for details.*

Unit General P

CREWE, Cheshire Map ref 4A2

★★★

SELF CATERING

Units **2**
Sleeps **2–6**
Low season per wk
£300.00–£350.00
High season per wk
£350.00–£400.00

Bank Farm Cottages, Crewe

contact Mrs Ann Vaughan, Bank Farm Cottages, Newcastle Road, Crewe CW2 5JG
t (01270) 841809 **f** (01270) 841809

Charming holiday cottages created from Victorian farm buildings, furnished to a high standard. Full gas central heating, washing machines, microwaves. Ample parking. Excellent base for North Wales potteries.

open All year
payment Cash/cheques

Unit General P Leisure Shop 1 mile Pub 0.5 miles

DENT, Cumbria Map ref 5B3

★★★

SELF CATERING

Units **2**
Sleeps **4**
Low season per wk
£190.00–£245.00
High season per wk
£255.00–£310.00

Middleton's Cottage and Fountain Cottage, Sedbergh

contact Mr & Mrs Ayers, Middleton's Cottage and Fountain Cottage, The Old Rectory, Polegate BN26 5RB
t (01323) 870032 **f** (01323) 870032 **e** candpayers@mistral.co.uk **w** dentcottages.co.uk

open All year
payment Cash/cheques

Modernised mid-17thC cottages in centre of small, quaint village, comfortably furnished and decorated to high standards. Quiet, unspoilt Dentdale offers a good base for walking, touring and exploring the Yorkshire Dales or the Lake District, with Kendal and Hawes nearby. Brochure available. Open all year.

⊕ *Dent is 10 miles from M6 jct 37. Follow A684 to Sedbergh, then minor road signposted to Dent, 5 miles. Cottages are in village centre.*

❤ *Short breaks from Oct-Mar, weekend or mid-week. Any combination, subject to availability.*

Unit General P S

Phone ahead

Even the most ardent pet lover would appreciate some advance warning of Rover's visit, so please phone ahead and check what facilities will be available.

ELTERWATER, Cumbria Map ref 5A3

★★★
SELF CATERING

Units **2**
Sleeps **3–4**
Low season per wk
£325.00–£348.00
High season per wk
£376.00–£433.00

Wistaria Cottage and 3 Main Street, Elterwater

contact Mr G & Mrs D Beardmore, 2 Beech Drive, Stoke-on-Trent ST7 1BA
t (01782) 783170 **f** (01782) 783170 **e** geoff.doreen.beardmore@ntlworld.com

Traditional 18thC cottages near village centre. Tastefully renovated, well equipped. Serviced and maintained by owners. Warm and comfortable, off-peak heating, open fires. Fell and valley walking.

open All year
payment Cash/cheques

Unit General 10 P Shop < 0.5 miles Pub < 0.5 miles

ESKDALE, Cumbria Map ref 5A3

★★★★
SELF CATERING

Units **1**
Sleeps **2–6**
Low season per wk
£280.00–£385.00
High season per wk
£415.00–£505.00

Old Brantrake, Holmrook

contact Mr & Mrs Tyson, Old Brantrake, Brant Rake, Eskdale CA19 1TT
t (01946) 723340 **f** (01946) 723340

open All year
payment Cash/cheques

17thC listed farmhouse in a quiet rural setting; ideal for walking, exploring the central fells or touring. Restored to high standard, three bedrooms, with two WCs, bath and shower, modern kitchen and woodfire. In winter, short lets (minimum three nights) are also available. Brochure.

From M6 jct 36, by A590, A5092 and A595, to lights after Broughton. Turn right for Ulpha and Eskale. Old Brantrake is 2nd house in Birkby Road.

Unit General P Leisure Shop 1.5 miles Pub 0.75 miles

ESKDALE, Cumbria Map ref 5A3

★★★★
SELF CATERING

Units **1**
Sleeps **2–4**
Low season per wk
£240.00–£350.00
High season per wk
£390.00–£450.00

Randle How, Eskdale Green

contact Susan Wedley, Randle How, c/o Long Yocking How, Eskdale Green, Holmrook CA19 1UA
t (01946) 723126 **f** (01946) 723490 **e** jswedley@btinternet.com

18thC cottage with modern facilities and a large, attractive garden. Situated in a quiet lane but only five minutes to shop. Walks from the door. Eskdale and Ravenglass railway station three minutes' walk.

open All year
payment Cash/cheques

Unit General P Leisure Shop 0.5 miles Pub 0.5 miles

FORTON, Lancashire Map ref 4A1

★-★★★
SELF CATERING

Units **3**
Sleeps **1–6**
Low season per wk
£350.00–£700.00
High season per wk
£450.00–£800.00

Cleveley Mere Fishing & Lodges., Forton, Preston

contact Peter & Lynne Brown, Cleveley Mere Fishing Lodges, Cleveley Lodge, Forton PR3 1BY
t (01524) 793644 **w** cleveleymere.com

open All year except Christmas
payment Cash/cheques

Cleveley Mere lies in the scenic Wyre Valley and is a beautiful, peaceful, 23-acre trout lake set in a private nature reserve and surrounded by fields, woodlands and River Wyre, with magnificent views of the neighbouring fells. Short breaks or weekly breaks available.

⊕ *Located between M6 and A6 at Forton, approx 1 mile south of Lancaster Forton Services exit and 2.5 miles south of Lancaster South jct 33 exit off M6.*

Unit General **P** Leisure Shop 1.5 miles Pub 1.5 miles

FORTON, Lancashire Map ref 4A1

★★★★
SELF CATERING

Units **3**
Sleeps **2–6**
Low season per wk
£210.00–£300.00
High season per wk
£315.00–£445.00

Shirebank Court, Preston

t (01524) 792179 **e** mail@shirebankcourt.co.uk **w** shirebankcourt.co.uk

open All year
payment Cash/cheques

Barn conversions on a working family farm. Very spacious and well equipped; maintained to a high standard. Wood burners in lounges, large car park and gardens. Village shop, pubs and restaurant within a five-minute walk. Pleasant walks in surrounding countryside. Lakes, Yorkshire Dales and seaside all within easy reach.

⊕ *M6 jct 33, turn south onto A6. Travel 1.5 miles to School Lane in Forton. Turn right into lane. Farm 20yds on right.*

Unit General **P** Leisure Shop 0.5 miles Pub 0.5 miles

GRANGE-OVER-SANDS, Cumbria Map ref 5A3

★★★
SELF CATERING

Units **1**
Sleeps **2–4**
Low season per wk
£300.00–£350.00
High season per wk
£350.00–£450.00

Cornerways Bungalow, Grange-over-Sands

contact Eunice Rigg, Cornerways Bungalow & Greaves Farm, Prospect House, Barber Green, Grange-over-Sands LA11 6HU
t (015395) 36329 & (015395) 36587

Pleasant bungalow in quiet situation, with double and twin bedroom. All-round views, private garden with parking. Ideal base for touring Lake District. Personal supervision. Open March to October.

payment Cash/cheques

Unit General 4 **P** Shop 2 miles Pub 2 miles

GRASMERE, Cumbria Map ref 5A3

★★★
SELF CATERING

Units **1**
Sleeps **2–5**
Low season per wk
£200.00–£300.00
High season per wk
£400.00–£600.00

1 Field Foot, Ambleside

contact Mrs J Morrison, 1 Field Foot, Park Crescent, Wigan WN1 1RZ
t (01942) 236350 & (015394) 45305 **e** jean-morrison@hotmail.co.uk

A large, cosy cottage in the middle of the village. Heating and electricity included. Top bedroom has wonderful views. Large kitchen/diner, separate TV lounge. Garage. Children and one dog welcome.

open All year
payment Cash/cheques

Unit General Shop < 0.5 miles Pub < 0.5 miles

GRASMERE, Cumbria Map ref 5A3

Rating Applied For
SELF CATERING

Units **1**
Sleeps **10**
Low season per wk
£500.00–£750.00
High season per wk
£750.00–£2,000.00

Bramrigg House, Grasmere

Lakeland Character Cottages, The Kings Head Hotel, Thirlmere CA12 4TN
t 0500 600 725 **f** (017687) 72309 **e** stay@lakedistrictinns.co.uk **w** lakedistrictinns.co.uk

open All year
payment Cash/cheques

This fine Lakeland house, dating from the early 1900s, is situated on the outskirts of the picturesque village of Grasmere, in the heart of the Lake District National Park. Standing in private gardens at the foot of Helvellyn, Bramrigg is one of the finest holiday homes in the Lake District.

⊕ *Bramrigg House is located on Dunmail Raise, on the outskirts of Grasmere on the A591.*

❤ *Permanent special offers on last-minute availability.*

Unit General Shop 1 mile Pub 0.5 miles

GRASMERE, Cumbria Map ref 5A3

★★★★
SELF CATERING

Units **3**
Sleeps **2–5**
Low season per wk
£265.00–£300.00
High season per wk
£435.00–£600.00

Broadrayne Farm Cottages, Grasmere

contact Mr Bev Dennison & Mrs Jo Dennison Drake, Broadrayne Farm, Grasmere, Ambleside LA22 9RU
t (015394) 35055 **f** (015394) 35733 **e** bev@grasmerehostel.co.uk **w** grasmere-accommodation.co.uk

open All year
payment Cash/cheques

With dramatic mountains, rolling fells, glorious lakes and peaceful valleys, Broadrayne Farm is at the heart of the Lake District, superbly located for wonderful views. The traditional farm properties have been lovingly renovated with today's creature comforts, including open coal fires, central heating and off-street parking. Pets welcome by arrangement.

⊕ *Our driveway is directly off the A591, we are 1.25 miles north of the village of Grasmere, 400m after the Travellers Rest Pub.*

❤ *A week booked in the year allows 10% off a second week booked in Mar (excl Easter holidays).*

Unit General Leisure Shop 1.3 miles Pub 1.25 miles

Place index

If you know where you want to stay the index at the back of the guide will give you the page number which lists accommodation in your chosen town, city or village. Check out the other useful indexes too.

GRASMERE, Cumbria Map ref 5A3

★★★★
SELF CATERING

Units **3**
Sleeps **2–6**
High season per wk
£315.00–£850.00

Grasmere Cottages, Grasmere

contact Martin Wood, Grasmere Cottages, Lane End, College Street LA22 9SZ
t (015394) 35395 **e** enquiries@grasmerecottageaccommodation.co.uk
w grasmerecottageaccommodation.co.uk

Traditional, stone-built Lakeland cottages that have been fully refurbished without losing their old-world charm.

open All year
payment Cash/cheques

Unit General P Leisure Shop 0.5 miles Pub 0.5 miles

GRASMERE, Cumbria Map ref 5A3

★★★★
SELF CATERING

Units **1**
Sleeps **2–4**
Low season per wk
£300.00–£370.00
High season per wk
£490.00–£610.00

Rothay Lodge Garden Apartment, Grasmere

contact Lindsay Rogers, Rothay Lodge Garden Apartment, c/o 54a Trevor Road, West Bridgford, Nottingham NG2 6FT
t (0115) 923 2618 **f** (0115) 923 3984 **e** enquiries@rothay-lodge.co.uk **w** rothay-lodge.co.uk

open All year
payment Cash/cheques, euros

In a peaceful riverside location, a short level stroll to village shops, pubs and restaurants, our spacious ground-floor garden apartment has two double en suite bedrooms, lounge with access to garden patio, large fully equipped kitchen/dining room. All services and linen included. Sorry, no pets, non-smoking.

⊕ *From M6 jct 36 follow A590/A591 to Ambleside. Continue on A591 to Grasmere and turn left at The Swan Hotel. Rothay Lodge is on the left.*

Unit General P Shop 0.6 miles Pub < 0.5 miles

GRASMERE, Cumbria Map ref 5A3

★★★
SELF CATERING

Units **1**
Sleeps **2–5**
Low season per wk
£170.00–£300.00
High season per wk
£375.00–£450.00

Silvergarth, Grasmere

contact Susan Coward, Silvergarth, c/o Low Riddings, Grasmere LA22 9QY
t (015394) 35828 **f** (015394) 35828 **e** cowards.silvergarth@btinternet.com
w cowards.silvergarth.btinternet.co.uk

payment Cash/cheques

A personal welcome awaits you at this attractive Lakeland house furnished to a high standard. Ideal situation on village outskirts, within minutes of local amenities. Three bedrooms, large, modern kitchen, dining room, comfortable lounge with magnificent views of fells. Spacious, yet cosy and warm in winter (coal fire optional). Attractive garden.

⊕ *From M6 jct 36 follow the A591 for 24 miles. Turn right at the foot of Hollens Farm Drive, 0.5 miles north of Dove Cottage.*

Unit General 10 P S Shop 0.5 miles Pub 0.5 miles

Using map references

The map references refer to the colour maps at the front of this guide. The first figure is the map number; the letter and figure that follow indicate the grid reference on the map.

GREAT ASBY, Cumbria Map ref 5B3

★★★★
SELF CATERING

Units 3
Sleeps 2–5
Low season per wk
£240.00–£305.00
High season per wk
£336.00–£460.00

Scalebeck Holiday Cottages, Great Asby, Appleby-in-Westmorland

contact Mr K J Budding, Scalebeck Holiday Cottages, Scalebeck, Appleby-in-Westmorland CA16 6TF
t (01768) 351006 **f** (01768) 353532 **e** mail@scalebeckholidaycottages.com
w scalebeckholidaycottages.co.uk

Self-catering cottages in barn conversion. Secluded valley, abundant wildlife. Non-smokers, pets welcome, games room, open all year.

open All year
payment Credit/debit cards, cash/cheques

Unit General Leisure Shop 5 miles Pub 1 mile

GRIZEDALE, Cumbria Map ref 5A3

★★★
SELF CATERING

Units 2
Sleeps 2–6
Low season per wk
£195.00–£445.00
High season per wk
£284.00–£650.00

High Dale Park Barn, Ulverston

contact Peter Brown, High Dale Park Barn, c/o High Dale Park Farm, High Dale Park, Satterthwaite, Ulverston LA12 8LJ
t (01229) 860226 **e** peter@lakesweddingmusic.com **w** lakesweddingmusic.com/accomm/

open All year
payment Cash/cheques

Come and enjoy the peace and tranquillity of Grizedale Forest. Delightfully situated, south-facing, 17thC converted barn attached to owner's farmhouse. Wonderful views down quiet, secluded valley, surrounded by beautiful, broadleaf woodland, rich in wildlife. Oak beams, log fire, central heating, patio. Hawkshead and Beatrix Potter's house three miles.

⊕ *High Dale Park Barn is approximately 40 minutes by car from jct 36 of the M6.*

❤ *Short breaks available, minimum 2 nights.*

Unit General Leisure Shop 3 miles Pub 2 miles

HAVERIGG, Cumbria Map ref 5A3

★★★
SELF CATERING

Units 1
Sleeps 2–5
Low season per wk
£150.00–£200.00
High season per wk
£300.00–£360.00

Quiet Cottage, Millom

contact Mr & Mrs Haston, Quiet Cottage, c/o 2 Pool Side, Haverigg LA18 4HW
t (01229) 772974 **e** quietcottage@tiscali.co.uk **w** quietcottage.golakes.co.uk

One single, two twins, 300yds to pub, shops, beach. On bus route. Private parking. Changeover day Saturday. Visitors are asked to arrive after 1500 and depart before 1000. Sorry, no pets.

open All year
payment Cash/cheques

Unit General Leisure Shop 0.5 miles Pub 0.5 miles

HAWKSHEAD, Cumbria Map ref 5A3

★★★
SELF CATERING

Units 9
Sleeps 2–6
Low season per wk
£220.00–£310.00
High season per wk
£312.00–£420.00

The Croft Holiday Flats, Ambleside

contact Mrs Barr, The Croft Holiday Flats, North Lonsdale Road, Hawkshead LA22 0NX
t (015394) 36374 **f** (015394) 36544 **e** enquiries@hawkshead-croft.com **w** hawkshead-croft.com

Large house, with garden and private parking, converted into holiday flats. In village of Hawkshead on B5286 from Ambleside.

open All year
payment Credit/debit cards, cash/cheques

Unit General Leisure

HAWKSHEAD, Cumbria Map ref 5A3

★★★
SELF CATERING

Units **1**
Low season per wk
£229.00–£274.00
High season per wk
£324.00–£448.00

Meadow View, Ambleside

Blakes Cottages, Earby, Barnoldswick BB94 0AA
t 0870 336 7777 **w** blakes.cottages.co.uk

Three-hundred-year-old cottage in the centre of Hawkshead. Entrance hall, bathroom, twin bedroom, double bedroom with wash basin and separate wc, kitchen and living accommodation. Central heating.

payment Credit/debit cards, cash/cheques

Unit General 11 P Leisure Shop < 0.5 miles Pub < 0.5 miles

HIGH LANE, Greater Manchester Map ref 4B2

★★★★
SELF CATERING

Units **1**
Sleeps **1–6**
Low season per wk
£250.00–£300.00
High season per wk
£350.00–£400.00

Ty Coch, Stockport

contact Mrs Jane Beard, Ty Coch, 1 Huron Crescent, Lakeside, Cardiff CF23 6DT
t (029) 2076 1888

Two-bedroom bungalow. The kitchen has all facilities with TVs in the lounge and bedrooms. Enclosed rear garden. Good local walks. Close to Lyme Park and Peak District National Park.

open All year
payment Cash/cheques

Unit General P Leisure

HIGH LORTON, Cumbria Map ref 5A3

★★★
SELF CATERING

Units **3**
Sleeps **2–8**
Low season per wk
£195.00–£420.00
High season per wk
£320.00–£745.00

High Swinside Holiday Cottages, High Lorton

contact Jacques Hankin, High Swinside Holiday Cottages, High Swinside Farm, High Lorton CA13 9UA
t (01900) 85206 **f** (01900) 85451 **e** bookings@highswinside.demon.co.uk
w highswinside.demon.co.uk

open All year
payment Credit/debit cards, cash/cheques

Former hill farm, overlooking Lorton Vale with stunning views and offering peace and tranquillity. Well-equipped cottages. Large groups (up to 14) can be catered for. Children welcome. Beams and log fires, together with meal service, make for a wonderful stay. Full details on our website.

⊕ *A66 to Braithwaite, Whinlatter Pass, past visitor centre, left along small road to Hopebeck and narrow-gated road. Left at fork, through gate, property below 1st gate.*

Unit General P Leisure Shop 2 miles Pub 2 miles

HIGH LORTON, Cumbria Map ref 5A3

★★★★
SELF CATERING

Units **1**
Sleeps **2**
Low season per wk
£225.00–£260.00
High season per wk
£295.00–£380.00

Holemire Barn, Cockermouth

contact Angela Fearfield, Holemire Barn, Holemire House, Cockermouth CA13 9TX
t (01900) 85225 **e** enquiries@lakelandbarn.co.uk **w** lakelandbarn.co.uk

open All year
payment Cash/cheques

Traditional Lakeland barn with exposed beams, converted to quality accommodation. In beautiful Lorton Vale, overlooking local fells. Close to Keswick and northern Lakes. Warm in winter, light and sunny in summer. Situated in the midst of superb walking country. All prices include electricity, central heating and linen. Tennis courts nearby.

⊕ *M6 jct 40, follow A66 to Keswick. Turn left onto Whinlatter pass B5292. Holemire House and Barn are on the right opposite turning to Low Lorton.*

Unit General **P** Leisure Shop < 0.5 miles Pub < 0.5 miles

HUTTON ROOF, Cumbria Map ref 5A2

★★★★★
SELF CATERING

Units **4**
Sleeps **2–20**
Low season per wk
£395.00–£1,495.00
High season per wk
£395.00–£1,495.00

Carrock Cottages, Penrith

contact Malcolm & Gillian Iredale, Carrock Cottages, Carrock House, How Hill, Hutton Roof CA11 0XY
t (01768) 484111 **f** (01768) 488850 **e** info@carrockcottages.co.uk **w** carrockcottages.co.uk

payment Credit/debit cards, cash/cheques

Luxury in a quiet, rural location near the lovely villages of Hesket Newmarket, Caldbeck and Greystoke. Explore the northern Lake District or head north to historic Carlisle and on to Hadrian's Wall. Restaurants, fell-walking and other activities. A warm welcome guaranteed. Prices differ at Christmas, New Year and Easter.

⊕ *From M6 jct 41, take B5305 for approx 8 miles; left into Lamonby Village. 1st right at 1st crossroads. Cottages on left, 800m after the wishing well.*

❤ *15% discount on second week of stay.*

Unit General **P** Leisure Shop 5 miles Pub 5 miles

KENDAL, Cumbria Map ref 5B3

★★★★
SELF CATERING

Units **4**
Sleeps **2–18**
Low season per wk
£200.00–£240.00
High season per wk
£255.00–£420.00

Shaw End Mansion, Kendal

contact Mr & Mrs Robinson, Haveriggs Farm, Kendal LA8 9EF
t (01539) 824220 **f** (01539) 824464 **e** robinson@fieldendholidays.co.uk **w** fieldendholidays.co.uk

open All year
payment Credit/debit cards, cash/cheques

Shaw End Mansion is set on a 200-acre farm in a beautiful location. Shaw End – a restored Georgian house – contains spacious and elegant apartments with fantastic views and walks from the doorstep. Why not rent the whole house, which is ideal for weddings and parties.

⊕ *From Kendal follow A685 to turning on the left towards Mealbank. Through village towards Patton. Follow road for 1.5 miles to turning on right to Shaw End.*

❤ *Short breaks from 2 nights available most of the year, prices from £100.*

Unit General **P** Leisure Shop 3 miles Pub 3 miles

Key to symbols

Open the back flap for a key to symbols.

KESWICK, Cumbria Map ref 5A3

★★★-★★★★★
SELF CATERING

Units **3**
Sleeps **1–4**
Low season per wk
£140.00–£210.00
High season per wk
£250.00–£395.00

Belle Vue, Keswick

contact Lexie Ryder, Belle Vue, c/o Hillside, Portinscale, Keswick CA12 5RS
t (01768) 771065 **f** (01769) 771065 **e** lexieryder@hotmail.co.uk

open All year
payment Cash/cheques

Close to the heart of Keswick, this lovely Lakeland-stone residence has been superbly converted, providing very spacious, comfortable, well-appointed suites. Tariff includes central heating. Carefully owner maintained. Personal welcome. Fell-top views of Catbells/Newlands Valley from lounges. Short walk to lake/parks/theatre. Double/separate twin bedrooms.

⊕ *Directions provided once booking is confirmed.*

♥ *Short breaks, min 3 nights. Reductions for less than 4 people.*

Unit General 4 P Leisure Shop < 0.5 miles Pub < 0.5 miles

KESWICK, Cumbria Map ref 5A3

★★★★★
SELF CATERING

Units **2**
Sleeps **1–2**
Low season per wk
£320.00–£420.00
High season per wk
£420.00–£460.00

The Coach House & Derwent Cottage Mews, Keswick

contact Sue Newman, Derwent Cottage, Portinscale, Keswick CA12 5RF
t (01768) 774838 **w** derwentcottage.co.uk

open All year
payment Credit/debit cards, cash/cheques

Derwent Cottage Mews and Coach House are both one-bedroom apartments, decorated to a high standard and fully equipped. Both have access to the garden, the Coach House having double doors opening out from the living room onto an awning-covered patio. Derwent Cottage is set back from the road in its own grounds, one mile from Keswick.

⊕ *Leave the M6 at jct 40, following the A66 towards Keswick, following signs for Portinscale.*

♥ *Any 3 consecutive days at a cost of £75pn reducing to £50pn during winter months, subject to availability.*

Unit General P Shop 1 mile Pub < 0.5 miles

KESWICK, Cumbria Map ref 5A3

★★★
SELF CATERING

Units **1**
Sleeps **1–4**
Low season per wk
Min £200.00
High season per wk
Max £340.00

The Cottage, Keswick

contact Mrs Margaret Beaty, The Cottage, Birkrigg, Newlands Valley, Keswick CA12 5TS
t (01768) 778278

open All year
payment Cash/cheques

Cosy, comfortable, oak-beamed cottage, converted from a stable, nestled between the farm guesthouse and adjoining barn. Very pleasantly situated five miles from Keswick in a peaceful valley with excellent view of the surrounding range of mountains. Ideal for fell-walking. Lounge, kitchen, one double room, one twin room, shower/toilet.

⊕ *From Penrith, A66 to Keswick and Workington. Two miles past Keswick, left into Braithwaite. Keep left through Braithwaite, following signs to Buttermere. Three miles from village.*

♥ *Short breaks welcome, out of season only, from Nov-Apr.*

Unit General 2 P Shop 3 miles Pub 2 miles

KESWICK, Cumbria Map ref 5A3

★★★★
SELF CATERING

Units **5**
Sleeps **2–8**
Low season per wk
£275.00–£505.00
High season per wk
£430.00–£940.00

Croft House Holidays, Keswick

contact Mrs Boniface, Croft House Holidays, Croft House, Applethwaite CA12 4PN
t (01768) 773693 **e** holidays@crofthouselakes.co.uk **w** crofthouselakes.co.uk

open All year
payment Cash/cheques

Escape to stunning, panoramic views of Derwentwater and Borrowdale. Peaceful, rural locations in Applethwaite village, one mile from Keswick. Cottage for four and ground-floor apartment for two in a Victorian country house. Two further cottages for four and six and spacious detached barn conversion for eight with snooker room.

⊕ *From A66 roundabout on northern outskirts of Keswick, take A591 to Carlisle. After 0.5 miles, right into lane (signposted Applethwaite and Skiddaw). Croft House is on the bend.*

♥ *Short breaks (min 2 nights) Nov-Mar and at other times at short notice. Special 2- and 4-person rates.*

Unit General P Leisure Shop 1 mile Pub 1 mile

KESWICK, Cumbria Map ref 5A3

★★★★★
SELF CATERING

Units **2**
Sleeps **1–4**
Low season per wk
£265.00–£330.00
High season per wk
£450.00–£535.00

Croftlands Cottages, Thornthwaite, Keswick

contact Susan McGarvie, Croftlands Cottages, Thornthwaite, Keswick CA12 5SA
t (01768) 778300 **f** (01768) 778300 **e** robmcgarvie@lineone.net **w** croftlands-cottages.co.uk

open All year
payment Credit/debit cards, cash/cheques

Stunning cottages surrounded by fells and forest. Luxuriously appointed with log stoves, old beams and antiques. Fox Howe has king-size and twin en suite bedrooms with bath or shower for two. Squirrel has king-size four-poster bed and very special bathroom. Walks from the doorstep. Seven minutes' drive to Keswick.

⊕ *M6 jct 40, A66 signed Keswick. After 17 miles, left for Thornthwaite. Proceed for approx 1 mile, pass gallery sign and bus stop, next driveway on left.*

♥ *Short breaks available Nov-Mar, min 3 nights (excl Christmas and New Year).*

Unit General P Leisure Shop 1.5 miles Pub 1 mile

KESWICK, Cumbria Map ref 5A3

★★★
SELF CATERING

Units **4**
Sleeps **1–6**
Low season per wk
£115.00–£220.00
High season per wk
£265.00–£390.00

Derwent House and Brandelhowe, Keswick

contact Oliver & Mary Bull, Derwent House Holidays, c/o Stone Heath, Hilderstone ST15 8SH
t (01889) 505678 **f** (01889) 505679 **e** thebulls@globalnet.co.uk **w** dhholidays-lakes.com

open All year
payment Cash/cheques

Traditional stone and slate Lakeland building of character in village on north shore of Derwentwater one mile from Keswick. Comfortable, well-equipped holiday suites, one retaining old cottage grate and range and another open beams. Various views over lake and to Skiddaw. Ideal centre for walking and resting.

⊕ *From M6 jct 40, A66 past Keswick, left for Portinscale etc. Past Farmers Arms on left. After 200yds turn left. We are 60yds on left.*

♥ *Short breaks available Nov-Mar (min 2 nights).*

Unit General 6 P Leisure Shop 1 mile Pub < 0.5 miles

KESWICK, Cumbria Map ref 5A3

★★★★
SELF CATERING

Units **19**
Sleeps **2–6**
Low season per wk
£240.00–£455.00
High season per wk
£410.00–£670.00

Derwent Manor, Keswick

contact Mr David Leighton, Derwentwater Hotel (Diament Ltd), Portinscale, Keswick CA12 5RE
t (017687) 72538 **f** (017687) 71002 **e** info@derwent-manor.co.uk **w** derwent-manor.co.uk

open All year
payment Credit/debit cards, cash/cheques

Enjoy village life at this former gentleman's residence. Refurbished to provide some of the most comfortable and well-equipped apartments available, or one-bedroomed cottage within grounds. Many extras including Sunday lunch, entry to local leisure club. Pets welcome. Lake on your doorstep, with 16 acres of conservation grounds.

⊕ *From M6 jct 40 follow A66 west of Keswick. Turn into village of Portinscale past pub and turn left at sign to hotel.*

♥ *Short breaks, subject to availability.*

Unit General P Leisure Shop 2 miles Pub < 0.5 miles

KESWICK, Cumbria Map ref 5A3

★★★
SELF CATERING

Units **3**
Sleeps **2–6**
Low season per wk
£240.00–£340.00
High season per wk
£360.00–£460.00

Hillside, Keswick

contact Dr & Mrs M J & D J Wright, Fisherfield, New Road, Portinscale, Keswick CA12 5TX
t (017687) 80256 **f** (017687) 80477 **e** sparkywright@btinternet.com
w keswickhillsideapartments.co.uk

Edwardian house converted into very comfortable, self-catering apartments. The ideal location for a flexible family holiday away from the madding crowds. Free parking facilities.

open All year
payment Cash/cheques

Unit General P Leisure Shop < 0.5 miles Pub < 0.5 miles

KING'S MEABURN, Cumbria Map ref 5B3

★★★★
SELF CATERING

Units **4**
Sleeps **3–6**
Low season per wk
£190.00–£280.00
High season per wk
£290.00–£470.00

Lyvennet Cottages, Penrith

contact Margaret, Wendy & Janet Addison, Lyvennet Cottages, Keld Farm, King's Meaburn, Penrith CA10 3BS
t (01931) 714226 **f** (01931) 714228 **e** wendyaddison@yahoo.com **w** lyvennetcottages.co.uk

open All year
payment Cash/cheques

Attractive, well-furnished cottages in quiet village, overlooking the beautiful Lyvennet Valley and Lakeland hills. Some log fires in winter. Fishing, fuel and linen inclusive. Children and pets welcome. Good pub. Own woodland walks and bird-watching. Bring your own horse – excellent livery or grass. Ideal centre for Lakes, Dales, Hadrian's Wall and Scottish Borders.

⊕ *M6 jct 38, 3 miles from the B6260 (Tebay to Appleby).*

♥ *Short breaks available Oct-Mar (excl Christmas and New Year). Minimum 2 nights.*

Unit General P Leisure

WALKERS WELCOME WELCOME WALKERS

Best foot forward

Walkers feel at home in accommodation participating in our Walkers Welcome scheme. Look out for the symbol. Consider walking all or part of a long-distance route – go online at nationaltrail.co.uk.

KIRKBY LONSDALE, Cumbria Map ref 5B3

★★★★
SELF CATERING

Units 1
Sleeps 4
Low season per wk
£300.00–£350.00
High season per wk
£420.00–£500.00

Nutshell Barn, Kirkby Lonsdale

contact Mr Stephen Wightman, Keerdale Barn, Capernwray, Carnforth LA6 1AD
t (01524) 733865 **f** (01524) 733948 **e** sj@nutshell-barn.co.uk **w** nutshell-barn.co.uk

open All year
payment Cash/cheques

Luxury, Grade II Listed barn in heart of the Lune Valley, situated between lakes and dales. Quiet location. The accommodation overlooks open countryside and comprises one twin, one double and first-floor dining/kitchen with separate lounge. Log-burner. Walking distance to historic market town of Kirkby Lonsdale with shops, pubs and restaurants.

⊕ *From A65, turn for Burton and Hutton Roof, follow for 0.3 miles, take right for Biggins, follow for 0.2 miles. Nutshell Barn drive on right.*

❤ *Mid-week and weekend breaks available.*

Unit General P Leisure Shop 0.7 miles Pub 1 mile

KIRKBY LONSDALE, Cumbria Map ref 5B3

★★★★
SELF CATERING

Units 3
Low season per wk
£260.00–£360.00
High season per wk
£400.00–£460.00

Sellet Hall Cottages, Carnforth, Kirkby Lonsdale

contact Mrs Hall, Sellet Hall Cottages, Sellet Hall, Carnforth LA6 2QF
t (01524) 271865 **f** (01524) 271865 **e** sellethall@hotmail.com **w** sellethall.com

open All year
payment Cash/cheques

Unique cottages converted from 17thC barn set in the grounds of Sellet Hall, surrounded by open countryside and complemented by far-distance views over the Lune Valley, Trough of Bowland and Yorkshire Dales. All have log fires, fitted kitchens, dishwasher, microwave etc. Own gardens, patio and parking.

⊕ *From M6 jct 36 take A65 (Kirkby Lonsdale). After Kirkby Motors Garage turn right (Hutton Roof, Burton). Cottages are approx 0.75 miles on the left.*

❤ *Short breaks, subject to availability, (excl Christmas and New Year). Pets welcome.*

Unit General P Leisure

KIRKOSWALD, Cumbria Map ref 5B2

★★★★
SELF CATERING

Units 5
Sleeps 2–4
Low season per wk
£220.00–£360.00
High season per wk
£320.00–£490.00

Howscales, Penrith

contact Liz Webster, Howscales, Kirkoswald, Penrith CA10 1JG
t (01768) 898666 **f** (01768) 898710 **e** liz@howscales.co.uk **w** howscales.co.uk

Cosy, well-equipped, converted 17thC farm cottages set in open, tranquil countryside with superb views. Touring base for Eden Valley, lakes, Pennines. Brochure. Short breaks. Resident owner.

open All year
payment Credit/debit cards, cash/cheques

Unit General P Leisure Shop 1.5 miles Pub 1.5 miles

Friendly help and advice

Tourist information centres offer friendly help with accommodation and holiday ideas as well as suggestions of places to visit and things to do. You'll find contact details at the beginning of each regional section.

KNUTSFORD, Cheshire Map ref 4A2

★★★★
SELF CATERING

Units **5**
Sleeps **1–6**
Low season per wk
£415.00–£650.00
High season per wk
£415.00–£650.00

Danebury Serviced Apartments, Knutsford

contact Mr & Mrs Stephen and Pauline West, Danebury Gardens Serviced Apartments, 8 Tabley Road, Knutsford WA16 0NB
t (01565) 755219 **e** info@daneburyapartments.co.uk **w** daneburyapartments.co.uk

open All year
payment Cash/cheques, euros

Set in the town's conservation area, these self-contained apartments have been thoughtfully created from an Edwardian property of character. Choice of one, two or three bedrooms with fully equipped kitchens, bathrooms, lounge/dining areas and parking spaces. Only a stroll from the pretty town of Knutsford's restaurants, bars and boutiques. Free broadband Internet access.

⊕ *M6 jct 19, take A556 (Knutsford). Immediately after roundabout at jct 19 left into Tabley Hill Lane. Danebury Apartments on left after approx 1.5 miles.*

Unit General P Leisure Shop 0.5 miles Pub 0.5 miles

LAMPLUGH, Cumbria Map ref 5A3

★★★★
SELF CATERING

Units **1**
Sleeps **1–4**
Low season per wk
£210.00
High season per wk
£330.00

2 Folly, Workington

contact Alison Wilson, 2 Folly, c/o Dockray Nook, Lamplugh CA14 4SH
t (01946) 861151 **f** (01946) 862367 **e** dockraynook@talk21.com **w** felldykecottageholidays.co.uk

A 19thC, mid-terraced cottage situated at the base of Knock Fell. It is owner maintained and well equipped with simple decor but warm and cosy – definitely a home from home. Quiet and peaceful.

open All year
payment Cash/cheques

Unit General P S Leisure Shop 2.5 miles Pub 1 mile

LANGDALE, Cumbria Map ref 5A3

★★★–★★★★
SELF CATERING

Units **2**
Sleeps **2–10**
Low season per wk
£240.00–£870.00
High season per wk
£320.00–£2,200.00

Meadow Bank, Ambleside

contact Patricia Locke, Langdale Cottages, 17 Shay Lane, Hale Barns WA15 8NZ
t 07854 960716 **e** lockemeadowbank@aol.com **w** langdalecottages.co.uk

open All year
payment Cash/cheques

In the centre of the unspoilt village of Elterwater, Meadow Bank has fine views towards the beck and fells. It is an exceptional property, completely renovated and beautifully furnished throughout. The house has four bedrooms and three bathrooms. There is also the Garden Cottage. Leisure club facilities are included.

⊕ *From Ambleside, A593 (Langdale and Coniston). Right at Skelwith Bridge towards Langdale. After 1.5 miles, left into Elterwater. Meadow Bank is last house on left.*

❤ *4-night winter mid-week breaks for the price of 2 (Garden Cottage £130, Meadow Bank £300).*

Unit General P S Leisure Shop < 0.5 miles Pub < 0.5 miles

CYCLISTS WELCOME WELCOME CYCLISTS

A holiday on two wheels

For a fabulous freewheeling break seek out accommodation participating in our Cyclists Welcome scheme. Look out for the symbol and plan your route online at nationalcyclenetwork.org.

LINDALE, Cumbria Map ref 5A3

★★★
SELF CATERING

Units **1**
Sleeps **4–5**
Low season per wk
£200.00–£300.00
High season per wk
£350.00–£400.00

7 New Cottages, Grange-over-Sands

contact Mr & Mrs David & Margaret Potts, Lindale Property, 37 Egerton Road, Davenport, Stockport SK3 8TQ
t (0161) 285 6867 **e** lindale.cottage@ntlworld.com **w** lindale-cottage.co.uk

payment Cash/cheques, euros

Three-bedroomed semi-detached cottage with wood-burning stove at the edge of a quiet village. Close to shop and pub. Cosy winter, mid-week breaks. One double bed, twin beds, one single plus cot. The Edwardian-style resort of Grange-over-Sands is 1.5 miles away. Closed New Year.

⊕ *M6 jct 36, follow signs for A590 Barrow for 10 miles. At roundabout take B5277 (towards Grange) into Lindale village. Right up side of Lindale Inn.*

♥ *Winter mid-week breaks, Nov-Mar, 3/4 nights, £85-£115.*

Unit General P Shop < 0.5 miles Pub < 0.5 miles

LITTLE STRICKLAND, Cumbria Map ref 5B3

★★★★
SELF CATERING

Units **1**
Sleeps **2–3**
Low season per wk
£200.00–£250.00
High season per wk
£250.00–£300.00

Spring Bank, Penrith

contact Mrs J Ostle, Spring Bank, Little Strickland, c/o Meadowfield, Penrith CA10 3EG
t (01931) 716246 **e** springbank17@hotmail.com **w** holidaycumbria.co.uk

Spacious, king-/twin-bedded bungalow in quiet location. Easy access to Lakes, Dales and Eden Valley. Satisfied clients reflect quality accommodation/location. All facilities, kitchen/diner, garden, rural views. Brochure available.

open All year
payment Cash/cheques

Unit General P S Leisure Shop 3 miles Pub 2 miles

LIVERPOOL, Merseyside Map ref 4A2

★★★
SERVICED APARTMENTS

Units **6**
Sleeps **2–6**
Low season per wk
£300.00–£850.00
High season per wk
£300.00–£900.00

International Inn Serviced Apartments, Liverpool

contact Leah Williams, 4 South Hunter Street, Off Hardman Street, Liverpool L1 9JG
t (0151) 709 8135 **f** (0151) 709 8135 **e** info@internationalinn.co.uk
w internationalinnapartments.co.uk

Award-winning team excelling in customer service. Fully furnished, city centre, one- or three-bedroom apartments, available daily or long term. Ideal for city attractions and nightlife. Internet cafe.

open All year except Christmas
payment Credit/debit cards, cash/cheques

Unit General S Leisure Shop < 0.5 miles Pub < 0.5 miles

LIVERPOOL, Merseyside Map ref 4A2

★★★★
SELF CATERING

Units **1**
Sleeps **1–4**
Low season per wk
Min £400.00
High season per wk
Max £450.00

Flat 1, Medici Building, Liverpool

Executive Short Stay Homes, The Old Workshops, Bruncombe Lane, Abingdon OX13 6QU
t (01865) 321106 **f** (01865) 321101 **e** greenhavenoxford@btconnect.com
w holidayhomeoxford.co.uk

A smart two-bedroom, two-bathroom apartment located in the city centre with private secure parking and views over the Anglican cathedral. See our website for more details. Please 'phone during office hours only.

open All year
payment Cash/cheques

Unit General P S Shop < 0.5 miles Pub < 0.5 miles

Check it out

Please check prices, quality ratings and other details when you book.

LIVERPOOL, Merseyside Map ref 4A2

★★★★
SELF CATERING

Units **2**
Sleeps **4–6**
Low season per wk
Min £309.00
High season per wk
£490.00–£515.00

Port Sunlight Village Trust, Port Sunlight, Wirral

contact Mrs Sandra Nicholls, 95 Greendale Road, Port Sunlight, Wirral CH62 4XE
t (0151) 644 4801 **f** (0151) 645 8973 **e** sandra.psvt@btconnect.com **w** portsunlightvillage.com

Grade II Listed cottages located in the heart of Port Sunlight garden village amid picturesque surroundings. Within easy reach of Chester, Liverpool and North Wales.

open All year
payment Credit/debit cards, cash/cheques

Unit General P Leisure Shop 0.5 miles Pub 0.5 miles

LIVERPOOL, Merseyside Map ref 4A2

★★★★
SELF CATERING

Units **2**
Sleeps **1–8**
Low season per wk
£400.00–£600.00
High season per wk
£500.00–£600.00

Trafalgar Warehouse Apartments, Liverpool

contact Mr Ray Gibson, Trafalgar Warehouse Apartments, Appt 9/10, 17-19 Lord Nelson Street, Liverpool L3 5QB
t 07715 118419 **f** (0151) 734 4924

Fully-furnished, open-plan apartments with character features and contemporary fittings. Two double beds in each apartment, one of which is on the mezzanine floor. Luxurious bathroom with jacuzzi.

open All year
payment Credit/debit cards, cash/cheques, euros

Unit General

LONGSLEDDALE, Cumbria Map ref 5B3

★★★
SELF CATERING

Units **1**
Sleeps **2**
Low season per wk
£150.00–£200.00
High season per wk
Min £250.00

The Coach House, Kendal

contact Jenny Farmer, The Coach House, c/o Capplebarrow House, Longsleddale, Kendal LA8 9BB
t (01539) 823686 **e** jenyfarmer@aol.com **w** capplebarrowcoachhouse.co.uk

Stone-built, converted coach house with ground-floor shower room and bedroom and open staircase to first-floor kitchen and lounge. Excellent views. Located in peaceful, picturesque valley.

open All year
payment Cash/cheques

Unit General P Shop 6 miles Pub 4 miles

LYTHAM ST ANNES, Lancashire Map ref 4A1

★★★
SELF CATERING

Units **4**
Sleeps **1–5**
Low season per wk
£185.00–£255.00
High season per wk
£220.00–£290.00

Merlewood Holiday Apartments, Lytham St Annes

contact Mrs Sharon Iqbal, Merlewood Holiday Apartments, 383 Clifton Drive North, Lytham St Annes FY8 2PA
t (01253) 726082 **w** merlewoodapartments.co.uk

Self-contained apartments for couples/families. Separate kitchens and bedrooms, sea views, 50yds from promenade and town centre. Private parking.

open All year
payment Cash/cheques

Unit General P

It's all quality-assessed accommodation

Our commitment to quality involves wide-ranging accommodation assessment. Ratings and awards were correct at the time of going to press but may change following a new assessment. Please check at the time of booking.

MACCLESFIELD, Cheshire Map ref 4B2

★★★★
SELF CATERING

Units **2**
Sleeps **4–10**
Low season per wk
£250.00–£450.00
High season per wk
£450.00–£550.00

Common Barn Cottages, Rainow, Macclesfield

contact Geoff & Rona Cooper, Common Barn Self-Catering Cottages, Common Barn Farm, Smith Lane, Rainow, Macclesfield SK10 5XJ
t (01625) 574878 **e** g-greengrass@hotmail.com **w** cottages-with-a-view.co.uk

open All year
payment Credit/debit cards, cash/cheques

A superb barn conversion situated on a working (sheep) hill farm 1,200ft above sea level. Set amongst the rolling hills of the Peak District National Park with breathtaking views of the Cheshire plain and across to the Welsh mountains.

Unit General P Leisure Shop 3 miles Pub 0.5 miles

MACCLESFIELD, Cheshire Map ref 4B2

★★★
SELF CATERING

Units **1**
Sleeps **6**
Low season per wk
£175.00–£190.00
High season per wk
£190.00–£280.00

Mill House Farm Cottage, Macclesfield

contact Mrs Lynne Whittaker, Mill House Farm Cottage, Mill House Farm, Macclesfield SK11 0NZ
t (01260) 226265 **e** lynne_whittaker@yahoo.co.uk **w** geocities.com/farm_cottage

Comfortable, spacious cottage on 130-acre dairy farm bordering the Peak District. Beautiful surrounding countryside and convenient for Alton Towers, Potteries, Chester, Manchester Airport.

open All year except Christmas and New Year
payment Cash/cheques

Unit General P Leisure

MANCHESTER AIRPORT

See under Knutsford

MAULDS MEABURN, Cumbria Map ref 5B3

★★★★
SELF CATERING

Units **1**
Sleeps **6**
Low season per wk
£260.00–£280.00
High season per wk
£440.00–£460.00

The Stable, Crosby Ravensworth, Penrith

contact Mrs Christine Jackson, Wickerslack Farm, Crosby Ravensworth, Penrith CA10 2LN
t (01931) 715236

Recently renovated, clean, warm and cosy cottage. Peaceful, rural setting with superb views. One king-size bedroom, one double and one twin (all on ground and first floor), two bathrooms. Patio and barbecue.

open All year
payment Cash/cheques

Unit General P Leisure Shop 3 miles Pub 2 miles

MIDDLEWICH, Cheshire Map ref 4A2

★★★–★★★★★
SELF CATERING

Units **2**
Sleeps **4–5**
Low season per wk
£250.00–£320.00
High season per wk
£375.00–£450.00

Forge Mill Farm Cottages, Warmingham

contact Mrs Susan Moss, Forge Mill Farm, Forge Mill Lane, Warmingham, Middlewich CW10 0HQ
t (01270) 526204 **f** (01270) 526204 **e** forgemill2@msn.com

open All year
payment Cash/cheques

Barn, recently converted to a high standard to create beautiful cottages. Located in a peaceful situation, ideal for a long-weekend break, peaceful holiday or business trip. Forge Masters is the larger cottage and is suitable for the partially disabled. Millers is smaller but has its own special charm. Equipped with all modern conveniences.

⊕ *M6 jct 18, A54 Middlewich. At lights, left (A533). After 40mph sign, right, then immediately left into Warmingham Lane. Right at T-junction (1.75 miles), then we're on right.*

❤ *3-night stays available all year.*

Unit General P Leisure

MOORHOUSE, Cumbria Map ref 5A2

★★★★
SELF CATERING

Units **1**
Sleeps **9**
Low season per wk
£490.00–£670.00
High season per wk
£730.00–£1,050.00

Low Moor House, Carlisle

contact Mr Ron Palmer, Low Moor House, Manor Croft, Moorhouse, Carlisle CA5 6EL
t (01228) 575153 **e** info@lowmoorhouse.co.uk **w** lowmoorhouse.co.uk

open All year
payment Cash/cheques

Charming Grade II Listed country house dating from 1734. Spacious, yet with the ambience of a cottage – beamed ceilings and cosy snug rooms. Altogether an ideal, quiet retreat for a relaxing self-contained holiday in a beautiful, little-known part of Cumbria.

⊕ *From Carlisle take A595 then B5307 (Kirkbride Road). Follow this road 4 miles to Moorhouse and turn left. Low Moor House on right.*

❤ *Short breaks available – call for details.*

Unit General P Leisure Shop 2 miles
Pub < 0.5 miles

MUNGRISDALE, Cumbria Map ref 5A2

Rating Applied For
SELF CATERING

Units **5**
Sleeps **2–7**
Low season per wk
£250.00–£375.00
High season per wk
£350.00–£575.00

Near Howe Cottages, Penrith

contact Steve & Jill Woolley, Near Howe Hotel and Cottages, Near Howe, Mungrisdale, Penrith CA11 0SH
t (01768) 779678 **f** (01768) 779462 **e** wswoolley@tiscali.co.uk **w** nearhowe.co.uk

open All year
payment Cash/cheques, euros

The ideal answer for a stress-free, away-from-it-all holiday, set amidst 350 acres of open moorland. All cottages have spectacular views over the Cumbrian Fells. Comfortable bar with real fire. Large garden with relaxation areas. Easily accessible, yet isolated enough to ensure peace and tranquillity.

⊕ *From M6 jct 40, travel west towards Keswick (A66). Pass Troutbeck after 9 miles. After 1 mile, turn right to Mungrisdale/Caldbeck. Near Howe is 1 mile on the right.*

Unit General P Leisure Shop 5 miles Pub 2 miles

Star ratings

Further information about star ratings can be found at the back of this guide.

NETHER KELLET, Lancashire Map ref 5B3

★★★
SELF CATERING

Units **1**
Sleeps **3–4**
Low season per wk
Min £155.00
High season per wk
Min £235.00

The Apartment, Nether Kellet

contact Mr Richardson, The Apartment, 10 Meadowcroft, Carnforth LA6 1HN
t (01524) 734969 & (01524) 736331

One-bedroomed, self-contained flat with extensive, private gardens in peaceful, rural village. Secluded cul-de-sac location.

open All year
payment Cash/cheques

Unit General Leisure Shop < 0.5 miles Pub < 0.5 miles

NEWBY BRIDGE, Cumbria Map ref 5A3

★★★★
SELF CATERING

Units **1**
Sleeps **2–4**
Low season per wk
£230.00–£365.00
High season per wk
£365.00–£500.00

Woodland Cottage, Newby Bridge

contact Mr Newton, Newby Bridge Country Caravan Park, c/o Fellside Lodge, Canny Hill LA12 8NF
t (015395) 31030 **f** (015395) 30105 **e** info@cumbriancaravans.co.uk **w** cumbriancaravans.co.uk

Detached cottage with two en suite bedrooms, in own private gardens within the award-winning Newby Bridge Caravan Park. All on one level.

open All year except Christmas and New Year
payment Credit/debit cards, cash/cheques, euros

Unit General Leisure Shop < 0.5 miles Pub 1 mile

NEWTON-IN-BOWLAND, Lancashire Map ref 4A1

Rating Applied For
SELF CATERING

Units **1**
Sleeps **5**
Low season per wk
Min £250.00
High season per wk
Max £470.00

Stonefold Holiday Cottage, Clitheroe

contact Mrs Helen Blanc, Stonefold Farm, Slaidburn Road, Newton-in-Bowland BB7 3DL
t 07966 582834 **w** stonefoldholidaycottage.co.uk

open All year
payment Cash/cheques

Idyllic, recently renovated barn with spectacular views. Beautifully maintained throughout with exposed beams and flagged floors. Spacious open-plan lounge with well-equipped oak kitchen, ground-floor twin bedroom and shower/wet room, first-floor en suite double bedroom and a cosy single bedroom. Ideally situated for walking, cycling and touring.

⊕ *From Clitheroe, take the B6478 (signposted Waddington). On reaching Waddington, follow signs to Newton. After approx 4 miles turn left at 'Stonefold' sign. Property 1 mile.*

Unit General Leisure Shop 5 miles Pub 3 miles

PATTERDALE, Cumbria Map ref 5A3

★★★★
SELF CATERING

Units **1**
Sleeps **12–15**
Low season per wk
£1,270.00–£1,500.00
High season per wk
£1,980.00–£2,200.00

Broad How, Penrith

contact Dr & Mrs Wynne-Willson, 28 Garland Way, Northfield B31 2BT
t (0121) 475 6508 **e** williamww@aol.com **w** broad-how.co.uk

open All year
payment Credit/debit cards, cash/cheques

Beautiful, large, 1850s family house, sensitively and comfortably modernised. Log fire, piano, pool table, books and games. In stunning Lakeland scenery, one mile from Ullswater with its steamer service (April to October), sailing, swimming etc. Marvellous fell walking, and within easy reach of small towns for non-walkers. Property number 8478.

⊕ *For travel directions please see our website.*

Unit General Leisure
Shop < 0.5 miles Pub < 0.5 miles

PENRITH, Cumbria Map ref 5B2

★★★★
SELF CATERING

Units 3
Sleeps 2–3
Low season per wk
£280.00–£340.00
High season per wk
£310.00–£390.00

Stonefold, Ullswater

contact Gill Harrington, Stonefold Cottages, Newbiggin, Stainton CA11 0HP
t (01768) 866383 **f** (01768) 866383 **e** gill@stonefold.co.uk **w** stonefold.co.uk

open All year
payment Credit/debit cards, cash/cheques

These superbly appointed self-catering holiday cottages offer the comfort you'd expect in a modern hotel, but with the addition of all the personal touches which go to make them a home from home. Situated in a beautiful panoramic position bordering the Lake District, Eden Valley and the majestic Pennines. Leisure facilities available nearby.

⊕ *Leave M6 at jct 40, take A66 Keswick road. Straight over roundabout at Rheged centre and turn right at sign, for Newbiggin. Stonefold one minute's drive on left.*

Unit General Leisure Shop 1 mile Pub 1 mile

RIBBLE VALLEY

See under Newton-in-Bowland

ROCHDALE, Greater Manchester Map ref 4B1

★★★
SELF CATERING

Units 1
Sleeps 5
Low season per wk
£220.00–£250.00
High season per wk
£240.00–£300.00

Pennine Cottages, Wardle, Rochdale

contact Mrs Joy Mitchell, 2 Pennine Cottages, Lower House Lane, Wardle, Rochdale OL12 9PL
t (01706) 379632 **w** hometown.aol.co.uk/penninecottage/myhomepage/business.html/

Stone-built farm cottage on a working sheep farm. Three bedrooms. Baby facilities on request, at no extra charge.

open All year
payment Cash/cheques, euros

Unit General Leisure Shop 1 mile Pub 1 mile

RYDAL, Cumbria Map ref 5A3

★★★
SELF CATERING

Units 1
Sleeps 2–6
Low season per wk
£250.00–£300.00
High season per wk
£450.00–£575.00

Hall Bank Cottage – Rydal Estate, Ambleside

contact Janet Horne, Carter Jonas, 52 Kirkland, Kendal LA9 5AP
t (01539) 814902 **f** (01539) 814902 **e** janet.horne@carterjonas.co.uk

open All year
payment Cash/cheques

Delightful 17thC detached cottage set centrally within a large rural estate, held by one family since 1480. Spacious, yet cosy with log fire. Large private garden and ample off-road parking. Superb location at foot of Nab Scar. Historic Rydal Mount, Rydal Hall and gardens immediately adjacent.

⊕ *Rydal is midway between Ambleside and Grasmere on A591. Hall Bank Cottage is situated on side road halfway up Rydal Hill opposite entrance to Rydal Hall.*

❤ *Short breaks available.*

Unit General Leisure

How many beds?

The minimum and maximum number of people that each property can accommodate is shown. If an entry includes details of more than one property the sleeping capacity may vary between them. Please check when you make your booking.

ST BEES, Cumbria Map ref 5A3

★★★★
SELF CATERING

Units 1
Sleeps 6
Low season per wk
Min £295.00
High season per wk
Min £395.00

Tarn Flatt Cottage, Whitehaven

contact Janice Telfer, Tarn Flatt Cottage, Tarn Flatt Hall, Sandwith CA28 9UX
t (01946) 692162 **e** stay@tarnflattfarm.co.uk **w** tarnflattfarm.co.uk

Charming three-bedroomed cottage with panoramic sea views. Quiet location.

open All year
payment Cash/cheques

Unit General Leisure **Shop** 2 miles **Pub** 1 mile

SAWREY, Cumbria Map ref 5A3

★★★★
SELF CATERING

Units 1
Sleeps 2
Low season per wk
£285.00–£385.00
High season per wk
£397.00–£496.00

West Vale Cottage, Sawrey

contact Glynn & Dee Pennington, West Vale Country House & Restaurant, Far Sawrey, Hawkshead LA22 0LQ
t (015394) 42817 **f** (015394) 45302 **e** enquiries@westvalecountryhouse.co.uk
w westvalecountryhouse.co.uk

West Vale is situated in the heart of Beatrix Potter Country, whose house, Hill Top, is a few minutes' walk away. Central to exploring all the Lake District has to offer. Cottage lets Saturday to Saturday. No children, no pets.

open All year
payment Cash/cheques

Unit General P Leisure **Shop** < 0.5 miles **Pub** < 0.5 miles

SEDBERGH, Cumbria Map ref 5B3

★★★
SELF CATERING

Units 1
Sleeps 6
Low season per wk
£245.00–£270.00
High season per wk
£345.00–£395.00

4 Railway Cottages, Sedbergh

contact Wendy Mills, 4 Railway Cottages, c/o 131 Glendale Gardens, Leigh-on-Sea SS9 2BE
t (01702) 478846 **e** trewen@clara.co.uk **w** dalescottages.com

Ex-railwayman's cottage alongside Garsdale Station. Two doubles, one bunk plus cot. Fully double glazed, comfortably furnished, panoramic views. Everything you need for a relaxing and enjoyable holiday.

open All year
payment Credit/debit cards, cash/cheques, euros

Unit General P **Shop** 5 miles **Pub** 1 mile

SOUTHPORT, Merseyside Map ref 4A1

★★★★
SELF CATERING

Units 2
Sleeps 1–6
Low season per wk
£285.00–£350.00
High season per wk
£325.00–£410.00

Martin Lane Farmhouse Holiday Cottages, Burscough

contact Mrs Stubbs, Martin Lane Farmhouse Holiday Cottages, Ormskirk L40 8JH
t (01704) 893527 **f** (01704) 893527 **e** mlfhc@btinternet.com
w martinlanefarmhouse.btinternet.co.uk

open All year
payment Cash/cheques, euros

Beautiful, award-winning country cottages, nestling in the rich arable farmland of West Lancashire and just four miles from Southport and the seaside. Our cottages have a friendly, relaxed, family atmosphere. The ideal base for visiting all the North West's major attractions.

⊕ *From A59 take B5242. After 2 miles turn right (Drummersdale Lane). 1st right (Merscar Lane). Right onto Martin Lane, over canal, 200yds.*

♥ *10% discount on 2-week bookings.*

Unit General P Leisure

SOUTHPORT, Merseyside Map ref 4A1

★★★
SELF CATERING

Units 5
Sleeps 2–6
Low season per wk
Min £150.00
High season per wk
Max £320.00

Sandy Brook Farm, Southport

contact Mr Core, Sandy Brook Farm, 52 Wyke Cop Road, Scarisbrick, Southport PR8 5LR
t (01704) 880337 & 07719 468712 **e** sandybrookfarm@lycos.co.uk **w** sandybrookfarm.co.uk

Converted barn offering self-catering apartments furnished in traditional style with all modern amenities. Three-and-a-half miles from Southport in rural area of Scarisbrick. Adapted apartment for disabled guests.

open All year
payment Cash/cheques

Unit General P Leisure Shop 2 miles Pub 1 mile

STAVELEY, Cumbria Map ref 5A3

★★★
SELF CATERING

Units 4
Sleeps 2–5
Low season per wk
£230.00–£260.00
High season per wk
£350.00–£500.00

Brunt Knott Farm Holiday Cottages, Kendal

contact William & Margaret Beck, Brunt Knott Farm Holiday Cottages, Brunt Knott Farm, Kendal LA8 9QX
t (01539) 821030 **f** (01539) 821221 **e** margaret@bruntknott.demon.co.uk
w bruntknott.demon.co.uk

open All year
payment Cash/cheques

Cosy cottages on small, secluded, 17thC hill farm. Peaceful, elevated, fellside location with superb panoramic views over Lakeland fells. Five miles from Windermere/Kendal. Cycling/lovely walks from your doorstep. Central heating. Three cottages with wood-burner/open fire. Parking. Laundry facilities. Winter short breaks available. Brochure available.

⊕ *M6 jct 36, A590/A591 to Staveley, 10 miles. Right into Staveley.*

Unit General P Leisure Shop 1.5 miles Pub 1.5 miles

THORNLEY, Lancashire Map ref 4A1

★★★★
SELF CATERING

Units 2
Sleeps 4–10
Low season per wk
£240.00–£470.00
High season per wk
£345.00–£700.00

Loudview Barn, Preston

contact Mr & Mrs Oliver & Ness Starkey, Loudview Barn, Rams Clough Farm, Thornley, Preston PR3 2TN
t (01995) 61476 **e** loudview@ic24.net

open All year
payment Cash/cheques

Stone barn conversion in peaceful location on fellside in Forest of Bowland, enjoying exceptional views across unspoilt countryside. Accommodation in two units that can be combined. Unit 1 comprises one double, one twin and pair of bunk beds. Unit 2 comprises one double and one twin.

⊕ *Easy access from M6, mainline rail and airports (Manchester and Liverpool in 1 hour).*

Unit General P Leisure Shop 4 miles Pub 2 miles

Pool search

If a swimming pool is an essential element of your holiday accommodation check out the special index at the back of this guide.

THRELKELD, Cumbria Map ref 5A3

★★★
SELF CATERING

Units 2
Sleeps 2–6
Low season per wk
£200.00–£275.00
High season per wk
£325.00–£475.00

Blencathra Centre, Keswick

contact Tim Foster, Blencathra Centre, Threlkeld, Keswick CA12 4SG
t (01768) 779601 **f** (01768) 779264 **e** enquiries.bl@field-studies-council.org

Cottages high on the slopes of Blencathra, in grounds of award-winning Eco-Centre. Walking from the door. Brochure available, dogs welcome.

open All year except Christmas
payment Credit/debit cards, cash/cheques

Unit General Leisure Shop 6 miles Pub 1 mile

THURSTONFIELD, Cumbria Map ref 5A2

★★★★–★★★★★
SELF CATERING

Units 7
Sleeps 2–6
Low season per wk
£318.00–£589.00
High season per wk
£552.00–£1,076.00

The Tranquil Otter, Thurstonfield, Carlisle

contact Richard & Wendy Wise, The Tranquil Otter Ltd, The Lough, Thurstonfield CA5 6HB
t (01228) 576661 **f** (01228) 576662 **e** info@thetranquilotter.co.uk **w** thetranquilotter.co.uk

open All year
payment Credit/debit cards, cash/cheques, euros

Well-equipped lodges with picture-book views set in private nature reserve right on the lakeshore in peaceful beauty spot. Log-burner, jacuzzi bath/sauna or hot tub. Wonderful nature (including otters). Private lakeside walks. Own rowing boat. Fly fishing. Outstanding wheelchair access with wheely boat and mobility scooter.

⊕ *Adjacent to the village of Thurstonfield in North Cumbria. Five miles west of Carlisle on the B5307.*

Unit General Leisure
Shop < 0.5 miles Pub 2 miles

TIRRIL, Cumbria Map ref 5B2

★★★★
SELF CATERING

Units 5
Sleeps 1–9
Low season per wk
£120.00–£470.00
High season per wk
£220.00–£890.00

Tirril Farm Cottages, Penrith

contact David Owens, Tirril Farm Cottages, Tirril View, Penrith CA10 2JE
t (01768) 864767 **f** (01768) 864767 **e** enquiries@tirrilfarmcottages.co.uk **w** tirrilfarmcottages.co.uk

open All year
payment Cash/cheques

Easily accessible, two miles from Ullswater, these tasteful barn conversions enjoy a quiet courtyard setting with outstanding views over the fells. Tirril is an attractive village with prize-winning pub/restaurant. Ideal for visiting the Lakes and Eden Valley. Short breaks welcome.

⊕ *M6 jct 40, A66 Scotch Corner for 1 mile then A6 Shap for 0.5 miles. Right onto B5320 to Tirril. Left at village green – Tirril Farm Cottages 100m.*

Unit General Leisure Shop 2 miles Pub < 0.5 miles

Prices

These are shown for one week's accommodation. If an entry includes details of more than one property it is usual that the minimum price is for low season in the smallest property and the maximum price is for high season in the largest property.

TORVER, Cumbria Map ref 5A3

★★★
SELF CATERING

Units **3**
Sleeps **2–5**
Low season per wk
£280.00
High season per wk
£375.00–£525.00

Sunny Bank Mill, Coniston

contact Claire Wildsmith, Sunny Bank Mill, c/o Fayrer Garden House Hotel, Lyth Valley Road, Bowness-on-Windermere LA23 3JP
t (015394) 47474 **f** (015394) 45986 **e** lakescene@fayrergarden.com **w** sunnybankmill.com

Delightful conversion of typical Lakeland watermill in idyllic setting beside Torver Beck. Wooded grounds include private access to Coniston Water. Four miles from Coniston village, the perfect base for walking.

open All year
payment Credit/debit cards, cash/cheques

Unit General P Shop 2 miles Pub 2 miles

ULLSWATER, Cumbria Map ref 5A3

★★★
SELF CATERING

Units **4**
Sleeps **1–5**
Low season per wk
£290.00–£550.00
High season per wk
£350.00–£560.00

Land Ends Cabins, Watermillock

contact Mrs B Murphy, Land Ends Country Lodge, Watermillock, Ullswater CA11 0NB
t (01768) 486438 **f** (01768) 486903 **e** infolandends@btinternet.com **w** landends.co.uk

open All year
payment Cash/cheques, euros

For those seeking total relaxation, Land Ends is ideal. Only one mile from Ullswater, our detached log cabins have a peaceful, fellside location in 25-acre grounds with two pretty lakes, red squirrels, ducks and wonderful birdlife. Inside, exposed logs and comfortable furnishings give a cosy, rustic appeal. Dogs welcome.

⊕ *M6 jct 40, A66 towards Keswick for 4 miles. Left at 1st sign for Hutton. Keep straight on for 2 miles, entrance is on the right.*

♥ *Short breaks available.*

Unit General P S Leisure Shop 3 miles Pub 1.5 miles

ULLSWATER, Cumbria Map ref 5A3

★★★
SELF CATERING

Units **5**
Sleeps **6–14**
Low season per wk
£195.00–£668.00
High season per wk
£245.00–£1,430.00

Swarthbeck Farm Holiday Cottages, Howtown-on-Ullswater, Penrith

contact Mr & Mrs W H Parkin, Swarthbeck Farm Holiday Cottages, Swarthbeck Farm, Howtown-on-Ullswater, Penrith CA10 2ND
t (017684) 86432 **e** whparkin@ukonline.co.uk

Properties on 160-acre farm overlooking Ullswater. Private access to lake. Visitors may bring own boats and horses. Owners' boats and mountain bikes available for visitors' use.

open All year
payment Cash/cheques

Unit General P S Leisure Shop 2 miles Pub 2 miles

ULVERSTON, Cumbria Map ref 5A3

★★★★
SELF CATERING & SERVICED APARTMENTS

Units **5**
Sleeps **2–17**
Low season per wk
£265.00–£890.00
High season per wk
£499.00–£1,950.00

Ashlack Cottages, Kirkby-in-Furness

t (01229) 889888 **f** (01229) 889111 **e** enquiries@ashlackcottages.co.uk **w** ashlackcottages.co.uk

Luxury holiday cottages, surrounded by farmland, overlooking the Duddon estuary, providing excellent accommodation.

open All year
payment Credit/debit cards, cash/cheques

Unit General P S Leisure Shop 2 miles Pub 1 mile

ULVERSTON, Cumbria Map ref 5A3

★★★
SELF CATERING

Units **3**
Sleeps **2–6**
Low season per wk
£240.00–£400.00
High season per wk
£350.00–£550.00

The Falls, Ulverston

contact Hilary Cheetham & Jane Unger, The Falls, Mansriggs, Ulverston LA12 7PX
t (01229) 583781 **w** thefalls.co.uk

17thC farmstead in beautiful surroundings, converted into holiday homes in traditional Lakeland style. Resident proprietors. Children and dogs welcome.

open All year
payment Cash/cheques, euros

Unit General P Leisure Shop 1 mile Pub 1 mile

WHITEHAVEN, Cumbria Map ref 5A3

★★★★
SELF CATERING

Units **2**
Sleeps **4–6**
Low season per wk
£240.00–£360.00
High season per wk
£290.00–£480.00

Rosmerta & Brighida Cottages, Whitehaven

contact David & Jane Saxon, Moresby Hall, Moresby, Whitehaven CA28 6PJ
t (01946) 696317 **f** (01946) 694385 **e** ctb@moresbyhall.co.uk **w** moresbyhall.co.uk

open All year
payment Credit/debit cards, cash/cheques, euros

Cottages adjacent to Moresby Hall, a historical, Grade I Listed building (circa 1620), managed by the owners of Moresby Hall with care and attention. Superbly equipped, delightful decor, quality furnishings and deceptively spacious. Our fine reputation brings many recommendations and repeat visits from satisfied guests each year. Many extras, including a welcome grocery pack.

⊕ *M6 jct 40, A66 past Keswick. A595 for Whitehaven. After 7 miles go past Howgate Inn on left, 1st right (Lowca/Parton). Moresby Hall 50yds on right.*

❤ *Short breaks (3 nights for the price of 2) available Nov-Mar (excl Christmas and New Year).*

Unit General P Leisure Shop 2 miles Pub 0.5 miles

WINDERMERE, Cumbria Map ref 5A3

★★★
SELF CATERING

Units **7**
Sleeps **2–6**
Low season per wk
£240.00–£350.00
High season per wk
£320.00–£600.00

Birthwaite Edge, Windermere

contact Mr Bruce Dodsworth, Birthwaite Edge, Birthwaite Road, Windermere LA23 1BS
t (015394) 42861 **e** dms@lakedge.com **w** lakedge.com

The perfect holiday base from which to explore the north. Public transport and tours nearby. In an exclusive area ten minutes' stroll from village and lake. Central for restaurants, cafes and inns.

open All year except Christmas
payment Credit/debit cards, cash/cheques, euros

Unit General P Leisure Shop 1 mile Pub 1 mile

WINDERMERE, Cumbria Map ref 5A3

★★★★
SELF CATERING

Units **1**
Sleeps **1–4**
Low season per wk
£265.00–£420.00
High season per wk
£445.00–£495.00

Gavel Cottage, Windermere

contact Mr Screeton, Screetons, 25 Bridgegate, Howden DN14 7AA
t (01430) 431201 **f** (01430) 432114 **e** howden@screetons.co.uk **w** screetons.co.uk

Secluded period cottage situated in an elevated position close to the marina. Entrance hall, open-plan lounge (with open fire), dining area and kitchen, two bedrooms, bathroom, large garden and summer house.

open All year
payment Cash/cheques

Unit General P

WINDERMERE, Cumbria Map ref 5A3

★★★
SELF CATERING

Units **4**
Sleeps **2–6**
Low season per wk
£180.00–£280.00
High season per wk
£280.00–£475.00

Langdale View Apartments, Windermere

contact Julie Marsh, Langdale View Apartments, 112 Craig Walk, Windermere LA23 3AX
t (015394) 46655 **e** enquiries@langdale-view.co.uk **w** langdale-view.co.uk

Attractive, comfortable holiday apartments with car parking. Quiet position close to village centre, lake, steamers, shops and restaurants. The apartments have fully equipped kitchens and spacious living areas.

open All year
payment Credit/debit cards, cash/cheques

Unit General Leisure Shop < 0.5 miles Pub < 0.5 miles

WINDERMERE, Cumbria Map ref 5A3

★★★
SELF CATERING

Units **3**
Sleeps **1–2**
Low season per wk
£200.00–£240.00
High season per wk
£270.00–£295.00

Winster House, Windermere

contact Mr and Mrs Whalley, Winster House, Sunny Bank Road, Windermere LA23 2EN
t (015394) 44723 **e** enquiries@winsterhouse.co.uk **w** winsterhouse.co.uk

Private parking and use of secluded garden. Five minutes' walk to shops and restaurants, ten minutes' walk to Lake Windermere. Brochure available.

open All year
payment Cash/cheques

Unit General Shop < 0.5 miles Pub < 0.5 miles

WORSTON, Lancashire Map ref 4A1

★★★★
SELF CATERING

Units **2**
Sleeps **1–4**
Low season per wk
£245.00–£275.00
High season per wk
£330.00–£400.00

Angram Green Holiday Cottages, Clitheroe

contact Ms Christine Gorrill, Worston, Clitheroe BB7 1QB
t (01200) 441455 **e** info@angramgreen.co.uk **w** angramgreen.co.uk

Farm-based cottages in rural Lancashire. Open beams and wood-burning stove. Stunning views across open countryside. Ideal base for walkers and cyclists. One double bedroom, one pair of child-size bunks.

open All year
payment Cash/cheques

Unit General Leisure Shop 2 miles Pub 0.5 miles

Take a break

Look out for special promotions and themed breaks. This could be your chance to indulge an interest, find a new one, or just relax and enjoy exceptional value! Offers are highlighted in colour (and are subject to availability).

LAKELOVERS

The Countryside Rights of Way Act gives people new rights to walk on areas of open countryside and registered common land.

To find out where you can go and what you can do, as well as information about taking your dog to the countryside, go online at countrysideaccess.gov.uk.

And when you're out and about...

Always follow the Country Code

- **Be safe – plan ahead and follow any signs**
- **Leave gates and property as you find them**
- **Protect plants and animals, and take your litter home**
- **Keep dogs under close control**
- **Consider other people**

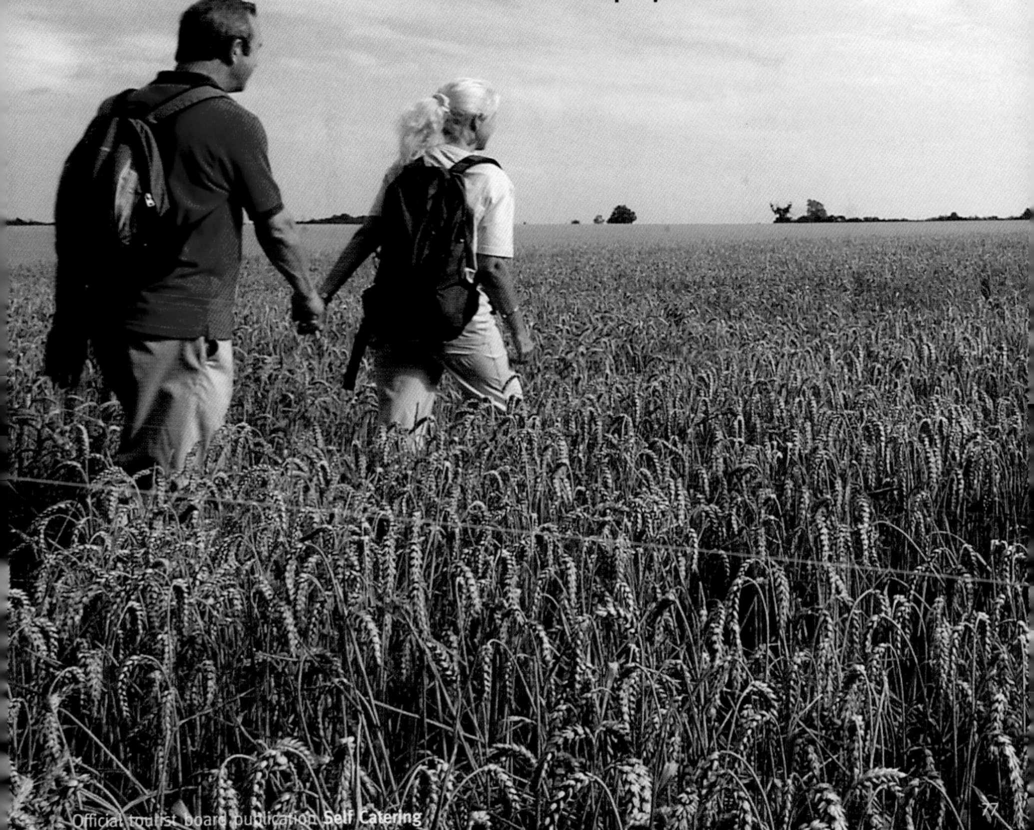

North East England

County Durham › Northumberland
Tees Valley › Tyne and Wear

Strolling through the waves towards Bamburgh Castle, Northumbria

One NorthEast Tourism Team
Stella House, Gold Crest Way, Newburn
Riverside, Newcastle upon Tyne NE15 8NY
0870 160 1781
visitnorthumbria.com

Main Stunning night-time views of The Sage Gateshead
Left The powerful beauty of High Force, near Middleton-in-Teesdale; Up for the challenge on the Hadrian's Wall Path; dazzling fountains at The Alnwick Garden, Northumberland; fantastic views of Durham Cathedral

Discover the beauty of unspoilt coastlines and breathtaking countryside, feel revived by the crisp, fresh air and experience limitless nightlife in the cities. **There's so much diversity, you'll want to come back for more.**

Explore North East England

Outdoor living

Feel exhilarated by the vast wide-open spaces of the North East. Feel the refreshing spray on your face at High Force – the highest unbroken waterfall in the country. Take up the challenge and walk one of the many National Trails through either of the National Parks. Feeling strong? Follow in Roman footsteps along the 84-mile Hadrian's Wall Path. If you're with the kids, why not walk a section of it and call in at Segedunum Roman Fort, Baths & Museum, then hop on the Hadrian's Wall Bus for a scenic tour.

Watch red squirrels scavenging the undergrowth and admire the stunning simple beauty of Kielder Water. Lose yourself in the enchantment of the surrounding forest and be inspired by the impressive visual arts and sculpture trail. Stand and gaze in awe from the base of the magnificent Angel of the North or take a day trip to The Alnwick Garden in Northumberland for a truly magical experience within the walls of this redeveloped haven.

Bright lights, big city

Treat yourself to a spending spree in Newcastle: browse Europe's largest indoor shopping complex, the MetroCentre, find all the high street shops at Eldon Square, or seek out something individual in the boutiques and markets. Relax in one of the numerous pavement cafes – cappuccino in hand – and treat yourself to an exquisite meal, taking your pick from dishes spanning the globe.

Take in a play at The Sage Gateshead – a truly magnificent building staging outstanding theatrical performances and live music.

Head to NewcastleGateshead Quayside to see spectacular architecture, and party the night away in one of the many nightclubs.

Castle central

Admire the intricate carvings as you amble softly through the aisles of Durham Cathedral and visit Durham Castle – a Norman fortress that lies just behind it. View the fabulous art collection within Raby Castle or take a trip to Barnard Castle, and then wander the streets of the picturesque town that surround it.

Whisk the kids into a world where the past comes to life at Beamish, The North of England Open Air Museum. Give them a pioneering eco experience at Nature's World or allow them to be inspired at Seven Stories, the Centre for Children's Books in Ouseburn Valley.

Adventure seeking

Take your chances with the rapids at the Four Seasons Teesside White Water Centre; push the boat out and hire a log cabin in the grounds so you can really get a feel for white-water rafting. Relax with a pair of binoculars at Farne Island – perfect for birdwatching – or take a boat trip and spot wading puffins.

Spin those spokes in Hamsterley Forest – a veritable haven for mountain bikers and indeed all manner of cyclists. Varied colours mark routes in terms of difficulty, making this ideal for all levels of riders. Alternatively, kick off your shoes and relax on the stunning Northumberland or Durham Heritage Coasts. Appreciate the uncrowded beaches and sample a local dish in a cosy pub.

Places to **visit**

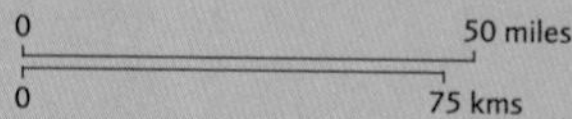

National Park

Area of Outstanding Natural Beauty

Heritage Coast

National Trails
nationaltrail.co.uk

National Trails approved but not yet open

3 Sections of the National Cycle Network
nationalcyclenetwork.org.uk

The Alnwick Garden
Northumberland
(01665) 511350
alnwickgarden.com
Magnificent and contemporary

The Angel of the North
NewcastleGateshead,
Tyne and Wear
(0191) 433 3000
gateshead.gov.uk/angel
Outstanding hillside sculpture

Baltic Centre for Contemporary Art
Gateshead, Tyne and Wear
(01914) 781810
balticmill.com
Diverse international art

Barnard Castle
County Durham
(01833) 690909
teesdalediscovery.com
Inspiring ruins of majestic Norman castle

Beamish, The North of England Open Air Museum
Stanley, County Durham
(01913) 704000
beamish.org.uk
Let the past come to life

Blue Reef Aquarium
Tynemouth, Tyne and Wear
(01912) 581031
bluereefaquarium.co.uk
Gaze from the underwater tunnel

Centre for Life
Newcastle upon Tyne,
Tyne and Wear
(01912) 438210
life.org.uk
A hands-on experience for all

Discovery Museum
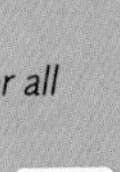
Newcastle upon Tyne,
Tyne and Wear
(01912) 326789
twmuseums.org.uk/discovery
Explore world-changing inventions

Durham Castle
(01913) 344106
durhamcastle.com
Fine example of motte and bailey

Durham Cathedral
(01913) 864266
durhamcathedral.co.uk
Beautiful Norman architecture

Four Seasons Teesside White Water Centre
Stockton-on-Tees, Tees Valley
(01642) 678000
4seasons.co.uk
Prepare for a white-knuckle ride

Hadrian's Wall Path National Trail
Hexham, Northumberland
(01912) 691600
nationaltrail.co.uk/hadrianswall
An essential and historic 84-mile trail

Hamsterley Forest
County Durham
(01388) 488312
hamsterley-trailblazers.co.uk
Cycling adventures for all ages and abilities

Kielder Water and Forest Park
Northumberland
(01434) 220643
kielder.org
Divine views and an abundance of nature

Nature's World
Middlesbrough,
County Durham
(01642) 594895
naturesworld.org.uk
A pioneering eco experience that could change you

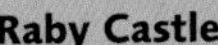

Raby Castle

Darlington, County Durham
(01833) 660202
rabycastle.com
Medieval castle with outstanding walled gardens and surrounding park

Seven Stories, the Centre for Children's Books
NewcastleGateshead,
Tyne and Wear
0845 271 0777
sevenstories.org.uk
Celebrating children's books

Segedunum Roman Fort Baths & Museum
Wallsend, Tynedale
(0191) 236 9347
twmuseums.org.uk
The most excavated fort in Britain

The Sage Gateshead
Tyne and Wear
(01914) 434666
thesagegateshead.org
Pioneering centre for musical discovery

Wet n' Wild
North Shields, Tyne and Wear
(01912) 961333
wetnwild.co.uk
Indoor waterpark with whirlpools

Tourist information centres 

When you arrive at your destination, visit a tourist information centre for help with accommodation and information about local attractions and events, or email your request before you go.

Adderstone	Adderstone Garage	(01668) 213678	adderstone@hotmail.com
Alnwick	2 The Shambles	(01665) 510665	alnwicktic@alnwick.gov.uk
Amble*	Queen Street Car Park	(01665) 712313	ambletic@alnwick.gov.uk
Barnard Castle	Woodleigh Flatts Road	(01833) 690909	tourism@teesdale.gov.uk
Bellingham	Main Street	(01434) 220616	bellinghamtic@btconnect.com
Berwick-upon-Tweed	106 Marygate	(01289) 330733	tourism@berwick-upon-tweed.gov.uk
Bishop Auckland	Market Place	(01388) 604922	bishopauckland.tourisminfo@durham.gov.uk
Corbridge*	Hill Street	(01434) 632815	corbridgetic@btconnect.com
Craster*	Craster Car Park	(01665) 576007	crastertic@alnwick.gov.uk
Darlington	13 Horsemarket	(01325) 388666	tic@darlington.gov.uk
Durham	2 Millennium Place	(0191) 384 3720	touristinfo@durhamcity.gov.uk
Gateshead (Central Library)	Prince Consort Road	(0191) 433 8400	tic@gateshead.gov.uk
Gateshead (Visitor Centre, Quayside)	St Mary's Church	(0191) 478 4222	tourism@gateshead.gov.uk
Guisborough	Church Street	(01287) 633801	guisborough_tic@redcar-cleveland.gov.uk
Haltwhistle	Station Road	(01434) 322002	haltwhistletic@btconnect.com
Hartlepool	Church Square	(01429) 869706	hpooltic@hartlepool.gov.uk
Hexham	Wentworth Car Park	(01434) 652220	hexham.tic@tynedale.gov.uk
Middlesbrough	99-101 Albert Road	(01642) 729700	middlesbrough_tic@middlesbrough.gov.uk
Middleton-in-Teesdale	10 Market Place	(01833) 641001	middletonplus@compuserve.com
Morpeth	Bridge Street	(01670) 500700	tourism@castlemorpeth.gov.uk
Newcastle International Airport		(0191) 214 4422	niatic@hotmail.com
Newcastle upon Tyne (Grainger St)	132 Grainger Street	(0191) 277 8000	tourist.info@newcastle.gov.uk
Newcastle upon Tyne (Guildhall)	Quayside	(0191) 277 8000	tourist.info@newcastle.gov.uk
North Shields	Royal Quays Outlet Shopping	(0191) 200 5895	ticns@northtyneside.gov.uk
Once Brewed*	Military Road	(01434) 344396	tic.oncebrewed@nnpa.org.uk
Otterburn	Otterburn Mill	(01830) 520093	tic@otterburnmill.co.uk
Peterlee	4 Upper Yoden Way	(0191) 586 4450	touristinfo@peterlee.gov.uk
Redcar	West Terrace	(01642) 471921	redcar_tic@redcar-cleveland.gov.uk
Rothbury*	Church Street	(01669) 620887	tic.rothbury@nnpa.org.uk
Saltburn-by-the-Sea	Station Square	(01287) 622422	saltburn_tic@redcar-cleveland.gov.uk
Seahouses*	Seafield car park	(01665) 720884	seahousestic@berwick-upon-tweed.gov.uk
South Shields	Ocean Road	(0191) 454 6612	museum.tic@southtyneside.gov.uk
South Shields (Amphitheatre)*	Sea Road	(0191) 455 7411	foreshore.tic@southtyneside.gov.uk
Stanhope	Durham Dales Centre	(01388) 527650	durham.dales.centre@durham.gov.uk
Stockton-on-Tees	Church Road	(01642) 528130	touristinformation@stockton.gov.uk
Sunderland	50 Fawcett Street	(0191) 553 2000	tourist.info@sunderland.gov.uk
Whitley Bay	Park Road	(0191) 200 8535	ticwb@northtyneside.gov.uk
Wooler*	12 Padgepool Place	(01668) 282123	woolertic@berwick-upon-tweed.gov.uk

* *seasonal opening*

Alternatively, you can text **TIC LOCATE** to **64118** to find your nearest tourist information centre

Find out **more**

Further publications are available from One NorthEast Tourism Team (unless otherwise stated) by logging on to **visitnorthumbria.com** or calling **0870 160 1781**:

› **Holiday and Short Breaks Guide**
Information on the region, including hotels, bed and breakfast and self-catering accommodation, caravan and camping parks and attractions. Call 0870 160 1781.

› **Cycling Guide**
For information on day rides, traffic-free trails and challenging routes call 0870 160 1778 for your free cycling guide.

› **Gardens Guide**
For your free guide to the region's inspirational gardens call 0870 225 5380.

› **Walking Guide**
For information on walking in North East England call 0870 225 0129 for your free walking guide.

› **Group Travel Guide**
Packed with everything tour planners need to know when planning a group visit – group hotels, attractions, destinations, itinerary suggestions, Blue Badge Guides, coach-parking locations and events. Call 0870 428 0810.

› **Educational Visits Guide**
Information for teachers planning school visits, including attractions with links to National Curriculum subjects, suitable accommodation, itinerary suggestions and events. Call (0191) 229 6845.

› **Tailored to Suit**
Aimed at group organisers, this guide includes a selection of themed itineraries offering suggestions for day tours, short breaks and long-stay holidays which can be tailored to suit the needs of the group. Call 0870 428 0810.

Travel **info**

By road:
There is excellent motorway access via the A1/A1M and A69 and A66 connecting to the M6. Within North East England you will find fast, modern interconnecting roads between all the main centres, a vast network of scenic, traffic-free country roads, which make motoring a pleasure, and frequent local bus services which operate to towns and villages.

By rail:
Direct train services operate from most cities in Britain to Newcastle's Central Station. The London to Edinburgh InterCity service stops at Darlington, Durham, Newcastle and Berwick upon Tweed. Trains make the journey between London and Newcastle in just over three hours. The London to Middlesbrough journey (changing at Darlington) takes three hours, Birmingham to Darlington just under three hours, Bristol to Durham five hours and Sheffield to Newcastle just over two hours. Regional services to areas of scenic beauty operate frequently, allowing the traveller easy access. The Tyne and Wear Metro makes it possible to travel to many destinations within the Tyne and Wear area, such as Gateshead, South Shields, Whitley Bay, Sunderland, Newcastle City Centre and Newcastle International Airport, in minutes.

By air:
Fly into Durham Tees Valley or Newcastle International airports.

where to stay in

North East England

All place names in the blue bands are shown on the maps at the front of this guide.

A complete listing of all Enjoy England assessed accommodation covered by this guide appears at the back.

Accommodation symbols
Symbols give useful information about services and facilities. Inside the back-cover flap you can find a key to these symbols. Keep it open for easy reference.

ALNMOUTH, Northumberland Map ref 5C1

★★–★★★
SELF CATERING

Units **4**
Sleeps **5**
Low season per wk
£200.00–£250.00
High season per wk
£250.00–£300.00

Wooden Farm Holiday Cottages, Alnmouth

contact Mr Gordon Farr, Wooden Farm Holiday Cottages, Lesbury, Alnmouth, Alnwick NE66 2TW
t (01665) 830342

Stone-built cottages in a quiet farm setting, overlooking the coast and the picturesque village of Alnmouth. Only four miles from Alnwick Castle/Garden.

open All year
payment Credit/debit cards, cash/cheques

Unit General P Leisure **Shop** 1 mile **Pub** 1 mile

ALNWICK, Northumberland Map ref 5C1

★★★★
SELF CATERING

Units **1**
Sleeps **1–8**
Low season per wk
£250.00–£350.00
High season per wk
£400.00–£500.00

3 Jubilee Court, Alnwick

contact Mrs Jenny Robinson, 8 Howick Street, Alnwick NE66 1UY
t (01665) 605153 **e** wwr@globalnet.co.uk

Within walking distance of Alnwick Garden and Castle. Three-bedroom townhouse (one double with en suite, one single, one triple bunk). Sofa bed in lounge. Quiet location, central situation. Covered, allocated parking.

open All year
payment Cash/cheques

Unit General P Leisure **Shop** < 0.5 miles **Pub** < 0.5 miles

ALNWICK, Northumberland Map ref 5C1

★★★
SELF CATERING

Units **3**
Sleeps **4–10**
Low season per wk
£250.00–£350.00
High season per wk
£350.00–£650.00

Harehope Hall, Alnwick

contact Ms Alison Wrangham, Harehope Hall, Eglingham, Alnwick NE66 2DP
t (01668) 217329 **f** (01688) 217346 **e** aliwrangham@btconnect.com

Self-catering wing of large secluded country house and riverside cottages. All facilities including linen. Spacious and comfortable. Beautiful views. Quiet and peaceful.

open All year
payment Cash/cheques

Unit General P Leisure **Shop** 4 miles **Pub** 2 miles

ALNWICK, Northumberland Map ref 5C1

★★★
SELF CATERING

Units **1**
Sleeps **1–5**
Low season per wk
£247.00–£285.00
High season per wk
£350.00–£499.00

The Pebble, Alnwick

contact Mrs Clare Laughton, Okelands,, Pickhurst Road, Chiddingfold GU8 4TS
t (01428) 683941 **e** clarelaughton@googlemail.com

Spacious, comfortable, warm, semi-detached cottage on family farm. Enclosed garden with barbecue, facing south over farmland. One double, one twin, one single. Ideal base for exploring Heritage Coast, beaches, castles and moors.

open All year
payment Cash/cheques

Unit General 4 P Leisure **Shop** < 0.5 miles **Pub** 2.5 miles

ALNWICK, Northumberland Map ref 5C1

★★★–★★★★★
SELF CATERING

Units **12**
Sleeps **1–12**
Low season per wk
£150.00–£510.00
High season per wk
£270.00–£1,650.00

Village Farm, Alnwick

contact Mrs Crissy Stoker, Town Foot Farm, Shilbottle, Alnwick NE66 2HG
t (01665) 575591 **f** (01665) 575591 **e** crissy@villagefarmcottages.co.uk **w** villagefarmcottages.co.uk

open All year
payment Credit/debit cards, cash/cheques

17thC farmhouse, cottages and beautifully appointed chalets complemented by excellent facilities – indoor heated swimming pool, health club, steam room, sauna, sunshower, beauty therapist, games room, tennis, riding, fishing and adventure playground. Situated between Alnwick and Heritage Coast. A warm, personal welcome.

⊕ *Travelling north – from A1 take Alnmouth/Shilbottle turn-off to right. Proceed for 1.5 miles to the village, take 1st right and 1st left. Proceed 200yds – near church.*

❤ *2-/3-night stays available Nov-Easter (excl Christmas, New Year and half-terms).*

Unit General P Leisure
Shop < 0.5 miles **Pub** < 0.5 miles

AMBLE, Northumberland Map ref 5C1

★★★
SELF CATERING

Units **1**
Sleeps **1–4**
Low season per wk
£190.00–£290.00
High season per wk
£300.00–£375.00

Acarsaid, Amble

contact Mrs Lynne Gray, 17 West Avenue, Amble NE65 0PD
t (01665) 711737

Cosy ground-floor apartment in peaceful area near the harbour and restored pier. Explore Northumberland's beautiful countryside and varied attractions.

open All year
payment Cash/cheques, euros

Unit General P Leisure **Shop** < 0.5 miles **Pub** < 0.5 miles

BAMBURGH, Northumberland Map ref 5C1

★★★–★★★★
SELF CATERING

Units **4**
Sleeps **2–6**
Low season per wk
£200.00–£400.00
High season per wk
£400.00–£600.00

Bradford Country Cottages, Bamburgh

contact Mr L W Robson, Bradford Country Cottages, Bradford House, Bamburgh NE70 7JT
t (01668) 213432 **f** (01668) 213891 **e** lwrob@tiscali.co.uk **w** bradford-leisure.co.uk

Stone-built cottages in a rural setting, two miles from Bamburgh village, full central heating and facilities, access to swimming pool included in tariff.

open All year
payment Credit/debit cards, cash/cheques

Unit General P Leisure **Shop** 2 miles **Pub** 2 miles

BAMBURGH, Northumberland Map ref 5C1

★★★★
SELF CATERING

Units **1**
Sleeps **4**
Low season per wk
Min £280.00
High season per wk
Max £585.00

The Cottage, Bamburgh

contact Mrs Turnbull, 1 Friars Court, Bamburgh NE69 7AE
t (01668) 214494 **e** theturnbulls2k@btinternet.com **w** holidaynorthumbria.co.uk

Charming, quality accommodation minutes from a beautiful sandy beach, with wonderful views of the magnificent Bamburgh Castle. Large, private gardens and parking.

open All year
payment Cash/cheques

Unit General

BAMBURGH, Northumberland Map ref 5C1

★★★★
SELF CATERING

Units **5**
Sleeps **2–8**
Low season per wk
£325.00–£795.00
High season per wk
£465.00–£1,175.00

Dukesfield Farm Holiday Cottages, Bamburgh

contact Mrs Maria Eliana Robinson, EMR Properties, The Glebe, Radcliffe Road, Bamburgh NE69 7AE
t (01668) 214456 **f** (01668) 214354 **e** eric_j_robinson@compuserve.com
w secretkingdom.com/dukes/field.htm

open All year
payment Cash/cheques

Situated just outside Bamburgh village, this attractive farmsteading offers easy access to coast, castle, beach and golf course. Spacious yet cosy cottages with first-class kitchens and bathrooms. Own paddocks. Children and household pets welcome. Ample parking. An ideal base for walking and exploring Northumberland's Heritage Coast.

⊕ *From A1 take B1341 10 miles north of Alnwick. Follow signs to Bamburgh, turn left at church (B1342). Dukesfield is located 0.75 miles on left.*

❤ *Short breaks available Nov-May.*

Unit General Leisure

BAMBURGH, Northumberland Map ref 5C1

★★★★★
SELF CATERING

Units **2**
Sleeps **2–8**
Low season per wk
£375.00–£895.00
High season per wk
£575.00–£1,395.00

Glebe House and Glebe Cottage, Bamburgh

contact Mrs Maria Eliana Robinson, EMR Properties, The Glebe, Radcliffe Road, Bamburgh NE69 7AE
t (01668) 214456 **f** (01668) 214354 **e** eric_j_robinson@compuserve.com
w secretkingdom.com/glebe/house.htm

open All year
payment Cash/cheques

This lovely 18thC vicarage has stunning views of church, castle and sea. Spacious and well furnished with full central heating included. First-class kitchen. Children and household pets welcome. Large, peaceful, private gardens. An ideal base for walking and exploring Northumberland's Heritage Coast.

⊕ *From A1, take B1341 10 miles north of Alnwick. Follow signs to Bamburgh, turn left at church (B1342). Glebe is located 300 yds on right.*

❤ *Short breaks available Nov-Mar.*

Unit General Leisure Shop < 0.5 miles
Pub < 0.5 miles

Check it out

Information on accommodation listed in this guide has been supplied by proprietors. As changes may occur you should remember to check all relevant details at the time of booking.

BAMBURGH, Northumberland Map ref 5C1

★★★★
SELF CATERING

Units 1
Sleeps 4
Low season per wk
£250.00–£320.00
High season per wk
£420.00–£500.00

Harelaw House, Bamburgh

contact Ms Zana Juppenlatz, 15 Church Hill, Chatton, Alnwick NE66 5PY
t (01668) 215494 **f** (01668) 215494 **e** zana.juppenlatz@ukonline.co.uk **w** harelawhouse.ntb.org.uk

Spacious, fully equipped house within historic Bamburgh village, five minutes from castle, village green, wide sandy beaches, restaurants, pubs and tea shops. Open-plan dining room/kitchen, wood-burning stove. South-facing conservatory, landscaped garden.

open All year
payment Credit/debit cards, cash/cheques

Unit General P Leisure Shop < 0.5 miles Pub < 0.5 miles

BAMBURGH, Northumberland Map ref 5C1

★★★★
SELF CATERING

Units 16
Sleeps 2–6
Low season per wk
£247.00–£440.00
High season per wk
£402.00–£737.00

Outchester & Ross Farm Cottages, Belford

contact Mrs Shirley McKie, 1 Cragview Road, Belford NE70 7NT
t (01668) 213336 **f** (01668) 219385 **e** enquiry@rosscottages.co.uk **w** rosscottages.co.uk

open All year
payment Cash/cheques

Outchester and Ross are both in unique, secluded coastal locations in one of the most beautiful areas of Northumberland between Bamburgh and Holy Island. Our cottages are warm, comfortable and well equipped – each double glazed and with its own private garden. Relax completely and just enjoy being here.

Maps supplied on booking.

Unit General P Leisure Shop 3 miles
Pub 3 miles

BAMBURGH, Northumberland Map ref 5C1

★★★
SELF CATERING

Units 5
Sleeps 5–17
Low season per wk
£195.00–£255.00
High season per wk
£430.00–£490.00

Point Cottages, Bamburgh

contact Mrs Sanderson, 30 The Oval, Benton, Newcastle upon Tyne NE12 9PP
t (0191) 266 2800 **f** (0191) 215 1630 **e** info@bamburgh-cottages.co.uk **w** bamburgh-cottages.co.uk

Cluster of cottages, with fine sea views, located next to golf course. Furnished to a high standard with log fires and large garden.

open All year
payment Cash/cheques

Unit General P Leisure Shop 1 mile Pub 1 mile

Accessible needs?

If you have special hearing, visual or mobility needs, there's an index of all National Accessible Scheme participants at the back of this guide. Or buy a copy of our guide – Britain's Accessible Places to Stay – available from good bookshops and online at visitbritaindirect.com.

BAMBURGH, Northumberland Map ref 5C1

★★★★★
SELF CATERING

Units **3**
Sleeps **2–28**
Low season per wk
£221.00–£1,666.00
High season per wk
£394.00–£2,362.00

Waren Lea Hall, Bamburgh

contact Carolynn and David Croisdale-Appleby, Abbotsholme, Hervines Road, Amersham HP6 5HS
t (01494) 725194 **f** (01494) 725474 **e** croisdaleappleby@aol.com **w** selfcateringluxury.co.uk

open All year
payment Cash/cheques

Imposing, spacious country house on shore of Budle Bay at Waren Mill near Bamburgh in two acres of waters-edge parkland. Breathtaking, panoramic views of Lindisfarne and the Cheviots. The holiday homes can be booked individually or together. Waren Lea Hall enjoys an unrivalled location with easy access for walking, golf, fishing etc.

⊕ *From A1, 15 miles north of Alnwick, turn towards Belford Station on B1342. On reaching Waren Mill turn towards Bamburgh. Cross bridge over river. Property is 100yds on left.*

♥ *Short breaks available from Nov-Mar. Weekend breaks, 3 nights, Fri-Mon. Mid-week breaks, 4 nights, Mon-Fri.*

Unit General P Leisure Shop 1.5 miles Pub 1.5 miles

BARNARD CASTLE, County Durham Map ref 5B3

★★★★
SELF CATERING

Units **2**
Sleeps **2–5**
Low season per wk
£190.00–£225.00
High season per wk
£270.00–£425.00

Staindrop House Mews & The Arches, Darlington

contact Mrs Dorothy Walton, 14 Front Street, Darlington DL2 3NH
t (01833) 660951 **e** harry-1937@hotmail.com

open All year
payment Cash/cheques

Converted stable units comprising one/two reception rooms, bathroom, shower room, fitted kitchen and small balcony. The unit with two reception rooms also has a beamed ceiling. Pretty countryside village. Use of large, landscaped garden with children's play area. All linen provided. No pets in Arches unit.

⊕ *Staindrop village is on the A688 between Bishop Auckland and Barnard Castle. Staindrop House is on left in the village 150yds past village church on main road.*

♥ *Coal fire (first bucket of coal free). Bottle of wine in fridge.*

Unit General P Shop < 0.5 miles Pub < 0.5 miles

BARNARD CASTLE, County Durham Map ref 5B3

★★★
SELF CATERING

Units **1**
Sleeps **1–4**
Low season per wk
£180.00–£220.00
High season per wk
£220.00–£320.00

Wackford Squeers Cottage, Barnard Castle

contact Mr John Braithwaite, Wackford Squeers Cottage, Wodencroft, Cotherstone, Barnard Castle DL12 9UQ
t (01833) 650032 **f** (01833) 650909 **e** wodencroft@freenet.co.uk

Open-beamed cottage on quiet Teesdale farm in unspoilt countryside. Easy access to long-distance paths. Easy drive to lakes and Yorkshire Dales.

open All year
payment Cash/cheques

Unit General P Leisure Shop 1 mile Pub 1 mile

Check the maps

Colour maps at the front pinpoint all the places you will find accommodation entries in the regional sections. Pick your location and then refer to the place index at the back to find the page number.

BEADNELL, Northumberland Map ref 5C1

★★★★
SELF CATERING

Units **1**
Sleeps **8**
Low season per wk
£400.00–£650.00
High season per wk
£650.00–£800.00

Beechley, Chathill

contact Mrs Deborah Baker, 22 Upper Green Way, Tingley, Wakefield WF3 1TA
t (0113) 218 9176 **f** (0113) 218 9176 **e** deb_n_ade@hotmail.com

Seafront house with four bedrooms and two bathrooms. Recently refurbished throughout. Enclosed south-facing rear garden with barbecue and furniture. Sea view from all bedrooms. Fuel and linen included.

open All year except Christmas
payment Cash/cheques

Unit General P Leisure **Shop** 1 mile **Pub** 1 mile

BEADNELL, Northumberland Map ref 5C1

★★★
SELF CATERING

Units **7**
Sleeps **2–5**
Low season per wk
£170.00–£200.00
High season per wk
£400.00–£460.00

Town Farm Cottages, Chathill

contact Mr & Mrs Paul & Marianne Thompson, Marshall Thompson, Swarland, Morpeth NE65 9HZ
t (01670) 783686 **f** (01670) 786188 **e** marianne@marishalthompson.co.uk
w heritagecoastholidays.com

17thC stable block converted to cottages and apartments. Close to the sea and beaches. Short distance to Bamburgh Castle and Holy Isle. Alnwick Gardens and Castle easily accessible, plus Heritage Coast and National Park.

open All year
payment Credit/debit cards, cash/cheques, euros

Unit General P Leisure

BEAMISH, County Durham Map ref 5C2

★★★
SELF CATERING

Units **4**
Sleeps **2**
Low season per wk
£180.00
High season per wk
£190.00

Chapel House Studio Apartments, Newcastle upon Tyne

contact Mr John MacLennan, Chapel House, Causey Row, Marley Hill, Newcastle upon Tyne NE16 5EJ
t (01207) 290992 **w** chapelhouseapartments.co.uk

Studio apartments located on a quiet country lane overlooking farmland. Beamish Museum and Tanfield Railway are a short drive away and the MetroCentre can be reached in 20 minutes.

payment Cash/cheques

Unit General P S Leisure **Shop** 2 miles **Pub** < 0.5 miles

BERWICK-UPON-TWEED, Northumberland Map ref 5B1

★★★
SELF CATERING

Units **1**
Sleeps **6–10**
Low season per wk
£300.00–£500.00
High season per wk
£500.00–£700.00

2 The Courtyard, Berwick-upon-Tweed

contact Mrs Morton, 1 The Courtyard, Church Street, Berwick-upon-Tweed TD15 1EE
t (01289) 308737 **f** (01706) 817382 **e** jvm@patmosphere.uklinux.net **w** berwickselfcatering.co.uk

Secluded townhouse in the heart of old Berwick. Minutes from historic ramparts, golf course, beaches and shopping. Generous sunny verandah. Accommodation includes studio flat, double room and family room.

open All year
payment Cash/cheques, euros

Unit General 8 Leisure **Shop** < 0.5 miles **Pub** < 0.5 miles

enjoy**England**.com

Big city buzz or peaceful panoramas? Take a fresh look at England and you may be surprised at what's right on your doorstep. Explore the diversity online at enjoyengland.com.

BERWICK-UPON-TWEED, Northumberland Map ref 5B1

★★
SELF CATERING

Units **1**
Sleeps **1–5**
Low season per wk
£150.00–£190.00
High season per wk
£200.00–£350.00

Broadstone Cottage, Berwick-upon-Tweed

contact Mr Edward Chantler, Broadstone Farm, Maidstone ME17 2AT
t (01622) 850207 **f** (01622) 851750

Village cottage. Ideal centre for touring, walking and fishing holidays. Twenty minutes to beach. Shops and pubs nearby. Full central heating. Bathroom with shower. One double, one twin.

open All year
payment Cash/cheques

Unit General P

BERWICK-UPON-TWEED, Northumberland Map ref 5B1

★★★
SELF CATERING

Units **2**
Sleeps **4–6**
Low season per wk
£240.00–£280.00
High season per wk
£340.00–£390.00

West Kyloe Cottages, Berwick-upon-Tweed

contact Mrs Teresa Smalley, Garden Cottage, 1 West Kyloe, Berwick-upon-Tweed TD15 2PG
t (01289) 381279 **f** (01289) 381279 **e** teresasmalley@westkyloe.demon.co.uk **w** westkyloe.co.uk

Comfortable, well-appointed cottages with views of Holy Island and the Farnes. Within easy reach of the Cheviots, and close to the beaches and golf course. Ideal for touring the historic border region. Lovely farm walks.

open All year
payment Cash/cheques

Unit General P Shop 2 miles Pub 2 miles

BLANCHLAND, Northumberland Map ref 5B2

★★
SELF CATERING

Units **2**
Sleeps **4**
Low season per wk
£170.00
High season per wk
£170.00

Boltsburn Holiday Cottages, Consett

contact Mrs Amanda Pearson, Prospect House, Watergate Road, Consett DH8 9QS
t (01207) 506194 & (01207) 583076

Self-contained cottages in picturesque countryside, two miles Blanchland, ten miles Hexham. Hadrian's Wall, Beamish Museum, Durham Cathedral all within driving distance. Open May to September.

payment Cash/cheques

Unit General P Leisure U Shop 2 miles Pub 2 miles

CASTLESIDE, County Durham Map ref 5B2

★★–★★★
SELF CATERING

Units **3**
Sleeps **1–5**
Low season per wk
£225.00–£250.00
High season per wk
£250.00–£275.00

Derwent Grange Cottages, Consett

contact Mr & Mrs Elliot, Derwent Grange Farm, Castleside, Consett DH8 9BN
t (01207) 508358 **e** ekelliot@aol.com **w** derwentgrange.co.uk

Charming cottages converted from farm buildings, set on a working sheep farm, provide a serene, relaxing holiday. Access to wonderful countryside and tourist attractions. Friendly hosts.

open All year
payment Cash/cheques

Unit General P S Leisure Shop 1 mile Pub 1 mile

If you have access needs...

Look for the National Accessible Scheme symbols if you have special hearing, visual or mobility needs. An index of all accommodation participating in the scheme can be found at the back of this guide.

CHATHILL, Northumberland Map ref 5C1

★★★★
SELF CATERING

Units **2**
Sleeps **6**
Low season per wk
£260.00–£375.00
High season per wk
£370.00–£595.00

The Lodge and Head Gardener's House, Chathill

contact Mrs J Shirley Burnie, The Lodge and Head Gardener's House, Doxford Hall, Chathill NE67 5DN
t (01665) 589499 **f** (01665) 589499 **e** doxfordhall@aol.com

open All year
payment Cash/cheques, euros

Grade II Listed Victorian gardener's house – one double and two twin-bedded rooms, open fire, central heating. Separate sitting and dining room. Modern breakfasting kitchen. Grade II Listed Victorian lodge – one double, one twin and one single bedroom, open fire, central heating, hexagonal lounge with surrounding verandah.

⊕ *North on the A1, turn at B1340 to Seahouses. Continue for approx 3 miles, left to Seahouses. Left again after about 100yds, signposted Doxford Hall.*

❤ *Weekend and mid-week breaks Oct-Mar.*

Unit General P Shop 2 miles Pub 2 miles

CHATTON, Northumberland Map ref 5B1

★★★
SELF CATERING

Units **1**
Sleeps **2**
Low season per wk
£150.00–£240.00
High season per wk
£260.00–£330.00

Percy Cottage, Alnwick

contact Miss Helen Cunningham, The Property Investments, Jamarus Lodge, Kirknewton, Wooler NE71 6XF
t (01668) 216556 **e** tonyreedjones@aol.com **w** percycottage.co.uk

Attractive stone cottage set in village of Chatton, beautifully refurbished and offering spacious, well-equipped accommodation.

open All year
payment Cash/cheques

Unit General P Shop < 0.5 miles Pub < 0.5 miles

COCKFIELD, County Durham Map ref 5B3

★★★★
SELF CATERING

Units **2**
Sleeps **4–5**
Low season per wk
Min £150.00
High season per wk
Max £340.00

Stonecroft and Swallows Nest, Bishop Auckland

contact Mrs Alison Tallentire, Low Lands Farm, Bishop Auckland DL13 5AW
t (01388) 718251 **f** (01388) 718251 **e** info@farmholidaysuk.com **w** farmholidaysuk.com

open All year
payment Cash/cheques

Award-winning cottages on a working livestock farm. Both cottages beautifully renovated and decorated to an exceptionally high standard. Beams, log fires, gas barbecue, own gardens and parking. Close to Durham City, Northumberland, Lakes, Hadrian's Wall. Pets and children most welcome, childminding available. Children's equipment, fuels, electric, linens and towels all included.

⊕ *Directions on request.*

❤ *Mid-week and weekend breaks available out of season. Open Christmas and New Year.*

Unit General P Leisure Shop 1 mile Pub 1 mile

Use your i's

Tourist information centres provide a wealth of information and friendly advice, both before you go and during your stay. Refer to the front of this section for a list of tourist information centres in the region.

CORBRIDGE, Northumberland Map ref 5B2

★★★★
SELF CATERING

Units 1
Sleeps 5
Low season per wk
£300.00–£350.00
High season per wk
£400.00

April Cottage, Corbridge

contact Mrs Kate Dean, 21 Woodland Close, Chelford, Macclesfield SK11 9BZ
t (01625) 861718 **e** peterandkatedean@btopenworld.com **w** aprilcottagecorbridge.co.uk

A 19thC cottage with living room, kitchen/dining room, two bedrooms (one with washbasin), bathroom and sheltered garden with patio area.

open All year
payment Cash/cheques

Unit **General** **Leisure** **Shop** < 0.5 miles **Pub** < 0.5 miles

CORBRIDGE, Northumberland Map ref 5B2

★★★
SELF CATERING

Units 1
Sleeps 6
Low season per wk
£295.00–£425.00
High season per wk
£495.00–£555.00

Granary Cottage, Newton

contact Mr Rob Harris, The Granary, Newton, Stocksfield NE43 7UL
t 07970 709632 **f** (01661) 843646 **e** robharris1951@hotmail.com

Superbly appointed detached cottage situated in beautiful Northumbrian village. Private garden and car parking. Ideal location for places of interest in northern England and southern Scotland.

open All year
payment Credit/debit cards, cash/cheques, euros

Unit **General** **Leisure** **Shop** 1 mile **Pub** < 0.5 miles

CORBRIDGE, Northumberland Map ref 5B2

★★★★
SELF CATERING

Units 1
Sleeps 6
Low season per wk
£300.00–£350.00
High season per wk
£400.00–£550.00

Oswald Cottage, Corbridge

contact Mrs Hannah Harriman, Oswald Cottage, Swarden House, Kyloe House Farm, Eachwick, Newcastle upon Tyne NE18 0BB
t (01661) 852909 **f** (01661) 854106 **e** hannahharriman@btinternet.com

open All year
payment Cash/cheques

Exceptional 18thC double-fronted large stone cottage. Carved external Latin inscription 'To the good all things are good' reflects interior ambience, beams and open fire. In heart of historic village but quiet. Stone's throw from river and superb local shops. Lovely patio garden. Perfect, winter or summer.

⊕ *Take B6530 from A69 signposted Corbridge. Head to Corbridge Bridge. Take right turn before bridge into Front Street.*

♥ *Weekends available.*

Unit **General** 5 **Shop** < 0.5 miles **Pub** < 0.5 miles

CORNHILL-ON-TWEED, Northumberland Map ref 5B1

★★★
SELF CATERING

Units 2
Sleeps 1–4
Low season per wk
£200.00–£220.00
High season per wk
£270.00–£300.00

Harelaw Cottages, Mindrum

contact Mr & Mrs Andy & Val Young, Harelaw, Mindrum TD12 4QP
t (01890) 850327 **f** (01890) 850327 **e** harelawcot@btinternet.com **w** harelaw.org

Harelaw is a rural property set in two acres of woodland gardens. Leveret and Hoolit are two-bedroom adjoining cottages. Ideal for touring and walking North Northumberland and the Scottish Borders.

open All year
payment Cash/cheques

Unit **General** **Leisure** **Shop** 2 miles **Pub** 2 miles

COTHERSTONE, County Durham Map ref 5B3

★★★
SELF CATERING

Units **1**
Sleeps **4–6**
Low season per wk
Min £110.00
High season per wk
Max £290.00

Farthings, Cotherstone, Barnard Castle

contact Mr Christopher John Bainbridge, Glen Leigh, Cotherstone, Barnard Castle DL12 9QW
t (01833) 650331

open All year
payment Cash/cheques

Shop/post office and two pubs (both serving meals) in village. Regular bus service. Many peaceful country walks. Easy access to coast and Lake District.

⊕ *Situated on the B6277, between Barnard Castle and Middleton-in-Teesdale.*

Unit General P Leisure

CRAMLINGTON, Northumberland Map ref 5C2

★★★★
SELF CATERING

Units **9**
Sleeps **2–36**
Low season per wk
£270.00–£520.00
High season per wk
£430.00–£840.00

Burradon Farm Houses & Cottages, Cramlington

contact Mrs Judith Younger, Burradon Farm Houses & Cottages, Burradon Farm, Cramlington NE23 7ND
t (0191) 268 3203 **e** judy@burradonfarm.co.uk **w** burradonfarm.co.uk

open All year
payment Credit/debit cards, cash/cheques

Burradon Farm is located only a few miles from the spectacular Northumbrian coastline and within easy reach of the cultural heritage and dynamic centre which is Newcastle-upon-Tyne. The new barn conversions have become characterful, high-quality houses and cottages boasting every amenity and facility to ensure an enjoyable visit. Dishwasher in houses.

⊕ *B1505 to Burradon. Travel 0.3 miles up hill and take 1st left onto Burradon Farm Road. Farmhouse is on right-hand side.*

❤ *3-4-night stays welcomed, all year round.*

Unit General P S Leisure Shop 0.5 miles
Pub 0.5 miles

CRASTER, Northumberland Map ref 5C1

★★★★
SELF CATERING

Units **2**
Sleeps **1–5**
Low season per wk
£230.00–£300.00
High season per wk
£330.00–£600.00

Harbourside House and 2 Old Farm Buildings, Low Newton-by-the-Sea, Alnwick

contact Mr Geoffrey Brewis-Levie, 10 The Severals, Bury Road, Newmarket CB8 7YN
t (01638) 604304 **f** (01638) 604304 **e** brewislevie@aol.com

Harbourside House has been completely refurbished and has views of the harbour. Old Farm Buildings is a cottage with garden leading directly onto a sandy beach.

open All year
payment Cash/cheques

Unit General P S Leisure Shop 2 miles
Pub < 0.5 miles

To your credit

If you book by phone you may be asked for your credit card number. If so, it is advisable to check the proprietor's policy in case you have to cancel your reservation at a later date.

DARLINGTON, Tees Valley Map ref 5C3

★★★
SELF CATERING

Units **1**
Sleeps **4–6**
Low season per wk
£220.00–£270.00
High season per wk
£270.00–£330.00

Pegasus Cottage, Darlington

contact Mr & Mrs Stuart and Denise Chapman, Pegasus Cottage, 4 Tees View, Hurworth Place, Darlington DL2 2DH
t (01325) 722542 **f** (01325) 722542 **e** stuart1948@msn.com **w** pegasuscottage.co.uk

Converted stable block of a Grade II Listed building, c1850. Local mayor's Design Award winner 1995. Set in small village three miles from Darlington.

open All year
payment Credit/debit cards, cash/cheques

Unit General P Leisure Shop 1 mile Pub < 0.5 miles

DURHAM, County Durham Map ref 5C2

★★★★
SELF CATERING

Units **1**
Sleeps **1–3**
Low season per wk
Min £400.00
High season per wk
Max £450.00

Durham4u.com, Durham

contact Mrs Gill Wray, 1 Cedar Drive, Farewell Hall, Durham DH1 3TF
t (0191) 383 2049 **f** (0191) 383 2049 **e** enquiries@durham4u.com **w** durham4u.com

payment Cash/cheques, euros

With a fabulous view of the cathedral from your back door, this luxurious new apartment (two bedrooms with master en suite) is perfect for short breaks in a romantic setting. Easy walking distance to the city centre, and an ideal location for exploring the surrounding area by foot or by car.

⊕ *Exit A1(M) at jct 62, take A690 to Durham. After 2 miles, at roundabout take 1st exit, Station Lane. Bear right, then take 1st right, The Sidings.*

Unit General P Leisure

EMBLETON, Northumberland Map ref 5C1

★★★–★★★★
SELF CATERING

Units **8**
Sleeps **2–7**
Low season per wk
£175.00–£250.00
High season per wk
£350.00–£550.00

Doxford Farm Cottages, Chathill

contact Mrs Sarah Shell, Doxford Farm, Doxford, Chathill NE67 5DY
t (01665) 579348 & (01665) 579477 **f** (01665) 579331 **e** doxfordfarm@hotmail.com
w doxfordfarmcottages.com

open All year
payment Credit/debit cards, cash/cheques

Set in wooded countryside four miles from sea, on a working mixed farm. Well-equipped and -furnished cottages with central heating and open fires. Wildlife trail, woodland walks. Doxford Country Store is nearby, with coffee shop, gift shop, country clothing and art gallery. Ideal base for Northumberland's castles and coastline and Alnwick Gardens.

⊕ *Turn off the A1(M) towards the coast on the B6347, 5 miles north of Alnwick. Keep left for 3 miles following signposts to Doxford Farm and Doxford Country Crafts.*

❤ *3-night stays available Oct-Mar (excl Christmas and New Year).*

Unit General P Leisure Shop 4 miles
Pub 4 miles

Town, country or coast?

The entertainment, shopping and innovative attractions of the big cities, the magnificent vistas of the countryside or the relaxing and refreshing coast – this guide will help you find what you're looking for!

EMBLETON, Northumberland Map ref 5C1

★★
SELF CATERING

Units **4**
Sleeps **2–4**
Low season per wk
£175.00–£195.00
High season per wk
£340.00–£460.00

Dunstanburgh Castle Courtyard Cottages, Alnwick

contact Mrs Marianne Thompson, Heritage Coast Holidays, 6g Greensfield Court, Greensfield Industrial Estate, Alnwick NE66 2DE
t (01665) 606022 **f** 0870 241 4339 **e** marianne@marishalthompson.co.uk
w heritagecoastholidays.com

17thC coach house converted to cottages. An easy walk to the superb Embleton Beach and Dunstanburgh Castle. Ideal for exploring Northumbria, the Heritage Coast, Holy island and Alnwick Castle and Gardens.

open All year
payment Cash/cheques

Unit General Leisure Shop < 0.5 miles Pub < 0.5 miles

FORD, Northumberland Map ref 5B1

★★★–★★★★★
SELF CATERING

Units **2**
Sleeps **2–13**
Low season per wk
£336.00–£594.00
High season per wk
£448.00–£931.00

Ford Castle, Ford and Etal

contact Mrs Karen Bartlett, Ford Castle, Ford Village, Berwick-upon-Tweed TD15 2PX
t (01890) 820257 **f** (01890) 820413 **e** kbartlett@northumberland.gov.uk **w** fordcastle.org.uk

open All year
payment Credit/debit cards, cash/cheques

Ford Castle is a residential activity centre, dating back to the 14thC, with two self-catering properties within the grounds. The Flag Tower has been refurbished to a very high standard. The Clock Tower cottage has three bedrooms, one with en suite facilities.

⊕ *From Berwick-upon-Tweed south on A1 turn off onto B6354 to Ford and Etal. From Morpeth north on A697 turn off onto B6353.*

❤ *Weekend and short breaks, min 2 nights, available throughout the year.*

Unit General Leisure Shop < 0.5 miles Pub 1.8 miles

HALTWHISTLE, Northumberland Map ref 5B2

★★★
SELF CATERING

Units **1**
Sleeps **1–5**
Low season per wk
£180.00–£250.00
High season per wk
£250.00–£350.00

Whitchester Farm Cottage, Haltwhistle

contact J M Hall, Whitchester Farm Cottage, Whitchester House, Haltwhistle NE49 0NF
t (01434) 320540 & 07957 862988 **e** whitchester@ukonline.co.uk **w** whitchester.co.uk

Farm cottage on working dairy farm in Roman Wall area. The accommodation comprises two bedrooms, shower room with wc, living room, kitchen and utility room.

open All year
payment Cash/cheques

Unit General Leisure Shop 1 mile Pub 1 mile

HAMSTERLEY FOREST

See under Barnard Castle, Tow Law, Wolsingham

Country Code Always follow the Country Code

- Be safe – plan ahead and follow any signs
- Leave gates and property as you find them
- Protect plants and animals, and take your litter home
- Keep dogs under close control
- Consider other people

HARWOOD, County Durham Map ref 5B2

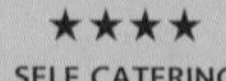

★★★★ SELF CATERING

Units 1
Sleeps 4
Low season per wk
Max £180.00
High season per wk
£280.00–£350.00

Frog Hall Cottage, Barnard Castle

contact Ms Kath Toward, Herd Ship Farm, Barnard Castle DL12 0YB
t (01833) 622215 **f** (01833) 622215 **e** kath.herdship@btinternet.com **w** herdship.co.uk

open All year
payment Cash/cheques

Secluded, stone-built dales cottage in spectacular setting in the centre of an award-winning environmental farm on the edge the Pennine moorland. Magnificent views of wading birds, flowering meadows, rare flowers and black grouse. Adjacent to National Nature Reserve. Private garden area.

⊕ *Take the Alston Road (B6277) and follow for 10 miles. After passing Langdon Beck, left at next telephone box, follow lane until you reach Frog Hall.*

Unit General P S Shop 10 miles Pub 3 miles

HEDDON-ON-THE-WALL, Northumberland Map ref 5B2

★★★ SELF CATERING

Units 1
Sleeps 2–7
Low season per wk
£250.00–£280.00
High season per wk
£350.00–£425.00

2 East Town House, Newcastle upon Tyne

contact Mr & Mrs Ridley and Beryl Amos, 1 East Town House, Heddon-on-the-Wall, Newcastle upon Tyne NE15 0DR
t (01661) 852277 **f** (01661) 853063

Stone-built, well-equipped house furnished to a high standard, in historic village on Hadrian's Wall. Only six miles to Newcastle, 20 minutes from Hexham.

open All year
payment Cash/cheques

Unit General P Leisure Shop < 0.5 miles Pub < 0.5 miles

HEXHAM, Northumberland Map ref 5B2

★★★★★ SELF CATERING

Units 1
Sleeps 3
Low season per wk
£250.00–£306.00
High season per wk
£354.00–£434.00

Holy Island House, Hexham

contact Mrs Judith Youens, Holy Island House, Gilesgate, Hexham NE46 3QL
t (01434) 609386 **e** stay@holyislandhouse.co.uk **w** holyislandhouse.co.uk

payment Cash/cheques

An 18thC wing of 17thC listed building. Beamed ceilings, flagged floors, feature fireplaces, period furnishings. Kitchen, living/dining room, single and double bedroom, bath with shower over, parking and small garden. Close to town centre, award-winning park and Hexham Abbey.

⊕ *Map and detailed directions will be sent on booking.*

❤ *3-night, off-season breaks available.*

Unit General 12 P S

Ancient and modern

Experience timeless favourites or discover the latest must-sees. Whatever your choice, be inspired by the places of interest highlighted for each region and the events listed towards the back of this guide.

HEXHAM, Northumberland Map ref 5B2

SELF CATERING

Units **1**
Sleeps **2–4**
Low season per wk
£270.00–£320.00
High season per wk
£320.00–£460.00

Sammy's Place, Hexham

contact Mr & Mrs Ian and Susan Sibbald, 9 Charlton Close, Beaumont Park, Hexham NE46 2QF
t (01434) 604143 **e** sammys-place@hotmail.com **w** sammyshideaways.com

Beautifully appointed two-bedroomed apartment, with both rooms being en suite. The property is situated in the heart of historic Hexham in Hadrian's Wall country.

open All year
payment Credit/debit cards

Unit General Leisure Shop < 0.5 miles Pub < 0.5 miles

HOLY ISLAND, Northumberland Map ref 5C1

★★★

SELF CATERING

Units **2**
Sleeps **4**
Low season per wk
£220.00–£350.00
High season per wk
£350.00–£535.00

Farne Court Cottage, Farne View Cottage, Holy Island

contact Mrs Batty, Waterside House, Dalton, Lockerbie DG11 1AT
t (01387) 840122 **e** angelabatty@ukonline.co.uk

18thC stone cottages with courtyard, private garden and parking. Very well equipped and furnished. Cosy in winter (woodburner). Close to beach and castle.

open All year
payment Cash/cheques

Unit General P Leisure Shop < 0.5 miles Pub < 0.5 miles

HOLY ISLAND, Northumberland Map ref 5C1

★★★

SELF CATERING

Units **1**
Sleeps **8**
Low season per wk
Min £475.00
High season per wk
Max £920.00

Links View, Berwick-upon-Tweed

contact Dr Rachel Pain, Sandham Lane, Holy Island, Berwick-upon-Tweed TD15 2SG
e linksviewholyisland@yahoo.co.uk **w** lindisfarne.org.uk/links-view

A Grade II Listed house in Holy Island village offering self-catering holiday accommodation.

open All year
payment Cash/cheques

Unit General P Shop < 0.5 miles Pub < 0.5 miles

HUMSHAUGH, Northumberland Map ref 5B2

★★★

SELF CATERING

Units **1**
Sleeps **3**
Low season per wk
Max £175.00
High season per wk
Max £225.00

East Farm Cottage, Hexham

contact Mrs Gwen Dodds, East Farm House, Humshaugh, Hexham NE46 4AT
t (01434) 689150 **e** charles.dodds2@btopenworld.com

Listed 18thC cottage. Lounge and kitchen with dining area on ground floor. Two bedrooms (double and single) and bathroom on first floor.

open All year
payment Cash/cheques

Unit General P Shop < 0.5 miles Pub 0.5 miles

KIELDER FOREST

See under Wark

Phone ahead

Even the most ardent pet lover would appreciate some advance warning of Rover's visit, so please phone ahead and check what facilities will be available.

MICKLETON, County Durham Map ref 5B3

★★★★
SELF CATERING

Units **1**
Sleeps **1–4**
Low season per wk
Max £215.00
High season per wk
Max £330.00

The Old Dairy, Mickleton, Barnard Castle

contact Mrs Tracey Cook, West Pasture Farm, Kelton Road, Mickleton, Barnard Castle DL12 0PW
t (01833) 640248 **f** (01833) 640491 **e** cookes@homecall.co.uk **w** teesdaleholidaycottages.co.uk

open All year
payment Cash/cheques

Set in the heart of the North Pennines, on the side of Grassholme Reservoir, surrounded by woods, fells and fields, this two-bedroom converted dairy is a haven for those wanting to escape the hustle and bustle of everyday living. Perfect for walking, fishing, cycling, sailing or just relaxing.

⊕ *From A1(M) Scotch Corner take the A66 (Brough). After 12 miles, B6277 through Cotherstone and Romaldkirk into Mickleton. After Rose and Crown turn left (Kelton). Cottage on left, 1.5 miles.*

♥ *Short breaks available.*

Unit **General** **Leisure** **Shop** 1.5 miles
Pub 1.5 miles

MICKLETON, County Durham Map ref 5B3

★★★★
SELF CATERING

Units **1**
Sleeps **8**
Low season per wk
£400.00–£535.00
High season per wk
£625.00–£850.00

Whitbridge, Nr Barnard Castle

contact Mr Raymond Taffurelli, Mickleton, Middleton-in-Teesdale, Nr Barnard Castle DL12 0LW
t (01833) 640100 **f** (01833) 640100 **e** taffurs@thetaffurellis.freeserve.co.uk

open All year
payment Cash/cheques

Lovely period house in 2.5-acre grounds. Magnificent views. Four en suite bedrooms (two kings, two twins), lounge, study, dining room, conservatory, large kitchen/diner. Excellent pubs and restaurants close by. Wonderful walking, fishing and horse-riding. Day trips to coast, lakes and cities.

⊕ *Short breaks available (3 nights). Reduced prices for 6 people (3-bedroom occupanacy).*

♥ *From Barnard Castle, take B6277 to Mickleton. On leaving Mickleton, Whitbridge is on right, 170m beyond village boundary.*

Unit **General** **Leisure** **Shop** 0.5 miles
Pub 0.5 miles

MIDDLETON-IN-TEESDALE, County Durham Map ref 5B3

★★★
SELF CATERING

Units **1**
Sleeps **2–6**
Low season per wk
Min £150.00
High season per wk
Max £350.00

Country Cottage, Middleton-in-Teesdale

contact Mr Burman, 1 Thorn Road, Stockport SK7 1HG
t (0161) 860 7123 **e** enquiries@robinburman.com

Two-hundred-year-old cottage in quiet, peaceful location with superb views, surrounded by farmland. Excellent walking countryside.

open All year
payment Cash/cheques

Unit **General**

Place index

If you know where you want to stay the index at the back of the guide will give you the page number which lists accommodation in your chosen town, city or village. Check out the other useful indexes too.

MIDDLETON-IN-TEESDALE, County Durham Map ref 5B3

★★★
SELF CATERING & SERVICED APARTMENTS

Units **1**
Sleeps **2**
Low season per wk
£120.00–£140.00
High season per wk
£150.00–£200.00

Firethorn Cottage, Middleton-in-Teesdale

contact Mrs June Thompson, Cutbush Farmhouse, Hardingham Road, Hingham, Norwich NR9 4LY
t (01953) 850364

Stone-built lead miner's cottage, one up/one down, flagstone floors, traditional rag rugs, beamed ceilings. Superb walking, fishing, pubs and restaurants.

open All year
payment Cash/cheques

Unit General

MORPETH, Northumberland Map ref 5C2

★★★
SELF CATERING

Units **1**
Sleeps **4**
Low season per wk
£250.00–£300.00
High season per wk
£375.00–£400.00

Meldon Park, Morpeth

contact Mrs Janet Wilson, Flat 1, Meldon Park, Morpeth NE61 3SW
t (01670) 772622 **f** (01670) 772341 **e** mrscookson@compuserve.com
w cottageguide.co.uk/meldonpark

Stunning, unique and peaceful location in rural Northumberland, centrally located for city, hills and coast. One double and one twin room, log-burning stove, central heating, spacious gardens and unrivalled views.

open All year
payment Cash/cheques

Unit General P Leisure **Shop** 5 miles **Pub** 0.5 miles

NEWBIGGIN-BY-THE-SEA, Northumberland Map ref 5C2

★★★★
SELF CATERING

Units **1**
Sleeps **10**
Low season per wk
£350.00–£650.00
High season per wk
£650.00–£900.00

Tahfay House, Newbiggin-by-the-Sea

contact Mr Stuart Dodds, 4 Fawdon House Farm, Longhirst, Morpeth NE61 3LQ
t (01670) 503597 **f** (01670) 503597 **e** cozydays@tiscali.co.uk **w** cozydays.co.uk

open All year
payment Cash/cheques

Tahfay House offers spacious accommodation just 50m from the sea, 30 minutes from Newcastle and is ideally located for exploring Northumberland. This refurbished, tastefully appointed Victorian town house has five bedrooms. Northumberland's Heritage Trail boasts wonderful castles and miles of exquisite beaches, bays and lovely seaside villages.

⊕ *From Newcastle, follow the A1 north, exit A197 (Morpeth). A197 to Newbiggin-by-the-Sea. Tahfay House is located opposite public library on Windsor Road.*

♥ *3-night stays available Oct-Mar (excl Christmas and New Year). Last-minute discounts available. Reduction for parties of up to 5 people.*

Unit General P Leisure **Shop** < 0.5 miles **Pub** < 0.5 miles

NEWCASTLE UPON TYNE, Tyne and Wear Map ref 5C2

★★★
SELF CATERING

Units **1**
Sleeps **1–6**
Low season per wk
£230.00–£350.00
High season per wk
£230.00–£350.00

135 Audley Road, Newcastle upon Tyne

contact Miss Linda Wright, 137 Audley Road, South Gosforth, Newcastle upon Tyne NE3 1QH
t (0191) 285 6374 **e** lkw@audleyender.fsnet.co.uk **w** audleyender.fsnet.co.uk

Self-contained flat, close to shops and Metro and with easy access to city centre. All amenities.

payment Cash/cheques

Unit General **Shop** < 0.5 miles **Pub** < 0.5 miles

NEWTON-BY-THE-SEA, Northumberland Map ref 5C1

★★★★
SELF CATERING

Units **1**
Sleeps **2–6**
Low season per wk
£295.00–£445.00
High season per wk
£370.00–£670.00

Seawinds, Alnwick

contact Miss Jo Park, Bygate, Black Heddon, Newcastle upon Tyne NE20 0JJ
t (01665) 714805 **f** (01665) 711345 **e** jopark@farming.co.uk **w** buston.co.uk

open All year
payment Cash/cheques

Situated within the picturesque village of Low Newton-by-the-Sea, this former fisherman's cottage is just 200m from a beautiful sandy beach which is part of Northumberland's Heritage Coast area. A high-quality cottage offering many home comforts, making it an exceptional base from which to discover the many secrets of the surrounding area.

⊕ *From A1 take B6347 to Christon Bank, continue until junction. Take road almost straight ahead to Low Newton-by-the-Sea. Continue until the coast, 2nd on right.*

Unit General P Pub < 0.5 miles

OVINGTON, Northumberland Map ref 5B2

★★★★
SELF CATERING

Units **1**
Sleeps **2–4**
Low season per wk
£280.00–£350.00
High season per wk
£350.00–£400.00

Westgarth Cottage, Ovington, Prudhoe

contact Mrs Claire Graham, Stonecroft, Ovington, Prudhoe NE42 6EB
t (01661) 832202 **e** west.cape@btinternet.com

Attractive stone-built cottage in a small, peaceful village surrounded by beautiful countryside, near the historic towns of Hexham and Corbridge.

open All year
payment Cash/cheques

Unit General 5 P Shop < 0.5 miles Pub 1 mile

ROTHBURY, Northumberland Map ref 5B1

★★★–★★★★
SELF CATERING

Units **4**
Sleeps **4–21**
Low season per wk
£200.00–£300.00
High season per wk
£320.00–£495.00

Low Alwinton Cottages, Nr Rothbury

contact Mr & Mrs Eamonn and Susan Gribben, 12 Parkshiel, South Shields NE34 8BU
t (0191) 420 4919 **f** (0191) 420 4919 **e** eamonngribben@blueyonder.co.uk **w** lowalwinton.co.uk

open All year
payment Credit/debit cards, cash/cheques, euros

Luxury cottages nestling in a spectacular wooded valley, amidst the glorious National Park. Located beside the River Coquet and ten minutes from Caistron trout fishery. Stunning panoramic views. Otters, birds, squirrel and deer are just some of the wildlife found here. Ideal for nature lovers, walkers, fishermen, cyclists and families.

❤ *If 4 people or less in Byre Cottage (sleeps 8), £50 off.*

Unit General P Leisure
Shop 1.5 miles Pub 1 mile

Using map references

The map references refer to the colour maps at the front of this guide. The first figure is the map number; the letter and figure that follow indicate the grid reference on the map.

ROTHBURY, Northumberland Map ref 5B1

★★★★
SELF CATERING

Units **4**
Sleeps **2–4**
Low season per wk
£197.00–£269.00
High season per wk
£214.00–£456.00

Riverside Lodges, Morpeth

contact Mr Eric Jensen, Edgecombe, Hillside Road, Rothbury, Morpeth NE65 7PT
t (01669) 620464 **f** (01669) 621031 **e** eric_jensen@tiscali.co.uk **w** theriversidelodge.com

open All year
payment Cash/cheques

Tastefully converted, stone-built schoolhouse overlooking the River Coquet. Fully equipped one- or two-bedroomed units. Coal fires, on-site parking, perfect centre for Northumberland National Park, walking, riding, fishing. Coast and beaches within easy reach. Situated in the beautiful town of Rothbury which provides ample shopping and eating facilities.

⊕ *Arriving from Weldon Bridge, turn left in the centre of Rothbury. Proceed over the bridge and turn left. Riverside Lodge is the 1st building on the left-hand side.*

Unit General P Leisure **Shop** < 0.5 miles
Pub < 0.5 miles

ROTHBURY, Northumberland Map ref 5B1

★★★★
SELF CATERING

Units **1**
Sleeps **6**
Low season per wk
£230.00–£260.00
High season per wk
£430.00–£575.00

Whitton Lodge, Rothbury

contact Mrs Maggie Monaghan, Whitton Grange, Whitton, Morpeth NE65 7RL
t (01669) 620929 **f** (01669) 620471 **e** maggie.monaghan@btinternet.com
w cottage-northumberland.co.uk

open All year
payment Cash/cheques

Listed lodge and garden. Idyllic, peaceful setting. Stunning views over Coquetdale. Recently refurbished. Children welcome. No pets. Non-smoking. Ten-minute walk to Rothbury with excellent shopping and eating. The recently restored grange Edwardian gardens will be a delight to gardeners, and may be viewed by arrangement with the owners. Walkers and cyclists welcome.

⊕ *In Rothbury turn left opposite Queens Head Hotel, cross river, right at end of bridge. Follow road 0.5 miles to give way, turn left, stone gate posts on left.*

❤ *3-night breaks available. Nov-Mar inclusive.*

Unit General P S Leisure **Shop** 0.6 miles
Pub 0.6 miles

SALTBURN-BY-THE-SEA, Tees Valley Map ref 5C3

★★★
SELF CATERING

Units **1**
Sleeps **4**
Low season per wk
£200.00–£275.00
High season per wk
£300.00–£325.00

The Zetland, Saltburn-by-the-Sea

contact Mrs Joan Carter, 1 Hawthorn Grove, Yarm TS15 9EZ
t (01642) 679831 & (01642) 782507 **f** (01642) 670346 **e** graham@howard95.freeserve.co.uk

Most famous building in Saltburn, the old Zetland Hotel, an imposing Victorian building. Second-floor, two-bedroom apartment with spectacular views of the sea, cliffs and surrounding countryside.

open All year
payment Cash/cheques

Unit General P Leisure **Shop** < 0.5 miles **Pub** < 0.5 miles

WALKERS WELCOME WELCOME WALKERS

Best foot forward

Walkers feel at home in accommodation participating in our Walkers Welcome scheme. Look out for the symbol. Consider walking all or part of a long-distance route – go online at nationaltrail.co.uk.

SEAHOUSES, Northumberland Map ref 5C1

★★★★
SELF CATERING

Units 1
Sleeps 1–6
Low season per wk
Min £225.00
High season per wk
Max £475.00

The Lobster Pots, Seahouses

contact Mrs Julia Steel, 10 Crofters Lea, Leeds LS19 7WE
t (0113) 239 1130 **e** julia@thelobsterpots.co.uk **w** thelobsterpots.co.uk

Beautifully furnished holiday home with sea views. Situated only five minutes' walk from breathtaking coastline. Ideal for children with enclosed garden and toys. Dogs welcome.

open All year
payment Cash/cheques

Unit General P Leisure Shop 0.5 miles Pub 0.5 miles

SEAHOUSES, Northumberland Map ref 5C1

★★★
SELF CATERING

Units 2
Sleeps 1–4
Low season per wk
£212.00–£266.00
High season per wk
£365.00–£482.00

North East Coast Holidays, Seahouses

contact Mrs Lesley Barnett, 7 Alnside Court, Lesbury, Alnwick NE66 3PD
t (01665) 833233 **f** (01665) 833233 **e** d_barnettuk@yahoo.co.uk **w** northeastcoastholidays.co.uk

open All year
payment Cash/cheques

Comfortable, well-equipped, two-bedroom cottages close to sea, beaches and golf courses. These cottages are the perfect base to explore Northumberland. Own garden and parking. Linen included. Families welcome. Non-smoking. Sea views. Houses next door to each other (ideal for two families).

⊕ *Travel directions given at time of booking.*

Unit General P Leisure Shop 1 mile Pub 1 mile

SLAGGYFORD, Northumberland Map ref 5B2

SELF CATERING

Units 1
Sleeps 5–6
Low season per wk
£160.00–£200.00
High season per wk
£390.00–£430.00

Town Green Cottage, Slaggyford

contact Miss Colleen Cairns, West Farm, Hall Road, Chopwell, Newcastle upon Tyne NE17 7AB
t (01207) 560115 & 07714 345766 **f** (01207) 560115 **e** colleen_cairns181@hotmail.com

Stone cottage with magnificent views of the Pennines. Furnished and equipped to high standards. Facilities for walkers/cyclists.

open All year
payment Cash/cheques

Unit General 5 P Leisure Shop 8 miles Pub < 0.5 miles

Check the maps

Colour maps at the front pinpoint all the cities, towns and villages where you will find accommodation entries in the regional sections. Pick your location and then refer to the place index at the back to find the page number.

STAINDROP, County Durham Map ref 5B3

★★★★
SELF CATERING

Units 1
Sleeps 4
Low season per wk
Min £200.00
High season per wk
Max £350.00

Fawnlea Cottage, Staindrop, Darlington

contact Mrs Gillian Sumpton, 10 Winston Road, Staindrop, Darlington DL2 3NN
t (01833) 660896 **e** gillian64@btinternet.com **w** fawnleacottage.co.uk

open All year
payment Cash/cheques

Fawnlea is a newly built modern cottage with traditional bedrooms (two twins), cosy open-plan kitchen/lounge and off-road parking. Three minutes' walk to village pubs and shops. Half a mile away is Raby Castle with its grounds, tea shop and gardens.

⊕ *From A66 take A688; from A688 take B6274; from A67 take B6274. The cottage is at no 10.*

❤ *Short stays available on request Oct-Mar.*

Unit General P Leisure Shop < 0.5 miles Pub < 0.5 miles

TOW LAW, County Durham Map ref 5B2

★★★★
SELF CATERING

Units 1
Sleeps 2–6
Low season per wk
£210.00
High season per wk
£295.00–£395.00

Binks Cottage, Bishop Auckland

contact Mrs Amanda Simpson, Oaklea, Thornley Village, Tow Law, Bishop Auckland DL13 4PA
t (01388) 731121 **f** (01388) 731121 **e** amanda.simpson@totalise.co.uk **w** binkscottage.co.uk

Stone cottage set on a working farm overlooking a picturesque village green. Equipped to a high standard. Central heating, towels and linen included in price.

open All year
payment Cash/cheques

Unit General P S Leisure Shop 1 mile Pub 1 mile

WAREN MILL, Northumberland Map ref 5C1

★★★★
SELF CATERING

Units 1
Sleeps 1–4
Low season per wk
£185.00–£295.00
High season per wk
£295.00–£495.00

Cove Cottage, Waren Mill, Belford

contact Mrs Anne Lawrence, 10 Woodpack Avenue, Whickham, Newcastle upon Tyne NE16 5YY
t (0191) 488 6414 & 07932 795251 **e** enquiries@northumberland-coast-holidays.co.uk
w northumberland-coast-holidays.co.uk

Two-bedroom stone barn conversion with pleasant courtyard and sitting area. Very cosy and comfortable. Within easy reach of all amenities, and a two-minute walk to Budle Bay.

open All year
payment Cash/cheques

Unit General P S Leisure Shop 2 miles Pub 2 miles

WAREN MILL, Northumberland Map ref 5C1

★★★★
SELF CATERING

Units 1
Sleeps 2–5
Low season per wk
Min £260.00
High season per wk
Max £550.00

Eider Cottage, Nr Bamburgh

contact Mrs S Turnbull, 1 Friars Court, Bamburgh NE69 7AE
t (01668) 214494 **e** theturnbulls2k@btinternet.com **w** holidaynorthumbria.co.uk

This charming, stone-built, former miller's cottage is situated yards from Budle Bay, a renowned bird-watching area near Bamburgh. Ideal base for exploring Northumberland.

open All year
payment Cash/cheques

Unit General P

Key to symbols

Open the back flap for a key to symbols.

WARK, Northumberland Map ref 5B2

★★★★
SELF CATERING

Units **1**
Sleeps **2–6**
Low season per wk
£260.00–£300.00
High season per wk
£475.00

The Hemmel, Hexham

contact Mrs Amanda Nichol, Hetherington, Wark, Hexham NE48 3DR
t (01434) 230260 **f** (01434) 230260 **e** alan_nichol@hotmail.com **w** hetheringtonfarm.co.uk

Excellent converted farm building, all mod cons. A lovely rural setting close to Hadrian's Wall. Ideal for walking, touring or a relaxing holiday. Well recommended.

open All year
payment Cash/cheques

Unit General P Leisure Shop 3 miles Pub 3 miles

WARK, Northumberland Map ref 5B2

★★★★
SELF CATERING

Units **2**
Sleeps **2–8**
Low season per wk
£160.00–£320.00
High season per wk
£240.00–£470.00

Roses Bower, Hexham

contact Mr & Mrs Lewis and Susan Watson, Roses Bower Farm, Wark, Hexham NE48 3DX
t (01434) 230779 **f** (01434) 230779 **e** sandlwatson@rosesbower.fsworld.co.uk **w** roses-bower.co.uk

A cosy cottage or a traditional farmhouse in the grounds of Roses Bower, a working sheep farm in a magnificent location on The Warksburn, within the Northumbrian National Park.

open All year
payment Cash/cheques

Unit General P Leisure Shop 5 miles Pub 5 miles

WARKWORTH, Northumberland Map ref 5C1

★★★★
SELF CATERING

Units **3**
Sleeps **2–4**
Low season per wk
£230.00–£330.00
High season per wk
£280.00–£480.00

Buston Farm Holiday Cottages, Warkworth

contact Miss Jo Park, Bygate, Black Heddon, Newcastle upon Tyne NE20 0JJ
t (01665) 714805 **e** jopark@farming.co.uk **w** buston.co.uk

open All year
payment Cash/cheques

Situated within the unique area of the Heritage Coast, between the historical village of Warkworth and picturesque Alnmouth, Buston Farm provides the ideal base from which to discover the secrets of rural Northumberland. We offer quality cottages, all superbly equipped, with many home comforts, four-poster beds and mostly en suite rooms.

⊕ *From A1 take A1068 coastal route, travel through Warkworth and over River Coquet. Turn left and follow National Cycle Route, over railbridge. Farm 0.5 miles along road.*

Unit General P Leisure Shop 2 miles Pub 2 miles

WARKWORTH, Northumberland Map ref 5C1

★★★★
SELF CATERING

Units 1
Sleeps 4
Low season per wk
£235.00–£295.00

Coquet Cottage, Warkworth

contact Mrs Barbara Jean Purvis, The Byres, Mouldshaugh Farm, Felton, Morpeth NE65 9NP
t (01670) 786088 & 07731 883657 **e** fenwickpurvis@virgin.net

open All year
payment Cash/cheques

Charming 19thC stone cottage situated next to the River Coquet in historic Warkworth village, dominated by its castle and 0.5 miles from sandy beaches. Restored to the highest standards, with attractive, co-ordinated furnishings, and well equipped. All the village amenities are just a few minutes' walk away.

⊕ *A1 North, right Felton, leaving Acklington turn left for Warkworth. Castle on left, drive down Castle Street, turn left past church, 300yds Coquet Cottage.*

Unit General Leisure Shop < 0.5 miles Pub < 0.5 miles

WOLSINGHAM, County Durham Map ref 5B2

★★★
SELF CATERING

Units 2
Sleeps 4
Low season per wk
Min £155.00
High season per wk
Max £235.00

Ardine and Elvet Cottage, Bishop Auckland

contact Mrs Gardiner, 3 Melbourne Place, Bishop Auckland DL13 3EQ
t (01388) 527538

Cosy, two-bedroomed terraced cottages overlooking small village green in old part of Wolsingham. Excellent walking and touring centre.

open All year
payment Cash/cheques

Unit General Shop < 0.5 miles Pub < 0.5 miles

WOLSINGHAM, County Durham Map ref 5B2

★★★
SELF CATERING

Units 4
Sleeps 1–7
Low season per wk
£190.00–£450.00
High season per wk
£280.00–£600.00

Bradley Burn Holiday Cottages, Bishop Auckland

contact Mrs Judith Stephenson, Bradley Burn Holiday Cottages, Bradley Burn Farm, Wolsingham, Bishop Auckland DL13 3JH
t (01388) 527285 **f** (01388) 527285 **e** jas@bradleyburn.co.uk **w** bradleyburn.co.uk

open All year
payment Cash/cheques, euros

Small complex of interesting barn conversions, with all modern amenities. Situated on our working farm in east Weardale. Ideal touring/walking base. Granary Cottage is ideal for families (three bedrooms, one en suite), whilst Stable Cottages and Harvest Cottage are perfect for couples.

⊕ *Bradley Burn is adjacent to A689, the main road through Weardale, between A68 junction and Wolsingham.*

Unit General Leisure

Friendly help and advice

Tourist information centres offer friendly help with accommodation and holiday ideas as well as suggestions of places to visit and things to do. You'll find contact details at the beginning of each regional section.

WOLSINGHAM, County Durham Map ref 5B2

★★★
SELF CATERING

Units **1**
Sleeps **7**
Low season per wk
£215.00–£350.00
High season per wk
£350.00–£470.00

Whitfield House Cottage, Bishop Auckland

contact Mrs Margaret Shepheard, 25 Front Street, Bishop Auckland DL13 3DF
t (01388) 527466 **e** enquiries@whitfieldhouse.clara.net **w** whitfieldhouse.clara.net

Spacious accommodation in part of an attractive Grade II* Listed Queen Anne house. Near the centre of this small town, in a designated Area of Outstanding Natural Beauty.

open All year
payment Cash/cheques, euros

Unit General Leisure Shop < 0.5 miles Pub < 0.5 miles

WOOLER, Northumberland Map ref 5B1

★★★
SELF CATERING

Units **1**
Sleeps **6**
Low season per wk
£220.00–£260.00
High season per wk
£300.00–£350.00

Rose Cottage, Wooler

contact Mrs Christine Andrews, 1 Littleworth Lane, Esher KT10 9PF
t (01372) 464284 **f** (01372) 467715 **e** andrews@playfactors.demon.co.uk

payment Cash/cheques, euros

Old stone cottage with superb views over Glendale Valley, set amid farmland. Beautiful Northumberland beaches, castles and gardens. Edinburgh and Newcastle within easy reach, plus all the Scottish Border land. Log fires and efficient heating make it a good spring or autumn break. Open April to October.

⊕ *Short distance from A697 as it goes through Wooler.*

Unit General Leisure Shop 1 mile Pub 1 mile

Walkers and cyclists welcome

Look out for quality-assessed accommodation displaying the Walkers Welcome and Cyclists Welcome signs.

Participants in this scheme actively encourage and support walking and cycling. In addition to special meal arrangements and helpful information, they'll provide a water supply to wash off the mud, an area for drying wet clothing and footwear, maps and books to look up cycling and walking routes and even an emergency puncture-repair kit! Bikes can also be locked up securely undercover.

The standards for the scheme have been developed in partnership with the tourist boards in Northern Ireland, Scotland and Wales, so wherever you're travelling in the UK you'll receive the same welcome.

Ratings
you can trust

Wherever you see a quality rating sign, you can be sure that one of Enjoy England's professional assessors has been there before you, checking the place on your behalf – and will be there again, because every place with a national rating is assessed annually.

The star ratings reflect the quality that you're looking for when booking accommodation. All properties have to meet an extensive list of minimum requirements to take part in the scheme. From there, increased levels of quality apply. For instance, you'll find acceptable quality at one star, good to very good quality at three star and exceptional quality at five star establishments.

Quite simply, the more stars, the higher the overall level of quality you can expect to find. Establishments at higher rating levels also have to meet some additional requirements for facilities.

Minimum entry requirements include the following:

- High standards of cleanliness throughout
- Clear pricing and booking conditions
- Local information to help you make the best of your stay
- Comfortable accommodation with a range of furniture to meet your needs
- Colour television (where signal available) at no extra charge
- Kitchen equipped to meet all essential requirements.

Many self-catering establishments have a range of accommodation units in the building or on the site, and in some cases the individual units may have different star ratings. In such cases, the entry shows the range available.

Yorkshire

East Yorkshire › North Yorkshire › South Yorkshire › West Yorkshire

Fascinating marine life at The Deep, Hull

Yorkshire Tourist Board
312 Tadcaster Road
York YO24 1GS
0870 609 0000
info@ytb.org.uk
yorkshirevisitor.com

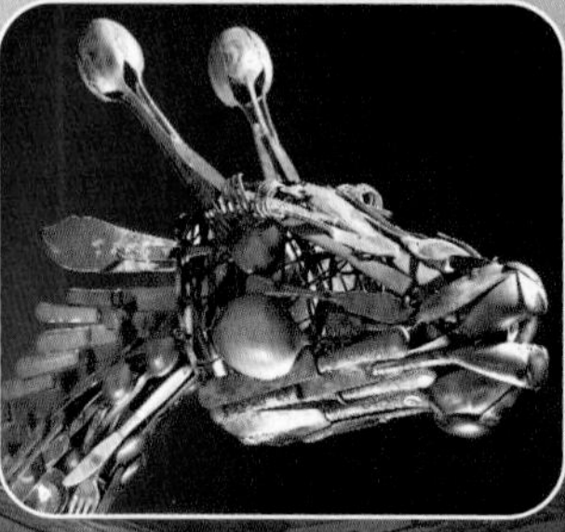

proud heritage, big attractions, lush dales

Main Stunning views across Yorkshire fields **Left** Come face to face with the past at Jorvik – The Viking City, York; family fun at Spurn Point Nature Reserve, Humberside; contemporary displays at Sheffield's Millennium Galleries; balancing on the limestone pavement at Malham Cove, North Yorkshire

With its rolling hills and dramatic, lush green landscapes, England's biggest county boasts some of the most picturesque pockets to be found in the country. Along with lively cities and ancient, ruined abbeys, **Yorkshire is rich in both history and culture**.

Explore Yorkshire

A sea of green

Experience the spine-tingling desolation of the Yorkshire moors as they sweep you into the world of Emily Brontë's Wuthering Heights. Coupled with a visit to the Brontë Parsonage Museum, where the works of the remarkable sisters came to life, Brontë Country is truly inspiring.

Lose yourself in the 30,000 acres of stunning countryside encompassing the Bolton Abbey Estate, traverse woodland and riverside paths and soak up the incredible vistas. Or head to the vibrant coastal town of Scarborough – the country's first seaside resort – and immerse yourself in marine life at the Sea Life Centre.

Eye it up

Allow the innovative space at Sheffield's Millennium Galleries to guide you on a journey of art throughout the ages. Or take a trip to Bradford and experience art of a different nature at the National Museum of Photography, Film & Television, the country's most visited museum outside the capital. Be amazed by the new interactive exhibition, Experience TV, and discover how television comes to life.

At Yorkshire Sculpture Park in West Bretton, you will discover that no two visits are ever the same. Changing weather and seasons will alter your perception of this unique park, where art is integrated into the landscape in a complementary fashion.

Take time to soak up some of the rich heritage that Yorkshire has to offer. Pay the 11th-century Middleham Castle a visit and discover the childhood home of Richard III, or hunt for ghosts in the ruins of the majestic Rievaulx Abbey and admire its graceful arches and elegant structure.

Put your boots on

Pull on your hiking boots and explore the 1,000 square miles of National Parks (the Yorkshire Dales, the North York Moors and the Peak District). Stride out along the Pennine or Dales Way or take a leisurely stroll along one of the many trails across this vast expanse of beautiful countryside.

Gaze in awe at the mighty Malham Cove – a curved crag of limestone formed after the last ice age – and attempt to understand this truly magnificent spectacle. Pick your way across the disected limestone pavement running across the surface of the cove – a result of chemical weathering – and admire the simplistic beauty of the eroded channels.

The charming fishing village of Robin Hood's Bay near Whitby is the perfect place to relax and dip into the rock pools that surround the delightful sandy beaches. Or take your binoculars up the 400-feet chalk cliffs of the Flamborough Headland Heritage Coast and spot the intriguing selection of wildlife.

But above all, don't forget about the wonderful tastes the region has to offer. Sup a true pint of Yorkshire bitter and nibble on a chunk of Wensleydale, or warm your cockles with a selection of traditional pies and Yorkshire pudding. And, for that sweet tooth, there's always Bakewell tart for dessert.

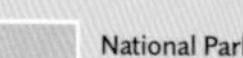

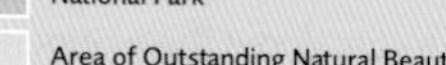

National Park

Area of Outstanding Natural Beauty

Heritage Coast

National Trails
nationaltrail.co.uk

National Trails approved
but not yet open

Sections of the
National Cycle Network
nationalcyclenetwork.org.uk

Aerial Extreme
Bedale, North Yorkshire
(01845) 567100
aerialextreme.co.uk
Swing high above the forest floor

Bolton Abbey Estate
North Yorkshire
(01756) 718009
boltonabbey.com
Beautiful setting, ruins and stepping stones

Brontë Parsonage Museum
Haworth, West Yorkshire
(01535) 642323
bronte.info
Former home of the inspiring literary sisters in quaint village setting

The Deep
Hull, East Yorkshire
(01482) 381000
thedeep.co.uk
Learn the history of the oceans

The Henry Moore Institute
Leeds, West Yorkshire
(0113) 246 7467
henry-moore-fdn.co.uk
Unique building housing art exhibitions

Jorvik – The Viking City
York, North Yorkshire
(01904) 543402
vikingjorvik.com
Viking history comes to life

Magna Science Adventure Centre

Rotherham, South Yorkshire
(01709) 723123
magnatrust.org.uk
An extraordinary science adventure

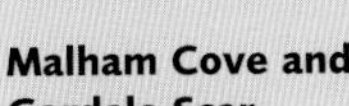

Malham Cove and Gordale Scar
North Yorkshire
(01729) 830363
malhamdale.com
Awe-inspiring rock formations

Middleham Castle
North Yorkshire
0870 333 1181
english-heritage.org.uk
Impressive 11th-century ruined castle

Millennium Galleries
Sheffield, South Yorkshire
(0114) 278 2600
sheffieldgalleries.org.uk
Innovative and diverse art space

National Museum of Photography, Film & Television
Bradford, West Yorkshire
0870 701 0200
nmpft.org.uk
With a spectacular 3D IMAX cinema and interactive television gallery

North Yorkshire Moors Railway
(01751) 473799
northyorkshiremoorsrailway.com
Heritage railway steaming through stunning scenery

Rievaulx Abbey
near Helmsley, North Yorkshire
(01439) 798228
yorkshirevisitor.com
Awe-inspiring ruined abbey in tranquil valley

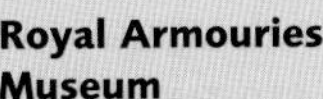

Royal Armouries Museum
Leeds, West Yorkshire
(0113) 220 1916
armouries.org.uk
Jousting tournaments and fabulous exhibitions

Sea Life Centre
Scarborough, East Yorkshire
(01723) 373414
sealife.co.uk
Marine life at your fingertips

Sheffield Botanical Gardens
South Yorkshire
(0114) 267 6496
sbg.org.uk
Lanscaped gardens of historical interest

Sheffield Ski Village
South Yorkshire
(0114) 276 9459
sheffieldskivillage.co.uk
Europe's largest artificial ski complex

Underground RAF Bunker Tours
Withernsea, East Yorkshire
(01964) 630208
rafholmpton.co.uk
Explore the past, deep underground

York Minster
North Yorkshire
(01904) 557216
yorkminster.org
Huge, stunning, medieval gothic cathedral

Yorkshire Sculpture Park
West Bretton, West Yorkshire
(01924) 832631
ysp.co.uk
Open-air gallery in beautiful grounds

Tourist information centres

When you arrive at your destination, visit a tourist information centre for help with accommodation and information about local attractions and events, or email your request before you go.

Aysgarth Falls	Aysgarth Falls National Park Centre	(01969) 662910	aysgarth@ytbtic.co.uk
Barnsley	Central Library	(01226) 206757	barnsley@ytbtic.co.uk
Batley	Bradford Road	(01924) 426670	batley@ytbtic.co.uk
Beverley	34 Butcher Row	(01482) 867430	beverley.tic@eastriding .gov.uk
Bradford	City Hall	(01274) 739067	tourist.information@bradford.gov.uk
Bridlington	25 Prince Street	(01262) 673474	bridlington.tic@eastriding.gov.uk
Brigg	Market Place	(01652) 657053	brigg.tic@northlincs.gov.uk
Cleethorpes	42-43 Alexandra Road	(01472) 323111	cleethorpes@ytbtic04.freeserve.co.uk
Danby*	Lodge Lane	(01439) 772737	moorscentre@northyorkmoors-npa.gov.uk
Doncaster	38-40 High Street	(01302) 734309	tourist.information@doncaster.gov.uk
Filey*	John Street	(01723) 383637	fileytic@scarborough.gov.uk
Grassington	Hebden Road	(01756) 752774	grassington@ytbtic.co.uk
Guisborough	Church Street	(01287) 633801	guisborough_tic@redcar-cleveland.gov.uk
Halifax	Piece Hall	(01422) 368725	halifax@ytbtic.co.uk
Harrogate	Crescent Road	(01423) 537300	tic@harrogate.gov.uk
Hawes	Station Yard	(01969) 666210	hawes@ytbtic.co.uk
Haworth	2/4 West Lane	(01535) 642329	haworth@ytbtic.co.uk
Hebden Bridge	New Road	(01422) 843831	hebdenbridge@ytbtic.co.uk
Helmsley	Castlegate	(01439) 770173	helmsley@ytbtic.co.uk
Holmfirth	49-51 Huddersfield Road	(01484) 222444	holmfirth.tic@kirklees.gov.uk
Hornsea*	120 Newbegin	(01964) 536404	hornsea.tic@eastriding.gov.uk
Horton in Ribblesdale	Pen-y-ghent Cafe	(01729) 860333	horton@ytbtic.co.uk
Huddersfield	3 Albion Street	(01484) 223200	huddersfield.tic@kirklees.gov.uk
Hull	1 Paragon Street	(01482) 223559	tourist.information@hullcc.gov.uk
Humber Bridge	Ferriby Road	(01482) 640852	humberbridge.tic@eastriding.gov.uk
Ilkley	Station Road	(01943) 602319	ilkley@ytbtic.co.uk
Ingleton*	The Community Centre Car Park	(015242) 41049	ingleton@ytbtic.co.uk
Knaresborough	9 Castle Courtyard	08453 890177	kntic@harrogate.gov.uk
Leeds	The Arcade, City Station	(0113) 242 5242	tourinfo@leeds.gov.uk
Leeming Bar	The Great North Road	(01677) 424262	leeming@ytbtic.co.uk
Leyburn	4 Central Chambers	(01969) 623069	leyburn@ytbtic.co.uk
Malham		(01969) 652380	malham@ytbtic.co.uk
Malton	58 Market Place	(01653) 600048	maltontic@btconnect.com
Otley	Nelson Street	(01943) 462485	otleytic@leedslearning.net
Pateley Bridge*	18 High Street	08453 890179	pbtic@harrogate.gov.uk
Pickering	The Ropery	(01751) 473791	pickering@ytbtic.co.uk
Redcar	West Terrace	(01642) 471921	redcar_tic@redcar-cleveland.gov.uk

Reeth	The Green	(01748) 884059	reeth@ytbtic.co.uk
Richmond	Friary Gardens	(01748) 850252	richmond@ytbtic.co.uk
Ripon*	Minster Road	08453 890178	ripontic@harrogate.gov.uk
Rotherham Visitor Centre	40 Bridgegate	(01709) 835904	tic@rotherham.gov.uk
Saltburn-by-the-Sea	Station Square	(01287) 622422	saltburn_tic@redcar-cleveland.gov.uk
Scarborough	Brunswick Centre	(01723) 383636	tourismbureau@scarborough.gov.uk
Scarborough (Harbourside)	Sandside	(01723) 383636	harboursidetic@scarborough.gov.uk
Scunthorpe	Carlton Street	(01724) 297354	brigg.tic@northlincs.gov.uk
Selby	52 Micklegate	(01757) 212181	selby@ytbtic.co.uk
Settle	Cheapside	(01729) 825192	settle@ytbtic.co.uk
Sheffield	Winter Garden	(0114) 221 1900	visitor@sheffield.gov.uk
Skipton	35 Coach Street	(01756) 792809	skipton@ytbtic.co.uk
Sutton Bank	Sutton Bank	(01845) 597426	suttonbank@ytbtic.co.uk
Thirsk	49 Market Place	(01845) 522755	thirsktic@hambleton.gov.uk
Todmorden	15 Burnley Road	(01706) 818181	todmorden@ytbtic.co.uk
Wakefield	9 The Bull Ring	0845 601 8353	tic@wakefield.gov.uk
Wetherby	17 Westgate	(01937) 582151	wetherbytic@leedslearning.net
Whitby	Langborne Road	(01723) 383637	whitbytic@scarborough.gov.uk
Withernsea*	131 Queen Street	(01964) 615683	withernsea.tic@eastriding.gov.uk
York (De Grey Rooms)	Exhibition Square	(01904) 621756	tic@york-tourism.co.uk
York (Railway Station)	Station Road	(01904) 621756	kg@ytbyork.swiftserve.net

**seasonal opening*

Alternatively, you can text **TIC LOCATE** to **64118** to find your nearest tourist information centre

Find out **more**

The following publications are available from Yorkshire Tourist Board by logging on to **yorkshirevisitor.com** or calling **0870 609 0000**

Yorkshire Accommodation Guide 2007

Information on Yorkshire and northern Lincolnshire, including hotels, self catering, camping and caravan parks.

Make Yorkshire Yours Magazine

This entertaining magazine is full of articles and features about what's happening in Yorkshire, including where to go and what to do.

Travel **info**

By road:

Motorways: M1, M62, M606, M621, M18, M180, M181, A1(M). Trunk roads: A1, A19, A57, A58, A59, A61, A62, A63, A64, A65, A66.

By rail:

InterCity services to Bradford, Doncaster, Harrogate, Kingston upon Hull, Leeds, Sheffield, Wakefield and York. Frequent regional railway services city centre to city centre, including Manchester Airport service to Scarborough, York and Leeds.

By air:

Fly into Durham Tees Valley, Humberside, Leeds/Bradford International or Robin Hood, Doncaster, Sheffield.

where to stay in
Yorkshire

All place names in the blue bands are shown on the maps at the front of this guide.

A complete listing of all Enjoy England assessed accommodation covered by this guide appears at the back.

Accommodation symbols
Symbols give useful information about services and facilities. Inside the back-cover flap you can find a key to these symbols. Keep it open for easy reference.

ARRATHORNE, North Yorkshire Map ref 5C3

★★★★
SELF CATERING

Units **2**
Sleeps **2–4**
Low season per wk
£145.00–£305.00
High season per wk
£355.00–£440.00

Elmfield Cottages, Bedale

contact Mr & Mrs Lillie, Elmfield Cottages, Arrathorne, Bedale DL8 1NE
t (01677) 450052 **e** elmfieldcottages@hotmail.com **w** elmfieldcottages.co.uk

open All year
payment Cash/cheques

Newly refurbished cottages next to each other. Open-plan lounge/dining/kitchen area, two en suite bedrooms in each cottage, plus one has full wheelchair-accessible shower and level access throughout. Excellent country location between Bedale and Richmond in Yorkshire Dales. Walking, fishing, races. All bedding etc included.

⊕ *From A1 take A684 through Bedale towards Leyburn. After village of Patrick Brompton turn right towards Richmond. Elmfield is then 1.5 miles on right.*

❤ *Short breaks available Oct-Mar – weekends or 3 nights.*

Unit General P Leisure Shop 1.5 miles Pub 1.5 miles

ASKRIGG, North Yorkshire Map ref 5B3

★★★
SELF CATERING

Units **1**
Sleeps **2–6**
Low season per wk
£250.00–£275.00
High season per wk
£350.00–£450.00

Faith Hill Cottage, Askrigg

contact Jennifer Kirkbride, Faith Hill Cottage, Moor Road, Askrigg DL8 3HH
t (01969) 650325 **e** allenkirkbride@hotmail.com

Three-bedroom cottage (one double, two twin) with central heating and coal fire. Fully equipped kitchen, comfortable furnishings, ample parking for three cars.

open All year
payment Cash/cheques

Unit General P

Check it out

Information on accommodation listed in this guide has been supplied by proprietors. As changes may occur you should remember to check all relevant details at the time of booking.

BARMBY MOOR, East Riding of Yorkshire Map ref 4C1

★★★★
SELF CATERING

Units **1**
Sleeps **1–6**
Low season per wk
£375.00–£400.00
High season per wk
£440.00–£600.00

Northwood Coach House, York

contact Ann Gregory, Northwood Coach House, St Helens Square, Barmby Moor YO42 4HF
t (01759) 302305 **e** annjgregory@hotmail.com **w** northwoodcoachhouse.co.uk

open All year
payment Cash/cheques, euros

This pretty, three-bedroomed, converted Victorian coach house overlooks open countryside. Warm and cosy in winter, it is ideally situated in a picturesque village on the edge of the Wolds, only 12 miles from York and convenient for the coast and moors. Pubs, shops and restaurants nearby.

⊕ *At main crossroads in village take road between the pub and general store. House is up a long drive after sharp bend before school field.*

❤ *Short breaks (3 days), bookable 28 days in advance, 60% normal weekly rate.*

Unit **General** P S **Leisure** **Shop** < 0.5 miles **Pub** < 0.5 miles

BEVERLEY, East Riding of Yorkshire Map ref 4C1

★★★★
SELF CATERING

Units **1**
Sleeps **4**
Low season per wk
£265.00–£285.00
High season per wk
£290.00–£350.00

The Cottage, Beverley

contact Kenneth Hearne, The Cottage, 25 Allhallows Road, Walkington HU17 8SH
t (01482) 868310 **e** knhearne@talk21.com **w** akcottage.com

Cottage with two bedrooms (one double, one twin). Furnished to a very high standard. All mod cons and safety requirements. Private parking. Rural, picturesque environment.

open All year
payment Cash/cheques

Unit **General** 5 P **Leisure** **Shop** < 0.5 miles **Pub** < 0.5 miles

BISHOP WILTON, East Riding of Yorkshire Map ref 4C1

★★★
SELF CATERING

Units **2**
Sleeps **2–4**
Low season per wk
£150.00–£220.00
High season per wk
£250.00–£350.00

Grange Farm Holiday Cottages, Bishop Wilton

contact Mr Richard & Mrs Judith Davy, Grange Farm Holiday Cottages, The Grange, Bishop Wilton YO42 1SA
t (01759) 369500 **e** richarddavy@supanet.com **w** thegrangefarm.com

Well-equipped, comfortable cottages on working farm. One double bed and one zip-linked twin bed. Peaceful, with panoramic views. Easy reach of York, coast and moors. Open all year. Pets and children welcome.

open All year
payment Cash/cheques

Unit **General** P S **Leisure** **Shop** 1 mile **Pub** 1 mile

BRIDLINGTON, East Riding of Yorkshire Map ref 5D3

★–★★
SELF CATERING

Units **5**
Sleeps **2–6**
Low season per wk
£140.00–£210.00
High season per wk
£210.00–£420.00

Hemsley Holiday Flats, Bridlington

contact Mr E Halliday, Helmsley Holiday Flats, 5 Alexandra Drive, Bridlington YO15 2HZ
t (01262) 672603

open All year
payment Cash/cheques

Hemsley Holiday Flats enjoy a quiet location on a private road, overlooking the North Bay seafront, bowling green and Flamborough Head. Accommodation is self-contained with fridge, cooker and colour TV. Scooter- and wheelchair-charging facilities. We are close to shops, cafes and the Leisure World complex. Dogs are welcome by arrangement.

⊕ *From M62 via Bridlington promenade.*

Unit General P Shop 0.5 miles Pub 0.5 miles

BRIDLINGTON, East Riding of Yorkshire Map ref 5D3

★–★★★
SELF CATERING

Units **4**
Sleeps **1–5**
Low season per wk
£70.00–£200.00
High season per wk
£200.00–£380.00

Highcliffe Holiday Apartments, Bridlington

contact Mrs Pat Willcocks, Highcliffe Holiday Apartments, 19 Albion Terrace, Bridlington YO15 2PJ
t (01262) 674127 **e** john.willcocks@fsmail.net **w** highcliffe.net

open All year
payment Cash/cheques

On the seafront, south facing, only 50m from sandy beach and promenade. All apartments have uninterrupted views along the beach to the harbour. Ideal position for main shopping centre, restaurants and Leisure World complex. Fully equipped, with high standard of furnishing, each with own private bathroom facilities.

⊕ *In North Bay area of Bridlington, 300m north of well-signposted Leisure World complex.*

Unit General P Leisure Shop < 0.5 miles Pub < 0.5 miles

Check the maps

Colour maps at the front pinpoint all the places you will find accommodation entries in the regional sections. Pick your location and then refer to the place index at the back to find the page number.

BRIDLINGTON, East Riding of Yorkshire Map ref 5D3

★★★★★
SELF CATERING

Units **3**
Sleeps **2–5**
Low season per wk
£300.00–£500.00
High season per wk
£500.00–£800.00

North Kingsfield Holiday Cottages, Fraisthorpe, Bridlington

contact Peter and Helen Milner, North Kingsfield Holiday Cottages, North Kingsfield Farm, Fraisthorpe YO15 3QP
t (01262) 673743 **e** helen@northkingsfield.co.uk **w** northkingsfield.co.uk

open All year
payment Cash/cheques

The Stable features a spacious living area, wood-burning stove, farmhouse-style kitchen and two en suite bedrooms. The Mill House is a beautiful ground-floor apartment with two en suite bedrooms. The Grainary, ideal for couples, features a whirlpool spa bath. Free use of private leisure club two miles away.

⊕ *Look for the brown road signs between Bridlington (approx 3 miles) and Fraisthorpe village (approx 2 miles) on the main A165 Bridlington to Hull road.*

Unit General P Leisure
Shop 4 miles Pub 2 miles

BURNSALL, North Yorkshire Map ref 5B3

★★★★
SELF CATERING

Units **1**
Sleeps **1–6**
Low season per wk
£220.00–£340.00
High season per wk
£400.00–£475.00

The Sycamores, Skipton

contact Sheila Carr, DSC Holiday Lettings Ltd, Moor Green Farm, Skipton BD23 5NR
t (01756) 752435 **f** (01756) 752435 **e** carr@totalise.co.uk
w yorkshirenet.co.uk/stayat/mannacottage

open All year
payment Cash/cheques

Overlooking the village green and river, this large family cottage offers a high standard of accommodation. Its well-equipped kitchen, comfortable bedrooms and cosy lounge with open fire make it ideal for any time of the year. Patio with barbecue and garden furniture. Excellently situated for walking or touring the Dales.

⊕ *From Skipton take B6265, Grassington road. In Threshfield take the B6160 to Burnsall.*

♥ *Weekends and short breaks available Oct-Mar.*

Unit General Leisure Shop < 0.5 miles Pub < 0.5 miles

CHOP GATE, North Yorkshire Map ref 5C3

★★★★
SELF CATERING

Units **1**
Sleeps **2–7**
Low season per wk
£325.00–£400.00
High season per wk
£400.00–£500.00

Broadfields Cottage, Middlesbrough

contact Mrs Judith Staples, Broadfields Cottage, Broadfields, Chop Gate, Middlesborough TS9 7JB
t (01642) 778384 **w** diamond.org/broadfields

Stone-built, semi-detached, four-bedroom cottage of character with one four-foot bed, one double, one single and a bunk bed. Outstanding views; set in the National Park.

open All year
payment Cash/cheques

Unit General P Leisure Shop 2 miles Pub 1 mile

DALTON, North Yorkshire Map ref 5B3

★★★
SELF CATERING

Units 1
Sleeps 4
Low season per wk
£200.00–£300.00
High season per wk
£300.00–£400.00

Keepers Cottage, Dalton

contact Dorothy Lewis, Keepers Cottage, Dalton Hall, Dalton, Richmond DL11 7GU
t (01833) 621446 **e** peter.lewis63@btinternet.com

Lovingly restored Georgian gamekeeper's cottage. Lounge, eat-in kitchen, two bedrooms. Beautiful views across open countryside.

open All year
payment Cash/cheques, euros

Unit General P Leisure Shop 8 miles Pub 0.5 miles

DANBY, North Yorkshire Map ref 5C3

★★
SELF CATERING

Units 1
Sleeps 1–7
Low season per wk
£160.00–£260.00
High season per wk
£190.00–£300.00

Clitherbecks Farm, Whitby

contact Catherine Harland, Clitherbecks Farm, Clitherbecks, Danby YO21 2NT
t (01287) 660321 **e** nharland@clitherbecks.freeserve.co.uk **w** clitherbecks.freeserve.co.uk

Get away from it all in this 18thC farmhouse at the head of its own valley in the North York Moors National Park.

open All year
payment Cash/cheques

Unit General P Shop 1 mile Pub 1 mile

EGTON BRIDGE, North Yorkshire Map ref 5D3

★★★★
SELF CATERING

Units 3
Sleeps 2–4
Low season per wk
£194.00–£324.00
High season per wk
£324.00–£648.00

Broom House Cottages, Egton Bridge, Whitby

contact Mrs Maria White, Broom Cottage, Whitby YO21 1XD
t (01947) 895279 **f** (01947) 895657 **e** mw@broom-house.co.uk

open All year
payment Credit/debit cards, cash/cheques

Recently refurbished stone cottages situated in Egton Bridge village in the beautiful Esk Valley, in the North York Moors National Park. Excellent walking etc. Shop and pub within walking distance. Visit website for virtual tour.

Unit General P Leisure Shop 1 mile Pub 0.75 miles

FILEY, North Yorkshire Map ref 5D3

★★★
SELF CATERING

Units 5
Sleeps 1–5
Low season per wk
£295.00–£365.00
High season per wk
£450.00–£555.00

The Cottages, Filey

contact Mr & Mrs David Teet, The Cottages, Muston Grange Farm, Muston Road, Filey YO14 0HU
t (01723) 516620 **f** (01723) 516620

open All year
payment Cash/cheques, euros

Situated between Muston and Filey, the cottages are a range of converted, traditional, ex-farm buildings providing quality accommodation in a private courtyard setting. One ground-floor cottage is suitable for wheelchair access. Twenty minutes' walk to beach or town. Ideal spot for access to many of Yorkshire's attractions and countryside.

Unit General P Leisure Shop 1 mile Pub 1 mile

GIGGLESWICK, North Yorkshire Map ref 5B3

★★★
SELF CATERING

Units 1
Sleeps 2–4
Low season per wk
£185.00–£255.00
High season per wk
£255.00–£350.00

Black Horse Cottage, Giggleswick

contact Anthony & Ann Haygarth, Black Horse Cottage, 12 Barfield Grove, Alwoodley LS17 8TF
t (0113) 269 3960 **e** haygarthtony@aol.com **w** black-horse-cottage.co.uk

18thC character cottage, renovated and refurbished to provide cosy family accommodation, while retaining much of its original character, including beamed ceilings. Ideal for touring/walking the Dales and the Lakes.

open All year
payment Cash/cheques, euros

Unit General Leisure Shop < 0.5 miles Pub < 0.5 miles

GILLING WEST, North Yorkshire Map ref 5C3

★★★★
SELF CATERING

Units 6
Sleeps 2–10
Low season per wk
£177.00–£450.00
High season per wk
£265.00–£725.00

Gilling Old Mill Cottages, Richmond

contact Mr & Mrs Hugh & Joyce Bird, Gilling Old Mill, Waters Lane, Gilling West, Richmond DL10 5JD
t (01748) 822771 **f** (01748) 821734 **e** admin@yorkshiredales-cottages.com
w yorkshiredales-cottages.com

Magnificent properties converted from traditional stone barns situated in idyllic courtyard setting, overlooking delightful open countryside. An ideal base from which to explore Swaledale and surrounding area.

open All year
payment Cash/cheques

Unit General P Leisure Shop < 0.5 miles Pub < 0.5 miles

GRASSINGTON, North Yorkshire Map ref 5B3

★★★★
SELF CATERING

Units 1
Sleeps 1–4
Low season per wk
£220.00–£340.00
High season per wk
£400.00–£475.00

Manna Cottage, Skipton

contact Mrs Sheila Carr, Moor Green Farm, Tarns Lane, Threshfield, Skipton BD23 5NR
t (01756) 752435 **f** (01756) 752435 **e** carr@totalise.co.uk
w yorkshirenet.co.uk/stayat/mannacottage

open All year
payment Cash/cheques

An 18thC former lead miner's cottage which has been renovated to a high standard and now boasts many original features including beams and fireplaces. Being situated in Grassington, this cosy and comfortable cottage is ideal as a base from which to explore the Dales. Parking, excellent facilities. Shops and pubs two minutes' walk.

⊕ *Grassington is on the B6265. Turn into main square, carry on up main street until town hall. The cottage is to the left of Art Garden shop.*

♥ *Weekend breaks available Oct-Mar.*

Unit General 3 P Leisure Shop < 0.5 miles Pub < 0.5 miles

Friendly help and advice

Did you know there are more than 500 tourist information centres throughout England? It adds up to a lot of friendly help and advice. You'll find contact details at the beginning of each regional section.

GRINTON, North Yorkshire Map ref 5B3

★★★★
SELF CATERING

Units **3**
Sleeps **2–13**
Low season per wk
£305.00–£395.00
High season per wk
£415.00–£580.00

Feetham Holme, Richmond

contact Mr Ian Robinson, Plantation Business Services, Plantation House, Chipping Road, Clitheroe BB7 3LX
t (01254) 826546 **f** (01254) 826880 **e** plantation@talk21.com

open All year
payment Cash/cheques

Fully renovated cottages in the heart of the National Park, beautiful secluded location. Tastefully finished and fully equipped accommodation. Wood-burning stoves and original features make the cottages a delight to enjoy. Design award for renovation. Quote VB7 when booking.

⊕ *Pass through Heelaugh, take 1st left (Askrigg), cross River Swale, right at T-junction. Feetham Holme is on right after approx 0.75 miles.*

❤ *Weekend and mid-week breaks available. Discount for booking all units together.*

Unit General P Shop 5 miles Pub 5 miles

GRISTHORPE BAY, North Yorkshire Map ref 5D3

★★★
SELF CATERING

Units **1**
Sleeps **1–5**
Low season per wk
£100.00–£200.00
High season per wk
£350.00–£410.00

58 Clarence Drive, Filey

contact Mrs Mary Graves, 5 Whiston Drive, Filey YO14 0DB
t (01723) 512791 **e** marygraves5@tiscali.co.uk

Two-bedroomed bungalow; two singles in one, double in other. Fully fitted kitchen. Enclosed back garden safe for children and pets. Off-street parking. Close to shops and crescent.

open All year
payment Cash/cheques, euros

Unit General P Shop 1 mile Pub 1 mile

HALIFAX, West Yorkshire Map ref 4B1

★★★★
SELF CATERING

Units **2**
Sleeps **2–4**
Low season per wk
£270.00–£290.00
High season per wk
£380.00–£435.00

Cherry Tree Cottages, Barkisland, Nr Halifax

contact Stan & Elaine Shaw, Cherry Tree Cottages, Wall Nook, Barkisland, Halifax HX4 0BL
t (01422) 372662 **f** (01422) 372662 **e** cherrytree@yorkshire-cottages.co.uk
w yorkshire-cottages.co.uk

open All year
payment Credit/debit cards, cash/cheques

Warm, comfortable, stone-built cottages set in two acres of natural woodland/heather garden with superb Pennine views and direct access to open countryside and footpaths. Close to a quiet Calderdale village with good pubs and restaurants nearby. Ideal location for exploring Brontë Country and Pennine Yorkshire. Pets and children welcome.

⊕ *Ten-minute drive from either jct 22 or 24 on M62. Two miles from Ripponden on B6113, and 400yds from the Spring Rock Tavern.*

❤ *Short breaks available, minimum 3 nights. Check our website for late availability.*

Unit General P Leisure Shop 1 mile Pub < 0.5 miles

If you have access needs...

Look for the National Accessible Scheme symbols if you have special hearing, visual or mobility needs. An index of all accommodation participating in the scheme can be found at the back of this guide.

HARROGATE, North Yorkshire Map ref 4B1

★★★★
SELF CATERING

Units **23**
Sleeps **2–4**
Low season per wk
£325.00–£455.00
High season per wk
£370.00–£535.00

Ashness Apartments, Harrogate

contact Mr Spinlove & Miss H Spinlove, Ashness Apartments, 15 St Marys Avenue HG2 0LP
t (01423) 526894 **f** (01423) 700038 **e** office@ashness.com **w** ashness.com

open All year
payment Credit/debit cards, cash/cheques

High-quality apartments, superbly situated in a nice, quiet road of fine Victorian townhouses very near the town centre of Harrogate. Excellent shops, restaurants and cafes are a short walk away through Montpellier Gardens with the Stray and Valley Gardens just around the corner.

⊕ *From the centre of Harrogate proceed down Montpellier Hill to roundabout. Left onto Cold Bath Road. St Marys Avenue is 2nd road on left-hand side.*

❤ *Short breaks available from £60pn, minimum 2 nights.*

Unit General P S

HARROGATE, North Yorkshire Map ref 4B1

★★★★
SELF CATERING

Units **1**
Sleeps **1–5**
Low season per wk
£300.00–£400.00
High season per wk
£350.00–£450.00

Ashrigg, Harrogate

contact Mr & Mrs Peter & Angela Holt, 39 Spring Lane, Harrogate HG3 1NP
t (01423) 871177 **f** (01423) 871177 **e** pholt@westrigg.freeserve.co.uk **w** ashrigg.co.uk

Fully furnished/equipped first-floor apartment. One double, one twin and one single. Full central heating, fully fitted kitchen. Garden for guests' use. Off-road parking.

open All year
payment Cash/cheques

Unit General P S **Shop** < 0.5 miles **Pub** < 0.5 miles

HARROGATE, North Yorkshire Map ref 4B1

★★★★
SELF CATERING

Units **1**
Sleeps **1–5**
Low season per wk
£175.00–£295.00
High season per wk
£250.00–£495.00

The Barn @ Fir Tree Farm, Harrogate

contact Mrs Rebecca Donnelly, High Winsley, Brimham Rocks Road, Burnt Yates, Harrogate HG3 3EP
t (01423) 779708 **e** thebarninharrogate@hotmail.com **w** thebarninharrogate.co.uk

open All year
payment Cash/cheques

Recently converted, The Barn offers stylish accommodation comprising two luxurious en suite bedrooms, fully equipped kitchen, cosy lounge and dining area. Features include widescreen TV and CD player. The Barn is situated just 15 minutes from Harrogate and overlooks the scenic Nidderdale Valley. Children's ball pool and toys available on request.

⊕ *Located just outside Burnt Yates; please call us or see our website for directions and map.*

❤ *Complimentary welcome hamper provided on arrival.*

Unit General P S **Leisure** **Shop** 4 miles **Pub** 1 mile

CYCLISTS WELCOME WELCOME CYCLISTS

A holiday on two wheels

For a fabulous freewheeling break seek out accommodation participating in our Cyclists Welcome scheme. Look out for the symbol and plan your route online at nationalcyclenetwork.org.

HARROGATE, North Yorkshire Map ref 4B1

★★★
SELF CATERING

Units **14**
Sleeps **2–7**
Low season per wk
Min £300.00
High season per wk
Max £885.00

Rudding Holiday Park, Harrogate

Rudding Holiday Park, Follifoot, Harrogate HG3 1JH
t (01423) 870439 **f** (01423) 870859 **e** holiday-park@ruddingpark.com **w** ruddingpark.com

open All year
payment Credit/debit cards, cash/cheques, euros

Choose from our traditional stone-built houses in the beautiful grounds of Rudding Park or our timber lodges, set in delightful woodland clearings, many overlooking a small lake. Three miles south of Harrogate, Deer House family pub, shop, swimming pool, children's playground, games room, 18-hole golf course and driving range.

⊕ *Three miles south of Harrogate to the north of A658 between its junction with the A61 to Leeds and the A661 to Wetherby.*

❤ *Receive £20 off your booking if you mention this advert when making your reservation.*

Unit General P Leisure Shop < 0.5 miles Pub < 0.5 miles

HAWKSWICK, North Yorkshire Map ref 5B3

★★★★★
SELF CATERING

Units **1**
Sleeps **9**
Low season per wk
£750.00
High season per wk
£970.00–£1,600.00

Redmire Farm, Hawkswick, Skipton

contact Neil Tomlinson, Shaw Farm, Shaw Lane, Oxenhope BD22 9QL
t (01535) 648791 & 07768 230522 **f** (01535) 643671 **e** info@mckeighley.co.uk **w** redmire-farm.com

Recently renovated, detached, Grade II Listed farmhouse dating from 1711. Idyllically situated in the heart of the Dales National Park.

open All year
payment Cash/cheques, euros

Unit General P Leisure
Shop 0.5 miles Pub 1.5 miles

HAWORTH, West Yorkshire Map ref 4B1

★★★★
SELF CATERING

Units **1**
Sleeps **1–4**
Low season per wk
Max £260.00
High season per wk
Max £395.00

Heron Cottage, Haworth, Keighley

contact Mr & Mrs Richard and Jan Walker, Heron Cottage, Vale Barn, Mytholmes Lane, Haworth BD22 0EE
t (01535) 648537 **e** jan.w@virgin.net

Comfortable two-bedroom cottage in peaceful location beside River Worth. Set in paddocks and woodland with abundant walks. Haworth village, Yorkshire Dales and steam trains nearby.

open All year
payment Cash/cheques, euros

Unit General P Shop 1 mile Pub 1 mile

A holiday for Fido?

Some proprietors welcome well-behaved pets. Look for the symbol in the accommodation listings. You can also buy a copy of our new guide – Pets Come Too! – available from good bookshops and online at enjoyenglanddirect.com.

HAWORTH, West Yorkshire Map ref 4B1

★★★★-★★★★★
SELF CATERING

Units **9**
Sleeps **1–7**
Low season per wk
£275.00–£500.00
High season per wk
£330.00–£660.00

Hewenden Mill Cottages, Cullingworth

contact Janet Emanuel, Hewenden Mill Cottages, Cullingworth BD13 5BP
t (01535) 274259 **f** (01535) 273943 **e** info@hewendenmillcottages.co.uk
w hewendenmillcottages.co.uk

open All year
payment Credit/debit cards, cash/cheques

Ideally located in idyllic Brontë Country, our cottages provide a perfect base for exploring northern England. Set in ten acres of ancient woodland, they form part of an old water-mill complex and have been recently renovated to provide luxury, self-catering accommodation. Ideal for lovers of walking, wildlife and Wuthering Heights!

⊕ *Situated on the B6144, Bradford to Haworth road, 1 mile from Cullingworth, at the bottom of Hewenden Valley, opposite the viaduct.*

❤ *Short breaks our speciality: 3-night weekend and 4-night mid-week (excl Bank Holidays).*

Unit General P Leisure Shop 1 mile Pub 1 mile

HAWORTH, West Yorkshire Map ref 4B1

★★★
SELF CATERING

Units **2**
Sleeps **2**
Low season per wk
£165.00–£215.00
High season per wk
£170.00–£350.00

Weavers Cottage and Loft, Keighley

contact Gaye Bond, Weavers Cottage & Weavers Loft, 10 & 8 Mill Hill, Haworth BD22 8QT
t (01535) 211184 **f** (01535) 211184 **e** g.j.bond@blueyonder.co.uk **w** weaverscottage-web.co.uk

The weavers' cottage and loft, built in 1780, is a Grade II Listed building of special historic interest. There are many original features including mullion windows.

open All year
payment Cash/cheques

Unit General P Shop < 0.5 miles Pub < 0.5 miles

HAWORTH, West Yorkshire Map ref 4B1

★★★
SELF CATERING

Units **1**
Sleeps **1–4**
Low season per wk
£300.00–£325.00
High season per wk
£325.00–£350.00

Woolcombers Cottage, Haworth, Keighley

contact Ms Kay Doyle Johnson, 276 Broad Street, San Luis Obispo, California 93405, USA
t (01535) 646778 **e** woolcombers@clara.co.uk **w** bronte-country.com/accomm/woolcombers

Cosy, beautiful, charming, three-storey cottage in ultimate Brontë location. Situated in cobbled main street, yards from Parsonage. Built 1820, original beams, fully modernised. All our delighted guests come again!

open All year
payment Cash/cheques

Unit General 6 Shop < 0.5 miles Pub < 0.5 miles

HEBDEN BRIDGE, West Yorkshire Map ref 4B1

SELF CATERING

Units **1**
Sleeps **3**
Low season per wk
£110.00–£140.00
High season per wk
£120.00–£190.00

3 Birks Hall Cottage, Cragg Vale, Hebden Bridge

contact Hilda Wilkinson, 3 Birks Hall Cottage, Upper Birks, Cragg Vale HX7 5SB
t (01422) 882064

Country cottage with two bedrooms, bathroom, kitchen and lounge with Georgian windows. In a small, picturesque village near the Pennine centre of Hebden Bridge.

open All year
payment Cash/cheques

Unit General P Shop 1.25 miles Pub < 0.5 miles

HELMSLEY, North Yorkshire Map ref 5C3

★★★★
SELF CATERING

Units **1**
Sleeps **1–4**
Low season per wk
Min £190.00
High season per wk
£285.00–£350.00

Townend Cottage, Beadlam

contact Mrs Margaret Begg, Townend Farmhouse, High Lane, Beadlam, Nawton, York YO62 7SY
t (01439) 770103 **e** margaret.begg@ukgateway.net **w** visityorkshire.com

open All year
payment Cash/cheques

Originally part of an 18thC farmhouse, this is a very warm, comfortable, two-bedroomed stone cottage with oak beams. Situated off the main road in a village three miles from the charming market town of Helmsley. Ideal for walking or touring Moors, coast and York. Central heating and log fire included in price.

⊕ *Enter Beadlam on the A170 from Helmsley. Take 1st left turning into High Lane and then 1st right turning into Townend Cottage Drive.*

Unit General P Leisure Shop 3 miles Pub < 0.5 miles

HIGH BENTHAM, North Yorkshire Map ref 5B3

★★★★
SELF CATERING

Units **1**
Sleeps **1–4**
High season per wk
£190.00–£270.00

Holmes Farm Cottage, Lancaster

contact Mrs Story, Holmes Farm Cottage, Holmes Farm, Lower Bentham, Lancaster LA2 7DE
t (015242) 61198 **e** lucy@clucy.demon.co.uk

open All year
payment Cash/cheques

Tastefully converted stone cottage with large, landscaped garden, surrounded by 127 acres of beautiful pastureland. Ideal base for visiting Lake District, Dales and coast.

Unit General P Leisure Shop 1 mile Pub 0.5 miles

HOLMFIRTH, West Yorkshire Map ref 4B1

★★★★
SELF CATERING

Units **1**
Sleeps **1–6**
Low season per wk
£200.00–£300.00
High season per wk
£300.00–£400.00

Mytholmbridge Studio Cottage, Holmfirth

contact Sue Clay, Mytholmbridge Studio Cottage, Luke Lane, Holmfirth HD9 7TB
t (01484) 686642 **e** cottages@mytholmbridge.co.uk **w** mytholmbridge.co.uk

Secluded 250-year-old stone barn situated in 'Last of the Summer Wine' country. Original beams retained within the contemporary open space. Garden, large car park, close to local amenities.

open All year
payment Cash/cheques, euros

Unit General P Leisure Shop < 0.5 miles Pub < 0.5 miles

It's all quality-assessed accommodation

Our commitment to quality involves wide-ranging accommodation assessment. Ratings and awards were correct at the time of going to press but may change following a new assessment. Please check at the time of booking.

HORNSEA, East Riding of Yorkshire Map ref 4D1

★★★
SELF CATERING

Units **1**
Sleeps **1–4**
Low season per wk
£200.00–£300.00
High season per wk
£300.00–£400.00

Cherry Tree, Hornsea

contact Mrs Rita Leonard, Cherry Tree, 11 Willows Drive, Off Newbegin, Hornsea HU18 1DA
t (01964) 527245 **f** (01964) 527521 **e** ritaleonard@serverX1.net

A semi-detached bungalow in a cul-de-sac off the main shopping area of the town, with gardens backing onto the junior-school grounds. There are two golf courses and a leisure centre with heated pool nearby.

open All year
payment Cash/cheques, euros

Unit General Leisure Shop < 0.5 miles Pub < 0.5 miles

HUDDERSFIELD, West Yorkshire Map ref 4B1

★★★★
SELF CATERING

Units **1**
Sleeps **1–4**
Low season per wk
£150.00–£200.00
High season per wk
£220.00–£400.00

1535 Melting Point, Huddersfield

contact Ms Karen Bonnett, Mapleton Farm, Mead Lane, Lower Basildon, Reading RG8 9NY
t (0118) 984 5800 **f** (0118) 984 5621 **e** karen.bonnett@bt.com **w** meltingpointcottage.co.uk

Brand new, fully furnished, two-bedroom ground-floor apartment with swimming and gym facilities included. Concierge service available.

open All year
payment Cash/cheques

Unit General Leisure Shop < 0.5 miles Pub < 0.5 miles

HULL, East Riding of Yorkshire Map ref 4C1

★★★
SELF CATERING

Units **1**
Sleeps **2–5**
Low season per wk
£275.00–£300.00
High season per wk
£300.00–£375.00

Cottage in the Pond, Garton

contact Mr Adrian Fisher, Middle Keld Countryside Experience, North Field Farm, Garton HU11 4QB
t (01964) 527256 **f** (01964) 529029 **e** info@middlekeld.co.uk **w** middlekeld.co.uk

The cottage is located on a farm in a quiet location. Completely refurbished to a high standard, this 300-year-old cottage still retains its original character. Woodland and paddock walk on site.

open All year
payment Credit/debit cards, cash/cheques

Unit General Leisure Shop 2 miles Pub 2 miles

HUSTHWAITE, North Yorkshire Map ref 5C3

★★★
SELF CATERING

Units **3**
Low season per wk
£120.00–£200.00
High season per wk
£200.00–£300.00

Greg's Cottage, York

contact Mr Greg Harrand, Hedley House Hotel, 3 Bootham Terrace, York YO30 7DH
t (01904) 637404 **f** (01904) 639774 **e** greg@hedleyhouse.com **w** hedleyhouse.com

A one-bedroom cottage and two one-bedroom apartments in Easingwold town centre. Recently renovated to a high standard.

open All year
payment Credit/debit cards, cash/cheques

Unit General Leisure

How many beds?

The minimum and maximum number of people that each property can accommodate is shown. If an entry includes details of more than one property the sleeping capacity may vary between them. Please check when you make your booking.

KETTLEWELL, North Yorkshire Map ref 5B3

★★★★
SELF CATERING

Units **4**
Sleeps **1–4**
Low season per wk
Min £220.00
High season per wk
Max £440.00

Fold Farm Cottages, Kettlewell

contact Mrs Barbara Lambert, Fold Farm Cottages, Fold Farm, Kettlewell, Skipton BD23 5RH
t (01756) 760886 **f** (01756) 760464 **e** info@foldfarm.co.uk **w** foldfarm.co.uk

open All year
payment Cash/cheques, euros

Stone-built cottages beside village stream. Beamed ceilings, open fires, fully fitted kitchens with dishwashers and washer/dryer machines. Private off-road parking. Each cottage has a double and twin bedroom. Easy walking distance to pubs, shops and church.

Unit General Leisure

KIRKBYMOORSIDE, North Yorkshire Map ref 5C3

★★★★
SELF CATERING

Units **1**
Sleeps **6**
Low season per wk
£350.00–£385.00
High season per wk
£400.00–£450.00

Cherry View Cottage, York

contact Mrs Sylvianne Drinkel, Cherry View Cottage, Hagg Road, Off Starfitts Lane, Kirkbymoorside YO62 7JF
t (01751) 431714 **f** (01751) 430130 **e** sylvianne@talktalkbusiness.net

open All year
payment Cash/cheques

Cottage set at edge of farm with breathtaking views across the Vale of Pickering. Spacious, self-contained, three-bedroomed accommodation, furnished to a high standard. Lawned garden, ample parking. Pets welcome by prior arrangement.

⊕ *Follow A170 Helmsley to Scarborough road. Left for Fadmoor, continue for 1 mile. Right past the farm entrance to cottage on left with wrought iron gates.*

Unit General Leisure Shop 1 mile Pub 1.5 miles

KIRKBYMOORSIDE, North Yorkshire Map ref 5C3

★★★★
SELF CATERING

Units **2**
Sleeps **2–4**
Low season per wk
£275.00–£350.00
High season per wk
£350.00–£375.00

The Cornmill, Kirkbymoorside

contact Chris & Karen Tinkler, The Cornmill, Kirkby Mills, Kirkbymoorside YO62 6NP
t (01751) 432000 **e** cornmill@kirbymills.demon.co.uk **w** kirbymills.demon.co.uk

open All year
payment Credit/debit cards, cash/cheques

Sympathetically restored stable mews cottages in 18thC watermill complex on the River Dove. Well-appointed accommodation with linen and towels, TV, video, mini hi-fi and central heating included. Bed and bath downstairs, living room upstairs. Garden and barbecue. Meals in the millhouse by arrangement.

⊕ *A170 towards Scarborough. After Kirkbymoorside roundabout take left turn (after Kedholme-only exit) into Kirkby Mills. Entrance to car park is 20m on right.*

Unit General Leisure Shop 0.5 miles
Pub 0.75 miles

Key to symbols

Open the back flap for a key to symbols.

KIRKBYMOORSIDE, North Yorkshire Map ref 5C3

★★★★
SELF CATERING

Units **2**
Sleeps **4**
Low season per wk
£230.00–£360.00
High season per wk
£370.00–£430.00

Surprise View Cottage & Field Barn Cottage,
Kirkbymoorside

contact Mrs Ruth Wass, Sinnington Lodge, Sinnington, York YO62 6RB
t (01751) 431345 **f** (01751) 431345 **e** info@surpriseviewcottages.co.uk
w surpriseviewcottages.co.uk

open All year
payment Cash/cheques

Historic barn conversions on farmstead (originally an old mill and tannery) giving panoramic views over moorland edge, and immediate access to field and woodland walks. Warm, roomy accommodation with excellent-quality furnishings and fittings. A wealth of beams and original stone and brick features. 'Comfort' is the key word.

⊕ *From the A1 take York intersection, then A64 to Malton, north on A169 to Pickering, west along A170 to Kirkbymoorside. Then turn north to Gillamoor.*

❤ *Short breaks available Nov-Mar – 3-night stay (excluding Christmas and half-terms).*

Unit General P Leisure Shop 3 miles
Pub 1 mile

KNARESBOROUGH, North Yorkshire Map ref 4B1

★★★★
SELF CATERING

Units **1**
Sleeps **1–2**
Low season per wk
£235.00–£260.00
High season per wk
£260.00–£295.00

The Granary, Knaresborough

contact Mrs Rachel Thornton, Gibbet House Farm, Farnham Lane, Knaresborough HG5 9JP
t (01423) 862325 & 07970 000068 **f** (01423) 862271

open All year
payment Cash/cheques, euros

Traditional, converted granary adjacent to farmhouse. Situated in 30 acres of parkland with stunning views of the Nidderdale Valley. Furnished to a high standard. Five miles Harrogate, two miles Knaresborough. Central for Dales, Yorkshire coast, Herriot and Heartbeat Country. The perfect setting for a peaceful and comfortable holiday.

⊕ *From A1(M) Boroughbridge, A6055, short distance from Knaresborough. Right down Farnham Lane, property on the right, 0.25 miles to 1st gate.*

❤ *Short breaks available. 3-night stays Oct-Mar.*

Unit General P S Leisure

LEYBURN, North Yorkshire Map ref 5B3

★★★-★★★★
SELF CATERING

Units **6**
Sleeps **2–6**
Low season per wk
£140.00–£215.00
High season per wk
£215.00–£350.00

Dales View Holiday Homes, Leyburn

contact Messrs John Chilton, Dales View Holiday Homes, Jenkins Garth, Leyburn DL8 5SP
t (01969) 623707 & (01969) 622808 **f** (01969) 623707 **e** daleshols@aol.com **w** daleshols.co.uk

open All year
payment Cash/cheques

Stone-built period cottages and self-contained apartments form a secluded courtyard only 80m from Leyburn marketplace. Ideal touring and walking centre for the Dales. Comfortable, well-maintained properties, heated throughout winter. Private parking, garden and play area. Some properties with panoramic views over Wensleydale.

⊕ *A1(M) jct 56. The properties are down a lane off the south-east corner of Leyburn marketplace.*

❤ *Short breaks available Oct-Apr.*

Unit General P S Leisure **Shop** < 0.5 miles **Pub** < 0.5 miles

LOCKTON, North Yorkshire Map ref 5D3

★★★
SELF CATERING

Units **1**
Sleeps **2–4**
Low season per wk
Min £295.00
High season per wk
Max £295.00

The Little Barn, Pickering

contact Mr James Fisk, The Little Barn, The Courtyard, Ivy Cottage, Lockton YO18 7PY
t (01751) 460325 **e** judi@btinternet.com

This charming 17thC barn is peacefully situated in a spacious cottage garden between moors and forest. Oak beams throughout. Ideal for steam train, 'Heartbeat' Country, York and east coast.

open All year
payment Cash/cheques

Unit General P Leisure Pub 0.5 miles

LOW ROW, North Yorkshire Map ref 5B3

★★★★
SELF CATERING

Units **2**
Sleeps **2–3**
Low season per wk
£229.00–£257.00
High season per wk
£357.00–£378.00

Birds Nest Cottages, Low Row, Richmond

contact Charles & Julie Folkes, Birds Nest Cottages, Low Row, Richmond DL11 6PP
t (01748) 886858 **f** (01748) 886858 **e** info@yorkshiredales-cottages.net
w yorkshiredales-cottages.net

open All year
payment Cash/cheques

Beautifully renovated lead-miners' cottages with panoramic views over Swaledale and outside terrace with eating facilities and barbecue. Furnished and equipped to a high standard with king-size bed in open-beamed bedroom. Within easy reach of lovely market towns with excellent shopping, great pubs and outstanding restaurants. Walks from the door. An ideal romantic retreat.

⊕ *Leave A1 at Scotch Corner to Richmond. Take A6108, then B6270 to Reeth. Continue to Low Row. Turn right into Langthwaite. Turn left 250yds after cattle grid.*

Unit General P Leisure Shop 3 miles Pub 3 miles

MALTON, North Yorkshire Map ref 5D3

★★★★
SELF CATERING

Units **1**
Sleeps **2–3**
Low season per wk
£205.00–£275.00
High season per wk
£305.00–£355.00

Swans Nest Cottage, Malton

contact Yvonne Dickinson, Swans Nest Cottage, Abbotts Farm House, Ryton YO17 6SA
t (01653) 694970 **e** swansnestcottage@hotmail.com **w** uk-holiday-cottages.co.uk/swans-nest

open All year
payment Credit/debit cards, cash/cheques

A cosy, two-bedroomed, fully equipped old farm cottage, caringly modernised to a very high standard, situated in the heart of rural Ryedale. Ideally located, being central to the North York Moors, Yorkshire Wolds, east coast seaside and the old City of York. Price includes logs and coal for multi-fuel stove.

⊕ *A64, turn onto A169 Whitby/Pickering road. Left after approx 200yds (Ryton/Eden Camp). Abbotts Farm is signposted approx 2.5 miles along on the right.*

♥ *Mid-week and weekend breaks generally available.*

Unit General 3 P Shop 5 miles Pub 2.5 miles

Pool search

If a swimming pool is an essential element of your holiday accommodation check out the special index at the back of this guide.

MALTON, North Yorkshire Map ref 5D3

★★★★
SELF CATERING

Units **1**
Sleeps **1–4**
Low season per wk
£202.00–£246.00
High season per wk
£280.00–£440.00

Walnut Garth, Nr Malton

t (01751) 434261 **f** (01653) 691293 **e** cas@radfords.org **w** radfords.org

open All year
payment Cash/cheques

Tastefully decorated, two-bedroom cottage furnished to a high standard with all modern conveniences. Walnut Garth is set in the grounds of owner's property at edge of village, yet only two miles from market town of Malton and excellent selection of local amenities and attractions. Easy access to York and coast.

⊕ *From A64, take Malton turn-off, turn onto B1257 toward Hovingham. Travel for 2 miles. Last house on left in Swinton village.*

❤ *10% discount for stays of 2 weeks or longer.*

Unit General Leisure Shop < 0.5 miles Pub < 0.5 miles

NEWSHAM, North Yorkshire Map ref 5B3

★★★★
SELF CATERING

Units **1**
Sleeps **2–6**
Low season per wk
£230.00–£450.00
High season per wk
£360.00–£450.00

Dyson House Barn, Richmond

contact Mr & Mrs Clarkson, Dyson House, Newsham, Richmond DL11 7QP
t (01833) 627365 **e** dysonbarn@tinyworld.co.uk **w** cottageguide.co.uk/dysonhousebarn

open All year
payment Cash/cheques

Between Richmond and Barnard Castle this spacious, well-equipped, converted farm barn makes an ideal base for touring Teesdale, Swaledale, North Yorkshire, Durham and Cumbria. Retaining many original features there are three large bedrooms including one on ground floor with shower room. Patio with barbecue. Two public house/restaurants 10 minutes' walk. Brochure available.

⊕ *Leave A1(M); travel west on A66 from Scotch Corner (8 miles). A66 motel, left (Newsham). After approx 200yds, at Smallways Inn, branch right. We are at end of road.*

❤ *Short stays available 4 Nov-31 Mar (excl school holidays), minimum 2 nights.*

Unit General P Leisure Shop 6 miles Pub < 0.5 miles

NORTH DALTON, East Riding of Yorkshire Map ref 4C1

★★★
SELF CATERING

Units **1**
Sleeps **3–4**
Low season per wk
£182.00–£310.00
High season per wk
£300.00–£410.00

Old Cobbler's Cottage, Driffield, North Dalton

t (01377) 217523 & (01377) 217662 **f** (01377) 217754 **e** chris@adastra-music.co.uk
w waterfrontcottages.co.uk

open All year
payment Credit/debit cards, cash/cheques

19thC, mid-terraced, oak-beamed cottage overlooking picturesque pond in a peaceful and friendly farming village, between York and Yorkshire's Heritage Coast. Ideally located for walking, visiting the coast, historic houses, races at York and Beverley or just relaxing. Excellent inn/restaurant adjacent, shops 1.5 miles. Pets welcome.

⊕ *On entering North Dalton, take narrow lane up the side of The Star pub car park. Old Cobbler's is a mid-terraced cottage in the row.*

❤ *Short breaks available, 2 nights (excl Christmas, New Year, Easter and Bank Holidays).*

Unit General P Leisure Shop 1.5 miles Pub < 0.5 miles

OXENHOPE, West Yorkshire Map ref 4B1

★★★
SELF CATERING

Units **1**
Sleeps **2–3**
Low season per wk
£100.00–£120.00
High season per wk
£180.00–£200.00

Yate Cottage, Oxenhope, Keighley

contact Mrs Jean M M Dunn, Yate House, Yate Cottage, Yate Lane, Oxenhope, Keighley BD22 9HL
t (01535) 643638 **e** jeanandhugh@dunnyate.freeserve.co.uk
w uk-holiday-cottages.co.uk/yatecottage

18thC cottage adjoining Yate House, a 'yeoman' house of striking architectural appearance. South-facing view over beautiful garden to hills. No short breaks.

open All year except Christmas and New Year
payment Cash/cheques

Unit General 8 P Shop < 0.5 miles Pub < 0.5 miles

PATELEY BRIDGE, North Yorkshire Map ref 5C3

★★★★
SELF CATERING & SERVICED APARTMENTS

Units **4**
Sleeps **2–10**
Low season per wk
£195.00–£385.00
High season per wk
£335.00–£710.00

Helme Pasture, Old Spring Wood, Harrogate

contact Mrs Rosemary Helme, Hartwith Bank, Summerbridge, Harrogate HG3 4DR
t (01423) 780279 **f** (01423) 780994 **e** info@helmepasture.co.uk **w** helmepasture.co.uk

open All year
payment Credit/debit cards, cash/cheques, euros

Scandinavian lodges and converted Dales barn. Award-winning conservation woodland. Holiday in tranquil surroundings. Country walks. Close to a multitude of attractions including Fountains Abbey, castles, Yorkshire villages and floral towns – Harrogate, Skipton, Ripon, York. Traditional markets. Pet friendly, and a warm family welcome.

⊕ *Harrogate, B6165 towards Pateley Bridge. At Summerbridge (Flying Dutchman pub), turn up Hartwith Bank. Helme Pasture is 0.3 miles on left.*

❤ *Short breaks available.*

Unit General P Leisure Shop < 0.5 miles Pub < 0.5 miles

PICKERING, North Yorkshire Map ref 5D3

★★★★–★★★★★
SELF CATERING

Units **8**
Sleeps **2–10**
Low season per wk
£255.00–£855.00
High season per wk
£495.00–£1,835.00

Beech Farm Cottages, Nr Pickering

contact Mrs Pat Massara, Beech Farm Cottages, Wrelton YO18 8PG
t (01751) 476612 **f** (01751) 475032 **e** holiday@beechfarm.com **w** beechfarm.com

open All year
payment Credit/debit cards, cash/cheques, euros

Award-winning, luxury stone cottages with heated indoor pool, sauna, children's play area, gardens and paddock. Horse, pony and llama in field. Delightful location in quiet village on edge of North York Moors National Park. Also convenient for coast and York. The cottages are in a courtyard setting backing onto fields. Brochure available or please phone.

⊕ *The village of Wrelton is just off the A170, 3 miles west of Pickering.*

❤ *4-times winner of Yorkshire Tourist Board's Self-Catering Holiday of the Year award.*

Unit General P Leisure Shop 2 miles Pub < 0.5 miles

Prices

These are shown for one week's accommodation. If an entry includes details of more than one property it is usual that the minimum price is for low season in the smallest property and the maximum price is for high season in the largest property.

PICKERING, North Yorkshire Map ref 5D3

★★★★
SELF CATERING

Units **8**
Sleeps **1–11**

Low season per wk
£190.00–£385.00
High season per wk
£410.00–£1,005.00

Easthill Farm House and Lodges, Pickering

contact Mrs Diane Stenton, Easthill Farm House and Lodges, Wilton Road, Thornton Dale, Pickering YO18 7QP
t (01751) 474561 **e** info@easthill-farm-holidays.co.uk **w** easthill-farm-holidays.co.uk

open All year
payment Credit/debit cards, cash/cheques

Beautifully equipped/furnished farmhouse divided into apartments (separate entrances) with adjoining cottage. Also pine lodges (one fully wheelchair accessible) nestled in woodland bordering landscaped gardens. Enjoy all-weather tennis, jacuzzi, putting, barbecue, play areas, games room and some farm animals. Friendly, personal supervision throughout. Central for North York Moors, forestry, coast and York.

⊕ *From York take A64 (Scarborough) road. At Pickering (Whitby) exit onto A169. At Pickering roundabout, right onto A170. Through Thornton-le-Dale. Easthill is last house on right.*

♥ *Short breaks available. Finalist in White Rose 'Self-Catering Holiday of the Year' award.*

Unit General Leisure
Shop 0.75 miles Pub 0.75 miles

PICKERING, North Yorkshire Map ref 5D3

★★★–★★★★★
SELF CATERING

Units **11**
Sleeps **4–12**

Low season per wk
£350.00–£750.00
High season per wk
£500.00–£1,500.00

Hungate Cottages, Pickering

contact Mr Richard Robertson, Hungate Cottages, Recreation Road, Pickering YO18 7ET
t (01751) 476382 **f** (01751) 476382 **e** holidays@hungatecottages.co.uk **w** hungatecottages.co.uk

open All year
payment Credit/debit cards, cash/cheques, euros

Luxury, highly individual holiday cottages which have the unique appeal of being a short walk from the town centre, whilst retaining the tranquillity and peacefulness of the countryside. Easy access to the Moors, York, Castle Howard, steam railway and the beautiful port towns of Whitby and Scarborough. See website for further information.

⊕ *In Pickering locate roundabout where A169 and A170 cross, 50yds south take turning to west (cricket field on left). Arched entrance to Hungate Cottages 50yds on right.*

Unit General P Leisure
Shop < 0.5 miles Pub < 0.5 miles

PICKERING, North Yorkshire Map ref 5D3

★★★★
SELF CATERING

Units **9**
Sleeps **2–8**

Low season per wk
£189.00–£380.00
High season per wk
£424.00–£1,050.00

Keld Head Farm Cottages, Pickering

contact Julian & Penny Fearn, Keld Head Farm Cottages, Keld Head, Pickering YO18 8LL
t (01751) 473974 **e** julian@keldheadcottages.com **w** keldheadcottages.com

open All year
payment Cash/cheques, euros

On the edge of Pickering, in open countryside overlooking fields where sheep and cows graze. Beautiful, spacious, character stone cottages with pantile roofs, traditional stone fireplaces and beamed ceilings, tastefully furnished with the emphasis on comfort and relaxation. Some rooms with four-poster beds. Award-winning gardens with garden house. York, moors and coast easily accessible.

⊕ *Cottages are on western periphery of Pickering, at corner of A170 and road signposted Marton. Turn into this road and the entrance is on the left.*

♥ *Senior citizen and 2-person discounts. Short breaks.*

Unit General P Leisure Shop < 0.5 miles
Pub 0.5 miles

PICKERING, North Yorkshire Map ref 5D3

★★★★
SELF CATERING

Units **3**
Sleeps **4–6**
Low season per wk
£282.00–£346.00
High season per wk
£610.00–£790.00

Let's Holiday, Pickering

contact Mr John Wicks, Let's Holiday, Pickering YO18 8QA
t (01751) 475396 **e** holiday@letsholiday.com **w** letsholiday.com

open All year
payment Credit/debit cards, cash/cheques

Comfortable and fully equipped offering indoor pool, spa and sauna, and set in extensive level grounds at the heart of our National Park village. Paddocks and stabling for DIY livery. Village pub, play area and duck pond nearby. Perfect for exploring North York Moors, the coast and City of York.

⊕ *In Pickering turn left at roundabout along A170. After approx 300m turn right at traffic lights. Follow road for approx 4 miles to reach Newton-on-Rawcliffe.*

♥ *Low season short breaks: 2 or 3 nights over the weekend and 4 nights for the price of 3 mid-week.*

Unit General Leisure Shop 4 miles Pub < 0.5 miles

PICKERING, North Yorkshire Map ref 5D3

★★★
SELF CATERING

Units **2**
Sleeps **2**
Low season per wk
£190.00–£260.00
High season per wk
£260.00–£310.00

The Old Forge Cottages, Pickering

contact Judy French, The Old Forge, Wilton, Pickering YO18 7JY
t (01751) 477399 **e** theoldforge1@aol.com **w** forgecottages.co.uk

open All year
payment Cash/cheques

Cosy cottages for two, all year round. Forge stable conversions providing comfortable, well-equipped accommodation with patio and barbecue. Private parking, easy access to bus route. Local attractions include steam railway, Dalby Forest, Yorkshire Moors, Eden Camp, Flamingo Land and Langdale Quest.

⊕ *Follow the A170 Pickering-Scarborough road. Turn left in Wilton, just after bus stop. Park in courtyard behind The Old Forge. Sign on building.*

Unit General Leisure Shop 1 mile Pub 1 mile

RAVENSCAR, North Yorkshire Map ref 5D3

★★★-★★★★
SELF CATERING

Units **3**
Sleeps **2–4**
Low season per wk
£215.00–£260.00
High season per wk
£437.00–£550.00

Smugglers Rock Country House, Ravenscar, Scarborough

contact Mrs Sharon Gregson, Smugglers Rock Country House, Staintondale Road, Ravenscar, Scarborough YO13 0ER
t (01723) 870044 **e** info@smugglersrock.co.uk **w** smugglersrock.co.uk

open All year
payment Cash/cheques

Beautiful cottages furnished to a very high standard and fully equipped for maximum comfort and relaxation. Situated in the North York Moors National Park with wonderful views and friendly farm animals, the cottages are an ideal base for country and coastal holidays. B&B also available.

⊕ *Take road signposted Ravenscar from A171 (Scarborough to Whitby). 0.5 miles before village, take left fork after Smugglers Rock (on left) and turn into car park.*

♥ *3-night and last-minute breaks available Oct-Mar.*

Unit General Leisure Shop 2 miles Pub 2 miles

Check it out

Please check prices, quality ratings and other details when you book.

REETH, North Yorkshire Map ref 5B3

★★★★
SELF CATERING

Units **3**
Sleeps **2–5**
Low season per wk
£255.00–£275.00
High season per wk
£400.00–£440.00

Burton House, Greystones and Charlie's Stable, Reeth

contact Mrs Patricia Procter, Hill Cottage, Reeth, Richmond DL11 6SQ
t (01748) 884273 **w** uk-cottages.com

Stone-built cottages, beautifully situated near the River Arkle, providing every comfort and amenity at no extra cost.

open All year
payment Cash/cheques

Unit General Leisure Shop < 0.5 miles Pub < 0.5 miles

RIPON, North Yorkshire Map ref 5C3

★★★★
SELF CATERING

Units **1**
Sleeps **8**
Low season per wk
Min £300.00
High season per wk
Max £600.00

Intake, Ripon

contact Fiona McConnell, 3 Hippingstones Lane, Corbridge NE45 5JP
e kfiona@tiscali.co.uk **w** intakefarmhouse.co.uk

Traditional stone farmhouse, newly renovated. Furnished to high standard. Log fire, Stanley cooker. Lovely view over fields – listen to curlews. Many diverse attractions within easy reach.

open All year except Christmas and New Year
payment Cash/cheques

Unit General Shop 0.75 miles Pub 0.75 miles

ROBIN HOOD'S BAY, North Yorkshire Map ref 5D3

★★★
SELF CATERING

Units **1**
Sleeps **2–4**
Low season per wk
£190.00–£250.00
High season per wk
£270.00–£355.00

Lingers Hill, Whitby

contact Frances Harland, Lingers Hill, Thorpe Lane, Robin Hood's Bay, Whitby YO22 4TQ
t (01947) 880608 **e** info@ytb.org.uk

Cosy character cottage situated on the edge of the village at Robin Hood's Bay. Close to amenities, ideal walking and cycling area. Lovely views. Two double-bedded rooms.

open All year
payment Cash/cheques

Unit General Leisure Shop < 0.5 miles Pub < 0.5 miles

ROSEDALE ABBEY, North Yorkshire Map ref 5C3

★★★★
SELF CATERING

Units **1**
Sleeps **2–8**
Low season per wk
£300.00–£550.00
High season per wk
£550.00–£850.00

Woodlea, Pickering

contact Pauline Belt, Woodlea, 2 Low Green, Copmanthorpe YO23 3SB
t (01904) 705549 **f** (01937) 831296 **e** p.belt@daviscoleman.com **w** rosedaleholidaycottage.co.uk

Delightful house with stunning views. Three twin bedrooms and one double. Beautiful, well-maintained garden. New kitchen recently fitted. Log fire in the lounge. Village shop, pubs and restaurants within five minutes' walk.

open All year
payment Cash/cheques

Unit General Leisure Shop 0.75 miles Pub 0.5 miles

Take a break

Look out for special promotions and themed breaks. This could be your chance to indulge an interest, find a new one, or just relax and enjoy exceptional value! Offers are highlighted in colour (and are subject to availability).

SCARBOROUGH, North Yorkshire Map ref 5D3

★★★★
SELF CATERING

Units **1**
Sleeps **1–4**
Low season per wk
Min £250.00
High season per wk
Max £450.00

Lendal House, Scarborough

contact Petra Scott, Lendal House, 34 Trafalgar Square, Scarborough YO12 7PY
t (01723) 372178 **e** info@lendalhouse.co.uk **w** lendalhouse.co.uk

Luxury, self-contained ground-floor flat with four-poster bed. Near cricket ground; five minutes' walk to North Bay Beach and town centre. Also great for walks on the North York Moors.

open All year
payment Cash/cheques

Unit General

SCARBOROUGH, North Yorkshire Map ref 5D3

★★★★
SELF CATERING

Units **4**
Sleeps **1–7**
Low season per wk
£255.00–£350.00
High season per wk
£450.00–£600.00

Lingholm Court, Lebberston, Scarborough

contact Mrs Caroline Woodhouse, Lingholm Lane, Lebberston, Scarborough YO11 3PG
t (01723) 586365 **f** (01723) 585838 **e** info@lingholm.co.uk **w** lingholm.co.uk

open All year
payment Cash/cheques, euros

Barn conversions and original farmhouse situated in beautiful countryside, down peaceful lane. Attractively furnished, excellently equipped, providing every comfort. Set around stunning enclosed courtyard. Pool table. Play house. Farmhouse has superb enclosed garden and log fires. Ideal for families, bird-watchers, walkers or a romantic getaway. Short breaks. Brochure.

⊕ *Between Scarborough (5 miles) and Filey (3.5 miles).*

❤ *Discount for 2 people on weekly lets. Mid-week short breaks: 4 nights for the price of 3.*

Unit General P Leisure Shop 2 miles
Pub 1.5 miles

SCARBOROUGH, North Yorkshire Map ref 5D3

★★★★
SELF CATERING

Units **9**
Sleeps **1–8**
Low season per wk
£270.00–£580.00
High season per wk
£565.00–£1,460.00

Wrea Head Cottage Holidays, Scarborough

contact Mr Steve Marshall, Wrea Head Cottage Holidays, Barmoor Lane, Scarborough YO13 0PG
t (01723) 375844 **e** ytb@wreahead.co.uk **w** wreahead.co.uk

open All year
payment Credit/debit cards, cash/cheques

A rural heaven inspiring charm, character and tranquillity. National winners of VisitBritain 'England for Excellence' award for Best Self-Catering Holiday of the Year. Superb indoor heated swimming pool, jacuzzi and sauna. Stunning panoramic sea views and beautiful countryside on edge of National Park. Lovely, award-winning gardens. Picnic park.

⊕ *From Scarborough take A171 towards Whitby, past Newby village into Scalby. Turn left into Barmoor Lane, continuing for 0.5 miles. Turn left at Wrea Head Holidays Cottages.*

❤ *Excellent-value short breaks available Nov-Apr, including 4 nights for the price of 3.*

Unit General P Leisure

Use your i's

Tourist information centres provide a wealth of information and friendly advice, both before you go and during your stay. Refer to the front of this section for a list of tourist information centres in the region.

SELBY, North Yorkshire Map ref 4C1

★★★
SELF CATERING & SERVICED APARTMENTS

Units **1**
Sleeps **1–6**
Low season per wk
£210.00–£300.00
High season per wk
£360.00–£380.00

Rusholme Grange Cottage, Drax, Selby

contact Anne Roberts, Rusholme Cottage, Rusholme Grange, Drax YO8 8PW
t (01757) 618257 **e** anne@rusholmegrange.co.uk **w** rusholmegrange.co.uk

A delightful cosy cottage on our rural family farm which boasts a fully fitted kitchen, two generous bedrooms (double and twin) and separate sitting room with log fire.

open All year
payment Cash/cheques

Unit General Leisure Shop 1.5 miles Pub 1.5 miles

SETTLE, North Yorkshire Map ref 5B3

★★★★
SELF CATERING

Units **1**
Sleeps **5**
Low season per wk
£185.00–£290.00
High season per wk
£375.00–£390.00

Cragdale Cottage, Settle

contact Mr Paul Whitehead, Cragdale Cottage, 139 Hitchings Way, Reigate RH2 8EP
t (020) 8647 8397 & (01737) 247179 **e** paul@cragdalecottage.co.uk **w** cragdalecottage.co.uk

Stone cottage in heart of traditional market town. Three bedrooms, open fire, refurbished 2003, well equipped. Excellent walking/touring base.

open All year
payment Cash/cheques

Unit General

SETTLE, North Yorkshire Map ref 5B3

★★★
SELF CATERING

Units **1**
Sleeps **1–5**
Low season per wk
£191.00–£228.00
High season per wk
£293.00–£368.00

Middle Cottage, Settle

contact Ms Anna Greenhalgh, Suncroft, Austwick, Via Lancaster LA2 8DA
t (01524) 251735 & 07967 890043 **f** (01524) 251735 **e** agreenhalgh@austwick.org

A stone terraced cottage decorated to a high standard. Modern fitted kitchen, spacious beamed sitting room, open fire, patio area, three bedrooms (one double, one twin, one single).

open All year
payment Cash/cheques, euros

Unit General Leisure Shop < 0.5 miles Pub < 0.5 miles

SIGGLESTHORNE, East Riding of Yorkshire Map ref 4D1

★★★★
SELF CATERING

Units **1**
Sleeps **1–4**
Low season per wk
£150.00–£250.00
High season per wk
£250.00–£350.00

Peggy's Cottage, Hornsea

contact Ms Jude Collingwood, Peggy's Cottage, Hall Farm, Hull HU11 5QH
t (01964) 535395 **e** p.collingwood@btinternet.com

Once a stable, now a comfortable and pretty cottage enjoying a peaceful, rural setting four miles from the sea and Hornsea Mere.

open All year
payment Cash/cheques, euros

Unit General Leisure Shop 1 mile Pub 1 mile

To your credit

If you book by phone you may be asked for your credit card number. If so, it is advisable to check the proprietor's policy in case you have to cancel your reservation at a later date.

SKIPTON, North Yorkshire Map ref 4B1

★★★-★★★★★
SELF CATERING

Units **7**
Sleeps **1–4**
Low season per wk
£150.00–£260.00
High season per wk
£230.00–£400.00

Cawder Hall Cottages, Skipton

contact Graham Pearson, Cawder Hall Cottages, Cawder Lane, Skipton BD23 2TD
t (01756) 791579 **f** (01756) 797036 **e** info@cawderhallcottages.co.uk **w** cawderhallcottages.co.uk

open All year
payment Credit/debit cards, cash/cheques

Peaceful, tastefully converted farm cottages in open countryside, one mile from castle and historic market town of Skipton. Suitable for disabled.

⊕ *Follow Keighley Road from Skipton town centre. After 0.5 miles you will reach some 'keep left' bollards. Here turn left over canal bridge. Cawder Lane is 100yds on right.*

Unit General P Leisure Shop 1 mile Pub 0.5 miles

SKIPTON, North Yorkshire Map ref 4B1

SOWERBY BRIDGE, West Yorkshire Map ref 4B1

★★★
SELF CATERING

Units **1**
Sleeps **4**
Low season per wk
£180.00–£250.00
High season per wk
£250.00–£350.00

Lane Ends Barn, Sowerby Bridge

contact Ms Carola Ibbotson, Steep Lane, Sowerby Bridge HX6 1PE
t (01422) 833267 **e** carolalubk@hotmail.com **w** laneends-selfcatering.co.uk

Modern apartment in a modernised farmhouse in stunning rural location. Two bedrooms, two bathrooms, fully equipped kitchen. Superb local walks/bike rides. Near restaurants. On-site parking. Great transport links.

open All year except Christmas and New Year
payment Cash/cheques, euros

Unit General P Leisure Shop 1 mile Pub < 0.5 miles

Take a break

Many establishments offer special promotions and themed breaks. It's a golden opportunity to indulge an interest or find a new one, or just relax and enjoy exceptional value! Offers and promotions are highlighted in colour (and are subject to availability).

STAINTONDALE, North Yorkshire Map ref 5D3

★★★
SELF CATERING

Units 4
Sleeps 1–6
Low season per wk
£165.00–£240.00
High season per wk
£280.00–£450.00

White Hall Farm Holiday Cottages, Scarborough

contact Mr & Mrs James and Celia White, White Hall Farm Holiday Cottages, White Hall Farm, Scarborough YO13 0EY
t (01723) 870234 **e** celia@white66.fsbusiness.co.uk **w** whitehallcottages.co.uk

open All year
payment Cash/cheques

Peace and tranquillity found on our 130-acre sheep farm with stunning coastal and rural views. Walks from your door amid woodland, streams and coastal path. Home from home, well-equipped, welcoming cottages, which are separate from the farm. Ideally located to explore North Yorkshire. Dogs/horses made welcome.

⊕ *Scarborough to Whitby (A171). At Cloughton, right turn to Shire Horse Farm. Go straight on for 1 mile on country lane. Cottages at end of lane.*

Unit General P Leisure Shop 6 miles Pub 4 miles

STAITHES, North Yorkshire Map ref 5C3

★★★
SELF CATERING

Units 1
Sleeps 4
Low season per wk
£230.00–£275.00
High season per wk
£275.00–£370.00

Glencoe Cottage, Staithes

contact David Purdy, The Vicarage, Church Street, Kirkbymoorside, York YO62 6AZ
t (01751) 431452

Cosy, harbourside, mid-terrace former fisherman's cottage with open fire, situated in a picturesque fishing village steeped in history. Two bedrooms (one double, one twin). Close to beach, shops, pubs and restaurants.

open All year
payment Cash/cheques

Unit General Leisure Shop < 0.5 miles Pub < 0.5 miles

STAITHES, North Yorkshire Map ref 5C3

★★★
SELF CATERING

Units 1
Sleeps 5
Low season per wk
£237.00–£325.00
High season per wk
£330.00–£595.00

Pennysteel Cottage, Staithes

contact Chris Wade, Waterfront Cottages, 2 Star Row, North Dalton, Driffield YO25 9UX
t (01377) 217662 & (01377) 217523 **f** (01377) 217754 **e** chris@adastra-music.co.uk
w waterfrontcottages.co.uk

open All year
payment Credit/debit cards, cash/cheques

Old fisherman's cottage of unique character with beamed ceilings, wood-panelled walls and wood-burning stove. All windows and terrace overlook the picturesque harbour of Staithes. Ideal for the coast and walking. Top-quality restaurant, pub serving food, cafes, art gallery and craft and local shops all within a few yards.

⊕ *Go down hill into the old village. Bear right at the bottom. Take the 2nd passage on the left after the pub. Take left fork.*

❤ *5% discount for repeat booking for 2007.*

Unit General Leisure Shop < 0.5 miles Pub < 0.5 miles

Town, country or coast?

The entertainment, shopping and innovative attractions of the big cities, the magnificent vistas of the countryside or the relaxing and refreshing coast – this guide will help you find what you're looking for!

THIRSK, North Yorkshire Map ref 5C3

★★★★★
SELF CATERING

Units 1
Sleeps 1–6
Low season per wk
£350.00–£450.00
High season per wk
£500.00–£575.00

Church Garth, Maunby

contact Vicky Hudson, Church Garth, Birkdale Cottage, The Green, York YO7 4HG
t (01845) 587215 **f** (01642) 437921 **e** svhudson@btinternet.com

Beautiful detached bungalow close to the River Swale, on the edge of Maunby village green. Perfect for walking or sightseeing holidays; also fishing rights available. Good food pub in village.

open All year
payment Cash/cheques

Unit General P Leisure Shop 6 miles Pub < 0.5 miles

TODMORDEN, West Yorkshire Map ref 4B1

★★★
SELF CATERING

Units 1
Sleeps 4
Low season per wk
£145.00–£175.00
High season per wk
£175.00–£205.00

The Cottage, Todmorden

contact Mr & Mrs Bentham, The Cottage, Causeway East Farmhouse, Lee Bottom Road, Todmorden OL14 6HH
t (01706) 815265 **e** andrew-b_5@tiscali.co.uk

Part of a 17thC farmhouse beneath the Pennine Way. Ideal for walking and touring.

open All year
payment Cash/cheques

Unit General P Leisure Shop 2 miles Pub 0.5 miles

TODMORDEN, West Yorkshire Map ref 4B1

★★★
SELF CATERING

Units 1
Sleeps 10
Low season per wk
Max £600.00
High season per wk
Max £900.00

Shoebroad Barn, Todmorden

contact Mrs Horsfall, Pennine House, Pennine Grove, Todmorden OL14 8AU
t (01706) 817015 **e** thehorsfalls@beeb.net **w** shoebroadbarn.co.uk

Large, well-contained barn in lovely open area with commanding views and only one mile from town centre. Secluded, yet close to all amenities.

open All year
payment Cash/cheques

Unit General P Leisure Shop 1 mile Pub 1 mile

WHITBY, North Yorkshire Map ref 5D3

★★★★
SELF CATERING

Units 1
Sleeps 1–5
Low season per wk
Min £280.00
High season per wk
Max £430.00

Allum Garth Cottage, Sleights

contact Barbara Tyerman, Allum Garth Cottage, Partridge Nest Farm, Eskdaleside, Sleights YO22 5ES
t (01947) 810450 **f** (01947) 811413 **e** barbara@partridgenestfarm.com **w** partridgenestfarm.com

Allum Garth Cottage is situated within the heart of Partridge Nest Farm. The cottage is attractive and comfortable with all modern conveniences. One double and one twin with extra bed.

open All year
payment Cash/cheques

Unit General Leisure Shop 2.5 miles Pub 1.5 miles

Ancient and modern

Experience timeless favourites or discover the latest must-sees. Whatever your choice, be inspired by the places of interest highlighted for each region and the events listed towards the back of this guide.

WHITBY, North Yorkshire Map ref 5D3

★★★
SELF CATERING

Units **1**
Sleeps **2**
Low season per wk
£200.00–£250.00
High season per wk
£300.00–£400.00

Bolthole Cottage, Whitby

t (01947) 880063 **e** kaaren@noble47.freeserve.co.uk **w** boltholecottage.co.uk

Quiet, warm, comfortable cottage. Two minutes from harbour. Good base for walking. Bath, shower, TV, DVD and modern kitchen.

open All year
payment Cash/cheques

Unit General Leisure Shop < 0.5 miles Pub < 0.5 miles

WHITBY, North Yorkshire Map ref 5D3

★–★★★★
SELF CATERING

Units **8**
Sleeps **2–4**
Low season per wk
£145.00–£380.00
High season per wk
£185.00–£510.00

Carlton House Holiday Accommodation, Whitby

contact Susan Brookes, Carlton House Holiday Accommodation, 5 Royal Crescent West Cliff, Whitby YO21 3EJ
t (01947) 602868 & (01947) 603456 **e** info@carltonhouseapartments.co.uk
w northstaraccommodation.co.uk

The accommodation is located on West Cliff with stunning views out to sea from all the front rooms. Convenient for all amenities Whitby has to offer. Refurbished 2005.

open All year
payment Credit/debit cards, cash/cheques

Unit General Leisure Shop < 0.5 miles Pub < 0.5 miles

WHITBY, North Yorkshire Map ref 5D3

★★–★★★
SELF CATERING

Units **5**
Sleeps **1–7**
Low season per wk
£160.00–£340.00
High season per wk
£280.00–£495.00

Glencoe Holiday Flats, Whitby

contact Julie Charlton, Glencoe Holiday Flats, 18 Linden Close, Briggswath YO21 1TA
t (01947) 811531 & (01947) 602474 **w** holidayflat.co.uk

Spacious, comfortably furnished flats, two with sunny balconies, one with four-poster bed. Westcliff area, close to all amenities. Send SAE for brochure.

open All year
payment Cash/cheques

Unit General P Shop < 0.5 miles Pub < 0.5 miles

WHITBY, North Yorkshire Map ref 5D3

SELF CATERING

Units **1**
Sleeps **1–5**
Low season per wk
£225.00–£340.00
High season per wk
£440.00–£540.00

Kingfisher Cottage, Whitby

contact Ingrid Flute, Holiday Accommodation Agency, 1 Hillcrest Avenue,, Scarborough YO12 6RQ
t (01723) 376777 **f** (01723) 376777 **e** info@ingridflute.co.uk **w** ingridflute.co.uk

Close to water's edge with unrivalled views on redevelopment of an old fishing wharf in Whitby. Within walking distance of all amenities. Ideal for all east coast and North Yorkshire Moors. Cottage ref: 2588.

open All year
payment Credit/debit cards, cash/cheques

Unit General P Leisure Shop < 0.5 miles
Pub < 0.5 miles

WHITBY, North Yorkshire Map ref 5D3

NorthStar Accommodation, Whitby

Open: All Year. Payment: Credit/debit card - Book Online.

An exclusive collection of luxury holiday accommodation in and around the ancient sea port of Whitby. Three cottages and one town apartment are available (4-star), and Carlton House, offering 2 apartments (4-star), and six flats (1-3 stars).

Philip Moore, Hildegarde House, 27 Skinner Street, Whitby, North Yorkshire, YO21 3AH

Tel: +44 (0)1947 603456 Mob: +44 (0)7990 972858
email: info@northstaraccommodation.co.uk
web site: www.northstaraccommodation.co.uk

Units 12
Sleeps 1-10
Low season per week
£145 - £650
High season per week
£185 - £1050

WHITBY, North Yorkshire Map ref 5D3

★★★★
SELF CATERING

Units **1**
Sleeps **2–4**
Low season per wk
£280.00–£380.00
High season per wk
£380.00–£500.00

The Old Granary, Whitby

contact Mrs Jackie Richardson, Raven Hill Farm, Dunsley, Nr Sandsend, Whitby YO21 3TJ
t (01947) 893331 **f** (01947) 893331 **e** jackie.richardson6@btopenworld.com

open All year
payment Cash/cheques, euros

Recently restored, 17thC former granary overlooking Sandsend Bay. Set on a working farm with one of the finest views in North Yorkshire, possibly the country. Facilities include one double and one twin bedroom, comfortable lounge, exposed beams, oak floors and fully equipped kitchen. The perfect base for exploring Yorkshire.

⊕ *Go through Sandsend, take right turn for Dunsley on leaving the village. We are about 800yds up the hill, the 1st farm on the left.*

❤ *Mid-week and weekend breaks available in low season.*

Unit General P Leisure Shop < 0.5 miles Pub < 0.5 miles

WHITBY, North Yorkshire Map ref 5D3

SELF CATERING

Units **8**
Sleeps **2–7**
Low season per wk
£150.00–£275.00
High season per wk
£230.00–£440.00

Swallow Holiday Cottages, Whitby

contact Jillian McNeil, Swallow Holiday Cottages, Long Leas Farm, Hawsker YO22 4LA
t (01947) 603790 **f** 0870 705 2362 **e** Jillian@swallowcottages.co.uk **w** swallowcottages.co.uk

open All year
payment Credit/debit cards, cash/cheques

Swallow Cottages, regarded by many as the premier rural cottages in the area, converted listed buildings and others in two groups. Ample parking. Some wheelchair-friendly. Situated in North York Moors National Park. All have stunning views. Two miles to Whitby centre.

⊕ *One-and-a-half miles south of Whitby on the A171. Turn off into Stainsacre.*

❤ *Short breaks available in winter.*

Unit General 1 P Leisure Shop 2 miles Pub < 0.5 miles

WHITBY, North Yorkshire Map ref 5D3

★★★
SELF CATERING

Units **1**
Sleeps **1–6**
Low season per wk
£200.00–£250.00
High season per wk
£250.00–£350.00

White Horse Cottage, Whitby

contact George & Steven Walker, White Horse Cottage, 5 White Horse Yard, Church Street, Whitby YO22 4BW
t (01709) 367031

Grade II Listed building with period features situated at the rear of the Old White Horse and Griffin pub near market square. Gas-fired central heating.

open All year
payment Cash/cheques

Unit General Leisure Shop < 0.5 miles Pub < 0.5 miles

Phone ahead

Even the most ardent pet lover would appreciate some advance warning of Rover's visit, so please phone ahead and check what facilities will be available.

YORK, North Yorkshire Map ref 4C1

★★★
SELF CATERING

Units **1**
Sleeps **1–4**
Low season per wk
£265.00–£355.00
High season per wk
£405.00–£440.00

17 Escrick Street, York

contact Helen Jones, Holidayork, 11 Walmgate, York YO1 9TX
t (01904) 632660 **f** (01904) 632434 **e** agents@holidayork.co.uk **w** holidayork.co.uk

A very nice apartment situated near the centre and shops. Two second-floor bedrooms (one double, one twin), first-floor lounge/diner, fully fitted and equipped kitchen and bathroom. Private parking.

open All year
payment Credit/debit cards, cash/cheques

Unit General P Shop < 0.5 miles Pub < 0.5 miles

YORK, North Yorkshire Map ref 4C1

★★★★
SELF CATERING

Units **7**
Low season per wk
£265.00–£375.00
High season per wk
£395.00–£440.00

24 Woodsmill Quay, York

contact Mrs Helen Jones, Holidayork, 11 Walmgate, York YO1 9TX
t (01904) 632660 **f** (01904) 632434 **e** agents@holidayork.co.uk **w** holidayork.co.uk

open All year
payment Credit/debit cards, cash/cheques

Woodsmill Quay is on the riverside and is a beautiful flat with one bedroom which overlooks the Ouse. Quietly situated, but within easy reach of the centre of York and its attractions. Private parking.

Directions given at time of booking.

Unit General P

YORK, North Yorkshire Map ref 4C1

★★★★★
SELF CATERING

Units **1**
Sleeps **2–8**
Low season per wk
Min £295.00

Abbeygate House, York

contact Mr & Mrs Halliday, 1 Grange Drive, Leeds LS18 5EQ
t (0113) 258 9833

open All year
payment Credit/debit cards, cash/cheques

Superior new Georgian-style townhouse situated on the prestigious Bishops Wharf riverside development overlooking the medieval city walls and only a few minutes' walk along the river into York. Stunning new dining-kitchen, spacious lounge with four luxurious leather sofas and south-facing balcony. Three bathrooms, one with jacuzzi bath. Private parking.

A1036 (York), past racecourse to city walls, right into Nunnery Lane. Take right-hand lane at junction into Clementhorpe. 2nd left, then left past Cherry Hill House.

Short breaks available. Discounts for smaller groups.

Unit General 6 P Leisure Shop < 0.5 miles Pub < 0.5 miles

Place index

If you know where you want to stay the index at the back of the guide will give you the page number which lists accommodation in your chosen town, city or village. Check out the other useful indexes too.

YORK, North Yorkshire Map ref 4C1

★★★★
SELF CATERING

Units 1
Sleeps 1–3
Low season per wk
£285.00–£350.00
High season per wk
£360.00–£490.00

Ambler York Riverside Apartment, York

contact Peter & Elizabeth Jackson, Ambler York Riverside Apartment, 17 Great Close, Cawood YO8 3UG
t (01757) 268207 & 07885 921691 **e** pajack@lineone.net **w** yorkriversideholidayflat.co.uk

Luxury first-floor city-centre apartment overlooking river with fine views of the city. Double-bedded room. Bathroom with bath and shower. Fitted kitchen, designated car parking space, CCTV.

open All year
payment Cash/cheques

Unit General 8 P Leisure Shop < 0.5 miles Pub < 0.5 miles

YORK, North Yorkshire Map ref 4C1

★★★
SELF CATERING

Units 1
Sleeps 1–5
Low season per wk
£150.00–£263.00
High season per wk
£263.00–£399.00

Baile Hill Cottage, York

contact Paul Hodgson, Baile Hill Cottage, Avalon, 19 North Lane, Wheldrake YO19 6AY
t (01904) 448670 **e** enquiries@holiday-cottage.org.uk **w** holiday-cottage.org.uk

open All year
payment Cash/cheques

Victorian town cottage with two bedrooms, dining room, lounge and modern fitted kitchen. Many original features and a four-poster bed. Peaceful, central location overlooking the city walls. Private patio garden. Car parking.

⊕ *Given with booking confirmation.*

❤ *3-night stays and short breaks available all year round. Please phone for details.*

Unit General P Shop < 0.5 miles Pub < 0.5 miles

YORK, North Yorkshire Map ref 4C1

★★★★
SELF CATERING

Units 1
Sleeps 4
Low season per wk
£380.00–£420.00
High season per wk
£460.00–£500.00

Bay Tree House, York

contact Clare Arnold, 92 Bishopthorpe Road, York YO23 1JS
t (01904) 659462 **e** info@baytree-york.co.uk **w** baytreehouse-york.co.uk

Charming Victorian terraced house offering quality accommodation in the heart of York. One double and one twin room. Luxury bathroom. Free parking for guests.

open All year
payment Credit/debit cards, cash/cheques

Unit General P Leisure Shop < 0.5 miles Pub < 0.5 miles

Don't forget www.

Web addresses throughout this guide are shown without the prefix www. Please include www. in the address line of your browser. If a web address does not follow this style it is shown in full.

YORK, North Yorkshire Map ref 4C1

★★★★
SELF CATERING

Units **4**
Sleeps **1–4**
Low season per wk
£700.00–£1,400.00
High season per wk
£700.00–£1,400.00

The Blue Rooms, York

contact Miss Kirsty Reid, The Blue Bicycle York Ltd, 34 Fossgate, York YO1 9TA
t (01904) 673990 **f** (01904) 677688 **e** blue-rooms@thebluebicycle.com **w** thebluebicycle.com

open All year
payment Credit/debit cards, cash/cheques

Overlooking the River Foss, The Blue Rooms occupy a secluded mews position and are equipped to the very highest standards. They offer luxury, convenience, privacy and comfort for that short romantic break or business trip. You will be welcomed on arrival with a bottle of champagne and fresh fruit basket, with our compliments.

⊕ *Please request directions at time of booking.*

Unit General P Leisure Shop < 0.5 miles Pub < 0.5 miles

YORK, North Yorkshire Map ref 4C1

★★★★★
SELF CATERING

Units **1**
Sleeps **1–2**
Low season per wk
£300.00–£500.00
High season per wk
£350.00–£600.00

Castlegate Apartment, York

contact Maureen Hardy, Unique Stays, PO Box 490, York YO1 0AU
t (01904) 652664 & 07786 065286 **e** info@unique-stays.co.uk **w** unique-stays.co.uk

A luxury, period duplex residence within a Georgian house, tucked away in the heart of the city centre. Recently refurbished to a very high standard with tasteful furnishings, decor and communal walled garden.

open All year
payment Cash/cheques

Unit General Leisure Shop < 0.5 miles Pub < 0.5 miles

YORK, North Yorkshire Map ref 4C1

★★★
SELF CATERING

Units **4**
Sleeps **2–5**
Low season per wk
£133.00–£256.00
High season per wk
£206.00–£364.00

Classique Select Holiday Apartments, York

contact Mr Rodney Inns, 21 Larchfield, Stockton Lane, York YO31 1JS
t (01904) 421339 **f** (01904) 421339 **e** rodela_2194_inns@hotmail.com **w** classique-york.co.uk

Comfortable, self-contained apartments approximately 20 minutes' walk to York Minster and historic attractions. Modern kitchens, double beds with coronet drapes, night-storage heating, parking, garden. High standards maintained. No pets. Four nights for price of three.

open All year
payment Cash/cheques

Unit General P Leisure Shop < 0.5 miles Pub < 0.5 miles

YORK, North Yorkshire Map ref 4C1

★★★★
SELF CATERING

Units **1**
Sleeps **1–4**
Low season per wk
£380.00–£480.00
High season per wk
£500.00–£650.00

Crambeck Court, York

contact Mrs Helen Jones, Holidayork, 11 Walmgate, York YO1 9TX
t (01904) 632660 **f** (01904) 632434 **e** agents@holidayork.co.uk **w** holidayork.co.uk

A very attractive first-floor flat in the centre of York. En suite shower room, main bathroom, lounge with DVD, TV, CD player and video. One double, one twin. Private parking for one car.

open All year
payment Credit/debit cards, cash/cheques

Unit General P Shop < 0.5 miles Pub < 0.5 miles

Star ratings

Further information about star ratings can be found at the back of this guide.

YORK, North Yorkshire Map ref 4C1

★★
SELF CATERING
Units **6**
Sleeps **2–4**
Low season per wk
£200.00–£300.00
High season per wk
£250.00–£550.00

Knowle House Apartments, York

contact Greg Harrand, Hedley House Hotel, 3-4 Bootham Terrace, York YO30 7DH
t 0800 583 6374 **f** (01904) 639774 **e** greg@hedleyhouse.com **w** hedleyhouse.com

City-centre apartments next door to owner's hotel. Off-street parking. See website for more information.

open All year
payment Credit/debit cards, cash/cheques

Unit General P Leisure

YORK, North Yorkshire Map ref 4C1

★★★
SELF CATERING
Units **8**
Sleeps **2–8**
Low season per wk
£210.00–£390.00
High season per wk
£315.00–£640.00

Merricote Cottages, York

contact Andrew Williamson, Merricote Cottages, Malton Road, Stockton on the Forest YO32 9TL
t (01904) 400256 **f** (01904) 400846 **e** merricote@hotmail.com **w** merricote-holiday-cottages.co.uk

A beautiful spot from which to explore the historic city of York (three miles), the Moors and coast. The cottages and bungalow are well appointed. Many amenities nearby.

open All year
payment Credit/debit cards, cash/cheques

Unit General P S Leisure Shop 2 miles Pub 1 mile

YORK, North Yorkshire Map ref 4C1

★★★★★
SELF CATERING
Units **1**
Sleeps **1–5**
Low season per wk
£400.00–£500.00
High season per wk
£520.00–£670.00

Number 22 Bootham Terrace, York

contact Mrs Helen Jones, Homefinders Holidays, 11 Walmgate, York YO1 9TJ
t (01904) 632660 **f** (01904) 632434 **e** agents@holidayork.co.uk **w** holidayork.co.uk

open All year
payment Credit/debit cards, cash/cheques

Bootham Terrace is a superb house; it has lots of room and is beautifully furnished and decorated. There is a large lounge and separate dining room. It has a very nice garden to sit in and is very central. There is one double, one twin and one single bedroom.

⊕ *Directions given at time of booking.*

Unit General P

YORK, North Yorkshire Map ref 4C1

★★★★–★★★★★
SELF CATERING
Units **16**
Sleeps **2–7**
Low season per wk
£225.00–£325.00
High season per wk
£480.00–£790.00

York Lakeside Lodges, York

contact Mr Manasir, York Lakeside Lodges Ltd, Moor Lane, York YO24 2QU
t (01904) 702346 **f** (01904) 701631 **e** neil@yorklakesidelodges.co.uk **w** yorklakesidelodges.co.uk

Self-catering lodges and cottages in mature parkland around large fishing lake. Superstore across the road, coach to York centre every ten minutes.

open All year
payment Cash/cheques, euros

Unit General P Leisure Shop < 0.5 miles Pub 0.6 miles

Mention our name

Please mention this guide when making your booking.

YORK, North Yorkshire Map ref 4C1

★★★★
SELF CATERING

Units **1**
Sleeps **5**
Low season per wk
£360.00–£420.00
High season per wk
£420.00–£480.00

York Luxury Breaks, York

contact Mrs Linda Waddington, York Luxury Breaks, 166 York Road, Haxby, York YO32 3EP
t (01904) 768569 **f** (01904) 768569 **w** yorkluxurybreaks.co.uk

Luxury two-bedroomed apartment five minutes' walk to city centre. Private parking and all mod cons. Private patio with seating. Mid-week special offers available.

open All year
payment Cash/cheques

Unit General P Leisure Shop < 0.5 miles Pub < 0.5 miles

Heart of England

Birmingham › Black Country › Coventry & Warwickshire
Herefordshire & the Wye Valley › Shakespeare Country
Shropshire & the Welsh Borders › Staffordshire & the Peak District
Stoke & The Potteries › Worcestershire

Soak up the drama of Shakespeare Country

Heart of England Tourism
Larkhill Road, Worcester WR5 2EZ
(01905) 761100
visitheartofengland.com

gritstone heights, colourful canals, pioneering heritage

Main Sweeping views of the River Wye and The Forest of Dean from Symonds Yat
Left Shop until you drop at Birmingham's Bullring; take up the challenge at The Roaches, Staffordshire; alongside the Grand Union Canal, Hatton; impressive birds of prey at Warwick Castle

Cruise the inland waterways, discover rich industrial heritage and explore ruined castles. Home of the country's second biggest city, one of the world's leading theme parks and inspiring Shakespeare country, **the Heart of England is action packed.**

Explore Heart of England

A Tale of Two Cities

You'll find yourself in shopping heaven in Birmingham's Bullring. With hundreds of outlets covering the space of 26 football pitches, this shoppers' paradise will satisfy your every retail need! Party 'til dawn in this City of Entertainment, with lively chatter in canal-side cafes and non-stop nightlife. Indulge in a visit to Cadbury World, learn the history of the nation's favourite treat and, if you're lucky, sample steaming liquid chocolate straight from the vat. Marvel at ruffled Pufferfish and explore AmaZonia at the Sea Life Centre.

Get in gear for a visit to Coventry Transport Museum where the fantastic collection of motor vehicles rivals any in the country. Tread softly around the awe-inspiring cathedral – a remarkable modern structure built upon ruins from World War II. Hop on a boat and cruise down the Canal Art Trail, or wander around Millennium Place where the stunning glass bridge and use of public space for artistic purposes will leave you speechless.

Historic times

Test your literary knowledge with a trip to the black-and-white town of Stratford-upon-Avon. Visit the birthplace of its most famous inhabitant – William Shakespeare – and gain an insight into the Tudor world in which the bard lived. Discover the horrors of the oubliette at Warwick Castle and learn the grizzly past of the historic fortress. Get your mind racing at the Ironbridge Gorge Museums and interactive technology centre in Shropshire – stroll amongst working Victorians at Blists Hill or let your imagination run wild at Enginuity.

Discover the story of Stoke-on-Trent's people, industry, products and landscapes at The Potteries – the world's finest collection of Staffordshire ceramics. Or explore the remarkable ruins of Witley Court, a once great Jacobean manor-house, near Worcester. Take a picnic and spend a day in the picturesque and historic Shropshire market town of Ludlow: peer from the ruins of the cliff-top castle or stroll the banks of the sleepy River Teme.

Rolling hills

Gaze out from Worcestershire Beacon across the undulating Malvern Hills for spectacular views of the Cotswolds. Admire differing landscapes and explore geological variety and patchwork fields. Follow the Wye Valley through breathtaking scenery, and take time to enjoy the outstanding views from Symonds Yat and spot peregrines.

Step up the pace and head out on foot across the Shropshire Hills. Challenge yourself to a section of the hundreds of miles of footpaths leading you along ancient trackways, through river valleys and down sunken lanes.

Goblins and grassland

Hold on tight and feel your senses spin at the ever-popular Alton Towers theme park. Or go on a journey across Middle-earth (Birmingham) on the Tolkien Trail and explore the local landmarks that inspired the many settings for The Lord of the Rings.

Tee off in the glorious setting of Trentham Park in Staffordshire, or wander into the National Forest, relax amongst the trees and spot abundant wildlife.

Places to **visit**

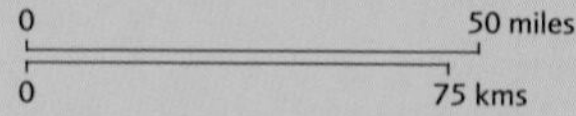

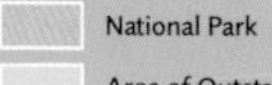

National Park

Area of Outstanding Natural Beauty

National Trails
nationaltrail.co.uk

Sections of the National Cycle Network
nationalcyclenetwork.org.uk

Alton Towers Theme Park
Stoke-on-Trent, Staffordshire
0870 520 4060
altontowers.com
Britain's number one theme park

Black Country Living Museum
Dudley, West Midlands
(0121) 557 9643
bclm.co.uk
Twenty-six acres of fascinating living history

Bullring
Birmingham, West Midlands
(0121) 632 1500
bullring.co.uk
Hundreds of outlets – a shopper's paradise

Cadbury World
Birmingham,
West Midlands
0845 450 3599
cadburyworld.co.uk
Chocolate-making demonstrations and samples

Canal Art Trail
Coventry, West Midlands
(024) 7678 5507
covcanalsoc.org.uk
Cruise through five miles of inspiring work

Cider Museum and King Offa Distillery
Hereford
(01432) 354207
cidermuseum.co.uk
Be sure to sample a free tasting of distillery products

Coventry Cathedral
Coventry, West Midlands
(024) 7652 1200
coventrycathedral.org
Glorious and unique 20th-century arcitecture to both inspire and enthrall

Coventry Transport Museum
Coventry, West Midlands
(024) 7623 4270
transport-museum.com
Fascinating and immense collection of vehicles spanning the ages

Hawkstone Hall and Gardens
Shrewsbury, Shropshire
(01630) 685242
hawkstone-hall.com
Beautiful Georgian mansion in spacious parkland with outstanding rose gardens and a stunning lilly pool

Ironbridge Gorge Museums
Shropshire
(01952) 435900
ironbridge.org.uk
Revolutionary inventions in inspiring museums

Millennium Place
Coventry, West Midlands
(024) 7622 7264
coventryinspires.com
Stunning public art space

National Motorcycle Museum
Solihull, West Midlands
(01675) 443311
nationalmotorcyclemuseum.co.uk
Largest of its kind in the world

The Potteries
Stoke-on-Trent, Staffordshire
(01782) 236000
visitstoke.co.uk
Finest collection of Staffordshire ceramics

Sea Life Centre
Birmingham, West Midlands
(0121) 643 6777
sealife.co.uk
Marine life at your fingertips

Shakespeare's Birthplace
Stratford-upon-Avon, Warwickshire
(01789) 201822
shakespeare.org.uk
The bard's inspiring dwelling place

Tolkien Trail
Birmingham, West Midlands
(0121) 777 6612
bmag.org.uk/sarehole_mill
Journey through Middle-earth

Trentham Leisure
Stoke-on-Trent, Staffordshire
(01782) 657341
trenthamleisure.co.uk
Incredibly scenic, outstanding leisure complex

Warwick Castle
0870 442 2000
warwick-castle.co.uk
Historic fortress with grizzly past

West Midland Safari and Leisure Park
Bewdley, Worcestershire
(01299) 402114
wmsp.co.uk
Observe rare white lions

Witley Court

Worcestershire
0870 333 1181
english-heritage.co.uk
Country house with stunning grounds

Tourist information centres 

When you arrive at your destination, visit a tourist information centre for help with accommodation and information about local attractions and events, or email your request before you go.

Bewdley	Load Street	(01299) 404740	bewdleytic@btconnect.com
Birmingham (NEC)	The Atrium	(0121) 202 5099	atrium@marketingbirmingham.com
Birmingham (NEC)	The Piazza	(0121) 202 5099	piazza@marketingbirmingham.com
Birmingham Rotunda	150 New Street	(0121) 202 5099	ticketshop@marketingbirmingham.com
Bridgnorth	Listley Street	(01746) 763257	bridgnorth.tourism@shropshire-cc.gov.uk
Bromsgrove	26 Birmingham Road	(01527) 831809	
Bromyard	Cruxwell Street	(01432) 260280	tic-bromyard@herefordshire.gov.uk
Burton upon Trent	Horninglow Street	(01283) 508111	tic@eaststaffsbc.gov.uk
Church Stretton	Church Street	(01694) 723133	churchstretton.tourism@shropshire-cc.gov.uk
Coventry	4 Priory Row	(024) 7622 7264	tic@cvone.co.uk
Droitwich Spa	Victoria Square	(01905) 774312	heritage@droitwichspa.gov.uk
Dudley	St James's Road	(01384) 812830	information.centre@dudley.gov.uk
Ellesmere, Shropshire*	Mereside	(01691) 622981	ellesmere.tourism@shropshire-cc.gov.uk
Evesham	Abbey Gate	(01386) 446944	tic@almonry.ndo.co.uk
Hereford	1 King Street	(01432) 268430	tic-hereford@herefordshire.gov.uk
Ironbridge	Ironbridge Gorge Museum Trust	(01952) 884391	tic@ironbridge.org.uk
Kenilworth	11 Smalley Place	(01926) 748900	kenilworthlibrary@warwickshire.gov.uk
Leamington Spa	The Parade	(01926) 742762	leamington@shakespeare-country.co.uk
Ledbury	3 The Homend	(01531) 636147	tic-ledbury@herefordshire.gov.uk
Leek	Stockwell Street	(01538) 483741	tourism.services@staffsmoorlands.gov.uk
Leominster	1 Corn Square	(01568) 616460	
Lichfield	Bore Street	(01543) 308209	info@visitlichfield.com
Ludlow	Castle Street	(01584) 875053	ludlow.tourism@shropshire-cc.gov.uk
Malvern	21 Church Street	(01684) 892289	malvern.tic@malvernhills.gov.uk
Market Drayton	49 Cheshire Street	(01630) 653114	marketdrayton.tourism@shropshire-cc.gov.uk
Merry Hill	Merry Hill	(01384) 487900	
Much Wenlock*	High Street	(01952) 727679	muchwenlock.tourism@shropshire-cc.gov.uk
Newcastle-under-Lyme	Ironmarket	(01782) 297313	tic.newcastle@staffordshire.gov.uk
Nuneaton	Church Street	(024) 7634 7006	nuneatonlibrary@warwickshire.gov.uk
Oswestry (Mile End)	Mile End	(01691) 662488	tic@oswestry-bc.gov.uk
Oswestry Town (Heritage Centre)	2 Church Terrace	(01691) 662753	ot@oswestry-welshborders.org.uk
Queenswood*	Dinmore Hill	(01568) 797842	
Redditch	Alcester Street	(01527) 60806	info.centre@redditchbc.gov.uk
Ross-on-Wye	Edde Cross Street	(01989) 562768	tic-ross@herefordshire.gov.uk
Rugby	Little Elborow Street	(01788) 534970	visitor.centre@rugby.gov.uk
Shrewsbury	The Square	(01743) 281200	tic@shrewsburytourism.co.uk

Solihull	Homer Road	(0121) 704 6130	ckelly@solihull.gov.uk
Stafford	Market Street	(01785) 619619	tic@staffordbc.gov.uk
Stoke-on-Trent	Bagnall Street	(01782) 236000	stoke.tic@stoke.gov.uk
Stratford-upon-Avon	Bridgefoot	0870 160 7930	stratfordtic@shakespeare-country.co.uk
Tamworth	29 Market Street	(01827) 709581	tic@tamworth.gov.uk
Telford	The Telford Centre	(01952) 238008	tourist-info@telfordshopping.co.uk
Upton-upon-Severn	4 High Street	(01684) 594200	upton.tic@malvernhills.gov.uk
Walsall	St Pauls Street	(01922) 625540	walsalltt&i@travelwm.co.uk
Warwick	Jury Street	(01926) 492212	touristinfo@warwick-uk.co.uk
Whitchurch (Shropshire)	12 St Mary's Street	(01948) 664577	whitchurch.heritage@ukonline.co.uk
Wolverhampton	18 Queen Square	(01902) 556110	wolverhampton.tic@dial.pipex.com
Worcester	High Street	(01905) 726311	touristinfo@cityofworcester.gov.uk

* *seasonal opening*

Alternatively, you can text **TIC LOCATE** to **64118** to find your nearest tourist information centre

Find out **more**

The following publications are available from Heart of England Tourism by logging on to **visitheartofengland.com** or calling **(01905) 761100**:

Bed & Breakfast Touring Map including Camping and Caravan Parks 2007

Visit the Heart of England 2007
Attractions in the Heart of England.

Gardens of the Heart
Details of over 100 from around the region, from small cottage gardens to grand formal affairs.

Heart of England in Bloom Floral Trail
A guide to cities, towns and villages involved in the regional Britain in Bloom competition.

Touring the Heart
Ideas for driving, cycling, boating and walking.

Heroes of the Heart
Attractions associated with some of the famous people from the region.

Heritage of the Heart
Detailed information on the historic properties in the Heart of England.

Family Fun in the Heart
A guide to family friendly attractions.

Travel **info**

By road:
Britain's main motorways (M1/M6/M5) meet in the Heart of England; the M40 links with the M42 south of Birmingham while the M4 provides fast access from London to the south of the region. These road links ensure that the Heart of England is more accessible by road than any other region in the UK.

By rail:
The Heart of England is served by an excellent rail network. InterCity rail services are fast and frequent from London and other major cities into the region. Trains run from Euston to Birmingham, Coventry and Rugby; from Paddington to the Cotswolds, Stratford-upon-Avon and Worcester; and from Marylebone to Birmingham and Stourbridge. From the main stations a network of regional routes take you around the Heart of England.

By air:
Fly into Birmingham, Coventry or Nottingham East Midlands.

where to stay in
Heart of England

All place names in the blue bands are shown on the maps at the front of this guide.

A complete listing of all Enjoy England assessed accommodation covered by this guide appears at the back.

Accommodation symbols
Symbols give useful information about services and facilities. Inside the back-cover flap you can find a key to these symbols. Keep it open for easy reference.

ABBERLEY, Worcestershire Map ref 4A3

★★★
SELF CATERING

Units 4
Sleeps 1–4
Low season per wk
£165.00–£215.00
High season per wk
£280.00–£380.00

Old Yates Cottages, Worcester

contact Mr & Mrs Richard & Sarah Goodman, Old Yates Cottages, Stockton Road, Abberley, Worcester WR6 6AT
t (01299) 896500 **f** (01299) 896065 **e** oldyates@aol.com **w** oldyatescottages.co.uk

open All year
payment Credit/debit cards, cash/cheques

Cosy cottages in tranquil surroundings amidst beautiful countryside. A personal welcome awaits you. Convenient for exploring the Midlands and Welsh Borders. Contact us for colour brochure.

⊕ *Entrance off A443, 1 mile west of Abberley village.*

Unit General Leisure Shop 1 mile Pub 2 miles

ABBOTS BROMLEY, Staffordshire Map ref 4B3

★★★★
SELF CATERING

Units 6
Sleeps 2–10
Low season per wk
£190.00–£400.00
High season per wk
£350.00–£850.00

Blithfield Lakeside Barns, Rugeley

contact Mrs Maxine Brown, PG & RG Brown & Partners, St Stephens Hill Farm, Admaston, Rugeley WS15 3NQ
t (01889) 500234 **f** (01889) 500288 **e** maxine.brown@lineone.net **w** blithfieldlakesidebarns.co.uk

open All year
payment Cash/cheques, euros

Superb lakeside barn conversions on organic dairy farm overlooking Blithfield Reservoir, two miles from Abbots Bromley. All units have breathtaking views of the water, lakeside patios, en suite facilities and oak beams. Close to Alton Towers and Peak District. Trout and carp fishing. Walking on site, cycling and riding nearby. Excellent local pubs/restaurants.

⊕ *From A51, take B5013 Rugeley to Uttoxeter road; we are situated on banks of Blithfield Reservoir.*

Unit General Leisure Shop 2 miles Pub 2 miles

ADMINGTON, Warwickshire Map ref 2B1

★★★★
SELF CATERING

Units **1**
Sleeps **1–4**
Low season per wk
£350.00–£395.00
High season per wk
£395.00–£420.00

Mole End, Admington, Shipston-on-Stour

contact Mrs Liz Hale, Willow Tree Farm, Admington Lane, Admington, Shipston-on-Stour CV36 4JJ
t (01789) 450881 **e** liz-hale@willowtreefarm.fslife.co.uk **w** mole-end-cottage.co.uk

Self-contained, large kitchen/diner, lounge, utility, bathroom, two bedrooms (one twin and one double). Centrally heated, large garden area. No smoking and no pets.

open All year
payment Cash/cheques

Unit General Shop 1.5 miles Pub 1.5 miles

ALSTONEFIELD, Staffordshire Map ref 4B2

★★★★★
SELF CATERING

Units **1**
Sleeps **5–6**
Low season per wk
£345.00–£540.00
High season per wk
£750.00–£1,305.00

Dove Cottage Fishing Lodge, Unknown

contact Mr Rupert Hignett, Dove Cottage Fishing Lodge, c/o 112 High Street, Burford OX18 4QJ
t (01993) 825900 & (01285) 850779 **f** (01993) 824241 **e** info@dovecottages.co.uk
w dovecottages.co.uk

open All year
payment Cash/cheques

Situated in a beautiful and idyllic part of Wolfscote Dale, enjoying stunning views along the River Dove. Relax in a comfortable and highly maintained family home. Let us spoil you with fires laid daily, welcome grocery basket, electric blankets and hand cream! Large gardens, toys, videos.

⊕ *From Ashbourne, A515 for 5 miles, 1 mile after Tissington, left (signed Alstonefield). Follow road down hill, just before bridge is gate to Dove Cottage. Cottage 1st on right.*

❤ *2-rods fishing on River Dove (Apr-Oct). Short breaks available Oct-Apr (incl Christmas and New Year).*

Unit General Leisure Shop 6 miles Pub 1 mile

BEWDLEY, Worcestershire Map ref 4A3

★★★
SELF CATERING

Units **1**
Sleeps **1–4**
Low season per wk
Min £190.00
High season per wk
Max £390.00

Manor Holding, Bewdley

contact Mr & Mrs Nigel & Penny Dobson-Smyth, 32 Church Street, Hagley, Stourbridge DY9 0NA
t 07970 260010 **e** nds@landscapeconsultancy.freeserve.co.uk

Secluded 17thC farmhouse in tranquil, ancient forest (National Nature Reserve) laced with traffic-free foot, cycle and bridle paths. Enchanting, rolling countryside sprinkled with historic market towns. Near Birmingham, Ironbridge and Ludlow.

open All year
payment Cash/cheques, euros

Unit General Leisure Shop 2 miles
Pub 2 miles

BEWDLEY, Worcestershire Map ref 4A3

★★★★
SELF CATERING & SERVICED APARTMENTS

Units **1**
Sleeps **1–5**
Low season per wk
£285.00–£335.00
High season per wk
£345.00–£450.00

Peacock Coach House, Bewdley

contact Mrs Prisca Hall, Peacock House, Lower Park, Bewdley DY12 2DP
t (01299) 400149 **e** priscahall@hotmail.com

Restored, 17thC, oak-beamed coach house, five minutes from Bewdley town centre and River Severn. Private walled garden with patio and barbecue.

open All year
payment Cash/cheques

Unit General Leisure Shop < 0.5 miles Pub < 0.5 miles

BISHOP'S CASTLE, Shropshire Map ref 4A3

★★★★
SELF CATERING

Units **1**
Sleeps **4**
Low season per wk
£195.00–£260.00
High season per wk
£260.00–£330.00

Mount Cottage, Bishop's Castle

contact Mrs Heather Willis, Mount Cottage, Bull Lane, Bishop's Castle SY9 5DA
t (01588) 638288 **f** (01588) 638288 **e** heather@mountcottage.co.uk **w** mountcottage.co.uk

Converted 17thC barn. Very short walk to town. Well-equipped, modern fitted kitchen. Bathroom/wc with over-bath shower and second wc. Beams throughout.

open All year
payment Cash/cheques

Unit General Leisure Shop < 0.5 miles Pub < 0.5 miles

BISHOPS FROME, Herefordshire Map ref 2B1

★★★
SELF CATERING

Units **1**
Sleeps **3–4**
Low season per wk
£175.00–£225.00
High season per wk
£250.00–£300.00

Cheyney Chapel, Worcester

contact Mrs D H Harrison, Bishops Frome, Worcester WR6 5AS
t (01531) 640846 **f** (01531) 640846 **e** bjharrison@tiscali.co.uk

16thC chapel, peacefully situated on farm, overlooking large lawn and lake with variety of wildlife and wonderful sunsets. Double bedroom up steep stairs, shower room, modern kitchen, dining area, sofa/futon, easy chair.

open All year
payment Cash/cheques

Unit General P Leisure Shop 1 mile Pub 1 mile

BRIDGNORTH, Shropshire Map ref 4A3

★★★
SELF CATERING & SERVICED APARTMENTS

Units **1**
Sleeps **1–2**
Low season per wk
Min £140.00
High season per wk
Min £180.00

The Granary, Bridgnorth

contact Mrs Sarah Allen, The Granary, The Old Vicarage, Vicarage Road, Dittons Priors, Bridgnorth WV16 6SP
t (01746) 712272 **f** (01746) 712288 **e** allens@oldvicditton.freeserve.co.uk

Farm granary in unspoilt South Shropshire countryside. Bridgnorth within easy reach, Ludlow 16 miles. Studio sitting room, bedroom, kitchen, bathroom. Excellent walking.

open All year
payment Cash/cheques

Unit General P Leisure Shop 0.5 miles Pub 0.5 miles

CHURCH STRETTON, Shropshire Map ref 4A3

★★★★
SELF CATERING

Units **2**
Sleeps **4–5**
Low season per wk
£220.00–£275.00
High season per wk
£275.00–£375.00

Granary Cottage, Church Stretton

contact Mr & Mrs Kirkwood, Lower Day House, Church Preen, Church Stretton SY6 7LH
t (01694) 771521 **e** bookings@lowerdayhouse.com **w** lowerdayhouse.com

open All year
payment Cash/cheques

Part of an 18thC farm courtyard, sited next to an oak-framed threshing barn. The cottages are tastefully furnished, retaining many original beams and features, with magnificent views of Wenlock Edge. Ideally suited to those seeking the real 'heart of the country'. Sorry, no smoking or pets.

⊕ *Please request travel directions at time of booking.*

❤ *Short breaks available from end Oct–Easter.*

Unit General P Leisure

CLUN, Shropshire Map ref 4A3

★★★★–★★★★★
SELF CATERING

Units **3**
Sleeps **2**
Low season per wk
£275.00–£340.00
High season per wk
£360.00–£425.00

Pooh Hall Cottages, Clun

contact Mrs Sue Murray, Woodside, Clun, Craven Arms SY7 0JB
t (01588) 640075 **e** pooh-hall@realemail.co.uk **w** pooh-hallcottages.co.uk

open All year
payment Cash/cheques

Beautifully designed stone cottage retreats, each having outdoor seating with wonderful views across the Clun Valley. One mile from Clun centre for pubs and shops; many other places of interest within easy reach. Wood-burning stoves, walks from the door and a fresh-meal service make a perfect holiday. Heart of England 2005 Excellence in Tourism Gold Winner.

⊕ *One mile from the centre of Clun. For detailed directions see website.*

♥ *3-/4-night breaks available. Kennel available for occasional use (no charge).*

Unit General P Shop 1 mile Pub 1 mile

CRAVEN ARMS, Shropshire Map ref 4A3

★★★★
SELF CATERING

Units **5**
Sleeps **4–12**
Low season per wk
Min £366.00
High season per wk
Min £1,400.00

Upper Onibury Cottages, Craven Arms

contact Mrs Hickman, Upper Onibury, Craven Arms SY7 9AW
t (01584) 856206 **f** (01584) 856236 **e** info@shropshirecottages.com **w** shropshirecottages.com

Charming stone barns beautifully furnished, set around central courtyard. Pretty gardens with furniture and gas barbecues. Use of heated indoor swimming pool and tennis court.

open All year
payment Cash/cheques

Unit General P Leisure Shop 1.5 miles Pub 0.5 miles

DOCKLOW, Herefordshire Map ref 2A1

★★★
SELF CATERING

Units **2**
Sleeps **2–4**
Low season per wk
£275.00–£325.00
High season per wk
£375.00–£475.00

Docklow Manor Holiday Cottages, Leominster

contact Mrs Jane Viner, Docklow Manor Holiday Cottages, Docklow Manor, Docklow, Leominster HR6 0RX
t (01568) 760668 **f** (01568) 760572 **e** jane498@btinternet.com **w** docklow-manor.co.uk

open All year
payment Cash/cheques

Traditional stone cottages set in five acres of Victorian gardens and woodland at Docklow Manor. The location is outstanding – in the heart of the idyllic Herefordshire countryside with unspoilt views towards Wales. The pretty market towns of Leominster, Ledbury and Ludlow are all nearby. Good home cooking available.

⊕ *Forty minutes from jct 7 of the M5. After leaving the motorway, follow signs for Leominster and the A44.*

♥ *Short breaks available all year round.*

Unit General Leisure Shop 4.5 miles Pub < 0.5 miles

Key to symbols

Open the back flap for a key to symbols.

DUNCHURCH, Warwickshire Map ref 4C3

★★★★
SELF CATERING

Units **1**
Sleeps **4**
Low season per wk
Min £450.00
High season per wk
Min £650.00

Toft Manor Cottage, Rugby

contact Ms Shirley Bettinson, Toft Manor Cottage, Dunchurch, Rugby CV22 6NR
t (01788) 810626 **f** (01788) 522347 **e** shirley@toft-alpacas.co.uk **w** toft-alpacas.co.uk

Set in the grounds of Toft Manor amongst a prize-winning herd of Toft Alpacas, offering outstanding views across Draycote Water.

open All year
payment Cash/cheques

Unit General P Leisure Shop 0.5 miles
Pub 0.5 miles

ELMLEY CASTLE, Worcestershire Map ref 2B1

★★
SELF CATERING

Units **1**
Sleeps **1–2**
Low season per wk
£130.00–£150.00
High season per wk
£160.00–£190.00

The Cottage Manor Farm House, Pershore

contact Mr & Mrs Brian and Pat Lovett, Manor Farm House, Main Street, Elmley Castle, Pershore WR10 3HS
t (01386) 710286 **f** (01386) 710112

Small cottage attached to original village farmhouse and beautiful garden, at the foot of Bredon Hill. Excellent for trekking and touring the Cotswolds and Malverns.

open All year
payment Cash/cheques

Unit General P

EVESHAM, Worcestershire Map ref 2B1

★★★★
SELF CATERING

Units **1**
Sleeps **2–6**
Low season per wk
£425.00–£495.00
High season per wk
£495.00–£575.00

Thatchers End, Evesham

contact Mr & Mrs Wilson, 60 Pershore Road, Evesham WR11 2PQ
t (01386) 446269 **f** (01386) 446269 **e** trad.accom@virgin.net
w http://freespace.virgin.net/trad.accom

open All year
payment Credit/debit cards, cash/cheques, euros

Delightful Grade II Listed thatched black and white cottage with many traditional and original period features. Spacious, tastefully furnished, all modern facilities. Large enclosed garden, patio area, garden furniture. Private and peacefully situated. Ample parking. Ideal touring base. Family supervised. No pets. Brochures available.

⊕ *Private drive off B4084 (was A44) in parish of Hampton. Signpost at bottom of drive on right past church.*

Unit General P Leisure Shop < 0.5 miles
Pub < 0.5 miles

HEREFORD, Herefordshire Map ref 2A1

★★★★
SELF CATERING

Units **1**
Sleeps **6**
Low season per wk
£350.00–£550.00
High season per wk
£600.00–£850.00

Castle Cliffe East, Hereford

contact Mr Mark Hubbard & Mr Phil Wilson, Castle Cliffe West, 14 Quay Street, Hereford HR1 2NH
t (01432) 272096 **e** mail@castlecliffe.net **w** castlecliffe.net

open All year
payment Cash/cheques

Originally a medieval watergate, Castle Cliffe provides luxury accommodation which is both tranquil and convenient. Set in parkland, it has period furniture, open fires and a south-facing riverside garden. And with shops, restaurants and the cathedral within a few minutes' walk, it is the ideal place to relax and unwind.

⊕ *Follow signs for city centre, past train station to traffic lights. Left into Union Street, into Offa Street, 1st left (East Street), right (Ethelbert Street), into Castle Street.*

♥ *Short breaks available all year. Claim a 10% discount by mentioning 'Where to Stay' or VisitBritain.*

Unit General P S Leisure Shop 0.5 miles
Pub 0.5 miles

HEREFORD, Herefordshire Map ref 2A1

★★★★
SELF CATERING

Units **1**
Sleeps **1–7**
Low season per wk
£211.00–£317.00
High season per wk
£317.00–£489.00

The Green Farm Cottage, Felton, Hereford

contact Mrs Shirley Simcock, The Green Farm, Felton, Hereford HR1 3PH
t (01432) 820234 **f** (01432) 820437

open All year
payment Cash/cheques

Spacious cottage with oil-fired central heating throughout. Electricity, bedding and towels included. Open all year.

Unit General P S Leisure Shop 2 miles
Pub 3 miles

HEREFORD, Herefordshire Map ref 2A1

★★★★
SELF CATERING

Units **5**
Sleeps **2–6**
Low season per wk
£300.00–£450.00
High season per wk
£395.00–£625.00

Hermit Holidays, Hereford

contact Mr Ron Zahl, The Hermitage, Canon Pyon, Hereford HR4 8NR
t (01432) 760022 **e** info@hermitholidays.co.uk **w** hermitholidays.co.uk

Lots of 'air smiles', woodland walks, spring water, organic gardens. Self-catering, with optional Japanese and vegetarian meals on request. Lovely secluded setting. Perfect for couples and families seeking a get-away break.

open All year
payment Cash/cheques, euros

Unit General P S Leisure Shop 1 mile
Pub 1 mile

Check it out

Information on accommodation listed in this guide has been supplied by proprietors. As changes may occur you should remember to check all relevant details at the time of booking.

HONEYBOURNE, Worcestershire Map ref 2B1

★★★
SELF CATERING

Units **7**
Sleeps **2–4**
Low season per wk
Min £336.00
High season per wk
Max £420.00

Peace Haven Holiday Lets, Evesham

contact Mrs Fiona Humphrys, Buckle Street, Evesham WR11 8QQ
t (01386) 832785 **f** (01386) 830937 **e** peace.haven@btconnect.com **w** peacehavenlets.com

Peace Haven is situated at the foot of the Cotswolds, an ideal base from which to explore Worcestershire, Gloucestershire and Warwickshire.

open All year
payment Credit/debit cards, cash/cheques, euros

Unit General Leisure Shop 0.5 miles Pub 0.5 miles

ILAM, Staffordshire Map ref 4B2

SELF CATERING

Units **3**
Sleeps **6–24**
Low season per wk
£290.00–£450.00
High season per wk
£640.00–£800.00

Lower Damgate Barns, Reuben's Roost, Bremen's Barn, Hope's Hideaway, Ilam, Ashbourne

contact Mrs Carolyn Wilderspin, Lower Damgate Farm, Stanshope, Ashbourne DE6 2AD
t (01335) 310367 & 07779 210791 **e** damgate@hotmail.com **w** damgate.com

open All year
payment Cash/cheques

A 16thC, Grade II Listed rural farm in a stunning setting in the Peak District National Park. The farm is surrounded by National Trust land, and there is excellent walking from the door. The barns retain individuality and have luxury fittings. Games room, patio, barbecue, picnic and playing field. Pet sheep, ducks and chickens.

⊕ *Directions provided once booking is confirmed.*

Unit General Leisure
Shop 4 miles Pub 1 mile

ILMINGTON, Warwickshire Map ref 2B1

★★★★
SELF CATERING

Units **1**
Sleeps **1–4**
Low season per wk
£205.00–£225.00
High season per wk
£240.00–£290.00

Featherbed Cottage, Shipston-on-Stour

contact Mr David Price, 8 Nellands Close, Ilmington, Shipston-on-Stour CV36 4NF
t (01608) 682215 **e** featherbedcottage@hotmail.com

Comfortable, well-equipped, two-bedroomed house in village on the edge of Cotswolds overlooking open country. Small garden. Off-season short breaks.

open All year
payment Cash/cheques

Unit General Shop < 0.5 miles Pub < 0.5 miles

Suit yourself

The symbols at the end of each entry mean you can enjoy virtually made-to-measure accommodation with the services and facilities most important to you. A key to the symbols can be found inside the back-cover flap. Keep this open for easy reference.

IRONBRIDGE, Shropshire Map ref 4A3

★★★–★★★★★
SELF CATERING

Units **6**
Sleeps **2–7**
Low season per wk
£180.00–£385.00
High season per wk
£210.00–£435.00

Eleys of Ironbridge, Ironbridge

Eleys of Ironbridge, 13 Tontine Hill, Ironbridge TF8 7AL
t (01952) 432030 **f** (01952) 432382 **e** info@eleys-ironbridge.co.uk **w** eleys-ironbridge.co.uk

open All year
payment Credit/debit cards, cash/cheques

One of Ironbridge's premier holiday/letting companies offering a wide range of accommodation to suit all. Central Ironbridge, riverside or rural locations. Some with views of the 'iron bridge' itself, all with private parking. 3/4/7 night breaks available all year round. Holiday or business lets. Free colour brochure and fantastic new website.

⊕ *Full directions and your property keys will be given to you on your arrival at our shop, which you will find opposite the 'iron bridge'.*

♥ *Weekend and mid-week breaks available. Check out our website for special offers and free museum tickets.*

Unit General P Leisure

KINETON, Warwickshire Map ref 2C1

★★★★★
SELF CATERING

Units **1**
Sleeps **6**
Low season per wk
Min £360.00
High season per wk
Max £680.00

Long Ground Barn, Kineton, Warwick

contact Mrs Carolyn Gasson, Hampton House Farm, Combrook Road, Kineton CV35 0JH
t (01926) 641829 **f** (01926) 641829 **e** carolyn@heartofthecountryholidays.co.uk
w heartofthecountryholidays.co.uk

open All year
payment Cash/cheques

Three quarters of a mile from the road, this recently converted barn, with traditional features, has stunning views from Edgehill to the Cotswolds. The three en suite bedrooms and open-plan kitchen/diner/sitting room provide quality accommodation, with linen, towels and services included. Only 15 minutes from Stratford-upon-Avon, Warwick and Banbury.

⊕ *M40 jct 12 to Kineton. Take B4086 towards Wellesbourne. One mile from Kineton take left turn to Combrook. After 0.25 miles, right-hand bend. Take last drive on left.*

♥ *Short breaks available.*

Unit General P Leisure Shop 1.5 miles Pub 1.5 miles

LEAMINGTON SPA, Warwickshire Map ref 4B3

★★★★
SELF CATERING

Units **1**
Sleeps **1–2**
Low season per wk
£250.00–£280.00
High season per wk
£280.00–£300.00

Barn Owl Cottage, Leamington Spa

contact Mrs Beatrice Norman, Fosseway Barns, Fosse Way, Leamington Spa CV33 9BQ
t (01926) 614647 **f** (01926) 614647 **e** bnorman@fossebarn.prestel.co.uk **w** barnowlcottage.co.uk

open All year
payment Cash/cheques, euros

Superbly appointed luxury cottage in delightful rural setting close to Warwick, Stratford and the Cotswolds. Tastefully decorated living/dining room, modern, well-equipped fitted kitchen and attractive twin-bedded room. Delightful, landscaped cottage garden with patio. Open views and nearby public right of way.

⊕ *From M40 jct 12, B4100 to roundabout, then B4455 towards Leicester over next roundabout, over canal then left at top of hill signposted Barn Owl Cottage.*

♥ *Short breaks available. 10% discount if booking 2 weeks.*

Unit General P Leisure Shop 3 miles Pub 0.5 miles

LEAMINGTON SPA, Warwickshire Map ref 4B3

★★★–★★★★ SELF CATERING

Units 4
Sleeps 2–6
Low season per wk Min £220.00
High season per wk Max £425.00

Furzen Hill Farm, Leamington Spa

contact Mrs Christine Whitfield, Furzen Hill Farm, Coventry Road, Cubbington Heath, Leamington Spa CV32 7UJ
t (01926) 424791 **f** (01926) 424791 **e** christine.whitfield1@btopenworld.com
w furzenhillfarmcottages.co.uk

Cottages at Cubbington, ideally situated for Warwick, Stratford-upon-Avon and NEC. Large garden. Use of hard tennis court.

open All year
payment Cash/cheques

Unit General Leisure Shop 1.25 miles Pub 1.25 miles

LEDBURY, Herefordshire Map ref 2B1

★★★–★★★★ SELF CATERING

Units 5
Sleeps 2–5
Low season per wk £190.00–£380.00
High season per wk £240.00–£499.00

White House Cottages, Ledbury

contact Mrs Marianne Hills, The White House, Aylton, Ledbury HR8 2RQ
t (01531) 670349 **e** bookings@whitehousecottages.co.uk **w** whitehousecottages.co.uk

open All year
payment Cash/cheques

Well-equipped, self-catering cottages situated in a small hamlet four miles west of Ledbury. Surrounded by Herefordshire's idyllic countryside, these former farm buildings have been carefully adapted to create very comfortable and individual holiday accommodation. Perfect for exploring the Wye Valley, the Malverns and surrounding area. Resident owners.

⊕ *From Ledbury take A438 to Hereford. At the Trumpet crossroads turn left onto A4172. After 1 mile turn right to Aylton, White House approx 0.25 miles on left.*

♥ *3-night short breaks available all year, subject to certain booking restrictions. Please ring for details.*

Unit General Leisure Shop 4 miles Pub 2 miles

LEDBURY, Herefordshire Map ref 2B1

★★★★★ SELF CATERING

Units 2
Sleeps 2–6
Low season per wk £250.00–£500.00
High season per wk £450.00–£1,000.00

The Woodhouse Farm Cottages, Ledbury

contact Mrs Susan Furnival, The Woodhouse, Staplow, Ledbury HR8 1NP
t (01531) 640030 **f** (01531) 640030 **e** sue@thewoodhousefarm.co.uk **w** thewoodhousefarm.co.uk

open All year
payment Credit/debit cards, cash/cheques

Tranquil retreats. Barn Croft and The Wainhouse share 15 acres of grounds with The Woodhouse, a medieval, Grade II Listed, semi-moated hall house. Comfortably furnished to very high standards with antiques and prints. All bedrooms are en suite. Each cottage has a private garden. Choice of dining solutions and food hampers.

⊕ *Within 5 minutes of Ledbury, off the B4214 in Staplow, between Ledbury and Bosbury.*

♥ *Romantic breaks. 3- and 4-night breaks available.*

Unit General Leisure Shop 2 miles Pub < 0.5 miles

Check the maps

Colour maps at the front pinpoint all the places you will find accommodation entries in the regional sections. Pick your location and then refer to the place index at the back to find the page number.

LEEK, Staffordshire Map ref 4B2

★★★★
SELF CATERING

Units **1**
Sleeps **1–4**
Low season per wk
£200.00–£350.00
High season per wk
£350.00–£500.00

Deansgate, Leek

contact Victoria Heath, 1 Bridge Houses, Bridge End, Leek ST13 8LG
t 07989 337973 **f** (01538) 387784 **e** deansgate@fsmail.net

Superior Victorian terrace. Luxury serviced accommodation. Antique furniture, granite surfaces and Egyptian-cotton linen. Ideally located in the heart of the market town of Leek. Weekend stays all year: £130.

open All year
payment Credit/debit cards, cash/cheques, euros

Unit General P Leisure Shop < 0.5 miles Pub < 0.5 miles

LEEK, Staffordshire Map ref 4B2

★★★★
SELF CATERING

Units **3**
Sleeps **4–10**
Low season per wk
£233.00–£538.00
High season per wk
£381.00–£939.00

Foxtwood Cottages, Foxt, Froghall

contact Mr & Mrs Clive & Alison Worrall, Foxtwood Cottages, Foxt Road, Foxt, Stoke-on-Trent ST10 2HJ
t (01538) 266160 **e** info@foxtwood.co.uk **w** foxtwood.co.uk

open All year
payment Cash/cheques, euros

Orchids in the flower meadow, a kingfisher flashing by, a fleeting glimpse of a deer in the woods. Relax and watch canal boats chug past, hear the steam trains whistle along the valley. Come and explore this fascinating area. Foxtwood is unique and stunning.

⊕ *Between Derby and Stoke-on-Trent on the A52. At Froghall take local road to Foxt for 0.25 miles. We are on the left past the canal.*

♥ *Special winter breaks for the retired. 4 nights mid-week for less than a 3-night weekend.*

Unit General P Leisure Shop 2 miles Pub < 0.5 miles

LEINTWARDINE, Herefordshire Map ref 4A3

★★★
SELF CATERING

Units **1**
Sleeps **2–4**
Low season per wk
Min £220.00
High season per wk
Max £330.00

Oak Cottage, Leintwardine

contact Mrs Vivienne Faulkner, 24 Watling Street, Leintwardine SY7 0LW
t (01547) 540629 **f** (01547) 540181 **e** francism-jones@virgin.net

16thC, Grade II Listed, timber-framed cottage, carefully restored and equipped, in borderland village on River Teme. Glorious walking, fishing, good food. You can even coracle.

open All year
payment Cash/cheques

Unit General P Leisure Shop < 0.5 miles Pub < 0.5 miles

Don't forget www.

Web addresses throughout this guide are shown without the prefix www. Please include www. in the address line of your browser. If a web address does not follow this style it is shown in full.

LEOMINSTER, Herefordshire Map ref 2A1

★★★
SELF CATERING

Units **2**
Sleeps **5–8**
Low season per wk
£150.00–£230.00
High season per wk
£230.00–£280.00

Ashton Court Farm, Leominster

contact Mrs Pam Edwards, Ashton Court Farm, Ashton, Leominster HR6 0DN
t (01584) 711245 **e** Griffithsbrooches@btinternet.com

open All year
payment Cash/cheques

Our spacious farmhouse apartment and semi-detached cottage, converted from an old granary, are situated in a large garden with swings, play equipment and garden games. Table tennis and pool tables in the barn. Situated between Leominster and Ludlow, the location is central for touring the Welsh Borders, Shropshire and Worcestershire.

⊕ *Close to A49, 4 miles north of Leominster, 7 miles south of Ludlow.*

Unit General P Shop 4 miles Pub 2 miles

LITTLE TARRINGTON, Herefordshire Map ref 2A1

★★★★
SELF CATERING

Units **1**
Sleeps **1–6**
Low season per wk
£300.00–£550.00
High season per wk
£300.00–£550.00

Stock's Cottage, Little Tarrington, Hereford

contact Mrs Angela Stock, Stock's Cottage, Little Tarrington, Hereford HR1 4JA
t (01432) 890243 **f** (01432) 890243 **e** stay@stockscottage.co.uk **w** stockscottage.co.uk

Modern, one-story, brick-built accommodation with three bedrooms. All mod cons, disabled friendly. Rural setting.

open All year
payment Cash/cheques, euros

Unit General P Leisure Shop 4 miles Pub 0.5 miles

LUDLOW, Shropshire Map ref 4A3

★★★★
SELF CATERING

Units **1**
Sleeps **6**
Low season per wk
£180.00–£250.00
High season per wk
£220.00–£375.00

The Avenue Flat, Ludlow

contact Mr Meredith, The Avenue Flat, Donkey Lane, Ashford Carbonell, Ludlow SY8 4DA
t (01584) 831616 **e** ronmeredithavenue@talk21.com **w** theavenueflat.co.uk

Second floor of large, attractive, peaceful country residence set in six acres. Completely independent access with fine views and very comfortable, well-equipped accommodation.

open All year
payment Cash/cheques

Unit General P

Our quality rating schemes

For a detailed explanation of the quality and facilities represented by the stars please refer to the information pages at the back of this guide.

LUDLOW, Shropshire Map ref 4A3

★★
SELF CATERING

Units 1
Sleeps 5
Low season per wk
Max £190.00
High season per wk
Max £220.00

Church Bank, Burrington, Ludlow

contact Mrs Rosemary Laurie, Church Bank, Burrington, Ludlow SY8 2HT
t (01568) 770426 **e** alan@alaurie5.wanadoo.co.uk

payment Cash/cheques

This stone cottage lies in a beautiful, peaceful valley near River Teme. There are excellent walks on the hills and forest trails. Wildlife abounds. Historic Ludlow is five winding miles away. Large, comfortable sitting room with wood-burner and many books. Dinner can be provided by arrangement. Available March to October.

⊕ *Having crossed the bridge going south out of Ludlow, take road on the right signposted Burrington, 5 miles.*

Unit General Leisure Shop 3 miles Pub 3 miles

LUDLOW, Shropshire Map ref 4A3

★★★★
SELF CATERING

Units 1
Sleeps 1–6
Low season per wk
£300.00–£400.00
High season per wk
£500.00–£600.00

Counties View, Ludlow

contact Mrs Marguerite Maclean, Witley House, Old Swinford Hospital, Heath Lane, Stourbridge DY8 1QX
t (01384) 817333 **e** margueritemusic@hotmail.com **w** sykescottages.co.uk/cottages/1355.php

open All year
payment Credit/debit cards, cash/cheques

Charming 230-year-old cottage, renovated to a high standard of comfort and very centrally situated for the best of Ludlow's cuisine, history and walks. Three bedrooms, all with en suite bath or shower, TVs in all rooms, large kitchen, cosy lounge with open fireplace, excellent heating.

⊕ *From A49 take last exit on right into Ludlow. At traffic lights by Tesco, left. Go straight to T-junction; turn right. Left opposite Somerfield. Property last on left opposite the church.*

Unit General Shop < 0.5 miles Pub < 0.5 miles

LUDLOW, Shropshire Map ref 4A3

★★★★
SELF CATERING

Units 1
Sleeps 2–4
Low season per wk
£325.00–£450.00
High season per wk
£450.00–£525.00

Glebe Farm Cottage, Clee St Margaret

contact Mr & Mrs John & Lesley Thirlwell, Glebe Farm, Clee St Margaret SY7 9DT
t (01584) 823349 **e** cottage@glebefarm.info **w** glebefarm.info

open All year
payment Cash/cheques

Converted detached stone granary with inglenook, exposed beams and woodburner, plus all modern comforts. In the heart of the Shropshire Hills, yet less than 20 minutes from Ludlow. Enjoy our 12 acres of flower-rich hay meadows, wildlife, stream and ponds – designated an Environmentally Sensitive Area and managed for conservation.

⊕ *Under an hour from the motorways (M5/M6/M54), 7 miles north east of Ludlow.*

♥ *Want to unwind for just a few days? 3-night weekend, 4-night mid-week, or breaks tailored to your individual requirements.*

Unit General Leisure Shop 4.5 miles Pub 3.3 miles

LUDLOW, Shropshire Map ref 4A3

★★★★
SELF CATERING

Units 1
Sleeps 1–4
Low season per wk
Min £205.00
High season per wk
Max £440.00

Hazel Cottage, Craven Arms

contact Mrs Rachel Sanders, Hazel Cottage, Duxmoor Farm, Craven Arms SY7 9BQ
t (01584) 856342 **f** (01584) 856696 **e** rachelsanders@mac.com **w** stmem.com/hazelcottage

open All year
payment Cash/cheques

Beautifully restored period cottage retaining its original features, including antiques. It comprises a living room with Victorian range (working perfectly), dining room, kitchen, hall, Victorian bathroom, two bedrooms with washbasins. Set in its own peaceful and private cottage garden with panoramic views of the surrounding countryside. Five miles north of historic Ludlow.

On A49 5 miles north of Ludlow, left at Onibury sign. Left at crossroads. Drive 1.5 miles. Cottage 1st on right after 2nd right turning.

Short breaks available.

Unit General Leisure Shop 5 miles Pub 1.5 miles

LUDLOW, Shropshire Map ref 4A3

★★
SELF CATERING

Units 1
Sleeps 1–4
Low season per wk
£180.00–£200.00
High season per wk
£225.00–£250.00

Posthorn Cottage, Ludlow

contact Ms Helen Davis, 32 Leamington Drive, Chilwell, Nottingham NG9 5LJ
t (0115) 922 2383 **w** posthorncottage.co.uk

Charming two-storey cottage in historic town-centre building with exposed beams and small, private patio. In quiet courtyard off Broad Street.

open All year
payment Cash/cheques

Unit General Shop < 0.5 miles Pub < 0.5 miles

LUDLOW, Shropshire Map ref 4A3

★★★★
SELF CATERING

Units 6
Sleeps 2–6
Low season per wk
£208.00–£430.00
High season per wk
£345.00–£500.00

Sutton Court Farm Cottages, Ludlow

contact Mrs Jane Cronin, Sutton Court Farm, Little Sutton, Stanton Lacy, Ludlow SY8 2AJ
t (01584) 861305 **f** (01584) 861441 **e** suttoncourtfarm@hotmail.com **w** suttoncourtfarm.co.uk

open All year
payment Cash/cheques

Comfortable cottages set around a peaceful courtyard in the beautiful Corvedale, just five miles from historic Ludlow. World Heritage Ironbridge Gorge, Shrewsbury, Hereford and the Welsh borders all within easy reach. Short breaks available all year. Cream teas and evening meals can be ordered in advance.

From A49 north of Ludlow, B4365 across golf/racecourse. Right into Stanton Lacy, left at postbox. Left at T-junction (signed Hayton). Follow for 2.5 miles until hanging sign on right.

Short breaks from Oct-Mar (excl holidays). 3 nights for 2, 4 nights for 3.

Unit General Leisure Shop 6 miles Pub 6 miles

LYDBURY NORTH, Shropshire Map ref 4A3

★★★-★★★★ SELF CATERING

Units **6**
Sleeps **2–8**
Low season per wk £250.00–£450.00
High season per wk £400.00–£700.00

Walcot Hall Holiday apartments, Lydbury North

contact Miss Maria Higgs, Walcot Hall Administration Office, Walcot Hall, Lydbury North SY7 8AZ
t (01588) 680570 **f** (01568) 681030 **e** maria@walcotthall.com **w** walcothall.com

Spacious apartments with character in stately home once owned by Clive of India. Idyllic country setting with lakes, gardens and arboretum to explore. Doubles, twins and family room.

open All year
payment Cash/cheques

Unit General P S Leisure Shop 1.5 miles Pub 1 mile

MALVERN, Worcestershire Map ref 2B1

★★★★-★★★★★ SELF CATERING

Units **6**
Sleeps **2–9**
Low season per wk £259.00–£559.00
High season per wk £562.00–£1,272.00

Hidelow House Cottages, Worcester

contact Mr & Mrs Stuart & Pauline Diplock, Hidelow House Cottages, Hidelow House, Acton Green, Acton Beauchamp, Worcester WR6 5AH
t (01886) 884547 **f** (01886) 884658 **e** hwv@hidelow.co.uk **w** hidelow.co.uk

open All year
payment Credit/debit cards, cash/cheques, euros

Relax and unwind in luxury for a short break or longer. A peaceful, rural retreat with exceptional views, on the edge of an Area of Outstanding Natural Beauty, yet only 2.5 hours from London and Manchester. Former hop kilns and a tithe barn, now with four-poster beds, log fires, private gardens and barbecues.

⊕ *M5 jct 7. A4103 Worcester to Hereford. Turn right at B4220, signposted Bromyard. Hidelow House is 2 miles from this junction on left.*

♥ *Honeymoons and romantic breaks a speciality (champagne and roses). Personal transport service.*

WALKERS WELCOME CYCLISTS WELCOME

Unit General P S Leisure
Shop < 0.5 miles Pub 3 miles

MALVERN, Worcestershire Map ref 2B1

★★★★ SELF CATERING

Units **1**
Sleeps **6–8**
Low season per wk Max £295.00
High season per wk £495.00–£550.00

Holly Lodge, Earl's Croome, Worcester

contact Mrs Sandra Goodwin, c/o Hollybeds Farm, Worcester Road, Earls Croome, Worcester WR8 9DA
t (01684) 592877 **e** sandra@hollylodge.biz **w** hollylodge.biz

A new, well-equipped luxury log cabin with wheelchair access and private garden. Idyllic surroundings overlooking the Severn Valley in the shadow of the Malvern Hills. Close to local pubs. Closed January.

payment Cash/cheques

Unit General P S Shop 2 miles Pub 0.5 miles

Friendly help and advice

Did you know there are more than 500 tourist information centres throughout England? It adds up to a lot of friendly help and advice. You'll find contact details at the beginning of each regional section.

MALVERN, Worcestershire Map ref 2B1

★★★
SELF CATERING

Units **1**
Sleeps **9**
Low season per wk
£320.00–£430.00
High season per wk
£580.00–£830.00

Wayfarers Cottage, Malvern

contact Mr & Mrs John & Caroline Roslington, Wayfarers, Park Road, Malvern WR14 4BJ
t (01684) 575758 **e** jroslington@mac.com **w** wayfarerscottage.co.uk

open All year except Christmas
payment Cash/cheques

A real treat for family and friends, in attractive area rich in history and leisure activities. Spacious, extended cottage on Malvern Hills, superb views towards Wales. Parking for three cars. Established garden with barbecue. Quiet pub with good food. One single, two double and two twin bedrooms, bathroom, shower room, three toilets.

⊕ *Please request travel directions at time of booking, and we will send a map.*

Unit General P Leisure Shop 1 mile Pub < 0.5 miles

MUCH WENLOCK, Shropshire Map ref 4A3

★★★
SELF CATERING

Units **1**
Sleeps **1–4**
Low season per wk
£190.00–£250.00
High season per wk
£270.00–£310.00

3 Queen Street, Much Wenlock

contact Mrs E A Williams, 3 Queen Street, c/o 68 Church Hill, Penn, Wolverhampton WV4 5JD
t (01902) 341399 & (01743) 362315 **e** williams_letting@hotmail.com **w** stmem.com/3queenstreet

Secluded, detached cottage in heart of small medieval market town. Spacious, comfortable rooms including one double and one twin bedroom. Sunny walled garden. Short walk to Wenlock Priory, museum, Tourist Information Centre, shops and pubs.

open All year
payment Cash/cheques

Unit General P Leisure Shop < 0.5 miles Pub < 0.5 miles

MUCH WENLOCK, Shropshire Map ref 4A3

★★★★★
SELF CATERING

Units **1**
Sleeps **1–6**
Low season per wk
Max £350.00
High season per wk
Max £510.00

The Owl's House, Much Wenlock

contact Mrs Samantha Gray, The Owl's House, c/o Penkridge Cottage, Sheinton Road, Much Wenlock TF13 6NS
t (01952) 728169 **e** dgray@dgray96.fsnet.co.uk **w** owlshouse.co.uk

open All year
payment Cash/cheques

Set in the heart of the Shropshire countryside, only two miles from Much Wenlock, this recently renovated and beautifully refurbished holiday cottage offers an idyllic location in which to relax and unwind. There is a herb garden and patio area, sitting amongst woodland views over the Wenlock Edge, Long Mynd and Wrekin.

⊕ *Please contact Samantha or Duncan Gray for directions or see website for full details.*

Unit General 10 P Shop 2 miles Pub 2 miles

If you have access needs...

Look for the National Accessible Scheme symbols if you have special hearing, visual or mobility needs. An index of all accommodation participating in the scheme can be found at the back of this guide.

NORTON LINDSEY, Warwickshire Map ref 2B1

★★★★
SELF CATERING

Units **1**
Sleeps **5**
Low season per wk
£284.00–£369.00
High season per wk
£426.00–£586.00

Willow Cottage, Norton Lindsey, Warwick

contact Mrs Helen Phillips, Lower House Farm, Canada Lane, Warwick CV35 8JH
t (01926) 842394 **e** canadalanefarm@yahoo.co.uk **w** willow-cottage.org.uk

Centrally heated cottage set in a quiet, rural location. Linen and heating provided. Ample parking. Lawned garden and patio.

open All year
payment Cash/cheques

Unit General P Shop 2.5 miles Pub 0.75 miles

OSWESTRY, Shropshire Map ref 4A3

★★★
SELF CATERING

Units **1**
Sleeps **3**
Low season per wk
Min £210.00
High season per wk
Max £240.00

Cross Keys Cottage, Selattyn, Oswestry

contact Mr & Mrs Philip Rothera, Glyn Road, Selattyn, Oswestry SY10 7DH
t (01691) 650247 **e** hildarothera@tiscali.co.uk **w** thecrosskeys-selattyn.co.uk

Converted shop and granary attached to pub, regularly featured in the Good Beer Guide. Situated in beautiful walking country. Easy access to Oswestry, Shrewsbury and Chester.

open All year
payment Cash/cheques

Unit General P Shop 1 mile Pub < 0.5 miles

OSWESTRY, Shropshire Map ref 4A3

★★★★
SELF CATERING

Units **1**
Sleeps **2–4**
Low season per wk
£150.00–£200.00
High season per wk
£250.00–£300.00

The Stables, Morton, Oswestry

contact Mrs L M Frank, The Stables, Morton Farm, Morton, Oswestry SY10 8BE
t (01691) 682218 **e** bookings@mortonstables.co.uk **w** mortonstables.co.uk

open All year
payment Cash/cheques

Delightful converted stable facing open countryside, across the road from our working farm. Charming bedroom with antique brass bed, French windows onto patio, and en suite shower room. Excellent fitted kitchen with washer/dryer. Comfortable sofa bed. Underfloor heating and all services included. Cosy ground-floor accommodation suitable for people with limited mobility.

⊕ *Midlands – M6, M54, A5 past Shrewsbury. At roundabout, B4396 to Knockin. Through Knockin, continue for 1 mile, over hump-back bridge. Next right for Maesbury – 2nd on right.*

Unit General P Leisure Shop 2 miles Pub 1 mile

PEAK DISTRICT

See under Alstonefield

PEMBRIDGE, Herefordshire Map ref 2A1

★★★
SELF CATERING

Units **2**
Sleeps **1–4**
Low season per wk
£175.00–£270.00
High season per wk
£270.00–£320.00

The Granary and The Dairy, Leominster

contact Mrs Nancy Owens, The Granary and The Dairy, The Grove, Noke Lane, Pembridge, Leominster HR6 9HP
t (01544) 388268 **f** (01544) 388154 **e** nancy@grovedesign.co.uk

open All year
payment Cash/cheques

Set in spectacular, peaceful Herefordshire countryside. Ideal for walks on Offa's Dyke, Mortimer Trail or around the farm itself. Many interesting places to visit, eg Mappa Mundi, Hereford and National Trust properties. Local horse-riding, fishing, go-karting. Warm welcome with tea tray and home bakes.

Unit General P Leisure Shop 3 miles Pub 3 miles

RICHARDS CASTLE, Shropshire Map ref 4A3

★★★★
SELF CATERING

Units **1**
Sleeps **2–3**
Low season per wk
£180.00–£220.00
High season per wk
£220.00–£260.00

Stables Flat, Richards Castle, Ludlow

contact Mrs Sandra English, Woodhouse Farm, Richards Castle, Ludlow SY8 4EU
t (01584) 831265 **f** (01584) 831265 **e** english.david@tiscali.co.uk

Upstairs beamed Stables Flat, fully fitted, all linen provided. Overlooks attractive garden and distant views. Ideal base for cycling, walking, bird-watching and touring. Near Ludlow and Leominster.

open All year
payment Cash/cheques

Unit General P Leisure Shop 2 miles Pub 2 miles

ROSS-ON-WYE, Herefordshire Map ref 2A1

★★★
SELF CATERING

Units **2**
Sleeps **2–4**
Low season per wk
Max £185.00
High season per wk
Max £240.00

Benhall Farm, Ross-on-Wye

contact Mrs Carol Brewer, Benhall Farm, Wilton, Ross-on-Wye HR9 6AG
t (01989) 563900 **f** (01989) 563900 **e** info@benhallfarm.co.uk **w** benhallfarm.co.uk

open All year
payment Credit/debit cards, cash/cheques

A peaceful haven in a busy world! Comfortable, well-equipped accommodation with picturesque views on a working dairy and arable farm. Historic market town of Ross-on-Wye close by. Ideal for touring Wye Valley, Forest of Dean and Welsh Borders. Walking, canoeing, fishing and golf nearby.

⊕ *Junction A40 with A49 Wilton roundabout, take A40 direction of M50. Turn immediately left into no-through road (Benhall Lane). Farm is at end.*

Unit General P Leisure Shop < 0.5 miles Pub < 0.5 miles

Using map references

The map references refer to the colour maps at the front of this guide. The first figure is the map number; the letter and figure that follow indicate the grid reference on the map.

ROSS-ON-WYE, Herefordshire Map ref 2A1

★★★
SELF CATERING

Units **2**
Sleeps **2–4**
Low season per wk
£195.00–£230.00
High season per wk
£250.00–£350.00

The Game Larders and The Old Bakehouse, Ross-on-Wye

contact Miss Anthea McIntyre, The Game Larders and The Old Bakehouse, Wythall Estate, Bulls Hill, Ross-on-Wye HR9 5SD
t (01989) 562688 **f** (01989) 763225 **e** wythall@globalnet.co.uk **w** wythallestate.co.uk

open All year
payment Cash/cheques

Self-contained cottages in the wing of a 16thC manor-house in a secluded setting with garden, duck pond and wooded grounds. You will enjoy peace and quiet here and see an abundance of wildlife. Well equipped and furnished in period style, the cottages are warm and comfortable.

⊕ *Please contact us for directions.*

❤ *Short breaks available Oct-Mar. 3-night stay.*

Unit General Shop 2 miles Pub 1 mile

ROSS-ON-WYE, Herefordshire Map ref 2A1

★★★★★
SELF CATERING

Units **3**
Sleeps **2–4**
Low season per wk
£420.00–£485.00
High season per wk
£635.00–£730.00

Wharton Lodge Cottages, Ross-on-Wye

contact Mrs Nicky Cross, Weston under Penyard, Ross-on-Wye HR9 7JX
t (01989) 750140 **f** (01989) 750140 **e** ncross@whartonlodge.co.uk **w** whartonlodge.co.uk

Beautifully appointed cottages. Idyllic setting in 14-acre parkland of country house, overlooking Forest of Dean, adjacent to Wye Valley. Fabulous Italianate garden and furnished greenhouse/orangery.

open All year
payment Credit/debit cards, cash/cheques

Unit General Leisure Shop 1 mile Pub 1 mile

RUGBY, Warwickshire Map ref 4C3

★★★★
SELF CATERING

Units **3**
Sleeps **4–8**
Low season per wk
£400.00–£450.00
High season per wk
£450.00–£600.00

Lawford Hill Farm, Rugby

contact Mr & Mrs Susan Moses, Lawford Hill Farm, Lawford Heath Lane, Rugby CV23 9HG
t (01788) 542001 **f** (01788) 537880 **e** lawford.hill@talk21.com **w** lawfordhill.co.uk

Attractive converted barns set within a farmyard. Fully equipped to ensure you are cosy and comfortable. Short breaks by arrangement. Fishing available. Located three miles from Rugby on Lawford Heath Lane.

open All year
payment Credit/debit cards, cash/cheques

Unit General Leisure Shop 1.5 miles Pub 1 mile

STONE, Staffordshire Map ref 4B2

★★★★
SELF CATERING

Units 1
Sleeps 4
Low season per wk
£300.00–£350.00
High season per wk
£300.00–£350.00

Fox Hollow, Hilderstone, Stone

contact Ms Michelle Monaghan, Cresswell Road, Hilderstone, Stone ST15 8SL
t (01889) 505045 **e** mcmahon605@hotmail.com **w** foxhollowbarnes.co.uk

open All year
payment Cash/cheques

A converted cowshed, comprising two double bedrooms, upstairs family bathroom, farmhouse-style kitchen, lounge, through dining room and downstairs wc. Central heating. Set in eight acres. Manicured gardens, stream. We have chickens, goats and rabbits – lovely for children.

Discounts available for Senior Citizens.

Unit General Leisure Shop 4 miles Pub 0.5 miles

STRATFORD-UPON-AVON, Warwickshire Map ref 2B1

★★★★
SELF CATERING

Units 2
Sleeps 1–3
Low season per wk
£265.00–£300.00
High season per wk
£300.00–£385.00

1 College Mews, Stratford-upon-Avon

contact Mr Reid, Inwood House, New Road, Stratford-upon-Avon CV37 8PE
t (01789) 450266 **f** (01789) 450266

Quietly situated ground-floor apartment in old town, within easy walking distance of theatres, shops and riverside parks. Owner supervised.

open All year
payment Cash/cheques

Unit

STRATFORD-UPON-AVON, Warwickshire Map ref 2B1

★★★
SELF CATERING

Units 1
Sleeps 1–3
Low season per wk
£180.00–£190.00
High season per wk
£220.00–£260.00

Chestnut Cottage, Pathlow, Stratford-upon-Avon

contact Mrs Joyce Rush, Chestnut Cottage, Gospel Oak House, Gospel Oak Lane, Pathlow, Stratford-upon-Avon CV37 0JA
t (01789) 292764

Set in splendid, secluded grounds by woodland, with far-reaching views. Well appointed, attractively furnished, ample parking. Two and a half miles from Stratford-upon-Avon.

open All year except Christmas and New Year
payment Cash/cheques

Unit General Shop 2 miles Pub < 0.5 miles

STRATFORD-UPON-AVON, Warwickshire Map ref 2B1

★★★★
SELF CATERING

Units 1
Sleeps 2–8
Low season per wk
Min £400.00
High season per wk
Min £625.00

Holtom Mews, Stratford-upon-Avon

contact Ms Jan Brady, 35 Bracebridge Road, Sutton Coldfield B74 2QL
t (0121) 308 7050 **f** (0121) 308 0626 **e** ardenproperties@btinternet.com **w** ardenproperties.co.uk

Modern townhouse, appealing to families or friends, within easy walk of Stratford's attractions. Three double bedrooms, plus bed-settee, patio garden and scarce off-road parking. Visit our website for more information.

open All year
payment Cash/cheques

Unit General Shop < 0.5 miles Pub < 0.5 miles

Check it out

Please check prices, quality ratings and other details when you book.

STRATFORD-UPON-AVON, Warwickshire Map ref 2B1

★★★★
SELF CATERING

Units **1**
Sleeps **1–6**
Low season per wk
£595.00–£630.00
High season per wk
£630.00–£750.00

Riverview Lodge, Stratford-upon-Avon

t 07802 640372 **f** (01676) 532911 **e** info@luxurylifestylelodges.co.uk **w** luxurylifestylelodges.co.uk

open All year
payment Cash/cheques

Riverview Lodge is a luxury holiday retreat with decked area overlooking the River Avon, only 0.75 miles from Stratford-upon-Avon town. A perfect base for exploring the many historical and beautiful sites of Warwickshire and the Cotswolds. Designed and decorated with style and comfort in mind.

⊕ *M40 jct 15, then follow A46 (Stratford). At island, bear left onto A439, follow for 3.5 miles. Entrance to Avon Estates on left (opposite Welcome Golf Club).*

Unit General P Leisure Shop < 0.5 miles Pub < 0.5 miles

TENBURY WELLS, Worcestershire Map ref 4A3

★★★–★★★★
SELF CATERING

Units **2**
Sleeps **3–8**
Low season per wk
Min £180.00
High season per wk
Max £600.00

Rochford Park Cottages, Tenbury Wells

contact Mrs J Robinson, Rochford Park, Tenbury Wells WR15 8SP
t (01584) 781392 **f** (01584) 781392 **e** mrs.j.robinson@fwi.co.uk **w** rochfordpark.co.uk

Former stable and barn, now stylish, comfortable accommodation for an active family in one or a group of friends/family in the other. Bookable together.

open All year
payment Cash/cheques

Unit General P Leisure Shop 3 miles Pub 1.5 miles

UPTON UPON SEVERN, Worcestershire Map ref 2B1

★★★★
SELF CATERING

Units **1**
Sleeps **1–2**
Low season per wk
£150.00–£250.00
High season per wk
£250.00–£500.00

Captains Retreat, Worcester

contact Mr & Mrs Michael & Julie-Ann Cranton, White Cottage, Church End, Hanley Castle, Worcester WR8 0BL
t (01684) 592023 **f** (01684) 592328 **e** michael@cranton.freeserve.co.uk

open All year
payment Cash/cheques

Converted from a 17thC inn, this fully renovated and spacious first-floor apartment offers the perfect base for exploring and relaxing in this beautiful part of the country. Two hundred yards from open countryside, just off the centre of Upton, this beautiful timber-framed accommodation offers the perfect retreat.

⊕ *M50 jct1 onto A38 (Worcester). After 4 miles, left to Upton upon Severn. After 1 mile left at mini-roundabout into town centre. Right into New Street.*

❤ *Short 3-day breaks available, from £120.*

Unit General P Leisure Shop < 0.5 miles Pub < 0.5 miles

WALKERS WELCOME WALKERS WELCOME

Best foot forward

Walkers feel at home in accommodation participating in our Walkers Welcome scheme. Look out for the symbol. Consider walking all or part of a long-distance route – go online at nationaltrail.co.uk.

WELLINGTON, Shropshire Map ref 4A3

★★★★
SELF CATERING

Units 1
Sleeps 4
Low season per wk
£250.00–£300.00
High season per wk
£350.00–£450.00

The Coach House, Wrockwardine

contact Mrs Fellows, Old Vicarage, Wrockwardine, Telford TF6 5DG
t (01952) 244859 **f** (01952) 255066 **e** mue@mfellows0.freeserve.co.uk

Detached private house providing centrally heated, two-bedroomed accommodation. Pleasant location, surrounded by farms yet close to Ironbridge, Shrewsbury and the Welsh Marches.

open All year
payment Cash/cheques

Unit General Shop 1 mile Pub 1 mile

WESTON RHYN, Shropshire Map ref 4A2

★★★
SELF CATERING

Units 1
Sleeps 4
Low season per wk
£180.00–£190.00
High season per wk
£190.00–£200.00

Mill Cottage, Oswestry

contact Mr & Mrs H Brannick, Mill Cottage, Mill House, The Wern, Weston Rhyn, Oswestry SY10 7ER
t (01691) 659738

Mill Cottage is a converted 18thC barn. Set in rural surroundings with stream, very peaceful, four miles from Oswestry and the Welsh border.

open All year except Christmas and New Year
payment Cash/cheques

Unit General Leisure Shop 1 mile Pub 0.5 miles

WHITBOURNE, Herefordshire Map ref 2B1

★★★
SELF CATERING

Units 1
Sleeps 2–11
Low season per wk
£390.00–£970.00
High season per wk
£440.00–£690.00

Crumplebury Farmhouse, Whitbourne

contact Mrs Anne Evans, Dial House, Whitbourne Hall Park, Whitbourne, Worcester WR6 5SG
t (01886) 821534 **e** a.evans@candaevans.fsnet.co.uk **w** whitbourne-estate.co.uk/crumplebury

Owner-maintained, comfortable and cosy five-bedroom farmhouse on family farm. Ideal for reunions, family gatherings, walking. Enclosed garden. Quiet. Coarse fishing available.

open All year
payment Cash/cheques

Unit General Leisure Shop 2 miles Pub 1.5 miles

WORCESTER, Worcestershire Map ref 2B1

★★★★
SELF CATERING

Units 1
Low season per wk
£200.00–£250.00
High season per wk
Max £300.00

The Whitehouse, Worcester

contact Mrs Susan O'Neill, The Whitehouse, Monkwood Green, Hallow, Worcester WR2 6NX
t (01886) 888743 **f** (01886) 888743

Detached, one-bedroom cosy cottage in a peaceful location, offering a garden, off-road parking and many places of interest within easy reach.

open All year
payment Cash/cheques

Unit General Leisure

WYE VALLEY

See under Hereford, Ross-on-Wye

Friendly help and advice

Tourist information centres offer friendly help with accommodation and holiday ideas as well as suggestions of places to visit and things to do. You'll find contact details at the beginning of each regional section.

WYTHALL, Worcestershire Map ref 4B3

★★★-★★★★
SELF CATERING

Units **7**
Sleeps **4–6**
Low season per wk
£195.00–£365.00
High season per wk
£200.00–£365.00

Inkford Court Cottages, Whythall

contact Mr Bedford, Inkford Court Cottages, Alcester Road, Wythall, Worcester B47 6DL
t (01564) 822304 **f** (01564) 829618

Cottages, part of a restoration and conversion of 18thC period farm buildings, set in 6.5 acres. Ideally located for Heart of England.

open All year
payment Cash/cheques

Unit General **P**

Bank holiday
dates for your diary

holiday	2007	2008
New Year's Day	1 January	1 January
Good Friday	6 April	21 March
Easter Monday	9 April	24 March
Early May Bank Holiday	7 May	5 May
Spring Bank Holiday	28 May	26 May
Summer Bank Holiday	27 August	25 August
Christmas Day	25 December	25 December
Boxing Day	26 December	26 December

East Midlands

Derbyshire & the Peak District › Leicestershire & Rutland
Lincolnshire › Northamptonshire › Nottinghamshire

On target at Sherwood Forest Country Park

England's East Midlands
enjoyeastmidlands.com
Leicester Shire Promotions
0906 294 1113
goleicestershire.com
Lincolnshire Tourism
(01522) 526450
visitlincolnshire.com
Explore Northamptonshire
(01604) 838800
explorenorthamptonshire.co.uk
Experience Nottinghamshire
(0115) 962 8300
visitnottingham.com
Peak District and Derbyshire
0870 444 7275
derbyshirethepeakdistrict.com
visitpeakdistrict.com

Pleasurable peaks, forest adventure, vibrant cities

Main Live the high life in the Peak District **Left** There's always time for adventure at Rockingham Castle, Market Harborough; celebrate Diwali in style in Leicester; cruising along the Grand Union Canal; time for lift-off at the National Space Centre, Leicester

From the adventurous trails of the Peak District and the gentle waters of the Leicestershire canals to the vibrant, cosmopolitan buzz of the cities – **the East Midlands may surprise you.**

Explore East Midlands

Picture the scene

Take up the challenge and scale the face of a weathered crag in the Peak District, or find your feet on a section of the Pennine Way where spectacular scenery will spur you on. Disappear underground and try potholing, or get those bicycle wheels spinning and head out across Derwent Valley past historic reservoirs and enchanting woodland.

The National Forest is crying out for a visit: take to the water and sail across one of its beautiful lakes, or don your green fingers and plant a tree, and become involved in the future of the forest. Let the kids go nuts for Conkers at the heart of the forest for unforgettable outdoor experiences.

Lose yourself in legend in Sherwood Forest, home of the notorious Robin Hood, try your hand at a spot of archery and hunt for the Major Oak. Explore the rich heritage and natural beauty of the fens, and keep your eyes peeled for the vast array of wildlife at Rutland Water Nature Reserve.

City diversity

Let your senses guide you down Belgrave Road in Leicester to sample the vast range of curried delights. Explore the city's historic quarter, and drop in on the National Space Centre for an experience, quite literally, out of this world! Travel through centuries of crime and punishment at Nottingham's Galleries of Justice, or slip on some headphones for an audio tour in the preserved workhouse in Southwell and listen to the forgotten inhabitants.

Indulge in a treat as you stroll around the unique shopping areas of Lincoln and gaze up in awe from the base of the hilltop cathedral. Unravel 250,000 years of history at The Collection – the city's museum of art and archaeology – where the exhibitions are continually growing, or head 'downhill' – as the locals call it – for the vibrant nightlife and cafe culture.

Fun for all the family

Watch your knuckles turn white on the Boomerang at Pleasure Island in Cleethorpes, or observe seals and penguins playfully scrambling for fish at Natureland on the 'Fun Coast' in Skegness.

Rifle your way through one of the oldest markets in the region in Bakewell and sample one of the local tarts. Catch a glimpse of the traditional and decorative well dressing, on display throughout Derbyshire. Watch the sun sparkle off the jets from the beautiful fountains at Chatsworth House, or take a step back in time at delightful medieval manor-house, Haddon Hall.

Sights to behold

Pull your boots on and follow the enthralling five-mile Bamford Touchstones Sculpture Trail in Derbyshire, or roll out a picnic rug in the beautiful gardens of Althorp in Northamptonshire – home of the Spencer family for over 500 years. Wander through the grounds of the remarkable Rockingham Castle, built on the instruction of William the Conqueror, and fill your lungs with the sweet scent of the stunning 19th-century rose garden.

Places to **visit**

National Park

Area of Outstanding Natural Beauty

National Trails
nationaltrail.co.uk

Sections of the National Cycle Network
nationalcyclenetwork.org.uk

Regional Route

Althorp
Northampton
(01604) 770107
althorp.com
Spencer family home since 1508

Bamford Touchstones Sculpture Trail
Derbyshire
bamfordvillage.co.uk
Encompassing all the natural elements

Bradgate Country Park
Newtown Linford, Leicestershire
(0116) 236 2713
nationalforest.org
Historic heather-covered parkland

Buxton Opera House
Buxton, Derbyshire
0845 127 2190
buxton-opera.co.uk
Beautifully restored Edwardian theatre

Chatsworth House, Garden, Farmyard & Adventure Playground
Bakewell, Derbyshire
(01246) 582204
chatsworth.org
Beautiful house and fountains

The Collection
Lincoln
(01522) 550990
thecollection.lincoln.museum
Museum of art and archaeology

Conkers
near Ashby-de-la-Zouch, Derbyshire
(01283) 216633
visitconkers.com
Interactive exhibits and woodland trails in The National Forest

Creswell Crags Museum and Education Centre, Picnic Site, Caves & Gorge
Worksop, Derbyshire
(01909) 720378
creswell-crags.org.uk
Limestone gorge, caves and lake

Crich Tramway Village
Matlock, Derbyshire
0870 758 7267
tramway.co.uk
Street scenes, rides and exhibits in a charming setting

Derwent Valley Visitor Centre
Belper, Derbyshire
(01773) 880474
belpernorthmill.org.uk
Industrial exhibits, models and machinery

The Galleries of Justice
Nottingham
(0115) 952 0555
galleriesofjustice.org.uk
Delve into the history of crime and punishment throughout the ages

Gibraltar Point National Nature Reserve and Visitor Centre
Skegness, Lincolnshire
(01754) 762677
lincstrust.org.uk
1,500 acres of glorious sand dunes, salt marsh and muddy shores

Haddon Hall

Bakewell, Derbyshire
(01629) 812855
haddonhall.co.uk
Medieval and Tudor manor-house

National Space Centre

Leicester
0870 607 7223
spacecentre.co.uk
The UK's largest space attraction

Natureland
Skegness, Lincolnshire
(01754) 764345
skegnessnatureland.co.uk
Watch seals and penguins feeding

Pleasure Island Family Theme Park
Cleethorpes, Lincolnshire
(01472) 211511
pleasure-island.co.uk
Featuring rides for all ages

Rockingham Castle

Market Harborough, Northamptonshire
(01536) 770240
rockinghamcastle.com
Rose gardens and exquisite art

Rutland Water
Oakham
(01572) 653026
rutlandwater.net
Vast, stunning man-made lake

Sherwood Forest Country Park
Mansfield, Nottinghamshire
(01623) 821327
sherwood-forest.org.uk
Native woodland packed with adventure

The Workhouse
Nottingham
(01636) 817250
nationaltrust.org.uk
Fascinating 19th-century preserved workhouse

Tourist information centres 

When you arrive at your destination, visit a tourist information centre for help with accommodation and information about local attractions and events, or email your request before you go.

Ashbourne	13 Market Place	(01335) 343666	ashbourneinfo@derbyshiredales.gov.uk
Ashby-de-la-Zouch	North Street	(01530) 411767	ashby.tic@nwleices.gov.uk
Bakewell	Bridge Street	(01629) 816558	bakewell@peakdistrict-npa.gov.uk
Boston	Market Place	(01205) 356656	ticboston@boston.gov.uk
Brackley	2 Bridge Street	(01280) 700111	tic@southnorthants.gov.uk
Buxton	The Crescent	(01298) 25106	tourism@highpeak.gov.uk
Chesterfield	Rykneld Square	(01246) 345777	tourism@chesterfield.gov.uk
Corby	George Street	(01536) 407507	tic@corby.gov.uk
Derby City	Market Place	(01332) 255802	tourism@derby.gov.uk
Glossop	Victoria Street	(01457) 855920	info@glossoptouristcentre.co.uk
Grantham	St Peter's Hill	(01476) 406166	granthamtic@southkesteven.gov.uk
Hinckley	Lancaster Road	(01455) 635106	hinckleytic@leics.gov.uk
Horncastle	14 Bull Ring	(01507) 526636	horncastleinfo@e-lindsey.gov.uk
Kettering	Sheep Street	(01536) 410266	tic@kettering.gov.uk
Leicester City	7/9 Every Street	0906 294 1113**	info@goleicestershire.com
Lincoln Castle Hill	9 Castle Hill	(01522) 873213	tourism@lincoln.gov.uk
Lincoln Corn Hill	21 Cornhill	(01522) 873256	tourism@lincoln.gov.uk
Loughborough	Market Place	(01509) 218113	tic@charnwoodbc.gov.uk
Louth	The Market Hall	(01507) 609289	louthinfo@e-lindsey.gov.uk
Mablethorpe	The Dunes Centre	(01507) 474939	mablethorpeinfo@e-lindsey.gov.uk
Market Harborough	Adam & Eve Street	(01858) 828282	customer.services@harborough.gov.uk
Matlock	Crown Square	(01629) 583388	matlockinfo@derbyshiredales.gov.uk
Matlock Bath*	The Pavillion	(01629) 55082	matlockbathinfo@derbyshiredales.gov.uk
Melton Mowbray	7 King Street	(01664) 480992	tic@melton.gov.uk
Newark	Castlegate	(01636) 655765	gilstrap@nsdc.info
Northampton	St Giles Street	(01604) 838800	northampton.tic@explorenorthamptonshire.co.uk
Nottingham	1-4 Smithy Row	0844 477 5678	tourist.information@nottinghamcity.gov.uk
Oakham	39 High Street	(01572) 758441	oakhamtic@biz-dial.co.uk
Ollerton	Sherwood Heath	(01623) 824545	sherwoodheath@nsdc.info
Oundle	14 West Street	(01832) 274333	oundle@east-northamptonshire.gov.uk
Retford	40 Grove Street	(01777) 860780	retford.tourist@bassetlaw.gov.uk
Ripley	Market Place	(01773) 841488	touristinformation@ambervalley.gov.uk
Rutland Water*	Sykes Lane	(01572) 653026	tic@anglianwater.co.uk
Skegness	Grand Parade	(01754) 899887	skegnessinfo@e-lindsey.gov.uk
Sleaford	Carre Street	(01529) 414294	tic@n-kesteven.gov.uk
Spalding	Market Place	(01775) 725468	tic@sholland.gov.uk
Stamford	27 St Mary's Street	(01780) 755611	stamfordtic@southkesteven.gov.uk
Woodhall Spa*	Iddesleigh Road	(01526) 353775	woodhallspainfo@e-lindsey.gov.uk
Worksop	Memorial Avenue	(01909) 501148	worksop.tourist@bassetlaw.gov.uk

** seasonal opening ** calls to this number are charged at premium rate*

Alternatively, you can text **TIC LOCATE** to **64118** to find your nearest tourist information centre

Find out **more**

Further publications are available from the following organisations:

Experience Nottinghamshire

w visitnotts.com

- **Nottinghamshire Essential Guide**
- **Nottinghamshire Where to Stay Guide**
- **Nottinghamshire Stay Somewhere Different**
- **Nottinghamshire City Breaks**
- **Nottinghamshire Attractions – A Family Day Out**

Peak District and Derbyshire

w derbyshirethepeakdistrict.com or visitpeakdistrict.com

- **Peak District Visitor Guide**
- **Savour the Flavour of the Peak District**
- **Derbyshire – the Peak District Visitor Guide**
- **Derbyshire – the Peak District Attractions Guide**
- **Camping and Caravanning Guide**
- **What's on Guide**

Lincolnshire

w visitlincolnshire.com

- **Visit Lincolnshire – Destination Guide**
- **Visit Lincolnshire – Great days out**
- **Visit Lincolnshire – Gardens & Nurseries**
- **Visit Lincolnshire – Aviation Heritage**
- **Tastes of Lincolnshire – Good Taste**

Explore Northamptonshire

w explorenorthamptonshire.co.uk

- **Explore Northamptonshire Visitor Guide**
- **Explore Northamptonshire County Map**
- **Explore Northamptonshire Food and Drink**

Leicestershire and Rutland

w goleicestershire.com

- **Rutland Visitor Guide**
- **Market Harborough & Lutterworth Guide**
- **Leicester City Guide**
- **Ashby de la Zouch and The National Forest Guide**
- **Belgrave Guide**
- **Melton Mowbray and the Vale of Belvoir**
- **Hinkley and Market Bosworth Guide**
- **Loughborough and Charnwood Forest**

Travel **info**

The central location of the East Midlands makes it easily accessible from all parts of the UK.

By road:

From the north and south, the M1 bisects the East Midlands with access to the region from junctions 14 through to 31. The A1 offers better access to the eastern part of the region, particularly Lincolnshire and Rutland. From the west, the M69, M/A42 and A50 provide easy access.

By rail:

The region is well served by three main line operators – GNER, Midland Mainline and Virgin Trains, each offering direct services from London and the north of England and Scotland to the East Midlands' major cities and towns. East/west links are provided by Central Trains, offering not only access to the region but also travel within it.

By air:

Nottingham East Midlands airport is located centrally in the region, with scheduled domestic flights from Aberdeen, Belfast, Edinburgh, Glasgow, Isle of Man and the Channel Islands. Manchester, Birmingham, Luton, Stansted and Humberside airports also offer domestic scheduled routes, with easy access to the region by road and rail.

where to stay in
East Midlands

All place names in the blue bands are shown on the maps at the front of this guide.

A complete listing of all Enjoy England assessed accommodation covered by this guide appears at the back.

Accommodation symbols
Symbols give useful information about services and facilities. Inside the back-cover flap you can find a key to these symbols. Keep it open for easy reference.

ALFORD, Lincolnshire Map ref 4D2

★★★★
SELF CATERING

Units **4**
Sleeps **2–6**
Low season per wk
£120.00–£250.00
High season per wk
£220.00–£450.00

Woodthorpe Hall Country Cottage, Alford

contact Mrs Stubbs, Woodthorpe Hall Country Cottage, Woodthorpe, Alford LN13 0DD
t (01507) 450294 **f** (01507) 450885 **e** enquiries@woodthorpehallleisure.co.uk
w woodthorpehallleisure.co.uk

Cottages overlooking golf course. Central heating, TV and video, dishwasher, washer/dryer, fridge/freezer, microwave and telephone. Fishing, garden and aquatic centre, restaurant and bar etc.

open All year
payment Credit/debit cards, cash/cheques

Unit General P Leisure Shop < 0.5 miles Pub < 0.5 miles

ALPORT, Derbyshire Map ref 4B2

★★★★
SELF CATERING

Units **1**
Sleeps **4**
Low season per wk
£416.00–£500.00
High season per wk
£816.00–£900.00

Rock Cottage, Bakewell

contact Ms Janet O'Sullivan, Estate Office, Haddon Hall, Bakewell DE45 1LA
t (01629) 810910 **f** (01629) 814379 **e** janet@haddonhall.co.uk

Rock Cottage provides a very comfortable and beautifully furnished holiday home, situated on the Haddon Estate. Conveniently located for visiting Haddon Hall and Chatsworth.

open All year
payment Credit/debit cards, cash/cheques

Unit General P S Leisure Shop 1 mile Pub 1 mile

ARNOLD, Nottinghamshire Map ref 4C2

★★★
SELF CATERING

Units **1**
Sleeps **3**
Low season per wk
£260.00–£295.00
High season per wk
£260.00–£300.00

The Grannary, Nottingham

contact Mrs Lamin, The Grannary, Top House Farm, Mansfield Road, Arnold, Nottingham NG5 8PH
t (0115) 926 8330

A charming granny flat with beams, an open fireplace and patio doors leading onto a garden. Within easy reach of Newstead Abbey, Nottingham, Southwell Minster and Sherwood Forest.

open All year
payment Cash/cheques

Unit General P Leisure Shop 2 miles Pub 0.5 miles

ASHBOURNE, Derbyshire Map ref 4B2

★★★★
SELF CATERING

Units **1**
Sleeps **2–6**
Low season per wk
Max £298.00
High season per wk
Max £575.00

Croft House Barn, Nr Ashbourne

contact Stephanie Cadenhead, Waterfall, Waterhouses ST10 3HZ
t (01538) 308125 **e** stephanie@crofthousebarn.co.uk **w** crofthousebarn.co.uk

Comfortable, beautifully renovated, 400-year-old, Peak District stone cottage in rural Waterfall. Three en suite bedrooms provide luxurious accommodation, doorstep walks/cycling. Quality pub meals – a two-minute stroll!

open All year
payment Credit/debit cards, cash/cheques

Unit General P Leisure Shop 1 mile Pub < 0.5 miles

ASHBOURNE, Derbyshire Map ref 4B2

★★★★
SELF CATERING

Units **1**
Sleeps **14**
Low season per wk
£850.00–£950.00
High season per wk
£1,075.00–£1,850.00

Greenacres, Ashbourne

contact Ms Frances Williamson, Luxury Location Lets, 34a Derby Road, Borrowash, Derby DE72 3HA
t (01332) 723192 **f** (01332) 723192 **e** frances2@ntlworld.com

open All year
payment Cash/cheques

This magnificent house is in the heart of Ashbourne, tucked away in two acres of garden, providing a quiet, secluded holiday home of real quality. The beautiful garden, with a variety of places to explore, has a very large lawn, a wooded area with stream and bridge, and much more.

⊕ *From Derby, follow the A52 to Ashbourne. Follow signs for Buxton (A515), past the market square, taking the 1st right.*

Unit General P Leisure

ASHBOURNE, Derbyshire Map ref 4B2

★★★★★
SELF CATERING

Units **1**
Sleeps **6–8**
Low season per wk
£410.00–£595.00
High season per wk
£595.00–£795.00

The Grooms Quarters, Ashbourne

contact Mr & Mrs Ray & Ann Thompson, The Old Coach House, Hall Lane, Wootton, Ellastone, Ashbourne DE6 2GW
t (01335) 324549 **e** ann@groomsquarters.co.uk **w** groomsquarters.co.uk

open All year
payment Cash/cheques

Part of 18thC coach house, many original features, converted into a spacious and cosy retreat. Elevated and tranquil with superb views. Good walking from the door, cycling on the trails. Bordering Dovedale and Peak Park. Alton Towers three miles. Wood-burning stove, super-king beds, farmhouse-style kitchen, enclosed, lawned garden and pool table.

⊕ *When entering Wootton, proceed into centre, look for Hall Lane and follow this until you see stone pillars, go through and down the drive into yard at the end.*

♥ *Short breaks available. 'Just for Two' discounts. Mon–Fri: 4 nights for the price of 3.*

Unit General P Leisure
Shop 2 miles Pub 2 miles

Check it out

Information on accommodation listed in this guide has been supplied by proprietors. As changes may occur you should remember to check all relevant details at the time of booking.

ASHBOURNE, Derbyshire Map ref 4B2

★★★★
SELF CATERING

Units **5**
Sleeps **2–6**
Low season per wk
£234.00–£430.00
High season per wk
£430.00–£677.00

Paddock House Farm Holiday Cottages, Alstonefield, Ashbourne

contact Mr & Mrs Mark & Melissa Redfern, Paddock House Farm Holiday Cottages, Alstonefield, Ashbourne DE6 2FT
t 0870 027 2500 **f** 0870 027 2400 **e** info@paddockhousefarm.co.uk **w** paddockhousefarm.co.uk

open All year
payment Cash/cheques

Luxury holiday cottages in the heart of the Peak District National Park. Cottages have either three bedrooms, two bedrooms or one bedroom. Wonderful views of the open countryside in a very peaceful location. Excellent attractions, including Alton Towers, Chatsworth and Dovedale.

⊕ *From Alstonefield village head for Hulme End, 1.5 miles on the left. At the end of our drive turn left to the main courtyard.*

❤ *20% reduction for 2 adults booking a 3-bedroom cottage only using 1 bedroom (off-peak only).*

Unit General P Leisure
Shop 1.5 miles Pub 1.5 miles

ASHBOURNE, Derbyshire Map ref 4B2

★★★–★★★★
SELF CATERING

Units **41**
Sleeps **2–8**
Low season per wk
£270.00–£530.00
High season per wk
£370.00–£995.00

Sandybrook Country Park, Ashbourne

contact Reception, Pinelodge Holidays, Sandybrook Country Park, Buxton Road, Ashbourne DE6 2AQ
t (01335) 300000 **f** (01335) 342679 **e** enquiries@pinelodgeholidays.co.uk
w pinelodgeholidays.co.uk/sandybrook.ihtml

open All year
payment Credit/debit cards, cash/cheques

Set in the former grounds of Sandybrook Hall, an elegant, 19thC manor-house with woodland walks and wonderful views. Luxurious, fully equipped pine lodges furnished to the highest standards. Heated indoor swimming pool, indoor and outdoor play areas, restaurant and bar.

⊕ *Take A52 through Derby, then to Ashbourne. In Ashbourne take the A515 towards Buxton. Park is 1 mile out of town on the right-hand side.*

❤ *Mid-week and weekend breaks available all year round (excl Christmas and New Year).*

Unit General P Leisure Shop 1 mile
Pub < 0.5 miles

ASHBOURNE, Derbyshire Map ref 4B2

★★★★★
SELF CATERING

Units **1**
Sleeps **2–4**
Low season per wk
£250.00–£300.00
High season per wk
£375.00–£500.00

Thorpe Cloud View, Ashbourne

contact Mr Raymond Neilson, Thorpe Cloud View, Thorpe House, Thorpe, Ashbourne DE6 2AW
t (01335) 350215 **e** rayneilson@aol.com **w** peakdistrictcottage.com

open All year
payment Cash/cheques

You are invited to a luxury, 18thC, detached stone barn conversion on a beautiful four-acre estate. Enjoy exclusive use of the opulent indoor swimming pool and jacuzzi. Breathtaking views of the mountains at Dovedale. Ideally located for walking, cycling, watersports, Alton Towers and many historic houses.

⊕ *Please contact us for directions.*

Unit General P Leisure Shop 3 miles
Pub 0.5 miles

ASHBOURNE, Derbyshire Map ref 4B2

★★★★
SELF CATERING

Units 1
Sleeps 1–2
Low season per wk
£140.00–£200.00
High season per wk
£210.00–£385.00

Turlow Fields Farm, Hognaston, Ashbourne

contact Mandy & Adrian Hunter, Barnclose Cottage, Turlow Fields Farm, Ashbourne DE6 1PW
t (01335) 370834 **e** aahunter@uk2.net

open All year
payment Cash/cheques

Cottage on small organic farm. Double bedroom with bunk bed (can be separated), full underfloor heating, private garden with beautiful views, private picnic areas (picnics prepared by arrangement), farm walks (cattle, sheep, pigs and more to see). Carsington Water is a short, quiet walk away, and Ashbourne and Dovedale a five- to ten-minute drive.

⊕ *A517 towards Belper. After 4.5 miles, turn left (signposted Carsington Water and Hognaston). After 1.3 miles, Turlow Fields Farm on right.*

Unit General P Leisure Shop 1.5 miles Pub 1 mile

ASHBOURNE, Derbyshire Map ref 4B2

★★★★–★★★★★
SELF CATERING

Units 4
Sleeps 2–4
Low season per wk
£200.00–£450.00
High season per wk
£250.00–£500.00

Yeldersley Hall, Ashbourne

contact Mr Andrew Bailey, Yeldersley Hall, Yeldersley, Ashbourne DE6 1LS
t (01335) 343432

Flats in a stable block and east wing of a Georgian country house, standing in 12 acres of grounds. Ashbourne is two miles away.

open All year
payment Cash/cheques

Unit General P Leisure

ASHBY-DE-LA-ZOUCH, Leicestershire Map ref 4B3

★★★★
SELF CATERING

Units 1
Sleeps 2–5
Low season per wk
£250.00–£390.00
High season per wk
£290.00–£450.00

Norman's Barn, Ashby-de-la-Zouch

contact Mrs Isabel Stanley, Norman's Barn, Ingles Hill Farm, Burton Road, Ashby-de-la-Zouch LE65 2TE
t (01530) 412224 **e** isabel_stanley@hotmail.com **w** normansbarn.co.uk

open All year
payment Cash/cheques

Luxuriously appointed barn conversion incorporating minstrels' gallery. Both double bedrooms en suite. On working farm including 130 acres of woodland walks. Easy access to M42, NEC, Calke Abbey and Castle Donington Park/Airport.

⊕ *Exit A42 at junction 13, take A511 towards Burton-on-Trent. At 3rd roundabout turn left (Ashby). We are 1 mile from there on the left-hand side on top of the hill. Take 1st entrance gate opposite Caravan Club sign.*

Unit General P Leisure Shop 0.5 miles Pub 0.5 miles

Check the maps

Colour maps at the front pinpoint all the places you will find accommodation entries in the regional sections. Pick your location and then refer to the place index at the back to find the page number.

ASHBY-DE-LA-ZOUCH, Leicestershire Map ref 4B3

★★★★★
SELF CATERING

Units **6**
Sleeps **2–8**
Low season per wk
£300.00–£825.00
High season per wk
£340.00–£980.00

Upper Rectory Farm Cottages, Ashby de la Zouch

contact Mrs Jean Corbett, Upper Rectory Farm Cottages, Cottage Farm, Norton-Juxta-Twycross CV9 3QH
t (01827) 880448 **f** (01827) 830621 **e** info@upperrectoryfarmcottages.co.uk
w upperrectoryfarmcottages.co.uk

open All year
payment Credit/debit cards, cash/cheques

Multi-award-winning, beautifully converted luxury cottages set around adjoining courtyards. En suite facilities throughout, splendid panoramic views, lovely old oak beams, luxurious, yet homely atmosphere – and a warm welcome! So much to do for all the family locally. Central for touring Warwickshire, Leicestershire, Derbyshire and Staffordshire.

⊕ *From jct 11, M42 take A444 towards Nuneaton. Take 2nd left turn to Appleby Magna. At telephone box turn right into Snarestone Road. Farm drive on right.*

Unit General Leisure Shop 1 mile Pub 0.5 miles

BAKEWELL, Derbyshire Map ref 4B2

★★★★
SELF CATERING

Units **1**
Sleeps **1–4**
Low season per wk
£220.00–£260.00
High season per wk
£295.00–£420.00

Braemar Cottage, Youlgrave, Nr Bakewell

contact c/o Mrs Irene Shimwell, Braemar Cottage, Crimble House, Main Street, Youlgrave DE45 1UW
t (01629) 636568 & 07929 396525 **e** braemarcottage@fsmail.net **w** braemarcottage.co.uk

Recently restored, luxuriously appointed cottage lying in the heart of the beautiful village of Youlgrave – an ideal base for walking and sightseeing. Pubs and shops close by.

open All year
payment Cash/cheques

Unit General Shop < 0.5 miles Pub < 0.5 miles

BAKEWELL, Derbyshire Map ref 4B2

★★★
SELF CATERING

Units **1**
Sleeps **1–4**
Low season per wk
£204.00–£272.00
High season per wk
£390.00–£448.00

Cartwheels, Bakewell

Sykes Cottages, York House, York Street, Chester CH1 3LR
t (01244) 345700 **f** (01244) 321442 **e** info@sykescottages.co.uk **w** sykescottages.co.uk

open All year
payment Credit/debit cards, cash/cheques, euros

Elegantly furnished, stone-built cottage in heart of Derbyshire's Peak District. In beautiful Bakewell, a peaceful backwater overlooking the town, but only five minutes' walk to the centre. Two bedrooms, multi-fuel burner, big, exposed oak beam in lounge. Special parking permit provided.

⊕ *From Bakewell's only roundabout, go up North Church Street, with Bakewell church spire on left. After right-angled bend, Cartwheels is left, up Cunningham Place.*

Unit General Leisure Shop < 0.5 miles Pub < 0.5 miles

BAKEWELL, Derbyshire Map ref 4B2

★★★★
SELF CATERING

Units **1**
Sleeps **1–4**
Low season per wk
£250.00–£350.00
High season per wk
£360.00–£450.00

The Cottage, Bakewell

contact Mrs Catherine Harrison, Riversdale, Castle Street, Bakewell DE45 1DU
t (01629) 813768 & 07801 598720

Luxury converted two-bedroom, two-bathroom terraced cottage in quiet backwater, within 100yds of town centre. Parking.

open All year
payment Cash/cheques

Unit General P Leisure Shop < 0.5 miles Pub < 0.5 miles

BAKEWELL, Derbyshire Map ref 4B2

Rating Applied For
SELF CATERING

Units **1**
Sleeps **1–2**
Low season per wk
£140.00–£180.00
High season per wk
£220.00–£280.00

The Garden Lodge, Youlgrave, Nr Bakewell

contact c/o Mrs Irene Shimwell, The Garden Lodge, Crimble House, Main Street, Youlgrave, Bakewell DE45 1UW
t (01629) 636568 **e** braemarcottage@fsmail.net **w** braemarcottage.co.uk

Recently refurbished converted architect's studio set in a private garden with views over Bradford Dale. All mod cons.

open All year
payment Cash/cheques

Unit General Shop < 0.5 miles Pub < 0.5 miles

BAKEWELL, Derbyshire Map ref 4B2

★★★
SELF CATERING

Units **10**
Sleeps **2–7**
Low season per wk
£185.00–£450.00
High season per wk
£300.00–£900.00

Haddon Grove Farm Cottages, Bakewell

contact Mr & Mrs John Boxall, Haddon Grove Farm Cottages, Haddon Grove Farm, Monyash Road DE45 1JF
t (01629) 813551 **f** (01629) 815684 **w** haddongrovefarmcottages.co.uk

Cottages in courtyard setting overlooking Lathkill Dale. Additional facilities include barbecue area, games room and heated indoor swimming pool. We offer a superb base for cycling, riding, walking and the local visitor attractions.

open All year
payment Cash/cheques

Unit General Leisure Shop 3 miles Pub 2 miles

BAMFORD, Derbyshire Map ref 4B2

★★★★
SELF CATERING

Units **3**
Sleeps **1–6**
Low season per wk
£275.00–£300.00
High season per wk
£400.00–£475.00

Shatton Hall Farm Cottages, Hope Valley

contact Mrs Angela Kellie, Shatton Hall Farm Cottages, Shatton Hall Farm, Shatton, Hope Valley S33 0BG
t (01433) 620635 **f** (01433) 620689 **e** ahk@peakfarmholidays.co.uk **w** peakfarmholidays.co.uk

open All year
payment Credit/debit cards, cash/cheques, euros

Comfortable barn-converted cottages, each with own garden or terrace, on this 'out of the way', beautifully situated farmstead, with good access. Waymarked woodland walks, trout lake, tennis court and gardens of interest, open National Garden Scheme. Each cottage has double and twin-bedded rooms and good-size living areas with open fires.

⊕ *Apply for directions to the farm or find location maps on our website.*

Unit General P Leisure Shop 1.5 miles Pub 1.5 miles

BAMFORD, Derbyshire Map ref 4B2

★★★★★
SELF CATERING

Units **2**
Sleeps **2–6**
Low season per wk
£350.00–£500.00
High season per wk
£650.00–£800.00

Yorkshire Bridge Inn, Hope Valley

contact Mr John Illingworth, Yorkshire Bridge Inn, Ashopton Road, Hope Valley S33 0AZ
t (01433) 651361 **f** (01433) 651361 **e** enquiries@ladybowerapartments.co.uk
w yorkshire-bridge.co.uk

open All year
payment Credit/debit cards, cash/cheques

Set in a glorious location, Ladybower apartments offer all the ingredients for a memorable holiday in the heart of the beautiful Peak District National Park. These stunning new apartments offer guests the luxury of material comforts on the inside and nature's wonderful landscape outside.

⊕ *Sheffield, west on A57 for about 15 miles. Ladybower Reservoir on left, turn left over viaduct onto A6103, Ladybower Lodge on left, Yorkshire Bridge Inn on right.*

Unit General Leisure **Shop** 0.5 miles **Pub** < 0.5 miles

BARNOLDBY LE BECK, North East Lincolnshire Map ref 4D1

★★★–★★★★
SELF CATERING

Units **3**
Sleeps **2–6**
Low season per wk
£175.00–£200.00
High season per wk
£250.00–£320.00

Grange Farm Cottages & Riding School, Grimsby

contact Jo & Sue Jenkins, Grange Farm Cottages & Riding School, Waltham Road, Barnoldby le Beck DN37 0AR
t (01472) 822216 **f** (01472) 233550 **e** sueuk4000@netscape.net **w** grangefarmcottages.com

The holiday cottages are equipped with one double and one twin room. Take advantage of our all-weather-surface riding school, with fully qualified instructors.

open All year
payment Cash/cheques

Unit General P Leisure **Shop** 2 miles **Pub** 0.5 miles

BARROW UPON SOAR, Leicestershire Map ref 4C3

★★★
SELF CATERING

Units **1**
Sleeps **4–6**
Low season per wk
£360.00–£390.00
High season per wk
£360.00–£450.00

Kingfisher Cottage, Loughborough

contact Mr Matthews, 114 Main Street, Woodhouse Eaves, Loughborough LE12 8RZ
t (01509) 890244 **e** nikkidavid@aol.com

Semi-detached roadside cottage comprising two reception rooms, two bedrooms, two bathrooms and rear garden to canal. Quiet part of village, convenient for shops and transport. Friendly pub nearby.

open All year
payment Cash/cheques

Unit General 3 P Leisure **Shop** < 0.5 miles **Pub** < 0.5 miles

BASLOW, Derbyshire Map ref 4B2

★★★★
SELF CATERING

Units **1**
Sleeps **6–8**
Low season per wk
£400.00–£550.00
High season per wk
£600.00–£700.00

Stable Cottage, Bakewell

contact Mrs Anne O' Connor, Stable Cottage, Nether End, Baslow DE45 1SR
t (01246) 582285 **e** ourstablecottage@aol.com **w** stablecottagebaslow.com

Self-catering 18thC farmhouse/stable conversion within walking distance of Chatsworth House. Ideal base for exploring the Peak District or simply a haven for relaxation. Two doubles, one twin.

open All year
payment Cash/cheques

Unit General P Leisure **Shop** < 0.5 miles **Pub** < 0.5 miles

BEESBY, Lincolnshire Map ref 4D2

★★★
SELF CATERING

Units **1**
Sleeps **6**
Low season per wk
£220.00–£330.00
High season per wk
£330.00–£425.00

Walk Villa, Alford

contact Mrs Joanne White, Manor Farm, Beesby, Alford LN13 0JG
t (01507) 450323 & (01507) 450392

open All year
payment Cash/cheques

Countryside house with full central heating and open fire. Views over arable fields and green pasture. Rural village setting, parking for three cars. Feature half-tester bed complete with drapes. Beautifully equipped kitchen. Close to market town of Alford and four miles from the beach.

Follow A1104 through Alford. In Beesby turn right at junction (phone box) into Pinfold Lane. Walk Villa is approx 0.5 miles down this road on the right.

Short breaks available.

Unit General P

BOSTON, Lincolnshire Map ref 3A1

★★★★
SELF CATERING

Units **8**
Sleeps **1–6**
Low season per wk
£290.00–£320.00
High season per wk
£370.00–£395.00

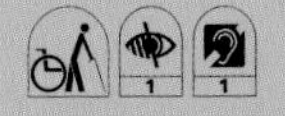

Elms Farm Cottages, Boston

contact Carol Emerson, Elms Farm Cottages, The Elms, Hubberts Bridge, Boston PE20 3QP
t (01205) 290840 & 07887 652021 **f** (01205) 290840 **e** carol@elmsfarmcottages.co.uk
w elmsfarmcottages.co.uk

open All year
payment Credit/debit cards, cash/cheques

Award-winning barn conversion of high-quality cottages, some with wood-burning stoves. Private patio with picnic bench. All cottages are accessible, four with disabled shower rooms especially suitable for wheelchair users. Grass field with wild-flower meadow for guests to enjoy. Communal laundry and built-in barbecue.

On A1121 (Boston side), 250m from Hubberts Bridge crossroads.

Tastes of Lincolnshire welcome pack on weekly stays.

Unit General P S Leisure Shop 2 miles
Pub < 0.5 miles

BRAILSFORD, Derbyshire Map ref 4B2

★★★★
SELF CATERING

Units **1**
Sleeps **1–4**
Low season per wk
£200.00–£375.00
High season per wk
£275.00–£375.00

The Cottage at Culland Mount Farm, Ashbourne

contact Ms Phillips, The Cottage at Culland Mount Farm, Culland Mount Farm, Culland Lane, Ashbourne DE6 3BW
t (01335) 360313 **e** cullandmount@tiscali.co.uk **w** cullandmount.co.uk

Enjoy a quiet, relaxing holiday at Culland Mount Farm with superb views of undulating countryside. Two-bedroomed holiday home is half of the farmhouse with large bay windows and open log fire. Fully heated and double-glazed windows.

open All year
payment Cash/cheques

Unit General P

If you have access needs...

Look for the National Accessible Scheme symbols if you have special hearing, visual or mobility needs. An index of all accommodation participating in the scheme can be found at the back of this guide.

BRASSINGTON, Derbyshire Map ref 4B2

★★★★
SELF CATERING

Units **2**
Sleeps **2–6**
Low season per wk
£330.00–£500.00
High season per wk
£580.00–£800.00

Hoe Grange Holidays, Matlock

contact Felicity Brown, Hoe Grange, Matlock DE4 4HP
t (01629) 540262 **f** (01629) 540262 **e** info@hoegrangeholidays.co.uk **w** hoegrangeholidays.co.uk

open All year
payment Cash/cheques, euros

Secluded log cabins furnished to a high standard with spacious outdoor decking – a real home from home. Near Dovedale, Chatsworth and Carsington Water, Hoe Grange is an idyllic base for all outdoor pursuits and sightseeing. Bring your horse on holiday to ride the Pennine Bridleway. Excellent disabled facilities.

⊕ *From Ashbourne take A515 for Buxton. Turn right onto B5056 towards Bakewell. Hoe Grange is on left, 5 miles from this junction, past turn for Parwich.*

♥ *Short breaks available.*

Unit General Leisure Shop 3 miles
Pub 2 miles

CALDECOTT, Rutland Map ref 4C3

★★★
SELF CATERING

Units **2**
Sleeps **1–8**
Low season per wk
£190.00–£385.00
High season per wk
£215.00–£550.00

Wisteria Cottage, Caldecott

contact Mrs Hudson, 22 Main Street, Caldecott LE16 8RS
t (01536) 771357 **e** enquiries@rutland-cottages.co.uk **w** rutland-cottages.co.uk

open All year
payment Cash/cheques, euros

A charming stone-built cottage in historic Rutland, overlooking the rolling hills of the Welland valley. The cottage can be used as one or two dwellings, offering high-quality accommodation, a secluded garden and secure parking – an ideal location for watersports, walking, cycling, fishing and bird-watching.

⊕ *Leave A14 at jct 7. Follow A43 towards Stamford. At next island take A6003 towards Oakham. Stay on A6003 through Rockingham village and on towards Caldecott.*

♥ *Open Christmas and New Year. 2/3-night weekend breaks. Special rates for long-term stays.*

Unit General Leisure Shop 2 miles
Pub < 0.5 miles

CARSINGTON, Derbyshire Map ref 4B2

★★★
SELF CATERING

Units **1**
Sleeps **8**
Low season per wk
£450.00–£700.00
High season per wk
£500.00–£1,000.00

Owslow, Matlock

contact Mr Peter Oldfield, Owslow, Owslow Farm, Carsington, Matlock DE4 4DD
t (01629) 540510 **f** (01629) 540445 **e** peter.oldfield@ukonline.co.uk **w** peakdistrictfarmhols.co.uk

open All year
payment Cash/cheques

A 16thC farmhouse with flagstone dining room, modern kitchen, downstairs wc, utility room, two sitting rooms, two double bedrooms, two twin bedrooms and a bathroom.

⊕ *Follow signs for Carsington Water along B5035. After 2nd hill pass signs for the Visitors Centre, pass Knockerdown pub, we are on next corner on left.*

Unit General Leisure Shop 4 miles
Pub 1 mile

CASTLETON, Derbyshire Map ref 4B2

★★★★★
SELF CATERING

Units **2**
Sleeps **2–4**
Low season per wk
£170.00–£430.00
High season per wk
£440.00–£500.00

Riding House Farm Cottages, Hope Valley

contact Mrs Denise Matthews, Castleton, Hope Valley S33 8WB
t (01433) 620257 **e** denise@riding-house-cottages.co.uk **w** riding-house-cottages.co.uk

open All year
payment Cash/cheques

Newly converted farm cottages in the heart of the Peak District National Park. One cottage has a queen-size bed, the other has one double and one twin bedroom. Both cottages have two bathrooms and are equipped to a very high standard, with charm, character, stunning location and views.

⊕ *From westerly direction via A6187, drive through Hope until Castleton village 30mph sign. Turn right into narrow lane. Up lane, bear left through gateway to Riding House.*

♥ *Short breaks available late Sep-Apr (excl Christmas and New Year). Last-minute short breaks may be available in high season – please phone.*

Unit General Leisure Shop 1 mile
Pub 1 mile

CHESTERFIELD, Derbyshire Map ref 4B2

★★★★
SELF CATERING

Units **1**
Sleeps **2–4**
Low season per wk
£175.00–£250.00
High season per wk
£250.00–£450.00

Pear Tree Farm Barn, Rowthorne Village, Chesterfield

contact Mel Copley, Pear Tree Farm House, Rowthorne Village, Glapwell, Chesterfield S44 5QQ
t (01623) 811694 **e** enquiries@peartreefarmbarn.co.uk **w** peartreefarmbarn.co.uk

open All year
payment Cash/cheques

Grade II Listed barn conversion in quiet conservation village. Double bedroom with en suite (extra beds available), lounge/diner and kitchen. Full central heating with wood-burning stove. Ten minutes' walk to Hardwick Hall (National Trust). Ideally situated for visiting Peak District (Chatsworth 40 minutes). Pub and shop within walking distance.

⊕ *Ten minutes from jct 29, M1, follow A617 towards Mansfield, turn right at pub (The Young Vanish).*

♥ *Special offers Nov, Dec, Jan and Feb (excl Christmas and New Year). Short breaks all year.*

Unit General Leisure Shop 0.5 miles
Pub 0.5 miles

CHESTERFIELD, Derbyshire Map ref 4B2

★★★★
SELF CATERING

Units **1**
Sleeps **1–5**
Low season per wk
£250.00–£260.00
High season per wk
£260.00–£280.00

Ploughmans Cottage, Chesterfield

contact Mrs Margaret Fry, Ploughmans Cottage, Low Farm, Main Road, Marsh Lane S21 5RH
t (01246) 435328 **e** ploughmans.cottage@virgin.net **w** ploughmanscottage.com

open All year
payment Cash/cheques, euros

Fresh eggs from our hens, kisses from our llamas, skylarks and woodland walks. This delightful cottage is carefully and attractively maintained. It has a fenced garden with orchard, lawns, flower beds, patio and sandpit. Lovely open views and many places of interest within easy reach.

⊕ *From jct 30 of the M1 take the A6135 to Eckington. Take left to B6052 leading to B6056, 2nd on left. After filling station, beside poplar trees.*

♥ *Short breaks available Oct-Mar (excl Christmas).*

Unit General Leisure Shop 0.5 miles Pub 0.5 miles

COMBS, Derbyshire Map ref 4B2

★★★★★
SELF CATERING

Units **1**
Sleeps **1–2**
Low season per wk
£290.00–£320.00
High season per wk
£340.00–£405.00

Pyegreave Cottage, High Peak

contact Mr & Mrs Noel & Rita Pollard, Pyegreave Cottage, High Peak SK23 9UX
t (01298) 813444 **f** (01298) 815381 **e** n.pollard@allenpollard.co.uk **w** holidayapartments.org

open All year
payment Credit/debit cards, cash/cheques, euros

Situated within the Peak District National Park and enjoying spectacular views, this cottage is finished and furnished to a very high standard whilst retaining original oak beams and many other interesting features. Ideal location for walking, golfing, the theatre (Buxton) or simply as an idyllic hideaway.

⊕ *From Combs village at T-junction turn left, follow road for 0.6 miles, farm road on the right-hand side, farm name sign on the wall.*

Unit General Leisure Shop 3 miles Pub 0.5 miles

CRESSBROOK, Derbyshire Map ref 4B2

★★★★
SELF CATERING

Units **3**
Sleeps **1–14**
Low season per wk
£295.00–£595.00
High season per wk
£425.00–£925.00

Cressbrook Hall Self-catering Cottages, Nr Buxton

contact Mrs Bobby Hull-Bailey, Cressbrook Hall, Cressbrook, Nr Buxton SK17 8SY
t (01298) 871289 **f** (01298) 871845 **e** stay@cressbrookhall.co.uk **w** cressbrookhall.co.uk

Accommodation with a difference! Self-catering or B&B in magnificent surroundings. Special catering services and leisure facilities ensure a carefree holiday. Colour brochure.

open All year
payment Credit/debit cards, cash/cheques

Unit General Leisure Shop 2 miles Pub 1 mile

CRESSBROOK, Derbyshire Map ref 4B2

★★★★★
SELF CATERING

Units **1**
Sleeps **5**
Low season per wk
£300.00–£500.00
High season per wk
£400.00–£600.00

Monsal Dale Apartment, Buxton

contact Dr P Howard, Heritage Holiday Homes, The White House, 3 Sandygate Park, Sheffield S10 5TZ
t (0114) 230 8456 **f** (0114) 238 0443 **e** Dr.Howard@btconnect.com **w** heritageholidayhomes.co.uk

open All year
payment Cash/cheques, euros

A spacious two-bedroom, one-and-a-half bathroom, first-floor apartment in a tastefully renovated historic cotton mill. Large lounge/dining room, fully fitted kitchen, utility room. All rooms face south. Unrestricted views of Monsal Dale, one of the most beautiful dales in Derbyshire. Gardens. Parking. Ideal for walking, riding and country pursuits. Excellent pubs.

⊕ *M1, exit 29 (Chesterfield). Road to Baslow (Chatsworth) and Bakewell. Buxton Road for 0.75 miles. Right to Ashford. Ashford to Monsal Head. Steep road into dale. Cressbrook Mill at end.*

Unit General Leisure
Shop 2 miles Pub 1 mile

A holiday on two wheels

For a fabulous freewheeling break seek out accommodation participating in our Cyclists Welcome scheme. Look out for the symbol and plan your route online at nationalcyclenetwork.org.

CURBAR, Derbyshire Map ref 4B2

Rating Applied For
SELF CATERING

Units **2**
Sleeps **2–6**
Low season per wk
£180.00–£200.00
High season per wk
£230.00–£290.00

Upper Barn and Lower Barn, Hope Valley

contact Dr J Morrissy & Dr P Cox, Upper Barn and Lower Barn, Orchard House, The Hillock, Curbar, Calver, Hope Valley S32 3YJ
t (01433) 631885 **w** curbarcottages.com

A recent conversion of a 200-year-old barn into cottages. Linked to let as one if required.

open All year
payment Cash/cheques, euros

Unit General Leisure **Shop** 1 mile **Pub** < 0.5 miles

CUTTHORPE, Derbyshire Map ref 4B2

★★★
SELF CATERING

Units **2**
Sleeps **2–3**
Low season per wk
£170.00–£240.00
High season per wk
£240.00–£275.00

Cow Close Farm Cottages, Chesterfield

contact Mrs Caroline Burke, Cow Close Farm, Overgreen, Cutthorpe, Chesterfield S42 7BA
t (01246) 232055 **e** cowclosefarm@aol.com **w** cowclosefarm.com

Set in beautiful countryside, on the doorstep of the Peak District. The cottages are converted outbuildings, surrounding a 17thC farmhouse. Many places of interest within easy reach.

open All year
payment Cash/cheques

Unit General **Shop** 2 miles **Pub** < 0.5 miles

EAST HADDON, Northamptonshire Map ref 4C3

★★★★
SELF CATERING

Units **4**
Sleeps **2–5**
Low season per wk
£245.00–£415.00
High season per wk
£275.00–£560.00

East Haddon Grange Country Cottages, East Haddon

contact Gerald Pike, East Haddon Grange Country Cottages, East Haddon Grange, East Haddon NN6 8DR
t (01604) 770368 & 07979 661122 **f** (01604) 770368 **e** enquiries@easthaddongrange.co.uk
w easthaddongrange.co.uk

open All year
payment Cash/cheques

Relax in these traditional stone cottages on a family farm surrounded by open countryside. The cottages, lovingly converted from an old barn, offer spacious beautifully presented accommodation in an idyllic rural setting only six miles from Northampton. Perfect for weekend breaks, holidays or longer stays, business or relocating home.

⊕ *Located 1.5 miles from East Haddon village – off the A428 Northampton to Rugby road between the Althorpe railway bridge and the East Haddon/Great Brington crossroads.*

❤ *Discounts available for longer stays. Special rates for mid-week/weekend breaks.*

Unit General Leisure **Shop** 1.5 miles **Pub** 1.5 miles

EDALE, Derbyshire Map ref 4B2

★★★
SELF CATERING

Units **1**
Sleeps **12**
Low season per wk
£700.00–£800.00
High season per wk
£1,000.00–£1,200.00

Grindslow House, Hope Valley

contact Mrs S Crook, c/o Meller Braggins, The Estate Office, Rostherne, Knutsford WA16 6SW
t (01565) 830395 **f** (01565) 830241

A beautiful six-bedroom Derbyshire stone manor-house, in a private, secluded, elevated position, overlooking the village of Edale.

open All year
payment Cash/cheques

Unit General **Shop** 0.5 miles **Pub** 0.5 miles

EYAM, Derbyshire Map ref 4B2

★★★★
SELF CATERING

Units **1**
Sleeps **1–4**
Low season per wk
£300.00–£350.00
High season per wk
£375.00–£425.00

Beck Cottage, Eyam, Hope Valley

contact Mr & Mrs R Burton, Clifford Road, Sheffield S11 9AQ
t (0114) 250 9357 **f** (0114) 255 1058 **e** rburton04@tiscali.co.uk **w** ukpeakretreats.com

open All year
payment Cash/cheques

Beck Cottage is set in the heart of Eyam, in the Peak District. This two-bedroom, detached, 400-year-old cottage has recently undergone extensive and sympathetic refurbishment and is situated on a quiet and peaceful lane, standing just a minute's walk from the village square.

⊕ *M1 jct 29. Follow A617 (Chesterfield), then follow A619 (signposted Bakewell) until A623 (Stockport and Manchester). Turn right onto B6521 (signposted Eyam).*

♥ *Short breaks available (min 3 nights).*

Unit General Shop < 0.5 miles Pub < 0.5 miles

FENNY BENTLEY, Derbyshire Map ref 4B2

★★★
SELF CATERING

Units **1**
Sleeps **4–6**
Low season per wk
£140.00–£230.00
High season per wk
£325.00–£475.00

The Priory, Ashbourne

contact Mrs A Hughes, Woodeaves, Fenny Bentley, Ashbourne DE6 1LF
t (01335) 350238 **e** hughes.priory@virgin.net

In the Peak District National Park, a peaceful, comfortable stone cottage with central heating, open fire, games room and garden.

open All year
payment Cash/cheques

Unit General P Leisure Shop 2.5 miles Pub 0.5 miles

FLAGG, Derbyshire Map ref 4B2

★★★★
SELF CATERING

Units **3**
Sleeps **2–12**
Low season per wk
£260.00–£425.00
High season per wk
£400.00–£695.00

Taddington Barns, Buxton

contact Mrs Elizabeth Charboneau, Taddington Barns, Moor Grange Farm, Moor Lane, Flagg SK17 9RA
t (01298) 85020 & 07974 258765 **e** tony@moorgrangefarm.co.uk **w** moorgrangefarm.co.uk

open All year
payment Credit/debit cards, cash/cheques

A beautiful rural retreat with stunning views and indoor, 37ft swimming pool. Ideal for family gatherings. Badger's Wood has two en suite bedrooms (one double, one twin), bunk room and bathroom. Robin's Nest has two en suite bedrooms (one double, one twin). Chicken Coop has one bedroom (king-size bed) and bathroom.

⊕ *Five miles equidistant Bakewell and Buxton, off A6. Into Taddington village, onto School Lane, onto Slipperlow Lane. Follow to top, bends to right, 1st farm on right.*

♥ *Short breaks available.*

Unit General P Leisure Shop 4.5 miles Pub 1.2 miles

It's all quality-assessed accommodation

Our commitment to quality involves wide-ranging accommodation assessment. Ratings and awards were correct at the time of going to press but may change following a new assessment. Please check at the time of booking.

FROGGATT, Derbyshire Map ref 4B2

★★★★★
SELF CATERING

Units **1**
Sleeps **4**
Low season per wk
Min £560.00
High season per wk
Max £960.00

Bridgefoot Cottage, Hope Valley

contact Mrs Marsha North, Bridgefoot Cottage, c/o Green Farm, Curbar S32 3YH
t (01433) 630120 **f** (01433) 631829 **e** enquiries@peakdistrictholiday.plus.com
w peakdistrictholiday.co.uk

Historic, detached stone cottage in central village location. Good local pubs. Beautifully furnished. Oak beams, antiques, four-poster bed, Aga, real log fires. Romantic luxury. Ideal for those in search of perfect peace.

open All year
payment Cash/cheques

Unit General **P** Leisure
Shop 1 mile Pub < 0.5 miles

GREAT CARLTON, Lincolnshire Map ref 4D2

★★★
SELF CATERING

Units **1**
Sleeps **5**
Low season per wk
£150.00–£190.00
High season per wk
£200.00–£300.00

Willow Farm, Louth

contact Mr James Clark, Willow Farm, Louth LN11 8JT
t (01507) 338540

open All year
payment Cash/cheques

Cosy, detached bungalow in quiet, rural location. High standard of accommodation comprising one single and two twin bedrooms. Fly and coarse fishing available on site. Touring caravans welcome by arrangement. Approximately eight miles from the market town of Louth and the lovely Lincolnshire Wolds. Well situated for Cadwell Park and several golf courses.

⊕ *From Louth bypass, take B1200 to Saltfleetby church on crossroads. Turn right then 2nd right towards Great Carlton (0.5 miles).*

Unit General **P** Leisure Shop 1.5 miles Pub 2 miles

GREAT LONGSTONE, Derbyshire Map ref 4B2

★★
SELF CATERING

Units **1**
Sleeps **1–2**
Low season per wk
£150.00–£230.00
High season per wk
£240.00–£260.00

Field House Cottage, Great Longstone, Nr Bakewell

contact Julia Spink, Field House, Moor Road, Great Longstone DE45 1UA
t (01629) 640103 **e** juliag@lumina-solns.com

open All year except Christmas
payment Cash/cheques

Delightful, open-plan, compact cottage in heart of Peak District. Fabulous doorstep walks/cycling on Longstone Edge, Monsal Trail etc. Visit Chatsworth, Castleton, Bakewell, Dovedale. Fully equipped kitchen, large, modern shower room, spiral stairs to galleried double sleeping platform over lounge, shared garden. Three pubs and shop within ten minutes' walk.

⊕ *Bakewell to Ashford in the Water. A6020 1 mile; left turn Great Longstone, past Crispin pub, right turn into Moor Road, 400yds on left.*

❤ *Short breaks available – 3/4 nights.*

Unit General **P** Leisure Shop 0.5 miles Pub < 0.5 miles

How many beds?

The minimum and maximum number of people that each property can accommodate is shown. If an entry includes details of more than one property the sleeping capacity may vary between them. Please check when you make your booking.

HARTINGTON, Derbyshire Map ref 4B2

★★★★
SELF CATERING

Units **2**
Sleeps **6**
Low season per wk
£300.00–£400.00
High season per wk
£400.00–£550.00

1 Staley Cottage and Victoria House, Buxton

contact Mr & Mrs Oliver, Carr Head Farm, Carr Head Lane, Penistone, Sheffield S36 7GA
t (01226) 762387

Spacious cottage with three bedrooms (two double, one twin), dining room, lounge, bathroom, shower room/wc and garden. In a pretty village near amenities, shops and restaurants. Also second property. Owner maintained, established 22 years.

open All year
payment Cash/cheques

Unit General P Leisure Shop < 0.5 miles Pub < 0.5 miles

HARTINGTON, Derbyshire Map ref 4B2

★★★
SELF CATERING

Units **1**
Sleeps **5**
Low season per wk
£170.00–£195.00
High season per wk
£195.00–£250.00

Church View, Buxton

contact Miss Kathleen Bassett, Digmer, Dig Street, Buxton SK17 0AQ
t (01298) 84660

open All year
payment Cash/cheques

Stone-built cottage with lawns to the front and side. Storage heaters. Spacious, comfortable interior. Lounge, dining room, utility room, recently fitted kitchen. Three bedrooms, upstairs bathroom consisting of bath, toilet, wash basin and new walk-in shower. Open fire optional. Close to amenities. Owner maintained. Established 22 years.

⊕ *From A515 Buxton to Ashbourne turn for Hartington B5054.*

Unit General P Shop < 0.5 miles Pub < 0.5 miles

HARTINGTON, Derbyshire Map ref 4B2

★★★★
SELF CATERING

Units **4**
Sleeps **2–7**
Low season per wk
£180.00–£320.00
High season per wk
£480.00–£650.00

Cruck & Wolfscote Grange Cottages, Buxton

contact Mrs Jane Gibbs, Cruck & Wolfscote Grange Cottages, Wolfscote Grange Farm, Hartington, Buxton SK17 0AX
t (01298) 84342 **e** wolfscote@btinternet.com **w** wolfscotegrangecottages.co.uk

open All year
payment Cash/cheques

The unique setting overlooking Dove Valley/Dale, with miles of rolling countryside and picture views, sells Wolfcote Cottages as the perfect place to stay. Cruck Cottage – an oak-beamed hideaway. 'No neighbours, only sheep'. Swallows Cottage – en suites, spa bathroom. Both offer comfort and character. Farm trail with freedom to roam. Central to Peak District.

⊕ *From A515 – B5054 to Hartingdon, left at telephone box, up hill. Sharp right 20yds after passing chapel. Follow signs for Wolfscote Grange Farm.*

❤ *Private farm trail weekend and short breaks available (especially Oct-Easter).*

Unit General P S Leisure Shop 2 miles Pub 2 miles

Pool search

If a swimming pool is an essential element of your holiday accommodation check out the special index at the back of this guide.

HATHERSAGE, Derbyshire Map ref 4B2

★★★
SELF CATERING

Units **1**
Sleeps **4–6**
Low season per wk
Min £245.00
High season per wk
£245.00–£370.00

Pat's Cottage, Sheffield

contact Mr John Drakeford, Pat's Cottage, 110 Townhead Road, Dore, Sheffield S17 3GB
t (0114) 236 6014 & 07850 200711 **f** (0114) 236 6014 **e** johnmdrakeford@hotmail.com
w patscottage.co.uk

An attractive 18thC stone cottage, sympathetically refurbished, retaining original features including black beams. On the edge of the Peak District, close to Hathersage and the city of Sheffield.

open All year
payment Cash/cheques

Unit **General** P **Leisure** **Shop** < 0.5 miles **Pub** < 0.5 miles

HATHERSAGE, Derbyshire Map ref 4B2

★★★
SELF CATERING

Units **1**
Sleeps **4**
Low season per wk
£195.00–£225.00
High season per wk
£265.00–£340.00

St Michael's Cottage, Hope Valley

contact Miss Turton, Saint Michael's Environmental Education Centre, Main Road, Hathersage, Hope Valley S32 1BB
t (01433) 650309 **f** (01433) 650089 **e** stmichaels@education.nottscc.gov.uk **w** eess.org.uk

Cosy character cottage with one double and one twin bedroom. Dramatic scenery, walks from the door, close to all amenities.

open All year
payment Cash/cheques

Unit **General** 3 P **Shop** < 0.5 miles **Pub** < 0.5 miles

HOPE, Derbyshire Map ref 4B2

★★★★
SELF CATERING

Units **2**
Sleeps **2–4**
Low season per wk
£220.00–£320.00
High season per wk
£320.00–£420.00

Chapman Farm Cottages, Hope Valley

contact Mrs Dorothy Vernon, Chapman Farm Cottages, Chapman Farm, Edale Road, Hope S33 6ZF
t (01433) 620297

open All year
payment Cash/cheques

These charming cottages have been tastefully converted to combine old-world charm and original features with modern, comfortable accommodation to make your stay relaxing and comfortable.

⊕ *From Hope village church turn right onto the Edale road. Chapman Farm is on the left just before the Cheshire Cheese Inn.*

Unit **General** S **Leisure** **Shop** < 0.5 miles
Pub < 0.5 miles

HORNCASTLE, Lincolnshire Map ref 4D2

★★★
SELF CATERING

Units **2**
Sleeps **4–6**
Low season per wk
£220.00–£290.00
High season per wk
£365.00–£400.00

Green Court, Fulletby, Nr Horncastle

contact Mr John Robinson, 401 Brant Road, Waddington, Lincoln LN5 9AH
t (01522) 876994 **w** woldscottages.co.uk

open All year
payment Cash/cheques

Very pleasant converted buildings in the centre of the Lincolnshire Wolds, approximately 25 miles from the coast and Lincoln. The master bedrooms in both cottages have four-poster beds and en suites. Carpenters has its own games room. Seating is available outside with grassed areas for children to play on.

⊕ *Take A153 from Horncastle towards Louth. Pass through West Ashby. Turn right for Fulletby. Past Fulletby Motors. Tale 3rd lane on left. Cottages on right.*

♥ *Special rates for booking both cottages for Christmas, New Year or any other week of the year.*

Unit General P Leisure Shop 3.5 miles Pub 1.5 miles

KING'S CLIFFE, Northamptonshire Map ref 3A1

★★★★
SELF CATERING

Units **1**
Sleeps **1–2**
Low season per wk
£130.00–£150.00
High season per wk
£180.00–£250.00

Maltings Cottage, King's Cliffe, Peterborough

contact Mrs Jenny Dixon, 19 West Street, Kings Cliffe, Peterborough PE8 6XB
t (01780) 470365 **f** (01780) 470623 **e** kjhl_dixon@hotmail.com **w** kingjohnhuntinglodge.co.uk

open All year
payment Cash/cheques

Cosy stone cottage situated in centre of beautiful historic village with shops, pub and post office. Attractively furnished and well equipped. Central heating. Surrounded by stately homes, all within 45 minutes' drive. Wonderful rolling countryside for walking. Near Rutland Water for sailing and bird-watching. Rockingham Motor Speedway six miles.

⊕ *A1 junction with A47 Wansford, go towards Leicester, next left (King's Cliffe) then right at Cattery. At T-junction left to centre of village. At crossroads turn right.*

Unit General P Shop < 0.5 miles Pub < 0.5 miles

KNIVETON, Derbyshire Map ref 4B2

★★★★
SELF CATERING

Units **1**
Sleeps **2–4**
Low season per wk
£275.00–£300.00
High season per wk
£300.00–£400.00

Willow Bank, Ashbourne

contact Mrs Mary Vaughan, Willow Bank, Kniveton, Ashbourne DE6 1JJ
t (01335) 343308 **f** (01335) 347859 **e** willowbank@kniveton.net **w** kniveton.net

Luxurious, recently fitted ground-floor accommodation, one double bedroom, one twin. An acre of garden, summerhouse, stream, barbecue, lovely views. CD player, Freeview, Internet access. Pretty Peak District village, Ashbourne 15 minutes.

open All year
payment Cash/cheques

Unit General 5 P S Leisure Shop 3 miles Pub 0.5 miles

Prices

These are shown for one week's accommodation. If an entry includes details of more than one property it is usual that the minimum price is for low season in the smallest property and the maximum price is for high season in the largest property.

LAMBLEY, Nottinghamshire Map ref 4C2

★★★
SELF CATERING & SERVICED APARTMENTS

Units **1**
Sleeps **4**
Low season per wk
£180.00–£200.00
High season per wk
£245.00–£265.00

Dickman's Cottage, Lambley, Nottingham

contact Mr William Marshall Smith, Springsyde, Birdcage Walk, Otley LS21 3HB
t (01943) 462719 **f** (01943) 850925 **e** marshallsmithuk@hotmail.com
w http://mywebpage.netscape.com/wmarshallsmith/default.html

open All year
payment Cash/cheques, euros

Five miles north-east of Nottingham. Beamed cottage with garden. Two bedrooms – one double, one twin. TV/video, dishwasher, washer/dryer. Private parking.

⊕ *M1 jct 26. Follow the signs for Arnold and from there for Lambley then turn into Mill Lane from Main Street.*

❤ *Short and weekend breaks available. Prices on application.*

Unit General Shop < 0.5 miles Pub < 0.5 miles

LINCOLN, Lincolnshire Map ref 4C2

★★★★
SELF CATERING

Units **1**
Sleeps **1–4**
Low season per wk
£200.00–£250.00
High season per wk
£300.00–£400.00

5 Francis Hill Court, Lincoln

contact Mr Stephen Layton, Sycamore Cottage, Clint Lane, Navenby, Lincoln LN5 0EX
t (01522) 810321 **f** 0870 094 0333 **e** layton@doctors.org.uk **w** francishillcourt.co.uk

Modern, well-appointed ground-floor apartment providing comfortable accommodation for up to two couples, each with separate bathroom facilities. Situated in uphill Lincoln near cathedral, castle and popular Bailgate.

open All year
payment Cash/cheques, euros

Unit General Shop 0.5 miles Pub 0.5 miles

LINCOLN, Lincolnshire Map ref 4C2

★★★
SELF CATERING

Units **1**
Sleeps **3**
Low season per wk
£220.00–£260.00
High season per wk
£270.00–£340.00

Ashleigh, Lincoln

contact Mr Colin Ashton, 18 De Braose Way, Bramber, Steyning BN44 3FD
t (01903) 814305 **e** colinashton@dsl.pipex.com **w** lincolnselfcatering.co.uk

Modernised, comfortable Victorian terraced house within ten to fifteen minutes' walk of the city centre. Recently fitted kitchen and bathroom. Warm and cosy in winter. Many places of interest within easy reach.

open All year
payment Cash/cheques

Unit General 1 Leisure Shop 0.5 miles Pub 0.5 miles

LINCOLN, Lincolnshire Map ref 4C2

★★★
SELF CATERING

Units 1
Sleeps 2
Low season per wk
Min £140.00
High season per wk
Max £200.00

Martingale Cottage, Lincoln

contact Mrs Patsy Pate, 19 East Street, Nettleham, Lincoln LN2 2SL
t (01522) 751795 **e** patsy.pate@ntlworld.com

open All year
payment Cash/cheques

An 18thC stone cottage near the centre of the attractive village of Nettleham, 2.5 miles from Lincoln. Very comfortable, well-equipped accommodation with private parking. Use of owner's spacious, secluded garden. Good local shops and pubs, post office and library. Picturesque beckside and bus service to Lincoln. Personal attention and a warm welcome.

⊕ *A46 (Lincoln to Grimsby), 2nd turning to Nettleham (Deepdale Lane) to end. Turn right and the cottage is 50yds on the right.*

Unit General P Shop < 0.5 miles Pub < 0.5 miles

LINCOLN, Lincolnshire Map ref 4C2

★★★★
SELF CATERING

Units 2
Sleeps 2–4
Low season per wk
Min £155.00
High season per wk
Max £340.00

Old Vicarage Cottages, Nettleham

contact Mrs Susan Downs, The Old Vicarage, East Street, Lincoln LN2 2SL
t (01522) 750819 **f** (01522) 750819 **e** susan@oldvic.net **w** oldvic.net

open All year
payment Cash/cheques

Delightful old stone cottages offering spacious accommodation, equipped with everything you need including a whirlpool bath. Private gardens and off-road parking/garage. Close to the centre of this award-winning village with shops, pubs, green and picturesque beckside. Good bus service. Four miles from Lincoln – the perfect holiday location.

⊕ *Follow A46 from Lincoln towards Grimsby. Take 2nd right turn to Nettleham, entrance is on the right-hand side, 20m before crossroads.*

Unit General P Leisure Shop < 0.5 miles Pub < 0.5 miles

LINCOLN, Lincolnshire Map ref 4C2

★★★
SELF CATERING

Units 3
Sleeps 1–2
Low season per wk
Min £150.00
High season per wk
Min £210.00

Saint Clements, Lincoln

contact Mrs Gill Marshall, Saint Clements, Langworthgate, Lincoln LN2 4AD
t (01522) 538087 **f** (01522) 560642 **e** jroywood@aol.com **w** stayatstclements.co.uk

open All year
payment Cash/cheques

Well-equipped, centrally heated apartments in comfortable Victorian rectory; one is twin-bedded, two are doubles. Situated down quiet drive lined with mature trees. Cathedral views, and only five minutes' walk from historic up-hill area. Plenty of car parking. A peaceful retreat in the heart of the city. Short breaks when available.

⊕ *Situated in central Lincoln.*

Unit General P Shop < 0.5 miles Pub < 0.5 miles

Key to symbols

Open the back flap for a key to symbols.

LINCOLN, Lincolnshire Map ref 4C2

★★★★
SELF CATERING

Units **1**
Sleeps **2–4**
Low season per wk
£190.00–£250.00
High season per wk
£250.00–£375.00

The Stable, Lincoln

contact Jerry & Chris Scott, Sunnyside, Lincoln Road, Lincoln LN1 2SQ
t (01522) 730561 **e** jerry@lincolncottages.co.uk **w** lincolncottages.co.uk

open All year
payment Cash/cheques, euros

300-year-old cottage of character converted from a former stone and pantile stable. Peace and tranquillity in a conservation village, yet only six miles from the historic cathedral city of Lincoln. Tastefully furnished and decorated. Own enclosed cottage garden and views over open fields.

From M180 jct 4, south towards Lincoln. From Lincoln, A15 north, A1500 west, B1398 north.

4 nights for the price of 3 in low season.

Unit General P Leisure Shop 1.5 miles Pub 1 mile

LONG WHATTON, Leicestershire Map ref 4C3

★★★
SELF CATERING

Units **1**
Sleeps **5**
Low season per wk
£245.00–£420.00
High season per wk
£490.00–£630.00

Oscar House, Long Whatton, Loughborough

contact Ms Emma Blessed, 9 Main Street, Long Whatton, Loughborough LE12 5DF
t (01509) 842529 **e** enquiries@oscarhouse.co.uk **w** oscarhouse.co.uk

Property in excellent location, situated in a quaint village with superb facilities. Private rear garden. Close to NEMA and Donington Park. Very accessible for Nottingham, Derby and Leicester.

open All year
payment Credit/debit cards, cash/cheques

Unit General P Leisure Shop 0.5 miles Pub 0.5 miles

LOUTH, Lincolnshire Map ref 4D2

★★★
SELF CATERING

Units **1**
Sleeps **1–4**
Low season per wk
£200.00–£300.00
High season per wk
£250.00–£350.00

Mill Lodge, Louth

contact Mrs Cade, Mill Lodge, Benniworth House Farm, Donington on Bain, Louth LN11 9RD
t (01507) 343265

open All year
payment Cash/cheques

Ezra and Pamela Cade welcome you to a comfortable, warm, detached cottage, with conservatory, garden and garage, on lovely farm/nature reserve. Fitted kitchen, open log fire. Free first snack with home-produced honey. Good footpaths join the Viking Way, open access to countryside stewardship area. Children welcome.

From B1225 between Caistor and Horncastle, take Donington on Bain road with Belmont Mast on right. Drive down hill to T-junction, Mill Lodge is opposite.

Special rates for just 2 visitors. Discounted honey available.

Unit General 3 P Leisure Shop 0.75 miles Pub 1 mile

Take a break

Look out for special promotions and themed breaks. This could be your chance to indulge an interest, find a new one, or just relax and enjoy exceptional value! Offers are highlighted in colour (and are subject to availability).

LOUTH, Lincolnshire Map ref 4D2

★★★
SELF CATERING

Units **1**
Sleeps **2–8**
Low season per wk
£325.00–£479.00
High season per wk
£479.00–£649.00

Station Masters House, Ludborough, Nr Louth

t (01507) 363470 **f** (01507) 363633 **e** info@raileisure.com **w** raileisure.com

open All year
payment Credit/debit cards, cash/cheques

High-quality self-catering accommodation within the Lincolnshire Wolds. Peace and tranquillity, ideal for railway, walking and cycling enthusiasts. A most unique holiday home, ideal for the larger family or family reunions, within picturesque surroundings.

⊕ *Please see our website for comprehensive travel directions.*

❤ *Off-season short breaks available for a whistle-stop holiday.*

Unit General P Leisure Shop 2 miles Pub 2 miles

MABLETHORPE, Lincolnshire Map ref 4D2

SELF CATERING

Units **1**
Sleeps **1–6**
Low season per wk
Min £280.00
High season per wk
Max £500.00

Dunes Cottage, Theddlethorpe St Helen

Dunes cottage, Brickyard Lane, Theddlethorpe St Helen LN12 1NR
t (01507) 338342 **f** (01507) 338359 **e** Sheila.a.morrison@btopenworld.co.uk
w dunesholidaycottage.co.uk

This charming 19thC cottage, nestling on the edge of a National Nature Reserve, offers visitors peace and tranquillity, a place to get away from the stresses and strains of modern life.

open All year
payment Cash/cheques

Unit General P Shop 4 miles Pub 2 miles

MABLETHORPE, Lincolnshire Map ref 4D2

★★★★
SELF CATERING

Units **6**
Sleeps **4–6**
Low season per wk
Min £250.00
High season per wk
Max £550.00

Grange Cottages, Maltby le Marsh, Alford

contact Ann Graves, Grange Cottages, Main Road, Alford LN13 0JP
t (01507) 450267 **f** (01507) 450180 **w** grange-cottages.co.uk

Luxuriously and beautifully appointed holiday cottages (new in 2005) on working farm, three miles from the coast. Private fishing, play area.

open All year
payment Cash/cheques

Unit General P Leisure Shop < 0.5 miles Pub < 0.5 miles

MANSFIELD, Nottinghamshire Map ref 4C2

★★★★
SELF CATERING

Units **2**
Sleeps **6**
Low season per wk
£80.00–£180.00
High season per wk
£80.00–£180.00

Watson Avenue, Mansfield

contact Dionne Miller, David Blount Ltd, 44 Station Street, Kirkby-in-Ashfield, Mansfield NG17 7AS
t (01623) 721155 **f** (01623) 758112 **e** lettings@davidblount.co.uk **w** nottshouse.co.uk

open All year
payment Cash/cheques, euros

High-quality living in 2004-built houses. Ideal for visiting Sherwood Forest, numerous nearby historic houses, cycling, golfing, walks. Few minutes' walk to town's cultural quarter with restaurants and pubs. Three double bedrooms (one en suite), lounge, dining room, kitchen, bathroom, contemporary furnishings, multi media to all main rooms, security, parking, gardens, patio.

⊕ *Fifteen minutes from M1, jct 28 or 29. Follow Mansfield town centre. Situated in residential area just north of inner ring road between Woodhouse Road and Bath Lane.*

❤ *Book for just a day or a week. Discounts for stays of 1 week or more.*

Unit **General** P S **Leisure** **Shop** < 0.5 miles **Pub** < 0.5 miles

MATLOCK, Derbyshire Map ref 4B2

SELF CATERING

Units **9**
Sleeps **4–7**
Low season per wk
£360.00–£470.00
High season per wk
£699.00–£876.00

Darwin Lake, Matlock

contact Miss Nikki Manning, Darwin Lake, The Lodge, Jaggers Lane, Matlock DE4 5LH
t (01629) 735859 **f** (01629) 735859 **e** enquiries@darwinlake.co.uk **w** darwinlake.co.uk

open All year
payment Credit/debit cards, cash/cheques

Set in ten acres of private, wooded grounds surrounding Darwin Lake, these superb, luxury, stone-built cottages provide a perfect setting for a tranquil, relaxing holiday or for exploring the peaks and dales. Bustling market towns, stately homes, quaint villages and many family attractions. Village shops and pub two miles. Pets welcome in selected cottages.

⊕ *Details will be sent upon booking.*

❤ *Larger detached cottages also available. Short breaks of 3 and 4 nights available (excl peak times). Late-booking discount.*

Unit **General** P S **Leisure** **Shop** 2 miles **Pub** 2 miles

MATLOCK, Derbyshire Map ref 4B2

★★★★
SELF CATERING

Units **1**
Sleeps **1–5**
Low season per wk
£200.00–£250.00
High season per wk
£250.00–£300.00

Eagle Cottage, Birchover, Matlock

contact Mrs Mary Prince, Eagle Cottage, c/o Haresfield House, Keeling Lane, Birchover, Matlock DE4 2BL
t (01629) 650634 **e** maryprince@msn.com **w** cressbrook.co.uk/youlgve/eagle/

open All year
payment Cash/cheques

A quiet end cottage in the centre of a small Peak District village having two pubs and a shop. The village is surrounded by a network of public footpaths and stunning scenery in an Area of Outstanding Natural Beauty. Many attractions, including stately Chatsworth House and Haddon Hall, are nearby.

⊕ *From the A6, take the B5056 towards Ashbourne. After 2.2 miles, take a left turn up to Birchover.*

Unit **General** P **Leisure** **Shop** < 0.5 miles **Pub** < 0.5 miles

MATLOCK, Derbyshire Map ref 4B2

★★★★-★★★★★
SELF CATERING

Units **3**
Sleeps **4–18**
Low season per wk
£270.00–£630.00
High season per wk
£385.00–£880.00

Mooredge Barns, Matlock

contact Mr Barratt, Mooredge Farm, Knabb Hall Lane, Tansley, Matlock DE4 5FS
t (01629) 583701 & 07766 074585 **f** (01629) 583701 **e** enquiries@mooredgefarmcottages.co.uk
w mooredgefarmcottages.co.uk

open All year
payment Cash/cheques

These barns are set in a very rural location down a quiet country lane, having splendid panoramic views from the grounds of the whole surrounding area with Riber Castle sitting on the horizon overlooking Matlock. Choice of cottages. Heated indoor pool.

⊕ *A38 to Alfreton, then A615 to Matlock, passing through Wessington. Continue on main road for 5 miles, down hill, at garden centre right, 1st lane on left.*

❤ *Enjoy swimming in our heated indoor pool all year round, free to cottage guests.*

Unit General Leisure Shop 1 mile
Pub 0.5 miles

MEASHAM, Leicestershire Map ref 4B3

★★★
SELF CATERING

Units **1**
Sleeps **6**
Low season per wk
Max £200.00
High season per wk
Max £300.00

105 Bosworth Road, Swadlincote

contact Alan and Christine Cornell, 'Omega', Ashby Road, Measham, Swandlicote DE12 7JR
t (01530) 271245

open All year
payment Cash/cheques

Semi-detached property with two double bedrooms and sofa bed. Central heating, dishwasher, washing machine, TV, video, DVD and CD player. Bath, shower, sitting room and dining room. Garden and patio.

⊕ *Five minutes from jcts 11 and 12, M42.*

Unit General Leisure Shop < 0.5 miles
Pub < 0.5 miles

MONYASH, Derbyshire Map ref 4B2

★★★
SELF CATERING

Units **1**
Sleeps **1–3**
Low season per wk
Max £150.00
High season per wk
Max £260.00

Rose Cottage, Monyash

contact Mrs Heather Read, Rose Cottage, Church Street DE45 1JH
t (01629) 813629

Traditional stone cottage with views over fields at front. Quality furnishings, warm, clean and comfortable. One single, two twins, private rear patio with garden furniture. Short walk to pub.

open All year except Christmas and New Year
payment Cash/cheques

Unit General

Use your i's

Tourist information centres provide a wealth of information and friendly advice, both before you go and during your stay. Refer to the front of this section for a list of tourist information centres in the region.

MONYASH, Derbyshire Map ref 4B2

★★★★
SELF CATERING & SERVICED APARTMENTS

Units **2**
Sleeps **2–5**
Low season per wk
£216.00–£281.00
High season per wk
£367.00–£478.00

Sheldon Cottages, Bakewell

contact Mrs Louise Fanshawe, Sheldon Cottages, Sheldon House, Chapel Street, Bakewell DE45 1JJ
t (01629) 813067 **f** (01629) 815768 **e** info@sheldoncottages.co.uk **w** sheldoncottages.co.uk

Detached, self-catering cottage and flat in the heart of the Peak District; ideal for touring and walking. Dogs welcome in cottage by arrangement.

open All year
payment Cash/cheques

Unit General Leisure Shop 4 miles
Pub < 0.5 miles

NEW MILLS, Derbyshire Map ref 4B2

★★
SELF CATERING

Units **4**
Sleeps **6–8**
Low season per wk
£270.00–£320.00
High season per wk
£360.00–£500.00

Shaw Farm Cottage, High Peak

contact Mrs Nicky Burgess, Shaw Farm Cottage, Shaw Marsh, New Mills SK22 4QE
t (0161) 427 1841 **e** nicky.burgess@talk21.com **w** shawfarmholidays.co.uk

A three-bedroomed farmhouse with character, set in open countryside. Price reduced if family bedroom not required. Garden with patio. Children's play area. Please apply for brochure or see website.

open All year
payment Cash/cheques, euros

Unit General Leisure

OAKHAM, Rutland Map ref 4C3

★★★★
SELF CATERING

Units **1**
Sleeps **1–3**
Low season per wk
£275.00–£350.00
High season per wk
£400.00–£450.00

Old School Cottage, North Luffenham, Nr Oakham

contact Mrs E Handley, Wytchley House, Empingham Road, Ketton, Stamford PE9 3UP
t (01780) 721768 **f** (01780) 720214 **e** rhandley@supanet.com **w** rutnet.co.uk/oldschoolcottage

Immaculate, spacious stone cottage in peaceful location close to Rutland Water. One double, one single, garage, facility for bike storage. An ideal base for sightseeing.

open All year
payment Cash/cheques

Unit General Leisure Shop 2 miles Pub < 0.5 miles

OUNDLE, Northamptonshire Map ref 3A1

★★★★
SELF CATERING

Units **1**
Sleeps **1–4**
Low season per wk
Min £300.00
High season per wk
Min £300.00

The Bolt Hole, Oundle

contact Mrs Anita Spurrell, Rose Cottage, 70 Glapthorne Road, Oundle, Peterborough PE8 4PT
t (01832) 272298 & 07850 388109 **e** nanda@spurrell.ocs-uk.com

open All year
payment Cash/cheques

Well-appointed bungalow in quiet cul-de-sac, near town centre and countryside. Lounge/diner, fitted kitchen. Garden room/second bedroom. Double bedroom with large en suite shower. Separate cloaks/utility room. Basic stores/fresh breakfast ingredients supplied. Fenced rear garden with patio, lawn, vegetables and herbs. Parking on private drive outside front door.

⊕ *In Oundle, right into New Street, 0.75 miles on left is the George pub. Right into Cotterstock Road, 150yds on left is Ray Close.*

Unit General Leisure Shop 1 mile
Pub < 0.5 miles

OUNDLE, Northamptonshire Map ref 3A1

★★★–★★★★★
SELF CATERING

Units 4
Sleeps 1–4
Low season per wk
£230.00–£325.00
High season per wk
£230.00–£325.00

Oundle Cottage Breaks, Peterborough

contact Mr & Mrs Simmonds, Oundle Cottage Breaks, Market Place, Oundle, Peterborough PE8 4BE
t (01832) 275508 **e** richard@simmondsatoundle.co.uk **w** oundlecottagebreaks.co.uk

Self-contained units providing accommodation which forms part of the curtilage of a Listed building. Non-smokers only please.

open All year except Christmas and New Year
payment Credit/debit cards, cash/cheques

Unit General Leisure Pub < 0.5 miles

PEAK DISTRICT

See under Ashbourne, Bakewell, Bamford, Baslow, Castleton, Cressbrook, Edale, Eyam, Hartington, Hathersage, Hope, Monyash, New Mills, Tideswell, Winster, Youlgreave

RETFORD, Nottinghamshire Map ref 4C2

★★★
SELF CATERING

Units 1
Sleeps 4
Low season per wk
£250.00–£300.00
High season per wk
£300.00–£360.00

Westhill Cottage, Retford

t (01777) 707034 **e** doreen@holly23.freeserve.co.uk **w** westhillcottage.co.uk

Detached bungalow with two twin bedrooms and full central heating. Fully equipped to a very comfortable standard. Four pubs and a sports centre nearby.

open All year
payment Cash/cheques

Unit General P Leisure Shop 1 mile Pub 1 mile

RUTLAND WATER

See under Oakham

SHERWOOD FOREST

See under Mansfield, Retford, Southwell

SOUTH COCKERINGTON, Lincolnshire Map ref 4D2

★★★★
SELF CATERING

Units 2
Sleeps 4–5
Low season per wk
£250.00–£300.00
High season per wk
£300.00–£425.00

Grasswells Farm Holiday Cottages, Louth

contact Ms Janice Foster, Grasswells Holiday Cottages (Saddleback Leisure Ltd), Saddleback Road, Howdales, South Cockerington, Louth LN11 7DJ
t (01507) 338508 **e** thefosters2002@aol.com

Single barn conversions, spacious, comfortable and well equipped. Set in three acres of grounds with private fishing lake.

open All year
payment Cash/cheques

Unit General P Leisure

Country Code Always follow the Country Code

- Be safe – plan ahead and follow any signs
- Leave gates and property as you find them
- Protect plants and animals, and take your litter home
- Keep dogs under close control
- Consider other people

SOUTH COCKERINGTON, Lincolnshire Map ref 4D2

★★★
SELF CATERING

Units **3**
Sleeps **2–4**
Low season per wk
£230.00–£270.00
High season per wk
£320.00–£360.00

West View Cottages, Louth

contact Mr Richard Nicholson and Mrs J Hand, West View, South View Lane, Louth LN11 7ED
t (01507) 327209 **e** enquiries@west-view.co.uk **w** west-view.co.uk

open All year
payment Cash/cheques

Beautifully converted, single-storey farm buildings tastefully decorated to a high standard. Ideally located in a quiet village with the market town of Louth four miles away. There are numerous quiet beaches along the coast (six miles). Suitable walking and cycling routes are close by. Come and relax in pleasant surroundings.

⊕ *Take the A157, go straight onto the B1200 signposted Manby. In 2 miles at lights left through Grimoldby, at South Cockerington left into South View Lane, entrance on left.*

Unit General P Leisure Shop 2 miles Pub 2 miles

SOUTHWELL, Nottinghamshire Map ref 4C2

★★★
SELF CATERING

Units **3**
Sleeps **2–6**
Low season per wk
£180.00–£350.00
High season per wk
£180.00–£350.00

The Hayloft, Little Tithe & Dovecote, Southwell

contact Mrs Wilson, Lodge Farm, Gorsy Lane, Morton, Fiskerton, Southwell NG25 0XH
t (01636) 830497 **w** lodgebarns.com

open All year
payment Cash/cheques

Situated on working farm in country village of Morton, these 18thC barn conversions offer you a high standard of self-contained facilities. Twin-bedded rooms, each with shower room, fully fitted kitchen, lounge. Set in an orchard courtyard and farmland. Within walking distance of village shop, local pubs and River Trent.

⊕ *Please request at time of booking or visit our website.*

Unit General P Leisure Shop 1 mile
Pub 0.5 miles

STAMFORD, Lincolnshire Map ref 3A1

★★★
SELF CATERING

Units **1**
Sleeps **4**
Low season per wk
£200.00–£300.00
High season per wk
£300.00–£400.00

Elder Flower Cottage, Belmesthorpe, Stamford

contact Mr P and Mrs D Wilkinson, Elder Flower Cottage, Shepherds Walk, Belmesthorpe PE9 4JG
t (01780) 757188 & 07711 533204 **f** (01780) 757188 **e** philanddawn@tiscali.co.uk

This recently built, spacious, detached, high quality bungalow has been very well decorated and furnished, and is equipped to a high standard.

open All year
payment Cash/cheques

Unit General P Leisure

To your credit

If you book by phone you may be asked for your credit card number. If so, it is advisable to check the proprietor's policy in case you have to cancel your reservation at a later date.

STAMFORD, Lincolnshire Map ref 3A1

★★★★
SELF CATERING

Units **2**
Sleeps **1–14**
Low season per wk
£260.00–£550.00
High season per wk
£550.00–£650.00

Granary Cottages, Stamford

contact Mrs Katie Maitland, Aunby Manor, Aunby, Stamford PE9 4EE
t (01778) 590085 **e** mkmaitland@hotmail.com **w** aunby.co.uk

Converted, traditional stone buildings available separately or combined. Light, airy, loft-style granary comprises three double bedrooms and 50ft reception room. Cottage has two double bedrooms, lake/meadow views, stables and garden.

open All year
payment Cash/cheques, euros

Unit General Leisure Shop 2 miles Pub 2 miles

STAMFORD, Lincolnshire Map ref 3A1

★★★★
SELF CATERING

Units **1**
Sleeps **1–8**
Low season per wk
£250.00–£350.00
High season per wk
£375.00–£600.00

Wyandotte Cottage, Stamford

contact Mrs Jane Thorpe-Codman, Frog Hall, Northfields Lane, Nassington PE8 6QJ
t (01780) 784394 & 07833 680110 **f** (01780) 784394 **e** bookings@stamfordcottages.co.uk
w stamfordcottages.co.uk

Conveniently located in stunning Stamford, three- to four-bedroom cosy townhouse. Burghley Park and Rutland Water close by. Available from one night to many nights. Easy access to A1. A warm welcome awaits.

open All year
payment Cash/cheques, euros

Unit General Leisure Shop 0.5 miles Pub < 0.5 miles

SUTTERTON, Lincolnshire Map ref 3A1

★★★
SELF CATERING

Units **1**
Sleeps **1–4**
Low season per wk
Max £160.00
High season per wk
Max £400.00

Somercotes, Boston

contact Dr J V Sharp, Inish Fail, Orchard Close, East Hendred, Wantage OX12 8JJ
t (01235) 833367 **f** (01235) 833367 **e** J.V.Sharp@btinternet.com **w** somercotes.biz

A comfortable bungalow with its own large, private garden and ample parking. Near to local shops and public houses. Restaurant in village.

open All year
payment Cash/cheques

Unit General Leisure Shop 0.5 miles Pub < 0.5 miles

SUTTON ST JAMES, Lincolnshire Map ref 3A1

SELF CATERING

Units **2**
Sleeps **2–4**
Low season per wk
£199.00–£240.00
High season per wk
£210.00–£289.00

Foreman's Bridge Caravan Park, Spalding

contact Mr John Hoey, Foreman's Bridge Caravan Park, Sutton Road, Sutton St. James, Spalding PE12 0HU
t (01945) 440346 **f** (01945) 440346 **e** foremansbridge@btconnect.com **w** foremans-bridge.co.uk

payment Cash/cheques

Holiday cottages, one suitable for the disabled, and luxury static caravans set in rural location adjacent to tranquil fen waterway. Ideal for fishing. Open 1 March to 15 January.

Unit General Leisure Shop 1 mile Pub 1 mile

SUTTON-ON-SEA, Lincolnshire Map ref 4D2

★★★-★★★★
SELF CATERING

Units **2**
Sleeps **2–8**
Low season per wk
£100.00–£300.00
High season per wk
£400.00–£500.00

Country Retreat Equestrian Lodges, Sutton-on-Sea

contact Ms Maria Spradbury, Country Retreat Equestrian Lodges, Huttoft Road, Mablethorpe, Sutton-on-Sea LN12 2QY
t (01507) 442631 **f** (01507) 442631 **e** mariaequestrian@aol.com **w** blackcatequestriancentre.co.uk

open All year
payment Cash/cheques

Ideally situated near the sandy beaches of Sutton-on-Sea, enjoy a 'get away from it all' holiday in our handmade luxury Scandinavian log cabins. Explore the coast and countryside, or relax in the landscaped grounds of the Black Cat Equestrian Centre. A holiday to remember.

⊕ *A52, 1.5 miles south of Sutton-on-Sea.*

❤ *3-night breaks available during non-peak periods.*

Unit **General** **Leisure** **Shop** 0.5 miles **Pub** 0.5 miles

SWADLINCOTE, Derbyshire Map ref 4B3

★★★★
SELF CATERING

Units **4**
Sleeps **6–10**
Low season per wk
£359.00–£419.00
High season per wk
£419.00–£798.00

Forest Lodges, Rosliston, Swadlincote

contact Mrs Marie Hall, Rosliston Forest Centre, Burton Road, Rosliston, Swadlincote DE12 8JX
t (01283) 519119 **f** (01283) 565494 **e** enquiries@roslistonforestrycentre.co.uk
w roslistonforestrycentre.co.uk

open All year
payment Credit/debit cards, cash/cheques

Luxury, fully equipped lodges nestling in a 154-acre young woodland. Our lodges are fully accessible, with additional features including electric beds, hoist and extra-large shower rooms. Large range of activities available on site from fishing, walking and cycling to archery, falconry and laser combat. Pets welcome by arrangement in one lodge.

⊕ *Nearest train station Burton on Trent. Bus service (Arriva, No. 22) from Burton and Swadlincote.*

Unit **General** **Leisure** **Shop** < 0.5 miles
Pub < 0.5 miles

TIDESWELL, Derbyshire Map ref 4B2

★★★
SELF CATERING

Units **1**
Sleeps **4**
Low season per wk
Min £200.00
High season per wk
£210.00–£225.00

Geil Torrs, Buxton

contact Mr Harry Buttle, Geil Torrs, Buxton Road, Buxton SK17 8QJ
t (01298) 871302

Situated in Tideswell Dale, about 0.5 miles from the village of Tideswell, a village at the heart of the Peak District National Park.

open All year
payment Cash/cheques

Unit **General** **Shop** 0.5 miles **Pub** 0.5 miles

Town, country or coast?

The entertainment, shopping and innovative attractions of the big cities, the magnificent vistas of the countryside or the relaxing and refreshing coast – this guide will help you find what you're looking for!

WELLINGBOROUGH, Northamptonshire Map ref 3A2

★★★★
SELF CATERING

Units **1**
Sleeps **6**
Low season per wk
Min £350.00
High season per wk
Max £400.00

Friendly Lodge Cottage, Wellingborough

contact Mrs Kaye Saunders, Friendly Lodge Farm, Station Road, Raunds, Wellingborough NN9 6BT
t (01933) 461102 **f** (01933) 461102

open All year
payment Cash/cheques

New, spacious, luxury self-catering cottage on arable farm in rolling countryside. Lounge/diner, fully equipped kitchen and utility room, three bedrooms, including ground-floor double with en suite disabled facilities. Ideally situated for many attractions and places of interest in the Heart of England.

⊕ *Two miles east of Raunds on B663. Easy access from A14 and A45.*

♥ *3-night weekend breaks: £150.*

Unit General P Leisure Shop 2 miles Pub 1 mile

WELTON, Lincolnshire Map ref 4C2

★★★★
SELF CATERING

Units **1**
Low season per wk
£1,695.00–£1,995.00
High season per wk
£1,995.00–£3,000.00

Athina, Lincoln

contact Mrs Michelle Billington, 33 Hill Drive, Whaley Bridge, High Peak SK23 7BH
t (01663) 719661 **f** (01908) 320934 **e** athinabookings@aol.com **w** athinacottage.co.uk

Luxury, spacious ten-bedroom house, village location. Indoor heated swimming pool, jacuzzi, sauna, pool table and secluded gardens. Ideal for family parties and holidays.

open All year
payment Cash/cheques

Unit General P Leisure
Shop 0.5 miles Pub 0.5 miles

WINSTER, Derbyshire Map ref 4B2

★★★★
SELF CATERING

Units **1**
Sleeps **2**
Low season per wk
Min £190.00
High season per wk
£290.00–£340.00

Briar Cottage, Matlock

contact Mrs Anne Walters, Briar Cottage, c/o Heathcote House, Main Street DE4 2DJ
t (01629) 650342 **e** etegfan@clara.co.uk

A small, cosy, tastefully furnished cottage featuring an inglenook fireplace with gas coals, beamed ceiling and central heating throughout. Ideal base for walking.

open All year except Christmas
payment Cash/cheques

Unit General P Shop < 0.5 miles Pub < 0.5 miles

YOULGREAVE, Derbyshire Map ref 4B2

★★★
SELF CATERING

Units **1**
Sleeps **2**
Low season per wk
Min £190.00
High season per wk
Max £315.00

Sunnyside, Youlgreave, Bakewell

contact Ms J Steed, Falkland House, 10 New Road, Bakewell DE45 1WP
t (01629) 636195

open All year
payment Cash/cheques

Sunnyside is a homely, self-contained, very private apartment. From its patio, which is well-stocked with hanging baskets, various old farm implements and stone troughs, there are lovely views to the hills. Close to local amenities (including good pubs!), long/short walks from the door and tourist attractions (Chatsworth, Bakewell etc). Off-street parking.

⊕ *From A6 approx 3 miles south of Bakewell, B5056 signposted Ashbourne. Keep on same road for about 2 miles to reach Youlgreave, 1st turning on left, Sunnyside on right.*

❤ *3-night breaks available Nov-Apr.*

Unit General P Shop < 0.5 miles Pub < 0.5 miles

East of England

Bedfordshire › Cambridgeshire › Essex
Hertfordshire › Norfolk › Suffolk

The stunning Scallop sculpture at Aldeburgh

East of England Tourist Board
Toppesfield Hall, Hadleigh
Suffolk IP7 5DN
0870 225 4800
visiteastofengland.com

timeless pleasures, unspoilt coastline, treetop action

Main Spot spiralling birdlife at Minsmere Nature Reserve, Suffolk **Left** Enjoy the beautiful gardens at Audley End House, Essex; admire the breathtaking cathedral at Ely; revel in the excitement of an air show at the Imperial War Museum Duxford; stroll through the evening glow of cornfields on the Norfolk Broads

Rich in heritage, and scattered with market towns, fishing villages and seaside resorts, the East of England makes **a great escape for a quintessential English break.**

Explore East of England

Coasting along

Traverse the shingle beaches of the tranquil town of Felixstowe, relax in the award-winning gardens and stroll along the promenade staring wistfully out to sea. Admire the contours of the Scallop sculpture in Aldeburgh, explore the wide, Georgian high street and watch the fishermen arrive with their daily catch. If you're here in June, sample the delights of the Aldeburgh Festival – a concoction of art, literature and classical music to both tantalise and entertain.

Amble past brightly coloured beach huts in Southwold and sup a pint of the local brew, climb the lighthouse for fantastic views and try your luck on the vintage arcade machines on the pier. For an action-packed break, head to the popular resort of Great Yarmouth, enjoy the buzz of the nightlife and take your chances on the towering Sky-Drop at the Pleasure Beach.

Two legs, two wheels

Get your spokes spinning and feel the country air fill your lungs on one of the many cycling routes. Explore the vast, flat landscape of The Fens Cycle Way and imagine the Romans cultivating the land, or admire the re-created 19th-century Swiss village surroundings of the Old Warden cycle route in Bedfordshire. Pull on your boots and spot lizards and crabs along the Peddars Way National Trail on the Norfolk Coast Path from Knettishall to Cromer.

Breathe deeply at Norfolk Lavender farm and be enthralled by the dramatic, sweeping purple landscape. Relax on a chequered rug in the gardens of Audley End House and enjoy an excerpt from the Music on a Summer Evening concert programme.

Experience stunning sunsets across glowing Norfolk cornfields and fantastic panoramas throughout the Norfolk Broads. Explore the Broads (the country's largest wetland), meander between restored windmills, medieval churches and magnificent gardens, or hire a boat and discover the 125 miles of rivers snaking their way through the lush green countryside.

Unforgettable experiences

Feel the harmony between the extraordinary sculptures and glorious landscapes at the Henry Moore Foundation at Perry Green. Take time to explore the fruitful heritage of the region and visit the royal Anglo-Saxon burial ground of Sutton Hoo. Find yourself transfixed by the elegant beauty of the Cathedral and Abbey Church of St Alban, or settle down for an outstanding performance from one of the most famous choirs in the world at King's College Chapel in Cambridge.

Out and about

Shadow a ranger for a day at the Woburn Safari Park, or explore the extensive leisure area and meet the animals in residence. Allow the Nene Valley Railway in Peterborough to whisk you back in time as you steam along the tracks in a preserved locomotive. Descend into an excavation shaft at Grimes Graves Neolithic flint mine in Norfolk, or snap up a prize at The British Open Crabbing Championships in the charming coastal village of Walberswick in Suffolk.

Places to **visit**

Cromer
Hunstanton
Norfolk Coast
King's Lynn
PEDDARS WAY & NORFOLK COAST PATH
Great Yarmouth
Norwich
THE BROADS
Peterborough
Lowestoft
Welney
Ely
Thetford
Southwold
Suffolk Coast & Heaths
Newmarket
Bury St Edmunds
Aldeburgh
Bedford
Cambridge
Lavenham
Ipswich
Saffron Walden
Dedham Vale
Royston
Stevenage
Colchester
Harwich
Coggeshall
Dunstable
Hertford
Clacton-on-Sea
Brightlingsea
St Albans
Chelmsford
Epping
Southend-on-Sea

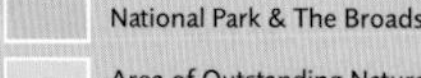

National Park & The Broads
Area of Outstanding Natural Beauty
Heritage Coast
National Trails nationaltrail.co.uk
Sections of the National Cycle Network nationalcyclenetwork.org.uk

Audley End House and Gardens
Saffron Walden,
Essex
(01799) 522842
english-heritage.org.uk
One of England's grandest stately homes

Bodyflight Bedford
Clapham, Bedfordshire
0845 200 2960
bodyflight.co.uk
Learn to sky dive indoors

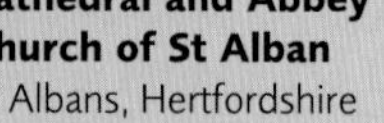

Cathedral and Abbey Church of St Alban
St Albans, Hertfordshire
(01727) 864511
stalbans.gov.uk/tourism
Witness the stunning medieval architecture

Colchester Castle
Essex
(01206) 282939
colchestermuseums.org.uk
Spectacular displays of Colchester history

Colchester Zoo

Essex
(01206) 331292
colchester-zoo.com
Impressive specimens, plus gardens and lakes

Grimes Graves

near Thetford, Norfolk
0870 333 1181
english-heritage.org.uk
Climb into the flint mine and explore

New Pleasurewood Hills Leisure Park
Lowestoft, Suffolk
(01502) 586000
pleasurewoodhills.com
An abundance of rides for all

Norfolk Lavender

near King's Lynn, Norfolk
(01485) 570384
norfolk-lavender.co.uk
Learn about lavender in a beautiful location

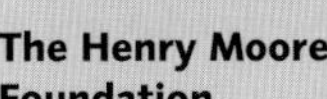

The Henry Moore Foundation
Perry Green, Hertfordshire
(01279) 843333
henry-moore-fdn.co.uk
Provocative artworks in beautiful setting

King's College Chapel
Cambridge
0906 58602526
visitcambridge.org
Listen to the famous choir

Knebworth House, Gardens and Park
Hertfordshire
(01438) 812661
knebworthhouse.com
View exhibits and explore parkland

Nene Valley Railway
Peterborough, Cambridgeshire
(01780) 784444
nvr.org.uk/thomas
Ride in a preserved locomotive

Oliver Cromwell's House
Ely, Cambridgeshire
(01353) 662062
ely.org.uk/tic
Step into his haunted bedroom

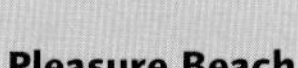

Pleasure Beach
Great Yarmouth, Norfolk
(01493) 844585
pleasure-beach.co.uk
A classic coastal fun park

RSPB Minsmere Nature Reserve
Saxmundham, Suffolk
(01728) 648281
rspb.org.uk
Bird-watching hides and trails

Sainsbury Centre for Visual Arts
Norwich, Norfolk
(01603) 593199
scva.org.uk
Featuring works by Picasso and Henry Moore

Shuttleworth Collection
near Bedford
(01767) 627927
shuttleworth.org
A unique and historical collection of aircraft out on display

Sutton Hoo Burial Site
Woodbridge, Suffolk
(01394) 389700
suttonhoo.org
Grassy mounds overlooking River Deben, and fascinating exhibition hall

West Stow Anglo-Saxon Village
Bury St Edmunds, Suffolk
(01284) 728718
stedmundsbury.gov.uk
A fascinating reconstructed piece of history, bringing the past to life

Woburn Safari Park
Bedfordshire
(01525) 290407
discoverwoburn.co.uk
Observe and interact with an impressive selection of animals in a natural setting

Tourist information centres 

When you arrive at your destination, visit a tourist information centre for help with accommodation and information about local attractions and events, or email your request before you go.

Aldeburgh	152 High Street	(01728) 453637	atic@suffolkcoastal.gov.uk
Aylsham	Norwich Road	(01263) 733903	aylsham.tic@broadland.gov.uk
Beccles*	Fen Lane	(01502) 713196	becclesinfo@broads-authority.gov.uk
Bedford	St Pauls Square	(01234) 215226	TouristInfo@bedford.gov.uk
Birchanger Green	Welcome Break Service Area	(01279) 508656	
Bishop's Stortford	Windhill	(01279) 655831	tic@bishopsstortford.org
Braintree	Market Place	(01376) 550066	tic@braintree.gov.uk
Brentwood	44 High Street	(01277) 200300	michelle.constable@brentwood.gov.uk
Burnham Deepdale	Deepdale Farm	(01485) 210256	info@deepdalefarm.co.uk
Bury St Edmunds	6 Angel Hill	(01284) 764667	tic@stedsbc.gov.uk
Cambridge	Wheeler Street	0871 226 8006	tourism@cambridge.gov.uk
Clacton-on-Sea	Station Road	(01255) 423400	emorgan@tendringdc.gov.uk
Colchester	1 Queen Street	(01206) 282920	vic@colchester.gov.uk
Cromer	Prince of Wales Road	0871 200 3071	cromertic@north-norfolk.gov.uk
Diss	Mere Street	(01379) 650523	dtic@s-norfolk.gov.uk
Downham Market	78 Priory Road	(01366) 383287	downham-market.tic@west-norfolk.gov.uk
Ely	29 St Mary's Street	(01353) 662062	tic@eastcambs.gov.uk
Felixstowe	91 Undercliff Road West	(01394) 276770	ftic@suffolkcoastal.gov.uk
Flatford	Flatford Lane	(01206) 299460	flatfordvic@babergh.gov.uk
Great Yarmouth	25 Marine Parade	(01493) 846345	tourism@great-yarmouth.gov.uk
Harwich Connexions	Iconfield Park	(01255) 506139	tic@harwichticconnexions.co.uk
Hemel Hempstead	Marlowes	(01442) 234222	stephanie.canadas@dacorum.gov.uk
Hertford	10 Market Place	(01992) 584322	tic@hertford.gov.uk
Holt*	3 Pound House	0871 200 3071	holttic@north-norfolk.gov.uk
Hoveton*	Station Road	(01603) 782281	hovetoninfo@broads-authority.gov.uk
Hunstanton	The Green	(01485) 532610	hunstanton.tic@west-norfolk.gov.uk
Huntingdon	Princes Street	(01480) 388588	hunts.tic@huntsdc.gov.uk
Ipswich	St Stephens Lane	(01473) 258070	tourist@ipswich.gov.uk
King's Lynn	Purfleet Quay	(01553) 763044	kings-lynn.tic@west-norfolk.gov.uk
Lavenham*	Lady Street	(01787) 248207	lavenhamtic@babergh.gov.uk
Letchworth Garden City	33-35 Station Road	(01462) 487868	tic@letchworth.com
Lowestoft	Royal Plain	(01502) 533600	touristinfo@waveney.gov.uk
Luton	St George's Square	(01582) 401579	tourist.information@luton.gov.uk
Maldon	Coach Lane	(01621) 856503	tic@maldon.gov.uk
Newmarket	Palace Street	(01638) 667200	tic.newmarket@forest-heath.gov.uk
Norwich	Millennium Plain	(01603) 727927	tourism@norwich.gov.uk

Peterborough	3-5 Minster Precincts	(01733) 452336	tic@peterborough.gov.uk
Saffron Walden	1 Market Place	(01799) 510444	tourism@uttlesford.gov.uk
Sandy	5 Shannon Court	(01767) 682728	tourism@sandytowncouncil.gov.uk
Sheringham*	Station Approach	0871 200 3071	sheringhamtic@north-norfolk.gov.uk
Southend-on-Sea	Western Esplanade	(01702) 215620	vic@southend.gov.uk
Southwold	69 High Street	(01502) 724729	southwold.tic@waveney.gov.uk
St Albans	Market Place	(01727) 864511	tic@stalbans.gov.uk
St Neots	8 New Street	(01480) 388788	stneots.tic@huntsdc.gov.uk
Stowmarket	Museum of East Anglican Life	(01449) 676800	tic@midsuffolk.gov.uk
Sudbury	Market Hill	(01787) 881320	sudburytic@babergh.gov.uk
Swaffham*	Market Place	(01760) 722255	swaffham@eetb.info
Thetford	4 White Hart Street	(01842) 820689	info@thetfordtourism.co.uk
Waltham Abbey	2-4 Highbridge Street	(01992) 652295	tic@walthamabbey.org.uk
Wells-next-the-Sea*	Staithe Street	0871 200 3071	wellstic@north-norfolk.gov.uk
Wisbech	2-3 Bridge Street	(01945) 583263	tourism@fenland.gov.uk
Woodbridge	Station Buildings	(01394) 382240	wtic@suffolkcoastal.gov.uk
Wymondham	Market Place	(01953) 604721	wymondhamtic@btconnect.com

* *seasonal opening*

Alternatively, you can text **TIC LOCATE** to **64118** to find your nearest tourist information centre

Find out **more**

The following publications are available from East of England by logging on to **visiteastofengland.com** or calling **0870 225 4800**:

› East of England 2007

A great flavour of what the East of England has to offer – vibrant cities, coastal escapes, seaside fun and so much more. This free publication is a gateway for holiday ideas, promoting a wide range of more detailed printed matter and websites.

› Let's Go East of England 2007

A region so diverse, right on London's doorstep – the East of England has so much to offer for short breaks and day trips. A free A5 publication packed full of great ideas, linking to a fine array of special offers. Suggestions for trips by rail are included, but this is also one you'll want to keep in your glove box!

› East of England – Cycling

The East of England offers perfect cycling country, from quiet country lanes to ancient trackways. This free publication promotes the many Cycling Discovery Maps that are available, as well as providing useful information for anyone planning a cycling tour of the region.

› East of England – Gardens

The East of England has English country gardens to inspire. This free publication is more than a just directory for gardens to visit – its features, behind-the-scenes insights and masterclass tips make it a gardening inspiration in itself.

Travel **info**

By road:

The region is easily accessible: from London and the South via the A1(M), M11, M25, A10, M1 and A12; from the North via the A1(M), A17, A15, A5, M1 and A6; from the West via the A14, A47, A421, A428, A418, A41, A422 and A427.

By rail:

Regular fast and frequent trains run to all major cities and towns. London stations which serve the region are Liverpool Street, King's Cross, Fenchurch Street, Marylebone and Euston. Bedford, Luton and St Albans are on the Thameslink line which runs to King's Cross and on to London Gatwick Airport. There is also a direct link between London Stansted Airport and Liverpool Street. Through the Channel Tunnel, there are trains direct from Paris and Brussels to Waterloo Station, London. A short journey on the Underground will bring passengers to those stations operating services into the East of England. Further information on rail journeys in the East of England can be obtained on 0845 748 4950.

By air:

Fly into London Luton, London Stansted or Norwich International.

Striking sculptures at The Henry Moore Foundation, Perry Green

where to stay in

East of England

All place names in the blue bands are shown on the maps at the front of this guide.

A complete listing of all Enjoy England assessed accommodation covered by this guide appears at the back.

Accommodation symbols
Symbols give useful information about services and facilities. Inside the back-cover flap you can find a key to these symbols. Keep it open for easy reference.

ALDEBURGH, Suffolk Map ref 3C2

★★★★
SELF CATERING

Units 1
Sleeps 1–6
Low season per wk
£345.00–£465.00
High season per wk
£725.00–£899.00

Lower Thellusson, Aldeburgh

contact Mrs Claire Gawthrop, East Green Farm, Kelsale, Saxmundham IP17 2PH
t (01728) 602316 **f** (01728) 604408 **e** claire@eastgreenproperty.co.uk **w** eastgreencottages.co.uk

Situated in the heart of Aldeburgh, just 40yds from the beach. A spacious, secluded, south-facing house set in its own mature gardens with sun terrace, conservatory and ample parking. Three twin bedrooms.

open All year
payment Cash/cheques

Unit General Leisure Shop < 0.5 miles Pub < 0.5 miles

ALDEBURGH, Suffolk Map ref 3C2

★★★
SELF CATERING & SERVICED APARTMENTS

Units 1
Sleeps 12–15
Low season per wk
£800.00–£1,300.00
High season per wk
£1,300.00–£1,700.00

Orlando, Aldeburgh

contact Mr Peter Hatcher, Martlesham Hall, Church Lane, Woodbridge IP12 4PQ
t (01394) 382126 **f** (01394) 278600 **e** orlando@hatcher.co.uk **w** hatcher.co.uk/orlando

payment Cash/cheques, euros

Orlando is a spacious, six-bedroom house adjacent to the beach with magnificent, panoramic views of the sea. The house is well equipped with all modern facilities. Open-plan kitchen with Aga and dining area. Two living rooms on two floors, four bathrooms. Ideal for three families.

From Moot Hall, follow road south and turn left after Ye Olde Cross Keys pub. Then right into King Street. Orlando is on right after 200m.

Unit General Leisure Shop < 0.5 miles Pub < 0.5 miles

Check it out

Information on accommodation listed in this guide has been supplied by proprietors. As changes may occur you should remember to check all relevant details at the time of booking.

ALRESFORD, Essex Map ref 3B2

★★★
SELF CATERING

Units **1**
Sleeps **1–2**
Low season per wk
Min £150.00
High season per wk
Min £230.00

Creek Lodge, Colchester

contact Mrs Patricia Mountney, Creek Lodge, Ford Lane, Colchester CO7 8BE
t (01206) 825411

Tranquil riverside cottage set in extensive landscaped gardens, perfectly situated for sailing, walking and bird-watching. Only five miles from historic Colchester.

open All year
payment Cash/cheques

Unit General Shop 0.75 miles Pub 0.75 miles

BILLERICAY, Essex Map ref 3B3

★★★★★
SELF CATERING

Units **1**
Sleeps **1–6**
Low season per wk
£475.00–£950.00
High season per wk
£600.00–£1,050.00

Pump House Apartment, Billericay

contact Mr John Bayliss, Pump House, Church Street, Billericay CM11 2TR
t (01277) 656579 **f** (01277) 631160 **e** johnwbayliss@btinternet.com
w thepumphouseapartment.co.uk

open All year
payment Credit/debit cards, cash/cheques, euros

The apartment is on two floors and luxuriously furnished, with air-conditioning. The accommodation comprises two living rooms, fully fitted kitchen/diner and the option of one, two or three bedrooms with one, two or three bath/shower rooms. Guests have use of heated outdoor pool (May to September), hot tub, gazebo and gardens. Personal supervision.

Turn off M25 at jct 29. Take A127 towards Southend-on-Sea then A176 to Billericay, right to Great Burstead.

5% discount for stays of 4 weeks/10% discount for stays of 8 weeks against 2-/3-bedroom options.

Unit General Leisure
Shop 0.75 miles Pub 0.5 miles

BRANCASTER, Norfolk Map ref 3B1

★★★
SELF CATERING

Units **1**
Sleeps **1–6**
Low season per wk
£299.00–£545.00
High season per wk
£399.00–£659.00

Cheal Cottage, Brancaster, King's Lynn

contact Mrs Janet Harrison, Field House, Little Lane, Surfleet PE11 4AZ
t (01775) 680513 **f** (01775) 680613

Modern, well-appointed and -equipped cottage with three bedrooms, two bathrooms and enclosed south-facing garden and patio. Quiet location, ample parking. Beach and sailing nearby.

open All year
payment Cash/cheques

Unit General Leisure Shop 0.5 miles Pub 0.5 miles

BRANCASTER, Norfolk Map ref 3B1

★★★
SELF CATERING

Units **1**
Sleeps **1–8**
Low season per wk
£330.00–£410.00
High season per wk
£470.00–£700.00

Lindum, Brancaster, King's Lynn

contact Mrs Sally Blyth, Corner Cottage, 34 The Street, Honingham, Norwich NR9 5BL
t (01603) 880286 **f** (01603) 881404 **e** paul_sally@tiscali.co.uk **w** lindum-brancaster.co.uk

Spacious end-of-terrace house. Two double rooms, two twin-bedded rooms. Enclosed garden; non-smoking. Near sandy beach, nature reserves and stately homes. Parking.

open All year
payment Cash/cheques, euros

Unit General Leisure Shop < 0.5 miles
Pub < 0.5 miles

BRANCASTER STAITHE, Norfolk Map ref 3B1

★★★
SELF CATERING

Units 2
Sleeps 2–6
Low season per wk
£210.00–£300.00
High season per wk
£300.00–£750.00

Vista And Carpenters Cottage, Brancaster Staithe

contact Mrs Gloria Smith, Dale View, Main Road, Brancaster Staithe, King's Lynn PE31 8BY
t (01485) 210497 **f** (01485) 210497

open All year
payment Cash/cheques

These lovely cottages enjoy one of the best views along the Norfolk coast (see picture). Walking down the cottage gardens you meet the saltmarsh and the Norfolk coastal path. The cottages have exposed beams and open fires as well as central heating throughout. Close to amenities. Pets welcome.

Situated on the sea side of the A149 coast road.

Short breaks (weekend and mid-week) available during low season or at short notice; minimum 3 nights.

Unit General P Leisure Shop 0.5 miles Pub 0.5 miles

BRANTHAM, Suffolk Map ref 3B2

★★★★
SELF CATERING

Units 1
Sleeps 6
Low season per wk
Max £300.00
High season per wk
£400.00–£600.00

Hall Cottage, Manningtree

contact Ms Caroline Williams, Brantham Lodge, Manningtree CO11 1PT
t (01473) 327090 **f** (01473) 327090 **e** hwilliams@branmann.freeserve.co.uk

open All year
payment Cash/cheques

18thC cottage on South Suffolk farm overlooking Stour estuary (bird-watching). Full of character, two narrow staircases, four walk-through bedrooms. Enclosed garden, paved terrace. Footpaths to Flatford, Dedham and Shotley Peninsula. Peaceful spot, but pubs, shops and Alton Water nearby. Easy access to Ipswich, Colchester and Suffolk coast.

Situated 200yds west of Brantham railway bridge on A137. Turn left through white gates. Follow farm drive for 400yds to Brantham Hall.

Short breaks available.

Unit General P Leisure Shop 2 miles Pub 0.5 miles

BURY ST EDMUNDS, Suffolk Map ref 3B2

★★★
SELF CATERING

Units 1
Sleeps 2
Low season per wk
Min £165.00
High season per wk
Max £230.00

Oliver's Retreat, Bury St Edmunds

contact Mrs C Titcombe, 95 Oliver Road, Bury St Edmunds IP33 3JG
t (01284) 766432 **w** tiscover.co.uk

Oliver's Retreat is a well-equipped and tastefully decorated cosy, ground-floor, detached studio overlooking a beautiful view of the scenic countryside. Pets welcome by arrangement.

open All year
payment Cash/cheques

Unit General P Leisure Shop < 0.5 miles Pub 0.5 miles

CAISTER-ON-SEA, Norfolk Map ref 3C1

★★
SELF CATERING

Units 8
Sleeps 1–5
Low season per wk
£164.00–£265.00
High season per wk
£164.00–£345.00

Sand Dune Cottages, Great Yarmouth

contact Mr Miles Rainer, Rear of 57a Tan Lane, Caister-on-Sea, Great Yarmouth NR30 5DT
t (01493) 720352 **e** sand.dune.cottages@amserve.net
w netsalesuk.co.uk/gt-yarmouth/cottages/sanddune.htm

Modern cottages that you'll fall in love with, fronting onto golf course and overlooking sand dunes 150yds away. Private car park. Pets welcome. Open March to October and Christmas and New Year's Eve.

payment Cash/cheques

Unit General P Leisure Shop < 0.5 miles Pub < 0.5 miles

CAMBRIDGE, Cambridgeshire Map ref 2D1

★★★★
SELF CATERING

Units **1**
Sleeps **1–6**
Low season per wk
£350.00–£650.00
High season per wk
£450.00–£700.00

School House, Cambridge

contact Mr Terry & Nicola Mann, School House, High Street, Horningsea CB5 9JG
t (01223) 440077 **f** (01223) 441414 **e** schoolhse1@btinternet.com **w** schoolhouse-uk.com

open All year except Christmas and New Year
payment Credit/debit cards, cash/cheques, euros

A wonderful Victorian headmaster's house situated in an unspoilt village four miles from Cambridge city centre. Beautiful interior and very well equipped. Two bedrooms (one double, one king-size), bathroom with roll-top bath, sofa bed for additional guests, patio garden. Local riverside walks and traditional pubs.

M11 jct 14 onto A14 eastbound, 3rd exit (Fendítton, Horningsea B1047). Turn left, 0.5 miles to Horningsea. School House on right-hand-side in centre of village.

Weekend breaks can be offered. Any length of stay considered.

Unit General P Leisure Shop < 0.5 miles Pub < 0.5 miles

CASTLE HEDINGHAM, Essex Map ref 3B2

★★★★
SELF CATERING

Units **2**
Low season per wk
Min £220.00
High season per wk
Max £360.00

Rosemary Farm, Halstead

contact Mr Garry Ian Henderson, Rosemary Farm, Rosemary Lane, Halstead CO9 3AJ
t (01787) 461653

open All year
payment Cash/cheques

Rosemary Farm is situated in a quiet country lane within view of Hedingham Castle, former home of the De Veres, Earls of Oxford, and is a convenient base for visiting the many nearby attractions. Cottages in barn conversion offering lounge, kitchen, one and two bedrooms, shower/toilet, tiled flooring throughout, patio area, parking.

Go past shops in Sible Hedingham, turn right into Station Road and through Castle Hedingham village towards Sudbury (B1058). Rosemary Lane is approximately 200yds on the left.

Unit General P

CLEY NEXT THE SEA, Norfolk Map ref 3B1

★★★
SELF CATERING

Units **1**
Sleeps **1–7**
Low season per wk
£230.00–£310.00
High season per wk
£340.00–£500.00

Archway Cottage, Holt

contact Mrs Vickey Jackson, 3a Brickendon Lane, Hertford SG13 8NU
t (01992) 511303 & (01992) 503196 **f** (01992) 511303

open All year
payment Cash/cheques

Pretty 18thC flint cottage, well furnished and comfortable, with four bedrooms, two bathrooms and garage. Near village centre, bird sanctuaries and the sea. Also Chantry, another similar cottage in Wells-next-the-Sea. Illustrated brochures available for both cottages.

Situated in the centre of Cley next the Sea.

Unit General

Key to symbols

Open the back flap for a key to symbols.

COLCHESTER, Essex Map ref 3B2

★★★
SELF CATERING

Units 1
Sleeps 5
Low season per wk
£200.00–£220.00
High season per wk
£240.00–£270.00

50 Rosebery Avenue, Colchester

contact Mrs Katharine Webb, 51 Rosebery Avenue, Colchester CO1 2UP
t (01206) 866888 **e** rosebery.avenue@btinternet.com

Modernised house in quiet town-centre location. Castle, park, shops, museums and sports centre within walking distance. Ideal for east coast. Bus/trains close by.

open All year
payment Cash/cheques, euros

Unit General P Shop < 0.5 miles Pub < 0.5 miles

COLTISHALL, Norfolk Map ref 3C1

★★★
SELF CATERING

Units 1
Sleeps 2–3
Low season per wk
Min £190.00
High season per wk
Max £300.00

Broadgates, Coltishall

contact Mrs Dack, Broadgates, Coltishall NR12 7DU
t (01603) 737598 **e** 2.richard@4broads.fsnet.co.uk **w** broadgates-coltishall.com

Broadgates is situated in the heart of Coltishall, which is said to be one of the prettiest villages in Norfolk. Ideally situated for exploring.

open All year
payment Cash/cheques

Unit General P S Leisure Shop < 0.5 miles Pub < 0.5 miles

CRATFIELD, Suffolk Map ref 3C2

★★★★
SELF CATERING

Units 3
Sleeps 2–10
Low season per wk
£225.00–£350.00
High season per wk
£295.00–£515.00

Holly Tree Farm Barns, Halesworth

contact Ms Rachel Boddy, Holly Tree Farm, Bell Lane, Cratfield, Halesworth IP19 0DN
t (01986) 798062 **e** hollytreebarns@lycos.co.uk **w** hollytreebarns.co.uk

open All year
payment Cash/cheques

Unrivalled tranquillity in recently converted barns. Private gardens offer unbroken farmland views. Heritage Coast and unspoiled delights of Suffolk nearby. Short walk to village pub. Eleven acres of meadowland. Dogs welcome. Ample parking. Sky TV. Each cottage has a sofa bed sleeping two.

⊕ *Leave centre of Cratfield village with The Poacher (pub) on your right-hand side – we are one of the last places on the left.*

❤ *Short breaks available by arrangement.*

Unit General P S Leisure Shop 3 miles Pub 0.5 miles

CRATFIELD, Suffolk Map ref 3C2

★★★★
SELF CATERING

Units 4
Sleeps 2–6
Low season per wk
£155.00–£275.00
High season per wk
£360.00–£495.00

School Farm Cottages, Halesworth

contact Mrs Claire Sillett, School Farm, Church Road, Cratfield, Halesworth IP19 0BU
t (01986) 798844 **e** schoolfarmcotts@aol.com **w** schoolfarmcottages.com

High-quality, well-equipped cottages converted from traditional farm buildings. Attractive setting on working farm in beautiful Suffolk countryside. Near Heritage Coast.

open All year
payment Cash/cheques

Unit General P S Leisure Shop 3 miles Pub < 0.5 miles

Check it out

Please check prices, quality ratings and other details when you book.

CROMER, Norfolk Map ref 3C1

★★
SELF CATERING

Units 1
Sleeps 6
High season per wk
Min £275.00

Cliff Hollow, Cromer

contact Miss L Willins, Cliff Hollow, Cromer NR27 0AL
t (01263) 512447 **f** (01263) 512447

Family home, secluded area, own garden, four bedrooms, combined bathroom/wc, lounge, dining room and kitchen. Cot and highchair. Open April to October and Christmas and New Year.

payment Cash/cheques

Unit General P Leisure Shop 0.5 miles Pub 1 mile

CROMER, Norfolk Map ref 3C1

★★★★
SELF CATERING

Units 7
Sleeps 2–6
Low season per wk
£165.00–£255.00
High season per wk
£285.00–£599.00

Poppyland Holiday Cottages, Overstrand, Nr Cromer

contact Mr & Mrs Riches, 21 Regent Street, Wickmere, Norwich NR11 7ND
t (01263) 577473 **e** poppyland@totalise.co.uk

open All year
payment Credit/debit cards

Individual, award-winning properties, five of which are in Overstrand, a fishing village with safe sandy beaches, one mile east of Cromer. The remaining properties are in the rural hamlet of Wickmere, surrounded by open countryside within a conservation area seven miles south of Sheringham. Ideal for walking, cycling and bird-watching.

Short breaks available Sep-May. Senior Citizens: 10% discount low season. Phone for late-availability reduced rates.

Unit General P S Shop 0.5 miles Pub 0.5 miles

DUDDENHOE END, Essex Map ref 2D1

★★★★
SELF CATERING

Units 1
Sleeps 2–4
Low season per wk
£200.00–£225.00
High season per wk
£225.00–£250.00

Cosh Cottage, Duddenhoe End, Saffron Walden

contact Mrs Susan Perks, The Cosh, Duddenhoe End, Saffron Walden CB11 4UX
t (01763) 838880 **f** (01763) 838880 **e** susan.perks@virgin.net

A two-bedroom cottage close to the owner's own house. Surrounded by Essex cornfields. Equipped kitchen: cooker, fridge, dishwasher, washer/dryer and microwave. Summer use of swimming pool and tennis court.

open All year
payment Cash/cheques, euros

Unit General P Leisure Shop 6 miles Pub 3 miles

EDWARDSTONE, Suffolk Map ref 3B2

★★★★
SELF CATERING

Units 2
Sleeps 2–6
Low season per wk
£300.00–£400.00
High season per wk
£425.00–£650.00

Sherbourne Farm Lodge Cottages, Sudbury

contact Mrs Anne Suckling, Sherbourne House Farm, Edwardstone, Sudbury CO10 5PD
t (01787) 210885 **e** enquiries@sherbournelodgecottages.co.uk **w** sherbournelodgecottages.co.uk

open All year
payment Cash/cheques

Located on a family farm in picturesque Suffolk, single-storey barn conversions offering quality accommodation. Each comprises kitchen/living area, wet room with bath and shower, two bedrooms (double or twin), courtyard and games barn. Discover a world of nature in our unique wildlife valley. Disabled facilities throughout.

From A12 take A134 (Sudbury). A1071 to Boxford. Boxford village turn into Swan Street, next left into Sherbourne Street. Cottages are signposted approx 500yds on left.

Unit General P S Leisure
Shop < 0.5 miles Pub < 0.5 miles

ELY, Cambridgeshire Map ref 3A2

★★★
SELF CATERING

Units **1**
Sleeps **1–5**
Low season per wk
Min £360.00
High season per wk
Min £360.00

7 Lisle Lane, Ely

contact Judy Jones & Ken Davis, 9 Lisle Lane, Ely CB7 4AS
t (01353) 615406 & (01353) 675249 **e** fortyfarmhouse@aol.com

Ideally placed, modern but traditional, three-bedroom terrace townhouse with enclosed patio garden. Close to river, cathedral and market square. Private parking and walking distance to railway station. Reductions for long stays.

open All year
payment Cash/cheques

Unit General Leisure Shop < 0.5 miles Pub < 0.5 miles

EPPING, Essex Map ref 2D1

Rating Applied For
SELF CATERING

Units **1**
Sleeps **2–4**
Low season per wk
£280.00
High season per wk
£280.00–£340.00

Mandalay, Epping

contact Ms Brenda Foster, Kingsway Cottage, Epping Green CM16 6PX
t (01992) 571828 **f** (01992) 570216 **e** kingsway@tesco.net **w** ukholidaycottages.biz

Self-contained bungalow in Essex village near Epping. Ideal for visiting London. One twin bedroom with en suite shower, lounge with sofa bed. Small garden with patio set and barbecue.

open All year
payment Credit/debit cards, cash/cheques

Unit General Leisure Shop 3 miles Pub < 0.5 miles

ERPINGHAM, Norfolk Map ref 3B1

★★★
SELF CATERING

Units **4**
Sleeps **2–7**
Low season per wk
£200.00–£400.00
High season per wk
£380.00–£650.00

Grange Farm, Erpingham, Norwich

contact Mrs Jane Bell, Grange Farm Holidays, Scarrow Beck Farm, Erpingham, Norwich NR11 7QU
t (01263) 761241 **f** (01263) 768398 **e** jane.bell5@btopenworld.com **w** grangefarmholidays.co.uk

open All year
payment Cash/cheques

A 17thC farmhouse and converted period farm buildings around a courtyard, all in a large garden, in the middle of an 80-acre farm beside a river. Heated indoor swimming pool. Open Christmas and New Year.

⊕ *From A140, turn west at brown tourist sign for Wolterton Park. 1st right then 1st left (Scarrow Beck Road). Farm is 0.5 miles on right.*

❤ *Weekends (up to 4 nights) from £150 in low season.*

Unit General Leisure Shop 2 miles Pub 0.75 miles

EYE, Suffolk Map ref 3B2

★★★★
SELF CATERING

Units **4**
Sleeps **2–6**
Low season per wk
£265.00–£325.00
High season per wk
£385.00–£640.00

Athelington Hall, Eye

contact Mr Peter Havers, Athelington Hall, Eye IP21 5EJ
t (01728) 628233 **f** (01379) 384491 **e** peter@logcabinholidays.co.uk **w** logcabinholidays.co.uk

Situated in an idyllic location, spacious two-bedroom lodge: one double with en suite shower and one twin with verandah and fantastic view. Breathtaking Suffolk Heritage Coast only 25 minutes away.

open All year
payment Credit/debit cards, cash/cheques

Unit General Leisure Shop 1 mile Pub 3 miles

Star ratings

Further information about star ratings can be found at the back of this guide.

EYE, Suffolk Map ref 3B2

★★★
SELF CATERING

Units **1**
Sleeps **2**
Low season per wk
£175.00–£200.00
High season per wk
£225.00–£250.00

Orchard Cottage, Thornham Magna

contact Mrs Caroline Coles, Water House, Water Lane, Eye IP23 8LH
t (01379) 678656 **f** (01379) 672900 **e** tonyatthornham@btinternet.com

Modern, well equipped, detached cottage in walled area of riverside garden. Secluded location with views over water meadows. Picturesque hamlet, thatched pub nearby. Double bedroom. Open March to October; Christmas and New Year.

payment Cash/cheques, euros

Unit General **P** Shop 4 miles Pub < 0.5 miles

FAKENHAM, Norfolk Map ref 3B1

★★★–★★★★
SELF CATERING

Units **14**
Sleeps **2–7**
Low season per wk
£315.00–£603.00
High season per wk
£666.00–£1,488.00

Idyllic Cottages at Vere Lodge, Fakenham

contact Mrs Jane Bowlby, Holiday Complex, Fakenham NR21 7HE
t (01328) 838261 **f** (01328) 838300 **e** major@verelodge.co.uk **w** idylliccottages.co.uk

open All year
payment Credit/debit cards, cash/cheques

Superbly equipped cottages in eight acres of secluded grounds. Leisure centre with heated indoor pool, sauna, solarium and games room. Animal farm, children's play area, tennis court and enchanted wood. Plenty to do for adults and children with Norfolk's wonderful beaches a short drive away. Pets welcome.

⊕ *From Swaffham take A1065 towards Fakenham. After 11 miles, left in South Raynham. Vere Lodge is the large white house 400yds ahead across a shallow valley.*

♥ *Short breaks available.*

Unit General **P** Leisure Shop 0.5 miles Pub 4.5 miles

FAKENHAM, Norfolk Map ref 3B1

★★★★
SELF CATERING

Units **1**
Sleeps **1–8**
Low season per wk
£290.00–£560.00
High season per wk
£450.00–£800.00

Pollywiggle Cottage, West Raynham, Fakenham

contact Mrs Marilyn Farnham-Smith, 79 Earlham Road, Norwich NR2 3RE
t (01603) 471990 **f** (01603) 612221 **e** marilyn@pollywigglecottage.co.uk **w** pollywigglecottage.co.uk

open All year
payment Cash/cheques

Brimming with character, this pretty, well-equipped home wraps you in its cosy, comfortable interior. Nestled in secluded, rambling flower gardens, Pollywiggle lies on the fringe of a tranquil village 15 miles from the North Norfolk coast. A wealth of amenities and attractions are within an easy drive. Ramblers/cyclists are welcome.

⊕ *A1065 (Swaffham to Fakenham) for 14 miles. Left to West Raynham, through village, left at childrens playground to East Rudham. After 100m left up narrow lane.*

♥ *Small-party reductions and short breaks available – minimum 2 nights – during non-peak times.*

Unit General **P** Leisure Shop 4 miles Pub 3 miles

Check the maps

Colour maps at the front pinpoint all the places you will find accommodation entries in the regional sections. Pick your location and then refer to the place index at the back to find the page number.

FIELD DALLING, Norfolk Map ref 3B1

★★★★
SELF CATERING

Units 1
Sleeps 1–5
Low season per wk
£300.00–£400.00
High season per wk
£500.00–£550.00

Eastcote Cottage, Field Dalling

contact Ms Sally Grove, Eastcote Farm, Field Dalling NR25 7LE
t (01328) 830359 **e** sally@eastcotecottage.co.uk **w** eastcotecottage.co.uk

open All year
payment Cash/cheques

An excellent renovation offering rural charm in relaxing and snug surroundings. Tastefully decorated and furnished. Fully equipped with all mod cons and two bathrooms. Underfloor heating throughout plus woodburner. Secure, private garden with patio, garden furniture and barbecue. Pets considered. Tennis court available. Ample off-road parking.

⊕ *Map provided when booking is made.*

❤ *3-night stays available Oct-Jan (excl Christmas and New Year).*

Unit General Leisure Shop 3 miles Pub 2 miles

FOXLEY, Norfolk Map ref 3B1

★★-★★★★
SELF CATERING

Units 12
Sleeps 3–10
Low season per wk
£200.00–£550.00
High season per wk
£350.00–£860.00

Moor Farm Stable Cottages, Dereham

contact Mr Paul Davis, Moor Farm, Foxley, Dereham NR20 4QP
t (01362) 688523 **f** (01362) 688523 **e** mail@moorfarmstablecottages.co.uk
w moorfarmstablecottages.co.uk

open All year
payment Cash/cheques

Located on working farm, a courtyard of two- and three-bedroomed self-catering cottages, all fully equipped and centrally heated, two specially adapted for disabled. Ideally situated for coast, Broads, Norwich, Sandringham. 365 acres of mature woodland adjoining owners' farm in which to walk. Fishing available in owners' lake close by. Pets welcome.

⊕ *From King's Lynn take A148 to Fakenham, then A1067 to Norwich. Moor Farm is situated at the bottom of Foxley Street which is signposted off the A1067.*

❤ *2-/3-night breaks available (mid-week or weekend) Oct-May, 5 nights Christmas/New Year.*

Unit General Leisure Shop 1 mile Pub 0.5 miles

FRETTENHAM, Norfolk Map ref 3C1

★★★
SELF CATERING

Units 3
Sleeps 4–7
Low season per wk
£210.00–£750.00

Glebe Farm, Norwich

contact Mrs Rona Norton, Beck Farm, Off Pound Hill, Frettenham, Norwich NR12 7NF
t (01603) 897641 **e** rona.norton@btinternet.com **w** glebefarm-cottages.co.uk

We offer very different-sized cottages on our farm. All are set in large gardens and offer well-equipped, comfortable, modern facilities in a picturesque rural setting with views over open countryside.

open All year
payment Cash/cheques

Unit General Leisure Shop 2 miles Pub 1 mile

GAYTON, Norfolk Map ref 3B1

★★★
SELF CATERING

Units **1**
Sleeps **1–4**
Low season per wk
£180.00–£240.00
High season per wk
£240.00–£310.00

Field View, King's Lynn

contact Mrs Rachel Steel, Aramir, Lynn Road, Gayton, King's Lynn PE32 1QJ
t (01553) 636813 **w** fieldviewcottage.mysite.wanadoo-members.co.uk

open All year
payment Cash/cheques

Set in the very popular rural village of Gayton, this well-presented, semi-detached, two-bedroomed cottage is an ideal base for exploring all Norfolk has to offer. Ample off-road parking and unspoilt views over open countryside. The village boasts many amenities, including two highly recommended public houses.

⊕ *From King's Lynn, A149 (Cromer and Hunstanton) to roundabout adjacent to hospital. B1145 (Gayton and Crematorium) to Gayton village. On left opposite C E Grimes (butchers).*

Unit General P Shop < 0.5 miles Pub < 0.5 miles

GORLESTON-ON-SEA, Norfolk Map ref 3C1

★★★
SELF CATERING

Units **1**
Sleeps **4**
Low season per wk
£110.00–£170.00
High season per wk
£220.00–£300.00

Manor Cottage, Gorleston, Great Yarmouth

contact Mrs Margaret Ward, North Manor House, 12 Pier Plain, Gorleston, Great Yarmouth NR31 6PE
t (01493) 669845 **f** (01493) 669845 **e** manorcottage@wardm4.fsnet.co.uk **w** wardm4.fsnet.co.uk

Edwardian two-bedroomed cottage attached to manor-house. Quiet location between high street, beach and harbour. Parking. Near Yarmouth, Hopton, Lowestoft, Broads and nature reserves.

open All year except Christmas and New Year
payment Cash/cheques

Unit General P

GREAT PLUMSTEAD, Norfolk Map ref 3C1

★★★
SELF CATERING

Units **1**
Sleeps **2–6**
Low season per wk
£295.00–£395.00
High season per wk
£350.00–£630.00

Windfalls, Norwich

contact Mrs Jane Jones, Hall Farm, Great Plumstead NR13 5EF
t (01603) 720235 **f** (01603) 722008 **e** hall.farm@btinternet.com

Close to Norwich city centre, located in open countryside. Comfortable, three-bedroomed detached house, surrounded by a large garden including toy-filled Wendy House.

open All year
payment Cash/cheques

Unit General P S Leisure Shop 1 mile Pub 1 mile

GREAT YARMOUTH, Norfolk Map ref 3C2

HADLEIGH, Suffolk Map ref 3B2

★★★★
SELF CATERING

Units **3**
Sleeps **1–8**
Low season per wk
£350.00–£470.00
High season per wk
£580.00–£1,000.00

Wattisham Hall Holiday Cottages, Wattisham, Ipswich

contact Mrs Jo Squirrell, Wattisham Hall, Wattisham, Ipswich IP7 7JX
t (01449) 740240 **f** (01449) 744535 **e** jhsquirr@farming.co.uk **w** wattishamhall.co.uk

open All year
payment Cash/cheques

Charming barn conversion within an ancient moat, surrounded by tranquil countryside. The cottages are beautifully furnished, having exposed beams, oak floors, wood-burning stoves and plenty of character. Enclosed patio gardens, shared games room and outdoor play area. Within easy reach of Constable Country and many picturesque villages such as Lavenham.

⊕ *For full travel directions please visit our website or contact us.*

❤ *Short breaks available all year excl May and Oct half-terms, school summer holidays, Christmas and New Year.*

Unit General P Leisure Shop 2 miles Pub 2 miles

HALSTEAD, Essex Map ref 3B2

★★★★
SELF CATERING

Units **1**
Sleeps **2–9**
High season per wk
£650.00–£995.00

Froyz Hall Barn, Halstead

contact Mrs Judi Butler, Froyz Hall Farm, Halstead CO9 1RS
t (01787) 476684 **f** 07977 870138 **e** judibutler@dsl.pipex.com

open All year
payment Credit/debit cards, cash/cheques

Beautifully converted granary barn (2,500 sq ft) set on country estate two miles from Halstead, where you can enjoy swimming (in summer), tennis, woodland walks and fishing. This peaceful location is on the doorstep of Constable Country, and within easy reach of Cambridge and Colchester.

⊕ *From Halstead, A131 to Chelmsford. After leaving Halstead, follow bendy country roads until phone box on left. Continue for 0.25 miles, turn right into Froyz Hall Farm, drive to barn.*

Unit General P Leisure Shop 2 miles Pub 2 miles

HAUGHLEY, Suffolk Map ref 3B2

★★★
SELF CATERING

Units **3**
Sleeps **8**
Low season per wk
£225.00–£300.00
High season per wk
£300.00–£420.00

Cottage, Stowmarket

contact Mrs Mary Noy, Red House Farm, Stowmarket IP14 3QP
t (01449) 673323 **f** (01449) 675413 **e** mary-n@tiscali.co.uk

Delightful, well-equipped cottage adjoining farmhouse on small grassland farm. Ideal for exploring the many attractions in Suffolk, Norfolk and Essex.

open All year except Christmas and New Year
payment Credit/debit cards, cash/cheques

Unit General P Leisure Shop 1 mile Pub 1 mile

If you have access needs...

Look for the National Accessible Scheme symbols if you have special hearing, visual or mobility needs. An index of all accommodation participating in the scheme can be found at the back of this guide.

HEACHAM, Norfolk Map ref 3B1

★★
SELF CATERING

Units **4**
Sleeps **4**
Low season per wk
£85.00–£130.00
High season per wk
£130.00–£185.00

Cedar Springs Chalets, Heacham

contact Michael & Ann Chestney, The Street, West Raynham, Fakenham NR21 7EY
t (01328) 838341 **f** (01328) 838341 **w** tiscover.co.uk

Two-bedroomed chalets on quiet garden site 300yds from beach. Conservation Area of Outstanding Natural Beauty. Sandringham within six miles. Open 1 April to 30 September. No dogs, please.

payment Cash/cheques

Unit General P

HINGHAM, Norfolk Map ref 3B1

★★★
SELF CATERING

Units **1**
Sleeps **4**
Low season per wk
£190.00–£295.00
High season per wk
£295.00–£345.00

The Granary, Norwich

contact Mrs Dunnett, College Farm, Hingham, Norwich NR9 4PP
t (01953) 850596 **e** christine.dunnett@lineone.net

open All year
payment Cash/cheques

Tastefully converted 18thC granary. Peaceful location on small stud farm with pets galore. Very attractive, well-equipped accommodation with original oak beams throughout. Warm and cosy in winter. Perfect location to explore Norfolk.

⊕ *Take B1108 westwards, take 1st right signposted Shipdham and Cranworth. 1st right again signposted Southburgh. 3rd property on right round left-hand bend, set back from the road.*

♥ *3-night low-season breaks available for only £120.*

Unit General P Leisure Shop 1 mile Pub 1 mile

HOLME NEXT THE SEA, Norfolk Map ref 3B1

★★★★
SELF CATERING

Units **1**
Sleeps **6**
Low season per wk
£240.00–£300.00
High season per wk
£400.00–£680.00

Broadwater Cottage, Holme next the Sea, Hunstanton

contact Mrs Jayne Ransom, Vine Farm, 38 Church Street, Cambridge CB2 5DS
t (01223) 524821 **f** (01223) 524821 **e** vine.farm@ntlworld.com **w** broadwatercottage.co.uk

open All year
payment Cash/cheques

Comfortable flint, chalk and carrstone cottage in the village centre close to an excellent pub/restaurant with garden. The beach is a short walk across open fields and sand dunes with salt marshes beyond. Enclosed garden overlooking fields, conservatory and woodburner. One double, two twins, shower room and bathroom. Off-road parking.

⊕ *Off A149 between Hunstanton and Thornham. Take Peddars Way to centre of village, turn right and cottage is 50yds on the right, close to pub.*

♥ *Ideal for summer and winter. Discounts for off-season short breaks, long weekends and two-person occupancy. Pets by arrangement at additional cost.*

Unit General P Leisure Shop 3 miles Pub < 0.5 miles

Ancient and modern

Experience timeless favourites or discover the latest must-sees. Whatever your choice, be inspired by the places of interest highlighted for each region and the events listed towards the back of this guide.

HOLT, Norfolk Map ref 3B1

★★★
SELF CATERING

Units **1**
Sleeps **4**
Low season per wk
£215.00–£280.00
High season per wk
£325.00–£400.00

5 Carpenters Cottages, Holt

contact Mr Christopher Knights, The Hollies Farmhouse, Rushmere, Lowestoft NR33 8EP
t (01493) 842289 & (01502) 742022 **f** (01502) 742022

Attractive 18thC flint and pantile cottage with gravelled garden area, on the edge of a pleasant market town four miles from the coast. Open April to October and Christmas.

payment Cash/cheques

Unit General 5 P Shop < 0.5 miles Pub < 0.5 miles

HOLT, Norfolk Map ref 3B1

★★★★
SELF CATERING

Units **1**
Sleeps **4**
Low season per wk
£200.00–£300.00
High season per wk
£350.00–£400.00

Maple Cottage, Stody, Melton Constable

contact Mrs Stephanie Moore, Stody Cottage, Brinton Road, Stody, Melton Constable NR24 2ED
t (01263) 861590 **f** (01263) 862158 **e** maplecottage1@btinternet.com

Lovely, quiet cottage in idyllic village location, with gardens on three sides, off-road parking and garage, both bedrooms with en suites. Woodburner and central heating. Personally supervised. Pets by arrangement.

open All year
payment Cash/cheques

Unit General P Shop 1.5 miles Pub 1 mile

HORHAM, Suffolk Map ref 3B2

★★★
SELF CATERING

Units **2**
Sleeps **4–5**
Low season per wk
£216.00–£290.00
High season per wk
£496.00–£548.00

Alpha Cottages, Eye

Alpha Cottages, Lodge Farm, Horham, Eye IP21 5DX
t (01379) 384424 **f** (01379) 384424

open All year
payment Cash/cheques

Beautifully converted, well-equipped cottages in the heart of rural East Anglia. Fenced garden, patio with meadow and play equipment. Leisure facilities and good inns two miles. Welcome pack on arrival.

B1117 from Eye to Horham. Lodge Farm is 5 houses before church on left. Alpha Cottages are 50m to the right on farm drive.

Unit General P Shop < 0.5 miles Pub 2 miles

HUNSTANTON, Norfolk Map ref 3B1

★★★★
SELF CATERING

Units **1**
Sleeps **2–8**
Low season per wk
£295.00–£395.00
High season per wk
£625.00–£825.00

Blue Skies, Hunstanton

contact Ms Debbie Harrington, 45 Burrettgate Road, Walsoken, Wisbech PE14 7BN
t (01945) 588055 **f** (01945) 474397 **e** debs.harrington@btinternet.com
w hunstantonholidaycottages.co.uk

Spacious Victorian house in a peaceful, residential area between town and Old Hunstanton, only a five-minute walk from a beautiful sandy beach. Everything for a family holiday, including Sky TV.

open All year
payment Cash/cheques, euros

Unit General S Leisure Shop < 0.5 miles Pub 0.5 miles

Mention our name

Please mention this guide when making your booking.

HUNTSTANTON, Norfolk Map ref 3B1

★★★
SELF CATERING

Units 1
Sleeps 2
Low season per wk
Min £180.00
High season per wk
Max £280.00

Jaskville, Hunstanton

contact Mr John Smith, Jaskville, Hunstanton PE36 5BZ
t (01485) 533404 **w** tiscover.co.uk

The holiday flat is quietly situated within easy reach of the promenade and beach.

open All year except Christmas and New Year
payment Cash/cheques, euros

Unit General P

HUNSTANTON, Norfolk Map ref 3B1

★★★
SELF CATERING

Units 1
Sleeps 5
Low season per wk
£330.00–£400.00
High season per wk
£400.00–£465.00

Minna Cottage, Hunstanton

contact Mr Tony Cassie, Cassie's Restaurant, Hunstanton PE36 5AH
t (01485) 532448 **e** tonycassie@btconnect.com **w** minnacottage.com

This fully modernised coachman's cottage provides comfortable, private accommodation with views of The Wash. Convenient for shops, 200yds to beach.

open All year
payment Cash/cheques

Unit General P Leisure

HUNSTANTON, Norfolk Map ref 3B1

★★★
SELF CATERING

Units 1
Sleeps 2
Low season per wk
Min £200.00
High season per wk
Max £320.00

West Lodge, Hunstanton

contact Mrs Geraldine Tibbs, Cole Green Cottage, Cole Green, Sedgeford, Hunstanton PE36 5LS
t (01485) 571770 **f** (01485) 571770

Colonial-style gate cottage built in 1908 at the former entrance to Sedgeford Hall. Restored and furnished to a high standard. Garden and own parking area.

open All year
payment Cash/cheques

Unit General P Leisure Shop < 0.5 miles Pub < 0.5 miles

KELSALE, Suffolk Map ref 3C2

★★★★
SELF CATERING

Units 4
Sleeps 4–6
Low season per wk
£225.00–£355.00
High season per wk
£345.00–£665.00

East Green Farm Cottages, Saxmundham

contact Claire & Robbie Gawthrop, East Green Farm Cottages, Kelsale IP17 2PH
t (01728) 602316 **f** (01728) 604408 **e** claire@eastgreenproperty.co.uk **w** eastgreencottages.co.uk

open All year
payment Cash/cheques

Between Southwold and Aldeburgh and only two miles from the beautiful Heritage Coast. The Granary, The Old Stables, The Hayloft and The Dairy are charming, spacious, fully equipped, converted barns set in the grounds of a 500-year-old farmhouse. Thirteen acres of paddocks, tennis court and outdoor swimming pool. Tennis coaching available.

⊕ *From A12 take B1121 after Saxmundham to Kelsale. After 0.25 miles turn left into town. Continue until turning left into East Green. Farm is 2nd on left.*

♥ *Short breaks and weekends available from £165. Tennis weekends for groups.*

Unit General P Leisure Shop 2 miles Pub 2 miles

KERSEY, Suffolk Map ref 3B2

★★★★★
SELF CATERING

Units **1**
Sleeps **8**
Low season per wk
£260.00–£875.00
High season per wk
£570.00–£1,800.00

Old Drift House, Ipswich

contact Mrs Jill Black, 11 Poynings Close, Harpenden AL5 1JD
t (01582) 763533 **f** (01582) 763955 **e** ejblk@talk21.com **w** olddrifthouse.co.uk

open All year
payment Cash/cheques

15thC, Grade II Listed thatched cottage, beamed throughout, with inglenook fireplaces, bread oven and secluded garden with well – a quintessential 'chocolate-box' cottage. Set in the most picturesque village with ford and ducks by the pub. Access to Suffolk coast, Constable Country, Lavenham, Long Melford and Colchester.

⊕ *London: A12, B1070 to Hadleigh. Bury St Edmunds: A134 to Sudbury, A1071 to Hadleigh, A1141 signposted Lavenham. Kersey 1 mile on left, right past church, 1st left turn, 1st house left*

♥ *Short breaks available for 3 or 4 nights.*

Unit General P Leisure Shop 2 miles Pub < 0.5 miles

KESSINGLAND, Suffolk Map ref 3C1

★★★
SELF CATERING

Units **1**
Sleeps **4–5**
Low season per wk
£180.00–£190.00
High season per wk
£200.00–£260.00

Kew Cottage, Lowestoft

contact Mrs Joan Gill, 46 St Georges Avenue, Northampton NN2 6JA
t (01604) 717301 **f** (01604) 791424 **e** b.s.g@btinternet.com

payment Cash/cheques, euros

Modernised, two-bedroomed, semi-detached cottage in the middle of village, ten minutes' walk from the sea. Large back garden with patio and seating area. Norfolk Broads three miles, Lowestoft three miles, Southwold five miles, Norwich 30 miles.

⊕ *From A12 (London to Lowestoft) take signs for Kessingland. From Midlands, A14 to Bury St Edmunds, A143 (Beccles).*

Unit General P Shop < 0.5 miles Pub < 0.5 miles

LAVENHAM, Suffolk Map ref 3B2

★★★★★
SELF CATERING

Units **2**
Sleeps **2–4**
Low season per wk
£350.00–£460.00
High season per wk
£550.00–£740.00

Blaize Cottages, Sudbury

contact Mr & Mrs Jim & Carol Keohane, Blaize Cottages, Blaize House, Church Street, Sudbury CO10 9QT
t (01787) 247402 **f** (01787) 247402 **e** info@blaizecottages.com **w** blaizecottages.com

open All year
payment Credit/debit cards, cash/cheques

Enjoy England Excellence Awards 2005/2006: Top three Self-Catering Holiday of the Year. Blaize Barn and Lady Cottage are luxury cottages in the heart of Lavenham, England's finest medieval village. Within 200m of excellent pubs, restaurants and village shops. Sky TV, DVD library, large beds, baths, landscaped private gardens and luxury furnishings.

⊕ *Blaize Barn is tucked behind houses on Church Street, 20yds up in Bears Lane. Lady Cottage is located in Lady Street, which is behind the Swan.*

♥ *3-day weekend breaks or 4-day mid-week breaks throughout the year. Romantic breaks and gift vouchers available.*

Unit General 10 P Shop < 0.5 miles Pub < 0.5 miles

LAVENHAM, Suffolk Map ref 3B2

★★★
SELF CATERING

Units 1
Sleeps 2–6
Low season per wk
Min £275.00
High season per wk
Max £395.00

Old Wetherden Hall, Ipswich

contact Mrs Julie Elsden, Old Wetherden Hall, Hitcham IP7 7PZ
t (01449) 740574 **f** (01449) 740574 **e** julie.elsden@btconnect.com **w** oldwetherdenhall.co.uk

open All year
payment Cash/cheques

15thC oak-beamed house, enclosed moated site on arable farm. Beautiful, secluded setting, large garden, abundance of wildlife. Inglenook fireplace. Moat stocked with carp and other fish. Fishing available.

⊕ *Turn off B1115 at Hitcham White Horse. Then 1st left up hill, 1 mile on right set back from the road.*

Unit General P Leisure Shop 2 miles Pub 1 mile

LAVENHAM, Suffolk Map ref 3B2

★★★
SELF CATERING

Units 1
Sleeps 2
Low season per wk
£294.00–£322.00
High season per wk
£326.00–£364.00

The Rector's Retreat, Ipswich

contact Mr & Mrs Peter Gutteridge, The Rector's Retreat, The Old Convent, The Street, Kettlebaston, Ipswich IP7 7QA
t (01449) 741557 **e** holidays@kettlebaston.fsnet.co.uk **w** kettlebaston.fsnet.co.uk

open All year
payment Cash/cheques

Timber building within the curtilage of a Grade II Listed thatched cottage. Recently refurbished and renovated to provide wheelchair access. Complimentary basic provisions (milk/beverages and toiletries). The Retreat comprises a double bedroom with en suite shower, lounge/diner, kitchen, electric storage heaters. Electricity and linen included. Brochure available.

⊕ *Exit M25 jct 28 onto A12 (Ipswich); B1070 to Hadleigh; A1071, then B1115 (Stowmarket). At Hitcham turn left at White Horse and left again to Kettlebaston.*

♥ *Jun and Sep: 7 nights for £294. Minimum 3 nights' stay from £44 per couple, per night.*

Unit General P Leisure Shop 2 miles Pub 1 mile

LAXFIELD, Suffolk Map ref 3C2

★★★★
SELF CATERING

Units 1
Sleeps 1–5
Low season per wk
£200.00–£350.00
High season per wk
£360.00–£525.00

Meadow Cottage, Laxfield, Woodbridge

contact Mr William Ayers, Meadow Cottage Leisure, Quinton House, Laxfield IP13 8DN
t (01986) 798345 **f** (01986) 798345 **e** will.ayers@btinternet.com

open All year
payment Cash/cheques

Pretty Victorian cottage offering spacious accommodation in the centre of Laxfield. Ideal base for exploring Suffolk's Heritage Coast or the heart of Suffolk. Extremely well appointed, the cottage is cosy and comfortable all year round and overlooks peaceful meadowland. Two pubs/restaurants within 100yds.

⊕ *B1116 to Framlingham. Through Framlingham to Dennington. Left at B1117 to Harleston/Laxfield for 3 miles. Right at Les Cottons. Through High Street, cottage on right.*

♥ *First basket of logs for woodburner free from 1 Oct 2006 to 1 Apr 2007; further logs available from owner.*

Unit General P Leisure Shop < 0.5 miles
Pub < 0.5 miles

LITTLE BENTLEY, Essex Map ref 3B2

★★★★
SELF CATERING

Units 1
Sleeps 4

Low season per wk
£200.00–£295.00
High season per wk
£300.00–£400.00

Spring Hall Cottage, Colchester

contact Mrs Tricia Maestrani, Spring Hall, Little Bentley CO7 8SR
t (01206) 251619 & 07779 264679 **f** (01206) 251619 **e** triciamaestrani@hotmail.co.uk

open All year
payment Cash/cheques, euros

Grade II Listed, 17thC thatched cottage with a wealth of character and original features including exposed beams and inglenook fireplace. Two double bedrooms, double cart lodge, 0.33-acre enclosed garden, patio area and barbecue. Ideal location for Constable Country, Manningtree, historical Harwich/ Colchester and Essex coast. Excellent selection of pubs/restaurants nearby.

From Colchester, take A120 to Harwich. After approx 6 miles, take 2nd turning (signposted Little Bentley), then 1st right into Harwich Road. Property is 400yds on right.

Short breaks available (min 3 nights). Welcome pack and complimentary bottle of wine per couple for your enjoyment.

Unit General 5 P Leisure Shop 2 miles
Pub 0.5 miles

LITTLE SNORING, Norfolk Map ref 3B1

★★★★
SELF CATERING

Units 2
Sleeps 5–7

Low season per wk
Min £250.00
High season per wk
£580.00–£730.00

Jex Farm Barns, Fakenham

contact Mr Stephen Harvey, Jex Farm, Little Snoring, Fakenham NR21 0JJ
t (01328) 878257 & 07979 495760 **f** (01328) 878257 **e** farmerstephen@jexfarm.wanadoo.co.uk
w jefarm.co.uk

Recently converted detached barns with many traditional features, including wooden floors and beams. The barns have private gardens and enjoy a rural location. Close to the North Norfolk coast.

open All year
payment Cash/cheques

Unit General P Leisure Shop 0.5 miles
Pub 0.5 miles

LONG MELFORD, Suffolk Map ref 3B2

★★★★
SELF CATERING

Units 1
Sleeps 4

Low season per wk
Min £250.00
High season per wk
Max £400.00

Hope Cottage, Long Melford

contact Ms S Jamil, Hill Farm Cottage, Duffs Hill, Glemsford, Sudbury CO10 7PP
t (01787) 282338 & 07970 808701 **f** (01787) 282338 **e** sns.jam@tesco.net
w hope-cottage-suffolk.co.uk

open All year
payment Cash/cheques, euros

Delightful Grade II Listed flint cottage in the heart of this historic and picturesque village. Recently renovated, retaining many traditional features. Attractively furnished to high levels of comfort. Secluded garden backing onto meadowlands. All amenities in the village are close by, including restaurants and shops.

Leave A14 at Bury St Edmunds east. Take A134 to Sudbury, after approximately 15 miles take right turn into Long Melford village. End cottage in Park Terrace.

Short breaks available all year (subject to availability in high season).

Unit General P Leisure Shop < 0.5 miles Pub < 0.5 miles

What's in a quality rating?

Information about ratings can be found at the back of this guide.

LOWESTOFT, Suffolk Map ref 3C1

★
SELF CATERING

Units 1
Sleeps 2–4
Low season per wk
£125.00–£175.00
High season per wk
£250.00–£350.00

Marine House, Lowestoft

contact Mr & Mrs David & Teresa Conway, 416 Ashingdon Road, Rochford SS4 3EW
t (01702) 545495 **f** (01702) 542865 **e** davidfconway@hotmail.co.uk **w** 10marineparade.co.uk

Holiday flat overlooking the sea, close to all amenities. Lounge, bedroom, kitchen, shower, separate wc, reasonable rates, non-smoking, all-inclusive. Parking.

open All year
payment Cash/cheques, euros

Unit General 1 Shop < 0.5 miles Pub < 0.5 miles

LOWESTOFT, Suffolk Map ref 3C1

★★★★
SELF CATERING

Units 1
Sleeps 1–4
Low season per wk
Min £255.00
High season per wk
Max £480.00

Pippin Cottage, Lowestoft

contact Mr Ian Crocker, Somerton House, Lowestoft NR33 0BY
t (01502) 565665 **f** (01502) 501176 **e** somerton@screaming.net **w** pippin-cottage.co.uk

Pippin Cottage, c1749, is set in a secluded area with private parking. Oak beams, log stove, central heating. Close to South Beach. Summer or winter, Pippin has it all.

open All year
payment Credit/debit cards, cash/cheques

Unit General P Leisure Shop < 0.5 miles Pub < 0.5 miles

LOWESTOFT, Suffolk Map ref 3C1

★★★
SELF CATERING

Units 1
Sleeps 5
Low season per wk
£230.00–£250.00
High season per wk
£280.00–£370.00

Suffolk Seaside & Broadlands, Lowestoft

contact Mrs Collecott, 282 Gorleston Road, Oulton, Lowestoft NR32 3AJ
t (01502) 564396 **f** (01502) 564396

Beautifully furnished, well-equipped bungalow with conservatory, garden and garage. Two bedrooms, two bathrooms, sitting room, dining room and large, fully fitted kitchen.

open All year
payment Cash/cheques

Unit General P Leisure Shop 1 mile Pub < 0.5 miles

LYNG, Norfolk Map ref 3B1

★★★★
SELF CATERING

Units 1
Sleeps 5
Low season per wk
£265.00–£295.00
High season per wk
£330.00–£415.00

Utopia Paradise, Lyng, Norwich

contact Mrs Suzan Jarvis, The Mallards, Farman Close, Lyng, Norwich NR9 5RD
t (01603) 870812 **e** holidays@utopia-paradise.co.uk

open All year
payment Cash/cheques, euros

A traditional brick and flint cottage nestling beside a willow-clad, mixed coarse-fishing lake in the picturesque village of Lyng, 13 miles from Norwich. One double, one twin, one single. Linen, towels, fishing and electricity included. Shop, post office, pub, garage and public telephone are all within five minutes' walk.

⊕ *A47 Dereham to Norwich, slip road to North Tuddenham, right at T-junction, Lyng crossroads right, 2nd left, then left into Utopia Paradise Caravan Park. Cottage at top.*

❤ *Short breaks available Oct-Mar (excl Christmas and New Year).*

Unit General P Leisure

MIDDLETON, Suffolk Map ref 3C2

★★★★
SELF CATERING

Units **1**
Sleeps **2–6**
Low season per wk
£300.00–£370.00
High season per wk
£420.00–£470.00

The Cottage at Red Lodge Barn, Nr Saxmundham

contact Mrs Patricia Dowding, The Cottage at Red Lodge Barn, Middleton Moor, Middleton, Saxmundham IP17 3LN
t (01728) 668100 **f** (01728) 668100 **e** pat_roy16@hotmail.com **w** redlodgebarnsuffolk.co.uk

open All year
payment Cash/cheques, euros

Spacious, well-equipped accommodation, in an acre of grounds. Large, freshwater pond frequented by many birds. Full central heating and wood-burning stove. Many places of interest within easy reach. Five miles from Heritage Coast.

⊕ *From Yoxford on A12, take B1122 (signposted Leiston). Go over level crossing, and 1 mile on, just after 30mph and Middleton Moor sign, turn right after pond.*

❤ *Short breaks available (excl Aug), min 2 nights.*

Unit General 5 P Leisure Shop 1 mile Pub 1 mile

NAYLAND, Suffolk Map ref 3B2

★★★★–★★★★★
SELF CATERING

Units **9**
Sleeps **2–8**
Low season per wk
£260.00–£875.00
High season per wk
£570.00–£1,800.00

Gladwins Farm, Nayland

contact Mr Pauline Dossor, Gladwins Farm, Harpers Hill, Colchester CO6 4NU
t (01206) 262261 **f** (01206) 263001 **e** gladwinsfarm@aol.com **w** gladwinsfarm.co.uk

open All year
payment Credit/debit cards, cash/cheques

Extensive wooded grounds in Suffolk's rolling Constable Country with marvellous views make ours a wonderful location. Charming villages and gardens to explore – not far from the sea. Heated indoor pool, sauna, hot tub, tennis, fishing, animals and playground. Pets welcome. Chelsworth and Melford cottages have private hot tubs.

⊕ *From A12 take A133 to Colchester. Follow signs to A134 Sudbury. Nayland is 6 miles out. Entrance to farm approximately 800m past village.*

❤ *Short breaks Oct-Easter. 3-night weekends or 4-night mid-week breaks at 70% full-week rate.*

Unit General P Leisure Shop 0.5 miles
Pub < 0.5 miles

NORFOLK BROADS

See under Caister-on-Sea, Coltishall, Gorleston-on-Sea, Lowestoft, Norwich, Wroxham

NORWICH, Norfolk Map ref 3C1

★★★★
SELF CATERING

Units **1**
Sleeps **1–4**
Low season per wk
£250.00–£300.00
High season per wk
£300.00–£480.00

The Apartment at City Heights, Norwich

contact Mrs Susan Potter, 6 Stanley Avenue, Norwich NR7 0BE
t (01603) 700438 **e** sueno6p@aol.com **w** number-6.co.uk

open All year
payment Cash/cheques

New two-bedroom executive apartment within walking distance of the city centre, riverside inns and restaurants. Ultra-modern interior with new facilities.

⊕ *A47, signs for Norwich football ground. Go around Carrow Road Stadium, take right-hand lane round one-way system onto Yarmouth Road. City Heights left-hand side.*

Unit General P Leisure Shop 0.5 miles
Pub < 0.5 miles

NORWICH, Norfolk Map ref 3C1

★★★–★★★★
SELF CATERING

Units **8**
Sleeps **3–10**
Low season per wk
£250.00–£490.00
High season per wk
£330.00–£990.00

Spixworth Hall Cottages, Norwich

contact Mrs Sheelah Cook, Spixworth Hall Cottages, Buxton Road, Spixworth, Norwich NR10 3PR
t (01603) 898190 **f** (01603) 897176 **e** hallcottages@btinternet.com **w** hallcottages.co.uk

open All year
payment Credit/debit cards, cash/cheques, euros

These delightful cottages, situated in seclusion on our farm, are ideal for exploring Norwich, the Broads and coast. They have quality furnishings and equipment, log fires and attractive gardens. We offer a warm welcome, farm and woodland walks, swimming, tennis, fishing, a games barn and space to relax and unwind.

⊕ *A140 to Cromer. Right to Horsham St Faith after 2.5 miles. Right to Spixworth after church. Right at next junction. After pub on left, take farm track on right.*

❤ *3-night breaks Oct-Mar from £150. 4 nights for the price of 3, Mon-Thu. Snowdrop and bluebell walks.*

Unit General P Leisure
Shop 0.8 miles Pub < 0.5 miles

PELDON, Essex Map ref 3B3

★★★★
SELF CATERING

Units **1**
Sleeps **6**
Low season per wk
£250.00–£300.00
High season per wk
£350.00–£450.00

Rose Barn Cottage, Peldon, Colchester

contact Mrs Ariette Everett, Rose Barn, Mersea Road/Colchester Road, Peldon, Colchester CO5 7QJ
t (01206) 735317 **f** (01206) 735311 **e** everettaj@aol.com

Self-catering annexe to a converted barn-type property, set in four acres. Five Lakes Country Club golf ten minutes, Colchester ten minutes, beach five minutes. Brochure available.

open All year except Christmas and New Year
payment Cash/cheques, euros

Unit General P Leisure Shop 2 miles
Pub < 0.5 miles

PIN MILL, Suffolk Map ref 3C2

★★★
SELF CATERING

Units **1**
Sleeps **4**
Low season per wk
£230.00–£360.00
High season per wk
£350.00–£400.00

Alma Cottage, Ipswich

contact Mr John Pugh, Culver End, Stroud GL5 5AG
t (01453) 872551 **e** john.pugh@talk21.com

open All year
payment Cash/cheques, euros

Located in the centre of Pin Mill, 25m from high water with uninterrupted views over the unspoilt Orwell Estuary. Pin Mill is a traditional sailing village with free public access to water. The tidal estuary and the nearby coast are ideal for families, walkers, bird-watchers and painters.

⊕ *At jct A14 and A137 turn towards Ipswich. Next roundabout, B1456 towards Chelmondiston and Shotley. In Chelmondiston right to Pin Mill, at bottom of lane, last on right.*

Unit General P Leisure Shop 0.75 miles Pub < 0.5 miles

Phone ahead

Even the most ardent pet lover would appreciate some advance warning of Rover's visit, so please phone ahead and check what facilities will be available.

REDBOURN, Hertfordshire Map ref 2D1

★★★
SELF CATERING

Units **1**
Sleeps **3–4**
Low season per wk
£360.00–£410.00
High season per wk
£360.00–£410.00

The Beeches, St Albans

contact Mrs June Surridge, The Beeches, Hemel Hempstead Road, Redbourn, St Albans AL3 7AG
t (01582) 792638 **f** (01582) 792638

House set in acre of garden, with adjoining fields. Easy access to major shopping centre.

open All year
payment Cash/cheques

Unit General P Leisure Shop 1 mile Pub 1 mile

REDE, Suffolk Map ref 3B2

★★★★
SELF CATERING & SERVICED APARTMENTS

Units **2**
Sleeps **2–6**
Low season per wk
£225.00–£300.00
High season per wk
£500.00–£650.00

Rede Hall Farm Park, Bury St Edmunds

t (01284) 850695 **f** (01284) 850345 **e** oakley@soils.fsnet.co.uk **w** redehallfarmpark.co.uk

Ideal country retreat in old-fashioned farmyard. Jenny Wren has two double bedrooms and galleried twin room with its own sitting room. Nuthatch has two double en suite bedrooms and a sofa bed.

open All year
payment Cash/cheques

Unit General P Leisure Shop 2 miles Pub 2 miles

SAXMUNDHAM, Suffolk Map ref 3C2

★★★★
SELF CATERING

Units **1**
Sleeps **4**
Low season per wk
£350.00–£400.00
High season per wk
£450.00–£475.00

Rookery Park, Saxmundham

contact Mrs Eden McDonald, Rookery Park, Yoxford IP17 3HQ
t (01728) 668740 **f** (01728) 668102 **w** tiscover.co.uk

open All year except Christmas
payment Cash/cheques

Convenient Heritage Coast (Southwold, Dunwich, Minsmere, Snape, Aldeburgh) and rural Suffolk. Attractively furnished. Clean, spacious lounge/diner/kitchen (dishwasher, washing machine, dryer, microwave etc). One double, one twin. Large patio. Panoramic parkland views. Own grounds on 120-acre country estate. Linen, heating and lighting included. Parking.

⊕ *Rookery Park entrance by lodge cottage at junction of A12 and B1122. Through white gateway past lodge, tarmac drive, 1st big house on right. Ring bell.*

Unit General P Shop 0.5 miles Pub 0.5 miles

Check the maps

Colour maps at the front pinpoint all the cities, towns and villages where you will find accommodation entries in the regional sections. Pick your location and then refer to the place index at the back to find the page number.

SEDGEFORD, Norfolk Map ref 3B1

★★★★
SELF CATERING

Units **1**
Sleeps **8**
Low season per wk
£414.00–£511.00
High season per wk
£556.00–£673.00

Cobble Cottage, Sedgeford

Norfolk Country Cottages, Carlton House, Market Place, Reepham, Norwich NR10 4JJ
t (01603) 871872 **f** (01603) 870304 **e** info@norfolkcottages.co.uk
w norfolkcottages.co.uk/properties/841

open All year
payment Credit/debit cards, cash/cheques, euros

Sedgeford is close to both the sandy beaches of the North Norfolk Heritage Coast and the west-facing coastline of the Wash, and the RSPB reserves of Titchwell Marsh and Snettisham. Recently refurbished with two car-parking bays, parts of the cottage are thought to date from the late 1700s.

⊕ *Take A149 from King's Lynn, then B1454 towards Docking. Left onto gravel track 200yds past 30mph sign. Access to cottage at the rear.*

♥ *3- to 6-night stays available Oct-Apr (excl Bank Holidays and school half-terms) and sometimes from Apr-Oct.*

Unit General P Leisure Shop 2 miles
Pub < 0.5 miles

SHARRINGTON, Norfolk Map ref 3B1

★★★★
SELF CATERING

Units **1**
Sleeps **2–4**
Low season per wk
£230.00–£320.00
High season per wk
£375.00

Garden Cottage, Chequers, Sharrington

contact Mrs R M Kimmins, Chequers, Bale Road, Sharrington NR24 2PG
t (01263) 860308 **e** rosemary@kimmins1.wanadoo.co.uk **w** tiscover.co.uk

Super-comfortable conversion of 18thC building overlooking large, quiet garden of period private house. Convenient for Holt and North Norfolk coast. Double and twin rooms.

open All year except Christmas and New Year
payment Cash/cheques

Unit General 15 P Shop 1 mile Pub 3 miles

SIBTON, Suffolk Map ref 3C2

★★★★
SELF CATERING

Units **1**
Sleeps **1–5**
Low season per wk
£220.00–£370.00
High season per wk
£340.00–£540.00

Cardinal Cottage, Sibton, Saxmundham

contact Mr & Mrs Eric Belton, Cardinal Cottage, Pouy Street, Sibton, Saxmundham IP17 2JH
t (01728) 660111 **e** jan.belton@btinternet.com **w** cardinalcottageholidays.co.uk

open All year
payment Cash/cheques

Delightfully cosy, period, timber-framed cottage with spectacular beams. Three bedrooms, sitting room, dining room, kitchen and bathroom, all fully equipped to high standard. Enclosed private garden with car park. Close Heritage Coast, Minsmere, Aldeburgh and Southwold. Ideal base for walkers and bird-watchers, or those after a quiet country retreat.

⊕ *From A12 at Yoxford, A1120 to Peasenhall. Through Yoxford into Sibton. At signposted nursery school turn right, over junction to right-hand bend. Cardinal Cottage on left.*

♥ *3- and 4-night breaks available Nov-Mar (excl Christmas, New Year and Easter).*

Unit General P Leisure Shop 0.75 miles
Pub < 0.5 miles

Confirm your booking

It's always advisable to confirm your booking in writing.

SOUTH MIMMS, Hertfordshire Map ref 2D1

★★–★★★
SELF CATERING

Units **3**
Sleeps **2–6**
Low season per wk
£210.00–£260.00
High season per wk
£240.00–£300.00

The Black Swan, Potters Bar

contact Mr Marsterson, The Black Swan, Blanche Lane, Potters Bar EN6 3PD
t (01707) 644180 **f** (01707) 642344

Cottage and self-contained flats, 16thC listed building. Rail connections at Potters Bar and London Underground at Barnet allow travel to London within 45 minutes.

open All year
payment Cash/cheques

Unit General **P** Shop < 0.5 miles Pub < 0.5 miles

SOUTHWOLD, Suffolk Map ref 3C2

★★★
SELF CATERING

Units **1**
Sleeps **6**
Low season per wk
£340.00–£420.00
High season per wk
£440.00–£650.00

11 Chester Road, Southwold

contact H A Adnams, 98 High Street, Southwold IP18 6DP
t (01502) 723292 **f** (01502) 724794 **w** haadnams.com

Three-bedroom house close to beach and shops. Small patio at rear. Outlook to lighthouse. Two double beds and two full-size bunk beds.

open All year
payment Cash/cheques

Unit General **P** Leisure Shop < 0.5 miles Pub < 0.5 miles

SOUTHWOLD, Suffolk Map ref 3C2

★★★
SELF CATERING

Units **1**
Sleeps **1–6**
Low season per wk
Min £400.00
High season per wk
Max £800.00

15 Stradbroke Road, Southwold

contact H A Adnams, 89 High Street, Southwold IP18 6DP
t (01502) 723292 **f** (01502) 724794 **w** haadnams.com

A delightful family house, sympathetically modernised to a high standard. Situated close to the sea and within easy reach of the shops and town centre. Strictly non-smoking.

open All year
payment Credit/debit cards

Unit General **P** Leisure Shop < 0.5 miles Pub < 0.5 miles

SOUTHWOLD, Suffolk Map ref 3C2

★★★★
SELF CATERING

Units **1**
Sleeps **1–3**
Low season per wk
£180.00–£190.00
High season per wk
£300.00–£350.00

The Cottage, Southwold

contact Mr Thomas, 2 Pier Court, Pier Avenue, Southwold IP18 6BL
t (01502) 723561

Lounge/diner, one twin and one single bedroom, bathroom, cloakroom, radio and TV/video. Fully fitted kitchen with washer/drier, fridge, freezer and microwave.

open All year
payment Cash/cheques

Unit General 5 **P** Shop < 0.5 miles Pub < 0.5 miles

Place index

If you know where you want to stay the index at the back of the guide will give you the page number which lists accommodation in your chosen town, city or village. Check out the other useful indexes too.

SOUTHWOLD, Suffolk Map ref 3C2

★★★
SELF CATERING

Units **1**
Sleeps **6**
Low season per wk
Min £467.00
High season per wk
Min £798.00

Fisherman's Cottage, Southwold

contact H A Adnams, 98 High Street, Southwold IP18 6DP
t (01502) 723292 **f** (01502) 724794

open All year
payment Cash/cheques

Bright, cosy, terraced cottage 100yds from Southwold beach. Two reception rooms plus dining room. Three bedrooms (two double, one twin), one with en suite shower and wc. Small bathroom with full-size bath, separate shower and wc. Wood-burning stoves in two bedrooms, both reception rooms and dining room.

Unit General Shop < 0.5 miles Pub < 0.5 miles

SOUTHWOLD, Suffolk Map ref 3C2

★★★★
SELF CATERING

Units **2**
Sleeps **1–6**
Low season per wk
£190.00–£250.00
High season per wk
£320.00–£450.00

Poplar Hall, Southwold

contact Mrs Anna Garwood, Poplar Hall, Frostenden, Nr Southwold NR34 7JA
t (01502) 578549 **w** southwold.ws/poplar-hall

open All year
payment Cash/cheques

Excellent self-catering accommodation in the grounds of 16thC thatched Poplar Hall, surrounded by quiet lanes, woods, meadows and secluded beaches. The Cottage (with double bedroom) and Lofthouse (with a double and twin) are characterful and welcoming, fully equipped and tastefully and comfortably decorated. Private gardens/patio, private parking close to units.

⊕ *A12 to Wangford, after 0.5 miles past garage and Plough Inn on left. Right to Frostenden/South Cove. Keep left fork for 0.5 miles. We are on left, past the green.*

❤ *Off-peak, 3- or 4-day short breaks available throughout the year (excl Bank Hols).*

Unit General P Leisure Shop 1.5 miles Pub 1.5 miles

SOUTHWOLD, Suffolk Map ref 3C2

★★★
SELF CATERING

Units **1**
Sleeps **4–6**
Low season per wk
£240.00–£305.00
High season per wk
£320.00–£530.00

Weavers Cottage, Southwold

contact H A Adnams, 98 High Street, Southwold IP18 6DP
t (01502) 723292 **f** (01502) 724794 **e** haadnams-sales@ic24.net **w** haadnams.com

open All year
payment Cash/cheques

Charming semi-detached cottage, well furnished and equipped with very comfortable rooms and patio area with seating. Located in an idyllic spot in a private road (parking available) leading onto the common and golf course. Lovely scenery and walks. Five minutes' walk to beach, pubs and shops. Many places of interest nearby.

⊕ *Follow signs to Southwold and Reydon from A12. Through Reydon over Mights Bridge. Up Station Road into high street. Right (before King's Head pub) into Spinners Lane.*

❤ *Short breaks available Nov-end Mar.*

Unit General Leisure Shop < 0.5 miles Pub < 0.5 miles

THETFORD, Norfolk Map ref 3B2

Rating Applied For
SELF CATERING

Units **1**
Sleeps **6**
Low season per wk
£250.00–£350.00
High season per wk
£350.00–£500.00

Forest Lodge Holidays, Santon Downham, Brandon

contact Mr & Mrs Jeff & Hannah Hibbs, Little Lodge Farm, Brandon IP27 0TX
t (01842) 813438 **e** info@littlelodgefarm.co.uk **w** littlelodgefarm.co.uk

Forest log cabin overlooking meadows and river, set in Thetford forest. One double, en suite bedroom, one twin bedroom, plus sofa beds.

open All year
payment Cash/cheques

Unit General P Leisure Shop 2 miles Pub 3 miles

THORNHAM, Norfolk Map ref 3B1

★★
SELF CATERING

Units **1**
Sleeps **5**
Low season per wk
£200.00–£280.00
High season per wk
£320.00–£450.00

Malthouse Cottages, Thornham, Hunstanton

contact Mrs Leslie Rigby, Brindle Cottage, Castor PE5 7AU
t (01733) 380399 **f** (01733) 380399 **e** leslierigby@castor.freeserve.co.uk

Charming, traditional Norfolk cottage with open fire in lovely coastal village with three pubs and beautiful beach. Area renowned for sailing, walking, bird-watching and golfing. Two double rooms and put-u-up.

open All year
payment Cash/cheques

Unit General Leisure Shop < 0.5 miles

THORPENESS, Suffolk Map ref 3C2

★★★
SELF CATERING

Units **1**
Sleeps **12**
Low season per wk
£1,900.00–£2,400.00
High season per wk
£2,600.00–£2,900.00

House in the Clouds, Thorpeness

contact Mrs Le Comber, The House in the Clouds, 4 Hinde House, 14 Hinde Street, London W1U 3BG
t (020) 7224 3615 **f** (020) 7224 3615 **e** houseintheclouds@btopenworld.com
w houseintheclouds.co.uk

open All year
payment Cash/cheques

A true family holiday in this wonderfully eccentric 'fantasy unmatched in England'. The House in the Clouds has five bedrooms, three bathrooms and unrivalled views from the 'Room at the Top'. Play billiards, snooker, table tennis, tennis and boules. Overlooking sea, golf course and Meare. Bird-watching on RSPB reserves.

⊕ *From A12 take A1094 to Aldeburgh, turn left at seafront. Continue for 2 miles to Thorpeness. 1st left (private road and golf club), entrance opposite windmill.*

Unit General P Leisure Shop 0.5 miles
Pub 0.5 miles

WELLS-NEXT-THE-SEA, Norfolk Map ref 3B1

★★★
SELF CATERING

Units **1**
Sleeps **1–4**
Low season per wk
£220.00–£300.00
High season per wk
£330.00–£450.00

14 Church Street, Wells-next-the-Sea

contact Mrs Rita Piesse, Convent House, 1 Longwater Lane, Costessey, Norwich NR8 5AH
t (01603) 744233 **e** randjp2004@yahoo.com

Detached house with garage and garden. Two bedrooms with double beds, upstairs bathroom. Lounge/diner, electric or solid fuel heating, TV/VCR. Kitchen with electric cooker, fridge/freezer, microwave. Bicycles.

open All year
payment Cash/cheques

Unit General P Leisure Shop < 0.5 miles Pub < 0.5 miles

WELLS-NEXT-THE-SEA, Norfolk Map ref 3B1

★★★
SELF CATERING

Units **1**
Sleeps **7**
Low season per wk
£360.00–£490.00
High season per wk
£410.00–£500.00

Harbour Cottage, Wells-next-the-Sea

contact Mr & Mrs Simon & Trish Jackson, 233 Melton Road, Edwalton NG12 4DB
t (0115) 923 4545 **f** (0115) 923 4545 **e** simonjackson@btinternet.com **w** harbourcottagewells.co.uk

open All year
payment Cash/cheques, euros

Charming, traditional, 180-year-old three-bedroom luxury home, sensitively refurbished to a high standard. Lounge with log-burner, cloakroom off, modern oak dining kitchen. Rear bedrooms and bathroom have fabulous sea views. Attractive south-facing patio garden. Close to all amenities. Ideal for families wishing to walk, bird-watch or just relax.

⊕ *From A149 take signs to Wells quay. Cottage is located down private lane next to Wells Tandoori, opposite Ark Royal pub.*

♥ *Short stays available Oct-Feb (excl Christmas and New Year). Last-minute bookings sometimes available – contact owners for details.*

Unit General Leisure Shop < 0.5 miles Pub < 0.5 miles

WELLS-NEXT-THE-SEA, Norfolk Map ref 3B1

★★★
SELF CATERING

Units **1**
Sleeps **4**
Low season per wk
£250.00–£450.00

Honeypot Cottage, Wells-next-the-Sea

contact Mrs Joan Price, Shingles, Wells-next-the-Sea NR23 1HG
t (01328) 711982 **f** (01328) 711982 **e** walker.al@talk21.com **w** wells-honeypot.co.uk

Honeypot Cottage offers comfortable accommodation on the picturesque North Norfolk coast, with quaint shopping streets and harbour within easy walking distance. Ideally situated for bird-watching, walking, sightseeing etc.

open All year
payment Cash/cheques

Unit General P

WEYBOURNE, Norfolk Map ref 3B1

★★★-★★★★
SELF CATERING

Units **7**
Sleeps **2–7**
Low season per wk
£186.00–£565.00
High season per wk
£366.00–£755.00

Home Farm Cottages, Weybourne

contact Mrs Sally Middleton, Home Farm, Holt Road, Weybourne, Holt NR25 7ST
t (01263) 588334 **e** sallymiddleton@virgin.com **w** weybourne-holiday-cottages.co.uk

open All year
payment Cash/cheques

Converted flint barn cottages and houses built in traditional flint style situated on edge of village and small, working, arable farm. New indoor heated pool, games room, play area, laundry facilities, ample off-road parking. The owners live on site and can resolve any problems and share local knowledge. Some ground-floor bedrooms and showers/toilets.

⊕ *A148 to Holt. Go through town centre, passing garage. 2nd left to Weybourne and follow for 3 miles. Home Farm is the 1st farm on the left.*

Unit General P S Leisure U Shop < 0.5 miles
Pub < 0.5 miles

Using map references

The map references refer to the colour maps at the front of this guide. The first figure is the map number; the letter and figure that follow indicate the grid reference on the map.

WICKHAM SKEITH, Suffolk Map ref 3B2

★★★
SELF CATERING

Units **1**
Sleeps **1–4**
Low season per wk
£195.00–£235.00
High season per wk
£250.00–£270.00

The Netus Barn, Wickham Skeith, Eye

contact Mrs Joy Homan, Street Farm, Eye IP23 8LP
t (01449) 766275 **e** joygeoff@homansf.freeserve.co.uk

Single-storey period barn, well-equipped kitchen-cum-living room, bathroom (shower), two twin bedrooms, disabled friendly, parking, patio garden. Rural views. Dogs welcome.

open All year
payment Cash/cheques

Unit General Leisure Shop 2 miles Pub 2 miles

WOODBRIDGE, Suffolk Map ref 3C2

★★★
SELF CATERING

Units **1**
Sleeps **4**
Low season per wk
£220.00–£250.00
High season per wk
£270.00–£350.00

The Coach House, Framsden

contact Ms Nicola Deller, Hill House, Mill Hill, Framsden IP14 6HB
t (01473) 890891 **e** nicoladeller@yahoo.com

open All year
payment Cash/cheques

In glorious Suffolk countryside, in front of Framsden windmill. Close to many walks/attractions and within easy reach of the coast (30 minutes) and historic market towns. Exceptionally spacious, clean, warm and well equipped. Modern kitchen with washer/dryer. Lovely views. Shared garden. Short walk to village pub. Grocery delivery by arrangement.

A14 to A140 – follow signs to Diss. At junction with A1120 'Tourist Route', right towards Yoxford. After 5 miles, right onto B1077. We are on left by windmill.

Unit General Leisure Shop 3 miles Pub 0.5 miles

WOODBRIDGE, Suffolk Map ref 3C2

★★★★
SELF CATERING

Units **6**
Sleeps **2–8**
Low season per wk
£254.00–£414.00
High season per wk
£484.00–£750.00

Windmill Lodges, Woodbridge

Windmill Lodges Ltd, Windmill Lodges Holidays, Saxtead, Woodbridge IP13 9RD
t (01728) 685338 **f** (01728) 684850 **e** holidays@windmilllodges.co.uk **w** windmilllodges.co.uk

open All year
payment Credit/debit cards, cash/cheques

Cosy log cabins nestled around our small, private fishing lake in beautiful countryside. Each lodge is extremely well equipped and features a secluded outdoor hot tub to relax in! Guests have use of our covered, heated swimming pool. Village location within walking distance of pub. Close to coast and attractions.

Turn off A1120 in the centre of Saxtead Green towards Tannington/Worlingworth. Entrance is directly in front of you on the 1st bend.

Off-peak short breaks available (weekend – 3 nights, or mid-week – 4 nights).

Unit General Leisure Shop 3 miles
Pub 0.5 miles

Best foot forward

Walkers feel at home in accommodation participating in our Walkers Welcome scheme. Look out for the symbol. Consider walking all or part of a long-distance route – go online at nationaltrail.co.uk.

WROXHAM, Norfolk Map ref 3C1

★★★★
SELF CATERING

Units **6**
Sleeps **2–6**
Low season per wk
£270.00–£580.00
High season per wk
£670.00–£893.00

Old Farm Cottages, Tunstead, Nr Wroxham

contact Mrs Kay Paterson, Old Farm Cottages, Tunstead, Norwich NR12 8HS
t (01692) 536612 **e** kay@oldfarmcottages.fsnet.co.uk **w** oldfarmcottages.com

payment Cash/cheques

Beautifully furnished cottage barn conversions, providing outstandingly comfortable and well-appointed accommodation. Indoor swimming pool, spa, fitness room, play area and games room. Perfectly situated for coast, countryside, riverside pubs, boat/canoe hire, stately homes and Norwich. Closed 18 November to 22 December, open Christmas and New Year. Closed 6 January to 10 February.

⊕ *A1151 through Wroxham. After 4 miles branch left, signposted Dilham. Left at crossroad and follow this road until you come to Old Farm Cottages.*

♥ *See website.*

Unit General **P** Leisure
Shop 1.5 miles Pub 1.5 miles

Country ways

The Countryside Rights of Way Act gives people new rights to walk on areas of open countryside and registered common land.

To find out where you can go and what you can do, as well as information about taking your dog to the countryside, go online at countrysideaccess.gov.uk.

And when you're out and about...

Always follow the Country Code

- Be safe – plan ahead and follow any signs
- Leave gates and property as you find them
- Protect plants and animals, and take your litter home
- Keep dogs under close control
- Consider other people

London

Including Greater London

Lose yourself in the romance of Tate Modern

Visit London
6th Floor, 2 More London Riverside
London SE1 2RR
(020) 7234 5800
visitlondon.com

sensational, refreshing, historic and contemporary

Main Feel the drama at The Lion King **Left** Admire canal boats in Little Venice; absorb untold ancient history at The British Museum; feel a chill as you walk through the Tower of London; choose from unrivalled variety at Borough Market

Enjoy the culture, the sights and the entertainment of one of the most lively and cosmopolitan cities in the world, **or take the chance to explore its greener corners.**

Explore London

History in the making

Take a ferry along the Thames and race to the centre of the maze at the magnificent red-bricked Hampton Court Palace. Marvel at the Crown Jewels and feel a chill run down your spine as you walk the grounds of the Tower of London. Many a nobleman suffered at the hands of the high executioner – can you still hear their screams?

Head to the Museum in Docklands and absorb 2,000 years of the city's remarkable history, sign up for a guided tour of the docks and hear echoes of the past when the Thames was alive with bustling trade. Take a ride above the city on the British Airways London Eye for a capital view and pick out your favourite landmarks, then step into the London Aquarium and witness divers hand-feeding rays and sharks amid the colourful marine life.

Markets and museums

Discover the many markets London has to offer and get a feel for the diversity of the city. At Borough Market your taste buds will tingle at the sight of the eclectic selection of foods from all corners of the globe. Snap up a bargain at the world's largest antiques market on Portobello Road, or have your palm read at Camden Lock and browse the colourful stalls at the Stables Market. A trip to London wouldn't be complete without venturing into the Harrods Food Hall and seeing the delectable and flavoursome wares, or wandering through the bustling crowds on Oxford Street.

Enjoy a calming day out discovering museums at your leisure. Allow yourself to be swept off your feet at Tate Modern, where the passionate embrace of The Kiss by Rodin is enough to make the coolest of hearts flutter. Try the Science Museum and keep the kids amused at Launch Pad and head to the Natural History Museum to inspect the impressive dinosaurs.

The grass is greener

Relax with a picnic in one of London's many parks. Spot the roaming deer in Richmond Park, don your swimmers and take a dip in the pond at Hampstead Heath, or take in a play at the Open Air Theatre, Regents Park.

Give the kids a treat and visit London Wetland Centre in Barnes to admire the spectacular and rare breeds of bird life wandering the grounds. Make a day of it at London Zoo where you can discover far-off climates at the new exhibit Into Africa and be dazzled by the flitting colours throughout Butterfly Paradise.

The main event

Seek out one of the many theatres in the nearby West End, or enjoy a play at Shakespeare's Globe – described as 'the beating heart of theatrical London'. With no end of variety, from musicals to Chekhov, and the famous to the little known, there is something to entertain everyone.

Places to **visit**

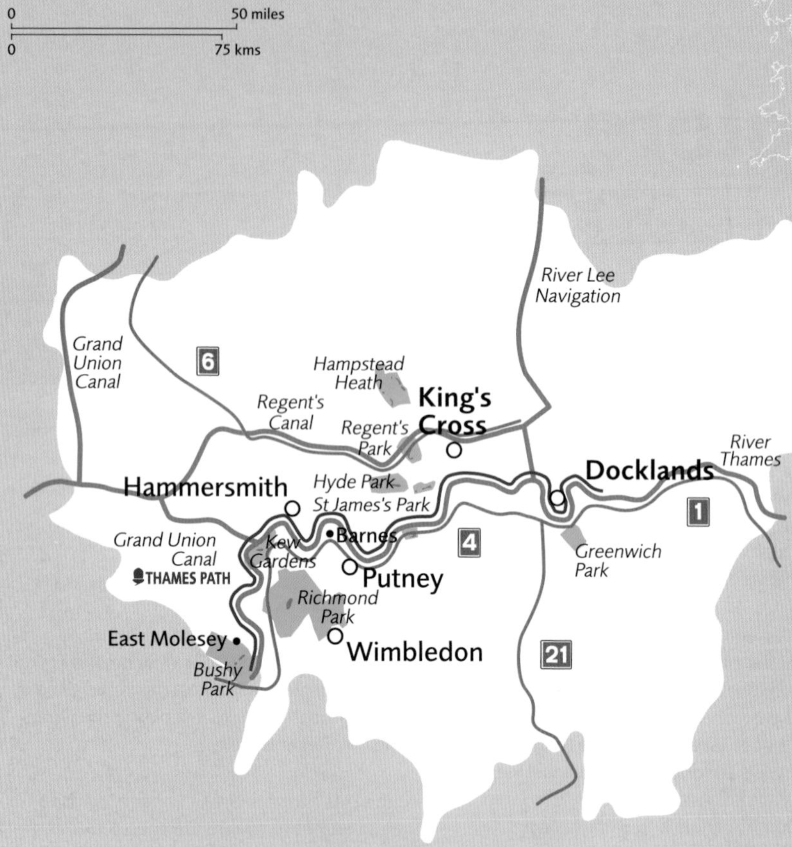

Grand Union Canal
6
River Lee Navigation
Hampstead Heath
King's Cross
Regent's Canal
Regent's Park
River Thames
Docklands
Hammersmith
Hyde Park
St James's Park
1
Grand Union Canal
Kew Gardens
Barnes
4
Greenwich Park
THAMES PATH
Putney
Richmond Park
East Molesey
Wimbledon
21
Bushy Park

National Trails
nationaltrail.co.uk

3 Sections of the National Cycle Network
nationalcyclenetwork.org.uk

British Airways London Eye
0870 500 0600
ba-londoneye.com
View the capital from above

The British Museum
London
(020) 7323 8299
thebritishmuseum.ac.uk
Outstanding and famous exhibits

Buckingham Palace
London
(020) 7766 7300
royalcollection.org.uk
The Queen's official London residence

Cabinet War Rooms and Churchill Museum

London
(020) 7930 6961
iwm.org.uk
Preserved rooms and fascinating exhibition detailing the former Prime Minister's term

Cutty Sark Clipper Ship
London
(020) 8858 3445
cuttysark.org.uk
Climb aboard the world's last and most famous tea-clipper ever built

Hampton Court Palace

East Molesey,
Greater London
0870 752 7777
hrp.org.uk
Outstanding Tudor palace with famous maze

Kew Gardens (Royal Botanic Gardens)

Greater London
(020) 8332 5655
kew.org
Stunning vistas and magnificent glasshouses

London Aquarium
(020) 7967 8000
londonaquarium.co.uk
Come face to face with zebra sharks

The London Dungeon
(020) 7403 7221
thedungeons.com
Gruesome British events re-enacted

London Wetland Centre

Barnes, Greater London
(020) 8409 4400
wwt.org.uk
Observe wildlife in recreated natural habitats

London Zoo
(020) 7722 3333
londonzoo.co.uk
Walk-through enclosures and beautiful gardens

Madame Tussauds and the London Planetarium
0870 400 3000
madame-tussauds.com
Spot many a famous face

Museum in Docklands
London
0870 444 3857
museumindocklands.org.uk
Learn the history of London

Natural History Museum
London
(020) 7942 5000
nhm.ac.uk
Highlighting the earth's natural treasures

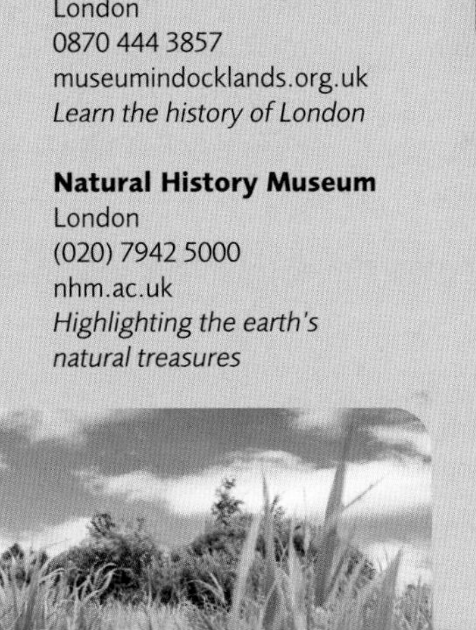

Royal Observatory Greenwich
London
(020) 8858 4422
nmm.ac.uk
Treat yourself to a guided tour and explore the history of astronomy and time

Science Museum
London
0870 870 4868
sciencemuseum.org.uk
With fantastic interactive features at Launch Pad

Shakespeare's Globe Exhibition and Tour
London
(020) 7902 1500
shakespeares-globe.org
A fascinating introduction to William Shakespeare's London

St Paul's Cathedral
London
(020) 7246 8357
stpauls.co.uk
Sir Christopher Wren's stunning masterpiece

Tate Modern
London
(020) 7887 8008
tate.org.uk
The UK's largest modern art gallery

Tower of London
0870 756 6060
hrp.org.uk
Resting place of the Crown Jewels, with a tortured history

Tourist information centres 

When you arrive at your destination, visit a tourist information centre for help with accommodation and information about local attractions and events, or email your request before you go.

Bexley (Hall Place)	Bourne Road	(01322) 558676	hallplaceshoptic@tiscali.co.uk
Britain & London Visitor Centre	1 Regent Street		blvcinfo@visitbritain.org
Croydon	Katharine Street	(020) 8253 1009	tic@croydon.gov.uk
Greenwich	2 Cutty Sark Gardens	0870 608 2000	tic@greenwich.gov.uk
Harrow	Station Road	(020) 8424 1102	info@harrow.gov.uk
Hillingdon	14-15 High Street	(01895) 250706	libraryinfoteam@hillingdongrid.org
Hounslow	High Street	0845 456 2929	tic@cip.org.uk
Kingston	Market Place	(020) 8547 5592	tourist.information@rbk.kingston.gov.uk
Lewisham	199-201 Lewisham High Street	(020) 8297 8317	tic@lewisham.gov.uk
Richmond	Whittaker Avenue	(020) 8940 9125	info@visitrichmond.co.uk
Southwark	1 Bank End	(020) 7357 9168	tourisminfo@southwark.gov.uk
Swanley	London Road	(01322) 614660	touristinfo@swanley.org.uk
Twickenham	44 York Street	(020) 8891 7272	info@visitrichmond.co.uk
Waterloo International	Arrivals Hall	(020) 7620 1550	london.visitorcentre@iceplc.com

Alternatively, you can text **TIC LOCATE** to **64118** to find your nearest tourist information centre

Find out **more**

By logging on to **visitlondon.com** or calling **0870 1 LONDON** for the following:

› **A London tourist information pack**

› **Tourist information on London**
Speak to an expert for information and advice on museums, galleries, attractions, riverboat trips, sightseeing tours, theatre, shopping, eating out and much more! Or simply visit www.visitlondon.com.

› **Accommodation reservations**

Or visit one of London's tourist information centres listed above.

Which part of London?

The majority of tourist accommodation is situated in the central parts of London and is therefore very convenient for most of the city's attractions and nightlife.

However, there are many establishments in Outer London which provide other advantages, such as easier parking. In the accommodation pages which follow, you will find establishments listed under INNER LONDON (covering the E1 to W14 London Postal Area) and OUTER LONDON (covering the remainder of Greater London). Colour maps 6 and 7 at the front of the guide show place names and London postal area codes and will help you to locate accommodation in your chosen area.

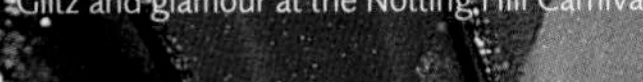

Glitz and glamour at the Notting Hill Carnival

Travel **info**

By road:
Major trunk roads into London include: A1, M1, A5, A10, A11, M11, A13, A2, M2, A23, A3, M3, A4, M4, A40, M40, A41, M25 (London orbital).

Transport for London is responsible for running London's bus services, the underground rail network and the DLR (Docklands Light Railway) and river services. (020) 7222 1234 (24-hour telephone service; calls answered in rotation).

By rail:
Main rail terminals: Victoria/Waterloo/Charing Cross – serving the South/South East; King's Cross – serving the North East; Euston – serving the North West/Midlands; Liverpool Street – serving the East; Paddington – serving the Thames Valley/West.

By air:
Fly into London City, London Gatwick, London Heathrow, London Luton and London Stansted.

where to stay in
London

All place names in the blue bands are shown on the maps at the front of this guide.

A complete listing of all Enjoy England assessed accommodation covered by this guide appears at the back.

Accommodation symbols
Symbols give useful information about services and facilities. Inside the back-cover flap you can find a key to these symbols. Keep it open for easy reference.

INNER LONDON

LONDON E1

★★★
SELF CATERING

Units **4**
Sleeps **4–6**
Low season per wk
£540.00–£720.00
High season per wk
£595.00–£775.00

Hamlet UK, St Katharine Docks, Tower Hill, London
contact Ms Renata Naufal, Hamlet UK, 47 Willian Way, Letchworth SG6 2HJ
t (01462) 678037 **f** (01462) 679639 **e** hamlet_uk@globalnet.co.uk **w** hamletuk.com

open All year
payment Credit/debit cards, cash/cheques, euros

Friendly and personal service. Very attractive surroundings. Comfortable and clean accommodation close to public transport, supermarket, the Tower of London, Tower Bridge and the ExCeL exhibition centre. Fully fitted kitchen, full bathroom, linen and towels provided, TV, direct-dial phone, wireless broadband connection, washer/dryer, off-street parking. See guests' feedback on our website.

⊕ *Take the A13 off the A406 towards Whitechapel and Tower Bridge. Follow signs to St Katharine Docks.*

❤ *Discounted last-minute and long-term lets.*

Unit General P Shop < 0.5 miles Pub < 0.5 miles

LONDON E14

★★★★★
SELF CATERING

Units **1**
Sleeps **1–4**
Low season per wk
Min £770.00
High season per wk
Min £833.00

Bridge House, London
contact Mr John Graham, 31 Falcon Way, London E14 9UP
t 07973 857187 **e** john@johnkgraham.com **w** johnkgraham.com

Two-bedroomed luxury house. Spectacular waterside location in a tranquil oasis in the heart of Docklands. Sunny waterside garden and master bedroom with balcony over the water. Direct-dial telephone and wireless broadband.

open All year
payment Credit/debit cards, cash/cheques, euros

Unit General P S Leisure Shop < 0.5 miles Pub < 0.5 miles

Key to symbols
Open the back flap for a key to symbols.

LONDON N7

★★★
SELF CATERING

Units **2**
Sleeps **1–5**
Low season per wk
£300.00–£500.00
High season per wk
£350.00–£550.00

Carena Holiday Apartments, London

contact Mr M Chouthi, 98 St George's Avenue, London N7 0AH
t (020) 7607 7453 **f** (020) 7607 7453 **e** deo.chouthi@btopenworld.com **w** carena-apartments.co.uk

Situated in quiet road. Comfortable apartments with a range of quality facilities and services. Easy access to central London. Dishwasher and laundry room in one unit. The apartments are non-smoking.

open All year
payment Cash/cheques

Unit General 10 Shop < 0.5 miles Pub < 0.5 miles

LONDON SE10

★★★★
SELF CATERING

Units **1**
Sleeps **1–4**
Low season per wk
£595.00–£665.00
High season per wk
£595.00–£665.00

Harbour Master's House, London

contact Prof Chris French, 20 Ballast Quay, London SE10 9PD
t (020) 8293 9597 **e** harbourmaster@lineone.net **w** http://website.lineone.net/~harbourmaster

Superb self-contained flat, part of the historic Harbour Master's House (Grade II Listed). Situated on attractive riverside enclave on the Thames in maritime Greenwich.

open All year
payment Cash/cheques

Unit General P Shop 0.5 miles Pub < 0.5 miles

LONDON SW3

★★★★
SELF CATERING

Units **42**
Sleeps **2–6**
Low season per wk
£746.00–£1,645.00
High season per wk
£746.00–£1,645.00

The Apartments, London

contact Ms Maureen Boyle, 'The Apartments', Panorama Property Services Ltd, The Garage, 22 Queensgate Place Mews, London SW7 5BQ
t (020) 7589 3271 **f** (020) 7589 3274 **e** sales@theapartments.co.uk **w** theapartments.co.uk

open All year
payment Credit/debit cards, cash/cheques

A selecton of elegant, serviced studios and one- to two-bedroom apartments housed in prestigious Victorian buildings. Individually designed with a full range of modern amenities including broadband Internet access, for the discerning, independent traveller. The apartments offer you a unique, luxurious environment combining privacy, independence and the relaxed atmosphere of home.

Tube: Five minutes' walk from South Kensington Underground and 3 minutes' walk from Sloane Square. Road: A4 Cromwell Road, turning right into Sloane Street, down to Sloane Square.

Unit General Leisure Shop < 0.5 miles Pub < 0.5 miles

A holiday for Fido?

Some proprietors welcome well-behaved pets. Look for the symbol in the accommodation listings. You can also buy a copy of our new guide – Pets Come Too! – available from good bookshops and online at enjoyenglanddirect.com.

LONDON SW7

★★★
SELF CATERING

Units **14**
Sleeps **1–4**
Low season per wk
£740.00–£1,020.00
High season per wk
£800.00–£1,100.00

Snow White Properties, London

contact Ms Maxine White, 55 Ennismore Gardens, London SW7 1AJ
t (020) 7584 3307 **f** (020) 7581 4686 **e** snow.white@virgin.net **w** snowwhitelondon.com

open All year
payment Credit/debit cards, cash/cheques, euros

Elegant 19thC house situated in beautiful, quiet garden square close to Harrods, Hyde Park, museums and public transport. Your home away from home – a gem. Several flats have own patios and views overlooking charming gardens. Staff happy to help with any queries.

⊕ *Situated between two main arteries: the A4 at Brompton Road and the A315 at Knightsbridge Road.*

Unit General Shop < 0.5 miles Pub < 0.5 miles

LONDON SW18

★★★★
SELF CATERING

Units **2**
Sleeps **1–8**
Low season per wk
£490.00–£690.00
High season per wk
£510.00–£810.00

Beaumont Apartments, London

contact Mr & Mrs Alan & Monica Afriat, Beaumont Apartments, 24 Combemartin Road, London SW18 5PR
t (020) 8789 2663 **f** (020) 8265 5499 **e** alan@beaumont-london-apartments.co.uk
w beaumont-london-apartments.co.uk

Well-appointed flats in leafiest suburb within 25 minutes of West End. Close to Zone 3 Underground and Wimbledon tennis and convenient for A3, M4, M41, M25, Heathrow and Gatwick.

open All year
payment Credit/debit cards, cash/cheques, euros

Unit General P Leisure

LONDON SW20

★★★★
SELF CATERING

Units **2**
Sleeps **5–6**
High season per wk
£630.00–£735.00

Thalia & Hebe Holiday Homes, Wimbledon, London

contact Mr Peter Briscoe-Smith, 150 Westway, Wimbledon, London SW20 9LS
t (020) 8542 0505 **f** (020) 8287 0637 **e** peter@briscoe-smith.org.uk **w** briscoe-smith.org.uk

Thalia and Hebe are both three-bedroomed houses in the residential suburban area of West Wimbledon. Home from home, with easy access to central London.

open All year
payment Cash/cheques

Unit General P Shop 0.5 miles Pub 0.5 miles

LONDON W1

★★–★★★
SELF CATERING

Units **10**
Sleeps **2–6**
Low season per wk
£380.00–£690.00
High season per wk
£390.00–£700.00

Tustin Holiday Flats, London

contact Mr C Vaughan-Jones, 94 York Street, London W1H 1QX
t (020) 7723 9611 **f** (020) 7724 0224 **e** pctustinuk@btconnect.com **w** pctustin.com

Fully furnished, self-contained flats in central London, offering easy access to Oxford Street, places of interest and public transport.

open All year
payment Credit/debit cards, cash/cheques

Unit General

Check it out

Please check prices, quality ratings and other details when you book.

OUTER LONDON

BECKENHAM

★★–★★★
SELF CATERING

Units **8**
Sleeps **2–6**
Low season per wk
£250.00–£625.00
High season per wk
£250.00–£625.00

Oakfield Apartments, Beckenham

t (020) 8658 4441 f (020) 8658 9198 e enquiries@oakfield.co.uk w oakfield.co.uk

open All year
payment Credit/debit cards, cash/cheques, euros

Victorian mansion with a large garden in a semi-rural setting, three minutes' walk to Eden Park rail station, 25 minutes by rail or nine miles by road to central London. Mr and Mrs Deane live on the premises and welcome children but not pets.

⊕ *Take A214 to Eden Park station, turn left under bridge, then left again and continue for 400yds. Driveway to house is between numbers 103 and 105.*

Unit General P Leisure Shop < 0.5 miles Pub < 0.5 miles

HAMPTON COURT

★★
SELF CATERING & SERVICED APARTMENTS

Units **1**
Sleeps **4**
Low season per wk
Min £450.00
High season per wk
Max £550.00

Moores Place, East Molesey

contact Mr Mark Barnes, 4 King Charles Road, Surbiton KT5 8PY
t (020) 8979 1792 f (020) 8399 6639

18thC cottage overlooking Hampton Court Palace and River Thames. Twenty minutes to central London, 30 minutes to Heathrow and Gatwick, ten minutes to Kingston shopping. Host of original features.

open All year
payment Cash/cheques, euros

Unit General P Leisure Shop < 0.5 miles Pub < 0.5 miles

SOUTH CROYDON

★★
SELF CATERING

Units **1**
Sleeps **1–2**
Low season per wk
£180.00–£210.00
High season per wk
£180.00–£240.00

The Studio, South Croydon

contact Mrs Lynn Starling, South Croydon CR2 6JJ
t (020) 8760 0371

Newly decorated, self-contained studio apartment with large, bright room, separate kitchen and bathroom.

open All year
payment Cash/cheques

Unit General Shop < 0.5 miles Pub < 0.5 miles

Take a break

Many establishments offer special promotions and themed breaks. It's a golden opportunity to indulge an interest or find a new one, or just relax and enjoy exceptional value! Offers and promotions are highlighted in colour (and are subject to availability).

South East England

Berkshire › Buckinghamshire › East Sussex › Hampshire
Isle of Wight › Kent › Oxfordshire › Surrey › West Sussex

Step back in time at Dinosaur Isle, Isle of Wight

Tourism South East
40 Chamberlayne Road,
Eastleigh, Hampshire SO50 5JH
(023) 8062 5400
visitsoutheastengland.com

classic sites, glorious gardens, retail therapy

Main Speeding through the grounds of Hever Castle, Kent **Left** Dizzy heights at the Spinnaker Tower, Portsmouth; take part in the history at Bodiam Castle, East Sussex; take a walk with the Surrey Hills Llamas, near Guildford; awe-inspiring architecture at Winchester Cathedral, Hampshire

Stroll around a true English country garden, set sail on one of the many splendid waters, wander by spectacular coastlines and **soak up the rich history the South East has to offer.**

Explore South East England

On the coast

Take a day trip to the seaside – wander around vibrant Brighton & Hove, delve into the unique shops in The Lanes, stop by The Royal Pavilion and marvel at the intricate Chinese furnishings, or tuck into a bag of fish and chips on the pier.

Head to Portsmouth and tentatively ascend the elegant Spinnaker Tower for views stretching over 23 miles on a clear day. Then explore the historic dockyard: climb aboard Nelson's HMS Victory and be amazed by the remarkable shipwreck, and Henry VIII's favourite vessel, The Mary Rose. For a breath of fresh salty air, stroll along the chalky white cliffs of Dover and wonder if bluebirds ever gracefully flew over their jagged edges.

For all the family

Treat the kids and revisit your youth with a trip to the enchanting Ashdown Forest, within the stunning High Weald. Allow A A Milne's creations to come to life – enjoy a game of Poohsticks and step into Pooh Corner. Continuing the storybook theme, lose yourself in a world of extraordinary fairytales at The Roald Dahl Museum and Story Centre in Buckinghamshire. Or get the adrenalin pumping as you prepare for a white-knuckle ride and defy gravity aboard Nemesis Inferno at Tussauds Thorpe Park.

Historical times

Visit the historic cities and towns of Windsor, Oxford and Canterbury. Discover elegant cathedrals and sturdy castles and relax in one of the many charming pavement cafes. Explore 5,000 sweeping acres of Windsor Great Park and marvel at the mysterious Uffington White Horse, chalked into an Oxfordshire hillside.

Take time to stride around Leeds and Hever castles in Kent and explore their outstanding gardens and grounds, or head to the impressive 11th-century Carisbrooke Castle on the Isle of Wight. Be sure to catch a boat around the mighty Needles at Alum Bay, where the multi-coloured cliffs prove a worthy spectacle.

English country gardens

The South East is blessed with outstanding gardens and scenery. Follow in the footsteps of poet John Keats through Winchester's Water Meadows, or wander through the calming Royal Botanic Gardens, Wakehurst Place in West Sussex. Feel inspired by the changing of the seasons and the natural beauty to be found in each one.

Escape on horseback into the New Forest, past blankets of heather, grazing deer and foraging pigs, or hike past glorious landscapes peppered with colour and spot scurrying wildlife. And take a trip to the stunning Blenheim Palace in Oxfordshire to achieve what Sir Winston Churchill's mother described as 'the finest view in England'.

Places to **visit**

Blenheim Palace
Woodstock, Oxfordshire
(01993) 811091
blenheimpalace.com
Beautiful palace surrounded by parkland

Carisbrooke Castle
Newport, Isle of Wight
(01983) 522107
english-heritage.org.uk
Splendid Norman castle

Dinosaur Isle
Sandown, Isle of Wight
(01983) 404344
dinosaurisle.com
Walk back through fossilized time

Go Ape! High Ropes Forest Adventure
near Bracknell, Berkshire
0870 444 5562
goape.co.uk
Swing through the forest trees

Hever Castle
Kent
(01732) 865224
hever-castle.co.uk
Anne Boleyn's beautiful childhood home

Leeds Castle and Gardens
Maidstone, Kent
(01622) 765400
leeds-castle.com
Ninth-century, lovingly restored castle

Legoland Windsor
Berkshire
0870 504 0404
legoland.co.uk
Witness Lego creations come to life

National Park
South Downs National Park (designated but not yet confirmed)
Area of Outstanding Natural Beauty
Heritage Coast
National Trails nationaltrail.co.uk
Sections of the National Cycle Network nationalcyclenetwork.org.uk
Regional route
Ferry routes

Marwell Zoological Park
Winchester, Hampshire
(01962) 777407
marwell.org.uk
Observe many endangered species

The Needles Park
Totland Bay, Isle of Wight
0870 458 0022
theneedles.co.uk
Catch a chairlift over Alum Bay

Portsmouth Historic Dockyard
Hampshire
(023) 9283 9766
historicdockyard.co.uk
Home of historically important warships

The Roald Dahl Museum and Story Centre
Great Missenden, Buckinghamshire
(01494) 892192
roalddahlmuseum.org
Step inside his imaginative world

Royal Pavilion
Brighton, East Sussex
(01273) 290900
royalpavilion.org.uk
Magnificent former royal seaside residence

Royal Botanic Gardens, Wakehurst Place
near Haywards Heath, West Sussex
(01444) 894000
rbgkew.org.uk
Beautiful gardens throughout the seasons

The Savill Garden, Windsor Great Park
Berkshire
(01753) 847518
savillgarden.co.uk
Beautiful gardens with royal connections

Spinnaker Tower
Portsmouth, Hampshire
(023) 9285 7520
spinnakertower.co.uk
Striking viewing tower with three platforms

Smugglers Adventure
Hastings, East Sussex
(01424) 422964
discoverhastings.co.uk
Dramatic interactive adventure and exhibition

Tussauds Thorpe Park
Chertsey, Surrey
0870 444 4466
thorpepark.co.uk
Thrilling rides for the whole family

Uffington White Horse
Oxfordshire
0870 333 1181
wiltshirewhitehorses.org.uk
Mysterious chalk markings in the hillside

Water Meadows
Winchester, Hampshire
(01962) 840500
visitwinchester.co.uk
Meander along the Keats Walk

Winchester Cathedral
Hampshire
(01962) 857225
winchester-cathedral.org.uk
Magnificent cathedral, and Jane Austen's tomb

Tourist information centres 

When you arrive at your destination, visit a tourist information centre for help with accommodation and information about local attractions and events, or email your request before you go.

Aldershot	39 High Street	(01252) 320968	mail@rushmoorvic.com
Alton	7 Cross and Pillory Lane	(01420) 88448	altoninfo@btconnect.com
Andover	6 Church Close	(01264) 324320	andovertic@testvalley.gov.uk
Arundel	61 High Street	(01903) 882268	arundel.vic@arun.gov.uk
Ashford	18 The Churchyard	(01233) 629165	tourism@ashford.gov.uk
Aylesbury	Kings Head Passage	(01296) 330559	tic@aylesburyvaledc.gov.uk
Banbury	Spiceball Park Road	(01295) 259855	banbury.tic@cherwell-dc.gov.uk
Basingstoke	Market Place	(01256) 817618	basingstoket.i.c@btconnect.com
Battle	High Street	(01424) 773721	battletic@rother.gov.uk
Bicester	Bicester Village	(01869) 369055	bicester.vc@cherwell-dc.gov.uk
Bognor Regis	Belmont Street	(01243) 823140	bognorregis.vic@arun.gov.uk
Bracknell	Nine Mile Ride	(01344) 354409	TheLookOut@bracknell-forest.gov.uk
Brighton	10 Bartholomew Square	0906 711 2255**	brighton-tourism@brighton-hove.gov.uk
Broadstairs	2 Victoria Parade	0870 2646111	
Buckingham	Market Hill	(01280) 823020	buckingham.t.i.c@btconnect.com
Burford	Sheep Street	(01993) 823558	burford.vic@westoxon.gov.uk
Burgess Hill	96 Church Walk	(01444) 238202	touristinformation@burgesshill.gov.uk
Canterbury	12/13 Sun Street	(01227) 378100	canterburyinformation@canterbury.gov.uk
Chichester	29a South Street	(01243) 775888	chitic@chichester.gov.uk
Cowes	9 The Arcade	(01983) 813818	info@islandbreaks.co.uk
Crawley	County Mall	(01293) 846968	vip@countymall.co.uk
Deal	129 High Street	(01304) 369576	tic@doveruk.com
Didcot	118 Broadway	(01235) 813243	didcottic@tourismse.com
Dover	Biggin	(01304) 205108	tic@doveruk.com
Eastbourne	Cornfield Road	0906 711 2212**	tic@eastbourne.gov.uk
Fareham	West Street	(01329) 221342	touristinfo@fareham.gov.uk
Faringdon	5 Market Place	(01367) 242191	tourism@faringdontowncouncil.org.uk
Faversham	13 Preston Street	(01795) 534542	fata@visitfaversham.com
Fleet	236 Fleet Road	(01252) 811151	
Folkestone	Harbour Street	(01303) 258594	
Fordingbridge*	Salisbury Street	(01425) 654560	fordingbridgetic@tourismse.com
Gosport	South Street	(023) 9252 2944	tourism@gosport.gov.uk
Gravesend	18a St George's Square	(01474) 337600	info@towncentric.co.uk
Guildford	14 Tunsgate	(01483) 444333	tic@guildford.gov.uk
Hastings (Old Town)*	The Stade	(01424) 781111	hic@hastings.gov.uk
Hastings	Queens Square	(01424) 781111	hic@hastings.gov.uk
Havant	1 Park Road South	(023) 9248 0024	tourism@havant.gov.uk
Hayling Island*	Seafront	(023) 9246 7111	tourism@havant.gov.uk
Henley-on-Thames	Kings Road	(01491) 578034	henleytic@hotmail.com
Herne Bay	Central Parade	(01227) 361911	hernebayinformation@canterbury.gov.uk
High Wycombe	Paul's Row	(01494) 421892	tourism_enquiries@wycombe.gov.uk

Horsham	9 The Causeway	(01403) 211661	tourist.information@horsham.gov.uk
Hythe	Scanlons Bridge Road	(01303) 266421	
Lewes	187 High Street	(01273) 483448	lewes.tic@lewes.gov.uk
Littlehampton	63-65 Surrey Street	(01903) 721866	littlehampton.vic@arun.gov.uk
Lymington	New Street	(01590) 689000	information@nfdc.gov.uk
Lyndhurst & New Forest	Main Car Park	(023) 8028 2269	information@nfdc.gov.uk
Maidenhead	St Ives Road	(01628) 796502	maidenhead.tic@rbwm.gov.uk
Maidstone	High Street	(01622) 602169	tourism@maidstone.gov.uk
Margate	12-13 The Parade	0870 264 6111	margate.tic@visitor-centre.net
Marlow	31 High Street	(01628) 483597	tourism_enquiries@wycombe.gov.uk
Midhurst	North Street	(01730) 817322	midtic@chichester.gov.uk
New Romney	New Romney Station	(01797) 362353	
Newbury	The Wharf	(01635) 30267	tourism@westberks.gov.uk
Newport	High Street	(01983) 813818	info@islandbreaks.co.uk
Oxford	15/16 Broad Street	(01865) 726871	tic@oxford.gov.uk
Petersfield	27 The Square	(01730) 268829	petersfieldinfo@btconnect.com
Petworth*	The Old Bakery	(01798) 343523	
Portsmouth	Clarence Esplanade	(023) 9282 6722	vis@portsmouthcc.gov.uk
Portsmouth	The Hard	(023) 9282 6722	vis@portsmouthcc.gov.uk
Ramsgate	17 Albert Court	0870 2646111	ramsgate.tic@visitor-centre.net
Reading	Chain Street	(0118) 956 6226	touristinfo@reading.gov.uk
Ringwood	The Furlong	(01425) 470896	information@nfdc.gov.uk
Rochester	95 High Street	(01634) 843666	visitor.centre@medway.gov.uk
Romsey	13 Church Street	(01794) 512987	romseytic@testvalley.gov.uk
Royal Tunbridge Wells	The Pantiles	(01892) 515675	touristinformationcentre@tunbridgewells.gov.uk
Ryde	81-83 Union Street	(01983) 813818	info@islandbreaks.co.uk
Rye	Strand Quay	(01797) 226696	ryetic@rother.gov.uk
Sandown	8 High Street	(01983) 813818	info@islandbreaks.co.uk
Sandwich*	Cattle Market	(01304) 613565	info@ticsandwich.wanadoo.co.uk
Seaford	25 Clinton Place	(01323) 897426	seaford.tic@lewes.gov.uk
Sevenoaks	Buckhurst Lane	(01732) 450305	tic@sevenoakstown.gov.uk
Shanklin	67 High Street	(01983) 813818	info@islandbreaks.co.uk
Southampton	9 Civic Centre Road	(023) 8083 3333	tourist.information@southampton.gov.uk
Southsea	Clarence Esplanade	(023) 9282 6722	vis@portsmouthcc.gov.uk
Tenterden*	High Street	(01580) 763572	tentic@ashford.gov.uk
Tonbridge	Castle Street	(01732) 770929	tonbridge.castle@tmbc.gov.uk
Wendover	High Street	(01296) 696759	tourism@wendover-pc.gov.uk
Whitstable	7 Oxford Street	(01227) 275482	whitstableinformation@canterbury.gov.uk
Winchester	High Street	(01962) 840500	tourism@winchester.gov.uk
Windsor	24 High Street	(01753) 743900	windsor.tic@rbwm.gov.uk
Witney	26a Market Square	(01993) 775802	witney.vic@westoxon.gov.uk
Woodstock	Park Street	(01993) 813276	woodstock.vic@westoxon.gov.uk
Worthing	Chapel Road	(01903) 221307	tic@worthing.gov.uk
Worthing*	Marine Parade	(01903) 221307	tic@worthing.gov.uk
Yarmouth	The Quay	(01983) 813818	info@islandbreaks.co.uk

** seasonal opening ** calls to this number are charged at premium rate*

Alternatively, you can text **TIC LOCATE** to **64118** to find your nearest tourist information centre

Find out **more**

The following publications are available from Tourism South East by logging on to **visitsouthernengland.com** or calling **(023) 8062 5400**:

- **Escape into the Countryside**
- **Cities**
- **Favourite Gardens and Garden Stays**
- **Great Days Out in Berkshire, Buckinghamshire and Oxfordshire**
- **Distinctive Country Inns**
- **We Know Just the Place**

Travel **info**

By road:
From the North East – M1 & M25;
the North West – M6, M40 & M25;
the West and Wales – M4 & M25;
the East – M25;
the South West – M5, M4 & M25;
London – M25, M2, M20, M23, M3, M4 or M40.

By rail:
Regular services from London's Charing Cross, Victoria, Waterloo and Waterloo East stations to all parts of the South East. Further information on rail journeys in the South East can be obtained on 0845 748 4950.

By air:
Fly into London City, London Heathrow, London Gatwick, London Southend, Southampton or Shoreham (Brighton City).

Relaxing on the River Thames at Cookham Dean, Berkshire

where to stay in

South East England

All place names in the blue bands are shown on the maps at the front of this guide.

A complete listing of all Enjoy England assessed accommodation covered by this guide appears at the back.

Accommodation symbols
Symbols give useful information about services and facilities. Inside the back-cover flap you can find a key to these symbols. Keep it open for easy reference.

ADDERBURY, Oxfordshire Map ref 2C1

★★★★
SELF CATERING

Units 1
Sleeps 2

Low season per wk
£270.00–£290.00
High season per wk
£300.00–£350.00

Hannah's Cottage at Fletcher's, Banbury

contact Mrs Charlotte Holmes, Fletcher's, High Street, Adderbury, Banbury OX17 3LS
t (01295) 810308 **e** charlotteaholmes@hotmail.com **w** holiday-rentals.com

Hannah's, a recently restored Victorian garden cottage which incorporates a former hayloft as first-floor lounge, is cosy and quiet although in the centre of this lovely village.

open All year
payment Cash/cheques, euros

Unit General P Shop < 0.5 miles Pub < 0.5 miles

ALTON, Hampshire Map ref 2C2

★★★★
SELF CATERING

Units 1
Sleeps 4

Low season per wk
£300.00–£350.00
High season per wk
£400.00–£525.00

Green Farm, Bentley, Farnham

contact Mrs Glenda Powell, The Drift, Bentley, Farnham GU10 5JX
t (01420) 23246 **f** (01252) 737916 **e** chris@powellmessenger.co.uk **w** greenfarm.org.uk

Luxury self-contained accommodation in newly built annexe of listed farmhouse. Fully fitted and very spacious. Terrace and ample parking. Full details on website.

open All year
payment Cash/cheques, euros

Unit General P Leisure Shop 0.5 miles Pub 0.5 miles

ALVERSTOKE, Hampshire Map ref 2C3

★★
SELF CATERING

Units 1
Sleeps 6
Low season per wk
£330.00–£380.00
High season per wk
£380.00–£410.00

28 The Avenue, Alverstoke

contact Mr Martin Lawson, 18 Upper Paddock Road, Watford WD19 4DZ
t (01923) 244042 **f** (01923) 244042 **e** martinlawson8400@aol.com

Three-bedroomed house with pleasant garden, five minutes from Stokes Bay. Opportunities for fishing, sailing and windsurfing. Close to Portsmouth, Southampton and New Forest. On-site parking provided.

open All year
payment Cash/cheques

Unit General Shop < 0.5 miles Pub < 0.5 miles

AMBERLEY, West Sussex Map ref 2D3

★★
SELF CATERING

Units 1
Sleeps 4
Low season per wk
£400.00–£500.00
High season per wk
£600.00

Culver Cottage, Arundel

contact Mrs Howell-Hughes, Swallow Barn, The Sqaure, Amberley BN18 9SR
t (01798) 831312 & +33 05659 96950 **e** stellainamberley@yahoo.co.uk **w** visitbritain.com

A secluded cottage in the heart of Amberley, hidden up a twitten. Beautiful South Downs views, thatched houses, flowering stone walls, Norman church and castle. Pubs and restaurants within walking distance.

open All year
payment Cash/cheques, euros

Unit General Leisure Shop < 0.5 miles Pub < 0.5 miles

AMERSHAM, Buckinghamshire Map ref 2D1

★★★★
SELF CATERING

Units 1
Sleeps 8
Low season per wk
£1,000.00
High season per wk
£1,000.00–£1,400.00

Chiltern Cottages, Amersham

contact Mr Stephen Hinds, Chiltern Cottages, Hill Farm Lane, Chalfont St Giles HP8 4NT
t (01494) 874826 **e** bookings@chilterncottages.org **w** chilterncottages.org

open All year
payment Cash/cheques

This fine 15thC residence, in the heart of Amersham old town, boasts a large dining room with 16thC wall paintings, a fully equipped kitchen, comfortable, high-quality living room and a four-poster bed in the master bedroom. Free car parking. Approximately one mile from London Underground station.

Head for Amersham Old Town and the Old Town Centre. The Old House is about 250m after the marketplace (in the centre of the road).

Short-break bookings permitted 2 months before start date. Price: weekly rate less 10% per day not used.

Unit General Leisure Shop < 0.5 miles Pub < 0.5 miles

ANDOVER, Hampshire Map ref 2C2

★★★★
SELF CATERING

Units 1
Sleeps 4
Low season per wk
£300.00–£400.00
High season per wk
£400.00–£540.00

Westmead, Weyhill, Nr Andover

contact Mrs Dianna Leighton, Westmead, Amesbury Road, Weyhill, Andover SP11 8DU
t (01264) 772513 **f** (01204) 773003 **e** westmeadweyhill@aol.com **w** westmeadweyhill.co.uk

Spacious two-bedroom bungalow with modern facilities. Large garden, terrace and tennis court. Off-road parking. All linen and towels provided.

open All year except Christmas and New Year
payment Cash/cheques, euros

Unit General Leisure Shop 1 mile Pub 1 mile

ARUNDEL, West Sussex Map ref 2D3

★★
SELF CATERING

Units **1**
Sleeps **1–4**
Low season per wk
£350.00
High season per wk
£450.00

The Garden Room, Wepham, Nr Arundel

contact Mrs J Ramseyer, Thomas Cottage, Wepham, Arundel BN18 9RG
t (01903) 883222 **e** info@thomascottage.co.uk **w** thomascottage.co.uk

open All year
payment Cash/cheques

A New England-style detached studio in the garden of a 500-year-old, thatched, box-framed Tudor cottage in a rural hamlet. Light and airy, decorated in fresh pastel colours, facing the main house across a small front lawn, standing in about an acre. ' ... it exceeded our expectations ... '

Entering Wepham, road rises up short hill. Go left to Splash Farm, passing telephone box. Thomas Cottage 100yds on left. Park in drive behind house.

Unit General Leisure Shop 3 miles Pub 0.5 miles

ASHDOWN FOREST

See under Nutley

ASHFORD, Kent Map ref 3B4

★★★
SELF CATERING

Units **6**
Sleeps **1–4**
Low season per wk
£255.00–£460.00
High season per wk
£460.00–£645.00

Eversleigh Woodland Lodges, Ashford

contact Mrs Christine Drury, Eversleigh Woodland Lodges, Hornash Lane, Shadoxhurst, Ashford TN26 1HX
t (01233) 733248 **f** (01233) 733248 **e** enquiries@eversleighlodges.co.uk **w** eversleighlodges.co.uk

Spacious, detached lodges in woodland setting. One double, one twin. Heated indoor swimming pool, games room, gymnasium, solarium, gardens. Easy access south coast, London, Canterbury, Channel ports and tunnel.

open All year
payment Credit/debit cards, cash/cheques

Unit General Leisure Shop 2 miles Pub 1.5 miles

ASHFORD, Kent Map ref 3B4

★★★★★
SELF CATERING

Units 1
Sleeps 4
Low season per wk
£350.00–£400.00
High season per wk
£450.00–£600.00

Hazelhope Barn, Stalisfield, Nr Ashford

contact Mandy Southern, Hazelhope Barn, Hazelhope, Stalisfield Green, Faversham ME13 0HY
t (01233) 713806 **f** (01233) 714840 **e** mandy@hazelhopebarn.co.uk **w** hazelhopebarn.co.uk

open All year
payment Credit/debit cards, cash/cheques, euros

Excellent location. Luxury, new first-floor apartment with stunning views. Built over stables in a Kent barn. Double with large, en suite shower and broadband Internet access. Large twin with adjacent bathroom. Fully fitted kitchen and separate utility room with washer/dryer. Very comfortable living/ dining areas. Secure parking. Private garden with barbecue.

M20 jct 8. A20 towards Ashford. Turn left at static-mobile-home park (signposted Stalisfield Green). Approx 1 mile on right.

Unit General Shop 2 miles Pub 0.5 miles

BANBURY, Oxfordshire Map ref 2C1

★★★★
SELF CATERING

Units 1
Sleeps 2–4
Low season per wk
£280.00–£310.00
High season per wk
£360.00–£450.00

Mill Wheel Cottage, Banbury

contact Mrs Sheila Nichols, Mill House Farm, Kings Sutton, Banbury OX17 3QP
t (01295) 811637 **f** (01295) 811637 **w** holiday-rentals.com

open All year
payment Cash/cheques

Idyllic, private, very comfortable, well-equipped cottage on River Cherwell, converted to a high standard with original beams. Full of character, surrounded by water meadows with abundant wildlife, the ultimate in tranquillity and relaxation. Canal close by. Ideal for exploring the Cotswolds, Stratford and Oxford. Enjoy a warm welcome and personal attention.

From M40 jct 10, B4100 between Adderbury and Aynho, off B4100 turning to King's Sutton, 100yds left-hand side, entrance to farm through double gates.

Unit General Leisure Shop 2 miles Pub 2 miles

BARNHAM, West Sussex Map ref 2C3

★★★★★
SELF CATERING

Units 1
Sleeps 2
Low season per wk
Min £325.00
High season per wk
Max £425.00

Welldiggers, Bognor Regis

contact Mrs Penelope Crawford, Church Farm Barns, Hill Lane, Bognor Regis PO22 0BN
t (01243) 555119 **f** (01243) 552779 **e** welldiggers@hotmail.com **w** welldiggers.co.uk

A converted barn with all facilities. Private garden. Pub ten minutes' walk. One pet welcomed.

open All year
payment Cash/cheques

Unit General Shop 1.5 miles Pub 1 mile

CYCLISTS WELCOME

A holiday on two wheels

For a fabulous freewheeling break seek out accommodation participating in our Cyclists Welcome scheme. Look out for the symbol and plan your route online at nationalcyclenetwork.org.

BEMBRIDGE, Isle of Wight Map ref 2C3

★★★
SELF CATERING

Units **1**
Sleeps **10**
Low season per wk
£260.00–£390.00
High season per wk
£400.00–£850.00

Nine, Bembridge

contact Mrs Ann Hayward, Homewood, 37 Cross Lane, Findon BN14 0UB
t (01903) 873699 **f** (01903) 873819

Ideal holiday home 400yds from sea. Five double bedrooms, sun parlour, good garden. TV, video, washing machine/drier, dishwasher, fridge/freezer. Parking. Dogs welcome.

open All year
payment Cash/cheques

Unit **General** **Shop** < 0.5 miles **Pub** 0.5 miles

BEMBRIDGE, Isle of Wight Map ref 2C3

★★★-★★★★
SELF CATERING

Units **2**
Sleeps **4–6**
Low season per wk
£405.00–£540.00
High season per wk
£615.00–£660.00

Princessa Cottage & Coastwatch Cottage, Bembridge

contact Mrs Hargreaves, 1 Norcott Drive, Bembridge PO35 5TX
t (01983) 874403 **f** (01983) 874403 **e** ssnharg@aol.com

Former coastguard cottages near sandy beach with rock pools at low tide. Well furnished and equipped to high standard. Private parking and gardens. Linen provided.

open All year
payment Cash/cheques

Unit **General** P **Leisure** **Shop** 1 mile **Pub** < 0.5 miles

BEMBRIDGE, Isle of Wight Map ref 2C3

★★
SELF CATERING

Units **1**
Sleeps **4**
Low season per wk
£180.00–£230.00
High season per wk
£240.00–£300.00

Will-o-Cott, Bembridge

contact Mrs Ann Hayward, Homewood, 37 Cross Lane, Findon BN14 0UB
t (01903) 873699 **f** (01903) 873819

Chalet-type bungalow, with pleasant garden, three minutes from sea. Open March to October.

payment Cash/cheques

Unit **General** **Shop** < 0.5 miles **Pub** 0.5 miles

BICESTER, Oxfordshire Map ref 2C1

★★★★
SELF CATERING

Units **5**
Sleeps **2–6**
Low season per wk
£274.00–£410.00
High season per wk
£370.00–£570.00

Pimlico Farm Country Cottages, Bicester

contact Mr & Mrs John & Monica Harper, Pimlico Farm Country Cottages, Pimlico Farm, Tusmore, Bicester OX27 7SL
t (01869) 810306 **f** (01869) 810309 **e** enquiries@pimlicofarm.co.uk

Top-quality Cotswold-stone barn conversions situated on a 500-acre working farm. Free, on-farm fishing. Close to Oxford, Stratford-upon-Avon, Warwick. Wealth of historic houses nearby. Resident owners will make guests welcome.

open All year
payment Credit/debit cards, cash/cheques

Unit **General** P **Leisure** **Shop** 2 miles **Pub** 2 miles

BICESTER, Oxfordshire Map ref 2C1

★★★★
SELF CATERING

Units **2**
Sleeps **2**

Low season per wk
£285.00–£325.00
High season per wk
£365.00–£370.00

Stoke Lyne Farm Cottages, Stoke Lyne, Bicester

contact Mrs Julie Adams, Stoke Lyne Farm Cottages, Lower Farm, Bicester OX27 8SD
t (01869) 345306 **f** (01869) 346705 **e** info@stokelynefarmcottages.co.uk
w stokelynefarmcottages.co.uk

Beautiful stone barn conversion on a working farm in North Oxfordshire. Lovely original features, oak furniture and wooden flooring. Pretty courtyard gardens. Broadband internet access. Horse accommodation. Near to Blenheim Palace and Silverstone.

open All year
payment Cash/cheques

Unit General P Leisure Shop 1.5 miles
Pub < 0.5 miles

BISHOPSTONE, East Sussex Map ref 2D3

★★★
SELF CATERING

Units **1**
Sleeps **1–5**

Low season per wk
£140.00–£190.00
High season per wk
£190.00–£335.00

144 Norton Cottage, Seaford

contact Mrs Carol Collinson, Inces Barn, Norton Farm, Bishopstone, Seaford BN25 2UW
t (01323) 897544 **f** (01323) 897544 **e** norton.farm@farmline.com
w http://members.farmline.com/collinson/

Comfortably furnished, semi-detached cottage situated on a working farm in a peaceful, rural location on the South Downs. Ideal for touring South East.

open All year
payment Cash/cheques

Unit General P

BOGNOR REGIS, West Sussex Map ref 2C3

Rating Applied For
SELF CATERING

Units **1**
Sleeps **5–6**

Low season per wk
£450.00–£700.00
High season per wk
£700.00–£1,200.00

Gabriels Hall, Bognor Regis

contact Sian ,Irvine, 94 Nightingale Road, London E5 8NB
t (020) 7923 3678 & 07931 505696 **f** (020) 7254 7694 **e** info@gabrielshall.com **w** gabrielshall.com

open All year
payment Credit/debit cards, cash/cheques, euros

Gabriels Hall is a Grade II Listed Regency town house, refurbished to a high standard, with sea views. One single and two double bedrooms, one with en suite bathroom, second bathroom plus shower (wet room). A great base from which to explore country pursuits, eg Festival of Speed. Enjoy Bognor's clean beaches, with Chichester, Arundel and Brighton nearby.

Unit General 10 Leisure Shop < 0.5 miles
Pub < 0.5 miles

BOWLHEAD GREEN, Surrey Map ref 2C2

★★
SELF CATERING

Units **1**
Sleeps **1–2**

Low season per wk
Max £120.00
High season per wk
Min £140.00

The Barn Flat, Godalming

contact Mrs Grace Ranson, Bowlhead Green Farm, Bowlhead Green, Godalming GU8 6NW
t (01428) 682687 **e** ranson@bowlhead.fsnet.co.uk

In delightful hamlet, 16thC barn conversion with exposed oak beams. Attractive, small, self-contained flat overlooking farmhouse garden. Double sofa bed, kitchenette, shower and wc. No pets.

open All year
payment Cash/cheques

Unit General P Shop 1.25 miles

Key to symbols

Open the back flap for a key to symbols.

BRACKLESHAM BAY, West Sussex Map ref 2C3

Rating Applied For
SELF CATERING

Units **1**
Sleeps **1–6**
Low season per wk
£230.00–£310.00
High season per wk
£420.00–£500.00

Windrush, Bracklesham Bay

contact Andy Stevens, Windrush Holidays, Windrush, Farm Road, Bracklesham Bay PO20 8JT
t 0845 644 0717 **f** 0870 766 2713 **e** enquiries@windrush-holidays.com **w** bracklesham-bay.co.uk

payment Cash/cheques

A two-bedroom, well-appointed chalet on quiet, landscaped, 90-acre site with stream and two large ponds. Site includes outdoor pool, shop, children's play area. Walk to unspoilt pebble/wet-sand beach. Good for touring, walking, cycling or just relaxing. The historic city of Chichester is about eight miles away. Open March to October.

⊕ *From A27 exit roundabout, A286 Witterings. Left at Birdham roundabout. B2198 East Wittering. Bracklesham Bay turn left. Clappers Lane. Enter Sussex beach after 1 mile.*

♥ *Short breaks available low season. Also discount for full-time Christian workers.*

Unit General Leisure **Shop** < 0.5 miles **Pub** < 0.5 miles

BRIGHTON & HOVE, East Sussex Map ref 2D3

BRIGHTON & HOVE, East Sussex Map ref 2D3

★★★★
SELF CATERING

Units **3**
Sleeps **2–4**
Low season per wk
Max £425.00
High season per wk
Max £625.00

Brighton Marina Holiday Apartments, Brighton

contact Mrs A Wills, 5 Marlborough Road, Richmond TW10 6JT
t (020) 8940 6945 **f** (020) 8241 1191 **e** keith.wills@london.com
w brightonmarinaholidayapartments.co.uk

open All year
payment Cash/cheques, euros

Overlooking the inner harbour with private waterside terrace/balcony, luxury two-bedroom apartments. One twin, one double with en suite shower, bathroom, lounge/dining room and fully equipped kitchen. Satellite TV, DVD, telephone, private parking. Situated a mile east of Brighton, the marina boasts an extensive range of restaurants, leisure and dining facilities.

⊕ *From A27 take the Brighton coast road going east signposted to Brighton Marina. At 1st roundabout within marina, take 2nd exit signposted to Mariners Quay.*

Unit **General** **Shop** < 0.5 miles **Pub** < 0.5 miles

BRIGHTON & HOVE, East Sussex Map ref 2D3

★★★★★
SELF CATERING

Units **1**
Sleeps **2–6**
Low season per wk
£500.00–£650.00
High season per wk
£700.00–£850.00

Kilcolgan Bungalow, Rottingdean, Brighton

contact Mr J C St George, 22 Baches Street, London N1 6DL
t (020) 7250 3678 **f** (020) 7250 1955 **e** jc.stgeorge@virgin.net **w** holidaybungalowsbrightonuk.com

open All year
payment Cash/cheques, euros

Welcome to excellence in self-catering accommodation. Exceptional, detached, three-bedroomed bungalow comprehensively equipped, with emphasis on comfort. Secluded, landscaped garden overlooking farmland. Garage parking for two vehicles. Accessible to the disabled. Rottingdean is a delightful seaside village with seafront and promenade, four miles from Brighton. Ideal, quiet retreat. Pets by arrangement (small charge).

⊕ *Left at Brighton Pier onto A259 towards Newhaven. At Rottingdean traffic lights, left onto High Street. Bear right around Kipling gardens, then left into Dean Court Road.*

♥ *Short breaks (min 3 nights) possible during low season (excl Christmas and New Year). Terms on request.*

Unit **General** **Leisure** **Shop** 0.75 miles **Pub** 0.75 miles

BRIGHTON & HOVE, East Sussex Map ref 2D3

★★★★
SELF CATERING

Units **1**
Sleeps **4**
Low season per wk
Min £600.00
High season per wk
Min £900.00

Spell Self-Catering, Brighton

contact Ms Susan Ellis, Bramley Fell, Church Road, Old Beetley, Dereham NR20 4AB
t 07707 813012 **e** spell.let@virgin.net **w** spellsc.co.uk

In central Brighton, an immaculate airy apartment in private Regency house. Two double rooms, lounge/diner, only one minute from the beach and five minutes from the town centre.

open All year
payment Cash/cheques

Unit **General** **Leisure** **Shop** < 0.5 miles **Pub** < 0.5 miles

Check it out

Information on accommodation listed in this guide has been supplied by proprietors. As changes may occur you should remember to check all relevant details at the time of booking.

BROADSTAIRS, Kent Map ref 3C3

★★★
SELF CATERING

Units **1**
Sleeps **4**
Low season per wk
£220.00–£280.00
High season per wk
£300.00–£350.00

11 Inverness Terrace, Broadstairs

contact Mrs Beatrice Jones, 11 Inverness Terrace, The Vale, Broadstairs CT10 1QZ
t (01843) 867116 **e** rhys.maps@dsl.pipex.com

Comfortable garden flat, newly refurbished throughout, convenient for beach and town centre in quiet part of Broadstairs. Open Easter to October.

payment Cash/cheques

Unit General P Leisure Shop 0.5 miles Pub < 0.5 miles

BROADSTAIRS, Kent Map ref 3C3

★★★★
SELF CATERING

Units **1**
Sleeps **6**
Low season per wk
£250.00–£400.00
High season per wk
£350.00–£550.00

Beacon Light Cottage, Broadstairs

contact Mr Patrick Vandervorst, Duinhelmlaan 11, B-8420 Wenduine, Belgium
e beaconlight.cottage@scarlet.be **w** beaconlightcottage.com

We welcome you with a bottle of wine in our spacious cottage with garden, conservatory, parking space and sea views. Near beaches and shops. One double, two twins. Ground-floor bedroom.

open All year
payment Cash/cheques, euros

Unit TV General P S Leisure Shop < 0.5 miles Pub < 0.5 miles

BROADSTAIRS, Kent Map ref 3C3

★★★★
SELF CATERING

Units **1**
Sleeps **2–6**
Low season per wk
£320.00–£450.00
High season per wk
£480.00–£630.00

Fisherman's Cottage, Broadstairs

contact Ms Linda Spillane, 33 St James' Drive, Wandsworth, London SW17 7RN
t (020) 8672 4150 **e** linda.spillane@virgin.net **w** fishermanscottagebroadstairs.co.uk

open All year
payment Cash/cheques

Delightfully converted, four-storey, Grade II Listed flint cottage in Broadstairs conservation area. One minute to harbour and beach. The cottage has three bedrooms, a well-equipped kitchen and spacious living areas. The floors are linked by a wooden spiral staircase – see virtual tour on our website.

⊕ *From Broadstairs town centre follow directions to the harbour, continuing on Harbour Street. Fisherman's Cottage is on the left after 100m, behind the cafe.*

Unit TV General

Suit yourself

The symbols at the end of each entry mean you can enjoy virtually made-to-measure accommodation with the services and facilities most important to you. A key to the symbols can be found inside the back-cover flap. Keep this open for easy reference.

BUCKINGHAM, Buckinghamshire Map ref 2C1

★★★★
SELF CATERING

Units **6**
Sleeps **1–9**
Low season per wk
£225.00–£500.00
High season per wk
£300.00–£600.00

Huntsmill Holidays, Buckingham

contact Mrs Fiona Hilsdon, Huntsmill Holidays, Huntsmill Farm, Buckingham MK18 5ND
t (01280) 704852 & 07974 122578 **f** (01280) 704852 **e** fiona@huntsmill.com **w** huntsmill.com

open All year
payment Credit/debit cards, cash/cheques, euros

Courtyard of traditional stone, timber and slate barns, imaginatively converted from former calf sheds and pig sties, offering a high standard of accommodation. Set on a working farm in a quiet location with views of open countryside. Large gardens with easy access to footpaths. Close to Silverstone and many National Trust properties.

⊕ *We are between Buckingham and Brackley, about 0.33 miles off the A422, to the south, along road marked Finmere and Mixbury.*

❤ *Additional rooms may be added from B&B on special room-only rate.*

Unit General P Leisure Shop 2 miles
Pub 2 miles

CANTERBURY, Kent Map ref 3B3

★★★★★
SELF CATERING

Units **3**
Sleeps **2–14**
Low season per wk
£400.00–£700.00
High season per wk
£700.00–£1,200.00

Canterbury Country Houses, Canterbury

contact Mr Mark Mount, Canterbury Country Houses, Woolton Farm, Bekesbourne, Canterbury CT4 5EA
t (01227) 830126 **f** (01227) 831969 **e** info@canterburyholidays.com
w canterburycountryhouses.co.uk

open All year
payment Credit/debit cards, cash/cheques, euros

Choice of houses within three miles of Canterbury. The Oast and The Old Tannery are Grade II Listed and are situated in the village of Littlebourne. Ellen's Cottage is a typical Kentish house on a fruit farm with large garden overlooking the fields.

⊕ *M2/A2 southbound. Next slip road after Canterbury. Follow signs to Bekesbourne and Littlebourne.*

❤ *Short breaks of 3 or 4 nights (excl Jun, Jul and Aug). The Oast and Tannery can be combined for groups of up to 14.*

Unit General P Leisure
Shop < 0.5 miles Pub < 0.5 miles

CANTERBURY, Kent Map ref 3B3

★★★★★
SELF CATERING

Units **1**
Sleeps **8**
Low season per wk
£400.00–£500.00
High season per wk
£500.00–£550.00

Canterbury Self-catering, Canterbury

contact Mrs Kathryn Nevell, Canterbury Holiday Lets, 4 Harbledown Park, Harbledown, Canterbury CT2 8NR
t (01227) 763308 & 07941 969110 **e** rnevell@aol.com **w** canterburyselfcatering.com

Five-bedroomed, detached, well-equipped accommodation. Sports facilities and woodland walks. Half a mile to nature reserve, 1.5 miles from city centre. Excellent value for money. Use of outdoor swimming pool by private arrangement.

payment Credit/debit cards, cash/cheques

Unit General P Leisure Shop < 0.5 miles
Pub < 0.5 miles

Check it out

Please check prices, quality ratings and other details when you book.

CANTERBURY, Kent Map ref 3B3

★★★-★★★★★
SELF CATERING

Units **7**
Sleeps **2–19**
Low season per wk
£200.00–£1,600.00
High season per wk
£285.00–£2,300.00

Knowlton Court, Canterbury

contact Miss Amy Froggatt, Knowlton Court, Knowlton, Canterbury CT3 1PT
t (01304) 842402 **f** (01304) 842403 **e** cottages@knowltoncourt.co.uk **w** knowltoncourt.co.uk

Elizabethan house and former farm cottages. Golf courses at Sandwich, Channel Tunnel at Folkestone, port of Dover and cathedral city of Canterbury all easily accessible.

open All year
payment Credit/debit cards, cash/cheques

Unit General P S Leisure Shop 3 miles Pub < 0.5 miles

CANTERBURY, Kent Map ref 3B3

★★★★
SELF CATERING

Units **3**
Sleeps **1–3**
Low season per wk
£220.00–£340.00
High season per wk
£300.00–£390.00

Oriel Lodge Holiday Apartments, Canterbury

contact Mr Keith Rishworth, Oriel Lodge, 3 Queens Avenue, Canterbury CT2 8AY
t (01227) 462845 **f** (01227) 462845 **e** info@oriel-lodge.co.uk **w** oriel-lodge.co.uk

High-grade apartments in a peaceful Edwardian house, set in a residential area with private parking, five minutes' walk from the city centre. Weekend and short breaks all year.

open All year
payment Credit/debit cards, cash/cheques

Unit General 6 P S Leisure Shop < 0.5 miles Pub < 0.5 miles

CHICHESTER, West Sussex Map ref 2C3

★★★★★
SELF CATERING

Units **1**
Sleeps **4**
Low season per wk
£400.00–£500.00
High season per wk
£525.00–£625.00

Apple Barn, Runcton, Chichester

contact Mrs R Kendall, Saltham House, Saltham Lane, Runcton, Chichester PO20 1XJ
t (01243) 775997 **e** applebarn@salthamhouse.co.uk **w** salthamhouse.co.uk

Apple Barn is an old single-storey barn which has been converted into a luxury two-bedroom holiday cottage. Set in open farmland, it is well situated for Chichester and the surrounding area.

open All year
payment Credit/debit cards, cash/cheques

Unit General P Leisure Shop < 0.5 miles Pub 1 mile

CHICHESTER, West Sussex Map ref 2C3

★★★★
SELF CATERING

Units **1**
Sleeps **1–6**
Low season per wk
£385.00–£555.00
High season per wk
£555.00–£645.00

Cornerstones, Chichester

contact Mrs Higgins, Goodwood Gardens, Chichester PO20 1SP
t (01243) 839096 **e** v.r.higgins@dsl.pipex.com **w** cornercottages.com

open All year
payment Cash/cheques

Sussex-style house. Two bedrooms upstairs, one downstairs. Bathroom. Separate shower room. Equipped to high standard. Double garage. Enclosed gardens. Village between Chichester and coast. Easy walks to pub/restaurant, post office/shop, church and Pagham nature reserve. Five-minute drive to Chichester. Ten minutes to Goodwood Racecourse.

⊕ *A27 Chichester bypass. Roundabout with A259 Bognor take minor road (Pagham and Runcton). Next mini-roundabout left (Pagham). After 0.25 miles right into Brookside Lane, right into Brookside Close.*

❤ *Short breaks available Oct-May. Reduced rates for couples Oct-May.*

Unit General P Shop 0.5 miles Pub < 0.5 miles

CHICHESTER, West Sussex Map ref 2C3

★★★★
SELF CATERING

Units **1**
Sleeps **1–2**
Low season per wk
£215.00–£285.00
High season per wk
£285.00–£330.00

Cygnet Cottage, Chichester

contact Mrs Higgins, Greenacre, Goodwood Gardens, Chichester PO20 1SP
t (01243) 839096 **e** v.r.higgins@dsl.pipex.com **w** cornercottages.com

open All year
payment Cash/cheques

Cosy one-bedroom detached cottage in village between Chichester and coast. Easy country walks to pub/restaurant, post office/shop, church and Pagham nature reserve. Fully equipped to high standard. Suntrap patio. Off-road parking. Canalside walk or five minutes' drive to historic Chichester. Ten minutes' drive to Goodwood racecourse.

⊕ *A27 Chichester bypass. Roundabout with A259 Bognor take minor road (Pagham and Runcton). After 1 mile at next mini-roundabout straight across. Cottage 0.25 miles on right.*

♥ *Short breaks available Oct-Apr. Minimum 3 nights.*

Unit General Shop 0.5 miles Pub < 0.5 miles

CHICHESTER, West Sussex Map ref 2C3

★★★
SELF CATERING

Units **5**
Sleeps **2–5**
Low season per wk
£234.00–£321.00
High season per wk
£312.00–£514.00

Hunston Mill Cottages, Chichester

contact Mr & Mrs Ian & Lyn Potter, Hunston Mill, Selsey Road, Hunston, Chichester PO20 1AU
t (01243) 783375 **f** (01243) 785179 **e** hunstonmillcottages@bushinternet.com **w** hunstonmill.co.uk

open All year
payment Cash/cheques

18thC windmill and adjoining buildings converted into comfortable holiday homes, set in nearly an acre of attractive gardens with putting and barbecue. Situated in the country between the historic city of Chichester and the sea, with views over farmland, golf course and to the Downs.

⊕ *From A27, turn off onto the B2145 Selsey road. Hunston Mill is on left after 2 miles, south of Hunston village.*

Unit General Leisure Shop 0.5 miles Pub 0.5 miles

CHICHESTER, West Sussex Map ref 2C3

★★★★
SELF CATERING

Units **2**
Sleeps **8–20**
Low season per wk
£600.00–£800.00
High season per wk
£1,000.00–£1,400.00

Poplars Farm House, Chichester

contact Mr & Mrs T Kinross, Poplars Farm House, Batchmere Road, Chichester PO20 7LD
t (01243) 602250 **e** poplarsfarmhouse@tiscali.co.uk **w** poplarsfarmhouse.co.uk

open All year
payment Credit/debit cards, cash/cheques

Set in 2.5 acres, well back from the road, a 17thC farmhouse and dairy cottage conversion. The farmhouse sleeps eight in four bedrooms, the dairy cottage sleeps six in three bedrooms and the studio annexe sleeps six. The farmhouse has an Aga kitchen and a dining room to seat 14.

⊕ *South from Chichester towards The Witterings. After Birdham sign turn left towards Almodington. Continue past Second Avenue to driveway on left after hedge with black posts.*

♥ *Short breaks available outside Jul and Aug.*

Unit General Leisure Shop 2 miles Pub 1.5 miles

Star ratings

Further information about star ratings can be found at the back of this guide.

CHIPPING NORTON, Oxfordshire Map ref 2C1

★★★★★
SELF CATERING

Units **1**
Sleeps **2–20**
Low season per wk
£2,300.00–£2,500.00
High season per wk
£2,500.00–£3,000.00

Beech House, Old Chalford, Chipping Norton

contact Mrs Dorothy Canty, Oak House, Chalford Park, Old Chalford,
t (01608) 641435 **f** (01608) 641435 **e** beechhouse@chalfordpark.co.u

open All year
payment Cash/cheques

Situated in an Area of Outstanding Natural Beauty, an elegant and relaxing base for exploring the lovely Cotswold Hills and villages nearby. A great party house for family get-togethers, anniversaries, birthdays, reunions and holidays. London only 90 minutes by rail or car. Within easy reach of Oxford, Blenheim Palace, Stratford-upon-Avon, Warwick and Cheltenham.

⊕ *M40 jct 11, follow A361 to roundabout before Chipping Norton, turn left on A44 towards Oxford. After traffic lights Chalford Park Barns signposted on left.*

Unit General P Shop 2 miles Pub 2 miles

CLIFTONVILLE

See under Margate

COTSWOLDS

See under Chipping Norton, Witney
See also Cotswolds in South West England section

COWES, Isle of Wight Map ref 2C3

★★★★
SELF CATERING

Units **1**
Sleeps **2–10**
Low season per wk
£355.00–£430.00
High season per wk
£500.00–£630.00

The Old School House, Cowes

t 07831 514108 **e** tim@coweshouse.co.uk **w** coweshouse.co.uk

open All year
payment Cash/cheques

Unique upside-down property offering a first-floor, wooden beamed, loft-style, open-plan sitting/dining and kitchen area. One double, one twin, one bunk, two bathrooms plus two double sofa beds. Recently redecorated in a contemporary style. Conveniently located for Cowes shops, restaurants, bars and marina. Easy access to rest of island by car.

⊕ *Located in East Cowes, in no-through road opposite chain ferry. Easy access by car and passenger ferries from Southampton or Portsmouth.*

❤ *Short breaks available on request.*

Unit General P Leisure Shop < 0.5 miles
Pub < 0.5 miles

CROWBOROUGH, East Sussex Map ref 2D2

★★★★
SELF CATERING

Units **2**
Sleeps **2–4**
Low season per wk
£210.00–£250.00
High season per wk
£335.00–£395.00

Cleeve Lodge & Belle Croix, Crowborough

contact Mr & Mrs Edward & Nina Sibley, The Old House, Harlequin Lane, Crowborough TN6 1HS
t (01892) 654331 **e** nina@the-old-house.co.uk **w** the-old-house.co.uk

Delightful self-catering accommodation either in a Victorian lodge – the separate end of period property dating back to the 1700s – or in a new, high-quality apartment. Fully equipped with lovely views!

open All year
payment Cash/cheques, euros

Unit General P Leisure Shop 1 mile
Pub 0.5 miles

Mention our name

Please mention this guide when making your booking.

NG, Surrey Map ref 2D2

★★★
SELF CATERING

Units 2
Sleeps 2–4
Low season per wk
£250.00–£330.00
High season per wk
£310.00–£400.00

Bulmer Farm, Holmbury St Mary, Dorking

contact Mrs Gill Hill, Bulmer Farm, Holmbury St Mary, Dorking RH5 6LG
t (01306) 730210

Thirty-acre beef farm. Single-storey units converted from 17thC farm building. Two-person unit, suitable for disabled, and four-person unit together form a courtyard to the farmhouse. Brochure available.

open All year
payment Cash/cheques

Unit General P Leisure Shop 3 miles Pub < 0.5 miles

DORKING, Surrey Map ref 2D2

★★★
SELF CATERING

Units 1
Sleeps 1–2
Low season per wk
Max £285.00
High season per wk
Max £285.00

The Little Cottage, Dorking

contact Mrs Susan Scarrott
t (01306) 877256 **e** abacusue@aol.com **w** surreyhills-holiday-cottage.co.uk

Studio accommodation in a detached annexe to an 18thC cottage with its back gate leading into a bluebell wood. Easy walk to town.

open All year
payment Cash/cheques

Unit General P Leisure

DYMCHURCH, Kent Map ref 3B4

★★★★★
SELF CATERING

Units 1
Sleeps 2–8
Low season per wk
£350.00–£500.00
High season per wk
£500.00–£700.00

Dymchurch House, Dymchurch

contact Mrs Uden, 53 Crescent Road, Sidcup DA15 7HW
t (020) 8300 2100 **e** dymchurchhouse@btopenworld.com

open All year
payment Cash/cheques

Luxury, spacious, detached property in a prime position. Equipped to a very high standard. Ideal for superb sandy beach accessed directly via footpath. An indoor swimming pool and the famous miniature railway and village, with its children's amusement park, are all within easy walking distance. Excellent location for visiting tourist attractions.

⊕ *Full directions are given at time of booking.*

Unit General P Leisure

EAST MOLESEY, Surrey Map ref 2D2

★★★★
SELF CATERING

Units 1
Sleeps 6
Low season per wk
£1,000.00
High season per wk
£1,000.00

Wisteria Cottage, East Molesey

contact Jenny Bailey, 11 Riverside Avenue, East Molesey KT8 0AE
t (020) 8339 1278 **f** (020) 8339 1278 **e** jenny@riversiderentals.co.uk **w** riversiderentals.co.uk

Newly renovated cottage with three double bedrooms, two bathrooms and beautiful private gardens backing on to river. Eight minutes' walk to Hampton Court Palace, 35 minutes' direct train journey to London.

open All year
payment Credit/debit cards, cash/cheques

Unit General P Leisure Shop < 0.5 miles
Pub < 0.5 miles

What's in a quality rating?

Information about ratings can be found at the back of this guide.

EMSWORTH, Hampshire Map ref 2C3

★★★
SELF CATERING

Units 1
Sleeps 2–6
Low season per wk
£300.00–£350.00
High season per wk
£360.00–£475.00

Delta House, Emsworth

contact Mr Ben Francis, Flat 1, 38 Mayfield Road, Finsbury Park, London N8 9LP
t (020) 8340 8074 **e** ben@deltahouse-emsworth.co.uk **w** deltahouse-emsworth.co.uk

Delta House is a spacious, three-bedroom townhouse located in the centre of the beautiful fishing village of Emsworth. Located 100m from the harbour.

open All year
payment Cash/cheques

Unit General P Leisure Shop < 0.5 miles Pub < 0.5 miles

EPSOM, Surrey Map ref 2D2

★★★
SELF CATERING

Units 1
Sleeps 1–5
Low season per wk
£190.00–£215.00
High season per wk
£240.00–£265.00

7 Great Tattenhams, Epsom

contact Mrs Mary Willis, 7 Great Tattenhams, Epsom KT18 5RF
t (01737) 354112

Modern, spacious, comfortably furnished first-floor flat. A good touring centre for London and the South East. Superstore nearby.

open All year
payment Cash/cheques

Unit General P Leisure Shop < 0.5 miles Pub 0.75 miles

ESHER, Surrey Map ref 2D2

★★★
SELF CATERING

Units 1
Sleeps 2
Low season per wk
£175.00
High season per wk
£175.00

Lynwood Studio, Thames Ditton

contact Ms Rebecca Hughes, 18 Lynwood Road, Thames Ditton KT7 0DN
t (020) 8339 3739 **e** hughesbex@aol.com **w** lynwoodstudio.co.uk

Large ground-floor studio apartment. Quiet location within private cul-de-sac. Large living area with double bed and sofa, fully equipped kitchen area, bathroom with power shower and wc. TV and DVD player.

open All year
payment Cash/cheques

Unit General P Shop 1 mile Pub 1 mile

ETCHINGHAM, East Sussex Map ref 3B4

★★★★
SELF CATERING

Units 1
Sleeps 5
Low season per wk
Min £300.00
High season per wk
Max £550.00

Moon Cottage, Etchingham, Wadhurst

contact Mrs Jan Harrison, Union Street, Flimwell, Wadhurst TN5 7NT
t (01580) 879328 **f** (01580) 879729 **e** enquiries@harrison-holidays.co.uk **w** harrison-holidays.co.uk

open All year
payment Cash/cheques, euros

Beautifully refurbished/equipped cottage in quiet lane. Country walks in Area of Outstanding Natural Beauty. Convenient for many places of interest, National Trust properties and coastal resorts. Station two miles, with trains to London (one hour). Cosy living room with log-burning stove, conservatory, pretty cottage garden, spacious patio, off-road parking. Pets welcome.

⊕ *From A21 London/Hastings, turn right onto A265 (Heathfield/Lewes). Go to Etchingham village, over level crossing, 1st right after church. Over railway bridge, up hill, sharp left, Sheepstreet Lane.*

❤ *Short breaks available. Please contact us for details.*

Unit General P Leisure Shop 2 miles Pub 2 miles

EXTON, Hampshire Map ref 2C3

★★★★
SELF CATERING

Units 5
Sleeps 1–5
Low season per wk
Max £330.00
High season per wk
Max £485.00

Beacon Hill Farm Cottages, Southampton

contact Mrs Catherine Dunford, Farm Office, Beacon Hill Farm, Alton Road, Warnford, Southampton SO32 3LA
t (01730) 829724 **f** (01730) 829833 **e** info@beaconhillcottages.co.uk **w** beaconhillcottages.co.uk

Barn conversion, comprising studio and cottages, each with garden and barbecue. Farmland views and safe play area. Market towns, Winchester and Portsmouth easily accessible. Excellent village pub. Ideal for cyclists and walkers.

open All year
payment Cash/cheques

Unit General P Leisure Shop 2 miles Pub 2 miles

FARNHAM, Surrey Map ref 2C2

★★
SELF CATERING

Units 2
Sleeps 1–5
Low season per wk
£175.00–£350.00
High season per wk
£210.00–£450.00

High Wray, Farnham

contact Mrs Alexine G N Crawford, High Wray, 73 Lodge Hill Road, Farnham GU10 3RB
t (01252) 715589 **e** crawford@highwray73.co.uk **w** highwray73.co.uk

open All year
payment Cash/cheques

Ground-floor flats ideal for wheelchair users. Dorcy has double and triple bedrooms, kitchen/dining room and wheel-in shower. Rose has similar facilities with twin bed/sitting room. Open-plan studio with barn roof in corner of large garden sleeps two in gallery plus double sofa bed in living area.

⊕ *A31, south at traffic lights to station; over level crossing, immediately bear right into Tilford Road. At top of 2nd hill turn right at crossroads. House 1st on right.*

Unit General P Leisure Shop 0.5 miles Pub 0.5 miles

FAVERSHAM, Kent Map ref 3B3

★★★
SELF CATERING

Units 1
Sleeps 5
High season per wk
Max £450.00

Old Dairy, Selling, Faversham

contact Mrs Gillian Falcon, Shepherds Hill, Selling, Faversham ME13 9RS
t (01227) 752212 **f** (01227) 752212 **e** ag@agfalcon.f9.co.uk

The Old Dairy is a secluded, rural, modernised property with two bedrooms, a 30ft living room and central heating. Within easy reach of beaches, Canterbury, castles and famous gardens. Walking, bird-watching.

open All year
payment Cash/cheques

Unit General P Leisure Shop 4 miles
Pub 1 mile

FORDINGBRIDGE, Hampshire Map ref 2B3

★★★
SELF CATERING

Units 3
Sleeps 2–6
Low season per wk
£250.00–£300.00
High season per wk
£320.00–£500.00

Alderholt Mill, Fordingbridge

contact Mr & Mrs Richard & Sandra Harte, Alderholt Mill, Fordingbridge SP6 1PU
t (01425) 653130 **f** (01425) 652868 **e** alderholt-mill@zetnet.co.uk **w** alderholtmill.co.uk

open All year
payment Credit/debit cards, cash/cheques

Picturesque working water mill. The grain store has been sympathetically converted into delightful holiday apartments comprising two small ground-floor units and one large, air-conditioned, first- and second-floor apartment, all with a wealth of oak beams and modern-day facilities. Idyllic, rural setting. Lovely gardens, private fishing on site. Off-road parking.

⊕ *Directions given at time of booking.*

Unit General 10 Leisure Shop 2 miles Pub 2 miles

FORDINGBRIDGE, Hampshire Map ref 2B3

★★★★–★★★★★
SELF CATERING

Units 8
Sleeps 2–18
Low season per wk
£266.00–£1,414.00
High season per wk
£288.00–£2,952.00

Burgate Manor Farm Holidays, Fordingbridge

contact Mrs Bridget Stallard, Burgate Manor Farm Holidays, Burgat Manor Farm, Burgate, Fordingbridge SP6 1LX
t (01425) 653908 **f** (01425) 653908 **e** info@newforestcottages.com **w** newforestcottages.com

New Forest/Avon Valley. Small- and medium-sized farm cottages and large, recently converted, galleried, beamed barn. Short walk pub/restaurant. Games barn. Fishing. Grazing. Beach 15 miles.

open All year
payment Cash/cheques

Unit General P Leisure Shop 1 mile Pub < 0.5 miles

FORDINGBRIDGE, Hampshire Map ref 2B3

★★★
SELF CATERING

Units 1
Sleeps 4
Low season per wk
£225.00–£300.00
High season per wk
£300.00–£445.00

Glencairn, Fordingbridge

contact Mrs Catriona Tiller, 2 Fernlea, Fordingbridge SP6 1PN
t (01425) 652506

Detached cottage in pleasant, friendly village close to New Forest. Comfortably furnished and well maintained. Three bedrooms, well-equipped kitchen, large, quiet garden. Brochure available. Open March to October and Christmas.

payment Cash/cheques

Unit General P Shop 2 miles Pub < 0.5 miles

Key to symbols

Symbols at the end of each entry help you pick out the services and facilities which are most important for your stay. A key to the symbols can be found inside the back-cover flap. Keep this open for easy reference.

FRESHWATER, Isle of Wight Map ref 2C3

★★★
SELF CATERING

Units **29**
Sleeps **2–7**
Low season per wk
£270.00–£430.00
High season per wk
£440.00–£900.00

Farringford Hotel, Freshwater

contact Miss Lisa Hollyhead, Farringford Hotel, Bedbury Lane, Freshwater PO40 9PE
t (01983) 752500 **f** (01983) 756515 **e** enquiries@farringford.co.uk **w** farringford.co.uk

open All year
payment Euros

Once the home of Alfred Lord Tennyson, now a country-style house with self-catering units of three different styles to suit individual needs. Set within 35 acres of mature pastureland incorporating a 9-hole par 3 golf course, tennis, outdoor heated pool, Bistro Bar and bowls.

⊕ *From A3054 turn left down Pixlie Hill. At roundabout, left to Bay At Bay. Right onto Bedbury Lane.*

❤ *Fully inclusive Christmas packages available. Ferry-inclusive deals available. Subsidised child and pet rates available.*

Unit General P Leisure Shop 0.5 miles Pub 0.5 miles

GLYNDE, East Sussex Map ref 2D3

★★★★
SELF CATERING

Units **8**
Sleeps **2–6**
Low season per wk
£200.00–£480.00
High season per wk
£200.00–£520.00

Caburn Cottages, Glynde

contact Mrs Rosemary Norris, Ranscombe Farm, Glynde BN8 6AA
t (01273) 858062

Lovely flint and brick cottages on working farm. Very comfortable. Non-smoking. Downland walks. Close to Glyndebourne, Lewes and Brighton. Friendly welcome.

open All year
payment Cash/cheques, euros

Unit General P Shop 1.5 miles Pub 1.5 miles

GOSPORT, Hampshire Map ref 2C3

★★★
SELF CATERING

Units **1**
Sleeps **2–4**
Low season per wk
£420.00–£840.00

26 The Quarterdeck, Gosport

contact Mr & Mrs Gibbs, 1 Ellachie Road, Alverstoke, Gosport PO12 2DP
t (023) 9258 6258 **e** info@ellachie.co.uk **w** ellachie.co.uk

Situated in Gosport Marina overlooking Portsmouth Harbour to the Historic Dockyard, naval shipping, ferries, Gunwharf Quays and the Spinnaker Tower.

open All year
payment Cash/cheques

Unit General 1 Leisure Shop < 0.5 miles Pub < 0.5 miles

GOSPORT, Hampshire Map ref 2C3

★★★
SELF CATERING

Units **1**
Sleeps **1–2**
Low season per wk
Min £190.00
High season per wk
Min £260.00

Linden House, Gosport

contact Mrs F Slaven
t (023) 9258 7887 **e** enquiries@harringtonhouses.co.uk **w** harringtonhouses.co.uk

Fully furnished, self-contained apartment on the south coast. Attractive private patio garden. Exclusive access to beach hut. Offers easy access to Portsmouth.

open All year
payment Credit/debit cards, cash/cheques

Unit General Leisure Shop < 0.5 miles Pub < 0.5 miles

Using map references

Map references refer to the colour maps at the front of this guide.

GOSPORT, Hampshire Map ref 2C3

★★★
SELF CATERING

Units 1
Sleeps 1–7
Low season per wk
£285.00–£489.00
High season per wk
£445.00–£645.00

Park House, Gosport

contact Mrs F Slaven
t (023) 9258 7887 **e** enquiries@harringtonhouses.co.uk **w** harringtonhouses.co.uk

Three-bedroom house in a quiet cul-de-sac on the south coast. Near Stokes Bay Beach. Beach hut provided (subject to availability).

open All year
payment Credit/debit cards, cash/cheques

Unit General Leisure Shop < 0.5 miles Pub < 0.5 miles

GOUDHURST, Kent Map ref 3B4

★★★★
SELF CATERING

Units 4
Sleeps 2–8
Low season per wk
£285.00–£550.00
High season per wk
£320.00–£800.00

Three Chimneys Farm, Cranbrook

contact Mrs Marion Fuller, Three Chimneys Farm, Bedgebury Road, Goudhurst, Cranbrook TN17 2RA
t (01580) 212175 **f** (01580) 212175 **e** marionfuller@threechimneysfarm.co.uk
w threechimneysfarm.co.uk

Eighty-acre mixed farm. Spacious cottages in a beautiful location, very quiet but not isolated. Stabling available for two horses.

open All year
payment Credit/debit cards, cash/cheques

Unit General P Leisure Shop 2 miles Pub 2 miles

GUILDFORD, Surrey Map ref 2D2

★★★
SELF CATERING

Units 1
Sleeps 2–6
Low season per wk
Min £500.00
High season per wk
Min £500.00

Lavender, Guildford

contact Mr & Mrs Liew, Mandarin, Pewley Point, Guildford GU1 3SP
t (01483) 506819 & 07906 179084 **f** (01483) 506819 **e** shirleyliew9@hotmail.com

Well-presented, fully furnished, comfortable house, conveniently situated in town centre, close to high street shops, river, theatre, leisure facilities and railway station. Airports 40 minutes.

open All year
payment Cash/cheques

Unit General P

GUILDFORD, Surrey Map ref 2D2

★★–★★★
SELF CATERING

Units 20
Sleeps 4–5
Low season per wk
£380.00–£440.00
High season per wk
£380.00–£440.00

University of Surrey, Guildford

contact Conference Office, University of Surrey, Guildford GU2 7XH
t (01483) 686767 **f** (01483) 579266 **e** conferences@surrey.ac.uk **w** surrey.ac.uk/conferences

Modern, self-contained accommodation for self-catering holidays on attractive campus. One mile from Guildford centre. Ideal base to enjoy London and South East England. Open June, July and August.

payment Credit/debit cards, cash/cheques

Unit General Leisure Shop 0.5 miles Pub 1 mile

Check the maps

Colour maps at the front pinpoint all the places you will find accommodation entries in the regional sections. Pick your location and then refer to the place index at the back to find the page number.

GUILDFORD, Surrey Map ref 2D2

★★★
SELF CATERING

Units **1**
Sleeps **1–5**
Low season per wk
Min £260.00
High season per wk
Min £275.00

West View, West Horsley, Guildford

contact Mrs Janet Steer, West View, Shere Road, Leatherhead KT24 6EW
t (01483) 284686 **e** cliveandjan@aol.com **w** homestead.com/2westview

Apartment attached to country house in woodland of exceptional beauty. Patio, large double bedroom, bathroom with shower, lounge with double sofa bed, futon and cot, kitchen, ample parking, quiet location.

open All year
payment Cash/cheques

Unit General P Shop 0.5 miles Pub 0.5 miles

HAILSHAM, East Sussex Map ref 2D3

★★★–★★★★★
SELF CATERING

Units **5**
Sleeps **4–11**
Low season per wk
Min £385.00
High season per wk
Max £1,586.00

Pekes, Chiddingly

contact Ms Eva Morris, 124 Elm Park Mansions, Park Walk, London SW10 0AR
t (020) 7352 8088 **f** (020) 7352 8125 **e** pekes.afa@virgin.net **w** pekesmanor.com

open All year
payment Cash/cheques

Spacious oast house, cottages and wing of Tudor manor in extensive grounds. Hard tennis court, indoor heated pool, sauna, jacuzzi, badminton. Children and pets welcome. Prices shown are for the cottages; oast house is £1,220.00-£1,586.00.

⊕ *Directions given at time of booking.*

❤ *Off-peak and short breaks available (excl school holidays). Cottages £235-£650, oast house £825-£1,045.*

Unit General P S Leisure U Shop 1.25 miles
Pub 1.25 miles

HASTINGLEIGH, Kent Map ref 3B4

★★★★
SELF CATERING

Units **1**
Sleeps **1–2**
Low season per wk
£300.00
High season per wk
£300.00

Staple Farm, Hastingleigh, Ashford

contact Mr & Mrs Cliff & Betty Martindale, Staple Farm, Hastingleigh, Ashford TN25 5HF
t (01233) 750248 **f** (01233) 750249

payment Cash/cheques

Stable conversion displaying beams and original features, yet offering all modern amenities. Situated in Area of Outstanding Natural Beauty with excellent walks from front door, including the North Downs Way. Within easy reach of Canterbury, Eurostar terminals, Channel ports of Dover and Folkestone, plus many places of historic interest.

⊕ *From M20 jct 9 take A28 towards Wye. At 3rd set of crossroads, 2.8 miles from Wye parish church, turn right.*

Unit General P Shop 2.8 miles Pub 1 mile

HAWKHURST, Kent Map ref 3B4

★★★★
SELF CATERING

Units **1**
Sleeps **2–4**
Low season per wk
£200.00–£250.00
High season per wk
£250.00–£350.00

4 Alma Terrace, Hawkhurst

contact Ms Rachel Barton, Southdowns, Burwash Road, Broad Oak, Heathfield TN21 8TE
t (01435) 868333 **e** bartonrachel@yahoo.co.uk
w holiday-rentals.com/england/holiday-house-kent/p52466.htm

Victorian terrace with country views, garden, patio and shed. Bedrooms: one double, one twin. Near village shop and pubs. Off-street parking. Ideal for cycling, walking, historic sites, houses, gardens.

open All year
payment Cash/cheques

Unit General P Leisure Shop < 0.5 miles Pub < 0.5 miles

HAYLING ISLAND, Hampshire Map ref 2C3

HENFIELD, West Sussex Map ref 2D3

★★★
SELF CATERING

Units **2**
Sleeps **3–5**
Low season per wk
£260.00–£320.00
High season per wk
£320.00–£440.00

New Hall Cottage & New Hall Holiday Flat, Henfield

contact Mrs Marjorie Carreck, New Hall Cottage & New Hall Holiday Flat, New Hall Lane, Small Dole, Henfield BN5 9YJ
t (01273) 492546

open All year
payment Cash/cheques

Self-contained flat and 17thC cottage attached to manor house. Set in 3.5 acres of mature gardens and surrounded by farmland. Within easy reach of famous Sussex gardens – Nymans, High Beeches, Wakehurst Place, Leonardslee – and less than an hour from Wisley. Or visit the towns of Brighton, Arundel, Lewes and Chichester, the South Downs and the coast.

⊕ *Leave A23 at Henfield and Hurstpierpoint sign. Take A2037 south from Henfield for 2 miles. New Hall Lane is 2nd turning on right after Woods Mill.*

♥ *Short breaks available: £150 for 2 nights, each extra night £45.*

Unit General P Leisure Shop 0.5 miles Pub 0.5 miles

If you have access needs...

Look for the National Accessible Scheme symbols if you have special hearing, visual or mobility needs. An index of all accommodation participating in the scheme can be found at the back of this guide.

HENLEY-ON-THAMES, Oxfordshire Map ref 2C2

★★
SELF CATERING

Units **1**
Sleeps **2**
Low season per wk
£190.00
High season per wk
£220.00–£250.00

The Studio, Henley-on-Thames

contact Mrs Kuipers, 2 Bell Lane, Henley-on-Thames RG9 2HP
t (01491) 574760

In a quiet residential cul-de-sac, close to town centre and Phyllis Court Club. Charmingly decorated studio with central heating, garden view and parking.

open All year
payment Cash/cheques, euros

Unit General P

HIGH HALDEN, Kent Map ref 3B4

★★★★
SELF CATERING

Units **2**
Sleeps **2–8**
Low season per wk
£315.00–£455.00
High season per wk
£480.00–£520.00

The Granary & The Stables, Nr Tenterden

contact Mrs Serena Maundrell, Vintage Years Company Ltd, High Halden, Ashford TN26 3JQ
t (01233) 850871 & 07715 488804 **f** (01233) 850717 **e** serena@vintage-years.co.uk
w vintage-years.co.uk

open All year
payment Cash/cheques, euros

The Granary is beautifully converted and heavily beamed, with one double and one twin. The Stables has two en suite bedrooms on one level, one designed for wheelchair access. Both units are comfortably furnished and fully equipped. Set in ten acres of gardens, they provide tranquillity and an excellent touring base.

⊕ *Details given at time of booking.*

❤ *Swim for free at Tenterden Leisure Centre. Enjoy dinner and cinema evenings. Details on request.*

Unit General P Leisure Shop 2 miles Pub 1 mile

HIGHCLERE, Hampshire Map ref 2C2

★★★
SELF CATERING

Units **1**
Sleeps **3**
Low season per wk
£300.00
High season per wk
£300.00

Glencross Annexe, Highclere, Newbury

Glencross Annexe, Mount Road, Highclere, Newbury RG20 9QZ
t (01635) 253244 **e** annexe@owenalex.freeserve.co.uk

Lounge with french window, kitchen/diner, upstairs bathroom/shower, one twin, one single bedroom, storage heaters, payphone and parking for two cars.

open All year
payment Cash/cheques

Unit General 12 P S Leisure Shop 1 mile Pub 1 mile

HILDENBOROUGH, Kent Map ref 2D2

★★★
SELF CATERING

Units **1**
Sleeps **2**
Low season per wk
£190.00–£210.00
High season per wk
£220.00–£240.00

The Cottage, Tonbridge

contact Mr Dudley Hurrell, The Cottage, Coldharbour Lane, Hildenborough, Tonbridge TN11 9LE
t (01732) 832081 **f** (01732) 832081

Attractive cottage-style self-contained extension to converted stable block set in mature garden in a rural situation. One mile along quiet lane from main road (B254). Open June to September inclusive.

payment Cash/cheques

Unit General P Shop 0.5 miles Pub 0.5 miles

Make it a date

Check out the events listing at the back of the guide, or for latest information go online at enjoyengland.com.

HOLLINGBOURNE, Kent Map ref 3B3

★★★★★
SELF CATERING

Units 1
Sleeps 7
Low season per wk
£625.00–£795.00
High season per wk
£850.00–£1,195.00

Well Cottage, Hollingbourne

contact Mr & Mrs Paul & Angela Dixon, North Downs Country Cottages, The Courtyard, Hollingbourne House, Hollingbourne, Maidstone ME17 1QJ
t (01622) 880991 **f** (01622) 880991 **e** info@wellcottagekent.co.uk **w** wellcottagekent.co.uk

open All year
payment Credit/debit cards, cash/cheques

Situated on top of the North Downs, an Area of Outstanding Natural Beauty, Well Cottage is Grade II Listed and restored to the highest standards. Large farmhouse kitchen/diner, characterful lounge with wood-burning stove, atmospheric dining room, two double bedrooms with en suites, a twin and single bedroom and family bathroom.

⊕ *M20 jct 8, follow A20 towards Lenham, at roundabout turn left. Go through Hollingbourne, up Hollingbourne Hill. On brow turn right into Hollingbourne House, take left fork to cottage.*

❤ *Short breaks available all year (excl Christmas and New Year).*

Unit General P Leisure Shop 1.5 miles Pub 0.5 miles

HOVE

See under Brighton & Hove

IBSLEY, Hampshire Map ref 2B3

★★★★★
SELF CATERING

Units 1
Sleeps 6
Low season per wk
£450.00–£650.00
High season per wk
£695.00–£795.00

Chocolate Box Cottage, Ringwood

contact Mrs Frances Higham
t (01268) 741036 & 07768 075761 **f** (01268) 741990 **e** chocolateboxcottage@btinternet.com
w chocolateboxcottage.co.uk

Beautiful 'chocolate box' cottage set in 0.5-acre grounds, on the edge of the New Forest. High-standard accommodation. Pets welcome. Smoking permitted. Ideal for exploring the New Forest.

open All year
payment Cash/cheques

Unit General P Leisure Shop 1 mile Pub < 0.5 miles

ISLE OF WIGHT

See under Bembridge, Cowes, Freshwater, Ryde, Shanklin, Totland Bay, Ventnor, Whitwell

ITCHEN ABBAS, Hampshire Map ref 2C2

★★★–★★★★
SELF CATERING

Units 2
Sleeps 2–4
Low season per wk
Min £395.00
High season per wk
Max £600.00

Itchen Down Farm, Winchester

contact Mrs Brenda Hulme, Itchen Down Farm, Itchen Down, Winchester SO21 1BS
t (01962) 779388 **e** itchendownfarm@farming.co.uk **w** itchendownfarm.co.uk

Converted brick and flint traditional farm courtyard adjacent to farmhouse, situated in idyllic Hampshire downland. WI-FI Internet in both units for guests' use.

open All year
payment Cash/cheques

Unit General P Leisure Shop 3 miles Pub 1 mile

It's all quality-assessed accommodation

Our commitment to quality involves wide-ranging accommodation assessment. Ratings and awards were correct at the time of going to press but may change following a new assessment. Please check at the time of booking.

LEE-ON-THE-SOLENT, Hampshire Map ref 2C3

★★★
SELF CATERING

Units **1**
Sleeps **5–6**
Low season per wk
£280.00–£350.00
High season per wk
£380.00–£450.00

The Chart House, Lee-on-the-Solent

contact Mr Brook White, 6 Cambridge Road, Lee-on-the-Solent PO13 9DH
t (023) 9255 4145 **f** (023) 9255 3847 **e** brook.white1@btopenworld.com
w brook.white1.btinternet.co.uk

Comfortable, detached, three-bedroomed family home, close to seafront. Enclosed patio/garden. Off-road parking. Private indoor heated pool available by arrangement.

open All year
payment Cash/cheques

Unit General **P** Leisure Shop 0.5 miles Pub < 0.5 miles

LEWES, East Sussex Map ref 2D3

★★★
SELF CATERING

Units **1**
Sleeps **1–4**
Low season per wk
£220.00–£265.00
High season per wk
£265.00–£290.00

5 Buckhurst Close, Lewes

contact Mrs S Foulds, 66 Houndean Rise, Lewes BN7 1EJ
t (01273) 474755 **f** (01273) 474755

Modern terraced house, fully equipped. Small garden, parking space. Easy walking distance to town. Five minutes' drive to station or Glyndebourne.

open All year
payment Cash/cheques

Unit TV General **P** Shop 1 mile Pub 2 miles

LEWES, East Sussex Map ref 2D3

★★★★–★★★★★
SELF CATERING

Units **4**
Sleeps **2–6**
Low season per wk
£283.00–£465.00
High season per wk
£400.00–£850.00

Mill Laine Farm, Offham, Lewes

contact Mrs Susan Harmer, Offham, Lewes BN7 3QB
t (01273) 475473 **e** harmer@farming.co.uk **w** milllainebarns.co.uk

Near historic Lewes, luxuriously converted, comfortable, well-equipped barns with central heating and wood stove. Outstanding views. Walking and riding in a secluded valley.

open All year
payment Cash/cheques

Unit TV General **P** S Leisure Shop 1 mile Pub < 0.5 miles

LEWES, East Sussex Map ref 2D3

★★★★
SELF CATERING

Units **2**
Sleeps **1–4**
Low season per wk
£300.00–£400.00
High season per wk
£400.00–£600.00

Sussex Countryside Accommodation, Barcombe, Lewes

contact Mrs Hazel Gaydon, Sussex Countryside Accommodation, Crink House, Barcombe Mills, Lewes BN8 5BJ
t (01273) 400625 **e** info@crinkhouse.co.uk **w** sussexcountryaccommodation.co.uk

Well-appointed holiday cottages with panoramic views, four miles from Lewes. Two bathrooms, two showers. Some ground-floor bedrooms. Parking. Garden. No smoking. Friday to Friday lets.

open All year
payment Cash/cheques

Unit TV General **P** Shop 0.5 miles Pub 0.5 miles

How many beds?

The minimum and maximum number of people that each property can accommodate is shown. If an entry includes details of more than one property the sleeping capacity may vary between them. Please check when you make your booking.

LYMINGTON, Hampshire Map ref 2C3

★★★★
SELF CATERING

Units **1**
Sleeps **1–4**
Low season per wk
£350.00–£450.00
High season per wk
£500.00–£600.00

No 17 Southampton Road, Lymington

contact Miss Julie Stevens & Andrew Baxendine, Elm Cottage, Pilley Bailey, Lymington SO41 5QT
t (01590) 676445 **e** juleestevens@aol.com **w** 17southamptonroad.co.uk

Beautifully presented three-bedroom Georgian townhouse. Close proximity to shops, restaurants and pretty town quay. Secluded patio garden. Isle of Wight ferry nearby. Welcome pack.

open All year
payment Cash/cheques

Unit General 10 P

LYMINGTON, Hampshire Map ref 2C3

★★★
SELF CATERING

Units **1**
Sleeps **1–8**
Low season per wk
£420.00–£590.00
High season per wk
£640.00–£875.00

2 Uplay Cottages, Lymington

contact Ms Jacquie Taylor, Three Corners, Centre Lane, Everton, Lymington SO41 0JP
t (01590) 641810 **f** (01590) 673633 **e** bookings@halcyonholidays.com **w** halcyonholidays.com

A beautifully refurbished, comfortable Edwardian cottage set at the end of a quiet, no-through lane in the heart of the village with shops, pub, coast and forest nearby.

open All year
payment Credit/debit cards, cash/cheques

Unit General P Leisure Shop < 0.5 miles
Pub < 0.5 miles

LYMINGTON, Hampshire Map ref 2C3

★★★
SELF CATERING

Units **1**
Sleeps **12**
Low season per wk
£420.00–£800.00
High season per wk
£840.00–£1,280.00

Wheathill, Lymington

contact Mrs Jacquie Taylor, Three Corners, Centre Lane, Everton, Lymington SO41 0JP
t (01590) 641810 **f** (01590) 671325 **e** jacquie@halcyonholidays.com **w** halcyonholidays.com

open All year
payment Credit/debit cards, cash/cheques, euros

In a semi-rural location on the outskirts of Lymington, on a leafy road leading to the New Forest, this beautifully refurbished house has mature gardens. An ideal base for exploring Lymington Quay, the New Forest, coastal walks and marshes. See website for further pictures and information/guest comments.

⊕ *Directions given at time of booking.*

❤ *Discounted weekend/mid-week bookings available all year round.*

Unit General P Leisure Shop 0.5 miles
Pub 0.5 miles

Our quality rating schemes

For a detailed explanation of the quality and facilities represented by the stars please refer to the information pages at the back of this guide.

LYNDHURST, Hampshire Map ref 2C3

★★★★
SELF CATERING

Units **1**
Sleeps **5**
Low season per wk
£300.00–£495.00
High season per wk
£520.00–£675.00

Bay Tree Cottage, Lyndhurst

contact Mrs Katrina Long, 12 Princes Crescent, Lyndhurst SO43 7BS
t (023) 8028 2821 **f** (023) 8028 2821 **w** baytreecottage.co.uk

open All year
payment Credit/debit cards, cash/cheques

New Forest. Delightful, well-equipped cottage close to Lyndhurst village centre. Short walk to shops, pubs and restaurants. Three bedrooms: one double, one twin and one single. Sitting room, separate dining room, kitchen, cloakroom. Enclosed garden with shed for bicycles. Near open forest for scenic drives, walking and cycling.

Unit General Leisure

LYNDHURST, Hampshire Map ref 2C3

★★★
SELF CATERING

Units **1**
Sleeps **1–6**
Low season per wk
£170.00–£350.00
High season per wk
£350.00–£575.00

Fern Cottage, Lyndhurst

contact Mr Robin Austin, The Hollies, Sandy Lane, Belbins, Romsey SO51 0PE
t 07717 796156 **f** (023) 8033 3881 **e** robaust@aol.com **w** lyndhurstholidays.com

An attractive renovated Victorian cottage within walking distance of Lyndhurst village centre and the New Forest.

open All year
payment Cash/cheques

Unit General Shop 0.5 miles Pub 0.5 miles

LYNDHURST, Hampshire Map ref 2C3

★★★
SELF CATERING

Units **1**
Sleeps **8–28**
Low season per wk
£480.00–£1,680.00
High season per wk
£1,200.00–£4,480.00

The Old Stables, Lyndhurst

contact Jacquie Taylor, Halcyon Holiday Cottages, Three Corners, Centre Lane, Everton, Lymington SO41 0JP
t (01590) 641810 **f** (01590) 671325 **e** booking@halcyonholidays.com **w** halcyonholidays.com

Holiday cottage situated off the High Street in Lyndhurst village – the traditional capital of the New Forest.

open All year
payment Credit/debit cards, cash/cheques

Unit General Leisure Shop < 0.5 miles
Pub < 0.5 miles

MAIDSTONE, Kent Map ref 3B3

★★★★
SELF CATERING

Units **1**
Sleeps **4**
Low season per wk
£375.00–£395.00
High season per wk
£410.00–£425.00

The Old Wagon Lodge, Maidstone

contact Sarah Sunnucks, Linton Hill, Linton, Maidstone ME17 4AU
t (01622) 745631 **f** (01622) 741512 **e** scarytoe@kentit.net **w** rankinsfarm.co.uk

open All year
payment Cash/cheques

Beautiful two-bedroom cottage, vaulted, open-plan living/dining with kitchen area and bathroom. Situated in heart of working fruit farm. Farm shop on site, open April to October. Spectacular countryside. Ideal base for sightseeing. Leeds/Sissinghurst Castle nearby. London one hour by train. DEFRA/EU supported.

⊕ *On main A229 Maidstone to Hastings road. Down Linton Hill, passing The Bull public house on right. Approx 0.5 miles on right, turn into Rankins Farm.*

Unit TV General P Leisure Shop 2 miles Pub 0.5 miles

MARGATE, Kent Map ref 3C3

★★★★
SELF CATERING

Units **3**
Sleeps **4–6**
Low season per wk
£400.00–£600.00
High season per wk
£400.00–£600.00

Salmestone Grange, Margate

Salmestone Grange, Nash Road, Margate CT9 4BX
t (01843) 231161 **f** (01843) 231161 **e** salmestonegrange@aol.com **w** salmestonegrange.co.uk

open All year
payment Credit/debit cards, cash/cheques

Unique 14thC monastic grange set in beautiful gardens. The lovingly restored apartments have many original features which capture a 'modern meets medieval' experience. Salmestone Grange is centrally located to the area's five main sandy beaches, with other tourist attractions, festivals, shopping centre and public transport also close by.

⊕ *From M25, follow M2 then A299 onto A28 into Margate. Turn off onto B2052, following signposts to QEQM hospital. Straight ahead at traffic lights, 300yds on right-hand side.*

♥ *Mid-week and nightly stay visitors are also welcome (a nightly tariff applies). Please call for further information.*

Unit TV General P S Leisure Shop < 0.5 miles Pub < 0.5 miles

MEOPHAM, Kent Map ref 3B3

★★★★
SELF CATERING

Units **1**
Sleeps **2**
Low season per wk
Min £300.00
High season per wk
Max £350.00

Feathercot Lodge, Gravesend

contact Mrs S Smith, New Street Road, Meopham, Gravesend DA13 0JS
t (01474) 872265 & 07764 784370 **e** feathercot@hotmail.com **w** holidayhomeandaway.com

Fully equipped luxury log cabin with double bedroom, walk-in shower, TV, DVD, Freeview, dishwasher, microwave, washing machine etc. Rural location, near Brands Hatch. Secure parking.

open All year
payment Cash/cheques

Unit TV General P Leisure Shop 2 miles Pub 2 miles

Pool search

If a swimming pool is an essential element of your holiday accommodation check out the special index at the back of this guide.

MILFORD ON SEA, Hampshire Map ref 2C3

★★★
SELF CATERING

Units 1
Sleeps 5
Low season per wk
£225.00–£250.00
High season per wk
£295.00–£525.00

Windmill Cottage, Milford on Sea

contact Mrs Perham, 14 Kivernell Road, Milford on Sea, Lymington SO41 0PQ
t (01590) 643516 **f** (01590) 641255

open All year
payment Cash/cheques

Delightful Georgian-style house in quiet residential area close to village, sea and the New Forest. Three bedrooms – one double, one twin and one single. Recently refitted kitchen. Garage and easy parking. Five minutes' walk to village centre, good restaurants and pubs. Many places of interest nearby.

⊕ *Directions provided in advance to every visitor.*

Unit General P Leisure Shop < 0.5 miles
Pub < 0.5 miles

MOLLINGTON, Oxfordshire Map ref 2C1

★★★–★★★★
SELF CATERING

Units 3
Sleeps 2–8
Low season per wk
£160.00–£595.00
High season per wk
£240.00–£795.00

The Stables, The Shippon, The Byre – Anita's Holiday Cottages, Mollington

contact Mr & Mrs Darrel & Anita Gail Jeffries, Anita's Holiday Cottages, The Yews, Church Farm, Banbury OX17 1AZ
t (01295) 750731 **f** (01295) 750731 **e** anitagail@btopenworld.com

open All year
payment Cash/cheques

Converted from an old cow byre, these cottages are superbly finished to a high standard. Situated in the lovely village of Mollington, within walking distance of the pub. Central to Oxford, Stratford-on-Avon, Blenheim, Warwick and the Cotswolds. Lovely walks and cycling, even fishing close by.

⊕ *M40 jct 11, follow sign to Chipping Norton. Over 2 roundabouts to 3rd roundabout onto A423 to Southam. Mollington after four miles. The Yews 200yds past turning on left.*

❤ *Short breaks available on request.*

Unit General P Leisure Shop 1 mile
Pub < 0.5 miles

NEW FOREST

See under Fordingbridge, Lymington, Lyndhurst, Milford on Sea, Woodgreen

NEWBURY, Berkshire Map ref 2C2

Rating Applied For
SELF CATERING

Units 2
Sleeps 2–8
Low season per wk
Min £260.00

Yaffles, Newbury

contact Mr & Mrs Steve & Nikki Absolom, Yaffles, Red Shute Hill, Hermitage, Thatcham RG18 9QH
t (01635) 201100 **f** (01635) 201100 **e** yaffles@ukonline.co.uk **w** yaffles.org

Comfortable, secluded, self-contained garden flat and studio set in spacious, peaceful grounds just north of Newbury yet near junction 13 of M4. Prices are for two people.

open All year
payment Cash/cheques

Unit General P Leisure Shop 0.5 miles Pub 0.5 miles

Prices

These are shown for one week's accommodation. If an entry includes details of more than one property it is usual that the minimum price is for low season in the smallest property and the maximum price is for high season in the largest property.

NITON, Isle of Wight Map ref 2C3

★★
SELF CATERING

Units **1**
Low season per wk
£165.00–£220.00
High season per wk
£255.00–£330.00

Wight Heaven, Ventnor

contact Mr & Mrs John Sheppard, 4 Withers Road, Chale Green, Ventnor PO38 2JJ
t (01983) 551501 **e** dadshep@dial.pipex.com **w** wightheaven.co.uk

Comfortable chalet on small, peaceful, gated, gardened site in Area of Outstanding Natural Beauty at island's southern tip. Suit peacelovers, honeymooners, walkers or cyclists.

open All year
payment Cash/cheques

Unit General Shop 0.5 miles Pub 0.5 miles

NORTHIAM, East Sussex Map ref 3B4

Rating Applied For
SELF CATERING

Units **1**
Sleeps **2–5**
Low season per wk
£250.00–£325.00
High season per wk
£325.00–£375.00

Hop Press Cottage, Rye

contact Ms Brenda Haines, Hop Press Cottage, Morley Farm, Beckley Road, Rye TN31 6JB
t (01797) 252011 **e** brenda@curtishaines.co.uk **w** froglets.uk.com

An idyllic Grade II Listed cottage, perfect for a special break. Full gas central heating, inglenook fireplace, vaulted ceilings and pretty barbecue terrace.

open All year
payment Credit/debit cards, cash/cheques

Unit General P Leisure Shop 1 mile Pub 1 mile

NUTLEY, East Sussex Map ref 2D3

★★★★
SELF CATERING

Units **1**
Sleeps **1–4**
Low season per wk
£300.00–£400.00
High season per wk
£400.00–£500.00

The Old Cart Lodge, Uckfield

contact Mrs Pauline Graves, 2 Victoria Cottages, Bell Lane, Nutley, Uckfield TN22 3PD
t (01825) 712475 **f** (01825) 712475 **e** grapauline@aol.com

open All year
payment Cash/cheques, euros

Ashdown Forest, in the beautiful Sussex countryside. With fourteen years' experience of providing first-class accommodation, we offer The Old Cart Lodge, our latest venture. One king-size room, one twin, and a secluded garden in a peaceful location. Wakehurst Place, Sheffield Park and Bluebell Railway nearby, plus many other National Trust gardens and houses.

⊕ *Follow A22 from East Grinstead to Nutley for approx 7 miles. Turn right by church wall. Travel 0.75 miles down hill. Climb hill. Farm and lodge on right.*

Unit General P Leisure Shop 1 mile Pub 1.5 miles

NUTLEY, East Sussex Map ref 2D3

★★-★★★
SELF CATERING

Units 10
Sleeps 1–5
Low season per wk
£249.00–£449.00
High season per wk
£336.00–£449.00

Whitehouse Farm Holiday Cottages, Nutley

contact Mr Keith Wilson, Whitehouse Farm Holiday Cottages, Whitehouse Farm, Uckfield TN22 3EE
t (01825) 712377 **f** (01825) 712377 **e** keith.g.r.wilson@btinternet.com
w streets-ahead.com/whitehousefarm

open All year
payment Credit/debit cards, cash/cheques

Former smallholding overlooking open countryside and Ashdown Forest. Shower room, kitchen/diner/lounge. Fully equipped. Wheelchair-, pet- and smoker-friendly cottages available. Spare camp-beds. Ideally situated for London, castles, gardens and coast. Both Friday and Saturday turnaround.

⊕ *From M23 jct 10. Access from A22, 1 mile south of Nutley, on left.*

Unit General P Leisure Shop 1.25 miles Pub 1.25 miles

OXFORD, Oxfordshire Map ref 2C1

★★★
SELF CATERING

Units 1
Sleeps 4
Low season per wk
£500.00–£575.00
High season per wk
£575.00

48 St Bernards Road, Oxford

contact Ms Julie Gardiner, St Bernards Road, Oxford OX2 6EH
t (01865) 321101 **e** greenhavenoxford@btconnect.com **w** holidayhomeoxford.co.uk

Two-bedroom terraced house in central location. Spacious lounge and kitchen/diner. Small, paved private garden area. Recently renovated and decorated.

open All year
payment Cash/cheques

Unit General P Shop < 0.5 miles Pub < 0.5 miles

OXFORD, Oxfordshire Map ref 2C1

★★★★★
SELF CATERING

Units 1
Sleeps 1–5
High season per wk
£700.00–£900.00

Cherbridge Cottage, Oxford

contact Ms Laura Colman, Hill Farm, Mill Lane, Marston OX3 0QG
t (01865) 512920 & 07976 288329 **e** laura@cherbridgecottages.co.uk **w** cherbridgecottages.co.uk

open All year
payment Credit/debit cards, cash/cheques

Cherbridge Cottage is part of a 1930s punting station, providing spacious holiday accommodation with en suite facilities. The secluded garden has extensive river frontage. Private punts are available, or guests are welcome to bring their own boat. Oxford city centre is easily accessible, being just two miles distant.

⊕ *For location and directions please contact us by telephone or visit our website.*

Unit General P Leisure Shop 1.5 miles
Pub 1.5 miles

Take a break

Look out for special promotions and themed breaks. This could be your chance to indulge an interest, find a new one, or just relax and enjoy exceptional value! Offers are highlighted in colour (and are subject to availability).

PANGBOURNE, Berkshire Map ref 2C2

★★★
SELF CATERING

Units **1**
Sleeps **5**
Low season per wk
Min £395.00
High season per wk
Max £475.00

Brambly Thatch, Nr Reading

contact Mr & Mrs Hatt, Merricroft Farming, Goring Heath, Reading RG8 7TA
t (0118) 984 3121 **f** (0118) 984 4662 **e** merricroft@yahoo.co.uk

open All year
payment Credit/debit cards, cash/cheques

Picturebook brick and flint thatched cottage on 300-acre beef and arable farm. Ideal base for visiting London, Oxford, Stonehenge and Stratford, and for sightseeing in the Thames Valley, Chilterns, Cotswolds and beyond. A warm and friendly home from home for a holiday to remember. Please telephone for quickest response.

⊕ *From M4 jct 12 or M40 jcts 6-9, or by train to Reading, Pangbourne or Goring.*

❤ *Pay by credit card free of charge if you mention this advert. Also special monthly rates in winter.*

Unit General P Leisure Shop 2 miles Pub 1 mile

PLAXTOL, Kent Map ref 2D2

★★★
SELF CATERING

Units **1**
Sleeps **1–6**
Low season per wk
Min £220.00
High season per wk
Max £430.00

Golding Hop Farm Cottage, Sevenoaks

contact Mrs Jacqueline Vincent, Golding Hop Farm, Bewley Lane, Plaxtol, Sevenoaks TN15 0PS
t (01732) 885432 **e** info@goldinghopfarm.com **w** goldinghopfarm.com

South-facing cottage on 12-acre cobnut farm. Quiet position, but not isolated. Three bedrooms (two twin, one single), garden, all modern conveniences.

open All year
payment Cash/cheques

Unit General P Leisure Shop 1.5 miles Pub < 0.5 miles

PORTSMOUTH & SOUTHSEA, Hampshire Map ref 2C3

★★★
SELF CATERING

Units **6**
Sleeps **1–7**
Low season per wk
£100.00–£300.00
High season per wk
£200.00–£400.00

Atlantic Apartments, Southsea

contact Mrs Dawn Sait, Atlantic Apartments, 63a Festing Road, Southsea PO4 0NQ
t (023) 9282 3606 **f** (023) 9229 7046 **w** portsmouth-apartments.co.uk/atlantic.htm

Situated in one of the most attractive areas of Southsea, only a few yards from the canoe lake and seafront. All apartments are fully self-contained. Large car park.

open All year
payment Cash/cheques, euros

Unit General P Leisure Shop < 0.5 miles Pub < 0.5 miles

PORTSMOUTH & SOUTHSEA, Hampshire Map ref 2C3

★★★
SELF CATERING

Units **6**
Sleeps **1–8**
Low season per wk
£200.00–£350.00
High season per wk
£250.00–£600.00

Ocean Apartments, Southsea

contact Mrs Dawn Sait, 8-10 St Helens Parade, Southsea PO4 0RW
t (023) 9273 4233 **f** (023) 9229 7046 **e** ocean@portsmouth-apartments.co.uk
w portsmouth-apartments.co.uk/ocean.htm

Imposing seafront building with magnificent views. Recently refurbished. Very spacious one- to four-bedroomed self-contained apartments, lift, private car parking. Executive suites available. Short- and long-term bookings welcome.

open All year
payment Cash/cheques, euros

Unit General P Leisure Shop 1 mile Pub < 0.5 miles

Pool search

If a swimming pool is an essential element of your holiday accommodation check out the special index at the back of this guide.

ROCHESTER, Kent Map ref 3B3

★★★★
SELF CATERING

Units 6
Sleeps 5–8
Low season per wk
£250.00–£450.00
High season per wk
£400.00–£600.00

Stable Cottages, Rochester

contact Mrs Debbie Symonds, Stable Cottages, Fenn Croft, Newland Farm Road, St Mary Hoo, Rochester ME3 8QS
t (01634) 272439 & 07802 662702 **f** (01634) 272205 **e** stablecottages@btinternet.com
w stable-cottages.com

open All year
payment Cash/cheques

These luxury, oak-beamed cottages are set in 20 acres of secluded farmland close to RSPB reserve with panoramic views of the Thames. Access to motorways and ports. London/Canterbury 45 minutes. Perfect base for walking, bird-watching, sightseeing or just getting away from it all. Warm welcome. Family run. Indoor pool.

⊕ *From M2 jct 1, follow A228 towards Grain, turn off towards Allhallows. 1st left, follow lane to end, bear right at pond and follow track to end.*

❤ *Short breaks and split weeks available.*

Unit General Leisure Shop 3 miles Pub 1 mile

ROTHERFIELD, East Sussex Map ref 2D2

★★★★
SELF CATERING

Units 1
Sleeps 1–4
Low season per wk
£300.00–£350.00
High season per wk
£500.00–£560.00

Medway Farm Barn Cottage, Rotherfield, Crowborough

contact Mr & Mrs Mark & Sue Playford, Medway Farm Barn, Catts Hill, Crowborough TN6 3NQ
t (01892) 852802 **f** (01892) 752062 **e** contact@medwayfarmbarn.co.uk **w** medwayfarmbarn.co.uk

open All year
payment Cash/cheques, euros

Delightful, detached, newly converted two-bedroom cottage in the heart of Sussex, close to local amenities. London and coastal towns within easy reach. Superb woodland walks surround the property. Children and pets welcome.

⊕ *Take A259 south from Tunbridge Wells to Eastbourne. After approx 6 miles turn right at Mark Cross. 0.7 miles Medway Farm Barn on right.*

❤ *Equestrian facilities available to include stable, grazing, sand and school hacking on local bridle paths.*

Unit General Leisure Shop < 0.5 miles Pub 0.7 miles

ROYAL TUNBRIDGE WELLS, Kent Map ref 2D2

★★★
SELF CATERING

Units 1
Sleeps 4
Low season per wk
£240.00–£260.00
High season per wk
£250.00–£260.00

22 Hawkenbury Mead, Royal Tunbridge Wells

contact Mr R H Wright, Hawkenbury Farm, Hawkenbury Road, Royal Tunbridge Wells TN3 9AD
t (01892) 536977 **f** (01892) 536200 **e** rhwright1@aol.com

A charming furnished cottage set on the outskirts of the historic spa town of Royal Tunbridge Wells.

open All year
payment Credit/debit cards, cash/cheques

Unit General Leisure Shop < 0.5 miles Pub < 0.5 miles

Use your i's

Tourist information centres provide a wealth of information and friendly advice, both before you go and during your stay. Refer to the front of this section for a list of tourist information centres in the region.

ROYAL TUNBRIDGE WELLS, Kent Map ref 2D2

★★★
SELF CATERING

Units **2**
Sleeps **2–4**
Low season per wk
Min £240.00
High season per wk
Max £350.00

Ford Cottage, Royal Tunbridge Wells

contact Mrs Wendy Cusdin, Ford Cottage, Linden Park Road, Tunbridge Wells TN2 5QL
t (01892) 531419 **e** FordCottage@tinyworld.co.uk **w** fordcottage.co.uk

open All year except Christmas
payment Cash/cheques, euros

Ford Cottage is a picturesque Victorian cottage three minutes' walk from the Pantiles. Self-contained studio flats with own front doors, fully fitted kitchens, en suites and showers. Off-street parking. Ideal for visiting many local gardens, castles and historic houses. Prices are for two or four people.

⊕ *M25 jct 5, A21 towards Hastings. After 10 miles take A26 to Tunbridge Wells. Follow signs to Pantiles. At end turn immediately into Linden Park Road.*

❤ *Short breaks available – terms on request.*

Unit General 1 P Leisure Shop < 0.5 miles Pub < 0.5 miles

ROYAL TUNBRIDGE WELLS, Kent Map ref 2D2

★★★★
SELF CATERING

Units **6**
Sleeps **2–4**
Low season per wk
£252.00–£288.00
High season per wk
£375.00–£430.00

Itaris Properties Limited, Royal Tunbridge Wells

contact Mrs Angela May, Itaris Properties Ltd, 12 Mount Ephraim, Royal Tunbridge Wells TN4 8AS
t (01892) 511065 **f** (01892) 540171 **e** enquiries@itaris.co.uk **w** itaris.co.uk

open All year
payment Cash/cheques

Royal Tunbridge Wells is surrounded by beautiful and unspoilt countryside and is the ideal location for a short break or relaxing holiday. Our self-contained and fully equipped holiday apartments are situated in the very heart of Tunbridge Wells within walking distance of its many amenities.

⊕ *From M25 jct 5 A21 and A26 to Tunbridge Wells.*

Unit General P

RUCKINGE, Kent Map ref 3B4

★★★
SELF CATERING

Units **1**
Sleeps **1–7**
Low season per wk
£295.00–£375.00
High season per wk
£400.00–£525.00

The Old Post Office, Ashford

contact Mr Chris Cook, 121 The Drive, Beckenham BR3 1EF
t (020) 8655 4466 **f** (020) 8656 7755 **e** c.cook@btinternet.com **w** ruckinge.info

open All year
payment Credit/debit cards, cash/cheques

A comprehensively equipped large house, very suitable for two families holidaying together. Four bedrooms, two kitchens, two bathrooms, a huge garden from which public footpaths lead off, canal walks 100yds. Full central heating, digital TV and many books and guides. Website has pictures of all the rooms.

⊕ *M20 jct 10, south on A2070 (Brenzett). After 4 miles onto B2067 through Ham Street. Property on left after 1.5 miles – follow Ruckinge direction signs.*

❤ *Short breaks Sep-Jun.*

Unit General P Leisure Shop 1.5 miles
Pub < 0.5 miles

Travel update

Get the latest travel information – just dial the RAC on 1740 from your mobile phone.

RYDE, Isle of Wight Map ref 2C3

★★★★
SELF CATERING

Units **2**
Sleeps **2–3**
Low season per wk
£150.00–£200.00
High season per wk
£300.00–£350.00

Claverton House, Ryde

contact Dr Hartwig Metz, Claverton, 12 The Strand, Ryde PO33 1JE
t (01983) 613015 **f** (01983) 613015 **e** clavertonhouse@aol.com
w hometown.aol.co.uk/clavertonhouse

Beautiful holiday residence on Ryde's seafront, overlooking the Solent. Ten minutes' walk to town centre, bus station and passenger ferries.

open All year
payment Cash/cheques, euros

Unit General P Shop < 0.5 miles Pub < 0.5 miles

RYE, East Sussex Map ref 3B4

★★★
SELF CATERING

Units **1**
Sleeps **3–4**
Low season per wk
£240.00–£305.00
High season per wk
£310.00–£480.00

Chesterfield Cottage, Rye

contact Ms Sally Bayly, 44 1/2 The Mint, Rye TN31 7EN
t (01797) 222498 & 07956 280257 **e** chesterfieldcottage@virgin.net **w** country-holidays.co.uk

open All year
payment Cash/cheques

Charming 15thC Grade II Listed cottage situated by the Landgate old town wall and centre of Rye. Exposed beams, open hearth, central heating and private courtyard garden. Fabulous country walks on the doorstep and a choice of beautiful beaches ten minutes away. Not suitable for very elderly or infirm. Website: property ref.16230.

⊕ *From M20 jct 9, or M25/M26/A21 towards Hastings. Detailed directions given at time of booking.*

Unit General Shop < 0.5 miles Pub < 0.5 miles

RYE, East Sussex Map ref 3B4

★★★★
SELF CATERING

Units **1**
Sleeps **2–6**
Low season per wk
£320.00–£425.00
High season per wk
£425.00–£550.00

Froglets Cottage, Rye

contact Mrs Brenda Haines, Morley Farm, Beckley Road, Northiam, Cranbrook TN31 6JB
t (01797) 252011 **e** brenda@curtishaines.co.uk **w** froglets.uk.com

A characterful Grade II Listed cottage in the heart of the conservation area and attracting many return visitors. Full gas central heating, large open log fire and personally cared for.

open All year
payment Credit/debit cards, cash/cheques

Unit General P Leisure

RYE, East Sussex Map ref 3B4

★★★★
SELF CATERING

Units **1**
Sleeps **6**
Low season per wk
£400.00–£700.00
High season per wk
£400.00–£700.00

Oak Cottage, Rye

contact Mike Fowler, Priors Barn, Magreed Lane, Broad Oak, Heathfield TN21 8TR
t (01435) 862535 & 07802 195644 **f** (01435) 862535 **e** m.fowler1@btopenworld.com

Period cottage, approximately 400 years old, in medieval town of Rye. Oak beams, inglenook fireplace. Three double bedrooms (one en suite), shower room.

open All year
payment Cash/cheques, euros

Unit General Leisure

Take a break

Look out for special promotions and themed breaks highlighted in colour. (Offers subject to availability.)

ST LEONARDS, East Sussex Map ref 3B4

★★★
SELF CATERING

Units **6**
Sleeps **1–6**
Low season per wk
£160.00–£300.00
High season per wk
£200.00–£400.00

Glastonbury Self-Catering, Hastings

contact Mr Campbell, Glastonbury Self-Catering, 45 Eversfield Place, St Leonards-on-Sea TN37 6DB
t (01424) 436186 **e** glastonburyselfcatering@btinternet.com **w** hastings.gov.uk

Situated on the seafront close to Hastings, pier and town centre. Tourist attractions within walking distance. Ideal location for family summer holidays and short breaks.

open All year
payment Cash/cheques, euros

Unit General 1 Leisure Shop < 0.5 miles Pub < 0.5 miles

SEAFORD, East Sussex Map ref 2D3

★★★★
SELF CATERING

Units **1**
Sleeps **1–5**
Low season per wk
£400.00–£450.00
High season per wk
£400.00–£450.00

2 Kingsway Court, Seaford

contact Mrs Pauline Gower, 6 Sunningdale Close, Southdown Road, Seaford BN25 4PF
t (01323) 895233 & 07889 310414 **e** sific@bgower.f9.co.uk

Fully equipped, spacious, semi-detached house. Gardens, balcony, parking. Five minutes from sea, open country, station and town centre. One single and two double bedrooms.

open All year except Christmas and New Year
payment Cash/cheques

Unit General P Leisure Shop < 0.5 miles Pub < 0.5 miles

SHANKLIN, Isle of Wight Map ref 2C3

★★★
SELF CATERING

Units **8**
Sleeps **2–6**
Low season per wk
£190.00–£320.00
High season per wk
£425.00–£710.00

Lyon Court, Shanklin

contact Mrs Sandra Humphreys, Lyon Court, Westhill Road, Shanklin PO37 6PZ
t (01983) 865861 **e** info@lyoncourtshanklin.co.uk **w** lyoncourtshanklin.co.uk

open All year
payment Cash/cheques

Charming Victorian country house with eight self-catering apartments. Delightful gardens, heated outdoor swimming pool and spa pool, garden sauna, children's play area. Situated on the edge of the downs, near Shanklin Old Village and beaches. Easy access to Shanklin Down, Worsley Trail and Coastal path. Good bus and rail links.

⊕ *From Newport follow the A3020 to Shanklin. Half a mile after entering Shanklin, turn right into Westhill Road. Lyon Court is 2nd property on the left.*

♥ *Short breaks available Oct-May.*

Unit General Leisure Shop 0.5 miles Pub 0.5 miles

SHANKLIN, Isle of Wight Map ref 2C3

★★★
SELF CATERING

Units **7**
Sleeps **1–6**
Low season per wk
£170.00–£430.00
High season per wk
£370.00–£750.00

Luccombe Villa, Shanklin

contact Mrs Fiona Seymour, Luccombe Villa, 9 Popham Road, Shanklin PO37 6RF
t (01983) 862825 **e** info@luccombevilla.co.uk **w** luccombevilla.co.uk

open All year
payment Cash/cheques

Seven self-contained holiday apartments. One to three bedrooms with en suite facilities. Comfortably furnished with digital TV and DVD players. Well-equipped kitchens and separate laundry room. Plenty of parking. Guests may use the facilities at nearby Luccombe Hall Hotel free of charge. These include pools, jacuzzi, gym, squash etc.

⊕ *From A3055 through Shanklin Old Village, 1st left into Luccombe. First left down to Rylstone Gardens.*

Unit General **P** Leisure Shop < 0.5 miles Pub < 0.5 miles

SHELDWICH, Kent Map ref 3B3

★★★★
SELF CATERING

Units **1**
Sleeps **2**
Low season per wk
£260.00–£325.00
High season per wk
£350.00–£400.00

Littles Manor Farmhouse, Faversham

contact Tim Bourne, Littles Manor Farmhouse, North Street, Faversham ME13 0LP
t (01233) 820425 **f** (01233) 820746

open All year
payment Cash/cheques

Converted, fully equipped, award-winning Victorian barn in the grounds of Littles Manor Farmhouse, overlooking beautiful countryside and the sea. Easy reach of Canterbury, Calais, historic castles, golf, sea. Ideal base for walking, bird-watching and exploring the countryside. Excellent access to London and the Channel port by road and rail.

⊕ *Take the A251 from Faversham to Ashford. After 1.5 miles you will reach North Street, Sheldwich.*

Unit General **P** Leisure

SOUTHAMPTON, Hampshire Map ref 2C3

★★★
SELF CATERING

Units **2**
Sleeps **2**
Low season per wk
Max £155.00
High season per wk
Max £190.00

Pinewood Lodge Apartments, Southampton

contact Dr Bradberry, Kanes Hill, Southampton SO19 6AJ
t (023) 8040 2925 **e** stan.bradberry@tesco.net **w** self-catering-apartments-southampton.co.uk

Double- or twin-bedded, fully equipped, self-contained apartments, in pleasant wooded area, each with separate kitchen, bathroom and lounge. Private verandah or patio.

open All year
payment Cash/cheques

Unit General **P**

SOUTHSEA

See under Portsmouth & Southsea

To your credit

If you book by phone you may be asked for your credit card number. If so, it is advisable to check the proprietor's policy in case you have to cancel your reservation at a later date.

STONEGATE, East Sussex Map ref 3B4

★★★★★
SELF CATERING

Units 3
Sleeps 4
Low season per wk
Min £385.00
High season per wk
Max £795.00

Bardown Farm Holiday Cottages, Wadhurst

contact Mrs A Watkins, Bardown Road, Stonegate, Wadhurst TN5 7EL
t (01580) 200452 **f** (01580) 200452 **e** info@bardownfarm.co.uk **w** bardownfarm.co.uk

open All year
payment Cash/cheques

Recently converted Sussex barn. Luxury cottages with oak beams and bespoke kitchens. From the private patios and superb outdoor pool are stunning, panoramic views across peaceful Wealden countryside. Explore the woods and meadows on the farm or visit Bewl Water, Tunbridge Wells, Camber Sands and much more.

Directions given at time of booking.

Unit General Leisure
Shop 3 miles Pub 3 miles

STONEGATE, East Sussex Map ref 3B4

★★★★★
SELF CATERING

Units 1
Sleeps 4
Low season per wk
£380.00–£480.00
High season per wk
£480.00–£680.00

Coopers Farm Cottage, Stonegate

contact Ms Jane Howard, Coopers Farm Cottage, Bardown Road, Stonegate, Wadhurst TN5 7EH
t (01580) 200386 **e** jane@coopersfarmstonegate.co.uk **w** coopersfarmstonegate.co.uk

open All year except Christmas
payment Cash/cheques, euros

Coopers Cottage combines the charm of an ancient building – huge inglenook fireplace and a wealth of beams – with the comfort of five-star accommodation. Enjoy the peace and seclusion of this traditional working farm situated in the High Weald Area of Outstanding Natural Beauty. Horses welcome.

Take A21 to Hastings. At Lamberhurst, turn right to Wadhurst. About 0.75 miles the other side turn right to Stonegate. After 1 mile Coopers Farm is on right.

From Nov-Mar: £300 for the weekend or a 4-night, mid-week break.

Unit General Leisure Shop 3 miles
Pub 3 miles

TENTERDEN, Kent Map ref 3B4

★★★★
SELF CATERING

Units 2
Sleeps 4–5
Low season per wk
Min £195.00
High season per wk
Max £475.00

Meadow Cottage & Tamworth Cottage, Tenterden

contact Mrs Cooke, Great Prawls Farm, Stone, Tenterden TN30 7HB
t (01797) 270539 **e** info@prawls.co.uk **w** prawls.co.uk

open All year
payment Cash/cheques

Lovely, detached, single-storey cottages on peaceful grass farm with views in Area of Outstanding Natural Beauty. Sandy beaches, medieval Rye and Tenterden 15 minutes. Castles, National Trust properties, bird reserves and steam trains nearby – France for a day trip! Personally supervised. Short breaks. Brochure. See website for photos/prices/ booking form.

From M20 jct 10 to Hamstreet. On to Kenardington and Stone, fork right at Crown pub. Farm gate on left, 0.75 miles.

Unit General Leisure Pub 0.75 miles

TENTERDEN, Kent Map ref 3B4

★★★★
SELF CATERING

Units 1
Sleeps 5
Low season per wk
£250.00–£365.00
High season per wk
£410.00–£450.00

Quince Cottage, Tenterden

contact Mrs Heather E S Crease, 38 Ashford Road, Tenterden TN30 6LL
t (01580) 765636 **e** quincott@zetnet.co.uk **w** quincecottage.co.uk

open All year
payment Cash/cheques, euros

Listed, beamed cottage on residential side of tree-lined high street. Comfortable home from home. One single, two double bedrooms, cot available. Rear secluded courtyard. Close to all amenities, including steam railway and leisure centre. Children welcome. Sorry no pets, no smoking. Good centre for exploring Kent and East Sussex. Brochure available.

⊕ *From M20, jct 8 to Leeds village, A274 Headcorn-Tenterden.*

❤ *10% discount on bookings for 2 or more consecutive weeks. Short breaks (minimum 3 nights) possible Oct-Mar.*

Unit General P Leisure

THAME, Oxfordshire Map ref 2C1

★★★★
SELF CATERING

Units 1
Sleeps 6
Low season per wk
£375.00–£395.00
High season per wk
£425.00–£475.00

The Hollies, Thame

contact Ms Julia Tanner, Little Acre, 4 High Street, Tetsworth, Thame OX9 7AT
t (01844) 281423 **e** info@theholliesthame.co.uk **w** theholliesthame.co.uk

Beautifully appointed, luxury cottage-style bungalow with peaceful gardens, situated in a secluded backwater near the oldest part of Thame, five minutes' walk from the centre of our historic market town.

open All year
payment Cash/cheques

Unit General P Leisure Shop < 0.5 miles Pub < 0.5 miles

THAME, Oxfordshire Map ref 2C1

★★★★
SELF CATERING

Units 4
Sleeps 2–7
Low season per wk
Min £230.00
High season per wk
Max £450.00

Meadowbrook Farm Holiday Cottages, Thame

contact Mrs Diana Wynn, Meadowbrook Farm Holiday Cottages, Moreton, Thame OX9 2HY
t (01844) 212116 **f** (01844) 217503 **e** rdwynn@ukonline.co.uk **w** meadowbrookfarm.co.uk

Characterful, spacious, luxurious cottages with exposed beams, private gardens, ample parking. Peaceful retreat in Area of Outstanding Natural Beauty. Situated in pretty hamlet without passing traffic. Ten-minute walk to Thame, and walks on farm.

open All year
payment Cash/cheques

Unit General P S Leisure Shop 1 mile Pub 1 mile

TONBRIDGE, Kent Map ref 2D2

★★★★
SELF CATERING

Units **1**
Sleeps **1–4**
Low season per wk
£300.00–£395.00
High season per wk
£450.00–£500.00

Oast Barn, Tonbridge

contact Mr Trevor Bartle, Oast Barn, 5 Bourne Lane, Tonbridge TN9 1LG
t (01732) 353298 **f** (01732) 353298 **e** trevor@kentcottage.co.uk **w** kentcottage.co.uk

open All year
payment Cash/cheques, euros

Character, detached, converted barn in quiet lane within ten minutes' walk of central Tonbridge. Comfortably furnished, fully equipped, own garden, welcome pack. Every effort made to ensure your stay is as comfortable and relaxing as possible. Ideal location for touring Kent and Sussex, with many places of historical interest nearby.

⊕ *Hildenborough exit A21 to Tonbirdge. Left into Dry Hill Park Road/Yardley Park Road. Right at T-junction. Bourne Lane is 1st right.*

❤ *Weekend or short breaks of up to 4 nights offered at 75% of weekly rate (subject to availablility).*

Unit General P Leisure Shop 1 mile Pub 0.5 miles

TOTLAND BAY, Isle of Wight Map ref 2C3

★★★
SELF CATERING

Units **1**
Sleeps **6**
Low season per wk
Min £200.00
High season per wk
Max £550.00

Stonewind Farm, Totland Bay

contact Mrs Pat Hayles, Barn Cottage, Middleton, Freshwater PO40 9RW
t (01983) 752912 **f** (01983) 752912

Charming two-bedroomed farmhouse in peaceful area with fine views. Secluded gardens with barbecue. Ten minutes' walk from villages of Totland Bay and Freshwater. The island has lots of interesting walks.

open All year
payment Cash/cheques

Unit General P Shop 1 mile Pub 1 mile

TUNBRIDGE WELLS

See under Royal Tunbridge Wells

VENTNOR, Isle of Wight Map ref 2C3

★★★★
SELF CATERING

Units **1**
Sleeps **2–8**
Low season per wk
£500.00–£750.00
High season per wk
£800.00–£1,000.00

Garden House, Ventnor

contact Mr Philip Barton, 67 Strode Road, London SW6 6BL
t (01983) 854451 & 07887 848146 **e** philip@peoplesense.co.uk
w holidaylets.net/prop_detail.asp?id=13874

open All year
payment Cash/cheques

Comfortable and spacious family house with pretty, secluded garden, children's playhouse, barbecue and outside eating area. Garden House provides a perfect holiday setting for families and walkers. A few minutes' walk from pretty beaches, the stunning South Wight Coastal Path, Bonchurch village and the quiet Victorian resort of Ventnor.

⊕ *At the junction of the A3055 and B3327 in Ventnor, turn left into St Boniface Road towards Bonchurch. Garden House is directly opposite Maples Drive.*

❤ *Long weekends and short breaks (ideal for families and walkers) available off-peak.*

Unit General Shop 0.5 miles Pub 0.5 miles

Tourist information centres

To find the nearest one during your stay text TIC LOCATE to 64118.

VENTNOR, Isle of Wight Map ref 2C3

★★★★
SELF CATERING

Units 1
Sleeps 4
Low season per wk
Min £180.00
High season per wk
Max £695.00

Maple Cottage, Ventnor

contact Mr & Mrs Stuart & Sarah Merry, White Cottage, 82 Nutley Lane, Reigate RH2 9HS
t 07970 073339 **e** s.merry2@ntlworld.com **w** ventnorholidaycottage.co.uk

An idyllic cottage situated in Ventnor, with pretty gardens and sea views. Recently refurbished, with all mod cons. Short walk to shops and beach.

open All year
payment Cash/cheques

Unit General Shop < 0.5 miles Pub < 0.5 miles

WALTON ON THE HILL, Surrey Map ref 2D2

★★★★★
SELF CATERING

Units 1
Sleeps 20
Low season per wk
£2,900.00–£3,200.00
High season per wk
£3,900.00–£4,500.00

Far End, Walton on the Hill

contact Jacquelyn Beesley, Streele Farm, Dewlands Hill, Crowborough TN6 3RU
t (01892) 852579 **e** stay@compasscottages.co.uk **w** compasscottages.co.uk

open All year
payment Cash/cheques, euros

Beautiful Edwardian mansion with many original period features. Luxury accommodation including eight double bedrooms (three master suites), six bathrooms, huge oak-panelled dining room, two surround-sound TV rooms, pool table, play room, gas barbecue. Ideal for family reunions, group holidays and celebrations. Pubs, restaurants, shops, golf, horse-riding, London and south-east attractions within easy reach.

M25 jct 8. A217 (Sutton). Left onto B2032 (Walton on the Hill). At T-junction, left (Dorking Road). After one mile, right (Deans Lane), past golf course, next left.

3-night weekend and 4-night mid-week breaks available year round from £2,000.

Unit General Leisure
Shop < 0.5 miles Pub < 0.5 miles

WALTON-ON-THAMES, Surrey Map ref 2D2

★★★★
SELF CATERING

Units 1
Sleeps 1–3
Low season per wk
£260.00–£310.00
High season per wk
£310.00–£340.00

Guest Wing, Walton-on-Thames

contact Mr Richard Dominy, Guest Wing, 30 Mayfield Gardens, Walton-on-Thames KT12 5PP
t (01932) 241223

Attractive, two-bedroomed, self-contained wing of neo-Georgian house in residential cul-de-sac, adjacent to Walton station. Ideal for London, Hampton Court, Windsor and motorway network.

open All year
payment Cash/cheques

Unit General

WANTAGE, Oxfordshire Map ref 2C2

SELF CATERING

Units 1
Sleeps 4–5
Low season per wk
£325.00–£365.00
High season per wk
£405.00–£445.00

Cartwheel Cottage, Woolstone, Faringdon

t (01367) 820116 **e** ridgewayholidays@amserve.net

Comfortable, cosy, converted cart-barn. Quiet, sunny courtyard with patio and parking. The ancient Ridgeway and famous White Horse Hill provide panoramic views. Historic houses, market towns and River Thames nearby.

open All year
payment Cash/cheques

Unit General Leisure Shop 1 mile Pub 1 mile

WARTLING, East Sussex Map ref 3B4

★★★★
SELF CATERING

Units **1**
Sleeps **1–4**
Low season per wk
£295.00–£495.00
High season per wk
£550.00–£695.00

The Coach House, Nr Herstmonceux

contact Mrs Helen Enock, Tremayne House, Wartling, Hailsham BN27 1RY
t (01323) 832131 **f** (01323) 832876 **e** helen.enock@btinternet.com **w** thecoachhousewartling.com

open All year
payment Cash/cheques

Victorian coach house, recently renovated to a very high standard, including underfloor heating, TV/DVD, dishwasher, washer/drier and four-poster bed. Two double bedrooms, both with en suite facilities. Off-road parking and private terrace and garden. Wartling is a charming little village a few miles from the sea at Pevensey.

⊕ *Follow A271 through Herstmonceux to Windmill Hill. Turn right to Wartling.*

♥ *Phone for details or check website.*

Unit General 10 P Leisure Shop 2 miles Pub < 0.5 miles

WEST MARDEN, West Sussex Map ref 2C3

★★★★
SELF CATERING

Units **1**
Sleeps **2–5**
Low season per wk
£325.00–£475.00
High season per wk
£525.00–£675.00

Cabragh Cottage, Chichester

contact Mrs Lesley Segrave, Cabragh House, West Marden, Chichester PO18 9EJ
t (023) 9263 1267 **e** lsegrave@tinyworld.co.uk

open All year
payment Cash/cheques

This attractive former coach house offers excellent self-catering accommodation in a lovely woodland setting of 65 acres where peacocks freely roam. There are many public footpaths in the vicinity and four delightful country pubs ten minutes away.

⊕ *On B2146 turn to the west 1 mile south of West Marden, signposted Rowlands Castle. Cabragh House is the only house on this lane.*

Unit General P Leisure Shop 2 miles Pub 1 mile

WHITWELL, Isle of Wight Map ref 2C3

★★★★
SELF CATERING

Units **1**
Sleeps **6**
Low season per wk
£340.00–£400.00
High season per wk
£480.00–£750.00

Maytime Cottage, Ventnor

contact Mr Jonathan McCulloch, 5 King Edward Road, Horsham RH13 0ND
t (01403) 211052 **f** (01403) 211603 **e** jonty@bpmd.co.uk **w** maytimecottage.co.uk

Spacious, well-equipped 19thC stone cottage in beautiful rural setting in South Wight. Three bedrooms, two bathrooms, superb garden room, enclosed rear garden and lovely views. Ideal cycling/walking base.

open All year
payment Cash/cheques

Unit General P Leisure Shop 2 miles Pub 1 mile

Town, country or coast?

The entertainment, shopping and innovative attractions of the big cities, the magnificent vistas of the countryside or the relaxing and refreshing coast – this guide will help you find what you're looking for!

WINCHESTER, Hampshire Map ref 2C3

★★★★
SELF CATERING

Units **1**
Sleeps **4**
Low season per wk
£350.00–£420.00
High season per wk
£350.00–£490.00

Burwood, Winchester

contact Mrs Alice Lowery, Burwood, 128 Downs Road, South Wonston, Winchester SO21 3EH
t (01962) 881690 **e** lowery2@btinternet.com

A tastefully furnished bungalow annexe in the village of South Wonston, north of the historic city of Winchester. Easy access to the south coast, New Forest, Oxford and London.

open All year
payment Cash/cheques, euros

Unit General 8 P Leisure Shop < 0.5 miles Pub 2 miles

WINCHESTER, Hampshire Map ref 2C3

★★★★
SELF CATERING

Units **1**
Sleeps **4**
Low season per wk
£308.00–£409.00
High season per wk
£435.00–£451.00

Gyleen, Winchester

contact Mr & Mrs Paul & Elizabeth Tipple, 9 Mount View Road, Olivers Battery, Winchester SO22 4JJ
t (01962) 861918 **e** pauliz@tipple.co.uk **w** cottageguide.co.uk/gyleen

Detached, secluded, well-equipped, two-bedroom bungalow (one double, one twin) set in large, peaceful, mature garden overlooking golf course. Two miles west of Winchester on a bus route. Ample parking in drive.

open All year
payment Cash/cheques

Unit General P Leisure Shop 0.5 miles Pub 1 mile

WINCHESTER, Hampshire Map ref 2C3

★★★★★
SELF CATERING

Units **2**
Sleeps **6**
Low season per wk
£385.00–£520.00
High season per wk
£590.00–£740.00

South Winchester Lodges, Winchester

contact Mr Laurence Ross, 18 The Green, South Winchester Golf Club, Romsey Road, Winchester SO22 5QX
t (01962) 820490 **f** (01962) 844161 **e** info@golfholidaywinchester.com
w golfholidaywinchester.com

open All year
payment Cash/cheques

Luxury three-bedroom, two-bathroom log cabins with spacious, open-plan living area and large decked balcony overlooking private putting green. Tranquil setting at the heart of South Winchester Golf Club. Two miles from the centre of historic Winchester and close to tourist attractions of the south coast and New Forest.

⊕ *M3 jct 11. Continue on A3090 towards Romsey. At 4th roundabout by Murco petrol station follow brown signs to South Winchester Golf Club.*

♥ *10% discount for bookings made before 1 Apr 2007. See website for other current offers.*

Unit General P Leisure Shop < 0.5 miles Pub < 0.5 miles

WINDSOR, Berkshire Map ref 2D2

★★
SELF CATERING

Units **3**
Sleeps **1–14**
Low season per wk
£420.00–£966.00
High season per wk
£420.00–£966.00

Dorney Self-Catering Apartments, Windsor

contact Sarah Everitt, Wisteria & Gardeners Bothy, The Old Place, Lock Path Dorney, Windsor SL4 6QQ
t (01753) 827037 **f** (01753) 855022 **e** enquiries@troppo.uk.com **w** troppo.uk.com

Apartments set in rural location. Close to Windsor, Legoland, Dorney Lake, trains to London. Rowers welcome. Book by the night, from £60.

open All year
payment Credit/debit cards, cash/cheques

Unit General P Leisure Shop 3 miles Pub 1 mile

WINDSOR, Berkshire Map ref 2D2

★★★
SELF CATERING

Units **1**
Sleeps **1–4**
Low season per wk
Min £475.00
High season per wk
£500.00–£550.00

Flat 6 The Courtyard, Windsor

contact Mr Gavin Gordon, 5 Temple Mill Island, Marlow SL7 1SG
t (01628) 824267 **e** gavingordon@totalise.co.uk **w** windsor-selfcatering.co.uk

open All year
payment Cash/cheques

An elegant, well-equipped, first-floor (lift) apartment centrally situated in a quiet courtyard almost opposite Windsor Castle. One double and one twin bedroom. With direct access to Windsor High Street, the many restaurants, excellent shops, Theatre Royal and castle are only minutes away. London approximately 30 minutes. Exclusive parking.

⊕ *From M4 jct 6 take A355 (Windsor). At roundabout take 1st exit. Continue until Madeira Walk just before T-junction. Car park access immediately on right.*

Unit General P

WITNEY, Oxfordshire Map ref 2C1

★★★
SELF CATERING

Units **1**
Sleeps **2**
Low season per wk
Max £185.00
High season per wk
Max £255.00

Lovegrove Cottage, Witney

contact Mrs Olive Harris, Lovegrove Farm, Fordwells, Witney OX29 9PP
t (01993) 878747

Small cottage for two in quiet hamlet, situated in an Area of Outstanding Natural Beauty. Owner maintained. No pets or smokers. Minimum three-night breaks.

open All year except Christmas and New Year
payment Cash/cheques

Unit General P Leisure Shop 1 mile Pub 1 mile

WOODGREEN, Hampshire Map ref 2B3

★★★★
SELF CATERING

Units **1**
Sleeps **2**
Low season per wk
Min £270.00
High season per wk
Min £380.00

Sunset Place, Fordingbridge

contact Mrs Lupita Cadman, Castle Hill, Woodgreen, Fordingbridge SP6 2AX
t (01725) 512009 **e** lupita_cadman@yahoo.co.uk **w** cottage-crest.co.uk

Comfortable, well-equipped cottage in delightful surroundings on edge of New Forest with lovely views over the River Avon valley.

open All year
payment Cash/cheques

Unit General 4 P Leisure Shop 0.75 miles Pub 0.5 miles

WOOTTON BRIDGE, Isle of Wight Map ref 2C3

SELF CATERING

Units **23**
Sleeps **4–6**
Low season per wk
£250.00–£600.00
High season per wk
£450.00–£700.00

Creek Gardens, Ryde

contact Mr S Catton, Creek Gardens, New Road, Wootton Bridge PO33 4JX
t (01564) 777711

One-, two- and three-bedroom units in tranquil setting overlooking picturesque Wootton Creek on the Isle of Wight. Weekly servicing of units. Three-bedroom units include washing machine and fridge/freezer.

open All year
payment Credit/debit cards, cash/cheques

Unit General Leisure Shop 0.5 miles Pub 0.5 miles

Stay focused

Don't forget your camera. Take home some shots of the greatest scenery, super seascapes and family fun.

South West England

Bath & Bristol › Cornwall & the Isles of Scilly › Devon › Dorset
Gloucestershire & the Cotswolds › Somerset › Wiltshire

Surf's up at Polzeath, Cornwall

South West Tourism
Woodwater Park
Exeter EX2 5WT
0870 442 0800
visitsouthwest.co.uk

sheltered bays, wild moors, relaxing resorts

Main Find yourself inspired by The Forest of Dean Sculpture Trail
Left Venturing through the Eden Project, near St Austell; sweeping views across the Jurassic Coast World Heritage Site; breathtaking colours at the Balloon Festival, Bristol; free spirits at Glastonbury Festival

Ride on the crest of a wave, then relax on a beautiful sandy beach, feel inspired by sweeping moors and wooded valleys, and **enjoy the party atmosphere in the coastal resorts.**

Explore South West England

Surf's up

It's hard to beat the dramatic stretching beaches and magnificent coastlines of the South West. Learn to surf, or simply improve your skills atop the crashing waves in Croyde or Woolacombe. Dive in and explore the artificial reef at Whitsand Bay, created by the sinking of a disused naval ship, and hunt for marine life aboard its many decks. Have your senses shaken at the Extreme Academy in Watergate Bay – try your hand at waveskiing, mountain boarding or kite surfing, and feel your adrenalin levels hit an all-time high.

Lose yourself in a daydream staring out from one of the many beautiful shorelines on the Isles of Scilly. Observe flower fields ablaze with colour and spot puffins diving for unsuspecting fish. Find your bearings along a section of the 630-mile South West Coast Path and enjoy breathtaking views along the way.

Lost worlds

Sense the magic of the mysterious Lost Gardens of Heligan in Pentewan, Cornwall, and unlock the secrets held within its walls. For more inspiration, follow The Forest of Dean Sculpture Trail where you can find thought-provoking work nestling between the trees.

The mighty Stonehenge and Avebury World Heritage Site on Salisbury Plain never ceases to amaze: revel in its 5,000-year history and feel truly humbled by the size of these prehistoric archaeological monuments. Take a stroll around Westonbirt: The National Arboretum in Gloucestershire and allow the colours to mesmerise you whatever the season.

Catch a glimpse of wild red deer or grazing ponies in the stunning Exmoor National Park and gaze at reflections in beautiful lake-like reservoirs on heather-clad Dartmoor. Take your own piece of history home – search for fossils along the Jurassic Coast World Heritage Site in Dorset and East Devon.

Get up and go

Be transported to far-off climates in the transparent biomes of the Eden Project near St Austell. Wander amongst prairie flowers and olive trees and peel back tropical leaves as you pick your way through this remarkable educational centre. Take your chances at the UK's first safari park at Longleat in Warminster, drive amongst prowling tigers and towering giraffes and take a boat trip to Gorilla Island.

Unleash your wild side and try zorbing down a hillside in Dorset. Strap yourself into a large transparent PVC ball (add water for the hydro-zorbing experience), take a deep breath and think of England as you tumble down the hill!

City culture

Head to the vibrant city of Bristol and experience the superb Harbourside complex – admire the water sculpture and pull up a chair at a pavement cafe. Explore At-Bristol, where science, nature and art spring to life in this unique centre of discovery.

Indulge in a Cornish cream tea, tuck into a hearty pub lunch, sample the seafood and don't forget to savour the local pasties. But above all, eat well in this region laden with culinary delights – you're on holiday after all!

Places to **visit**

At-Bristol
Bristol
0845 345 1235
at-bristol.org.uk
Interactive adventure of a lifetime

Bristol Zoo Gardens
Bristol
(0117) 974 7399
bristolzoo.org.uk
Over 400 exotic and endangered species

Cheddar Caves & Gorge
Somerset
(01934) 742343
cheddarcaves.co.uk
A place of wild, rugged beauty

Corfe Castle
Dorset
0870 458 4000
purbeck.gov.uk
Majestic hilltop ruins

Flambards Experience
Helston, Cornwall
(01326) 573404
flambards.co.uk
Fantastic family theme park

Eden Project
near St Austell, Cornwall
(01726) 811911
edenproject.com
A gateway into the plant world

Extreme Academy
near Newquay, Cornwall
(01637) 860840
extremeacademy.co.uk
A Mecca for adventure enthusiasts

The Forest of Dean Sculpture Trail
Gloucestershire
(01594) 833057
forestofdean-sculpture.org.uk
Spot artworks amid the trees

Longleat
Warminster, Wiltshire
(01985) 844400
longleat.co.uk
Beautiful stately home, plus safari park

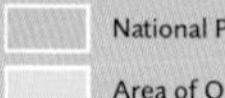
National Park
Area of Outstanding Natural Beauty

Heritage Coast

National Trails
nationaltrail.co.uk

Sections of the National Cycle Network
nationalcyclenetwork.org.uk
Ferry routes

Roman Baths
Bath, Somerset
(01225) 477785
romanbaths.co.uk
Fascinating ancient temple and baths

St Michael's Mount
Penzance, Cornwall
(01736) 710507
stmichaelsmount.co.uk
Island crowned by medieval church

Stonehenge and Avebury World Heritage Site
Salisbury, Wiltshire
0870 333 1181
english-heritage.org.uk/stonehenge
World-famous prehistoric monument

The Lost Gardens of Heligan
near St Austell, Cornwall
(01726) 845100
heligan.com
Beautifully restored gardens

Monkey World – Ape Rescue Centre
Wareham, Dorset
(01929) 462537
monkeyworld.org
Internationally acclaimed primate rescue centre

Oceanarium
Bournemouth, Dorset
(01202) 311993
oceanarium.co.uk
Embark on an underwater journey

Paignton Zoo Environmental Park
Devon
(01803) 697500
paigntonzoo.org.uk
Set in beautiful botanical gardens

Tate St Ives
Cornwall
(01736) 796226
tate.org.uk/stives
A unique introduction to modern art

Westonbirt: The National Arboretum
Tetbury, Gloucestershire
(01666) 880220
forestry.gov.uk/westonbirt
A divine collection of trees

Zorb South UK
Dorchester, Dorset
(01929) 426595
zorbsouth.co.uk
Strap in to a PVC ball and let go!

Tourist information centres 

When you arrive at your destination, visit a tourist information centre for help with accommodation and information about local attractions and events, or email your request before you go.

Amesbury	Smithfield Street	(01980) 622833	amesburytic@salisbury.gov.uk
Avebury	Green Street	(01672) 539425	all.atic@kennet.gov.uk
Axminster*	Church Street	(01297) 34386	axminstertic@btopenworld.com
Barnstaple	The Square	(01271) 375000	info@staynorthdevon.co.uk
Bath	Abbey Church Yard	0906 711 2000**	tourism@bathnes.gov.uk
Bideford	Victoria Park	(01237) 477676	bidefordtic@torridge.gov.uk
Blandford Forum	1 Greyhound Yard	(01258) 454770	blandfordtic@north-dorset.gov.uk
Bodmin	Mount Folly Square	(01208) 76616	bodmintic@visit.org.uk
Bournemouth	Westover Road	(01202) 451700	info@bournemouth.gov.uk
Bourton-on-the-Water	Victoria Street	(01451) 820211	bourtonvic@cotswold.gov.uk
Bradford-on-Avon	50 St Margaret's Street	(01225) 865797	tic@bradfordonavon2000.fsnet.co.uk
Braunton	Caen Street	(01271) 816400	info@brauntontic.co.uk
Bridgwater	King Square	(01278) 436438	bridgwater.tic@sedgemoor.gov.uk
Bridport	47 South Street	(01308) 424901	bridport.tic@westdorset-dc.gov.uk
Bristol	Harbourside	0906 711 2191**	ticharbourside@destinationbristol.co.uk
Brixham	The Quay	0870 707 0010	brixham.tic@torbay.gov.uk
Bude	The Crescent	(01288) 354240	budetic@visitbude.info
Budleigh Salterton	Fore Street	(01395) 445275	budleigh.tic@btconnect.com
Burnham-on-Sea	South Esplanade	(01278) 787852	burnham.tic@sedgemoor.gov.uk
Camelford*	The Clease	(01840) 212954	manager@camelfordtic.eclipse.co.uk
Cartgate	A303/A3088 Cartgate Picnic Site	(01935) 829333	cartgate.tic@southsomerset.gov.uk
Chard	Fore Street	(01460) 65710	chardtic@chard.gov.uk
Cheddar*	The Gorge	(01934) 744071	cheddar.tic@sedgemoor.gov.uk
Cheltenham	77 Promenade	(01242) 522878	tic@cheltenham.gov.uk
Chippenham	Market Place	(01249) 665970	tourism@chippenham.gov.uk
Christchurch	49 High Street	(01202) 471780	enquiries@christchurchtourism.info
Cirencester	Market Place	(01285) 654180	cirencestervic@cotswold.gov.uk
Coleford	High Street	(01594) 812388	tourism@fdean.gov.uk
Combe Martin*	Cross Street	(01271) 883319	mail@visitcombemartin.co.uk
Corsham	31 High Street	(01249) 714660	corshamheritage@northwilts.gov.uk
Crediton	High Street	(01363) 772006	info@devonshireheartland.co.uk
Dartmouth	Mayor's Avenue	(01803) 834224	holidays@discoverdartmouth.com
Dawlish	The Lawn	(01626) 215665	dawtic@Teignbridge.gov.uk
Devizes	Market Place	(01380) 729408	all.dtic@kennet.gov.uk
Dorchester	11 Antelope Walk	(01305) 267992	dorchester.tic@westdorset-dc.gov.uk
Exeter	Paris Street	(01392) 265700	tic@exeter.gov.uk
Exmouth	Alexandra Terrace	(01395) 222299	info@exmouthtourism.co.uk

Falmouth	28 Killigrew Street	(01326) 312300	info@falmouthtic.co.uk
Fowey	5 South Street	(01726) 833616	info@fowey.co.uk
Frome	Justice Lane	(01373) 467271	frome.tic@ukonline.co.uk
Glastonbury	9 High Street	(01458) 832954	glastonbury.tic@ukonline.co.uk
Gloucester	28 Southgate Street	(01452) 396572	tourism@gloucester.gov.uk
Helston and Lizard Peninsula	79 Meneage Street	(01326) 565431	info@helstontic.demon.co.uk
Honiton	Lace Walk Car Park	(01404) 43716	honitontic@honitontic.freeserve.co.uk
Ilfracombe	The Seafront	(01271) 863001	info@ilfracombe-tourism.co.uk
Isles of Scilly	Hugh Street, Hugh Town	(01720) 422536	tic@scilly.gov.uk
Ivybridge	Leonards Road	(01752) 897035	bookends.ivybridge@virgin.net
Kingsbridge	The Quay	(01548) 853195	advice@kingsbridgeinfo.co.uk
Launceston	Market Street	(01566) 772321	launcestontica@btconnect.com
Looe*	Fore Street	(01503) 262072	looetic@btconnect.com
Lyme Regis	Church Street	(01297) 442138	lymeregis.tic@westdorset-dc.gov.uk
Lynton and Lynmouth	Lee Road	0845 660 3232	info@lyntourism.co.uk
Malmesbury	Market Lane	(01666) 823748	malmesburyip@northwilts.gov.uk
Marlborough	High Street	(01672) 513989	all.tic's@kennet.gov.uk
Melksham	Church Street	(01225) 707424	visitmelksham2@tiscali.co.uk
Mere	Barton Lane	(01747) 861211	MereTIC@Salisbury.gov.uk
Minehead	17 Friday Street	(01643) 702624	info@mineheadtic.co.uk
Modbury*	5 Modbury Court	(01548) 830159	modburytic@lineone.net
Newent	7 Church Street	(01531) 822468	newent@fdean.gov.uk
Newquay	Marcus Hill	(01637) 854020	info@newquay.co.uk
Newton Abbot	6 Bridge House	(01626) 215667	natic@Teignbridge.gov.uk
Okehampton	3 West Street	(01837) 53020	okehamptontic@westdevon.gov.uk
Ottery St Mary	10a Broad Street	(01404) 813964	info@otterytourism.org.uk
Padstow	North Quay	(01841) 533449	padstowtic@btconnect.com
Paignton	The Esplanade	0870 707 0010	paignton.tic@torbay.gov.uk
Penzance	Station Road	(01736) 362207	pztic@penwith.gov.uk
Plymouth (Discovery Centre)	Crabtree	(01752) 266030	mtic@plymouth.gov.uk
Plymouth (Plymouth Mayflower)	3-5 The Barbican	(01752) 306330	barbicantic@plymouth.gov.uk
Poole	Poole Quay	(01202) 253253	info@poole.gov.uk
St Austell	Southbourne Road	0845 094 0428	tic@cornish-riviera.co.uk
St Ives	Street-an-Pol	(01736) 796297	ivtic@penwith.gov.uk
Salcombe	Market Street	(01548) 843927	info@salcombeinformation.co.uk
Salisbury	Fish Row	(01722) 334956	visitorinfo@salisbury.gov.uk
Seaton	The Underfleet	(01297) 21660	info@seatontic.freeserve.co.uk
Sedgemoor Services	M5 Southbound	(01934) 750833	somersetvisitorcentre@somerserset.gov.uk
Shaftesbury	8 Bell Street	(01747) 853514	shaftesburytic@north-dorset.gov.uk
Shepton Mallet	48 High Street	(01749) 345258	sheptonmallet.tic@ukonline.co.uk
Sherborne	3 Tilton Court	(01935) 815341	sherborne.tic@westdorset-dc.gov.uk
Sidmouth	Ham Lane	(01395) 516441	sidmouthtic@eclipse.co.uk

South Molton	1 East Street	(01769) 574122	visitsouthmolton@btconnect.com
Stow-on-the-Wold	The Square	(01451) 831082	stowvic@cotswold.gov.uk
Street	Farm Road	(01458) 447384	street.tic@ukonline.co.uk
Stroud	George Street	(01453) 760960	tic@stroud.gov.uk
Swanage	Shore Road	(01929) 422885	mail@swanage.gov.uk
Swindon	37 Regent Street	(01793) 530328	infocentre@swindon.gov.uk
Taunton	Paul Street	(01823) 336344	tauntontic@tauntondeane.gov.uk
Tavistock	Bedford Square	(01822) 612938	tavistocktic@westdevon.gov.uk
Teignmouth	Sea Front	(01626) 215666	teigntic@teignbridge.gov.uk
Tetbury	33 Church Street	(01666) 503552	tourism@tetbury.org
Tewkesbury	64 Barton Street	(01684) 295027	tewkesburytic@tewkesburybc.gov.uk
Tiverton	Phoenix Lane	(01884) 255827	tivertontic@btconnect.com
Torquay	Vaughan Parade	0870 707 0010	torquay.tic@torbay.gov.uk
Torrington	Castle Hill	(01805) 626140	info@great-torrington.com
Totnes	Coronation Road	(01803) 863168	enquire@totnesinformation.co.uk
Trowbridge	St Stephen's Place	(01225) 710530	tic@trowbridge.gov.uk
Truro	Boscawen Street	(01872) 274555	tic@truro.gov.uk
Wadebridge	Eddystone Road	0870 122 3337	wadebridgetic@btconnect.com
Wareham	South Street	(01929) 552740	tic@purbeck-dc.gov.uk
Warminster	off Station Rd	(01985) 218548	visitwarminster@btconnect.com
Wellington	30 Fore Street	(01823) 663379	wellingtontic@tauntondeane.gov.uk
Wells	Market Place	(01749) 672552	touristinfo@wells.gov.uk
Westbury	Edward Street	(01373) 827158	visitwestbury@westwiltshire.gov.uk
Weston-super-Mare	Beach Lawns	(01934) 888800	westontouristinfo@n-somerset.gov.uk
Weymouth	The Esplanade	(01305) 785747	tic@weymouth.gov.uk
Wimborne Minster	29 High Street	(01202) 886116	wimbornetic@eastdorset.gov.uk
Winchcombe*	High Street	(01242) 602925	winchcombetic@tewkesbury.gov.uk
Woolacombe	The Esplanade	(01271) 870553	info@woolacombetourism.co.uk
Yeovil Heritage & Visitor Information Centre	Hendford	(01935) 845946	yeoviltic@southsomerset.gov.uk

* *seasonal opening* ** *calls to this number are charged at premium rate*

Alternatively, you can text **TIC LOCATE** to **64118** to find your nearest tourist information centre

Find out **more**

Visit the following websites for further information on South West England (or call **0870 442 0800**):

- **visitsouthwest.co.uk**
- **swcp.org.uk**

Also available from South West Tourism:

- **The Trencherman's Guide to Fine Food in South West England**

Gaze in awe at the mighty Stonehenge on Salisbury Plain

Travel **info**

By road:

The region is easily accessible from London, the South East, the North and the Midlands by the M6/M5 which extends just beyond Exeter, where it links in with the dual carriageways of the A38 to Plymouth, the A380 to Torbay and the A30 into Cornwall. The North Devon Link Road A361 joins junction 27 with the coast of North Devon and the A39, which then becomes the Atlantic Highway into Cornwall.

By rail:

The main towns and cities in the South West are served throughout the year by fast, direct and frequent rail services from all over the country. Trains operate from London (Paddington) to Chippenham, Swindon, Bath, Bristol, Weston-super-Mare, Taunton, Exeter, Plymouth and Penzance. A service runs from London (Waterloo) to Exeter, via Salisbury, Yeovil and Crewkerne.

By air:

Daily flights into Bristol, Bournemouth, Exeter, Gloucester, Isles of Scilly, Newquay and Plymouth operate from airports around the UK and Europe. For schedules, log on to visitsouthwest.co.uk/flights.

where to stay in

South West England

All place names in the blue bands are shown on the maps at the front of this guide.

A complete listing of all Enjoy England assessed accommodation covered by this guide appears at the back.

Accommodation symbols
Symbols give useful information about services and facilities. Inside the back-cover flap you can find a key to these symbols. Keep it open for easy reference.

ALLERFORD, Somerset Map ref 1D1

★★★
SELF CATERING

Units **1**
Sleeps **2–6**
Low season per wk
£280.00–£320.00
High season per wk
£340.00–£370.00

Orchard Cottage, Allerford

contact Mrs Diana Williams, Orchard Cottage, Brandish Street Farm, Brandish Street, Minehead TA24 8HR
t (01643) 862383

open All year
payment Cash/cheques

Delightful, character, National Trust cottage on a traditional working farm, surrounded by beautiful scenery. Old beams, log fire, cosy, clean and comfortable. Situated near Allerford and Minehead, and central for exploring the Exmoor coast and countryside. Many attractions nearby. Village shops, pubs and restaurants five minutes' drive away. Colour brochure available.

⊕ *A358 (Taunton to Williton), then A39 (Williton to Minehead), then follow sign for Porlock. After 3.5 miles, right. Follow sign for Brandish Street Farm.*

Unit General 4 P Leisure

ASHBURTON, Devon Map ref 1C2

★★★–★★★★★
SELF CATERING

Units **7**
Sleeps **2–12**
Low season per wk
£180.00–£650.00
High season per wk
£300.00–£1,050.00

Wooder Manor Holiday Homes, Widecombe-in-the-Moor

contact Mrs Angela Bell, Wooder Manor Holiday Homes, Widecombe-in-the-Moor, Newton Abbot TQ13 7TR
t (01364) 621391 **f** (01364) 621391 **e** angela@woodermanor.com **w** woodermanor.com

open All year
payment Credit/debit cards, cash/cheques

Cottages nestled in picturesque valley in Dartmoor National Park. Peaceful location, beautiful views of woodland, moors and granite tors. Explore Devon, Dartmoor, the coast, National Trust properties and attractions. Clean and very well equipped. Gardens. Off-road parking. Good food at two local inns 0.5 and 0.75 miles. Colour brochure. Units sleep 2-4, 4-6 and 8-12.

⊕ *A38 towards Plymouth, A382 to Bovey Tracey. Left at Bovey Tracey (B3387 to Widecombe). At village green take Natsworthy and Wooder Manor sign for 0.6 miles.*

❤ *Short breaks available.*

Unit General P S Leisure Shop 0.5 miles
Pub 0.5 miles

The largest selection
of Visit Britain Inspected
holiday cottages in North Devon.

Choose from over 300 cottages,
sleeping from 2 to 28,
some with swimming pools.

www.marsdens.co.uk
for information and 24 hour on line booking

For a free brochure, contact holidays@marsdens.co.uk, phone
01271 813777 or write 2 The Square, Braunton, Devon EX33 2JB

freedom
of choice

Enjoy the freedom and the beauty of this delightful corner of South West England with over 750 of the finest holiday cottages throughout Cornwall, Devon, Somerset and Dorset. All situated in superb coastal & rural locations. View our full collection, search availability and book securely online. The perfect holiday is yours to choose!

holidaycottages.co.uk

01237 479698

• Log Cabins • Luxury Riverside Apartments
• Fisherman's Cottages • Barn Conversions

ASHBURTON, Devon Map ref 1C2

★★★★
SELF CATERING

Units **2**
Sleeps **2–4**
Low season per wk
Min £210.00
High season per wk
Max £430.00

Wren & Robin Cottages, Newton Abbot

contact Mrs Margaret Phipps, Wren & Robin Cottages, New Cott Farm, Newton Abbot TQ13 7PD
t (01364) 631421 **f** (01364) 631421 **e** enquiries@newcott-farm.co.uk **w** newcott-farm.co.uk

Enjoy Dartmoor National Park with tors, moors and tiny villages. Stress free, plenty of fresh air. Wren/Robin Cottages are peacefully situated and beautifully furnished. Prices all-inclusive.

open All year
payment Credit/debit cards, cash/cheques

Unit General 3 P Leisure Shop 4 miles Pub 1 mile

ASHWATER, Devon Map ref 1C2

SELF CATERING

Units **8**
Sleeps **2–6**
Low season per wk
£225.00–£554.00
High season per wk
£612.00–£895.00

Blagdon Farm Country Holidays, Beaworthy

contact Mr & Mrs M Clark & Mr & Mrs H O'Brien, Blagdon Farm Country Holidays, Ashwater, Beaworthy EX21 5DF
t (01409) 211509 **f** (01409) 211510 **e** info@blagdon-farm.co.uk **w** blagdon-farm.co.uk

open All year
payment Cash/cheques

Fully accessible, award-winning cottages set in 11 acres of west Devon countryside. All cottages are south facing, in a parkland setting with outstanding views over a two-acre coarse-fishing lake, forest and fields beyond. Heated indoor hydrotherapy swimming pool, licensed bistro, children's play area.

⊕ *From the A30 at Launceston, take the A388 Holsworthy Road. After 8 miles, take the 2nd Ashwater turning, following the brown tourist signs.*

♥ *Weekend and mid-week breaks available Oct-May.*

Unit General P Leisure Shop 1.5 miles Pub 1.5 miles

ASHWATER, Devon Map ref 1C2

★★–★★★
SELF CATERING

Units **6**
Sleeps **2–16**
Low season per wk
£100.00–£400.00
High season per wk
£420.00–£1,350.00

Braddon Cottages and Forest, Ashwater

contact Mr & Mrs George & Anne Ridge, Braddon Cottages, Ashwater, Beaworthy EX21 5EP
t (01409) 211350 **e** holidays@braddoncottages.co.uk **w** braddoncottages.co.uk

For country lovers, cottages in secluded location. Games field, adults' snooker and children's games rooms. Wood fires. New three-mile path suitable for pedestrians and bicycles. Colour brochure, extensive website.

open All year
payment Credit/debit cards, cash/cheques

Unit General P Leisure Shop 2 miles Pub 2 miles

AXMINSTER, Devon Map ref 1D2

★★★★
SELF CATERING

Units **1**
Sleeps **6**
Low season per wk
£800.00
High season per wk
£1,000.00–£1,200.00

Trout Lodge, Weycroft, Axminster

contact Miss Caroline Cross, 19 Hylton Road, Petersfield GU32 3JY
t (01730) 263732 **e** caroline@troutlodge.co.uk **w** troutlodge.co.uk

open All year
payment Cash/cheques

In a designated Area of Outstanding Natural Beauty, this beautiful lodge is set on its own little island with 600yds of fishing on the River Axe. The accommodation comprises two twin bedrooms and one double (all en suite), an enormous living room, dining room, terrace and a well-equipped kitchen. Dogs welcome.

⊕ *Trout Lodge is off the A358 Axminster/Chard road at Weycroft. The entrance is between 2 sets of traffic lights each side of the bridge.*

Unit General P Leisure Shop 1 mile Pub 1 mile

BAMPTON, Devon Map ref 1D1

★★★★
SELF CATERING

Units **5**
Sleeps **2–6**
Low season per wk
£150.00–£285.00
High season per wk
£355.00–£910.00

Three Gates Farm, Tiverton

contact Mrs Alison Spencer, Three Gates Farm, Huntsham, Tiverton EX16 7QH
t (01398) 331280 **e** threegatesfarm@hotmail.com **w** threegatesfarm.co.uk

open All year
payment Cash/cheques

Relax in one of our excellent converted barns, in the beautiful Devonshire countryside. Spend hours in our superb indoor heated pool, sauna or fitness room. Play in the grounds, with play tower and games rooms. The perfect place to unwind and explore the beaches, river valleys and attractions of Devon.

Jct 27 M5 A362. 1st Tiverton exit. Right Chettiscombe. Over A361 right, 3.5 miles right Huntsham, 1 mile Three Gates on right.

Short breaks available Oct-May (excl school holidays).

Unit General P Leisure

BAMPTON, Devon Map ref 1D1

★★★
SELF CATERING

Units **1**
Sleeps **4–6**
Low season per wk
£200.00–£360.00
High season per wk
£360.00–£400.00

Wonham Barton, Bampton, Tiverton

contact Mrs Anne McLean Williams, Wonham Barton, Bampton, Tiverton EX16 9JZ
t (01398) 331312 **f** (01398) 331312 **w** wonham-country-holidays.co.uk

open All year
payment Credit/debit cards, cash/cheques

From friendly accommodation overlooking Exe Valley, conveniently explore secretive, historic Devon, rolling moorlands and dramatic coastlines; enjoy country pursuits and leisurely cream teas. Savour 300 tranquil acres, glimpsing Exmoor red deer, soaring buzzards and traditional shepherding; share romantic scenes from TV drama and 'Landgirls', filmed here. Tell us when you're coming!

M5 jct 27, A361 to Tiverton. A396 (north) to Bampton. Follow signs for Dulverton and Exebridge and fork left to Oakford Bridge. Farm is 2nd on left.

Short breaks available Oct-Mar. Min 2 nights. Prices on request. Dogs accepted by arrangement.

Unit General P Leisure Shop 2.5 miles
Pub 2.5 miles

BARNSTAPLE, Devon Map ref 1C1

★★★★
SELF CATERING

Units **1**
Sleeps **4–5**
Low season per wk
£300.00–£400.00
High season per wk
£475.00–£600.00

Coombe Cottage, Goodleigh, Barnstaple

contact Karen and John Talbot, 4 Garden Cottages, Bearwood College, Wokingham RG41 5DP
t (0118) 976 0449 **e** karen@coombecottage.co.uk **w** coombecottage.co.uk

Two-hundred-year-old updated cottage. Farmland views, picturesque village, exposed beams, pine flooring, woodburner. Large garden with patio furniture. Lounge, garden room, fully equipped kitchen, utility room, three bedrooms, two bathrooms.

open All year
payment Cash/cheques

Unit General P Leisure Shop 3 miles
Pub < 0.5 miles

Check it out

Information on accommodation listed in this guide has been supplied by proprietors. As changes may occur you should remember to check all relevant details at the time of booking.

BARNSTAPLE, Devon Map ref 1C1

★★★★ SELF CATERING

Units **11**
Sleeps **2–8**
Low season per wk £330.00–£550.00
High season per wk £775.00–£1,350.00

Corffe Holiday Cottages, Barnstaple

contact Mr Christopher Wheeler-Grix, Tawstock, Barnstaple EX31 3NZ
t (01271) 342588 **f** (01271) 342588 **e** corffe@tiscali.co.uk **w** corffe.co.uk

Luxury self-catering cottages. Award-winning indoor heated swimming pool and jacuzzi. LTA-standard tennis court. Excellent countryside views.

open All year
payment Cash/cheques

Unit General P Leisure
Shop 1.5 miles Pub 1.5 miles

BARNSTAPLE, Devon Map ref 1C1

★★★ SELF CATERING

Units **8**
Sleeps **2–8**
Low season per wk £200.00–£300.00
High season per wk £300.00–£800.00

North Hill Cottages, Barnstaple

contact Mrs Carol Ann Black, North Hill Cottages, North Hill, Shirwell, Barnstaple EX31 4LG
t (01271) 850611 **f** (01271) 850693 **e** info@north-hill.co.uk **w** north-hill.co.uk

Converted 17thC farm buildings set in eight acres of secluded gardens and meadows. Ten minutes from Barnstaple town centre.

open All year
payment Cash/cheques

Unit General P Leisure Shop 3 miles Pub 3 miles

BATH, Somerset Map ref 2B2

★★★★ SELF CATERING

Units **7**
Sleeps **2–4**
Low season per wk £275.00–£645.00
High season per wk £465.00–£875.00

Church Farm Country Cottages, Bradford-on-Avon

contact Mrs Trish Bowles, Church Farm, Winsley, Bradford-on-Avon BA15 2JH
t (01225) 722246 **f** (01225) 722246 **e** stay@churchfarmcottages.com **w** churchfarmcottages.com

open All year
payment Credit/debit cards, cash/cheques, euros

Well-equipped, single-storey, traditional cow byres. Bath four miles. Working farm with sheep, free-range hens and horses. Swim in our luxurious, heated indoor pool (12m x 5m), whatever the weather! Pub/shop 500m. Kennet & Avon Canal nearby for boating, cycling and walking. Regular buses. Welcome cream tea.

⊕ *M4 jct 18, take A46 to Bath, then A363 to Bradford-on-Avon. B3108 to Winsley (2 miles). At roundabout, 2nd exit to Bath/Limpley Stoke. Farm 0.75 miles on right.*

❤ *4-night mid-week break (Mon-Thu) available at same price as 3-night weekend break (Fri-Sun), excl school holidays.*

Unit General P Leisure
Shop < 0.5 miles Pub < 0.5 miles

BATH, Somerset Map ref 2B2

★★★★★ SELF CATERING

Units **1**
Sleeps **2–4**
Low season per wk Min £800.00
High season per wk Min £1,000.00

The Garden House, Bath

contact Ms Elizabeth Orchard, St Catherines End House, St Catherine, Bath BA1 8HE
t (01225) 852340 **f** (01225) 852551 **e** elizabeth@elizabethorchard.com **w** lakeorchard.com

Luxurious 17thC barn conversion overlooking stunning countryside, five miles from Bath. Renovated to a very high standard and retaining character, with exposed beams. Secluded terrace with hot tub.

open All year
payment Cash/cheques, euros

Unit General P Leisure Shop 1.5 miles Pub 1.5 miles

BATH, Somerset Map ref 2B2

★★★★★
SELF CATERING

Units 5
Sleeps 2–4
Low season per wk
£211.00–£311.00
High season per wk
£341.00–£462.00

Greyfield Farm Cottages, High Littleton

contact Mrs June Merry, Greyfield Farm Cottages, Greyfield Road, High Littleton, Bristol BS39 6YQ
t (01761) 471132 **f** (01761) 471132 **e** june@greyfieldfarm.com **w** greyfieldfarm.com

open All year
payment Cash/cheques, euros

Attractive stone cottages in peaceful, private, 3.5-acre setting overlooking the Mendips. The cottages are spacious, fully equipped, warm and very comfortable. Each enjoys its own garden/patio and adjacent safe parking. Free facilities include hot tub, sauna, fitness and barbecue centres plus video/DVD library.

⊕ *A4 through Bath towards Bristol. Just after leaving Bath, left onto A39 to High Littleton. Greyfield Road for 200yds, bear right. Farm 3rd entrance on left.*

♥ *Fully flexible bookings and short breaks available all year round. Availability calendar and full details available on our website.*

Unit General Leisure
Shop 0.5 miles Pub 0.5 miles

BATHEASTON, Somerset Map ref 2B2

★★★★–★★★★★
SELF CATERING

Units 2
Sleeps 1–8
Low season per wk
£350.00–£580.00
High season per wk
£475.00–£850.00

Avondale Riverside, Bath

contact Mr & Mrs Pecchia, Avondale Riverside, 104 Lower Northend, North End, Batheaston, Bath BA1 7HA
t (01225) 852226 **f** (01225) 852226 **e** sheilapex@questmusic.co.uk **w** riversapart.co.uk

Balconied riverside apartments overlooking nature reserve. Private garden, secure parking, widescreen TV, whirlpool bath, en suite bedrooms, hot tub. Short breaks. Special rates for parties of eight. Ten minutes' drive to city centre.

open All year
payment Cash/cheques

Unit General Leisure Shop < 0.5 miles
Pub < 0.5 miles

BEAMINSTER, Dorset Map ref 2A3

★★★
SELF CATERING

Units 3
Sleeps 4
Low season per wk
£100.00–£210.00
High season per wk
£210.00–£320.00

Greens Cross Farm, Beaminster

contact Mr & Mrs David & Lora Baker, Greens Cross Farm, Stoke Road, Beaminster DT8 3JL
t (01308) 862661 **f** (01308) 863800 **e** greenscross@btopenworld.com

Well-equipped holiday units within walking distance of Beaminster in heart of Dorset and close to coast. Short winter breaks. Nearby woods and walking paths to countryside.

open All year
payment Cash/cheques

Unit General Leisure Shop 0.75 miles Pub 0.75 miles

BEAMINSTER, Dorset Map ref 2A3

★★★★
SELF CATERING

Units **1**
Sleeps **2–8**

Low season per wk
£300.00–£425.00
High season per wk
£475.00–£650.00

Orchard End, Hooke, Beaminster

contact Mrs Pauline Wallbridge, Watermeadow House, Bridge Farm, Beaminster DT8 3PD
t (01308) 862619 **f** (01308) 862619 **e** enquiries@watermeadowhouse.co.uk
w watermeadowhouse.co.uk

open All year
payment Cash/cheques

Bungalow on our family-run dairy farm in the small village of Hooke. Spacious accommodation with four bedrooms and two bathrooms. Well equipped, with dishwasher, washing machine etc. Fenced garden, off-road parking. Lovely walking area nine miles from coast and four miles from the small town of Beaminster.

⊕ *Approx 9 miles east of Crewkerne on A356, and 3.5 miles west of Maiden Newton on A356.*

Unit General Leisure

BEAMINSTER, Dorset Map ref 2A3

★★★★
SELF CATERING

Units **1**
Sleeps **2–3**

Low season per wk
Min £150.00
High season per wk
Max £400.00

Stable Cottage, Beaminster

contact Mrs Diana Clarke, Stable Cottage, Meerhay Manor, Beaminster DT8 3SB
t (01308) 862305 **f** (01308) 863972 **e** meerhay@aol.com **w** meerhay.co.uk

Ground-floor conversion of old barn in grounds of old manor. Wheelchair accessible. Idyllic setting in 40 acres of farmland. Plantsman's garden, tennis court, stabling. Seven miles coast.

open All year
payment Cash/cheques

Unit General P Leisure Shop 1 mile Pub 1 mile

BENTHAM, Gloucestershire Map ref 2B1

★★★★★
SELF CATERING

Units **1**
Sleeps **1–4**

Low season per wk
£250.00–£300.00
High season per wk
£300.00–£550.00

Bridge House Cottage, Cheltenham

contact Mrs Yvonne Hodges, Bridge House, Church Lane, Bentham, Cheltenham GL51 4TZ
t (01452) 862998 **e** yvonne@hodges0.wanadoo.co.uk **w** benthamcottage.co.uk

Cotswolds location. Wing of barn conversion. Heavily beamed and beautifully furnished. Own enclosed grounds including 16thC dovecote.

open All year
payment Cash/cheques

Unit General P Leisure Shop 0.5 miles
Pub 0.5 miles

BERRYNARBOR, Devon Map ref 1C1

★★★
SELF CATERING

Units **5**
Sleeps **2–8**
Low season per wk
£110.00–£320.00
High season per wk
£550.00–£900.00

Smythen Farm Coastal Holiday Cottages, Ilfracombe

contact Mr & Ms Thompson & Elstone, Smythen Farm Coastal Holiday Cottages, Symthen, Sterridge Valley, Berrynarbor, Ilfracombe EX34 9TB
t (01271) 882875 **f** (01271) 882875 **e** jayne@smythenfarmholidaycottages.co.uk
w smythenfarmholidaycottages.co.uk

open All year except Christmas and New Year
payment Cash/cheques

Near golden sands with sea and coastal views. Heated, covered swimming pool in a suntrap enclosure, gardens and games room with pool table, table tennis, football machine. Tree-house on two levels. Free pony rides, ball pond and bouncy castle, 14-acre recreation field and dog walk. For colour brochure phone Jayne.

⊕ *A361 to Barnstaple then A39 for 1 mile towards Lynton. Left onto B3230, through Muddiford and Milltown. Right by garage onto A3123, next left to Sterridge Valley.*

Unit General P Leisure
Shop 1.5 miles Pub 1.5 miles

BIBURY, Gloucestershire Map ref 2B1

★★★★
SELF CATERING

Units **2**
Sleeps **4**
Low season per wk
£240.00–£290.00
High season per wk
£310.00–£375.00

Cotteswold House Cottages, Bibury

contact Mrs Judith Underwood, Cotteswold House, Arlington, Bibury, Cirencester GL7 5ND
t (01285) 740609 **f** (01285) 740609 **e** enquiries@cotteswoldhouse.org.uk **w** cotteswoldhouse.org.uk

open All year
payment Credit/debit cards, cash/cheques

Situated in this picturesque village, these delightful cottages offer tastefully furnished, spacious accommodation. Equipped to a high standard to include all the comforts of home. Heating, linen and electricity included. Private parking. No smoking/ pets. An ideal centre for touring the Cotswolds and surrounding areas.

⊕ *As you enter the village of Bibury from Cirencester on the B4425 Cotteswold House Cottages are on the left before descending the hill.*

Unit General P Shop 1 mile Pub 0.5 miles

BIDEFORD, Devon Map ref 1C1

★★★★
SELF CATERING

Units **6**
Sleeps **4–6**
Low season per wk
£325.00–£450.00
High season per wk
£790.00–£1,060.00

Robin Hill Farm Cottages, Bideford

contact Mr & Mrs Rob & Sue Williams, Robin Hill Farm, Littleham, Bideford EX39 5EG
t (01237) 473605 **e** r.hillcotts@amserve.net **w** robinhillcottages.co.uk

open All year
payment Cash/cheques

Cottages approached by a 0.5-mile leafy lane through 14 acres of woodland and pasture. Set away from the cottages is a leisure complex with an indoor pool and games room. Enjoy the peace and tranquillity, with spectacular views to Exmoor, in rolling countryside close to the coast.

⊕ *Full directions will be sent on receipt of final payment for holiday.*

♥ *Short breaks available all year (excl school holidays).*

Unit General P Leisure Shop 1.5 miles
Pub 1.5 miles

BIDEFORD, Devon Map ref 1C1

★★★–★★★★ SELF CATERING

Units **2**
Sleeps **2–10**
Low season per wk
£230.00–£370.00
High season per wk
£370.00–£824.00

West Hele, Bideford

contact Mrs Lorna Hicks, Buckland Brewer, Bideford EX39 5LZ
t (01237) 451044 **f** (01237) 451309 **e** lorna.hicks@virgin.net **w** westhele.co.uk

open All year
payment Cash/cheques

Peaceful beef farm in beautiful rolling countryside. Watch the wild birds, gaze at exceptional stars. Stay in the Garden Wing, part of the traditional farmhouse, or in Orchard Barn (illustrated), a character cottage with spacious rooms and level access.

⊕ *Please see website.*

Unit General P Leisure Shop 2 miles Pub 2 miles

BIGBURY-ON-SEA, Devon Map ref 1C3

★★★★★ SELF CATERING & SERVICED APARTMENTS

Units **1**
Sleeps **1–4**
Low season per wk
£429.00–£958.00
High season per wk
£1,068.00–£1,497.00

Apartment 5, Burgh Island Causeway, Bigbury-on-Sea

contact Helpful Holidays, Mill Street, Chagford, Newton Abbot TQ13 8AW
t (01647) 433593 **f** (01647) 433694 **e** help@helpfulholidays.com

open All year
payment Credit/debit cards, cash/cheques

Luxury, modern, ground-floor apartment set into cliff with panoramic southerly views from large patio. Facilities include pool, gym, sauna, cafe/bar, grassy cliff-top grounds and direct access to beautiful large sandy beach and coastal path. Popular for surfing and near golf course and village shop/post office.

⊕ *From A38 at Ivybridge, take the 'B' road to Modbury then the A379 towards Kingsbridge. Very soon leave on B3392 for Bigbury-on-Sea.*

❤ *Bargain weekend and short-stay breaks available in autumn and winter months.*

Unit General P Leisure Shop < 0.5 miles Pub < 0.5 miles

BIGBURY-ON-SEA, Devon Map ref 1C3

★★★★ SELF CATERING

Units **1**
Sleeps **1–6**
Low season per wk
£270.00–£470.00
High season per wk
£570.00–£870.00

Ferrycombe, Kingsbridge

contact Mrs Juliet Fooks, Little Grassington, The Spinneys, Heathfield TN21 8YN
t (01435) 863045 & 07050 030231

Unique, old Devon-stone barn in small courtyard with private gardens. Spectacular sea views of Bigbury Bay with its sandy beaches. Ideal for families with children and dogs.

open All year
payment Cash/cheques

Unit General P Leisure Shop 0.5 miles Pub 0.5 miles

Check the maps

Colour maps at the front pinpoint all the places you will find accommodation entries in the regional sections. Pick your location and then refer to the place index at the back to find the page number.

BIRDLIP, Gloucestershire Map ref 2B1

★★★★
SELF CATERING

Units **1**
Sleeps **4**
Low season per wk
£250.00–£350.00
High season per wk
£400.00–£475.00

Sidelands Farm, Gloucester

contact Ms Harriet Saunders, Sidelands Farm Holidays, Sidelands Farm, Brimpsfield Road, Gloucester GL4 8LJ
t (01452) 864826 **e** saunders@sidelands.fsnet.co.uk **w** sidelandsfarm.co.uk

Self-catering accommodation providing spacious family cottage in a rural but well-connected location in the heart of the beautiful Cotswolds.

open All year
payment Cash/cheques

Unit General P Leisure Shop 4 miles Pub 1 mile

BLUE ANCHOR, Somerset Map ref 1D1

★★★★
SELF CATERING

Units **3**
Sleeps **2–5**
Low season per wk
£255.00–£285.00
High season per wk
£320.00–£495.00

Huntingball Lodge, Blue Anchor

contact Mr & Mrs Brian & Kim Hall, Huntingball Lodge, Blue Anchor, Minehead TA24 6JP
t (01984) 640076 **f** (01984) 640076 **w** huntingball-lodge.co.uk

open All year
payment Cash/cheques

Elegant, quiet country house with spectacular views over the Somerset coastline and Exmoor countryside. Luxurious and spacious self-catering apartments furnished and equipped to a very high standard, each with own private terrace or balcony. Pub/restaurant, farm shop/tea rooms and convenience store within easy walking distance. Guaranteed warm welcome from the resident owners.

⊕ *From Taunton, A358 then A39 to Minehead. At Carhampton, right (signed Blue Anchor). Go along seafront, 1st right to Chapel Cleeve. We are 1st on left.*

❤ *Short breaks available Nov-Mar (excl Christmas and New Year).*

Unit General P Shop < 0.5 miles Pub < 0.5 miles

BOSCASTLE, Cornwall Map ref 1B2

★★★★
SELF CATERING

Units **5**
Sleeps **4–6**
Low season per wk
£180.00–£275.00
High season per wk
£275.00–£610.00

Cargurra Farm, Boscastle

contact Mrs Gillian Elson, Hennett, St Juliot, Boscastle PL35 0BT
t (01840) 261206 **f** (01840) 261206 **e** gillian@cargurra.co.uk **w** cargurra.co.uk

open All year
payment Credit/debit cards, cash/cheques

Secluded farm setting within the beautiful Valency Valley where Thomas Hardy met his love. Well-appointed, traditional cottage, log fire, central heating. Spacious gardens, barbecue, games room with pool and table tennis. WI-FI Internet access, communal computer. Private road, ample parking. Country and coastal walks. Also, cottages converted from Victorian barn.

⊕ *Travel directions provided once booking is confirmed.*

Unit General P Leisure Shop 2 miles Pub 2 miles

BOURTON-ON-THE-WATER, Gloucestershire Map ref 2B1

★★★★
SELF CATERING

Units **1**
Sleeps **1–6**
Low season per wk
Min £300.00
High season per wk
Min £740.00

Cloisters, Bourton-on-the-Water, Cheltenham

contact Mrs Harmer, Charts Edge, Hosey Hill, Westerham TN16 1PL
t (01959) 569096 & 07866 477545 **f** (01959) 565641 **e** enquiries@prestigeholidaycottages.co.uk
w prestigeholidaycottages.co.uk

open All year
payment Cash/cheques

Charming Grade II Listed period stone cottage situated in the heart of this famous village. Beautifully furnished with beams, stone walls and fire. Secluded south-facing garden, garage and parking. One double, two twins. Pets welcome. Ideally located for exploring the Cotswolds. Short breaks welcome.

⊕ *A420 to Bourton-on-the-Water. Right onto Rissington Road, then left onto High Street. 1st left then 2nd left onto Victoria Street. The cottage is on left.*

Unit General **P** Shop < 0.5 miles Pub < 0.5 miles

BOURTON-ON-THE-WATER, Gloucestershire Map ref 2B1

★★★
SELF CATERING

Units **1**
Sleeps **1–6**
Low season per wk
£295.00
High season per wk
£295.00

Inglenook Cottage, Cheltenham

contact Mrs Vicki Garland, Ratcliffe House Farm, Ratcliffe House Lane, Ratcliffe Culey, Atherstone CV9 3LZ
t (01827) 712367 & 07751 801508

Inglenook Cottage is an old stone-built cottage, built in the Victorian era, with private courtyard garden. Centrally situated near the river. One twin, one double and downstairs toilet/cloakroom.

open All year
payment Cash/cheques

Unit General **P** Leisure

BOVEY TRACEY, Devon Map ref 1D2

★★★★
SELF CATERING

Units **1**
Sleeps **1–12**
Low season per wk
£400.00–£700.00
High season per wk
£900.00–£1,250.00

Warmhill Farm, Bovey Tracey

contact Mr W B Marnham, Warmhill Farm, Hennock, Bovey Tracey, Newton Abbot TQ13 9QH
t (01626) 833229 **f** (01626) 835187 **e** marnham@agriplus.net

A 100-acre working farm. Superb thatched farmhouse in Dartmoor National Park. Ideal for moor and sea. Spacious and comfortable, with many old features preserved.

open All year
payment Cash/cheques

Unit General **P** Leisure Shop 2 miles
Pub 0.5 miles

Country Code Always follow the Country Code

- Be safe – plan ahead and follow any signs
- Leave gates and property as you find them
- Protect plants and animals, and take your litter home
- Keep dogs under close control
- Consider other people

BRADFORD-ON-AVON, Wiltshire Map ref 2B2

★★★★★
SELF CATERING

Units **2**
Sleeps **11**

Low season per wk
£700.00–£925.00
High season per wk
£1,040.00–£1,386.00

Fairfield Barns, Atworth

contact Mr & Mrs Taff & Gilly Thomas, Bradford Road, Atworth, Melksham SN12 8HZ
t (01225) 703585 **f** 0870 051490 **e** gilly@fairfieldbarns.com **w** fairfieldbarns.com

open All year
payment Credit/debit cards, cash/cheques

In a quiet village near Bath, luxurious barn conversions. Panoramic views of the Wiltshire countryside. Superbly equipped, wood-burning stoves, beamed throughout, en suite bedrooms with foreign theme. Indoor swimming pool, gym, tennis court, sauna and children's playhouse and adventure playground. Perfect for touring and sightseeing.

⊕ *A350 to Chippenham, then A4 to Atworth. Right after BP garage (Bradford Road). Pass school on left. Follow road to left. Fairfield Barns is last driveway on left.*

❤ *Short breaks available Sep-Jun.*

Unit General Leisure
Shop < 0.5 miles Pub 0.5 miles

BRATTON, Somerset Map ref 1D1

★★★★
SELF CATERING

Units **8**
Sleeps **2–11**

Low season per wk
£170.00–£700.00
High season per wk
£270.00–£1,250.00

Woodcombe Lodges, Minehead

contact Mrs Nicola Hanson, Woodcombe Lodges, Bratton Lane, Minehead TA24 8SQ
t (01643) 702789 & 07860 667325 **f** (01643) 702789 **e** nicola@woodcombelodge.co.uk
w woodcombelodge.co.uk

open All year
payment Credit/debit cards, cash/cheques

Timber lodges and stone cottages in a tranquil, rural setting on the edge of Exmoor National Park. Standing in a beautiful, 2.5-acre garden with wonderful views towards the wooded slopes of Exmoor. Minehead's seafront, harbour, shops etc 1.5 miles. Close to Dunster, Selworthy, Porlock and many local beauty spots.

⊕ *M5 jct 24, A39 to Minehead. Follow road out of Minehead towards Porlock then turn west into Woodcombe Lane, then Bratton Lane. Lodges on right just before open country.*

❤ *Short breaks available Nov-Easter, min 3 nights.*

Unit General Leisure Shop 1 mile Pub 1 mile

BRAYFORD, Devon Map ref 1C1

★★★
SELF CATERING

Units **1**
Sleeps **6**

Low season per wk
Min £165.00
High season per wk
Max £350.00

Muxworthy Cottage, Barnstaple

contact Mrs G M Bament, Muxworthy Farm, Brayford, Barnstaple EX32 7QP
t (01598) 710342

Secluded old-world cottage in idyllic rural location, fully equipped, with wood-burning stove. Unspoilt countryside, ideal for a peaceful holiday in the heart of Exmoor. Weekends and short breaks available.

open All year
payment Cash/cheques

Unit General Leisure Shop 3 miles Pub 3 miles

If you have access needs...

Look for the National Accessible Scheme symbols if you have special hearing, visual or mobility needs. An index of all accommodation participating in the scheme can be found at the back of this guide.

BRIDGWATER, Somerset Map ref 1D1

★★★★
SELF CATERING

Units **1**
Sleeps **5**
Low season per wk
£230.00–£270.00
High season per wk
£280.00–£360.00

Nelson Cottage, Nr Bridgwater

contact Mr & Mrs Robbins, Nelson Lodge, Chedzoy Lane, Bridgwater TA7 8QR
t (01278) 453492 **e** robbinsm@bridgwater.ac.uk

Single-storey cottage on the edge of the Somerset Levels offering two bedrooms, living area, kitchen and shower room. Well placed for the Somerset coast and beaches, the Quantocks and the Mendips.

open All year
payment Cash/cheques

Unit General P Shop 1 mile Pub 0.5 miles

BRIDPORT, Dorset Map ref 2A3

★★★★
SELF CATERING

Units **10**
Sleeps **2–6**
Low season per wk
£270.00–£445.00
High season per wk
£460.00–£795.00

Rudge Farm, Bridport

contact Mr Michael Hamer, Rudge Farm, Chilcombe, Bridport DT6 4NF
t (01308) 482630 **e** enquiries@rudgefarm.co.uk **w** rudgefarm.co.uk

open All year
payment Credit/debit cards, cash/cheques

Rudge Farm provides a beautiful countryside location for a stress-free holiday, a short distance away from the World Heritage Coastline. The old farm buildings have been converted into comfortable and cosy cottages, ranging from one to three bedrooms. There are a number of leisure facilities on the farm, including a tennis court and games barn.

⊕ *From Dorchester, take the A35 towards Bridport for 10 miles, turning left 2 miles before Bridport. Follow road for 1 mile. Rudge Farm is on your left.*

❤ *Short breaks available all year.*

Unit General P Leisure Shop 2 miles Pub 1 mile

BRIMPSFIELD, Gloucestershire Map ref 2B1

★★★
SELF CATERING

Units **1**
Sleeps **4**
Low season per wk
£180.00–£200.00
High season per wk
Max £300.00

Brimpsfield Farmhouse (West Wing), Gloucester

contact Mrs Valerie Partridge, Brimpsfield Farmhouse (West Wing), Brimpsfield Farm, Brimpsfield, Gloucester GL4 8LD
t (01452) 863568

Self-contained modern annexe adjoining farmhouse, comfortably furnished and well equipped, village location, central Cotswolds, well placed for touring and walking.

open All year
payment Cash/cheques

Unit General P

Check the maps

Colour maps at the front pinpoint all the cities, towns and villages where you will find accommodation entries in the regional sections. Pick your location and then refer to the place index at the back to find the page number.

BRIXHAM, Devon Map ref 1D2

★★
SELF CATERING

Units **6**
Sleeps **1–5**
Low season per wk
£299.00–£300.00
High season per wk
£299.00–£499.00

Devoncourt Holiday Flats, Brixham

contact Mr Robin Hooker, Devoncourt Holiday Flats, Berry Head Road, Brixham TQ5 9AB
t (01803) 853748 **e** bookings@devoncourt.net **w** devoncourt.info

open All year
payment Credit/debit cards, cash/cheques, euros

Panoramic sea views from your balcony and lounge over Torbay, Brixham harbour and marina. The beach is opposite, only 50m. Each flat is fully self-contained and carpeted, with colour TV and full cooker. Private gardens. Car park. Children, pets and credit cards welcome. For colour brochure telephone (01803) 853748 or 07050 853748.

Follow main road from Paignton into Brixham. Follow the Berry Head road, with the sea on your left, until white block of flats on right marked 'Devoncourt'.

10% discount for Senior Citizens.

Unit General P Leisure Shop 0.5 miles Pub 0.5 miles

BRIXHAM, Devon Map ref 1D2

★★★
SELF CATERING

Units **1**
Sleeps **6**
Low season per wk
£200.00–£255.00
High season per wk
£255.00–£410.00

Windjammer Apartment, Brixham

contact Mr & Mrs Skeggs, Windjammer Apartment, Windjammer Lodge, Parkham Road, Brixham TQ5 9BU
t (01803) 854279 **e** windjammerapartments@yahoo.co.uk **w** holiday-brixham.co.uk

Large top-floor apartment in detached Victorian house. Three bedrooms: one double, two twin. Heating, H/C water all rooms, garden, barbecue, parking. Town and sea view; ten minutes' walk to harbour.

open All year
payment Cash/cheques

Unit General P S Leisure Shop < 0.5 miles Pub < 0.5 miles

BROAD CAMPDEN, Gloucestershire Map ref 2B1

★★★
SELF CATERING

Units **1**
Sleeps **1–6**
Low season per wk
£265.00–£300.00
High season per wk
£320.00–£390.00

Lion Cottage, Broad Campden

contact Mrs Barbara Rawcliffe, Lion Cottage, Broad Campden, Chipping Campden GL55 6UR
t (01386) 840077

open All year
payment Cash/cheques

Cotswold-stone cottage, beamed ceilings, open fireplace, open plan sitting/dining/kitchen. One twin, one double, one single bedroom. Bathroom, shower room. Broad Campden, with its excellent pub, is an ideal base for exploring the beautiful Cotswold countryside. Nearby is historic Chipping Campden, with Cheltenham, Oxford and Stratford within an hour's drive.

From A44 take B4081 (Chipping Campden). At 1st main junction bear right (Broad Campden). Continue for approx 1 mile and cottage is beside red phone box on left.

Unit General P Leisure Shop 1 mile Pub < 0.5 miles

Ancient and modern

Experience timeless favourites or discover the latest must-sees. Whatever your choice, be inspired by the places of interest highlighted for each region and the events listed towards the back of this guide.

BUCKFASTLEIGH, Devon Map ref 1C2

★★★★
SELF CATERING

Units **1**
Sleeps **5–6**
Low season per wk
£350.00–£500.00
High season per wk
£600.00–£750.00

Spindle Cottage, Moor's Court, Buckfastleigh

contact Ms Dawn Riggs, Bellamarsh Barton, Kingsteignton Road, Chudleigh TQ13 0AJ
t (01626) 853995 **e** dawnriggs@threads-of-time.co.uk

open All year
payment Cash/cheques

17thC wool-worker's cottage situated in a tranquil, cobbled courtyard, nestling on the edge of Dartmoor. High-quality accommodation comprising three bedrooms and excellently equipped kitchen. Digital weather station. Focus on natural fibres and local, organic produce. Five minutes' walk from shops and pubs. Many places of interest within easy reach.

⊕ *Leave A38 at Dartbridge. Follow signs for Buckfastleigh. Turn left at roundabout, then 2nd right. Moor's Court is through archway opposite Station Road car park.*

❤ *Please phone for information.*

Unit General Leisure Shop < 0.5 miles Pub < 0.5 miles

BUCKLAND NEWTON, Dorset Map ref 2B3

★★★★
SELF CATERING

Units **3**
Sleeps **4**
Low season per wk
£200.00–£330.00
High season per wk
£360.00–£490.00

Domineys Cottages, Buckland Newton, Nr Dorchester

contact Mrs Jeanette Gueterbock, Domineys Cottages, Domineys Yard, Buckland Newton, Dorchester DT2 7BS
t (01300) 345295 **f** (01300) 345596 **e** cottages@domineys.com **w** domineys.com

open All year
payment Cash/cheques

Delightful, Victorian, two-bedroomed cottages, comfortably furnished and equipped and maintained to highest standards. Surrounded by beautiful gardens with patios. Heated summer swimming pool. Peaceful location on village edge in heart of Hardy's Dorset. Well situated for touring Wessex, walking and country pursuits. Regret no pets. Children 5+ and babies welcome.

⊕ *A352 Dorchester. Left on B3146, follow signs for Buckland Newton. In village take no-through road on left just past pub and telephone box.*

Unit General 5 P Leisure Shop 1 mile Pub < 0.5 miles

BUDE, Cornwall Map ref 1C2

★★★★
SELF CATERING

Units **7**
Sleeps **2–6**
Low season per wk
£275.00–£405.00
High season per wk
£425.00–£940.00

Glebe House Cottages, Holsworthy

contact Mr & Mrs James Varley, Glebe House Cottages Limited, Bridgerule, Holsworthy EX22 7EW
t (01288) 381272 **e** etc@glebehousecottages.co.uk **w** glebehousecottages.co.uk

open All year
payment Credit/debit cards, cash/cheques

Beautiful period cottages with exposed beams, some four-poster beds, en suite facilities and double whirlpool baths. Set in five acres of beautiful gardens and woodland on Grade II Listed Georgian estate overlooking the Tamar Valley. Only ten minutes' drive to Bude's sandy beaches and spectacular North Cornish coast.

⊕ *A30 to Okehampton, then A3079 and A3072 to Bude. Two miles beyond Holsworthy, left signed Bridgerule. Three miles to T-junction and left again. 300yds on right.*

❤ *Short breaks available most of the year (excl school summer holidays). Special offers for celebration weekends.*

Unit General P Leisure Shop < 0.5 miles Pub < 0.5 miles

BUDE, Cornwall Map ref 1C2

★★★★-★★★★★
SELF CATERING

Units **6**
Sleeps **2–8**
Low season per wk
£200.00–£600.00
High season per wk
£460.00–£1,450.00

Ivyleaf Barton Cottages, Bude

t (01283) 321237 **e** info@ivyleafbarton.co.uk **w** ivyleafbarton.co.uk

Well-equipped, cosy cottages converted from stone barns. Two sleeping two people, one sleeping four, two sleeping seven and one sleeping eight. Tennis court, adjacent golf course. Three miles to Bude. Short breaks welcome.

open All year
payment Credit/debit cards, cash/cheques, euros

Unit General P Leisure Shop 1.5 miles Pub 1.5 miles

BUDE, Cornwall Map ref 1C2

★★★★
SELF CATERING

Units **10**
Sleeps **4–6**
Low season per wk
£295.00–£335.00
High season per wk
£645.00–£810.00

Ivyleaf Combe, Bude

contact Mr Cheeseman, Ivyleaf Combe, Ivyleaf Hill, Stratton EX23 9LD
t (01288) 321323 **f** (01288) 321323 **e** tony@ivyleafcombe.com **w** ivyleafcombe.com

open All year
payment Cash/cheques

Discover this superbly appointed selection of lodges in a tranquil and beautiful setting. These spacious and contemporary lodges offer the perfect place in which to unwind and relax. All have their own deck/patio, and some have hot tubs. Large, safe play area. Ivyleaf Combe is perfect for that romantic break or the family holiday.

⊕ *M5 jct 27, A361 to Barnstaple, left onto A39 towards Bude. Through Kilkhampton. Turn off A39 left towards Ivyleaf golf course. Ivyleaf Combe at bottom of hill on left.*

♥ *3- and 4-night stays available. Romantic-break packages in lodges with 4-poster bed and hot tub.*

Unit General P S Leisure Shop 1 mile Pub 1.5 miles

BUDE, Cornwall Map ref 1C2

★★★★★
SELF CATERING

Units **19**
Sleeps **2–10**
Low season per wk
£276.00–£849.00
High season per wk
£597.00–£2,583.00

Kennacott Court, Bude

contact Mr & Mrs Myers, Kennacott Court, Widemouth, Bude EX23 0ND
t (01288) 362000 **f** (01288) 361434 **e** phil@kennacottcourt.co.uk **w** kennacottcourt.co.uk

open All year
payment Credit/debit cards, cash/cheques

An outstanding collection of cottages which are beautifully furnished, very comfortable and comprehensively equipped. Kennacott Court has a wide range of activities: indoor swimming pool, games room, badminton, snooker and children's room, together with tennis courts and our own golf course. All set in 70 acres overlooking the sea at Widemouth Bay.

⊕ *Travel south of Bude on A39 until 1st turning on right to Widemouth Bay. Turn right, and entrance is 50m on right.*

♥ *Open all year with attractive out-of-season short breaks. Please contact us with your requirements.*

Unit General S Leisure
Shop 3 miles Pub 1 mile

Phone ahead

Even the most ardent pet lover would appreciate some advance warning of Rover's visit, so please phone ahead and check what facilities will be available.

BUDE, Cornwall Map ref 1C2

★★★
SELF CATERING

Units **8**
Sleeps **2–6**
Low season per wk
£185.00–£320.00
High season per wk
£320.00–£775.00

Langfield Manor, Bude

Langfield Manor, Broadclose, Bude EX23 8DP
t (01288) 352415 e info@langfieldmanor.co.uk w langfieldmanor.co.uk

open All year
payment Credit/debit cards, cash/cheques

Quality apartments within fine Edwardian house. Games room with full-sized snooker table, pool and table-tennis tables. Three minutes' walk to the shops and ten to beautiful sandy beaches, yet peacefully situated in delightful, sheltered, south-facing gardens with heated outdoor swimming pool. Golf course adjacent.

From Stratton and A39 take Stratton Road past Morrisons and Esso garage. Take 1st right, 1st left, 1st right, 1st left, then right and right again after 30yds.

Unit General P Leisure

BUDE, Cornwall Map ref 1C2

★★★★
SELF CATERING

Units **4**
Sleeps **2–7**
Low season per wk
£250.00–£450.00
High season per wk
£450.00–£880.00

West Woolley Barns, Bude

contact Mrs Jan Everard, West Woolley Barns, Woolley, Morwenstow EX23 9PP
t (01288) 331202 e info@westwoolleyfarm.co.uk w westwoolleyfarm.co.uk

Beautiful, individually designed barn conversions on small farm near the spectacular North Cornish coast in historical Morwenstow. Horses, alpacas, great beaches and stunning walks.

open All year
payment Cash/cheques

Unit General P Leisure **Shop** 2 miles **Pub** 3 miles

BURNHAM-ON-SEA, Somerset Map ref 1D1

★★★-★★★★
SELF CATERING

Units **4**
Sleeps **2–9**
Low season per wk
£100.00–£175.00
High season per wk
£235.00–£595.00

Prospect Farm Holidays, Highbridge

contact Mrs Gillian Wall, Prospect Farm Holidays, Strowlands, East Brent, Highbridge TA9 4JH
t (01278) 760507

open All year
payment Cash/cheques

17thC, tastefully restored country cottages set amidst flower gardens and surrounded by the natural West Country beauty of the Somerset Levels, near the legendary Brent Knoll, with remains of Iron Age and Roman settlements. Two miles junction 22 M5, three miles Burnham-on-Sea. Variety of small farm animals and pets. Children welcome.

M5 jct 22, take A38 for Weston-super-Mare/Bristol, then A370 for Weston-super-Mare. At war memorial, 1st right, then 1st left, then immediately right into Strowlands. Farm 300yds on right.

Special tariffs quoted for mid-week and weekend breaks in low season.

Unit General P Leisure
Shop < 0.5 miles **Pub** < 0.5 miles

Place index

If you know where you want to stay the index at the back of the guide will give you the page number which lists accommodation in your chosen town, city or village. Check out the other useful indexes too.

BURROWBRIDGE, Somerset Map ref 1D1

★★★
SELF CATERING

Units **1**
Sleeps **2**
Low season per wk
£185.00
High season per wk
£210.00

Hillview, Bridgwater

contact Mrs Rosalind Griffiths, Hillview, Stanmoor Road, Burrowbridge, Bridgwater TA7 0RX
t (01823) 698308 **f** (01823) 698308

Compact bungalow, fully equipped and centrally heated, in its own grounds. Conservatory. Short breaks available in low season.

open All year
payment Cash/cheques

Unit **General** P **Shop** 2 miles **Pub** 0.75 miles

BURTON BRADSTOCK, Dorset Map ref 2A3

★★★
SELF CATERING

Units **1**
Sleeps **2**
Low season per wk
Max £385.00
High season per wk
Max £399.00

Pebble Beach Lodge, Bridport

contact Mrs Jan Hemingway, Pebble Beach Lodge, Burton Bradstock, Bridport DT6 4RJ
t (01308) 897428 **w** burtonbradstock.org.uk

Self-catering apartment within modern building, affording panoramic views of Heritage Coastline with direct access to beach.

open All year
payment Cash/cheques

Unit **General** P **Leisure**

CAMELFORD, Cornwall Map ref 1B2

★★★★–★★★★★
SELF CATERING

Units **4**
Sleeps **2–7**
Low season per wk
£500.00–£750.00
High season per wk
£750.00–£1,400.00

Helsbury Park, Camelford

contact Mrs Leza Wilson, 42 Easthorpe Street, Ruddington, Nottingham NG11 6LA
t (0115) 914 7212 **e** leza.w@ntlworld.com **w** helsburypark.co.uk

Award-winning, luxury accommodation set in parkland with woods and river frontage. The cottages mix traditional character with modern comfort, including well-equipped kitchens, ample bathrooms, log fires and four-poster beds.

open All year
payment Credit/debit cards, cash/cheques

Unit **General** P **Leisure** **Shop** 2 miles **Pub** 2 miles

CAMELFORD, Cornwall Map ref 1B2

★★★★
SELF CATERING

Units **5**
Sleeps **1–6**
Low season per wk
Max £199.00
High season per wk
Max £720.00

Juliot's Well Cottages, Camelford

contact Mr & Mrs Boundy, Juliot's Well Cottages, Camelford PL32 9RF
t (01840) 213302 **f** (01840) 212700 **e** juliotswell@holidaysincornwall.net **w** holidaysincornwall.net

Stone-built cottages with a very high specification throughout, situated within 31 acres of beautiful woodland and meadows. Outdoor heated pool, bar, restaurant. Close to the coast/beach and Bodmin Moor.

open All year
payment Credit/debit cards, cash/cheques

Unit **General** P **Leisure** **Shop** < 0.5 miles **Pub** < 0.5 miles

Using map references

The map references refer to the colour maps at the front of this guide. The first figure is the map number; the letter and figure that follow indicate the grid reference on the map.

CARBIS BAY, Cornwall Map ref 1B3

★★★★
SELF CATERING

Units **8**
Sleeps **4–6**
Low season per wk
£240.00–£350.00
High season per wk
£350.00–£720.00

Rotorua Apartments, Carbis Bay

contact Mrs Linda Roach, Rotorua Apartments, Trencrom Lane, Carbis Bay TR26 2TD
t (01736) 795419 **f** (01736) 795419 **e** rotorua@btconnect.com **w** stivesapartments.com

Holiday apartments situated in quiet wooded lane, with heated outdoor swimming pool and gardens. All apartments are furnished and equipped to a very high standard, including dishwasher, microwave, fridge/freezer and electric cooker.

open All year
payment Credit/debit cards, cash/cheques

Unit General P Leisure Shop 0.5 miles Pub 1 mile

CASTLE CARY, Somerset Map ref 2B2

★★★
SELF CATERING

Units **2**
Sleeps **4**
Low season per wk
£175.00–£225.00
High season per wk
£275.00–£320.00

Orchard Farm Cottages, Castle Cary

contact Mr & Mrs Dave & Helen Boyer, Orchard Farm Cottages, Cockhill, Castle Cary BA7 7NY
t (01963) 350418 **e** boyer@orchard-farm.co.uk **w** orchard-farm.co.uk

open All year
payment Cash/cheques, euros

Traditional Somerset byre converted into cosy cottages providing fully equipped and comfortably furnished accommodation at a reasonable price. One cottage suitable for wheelchairs. Relax in the lawned garden or enjoy quiet country walks. Less than two miles from picturesque Castle Cary's pubs and shops. Many attractions nearby. Ideal for exploring the West Country.

⊕ *From A303 take A359 at Sparkford for Castle Cary. After about 3 miles, left onto B3152 then left to Cockhill; 2nd farm on right after 0.5 miles.*

Unit General P S Leisure Shop 1.5 miles Pub 1 mile

CHARDSTOCK, Devon Map ref 1D2

★★★★
SELF CATERING

Units **1**
Sleeps **2**
Low season per wk
£200.00–£275.00
High season per wk
£250.00–£345.00

Barn Owls Cottage, Axminster

contact Mrs Jean Hafner, Barn Owls Cottage, Chardstock, Axminster EX13 7BY
t (01460) 220475 **f** (01460) 220475 **e** jean.hafner1@btinternet.com
w cottageguide.co.uk/barnowlscottage

open All year
payment Cash/cheques

Peaceful and relaxing cottage with emphasis on quality and comfort. King-size posture-sprung bed. Beautiful views over River Axe valley. Bird-watching, large garden, conservatory. Near Lyme Regis, Beer, Branscombe, Forde Abbey (National Trust). Located within Blackdown Hills, an area designated as an Area of Outstanding Natural Beauty. Local walks. Faces south/south-west. Owner's personal attention.

⊕ *M5 jct 25 to A358 (Chard) or A303 to Chard. Then A358 to Tytherleigh. One mile to Chardstock.*

❤ *3-night short breaks Mar or Oct.*

Unit General P Leisure Shop 0.5 miles Pub < 0.5 miles

Best foot forward

Walkers feel at home in accommodation participating in our Walkers Welcome scheme. Look out for the symbol. Consider walking all or part of a long-distance route – go online at nationaltrail.co.uk.

CHARMOUTH, Dorset Map ref 1D2

★★★
SELF CATERING

Units 1
Sleeps 4
Low season per wk
Min £210.00
High season per wk
Max £550.00

The Poplars, Charmouth

contact Mrs Jane Bremner, Wood Farm Caravan Park, Axminster Road, Bridport DT6 6BT
t (01297) 560697 **f** (01297) 561243 **e** holiday@woodfarm.co.uk **w** woodfarm.co.uk

payment Credit/debit cards, cash/cheques

With breathtaking views and superb facilities, The Poplars offers spacious, comfortable accommodation specifically designed for disabled guests. See our Heritage Coast and spectacular rural scenery. Open Easter to end of October.

⊕ *Approx midway between Axminster and Bridport, turn off roundabout on A35 for Charmouth. Located 0.5 miles west of the village.*

❤ *10% discount for 2-week stays. Early Bird offer for bookings received before 1 Mar.*

Unit General P Leisure

CHAXHILL, Gloucestershire Map ref 2B1

★★★
SELF CATERING

Units 1
Sleeps 1–3
Low season per wk
£150.00–£250.00
High season per wk
£150.00–£450.00

Laurel Cottage, Westbury-on-Severn

contact Mr & Mrs Mark & Tasmin Terry-Lush, The Rowans, Chaxhill, Westbury-on-Severn GL14 1QP
t (01452) 760147 **f** (01452) 762006 **e** enjoyengland@laurel-cottage.com **w** laurel-cottage.com

open All year except Christmas and New Year
payment Cash/cheques

Near the Forest of Dean, Severn and Wye valleys, Laurel Cottage is attached to an 18thC farmhouse in the sleepy hamlet of Chaxhill. Modern facilities and old-world charm await couples or families.

Unit General P S Leisure
Shop < 0.5 miles Pub 1 mile

CHEDDAR, Somerset Map ref 1D1

★★★★
SELF CATERING

Units 4
Sleeps 2–7
Low season per wk
£240.00–£450.00
High season per wk
£350.00–£695.00

Home Farm Cottages, Winscombe

contact Mr Chris Sanders, Home Farm Cottages, Barton, Winscombe BS25 1DX
t (01934) 842078 **f** (01934) 842500 **e** enquiries@homefarmcottages.com **w** homefarmcottages.com

open All year
payment Credit/debit cards, cash/cheques

Characterful, beamed, converted farm buildings, providing an ideal place to relax and an excellent base for Cheddar, Bath, Wells, Bristol and Weston-super-Mare. Many lovely walks in the area and comfortable, well-equipped cottages to return to. Set in two acres adjacent to farmhouse.

⊕ *A371 to Banwell; through Banwell to Winscombe. Right into Church Road. Right into Barton Road. Home Farm Cottages is 1.3 miles on right.*

❤ *Short breaks available.*

Unit General P S Leisure Shop 2 miles Pub 2 miles

Key to symbols

Open the back flap for a key to symbols.

CHEDDAR, Somerset Map ref 1D1

★★★★
SELF CATERING

Units **3**
Sleeps **2**
Low season per wk
£220.00–£240.00
High season per wk
£300.00–£320.00

Spring Cottages, Cheddar

contact Mrs Jennifer Buckland, Spring Cottage, Venns Gate, Cheddar BS27 3LW
t (01934) 742493 **f** (01934) 742493 **e** buckland@springcottages.co.uk **w** springcottages.co.uk

open All year
payment Credit/debit cards, cash/cheques

Charming one-bedroomed cottages in converted barn in two acres of gardens/grounds between the Mendip Hills and Somerset Levels. The famous Cheddar Gorge and caves are within walking distance. Ideally situated for touring the West Country. Nearby opportunities for most sports/interests. No smoking. Ample off-road parking. Dogs by arrangement.

⊕ *Take A38 towards Bristol then A371 to Cheddar. On outskirts of Cheddar turn off at BP garage to Gorge. Venns Gate is 1st left.*

♥ *See our website for special offers.*

Unit General P Leisure Shop 0.5 miles Pub < 0.5 miles

CHEDDAR, Somerset Map ref 1D1

★★★
SELF CATERING

Units **4**
Sleeps **1–4**
Low season per wk
£140.00–£160.00
High season per wk
£160.00–£185.00

Sungate Holiday Apartments, Cheddar

contact Mrs M M Fieldhouse, Pyrenmount, Parsons Way, Winscombe BS25 1BU
t (01934) 842273 & (01934) 742264 **w** sungateholidayapartments.co.uk

Delightful apartments in listed Georgian house. Well furnished and equipped. Level rear entrance. In the centre of Cheddar village close to gorge and caves. Well-behaved children and pets welcome.

open All year
payment Cash/cheques, euros

Unit General P Shop < 0.5 miles Pub < 0.5 miles

CHELTENHAM, Gloucestershire Map ref 2B1

★★★★
SELF CATERING

Units **3**
Sleeps **8–10**
Low season per wk
£190.00–£260.00
High season per wk
£290.00–£370.00

Holmer Cottages, Cheltenham

contact Mrs Jill Collins, Holmer Cottages, Haines Orchard, Woolstone, Cheltenham GL52 9RG
t (01242) 672848 **f** (01242) 672848 **e** holmercottages@talk21.com
w cottageguide.co.uk/holmercottages

Numbers 1 and 2 are charming, comfortable, rural, Edwardian cottages. Number 3 is a luxurious, independent wing of the owner's house in a peaceful hamlet.

open All year
payment Cash/cheques

Unit General P Leisure Shop 1 mile Pub 0.5 miles

CHELTENHAM, Gloucestershire Map ref 2B1

★★★
SELF CATERING

Units **1**
Sleeps **1–4**
Low season per wk
£250.00–£280.00
High season per wk
£280.00–£350.00

Priory Cottage, Southam

contact Mr Mant, Church Gate, Southam Lane, Cheltenham GL52 3NY
t (01242) 584693 **f** (01242) 584693 **e** iansmant@hotmail.com **w** countrycottagesonline.net

open All year except Christmas
payment Cash/cheques

Old Cotswold-stone cottage in own garden overlooking apple orchard. Cosy and warm in winter with wood-burning stove. Two bedrooms, one double, one twin; sitting room, dining room, modern fitted kitchen. Ideal base for Cotswolds, Cheltenham and Area of Outstanding Natural Beauty. Good walking country including Cotswold Way.

M40/A40 or M5 to Cheltenham, leave Cheltenham on B4632. Three miles north of Cheltenham at Southam turn left into Southam Lane. Priory Cottage is on the right.

Short breaks available all year from £150.

Unit General 10 P Shop 1 mile Pub 1 mile

CHIPPENHAM, Wiltshire Map ref 2B2

★★★★
SELF CATERING

Units **2**
Sleeps **4–6**
Low season per wk
£225.00–£300.00
High season per wk
£350.00–£450.00

Olivemead Farm Holidays, Chippenham

contact Mrs Suzanne Candy, Olivemead Farm, Olivemead Lane, Chippenham SN15 4JQ
t (01666) 510205 **e** enquiries@olivemeadfarmholidays.com **w** olivemeadfarmholidays.com

open All year
payment Credit/debit cards, cash/cheques

Imagine two delightful, comfortable, well-equipped cottages on a working farm, converted to offer the luxuries of modern living but retaining traditional features. Bed-settees available for extra guests. Perfectly positioned for days out in Wiltshire, Bath and the Cotswolds. Convenient M4. Brochure available.

M4 jct 17, roundabout onto B4122, left onto B4069. Follow signs for Dauntsey; over motorway bridge, 1st right, 2nd right. Cottage is at end of the lane.

Unit General P Leisure Shop 3 miles
Pub 3 miles

CHIPPING CAMPDEN, Gloucestershire Map ref 2B1

★★★★
SELF CATERING

Units **6**
Sleeps **2–6**
Low season per wk
£320.00–£360.00
High season per wk
£500.00–£1,030.00

Cotswold Charm, Chipping Campden

contact Mr & Miss Michael & Margaret Haines, Cotswold Charm, Top Farm, Blind Lane, Chipping Campden GL55 6ED
t (01386) 840164 **f** (01386) 841883 **e** info@cotswoldcharm.co.uk **w** cotswoldcharm.co.uk

open All year
payment Credit/debit cards, cash/cheques

Cotswold Charm – Top Farm's delightful farm cottages in Chipping Campden's tranquil Westington hamlet, just a five minute walk to High Street restaurants. Year-round idyllic holiday location for the Cotswolds, the Malverns, Oxford, Stratford, Warwick and Worcester. Level access, ground-floor bedroom, supports independent living. Low-allergen air filtration. No smoking/pets.

Unit General P Leisure
Shop < 0.5 miles Pub < 0.5 miles

Check it out

Please check prices, quality ratings and other details when you book.

CHIPPING CAMPDEN, Gloucestershire Map ref 2B1

★★★★
SELF CATERING

Units **1**
Sleeps **6**
Low season per wk
Min £525.00
High season per wk
Max £850.00

Orchard Cottage, Saintbury

contact Ms Sheila Rolland, Campden Cottages, Folly Cottage, Paxford, Chipping Campden GL55 6XG
t (01386) 593315 **f** (01386) 593057 **e** info@campdencottages.co.uk **w** campdencottages.co.uk

open All year
payment Credit/debit cards, cash/cheques

A 16thC Cotswold-stone cottage overlooking beautiful, peaceful countryside. Chipping Campden or Broadway three miles. Many original features including exposed beams, flagstone floor downstairs, wood floors upstairs, inglenook fireplace in sitting room (with logs supplied), separate dining room, three bedrooms, two bathrooms. Garden, barbecue, parking. We regret no dogs.

❤ *Short breaks out of season/close to date – min 3 nights. Other cottages available Chipping Campden/Broadway area – sleeping 2-6, from £290.*

Unit General P Leisure Shop 1 mile Pub 1 mile

CHRISTCHURCH, Dorset Map ref 2B3

★★★
SELF CATERING

Units **1**
Sleeps **6**
Low season per wk
£185.00–£315.00
High season per wk
£365.00–£495.00

Mude Lane, Christchurch

contact Mrs Brickell, 179 Burley Road, Bransgore, Christchurch BH23 8DE
t (01425) 672541

Situated in a quiet area, one mile from Mudeford Quay, two miles from Christchurch, five miles from New Forest. Spacious living area, three bedrooms (two double), bathroom and shower room, attractive garden.

open All year
payment Cash/cheques

Unit General P Leisure Shop < 0.5 miles Pub < 0.5 miles

CHRISTCHURCH, Dorset Map ref 2B3

★★★★
SELF CATERING

Units **1**
Sleeps **10**
Low season per wk
£600.00–£700.00
High season per wk
£850.00–£1,300.00

Riverbank House, Christchurch

contact Mrs Sall Burrows, Oakdene Orchard, Ringwood Road, Three Legged Cross, Wimborne BH21 6RB
t (01202) 813723 & 07796 402912 **f** (01202) 828487 **e** handbleisure@amserve.net
w riverbankholidays.co.uk

Three-storey, south-facing property fronting River Stour. Magnificent views. Available mooring. Family accommodation. Outdoor hot spa overlooking the river.

open All year
payment Cash/cheques

Unit General P Leisure Shop < 0.5 miles Pub < 0.5 miles

CHRISTCHURCH, Dorset Map ref 2B3

★★★
SELF CATERING & SERVICED APARTMENTS

Units **8**
Sleeps **2–6**
Low season per wk
£200.00–£340.00
High season per wk
£340.00–£720.00

Riverside Park, Christchurch

contact Mrs Lisa Booth, Riverside Park, Paddlegrade Limited, 28 Willow Way, Christchurch BH23 1JJ
t (01202) 471090 **e** holidays@riversidepark.biz **w** riversidepark.biz

open All year
payment Cash/cheques

Select, individual holiday houses on the River Stour, each with a balcony and patio overlooking private gardens and river. Ample car parking, riverside picnic and barbecue area. Ideally situated for riverside walks, Priory Church, quay, shops, safe sandy beaches, the New Forest, golfing and horse-riding.

⊕ *See website.*

❤ *Short breaks available Oct-mid-Mar (excl Christmas and New Year). Minimum stay 3 nights.*

Unit General P Leisure Shop < 0.5 miles Pub < 0.5 miles

CHULMLEIGH, Devon Map ref 1C2

★★★★
SELF CATERING

Units 1
Sleeps 2
Low season per wk
Min £224.00
High season per wk
£231.00–£378.00

Deer Cott, Chulmleigh

contact Mr & Mrs George Simpson, Deer Cott, Middle Garland, Chulmleigh EX18 7DU
t (01769) 580461 **f** (01769) 580461 **e** enquiries@deercott.co.uk **w** deercott.co.uk

open All year
payment Cash/cheques

Discover the peace and beauty of the Devonshire countryside and relax in comfortable accommodation offering every convenience for two at any time of the year. In a park-like setting of 20 acres within the Devon heartland, handy for the moors and shores. Amenities at South Molton/Barnstaple a short drive away.

⊕ *M5 jct 27 onto A361 for 17 miles. Left at Knowstone picnic area towards Chulmleigh. Right signposted King's Nympton to Garland crossroads. Turn left, 1st drive on left.*

Unit General P Leisure Shop 4 miles Pub 3 miles

CHURCHINFORD, Somerset Map ref 1D2

★★★★
SELF CATERING

Units 1
Sleeps 6
Low season per wk
£100.00–£250.00
High season per wk
£250.00–£510.00

South Cleeve Bungalow, Taunton

contact Mrs V D Manning, Churchinford, Taunton TA3 7PR
t (01823) 601378 **e** enquiries@timbertopbungalows.co.uk **w** timbertopbungalows.co.uk

Relax in a well-appointed bungalow, lovingly cared for by owners. Watch the birds that come to the large, secluded garden. High-standard accommodation with two doubles (one en suite) and one twin.

open All year
payment Cash/cheques

Unit General P Shop 1 mile Pub 1 mile

CHURSTON FERRERS, Devon Map ref 1D2

★★★★★
SELF CATERING

Units 2
Sleeps 4–7
Low season per wk
£290.00–£390.00
High season per wk
£730.00–£960.00

Alston Farm Cottages, Brixham

contact Mrs Claire Hockaday, Alston Lane, Churston Ferrers, Brixham TQ5 0HT
t (01803) 845388 **f** (01803) 842065 **e** alstonnch@aol.com **w** alstonfarm.co.uk

open All year
payment Cash/cheques

Delightfully furnished accommodation in converted, Grade II Listed barns. Baytree comprises two en suite bedrooms and cloakroom; Laurel comprises three bedrooms and two bathrooms. Designed for year-round comfort. Welcome tray, fresh flowers.

⊕ *Please phone or see website.*

❤ *Short breaks available off season: 2 nights from £205, 3 nights from £215.*

Unit General Leisure Shop 1.5 miles Pub 0.75 miles

CIRENCESTER, Gloucestershire Map ref 2B1

★★★★
SELF CATERING

Units **5**
Sleeps **2–6**
Low season per wk
£170.00–£275.00
High season per wk
£245.00–£540.00

Glebe Farm Holiday Lets, Cirencester

contact Mrs Polly Handover, Glebe Farm Holiday Lets, Barnsley Road, Ampney Crucis, Cirencester GL7 5DY
t (01285) 659226 **f** (01285) 642622 **e** enquiries@glebefarmcottages.co.uk
w glebefarmcottages.co.uk

open All year
payment Cash/cheques

Very high standard and spacious barn conversions in the centre of the Cotswolds, two miles from Cirencester, one hour from Stratford, Bath and Oxford. Located in the grounds of the owner's house, they are beautifully furnished with antiques and pine, and retain old beams and exposed stone walls.

⊕ *From Cirencester take the B4425 for 3 miles. The entrance is on the left beyond a large layby. White posts either side of the entrance; long drive.*

Unit General P Leisure Shop 2 miles Pub 1 mile

CIRENCESTER, Gloucestershire Map ref 2B1

★★★
SELF CATERING

Units **1**
Sleeps **2**
Low season per wk
Min £170.00
High season per wk
Max £240.00

The Tallet, Cirencester

contact Mrs Susan Spivey, The Tallet, The Old Farmhouse, Preston, Cirencester GL7 5PR
t (01285) 653405 **f** (01285) 651152 **e** howard@spiveyfarm.co.uk

An attractive Cotswold-barn conversion approached by oustide stone steps. Beams in all rooms which overlook farmland with a small number of livestock. Perfect for touring.

payment Cash/cheques, euros

Unit General P

COLD ASHTON, Gloucestershire Map ref 2B2

Rating Applied For
SELF CATERING

Units **1**
Sleeps **12**
Low season per wk
£1,880.00–£2,480.00
High season per wk
£2,600.00–£3,280.00

Sayres House, Nr Bath, Chippenham

contact Ms Pamela Skinner, Dunster Living, The Old Cart House, Lower Street, Winterborne Whitechurch DT11 9AW
t 0870 620 1066 **f** (01258) 881780 **e** info@dunsterliving.co.uk **w** sayreshouse.co.uk

Elegant, period Cotswold-stone house with excellent facilities and one acre of beautiful gardens with terrace and barbecue. Three double bedrooms, two triple, Aga, indoor heated swimming pool.

open All year
payment Credit/debit cards, cash/cheques, euros

Unit General P Leisure
Shop 2 miles Pub 2 miles

Friendly help and advice

Did you know there are more than 500 tourist information centres throughout England? It adds up to a lot of friendly help and advice. You'll find contact details at the beginning of each regional section.

COLEFORD, Gloucestershire Map ref 2A1

★★★
SELF CATERING

Units **1**
Sleeps **6**
Low season per wk
Min £225.00
High season per wk
Max £325.00

32 Tudor Walk, Coleford

contact Mrs Beale, 82 Park Road, Christchurch, Coleford GL16 7AZ
t (01594) 832061

open All year
payment Cash/cheques

Three-bedroomed bungalow set 100yds from the Forest of Dean in its own garden, on a flat site with off-road parking. Ideal for relaxing, walking and cycling in the forest. All services provided. Golf courses and leisure facilities nearby. Well-behaved dogs welcome.

⊕ *M50 jct 1. Follow signs from Gloucester, Ross-on-Wye or Monmouth to Forest of Dean and Coleford. One mile from town to Christchurch.*

Unit General P Leisure

COLYTON, Devon Map ref 1D2

★★★★
SELF CATERING

Units **4**
Sleeps **2–6**
Low season per wk
£175.00–£295.00
High season per wk
£395.00–£725.00

Smallicombe Farm, Colyton

contact Mrs Todd, Smallicombe Farm, Colyton EX24 6BU
t (01404) 831310 **f** (01404) 831431 **e** maggie_todd@yahoo.com **w** smallicombe.com

open All year
payment Credit/debit cards, cash/cheques

Relax in well-equipped, award-winning converted barns enjoying idyllic views over grazing sheep and cattle. Roam our ancient woodland abounding in wildlife with only the sights and sounds of the countryside. Close to the World Heritage Coastline. Meet prize-winning Berkshire sows and piglets.

⊕ *From Honiton High Street take New Street past station, up hill, left at mini-roundabout, then 1st right to top of hill. Left after 2 miles signed 'Slade'.*

♥ *Short breaks or 'piggy weekends' from £99. 'Introduction to pig-keeping' courses. Monthly rates or longer lets Nov-Mar.*

Unit TV General P S Leisure Shop < 0.5 miles
Pub 2 miles

CONSTANTINE BAY, Cornwall Map ref 1B2

★★★
SELF CATERING

Units **1**
Sleeps **1–8**
Low season per wk
£275.00–£525.00
High season per wk
£525.00–£750.00

Bumblers, Constantine Bay, Nr Padstow

contact The Proprietor, Bumblers, 17 Crescent Rise, Constantine Bay PL28 8JE
t (01732) 863121 **e** partridgefarm@talk21.com

Bumblers is a detached, modern, well-equipped house, with open fire, close to the beach, golf course and local shop. Bedrooms consist of one double, two twins and a bunk room.

open All year
payment Cash/cheques

Unit TV General P S Leisure
Shop 0.5 miles Pub 3 miles

CYCLISTS WELCOME WELCOME CYCLISTS

A holiday on two wheels

For a fabulous freewheeling break seek out accommodation participating in our Cyclists Welcome scheme. Look out for the symbol and plan your route online at nationalcyclenetwork.org.

CONSTANTINE BAY, Cornwall Map ref 1B2

★★★
SELF CATERING

Units **3**
Sleeps **2–4**
Low season per wk
£170.00–£210.00
High season per wk
£350.00–£560.00

The Garden Cottage Holiday Flats, Padstow

contact Mrs Elizabeth Harris, Constantine Bungalow, Constantine Bay, Padstow PL28 8JJ
t (01841) 520262 **f** (01841) 520262 **e** gardencottage@cornwall-county.com

Property surrounded by large garden and field, part of which is car park. Two hundred yards from beach and four miles from Padstow. Adjoins golf course and coastal path. Open March to November.

payment Cash/cheques

Unit **General** **Leisure** **Shop** < 0.5 miles **Pub** 1 mile

CORFE CASTLE, Dorset Map ref 2B3

★★★★
SELF CATERING

Units **3**
Sleeps **2–10**
Low season per wk
£225.00–£400.00
High season per wk
£650.00–£1,100.00

Scoles Manor, Wareham

contact Peter and Belinda Bell, Scoles Manor, Kingston, Corfe Castle, Wareham BH20 5LG
t (01929) 480312 **e** peter@scoles.co.uk **w** scoles.co.uk

open All year
payment Cash/cheques

Scoles Manor barns are next to historic Scoles Manor (Grade II Listed) and have been converted into beautifully appointed units. They are in a superb rural setting with 30 acres of meadows and woodlands with spectacular views over Corfe Castle and the Purbeck countryside.

⊕ *A351 through Corfe Castle village, onto B3069 (Kingston). Left onto private lane 100yds after 3 road signs for steep hill, bends and horse. Scoles Manor 0.5 miles.*

Unit **General** **Shop** 2 miles **Pub** 0.5 miles

COTSWOLDS

See under Bibury, Birdlip, Bourton-on-the-Water, Broad Campden, Cheltenham, Chipping Campden, Cirencester, Daglingworth, Dursley, Gloucester, Miserden, Moreton-in-Marsh, Northleach, Nympsfield, Slimbridge, Stow-on-the-Wold, Upton St Leonards, Winchcombe
See also Cotswolds in South East England section

COVERACK, Cornwall Map ref 1B3

★★★★
SELF CATERING

Units **1**
Sleeps **1–2**
Low season per wk
£170.00–£280.00
High season per wk
£290.00–£370.00

14 Coverack Headland, Helston

contact Mrs Anne Bradley-Smith, Dorland Cottage, The Mint, Church Lane, Bletchingley, Redhill RH1 4LP
t (01883) 743442 **w** coverack.org

Beautiful two-person apartment. Panoramic sea views. Linen supplied. TV, VCR and tennis court. Gardens lead down to beach below.

open All year
payment Cash/cheques

Unit **General** P **Leisure** **Shop** 0.5 miles **Pub** 0.5 miles

A holiday for Fido?

Some proprietors welcome well-behaved pets. Look for the symbol in the accommodation listings. You can also buy a copy of our new guide – Pets Come Too! – available from good bookshops and online at enjoyenglanddirect.com.

CRAPSTONE, Devon Map ref 1C2

★★★★
SELF CATERING

Units **1**
Sleeps **2–6**
Low season per wk
£275.00–£400.00
High season per wk
£400.00–£600.00

Midway, Yelverton

contact Mrs Susan Eggins, Leigh Farm, Roborough, Plymouth PL6 7BS
t (01752) 733221 **e** sueandmikeeggins@hotmail.co.uk **w** midwayhouse.co.uk

Ground-floor, self-contained apartment in a large, detached house on the edge of Dartmoor. Large, fully fitted kitchen, dining room, lounge with french doors, two double bedrooms and smaller room with bunk beds.

open All year
payment Cash/cheques

Unit General P Leisure Shop < 0.5 miles
Pub 1 mile

CROWLAS, Cornwall Map ref 1B3

★★★
SELF CATERING

Units **1**
Sleeps **1–5**
Low season per wk
£230.00–£260.00
High season per wk
£570.00–£600.00

Millers Loft, Penzance

contact Mr & Mrs Taylor, Millers Loft, Truthwall Mill, Gwallon TR20 9BL
t (01237) 479146 **f** (01237) 421512 **e** enquiries@farmcott.co.uk **w** farmcott.co.uk

Spacious loft apartment in Grade II Listed mill. Comfortable lounge/kitchen/dining room with original features. One single and two double bedrooms. Secluded orchard garden. One and a half miles from Marazion and St Michael's Mount.

open All year
payment Cash/cheques, euros

Unit General P Shop 0.75 miles Pub 0.75 miles

DAGLINGWORTH, Gloucestershire Map ref 2B1

★★★★
SELF CATERING

Units **1**
Sleeps **2**
Low season per wk
Min £235.00
High season per wk
Min £235.00

Corner Cottage, Cirencester

contact Mrs Mary Bartlett, Brook Cottage, 23 Farm Court, Daglingworth, Cirencester GL7 7AF
t (01285) 653478 **f** (01285) 653478

open All year
payment Cash/cheques, euros

Well-equipped, cosy cottage in small village. Excellent centre for exploring the Cotswolds Area of Outstanding Natural Beauty and glorious Gloucestershire. All-inclusive tariff. No hidden extras. All you need provide is food and transport. Allergy-friendly accommodation free from fur, feathers and tobacco smoke.

⊕ *Three miles north of Cirencester. Full directions given when booking is confirmed.*

♥ *No high-season charges. Single, flat-rate tariff throughout the year.*

Unit General P Shop 2 miles Pub 2 miles

Take a break

Many establishments offer special promotions and themed breaks. It's a golden opportunity to indulge an interest or find a new one, or just relax and enjoy exceptional value! Offers and promotions are highlighted in colour (and are subject to availability).

DARTMEET, Devon Map ref 1C2

★★★★
SELF CATERING

Units **1**
Sleeps **2–4**
Low season per wk
£210.00–£285.00
High season per wk
£315.00–£395.00

Coachman's Cottage, Dartmeet

contact Mr John Evans, Coachman's Cottage, Hunter's Lodge, Dartmeet, Yelverton PL20 6SG
t (01364) 631173 **e** mail@dartmeet.com **w** dartmeet.com

open All year
payment Credit/debit cards, cash/cheques, euros

In the heart of Dartmoor National Park, this granite cottage, converted from an old coach house, enjoys a breathtaking view of the Dart Valley and surrounding tors. Fully equipped kitchen/dining room. Spacious double/twin bedroom plus another large lounge/bedroom. Immediate access to riverbank, woodland and open moorland.

From Pear Tree exit at Ashburton, B3357 towards Two Bridges for 7 miles. Hunter's Lodge is 1st building on right after bridge in Dartmeet.

Short breaks available (excl school holidays).

Unit General P Leisure Shop 4 miles Pub 1 mile

DARTMOOR

See under Ashburton, Bovey Tracey, Buckfastleigh, Dartmeet, Didworthy, Drewsteignton, Moretonhampstead, Okehampton, Tavistock

DARTMOUTH, Devon Map ref 1D3

★★★
SELF CATERING

Units **4**
Sleeps **2–6**
Low season per wk
£255.00–£455.00
High season per wk
£355.00–£660.00

The Old Bakehouse, Dartmouth

contact Mrs Sylvia Ridalls, The Old Bakehouse, 7 Broadstone, Dartmouth TQ6 9NR
t (01803) 834585 **f** (01803) 834585 **e** gparker@pioneerps.co.uk **w** oldbakehousedartmouth.co.uk

Character cottages, some with beams and old stone fireplaces. In a conservation area, two minutes from historic town centre and river. Free parking. Beach 15 minutes' drive.

open All year
payment Credit/debit cards, cash/cheques

Unit General Leisure Shop < 0.5 miles Pub < 0.5 miles

DAWLISH, Devon Map ref 1D2

★★★★
SELF CATERING

Units **5**
Sleeps **4–6**
Low season per wk
£285.00–£325.00
High season per wk
£675.00–£735.00

Cofton Country Holiday Park, Dawlish

contact Mrs Valerie Jeffery, Cofton Country Cottage Holidays, Cofton, Starcross, Exeter EX6 8RP
t (01626) 890111 **f** (01626) 891572 **e** info@coftonholidays.co.uk **w** coftonholidays.co.uk

open All year
payment Credit/debit cards, cash/cheques

On the edge of privately owned Cofton Country Holiday Park, converted 100-year-old farm buildings overlooked by ancient Cofton church. Coarse-fishing lakes. Woodland walks. Within a short drive of the Exe Estuary and Dawlish Warren. All amenities of the park available during season, including swimming pool and pub.

From M5 jct 30 take A379 for Dawlish; 3 miles Exeter side of Dawlish.

Short breaks early and late season. 3- or 4-night breaks at most times. Free coarse fishing Nov-Mar.

Unit General P Leisure Shop < 0.5 miles Pub < 0.5 miles

Star ratings

Further information about star ratings can be found at the back of this guide.

DAWLISH WARREN, Devon Map ref 1D2

★★★★
SELF CATERING

Units 5
Sleeps 4–6
Low season per wk
£285.00–£339.00
High season per wk
£675.00–£769.00

Eastdon House, Dawlish Warren

contact Mrs Valerie Jeffery, Cofton Country Holidays, Cofton, Starcross, Exeter EX6 8RP
t (01626) 890111 **f** (01626) 891572 **e** info@coftonholidays.co.uk **w** coftonholidays.co.uk

payment Credit/debit cards, cash/cheques

Magnificent 18thC house converted into luxury apartments. Woodside Cottages – estate workers' cottage conversions. Exe Estuary views, surrounded by fields and 50 acres of unspoilt woodlands. Quiet and restful holidays in a perfect setting. Amenities at Cofton during season.

⊕ *From M5 jct 30, take A379 towards Dawlish. Location is 3 miles from the Exeter side of Dawlish.*

❤ *Short breaks early and late season. 3- or 4-night breaks at most times. Free coarse fishing Nov-Mar.*

Unit General Leisure Shop 0.5 miles Pub 1 mile

DEERHURST, Gloucestershire Map ref 2B1

★★★★
SELF CATERING

Units 2
Sleeps 2–4
Low season per wk
Min £200.00
High season per wk
Max £465.00

Deerhurst Cottages, Gloucester

contact Mrs Nicole Samuel, Abbots Court Farm, Deerhurst, Gloucester GL19 4BX
t (01684) 275845 **f** (01684) 275845 **e** enquiries@deerhurstcottages.co.uk
w deerhurstcottages.co.uk

open All year
payment Credit/debit cards, cash/cheques

Relax on our traditional dairy farm surrounded by beautiful countryside with miles of walks along the River Severn. Hazelgrove and Swanlands cottages have been lovingly converted, offering comfortable, spacious and well-equipped holiday accommodation. The perfect base for exploring the Cotswolds, Forest of Dean and the Malvern Hills.

⊕ *Provided upon booking.*

❤ *Short breaks available Nov-Mar (excl Christmas and New Year), min 3-night stay.*

Unit General Leisure Shop 3 miles Pub 1.5 miles

DEVIZES, Wiltshire Map ref 2B2

★★★★
SELF CATERING

Units 1
Sleeps 1–5
Low season per wk
£275.00–£335.00
High season per wk
£395.00–£495.00

Owls Cottage, Devizes

contact Mrs Gill Whittome, Owls Cottage, 48 White Street, Easterton, Devizes SN10 4PA
t (01380) 818804 **f** (01380) 818804 **e** gill@owls-cottage.com **w** owls-cottage.com

open All year
payment Credit/debit cards, cash/cheques

Really comfortable cottage, tastefully furnished to a high standard. Situated in private and spacious location, with outstanding downland views. Village shops and good pub within easy walking distance. Good access to White Horse/Ridgeway cycleway. Convenient Longleat, Bath, Stonehenge. Fully inclusive. A really special place to stay. Winter breaks. Brochure.

Unit General Leisure Shop 1 mile
Pub < 0.5 miles

Mention our name

Please mention this guide when making your booking.

DEVIZES, Wiltshire Map ref 2B2

★★★★
SELF CATERING

Units **3**
Sleeps **2–4**
Low season per wk
Max £266.00
High season per wk
Max £476.00

Tichborne's Farm Cottages, Devizes

contact Mr & Mrs Jon & Judy Nash, Tichborne's Farm, Etchilhampton, Devizes SN10 3JL
t (01380) 862971 **f** (01380) 862971 **e** info@tichbornes.co.uk **w** tichbornes.co.uk

Luxury single-storey cottages, converted from former stables, within a courtyard setting in an Area of Outstanding Natural Beauty on the edge of Pewsey Vale. Between Bath, Stonehenge and Avebury.

open All year
payment Credit/debit cards

Unit General Leisure Shop 1 mile Pub 1 mile

DIDWORTHY, Devon Map ref 1C2

★★★★
SELF CATERING

Units **3**
Sleeps **2–6**
Low season per wk
£240.00–£365.00
High season per wk
£410.00–£700.00

Didworthy House, Didworthy, South Brent

contact Mr & Mrs J Beer, Didworthy, South Brent TQ10 9EF
t (01364) 72655 **f** (01364) 72655 **e** info@didworthyhouse.co.uk **w** didworthyhouse.co.uk

Delightful accommodation in wings of large Victorian country house set in two acres of garden on southern fringes of Dartmoor, in the beautiful Avon Valley. Heated outdoor swimming pool. Wonderful walks and scenery.

open All year
payment Cash/cheques

Unit General Leisure Shop 2 miles Pub 2 miles

DREWSTEIGNTON, Devon Map ref 1C2

★★★
SELF CATERING

Units **2**
Sleeps **6**
High season per wk
£300.00–£600.00

Clifford Barton Holiday Cottages, Exeter

contact Mrs Susan Butler-Cole, Drewsteignton, Exeter EX6 6QB
t (01647) 24763 & (01647) 24266 **e** mail@cliffordbarton.co.uk **w** cliffordbarton.co.uk

Comfortable cottages on peaceful farm in Dartmoor National Park. Pretty south-facing gardens. Accessible to disabled visitors. Children welcome. Pets welcome. Trout fishing on private lake and in River Teign.

open All year
payment Credit/debit cards, cash/cheques, euros

Unit General Leisure Shop 3 miles Pub 3 miles

DRIFFIELD, Gloucestershire Map ref 2B1

★★★★
SELF CATERING

Units **1**
Sleeps **1–4**
Low season per wk
£225.00
High season per wk
£325.00

The Stables, Cirencester

contact Mrs Margaret Smith, The Grange, Driffield, Cirencester GL7 5PY
t (01285) 850641 **e** me_smith@btinternet.com

open All year
payment Cash/cheques

This spacious stable conversion is situated in a quiet, rural village, yet only five miles from Cirencester and two miles from Cotswold Water Parks. Furnished to a high standard and immaculately maintained with sofa bed in lounge. Owners live opposite property. No pets.

⊕ *On entering Driffield, the property is to be found within the grounds of The Grange on the right, just before a left-hand sharp bend.*

Unit General Leisure Shop 4 miles Pub 2 miles

Confirm your booking

It's always advisable to confirm your booking in writing.

EAST BUDLEIGH, D

★★★ SELF CATERI

Units
Sleeps

DULVERTON, Somerset Map ref 1D1

★★★★
SELF CATERING

Units **4**
Sleeps **2–18**
Low season per wk
Min £250.00
High season per wk
Min £350.00

Deer's Leap Country Cottages

contact Mrs Heather Fuidge, Deer's Leap Country Cotta
t (01398) 341407 **f** (01398) 341407 **e** deersleapcottage

paymen

Cottage
intimate
Exmoor
stars, th
decking
February to December and New Year.

⊕ *Detailed directions on application.*

Unit General P S Leisure Shop 0.75 miles
Pub 2.5 miles

DUNSTER, Somerset Map ref 1D1

★★★★
SELF CATERING

Units **12**
Sleeps **2–12**
Low season per wk
£220.00–£1,100.00
High season per wk
£420.00–£2,010.00

Duddings Country Cottages, Minehead

contact Mr Richard Tilke, Duddings Country Holidays, Timberscombe, Minehead TA24 7TB
t (01643) 841123 **f** (01643) 841165 **e** richard@duddings.co.uk **w** duddings.co.uk

open All year
payment Cash/cheques

Thatched longhouse and eleven cottages, tastefully converted from old stone barns on small country estate in stunning location in Exmoor National Park. Heated indoor pool, tennis court, putting green, pool, table tennis, football net, trampoline, swings and slide. Families and pets welcome. Attentive resident owners.

⊕ *From Dunster, take the A396 (signposted Tiverton). Duddings is on the right just before Timberscombe (approx 2 miles).*

❤ *Short breaks available (excl main school holidays).*

Unit General P S Leisure Shop 2 miles
Pub 0.5 miles

DURSLEY, Gloucestershire Map ref 2B2

★★★
SELF CATERING

Units **1**
Sleeps **1–4**
Low season per wk
£174.00–£213.00
High season per wk
£213.00–£246.00

Two Springbank, Dursley

contact Mrs Freda Jones, 32 Everlands, Cam, Dursley GL11 5NL
t (01453) 543047 **e** lhandfaj32lg@surefish.co.uk

Victorian, mid-terraced cottage in a pleasant, rural location near to a 14thC village church with open fields to rear and within easy reach of the Cotswold Way.

open All year
payment Cash/cheques

Unit General P S Leisure Shop 0.75 miles
Pub 0.75 miles

It's all quality-assessed accommodation

Our commitment to quality involves wide-ranging accommodation assessment. Ratings and awards were correct at the time of going to press but may change following a new assessment. Please check at the time of booking.

...evon Map ref 1D2

...NG

1
6–8

...ason per wk
...5.00–£495.00
...igh season per wk
£545.00–£750.00

Brook Cottage, Budleigh Salterton

contact Mrs Jo Simons, Foxcote, Noverton Lane, Prestbury, Cheltenham GL52 5BB
t (01242) 574031 **e** josimons@tesco.net **w** brookcottagebudleigh.co.uk

open All year
payment Cash/cheques

Spacious thatched cottage. Two showers and bathroom. Beaches, walking, golf, karting, bird-watching, riding nearby – but the cottage is so comfortable it's a pleasure to be indoors. Two living rooms with TVs, one for the adults, and a snug, with sofa bed, for the children! Visit our website for more photos.

⊕ *From A376 take B3179 signed for Woodbury and Budleigh Salterton; proceed through Woodbury and Yettington; right after Bicton gates and again on entering East Budleigh.*

❤ *Reduced-rate winter breaks for 3-night stays with or without linen (excl Christmas and New Year).*

Unit General P Leisure Shop 1 mile
Pub < 0.5 miles

EAST LOOE, Cornwall Map ref 1C3

★★★★★
SELF CATERING

Units 1
Sleeps 1–10
Low season per wk
£450.00–£840.00
High season per wk
£840.00–£2,360.00

Endymion, Looe

contact Mr David Pearn, 2 Lower Street, Looe PL13 1DA
t (01503) 262244 & 07768 333924 **f** (01503) 262244 **e** endymion@exclusivevacations.co.uk
w exclusivevactions.co.uk/endymion

open All year
payment Cash/cheques

Luxurious detached cliff-top property, offering a high standard of accommodation. Bathroom and one double bedroom on ground-floor level. Separate shower room. Stunning coastal views. Private footpath to beach. Superb patio area with barbecue. Parking. Within easy reach of local amenities and places of interest.

⊕ *From A38 follow signs to Looe at Trerulefoot roundabout. Take left hand turn after sign 'Welcome to Looe'.*

Unit General P Leisure Shop 0.5 miles
Pub 0.5 miles

EAST LOOE, Cornwall Map ref 1C3

★★★–★★★★★
SELF CATERING

Units 11
Sleeps 2–6
Low season per wk
£175.00–£330.00
High season per wk
£600.00–£1,470.00

Fox Valley Cottages, Looe

contact Mr & Mrs Andy & Linda Brown, Lanlawren, Trenewan, Looe PL13 2PZ
t (01726) 870115 **e** lanlawren@lycos.com **w** foxvalleycottages.co.uk

open All year
payment Credit/debit cards, cash/cheques

The cottages are set in beautiful countryside – an idyllic location for your holiday in Cornwall. Indoor heated pool, spa, sauna, solarium, games room. Open fires in most of the cottages for those cosy or romantic nights in winter. Dishwashers in large cottages.

⊕ *Three miles west of Polperro. Map sent with directions.*

❤ *Out-of-season short breaks (mid-week or long weekends).*

Unit General P Leisure Shop 3 miles Pub 3 miles

EXETER, Devon Map ref 1D2

★★★★
SELF CATERING

Units **7**
Sleeps **6–7**
Low season per wk
£340.00–£480.00
High season per wk
£465.00–£835.00

Bussells Farm Cottages, Exeter

contact Andy and Lucy Hines, Bussells Farm, Huxham, Nr Stoke Canon, Exeter EX5 4EN
t (01392) 841238 **f** (01392) 841345 **e** bussellsfarm@aol.com **w** bussellsfarm.co.uk

open All year
payment Credit/debit cards, cash/cheques

Lovely barn-conversion cottages, heated outdoor swimming pool from May to September, adventure playground, well-equipped games room and excellent coarse fishing in the private lakes. We offer a wonderful base from which to explore the beautiful Exe Valley, Dartmoor, the South Devon beaches and the ancient city of Exeter.

⊕ *At Stoke Canon, take road next to church signposted Huxham and Poltimore; just after Barton Cross Hotel (0.5 miles) turn left. Bussells Farm is 0.5 miles on left.*

❤ *3-night stays available. Low season discounts for 1 or 2 people. Pets welcome.*

Unit General P Leisure Shop 1 mile Pub 1 mile

EXETER, Devon Map ref 1D2

★★★★★
SELF CATERING

Units **1**
Sleeps **4**
Low season per wk
£195.00–£380.00
High season per wk
£410.00–£520.00

Coach House Farm, Exeter

contact Mr & Miss John & Polly Bale, Coach House Farm, Exeter EX5 3JH
t (01392) 461254 **f** (01392) 460931 **e** selfcatering@mpprops.co.uk

open All year
payment Credit/debit cards, cash/cheques, euros

Surrounded by the National Trust Killerton estate, the converted stables of our Victorian coach house provide comfortable ground-floor accommodation (no steps) with private entrance and garden overlooking sheep meadows. Working arable and sheep farm. Spectacular East Devon coastline, Exmoor, Dartmoor and Exeter are easily reached. Good access from M5/A30.

⊕ *Information on the location will be given on confirmation of the booking.*

Unit General P Shop 1 mile Pub 1 mile

EXFORD, Somerset Map ref 1D1

★★★
SELF CATERING

Units **1**
Sleeps **6**
Low season per wk
Max £285.00
High season per wk
Max £385.00

No 2 Auction Field Cottage, Exford

contact Mr & Mrs Keith & Gill Batchelor, Bulbarrow Farm, Bulbarrow, Blandford Forum DT11 0HQ
t (01258) 817801 **f** (01258) 817004

Available all year. Short walk from village. Superb woodland and moorland walking. Very well equipped, comfortable and relaxing. An ideal base for exploring Exmoor.

open All year
payment Cash/cheques

Unit General P Leisure Shop < 0.5 miles Pub < 0.5 miles

How many beds?

The minimum and maximum number of people that each property can accommodate is shown. If an entry includes details of more than one property the sleeping capacity may vary between them. Please check when you make your booking.

EXFORD, Somerset Map ref 1D1

★★★★
SELF CATERING

Units **4**
Sleeps **2–7**
Low season per wk
£110.00–£230.00
High season per wk
£265.00–£595.00

Riscombe Farm Holiday Cottages and Stabling, Exford, Minehead

contact Mr & Mrs Brian & Leone Martin, Riscombe Farm Holiday Cottages and Stabling, Exford, Minehead TA24 7NH
t (01643) 831480 **f** (01643) 831480 **e** info@riscombe.co.uk **w** riscombe.co.uk

open All year
payment Cash/cheques

Relax beside the River Exe in the centre of Exmoor National Park. Our charming cottages are converted from stone barns and are set beside an attractive courtyard. Log fires and exposed beams. Meet our friendly animals, chickens and ducks. Enjoy excellent walking in the valleys, on the Moors or along the nearby spectacular coast.

⊕ *A39 to Minehead. At Dunster, left onto A396. Right at Wheddon Cross (B3224) via Exford towards Simonsbath. After 1 mile turn right, 0.5 miles down lane.*

♥ *Short breaks available Nov-Dec and Jan-Mar (excl Christmas and New Year) and at other times when vacancies allow.*

Unit General P Leisure **Shop** 1.5 miles **Pub** 1.5 miles

EXMOOR

See under Allerford, Bratton, Brayford, Dulverton, Dunster, Exford, Lynton, Minehead, North Molton, Parracombe, Porlock, Simonsbath

FALMOUTH, Cornwall Map ref 1B3

★★
SELF CATERING

Units **1**
Sleeps **7**
High season per wk
£450.00–£550.00

8 Marine Crescent, Falmouth

contact Mrs Pauline Spong, 42 Westleigh Avenue, Leigh-on-Sea SS9 2LF
t (01702) 712596 **f** (01702) 712596 **e** rcspong@hotmail.com
w cornwall-online.co.uk/self-catering/falmouth/8marinecrescent

Comfortable harbourside house. Ideally located near Maritime Museum, beach, shops and restaurants. Fully equipped. Regret no singles, no pets. Open early July to late September.

payment Cash/cheques

Unit General P Leisure **Shop** < 0.5 miles **Pub** < 0.5 miles

FALMOUTH, Cornwall Map ref 1B3

★★★
SELF CATERING

Units **6**
Sleeps **2–5**
Low season per wk
£205.00–£360.00
High season per wk
£385.00–£460.00

Good-Winds Holiday Apartments, Falmouth

contact Mrs Goodwin, Good-Winds Holiday Apartments, 13 Stratton Terracce, Falmouth TR11 2SY
t (01326) 313200 **f** (01326) 313200 **e** goodwinds13@aol.com

open All year
payment Cash/cheques, euros

Modern, two-bedroom apartments with balconies having marvellous views over the harbour, River Pen and the quaint fishing village of Flushing. Under-cover parking for two cars. Walking distance to town. One double bed, two singles and extra single in three units.

⊕ *Please request travel directions at time of booking.*

Unit General P **Shop** 0.5 miles **Pub** 0.75 miles

Make it a date

Check out the events listing at the back of the guide, or for latest information go online at enjoyengland.com.

FALMOUTH, Cornwall Map ref 1B3

★★★
SELF CATERING

Units **8**
Sleeps **2–6**
Low season per wk
£225.00–£345.00
High season per wk
£395.00–£515.00

Pantiles, Falmouth

contact Mr & Mrs Kemp, Pantiles, 6 Stracey Road, Falmouth TR11 4DW
t (01326) 211838 **f** (01326) 211668 **e** colinkemp@lineone.net **w** colinkemp.plus.com

open All year
payment Cash/cheques

These delightful one- and two-bedroom apartments offer home-from-home comfort. All apartments are spacious and have windows overlooking beautiful gardens to the front and rear. Quiet location, yet only three minutes' walk from beach and fifteen minutes to harbour and main shopping areas. Beautiful coastal walks on your doorstep. Wireless broadband in all apartments.

⊕ *Follow signs to the beaches. Turn left into Stracey Road immediately after passing tennis courts on your right. Pantiles is situated 100yds on left-hand side.*

Unit General P Leisure Shop 1 mile Pub 1 mile

FOLKE, Dorset Map ref 2B3

★★★★
SELF CATERING

Units **4**
Sleeps **4–8**
Low season per wk
£200.00–£500.00
High season per wk
£400.00–£1,000.00

Folke Manor Farm Cottages, Sherborne

contact Mr & Mrs John & Carol Perrett, Folke Manor Farm, Folke, Sherborne DT9 5HP
t (01963) 210731 **e** folkemanorfarm@aol.com

Folke Manor Farm Cottages are spacious barn conversions in a quiet part of the Blackmore Vale close to Sherborne. Ideal place for walking and to relax in our beautiful gardens.

open All year
payment Cash/cheques

Unit General P S Leisure Shop 0.5 miles Pub 0.5 miles

FOREST OF DEAN

See under Coleford, Lydney, St Briavels

FROME, Somerset Map ref 2B2

★★★★★
SELF CATERING

Units **10**
Sleeps **2–22**
Low season per wk
£200.00–£1,680.00
High season per wk
£360.00–£3,360.00

Executive Holidays, Frome

contact Mr R A Gregory, Executive Holidays, Whitemill Farm, Iron Mill Lane, Oldford, Frome BA11 2NR
t (01373) 452907 & 07860 147525 **f** (01373) 453253 **e** info@executiveholidays.co.uk
w executiveholidays.co.uk

16thC mill and cottage, courtyard cottages and 16thC farmhouse. Country setting in own grounds with private trout stream. Twelve miles from Bath. Free brochure on request.

open All year
payment Credit/debit cards, cash/cheques, euros

Unit General P S Leisure Shop 1 mile Pub < 0.5 miles

GILLINGHAM, Dorset Map ref 2B3

★★★★
SELF CATERING

Units **1**
Sleeps **2**
Low season per wk
£185.00–£220.00
High season per wk
Max £320.00

Woolfields Barn, Gillingham

contact Mr & Mrs Thomas, Woolfields Barn, Woolfields Farm, Milton on Stour, Gillingham SP8 5PX
t (01747) 824729 **f** (01747) 824986 **e** OThomas453@aol.com **w** woolfieldsbarn.co.uk

Fully equipped barn conversion. Extremely comfortable and peaceful. Centrally heated. Linen provided.

open All year
payment Cash/cheques

Unit General P Leisure Shop 0.5 miles Pub 1 mile

GLASTONBURY, Somerset Map ref 2A2

★★★★
SELF CATERING

Units 8
Sleeps 2–6
Low season per wk
£205.00–£300.00
High season per wk
£430.00–£770.00

MapleLeaf Middlewick Holiday Cottages, Glastonbury

Middlewick Holiday Cottages, Wick Lane, Glastonbury BA6 8JW
t (01458) 832351 **f** (01458) 832351 **e** middlewick@btconnect.com
w middlewickholidaycottages.co.uk

open All year
payment Credit/debit cards, cash/cheques

The cottages within this Grade II Listed farmstead have been restored to provide comfortable, well-equipped accommodation. Walk to Glastonbury Tor from the back door, and after a day of exercising, sight-seeing or just communing, relax in the heated indoor swimming pool. WI-FI Internet access.

⊕ *Wick Lane runs between A361 and A39. From A39 we are 1 mile on your right. From A361 1.5 miles on your left.*

❤ *Online booking for last-minute discounts for weekly or short breaks. Optional breakfasts available in the Meadow Barn dining room.*

Unit General Leisure Shop 2 miles Pub 3 miles

GLOUCESTER, Gloucestershire Map ref 2B1

★★★★★
SELF CATERING

Units 1
Sleeps 4–10
Low season per wk
£884.00–£909.00
High season per wk
£955.00–£2,038.00

Barncastle, Pitchcombe, Stroud

contact Mrs Valerie King, Brook Farm, Stroud Road, Brookthorpe GL4 0UQ
t (01452) 814207 **w** barncastle.co.uk

open All year
payment Cash/cheques

Barncastle is a large, recently converted Cotswold-stone barn in the beautiful Painswick Valley with outstanding views. It offers fitted kitchen, dining room with gallery and woodburner, beamed living room with views and Sky TV. Large, secluded garden. Five minutes walk to local pub.

⊕ *From Gloucester, take A4173 towards Stroud. Travel through Brookthorpe and Edge. After Edgemoor Inn take 2nd left into Wragg Castle lane. Barnside is on the right.*

❤ *Short breaks available (excl Christmas and New Year). Special rates for Cheltenham Gold Cup race week.*

Unit General P Leisure Shop 2 miles Pub .5 miles

GLOUCESTER, Gloucestershire Map ref 2B1

★★★★
SELF CATERING

Units 2
Sleeps 2
Low season per wk
£200.00–£265.00
High season per wk
£265.00–£345.00

Middletown Farm Cottages, Upleadon, Nr Newent

contact Mrs Judy Elkins, Middletown Farm, Middletown Lane, Upleadon, Newent GL18 1EQ
t (01531) 828237 **f** (01531) 822850 **e** cottages@middletownfarm.co.uk **w** middletownfarm.co.uk

open All year
payment Cash/cheques

Delightful cottages surrounded by tranquil countryside. Refurbished to a high standard and very well equipped with everything you could need for a relaxing break in the country. Easy access to Gloucester, the Malvern Hills, the enchanting Royal Forest of Dean, the scenic Cotswolds and much more.

⊕ *Travel directions given on confirmation of booking.*

❤ *3-/4-night stays available Nov-Mar.*

Unit General P Leisure Shop 3 miles Pub 2 miles

Look at the maps

Colour maps at the front pinpoint the location of all accommodation found in the regional sections.

GORRAN HAVEN, Cornwall Map ref 1B3

★★★
SELF CATERING

Units **2**
Sleeps **2–4**
Low season per wk
£150.00–£220.00
High season per wk
£280.00–£480.00

Tregillan, St Austell

contact Mrs Sally Pike, Tregillan, Trewollock Lane, Gorran Haven PL26 6NT
t (01726) 842452 **e** tregillanapartment@tiscali.co.uk **w** tregillanapartments.co.uk

Self-contained apartments, 600yds to beach, harbour and village shops. The apartments are fully equipped and have sea views, large, secluded garden and patio and secure parking. Open all year.

open All year
payment Cash/cheques

Unit General P S Leisure Shop < 0.5 miles Pub < 0.5 miles

GREAT CHEVERELL, Wiltshire Map ref 2B2

★
SELF CATERING

Units **1**
Sleeps **1–4**
Low season per wk
Max £220.00
High season per wk
Max £240.00

Downswood, Devizes

contact Mrs Ros Shepherd, Downswood, Great Cheverell, Devizes SN10 5TW
t (01380) 813304

Seven-acre stud farm. Annexe to small country house. Gardens, lovely surroundings. Adjacent to Salisbury Plain and ideal for touring, walking or riding. Dogs/horses welcome.

payment Cash/cheques

Unit General 8 P S Leisure Shop 1 mile Pub 1 mile

HELSTON, Cornwall Map ref 1B3

★★★★
SELF CATERING

Units **1**
Sleeps **4**
Low season per wk
£230.00–£325.00
High season per wk
£400.00–£540.00

Carminowe View, Helston

contact Mr Huddleston, Carminowe View, 3 Northfield Road, Portishead BS20 8LE
t (01275) 848899 **e** jhuddl2144@aol.com

open All year
payment Cash/cheques

Overlooking Carminowe Valley and close to Loe Pool. An inverted, two-storey barn conversion with two en suite bedrooms, separate fitted kitchen and lounge and dining area. Washing/drying facilities. Central heating and wood-burning stove. Linen and towels supplied. Walled, secluded garden with seating and barbecue.

Unit General P S Leisure Shop 2.5 miles Pub 3 miles

Don't forget www.

Web addresses throughout this guide are shown without the prefix www. Please include www. in the address line of your browser. If a web address does not follow this style it is shown in full.

HELSTON, Cornwall Map ref 1B3

★★★
SELF CATERING

Units **3**
Sleeps **1–6**
Low season per wk
£150.00–£250.00
High season per wk
£250.00–£425.00

Mudgeon Vean Farm Holiday Cottages, Helston

contact Mr & Mrs Trewhella, Mudgeon Vean Farm Holiday Cottages, St Martin, Helston TR12 6DB
t (01326) 231341 **f** (01326) 231341 **e** mudgeonvean@aol.com
w cornwall-online.co.uk/mudgeon-vean/ctb.htm

open All year
payment Cash/cheques

Cosy cottages on small 18thC farm producing apple juice and cider, near Helford River. Equipped to high standard and personally supervised. Night storage heaters and log fires. National Trust walk to the river, outdoor play area for children, games room. Peaceful location in an Area of Outstanding Natural Beauty.

⊕ *A3083 Helston, B3293 Mawgan village. Through Mawgan to St Martins Green. Left at St Martins Green, to next crossroads. Turn left. We are 2nd turning on right down lane.*

Unit General P Leisure Shop 1 mile Pub 2 miles

HELSTON, Cornwall Map ref 1B3

★★★★
SELF CATERING

Units **1**
Sleeps **9**
Low season per wk
Min £878.00
High season per wk
Max £2,117.00

Tregoose Farmhouse, Helston

contact Mrs Hazel Bergin, Tregoose Farmhouse, The Downes, Foundry Hill, Hayle TR27 4HW
t (01736) 751749 **e** arcj88@dsl.pipex.com **w** tregooselet.co.uk

open All year
payment Cash/cheques

A spacious and luxuriously renovated farmhouse in a peaceful, rural setting. Indoor swimming pool, games room, ground-floor bedroom and wet room, far-reaching views. Conveniently positioned for touring South and West Cornwall's coastline, gardens and attractions.

⊕ *From A394 (Helston to Penzance), turn right onto B3302. Take 2nd right signposted Gwavas/Lowertown. Left at crossroad. 30yds turn right. Top of hill on left.*

Unit General P Leisure Shop 1 mile
Pub 2 miles

HELSTONE, Cornwall Map ref 1B2

★★★
SELF CATERING

Units **6**
Sleeps **1–6**
Low season per wk
£285.00–£500.00
High season per wk
£682.00–£915.00

Mayrose Farm, Camelford

contact Mrs Jane Maunder, Mayrose Farm, Camelford PL32 9RN
t (01840) 213509 **f** (01840) 213509 **e** info@mayrosefarmcottages.co.uk
w mayrosefarmcottages.co.uk

open All year
payment Credit/debit cards, cash/cheques

Off quiet country lane, Cornish-stone farm cottages overlooking 18 acres of fields with views down picturesque Allen Valley. Cosy whitewashed interiors, some log-burners. Linen and towels provided. Heated outdoor pool, friendly farm animals for the children. Close to coast and moor. In low season various courses available – please enquire.

⊕ *Take signs for North Cornwall, join A39 at Davidstow, then through Camelford and Helstone, then left signed Mayrose Farm.*

❤ *Ideal for family reunions, group holidays etc. Catering help available. Short breaks available Oct-Mar. Alternative-therapy courses in autumn.*

Unit General P Leisure Shop 1 mile
Pub 2 miles

HIGHBRIDGE, Somerset Map ref 1D1

★★★★
SELF CATERING

Units **1**
Sleeps **5**
Low season per wk
£195.00–£285.00
High season per wk
£270.00–£435.00

The Cottage, Highbridge

contact Mrs Sarah Alderton, Greenacre Place, Bristol Road, Edithmead, Highbridge TA9 4HA
t (01278) 785227 **f** (01278) 785227 **e** sm.alderton@btopenworld.com **w** greenacreplace.com

open All year
payment Cash/cheques

Beautifully furnished and equipped cottage with one double and one twin bedroom, two bathrooms and private patio with furniture and barbecue. Linen, towels and electricity included.

Unit General P Leisure Shop 2 miles Pub 1 mile

HONITON, Devon Map ref 1D2

★★★★★
SELF CATERING

Units **2**
Sleeps **7**
Low season per wk
Min £275.00
High season per wk
Max £875.00

The Haybarton, Honiton

contact Mrs Patricia Wells, The Haybarton, Bidwell Farm, Upottery, Honiton EX14 9PP
t (01404) 861122 **e** pat@bidwellfarm.co.uk **w** bidwellfarm.co.uk

open All year
payment Credit/debit cards, cash/cheques, euros

Nestling in beautiful Blackdown Hills, this award-winning cottage offers three large, en suite bedrooms and a fantastic farmhouse kitchen opening onto picnic/barbecue/play area with unbeatable views. Large, comfortable sitting room with log fire/Sky programmes. Explore Blackdown Hills, Dartmoor, Exmoor, Jurassic Coastline. Fish free in our on-stream trout pond. Second cottage available – awaiting grading.

⊕ *A303 merges with A30, 4.5 miles east of Honiton. Immediately after the merge, turn right (Upottery). In village at T-junction, left. Look for 1st farm on left.*

❤ *B&B available – see website.*

Unit General P S Leisure Shop 4 miles Pub 1 mile

HOPE COVE, Devon Map ref 1C3

★★★
SELF CATERING

Units **1**
Sleeps **1–6**
Low season per wk
£195.00–£380.00
High season per wk
£380.00–£630.00

Sanderlings, Kingsbridge

contact Mrs Diana Middleton, 6 Reading Road, Reading RG5 3DB
t (0118) 969 0958 **e** diana_middleton@yahoo.com

open All year
payment Cash/cheques

This three-bedroom detached bungalow, with separate cloakroom and wc, is situated in a quiet location on the outskirts of the village of Hope Cove but within walking distance of the beaches. It is approximately six miles from Kingsbridge and Salcombe, and particularly suitable for families and those who enjoy the outdoors.

⊕ *Travel directions provided once booking is confirmed.*

Unit General P S Shop < 0.5 miles Pub < 0.5 miles

HUNTLEY, Gloucestershire Map ref 2B1

★★★
SELF CATERING

Units **1**
Sleeps **6**
Low season per wk
£180.00–£200.00
High season per wk
£200.00–£270.00

The Vineary, Gloucester

contact Mrs Ann Snow, The Vineary, Vinetree Cottage, Solomons Tump, Huntley, Gloucester GL19 3EB
t (01452) 830006

The Vineary is a self-catering annexe to Vinetree Cottage in a quiet country lane with open views. Easy access to shop, post office and country inns.

open All year
payment Cash/cheques

Unit General P Leisure Shop < 0.5 miles Pub < 0.5 miles

ILFRACOMBE, Devon Map ref 1C1

★★★★
SELF CATERING

Units **5**
Sleeps **2–4**
Low season per wk
£225.00–£425.00
High season per wk
£350.00–£710.00

The Admirals House, Ilfracombe

contact Miss Marshall, Admirals House, Quayfield Road, Ilfracombe EX34 9EN
t (01271) 864666 **f** (01271) 864666 **e** enquiries@theadmiralshouse.co.uk **w** theadmiralshouse.co.uk

open All year
payment Cash/cheques

Georgian manor-house converted into stunning apartments and cottage, situated right on Ilfracombe's famous heritage harbourside. Superb views, great location near restaurants, pubs, theatre, coastal paths and the sea. Watch the fishing boats land lobsters and crabs and buy one for your supper!

⊕ *M5 jct 27 (A361). Continue through Barnstaple to Ilfracombe harbour.*

❤ *Short breaks off-season. Special discounts for couples.*

Unit General P Leisure Shop < 0.5 miles Pub < 0.5 miles

ISLES OF SCILLY, Isles of Scilly Map ref 1A3

★★★
SELF CATERING

Units **6**
Sleeps **2–6**
Low season per wk
£280.00–£420.00
High season per wk
£480.00–£800.00

Moonrakers Holiday Flats, St Mary's

contact Mr & Mrs R J Gregory, Moonrakers Holiday Flats, Garrison Lane, St Mary's, Isles of Scilly TR21 0JF
t (01720) 422717 **w** moonrakersholidayflats.co.uk

Modern flats with superb sea views and quiet location away from main street, but only two minutes from shops, quay, beaches and inter-island passenger boats. Cleanliness guaranteed. Resident proprietors. Open March to October.

payment Cash/cheques, euros

Unit General 3 Shop < 0.5 miles Pub < 0.5 miles

ISLES OF SCILLY, Isles of Scilly Map ref 1A3

★★★★
SELF CATERING

Units **1**
Sleeps **4**
Low season per wk
£250.00–£500.00
High season per wk
£575.00–£675.00

The Stable, St Martin's

contact Mrs D Williams, The Stable, Middle Town, St Martin's TR25 0QN
t (01720) 422810 **f** (01720) 422810 **e** fiestydee2002@yahoo.co.uk

Converted stable offering very comfortable, well-equipped and beautifully presented accommodation in quiet location. Two bedrooms (one double, one twin).

open All year
payment Cash/cheques

Unit General 10 Shop 0.5 miles Pub < 0.5 miles

What's in an award

Further information about awards can be found at the front of this guide.

ISLES OF SCILLY, Isles of Scilly Map ref 1A3

★★★★
SELF CATERING

Units **1**
Sleeps **8**
Low season per wk
£1,100.00–£1,300.00
High season per wk
£1,400.00–£1,650.00

Trevean, St Mary's

contact Mrs Rosemary Sharman, Robinswood Farm, Wareham, Bere Regis BH20 7JJ
t (01929) 471210 **f** (01929) 472182 **e** robin@sharman0848.freeserve.co.uk

Large three-storey granite house in town centre, two minutes to beaches. Four bedrooms (one double, three twins), 31ft lounge/diner on third floor with oblique view over harbour.

open All year
payment Cash/cheques

Unit General Leisure

KINGSBRIDGE, Devon Map ref 1C3

★★★
SELF CATERING

Units **2**
Sleeps **2–4**
Low season per wk
£175.00–£250.00
High season per wk
£250.00–£400.00

Reads Farm, Kingsbridge

contact Mrs Pethybridge, Reads Farm, Loddiswell, Kingsbridge TQ7 4RT
t (01548) 550317 **f** (01548) 550317

Flats are part of farmhouse in an Area of Outstanding Natural Beauty. Farmland adjoins River Avon. Fishing. Heated swimming pool. Bedrooms en suite. No through traffic. Open April to September.

payment Cash/cheques

Unit General P Leisure Shop 0.5 miles Pub 0.5 miles

LACOCK, Wiltshire Map ref 2B2

★★★★
SELF CATERING

Units **2**
Sleeps **2–5**
Low season per wk
£290.00–£440.00
High season per wk
£445.00–£615.00

Cyder House and Cheese House, Lacock

contact Mr & Mrs Philip & Susan King, Cyder House and Cheese House, Wick Farm, Wick Lane, Chippenham SN15 2LU
t (01249) 730244 **f** (01249) 730072 **e** kingsilverlands2@btinternet.com
w cheeseandcyderhouses.co.uk

open All year
payment Credit/debit cards, cash/cheques

Tastefully converted, beamed farm building with many original features, 1.5 miles from National Trust village. Private garden with furniture and barbecue. Good location for Bath (12 miles), Stonehenge, Stourhead, Longleat and Wiltshire chalk horses.

⊕ *Take A350. At Lacock, between Chippenham and Melksham, turn right into Foly Lane West. Travel approx 1 mile, go under railway bridge, turn down no-through road.*

♥ *Anglers welcome at our coarse-fishing lake. Short breaks low season.*

Unit General P S Leisure Shop 1.5 miles Pub 1.5 miles

Country Code

Always follow the Country Code

- Be safe – plan ahead and follow any signs
- Leave gates and property as you find them
- Protect plants and animals, and take your litter home
- Keep dogs under close control
- Consider other people

LANGTON MATRAVERS, Dorset Map ref 2B3

★★
SELF CATERING

Units **1**
Sleeps **4–5**
Low season per wk
£210.00–£280.00
High season per wk
£280.00–£350.00

Flat 5 Garfield House, Swanage

contact Miss Susan Inge, Flat A, 147 Holland Road, London W14 8AS
t (020) 7602 4945 & 07798 500437 **e** sueinge@hotmail.com **w** langton-matravers.co.uk

open All year except Christmas and New Year
payment Cash/cheques

The village of Langton Matravers is built almost entirely of the local Purbeck stone. The flat in Garfield House is spacious, traditionally furnished and homely. It has spectacular views to the Purbeck Hills and over the sea to the Isle of Wight, and is a ten-minute walk to the Jurassic Coastline.

From M27 jct 1, take A31 towards Ringwood and Dorchester, then A35 to Wareham. Follow road to Swanage, and after 10 miles turn south to Langton Matravers.

Unit General P Leisure Shop < 0.5 miles Pub < 0.5 miles

LANIVET, Cornwall Map ref 1B2

★★★★
SELF CATERING

Units **1**
Sleeps **2–5**
Low season per wk
£300.00–£450.00
High season per wk
£450.00–£800.00

Owls Reach, Roche, St Austell

contact Diana Pride, Owls Reach, Colbiggan Farm, Roche PL26 8LJ
t (01208) 831597 **e** info@owlsreach.co.uk **w** owlsreach.co.uk

open All year
payment Cash/cheques, euros

A quiet, comfortable and elegant setting for your holiday. Detached, single-storey cottage, double glazed and centrally heated, with abundant natural light. Double/twin/single bedrooms, bathroom and shower room. Central location in peaceful countryside, adjacent to moorland – pheasants on lawn! Includes subscription to Country Club, with large indoor pool.

A30 to Innis Downs junction. Follow signs to Lanivet and in centre of village turn left. Turn left at next crossroads, past Lakeview.

Unit General P Leisure Shop 2 miles Pub 2 miles

LANREATH-BY-LOOE, Cornwall Map ref 1C2

★★★
SELF CATERING

Units **6**
Sleeps **2–8**
Low season per wk
£180.00–£345.00
High season per wk
£385.00–£830.00

The Old Rectory, Lanreath, Looe

contact Mr & Mrs Chris and Julie Edge, The Old Rectory, Lanreath, Looe PL13 2NU
t (01503) 220247 **e** ask@oldrectory-lanreath.co.uk **w** oldrectory-lanreath.co.uk

open All year
payment Credit/debit cards, cash/cheques

Gracious Georgian mansion with spacious, fully-equipped apartments reflecting the elegance of the period. Large, beautiful, secluded gardens with heated outdoor pool. Picturesque, tranquil village in breathtaking countryside, minutes from pretty fishing villages and beaches. Superb stately homes and lovely gardens to visit. Excellent village shop two miles. On-site parking.

Leave Liskeard on A38. At Dobwalls, left onto A390, then left onto B3359 after East Taphouse. After 5 miles, right at sign 'Lanreath 0.5 miles'.

Weekend and mid-week short breaks available (excl Jun-Sep). Please telephone for further information.

Unit General Leisure Shop 2 miles Pub < 0.5 miles

LAUNCESTON, Cornwall Map ref 1C2

★★★★
SELF CATERING

Units **8**
Sleeps **2–8**
Low season per wk
£210.00–£320.00
High season per wk
£535.00–£1,185.00

Bamham Farm Cottages, Launceston

contact Mrs Jackie Chapman, Bamham Farm Cottages, Higher Bamham Farm, Launceston PL15 9LD
t (01566) 772141 **f** (01566) 775266 **e** jackie@bamhamfarm.co.uk **w** bamhamfarm.co.uk

open All year
payment Credit/debit cards, cash/cheques

Individually designed cottages, ideally situated in beautiful countryside one mile from Launceston, the ancient capital of Cornwall, dominated by its Norman castle. The north and south coasts are easily accessible as are both Dartmoor and Bodmin Moor. Facilities include a heated indoor swimming pool, sauna, solarium, video recorders and trout fishing.

⊕ *Leave A30 at Launceston. Farm situated on the Polson Road just 1 mile from the town.*

❤ *For special offers see our website.*

Unit General P Leisure Shop 1 mile
Pub 1 mile

LAUNCESTON, Cornwall Map ref 1C2

★★★★
SELF CATERING

Units **3**
Sleeps **4–6**
Low season per wk
£150.00–£300.00
High season per wk
£250.00–£600.00

Frankaborough Farm Cottages, Lifton

contact Mrs Linda Banbury, Frankaborough Farm Cottages, Lifton PL16 0JS
t (01409) 211308 **f** (01409) 211308 **e** banbury960@aol.com **w** devonfarmcottage.co.uk

Close to Devon/Cornwall border, 260-acre mixed dairy farm offering imaginative barn conversions decorated to a high standard, set in a rural location but easily accessible to the A30.

open All year
payment Cash/cheques, euros

Unit General P Leisure Shop 4 miles
Pub 4 miles

LAUNCESTON, Cornwall Map ref 1C2

★★★–★★★★
SELF CATERING

Units **4**
Sleeps **2–4**
Low season per wk
£140.00–£260.00
High season per wk
£260.00–£425.00

Langdon Farm Holiday Cottages, Launceston

contact Mrs Fleur Rawlinson, Langdon Farm Holiday Cottages, Langdon Farm, Launceston PL15 8NW
t (01566) 785389 **e** g.f.rawlinson@btinternet.com **w** langdonholidays.com

One- and two-bedroom, well-equipped cottages, four-poster beds, countryside setting, near pub, ten miles from sea. Easy drive to Eden Project. Short breaks available.

open All year
payment Credit/debit cards, cash/cheques

Unit General P Leisure Shop 4 miles
Pub 1 mile

Suit yourself

The symbols at the end of each entry mean you can enjoy virtually made-to-measure accommodation with the services and facilities most important to you. A key to the symbols can be found inside the back-cover flap. Keep this open for easy reference.

LAUNCESTON, Cornwall Map ref 1C2

★★★
SELF CATERING

Units **2**
Sleeps **2–8**
Low season per wk
£185.00–£350.00
High season per wk
£380.00–£620.00

Lower Dutson Farm, Launceston

contact Mrs Kathryn Broad, Lower Dutson Farm, Dutson, Launceston PL15 9SP
t (01566) 776456 **f** (01566) 776456 **e** holidays@farm-cottage.co.uk **w** farm-cottage.co.uk

open All year
payment Cash/cheques

Play fetch with Fly, our sheepdog. Watch for the kingfisher when relaxing or fishing by the lake or Tamar Valley riverside. Get up late and enjoy lunch at Homeleigh Garden Centre (400m). Two miles from historic Launceston with Norman castle. Central for coasts, beaches, moors, National Trust houses and gardens.

⊕ *M5 jct 31, A30 to Launceston, then A388 towards Holsworthy. We are located 2 miles from Launceston on right.*

♥ *Free coarse fishing on lake and River Tamar (trout, salmon and grayling) for 2 people per cottage.*

Unit General P Leisure Shop 1 mile Pub 1 mile

LEE, Devon Map ref 1C1

★★★–★★★★
SELF CATERING

Units **8**
Sleeps **2–8**
Low season per wk
£195.00–£475.00
High season per wk
£415.00–£980.00

Lower Campscott Farm, Ilfracombe

contact Mrs Margaret Cowell, Lower Campscott Farm, Lee, Ilfracombe EX34 8LS
t (01271) 863479 **f** (01271) 867639 **e** holidays@lowercampscott.co.uk **w** lowercampscott.co.uk

open All year
payment Credit/debit cards, cash/cheques

Charming, tastefully furnished character cottages converted from our farm buildings. Everything supplied to make your stay special. Also holiday homes and lodges. Peaceful farm setting with views across the Bristol Channel. Lee and Woolacombe beaches are easily accessible.

⊕ *Information on the location will be sent when the booking is confirmed.*

♥ *Short breaks available out of school holidays. Residential craft and hobby courses second and third weeks of the month.*

Unit General P Leisure Shop 1.5 miles Pub 1.5 miles

LISKEARD, Cornwall Map ref 1C2

★★★★
SELF CATERING

Units **3**
Sleeps **4–6**
Low season per wk
£205.00–£265.00
High season per wk
£390.00–£540.00

Hopsland Holidays, Liskeard

contact Mr & Mrs Hosken, Hopsland Holidays, Common Moor, Liskeard PL14 6EJ
t (01579) 344480 **f** (01579) 344480 **e** hopslandholidays@aol.com **w** hopslandholidays.co.uk

A beautifully renovated barn, converted into three well-equipped cottages. Purposely converted upside down to maximize the beautiful views. All cottages have oil-fired central heating, first £5 electricity, bed linen (including duvets).

open All year
payment Cash/cheques

Unit General P Leisure Shop 2 miles Pub 2 miles

Pool search

If a swimming pool is an essential element of your holiday accommodation check out the special index at the back of this guide.

LISKEARD, Cornwall Map ref 1C2

★★★
SELF CATERING

Units **2**
Sleeps **2–5**
Low season per wk
Min £160.00
High season per wk
Max £540.00

Lodge Barton, Liskeard

contact Mr & Mrs Hodin, Lodge Barton, Lodge Hill, Liskeard PL14 4JX
t (01579) 344432 **e** lodgebart@aol.com **w** selectideas.co.uk/lodgebarton

Idyllic farm setting with river valley and woods. Sunny character cottages, well equipped and within easy reach of beaches and moors.

open All year
payment Cash/cheques

Unit General P Leisure

LISKEARD, Cornwall Map ref 1C2

★★★
SELF CATERING

Units **1**
Sleeps **4**
Low season per wk
Max £350.00
High season per wk
Max £500.00

Trelyn Cottage, Liskeard

contact Ms Angie Fisher, Trelyn Cottage, Trelyn, Keason, St Ive, Liskeard PL14 3NE
t (01579) 383881 **f** (01579) 383881 **e** trelyn@kingfisher-training.freeserve.co.uk
w http://trelyncottage.mysite.wanadoo-members.co.uk

open All year
payment Cash/cheques

One double and one twin bedroom, both en suite. Edge of village location, stunning countryside views. An ideal base for touring Cornwall and West Devon. Within easy reach of local Heritage sites, good walking country, golf courses, National Trust properties, the Eden Project and popular towns such as Looe and Polperro.

⊕ *M5/A38 to Plymouth, A388 Saltash-Callington, then A390. Or M5/A30 to Launceston, A388 to Callington, then A390. Or across Dartmoor: A390 from Tavistock.*

Unit General P S Leisure Shop 2.5 miles Pub 0.75 miles

LOOE, Cornwall Map ref 1C3

★★★★
SELF CATERING

Units **3**
Sleeps **4–5**
Low season per wk
£200.00–£345.00
High season per wk
£350.00–£560.00

Bocaddon Holiday Cottages, Looe

contact Mrs Alison Maiklem, Bocaddon Holiday Cottages, Bocaddon Farm, Lanreath PL13 2PG
t (01503) 220192 **e** holidays@bocaddon.com **w** bocaddon.com

open All year
payment Credit/debit cards, cash/cheques

Warm, welcoming and peaceful, these tastefully converted barns on a working farm nestle deep in beautiful Cornish countryside, yet are near the famous beaches and fishing harbours of Looe, Polperro and Fowey. Walking, fishing, wonderful houses and gardens are easily available, or just relax in comfort. Very wheelchair friendly.

⊕ *From A38, take A390 (East Taphouse). Left onto B3359. After 4 miles, right (Shillamill Lakes). We are 0.25 miles on left-hand side.*

❤ *Short breaks available Oct-Mar.*

Unit General P Leisure Shop 2 miles Pub 2 miles

Prices

These are shown for one week's accommodation. If an entry includes details of more than one property it is usual that the minimum price is for low season in the smallest property and the maximum price is for high season in the largest property.

LOOE, Cornwall Map ref 1C3

★★★★-★★★★★
SELF CATERING

Units **5**
Sleeps **2–8**
Low season per wk
£180.00–£275.00
High season per wk
£275.00–£975.00

Bucklawren Farm, Looe

contact Mrs Henly, Bucklawren Farm, St Martins, Looe PL13 1NZ
t (01503) 240738 **f** (01503) 240481 **e** bucklawren@btopenworld.com **w** bucklawren.com

open All year
payment Credit/debit cards, cash/cheques

Set deep in unspoilt countryside, with a large garden and exceptional sea views, these delightful stone cottages on an award-winning farm are just one mile from the beach and three miles from the fishing port of Looe. The Granary Restaurant is on site.

⊕ *Leave A38 at Trerulefoot roundabout, follow sign for Looe. At Shorta, left onto B3253. After 1 mile left to Monkey Sanctuary. Right to Bucklawren, down lane past restaurant.*

♥ *Short breaks from Nov-Apr (excl Christmas and New Year).*

Unit General P Leisure Shop 1 mile Pub 3 miles

LOOE, Cornwall Map ref 1C3

★★★★
SELF CATERING & SERVICED APARTMENTS

Units **8**
Sleeps **4–8**
Low season per wk
£203.00–£355.00
High season per wk
£546.00–£985.00

Rock Towers Apartments, Looe

contact Mr Dixon, Rock Towers Apartments, Marine Drive, Hannafore PL13 2DQ
t (01503) 262736 **f** (01503) 265913 **e** cornishcol@aol.com **w** cornishcollection.co.uk

open All year
payment Credit/debit cards, cash/cheques

Situated in a commanding position right on the seafront in Looe, these apartments provide high-quality accommodation with a very high level of facilities. The views from each apartment are stunning, and the location is an ideal base for exploring the rest of Cornwall and South Devon.

⊕ *Leave A38 at Trerulefoot roundabout and follow signs for Looe. Rock Towers Apartments will be found on west side of town at Hannafore, overlooking main Looe beach.*

Unit General P Leisure Shop < 0.5 miles Pub < 0.5 miles

LOOE, Cornwall Map ref 1C3

★★★★
SELF CATERING

Units **6**
Sleeps **2–5**
Low season per wk
£175.00–£350.00
High season per wk
£350.00–£595.00

Summercourt Coastal Cottages, Looe

contact Mr Hocking, Summercourt Coastal Cottages, Bodigga Cliff, St Martin PL13 1NZ
t (01503) 263149 **e** sccottages@freenet.co.uk **w** holidaycottagescornwall.tv

Stone barns converted to comfortable and well-equipped cottages in a rural Area of Outstanding Natural Beauty. Close to sea and beaches.

open All year
payment Credit/debit cards, cash/cheques

Unit General P Leisure Shop 2 miles Pub 2 miles

Take a break

Look out for special promotions and themed breaks. This could be your chance to indulge an interest, find a new one, or just relax and enjoy exceptional value! Offers are highlighted in colour (and are subject to availability).

LOOE, Cornwall Map ref 1C3

★★★★
SELF CATERING

Units **5**
Sleeps **2–5**
Low season per wk
£165.00–£450.00
High season per wk
£319.00–£665.00

Talehay, Looe

contact Neil & Theresa Dennett, Talehay, Tremaine, Looe PL13 2LT
t (01503) 220252 **e** infobooking@talehay.co.uk **w** talehay.co.uk

open All year
payment Credit/debit cards, cash/cheques

Tastefully converted and very comfortable stone holiday cottages set around 17thC non-working farmstead. Set in unspoilt, peaceful countryside with breathtaking coastal walks and beaches nearby. Close to Eden Project, Lost Gardens of Heligan and many National Trust properties. An ideal base for exploring the many varied delights of Cornwall.

⊕ *Over Tamar bridge, A38 for 16 miles. Dobwalls traffic lights, A390 St Austell road (2.5 miles). B3359, left on Looe road. After 6 miles right at crossroads.*

♥ *Short breaks available Oct-Mar (excl Christmas and New Year), minimum 2 nights.*

Unit General P Leisure **Shop** 1 mile **Pub** 1 mile

LOOE, Cornwall Map ref 1C3

★★★-★★★★
SELF CATERING

Units **3**
Sleeps **2–5**
Low season per wk
Min £175.00
High season per wk
Max £660.00

Trehalvin Cottages, Liskeard

contact Mrs Catherine Woollard, Trehalvin Cottages, Trehalvin, Trewidland PL14 4ST
t (01503) 240334 **f** (01503) 240334 **e** cottages@trehalvin.co.uk **w** trehalvin.co.uk

open All year
payment Credit/debit cards, cash/cheques

Pretty cottages set in a beautiful, peaceful location with superb views over the Looe Valley. Facilities include heated pool and hot tub. Within easy reach of the Eden Project, beaches and many local attractions. The cottages are very comfortably furnished and are a perfect retreat for families and couples.

⊕ *Directions provided once booking is confirmed.*

♥ *Special offers often available.*

Unit General P S Leisure **Shop** < 0.5 miles
Pub 3 miles

LOOE, Cornwall Map ref 1C3

★★★★
SELF CATERING

Units **4**
Sleeps **2–8**
Low season per wk
Min £220.00
High season per wk
Max £900.00

Woodsaws Farm, Looe

contact Mrs Ann Wills, Woodsaws Cross, Lanreath, Looe PL13 2NT
t (01503) 220190 **e** ann@woodsawsfarm.co.uk

A stone-built, 19thC working mill converted into spacious and comfortable cottages, one reverse-level cottage and a bungalow-style cottage in rural countryside.

open All year
payment Cash/cheques

Unit General P S Leisure **Shop** 0.5 miles
Pub 0.5 miles

Use your i's

Tourist information centres provide a wealth of information and friendly advice, both before you go and during your stay. Refer to the front of this section for a list of tourist information centres in the region.

LOSTWITHIEL, Cornwall Map ref 1B2

★★★★
SELF CATERING

Units **5**
Sleeps **2–4**
Low season per wk
£200.00–£360.00
High season per wk
£300.00–£510.00

Chark Country Holidays, Lostwithiel

contact Mrs Littleton, Chark Country Holidays, Redmoor, Bodmin PL30 5AR
t (01208) 871118 **e** charkholidays@tiscali.co.uk **w** charkcountryholidays.co.uk

Delightful barn conversions in beautiful rural location, yet near Eden Project and many other attractions and beaches. Ideal base for touring, walking, cycling and riding.

open All year
payment Cash/cheques

Unit General Leisure Shop 2 miles Pub 1.5 miles

LOSTWITHIEL, Cornwall Map ref 1B2

★★★–★★★★
SELF CATERING

Units **8**
Sleeps **1–6**
Low season per wk
Min £200.00
High season per wk
Max £855.00

Lanwithan Cottages, Lostwithiel

contact Mr V B Edward-Collins, Lanwithan Cottages, Lerryn Road, Lostwithiel PL22 0LA
t (01208) 872444 **f** (01208) 872444 **e** lanwithan@btconnect.com **w** lanwithancottages.co.uk

open All year
payment Cash/cheques, euros

Charming selection of Georgian estate cottages nestling in the Fowey Valley with two delightful waterside properties. Cottages with leaded-light windows, crackling log fires, four-poster bed and glass-topped well. Parkland, river frontage and boat. Woodland and riverside walks from your garden gate. Come and relax and soak up the Cornish atmosphere.

Liskeard to Lostwithiel on A390, pass National garage on left. 1st left, Great Western units, and 1st left again. Sign after 300yds – follow to house, not farm.

Short breaks out of season. Reduced green fees. Pets accepted in some cottages. Canoe trips available with safety boat.

Unit General Leisure
Shop 0.5 miles Pub 0.5 miles

LOWER APPERLEY, Gloucestershire Map ref 2B1

★★★★★
SELF CATERING

Units **1**
Sleeps **1–8**
Low season per wk
£675.00–£775.00
High season per wk
£810.00–£980.00

Rofield Barn, Gloucester

contact Mrs Hazel Lewis, Lower Apperley, Gloucester GL19 4DR
t (01452) 780323 **f** (01452) 780777 **e** jeremy@tewkbury.freeserve.co.uk **w** rofieldbarn.com

Recently converted from a 300-year-old barn, this outstanding property has four double bedrooms, is attractively furnished and offers every amenity in a spacious, light and airy environment. Private garden with outstanding views to the Cotswold Hills.

open All year
payment Cash/cheques

Unit General Leisure Pub < 0.5 miles

LUDGVAN, Cornwall Map ref 1A3

★★★
SELF CATERING

Units **1**
Sleeps **2–6**
Low season per wk
Min £300.00
High season per wk
Max £450.00

Nanceddan, Penzance

contact Mrs Richards, Nanceddan, Ludgvan, Penzance TR20 8AN
t (01736) 740165 **e** nanceddan@hotmail.com **w** nanceddan.com

Spacious farmhouse apartment in tranquil valley setting, midway between St Ives and Penzance. Superb views of St Michael's Mount, Mounts Bay and surrounding countryside. An ideal holiday destination.

open All year except Christmas and New Year
payment Cash/cheques

Unit General Leisure Shop 2 miles Pub 1 mile

LYDNEY, Gloucestershire Map ref 2B1

★★★
SELF CATERING

Units **3**
Sleeps **2–5**
Low season per wk
£140.00–£190.00
High season per wk
£220.00–£320.00

Highbury Coach House, Lydney

contact Mr Anthony Midgley, Highbury Coach House, Bream Road, Lydney GL15 5JH
t (01594) 842339 **f** (01594) 842339 **e** midgleya1@aol.com

Apartments in a listed coach house close to Lydney with panoramic views over the Forest of Dean and Severn Valley. Gardens, snooker and games rooms.

open All year
payment Cash/cheques, euros

Unit General Leisure Shop 0.5 miles
Pub 0.5 miles

LYME REGIS, Dorset Map ref 1D2

★★★
SELF CATERING

Units **3**
Sleeps **4–6**
Low season per wk
Min £200.00
High season per wk
Max £620.00

Harbour House Flats, Lyme Regis

contact Mrs Monica Cary, Briseham,, Broadway Road, Kingsteignton, Newton Abbot TQ12 3EH
t (01626) 364779

Harbour House Flats are situated 50yds from the harbour, and command superb views over Lyme Bay.

open All year
payment Cash/cheques

Unit General P

LYME REGIS, Dorset Map ref 1D2

★★★
SELF CATERING

Units **1**
Sleeps **8**
Low season per wk
£400.00–£600.00
High season per wk
£600.00–£900.00

Marmalade House, Lyme Regis

contact Mrs Pam Corbin, Whitty Down, Rocombe, Lyme Regis DT7 3RR
t (01297) 442378 **f** (01297) 445911 **e** ozonepam@aol.com

open All year
payment Cash/cheques, euros

With stunning views from all three floors over the World Heritage Coastline, Marmalade House, recently refurbished, provides spacious and contemporary living. It offers well-equipped accommodation with Aga. Centrally located in historic Lyme Regis and a few minutes' walk from The Cobb, beaches, shops, restaurants and cinema.

❤ *Short breaks available out of season. Min 3 nights.*

Unit General

LYME REGIS, Dorset Map ref 1D2

★★★★
SELF CATERING

Units **2**
Sleeps **2–4**
Low season per wk
£295.00–£420.00
High season per wk
£465.00–£595.00

Sea Tree House, Lyme Regis

contact Mr David Parker, Sea Tree House, 18 Broad Street, Lyme Regis DT7 3QE
t (01297) 442244 **f** (01297) 442244 **e** seatree.house@ukonline.co.uk
w lymeregis.com/seatreehouse

open All year
payment Cash/cheques

Romantic, elegant apartments overlooking the sea, three minutes from the beach. Spacious living room with dining area overlooking the sea. Central position giving easy access to restaurants, pubs and walks in Area of Outstanding Natural Beauty. Warm, friendly welcome from owners.

⊕ *Approach Lyme Regis from either A35 or A3052. Sea Tree House is on Broad Street, the main street, just before you reach the sea.*

❤ *Short breaks available in the low season.*

Unit General P Leisure Shop 0.5 miles
Pub 0.5 miles

LYME REGIS, Dorset Map ref 1D2

★★★
SELF CATERING

Units **4**
Sleeps **6–8**
Low season per wk
£180.00–£290.00
High season per wk
£295.00–£750.00

Westover Farm Cottages, Bridport

contact Mrs Debby Snook, Westover Farm Cottages, Westover Farm, Wootton Fitzpaine, Bridport DT6 6NE
t (01297) 560451 **e** wfcottages@aol.com **w** westoverfarmcottages.co.uk

open All year
payment Cash/cheques, euros

Lovely three-bedroomed cottages with wood-burning stoves, inglenook and open fires on edge of picturesque village. Additional three-bedroomed, stone-built cottages with adjoining games room overlooking gentle valley. Parking and large garden at all cottages. In an Area of Outstanding Natural Beauty, 1.5 miles from World Heritage Coastline.

⊕ *A35 from Dorchester. Right to Wootton Fitzpaine 0.75 miles beyond Charmouth roundabout. Westover Farm is 1st house on left. From Axminster turn left 0.75 miles before roundabout.*

❤ *Short-break bookings a speciality and very welcome.*

Unit General P S Leisure Shop 1.5 miles Pub 1.5 miles

LYMPSHAM, Somerset Map ref 1D1

★★
SELF CATERING

Units **4**
Sleeps **2–7**
Low season per wk
£130.00–£249.00
High season per wk
£195.00–£350.00

Dulhorn Farm Holiday Park, Weston-super-Mare

contact Mr & Mrs Bowden, Dulhorn Farm Holiday Park, Weston Road, Weston-super-Mare BS24 0JQ
t (01934) 750298 **f** (01934) 750913

On working farm. Ideal touring and fishing, country surroundings. Beaches approximately four miles. Easy access to motorway. Pets welcome. Also campsite etc. Open mid-February to mid-December.

payment Cash/cheques

Unit General P S Leisure Shop 1.5 miles Pub 1 mile

LYNTON, Devon Map ref 1C1

★★★★
SELF CATERING

Units **3**
Sleeps **2–8**
Low season per wk
£210.00–£440.00
High season per wk
£470.00–£895.00

Cloud Farm, Lynton

contact Mrs Jill Harman, Oare, Lynton EX35 6NU
t (01598) 741234 **f** (01598) 741154 **e** doonevalleyholidays@hotmail.com
w doonevalleyholidays.co.uk

open All year
payment Credit/debit cards, cash/cheques

Cloud Farm is a lovely riverside farmhouse in the heart of Exmoor's beautiful Doone Valley. The cottages, with tea room, shop, off-licence and gardens, provide an idyllic base for families and children, walkers and tourers seeking an 'away-from-it-all' break at any time of year. Riding for all ages and abilities.

⊕ *A39, Porlock towards Lynton. Four miles beyond Porlock Hill, left to Oare and Malmsmead. Right at Oare Church, Cloud Farm 1 mile on left.*

❤ *Short breaks and weekend breaks available during off-peak seasons. Special rates for advanced and late bookings.*

Unit General P S Leisure Shop < 0.5 miles Pub 3 miles

To your credit

If you book by phone you may be asked for your credit card number. If so, it is advisable to check the proprietor's policy in case you have to cancel your reservation at a later date.

LYNTON, Devon Map ref 1C1

★★★★
SELF CATERING

Units **1**
Sleeps **2–4**
Low season per wk
£250.00–£400.00
High season per wk
£450.00–£600.00

Hollowbrook Cottage, Martinhoe, Barnstaple

contact Mr Christopher Legg, Martinhoe, Parracombe, Barnstaple EX31 4QT
t (01598) 763368 **e** info@oldrectoryhotel.co.uk **w** exmoorcottages.co.uk

Attractive stone-built cottage, tastefully furnished, idyllically situated in peaceful surroundings within Exmoor National Park, near the coastal path.

open All year
payment Credit/debit cards, cash/cheques

Unit General 12 P Leisure Shop 4 miles Pub 1 mile

LYNTON, Devon Map ref 1C1

★★★★
SELF CATERING

Units **1**
Sleeps **1–2**
Low season per wk
Min £245.00
High season per wk
Max £570.00

Royal Castle Lodge, Lynton

contact Mr M Wolverson, Primespot Character Cottages, c/o Stag Cottage, Holdstone Down, Combe Martin EX34 0PF
t (01271) 882449

open All year
payment Cash/cheques, euros

Something special! High-quality, 16thC, detached, thatched stone cottage with rustic balcony, stable door, real fire, garden. Idyllic coastal setting in England's 'Little Switzerland'. Exmoor National Park, wooded outlook with harbour, pubs, restaurants, shops within walking distance. Spectacular walks. Spotless, warm and cosy. Off-season short breaks. Perfect honeymoon/anniversaries.

⊕ *Follow A39 via Minehead for Lynton and Lynmouth. Telephone from anywhere in Lynton/Lynmouth and we will come and meet you.*

❤ *De-stressing breaks Nov-Mar.*

Unit General P Leisure Shop < 0.5 miles Pub < 0.5 miles

MAIDENCOMBE, Devon Map ref 1D2

★★★
SELF CATERING

Units **6**
Sleeps **2–4**
Low season per wk
£200.00–£360.00
High season per wk
£290.00–£560.00

Bowden Close House, Maidencombe

contact Mrs Sarah Farquharson, Bowden Close House, Teignmouth Road, Maidencombe, Torquay TQ1 4TJ
t (01803) 328029 **e** enquiries@bowdenclose.co.uk **w** bowdenclose.co.uk

open All year
payment Cash/cheques, euros

Relax in very comfortable apartments or two-storey, self-contained wings of large Victorian house overlooking Lyme Bay, four miles from Torquay. Acre of gardens with stunning views. Minutes from sheltered Maidencombe Cove and the South West Coast Path. Easy access to Dartmoor and the lovely South Devon countryside.

⊕ *M5 south, A38 Plymouth/Torquay. A380 Torquay. B3192 Teignmouth, follow signs for Torquay, over Shaldon Bridge. Coast road to Maidencombe, Bowden Close House on left.*

❤ *Short breaks available. Low season: 20% discount for couples (except for 'Poppy' unit).*

Unit General Leisure Shop 3 miles Pub 0.5 miles

Out and about

For ideas on places to visit see the beginning of this regional section or go online at enjoyengland.com.

MALMESBURY, Wiltshire Map ref 2B2

★★★★
SELF CATERING

Units **1**
Sleeps **5**
Low season per wk
£250.00–£350.00
High season per wk
£400.00–£500.00

The Cottage, Malmesbury

contact Mrs Ross Eavis, Manor Farm, Corston, Malmesbury SN16 0HF
t (01666) 822148 **f** (01666) 826565 **e** ross@johneavis.wanadoo.co.uk **w** manorfarmbandb.co.uk

Relax and unwind in farm surroundings. The Cottage is full of character and furnished to a very high standard. Easy access to the M4, the Cotswolds and Bath.

open All year
payment Credit/debit cards, cash/cheques

Unit General P Shop 2 miles Pub < 0.5 miles

MANACCAN, Cornwall Map ref 1B3

★★–★★★★
SELF CATERING

Units **3**
Sleeps **2–18**
Low season per wk
Min £150.00
High season per wk
Max £720.00

Lestowder Farm, Helston

contact Mrs Martin, Lestowder Farm, Manaccan, Helston TR12 6ES
t (01326) 231400 **e** lestowderfarm@hotmail.com **w** lestowderfarmcottages.co.uk

Lestowder Farm cottages nestle in a very quiet, unspoilt part of Cornwall, on the south of River Helford, near coastal footpath and beach.

open All year
payment Cash/cheques, euros

Unit General P Leisure Shop 2.5 miles Pub 2.5 miles

MARAZION, Cornwall Map ref 1B3

★★★
SELF CATERING

Units **13**
Sleeps **1–5**
Low season per wk
£166.00–£391.00
High season per wk
£395.00–£795.00

Trevarthian Holiday Homes, Marazion

contact Mrs Sally Cattran, Trevarthian Holiday Homes, Trevarthian House, West End TR17 0EG
t (01736) 710100 **f** (01736) 710111 **e** info@trevarthian.co.uk **w** trevarthian.co.uk

open All year
payment Credit/debit cards, cash/cheques

Converted from a Victorian hotel in Mount's Bay location, 50yds from beach. Superb views of St Michael's Mount, Mousehole, Newlyn, Penzance. A selection of the finest self-catering accommodation available. One- to five-minute walk to safe sandy beach. Playground, pubs, restaurants, galleries, shops, bus routes for Land's End, St Ives, Penzance.

⊕ *Enter Marazion and you will find our signs at the bottom of our drive opposite the folly field before you reach the children's playground.*

♥ *£100 for 2 nights per unit in off-peak time.*

Unit General P Leisure

Key to symbols

Symbols at the end of each entry help you pick out the services and facilities which are most important for your stay. A key to the symbols can be found inside the back-cover flap. Keep this open for easy reference.

MARLBOROUGH, Wiltshire Map ref 2B2

★★–★★★
SELF CATERING

Units **1**
Sleeps **1–8**
Low season per wk
£300.00–£490.00
High season per wk
£525.00–£650.00

Dairy Cottage, Marlborough

contact Mr & Mrs Mark and Hazel Crockford, Dairy Cottage, Browns Farm, Marlborough SN8 4ND
t (01672) 515129 & 07931 311985 **e** crockford@farming.co.uk

open All year
payment Credit/debit cards, cash/cheques

Dairy Cottage is situated on Browns Farm which is a working dairy/arable farm set on the edge of Savernake Forest overlooking open farmland. The cottage offers peace and tranquillity for a true North Wiltshire holiday. A modern, spacious, well-equipped bungalow with open fire awaits your arrival.

⊕ *From Marlborough, A346 south (Salisbury). Proceed over new roundabout and travel up steep hill. Dairy Cottage is 300yds past Browns Farm on the right.*

Unit General P Leisure Shop 2 miles Pub 2 miles

MARLDON, Devon Map ref 1D2

★★★★
SELF CATERING

Units **1**
Sleeps **5**
Low season per wk
£250.00–£320.00
High season per wk
£285.00–£600.00

Lower Tor Cot, Paignton

contact Mrs Sally Wetherbee, Thorn Cottage, Burn Lane, Brentor, Tavistock PL19 0ND
t (01822) 810285 **e** sally@wetherbee.fsnet.co.uk **w** sallysholidaycottages.co.uk

open All year
payment Cash/cheques

Situated on a steep lane, this comfortable, well-equipped cottage offers panoramic views across fields and towards Dartmoor. Three bedrooms (double, twin and single). Multi-fuel stove and night-storage heaters for winter warmth. Patio/garden. Maximum of two dogs very welcome. Network of footpaths from door. Torbay, beaches, Dartmouth and Totnes very accessible.

⊕ *Newton Abbot, then A381 towards Totnes. Turn left in Ipplepen, signposted Compton and Marldon. Detailed directions and map sent with booking confirmation.*

❤ *Short breaks available Nov-Mar inclusive, min 2 nights (excl main school holiday dates).*

Unit General Leisure Shop 0.5 miles Pub < 0.5 miles

MELCOMBE BINGHAM, Dorset Map ref 2B3

★★★★
SELF CATERING

Units **1**
Sleeps **1–7**
Low season per wk
£450.00–£550.00
High season per wk
£600.00–£800.00

Greygles, Melcombe Bingham, Dorchester

contact Mr Paul Sommerfeld, 22 Tiverton Road, London NW10 3HL
t (020) 8969 4830 **f** (020) 8960 0069 **e** enquiry@greygles.co.uk **w** greygles.co.uk

open All year
payment Cash/cheques, euros

Rural peace in spacious, well-equipped stone cottage with delightful views. Hardy Country, on edge of friendly village with well-known pub. Four bedrooms, one on ground floor. Log fire. Wendy house in garden. In an Area of Outstanding Natural Beauty, just off Wessex Ridgeway walkers' path. Coast, abbeys, castles, gardens, many attractions within 30 minutes' drive.

⊕ *From Winterbourne Whitechurch on A354 Blandford/Dorchester road, follow sign to Milton Abbas, then through Milton, Hilton and Ansty to Melcombe Bingham.*

❤ *Short breaks available outside summer peak, Christmas and Easter. Min 3-night stay. Linen, towels and heating included.*

Unit General P Leisure Shop 0.5 miles Pub 0.5 miles

MENHENIOT, Cornwall Map ref 1C2

★★★★
SELF CATERING

Units **5**
Sleeps **2–5**
Low season per wk
£198.00–£305.00
High season per wk
£260.00–£750.00

Hayloft Courtyard Cottages, Liskeard

contact Michele & Stephen Hore, Hayloft Courtyard Cottages, Lower Clicker Road, Menheniot, Liskeard PL14 3PU
t (01503) 240879 **e** courtyardcottage@btconnect.com **w** hayloftcourtyardcottages.com

open All year
payment Credit/debit cards, cash/cheques

A warm welcome and Cornish cream tea await your arrival at our family-run cottages, lovingly converted from original stone barns and retaining many character features. Each cottage is equipped to a high standard with many home-from-home comforts. Ideally situated for touring coast, moors and attractions. Renowned Hayloft Restaurant on site.

Tamar Bridge, A38 for Liskeard. Three miles from 2nd roundabout, up hill on dual carriageway. Sign right for Menheniot. Cross dual carriageway. Hayloft opposite (2nd entrance for cottage).

Short breaks – off-peak. Special offers spring/autumn.

Unit General P S Leisure Shop 1 mile Pub < 0.5 miles

MENHENIOT, Cornwall Map ref 1C2

★★★–★★★★
SELF CATERING

Units **3**
Sleeps **1–5**
Low season per wk
£150.00–£275.00
High season per wk
£400.00–£600.00

Trewint Farm, Liskeard

contact Mrs Rowe, Trewint Farm, Menheniot, Liskeard PL14 3RE
t (01579) 347155 **f** (01579) 347155 **e** holidays@trewintfarm.co.uk **w** trewintfarm.co.uk

Recently converted cottages with all the extras to make your holiday special. Cornish cream tea on arrival. Children can enjoy the games room, play area and pet corner. Ideal for exploring Looe and Polperro.

open All year
payment Credit/debit cards, cash/cheques

Unit General P Leisure Shop 1 mile Pub 1 mile

MEVAGISSEY, Cornwall Map ref 1B3

★★★
SELF CATERING

Units **1**
Sleeps **4**
Low season per wk
£250.00–£350.00
High season per wk
£350.00–£550.00

Blue Waters, Mevagissey, St Austell

contact Mrs D Kendall, 13 Kiln Close, Mevagissey, St Austell PL26 6TP
t (01726) 843164 **e** edwin.kendall@btinternet.com

Comfortable, well-equipped cottage with panoramic views of harbour and bay. Short stroll to village. Linen provided. Private parking.

open All year
payment Cash/cheques, euros

Unit General P S Leisure Shop < 0.5 miles Pub < 0.5 miles

MEVAGISSEY, Cornwall Map ref 1B3

★★★
SELF CATERING

Units **13**
Sleeps **2–6**
Low season per wk
£185.00–£265.00
High season per wk
£399.00–£690.00

Treloen Holiday Apartments, Mevagissey

contact Mrs Seamark, Treloen Holiday Apartments, Polkirt Hill, Mevagissey, Unknown PL26 6UX
t (01726) 842406 **f** (01726) 842406 **e** holidays@treloen.co.uk **w** treloen.co.uk

Quality apartments in secluded cliff-top setting, all with spectacular sea views and private balconies/patios. Picturesque harbour, shops and beach 450m. Ten miles Eden Project.

open All year
payment Credit/debit cards, cash/cheques

Unit General P S Leisure Shop < 0.5 miles Pub < 0.5 miles

MILTON ABBAS, Dorset Map ref 2B3

★★★★
SELF CATERING

Units **6**
Sleeps **1–7**
Low season per wk
£280.00–£495.00
High season per wk
£415.00–£895.00

Luccombe Farm, Blandford Forum

contact Mr & Mrs Murray & Amanda Kayll, Luccombe Farm, Milton Abbas, Blandford Forum DT11 0BE
t (01258) 880558 **f** (01258) 881384 **e** mkayll@aol.com **w** luccombeholidays.co.uk

open All year
payment Credit/debit cards, cash/cheques

Comfortably converted cottages, with traditional character. Idyllic, peaceful setting in middle of proper working farm close to the historic village of Milton Abbas. Many facilities, including indoor pool.

⊕ *From the A354 between Blandford and Dorchester, at Winterbourne Whitechurch, head north towards Milton Abbas. Turn left into Farm Lane after 1.5 miles. Continue for 0.75 miles.*

Unit General Leisure
Shop 2 miles Pub 2 miles

MILTON ABBAS, Dorset Map ref 2B3

★★★★
SELF CATERING

Units **1**
Sleeps **2–6**
Low season per wk
£220.00–£280.00
High season per wk
£320.00–£510.00

Primrose Cottage, Blandford Forum

contact Mrs Therese Clemson, 22 Kerrfield, Winchester SO22 5EX
t (01962) 865786 **f** (01962) 865786 **e** therese.clemson@btinternet.com
w miltonabbas-primrosecottage.co.uk

open All year
payment Cash/cheques

Grade II Listed, 18thC, thatched cob cottage set on the street in the unique village of Milton Abbas, created by Lord Milton. Centre of Hardy Country. Ideal for walkers and romantics.

⊕ *From A354 follow signs to Milton Abbas.*

Unit General Leisure

MILVERTON, Somerset Map ref 1D1

★★★★★
SELF CATERING

Units **1**
Sleeps **14**
Low season per wk
Min £1,243.00
High season per wk
Max £2,779.00

Wellisford Manor Barn, Wellisford

contact Ms Sarah Campos, Wellisford Manor Barn, Wellington TA21 0SB
t (01823) 672794 **f** (01823) 673229 **e** sjcampos.martyn@btinternet.com **w** wellisfordmanorbarn.com

Luxury, contemporary, converted barn/coach house set around private landscaped garden with hot tub and barbecue. Three bathrooms (two en suite), media room with four-foot plasma screen, kitchen and utility room. All bedrooms have real linen bedlinen and plasma TVs.

open All year
payment Cash/cheques, euros

Unit General
Leisure Shop 6 miles Pub 1 mile

Town, country or coast?

The entertainment, shopping and innovative attractions of the big cities, the magnificent vistas of the countryside or the relaxing and refreshing coast – this guide will help you find what you're looking for!

MINEHEAD, Somerset Map ref 1D1

★★★
SELF CATERING

Units **1**
Sleeps **5**
Low season per wk
£200.00–£280.00
High season per wk
£380.00–£400.00

Fishermans Cottage, Minehead

contact Mrs Martin, 57 Quay Street, Minehead TA24 5UL
t (01643) 704263

Situated overlooking Minehead bay and harbour. Near town centre, a few minutes' walk from walks on North Hill. Two bedrooms, bathroom with shower unit and wash basin, lounge/dining room.

open All year
payment Cash/cheques

Unit General 5 P Leisure Shop 1 mile Pub < 0.5 miles

MINEHEAD, Somerset Map ref 1D1

★★★–★★★★
SELF CATERING

Units **2**
Sleeps **2–7**
Low season per wk
£160.00–£270.00
High season per wk
£370.00–£470.00

Merlin House Holiday Apartments, Blue Anchor, Minehead

contact Ms Penny Marshall-Rush, Carhampton Road, Blue Anchor, Minehead TA24 6LB
t (01643) 822014 **e** merlinhouseholidayapartments@fsmail.net
w merlinhouseholidayapartments.co.uk

Self-contained holiday apartments with panoramic views, 100yds from beach. Fifty yards from West Somerset Railway station at Blue Anchor.

open All year
payment Credit/debit cards, cash/cheques

Unit General P Leisure Shop 0.5 miles Pub < 0.5 miles

MISERDEN, Gloucestershire Map ref 2B1

★★★
SELF CATERING

Units **3**
Sleeps **2–6**
Low season per wk
£240.00–£350.00
High season per wk
£300.00–£430.00

Sudgrove Cottages, Stroud

contact Mr & Mrs Martin & Carol Ractliffe, Sudgrove Cottages, Sudgrove, Miserden, Stroud GL6 7JD
t (01285) 821322 **f** (01285) 821322 **e** enquiries@sudgrovecottages.co.uk **w** sudgrovecottages.co.uk

open All year
payment Cash/cheques

Attractive Cotswold-stone cottages with views across fields, in a peaceful hamlet on a no-through road. Footpaths lead through valleys, woods and pasture to picturesque villages, while Cirencester, Stroud, Cheltenham and Gloucester are easily reached by car. You will find Sudgrove a place to relax and unwind.

⊕ *Sudgrove lies at the centre of a triangle formed by linking Cheltenham, Cirencester and Stroud. Full travel directions are supplied on booking.*

♥ *Short breaks available Nov-Mar, min 2 nights. Special offer: 3 nights for the price of 2.*

Unit General P Leisure Shop 0.5 miles
Pub 0.5 miles

MODBURY, Devon Map ref 1C3

★★★★
SELF CATERING

Units **4**
Sleeps **2–6**
Low season per wk
£210.00–£305.00
High season per wk
£415.00–£610.00

Oldaport Farm Cottages, Ivybridge

contact Miss C M Evans, Oldaport Farm Cottages, Modbury, Nr Ivybridge PL21 0TG
t (01548) 830842 **f** (01548) 830998 **e** cathy@oldaport.com **w** oldaport.com

Comfortable cottages converted from redundant stone barns sited on historic, working sheep farm in beautiful South Hams valley.

open All year
payment Cash/cheques

Unit General

MOORSHOP, Devon Map ref 1C2

★★★
SELF CATERING

Units **2**
Sleeps **1–4**
Low season per wk
£150.00–£250.00
High season per wk
£220.00–£400.00

Higher Longford, Tavistock

Higher Longford, Tavistock PL19 9LQ
t (01822) 613360 **f** (01822) 618722 **e** stay@higherlongford.co.uk **w** higherlongford.co.uk

Excellently presented, comfortable, stone-built cottages with all the comforts from home, set within the Dartmoor National Park. Ideal for touring Devon and Cornwall.

open All year
payment Credit/debit cards, cash/cheques

Unit General P Leisure **Shop** < 0.5 miles **Pub** 1 mile

MORCOMBELAKE, Dorset Map ref 1D2

★★★
SELF CATERING

Units **1**
Sleeps **7**
Low season per wk
Min £295.00
High season per wk
Min £595.00

Norchard Farmhouse, Bridport

contact Mrs Mary Ollard, Norchard Farmhouse, Norchard Barn, Morcombelake, Bridport DT6 6EP
t (01297) 489263 **e** norchardbarn@btinternet.com

Converted barn in beautiful west Dorset. Half a mile from the coast. Comfortable, spacious and isolated. Closed January.

payment Credit/debit cards, cash/cheques

Unit General 2 P Leisure **Shop** 1 mile **Pub** 2 miles

MORETONHAMPSTEAD, Devon Map ref 1C2

★★–★★★
SELF CATERING

Units **7**
Sleeps **2–6**
Low season per wk
Min £145.00
High season per wk
Max £495.00

Budleigh Farm, Moretonhampstead

contact Mrs Judith Harvey, Budleigh Farm, Moretonhampstead TQ13 8SB
t (01647) 440835 **f** (01647) 440436 **e** harvey@budleighfarm.co.uk **w** budleighfarm.co.uk

open All year
payment Credit/debit cards, cash/cheques

Properties created with flair from granite barns, on a farm at the end of a stunning valley – rural but not remote. Easy to find. Superb gardens, pubs of character, beaches and castles are all accessible. Superb walking country. In Dartmoor National Park.

⊕ *From M5, A38 towards Plymouth. Right onto A382 (Bovey Tracey and Moretonhampstead). Farm is 0.5 miles from Moretonhampstead, in the direction of Bovey Tracey.*

Unit General P Leisure **Shop** 0.5 miles **Pub** 0.5 miles

MORETON-IN-MARSH, Gloucestershire Map ref 2B1

★★★
SELF CATERING

Units **1**
Sleeps **1–4**
Low season per wk
£230.00–£295.00
High season per wk
£295.00–£380.00

Little Pinners, Moreton-in-Marsh

contact Mrs Mariam Gilbert, Country House Interiors, High Street, Moreton-in-Marsh GL56 0AT
t (01608) 650007 **f** (01608) 650007

A 200-year-old Cotswold-stone cottage with double and twin bedrooms and a beautiful garden. In a quiet location but within walking distance of all town facilities.

open All year
payment Cash/cheques

Unit General P Leisure **Shop** < 0.5 miles **Pub** < 0.5 miles

Rest assured

All accommodation in this guide has been rated, or is awaiting assessment, by a professional assessor.

MOTHECOMBE, Devon Map ref 1C3

★★★★–★★★★★
SELF CATERING

Units **7**
Sleeps **5–12**
Low season per wk
£530.00–£965.00
High season per wk
£1,290.00–£1,975.00

The Flete Estate Holiday Cottages, Plymouth

contact Miss Josephine Webb, The Flete Estate Holiday Cottages, Pamflete, Plymouth PL8 1JR
t (01752) 830234 **f** (01752) 830513 **e** cottages@flete.co.uk **w** flete.co.uk

open All year
payment Cash/cheques

The Flete Estate is undoubtedly the Jewel in the Crown of the beautiful South Hams. This private, 5,000-acre estate is designated an Area of Outstanding Natural Beauty, encompassing large, broadleaf woodlands, rolling pastures, cliff paths and sandy beaches, secluded cottages, little hamlets and a tantalising lacework of private drives and pathways.

⊕ *From M5 jct 31, A38 left to Ermington on A3121, right to A379. One mile left to Mothecombe, follow road for 3 miles.*

♥ *Winter breaks Nov-Mar (excl Christmas and New Year) from £150pn, minimum 3 nights.*

Unit **General** P **Leisure** **Shop** 1 mile **Pub** 1 mile

MOUSEHOLE, Cornwall Map ref 1A3

★★★
SELF CATERING

Units **1**
Sleeps **4**
Low season per wk
£300.00–£400.00
High season per wk
£450.00–£550.00

Penzer Cottage, Mousehole

contact Mrs MacDonald, Penzer Cottage, 1 Franklyn Crescent, Windsor SL4 4YT
t (01753) 854395 & 07769 741018 **e** info@penzercottage.co.uk **w** penzercottage.co.uk

open All year
payment Cash/cheques

Penzer Cottage is a delightful Cornish cottage 75yds from Mousehole Harbour with double and twin bedrooms, bathroom, downstairs shower/toilet/utility, kitchen/diner/lounge (with woodburner) and courtyard with barbecue. Bed linen, towels, electricity and welcome pack of cream tea/wine are included in the price. Book early for 2007 to avoid disappointment.

⊕ *Follow A30 to Land's End, then Mousehole. At Mousehole pull in beyond the Harbour Mouth Cafe. Walk between the two cottages opposite The British Legion. Cottage on left.*

Unit **General** **Shop** < 0.5 miles **Pub** < 0.5 miles

MYLOR CHURCHTOWN, Cornwall Map ref 1B3

★★★★
SELF CATERING

Units **1**
Sleeps **8**
Low season per wk
£515.00–£700.00
High season per wk
£800.00–£1,090.00

Penarrow Cottage, Falmouth

contact Mrs Penelope Warner, 54 Lemon Street, Truro TR1 2PE
t (01872) 270199 **f** (01872) 277267 **e** lemonstreetlady@aol.com

Lovely well-equipped waterside cottage in private gardens. Ample parking. Children and dogs welcome. The harbour, with restaurants, cafe/grocery, boat hire and sailing schools, is 150yds away.

open All year
payment Cash/cheques

Unit **General** P **Leisure** **Shop** < 0.5 miles **Pub** 3 miles

Check it out

Information on accommodation listed in this guide has been supplied by proprietors. As changes may occur you should remember to check all relevant details at the time of booking.

NEW POLZEATH, Cornwall Map ref 1B2

★★★
SELF CATERING

Units 1
Sleeps 6
Low season per wk
£350.00–£450.00
High season per wk
£580.00–£730.00

Treheather, Wadebridge

contact Dr Elizabeth Mayall, Osmond House, Chestnut Crescent, Exeter EX5 4AA
t (01392) 841219

Spacious, modern bungalow. About 200yds from sandy surfing beach with rock pools. Garden, coastal walks. Open March to November. One double bedroom, one twin with 3ft beds, one twin with 2ft6in beds.

payment Cash/cheques

Unit General P Leisure Shop 0.5 miles

NEWQUAY, Cornwall Map ref 1B2

★★★★
SELF CATERING

Units 4
Sleeps 2–8
Low season per wk
£190.00–£720.00
High season per wk
£360.00–£1,195.00

Cheviot Holiday Apartments, Newquay

contact Mr & Mrs Brian & Jill Biscard, 26 Chyverton Close, Newquay TR7 2AR
t (01637) 872712 **f** (01637) 872712 **e** info@cheviotnewquay.co.uk **w** cheviotnewquay.co.uk

The Cheviot Holiday Apartments are set in their own grounds and are spacious, comfortable, self-contained and of a good quality.

open All year
payment Credit/debit cards, cash/cheques

Unit General P Leisure Shop < 0.5 miles
Pub < 0.5 miles

NEWQUAY, Cornwall Map ref 1B2

SELF CATERING

Units 4
Sleeps 2–6
Low season per wk
£300.00–£495.00
High season per wk
£795.00–£1,185.00

Cornwall Coast Holidays, Newquay

contact Mrs Deborah Spencer-Smith, Cornwall Coast Holidays
t (020) 8440 7518 & 07910 583050 **e** debbie@cornwallcoastholidays.com
w cornwallcoastholidays.com

open All year
payment Cash/cheques

Cornwall Coast Holidays offer apartments and cottages that are in the perfect location for wonderful beach holidays. The cottages are modern, and the apartments have stunning sea views. Both apartments and cottages have one en suite bathroom and are close to the town centre, golf course and other amenities.

Unit General P

Our quality rating schemes

For a detailed explanation of the quality and facilities represented by the stars please refer to the information pages at the back of this guide.

NEWQUAY, Cornwall Map ref 1B2

★★
SELF CATERING

Units **9**
Sleeps **2–6**
Low season per wk
£150.00–£250.00
High season per wk
£320.00–£750.00

Croftlea Holiday Flats, Newquay

Croftlea Holiday Flats, Wildflower Lane, Newquay TR7 2QB
t (01637) 852505 **f** (01637) 877183 **e** info@croftlea.co.uk **w** croftlea.co.uk

open All year
payment Credit/debit cards, cash/cheques, euros

Croftlea Holiday Flats are fully self-contained and are ideally situated close to beaches, shops, station, leisure and sports facilities. Croftlea overlooks Trenance Leisure Park with zoo, tennis courts, bowls, boating, crazy golf and skateboarding. The property stands in its own grounds with swimming pool, barbecue area, gardens and ample car parking.

⊕ *From A30 leave on A392 for Newquay. Turn right at roundabout by boating lake and keep lake on your left. Pass under viaduct. Croftlea is 1st house on right.*

❤ *Short breaks available Oct-Mar, 3 nights min.*

Unit General Leisure **Shop** 0.5 miles **Pub** < 0.5 miles

NEWQUAY, Cornwall Map ref 1B2

★★★★
SELF CATERING

Units **2**
Sleeps **2**
Low season per wk
£240.00
High season per wk
£240.00–£610.00

Degembris Cottage, Nr Newquay

contact Mrs Kathy Woodley, St Newlyn East, Newquay TR8 5HY
t (01872) 510555 **f** (01872) 510230 **e** kathy@degembris.co.uk **w** degembris.co.uk

open All year
payment Credit/debit cards, cash/cheques

Self-catering cottages situated in the heart of Cornwall, providing an ideal base from which to explore the whole of the county. Individual design and extensive use of natural wood and carefully chosen furnishings create a warm, homely atmosphere. The views from the french windows stretch for several miles, enabling nature to boast its glory!

⊕ *A30 to Summercourt village. At traffic lights turn right (A3058) to Newquay. 3rd left to Newlyn East. 2nd left signposted Degembris Major Farm.*

❤ *3-night short breaks Nov-Mar.*

Unit General **Shop** 2 miles **Pub** 2 miles

NEWQUAY, Cornwall Map ref 1B2

★★★
SELF CATERING

Units **4**
Sleeps **2–8**
Low season per wk
£180.00–£600.00
High season per wk
£600.00–£950.00

Eton Court, Newquay

contact Mr Allan O'Dell, 2 Playingfield Lane, Newquay TR7 2DB
t (01637) 852545 **e** fiona@holidaysinnewquay.com **w** holidaysinnewquay.com

open All year
payment Credit/debit cards, cash/cheques, euros

Luxury two-bedroom apartment and three-bedroom penthouses with superb sea views. Fully fitted kitchen, two bathrooms, lounges with balconies, TV, Freeview, DVD, radio/cassette/CD player. Fully equipped. Internet room and laundry room. Five minutes' walk to town and beaches.

⊕ *A392 to Newquay, follow signs for Newquay town centre. Top of Gannel Road, right at roundabout onto Mount Wise. Eton Court on right 100 yds from traffic lights.*

❤ *Short breaks available. Special rates low and mid season (excl Christmas and New Year).*

Unit General Leisure
Shop < 0.5 miles **Pub** < 0.5 miles

NEWQUAY, Cornwall Map ref 1B2

★★★★
SELF CATERING

Units **3**
Sleeps **1–6**
Low season per wk
£300.00–£450.00
High season per wk
£570.00–£960.00

Tregurrian Villas, Newquay

Tregurrian Villas, Watergate Bay, Newquay TR8 4AB
t (01637) 873274 **f** (01637) 879572 **e** enquiries@tregurrianhotel.com **w** tegurrianhotel.com

Superb villas just 100yds from beach, four miles from Newquay. Access to hotel amenities (same ownership), including bar, restaurant and pool, 50yds away.

open All year
payment Credit/debit cards, cash/cheques, euros

Unit TV General P S Leisure

NORTH MOLTON, Devon Map ref 1C1

★★–★★★
SELF CATERING

Units **3**
Sleeps **2–8**
Low season per wk
Min £90.00
High season per wk
Max £420.00

West Millbrook Farm, South Molton

contact Mrs Rosemarie Courtney, West Millbrook Farm, West Millbrook, Twitchen, South Molton EX36 3LP
t (01598) 740382 **e** wmbselfcatering@aol.com **w** westmillbrook.co.uk

open All year
payment Cash/cheques

Farm bordering Exmoor, surrounded by pleasant gardens and beautiful, peaceful countryside. Situated a mile from North Molton village with easy access from North Devon link road. Ideal for touring Exmoor and North Devon/Somerset coast and beaches. Games room, play area. Out-of-season short breaks. Colour brochure available.

⊕ *A361 towards Barnstaple, leave at North Molton junction. Through village, over bridge, up hill to Y-junction, right fork. West Millbrook approx 0.5 miles on right.*

Unit TV General P Leisure

NORTHLEACH, Gloucestershire Map ref 2B1

★★★
SELF CATERING

Units **1**
Sleeps **4**
Low season per wk
Min £200.00
High season per wk
Max £433.00

Cotteswold Cottage, Northleach, Cheltenham

contact Mr David Atkinson, Cotteswold House B&b, Market Place, Northleach, Cheltenham GL54 3EG
t (01451) 860493 **f** (01451) 860493 **e** cotteswoldhouse@aol.com

Small stone cottage attached to Grade II Listed B&B. Beautifully furnished. Stone floor with underfloor heating. Double and twin bedroom, each with shower room. Pubs and shops within easy walking distance.

open All year
payment Credit/debit cards

Unit TV General 10 Shop < 0.5 miles Pub < 0.5 miles

NYMPSFIELD, Gloucestershire Map ref 2B1

★★★
SELF CATERING

Units **1**
Sleeps **1–4**
Low season per wk
£150.00
High season per wk
£170.00

Crossways, Stonehouse

contact Mr & Mrs Bowen, Crossways, Tinkley Lane, Stonehouse GL10 3TU
t (01453) 860309

Annexe to house, large living room, french window onto garden, fitted kitchen/diner. Twin-bedded room, bathroom. Own entrance. Fully self-contained. Private garden. Adjacent to the Cotswold Way.

open All year except Christmas and New Year
payment Cash/cheques

Unit TV General P Leisure Shop 2 miles Pub < 0.5 miles

To your credit

If you book by credit card it's advisable to check the proprietor's policy in case you have to cancel.

OKEHAMPTON, Devon Map ref 1C2

★★★★
SELF CATERING

Units **4**
Sleeps **4–6**
Low season per wk
£190.00–£360.00
High season per wk
£370.00–£650.00

Beer Farm, Okehampton

contact Bob & Sue Annear, Beer Farm, Okehampton EX20 1SG
t (01837) 840265 **f** (01837) 840245 **e** info@beerfarm.co.uk **w** beerfarm.co.uk

open All year
payment Cash/cheques

Enjoy a peaceful holiday on our small farm situated on the northern edge of Dartmoor in mid-Devon. Comfortable and well-equipped two- and three-bedroomed cottages with DVDs and CD players. One offers accessibility for the less mobile. Games room, some covered parking. Dogs/horses by arrangement. Good walking, cycling and touring base.

⊕ *A30 towards Okehampton. Leave at Sticklepath, Belstone junction. Take old A30 towards Sticklepath. Left at Tongue End crossroads. Right to Taw Green. After 800yds, Beer Farm on left.*

❤ *5% discount on second (lower price) cottage if booked together. Short breaks often available (minimum 3 nights).*

Unit General Leisure Shop 1 mile
Pub 1.5 miles

OKEHAMPTON, Devon Map ref 1C2

★★★★
SELF CATERING

Units **3**
Sleeps **2–9**
Low season per wk
Min £195.00
High season per wk
Max £995.00

Bowerland, Okehampton

contact Mr Ray Quirke, East Bowerland Farm, Okehampton EX20 4LZ
t (01837) 55979 **e** bowerland@devonhols.com **w** devonhols.com

payment Credit/debit cards, cash/cheques

Bowerland is an ancient farmhouse and courtyard conversion on Dartmoor's doorstep. Ideally situated for a relaxing holiday in beautiful countryside but within easy reach of the many attractions of Devon and Cornwall. Good local food, superb walking, fishing, golf, cycling, tennis etc.

⊕ *For simple directions please refer to our website, or ring us on our local-call line: 0845 225 5608.*

❤ *Short breaks available out of high season.*

Unit General Leisure Shop 1 mile

OKEHAMPTON, Devon Map ref 1C2

★★★★
SELF CATERING

Units **4**
Sleeps **4–8**
Low season per wk
£300.00–£460.00
High season per wk
£360.00–£920.00

Week Farm Country Holidays, Okehampton

contact Mrs Margaret Hockridge, Week Farm Country Holidays, Bridestowe, Okehampton EX20 4HZ
t (01837) 861221 **f** (01837) 861221 **e** accom@weekfarmonline.com **w** weekfarmonline.com

open All year
payment Credit/debit cards, cash/cheques

Delightful barn conversions on working sheep farm, furnished to high standards. Lounge, well-equipped fitted kitchens/dining areas, outdoor heated swimming pool, gardens and patio, barbecue areas. Dartmoor just a walk away. Pony-trekking, walking, cycling, fishing or just simply relaxing. Home from home. Three coarse-fishing lakes.

⊕ *Pass Okehampton. Leave A30 Sourton Cross. Follow signs towards Bridestowe. Tescott Way and Week, turn right. End of three-lane traffic, follow signs to Week.*

❤ *Fishing weekends based on 3 well-stocked coarse-fishing lakes.*

Unit General Leisure
Shop 1.25 miles Pub 1.25 miles

OTTERFORD, Somerset Map ref 1D2

★★★★
SELF CATERING

Units **1**
Sleeps **1–11**
Low season per wk
£195.00–£405.00
High season per wk
£550.00–£705.00

Tamarack Lodge, Chard

contact Matthew Sparks, Tamarack Lodge, Fyfett Farm, Chard TA20 3QP
t (01823) 601270 **e** matthew.sparks@tamaracklodge.co.uk **w** tamaracklodge.co.uk

open All year
payment Cash/cheques

Luxurious log cabin-style ranch house on beautiful Blackdown Hills of Somerset. As seen on TV and in Daily Telegraph article. Suitable for disabled. Stabling available. Situated on organic family livestock farm. Two wildlife sites. Coast 35 minutes away.

⊕ *B3170 to Corfe. Pass through Corfe, travel up hill for 3 miles. At top of hill, pass over crossroads and take 2nd left to Fyfett Farm.*

Unit **General** **Leisure** **Shop** 1 mile **Pub** 0.5 miles

PADSTOW, Cornwall Map ref 1B2

★★★
SELF CATERING

Units **1**
Sleeps **1–5**
Low season per wk
£200.00–£250.00
High season per wk
£300.00–£460.00

34 Sarah's View, Padstow

contact Mrs Margaret Thomas, 31 Dennis Road, Padstow PL28 8DF
t (01841) 532243

Modern, well-equipped cottage on edge of town (Tesco nearby). Owner supervised. Close to Camel Trail, lovely coastal walks. Off-street parking.

open All year except Christmas
payment Cash/cheques

Unit **General** 3 **Leisure** **Shop** < 0.5 miles **Pub** 0.5 miles

PADSTOW, Cornwall Map ref 1B2

★★–★★★
SELF CATERING

Units **1**
Sleeps **5**
Low season per wk
£250.00–£300.00
High season per wk
£500.00–£750.00

Bloomfield, Trevone, Padstow

t (01841) 533804 **f** (01841) 533804 **e** garsladeguest@btconnect.com **w** bloomfieldcottage.com

Bloomfield is a 19thC cottage situated in the heart of Trevone, with the post office and shop just down the road and a farm shop opposite. Beach, with lifeguards, less than a ten-minute walk. Open April to September.

payment Cash/cheques

Unit **General** **Leisure** **Shop** < 0.5 miles **Pub** < 0.5 miles

PADSTOW, Cornwall Map ref 1B2

★★★★
SELF CATERING

Units **1**
Low season per wk
£300.00–£350.00
High season per wk
£400.00–£525.00

Catherine, Padstow

contact Mr & Mrs Lovell, Catherine, 13a Duke Street, Padstow PL28 8AB
t (01841) 533859 **e** bob@padstow.force9.co.uk

Situated minutes from harbour and all amenities. A large, self-contained flat in Padstow town centre with two bedrooms (one large double and one twin). Large, fully equipped kitchen with dining area.

open All year
payment Cash/cheques

Unit **General** **Leisure** **Shop** < 0.5 miles **Pub** < 0.5 miles

What's in a quality rating?

Information about ratings can be found at the back of this guide.

PADSTOW, Cornwall Map ref 1B2

★★★★
SELF CATERING

Units **2**
Sleeps **2–6**
Low season per wk
£250.00–£670.00
High season per wk
£440.00–£850.00

Sunday Cottage & School Cottage, Padstow

contact Mrs Diane Hoe, Lower Cottage, Preston on Stour, Stratford-upon-Avon CV37 8NG
t (01789) 450214 **f** (01789) 450284 **e** mail@sundaycottage.co.uk **w** sundaycottage.co.uk

open All year
payment Cash/cheques

Beautifully restored, tastefully furnished cottages in old part of Padstow. Only three minutes' walk to the delightful harbour. Ideal location for those who appreciate comfort and quality. School Cottage has a lovely private, walled garden. Beautiful unspoilt coastline and beaches all around and many fine restaurants including four Rick Stein establishments.

Unit General 8 **P**

PADSTOW, Cornwall Map ref 1B2

★★★–★★★★
SELF CATERING

Units **6**
Sleeps **1–6**
Low season per wk
£220.00–£320.00
High season per wk
£630.00–£750.00

Yellow Sands Cottages, Padstow

contact Mrs Sharon Keast, Yellow Sands Cottages, Harlyn Bay, Padstow PL28 8SE
t (01637) 881548 **e** yellowsands@btinternet.com **w** yellowsands.co.uk

open All year
payment Cash/cheques

Cottages set in well-kept grounds, ideally situated just 250m to Harlyn's sandy shore and coastal path. Local amenities and eating houses within one mile, Padstow 2.5 miles. The cottages are fully equipped and furnished, and serviced to a high standard, providing an environment in which to sit back, relax and enjoy!

Unit General **P** Shop 1 mile Pub 0.5 miles

PAIGNTON, Devon Map ref 1D2

★★★
SELF CATERING

Units **9**
Sleeps **1–6**
Low season per wk
£90.00–£180.00
High season per wk
£200.00–£385.00

Hudson's Bay, Paignton

contact Mr & Mrs J & T Somers, 12 Adelphi Road, Paignton TQ4 6AW
t (01803) 664455 **f** (0116) 257 1740 **e** jsomer8@aol.com

Superb level location, close to beaches, shops and attractions. Train and coach stations five minutes' walk. Parking. Ground-floor apartments.

open All year
payment Cash/cheques

Unit General **P**

Check the maps

Colour maps at the front pinpoint all the places you will find accommodation entries in the regional sections. Pick your location and then refer to the place index at the back to find the page number.

PAIGNTON, Devon Map ref 1D2

★★★
SELF CATERING

Units **10**
Sleeps **2–8**
Low season per wk
£150.00–£250.00
High season per wk
£300.00–£495.00

Julie Court Holiday Apartments, Paignton

Julie Court Holiday Apartments, 5 Colin Road, Preston, Paignton TQ3 2NR
t (01803) 551012 **e** info@juliecourt.co.uk **w** juliecourt.co.uk

open All year
payment Credit/debit cards, cash/cheques

Finalist for the English Riviera Best Self-catering award for last two years. Regularly quoted by our guests as 'Best in Paignton' and 'Great for location'. Seafront location, close to all beaches, attractions, piers, cinema, coastal walks and local amenities. Quality self-catering apartments with private car park, situated on a level and quiet cul-de-sac.

⊕ *From Exeter take A380 to Torquay, then A3022 to Paignton seafront via Torquay seafront. On passing under the railway bridge, Colin Road is 2nd right off Marine Drive.*

♥ *3-night stays available Oct-Jan (excl Christmas and New Year).*

Unit General P Leisure Shop < 0.5 miles
Pub < 0.5 miles

PAIGNTON, Devon Map ref 1D2

★★★★
SELF CATERING

Units **7**
Sleeps **2–12**
Low season per wk
£190.00–£280.00
High season per wk
£315.00–£1,590.00

Newbarn Farm Cottages and Angling Centre, Paignton

contact Catherine Soley, Newbarn Farm Cottages and Angling Centre, Totnes Road, Collaton St Mary, Paignton TQ4 7PT
t (01803) 553602 **f** (01803) 553603 **e** swt@newbarnfarm.com **w** newbarnfarm.com

open All year
payment Credit/debit cards, cash/cheques

A selection of well-equipped, self-catering cottages set in 40 acres of pasture and woodland. Magnificent hill-top views of Dartmoor and the South Hams. Peaceful and tranquil, with on-site fishing lakes. Close to Paignton, Totnes and Torquay. Many places of interest within easy reach. Beach 2.5 miles.

⊕ *A38 southbound, take the A385 (signposted Totnes). Pass Totnes and head towards Paignton. Newbarn Farm is on the right 3 miles from Totnes.*

♥ *Short breaks available Oct-Apr – 3-, 4-, and 5-night stays.*

Unit General P Leisure Shop 1.5 miles
Pub 0.5 miles

PANCRASWEEK, Devon Map ref 1C2

★★★
SELF CATERING

Units **1**
Sleeps **7**
Low season per wk
Min £265.00
High season per wk
Max £560.00

Tamarstone Farm, Holsworthy

contact Mrs Megan Daglish, Tamarstone Farm, Bude Road, Pancrasweek, Holsworthy EX22 7JT
t (01288) 381734 **e** cottage@tamarstone.co.uk **w** tamarstone.co.uk

Tastefully extended, centrally heated, three-bedroomed cob cottage. Peacefully situated on the Devon/Cornwall borders, ideal for touring both counties. One double, one twin, one with bunks and a single.

open All year
payment Cash/cheques

Unit General P Leisure Shop 1.25 miles
Pub 1.25 miles

Rest assured

All accommodation in this guide has been rated, or is awaiting assessment, by a professional assessor.

PARRACOMBE, Devon Map ref 1C1

★★★★
SELF CATERING

Units **3**
Sleeps **1–2**
Low season per wk
£225.00–£300.00
High season per wk
£365.00–£440.00

Martinhoe Cleave Cottages, Parracombe, Barnstaple

contact Mr & Mrs R M J Deville, Parracombe, Barnstaple EX31 4PZ
t (01598) 763313 **e** info@exmoorhideaway.co.uk **w** exmoorhideaway.co.uk

Delightful cottages within the Exmoor National Park and adjoining the South West Coast Path. Of the highest standard throughout, with many extras included. Dogs welcome at no additional cost.

open All year
payment Cash/cheques

Unit General **P** Leisure Shop 7 miles Pub 1 mile

PENDOGGETT, Cornwall Map ref 1B2

★★★★★
SELF CATERING

Units **1**
Sleeps **6**
Low season per wk
£300.00–£500.00
High season per wk
£750.00–£900.00

Mays Cottage, Bodmin

contact Mrs Julia Payne, Manor Farm, Taunton TA4 1DL
t (01823) 432615 **f** (01823) 432615 **e** enquiries@scarletgreen.com **w** scarletgreen.com

Traditional cottage with large, sunny garden set in stunning open country but ten minutes from the surf at Polzeath. Beautifully furnished and comprehensively equipped. Double, twin and bunks. Secure parking.

open All year
payment Cash/cheques

Unit General 5 **P** Shop 3 miles Pub 3 miles

PENRYN, Cornwall Map ref 1B3

★★★
SELF CATERING

Units **1**
Sleeps **2**
Low season per wk
£216.00–£280.00
High season per wk
£320.00–£440.00

Bell Cottage, Penryn

contact Mrs Penny Snow, Bell Cottage, Kernick Park, Penryn TR10 9DG
t (01326) 376466 **e** alpensnow@btinternet.com **w** bellcottagecornwall.co.uk

Pretty character cottage in quiet courtyard and parkland setting, three miles from Falmouth. Spacious, comfortable and well furnished. Double bedroom, all inclusive. Sunny garden, parking, shops nearby. Illustrated brochure.

open All year
payment Cash/cheques

Unit General **P** Leisure Shop 0.5 miles Pub 1 mile

PENZANCE, Cornwall Map ref 1A3

★★★
SELF CATERING

Units **1**
Sleeps **2–4**
Low season per wk
£155.00–£200.00
High season per wk
£200.00–£300.00

Crankan Flat, Penzance

contact Mr & Mrs Braybrooks, Crankan Flat, Crankan, Bone Valley TR20 8UJ
t (01736) 351388

Peaceful three-roomed ground-floor flat in quiet gardens. Heamoor village is 0.25 miles distant, with shops, bakery, pub and post office. Excellent centre for sandy beaches, good walks and rugged coast.

open All year
payment Cash/cheques

Unit General **P** Leisure Shop < 0.5 miles Pub < 0.5 miles

PENZANCE, Cornwall Map ref 1A3

★★★
SELF CATERING

Units **2**
Sleeps **3–8**
Low season per wk
£200.00–£300.00
High season per wk
£350.00–£450.00

Rospannel Farm, Penzance

contact Mr Hocking, Rospannel Farm, Crows-An-Wra, Penzance TR19 6HS
t (01736) 810262 **e** gbernard@v21.me.uk **w** rospannel.com

Old-fashioned, very quiet and peaceful farm. Own pool and hide for bird-watchers. Moth light for insect enthusiasts. Badgers, foxes and lots of wildlife.

open All year
payment Cash/cheques

Unit General

PERRANPORTH, Cornwall Map ref 1B2

★★★★★
SELF CATERING

Units **1**
Sleeps **8**
Low season per wk
£495.00–£795.00
High season per wk
£995.00–£1,295.00

2 Lower Hill Crest, Perranporth

contact Mike & Jo Williams, Goonpiper Lodge, Feock TR3 6RA
t (01872) 862573 **e** fiveatuplands@aol.co.uk

open All year
payment Credit/debit cards, cash/cheques

Brand new, purpose-built, four-bedroom detached house within walking distance of beach and shops, and 100m from park (football pitch, play area, tennis court). Two bathrooms, large open-plan kitchen/diner and separate spacious, comfortable living room. Very large patio area. Parking for three cars.

⊕ *B3284: Proceed down Liskey Hill. At bottom, go straight on, across small bridge. Left up St Georges Hill. Lower Hill Crest on left after park.*

♥ *Short breaks available in low season.*

Unit General Leisure Shop < 0.5 miles
Pub < 0.5 miles

PERRANPORTH, Cornwall Map ref 1B2

★★★★
SELF CATERING

Units **1**
Sleeps **1–6**
Low season per wk
£250.00–£475.00
High season per wk
£475.00–£650.00

Treth Cottage, Perranporth

contact Mr & Mrs John & Jenny Cuthill, Claremont, St Georges Hill, Perranporth TR6 0JS
t (01872) 573624

Early-Victorian cottage in a quiet, private location with a sheltered garden, 150m from a sandy surfing beach. Close to all amenities. Parking.

open All year
payment Cash/cheques

Unit General Leisure Shop < 0.5 miles Pub < 0.5 miles

PLYMOUTH, Devon Map ref 1C2

SELF CATERING

Units **3**
Sleeps **1–6**
Low season per wk
£225.00–£695.00
High season per wk
£245.00–£750.00

Carsons Plymouth Hoe Holiday Apartments, Plymouth

contact Mr Sean Carson, Carsons Plymouth Hoe Holiday Apartments, 5 Regent Street, Plymouth PL4 8BA
t (01752) 254425 **e** sajrcarson@aol.com **w** plymouth-hoe-apartments.co.uk

Superb self-contained apartments within walking distance of the seafront and city centre. Parking. Please take a look at our website.

open All year
payment Cash/cheques, euros

Unit General Shop < 0.5 miles Pub < 0.5 miles

Out and about

For ideas on places to visit see the beginning of this regional section or go online at enjoyengland.com.

PLYMOUTH, Devon Map ref 1C2

★★★★
SELF CATERING

Units **5**
Sleeps **1–6**
Low season per wk
£225.00–£305.00
High season per wk
£265.00–£325.00

Haddington House Apartments, Plymouth

contact Mr Fairfax Luxmoore, 42 Haddington Road, Plymouth PL2 1RR
t (01752) 500383 **w** abudd.co.uk

Elegant, self-contained apartments set within a large Victorian house, offering well-appointed modern facilities, tasteful decoration and furnishings. Complimentary pick-up service at Plymouth stations, secure parking, courtyard gardens.

open All year
payment Cash/cheques

Unit General Leisure

POLPERRO, Cornwall Map ref 1C3

★★★–★★★★
SELF CATERING

Units **7**
Sleeps **1–5**
Low season per wk
£185.00–£245.00
High season per wk
£355.00–£630.00

Crumplehorn Cottages, Looe

contact Mr & Mrs Collings, Crumplehorn Cottages, c/o The Anchorage, Portuan Road PL13 2DN
t (01503) 262523 **f** (01503) 262523 **e** enquiries@crumplehorncottages.co.uk
w crumplehorncottages.co.uk

open All year
payment Cash/cheques

Individual Cornish cottages with lots of charm, situated in the beautiful coastal resorts of Polperro and Looe. Just minutes from the harbour, safe sandy beaches and spectacular coastal paths.

⊕ *Head towards Plymouth, Tamar toll bridge. Follow the A38 to Looe. Continue across Looe bridge to West Looe, or on to Polperro.*

♥ *3-day breaks Nov-Mar: £135 for 2 people (excl Christmas and New Year).*

Unit General Leisure

POLZEATH, Cornwall Map ref 1B2

★★
SELF CATERING

Units **1**
Sleeps **8**
Low season per wk
£250.00–£375.00
High season per wk
£500.00–£825.00

Polmeor & Trehenlie, Polzeath

contact Mrs Angwin, Polmeor & Trehenlie, Lower Boscarne, Nanstallon PL30 5LG
t (01208) 72684 & (01208) 75243 **e** steve@angwin.fsnet.co.uk

A very comfortable house equipped to a high standard. Double bedrooms with hot and cold, two bathrooms and shower. Washing machine, tumble dryer, dishwasher, microwave, heaters, TV, telephone. Beach two minutes.

open All year
payment Cash/cheques

Unit General P Leisure Shop < 0.5 miles Pub 0.5 miles

POLZEATH, Cornwall Map ref 1B2

★★★
SELF CATERING

Units **1**
Sleeps **2–8**
Low season per wk
Min £250.00
High season per wk
Max £800.00

Trehenlie, Polzeath, Wadebridge

contact Mrs Julie Angwin, Sunrise, Lower Boscarne, Nanstallon, Bodmin PL30 5LG
t (01208) 75243 **f** (01208) 75243 **e** steve@angwin.fsnet.co.uk

Spacious, detached bungalow, excellently furnished and equipped. Central heating. Minutes from local amenities and wonderful surfing. Beach perfect for children. Glorious coastal walks, golf, tennis, riding. Quiet location.

open All year
payment Cash/cheques

Unit General P Leisure Shop < 0.5 miles
Pub < 0.5 miles

POOLE, Dorset Map ref 2B3

★★★★★
SELF CATERING

Units **1**
Sleeps **1–5**
Low season per wk
Min £475.00
High season per wk
Max £850.00

Dolphin Quays, Poole

contact Mrs Helen Challis, West End House, 2 St James Close, Poole BH15 1JL
t (01202) 649228 & 07867 786872 **f** (01202) 649228 **e** dolphin.quays@btinternet.com

open All year
payment Credit/debit cards, cash/cheques

Spacious and luxurious two-bedroom, two-bathroom apartment located on Poole Quay. Two balconies with oblique harbour views. Comprehensively equipped including Sky, plasma, DVD/CD. Secure parking. All linen and beach towels included. Ferries from Poole Quay to Brownsea Island, Sandbanks and beyond. Fishing trips. Quayside seasonal leisure activities. Beaches are a 15-minute drive.

❤ *Flexible dates and rates available.*

Unit General Leisure Shop < 0.5 miles Pub < 0.5 miles

POOLE, Dorset Map ref 2B3

★★★★★
SELF CATERING

Units **10**
Sleeps **2–8**
Low season per wk
£345.00–£550.00
High season per wk
£725.00–£1,140.00

The Dorset Resort, Hyde, Wareham

contact Miss Jackie Langworthy, The Dorset Resort, Hyde, Wareham BH20 7NT
t (01929) 472244 **f** (01929) 471294 **e** resort@dorsetresort.com **w** dorsetresort.com

open All year
payment Credit/debit cards, cash/cheques

The Scandinavian-style log homes at the Dorset Resort are both beautiful and luxurious. Superbly well crafted, they are set in tranquil woodland in the heart of Dorset's stunning countryside. Each has its own sauna, log-burning stove and balcony. We are minutes from Blue Flag beaches, Jurassic Coast etc.

⊕ *See website for details.*

❤ *Special offers will appear from time to time on our website.*

Unit General Leisure
Shop 3 miles Pub 3 miles

POOLE, Dorset Map ref 2B3

★★★★
SELF CATERING

Units **1**
Sleeps **4**
Low season per wk
£210.00–£350.00
High season per wk
£350.00–£595.00

Fripps Cottage, Wimborne

contact Mrs Helen Edbrooke, Stoneleigh House, 2 Rowlands Hill, Wimborne BH21 1AN
t (01202) 848312 **f** (01202) 848312 **e** helen@stoneleighhouse.com
w stoneleighhouse.com/frippscottage

Two-bedroom detached bungalow set in five acres in beautiful country location, close to town and coast. Large, enclosed, well-maintained garden. All mod cons, and fully equipped for a very comfortable stay.

open All year
payment Cash/cheques

Unit General Leisure Shop 1.5 miles Pub 1 mile

If you have access needs...

Look for the National Accessible Scheme symbols if you have special hearing, visual or mobility needs. An index of all accommodation participating in the scheme can be found at the back of this guide.

POOLE, Dorset Map ref 2B3

★★
SELF CATERING

Units **2**
Sleeps **6–8**
Low season per wk
£250.00–£420.00
High season per wk
£600.00–£735.00

Harbour Holidays, Poole

contact Mrs Beryl Saunders, Harbour Holidays, 1 Harbour Shallows, 15 Whitecliff Road, Poole BH14 8DU
t (01202) 741637

Bungalow with three bedrooms, wheelchair access, garden and ample parking. Waterside townhouse with three bedrooms, balcony, harbour view, patio, barbecue and ample parking.

open All year
payment Cash/cheques, euros

Unit General P Shop 0.5 miles Pub 0.5 miles

PORLOCK, Somerset Map ref 1D1

★★★★
SELF CATERING

Units **4**
Sleeps **2**
Low season per wk
Min £151.00
High season per wk
Max £433.00

The Ships Mews, Porlock

contact Mr & Mrs Alan & Jacqueline Cottrell, Ship Bungalow, West End, High Street, Porlock TA24 8QD
t 07979 278466 **w** shipsmews.co.uk

Designed to a very high specification, each apartment is fitted with a mini-kitchen, TV/DVD, shower/wc, double bed and quality sofa bed. There is allocated parking and stunning sea views.

open All year
payment Cash/cheques

Unit General P Leisure Shop < 0.5 miles Pub < 0.5 miles

PORT GAVERNE, Cornwall Map ref 1B2

★★★–★★★★
SELF CATERING

Units **10**
Sleeps **2–8**
Low season per wk
£323.00–£515.00
High season per wk
£546.00–£1,124.00

Green Door Cottages, Port Isaac

contact Mrs Ross, Green Door Cottages, Port Isaac PL29 3SQ
t (01208) 880293 **f** (01208) 880151 **e** enquiries@greendoorcottages.co.uk
w greendoorcottages.co.uk

open All year
payment Credit/debit cards, cash/cheques

A delightful collection of restored 18thC Cornish buildings built around a sunny enclosed courtyard and two lovely apartments with stunning sea views. Picturesque, tranquil cove ideal for children. Half a mile from Port Isaac, on the South West Coast Path. Polzeath beach and Camel Trail nearby. Traditional pub opposite. Dogs welcome.

⊕ *From A30 right onto A395 at Kennards House. Right at T-junction with A39. After 1 mile right onto B3314, signposted Boscastle. Two miles after Delabole, right to Port Gaverne.*

♥ *3-night weekend or 4-night mid-week short breaks available Jan-May, Sep-Dec.*

Unit General P Leisure Shop 0.5 miles Pub < 0.5 miles

PORT ISAAC, Cornwall Map ref 1B2

★★★★–★★★★★
SELF CATERING

Units **10**
Sleeps **2–14**
Low season per wk
£100.00–£500.00
High season per wk
£540.00–£1,300.00

Trevathan Farm, Port Isaac

contact Mrs Jo Symons, Trevathan Farm, St Endellion, Port Isaac PL29 3TT
t (01208) 880248 **f** (01208) 880248 **e** symons@trevathanfarm.com **w** trevathanfarm.com

Beautiful cottages with countryside views, games room, fishing lake, tennis court, set on working farm. Beaches, golf, riding within three miles. Also large period house available.

open All year
payment Cash/cheques

Unit General P Leisure Shop 3 miles Pub 2 miles

PORTLAND, Dorset Map ref 2B3

★★★
SELF CATERING

Units **1**
Sleeps **6**
Low season per wk
£200.00–£230.00
High season per wk
£370.00–£420.00

Farion Cottage, Portland

contact Mrs Jenny Greenwood, 7 St Hubert Road, Andover SP10 3QA
t (01264) 394164 **e** jenny.greenwood6@btinternet.com

Three-bedroom, traditional Portland-stone cottage ideally situated on the Jurassic Coast.

open All year
payment Cash/cheques

Unit General Leisure

PORTLAND, Dorset Map ref 2B3

★★★
SELF CATERING

Units **1**
Sleeps **1–4**
Low season per wk
Min £135.00
High season per wk
Max £365.00

Lilac Cottage, Portland

contact Ms Shelagh Hepple, 9 Kestrel Drive, Sandal, Wakefield WF2 6SB
t (01924) 252522 **e** hepple@lilaccott171.fs.co.uk **w** portlandholiday.co.uk

A delightful Victorian terraced cottage with modern amenities but which retains many of its original features. Located in a highly scenic area five minutes from Church Ope Cove.

open All year
payment Cash/cheques

Unit General

PORTREATH, Cornwall Map ref 1B3

★★★★★
SELF CATERING

Units **3**
Sleeps **1–6**
Low season per wk
£220.00–£300.00
High season per wk
£300.00–£700.00

Higher Laity Farm, Redruth

contact Mrs Lynne Drew, Higher Laity Farm, Portreath Road, Redruth TR16 4HY
t (01209) 842317 **f** (01209) 842317 **e** info@higherlaityfarm.co.uk **w** higherlaityfarm.co.uk

open All year
payment Cash/cheques

Come and relax in our tastefully converted luxury barns. En suite bedrooms, central heating, linen provided, gas cooker, fridge/freezer, microwave, dishwasher, washer/dryer, hi-fi, video, DVD. Close to beaches and the breathtaking North Cornish coast. Ideal for walking, relaxing and exploring Cornwall. A friendly welcome is guaranteed. One cottage wheelchair accessible.

⊕ *From M5 take A30 to Redruth/Porthtowan slip road towards Redruth. For full travel directions please contact us directly.*

❤ *Short breaks available Oct-Mar, also discounted rates for couples, out of season.*

Unit General P Leisure Shop 1 mile
Pub 0.5 miles

PORTREATH, Cornwall Map ref 1B3

★★★-★★★★★
SELF CATERING

Units **7**
Sleeps **2–6**
Low season per wk
£200.00–£300.00
High season per wk
£300.00–£720.00

Trengove Farm Cottages, Redruth

contact Mrs Richards, Trengove Farm Cottages, Trengove Farm, Cot Road, Illogan, Redruth TR16 4PU
t (01209) 843008 **f** (01209) 843682 **e** richards@farming.co.uk

open All year
payment Credit/debit cards, cash/cheques, euros

Traditional, well-equipped cottages and farmhouse on a 140-acre arable farm. Close to beautiful beaches, cliffs and countryside park, yet within easy reach of the main towns. Centrally heated, some with wood-burners – ideal for winter breaks. A superb location for walking, swimming, touring or just switching off.

⊕ *Follow signs to Portreath. Turn right, back under dual carriageway, 2nd left. Straight over roundabout, right at T-junction. Left, then right into farm drive after Alexandra Road.*

♥ *Short breaks available from £100 during low season.*

Unit General Leisure Shop 1 mile Pub 1 mile

PUNCKNOWLE, Dorset Map ref 2A3

★★★★-★★★★★
SELF CATERING

Units **2**
Sleeps **11–16**
Low season per wk
£1,000.00–£1,500.00
High season per wk
£1,500.00–£2,200.00

Berwick Manor and Puncknowle Manor Farmhouse, Dorchester

contact Ms Rebecca Hutchings, Puncknowle Manor Cottages, Puncknowle Manor Estate, Puncknowle, Dorchester DT2 9BX
t (01308) 897706 **f** (01308) 898022 **e** cottages@pknlest.com **w** dorset-selfcatering.co.uk

Manor and farmhouse in idyllic position overlooking the peaceful Bride Valley. Just two minutes' drive from the Jurassic Coast. Both are bright, and adaptable for large family holidays.

open All year
payment Cash/cheques

Unit General Leisure

RAME, Cornwall Map ref 1C3

★★★
SELF CATERING

Units **1**
Sleeps **20**
Low season per wk
£6,500.00–£9,645.00
High season per wk
£10,135.00–£18,625.00

Polhawn Fort, Torpoint

contact Miss Kathryn Deakin, Polhawn Fort, Rame, Polhawn, Torpoint PL10 1LL
t (01752) 822864 **f** (01752) 822341 **w** polhawnfort.com

Napoleonic fort for exclusive hire for holidays, parties and weddings – the fort has a civil wedding licence. Prices for shorter stays range from £2,595 for mid-week stays to £6,795 for a summer weekend.

open All year
payment Credit/debit cards, cash/cheques

Unit General Leisure Shop 2 miles
Pub 2 miles

REDRUTH, Cornwall Map ref 1B3

★★★
SELF CATERING

Units **1**
Sleeps **2–6**
Low season per wk
£210.00–£250.00
High season per wk
£350.00–£500.00

The Barn at Little Trefula, Redruth

contact Mr & Mrs Higgins, The Barn at Little Trefula, Little Trefula Farm, Trefula TR16 5ET
t (01209) 820572 **e** barn@trefula.com **w** trefula.com

The Barn at Little Trefula, in Cornwall's historical mining country yet surrounded by fields, is an architect-designed recent conversion offering panoramic views and the perfect base for a peaceful and comfortable family holiday.

open All year
payment Cash/cheques, euros

Unit General Leisure Shop 1 mile Pub < 0.5 miles

REDRUTH, Cornwall Map ref 1B3

★★★★
SELF CATERING

Units **1**
Sleeps **2–3**
Low season per wk
£170.00–£214.00
High season per wk
£236.00–£360.00

The Gables Cottage, Redruth

contact Mrs Shiona King, The Gables Cottage, The Gables, Higher Trevethan TR16 5HJ
t (01209) 822294 **e** enquiries@higher-trevethan.co.uk **w** higher-trevethan.co.uk

open All year
payment Cash/cheques

A peaceful yet central retreat, surrounded by fields, moorland, ancient stone hedges, fresh air and acres of sky. High on Carn Marth, close to historic Gwennap Pit. Cosy, refurbished and homely. One single and one twin/large double. A warm welcome awaits at any time of the year.

⊕ *From A30, take A3047 to Scorrier, then B3298 to Falmouth. Turn right in Carharrack to Gwennap Pit. Left opposite postbox, 1st right, 2nd property along lane.*

Unit General Shop 1 mile Pub 1 mile

REDRUTH, Cornwall Map ref 1B3

★★–★★★
SELF CATERING

Units **2**
Sleeps **4**
Low season per wk
£200.00–£270.00
High season per wk
£300.00–£415.00

Morthana Farm Holidays, Redruth

contact Mrs Pearce, Morthana Farm Holidays, Wheal Rose, Scorrier TR16 5DF
t (01209) 890938 **f** (01209) 890938

Modern, semi-detached cottages. Equipped to a high standard. Suntrap patios and rural views. Friendly animals. Central for all attractions. Beaches nearby. Couples and children welcome. Open May to October.

payment Cash/cheques

Unit General Shop 2 miles Pub 1 mile

ROCK, Cornwall Map ref 1B2

★★★–★★★★★
SELF CATERING

Units **5**
Sleeps **2–6**
Low season per wk
£475.00–£600.00
High season per wk
£900.00–£1,200.00

Mariners Lettings, Rock

contact Miss Claire Tordoff, Mariners Lettings Ltd, 41 Abingdon Road, London W8 6AH
t (020) 7938 2019 **w** marinersrock.com

Luxury self-catering houses with sea views. Two minutes' walk to the beautiful Camel estuary. Fully equipped including bed linen. Dogs welcome.

open All year
payment Credit/debit cards, cash/cheques

Unit General Leisure

RODNEY STOKE, Somerset Map ref 2A2

★★★★
SELF CATERING

Units **1**
Sleeps **4**
Low season per wk
Min £200.00
High season per wk
Min £400.00

Cider Barrel Cottage, Cheddar

contact Mrs Kathy Longhurst, Cider Barrel Cottage, Honeyhurst Farm, Rodney Stoke, Cheddar BS27 3UJ
t (01749) 870322 **e** don@longhurst16.freeserve.co.uk

open All year
payment Cash/cheques, euros

Nestling under the Mendip Hills, amid pastureland with babbling brook, in an idyllic setting. The two-bedroom cottage, formerly a farm store, is set within a 0.5-acre, part-walled garden and four-acre traditional working cider orchard with ample seating for quiet enjoyment. Wells, Cheddar and Glastonbury nearby, Bath 25 miles.

M5 jct 21; A371 towards Wells; through Cheddar. At Red Lion, Draycott, right for Wedmore. Pass village and 2 farms. Left at T-junction. Farm on left.

Unit General Leisure **Shop** 1 mile **Pub** 1 mile

RUAN HIGH LANES, Cornwall Map ref 1B3

★★★
SELF CATERING

Units **1**
Sleeps **2**
Low season per wk
£175.00–£280.00
High season per wk
£300.00–£410.00

The Old Loft, Ruan High Lanes

contact Mrs Delia Collins, The Old Loft, Higher Treluggan, Ruan High Lanes TR2 5LP
t (01872) 580732 **e** dee@roselandrentals.co.uk **w** roselandrentals.co.uk

Coach house, recently converted to a high standard. Slate patio area to front for barbecues, parking space. Located on the beautiful Roseland Peninsula, close to Portscatho, restaurants and pubs.

open All year
payment Cash/cheques

Unit General 1 P **Shop** 1.5 miles **Pub** 1.5 miles

ST AGNES, Cornwall Map ref 1B3

★★★★★
SELF CATERING

Units **1**
Sleeps **1–5**
Low season per wk
£295.00–£395.00
High season per wk
£450.00–£825.00

The Owl House, St Agnes

contact Ms Hicks, The Owl House, Chy Ser Rosow, Barkla Shop, St Agnes TR5 0XN
t (01872) 553644 **e** enquiries@the-owl-house.co.uk **w** the-owl-house.co.uk

open All year
payment Credit/debit cards, cash/cheques

Spacious detached cottage enjoying the seclusion of woodland with meandering stream. Superbly equipped and with its own private patio, The Owl House is a luxurious base from which to explore Cornwall, with many walks from the doorstep. The lovely village of St Agnes is less than one mile away. Brochure available.

See website for map.

Short breaks available in low season from £195.

Unit General P Leisure **Shop** 1 mile **Pub** 0.5 miles

Ancient and modern

Experience timeless favourites or discover the latest must-sees. Whatever your choice, be inspired by the places of interest highlighted for each region and the events listed towards the back of this guide.

ST AUSTELL, Cornwall Map ref 1B3

★★★–★★★★★
SELF CATERING

Units **19**
Sleeps **3–12**
Low season per wk
£275.00–£900.00
High season per wk
£600.00–£2,000.00

Bosinver Farm Cottages, St Austell

contact Mrs Smith, Bosinver Farm Cottages, Trelowth, St Austell PL26 7DT
t (01726) 72128 **f** (01726) 72128 **e** reception@bosinver.co.uk **w** bosinver.co.uk

open All year
payment Credit/debit cards, cash/cheques, euros

Best Self-Catering Establishment 2005 – Cornwall Tourism Awards. Bosinver Farm Cottages are so nice our guests often don't want to leave. Here you can relax in real comfort, enjoy your own private garden, splash in the pool, feed the chickens, watch the wildlife, love the village feel and explore the Cornish coast and countryside.

⊕ *Take A390 from St Austell towards Truro. Approx 1 mile from town, take 2nd left signposted Sticker, Polgooth and Trelowth. Follow for approx 50yds, then 1st left.*

❤ *Short breaks Sep-May, £50 per night for 2 persons (min 3 nights).*

Unit General Leisure
Shop 1 mile Pub 1.5 miles

ST AUSTELL, Cornwall Map ref 1B3

★★★★
SELF CATERING

Units **2**
Sleeps **3**
Low season per wk
Min £245.00
High season per wk
Max £510.00

Lanjeth Farm Holiday Cottages, St Austell

contact Mrs Anita Webber, Lanjeth Farm, Lanjeth, St Austell PL26 7TN
t (01726) 68438 **e** anita@cornwall-holidays.uk.com **w** cornwall-holidays.uk.com

Gardens and art interests. Peaceful, quality, fully equipped cottages overlooking plantsman's garden on smallholding. Double and single bedroom in each. Cornish etchings throughout. Eden, Heligan and coast nearby.

open All year
payment Cash/cheques

Unit General 12 P Leisure

ST AUSTELL, Cornwall Map ref 1B3

★★★★
SELF CATERING

Units **7**
Sleeps **2–6**
Low season per wk
Min £350.00
High season per wk
Max £1,025.00

Tregongeeves Farm Cottages, St Austell

contact Mr & Mrs John & Judith Clemo, Tregongeeves Farm Holiday Cottages, St. Austell PL26 7DS
t (01726) 68202 **f** (01726) 68202 **w** cornwall-holidays.co.uk

open All year
payment Credit/debit cards, cash/cheques, euros

Tregongeeves combines quality accommodation with excellent leisure facilities. Guests enjoy exclusive, all year round use of the indoor heated swimming pool, spa bath, gym, recreation room and a professional tennis court. Being located in mid-Cornwall just off the A390 at St Austell, both coastlines are within easy reach.

⊕ *Take A390 for 1.5 miles from St Austell, turn left into Tregongeeves Lane. Proceed for 250yds. The cottages are the 1st properties on the right.*

❤ *Short breaks available Nov-Mar inclusive. Free wireless broadband available in all the cottages.*

Unit General Leisure
Shop 1 mile Pub 1 mile

Phone ahead

Even the most ardent pet lover would appreciate some advance warning of Rover's visit, so please phone ahead and check what facilities will be available.

ST BLAZEY, Cornwall Map ref 1B2

★★★★
SELF CATERING

Units **5**
Sleeps **2**
Low season per wk
Min £150.00
High season per wk
Max £350.00

The Mill, Par

contact Mr John Tipper & Ms Caroline Ivey, Woodmill Farm - The Mill, Prideaux Road, St Blazey, Par PL24 2SR
t (01726) 810171 **f** (01726) 810171 **e** enquiries@woodmill-farm.co.uk **w** woodmill-farm.co.uk

Tastefully converted, one-bedroom cottages in former 17thC flour mill. Eden one mile, Lost Gardens six miles. Two local pubs within easy walking distance. Ideally situated to tour Cornwall.

open All year
payment Credit/debit cards, cash/cheques

Unit General Leisure

ST BRIAVELS, Gloucestershire Map ref 2A1

★★★★
SELF CATERING

Units **1**
Sleeps **2**
Low season per wk
£190.00–£230.00
High season per wk
£290.00–£340.00

Brook Farm Cottage, St Briavels, Lydney

contact Mrs Barbara Smith, Brook Farm, Mork, St Briavels, Lydney GL15 6QH
t (01594) 530995 **e** brookfarm@dial.pipex.com **w** brookfarmcottage.co.uk

Comfortable stone barn conversion in rolling Wye Valley/Forest of Dean countryside. Our nine acres feature wildlife ponds, waterfalls and footpaths. Superb views. One double en suite with beams. Private terrace and parking.

open All year
payment Cash/cheques

Unit General P Leisure Shop 2 miles Pub 1 mile

ST CLETHER, Cornwall Map ref 1C2

★★★★
SELF CATERING

Units **2**
Sleeps **4–6**
Low season per wk
£280.00–£350.00
High season per wk
£350.00–£750.00

Forget-me-not Farm Holidays, Launceston

contact Mr & Mrs James & Sheila Kempthorne, Forget-me-not Farm Holidays, Trefranck, St Clether PL15 8QN
t (01566) 86284 **f** (01566) 86284 **e** holidays@trefranck.co.uk **w** forget-me-not-farm-holidays.co.uk

open All year
payment Cash/cheques

Superb location between Bodmin Moor and spectacular North Cornwall Heritage Coast on our 300-year-old family working farm. The cottage and barn are superbly equipped and spacious, yet warm and cosy with real log fire, romantic four-poster bed and secluded garden. Ideal base for outdoor activities. A welcome retreat all year round.

From M5 turning off to A30, onto A395, travel through Pipers Pool. Pass Moorview Garage. 1st left at Coldnorthcott. One mile to crossroads; cottage on left.

Long weekends or short breaks welcome – out of school holidays at short notice.

Unit General P Leisure Shop 5 miles Pub 3 miles

ST EWE, Cornwall Map ref 1B3

★★★★
SELF CATERING

Units **1**
Sleeps **2–6**
Low season per wk
£350.00–£450.00
High season per wk
£600.00–£800.00

Galowras Farm Cottage, St Austell

contact Dr Dunne, Galowras Farm Cottage, Galowras Farm, St Ewe PL26 6EW
t (01726) 842373 **f** (01726) 842373 **e** galowrasfarm@eircom.net **w** galowrasfarm.co.uk

A barn conversion providing high-quality accommodation in an idyllic situation. This is a special place in which to relax and unwind. Heligan Gardens, Eden, beaches and coastal path nearby.

open All year
payment Cash/cheques

Unit General P Leisure Shop 2 miles Pub 2 miles

ST IVES, Cornwall Map ref 1B3

★★★
SELF CATERING

Units **1**
Sleeps **1–4**
Low season per wk
£200.00–£325.00
High season per wk
£330.00–£550.00

9 Ayr Lane, St Ives

contact Ms Sue Kibby, 115 Earlsfield Road, London SW18 3DD
t (020) 8870 3228 **e** sue.kibby@btinternet.com **w** btinternet.com/~stives.cottage

open All year
payment Cash/cheques

Cosy, modernised, ancient, granite, three-storey cottage overlooking town and harbour. Central location. Self-guided walking pack available. Also local history books and maps. Easily accessible by car, train or coach. Perfect all year round. Linen and electricity included.

⊕ *From Carbis Bay, right at Porthminster Hotel down Tregunna Hill into Tregunna Place. Then towards harbour, and at market building towards Hepworth Museum and into Ayr Lane.*

♥ *Low-season discounts for short breaks of 4 days or less.*

Unit General Leisure Shop < 0.5 miles Pub < 0.5 miles

ST IVES, Cornwall Map ref 1B3

★★★★
SELF CATERING

Units **1**
Sleeps **10**
Low season per wk
£595.00–£895.00
High season per wk
£995.00–£1,995.00

Accommodation Orla-Mo, St Ives

19 Salter Road, Poole BH13 7RQ
t 0845 644 2833 **f** 0871 277 2773 **e** info@surfives.co.uk **w** surfives.co.uk

Stunning, luxuriously refurbished captain's house, centrally located, with breathtaking harbour/bay views. Three king-size beds, two twin beds, three en suites, bathroom, designer kitchen, parking. Spacious and well equipped. WI-FI Internet access (2Mb).

open All year
payment Cash/cheques, euros

Unit General P Leisure Shop < 0.5 miles Pub < 0.5 miles

ST IVES, Cornwall Map ref 1B3

★★★
SELF CATERING

Units **7**
Sleeps **1–7**
Low season per wk
£185.00–£300.00
High season per wk
£490.00–£675.00

Chy Mor and Premier Apartments, St Ives

contact Michael Gill, Chy Mor and Premier Apartments, Beach House, The Wharf, St Ives TR26 1QA
t (01736) 798798 **f** (01736) 796831 **e** enquiry@stivesharbour.com **w** stivesharbour.com

Situated on St Ives harbour front with uninterrupted views of the harbour and bay. Visit our website, www.stivesharbour.com.

open All year
payment Credit/debit cards, cash/cheques

Unit General Leisure Shop < 0.5 miles Pub < 0.5 miles

ST IVES, Cornwall Map ref 1B3

★★
SELF CATERING

Units **1**
Sleeps **7–9**
Low season per wk
£310.00–£450.00
High season per wk
£500.00–£685.00

The Studio, St Ives

contact Carol Holland, Little Parc Owles, Pannier Lane, Carbis Bay, St Ives TR26 2RQ
t (01736) 793015

Well-equipped five-bedroom cottage in the picturesque old fishermen's and artists' quarter of St Ives. This converted sail loft also has a spacious living room, kitchen, bath/wc and shower/wc.

open All year
payment Cash/cheques

Unit General Shop < 0.5 miles Pub < 0.5 miles

Pool search

If a swimming pool is an essential element of your holiday accommodation check out the special index at the back of this guide.

ST IVES, Cornwall Map ref 1B3

★★★–★★★★★
SELF CATERING

Units **67**
Sleeps **2–8**
Low season per wk
£280.00–£560.00
High season per wk
£500.00–£750.00

Tregenna Castle Self-Catering, St Ives

contact Mrs Sheila Barker, Tregenna Castle Self-Catering, Treloyhan Avenue, St Ives TR26 2DE
t (01736) 795588 **f** (01736) 796066 **e** hotel@tregenna-castle.co.uk **w** tregenna-castle.co.uk

Range of individual traditional cottages and modern apartments with full use of Tregenna Estate's leisure facilities, including golf, squash, tennis, badminton, croquet, gym, sauna, solarium, jacuzzi, steam room and indoor and outdoor swimming pools.

open All year
payment Credit/debit cards, cash/cheques

Unit General P Leisure Shop 0.5 miles Pub < 0.5 miles

ST IVES, Cornwall Map ref 1B3

★★★★
SELF CATERING

Units **4**
Sleeps **2–6**
Low season per wk
£195.00–£370.00
High season per wk
£230.00–£600.00

Trevalgan Holiday Farm, St Ives

contact Mrs Melanie Osborne, Trevalgan Holiday Farm, Trevalgan, St Ives TR26 3BJ
t (01736) 796529 **f** (01736) 796529 **e** holidays@trevalgan.co.uk **w** trevalgan.co.uk

open All year
payment Cash/cheques

Set in an idyllic location, this working farm combines first-class accommodation and breathtaking scenery with a friendly atmosphere. Attention to detail means the cottages are decorated, furnished and equipped to a very high standard. The farm trail joins the South West Coast Path, and the A30 is close, making it easy to explore.

⊕ *Leave A30 for St Ives. Follow day visitors' route for B3311. At 2nd T-junction turn left onto B3306 – follow signs for Trevalgan Holiday Farm.*

❤ *Short breaks available Oct-Apr. Special packages for families with pre-school children.*

Unit General P Leisure Shop 1.5 miles Pub 1.5 miles

ST IVES, Cornwall Map ref 1B3

★★★
SELF CATERING

Units **1**
Sleeps **6**
Low season per wk
£500.00–£600.00
High season per wk
£700.00

Well Cottage, Carbis Bay

contact Mrs Linda Dodwell, Well Cottage, Belevedere, Treloyhan Park Road TR26 2AH
t (01736) 796846

open All year
payment Cash/cheques

Well Cottage is a single-storey converted barn, dating from the early 19th century, in a secluded position. Three bedrooms (two double, one twin), parking for two cars.

Unit General P Leisure Shop 0.5 miles Pub 0.5 miles

Place index

If you know where you want to stay the index at the back of the guide will give you the page number which lists accommodation in your chosen town, city or village. Check out the other useful indexes too.

ST JUST, Cornwall Map ref 1A3

★★★★
SELF CATERING

Units 1
Sleeps 5
Low season per wk
£250.00–£350.00
High season per wk
£400.00–£625.00

Churchgate Cottage, St Just

contact Mrs Coral Senior, Churchgate Cottage, 2 Trevear Cottage, Sennen TR19 7BH
t (01736) 871120 **e** matt.senior@virgin.net **w** churchgatecottage.co.uk

Stone cottage in conservation area opposite St Just Church, one mile from Cape Cornwall and stunning beaches. Newly furnished accommodation comprising double, twin and single bedroom, family bathroom, en suite shower. Secluded courtyard.

open All year
payment Cash/cheques

Unit General P Shop < 0.5 miles Pub < 0.5 miles

ST MABYN, Cornwall Map ref 1B2

★★★★★
SELF CATERING

Units 1
Sleeps 4
Low season per wk
£262.00–£348.00
High season per wk
£297.00–£714.00

Polglynn Cottage, St Mabyn, Bodmin

contact Mr William Wareham, Polglynn Cottage, St Mabyn, Bodmin PL30 3DE
t (01208) 850538 **f** (01208) 850538 **e** bill@polglaze.freeserve.co.uk

open All year
payment Cash/cheques

Private, luxuriously appointed, two-bedroom cottage. Stunning panoramic views over valley. Central location for sea and all other attractions. One double bedroom with 5ft bed and en suite bathroom with bath and power shower over. Bedroom two has twin 3ft beds and en suite bathroom with power shower. Ideal location to relax.

⊕ *At Launceston take A39 to Camelford. Follow B3266 to Longstone, turn right at crossroads, take 1st right. Go 0.75 miles. Polglynn Cottage on left.*

Unit General P S Leisure
Shop 1.8 miles Pub 1.8 miles

ST MERRYN, Cornwall Map ref 1B2

★★★
SELF CATERING

Units 1
Sleeps 1–6
Low season per wk
£250.00–£450.00
High season per wk
£350.00–£700.00

138 Jasmine Way, St Merryn

contact Miss Morgan, 138 Jasmine Way, Flat 2, 13 Pinfold Road, London SW16 2SL
t (020) 8355 9773 **f** (020) 8355 9773 **e** haha.films@virgin.net **w** cornishselfcateringhols.com

open All year
payment Cash/cheques, euros

In the countryside, near local shops, bars, and restaurants (including those with Michelin stars). Surf off the very nearby beaches, play golf on the championship course, Trevose. Ten minutes to Padstow. Three bedrooms (including two doubles), fully fitted kitchen equipped with washing machine and microwave. Bath with electric shower. Parking. Front and rear garden.

⊕ *Please see website for full details.*

❤ *10% off today's rate if you book now.*

Unit General P S Leisure Shop 0.5 miles Pub 1.5 miles

Using map references

The map references refer to the colour maps at the front of this guide. The first figure is the map number; the letter and figure that follow indicate the grid reference on the map.

SALCOMBE, Devon Map ref 1C3

★★★★★
SELF CATERING

Units **3**
Sleeps **4–6**
Low season per wk
£310.00–£440.00
High season per wk
£690.00–£820.00

Bolberry Farm Cottages, Bolberry Salcombe

contact Mrs Hazel Hassall, Bolberry Farm Cottages, Bolberry, Kingsbridge TQ7 3DY
t (01548) 561384 **e** info@bolberryfarmcottages.co.uk **w** bolberryfarmcottages.co.uk

open All year
payment Credit/debit cards, cash/cheques

Luxury two- and three-bedroom, tasteful barn-conversion cottages. Each individually designed, retaining true character whilst creating modern, high-quality living accommodation. Hand-crafted furniture, TV, video, washer/dryer, microwave, dishwasher. Full central heating and coal-effect gas open fire. Enclosed garden, car park and pet/boot wash area.

❤ *Short breaks out of season; discount off evening meals taken at our nearby Port Light hotel.*

Unit General P Leisure Shop 2 miles Pub 0.5 miles

SALCOMBE, Devon Map ref 1C3

★★★★
SELF CATERING

Units **1**
Sleeps **1–6**
Low season per wk
£650.00–£1,150.00
High season per wk
£1,550.00–£1,800.00

Coxswain's Watch, Salcombe

contact Mrs Julie Powell, Robert Oulsnam & Co, 79 Hewell Road, Barnt Green, Birmingham B45 8NL
t (0121) 445 3311 **f** (0121) 445 6026 **e** barntgreen@oulsnam.net **w** oulsnam.net

open All year
payment Credit/debit cards, cash/cheques

Delightfully appointed period residence in superb sailing resort, with magnificent views over harbour and estuary and lying close to shops, pubs, restaurants and ferry to beaches. Hall, cloaks/shower room, lounge, kitchen/breakfast room, laundry, three bedrooms, bathroom, patio, central heating. Free use of indoor swimming pool. Refurbished in 2005.

⊕ *A384 to Totnes, then A381 to Kingsbridge and Salcombe. Enter Salcombe at top of hill, pass school on left and turn left into Onslow Road. Right into Fore Street.*

Unit General Leisure

SALISBURY, Wiltshire Map ref 2B3

★★★★
SELF CATERING

Units **2**
Sleeps **1–2**
Low season per wk
£420.00–£455.00
High season per wk
£420.00–£455.00

4TEEN, Salisbury

contact Mrs Mary Webb, 4TEEN, Hartington Road, Salisbury SP2 7LG
t (01722) 340892 & 07759 474115 **f** (01722) 421903 **e** enquiries@4teen.biz **w** 4teen.biz

open All year
payment Credit/debit cards, cash/cheques

Freedom to do as you please, in your own time, in your own space, for business, for pleasure, for visiting friends and family or escaping for two days, two weeks or longer – 4TEEN has it all. Rachel said: 'It was a pleasure to return home to 4TEEN each day.' Now with broadband connection.

⊕ *From A360 400yds up Devizes Road (A360) from the city. Turn left into Hartington Road. Number 14 is at end of road on right-hand side.*

Unit General P Leisure Shop < 0.5 miles
Pub < 0.5 miles

Travel update

Get the latest travel information – just dial the RAC on 1740 from your mobile phone.

SALISBURY, Wiltshire Map ref 2B3

★★★★
SELF CATERING

Units **1**
Sleeps **1–2**
Low season per wk
£300.00–£350.00
High season per wk
£450.00–£495.00

The Hayloft, Ebblesway Courtyard, Salisbury

contact Mrs Gail Smalley, High Road, Broad Chalke, Salisbury SP5 5EF
t (01722) 780182 **e** gail@ebbleswaycourtyard.co.uk **w** ebbleswaycourtyard.co.uk

open All year
payment Credit/debit cards, cash/cheques, euros

Luxury cottage in award-winning courtyard. Beautiful location seven miles from Salisbury. Retaining the charm and character of the original farm building, yet providing the latest modern luxury fittings. Spa bath, digital TV, DVD, WI-FI. Private gardens. Excellent walking, cycling, pubs, restaurants and tourist attractions, including Stonehenge and Salisbury Cathedral.

⊕ *A354 signed Blandford. After 3 miles right turn coming into Coombe Bissett. Continue for 3 miles and establishment is on right (1 mile past White Hart Pub).*

❤ *Short breaks all year: 4 nights mid-week, 3 nights weekend. Gift vouchers available. Special romantic breaks – see website.*

Unit **General** P **Leisure** **Shop** 1 mile **Pub** 1 mile

SALISBURY, Wiltshire Map ref 2B3

★★★★
SELF CATERING

Units **1**
Sleeps **2**
Low season per wk
£350.00–£375.00
High season per wk
£410.00–£435.00

Little Till Cottage, Salisbury

contact Mr & Mrs Hearn, Winterbourne Stoke, Salisbury SP3 4TG
t (01980) 620396 **e** mikehearn@onetel.com **w** littletillcottage.com

Located in a tranquil setting, down a 0.25-mile track, beside a clear river. Kitchen/dining room, twin/double bedroom, sitting room, dressing room, shower room and wc, garden.

open All year
payment Cash/cheques

Unit **General** P **Shop** 1 mile **Pub** < 0.5 miles

SALISBURY, Wiltshire Map ref 2B3

★★★★
SELF CATERING

Units **1**
Sleeps **2–5**
Low season per wk
£250.00–£300.00
High season per wk
£300.00–£375.00

Sycamore Cottage, Salisbury

contact Mr & Mrs Richard & Cilla Pickett, Melrose Cottage, Lower Road, Quidhampton, Salisbury SP2 9AS
t (01722) 743160 **e** cilla@sycamorecottage.biz **w** sycamorecottage.biz

A recently converted stable offering high-quality accommodation in a lovely countryside setting. Salisbury city centre very easily accessible.

open All year
payment Cash/cheques

Unit **General** P **Shop** 1 mile **Pub** < 0.5 miles

SALISBURY, Wiltshire Map ref 2B3

★★★★
SELF CATERING

Units **1**
Sleeps **1–2**
Low season per wk
£190.00–£220.00
High season per wk
£245.00–£325.00

Wich Hazel's Apartment, Woodfalls, Salisbury

contact Mrs Ann Eveleigh, Wich Hazel's Apartment, Witch Hazel, Slab Lane, Salisbury SP5 2NE
t (01725) 511599 **e** anneveleigh@aol.com **w** wichhazel.co.uk

open All year except Christmas and New Year
payment Cash/cheques

We are ideally situated between the beautiful city of Salisbury and the New Forest National Park. Wich Hazel's Apartment is modern, spacious and well equipped, offering one double bedroom and own private garden. Located in a peaceful country lane, it's an ideal base for walking, cycling, golfing and horse-riding.

⊕ *Eight miles from Salisbury and Fordingbridge, 1 mile from New Forest boundary. Detailed directions given at time of booking.*

❤ *Short breaks available all year round.*

Unit General P Leisure Shop 0.75 miles Pub 0.75 miles

SALISBURY PLAIN

See under Great Cheverell, Salisbury, Warminster

SANDHURST, Gloucestershire Map ref 2B1

SELF CATERING

Units **3**
Sleeps **4–6**
Low season per wk
Min £260.00
High season per wk
Min £600.00

Great Coverden, Gloucester

contact Mrs Deb Warren, Bengrove Farm, Base Lane, Gloucester GL2 9NU
t (01452) 730231 **f** (01452) 730895 **e** Debs@bengrovefarm.fsnet.co.uk **w** greatcoverden.com

Located on a farm, these converted barns with oak beams offer a high standard of spacious, well-equipped accommodation. Large gardens with fantastic views, close to many places of interest.

open All year
payment Cash/cheques, euros

Unit General P Leisure Shop 3 miles Pub 3 miles

SEATON, Devon Map ref 1D2

★★★
SELF CATERING

Units **1**
Sleeps **1–4**
Low season per wk
£195.00–£295.00
High season per wk
£315.00–£525.00

West Ridge Bungalow, Seaton

contact Mrs Hildegard Fox, West Ridge Bungalow, Harepath Hill, Seaton EX12 2TA
t (01297) 22398 **f** (01297) 22398 **e** foxfamily@westridge.fsbusiness.co.uk
w cottageguide.co.uk/westridge

payment Cash/cheques

Comfortably furnished bungalow on elevated ground in 1.5 acres of gardens. Beautiful, panoramic views of Axe Estuary and sea. Close by are Beer and Branscombe. Lyme Regis seven miles, Sidmouth ten miles. Excellent centre for touring, walking, sailing, fishing, golf. Full gas central heating, double glazing throughout. Open March to October.

⊕ *From M5 jct 25 (Taunton exit) take A358 southwards for 25 miles. At A3052 turn right. West Ridge is 400m to the west of Colyford.*

❤ *10% reduction for 2 persons only, throughout booking period.*

Unit General P Leisure Shop 0.5 miles Pub 1 mile

Best foot forward

Walkers feel at home in accommodation participating in our Walkers Welcome scheme. Look out for the symbol. Consider walking all or part of a long-distance route – go online at nationaltrail.co.uk.

SENNEN, Cornwall Map ref 1A3

★★★
SELF CATERING

Units **2**
Sleeps **1–5**
Low season per wk
£200.00–£230.00
High season per wk
£400.00–£440.00

3 & 4 Wesley Cottages, St Just, Penzance

contact Mrs J Davey, Rosteague, Raginnis Farm, Penzance TR19 6NJ
t (01736) 731933 **f** (01736) 732344 **e** wesley@raginnis.demon.co.uk **w** wesleyatnanquidno.co.uk

Single-storey cosy cottages with open fires. In peaceful valley with countryside/sea views. Wonderful walks/beaches. Attractions include Minack Theatre, art galleries, archaeological sites, golf, fishing, wildlife havens, theme parks and more.

open All year
payment Cash/cheques

Unit **General** P **Leisure** **Shop** 2.5 miles **Pub** 2.5 miles

SENNEN, Cornwall Map ref 1A3

★★★
SELF CATERING

Units **1**
Sleeps **2–5**
Low season per wk
£195.00–£270.00
High season per wk
£290.00–£435.00

Surfers, Penzance

contact Mr & Mrs Bishop, Surfers, 311 Longford Road, Cannock WS11 1NF
t (01543) 570901 **e** bbishop1@onetel.com

open All year
payment Cash/cheques

A modern, granite, two-bedroom bungalow in a group of converted farm buildings. Bedroom one has three single beds, bedroom two has a double bed, shower and basin. Bathroom with shower over bath, well-equipped kitchen. Quiet location near Sennen Cove's surfing beach and cliff walks and Land's End.

⊕ *Take bypass in Penzance to Sennen and Land's End. Just after passing Cove Road, left opposite petrol station and post office, up private drive to Mayon Farm.*

❤ *Short breaks available Oct-Apr. Discount for 2 people. 10% discount for early booking before 31 Jan.*

Unit **General** P **Leisure** **Shop** < 0.5 miles **Pub** < 0.5 miles

SENNEN, Cornwall Map ref 1A3

★★★★
SELF CATERING

Units **1**
Sleeps **2–10**
Low season per wk
Min £310.00
High season per wk
Max £1,100.00

Trevear Farm, Penzance

contact Mrs Thomas, Trevear Farm, Sennen, Penzance TR19 7BH
t (01736) 871205 **f** (01736) 871205 **e** trevear.farm@farming.co.uk **w** trevearfarm.co.uk

open All year
payment Cash/cheques

Large farmhouse, completely refurbished; very clean and well equipped; central heating and woodburner. Five minutes' drive to beautiful Sennen Cove. Ample parking, enclosed garden. Great for walking, beaches, cycling and culture. Activity or relaxation – the choice is yours! Also, stunning house for six at Lamorna.

⊕ *From Penzance, take A30 towards Land's End. Private drive is on the left, just outside Sennen.*

❤ *Weekend breaks and discount for unit occupancy (excl school and Bank Holidays).*

Unit **General** P S **Leisure** **Shop** 1.5 miles **Pub** 1.5 miles

Friendly help and advice

Tourist information centres offer friendly help with accommodation and holiday ideas as well as suggestions of places to visit and things to do. You'll find contact details at the beginning of each regional section.

SHEPTON MALLET, Somerset Map ref 2A2

SELF CATERING

Units **4**
Sleeps **2–6**
Low season per wk
£175.00–£365.00
High season per wk
£325.00–£575.00

Knowle Farm Cottages, Shepton Mallet

contact Lisa Sharp, Knowle Farm Cottages, Knowle Farm, West Compton, Shepton Mallet BA4 4PD
t (01749) 890482 **f** (01749) 890405 **e** mail@knowle-farm-cottages.co.uk
w knowle-farm-cottages.co.uk

open All year
payment Cash/cheques, euros

Self-catering cottages converted from traditional farm buildings set around a pretty communal garden, located in a peaceful, secluded valley. All cottages fully equipped, central heating and open fires. Ideal centre for exploring Somerset. Close to Wells, Glastonbury, Bath and local family attractions. No pets.

⊕ *A371 to Shepton Mallet; left onto A361 towards Glastonbury; at Pilton, right for West Compton. After approx 1 mile, turn left (our sign is on a wall).*

Unit General P Leisure Shop 2 miles Pub 2 miles

SHEPTON MONTAGUE, Somerset Map ref 2B2

★★★★
SELF CATERING

Units **1**
Sleeps **1–3**
Low season per wk
£200.00–£250.00
High season per wk
£300.00–£350.00

Seed House, Wincanton

contact Mrs Christina Dimond, Higher Farm, Wincanton BA9 8JJ
t (01749) 812373 **f** (01749) 812373 **e** dimond@farm24771.fsnet.co.uk

Tastefully converted from an old seed house with oak beams and stone and brick features, this cottage is situated in a delightfully rural village. One double, one single. Fully equipped.

open All year
payment Cash/cheques

Unit General P Leisure Shop 3 miles Pub < 0.5 miles

SIDMOUTH, Devon Map ref 1D2

★★★★
SELF CATERING

Units **7**
Sleeps **4–6**
Low season per wk
£264.00–£364.00
High season per wk
£754.00–£1,038.00

Boswell Farm Cottages, Sidmouth

contact Mr & Mrs Brian & Linda Dillon, Boswell Farm Holiday Cottages, Boswell Farm, Harcombe, Sidmouth EX10 0PP
t (01395) 514162 **f** (01395) 514162 **e** dillon@boswell-farm.co.uk **w** boswell-farm.co.uk

open All year
payment Credit/debit cards, cash/cheques

Two miles from the World Heritage Coastline and beaches, cradled in 45 acres of peaceful valley. Listed, 17thC farmhouse with period cottages, lovingly converted from original farm buildings, each with own enclosed flower-filled cottage garden. Idyllic walks, ideal touring base. Tennis court, trout pond. 14thC inn and amenities within walking distance.

⊕ *M5 jct 30 onto A3052 Exeter to Lyme Regis road, follow signs to Harcombe at Sidford. Farm signed at 1st crossroads where you turn right.*

♥ *25% reduction – 2 people (or 2 people and baby) Nov-Mar (for full week only, excl Bank Holidays).*

Unit General P Leisure Shop 1 mile Pub 0.5 miles

SIDMOUTH, Devon Map ref 1D2

★★★★
SELF CATERING

Units **5**
Sleeps **2–4**
Low season per wk
£174.00–£216.00
High season per wk
£243.00–£544.00

Leigh Farm, Sidmouth

contact Mr & Mrs Geoff & Gill Davis, Leigh Farm, Weston, Sidmouth EX10 0PH
t (01395) 516065 **f** (01395) 579582 **e** leigh.farm@virgin.net **w** streets-ahead.com/leighfarm

open All year except Christmas and New Year
payment Credit/debit cards

We are 150yds from a National Trust valley which leads to the South West Coast Path and Weston beach. Excellent walking and touring area. Our bungalows face south onto a lawn, and each has a patio table and chairs for your use. The perfect location for an interesting and relaxing holiday.

M5 jct 30, join A3052. At Sidford straight on then right at top of hill, signposted Weston. Follow signs to hamlet, 1st property on right.

Unit General P Leisure Shop 1.5 miles Pub 1.5 miles

SIMONSBATH, Somerset Map ref 1C1

★★★★
SELF CATERING

Units **5**
Sleeps **1–6**
Low season per wk
£250.00–£410.00
High season per wk
£295.00–£675.00

Wintershead Farm, Minehead

contact Mrs Styles, Wintershead Farm, Simonsbath, Minehead TA24 7LF
t (01643) 831222 **w** wintershead.co.uk

Off the beaten track, converted stone cottages, perfectly situated for exploring the moor. A lot of the traffic has four legs, and the only street lighting comes from the stars above. Colour brochure. Open March to November and Christmas and New Year.

payment Cash/cheques

Unit General P Leisure Shop 7 miles Pub 3 miles

SLIMBRIDGE, Gloucestershire Map ref 2B1

★★★★★
SELF CATERING

Units **1**
Sleeps **13**
Low season per wk
£1,880.00–£2,480.00
High season per wk
£2,600.00–£3,280.00

Rectory Park, Gloucester

contact Ms Pamela Skinner, Dunster Living, The Old Cart House, Lower Street, Winterborne Whitechurch DT11 9AW
t 0870 620 1066 **f** (01258) 881780 **e** info@dunsterliving.co.uk **w** rectorypark.co.uk

Elegant Regency rectory with excellent facilities. Six double bedrooms, one single. Extensive grounds, hot tub, croquet lawn, swings and barbecue. Home cinema, snooker table and table tennis.

open All year
payment Credit/debit cards, cash/cheques, euros

Unit General P Leisure
Shop 3 miles Pub 1 mile

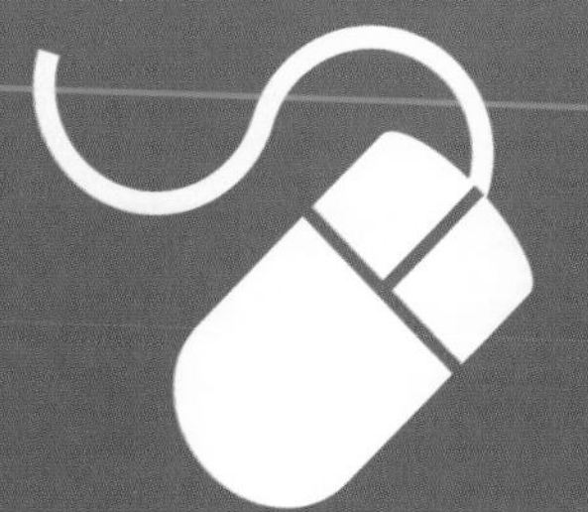

Don't forget www.

Web addresses throughout this guide are shown without the prefix www. Please include www. in the address line of your browser. If a web address does not follow this style it is shown in full.

SOUTH MILTON, Devon Map ref 1C3

★★★
SELF CATERING

Units **1**
Sleeps **10**
Low season per wk
£450.00–£600.00
High season per wk
£700.00–£1,200.00

Savernake, South Milton

contact Mr Andrew Dawson, Hall Wells Barn, Appletreewick, Skipton BD23 6DD
t (01756) 720450 **e** e.dawson@zoom.co.uk **w** savernake-devon.com

open All year
payment Cash/cheques

Wonderful 1920s detached family house, 100m from the beach. Large gardens with beautiful unobstructed views of Thurlestone Rock and the sea. Fully equipped kitchen, large roll-top bath, log fire and original features throughout. One king-size bed, three twins and two singles. Fifteen minutes' walk from village shop and pub.

⊕ *Follow signs to Loddiswell, then Kingsbridge, then South Milton, then Thurlestone Sands. Savernake is the pink house at the bottom of the cul-de-sac.*

♥ *Short breaks available Oct-Mar.*

Unit General P Leisure Shop 1 mile Pub 1 mile

SOUTH PETHERTON, Somerset Map ref 1D2

★★★★
SELF CATERING

Units **1**
Sleeps **4**
Low season per wk
£200.00–£250.00
High season per wk
£260.00–£360.00

Tanwyn, South Petherton

contact Mr & Mrs Rodney & Ann Tanswell, St Brides Major, Bridgend CF32 0SB
t (01656) 880524 **f** (01656) 880524 **e** rodney.tanswell@btinternet.com **w** freewebs.com/tanwyn

Delightful semi-detached cottage in quiet picturesque village. Three bedrooms, bathroom and shower room. Well-equipped kitchen. Large garden and orchard. Good restaurant and pub nearby.

open All year except Christmas and New Year
payment Cash/cheques

Unit General 10 P Shop 1 mile Pub < 0.5 miles

STITHIANS, Cornwall Map ref 1B3

★★★
SELF CATERING

Units **9**
Sleeps **2–8**
Low season per wk
£175.00–£250.00
High season per wk
£430.00–£750.00

Higher Trewithen Holiday Cottages, Truro

contact Mr Burgess, Higher Trewithen Holiday Cottages, Stithians, Truro TR3 7DR
t (01209) 860863 **e** trewithen@talk21.com **w** trewithen.com

open All year
payment Cash/cheques, euros

Converted cottages and apartments, peacefully situated deep in the Cornish countryside. Central location within easy reach of most of Cornwall's tourist attractions. A few miles from both north and south coasts. Stithians village is five minutes by car or fifteen minutes' walk across open fields for shops and friendly pub. Dogs welcome.

⊕ *From IMP garage at Ponsanooth (A393), turn left towards Stithians, then 2nd right, 2nd right again, then 1st right. Situated 200yds on the left.*

Unit General P Leisure Shop 2 miles Pub 2 miles

It's all quality-assessed accommodation

Our commitment to quality involves wide-ranging accommodation assessment. Ratings and awards were correct at the time of going to press but may change following a new assessment. Please check at the time of booking.

STOKE GABRIEL, Devon Map ref 1D2

★★★★★
SELF CATERING

Units 1
Sleeps 1–6
Low season per wk
£420.00–£595.00
High season per wk
£610.00–£895.00

Aish Cross Holiday Cottages, Totnes

contact Mrs Angela Pavey, Aish Cross House, Aish, Stoke Gabriel, Totnes TQ9 6PT
t (01803) 782022 **f** (01803) 211307 **e** info@aishcross.co.uk **w** aishcross.co.uk

open All year
payment Cash/cheques

Original coach house attached to lovely Regency home. Set in tranquil countryside and offering spacious, character, all-year accommodation in Area of Outstanding Natural Beauty close to River Dart and Totnes. Two king-size/twin-bedded rooms with en suite (third twin/double available), large lounge/conservatory, separate kitchen/dining area. See website for pictures etc.

⊕ *Totnes: A385 to Paignton (1.5 miles). At Longcombe Cross turn right to Stoke Gabriel. Aish is 1 mile. Aish Cross House is on left, just after postbox.*

Unit General P Leisure Shop 1.5 miles Pub 1.5 miles

STOKE SUB HAMDON, Somerset Map ref 1D2

★★★
SELF CATERING

Units 1
Sleeps 2
Low season per wk
£100.00–£150.00
High season per wk
£160.00–£200.00

Top o Hill, Stoke sub Hamdon

contact Mrs Mary Gane, Top o Hill, Stoke-sub-Hamdon TA14 6RD
t (01935) 822089

Annexe of 150-year-old house in private road, close to A303. Excellent touring base for many places of interest. Garden with garden furniture, own entrance. Open spring to autumn.

payment Cash/cheques

Unit General P Leisure Shop 1 mile Pub 1 mile

STOW-ON-THE-WOLD, Gloucestershire Map ref 2B1

★★★★
SELF CATERING

Units 1
Sleeps 4
Low season per wk
Min £280.00
High season per wk
Min £490.00

Bottom End Cottage, Stow-on-the-Wold

contact Ms Karen Hawkes, Cottage in the Country and Cottage Holidays, Forest Gate, Frog Lane, Milton-under-Wychwood, Chipping Norton OX7 6JZ
t (01993) 831495 **f** (01993) 831095 **e** enquiries@cottageinthecountry.co.uk
w cottageinthecountry.co.uk

open All year
payment Credit/debit cards, cash/cheques

Delightful Victorian Cotswold-stone semi-detached cottage, in a quiet street just five minutes' walk from the Market Square. Recently renovated and comfortably furnished, but retaining many original features including stripped pine doors, flagstone floors and an original range in the breakfast kitchen. Conservatory at the rear overlooks pleasant enclosed garden.

⊕ *A429 south to Stow. Left at 3rd set of traffic lights. Into Sheep Street, which leads into Park Street. Opposite the Bell Pub, left into Union Street.*

Unit General P Shop < 0.5 miles Pub < 0.5 miles

How many beds?

The minimum and maximum number of people that each property can accommodate is shown. If an entry includes details of more than one property the sleeping capacity may vary between them. Please check when you make your booking.

STOW-ON-THE-WOLD, Gloucestershire Map ref 2B1

★★★★★
SELF CATERING

Units 4
Sleeps 1–4
Low season per wk
Min £285.00
High season per wk
Max £575.00

Broad Oak Cottages, Stow-on-the-Wold, Cheltenham

contact Mrs Wilson, Broad Oak Cottages, The Counting House, Oddington Road, Stow on the Wold, Cheltenham GL54 1AL
t (01451) 830794 **f** (01451) 830794 **e** mary@broadoakcottages.co.uk **w** broadoakcottages.co.uk

open All year
payment Cash/cheques, euros

Delightful cottages situated within a few minutes' walk of the centre of Stow. The cottages are furnished and equipped to the highest standard comprising both double and twin bedrooms, full central heating, log fires and fully modernised bathrooms and kitchens. Parking, south-facing patios, gardens and lovely views.

⊕ *From the A429 Fosseway turn east onto the A436 at the traffic lights in centre of Stow. All cottages are adjacent to this road.*

❤ *Short breaks available (except in high season).*

Unit General P Leisure Shop 0.5 miles Pub 0.5 miles

STOW-ON-THE-WOLD, Gloucestershire Map ref 2B1

★★★★
SELF CATERING

Units 1
Sleeps 2
Low season per wk
£270.00–£290.00
High season per wk
£290.00–£340.00

Rose's Cottage, Broadwell, Stow-on-the-Wold

contact Mr Richard Drinkwater, Rose's Cottage, The Green, Broadwell, Moreton-in-Marsh GL56 0UF
t (01451) 830007 **e** richard.drinkwater@ukonline.co.uk

Delightful garden cottage overlooking the green of charming Cotswold village. One-and-a-half miles from Stow-on-the-Wold in an Area of Outstanding Natural Beauty. Children with maximum age of two accepted.

open All year
payment Cash/cheques

Unit General P Leisure Shop 1.25 miles Pub < 0.5 miles

STRATTON-ON-THE-FOSSE, Somerset Map ref 2B2

★★★★
SELF CATERING

Units 2
Sleeps 4–8
Low season per wk
£300.00–£395.00
High season per wk
£365.00–£630.00

Pitcot Farm Barn Cottages, Stratton-on-the-Fosse, Radstock

contact Mrs Mary Coles, Pitcot Lane, Stratton-on-the-Fosse, Radstock BA3 4SX
t (01761) 233108 **f** (01761) 417710 **e** info@pitcotfarm.co.uk **w** pitcotfarm.co.uk

Between Bath and Wells, on the edge of the Mendip Hills, well-equipped and comfortable single-storey barn cottages with log-burning stoves and exposed beams. Rural situation with beautiful views. Convenient for Longleat, Stourhead and Cheddar.

open All year
payment Cash/cheques

Unit General P S Leisure Shop 1 mile Pub 1 mile

SUTTON WALDRON, Dorset Map ref 2B3

Rating Applied For
SELF CATERING

Units 1
Sleeps 1–4
Low season per wk
Min £260.00
High season per wk
Min £310.00

Dairy Cottage, Blandford Forum

contact Mr and Mrs Stuart Asbury, Broadlea Farm, Sutton Waldron, Blandford Forum DT11 8NS
t (01747) 811330

Fully equipped cottage amidst lovely countryside, south of Shaftesbury. Two bedrooms (double and twin), triple-aspect lounge/dining room, separate kitchen and bathroom. All on one level.

open All year
payment Cash/cheques

Unit General P Shop 0.5 miles Pub 0.5 miles

SWANAGE, Dorset Map ref 2B3

★★★
SELF CATERING

Units **1**
Sleeps **4**
Low season per wk
£240.00–£350.00
High season per wk
£350.00–£495.00

11 Wordsworth Court, Swanage

contact Ms Lyn Whaley, Hidden Cottage, 20 Sidbury Close
t (01344) 873615 **e** lyn@whaley.uk.com

open All
payment Cash

South-facing, two-bedroo... position adjacent to the Downs. ... Swanage beach, pier and town centre. Bea... top walks to Durleston Country Park and the Juras... Coast. Sea views from balcony, lounge and kitchen. Central heating. Fully equipped kitchen. Communal gardens. Off-road parking.

⊕ *From town centre (Station Road), bear right Institute Road, left High Street, 3rd turning right Seymer Road, left Durleston Road, 2nd left Belle Vue Road.*

♥ *Short breaks available from £50 per night Sep-Jun (min 2 nights).*

Unit General P Leisure Shop < 0.5 miles Pub < 0.5 miles

SWANAGE, Dorset Map ref 2B3

★★★
SELF CATERING & SERVICED APARTMENTS

Units **4**
Sleeps **2–6**
Low season per wk
£180.00–£320.00
High season per wk
£390.00–£470.00

Alrose Villa Holiday Apartements, Swanage

contact Mrs Jacqueline Wilson, Alrose Villa Holiday Apartments, 2 Highcliffe Road, Swanage BH19 1LW
t (01929) 426318 **e** enquiry@alrosevilla.co.uk **w** alrosevilla.co.uk

open All year except Christmas and New Year
payment Cash/cheques

Charming Victorian villa, 100m from Swanage beach, comprising recently refurbished holiday apartments, some with balconies and sea views. Attractive garden with barbecue, private car parking. Whether you're looking for a relaxing break, a seaside holiday with the family, or just want to explore the beautiful countryside, Alrose Villa offers the perfect location.

⊕ *From A351 to Swanage, turn left along seafront, then 1st turning on right.*

Unit General P Shop < 0.5 miles Pub < 0.5 miles

SWANAGE, Dorset Map ref 2B3

★★★–★★★★★
SELF CATERING

Units **3**
Sleeps **5–8**
Low season per wk
£200.00–£500.00
High season per wk
£500.00–£1,000.00

Swanage Cottage Holidays, Swanage

contact Mr & Mrs B Howells, Swanage Cottage Holidays, 60 Bell Street, Swanage BH19 2SB
t (01929) 421601 & 07971 552082 **e** bjhowells@hotmail.com **w** swanagecottageholidays.co.uk

open All year
payment Cash/cheques, euros

Comfortable, well-equipped stone cottages in old seaside resort near World Heritage Coastline and outstanding countryside. The Grade II Listed Plum Tree Cottage has four bedrooms and a large garden. Others have three bedrooms and small, south-west facing gardens. We provide everything possible to make your holiday successful. Your home away from home.

⊕ *From A35 Poole take A351 through Wareham and Corfe Castle to Swanage. Fork right, signposted High Street. Go immediately right up Bell Street past Globe pub.*

♥ *£50 discount if couple and baby. 3/4-night stays Oct-Apr (excl school/public holidays).*

Unit General P Leisure Shop < 0.5 miles Pub < 0.5 miles

... Devon Map ref 1C1

★
...TERING

Units **4**
...s **2–9**
... season per wk
...90.00–£443.00
High season per wk
£355.00–£959.00

Lower Hearson Farm, Barnstaple

contact Mr & Mrs G Pelling, Swimbridge, Barnstaple EX32 0QH
t (01271) 830702 **e** info@hearsoncottagesdevon.co.uk **w** hearsoncottagesdevon.co.uk

open All year
payment Cash/cheques

Former dairy farm set in 13 acres of gardens, field and woodland. Tucked away in the heart of the North Devon countryside, it's perfect for a relaxing holiday. Our holiday cottages, games facilities and pool are surrounded by two acres of gardens, making this a safe place for children.

Unit General Leisure Shop 2 miles
Pub 1.5 miles

TAUNTON, Somerset Map ref 1D1

★★★★
SELF CATERING

Units **1**
Sleeps **7**
Low season per wk
Max £499.00
High season per wk
Max £793.00

Linnets, Fitzhead, Taunton

contact Mrs Patricia Grabham, Linnets, Taunton TA4 3JX
t (01823) 400658 **f** (01823) 400658 **e** patricia.grabham@onetel.net

open All year except Christmas and New Year
payment Cash/cheques

Linnets enjoys a tranquil environment with spacious accommodation. The village inn, less than a five-minute walk away, serves wonderful food and wine. Three bedrooms, fully equipped kitchen, wet room, upstairs oak-floored bathroom, sitting/dining room with patio doors opening on to the secluded garden with heated swimming pool and summerhouse. All windows overlook the garden.

M5 jct 25 to Taunton. B3227 to Norton Fitzwarren and Wiveliscombe. Take 1st right turn out of Preston Bowyer to Fitzhead. Please call for further directions.

Unit General Leisure Shop 2.5 miles
Pub 0.5 miles

TAVISTOCK, Devon Map ref 1C2

★★★★
SELF CATERING

Units **1**
Sleeps **1–4**
Low season per wk
£200.00–£300.00
High season per wk
£300.00–£400.00

Edgemoor Cottage, Tavistock

contact Mrs Mary Susan Fox, Edgemoor, Middlemoor, Tavistock PL19 9DY
t (01822) 612259 **f** (01822) 617625 **e** Foxes@dartmoorcottages.info **w** edgemoorcottage.co.uk

open All year
payment Cash/cheques, euros

Attractive country cottage in peaceful hamlet. Two en suite bedrooms (one twin, one double, both with TV), kitchen/dining room, upstairs living room leading into a sun lounge/diner with patio overlooking fields. Perfect base to explore Dartmoor, Devon and Cornwall. North and south coasts are within an hour's drive.

At Tavistock follow road signs to Whitchurch. At Whitchurch Post Office turn up the hill, turn right at the cattle grid to Middlemoor.

£25 discount to holidaymakers booking a second week with us. £25 discount to holidaymakers booking a subsequent holiday with us.

Unit General Leisure Shop < 0.5 miles
Pub < 0.5 miles

TAVISTOCK, Devon Map ref 1C2

★★★
SELF CATERING

Units 1
Sleeps 2
Low season per wk
£150.00
High season per wk
£150.00

Higher Chaddlehanger Farm, Tavistock

contact Mrs Ruth Cole, The Annexe, Higher Chaddlehanger Farm, Tavistock PL19 0LG
t (01822) 810268 **f** (01822) 810268

Holiday flatlet in farmhouse on beef and sheep farm, close to Moors. Own entrance, private garden.

open All year
payment Cash/cheques

Unit General

TAVISTOCK, Devon Map ref 1C2

★★★★
SELF CATERING

Units 1
Sleeps 1–6
Low season per wk
£260.00–£300.00
High season per wk
£500.00–£600.00

Moorview Cottage, Peter Tavy

contact Mrs Elaine Mackintosh, Moorview, Cudlipptown, Peter Tavy, Tavistock PL19 9LZ
t (01822) 810271 **f** (01822) 810082 **e** ejm@dartmoor-holidays.fsnet.co.uk **w** dartmoor-holidays.com

open All year
payment Cash/cheques

An ideal base for walking, or exploring, enjoying the countryside, views and wildlife or simply relaxing with a good book. Moorview is well located, offering the opportunity to explore all of Devon and Cornwall. Good food served at local pubs and restaurants. The historic market town of Tavistock is close by.

⊕ *Go through Peter Tavy village. On leaving village go past church on the left-hand side. Drive a further mile, and Moorview is on the left-hand side.*

♥ *Short breaks available in low season. Reduced rates when only 2 people occupying the cottage – please quote 7VDSWT.*

Unit General P Leisure Shop 3 miles
Pub 1 mile

TAYNTON, Gloucestershire Map ref 2B1

★★★★
SELF CATERING

Units 1
Sleeps 1–2
Low season per wk
Min £195.00
High season per wk
£195.00–£300.00

Owls Barn, Gloucester

contact Mrs Barbara Goodwin, Coldcroft Farm, Glasshouse Lane, Gloucester GL19 3HJ
t (01452) 831290 **f** (01452) 831290 **e** goodies@coldcroft.freeserve.co.uk
w coldcroft.freeserve.co.uk

Owls Barn is a tastefully converted twin-bedded barn with shower, kitchen/diner and sitting room. Excellent views. Within one hour's drive of Bath, Bristol, Hereford and Worcester.

open All year
payment Cash/cheques

Unit General P Leisure Shop < 0.5 miles
Pub < 0.5 miles

TEIGNGRACE, Devon Map ref 1D2

SELF CATERING

Units 2
Sleeps 4–5
Low season per wk
£250.00–£300.00
High season per wk
£350.00–£470.00

Twelve Oaks Holiday Cottages, Newton Abbot

contact Mrs Gale, Twelve Oaks Holiday Cottages, Twelve Oaks Farm, Newton Abbot TQ12 6QT
t (01626) 352769 **f** (01626) 352769

Working 220-acre beef farm bordered by the River Teign, on the edge of the village of Teigngrace. Carefully converted cottages, each with own patio. Outdoor heated swimming pool. Open May to October.

payment Credit/debit cards, cash/cheques

Unit General P Leisure Shop 2 miles Pub 1.5 miles

THREE LEGGED CROSS, Dorset Map ref 2B3

★★★★
SELF CATERING

Units **1**
Sleeps **4–5**
Low season per wk
£280.00–£480.00
High season per wk
£400.00–£690.00

Foresters, Nr Ringwood

contact Mrs Jean Baylis, Cottage Farm, Verwood Road, Three Legged Cross BH21 6RN
t (01202) 820203 **e** cottagefarm@sagainternet.co.uk

Detached, ground-level cottage on farm. Gas central heating, double/twin bedrooms, both en suite, linen and towels included, washer/dryer, DVD, video, CD, radio, TV. Close to sea and New Forest. Dogs and horses by arrangement.

open All year
payment Cash/cheques, euros

Unit General P Leisure Shop 0.5 miles Pub 0.5 miles

TINTAGEL, Cornwall Map ref 1B2

★★★
SELF CATERING

Units **1**
Sleeps **1–4**
Low season per wk
Min £110.00
High season per wk
Max £410.00

Tregeath, Tintagel

contact Mrs Edwina Broad, Davina, Trevillett, Tintagel PL34 0HL
t (01840) 770217 **f** (01840) 770217

Old modernised detached cottage, built of stone and slate. Coal grate, six night-storage heaters, TV/video, payphone, microwave. One dog, no cats. Parking space. Washing machine. Separate tumble dryer.

open All year
payment Cash/cheques

Unit General P Shop 1 mile Pub 1 mile

TIVERTON, Devon Map ref 1D2

★★★★
SELF CATERING

Units **13**
Sleeps **2–10**
Low season per wk
Min £235.00
High season per wk
Max £1,058.00

Old Bridwell Holiday Cottages, Cullompton

contact Ms Jackie Kind, Old Bridwell Holiday Cottages, Uffculme, Cullompton EX15 3BU
t (01884) 841464 **e** jackie@oldbridwell.co.uk **w** oldbridwell.co.uk

Clustered around the thatched pumphouse, each of our spacious, individually styled cottages offers home-from-home comfort. Our extensive grounds have a safe children's play area and restored, walled fruit garden.

open All year
payment Cash/cheques, euros

Unit General P Leisure Shop 1 mile Pub 1 mile

TIVERTON, Devon Map ref 1D2

★★★–★★★★
SELF CATERING

Units **5**
Sleeps **1–9**
Low season per wk
£280.00–£530.00
High season per wk
£390.00–£930.00

West Pitt Farm, Tiverton

contact Ms Susanne Westgate, West Pitt Farm, Whitnage, Tiverton EX16 7DU
t (01884) 820296 **f** (01884) 820818 **e** susannewestgate@yahoo.com

open All year
payment Cash/cheques, euros

Delightful stable conversions and 16thC cottage with lovely farmhouse kitchen and living room with open fireplace. Set in glorious farmland, West Pitt offers an indoor heated pool and sauna, fishing, walking, tennis and an excellent games room. Well placed for Exmoor, Dartmoor and North and South Devon.

⊕ *M5 jct 27, A361 (Barnstaple). Fork immediately left (Sampford Peverell). Right at mini-roundabout. Straight over 2nd roundabout. 1st left (Whitnage). Right at Stonesland Cross, left at Pitt crossroads.*

❤ *Short breaks available – 3 or 4 nights.*

Unit General Leisure Shop 3 miles Pub 2 miles

TOLLER PORCORUM, Dorset Map ref 2A3

★★★
SELF CATERING

Units **3**
Sleeps **4**
Low season per wk
£170.00–£380.00
High season per wk
£390.00–£480.00

Old School Cottage, Dorchester

contact Mrs Jean Wallbridge, The Old School, 2 School Lane, Toller Porcorum, Dorchester DT2 0DF
t (01300) 320046 **e** oldschooltoller@aol.com **w** oldschooltoller.co.uk

open All year
payment Credit/debit cards, cash/cheques, euros

Set in a tranquil village, The Old School offers relaxing, well-equipped accommodation with fantastic views, ideal for walkers and nature lovers. Within easy reach of West Bay, Burton Bradstock and Abbotsbury on the stunning Jurassic Coast. All properties have one double and one twin room, one with both bedrooms en suite.

⊕ *From A356, north of Maiden Newton, turn to Toller Porcorum. In village, 2nd right into School Lane. The Old School is past Church Mead and The Owls.*

❤ *3-night stays available Nov-Apr (excl Christmas, Easter and Bank Holidays).*

Unit General P Leisure Shop 2 miles Pub 2 miles

TORQUAY, Devon Map ref 1D2

★★★
SELF CATERING

Units **5**
Sleeps **2–6**
Low season per wk
£165.00–£225.00
High season per wk
£320.00–£445.00

Bedford House, Torquay

contact Mrs MacDonald-Smith, Bedford House, 517 Babbacombe Road, Torquay TQ1 1HJ
t (01803) 296995 **e** bedfordhotorquay@btconnect.com **w** bedfordhousetorquay.co.uk

open All year
payment Credit/debit cards, cash/cheques

An elegant, Tudor-style house built in 1888 and set in a sunny, pleasant garden. Well situated in a conservation area, only 500m from harbour, shops and entertainment. Comfortable, self-contained and well-equipped apartments. Colour TV and microwaves. Bath or shower room. Bed linen. Guest laundry. Central heating. Private car park.

⊕ *From A380, A3022, follow signs to harbour, then left to Babbacombe.*

❤ *Short breaks available Oct-Apr, min 3 nights.*

Unit General P

TORQUAY, Devon Map ref 1D2

★★★
SELF CATERING

Units **24**
Sleeps **1–6**
Low season per wk
£195.00–£290.00
High season per wk
£320.00–£715.00

Maxton Lodge Holiday Apartments, Torquay

contact Mark Shephard and Alex Brook, Maxton Lodge Holiday Apartments, Rousdown Road, Torquay TQ2 6PB
t (01803) 607811 **f** (01803) 605357 **e** stay@redhouse-hotel.co.uk **w** redhouse-hotel.co.uk

Well-appointed, self-contained apartments providing superior accommodation. Close to shops and seafront and an ideal base for touring. Indoor/outdoor pools, spa, sauna, gymnasium. Beauty salon, solarium, games room, licensed bar, restaurant.

open All year
payment Credit/debit cards, cash/cheques

Unit General P Leisure Shop < 0.5 miles
Pub < 0.5 miles

Pool search

If a swimming pool is an essential element of your holiday accommodation check out the special index at the back of this guide.

TORQUAY, Devon Map ref 1D2

★★★★★
SELF CATERING

Units **1**
Sleeps **2–10**
Low season per wk
£500.00–£900.00
High season per wk
£1,000.00–£1,700.00

St Christophers Holiday Home, Torquay

contact Mr David Perry, Wildewood, Meadfoot Road, Torquay TQ1 2JP
t (01803) 297471 **e** cperry@lineone.net **w** torquayholiday.com

Luxury, detached holiday home within walking distance of three beaches, town and harbour. Warm and cosy in winter with central heating and woodburner. Patio and parking.

open All year
payment Cash/cheques

Unit General P Leisure Shop < 0.5 miles Pub < 0.5 miles

TORQUAY, Devon Map ref 1D2

★★★
SELF CATERING

Units **18**
Sleeps **1–5**
Low season per wk
£130.00–£220.00
High season per wk
£260.00–£490.00

South Sands Apartments, Torquay

contact Mr & Mrs Paul & Deborah Moorhouse, South Sands Apartments, Torbay Road, Livermead, Torquay TQ2 6RG
t (01803) 293521 **f** (01803) 293502 **e** info@southsands.co.uk **w** southsands.co.uk

open All year
payment Credit/debit cards, cash/cheques, euros

Specifically designed holiday apartments offering a high degree of comfort and cleanliness. Spacious and tastefully decorated with fitted kitchens. Apartments with bath or shower. No meters. Towels available upon request. Ground and first floor only. Seafront location. Beach 100yds. Main bus route. Families and couples only. Parking on site.

Follow signs to Torquay seafront. Turn right towards Paignton. Situated on right-hand side of road after approx 0.5 miles.

Short breaks and mid-week bookings in low season. Discount available 2 consecutive weeks or more.

Unit General 1 P Leisure Shop 0.5 miles Pub 0.5 miles

TORQUAY, Devon Map ref 1D2

★★★
SELF CATERING

Units **19**
Sleeps **1–6**
Low season per wk
£100.00–£190.00
High season per wk
£355.00–£650.00

Sunningdale Apartments, Torquay

contact Mr Allan Carr, Sunningdale Apartments, 11 Babbacombe Downs Road, Torquay TQ1 3LF
t (01803) 325786 **e** allancarr@yahoo.com **w** sunningdaleapartments.co.uk

open All year
payment Cash/cheques, euros

Spacious apartments, many overlooking beach with stunning sea views. Self-contained with bathroom and shower, fitted kitchen and lounge with dining area. Large car park, laundry room, gardens. All double glazed with central heating. Level walk to shops, restaurants, bar and theatre. Excellent touring/walking/sports centre.

From M5 jct 31 onto A380 signposted Torquay. Follow signs for Babbacombe then signs for Babbacombe Cliff Railway and Model Village. Onto Babbacombe Downs Road.

Unit General P Leisure Shop 0.5 miles Pub 0.5 miles

Prices

These are shown for one week's accommodation. If an entry includes details of more than one property it is usual that the minimum price is for low season in the smallest property and the maximum price is for high season in the largest property.

TORRINGTON, Devon Map ref 1C2

★★★
SELF CATERING

Units **4**
Sleeps **4–6**
Low season per wk
£260.00–£310.00
High season per wk
£340.00–£590.00

Stowford Lodge, Torrington

contact Mr & Mrs R Jones, Stowford Lodge, Langtree, Torrington EX38 8NU
t (01805) 601540 **f** (01805) 601487 **e** enq@stowfordlodge.co.uk **w** stowfordlodge.co.uk

Delightful stone cottages converted from Victorian farm buildings, set in six acres. Heated indoor pool. Safe and peaceful setting. Children's play area. Dogs welcome.

open All year
payment Credit/debit cards, cash/cheques

Unit General P Leisure Shop 3 miles Pub 3 miles

TRURO, Cornwall Map ref 1B3

★★★★
SELF CATERING

Units **1**
Sleeps **1–6**
Low season per wk
Min £250.00
High season per wk
Max £750.00

Trelowthas, Truro

contact Mr Chris Churm, 16 Morleys Close, Lowdham, Nottingham NG14 7HN
t (0115) 966 5611 **f** (0115) 966 5611

Quality, luxurious accommodation ideal for couples and families. Set in the picturesque riverside village of Malpas, two miles from Truro. Magnificent views and walks, very peaceful, excellent facilities. Mahogany four-poster bed.

open All year
payment Cash/cheques, euros

Unit General P Leisure Shop < 0.5 miles Pub < 0.5 miles

TRURO, Cornwall Map ref 1B3

★★★★★
SELF CATERING

Units **46**
Sleeps **1–7**
Low season per wk
£450.00–£955.00
High season per wk
£995.00–£1,400.00

The Valley, Carnon Downs, Truro

contact Mr & Mrs Keith & Julie Horsfall, Bissoe Road, Carnon Downs, Truro TR3 6LQ
t (01872) 862194 **f** (01872) 864343 **e** info@valleycottages.net **w** the-valley.co.uk

open All year
payment Credit/debit cards, cash/cheques, euros

A secluded hamlet of contemporary holiday cottages in the centre of Cornwall's beauty and life. Relax in architect-designed luxury with an ambience of contemporary living. In spectacular countryside, with indoor and outdoor pools, squash and tennis courts, gym and the stylish Cafe Azur with exquisite cuisine on your doorstep.

⊕ *A30 from Exeter to A39/A3076 (Truro). Bypass Truro to A39 (Falmouth). The Valley is signposted from A39 Falmouth road at Carnon Downs roundabout, about 3 miles outside Truro.*

♥ *Call for short-break special offers and out-of-season discounts at Cornwall's chic country retreat.*

Unit General P Leisure
Shop 0.5 miles Pub 0.5 miles

UPLYME, Devon Map ref 1D2

★★★★
SELF CATERING

Units **1**
Sleeps **6**
Low season per wk
£300.00–£400.00
High season per wk
£550.00–£650.00

Higher Holcombe Farm Cottage, Lyme Regis

contact Mrs Rosamund Duffin, Higher Holcombe Farm Cottage, Holcombe Lane, Uplyme, Lyme Regis DT7 3SN
t (01297) 444078 **e** rozduffin@hotmail.com **w** higherholcombe.com

A self-contained annexe to a period farmhouse, one mile from Lyme Regis. Private garden and ample parking in a beautiful setting.

open All year except Christmas
payment Cash/cheques

Unit General P Leisure Shop 1 mile Pub 1 mile

UPTON ST LEONARDS, Gloucestershire Map ref 2B1

★★
SELF CATERING

Units **2**
Sleeps **1–4**
Low season per wk
Min £190.00
High season per wk
Min £270.00

Hill Farm Cottages, Gloucester

contact Mrs Margaret McLellan, Hill Farm Cottages, Hill Farm, Upton Hill, Upton St. Leonards, Gloucester GL4 8DA
t (01452) 614081

open All year
payment Cash/cheques

Two miles from Gloucester with panoramic views of the Cotswolds. Close to dry ski slope and golfing facilities. Ideal for walking. Country pub nearby providing food.

⊕ *From the A38 take the B4073 for approx 2 miles, the Kings Head pub is on the left, 300yds up hill on same side of pub.*

Unit General P Leisure Shop < 0.5 miles Pub < 0.5 miles

VERYAN, Cornwall Map ref 1B3

★★★★
SELF CATERING

Units **2**
Sleeps **6**
Low season per wk
£240.00–£470.00
High season per wk
£470.00–£760.00

Trenona Farm Holidays, Veryan

contact Mrs Pamela Carbis, Trenona Farm, Ruan High Lanes, Truro TR2 5JS
t (01872) 501339 **f** (01872) 501253 **e** pam@trenonafarmholidays.co.uk
w trenonafarmholidays.co.uk

open All year
payment Credit/debit cards, cash/cheques

The former farmhouse, and old stone workshop, have been tastefully converted to provide quality accommodation with modern furnishings and appliances for relaxing holidays on a mixed working farm on the beautiful Roseland Peninsula. Private gardens and patios. Many public gardens and attractions nearby. Children/pets welcome. Disabled access.

⊕ *A30 past Bodmin, A391 to St Austell, A390 towards Truro. Just beyond Probus take A3078 to St Mawes. After 8 miles pass Esso garage, Trenona Farm 2nd on left.*

♥ *Short breaks available Oct-Mar.*

Unit General P Leisure Shop 1 mile Pub 2 miles

WADEBRIDGE, Cornwall Map ref 1B2

★★
SELF CATERING

Units **115**
Sleeps **2–8**
Low season per wk
£85.00–£315.00
High season per wk
£425.00–£795.00

Michaelstow Manor Holiday Park, Bodmin

contact Mr Jesson, Michaelstow Manor Holiday Park, St Tudy, Bodmin PL30 3PB
t (01208) 850244 **f** (01208) 851420 **e** michaelstow@eclipse.co.uk **w** michaelstow-holidays.co.uk

Chalets and apartments set within picturesque grounds of Victorian Manor. Full use of all facilities. Situated on edge of Bodmin Moor, yet only a short drive from the coast. March to October.

payment Credit/debit cards, cash/cheques

Unit General P Leisure

Take a break

Look out for special promotions and themed breaks. This could be your chance to indulge an interest, find a new one, or just relax and enjoy exceptional value! Offers are highlighted in colour (and are subject to availability).

WADEBRIDGE, Cornwall Map ref 1B2

★★★★
SELF CATERING

Units **4**
Sleeps **2–8**
Low season per wk
£225.00–£435.00
High season per wk
£435.00–£850.00

Tregolls Farm Cottages, Bodmin

contact Mrs Hawkey, Tregolls Farm Cottages, St Wenn, Bodmin PL30 5PG
t (01208) 812154 **e** tregollsfarm@btclick.com **w** tregollsfarm.co.uk

open All year
payment Credit/debit cards, cash/cheques

Well-equipped holiday cottages, tastefully converted from redundant stone barns. Charming, mellow oak beams, slate window sills, fire hearths, and wonderful views of the open countryside with fields of cows and sheep grazing and a stream meandering through the valley. Pets' corner, games room, farm trail and barbecues.

⊕ *Four miles south of Wadebridge. O.S. map 200, ref. 983661 or phone for directions.*

♥ *3- and 4-night breaks Oct-Apr.*

Unit General P Leisure Shop 4 miles
Pub 4 miles

WAREHAM, Dorset Map ref 2B3

★
SELF CATERING

Units **1**
Sleeps **5**
Low season per wk
£295.00–£355.00
High season per wk
£425.00–£450.00

Dormer Cottage, Hyde, Wareham

contact Mrs Madeleine Constantinides, Hyde, Wareham BH20 7NT
t (01929) 471239

Converted 400-year-old barn in the lovely Dorset countryside – perfect for relaxation and peace. Large wood and play areas. Children and pets welcome.

open All year
payment Cash/cheques

Unit General P Leisure Shop 3.5 miles Pub 3.5 miles

WARMINSTER, Wiltshire Map ref 2B2

★★★★
SELF CATERING

Units **3**
Sleeps **2–9**
Low season per wk
£225.00–£300.00
High season per wk
£280.00–£650.00

Eastleigh Farm, Bishopstrow, Warminster

contact Mrs Roz Walker, Eastleigh Farm, Bishopstrow, Warminster BA12 7BE
t (01985) 212325

This former cow byre has been sympathetically converted into cottages of an exceptionally high standard, providing well-equipped, comfortable, spacious accommodation. Within easy reach of Bath, Salisbury, Longleat, Stonehenge, Glastonbury and Cheddar Gorge.

open All year
payment Cash/cheques

Unit General P Leisure Shop 3 miles
Pub 3 miles

WATERROW, Somerset Map ref 1D1

★★★★
SELF CATERING

Units **8**
Sleeps **1–9**
Low season per wk
Min £160.00
High season per wk
Max £595.00

Exmoor Gate Lodges, Waterrow, Nr Taunton

contact Mrs Sue Gallagher, Whipcott Heights, Holcombe Rogus, Wellington TA21 0NA
t (01823) 672339 **f** (01823) 672339 **e** bookings@oldlimekiln.freeserve.co.uk

open All year
payment Credit/debit cards, cash/cheques, euros

Lodges set on wooded hillside with panoramic views, stream and abundant wildlife. Modern interiors, fully equipped to a high standard. Central heating, double glazing. Open-plan lounge/kitchen/diner with bedroom and bathroom on the ground floor, further bedrooms and bathrooms upstairs in larger units. Ideal base for exploring Exmoor and the Somerset coast.

⊕ *Leave M5 at jct 25, following A358/B3227 to Minehead. At Staplegrove follow B3227 to Wiveliscombe. Exmoor Gate is 2 miles beyond Wiveliscombe on the left.*

❤ *Short breaks available all year round – please contact owner for details*

Unit General Leisure Shop 2 miles
Pub 0.5 miles

WELLS, Somerset Map ref 2A2

★★★★
SELF CATERING

Units **1**
Sleeps **1–5**
Low season per wk
£295.00–£450.00
High season per wk
£475.00–£650.00

Honeysuckle Cottage, Wells

contact Mrs Luana Law, Honeysuckle Cottage, Worth, Wookey, Wells BA5 1LW
t (01749) 678971 **e** honeycroft2@aol.com

open All year
payment Cash/cheques

Barn conversion on working farm in beautiful countryside. One double en suite and one double with adjoining single bedrooms. Bath and shower room. Spacious kitchen/diner/lounge leading to large patio and garden overlooking stunning Mendip Hills. All modern equipment from dishwasher to DVD.

⊕ *M5 jct 22. A38 towards Bristol for 500m. Right at Fox and Goose to Mark. Two miles, left towards Wells/Wedmore. Ten miles, Worth village. Cottage on left.*

❤ *Short stays available.*

Unit General P Leisure Shop 0.5 miles
Pub < 0.5 miles

WELLS, Somerset Map ref 2A2

★★★★
SELF CATERING

Units **1**
Sleeps **1–4**
Low season per wk
£300.00–£400.00
High season per wk
£450.00–£650.00

Wrinkle Mead, Wells

contact Mrs Cynthia Glass, Wrinkle Mead, Islington Farm, Wells BA5 1US
t (01749) 673445 **f** (01749) 673445 **e** islingtonfarm2004@yahoo.co.uk **w** islingtonfarmatwells.co.uk

open All year
payment Credit/debit cards, cash/cheques

Uniquely situated adjacent to The Bishop's Palace, a recent stable conversion overlooking fields and parkland, standing detached within the grounds of owner's property. Three minutes' walk to city centre. Ideal base for visiting Cheddar, Wookey Hole, Georgian Bath and National Trust properties. Excellent walking, cycling and riding on the Mendip Hills.

⊕ *A39 to Wells, straight across roundabout, immediately right by Sherston Inn into Southover. Right opposite Full Moon pub into Silver Street. Islington Farm on right.*

Unit General 5 P Leisure Shop < 0.5 miles
Pub < 0.5 miles

WEST BAY, Dorset Map ref 2A3

★★★
SELF CATERING

Units **1**
Sleeps **4**
Low season per wk
£200.00
High season per wk
£370.00

Jurassic View, Bridport

contact Mrs Frances Hunt, Spices, Stoney Lane, Curry Rivel, Langport TA10 0HY
t (01458) 251203 **f** (01458) 251203 **e** frances.kitchin.@somersetcook.freeserve.co.uk
w holsindorset.co.uk

A spacious two-bedroom, south-facing apartment with a balcony overlooking the sea. Lift and own parking space. Short stroll to harbour, shops, pubs, buses etc.

open All year
payment Cash/cheques

Unit General P Shop < 0.5 miles Pub < 0.5 miles

WEST BAY, Dorset Map ref 2A3

★★★-★★★★
SELF CATERING

Units **7**
Sleeps **2–8**
Low season per wk
£190.00–£340.00
High season per wk
£365.00–£590.00

Westpoint Apartments, Bridport

contact Mr & Mrs Slade, Westpoint Apartments, Esplanade, Bridport DT6 4HE
t (01308) 423636 **f** (01308) 458871 **e** bea@westpoint-apartments.co.uk
w westpointapartments.co.uk

Quality self-catering apartments on seafront overlooking sea and harbour. Fishing, 18-hole golf course, beautiful cliff walks, Thomas Hardy Country. Three- and four-day breaks available.

open All year
payment Credit/debit cards, cash/cheques

Unit General 5 P Leisure

WEST BEXINGTON, Dorset Map ref 2A3

★★★-★★★★
SELF CATERING

Units **6**
Sleeps **4–7**
Low season per wk
Min £250.00
High season per wk
Max £940.00

Tamarisk Farm Cottages, Dorchester

contact Mrs Josephine Pearse, Tamarisk Farm Cottages, Beach Road, West Bexington, Dorchester DT2 9DF
t (01308) 897784 **f** (01308) 897784 **e** holidays@tamariskfarm.com **w** holidays/tamariskfarm.co.uk

Cottages on organic farm sloping down to Chesil Beach, each with own garden and glorious sea views. Excellent walking country, abundant bird life, fossil-hunting on Jurassic Coast, tourist attractions. Not all facilities present in all units.

open All year
payment Credit/debit cards, cash/cheques, euros

Unit General P Leisure Shop 3 miles Pub < 0.5 miles

WEST LULWORTH, Dorset Map ref 2B3

★★★★
SELF CATERING

Units **1**
Sleeps **2–8**
Low season per wk
£420.00–£600.00
High season per wk
£600.00–£1,050.00

Seavale, West Lulworth

contact Mr Eric Symes, Seavale, Lulworth Lodge, Main Road, Wareham BH20 5RJ
t (01929) 406110 **f** (01929) 406110 **e** info@lulworthcove.org.uk **w** lulworthcove.org.uk

open All year
payment Cash/cheques

Situated amid the Jurassic Coast at Lulworth Cove. This comfortable architect-designed bungalow has lovely sea and country views and is set in an elevated position with steps up from parking area. Seavale has a garden, patio, balconies, log fire and three bathrooms.

Take the B3071 to West Lulworth. Drive towards the cove, taking small slip road on left. Seavale is past the high red-brick building.

Unit General S Leisure Shop < 0.5 miles Pub < 0.5 miles

Take a break

Look out for special promotions and themed breaks highlighted in colour. (Offers subject to availability.)

WESTON-SUPER-MARE, Somerset Map ref 1D1

★★★★
SELF CATERING

Units **4**
Sleeps **1–5**
Low season per wk
£187.00–£377.00
High season per wk
£392.00–£635.00

Hope Farm Cottages, Lympsham, Nr Weston-super-Mare

contact Mrs Liz Stirk, Hope Farm Cottages, Brean Road, Lympsham, Weston-super-Mare BS24 0HA
t (01934) 750506 **f** (01934) 750506 **e** stirkhopefarm@aol.com **w** hopefarmcottages.co.uk

Tranquil ground-floor cottages, each with two en suites, overlooking level, landscaped courtyard. Wheelchair and other aids available. Play areas, games room, laundry. Dogs welcomed.

open All year
payment Cash/cheques, euros

Unit General Leisure Shop 1 mile Pub 2 miles

WEYMOUTH, Dorset Map ref 2B3

★★★★★
SELF CATERING

Units **5**
Sleeps **4–8**
Low season per wk
Min £250.00

Bay Lodge Self-Catering Accommodation, Weymouth

contact Mr & Mrs Graham & Barbara Dubben, Bay Lodge Self-Catering Accommodation, 27 Greenhill, Weymouth DT4 7SW
t (01305) 787815 **e** barbara@baylodge.co.uk **w** baylodge.co.uk

open All year
payment Credit/debit cards, cash/cheques, euros

Seaside and country cottages, all with complimentary parking. Majority of bedrooms en suite with bath and shower; some with king-size double beds and jacuzzi. Newly fitted, fully equipped kitchens. Comfy lounges with colour TV, video and music centre. Most cottages with enclosed gardens. Indoor and outdoor swimming, and tennis courts nearby.

Unit General Leisure Shop < 0.5 miles Pub < 0.5 miles

WHIMPLE, Devon Map ref 1D2

★★★
SELF CATERING

Units **3**
Sleeps **4–6**
Low season per wk
£190.00–£265.00
High season per wk
£315.00–£420.00

LSF Holiday Cottages, Exeter

contact Mrs Angela Lang, LSF Holiday Cottages, Lower Southbrook Farm, Southbrook Lane, Exeter EX5 2PG
t (01404) 822989 **f** (01404) 822989 **e** lowersouthbrookfarm@btinternet.com
w lowersouthbrookfarm.co.uk

open All year
payment Cash/cheques, euros

Clean, comfortable, well-equipped cottages in the beautiful East Devon countryside. Set in a peaceful location, yet convenient for the cathedral city of Exeter, beaches and other popular tourist attractions. Heated swimming pool and large play area for children. Fully centrally heated for early/late holidays. Brochure available.

From the new A30 towards Honiton, follow signs to Whimple/Rockbeare. Take turning off Rockbeare opposite Oriental Promise.

Short breaks available throughout the year. Please ring for availability.

Unit General Leisure Shop 2 miles Pub 1 mile

Tourist information centres

To find the nearest one during your stay text TIC LOCATE to 64118.

WHITCHURCH, Devon Map ref 1C2

★★★★
SELF CATERING

Units 1
Sleeps 8
Low season per wk
£400.00–£600.00
High season per wk
£600.00–£800.00

Challonsleigh, Tavistock

contact Mary Susan Fox, Edgemoor, Middlemoor, Tavistock PL19 9DY
t (01822) 612259 **e** vicky@dartmoorcottages.info **w** challonsleigh.co.uk

open All year
payment Cash/cheques

Spacious, detached family house surrounded by gardens with spectacular views overlooking fields adjacent to extensive moorland. Two double and two twin bedrooms. Within an hour of both South and North Devon and Cornish beaches, the Eden Project, the aquarium, gardens and places of historic interest. Wonderful walking, riding and cycling over Dartmoor.

⊕ *From A30, take A386 to Tavistock. Take the Whitchurch road to the post office/shop crossroads. Turn left past pub and church. Last house on right before cattlegrid.*

Unit General P Leisure Shop < 0.5 miles Pub < 0.5 miles

WILLAND, Devon Map ref 1D2

★★★★
SELF CATERING

Units 2
Sleeps 4
Low season per wk
£340.00–£475.00
High season per wk
£475.00–£720.00

Bradfield Cottages, Cullompton

contact Jodee Culver Evans, Bradfield, Willand, Cullompton EX15 2RA
t (01884) 840222 **e** reservations@bradfieldcottages.co.uk **w** bradfieldcottages.co.uk

open All year
payment Cash/cheques

Stylish and extremely comfortable single-storey cottages, set in 18 acres of beautiful Devon countryside, with private gardens, woodland and a fishing lake. Each cottage has direct access to its own patio and walled garden. Easy access to all of Devon's activities and attractions. The perfect place for relaxing.

⊕ *From M5 jct 28 turn towards Honiton. Take the 1st left turn. Property is exactly 2.5 miles up this lane on the right.*

❤ *Short breaks available Oct-Mar and at short notice Mar-Oct.*

Unit General P S Leisure Shop 3 miles Pub 3 miles

WILLERSEY, Gloucestershire Map ref 2B1

★★
SELF CATERING

Units 1
Sleeps 3
Low season per wk
£200.00–£250.00
High season per wk
£270.00–£300.00

3 Cheltenham Cottages, Broadway

contact Mrs Gillian Malin, 28 Bibsworth Avenue, Broadway WR12 7BQ
t (01386) 853248 **e** g.malin@virgin.net

Grade II Listed Cotswold-stone cottage with countryside views. Award-winning village with excellent shops and pubs. Ideal for exploring the Cotswolds and Shakespeare country.

open All year
payment Cash/cheques

Unit General 5 Leisure Shop < 0.5 miles Pub < 0.5 miles

To your credit

If you book by phone you may be asked for your credit card number. If so, it is advisable to check the proprietor's policy in case you have to cancel your reservation at a later date.

WINCHCOMBE, Gloucestershire Map ref 2B1

★★★★
SELF CATERING

Units 1
Sleeps 1–4
Low season per wk
£225.00–£375.00
High season per wk
£375.00–£575.00

Misty View, Cheltenham

contact Mr Bob Turner, 32 North Street, Winchcombe, Cheltenham GL54 5PS
t (01242) 603583 & 07831 212501 **e** bobturner@mistyview.wannadoo.co.uk

open All year
payment Cash/cheques, euros

Modern Cotswold-stone cottage, close to heart of the delightful Saxon town of Winchcombe. Farmhouse-style kitchen, stone floors, beamed ceilings. One twin en suite bedroom, one 5ft king-size en suite bedroom. Five minutes' walk to historic pubs, restaurants and beautiful Sudeley Castle, once home of an English queen.

Railway station: Ashchurch for Tewkesbury, 7 miles. Motorway: M5 jct 9, 7.3 miles. Airport: Birmingham, 35.7 miles.

Short breaks available – email or phone for details and brochure.

Unit General Leisure Shop < 0.5 miles Pub < 0.5 miles

WINCHCOMBE, Gloucestershire Map ref 2B1

★★★★
SELF CATERING

Units 1
Sleeps 2–6
Low season per wk
£225.00–£275.00
High season per wk
£375.00–£450.00

Muir Cottage, Winchcombe, Cheltenham

contact Mark Grassick, Postlip Estate Co, Muir Cottage, Postlip, Winchcombe, Cheltenham GL54 5AQ
t (01242) 603124 **f** (01242) 603602 **e** enquiries@thecotswoldretreat.co.uk
w thecotswoldretreat.co.uk

Attractive, high-quality, Arts and Crafts-inspired, Cotswold-stone cottage converted from 18thC barn. Quietly located on historic country estate adjacent to Cotswold Way. Log fire, satellite TV. The ideal hideaway.

open All year
payment Cash/cheques, euros

Unit General Leisure Shop 1.5 miles Pub 1.5 miles

WINCHCOMBE, Gloucestershire Map ref 2B1

★★★
SELF CATERING

Units 1
Sleeps 4
Low season per wk
£200.00–£285.00
High season per wk
£285.00–£350.00

The Old Stables, Cheltenham

contact Miss Jane Eayrs, Hill View, Farmcote, Winchcombe, Cheltenham GL54 5AU
t (01242) 603860 **e** janeaycote@tesco.net

A delightful stable conversion on a working farm, set in beautiful countryside. Garden with magnificent views toward the Malvern Hills.

open All year
payment Cash/cheques

Unit General Shop 3.5 miles Pub 2 miles

Accessible needs?

If you have special hearing, visual or mobility needs, there's an index of all National Accessible Scheme participants at the back of this guide. Or buy a copy of our guide – Britain's Accessible Places to Stay – available from good bookshops and online at visitbritaindirect.com.

WINCHCOMBE, Gloucestershire Map ref 2B1

★★★★-★★★★★
SELF CATERING

Units 2
Sleeps 2–4
Low season per wk
£350.00–£450.00
High season per wk
£450.00–£495.00

Traditional Accommodation, Winchcombe, Cheltenham

contact Mr & Mrs Wilson, 60 Pershore Road, Evesham WR11 2PQ
t (01386) 446269 **f** (01386) 446269 **e** trad.accom@virgin.net
w http://freespace.virgin.net/trad.accom

open All year
payment Credit/debit cards, cash/cheques, euros

Courtyard setting of old traditional barns of individual style and character, finely restored to provide spacious, high-quality accommodation. Original features, quality facilities and furnishings. Gardens and patios, countryside views and private parking. Family supervised. Ideal touring base. Regret no pets. Brochures available.

⊕ *Midway between village of Greet and town of Winchcombe on B4078.*

Unit General **P** Leisure Shop 0.5 miles Pub < 0.5 miles

WINFORD, Somerset Map ref 2A2

★★★
SELF CATERING

Units 2
Sleeps 2–4
Low season per wk
£185.00–£255.00
High season per wk
£315.00–£445.00

Regilbury Farm, Bristol

contact Mrs Keedwell, Regilbury Farm, The Street, Regil, Winford, Bristol BS40 8BB
t (01275) 472369 **e** janekeedwell@yahoo.co.uk **w** regilburyfarm.co.uk

A working farm with cattle, sheep and chickens, all set in a beautiful, quiet hamlet. Wonderful rambling and lots to see. Guided walks available. Cowshed – double, Parlour – double and twin.

open All year
payment Cash/cheques

Unit General **P** Leisure Shop 2 miles Pub 1 mile

WOOLACOMBE, Devon Map ref 1C1

★★
SELF CATERING

Units 1
Sleeps 5
Low season per wk
£200.00–£250.00
High season per wk
£300.00–£525.00

Cove Cottage Flat, Woolacombe

contact Mrs Vivien Lawrence, Sharp Rock, Mortehoe, Woolacombe EX34 7EA
t (01271) 870403 **f** (01271) 870403 **e** vlawrence05@aol.com

Self-contained flat overlooking sandy beach (ten-minute walk). Washer/dryer, fridge/freezer, microwave, TV/video/DVD, garden. Pets welcome. Open all year. Central heating included early/late season. Parking.

open All year
payment Cash/cheques

Unit General **P** Leisure Shop 0.5 miles Pub 0.5 miles

Country Code Always follow the Country Code

- Be safe – plan ahead and follow any signs
- Leave gates and property as you find them
- Protect plants and animals, and take your litter home
- Keep dogs under close control
- Consider other people

Self-catering **agencies**

This section of the guide lists agencies that have a selection of accommodation to let in various parts of the country. Some agencies specialise in a particular area or region while others have properties in all parts of England.

The agencies listed here are grouped first into those who have had all properties assessed by Enjoy England, secondly into those who have had at least 75% of their properties assessed and thirdly those who have had at least 50% of their properties assessed.

To obtain further information on individual properties please contact the agency or agencies direct, indicating the time of year when the accommodation is required, the number of people to be accommodated and any preferred locations.

* The agencies printed in bold have an advertisement in this guide.

Quality Accredited Agency Standard

As a further step towards achieving quality not only in accommodation, Enjoy England has recently launched a Quality Accredited Agency Standard. Agencies who are awarded the Quality Accredited Agency Marque by Enjoy England are recognised as offering good customer service and peace of mind, following an assessment of their office policies, practices and procedures.

Quality Accredited Agency

Policies, Practices & Procedures Assessed

Totally quality assessed

These agencies only promote properties that have been assessed under Enjoy England's Quality Rose assessment scheme

Acanthus Property Letting Services
t (01502) 724033
w southwold-holidays.co.uk
Offering accommodation in Southwold, Walberswick and Dunwich, Suffolk

Ayia Napa Holidays
t (01736) 757237
w carbisbeachaparts.co.uk
Offering accommodation in Carbis Bay and St Ives, Cornwall

Bath Centre-Stay Holidays
t (01225) 313205
w bcsh.co.uk
Offering accommodation in Bath, Somerset

Bath Holiday Homes
t (01225) 830830
w bathholidayhomes.co.uk
Offering accommodation in Bath, Somerset

Blakes Cottages
t 0870 197 1000
w blakes-cottages.co.uk
Offering accommodation throughout England

Combermere Abbey Cottages
t (01948) 662876
w combermereabbey.co.uk
Offering accommodation in Combermere Abbey Estate, Cheshire/ Shropshire border

The Coppermines & Coniston Lake Cottages

t (015394) 41765
w coppermines.co.uk
Offering accommodation in Cumbria – The Lake District

Cornish Horizons Holiday Cottages
t (01841) 520889
w cornishhorizons.co.uk
Offering accommodation in North Cornwall

Cottages South West
t (01626) 872314
w cottagessw.vir.co.uk
Offering accommodation in Shaldon and Teignmouth, Devon

Country Hideaways
t (01969) 663559
w countryhideaways.co.uk
Offering accommodation in the Yorkshire Dales

Country Holidays
t 0870 197 1000
w country-holidays.co.uk
Offering accommodation throughout England

Cumbrian Cottages Ltd
t (01228) 599950
w cumbrian-cottages.co.uk
Offering accommodation in Cumbria – The Lake District

Diana Bullivant Holidays
t (01208) 831336
w cornwall-online.co.uk/diana-bullivant
Offering accommodation in North Cornwall

Dorset Cottage Holidays
t (01929) 553443
Offering accommodation in Dorset

Dream Cottages
t (01305) 789000
w dream-cottages.co.uk
Offering accommodation in Dorset, Devon, Wiltshire and Hampshire

Duchy Holidays Ltd
t (01872) 572971
w duchyholidays.co.uk
Offering accommodation in Perranporth and St Agnes, Cornwall

Fowey Harbour Cottages (W J B Hill & Son)
t (01726) 832211
Offering accommodation in and around Fowey, Cornwall

Freedom Holiday Homes
t (01580) 720770
w freedomholidayhomes.co.uk
Offering accommodation in Kent and East Sussex

Garden of England Cottages Limited
t (01732) 369168
w gardenofenglandcottages.co.uk
Offering accommodation in Kent and East Sussex

Harbour Holidays, Padstow
t (01841) 533402
w harbourholidays.co.uk
Offering accommodation in Padstow, Cornwall

Harrogate Holiday Cottages
t (01423) 523333
w harrogateholidays.co.uk
Offering accommodation in and around Harrogate, North Yorkshire

---

Heart of the Lakes and Cottage Life
t (015394) 32321
w heartofthelakes.co.uk
Offering accommodation in Cumbria – The Lake District

Helford River Cottages
t (01326) 231666
w helfordcottages.co.uk
Offering accommodation in and around Helford, Cornwall

Holiday Home Services (Seaview)
t (01983) 811418
w seaview-holiday-homes.co.uk
Offering accommodation in Seaview, Isle of Wight

Holiday Homes and Cottages SW
t (01803) 663650
w swcottages.co.uk
Offering accommodation in Devon and Cornwall

Holiday Homes Owners Services (West Wight)
t (01983) 753423
Offering accommodation on the Isle of Wight

Home from Home Holidays
t (01983) 854340
w hfromh.co.uk
Offering accommodation on the Isle of Wight

Island Cottage Holidays
t (01929) 480080
w islandcottageholidays.com
Offering accommodation on the Isle of Wight

Island Holiday Homes
t (01983) 521113
w island-holiday.homes.net
Offering accommodation on the Isle of Wight

Island Properties
t (01720) 422082
w islesofscillyholidays.com
Offering accommodation on the Isles of Scilly

Jean Bartlett Cottage Holidays Ltd
t (01297) 23221
w jeanbartlett.com
Offering accommodation in East Devon and West Dorset

Keswick Cottages
t (017687) 73895
w keswickcottages.co.uk
Offering accommodation in and around Keswick, Cumbria – The Lake District

---

Lakeland Cottage Company
t 0870 442 5814
w lakelandcottageco.com
Offering accommodation in Cumbria – The Lake District

Lakeland Cottage Holidays
t (017687) 76065
w lakelandcottages.co.uk
Offering accommodation in Cumbria – The Lake District

Agencies printed in bold have an advertisement in this guide

Lakelovers
t (015394) 88855
w lakelovers.co.uk
Offering accommodation in Cumbria – The Lake District

Linstone Chine Holiday Services Ltd
t (01983) 755933
w linstone-chine.co.uk
Offering accommodation on the Isle of Wight

Lyme Bay Holidays
t (01297) 443363
w lymebayholidays.co.uk
Offering accommodation in and around Lyme Regis, Dorset

Marsdens Cottage Holidays
t (01271) 813777
w marsdens.co.uk
Offering accommodation in North Devon

Milkbere Cottage Holidays
t (01297) 20729
w milkberehols.com
Offering accommodation in Devon

Millers of Hayling
t (023) 9246 5951
w haylingproperty.co.uk
Offering accommodation on Hayling Island, Hampshire

Miraleisure Ltd
t (01424) 730298
Offering accommodation in Bexhill-on-Sea, East Sussex

Red Rose Cottages
t (01200) 420101
w redrosecottages.co.uk
Offering accommodation in Yorkshire, Cumbria – The Lake District, the Peak District and Lancashire

Roseland Holiday Cottages
t (01872) 580480
w roselandholidaycottages.co.uk
Offering accommodation in St Mawes and Portscatho, Cornwall

Special Places in Cornwall
t (01872) 864400
w specialplacescornwall.co.uk
Offering accommodation in Cornwall

Suffolk Country Cottages
t (01603) 873378
w suffolkcountrycottages.co.uk
Offering accommodation in Suffolk and South Norfolk

Suffolk Holidays Limited
t (01502) 723571
w holidaysinsuffolk.co.uk
Offering accommodation in Southwold, Aldeburgh and Walberswick, Suffolk

Suffolk Secrets
t (01379) 651297
w suffolk-secrets.co.uk
Offering accommodation in Suffolk

Town or Country Serviced Apartments and Houses
t (023) 8088 1000
w town-or-country.co.uk
Offering accommodation in and around Southampton, Hampshire

Valley Villas Ltd
t (01752) 774900
w valleyvillas.com
Offering accommodation in Cornwall

Wheelwrights
t (015394) 37635
w wheelwrights.com
Offering accommodation in Cumbria – The Lake District

Whitby Holiday Cottages
t (01947) 603010
w whitby-cottages.co.uk
Offering accommodation in Yorkshire

Yealm Holidays
t 0870 747 2987
w yealm-holidays.co.uk
Offering accommodation in South West Devon

York Holiday Homes
t (01904) 641997
w yorkshirenet.co.uk/accgde/yorkholidayhomes
Offering accommodation in York, North Yorkshire

At least 75% quality assessed

Birds Norfolk Holiday Homes
t (01485) 534267
w norfolkholidayhomes-birds.co.uk
Offering accommodation in Norfolk

Homefinders Holidays
t (01904) 632660
w letters-of-york.co.uk
Offering accommodation in York, North Yorkshire

Rock Holidays
t (01208) 863399
w rockholidays.co.uk
Offering accommodation in Cornwall

Rumsey Holiday Homes
t 0845 644 4852
w rhh.org
Offering accommodation in Poole, Bournemouth and South Dorset

Shoreline Cottages Ltd
t (0113) 244 8410
w shoreline-cottages.com
Offering accommodation in and around Whitby, North Yorkshire

At least 50% quality assessed

Albion Rose Properties
t (01763) 249999
w albionrose.co.uk
Offering accommodation in Norfolk and Suffolk

Cottage in the Country & Cottage Holidays
t (01993) 831495
w cottageinthecountry.co.uk
Offering accommodation throughout England

Dales Holiday Cottages
t (01756) 799821
w dalesholcot.com
Offering accommodation in the north of England

Holiday Cottages Yorkshire
t (01756) 700510
w holidaycotts.co.uk
Offering accommodation in the north of England

Ingrid Flute Holiday Cottages
t (01723) 376777
w ingridflute.co.uk
Offering accommodation in Yorkshire

Lambert & Russell
t (01263) 513139
Offering accommodation in Norfolk

Manor Cottages
t (01993) 824252
Offering accommodation in the Cotswolds

Mullion Cottages
t (01326) 240315
w mullioncottages.com
Offering accommodation in Cornwall

Peak Cottages
t (0114) 262 0777
w peakcottages.com
Offering accommodation in the Peak District

Agencies printed in bold have an advertisement in this guide

Enjoy England's assessed accommodation

On the following pages you will find an exclusive listing of every self-catering establishment in England that has been assessed for quality by Enjoy England.

The information includes brief contact details for each place to stay, together with its star rating and designator. The listing also shows if an establishment has a National Accessible rating or participates in the Walkers and Cyclists Welcome schemes (see the front of the guide for further information). Accommodation is listed by region and then alphabetically by place name. Establishments may be located in, or a short distance from, the places in blue bands.

More detailed information on all the properties shown in bold can be found in the regional sections (where establishments have paid to have their details included). To find these entries please refer to the property index at the back of this guide.

The list which follows was compiled slightly later than the regional sections. For this reason you may find that, in a few instances, a star rating and quality award may differ between the two sections. This list contains the most up-to-date information and was correct at the time of going to press.

Boat accommodation

Towards the end of this section you will find details of boat accommodation quality-assessed by Enjoy England.

Approved caravan holiday homes

At the end of this section you will find details of individual, quality-assessed caravans.

ENGLAND'S NORTHWEST

ACCRINGTON
Lancashire

Low Moorside Farm Cottage ★★★ *Self Catering*
Contact: Mr & Mrs C & E Hallworth
t (01254) 237053

ADLINGTON
Cheshire

Carr Cottage ★★★★
Self Catering
Contact: Mrs Isobel Worthington
t (01625) 828337
e isobel@carrhousefarm.fsnet.co.uk
w topfarms.co.uk

AINSTABLE
Cumbria

Eden House ★★★
Self Catering
Contact: Peter Durbin
Cumbrian Cottages Ltd
t (01228) 599950
e enquiries@cumbrian-cottages.co.uk
w cumbrian-cottages.co.uk

ALLITHWAITE
Cumbria

Fair View ★★★ *Self Catering*
Contact: Peter Durbin
Cumbrian Cottages Ltd
t (01228) 599950
e enquiries@cumbrian-cottages.co.uk
w cumbrian-cottages.co.uk

ALLONBY
Cumbria

Crookhurst Farm ★★★★
Self Catering
Contact: Brenda Wilson
t (01900) 881228
e brenda@crookhurst.com
w crookhurst.com

Dickinson Place Holiday Cottages ★★★-★★★★
Self Catering
Contact: James Williamson
Dickinson Place Holiday Cottages
t (01900) 881440
e holidays@dickinsonplace.co.uk
w dickinsonplace.co.uk

The Old Coachmans Cottage ★★★ *Self Catering*
Contact: Peter Durbin
Cumbrian Cottages Ltd
t (01228) 599950
e enquiries@cumbrian-cottages.co.uk
w cumbrian-cottages.co.uk

Spring Lea ★★★★
Self Catering
Contact: John Williamson
Spring Lea Caravan Park
t (01900) 881331
e mail@springlea.co.uk
w springlea.co.uk

ALSTON
Cumbria

Back O' The Burn ★★★★
Self Catering
Contact: Peter Durbin
Cumbrian Cottages Ltd
t (01228) 599950
e enquiries@cumbrian-cottages.co.uk
w cumbrian-cottages.co.uk

Ghyll Burn Cottage ★★★
Self Catering
t (01434) 381372
e ghyllburn@macunlimited.net

Palace Cottage ★★★
Self Catering
Contact: Richard Leon
t 07801 258490

Rock House Estate ★★★★
Self Catering
Contact: Paul & Carol Huish
t (01434) 382684
e paul@rockhouseestate.co.uk
w rockhouseestate.co.uk

Stone Barn Cottage ★★★★★ *Self Catering*
Contact: Mrs Dee Ellis
Stone Barn Cottage
t (01434) 381672
e tim@hillfarmer.com
w hillfarmer.com

AMBLESIDE
Cumbria

1 Tom Fold ★★★
Self Catering
Lakelovers
t (015394) 88855
e bookings@lakelovers.co.uk
w lakelovers.co.uk

1 West View ★★★★
Self Catering
Contact: Peter Durbin
Cumbrian Cottages Ltd
t (01228) 599960
e enquiries@cumbrian-cottages.co.uk
w cumbrian-cottages.co.uk

10 Badgers Rake ★★★★
Self Catering
Contact: Peter Durbin
Cumbrian Cottages Ltd
t (01228) 599950
e enquiries@cumbrian-cottages.co.uk
w cumbrian-cottages.co.uk

11 Badgers Rake ★★★
Self Catering
Contact: Peter Durbin
Cumbrian Cottages Ltd
t (01228) 599950
e enquiries@cumbrian-cottages.co.uk
w cumbrian-cottages.co.uk

12 Badgers Rake ★★★★
Self Catering
Contact: Peter Durbin
Cumbrian Cottages Ltd
t (01228) 599950
e enquiries@cumbrian-cottages.co.uk
w cumbrian-cottages.co.uk

1,2,3 Riverside Cottages ★★★-★★★★ *Self Catering*
Contact: Mr Paul Liddell
Lakelovers
t (015394) 88855
e bookings@lakelovers.co.uk
w lakelovers.co.uk

19 The Lakelands ★★★★
Self Catering
Contact: Mr Paul Liddell
Lakelovers
t (015394) 88855
e bookings@lakelovers.co.uk
w lakelovers.co.uk

20 and 21 The Falls ★★★
Self Catering
Contact: Mr Paul Liddell
Lakelovers
t (015394) 88855
e bookings@lakelovers.co.uk
w lakelovers.co.uk

5 Lowfield ★★★★
Self Catering
Contact: Peter Durbin
Cumbrian Cottages Ltd
t (01228) 599950
e enquiries@cumbrian-cottages.co.uk
w cumbrian-cottages.co.uk

7 Badgers Rake ★★★★
Self Catering
Contact: Peter Durbin
Cumbrian Cottages Ltd
t (01228) 599950
e enquiries@cumbrian-cottages.co.uk
w cumbrian-cottages.co.uk

9 Badgers Rake ★★★★
Self Catering
Contact: Peter Durbin
Cumbrian Cottages Ltd
t (01228) 599950
e enquiries@cumbrian-cottages.co.uk
w cumbrian-cottages.co.uk

Above Stock ★★★★
Self Catering
Contact: Mr Paul Liddell
Lakelovers
t (015394) 88855
e bookings@lakelovers.co.uk
w lakelovers.co.uk

Acorns ★★★★ *Self Catering*
Heart of the Lakes
t (015394) 32321
e info@heartofthelakes.co.uk
w heartofthelakes.co.uk

Altar End ★★★★
Self Catering
Contact: Susan Jackson
Heart of the Lakes
t (015394) 32321
e info@heartofthelakes.co.uk
w heartofthelakes.co.uk

Amblers Rest ★★★★
Self Catering
Contact: Peter Durbin
Cumbrian Cottages Ltd
t (01228) 599950
e enquiries@cumbrian-cottages.co.uk
w cumbrian-cottages.co.uk

Angela's Cottage ★★★
Self Catering
Contact: Jo Tomlinson
t (015394) 32383
e martin@waltonmount.plus.com

Appletree Cottage ★★★★
Self Catering
Contact: Mrs Susan Jackson
Heart of the Lakes
t (015394) 32321
e info@heartofthelakes.co.uk
w heartofthelakes.co.uk

Appletree Cottage ★★★
Self Catering
Contact: Peter Durbin
Cumbrian Cottages Ltd
t (01228) 599950
e enquiries@cumbrian-cottages.co.uk
w cumbrian-cottages.co.uk

Ashburne Cottage ★★★
Self Catering
Contact: Mrs Susan Jackson
Heart of the Lakes
t (015394) 32321
e info@heartofthelakes.co.uk
w heartofthelakes.co.uk

Ashness ★★★★
Self Catering
Contact: Mrs Susan Jackson
Heart of the Lakes
t (015394) 32321
e info@heartofthelakes.co.uk
w heartofthelakes.co.uk

Babbling Brook ★★★★
Self Catering
Contact: Susan Jackson
Heart of the Lakes
t (015394) 32321
e info@heartofthelakes.co.uk
w heartofthelakes.co.uk

Bakers Rest ★★★★
Self Catering
Contact: Peter Durbin
Cumbrian Cottages Ltd
t (01228) 599950
e enquiries@cumbrian-cottages.co.uk
w cumbrian-cottages.co.uk

Bakestones Cottage ★★★★
Self Catering
Contact: Susan Jackson
Heart of the Lakes
t (015394) 32321
e info@heartofthelakes.co.uk
w heartofthelakes.co.uk

The Barn ★★★★
Self Catering
Contact: Susan Jackson
Heart of the Lakes
t (015394) 32321
e info@heartofthelakes.co.uk
w heartofthelakes.co.uk

Beck, Hillside and Couter Cottages ★★★ *Self Catering*
Contact: Mrs Morris
t (0161) 790 8023
w amblesideselfcatering.co.uk

Birch Cottage ★★★
Self Catering
Contact: Dr Nash
Birch Cottage
t (020) 8888 1252 & 07974 817787
e birch@drnash.wanadoo.co.uk
w cottage-lakedistrict.mysite.wanadoo-members.co.uk

Birch Knoll ★★★★
Self Catering
Contact: Mr Paul Liddell
Lakelovers
t (015394) 88855
e bookings@lakelovers.co.uk
w lakelovers.co.uk

Birchcroft ★★★★
Self Catering
Contact: Susan Jackson
Heart of the Lakes
t (015394) 32321
e info@heartofthelakes.co.uk
w heartofthelakes.co.uk

Blelham Tarn at Neaum Crag ★★★★ *Self Catering*
Contact: Andy Witts
PAD-LOK Products Ltd
t 07740 486947
e enquiries@logcabin.bz
w logcabin.bz

Blencathra ★★★
Self Catering
Contact: Mrs Susan Jackson
Heart of the Lakes
t (015394) 32321
e info@heartofthelakes.co.uk
w heartofthelakes.co.uk

Blue Hill Cottage ★★★
Self Catering
Contact: Peter Durbin
Cumbrian Cottages Ltd
t (01228) 599950
e enquiries@cumbrian-cottages.co.uk
w cumbrian-cottages.co.uk

Bluebell Cottage ★★★★
Self Catering
Contact: Ms Sue Jackson
Heart of the Lakes
t (015394) 32321
e info@heartofthelakes.co.uk
w heartofthelakes.co.uk

Bobbin Cottage ★★★
Self Catering
Contact: Mr Paul Liddell
Lakelovers
t (015394) 88855
e bookings@lakelovers.co.uk
w lakelovers.co.uk

Brackenrigg ★★★
Self Catering
Contact: Mr Paul Liddell
Lakelovers
t (015394) 88855
e bookings@lakelovers.co.uk
w lakelovers.co.uk

Brae Cottage ★★★
Self Catering
Contact: Mr Paul Liddell
Lakelovers
t (015394) 88855
e bookings@lakelovers.co.uk
w lakelovers.co.uk

Braebeck ★★★ *Self Catering*
Contact: Mr Paul Liddell
Lakelovers
t (015394) 88855
e bookings@lakelovers.co.uk
w lakelovers.co.uk

Briar Nook ★★★★
Self Catering
Contact: Peter Durbin
Cumbrian Cottages Ltd
t (01228) 599950
e enquiries@cumbrian-cottages.co.uk
w cumbrian-cottages.co.uk

Briardale Cottage ★★★
Self Catering
Contact: Susan Jackson
Heart of the Lakes
t (015394) 32321
e info@heartofthelakes.co.uk
w heartofthelakes.co.uk

Brookfield ★★★★
Self Catering
Contact: Peter Durbin
Cumbrian Cottages Ltd
t (01228) 599950
e enquiries@cumbrian-cottages.co.uk
w cumbrian-cottages.co.uk

Brunt How ★★★
Self Catering
Contact: Mrs Susan Jackson
Heart of the Lakes
t (015394) 32321
e info@heartofthelakes.co.uk
w heartofthelakes.co.uk

Brydewood ★★★★
Self Catering
Contact: Mrs Susan Jackson
Heart of the Lakes
t (015394) 32321
e info@heartofthelakes.co.uk
w heartofthelakes.co.uk

Buttermere ★★★
Self Catering
Contact: Mr Paul Liddell
Lakelovers
t (015394) 88855
e bookings@lakelovers.co.uk
w lakelovers.co.uk

Byways ★★ *Self Catering*
Contact: Susan Jackson
Heart of the Lakes
t (015394) 32321
e info@heartofthelakes.co.uk
w heartofthelakes.co.uk

Cairn Cottage ★★★★
Self Catering
Contact: Peter Durbin
Cumbrian Cottages Ltd
t (01228) 599950
e enquiries@cumbrian-cottages.co.uk
w cumbrian-cottages.co.uk

Candleberry Cottage ★★★★ *Self Catering*
Lakelovers
t (015394) 88855
e bookings@lakelovers.co.uk
w lakelovers.co.uk

Cedar House ★★★★
Self Catering
Lakelovers
t (015394) 88855
e bookings@lakelovers.co.uk
w lakelovers.co.uk

Chestnuts, Beeches and The Granary ★★★★ *Self Catering*
Contact: Mr Benson
Chestnuts, Beeches and The Granary
t (015394) 42731
e info@accommodationlakedistrict.com
w accommodationlakedistrict.com

Church View ★★★★
Self Catering
Contact: Peter Durbin
Cumbrian Cottages Ltd
t (01228) 599950
e enquiries@cumbrian-cottages.co.uk
w cumbrian-cottages.co.uk

Clover Cottage ★★★
Self Catering
Contact: Susan Jackson
Heart of the Lakes
t (015394) 32321
e info@heartofthelakes.co.uk
w heartofthelakes.co.uk

The Coach House ★★★★★
Self Catering
Contact: Mrs Susan Jackson
Heart of the Lakes
t (015394) 32321
e info@heartofthelakes.co.uk
w heartofthelakes.co.uk

Cobblestones ★★★★
Self Catering
Contact: Peter Durbin
Cumbrian Cottages Ltd
t (01228) 599950
e enquiries@cumbrian-cottages.co.uk
w cumbrian-cottages.co.uk

Cobblestones House ★★★★ *Self Catering*
Contact: Peter Durbin
Cumbrian Cottages Ltd
t (01228) 599950
e enquiries@cumbrian-cottages.co.uk
w cumbrian-cottages.co.uk

Conifers ★★★ *Self Catering*
Contact: Mrs Susan Jackson
Heart of the Lakes
t (015394) 32321
e info@heartofthelakes.co.uk
w heartofthelakes.co.uk

Cooksons Garth ★★★★
Self Catering
Contact: Mrs Susan Jackson
Heart of the Lakes
t (015394) 32321
e info@heartofthelakes.co.uk
w heartofthelakes.co.uk

Copper Tops ★★★★
Self Catering
Contact: Anne Gallagher
Hideaways
t (015394) 42435
e bookings@lakeland-hideaways.co.uk
w lakeland-hideaways.co.uk

Copt How ★★★★
Self Catering
Lakelovers
t (015394) 88855
e bookings@lakelovers.co.uk
w lakelovers.co.uk

Cornerstones ★★★★
Self Catering
Contact: Peter Durbin
Cumbrian Cottages Ltd
t (01228) 599950
e enquiries@cumbrian-cottages.co.uk
w cumbrian-cottages.co.uk

Couter Cottage ★★★
Self Catering
Lakelovers
t (015394) 88855
e bookings@lakelovers.co.uk
w lakelovers.co.uk

Crag View ★★★★
Self Catering
Contact: Mrs Davies
t (0151) 924 6995
e pfdavies@blueyonder.co.uk
w amblesidecottage.net

Cranford Cottage ★★★
Self Catering
Contact: Mr Clive Sykes
Sykes Cottages
t (01244) 345700
e info@sykescottages.co.uk
w sykescottages.co.uk

Cringol Cottage ★★★
Self Catering
Contact: Susan Jackson
Heart of the Lakes
t (015394) 32321
e info@heartofthelakes.co.uk
w heartofthelakes.co.uk

Crinkle Crags ★★★
Self Catering
Contact: Susan Jackson
Heart of the Lakes
t (015394) 32321
e info@heartofthelakes.co.uk
w heartofthelakes.co.uk

Croft Cottage ★★★★
Self Catering
Contact: Ms Sue Jackson
Heart of the Lakes
t (015394) 32321
e info@heartofthelakes.co.uk
w heartofthelakes.co.uk

Cuckoo's Nest ★★★★★
Self Catering
Contact: Anthony & Christine Harrison
Smallwood House Hotel
t (015394) 32330
e cuckoosnest@cottagesambleside.co.uk
w cottagesambleside.co.uk

Derby Cottage ★★★
Self Catering
Contact: Peter Durbin
Cumbrian Cottages Ltd
t (01228) 599950
e enquiries@cumbrian-cottages.co.uk
w cumbrian-cottages.co.uk

Dower House Cottage ★★★
Self Catering
Contact: Mrs Margaret Rigg
The Dower House
t (015394) 33211

Dwarf Hall Studio ★★★★
Self Catering
Contact: Peter Durbin
Cumbrian Cottages Ltd
t (01228) 599950
e enquiries@cumbrian-cottages.co.uk
w cumbrian-cottages.co.uk

Ecclerigg Cottage ★★★★
Self Catering
Contact: Susan Jackson
Heart of the Lakes
t (015394) 32321
e info@heartofthelakes.co.uk
w heartofthelakes.co.uk

Ecclerigg Old Farm ★★★
Self Catering
Contact: Susan Jackson
Heart of the Lakes
t (015394) 32321
e info@heartofthelakes.co.uk
w heartofthelakes.co.uk

Edelweiss ★★★★
Self Catering
Heart of the Lakes
t (015394) 32321
e info@heartofthelakes.co.uk
w heartofthelakes.co.uk

Edelweiss ★★★★
Self Catering
Contact: Peter Durbin
Cumbrian Cottages Ltd
t (01228) 599950
e enquiries@cumbrian-cottages.co.uk
w cumbrian-cottages.co.uk

Edenbridge ★★★
Self Catering
Heart of the Lakes
t (015394) 32321
e info@heartofthelakes.co.uk
w heartofthelakes.co.uk

Ellerview ★★★ *Self Catering*
Contact: Mr Paul Liddell
Lakelovers
t (015394) 88855
e bookings@lakelovers.co.uk
w lakelovers.co.uk

Eskdale ★★★★ *Self Catering*
Contact: Peter Durbin
Cumbrian Cottages Ltd
t (01228) 599950
e enquiries@cumbrian-cottages.co.uk
w cumbrian-cottages.co.uk

Fairview ★★★★★
Self Catering
Contact: Mrs Susan Jackson
Heart of the Lakes
t (015394) 32321
e info@heartofthelakes.co.uk
w heartofthelakes.co.uk

Falls View Cottage ★★★
Self Catering
Contact: Susan Jackson
Heart of the Lakes
t (015394) 32321
e info@heartofthelakes.co.uk
w heartofthelakes.co.uk

Fell View ★★★★
Self Catering
Contact: Peter Durbin
Cumbrian Cottages Ltd
t (01228) 599950
e enquiries@cumbrian-cottages.co.uk
w cumbrian-cottages.co.uk

Fellcroft ★★★★
Self Catering
Contact: Mrs Susan Jackson
Heart of the Lakes
t (015394) 32321
e info@heartofthelakes.co.uk
w heartofthelakes.co.uk

Fellmere ★★★★★
Self Catering
Contact: Peter Durbin
Cumbrian Cottages Ltd
t (01228) 599950
e enquiries@cumbrian-cottages.co.uk
w cumbrian-cottages.co.uk

Fellside ★★★ *Self Catering*
Lakelovers
t (015394) 88855
e bookings@lakelovers.co.uk
w lakelovers.co.uk

Fellside ★★★★ *Self Catering*
Contact: Mrs Susan Jackson
Heart of the Lakes
t (015394) 32321
e info@heartofthelakes.co.uk
w heartofthelakes.co.uk

Fern Ghyll ★★★★
Self Catering
Contact: Susan Jackson
Heart of the Lakes
t (015394) 32321
e info@heartofthelakes.co.uk
w heartofthelakes.co.uk

Field Foot Cottage ★★★★
Self Catering
Contact: Susan Jackson
Heart of the Lakes
t (015394) 32321
e info@heartofthelakes.co.uk
w heartofthelakes.co.uk

The Flat ★★★ *Self Catering*
Contact: Susan Jackson
Heart of the Lakes
t (015394) 32321
e info@heartofthelakes.co.uk
w heartofthelakes.co.uk

Forge Side ★★★
Self Catering
Contact: Susan Jackson
Heart of the Lakes
t (015394) 32321
e info@heartofthelakes.co.uk
w heartofthelakes.co.uk

Four Seasons Cottage ★★★
Self Catering
Contact: Susan Jackson
Heart of the Lakes
t (015394) 32321
e info@heartofthelakes.co.uk
w heartofthelakes.co.uk

Gable End & Amblers Rest ★★★★ *Self Catering*
Contact: Peter Durbin
Cumbrian Cottages Ltd
t (01228) 599950
e enquiries@cumbrian-cottages.co.uk
w cumbrian-cottages.co.uk

The Gables ★★★★
Self Catering
Contact: Susan Jackson
Heart of the Lakes
t (015394) 32321
e info@heartofthelakes.co.uk
w heartofthelakes.co.uk

Galava Sheil ★★★★
Self Catering
Contact: Ms Sue Jackson
Heart of the Lakes
t (015394) 32321
e info@heartofthelakes.co.uk
w heartofthelakes.co.uk

Gale House Cottage ★★★★
Self Catering
Contact: Mrs Susan Jackson
Heart of the Lakes
t (015394) 32321
e info@heartofthelakes.co.uk
w heartofthelakes.co.uk

Gale Howe Barn ★★★★
Self Catering
Contact: Mrs Susan Jackson
Heart of the Lakes
t (015394) 32321
e info@heartofthelakes.co.uk
w heartofthelakes.co.uk

Gale Lodge Cottage ★★★★
Self Catering
Contact: Mrs Vivien Bass
Wheelwrights Holiday Cottages
t (015394) 37635
e enquiries@wheelwrights.com

Gale Lodge Stables ★★★★
Self Catering
Contact: Mr Paul Liddell
Lakelovers
t (015394) 88855
e bookings@lakelovers.co.uk
w lakelovers.co.uk

Gale Mews ★★★★
Self Catering
Contact: Susan Jackson
Heart of the Lakes
t (015394) 32321
e info@heartofthelakes.co.uk
w heartofthelakes.co.uk

The Garden Flat ★★★
Self Catering
Contact: Alan & Margaret Wardle
Lake District Holidays
t (015395) 68103
e lakedistricthols@aol.com
w lakedistrictholidays.net

The Gate ★★★★
Self Catering
Contact: Susan Jackson
Heart of the Lakes
t (015394) 32321
e info@heartofthelakes.co.uk
w heartofthelakes.co.uk

Ghyll Bank ★★★★
Self Catering
Contact: Susan Jackson
Heart of the Lakes
t (015394) 32321
e info@heartofthelakes.co.uk
w heartofthelakes.co.uk

Ghyll Heights ★★★
Self Catering
Contact: Peter Durbin
Cumbrian Cottages Ltd
t (01228) 599950
e enquiries@cumbrian-cottages.co.uk
w cumbrian-cottages.co.uk

Ghyll View ★★★
Self Catering
Contact: Susan Jackson
Heart of the Lakes
t (015394) 32321
e info@heartofthelakes.co.uk
w heartofthelakes.co.uk

Ghyllside 3 ★★★
Self Catering
Contact: Peter Durbin
Cumbrian Cottages Ltd
t (01228) 599950
e enquiries@cumbrian-cottages.co.uk
w cumbrian-cottages.co.uk

Ghyllstead ★★★★
Self Catering
Contact: Ms Sue Jackson
Heart of the Lakes
t (015394) 32321
e info@heartofthelakes.co.uk
w heartofthelakes.co.uk

Gilbertscar Foot ★★★★
Self Catering
Contact: Mr David Milne
t (015394) 32395

Gillybeck, The Falls ★★★★
Self Catering
Contact: Susan Jackson
Heart of the Lakes
t (015394) 32321
e info@heartofthelakes.co.uk
w heartofthelakes.co.uk

Glenmore Cottage ★★★★
Self Catering
Contact: Peter Durbin
Cumbrian Cottages Ltd
t (01228) 599950
e enquiries@cumbrian-cottages.co.uk
w cumbrian-cottages.co.uk

The Granary ★★★★
Self Catering
Contact: Ms Sue Jackson
Heart of the Lakes
t (015394) 32321
e info@heartofthelakes.co.uk
w heartofthelakes.co.uk

The Granny Flat ★★★
Self Catering
Contact: Susan Jackson
Heart of the Lakes
t (015394) 32321
e info@heartofthelakes.co.uk
w heartofthelakes.co.uk

Green Moss ★★★★
Self Catering
Contact: Mrs Susan Jackson
Heart of the Lakes
t (015394) 32321
e info@heartofthelakes.co.uk
w heartofthelakes.co.uk

Greenways ★★★★
Self Catering
Contact: Mr Paul Liddell
Lakelovers
t (015394) 88855
e bookings@lakelovers.co.uk
w lakelovers.co.uk

The Grove Cottages ★★★★-★★★★★
Self Catering
Contact: Zee Thompson
t (015394) 33074
e grovecottages@clara.co.uk
w grovecottages.com

Halfway House ★★★★
Self Catering
Contact: Peter Durbin
Cumbrian Cottages Ltd
t (01228) 599950
e enquiries@cumbrian-cottages.co.uk
w cumbrian-cottages.co.uk

Hayrake ★★★ *Self Catering*
Contact: Peter Durbin
Cumbrian Cottages Ltd
t (01228) 599950
e enquiries@cumbrian-cottages.co.uk
w cumbrian-cottages.co.uk

Hazelnut Cottage ★★★★
Self Catering
Contact: Susan Jackson
Heart of the Lakes
t (015394) 32321
e sue@heartofthelakes.co.uk
w heartofthelakes.co.uk

Heather Cottage ★★★
Self Catering
Contact: Mr Paul Liddell
Lakelovers
t (015394) 88855
e bookings@lakelovers.co.uk
w lakelovers.co.uk

Herald Cottage ★★★★
Self Catering
Contact: Peter Durbin
Cumbrian Cottages Ltd
t (01228) 599950
e enquiries@cumbrian-cottages.co.uk
w cumbrian-cottages.co.uk

Heron Cottage ★★★
Self Catering
Contact: Peter Durbin
Cumbrian Cottages Ltd
t (01228) 599950
e enquiries@cumbrian-cottages.co.uk
w cumbrian-cottages.co.uk

Hideaway Cottage ★★★
Self Catering
Contact: Ms Sue Jackson
Heart of the Lakes
t (015394) 32321
e info@heartofthelakes.co.uk
w heartofthelakes.co.uk

High Bank ★★★
Self Catering
Contact: Susan Jackson
Heart of the Lakes
t (015394) 32321
e info@heartofthelakes.co.uk
w heartofthelakes.co.uk

High Bank Cottage ★★★
Self Catering
Contact: Mrs Susan Jackson
Heart of the Lakes
t (015394) 32321
e info@heartofthelakes.co.uk
w heartofthelakes.co.uk

High Pike Cottage ★★★
Self Catering
Contact: Susan Jackson
Heart of the Lakes
t (015394) 32321
e info@heartofthelakes.co.uk
w heartofthelakes.co.uk

High Spy ★★★★
Self Catering
Contact: Ms Sue Jackson
Heart of the Lakes
t (015394) 32321
e info@heartofthelakes.co.uk
w heartofthelakes.co.uk

High View ★★★
Self Catering
Contact: Ms Sue Jackson
Heart of the Lakes
t (015394) 32321
e info@heartofthelakes.co.uk
w heartofthelakes.co.uk

High White Stones ★★★★
Self Catering
Contact: Peter Durbin
Cumbrian Cottages Ltd
t (01228) 599950
e enquiries@cumbrian-cottages.co.uk
w cumbrian-cottages.co.uk

Hilber Cottage ★★★
Self Catering
Contact: Mrs Susan Jackson
Heart of the Lakes
t (015394) 32321
e info@heartofthelakes.co.uk
w heartofthelakes.co.uk

Hillandale ★★★ *Self Catering*
Contact: Mr Paul Liddell
Lakelovers
t (015394) 88855
e bookings@lakelovers.co.uk
w lakelovers.co.uk

Hillcrest Cottage ★★★★
Self Catering
Contact: Mr Paul Liddell
Lakelovers
t (015394) 88855
e bookings@lakelovers.co.uk
w lakelovers.co.uk

Hillside Cottage ★★★
Self Catering
Contact: Susan Jackson
Heart of the Lakes
t (015394) 32321
e info@heartofthelakes.co.uk
w heartofthelakes.co.uk

Holbeck ★★★★
Self Catering
Contact: Susan Jackson
Heart of the Lakes
t (015394) 32321
e info@heartofthelakes.co.uk
w heartofthelakes.co.uk

Hole House ★★★
Self Catering
Contact: Clare Irvine
Tock How Farm
t (015394) 36106
e info@tock-how-farm.com
w tock-how-farm.com

The Hollies ★★★
Self Catering
Contact: Peter Durbin
Cumbrian Cottages Ltd
t (01228) 599950
e enquiries@cumbrian-cottages.co.uk
w cumbrian-cottages.co.uk

Holly Cottage ★★★
Self Catering
Contact: Mrs Susan Jackson
Heart of the Lakes
t (015394) 32321
e info@heartofthelakes.co.uk
w heartofthelakes.co.uk

Hollybrook ★★★★
Self Catering
Contact: Peter Durbin
Cumbrian Cottages Ltd
t (01228) 599950
e enquiries@cumbrian-cottages.co.uk
w cumbrian-cottages.co.uk

Honey Pot Cottage ★★★★
Self Catering
Contact: Mrs Susan Jackson
Heart of the Lakes
t (015394) 32321
e info@heartofthelakes.co.uk
w heartofthelakes.co.uk

Honeypot Cottage ★★★★
Self Catering
Contact: Susan Jackson
Heart of the Lakes
t (015394) 32321
e info@heartofthelakes.co.uk
w heartofthelakes.co.uk

Horseshoe Cottage ★★★
Self Catering
Contact: Susan Jackson
Heart of the Lakes
t (015394) 32321
e info@heartofthelakes.co.uk
w heartofthelakes.co.uk

How Head Barn S/C ★★★
Self Catering
Contact: Val Walker
How Head Barn
t (015394) 32948
e howhead@btopenworld.com

How Head Cottage ★★★
Self Catering
Contact: Susan Jackson
Heart of the Lakes
t (015394) 32321
e info@heartofthelakes.co.uk
w heartofthelakes.co.uk

Iona ★★★ *Self Catering*
Contact: Susan Jackson
Heart of the Lakes
t (015394) 32321
e info@heartofthelakes.co.uk
w heartofthelakes.co.uk

Juniper Cottage ★★★
Self Catering
Contact: Mr Paul Liddell
Lakelovers
t (015394) 88855
e bookings@lakelovers.co.uk
w lakelovers.co.uk

Kelsick Court ★★★
Self Catering
Contact: Peter Durbin
Cumbrian Cottages Ltd
t (01228) 599950
e enquiries@cumbrian-cottages.co.uk
w cumbrian-cottages.co.uk

Kelsick Heights ★★★★
Self Catering
Contact: Peter Durbin
Cumbrian Cottages Ltd
t (01228) 599950
e enquiries@cumbrian-cottages.co.uk
w cumbrian-cottages.co.uk

Kiln Cottage ★★★★
Self Catering
Lakelovers
t (015394) 88855
e bookings@lakelovers.co.uk
w lakelovers.co.uk

Kirkstone Cottage ★★★
Self Catering
Contact: Peter Durbin
Cumbrian Cottages Ltd
t (01228) 599950
e enquiries@cumbrian-cottages.co.uk
w cumbrian-cottages.co.uk

Kirkstone Foot Cottages and Apartments
★★★★–★★★★★
Self Catering
Contact: Mr Norfolk
t (015394) 32232
e info@kirkstonefoot.co.uk
w kirkstonefoot.co.uk

Lakefield House ★★★★
Self Catering
Contact: Susan Jackson
Heart of the Lakes
t (015394) 32321
e info@heartofthelakes.co.uk
w heartofthelakes.co.uk

Lakeland Cottage ★★★★
Self Catering
Contact: Mr Paul Liddell
Lakelovers
t (015394) 88855
e bookings@lakelovers.co.uk
w lakelovers.co.uk

The Lakelands ★★★★
Self Catering
Contact: Jackie Kingdom
The Lakelands
t (015394) 33777
e enquiry@the-lakelands.com
w the-lakelands.com

Langdale ★★★ *Self Catering*
Contact: Mrs Susan Jackson
Heart of the Lakes
t (015394) 32321
e info@heartofthelakes.co.uk
w heartofthelakes.co.uk

The Larches ★★★★
Self Catering
Contact: Mrs Susan Jackson
Heart of the Lakes
t (015394) 32321
e info@heartofthelakes.co.uk
w heartofthelakes.co.uk

Leafy Nook ★★★★
Self Catering
Contact: Susan Jackson
Heart of the Lakes
t (015394) 32321
e info@heartofthelakes.co.uk
w heartofthelakes.co.uk

Lingmell ★★★★
Self Catering
Lakelovers
t (015394) 88855
e bookings@lakelovers.co.uk
w lakelovers.co.uk

Little Robin Cottage ★★★
Self Catering
Contact: Peter Durbin
Cumbrian Cottages Ltd
t (01228) 599950
e enquiries@cumbrian-cottages.co.uk
w cumbrian-cottages.co.uk

Littlegarth ★★★★
Self Catering
Contact: Mrs Vivien Bass
Wheelwrights Holiday Cottages
t (015394) 37635
e enquiries@wheelwrights.com

Long Mynd ★★★
Self Catering
Contact: Peter Durbin
Cumbrian Cottages Ltd
t (01228) 599950
e enquiries@cumbrian-cottages.co.uk
w cumbrian-cottages.co.uk

Longmeadow ★★★★
Self Catering
Contact: Peter Durbin
Cumbrian Cottages Ltd
t (01228) 599950
e enquiries@cumbrian-cottages.co.uk
w cumbrian-cottages.co.uk

The Lookout ★★★★★
Self Catering
Contact: Susan Jackson
Heart of the Lakes
t (015394) 32321
e info@heartofthelakes.co.uk
w heartofthelakes.co.uk

Loughrigg ★★★★
Self Catering
Contact: Peter Durbin
Cumbrian Cottages Ltd
t (01228) 599950
e enquiries@cumbrian-cottages.co.uk
w cumbrian-cottages.co.uk

Loughrigg ★★★★
Self Catering
Contact: Mrs Susan Jackson
Heart of the Lakes
t (015394) 32321
e info@heartofthelakes.co.uk
w heartofthelakes.co.uk

Loughrigg Suite ★★★★★
Self Catering
Heart of the Lakes
t (015394) 32321
e info@heartofthelakes.co.uk
w heartofthelakes.co.uk

Loughrigg View ★★★★
Self Catering
Contact: Peter Durbin
Cumbrian Cottages Ltd
t (01228) 599950
e enquiries@cumbrian-cottages.co.uk
w cumbrian-cottages.co.uk

Loughrigg View ★★★
Self Catering
Contact: Mrs Susan Jackson
Heart of the Lakes
t (015394) 32321
e info@heartofthelakes.co.uk
w heartofthelakes.co.uk

Low Fold ★★★★
Self Catering
Contact: Ms Sue Jackson
Heart of the Lakes
t (015394) 32321
e info@heartofthelakes.co.uk
w heartofthelakes.co.uk

Low Grove Cottage ★★★★
Self Catering
Contact: Susan Jackson
Heart of the Lakes
t (015394) 32321
e info@heartofthelakes.co.uk
w heartofthelakes.co.uk

Low White Stones ★★★★
Self Catering
Contact: Peter Durbin
Cumbrian Cottages Ltd
t (01228) 599950
e enquiries@cumbrian-cottages.co.uk
w cumbrian-cottages.co.uk

Lyndhurst ★★★
Self Catering
Contact: Mrs Susan Jackson
Heart of the Lakes
t (015394) 32321
e info@heartofthelakes.co.uk
w heartofthelakes.co.uk

Martin's Nest ★★★★
Self Catering
Heart of the Lakes
t (015394) 32321
e info@heartofthelakes.co.uk
w heartofthelakes.co.uk

Melverley ★★★ *Self Catering*
Contact: Susan Jackson
Heart of the Lakes
t (015394) 32321
e info@heartofthelakes.co.uk
w heartofthelakes.co.uk

Mickle Moss ★★★
Self Catering
Contact: Peter Durbin
Cumbrian Cottages Ltd
t (01228) 599950
e enquiries@cumbrian-cottages.co.uk
w cumbrian-cottages.co.uk

Milestones ★★★
Self Catering
Contact: Mr Paul Liddell
Lakelovers
t (015394) 88855
e bookings@lakelovers.co.uk
w lakelovers.co.uk

Mill Brow Farm Cottage
★★★★ *Self Catering*
Contact: Pat Long
t (015394) 33253

Mountain View Cottage
★★★ *Self Catering*
Lakelovers
t (015394) 88855
e bookings@lakelovers.co.uk
w lakelovers.co.uk

Nook End Annexe ★★★
Self Catering
Contact: Mr John Serginson
The Lakeland Cottage Company
t (015395) 30024
e john@lakelandcottageco.com

Nook End Farm ★★★★
Self Catering
Contact: Barbara Humphreys
t (015394) 31324

Nook End Garden Room ★★
Self Catering
The Lakeland Cottage Company
t 0870 442 5814
e john@lakelandcottageco.com
w lakelandcottageco.com

Nook End Studio ★★★
Self Catering
Contact: Mr John Serginson
The Lakeland Cottage Company
t (015395) 30024
e john@lakelandcottageco.com

North Cottage ★★★★
Self Catering
Contact: Susan Jackson
Heart of the Lakes
t (015394) 32321
e info@heartofthelakes.co.uk
w heartofthelakes.co.uk

Number Seven ★★★★
Self Catering
Contact: Ms Sue Jackson
Heart of the Lakes
t (015394) 32321
e info@heartofthelakes.co.uk
w heartofthelakes.co.uk

Oak Bank (Merewood)
★★★★★ *Self Catering*
Heart of the Lakes
t (015394) 32321
e info@heartofthelakes.co.uk
w heartofthelakes.co.uk

Oaklands ★★★ *Self Catering*
Contact: Peter Durbin
Cumbrian Cottages Ltd
t (01228) 599950
e enquiries@cumbrian-cottages.co.uk
w cumbrian-cottages.co.uk

Old Coach House ★★★
Self Catering
Contact: Peter Durbin
Cumbrian Cottages Ltd
t (01228) 599950
e enquiries@cumbrian-cottages.co.uk
w cumbrian-cottages.co.uk

Old Coachman's Cottage
★★★★ *Self Catering*
Lakelovers
t (015394) 88855
e bookings@lakelovers.co.uk
w lakelovers.co.uk

Old Mill Cottage ★★★
Self Catering
Contact: Susan Jackson
Heart of the Lakes
t (015394) 32321
e info@heartofthelakes.co.uk
w heartofthelakes.co.uk

Old Mill Cottage & Squirrel Bank ★★★ *Self Catering*
Contact: Susan Jackson
Heart of the Lakes
t (015394) 32321
e info@heartofthelakes.co.uk
w heartofthelakes.co.uk

Old Oak Cottage ★★★★
Self Catering
Lakelovers
t (015394) 88855
e bookings@lakelovers.co.uk
w lakelovers.co.uk

The Old Wash House
★★★★ *Self Catering*
Lakelovers
t (015394) 88855
e bookings@lakelovers.co.uk
w lakelovers.co.uk

Orchard House ★★★★★
Self Catering
Contact: Susan Jackson
Heart of the Lakes
t (015394) 32321
e info@heartofthelakes.co.uk
w heartofthelakes.co.uk

Otters Holt ★★★★
Self Catering
Contact: Lynne Bush
Brackenrigg Lodge
t (015394) 47770
e lynne@brackenriggs.co.uk
w brackenriggs.co.uk

Overghyll ★★★★
Self Catering
Heart of the Lakes
t (015394) 32321
e info@heartofthelakes.co.uk
w heartofthelakes.co.uk

Parkwood ★★★★
Self Catering
Contact: Susan Jackson
Heart of the Lakes
t (015394) 32321
e info@heartofthelakes.co.uk
w heartofthelakes.co.uk

Primrose Cottage ★★★
Self Catering
Contact: Ms Sue Jackson
Heart of the Lakes
t (015394) 32321
e info@heartofthelakes.co.uk
w heartofthelakes.co.uk

Printers Cottage ★★★
Self Catering
Contact: Susan Jackson
Heart of the Lakes
t (015394) 32321
e info@heartofthelakes.co.uk
w heartofthelakes.co.uk

Pudding Cottage ★★★★★
Self Catering
Contact: Jacky Morrison
t (0151) 342 1234
e jacky.morrison@btinternet.com
w pudding-cottage.com

Raaesbeck ★★★★
Self Catering
Lakelovers
t (015394) 88855
e bookings@lakelovers.co.uk
w lakelovers.co.uk

Ramsteads ★ *Self Catering*
Contact: Mr Evans
t (015394) 36583

Red Screes Cottage ★★★★
Self Catering
Contact: Mr Paul Liddell
Lakelovers
t (015394) 88855
e bookings@lakelovers.co.uk
w lakelovers.co.uk

Redwoods ★★★★
Self Catering
Contact: Mrs Susan Jackson
Heart of the Lakes
t (015394) 32321
e info@heartofthelakes.co.uk
w heartofthelakes.co.uk

The Retreat ★★★★
Self Catering
Heart of the Lakes
t (015394) 32321
e info@heartofthelakes.co.uk
w heartofthelakes.co.uk

River Falls View ★★★★
Self Catering
Contact: Mr Paul Liddell
Lakelovers
t (015394) 88855
e bookings@lakelovers.co.uk
w lakelovers.co.uk

Riverside Lodge ★★★★
Self Catering
Contact: Alan Rhone
t (015394) 34208
e alanrhone@riversidelodge.co.uk
w riversidelodge.co.uk

Riverside Retreat ★★★★
Self Catering
Lakelovers
t (015394) 88855
e bookings@lakelovers.co.uk
w lakelovers.co.uk

Rock Shop Flat ★★★★
Self Catering
Contact: Louise Burhouse
Burhouse Lettings
t (01484) 485104
e flat@rock-shop.co.uk
w rock-shop.co.uk/flat

Rose Cottage ★★★★
Self Catering
Contact: Susan Jackson
Heart of the Lakes
t (015394) 32321
e info@heartofthelakes.co.uk
w heartofthelakes.co.uk

Roselea ★★★★ *Self Catering*
Contact: Peter Durbin
Cumbrian Cottages Ltd
t (01228) 599950
e enquiries@cumbrian-cottages.co.uk
w cumbrian-cottages.co.uk

Rothay 18 ★★★
Self Catering
Contact: Mrs Susan Jackson
Heart of the Lakes
t (015394) 32321
e info@heartofthelakes.co.uk
w heartofthelakes.co.uk

Rushbrook Cottage ★★★★
Self Catering
Contact: Susan Jackson
Heart of the Lakes
t (015394) 32321
e info@heartofthelakes.co.uk
w heartofthelakes.co.uk

Rydal ★★★★ *Self Catering*
Contact: Mrs Susan Jackson
Heart of the Lakes
t (015394) 32321
e info@heartofthelakes.co.uk
w heartofthelakes.co.uk

Rydale ★★★★ *Self Catering*
Contact: Mrs Susan Jackson
Heart of the Lakes
t (015394) 32321
e info@heartofthelakes.co.uk
w heartofthelakes.co.uk

Sarum ★★★ *Self Catering*
t (01704) 831558

Scafell ★★★★ *Self Catering*
Heart of the Lakes
t (015394) 32321
e info@heartofthelakes.co.uk
w heartofthelakes.co.uk

Scandale Bridge Cottage
★★★ *Self Catering*
Lakeland Character Cottages
t 0500 600725
e stay@lakedistrictinns.co.uk
w lakedistrictinns.co.uk

Sheenfell ★★★ *Self Catering*
Contact: Mrs Susan Jackson
Heart of the Lakes
t (015394) 32321
e info@heartofthelakes.co.uk
w heartofthelakes.co.uk

Shepherds Fold ★★★★
Self Catering
Contact: Mrs Susan Jackson
Heart of the Lakes
t (015394) 32321
e info@heartofthelakes.co.uk
w heartofthelakes.co.uk

Silver How ★★★★★
Self Catering
Contact: Mrs Susan Jackson
Heart of the Lakes
t (015394) 32321
e info@heartofthelakes.co.uk
w heartofthelakes.co.uk

The Spinney ★★★★
Self Catering
Lakelovers
t (015394) 88855
e bookings@lakelovers.co.uk
w lakelovers.co.uk

Spring Cottage ★★★★
Self Catering
Contact: Susan Jackson
Heart of the Lakes
t (015394) 32321
e info@heartofthelakes.co.uk
w heartofthelakes.co.uk

Spring Cottage ★★★
Self Catering
Contact: Mr Paul Liddell
Lakelovers
t (015394) 88855
e bookings@lakelovers.co.uk
w lakelovers.co.uk

The Stables ★★★★★
Self Catering
Contact: Susan Jackson
Heart of the Lakes
t (015394) 32321
e info@heartofthelakes.co.uk
w heartofthelakes.co.uk

Steeple View ★★★
Self Catering
Contact: Susan Jackson
Heart of the Lakes
t (015394) 32321
e info@heartofthelakes.co.uk
w heartofthelakes.co.uk

Stockghyll Court ★★★
Self Catering
Contact: Peter Durbin
Cumbrian Cottages Ltd
t (01228) 599950
e enquiries@cumbrian-cottages.co.uk
w cumbrian-cottages.co.uk

Stonebank ★★★★
Self Catering
Contact: Susan Jackson
Heart of the Lakes
t (015394) 32321
e info@heartofthelakes.co.uk
w heartofthelakes.co.uk

Striding Home ★★★★
Self Catering
Contact: Mrs Susan Jackson
Heart of the Lakes
t (015394) 32321
e info@heartofthelakes.co.uk
w heartofthelakes.co.uk

Studio Cottage ★★★★
Self Catering
Contact: Mrs Susan Jackson
Heart of the Lakes
t (015394) 32321
e info@heartofthelakes.co.uk
w heartofthelakes.co.uk

Sunset Cottage ★★★★
Self Catering
Lakelovers
t (015394) 88855
e bookings@lakelovers.co.uk
w lakelovers.co.uk

Swallowdale ★★★★
Self Catering
Contact: Susan Jackson
Heart of the Lakes
t (015394) 32321
e info@heartofthelakes.co.uk
w heartofthelakes.co.uk

Sweden Bank ★★★
Self Catering
Contact: Susan Jackson
Heart of the Lakes
t (015394) 32321
e info@heartofthelakes.co.uk
w heartofthelakes.co.uk

Sycamore House ★★★
Self Catering
Contact: Peter Durbin
Cumbrian Cottages Ltd
t (01228) 599950
e enquiries@cumbrian-cottages.co.uk
w cumbrian-cottages.co.uk

Tethera ★★★ *Self Catering*
Contact: Peter Durbin
Cumbrian Cottages Ltd
t (01228) 599950
e enquiries@cumbrian-cottages.co.uk
w cumbrian-cottages.co.uk

Thomas Fold Cottage
★★★★ *Self Catering*
Contact: Susan Jackson
Heart of the Lakes
t (015394) 32321
e info@heartofthelakes.co.uk
w heartofthelakes.co.uk

Tottlebank ★★★
Self Catering
Contact: Peter Durbin
Cumbrian Cottages Ltd
t (01228) 599950
e enquiries@cumbrian-cottages.co.uk
w cumbrian-cottages.co.uk

Troutbeck ★★★★
Self Catering
Contact: Mrs Susan Jackson
Heart of the Lakes
t (015394) 32321
e info@heartofthelakes.co.uk
w heartofthelakes.co.uk

Upper Sycamore Cottage
★★★★ *Self Catering*
Heart of the Lakes
t (015394) 32321
e info@heartofthelakes.co.uk
w heartofthelakes.co.uk

Valentine Cottage ★★★★★
Self Catering
Contact: Mr Paul Liddell
Lakelovers
t (015394) 88855
e bookings@lakelovers.co.uk
w lakelovers.co.uk

Violet Cottage ★★★★
Self Catering
Contact: Peter Durbin
Cumbrian Cottages Ltd
t (01228) 599950
e enquiries@cumbrian-cottages.co.uk
w cumbrian-cottages.co.uk

Walkers Cottage ★★★
Self Catering
Contact: Peter Durbin
Cumbrian Cottages Ltd
t (01228) 599950
e enquiries@cumbrian-cottages.co.uk
w cumbrian-cottages.co.uk

Wansfell ★★★★★
Self Catering
Contact: Mrs Susan Jackson
Heart of the Lakes
t (015394) 32321
e info@heartofthelakes.co.uk
w heartofthelakes.co.uk

Waterfalls ★★★★
Self Catering
Contact: Mrs Susan Jackson
Heart of the Lakes
t (015394) 32321
e info@heartofthelakes.co.uk
w heartofthelakes.co.uk

Wayside Cottage ★★★★
Self Catering
Contact: Dr Leech
t (024) 7667 7549
e waysidecottage@lineone.net
w toddcrag.co.uk

Wendin Cottage ★★★
Self Catering
Contact: Ms Sue Jackson
Heart of the Lakes
t (015394) 32321
e info@heartofthelakes.co.uk
w heartofthelakes.co.uk

Wetherlam ★★★★
Self Catering
Contact: Mr Paul Liddell
Lakelovers
t (015394) 88855
e bookings@lakelovers.co.uk
w lakelovers.co.uk

Willow Hill ★★★★
Self Catering
Contact: Mr Peter Liddell
Lakelovers
t (015394) 88855
e bookings@lakelovers.co.uk
w lakelovers.co.uk

Wilmar Cottage ★★
Self Catering
Contact: Susan Jackson
Heart of the Lakes
t (015394) 32321
e info@heartofthelakes.co.uk
w heartofthelakes.co.uk

Winander ★★★★★
Self Catering
Contact: Mrs Susan Jackson
Heart of the Lakes
t (015394) 32321
e info@heartofthelakes.co.uk
w heartofthelakes.co.uk

Windermere Suite ★★★★
Self Catering
Contact: Susan Jackson
Heart of the Lakes
t (015394) 32321
e info@heartofthelakes.co.uk
w heartofthelakes.co.uk

Woodside Cottage
★★★★★ *Self Catering*
Contact: Gillian Lane
t (015394) 33215
e email@fisherbeckhotel.co.uk

Woolly End ★★★★
Self Catering
Contact: Mr Paul Liddell
Lakelovers
t (015394) 88855
e bookings@lakelovers.co.uk
w lakelovers.co.uk

Wren Cottage ★★★★
Self Catering
Contact: Susan Jackson
Heart of the Lakes
t (015394) 32321
e info@heartofthelakes.co.uk
w heartofthelakes.co.uk

Yew Tree Cottage ★★★
Self Catering
Contact: Mrs Susan Jackson
Heart of the Lakes
t (015394) 32321
e info@heartofthelakes.co.uk
w heartofthelakes.co.uk

APPLEBY-IN-WESTMORLAND
Cumbria

Ivy Cottage ★★★
Self Catering
t (01768) 361233

The Little House ★★★★
Self Catering
Contact: Mr & Mrs Hiscox
t (01673) 860047
e rogerhiscox@beeb.net
w thelittlehouseappleby.com

Milburn Grange Holiday Cottages ★★★ *Self Catering*
Contact: Peter G Baker
t (01768) 361867
e holidays@milburngrange.co.uk
w milburngrange.co.uk

The Old Smithy ★★★★
Self Catering
Contact: Kay E Smith
t (01768) 361333
e smithies.com@talk21.com

Owl Cottage ★★★
Self Catering
Dales Holiday Cottages
t 0870 909 9500
e info@dales-holiday-cottages.com
w dalesholcot.com

Wray Cottage ★★★
Self Catering
Contact: Mrs Cowey
t (01768) 352485

APPLETHWAITE
Cumbria

Applethwaite Country House ★★★★ *Self Catering*
Contact: Tom & Gail Ryan
t (01768) 772413
e ryan@applethwaite.com
w geocities.com/deanedna

The Manesty ★★★★
Self Catering
Contact: Peter Durbin
Cumbrian Cottages Ltd
t (01228) 599950
e enquiries@cumbrian-cottages.co.uk
w cumbrian-cottages.co.uk

Somervell ★★★ *Self Catering*
Contact: Peter Durbin
Cumbrian Cottages Ltd
t (01228) 599950
e enquiries@cumbrian-cottages.co.uk
w cumbrian-cottages.co.uk

Whiteside ★★★
Self Catering
Contact: David Burton
Lakeland Cottage Holidays
t (01768) 776065
e info@lakelandcottages.co.uk
w lakelandcottages.co.uk

ARKHOLME
Lancashire

Redwell Fisheries ★★★
Self Catering
Contact: Mrs Campbell-Barker & Mr Hall
t (01524) 221979
e kenanddiane@redwellfisheries.co.uk
w redwellfisheries.co.uk

ARMATHWAITE
Cumbria

Coombs Cottage ★★★★
Self Catering
Contact: Peter Durbin
Cumbrian Cottages Ltd
t (01228) 599950
e enquiries@cumbrian-cottages.co.uk
w cumbrian-cottages.co.uk

Longdales Cottage ★★★
Self Catering
Contact: Peter Durbin
Cumbrian Cottages Ltd
t (01228) 599950
e enquiries@cumbrian-cottages.co.uk
w cumbrian-cottages.co.uk

ARNSIDE
Cumbria

Bay View House ★★★
Self Catering
Contact: Mr Jackson
t (01524) 762131
e john@jackson5459.fsnet.co.uk

ASKHAM
Cumbria

Park View ★★★★
Self Catering
Contact: Mrs Lyn Page
t (01931) 712577
e lyn.page@lowther.co.uk

Scarr View ★★★
Self Catering
Contact: Peter Durbin
Cumbrian Cottages Ltd
t (01228) 599950
e enquiries@cumbrian-cottages.co.uk
w cumbrian-cottages.co.uk

Sycamore Barn Holiday Cottage ★★★★ *Self Catering*
Contact: Ellen Pickup
t (01931) 712410
e pickupaskham@btinternet.com
w sycamorehousebarn.com

ASPATRIA
Cumbria

Big White House ★★★
Self Catering
Contact: Philip Carr
Skiddaw View Holiday Home Park Ltd
t (01697) 320919
e info@bigwhitehouse.co.uk
w bigwhitehouse.co.uk

Inglecroft ★★★ *Self Catering*
Contact: Peter Durbin
Cumbrian Cottages Ltd
t (01228) 599950
e enquiries@cumbrian-cottages.co.uk
w cumbrian-cottages.co.uk

AUDLEM
Cheshire

Berry Cottage ★★★
Self Catering
Contact: Jane Hardwick
t (01270) 811573
e hardwork@tesco.net

Field View Cottage Holidays
★★★★ *Self Catering*
Contact: Mr & Mrs Liles
t (01270) 811208

BACKBARROW
Cumbria

Cark Cottage ★★★
Self Catering
Contact: Peter Durbin
Cumbrian Cottages Ltd
t (01228) 599950
e enquiries@cumbrian-cottages.co.uk
w cumbrian-cottages.co.uk

Glenfinnan ★★★★
Self Catering
Contact: Philip Brewer
t 07710 466702
e phil.brewer2@btopenworld.com
w southlakesholidaycottage.co.uk

Lynwood Cottage ★★★
Self Catering
Contact: Peter Durbin
Cumbrian Cottages Ltd
t (01228) 599950
e enquiries@cumbrian-cottages.co.uk
w cumbrian-cottages.co.uk

BACUP
Lancashire

Oakenclough Farm ★★★
Self Catering
Contact: Mr Martin Mcshane
Red Rose Cottages
t (01200) 420101
e info@redrosecottages.co.uk

BAILEY
Cumbria

Saughs Farm Cottages
★★★★ *Self Catering*
Contact: Kevin & Jane Gray
t (01697) 748346
e kevin.graykm@btopenworld.com

BAMPTON
Cumbria

Tethera ★★★★ *Self Catering*
Contact: Paul Durbin
Cumbrian Cottages Ltd
t (01228) 599950
e enquiries@cumbrian-cottages.co.uk
w cumbrian-cottages.co.uk

Wheat Close ★★★★
Self Catering
Contact: Peter Durbin
Cumbrian Cottages Ltd
t (01228) 599950
e enquiries@cumbrian-cottages.co.uk
w cumbrian-cottages.co.uk

BARNOLDSWICK
Lancashire

Hill Top Barn ★★★★★
Self Catering
Contact: Mr & Mrs Sharples
Hill Top Farm
t (01282) 812460
e info@hilltopbarn.com
w hilltopbarn.com

BARROWFORD
Lancashire

Alondra ★★★★ *Self Catering*
t (01282) 601604

BARROWS GREEN
Cumbria

High Meadows ★★★★★
Self Catering
Contact: Peter Durbin
Cumbrian Cottages Ltd
t (01228) 599950
e enquiries@cumbrian-cottages.co.uk
w cumbrian-cottages.co.uk

BASHALL EAVES
Lancashire

Clough Bottom Farm Cottages
Rating Applied For
Self Catering
Contact: Mrs Jane Backhouse
t (01254) 826285
e info@cloughbottom.co.uk
w cloughbottom.co.uk

BASSENTHWAITE
Cumbria

6 Low Kiln Court ★★★
Self Catering
Contact: Peter Durbin
Cumbrian Cottages Ltd
t (01228) 599950
e enquiries@cumbrian-cottages.co.uk
w cumbrian-cottages.co.uk

Apple Tree Cottage ★★★★
Self Catering
Contact: Jill Pointon
t (01900) 85011

Brook Cottage ★★★★
Self Catering
Contact: Peter Durbin
Cumbrian Cottages Ltd
t (01228) 599950
e enquiries@cumbrian-cottages.co.uk
w cumbrian-cottages.co.uk

Look out for establishments participating in the Walkers and Cyclists Welcome Schemes

Brookfield ★★★★
Self Catering
Contact: Peter Durbin
Cumbrian Cottages Ltd
t (01228) 599950
e enquiries@cumbrian-cottages.co.uk
w cumbrian-cottages.co.uk

Garries Cottage ★★★
Self Catering
Contact: Peter Durbin
Cumbrian Cottages Ltd
t (01228) 599950
e enquiries@cumbrian-cottages.co.uk
w cumbrian-cottages.co.uk

The Granary ★★★
Self Catering
Contact: Margaret Crooks
t (01697) 371524
e mcrooks.roadfarm@btopenworld.com

High Spy Cottage ★★★
Self Catering
Contact: Peter Durbin
Cumbrian Cottages Ltd
t (01228) 599950
e enquiries@cumbrian-cottages.co.uk
w cumbrian-cottages.co.uk

Hill Cottage ★★★★
Self Catering
Contact: Mrs Susan Jackson
Heart of the Lakes
t (015394) 32321
e info@heartofthelakes.co.uk
w heartofthelakes.co.uk

Irton House Farm ★★★★
Self Catering
Contact: Mrs Almond
Irton House Farm
t (01768) 776380
e almond@farmersweekly.net
w irtonhousefarm.com

Melbecks Holidays Homes: Skiddaw, Dodd, Dash, Randel ★★★-★★★★
Self Catering
Contact: Mr Burton
Lakeland Cottage Holidays
t (01768) 776065
e info@lakelandcottages.co.uk

Mill Cottage ★★★
Self Catering
Contact: Peter Durbin
Cumbrian Cottages Ltd
t (01228) 599950
e enquiries@cumbrian-cottages.co.uk
w cumbrian-cottages.co.uk

Random Stones ★★★★
Self Catering
Contact: Mrs Susan Jackson
Heart of the Lakes
t (015394) 32321
e info@heartofthelakes.co.uk
w heartofthelakes.co.uk

Riggs Cottage ★★★★
Self Catering
Contact: Peter Durbin
Cumbrian Cottages Ltd
t (01228) 599950
e enquiries@cumbrian-cottages.co.uk
w cumbrian-cottages.co.uk

The Ruddings ★★★
Self Catering
Contact: Peter Durbin
Cumbrian Cottages Ltd
t (01228) 599950
e enquiries@cumbrian-cottages.co.uk
w cumbrian-cottages.co.uk

South View ★★★
Self Catering
Contact: Peter Durbin
Cumbrian Cottages Ltd
t (01228) 599950
e enquiries@cumbrian-cottages.co.uk
w cumbrian-cottages.co.uk

Uldale ★★★★ *Self Catering*
Contact: Mr David Burton
Lakeland Cottage Holidays
t (01768) 776065
e info@lakelandcottages.co.uk

BASSENTHWAITE LAKE
Cumbria

Park View Cottage ★★★
Self Catering
Contact: Peter Durbin
Cumbrian Cottages Ltd
t (01228) 599950
e enquiries@cumbrian-cottages.co.uk
w cumbrian-cottages.co.uk

BECKFOOT, SILLOTH
Cumbria

Seaview Farmhouse
★★★★★ *Self Catering*
Contact: Mr & Mrs Graham & Betty Walton
t (01697) 331030
w english-country-cottages.co.uk

BEESTON
Cheshire

The Lodge – Whitegate Farm ★★★★ *Self Catering*
t (01829) 261601
e stevedavies@euphony.net

BENTHAM
Lancashire

Borrans Cottage Ref:2895
★★★ *Self Catering*
Contact: Ms Lorraine Kidd
Dales Holiday Cottages
t 0870 909 9500
e info@dales-holiday-cottages.com
w dalesholcot.com

BERRIER
Cumbria

Bells Farm ★★★
Self Catering
Contact: Peter Durbin
Cumbrian Cottages Ltd
t (01228) 599950
e enquiries@cumbrian-cottages.co.uk
w cumbrian-cottages.co.uk

The Cruck Barn ★★★
Self Catering
Contact: Peter Durbin
Cumbrian Cottages Ltd
t (01228) 599950
e enquiries@cumbrian-cottages.co.uk
w cumbrian-cottages.co.uk

Whitbarrow Holiday Village
★★★ *Self Catering*
Contact: Peter Durbin
Cumbrian Cottages Ltd
t (01228) 599950
e enquiries@cumbrian-cottages.co.uk
w cumbrian-cottages.co.uk

Whitbarrow Lodge 1 ★★★
Self Catering
Contact: Peter Durbin
Cumbrian Cottages Ltd
t (01228) 599950
e enquiries@cumbrian-cottages.co.uk
w cumbrian-cottages.co.uk

Whitbarrow Lodge 10 ★★★
Self Catering
Contact: Peter Durbin
Cumbrian Cottages Ltd
t (01228) 599950
e enquiries@cumbrian-cottages.co.uk
w cumbrian-cottages.co.uk

Whitbarrow Lodge 14 ★★★
Self Catering
Contact: Peter Durbin
Cumbrian Cottages Ltd
t (01228) 599950
e enquiries@cumbrian-cottages.co.uk
w cumbrian-cottages.co.uk

BEWCASTLE
Cumbria

Arch View Cottages ★★★★
Self Catering
Contact: Jean James
Arch View
t (01697) 748213
e jjames@v21mail.co.uk
w holidaycottagescarlisle.co.uk

BILLINGTON
Lancashire

Snowdrop Cottage
Rating Applied For
Self Catering
Contact: Mrs Jenny Goldsmith
t (01769) 580315
e jennygoldsmith@hotmail.co.uk

Weavers Cottage ★★★
Self Catering
t (01254) 825772

BISPHAM
Lancashire

Burbage Holiday Lodge
★★★★-★★★★★
Self Catering
t (01253) 356657
e enquiries@burbageholidaylodge.co.uk
w burbageholidaylodge.co.uk

BLACKO
Lancashire

Malkin Tower Farm Cottages
★★★★ *Self Catering*
Contact: Mrs Rachel Turner
t (01282) 699992
e info@malkintowerfarm.co.uk

BLACKPOOL
Lancashire

Abingdon Holiday Flats ★★
Self Catering
Contact: Mr Douglas Nelson
t (01253) 356181

Beach House The ★★★★★
Self Catering
Contact: Mrs Livesey
The Beach House
t (01253) 352699
e info@thebeachhouse.co.uk
w thebeachhouseblackpool.co.uk

Beachcliffe Holiday Flats
★★★ *Self Catering*
Contact: Mrs Maureen Checklin
t (01253) 357147
w beachcliffe.com

Bridle Lodge Apartments
★★★ *Self Catering*
Contact: Mrs Anne Oxley
t (01253) 404117
w bridlelodgeapartments.co.uk

Coast Apartments
Rating Applied For
Self Catering
Contact: Steven & Karen Livesey
t (01253) 351377
e enquiries@coastapartments.co.uk
w coastapartments.co.uk

Crystal Lodge Holiday Flats
★★-★★★ *Self Catering*
Contact: Mr & Mrs Askham
t (01253) 346691

Donange Holiday Flats
★★-★★★ *Self Catering*
Contact: Mr M Hasson
t (01253) 355051
w donange.cjb.net

The Holiday Lodge ★★
Self Catering
Contact: Ms Kathrine Drakley
t (01253) 352934
w holidaylodge.co.uk

Jade (South Shore)
★★★-★★★★ *Self Catering*
Contact: Jean Long
t (01253) 341500
w jadeapartments.com

San Remo Holiday Flats ★★
Self Catering
Contact: Mrs June Morgan
t (01253) 353487
e sanremoapartment@aol.com

Sea Cote Holiday Flats ★★★
Self Catering
Contact: Mr Anne Cunningham
Sea Cote Holiay Flats
t (01253) 354435

Stratford Holiday Apartments ★★-★★★
Self Catering
Contact: Mr Chris Taylor
t (01253) 500150
e tonorthdene@hotmail.com

BLAWITH
Cumbria

Birchbank Cottage ★★★★
Self Catering
Contact: Linda Nicholson
t (01229) 885277
e birchbank@btinternet.com
w lakedistrictfarmhouseholidays.co.uk/birchbankcottage

Blea Brows Cottage ★★★
Self Catering
Contact: Mr Philip Johnston
The Coppermines & Coniston Lake Cottages
t (015394) 41765
e info@coppermines.co.uk
w coppermines.co.uk

Brown Howe Cottage ★★★
Self Catering
Contact: Mr Philip Johnston
The Coppermines & Coniston Lake Cottages
t (015394) 41765
e info@coppermines.co.uk
w coppermines.co.uk

BOLLINGTON
Cheshire

Higher Ingersley Barn ★★★★★ *Self Catering*
Contact: Mr Peacock
Higher Ingersley Barn
t (01625) 572245
e bw.peacock@ntlword.com
w higheringerleyfarm.co.uk

BOLTON-BY-BOWLAND
Lancashire

Springhead Farm Holiday Cottages ★★★★
Self Catering
Contact: Mrs Susan Lund
t (01200) 447245

BOLTON-LE-SANDS
Lancashire

Bay View ★★★ *Self Catering*
Contact: Mr John Sharples
t (01524) 822783
e acsjohn@tiscali.co.uk
w freewebs.com/bayviewlimited

Jasmine Cottage ★★★
Self Catering
Contact: Mr & Mrs Baker
Rosedene
t (01524) 733532

Waterside ★★★★
Self Catering
Contact: Mrs Hazel Wilson
t (01204) 882580
e joe@wilson882.freeserve.co.uk

BOOTLE STATION
Cumbria

Station Cottage ★★★
Self Catering
Contact: Vicky & David Rowe
t (01229) 718258
e bootlestation@aol.com
w bootlestation.co.uk

BORROWDALE
Cumbria

Barrowgate ★★★
Self Catering
Contact: Mr David Burton
Lakeland Cottage Holidays
t (01768) 776065
e info@lakelandcottages.co.uk

Derwent Farmhouse ★★★
Self Catering
Contact: Mr David Burton
Lakeland Cottage Holidays
t (01768) 776065
e info@lakelandcottages.co.uk

Dove's Nest ★★★
Self Catering
Contact: Peter Durbin
Cumbrian Cottages Ltd
t (01228) 599950
e enquiries@cumbrian-cottages.co.uk
w cumbrian-cottages.co.uk

Grange Cottage ★★★
Self Catering
Contact: Peter Durbin
Cumbrian Cottages Ltd
t (01228) 599950
e enquiries@cumbrian-cottages.co.uk
w cumbrian-cottages.co.uk

Hazel Bank Cottage ★★★★
Self Catering
Contact: Glen & Brenda Davies
t (01768) 777248
e enquiries@hazelbankhotel.co.uk
w hazelbankhotel.co.uk

The Hollies ★★★★
Self Catering
Contact: Peter Durbin
Cumbrian Cottages Ltd
t (01228) 599950
e enquiries@cumbrian-cottages.co.uk
w cumbrian-cottages.co.uk

Maiden Moor ★★★
Self Catering
Contact: Peter Durbin
Cumbrian Cottages Ltd
t (01228) 599950
e enquiries@cumbrian-cottages.co.uk
w cumbrian-cottages.co.uk

Rose Cottage Holiday Apartments ★★★
Self Catering
Contact: Steve Cooke
Rose Cottage Holidays
t (01768) 777678
e steve.cooke1@tiscali.co.uk
w borrowdalecottages.co.uk

Scale Force ★★★
Self Catering
Contact: Mr David Burton
Lakeland Cottage Holidays
t (01768) 776065
e info@lakelandcottages.co.uk

BORWICK
Lancashire

Borwick Hall ★★–★★★
Self Catering
t (01524) 732508
e borwickhall.bookings@ed.lancscc.gov.uk

BOSLEY
Cheshire

The Old Byre ★★★
Self Catering
Contact: Mrs Dorothy Gilman
t (01260) 223293
e d.gilman@hotmail.co.uk

Strawberry Duck Holidays ★★★ *Self Catering*
Contact: Mr Bruce Carter
t (01260) 223591

BOTHEL
Cumbria

The Lodge ★★★★
Self Catering
Contact: Diane Shankland
t (01697) 321674
e lodge.bothel@tiscali.co.uk
w lodge-bothel.co.uk

BOUTH
Cumbria

2 Kiln Houses ★★★★
Self Catering
Contact: Mr John Serginson
The Lakeland Cottage Company
t (015395) 30024
e john@lakelandcottageco.com

Kiln Cottage ★★★
Self Catering
Contact: Mr John Serginson
The Lakeland Cottage Company
t (015395) 30024
e john@lakelandcottageco.com

No 1 & 2 Rose Cottages ★★★★ *Self Catering*
Contact: Mr John Serginson
The Lakeland Cottage Company
t (015395) 30024
e john@lakelandcottageco.com

BOWLAND BRIDGE
Cumbria

Chase Cottage ★★★★
Self Catering
Contact: Susan Jackson
Heart of the Lakes
t (015394) 32321
e info@heartofthelakes.co.uk
w heartofthelakes.co.uk

Ramblers Lodge ★★★★
Self Catering
Contact: Peter Durbin
Cumbrian Cottages Ltd
t (01228) 599950
e enquiries@cumbrian-cottages.co.uk
w cumbrian-cottages.co.uk

BOWMANSTEAD
Cumbria

No 2 Lake View ★★★★
Self Catering
Contact: Mr Philip Johnston
The Coppermines & Coniston Lake Cottages
t (015394) 41765
e info@coppermines.co.uk
w coppermines.co.uk

Number 1 Lake View Cottages ★★★★
Self Catering
Contact: Mr Philip Johnston
The Coppermines & Coniston Lake Cottages
t (015394) 41765
e info@coppermines.co.uk
w coppermines.co.uk

BOWNESS-ON-WINDERMERE
Cumbria

Lake View Apartment ★★★
Self Catering
Contact: Peter Durbin
Cumbrian Cottages Ltd
t (01228) 599950
e enquiries@cumbrian-cottages.co.uk
w cumbrian-cottages.co.uk

BRAITHWAITE
Cumbria

1 Skiddaw View ★★★
Self Catering
Contact: Peter Durbin
Cumbrian Cottages Ltd
t (01228) 599950
e enquiries@cumbrian-cottages.co.uk
w cumbrian-cottages.co.uk

Beech End ★★ *Self Catering*
Contact: Mr David Burton
Lakeland Cottage Holidays
t (01768) 776065
e info@lakelandcottages.co.uk

Bridge End ★★★★
Self Catering
Contact: Denise McAdam
t (01768) 778481
w bridge-end-holidaycottage.co.uk

Brookside Cottage ★★★★
Self Catering
Contact: Peter Durbin
Cumbrian Cottages Ltd
t (01228) 599950
e enquiries@cumbrian-cottages.co.uk
w cumbrian-cottages.co.uk

Catbells Cottage ★★★★
Self Catering
Contact: Peter Durbin
Cumbrian Cottages Ltd
t (01228) 599950
e enquiries@cumbrian-cottages.co.uk
w cumbrian-cottages.co.uk

Cosy Cottage ★★★
Self Catering
Contact: Mr David Burton
Lakeland Cottage Holidays
t (01768) 776065
e info@lakelandcottages.co.uk

Doves Nest ★★★
Self Catering
Contact: Ms Sheena Holden
Cumbrian Cottages Ltd
t (01228) 599950
e enquiries@cumbrian-cottages.co.uk
w cumbrian-cottages.co.uk

Ghyll Bank ★★★
Self Catering
Contact: Mrs Susan Jackson
Heart of the Lakes
t (015394) 32321
e info@heartofthelakes.co.uk
w heartofthelakes.co.uk

Highbridge Cottages ★★★★ *Self Catering*
Contact: Peter Rigg
t (01768) 780561
e riggpeter@tiscali.co.uk
w braithwaite-cottage.co.uk

The Island ★★★
Self Catering
Contact: Mrs Susan Jackson
Heart of the Lakes
t (015394) 32321
e info@heartofthelakes.co.uk
w heartofthelakes.co.uk

Olives Cottage & Rosebank
★★★★ *Self Catering*
Contact: Anthony Fearns
Keswick Cottages
t (01768) 778555
e info@keswickcottages.co.uk
w keswickcottages.co.uk

The Shieling ★★★
Self Catering
Contact: Mr David Burton
Lakeland Cottage Holidays
t (01768) 776065
e info@lakelandcottages.co.uk

Windrush ★★★★
Self Catering
Contact: Mr David Burton
Lakeland Cottage Holidays
t (01768) 776065
e info@lakelandcottages.co.uk

Wychwood ★★★
Self Catering
Contact: David Burton
Lakeland Cottage Holidays
t (01768) 776065
e info@lakelandcottages.co.uk
w lakelandcottages.co.uk

BRAMPTON
Cumbria

Clematis Cottage ★★★★
Self Catering
Contact: Peter Durbin
Cumbrian Cottages Ltd
t (01228) 599950
e enquiries@cumbrian-cottages.co.uk
w cumbrian-cottages.co.uk

Hay Barn Cottage ★★★★
Self Catering
Contact: Paul & Judith Barton
Bush Nook
t (01697) 747194
e info@bushnook.co.uk
w bushnook.co.uk

Long Byres at Talkin Head
★★★ *Self Catering*
Contact: Harriet Sykes
t (01697) 73435
e harriet@talkinhead.demon.co.uk
w longbyres.co.uk

South View Cottage ★★★★
Self Catering
Contact: Marie Hodgson
t (0161) 374 0110
e mariehodgson@southviewbanks.f9.co.uk

Warren Bank Cottage
★★★★★ *Self Catering*
Contact: Margie Douglas
Warren Bank Cottage
t (01434) 607544
e margie@warrenbankcottage.com
w warrenbankcottage.com

BRIDEKIRK
Cumbria

Anns Hill ★★★★★
Self Catering
Contact: Vanessa Steel
t 07710 388180
e vanessa@annshill.co.uk
w annshill.co.uk

Ellwood ★★★★★
Self Catering
Contact: Peter Durbin
Cumbrian Cottages Ltd
t (01228) 599950
e enquiries@cumbrian-cottages.co.uk
w cumbrian-cottages.co.uk

BRIERCLIFFE
Lancashire

Delph Cottage ★★★
Self Catering
Contact: Mr Martin McShane
Red Rose Cottages
t (01200) 420101

BRIGSTEER
Cumbria

Garden Cottage ★★★★
Self Catering
Contact: Peter Durbin
Cumbrian Cottages Ltd
t (01228) 599950
e enquiries@cumbrian-cottages.co.uk
w cumbrian-cottages.co.uk

Moss Rigg ★★★
Self Catering
Contact: Peter Durbin
Cumbrian Cottages Ltd
t (01228) 599950
e enquiries@cumbrian-cottages.co.uk
w cumbrian-cottages.co.uk

The Old Barn ★★★★
Self Catering
Contact: Mr Paul Liddell
Lakelovers
t (015394) 88855
e bookings@lakelovers.co.uk
w lakelovers.co.uk

Sunnyhill ★★★★
Self Catering
Contact: Peter Durbin
Cumbrian Cottages Ltd
t (01228) 599950
e enquiries@cumbrian-cottages.co.uk
w cumbrian-cottages.co.uk

BRINSCALL
Lancashire

Moors View Cottage ★★★
Self Catering
Contact: Mrs Sheila Smith
Moors View Cottage
t (01253) 853537 & 07747 808406

BROUGHTON IN FURNESS
Cumbria

Holebeck Farm Cottages
★★★-★★★★ *Self Catering*
Contact: Mr Philip Johnston
The Coppermines & Coniston Lake Cottages
t (015394) 41765
e info@coppermines.co.uk
w coppermines.co.uk

The Old Millers Cottage
★★★★ *Self Catering*
Contact: Mr Philip Johnston
The Coppermines & Coniston Lake Cottages
t (015394) 41765
e info@coppermines.co.uk
w coppermines.co.uk

Ring House Cottages
★★★-★★★★ *Self Catering*
Contact: Stuart & Lynda Harrison
t (01229) 716578
e info@ringhouse.co.uk
w ringhouse.co.uk

Thornthwaite Farm ★★★
Self Catering
Contact: Jean Jackson
t (01229) 716340
e info@lakedistrictcottages.co.uk
w lakedistrictcottages.co.uk

BROUGHTON MILLS
Cumbria

Hobkin Cottage ★★★
Self Catering
Contact: Mr Philip Johnston
The Coppermines & Coniston Lake Cottages
t (015394) 41765
e info@coppermines.co.uk
w coppermines.co.uk

BULLGILL
Cumbria

Barn Cottage & Loft Cottage
★★★★ *Self Catering*
Contact: Peter Durbin
Cumbrian Cottages Ltd
t (01228) 599950
e enquiries@cumbrian-cottages.co.uk
w cumbrian-cottages.co.uk

Row Moor Farm ★★★★
Self Catering
Contact: Peter Durbin
Cumbrian Cottages Ltd
t (01228) 599950
e enquiries@cumbrian-cottages.co.uk
w cumbrian-cottages.co.uk

BURLAND
Cheshire

The Stables ★★★★
Self Catering
t (01270) 524535

BURNESIDE
Cumbria

Mirefoot Cottages ★★★★★
Self Catering
Contact: Kate Curwen
t (01539) 720015
e kate@mirefoot.co.uk
w mirefoot.co.uk

BURSCOUGH
Lancashire

Moss Farm Barn ★★★★
Self Catering
t (01704) 897944
e rosebowman@tiscali.co.uk

BURTON-IN-KENDAL
Cumbria

East Wing ★★★★
Self Catering
Contact: Peter Durbin
Cumbrian Cottages Ltd
t (01228) 599950
e enquiries@cumbrian-cottages.co.uk
w cumbrian-cottages.co.uk

BURY
Greater Manchester

Top o' th' Moor Cottage
★★★★ *Self Catering*
Contact: Mrs Michelle Richardson
t 07976 034196
e info@topofthemoorcottage.com
w topofthemoorcottage.com

BUTTERMERE
Cumbria

Bridge Hotel & Self Catering Apartments ★★★★
Self Catering
Contact: John McGuire
Bridge Hotel & Self Catering Apartments
t (01768) 770252
e enquiries@bridge-hotel.com
w bridge-hotel.com

Lanthwaite Green Farm Cottage ★★★★ *Self Catering*
Contact: John McGuire
Bridge Hotel & Self Catering Apartments
t (01768) 770252
e enquiries@bridge-hotel.com
w bridge-hotel.com

BUTTERWICK
Cumbria

Gill Barn ★★★ *Self Catering*
Contact: Peter Durbin
Cumbrian Cottages Ltd
t (01228) 599950
e enquiries@cumbrian-cottages.co.uk
w cumbrian-cottages.co.uk

CALDBECK
Cumbria

The Barn, Manor Cottage
★★★★ *Self Catering*
Contact: Ann Wade
Manor Cottage
t (01697) 478214
e walterwade@tiscali.co.uk

Ellwood House ★★★
Self Catering
Contact: Peter Durbin
Cumbrian Cottages Ltd
t (01228) 599950
e enquiries@cumbrian-cottages.co.uk
w cumbrian-cottages.co.uk

Greenside Cottage ★★★
Self Catering
Contact: Peter Durbin
Cumbrian Cottages Ltd
t (01228) 599950
e enquiries@cumbrian-cottages.co.uk
w cumbrian-cottages.co.uk

High Greenrigg House Country Cottages ★★★★★
Self Catering
Contact: Mrs Sonia Hill
t (01697) 478430
e info@highgreenrigghouse.co.uk

Little Orchard ★★★
Self Catering
Contact: Peter Durbin
Cumbrian Cottages Ltd
t (01228) 599950
e enquiries@cumbrian-cottages.co.uk
w cumbrian-cottages.co.uk

Monkhouse Hill Cottages ★★★★-★★★★★
Self Catering
Contact: Andy & Jennifer Collard
t (01697) 476254
e cottages@monkhousehill.co.uk
w monkhousehill.co.uk

CARK IN CARTMEL
Cumbria

Batters Cottage ★★★
Self Catering
Contact: Mr John Serginson
The Lakeland Cottage Company
t (015395) 30024
e john@lakelandcottageco.com

Salesbrook ★★★★
Self Catering
Contact: Mr John Serginson
The Lakeland Cottage Company
t (015395) 30024
e john@lakelandcottageco.com

CARLETON
Cumbria

Newbiggin Hall ★★★★
Self Catering
Contact: Mr & Mrs David & June Bates
t (01228) 527549
e all.bates@virgin.net

CARLISLE
Cumbria

Bessiestown Farm Country Cottages ★★★★
Self Catering
Contact: John Sisson
Bessiestown Farm
t (01228) 577219
e info@bessiestown.co.uk
w bessiestown.co.uk

The Gables ★★★
Self Catering
t (01228) 599960
e enquiries@cumbrian-cottages.co.uk
w cumbrian-cottages.co.uk

Meadow View, Burn Cottage & Ald Pallyards ★★★★
Self Catering
Contact: Mrs Elwen
t (01228) 577308
e info@newpallyards.freeserve.co.uk
w newpallyards.freeserve.co.uk

Old Brewery Residences ★★★ *Self Catering*
Contact: Dee Carruthers
Impact Housing Association
t (01228) 597352
e deec@impacthousing.org.uk
w impacthousing.org.uk

West Cottage ★★★★
Self Catering
Contact: Mrs Allison Stamper
West Cottage
t (01228) 561600

CARNFORTH
Lancashire

Coppernob Mews ★★★★
Self Catering
Contact: Peter Durbin
Cumbrian Cottages Ltd
t (01228) 599950
e enquiries@cumbrian-cottages.co.uk
w cumbrian-cottages.co.uk

Deroy Cottage ★★★
Self Catering
t (01524) 733196

Mansergh Farmhouse Cottages ★★★★
Self Catering
Contact: Mrs Linda Rigby
t (01524) 720129

Pine Lake Lodges ★★★★
Self Catering
Contact: Mr Tony Commons
Cumbrian Cottages Ltd
t (01228) 599950
e enquiries@cumbrian-cottages.co.uk
w cumbrian-cottages.co.uk

CARTMEL
Cumbria

Bradlea ★★★ *Self Catering*
Contact: Peter Durbin
Cumbrian Cottages Ltd
t (01228) 599950
e enquiries@cumbrian-cottages.co.uk
w cumbrian-cottages.co.uk

Clogger Beck Cottage ★★★★ *Self Catering*
Contact: Peter Durbin
Cumbrian Cottages Ltd
t (01228) 599950
e enquiries@cumbrian-cottages.co.uk
w cumbrian-cottages.co.uk

Grange End Cottage ★★★★
Self Catering
Contact: Simon Cleasby
Grange End Cottages
t (01524) 702955 & 07770 301709
e stc@f2s.com
w holidaycottagescumbria.com

Longlands at Cartmel ★★★-★★★★ *Self Catering*
Contact: Martin Ainscough
Longlands at Cartmel
t (015395) 36475
e longlands@cartmel.com
w cartmel.com

Longlands Farm Cottage ★★★ *Self Catering*
Contact: Valerie Dixon
t (015395) 36406
e longlandsfarm@freeuk.com
w longlandsfarmcottage.co.uk

The Old Telephone Exchange ★★★ *Self Catering*
Contact: Peter Durbin
Cumbrian Cottages Ltd
t (01228) 599950
e enquiries@cumbrian-cottages.co.uk
w cumbrian-cottages.co.uk

The Old Vicarage, Field Broughton ★★★★
Self Catering
Contact: Mrs Sharphouse
The Old Vicarage Flat
t (015395) 36540
e theflat@sharphouse.co.uk
w sharphouse.co.uk/theflat

Wharton Barn ★★★★★
Self Catering
Contact: Mr John Serginson
The Lakeland Cottage Company
t (015395) 30024
e john@lakelandcottageco.com
w lakelandcottageco.com

Wharton Cottage
Rating Applied For
Self Catering
Contact: Peter Durbin
Cumbrian Cottages Ltd
t (01228) 599950
e enquiries@cumbrian-cottages.co.uk
w cumbrian-cottages.co.uk

CASTLE CARROCK
Cumbria

Tottergill Farm ★★★★-★★★★★
Self Catering
Contact: Alison Bridges
t (01228) 670615
e alison@tottergill.demon.co.uk
w tottergill.demon.co.uk

CATON
Lancashire

Croft (The) – Ground Floor Apartment ★★★★ *Self Catering & Serviced Apartments*
Contact: Miss Sue Brierly-Hampton
t (01524) 770725

CHAPEL STILE
Cumbria

1 Lingmoor View ★★★
Self Catering
Contact: Pauline Robinson
t (01229) 583889
e paulinerobinson@lakelandcottage.com
w lakelandcottage.com

10 Lingmoor View ★★★
Self Catering
Contact: Mrs Vivien Bass
Wheelwrights Holiday Cottages
t (015394) 37635
e enquiries@wheelwrights.com

14 Fir Garth ★★★
Self Catering
Contact: Peter Durbin
Cumbrian Cottages Ltd
t (01228) 599950
e enquiries@cumbrian-cottages.co.uk
w cumbrian-cottages.co.uk

16 Fir Garth ★★★
Self Catering
Contact: Mrs Vivien Bass
Wheelwrights Holiday Cottages
t (015394) 37635
e enquiries@wheelwrights.com

16 Thrang Brow ★★★
Self Catering
Contact: Mrs Vivien Bass
Wheelwrights Holiday Cottages
t (015394) 37635
e enquiries@wheelwrights.com

18 Thrang Brow ★★★
Self Catering
Contact: Mrs Vivien Bass
Wheelwrights Holiday Cottages
t (015394) 37635
e enquiries@wheelwrights.com

2 Undergarth ★★★
Self Catering
Contact: Peter Durbin
Cumbrian Cottages Ltd
t (01228) 599950
e enquiries@cumbrian-cottages.co.uk
w cumbrian-cottages.co.uk

20 Thrang Brow ★★★
Self Catering
Contact: Mrs Vivien Bass
Wheelwrights Holiday Cottages
t (015394) 37635
e enquiries@wheelwrights.com

3 Lingmoor View ★★★
Self Catering
Contact: Mr & Mrs Geoffrey & Sheila Smith
t (01756) 791779
e g.s.smith@btinternet.com

5 Lingmoor View ★★★
Self Catering
Contact: Mrs Vivien Bass
Wheelwrights Holiday Cottages
t (015394) 37635
e enquiries@wheelwrights.com

7 Fir Garth ★★★★
Self Catering
Contact: Mrs Vivien Bass
Wheelwrights Holiday Cottages
t (015394) 37635
e enquiries@wheelwrights.com

7 Thrang Brow ★★★
Self Catering
Contact: Mrs Vivien Bass
Wheelwrights Holiday Cottages
t (015394) 37635
e enquiries@wheelwrights.com

9 Lingmoor View ★★★★
Self Catering
Contact: Mrs Vivien Bass
Wheelwrights Holiday Cottages
t (015394) 37635
e enquiries@wheelwrights.com
w wheelwrights.com

Anns Cottage ★★★
Self Catering
Contact: Mrs Vivien Bass
Wheelwrights Holiday Cottages
t (015394) 37635
e enquiries@wheelwrights.com

Ann's Cottage ★★★
Self Catering
Lakelovers
t (015394) 88855
e bookings@lakelovers.co.uk
w lakelovers.co.uk

Bank View ★★★
Self Catering
Contact: Peter Durbin
Cumbrian Cottages Ltd
t (01228) 599950
e enquiries@cumbrian-cottages.co.uk
w cumbrian-cottages.co.uk

Birdie Fell ★★★ *Self Catering*
Contact: Mrs Vivien Bass
Wheelwrights Holiday Cottages
t (015394) 37635
e enquiries@wheelwrights.com

Christmas Cottage ★★★
Self Catering
Contact: Peter Durbin
Cumbrian Cottages Ltd
t (01228) 599950
e enquiries@cumbrian-cottages.co.uk
w cumbrian-cottages.co.uk

Church Bank ★★★
Self Catering
Contact: Mrs Vivien Bass
Wheelwrights Holiday Cottages
t (015394) 37635
e enquiries@wheelwrights.com

Cottage Walthwaite ★★★★
Self Catering
Contact: Mrs Vivien Bass
Wheelwrights Holiday Cottages
t (015394) 37635
e enquiries@wheelwrights.com

Daw Bank ★★★ *Self Catering*
Contact: Mrs Vivien Bass
Wheelwrights Holiday Cottages
t (015394) 37635
e enquiries@wheelwrights.com

Dulcanter ★★★★
Self Catering
Contact: Peter Durbin
Cumbrian Cottages Ltd
t (01228) 599950
e enquiries@cumbrian-cottages.co.uk
w cumbrian-cottages.co.uk

End Cottage ★★
Self Catering
Contact: Mrs Vivien Bass
Wheelwrights Holiday Cottages
t (015394) 37635
e enquiries@wheelwrights.com

Fir Garth ★★★ *Self Catering*
Contact: Peter Durbin
Cumbrian Cottages Ltd
t (01228) 599950
e enquiries@cumbrian-cottages.co.uk
w cumbrian-cottages.co.uk

Fold Cottage ★★★
Self Catering
Contact: Mrs Vivien Bass
Wheelwrights Holiday Cottages
t (015394) 37635
e enquiries@wheelwrights.com

Greenmire ★★★★
Self Catering
Contact: Mrs Vivien Bass
Wheelwrights Holiday Cottages
t (015394) 37635
e enquiries@wheelwrights.com

Inglewood Cottage ★★★
Self Catering
Contact: Mrs Vivien Bass
Wheelwrights Holiday Cottages
t (015394) 37635
e enquiries@wheelwrights.com

Inglewood House ★★★★
Self Catering
Contact: Mrs Vivien Bass
Wheelwrights Holiday Cottages
t (015394) 37635
e enquiries@wheelwrights.com

Jacks Nook ★★★
Self Catering
Contact: Mrs Vivien Bass
Wheelwrights Holiday Cottages
t (015394) 37635
e enquiries@wheelwrights.com

Jenny's Cottage ★★★
Self Catering
Contact: Mrs Vivien Bass
Wheelwrights Holiday Cottages
t (015394) 37635
e enquiries@wheelwrights.com
w wheelwrights.com

Meadow View ★★★
Self Catering
Contact: Mrs Vivien Bass
Wheelwrights Holiday Cottages
t (015394) 37635
e enquiries@wheelwrights.com

Myrtle Cottage ★★★
Self Catering
Contact: Mrs Vivien Bass
Wheelwrights Holiday Cottages
t (015394) 37635
e enquiries@wheelwrights.com

Oak Cottage ★★★★
Self Catering
Contact: Mrs Vivien Bass
Wheelwrights Holiday Cottages
t (015394) 37635
e enquiries@wheelwrights.com

Oakdene Cottage ★★★★
Self Catering
Contact: Mrs Vivien Bass
Wheelwrights Holiday Cottages
t (015394) 37635
e enquiries@wheelwrights.com

Oakdene House ★★★★
Self Catering
Contact: Mrs Vivien Bass
Wheelwrights Holiday Cottages
t (015394) 37635
e enquiries@wheelwrights.com

The Old Post Office ★★★★
Self Catering
Contact: Mrs Vivien Bass
Wheelwrights Holiday Cottages
t (015394) 37635
e enquiries@wheelwrights.com

Old White Lion ★★★
Self Catering
Contact: Mrs Vivien Bass
Wheelwrights Holiday Cottages
t (015394) 37635
e enquiries@wheelwrights.com

Orchard Cottage ★★★
Self Catering
Contact: Mrs Vivien Bass
Wheelwrights Holiday Cottages
t (015394) 37635
e enquiries@wheelwrights.com
w wheelwrights.com

Plumblands ★★★★
Self Catering
Contact: Peter Durbin
Cumbrian Cottages Ltd
t (01228) 599950
e enquiries@cumbrian-cottages.co.uk
w cumbrian-cottages.co.uk

Priest End ★★★
Self Catering
Contact: Mrs Vivien Bass
Wheelwrights Holiday Cottages
t (015394) 37635
e enquiries@wheelwrights.com

Spedding Fold ★★★
Self Catering
Contact: Mrs Vivien Bass
Wheelwrights Holiday Cottages
t (015394) 37635
e enquiries@wheelwrights.com

White Lion Cottage ★★★★
Self Catering
Contact: Mrs Vivien Bass
Wheelwrights Holiday Cottages
t (015394) 37635
e enquiries@wheelwrights.com

CHESTER
Cheshire

The Almshouse ★★★★
Self Catering
t (01928) 733096
e thealmshouse@fsmail.net
w thealmshouseholidaycottage.co.uk

Cherry Tree Cottage & Damson Cottage ★★★★
Self Catering
Cheshire Country Cottages
t (01829) 740732
e info@cheshirecottages.com

Chester Gems Garden Cottage ★★★★ *Self Catering*
Contact: Mrs Sue Byrne
Walnut Cottage
t (01244) 379824
e sue@chestergems.freeserve.co.uk

The City Apartments ★★★★ *Self Catering*
t (01244) 372091
e chesterhols@btinternet.com
w chesterholidays.co.uk

City Walls Apartments ★★★ *Self Catering*
Thompson Cox Partnership
t (01244) 313400
e admin@rufuscourt.co.uk

Domini Mews ★★★
Self Catering
t (01244) 815664

Duchess Apartment ★★★★★ *Self Catering*
t (01928) 788355
e cheswilliamj99@freeserve.co.uk
w wickentreefarm.co.uk

Fir Tree Cottage ★★★
Self Catering
t (01244) 382681

Handbridge Village ★★★
Self Catering
Contact: Mrs R A Owen
t (01244) 676159

Ivy Cottage ★★★
Self Catering
t (01244) 403630
e rmd.heritage@btconnect.com
w rmd-heritage.co.uk

Kingswood Coach House ★★★ *Self Catering*
Contact: Mrs C Perry
Kingswood Coach House
t (01244) 851204
e caroline.m.perry@btopenworld.com

The Lodge ★★★
Self Catering
Highfield Cottage
t (01244) 678109

Mews Style Cottages ★★★★★ *Self Catering*
t (01745) 825880
e k.buchan@btinternet.com
w chesterholidaycottages.com

Queen's Park ★★★
Self Catering
t (01244) 676141

St James Apartments
★★★★ *Self Catering*
Contact: Mrs Davies
t (01244) 323204

Stapleford Hall Cottage
★★★ *Self Catering*
t (01829) 740202
e staplefordcottage@hotmail.com
w staplefordhallcottage.com

Westminster House ★★★★
Self Catering
Contact: Mr Neil Graham
Passion For Property
t (01244) 350300
e neil@passionforproperty.com
w chestershortlets.com

Wharton Court ★★★★
Self Catering
t (01745) 822113
e peterdavies800@hotmail.com

Woodfield ★★★
Self Catering
t (01244) 880560
e churchfarmdairiesltd@supanet.com
w selfcateringchester.co.uk

CHIPPING
Lancashire

Fell View ★★★★
Self Catering
Contact: Mrs Joan Porter
t (01995) 61160

Judd Holmes BArn ★★★★
Self Catering
t (01995) 61655
w juddholmesbarn.co.uk

Pale Farm Cottages ★★★★
Self Catering
Contact: Mrs Lynn Ollerton
t (01772) 783082

Rakefoot Barn, Chaigley
★★★-★★★★ *Self Catering*
t (01995) 61332

The Waterwheel ★★★★
Self Catering
Contact: Mrs Carol Grant
t (01995) 61553
e carol.grant@virgin.net

Wolfen Mill Country Retreats ★★★★-★★★★★
Self Catering
Contact: Mr Michael Lawson
t (01995) 61574
e information@wolfenmill.co.uk
w wolfenmill.co.uk

CHURCHTOWN
Merseyside

Mews Cottage ★★★
Self Catering
Contact: Ms Sheena Brown
t (01704) 227222

CLAPPERSGATE
Cumbria

Ashley Green ★★★
Self Catering
Contact: Peter Durbin
Cumbrian Cottages Ltd
t (01228) 599950
e enquiries@cumbrian-cottages.co.uk
w cumbrian-cottages.co.uk

Blackcombe, Whitecraggs
★★★★ *Self Catering*
Heart of the Lakes
t (015394) 32321
e info@heartofthelakes.co.uk
w heartofthelakes.co.uk

The Clock ★★★★
Self Catering
Contact: Mr Paul Liddell
Lakelovers
t (015394) 88855
e bookings@lakelovers.co.uk
w lakelovers.co.uk

Courtyard Cottage ★★★★
Self Catering
Contact: Susan Jackson
Heart of the Lakes
t (015394) 32321
e info@heartofthelakes.co.uk
w heartofthelakes.co.uk

Crag Head Cottage
★★★★★ *Self Catering*
Lakelovers
t (015394) 88855
e bookings@lakelovers.co.uk
w lakelovers.co.uk

Dove Cot ★★★★
Self Catering
Contact: Peter Durbin
Cumbrian Cottages Ltd
t (01228) 599950
e enquiries@cumbrian-cottages.co.uk
w cumbrian-cottages.co.uk

Fell View ★★★ *Self Catering*
Contact: Susan Jackson
Heart of the Lakes
t (015394) 32321
e info@heartofthelakes.co.uk
w heartofthelakes.co.uk

The Hayloft ★★★
Self Catering
Contact: Susan Jackson
Heart of the Lakes
t (015394) 32321
e info@heartofthelakes.co.uk
w heartofthelakes.co.uk

The Mounting Steps ★★★★
Self Catering
Contact: Mr Paul Liddell
Lakelovers
t (015394) 88855
e bookings@lakelovers.co.uk
w lakelovers.co.uk

Park Cottage ★★★
Self Catering
Heart of the Lakes
t (015394) 32321
e info@heartofthelakes.co.uk
w heartofthelakes.co.uk

The Pavilion ★★★★
Self Catering
Contact: Peter Durbin
Cumbrian Cottages Ltd
t (01228) 599950
e enquiries@cumbrian-cottages.co.uk
w cumbrian-cottages.co.uk

Rock Cottage ★★★
Self Catering
Contact: Susan Jackson
Heart of the Lakes
t (015394) 32321
e info@heartofthelakes.co.uk
w heartofthelakes.co.uk

Scafell Pike, White Craggs
★★★★ *Self Catering*
Contact: Susan Jackson
Heart of the Lakes
t (015394) 32321
e info@heartofthelakes.co.uk
w heartofthelakes.co.uk

Skiddaw, Whitecrags
★★★★ *Self Catering*
Contact: Mrs Susan Jackson
Heart of the Lakes
t (015394) 32321
e info@heartofthelakes.co.uk
w heartofthelakes.co.uk

CLIBURN
Cumbria

The Coach House ★★★★
Self Catering
Contact: Ms Fiona Sheen
Dales Holiday Cottages
t 0870 909 9500
e fiona@dales-holiday-cottages.com
w dalesholcot.com

CLITHEROE
Lancashire

Brownhills Cottage
★★★★★ *Self Catering*
Contact: Mr Roger Wales
Holiday Cottages Yorkshire Ltd
t (01756) 700510
e info@holidaycotts.co.uk

Chestnut Cottage ★★★★
Self Catering
Contact: Mr Roger Wales
Holiday Cottages Yorkshire Ltd
t (01756) 700510
e info@holidaycotts.co.uk

Five Fells Cottage ★★★
Self Catering
t (01200) 424240
e roland.hailwood@talk21.com

Hawk Cottage ★★★★
Self Catering
Contact: Mr Martin Mcshane
Red Rose Cottages
t (01200) 420101
e info@redrosecottages.co.uk

Higher Gills Farm ★★★★
Self Catering
Contact: Mrs Freda Pilkington
t (01200) 445370

Hunters Rest ★★★★
Self Catering
Contact: Mrs Mary Kay
t (01254) 826304
e thekays@greengore.fsbusiness.co.uk
w huntersrestcottage.co.uk

Hydes Farm Holiday Cottages ★★★ *Self Catering*
t (01200) 446353

Saetr Cottage ★★★
Self Catering
Contact: Mrs Victoria Wood
t (01200) 447600

COCKERHAM
Lancashire

Near Moss Farm Holidays
★★★ *Self Catering*
Contact: Mr Sutcliffe
t (01253) 790504
e enquiry@nearmossfarm.co.uk
w nearmossfarm.co.uk

Patty's Farm Barn ★★★★
Self Catering
t (01524) 751285
w pattysfarm.co.uk

COCKERMOUTH
Cumbria

37 Kirkgate ★★★
Self Catering
Contact: Nelson & Val Chicken
39 Kirkgate
t (01900) 823236
e valandnelson@btopenworld.com
w 37kirkgate.com

Berrymeade ★★★
Self Catering
Contact: Peter Durbin
Cumbrian Cottages Ltd
t (01228) 599950
e enquiries@cumbrian-cottages.co.uk
w cumbrian-cottages.co.uk

Chestnut Cottage ★★★
Self Catering
Contact: Peter Durbin
Cumbrian Cottages Ltd
t (01228) 599950
e enquiries@cumbrian-cottages.co.uk
w cumbrian-cottages.co.uk

Corner Cottage ★★★
Self Catering
Contact: Susan Hannah
W. S & S Hannah
t (01900) 822480
e suehannah@limelighting.co.uk
w cottageguide.co.uk/greatbroughton

Corner House ★★★
Self Catering
Contact: Peter Durbin
Cumbrian Cottages Ltd
t (01228) 599950
e enquiries@cumbrian-cottages.co.uk
w cumbrian-cottages.co.uk

Garden Cottage ★★★
Self Catering
Contact: Colin Wornham
Dower Cottage
t (01900) 823531
e wornham2@aol.com
w lakesnw.co.uk/gardencottage

Ghyll Yeat ★★★★
Self Catering
Contact: Anne Haworth
t (01768) 780321
e peter_anneghyllyeat@lineone.net
w ghyllyeat.co.uk

The Hayloft 2 Hall Court ★★
Self Catering
Contact: Mr & Mrs Jackson
Two Hall Court
t (0118) 956 8330
e mjack2bl@aol.com

Highside Cottage ★★★★
Self Catering
Contact: Peter Durbin
Cumbrian Cottages Ltd
t (01228) 599950
e enquiries@cumbrian-cottages.co.uk
w cumbrian-cottages.co.uk

Jenkin Cottage ★★★★
Self Catering
Contact: Mrs Teasdale
t (01768) 776387
e janet@sheepsnet.demon.co.uk
w jenkinfarm.co.uk

Moorside ★★★ *Self Catering*
Contact: Peter Durbin
Cumbrian Cottages Ltd
t (01228) 599950
e enquiries@cumbrian-cottages.co.uk
w cumbrian-cottages.co.uk

Southwaite Mill Cottages
★★★★ *Self Catering*
Contact: David & Noreen Warner
Southwaite Holidays Ltd
t (01900) 827270

The Stables, Dean ★★★
Self Catering
Contact: Veronica Roper
Sunnyside
t (01254) 852027
e veronica@vroper.fsnet.co.uk
w vholidays.moonfruit.com

Stoneygate ★★★★
Self Catering
Contact: Dr & Mrs Pearson
Stoneygate
t (01900) 823595
e g.w.pearson@btinternet.com

COLNE
Lancashire

Alma Inn ★★★ *Self Catering*
Contact: Ms Janice Waters
t (01282) 863447
e thealmainncolne@btopenworld.com

White Syke Farm ★★★
Self Catering
t (01282) 815731

COLTHOUSE
Cumbria

Croft Foot Barn ★★★
Self Catering
Contact: Susan Jackson
Heart of the Lakes
t (015394) 32321
e info@heartofthelakes.co.uk
w heartofthelakes.co.uk

Croft Head ★★★★
Self Catering
Contact: Peter Durbin
Cumbrian Cottages Ltd
t (01228) 599950
e enquiries@cumbrian-cottages.co.uk
w cumbrian-cottages.co.uk

COLTON
Cumbria

Bracken Ground ★★★★
Self Catering
Contact: Peter Durbin
Cumbrian Cottages Ltd
t (01228) 599950
e enquiries@cumbrian-cottages.co.uk
w cumbrian-cottages.co.uk

Forest Field ★★★★
Self Catering
Contact: Mary Postle
t (01229) 861685
e info@forest-field.co.uk
w forest-field.co.uk

CONGLETON
Cheshire

Acorn Cottages ★★★★
Self Catering
Contact: Mr & Mrs Mark Bullock
t (01260) 223388
e mark.bullock@lineone.net

Yew Tree Farm Cottage, North Rode ★★★★
Self Catering
t (01260) 223547
e syson@ukonline.co.uk

CONISTON
Cumbria

1 & 4 Dixon Ground
★★★-★★★★ *Self Catering*
Contact: Mr Philip Johnston
The Coppermines & Coniston Lake Cottages
t (015394) 41765
e info@coppermines.co.uk
w coppermines.co.uk

1 and 2 Ash Gill Cottages, Torver ★★★★ *Self Catering*
Contact: Dorothy Cowburn
Lyndene
t (01772) 612832

1 Far End Cottages ★★★
Self Catering
Contact: Michael & Andrea Batho
Cottages Cumbria
t (015394) 41680
e a.batho@virgin.net
w cottagescumbria.com

10 Green Cottages ★★★★
Self Catering
Contact: Mr Philip Johnston
The Coppermines & Coniston Lake Cottages
t (015394) 41765
e info@coppermines.co.uk
w coppermines.co.uk

4 Coppermines Cottages
★★★ *Self Catering*
Contact: Mr Philip Johnston
The Coppermines & Coniston Lake Cottages
t (015394) 41765
e info@coppermines.co.uk
w coppermines.co.uk

5 Holme Ground Cottages
★★★ *Self Catering*
Contact: Mrs Kate Bradshaw
t (01434) 682526
e rookery1@tiscali.co.uk

Acorn Cottage ★★★★
Self Catering
Contact: Mrs Susan Jackson
Heart of the Lakes
t (015394) 32321
e info@heartofthelakes.co.uk
w heartofthelakes.co.uk

Atkinson Ground Cottage
★★★ *Self Catering*
Contact: Mr John Serginson
The Lakeland Cottage Company
t (015395) 30024
e john@lakelandcottageco.com

Bank Ground Farm Cottages
★★★★ *Self Catering*
Contact: Mr J Batty
t (015394) 41264
e info@bankground.com
w bankground.com

Banks Ghyll Cottage ★★★★
Self Catering
Contact: Mr Philip Johnston
The Coppermines & Coniston Lake Cottages
t (015394) 41765
e info@coppermines.co.uk
w coppermines.co.uk

The Barn ★★★★
Self Catering
Contact: Susan Jackson
Heart of the Lakes
t (015394) 32321
e info@heartofthelakes.co.uk
w heartofthelakes.co.uk

Beck Yeat Cottage ★★★
Self Catering
Contact: Mr Philip Johnston
The Coppermines & Coniston Lake Cottages
t (015394) 41765
e info@coppermines.co.uk
w coppermines.co.uk

Beech Grove ★★★★
Self Catering
Coniston Holidays
t (015394) 41319
e jean.orchardcottage@virgin.net

The Bridge Cottages ★★★★
Self Catering
Contact: Mr Philip Johnston
The Coppermines & Coniston Lake Cottages
t (015394) 41765
e info@coppermines.co.uk
w coppermines.co.uk

Bridge End Cottage ★★★★
Self Catering
Contact: Mr Philip Johnston
The Coppermines & Coniston Lake Cottages
t (015394) 41765
e info@coppermines.co.uk
w coppermines.co.uk

Brow Close Cottage ★★★
Self Catering
Contact: Mr Philip Johnston
The Coppermines & Coniston Lake Cottages
t (015394) 41765
e info@coppermines.co.uk
w coppermines.co.uk

Campbell Apartment ★★★
Self Catering
Contact: John & Clare Sergison
The Lakeland Cottage Company
t 0870 442 5814
w lakelandcottageco.com

The Caravan at Townson Ground ★★★★ *Self Catering*
Contact: Ms Jayne Nelson
t (01371) 872804
e barbara@townsonground.co.uk

Carries Gate ★★★★
Self Catering
Contact: Mrs Susan Jackson
Heart of the Lakes
t (015394) 32321
e info@heartofthelakes.co.uk
w heartofthelakes.co.uk

Cherry Tree Cottage ★★★
Self Catering
Contact: Mr Philip Johnston
The Coppermines & Coniston Lake Cottages
t (015394) 41765
e info@coppermines.co.uk
w coppermines.co.uk

Coniston Country Cottages
★★★★ *Self Catering*
Contact: Steve Abbott
t (015394) 41114
e enquiry@conistoncottages.co.uk
w conistoncottages.co.uk

Coniston Holidays ★★★
Self Catering
Contact: Jean Johnson
t (015394) 41319
e enquiries@conistonholidays.co.uk
w conistonholidays.co.uk

Coniston View Cottage
★★★ *Self Catering*
Contact: Susan Jackson
Heart of the Lakes
t (015394) 32321
e info@heartofthelakes.co.uk
w heartofthelakes.co.uk

The Coppermines Coniston Cottages ★★★-★★★★
Self Catering
Contact: Mr Philip Johnston
The Coppermines & Coniston Lake Cottages
t (015394) 41765
e info@coppermines.co.uk
w coppermines.co.uk

The Cottage ★★★
Self Catering
Contact: Mr & Mrs Serginson
The Lakeland Cottage Company
t 0870 442 5814
w lakeland-cottage-company.co.uk

Curdle Dub ★★ *Self Catering*
Contact: Mr Paul Liddell
Lakelovers
t (015394) 88855
e bookings@lakelovers.co.uk
w lakelovers.co.uk

Damson Cottage ★★★★
Self Catering
Contact: Peter Durbin
Cumbrian Cottages Ltd
t (01228) 599950
e enquiries@cumbrian-cottages.co.uk
w cumbrian-cottages.co.uk

Fair Snape Cottage ★★★★
Self Catering
Contact: Mr Philip Johnston
The Coppermines & Coniston Lake Cottages
t (015394) 41765
e info@coppermines.co.uk
w coppermines.co.uk

Fell Foot Cottage ★★★
Self Catering
Contact: Mr Philip Johnston
The Coppermines & Coniston Lake Cottages
t (015394) 41765
e info@coppermines.co.uk
w coppermines.co.uk

Fisherbeck Fold & Fisherbeck Nest ★★★
Self Catering
Lakelovers
t (015394) 88855
e bookings@lakelovers.co.uk
w lakelovers.co.uk

Forest Cottage ★★★★
Self Catering
Contact: Mr John Serginson
The Lakeland Cottage Company
t (015395) 30024
e john@lakelandcottageco.com

Gable Cottage ★★★
Self Catering
Contact: Mr Philip Johnston
The Coppermines & Coniston Lake Cottages
t (015394) 41765
e info@coppermines.co.uk
w coppermines.co.uk

Gable End ★★★★
Self Catering
Contact: Mr John Serginson
The Lakeland Cottage Company
t (015395) 30024
e john@lakelandcottageco.com

The Gallery ★★★★
Self Catering
Contact: Mr Philip Johnston
The Coppermines & Coniston Lake Cottages
t (015394) 41765
e info@coppermines.co.uk
w coppermines.co.uk

Gate House ★★★★
Self Catering
Contact: Mr Philip Johnston
The Coppermines & Coniston Lake Cottages
t (015394) 41765
e info@coppermines.co.uk
w coppermines.co.uk

Grange Cottage ★★★
Self Catering
Contact: Mr Philip Johnston
The Coppermines & Coniston Lake Cottages
t (015394) 41765
e info@coppermines.co.uk
w coppermines.co.uk

Grizedale ★★★ *Self Catering*
Contact: Mr John Serginson
The Lakeland Cottage Company
t (015395) 30024
e john@lakelandcottageco.com

Heathwaite Farm Cottages Heathwaite Farm House, The Old
Rating Applied For
Self Catering
Contact: Mr Philip Johnston
The Coppermines & Coniston Lake Cottages
t (015394) 41765
e info@coppermines.co.uk
w coppermines.co.uk

Hidden Cottage ★★★★
Self Catering
Contact: Mr Philip Johnston
The Coppermines & Coniston Lake Cottages
t (015394) 41765
e info@coppermines.co.uk
w coppermines.co.uk

High Arnside ★★★
Self Catering
Contact: Jan Meredith
t (015394) 32261
e jmeredith@beeb.net
w higharnsidefarm.co.uk

Hollin Bank Barn ★★★
Self Catering
Contact: Peter Durbin
Cumbrian Cottages Ltd
t (01228) 599950
e enquiries@cumbrian-cottages.co.uk
w cumbrian-cottages.co.uk

Holly Cottage ★★★★
Self Catering
Contact: Mr Philip Johnston
The Coppermines & Coniston Lake Cottages
t (015394) 41765
e info@coppermines.co.uk
w coppermines.co.uk

Holly Garth ★★★★
Self Catering
Contact: Susan Jackson
Heart of the Lakes
t (015394) 32321
e info@heartofthelakes.co.uk
w heartofthelakes.co.uk

How Head Cottage ★★★
Self Catering
Contact: Mr & Mrs Holland
How Head Cottages
t (015394) 41594
e howhead@lineone.net
w howheadcottages.co.uk

Howhead ★★★★
Self Catering
Contact: Mr John Serginson
The Lakeland Cottage Company
t (015395) 30024
e john@lakelandcottageco.com

Lake View Cottage ★★★
Self Catering
Contact: Susan Jackson
Heart of the Lakes
t (015394) 32321
e info@heartofthelakes.co.uk
w heartofthelakes.co.uk

Low Brow ★★★ *Self Catering*
Contact: Mrs Susan Jackson
Heart of the Lakes
t (015394) 32321
e info@heartofthelakes.co.uk
w heartofthelakes.co.uk

Lower Barn ★★★
Self Catering
Contact: Mr John Serginson
The Lakeland Cottage Company
t (015395) 30024
e john@lakelandcottageco.com
w lakelandcottageco.com

Mart Crag View ★★★★
Self Catering
Wheelwrights Holiday Cottages
t (015394) 37635
e enquiries@wheelwrights.com
w wheelwrights.com

Middlefield Cottage ★★★★
Self Catering
Contact: Mr Philip Johnston
The Coppermines & Coniston Lake Cottages
t (015394) 41765
e info@coppermines.co.uk
w coppermines.co.uk

Mountain Ash Cottage ★★★★ *Self Catering*
Contact: Mr Philip Johnston
The Coppermines & Coniston Lake Cottages
t (015394) 41765
e info@coppermines.co.uk
w coppermines.co.uk

No 1 Silverbank ★★★★★
Self Catering
Contact: Mr Anthony Hext
t (020) 704 9071
e no1silverbank@aol.com

Pear Tree House ★★★
Self Catering
Contact: Mr Philip Johnston
The Coppermines & Coniston Lake Cottages
t (015394) 41765
e info@coppermines.co.uk
w coppermines.co.uk

Potters Wheel ★★★★
Self Catering
Contact: Peter Durbin
Cumbrian Cottages Ltd
t (01228) 599950
e enquiries@cumbrian-cottages.co.uk
w cumbrian-cottages.co.uk

Rascal Howe Cottage ★★★
Self Catering
Contact: Mr Philip Johnston
The Coppermines & Coniston Lake Cottages
t (015394) 41765
e info@coppermines.co.uk
w coppermines.co.uk

Red Dell Cottage ★★★★
Self Catering
Contact: Mr Philip Johnston
The Coppermines & Coniston Lake Cottages
t (015394) 41765
e info@coppermines.co.uk
w coppermines.co.uk

River Cottage ★★★
Self Catering
Contact: Mr Philip Johnston
The Coppermines & Coniston Lake Cottages
t (015394) 41765
e info@coppermines.co.uk
w coppermines.co.uk

Rivington ★★★ *Self Catering*
Contact: Peter Durbin
Cumbrian Cottages Ltd
t (01228) 599950
e enquiries@cumbrian-cottages.co.uk
w cumbrian-cottages.co.uk

Rock Cottage ★★★
Self Catering
Contact: Mr Philip Johnston
The Coppermines & Coniston Lake Cottages
t (015394) 41765
e info@coppermines.co.uk
w coppermines.co.uk

Rockleigh ★★★ *Self Catering*
Lakelovers
t (015394) 88855
e bookings@lakelovers.co.uk
w lakelovers.co.uk

Rose Bank Cottage ★★★★
Self Catering
Contact: Mr Philip Johnston
The Coppermines & Coniston Lake Cottages
t (015394) 41765
e info@coppermines.co.uk
w coppermines.co.uk

Ruskin Apartment ★★★★
Self Catering
Contact: John & Clare Serginson
The Lakeland Cottage Company
t 0870 442 5814

Shelt Gill ★★★ *Self Catering*
Contact: Rosalind Dean
Shelt Gill
t 0845 009 3998
e holiday@sheltgill.co.uk
w sheltgill.co.uk

The Shieling ★★★
Self Catering
Contact: Mr Paul Liddell
Lakelovers
t (015394) 88855
e bookings@lakelovers.co.uk
w lakelovers.co.uk

Sunbeam Cottage ★★★
Self Catering
Contact: Mr Paul Liddell
Lakelovers
t (015394) 88855
e bookings@lakelovers.co.uk
w lakelovers.co.uk

Sunny Bank Farm ★★★★
Self Catering
Contact: Daphne Libby
t (01228) 515639
e daphne@sunnybankfarm.co.uk
w sunnybankfarm.co.uk

Sunny Brae Cottage ★★★
Self Catering
Contact: Mrs Marie Holland
The Coppermines & Coniston Lake Cottages
t (015394) 41765
e info@coppermines.co.uk
w coppermines.co.uk

Tent Lodge Cottage ★★★★
Self Catering
Contact: Mr John Serginson
The Lakeland Cottage Company
t (015395) 30024
e john@lakelandcottageco.com

Three Springs ★★★
Self Catering
Contact: Mr John Serginson
The Lakeland Cottage Company
t (015395) 30024
e john@lakelandcottageco.com

Thurston House & Thurston View ★★-★★★★
Self Catering
Contact: Alan Jefferson
Thurston House & Thurston View
t (01204) 419261
e alan@jefferson99.freeserve.co.uk
w jefferson99.freeserve.co.uk

Tilberthwaite Farm Cottage
★★★ *Self Catering*
Contact: Mrs D Wilkinson
t (015394) 37281
e tilberthwaite.farm@lineone.net
w tilberthwaitefarmcottage.com

Tinkler Beck Cottage
★★★★ *Self Catering*
Contact: Mr John Serginson
The Lakeland Cottage Company
t 0870 442 5814
e john@lakelandcottageco.com
w lakelandcottageco.com

Tinkler Beck Farm ★★★★★
Self Catering
Contact: Mr John Serginson
The Lakeland Cottage Company
t (015395) 30024
e john@lakelandcottageco.com

Townson Ground House
★★★★ *Self Catering*
Contact: Mr John Serginson
The Lakeland Cottage Company
t (015395) 30024
e john@lakelandcottageco.com

Wetherlam ★★★
Self Catering
Contact: Mr John Serginson
The Lakeland Cottage Company
t (015395) 30024
e john@lakelandcottageco.com

Windrush ★★★★
Self Catering
Contact: Mr John Sergison
The Lakeland Cottage Company
t (015395) 30024
e john@lakelandcottageco.com
w lakelandcottageco.com

Yewdale Cottage ★★★★
Self Catering
Contact: Peter Durbin
Cumbrian Cottages Ltd
t (01228) 599950
e enquiries@cumbrian-cottages.co.uk
w cumbrian-cottages.co.uk

COWAN HEAD
Cumbria

River View Cottage ★★★
Self Catering
Contact: Peter Durbin
Cumbrian Cottages Ltd
t (01228) 599950
e enquiries@cumbrian-cottages.co.uk
w cumbrian-cottages.co.uk

CRACKENTHORPE
Cumbria

Meadow Ing ★★★
Self Catering
Contact: Peter Durbin
Cumbrian Cottages Ltd
t (01228) 599950
e enquiries@cumbrian-cottages.co.uk
w cumbrian-cottages.co.uk

CREWE
Cheshire

Bank Farm Cottages ★★★
Self Catering
Contact: Mrs Ann Vaughan
Bank Farm Cottages
t (01270) 841809

CROOK
Cumbria

Brackenrigg ★★★
Self Catering
Contact: Peter Durbin
Cumbrian Cottages Ltd
t (01228) 599950
e enquiries@cumbrian-cottages.co.uk
w cumbrian-cottages.co.uk

Bronte Cottage ★★★
Self Catering
Contact: Peter Durbin
Cumbrian Cottages Ltd
t (01228) 599950
e enquiries@cumbrian-cottages.co.uk
w cumbrian-cottages.co.uk

Mitchelland Farm Bungalow
★★★★ *Self Catering*
Contact: Stuart Higham
t (015394) 47421

Tan Smithy Cottage ★★★★
Self Catering
Contact: Peter Durbin
Cumbrian Cottages Ltd
t (01228) 599950
e enquiries@cumbrian-cottages.co.uk
w cumbrian-cottages.co.uk

CROOKLANDS
Cumbria

Hillview Cottage ★★★★
Self Catering
Contact: Wendy Simpson
t (015395) 67467
e bouncershire6746@aol.com
w cottageguide.co.uk/hillviewcottage

CROSBY
Cumbria

Galloway Cottage ★★★
Self Catering
Contact: Peter Durbin
Cumbrian Cottages Ltd
t (01228) 599950
e enquiries@cumbrian-cottages.co.uk
w cumbrian-cottages.co.uk

Hill Farm House ★★
Self Catering
Contact: Peter Durbin
Cumbrian Cottages Ltd
t (01228) 599950
e enquiries@cumbrian-cottages.co.uk
w cumbrian-cottages.co.uk

CROSTHWAITE
Cumbria

Acorn Lodge ★★★★
Self Catering
Contact: Peter Durbin
Cumbrian Cottages Ltd
t (01228) 599950
e enquiries@cumbrian-cottages.co.uk
w cumbrian-cottages.co.uk

Barf Lodge ★★★★
Self Catering
Contact: Peter Durbin
Cumbrian Cottages Ltd
t (01228) 599950
e enquiries@cumbrian-cottages.co.uk
w cumbrian-cottages.co.uk

Bega ★★★★ *Self Catering*
Contact: Peter Durbin
Cumbrian Cottages Ltd
t (01228) 599950
e enquiries@cumbrian-cottages.co.uk
w cumbrian-cottages.co.uk

Bobbin Mill Cottage ★★★★
Self Catering
Contact: Roger Green
t (015395) 68057
e holidays@enjoythelakes.com
w enjoythelakes.com

Corner Cottage ★★★★
Self Catering
Contact: Mary Smith
t (01744) 894196
e mary@sgcornercottage.co.uk
w sgcornercottage.co.uk

Crosthwaite Cottages ★★★
Self Catering
Contact: Mr John Serginson
The Lakeland Cottage Company
t (015395) 30024
e john@lakelandcottageco.com

Crosthwaite Spring Cottage
★★★ *Self Catering*
Contact: Mr Paul Liddell
Lakelovers
t (015394) 88855
e bookings@lakelovers.co.uk
w lakelovers.co.uk

Damson Barn ★★★★
Self Catering
Contact: Peter Durbin
Cumbrian Cottages Ltd
t (01228) 599950
e enquiries@cumbrian-cottages.co.uk
w cumbrian-cottages.co.uk

Damson Fold ★★★
Self Catering
Contact: Peter Durbin
Cumbrian Cottages Ltd
t (01228) 599950
e enquiries@cumbrian-cottages.co.uk
w cumbrian-cottages.co.uk

Ennerdale ★★★★
Self Catering
Contact: Peter Durbin
Cumbrian Cottages Ltd
t (01228) 599950
e enquiries@cumbrian-cottages.co.uk
w cumbrian-cottages.co.uk

Ghyllbank ★★★★
Self Catering
Contact: Mr Paul Liddell
Lakelovers
t (015394) 88855
e bookings@lakelovers.co.uk
w lakelovers.co.uk

Gilpin View ★★★
Self Catering
Lakelovers
t (015394) 88855
e bookings@lakelovers.co.uk
w lakelovers.co.uk

Greenbank ★★★★
Self Catering
Contact: Jackie Gaskell
t (015395) 68598
e greenbank@nascr.net
w greenbank-cumbria.co.uk

High Beck Cottage ★★★★
Self Catering
Contact: Mr Paul Liddell
Lakelovers
t (015394) 88855
e bookings@lakelovers.co.uk
w lakelovers.co.uk

Hill Cottage ★★★★
Self Catering
Contact: Peter Durbin
Cumbrian Cottages Ltd
t (01228) 599950
e enquiries@cumbrian-cottages.co.uk
w cumbrian-cottages.co.uk

Low Cartmell Fold ★★★★
Self Catering
Contact: Peter Durbin
Cumbrian Cottages Ltd
t (01228) 599950
e enquiries@cumbrian-cottages.co.uk
w cumbrian-cottages.co.uk

Middlebank ★★★
Self Catering
Contact: Mr & Mrs Serginson
The Lakeland Cottage Company
t 0870 442 5814
w lakeland-cottage-company.co.uk

Top Bank ★★★ *Self Catering*
Contact: Mr & Mrs Serginson
The Lakeland Cottage Company
t 0870 442 5814
w lakeland-cottage-company.com

CROSTON
Lancashire

Cockfight Barn ★★★★
Self Catering
Contact: Ms Diane McMillan
t (01772) 600222
e diane@cockfightbarn.com
w cockfightbarn.com

CROWLEY
Cheshire

Fir Tree Barn Cottages
★★★★ *Self Catering*
t (01565) 777327
e info@firtreebarn.co.uk
w firtreebarn.co.uk

CUDDINGTON
Cheshire

The Coach House on The Mount ★★★★ *Self Catering*
Contact: Ms Annette Elwell
t (01606) 883254
e annette.elwell@btconnet.com
w thecoach-house.co.uk

CUMWHINTON
Cumbria

Rosecote ★★★★
Self Catering
Contact: Peter Durbin
Cumbrian Cottages Ltd
t (01228) 599950
e enquiries@cumbrian-cottages.co.uk
w cumbrian-cottages.co.uk

CUNSEY
Cumbria

Deer Holm ★★★★
Self Catering
Contact: Mr John Serginson
The Lakeland Cottage Company
t (015395) 30024
e john@lakelandcottageco.com

DACRE
Cumbria

2 Rose Cottages ★★★
Self Catering
Contact: Rose Hadden
Icon Marketing
t (0151) 342 3533
e enquiries@2rosecottages.co.uk
w 2rosecottages.co.uk

Blaes Crag Cottage ★★★
Self Catering
Contact: Peter Durbin
Cumbrian Cottages Ltd
t (01228) 599950
e enquiries@cumbrian-cottages.co.uk
w cumbrian-cottages.co.uk

Dacre Cottage ★★★★
Self Catering
Contact: Peter Durbin
Cumbrian Cottages Ltd
t (01228) 599950
e enquiries@cumbrian-cottages.co.uk
w cumbrian-cottages.co.uk

Farriers Lodge ★★★
Self Catering
Contact: Peter Durbin
Cumbrian Cottages Ltd
t (01228) 599950
e enquiries@cumbrian-cottages.co.uk
w cumbrian-cottages.co.uk

DEARHAM
Cumbria

Bendale Cottage ★★★★
Self Catering
Contact: Susan Harper
t (01900) 816763
e stay@bendalecottage.co.uk
w bendalecottage.co.uk

DEEPDALE
Cumbria

Willans ★★ *Self Catering*
Contact: Kathleen Bentham
t (015396) 25285
e kathbentham@hotmail.com
w cottageguide.co.uk/willans

DELAMERE
Cheshire

Wicken Tree Farm ★★★
Self Catering
t (01928) 788355
e ches@williamj99.freeserve.co.uk
w wickentreefarm.co.uk

DELPH
Greater Manchester

Millstone Apartment
★★★★ *Self Catering*
Contact: Mr Hugh Broadbent
Mill Barn
t (01457) 874053

The Stables, Delph ★★★★
Self Catering
Contact: Mrs G Whipp
Sandbed Farm Cottage
t (01457) 871668
e gwynethwhipp@compuserve.co.uk

DENSHAW
Greater Manchester

Home Cottage ★★★
Self Catering
Contact: Mrs Hazel Billing
Top O'Th Fold
t (01457) 876527
e hazel_billi@hotmail.com

DENT
Cumbria

Buzzards Cottage ★★★★
Self Catering
Contact: Mr & Mrs Stephenson
Dent Crafts Centre
t (015396) 25400

High Chapel Cottage
★★★★ *Self Catering*
Dales Hol Cot Ref:2074
t (01756) 799821
e info@dalesholcot.com

Middleton's Cottage and Fountain Cottage ★★★
Self Catering
Contact: Mr & Mrs Ayers
Middleton's Cottage and Fountain Cottage
t (01323) 870032
e candpayers@mistral.co.uk
w dentcottages.co.uk

Mire Garth ★★★
Self Catering
Contact: Jean Middleton
t (015396) 25235

Stonecroft ★★★
Self Catering
Croft House
t (015396) 25219

Wilsey House ★★★
Self Catering
Contact: Joan Saunders
t (01487) 841556
e enquiries@wilsey.co.uk
w wilsey.co.uk

DIGGLE
Greater Manchester

Diggle House Farm ★★★
Self Catering
Contact: Nigel Shaw
t (01457) 872340
e stay@digglehousefarm.co.uk
w digglehousefarm.co.uk

DOCKRAY
Cumbria

High Brow ★★★
Self Catering
Contact: Peter Durbin
Cumbrian Cottages Ltd
t (01228) 599950
e enquiries@cumbrian-cottages.co.uk
w cumbrian-cottages.co.uk

Lookin How ★★★★★
Self Catering
Contact: Peter Durbin
Cumbrian Cottages Ltd
t (01228) 599950
e enquiries@cumbrian-cottages.co.uk
w cumbrian-cottages.co.uk

DOVENBY
Cumbria

Sunnybrae Bungalow ★★★
Self Catering
Contact: Peter Durbin
Cumbrian Cottages Ltd
t (01228) 599950
e enquiries@cumbrian-cottages.co.uk
w cumbrian-cottages.co.uk

DOWNHAM
Lancashire

Stables Lodge Cottage ★★★
Self Catering
Contact: Mr Taylor
t (01200) 441242
e stableslodgecottage@yahoo.co.uk
w stableslodgecottage downham.co.uk

DRUMBURGH
Cumbria

The Grange ★★★-★★★★
Self Catering
Contact: Sarah Hodgson
Grange Cottages
t (01228) 576551
e messrs.hodgson@tesco.net
w thegrangecottage.co.uk

DUFTON
Cumbria

Brow Farm Bed & Breakfast
Rating Applied For
Self Catering
Contact: Mrs Wendy Swinbank
t (01768) 352865
e stay@browfarm.com
w browfarm.com

Holly Dene ★★★★
Self Catering
Contact: Peter Durbin
Cumbrian Cottages Ltd
t (01228) 599950
e enquiries@cumbrian-cottages.co.uk
w cumbrian-cottages.co.uk

EDDERSIDE
Cumbria

Centre Farm ★★★
Self Catering
Contact: Peter Durbin
Cumbrian Cottages Ltd
t (01228) 599950
e enquiries@cumbrian-cottages.co.uk
w cumbrian-cottages.co.uk

EDENHALL
Cumbria

Eden House Loft ★★★★
Self Catering
Contact: Mr Dominic Finn
Elfino Ltd.
t (01786) 451155
e dom@elfino.com
w edenhouseloft.com

EGERTON
Cheshire

Manor Farm Holiday Cottages ★★★★
Self Catering
t (01829) 720261

ELTERWATER
Cumbria

Ben's ★★★★ *Self Catering*
Contact: Ms Vivien Bass
Wheelwrights Holiday Cottages
t (015394) 37635
e enquiries@wheelwrights.com

Bottom Shop ★★★★
Self Catering
Contact: Mrs Vivien Bass
Wheelwrights Holiday Cottages
t (015394) 37635
e enquiries@wheelwrights.com
w wheelwrights.com

Bridge End Cottage ★★★★
Self Catering
Contact: Mr Paul Liddell
Lakelovers
t (015394) 88855
e bookings@lakelovers.co.uk
w lakelovers.co.uk

Bridge Syke Cottage ★★★★
Self Catering
Lakelovers
t (015394) 88855
e bookings@lakelovers.co.uk
w lakelovers.co.uk

Brooklands ★★★★
Self Catering
Contact: Mrs Vivien Bass
Wheelwrights Holiday Cottages
t (015394) 37635
e enquiries@wheelwrights.com

Eltermere Old Barn ★★★
Self Catering
Contact: Mrs Susan Jackson
Heart of the Lakes
t (015394) 32321
e info@heartofthelakes.co.uk
w heartofthelakes.co.uk

Fell View ★★★★
Self Catering
Contact: Ms Vivien Bass
Wheelwrights Holiday Cottages
t (015394) 37635
e enquiries@wheelwrights.com

Gunpowder Cottage ★★★★
Self Catering
Lakelovers
t (015394) 88855
e bookings@lakelovers.co.uk
w lakelovers.co.uk

Jonty's ★★★★ *Self Catering*
Contact: Ms Vivien Bass
Wheelwrights Holiday Cottages
t (015394) 37635
e enqireies@wheelwrights.com

Maple Tree Corner ★★★★
Self Catering
Contact: Mrs Susan Jackson
Heart of the Lakes
t (015394) 32321
e info@heartofthelakes.co.uk
w heartofthelakes.co.uk

Mill Race Cottage ★★★
Self Catering
Contact: Mrs Susan Jackson
Heart of the Lakes
t (015394) 32321
e info@heartofthelakes.co.uk
w heartofthelakes.co.uk

Nan's Cottage ★★★★
Self Catering
Contact: Ms Vivien Bass
Wheelwrights Holiday Cottages
t (015394) 37635
e enquiries@wheelwrights.com

Oak Bank ★★★★
Self Catering
Contact: Susan Jackson
Heart of the Lakes
t (015394) 32321
e info@heartofthelakes.co.uk
w heartofthelakes.co.uk

The Old Sawpit ★★★★
Self Catering
Contact: Mrs Vivien Bass
Wheelwrights Holiday Cottages
t (015394) 37635
e enquiries@wheelwrights.com
w wheelwrights.com

Peter Place ★★★
Self Catering
Contact: Mrs Vivien Bass
Wheelwrights Holiday Cottages
t (015394) 37635
e enquiries@wheelwrights.com

Pippins Cottage ★★★★
Self Catering
Contact: Mrs Vivien Bass
Wheelwrights Holiday Cottages
t (015394) 37635
e enquiries@wheelwrights.com

Rose Cottage ★★★★
Self Catering
Contact: Mrs Vivien Bass
Wheelwrights Holiday Cottages
t (015394) 37635
e enquiries@wheelwrights.com

St Giles ★★★ *Self Catering*
Contact: Susan Jackson
Heart of the Lakes
t (015394) 32321
e info@heartofthelakes.co.uk
w heartofthelakes.co.uk

The Stables ★★★★
Self Catering
Wheelwrights Holiday Cottages
t (015394) 37635
e enquiries@wheelwrights.com
w wheelwrights.com

Wistaria Cottage and 3 Main Street ★★★ *Self Catering*
Contact: Mr G & Mrs D Beardmore
t (01782) 783170
e geoff.doreen.beardmore@ntlworld.com

The Woodloft ★★★★
Self Catering
Contact: Ms Vivien Bass
Wheelwrights Holiday Cottages
t (015394) 37635
e enquiries@wheelwrights.com

EMBLETON
Cumbria

Morningside ★★★
Self Catering
Contact: Peter Durbin
Cumbrian Cottages Ltd
t (01228) 599950
e enquiries@cumbrian-cottages.co.uk
w cumbrian-cottages.co.uk

Sunny Bank Cottage ★★★
Self Catering
Contact: Margaret Bell
t (01768) 776273

ENDMOOR
Cumbria

Calvert Cottage ★★★★
Self Catering
Contact: Peter Durbin
Cumbrian Cottages Ltd
t (01228) 599950
e enquiries@cumbrian-cottages.co.uk
w cumbrian-cottages.co.uk

Sunrise ★★★★ *Self Catering*
Contact: Peter Durbin
Cumbrian Cottages Ltd
t (01228) 599950
e enquiries@cumbrian-cottages.co.uk
w cumbrian-cottages.co.uk

ESKDALE
Cumbria

Bridge End Farm Cottages ★★★★-★★★★★
Self Catering
t 0870 073 5328
w selectcottages.com

The Chalets ★★★★
Self Catering
Contact: Lisa Borrowdale & Philip Hayden
t (01946) 723128
e info@thechalets.co.uk
w thechalets.co.uk

Fisherground Farm Holidays ★★★ *Self Catering*
Contact: Ian Hall
Orchard House Holidays
t (01768) 773175
e ian@fisherground.co.uk
w fisherground.co.uk

Old Brantrake ★★★★
Self Catering
Contact: Mr & Mrs Tyson
Old Brantrake
t (01946) 723340

Randle How ★★★★
Self Catering
Contact: Susan Wedley
Randle How
t (01946) 723126
e jswedley@btinternet.com

ETTERBY
Cumbria

Etterby Country House ★★★ *Self Catering*
Contact: Mr Allan Atkinson
t (01228) 510472

FADDILEY
Cheshire

Old Cart House ★★★★★
Self Catering
t (01270) 524215

FAR SAWREY
Cumbria

1 & 2 Church Cottage ★★★★ *Self Catering*
Contact: Mrs Susan Jackson
Heart of the Lakes
t (015394) 32321
e info@heartofthelakes.co.uk
w heartofthelakes.co.uk

Brimstock Cottage ★★★★
Self Catering
Contact: Mr Philip Johnston
The Coppermines & Coniston Lake Cottages
t (015394) 41765
e info@coppermines.co.uk
w coppermines.co.uk

Claife Cottage ★★★
Self Catering
Contact: Peter Durbin
Cumbrian Cottages Ltd
t (01228) 599950
e enquiries@cumbrian-cottages.co.uk
w cumbrian-cottages.co.uk

Hayloft Cottage ★★★★
Self Catering
Contact: Mr Philip Johnston
The Coppermines & Coniston Lake Cottages
t (015394) 41765
e info@coppermines.co.uk
w coppermines.co.uk

Letterbox Cottage ★★★★
Self Catering
Contact: Peter Durbin
Cumbrian Cottages Ltd
t (01228) 599950
e enquiries@cumbrian-cottages.co.uk
w cumbrian-cottages.co.uk

The Morning Room ★★★★
Self Catering
Contact: Ms Anna Gallagher
Hideaways
t (015394) 42435
e bookings@lakeland-hideaways.co.uk
w lakeland-hideaways.co.uk

Rowan Cottage ★★★★
Self Catering
Contact: Mrs Susan Jackson
Heart of the Lakes
t (015394) 32321
e info@heartofthelakes.co.uk
w heartofthelakes.co.uk

Stables Cottage ★★★★
Self Catering
Lakelovers
t (015394) 88855
e bookings@lakelovers.co.uk
w lakelovers.co.uk

Tower Cottage ★★★★
Self Catering
Contact: Mr Philip Johnston
The Coppermines & Coniston Lake Cottages
t (015394) 41265
e info@coppermines.co.uk
w coppermines.co.uk

Writing Room ★★★★
Self Catering
Contact: Ms Anne Gallagher
Hideaways
t (015394) 42435
e bookings@lakeland-hideaways.co.uk
w lakeland-hideaways.co.uk

FARLAM
Cumbria

Calf Close Cottage ★★★★★
Self Catering
Contact: Peter Durbin
Cumbrian Cottages Ltd
t (01228) 599950
e enquiries@cumbrian-cottages.co.uk
w cumbrian-cottages.co.uk

FARNDON
Cheshire

Woodpecker Cottage ★★★★ *Self Catering*
Contact: Mrs Sue Heyworth
t (01829) 270927

FINSTHWAITE
Cumbria

The Barn ★★★★★
Self Catering
Contact: Mr John Serginson
The Lakeland Cottage Company
t (015395) 30024
e john@lakelandcottageco.com

Sheiling Barn ★★★★
Self Catering
Contact: Mr Paul Liddell
Lakelovers
t (015394) 88855
e bookings@lakelovers.co.uk
w lakelovers.co.uk

FIRBANK
Cumbria

Goodies Farmhouse
Rating Applied For
Self Catering
Contact: Peter Durbin
Cumbrian Cottages Ltd
t (01228) 599950
e enquiries@cumbrian-cottages.co.uk
w cumbrian-cottages.co.uk

Newbarn Cottage ★★★
Self Catering
Contact: Pamela Anne Thompson
t (015396) 21278
e newfield@pentalk.org
w newbarncottage.co.uk

FLOOKBURGH
Cumbria

Stockdale Farm ★★★
Self Catering
Contact: Janet Fallon
South Lakes Cottages
t (01229) 889601
e enquiries@southlakes-cottages.com
w southlakes-cottages.com

FORTON
Lancashire

Cleveley Mere Fishing & Lodges., Forton ★–★★★
Self Catering
Contact: Peter & Lynne Brown
Cleveley Mere Fishing Lodges
t (01524) 793644
w cleveleymere.com

Shirebank Court ★★★★
Self Catering
t (01524) 792179
e mail@shirebankcourt.co.uk
w shirebankcourt.co.uk

FOXFIELD
Cumbria

Thistle Cottage ★★★★
Self Catering
Contact: Peter Durbin
Cumbrian Cottages Ltd
t (01228) 599950
e enquiries@cumbrian-cottages.co.uk
w cumbrian-cottages.co.uk

GALGATE
Lancashire

Lakewood Cottages ★★★★
Self Catering
Contact: Mr Alec Sayer
t (01524) 757053
e lakewoodcottages@fsmail.net

GAMBLESBY
Cumbria

Church Court Cottages ★★★–★★★★ *Self Catering*
Contact: Mark Cowell
t (01768) 881682
e markcowell@tiscali.co.uk
w gogamblesby.co.uk

GARNETT BRIDGE
Cumbria

Cocks Close ★★★
Self Catering
Contact: Mrs Denny
Cumbrian Cottages Ltd
t (01932) 246432
e cocksclose@ntlworld.com
w freewebs.com/cocksclose/frames.htm

The Mill Cottage ★★★★
Self Catering
Country Holidays
t 0870 336 7800

GARSDALE
Cumbria

Cloughside Cottage ★★★★
Self Catering
Contact: Ms Lorraine Kidd
Dales Holiday Cottages
t 0870 909 9500
e info@dales-holiday-cottages.com
w dalesholcot.com

Far End Farm ★★★★
Self Catering
Contact: Chris Cooper
t (015396) 21906
e info@farendfarm.com
w farendfarm.com

GARSTANG
Lancashire

Barnacre Cottages ★★★★★
Self Catering
t (01995) 600918
w barnacre-cottages.co.uk

GILCRUX
Cumbria

Ellen Hall ★★–★★★★
Self Catering
Contact: Alison Dunlop
t (01697) 321439
e data.dunlop@virgin.net
w cottagesmadefortwo.co.uk

GILSLAND
Cumbria

Irthing House Cottage ★★★
Self Catering
Contact: Mr Chris Tweddle
t (01697) 747983
w cottagesinnorthumberland.com

The Ostlers ★★★
Self Catering
Contact: Peter Durbin
Cumbrian Cottages Ltd
t (01228) 599950
e enquiries@cumbrian-cottages.co.uk
w cumbrian-cottages.co.uk

Working Dales Pony Centre ★★★ *Self Catering*
Contact: Mr & Mrs Parker
t (01697) 747208

GISBURN
Lancashire

Coverdale Farm ★★★★
Self Catering
Contact: Mrs Mandy Pilkington
t (01200) 445265

GLASSONBY
Cumbria

Chapel House ★★★★
Self Catering
Contact: Mr Lowis
t (01768) 898747
e enquiries@glassonbycottages.co.uk
w glassonbycottages.co.uk

GLENRIDDING
Cumbria

3 High Rake ★★★
Self Catering
Contact: Peter Durbin
Cumbrian Cottages Ltd
t (01228) 599950
e enquiries@cumbrian-cottages.co.uk
w cumbrian-cottages.co.uk

Beech House Apartments 1 & 2 ★★★ *Self Catering*
Lakelovers
t (015394) 88855
e bookings@lakelovers.co.uk
w lakelovers.co.uk

Birkside Cottage ★★★
Self Catering
Contact: Peter Durbin
Cumbrian Cottages Ltd
t (01228) 599950
e enquiries@cumbrian-cottages.co.uk
w cumbrian-cottages.co.uk

Chapel Cottage ★★★★
Self Catering
Contact: Susan Jackson
Heart of the Lakes
t (015394) 32321
e info@heartofthelakes.co.uk
w heartofthelakes.co.uk

Chapel House ★★★★
Self Catering
Contact: Susan Jackson
Heart of the Lakes
t (015394) 32321
e info@heartofthelakes.co.uk
w heartofthelakes.co.uk

Fell View Holidays ★★★★
Self Catering
Contact: Mr J Burnett
t (01768) 867420 & (017688) 67420
e enquiries@fellviewholidays.com
w fellviewholidays.com

Grassthwaite How ★★★★
Self Catering
Contact: Susan Jackson
Heart of the Lakes
t (015394) 32321
e info@heartofthelakes.co.uk
w heartofthelakes.co.uk

Grisedale Cottage ★★★★
Self Catering
Contact: Mrs Susan Jackson
Heart of the Lakes
t (015394) 32321
e info@heartofthelakes.co.uk
w heartofthelakes.co.uk

Halton Cottage ★★★
Self Catering
Contact: Peter Durbin
Cumbrian Cottages Ltd
t (01228) 599950
e enquiries@cumbrian-cottages.co.uk
w cumbrian-cottages.co.uk

Keldas View Cottage ★★★★ *Self Catering*
Contact: Ruth Teasdale
t (01768) 864204
e info@keldasviewcottage.co.uk
w keldasviewcottage.co.uk

Middle Rake ★★★
Self Catering
Contact: Peter Durbin
Cumbrian Cottages Ltd
t (01228) 599950
e enquiries@cumbrian-cottages.co.uk
w cumbrian-cottages.co.uk

Mistal Cottage ★★★★
Self Catering
Contact: Susan Jackson
Heart of the Lakes
t (015394) 32321
e info@heartofthelakes.co.uk
w heartofthelakes.co.uk

The Old Coach House ★★★★ *Self Catering*
Contact: Peter Durbin
Cumbrian Cottages Ltd
t (01228) 599950
e enquiries@cumbrian-cottages.co.uk
w cumbrian-cottages.co.uk

Rathmore ★★★ *Self Catering*
Heart of the Lakes
t (015394) 32321
e info@heartofthelakes.co.uk
w heartofthelakes.co.uk

Stybarrow View Cottage ★★★ *Self Catering*
Contact: Peter Durbin
Cumbrian Cottages Ltd
t (01228) 599950
e enquiries@cumbrian-cottages.co.uk
w cumbrian-cottages.co.uk

Walkers Retreat ★★★★
Self Catering
Contact: Peter Durbin
Cumbrian Cottages Ltd
t (01228) 599950
e enquiries@cumbrian-cottages.co.uk
w cumbrian-cottages.co.uk

Whiteside Lodge ★★★★
Self Catering
Contact: Peter Durbin
Cumbrian Cottages Ltd
t (01228) 599950
e enquiries@cumbrian-cottages.co.uk
w cumbrian-cottages.co.uk

GOSFORTH
Cumbria

Pine Lodge Barn ★★★★
Self Catering
Contact: Peter Durbin
Cumbrian Cottages Ltd
t (01228) 599950
e enquiries@cumbrian-cottages.co.uk
w cumbrian-cottages.co.uk

Potters Barn & Well Cottage ★★★★ *Self Catering*
Contact: Barbara & Dick Wright
t (01946) 725296
e mail@potterycourses.co.uk
w potters-barn.co.uk

GRANGE-OVER-SANDS
Cumbria

The Chalet Studio & Chalet Garden Flat ★★★
Self Catering
Contact: Margaret Wilson
t (015395) 34695
e thechalet@freeuk.com
w lakelandchalet.co.uk

Cornerways Bungalow ★★★
Self Catering
Contact: Eunice Rigg
Cornerways Bungalow & Greaves Farm
t (015395) 36329 & (015395) 36587

Dyer Dene ★★★
Self Catering
Contact: Mrs Andrews
t (01995) 602769
e dyerdene@fish.co.uk
w dyerdene.com

Hazelwood Court Self-Catering ★★★★
Self Catering
Contact: Martin Stilling
t (015395) 34196
w hazelwoodcourt.co.uk

Spring Bank Cottage ★★★★
Self Catering
Contact: Mrs Brocklebank
t (015395) 32606

Swimmers Farm ★★★★★
Self Catering
Contact: Peter Durbin
Cumbrian Cottages Ltd
t (01228) 599950
e enquiries@cumbrian-cottages.co.uk
w cumbrian-cottages.co.uk

Wycombe Holiday Flats
★★★ *Self Catering*
Contact: Geoff & Auriel Benson
t (015395) 32297
e enq@whf.info
w whf.info

GRASMERE
Cumbria

1 Field Foot ★★★
Self Catering
Contact: Mrs J Morrison
1 Field Foot
t (01942) 236350 & (015394) 45305
e jean-morrison@hotmail.co.uk

14 Meadowcroft ★★★★
Self Catering
Contact: Mr Paul Liddell
Lakelovers
t (015394) 88855
e bookings@lakelovers.co.uk
w lakelovers.co.uk

2 Town Head Cottage ★★★
Self Catering
Contact: Peter Durbin
Cumbrian Cottages Ltd
t (01228) 599950
e enquiries@cumbrian-cottages.co.uk
w cumbrian-cottages.co.uk

3 Dale End ★★★
Self Catering
Contact: Anne Truelove
t (015394) 35200
e paul.truelove@btinternet.com
w daleend.co.uk

3 Tarn Cottages ★★★
Self Catering
Contact: Isobel Yates
t (015395) 68843
e iayates@btopenworld.com
w tarncottage.co.uk

Acorn Cottage ★★★★
Self Catering
Contact: Mr Paul Liddell
Lakelovers
t (015394) 88855
e bookings@lakelovers.co.uk
w lakelovers.co.uk

April Cottage ★★★
Self Catering
Lakelovers
t (015394) 88855
e bookings@lakelovers.co.uk
w lakelovers.co.uk

Badger Cottage ★★
Self Catering
Contact: Mrs Vivien Bass
Wheelwrights Holiday Cottages
t (015394) 37635
e enquiries@wheelwrights.com

Beck Allans Self Catering Apartments ★★★–★★★★
Self Catering
Contact: Brian & Pat Taylor
Beck Allans
t (015394) 35563
e mail@beckallans.com
w beckallans.com

Becksteps ★★★★
Self Catering
t (015394) 32321
e info@leisuretime.co.uk

Beechghyll ★★★★
Self Catering
Contact: Mrs Susan Jackson
Heart of the Lakes
t (015394) 32321
e info@heartofthelakes.co.uk
w heartofthelakes.co.uk

Bellfoot ★★★★ *Self Catering*
Contact: Mrs Susan Jackson
Heart of the Lakes
t (015394) 32321
e info@heartofthelakes.co.uk
w heartofthelakes.co.uk

Blind Tarn ★★★
Self Catering
Contact: Mrs Susan Jackson
Heart of the Lakes
t (015394) 32321
e info@heartofthelakes.co.uk
w heartofthelakes.co.uk

Bramrigg House
Rating Applied For
Self Catering
Lakeland Character Cottages
t 0500 600 725
e stay@lakedistrictinns.co.uk
w lakedistrictinns.co.uk

Broad Oak ★★★★
Self Catering
Contact: Susan Jackson
Heart of the Lakes
t (015394) 32321
e info@heartofthelakes.co.uk
w heartofthelakes.co.uk

Broadrayne Farm Cottages
★★★★ *Self Catering*
Contact: Mr Bev Dennison & Mrs Jo Dennison Drake
Broadrayne Farm
t (015394) 35055
e bev@grasmerehostel.co.uk
w grasmere-accommodation.co.uk

Coachmans Cottage ★★★★
Self Catering
Contact: Mrs Susan Jackson
Heart of the Lakes
t (015394) 32321
e info@heartofthelakes.co.uk
w heartofthelakes.co.uk

The Cottage ★★★
Self Catering
Contact: Peter Durbin
Cumbrian Cottages Ltd
t (01228) 599950
e enquiries@cumbrian-cottages.co.uk
w cumbrian-cottages.co.uk

Crummock Cottage ★★★★
Self Catering
Contact: Mrs Vivien Bass
Wheelwrights Holiday Cottages
t (015394) 37635
e enquiries@wheelwrights.com

Curlew Cottage ★★★
Self Catering
Contact: Ms Sue Jackson
Heart of the Lakes
t (015394) 32321
e info@heartofthelakes.co.uk
w heartofthelakes.co.uk

The Daffodils Studio ★★★★
Self Catering
Lakelovers
t (015394) 88855
e bookings@lakelovers.co.uk
w lakelovers.co.uk

Dale End Barn ★★★★
Self Catering
Contact: Mrs Vivien Bass
Wheelwrights Holiday Cottages
t (015394) 37635
e enquiries@wheelwrights.com

Dale End Cottage ★★★★★
Self Catering
Contact: Susan Jackson
Heart of the Lakes
t (015394) 32321
e info@heartofthelakes.co.uk
w heartofthelakes.co.uk

Dale End Farm ★★★★
Self Catering
Contact: Mrs Vivien Bass
Wheelwrights Holiday Cottages
t (015394) 37635
e enquiries@wheelwrights.com

Dale Head Cottage ★★★
Self Catering
Contact: Mrs Susan Jackson
Heart of the Lakes
t (015394) 32321
e info@heartofthelakes.co.uk
w heartofthelakes.co.uk

Dippers Bank ★★★★
Self Catering
Contact: Susan Jackson
Heart of the Lakes
t (015394) 32321
e info@heartofthelakes.co.uk
w heartofthelakes.co.uk

Dove Holme ★★★
Self Catering
Contact: Peter Durbin
Cumbrian Cottages Ltd
t (01228) 599950
e enquiries@cumbrian-cottages.co.uk
w cumbrian-cottages.co.uk

Dovecot Cottage ★★★★
Self Catering
Contact: Mr Philip Johnston
The Coppermines & Coniston Lake Cottages
t (015394) 41765
e info@coppermines.co.uk
w coppermines.co.uk

Dunnabeck ★★★★
Self Catering
Contact: Susan Jackson
Heart of the Lakes
t (015394) 32321
e info@heartofthelakes.co.uk
w heartofthelakes.co.uk

Easedale Cottage ★★★
Self Catering
Contact: Susan Jackson
Heart of the Lakes
t (015394) 32321
e info@heartofthelakes.co.uk
w heartofthelakes.co.uk

Eller Close House
Rating Applied For
Self Catering
Holiday Cottages Group
t (01282) 844284

Eller Close, Wisteria & Garden Cottage ★★★
Self Catering
Lakelovers
t (015394) 88855
e bookings@lakelovers.co.uk
w lakelovers.co.uk

Fairfield ★★★★
Self Catering
Contact: Susan Jackson
Heart of the Lakes
t (015394) 32321
e info@heartofthelakes.co.uk
w heartofthelakes.co.uk

Fairfield Cottage ★★★★
Self Catering
Heart of the Lakes
t (015394) 32321
e info@heartofthelakes.co.uk
w heartofthelakes.co.uk

Fellside Cottage ★★★★
Self Catering
Heart of the Lakes
t (015394) 32321
e info@heartofthelakes.co.uk
w heartofthelakes.co.uk

Fir Tree Cottage ★★★★
Self Catering
Contact: Mrs Marie Holland
The Coppermines & Coniston Lake Cottages
t (015394) 41765
e info@coppermines.co.uk
w coppermines.co.uk

Ghyllside Cottage
Rating Applied For
Self Catering
Contact: Derek Sweeney
The Kings Head Hotel
t (01768) 772393
e stay@lakedistrictinns.co.uk
w lakedistrictinns.co.uk

Glen Dene ★★★★
Self Catering
Contact: Susan Jackson
Heart of the Lakes
t (015394) 32321
e info@heartofthelakes.co.uk
w heartofthelakes.co.uk

Glen View Cottage ★★★★
Self Catering
Lakelovers
t (015394) 88855
e bookings@lakelovers.co.uk
w lakelovers.co.uk

Goody Bridge Barn ★★★★
Self Catering
Heart of the Lakes
t (015394) 32321
e infor@heartofthelakes.co.uk
w heartofthelakes.co.uk

Goody Bridge Cottage ★★★★ *Self Catering*
Heart of the Lakes
t (015394) 32321
e info@heartofthelakes.co.uk
w heartofthelakes.co.uk

Grasmere Cottages ★★★★
Self Catering
Contact: Martin Wood
Grasmere Cottages
t (015394) 35395
e enquiries@grasmerecottage accommodation.co.uk
w grasmerecottage accommodation.co.uk

Grasmere Self Catering ★★★★ *Self Catering*
Contact: Ann Dixon
Grasmere Self Catering Accommodation
t (015394) 35571
e ann@grasmere-holidays.co.uk
w grasmere-holidays.co.uk

Grasmere View ★★★
Self Catering
Contact: Peter Durbin
Cumbrian Cottages Ltd
t (01228) 599950
e enquiries@cumbrian-cottages.co.uk
w cumbrian-cottages.co.uk

Grey Crag Barn ★★★★★
Self Catering
Contact: Mr Paul Liddell
Lakelovers
t (015394) 88855
e bookings@lakelovers.co.uk
w lakelovers.co.uk

Helm Crag ★★★
Self Catering
Contact: Alan & Margaret Wardle
Lake District Holidays
t (015395) 68103
e lakedistricthols@aol.com
w lakedistrictholidays.net

Heron View ★★★★
Self Catering
Contact: Peter Durbin
Cumbrian Cottages Ltd
t (01228) 599950
e enquiries@cumbrian-cottages.co.uk
w cumbrian-cottages.co.uk

Heronsyde ★★★★
Self Catering
Contact: Susan Jackson
Heart of the Lakes
t (015394) 32321
e info@heartofthelakes.co.uk
w heartofthelakes.co.uk

Hollens Farmhouse ★★★★
Self Catering
Contact: Peter Durbin
Cumbrian Cottages Ltd
t (01228) 599950
e enquiries@cumbrian-cottages.co.uk
w cumbrian-cottages.co.uk

Holly Cottage ★★★★
Self Catering
Contact: Peter Durbin
Cumbrian Cottages Ltd
t (01228) 599950
e enquiries@cumbrian-cottages.co.uk
w cumbrian-cottages.co.uk

Huntingstile South ★★★★
Self Catering
Contact: Susan Jackson
Heart of the Lakes
t (015394) 32321
e info@heartofthelakes.co.uk
w heartofthelakes.co.uk

Juniper Cottage ★★★★
Self Catering
Contact: Susan Jackson
Heart of the Lakes
t (015394) 32321
e info@heartofthelakes.co.uk
w heartofthelakes.co.uk

Lake View Holiday Apartments, Grasmere ★★★ *Self Catering*
Contact: Stephen & Michelle King
Lake View Country House
t (015394) 35384
e dms@lakeview-grasmere.com
w lakeview-grasmere.com

Lamb Cottage ★★★★
Self Catering
Contact: Susan Jackson
Heart of the Lakes
t (015394) 32321
e info@heartofthelakes.co.uk
w heartofthelakes.co.uk

Langdale Apartment ★★★
Self Catering
Contact: Peter Durbin
Cumbrian Cottages Ltd
t (01228) 599950
e enquiries@cumbrian-cottages.co.uk
w cumbrian-cottages.co.uk

Lion Cottage ★★★★
Self Catering
Contact: Susan Jackson
Heart of the Lakes
t (015394) 32321
e info@heartofthelakes.co.uk
w heartofthelakes.co.uk

Little Beeches ★★★
Self Catering
Contact: Susan Jackson
Heart of the Lakes
t (015394) 32321
e info@heartofthelakes.co.uk
w heartofthelakes.co.uk

Mews Cottage ★★★★
Self Catering
Contact: David Perrem
t (015394) 35033
e dperrem@tiscali.co.uk

North Lodge ★★★★
Self Catering
Contact: Susan Jackson
Heart of the Lakes
t (015394) 32321
e info@heartofthelakes.co.uk
w heartofthelakes.co.uk

Oak Bank Apartment ★★★
Self Catering
Contact: Peter Durbin
Cumbrian Cottages Ltd
t (01228) 599950
e enquiries@cumbrian-cottages.co.uk
w cumbrian-cottages.co.uk

Old Bakers Cottage ★★★★
Self Catering
Contact: Peter Durbin
Cumbrian Cottages Ltd
t (01228) 599950
e enquiries@cumbrian-cottages.co.uk
w cumbrian-cottages.co.uk

Old Hallsteads ★★★★
Self Catering
Contact: Mr Paul Liddell
Lakelovers
t (015394) 88855
e bookings@lakelovers.co.uk
w lakelovers.co.uk

The Old Police House ★★★★ *Self Catering*
Contact: Mrs Susan Jackson
Heart of the Lakes
t (015394) 32321
e info@heartofthelakes.co.uk
w heartofthelakes.co.uk

Overmere ★★★★
Self Catering
Heart of the Lakes
t (015394) 32321
e info@heartofthelakes.co.uk
w heartofthelakes.co.uk

Poets View Cottage ★★★★
Self Catering
Contact: Peter Durbin
Cumbrian Cottages Ltd
t (01228) 599950
e enquiries@cumbrian-cottages.co.uk
w cumbrian-cottages.co.uk

Riverbank ★★★★
Self Catering
Lakelovers
t (015394) 88855
e bookings@lakelovers.co.uk
w lakelovers.co.uk

Rockwood ★★★
Self Catering
Contact: Mr Paul Liddell
Lakelovers
t (015394) 88855
e bookings@lakelovers.co.uk
w lakelovers.co.uk

Rothay Lodge Garden Apartment ★★★★
Self Catering
Contact: Lindsay Rogers
Rothay Lodge Garden Apartment
t (0115) 923 2618
e enquiries@rothay-lodge.co.uk
w rothay-lodge.co.uk

Rowan Cottage ★★★★
Self Catering
Contact: Peter Durbin
Cumbrian Cottages Ltd
t (01228) 599950
e enquiries@cumbrian-cottages.co.uk
w cumbrian-cottages.co.uk

Rowanberry Cottage ★★★
Self Catering
Lakelovers
t (015394) 88855
e bookings@lakelovers.co.uk
w lakelovers.co.uk

Silvergarth ★★★
Self Catering
Contact: Susan Coward
Silvergarth
t (015394) 35828
e cowards.silvergarth@btinternet.com
w cowards.silvergarth.btinternet.co.uk

Spinners ★★★★
Self Catering
Contact: Susan Jackson
Heart of the Lakes
t (015394) 32321
e info@heartofthelakes.co.uk
w heartofthelakes.co.uk

Stonebeck ★★★★
Self Catering
Contact: Susan Jackson
Heart of the Lakes
t (015394) 32321
e info@heartofthelakes.co.uk
w heartofthelakes.co.uk

Swallows Cottage ★★★★
Self Catering
Contact: Mr Paul Liddell
Lakelovers
t (015394) 88855
e bookings@lakelovers.co.uk
w lakelovers.co.uk

Thirlmere Cottage ★★★★
Self Catering
Contact: Susan Jackson
Heart of the Lakes
t (015394) 32321
e info@heartofthelakes.co.uk
w heartofthelakes.co.uk

Le Tholonet ★★★★
Self Catering
Contact: Susan Jackson
Heart of the Lakes
t (015394) 32321
e info@heartofthelakes.co.uk
w heartofthelakes.co.uk

Tilly's Cottage ★★★★
Self Catering
Lakelovers
t (015394) 88855
e bookings@lakelovers.co.uk
w lakelovers.co.uk

Underheron ★★★★
Self Catering
Contact: Susan Jackson
Heart of the Lakes
t (015394) 32321
e info@heartofthelakes.co.uk
w heartofthelakes.co.uk

Weavers ★★★★
Self Catering
Contact: Susan Jackson
Heart of the Lakes
t (015394) 32321
e info@heartofthelakes.co.uk
w heartofthelakes.co.uk

The West House ★★★
Self Catering
Contact: Susan Jackson
Heart of the Lakes
t (015394) 32321
e info@heartofthelakes.co.uk
w heartofthelakes.co.uk

Willow Bank ★★★
Self Catering
Contact: Susan Jackson
Heart of the Lakes
t (015394) 32321
e info@heartofthelakes.co.uk
w heartofthelakes.co.uk

Woodland Crag Cottage
★★★★ *Self Catering*
Contact: Susan Jackson
Heart of the Lakes
t (015394) 32321
e info@heartofthelakes.co.uk
w heartofthelakes.co.uk

GRAYRIGG
Cumbria

Punchbowl House ★★★
Self Catering
Contact: Mrs Johnson
t (01539) 824345
e enquiries@punchbowlhouse.co.uk

GREAT ASBY
Cumbria

Scalebeck Holiday Cottages, Great Asby ★★★★
Self Catering
Contact: Mr K J Budding
Scalebeck Holiday Cottages
t (01768) 351006
e mail@scalebeckholidaycottages.com
w scalebeckholidaycottages.co.uk

Town Head Farm Cottages
★★★★ *Self Catering*
Contact: Ms Debbie Lucas
t (01768) 351499
e info@townheadfarm.co.uk

GREAT BARROW
Cheshire

Hawthorn Cottage ★★★
Self Catering
Contact: Mrs Pratt
t (01244) 317287

GREAT CORBY
Cumbria

Clint Head Cottage ★★★★
Self Catering
Contact: Peter Durbin
Cumbrian Cottages Ltd
t (01228) 599950
e enquiries@cumbrian-cottages.co.uk
w cumbrian-cottages.co.uk

Thackmoor House ★★★★
Self Catering
Contact: Anne McDowall
Whitehall Properties
t (01228) 514004
e anne_635@fsmail.net
w northcumbriancottages.co.uk

GREAT ECCLESTON
Lancashire

Townside House ★★★
Self Catering
Contact: Mrs Judith Arnold
t (01995) 670086

GREAT LANGDALE
Cumbria

Elterwater Hall ★★★★★
Self Catering
Contact: Matthew Hartnett
Langdale Leisure Limited
t (015394) 38012
e marketing@langdale.co.uk
w langdale.co.uk

Harry's Place Farm Cottage
★★★ *Self Catering*
Contact: Susan Jackson
Heart of the Lakes
t (015394) 32321
e info@heartofthelakes.co.uk
w heartofthelakes.co.uk

Heron Place ★★★★★
Self Catering
Contact: Mrs Vivien Bass
Wheelwrights Holiday Cottages
t (015394) 37635
e enquiries@wheelwrights.com

Langdale Estate Chapel Stile Apartments ★★★★
Self Catering
Contact: Matthew Hartnett
Langdale Leisure Limited
t (015394) 38012
e marketing@langdale.co.uk

Langdale Estate Lodges
★★★★★ *Self Catering*
Contact: Matthew Hartnett
Langdale Leisure Limited
t (015394) 38012
e marketing@langdale.co.uk
w langdale.co.uk

Middlefell Farm Cottage
★★★ *Self Catering*
Contact: Susan Jackson
Heart of the Lakes
t (015394) 32321
e info@heartofthelakes.co.uk
w heartofthelakes.co.uk

Rawfell ★★★★ *Self Catering*
Contact: Susan Jackson
Heart of the Lakes
t (015394) 32321
e info@heartofthelakes.co.uk
w heartofthelakes.co.uk

Stickle Cottage ★★★★
Self Catering
Contact: Mrs Vivien Bass
Wheelwrights Holiday Cottages
t (015394) 37635
e enquiries@wheelwrights.com

GREAT MUSGRAVE
Cumbria

Blandswath Cottage ★★★
Self Catering
Contact: Mrs Watson
t (01768) 341842
e watson@blandswath.freeserve.co.uk

GREAT STRICKLAND
Cumbria

The Old Cow Byre ★★★★
Self Catering
Contact: Mr Mark Melling
Taylors Farm Cottages
t (01931) 712205
e info@taylorsfarm.co.uk

GRESSINGHAM
Lancashire

Garden Cottage ★★★
Self Catering
Contact: Mrs Margaret Burrow
t (01524) 221347
e gardencottage@highsnab.freeserve.co.uk

GREYSOUTHEN
Cumbria

Swallow Barn Cottage
★★★★ *Self Catering*
Contact: Mr & Mrs James
t (01900) 823016
e enquiry@swallowbarn.co.uk
w swallowbarn.co.uk

GREYSTOKE
Cumbria

The Orchard & The Granary
★★★★ *Self Catering*
Dales Holiday Cottages
t 0870 909 9500
e fiona@dalesholcot.com
w dalesholcot.com

Pelican Dairy ★★★★
Self Catering
Contact: Ms Fiona Sheen
Dales Holiday Cottages
t 0870 909 9500
e fiona@dales-holiday-cottages.com
w dalesholcot.com

Thanetwell Lodge ★★★★
Self Catering
Contact: Peter Durbin
Cumbrian Cottages Ltd
t (01228) 599950
e enquiries@cumbrian-cottages.co.uk
w cumbrian-cottages.co.uk

GRINDLETON
Lancashire

Crossfold House Holiday Cottage ★★★ *Self Catering*
Contact: Mrs Sheila Hailwood
t (01200) 440178
e rodney@rhailwood.freeserve.co.uk

GRIZEDALE
Cumbria

High Dale Park Barn ★★★
Self Catering
Contact: Peter Brown
High Dale Park Barn
t (01229) 860226
e peter@lakesweddingmusic.com
w lakesweddingmusic.com/accomm/

HARROP FOLD
Lancashire

Harrop Fold Cottages ★★★
Self Catering
Contact: Mr Frank Robinson
t (01200) 447665

HARTLEY
Cumbria

Hartley Castle Barn ★★★★
Self Catering
Contact: Sally Dixon
Hartley Castle
t (01768) 371331
e djs@hartleycastle.freeserve.co.uk
w hartleycastle.co.uk

HARTSOP
Cumbria

Caudale Beck ★★★
Self Catering
Contact: Susan Jackson
Heart of the Lakes
t (015394) 32321
e info@heartofthelakes.co.uk
w heartofthelakes.co.uk

Dovedale ★★★ *Self Catering*
Contact: Susan Jackson
Heart of the Lakes
t (015394) 32321
e info@heartofthelakes.co.uk
w heartofthelakes.co.uk

Greenbank ★★★★
Self Catering
Contact: Susan Jackson
Heart of the Lakes
t (015394) 32321
e info@heartofthelakes.co.uk
w heartofthelakes.co.uk

High Beckside ★★★
Self Catering
Contact: Susan Jackson
Heart of the Lakes
t (015394) 32321
e info@heartofthelakes.co.uk
w heartofthelakes.co.uk

Low Beckside ★★★
Self Catering
Contact: Shirley Thompson
Absolute Escapes
t (01768) 868989
e shirley@absolute-escapes.com
w absolute-escapes.com

Weavers Cottage ★★★
Self Catering
Contact: Susan Jackson
Heart of the Lakes
t (015394) 32321
e info@heartofthelakes.co.uk
w heartofthelakes.co.uk

HAUGHTON
Cheshire

Rookery Cottage ★★★
Self Catering
Contact: Mrs G.D Burdett
t (01829) 260069
e geoff.burdett@tesco.net

HAVERIGG
Cumbria

Lazey Cottage ★★★★★
Self Catering
Contact: Gloria Parsons
t (01229) 772515 & (01229) 773291

Quiet Cottage ★★★
Self Catering
Contact: Mr & Mrs Haston
Quiet Cottage
t (01229) 772974
e quietcottage@tiscali.co.uk
w quietcottage.golakes.co.uk

HAVERTHWAITE
Cumbria

Close Cottage ★★★★
Self Catering
Contact: Mr John Serginson
The Lakeland Cottage Company
t (015395) 30024
e john@lakelandcottageco.com

HAWKSHAW
Greater Manchester

The Loelands ★★★
Self Catering
t (01204) 882113

HAWKSHEAD
Cumbria

Above Beck ★★★
Self Catering
Contact: Peter Durbin
Cumbrian Cottages Ltd
t (01228) 599950
e enquiries@cumbrian-cottages.co.uk
w cumbrian-cottages.co.uk

The Barn, Stable & Crosslands Cottages ★★★
Self Catering
Contact: Mrs J Haddow
Broomriggs
t (015394) 36280
e info@broomriggs.co.uk

Barn Syke ★★★★
Self Catering
Contact: Mr Paul Liddell
Lakelovers
t (015394) 88855
e bookings@lakelovers.co.uk
w lakelovers.co.uk

Bettys Loft ★★★★
Self Catering
Contact: Gary Thomason
Hideaways
t (015394) 42435
w lakeland-hideaways.co.uk

Birkwray Farmhouse ★★★★ *Self Catering*
Contact: Mr Paul Liddell
Lakelovers
t (015394) 88855
e bookings@lakelovers.co.uk
w lakelovers.co.uk

The Briars ★★★★★
Self Catering
Contact: Anne Gallagher
Hideaways
t (015394) 42435
e bookings@lakeland-hideaways.co.uk
w lakeland-hideaways.co.uk

Bridge View ★★★
Self Catering
Contact: Mrs Dewhurst
t (015394) 36340

Broomriggs ★★★
Self Catering
Contact: Judi Haddow
t (015394) 36280
e broomriggs@zoom.co.uk
w broomriggs.co.uk

Columbine Cottage ★★★
Self Catering
Contact: Mr Paul Liddell
Lakelovers
t (015394) 88855
e bookings@lakelovers.co.uk
w lakelovers.co.uk

Cowpers Barn ★★★★★
Self Catering
Contact: Anne Gallagher
Hideaways
t (015394) 42435
e bookings@lakeland-hideaways.co.uk
w lakeland-hideaways.co.uk

The Croft Holiday Flats ★★★ *Self Catering*
Contact: Mrs Barr
The Croft Holiday Flats
t (015394) 36374
e enquiries@hawkshead-croft.com
w hawkshead-croft.com

Fair Cop ★★★★
Self Catering
Contact: Susan Jackson
Heart of the Lakes
t (015394) 32321
e info@heartofthelakes.co.uk
w heartofthelakes.co.uk

Greenbank House ★★★
Self Catering
Contact: Mrs Susan Jackson
Heart of the Lakes
t (015394) 32321
e info@heartofthelakes.co.uk
w heartofthelakes.co.uk

Hannakin Barn ★★★★★
Self Catering
Contact: Ms Sue Jackson
Heart of the Lakes
t (015394) 32321
e info@heartofthelakes.co.uk
w heartofthelakes.co.uk

Hatter's Cottage ★★★
Self Catering
Contact: Mr & Mrs Gunner
t (015394) 36203
e mail22@hatterscottage.co.uk
w hatterscottage.co.uk

Helm Cottage ★★★★
Self Catering
Contact: Mr Paul Liddell
Lakelovers
t (015394) 88855
e bookings@lakelovers.co.uk
w lakelovers.co.uk

Heron Cottage ★★★★
Self Catering
Contact: Mrs Susan Jackosn
Heart of the Lakes
t (015394) 32321
e info@heartofthelakes.co.uk
w heartofthelakes.co.uk

High Cross ★★★★
Self Catering
Contact: Peter Durbin
Cumbrian Cottages Ltd
t (01228) 599950
e enquiries@cumbrian-cottages.co.uk
w cumbrian-cottages.co.uk

High Orchard ★★★★
Self Catering
Contact: Anne Gallagher
Hideaways
t (015394) 42435
e bookings@lakeland-hideaways.co.uk
w lakeland-hideaways.co.uk

Hillcrest ★★★★★
Self Catering
Contact: Susan Jackson
Heart of the Lakes
t (015394) 32321
e info@heartofthelakes.co.uk
w heartofthelakes.co.uk

Keen Ground Cottage ★★★
Self Catering
Contact: Mr John Serginson
The Lakeland Cottage Company
t (015395) 30024
e john@lakelandcottageco.com

Kings Yard Cottage ★★★
Self Catering
Contact: Peter Durbin
Cumbrian Cottages Ltd
t (01228) 599950
e enquiries@cumbrian-cottages.co.uk
w cumbrian-cottages.co.uk

Lantern Cottage ★★★
Self Catering
Contact: Peter Durbin
Cumbrian Cottages Ltd
t (01228) 599950
e enquiries@cumbrian-cottages.co.uk
w cumbrian-cottages.co.uk

Larch Cottage ★★★★
Self Catering
Contact: Susan Jackson
Heart of the Lakes
t (015394) 32321
e info@heartofthelakes.co.uk
w heartofthelakes.co.uk

Meadow View ★★★
Self Catering
Blakes Cottages
t 0870 336 7777
w blakes.cottages.co.uk

The Nook Cottage ★★★★
Self Catering
Contact: Mrs Vivien Bass
Wheelwrights Holiday Cottages
t (015394) 37635
e enquiries@wheelwrights.com

Nurses Cottage ★★★★★
Self Catering
Contact: Mrs Susan Jackson
Heart of the Lakes
t (015394) 32321
e info@heartofthelakes.co.uk
w heartofthelakes.co.uk

Oak Apple Barn ★★★★
Self Catering
Contact: Nancy Penrice
t (015394) 36222
e chp@violetbank.freeserve.co.uk
w oak-apple.co.uk

Old Barn & Barn End ★★★★ *Self Catering*
Contact: Anne Gallagher
Hideaways
t (015394) 42435
e bookings@lakeland-hideaways.co.uk
w lakeland-hideaways.co.uk

Old Farm ★★★★
Self Catering
Contact: Mr John Serginson
The Lakeland Cottage Company
t (015395) 30024
e john@lakelandcottageco.com

The Old Loft ★★★★
Self Catering
Lakelovers
t (015394) 88855
e bookings@lakelovers.co.uk
w lakelovers.co.uk

Ramblers Roost
Rating Applied For
Self Catering
Contact: Howard King
Talcomb & Ramblers Roost
t 07973 420179
e hk.developments@virgin.net
w hkdevelopmentslakes.co.uk

Riggeswood Cottage ★★★
Self Catering
Contact: Mr Paul Liddell
Lakelovers
t (015394) 88855
e bookings@lakelovers.co.uk
w lakelovers.co.uk

The Rockery Suite ★★★★
Self Catering
Contact: Mrs Susan Jackson
Heart of the Lakes
t (015394) 32321
e info@heartofthelakes.co.uk
w heartofthelakes.co.uk

Rose Cottage ★★★★
Self Catering
Contact: Anne Gallagher
Hideaways
t (015394) 42435
e bookings@lakeland-hideaways.co.uk
w lakeland-hideaways.co.uk

Rose Howe ★★★★
Self Catering
Contact: Susan Jackson
Heart of the Lakes
t (015394) 32321
e info@heartofthelakes.co.uk
w heartofthelakes.co.uk

Sand Ground Barn ★★★
Self Catering
Contact: Susan Jackson
Heart of the Lakes
t (015394) 32321
e info@heartofthelakes.co.uk
w heartofthelakes.co.uk

Sergeant Man ★★★★
Self Catering
Contact: Susan Jackson
Heart of the Lakes
t (015394) 32321
e info@heartofthelakes.co.uk
w heartofthelakes.co.uk

Shepherds Cottage ★★★★
Self Catering
Contact: Peter Durbin
Cumbrian Cottages Ltd
t (01228) 599950
e enquiries@cumbrian-cottages.co.uk
w cumbrian-cottages.co.uk

Skelwith Force ★★★★
Self Catering
Contact: Susan Jackson
Heart of the Lakes
t (015394) 32321
e info@heartofthelakes.co.uk
w heartofthelakes.co.uk

Swallow's Nest ★★★
Self Catering
Heart of the Lakes
t (015394) 32321
e info@heartofthelakes.co.uk
w heartofthelakes.co.uk

Tarn Hows ★★★
Self Catering
Heart of the Lakes
t (015394) 32321
e info@heartofthelakes.co.uk
w heartofthelakes.co.uk

Walker Ground Barn
★★★★ *Self Catering*
Contact: Susan Jackson
Heart of the Lakes
t (015394) 32321
e info@heartofthelakes.co.uk
w heartofthelakes.co.uk

Walker Ground Cottage
★★★★ *Self Catering*
Contact: Peter Durbin
Cumbrian Cottages Ltd
t (01228) 599950
e enquiries@cumbrian-cottages.co.uk
w cumbrian-cottages.co.uk

Woodlands, Roger Ground
★★★★ *Self Catering*
Contact: Susan Jackson
Heart of the Lakes
t (015394) 32321
e info@heartofthelakes.co.uk
w heartofthelakes.co.uk

Yew Trees ★★★
Self Catering
Heart of the Lakes
t (015394) 32321
e info@heartofthelakes.co.uk
w heartofthelakes.co.uk

HAWKSHEAD HILL
Cumbria

The Coachman's Loft ★★★
Self Catering
Contact: Susan Jackson
Heart of the Lakes
t (015394) 32321
e info@heartofthelakes.co.uk
w heartofthelakes.co.uk

The Old Farmhouse ★★★★
Self Catering
Contact: Mr & Mrs Serginson
The Lakeland Cottage Company
t 0870 442 5814
w lakeland-cottage-company.co.uk

HAWS BANK
Cumbria

Beckside House ★★★★
Self Catering
Contact: Miss K Walton
Coniston Breaks
t (015394) 37379
e info@conistonbreaks.com
w conistonbreaks.com

HELTON
Cumbria

Chapel Cottage ★★★★
Self Catering
Contact: Peter Durbin
Cumbrian Cottages Ltd
t (01228) 599950
e enquiries@cumbrian-cottages.co.uk
w cumbrian-cottages.co.uk

Talbot House & Talbot Studio ★★★★ *Self Catering*
Contact: Mark Cowell
Church Court Cottages
t (01768) 881682
e markcowell@tiscali.co.uk
w gogamblesby.co.uk

HESKET NEWMARKET
Cumbria

Bannest Hill Cottage ★★★
Self Catering
Contact: Dr & Mrs Preston
Bannest Hill Cottage & Fountain Cottage
t (01768) 484394
e stay@bannesthill.co.uk
w bannesthill.co.uk

Beckend Barn ★★★
Self Catering
Contact: Peter Durbin
Cumbrian Cottages Ltd
t (01228) 599950
e enquiries@cumbrian-cottages.co.uk
w cumbrian-cottages.co.uk

Oak View ★★★★
Self Catering
Contact: Peter Durbin
Cumbrian Cottages Ltd
t (01228) 599950
e enquiries@cumbrian-cottages.co.uk
w cumbrian-cottages.co.uk

Ostlers Barn ★★★★★
Self Catering
Contact: Peter Durbin
Cumbrian Cottages Ltd
t (01228) 599950
e enquiries@cumbrian-cottages.co.uk
w cumbrian-cottages.co.uk

Syke House ★★★
Self Catering
Contact: Mr Clive Sykes
Sykes Cottages
t (01244) 345700
e info@sykescottages.co.uk
w sykescottages.co.uk

HETHERSGILL
Cumbria

Newlands Farmhouse
★★★★ *Self Catering*
Contact: Peter Durbin
Cumbrian Cottages Ltd
t (01228) 599950
e enquiries@cumbrian-cottages.co.uk
w cumbrian-cottages.co.uk

HIGH LANE
Greater Manchester

Ty Coch ★★★★
Self Catering
Contact: Mrs Jane Beard
Ty Coch
t (029) 2076 1888

HIGH LORTON
Cumbria

1 & 2 Midtown Cottages
★★★★ *Self Catering*
Contact: Mr Burrell
Midtown Cottages
t (01264) 710165
e info@midtowncottages.co.uk
w midtowncottages.co.uk

Brewery House ★★★★★
Self Catering
Contact: Peter Durbin
Cumbrian Cottages Ltd
t (01228) 599950
e enquiries@cumbrian-cottages.co.uk
w cumbrian-cottages.co.uk

Dale House ★★★
Self Catering
Contact: Peter Durbin
Cumbrian Cottages Ltd
t (01228) 599950
e enquiries@cumbrian-cottages.co.uk
w cumbrian-cottages.co.uk

Grooms Cottage ★★★
Self Catering
Contact: Peter Durbin
Cumbrian Cottages Ltd
t (01228) 599950
e enquiries@cumbrian-cottages.co.uk
w cumbrian-cottages.co.uk

High Swinside Holiday Cottages ★★★ *Self Catering*
Contact: Jacques Hankin
High Swinside Holiday Cottages
t (01900) 85206
e bookings@highswinside.demon.co.uk
w highswinside.demon.co.uk

Holemire Barn ★★★★
Self Catering
Contact: Angela Fearfield
Holemire Barn
t (01900) 85225
e enquiries@lakelandbarn.co.uk
w lakelandbarn.co.uk

HIGH WRAY
Cumbria

Claife View ★★★★★
Self Catering
Contact: Ruth Thomason
Hideaways
t (015394) 42435
e bookings@lakeland-hideaways.co.uk

Stable Cottage ★★★★
Self Catering
Contact: Sheila Briggs
High Wray Farm
t (015394) 32280
e sheila@highwrayfarm.co.uk
w highwrayfarm.co.uk

HOLMROOK
Cumbria

Yattus ★★★★★
Self Catering
Contact: Peter Durbin
Cumbrian Cottages Ltd
t (01228) 599950
e enquiries@cumbrian-cottages.co.uk
w cumbrian-cottages.co.uk

HOOLE
Cheshire

St James Apartments
★★★★ *Self Catering*
Contact: June & William Smith
Ba Ba Guest House
t (01244) 315047
e reservations@chesterholidayrentals.co.uk
w chesterholidayrentals.co.uk

HOWGILL
Cumbria

Ash Hining Farm ★★★★
Self Catering
Contact: Peter Durbin
Cumbrian Cottages Ltd
t (01228) 599950
e enquiries@cumbrian-cottages.co.uk
w cumbrian-cottages.co.uk

Blandsgill Cottage ★★★
Self Catering
Contact: Peter Durbin
Cumbrian Cottages Ltd
t (01228) 599950
e enquiries@cumbrian-cottages.co.uk
w cumbrian-cottages.co.uk

Drawell ★★★★ *Self Catering*
Contact: Janet Postlethwaite
t (015396) 21529
e drawell@pentalk.org
w drawellcottage.co.uk

Primrose Cottage
Rating Applied For
Self Catering
Contact: Helen Beare
t (015396) 21339
e helen@netherb.freeserve.co.uk
w primroseholiday.co.uk

The Whins
Rating Applied For
Self Catering
Contact: Miss Blades
t (015396) 20581

HOYLAKE
Merseyside

AAA North Villa Apartments
★★★★ *Self Catering*
t (0151) 632 3982
e sandra@northvilla.com
w northvilla.com

HUTTON ROOF
Cumbria

Carrock Cottages ★★★★★
Self Catering
Contact: Malcolm & Gillian Iredale
Carrock Cottages
t (01768) 484111
e info@carrockcottages.co.uk
w carrockcottages.co.uk

Dukes Meadow ★★★
Self Catering
Contact: Jane Hounsome
t (0121) 705 4381
e janeandben@hotmail.co.uk
w dukesmeadow.co.uk

Moor Cottage
Rating Applied For
Self Catering
Contact: Mrs Booth
t (01524) 702000

INGS
Cumbria

Ings Mill Park Cottages
★★★★ *Self Catering*
Contact: Peter Durbin
Cumbrian Cottages Ltd
t (01228) 599950
e enquiries@cumbrian-cottages.co.uk
w cumbrian-cottages.co.uk

Little Ghyll Cottage ★★★
Self Catering
Contact: Christine Omerod
t (01539) 821274
e alexormerod@hotmail.com

St Annes Cottage ★★★
Self Catering
Contact: Peter Durbin
Cumbrian Cottages Ltd
t (01228) 599950
e enquiries@cumbrian-cottages.co.uk
w cumbrian-cottages.co.uk

Topiary Cottage ★★★★
Self Catering
Contact: Mr Paul Liddell
Lakelovers
t (015394) 88855
e bookings@lakelovers.co.uk
w lakelovers.co.uk

IREBY
Cumbria

Barn Roost ★★★
Self Catering
Contact: Peter Durbin
Cumbrian Cottages Ltd
t (01228) 599950
e enquiries@cumbrian-cottages.co.uk
w cumbrian-cottages.co.uk

Daleside Farm ★★★★
Self Catering
t (01697) 371268
e info@dalesidefarm.co.uk

Fell Cottage ★★★★★
Self Catering
Contact: Peter Durbin
Cumbrian Cottages Ltd
t (01228) 599950
e enquiries@cumbrian-cottages.co.uk
w cumbrian-cottages.co.uk

Laundry Cottage ★★★★
Self Catering
Contact: Peter Durbin
Cumbrian Cottages Ltd
t (01228) 599950
e enquiries@cumbrian-cottages.co.uk
w cumbrian-cottages.co.uk

New Park Holiday Cottages ★★★★ *Self Catering*
Contact: Susan Swainson
Cumbrian Cottages Ltd
t (01697) 345476
e info@newparkfarm.co.uk
w newparkfarm.co.uk

Old Saddler's Cottage
Rating Applied For
Self Catering
Contact: Catherine Perry
t (01522) 532232
e nick.perry2@btinternet.com
w oldsaddlerscottage.com

The Old Stables ★★★★
Self Catering
Contact: Peter Durbin
Cumbrian Cottages Ltd
t (01228) 599950
e enquiries@cumbrian-cottages.co.uk
w cumbrian-cottages.co.uk

Overwater Lodge ★★★★
Self Catering
Contact: Peter Durbin
Cumbrian Cottages Ltd
t (01228) 599950
e enquiries@cumbrian-cottages.co.uk
w cumbrian-cottages.co.uk

Woodlands Cottage ★★★
Self Catering
Contact: Mr Ort & Ms Willis
t (01697) 371791
e stay@woodlandsatireby.co.uk
w woodlandsatireby.co.uk

IREBY
Lancashire

Springfield ★★★★
Self Catering
Contact: Miss Heather Bavin
t (01524) 242501
e heather.bavin@btinternet.com

IVEGILL
Cumbria

Stable Cottage ★★★
Self Catering
Contact: Messrs Wilson
t (01697) 473327
e jeanettewilson284@hotmail.com

KENDAL
Cumbria

14 Printers Croft ★★★★
Self Catering
Contact: Peter Durbin
Cumbrian Cottages Ltd
t (01228) 599950
e enquiries@cumbrian-cottages.co.uk
w cumbrian-cottages.co.uk

Barkinbeck Cottage ★★★
Self Catering
Contact: Mrs Hamilton
t (015395) 67122
e barkinhouse@yahoo.co.uk
w barkinbeck.co.uk

Harwood Dale Cottage
★★★★ *Self Catering*
Contact: Peter Durbin
Cumbrian Cottages Ltd
t (01228) 599950
e enquiries@cumbrian-cottages.co.uk
w cumbrian-cottages.co.uk

High Swinklebank Farm
★★★ *Self Catering*
Contact: Olive Simpson
t (01539) 823682
w lakedistrictfarmhouseholidays.co.uk/highswinklebank

Moresdale Bank Cottage
★★★★ *Self Catering*
Contact: Helen Parkins
t (01539) 824227
e mclamb@ukonline.co.uk
w moresdale-bank-cottage.co.uk

Shaw End Mansion ★★★★
Self Catering
Contact: Mr & Mrs Robinson
Haveriggs Farm
t (01539) 824220
e robinson@fieldendholidays.co.uk
w fieldendholidays.co.uk

Todd Meadow ★★★★ *Self Catering & Serviced Apartments*
Contact: Peter Durbin
Cumbrian Cottages Ltd
t (01228) 599950
e enquiries@cumbrian-cottages.co.uk
w cumbrian-cottages.co.uk

Toffeepot Cottage ★★★
Self Catering
Contact: Peter Durbin
Cumbrian Cottages Ltd
t (01228) 599950
e enquiries@cumbrian-cottages.co.uk
w cumbrian-cottages.co.uk

The Warren Cottage ★★★★
Self Catering
Lakelovers
t (015394) 88855
e bookings@lakelovers.co.uk
w lakelovers.co.uk

KENTMERE
Cumbria

High Fold ★★★★
Self Catering
Contact: Peter Durbin
Cumbrian Cottages Ltd
t (01228) 599950
e enquiries@cumbrian-cottages.co.uk
w cumbrian-cottages.co.uk

Nook Cottage – Kentmere Valley ★★★ *Self Catering*
Contact: Mr John Serginson
The Lakeland Cottage Company
t (015395) 30024
e john@lakelandcottageco.com

Rawe Cottage ★★★★
Self Catering
Contact: John Serginson
The Lakeland Cottage Company
t 0870 442 5814
e john@lakelandcottageco.com
w lakeland-cottage-company.co.uk

KESWICK
Cumbria

1 Balmoral House ★★★
Self Catering
Contact: Peter Durbin
Cumbrian Cottages Ltd
t (01228) 599950
e enquiries@cumbrian-cottages.co.uk
w cumbrian-cottages.co.uk

1 Lonsdale House ★★★★
Self Catering
Contact: Peter Durbin
Cumbrian Cottages Ltd
t (01228) 599950
e enquiries@cumbrian-cottages.co.uk
w cumbrian-cottages.co.uk

10 The Plosh ★★★★
Self Catering
Contact: Peter Durbin
Cumbrian Cottages Ltd
t (01228) 599950
e enquiries@cumbrian-cottages.co.uk
w cumbrian-cottages.co.uk

11 Burnside Park ★★★★
Self Catering
Contact: Peter Durbin
Cumbrian Cottages Ltd
t (01228) 599950
e enquiries@cumbrian-cottages.co.uk
w cumbrian-cottages.co.uk

11 Howrah's Court ★★★★
Self Catering
Contact: Peter Durbin
Cumbrian Cottages Ltd
t (01228) 599950
e enquiries@cumbrian-cottages.co.uk
w cumbrian-cottages.co.uk

11 The Plosh ★★★
Self Catering
Contact: Peter Durbin
Cumbrian Cottages Ltd
t (01228) 599950
e enquiries@cumbrian-cottages.co.uk
w cumbrian-cottages.co.uk

13 Greta Grove House ★★★
Self Catering
Contact: Jean Pechartscheck
Chaucer Lodge
t (01768) 778091
e info@chaucer-selfcatering.co.uk
w chaucer-selfcatering.co.uk

14 Elm Court ★★★
Self Catering
Contact: Peter Durbin
Cumbrian Cottages Ltd
t (01228) 599950
e enquiries@cumbrian-cottages.co.uk
w cumbrian-cottages.co.uk

14 Elm Court ★★★★
Self Catering
Contact: Peter Durbin
Cumbrian Cottages Ltd
t (01228) 599950
e enquiries@cumbrian-cottages.co.uk
w cumbrian-cottages.co.uk

17 Greta Grove ★★★★
Self Catering
Contact: Peter Durbin
Cumbrian Cottages Ltd
t (01228) 599950
e enquiries@cumbrian-cottages.co.uk
w cumbrian-cottages.co.uk

24 Ratcliffe Place ★★★
Self Catering
Contact: Mrs W Plant
t (0113) 286 3737
e nickplant@plant.go-legend.net

27 Lake Road ★★★★
Self Catering
Contact: Pete & Sharon Garner
Burnside B&B
t (01768) 772639
e stay@burnside-keswick.co.uk
w 27keswickcottages.co.uk

3 Balmoral House ★★★
Self Catering
Contact: Peter Durbin
Cumbrian Cottages Ltd
t (01228) 599950
e enquiries@cumbrian-cottages.co.uk
w cumbrian-cottages.co.uk

3 Catherine Cottages
★★★★ *Self Catering*
Contact: Peter Durbin
Cumbrian Cottages Ltd
t (01228) 599950
e enquiries@cumbrian-cottages.co.uk
w cumbrian-cottages.co.uk

3 Greta Grove ★★★★
Self Catering
Contact: Peter Durbin
Cumbrian Cottages Ltd
t (01228) 599950
e enquiries@cumbrian-cottages.co.uk
w cumbrian-cottages.co.uk

5 Londsdale House ★★★★
Self Catering
Contact: Peter Durbin
Cumbrian Cottages Ltd
t (01228) 599950
e enquiries@cumbrian-cottages.co.uk
w cumbrian-cottages.co.uk

8 Greta Grove ★★★★
Self Catering
Contact: Peter Durbin
Cumbrian Cottages Ltd
t (01228) 599950
e enquiries@cumbrian-cottages.co.uk
w cumbrian-cottages.co.uk

8 Lydia's Cottages ★★★★
Self Catering
Contact: Jean Hutchinson
t (01768) 777631
e jean@jhutch.demon.co.uk
w jhutch.demon.co.uk/jean/lydias.htm

9 Howrah's Court ★★★
Self Catering
Contact: Peter Durbin
Cumbrian Cottages Ltd
t (01228) 599950
e enquiries@cumbrian-cottages.co.uk
w cumbrian-cottages.co.uk

Acorn Apartments and Acorn View ★★★★
Self Catering
t (01768) 480310
e info@acornselfcatering.co.uk
w acornselfcatering.co.uk

Alice's Nook ★★★
Self Catering
Contact: Peter Durbin
Cumbrian Cottages Ltd
t (01228) 599950
e enquiries@cumbrian-cottages.co.uk
w cumbrian-cottages.co.uk

Alison's Cottage/View/Laal Yan/High Spy ★★★★
Self Catering
Contact: Alison Milner
Alison's Cottage and Alison's View
t (0115) 966 4049
e milner@fearon9.fsnet.co.uk
w alisonscottages.co.uk

Amba ★★★★ *Self Catering*
Contact: Peter Durbin
Cumbrian Cottages Ltd
t (01228) 599950
e enquiries@cumbrian-cottages.co.uk
w cumbrian-cottages.co.uk

Amphora ★★★ *Self Catering*
Contact: Peter Durbin
Cumbrian Cottages Ltd
t (01228) 599950
e enquiries@cumbrian-cottages.co.uk
w cumbrian-cottages.co.uk

Applecroft ★★★
Self Catering
Contact: Peter Durbin
Cumbrian Cottages Ltd
t (01228) 599950
e enquiries@cumbrian-cottages.co.uk
w cumbrian-cottages.co.uk

Applemere ★★★★
Self Catering
Contact: Peter Durbin
Cumbrian Cottages Ltd
t (01228) 599950
e enquiries@cumbrian-cottages.co.uk
w cumbrian-cottages.co.uk

Appleside ★★★
Self Catering
Contact: Peter Durbin
Cumbrian Cottages Ltd
t (01228) 599950
e enquiries@cumbrian-cottages.co.uk
w cumbrian-cottages.co.uk

Appletree ★★★★
Self Catering
Contact: Peter Durbin
Cumbrian Cottages Ltd
t (01228) 599950
e enquiries@cumbrian-cottages.co.uk
w cumbrian-cottages.co.uk

Ashbrooke ★★★
Self Catering
Contact: Peter Durbin
Cumbrian Cottages Ltd
t (01228) 599950
e enquiries@cumbrian-cottages.co.uk
w cumbrian-cottages.co.uk

Ashness ★★★★
Self Catering
Contact: Peter Durbin
Cumbrian Cottages Ltd
t (01228) 599950
e enquiries@cumbrian-cottages.co.uk
w cumbrian-cottages.co.uk

Ashness Apartment ★★★
Self Catering
Contact: Val Hewer
The Paddock Guest House
t (01768) 772510
e info@ashnet.net
w ashness.net

Bannerdale ★★★★
Self Catering
Contact: Hazel Hutton
Courtyard Cottages
t 07816 824253
e info@springs-farm.co.uk
w bannerdale.co.uk

Bay Tree ★★★ *Self Catering*
Contact: Peter Durbin
Cumbrian Cottages Ltd
t (01228) 599950
e enquiries@cumbrian-cottages.co.uk
w cumbrian-cottages.co.uk

Beagle Cottage ★★★
Self Catering
Contact: Peter Durbin
Cumbrian Cottages Ltd
t (01228) 599950
e enquiries@cumbrian-cottages.co.uk
w cumbrian-cottages.co.uk

Beech Nut ★★★
Self Catering
Contact: Peter Durbin
Cumbrian Cottages Ltd
t (01228) 599950
e enquiries@cumbrian-cottages.co.uk
w cumbrian-cottages.co.uk

Belle Vue ★★★-★★★★
Self Catering
Contact: Lexie Ryder
Belle Vue
t (01768) 771065
e lexieryder@hotmail.co.uk

Bessy Boot ★★★★
Self Catering
Contact: David Burton
Lakeland Cottage Holidays
t (01768) 776065
e info@lakelandcottages.co.uk
w lakelandcottages.co.uk

The Bield ★★★ *Self Catering*
Contact: Peter Durbin
Cumbrian Cottages Ltd
t (01228) 599950
e enquiries@cumbrian-cottages.co.uk
w cumbrian-cottages.co.uk

Bleach Green Cottages No 11 ★★★ *Self Catering*
Contact: Peter Durbin
Cumbrian Cottages Ltd
t (01228) 599950
e enquiries@cumbrian-cottages.co.uk
w cumbrian-cottages.co.uk

The Blencathra ★★★
Self Catering
Contact: Peter Durbin
Cumbrian Cottages Ltd
t (01228) 599950
e enquiries@cumbrian-cottages.co.uk
w cumbrian-cottages.co.uk

Blencathra
Rating Applied For
Self Catering
Contact: Mr David Burton
Lakeland Cottage Holidays
t (01768) 776065
e info@lakelandcottages.co.uk
w lakelandcottages.co.uk

Blencathra Bank ★★★
Self Catering
Contact: Peter Durbin
Cumbrian Cottages Ltd
t (01228) 599950
e enquiries@cumbrian-cottages.co.uk
w cumbrian-cottages.co.uk

Blencathra Cottage ★★★★
Self Catering
Contact: Peter Durbin
Cumbrian Cottages Ltd
t (01228) 599950
e enquiries@cumbrian-cottages.co.uk
w cumbrian-cottages.co.uk

Blencathra House ★★★★
Self Catering
Contact: Peter Durbin
Cumbrian Cottages Ltd
t (01228) 599950
e enquiries@cumbrian-cottages.co.uk
w cumbrian-cottages.co.uk

Bobbin Cottage ★★★★
Self Catering
Contact: Peter Durbin
Cumbrian Cottages Ltd
t (01228) 599950
e enquiries@cumbrian-cottages.co.uk
w cumbrian-cottages.co.uk

Bonshaw ★★★ *Self Catering*
Contact: Peter Durbin
Cumbrian Cottages Ltd
t (01228) 599950
e enquiries@cumbrian-cottages.co.uk
w cumbrian-cottages.co.uk

Bracken Lodge ★★★★
Self Catering
Contact: Peter Durbin
Cumbrian Cottages Ltd
t (01228) 599950
e enquiries@cumbrian-cottages.co.uk
w cumbrian-cottages.co.uk

Brandelhow ★★★★
Self Catering
Contact: Susan Jackson
Heart of the Lakes
t (015394) 32321
e info@heartofthelakes.co.uk
w heartofthelakes.co.uk

Brandelhowe ★★★★
Self Catering
Contact: Peter Durbin
Cumbrian Cottages Ltd
t (01228) 599950
e enquiries@cumbrian-cottages.co.uk
w cumbrian-cottages.co.uk

Brantside ★★★★
Self Catering
Contact: Ms Sue Jackson
Heart of the Lakes
t (015394) 32321
e info@heartofthelakes.co.uk
w heartofthelakes.co.uk

Brigham Farm ★★★★
Self Catering
Contact: Mr Green
The Studio
t (01768) 779666
e selfcatering@keswickholidays.co.uk
w keswickholidays.co.uk

Brow Riding ★★★
Self Catering
Contact: Peter Durbin
Cumbrian Cottages Ltd
t (01228) 599950
e enquiries@cumbrian-cottages.co.uk
w cumbrian-cottages.co.uk

Brundholme ★★★★
Self Catering
Contact: Peter Durbin
Cumbrian Cottages Ltd
t (01228) 599950
e enquiries@cumbrian-cottages.co.uk
w cumbrian-cottages.co.uk

Brundholme Glen ★★★★
Self Catering
Contact: Peter Durbin
Cumbrian Cottages Ltd
t (01228) 599950
e enquiries@cumbrian-cottages.co.uk
w cumbrian-cottages.co.uk

Bunbury Cottage ★★★★
Self Catering
Contact: Peter Durbin
Cumbrian Cottages Ltd
t (01228) 599950
e enquiries@cumbrian-cottages.co.uk
w cumbrian-cottages.co.uk

Cairnway ★★★★
Self Catering
Contact: Peter Durbin
Cumbrian Cottages Ltd
t (01228) 599950
e enquiries@cumbrian-cottages.co.uk
w cumbrian-cottages.co.uk

Candlemas ★★★
Self Catering
Contact: David Burton
Lakeland Cottage Holidays
t (01768) 776065
e info@lakelandcottages.co.uk

Carlton Cottage ★★★★
Self Catering
Contact: Peter Durbin
Cumbrian Cottages Ltd
t (01228) 599950
e enquiries@cumbrian-cottages.co.uk
w cumbrian-cottages.co.uk

Carolyn's Cottage ★★★
Self Catering
Contact: Peter Durbin
Cumbrian Cottages Ltd
t (01228) 599950
e enquiries@cumbrian-cottages.co.uk
w cumbrian-cottages.co.uk

Castlerigg Manor Lodge
★★★★ *Self Catering*
Contact: Peter Durbin
Cumbrian Cottages Ltd
t (01228) 599950
e enquiries@cumbrian-cottages.co.uk
w cumbrian-cottages.co.uk

Causey View ★★★
Self Catering
Contact: Stephen & Joanne Laker
Laker District
t (01737) 247345
e lakerdistrict@ntlworld.com
w lakerdistrict.com

Chaucer House Apartments
★★★ *Self Catering*
Contact: Peter Durbin
Cumbrian Cottages Ltd
t (01228) 599950
e enquiries@cumbrian-cottages.co.uk
w cumbrian-cottages.co.uk

Chevin Lodge ★★★★
Self Catering
Contact: Peter Durbin
Cumbrian Cottages Ltd
t (01228) 599950
e enquiries@cumbrian-cottages.co.uk
w cumbrian-cottages.co.uk

The Coach House ★★★★★
Self Catering
Contact: Mrs Susan Jackson
Heart of the Lakes
t (015394) 32321
e info@heartofthelakes.co.uk
w heartofthelakes.co.uk

The Coach House & Derwent Cottage Mews
★★★★★ *Self Catering*
Contact: Sue Newman
Derwent Cottage
t (01768) 774838
w derwentcottage.co.uk

The Conservatory ★★★★
Self Catering
Contact: Mrs Susan Jackson
Heart of the Lakes
t (015394) 32321
e info@heartofthelakes.co.uk
w heartofthelakes.co.uk

Cosy Nook ★★★
Self Catering
Contact: Peter Durbin
Cumbrian Cottages Ltd
t (01228) 599950
e enquiries@cumbrian-cottages.co.uk
w cumbrian-cottages.co.uk

The Cottage ★★★★
Self Catering
Contact: Michael Poole
Heart of the Lakes
t (015394) 32321
e info@heartofthelakes.co.uk
w heartofthelakes.co.uk

The Cottage ★★★
Self Catering
Contact: Mrs Margaret Beaty
The Cottage
t (01768) 778278

Courtyard Cottages ★★★★
Self Catering
Contact: Hazel Hutton
t (01768) 772144
e info@springs-farm.co.uk
w springs-farm.co.uk

Crag View ★★★
Self Catering
Contact: Peter Durbin
Cumbrian Cottages Ltd
t (01228) 599950
e enquiries@cumbrian-cottages.co.uk
w cumbrian-cottages.co.uk

The Croft ★★★ *Self Catering*
Contact: Peter Durbin
Cumbrian Cottages Ltd
t (01228) 599950
e enquiries@cumbrian-cottages.co.uk
w cumbrian-cottages.co.uk

Croft House Holidays
★★★★ *Self Catering*
Contact: Mrs Boniface
Croft House Holidays
t (01768) 773693
e holidays@crofthouselakes.co.uk
w crofthouselakes.co.uk

Croftlands Cottages, Thornthwaite ★★★★★
Self Catering
Contact: Susan McGarvie
Croftlands Cottages
t (01768) 778300
e robmcgarvie@lineone.net
w croftlands-cottages.co.uk

Dale Head Hall Lakeside Self Catering ★★★★–★★★★★
Self Catering
Contact: Marie Hill
Dale Head Hall Lakeside Hotel
t (01768) 772478
e info@daleheadhall.co.uk
w daleheadhall.co.uk

Dalrymple ★★★
Self Catering
Contact: Mr David Burton
Lakeland Cottage Holidays
t (01768) 776065
e info@lakelandcottages.co.uk

Darwin Cottage ★★★
Self Catering
Contact: Peter Durbin
Cumbrian Cottages Ltd
t (01228) 599950
e enquiries@cumbrian-cottages.co.uk
w cumbrian-cottages.co.uk

Denholm ★★★ *Self Catering*
Contact: Peter Durbin
Cumbrian Cottages Ltd
t (01228) 599950
e enquiries@cumbrian-cottages.co.uk
w cumbrian-cottages.co.uk

Derwent Cottage ★★★
Self Catering
Contact: Susan Jackson
Heart of the Lakes
t (015394) 32321
e info@heartofthelakes.co.uk
w heartofthelakes.co.uk

Derwent House and Brandelhowe ★★★
Self Catering
Contact: Oliver & Mary Bull
Derwent House Holidays
t (01889) 505678
e thebulls@globalnet.co.uk
w dhholidays-lakes.com

Derwent Manor ★★★★
Self Catering
Contact: Mr David Leighton
Derwentwater Hotel (Diament Ltd)
t (017687) 72538
e info@derwent-manor.co.uk
w derwent-manor.co.uk

Derwentwater ★★★★
Self Catering
Contact: Peter Durbin
Cumbrian Cottages Ltd
t (01228) 599950
e enquiries@cumbrian-cottages.co.uk
w cumbrian-cottages.co.uk

Dove House ★★★★
Self Catering
Contact: Peter Brackley
t 07731 398938
e dove@parkcottages.co.uk
w parkcottages.co.uk

Dowthwaite ★★★★
Self Catering
Contact: Susan Jackson
Heart of the Lakes
t (015394) 32321
e info@heartofthelakes.co.uk
w heartofthelakes.co.uk

Duck Pool ★★★
Self Catering
Contact: Mr David Burton
Lakeland Cottage Holidays
t (01768) 776065
e info@lakelandcottages.co.uk

Dunmallet ★★★
Self Catering
Contact: Peter Durbin
Cumbrian Cottages Ltd
t (01228) 599950
e enquiries@cumbrian-cottages.co.uk
w cumbrian-cottages.co.uk

Elm Court 11 ★★★
Self Catering
Contact: Peter Durbin
Cumbrian Cottages Ltd
t (01228) 599950
e enquiries@cumbrian-cottages.co.uk
w cumbrian-cottages.co.uk

Elmcot & Little Haven
★★★★ *Self Catering*
Contact: Mr Arun & Ajoy Roy
t (020) 8452 3695
e info.keswickholiday@btopenworld.com

Fell View ★★★ *Self Catering*
Contact: Peter Durbin
Cumbrian Cottages Ltd
t (01228) 599950
e enquiries@cumbrian-cottages.co.uk
w cumbrian-cottages.co.uk

Fell View Lodge ★★★★
Self Catering
Contact: Peter Durbin
Cumbrian Cottages Ltd
t (01228) 599950
e enquiries@cumbrian-cottages.co.uk
w cumbrian-cottages.co.uk

The Fells ★★★★
Self Catering
Contact: Peter Durbin
Cumbrian Cottages Ltd
t (01228) 599950
e enquiries@cumbrian-cottages.co.uk
w cumbrian-cottages.co.uk

Fernbank House ★★★★
Self Catering
Contact: Stephen Mason
Stonegarth Guest House
t (01768) 772436
e info@stonegarth.com
w fernbankhouse.com

Ferndale ★★★ *Self Catering*
Contact: Mr David Burton
Lakeland Cottage Holidays
t (01768) 776065
e info@lakelandcottages.co.uk

Fieldside Grange
★★★–★★★★ *Self Catering*
Kingstarn
t (01727) 853531

Fieldside Lodge ★★★★★
Self Catering
Contact: Peter Durbin
Cumbrian Cottages Ltd
t (01228) 599950
e enquiries@cumbrian-cottages.co.uk
w cumbrian-cottages.co.uk

Fornside Farm Cottages
★★★★ *Self Catering*
Contact: Mr & Mrs Hall
t (01768) 779173
e cottages@fornside.co.uk
w fornside.co.uk

Fountain Cottage ★★★
Self Catering
Contact: Dr & Mrs Preston
Bannest Hill Cottage & Fountain Cottage
t (01768) 484394
e stay@bannesthill.co.uk
w bannesthill.co.uk

Friars Cottage ★★★★
Self Catering
Contact: Peter Durbin
Cumbrian Cottages Ltd
t (01228) 599950
e enquiries@cumbrian-cottages.co.uk
w cumbrian-cottages.co.uk

Friars Crag ★★★
Self Catering
Contact: Peter Durbin
Cumbrian Cottages Ltd
t (01228) 599950
e enquiries@cumbrian-cottages.co.uk
w cumbrian-cottages.co.uk

Gable Cottage ★★★
Self Catering
Contact: Peter Durbin
Cumbrian Cottages Ltd
t (01228) 599950
e enquiries@cumbrian-cottages.co.uk
w cumbrian-cottages.co.uk

Gabriels Cottage ★★★★
Self Catering
Contact: Peter Durbin
Cumbrian Cottages Ltd
t (01228) 599950
e enquiries@cumbrian-cottages.co.uk
w cumbrian-cottages.co.uk

Gabriel's Cottage ★★★★
Self Catering
Contact: Tony Fearns
Keswick Cottages
t (01768) 773895
e info@keswickcottages.co.uk
w keswickcottages.co.uk

Gallery Mews Cottages ★★★ *Self Catering*
Contact: Ron & Anne Monk
t (01768) 778250
e enquiries@thornthwaite.net
w thornthwaite.net

Glaramara ★★★★
Self Catering
Contact: Peter Durbin
Cumbrian Cottages Ltd
t (01228) 599950
e enquiries@cumbrian-cottages.co.uk
w cumbrian-cottages.co.uk

Glenburn ★★★★
Self Catering
Contact: Ms Sue Jackson
Heart of the Lakes
t (015394) 32321
e info@heartofthelakes.co.uk
w heartofthelakes.co.uk

Glendera ★★★ *Self Catering*
Contact: Mr David Burton
Lakeland Cottage Holidays
t (01768) 776065
e info@lakelandcottages.co.uk

Glenmore ★★★ *Self Catering*
Contact: Peter Durbin
Cumbrian Cottages Ltd
t (01228) 599950
e enquiries@cumbrian-cottages.co.uk
w cumbrian-cottages.co.uk

Grandy View & Grandy Nook ★★★ *Self Catering*
Contact: Peter Durbin
Cumbrian Cottages Ltd
t (01228) 599950
e enquiries@cumbrian-cottages.co.uk
w cumbrian-cottages.co.uk

Grange Cottage Keswick ★★★ *Self Catering*
Contact: Peter Durbin
Cumbrian Cottages Ltd
t (01228) 599950
e enquiries@cumbrian-cottages.co.uk
w cumbrian-cottages.co.uk

Greenbank ★★★
Self Catering
Contact: Peter Durbin
Cumbrian Cottages Ltd
t (01228) 599950
e enquiries@cumbrian-cottages.co.uk
w cumbrian-cottages.co.uk

Greta Hall ★★★★
Self Catering
Contact: Peter Durbin
Cumbrian Cottages Ltd
t (01228) 599950
e enquiries@cumbrian-cottages.co.uk
w cumbrian-cottages.co.uk

Greta Side 1 ★★★
Self Catering
Contact: Peter Durbin
Cumbrian Cottages Ltd
t (01228) 599950
e enquiries@cumbrian-cottages.co.uk
w cumbrian-cottages.co.uk

Greta Side 2 ★★★
Self Catering
Contact: Peter Durbin
Cumbrian Cottages Ltd
t (01228) 599950
e enquiries@cumbrian-cottages.co.uk
w cumbrian-cottages.co.uk

Greta Side 4 ★★★
Self Catering
Contact: Peter Durbin
Cumbrian Cottages Ltd
t (01228) 599950
e enquiries@cumbrian-cottages.co.uk
w cumbrian-cottages.co.uk

Greta Side Court ★★★
Self Catering
Contact: John & Laura Atkinson
t (01204) 493138
e johnlaura3@btopenworld.com

Grizedale View ★★★★
Self Catering
Contact: Ms Sue Jackson
Heart of the Lakes
t (015394) 32321
e info@heartofthelakes.co.uk
w heartofthelakes.co.uk

Haystacks ★★★
Self Catering
Contact: Peter Durbin
Cumbrian Cottages Ltd
t (01228) 599950
e enquiries@cumbrian-cottages.co.uk
w cumbrian-cottages.co.uk

Heckberry & Knott House Farm ★★★★ *Self Catering*
Contact: Anthony Fearns
Keswick Cottages
t (01768) 773895
e info@keswickcottages.co.uk
w keswickcottages.co.uk

Helvellyn Rise ★★★
Self Catering
Contact: Peter Durbin
Cumbrian Cottages Ltd
t (01228) 599950
e enquiries@cumbrian-cottages.co.uk
w cumbrian-cottages.co.uk

Herries ★★★ *Self Catering*
Contact: Mr David Burton
Lakeland Cottage Holidays
t (01768) 776065
e info@lakelandcottages.co.uk

High Hill Farm Cottage ★★★★ *Self Catering*
Contact: Peter Durbin
Cumbrian Cottages Ltd
t (01228) 599950
e enquiries@cumbrian-cottages.co.uk
w cumbrian-cottages.co.uk

High Rigg ★★★★
Self Catering
Contact: Mr Sayer
t (01582) 872574

High Spy ★★★ *Self Catering*
Contact: Mr David Burton
Lakeland Cottage Holidays
t (01768) 776065
e info@lakelandcottages.co.uk

Highbank ★★★★
Self Catering
Contact: Peter Durbin
Cumbrian Cottages Ltd
t (01228) 599950
e enquiries@cumbrian-cottages.co.uk
w cumbrian-cottages.co.uk

Highcrest ★★★ *Self Catering*
Contact: Peter Durbin
Cumbrian Cottages Ltd
t (01228) 599950
e enquiries@cumbrian-cottages.co.uk
w cumbrian-cottages.co.uk

Hillside ★★★ *Self Catering*
Contact: Dr & Mrs M J & D J Wright
t (017687) 80256
e sparkywright@btinternet.com
w keswickhillsideapartments.co.uk

Hillview ★★★★ *Self Catering*
Contact: Peter Durbin
Cumbrian Cottages Ltd
t (01228) 599950
e enquiries@cumbrian-cottages.co.uk
w cumbrian-cottages.co.uk

Holly Bank Cottage ★★★-★★★★ *Self Catering*
Contact: Kate Danchin
Holly Bank & Jasmine Cottages
t (01900) 822001
e enquiries@hollybankcottage.co.uk
w hollybankcottage.co.uk

Holly Cottage ★★★★
Self Catering
t (0114) 296 0491
e r.e.t.wilson@btinternet.com
w hollycottage.info

Ivy Cottage ★★★★
Self Catering
Contact: Tony Fearns
Keswick Cottages
t (01768) 773895
e info@keswickcottages.co.uk
w keswickcottages.co.uk

Jane Eyres Cottage ★★★★
Self Catering
Contact: Peter Durbin
Cumbrian Cottages Ltd
t (01228) 599950
e enquiries@cumbrian-cottages.co.uk
w cumbrian-cottages.co.uk

Keswick Boat House ★★★★
Self Catering
Contact: Peter Durbin
Cumbrian Cottages Ltd
t (01228) 599950
e enquiries@cumbrian-cottages.co.uk
w cumbrian-cottages.co.uk

Keswick Timeshare Limited ★★★★ *Self Catering*
Contact: Mr David Etherden
t (01768) 773591
e enquiries@keswickb.com

Kingsfell ★★★★
Self Catering
Contact: Christine Leach
t (01462) 627291
e theleaches99@ntlworld.com
w gotothelakes.co.uk

Kingstarn ★★★★ *Self Catering & Serviced Apartments*
t (01727) 853531

Kinnear ★★★★ *Self Catering*
Contact: Mrs Susan Jackson
Heart of the Lakes
t (015394) 32321
e info@heartofthelakes.co.uk
w heartofthelakes.co.uk

Kintail ★★★★★
Self Catering
Contact: Peter Durbin
Cumbrian Cottages Ltd
t (01228) 599950
e enquiries@cumbrian-cottages.co.uk
w cumbrian-cottages.co.uk

Kylesku ★★★ *Self Catering*
Contact: Peter Durbin
Cumbrian Cottages Ltd
t (01228) 599950
e enquiries@cumbrian-cottages.co.uk
w cumbrian-cottages.co.uk

Lakeland House ★★★
Self Catering
Contact: Peter Durbin
Cumbrian Cottages Ltd
t (01228) 599950
e enquiries@cumbrian-cottages.co.uk
w cumbrian-cottages.co.uk

Latrigg View ★★★★
Self Catering
Contact: Ms Sue Jackson
Heart of the Lakes
t (015394) 32321
e info@heartofthelakes.co.uk
w heartofthelakes.co.uk

Latrigg View ★★★
Self Catering
Contact: Peter Durbin
Cumbrian Cottages Ltd
t (01228) 599950
e enquiries@cumbrian-cottages.co.uk
w cumbrian-cottages.co.uk

Lavender Cottage ★★★
Self Catering
Contact: Peter Durbin
Cumbrian Cottages Ltd
t (01228) 599950
e enquiries@cumbrian-cottages.co.uk
w cumbrian-cottages.co.uk

Leander ★★★★ *Self Catering*
Contact: Peter Durbin
Cumbrian Cottages Ltd
t (01228) 599950
e enquiries@cumbrian-cottages.co.uk
w cumbrian-cottages.co.uk

Little Chestnut Hill ★★★
Self Catering
Contact: Mr David Burton
Lakeland Cottage Holidays
t (01768) 776065
e info@lakelandcottages.co.uk

Low Briery Cottages ★★★★
Self Catering
Contact: Michael Atkinson
Low Briery Holiday Village
t (01768) 772044

Loweswater ★★★★
Self Catering
Contact: Peter Durbin
Cumbrian Cottages Ltd
t (01228) 599950
e enquiries@cumbrian-cottages.co.uk
w cumbrian-cottages.co.uk

Manesty View ★★★
Self Catering
Contact: Peter Durbin
Cumbrian Cottages Ltd
t (01228) 599950
e enquiries@cumbrian-cottages.co.uk
w cumbrian-cottages.co.uk

Meadow Cottage ★★★
Self Catering
Contact: Mr David Burton
Lakeland Cottage Holidays
t (01768) 776065
e info@lakelandcottages.co.uk

Michaels Cottage ★★★★
Self Catering
Contact: Peter Durbin
Cumbrian Cottages Ltd
t (01228) 599950
e enquiries@cumbrian-cottages.co.uk
w cumbrian-cottages.co.uk

Millbeck Cottage ★★★★
Self Catering
Contact: Peter Durbin
Cumbrian Cottages Ltd
t (01228) 599950
e enquiries@cumbrian-cottages.co.uk
w cumbrian-cottages.co.uk

Mountain View ★★★
Self Catering
Contact: Peter Durbin
Cumbrian Cottages Ltd
t (01228) 599950
e enquiries@cumbrian-cottages.co.uk
w cumbrian-cottages.co.uk

Newlands View ★★★★
Self Catering
Contact: Mr David Burton
Lakeland Cottage Holidays
t (01768) 776065
e info@lakelandcottages.co.uk

The Old Betting Shop ★★★
Self Catering
Contact: Peter Durbin
Cumbrian Cottages Ltd
t (01228) 599950
e enquiries@cumbrian-cottages.co.uk
w cumbrian-cottages.co.uk

Olivet ★★★ *Self Catering*
Contact: Peter Durbin
Cumbrian Cottages Ltd
t (01228) 599950
e enquiries@cumbrian-cottages.co.uk
w cumbrian-cottages.co.uk

Orchard Barn ★★★
Self Catering
Contact: Mr & Mrs Hall
t (01946) 723319
e holidays@fisherground.co.uk

Packhorse ★★★
Self Catering
Contact: Peter Durbin
Cumbrian Cottages Ltd
t (01228) 599950
e enquiries@cumbrian-cottages.co.uk
w cumbrian-cottages.co.uk

Peak View ★★★★
Self Catering
Contact: Peter Durbin
Cumbrian Cottages Ltd
t (01228) 599950
e enquiries@cumbrian-cottages.co.uk
w cumbrian-cottages.co.uk

Poet's Corner ★★★★
Self Catering
Contact: Mr Paul Liddell
Lakelovers
t (015394) 88855
e bookings@lakelovers.co.uk
w lakelovers.co.uk

Poplar Cottage ★★★
Self Catering
Contact: Peter Durbin
Cumbrian Cottages Ltd
t (01228) 599950
e enquiries@cumbrian-cottages.co.uk
w cumbrian-cottages.co.uk

Primrose Cottage ★★★★
Self Catering
Contact: Geoff & Julia Holloway
t (01473) 890035
e primrose.cott@btinternet.com
w primrose.cott.btinternet.co.uk

Ptarmigan House ★★★
Self Catering
Contact: Mrs Fursman
Cumbrian Cottages Ltd
t (01491) 681623
e jeanfursman@hotmail.com
w ptarmiganhouse.com

Quintok ★★★★ *Self Catering*
Contact: Mr David Burton
Lakeland Cottage Holidays
t (01768) 776065
e info@lakelandcottages.co.uk

The Retreat ★★★
Self Catering
Contact: Peter Durbin
Cumbrian Cottages Ltd
t (01228) 599950
e enquiries@cumbrian-cottages.co.uk
w cumbrian-cottages.co.uk

Rivendell ★★★ *Self Catering*
Contact: Mr David Burton
Lakeland Cottage Holidays
t (01768) 776065
e info@lakelandcottages.co.uk

River Cottage ★★★★
Self Catering
Contact: Peter Durbin
Cumbrian Cottages Ltd
t (01228) 599950
e enquiries@cumbrian-cottages.co.uk
w cumbrian-cottages.co.uk

Riverdale Cottage ★★★★
Self Catering
Contact: Mrs Susan Jackson
Heart of the Lakes
t (015394) 32321
e info@heartofthelakes.co.uk
w heartofthelakes.co.uk

Riverside Cottage ★★★
Self Catering
Contact: Mrs Susan Jackson
Heart of the Lakes
t (015394) 32321
e info@heartofthelakes.co.uk
w heartofthelakes.co.uk

Riverside Cottage ★★★★
Self Catering
Contact: Daphne Barron
t (01768) 776007
e info@riversideholidays.com
w riversideholidays.com

Robin's Nest ★★★★
Self Catering
Contact: Peter Durbin
Cumbrian Cottages Ltd
t (01228) 599950
e enquiries@cumbrian-cottages.co.uk
w cumbrian-cottages.co.uk

Rock House ★★★★
Self Catering
Contact: Mrs Susan Jackson
Heart of the Lakes
t (015394) 32321
e info@heartofthelakes.co.uk
w heartofthelakes.co.uk

Rose Cottage ★★
Self Catering
Contact: Peter Durbin
Cumbrian Cottages Ltd
t (01228) 599950
e enquiries@cumbrian-cottages.co.uk
w cumbrian-cottages.co.uk

Rosemary Cottage ★★★★
Self Catering
Contact: Mrs Susan Jackson
Heart of the Lakes
t (015394) 32321
e info@heartofthelakes.co.uk
w heartofthelakes.co.uk

The Rowans ★★★
Self Catering
Contact: Peter Durbin
Cumbrian Cottages Ltd
t (01228) 599950
e enquiries@cumbrian-cottages.co.uk
w cumbrian-cottages.co.uk

Rowanwood & Beechwood ★★★ *Self Catering*
Contact: Mr & Mrs Davison
Rowanwood
t (01623) 627370

Saddleback Cottage ★★★
Self Catering
Contact: Peter Durbin
Cumbrian Cottages Ltd
t (01228) 599950
e enquiries@cumbrian-cottages.co.uk
w cumbrian-cottages.co.uk

St Herbert's Cottage ★★★-★★★★ *Self Catering*
Contact: Stephen & Joanne Laker
Laker District
t (01737) 247345
e lakerdistrict@ntlworld.com
w lakerdistrict.com

St Johns View ★★★
Self Catering
Contact: Peter Durbin
Cumbrian Cottages Ltd
t (01228) 599950
e enquiries@cumbrian-cottages.co.uk
w cumbrian-cottages.co.uk

Sandburne Cottage ★★★★
Self Catering
Contact: Susan Jackson
Heart of the Lakes
t (015394) 32321
e info@heartofthelakes.co.uk
w heartofthelakes.co.uk

Scotts Court ★★★★
Self Catering
Contact: Mr & Mrs Peter & Pam Hodson
t (01204) 465631
e admin@6scottscourt.co.uk

Seat Howe ★★★
Self Catering
Contact: Peter Durbin
Cumbrian Cottages Ltd
t (01228) 599950
e enquiries@cumbrian-cottages.co.uk
w cumbrian-cottages.co.uk

Serendipity ★★★
Self Catering
Contact: Peter Durbin
Cumbrian Cottages Ltd
t (01228) 599950
e enquiries@cumbrian-cottages.co.uk
w cumbrian-cottages.co.uk

Shelter Stone ★★
Self Catering
Contact: Mr David Burton
Lakeland Cottage Holidays
t (01768) 776065
e info@lakelandcottages.co.uk

The Shieling ★★★★
Self Catering
Contact: Peter Durbin
Cumbrian Cottages Ltd
t (01228) 599950
e enquiries@cumbrian-cottages.co.uk
w cumbrian-cottages.co.uk

Shorley Lodge ★★★★
Self Catering
Contact: Peter Durbin
Cumbrian Cottages Ltd
t (01228) 599950
e enquiries@cumbrian-cottages.co.uk
w cumbrian-cottages.co.uk

Silene ★★★ *Self Catering*
Contact: David Burton
Lakeland Cottage Holidays
t (01768) 776065
e info@lakelandcottages.co.uk
w lakelandcottages.co.uk

Skiddaw Heights ★★★★
Self Catering
Contact: Peter Durbin
Cumbrian Cottages Ltd
t (01228) 599950
e enquiries@cumbrian-cottages.co.uk
w cumbrian-cottages.co.uk

Skiddaw View ★★★★
Self Catering
Contact: Peter Durbin
Cumbrian Cottages Ltd
t (01228) 599950
e enquiries@cumbrian-cottages.co.uk
w cumbrian-cottages.co.uk

Slate Cottage ★★★★
Self Catering
Contact: Peter Durbin
Cumbrian Cottages Ltd
t (01228) 599950
e enquiries@cumbrian-cottages.co.uk
w cumbrian-cottages.co.uk

South View ★★★★★
Self Catering
Contact: Mrs Susan Jackson
Heart of the Lakes
t (015394) 32321
e info@heartofthelakes.co.uk
w heartofthelakes.co.uk

Squirrel Cottage ★★★
Self Catering
Contact: David Burton
Lakeland Cottage Holidays
t (01768) 776065
e info@lakelandcottages.co.uk
w lakelandcottages.co.uk

Stables ★★★ *Self Catering*
Contact: Peter Watson
t (01768) 773478
e wattysam@wattys.wanadoo.co.uk

Stoneledges ★★★
Self Catering
Contact: Peter Durbin
Cumbrian Cottages Ltd
t (01228) 599950
e enquiries@cumbrian-cottages.co.uk
w cumbrian-cottages.co.uk

Sunnybank Cottage ★★★
Self Catering
Contact: Peter Durbin
Cumbrian Cottages Ltd
t (01228) 599950
e enquiries@cumbrian-cottages.co.uk
w cumbrian-cottages.co.uk

Thorndale ★★★★
Self Catering
Contact: Peter Durbin
Cumbrian Cottages Ltd
t (01228) 599950
e enquiries@cumbrian-cottages.co.uk
w cumbrian-cottages.co.uk

Threeways ★★★★
Self Catering
Contact: Peter Durbin
Cumbrian Cottages Ltd
t (01228) 599950
e enquiries@cumbrian-cottages.co.uk
w cumbrian-cottages.co.uk

The Tops ★★★★
Self Catering
Contact: Peter Durbin
Cumbrian Cottages Ltd
t (01228) 599950
e enquiries@cumbrian-cottages.co.uk
w cumbrian-cottages.co.uk

Topsey Turvey ★★★★
Self Catering
Contact: Peter Durbin
Cumbrian Cottages Ltd
t (01228) 599950
e enquiries@cumbrian-cottages.co.uk
w cumbrian-cottages.co.uk

Turners Retreat ★★★★
Self Catering
Contact: Peter Durbin
Cumbrian Cottages Ltd
t (01228) 599950
e enquiries@cumbrian-cottages.co.uk
w cumbrian-cottages.co.uk

Twentyman's Court ★★★
Self Catering
Contact: Peter Durbin
Cumbrian Cottages Ltd
t (01228) 599950
e enquiries@cumbrian-cottages.co.uk
w cumbrian-cottages.co.uk

Underne ★★★ *Self Catering*
Contact: Mr David Burton
Lakeland Cottage Holidays
t (01768) 776065
e info@lakelandcottages.co.uk

Underscar ★★★★★
Self Catering
Contact: Susan Jackson
Heart of the Lakes
t (015394) 32321
e info@heartofthelakes.co.uk
w heartofthelakes.co.uk

Upton Glen ★★★
Self Catering
Contact: Peter Durbin
Cumbrian Cottages Ltd
t (01228) 599950
e enquiries@cumbrian-cottages.co.uk
w cumbrian-cottages.co.uk

Walla Crag ★★★
Self Catering
Contact: Peter Durbin
Cumbrian Cottages Ltd
t (01228) 599950
e enquiries@cumbrian-cottages.co.uk
w cumbrian-cottages.co.uk

Wendover ★★★
Self Catering
Contact: Peter Durbin
Cumbrian Cottages Ltd
t (01228) 599950
e enquiries@cumbrian-cottages.co.uk
w cumbrian-cottages.co.uk

Westies ★★★ *Self Catering*
Contact: Mr David Burton
Lakeland Cottage Holidays
t (01768) 776065
e info@lakelandcottages.co.uk

White Wicket ★★★
Self Catering
Contact: Peter Durbin
Cumbrian Cottages Ltd
t (01228) 599950
e enquiries@cumbrian-cottages.co.uk
w cumbrian-cottages.co.uk

Windsor House ★★★★
Self Catering
Contact: John & Jean Thompson
t (01388) 811006
e info@highviewcountryhouse.co.uk
w highviewcountryhouse.co.uk

Woodleigh ★★★★
Self Catering
Contact: Peter Durbin
Cumbrian Cottages Ltd
t (01228) 599950
e enquiries@cumbrian-cottages.co.uk
w cumbrian-cottages.co.uk

KETTLESHULME
Greater Manchester

Townfield Farm ★★★★
Self Catering
Contact: Mrs Christine Hallam
t (01663) 733450

KILLINGTON
Cumbria

Ghyll Stile Mill Cottage
★★★ *Self Catering*
Contact: Janet & Nick Chetwood
t (015396) 21715
e janetghyll@aol.com
w ghyll-stile-mill-cottage.co.uk

KING'S MEABURN
Cumbria

Lyvennet Cottages ★★★★
Self Catering
Contact: Margaret, Wendy & Janet Addison
Lyvennet Cottages
t (01931) 714226
e wendyaddison@yahoo.com
w lyvennetcottages.co.uk

KIRKBY-IN-FURNESS
Cumbria

Sunset Cottage ★★★★
Self Catering
Contact: Janet Fallon
South Lakes Cottages
t (01229) 889601
e enquiries@southlakes-cottages.com
w southlakes-cottages.com

KIRKBY LONSDALE
Cumbria

Clarks Cottage ★★★★
Self Catering
Contact: Peter Durbin
Cumbrian Cottages Ltd
t (01228) 599950
e enquiries@cumbrian-cottages.co.uk
w cumbrian-cottages.co.uk

Nutshell Barn ★★★★
Self Catering
Contact: Mr Stephen Wightman
t (01524) 733865
e sj@nutshell-barn.co.uk
w nutshell-barn.co.uk

The Old Stables ★★★★
Self Catering
Contact: Peter Durbin
Cumbrian Cottages Ltd
t (01228) 599950
e enquiries@cumbrian-cottages.co.uk
w cumbrian-cottages.co.uk

Sellet Hall Cottages, Carnforth ★★★★
Self Catering
Contact: Mrs Hall
Sellet Hall Cottages
t (01524) 271865
e sellethall@hotmail.com
w sellethall.com

Weavers Cottage ★★★
Self Catering
Contact: Peter Durbin
Cumbrian Cottages Ltd
t (01228) 599950
e enquiries@cumbrian-cottages.co.uk
w cumbrian-cottages.co.uk

KIRKBY STEPHEN
Cumbria

Artlegarth Country Lodges
★★★★ *Self Catering*
Contact: Michael Franks
t (0113) 232 3273
e mf@supanet.com
w lodgebreaks.co.uk

Pennistone Green ★★★★
Self Catering
t (01629) 815683
e jackson@ashmere.fsnet.co.uk

Swallow Barn (3399)
★★★★ *Self Catering*
Dales Holiday Cottages
t 0870 909 9500
e info@dales-holiday-cottages.com
w dalesholcot.com

KIRKBY THORE
Cumbria

Holme Lea ★★★
Self Catering
Contact: Alan Price
t (01603) 279713
e jprice@albatross.co.uk
w cumbriaselfcater.co.uk

KIRKLINTON
Cumbria

Dovecote ★★★★
Self Catering
Contact: Sherann Chandley
t (01228) 675650
e slc@cleughside.co.uk
w cleughside.co.uk

Keepers Cottage ★★★★
Self Catering
Contact: Pat Armstrong
t (01228) 791378
e info@keepers-cottage.co.uk
w keepers-cottage.co.uk

KIRKOSWALD
Cumbria

Bank House Apartment
★★★★★ *Self Catering*
Contact: Peter Durbin
Cumbrian Cottages Ltd
t (01228) 599950
e enquiries@cumbrian-cottages.co.uk
w cumbrian-cottages.co.uk

Crossfield Cottages ★★★
Self Catering
Contact: Susan Bottom
t (01768) 898711
e info@crossfieldcottages.co.uk
w crossfieldcottages.co.uk

Howscales ★★★★
Self Catering
Contact: Liz Webster
Howscales
t (01768) 898666
e liz@howscales.co.uk
w howscales.co.uk

KNUTSFORD
Cheshire

Danebury Serviced Apartments ★★★★
Self Catering
Contact: Mr & Mrs Stephen and Pauline West
Danebury Gardens Serviced Apartments
t (01565) 755219
e info@daneburyapartments.co.uk
w daneburyapartments.co.uk

LAITHES
Cumbria

Petterill View ★★★★
Self Catering
Contact: Peter Durbin
Cumbrian Cottages Ltd
t (01228) 599950
e enquiries@cumbrian-cottages.co.uk
w cumbrian-cottages.co.uk

LAKESIDE
Cumbria

2 Stock Park Mansion ★★★
Self Catering
Contact: Diane Watson
Mr & Mrs J R Watson
t (01704) 871144
e rogerwatson@ic24.net

Deer Rise ★★★★
Self Catering
Lakelovers
t (015394) 88855
e bookings@lakelovers.co.uk
w lakelovers.co.uk

Fir Tree Lodge ★★★★
Self Catering
Lakelovers
t (015394) 88855
e bookings@lakelovers.co.uk
w lakelovers.co.uk

Landing Howe ★★★★
Self Catering
Contact: Mr Peter Liddell
Lakelovers
t (015394) 88855
e bookings@lakelovers.co.uk
w lakelovers.co.uk

Nutwood ★★★★
Self Catering
Lakelovers
t (015394) 88855
e bookings@lakelovers.co.uk
w lakelovers.co.uk

LAMONBY
Cumbria

Half Crown Cottage ★★★★
Self Catering
Contact: Peter Durbin
Cumbrian Cottages Ltd
t (01228) 599950
e enquiries@cumbrian-cottages.co.uk
w cumbrian-cottages.co.uk

LAMPLUGH
Cumbria

2 Folly ★★★★ *Self Catering*
Contact: Alison Wilson
2 Folly
t (01946) 861151
e dockraynook@talk21.com
w felldykecottageholidays.co.uk

The Old Rectory ★★★★★
Self Catering
Contact: Peter Durbin
Cumbrian Cottages Ltd
t (01228) 599950
e enquiries@cumbrian-cottages.co.uk
w cumbrian-cottages.co.uk

The Spinney ★★★★★
Self Catering
Contact: Peter Durbin
Cumbrian Cottages Ltd
t (01228) 599950
e enquiries@cumbrian-cottages.co.uk
w cumbrian-cottages.co.uk

LANCASTER
Lancashire

Mulberry Cottage ★★★
Self Catering
Contact: Mrs Catherine Fatkin
t (01524) 64755

Parkside & Woodside
★★★★ *Self Catering*
Contact: Thomas & Jane Marshall
t (01524) 262163
e info@riversidecaravanpark.co.uk
w riversidecaravanpark.co.uk

Rose Cottage ★★★
Self Catering
Contact: Mrs Susan Atkinson
t (01524) 791283
e atkinsons@sykesfarm.wanadoo.co.uk
w stayatrosecottage.co.uk

The Stables ★★★
Self Catering
Contact: Mr & Mrs Quinn
t (01524) 751568

LANGDALE
Cumbria

2 & 7 Lingmoor View ★★★
Self Catering
Contact: Michael & Andrea Batho
Cottages Cumbria
t (015394) 41680
e a.batho@virgin.net
w cottagescumbria.com

Long House Cottages ★★★
Self Catering
Contact: Mr Grayston
Long House
t (015394) 37222
e enquiries@longhousecottages.co.uk
w longhousecottages.co.uk

The Maple Loft ★★★★
Self Catering
Contact: Mrs Susan Jackson
Heart of the Lakes
t (015394) 32321
e info@heartofthelakes.co.uk
w heartofthelakes.co.uk

Meadow Bank
★★★-★★★★ *Self Catering*
Contact: Patricia Locke
Langdale Cottages
t 07854 960716
e lockemeadowbank@aol.com
w langdalecottages.co.uk

Tabitha's Cottage ★★★★
Self Catering
Heart of the Lakes
t (015394) 32321
e info@heartofthelakes.co.uk
w heartofthelakes.co.uk

Weir Cottage ★★★
Self Catering
Contact: Mrs Susan Jackson
Heart of the Lakes
t (015394) 32321
e info@heartofthelakes.co.uk
w heartofthelakes.co.uk

LANGLEY
Cheshire

Pyegreave Farm Cottages
★★★ *Self Catering*
Contact: Sally Hammill
t (01260) 252325

LANGWATHBY
Cumbria

Byre Cottage ★★★★
Self Catering
Contact: Angela Campbell
t (01768) 773634
e angelakeswick@hotmail.co.uk
w byrecottage.co.uk

LEASGILL
Cumbria

Maple Cottage ★★★★ *Self Catering & Serviced Apartments*
Contact: Beverly Keatings
t (015395) 63008
e andrew.keatings@btinternet.com
w cottageguide.co.uk/maplecottage

LEVENS
Cumbria

The Beeches & Beeches Cottage ★★★★ *Self Catering*
Contact: Peter Durbin
Cumbrian Cottages Ltd
t (01228) 599950
e enquiries@cumbrian-cottages.co.uk
w cumbrian-cottages.co.uk

Gilpin Farmhouse Cottage
★★★ *Self Catering*
Contact: Ms Fiona Moody
Dales Holiday Cottages
t 0870 909 9500
e info@dales-holiday-cottages.com
w dalesholcot.com

The Orchard ★★★
Self Catering
Contact: Peter Durbin
Cumbrian Cottages Ltd
t (01228) 599950
e enquiries@cumbrian-cottages.co.uk
w cumbrian-cottages.co.uk

Underhill Cottage ★★★★
Self Catering
Contact: Christine Phillips
t (015395) 60298
e underhillcottage@aol.com
w cottage-in-cumbria.com

LINDALE
Cumbria

7 New Cottages ★★★
Self Catering
Contact: Mr & Mrs David & Margaret Potts
Lindale Property
t (0161) 285 6867
e lindale.cottage@ntlworld.com
w lindale-cottage.co.uk

Horseshoe Cottage ★★★★
Self Catering
Contact: Peter Durbin
Cumbrian Cottages Ltd
t (01228) 599950
e enquiries@cumbrian-cottages.co.uk
w cumbrian-cottages.co.uk

The Institute ★★★★
Self Catering
Contact: Mr John Serginson
The Lakeland Cottage Company
t (015395) 30024
e john@lakelandcottageco.com

Lavender Cottage ★★★★
Self Catering
Contact: Mr John Serginson
The Lakeland Cottage Company
t (015395) 30024
e john@lakelandcottageco.com

Millers Loft ★★★
Self Catering
Contact: Mr John Serginson
The Lakeland Cottage Company
t (015395) 30024
e john@lakelandcottageco.com

LITTLE ARROW
Cumbria

Mulberry Cottage ★★★★
Self Catering
Contact: Mr Paul Liddell
Lakelovers
t (015394) 88855
e bookings@lakelovers.co.uk
w lakelovers.co.uk

LITTLE ECCLESTON
Lancashire

Barn Owl Cottage ★★★★
Self Catering
Contact: Mr & Mrs J. A. Garnett
t (01253) 858293

LITTLE LANGDALE
Cumbria

The Bield ★★★★
Self Catering
Contact: Mrs Susan Jackson
Heart of the Lakes
t (015394) 32321
e info@heartofthelakes.co.uk
w heartofthelakes.co.uk

Birch House ★★★★
Self Catering
Lakelovers
t (015394) 88855
e bookings@lakelovers.co.uk
w lakelovers.co.uk

Farra Grain ★★★★
Self Catering
Heart of the Lakes
t (015394) 32321
e info@heartofthelakes.co.uk
w heartofthelakes.co.uk

Fell Foot Cottage ★★★★
Self Catering
Contact: Kerrie Benson
Fell Foot Farm
t (015394) 37149
w fellfootfarm.co.uk

Hacket Forge ★★★
Self Catering
Contact: Judith Amos
t (015394) 37630
w amblesideonline.co.uk/display/hacket/main.html

Highfold Cottage ★★★
Self Catering
Contact: Christine Blair
t (015394) 37686
w highfoldcottage.co.uk

Lang Parrock ★★★
Self Catering
Contact: Susan Jackson
Heart of the Lakes
t (015394) 32321
e info@heartofthelakes.co.uk
w heartofthelakes.co.uk

Wilson Place Farm ★★★★
Self Catering
Contact: Mr & Mrs Bass
Wheelwrights Holiday Cottages
t (015394) 37635
e enquiries@wheelwrights.com

LITTLE STRICKLAND
Cumbria

Spring Bank ★★★★
Self Catering
Contact: Mrs J Ostle
Spring Bank
t (01931) 716246
e springbank17@hotmail.com
w holidaycumbria.co.uk

LITTLEBOROUGH
Greater Manchester

Long Lees Farm Cottage
★★★★ *Self Catering*
Contact: Mrs Dawn Gumbley
t (01706) 372468
w cottageguide.co.uk/longlees

LIVERPOOL
Merseyside

28 Tower Buildings
Rating Applied For
Self Catering
Contact: Joan Olsen
t 07772 291849
e towerbooker@hotmail.co.uk

Apartment 58 ★★★
Self Catering
Contact: Mrs Dawn Williams
t (0151) 284 4932
e dwools2576@hotmail.co.uk
w liverpoolholidayrental.com

City Quay ★★★ *Self Catering*
Contact: Mr Henderson
t (0151) 428 5251
e billy-noodle@hotmail.com
w cityquayapartments.co.uk

Greenbank Sports Academy
Rating Applied For
Self Catering
t (0151) 280 7757
e jroberts@greenbank-project.org.uk

International Inn Serviced Apartments ★★★
Serviced Apartments
Contact: Leah Williams
4 South Hunter Street
t (0151) 709 8135
e info@internationalinn.co.uk
w internationalinnapartments.co.uk

The Manhattan Apartment
★★★★ *Self Catering*
Contact: Mrs J Tunstall
t (01744) 885239
e jeanette@tunstall.wanadoo.co.uk

Flat 1, Medici Building
★★★★ *Self Catering*
Executive Short Stay Homes
t (01865) 321106
e greenhavenoxford@btconnect.com
w holidayhomeoxford.co.uk

Mersey Waterfront Apartments ★★★★
Self Catering
Contact: Mr & Mrs Ian & Janet Shields
t (0151) 487 7440
e merseywaterfrontapartments@aol.com

Port Sunlight Village Trust, Port Sunlight ★★★★
Self Catering
Contact: Mrs Sandra Nicholls
t (0151) 644 4801
e sandra.psvt@btconnect.com
w portsunlightvillage.com

St. Lukes Court ★★★
Self Catering
Contact: Sarah Chaddick
t (01695) 420922
e sarah@apartmentliverpool.com
w apartmentliverpool.com

Trafalgar Warehouse Apartments ★★★★
Self Catering
Contact: Mr Ray Gibson
Trafalgar Warehouse Apartments
t 07715 118419

Waterfront Penthouse
★★★★ *Self Catering*
t 07860 351684
e rod+muir@stayinginliverpool.com

LONGSLEDDALE
Cumbria

The Coach House ★★★
Self Catering
Contact: Jenny Farmer
The Coach House
t (01539) 823686
e jenyfarmer@aol.com
w capplebarrowcoachhouse.co.uk

LONGTHWAITE
Cumbria

Castle Lodge ★★★
Self Catering
Contact: Susan Jackson
Heart of the Lakes
t (015394) 32321
e info@heartofthelakes.co.uk
w heartofthelakes.co.uk

LORTON
Cumbria

Swaledale Cottage ★★★
Self Catering
Contact: Miss Christine England
t (01900) 85226
e stay@hope-farm-holiday-cottages.co.uk

LOUGHRIGG
Cumbria

Badgers Walk ★★★
Self Catering
Contact: Mr Paul Liddell
Lakelovers
t (015394) 88855
e bookings@lakelovers.co.uk
w lakelovers.co.uk

Bleaberry Tarn Lodge – Neaum Crag ★★★★★
Self Catering
Contact: Peter Durbin
Cumbrian Cottages Ltd
t (01228) 599950
e enquiries@cumbrian-cottages.co.uk
w cumbrian-cottages.co.uk

The Coach House ★★★★
Self Catering
Contact: Mr Paul Liddell
Lakelovers
t (015394) 88855
e bookings@lakelovers.co.uk
w lakelovers.co.uk

Crummock Water – Neaum Crag ★★ *Self Catering*
Contact: Peter Durbin
Cumbrian Cottages Ltd
t (01228) 599950
e enquiries@cumbrian-cottages.co.uk
w cumbrian-cottages.co.uk

Lane Head ★★★★
Self Catering
Heart of the Lakes
t (015394) 32321
e info@heartofthelakes.co.uk
w heartofthelakes.co.uk

Neaum Crag-Boltons Tarn
★★★ *Self Catering*
t (01228) 599960
w cumbrian-cottages.co.uk

The Poppies ★★★
Self Catering
Contact: Mrs Susan Jackson
Heart of the Lakes
t (015394) 32321
e info@heartofthelakes.co.uk
w heartofthelakes.co.uk

The Poppies – Neaum Crag
★★★ *Self Catering*
Contact: Peter Durbin
Cumbrian Cottages Ltd
t (01228) 599950
e enquiries@cumbrian-cottages.co.uk
w cumbrian-cottages.co.uk

Rydal Holiday Lettings
★★★★ *Self Catering*
Contact: Amanda Rowley
t (015394) 31043
e info@steppingstonesambleside.co.uk
w steppingstonesambleside.co.uk

LOW COTEHILL
Cumbria

Oakville Cottage ★★★★★
Self Catering
Contact: Peter Durbin
Cumbrian Cottages Ltd
t (01228) 599950
e enquiries@cumbrian-cottages.co.uk
w cumbrian-cottages.co.uk

Oakville Cottages ★★★★★
Self Catering
Contact: Peter Durbin
Cumbrian Cottages Ltd
t (01228) 599950
e enquiries@cumbrian-cottages.co.uk
w cumbrian-cottages.co.uk

LOW LORTON
Cumbria

Bridge End Cottage ★★★★
Self Catering
Contact: Peter Durbin
Cumbrian Cottages Ltd
t (01228) 599950
e enquiries@cumbrian-cottages.co.uk
w cumbrian-cottages.co.uk

The Chalet ★★★
Self Catering
Contact: Peter Durbin
Cumbrian Cottages Ltd
t (01228) 599950
e enquiries@cumbrian-cottages.co.uk
w cumbrian-cottages.co.uk

LOWESWATER
Cumbria

The Coach House ★★★★★
Self Catering
Contact: Naomi Kerr
t (01900) 85660
e lookingstead@aol.com

Crummockwater Cottages
★★★★★ *Self Catering*
Contact: Joan Warren
t (01900) 85637
e jm@crummockwatercottages.co.uk
w crummockwatercottages.co.uk

The Howe ★★★★
Self Catering
Contact: Millie Townson
t (01900) 823660
e millie@mosserhowe.freeserve.co.uk
w mosserhowe.co.uk

Low Park Cottage ★★★
Self Catering
Contact: Robert Watkins
t (01900) 85242

LOWICK
Cumbria

Bark Cottage ★★★
Self Catering
Contact: Jenny Tancock
t (01229) 885416
e joeandjenny@tannerybarn.freeserve.co.uk
w tannerybarn.freeserve.co.uk

Tsukudu ★★★★
Self Catering
Contact: Paul Durbin
Cumbrian Cottages Ltd
t (01228) 599950
e enquiries@cumbrian-cottages.co.uk
w cumbrian-cottages.co.uk

LOWICK BRIDGE
Cumbria

Appletree Barn ★★★★
Self Catering
Contact: Mr Philip Johnston
The Coppermines & Coniston Lake Cottages
t (015394) 41765
e info@coppermines.co.uk
w coppermines.co.uk

Langholme Cottage ★★★
Self Catering
Contact: Peter Durbin
Cumbrian Cottages Ltd
t (01228) 599950
e enquiries@cumbrian-cottages.co.uk
w cumbrian-cottages.co.uk

Rose Cottage ★★★★
Self Catering
Contact: Mr John Serginson
The Lakeland Cottage Company
t (015395) 30024
e john@lakelandcottageco.com

LOWICK GREEN
Cumbria

Thorn Cottage ★★★
Self Catering
Contact: Peter Durbin
Cumbrian Cottages Ltd
t (01228) 599950
e enquiries@cumbrian-cottages.co.uk
w cumbrian-cottages.co.uk

LYTH
Cumbria

Fellside Farm ★★★
Self Catering
Bowness Lakeland Holidays
t (0161) 796 3896

The Peat House ★★★★
Self Catering
Contact: Steven Brierley
t (015395) 68172
e enquiries@peathouse.co.uk
w peathouse.co.uk

LYTHAM ST ANNES
Lancashire

The Chymes Holiday Flats
★★★ *Self Catering*
t (01253) 726942
e chymes@saint-annes.fsnet.co.uk

Merlewood Holiday Apartments ★★★
Self Catering
Contact: Mrs Sharon Iqbal
Merlewood Holiday Apartments
t (01253) 726082
w merlewoodapartments.co.uk

York House Holiday Apartments ★★★
Self Catering
Contact: Mrs Sykes
t (01253) 721701
e info@yorkhouse.gb.com
w yorkhouse.gb.com

MACCLESFIELD
Cheshire

Common Barn Cottages, Rainow ★★★★ *Self Catering*
Contact: Geoff & Rona Cooper
Common Barn Self-Catering Cottages
t (01625) 574878
e g-greengrass@hotmail.com
w cottages-with-a-view.co.uk

Holiday Cottages North East Cheshire ★★ *Self Catering*
Contact: Mr Longden
t (01625) 875137
e hcnecaccommodation@msn.com

Lower Pethills Farm Cottage, Sutton ★★★★ *Self Catering*
Contact: Mr & Mrs Greg Rowson
t (01260) 252410

Mellow Brook Cottage at Harrop Fold Farm ★★★★
Self Catering
Contact: Mrs Sue Stevenson
t (01625) 560085
e harropfold@hotmail.com
w harropfoldfarm.co.uk

Mill House Farm Cottage
★★★ *Self Catering*
Contact: Mrs Lynne Whittaker
Mill House Farm Cottage
t (01260) 226265
e lynne_whittaker@yahoo.co.uk
w geocities.com/farm_cottage

The Teachers Cottage ★★★
Self Catering
t (01260) 252674
e enquiries@peakcottages.com
w peakcottages.com

MANCHESTER
Greater Manchester

The Place Apartment Hotel, Piccadilly
Rating Applied For
Self Catering
t (0161) 778 7500
e emmaa@theplacehotel.com
w theplacehotel.com

Westview ★★★ *Self Catering*
Contact: Mr & Mrs Mr Clifford
Astley Gardens
t (01455) 284748
e rosalie.reeder@ukonline.co.uk

MANESTY
Cumbria

The Coppice ★★
Self Catering
Contact: Mr David Burton
Lakeland Cottage Holidays
t (01768) 776065
e info@lakelandcottages.co.uk

High Ground ★★★
Self Catering
Contact: Mr David Burton
Lakeland Cottage Holidays
t (01768) 776065
e info@lakelandcottages.co.uk

MARPLE
Greater Manchester

Top Lock Bungalow ★★
Self Catering
Contact: Mr & Mrs Allcard
t (0161) 427 5712

MARTINDALE
Cumbria

Townhead Farm ★★★
Self Catering
Contact: Mr John Serginson
The Lakeland Cottage Company
t 0870 442 5814
e john@lakelandcottageco.com
w lakelandcottageco.com

MARYPORT
Cumbria

Harbour Gates ★★★★
Self Catering
Contact: Peter Durbin
Cumbrian Cottages Ltd
t (01228) 599950
e enquiries@cumbrian-cottages.co.uk
w cumbrian-cottages.co.uk

Harbour Lights ★★★
Self Catering
Contact: Peter Durbin
Cumbrian Cottages Ltd
t (01228) 599950
e enquiries@cumbrian-cottages.co.uk
w cumbrian-cottages.co.uk

MATTERDALE END
Cumbria

Finkle Laithe ★★★★
Self Catering
Contact: Ms Sue Jackson
Heart of the Lakes
t (015394) 32321
e info@heartofthelakes.co.uk
w heartofthelakes.co.uk

MAULDS MEABURN
Cumbria

Chestnuts ★★★★
Self Catering
Contact: Annie Kindleysides
Meaburn Hill Farm House
t (01931) 715168
e kindleysides@btinternet.com
w cumbria-bed-and-breakfast.co.uk

Harrys Barn ★★★★
Self Catering
Contact: Mike Eden
t (01704) 220703
e harrysbarn@hotmail.com
w harrysbarn.co.uk

The Stable, Crosby Ravensworth ★★★★
Self Catering
Contact: Mrs Christine Jackson
t (01931) 715236

MELLOR
Greater Manchester

The Hayloft ★★ *Self Catering*
Contact: Mrs D Tuffin-Hines
Three Chimneys
t (0161) 449 7269

MELMERBY
Cumbria

Fellside Cottage ★★★★
Self Catering
Contact: Peter Durbin
Cumbrian Cottages Ltd
t (01228) 599950
e enquiries@cumbrian-cottages.co.uk
w cumbrian-cottages.co.uk

MIDDLETON
Cumbria

Northerdale, Southerdale and Mill Cottages
Rating Applied For
Self Catering
Contact: Richard & Sue Birtwistle
t (01524) 276500
e rsvpmillhouse@hotmail.com
w millhousecottages.co.uk

MIDDLEWICH
Cheshire

Forge Mill Farm Cottages
★★★–★★★★ *Self Catering*
Contact: Mrs Susan Moss
Forge Mill Farm
t (01270) 526204
e forgemill2@msn.com

MILBURN
Cumbria

Bramley Cottage ★★★★
Self Catering
Contact: Guy & Rose Heelis
t (01768) 361074
e guyheelis@aol.com
w uk-holiday-cottages.co.uk/bramley

Gullom Cottage ★★★
Self Catering
Contact: Peter Durbin
Cumbrian Cottages Ltd
t (01228) 599950
e enquiries@cumbrian-cottages.co.uk
w cumbrian-cottages.co.uk

High Slakes ★★★★
Self Catering
Contact: Mrs J Taylor
Low Howgill Farm
t (01768) 361595
e holidays@low-howgill.co.uk
w lowhowgill.f9.co.uk

MILLBECK
Cumbria

3 Millbeck Cottages ★★★★
Self Catering
Contact: Richard Watson
Millbeck Cottages
t (01438) 869286
e r.watson@bbwlaw.biz

Beck View ★★★★
Self Catering
Contact: Peter Durbin
Cumbrian Cottages Ltd
t (01228) 599950
e enquiries@cumbrian-cottages.co.uk
w cumbrian-cottages.co.uk

MILLOM
Cumbria

Duddon Villa ★★★★★
Self Catering
Contact: Jenny Brumby
t (01229) 775005
e mcmeekin1@btconnect.com
w duddon-villa.co.uk

MILLTHROP
Cumbria

Under Rigg
Rating Applied For
Self Catering
Contact: Peter Durbin
Cumbrian Cottages Ltd
t (01228) 599950
e enquiries@cumbrian-cottages.co.uk
w cumbrian-cottages.co.uk

MILNROW
Greater Manchester

Butterworth Hall ★★★★
Self Catering
Contact: Mrs Judith Hirst
t (01706) 882781
e judyhirst@btinternet.com
w springmill.co.uk

MILNTHORPE
Cumbria

Pickles Cottage ★★★
Self Catering
Contact: Angela Stubbs
t (01207) 528869

MOBBERLEY
Cheshire

5 The Cedars ★★★★
Self Catering
Contact: Ms Jenny Dawson
Interludes
t (01625) 599802

MOORHOUSE
Cumbria

Low Moor House ★★★★
Self Catering
Contact: Mr Ron Palmer
Low Moor House
t (01228) 575153
e info@lowmoorhouse.co.uk
w lowmoorhouse.co.uk

MORECAMBE
Lancashire

Eden Vale Luxury Holiday Flats ★★★ *Self Catering*
Contact: Mr John Coombs
t (01524) 415544

Northumberland House
★★-★★★ *Self Catering*
t (01524) 412039

St Ives and Rydal Mount ★
Self Catering
Contact: Mrs Holmes
t (01524) 411858

Sandown Holiday Flats ★★
Self Catering
Contact: Mr & Mrs Colin Matthews
t (01524) 410933

MORLAND
Cumbria

Crosbar Cottage ★★★
Self Catering
Contact: Georgina Perkins
t (01931) 716638
e jo@steppingoff.co.uk

Highgate Farm ★★★★
Self Catering
Contact: Peter Durbin
Cumbrian Cottages Ltd
t (01228) 599950
e enquiries@cumbrian-cottages.co.uk
w cumbrian-cottages.co.uk

MOTHERBY
Cumbria

Nettle How Cottage ★★★
Self Catering
Contact: Mr & Mrs Bamber
t (01768) 483544
e doreen@jims99.freeserve.co.uk

MUNGRISDALE
Cumbria

The Garth ★★★★
Self Catering
Contact: Mrs Susan Jackson
Heart of the Lakes
t (015394) 32321
e info@heartofthelakes.co.uk
w heartofthelakes.co.uk

Near Howe Cottages
Rating Applied For
Self Catering
Contact: Steve & Jill Woolley
Near Howe Hotel and Cottages
t (01768) 779678
e wswoolley@tiscali.co.uk
w nearhowe.co.uk

NADDLE
Cumbria

Brackenrigg ★★★★
Self Catering
Contact: Harry Marsland
t (01768) 772258
e info@brackenrigg.com
w brackenrigg.com

The Bungalow ★★★
Self Catering
Contact: Mrs Jane Nicholson
Causeway Foot Farm
t (01768) 772290
e jackie@causewayfoot.co.uk

NANTWICH
Cheshire

The Outlanes ★★★★
Self Catering
Contact: Mr & Mrs Robert & Andrea Parton
t (01270) 522284
e robert.parton@theoutlanes.com
w theoutlanes.com

Stoke Grange Farm Mews
★★★★ *Self Catering*
t (01270) 625525
e stokegrange@freeuk.com

NATLAND
Cumbria

Hawes Bank ★★★★
Self Catering
Contact: Peter Durbin
Cumbrian Cottages Ltd
t (01228) 599950
e enquiries@cumbrian-cottages.co.uk
w cumbrian-cottages.co.uk

NEAR SAWREY
Cumbria

Croft End Cottage ★★★★
Self Catering
Contact: Mr Peter Liddell
Lakelovers
t (015394) 88855
e bookings@lakelovers.co.uk
w lakelovers.co.uk

The Delft Suite ★★★★
Self Catering
Contact: Anne Gallagher
Hideaways
t (015394) 42435
e bookings@lakeland-hideaways.co.uk
w lakeland-hideaways.co.uk

Meadowcroft ★★★★
Self Catering
Contact: Mr John Serginson
The Lakeland Cottage Company
t 0870 442 5814
e john@lakelandcottageco.com
w lakelandcottageco.com

Smithy Cottage ★★★
Self Catering
Contact: Mr Paul Liddell
Lakelovers
t (015394) 88855
e bookings@lakelovers.co.uk
w lakelovers.co.uk

NENTHEAD
Cumbria

The Bothy (4313) ★★★★★
Self Catering
Contact: Ms Lorraine Kidd
t (01756) 790919
e lorraine@dales-holiday-cottages.com
w dales-holiday-cottages.com

The Stable & Keepers Cottage ★★★★-★★★★★
Self Catering
Contact: Ms Lorraine Kidd
Dales Holiday Cottages
t 0870 909 9500
e info@dales-holiday-cottages.com
w dalesholcot.com

NETHER KELLET
Lancashire

The Apartment ★★★
Self Catering
Contact: Mr Richardson
The Apartment
t (01524) 734969 & (01524) 736331

Ashlea Cottage ★★★★
Self Catering
Contact: Mrs Caroline Scarisbrick
t (01524) 563669

NEW HUTTON
Cumbria

Hollins Farm Barn ★★★★
Self Catering
Contact: Peter Durbin
Cumbrian Cottages Ltd
t (01228) 599950
e enquiries@cumbrian-cottages.co.uk
w cumbrian-cottages.co.uk

NEWBIGGIN-ON-LUNE
Cumbria

Green Bell View ★★★
Self Catering
Dales Hol Cot Ref: 2076
t (01756) 790919
e info@dalesholcot.com

Lock Leigh ★★★★
Self Catering
Contact: Ms Fiona Sheen
Dales Holiday Cottages
t 0870 909 9500
e fiona@dales-holiday-cottages.com
w dalesholcot.com

Pleasant & Green Bell View
★★★ *Self Catering*
Contact: Ms Fiona Sheen
Dales Holiday Cottages
t 0870 909 9500
e fiona@dales-holiday-cottages.com
w dalesholcot.com

The Tower House ★★★
Self Catering
Contact: Peter Durbin
Cumbrian Cottages Ltd
t (01228) 599950
e enquiries@cumbrian-cottages.co.uk
w cumbrian-cottages.co.uk

NEWBY
Cumbria

Midtown Cottage & Dairy Cottage ★★★★-★★★★★
Self Catering
Contact: Mrs M Brown
t (015395) 68102
e enquiries@goosemirecottages.co.uk
w members.aol.com/midtowncottages

NEWBY BRIDGE
Cumbria

Fellcroft Cottage ★★★★
Self Catering
Contact: Cath Hale
t (015395) 30316
e cath@fellcroft.fsnet.co.uk

Woodland Cottage ★★★★
Self Catering
Contact: Mr Newton
Newby Bridge Country Caravan Park
t (015395) 31030
e info@cumbriancaravans.co.uk
w cumbriancaravans.co.uk

NEWLAND
Cumbria

Curlew Rise and Heron Beck ★★★★ *Self Catering*
Contact: Mr John Serginson
The Lakeland Cottage Company
t (015395) 30024
e john@lakelandcottageco.com

NEWLANDS
Cumbria

Aikin ★★★ *Self Catering*
Contact: Peter Durbin
Cumbrian Cottages Ltd
t (01228) 599950
e enquiries@cumbrian-cottages.co.uk
w cumbrian-cottages.co.uk

Bawd Hall ★★★★★
Self Catering
Contact: Alison Evens
High Mosser Gate
t (01442) 825855
e alison@bawdhall.co.uk
w bawdhall.co.uk

Fell Cottage ★★★
Self Catering
Contact: Mr David Burton
Lakeland Cottage Holidays
t (01768) 776065
e info@lakelandcottages.co.uk

Gill Brow Cottage ★★★
Self Catering
Contact: Anne Wilson
Gill Brow Farm
t (01768) 778270
e wilson_gillbrow@hotmail.com
w gillbrow-keswick.co.uk

The Oaks Apartment ★★★
Self Catering
Contact: Peter Durbin
Cumbrian Cottages Ltd
t (01228) 599950
e enquiries@cumbrian-cottages.co.uk
w cumbrian-cottages.co.uk

NEWTON-IN-BOWLAND
Lancashire

Stonefold Holiday Cottage
Rating Applied For
Self Catering
Contact: Mrs Helen Blanc
Stonefold Farm
t 07966 582834
w stonefoldholidaycottage.co.uk

NEWTON REIGNY
Cumbria

Blencathra Barn & Saddleback Barn ★★★★
Self Catering
Contact: Peter Durbin
Cumbrian Cottages Ltd
t (01228) 599950
e enquiries@cumbrian-cottages.co.uk
w cumbrian-cottages.co.uk

Saddleback Barn ★★★
Self Catering
Contact: Peter Durbin
Cumbrian Cottages Ltd
t (01228) 599950
e enquiries@cumbrian-cottages.co.uk
w cumbrian-cottages.co.uk

NIBTHWAITE
Cumbria

Fell View ★★★ *Self Catering*
Contact: Mrs Susan Jackson
Heart of the Lakes
t (015394) 32321
e info@heartofthelakes.co.uk
w heartofthelakes.co.uk

The Hovel ★★★
Self Catering
Contact: Mr John Serginson
The Lakeland Cottage Company
t (015395) 30024
e john@lakelandcottageco.com

Nibthwaite Grange Studio ★★★★ *Self Catering*
Contact: Mr John Serginson
The Lakeland Cottage Company
t (015395) 30024
e john@lakelandcottageco.com

The Peat House ★★★★★
Self Catering
Contact: Mr John Serginson
The Lakeland Cottage Company
t (015395) 30024
e john@lakelandcottageco.com

NOMANS HEATH
Cheshire

Dairyman's Cottage ★★★★
Self Catering
Contact: Sally-Ann Chesters
Millmoor Farm
t (01948) 820304
e dave-sal@millmoor-farm.fsnet.co.uk

OLDHAM
Greater Manchester

Clifton Cottage ★★★ *Self Catering & Serviced Apartments*
t (01457) 872098
e ced117@aol.com
w saddleworth-vacations.co.uk/index.php

ORMSKIRK
Lancashire

Coachman's Cottage ★★★★ *Self Catering*
t (01695) 722023
e mark@hudson4067.freeserve.co.uk
w coachmanscottage.com

Tristrams Farm Holiday Cottages ★★★ *Self Catering*
Contact: Mr David Swift
t (01704) 840323

ORTON
Cumbria

Chapel Beck Cottage ★★★★ *Self Catering*
Contact: Leonne Hodgson
t (015396) 24379
e enquiries@chapelbeck.co.uk
w chapelbeck.co.uk

OUSBY
Cumbria

Hole Bank ★★★★
Self Catering
Contact: Mrs Lesley McVey
t (01768) 892247

OUTGATE
Cumbria

Borwick Fold Cottages ★★★★ *Self Catering*
Contact: Mr & Mrs Johnson
t (015394) 36742
e borwickfoldcottages@firenet.uk.net
w borwickfold.com

Claife Cottage ★★★★
Self Catering
Lakelovers
t (015394) 88855
e bookings@lakelovers.co.uk
w lakelovers.co.uk

Grizedale Cottage ★★★★
Self Catering
Contact: Mr Paul Liddell
Lakelovers
t (015394) 88855
e bookings@lakelovers.co.uk
w lakelovers.co.uk

Honey Pot Cottage (Currier) ★★★★ *Self Catering*
Contact: Mr Philip Johnston
The Coppermines & Coniston Lake Cottages
t (015394) 41765
e info@coppermines.co.uk
w coppermines.co.uk

Honister Cottage ★★★★
Self Catering
Lakelovers
t (015394) 88855
e bookings@lakelovers.co.uk
w lakelovers.co.uk

Kirkstone Cottage ★★★★
Self Catering
Lakelovers
t (015394) 88855
e bookings@lakelovers.co.uk
w lakelovers.co.uk

Latterbarrow ★★★★
Self Catering
Contact: Mrs Vivien Bass
Wheelwrights Holiday Cottages
t (015394) 37635
e enquiries@wheelwrights.com

Moss Beck ★★★★★
Self Catering
Contact: Mr John Serginson
The Lakeland Cottage Company
t (015395) 30024
e john@lakelandcottageco.com

Peacock ★★★ *Self Catering*
Contact: Mrs Susan Jackson
Heart of the Lakes
t (015394) 32321
e info@heartofthelakes.co.uk
w heartofthelakes.co.uk

Pepper Cottage ★★★
Self Catering
Contact: Mr Paul Liddell
Lakelovers
t (015394) 88855
e bookings@lakelovers.co.uk
w lakelovers.co.uk

OUTHGILL
Cumbria

Ing Hill Barn Apartments ★★★★ *Self Catering*
Country Holidays ref:14815
t (01282) 445096

The Lodge ★★★
Self Catering
Contact: Peter Durbin
Cumbrian Cottages Ltd
t (01228) 599950
e enquiries@cumbrian-cottages.co.uk
w cumbrian-cottages.co.uk

OVER KELLET
Lancashire

Lime Tree Cottage ★★
Self Catering
t (01524) 732165

PAPCASTLE
Cumbria

The Loft ★★★★
Self Catering
Contact: Peter Durbin
Cumbrian Cottages Ltd
t (01228) 599950
e enquiries@cumbrian-cottages.co.uk
w cumbrian-cottages.co.uk

PARK GATE
Cumbria

Line Cottage ★★★
Self Catering
Contact: Mr Philip Johnston
The Coppermines & Coniston Lake Cottages
t (015394) 41765
e info@coppermines.co.uk
w coppermines.co.uk

Look out for establishments participating in the Walkers and Cyclists Welcome Schemes

PATTERDALE
Cumbria

Bleaze End ★★★★
Self Catering
Contact: Susan Jackson
Heart of the Lakes
t (015394) 32321
e info@heartofthelakes.co.uk
w heartofthelakes.co.uk

Broad How ★★★★
Self Catering
Contact: Dr & Mrs Wynne-Willson
28 Garland Way
t (0121) 475 6508
e williamww@aol.com
w broad-how.co.uk

Deepdale Hall Cottage
★★★★ *Self Catering*
Contact: Chris Brown
Deepdale Hall Farmhouse
t (01768) 482369
e brown@deepdalehall.freeserve.co.uk
w deepdalehall.co.uk

Deer How Cotttages
★★★★★ *Self Catering*
Contact: Donna Rawling
Scottwood Developments
t 07963 342856
w deerhow.co.uk

Elm How, Cruck Barn & Eagle Cottage
★★★-★★★★ *Self Catering*
Contact: Miss M Scott
Matson Ground Estate Co Ltd
t (015394) 45756
e info@matsonground.co.uk
w matsonground.co.uk

Fellside Farm Cottage ★★★
Self Catering
Contact: Susan Jackson
Heart of the Lakes
t (015394) 32321
e info@heartofthelakes.co.uk
w heartofthelakes.co.uk

Hartsop Fold Holiday Lodges ★★★ *Self Catering*
Contact: Mrs L Hennedy
t (015396) 22069
e bookings@hartsop-fold.co.uk
w hartsop-fold.co.uk

Lower Grisedale Lodge
★★★ *Self Catering*
Contact: Christine Kenyon
t (01768) 482155
e johnvarley@patterda.globalnet.co.uk
w grisedalelodge.co.uk

PENRITH
Cumbria

Bankside ★★★★
Self Catering
Contact: Peter Durbin
Cumbrian Cottages Ltd
t (01228) 599950
e enquiries@cumbrian-cottages.co.uk
w cumbrian-cottages.co.uk

Barn End & Barn Croft
★★★★ *Self Catering*
Contact: Brenda Walton
t (01768) 486376
e brenda@waltoncottages.fsnet.co.uk
w barnend-cottages.co.uk

Daisy Cottage & Lavender Cottage ★★★★ *Self Catering*
Contact: David Burton
Lakeland Cottage Holidays
t (01768) 776065
e info@lakelandcottages.co.uk
w lakelandcottages.co.uk

Elind ★★★★ *Self Catering*
Contact: Mrs Susan Jackson
Heart of the Lakes
t (015394) 32321
e info@heartofthelakes.co.uk
w heartofthelakes.co.uk

Mell Fell ★★★★★
Self Catering
Contact: Ms Sue Jackson
Heart of the Lakes
t (015394) 32321
e info@heartofthelakes.co.uk
w heartofthelakes.co.uk

Oak View Cottage ★★★★
Self Catering & Serviced Apartments
Contact: Ms Dearling
t (01931) 713121
e oakviewcottage@aol.com
w oakviewcottage.co.uk

Skirwith Hall Cottage & Smithy Cottage ★★★★
Self Catering
Contact: Laura Wilson
Skirwith Hall Cottages
t (01768) 88241
e stay@skirwithhallcottages.co.uk
w skirwithhallcottages.co.uk

Smithy Cottage Penrith
Rating Applied For
Self Catering
Contact: Peter Durbin
Cumbrian Cottages Ltd
t (01228) 599950
e enquiries@cumbrian-cottages.co.uk
w cumbrian-cottages.co.uk

Stonefold ★★★★
Self Catering
Contact: Gill Harrington
Stonefold Cottages
t (01768) 866383
e gill@stonefold.co.uk
w stonefold.co.uk

Wetheral Cottages ★★★★
Self Catering
Contact: Mr J Lowry
t (01768) 898779
e wetheralcottages@btopenworld.com
w wetheralcottages.co.uk

PENRUDDOCK
Cumbria

Beckses Cottage ★★★★
Self Catering
Contact: Peter Durbin
Cumbrian Cottages Ltd
t (01228) 599950
e enquiries@cumbrian-cottages.co.uk
w cumbrian-cottages.co.uk

Green Barn ★★★
Self Catering
Contact: Peter Durbin
Cumbrian Cottages Ltd
t (01228) 599950
e enquiries@cumbrian-cottages.co.uk
w cumbrian-cottages.co.uk

Low Garth Cottage ★★★★
Self Catering
Contact: Ms Fiona Sheen
Dales Holiday Cottages
t 0870 909 9500
e info@dales-holiday-cottages.com
w dalesholcot.com

Nab End ★★★★
Self Catering
Contact: Mr David Burton
Lakeland Cottage Holidays
t (01768) 776065
e info@lakelandcottages.co.uk

Penrobin ★★★ *Self Catering*
Heart of the Lakes
t (015394) 32321
e info@heartofthelakes.co.uk
w heartofthelakes.co.uk

Poppy Cottage ★★★★
Self Catering
Contact: Ms Jo Burton
Lakeland Cottage Holidays
t (01768) 776065
e info@lakelandcottages.co.uk

PENTON
Cumbria

Liddel Park Country Cottages ★★★ *Self Catering*
Contact: Brian Wicklow
t (01228) 577440
e holiday@liddelpark.co.uk
w liddelpark.co.uk

POOLEY BRIDGE
Cumbria

Barton Hall Farm Holiday Cottages ★★★★
Self Catering
Barton Hall FarmHoliday Cottages
t (01768) 486034

Beauthorn Coach House
★★★ *Self Catering*
Contact: Paul Durbin
Cumbrian Cottages Ltd
t (01228) 599950
e enquiries@cumbrian-cottages.co.uk
w cumbrian-cottages.co.uk

Blacksmiths Cottage ★★★★
Self Catering
Contact: Peter Durbin
Cumbrian Cottages Ltd
t (01228) 599950
e enquiries@cumbrian-cottages.co.uk
w cumbrian-cottages.co.uk

Fell Croft ★★★ *Self Catering*
Contact: Peter Durbin
Cumbrian Cottages Ltd
t (01228) 599950
e enquiries@cumbrian-cottages.co.uk
w cumbrian-cottages.co.uk

Finkle Cottage ★★★
Self Catering
Contact: Peter Durbin
Cumbrian Cottages Ltd
t (01228) 599950
e enquiries@cumbrian-cottages.co.uk
w cumbrian-cottages.co.uk

High Winder Cottages
★★★★ *Self Catering*
Contact: R A & L M Moss
t (01768) 486997
e mosses@highwinderhouse.co.uk
w highwindercottages.co.uk

Primrose Cottage ★★★★
Self Catering
Contact: Peter Durbin
Cumbrian Cottages Ltd
t (01228) 599950
e enquiries@cumbrian-cottages.co.uk
w cumbrian-cottages.co.uk

Windy Nook ★★★
Self Catering
Contact: Peter Durbin
Cumbrian Cottages Ltd
t (01228) 599950
e enquiries@cumbrian-cottages.co.uk
w cumbrian-cottages.co.uk

Winn's Cottage ★★★★
Self Catering
Contact: Mrs C Fortescue
t (01768) 486304

PORTINSCALE
Cumbria

3 Harney Peak ★★★★
Self Catering
Contact: Peter Durbin
Cumbrian Cottages Ltd
t (01228) 599950
e enquiries@cumbrian-cottages.co.uk
w cumbrian-cottages.co.uk

5 Harney Peak ★★★
Self Catering
Contact: Peter Durbin
Cumbrian Cottages Ltd
t (01228) 599950
e enquiries@cumbrian-cottages.co.uk
w cumbrian-cottages.co.uk

The Beeches ★★★★
Self Catering
Contact: Judith Sanderson
t 077090 89982
e judith5tc@aol.com

The Beeches ★★★★
Self Catering
Contact: Peter Durbin
Cumbrian Cottages Ltd
t (01228) 599950
e enquiries@cumbrian-cottages.co.uk
w cumbrian-cottages.co.uk

Borrowdale Apartment
★★★ *Self Catering*
Contact: Julie Fearnes
Keswick Cottages
t (01768) 773895
e info@keswickcottages.co.uk
w keswickcottages.co.uk

Grizedale View ★★★
Self Catering
Contact: Peter Durbin
Cumbrian Cottages Ltd
t (01228) 599950
e enquiries@cumbrian-cottages.co.uk
w cumbrian-cottages.co.uk

Harney Peak ★★★★
Self Catering
Contact: Peter Durbin
Cumbrian Cottages Ltd
t (01228) 599950
e enquiries@cumbrian-cottages.co.uk
w cumbrian-cottages.co.uk

Ingley Cottage ★★★
Self Catering
Contact: Ms Sue Jackson
Heart of the Lakes
t (015394) 32321
e info@heartofthelakes.co.uk
w heartofthelakes.co.uk

Jasmine Cottage ★★★
Self Catering
Contact: Peter Durbin
Cumbrian Cottages Ltd
t (01228) 599950
e enquiries@cumbrian-cottages.co.uk
w cumbrian-cottages.co.uk

Middle Howe ★★★★
Self Catering
Contact: Peter Durbin
Cumbrian Cottages Ltd
t (01228) 599950
e enquiries@cumbrian-cottages.co.uk
w cumbrian-cottages.co.uk

Osprey Heights ★★★★
Self Catering
Contact: Peter Durbin
Cumbrian Cottages Ltd
t (01228) 599950
e enquiries@cumbrian-cottages.co.uk
w cumbrian-cottages.co.uk

Portinscale House
Rating Applied For
Self Catering
Contact: Mr David Burton
Lakeland Holiday Cottages
t (01768) 776065
e info@lakelandcottages.co.uk
w lakelandcottages.co.uk

Rickerby Cottage ★★★
Self Catering
Contact: Peter Durbin
Cumbrian Cottages Ltd
t (01228) 599950
e enquiries@cumbrian-cottages.co.uk
w cumbrian-cottages.co.uk

Roseworth ★★★★
Self Catering
Contact: Peter Durbin
Cumbrian Cottages Ltd
t (01228) 599950
e enquiries@cumbrian-cottages.co.uk
w cumbrian-cottages.co.uk

Smithy Cottage ★★★
Self Catering
Contact: Peter Durbin
Cumbrian Cottages Ltd
t (01228) 599950
e enquiries@cumbrian-cottages.co.uk
w cumbrian-cottages.co.uk

Stable Cottage ★★★
Self Catering
Contact: Margaret Pope
t (01768) 775161
e pscale@btinternet.com

Watendlath ★★★★
Self Catering
Contact: Peter Durbin
Cumbrian Cottages Ltd
t (01228) 599950
e enquiries@cumbrian-cottages.co.uk
w cumbrian-cottages.co.uk

Whitegates ★★★
Self Catering
Contact: Peter Durbin
Cumbrian Cottages Ltd
t (01228) 599950
e enquiries@cumbrian-cottages.co.uk
w cumbrian-cottages.co.uk

Woodside
Rating Applied For
Self Catering
Contact: Paul Carter
t (01768) 772702
e paulineandrew40@hotmail.com
w keswick.org

POULTON-LE-FYLDE
Lancashire

Hardhorn Breaks
Rating Applied For
Self Catering
Contact: Mr Nick Pawson
t (01253) 890422
e anna@rosewood81.freeserve.co.uk

Swans Rest Holiday Cottages ★★★★
Self Catering
Contact: Mrs Irene O'Connor
t (01253) 886617
e swansrest@btconnect.com
w swansrest.co.uk

PULL WOODS
Cumbria

Swallows Nest ★★★
Self Catering
Contact: Mr Philip Johnston
The Coppermines & Coniston Lake Cottages
t (015394) 41765
e info@coppermines.co.uk
w coppermines.co.uk

Woodside ★★★★
Self Catering
Lakelovers
t (015394) 88855
e bookings@lakelovers.co.uk
w lakelovers.co.uk

QUERNMORE
Lancashire

Lodge View Cottages
★★★★ *Self Catering*
Contact: Mr David Gardner
t (01524) 63109
e djkagardner@ukgateway.net

Shepherds Barn ★★★★★
Self Catering
Contact: Mrs Anne Longton
t (01524) 36867
e longton@leeend.fsnet.co.uk

RAINOW
Cheshire

The Coach House ★★★★★
Self Catering
t (01625) 424220
e info@kerridgeendholidaycottages.co.uk
w kerridgeendholidaycottages.co.uk

RAVENSTONEDALE
Cumbria

Moss Cottages ★★★
Self Catering
Contact: George & Doreen Moynihan
t (015396) 23316
e moymoss@btinternet.com
w cumbrianholidaycottages.co.uk

Oaklea Bungalow ★★★★
Self Catering
Contact: June Ellis
Oaklea
t (015396) 23415
e enquiries@westview-cumbria.co.uk
w westview-cumbria.co.uk

REAGILL
Cumbria

Yew Tree Farm ★★★★★
Self Catering
Contact: Peter Durbin
Cumbrian Cottages Ltd
t (01228) 599950
e enquiries@cumbrian-cottages.co.uk
w cumbrian-cottages.co.uk

REDMAIN
Cumbria

Huddlestone Cottage and The Hayloft ★★★★
Self Catering
Contact: Christine Neale
Country Ayres
t (01900) 825695
e hudcot@lakesnw.co.uk
w lakesnw.co.uk/hudcot

RIMINGTON
Lancashire

Raikes Barn ★★★★
Self Catering
Contact: Mrs Robinson
t (01200) 445287

Tewit and Badger Cottages
★★★★ *Self Catering*
Contact: Mrs Anne Smith
t (01200) 445598

ROCHDALE
Greater Manchester

Pennine Cottages, Wardle
★★★ *Self Catering*
Contact: Mrs Joy Mitchell
2 Pennine Cottages
t (01706) 379632
w hometown.aol.co.uk/penninecottage/myhomepage/business.html/

ROGER GROUND
Cumbria

Lydia's Loft ★★★★
Self Catering
Contact: Mr Paul Liddell
Lakelovers
t (015394) 88855
e bookings@lakelovers.co.uk
w lakelovers.co.uk

Roger Ground House
★★★★ *Self Catering*
Contact: Mr Paul Liddell
Lakelovers
t (015394) 88855
e bookings@lakelovers.co.uk
w lakelovers.co.uk

ROSSENDALE
Lancashire

The Cottage, Cronkshaw Fold Farm
Rating Applied For
Self Catering
Contact: Ms Joy McCarthy
t (01706) 218614
e sjm@cronkshaw.co.uk
w cronkshaw.co.uk

The Old Stables, Tippett Farm ★★★★ *Self Catering*
t (01706) 224741
e wendy.davison@btopenworld.com

ROSTHWAITE
Cumbria

Borrowdale Self Catering Holidays ★★★ *Self Catering*
Contact: Peter & Nicola Davis-Merry
Borrowdale Self-Catering Holidays
t (01768) 777356
e info@kilnhow.com
w kilnhow.com

Castle Howe ★★★★
Self Catering
Contact: Peter Durbin
Cumbrian Cottages Ltd
t (01228) 599950
e enquiries@cumbrian-cottages.co.uk
w cumbrian-cottages.co.uk

Clare's Cottage ★★
Self Catering
t (01204) 668681
e dms@clarescottage.com

High Knott ★★★★
Self Catering
Contact: Peter Durbin
Cumbrian Cottages Ltd
t (01228) 599950
e enquiries@cumbrian-cottages.co.uk
w cumbrian-cottages.co.uk

Larch Cottage ★★★
Self Catering
Contact: Mr David Burton
Lakeland Cottage Holidays
t (01768) 776065
e info@lakelandcottages.co.uk

Lobstone ★★★ *Self Catering*
Contact: Peter Durbin
Cumbrian Cottages Ltd
t (01228) 599950
e enquiries@cumbrian-cottages.co.uk
w cumbrian-cottages.co.uk

Nokka ★★★ *Self Catering*
Contact: Peter Durbin
Cumbrian Cottages Ltd
t (01228) 599950
e enquiries@cumbrian-cottages.co.uk
w cumbrian-cottages.co.uk

Thwaite How ★★★
Self Catering
Contact: Mr & Mrs Brewerton
t (01455) 290168
e cematproperties@hotmail.com

RUCKCROFT
Cumbria

Ruckcroft Cottage ★★★
Self Catering
Contact: Peter Durbin
Cumbrian Cottages Ltd
t (01228) 599950
e enquiries@cumbrian-cottages.co.uk
w cumbrian-cottages.co.uk

RUSLAND
Cumbria

Archways ★★★ *Self Catering*
Contact: Peter Durbin
Cumbrian Cottages Ltd
t (01228) 599950
e enquiries@cumbrian-cottages.co.uk
w cumbrian-cottages.co.uk

Wood View & Stable End
★★★★ *Self Catering*
Contact: Mr John Serginson
The Lakeland Cottage Company
t (015395) 30024
e john@lakelandcottageco.com

RYDAL
Cumbria

1 Hart Head Barn ★★★★
Self Catering
Contact: Mrs Vivien Bass
Wheelwrights Holiday Cottages
t (015394) 37635
e enquiries@wheelwrights.com

Daffodils ★★★ *Self Catering*
Contact: Mrs Susan Jackson
Heart of the Lakes
t (015394) 32321
e info@heartofthelakes.co.uk
w heartofthelakes.co.uk

Fox Cottage ★★★★
Self Catering
Contact: Susan Jackson
Heart of the Lakes
t (015394) 32321
e info@heartofthelakes.co.uk
w heartofthelakes.co.uk

Hall Bank Cottage – Rydal Estate ★★★ *Self Catering*
Contact: Janet Horne
Carter Jonas
t (01539) 814902
e janet.horne@carterjonas.co.uk

Hart Head Barn ★★★★
Self Catering
Contact: Mrs Susan Jackson
Heart of the Lakes
t (015394) 32321
e info@heartofthelakes.co.uk
w heartofthelakes.co.uk

Rydal Mount Cottage
★★★★ *Self Catering*
Contact: Susan Jackson
Heart of the Lakes
t (015394) 32321
e info@heartofthelakes.co.uk
w heartofthelakes.co.uk

Strawberry Cottage ★★★
Self Catering
Contact: Ms Sue Jackson
Heart of the Lakes
t (015394) 32321
e info@heartofthelakes.co.uk
w heartofthelakes.co.uk

SABDEN
Lancashire

Kingfisher Cottage ★★★
Self Catering
Contact: Mr Gordon Greenwood
Greenbank Farm
t (01254) 823064
e gordon.greenwood@virgin.net

ST BEES
Cumbria

Tarn Flatt Cottage ★★★★
Self Catering
Contact: Janice Telfer
Tarn Flatt Cottage
t (01946) 692162
e stay@tarnflattfarm.co.uk
w tarnflattfarm.co.uk

ST JOHNS-IN-THE-VALE
Cumbria

Lowthwaite Cottage ★★★★
Self Catering
Contact: Peter Durbin
Cumbrian Cottages Ltd
t (01228) 599950
e enquiries@cumbrian-cottages.co.uk
w cumbrian-cottages.co.uk

The Old Hayloft ★★★
Self Catering
Contact: Mrs Sarah Chaplin-Brice
t (01768) 779242
e lbe@sjitv.freeserve.co.uk

The Studio ★★★★
Self Catering
Contact: Mr Green
t (01768) 779666
e selfcatering@keswickholidays.co.uk
w keswickholidays.co.uk

SALFORD
Greater Manchester

30 The Gallery ★★★
Self Catering
Contact: Kash Ijaz
t (020) 738 8993
e info@kash.co.uk

SANDWITH
Cumbria

Quarry Cottage ★★★★
Self Catering
Contact: Peter Durbin
Cumbrian Cottages Ltd
t (01228) 599950
e enquiries@cumbrian-cottages.co.uk
w cumbrian-cottages.co.uk

SATTERTHWAITE
Cumbria

Brackenghyll ★★
Self Catering
Contact: Peter Durbin
Cumbrian Cottages Ltd
t (01228) 599950
e enquiries@cumbrian-cottages.co.uk
w cumbrian-cottages.co.uk

Church Cottage ★★★★
Self Catering
Contact: Susan Jackson
Heart of the Lakes
t (015394) 32321
e info@heartofthelakes.co.uk
w heartofthelakes.co.uk

Deer Leap ★★★★
Self Catering
Contact: Peter Durbin
Cumbrian Cottages Ltd
t (01228) 599950
e enquiries@cumbrian-cottages.co.uk
w cumbrian-cottages.co.uk

Force Mill ★★★ *Self Catering*
Contact: Peter Durbin
Cumbrian Cottages Ltd
t (01228) 599950
e enquiries@cumbrian-cottages.co.uk
w cumbrian-cottages.co.uk

Hawkrigg House ★★★★
Self Catering
Contact: Mrs Susan Jackson
Heart of the Lakes
t (015394) 32321
e info@heartofthelakes.co.uk
w heartofthelakes.co.uk

Tanwood Barn ★★★★
Self Catering
Contact: Susan Jackson
Heart of the Lakes
t (015394) 32321
e info@heartofthelakes.co.uk
w heartofthelakes.co.uk

Town End Barn ★★★★
Self Catering
Contact: Peter Durbin
Cumbrian Cottages Ltd
t (01228) 599950
e enquiries@cumbrian-cottages.co.uk
w cumbrian-cottages.co.uk

Wain Garth ★★★
Self Catering
Contact: Peter Durbin
Cumbrian Cottages Ltd
t (01228) 599950
e enquiries@cumbrian-cottages.co.uk
w cumbrian-cottages.co.uk

Winnowing Barn ★★★★
Self Catering
Contact: Peter Durbin
Cumbrian Cottages Ltd
t (01228) 599950
e enquiries@cumbrian-cottages.co.uk
w cumbrian-cottages.co.uk

SAWREY
Cumbria

Anvil Cottage ★★★★
Self Catering
Contact: Peter Durbin
Cumbrian Cottages Ltd
t (01228) 599950
e enquiries@cumbrian-cottages.co.uk
w cumbrian-cottages.co.uk

Apple Tree Cottage ★★★
Self Catering
Contact: Mr Paul Liddell
Lakelovers
t (015394) 88855
e bookings@lakelovers.co.uk
w lakelovers.co.uk

Derwentwater Cottage
★★★ *Self Catering*
Contact: Anne Gallagher
Hideaways
t (015394) 42435
e bookings@lakeland-hideaways.co.uk
w lakeland-hideaways.co.uk

The Forge ★★★ *Self Catering*
Lakelovers
t (015394) 88855
e bookings@lakelovers.co.uk
w lakelovers.co.uk

Fountain Cottage ★★★
Self Catering
Contact: Mr Paul Liddell
Lakelovers
t (015394) 88855
e bookings@lakelovers.co.uk
w lakelovers.co.uk

Lakefield ★★★ *Self Catering*
Contact: John Taylor
t (015394) 36635
e lakefieldacom@aol.com
w lakefield-lakedistrict.co.uk

Meadowside ★★★★
Self Catering
Contact: Mr Paul Liddell
Lakelovers
t (015394) 88855
e bookings@lakelovers.co.uk
w lakelovers.co.uk

Sawrey Stables ★★★★★
Self Catering
Contact: Anne Gallagher
Hideaways
t (015394) 42435
e bookings@lakeland-hideaways.co.uk
w lakeland-hideaways.co.uk

Sunnyside Cottage ★★★★
Self Catering
Contact: Mr John Serginson
The Lakeland Cottage Company
t (015395) 30024
e john@lakelandcottageco.com

Top Garden Suite ★★★★
Self Catering
Contact: Mrs Susan Jackson
Heart of the Lakes
t (015394) 32321
e info@heartofthelakes.co.uk
w heartofthelakes.co.uk

Town End Cottage ★★★
Self Catering
Lakelovers
t (015394) 88855
e bookings@lakelovers.co.uk
w lakelovers.co.uk

West Vale Cottage ★★★★
Self Catering
Contact: Glynn & Dee Pennington
West Vale Country House & Restaurant
t (015394) 42817
e enquiries@westvalecountryhouse.co.uk
w westvalecountryhouse.co.uk

SCARISBRICK
Lancashire

Shamrock Cottage ★★★★
Self Catering
t (01704) 880272

SEATHWAITE
Cumbria

2 High Moss House ★★★
Self Catering
Contact: Helen Barnard
t (0141) 423 1060
e helen@ainsdale.force9.co.uk

Cockley Beck Cottage ★★★
Self Catering
Contact: Mrs Vivien Bass
Wheelwrights Holiday Cottages
t (015394) 37635

Hall Dunnerdale Farm Holiday Cottages
★★★-★★★★ *Self Catering*
Contact: Ms Anne Brockbank
t (01229) 889281
e anne@hall-dunnerdale.co.uk

Rose Cottage ★★★★
Self Catering
Contact: Mr John Serginson
The Lakeland Cottage Company
t (015395) 30024
e john@lakelandcottageco.com

Tarn Foot Cottage ★★★
Self Catering
Contact: Mr Philip Johnston
The Coppermines & Coniston Lake Cottages
t (015394) 41765
e info@coppermines.co.uk
w coppermines.co.uk

SEATOLLER Cumbria

The Barn ★★★★
Self Catering
Contact: Peter Durbin
Cumbrian Cottages Ltd
t (01228) 599950
e enquiries@cumbrian-cottages.co.uk
w cumbrian-cottages.co.uk

Bell Crags ★★★ *Self Catering*
Contact: Mr David Burton
Lakeland Cottage Holidays
t (01768) 776065
e info@lakelandcottages.co.uk

Brasscam ★★★★
Self Catering
Contact: Peter Durbin
Cumbrian Cottages Ltd
t (01228) 599950
e enquiries@cumbrian-cottages.co.uk
w cumbrian-cottages.co.uk

Ghyllside ★★★★★
Self Catering
Contact: Peter Durbin
Cumbrian Cottages Ltd
t (01228) 599960
e enquiries@cumbrian-cottages.co.uk
w ghyllside.com

Hause Gill ★★★
Self Catering
Contact: Mr David Burton
Lakeland Cottage Holidays
t (01768) 776065
e info@lakelandcottages.co.uk

High Stile ★★★ *Self Catering*
Contact: Mr David Burton
Lakeland Cottage Holidays
t (01768) 776065
e info@lakelandcottages.co.uk

Littlebeck ★★★★
Self Catering
Contact: Peter Durbin
Cumbrian Cottages Ltd
t (01228) 599950
e enquiries@cumbrian-cottages.co.uk
w cumbrian-cottages.co.uk

SEBERGHAM Cumbria

Stockwell Hall Cottage
★★★★★ *Self Catering*
Contact: Peter Durbin
Cumbrian Cottages Ltd
t (01228) 599950
e enquiries@cumbrian-cottages.co.uk
w cumbrian-cottages.co.uk

SEDBERGH Cumbria

4 Railway Cottages ★★★
Self Catering
Contact: Wendy Mills
4 Railway Cottages
t (01702) 478846
e trewen@clara.co.uk
w dalescottages.com

Carriers Cottage ★★★
Self Catering
Contact: Mr & Mrs Ellis
t (015396) 20566

Cobble Country Holidays
★★★-★★★★ *Self Catering*
Contact: Mrs R. Elizabeth Close
t (015396) 21000
e cobblesedbergh@yahoo.co.uk
w cobblecountry.co.uk

Fell House ★★★★
Self Catering
Contact: Stephen Wickham
t (01277) 652746
e steve@higround.co.uk
w higround.co.uk

Ingmire Lodge ★★★★★
Self Catering
Contact: Tracy Fletcher
t 07930 481009
w ingmirelodge.co.uk

Low Foulsyke Cottage ★★★
Self Catering
Contact: Emma Middleton
t (015396) 25308
e emmalmiddleton@hotmail.com

Merlin Cottage ★★★★
Self Catering
Contact: Christine Linley
t (01539) 738677
e christine@merlincottage.com
w merlincottage.com

The Mount ★★★★
Self Catering
Contact: Suzan Sedgwick
W R M & S L Sedgwick
t (015396) 20252
e sedgwick665@btinternet.com
w holidaysedbergh.co.uk

Randall Hill Cottage ★★★
Self Catering
Contact: Ms Fiona Sheen
Dales Holiday Cottages
t 0870 909 9500
e fiona@dales-holiday-cottages.com
w dalesholcot.com

Thwaite Cottage ★★★★
Self Catering
Contact: Mrs D Parker
t (015396) 20493
e thwaitefarm@btinternet.com

Whernside View ★★★★
Self Catering
Contact: Peter Durbin
Cumbrian Cottages Ltd
t (01228) 599950
e enquiries@cumbrian-cottages.co.uk
w cumbrian-cottages.co.uk

SEDGWICK Cumbria

Coach House ★★★★
Self Catering
Contact: Peter Durbin
Cumbrian Cottages Ltd
t (01228) 599950
e enquiries@cumbrian-cottages.co.uk
w cumbrian-cottages.co.uk

High House Barn ★★★★★
Self Catering
Contact: Peter Durbin
Cumbrian Cottages Ltd
t (01228) 599950
e enquiries@cumbrian-cottages.co.uk
w cumbrian-cottages.co.uk

Woodside ★★★★
Self Catering
Contact: Peter Durbin
Cumbrian Cottages Ltd
t (01228) 599950
e enquiries@cumbrian-cottages.co.uk
w cumbrian-cottages.co.uk

SETMURTHY Cumbria

Derwent View ★★★
Self Catering
Contact: Peter Durbin
Cumbrian Cottages Ltd
t (01228) 599950
e enquiries@cumbrian-cottages.co.uk
w cumbrian-cottages.co.uk

SILECROFT Cumbria

Lowsha Cottage ★★★
Self Catering
Dales Hol Cot Ref:3126
t (01756) 799821
e info@dalesholcot.com

SILLOTH Cumbria

Glencaple ★★★★
Self Catering
Contact: Peter Durbin
Cumbrian Cottages Ltd
t (01228) 599950
e enquiries@cumbrian-cottages.co.uk
w cumbrian-cottages.co.uk

Silloth Love Shack ★★
Self Catering
Contact: John Reid
The Love Shack
t (01900) 823110
e info@sillothloveshack.co.uk
w sillothloveshack.co.uk

SILVERDALE Lancashire

The Old Cottage at Wolf House ★★★★-★★★★★
Self Catering
t (01524) 701405
e enquiries@wolfhousecottages.co.uk
w wolfhousecottages.co.uk

Old Waterslack Farm Cottages and Caravans
★★★ *Self Catering*
t (01524) 701108

Pheasant Field ★★★
Self Catering
Sykes Cottages Ref: 684
t (01244) 345700
e info@sykescottages.co.uk

The Stables at Silverdale
★★★★ *Self Catering*
Contact: Mrs Cathy Ranford
t (01524) 702121
e stables@lindethhouse.co.uk
w lindethhouse.co.uk

Swallows End ★★★
Self Catering
Contact: Ms Fiona Moody
Dales Holiday Cottages
t 0870 909 9500
e info@dales-holiday-cottages.com
w dalesholcot.com

SKELWITH BRIDGE Cumbria

3 Neaum Crag Court ★★★★
Self Catering
Contact: Mrs Vivien Bass
Wheelwrights Holiday Cottages
t (015394) 37635
e enquiries@wheelwrights.com
w wheelwrights.com

Brathay View ★★★★
Self Catering
Contact: Susan Jackson
Heart of the Lakes
t (015394) 32321
e info@heartofthelakes.co.uk
w heartofthelakes.co.uk

Brow Foot ★★★★
Self Catering
Contact: Mrs Susan Jackson
Heart of the Lakes
t (015394) 32321
e info@heartofthelakes.co.uk
w heartofthelakes.co.uk

Carr Crag Cottage ★★★★
Self Catering
Contact: Alistair MacDonald
MacDonald Greenwood Property
t (015394) 37635
e enquiries@wheelwrights.com
w lakelandretreat.co.uk

Carr Crag Heights ★★★★
Self Catering
Contact: Ms Vivien Bass
Wheelwrights Holiday Cottages
t (015394) 37635
e enquiries@wheelwrights.com
w wheelwrights.com

The Coach House ★★★★
Self Catering
Contact: Susan Jackson
Heart of the Lakes
t (015394) 32321
e info@heartofthelakes.co.uk
w heartofthelakes.co.uk

Ghyll Pool – Neaum Crag ★★★ *Self Catering*
Contact: Peter Durbin
Cumbrian Cottages Ltd
t (01228) 599950
e enquiries@cumbrian-cottages.co.uk
w cumbrian-cottages.co.uk

Heatherlea ★★★
Self Catering
Contact: Mrs Vivien Bass
Wheelwrights Holiday Cottages
t (015394) 37635
e enquiries@wheelwrights.com

Hunters Moon ★★★
Self Catering
Contact: Peter Durbin
Cumbrian Cottages Ltd
t (01228) 599950
e enquiries@cumbrian-cottages.co.uk
w cumbrian-cottages.co.uk

Ivy Cottage ★★★★
Self Catering
Contact: Peter Durbin
Cumbrian Cottages Ltd
t (01228) 599950
e enquiries@cumbrian-cottages.co.uk
w cumbrian-cottages.co.uk

Little Garth ★★★★★
Self Catering
Contact: Mrs Susan Jackson
Heart of the Lakes
t (015394) 32321
e info@heartofthelakes.co.uk
w heartofthelakes.co.uk

Merlins ★★★★ *Self Catering*
Contact: Susan Jackson
Heart of the Lakes
t (015394) 32321
e info@heartofthelakes.co.uk
w heartofthelakes.co.uk

Mockerkin Tarn – Neaum Crag ★★★ *Self Catering*
Contact: Peter Durbin
Cumbrian Cottages Ltd
t (01228) 599950
e enquiries@cumbrian-cottages.co.uk
w cumbrian-cottages.co.uk

Oak Dene ★★★★
Self Catering
Contact: Susan Jackson
Heart of the Lakes
t (015394) 32321
e info@heartofthelakes.co.uk
w heartofthelakes.co.uk

Ramblers Rest ★★★
Self Catering
Lakelovers
t (015394) 88855
e bookings@lakelovers.co.uk
w lakelovers.co.uk

Riverbank Cottage ★★★★
Self Catering
Contact: Mrs Vivien Bass
Wheelwrights Holiday Cottages
t (015394) 37635
e enquiries@wheelwrights.com

Silverthwaite Cottage ★★★
Self Catering
Contact: Ms Sue Jackson
Heart of the Lakes
t (015394) 32321
e info@heartofthelakes.co.uk
w heartofthelakes.co.uk

Spindle Coppice ★★★
Self Catering
Lakelovers
t (015394) 88855
e bookings@lakelovers.co.uk
w lakelovers.co.uk

Tarn Hows ★★ *Self Catering*
Contact: Mr Paul Liddell
Lakelovers
t (015394) 88855
e bookings@lakelovers.co.uk
w lakelovers.co.uk

Tarn Moss – Neaum Crag ★★★ *Self Catering*
Contact: Peter Durbin
Cumbrian Cottages Ltd
t (01228) 599950
e enquiries@cumbrian-cottages.co.uk
w cumbrian-cottages.co.uk

Tiplog ★★★ *Self Catering*
Contact: Mrs Susan Jackson
Heart of the Lakes
t (015394) 32321
e info@heartofthelakes.co.uk
w heartofthelakes.co.uk

Wordsworth – Neaum Crag ★★★ *Self Catering*
Contact: Susan Jackson
Heart of the Lakes
t (015394) 32321
e info@heartofthelakes.co.uk
w heartofthelakes.co.uk

SKELWITH FOLD
Cumbria

Crop Howe ★★★★★
Self Catering
Contact: Mrs Susan Jackson
Heart of the Lakes
t (015394) 32321
e info@heartofthelakes.co.uk
w heartofthelakes.co.uk

Rivendell ★★★ *Self Catering*
Contact: Susan Jackson
Heart of the Lakes
t (015394) 32321
e info@heartofthelakes.co.uk
w heartofthelakes.co.uk

Swallows House ★★★★★
Self Catering
Contact: Mrs Vivien Bass
Wheelwrights Holiday Cottages
t (015394) 37635
e enquiries@wheelwrights.com

SLAIDBURN
Lancashire

Burn Fell View ★★★
Self Catering
Red Rose Cottages
t (01200) 446654
e info@redrosecottages.co.uk

Laythams Farm Cottages ★★★ *Self Catering*
Contact: Mr Ian Roger Driver
t (01200) 446454
e iandriver@nildram.co.uk
w laythamsfarmcottages.co.uk

The Olde Stables ★★★★
Self Catering
Contact: Mrs Margaret Robinson
t (01200) 446240

SMARDALE
Cumbria

Leases ★★★ *Self Catering*
Contact: Mrs Christina Galloway
t (01768) 371198
e leasesgal@aol.com

SOUTHPORT
Merseyside

45 Alexandra Road ★★
Self Catering
t (01704) 870137

Barford House Apartments ★★★-★★★★ *Self Catering*
Contact: Mr Graham Watson
t (01704) 548119
e graham@barfordhouse.co.uk

Beaucliffe Holiday Flats ★★★ *Self Catering*
Contact: Mrs Linda Lewis
t (01704) 537207
e linda@beaucliffeholidayflats.co.uk

Carlmerl Apartments ★★★
Self Catering
Contact: Mr Harrison Clive
t (01704) 538758
e carlmerl@bushinternet.com

Castle Mews ★★★
Self Catering
t (01704) 548119
e graham@barfordhouse.co.uk

Clare ★★★ *Self Catering*
t (01704) 538778

Den-Rae Holiday Flats ★★
Self Catering
Contact: Mr & Mrs Erich & Romana Warscher
t (01704) 530918

Gilmount Holiday Flat ★★
Self Catering
Contact: Mr Paul Harrison
t (01704) 542150
e paul@gilmount.freeserve.co.uk

Holiday House ★★★
Self Catering
t (01704) 25872

Martin Lane Farmhouse Holiday Cottages ★★★★
Self Catering
Contact: Mrs Stubbs
Martin Lane Farmhouse Holiday Cottages
t (01704) 893527
e mlfhc@btinternet.com
w martinlanefarmhouse.btinternet.co.uk

Portland House ★★★★
Self Catering
Contact: Ms Sandra Koller
t (01704) 510509
e portland.house@rapid.co.uk

Promenade Apartments ★★★★ *Self Catering*
t (01704) 541719

Sandcroft Holidy Flats ★
Self Catering
Contact: Mr Ralph Best
t (01704) 537497

Sandy Brook Farm ★★★
Self Catering
Contact: Mr Core
Sandy Brook Farm
t (01704) 880337 & 07719 468712
e sandybrookfarm@lycos.co.uk
w sandybrookfarm.co.uk

Southport Holiday Apartments ★★-★★★
Self Catering
Contact: Mrs Susan Lea
t (01704) 530792
e susan-lea@btconnect.com

SOUTHWAITE
Cumbria

Serendipity Cottage ★★★
Self Catering
Dales Hol Cot Rf:2814
t (01756) 799821
e info@dalesholcot.com

SPARK BRIDGE
Cumbria

Bluebell Cottage ★★★★
Self Catering
Contact: Mr Philip Johnston
The Coppermines & Coniston Lake Cottages
t (015394) 41765
e info@coppermines.co.uk
w coppermines.co.uk

Riverside Cottage ★★★
Self Catering
Contact: Peter Durbin
Cumbrian Cottages Ltd
t (01228) 599950
e enquiries@cumbrian-cottages.co.uk
w cumbrian-cottages.co.uk

Summer Hill Holidays ★★★
Self Catering
Contact: Mrs R Campbell
t (01229) 861510
e rosemary@summerhill.co.uk
w summerhill.co.uk

The Turners Cottage ★★★
Self Catering
Contact: Mr Philip Johnston
The Coppermines & Coniston Lake Cottages
t (015394) 41765
e info@coppermines.co.uk
w coppermines.co.uk

STAFFIELD
Cumbria

Raven House ★★★★
Self Catering
t (01228) 599960
e enquiries@cumbrian-cottages.co.uk
w cumbrian-cottages.co.uk

Staffield Hall Country Retreats ★★★★★
Self Catering
Contact: Michael & Marie Lawson
Staffield Hall
t (01995) 61574
e information@staffieldhall.co.uk
w staffieldhall.co.uk

STAINTON
Cumbria

The Cottage at Andrew House ★★★ *Self Catering*
Dales Hol Cot Ref:2098
t (01756) 799821
e info@dalesholcot.com

Dacre Garth ★★★★
Self Catering
Contact: Lindsay Taylor
t (01793) 780422
e dacregarth@onetel.com
w dacregarth.co.uk

Fairy Glenn ★★★
Self Catering
Contact: Peter Durbin
Cumbrian Cottages Ltd
t (01228) 599950
e enquiries@cumbrian-cottages.co.uk
w cumbrian-cottages.co.uk

STAIR
Cumbria

Clairgarth ★★★ *Self Catering*
Contact: Peter Durbin
Cumbrian Cottages Ltd
t (01228) 599950
e enquiries@cumbrian-cottages.co.uk
w cumbrian-cottages.co.uk

Grisedale Cottage
Rating Applied For
Self Catering
Contact: Mr David Burton
Lakeland Cottage Holidays
t (01768) 776065
e info@lakelandcottages.co.uk
w lakelandcottages.co.uk

Stair Mill ★★★ *Self Catering*
Contact: Jacqueline Williams
t (01768) 778333
e peterwilliams@stairmill.com
w stairmill.com

Swinside Cottage ★★★★
Self Catering
Contact: Ms Jo Burton
Lakeland Cottage Hollidays
t (01768) 776065
e Info@lakelandcottages.co.uk

STANK
Cumbria

Glenfield Farm Holidays ★★★-★★★★ *Self Catering*
Contact: Linda Caine
t (01229) 826969
e linda@gcaine.plus.com
w southlakescottages.co.uk

STAPLETON
Cumbria

Drove Cottage ★★★
Self Catering
Contact: Kenneth & Anne Hope
Drove Inn
t (01697) 748202
e droveinn@hotmail.com

STAVELEY
Cumbria

Ashleigh ★★★★
Self Catering
Contact: Mr John Serginson
The Lakeland Cottage Company
t (015395) 30024
e john@lakelandcottageco.com

Avondale ★★★ *Self Catering*
Contact: Helen Hughes
t (015394) 45713
e enquiries@avondale.uk.net
w avondale.uk.net

Beck View ★★★★
Self Catering
Contact: Peter Durbin
Cumbrian Cottages Ltd
t (01228) 599950
e enquiries@cumbrian-cottages.co.uk
w cumbrian-cottages.co.uk

Bobbin Cottage ★★★
Self Catering
Dales Hol Cot Ref:2284
t (01756) 799821
e info@dalesholcot.com

Brunt Knott Farm Holiday Cottages ★★★ *Self Catering*
Contact: William & Margaret Beck
Brunt Knott Farm Holiday Cottages
t (01539) 821030
e margaret@bruntknott.demon.co.uk
w bruntknott.demon.co.uk

The Chapel ★★★
Self Catering
Contact: Peter Durbin
Cumbrian Cottages Ltd
t (01228) 599950
e enquiries@cumbrian-cottages.co.uk
w cumbrian-cottages.co.uk

Headswood Cottage ★★★★
Self Catering
Lakelovers
t (015394) 88855
e bookings@lakelovers.co.uk
w lakelovers.co.uk

Heywood ★★★ *Self Catering*
Contact: Peter Durbin
Cumbrian Cottages Ltd
t (01228) 599950
e enquiries@cumbrian-cottages.co.uk
w cumbrian-cottages.co.uk

Littlewood Cottages ★★★
Self Catering
Contact: Ann Noble
t (01539) 821474
e annnoble@ktdinternet.com
w littlewoodcottages.co.uk

Reston Mill ★★★★
Self Catering
Contact: Peter Durbin
Cumbrian Cottages Ltd
t (01228) 599950
e enquiries@cumbrian-cottages.co.uk
w cumbrian-cottages.co.uk

Staveley House Apartment ★★★★ *Self Catering*
Contact: Peter Durbin
Cumbrian Cottages Ltd
t (01228) 599950
e enquiries@cumbrian-cottages.co.uk
w cumbrian-cottages.co.uk

Weasel Cottage ★★★
Self Catering
Contact: Peter Durbin
Cumbrian Cottages Ltd
t (01228) 599950
e enquiries@cumbrian-cottages.co.uk
w cumbrian-cottages.co.uk

STAVELEY-IN-CARTMEL
Cumbria

April Cottage ★★★
Self Catering
Contact: Peter Durbin
Cumbrian Cottages Ltd
t (01228) 599950
e enquiries@cumbrian-cottages.co.uk
w cumbrian-cottages.co.uk

Croft Cottage ★★★
Self Catering
Contact: Mr Paul Liddell
Lakelovers
t (015394) 88855
e bookings@lakelovers.co.uk
w lakelovers.co.uk

STONYHURST
Lancashire

Alden Cottage ★★★★
Self Catering
Contact: Mrs Brenda Carpenter
t (01254) 826468
e carpenter@aldencottagef9.co.uk
w fp.aldencottage.f9.co.uk

TABLEY
Cheshire

2 Waterless Brook Cottages ★★★ *Self Catering*
Contact: Roger Thorp
Waterless Brook Cottages
t (01565) 734159
e rthorp@tinyworld.co.uk

TALLENTIRE
Cumbria

2 Bush Cottages ★★★★
Self Catering
Contact: Maggie Redfern
Bush Cottage
t (01946) 812091
e maggie@redfernp.freeserve.co.uk
w bushcottage.com

TARVIN
Cheshire

Cheese Makers Cottage ★★★ *Self Catering*
Cross Lanes Farm
t (01829) 740439
e sherwins.agricon@virgin.net

TATHAM
Lancashire

Swallow Cottage ★★★★
Self Catering
Contact: Gaynor Leach
Moorhead Barn
t (01524) 222599
e claphamtyke@hotmail.com

THORNLEY
Lancashire

Loudview Barn ★★★★
Self Catering
Contact: Mr & Mrs Oliver & Ness Starkey
Loudview Barn
t (01995) 61476
e loudview@ic24.net

Thornley Hall ★★★ *Self Catering & Serviced Apartments*
Contact: Mrs Airey
t (01995) 61243

THORNTHWAITE
Cumbria

7 Ladstock Hall ★★★★★
Self Catering
Contact: Peter Durbin
Cumbrian Cottages Ltd
t (01228) 599950
e enquiries@cumbrian-cottages.co.uk
w cumbrian-cottages.co.uk

Barf Cottage ★★★
Self Catering
Contact: Mrs Susan Jackson
Heart of the Lakes
t (015394) 32321
e info@heartofthelakes.co.uk
w heartofthelakes.co.uk

Beck View ★★★★
Self Catering
Contact: Peter Durbin
Cumbrian Cottages Ltd
t (01228) 599950
e enquiries@cumbrian-cottages.co.uk
w cumbrian-cottages.co.uk

Comb Beck ★★★
Self Catering
Contact: Jacqui Davies
t (01768) 778582
e jacquidmoss@aol.com
w lakedistrict-cottage.com

Cygnet Cottage ★★★★
Self Catering
Contact: Mrs Susan Jackson
Heart of the Lakes
t (015394) 32321
e info@heartofthelakes.co.uk
w heartofthelakes.co.uk

Hallgarth Barn ★★★★
Self Catering
Contact: Peter Durbin
Cumbrian Cottages Ltd
t (01228) 599950
e enquiries@cumbrian-cottages.co.uk
w cumbrian-cottages.co.uk

Harriet's Hideaway ★★★★
Self Catering
Contact: Mr David Miller
Lyndhurst
t (01914) 880549
e dm81@blueyonder.co.uk
w dm81.pwp.blueyonder.co.uk

Look out for establishments participating in the National Accessible Scheme 

Jasmine Cottage ★★★★
Self Catering
Contact: Kate Danchin
Holly Bank & Jasmine Cottages
t (01900) 822001
e enquiries@hollybankcottage.co.uk
w hollybankcottage.co.uk

Joan's Cottage ★★★★
Self Catering
Contact: Peter Durbin
Cumbrian Cottages Ltd
t (01228) 599950
e enquiries@cumbrian-cottages.co.uk
w cumbrian-cottages.co.uk

The Larches
Rating Applied For
Self Catering
Contact: Mr David Burton
Lakeland Cottage Holidays
t (01768) 776065
e info@lakelandcottages.co.uk
w lakelandcottages.co.uk

Oak Lea ★★★ *Self Catering*
Contact: Peter Durbin
Cumbrian Cottages Ltd
t (01228) 599950
e enquiries@cumbrian-cottages.co.uk
w cumbrian-cottages.co.uk

The Old School House ★★★
Self Catering
Contact: Peter Durbin
Cumbrian Cottages Ltd
t (01228) 599950
e enquiries@cumbrian-cottages.co.uk
w cumbrian-cottages.co.uk

Seat Howe ★★★
Self Catering
Contact: Mrs Dorothy Bell
t (01768) 778371

Swallows' Nest ★★★★
Self Catering
Contact: Mrs Susan Jackson
Heart of the Lakes
t (015394) 32321
e info@heartofthelakes.co.uk
w http://website.lineone.net/~beckstones

Talcomb ★★★ *Self Catering*
Contact: Howard King
Talcomb & Ramblers Roost
t 07973 420179
e hk.developments@virgin.net
w hkdevelopmentslakes.co.uk

Thwaite Hill Barn ★★★
Self Catering
Contact: Peter Durbin
Cumbrian Cottages Ltd
t (01228) 599950
e enquiries@cumbrian-cottages.co.uk
w cumbrian-cottages.co.uk

Thwaite Hill Cottage ★★★
Self Catering
Contact: Mr David Burton
Lakeland Cottage Holidays
t (01768) 776065
e info@lakelandcottages.co.uk

Willow ★★★★★
Self Catering
Contact: Ms Sue Jackson
Heart of the Lakes
t (015394) 32321
e info@heartofthelakes.co.uk
w heartofthelakes.co.uk

Woodside Cottage ★★★★
Self Catering
Contact: Peter Durbin
Cumbrian Cottages Ltd
t (01228) 599950
e enquiries@cumbrian-cottages.co.uk
w cumbrian-cottages.co.uk

THORNTON
Lancashire

Highcliffe Holiday Apartments ★★★
Self Catering
Contact: Ms Jeanette Dowber
t (01253) 854673
e info@highcliffeapartments.co.uk
w highcliffeapartments.co.uk

Seahawk Holiday Apartments ★★-★★★
Self Catering
Contact: Mr & Mrs Ball
t (01253) 823957
e micar.seahawk@gmail.com
w seahawk-apartments.co.uk

THRELKELD
Cumbria

Blease Barn ★★★★
Self Catering
Contact: Peter Durbin
Cumbrian Cottages Ltd
t (01228) 599950
e enquiries@cumbrian-cottages.co.uk
w cumbrian-cottages.co.uk

Blease Cottage ★★★★
Self Catering
Contact: Peter Durbin
Cumbrian Cottages Ltd
t (01228) 599950
e enquiries@cumbrian-cottages.co.uk
w cumbrian-cottages.co.uk

Blencathra Centre ★★★
Self Catering
Contact: Tim Foster
Blencathra Centre
t (01768) 779601
e enquiries.bl@field-studies-council.org

The Bungalows Country Guest House S/C ★★★
Self Catering
Contact: Paul Sunley
The Bungalows Country Guest House
t (01768) 779679
e paulsunley@msn.com
w thebungalows.co.uk

Chapmere
Rating Applied For
Self Catering
Contact: Mr David Burton
Lakeland Cottage Holidays
t (01768) 776065
e info@lakelandcottages.co.uk
w lakelandcottages.co.uk

Corner Cottage
Rating Applied For
Self Catering
Contact: Mrs J Taberner
t (01768) 780691
e josie.chris@virgin.net
w cornercottagekeswick.co.uk

Cropple How ★★★
Self Catering
Contact: Peter Durbin
Cumbrian Cottages Ltd
t (01228) 599950
e enquiries@cumbrian-cottages.co.uk
w cumbrian-cottages.co.uk

Fell View ★★★ *Self Catering*
Contact: Mr Clive Sykes
Sykes Cottages
t (01244) 345700
e info@sykescottages.co.uk
w sykescottages.co.uk

Heather View ★★★
Self Catering
Contact: Peter Durbin
Cumbrian Cottages Ltd
t (01228) 599950
e enquiries@cumbrian-cottages.co.uk
w cumbrian-cottages.co.uk

Kiln How Cottage ★★★★
Self Catering
Contact: Peter Durbin
Cumbrian Cottages Ltd
t (01228) 599950
e enquiries@cumbrian-cottages.co.uk
w cumbrian-cottages.co.uk

Latcrag Cottage and Caravan ★★★★
Self Catering
Contact: Mrs Benson
t (01768) 779256

Nightingale Cottage ★★★
Self Catering
Contact: Ms Sue Jackson
Heart of the Lakes
t (015394) 32321
e info@heartofthelakes.co.uk
w heartofthelakes.co.uk

The Old Manse Barn ★★★
Self Catering
Contact: Mrs L Deadman
t (01768) 779270
e jon@deadman.freeserve.co.uk
w deadman.freeserve.co.uk

The Old School House ★★★★ *Self Catering*
Contact: Lucy Swarbrick
t (0161) 928 6290
e info@cottageinthrelkeld.co.uk
w theoldschoolhousethrelkeld.co.uk

Scales View Cottages ★★★
Self Catering
Contact: Peter Durbin
Cumbrian Cottages Ltd
t (01228) 599950
e enquiries@cumbrian-cottages.co.uk
w cumbrian-cottages.co.uk

Sunnyside
Rating Applied For
Self Catering
Contact: Mr David Burton
Lakeland Cottage Holidays
t (01768) 776065
e info@lakelandcottages.co.uk
w lakelandcottages.co.uk

Townhead Barn ★★★
Self Catering
Contact: Mr David Burton
Lakeland Cottage Holidays
t (01768) 776065
e info@lakelandcottages.co.uk

Townhead Byre ★★★
Self Catering
Contact: Mr Burton
t (01768) 776065

White Pike ★★★
Self Catering
Contact: Peter Durbin
Cumbrian Cottages Ltd
t (01228) 599950
e enquiries@cumbrian-cottages.co.uk
w cumbrian-cottages.co.uk

THURSTONFIELD
Cumbria

The Tranquil Otter, Thurstonfield ★★★★-★★★★★
Self Catering
Contact: Richard & Wendy Wise
The Tranquil Otter Ltd
t (01228) 576661
e info@thetranquilotter.co.uk
w thetranquilotter.co.uk

TIRRIL
Cumbria

Tirril Farm Cottages ★★★★
Self Catering
Contact: David Owens
Tirril Farm Cottages
t (01768) 864767
e enquiries@tirrilfarmcottages.co.uk
w tirrilfarmcottages.co.uk

TORVER
Cumbria

Brigg House ★★★★
Self Catering
Contact: John Serginson
The Lakeland Cottage Company
t 0870 442 5814
e john@lakelandcottageco.com

Brocklebank Ground Cottages Old Pottery, Old Stable, Old Dairy
★★★-★★★★ *Self Catering*
Contact: Mr Philip Johnston
The Coppermines & Coniston Lake Cottages
t (015394) 41765
e info@coppermines.co.uk
w coppermines.co.uk

Ellice Howe ★★★★
Self Catering
Contact: Mr Paul Liddell
Lakelovers
t (015394) 88855
e bookings@lakelovers.co.uk
w lakelovers.co.uk

High Park Cottage ★★★★
Self Catering
Contact: Mr Philip Johnston
The Coppermines & Coniston Lake Cottages
t (015394) 41765
e info@coppermines.co.uk
w coppermines.co.uk

Scarr Head Cottage ★★★★
Self Catering
Contact: Peter Durbin
Cumbrian Cottages Ltd
t (01228) 599950
e enquiries@cumbrian-cottages.co.uk
w cumbrian-cottages.co.uk

Station House & Station Cottage ★★★ *Self Catering*
Contact: Mr Philip Johnston
The Coppermines & Coniston Lake Cottages
t (015394) 41765
e info@coppermines.co.uk
w coppermines.co.uk

Sunny Bank Mill ★★★
Self Catering
Contact: Claire Wildsmith
Sunny Bank Mill
t (015394) 47474
e lakescene@fayrergarden.com
w sunnybankmill.com

TOSSIDE
Lancashire

Primrose Cottage, Jenny Wren, Wagtail, Swallows, Lower Gill Farm ★★★★
Self Catering
t (01756) 700510
w holidaycotts.co.uk

TRAWDEN
Lancashire

Far Wanless Farm Stable Cottage
Rating Applied For
Self Catering
Contact: Mrs V.M or Paul Johnson
t (01282) 867514

TROUTBECK
Cumbria

1 and 2 Butt Hill Cottage ★★★-★★★★ *Self Catering*
Contact: Mr Paul Liddell
Lakelovers
t (015394) 88855
e bookings@lakelovers.co.uk
w lakelovers.co.uk

Barn Cottage ★★★
Self Catering
Contact: Peter Durbin
Cumbrian Cottages Ltd
t (01228) 599950
e enquiries@cumbrian-cottages.co.uk
w cumbrian-cottages.co.uk

Betty's Cottage ★★★★
Self Catering
Heart of the Lakes
t (015394) 32321
e info@heartofthelakes.co.uk
w heartofthelakes.co.uk

Fell Cottage ★★★★
Self Catering
Contact: Mr Paul Liddell
Lakelovers
t (015394) 88855
e bookings@lakelovers.co.uk
w lakelovers.co.uk

Fell Top Lodge ★★★★
Self Catering
Contact: Peter Durbin
Cumbrian Cottages Ltd
t (01228) 599950
e enquiries@cumbrian-cottages.co.uk
w cumbrian-cottages.co.uk

Glenside ★★★ *Self Catering*
Contact: Susan Jackson
Heart of the Lakes
t (015394) 32321
e info@heartofthelakes.co.uk
w heartofthelakes.co.uk

Granary Cottage ★★★
Self Catering
Contact: Peter Durbin
Cumbrian Cottages Ltd
t (01228) 599950
e enquiries@cumbrian-cottages.co.uk
w cumbrian-cottages.co.uk

High Fold ★★★ *Self Catering*
Contact: Susan Jackson
Heart of the Lakes
t (015394) 32321
e info@heartofthelakes.co.uk
w heartofthelakes.co.uk

Holbeck Ghyll Lodge ★★★★ *Self Catering*
Contact: Maggie Kaye
t (01484) 684605
e maggie@holbecklodge.com
w holbecklodge.com

Ivy Cottage ★★★
Self Catering
Contact: Mr Paul Liddell
Lakelovers
t (015394) 88855
e bookings@lakelovers.co.uk
w lakelovers.co.uk

Knotts Cottage ★★★
Self Catering
Contact: Susan Jackson
Heart of the Lakes
t (015394) 32321
e info@heartofthelakes.co.uk
w heartofthelakes.co.uk

Knotts Farmhouse ★★★
Self Catering
Contact: Susan Jackson
Heart of the Lakes
t (015394) 32321
e info@heartofthelakes.co.uk
w heartofthelakes.co.uk

Long Mire Yeat ★★★
Self Catering
Contact: Susan Jackson
Heart of the Lakes
t (015394) 32321
e info@heartofthelakes.co.uk
w heartofthelakes.co.uk

Low House & The Studio ★★★★ *Self Catering*
Contact: Eileen Dale
t (01768) 779388
e jon.dale1@virgin.net
w holidaycottages-lakedistrict.co.uk

Myley Ghyll ★★★★★
Self Catering
Lakelovers
t (015394) 88855
e bookings@lakelovers.co.uk
w lakelovers.co.uk

Old Coach House ★★★★
Self Catering
Contact: Mr Ben Price
Wheelwrights Holiday Cottages
t (015394) 37635
e enquiries@wheelwrights.com

Orchard Cottage ★★★★
Self Catering
Contact: Mr Paul Liddell
Lakelovers
t (015394) 88855
e bookings@lakelovers.co.uk
w lakelovers.co.uk

Riverside Farmhouse & Cottage ★★★★ *Self Catering*
Contact: Peter Durbin
Cumbrian Cottages Ltd
t (01228) 599950
e enquiries@cumbrian-cottages.co.uk
w cumbrian-cottages.co.uk

South View ★★★
Self Catering
Contact: Peter Durbin
Cumbrian Cottages Ltd
t (01228) 599950
e enquiries@cumbrian-cottages.co.uk
w cumbrian-cottages.co.uk

Stamp Howe ★★★★
Self Catering
Contact: Susan Jackson
Heart of the Lakes
t (015394) 32321
e info@heartofthelakes.co.uk
w heartofthelakes.co.uk

Station House ★★★★
Self Catering
Contact: Peter Durbin
Cumbrian Cottages Ltd
t (01228) 599950
e enquiries@cumbrian-cottages.co.uk
w cumbrian-cottages.co.uk

Storeythwaite ★★★★
Self Catering
Contact: Susan Jackson
Heart of the Lakes
t (015394) 32321
e info@heartofthelakes.co.uk
w heartofthelakes.co.uk

Syke Villa ★★★ *Self Catering*
Contact: Mr Paul Liddell
Lakelovers
t (015394) 88855
e bookings@lakelovers.co.uk
w lakelovers.co.uk

Troutbeck Mews ★★★★
Self Catering
Contact: Mr & Mrs Bowers
t (01768) 483635
e enquiries@troutbeck-inn.com
w troutbeck-inn.com

Wee Fell Cottage ★★★★
Self Catering
Contact: Mr Paul Liddell
Lakelovers
t (015394) 88855
e bookings@lakelovers.co.uk
w lakelovers.co.uk

Wetherlam ★★★
Self Catering
Contact: Susan Jackson
Heart of the Lakes
t (015394) 32321
e info@heartofthelakes.co.uk
w heartofthelakes.co.uk

TROUTBECK BRIDGE
Cumbria

Barn Cottage ★★★
Self Catering
Contact: Peter Durbin
Cumbrian Cottages Ltd
t (01228) 599950
e enquiries@cumbrian-cottages.co.uk
w cumbrian-cottages.co.uk

Beckside Cottage ★★★
Self Catering
Contact: Peter Durbin
Cumbrian Cottages Ltd
t (01228) 599950
e enquiries@cumbrian-cottages.co.uk
w cumbrian-cottages.co.uk

Briery Lodge ★★★★
Self Catering
Contact: Susan Jackson
Heart of the Lakes
t (015394) 32321
e info@heartofthelakes.co.uk
w heartofthelakes.co.uk

Claife Holme ★★★★
Self Catering
Contact: Peter Durbin
Cumbrian Cottages Ltd
t (01228) 599950
e enquiries@cumbrian-cottages.co.uk
w cumbrian-cottages.co.uk

Cregary ★★★ *Self Catering*
Contact: Peter Durbin
Cumbrian Cottages Ltd
t (01228) 599950
e enquiries@cumbrian-cottages.co.uk
w cumbrian-cottages.co.uk

Groom Cottage ★★★★
Self Catering
Contact: Peter Durbin
Cumbrian Cottages Ltd
t (01228) 599950
e enquiries@cumbrian-cottages.co.uk
w cumbrian-cottages.co.uk

Howarth Cottage ★★★
Self Catering
Contact: Peter Durbin
Cumbrian Cottages Ltd
t (01228) 599950
e enquiries@cumbrian-cottages.co.uk
w cumbrian-cottages.co.uk

Lowther Cottage ★★★
Self Catering
Contact: Mrs Susan Jackson
Heart of the Lakes
t (015394) 32321
e info@heartofthelakes.co.uk
w heartofthelakes.co.uk

School Cottage ★★★★
Self Catering
Contact: Susan Jackson
Heart of the Lakes
t (015394) 32321
e info@heartofthelakes.co.uk
w heartofthelakes.co.uk

ULDALE
Cumbria

Coach House ★★★
Self Catering
Contact: Peter Durbin
Cumbrian Cottages Ltd
t (01228) 599950
e enquiries@cumbrian-cottages.co.uk
w cumbrian-cottages.co.uk

Coach House and Groom Cottage ★★★ *Self Catering*
Contact: Peter Durbin
Cumbrian Cottages Ltd
t (01228) 599950
e enquiries@cumbrian-cottages.co.uk
w cumbrian-cottages.co.uk

Knaifan Cottage ★★★
Self Catering
Contact: Peter Durbin
Cumbrian Cottages Ltd
t (01228) 599950
e enquiries@cumbrian-cottages.co.uk
w cumbrian-cottages.co.uk

The Mews ★★★★
Self Catering
Contact: Peter Durbin
Cumbrian Cottages Ltd
t (01228) 599950
e enquiries@cumbrian-cottages.co.uk
w cumbrian-cottages.co.uk

The Old School House ★★★
Self Catering
Contact: Peter Durbin
Cumbrian Cottages Ltd
t (01228) 599950
e enquiries@cumbrian-cottages.co.uk
w cumbrian-cottages.co.uk

ULLOCK
Cumbria

Treetops Holiday Apartment
★★★★ *Self Catering*
Contact: Marion Wilson
t (01946) 861772
e wilson@americafield.fsnet.co.uk

ULLSWATER
Cumbria

Beckside Cottage ★★★★
Self Catering
Contact: Mrs Caroline Ivinson
A & C Ivinson
t (01768) 486239
e ivinson_becksidefarm@hotmail.com

Cherry Holm Bungalow
★★★★ *Self Catering*
Contact: Mrs S Sheard
t (01943) 830766

Lakefield ★★★★
Self Catering
Contact: Susan Jackson
Heart of the Lakes
t (015394) 32321
e info@heartofthelakes.co.uk
w heartofthelakes.co.uk

Land Ends Cabins ★★★
Self Catering
Contact: Mrs B Murphy
Land Ends Country Lodge
t (01768) 486438
e infolandends@btinternet.com
w landends.co.uk

Low Wood View ★★★
Self Catering
Contact: Mrs J Wear
t (01768) 482396
w ullswater-steamers.co.uk/lowwoodview

Patterdale Hall Estate, Glenridding ★★-★★★
Self Catering
Contact: Sue Kay
Patterdale Hall Estate Ltd.
t (01768) 482308
e mail@patterdalehallestate.com
w patterdalehallestate.com

Swarthbeck Farm Holiday Cottages, Howtown-on-Ullswater ★★★ *Self Catering*
Contact: Mr & Mrs W H Parkin
Swarthbeck Farm Holiday Cottages
t (017684) 86432
e whparkin@ukonline.co.uk

Townhead Cottage ★★★★
Self Catering
Contact: Mr John Serginson
The Lakeland Cottage Company
t (015395) 30024
e john@lakelandcottageco.com
w lakelandcottageco.com

ULPHA
Cumbria

Brigg House Cottage
★★★★ *Self Catering*
Contact: Mr Philip Johnston
The Coppermines & Coniston Lake Cottages
t (015394) 41765
e info@coppermines.co.uk
w coppermines.co.uk

Fishermans Cottage (Church House) ★★★★ *Self Catering*
Contact: Mr Philip Johnston
The Coppermines & Coniston Lake Cottages
t (015394) 41765
e info@coppermines.co.uk
w coppermines.co.uk

High Kiln Bank Cottage
★★★★ *Self Catering*
Contact: Mr Philip Johnston
The Coppermines & Coniston Lake Cottages
t (015394) 41765
e info@coppermines.co.uk
w coppermines.co.uk

ULVERSTON
Cumbria

Ashlack Cottages ★★★★
Self Catering & Serviced Apartments
t (01229) 889888
e enquiries@ashlackcottages.co.uk
w ashlackcottages.co.uk

The Falls ★★★ *Self Catering*
Contact: Hilary Cheetham & Jane Unger
The Falls
t (01229) 583781
w thefalls.co.uk

Lile Cottage at Gleaston Water Mill ★★★★
Self Catering
Contact: Vicky Brereton
t (01229) 869244
e info@watermill.co.uk
w watermill.co.uk

Orchard Cottage ★★★
Self Catering
Contact: Brian Martin
t (01229) 463591
e brianmartin@orchardcottageulverston.co.uk
w orchardcottageulverston.co.uk

Prospect Cottage ★★★
Self Catering
Contact: Peter Durbin
Cumbrian Cottages Ltd
t (01228) 599950
e enquiries@cumbrian-cottages.co.uk
w cumbrian-cottages.co.uk

Swarthmoor Hall
★★★-★★★★ *Self Catering*
t (01229) 480603
e swarthmrhall@gn.apc.org
w swarthmoorhall.co.uk

UNDERBARROW
Cumbria

Ellerbeck ★★★★
Self Catering
Contact: Peter Durbin
Cumbrian Cottages Ltd
t (01228) 599950
e enquiries@cumbrian-cottages.co.uk
w cumbrian-cottages.co.uk

Honey Pot & Nanny Goat
★★★★★ *Self Catering*
Contact: Peter Durbin
Cumbrian Cottages Ltd
t (01228) 599950
e enquiries@cumbrian-cottages.co.uk
w cumbrian-cottages.co.uk

Nanny Goat ★★★★★
Self Catering
Contact: Peter Durbin
Cumbrian Cottages Ltd
t (01228) 599950
e enquiries@cumbrian-cottages.co.uk
w cumbrian-cottages.co.uk

UNDERSKIDDAW
Cumbria

Artists View ★★★★
Self Catering
Contact: Peter Durbin
Cumbrian Cottages Ltd
t (01228) 599950
e enquiries@cumbrian-cottages.co.uk
w cumbrian-cottages.co.uk

Brook Lodge ★★★★
Self Catering
Contact: Peter Durbin
Cumbrian Cottages Ltd
t (01228) 599950
e enquiries@cumbrian-cottages.co.uk
w cumbrian-cottages.co.uk

Derwent Lodge ★★★★
Self Catering
Contact: Peter Durbin
Cumbrian Cottages Ltd
t (01228) 599950
e enquiries@cumbrian-cottages.co.uk
w cumbrian-cottages.co.uk

Ewe Howe ★★★★
Self Catering
Contact: Peter Durbin
Cumbrian Cottages Ltd
t (01228) 599950
e enquiries@cumbrian-cottages.co.uk
w cumbrian-cottages.co.uk

Garth Cottage ★★★★
Self Catering
Contact: Peter Durbin
Cumbrian Cottages Ltd
t (01228) 599950
e enquiries@cumbrian-cottages.co.uk
w cumbrian-cottages.co.uk

Ivy Crag ★★★ *Self Catering*
Contact: Peter Durbin
Cumbrian Cottages Ltd
t (01228) 599950
e enquiries@cumbrian-cottages.co.uk
w cumbrian-cottages.co.uk

Latrigg ★★★★ *Self Catering*
Contact: Peter Durbin
Cumbrian Cottages Ltd
t (01228) 599950
e enquiries@cumbrian-cottages.co.uk
w cumbrian-cottages.co.uk

Oakfield Lodge ★★★
Self Catering
Contact: Peter Durbin
Cumbrian Cottages Ltd
t (01228) 599950
e enquiries@cumbrian-cottages.co.uk
w cumbrian-cottages.co.uk

Skiddaw Lodge ★★★★
Self Catering
Contact: Peter Durbin
Cumbrian Cottages Ltd
t (01228) 599950
e enquiries@cumbrian-cottages.co.uk
w cumbrian-cottages.co.uk

Squirrels Leap ★★★★
Self Catering
Contact: Peter Durbin
Cumbrian Cottages Ltd
t (01228) 599950
e enquiries@cumbrian-cottages.co.uk
w cumbrian-cottages.co.uk

Whinny Brow ★★★★
Self Catering
Contact: Peter Durbin
Cumbrian Cottages Ltd
t (01228) 599950
e enquiries@cumbrian-cottages.co.uk
w cumbrian-cottages.co.uk

Whiteside Lodge ★★★★
Self Catering
Contact: Peter Durbin
Cumbrian Cottages Ltd
t (01228) 599950
e enquiries@cumbrian-cottages.co.uk
w cumbrian-cottages.co.uk

Whitestones ★★★★
Self Catering
Contact: Peter Durbin
Cumbrian Cottages Ltd
t (01228) 599950
e enquiries@cumbrian-cottages.co.uk
w cumbrian-cottages.co.uk

WADDINGTON
Lancashire

Hedgehog Cottage ★★★★
Self Catering
Contact: Mr Stephen Tasker
t (01200) 429557
e stephen_tasker@btinternet.com

WAITBY
Cumbria

Waitby Longbarn ★★★
Self Catering
Contact: Peter Durbin
Cumbrian Cottages Ltd
t (01228) 599950
e enquiries@cumbrian-cottages.co.uk
w cumbrian-cottages.co.uk

WALLASEY
Merseyside

Captains View ★★★★
Self Catering
Contact: Marilyn Panton
t (0151) 638 5057
e marilyn.pantoni@xerox.com

Smugglers Way ★★★★
Self Catering
Contact: Mrs S.A Symington
Mrs. S.A. Symington
t (0151) 513 0709
e s_a_holme@yahoo.co.uk
w wirralcoastproperties.co.uk

WARWICK-ON-EDEN
Cumbria

Warwick Hall
★★★★-★★★★★
Self Catering
Contact: Ms Val Marriner
t (01228) 561546
e vmarriner@warwickhall.org

WASDALE
Cumbria

Sundial Cottage ★★★
Self Catering
Contact: Michael & Christine McKinley
t (01946) 726267
e mckinley2112@aol.com
w galesyke.co.uk

WATENDLATH
Cumbria

Fold Head Farm ★★★
Self Catering
Contact: Ms Sue Jackson
Heart of the Lakes
t (015394) 32321
e info@heartofthelakes.co.uk
w heartofthelakes.co.uk

WATER YEAT
Cumbria

Bee Bole House/The Farmstead/The Garden Cottage/Horseshoe Cottage
★★★★ *Self Catering*
Contact: Mr Philip Johnston
The Coppermines & Coniston Lake Cottages
t (015394) 41765
e info@coppermines.co.uk
w coppermines.co.uk

WATERHEAD
Cumbria

Betamere ★★★★
Self Catering
Contact: Susan Jackson
Heart of the Lakes
t (015394) 32321
e info@heartofthelakes.co.uk
w heartofthelakes.co.uk

High Borrans ★★★★
Self Catering
Contact: Susan Jackson
Heart of the Lakes
t (015394) 32321
e info@heartofthelakes.co.uk
w heartofthelakes.co.uk

Jenkins Crag ★★★★★
Self Catering
Contact: Susan Jackson
Heart of the Lakes
t (015394) 32321
e info@heartofthelakes.co.uk
w heartofthelakes.co.uk

Lakeland View ★★★★
Self Catering
Contact: Mrs Susan Jackson
Heart of the Lakes
t (015394) 32321
e info@heartofthelakes.co.uk
w heartofthelakes.co.uk

Latterbarrow ★★★★
Self Catering
Contact: Susan Jackson
Heart of the Lakes
t (015394) 32321
e info@heartofthelakes.co.uk
w heartofthelakes.co.uk

Romney 17 ★★★★
Self Catering
Contact: Susan Jackson
Heart of the Lakes
t (015394) 32321
e info@heartofthelakes.co.uk
w heartofthelakes.co.uk

Romney Grange ★★★★
Self Catering
Lakelovers
t (015394) 88855
e bookings@lakelovers.co.uk
w lakelovers.co.uk

Romney Grange ★★★★★
Self Catering
Contact: Susan Jackson
Heart of the Lakes
t (015394) 32321
e info@heartofthelakes.co.uk
w heartofthelakes.co.uk

Skelghyll ★★★★
Self Catering
Contact: Susan Jackson
Heart of the Lakes
t (015394) 32321
e info@heartofthelakes.co.uk
w heartofthelakes.co.uk

WATERMILLOCK
Cumbria

Beauthorn Cottage ★★★
Self Catering
Contact: Paul Durbin
Cumbrian Cottages Ltd
t (01228) 599950
e enquiries@cumbrian-cottages.co.uk
w cumbrian-cottages.co.uk

Leeming Old Lodge ★★★★
Self Catering
Contact: Peter Durbin
Cumbrian Cottages Ltd
t (01228) 599950
e enquiries@cumbrian-cottages.co.uk
w cumbrian-cottages.co.uk

The Library ★★★★
Self Catering
Contact: Peter Durbin
Cumbrian Cottages Ltd
t (01228) 599950
e enquiries@cumbrian-cottages.co.uk
w cumbrian-cottages.co.uk

Low House ★★★★★
Self Catering
Contact: Susan Jackson
Heart of the Lakes
t (015394) 32321
e info@heartofthelakes.co.uk
w heartofthelakes.co.uk

Middlegate ★★★
Self Catering
Contact: Susan Jackson
Heart of the Lakes
t (015394) 32321
e info@heartofthelakes.co.uk
w heartofthelakes.co.uk

The Old Bothy ★★★
Self Catering
Contact: Peter Durbin
Cumbrian Cottages Ltd
t (01228) 599950
e enquiries@cumbrian-cottages.co.uk
w cumbrian-cottages.co.uk

WENNINGTON
Lancashire

Easter Cottage ★★★★
Self Catering
Contact: Mrs Jenny Herd
t (01524) 221690

WESTWARD
Cumbria

Clea Hall ★★★★
Self Catering
Contact: Peter Durbin
Cumbrian Cottages Ltd
t (01228) 599950
e enquiries@cumbrian-cottages.co.uk
w cumbrian-cottages.co.uk

High Hall Cottage ★★★
Self Catering
Contact: Jane Thompson
t (01697) 342584

WETHERAL
Cumbria

Eden View 3 ★★★
Self Catering
t (01228) 599960
e enquiries@cumbrian-cottages.co.uk
w cumbrian-cottages.co.uk

Eden View 4 ★★★
Self Catering
Den View 4
t (01228) 599960
e enquiries@cumbrian-cottages.co.uk
w cumbrian-cottages.co.uk

Geltsdale ★★★★★
Self Catering
Contact: Peter Durbin
Cumbrian Cottages Ltd
t (01228) 599950
e enquiries@cumbrian-cottages.co.uk
w cumbrian-cottages.co.uk

Hall Moor Court ★★★★
Self Catering
Contact: Peter Durbin
Cumbrian Cottages Ltd
t (01228) 599950
e enquiries@cumbrian-cottages.co.uk
w cumbrian-cottages.co.uk

Sarahs Cottage ★★★★★
Self Catering
Contact: Peter Durbin
Cumbrian Cottages Ltd
t (01228) 599950
e enquiries@cumbrian-cottages.co.uk
w cumbrian-cottages.co.uk

WHALE
Cumbria

Whale Farm Cottage
★★★★★ *Self Catering*
Contact: Mrs Lyn Page
Estate Office
t (01931) 712577
e lyn.page@lowther.co.uk

WHALLEY
Lancashire

Tabgha ★★★ *Self Catering*
Contact: Mr Roger Wales
Holiday Cottages Yorkshire Ltd
t (01756) 700510
e info@holidaycotts.co.uk

WHINFELL
Cumbria

Agnes Cottage ★★★★
Self Catering
Contact: Kerry Darbishire
t (01539) 824670
e stephen@stephen-darbishire.com
w agnescottage.co.uk

Topthorn Holiday Cottages
Rating Applied For
Self Catering
Contact: Mrs Diane Barnes
t (01539) 824252
e barnes.topthornfarm@btinternet.com
w topthornholidatycottages cumbria.co.uk

WHITE MOSS
Cumbria

Ladywood Lodge ★★★
Self Catering
Contact: Martin Morris
Claremont - Belair
t (015394) 88657
e claremontbelair@btinternet.com
w ladywood.ws

WHITEHAVEN
Cumbria

Rosmerta & Brighida Cottages ★★★★
Self Catering
Contact: David & Jane Saxon
Moresby Hall
t (01946) 696317
e ctb@moresbyhall.co.uk
w moresbyhall.co.uk

Swallows Return and Owls Retreat ★★★★ *Self Catering*
Contact: James & Joyce Moore
t (01946) 64078
e mhc.moresby@virgin.net
w cottageguide.co.uk/moresby

WIGAN
Greater Manchester

Oysterber Farm Cottage Holidays ★★★ *Self Catering*
Contact: Mrs Cathy Cartledge
t (01524) 261567

Look out for establishments participating in the National Accessible Scheme

WIGTON
Cumbria

Croftlands Court Self-Catering Cottages ★★★★
Self Catering
Contact: Kathleen Hughes
Cumbrian Cottages Ltd
t (01697) 361256
w croftlandscourt.co.uk

East and West Court Refs. 2075/2315 ★★★
Self Catering
Dales Holiday Cottages
t 0870 909 9500
e fiona@dales-holiday-cottages.com
w dalesholcot.com

Foxgloves, Greenrigg Farm
★★★★ *Self Catering*
Contact: Mr & Mrs Kerr
Sykes Cottages
t (01697) 342676
e kerr_greenrigg@hotmail.com

Lane Head Apartment
★★★★ *Self Catering*
Contact: David Colborn
t (01697) 343888
e david.colborn@homecall.co.uk
w laneheadapartment.co.uk

Leegate House Cottage
★★★ *Self Catering*
Dales Hol Cot Ref:2658
t (01756) 799821
e info@dalesholcot.com

Rose Cottage ★★★
Self Catering
Contact: Peter Durbin
Cumbrian Cottages Ltd
t (01228) 599950
e enquiries@cumbrian-cottages.co.uk
w cumbrian-cottages.co.uk

Westrigg ★★★★
Self Catering
Contact: Peter Durbin
Cumbrian Cottages Ltd
t (01228) 599950
e enquiries@cumbrian-cottages.co.uk
w cumbrian-cottages.co.uk

WILDBOARCLOUGH
Cheshire

Lower House Cottage ★★★
Self Catering
Contact: Mrs C Waller
t (01260) 227229
e sheeponthehill@aol.com
w lowerhousecottage.co.uk

WILLINGTON
Cheshire

Delamere Cottage ★★★★
Self Catering
Contact: Mr E Sidebotham
t (01829) 751628
e delamere.cottage@btinternet.com

WINCLE
Cheshire

Clough Brook Cottage
★★★★ *Self Catering*
t (01260) 227209
e henshalls@btinternet.com

WINDERMERE
Cumbria

1 Birchmill Cottages ★★★★
Self Catering
Contact: Mr Paul Liddell
Lakelovers
t (015394) 88855
e bookings@lakelovers.co.uk
w lakelovers.co.uk

1 Brantfield House ★★★
Self Catering
Contact: Peter Durbin
Cumbrian Cottages Ltd
t (01228) 599950
e enquiries@cumbrian-cottages.co.uk
w cumbrian-cottages.co.uk

1 Brantfield House ★★★
Self Catering
Contact: Peter Durbin
Cumbrian Cottages Ltd
t (01228) 599950
e enquiries@cumbrian-cottages.co.uk
w cumbrian-cottages.co.uk

1 Old College Cottage
★★★★ *Self Catering*
Contact: Mr Paul Liddell
Lakelovers
t (015394) 88855
e bookings@lakelovers.co.uk
w lakelovers.co.uk

11 Wansfell Lodge ★★★
Self Catering
Contact: Peter Durbin
Cumbrian Cottages Ltd
t (01228) 599950
e enquiries@cumbrian-cottages.co.uk
w cumbrian-cottages.co.uk

2 Hodge How ★★★
Self Catering
Contact: Mr John Serginson
The Lakeland Cottage Company
t (015395) 30024
e john@lakelandcottageco.com

2 Meadowcroft House
★★★★ *Self Catering*
Contact: Mr Paul Liddell
Lakelovers
t (015394) 88855
e bookings@lakelovers.co.uk
w lakelovers.co.uk

2 Priory Manor ★★★★
Self Catering
Contact: Mr Paul Liddell
Lakelovers
t (015394) 88855
e bookings@lakelovers.co.uk
w lakelovers.co.uk

24 Victoria Terrace ★★
Self Catering
Contact: Mrs Lishman
Lishmans
t (015394) 42982

27 Beechwood Close ★★★
Self Catering
Contact: Peter Durbin
Cumbrian Cottages Ltd
t (01228) 599950
e enquiries@cumbrian-cottages.co.uk
w cumbrian-cottages.co.uk

3 Woodland Grove ★★★
Self Catering
Contact: Mr Paul Liddell
Lakelovers
t (015394) 88855
e bookings@lakelovers.co.uk
w lakelovers.co.uk

4 College Court ★★★
Self Catering
Contact: Mr Paul Liddell
Lakelovers
t (015394) 88855
e bookings@lakelovers.co.uk
w lakelovers.co.uk

4 Rustic Cottage ★★★
Self Catering
Contact: Mr White
Cumbrian Cottages Ltd
t 07786 984946
e withington01@blueyonder.co.uk
w bownesscottage.co.uk

48A Quarry Rigg ★★★
Self Catering
Contact: Mr Paul Liddell
Lakelovers
t (015394) 88855
e bookings@lakelovers.co.uk
w lakelovers.co.uk

5 Helm Rigg ★★★
Self Catering
Contact: Mr Paul Liddell
Lakelovers
t (015394) 88855
e bookings@lakelovers.co.uk
w lakelovers.co.uk

6 Meadowcroft ★★★★
Self Catering
Contact: Mr Paul Liddell
Lakelovers
t (015394) 88855
e bookings@lakelovers.co.uk
w lakelovers.co.uk

8 College Court ★★★
Self Catering
Contact: Mr Paul Liddell
Lakelovers
t (015394) 88855
e bookings@lakelovers.co.uk
w lakelovers.co.uk

The Abbey Coach House
★★★ *Self Catering*
Contact: Mrs P Bell
t (015394) 44027
e abbeycoach@aol.com
w abbeycoachhouse.co.uk

Abbeydale ★★★
Self Catering
Contact: Peter Durbin
Cumbrian Cottages Ltd
t (01228) 599950
e enquiries@cumbrian-cottages.co.uk
w cumbrian-cottages.co.uk

Above Cot ★★★
Self Catering
Contact: Peter Durbin
Cumbrian Cottages Ltd
t (01228) 599950
e enquiries@cumbrian-cottages.co.uk
w cumbrian-cottages.co.uk

Alderbeck ★★★★★
Self Catering
Lakelovers
t (015394) 88855
e bookings@lakelovers.co.uk
w lakelovers.co.uk

Annie's View ★★★
Self Catering
Contact: Peter Durbin
Cumbrian Cottages Ltd
t (01228) 599950
e enquiries@cumbrian-cottages.co.uk
w cumbrian-cottages.co.uk

Annisgarth ★★★
Self Catering
Contact: Peter Durbin
Cumbrian Cottages Ltd
t (01228) 599950
e enquiries@cumbrian-cottages.co.uk
w cumbrian-cottages.co.uk

Annisgarth ★★★
Self Catering
Contact: Mr Paul Liddell
Lakelovers
t (015394) 88855
e bookings@lakelovers.co.uk
w lakelovers.co.uk

April Meadow Cottage
★★★ *Self Catering*
Contact: Mr Paul Liddell
Lakelovers
t (015394) 88855
e bookings@lakelovers.co.uk
w lakelovers.co.uk

Bank Cottage ★★★★
Self Catering
Contact: Capt & Mrs Beighton
t (01474) 533028

Bear's Den ★★★
Self Catering
Contact: Peter Durbin
Cumbrian Cottages Ltd
t (01228) 599950
e enquiries@cumbrian-cottages.co.uk
w cumbrian-cottages.co.uk

Beau Penny ★★★
Self Catering
Contact: Mr Paul Liddell
Lakelovers
t (015394) 88855
e bookings@lakelovers.co.uk
w lakelovers.co.uk

Beaumont Cottages ★★★
Self Catering & Serviced Apartments
Contact: Charles Walmsley
Beaumont
t (015394) 45521
e beaumontcottages@aol.com
w beaumont-cottages.co.uk

Bede's Cottage ★★★★
Self Catering
Contact: Peter Durbin
Cumbrian Cottages Ltd
t (01228) 599950
e enquiries@cumbrian-cottages.co.uk
w cumbrian-cottages.co.uk

Beech How Cottage ★★★
Self Catering
Contact: Mr Paul Liddell
Lakelovers
t (015394) 88855
e bookings@lakelovers.co.uk
w lakelovers.co.uk

Beechmount ★★★★
Self Catering
Contact: Mrs Susan Jackson
Heart of the Lakes
t (015394) 32321
e info@heartofthelakes.co.uk
w heartofthelakes.co.uk

Beechwood Apartment
★★★ *Self Catering*
Contact: Peter Durbin
Cumbrian Cottages Ltd
t (01228) 599950
e enquiries@cumbrian-cottages.co.uk
w cumbrian-cottages.co.uk

Belle View – Quarry Rigg
★★★ *Self Catering*
Contact: Peter Durbin
Cumbrian Cottages Ltd
t (01228) 599950
e enquiries@cumbrian-cottages.co.uk
w cumbrian-cottages.co.uk

The Birds Nest ★★★
Self Catering
Contact: Susan Jackson
Heart of the Lakes
t (015394) 32321
e info@heartofthelakes.co.uk
w heartofthelakes.co.uk

Birthwaite Edge ★★★
Self Catering
Contact: Mr Bruce Dodsworth
Birthwaite Edge
t (015394) 42861
e dms@lakedge.com
w lakedge.com

Biskey Howe ★★★
Self Catering
Contact: Peter Durbin
Cumbrian Cottages Ltd
t (01228) 599950
e enquiries@cumbrian-cottages.co.uk
w cumbrian-cottages.co.uk

Biskey Howe Cottage ★★★
Self Catering
Contact: Peter Durbin
Cumbrian Cottages Ltd
t (01228) 599950
e enquiries@cumbrian-cottages.co.uk
w cumbrian-cottages.co.uk

Biskey Rise ★★★★
Self Catering
Contact: Susan Jackson
Heart of the Lakes
t (015394) 32321
e info@heartofthelakes.co.uk
w heartofthelakes.co.uk

Black Beck Cottage
★★★★★ *Self Catering*
Contact: Peter Durbin
Cumbrian Cottages Ltd
t (01228) 599950
e enquiries@cumbrian-cottages.co.uk
w cumbrian-cottages.co.uk

Bluebells & Daffodils Cottage Apartment ★★★★
Self Catering
Lakelovers
t (015394) 88855
e bookings@lakelovers.co.uk
w lakelovers.co.uk

The Bothy ★★★
Self Catering
Contact: Peter Durbin
Cumbrian Cottages Ltd
t (01228) 599950
e enquiries@cumbrian-cottages.co.uk
w cumbrian-cottages.co.uk

Bowmere ★★★★
Self Catering
Contact: Peter Durbin
Cumbrian Cottages Ltd
t (01228) 599950
e enquiries@cumbrian-cottages.co.uk
w cumbrian-cottages.co.uk

Bowness Oaks ★★★★
Self Catering
Contact: Peter Durbin
Cumbrian Cottages Ltd
t (01228) 599950
e enquiries@cumbrian-cottages.co.uk
w cumbrian-cottages.co.uk

Brackenrigg Lodge
★★★★★ *Self Catering*
Contact: Miss Lynne Bush
Brackenrigg
t (015394) 47770
e lynne@brackenriggs.co.uk

Brantfell Cottage ★★★
Self Catering
Contact: Peter Durbin
Cumbrian Cottages Ltd
t (01228) 599950
e enquiries@cumbrian-cottages.co.uk
w cumbrian-cottages.co.uk

Brent Cottage
Rating Applied For
Self Catering
Contact: Kathryn Hutton
t (01274) 563088
e info@brentcottage.co.uk
w brentcottage.co.uk

Briarwood ★★★
Self Catering
Contact: Peter Durbin
Cumbrian Cottages Ltd
t (01228) 599950
e enquiries@cumbrian-cottages.co.uk
w cumbrian-cottages.co.uk

Briscoe Lodge ★★★
Self Catering
Contact: Margaret Cook
t (015394) 42928

Brook House ★★★★
Self Catering
Contact: Peter Durbin
Cumbrian Cottages Ltd
t (01228) 599950
e enquiries@cumbrian-cottages.co.uk
w cumbrian-cottages.co.uk

Brunton Lodge ★★★★
Self Catering
Lakelovers
t (015394) 88855
e bookings@lakelovers.co.uk
w lakelovers.co.uk

Burkesfield Cottage ★★★★
Self Catering
Contact: Mr Paul Liddell
Lakelovers
t (015394) 88855
e bookings@lakelovers.co.uk
w lakelovers.co.uk

Burnside Park ★★★★
Self Catering
Contact: Mr David Morton
Bowness Leisure Plc
t 0870 046 8624
e stay@burnsidepark.co.uk
w burnsidepark.co.uk

The Burrow ★★★
Self Catering
Contact: Peter Durbin
Cumbrian Cottages Ltd
t (01228) 599950
e enquiries@cumbrian-cottages.co.uk
w cumbrian-cottages.co.uk

Calgarth ★★★ *Self Catering*
Contact: Peter Durbin
Cumbrian Cottages Ltd
t (01228) 599950
e enquiries@cumbrian-cottages.co.uk
w cumbrian-cottages.co.uk

Canon's Craig ★★★★
Self Catering
Contact: Mr & Mrs Salter
t (024) 7645 7141
e dougie@freeneasy.net
w http://web.ukonline.co.uk/dougiedoo/Index.htm

The Carriage House
★★★★★ *Self Catering*
Contact: Mrs Susan Jackson
Heart of the Lakes
t (015394) 32321
e info@heartofthelakes.co.uk
w heartofthelakes.co.uk

Chapel House & Rest
★★★★ *Self Catering*
Contact: Mr Paul Liddell
Lakelovers
t (015394) 88855
e bookings@lakelovers.co.uk
w lakelovers.co.uk

Charlies Corner ★★★
Self Catering
Contact: Peter Durbin
Cumbrian Cottages Ltd
t (01228) 599950
e enquiries@cumbrian-cottages.co.uk
w cumbrian-cottages.co.uk

Cherry Tree Cottage ★★★★
Self Catering
Contact: Peter Durbin
Cumbrian Cottages Ltd
t (01228) 599950
e enquiries@cumbrian-cottages.co.uk
w cumbrian-cottages.co.uk

Cinnamon Cottage ★★★★
Self Catering
Contact: Mrs Susan Jackson
Heart of the Lakes
t (015394) 32321
e info@heartofthelakes.co.uk
w heartofthelakes.co.uk

Claife Heights Flat
Rating Applied For
Self Catering
Contact: Mr & Mrs Ray & Barbara Hood
t (015394) 46565
e ray&barb@the-fairfield.co.uk
w the-fairfield.co.uk

Claife View ★★★
Self Catering
Contact: Peter Durbin
Cumbrian Cottages Ltd
t (01228) 599950
e enquiries@cumbrian-cottages.co.uk
w cumbrian-cottages.co.uk

Claife View ★★★
Self Catering
Contact: Mrs Susan Jackson
Heart of the Lakes
t (015394) 32321
e info@heartofthelakes.co.uk
w heartofthelakes.co.uk

Clara's Cottage ★★★
Self Catering
Lakelovers
t (015394) 88855
e bookings@lakelovers.co.uk
w lakelovers.co.uk

Cleabarrow Cottage ★★★★
Self Catering
Contact: Peter Durbin
Cumbrian Cottages Ltd
t (01228) 599950
e enquiries@cumbrian-cottages.co.uk
w cumbrian-cottages.co.uk

The Coach House ★★★
Self Catering
Contact: Ms Fiona McCulloch
t (01438) 717077
e fiona99@ukonline.co.uk
w windermere-accommodation.co.uk

Cobblers Cottage ★★★★
Self Catering
Lakelovers
t (015394) 88855
e bookings@lakelovers.co.uk
w lakelovers.co.uk

Cobblestones ★★★
Self Catering
Contact: Mr Paul Liddell
Lakelovers
t (015394) 88855
e bookings@lakelovers.co.uk
w lakelovers.co.uk

Cockshott Wood ★★★★
Self Catering
Contact: Mrs Susan Jackson
Heart of the Lakes
t (015394) 32321
e info@heartofthelakes.co.uk
w heartofthelakes.co.uk

College Gate ★★★
Self Catering
Contact: Peter Durbin
Cumbrian Cottages Ltd
t (01228) 599950
e enquiries@cumbrian-cottages.co.uk
w cumbrian-cottages.co.uk

Coppice Corner ★★★★★
Self Catering
Contact: Mr Paul Liddell
Lakelovers
t (015394) 88855
e bookings@lakelovers.co.uk
w lakelovers.co.uk

Coppice View ★★★★
Self Catering
Lakelovers
t (015394) 88855
e bookings@lakelovers.co.uk
w lakelovers.co.uk

Corner Cottage ★★★★
Self Catering
Contact: Peter Durbin
Cumbrian Cottages Ltd
t (01228) 599950
e enquiries@cumbrian-cottages.co.uk
w cumbrian-cottages.co.uk

Cosy Nook ★★★
Self Catering
Contact: Mr Paul Liddell
Lakelovers
t (015394) 88855
e bookings@lakelovers.co.uk
w lakelovers.co.uk

Cosy Nook Cottage ★★★
Self Catering
Contact: Peter Durbin
Cumbrian Cottages Ltd
t (01228) 599950
e enquiries@cumbrian-cottages.co.uk
w cumbrian-cottages.co.uk

Craglands ★★★★
Self Catering
Lakelovers
t (015394) 88855
e bookings@lakelovers.co.uk
w lakelovers.co.uk

Craigside ★★★★
Self Catering
Contact: Mr Paul Liddell
Lakelovers
t (015394) 88855
e bookings@lakelovers.co.uk
w lakelovers.co.uk

Crinkle Crag ★★★★
Self Catering
Contact: Peter Durbin
Cumbrian Cottages Ltd
t (01228) 599950
e enquiries@cumbrian-cottages.co.uk
w cumbrian-cottages.co.uk

Cross Cottage ★★★
Self Catering
Contact: Peter Durbin
Cumbrian Cottages Ltd
t (01228) 599950
e enquiries@cumbrian-cottages.co.uk
w cumbrian-cottages.co.uk

Crowmire Wood ★★★★
Self Catering
Contact: Mrs Susan Jackson
Heart of the Lakes
t (015394) 32321
e info@heartofthelakes.co.uk
w heartofthelakes.co.uk

Curlew Crag ★★★
Self Catering
Contact: Ms Sue Jackson
Heart of the Lakes
t (015394) 32321
e info@heartofthelakes.co.uk
w heartofthelakes.co.uk

Daisy Bank Cottage ★★★
Self Catering
Contact: Peter Durbin
Cumbrian Cottages Ltd
t (01228) 599950
e enquiries@cumbrian-cottages.co.uk
w cumbrian-cottages.co.uk

December Cottage ★★★★
Self Catering
Lakelovers
t (015394) 88855
e bookings@lakelovers.co.uk
w lakelovers.co.uk

Deloraine ★★★-★★★★
Self Catering
Contact: Mrs Fanstone
t (015394) 45557
e info@deloraine.demon.co.uk
w deloraine.demon.co.uk

Ecclerigg ★★★ *Self Catering*
Contact: Peter Durbin
Cumbrian Cottages Ltd
t (01228) 599950
e enquiries@cumbrian-cottages.co.uk
w cumbrian-cottages.co.uk

Elim Cottage ★★★
Self Catering
Contact: Peter Durbin
Cumbrian Cottages Ltd
t (01228) 599950
e enquiries@cumbrian-cottages.co.uk
w cumbrian-cottages.co.uk

Elterwater ★★★★
Self Catering
Contact: Peter Durbin
Cumbrian Cottages Ltd
t (01228) 599950
e enquiries@cumbrian-cottages.co.uk
w cumbrian-cottages.co.uk

Esthwaite ★★★ *Self Catering*
Contact: Peter Durbin
Cumbrian Cottages Ltd
t (01228) 599950
e enquiries@cumbrian-cottages.co.uk
w cumbrian-cottages.co.uk

Evergreen Cottage ★★★
Self Catering
Contact: Peter Durbin
Cumbrian Cottages Ltd
t (01228) 599950
e enquiries@cumbrian-cottages.co.uk
w cumbrian-cottages.co.uk

Fair View ★★★★
Self Catering
Contact: Susan Jackson
Heart of the Lakes
t (015394) 32321
e info@heartofthelakes.co.uk
w heartofthelakes.co.uk

Fairfield ★★★ *Self Catering*
Contact: Peter Durbin
Cumbrian Cottages Ltd
t (01228) 599950
e enquiries@cumbrian-cottages.co.uk
w cumbrian-cottages.co.uk

Fairhaven ★★★ *Self Catering*
Contact: Mrs Susan Jackson
Heart of the Lakes
t (015394) 32321
e info@heartofthelakes.co.uk
w heartofthelakes.co.uk

Ferry View ★★★
Self Catering
Contact: Mr Paul Liddell
Lakelovers
t (015394) 88855
e bookings@lakelovers.co.uk
w lakelovers.co.uk

Fir Cones ★★★★
Self Catering
Contact: Peter Durbin
Cumbrian Cottages Ltd
t (01228) 599950
e enquiries@cumbrian-cottages.co.uk
w cumbrian-cottages.co.uk

Firbank – Quarry Rigg ★★★
Self Catering
Contact: Peter Durbin
Cumbrian Cottages Ltd
t (01228) 599950
e enquiries@cumbrian-cottages.co.uk
w cumbrian-cottages.co.uk

Fireside Cottage ★★★
Self Catering
Contact: Peter Durbin
Cumbrian Cottages Ltd
t (01228) 599950
e enquiries@cumbrian-cottages.co.uk
w cumbrian-cottages.co.uk

Flat 4 ★★★ *Self Catering*
Contact: Mrs S. M. Cherif
t (01912) 572901
e chemirif@hotmail.com

Foxgloves ★★★ *Self Catering*
Contact: Peter Durbin
Cumbrian Cottages Ltd
t (01228) 599950
e enquiries@cumbrian-cottages.co.uk
w cumbrian-cottages.co.uk

The Galley ★★★★★
Self Catering
Heart of the Lakes
t (015394) 32321
e info@heartofthelakes.co.uk
w heartofthelakes.co.uk

Garden Bungalows ★★★
Self Catering
Contact: Bob & Maureen Theobald
Beaumont Holidays
t (015394) 88242
e dms@beaumont-holidays.co.uk
w beaumont-holidays.co.uk

Gardens View ★★★
Self Catering
Contact: Mr Paul Liddell
Lakelovers
t (015394) 88855
e bookings@lakelovers.co.uk
w lakelovers.co.uk

Garthmere ★★★★★
Self Catering
Contact: Ms Sue Jackson
Heart of the Lakes
t (015394) 32321
e info@heartofthelakes.co.uk
w heartofthelakes.co.uk

Gavel Cottage ★★★★
Self Catering
Contact: Mr Screeton
Screetons
t (01430) 431201
e howden@screetons.co.uk
w screetons.co.uk

Gildabrook Cottage ★★★
Self Catering
Contact: Mrs Susan Jackson
Heart of the Lakes
t (015394) 32321
e info@heartofthelakes.co.uk
w heartofthelakes.co.uk

Gillercombe ★★★★
Self Catering
Contact: Mrs Susan Jackson
Heart of the Lakes
t (015394) 32321
e info@heartofthelakes.co.uk
w heartofthelakes.co.uk

Glebe Holme ★★★
Self Catering
Contact: Peter Durbin
Cumbrian Cottages Ltd
t (01228) 599950
e enquiries@cumbrian-cottages.co.uk
w cumbrian-cottages.co.uk

Grace Cottage ★★★★
Self Catering
Contact: Helen May
t (01539) 732602
e cottage@mays-in-grace.co.uk
w mays-in-grace.co.uk

Granary Nook ★★★
Self Catering
Contact: Peter Durbin
Cumbrian Cottages Ltd
t (01228) 599950
e enquiries@cumbrian-cottages.co.uk
w cumbrian-cottages.co.uk

Grange House ★★★★
Self Catering
Contact: Peter Durbin
Cumbrian Cottages Ltd
t (01228) 599950
e enquiries@cumbrian-cottages.co.uk
w cumbrian-cottages.co.uk

Greenrigg ★★★★
Self Catering
Contact: Peter Durbin
Cumbrian Cottages Ltd
t (01228) 599950
e enquiries@cumbrian-cottages.co.uk
w cumbrian-cottages.co.uk

Grey Cottage ★★★
Self Catering
Contact: Peter Durbin
Cumbrian Cottages Ltd
t (01228) 599950
e enquiries@cumbrian-cottages.co.uk
w cumbrian-cottages.co.uk

Greystones ★★★
Self Catering
Contact: Peter Durbin
Cumbrian Cottages Ltd
t (01228) 599950
e enquiries@cumbrian-cottages.co.uk
w cumbrian-cottages.co.uk

The Heaning ★★★
Self Catering
Contact: Hazel Moulding
t (015394) 43453
e info@theheaning.co.uk
w theheaning.co.uk

Helm Farm ★★-★★★
Self Catering
Contact: Miss M Scott
Matson Ground Estate Co Ltd
t (015394) 45756
e info@matsonground.co.uk
w matsonground.co.uk

Hermitage Cottage ★★★
Self Catering
Contact: Mr John Serginson
The Lakeland Cottage Company
t (015395) 30024
e john@lakelandcottageco.com

Hidden Depths ★★★★★
Self Catering
Lakelovers
t (015394) 88855
e bookings@lakelovers.co.uk
w lakelovers.co.uk

Highcroft ★★★★
Self Catering
Contact: Susan Jackson
Heart of the Lakes
t (015394) 32321
e info@heartofthelakes.co.uk
w heartofthelakes.co.uk

Hodge Howe ★★★★★
Self Catering
Contact: Mrs Susan Jackson
Heart of the Lakes
t (015394) 32321
e info@heartofthelakes.co.uk
w heartofthelakes.co.uk

Holburn House ★★★
Self Catering
Contact: Peter Durbin
Cumbrian Cottages Ltd
t (01228) 599950
e enquiries@cumbrian-cottages.co.uk
w cumbrian-cottages.co.uk

Hollin Field ★★★★
Self Catering
Contact: Susan Jackson
Heart of the Lakes
t (015394) 32321
e info@heartofthelakes.co.uk
w heartofthelakes.co.uk

Holly Cottage ★★★★
Self Catering
Lakelovers
t (015394) 88855
e bookings@lakelovers.co.uk
w lakelovers.co.uk

Honeysuckle ★★★★
Self Catering
Contact: Mr John Serginson
The Lakeland Cottage Company
t (015395) 30024
e john@lakelandcottageco.com

Honeysuckle Cottage ★★★★ *Self Catering*
Contact: Mr Paul Liddell
Lakelovers
t (015394) 88855
e bookings@lakelovers.co.uk
w lakelovers.co.uk

Honeysuckle Cottage ★★★
Self Catering
Contact: Peter Durbin
Cumbrian Cottages Ltd
t (01228) 599950
e enquiries@cumbrian-cottages.co.uk
w cumbrian-cottages.co.uk

Howe Cottage ★★★
Self Catering
Contact: Peter Durbin
Cumbrian Cottages Ltd
t (01228) 599950
e enquiries@cumbrian-cottages.co.uk
w cumbrian-cottages.co.uk

Hunters Moon ★★★★
Self Catering
Lakelovers
t (015394) 88855
e bookings@lakelovers.co.uk
w lakelovers.co.uk

Hydaway ★★★ *Self Catering*
Contact: Peter Durbin
Cumbrian Cottages Ltd
t (01228) 599950
e enquiries@cumbrian-cottages.co.uk
w cumbrian-cottages.co.uk

Ings Howe Cottage ★★★★
Self Catering
Contact: Peter Durbin
Cumbrian Cottages Ltd
t (01228) 599950
e enquiries@cumbrian-cottages.co.uk
w cumbrian-cottages.co.uk

Kent Cottage ★★★
Self Catering
Contact: Mr Paul Liddell
Lakelovers
t (015394) 88855
e bookings@lakelovers.co.uk
w lakelovers.co.uk

Kerris Place ★★★
Self Catering
Contact: Peter Durbin
Cumbrian Cottages Ltd
t (01228) 599950
e enquiries@cumbrian-cottages.co.uk
w cumbrian-cottages.co.uk

Knotts View ★★★★
Self Catering
Contact: Mr Paul Liddell
Lakelovers
t (015394) 88855
e bookings@lakelovers.co.uk
w lakelovers.co.uk

Laburnum Cottage ★★★
Self Catering
Contact: Peter Durbin
Cumbrian Cottages Ltd
t (01228) 599950
e enquiries@cumbrian-cottages.co.uk
w cumbrian-cottages.co.uk

Lake Lodge Studio ★★★★
Self Catering
Lakelovers
t (015394) 88855
e bookings@lakelovers.co.uk
w lakelovers.co.uk

Lake View ★★★★
Self Catering
Contact: Mr Paul Liddell
Lakelovers
t (015394) 88855
e bookings@lakelovers.co.uk
w lakelovers.co.uk

Lakeland Lodge ★★★
Self Catering
Contact: Peter Durbin
Cumbrian Cottages Ltd
t (01228) 599950
e enquiries@cumbrian-cottages.co.uk
w cumbrian-cottages.co.uk

Lakeside Cottage ★★★★★
Self Catering
Contact: Ms Sue Jackson
Heart of the Lakes
t (015394) 32321
e info@heartofthelakes.co.uk
w heartofthelakes.co.uk

Lakeside View ★★★
Self Catering
Contact: Mr Paul Liddell
Lakelovers
t (015394) 88855
e bookings@lakelovers.co.uk
w lakelovers.co.uk

Lakeview ★★★ *Self Catering*
Contact: Peter Durbin
Cumbrian Cottages Ltd
t (01228) 599950
e enquiries@cumbrian-cottages.co.uk
w cumbrian-cottages.co.uk

Lamb Cottage ★★★
Self Catering
Contact: Peter Durbin
Cumbrian Cottages Ltd
t (01228) 599950
e enquiries@cumbrian-cottages.co.uk
w cumbrian-cottages.co.uk

Langdale View Apartments ★★★ *Self Catering*
Contact: Julie Marsh
Langdale View Apartments
t (015394) 46655
e enquiries@langdale-view.co.uk
w langdale-view.co.uk

Langrigge Cottage & High Langrigge
★★★★–★★★★★
Self Catering
Lakelovers
t (015394) 88855
e bookings@lakelovers.co.uk
w lakelovers.co.uk

Langthwaite Cottage ★★★
Self Catering
Contact: Mr DM & Mrs SJ Soar
Squirrel Bank
t (015394) 43329
e soar@squirrelbank.com
w langthwaitecottage.co.uk

Larch House ★★★★
Self Catering
Contact: Mr Paul Liddell
Lakelovers
t (015394) 88855
e bookings@lakelovers.co.uk
w lakelovers.co.uk

Lilac Cottage ★★★
Self Catering
Contact: Peter Durbin
Cumbrian Cottages Ltd
t (01228) 599950
e enquiries@cumbrian-cottages.co.uk
w cumbrian-cottages.co.uk

Ling Howe ★★★★★
Self Catering
Contact: Peter Durbin
Cumbrian Cottages Ltd
t (01228) 599950
e enquiries@cumbrian-cottages.co.uk
w cumbrian-cottages.co.uk

Little Ivy & Rowan Cottages ★★★ *Self Catering*
Contact: Peter Durbin
Cumbrian Cottages Ltd
t (01228) 599950
e enquiries@cumbrian-cottages.co.uk
w cumbrian-cottages.co.uk

Little Loughrigg ★★★★
Self Catering
Contact: Ms Sue Jackson
Heart of the Lakes
t (015394) 32321
e info@heartofthelakes.co.uk
w heartofthelakes.co.uk

Little Rowan ★★★
Self Catering
Contact: Peter Durbin
Cumbrian Cottages Ltd
t (01228) 599950
e enquiries@cumbrian-cottages.co.uk
w cumbrian-cottages.co.uk

The Lodge ★★★★
Self Catering
Contact: Peter Durbin
Cumbrian Cottages Ltd
t (01228) 599950
e enquiries@cumbrian-cottages.co.uk
w cumbrian-cottages.co.uk

Longmire Lodge ★★★
Self Catering
Contact: Peter Durbin
Cumbrian Cottages Ltd
t (01228) 599950
e enquiries@cumbrian-cottages.co.uk
w cumbrian-cottages.co.uk

Low Fell Cottage ★★★
Self Catering
Contact: Peter Durbin
Cumbrian Cottages Ltd
t (01228) 599950
e enquiries@cumbrian-cottages.co.uk
w cumbrian-cottages.co.uk

Low How ★★★★
Self Catering
Contact: Mrs Susan Jackson
Heart of the Lakes
t (015394) 32321
e info@heartofthelakes.co.uk
w heartofthelakes.co.uk

Maple Court ★★★
Self Catering
Contact: Peter Durbin
Cumbrian Cottages Ltd
t (01228) 599950
e enquiries@cumbrian-cottages.co.uk
w cumbrian-cottages.co.uk

Marsh Cottage ★
Self Catering
Contact: Peter Durbin
Cumbrian Cottages Ltd
t (01228) 599950
e enquiries@cumbrian-cottages.co.uk
w cumbrian-cottages.co.uk

Meadowcroft 4 ★★★★
Self Catering
Contact: Peter Durbin
Cumbrian Cottages Ltd
t (01228) 599950
e enquiries@cumbrian-cottages.co.uk
w cumbrian-cottages.co.uk

Meadowcroft No 1 ★★★★
Self Catering
Contact: Peter Durbin
Cumbrian Cottages Ltd
t (01228) 599950
e enquiries@cumbrian-cottages.co.uk
w cumbrian-cottages.co.uk

Meadowcroft No 3 ★★★★
Self Catering
Contact: Peter Durbin
Cumbrian Cottages Ltd
t (01228) 599950
e enquiries@cumbrian-cottages.co.uk
w cumbrian-cottages.co.uk

Meadowcroft No 7 ★★★★
Self Catering
Contact: Peter Durbin
Cumbrian Cottages Ltd
t (01228) 599950
e enquiries@cumbrian-cottages.co.uk
w cumbrian-cottages.co.uk

Meadowcroft No 8 ★★★★
Self Catering
Contact: Peter Durbin
Cumbrian Cottages Ltd
t (01228) 599950
e enquiries@cumbrian-cottages.co.uk
w cumbrian-cottages.co.uk

Meadows End ★★★
Self Catering
Contact: Peter Durbin
Cumbrian Cottages Ltd
t (01228) 599950
e enquiries@cumbrian-cottages.co.uk
w cumbrian-cottages.co.uk

Megan's Cottage ★★★★
Self Catering
Contact: Peter Durbin
Cumbrian Cottages Ltd
t (01228) 599950
e enquiries@cumbrian-cottages.co.uk
w cumbrian-cottages.co.uk

Mere View ★★★★
Self Catering
Contact: Mr Paul Liddell
Lakelovers
t (015394) 88855
e bookings@lakelovers.co.uk
w lakelovers.co.uk

Merewood Stables
★★★★★ *Self Catering*
Contact: Mrs Susan Jackson
Heart of the Lakes
t (015394) 32321
e info@heartofthelakes.co.uk
w heartofthelakes.co.uk

Middlerigg ★★★★
Self Catering
Contact: Susan Jackson
Heart of the Lakes
t (015394) 32321
e info@heartofthelakes.co.uk
w heartofthelakes.co.uk

Mill Beck ★★★ *Self Catering*
Contact: Vicky Farmer
t (01827) 330941
e mill.beck@virgin.net
w millbeckcottage.co.uk

Moss Bank ★★★★
Self Catering
Contact: Peter Durbin
Cumbrian Cottages Ltd
t (01228) 599950
e enquiries@cumbrian-cottages.co.uk
w cumbrian-cottages.co.uk

Mylne Cottage ★★★★
Self Catering
Contact: Peter Durbin
Cumbrian Cottages Ltd
t (01228) 599950
e enquiries@cumbrian-cottages.co.uk
w cumbrian-cottages.co.uk

North Lodge & North Cottage ★★★★ *Self Catering*
Contact: Alan & Margaret Wardle
Lake District Holidays
t (015395) 68103
e lakedistricthols@aol.com
w lakedistrictholidays.net

Nu Holme ★★★ *Self Catering*
Contact: Peter Durbin
Cumbrian Cottages Ltd
t (01228) 599950
e enquiries@cumbrian-cottages.co.uk
w cumbrian-cottages.co.uk

Octavia Cottage ★★★
Self Catering
Contact: Mr Clive Sykes
Sykes Cottages
t (01244) 345700
e info@sykescottages.co.uk

Old Fallbarrow Cottage
★★★★ *Self Catering*
Contact: Mrs Susan Jackson
Heart of the Lakes
t (015394) 32321
e info@heartofthelakes.co.uk
w heartofthelakes.co.uk

The Old Stables ★★★★
Self Catering
Contact: Peter Durbin
Cumbrian Cottages Ltd
t (01228) 599950
e enquiries@cumbrian-cottages.co.uk
w cumbrian-cottages.co.uk

Olde Coach House and Stables ★★★ *Self Catering*
Contact: Alan & Margaret Wardle
Lake District Holidays
t (015395) 68103
e lakedistricthols@aol.com
w lakedistrictholidays.net

Orchard Fold ★★★
Self Catering
Contact: Peter Durbin
Cumbrian Cottages Ltd
t (01228) 599950
e enquiries@cumbrian-cottages.co.uk
w cumbrian-cottages.co.uk

Pan's Cottage ★★★
Self Catering
Contact: Peter Durbin
Cumbrian Cottages Ltd
t (01228) 599950
e enquiries@cumbrian-cottages.co.uk
w cumbrian-cottages.co.uk

Partridge Holme ★★★
Self Catering
Contact: Peter Durbin
Cumbrian Cottages Ltd
t (01228) 599950
e enquiries@cumbrian-cottages.co.uk
w cumbrian-cottages.co.uk

Pear Tree Cottage ★★★
Self Catering
Contact: Peter Durbin
Cumbrian Cottages Ltd
t (01228) 599950
e enquiries@cumbrian-cottages.co.uk
w cumbrian-cottages.co.uk

Penny Place ★★★★
Self Catering
Contact: Mr Paul Liddell
Lakelovers
t (015394) 88855
e bookings@lakelovers.co.uk
w lakelovers.co.uk

Penny's Nest ★★★★
Self Catering
Contact: Mr Paul Liddell
Lakelovers
t (015394) 88855
e bookings@lakelovers.co.uk
w lakelovers.co.uk

Pine Lodge ★★★★
Self Catering
Contact: Mr Paul Liddell
Lakelovers
t (015394) 88855
e bookings@lakelovers.co.uk
w lakelovers.co.uk

Pine Ridge ★★★
Self Catering
Contact: Peter Durbin
Cumbrian Cottages Ltd
t (01228) 599950
e enquiries@cumbrian-cottages.co.uk
w cumbrian-cottages.co.uk

Pine Rigg ★★★ *Self Catering*
Contact: Peter Durbin
Cumbrian Cottages Ltd
t (01228) 599950
e enquiries@cumbrian-cottages.co.uk
w cumbrian-cottages.co.uk

Pine View ★★★ *Self Catering*
Contact: Peter Durbin
Cumbrian Cottages Ltd
t (01228) 599950
e enquiries@cumbrian-cottages.co.uk
w cumbrian-cottages.co.uk

Pipers Howe ★★★★
Self Catering
Contact: Mr Paul Liddell
Lakelovers
t (015394) 88855
e bookings@lakelovers.co.uk
w lakelovers.co.uk

The Priory ★★★★★
Self Catering
Contact: Susan Jackson
Heart of the Lakes
t (015394) 32321
e info@heartofthelakes.co.uk
w heartofthelakes.co.uk

Priory Coach House ★★★★
Self Catering
Contact: Mr Paul Liddell
Lakelovers
t (015394) 88855
e bookings@lakelovers.co.uk
w lakelovers.co.uk

Priory Lodge ★★★★
Self Catering
Contact: Mr Paul Liddell
Lakelovers
t (015394) 88855
e bookings@lakelovers.co.uk
w lakelovers.co.uk

Rainbows End ★★★
Self Catering
Dales Hol Cot Ref: 3338
t (01756) 799821
e info@dalesholcot.com

Rattle Beck ★★★
Self Catering
Contact: Peter Durbin
Cumbrian Cottages Ltd
t (01228) 599950
e enquiries@cumbrian-cottages.co.uk
w cumbrian-cottages.co.uk

Rattlebeck ★★★-★★★★
Self Catering
Contact: Peter Durbin
Cumbrian Cottages Ltd
t (01228) 599950
e enquiries@cumbrian-cottages.co.uk
w cumbrian-cottages.co.uk

The Reverie ★★ *Self Catering*
Lakelovers
t (015394) 88855
e bookings@lakelovers.co.uk
w lakelovers.co.uk

Rivendell ★★★ *Self Catering*
Contact: Peter Durbin
Cumbrian Cottages Ltd
t (01228) 599950
e enquiries@cumbrian-cottages.co.uk
w cumbrian-cottages.co.uk

Rogerground ★★★★
Self Catering
Contact: Mr Paul Liddell
Lakelovers
t (015394) 88855
e bookings@lakelovers.co.uk
w lakelovers.co.uk

Rose Cottage ★★★
Self Catering
Contact: Alan & Margaret Wardle
Lake District Holidays
t (015395) 68103
e lakedistricthols@aol.com
w lakedistrictholidays.net

Rustic Cottage ★★★
Self Catering
Lakelovers
t (015394) 88855
e bookings@lakelovers.co.uk
w lakelovers.co.uk

Saw Mill Cottage ★★★
Self Catering
Contact: Mrs Susan Jackson
Heart of the Lakes
t (015394) 32321
e info@heartofthelakes.co.uk
w heartofthelakes.co.uk

The Secret Garden ★★★
Self Catering
Contact: Peter Durbin
Cumbrian Cottages Ltd
t (01228) 599950
e enquiries@cumbrian-cottages.co.uk
w cumbrian-cottages.co.uk

Skylark ★★★★ *Self Catering*
Contact: Peter Durbin
Cumbrian Cottages Ltd
t (01228) 599950
e enquiries@cumbrian-cottages.co.uk
w cumbrian-cottages.co.uk

Solstice Cottage ★★★
Self Catering
Contact: Mr Paul Liddell
Lakelovers
t (015394) 88855
e bookings@lakelovers.co.uk
w lakelovers.co.uk

Squirrels Nest ★★★★
Self Catering
Lakelovers
t (015394) 88855
e bookings@lakelovers.co.uk
w lakelovers.co.uk

Stable Cottage ★★★★★
Self Catering
Contact: Mrs Susan Jackson
Heart of the Lakes
t (015394) 32321
e info@heartofthelakes.co.uk
w heartofthelakes.co.uk

Storrs Hall Self-Catering
★★★ *Self Catering*
Contact: Peter Durbin
Cumbrian Cottages Ltd
t (01228) 599950
e enquiries@cumbrian-cottages.co.uk
w cumbrian-cottages.co.uk

Sunny Brow ★★★★
Self Catering
Lakelovers
t (015394) 88855
e bookings@lakelovers.co.uk
w lakelovers.co.uk

Swallows Rest ★★★
Self Catering
Lakelovers
t (015394) 88855
e bookings@lakelovers.co.uk
w lakelovers.co.uk

The Thimble ★★★
Self Catering
Lakelovers
t (015394) 88855
e bookings@lakelovers.co.uk
w lakelovers.co.uk

The Thistles ★★★
Self Catering
Contact: Ms Sue Jackson
Heart of the Lakes
t (015394) 32321
e info@heartofthelakes.co.uk
w heartofthelakes.co.uk

Thompson Cottage ★★★★
Self Catering
Contact: Susan Jackson
Heart of the Lakes
t (015394) 32321
e info@heartofthelakes.co.uk
w heartofthelakes.co.uk

Tinkerbells ★★★
Self Catering
Contact: Peter Durbin
Cumbrian Cottages Ltd
t (01228) 599950
e enquiries@cumbrian-cottages.co.uk
w cumbrian-cottages.co.uk

The Toffee Loft ★★★★
Self Catering
Contact: Mr Paul Liddell
Lakelovers
t (015394) 88855
e bookings@lakelovers.co.uk
w lakelovers.co.uk

Tourelle ★★★★
Self Catering
Lakelovers
t (015394) 88855
e bookings@lakelovers.co.uk
w lakelovers.co.uk

Tree Tops ★★★★
Self Catering
Contact: Mr Paul Liddell
Lakelovers
t (015394) 88855
e bookings@lakelovers.co.uk
w lakelovers.co.uk

Treetops ★★★★
Self Catering
Contact: John Alcock
t (015394) 32819
e treetops@lakedistrictcumbria.co.uk
w lakedistrictcumbria.co.uk

Troutbeck Barn ★★★
Self Catering
Contact: Mr Paul Liddell
Lakelovers
t (015394) 88855
e bookings@lakelovers.co.uk
w lakelovers.co.uk

Waterfall ★★★ *Self Catering*
Contact: Peter Durbin
Cumbrian Cottages Ltd
t (01228) 599950
e enquiries@cumbrian-cottages.co.uk
w cumbrian-cottages.co.uk

Waterhead Cottage ★★★★
Self Catering
Contact: Ms Sue Jackson
Heart of the Lakes
t (015394) 32321
e info@heartofthelakes.co.uk
w heartofthelakes.co.uk

Waters Edge Villa ★★★★
Self Catering
Contact: Robert & Maureen Judson
Windermere Lake Holidays
t (015394) 43415
e email@lakewindermere.net
w lakewindermere.net

Wayside Cottage ★★★★
Self Catering
Lakelovers
t (015394) 88855
e bookings@lakelovers.co.uk
w lakelovers.co.uk

The Wendy House ★★★
Self Catering
Lakelovers
t (015394) 88855
e bookings@lakelovers.co.uk
w lakelovers.co.uk

Westwood ★★★★★
Self Catering
Contact: Mr Paul Liddell
Lakelovers
t (015394) 88855
e bookings@lakelovers.co.uk
w lakelovers.co.uk

White Moss ★★★★
Self Catering
Heart of the Lakes
t (015394) 32321
e info@heartofthelakes.co.uk
w heartofthelakes.co.uk

Wind Force ★★★★
Self Catering
Contact: Mr Paul Liddell
Lakelovers
t (015394) 88855
e bookings@lakelovers.co.uk
w lakelovers.co.uk

Windermere Marina Village
★★★★ *Self Catering*
Contact: Jason Dearden
Windermere Marina Village
t 0800 262902
e info@wmv.co.uk
w wmv.co.uk

Winster Fields ★★★★★
Self Catering
Contact: Mrs Susan Jackson
Heart of the Lakes
t (015394) 32321
e info@heartofthelakes.co.uk
w heartofthelakes.co.uk

Winster House ★★★
Self Catering
Contact: Mr and Mrs Whalley
Winster House
t (015394) 44723
e enquiries@winsterhouse.co.uk
w winsterhouse.co.uk

Woodland View ★★★
Self Catering
Contact: Peter Durbin
Cumbrian Cottages Ltd
t (01228) 599950
e enquiries@cumbrian-cottages.co.uk
w cumbrian-cottages.co.uk

Woodside ★★★★
Self Catering
Contact: Mrs Susan Jackson
Heart of the Lakes
t (015394) 32321
e info@heartofthelakes.co.uk
w heartofthelakes.co.uk

WINSTER
Cumbria

All Seasons ★★★
Self Catering
Lakelovers
t (015394) 88855
e bookings@lakelovers.co.uk
w lakelovers.co.uk

Head of Winster ★★★
Self Catering
Lakelovers
t (015394) 88855
e bookings@lakelovers.co.uk
w lakelovers.co.uk

WINTON
Cumbria

The Manor House ★★★
Self Catering
Contact: Peter Durbin
Cumbrian Cottages Ltd
t (01228) 599950
e enquiries@cumbrian-cottages.co.uk
w cumbrian-cottages.co.uk

Manor House ★★★
Self Catering
Contact: Mrs E Beckwith
t (01768) 341366
w country-holidays.co.uk

WITHERSLACK
Cumbria

Spa Inn House ★★★
Self Catering
Contact: Peter Durbin
Cumbrian Cottages Ltd
t (01228) 599950
e enquiries@cumbrian-cottages.co.uk
w cumbrian-cottages.co.uk

Thornbarrow Hill Cottage
★★★ *Self Catering*
Contact: Mr John Serginson
The Lakeland Cottage Company
t (015395) 30024
e john@lakelandcottageco.com

WORSLEY
Greater Manchester

The Cottage – Worsley
★★★ *Self Catering*
Contact: Mr John Atherton
t (0161) 793 4157

WORSTON
Lancashire

Angram Green Holiday Cottages ★★★★
Self Catering
Contact: Ms Christine Gorrill
Worston
t (01200) 441455
e info@angramgreen.co.uk
w angramgreen.co.uk

WRENBURY
Cheshire

Jasmine Cottage ★★★
Self Catering
Contact: Ms Michelle Groom
t 0845 095 6539

YANWATH
Cumbria

Amber Nook ★★★★
Self Catering
Contact: Peter Durbin
Cumbrian Cottages Ltd
t (01228) 599950
e enquiries@cumbrian-cottages.co.uk
w cumbrian-cottages.co.uk

Beech Barn ★★★
Self Catering
Contact: Peter Durbin
Cumbrian Cottages Ltd
t (01228) 599950
e enquiries@cumbrian-cottages.co.uk
w cumbrian-cottages.co.uk

Copper Beech Cottage
★★★★ *Self Catering*
t (01768) 892855

Lyzzick Lodge ★★★★
Self Catering
Contact: Peter Durbin
Cumbrian Cottages Ltd
t (01228) 599950
e enquiries@cumbrian-cottages.co.uk
w cumbrian-cottages.co.uk

Meadow Lodge ★★★★
Self Catering
Contact: Peter Durbin
Cumbrian Cottages Ltd
t (01228) 599950
e enquiries@cumbrian-cottages.co.uk
w cumbrian-cottages.co.uk

Look out for establishments participating in the Walkers and Cyclists Welcome Schemes

Tillybardine Lodge ★★★★
Self Catering
Contact: Peter Durbin
Cumbrian Cottages Ltd
t (01228) 599950
e enquiries@cumbrian-cottages.co.uk
w cumbrian-cottages.co.uk

YEALAND CONYERS
Lancashire

Kilross Lodge ★★★★★
Self Catering
Contact: Mrs Christina Winder
t (01524) 732814

YEALAND REDMAYNE
Lancashire

Brackenthwaite Cottages ★★★–★★★★ *Self Catering*
Contact: Mrs Susan Clarke
t (015395) 63276

YEARNGILL
Cumbria

Hill House ★★★
Self Catering
Contact: Mary Kinsella
t (01697) 322399
e mary@mkinsella.fsbusiness.co.uk
w mkinsella.fsbusiness.co.uk

NORTH EAST ENGLAND

ACKLINGTON
Northumberland

The Railway Inn ★★★
Self Catering
Contact: Mrs Linda Osborne
t (01670) 760320
e linda.osborne@btopenworld.com
w wishingwellcottages.co.uk

AKELD
Northumberland

Akeld Manor & Country Club (Ivy Cottage) ★★★★
Self Catering
Contact: Mrs Patricia Allan
Border Rose Cottages
t (01665) 721035
e allan.group@virgin.net
w borderrose-holidays.co.uk

Akeld Manor & Country Club (Blueberry Cottage)
★★★★ *Self Catering*
Contact: Mrs Patricia Allan
Border Rose Cottages
t (01665) 721035
e allan.group@virgin.net
w borderrose-holidays.co.uk

Akeld Manor & Country Club (Catkin Cottage)
★★★★ *Self Catering*
Contact: Mrs Patricia Allan
Border Rose Cottages
t (01665) 721035
e allan.group@virgin.net
w borderrose-holidays.co.uk

Akeld Manor & Country Club (Foxglove) ★★★★
Self Catering
Contact: Mrs Patricia Allan
Border Rose Cottages
t (01665) 721035
e allan.group@virgin.net
w borderrose-holidays.co.uk

Akeld Manor & Country Club (Honeysuckle Haven)
★★★★ *Self Catering*
Contact: Mrs Patricia Allan
Border Rose Cottages
t (01665) 721035
e allan.group@virgin.net
w borderrose-holidays.co.uk

Akeld Manor & Country Club (Lavender Cottages)
★★★★ *Self Catering*
Contact: Mrs Patricia Allan
Border Rose Cottages
t (01665) 721035
e allan.group@virgin.net
w borderrose-holidays.co.uk

Akeld Manor & Country Club (Pansy Plot) ★★★★
Self Catering
Contact: Mrs Patricia Allan
Border Rose Cottages
t (01665) 721035
e allan.group@virgin.net
w borderrose-holidays.co.uk

Akeld Manor & Country Club (The Columbine)
★★★★ *Self Catering*
Contact: Mrs Patricia Allan
Border Rose Cottages
t (01665) 721035
e allan.group@virgin.net
w borderrose-holidays.co.uk

Akeld Manor & Country Club (Timberwick Green)
★★★★ *Self Catering*
Contact: Mrs Patricia Allan
Border Rose Cottages
t (01665) 721035
e allan.group@virgin.net
w borderrose-holidays.co.uk

Akeld Manor & Country Club (Bizzie Lizzie) ★★★★
Self Catering
Contact: Mrs Patricia Allan
Border Rose Cottages
t (01665) 721035
e allan-group@virgin.net
w borderrose-holidays.co.uk

Akeld Manor & Country Club (Perry Winkle) ★★★★
Self Catering
Contact: Mrs Patricia Allan
Border Rose Cottages
t (01665) 721035
w borderrose-holidays.co.uk

Akeld Manor & Country Club (Fresia Cottage)
★★★★ *Serviced Apartments*
Contact: Mrs Patricia Allan
Border Rose Cottages
t (01665) 721035
e allan.group@virgin.net
w borderrose-holidays.co.uk

Akeld Manor & Country Club (Primula Patch) ★★★★
Self Catering
Contact: Mrs Patricia Allan
Border Rose Holidays
t (01665) 721035
e allan.group@virgin.net
w borderrose-holidays.co.uk

Akeld Manor & Country Club (Holly Hocks) ★★★★
Self Catering
Contact: Mrs Patricia Allan
Border Rose Cottages
t (01665) 721035
e allan.group@virgin.net
w borderrose-holidays.co.uk

Akeld Manor & Country Club (Aubretia Trail)
★★★★ *Self Catering*
Contact: Mrs Patricia Allan
Border Rose Holidays
t (01665) 721035
e allan.group@virgin.net
w borderrose-holidays.co.uk

ALLENDALE
Northumberland

Allenmill Cottages ★★★★
Self Catering
Contact: Ms Emma Robson
t (01434) 683126
e info@allenmill.com
w allenmill.com

ALLENHEADS
Northumberland

Englewood ★★★
Self Catering
Sykes Cottages Ref:291
t (01244) 345700
e info@sykescottages.co.uk
w sykescottages.co.uk

ALNMOUTH
Northumberland

Bilton Barns ★★★★
Self Catering
Contact: Mrs Dorothy Jackson
t (01665) 830427
e dorothy@biltonbarns.com
w biltonbarns.com

Curlews Calling ★★★
Self Catering
Contact: Miss Jane Worsley
t (020) 7223 9941
e jane@jworsley.wanadoo.co.uk
w curlewscalling.co.uk

Garden Cottage ★★★★
Self Catering
Contact: Mr Robin Winder
t (01914) 408586
e robin75up@hotmail.com

Grange Cottages – Old Watch Tower & The Coach House ★★★★ *Self Catering*
Contact: Ms Nicola Brierley
t (01665) 830783
e cottages@nccc.demon.co.uk
w northumbria-cottages.co.uk

Old Hall Cottage, High Buston Hall ★★★★★
Self Catering
Contact: Mrs Therese Atherton
t (01665) 830606
e highbuston@aol.com
w highbuston.com

Paradise Lodge
Rating Applied For
Self Catering
Contact: Sandra MacDonald
Durham House
t (01913) 843904
e sa@heavenlyholidayhomes.co.uk
w heavenlyholidayhomes.co.uk

Shepherds House ★★★
Self Catering
Contact: Mrs Lyn Frater
t (01665) 830361
e lynpfrater@aol.com
w cottageguide.co.uk/shepherdshouse

Sunnyside Cottage ★★★★
Self Catering
Contact: Mrs Mary Hollins
t (01914) 883939
e sunnysidecott@lineone.net
w visitalnwick.org.uk

Wooden Farm Holiday Cottages ★★–★★★
Self Catering
Contact: Mr Gordon Farr
t (01665) 830342

ALNWICK
Northumberland

21C & 21D The Hotspur
★★★★ *Self Catering*
Contact: Mr & Mrs Trevor & Elizabeth Dunn
t 07930 405961
e stay@thehotspur.co.uk
w thehotspur.co.uk

3 Jubilee Court ★★★★
Self Catering
Contact: Mrs Jenny Robinson
t (01665) 605153
e wwr@globalnet.co.uk

Alndyke Farm Cottages
★★★★ *Self Catering*
Contact: Mrs Laura Davison
t (01665) 510252
e alndyke@fsmail.net
w alndyke.co.uk

Alnwick Angel ★★★
Self Catering
Contact: Mr Colin McLean
t (01665) 602315
e alnwickangel@tesco.net

The Bailiffgate Flat ★★★★
Self Catering
Contact: Mr Christopher Goodfellow
t (01668) 214412
e sylviamcs1@aol.com
w bailiffgate.co.uk

Barbican View ★★★★
Self Catering
Contact: Mrs Frances Draper
t (01484) 683705
e fran.draper@virgin.net
w barbicanview.co.uk

Bog Mill Farm Holiday Cottages ★★★★-★★★★★
Self Catering
Contact: Mrs Ann Mason
t (01665) 604529
e stay@bogmill.co.uk
w bogmill.co.uk

Braeside
Rating Applied For
Self Catering
Contact: Mrs Margaret McGregor
t (01665) 574460
e margaret@broomehillfarm.co.uk
w broomehillfarm.co.uk

The Buie ★★★ *Self Catering*
Contact: Ms Diana Norris
t (01599) 522365
e diana_norris@hotmail.com

Dene View Cottage and Moor Croft Cottage ★★★★
Self Catering
Contact: Mrs Margaret McGregor
t (01665) 574460
e margaret@broomehillfarm.co.uk
w broomehillfarm.co.uk

Dunelm ★★★ *Self Catering*
Contact: Mrs Val Greene
t (01529) 413148
e val.greene@btinternet.com

Farm Cottage ★★★
Self Catering
Contact: Mrs J A Renner
t (01665) 579266
w cottageguide.co.uk/shipleyhill

Folly Cottage ★★★
Self Catering
Contact: Mrs Joan Gilroy
t (01665) 579265

Garden Cottages ★★★★
Self Catering
Contact: Miss Andrea Tomkins
t (01665) 574129
e info@alnwickgardencottages.co.uk
w alnwickgardencottages.co.uk

Harehope Hall ★★★
Self Catering
Contact: Ms Alison Wrangham
Harehope Hall
t (01668) 217329
e aliwrangham@btconnect.com

Herring Sheds Cottage ★★★★★ *Self Catering*
Contact: Mrs Jane Mallen
t (01668) 219941
e jane@nehc.co.uk
w alnwickcastlecottages.co.uk

Juliet Cottage ★★★
Self Catering
Contact: Mrs Louise Sweeney
t (01912) 857794
e louise.sweeney@blueyonder.co.uk
w cottageguide.co.uk/juliet

Limpet Cottage ★★★★
Self Catering
Contact: Mrs Jane Mallen
t (01668) 219941
e jane@nehc.co.uk
w alnwickcastlecottages.co.uk

Lumbylaw & Garden Cottages ★★★★
Self Catering
Contact: Mrs S Lee
t (01665) 574277
e holidays@lumbylaw.co.uk
w lumbylaw.co.uk

Mole End ★★★ *Self Catering*
Hoseasons
t 0870 534 2342

The Old Smithy ★★★★
Self Catering
Contact: Miss Lee-Anne Keers
t 07970 210607
e k.keers@tiscali.co.uk

The Pebble ★★★
Self Catering
Contact: Mrs Clare Laughton
t (01428) 683941
e clarelaughton@googlemail.com

Reiver Cottage – Ref 3607 ★★★★ *Self Catering*
Contact: Ms Lorraine Kidd
Dales Holiday Cottages
t 0870 909 9500
e lorraine.k@dales-holiday-cottages.com
w dalesholcot.com

Stamford & Embleton Mill Farm Cottages ★★★-★★★★ *Self Catering*
Contact: Mrs Hazel Grahamslaw
t (01665) 579425

Village Farm ★★★-★★★★★
Self Catering
Contact: Mrs Crissy Stoker
t (01665) 575591
e crissy@villagefarmcottages.co.uk
w villagefarmcottages.co.uk

Walkergate House ★★★
Self Catering
Contact: Mr Keith Richardson
t (01665) 830139
e keith.richardson@economicpartnership.com
w alnwickcottages.co.uk

ALWINTON Northumberland

Fellside Cottage ★★★★
Self Catering
Contact: Mrs Denise Straughan
t (01670) 823042
e stay@fellsidecottcheviots.co.uk
w fellsidecottcheviots.co.uk

Stonecrop Cottage ★★★
Self Catering
Contact: Mrs Maureen Mason
t (01912) 570892

AMBLE Northumberland

Acarsaid ★★★ *Self Catering*
Contact: Mrs Lynne Gray
t (01665) 711737

Amblers Rest ★★★
Self Catering
Contact: Mrs Glenys Rudd
t (01665) 714869
e neil@neilandglenys.freeserve.co.uk

Seashells ★★★ *Self Catering*
Contact: Mr & Mrs Ian & Sue Rochester
t (01665) 713448
e ian@roch11.freeserve.co.uk
w seashellscottage.co.uk

AMBLE-BY-THE-SEA Northumberland

Coastguard Cottage ★★★★
Self Catering
Contact: Mr & Mrs N Aitchison
t (01904) 490408
e neville@aitchison.co.uk
w coastguardcottage.co.uk

BALDERSDALE County Durham

Clove Lodge Cottage ★★★
Self Catering
Contact: Mrs Caroline Carter
t (01833) 650030
e carolinecarter69@aol.com
w clovelodge.co.uk

BAMBURGH Northumberland

The Blacksmiths ★★★
Self Catering
Contact: Mrs Rachel Cole
t (01636) 830864
e rachelstevecole@hotmail.com

Bradford Country Cottages ★★★-★★★★ *Self Catering*
Contact: Mr L W Robson
Bradford Country Cottages
t (01668) 213432
e lwrob@tiscali.co.uk
w bradford-leisure.co.uk

Bridge End ★★★★
Self Catering
Contact: Mr & Mrs Roger & Linda Topping
t (0141) 334 4833

The Bungalow ★★★★
Self Catering
Contact: Miss Eve Humphreys
t (01668) 214213
e evehumphreys@aol.com
w burtonhall.co.uk

Castle View Bungalow ★★★★ *Self Catering*
Contact: Mr & Mrs I Nicol
t (01665) 720320
e ian@slatehall.freeserve.co.uk
w slatehallridingcentre.com

The Cottage ★★★★
Self Catering
Contact: Mrs Turnbull
t (01668) 214494
e theturnbulls2k@btinternet.com
w holidaynorthumbria.co.uk

Dukesfield Farm Holiday Cottages ★★★★
Self Catering
Contact: Mrs Maria Eliana Robinson
EMR Properties
t (01668) 214456
e eric_j_robinson@compuserve.com
w secretkingdom.com/dukes/field.htm

The Fairway ★★
Self Catering
Contact: Mrs Diana Middleton
t (01661) 852125
e rsmiddleton@talk21.com

Glebe House and Glebe Cottage ★★★★★
Self Catering
Contact: Mrs Maria Eliana Robinson
EMR Properties
t (01668) 214456
e eric_j_robinson@compuserve.com
w secretkingdom.com/glebe/house.htm

The Granary ★★★
Self Catering
Contact: Mrs Patricia Cowen
t (01228) 560245
e cowen_home@hotmail.com

Harelaw House ★★★★
Self Catering
Contact: Ms Zana Juppenlatz
t (01668) 215494
e zana.juppenlatz@ukonline.co.uk
w harelawhouse.ntb.org.uk

Hoppen Hall Farm Cottages ★★★★ *Self Catering*
Contact: Mrs Jane Mallen
t (01668) 219941
e jane@nehc.co.uk
w alnwickcastlecottages.co.uk

Inglenook Cottage ★★★
Self Catering
Contact: Mrs Amanda J Moore
t (01423) 772211
e inglenookcottage@aol.com
w inglenookcottage.info

Millhouse Cottage ★★★★
Self Catering
Contact: Mrs Sarah Nelson
t (01665) 578361
e stay@millhouse-cottage.co.uk
w millhouse-cottage.co.uk

Outchester & Ross Farm Cottages ★★★★
Self Catering
Contact: Mrs Shirley McKie
t (01668) 213336
e enquiry@rosscottages.co.uk
w rosscottages.co.uk

Point Cottages ★★★
Self Catering
Contact: Mrs Sanderson
t (0191) 266 2800
e info@bamburgh-cottages.co.uk
w bamburgh-cottages.co.uk

Saint Oswald's ★★
Self Catering
Contact: Mr Anthony Smith
t (020) 8248 9589
e anthontsmith@hotmail.com

Smugglers Court ★★★★
Self Catering
Contact: Mr Gordon Begg
t (01289) 302416
e gordonbegg@hotmail.co.uk
w budle-bay.com

Springhill Farm Holiday Accommodation ★★★★
Self Catering
Contact: Mrs Julie Gregory
t (01665) 721820
e enquiries@springhill-farm.co.uk
w springhill-farm.co.uk

Waren Lea Hall ★★★★★
Self Catering
Contact: Carolynn and David Croisdale-Appleby
t (01494) 725194
e croisdaleappleby@aol.com
w selfcateringluxury.co.uk

Whinstone Cottage ★★★
Self Catering
Contact: Mrs Philippa Tait
t (01912) 851363

Wynding Down ★★★★★
Self Catering
Contact: Mrs Dianne Stanger
t (01670) 511162
e distanger@hotmail.com

BARDON MILL
Northumberland

Brownside ★★★★★
Self Catering
Contact: Mrs Ann Oliver
t (01434) 344928
e relax@brownside.co.uk
w brownside.co.uk

The Hott ★★★ *Self Catering*
Northumbria Byways Self-catering Cottages
t (01697) 741600

Keepers Cottage ★★★★★
Self Catering
Contact: Ms Jane Rees
t (01434) 344021
e jane.rees@bonnyrigghall.co.uk
w bonnyrigghall.co.uk

BARNARD CASTLE
County Durham

5A Market Place ★★★
Self Catering
Contact: Mr & Mrs C Armstrong
t (01833) 690726
e joan.marketplace@gmail.com

Boot and Shoe Cottage
★★★★ *Self Catering*
Contact: Mrs Rachel Peat
t (01833) 627200
e info@bootandshoecottage.co.uk
w bootandshoecottage.co.uk

East Briscoe Farm Cottages
★★★★ *Self Catering*
Contact: Mr Chris Tarpey
t (01833) 650087
e one@eastbriscoe.co.uk
w eastbriscoe.co.uk

Hauxwell Grange Cottages (The Stone Byre and Curlew Cottage) ★★★★
Self Catering
Contact: Mrs Val Pearson
t (01833) 695022
e hauxwellvmp@supaworld.com
w hauxwellgrangecottages.co.uk

Lanquitts Cottage ★
Self Catering
Contact: Mrs Brenda Kidd
t (01833) 650345

Riverdale Cottage ★★★★
Self Catering
Contact: Mrs Allyson Bunn
t (01915) 110555
e stay@riverdale-cottage.co.uk
w riverdale-cottage.co.uk

Staindrop House Mews & The Arches ★★★★
Self Catering
Contact: Mrs Dorothy Walton
t (01833) 660951
e harry-1937@hotmail.com

Tees View (4156) ★★★★
Self Catering
Contact: Ms Lorraine Kidd
Dales Holiday Cottages
t 0870 909 9500
e lorraine.k@dales-holiday-cottages.com
w dalesholcot.com

Thorngate Coach House
★★★★ *Self Catering*
Contact: Mrs Clare Terry
t (01833) 637791
e info@thorngatecoachhouse.co.uk
w thorngatecoachhouse.co.uk

Wackford Squeers Cottage
★★★ *Self Catering*
Contact: Mr John Braithwaite
Wackford Squeers Cottage
t (01833) 650032
e wodencroft@freenet.co.uk

Waterside (4157) ★★★★
Self Catering
Contact: Ms Lorraine Kidd
Dales Holiday Cottages
t 0870 909 9500
e lorraine.k@dales-holiday-cottages.com
w dalesholcot.com

Woodland House Cottage
★★★ *Self Catering*
Contact: Mr Harding
t (01388) 710836
e cottage@woodland-house.freeserve.co.uk
w cottageguide.co.uk/woodlandhouse

BARNINGHAM
County Durham

Dove Cottage ★★★
Self Catering
Contact: Miss Sheila Catton
t (01833) 621374
e dove@smithj90.fsnet.co.uk
w cottageguide.co.uk/dove-cottage

BEADNELL
Northumberland

3 Alexandra House ★★★
Self Catering
Contact: Mr & Mrs Stephen & Ruth Lithgow
t (01912) 666440
e ruthlithgow@yahoo.ie
w beadnellholidays.co.uk

6 Benthall ★★★★
Self Catering
Contact: Mr & Mrs F Davidson
t (01665) 720269

Alexandra Cottage ★★★★
Self Catering
Contact: Mrs Charlotte Slater
t (01661) 822337
e alexandracottage@beadnellvillage.co.uk
w beadnellvillage.co.uk/ac

Annstead Farm ★★★★
Self Catering
Contact: Mrs Susan Mellor
t (01665) 720387
e susan@annstead.co.uk
w annstead.co.uk

Beechley ★★★★
Self Catering
Contact: Mrs Deborah Baker
t (0113) 218 9176
e deb_n_ade@hotmail.com

The Bothy ★★★★
Self Catering
Contact: Mrs Beryl Seaward-Birchall
t (01665) 720497
w thebothy.ntb.org.uk

The Dells ★★★ *Self Catering*
Contact: Mr & Mrs Iain & Andrea Slater
t (01912) 365415
e andreaslater@beadnell.fsnet.co.uk

Driftwood
Rating Applied For
Self Catering
Contact: Mrs Carole Field
t (01665) 720225
e info@beachcourt.com
w beachcourt.com/driftwood

Low Dover Beadnell Bay
★★★★ *Self Catering*
Contact: Mrs Kath Thompson
t (01665) 720291
e enquiries@lowdover.co.uk
w lowdover.co.uk

Mapleleaf Cottage ★★★
Self Catering
Contact: Mrs Susan McKenzie
t (01670) 738422 & 07950 173570

Nook End Cottage & Driftwood Cottage
★★★★★ *Self Catering*
Contact: Ms Fiona McKeith
t (01912) 851272
e info@coastalretreats.co.uk
w coastalretreats.co.uk

St Ebba's Peep ★★★★★
Self Catering
Contact: Mrs Julie Carr
t (01665) 720569
e juliecarrl@hotmail.co.uk
w beadnellhouselets.co.uk

Torwoodlee & Shorestone (ref: 1892, 1893) ★★★
Self Catering
Contact: Ms Lorraine Kidd
Dales Holiday Cottages
t 0870 909 9500
e lorraine.k@dales-holiday-cottages.com
w dalesholcot.com

Town Farm Cottages ★★★
Self Catering
Contact: Mr & Mrs Paul & Marianne Thompson
Marshall Thompson
t (01670) 783686
e marianne@marishalthompson.co.uk
w heritagecoastholidays.com

BEAL
Northumberland

Bee Hill Properties
★★★★-★★★★★
Self Catering
Contact: Mr David Nesbitt
t (01289) 303425
e info@beehill.co.uk
w beehill.co.uk

BEAMISH
County Durham

Chapel House Studio Apartments ★★★
Self Catering
Contact: Mr John MacLennan
Chapel House
t (01207) 290992
w chapelhouseapartments.co.uk

BELFORD
Northumberland

Chillingham Cottage ★★★
Self Catering
Contact: Mr Scott Carruthers
t (01912) 802484
e scarruthers@blueyonder.co.uk

Elwick Farm Cottages
★★★★ *Self Catering*
Contact: Mrs Roslyn Reay
t (01668) 213242
e w.r.reay@talk21.com
w elwickcottages.co.uk

Gardener's Cottage ★★★★
Self Catering
Contact: Mrs Susan Comber
t (01668) 215443
e thecombers@supanet.com
w gardeners-cott.co.uk

Hollyhock House ★★★★
Self Catering
Contact: Miss Alison Turnbull
t (020) 7733 4904
e ali_turnbull@hotmail.com
w hollyhockhouse.co.uk

Owls Rest ★★★★
Self Catering
Contact: Ms Christine Brown
t (01668) 215343
e chattonbb@aol.com
w owlsrestbelford.co.uk

Swinhoe Farm Cottages and Riding Centre ★★★
Self Catering
Contact: Mrs Valerie Nixon
t (01668) 213370
e valerie@swinhoecottages.co.uk
w swinhoecottages.co.uk

Teal Cottage ★★★-★★★★
Self Catering
Contact: Mrs Katie Burn
t (01668) 213247
e enquiries@fenham-le-moor.co.uk
w fenham-le-moor.co.uk

BELLINGHAM
Northumberland

Boat Farm Cottages (Heron Cottage and Otter Cottage) ★★★★ *Self Catering*
Contact: Mrs Barbara Young
t (01434) 220989
e barbaraattheboat@hotmail.com
w boatfarm.co.uk

Buteland Bothy ★★
Self Catering
Contact: Mrs Alison Williams
t (01434) 220389
e buteland@aol.com

Castle Hill View ★★★
Self Catering
Contact: Mr & Mrs Len & Joan Batey
t (01434) 220263

Conheath Cottage ★★★★
Self Catering
Contact: Mrs Zaina Riddle
t (01434) 220250
e stay@conheath.co.uk
w conheath.co.uk

BELSAY
Northumberland

Lake Cottage
Rating Applied For
Self Catering
English Heritage Holiday Cottages
t 0870 333 1187
w english-heritage.org.uk/holidaycottages

BERWICK-UPON-TWEED
Northumberland

2 The Courtyard ★★★
Self Catering
Contact: Mrs Morton
t (01289) 308737
e jvm@patmosphere.uklinux.net
w berwickselfcatering.co.uk

Broadstone Cottage ★★
Self Catering
Contact: Mr Edward Chantler
t (01622) 850207

Cliff Cottage ★★★
Self Catering
Contact: Mr & Mrs James Fairbairn
t (01289) 307375

Courtyard Cottage ★★★★
Self Catering
Contact: Mrs Susan Howard
t (01912) 680788
e enquiries@reiverproperties.com
w reiverproperties.com

Honeysuckle Cottage and Bluebell Cottage ★★★★
Self Catering
Contact: Mr Robert Whitten
t (01289) 331112
e robert@westlongridge.co.uk
w westlongridge.co.uk

Ivy Cottage ★★★
Self Catering
Contact: Mr Robert Ian Heslop
t (01661) 833071
e ian@riheslop.go-plus.net

Ivy Place (3854) ★★★★
Self Catering
Contact: Ms Lorraine Kidd
Dales Holiday Cottages
t 0870 909 9500
e lorraine.k@dales-holiday-cottages.com
w dalesholcot.com

Lark Rise ★★★★
Self Catering
Contact: Mrs Deirdre Dickson
t (01912) 130662
e stay@northumbrian-cottages.co.uk
w northumbrian-cottages.co.uk

Mariner House ★★★
Self Catering
Contact: Mrs Brenda Trobe
The Old Presbytery
t (01670) 786001
e lindpress@aol.com

Mill Lane Apartments ★★★★ *Self Catering*
Contact: Mr John Haswell
t (01289) 304492
e john@millane.co.uk
w millane.co.uk

Newt Cottage ★★★★
Self Catering
Contact: Mrs Karen Burn
t (01289) 388652
e kburn.huntinghall@btinternet.com

The Old Barn ★★★★
Self Catering
Contact: Mr & Mrs Richard & Susan Persse
t (01289) 306585
e r.persse-highl@amserve.com
w oldbarnhighletham.co.uk

South Ord Farm Bungalow REF: 2203 ★★★★
Self Catering
Contact: Ms Lorraine Kidd
Dales Holiday Cottages
t 0870 909 9500
e lorraine.k@dales-holiday-cottages.com
w dalesholcot.com

Tigh Na Rudh ★★★★
Self Catering
Contact: Mrs Rosemary Evans
t (01835) 823031
e b.wynn.evans@care4free.net

Trevone ★★★★
Self Catering
Contact: Mr Peter Herdman
t (01289) 307524

Wellington Terrace Apartment ★★★★★
Self Catering
Contact: Mrs Aicha Fagan
t (01289) 305000
e aichafagan@hotmail.co.uk
w wellingtonterraceapartment.com

West Kyloe Cottages ★★★
Self Catering
Contact: Mrs Teresa Smalley
Garden Cottage
t (01289) 381279
e teresasmalley@westkyloe.demon.co.uk
w westkyloe.co.uk

West Ord Holiday Cottages ★★★-★★★★★ *Self Catering*
Contact: Mrs Carol Lang
t (01289) 386631
e stay@westord.co.uk
w westord.co.uk

Whitecroft ★★★★
Self Catering
Contact: Mrs Moira Kay
t (01289) 386066
e enquiries@whitecroftcottage.co.uk
w whitecroftcottage.co.uk

BILTON
Northumberland

Rose Cottage ★★★
Self Catering
Contact: Mr Reservations
t (01665) 830783
e cottages@nccc.demon.co.uk
w alnmouth-cottage.co.uk

BINGFIELD
Northumberland

The Hytte ★★★★★
Self Catering
Contact: Mr & Mrs S R Gregory
t (01434) 672321
e sgregory001@tiscali.co.uk
w thehytte.com

BISHOP AUCKLAND
County Durham

Five Gables Cottage, Binchester ★★★★
Self Catering
Contact: Mr & Mrs Paul & Judy Weston
t (01388) 608204
e cottage@fivegables.co.uk
w fivegables.co.uk

Gill Bank Farm Cottage ★★★ *Self Catering*
Contact: Mrs Anne Marley
t (01388) 718614

Meadow View ref:1462 ★★★ *Self Catering*
Contact: Ms Lorraine Kidd
Dales Holiday Cottages
t 0870 909 9500
e lorraine.k@dales-holiday-cottages.com
w dalesholcot.com

West Cottage ★★★★
Self Catering
Contact: Mrs Elizabeth Wilkinson
t (01388) 720252
e carrsides@farming.co.uk

BISHOP MIDDLEHAM
County Durham

Bee-Eater-Cottage ★★★
Self Catering
Contact: Mrs Daphne Anderson
t (01913) 771428
e farnless@btopenworld.co.uk
w bee-eater-cottage.co.uk

BLANCHLAND
Northumberland

Bail Hill ★★★ *Self Catering*
Contact: Mrs Jennifer Graham
t (01434) 675274

Boltsburn Holiday Cottages ★★ *Self Catering*
Contact: Mrs Amanda Pearson
Prospect House
t (01207) 506194 & (01207) 583076

Boltslaw Cottage ★★★★
Self Catering
Contact: Mrs Nicola Smith
t (01914) 879456
e asmith6000@aol.com
w cottageguide.co.uk/boltslaw

BOLAM
County Durham

Leggs Cross Farm Cottage
Rating Applied For
Self Catering
Contact: J S Ward
t (01388) 765425
e jsward@leggscrossfarm.com

BOULMER
Northumberland

Coble Cottage ★★★★
Self Catering
Contact: Mrs Lorna McQueen
t (01665) 577695
e lornamac19@netbreeze.co.uk
w coblecottage.co.uk

North Cottage ★★★★
Self Catering
Contact: Mrs Madeleine Frater
t (01665) 577308
e frater19@hotmail.com
w northcottageboulmer.co.uk

BOWES
County Durham

Mellwaters Barn ★★★★
Self Catering
Contact: Mr Andrew Tavener
t (01833) 628181
e mellwatesbarn@aol.com
w mellwatersbarn.co.uk

BRANTON
Northumberland

Breamish Valley Cottages ★★★★-★★★★★
Self Catering
Contact: Mrs Michele Moralee
t (01665) 578263
e peter@breamishvalley.co.uk
w breamishvalley.co.uk

BURRADON
Northumberland

Laird's Cottage ★★★★★
Self Catering
Contact: Mr David Matthews
t (01912) 511087
e enquiries@lairdscottage.co.uk
w lairdscottage.co.uk

BYRNESS
Northumberland

The Old School House ★★★★ *Self Catering*
Contact: Mr Dales Holiday Cottages
t (01756) 799821

CALLALY
Northumberland

Dene Cottage ★★★★
Self Catering
Contact: Mrs Maureen Winn
t (01665) 574513

CARLTON IN CLEVELAND
Tees Valley

Stables Cottage ★★★
Self Catering
Dales Hol Cot Ref:2697
t (01756) 799821
e info@dalesholcot.com
w dalesholcot.com

CARRVILLE
County Durham

62 Wantage Road ★★
Self Catering
Contact: Mr & Mrs Norman & Anne Walker
t (01913) 862290
e flatapar@hotmail.co.uk

CASTLESIDE
County Durham

Derwent Grange Cottages ★★–★★★ *Self Catering*
Contact: Mr & Mrs Elliot
Derwent Grange Farm
t (01207) 508358
e ekelliot@aol.com
w derwentgrange.co.uk

Manor Park Cottage (Manor Park Ltd) ★★★ *Self Catering*
Contact: Mr Brian Elstrop
t (01207) 501000

Pondfield Villa Farm Cottages ★★★★
Self Catering
Contact: Mrs Margaret Steel
t (01207) 582703
e k.a.steel@btinternet.co.uk
w pondfieldvillafarm.ntb.org.uk

CATTON
Northumberland

Station House Flat ★★★
Self Catering
Contact: Mr & Ms Michael & Verona Woodhouse
t (01434) 683362
e info@allendale-holidays.co.uk
w allendale-holidays.co.uk

CAWBURN
Northumberland

Rowan Cottage ★★★★
Self Catering
Contact: Mrs Margaret Swallow
t (01434) 320352
e swallow@rowan78freeserve.co.uk
w rowan78.freeserve.co.uk

CHATHILL
Northumberland

Charlton Hall Holiday Cottages ★★★★
Self Catering
Contact: Mr Robert Thorp
t (01665) 579378
w charltonhall.co.uk

East Cuttles & Rafters
Rating Applied For
Self Catering
Contact: Ms Carloyn Algar
t (01668) 214307
e carolynalgar150@msn.com

The Lodge and Head Gardener's House ★★★★
Self Catering
Contact: Mrs J Shirley Burnie
The Lodge and Head Gardener's House
t (01665) 589499
e doxfordhall@aol.com

Newstead Cottage ★★
Self Catering
Contact: Mrs Riddell
t (01665) 589263

CHATTON
Northumberland

Cheviot Suite
Rating Applied For
Self Catering
Contact: Ms Tracy Fiddes
t (01289) 388830
e fid@alnwick92.fsnet.co.uk

Percy Cottage ★★★
Self Catering
Contact: Miss Helen Cunningham
The Property Investments
t (01668) 216556
e tonyreedjones@aol.com
w percycottage.co.uk

CHESTER-LE-STREET
County Durham

The Old Stables ★★★★
Self Catering
Contact: Mr & Mrs Alan Cutter
t (01913) 887088
e cutter@hollycroft11.freeserve.co.uk

Plawsworth Hall Farm ★★★★ *Self Catering*
Contact: Mr Harry Johnson
t (01913) 710251
e plawsworth@aol.com
w plawsworth.com

CHILLINGHAM
Northumberland

Chillingham Castle ★★–★★★ *Self Catering*
Contact: Mrs Val Day
t (01668) 215359
e enquiries@chillingham-castle.com
w chillingham-castle.com

CHRISTON BANK
Northumberland

Rock Mill Cottage and Croft Cottage
Rating Applied For
Self Catering
Contact: Jeremy & Elaine Holt
t 07714 896834
e jeremy@rockmill.eclipse.co.uk

COANWOOD
Northumberland

Mill Hill Farmhouse ★★★
Self Catering
Contact: Mrs Stephanie Wigham
t (01434) 320256
e millhill@fsmail.net
w cottageguide.co.uk/millhill

COCKFIELD
County Durham

New Cottage ★★★
Self Catering
Contact: Mrs Margaret Partridge
t (01388) 718567

Stonecroft and Swallows Nest ★★★★ *Self Catering*
Contact: Mrs Alison Tallentire
Low Lands Farm
t (01388) 718251
e info@farmholidaysuk.com
w farmholidaysuk.com

COLWELL
Northumberland

Lance-Surtees Cottage, Colwell
Rating Applied For
Self Catering
Contact: Miss Dorothea Nelson
t (01884) 841320

CORBRIDGE
Northumberland

April Cottage ★★★★
Self Catering
Contact: Mrs Kate Dean
21 Woodland Close
t (01625) 861718
e peterandkatedean@btopenworld.com
w aprilcottagecorbridge.co.uk

Granary Cottage ★★★
Self Catering
Contact: Mr Rob Harris
The Granary
t 07970 709632
e robharris1951@hotmail.com

The Hayes ★★★
Self Catering
Contact: Mrs Monica Matthews
t (01434) 632010
e camon@surfree.co.uk
w hayes-corbridge.co.uk

Nosbor Cottage ★★★
Self Catering
Contact: Mrs Veronica Robson
t (01661) 871135
e nosboruk@yahoo.co.uk
w nosbor.co.uk

Oswald Cottage ★★★★
Self Catering
Contact: Mrs Hannah Harriman
Oswald Cottage
t (01661) 852909
e hannahharriman@btinternet.com

Wallhouses South Farm Cottage ★★★★ *Self Catering*
Contact: Mrs Eileen Lymburn
t (01434) 672388
e loraip@aol.com

West Fell Cottage ★★★
Self Catering
Contact: Mrs Joan Smith
t (01434) 632044

CORNHILL-ON-TWEED
Northumberland

Harelaw Cottages ★★★
Self Catering
Contact: Mr & Mrs Andy & Val Young
Harelaw
t (01890) 850327
e harelawcot@btinternet.com
w harelaw.org

Herds Hoose, Cherry Cottage ★★★ *Self Catering*
Contact: Mrs Diana Tweedie
t (01890) 850286
e info@tithehill.co.uk
w tithehill.co.uk

Jasmine Cottage REF: 2257 ★★★ *Self Catering*
Contact: Ms Lorraine Kidd
Dales Holiday Cottages
t 0870 909 9500
e lorraine.k@dales-holiday-cottages.com
w dalesholcot.com

Melkington Lodge ★★★★★
Self Catering
Contact: Mrs Veronica Barber
t (01890) 882313
e melkington@ic24.net
w melkington.co.uk

Orchard Cottage ★★★★
Self Catering
Contact: Mrs Lucy Carroll
t (01890) 882177
e fish@till-fishing.co.uk
w till-fishing.co.uk

The Stables ★★★★
Self Catering
Contact: Mrs Margaret Buckle
t (01890) 882390
e david.buckle@btinternet.com
w thestables.cornhill.btinternet.co.uk

Tillmouth Cottage ★★★★
Self Catering
Contact: Mrs J A Binnie
t (01289) 382482

West Learmouth Cottages ★★★★ *Self Catering*
Contact: Mrs Jasmin Moore
t (01890) 882304
e jasminmoore@westlear.fsnet.co.uk
w westlearmouthcottages.co.uk

CORNRIGGS
County Durham

Cornriggs Cottages ★★★★
Self Catering
Contact: Mrs Janet Elliot
t (01388) 537600
e enquiries@lowcornriggsfarm.fsnet.co.uk
w alstonandkillhoperidingcentre.co.uk

COTHERSTONE
County Durham

Farthings, Cotherstone ★★★ *Self Catering*
Contact: Mr Christopher John Bainbridge
t (01833) 650331

Plovers (4185) ★★★★
Self Catering
Contact: Ms Lorraine Kidd
t 0870 909 9505
e lorraine.k@dales-holiday-cottages.com
w dales-holiday-cottages.com

Thwaite Hall ★★★
Self Catering
Contact: Mrs Audrey Wickham
t (01915) 293793
e keith@gate7.co.uk
w thwaitehall.com

COWSHILL
County Durham

Dales Farm Cottage ★★★
Self Catering
Dales Holiday Cottages
t 0870 909 9500
e info@dales-holiday-cottages.com
w dalesholcot.com

CRAMLINGTON
Northumberland

Burradon Farm Houses & Cottages ★★★★
Self Catering
Contact: Mrs Judith Younger
t (0191) 268 3203
e judy@burradonfarm.co.uk
w burradonfarm.co.uk

CRASTER
Northumberland

Craster Pine Lodges ★★★★
Self Catering
Contact: Mr & Mrs Robson
t (01665) 576286
e rockville@barkpots.co.uk
w crasterpinelodges.co.uk

Harbourside House and 2 Old Farm Buildings, Low Newton-by-the-Sea ★★★★
Self Catering
Contact: Mr Geoffrey Brewis-Levie
t (01638) 604304
e brewislevie@aol.com

Proctor's Stead Cottages ★★★ *Self Catering*
Contact: Mrs Ruth Anne Davidson
t (01665) 576613
w proctorsstead.ntb.org.uk

Rock Ville ★★★★
Self Catering
Contact: Mr & Mrs Robson
t (01665) 576286
e rockville@barkpots.co.uk
w rockvillecraster.co.uk

Seahaven ★★★ *Self Catering & Serviced Apartments*
Contact: Mrs Imrie
t (01665) 602275
e miriamimrie@sagainternet.co.uk

CROOKHAM
Northumberland

Askew Cottage ★★★★
Self Catering
Contact: Mrs Heather Pentland
t (01890) 820201
e hjpentland@waitrose.com

DADDRY SHIELD
County Durham

Auntie Bella's Cottage ★★★★ *Self Catering*
Contact: Mrs Catherine Mary Sewell
t (01388) 517211
e mine.house@virgin.net
w auntibellascottage.com

DARLINGTON
Tees Valley

63 Cumberland Street ★★
Self Catering
Contact: Mrs Kathleen Reeve
t (01933) 387945
e barry.reeve1@ntlworld.com

Pegasus Cottage ★★★
Self Catering
Contact: Mr & Mrs Stuart and Denise Chapman
Pegasus Cottage
t (01325) 722542
e stuart1948@msn.com
w pegasuscottage.co.uk

DUNSTAN
Northumberland

Beech Cottage ★★★★
Self Catering
Contact: Mr & Mrs Mick & Karen Oxley
t (01665) 576422
e enquiries@mickoxley.com
w beech-cottage.co.uk

DURHAM
County Durham

15 Mackintosh Court ★★★★ *Self Catering*
Contact: Mrs P Dooley
t (01697) 342446
e mikedooley@btinternet.com

Arbour House Bungalow and Cottage ★★★
Self Catering
Contact: Mrs Rena Hunter
t (01913) 842418
e enquiries@arbourhouse.co.uk
w arbourhouse.ntb.org.uk

Baxter Wood Cottages ★★★ *Self Catering*
Contact: Mr & Mrs Trevor & Tricia Jones
t (01913) 865820
e info@baxterwood.co.uk
w baxterwood.co.uk

Bourne Cottages ★★★★
Self Catering
Contact: Mrs Judith Heron
t (01913) 720730
e judithheron@aol.com
w bournecottagedurham.com

Dove Cottage ★★★★
Self Catering
Contact: Mrs Eileen Woods
t (01913) 864176
e durhamcottages@aol.com
w durhamcottages.com

Durham4u.com ★★★★
Self Catering
Contact: Mrs Gill Wray
t (0191) 383 2049
e enquiries@durham4u.com
w durham4u.com

Jubilee House ★★★
Self Catering
Contact: Mrs Lynn Harvey
t (01913) 844894

Moor End Cottage ★★★★
Self Catering
Contact: Mrs Mary Buchanan
t (01913) 842796
e marybnb@hotmail.com
w moorenddurham.co.uk

The Old Power House ★★★★ *Self Catering*
Contact: Mrs Anne Hall
t (01913) 873001
e g.s.hall@talk21.com

Sands Cottage ★★★
Self Catering
Contact: Mrs Greta Hodgson
t (01913) 844731
e greta@sandshouse.fsnet.co.uk

Stowhouse Farm Cottages ★★★★ *Self Catering*
Contact: Mr Peter Swinburne
t (01913) 739990
w durhamfarmcottages.co.uk

Swallow's Barn ★★★★
Self Catering
Contact: Mrs Caroline Broome
t (01913) 737864
w durhamholidaycottage.co.uk

Thimble Cottage ★★★
Self Catering
Contact: Mr & Mrs M Camplin
t (01302) 786524
e enquiries@oldpitcottage.co.uk
w oldpitcottage.co.uk

EAGLESCLIFFE
Tees Valley

Aislaby Grange Farm Cottages ★★★ *Self Catering*
Contact: Mr Andrew Hutchinson
t (01642) 782170

EASTFIELD
Northumberland

Seafield Lodge ★★★★
Self Catering
Contact: Mrs Jennifer Cossins
Seafield Holidays
t (01665) 830597
e jd.cossins@virgin.net

EDLINGHAM
Northumberland

Briar, Rose And Clematis Cottage ★★★★ *Self Catering*
Contact: Mrs Helen Wyld
t (01665) 574638
e stay@newmoorhouse.co.uk
w newmoorhouse.co.uk

EGGLESTON
County Durham

Balmer House ★★★
Self Catering
Contact: Mr Roger Wales
t (01756) 700510
e info@holidaycotts.co.uk
w balmerhouse.co.uk

The Granary ★★★★
Self Catering
Contact: Mrs R Gray
t (01833) 650403

Iris Cottage ★★ *Self Catering*
Contact: Mrs D Garrett
t (01708) 447260
e coldigar@btinternet.com
w teesdalecottages.co.uk

Stable Court ★★★★
Self Catering
Contact: Mrs J.D Broughton
t (01263) 862500

Swinkly Cottage ★★★
Self Catering
Contact: Mrs Mary Robinson
t (01388) 605620
e info@swinklycottage.co.uk
w swinklycottage.co.uk

ELSDON
Northumberland

Dunns Farm & Bilsmoorfoot ★★★-★★★★ *Self Catering*
Contact: Mrs Mary Carruthers
t (01669) 640219
w dunnsfarm.ntb.org.uk

EMBLETON
Northumberland

Cra-na-ge ★★ *Self Catering*
Sykes Cottages Ref: 694
t (01244) 345700
e info@sykescottages.co.uk
w sykescottages.co.uk

Doxford Farm Cottages ★★★-★★★★ *Self Catering*
Contact: Mrs Sarah Shell
Doxford Farm
t (01665) 579348 & (01665) 579477
e doxfordfarm@hotmail.com
w doxfordfarmcottages.com

Dunstanburgh Castle Courtyard Cottages ★★
Self Catering
Contact: Mrs Marianne Thompson
Heritage Coast Holidays
t (01665) 606022
e marianne@marishalthompson.co.uk
w heritagecoastholidays.com

Eider ★★★★ *Self Catering*
Contact: Mrs Jan Straughan
t (01665) 830032

Embleton Cottage & The Nook ★★★ *Self Catering*
Contact: Mrs Ella Unwin
t (01665) 576573

Glebe Cottage
Rating Applied For
Self Catering
Contact: Mrs Sybil Goldthorpe
t (01665) 576465

The Haberdashers 2A Front Street ★★★ *Self Catering*
Contact: Mrs Mary Axelby
t (0114) 230 5090
e mary.axelby@btinternet.com
w haberdashers-alnwick.co.uk

Mansard Cottage ★★★★
Self Catering
Contact: Mr & Mrs Nic & Pauline Grant
t (01661) 853513
e pauline.grant@btinternet.com
w mansard.cottage.btinternet.co.uk

Northumbrian Holiday Cottages ★★★★
Self Catering
Contact: Mr & Mrs Chris Seal
t (01912) 856930
e seal@northumbrian-holiday-cottages.co.uk
w northumbrian-holiday-cottages.co.uk

ESCOMB
County Durham

Muskoka ★★★★
Self Catering
Contact: Mrs Maureen Falandysz
Dales Holiday Cottages
t (01388) 601649
e info@dales-holiday-cottages.com
w dalesholcot.com

FALSTONE
Northumberland

Station Cottage ★★★★
Self Catering
Contact: Mrs June Banks
t (01434) 240311

Look out for establishments participating in the National Accessible Scheme

FELTON
Northumberland

Garden House ★★★
Self Catering
Dales Holiday Cottages
t 0870 909 9500
e info@dales-holiday-cottages.com
w dalesholcot.com

Granary Cottage ★★★★
Self Catering
Contact: Mrs Irene Adamson
t (01665) 570205
w thegranarycottage.co.uk

FORD
Northumberland

Ford Castle ★★★-★★★★
Self Catering
Contact: Mrs Karen Bartlett
t (01890) 820257
e kbartlett@northumberland.gov.uk
w fordcastle.org.uk

FOURSTONES
Northumberland

Rosebank Cottage ★★★
Self Catering
Contact: Ms Colette Winters
Rosebank Cottage Rental
t 07816 909737
e info@rosebankcottage.co.uk
w rosebankcottage.co.uk

FOXTON
Northumberland

Greybarns ★★★★
Self Catering
Contact: Ms Jane Mallen
t (01668) 219941
e jane@nehc.co.uk
w alnwickcastlecottages.co.uk

FROSTERLEY
County Durham

Innkeepers Cottage 4001
★★★★ *Self Catering*
Contact: Lorraine Kidd
Dales Holiday Cottages
t 0870 909 9500
e lorraine.k@dales-holiday-cottages.com
w dalesholcot.com

GAINFORD
County Durham

Barn House Mews ref:1285
★★★ *Self Catering*
Contact: Ms Lorraine Kidd
Dales Holiday Cottages
t 0870 909 9500
e lorraine.k@dales-holiday-cottages.com
w dalesholcot.com

East Greystone Farm Cottages ★★★★
Self Catering
Contact: Mrs Sue Hodgson
t (01325) 730236
e sue@holidayfarmcottages.co.uk
w holidayfarmcottages.co.uk

GATESHEAD
Tyne and Wear

The Riding Farm ★★★★
Self Catering
Contact: Mrs Louise Johnson
t (01913) 701868
e lou.johnson@virgin.net
w lowurpeth.co.uk

GILESGATE
County Durham

Fern Cottage and Rose Cottage ★★★★ *Self Catering*
Contact: Mrs Eileen Woods
t (01913) 864176
e durhamcottages@aol.com
w durhamcottages.com

GILSLAND
Northumberland

West Nichold Cottage
★★★★★ *Self Catering*
Contact: Mr Paul Jameson
t (01697) 747008
e stay@westnichold.co.uk
w westnichold.co.uk

GLANTON
Northumberland

Coniston Cottage ★★★
Self Catering
Contact: Mrs Helen Jean Mossman
t (01665) 578305

Garden Cottage ★★★★
Self Catering
Contact: Mrs Rachel Smith
t (01665) 578797
e one@redlioncottages.co.uk

GREENHAUGH
Northumberland

Bought-Hill Mill ★★★★
Self Catering
Contact: Mrs A Cowan
t (01434) 240373

GREENHEAD
Northumberland

Holmhead Cottage ★★★
Self Catering
Contact: Mr & Mrs Brian & Pauline Staff
t (01697) 747402
w holmhead.com

Stanegate Cottage ★★★★
Self Catering
Contact: Mrs Shelagh Potts
t (01697) 747443
e smpotts@talk21.com
w braeside-banktop.co.uk

GUISBOROUGH
Tees Valley

Argument Cottage ★★★★
Self Catering
Contact: Maria Wilcock
t (01287) 638716
e mariawilcock@hotmail.com
w argumentproperties.co.uk

HALTON LEA GATE
Northumberland

The Old Chapel ★★★★★
Self Catering
Contact: Mr Stephen Jackson
t (01912) 746125
e info@theoldcountrychapel.com
w theoldcountrychapel.com

HALTWHISTLE
Northumberland

Ald White Craig Farm Cottages ★★★-★★★★
Self Catering
Contact: Mrs Cherine Zard
t (01434) 320565
e whitecraigfarm@yahoo.co.uk

Kellah Farm Cottages
★★★-★★★★ *Self Catering*
Contact: Mrs Lesley Teasdale
t (01434) 320816
e teasdale@ukonline.co.uk
w kellah.co.uk

Old High House Chapel
★★★ *Self Catering*
Contact: Simon Williams
Broome Cottage
t (01670) 828956
e info@1750chapel.co.uk
w 1750chapel.co.uk

Scotchcoulthard ★★★★
Self Catering
Contact: Mr & Mrs Andrew & Susan Saunders
t (01434) 344470
e cottages@scotchcoulthard.co.uk
w scotchcoulthard.co.uk

Whitchester Farm Cottage
★★★ *Self Catering*
Contact: J M Hall
Whitchester Farm Cottage
t (01434) 320540 & 07957 862988
e whitchester@ukonline.co.uk
w whitchester.co.uk

HAMSTERLEY
County Durham

Jasmine Cottage ★★★
Self Catering
Contact: Mrs A E Roberts
t (01388) 488630

HARBOTTLE
Northumberland

Brackenlea Cottage ★★★
Self Catering
Contact: Mr & Mrs John & Helen Dalrymple
t (01670) 519629
e john@dalrymple.me.uk
w brackenleacottage.co.uk

Honeysuckle Cottage ★★★
Self Catering
Contact: Mrs Jackie Bickmore
t (01669) 650348
e jackyhoney01@aol.com
w honeysuckleharbottle.ntb.org.uk

Kidlandlee
Rating Applied For
Self Catering
Contact: Mrs Sue Finch
t (01444) 819081
e svfinch@btinternet.com
w kidlandlee.co.uk

Woodhall Farm Holiday Cottage ★★★ *Self Catering*
Contact: Mrs J D Blakey
t (01669) 650245
e blakey@woodhall65.freeserve.co.uk
w woodhallcottage.co.uk

HARPERLEY
County Durham

Bushblades Farm Cottage
★★★ *Self Catering*
Contact: Mrs Pamela Gibson
t (01207) 232722

HARTLEPOOL
Tees Valley

Waters Edge ★★★
Self Catering
Contact: Mrs Rosalie Reeder
t (01455) 284748
e rosalie.reeder@ukonline.co.uk
w cottageguide.co.uk/watersedge

HARWOOD
County Durham

Frog Hall Cottage ★★★★
Self Catering
Contact: Ms Kath Toward
t (01833) 622215
e kath.herdship@btinternet.com
w herdship.co.uk

HAYDON BRIDGE
Northumberland

Braemar ★★★★
Self Catering
Contact: Mrs Cynthia Bradley
t (01434) 684622
e edenholme@btinternet.com
w edenholme.btinternet.co.uk

Clematis Cottage ★★★
Self Catering
Contact: Mrs Francis Templer
t (01434) 684280
e ftempler@toucansurf.com
w clem-cottage.co.uk

Langdale Cottage ★★★★
Self Catering
Contact: Mr & Mrs Mike & Yvonne Dennison
t (01434) 688570
e yvonne@bywellhouse.fsnet.co.uk
w HolidayHomeRental.co.uk/langdalecottage

Scotch Corner ★★★★
Self Catering
Contact: Mrs Pauline Wallis
t (01434) 684061
e wallis@scotcharms.fsnet.co.uk
w scotcharms.com

HEBBURN
Tyne and Wear

26 Hazelmoor ★★★★
Self Catering
Contact: Mr Peter Goodall
t 07941 611551
e peter.goodall7@virgin.net
w stayinbritain.com/hazelmoor

HEDDON-ON-THE-WALL
Northumberland

2 East Town House ★★★
Self Catering
Contact: Mr & Mrs Ridley and Beryl Amos
1 East Town House
t (01661) 852277

HEPPLE
Northumberland

Beech Cottage ★★★
Self Catering
Contact: Mrs Elizabeth Rogerson
t (01669) 640216
e erogerson@btopenworld.com
w visitrothbury.co.uk

HEXHAM
Northumberland

Brokenheugh Lodge & Orchard Barn ★★★★
Self Catering
Contact: Mrs Renee Jamieson
t (01434) 684206
e stay@brokenheugh.co.uk
w brokenheugh.co.uk

Chapel House ★★★★★
Self Catering
Contact: Mrs Joan Liddle
t (01434) 673286
e info@chapel-house.info
w chapel-house.info

Holy Island House ★★★★★
Self Catering
Contact: Mrs Judith Youens
Holy Island House
t (01434) 609386
e stay@holyislandhouse.co.uk
w holyislandhouse.co.uk

Moorgair Cottage ★★★★
Self Catering
Contact: Mrs Vicki Ridley
t (01434) 673473
e g_ridley@lineone.net
w moorgair.co.uk

Old Church Cottages, Chollerton ★★★★
Self Catering
Contact: Mrs Marilyn Framrose
t (01434) 681930
e oldchurch@supanet.com
w chollerton.urscene.net

Sammy's Place ★★★★
Self Catering
Contact: Mr & Mrs Ian and Susan Sibbald
t (01434) 604143
e sammys-place@hotmail.com
w sammyshideaways.com

HOLY ISLAND
Northumberland

Britannia House and The Cottage ★★★★ *Self Catering*
Contact: Mrs Katharine Tiernan
t (01289) 309826
e ktiernan@onetel.com
w lindisfarne-cottages.co.uk

Farne Court Cottage, Farne View Cottage ★★★
Self Catering
Contact: Mrs Batty
Waterside House
t (01387) 840122
e angelabatty@ukonline.co.uk

Links View ★★★
Self Catering
Contact: Dr Rachel Paine linksviewholyisland@yahoo.co.uk
w lindisfarne.org.uk/links-view

Memnon Cottage ★★★★
Self Catering
Contact: Ms Shirley Douglas
t (0161) 941 1963
e shirleyandouglas@aol.com
w memnon-cottage.co.uk

HORNCLIFFE
Northumberland

Smiddy Cottage ★★★
Self Catering
Contact: Mrs June Simpson
t (01289) 386411
e june@smiddycottage.co.uk
w smiddycottage.co.uk

HOWICK
Northumberland

South Cottage ★★★
Self Catering
Sykes Cottages Ref:625
t (01244) 345700
e info@sykescottages.co.uk
w sykescottages.co.uk

HUMSHAUGH
Northumberland

East Farm Cottage ★★★
Self Catering
Contact: Mrs Gwen Dodds
t (01434) 689150
e charles.dodds2@btopenworld.com

Widdrington Holiday Cottage
Rating Applied For
Self Catering & Serviced Apartments
Contact: Mrs Karin Milligan
t 07866 929074
e karin_m1@hotmail.com
w accommodationonhadrianswall.com

ILDERTON
Northumberland

Coach House & Coach House Cottage ★★★
Self Catering
Contact: Mrs Margaret Sale
t (01668) 217293
e margaretsale@amserve.com

INGLETON
County Durham

The Mill Granary ★★★★★
Self Catering
Contact: Mr & Mrs Richard & Kate Hodgson
t (01325) 730339
e info@millgranary.co.uk
w millgranary.co.uk

INGRAM
Northumberland

Cheviot Holiday Cottages ★★★★★ *Self Catering*
Contact: Mrs Trysha Stephenson
t (01665) 578236
e trysha@cheviotholidaycottages.co.uk
w cheviotholidaycottages.co.uk

IRESHOPEBURN
County Durham

Hillside Cottage ★★★
Self Catering
Contact: Mrs Sadie McMullon
t (01733) 349612
e sasmc2000@yahoo.co.uk
w hillsidecottagedurham.co.uk

JESMOND
Tyne and Wear

Week2Week
★★★★-★★★★★
Self Catering
Contact: Miss Kerry Wilson
t (01912) 813129
e info@week2week.co.uk
w week2week.co.uk

KIELDER
Northumberland

Kielder Lodges
★★★★-★★★★★
Self Catering
Contact: Ms Tonia Reeve
t (01434) 250294
e kielder.holidays@nwl.co.uk
w nwl.co.uk/kielder

KIELDER WATER
Northumberland

Calvert Trust Kielder
★★★★ *Self Catering*
Contact: Mr Bookings
t (01434) 250232
e enquiries@calvert-kielder.com
w calvert-trust.org.uk

KIRKNEWTON
Northumberland

Coldburn Cottage ★★★★
Self Catering
Contact: Mrs Jane Matheson
t (01668) 217070
e macdonaldsmith@btinternet.com
w saleandpartners.co.uk

Hillview Cottage REF: 2043
★★★★ *Self Catering*
Contact: Ms Lorraine Kidd
Dales Holiday Cottages
t 0870 909 9500
e lorraine.k@dales-holiday-cottages.com
w dalesholcot.com

New Cottage (4024) ★★★
Self Catering
Contact: Ms Lorraine Kidd
Dales Holiday Cottages
t 0870 909 9500
e lorraine.k@dales-holiday-cottages.com
w dalesholcot.com

LANCHESTER
County Durham

Browney Cottage & Browney Close ★★★
Self Catering
Contact: Mrs Ann Darlington
t (01207) 521476
e ann@hallhillfarm.co.uk
w hallhillfarm.co.uk

Stable Cottage ★★★★
Self Catering
Contact: Mrs Fiona Sheen
Dales Holiday Cottages
t 0870 909 9500
e fiona@dales-holiday-cottages.com
w dalesholcot.com

LANGLEY-ON-TYNE
Northumberland

The Waiting Room ★★★★
Self Catering
Contact: Ms Deborah Humble
t (01434) 683030
e info@debhumble.co.uk

West Deanraw Bungalow
★★★ *Self Catering*
Contact: Mr John Drydon
t (01434) 684228

LESBURY
Northumberland

Lesbury Glebe Cottage
★★★★★ *Self Catering*
Contact: Mrs D. Gillian Brunton
t (01665) 830732
e gillieray@tiscali.co.uk
w cottageguide.co.uk/lesburyglebe

LONGFRAMLINGTON
Northumberland

Dene House Farm Cottages
★★★-★★★★ *Self Catering*
Contact: Mrs Vivien Mason
t (01665) 570665
w denehousefarm.com

Picklewood Cottage
★★★★★ *Self Catering*
Contact: Mrs Di Jevons
t (01665) 570221
e di@picklewood.info
w picklewood.info

LONGHORSLEY
Northumberland

Beacon Hill Farm
Rating Applied For
Self Catering
Contact: Mr Alun Moore
t (01670) 780900
e alun@beaconhill.co.uk
w beaconhill.co.uk

Beacon Hill Farm Holidays
★★★★-★★★★★
Self Catering
Contact: Mr Alun Moore
t (01670) 780900
e alun@beaconhill.co.uk
w beaconhill.co.uk

Cartwheel Cottage ★★★
Self Catering
Contact: Mr & Mrs James & Sarah Chisholm
t (01665) 570661
e sarah@cartwheelcottage.com
w cartwheelcottage.com

Garrett Lee Cottage and Stable House ★★★★
Self Catering
Contact: Mrs Linda Wilson
t (01670) 788474
e info@garrettleefarm.com
w garrettleefarm.com

Green Yard Cottage ★★★
Self Catering
Contact: Mr & Mrs Lowes
t (01670) 788416
e susanjlowes@fsmail.net

LONGHOUGHTON
Northumberland

The Northumberland House
★★★★★ *Self Catering*
Contact: Mr & Mrs Michael & Jean Cockerill
t 07834 620669
e stay@thenorthumberlandhouse.co.uk
w thenorthumberlandhouse.co.uk

Rose Cottage & Croft Cottage ★★★ *Self Catering*
Contact: Mrs Margaret Forsyth
t (01665) 577227
w lowsteads.co.uk

Look out for establishments participating in the Walkers and Cyclists Welcome Schemes

LONGWITTON
Northumberland

The Byre ★★★★
Self Catering
Contact: Mrs Jane Renwick
t (01670) 774443
e yorkie@marthamoo.co.uk

LOWICK
Northumberland

Barmoor Ridge Cottage
★★★★ *Self Catering*
Contact: Mrs Patricia Adrienne Reavley
t (01289) 388226
e jimpyreavley@aol.com

Barmoor South Moor ★★★
Self Catering
Contact: Mrs Ann Gold
t (01289) 388205
e barryandanngold@aol.com

Granary Cottage 1015
★★★★ *Self Catering*
Contact: Mr Clive Sykes
Sykes Cottages
t (01244) 345700
e info@sykescottages.co.uk
w sykescottages.co.uk

South View Cottage ★★★★
Self Catering
Contact: Mrs Carol Waugh
t (01289) 388640

LUCKER
Northumberland

Lucker Hall Steading
★★★★-★★★★★
Self Catering
Contact: Mrs Jane Mallen
t (01668) 219941
e jane@nehc.co.uk
w alnwickcastlecottages.co.uk

Lucker Mill ★★★★★
Self Catering
Contact: Mrs Jane Mallen
t (01668) 219941
e jane@nehc.co.uk
w alnwickcastlecottages.co.uk

MAINSFORTH
County Durham

Swallow Cottage ★★★★
Self Catering
Contact: Mrs Julie Maude
t (01740) 656709
e maudes@onetel.net
w swallowcottage.visitnorthumbria.com

MARSKE-BY-THE-SEA
Tees Valley

4 Church Street ★★★
Self Catering
Contact: Mrs Barbara Mosey
t (01277) 652778
e brmosey@yahoo.co.uk

White Rose Cottage ★★★
Self Catering
Contact: Mr & Mrs Philip Phillips
t (01642) 481064
e phillipspcp@aol.com

MELKRIDGE
Northumberland

Common House Farm Cottages ★★★ *Self Catering*
Contact: Mr & Mrs Richard & Louise Currie
t (01434) 321680
e stay@commonhousefarm.com
w commonhousefarm.com

Hightown Farm Cottage
★★★★ *Self Catering*
Contact: Mrs Amanda Smith Jackson
t (01434) 321432
e asmithjackson@fsmail.net

MICKLETON
County Durham

1 Syke Cottage ★★★
Self Catering
Contact: Mr John Foster
t (01833) 640132

Bankside Cottage ★★★
Self Catering
Contact: Mrs Helen Crooks
t (01912) 365163
e george.crooks@btinternet.com

Blackthorn Cottage ★★★
Self Catering
Contact: Mrs Diane Garrett
t (01708) 447260
e coldigar@btinternet.com
w teesdalecottages.co.uk

Kirkcarrion Cottage ★★★
Self Catering
Contact: Mr John Foster
t (01833) 640132

The Old Dairy, Mickleton
★★★★ *Self Catering*
Contact: Mrs Tracey Cook
West Pasture Farm
t (01833) 640248
e cookes@homecall.co.uk
w teesdaleholidaycottages.co.uk

West Tofts ★★★★
Self Catering
Contact: Mrs Stoddart
t (01833) 640379
e enquiries@wemmergill-farm.co.uk
w wemmergill-farm.co.uk

Whitbridge ★★★★
Self Catering
Contact: Mr Raymond Taffurelli
t (01833) 640100
e taffurs@thetaffurellis.freeserve.co.uk

MIDDLETON-IN-TEESDALE
County Durham

The Barn ★★★ *Self Catering*
Contact: Mrs Ann Whitfield
t (01833) 640759
w thebarn.4t.com

The Barn ★★★★
Self Catering
Contact: Mr Alan Kitchener
t (01937) 844657

Brock Scar Cottage ★★★★
Self Catering
Contact: Mrs Winfred Gargate
t (01833) 640495
e wyngargate@btopenworld.com
w brockscar.co.uk

Bunny Cottage ★★★★
Self Catering
Contact: Karen & Anthony Slater-Davison
t (01623) 456194
e ksd1@hotmail.co.uk
w bunnycottage.co.uk

The Coach House ★★★★
Self Catering
Contact: Mrs J A Finn
t (01833) 640884
e info@thecoachhouse.net
w thecoachhouse.net

Country Cottage ★★★
Self Catering
Contact: Mr Burman
t (0161) 860 7123
e enquiries@robinburman.com

Daisy Cottage (3729)
★★★★ *Self Catering*
Contact: Ms Lorraine Kidd
Dales Holiday Cottages
t 0870 909 9500
e lorraine.k@dales-holiday-cottages.com
w dalesholcot.com

Firethorn Cottage ★★★ *Self Catering & Serviced Apartments*
Contact: Mrs June Thompson
t (01953) 850364

Green Acres, Meadow's Edge, Shepherds Cottage
★★★ *Self Catering*
Contact: Mrs Glennis Scott
t (01833) 640506

Hush Cottage ★★
Self Catering
Contact: Mrs V Mulholland
t (01985) 850450
e mul.cort@btinternet.com

Laneside, Middleton-in-Teesdale ★★★★
Self Catering
Contact: Mrs N J Liddle
t (01833) 640209
e teesdaleestate@rabycastle.com
w rabycastle.com

North Wythes Hill ★★★
Self Catering
Contact: Mrs Eileen Dent
t (01833) 640349
e eileendent@teesdaleonline.co.uk

Snaisgill Farm Cottage ★★★
Self Catering
Contact: Mrs Susan Parmley
t (01833) 640343

Town View Cottage ★★★
Self Catering
Contact: Mrs R Marshall
t (01325) 730989

Westfield Cottage ★★★★
Self Catering
Contact: Mrs Doreen Scott
t (01833) 640942

Willow Cottage ★★
Self Catering
Contact: Mrs Diane Garrett
t (01708) 447260
e coldigar@btinternet.com
w teesdalecottages.co.uk

MILFIELD
Northumberland

Milfield Hill Cottage ★★★★
Self Catering
Contact: Mrs Judith Craig
t (01668) 216338
e craig@milfield1.freeserve.co.uk

MINDRUM
Northumberland

Bowmont Cottage ★★
Self Catering
Contact: Mr & Mrs C Orpwood
t (01890) 850266
e s.orpwood@farmline.com
w cottageguide.co.uk/bowmonthill

The Longknowe ★★★
Self Catering
Contact: Ms Josephine Andrews
t (020) 7281 9579
e longknowe@hotmail.com

MITFORD
Northumberland

The Old Blacksmiths Cottage ★★★★ *Self Catering*
Contact: Mrs Pat Glass
t (01670) 512074
e blacksmith@mitford100.wanadoo.co.uk

MOORSHOLM
Tees Valley

Honeysuckle Cottage
★★★★ *Self Catering*
Contact: Miss Margaret Snowden
The Stripe
t (01642) 713274
e msn0902390@aol.com

MORLEY
County Durham

Calf Close Cottage Ref:3836
★★★ *Self Catering*
Contact: Ms Lorraine Kidd
Dales Holiday Cottages
t 0870 909 9500
e lorraine.k@dales-holiday-cottages.com
w dalesholcot.com

MORPETH
Northumberland

Barnacre ★★★★
Self Catering
Contact: Mrs Linda Rudd
t (01670) 790116
e info@barnacre.com
w barnacre.com

The Carriage House
★★★★★ *Self Catering*
Contact: Mr Joseph Evans
t (01670) 790225
e joe@ulgham.demon.co.uk
w ulgham.demon.co.uk

Meldon Park ★★★
Self Catering
Contact: Mrs Janet Wilson
Flat 1
t (01670) 772622
e mrscookson@compuserve.com
w cottageguide.co.uk/meldonpark

Netherwitton Hall Cottages
★★★ *Self Catering*
Contact: Mrs Anne-Marie Trevelyan
t (01670) 772249
e anne-marie@netherwitton.com

Old Barn Cottages ★★★
Self Catering
Contact: Mrs Jo Mancey
t (01670) 518507
w benridge-cottages-uk.tripod.com

Peigh Hills Farm Cottages
★★★★ *Self Catering*
Contact: Mr Anthony Tench
t (01670) 790332
e eve@peighhills.wanadoo.co.uk
w peighhillsfarmcottages.co.uk

NEWBIGGIN-BY-THE-SEA
Northumberland

5 Sandridge ★★★
Self Catering
Contact: Mrs Karen Gilson
High Croft House Farm
t (01429) 823866
e karen@kgilson.wannadoo.co.uk

Tahfay House ★★★★
Self Catering
Contact: Mr Stuart Dodds
4 Fawdon House Farm
t (01670) 503597
e cozydays@tiscali.co.uk
w cozydays.co.uk

NEWCASTLE UPON TYNE
Tyne and Wear

135 Audley Road ★★★
Self Catering
Contact: Miss Linda Wright
t (0191) 285 6374
e lkw@audleyender.fsnet.co.uk
w audleyender.fsnet.co.uk

93A Grey Street Apartments
★★★-★★★★★
Serviced Apartments
Contact: Mr Sandro & Mr Michael Rea
t 07766 008498
e info@93agreystservicedapartments.co.uk

Bavington Hall, Stable Court
★★★ *Self Catering*
Contact: Mr Patrick
t (01830) 530394
e enquiries@bavingtonhall.co.uk
w bavingtonhall.co.uk

River View at Three Indian Kings ★★★ *Self Catering*
Contact: Ms Deborah Prence
t (0114) 268 2200
e threeindiankings@lycos.com

Walbottle Farm House
★★★★★ *Self Catering*
Contact: Mr & Mrs Dominic Aston
t (01912) 671368
e aston@walbottle.fsnet.co.uk
w walbottlefarmhouse.co.uk

NEWTON-BY-THE-SEA
Northumberland

3A & 3B Coastguard Cottages ★★★ *Self Catering*
Contact: Mrs Alison Cottam
t (01912) 512506
e coastguardcottages@hotmail.com
w geocities.com/coastguardcottages

The Joiners Arms ★★★
Self Catering
Contact: Mr William MacKinlay
t (01665) 576645
e mail@joiners-arms.co.uk
w joiners-arms.co.uk

Link House Farm ★★★★
Self Catering
Contact: Mrs Jayne Hellmann
Link House Farm Ltd
t (01665) 576820
e jayne.hellmann@btinternet.com
w linkhousefarm.com

Newton Hall Cottages ★★★
Self Catering
Contact: Mrs Shirley Patterson
t (01665) 576239
e patterson@newtonholidays.co.uk
w newtonholidays.co.uk

Seawinds ★★★★
Self Catering
Contact: Miss Jo Park
t (01665) 714805
e jopark@farming.co.uk
w buston.co.uk

NORHAM
Northumberland

The Boathouse ★★★
Self Catering
Contact: Miss Emma Crabtree
t (020) 7584 8996
e emma@crabtreeandcrabtree.com
w crabtreeandcrabtree.com/the_boathouse.php

Boathouse Cottage ★★★★
Self Catering
Contact: Mrs Susan Dalgety
t (01289) 382300
e susan@boathousecottage.co.uk
w boathousecottage.co.uk

Norcot Cottage ★★★★
Self Catering
Contact: Mr Roland Potter
t (01661) 844661
e cheryl@silverleafsoftware.co.uk
w northumberlandcountrycottages.co.uk

NORTH SUNDERLAND
Northumberland

The Shieling ★★★
Self Catering
Contact: Mrs Susanna Hodgson
t (01665) 721309

OAKENSHAW
County Durham

Stockley Fell Farm Cottages
★★★★ *Self Catering*
Contact: Mr Thomas Carter
t (01388) 745938
e carter-thomas@yahoo.com

OAKWOOD
Northumberland

The Granary ★★★★★
Self Catering
Contact: Mrs Eileen Willey
t (01434) 607314
e eileenwilley@lineone.net
w villafirst.com

OTTERBURN
Northumberland

Elishaw Farm Holiday Cottages ★★★★
Self Catering
Contact: Mrs Tina Brown
t (01830) 520942
e elishawfarm@btopenworld.com
w elishawfarmholidaycottages.co.uk

Woodhill Country House
★★★★★ *Self Catering*
Contact: Mrs Corrinne Knight
t (01830) 520657
e enquiries@woodhillcountryhouse.co.uk
w woodhillcountryhouse.co.uk

OUSTON
County Durham

Katie's Cottage ★★★★
Self Catering
Contact: Mrs Hilary Johnson
t (01914) 102901
e stay@lowurpeth.co.uk
w lowurpeth.co.uk

OVINGTON
County Durham

High Fewster Gill Cottage (ref: 3228) ★★★
Self Catering
Contact: Ms Lorraine Kidd
Dales Holiday Cottages
t 0870 909 9500
e lorraine.k@dales-holiday-cottages.com
w dalesholcot.com

OVINGTON
Northumberland

Appletree Cottage ★★★★
Self Catering
Contact: Mrs Lesley Rowell
t (01661) 832355

Westgarth Cottage, Ovington ★★★★
Self Catering
Contact: Mrs Claire Graham
t (01661) 832202
e west.cape@btinternet.com

PIERCEBRIDGE
Tees Valley

The Bungalow ★★★
Self Catering
Contact: Mrs Jean Lowe
t (01388) 832779

Rose Cottage ★★★★
Self Catering
Contact: Mrs Brown
Lime Kiln House
t (01325) 730416
e lesliebrown.agricon@btinternet.com

PONTELAND
Northumberland

The Old Stables/ The Old Tack Room ★★★
Self Catering
Contact: Clare Stephenson
The Old Stables / The Old Tack Room
t (01661) 822188
e elandgreen@msn.com

POWBURN
Northumberland

Shepherd's Cottage ★★★
Self Catering
Contact: Mrs Sarah Wilson
t (01665) 578243
e sarah@ingramfarm.co.uk
w ingramfarm.co.uk

QUEBEC
County Durham

Clydesdale Cottage
Rating Applied For
Self Catering
Contact: Mrs June Whitfield
t (01207) 520388
e june@hamsteelshall.co.uk
w hamsteelshall.co.uk

REDCAR
Tees Valley

Dove Houses ★★★
Self Catering
Contact: Mrs Carol McGovern
t (01642) 479311
e themcgoverns@ntlworld.com
w dovehouses.co.uk

ROMALDKIRK
County Durham

Romaldkirk Self Catering Cottages ★★★-★★★★★
Self Catering
Contact: Mrs Gwen Wall
t (01833) 650794
e richard@wall8309.freeserve.co.uk
w cottageguide.co.uk/romaldkirk

Sycamore Cottage ★★★★
Self Catering
Contact: Ms Lorraine Kidd
Dales Holiday Cottages
t 0870 909 9500
e lorraine.k@dales-holiday-cottages.com
w dalesholcot.com

ROTHBURY
Northumberland

April Cottage ★★★★
Self Catering
Contact: Mr & Mrs Peter & Karina Biggers
t (01665) 603233
e hope.biggers@tiscali.co.uk
w april-cottage-rothbury.com

The Cottage ★★★
Self Catering
Contact: Mrs Isabelle Anthea Wilbie-Chalk
t (01669) 620430
e visitors@wellclose.com
w wellclose.com

Garden Cottage ★★★★
Self Catering
Contact: Mr & Mrs Roger & Dorothy Newman
t (01844) 274101
e rogerdnewman@hotmail.com

The Granary ★★★★★
Self Catering
Contact: Ms Mandy Lance
t (01665) 714455
e mandy@charityhallfarm.com
w charityhallfarm.com

Low Alwinton Cottages
★★★-★★★★ *Self Catering*
Contact: Mr & Mrs Eamonn and Susan Gribben
12 Parkshiel
t (0191) 420 4919
e eamonngribben@blueyonder.co.uk
w lowalwinton.co.uk

Master's Lodge ★★★★
Self Catering
Contact: Mr & Mrs David & Heather Lister
t (01669) 621972
e heather.lister@silverton98.plus.com
w masterslodge-rothbury.co.uk

The Old Telephone Exchange ★★★★
Self Catering
Contact: Mrs Kath Scott-Foreman
t (01669) 621858
e info@theoldtelephoneexchange.com
w theoldtelephoneexchange.com

The Pele Tower (wing)
★★★★★ *Self Catering*
Contact: Mr David Malia
t (01669) 620410
e davidmalia@aol.com
w thepeletower.com

Riverside Lodges ★★★★
Self Catering
Contact: Mr Eric Jensen Edgecombe
t (01669) 620464
e eric_jensen@tiscali.co.uk
w theriversidelodge.com

Ryecroft Cottage ★★★
Self Catering
Contact: Mrs Rosalind Kerven
t (01669) 640291
e roskerven@hotmail.com

Tosson Tower Farm
★★★-★★★★ *Self Catering*
Contact: Mrs Ann Foggin
t (01669) 620228
e stay@tossontowerfarm.com
w tossontowerfarm.com

Whitton Lodge ★★★★
Self Catering
Contact: Mrs Maggie Monaghan
t (01669) 620929
e maggie.monaghan@btinternet.com
w cottage-northumberland.co.uk

RYHOPE
Tyne and Wear

Thompson + Son Housing
★★★ *Self Catering*
Contact: David Thompson
t (01915) 210116

ST JOHN'S CHAPEL
County Durham

Burnbrae ★★★★
Self Catering
Contact: Mrs Ann Robson
t (01670) 518129
e ann@robsonmorpeth.freeserve.co.uk

SALTBURN-BY-THE-SEA
Tees Valley

Tower Court ★★★★
Self Catering
Contact: Mr & Mrs Martin & Ginette Mitchell
t (01484) 530990
e mgmitchell@tower-court.co.uk
w tower-court.co.uk

Victorian Cottage ★★★
Self Catering
Contact: Mr & Mrs Stewart & Susan Morgan
t (01287) 625237
e sueandstew@saltburn-accommodation.co.uk
w saltburn-accommodation.co.uk

The Zetland ★★★
Self Catering
Contact: Mrs Joan Carter
t (01642) 679831 & (01642) 782507
e graham@howard95.freeserve.co.uk

SCREMERSTON
Northumberland

Composers at Woodlands
★★★★★ *Self Catering*
Contact: Mr & Mrs Martin & Dee Colam
t (01289) 332599
e info@composers-woodlands.co.uk
w composers-woodlands.co.uk

SEAHOUSES
Northumberland

31 Dunstan View ★★★
Self Catering
Contact: Mr & Mrs Mark & Amanda Butler
t (01665) 576586
e mrb911@hotmail.com

Cliff House Cottages ★★★
Self Catering
Contact: Mrs Jackie Forsyth
t (01665) 721380
e info@beadnellhouse.com
w cliffhousecottages.co.uk

Fahren House ★★★★
Self Catering
Contact: Mrs Rachel Shiel
t (01665) 721297
e rachel.dawson@virgin.net
w farne-islands.com

Fisherlasses Flat ★★★
Self Catering
Contact: Mrs Karen Wilkin
t (01665) 720470
e wilkin@swallowfish.co.uk
w swallowfish.co.uk

Fishermans Mid Cottage
★★★★ *Self Catering*
Contact: Mrs Dorothy Jackson
t (01665) 830427
e dorothy@biltonbarns.com
w biltonbarns.com

Fisherman's Retreat
★★★★★ *Self Catering*
Contact: Ms Fiona McKeith
t (01912) 851272
e info@coastalretreats.co.uk
w coastalretreats.co.uk

Harbourside ★★★★
Self Catering
Contact: Ms Juliet Hall
t 07711 039309
e juliet@juliethall.wanadoo.co.uk
w harboursidecottage.co.uk

Kipper Cottage ★★★★
Self Catering
Contact: Mr & Mrs Forsyth
t (01665) 721380
e enquiries@kippercottage.co.uk
w kippercottage.co.uk

The Lobster Pots ★★★★
Self Catering
Contact: Mrs Julia Steel
t (0113) 239 1130
e julia@thelobsterpots.co.uk
w thelobsterpots.co.uk

Lynbank ★★★ *Self Catering*
Contact: Mrs Louise Donaldson
t (01665) 721066
e islandproperties@uk6.net
w lynbank.ntb.org.uk

North East Coast Holidays
★★★ *Self Catering*
Contact: Mrs Lesley Barnett
t (01665) 833233
e d_barnettuk@yahoo.co.uk
w northeastcoastholidays.co.uk

Peregrine ★★★ *Self Catering*
Contact: Miss Ursula. Wanglin
t (01665) 574304

Puffin's Nest and Blue Horizon ★★★★ *Self Catering*
Contact: Ms Carolyn Algar
t (01668) 214307
e carolynalgar150@msn.com
w seahousesself-catering.com

Quarry Cottage ★★★
Self Catering
Contact: Mrs Mary Alston
t (01665) 720235
e george.alston@ic24.net

Rose Cottages ★★★★
Self Catering
Contact: Mr Michael Townsend
t (01665) 576111
e stay@dunstanburghcastlehotel.co.uk
w dunstanburghcastlehotel.co.uk

Sparrowhawk ★★★★
Self Catering
Contact: Miss Ursula D Wanglin
t (01665) 574304

Westfield Farmhouse
★★★★ *Self Catering*
Contact: Mrs Jackie Forsythe
t (01665) 721380
e info@westfieldfarmhouse.co.uk
w westfieldfarmhouse.co.uk

SEATON CAREW
Tees Valley

Ships Watch ★★★
Self Catering
Contact: Mr Glyn Sanderson
t (01429) 222660 & 07748 381943
e lynda.sanderson1@ntlworld.com

SEDGEFIELD
County Durham

The Granary ★★★
Self Catering
Contact: Mr & Mrs J.S & J.E Edgoose
t (01740) 620244
e mail@toddshousefarm.co.uk
w toddshousefarm.co.uk

Sprucely Farm Cottage ★★
Self Catering
Contact: Mr Stewart Harris
t (01740) 620378
e barbara-harris@btconnect.com
w sprucelyfarmcottage.co.uk

SHARPERTON
Northumberland

North Sharperton Farm Cottage ★★★★ *Self Catering*
Contact: Ms Carolyn Banks
t (01669) 650321
e ormnthsharperton@bushinternet.com
w northsharperton.co.uk

SHOTLEY BRIDGE
County Durham

Rivers Edge Cottage ★★★★
Self Catering
Contact: Mrs Jean Johnson
t (01207) 501194
e jean.johnson1@tesco.net

SKELTON
Tees Valley

Barn Cottage and Newbrook Cottage ★★★★ *Self Catering*
Contact: Mr Neil Goodenough
t (01287) 650288
e neilgoodenough@msn.com
w barncottage.net

SLAGGYFORD
Northumberland

Town Green Cottage
Self Catering
Contact: Miss Colleen Cairns
t (01207) 560115 & 07714 345766
e colleen_cairns181@hotmail.com

SLALEY
Northumberland

Clairmont Cottage ★★★★
Self Catering
Contact: Mrs Evelyn Allsop
t (01434) 673686
e david.allsop4@which.net
w clairmontslaley.freeserve.co.uk

Combhills Farm ★★★
Self Catering
Contact: Mrs Ogle
t (01434) 673475
e ma.ogle@tiscali.co.uk

SNITTER
Northumberland

Silverdale Cottage ★★★★
Self Catering
Contact: Mrs Judith Price
t 07787 515190
e the4farm@aol.com
w visit-rothbury.co.uk

SOUTH SHIELDS
Tyne and Wear

22 Hartington Terrace ★★★
Self Catering
Contact: Mrs Patricia Capps
t (01845) 578657
e mantonandpat@aol.com

Beach Haven Apartment
Rating Applied For
Self Catering
Contact: Mr V Cole
t (01914) 561802

Eccleston Road ★★★
Self Catering
Contact: Mrs Kath Cole
t (01914) 561802

Sandhaven Beach Chalets
★★★ *Self Catering*
Contact: Mrs Christine Rowell
t (01914) 558319
e crowell@btconnect.com
w sandhavenchalets.co.uk

Seawynnings ★★★★
Self Catering
Contact: Mrs Christine Whincop
t (01914) 541876

SPARTY LEA
Northumberland

Isaac's and Hannah's Cottages ★★★ *Self Catering*
Contact: Mrs Heather Robson
t (01434) 685312

SPITTAL
Northumberland

21 Billendean Terrace ★★★
Self Catering
Contact: Mrs Myra J. Ingham
t (020) 8747 0425
e inghamfive@hotmail.com
w 21billendeanterrace.co.uk

Seaview Cottage ★★★★
Self Catering
Contact: Mrs Brenda Crowcroft
t (01289) 304175
e b.crowcroft@talk21.com
w stunningseaviews.co.uk

STAINDROP
County Durham

Fawnlea Cottage, Staindrop
★★★★ *Self Catering*
Contact: Mrs Gillian Sumpton
10 Winston Road
t (01833) 660896
e gillian64@btinternet.com
w fawnleacottage.co.uk

Melrose House ★★★★
Self Catering
Contact: Mrs Hylene Bowman
t (01833) 660323
e hylene.bowman@btinternet.com

STAINTON
County Durham

The Old Granary (ref:1691)
★★★★ *Self Catering*
Contact: Ms Lorraine Kidd
Dales Holiday Cottages
t 0870 909 9500
e lorraine.k@dales-holiday-cottages.com
w dalesholcot.com

STANHOPE
County Durham

Primrose Cottage ★★
Self Catering
Contact: Mrs Reed
t (01697) 741600
e enquiries@northumbria-byways.com
w northumbria-byways.com

Stanhope Morningside
★★★ *Self Catering*
Contact: Mr William Stobbs
t (01388) 527045
e williamstobbs@aol.com
w stanhopemorningside.co.uk

STOCKSFIELD
Northumberland

The Old Bakery Cottages
★★★★ *Self Catering*
Contact: Vivien & Ron Bolton
t (01434) 633217

Old Ridley Hall ★★★
Self Catering
Contact: Mrs Josephine Aldridge
t (01661) 842816
e oldridleyhall@talk21.com

SUNDERLAND
Tyne and Wear

22 Topcliff ★★★
Self Catering
Contact: Mr & Mrs M B Farrar
t (020) 8850 4863
e cass.farrar@virgin.net
w stayinsunderland.co.uk

33 Alexandra House ★★★★
Self Catering
Contact: Mr & Mrs Ian & Pauline Donaldson
t (01915) 108282
e jonty.donaldson@btinternet.com

Mill View ★★★ *Self Catering*
Contact: Mrs Bethan Farrar
t (020) 8850 4863
e cass@stayinsunderland.co.uk
w stayinsunderland.co.uk

Parkside ★★★★
Self Catering
Contact: Mrs Christine Whincop
t (01914) 541876

SWARLAND
Northumberland

Swarland Old Hall Luxury Pine Lodges ★★★★
Self Catering
Contact: Mrs Dianne Proctor
t (01670) 787642
e proctor@swarlandoldhall.fsnet.co.uk
w swarlandoldhall.co.uk

TARSET
Northumberland

Greystead Coach House
★★★★ *Self Catering*
Contact: Mr William Monroe
t (01434) 240244
e wafm@greystead.fsnet.co.uk

THROPTON
Northumberland

Black Chirnells, The Cottage
★★★★ *Self Catering*
Contact: Ms Liz Juppenlatz
t 07747 734946
e blackchirnells@cs.com

Mordue's Cottage & Grandma's Cottage ★★★
Self Catering
Contact: Mrs Helen Farr
t (01665) 574672
e info@lorbottle.com
w lorbottle.com

North Croft ★★★★
Self Catering
Contact: Mrs Marilyn Chalk
t (01670) 788655
e northcroftMC@aol.com
w visit-rothbury.co.uk/accom/sc_northcroft.htm

Physic Cottage ★★★★
Self Catering
Contact: Mrs Helen Duffield
t (01669) 620450
e physiccottage@aol.com
w visit-rothbury.co.uk

Westfield Cottage ★★★★
Self Catering
Contact: Mr & Mrs Alastair & Catherine Hardie
t (01669) 640263
e alicat@btinternet.com
w visit-rothbury.co.uk/accom/sc_westfield.htm

TOW LAW
County Durham

Binks Cottage ★★★★
Self Catering
Contact: Mrs Amanda Simpson Oaklea
t (01388) 731121
e amanda.simpson@totalise.co.uk
w binkscottage.co.uk

Greenwell Farm Cottages
★★★ *Self Catering*
Contact: Mrs Linda Vickers
t (01388) 527248
e greenwell.farm@btinternet.com
w greenwellfarm.co.uk

Pennine View ★★★★
Self Catering
Contact: Mrs Dawn Paterson
t (01388) 731329

TUDHOE COLLIERY
County Durham

Miner's Cottage ★★★
Self Catering
Contact: Mrs Jacqueline Galvin
t (01388) 721913
e lgalvin@talk21.com
w miners.cottage.btinternet.co.uk

WALL
Northumberland

Kiln Rigg ★★★ *Self Catering*
Contact: Mr & Mrs Ian & Lisa Burrows
t (01434) 681018
e kilnrigg@beeb.net

WAREN MILL
Northumberland

Cove Cottage, Waren Mill
★★★★ *Self Catering*
Contact: Mrs Anne Lawrence
10 Woodpack Avenue
t (0191) 488 6414 & 07932 795251
e enquiries@northumberland-coast-holidays.co.uk
w northumberland-coast-holidays.co.uk

Eider Cottage ★★★★
Self Catering
Contact: Mrs S Turnbull
t (01668) 214494
e theturnbulls2k@btinternet.com
w holidaynorthumbria.co.uk

WARENFORD
Northumberland

Etive Cottage ★★★★
Self Catering
Contact: Mr & Mrs David & Jan Thompson
t (01668) 213233

WARK
Northumberland

Coachmans and Stable Cottages ★★★ *Self Catering*
Contact: Mr & Mrs Bruce & Sally Napier
t (01434) 230223
w northumberland-self-catering.co.uk

The Hemmel ★★★★
Self Catering
Contact: Mrs Amanda Nichol Hetherington
t (01434) 230260
e alan_nichol@hotmail.com
w hetheringtonfarm.co.uk

Rainbow Cottage ★★★
Self Catering
Contact: Mrs Susan Thorkildsen
t (01890) 882218
e winston44@uwclub.net

Riverside Cottage ★★★
Self Catering
Contact: Mrs Stella Jackson
t (01914) 876531
e jands@wrekenton.freeserve.co.uk

Roses Bower ★★★★
Self Catering
Contact: Mr & Mrs Lewis and Susan Watson
Roses Bower Farm
t (01434) 230779
e sandlwatson@rosesbower.fsworld.co.uk
w roses-bower.co.uk

Look out for establishments participating in the Walkers and Cyclists Welcome Schemes

WARKWORTH
Northumberland

Birling Vale ★★★
Self Catering
Contact: Mrs Janet Brewis
t (01665) 575222
w woodhousefarmholidays.co.uk

Buston Farm Holiday Cottages ★★★★
Self Catering
Contact: Miss Jo Park
t (01665) 714805
e jopark@farming.co.uk
w buston.co.uk

Coquet Cottage ★★★★
Self Catering
Contact: Mrs Barbara Jean Purvis
The Byres
t (01670) 786088 & 07731 883657
e fenwickpurvis@virgin.net

The Loft ★★★★
Self Catering
Contact: Mrs Marie Wraith
t (01665) 711389

Mahonia Lodge ★★★★
Self Catering
Contact: Mr Paul Smith
t (01325) 374070
e bookings@mahonialodge.co.uk
w mahonia-lodge.co.uk

Old Barns Farmhouse Holiday Cottage ★★★★
Self Catering
Contact: Mrs Jane Wilkes
t (01665) 713427
e jane.wilkes@virgin.net
w oldbarnsholidaycottage.co.uk

Rebecca House ★★★★★
Self Catering
Contact: Ms Sue Fenlon
t (01665) 713118
e suefenlon@hotmail.com
w rebeccahouse.co.uk

Riverview Cottage ★★★★★
Self Catering
Contact: Mr & Mrs Paul & Helen Skuse
t (01454) 775441
e pmskuse@hotmail.com
w riverview-warkworth.co.uk

The Shieling ★★★★
Self Catering
Contact: Mrs Carole Ann Whitefield
t (01912) 584347
e holidayshieling@hotmail.com
w holiday-shieling.co.uk

Southmede Cottage ★★★★
Self Catering
Contact: Mr & Mrs Mike & Carol Smith
t (01665) 711360
e info@southmede.co.uk
w southmede.co.uk

WHITLEY BAY
Tyne and Wear

Seafront Apartments, Cullercoats ★★★
Self Catering
Contact: Mrs Rosemary Webb
t 07977 203379
e stay@seafront.info
w seafront.info

Southcliff Apartments ★★★
Self Catering
Contact: Mr Alan Heslington
t (01912) 513121
e southcliffapartments@theseaside.co.uk
w southcliffapartments.com

WHITTINGHAM
Northumberland

Bluebell Cottage ★★★★
Self Catering
Contact: Mrs Marian Charleton
t (01665) 574380
e stay@alnvalleycottages.co.uk
w alnvalleycottages.co.uk

The Lodge and the Gatehouse ★★★★
Self Catering
Contact: Mrs Jenny Sordy
t (01669) 630210
e jenny@alnhamfarm.co.uk
w alnhamfarm.co.uk

WHORLTON
County Durham

Lavender Cottage ★★★★
Self Catering
Contact: Mr Anthony Johnson
t (01642) 483690
e enquiries@lavender-cottage.co.uk
w lavender-cottage.co.uk

WINSTON
County Durham

The Cottage at Alwent Mill
Rating Applied For
Self Catering
Contact: Libby Hampson
t (01325) 730479
e libby@alwentmill.co.uk

Strathmore Barns ★★★★
Self Catering
Contact: Mrs Marion Boyes
t (01833) 660302
e info@strathmorebarns.co.uk
w strathmorebarns.co.uk

WOLSINGHAM
County Durham

Ardine and Elvet Cottage
★★★ *Self Catering*
Contact: Mrs Gardiner
t (01388) 527538

Bradley Burn Holiday Cottages ★★★ *Self Catering*
Contact: Mrs Judith Stephenson
Bradley Burn Holiday Cottages
t (01388) 527285
e jas@bradleyburn.co.uk
w bradleyburn.co.uk

Pasture Cottage ★★★★
Self Catering
Contact: Mrs Carolyn Ramsbotham
t (01388) 527864
e carolyn.ramsbotham@btopenworld.com
w pasturecottage.co.uk

Sandycarr Farm Cottage
★★★★ *Self Catering*
Contact: Mrs Marjorie Love
t (01388) 527249
e william@lovefarm.wanadoo.co.uk

Whitfield House Cottage
★★★ *Self Catering*
Contact: Mrs Margaret Shepheard
t (01388) 527466
e enquiries@whitfieldhouse.clara.net
w whitfieldhouse.clara.net

Willow Cottage Ref 4161
★★★★ *Self Catering*
Contact: Ms Lorraine Kidd
Dales Holiday Cottages
t 0870 909 9500
e lorraine.k@dales-holiday-cottages.com
w dalesholcot.com

WOODLAND
County Durham

Mayland Farm Cottage
★★★ *Self Catering*
Contact: Mrs Susan Mortimer
t (01388) 718237
e john_mortimer@btinternet.com
w cottageguide.co.uk/maylandfarmcottage

WOOLER
Northumberland

Castle Hill Cottage ★★★
Self Catering
Contact: Mr James Nall-Cain
t (01582) 831083
e manussj@aol.com

Coldgate Mill ★★★–★★★★
Self Catering
Contact: Diana Stone
t (01668) 217259
e diana_coldgatemill@hotmail.com
w coldgatemill.co.uk

Fenton Hill Farm Cottages
★★★★ *Self Catering*
Contact: Mrs Margaret Logan
t (01668) 216228
e stay@fentonhillfarm.co.uk
w fentonhillfarm.co.uk

Hayloft & Yearle Tower
★★★–★★★★ *Self Catering*
Country Holidays
t 0870 336 7800
e sales@holidaycottagesgroup.com
w country-holidays.co.uk

Kimmerston Riding Centre
★★★–★★★★ *Self Catering*
Contact: Mr Richard Jeffreys
t (01668) 216283
e jane@kimmerston.com
w kimmerston.com

Milfield Hill Steading
★★★★–★★★★★
Self Catering
Contact: Mrs Liz Turnbull
t (01914) 276203
e turnbullliz@aol.com
w english-country-cottages.co.uk

The Old Mill ★★★★
Self Catering
Contact: Mr Patrick Sheard
t (01892) 837286
e pj.sheard@virgin.net
w theoldmillwooler.co.uk

Peth Head Cottage ★★★★
Self Catering
Contact: Mr & Mrs Peter & Clare Jeffreys
t (01670) 514900
e peter@pncjeffreys.freeserve.co.uk
w pethheadcottage.co.uk

Rose Cottage ★★★
Self Catering
Contact: Mrs Christine Andrews
t (01372) 464284
e andrews@playfactors.demon.co.uk

Swallowfields Country Cottage ★★★★ *Self Catering*
Contact: Mr Malcolm Pringle
t (01668) 283488
e stay@coldmartin.co.uk
w coldmartin.co.uk

Westnewton Estate ★★★
Self Catering
Contact: Mrs Jean Davidson
t (01668) 216077
e jd@westnewtonestate.com
w westnewtonestate.com

YARM
Tees Valley

Yarm Holiday Homes
★★★★ *Self Catering*
Contact: Mr Geoff Rowley
t (01642) 787017
w yarmholidayhomes.co.uk

YARROW
Northumberland

Kielder Cottage ★★★★
Self Catering
Contact: Mr & Mrs Thomas & Elaine Hunt-Vincent
t (01915) 487829
e ehuntvin@aol.com
w kieldercottage.co.uk

YORKSHIRE

ACKLAM
North Yorkshire

Beck Side Cottage @ Trout Pond Barn ★★★★
Self Catering
Contact: Margaret Phillips
t (01653) 658468
e troutpondbarn@aol.com
w troutpond.co.uk

ACOMB
North Yorkshire

Beacon House ★★★★
Self Catering
Contact: Ruby Turner
t (01904) 700809

ADDINGHAM
West Yorkshire

Number Nine ★★★★
Self Catering
Contact: Ian & Jean Francis
t (01943) 831254

AIKE
East Riding of Yorkshire

The Old Chapel Ref:323 ★★★ *Self Catering*
Contact: S Boardman
Sykes Cottages
t (01244) 345700
e info@sykescottages.co.uk
w sykescottages.co.uk

AISKEW
North Yorkshire

The Courtyard ★★★
Self Catering
Contact: Mr & Mrs James & Jill Cartman
t (01677) 423689
e jill@courtyard.ndirect.co.uk

AISLABY
North Yorkshire

Coopers Farm Cottage
Rating Applied For
Self Catering
Contact: Mrs FJ Swift
t (01947) 895277
w coopersfarmcottage.co.uk

Farm Cottage ★★★
Self Catering
Contact: Ms Vanessa Hicking
Whitby Holiday Cottages
t (01947) 821122
e enquiries@whitby-cottages.co.uk
w whitby-cottages.co.uk

Granary Cottage ★★★★
Self Catering
Contact: Ms Vanessa Hicking
Whitby Holiday Cottages
t (01947) 821122
e enquiries@whitby-cottages.co.uk
w whitby-cottages.co.uk

Low Newbiggin House ★★★–★★★★ *Self Catering*
Contact: Miss Charlotte Etherington
t (01947) 811811
e holidays@lownewbiggin.co.uk

Stable Cottage & Byre Cottage ★★★ *Self Catering*
Contact: Ms Vanessa Hicking
Whitby Holiday Cottages
t (01947) 821122
e enquiries@whitby-cottages.co.uk
w whitby-cottages.co.uk

Wren Cottage ★★★
Self Catering
Contact: Janet Hoyle
Yorkshire Cottages
t (01943) 885306
e enquiries@yorkshire-cottages.info
w yorkshire-cottages.info

ALDBROUGH
East Riding of Yorkshire

Lilac Cottage ★★★★
Self Catering
Contact: Helen Stubbs
t (01964) 527645
e helen@seasideroad.freeserve.co.uk
w aer96.dial.pipex.com/lilac-cottage

ALDBROUGH
North Yorkshire

Greencroft Cottage ★★★
Self Catering
Contact: Mary Baxter
t (01325) 374550
e ray.baxter@btinternet.com
w greencroft.org.uk

ALDFIELD
North Yorkshire

Trips Cottage ★★★
Self Catering
Contact: Valerie Leeming
t (01765) 620394
e btfarm@ppcmail.co.uk
w yorkshirebandb.co.uk

ALLERSTON
North Yorkshire

The Old Station ★★★★
Self Catering
Contact: Mark & Carol Benson
t (01723) 859024
e mcrbenson@aol.com
w theoldstationallerston.co.uk

Rains Farm ★★★★
Self Catering
Contact: Mrs L Allanson
t (01723) 859333
e allan@rainsfarm.freeserve.co.uk

AMPLEFORTH
North Yorkshire

2 Carmel Cottage ★★★
Self Catering
Contact: Clare Jennings
t (01439) 788467
e carmelcott@onetel.net.uk

Brackensyke Cottage ★★★★ *Self Catering*
Contact: Peter Davis
t (01904) 690465
e eazystreetpd@yahoo.co.uk
w brackensyke-ampleforth.com

Brook House ★★★★
Self Catering
Contact: Mary Sturges
t (01439) 788563
e mpsturge@aol.com

Hillside Cottage ★★★★
Self Catering
Contact: Pam Noble
t (01439) 788303
e hillsidecottage@westend-ampleforth.co.uk
w cottageguide.co.uk/hillsidecottage

APPERSETT
North Yorkshire

The Coach House ★★★
Self Catering
Contact: Walter Head
t (01969) 667375
e walterhead@rigghouse.freeserve.co.uk

APPLETON-LE-MOORS
North Yorkshire

Darley Cottage ★★★★
Self Catering
Contact: James Brooke
t (01751) 417514
e jbrooke@pottery1.fsnet.co.uk

Hamley Hagg Cottage ★★★
Self Catering
Contact: June Feaster
t (01751) 417413
w appletonlemoors.fsnet.co.uk

Three Faces Cottage ★★★
Self Catering
Contact: Beryl Firth
t (0113) 258 8940
e the3faces@hotmail.com
w cottageguide.co.uk/the3faces

APPLETREEWICK
North Yorkshire

Fell View Ref:817 ★★★
Self Catering
Contact: S Boardman
Sykes Cottages
t (01244) 345700
e info@sykescottages.co.uk
w sykescottages.co.uk

Fellside ★★★ *Self Catering*
Contact: Jayne Murphy
t (0116) 239 5713
e murphyjayne@hotmail.com
w http://mysite.freeserve.com/AppletreewickCottage

ARKENGARTHDALE
North Yorkshire

Low Lock Slack Cottage Ref:62 ★★★ *Self Catering*
Contact: S Boardman
Sykes Cottages
t (01244) 345700
e info@sykescottages.co.uk
w sykescottages.co.uk

ARNCLIFFE
North Yorkshire

Green Farm Cottage Ref:1523 ★★★ *Self Catering*
Contact: Ms Lorraine Kidd
Dales Holiday Cottages
t 0870 909 9500
e info@dales-holiday-cottages.com
w dalesholcot.com

ARRATHORNE
North Yorkshire

Elmfield Cottages ★★★★
Self Catering
Contact: Mr & Mrs Lillie
Elmfield Cottages
t (01677) 450052
e elmfieldcottages@hotmail.com
w elmfieldcottages.co.uk

ASKRIGG
North Yorkshire

Askrigg Cottages ★★★★
Self Catering
Contact: Kate Empsall
t (01228) 406701
e rentals@swaledalecottage.com
w askrigg-cottages.co.uk

Bear Cottage ★★★★
Self Catering
Contact: Mrs Nadine Bell
Country Hideaways
t (01969) 663559
e nadine@countryhideaways.co.uk
w countryhideaways.co.uk

Burn Cottage – Askrigg Cottage Holidays ★★★★
Self Catering
Contact: Ken Williamson
Askrigg Cottage Holidays
t (01969) 650022
e stay@askrigg.com
w askrigg.com

Carr End Cottage Ref:2467 ★★★ *Self Catering*
Contact: Ms Lorraine Kidd
Dales Holiday Cottages
t 0870 909 9500
e info@dales-holiday-cottages.com
w dalesholcot.com

Cowlingholme Cottage ★★★★ *Self Catering*
Contact: Mrs Nadine Bell
Country Hideaways
t (01969) 663559
e nadine@countryhideaways.co.uk
w countryhideaways.co.uk

Elm Hill Holiday Cottages ★★★ *Self Catering*
Contact: Mr & Mrs Peter Haythornthwaite
Hargill Garth
t (01969) 624252
e enquiries@elmhillholidaycottages.co.uk

Faith Hill Cottage ★★★
Self Catering
Contact: Jennifer Kirkbride
Faith Hill Cottage
t (01969) 650325
e allenkirkbride@hotmail.com

Greystones ★★★
Self Catering
Contact: Mrs Nadine Bell
Country Hideaways
t (01969) 663559
e nadine@countryhideaways.co.uk
w countryhideaways.co.uk

Lukes Barn Ref:1675 ★★★
Self Catering
Contact: Ms Lorraine Kidd
Dales Holiday Cottages
t 0870 909 9500
e info@dales-holiday-cottages.com
w dalesholcot.com

Meadowsweet ★★★★
Self Catering
Contact: Mr Alan Rose
t (01904) 626009
e acrose@waitrose.com

Old Mill II ★★★ *Self Catering*
Contact: Mrs Nadine Bell
Country Hideaways
t (01969) 663559
e nadine@countryhideaways.co.uk
w countryhideaways.co.uk

Rooks Cottage – Askrigg Cottage Holidays ★★★★
Self Catering
Contact: Ken Williamson
Askrigg Cottage Holidays
t (01969) 650022
e stay@askrigg.com
w askrigg.com

School House ★★★
Self Catering
Contact: Mrs Nadine Bell
Country Hideaways
t (01969) 663559
e nadine@countryhideaways.co.uk
w countryhideaways.co.uk

Shaw Cote Cottage Ref: 218
★★★ *Self Catering*
Contact: S Boardman
Sykes Cottages
t (01244) 345700
e info@sykescottages.co.uk
w sykescottages.co.uk

The Shippon ★★★★
Self Catering
Contact: Mrs Nadine Bell
Country Hideaways
t (01969) 663559
e nadine@countryhideaways.co.uk
w countryhideaways.co.uk

AUSTWICK
North Yorkshire

Eldroth House ★★★★
Self Catering
Contact: Roger Wales
Holiday Cottages Yorkshire Ltd
t (01756) 700510
e brochure@holidaycotts.co.uk
w holidaycotts.co.uk

Spoutscroft Cottage
★★★★★ *Self Catering*
Contact: Christine Hartland
t (01524) 251052
e chrishartland@austwick.org
w cottageguide.co.uk/spoutscroft

BAINBRIDGE
North Yorkshire

Courtyard Cottage Ref 3708
★★★★ *Self Catering*
t (01756) 799821
e info@dalesholcot.com
w dales-holiday-cottages.com

Pinfold Cottage (4092)
★★★★ *Self Catering*
Dales Holiday Cottages
t 0870 909 9500
e lorraine.k@dales-holiday-cottages.com
w dalesholcot.com

BARMBY MOOR
East Riding of Yorkshire

Northwood Coach House
★★★★ *Self Catering*
Contact: Ann Gregory
Northwood Coach House
t (01759) 302305
e annjgregory@hotmail.com
w northwoodcoachhouse.co.uk

BARTON-LE-WILLOWS
North Yorkshire

The Old Granary ★★★★
Self Catering
Contact: Janet Hudson
t (01653) 618387
e bartonlewillows@netscapeonline.co.uk
w oldgranary.com

BAYSDALE
North Yorkshire

Baysdale Abbey ★★★★
Self Catering
Contact: The Agent
Burwarton Estates Company Limited
t 0870 585 1155
w english-country-cottages.co.uk

BECKWITHSHAW
North Yorkshire

The Old Mistal Cottage
★★★★ *Self Catering*
Contact: Christine Williams
t (01423) 561385
e c.williams@mistal.fsnet.co.uk
w mistal.fsnet.co.uk

BEDALE
North Yorkshire

High Grange Holiday Cottages ★★★★
Self Catering
Contact: Caroline Cottam
t (01677) 422740
e highgrange@yorks.net
w high-grange.co.uk

BELLERBY
North Yorkshire

Boar Cottage ★★★★
Self Catering
Contact: Bernie Gray
t (01969) 622220
e graydales@aol.com
w boarcottage.co.uk

Rowan Cottage ★★★★
Self Catering
Dales Holiday Cottages
t 0870 909 9500
e info@dales-holiday-cottages.com
w dalesholcot.com

Scott Cottage ★★★
Self Catering
Contact: Anne Maughan
t (01969) 622498
e scottcottage@fsmail.net
w scottcottageleyburn.co.uk

BEMPTON
East Riding of Yorkshire

Primrose Cottage Ref:2122
★★★★ *Self Catering*
Contact: Ms Lorraine Kidd
Dales Holiday Cottages
t 0870 909 9500
e info@dales-holiday-cottages.com
w dalesholcot.com

BEVERLEY
East Riding of Yorkshire

Aragon House Cottage
★★★ *Self Catering*
Contact: Mrs G Bennett
t (01482) 868506

Chapel View ★★★
Self Catering
Contact: Philip Hillman
t (01482) 867465
e pcoliverhillman@hotmail.com

The Cottage ★★★★
Self Catering
Contact: Kenneth Hearne
The Cottage
t (01482) 868310
e knhearne@talk21.com
w akcottage.com

Foremans Cottage ★★★
Self Catering
Contact: Heather Hayward
t (01964) 550821
e heather90hayward@btinternet.com

Lempicka Cottage ★★★★
Self Catering
Contact: Linda Boyeson
t (01482) 863665
e steve@lempicka.wanadoo.co.uk

Old Walkergate & The Cabin
★★★ *Self Catering*
Contact: Margaret Abbey
t (01482) 860005
e margaretabbey@beverleyselfcatering.freeserve.co.uk
w beverleyselfcatering.freeserve.co.uk

Rudstone Walk Country Accommodation ★★★★
Self Catering
Contact: Sylvia Spinks
t (01430) 422230
e sylvia@rudstone-walk.co.uk
w rudstone-walk.co.uk

BEWERLEY
North Yorkshire

Bewerley Hall Farm ★★★★
Self Catering
Contact: Eileen Smith
t (01423) 711636
e chris@farmhouseholidays.freeserve.co.uk
w bewerleyhallfarm.co.uk

BEWHOLME
East Riding of Yorkshire

Fold Yard Cottage ★★★
Self Catering
Contact: Janet Hoyle
Yorkshire Cottages
t (01943) 885306
e enquiries@yorkshire-cottages.info
w yorkshire-cottages.info

BIELBY
East Riding of Yorkshire

Sunnyside Cottage ★★★
Self Catering
Contact: Debbie Britton
t (01759) 318611
e britton@supanet.com
w sunnysidecottage.co.uk

BIRSTWITH
North Yorkshire

3 The Square ★★★★
Self Catering
Contact: H.R. Wales
Holiday Cottages (Yorkshire) Ltd
t (01756) 700510
e brochure@holidaycotts.co.uk
w holidaycotts.co.uk

BISHOP MONKTON
North Yorkshire

Granary Cottage ★★
Self Catering
Contact: Allison Hewson
t (01765) 677677

Hall Farm Cottage ★★★★
Self Catering
Contact: Jennifer Barker
t (01765) 677200
e jenkenhallfarm@onetel.com
w yorkshirebandb.co.uk

BISHOP THORNTON
North Yorkshire

The Courtyard at 'Dukes Place' ★★★★ *Self Catering*
Contact: Jaki Moorhouse
t (01765) 620229
e enquiries@dukesplace-courtyard.co.uk

BISHOP WILTON
East Riding of Yorkshire

Grange Farm Holiday Cottages ★★★ *Self Catering*
Contact: Mr Richard & Mrs Judith Davy
Grange Farm Holiday Cottages
t (01759) 369500
e richarddavy@supanet.com
w thegrangefarm.com

Low Callis Granary ★★★★
Self Catering
Contact: Jayne Stringer & Sons
t (01759) 368831
e thegranary@lowcallis.plus.com

BISHOPDALE
North Yorkshire

The Rookery ★★★★
Self Catering
Contact: Mrs Nadine Bell
Country Hideaways
t (01969) 663559
e nadine@countryhideaways.co.uk
w countryhideaways.co.uk

BLACKSHAW HEAD
West Yorkshire

The Garden House ★★★
Self Catering
Contact: Mr Martin Robinson
t (01422) 842794
e robinson@woodrillel.freeserve.co.uk

BOLSTERSTONE
South Yorkshire

Nook Farm Holiday Cottage
★★★★ *Self Catering*
Contact: Jane Wainwright
t (0114) 288 3335

BOLTBY
North Yorkshire

The Coach House ★★★
Self Catering
t 0870 444 6603
w boltbytrekking.co.uk

BOLTON ABBEY
North Yorkshire

The Beamsley Project
★★★★ *Self Catering*
Contact: John & Margaret Tomlinson
t (01756) 710255
e info@beamsleyproject.org.uk
w beamsleyproject.org.uk

Low Laithe Barn ★★★★★
Self Catering
Contact: Susan Gray
t (01943) 609819
e info@beechhousebarns.co.uk
w beechhousebarns.co.uk

BOUTHWAITE
North Yorkshire

Granary Cottage ★★★
Self Catering
Contact: John Corfield
t (01423) 755306
e john@covillbarn.co.uk
w covillbarn.co.uk

BOYNTON
East Riding of Yorkshire

No. 8 Boynton ★★★★
Self Catering
Contact: Elizabeth Myhill
t (01262) 420201
e liz.myhill@scarborough.gov.uk
w no8boynton.co.uk

West Lawn Farm ★★★
Self Catering
Contact: Wendy Yates
t (01653) 691146
e info@westlawnfarm.co.uk
w westlawnfarm.co.uk

BRADFIELD
South Yorkshire

Cricket View ★★★
Self Catering
Contact: Miss Shaz Thompson
t (0114) 285 1235
e info@thepostcardcafe.com

BRADFIELD DALE
South Yorkshire

Thornseat Cottage ★★★
Self Catering
t (0114) 285 1062
w peakcottages.com

BRADSHAW
West Yorkshire

Popples Cottage ★★★★
Self Catering
Contact: Colin Huntley
t (01422) 244788
w popplescottage.co.uk

BRANDESBURTON
East Riding of Yorkshire

Struncheon Hill Farm Cottages
Rating Applied For
Self Catering
t (01377) 271486

BRAWBY
North Yorkshire

The Old Cart House ★★★★
Self Catering
Contact: Anne Muir
t (01653) 668252
e theoldcarthouse@aol.com

BRIDLINGTON
East Riding of Yorkshire

23 Mount Drive
Rating Applied For
Self Catering
Contact: Helen Gudgeon
t (0113) 226 1298
e rkgudgeon@hotmail.com

Acorn House ★★★
Self Catering
Contact: Tony Morton
t (01262) 672451
e marieoak24@hotmail.com

Angie's Imp-press Holiday Apartments ★★★
Self Catering
Contact: Angela Boxer
t (01262) 608838

Arncliffe ★-★★★
Self Catering
Contact: Shirley Drew
t (01262) 677945

Ash Lee Holiday Apartments
★★-★★★ *Self Catering*
Contact: Janet Greatorex
t (01262) 400485
e another@ytb.co.uk
w bridlington-flats.co.uk

Ashton Holiday Flats ★★
Self Catering
Contact: Samuel & Helen Levitt
t (01262) 675132

Bay Side Holidays ★★★★
Self Catering
Contact: Mr & Mrs Barry & Anne Hatfield
c/o 25 Victoria Road
t (01262) 673871
e victoria.hotel@virgin.net

Beach House ★★★★
Self Catering
Contact: Doreen Hirst
t (01226) 206847

Beaconsfield House ★★★
Self Catering
Contact: Loraine Stuart
t (01262) 401482
e info@beaconsfieldholidayapartments.co.uk
w beaconsfieldholidayapartments.co.uk

Bluebell Holiday Apartment
★★★ *Self Catering*
Contact: Lorna Shaw
t (01262) 401445

East Coast Holiday Cottages
★★★ *Self Catering*
Contact: Cynthia Dean
t (01262) 601543
e eastcoastholidaycottages@hotmail.com
w bridlington.net/business.eastcoast

Ellwyn Holiday Flats ★★
Self Catering
Contact: James & Susan Thornton
t (01262) 606896
e elliethodsq@supanet.com
w bridlington.net/ellwyn/business

Fairholme Holiday Flats
★-★★ *Self Catering*
Contact: Nicholas Geraghty
t (01262) 676269
e nicholasscott@geraghty2.fsnet.co.uk

Finley Cottages ★★★
Self Catering
Contact: Pauline Halstead
t (01377) 253985
e winston.halstead@virgin.net

Fir Lodge Holiday Apartments ★★★
Self Catering
Contact: Chris & Les Day
t (01262) 671400
e firlodgeapts@aol.com

Fountain House ★-★★
Self Catering
Contact: Mr Shuttleworth
t (01262) 604850
e reservations@fountainhouse.co.uk

The Grosvenor Holiday Flats
★★★★ *Self Catering*
Contact: Elizabeth Otulakowski
t (01729) 830959
e anton@otulakowski.freeserve.co.uk

Hemsley Holiday Flats
★-★★ *Self Catering*
Contact: Mr E Halliday
Helmsley Holiday Flats
t (01262) 672603

Highcliffe Holiday Apartments ★-★★★
Self Catering
Contact: Mrs Pat Willcocks
Highcliffe Holiday Apartments
t (01262) 674127
e john.willcocks@fsmail.net
w highcliffe.net

Lunbelle Holiday Accommodation ★★
Self Catering
Contact: Catherine Ciosi
t (01262) 676671
e flats@sdinardo.freeserve.co.uk
w lunbelle-accommodation.co.uk

Marina Holiday Apartments
★★★ *Self Catering*
Contact: Lorna Shaw
t (01262) 401445

Marina View ★-★★★
Self Catering
Contact: Geraldine Ross
t (01262) 676565

Marton Manor Cottages
★★★★ *Self Catering*
Contact: Jane Waind
t (01262) 672522
e martonmanor@btopenworld.com
w martonmanor.co.uk

North Kingsfield Holiday Cottages, Fraisthorpe
★★★★★ *Self Catering*
Contact: Peter and Helen Milner
North Kingsfield Holiday Cottages
t (01262) 673743
e helen@northkingsfield.co.uk
w northkingsfield.co.uk

Oakwell Aparthotel
★★★-★★★★ *Self Catering*
Contact: Kay Williams
t (01262) 403666
e oakwellholidays@aol.com

Pembroke Holiday Flats
★★★ *Self Catering*
Contact: Mr & Mrs Eaton
t (01262) 677376
e ampembroke@btopenworld.com

The Rialto ★-★★
Self Catering
Contact: Michelle Stoddard
t (01262) 677653

Rowntree Seafront Holiday Flats
Rating Applied For
Self Catering
Rowntree Holiday Flats
t (01262) 678181

Royal Court Apartments
★★★★ *Self Catering*
t (01262) 676024

San Marino Court Holiday Flats ★★-★★★ *Self Catering & Serviced Apartments*
Contact: Paul Sharpe
t (01262) 678372
e paul8sharpe@yahoo.co.uk
w sanmarinocourt.co.uk

San Remo ★★★ *Self Catering*
Contact: Ann Jackson
t (01262) 676585

Sea View Holiday Flats
★-★★ *Self Catering*
Contact: Stanley & Margaret Benson
t (01262) 676974
e flash2@tesco.net

Winston Court Holiday Apartments ★-★★
Self Catering
Contact: Ian Read
Egsproperty
t (01262) 677819
e enquiries@winston-court.co.uk
w winston-court.co.uk

BRIGHOUSE
West Yorkshire

Modern Apartment in Brighouse ★★★★
Self Catering
Contact: Kash Ijaz
Nomorehotels
t 0870 850 8514
e info@nomorehotels.co.uk
w nomorehotels.co.uk/leeds.html

BUCKDEN
North Yorkshire

Dalegarth and The Ghyll Cottages ★★★★
Self Catering
Contact: David & Susan Lusted
t (01756) 760877
e info@dalegarth.co.uk
w dalegarth.co.uk

East Farm Ref:1542 ★★★★
Self Catering
Contact: Ms Lorraine Kidd
Dales Holiday Cottages
t 0870 909 9500
e info@dales-holiday-cottages.com
w dalesholcot.com

The Old Chapel (4148)
★★★ *Self Catering*
Contact: Ms Lorraine Kidd
t (01756) 790919
e lorraine.k@dales-holiday-cottages.com
w dales-holiday-cottages.com

Woods Barn Ref:3164
★★★★ *Self Catering*
Contact: Ms Lorraine Kidd
Dales Holiday Cottages
t 0870 909 9500
e info@dales-holiday-cottages.com
w dalesholcot.com

BULMER
North Yorkshire

Ashwall House ★★★★★
Self Catering
Contact: Mr Tony Thomas
t (01845) 597614
e enquiriesytb@ashwallhouse.co.uk

BURNSALL
North Yorkshire

Oatcroft Farm Barn Apartment ★★★-★★★★
Self Catering
Contact: Jane Stockdale
t (01756) 720268

Riversyde Cottage Ref: 214
★★★★ *Self Catering*
Contact: S Boardman
Sykes Cottages
t (01244) 345700
e info@sykescottages.co.uk
w sykescottages.co.uk

The Sycamores ★★★★
Self Catering
Contact: Sheila Carr
DSC Holiday Lettings Ltd
t (01756) 752435
e carr@totalise.co.uk
w yorkshirenet.co.uk/stayat/mannacottage

BURTERSETT
North Yorkshire

Middlegate ★★★
Self Catering
Contact: Ken Williamson
Askrigg Cottage Holidays
t (01969) 650022
e stay@askrigg.com
w askrigg.com

BURTON-IN-LONSDALE
North Yorkshire

Brentwood Farm Cottages
★★★★ *Self Catering*
Contact: Anita Taylor
t (01524) 262155
e info@brentwoodfarmcottages.co.uk
w brentwoodfarmcottages.co.uk

Greta Cottage ★★★★
Self Catering
Contact: Jane Burns
t (01524) 261081
e jandaburns@ktdinternet.com

Riverside Cottage ★★★★★
Self Catering
Contact: Patricia Leverton
t (01274) 560542
e riversidecott@whsmith.net
w members.aol.com/riversidecott

BURYTHORPE
North Yorkshire

The Granary ★★★★
Self Catering
Contact: Margaret Raines
t (01653) 658201
e thegranary1994@btinternet.com

Primrose Cottage ★★★★
Self Catering
Contact: Chris Turner
t (01653) 658336
e LowPenhowe@btinternet.com
w countryholidaycottages.co.uk

CARLETON
North Yorkshire

Rombalds Cottage and Crookrise Cottage R ★★★
Self Catering
Contact: Ms Lorraine Kidd
Dales Holiday Cottages
t 0870 909 9500
e info@dales-holiday-cottages.com
w dalesholcot.com

Sally's Cottage Ref:3052
★★★ *Self Catering*
Dales Holiday Cottages
t 0870 909 9500
e fiona@dales-holiday-cottages.com
w dalesholcot.com

CARLTON MINIOTT
North Yorkshire

10 Thirlmere Close ★★★
Self Catering
Contact: Joan Pounder
t (01845) 511265

Holly Barn ★★★★
Self Catering
Contact: William Edward Lawson
t (01845) 522099
e billlawson@tiscali.co.uk

CARPERBY
North Yorkshire

Barnbrook Ref:567 ★★★
Self Catering
Contact: S Boardman
Sykes Cottages
t (01244) 345700
e info@sykescottages.co.uk
w sykescottages.co.uk

Manor Farm Cottage, Pencroft Cottage & The Granary ★★★★ *Self Catering*
Dales Holiday Cottages
t 0870 909 9500
e fiona@dales-holiday-cottages.com
w dalesholcot.com

The Old Post Office ★★★★
Self Catering
Contact: Mrs Nadine Bell
Country Hideaways
t (01969) 663559
e nadine@countryhideaways.co.uk
w countryhideaways.co.uk

Woodsomme Cottage Ref:3305 ★★★★
Self Catering
Contact: Ms Lorraine Kidd
Dales Holiday Cottages
t 0870 909 9500
e info@dales-holiday-cottages.com
w dalesholcot.com

CASTLETON
North Yorkshire

Moor House ★★★★
Self Catering
Contact: Jackie Byers
NorthStar Accommodation
t (01947) 603456
e info@northstaraccommodation.co.uk
w northstaraccommodation.co.uk

CAYTON
North Yorkshire

Eldin Hall Cottages ★★★
Self Catering
Contact: Mrs Diane Callaghan
t (01723) 516700
e info@bedwyns.co.uk
w bedwyns.co.uk

Killerby Old Hall ★★★★
Self Catering
Contact: Margery Middleton
t (01723) 583799
w killerby.com

CHAPEL LE DALE
North Yorkshire

4 Salt Lake Cottages ★★★
Self Catering
Contact: M.G Lees
t (01729) 860485

Netherscar Ref: 281 ★★
Self Catering
Contact: S Boardman
Sykes Cottages
t (01244) 345700
e info@sykescottages.co.uk
w sykescottages.co.uk

CHOP GATE
North Yorkshire

Broadfields Cottage ★★★★
Self Catering
Contact: Mrs Judith Staples
Broadfields Cottage
t (01642) 778384
w diamond.org/broadfields

Lavrock Hall Farmhouse Cottage ★★★ *Self Catering*
Contact: Jane Brack
t (01439) 798275
e info@lavrockhall.co.uk
w lavrockhall.co.uk

CLAPHAM
North Yorkshire

The Old Stable ★★★★
Self Catering
Contact: Michael & Gillian Fell
t (01524) 251331
e gill@coppyhouse.co.uk
w coppyhouse.co.uk

Sherwood ★★★★
Self Catering
Contact: Mr & Mrs Beresford
Beresmoor
t (01729) 840231
e mrberesford@farming.co.uk

CLOUGHTON
North Yorkshire

Gowland Farm Holiday Cottages ★★★★
Self Catering
t (01723) 870924
w gowlandfarm.co.uk

Station House ★★★★
Self Catering
Contact: Mr & Mrs Steve & Barbara Hargreaves
t (01723) 870896

COLDEN
West Yorkshire

Riverdene House
Rating Applied For
Self Catering
t (01422) 847447

COMMONDALE
North Yorkshire

Fowl Green Farm
★★★-★★★★ *Self Catering*
Contact: Susan Muir
t (01287) 660742
e info@fowlgreenfarm.com
w fowlgreenfarm.com

CONISBROUGH
South Yorkshire

Cosy Terrace Cottage ★★
Self Catering
Contact: John Perrin
t (01709) 580612
e john@cosyterrace.co.uk
w cosyterrace.fsnet.co.uk

CONONLEY
North Yorkshire

Causeway Cottage ★★★★
Self Catering
Contact: Mrs H M Freeman
t (01535) 644140
e hilaryanddave@yahoo.co.uk

CRAGG VALE
West Yorkshire

Robin Hood Cottage ★★★
Self Catering
Contact: Isabel Woznicki
t 07977 459913
e liz@robinhoodcottage.co.uk
w robinhoodcottage.co.uk

CROPTON
North Yorkshire

2 Corner Cottage ★★
Self Catering
Contact: Mary Rowlands
t (01751) 417562
e rowlands.mary@talk21.com

Beckhouse Cottages, Cropton ★★★★
Self Catering
Contact: Pam Smith
t (01751) 417235
e beckhousecottages@hotmail.com
w beckhousecottages.co.uk

High Farm Holiday Cottages
★★★★ *Self Catering*
Contact: Mrs Ruth Feaster
t (01751) 417461
e highfarmcropton@aol.com

Whitethorn Holiday Home
Rating Applied For
Self Catering
Contact: Samantha Barnes
t (01751) 417262

DACRE
North Yorkshire

Burns Farm ★★ *Self Catering*
t (01423) 780217

DALTON
North Yorkshire

Badgerway Stoop Cottage Ref:3119 ★★★ *Self Catering*
Contact: Ms Lorraine Kidd
Dales Holiday Cottages
t 0870 909 9500
e info@dales-holiday-cottages.com
w dalesholcot.com

Hilltop Cottage ★★★★
Self Catering
Contact: Richard Farr
t (01833) 621234
e sue@sjfarr.freeserve.co.uk
w hilltopcottage.co.uk

Keepers Cottage ★★★
Self Catering
Contact: Dorothy Lewis
Keepers Cottage
t (01833) 621446
e peter.lewis63@btinternet.com

DANBY
North Yorkshire

Ainthorpe Farm Cottage
★★★★ *Self Catering*
Contact: Sheila Hide
t (01287) 660358

Beckwith House ★★★
Self Catering
Contact: Heather Mather
t (01287) 669104
e chmather@onetel.com

Clitherbecks Farm ★★
Self Catering
Contact: Catherine Harland
Clitherbecks Farm
t (01287) 660321
e nharland@clitherbecks.freeserve.co.uk
w clitherbecks.freeserve.co.uk

Margold Cottage Ref:2505
★★★ *Self Catering*
Contact: Ms Lorraine Kidd
Dales Holiday Cottages
t 0870 909 9500
e info@dales-holiday-cottages.com
w dalesholcot.com

DONCASTER
South Yorkshire

The Green Gable ★★★★
Self Catering
Contact: Trevor Smeaton
t (01302) 327782
e qjs@btconnect.com

DRIFFIELD
East Riding of Yorkshire

Manor Farm Cottages ★★★
Self Catering
Contact: Antony & Jennie Byass
t (01377) 217324
e lanpulses@aol.com

DRINGHOUSES
North Yorkshire

Knavesmire Cottage ★★★
Self Catering
Contact: John Slater
t (01904) 798272

Mayfield ★★★★
Self Catering
Contact: Cheryl Leslie
t (01372) 272782
e davidleslie@mcmail.com
w cottageholidaysonline.co.uk

DUGGLEBY
North Yorkshire

Highbury Farm Cottage
★★★★ *Self Catering*
Contact: John & Christine Sawdon
t (01944) 738664
e john.sawdon@virgin.net
w highbury-farm-holiday-cottage.co.uk

DUNGWORTH, BRADFIELD
South Yorkshire

Rickett Field Farm ★★★★
Self Catering
Contact: Connie Shepherd
Rickett Field
t (0114) 285 1218
e shepherd@rickettlathe.freeserve.co.uk
w rickettfieldfarm.co.uk

DUNNINGTON
North Yorkshire

Ashfield Cottages ★★★
Self Catering
Contact: Mr Robert Lewis
t (01904) 488631
e info@ashfieldholidaycottages.co.uk
w ashfieldholidaycottages.co.uk

DUNSLEY
North Yorkshire

The Shippon & The Stable Ref:188&1989 ★★★
Self Catering
Contact: Ms H Cook
Dales Holiday Cottages
t 0870 909 9500
e info@dales-holiday-cottages.com
w dalesholcot.com

EASBY
North Yorkshire

Abbey House ★★★★★
Self Catering
Contact: John Martin
t (01748) 825311

EASINGWOLD
North Yorkshire

Allerton Cottage ★★★
Self Catering
Contact: Angela Thornton
t (01347) 821912

Mooracres Bungalow Ref:753 ★★★ *Self Catering*
Contact: Ms Lorraine Kidd
Dales Holiday Cottages
t 0870 909 9500
e info@dales-holiday-cottages.com
w dalesholcot.com

EAST AYTON
North Yorkshire

Cloggers Cottage ★★★
Self Catering
Dales Holiday Cottages
t 0870 909 9500
e fiona@dales-holiday-cottages.com
w dalesholcot.com

EBBERSTON
North Yorkshire

Cliff House, Ebberston
★★★★ *Self Catering*
Contact: Simon Morris
t (01723) 859440
e cliffhouseebberston@btinternet.com
w cliffhouse-cottageholidays.co.uk

Cow Pasture Cottage
★★★-★★★★ *Self Catering*
Contact: Mr Green
t (01723) 859285
e ernie@jhodgson.fsnet.co.uk
w studley-house.co.uk

Nesfield Cottage ★★★★
Self Catering
Contact: Janet Wood
t (01530) 416094
e chris.wood4@virgin.net

EGTON
North Yorkshire

The Hayloft ★★★
Self Catering
Contact: Hilary Walker
t (01947) 895640
e hilary_phenix@hotmail.com
w copper-beeches.com

Westonby Cottage ★★
Self Catering
Contact: Joan Flintoft
t (01947) 895296

EGTON BRIDGE
North Yorkshire

Broom House Cottages, Egton Bridge ★★★★
Self Catering
Contact: Mrs Maria White
Broom Cottage
t (01947) 895279
e mw@broom-house.co.uk

FARNLEY TYAS
West Yorkshire

Sycamore Farm Cottages
★★★-★★★★ *Self Catering*
t (01484) 661458
e info@sycamorefarmcottages.co.uk
w sycamorefarmcottages.co.uk

FEARBY
North Yorkshire

Chapel Byre ★★★★
Self Catering
Contact: Mrs Nadine Bell
Country Hideaways
t (01969) 663559
e nadine@countryhideaways.co.uk
w countryhideaways.co.uk

FEIZOR
North Yorkshire

Scar Close Barn Ref:2953
★★★★ *Self Catering*
Contact: Ms Lorraine Kidd
Dales Holiday Cottages
t 0870 909 9500
e info@dales-holiday-cottages.com
w dalesholcot.com

FELLBECK
North Yorkshire

1 and 2 North Oaks Farm Cottages ★★★★
Self Catering
Contact: Sue Loveless
t (01423) 712446
e cottages@loveless.co.uk
w northoakscottages.co.uk

FILEY
North Yorkshire

84 Queen Street ★★★★
Self Catering
Contact: Suzan Brown
t (01246) 200780
w filey.biz

Baxter House ★★★★
Self Catering
Contact: Anne Cooper
t (01723) 365263

Beach Holiday Flats
★★-★★★ *Self Catering*
Contact: Ann Tindall
t (01723) 513178
e anntindall@aol.com
w thebeach-holidayflats.co.uk

Cliff View / Wold View
Rating Applied For
Self Catering
Contact: Mrs Lillian Mason
t (01723) 514596

The Cottages ★★★
Self Catering
Contact: Mr & Mrs David Teet
The Cottages
t (01723) 516620

Crescent Apartment ★★★
Self Catering
Contact: Mr Jack Speight
t (0113) 277 5853

Ennerdale Holiday Flats
★–★★ *Self Catering*
Contact: Chris Thompson
t (01723) 513798

Fisherman Cottage ★★★
Self Catering
Contact: Mrs Annette Cavell
Teathill Cottage
t (01757) 290020

Four Seasons Holiday Flats
★★★ *Self Catering*
Contact: Christine Clarbour
t (01723) 515332
e reservations@fourseasons-filey.co.uk

Langford Villa ★★★
Self Catering
Contact: Mr & Mrs D.H Midgley
Langford Villa Holiday Flat
t (01723) 514813
e dhmidgley@ukonline.co.uk

FINGHALL
North Yorkshire

Rose Cottage ★★★★
Self Catering
Country Hideaways
t (01969) 663559
w countryhideaways.co.uk

FITLING
East Riding of Yorkshire

Stables Cottage ★★★★
Self Catering
Contact: Patricia Cockshutt
t (01964) 527114
e stablescottage@tiscali.co.uk
w scope.karoo.net/fitling

FLAMBOROUGH
East Riding of Yorkshire

Flamborough Rock Cottages
★★★ *Self Catering*
Contact: Jannice Geraghty
t (01262) 850996
e info@flamboroughrockcottages.co.uk
w flamboroughrockcottages.co.uk

The Viking Hotel ★★★
Self Catering
Contact: Karen Summers
Summers Seaside Homes
t (01262) 851455
e info@thevikinghotel.co.uk
w thevikinghotel.co.uk

FOGGATHORPE
East Riding of Yorkshire

Yellowtop Country Park
★★★★ *Self Catering*
Contact: Paula Jessop
t (01430) 860461
e yellowtopcountry@aol.com
w yellowtopcountry.co.uk

FOLLIFOOT
North Yorkshire

Marlin Cottage ★★★★
Self Catering
Contact: Evelyn Clayton
t (01423) 883696
e clayton.clayton@virgin.net

FYLINGDALES
North Yorkshire

Demesne Farm ★★★★
Self Catering
Contact: June & Alan Bancroft
t (01947) 880448
e jhb49@hotmail.com
w demesnefarm.co.uk

Swallows Cottage & The Granary ★★★ *Self Catering*
Contact: Ms Vanessa Hicking
Whitby Holiday Cottages
t (01947) 821122
e enquiries@whitby-cottages.co.uk
w whitby-cottages.co.uk

FYLINGTHORPE
North Yorkshire

Croft Farm Cottage ★★★
Self Catering
Contact: Joanne Braithwaite
t (01947) 880231
e croftfarmbb@aol.com
w robinhoodsbay.co.uk/croftfarm

The Peat House ★★★★
Self Catering
Contact: Ms Vanessa Hicking
Whitby Holiday Cottages
t (01947) 821122
e enquiries@whitby-cottages.co.uk
w whitby-cottages.co.uk

GALPHAY
North Yorkshire

West Leas Farm ★★★
Self Catering
Contact: Mrs Catherine Raw
t (01765) 658416
e raw@westleas.co.uk
w westleas.co.uk

GAYLE
North Yorkshire

Aysgill Cottage ★★★
Self Catering
Contact: Deborah Allen
t (01969) 667477

Foss Cottage ★★★
Self Catering
Contact: Brenda Watering
t (01969) 667518
e brendale@watering.wanadoo.co.uk

Gayle Farmhouse Ref:636
★★★ *Self Catering*
Contact: Ms Lorraine Kidd
Dales Holiday Cottages
t 0870 909 9500
e info@dales-holiday-cottages.com
w dalesholcot.com

GIGGLESWICK
North Yorkshire

2 Gildersleets ★★★★
Self Catering
Contact: Paul Griffiths
t (0161) 795 9713
e doctor.g@gconnect.com
w 2gildersleets.co.uk

Black Horse Cottage ★★★
Self Catering
Contact: Anthony & Ann Haygarth
Black Horse Cottage
t (0113) 269 3960
e haygarthtony@aol.com
w black-horse-cottage.co.uk

Bookend Cottage Ref: 713
★★★ *Self Catering*
Contact: S Boardman
Sykes Cottages
t (01244) 345700
e info@sykescottages.co.uk
w sykescottages.co.uk

Close House Cottage Holidays ★★★★
Self Catering
Contact: Sue Hargreaves
t (01729) 822778
e chcottages@aol.com
w close-house.co.uk

Foxholes Lodge ★★★
Self Catering
Contact: Lynn Scruton
t (01729) 823505

Ivy Cottage Ref:629 ★★★★
Self Catering
Contact: Ms Lorraine Kidd
Dales Holiday Cottages
t 0870 909 9500
e info@dales-holiday-cottages.com
w dalesholcot.com

Rowan House, Willow Cottage Ref: 398&652
★★★★ *Self Catering*
Contact: Mr S Boardman
Sykes Cottages
t (01244) 345700
e info@sykescottages.co.uk
w sykescottages.co.uk

Stanton Cottage ★★★
Self Catering
Contact: Alison Boswell
t (01729) 822400
e pboswell@ukonline.co.uk

Sutcliffe Cottage Ref: 31
★★ *Self Catering*
Contact: S Boardman
Sykes Cottages
t (01244) 345700
e info@sykescottages.co.uk
w sykescottages.co.uk

GILLAMOOR
North Yorkshire

Gales House Farm ★★★★
Self Catering
Contact: Mr & Mrs David & Kathy Ward
t (01751) 431258
e cottages@gillamoor.com
w gillamoor.com

Keepers Cottage ★★★
Self Catering
Contact: Joan Davies
t (01751) 433129
e keri-davies@lineone.net
w yorkshireselfcatering.co.uk

GILLING EAST
North Yorkshire

Sunset Cottages
★★★–★★★★ *Self Catering*
Contact: Sally Banks
t (01347) 888654
e info@sunsetcottages.co.uk
w sunsetcottages.co.uk

GILLING WEST
North Yorkshire

Gilling Old Mill Cottages
★★★★ *Self Catering*
Contact: Mr & Mrs Hugh & Joyce Bird
Gilling Old Mill
t (01748) 822771
e admin@yorkshiredales-cottages.com
w yorkshiredales-cottages.com

GILSTEAD
West Yorkshire

Thimble, Bobbin & Shuttle
★★★ *Self Catering*
Contact: L Jean Warin
t (01274) 487433
e jean.warin@nevisuk.net
w yorkshirenet.co.uk/accgde/marchcote

GLAISDALE
North Yorkshire

Lanes Cottage ★★★
Self Catering
Contact: John & Nancy Dale
t (01947) 897316

The Studio Flat ★★★★
Self Catering
Contact: John & Mary Thompson
t (01947) 897353
e j-m.thompson.bandb@talk21.com
w postgate-farm-holidays.co.uk

Tailors Cottage Ref:457
★★★ *Self Catering*
Contact: S Boardman
Sykes Cottages
t (01244) 345700
e info@sykescottages.co.uk
w sykescottages.co.uk

Underhill Cottage ★★★★
Self Catering
Contact: Ms Vanessa Hicking
Whitby Holiday Cottages
t (01947) 821122
e enquiries@whitby-cottages.co.uk
w whitby-cottages.co.uk

Yaffles Cottage
Rating Applied For
Self Catering
Contact: Ms Vanessa Hicking
Whitby Holiday Cottages
t (01947) 603010
e enquiries@whitby-cottages.co.uk

GOATHLAND
North Yorkshire

14 Oakfield Avenue ★★★
Self Catering
Contact: Ms Vanessa Hicking
Whitby Holiday Cottages
t (01947) 821122
e enquiries@whitby-cottages.co.uk
w whitby-cottages.co.uk

Eskholme Holiday Cottage
★★★★ *Self Catering*
Contact: Janet Hodgson
Eskholme
t (01924) 498154
e ffsjan@aol.com

Orchard Cottage Ref:1418
★★★★★ *Self Catering*
Contact: Ms Lorraine Kidd
Dales Holiday Cottages
t 0870 909 9500
e info@dales-holiday-cottages.com
w dalesholcot.com

The Stone Cottage ★★★
Self Catering
Dales Holiday Cottages
t 0870 909 9500
e info@dales-holiday-cottages.com
w dalesholcot.com

Woodpecker Cottage Ref:3125 ★★★★
Self Catering
Contact: Ms Lorraine Kidd
Dales Holiday Cottages
t 0870 909 9500
e info@dales-holiday-cottages.com
w dalesholcot.com

GOLCAR
West Yorkshire

The Old School House ★★★★ *Self Catering*
Contact: Dale Harley
t (01484) 655792
e daleharley@tiscali.co.uk

GRANSMOOR
East Riding of Yorkshire

The Wagon Shed ★★★★
Self Catering
Contact: Mr Garry Slingsby
t (01262) 490338
e gslingsby@fni.co.uk

GRASSINGTON
North Yorkshire

6a Garrs Lane ★★★
Self Catering
Contact: Paul Borrill
t (01756) 752436 & 07709 313716
e info@grassingtonapartment.co.uk
w grassingtonapartment.co.uk

Jasmine Cottage ★★★
Self Catering
Dales Holiday Cottages
t 0870 909 9500
e fiona@dales-holiday-cottages.com
w dalesholcot.com

Manna Cottage ★★★★
Self Catering
Contact: Mrs Sheila Carr
Moor Green Farm
t (01756) 752435
e carr@totalise.co.uk
w yorkshirenet.co.uk/stayat/mannacottage

Riverside Apartment ★★★
Self Catering
Contact: Marilyn Brown
Riverside
t (01756) 753886
e malcolbrown@aol.com
w dales.accommodation.com

Sunnyside Cottage ★★★★
Self Catering
Contact: Carolyn Butt
t (01756) 730391 & 07720 294391
e cosycottages@hotmail.com
w grassingtoncottages.co.uk

Theatre Cottage Ref:2214
★★★ *Self Catering*
Contact: Ms Lorraine Kidd
Dales Holiday Cottages
t 0870 909 9500
e info@dales-holiday-cottages.com
w dalesholcot.com

Wellhead Cottage & Hilltop Fold Cottage ★★★★
Self Catering
Contact: Lesley Halliday
t (0113) 258 4212
e lesleyhalliday@hotmail.com

GREAT AYTON
North Yorkshire

Flat 2 ★★ *Self Catering*
Contact: Margaret Farrow
t (01642) 722935
e mmetcalfe2004@aol.com

The Old Stables ★★★★
Self Catering
Contact: Catherine Harman
Old Stables
t (01642) 722560
e theoldstables@btopen.world.com
w cottageguide.co.uk/theoldstables

The Stable Cottage Ref:3490
★★★ *Self Catering*
Contact: Ms Lorraine Kidd
Dales Holiday Cottages
t 0870 909 9500
e info@dales-holiday-cottages.com
w dalesholcot.com

GREAT EDSTONE
North Yorkshire

Cowldyke Farm
★★★-★★★★ *Self Catering*
Contact: Mrs Janet Benton
t (01751) 431242
e info@cowldyke-farm.co.uk

GREAT LANGTON
North Yorkshire

Stanhow Bungalow ★★★★
Self Catering
Contact: Mary Furness
t (01609) 748614
e mary.stanhow@freenet.co.uk

GREETLAND
West Yorkshire

The Barn, Lower High Trees Farm ★★★ *Self Catering & Serviced Apartments*
Contact: Kate Griffiths
t (01422) 375205
e griffs@freeuk.com
w greetland.org.uk

GREWELTHORPE
North Yorkshire

Crown Cottage Ref:718
★★★ *Self Catering*
Contact: Ms Lorraine Kidd
Dales Holiday Cottages
t 0870 909 9500
e info@dales-holiday-cottages.com
w dalesholcot.com

Fir Tree Farm Holiday Homes ★★★★ *Self Catering*
Contact: Eric & Jane Simpson
t (01765) 658727
e firtreefarmhouse@aol.com
w firtree-farm-holidayhomes.co.uk

GRINDALE
East Riding of Yorkshire

Smithy Cottage, Grindale
★★★★ *Self Catering*
Contact: Charlotte Davey
t (01262) 602367
e scjrm@msn.com
w smithycottage.moonfruit.com

GRINTON
North Yorkshire

Feetham Holme ★★★★
Self Catering
Contact: Mr Ian Robinson
Plantation Business Services
t (01254) 826546
e plantation@talk21.com

GRISTHORPE
North Yorkshire

Anchorage Holiday Flats
★★ *Self Catering*
Contact: Mr John Haywood
t (01723) 513805

Dove Cottage Ref:3035
★★★★ *Self Catering*
Contact: H Cook
t (01756) 799821
e info@dalesholcot.com
w dalesholcot.com

GRISTHORPE BAY
North Yorkshire

58 Clarence Drive ★★★
Self Catering
Contact: Mrs Mary Graves
t (01723) 512791
e marygraves5@tiscali.co.uk

GROSMONT
North Yorkshire

East Farm Cottage ★★★
Self Catering
Contact: Ms Vanessa Hicking
Whitby Holiday Cottages
t (01947) 821122
e enquiries@whitby-cottages.co.uk
w whitby-cottages.co.uk

Engineman's Lodge ★★
Self Catering
Contact: Ms Vanessa Hicking
Whitby Holiday Cottages
t (01947) 821122
e enquiries@whitby-cottages.co.uk
w whitby-cottages.co.uk

Moorend ★★★ *Self Catering*
Contact: Janet Hoyle
Yorkshire Cottages
t (01943) 885306
e enquiries@yorkshire-cottages.info
w yorkshire-cottages.info

Porter's Lodge ★★
Self Catering
Contact: Ms Vanessa Hicking
Whitby Holiday Cottages
t (01947) 821122
e enquiries@whitby-cottages.co.uk
w whitby-cottages.co.uk

GUNNERSIDE
North Yorkshire

Croft Cottage ★★
Self Catering
Contact: Margaret Batty
t (01748) 886460
e shirlswake2@aol.com
w yorkshirecottage.org.uk

High Oxnop ★★★★
Self Catering
Contact: Annie Porter
t (01748) 886253

Sundale ★★ *Self Catering*
Contact: H.R. Wales
Holiday Cottages (Yorkshire) Ltd
t (01756) 700510
e brochure@holidaycotts.co.uk
w holidaycotts.co.uk

HALIFAX
West Yorkshire

Cherry Tree Cottages, Barkisland ★★★★
Self Catering
Contact: Stan & Elaine Shaw
Cherry Tree Cottages
t (01422) 372662
e cherrytree@yorkshire-cottages.co.uk
w yorkshire-cottages.co.uk

The Fall ★★★★ *Self Catering*
Contact: Ann Knight
t (01422) 363346

HALTON GILL
North Yorkshire

Swains Cottage (4170)
★★★ *Self Catering*
Contact: Ms Lorri Gilmour
t 0870 909 9500
e info@dales-holiday-cottages.com
w dales-holiday-cottages.com

HAMBLETON
North Yorkshire

Casten Cottage Ref:549
★★★ *Self Catering*
Contact: S Boardman
Sykes Cottages
t (01244) 345700
e info@sykescottages.co.uk
w sykescottages.co.uk

HARMBY
North Yorkshire

1,2,3 and 4 Harmby Grange Cottages ★★★★
Self Catering
t (01756) 799821

Hillfoot House ★★★
Self Catering
Contact: Mr Jones
t (01969) 623632

HARROGATE
North Yorkshire

Apartment 1, Holmedale
★★★★ *Self Catering*
Contact: Graham & Amanda Lloyd
Apartments of Distinction
t (01423) 538742
e info@harrogateholidayapartments.co.uk
w harrogateholidayapartments.co.uk

Ashness Apartments
★★★★ *Self Catering*
Contact: Mr Spinlove & Miss H Spinlove
Ashness Apartments
t (01423) 526894
e office@ashness.com
w ashness.com

Ashrigg ★★★★ *Self Catering*
Contact: Mr & Mrs Peter & Angela Holt
t (01423) 871177
e pholt@westrigg.freeserve.co.uk
w ashrigg.co.uk

The Barn @ Fir Tree Farm
★★★★ *Self Catering*
Contact: Mrs Rebecca Donnelly
t (01423) 779708
e thebarninharrogate@hotmail.com
w thebarninharrogate.co.uk

Brimham Rocks Cottages
★★★★ *Self Catering*
Contact: Jacqueline Martin
t (01765) 620284
e brimhamrc@yahoo.co.uk
w brimham.co.uk

Dinmore Cottages, Burnt Yates ★★★★ *Self Catering*
Contact: Susan Chapman
t (01423) 770860
e aib@dinmore-cottages.freeserve.co.uk
w dinmore-cottages.co.uk

Duchy Mews ★★★★
Self Catering
Contact: Sandra Sykes
Duchy Rentals
t (01423) 565109
e sandra.sykes@btopenworld.com
w duchyrentals.co.uk

The Garden Apartment
★★★★ *Self Catering*
Contact: Graham & Amanda Lloyd
Apartments of Distinction
t (01423) 538742
e info@harrogateholidayapartments.co.uk
w harrogateholidayapartments.co.uk

Holly House Farm Cottages
★★★ *Self Catering*
Contact: Mary Owen
t (01423) 780266
e hollyhousecottages@supanet.com
w hollyhousecottages.co.uk

Old Swan View ★★★★
Self Catering
Contact: Graham & Amanda Lloyd
Apartments of Distinction
t (01423) 538742
e info@harrogateholidayapartments.co.uk
w harrogateholidayapartments.co.uk

Regent Cottage ★★★★
Self Catering
Contact: Robert Blake
t (01394) 382565
e robert@blake.4110.fsbusiness.co.uk

Regent House ★★★★
Self Catering
Contact: Julie Stanton
t (01423) 858316
e info@harrogateservicedapartments.com
w harrogateservicedapartments.com

Rudding Estate Cottages
★★★-★★★★ *Self Catering*
t (01423) 844844
e lm@rudding.com
w rudding.com/cottages_home.htm

Rudding Gates ★★★★★
Self Catering
Rudding Park Estate Ltd.
t (01423) 844844
e lm@rudding.com
w rudding.com/gates

Rudding Holiday Park ★★★
Self Catering
Rudding Holiday Park
t (01423) 870439
e holiday-park@ruddingpark.com
w ruddingpark.com

Studley View Apartment
★★★★ *Self Catering*
Contact: Graham & Amanda Lloyd
Apartments of Distinction
t (01423) 538742
e info@harrogateholidayapartments.co.uk
w harrogateholidayapartments.co.uk

HARTWITH
North Yorkshire

Cow Close Barn ★★★★ *Self Catering & Serviced Apartments*
Contact: Diana Kitzing
t (01423) 770850
e rainerkitzing@aol.com
w cowclose-barn.co.uk

HARWOOD DALE
North Yorkshire

Murk Head Holiday Cottages ★★★★
Self Catering
Contact: Joanna Gray
t (01723) 871686
e joannagray@aol.com

HATFIELD WOODHOUSE
South Yorkshire

Cosy Executive Accommodation ★★★
Self Catering
Contact: John Perrin
t (01709) 580612
e john@cosyterrace.fsnet.co.uk
w cosyexecutive.fsnet.co.uk

HAWES
North Yorkshire

Aska House ★★★★
Self Catering
t (0121) 420 3269
e neil@askahouse.co.uk
w askahouse.co.uk

Cherry Tree Cottage ★★★
Self Catering
Contact: Mrs Nadine Bell
Country Hideaways
t (01969) 663559
e nadine@countryhideaways.co.uk
w countryhideaways.co.uk

Gaudy House Farm ★★★
Self Catering
Contact: Jane Allison
t (01969) 667231
e sjane.allison@virgin.net
w gaudyhousefarm.co.uk

Jane Ann Cottage ★★
Self Catering
Contact: E Irene Sunter
t (01969) 667186
e irene@overdales.co.uk
w overdales.co.uk

Swallowdale ★★★★
Self Catering
Contact: Ms Lorraine Kidd
Dales Holiday Cottages
t 0870 909 9500
e info@dales-holiday-cottages.com
w dalesholcot.com

Yore View ★★★
Self Catering
Contact: Elizabeth Pedley
t (01969) 667358
e yoreviewcottage@talk21.com

Yorkshire Dales Country Cottages ★★★ *Self Catering*
Contact: Brenda Stott
t (01969) 667359
e rogerstott@aol.com
w yorkshirenet.co.uk/accgde/ydcotts.htm

HAWKSWICK
North Yorkshire

Redmire Farm, Hawkswick
★★★★★ *Self Catering*
Contact: Neil Tomlinson
t (01535) 648791 & 07768 230522
e info@mckeighley.co.uk
w redmire-farm.com

HAWORTH
West Yorkshire

Balcony Farm ★★★★
Self Catering
Contact: Mr Raine
t (01535) 643627

Bottoms Farm Cottages
★★★★ *Self Catering*
Contact: Mr Littler
t (01535) 607720
e Bottomsfarm@btinternet.com

Cross Cottage ★★★
Self Catering
Contact: Nikki Carroll
t (01535) 643474

Heather, Bilberry Cottage
★★★★ *Self Catering*
Contact: Janet Milner
t (01535) 644755
e janet@bronteholidays.co.uk
w bronteholidays.co.uk

Heron Cottage, Haworth
★★★★ *Self Catering*
Contact: Mr & Mrs Richard and Jan Walker
Heron Cottage
t (01535) 648537
e jan.w@virgin.net

Hewenden Mill Cottages
★★★★-★★★★★
Self Catering
Contact: Janet Emanuel
Hewenden Mill Cottages
t (01535) 274259
e info@hewendenmillcottages.co.uk
w hewendenmillcottages.co.uk

Keepers Cottage ★★★★
Self Catering
Contact: Sally Townend
t (01535) 644223
e hhh@billandsally.supanet.com
w bronte-country.com/accomm/keepers-cottage

Little Nook ★★★
Self Catering
Contact: Barbara Clayton
t (01535) 646779
e info@littlenook.co.uk
w littlenook.co.uk

Number 66 ★★★★
Self Catering
Contact: Glenda Joy
t (01535) 643008
e glendajoyuk@yahoo.co.uk
w bronte-country.com/accomm/number66

Penrhyn ★★★ *Self Catering*
Dales Holiday Cottages
t 0870 909 9500
e lorraine.k@dales-holiday-cottages.com
w dalesholcot.com

September Cottage ★★★★
Self Catering
Contact: Joy Page
t (01535) 644091
e robjoypagecromer@supanet.com

Spaw Cottage, Laneshaw Bridge ★★★★ *Self Catering*
Contact: Mr & Mrs Charnley
t (01282) 865283
e ingheysfarm@btconnect.com

Spring Cottage Ref:2389
★★★★ *Self Catering*
Contact: H Cook
t (01756) 799821
e info@dalesholcot.com
w dalesholcot.com

Tanera Ref:751 ★★★
Self Catering
Contact: Ms Lorraine Kidd
Dales Holiday Cottages
t 0870 909 9500
e info@dales-holiday-cottages.com
w dalesholcot.com

Weavers Cottage and Loft
★★★ *Self Catering*
Contact: Gaye Bond
Weavers Cottage & Weavers Loft
t (01535) 211184
e g.j.bond@blueyonder.co.uk
w weaverscottage-web.co.uk

Woolcombers Cottage, Haworth ★★★ *Self Catering*
Contact: Ms Kay Doyle Johnson
t (01535) 646778
e woolcombers@clara.co.uk
w bronte-country.com/accomm/woolcombers

Yarnspinners Cottage
★★★★ *Self Catering*
Dales Holiday Cottages
t 0870 909 9500
e fiona@dales-holiday-cottages.com
w dalesholcot.com

HAWSKER
North Yorkshire

Ling Hill Farm ★★
Self Catering
Contact: B Tordoff
t (01947) 603914

Summerfield Cottage
★★★★ *Self Catering*
Contact: Richard Noble
Summerfield Cottage & Red Barn Caravan
t (01947) 602677
e info@summerfieldfarm.co.uk
w summerfieldfarm.co.uk

West End Farm Cottage Ref:1228 ★★★★
Self Catering
Contact: Ms Lorraine Kidd
Dales Holiday Cottages
t 0870 909 9500
e info@dales-holiday-cottages.com
w dalesholcot.com

HEALAUGH
North Yorkshire

Harker View ★★★★
Self Catering
Contact: Mrs Nadine Bell
Country Hideaways
t (01969) 663559
e nadine@countryhideaways.co.uk
w countryhideaways.co.uk

HEALEY
North Yorkshire

Agra Cottage
Rating Applied For
Self Catering
Contact: Mr Mark Richardson
t (01765) 688788
e enquiries@agracottage.co.uk
w agracottage.co.uk

Grange End. Ref (3446)
★★★ *Self Catering*
Contact: Ms H Cook
Dales Holiday Cottages
t 0870 909 9500
e info@dales-holiday-cottages.com
w dalesholcot.com

HEATON
West Yorkshire

Honeysuckle Cottage ★★★
Self Catering
Contact: Pamela Stobart
t (01274) 541181

HEBDEN BRIDGE
West Yorkshire

15 Oldgate ★★★
Self Catering
Contact: Jan Barker
t (01422) 886179
e janatcobweb@aol.com

3 Birks Hall Cottage, Cragg Vale *Self Catering*
Contact: Hilda Wilkinson
3 Birks Hall Cottage
t (01422) 882064

The Chalet, Cairnacre ★★
Self Catering
Contact: Mr & Mrs C Price
t (01422) 842861
e ruth-price@lineone.net

Old Town Hall Cottage
★★★★ *Self Catering*
Contact: S Milner
t (01422) 846559
e oldtownhallcottage@yahoo.co.uk
w cottageguide.co.uk/oldtownhallcottage

HELMSLEY
North Yorkshire

8 Villiers Court
Rating Applied For
Self Catering
Contact: Mr & Mrs Mason
t +1 905 569 1098
e remason@ican.net
w yorkshireholidayhome.com

Amy's Cottage ★★★★
Self Catering
Contact: Jane Dzierzek
t (01439) 770172
e amyscottage@hotmail.co.uk
w amys-cottage.co.uk

Beadlam Farm Cottage
★★★ *Self Catering*
Contact: Jenny Rooke
t (01439) 770303
e mark.rooke@farming.co.uk
w stayfarmnorth.co.uk

Bondgate Flat ★★★★
Self Catering
Contact: Margaret Kilby
t (01653) 691576
e wakilby@tiscali.co.uk

Bondgate Mews Cottage
★★★ *Self Catering*
t (01302) 708883

Church View ★★★★
Self Catering
Contact: Sally Ann Foster
t (01709) 852929
e sally@helmsleyhouse.co.uk
w helmsleyhouse.co.uk

Fleur-de-lys ★★★★
Self Catering
Contact: Mrs Pat Anderson
Mrs Anderson's Country Cottages
t (01751) 472172
e bookings@boonhill69.freeserve.co.uk

Honeysuckle Cottage ★★★
Self Catering
Contact: Margaret Stringer
t (01751) 431983
e stringer@cornfield.go-legend.net

Rose Beck ★★★★
Self Catering
Contact: Steph Woolhouse
t (01709) 852483
e steph.woolhouse@yahoo.co.uk
w rosebeckcottages.co.uk

Tapestry Garden ★★★
Self Catering
Contact: Mr Simon Laycock
t (01439) 771300
e info@tapestrygarden.co.uk

Townend Cottage ★★★★
Self Catering
Contact: Mrs Margaret Begg
Townend Farmhouse
t (01439) 770103
e margaret.begg@ukgateway.net
w visityorkshire.com

Wardy's ★★★ *Self Catering*
Contact: Joanne Ward
t (01439) 770124
e joward@aol.com

HELPERTHORPE
North Yorkshire

The Old Dairy & The Granary ★★★★ *Self Catering*
t (01944) 738613
e rozannestartup@aol.com
w peartreecottages.com

HEPTONSTALL
West Yorkshire

5 Draper Corner ★★
Self Catering
Contact: Shirley Taylor
t (01422) 844323

The Hayloft Flat ★★★
Self Catering
Contact: H M Harrison
t (01422) 843145

HEPWORTH
West Yorkshire

Uppergate Farm ★★★★
Self Catering
Contact: Alison Booth
t (01484) 681369
e info@uppergatefarm.co.uk
w uppergatefarm.co.uk

HETTON
North Yorkshire

Bramble Cottage (3841)
★★★★ *Self Catering*
Dales Holiday Cottages
t 0870 909 9500
e lorraine.k@dales-holiday-cottages.com
w dalesholcot.com

HIGH BENTHAM
North Yorkshire

Batty Farm Ref:1362 ★★★
Self Catering
Contact: Ms Lorraine Kidd
Dales Holiday Cottages
t 0870 909 9500
e info@dales-holiday-cottages.com
w dalesholcot.com

Holmes Farm Cottage
★★★★ *Self Catering*
Contact: Mrs Story
Holmes Farm Cottage
t (015242) 61198
e lucy@clucy.demon.co.uk

HIGH CATTON
East Riding of Yorkshire

The Courtyard
★★★★-★★★★★
Self Catering
Contact: Sheila Foster
High Catton Grange
t (01759) 371374
e sheila.foster@btclick.com
w yorkshirevisitor.com/thecourtyard

HINDERWELL
North Yorkshire

Dunroamin ★★★
Self Catering
Contact: Ms Vanessa Hicking
Whitby Holiday Cottages
t (01947) 821122
e enquiries@whitby-cottages.co.uk
w whitby-cottages.co.uk

West End Bungalow (2103)
★★★ *Self Catering*
Contact: Ms Lorraine Kidd
Dales Holiday Cottages
t 0870 909 9500
e info@dales-holiday-cottages.com
w dalesholcot.com

HOLMBRIDGE
West Yorkshire

Ivy Cottage ★★★
Self Catering
Contact: Ian & Joyce Bangham
t (01484) 682561
e bangham77@hotmail.com

HOLMBRIDGE, HOLMFIRTH
West Yorkshire

Weavers Cottage ★★★★
Self Catering
Contact: Gillian Blewett
t (01484) 666319
e martinblewett@aol.com

HOLMFIRTH
West Yorkshire

Cuish Cottages ★★★★
Self Catering
Contact: Mairi Binns
t (01484) 682722
e martin@crepes.freeserve.co.uk

Lane Farm Holiday Cottages
★★★★ *Self Catering*
Contact: Vivienne Howard
t (01484) 682290
e viv@lanefarmcottages.co.uk
w lanefarmcottages.co.uk

Mytholmbridge Studio Cottage ★★★★ *Self Catering*
Contact: Sue Clay
Mytholmbridge Studio Cottage
t (01484) 686642
e cottages@mytholmbridge.co.uk
w mytholmbridge.co.uk

Nora Batty's Cottage ★★★
Self Catering
Contact: N Worthington
Nora Batty Experience
t (01274) 603750
e nw@worthingtonbrown.co.uk
w nora-batty.co.uk

Upper Nabb Farm Holiday Cottage ★★★★ *Self Catering*
Contact: Michelle Blackburn
Upper Nabb Farm
t (01484) 686743
e mail@uppernabbfarm.co.uk
w uppernabbfarm.co.uk

HOLTBY
North Yorkshire

The Apple Barn ★★★★
Self Catering
Contact: Laura Bough
t (01904) 488819
e bookings@theapplebarn.co.uk
w theapplebarn.co.uk

Garden Cottage ★★★★
Self Catering
Contact: Ann Wilson
t (01904) 488089

Look out for establishments participating in the National Accessible Scheme 

HORNSEA
East Riding of Yorkshire

Cherry Tree ★★★
Self Catering
Contact: Mrs Rita Leonard
Cherry Tree
t (01964) 527245
e ritaleonard@serverX1.net

Cobble Cottage ★★★
Self Catering
Contact: Mary Everington
t (01964) 536159

Little Arram Barn ★★★★
Self Catering
Contact: Alan & Ann Coates
t (01964) 530424
e alan@arram-barn.co.uk

Westgate Mews ★★★
Self Catering
Contact: Mr Walker
t (01964) 533430
e lettings@walkerhornsea.plus.com
w cottagesdirect.co.uk

HORTON IN RIBBLESDALE
North Yorkshire

Blind Beck Holiday Cottage
★★★ *Self Catering*
Contact: Heather Huddleston
t (01729) 860396
e h.huddleston@daelnet.co.uk
w blindbeck.co.uk

Fourways Cottage ★★★
Self Catering
Contact: Dermot & Deborah Griffin
t (020) 8870 6784
e enquiries@escapetothedales.co.uk
w escapetothedales.co.uk

The Old Stable ★★★
Self Catering
Contact: Sheila Fleming
t (01729) 860394
e info@south-view.org.uk
w south-view.org.uk

Poppy Cottage ★★★
Self Catering
t (01729) 860311
e info@poppycottage.fsbusiness.co.uk
w poppycottage.net

Selside Farm Holiday Cottage ★★★★ *Self Catering*
Contact: Shirley Lambert
t (01729) 860367
e shirley@lam67.freeserve.co.uk
w cottageguide.co.uk/selsidefarm

HOWDEN
East Riding of Yorkshire

101 Hailgate ★★★
Self Catering
Contact: Karen Lesley Formon
t 07970 445357
e karen.formon@ntlworld.com

HUDDERSFIELD
West Yorkshire

1535 Melting Point ★★★★
Self Catering
Contact: Ms Karen Bonnett
t (0118) 984 5800
e karen.bonnett@bt.com
w meltingpointcottage.co.uk

Ashes Farm Cottages
★★★-★★★★ *Self Catering*
Contact: Barbara Lockwood
t (01484) 426507
e enquiries@ashescommonfarm.co.uk
w ashescommonfarm.co.uk

Castle House Farm Cottages
★★★★ *Self Catering*
Contact: Philip Coates
J P & A Coates
t (01484) 663808
e philip@castlehousefarm.co.uk
w castlehousefarm.co.uk

Elam Cottage ★★★
Self Catering
Contact: Anne Mullany
Elam & Coates Cottages
t (01484) 431432
e anne.mullany@onetel.com

Swallow Cottage ★★★★
Self Catering
Contact: Margaret Kucharczyk
t (01484) 607072
e swallow@care4free.net

Tyas Cottage ★★★★
Self Catering
t (01484) 841010
e vicky.berryman@gmail.com
w yorkshire-holiday.co.uk

HUDSWELL
North Yorkshire

Flowery Dell Luxury Lodges
★★★★ *Self Catering*
Contact: Sam Cullen
Flowery Dell Luxury Pine Lodges
t (01748) 822406
e info@flowerydell-lodges.com
w flowerydell-lodges.com

HULL
East Riding of Yorkshire

80 Queen's Court ★★★★
Self Catering
Contact: Mrs Janet Langton
t (01482) 853248
e janet-the-acorn@yahoo.co.uk

Cottage in the Pond ★★★
Self Catering
Contact: Mr Adrian Fisher
Middle Keld Countryside Experience
t (01964) 527256
e info@middlekeld.co.uk
w middlekeld.co.uk

Queens Court
Rating Applied For
Self Catering
Contact: Leigh Ann Clark
t (01482) 666460
e john@dock.karoo.co.uk

Walton House ★★
Self Catering
Contact: Mr David Bradley
t (01482) 352733
w englandsrose.net

Waters Edge Executive Apartments ★★★★
Self Catering
Contact: Mrs J L Langton
Acorn Guest House
t (01482) 853248

HUNMANBY
North Yorkshire

Courtside Cottage ★★★
Self Catering
Contact: Karen Cawthorn
t (01723) 892882
e karen@kcawthorn.fsnet.co.uk
w courtsidecottage.co.uk

Honeysuckle Cottage ★★★
Self Catering
Contact: Ms Lorraine Kidd
Dales Holiday Cottages
t 0870 909 9500
e info@dales-holiday-cottages.com
w dalesholcot.com

HUNTON
North Yorkshire

Colling Well Cottage
★★★★ *Self Catering*
Contact: Sue Tabiner
t (01677) 450742
e collingwell@hotmail.com
w collingwell.co.uk

Emberton ★★★ *Self Catering*
Contact: Trevor & Wendy Mills
t (01702) 478846
e info@dalescottages.com
w dalescottages.com

HURST
North Yorkshire

Shiney Row Cottage Ref:2786 ★★★ *Self Catering*
Contact: Ms Lorraine Kidd
Dales Holiday Cottages
t 0870 909 9500
e info@dales-holiday-cottages.com
w dalesholcot.com

HUSTHWAITE
North Yorkshire

Greg's Cottage ★★★
Self Catering
Contact: Mr Greg Harrand
Hedley House Hotel
t (01904) 637404
e greg@hedleyhouse.com
w hedleyhouse.com

Kate's Cottage ★★
Self Catering
Contact: Anne Cox
t (01347) 868346
e c.anne.cox@virgin.net

HUTTON-LE-HOLE
North Yorkshire

Halfway Cottages ★★★★
Self Catering
Contact: Ms Lorraine Kidd
Dales Holiday Cottages
t 0870 909 9500
e info@dales-holiday-cottages.com
w dalesholcot.com

Primrose Hill Farmhouse
★★★ *Self Catering*
t (01751) 417752
e nigelcustance@wayah.freeserve.co.uk

HUTTON SESSAY
North Yorkshire

White Rose Holiday Cottages ★★★ *Self Catering*
Contact: Zoe Williamson
t (01845) 501180

IBURNDALE
North Yorkshire

Lavender Cottage ★★★
Self Catering
Contact: Mrs Vanessa Hicking
Whitby Holiday Cottages
t (01947) 603010
e enquiries@whitby-cottages.co.uk

ILKLEY
West Yorkshire

The Grange
★★★★-★★★★★
Self Catering
Contact: Debbie Skinn
t (01943) 878777
e skinn@attglobal.net
w faweathergrange.com

Westwood Lodge, Ilkley Moor ★★★★-★★★★★
Self Catering
Contact: Tim & Paula Edwards
t (01943) 433430
e welcome@westwoodlodge.co.uk
w westwoodlodge.co.uk

INGLEBY CROSS
North Yorkshire

The Cottage at Hill House
★★★★ *Self Catering*
Contact: Richard & Vee Kitteridge
t (01609) 882109
e kitteridge@ukgateway.net

INGLEBY GREENHOW
North Yorkshire

Ingleby Manor ★★★★
Self Catering
Contact: Christine Bianco
t (01642) 722170
e christine@inglebymanor.co.uk
w inglebymanor.co.uk

INGLETON
North Yorkshire

Beech Tree Cottages
★★★★ *Self Catering*
Contact: Ms Sharon McDonald
t (01524) 241100
e beechtreecottage@aol.com
w travel.to/beechtreecottages

Doefoot ★★★★
Self Catering
Contact: Ms Pauline Leet
Dales Holiday Cottages
t (01756) 799821
w dalesholiday-cottages.com

Holmeview Ref:4095
★★★★ *Self Catering*
Contact: Ms Lorraine Kidd
Dales Holiday Cottages
t 0870 909 9500
e lorraine.k@dales-holiday-cottages.com
w dalesholcot.com

Little Storrs & Flaggs Cottage ★★★★ *Self Catering*
Contact: Mrs Debby Kuhlmann
t (01524) 241843
e debbykuhlmann@aol.com

Low Barn ★★★★
Self Catering
Contact: Ms Lorraine Kidd
Dales Holiday Cottages
t 0870 909 9500
e lorraine.k@dales-holiday-cottages.com
w dalesholcot.com

Primrose Cottage ★★★
Self Catering
Contact: John & Celia Jones
t (01524) 241407
e topclub.john@virgin.net

KEARBY WITH NETHERBY North Yorkshire

Nethercroft Cottage ★★★★
Self Catering
Contact: Catherine Webb
t (0113) 288 6234
e info@maustin.co.uk
w maustin.co.uk

KELD North Yorkshire

Hillcrest Holiday Cottage
★★★ *Self Catering*
Contact: Barbara Rukin
t (01748) 886274
e babrarukin@ukonline.co.uk

The Smithy
Rating Applied For
Self Catering
Contact: Mrs Annette Riley
t (01969) 663716
e thesmithy@oldgoatholidays.co.uk

KETTLEWELL North Yorkshire

Fold Farm Cottages ★★★★
Self Catering
Contact: Mrs Barbara Lambert
Fold Farm Cottages
t (01756) 760886
e info@foldfarm.co.uk
w foldfarm.co.uk

Ghyll Cottage
Rating Applied For
Self Catering
t (01743) 357001
e mail@rab59.fsnet.co.uk

Heathlands Ref:931 ★★★
Self Catering
Contact: Ms Lorraine Kidd
Dales Holiday Cottages
t 0870 909 9500
e info@dales-holiday-cottages.com
w dalesholcot.com

Wayside Cottage ★★★
Self Catering
Contact: Georgina Drew
t (01296) 620017
e craig.drew@tesco.net

KILHAM East Riding of Yorkshire

Raven Hill Holiday Farmhouse ★★★★
Self Catering
Contact: Patricia Savile
t (01377) 267217

KINGTHORPE North Yorkshire

High Kingthorpe Lodges
★★★★ *Self Catering*
Contact: John Tunnicliffe
t (01751) 476457
e info@kingthorpe.com
w kingthorpe.com

KIRBY MISPERTON North Yorkshire

2 Rose Cottages ★★★
Self Catering
Contact: Kathryn Greenwood
t (01422) 364880
e kathryngreenwood@tiscali.co.uk
w cottageguide.co.uk/kirbymisperton

KIRKBY MALZEARD North Yorkshire

Alma Cottage ★★★★
Self Catering
Contact: Janet Barclay
t (01621) 828576
e janet@lbarclay.demon.co.uk
w almacottage.co.uk

Ashknott Cottage ★★★
Self Catering
t (01423) 545787
e info@ashknottcottage.co.uk
w ashknottcottage.co.uk

The Woodpeckers ★★★
Self Catering
Contact: Elizabeth Drewery
t (01765) 658206

KIRKBYMOORSIDE North Yorkshire

Abbey Cottage ★★★★
Self Catering
English Heritage Holiday Cottages
t 0870 333 1187
w hritage.org.uk/holidaycottages

Bay Cottage ★★★
Self Catering
Contact: Mr Tritton
t (01845) 597987
e pinnacleracing@btconnect.com
w moor2seacottages.co.uk

Burton House ★★★★
Self Catering
Contact: Mrs J Susan Gozney
t (01777) 838246
e burtonhousekm@aol.com

Catterbridge Farm Cottage
★★★★ *Self Catering*
Contact: Jayne Peace
t (01751) 433271

Cherry View Cottage
★★★★ *Self Catering*
Contact: Mrs Sylvianne Drinkel
Cherry View Cottage
t (01751) 431714
e sylvianne@talktalkbusiness.net

The Cornmill ★★★★
Self Catering
Contact: Chris & Karen Tinkler
The Cornmill
t (01751) 432000
e cornmill@kirbymills.demon.co.uk
w kirbymills.demon.co.uk

Ellerslie ★★★ *Self Catering*
Contact: Elizabeth Davison
t (01751) 431112
e mail@lizdavison.co.uk

Feversham Arms ★★★★
Self Catering
Contact: Mrs Frances Debenham
t (01751) 433206
e fevershamfarndale@hotmail.com

Oak Lodge ★★★
Self Catering
Contact: Andrea Turnbull
t (01751) 431298
e turnbulls@whitehornfarm.fsnet.co.uk

The Retreat Apartment
★★★★ *Self Catering*
Contact: Mrs A J Schulze
Mill Cottage
t (01751) 430806
e kingfisher.mill@virgin.net

Sinnington Common Farm
★★★ *Self Catering*
Contact: Felicity Wiles
t (01751) 431719
e felicity@scfarm.demon.co.uk
w scfarm.demon.co.uk

Sleightholmedale Cottages
★★★★ *Self Catering*
Contact: Mrs James
t (01751) 431942
e info@shdcottages.co.uk
w shdcottages.co.uk

Surprise View Cottage & Field Barn Cottage ★★★★
Self Catering
Contact: Mrs Ruth Wass
t (01751) 431345
e info@surpriseviewcottages.co.uk
w surpriseviewcottages.co.uk

KIRKSTALL West Yorkshire

The Tops ★★★ *Self Catering*
Contact: Merton Miles
t (0113) 257 2197
e mertonmiles@thetops.co.uk
w thetops.co.uk

KNARESBOROUGH North Yorkshire

Garden Apartment ★★★
Self Catering
Contact: Antje Rowinski
t (01423) 860463
e david.rowinski@ntlworld.com

The Granary ★★★★
Self Catering
Contact: Mrs Rachel Thornton
t (01423) 862325 & 07970 000068

Uncle Tom's Holiday Cabins
★★★ *Self Catering*
Contact: Pat Ridsdale
t (01423) 861397
e uncletoms@rapidial.co.uk

Watergate Lodge Holiday Apartments ★★★
Self Catering
Contact: Mr & Mrs Peter & Lesley Guest
t (01423) 864627
e info@watergatehaven.com

LANGTHWAITE North Yorkshire

Arklehurst ★★★
Self Catering
Contact: Julie Bissicks
t (01748) 884912
w arkengarthdalecottage.co.uk

LASTINGHAM North Yorkshire

Lastingham Holiday Cottages ★★★★
Self Catering
Contact: Andrea Cattle
t (01751) 417223
e lastinghamhols@aol.com
w members.aol.com/lastinghamhols

LEALHOLM North Yorkshire

Greenhouses Farm Cottages
★★★ *Self Catering*
Contact: Nick Eddleston
t (01947) 897486
e n_eddleston@yahoo.com
w greenhouses-farm-cottages.co.uk

Poets Cottage Holiday Flat
★★ *Self Catering*
Contact: Blanche Rees
t (01642) 532413
e rees@btinternet.com

West Banks Farmhouse Ref:1671 ★★★ *Self Catering*
Contact: Ms Lorraine Kidd
Dales Holiday Cottages
t 0870 909 9500
e info@dales-holiday-cottages.com
w dalesholcot.com

LEEDS West Yorkshire

Harman Suites ★★★★
Self Catering
t (0113) 295 5886
e info@harmansuite.co.uk
w harmansuite.co.uk

Leeds Apartment 52 St. James Quay ★★★★
Self Catering
Contact: Kash Ijaz
Nomorehotels
t 0870 850 8514
e info@nomorehotels.co.uk
w nomorehotels.co.uk

LEVEN East Riding of Yorkshire

Leven Park Lake ★★★★
Self Catering
Contact: Graham & Lisa Skinner
t (01964) 544510
w levenparklake.co.uk

LEVISHAM North Yorkshire

Lilac Farm ★★★–★★★★
Self Catering
Contact: Mrs Heather Eddon
t (01751) 460281
e heather@lilacfarm.f9.co.uk

Moorlands Cottage
★★★★★ *Self Catering*
Contact: Ron & Gill Leonard
t (01751) 460229
e ronaldoleonardo@aol.com
w moorlandscottage.co.uk

LEYBURN
North Yorkshire

2 Crown Court Cottage
★★★ *Self Catering*
Contact: Roland & Diane Terry
t (01969) 624448
e dalescottages@uku.co.uk
w yorkshiredalesholiday cottages.co.uk

39 Dale Grove ★★★★
Self Catering
Contact: Susan Platts
Wensleydale Breaks
t (01274) 676886
e gplatts@ukonline.co.uk

Bramble Lodge, Thorney Cottages ★★★ *Self Catering*
Contact: Mrs Nadine Bell
Country Hideaways
t (01969) 663559
e nadine@countryhideaways.co.uk
w countryhideaways.co.uk

Craken House Farm ★★★
Self Catering
Contact: Marjorie Iveson
t (01969) 622204
e marjorie@miveson.fsnet.co.uk

Dales View Holiday Homes
★★★-★★★★ *Self Catering*
Contact: Messrs John Chilton
Dales View Holiday Homes
t (01969) 623707 & (01969) 622808
e daleshols@aol.com
w daleshols.co.uk

Demonicus Cottage
★★★★★ *Self Catering*
Contact: Ms Joan Macbeth
t (01912) 399866
e joan@willsmum.force9.co.uk
w middlehamcottage.com

Eastburn Cottage ★★★★
Self Catering
Contact: Mrs Nadine Bell
Country Hideaways
t (01969) 663559
e nadine@countryhideaways.co.uk
w countryhideaways.co.uk

Low Riseborough ★★
Self Catering
Contact: John Rowntree
t (020) 8994 9837

Shawl Cottage ★★★★
Self Catering
Contact: Mr & Mrs Ken & Sue Williamson
Thwaite House
t (01969) 650022
e stay@askrigg.com

Southfield Mews ★★★★
Self Catering
Contact: Mrs Andrea Baugh
Yorkshire Cottages
t (01228) 406701
e enquiries@yorkshire-cottages.info

Throstlenest Holiday Cottages ★★★ *Self Catering*
Contact: Tricia Smith
t (01969) 623694
e info@throstlenestcottages.co.uk
w throstlenestcottages.co.uk

LINTON
North Yorkshire

Wharfedene ★★★★
Self Catering
Contact: Elaine Liquorish
t (0115) 922 3239
e eliquorish@avernish.fsnet.co.uk

LINTON-ON-OUSE
North Yorkshire

Nursery View & Fuchsia Cottage Ref:1463&1464
★★★ *Self Catering*
Contact: Ms H Cook
Dales Holiday Cottages
t 0870 909 9500
e info@dales-holiday-cottages.com
w dalesholcot.com

LITTLE BARUGH
North Yorkshire

Stainers Farm Cottages
★★★★ *Self Catering*
t (01653) 668224
e info@stainersfarm.co.uk
w stainersfarm.co.uk

LITTLE OUSEBURN
North Yorkshire

Hawtree Cottage ★★★★
Self Catering & Serviced Apartments
Contact: Anne Llewellyn
t (01423) 331526
e cgllewellyn@fsmail.net

LITTLE THIRKLEBY
North Yorkshire

Old Oak Cottages ★★★★
Self Catering
Contact: Amanda Tattersall
t (01845) 501258
e amanda@oldoakcottages.com
w oldoakcottages.com

LITTLEBECK
North Yorkshire

Kelp House ★★★★
Self Catering
Contact: Ingrid Flute
Ingrid Flute Holiday Accommodation
t (01723) 376777
e ingrid@ingridflute.co.uk

LITTLETHORPE
North Yorkshire

Moor End Farm ★★★
Self Catering
t (01765) 677419

LITTON
North Yorkshire

Stonelands ★★★★
Self Catering
Contact: Brenda Cowan
Stonelands Farm Yard Cottages
t (01756) 770293
w stonelands.co.uk

LOCKTON
North Yorkshire

Ashfield Cottages
Rating Applied For
Self Catering
Contact: Simon & Carol Fisk
t (01751) 460218
e info@ashfieldcotages.com
w asgfieldcottages.com

Barn Cottage ★★★
Self Catering
Contact: Gill Grant
t (01673) 842283
e emmalouise.grant@btopenworld.co.uk

The Little Barn ★★★
Self Catering
Contact: Mr James Fisk
The Little Barn
t (01751) 460325
e judi@btinternet.com

Old Barn Cottage Ref:3237
★★★★ *Self Catering*
Contact: Ms Lorraine Kidd
Dales Holiday Cottages
t 0870 909 9500
e info@dales-holiday-cottages.com
w dalesholcot.com

LOFTHOUSE
North Yorkshire

Edge Farm ★★★★
Self Catering
Contact: Michael O'Byrne
t (01422) 240829
e info@edgefarm.co.uk
w edgefarm.co.uk

Thrope Farm Cottage ★★★
Self Catering
Contact: Stephen Harker
t (01423) 755607
e eileen@thrope.freeserve.co.uk

LONG MARSTON
North Yorkshire

The Cottage ★★★
Self Catering
t (01904) 738535
e bob.gilmour@btopenworld.com
w bob.gilmour.btinternet.co.uk

LOTHERSDALE
North Yorkshire

Great Gib Cottage Ref:1859
★★★ *Self Catering*
Contact: Ms Lorraine Kidd
Dales Holiday Cottages
t 0870 909 9500
e info@dales-holiday-cottages.com
w dalesholcot.com

Street Head Farm ★★★★★
Self Catering
Contact: James Gooch
t (01535) 632535
e streethead@towtop.fsnet.co.uk
w towtop.co.uk

LOW MARISHES
North Yorkshire

Sheepfoot Cottage Ref: 3721 ★★★ *Self Catering*
Contact: Mrs Fiona Moody
Dales Holiday Cottages
t 0870 909 9500
e fiona@dales-holiday-cottages.com
w dalesholcot.com

LOW ROW
North Yorkshire

Birds Nest Cottages, Low Row ★★★★ *Self Catering*
Contact: Charles & Julie Folkes
Birds Nest Cottages
t (01748) 886858
e info@yorkshiredales-cottages.net
w yorkshiredales-cottages.net

High Smarber ★★★
Self Catering
Contact: Kate Empsall
t (01228) 406701
e rentals@swaledalecottage.com
w swaledalecottage.com

Intake Cottage ★★★
Self Catering
t (01748) 821322
e info@kent.go-plus.net
w iknow-yorkshire.co.uk

LYTHE
North Yorkshire

Moor View
Rating Applied For
Self Catering
Contact: H Haigh
English Country Cottages
t 0870 444 1101

Oakdene Cottage
Rating Applied For
Self Catering
Contact: Ms Vanessa Hicking
Whitby Holiday Cottages
t (01947) 603010
e enquiries@whitby-cottages.co.uk

MALHAM
North Yorkshire

The Old School ★★★★
Self Catering
Contact: Victoria Spence
t (01729) 830445
e oldschoolmalham@btopenworld.com
w theoldschoolmalham.co.uk

Waterside Cottage Ref:641
★★★★ *Self Catering*
Contact: S Boardman
Sykes Cottages
t (01244) 345700
e info@sykescottages.co.uk
w sykescottages.co.uk

MALTON
North Yorkshire

4 Wellgarth ★★ *Self Catering*
Contact: Dianne Waudby
t (01653) 697548
e diannewaudby@onetel.com

The Flat ★★★-★★★★
Self Catering
Contact: Mrs Sue Redfern
t (01653) 691270
e sue.redfern@btclick.com

Rowgate Cottage ★★★★
Self Catering
Contact: Mrs Janet Clarkson
t (01944) 758277
e janet@rowgatecottage.fsnet.co.uk

Swans Nest Cottage ★★★★
Self Catering
Contact: Yvonne Dickinson
Swans Nest Cottage
t (01653) 694970
e swansnestcottage@hotmail.com
w uk-holiday-cottages.co.uk/swans-nest

Walnut Garth ★★★★
Self Catering
t (01751) 434261
e cas@radfords.org
w radfords.org

MARISHES
North Yorkshire

Bellafax Holiday Cottage Ref:2798 ★★★ *Self Catering*
Contact: Ms Lorraine Kidd
Dales Holiday Cottages
t 0870 909 9500
e info@dales-holiday-cottages.com
w dalesholcot.com

MARRICK
North Yorkshire

Curlew Cottage ★★★
Self Catering
Contact: Michael Petty
t (01740) 620723
e m.c.petty@btinternet.com
w petty.org.uk

MARSDEN
West Yorkshire

Crow Hill Cottage ★★★★★
Self Catering
Contact: Eve Wood
Design Intervention
t (01484) 843435
e eve@designinter.co.uk
w crowhillcottages.co.uk

MARSKE
North Yorkshire

Home Farm ★★★★
Self Catering
Contact: Valerie Simpson
t (01748) 824770

MARTON
North Yorkshire

Wildsmith Court ★★★★
Self Catering
Contact: Mr & Mrs David & Joan Milner
t (01751) 431358
e milner@wildsmithcourt.freeserve.co.uk

MARTON CUM SEWERBY
East Riding of Yorkshire

Grange Farm Cottages ★★★★ *Self Catering*
Contact: Richard & Jane Dibb
t (01262) 671137
e richard.dibb@btclick.com
w grangefarmcottages.net

MASHAM
North Yorkshire

Barn Owl Cottage Ref:1178 ★★★ *Self Catering*
Contact: Ms Lorraine Kidd
Dales Holiday Cottages
t 0870 909 9500
e info@dales-holiday-cottages.com
w dalesholcot.com

Chapel Post House, Masham ★★★ *Self Catering*
Contact: Andrew Mallett
t (01912) 412075 & (0191) 273 1147

The Cottage (0144) ★★★
Self Catering
Dales Holiday Cottages
t 0870 909 9500
e fiona@dales-holiday-cottages.com
w dalesholcot.com

Craigendale Cottage ★★★★
Self Catering
Contact: Mrs Nadine Bell
t (01969) 663559
e nadine@counrtyhideaway.co.uk

Daleside ★★★★★
Self Catering
Contact: Mrs Pam Usher
Allendale
t (01765) 688277
w self-catering-masham.com

Masham Cottages ★★★
Self Catering
Contact: John Airton
t (01765) 689327
e airton@bronco.co.uk
w mashamcottages.co.uk

The Mews ★★★★
Self Catering
Contact: Janet Jameson
t (01765) 689068
e jameson1@ukf.net
w themews-masham.com

MELMERBY
North Yorkshire

Field Cottage ★★★
Self Catering
Contact: Mrs Nadine Bell
Country Hideaways
t (01969) 663559
e nadine@countryhideaways.co.uk
w countryhideaways.co.uk

West Close Cottage ★★★
Self Catering
Contact: Mrs Nadine Bell
Country Hideaways
t (01969) 663559
e nadine@countryhideaways.co.uk
w countryhideaways.co.uk

MELTHAM
West Yorkshire

Constance Cottage ★★★★
Self Catering
Contact: Mr Esposito
t (01484) 851811

MIDDLEHAM
North Yorkshire

Briar Cottage ★★★
Self Catering
Contact: Mrs Nadine Bell
Country Hideaways
t (01969) 663559
e nadine@countryhideaways.co.uk
w countryhideaways.co.uk

The Garth ★★★ *Self Catering*
Contact: Mrs Nadine Bell
Country Hideaways
t (01969) 663559
e nadine@countryhideaways.co.uk
w countryhideaways.co.uk

Grange Cottage ★★★★
Self Catering
Contact: Mrs Nadine Bell
t (01969) 663559
e nadine@countryhideaways.co.uk
w countryhideaways.co.uk

Honeykiln Cottage Ref:3197 ★★★ *Self Catering*
Contact: Ms Lorraine Kidd
Dales Holiday Cottages
t 0870 909 9500
e info@dales-holiday-cottages.com
w dalesholcot.com

Jade Cottage Ref:805 ★★★★ *Self Catering*
Contact: S Boardman
Sykes Cottages
t (01244) 345700
e info@sykescottages.co.uk
w sykescottages.co.uk

Middle Cottage ★★★★
Self Catering
Contact: Jennie Perren
t (0113) 237 1817
e jennifer.perren@btinternet.com
w yorkshire-dales-holiday-cottage.co.uk

Stonecroft ★★★★
Self Catering
Contact: Joyce Best
t (01748) 884062
e chapelfarmbb@aol.com
w middlehamcottage.co.uk

Sunnyside Cottage Ref:2531 ★★★ *Self Catering*
Contact: Ms Lorraine Kidd
Dales Holiday Cottages
t 0870 909 9500
e info@dales-holiday-cottages.com
w dalesholcot.com

West Hill ★★★★
Self Catering
Contact: Mrs Nadine Bell
Country Hideaways
t (01969) 663559
e nadine@countryhideaways.co.uk
w countryhideaways.co.uk

MIDDLETON
North Yorkshire

Applestore Cottage ★★★★-★★★★★
Self Catering
Contact: Noelle Thornton
t (01751) 472283
e noelle@middletonhall.org.uk

MOOR MONKTON
North Yorkshire

Mistral Cotage
Rating Applied For
Self Catering
Contact: Elizabeth Wilson
t (01904) 738981
e mistralcottage@geoffwilsontraining.co.uk

MUKER
North Yorkshire

Corner Cottage Ref:914 ★★★ *Self Catering*
Contact: Ms Lorraine Kidd
Dales Holiday Cottages
t 0870 909 9500
e info@dales-holiday-cottages.com
w dalesholcot.com

MYTHOLMROYD
West Yorkshire

Higher Clough Foot SelfCatering Cottages ★★★★ *Self Catering*
t (01422) 882577
e cloughfootbarn@tiscali.co.uk
w cloughfootbarn.co.uk

NAFFERTON
East Riding of Yorkshire

Heapfield Cottage Ref:2047 ★★★ *Self Catering*
Contact: Ms Lorraine Kidd
Dales Holiday Cottages
t 0870 909 9500
e info@dales-holiday-cottages.com
w dalesholcot.com

NEWBIGGIN
North Yorkshire

School Cottage ★★★★
Self Catering
Contact: Mr & Mrs Ken & Sue Williamson
t (01969) 650022
e stay@askrigg.com

NEWSHAM
North Yorkshire

Dyson House Barn ★★★★
Self Catering
Contact: Mr & Mrs Clarkson
t (01833) 627365
e dysonbarn@tinyworld.co.uk
w cottageguide.co.uk/dysonhousebarn

High Dalton Hall Cottage ★★★★ *Self Catering*
Contact: Elizabeth Jopling
t (01833) 621450
e elizabeth.jopling@btinternet.com
w cottageguide.co.uk/highdaltonhallcottage

NEWTON-LE-WILLOWS
North Yorkshire

The Shippon ★★★★
Self Catering
Contact: Valerie Nelson
t (01677) 450227
e andrew.nelson3@virgin.net
w theshippon.co.uk

NEWTON-ON-OUSE
North Yorkshire

Village Farm Cottage ★★★★ *Self Catering*
Contact: H.R. Wales
Holiday Cottages (Yorkshire) Ltd
t (01756) 700510
e brochure@holidaycotts.co.uk
w holidaycotts.co.uk

NEWTON-ON-RAWCLIFFE
North Yorkshire

Hill Rise Cottage ★★★★
Self Catering
Contact: Mrs Jennifer Peirson
Dales Holiday Cottages
t (01751) 473183
e info@dales-holiday-cottages.com
w dalesholcot.com

Keldlands Farm Cottages
★★★★ *Self Catering*
Contact: Jill Thomas
Holiday Homes in Yorkshire
t (01845) 597660
w keldlansfarmcottages.co.uk

Manor Farm Cottages
★★★-★★★★ *Self Catering*
Contact: Elizabeth Kirk
t (01751) 472601
e emkirkmanorfarm@aol.com
w members.aol.com/ManorfarmNewton

Sunset Cottage ★★★★
Self Catering
Contact: Pat Anderson
Mrs Anderson's Country Cottages
t (01751) 472172
e bookings@boonhill.co.uk
w boonhill.co.uk/sunset.htm

NORTH COWTON
North Yorkshire

Millstone Ref:613 ★★★
Self Catering
Contact: S Boardman
Sykes Cottages
t (01244) 345700
e info@sykescottages.co.uk
w sykescottages.co.uk

NORTH DALTON
East Riding of Yorkshire

Old Cobbler's Cottage, Driffield ★★★ *Self Catering*
t (01377) 217523 & (01377) 217662
e chris@adastra-music.co.uk
w waterfrontcottages.co.uk

NORTHALLERTON
North Yorkshire

The Byre ★★★★
Self Catering
Contact: Mary Crowe
t (01609) 776072

Hill House Farm Cottages
★★★★ *Self Catering*
Contact: James Griffith
t (01609) 770643
e info@hillhousefarmcottages.com
w hillhousefarmcottages.com

NORTON
North Yorkshire

Anson House ★★★★
Self Catering
Contact: Susan Camacho
t (01653) 694901
e ansonhouse@lycos.co.uk
w ansonhouseholidays.co.uk

The Cottage ★★★★
Self Catering
Contact: Patricia Barber
t (01653) 693409
e Patricia.barber@Btinternet.com

NUN MONKTON
North Yorkshire

Lane End Barn ★★★★
Self Catering
Contact: Ms Madeline Orman
t (01423) 330217
e 1000@orman25.fsnet.co.uk

NUNNINGTON
North Yorkshire

Orchard Cottage ★★
Self Catering
Contact: Clifford & Mrs Christine Foxton
t (01439) 748226

OAKWORTH
West Yorkshire

Pine Cottage (4146)
Rating Applied For
Self Catering
Contact: Ms Lorraine Kidd
Dales Holiday Cottages
t 0870 909 9500
e info@dales-holiday-cottages.com
w dalesholcot.com

OLD BYLAND
North Yorkshire

Tylas Lodge ★★★
Self Catering
Contact: Jane & Ivan Holmes
t (01439) 798308
e holmesivan@btinternet.com

Valley View Farm ★★★★
Self Catering
Contact: Sally Robinson
t (01439) 798221
e sally@valleyviewfarm.com
w valleyviewfarm.com

OLD MALTON
North Yorkshire

Chestnut Cottage ★★★★
Self Catering
Contact: Mr David Beeley
Barn House
t (01653) 698251
e enquiries@forgevalleycottages.co.uk

Coronation Cottage ★★★★
Self Catering
Contact: Mr David Beeley
Forge Valley Cottages
t (01653) 698251
w forgevalleycottages.co.uk

OSGODBY
North Yorkshire

Sea Views and Sea Views Too
Rating Applied For
Self Catering
Contact: Mr O'Connor
t (01484) 401757
e pat@oconn100.freeserve.co.uk
w sea-views-scarborough.co.uk

OSMOTHERLEY
North Yorkshire

Monk's Walk Ref:2041
★★★★ *Self Catering*
Contact: Ms Lorraine Kidd
Dales Holiday Cottages
t 0870 909 9500
e info@dales-holiday-cottages.com
w dalesholcot.com

OSWALDKIRK
North Yorkshire

Angel Cottage ★★★★
Self Catering
Contact: Jane Sweeney
t (01439) 788493
e jane.sweeney@lineone.net
w pb-design.com/swiftlink/sc/1325.htm

OXENHOPE
West Yorkshire

2 Mouldgreave Cottages
★★★★ *Self Catering*
Contact: Norma Mackrell
t (01535) 642325
e 2mouldgreave@lineone.net
w mouldgreave.plus.com

The Cottage ★★★★
Self Catering
Contact: Anita Holland
t (01535) 643270

Hawksbridge Cottage ★★★
Self Catering
Contact: Hazel Holmes
t (01535) 642203
e hazel.holmes1@virgin.net
w oxenhopeaccommodation.co.uk

Honeysuckle Cottage, Oxenhope ★★★★★
Self Catering
Contact: Mrs Susan Mytum
Hardnaze Farm
t (01535) 645500
e suemytum@btinternet.com
w hardnaze.co.uk

Lynden Barn Cottage
★★★★ *Self Catering*
Contact: I Spencer
t (01535) 645074
e lyndenbarn@ukonline.co.uk
w members.netscapeonline.co.uk/lyndenbarn/index.html

Old Cote Cottage ★★★
Self Catering
Contact: Mrs Groves
t (01535) 644180

Well Head Cottage
★★★★★ *Self Catering*
Contact: Sheena McBryde
t (01535) 647966
e sheena@brontecottages.com
w brontecottages.com

Yate Cottage, Oxenhope
★★★ *Self Catering*
Contact: Mrs Jean M M Dunn
Yate House
t (01535) 643638
e jeanandhugh@dunnyate.freeserve.co.uk
w uk-holiday-cottages.co.uk/yatecottage

PATELEY BRIDGE
North Yorkshire

Ashfield House ★★★
Self Catering
Contact: Mr Myers
t (01423) 711491
e john.myers@virgin.net
w http://freespace.virgin.net/john.myers

Bruce Cottage ★★★★
Self Catering
Contact: Michael Jarosz
t (01943) 607392
e enquiries@brucecottage.co.uk
w brucecottage.co.uk

Helme Pasture, Old Spring Wood ★★★★ *Self Catering & Serviced Apartments*
Contact: Mrs Rosemary Helme
t (01423) 780279
e info@helmepasture.co.uk
w helmepasture.co.uk

Rainbows End Ref:61 ★★★
Self Catering
Contact: S Boardman
Sykes Cottages
t (01244) 345700
e info@sykescottages.co.uk
w sykescottages.co.uk

Rolling Mill Stable Ref: 244
★★★ *Self Catering*
Contact: S Boardman
Sykes Cottages
t (01244) 345700
e info@sykescottages.co.uk
w sykescottages.co.uk

Wren Cottage ★★★
Self Catering
Contact: Alison Hartwell
t (01423) 523333
e info@harrogateholidays.co.uk
w harrogateholidays.co.uk

PATRICK BROMPTON
North Yorkshire

Wren Cottage ★★★★
Self Catering
Contact: Mrs Nadine Bell
Country Hideaways
t (01969) 663559
e nadine@countryhideaways.co.uk
w countryhideaways.co.uk

PICKERING
North Yorkshire

1 Westgate ★★★★
Self Catering
Contact: Mr & Mrs S Toothill
t (01302) 770601

11 Potter Hill ★★★
Self Catering
Contact: Michael Jones
t (020) 8305 0401
e michael@cheese-board.co.uk
w cottageguide.co.uk/potterhill

2 Spring Gardens ★★★★
Self Catering
Contact: Sandra Pickering
t (01751) 474279
w spring-gardens-cottage.co.uk

27A Hungate ★★★
Self Catering
Contact: Diana Ellis
t (01564) 779575
e diana@tanneryholidays.co.uk
w tanneryholidays.co.uk

Amelia Cottage ★★
Self Catering
Contact: Jennifer MacDonald
t (01482) 441175
e jennymaddonald@mac.com

Appletree Cottage ★★★★
Self Catering
Contact: Mrs Paula Foster
t (01480) 810221

Beech Farm Cottages
★★★★-★★★★★
Self Catering
Contact: Mrs Pat Massara
Beech Farm Cottages
t (01751) 476612
e holiday@beechfarm.com
w beechfarm.com

Bramwood Cottages ★★★★
Self Catering
Contact: Mr John Butler
Bramwood Guest House & Cottages
t (01751) 473446
e bramwood@fsbdial.co.uk
w bramwoodguesthouse.co.uk/cottages.html

Castlegate Cottages ★★★
Self Catering
Contact: Heather Litten
t (01751) 472544
e bookings@castlegatecottages.co.uk
w castlegatecottages.co.uk

Eastgate Cottages ★★★★
Self Catering
Contact: Helen Eddon
t (01751) 471300
e helen.eddon@q-sys.co.uk
w eastgatecottages.co.uk

Easthill Farm House and Lodges ★★★★ *Self Catering*
Contact: Mrs Diane Stenton
Easthill Farm House and Lodges
t (01751) 474561
e info@easthill-farm-holidays.co.uk
w easthill-farm-holidays.co.uk

Eastside Cottage ★★★
Self Catering
Contact: E Evans
t (01751) 477204

The Hayloft ★★★★
Self Catering
Contact: Karen Auker
t (01851) 477075
e granaryhayloft@hotmail.com

Hungate Cottages
★★★–★★★★ *Self Catering*
Contact: Mr Richard Robertson
Hungate Cottages
t (01751) 476382
e holidays@hungatecottages.co.uk
w hungatecottages.co.uk

Karen's Cottages ★★★
Self Catering
Contact: Karen Hill
t (01751) 473258
e hill@newmeadows.fsnet.co.uk

Keld Head Farm Cottages
★★★★ *Self Catering*
Contact: Julian & Penny Fearn
Keld Head Farm Cottages
t (01751) 473974
e julian@keldheadcottages.com
w keldheadcottages.com

Let's Holiday ★★★★
Self Catering
Contact: Mr John Wicks
Let's Holiday
t (01751) 475396
e holiday@letsholiday.com
w letsholiday.com

Lilac Cottage ★★★
Self Catering
Contact: Richard & Dorothy Munn
t (01751) 472193

Loand House Court ★★★★
Self Catering
Contact: RF Howarth
t (01751) 472587
e loandhousecourt@tiscali.co.uk

Low Costa Mill Cottages
★★★★ *Self Catering*
Contact: Eileen Thomas
t (01751) 472050
e thomas@lowcostamill.freeserve.co.uk
w lowcostamill.co.uk

Lynton Cottage Ref:2800
★★★ *Self Catering*
Contact: Ms Lorraine Kidd
Dales Holiday Cottages
t 0870 909 9500
e info@dales-holiday-cottages.com
w dalesholcot.com

Mill Cottage ★★★★
Self Catering
Contact: Mr Derek Calvert
t (01423) 865279
e dcal208936@aol.com

Newton Cottage ★★★
Self Catering
Contact: Tony Danks
t (01751) 477913
e mal.danks@btinternet.com

The Old Forge Cottages
★★★ *Self Catering*
Contact: Judy French
The Old Forge
t (01751) 477399
e theoldforge1@aol.com
w forgecottages.co.uk

Pan Cottage ★★★
Self Catering
t (01751) 473618
e pancottage@hotmail.co.uk
w pancottage.co.uk

Prospect Farm Cottages
★★★ *Self Catering*
Contact: G Webster
t (01751) 476835
e enquiries@prospectfarmcottages.co.uk

Rawcliffe House Farm
★★★★ *Self Catering*
Contact: Duncan & Jan Allsopp
t (01751) 473292
e stay@rawcliffehousefarm.co.uk
w rawcliffehousefarm.co.uk

Sands Farm Cottages
★★★★ *Self Catering*
Contact: Mr & Mrs M & S Parkin
t (01751) 474405
e info@sandsfarmcottages.co.uk
w sandsfarmcottages.co.uk

The Sidings ★★★
Self Catering
Contact: Lloyd & Liz Varley
t (0115) 945 5543
e varleyfm@supanet.com
w pickeringcottages.co.uk

Skelton Cottage & Rowntree Cottage ★★★★ *Self Catering*
Contact: Helen Eddon
Eastgate Cottages
t (01751) 471300
e helen.eddon@q-sys.co.uk
w eastgatecottages.co.uk

South View Cottages
★★★–★★★★ *Self Catering*
Contact: Mr Simpson
t (01937) 832192
e info@southviewcottage.co.uk
w southviewcottages.co.uk

Town End Farm Cottage
★★★ *Self Catering*
Contact: Christine Fenwick
t (01751) 472713

Upper Carr Chalet and Touring Park ★★★
Self Catering
Contact: Martin Harker
t (01751) 473115
e harker@uppercarr.demon.co.uk
w upercarr.demon.co.uk

White Lodge Cottage ★★★
Self Catering
Contact: Elizabeth Briggs
t (01751) 473897

PRESTON-UNDER-SCAR
North Yorkshire

Anna's Cottage at Rocky View ★★★ *Self Catering*
Contact: Mrs Nadine Bell
Country Hideaways
t (01969) 663559
e nadine@countryhideaways.co.uk
w countryhideaways.co.uk

Croxford Cottage Ref:2034
★★★ *Self Catering*
Contact: Ms Lorraine Kidd
Dales Holiday Cottages
t 0870 909 9500
e info@dales-holiday-cottages.com
w dalesholcot.com

Mallyan Wynd ★★★
Self Catering
Contact: Mrs Nadine Bell
Country Hideaways
t (01969) 663559
e nadine@countryhideaways.co.uk
w countryhideaways.co.uk

PRIMROSE VALLEY
North Yorkshire

Calm Waters Bungalow Ref:2478 ★★★ *Self Catering*
Contact: Ms Lorraine Kidd
Dales Holiday Cottages
t 0870 909 9500
e info@dales-holiday-cottages.com
w dalesholcot.com

RATHMELL
North Yorkshire

Layhead Farm Cottages
★★★★ *Self Catering*
Contact: Mrs Hyslop
t (01729) 840234
e rosehyslop@layhead.co.uk

RAVENSCAR
North Yorkshire

Raven Lea ★★★★
Self Catering
Contact: Mr Turner
t (01723) 870949
e ravenlea@ic24.net
w ravenlea.co.uk

Smugglers Rock Country House, Ravenscar
★★★–★★★★ *Self Catering*
Contact: Mrs Sharon Gregson
Smugglers Rock Country House
t (01723) 870044
e info@smugglersrock.co.uk
w smugglersrock.co.uk

REDMIRE
North Yorkshire

Lightfoot House
Rating Applied For
Self Catering
t (01434) 607891

REETH
North Yorkshire

Barn End Cottage Ref:3639
★★★ *Self Catering*
Contact: Ms Lorraine Kidd
Dales Holiday Cottages
t 0870 909 9500
e info@dales-holiday-cottages.com
w dalesholcot.com

Burton House, Greystones and Charlie's Stable ★★★★
Self Catering
Contact: Mrs Patricia Procter
t (01748) 884273
w uk-cottages.com

Half Moon House
Rating Applied For
Self Catering
Contact: Ms Doris Reed
t (01642) 866628
e d-reed@ntlworld.com

Swaledale Cottages ★★★★
Self Catering
Contact: Janet Hughes
t (01748) 884526
e thiernswood@talk21.com
w swaledale-cottages.co.uk

Winmaur Cottage Ref:2995
★★★★ *Self Catering*
Contact: Ms Lorraine Kidd
Dales Holiday Cottages
t 0870 909 9500
e info@dales-holiday-cottages.com
w dalesholcot.com

Wraycroft Holiday Cottages
★★★★ *Self Catering*
Contact: F Hodgson
t (01748) 884497
e wraycroft@rhodgson.demon.co.uk
w rhodgson.demon.co.uk

REIGHTON
North Yorkshire

Lavender Cottage ★★★★
Self Catering
Contact: Mrs Caroline Wilson
t (01262) 606665
e reighton@btinternet.com
w yorkshireheritagecoast.co.uk

St Helen's Cottage ★★★★★
Self Catering
Contact: Janice T Carter
t (01723) 882274

RICCALL
North Yorkshire

Pound Cottage ★★★★
Self Catering
Contact: Peggy Swann
t (01757) 248203
e southnewlandsfarm@yahoo.co.uk
w southnewlands.co.uk

RICHMOND
North Yorkshire

16 Culloden Mews ★★★
Self Catering
Contact: Robert Holmes
t (01748) 823043

2 Westview ★★★
Self Catering
Contact: Caroline O'Neill
t (01748) 850909
e caroline@escape2richamond.co.uk
w escape2richmond.co.uk

Barn Owl Cottage and Kingfisher Cottage Ref:3225/2224 ★★★★
Self Catering
Contact: Ms Fiona Moody
Dales Holiday Cottages
t 0870 909 9500
e info@dales-holiday-cottages.com
w dalesholcot.com

Blacksmiths Cottage ★★★
Self Catering
Contact: James &Susan Melville
t (01925) 268691
e js.melville@virgin.net

The Bungalow ★★★ *Self Catering & Serviced Apartments*
Contact: R Delf
t (01748) 823122

Coach House ★★★★
Self Catering
t (01748) 822884
e whashtonsprings@btconnect.com
w whashtonsprings.co.uk

Croft Cottage ★★★
Self Catering
Contact: Shirley Ann Wakeling-Stretton
t (01926) 428784
e shirlswake2@aol.com
w yorkshirecottage.org.uk

Fox Cottage ★★★
Self Catering
Contact: Mr Fryer
t (01748) 811772

Fryers Cottage ★★★
Self Catering
Contact: Oliver & Valerie Blease
t (01748) 823344

High Leases Cottage ★★★★
Self Catering
Contact: Heather-Jane Hold
t (01748) 826908
e holdfamily@hotmail.com

Hillcrest (3967)
Rating Applied For
Self Catering
Contact: Ms Lorraine Kidd
Dales Holiday Cottages
t 0870 909 9500
e info@dales-holiday-cottages.com
w dalesholcot.com

Lions Leap Ref 4014 ★★★★
Self Catering
Contact: Clive Haddon
Dales Holiday Cottages
t 0870 909 9500
e clive_haddon@hotmail.com
w dalesholcot.com

Nuns Cottage ★★★
Self Catering
Contact: Mrs Judith Flint
t (01748) 822809
e nunscottage@richmond.org.uk
w nunscottage.co.uk

Thornlea Cottage Ref:249 ★★★ *Self Catering*
Contact: S Boardman
Sykes Cottages
t (01244) 345700
e info@sykescottages.co.uk
w sykescottages.co.uk

Tish Toms Cottages ★★★
Self Catering
Contact: Mrs Ann Hall
Mount Arrarat
t (01748) 822167
e pete@catermech.co.uk
w tishtomscottages.com

RILLINGTON
North Yorkshire

Thorpe-Rise ★★★
Self Catering
Contact: Marilyn Legard
t (01944) 758446

RIPON
North Yorkshire

Intake ★★★★ *Self Catering*
Contact: Fiona McConnell
3 Hippingstones Lane
e kfiona@tiscali.co.uk
w intakefarmhouse.co.uk

Mallorie Bungalow Ref:2176 ★★★★ *Self Catering*
Contact: Ms Lorraine Kidd
Dales Holiday Cottages
t 0870 909 9500
e info@dales-holiday-cottages.com
w dalesholcot.com

Waterfront House ★★★★★
Self Catering
Contact: CE Braddon
t (01423) 770704
e chris1.braddon@virgin.net

ROBIN HOOD'S BAY
North Yorkshire

1 and 2 Wragby Barn ★★★★ *Self Catering*
Contact: Marilyn Fenby
t (01947) 880719
e marilyn@fenby.fsbusiness.co.uk
w wragbycottages.co.uk

Farsyde Farm Cottages ★★★-★★★★ *Self Catering*
Contact: Angela Green
t (01947) 880249
e farsydestud@talk21.com
w farsydefarmcottages.co.uk

Heather Croft Ref:925 ★★
Self Catering
Contact: Mr S Boardman
Sykes Cottages
t (01244) 345700
e info@sykescottages.co.uk
w sykescottages.co.uk

Inglenook ★★★★
Self Catering
Contact: Lesley Abbott
t (01904) 622059
e info@inglenook-cottage.co.uk
w inglenook-cottage.co.uk

Lingers Hill ★★★
Self Catering
Contact: Frances Harland
Lingers Hill
t (01947) 880608
e info@ytb.org.uk

Meadowcroft ★★★★
Self Catering
Contact: Ms Vanessa Hicking
Whitby Holiday Cottages
t (01947) 821122
e enquiries@whitby-cottages.co.uk
w whitby-cottages.co.uk

South House Farmhouse & Cottages ★★★★
Self Catering
Contact: Mrs Nealia Pattinson
t (01947) 880243
e kmp@bogglehole.fsnet.co.uk

The White Owl Holiday Apartments ★★★
Self Catering
Contact: Mr David Higgins
t (01947) 880879
e higgins@whiteowlrhb.freeserve.co.uk
w smoothhound.co.uk/hotels/whiteowl.html

ROSEDALE ABBEY
North Yorkshire

Abbey House ★★★★
Self Catering
Contact: Geoff Sherwin
t (01904) 431004
e ghsherwin@aol.com
w cottagenorthyorks.co.uk

Coach House ★★★★
Self Catering
Contact: Linda Sugars
t (01751) 417283
e sevenford@aol.com
w sevenford.com

Craven Garth Holiday Cottages ★★★ *Self Catering*
Contact: Ena Dent
t (01751) 417506
e ena@cravengarth.com
w cravengarth.com

The Grange Farm Cottages ★★★★ *Self Catering*
Contact: David Brown
t (01751) 417329
e dbrown329@tiscali.co.uk
w thegrangecottages.co.uk

Stable Cottage ★★★
Self Catering
Contact: Christine Ewington
t (01751) 417583
e holidays@medds.co.uk
w medds.co.uk

Woodlea ★★★★
Self Catering
Contact: Pauline Belt
Woodlea
t (01904) 705549
e p.belt@daviscoleman.com
w rosedaleholidaycottage.co.uk

ROSEDALE EAST
North Yorkshire

East Coast Holiday Bungalows ★★★★
Self Catering
Contact: Lorraine Drake
t (01751) 417785
e lorraine.rosedale@virgin.net
w eastcoastholidaybungalows.co.uk

Hill Farm ★★★★ *Self Catering & Serviced Apartments*
Contact: Mr & Mrs Richard & Val Cook
t (01751) 417404
e holidays@hillfarm-rosedale.co.uk

ROTHERHAM
South Yorkshire

Whiston Annexe ★★★
Self Catering
Contact: Rodney Marshall
t (01709) 820871

RUSWARP
North Yorkshire

Brook Cottage ★★★★
Self Catering
Contact: Jackie Byers
North Star Accommodation
t (01947) 603456
e info@northstaraccommodation.co.uk
w northstaraccommodation.co.uk

Croft Farm Holiday Cottages ★★★★ *Self Catering*
Contact: Ms Emma Carpenter
t (01947) 825853
e emma@croftfarm.com

Egton Cottage Ref:734 ★★★ *Self Catering*
Contact: S Boardman
t (01244) 345700
e info@sykescottages.co.uk
w sykescottages.co.uk

Esk Moor Cottage ★★★
Self Catering
Contact: Marion Corner
t (01947) 605836

Esk View Cottage Ref:1912 ★★★ *Self Catering*
Contact: Ms Lorraine Kidd
Dales Holiday Cottages
t 0870 909 9500
e info@dales-holiday-cottages.com
w dalesholcot.com

Maybeck Cottage Ref:1674 ★★★ *Self Catering*
Contact: Ms Lorraine Kidd
Dales Holiday Cottages
t 0870 909 9500
e info@dales-holiday-cottages.com
w dalesholcot.com

Turnerdale Cottage
★★★★★ *Self Catering*
Contact: Mr David Haycox
Shoreline Cottages Ltd
t (0113) 244 8410
e reservations@shoreline-cottages.com
w shoreline-cottages.com

SALTAIRE
West Yorkshire

Glen Knoll ★★★★
Self Catering
t (01274) 825303
e helen@msunderland.fsnet.co.uk

Overlookers Cottage
★★★★ *Self Catering*
Contact: Anne Heald
t (01274) 774993
w saltaire.yorks.com/touristinfo/overlookers.html

SALTMARSHE
East Riding of Yorkshire

Saltmarshe Cottages
Rating Applied For
Self Catering
t (01430) 430677
e vivienne.sweeting@btinternet.com
w saltmarshe-cottages.co.uk

SANDSEND
North Yorkshire

Caedmon House ★★★★★
Self Catering
Contact: Mr David Haycox & Mrs Sue Brooks
Shoreline Cottages Ltd
t (0113) 244 8410
e reservations@shoreline-cottages.com

Eden Cottage
Rating Applied For
Self Catering
Contact: Ms Vanessa Hicking
Whitby Holiday Cottages
t (01947) 603010
e enquiries@whitby-cottages.co.uk

Flat 3, Peacehaven ★★
Self Catering
Contact: Ms Vanessa Hicking
Whitby Holiday Cottages
t (01947) 821122
e enquiries@whitby-cottages.co.uk
w whitby-cottages.co.uk

The Garden Flat Ref:3460
★★★ *Self Catering*
Dales Holiday Cottages
t 0870 909 9500
e fiona@dales-holiday-cottages.com
w dalesholcot.com

Harlow Cottage ★★★★
Self Catering
Contact: Mr David Haycox
Shoreline Cottages Ltd
t (0113) 244 8410
e reservations@shoreline-cottages.com
w shoreline-cottages.com

Howdale Cottage ★★★★
Self Catering
Contact: Ms Vanessa Hicking
Whitby Holiday Cottages
t (01947) 821122
e enquiries@whitby-cottages.co.uk
w whitby-cottages.co.uk

Melrose ★★★ *Self Catering*
Contact: Ms Vanessa Hicking
Whitby Holiday Cottages
t (01947) 821122
e enquiries@whitby-cottages.co.uk
w whitby-cottages.co.uk

Plovers Nest Ref:2785
★★★★ *Self Catering*
Contact: Ms Lorraine Kidd
Dales Holiday Cottages
t 0870 909 9500
e info@dales-holiday-cottages.com
w dalesholcot.com

Prospect House, Flat 1 & 3
★★★★ *Self Catering*
Contact: Ms Vanessa Hicking
Whitby Holiday Cottages
t (01947) 821122
e enquiries@whitby-cottages.co.uk
w whitby-cottages.co.uk

Sunnyside ★★★★
Self Catering
Contact: Ms Vanessa Hicking
Whitby Holiday Cottages
t (01947) 821122
e enquiries@whitby-cottages.co.uk
w whitby-cottages.co.uk

Vancouver Cottage
★★★★★ *Self Catering*
Contact: Mrs Vanessa Hicking
Whitby Holiday Cottages
t (01947) 603010
e enquiries@whitby-cottages.co.uk

SAWDON
North Yorkshire

Sawdon Country Cottages
★★★★ *Self Catering*
Contact: Mrs Jennifer Worsley
t (01723) 859794
e sawdoncottages@btinternet.com
w sawdoncottages.co.uk

SAWLEY
North Yorkshire

Sawley Arms Cottages
★★★★ *Self Catering*
Contact: June Hawes
t (01765) 620642

SCALBY
North Yorkshire

Away From The Madding Crowd ★★★★ *Self Catering*
Contact: Peter Ward
t (01723) 360502
e peterandstella@scalbynabs99.fsnet.co.uk

SCARBOROUGH
North Yorkshire

Abbey Holiday Flats ★★
Self Catering
Contact: Ian Read
Egsproperty
t (01262) 677819
e enquiries@winston-court.co.uk
w abbey-holiday-flats.co.uk

Apartment 15 Easby Hall
★★★★ *Self Catering*
Contact: Diane Crampton
Bedwyn's Holiday Accommodation
t (01723) 516700
e info@bedwyns.co.uk
w bedwyns.co.uk

Apartment 4 Easby Hall
★★★★ *Self Catering*
Contact: Mrs Carmel Daly-Fletcher
Skyrack
t (0113) 278 5836
e pauldalyfletcher@hotmail.com

Atlantis Holiday Flats ★★
Self Catering
Contact: Mr & Mrs EM Dyson Dyson
t (01723) 375087
e atlantisholiday@btconnect.com

Avenwood Apartments ★★
Self Catering
Contact: Mr David Atkinson
t (01723) 374640
e dave@avenwood.freeserve.co.uk

Bay View Cottage ★★★★
Self Catering
Bay View Cottages
t (01723) 378711
e bayview.cottages@btinternet.com

Bayview Holiday Flatlets
★★ *Self Catering*
Contact: Ellen Johnson
t (01723) 375139

Brialene Holiday Apartments ★★★
Self Catering
Contact: Marlene Witty
t (01723) 367158
e reservations@scarborough-brialene.co.uk
w scarborough-brialene.co.uk

Brompton Holiday Flats
★★★ *Self Catering*
Contact: Kenneth Broadbent
t (01723) 364964
e info@bromptonholidayflats.co.uk
w bromptonholidayflats.co.uk

Cherry Trees Holiday Flats
★–★★ *Self Catering*
Contact: Helen Sanderson
t (01723) 501433
e info@cherrytrees.vholiday.co.uk
w cherrytrees.vholiday.co.uk

Cravendale Holiday Flats
★–★★★ *Self Catering*
Contact: Shirley Smith
t (01274) 871069
e shirleysflats@hotmail.com
w cravendaleflats.co.uk

Cresta House Flats ★★★★
Self Catering
Contact: Mr Dobie
t 07711 641967
e cresta_house@yahoo.co.uk

Cromwell Court ★★★
Self Catering
Contact: Gloria & Mr Ra
Walker
t (01723) 376008
w yorkshirecoast.co.uk/cromwell

East Farm Country Co
Rating Applied For
Self Catering
Contact: Joanne Ireland
t (01723) 353635
e joeastfarmcottages@h
co.uk
w eastfarmcountrycotta
uk

Elizabethan Court ★★
Self Catering
Contact: Paula Randall
t (01423) 324274
e paularandall1@ntlwor

Glaisdale Holiday Flat Cottage ★★★ *Self Cat*
Contact: Mr Michael Hc
FHCIMA
t (01723) 372728
e michael.holliday@tesc
w s-h-a.co.uk/glaisdale

Green Gables Hotel H Flats ★★–★★★ *Self C*
Contact: Nick Jones
Green Gables Hotel
t (01723) 361005
e enquiries@greengablesscarborough
w greengablesscarborou
uk

Harbour View Holiday
★★ *Self Catering*
Contact: David Gordon Jenkinson
t (01723) 361162

The Hayloft ★★★★
Self Catering
Contact: Ingrid Flute
Ingrid Flute Holiday Accommodation
t (01723) 376777
e info@ingridflute.co.uk

Honeysuckle Cottage
★★★★ *Self Catering*
Contact: Mr David Beel
Forge Valley Cottages
t (01653) 698251
w forgevalleycottages.cc

Kimberley Holiday Fla
★★–★★★ *Self Caterin*
Contact: S Costello & M
Quilter
t (01723) 850552
e stagedoorsteve@yaho
uk

Lendal House ★★★★
Self Catering
Contact: Petra Scott
Lendal House
t (01723) 372178
e info@lendalhouse.co.u
w lendalhouse.co.uk

Lingholm Court, Lebb
★★★★ *Self Catering*
Contact: Mrs Caroline Woodhouse
t (01723) 586365
e info@lingholm.co.uk
w lingholm.co.uk

Look out for establishments participating in the National Accessible Scheme 

Marlborough Flats
★★-★★★ *Self Catering*
Contact: Mrs Julie Ellard
t (01723) 373116
e julieellard@hotmail.com

Meenagoland Holiday Flats
★★ *Self Catering*
Contact: Samantha Pickering
t 07956 842612
e flats@meenagoland.co.uk
w meenagoland.co.uk

The Mews ★★★
Self Catering
Contact: Diane Crampton
Bedwyn's Holiday Accommodation
t (01723) 516700
e info@bedwyns.co.uk
w bedwyns.co.uk

Moordale House ★★★★
Self Catering
Contact: Shirley Tomlinson
t (01977) 799056
e ackworthroad@aol.com

Neville House Apartments
★★★ *Self Catering*
Contact: Linda Smailes
t (01723) 366123
e lindasmailes@tiscali.co.uk
w nevillehouseapartments.co.uk

Parade Holiday Flats
★★-★★★ *Self Catering*
Contact: Sue Sayers
t (01723) 374307
e suesayers@tesco.net

Priory View Bungalow ★★★
Self Catering
Contact: Denise Pemberton
t (01723) 584665
e les.pemberton@tesco.net

Sea Vista Holiday Bungalow
★★★★ *Self Catering*
Contact: Alan Roper
t (01274) 564741
e info@sea-vista.com
w sea-vista.com

Seacliffe Holiday Flats ★★
Self Catering
Contact: Elizabeth Lumley
t (01944) 728277
e info@seaviewflats.co.uk
w seacliffeholidays.co.uk

Seascape ★★★★
Self Catering
Contact: Julie Eborall
t (01723) 379858
e seascapebungalow@aol.com

Shell Seekers Cottage
★★★★ *Self Catering*
Contact: Joe & Jennifer Scott
t (01723) 516700
e info@shellseekerscottage.co.uk
w shellseekerscottage.co.uk

Spikers Hill Country Cottages, West Ayton ★★★
Self Catering
Contact: Janet Hutchinson
t (01723) 862537
e janet@spikershill.ndo.co.uk
w spikershill.ndo.co.uk

Town Farm Cottages
★★★★ *Self Catering*
Contact: Joe & Mrs Debbie Green
t (01723) 870278
e mail@greenfarming.co.uk
w greenfarming.co.uk

Valley View Holiday Flats
★★ *Self Catering*
Contact: Mr David Wilkinson
t (01723) 364709
e valleyview@btconnect.com
w valleyview.org.uk

The Villa Esplanade – Holiday Apartment
★★-★★★★ *Self Catering*
Contact: Pauline Gent
t (01723) 375571

Vincent Holiday Complex
★★★ *Self Catering*
Contact: Alan & Sandra Hopkins
t (01723) 500997
e vincents.scarborough@btinternet.com
w cottageguide.co.uk/vincents

Wayside Farm Holiday Cottages ★★-★★★
Self Catering
Contact: Peter Halder
t (01723) 870519

White Acre ★★★-★★★★
Self Catering
Contact: J.G. Squire
JG Squire (holidays) Ltd
t (01723) 374220
e squiresc@clara.co.uk
w squiresc.clara.co.uk

White Gable ★★★★
Self Catering
Contact: Mr Squire
t (01723) 374220
e squiresc@clara.co.uk
w squiresc.clara.co.uk

Windsor Holiday Flats ★
Self Catering
Contact: Andrew Eadie
t (01723) 375986
e andrew@windsorholidayflats.com
w windsorholidayflats.com

Wrea Head Cottage Holidays ★★★★
Self Catering
Contact: Mr Steve Marshall
Wrea Head Cottage Holidays
t (01723) 375844
e ytb@wreahead.co.uk
w wreahead.co.uk

SCAWTON
North Yorkshire

Forresters Cottage ★★★★
Self Catering
Contact: Charlotte de Klee
t (01337) 828217
e charlotte@lcokhiehead.freeserve.co.uk

Manor Farm Cottage ★★★
Self Catering
t (01439) 770586

SCHOLES, HOLMFIRTH
West Yorkshire

1 Cross Barn ★★★★
Self Catering
Contact: John & Janet Armitage
t (01484) 683664

SCORTON
North Yorkshire

7 The Forest ★★★★
Self Catering
Contact: Dennis & Marcia McLuckie
t (01748) 812888
e marcia.scorton@btconnect.com
w yorkshirecountryholidays.com

SCOTCH CORNER
North Yorkshire

5 Cedar Grove ★★★
Self Catering
Contact: James P Lawson
t (01723) 870455
e jim@lawson5270fsnet.co.uk

SEDBUSK
North Yorkshire

The Coach House Ref:2016
★★★ *Self Catering*
Contact: Ms Lorraine Kidd
Dales Holiday Cottages
t 0870 909 9500
e info@dales-holiday-cottages.com
w dalesholcot.com

West Cottage ★★★
Self Catering
Contact: Mrs Nadine Bell
Country Hideaways
t (01969) 663559
e nadine@countryhideaways.co.uk
w countryhideaways.co.uk

SELBY
North Yorkshire

Lund Farm Cottages ★★★★
Self Catering
Contact: Mr & Mrs Chris & Helen Middleton
t (01757) 228775
e chris.middleton@farmline.com
w lundfarm.co.uk

Rusholme Grange Cottage, Drax ★★★ *Self Catering & Serviced Apartments*
Contact: Anne Roberts
Rusholme Cottage
t (01757) 618257
e anne@rusholmegrange.co.uk
w rusholmegrange.co.uk

SETTLE
North Yorkshire

4 St John's Row ★★★
Self Catering
Contact: Mary Sowerby
t (01943) 875552
e marysowerby@yahoo.com
w johnscottage.com

Cobweb Cottage ★★★
Self Catering
Contact: Stephen Shaw
t 07971 806627
e cobwebcottage@settle-holidays.com
w settle-holidays.com

Cragdale Cottage ★★★★
Self Catering
Contact: Mr Paul Whitehead
Cragdale Cottage
t (020) 8647 8397 & (01737) 247179
e paul@cragdalecottage.co.uk
w cragdalecottage.co.uk

Devonshire Flat ★★★
Self Catering
Contact: Allan Aspden
t (01729) 825781

The Folly at Settle ★★★★★
Self Catering
Contact: Pat Rand
t (01729) 822930
e m.rand@virgin.net
w the-folly.co.uk

Goldielands (4004) ★★★★
Self Catering
Dales Holiday Cottages
t 0870 909 9500
e fiona@dales-holiday-cottages.com
w dalesholcot.com

Harry's Cottage ★★★
Self Catering
Contact: Wendy Porter
t (01729) 824268
e wendylou63@hotmail.com

Hazel Cottage ★★★
Self Catering
Contact: Jennie Crawford
Moorside Services
t (01274) 832368
e rogercrawford@greenclough.freeserve.co.uk
w geocities.com/moorsideuk

Lock Cottage Ref:816
★★★★ *Self Catering*
Contact: S Boardman
Sykes Cottages
t (01244) 345700
e info@sykescottages.co.uk
w sykescottages.co.uk

Middle Cottage ★★★
Self Catering
Contact: Ms Anna Greenhalgh
Suncroft
t (01524) 251735 & 07967 890043
e agreenhalgh@austwick.org

Old Brew House, Brewhouse Cottage & Robin Hill
★★★-★★★★ *Self Catering*
Contact: Mrs Jeanne Carr
t (01729) 850319
e jmcarr@tesco.net

SEWERBY
East Riding of Yorkshire

Field House Farm Cottages
★★★★-★★★★★
Self Catering
Contact: Angela & John Foster
t (01262) 674932
e john.foster@farmline.com
w fieldhousefarmcottages.co.uk

Oakwood ★★★★
Self Catering
Contact: Josephine Hodgson
t (01977) 704942
w oakwood-sewerby.co.uk

Park Cottage & April Cottage ★★★-★★★★
Self Catering
Contact: Sue Ashby
Harbour Light Cottages
t (01977) 620359

SHEFFIELD
South Yorkshire

Coppice House Farm Cottage ★★★★ *Self Catering*
Contact: Pamela Revitt
t (0114) 230 1753

The Flat ★★★ *Self Catering*
Contact: Margaret Cox
t (0114) 221 5553

Foxholes Farm ★★–★★★
Self Catering
Contact: Jean & Rachel Hague
t (0114) 285 1710
e foxholes.farm@tiscali.co.uk
w foxholesfarm.co.uk

Hangram Lane Farmhouse
★★★★ *Self Catering*
Contact: Janet Clark
t (0114) 230 3570

Mill Lane Farm Cottage and Orchard Cottage ★★★★★
Self Catering
Contact: Miss Jayne Middleton
t (0114) 263 0188
e milllanefarmcottages@hotmail.com

Moor Royd House
★★★–★★★★ *Self Catering*
Contact: Janet Hird
t (01226) 763353
e janet@moorroydhouse.freeserve.uk
w moorroydhouse.com

Ranmoor Apartments ★★★
Self Catering
t (0114) 258 0514
e geraldine70@hotmail.com
w stayinsheffield.co.uk

Smallshaw Farm Cottages
★★★★ *Self Catering*
Contact: James & Mary Booth
t (01226) 764271
e bookings@smallshaw.com
w smallshaw.com

Spital Bridge (River Dale)
★★★★ *Self Catering*
Contact: Luke Carter Anne Merril
t (0114) 263 0066

SHERBURN
North Yorkshire

Housemartins ★★★
Self Catering
Contact: Anna Massie
t (01944) 710259

Westfield Granary
★★★–★★★★ *Self Catering*
Contact: H.R. Wales
Holiday Cottages (Yorkshire) Ltd
t (01756) 700510
e brochure@holidaycotts.co.uk
w holidaycotts.co.uk

SIGGLESTHORNE
East Riding of Yorkshire

Peggy's Cottage ★★★★
Self Catering
Contact: Ms Jude Collingwood
Peggy's Cottage
t (01964) 535395
e p.collingwood@btinternet.com

SILSDEN
West Yorkshire

Croft Cottage Ref:1622
★★★★ *Self Catering*
Contact: Ms Lorraine Kidd
Dales Holiday Cottages
t 0870 909 9500
e info@dales-holiday-cottages.com
w dalesholcot.com

Ford Cottage Ref:89 ★★★
Self Catering
Contact: Ms Lorraine Kidd
Dales Holiday Cottages
t 0870 909 9500
e info@dales-holiday-cottages.com
w dalesholcot.com

SINNINGTON
North Yorkshire

Goose End of Seven House Ref:1779 ★★★ *Self Catering*
Contact: Ms Lorraine Kidd
Dales Holiday Cottages
t 0870 909 9500
e info@dales-holiday-cottages.com
w dalesholcot.com

Pear Tree Barn Ref: 3427
★★★★ *Self Catering*
Contact: Ms Lorraine Kidd
Dales Holiday Cottages
t 0870 909 9500
e info@dales-holiday-cottages.com
w dalesholcot.com

Sevenside Holiday Bungalow ★★★ *Self Catering*
Contact: Elizabeth Allan
t (01751) 431812
e jdallan@care4free.net
w sevensidebungalow.co.uk

SKERNE
East Riding of Yorkshire

Mulberry Cottage ★★★★
Self Catering
Contact: Gemma Dixon
t (01377) 254073
e info@mulberry-whin.com
w mulberry-whin.com

SKIPTON
North Yorkshire

7 Elliot Street ★★★★
Self Catering
Contact: H.R. Wales
Holiday Cottages (Yorkshire) Ltd
t (01756) 700510
e brochure@holidaycotts.co.uk
w holidaycotts.co.uk

Beck and Brooklyn Cottages
★★★ *Self Catering*
Malhamdale Cottages
t (01943) 461092
e info@malhamdalecottages.co.uk

Cawder Hall Cottages
★★★–★★★★ *Self Catering*
Contact: Graham Pearson
Cawder Hall Cottages
t (01756) 791579
e info@cawderhallcottages.co.uk
w cawderhallcottages.co.uk

Dales Flat ★★ *Self Catering*
Contact: Margaret Little
t (01756) 791688

Fairfax Street
Rating Applied For
Self Catering
Contact: Roger Wales
Holiday Cottages
t (01756) 700510
e info@holidaycotts.co.uk
w holidaycotts.co.uk

Garden Cottage
Rating Applied For
Self Catering
Contact: Barbara Anne Ross
t 07951 055330

Ginnel Mews Ref:46 ★★★
Self Catering
Contact: S Boardman
Sykes Cottages
t (01244) 345700
e info@sykescottages.co.uk
w sykescottages.co.uk

The Hide Ref:617 ★★★
Self Catering
Contact: S Boardman
Sykes Cottages
t (01244) 345700
e info@sykescottages.co.uk
w sykescottages.co.uk

High Malsis Farmhouse
★★★ *Self Catering*
Contact: Sheila Fort
t (01535) 633309
e holiday@jfort.co.uk
w jfort.co.uk/holiday

The Lodge ★★★★
Self Catering
Contact: Mrs Edith Ann Thwaite
t (01200) 445300
e editthwaite@hotmail.com

Low Skibeden Farm Cottage
★★★ *Self Catering*
Contact: Heather Simpson
Low Skibeden Farmhouse
t (01756) 793849
w yorkshirenet.co.uk/accgde.lowskibeden

Lower Heugh Cottage
★★★★★ *Self Catering*
Contact: T Nash
t (01756) 793702
e heughcottage@talk21.com
w cottageguide.co.uk

Maypole Cottage ★★★★
Self Catering
Contact: Elizabeth Gamble
t (01756) 720609
e gamble@daelnet.co.uk

None-go-Bye Farm Cottage
★★★ *Self Catering*
Contact: Mr Lawn
t (01756) 793165
e booking.nonegobye@virgin.net
w yorkshiredales.net/stayat/nonegobyefarm/index.htm

The Old Barn ★★★
Self Catering
Contact: Steve Ward
t (01491) 613119
e s.c_ward@tiscali.co.uk

Thisledo ★★★★
Self Catering
Contact: Shelley Green
t (01756) 795024
e mail@thisledo.co.uk
w thisledo.co.uk

Whitham Cottage ★★★★
Self Catering
Contact: Janet Hoyle
Yorkshire Cottages
t (01943) 885306
e enquiries@yorkshire-cottages.info
w yorkshire-cottages.info

SLEDMERE
East Riding of Yorkshire

Life Hill Farm Cottage
★★★★ *Self Catering*
Contact: Fay Grace
Life Hill Farm
t (01377) 236224
e info@lifehillfarm.co.uk
w lifehillfarm.co.uk

SLEIGHTS
North Yorkshire

Bracken Edge Ref:887 ★★★
Self Catering
Contact: S Boardman
Sykes Cottages
t (01244) 345700
e info@sykescottages.co.uk
w sykescottages.co.uk

Groves Dyke Holiday Cottage ★★★ *Self Catering*
Groves Dyke
t (01947) 811404
e relax@grovesdyke.co.uk
w grovesdyke.co.uk

Rose Nook ★★★
Self Catering
Contact: Nicola Welford
Rose Nook Cottage
t (01947) 840726
e rosenookcottage@aol.com

The Stable Ref:2892 ★★★★
Self Catering
Contact: Ms Lorraine Kidd
Dales Holiday Cottages
t 0870 909 9500
e info@dales-holiday-cottages.com
w dalesholcot.com

SLINGSBY
North Yorkshire

Cherrygarth Cottages – Hay Barn Stables ★★★★★
Self Catering
Contact: Stuart & Mrs Tracey Prest
D R Prest & Son
t (01653) 628247
e s.prest@btconnect.com
w cherrygarthcottages.co.uk

Dawson Cottage ★★★
Self Catering
Contact: Julia Snowball
t (01653) 628136
e julia.snowball@amserve.com

Home Farm Holiday Cottages ★★★★
Self Catering
Contact: Stephen & Mrs Rachel Prest
t (01653) 628277
e sgprest@farming.co.uk
w yorkshire-holiday-cottage.co.uk

Keepers Cottage Holidays
★★★ *Self Catering*
Contact: Joanna Pavey
t (01653) 628656

SNAINTON
North Yorkshire

Bramble End Cottage
★★★★ *Self Catering*
Contact: Mr Peter Durbin
Yorkshire Cottages
t (01943) 885306
e janet@yorkshire-cottages.info

SNAPE
North Yorkshire

Jasmine Cottage ★★★
Self Catering
Contact: Colette Leyshon
t (01925) 413907
e jasminecottage@ntlworld.com

SNEATON
North Yorkshire

Raygill Cottage ★★★
Self Catering
Contact: John Knell
t (01423) 566280

Rose Cottage ★★★
Self Catering
Contact: Ms Vanessa Hicking
Whitby Holiday Cottages
t (01947) 821122
e enquiries@whitby-cottages.co.uk
w whitby-cottages.co.uk

Sycamore Cottage ★★★
Self Catering
Contact: Janet Hoyle
Yorkshire Cottages
t (01943) 885306
e enquiries@yorkshire-cottages.info
w yorkshire-cottages.info

SNEATON THORPE
North Yorkshire

Sorrel Cottage ★★★★★
Self Catering
Contact: Mr David Haycox
Shoreline Cottages Ltd
t (0113) 244 8410
e reservations@shoreline-cottages.com
w shoreline-cottages.com

SOWERBY
North Yorkshire

Long Acre Lodge ★★★★
Self Catering
Contact: Mr Dawson
t (01845) 522360
w longacrethirsk.co.uk

SOWERBY BRIDGE
West Yorkshire

Lane Ends Barn ★★★
Self Catering
Contact: Ms Carola Ibbotson
t (01422) 833267
e carolalubk@hotmail.com
w laneends-selfcatering.co.uk

SPEETON
North Yorkshire

Woodbine Farm Holiday Cottages ★★★★
Self Catering
Contact: Karen Dyson
t (01723) 890783

SPROXTON
North Yorkshire

Sproxton Hall Cottages
★★★ *Self Catering*
Contact: Mr David Bowens
t (01439) 770980
e sproxtonhallcottages@btopenworld.com

STACKHOUSE
North Yorkshire

Langcliffe Locks ★★★★
Self Catering
Contact: Catherine Hibbert
t (01943) 601729
e catherine.hibbert@blueyonder.co.uk
w holidaycottage.pwp.blueyonder.co.uk

STAINFORTH
North Yorkshire

Ingle Byre (3874)
Rating Applied For
Self Catering
Contact: Ms Lorraine Kidd
t (01756) 790919
w dales-holiday-cottages.com

STAINTONDALE
North Yorkshire

White Hall Farm Holiday Cottages ★★★ *Self Catering*
Contact: Mr & Mrs James and Celia White
White Hall Farm Holiday Cottages
t (01723) 870234
e celia@white66.fsbusiness.co.uk
w whitehallcottages.co.uk

STAITHES
North Yorkshire

Glencoe Cottage ★★★
Self Catering
Contact: David Purdy
The Vicarage
t (01751) 431452

Pennysteel Cottage ★★★
Self Catering
Contact: Chris Wade
Waterfront Cottages
t (01377) 217662 & (01377) 217523
e chris@adastra-music.co.uk
w waterfrontcottages.co.uk

STAMFORD BRIDGE
East Riding of Yorkshire

The Cottage ★★★★
Self Catering
Contact: Sheila Foster
t (01759) 371374

STANBURY
West Yorkshire

Higher Scholes Cottage
★★★★★ *Self Catering*
Contact: Catherine O'Leary
t (01535) 646793
e olly@mopsy66552.freeserve.co.uk

Sarah's Cottage ★★★
Self Catering
Contact: Brian Fuller
t (01535) 643015
e brian.fuller2@btinternet.com
w sarahs-cottage.co.uk

STAPE
North Yorkshire

Kale Pot Cottage ★★★★
Self Catering
Contact: Diane & Mike Steele
t (01751) 476654
e mike@kalepothole.fsnet.co.uk

STARBOTTON
North Yorkshire

Horseshoe Cottage ★★★
Self Catering
Contact: Kevin & Lynn May
t (015396) 20877
e kevin@may1561.fsnet.co.uk

Ivy Cottage Ref: 3390
★★★★ *Self Catering*
Contact: Ms Lorraine Kidd
Dales Holiday Cottages
t 0870 909 9500
e info@dales-holiday-cottages.com
w dalesholcot.com

STILLINGTON
North Yorkshire

The Old Forge Holiday Cottage ★★★★ *Self Catering*
Contact: Annie Stirk
t (01347) 810531
e anne.stirk@btopenworld.com
w yorkholidaycottage.co.uk

Rose Cottage ★★★★
Self Catering
Contact: Susie Hamilton
t (01347) 822631
e enquiries@stillingtongrangefarm.co.uk
w stillingtongrangefarm.co.uk

STIRTON
North Yorkshire

Cockpit Corner Ref:1699
★★★ *Self Catering*
Contact: Ms Lorraine Kidd
Dales Holiday Cottages
t 0870 909 9500
e info@dales-holiday-cottages.com
w dalesholcot.com

SUTTON-ON-THE-FOREST
North Yorkshire

K M Knowlson Holiday Cottages ★★★ *Self Catering*
Contact: Heather Knowlson
t (01347) 810225
e kmkholcottyksuk@aol.com
w holidayskmkholcotts-yks.uk.com

TERRINGTON
North Yorkshire

Terrington Holiday Cottages
★★★-★★★★ *Self Catering*
Contact: Sally Goodrick
t (01653) 648370
e goodrick@terrington10.freeserve.co.uk
w terrington.com/sallycottages.html

THIRKLEBY
North Yorkshire

Thirkleby Hall Holiday Cottages ★★★ *Self Catering*
Contact: Catherine Lumb
t (01845) 501492
e info@thirklebyhall.co.uk
w thirklebyhall.co.uk

THIRN
North Yorkshire

Violet Cottage ★★★★
Self Catering
Contact: Mrs Nadine Bell
t (01969) 663559
e nadine@countryhideaways.co.uk
w countryhideaways.co.uk

THIRSK
North Yorkshire

80 St James Green ★★★
Self Catering
Contact: Joanna Todd
t (01845) 523522

Briar Cottage & Bramble Cottage ★★★ *Self Catering*
Contact: Ms Audrey Saye
t (01845) 597309
e jim.dickinson@btinternet.com

Church Garth ★★★★★
Self Catering
Contact: Vicky Hudson
Church Garth
t (01845) 587215
e svhudson@btinternet.com

The Old School House ★★★
Self Catering
Contact: Gabrielle Readman
t (01845) 567308

Pasture Field House ★★
Self Catering
Contact: Emma Hunter
t (01845) 587230
e richardhunter@fwi.co.uk

Poplars Holiday Cottages
★★★★ *Self Catering*
Contact: Chris Chilton
The Poplars Cottages
t (01845) 522712
e the_poplars_cottages@btopenworld.com
w yorkshirebandb.co.uk

Shires Court ★★★
Self Catering
Contact: Judy Rennie
t (01845) 537494

THORALBY
North Yorkshire

Coach House ★★★★
Self Catering
Contact: Mrs Nadine Bell
Country Hideaways
t (01969) 663559
e nadine@countryhideaways.co.uk
w countryhideaways.co.uk

The Garden Flat, The Old Corn Mill ★★★ *Self Catering*
Contact: Mrs Nadine Bell
Country Hideaways
t (01969) 663559
e nadine@countryhideaways.co.uk
w countryhideaways.co.uk

High Green Cottage ★★★
Self Catering
Contact: Mr Clive Sykes
t (01244) 345700
e info@sykescottages.co.uk
w sykescottages.co.uk

Meadowcroft Cottage
★★★★ *Self Catering*
Meadowcroft
t (01792) 280068
e mcmason@globalnet.co.uk
w meadowcroftcottage.co.uk

Woodpecker Cottage
★★★★ *Self Catering*
Contact: Mrs Nadine Bell
Country Hideaways
t (01969) 663559
e nadine@countryhideaways.co.uk
w countryhideaways.co.uk

THORGILL
North Yorkshire

Appledore Cottage ★★★★
Self Catering
Contact: David Glover
t (01914) 162723
e david@apledorecottage.co.uk
w appledorecottage.co.uk

THORNTON DALE
North Yorkshire

Brookwood ★★★★
Self Catering
Contact: Claire Lealman
t (01751) 474272
e baldersons@hotmail.com

Hillcroft ★★★ *Self Catering*
Contact: Lily Brookfield
t (01751) 474342
w country-holidays.co.uk

Station House Holiday Cottages ★★★–★★★★
Self Catering
Contact: Mrs Hilary Scales
t (01751) 474417
e overbrook@breathe.com

THORNTON IN CRAVEN
North Yorkshire

The Cottage Ref:2166 ★★★
Self Catering
Contact: Ms Lorraine Kidd
Dales Holiday Cottages
t 0870 909 9500
e info@dales-holiday-cottages.com
w dalesholcot.com

THORNTON RUST
North Yorkshire

Barn House ★★★★
Self Catering
Contact: Ms Annette Riley
t (01969) 663716
e info@oldgoathouse.co.uk

Nettle Cottage ★★★★★
Self Catering
Contact: Mrs Annette Riley
t (01969) 663716
e info@nettle-cottage.co.uk

The Old Goat House ★★★★
Self Catering
Contact: Annette Riley
t (01969) 663716
e info@oldgoathouse.co.uk
w oldgoathouse.co.uk

Outgang Cottage Ref:1468
★★★ *Self Catering*
Contact: Ms Lorraine Kidd
Dales Holiday Cottages
t 0870 909 9500
e info@dales-holiday-cottages.com
w dalesholcot.com

West Cottage ★★★
Self Catering
Contact: Mrs Nadine Bell
Country Hideaways
t (01969) 663559
e nadine@countryhideaways.co.uk
w countryhideaways.co.uk

THORPE BASSETT
North Yorkshire

The Old Post Office ★★★★
Self Catering
Contact: Sandra Simpson
S Simpson Cottages
t (01944) 758047
e ssimpsoncottages@aol.com
w ssimpsoncottages.co.uk

THRESHFIELD
North Yorkshire

Wharfe Lodge ★★★
Self Catering
Contact: J Mitton
t (01494) 872572

THWAITE
North Yorkshire

The Cottage ★★★
Self Catering
Contact: Mrs Nadine Bell
Country Hideaways
t (01969) 663559
e nadine@countryhideaways.co.uk
w countryhideaways.co.uk

Greystones – Askrigg Cottage Holidays ★★★★
Self Catering
Contact: Ken Williamson
Askrigg Cottage Holidays
t (01969) 650022
e stay@askrigg.com
w askrigg.com

Thwaite Farm Cottages
★★★–★★★★ *Self Catering*
Contact: Gillian Whitehead
t (01748) 886444
e info@thwaitefarmcottages.co.uk
w thwaitefarmcottages.co.uk

Thwaitedale Cottages
★★★★ *Self Catering*
Contact: Valerie Hunter
t (01530) 272794
e valerie@theturret.freeserve.co.uk
w thwaitecottages.co.uk

Turfy Gill Hall ★★★★
Self Catering
Contact: Keith & Ivy Moseley
t (01748) 886369
e info@turfygill.com
w turfygill.com

TIBTHORPE
East Riding of Yorkshire

Village Farm Cottage
★★★★ *Self Catering*
Contact: Mr Peter Durbin
Yorkshire Cottages
t (01943) 885306
e janet@yorkshire-cottages.info
w yorkshire-cottages.info

TODMORDEN
West Yorkshire

Butterworth Cottage ★★★
Self Catering
Contact: Neil & Patricia Butterworth
t (01706) 813067
e bookings@cottage-holiday.co.uk
w cottage-holiday.co.uk

The Cottage ★★★
Self Catering
Contact: Mr & Mrs Bentham
The Cottage
t (01706) 815265
e andrew-b_5@tiscali.co.uk

Shoebroad Barn ★★★
Self Catering
Contact: Mrs Horsfall
t (01706) 817015
e thehorsfalls@beeb.net
w shoebroadbarn.co.uk

Stannally Farm Cottage
★★★★ *Self Catering*
Contact: Dineen Ann Brunt
t (01706) 813998
e Bruntdennis@aol.com

Staups Barn Holiday Cottage
★★★ *Self Catering*
Contact: Mr Crabtree
t (01706) 812730
e staups1@supanet.com

TOLLERTON
North Yorkshire

Gill Cottage Ref:1977
★★★★ *Self Catering*
Contact: Ms Lorraine Kidd
Dales Holiday Cottages
t 0870 909 9500
e info@dales-holiday-cottages.com
w dalesholcot.com

TOTLEY RISE
South Yorkshire

Swallow Cottage ★★★★
Self Catering
Contact: Debbie Hill
t (0114) 236 7806
w peakcottages.com

WARLEY
West Yorkshire

Greystones Farm Cottage
★★★★ *Self Catering*
Contact: Alison Phillips
t (01422) 882445

WELBURN
North Yorkshire

Castle View ★★★
Self Catering
Contact: Michael Cockerill
t (01653) 618344

Dene Cottage & Oak Tree Cottage ★★★★ *Self Catering*
Contact: Mr Mark Rees
t (01653) 698074
e mark.rees@northyorkshire.pnn.police.uk

WENSLEY STATION
North Yorkshire

The Waiting Rooms ★★★★
Self Catering
Contact: Mrs Nadine Bell
Country Hideaways
t (01969) 663559
e nadine@countryhideaways.co.uk
w countryhideaways.co.uk

WENSLEYDALE
North Yorkshire

Mile House Farm Country Cottages ★★★★
Self Catering
Contact: Mrs Anne Fawcett
t (01969) 667481
e milehousefarm@hotmail.com

WEST AYTON
North Yorkshire

Endeavour Loft
Rating Applied For
Self Catering
Contact: Mike Joseph
t (01653) 696941
e mikejoseph7615@hotmail.com

WEST BRETTON
West Yorkshire

Parkside Cottage ★★★★
Self Catering
Contact: Philip & Joyce Platts
t (01924) 830215
e jmplatts@hotmail.com
w parksidecottage.co.uk

WEST BURTON
North Yorkshire

Cherry Tree Cottage ★★★
Self Catering
Contact: Mrs Nadine Bell
Country Hideaways
t (01969) 663559
e nadine@countryhideaways.co.uk
w countryhideaways.co.uk

Craggley Cottage ★★★★
Self Catering
Contact: Mrs Nadine Bell
Country Hideaways
t (01969) 663559
e nadine@countryhideaways.co.uk
w countryhideaways.co.uk

First Floor Apartment, The Mill ★★★ *Self Catering*
Contact: Mrs Nadine Bell
Country Hideaways
t (01969) 663559
e nadine@countryhideaways.co.uk
w countryhideaways.co.uk

The Garden Level Apartment, The Mill ★★★
Self Catering
Contact: Mrs Nadine Bell
Country Hideaways
t (01969) 663559
e nadine@countryhideaways.co.uk
w countryhideaways.co.uk

Grange House ★★★★
Self Catering
Contact: Zoe Mort
t (01969) 663641
e zeepee@beeb.net
w yorkshireholidaycottage.co.uk

Green Bank ★★★
Self Catering
Contact: Mrs Nadine Bell
Country Hideaways
t (01969) 663559
e nadine@countryhideaways.co.uk
w countryhideaways.co.uk

The Ground Floor Apartment, The Mill ★★★★
Self Catering
Contact: Mrs Nadine Bell
Country Hideaways
t (01969) 663559
e nadine@countryhideaways.co.uk
w countryhideaways.co.uk

Ivy Cottage ★★★
Self Catering
Contact: Mrs Nadine Bell
Country Hideaways
t (01969) 663559
e nadine@countryhideaways.co.uk
w countryhideaways.co.uk

Jesmond Cottage ★★★
Self Catering
Contact: Mrs Nadine Bell
Country Hideaways
t (01969) 663559
e nadine@countryhideaways.co.uk
w countryhideaways.co.uk

Penny Farthings ★★★
Self Catering
Contact: Mrs Nadine Bell
Country Hideaways
t (01969) 663559
e nadine@countryhideaways.co.uk
w countryhideaways.co.uk

Studio Apartment, The Mill ★★ *Self Catering*
Contact: Mrs Nadine Bell
Country Hideaways
t (01969) 663559
e nadine@countryhideaways.co.uk
w countryhideaways.co.uk

WEST HESLERTON
North Yorkshire

Whin Moor Cottage Ref:1575 ★★★ *Self Catering*
Contact: Ms Lorraine Kidd
Dales Holiday Cottages
t 0870 909 9500
e info@dales-holiday-cottages.com
w dalesholcot.com

WEST WITTON
North Yorkshire

1 Chestnut Garth Ref: 779 ★★★ *Self Catering*
Contact: S Boardman
Sykes Cottages
t (01244) 345700
e info@sykescottages.co.uk
w sykescottages.co.uk

Arnoldsholidaycottages ★★★ *Self Catering*
Contact: Ingrid Arnold
t (01969) 624303
e holidaycottage2004@yahoo.com
w arnoldsholidaycottages.com

Coachman's Loft ★★★★
Self Catering
Contact: Ms Carol Grieve
t (01969) 622226
e carolandsteve66@hotmail.com
w coachmansloft.co.uk

Dairy Cottage ★★★
Self Catering
Contact: Mrs Nadine Bell
Country Hideaways
t (01969) 663559
e nadine@countryhideaways.co.uk
w countryhideaways.co.uk

WETHERBY
West Yorkshire

Chestnut Chase ★★★
Self Catering
Contact: Chris Gibson
t (01937) 845781
e bob@bramham.f9.co.uk

WHASHTON
North Yorkshire

Mount Pleasant Farm ★★★-★★★★★
Self Catering
Contact: Mrs Pittaway
t (01748) 822784
e info@mountpleasantfarmhouse.co.uk

WHITBY
North Yorkshire

108 Upgang Lane ★★★
Self Catering
Contact: Ms Vanessa Hicking
Whitby Holiday Cottages
t (01947) 821122
e enquiries@whitby-cottages.co.uk
w whitby-cottages.co.uk

14 Holt Court ★★★★
Self Catering
Contact: Mrs Vanessa Hicking
Whitby Holiday Cottages
t (01947) 603010
e enquiries@whitby-cottages.co.uk
w whitby-cottages.co.uk

16 Bagdale Court ★★★★
Self Catering
Contact: Ms Vanessa Hicking
Whitby Holiday Cottages
t (01947) 821122
e enquiries@whitby-cottages.co.uk
w whitby-cottages.co.uk

18 Hunton Court ★★★★
Self Catering
Contact: Mrs Vanessa Hicking
Whitby Holiday Cottages
t (01947) 603010
e enquiries@whitby.cottages.co.uk
w whitby-cottages.co.uk

2 Pear Tree Cottages ★★★★ *Self Catering*
Contact: Ms Vanessa Hicking
Whitby Holiday Cottages
t (01947) 821122
e enquiries@whitby-cottages.co.uk
w whitby-cottages.co.uk

4 Halls Place ★★★★
Self Catering
Contact: Peter Goff
Duck Cottage (4 Halls Place)
t (01462) 641651
e peter.goff@ntlworld.com

53 Cliff Street ★★★★
Self Catering
Contact: Mrs Janet Lockwood
The Farm House
t (01430) 810663
e denis@denislockwood.freeserve.co.uk

7 Esk Terrace ★★★
Self Catering
Contact: Ms Vanessa Hicking
Whitby Holiday Cottages
t (01947) 821122
e enquiries@whitby-cottages.co.uk
w whitby-cottages.co.uk

7 Henrietta Street ★★★
Self Catering
Contact: William Usher
t (01947) 605868

Abbey Peep ★★★
Self Catering
Contact: Ms Vanessa Hicking
Whitby Holiday Cottages
t (01947) 603010
e enquiries@whitby-cottages.co.uk

Abbey View ★★★
Self Catering
Contact: Peter Simpson
t (01947) 604406
e info@southviewcottages.co.uk

Abbey View ★★★★
Self Catering
Contact: Ms Vanessa Hicking
Whitby Holiday Cottages
t (01947) 821122
e enquiries@whitby-cottages.co.uk
w whitby-cottages.co.uk

Abbey View Cottage ★★★★ *Self Catering*
Contact: Mr David Haycox
Shoreline Cottages Ltd
t (0113) 244 8410
e reservations@shoreline-cottages.com
w shoreline-cottages.com

Acacia House ★★★★
Self Catering
Contact: Ms Vanessa Hicking
Whitby Holiday Cottages
t (01947) 821122
e enquiries@whitby-cottages.co.uk
w whitby-cottages.co.uk

Admirals Lookout ★★★★
Self Catering
Contact: Mrs Vanessa Hicking
Whitby Holiday Cottages
t (01947) 603010
e enquiries@whitby-cottages.co.uk

Albany House ★★★★
Self Catering
Contact: Ms Vanessa Hicking
Whitby Holiday Cottages
t (01947) 821122
e enquiries@whitby-cottages.co.uk
w whitby-cottages.co.uk

Allum Garth Cottage ★★★★ *Self Catering*
Contact: Barbara Tyerman
Allum Garth Cottage
t (01947) 810450
e barbara@partridgenestfarm.com
w partridgenestfarm.com

Ambler Mews ★★★
Self Catering
Contact: Ms Vanessa Hicking
Whitby Holiday Cottages
t (01947) 821122
e enquiries@whitby-cottages.co.uk
w whitby-cottages.co.uk

Ammonite Apartments ★★★★ *Self Catering*
t (01947) 820497
e enquiries@ammonite-apartments.co.uk

Apartment 2, Moss Brow House ★★★★ *Self Catering*
Contact: Mr & Mrs M & A Mandelj
t (01924) 860550
e info@mossbrow.co.uk
w mossbrow.co.uk

Appleton Cottage ★★★★
Self Catering
Contact: Ms Vanessa Hicking
Whitby Holiday Cottages
t (01947) 821122
e enquiries@whitby-cottages.co.uk
w whitby-cottages.co.uk

April Cottage ★★★
Self Catering
Contact: Ms Vanessa Hicking
Whitby Holiday Cottages
t (01947) 821122
e enquiries@whitby-cottages.co.uk
w whitby-cottages.co.uk

At Long Last
Rating Applied For
Self Catering
Contact: Ms Vanessa Hicking
Whitby Holiday Cottages
t (01947) 603010
e enquiries@whitby-cottages.co.uk

Bakehouse Cottage ★★★★
Self Catering
Contact: Mr David Haycox
Shoreline Cottages Ltd
t (0113) 244 8410
e reservations@shoreline-cottages.com
w shoreline-cottages.com

Beckside Holiday Cottage ★★★★ *Self Catering*
Contact: Kathryn Hogarth
Beckside Cottage
t (01947) 897259
e jhnhogarth@aol.com

The Boat House ★★★★
Self Catering
Contact: Ms Vanessa Hicking
Whitby Holiday Cottages
t (01947) 821122
e enquiries@whitby-cottages.co.uk
w whitby-cottages.co.uk

Bolthole Cottage ★★★
Self Catering
t (01947) 880063
e kaaren@noble47.freeserve.co.uk
w boltholecottage.co.uk

Borough House ★★★★
Self Catering
Contact: Julie Besford
Julie Besford (Sole Trader)
t (01430) 430963
e jdgreenhalgh@tiscali.co.uk

Brecon Cottage ★★★
Self Catering
Contact: Ms Vanessa Hicking
Whitby Holiday Cottages
t (01947) 821122
e enquiries@whitby-cottages.co.uk
w whitby-cottages.co.uk

Broadings Farm Cottages
★★★★ *Self Catering*
t (01947) 601542
e info@broadingsfarm.co.uk
w broadingsfarmcottages.co.uk

Brook House Farm Holiday Cottages ★★★★
Self Catering
Contact: Sallie White
t (01287) 660064
e white.j@lineone.net
w stablecottage.net

Camden House Holiday Apartments ★★★
Self Catering
t (01947) 820233
e zig.star@virgin.net

Captain Cook's Haven
★★★–★★★★ *Self Catering*
Contact: Anne Barrowman
t (01947) 893573
w whitbyholidayhomes.co.uk

Captain's Quarters
★★★★★ *Self Catering*
Contact: Mr David Haycox
Shoreline Cottages Ltd
t (0113) 244 8410
e reservations@shoreline-cottages.com
w shoreline-cottages.com

The Captains View ★★★
Self Catering
Contact: Ms Vanessa Hicking
Whitby Holiday Cottages
t (01947) 821122
e enquiries@whitby-cottages.co.uk
w whitby-cottages.co.uk

Carlton House Holiday Accommodation ★–★★★★
Self Catering
Contact: Susan Brookes
Carlton House Holiday Accommodation
t (01947) 602868 & (01947) 603456
e info@carltonhouseapartments.co.uk
w northstaraccommodation.co.uk

Casa Romantica
Rating Applied For
Self Catering
Contact: Ms Vanessa Hicking
Whitby Holiday Cottages
t (01947) 603010
e enquiries@whitby.cottages.co.uk

Chimes Apartment ★★★
Self Catering
Contact: Ms Vanessa Hicking
Whitby Holiday Cottages
t (01947) 821122
e enquiries@whitby-cottages.co.uk
w whitby-cottages.co.uk

Church Cottage ★★★
Self Catering
Contact: Ms Vanessa Hicking
Whitby Holiday Cottages
t (01947) 821122
e enquiries@whitby-cottages.co.uk
w whitby-cottages.co.uk

Clematis Cottage ★★
Self Catering
Contact: Ms Vanessa Hicking
Whitby Holiday Cottages
t (01947) 821122
e enquiries@whitby-cottages.co.uk
w whitby-cottages.co.uk

Cliff House ★★ *Self Catering*
Contact: Pat Beale
t (01947) 810534
w cliffhousewhitby.co.uk

Coble Cottage ★★★
Self Catering
Contact: Ms Vanessa Hicking
Whitby Holiday Cottages
t (01947) 821122
e enquiries@whitby-cottages.co.uk
w whitby-cottages.co.uk

Copper Beeches ★★–★★★
Self Catering
Contact: Hilary Walker
The Hayloft
t (01947) 895640
e hilary_phenix@hotmail.com
w copperbeeches.com

The Cottage
Rating Applied For
Self Catering
Contact: Ms Vanessa Hicking
Whitby Holiday Cottages
t (01947) 603010
e enquiries@whitby-cottages.co.uk

Crows Nest Apartments
★★★ *Self Catering*
Contact: Mr Eric Tayler
t (01642) 492144
e crowsnest.whitby@ntlworld.com

Cuddy Cottage ★★★★
Self Catering
Contact: Mr David Haycox
Shoreline Cottages Ltd
t (0113) 244 8410
e reservations@shoreline-cottages.com
w shoreline-cottages.com

Discovery Accommodation
★★★★ *Self Catering*
Contact: Pam Gilmore
t (01947) 821598
e pam@discoveryaccommodation.com
w discoveryaccommodation.com

East Cliff Cottages ★★★
Self Catering
Contact: Joe Crocker
t (01653) 658249
e j.crocker@lineone.net
w eastcliffcottages.co.uk

Elizabeth House Holiday Flats ★★★–★★★★
Self Catering
Contact: Rosaline Cooper
t (01947) 604168
e jakanann@btopenworld.com
w elizabeth-house.biz

Endeavour Cottage ★★★
Self Catering
Contact: Mrs Adele Thompson
Whitby Holiday Cottages
t (01947) 603010
e enquiries@whitby-cottages.co.uk
w whitby-cottages.co.uk

Evelyn House
Rating Applied For
Self Catering
Contact: Jennifer Redway
t (01947) 897282
e jennyredway@hotmail.com
w evelynhousewhitby.co.uk

Explorers Rest ★★★★
Self Catering
Contact: Mrs Vanessa Hicking
Whitby Holiday Cottages
t (01947) 603010
e enquiries@whitby-cottages.co.uk
w whitby-cottages.co.uk

Fayvan Holiday Apartments
★★★★ *Self Catering*
Contact: Ian & Pauline Moore
t (01947) 604813
e info@fayvan.co.uk
w fayvan.co.uk

Fishermans Warehouse
★★★★ *Self Catering*
Contact: Ms Vanessa Hicking
Whitby Holiday Cottages
t (01947) 603010
e enquiries@whitby-cottages.co.uk

Foresters House ★★★★
Self Catering
Dales Holiday Cottages
t 0870 909 9500
e fiona@dales-holiday-cottages.com
w dalesholcot.com

Glencoe – Garden Flat
★★★★ *Self Catering*
Contact: Julie Charlton
t (01947) 811531
w holidayflat.co.uk

Glencoe Holiday Flats
★★–★★★ *Self Catering*
Contact: Julie Charlton
Glencoe Holiday Flats
t (01947) 811531 & (01947) 602474
w holidayflat.co.uk

Grange Farm Holiday Cottage ★★★★ *Self Catering*
Contact: D Hooning
t (01947) 881080
e info@grangefarm.net
w grangefarm.net

Graymount House ★★★★
Self Catering
Contact: Jackie Byers
NorthStar Accommodation
t (01947) 603456
e info@northstaraccommodation.co.uk
w northstaraccommodation.co.uk

Griffin Cottage ★★★★
Self Catering
Contact: Ms Vanessa Hicking
Whitby Holiday Cottages
t (01947) 821122
e enquiries@whitby-cottages.co.uk
w whitby-cottages.co.uk

Harbour Lights ★★★★
Self Catering
Contact: Ms Vanessa Hicking
Whitby Holiday Cottages
t (01947) 821122
e enquiries@whitby-cottages.co.uk
w whitby-cottages.co.uk

Harbourside Apartments
★★★–★★★★ *Self Catering*
Contact: Ian & June Roberts
t (01947) 810763
e marketing@whiterosecottages.co.uk
w whitbyharbourapartments.co.uk

Harbourside Cottage ★★★
Self Catering
Contact: Ms Vanessa Hicking
Whitby Holiday Cottages
t (01947) 821122
e enquiries@whitby-cottages.co.uk
w whitby-cottages.co.uk

The Haven ★★★★ *Self Catering & Serviced Apartments*
Contact: Ms Vanessa Hicking
Whitby Holiday Cottages
t (01947) 821122
e enquiries@whitby-cottages.co.uk
w whitby-cottages.co.uk

Haven Cottage ★★★★
Self Catering
Contact: Ms Vanessa Hicking
Whitby Holiday Cottages
t (01947) 821122
e enquiries@whitby-cottages.co.uk
w whitby-cottages.co.uk

Henrietta Cottage ★★★★
Self Catering
Contact: Mr David Haycox
Shoreline Cottages Ltd
t (0113) 244 8410
e reservations@shoreline-cottages.com
w shoreline-cottages.com

Herons Reach ★★★★
Self Catering
Contact: Ms Vanessa Hicking
Whitby Holiday Cottages
t (01947) 603010
e enquiries@whitby-cottages.co.uk

The Hideaway ★★★
Self Catering
Contact: Ms Vanessa Hicking
Whitby Holiday Cottages
t (01947) 821122
e enquiries@whitby-cottages.co.uk
w whitby-cottages.co.uk

Hideaway Cottage ★★★
Self Catering
Contact: Mrs Vanessa Hicking
Whitby Holiday Cottages
t (01947) 603010
e enquiries@whitby-cottages.co.uk
w whitby-cottages.co.uk

Hightrees Garden Apartment ★★★★
Self Catering
Contact: Sarah Elizabeth Clancy
t (01947) 601926
e seclancy@yahoo.co.uk

Jet Apartment ★★★★
Self Catering
Contact: Ms Vanessa Hicking
Whitby Holiday Cottages
t (01947) 603010
e enquiries@whitby-cottages.co.uk

Jet Cottage ★★★
Self Catering
Contact: Mrs Vanessa Hicking
Whitby Holiday Cottages
t (01947) 603010
e enquiries@whitby-cottages.co.uk
w whitby-cottages.co.uk

Kauri Cottage ★★★★
Self Catering
Contact: Christine Holmes
t (01484) 720912
e stones1397@aol.com
w whitbyholidaycottages.org

Kiln Cottage ★★★★
Self Catering
Contact: Mr David Haycox
Shoreline Cottages Ltd
t (0113) 244 8410
e reservations@shoreline-cottages.com
w shoreline-cottages.com

Kingfisher Cottage
Self Catering
Holiday Accommodation Agency
t (01723) 376777
e info@ingridflute.co.uk
w ingridflute.co.uk

Kipper Cottage ★★★★
Self Catering
Contact: Ms Vanessa Hicking
Whitby Holiday Cottages
t (01947) 821122
e enquiries@whitby-cottages.co.uk
w whitby-cottages.co.uk

Ladybird Cottage ★★★
Self Catering
Contact: Ms Vanessa Hicking
Whitby Holiday Cottages
t (01947) 821122
e enquiries@whitby-cottages.co.uk
w whitby-cottages.co.uk

The Lamp House ★★★★
Self Catering
Contact: Ms Vanessa Hicking
Whitby Holiday Cottages
t (01947) 821122
e enquiries@whitby-cottages.co.uk
w whitby-cottages.co.uk

Lantern Cottage ★★★★
Self Catering
Contact: Ms Vanessa Hicking
Whitby Holiday Cottages
t (01947) 821122
e enquiries@whitby-cottages.co.uk
w whitby-cottages.co.uk

Little Whitehall ★★★★
Self Catering
Contact: Ms Vanessa Hicking
Whitby Holiday Cottages
t (01947) 821122
e enquiries@whitby-cottages.co.uk
w whitby-cottages.co.uk

The Lobster Pot ★★★
Self Catering
Contact: Mrs Vanessa Hicking
Whitby Holiday Cottages
t (01947) 603010
e enquiries@whitby-cottages.co.uk

Loen Cottage Ref:3418
★★★ *Self Catering*
Contact: Ms Lorraine Kidd
Dales Holiday Cottages
t 0870 909 9500
e info@dales-holiday-cottages.com
w dalesholcot.com

The Lookout ★★
Self Catering
Contact: Ms Vanessa Hicking
Whitby Holiday Cottages
t (01947) 821122
e enquiries@whitby-cottages.co.uk
w whitby-cottages.co.uk

Lupine Cottage ★★★
Self Catering
Contact: Mrs Vanessa Hicking
Whitby Holiday Cottages
t (01947) 603010
e enquiries@whitbh-cottages.co.uk

Manor Cottage
Rating Applied For
Self Catering
Contact: Jackie Byers
NorthStar Accommodation
t (01947) 603456
e info@northstaraccommodation.co.uk
w northstaraccommodation.co.uk

Manor Cottage Ref:2448
★★★★ *Self Catering*
Contact: Ms Lorraine Kidd
Dales Holiday Cottages
t 0870 909 9500
e info@dales-holiday-cottages.com
w dalesholcot.com

Margherita Cottage ★★★
Self Catering
t (01947) 825400
e info@margheritacottage.co.uk
w margheritacottage.co.uk

Marina Cottage ★★★
Self Catering
Contact: Mrs Vanessa Hicking
Whitby Holiday Cottages
t (01947) 603010
e enquiries@whitby-cottages.co.uk

Mariner Cottage ★★★
Self Catering
Contact: Ms Vanessa Hicking
Whitby Holiday Cottages
t (01947) 821122
e enquiries@whitby-cottages.co.uk
w whitby-cottages.co.uk

Mariner's Cottage ★★★★
Self Catering
Contact: Mr David Haycox
Shoreline Cottages Ltd
t (0113) 244 8410
e reservations@shoreline-cottages.com
w shoreline-cottages.com

Market Place Apartment
★★★ *Self Catering*
Contact: Ms Vanessa Hicking
Whitby Holiday Cottages
t (01947) 821122
e enquiries@whitby-cottages.co.uk
w whitby-cottages.co.uk

Midships ★★★ *Self Catering*
Contact: Ms Vanessa Hicking
Whitby Holiday Cottages
t (01947) 821122
e enquiries@whitby-cottages.co.uk
w whitby-cottages.co.uk

Minstead Cottage
Rating Applied For
Self Catering
Contact: Mrs Vanessa Hicking
Whitby Holiday Cottages
t (01947) 603010
e enquiries@whitby-cottages.co.uk
w whitby-cottages.co.uk

Moor Peep ★★★
Self Catering
Contact: Ms Vanessa Hicking
Whitby Holiday Cottages
t (01947) 603010
e enquiries@whitby-cottages.co.uk

The Moorings ★★★★
Self Catering
Contact: Ms Vanessa Hicking
Whitby Holiday Cottages
t (01947) 821122
e enquiries@whitby-cottages.co.uk
w whitby-cottages.co.uk

Nans Cottage ★★★★
Self Catering
Contact: Ms Vanessa Hicking
Whitby Holiday Cottages
t (01947) 821122
e enquiries@whitby-cottages.co.uk
w whitby-cottages.co.uk

New Hills Ref:2586 ★★★
Self Catering
Contact: Ms Lorraine Kidd
Dales Holiday Cottages
t 0870 909 9500
e info@dales-holiday-cottages.com
w dalesholcot.com

Nobles Cottage ★★★★
Self Catering
Contact: Ms Vanessa Hicking
Whitby Holiday Cottages
t (01947) 821122
e enquiries@whitby-cottages.co.uk
w whitby-cottages.co.uk

Old Boatman's Shelter
★★★★ *Self Catering*
Contact: Alison Halidu
t (01947) 811089
e oldboatshelter@aol.com

Old Brewery Cottage
★★★★ *Self Catering*
Contact: Mrs Vanessa Hicking
Whitby Holiday Cottages
t (01947) 603010
e enquiries@whitby-cottages.co.uk

The Old Granary ★★★★
Self Catering
Contact: Mrs Jackie Richardson
t (01947) 893331
e jackie.richardson6@btopenworld.com

Olive Tree Cottage ★★★★
Self Catering
Contact: Ms Vanessa Hicking
Whitby Holiday Cottages
t (01947) 821122
e enquiries@whitby-cottages.co.uk
w whitby-cottages.co.uk

Pantiles ★★★★ *Self Catering*
Contact: Peter & Alison Lawson
t (0131) 446 0225
e pantileswhitby@blueyonder.co.uk
w pantileswhitby.pwp.blueyonder.co.uk

Penny Hedge House Ref:2994 ★★★★
Self Catering
Contact: Ms Lorraine Kidd
Dales Holiday Cottages
t 0870 909 9500
e info@dales-holiday-cottages.com
w dalesholcot.com

Perkins Cottage ★★★
Self Catering
Contact: Ms Vanessa Hicking
Whitby Holiday Cottages
t (01947) 821122
e enquiries@whitby-cottages.co.uk
w whitby-cottages.co.uk

Prince of Wales Cottage
★★★★ *Self Catering*
Contact: Mr David Haycox
Shoreline Cottages Ltd
t (0113) 244 8410
e reservations@shoreline-cottages.com
w shoreline-cottages.com

Puzzle Corner Ref:1679
★★★ *Self Catering*
Contact: Ms Lorraine Kidd
Dales Holiday Cottages
t 0870 909 9500
e info@dales-holiday-cottages.com
w dalesholcot.com

Quayside Cottage ★★★★
Self Catering
Contact: Mr David Haycox
Shoreline Cottages Ltd
t (0113) 244 8410
e reservations@shoreline-cottages.com
w shoreline-cottages.com

The Red House ★★★
Self Catering
Contact: Ms Vanessa Hicking
Whitby Holiday Cottages
t (01947) 821122
e enquiries@whitby-cottages.co.uk
w whitby-cottages.co.uk

Riverside ★★★★
Self Catering
Contact: Mrs Vanessa Hicking
Whitby Holiday Cottages
t (01947) 603010
e enquiries@whitby-cottages.co.uk
w whitby-cottages.co.uk

Riverside View ★★★★
Self Catering
Contact: Ms Vanessa Hicking
Whitby Holiday Cottages
t (01947) 821122
e enquiries@whitby-cottages.co.uk
w whitby-cottages.co.uk

Robin Hood's Bay Cottages
★★★ *Self Catering*
Contact: Mrs Jean Speight
t (0113) 277 5853

Rope Cottage ★★★★
Self Catering
Contact: Mrs Vanessa Hicking
Whitby Holiday Cottages
t (01947) 603010
e enquiries@whitby-cottages.co.uk
w whitby-cottages.co.uk

Sailing By ★★★ *Self Catering*
Contact: Ms Vanessa Hicking
Whitby Holiday Cottages
t (01947) 821122
e enquiries@whitby-cottages.co.uk
w whitby-cottages.co.uk

St Joseph's Cottage
★★★★★ *Self Catering*
Contact: Mr David Haycox
Shoreline Cottages Ltd
t (0113) 244 8410
e reservations@shoreline-cottages.com
w shoreline-cottages.com

Sandglass Cottage ★★★★
Self Catering
Shoreline Cottages Ltd
t (01279) 324146
e trisha.young@ntlworld.com

Seagull Cottage ★★★
Self Catering
Contact: Ms Vanessa Hicking
Whitby Holiday Cottages
t (01947) 821122
e enquiries@whitby-cottages.co.uk
w whitby-cottages.co.uk

Seagull Cottage ★★★★
Self Catering
Contact: Ms Vanessa Hicking
Whitby Holiday Cottages
t (01947) 821122
e enquiries@whitby-cottages.co.uk
w whitby-cottages.co.uk

Seagull Cottage ★★★★
Self Catering
Contact: Mr David Haycox
Shoreline Cottages Ltd
t (0113) 244 8410
e reservations@shoreline-cottages.com
w shoreline-cottages.com

Seal Cottage ★★★
Self Catering
Contact: Ms Vanessa Hicking
Whitby Holiday Cottages
t (01947) 603010
e enquiries@whitby-cottages.co.uk

Southern Cross ★★★
Self Catering
Contact: Ms Vanessa Hicking
Whitby Holiday Cottages
t (01947) 821122
e enquiries@whitby-cottages.co.uk
w whitby-cottages.co.uk

Spring Vale ★★★★
Self Catering
Contact: Mr David Haycox
Shoreline Cottages Ltd
t (0113) 244 8410
e reservations@shoreline-cottages.com
w shoreline-cottages.com

Stable Cottage ★★★★
Self Catering
Contact: Martin & Chrissie Warner
t (01947) 602660
e info@sandfieldhousefarm.co.uk
w sandfieldhousefarm.co.uk

Steps Cottage ★★★
Self Catering
Contact: Ms Vanessa Hicking
Whitby Holiday Cottages
t (01947) 821122
e enquiries@whitby-cottages.co.uk
w whitby-cottages.co.uk

Storm Cottage ★★
Self Catering
Contact: Ms Vanessa Hicking
Whitby Holiday Cottages
t (01947) 821122
e enquiries@whitby-cottages.co.uk
w whitby-cottages.co.uk

Studio Flat 6 ★★★
Self Catering
Contact: Ms Vanessa Hicking
Whitby Holiday Cottages
t (01947) 821122
e enquiries@whitby-cottages.co.uk
w whitby-cottages.co.uk

Swallow Cottage ★★★★
Self Catering
Contact: Ms Vanessa Hicking
Whitby Holiday Cottages
t (01947) 821122
e enquiries@whitby-cottages.co.uk
w whitby-cottages.co.uk

Swallow Holiday Cottages
Self Catering
Contact: Jillian McNeil
Swallow Holiday Cottages
t (01947) 603790
e Jillian@swallowcottages.co.uk
w swallowcottages.co.uk

Swanning Off ★★★
Self Catering
Contact: Mrs Vanessa Hicking
Whitby Holiday Cottages
t (01947) 603010
e enquiries@whitby-cottages.co.uk

Thimble Cottage, 15 Loggerhead Yard ★★
Self Catering
Contact: Tony & Janice Hill
t (0114) 296 2383
e tony@tht.co.uk

The Two Belles ★★★
Self Catering
Contact: Mrs Vanessa Hicking
Whitby Holiday Cottages
t (01947) 603010
e enquiries@whitby-cottages.co.uk
w whitby-cottages.co.uk

Tyremans Return ★★★
Self Catering
Contact: Ms Vanessa Hicking
Whitby Holiday Cottages
t (01947) 821122
e enquiries@whitby-cottages.co.uk
w whitby-cottages.co.uk

Walkers Cottage ★★★★
Self Catering
Contact: Suzanne Walker
t (01293) 885285
e a&swalker@walkerscottage.com
w walkerscottage.com

The Waterfront ★★★★
Self Catering
Contact: Ms Vanessa Hicking
Whitby Holiday Cottages
t (01947) 603010
e enquiries@whitby-cottages.co.uk

The Watermark Apartments
Rating Applied For
Self Catering
Contact: Mrs Julie Anne Purcell
t (01947) 841191
e thewatermark@fsmail.net
w thewatermark.net

Waters Edge ★★★★
Self Catering
Contact: Ms Vanessa Hicking
Whitby Holiday Cootages
t (01947) 603010

Waverley ★★★★
Self Catering
Contact: Ms Vanessa Hicking
Whitby Holiday Cottages
t (01947) 821122
e enquiries@whitby-cottages.co.uk
w whitby-cottages.co.uk

West End Cottage ★★★★
Self Catering
Contact: Mr David Haycox
Shoreline Cottages Ltd
t (0113) 244 8410
e reservations@shoreline-cottages.com
w shoreline-cottages.com

Westlan Limited ★★★
Self Catering
Contact: Mr Trevor West
t (01977) 709328
e trev.aly@btopenworld.com

Whitby Lighthouse Cottages
★★★★★ *Self Catering*
Contact: Mary Garne
Rural Retreats
t (01386) 701177
e info@ruralretreats.co.uk
w ruralretreats.co.uk

Whitby Retreats – Grape Lane ★★★★ *Self Catering*
Contact: Mr & Mrs Nick & Emma Jaques
t (0113) 225 0798
e info@whitbyretreats.co.uk

White Cottages ★★★
Self Catering
Contact: Ms Vanessa Hicking
Whitby Holiday Cottages
t (01947) 821122
e enquiries@whitby-cottages.co.uk
w whitby-cottages.co.uk

White Horse Cottage ★★★
Self Catering
Contact: George & Steven Walker
White Horse Cottage
t (01709) 367031

White Rose Holiday Cottages ★★★–★★★★
Self Catering
Contact: June Roberts
t (01947) 810763
e enquiries@whiterosecottages.co.uk
w whiterosecottages.co.uk

WHITWELL-ON-THE-HILL
North Yorkshire

The Hay Loft ★★★
Self Catering
Contact: Anne Polley
t (01653) 618324
e anne.polley1@btopenworld.com

WILTON
North Yorkshire

Willow Bungalow (3941)
★★★★ *Self Catering*
Dales Holiday Cottages
t 0870 909 9500
e fiona@dales-holiday-cottages.com
w dalesholcot.com

WINKSLEY
North Yorkshire

Meadow View Cottage
★★★ *Self Catering*
Contact: Les Broadbent
t (01274) 541622

WOLD NEWTON
East Riding of Yorkshire

The Curate's Cottage Ref: 3669 ★★★★ *Self Catering*
Contact: Mrs Fiona Moody
Dales Holiday Cottages
t 0870 909 9500
e fiona@dalesholcot.com
w dalesholcot.com

WOMBLETON
North Yorkshire

Cruck Cottage ★★
Self Catering
Dales Holiday Cottages
t 0870 909 9500
e fiona@dales-holiday-cottages.com
w dalesholcot.com

Rosebud Cottage ★★★★
Self Catering
Contact: Christine Hartup
t (01751) 431033
e christine.hartup@rosebud-holiday-cottage.co.uk
w rosebud-holiday-cottage.co.uk

WORSBROUGH
South Yorkshire

Delf Cottage ★★★★
Self Catering
Contact: Julie Elmhirst
t (01226) 282430
e t.elmhirst@btinternet.com
w delfcottage.co.uk

WORTON
North Yorkshire

Stoney End Cottage ★★★★
Self Catering
Contact: Mike & Pamela Hague
Stoney End Holidays
t (01969) 650652
e pmh@stoneyend.co.uk
w stoneyend.co.uk

WRELTON
North Yorkshire

Croft Head Cottage ★★★★
Self Catering
Contact: Sue & Chris Halstead
t (01751) 477918
e crofthead2005@yahoo.co.uk

Hallgarth ★★★★
Self Catering
Contact: Carol Marsh
t (01751) 476081

Rocklands Lodges
★★★-★★★★ *Self Catering*
Contact: Jen & Paul Cusworth
t (01751) 477621
e info@rocklandslodges.co.uk
w rocklandslodges.co.uk

Vale Cottage ★★★★
Self Catering
Contact: Thomas & Jean Scaling
t (01751) 473792
e jeanscaling@btinternet.com
w cottageguide.co.uk/valecottage

Wayside ★★★ *Self Catering*
Contact: Mr & Mrs Kevin & Julie Honchardenko
t (01302) 770599
e khoncharenko@aol.com

WRESSLE
East Riding of Yorkshire

Grange Farm Cottages
★★★★ *Self Catering*
Contact: Neil & Jo Battye
t (01757) 630311
e grangecottages@aol.com
w grangefarmcottageswressle.co.uk

YAPHAM
East Riding of Yorkshire

Wolds View Holiday Cottages ★★★★-★★★★★
Self Catering
Contact: Margaret Woodliffe
t (01759) 302172
e info@woldsview.co.uk

YORK
North Yorkshire

1 Cloisters Walk ★★★
Self Catering
Contact: Helen Jones
Holidayork
t (01904) 632660
e agents@holidayork.com
w holidayork.com

145 Mount Vale ★★★★
Self Catering
Contact: Helen Jones
Holidayork
t (01904) 632660
e agents@holidayork.com
w holidayork.com

15 Stonegate Court
★★★★★ *Self Catering*
Contact: Susan Kitchener
York Luxury Holidays
t (01904) 766789
e sue@yorkluxuryholidays.co.uk
w yorkluxuryholidays.co.uk

17 Escrick Street ★★★
Self Catering
Contact: Helen Jones
Holidayork
t (01904) 632660
e agents@holidayork.co.uk
w holidayork.co.uk

24 Woodsmill Quay ★★★★
Self Catering
Contact: Mrs Helen Jones
Holidayork
t (01904) 632660
e agents@holidayork.co.uk
w holidayork.co.uk

29 Richardson Street ★★★
Self Catering
Contact: Helen Jones
Holidayork
t (01904) 632660
e agents@holidayork.com
w holidayork.co.uk

3 Cloisters Walk ★★★
Self Catering
Contact: Ms Vanessa Warn
t (01904) 331479
e vanessawarn@yahoo.com
w yorkholidaylets.com

414 Westgate ★★★★
Self Catering
Contact: Helen Jones
Holidayork
t (01904) 632660
e agents@holidayork.com
w holidayork.co.uk

43 Postern Close ★★★★★
Self Catering
Contact: Gordon & Hilary Jones
t (01904) 702043
e hilary@yorkcloisters.com
w yorkcloisters.com

44 Postern Close ★★★★
Self Catering
Contact: Christine Turner
t (01954) 201218
e c.turner@gurdon.cam.ac.uk
w yorkholidayflat.co.uk

6 Monkbridge Court ★★★★
Self Catering
Contact: Angela Bush
Burtonfields Hall
t (01759) 371308
e angelabush@monkbridge.co.uk
w monkbridge.co.uk

6 Stonegate Court ★★★★★
Self Catering
Contact: Susan Kitchener
York Luxury Holidays
t (01904) 766789
e sue@yorkluxuryholidays.co.uk
w yorkluxuryholidays.co.uk

9 & 10 Cloisters Walk
★★★★ *Self Catering*
Contact: Gordon & Hilary Jones
t (01904) 702043
e hilary@yorkcloisters.com

9 Waterfront House, York
★★★★★ *Self Catering*
Contact: Mrs Veronica Lotbiniere
t (01842) 814215
e info@lignacite.co.uk

Abbeygate House ★★★★★
Self Catering
Contact: Mr & Mrs Halliday
t (0113) 258 9833

Ambassador Court
★★★★★ *Self Catering & Serviced Apartments*
Contact: Ms Cathryn Houghton
City Lets
t (01904) 652729
e info@cityletsyork.co.uk
w pfp-group.co.uk

Ambler York Riverside Apartment ★★★★
Self Catering
Contact: Peter & Elizabeth Jackson
Ambler York Riverside Apartment
t (01757) 268207 & 07885 921691
e pajack@lineone.net
w yorkriversideholidayflat.co.uk

The Apartment in York
★★★★ *Self Catering*
t 07967 092726
e info@theapartmentinyork.co.uk
w theapartmentinyork.co.uk

Ashling House ★★★★★
Self Catering
Contact: Mr Ian Addyman
t (01904) 706083
e info@yorkselfcatering.fsnet.co.uk

Assam House ★★★★★
Self Catering
Contact: Clare Proctor
t (01904) 700610
e cap@whsmithnet.co.uk
w assamhouse.co.uk

Baile Hill Cottage ★★★
Self Catering
Contact: Paul Hodgson
Baile Hill Cottage
t (01904) 448670
e enquiries@holiday-cottage.org.uk
w holiday-cottage.org.uk

Baille Hill House ★★★★★
Self Catering
Contact: Tony Thomas
t (01845) 597614
e enquiries@baillehillhouse.co.uk
w baillehillhouse.co.uk

Barbican Mews ★★★
Self Catering
Contact: Helen Jones
Holidayork
t (01904) 632660
e agents@holidayork.com
w holidayork.co.uk

Bay Tree House ★★★★
Self Catering
Contact: Clare Arnold
t (01904) 659462
e info@baytree-york.co.uk
w baytreehouse-york.co.uk

Betty's York Holiday Flat
★★★ *Self Catering*
Contact: Mrs Betty Lutyens-Humphrey
t 07768 137088
e betty@holidayflatyork.co.uk
w holidayflatyork.co.uk

Bishopgate Pavilion-Bishops Wharf, York ★★★★★
Self Catering
Contact: John Graham
Bishopgate Pavilion-Bishops Wharf
t 07973 857187
e john@johnkgraham.com
w johnkgraham.com

The Blue Rooms ★★★★
Self Catering
Contact: Miss Kirsty Reid
The Blue Bicycle York Ltd
t (01904) 673990
e blue-rooms@thebluebicycle.com
w thebluebicycle.com

Carlton House ★★★★
Self Catering
Contact: Kathryn Nevell
York Self-catering Carlton House
t (01227) 763308
e knevell@aol.com

Castlegate Apartment
★★★★★ *Self Catering*
Contact: Maureen Hardy
Unique Stays
t (01904) 652664 & 07786 065286
e info@unique-stays.co.uk
w unique-stays.co.uk

Centre York Cottages
★★-★★★ *Self Catering*
Contact: William Richardson
t (01759) 388280
e william@centre-yorkcottages.fsnet.co.uk
w centre-yorkcottages.fsnet.co.uk

Chestnut Farm Holiday Cottages ★★★★
Self Catering
Contact: Alison Smith
t (01904) 704676
e enquiries@chestnutfarmholidaypark.co.uk
w yorkholidaycottages.co.uk

Classique Select Holiday Apartments ★★★
Self Catering
Contact: Mr Rodney Inns
t (01904) 421339
e rodela_2194_inns@hotmail.com
w classique-york.co.uk

Colonia Holidays ★★★
Self Catering
Contact: Margaret Booth
t (01904) 738579

Crambeck Court ★★★★
Self Catering
Contact: Mrs Helen Jones
Holidayork
t (01904) 632660
e agents@holidayork.co.uk
w holidayork.co.uk

Emperors Wharf ★★★★
Self Catering
Contact: Mrs Helen Jones
Homefinders Holidays
t (01904) 632660
e agent@homefindersholidays.co.uk

Fairfax Corner ★★★★
Self Catering
Contact: Bill & Shan Rigby
t (01482) 862085
e rigby@york.netkonect.co.uk

Flat 24 Middleton House
★★★★ *Self Catering*
Contact: Carole Bowes
t (01845) 597334
e rce.bowes@lineone.net
w yorkcityflat.co.uk

The Garden Cottage ★★★★
Self Catering
Contact: Ann Hart
t (01904) 413353
e ann@yorkgardencottage.co.uk
w yorkgardencottage.co.uk

Grosvenor and Grosvenor York Holiday Let ★★★
Self Catering
Contact: Faye Grosvenor
t (01904) 691171

Hilary's Holiday Homes (Riverhaven & The Moorings) ★★★★
Self Catering
Contact: Mrs Hilary Kernohan
Duncanne House
t 07710 147665
e hak@btconnect.com

The Juniper ★★★★★
Self Catering
Contact: Matthew Waite
t 07871 728319
e thejuniper@hotmail.co.uk
w thejuniper.co.uk

Knowle House Apartments
★★ *Self Catering*
Contact: Greg Harrand
Hedley House Hotel
t 0800 583 6374
e greg@hedleyhouse.com
w hedleyhouse.com

A Luxury Apartment in York
Rating Applied For
Self Catering
Contact: Rita Ardron
t (0161) 330 9303 & 07790 603767
e rita@aluxuryapartmentinyork.com
w aluxuryapartmentinyork.com

Mayfield Cottage ★★★
Self Catering
Contact: Lorraine McDonald
No.3 The Brae
t (01786) 818994
e losmcd@hotmail.com

Merchants Gate ★★★★
Self Catering
Contact: Stephen Osborne
t (01937) 574836
e oaklands.wetherby@btopenworld.com

Merricote Cottages ★★★
Self Catering
Contact: Andrew Williamson
Merricote Cottages
t (01904) 400256
e merricote@hotmail.com
w merricote-holiday-cottages.co.uk

No 13 York City Arms Apartment ★★★★★
Self Catering
Contact: Mrs Andrea Baugh
Yorkshire Cottages
t (01228) 599960
e andrea@yorkshire-cottages.info

No 14 York City Arms Apartment ★★★★
Self Catering
Contact: Janet Hoyle
Yorkshire Cottages
t (01943) 885306
e enquiries@yorkshire-cottages.info
w yorkshire-cottages.info

Number 22 Bootham Terrace ★★★★★
Self Catering
Contact: Mrs Helen Jones
Homefinders Holidays
t (01904) 632660
e agents@holidayork.co.uk
w holidayork.co.uk

Old Rectory ★★★
Self Catering
Contact: Mr & Mrs A.W Morley
t (01904) 423506
e awm@fish.co.uk

The Penthouse, Westgate
★★★★★ *Self Catering*
Contact: Ian Berg
t (0161) 439 8964
e rtib@currantbun.com

Roman Retreat ★★★ *Self Catering & Serviced Apartments*
Contact: Stephen Hedderick
t (01904) 331803
e hedderick@ntlworld.com

St Peter's Quarter ★★★★★
Self Catering
Contact: Jane Wilson
t (01473) 890056
e janem.wilson@btopenworld.com
w yorkcityhouse.com

Shambles Holiday Apartments ★★★★
Self Catering
Contact: Mr Fletcher
t (01904) 623898
e shamblesholiday-york@tinyworld.co.uk

Skeldergate Apartment
★★★★ *Self Catering*
Contact: Mrs M Kilby
The Bungalow
t (01653) 691576
e mskilby@tiscali.co.uk

Sparrow Hall Cottages ★★★
Self Catering
Contact: Nick & Pam Gaunt
t (01759) 372917
e holidays@sparrowhall.co.uk
w sparrowhall.co.uk

Swallow Hall ★★★
Self Catering
Contact: Christine Scutt
t (01904) 448219
e jtscores@hotmail.com
w swallowhall.co.uk

Talbot Court
Rating Applied For
Self Catering
t (01944) 758222
e talbotcourt@gmail.com

York Holiday Apartments
★★★★ *Self Catering*
Contact: Malcolm Bradley
t (01977) 683499
e malcolmbradley@btinternet.com
w yorkholidayapartments.co.uk

York Holiday Homes
★★★-★★★★ *Self Catering*
Contact: Dorothy Preece
t (01904) 641997
e yorkholidayhomes@btconnect.com
w yorkholidayhomes.co.uk

York Lakeside Lodges
★★★★-★★★★★
Self Catering
Contact: Mr Manasir
York Lakeside Lodges Ltd
t (01904) 702346
e neil@yorklakesidelodges.co.uk
w yorklakesidelodges.co.uk

York Luxury Breaks ★★★★
Self Catering
Contact: Mrs Linda Waddington
York Luxury Breaks
t (01904) 768569
w yorkluxurybreaks.co.uk

HEART OF ENGLAND

ABBERLEY
Worcestershire

Old Yates Cottages ★★★
Self Catering
Contact: Mr & Mrs Richard & Sarah Goodman
Old Yates Cottages
t (01299) 896500
e oldyates@aol.com
w oldyatescottages.co.uk

ABBOTS BROMLEY
Staffordshire

Blithfield Lakeside Barns
★★★★ *Self Catering*
Contact: Mrs Maxine Brown
PG & RG Brown & Partners
t (01889) 500234
e maxine.brown@lineone.net
w blithfieldlakesidebarns.co.uk

ABBOTS LENCH
Worcestershire

Abbots Court Cottages
★★★★ *Self Catering & Serviced Apartments*
t (01386) 870520
e holiday@abbotscourtcottages.co.uk
w abbotscourtcottages.co.uk

ABDON
Shropshire

Little Cobblers Dingle ★★★
Self Catering
Contact: Josephine Brooks
t (01746) 712244
e brooks@cobblersdingle.wanadoo.co.uk
w stmem.com/cobblers-dingle

ACTON BURNELL
Shropshire

Rosehay ★★★★
Self Catering
Contact: Mr S Boardman
Sykes Cottages
t (01244) 345700
e info@sykescottages.co.uk

ADMINGTON
Warwickshire

Mole End, Admington
★★★★ *Self Catering*
Contact: Mrs Liz Hale
Willow Tree Farm
t (01789) 450881
e liz-hale@willowtreefarm.fslife.co.uk
w mole-end-cottage.co.uk

AFFCOT
Shropshire

The Coach House ★★★
Self Catering
Contact: Dr Sal Riding
t (01694) 781235
e sal.riding@nhs.net

ALCESTER
Warwickshire

The Croft Cottage ★★★★
Self Catering
Contact: Mrs Catherine Harris
t (01789) 490543
e cathy@thecroftcottage.co.uk
w thecroftcottage.co.uk

Dorset House Cottage and Dorset House ★★★★ *Self Catering & Serviced Apartments*
Contact: Mrs Plummer
Dorset House
t (01789) 762856
e dorsethac@aol.com

The Granary ★★★
Self Catering
Contact: Mrs Susan Kinnersley
t (01789) 762554
e JohnandSusan@kinnersley.fsworld.co.uk

HeronView ★★★★
Self Catering
Contact: Heather & Mike Bosworth
t (01789) 766506
e heather@heronview.net
w heronview.net

ALSTONEFIELD
Staffordshire

Ancestral Barn
★★★★-★★★★★
Self Catering
Contact: Mrs Sue Fowler
t (01335) 310243
e sue@fowler89.fsnet.co.uk
w dovedalecottages.co.uk

Dove Cottage Fishing Lodge
★★★★★ *Self Catering*
Contact: Mr Rupert Hignett
Dove Cottage Fishing Lodge
t (01993) 825900 & (01285) 850779
e info@dovecottages.co.uk
w dovecottages.co.uk

The Gables ★★★
Self Catering
Contact: Mr McKee
Timewell Estates Plc
t (0151) 625 3264
e timewell@rtconnect.com
w dovedale.org.uk

Gateham Grange Cottage & The Coach House
★★★-★★★★ *Self Catering*
Contact: Mrs Teresa Flower
t (01335) 310349
e gateham.grange@btinternet.com
w cressbrook.co.uk/hartingt/gateham

The Haybarn ★★★★
Self Catering
Contact: Mrs Coralie Smith
t (01335) 310328
w cottageguide.co.uk/haybarn

Hope Farm House Barn
★★★★ *Self Catering*
Contact: Mrs Ruth Pitts-Tucker
t (01327) 811407

Rowlands Cottage ★★★★
Self Catering
Contact: Mrs Ellen Wibberley
t (01335) 310370
e rog@wibbs200.fsnet.co.uk
w cottageguide.co.uk/Rowlandscottage

ALTON
Staffordshire

The Homesteads ★★★
Self Catering
Contact: Mrs Ann Smith
t (01889) 590062

The Raddle Inn ★★-★★★
Self Catering
Contact: Mr Peter Wilkinson
t (01889) 507278
e peter@logcabin.co.uk
w logcabin.co.uk

Rowan House ★★★★
Self Catering
Contact: Maggies Peet/ Emily Whitehead
t (01538) 702502
e enquiries@simplystaffordshire.co.uk
w simplystaffordshire.co.uk

ASHFORD BOWDLER
Shropshire

Harvest Barn ★★★
Self Catering
t (01584) 831707
e keithblight@aol.com
w stmem.com/harvestbarn

ASTON CANTLOW
Warwickshire

Cantlow Cottage ★★★
Self Catering
Contact: Mr & Mrs John & Jane Nickless
The Corner House
t (01789) 488513
w stratford-upon-avon.co.uk/cantlow.htm

ASTON EYRE
Shropshire

West Farm Cottage ★★★★
Self Catering
Contact: Mrs Deborah Meredith
t (01746) 714406
e deborahwestfarm@aol.com
w westfarmcottage.co.uk

ATHERSTONE
Warwickshire

Hipsley Farm Cottages
★★★★ *Self Catering & Serviced Apartments*
Contact: Mrs Ann Prosser
Waste Farm
t (01827) 872437
e ann@hipsleyco.uk
w hipsley.co.uk

AVON DASSETT
Warwickshire

The Limes Cottage ★★★
Self Catering
Contact: Mrs Diane Anderson
t (01295) 690245
e andrsndiane@tiscali.co.uk

AYMESTREY
Herefordshire

The Bungalow ★★★
Self Catering
Contact: Mr & Mrs T. Price
t (01568) 770582
e price2k@fsmail.net

BAGNALL
Staffordshire

Cordwainer Cottage ★★★
Self Catering
Contact: Mrs Muriel Buckle
t (01782) 302575
w cordwainercottage.co.uk

BALLINGHAM
Herefordshire

Fishermans Cottage ★★★★
Self Catering
Contact: Mrs V Allen
t (01432) 840844
e fishermanscottage@hotmail.co.uk
w riverwyecottage.co.uk

BARFORD
Warwickshire

The Old Barn ★★★
Self Catering
Contact: Mr Paul Hunt
t (01926) 624775

BARNT GREEN
Worcestershire

Sandon Self Catering ★★★
Self Catering
Contact: Ms Valerie Price
t (0121) 445 6797
e sandon@apartments.fsworld.co.uk
w sandonselfcatering.co.uk

BAYTON
Worcestershire

The Mill House ★★★
Self Catering
Contact: Mrs Jane Chance
t (01299) 832608
e millhousebayton@aol.com
w themillhouse-bayton.co.uk

BEWDLEY
Worcestershire

The Brant ★★★★
Self Catering
Contact: Mrs Helen Robson
t (01299) 825603
e paulandhelen@hotmail.com

Manor Holding ★★★
Self Catering
Contact: Mr & Mrs Nigel & Penny Dobson-Smyth
t 07970 260010
e nds@landscapeconsultancy.freeserve.co.uk

Peacock Coach House
★★★★ *Self Catering & Serviced Apartments*
Contact: Mrs Prisca Hall
t (01299) 400149
e priscahall@hotmail.com

Riverview Cottage ★★★
Self Catering
Contact: Mr & Mrs Giles
t (01299) 403481
e jgilesm81@aol.com
w riverview-bdy.co.uk

The White Cottage Garden Flat ★★★★ *Self Catering*
Contact: Mrs Tallents
t (01299) 841238

BIDFORD-ON-AVON
Warwickshire

Corner Cottage and Pathway Cottage
★★★★-★★★★★
Self Catering
Contact: Mr W A Lucas
t (01789) 293932
e lucasstratford@aol.com
w lucasstratford.co.uk

BIRCHER
Herefordshire

Brook House Farm Flat
★★★ *Self Catering*
Contact: Mrs Shan Smith
Brook House Farm
t (01568) 780520
e shanmsmith@aol.com

BISHOP'S CASTLE
Shropshire

Claremont Holiday Cottages
★★★ *Self Catering*
Contact: Mrs Price
t (01588) 638170
e info@priceclaremont.co.uk
w priceclaremont.co.uk

The Firs ★★★ *Self Catering*
Contact: Mr Clive Sykes
Sykes Cottage
t (01244) 345700
e info@sykescottages.co.uk
w thefirscolebatch.co.uk

Mount Cottage ★★★★
Self Catering
Contact: Mrs Heather Willis
Mount Cottage
t (01588) 638288
e heather@mountcottage.co.uk
w mountcottage.co.uk

The Old Chapel ★★★
Self Catering
Contact: Mrs Jane Traies
Simply Shropshire Cottage Holidays
t (01743) 891117
e jane.traies@btopenworld.com

Walkmill Cottage Barn ★★★
Self Catering
t (01588) 650671
w stmem.com/walkmillcottage

BISHOPS FROME
Herefordshire

Cheyney Chapel ★★★
Self Catering
Contact: Mrs D H Harrison
t (01531) 640846
e bjharrison@tiscali.co.uk

Five Bridges Inn ★★★★
Self Catering
Contact: Mr Mark Chatterton
t (01531) 640340
e mark@5bridges.freeserve.co.uk
w fivebridgescottage.co.uk

BLACKBROOK
Staffordshire

Nags Head Farm Cottage
★★★ *Self Catering*
Contact: Mrs A Leathem
t (01782) 680334
e nagsheadfarm@aol.com
w nagsheadfarm.co.uk

BOCKLETON
Worcestershire

Grafton Grove ★★★★
Self Catering
t (01568) 750602
w stmem.com/grafton-grove

BODENHAM
Herefordshire

Bodenham Forge, Bodenham ★★★★ *Self Catering & Serviced Apartments*
Contact: Mrs Mary Nickols
t (01568) 797144
e sgnickols@yahoo.co.uk
w bodenhamforge.co.uk

BORESFORD
Herefordshire

Hicks Farm Holidays ★★★★
Self Catering
Contact: Mrs Susan Bywater
t (01544) 260237
e holidays@hicksfarm.fsbusiness.co.uk
w hicksfarmholidays.co.uk

BOSBURY
Herefordshire

The Bee House and The Hive ★★★★ *Self Catering*
Contact: Mrs Sandra Anderson
t (01531) 640021

BOURTON
Shropshire

Bourton Manor ★★★★ *Self Catering & Serviced Apartments*
Contact: Mrs Caroline Barr
t (01746) 785377

BRADNOP
Staffordshire

Millstones ★★★
Self Catering
Contact: Mrs Josephine Edwards
t (01538) 304548
e stephan@swepme.fsnet.co.uk
w millstones.uk.com

School House ★★★★★
Self Catering
Contact: Mr Clive Sykes
Sykes Cottages
t (01244) 345700
e info@sykescottages.co.uk
w sykescottages.co.uk

BREDON
Worcestershire

The Moretons Vacation Houses ★★★★★
Self Catering
Contact: Mrs Karon Webb
t (01684) 772294
e soutar@moretonsbredon.co.uk
w moretons-soutar.co.uk

BRIDGNORTH
Shropshire

Bulls Head Inn – Self Catering ★★★ *Self Catering*
Contact: Mrs Norma Jones
The Bulls Head
t (01746) 861469
e bull_chelmarsh@btconnect.com
w bullsheadchelmarsh.co.uk

Eudon Burnell Cottages ★★★★ *Self Catering*
Contact: Mrs Margaret Crawford Clarke
t (01746) 789235
e eudon-burnell@talk21.com
w eudon.co.uk

The Granary ★★★ *Self Catering & Serviced Apartments*
Contact: Mrs Sarah Allen
The Granary
t (01746) 712272
e allens@oldvicditton.freeserve.co.uk

Jacob's Cottage ★★★★
Self Catering
Contact: Mrs Gilly Wooldridge
t (01952) 730485
e peterwulf@lineone.net
w virtual-shropshire.co.uk/jacob

Lobby Stables ★★★★ *Self Catering & Serviced Apartments*
t (01746) 789218
e lobby_farm@lineone.net
w shropshire-cottage.co.uk

Severn Rest ★★★
Self Catering
Contact: Mrs Jacky Davies
t (01746) 718093
e jacky.cartwright@virgin.net
w stmem.com/severn-rest

Upton Cressett Hall
Rating Applied For
Self Catering
Contact: Mrs Bridget Cash
t (01746) 714307
e bridgetcash@aol.com
w uptoncressetthall.co.uk

BRIERLEY
Herefordshire

Walnut Tree Cottage ★★★★ *Self Catering*
Contact: Ms Elaine Johnson
t (01568) 620033
e elaine@walnuttreecottage.net
w walnuttreecottage.net

BROADWAY
Worcestershire

Old Post Office Apartment ★★★★ *Self Catering*
Contact: Miss Sheila Rolland
Folly Cottage
t (01386) 593315
e info@campdencottages.co.uk
w campdencottages.co.uk

BROBURY
Herefordshire

Brobury House Cottages ★★★–★★★★ *Self Catering*
Contact: Mrs Pru Cartwright
t (01981) 500229
e enquiries@broburyhouse.co.uk
w broburyhouse.co.uk

BROCKTON
Shropshire

Skimblescott Barn ★★★★
Self Catering
Contact: Mrs Rowena Jones
t (01746) 785664
e skimblescott@yahoo.co.uk
w stmem.com/skimblescott-barn

BROMYARD
Herefordshire

Boyce Caravan Park ★★★★
Self Catering
Contact: Miss Alison Richards
t (01886) 884248

Mintridge ★★★★
Self Catering
Hodgebatch Manor
t (01885) 483262
e hodgebatch@aol.com
w mintridge.co.uk

BROSELEY
Shropshire

Aynsley Cottages ★★★
Self Catering
Contact: Mr & Mrs Kieth & Elsie Elcock
t (01952) 882695
e aynsleycottages@hotmail.com
w aynsleycottages.co.uk

BURLEY GATE
Herefordshire

Holly Lodge ★★★
Self Catering
Contact: Mr & Mrs Nick & Trudie Meers
t (01432) 820493
e lodge@meersphoto.com
w cottageguide.co.uk/hollylodge.html

BURLTON
Shropshire

Grey Stones Barn Annex
Rating Applied For
Self Catering
Contact: Kotti Brewin
Grey Srones Barn Annex
t (01939) 270999
e kotti@btinternet.com

BURTON DASSETT
Warwickshire

Caudle Hill Farm ★★★★
Self Catering
Contact: Mrs Jane Perry
t (01295) 770255
e janeperry@another.com
w caudlehillfarm.co.uk

BUTTERTON
Staffordshire

Swainsley Farm ★★★★★
Self Catering
Contact: Mr & Mrs Chris Snook
t (01298) 84530
e info@swainsleyfarm.co.uk
w swainsleyfarm.co.uk

CALLOW
Herefordshire

The Loft at Cold Nose
Rating Applied For
Self Catering
Contact: Mr & Mrs J. Evans
Cottage Life
t (01432) 340954
e john@cottagelife.freeserve.co.uk
w cottagelife.freeserve.co.uk

CARDINGTON
Shropshire

Plaish Park Farm ★★★★★
Self Catering
Contact: Mrs Sara Jones
t (01694) 771262
e bextajones@hotmail.com
w plaishparkfarm.co.uk

CAREY
Herefordshire

Carey Dene and Rock House ★★★ *Self Catering*
Contact: Mrs Milly Slater
Ruxton Farm
t (01432) 840493
e milly@wyevalleycottages.com
w wyevalleycottages.com

CHELMARSH
Shropshire

Dinney Farm Self Catering – Cart Cottage ★★★
Self Catering
t (01746) 861070

CHERINGTON
Warwickshire

Steele's Cottage ★★★★
Self Catering
Contact: Mrs Russell
Home Farm House
t (01608) 686540

CHIRBURY
Shropshire

Kingswood Retreats
Rating Applied For
Self Catering
Contact: Joanne Cawardine
t (01938) 561246

CHURCH LAWFORD
Warwickshire

The Grange ★★★
Self Catering
Contact: Mrs Lilian Reay
t (024) 7654 2133

CHURCH STRETTON
Shropshire

Audrey's Parkgate Cottages ★★★ *Self Catering*
Contact: Mrs Audrey Hill
t (01694) 751303
e park-gate@lineone.net
w stmem.com/parkgatecottages

Botvyle Farm Holiday Cottages ★★★–★★★★
Self Catering
Contact: Mrs Gill Bebbington
t (01694) 722869
e enquiries@botvylefarm.co.uk
w botvylefarm.co.uk

Brook House Cottage ★★
Self Catering
t (01342) 870444
e worley2@ukonline.co.uk
w stmem.com/brook-house-cottage

Broome Farm Cottages ★★★★★ *Self Catering*
Contact: Mr & Mrs Cavendish
t (01694) 771778
e sarah@sarahcavendish.demon.co.uk
w broomefarm.co.uk

Caradoc Cottages ★★★–★★★★ *Self Catering*
Contact: Mrs Wendy Lewis
Caradoc House
t (01694) 751488
e w-lewis@lineone.net
w churchstrettoncottages.co.uk

The Garden Flat ★★★
Self Catering
Contact: Mrs Carol Hembrow
t (01694) 723715
e cj.hembrow@ukonline.co.uk
w thegardenflatchurchstretton.co.uk

Look out for establishments participating in the National Accessible Scheme

Granary Cottage ★★★★
Self Catering
Contact: Mr & Mrs Kirkwood
Lower Day House
t (01694) 771521
e bookings@lowerdayhouse.com
w lowerdayhouse.com

Hodghurst Cottage ★★★
Self Catering
t (01694) 751403
w stmem.com/hodghurstcottage

Leasowes ★★★★
Self Catering
t (01694) 751351
e pauleasowes@btinternet.com
w stmem.com/leasowes-cottage

Middle Farm Cottages
★★★★ *Self Catering*
Contact: Mr Clive Sykes
Sykes Cottages
t (01244) 345700
e info@sykescottages.co.uk
w middlefarmcottages.co.uk

The Old Stables ★★★★
Self Catering
Contact: Miss Kate Tory
Ye Olde Stables at Jinlye
t (01694) 723243
e info@jinlye.co.uk
w jinlye.co.uk

The Retreat ★★★
Self Catering
t (01694) 723370
e john@theretreatcs.co.uk
w stmem.com/theretreat

The Sapling ★★★
Self Catering
Contact: Mrs Jan Oram
t (01694) 781347
e oakwoodcottage01@aol.com

CLEHONGER Herefordshire

Carramar ★★★★
Self Catering
Contact: Mr & Mrs Q Davies
t (01981) 250544
e carramar@hotmail.com

CLEOBURY MORTIMER Shropshire

Hop Barn ★★★★
Self Catering
Contact: Mrs Birgit Jones
t (01299) 271204
e birgit.jones@onetel.net

Prescott Mill Cottage ★★★
Self Catering
Contact: Mrs Wendy Etchells
t (01746) 718721
e mail@prescott-mill-cottage.co.uk
w prescott-mill-cottage.co.uk

CLIFTON UPON TEME Worcestershire

Pitlands Farm Holidays
★★★★ *Self Catering*
Contact: Mrs Diane Mann
t (01886) 812220
e pitlandsfarmholidays@btopenworld.com
w pitlandsfarm.co.uk

CLUN Shropshire

Bramleys ★★★★
Self Catering
t (01588) 673302
e bentleyfiona@aol.com
w bramleysbarn.com

Cockford Hall ★★★★★
Self Catering
Contact: Mr Roger Wren
Dick Turpin Cottage at Cockford Hall
t (01588) 640327
e cockford.hall@virgin.net
w go2.co.uk/cockfordhall

Pooh Hall Cottages
★★★★-★★★★★
Self Catering
Contact: Mrs Sue Murray
t (01588) 640075
e pooh-hall@realemail.co.uk
w pooh-hallcottages.co.uk

Wagtail Cottages ★★★★
Self Catering
Contact: Mrs Joyce Williams
Wagtail Cottage
t (01588) 640224
e hurstmillholidays@tinyworld.co.uk
w clunholidays.co.uk

Woolbury Barn ★★★★
Self Catering
t (01588) 640481
w stmem.com/woolburybarn

CLUNTON Shropshire

Clunton Farm Granary ★★★
Self Catering
Clunton Farmhouse
t (01588) 660120
e info@clunvalleyretreat.com
w clunvalleyretreat.com

COALBROOKDALE Shropshire

Coalbrookdale Cottages
Cottages ★★★-★★★★ *Self Catering & Serviced Apartments*
Contact: Mrs Mary Jones
t (01952) 433202
e mary@teakettlecottages.co.uk

The Cottage
Rating Applied For
Self Catering
t (01952) 433640
e salcozon@aol.com

Old Wynd Cottage
Rating Applied For
Self Catering
Contact: Charlie Boyce
Old Wynd House
t (01952) 432427
e info@oldwynd.co.uk
w oldwynd.co.uk

COALPORT Shropshire

Station House Holiday Lets
★★★★ *Self Catering*
Contact: Mrs Lisa Rawlings
t (01952) 881106
e enquiries@coalportstation.com
w coalportstation.com

COLWALL Herefordshire

Threshing Barn ★★★★
Self Catering
Contact: Mr Robin Coates
Lower House Farm
t (01684) 540284
e robin@robincoates.com
w robincoates.com

CORLEY West Midlands

St Ives Lodge ★★★★
Self Catering
Contact: Mr Tim Ruffett
t (01676) 542994
e tim@ruffett.co.uk
w st-ives-lodge.co.uk

CRAVEN ARMS Shropshire

Gwynfa, Long Meadow End
★★★ *Self Catering*
Gwynfa
t (01588) 673375
w stmem.com/gwynfa

Halford Holiday Homes
★★★-★★★★ *Self Catering*
Contact: Mr & Mrs E James
t (01588) 672382
w stmem.com/halfordholidayhomes

Highgrove Barns ★★★★
Self Catering
Contact: Mrs Christine Tromans
t (01588) 673113
e barns@tromans.go-plus.net
w highgrovebarns.co.uk

The Malt House ★★★★★
Self Catering
Contact: Mrs Margaret Mellings
t (01584) 873315
e jeanmellings@hotmail.com
w shropshirecottage.co.uk

Orchard Cottage ★★★★
Self Catering
t (01588) 673340
e pdlewisuk@aol.com
w stmem.com/orchardcottage

Strefford Hall Self Catering – Robins & Swallows Nest
★★★★ *Self Catering*
Contact: Mrs Caroline Morgan
t (01588) 672383
w streffordhall.co.uk

Upper Onibury Cottages
★★★★ *Self Catering*
Contact: Mrs Hickman
t (01584) 856206
e info@shropshirecottages.com
w shropshirecottages.com

CULMINGTON Shropshire

Stud Farm Cottage ★★★
Self Catering
Contact: Mrs M A Burgoyne
t (01584) 861340

DARLINGSCOTT Warwickshire

Sundial Wing ★★★★
Self Catering
Contact: Miss Sheila Rolland
Campden Cottages
t (01386) 593315
e info@campdencottages.co.uk
w campdencottages.co.uk

DENSTONE Staffordshire

Keepers Cottage ★★★★
Self Catering
Contact: Mr Christopher Ball
t (01889) 590415
e cm_ball@yahoo.co.uk
w 4posteraccom.com

DILHORNE Staffordshire

Birchenfields Farm ★★★
Self Catering
Contact: Mr & Mrs Peter Edge
t (01538) 753972

DOCKLOW Herefordshire

Docklow Manor Holiday Cottages ★★★ *Self Catering*
Contact: Mrs Jane Viner
Docklow Manor Holiday Cottages
t (01568) 760668
e jane498@btinternet.com
w docklow-manor.co.uk

DORRINGTON Shropshire

Netley Hall Holidays
Rating Applied For
Self Catering
Contact: Mrs Teresa Keeling
Netley Hall Holidays Ltd
t (01743) 718339
e holidays@netleyhall.co.uk
w netleyhall.co.uk

DORSINGTON Warwickshire

Windmill Grange Cottage
★★★★ *Self Catering*
Contact: Mrs Lorna Hollis
t (01789) 720866
e lornah_windmillgrange@hotmail.com
w windmillgrange.co.uk

DRAYCOTT-IN-THE-CLAY Staffordshire

Granary Court Holiday Cottages ★★★★
Self Catering
Contact: Mrs Lynne Statham
t (01283) 820917
w granarycourt.demon.co.uk

DUNCHURCH Warwickshire

Toft Manor Cottage ★★★★
Self Catering
Contact: Ms Shirley Bettinson
t (01788) 810626
e shirley@toft-alpacas.co.uk
w toft-alpacas.co.uk

EARDISLAND Herefordshire

The Hopleys ★★★★
Self Catering
Contact: Mrs Elaine Lyke
t (01568) 709285
e elaine@lyke5502.freeserve.co.uk

The Stables ★★★★
Self Catering
Contact: Mr & Mrs A Priday
t (01544) 388570
e pridays@aol.com

EARLS CROOME
Worcestershire

The Jockey Inn ★★★
Self Catering
Contact: Mr Anthony Lumb
t (01684) 592153
e thejockey@aol.com
w thejockeyinn.com

EATON-UNDER-HEYWOOD
Shropshire

Eaton Manor ★★★★
Self Catering
Contact: Miss Nichola Madeley
Eaton Manor Rural Escapes
t (01694) 724814
e ruralescapes@eatonmanor.co.uk
w eatonmanor.co.uk

ELKSTONE
Staffordshire

Stable Cottage ★★★
Self Catering
Contact: Mrs Veronica Lawrenson
t (01538) 300487
e elkstone@btinternet.com
w cottageguide.co.uk/peakdistrictcottage

ELLERDINE
Shropshire

1 Oak House Farm Cottages ★★★★ *Self Catering*
Contact: Ms Jane Fryer
t (01606) 351521
e info@yourshropshirecottage.co.uk
w yourshropshirecottage.co.uk

ELMLEY CASTLE
Worcestershire

The Cottage Manor Farm House ★★ *Self Catering*
Contact: Mr & Mrs Brian and Pat Lovett
Manor Farm House
t (01386) 710286

ELMS GREEN
Herefordshire

Wharton Bank Cottages ★★★★–★★★★★
Self Catering
Contact: Miss Leisa Copp
t (01568) 615302
e leisacopp@yahoo.co.uk

EVESHAM
Worcestershire

Thatchers End ★★★★
Self Catering
Contact: Mr & Mrs Wilson
t (01386) 446269
e trad.accom@virgin.net
w http://freespace.virgin.net/trad.accom

EXHALL
Warwickshire

Glebe Farm Cottages ★★★
Self Catering
Contact: Mr Roger Albutt
t (01386) 830687
w glebefarmcottages.net

FORD
Shropshire

Longmore Cottage ★★★★
Self Catering
t (01743) 884201
w stmem.com/longmorecottage

FOWNHOPE
Herefordshire

Birds Farm Cottage ★★★
Self Catering
Contact: Mrs Margaret Edwards
t (01989) 740644
e birdscottage@yahoo.com

FOXT
Staffordshire

Badgers Cottage ★★★★
Self Catering
Contact: K & CA Lockwood
t (01538) 266611

FRODESLEY
Shropshire

The Haven ★★★
Self Catering
Contact: Mr & Mrs Richard & Jenifer Pickard
t (01694) 731672
e the-haven@frodesley.fsnet.co.uk
w cottageguide.co.uk/the-haven

GOODRICH
Herefordshire

Flanesford Priory ★★★
Self Catering
Contact: Mr & Mrs Roper
t (01989) 770157
e nwr500@hotmail.com
w flanesfordpriory.com

GREAT COMBERTON
Worcestershire

The Granary ★★★★
Self Catering
Contact: Mrs Jenny Newbury
t (01386) 710210

GRINSHILL
Shropshire

Amblewood Cottage ★★★★ *Self Catering*
t (01939) 220214
e vantomwood@hotmail.com
w stmem.com/amblewood-cottage

Barleycorn Barns ★★★★
Self Catering
Contact: Mr Neil Lewis
t (01939) 220333
e booking@barleycornbarns.co.uk
w barleycornbarns.co.uk

Chestnut Croft Cottages ★★★ *Self Catering*
Chestnut Croft
t (01939) 220573
e roger@goodrj.fsnet.co.uk
w chestnutcroft.co.uk

GUYS CLIFFE
Warwickshire

Rose Cottage ★★★★
Self Catering
Contact: Ms Tracey Forrester
t (01789) 290904
e loesfarm@tesco.net
w loesfarm.co.uk

HALLOW
Worcestershire

The New Cottage ★★★★
Self Catering
Contact: Mrs Doreen Jeeves
t (01905) 640953
e jeeves@thenewcottage.co.uk
w thenewcottage.co.uk

HAMPTON LOADE
Shropshire

One Lion Cottage ★★★
Self Catering
Contact: Mrs Juliet Browning
t (01746) 780404
e julietbrowning@hotmail.com

HANLEY SWAN
Worcestershire

Mere End Cabin ★★★★
Self Catering
Contact: Mr A Bishop
t (01684) 310899
e hanleyholidays@yahoo.co.uk

HARMER HILL
Shropshire

Newton Meadows Holiday Cottages 2 ★★★★
Self Catering
Newton Meadows Holiday Cottages
t (01939) 290346
e e.simcox@btopenworld.com

HATTON
Shropshire

The Stable ★★★
Self Catering
Contact: Mr & Mrs Hall
t (01694) 781202
e raysarahhall@aol.com

HENLEY-IN-ARDEN
Warwickshire

Irelands Farm ★★★★
Self Catering
Contact: Mr & Mrs Stephanie Williams
t (01564) 792476
e stephaniewilliams1@tiscali.co.uk
w irelandsfarmcottages.com

HENTLAND
Herefordshire

Criss Cross Cottage ★★★★
Self Catering
Contact: Dr & Mr Christine & David Peacock
t (01989) 730300
e peacock@doctors.org.uk
w peacocks-in-property.co.uk

HEREFORD
Herefordshire

Anvil Cottage, Apple Bough and Cider Press ★★★★
Self Catering
Contact: Mrs Jennie Layton
t (01432) 268689
e jennielayton@ereal.net
w graftonvilla.co.uk

Castle Cliffe East ★★★★
Self Catering
Contact: Mr Mark Hubbard & Mr Phil Wilson
Castle Cliffe West
t (01432) 272096
e mail@castlecliffe.net
w castlecliffe.net

Cross In Hand Farm Cottage ★★★★ *Self Catering*
Contact: Dr J. Thornton
Cross In Hand Farm
t (01981) 540957

The Green Farm Cottage, Felton ★★★★ *Self Catering*
Contact: Mrs Shirley Simcock
The Green Farm
t (01432) 820234

Hermit Holidays ★★★★
Self Catering
Contact: Mr Ron Zahl
t (01432) 760022
e info@hermitholidays.co.uk
w hermitholidays.co.uk

Longwood Cottage ★★★★
Self Catering
Contact: Mrs Veronica Harris
t (01989) 740248
e kenverharris@aol.com

Rushford ★★★★
Self Catering
Contact: Mrs M Roberts
t (01432) 273380

HIMBLETON
Worcestershire

Phepson Farm Cottages ★★★–★★★★
Self Catering
Contact: Mrs Trica Havard
t (01905) 391205
e havard@globalnet.co.uk
w phepsonfarm.co.uk

HOARWITHY
Herefordshire

Old Mill Cottage ★★★
Self Catering
Contact: Mrs Carol Probert
Old Mill
t (01432) 840602
e carol.probert@virgin.net

HOLLINGTON
Staffordshire

Old Wood Farm Barns ★★★★ *Self Catering*
Contact: Liz Bean
t (01889) 507077
e paul.bean@bt.com

Rowan Cottage ★★★
Self Catering
Contact: Mr & Mrs P Campbell
The Bungalow
t (01889) 594279

HONEYBOURNE
Worcestershire

Peace Haven Holiday Lets ★★★ *Self Catering*
Contact: Mrs Fiona Humphrys
t (01386) 832785
e peace.haven@btconnect.com
w peacehavenlets.com

HOPE-UNDER-DINMORE
Herefordshire

The Fold ★★★★
Self Catering
Contact: Mrs Zena Legge
t (01568) 611314

Look out for establishments participating in the Walkers and Cyclists Welcome Schemes

HOPESAY
Shropshire

Hesterworth ★★–★★★
Self Catering
Contact: Mr Roger Davies
t (01588) 660487
w hesterworth.co.uk

HORTON
Staffordshire

Coach House & Gardeners Cottage ★★★★ *Self Catering*
Contact: Mrs Jean Thompson
t (01538) 360891
e thommoreds@aol.com

HULME END
Staffordshire

East & West Cawlow Barn
★★★★ *Self Catering*
Contact: Mr Clive Sykes
Sykes Cottages
t (01244) 345700
e info@sykescottages.co.uk

HUNGERFORD
Shropshire

Green Gates Apartment
Rating Applied For
Self Catering
Contact: Ms Sue Walsh
t (01584) 841225
e suewalsh@tesco.net
w virtual-shropshire.co.uk/greengates

ILAM
Staffordshire

Beechenhill Farm Cottages
★★★★ *Self Catering*
Contact: Mrs Sue Prince
t (01335) 310274
e beechenhill@btinternet.com
w beechenhill.co.uk

Lower Damgate Barns, Reuben's Roost, Bremen's Barn, Hope's Hideaway, Ilam
★★★★ *Self Catering*
Contact: Mrs Carolyn Wilderspin
t (01335) 310367 & 07779 210791
e damgate@hotmail.com
w damgate.com

Throwley Moor Farm House & Cottages ★★★★
Self Catering
Contact: Mrs Muriel Richardson
t (01538) 308202
e throwleyhall@btinternet.com
w throwleyhallfarm.co.uk

ILMINGTON
Warwickshire

Featherbed Cottage ★★★★
Self Catering
Contact: Mr David Price
t (01608) 682215
e featherbedcottage@hotmail.com

Woodruff Cottage ★★★★
Self Catering
Contact: Mrs Julia Gajny
Ilmington Stores & Post Office
t (01608) 682334
w woodruffcottage.co.uk

IPSTONES
Staffordshire

Coltstone Heath Cottage
★★★★★ *Self Catering*
Contact: Mrs Morgan
t (01538) 266740
w coltstone.co.uk

Meadow Place ★★★★
Self Catering
Contact: Mr Clive Sykes
Sykes Cottages
t (01244) 345700
e info@sykescottages.co.uk
w sykescottages.co.uk

Old Hall Farm Holiday Cottages ★★★ *Self Catering*
Contact: Mrs Ann Glover
t (01538) 266465
w oldhallholidaycottages.co.uk

The Stables & The Cart Shed
★★★ *Self Catering*
Contact: Mr & Mrs Michael & Hilary Hall
t (01538) 266259
w cloughhead.co.uk

IRONBRIDGE
Shropshire

Eleys of Ironbridge
★★★–★★★★ *Self Catering*
Eleys of Ironbridge
t (01952) 432030
e info@eleys-ironbridge.co.uk
w eleys-ironbridge.co.uk

Langdale Cottage ★★★
Self Catering
t (01584) 831707
e keithblight@aol.com
w stmem.com/langdale

Marnwood House and School House ★★★★★
Self Catering
Marnwood Properties Ltd
t 07831 398763
e jm@marnwood.fsnet.co.uk
w marnwoodproperty.co.uk

Martha's Cottage ★★★★
Self Catering
Contact: Mr John Russell
Marthas Cottage
t (01902) 871777
e marthascottage@cfe.co.uk
w stmem.com/marthascottage

Paradise House Flats ★★
Self Catering
Contact: Mrs Gilbride
Paradise House
t (01952) 433379
e marjorie@gilbride.co.uk
w flats.gilbride.co.uk

River Cottages
Rating Applied For
Self Catering
Contact: Marion Cooper
t (01952) 432246
e info@ironbridgeholidaycottages.co.uk
w ironbridgeholidaycottages.co.uk

Uplands Flat ★★★
Self Catering
Contact: Mrs Beryl Eccleston
The Uplands
t (01952) 433408

Victoria Cottage
Rating Applied For
Self Catering
Contact: Mr Colin Thompson
t 07970 417497
e cthompson@bcs.org.uk
w ironbridgegorge.com

IVINGTON
Herefordshire

Hop Kiln Cottage
Rating Applied For
Self Catering
Contact: Ms Aubrey Greene
t (01568) 720471

KENILWORTH
Warwickshire

Castle Cottage ★★★★
Self Catering
Contact: Mrs Sheila Tomalin
t (01926) 852204
e sheilatomalin@tinyonline.co.uk
w castlecottagekenilworth.co.uk

Jackdaw Cottage ★★★★
Self Catering
Contact: Mrs Lynn Grierson
t (01926) 855616
e kgrierson@ukonline.co.uk

The Little Barn ★★★
Self Catering
Contact: Mrs Oliver
t (01926) 850692

The Old Church House
★★★★ *Self Catering*
Contact: Mr & Mrs T Bray
t (01926) 859290
e info@theoldchurchhouse.co.uk

KENLEY
Shropshire

Church Farm House
Rating Applied For
Self Catering
Contact: Mr John Clowes
t (01446) 772680
e clowesjd@yahoo.co.uk

Courtyard Cottages ★★★★
Self Catering
Contact: Mrs Annabel Gill
No. 1 & 2 Courtyard Cottages
t (01952) 510841
e a-gill@hotmail.co.uk
w stmem.com/courtyardcottages

KIMBOLTON
Herefordshire

Rowley Farm ★★★
Self Catering
Contact: Jean & Sue Pugh
A M & L T Pugh
t (01568) 616123
e rowley@farmersweekley.net
w rowleyholidaypark.co.uk

KINETON
Warwickshire

Long Ground Barn, Kineton
★★★★★ *Self Catering*
Contact: Mrs Carolyn Gasson
Hampton House Farm
t (01926) 641829
e carolyn@heartofthecountryholidays.co.uk
w heartofthecountryholidays.co.uk

KINGS CAPLE
Herefordshire

Ruxton Farm – Wye Valley Cottages ★★★★
Self Catering
Contact: Mrs Milly Slater
t (01432) 840493
e milly@wyevalleycottages.com
w wyevalleycottages.com

KINGTON
Herefordshire

Cider Press Cottage ★★★★
Self Catering
Contact: Mrs Lorraine Wright
t (01544) 231462

KNIGHTCOTE
Warwickshire

Arbor Holiday & Knightcote Farm Cottages ★★★★★
Self Catering
Contact: Fiona & Craig Walker
t (01295) 770637
e fionawalker@farmcottages.com
w farmcottages.com

KNOCKIN
Shropshire

The Croft ★★★★
Self Catering
Contact: Mrs Pamela Ward
t (01691) 682485
e pam@rolly.co.uk
w rolly.co.uk

KNOWBURY
Shropshire

Old Vicarage Coach House
★★★ *Self Catering*
Contact: Mr Adrian Phillips
t (01584) 891749
e adriangphillips@aol.com
w knowburyoldvicarage.co.uk

LEA
Herefordshire

Moorlands ★★★
Self Catering
Contact: Mrs White
t (01989) 750230

LEA CROSS
Shropshire

Ranulf Holiday Cottage
★★★ *Self Catering*
t (01939) 210873
e tcshouse@talk21.com
w ranulfholidaycottage.co.uk

LEAMINGTON SPA
Warwickshire

Barn Owl Cottage ★★★★
Self Catering
Contact: Mrs Beatrice Norman
Fosseway Barns
t (01926) 614647
e bnorman@fossebarn.prestel.co.uk
w barnowlcottage.co.uk

Blackdown Farm Cottages
★★ *Self Catering*
Contact: Mr & Mrs R Solt
t (01926) 422522
e bobby@solt.demon.co.uk

Furzen Hill Farm
★★★-★★★★ *Self Catering*
Contact: Mrs Christine Whitfield
Furzen Hill Farm
t (01926) 424791
e christine.whitfield1@btopenworld.com
w furzenhillfarmcottages.co.uk

Riplingham ★★★★
Self Catering
Contact: Ms Shevlin
t (01926) 633790
e riplingham@hotmail.com

LEATON
Shropshire

Vicarage Cottage ★★★★★
Self Catering
Contact: Mrs Joan Mansell-Jones
The Old Vicarage
t (01939) 290989
e m-j@oldvicleaton.com
w oldvicleaton.com

LEDBURY
Herefordshire

Coach House Apartment
★★★ *Self Catering*
Contact: Mr Mike Williams
t (01531) 631199
e leadon.house@amserve.net
w leadonhouse.net

Homend Bank Cottage
★★★ *Self Catering*
Contact: Mrs Hughes
R H & R W Clutton The Estate Office
t (01531) 640262

The Old Kennels Farm
★★★-★★★★ *Self Catering*
Contact: Mrs J.K. Wilce
t (01531) 635024
e wilceoldkennelsfarm@btinternet.com
w oldkennelsfarm.co.uk

Quarry Lodge ★★★★
Self Catering
Contact: Mr Peter Viner
t (01531) 670816

White House Cottages
★★★-★★★★ *Self Catering*
Contact: Mrs Marianne Hills
t (01531) 670349
e bookings@whitehousecottages.co.uk
w whitehousecottages.co.uk

The Woodhouse Farm Cottages ★★★★★
Self Catering
Contact: Mrs Susan Furnival
t (01531) 640030
e sue@thewoodhousefarm.co.uk
w thewoodhousefarm.co.uk

Woodside Lodges ★★★★
Self Catering
Contact: K C Davies
t (01531) 670269
e info@woodsidelodges.co.uk
w woodsidelodges.co.uk

LEEK
Staffordshire

Blackshaw Grange Holiday Cottages ★★★★
Self Catering
Contact: Mrs Carolyn Williams
t (01538) 300165
e kevwilliams@btinternet.com
w btinternet.com/~blackshawgrange

Broomyshaw Country Cottages ★★★ *Self Catering*
Contact: Mr & Mrs Saul
t (01538) 308298
e grahambroomyshaw@tiscali.co.uk
w broomyshaw.co.uk

Candy Cottage ★★★★
Self Catering
Contact: Mrs Sylvia Plant
t (01538) 266243
e splantuppercadlow@hotmail.com
w cottageguide.co.uk/candycottage

Deansgate ★★★★
Self Catering
Contact: Victoria Heath
1 Bridge Houses
t 07989 337973
e deansgate@fsmail.net

Foxtwood Cottages, Foxt
★★★★ *Self Catering*
Contact: Mr & Mrs Clive & Alison Worrall
Foxtwood Cottages
t (01538) 266160
e info@foxtwood.co.uk
w foxtwood.co.uk

Lark's Rise ★★★
Self Catering
Contact: Mrs Laura Melland
t (01538) 304350
e newhousefarm@btinternet.com
w staffordshiremoorlandsfarmholidays.co.uk

Rosewood Cottage & Rosewood Flat ★★★
Self Catering
Contact: Edith & Alwyn Mycock
t (01538) 308213
w rosewoodcottage.co.uk

Wren Cottage, Rudyard
★★★★ *Self Catering*
Contact: Mrs Elizabeth Lowe
t (01260) 226341
e fairboroughs@talk21.com
w fairboroughs.co.uk

LEINTWARDINE
Herefordshire

Badgers Bluff ★★★★
Self Catering
Contact: Mr Norton
t (01547) 540648
e reg@badgersbluff.co.uk

Cubieres Cottage
Rating Applied For
Self Catering
Contact: Margaret Sheppard
t (01547) 540323
e marsheppard@tiscali.co.uk

Dower Cottage ★★★★
Self Catering
Contact: Ms Anne & Susan Douthwaite
Dower House
t (01547) 540446
e info@dower-cottage.co.uk

Oak Cottage ★★★
Self Catering
Contact: Mrs Vivienne Faulkner
t (01547) 540629
e francism-jones@virgin.net

Oaklands Farm Cottages
★★-★★★ *Self Catering*
Contact: Mrs Sally Ann Swift
Oaklands Farm
t (01547) 540635
e mrpaswift@aol.com
w stmem.com/oaklandsfarm

LEOMINSTER
Herefordshire

Ashton Court Farm ★★★
Self Catering
Contact: Mrs Pam Edwards
Ashton Court Farm
t (01584) 711245
e Griffithsbrooches@btinternet.com

The Buzzards ★★★★
Self Catering
Contact: Ms E Povey
t (01568) 708941
e holiday@thebuzzards.co.uk
w thebuzzards.co.uk

Ford Abbey ★★★★★
Self Catering
Contact: Mr Kenneth Garrood-Bailey
t (01568) 760700
e info@fordabbey.co.uk
w fordabbey.co.uk

LITTLE DEWCHURCH
Herefordshire

The Granary ★★★★
Self Catering
Contact: Ms Karen Tibbetts
t (01432) 840826

LITTLE STRETTON
Shropshire

Jessamine Cottage ★★★
Self Catering
Contact: Ms Claire Alford
t (01743) 873608
e clairealford@hotmail.com
w strettoncottages.co.uk

LITTLE TARRINGTON
Herefordshire

Stock's Cottage, Little Tarrington ★★★★
Self Catering
Contact: Mrs Angela Stock
Stock's Cottage
t (01432) 890243
e stay@stockscottage.co.uk
w stockscottage.co.uk

LLANGARRON
Herefordshire

Langstone Court Farmhouse
★★ *Self Catering*
Contact: Mrs Sonia Davies
t 07815 046 064
e sonialangstone@aol.com

Little Trereece Holiday Cottages ★★★ *Self Catering*
Contact: Mr Mark Cinderey
t (01989) 770145
e trereece@nasuwt.net
w homepages.nasuwt.net/trereece

Upper Trereece ★★★★
Self Catering
Chadstone
t (01604) 696889

LLANYBLODWEL
Shropshire

The Coach House ★★★★
Self Catering
Contact: Mr & Mrs Malcolm & Sylvia Perks
t (01691) 828038
e coach.house@micro-plus-web.net
w thecoachhouse.micro-plus-web.net

LONG LAWFORD
Warwickshire

Lodge Farm ★★★
Self Catering
Contact: Mr & Mrs Alec & Jane Brown
t (01788) 560193
e alec@lodgefarm.com
w lodgefarm.com

LONGNOR
Staffordshire

Merril Grove Cottages
★★★★ *Self Catering*
Contact: Mrs Beverley Hardy
t (01298) 83621
e merrilgrovecottages@gmail.com
w merrilgrovecottages.com

LONGTOWN
Herefordshire

New Barns Farm ★★★★
Self Catering
Contact: Mrs Anglea Lloyd
t (01981) 250250
e lloydnew@tesco.net
w golden-valley.co.uk/newbarns

LUDLOW
Shropshire

10 Mill Street ★★★★
Self Catering
Contact: Mrs Sarah Pitt
t (01746) 781947
e sarahipitt@aol.com
w stmem.com/10-mill-street

24 Mill Street ★★★★
Self Catering
Contact: Mrs Debbie Brodie
Re: 24 Mill Street
t (01588) 672074
w stmem.com/24-mill-street

Angel Barn ★★★★
Self Catering
Contact: Ms Jennifer Roberts
t (01584) 890381
e angelgardens@sy83hz.fsnet.co.uk
w stmem.com/angelbarn

Ashford Farm Cottages
★★★★ *Self Catering*
Contact: Mr & Mrs Norman Tudge
t (01584) 831243
e ashfordfarms@aol.com
w ashfordfarms.co.uk

The Avenue Flat ★★★★
Self Catering
Contact: Mr Meredith
The Avenue Flat
t (01584) 831616
e ronmeredithavenue@talk21.com
w theavenueflat.co.uk

The Bakery Appartment
★★★ *Self Catering*
Contact: Ms Deborah Cook
SC Price & Sons
t (01584) 872815
e pricesthebakers@btinternet.com

Cariad Cottage
Rating Applied For
Self Catering
Contact: Mrs Margaret Leake
Countisbury
t (01584) 873418

Church Bank, Burrington
★★ *Self Catering*
Contact: Mrs Rosemary Laurie
Church Bank
t (01568) 770426
e alan@alaurie5.wanadoo.co.uk

Counties View ★★★★
Self Catering
Contact: Mrs Marguerite Maclean
Witley House
t (01384) 817333
e margueritemusic@hotmail.com
w sykescottages.co.uk/cottages/1355.php

Criterion Cottage ★★★
Self Catering
Contact: Mrs Christine Hodgson
Criterion House
t (01584) 890344
w stmem.com/criterion-cottage

Elm Lodge Self Catering
★★★–★★★★ *Self Catering*
Contact: Mrs Barbara Weaver
t (01584) 872308
e info@elm-lodge.org.uk
w elm-lodge.org.uk

Emily Place ★★★★
Self Catering
Contact: Mrs Melanie Chetwood
t (01298) 73807
e paul.chetwood@royalmail.com
w emilyplace.co.uk

Flat 3 ★★★★ *Self Catering*
Contact: Mrs Wendy Petrie
t (01584) 875301
e wendypetrie@hotmail.co.uk

Garden Cottage (Westbury)
★★★★ *Self Catering*
t (01743) 884270
e whittonhall@farmersweekly.net
w stmem.com/gardencottage

Garden Flat ★★★
Self Catering
t (01584) 841225
e suewalsh@tesco.net
w stmem.com/gardenflat

Glebe Farm Cottage ★★★★
Self Catering
Contact: Mr & Mrs John & Lesley Thirlwell
t (01584) 823349
e cottage@glebefarm.info
w glebefarm.info

Goosefoot Barn ★★★★
Self Catering
Contact: Mrs Sally Loft
Goosefoot Barn Cottages
t (01584) 861326
e sally@goosefoot.freeserve.co.uk
w goosefootbarn.co.uk

The Granary ★★★
Self Catering
Contact: Mr & Mrs Richard Mercer
t (01584) 823272
e r.mercer@tinyworld.co.uk

Hazel Cottage ★★★★
Self Catering
Contact: Mrs Rachel Sanders
Hazel Cottage
t (01584) 856342
e rachelsanders@mac.com
w stmem.com/hazelcottage

Horseshoe Cottage ★★★★
Self Catering
Contact: Mr & Mrs Gill
t (024) 7661 2073
e trgill@btinternet.com
w cottageguide.co.uk/horseshoecottage

Lilac Cottage ★★★★
Self Catering
t (01746) 785564
e cottagefarm@farmersweekly.net
w stmem.com/lilaccottage

Ludford View ★★★★
Self Catering
Contact: Mrs Laura Rutty
Ludlowlife
t (01584) 873249
e ludlowlet@aol.com
w ludlowlife.co.uk

The Mews Flat ★★★★
Self Catering
Contact: Mrs Linda Taylor
t (01584) 873609
e mrs.miggs@virgin.net
w mewsflat.co.uk

Mocktree Barns Holiday Cottages ★★★ *Self Catering*
Contact: Mr & Mrs Clive & Cynthia Prior
t (01547) 540441
e mocktreebarns@care4free.net
w mocktreeholidays.co.uk

No 9 Brand Lane ★★★★
Self Catering
Contact: Mrs Angela Smart
Trappe House
t (01547) 560436
e enquiries@9brandlane.co.uk
w 9brandlane.co.uk

Posthorn Cottage ★★
Self Catering
Contact: Ms Helen Davis
t (0115) 922 2383
w posthorncottage.co.uk

Ravenscourt Manor ★★★★
Self Catering
Contact: Mrs Elizabeth Purnell
t (01584) 711905
e ravenscourtmanor@amserve.com
w cottagesdirect.com

Sutton Court Farm Cottages
★★★★ *Self Catering*
Contact: Mrs Jane Cronin
Sutton Court Farm
t (01584) 861305
e suttoncourtfarm@hotmail.com
w suttoncourtfarm.co.uk

Toad Hall ★★★ *Self Catering*
Contact: Mrs Jean Taylor
Lindidfarne
t (01584) 874161

Wandering William ★★★★
Self Catering
Contact: Mr Richard Maddicott
t (01584) 877899
e richard@maddicott.com

Whitton Farm Holiday Cottages ★★★★
Self Catering
t (01584) 890234
e alan@awozencroft.wanadoo.co.uk
w whittonfarmholidaycottages.com

LYDBURY NORTH
Shropshire

Walcot Hall Holiday apartments ★★★–★★★★
Self Catering
Contact: Miss Maria Higgs
Walcot Hall Administration Office
t (01588) 680570
e maria@walcotthall.com
w walcothall.com

LYONSHALL
Herefordshire

Field Cottage, The Sherriffs & Gardeners Cottage, The Colloquy & The Forge
★★★★–★★★★★
Self Catering
Contact: Mrs Joanna Hilditch
Field Cottage & The Sherriffs
t (01544) 340241 & (01544) 340241
e info@whiteheronproperties.com
w whiteheronproperties.com

Rosehill Guest House
Rating Applied For
Self Catering
Contact: Debbie Cambridge
t (01544) 340053
w rosehillguesthouse.co.uk

MADLEY
Herefordshire

Canon Bridge House ★★★★
Self Catering
Contact: Mrs Alison Anscomb
t (01981) 251104
e timothy.anscomb4@virgin.net
w cottageguide.co.uk/canonbridge

MALVERN
Worcestershire

Annexe to Blue Cedars
★★★ *Self Catering*
Contact: Mrs P M Longmire
Blue Cedars Annexe
t (01684) 566689
e pml@peachfield.freeserve.co.uk

April Cottage ★★★
Self Catering
Contact: Mrs Longmire
t (01684) 566689
e pml@peachfield.freeserve.co.uk

Clouds End ★★★
Self Catering
Contact: Suzie Neill
t (01684) 578834
e suzie@cloudsend.co.uk
w cloudsend.co.uk

Como House
Rating Applied For
Self Catering
Contact: Mr Kevin Austin
t (01684) 561486
e kevin@comohouse.co.uk
w comohouse.co.uk

The Dell House ★★★
Self Catering
Contact: Mr Ian Burrage
t (01684) 564448
e ian@dellhouse.co.uk
w dellhouse.co.uk

Farmhouse Cottage ★★★★
Self Catering
Contact: Mrs Sue Stringer
t (01684) 566750
e cowleighpark@ukonline.co.uk
w cowleighparkfarm.co.uk

Greenbank Garden Flat
★★★ *Self Catering*
Contact: Mr David Matthews
Greenbank House Garden Flat
t (01684) 567328
e matthews.greenbank@virgin.net

Hidelow House Cottages
★★★★–★★★★★
Self Catering
Contact: Mr & Mrs Stuart & Pauline Diplock
Hidelow House Cottages
t (01886) 884547
e hwv@hidelow.co.uk
w hidelow.co.uk

Holly Lodge, Earl's Croome
★★★★ *Self Catering*
Contact: Mrs Sandra Goodwin
c/o Hollybeds Farm
t (01684) 592877
e sandra@hollylodge.biz
w hollylodge.biz

Maynard Lodge ★★★★★
Self Catering
Contact: Mr Michael & Elaine Roberts
t (01684) 564568
e info@maynardlodge.co.uk

The Old Bakery ★★★
Self Catering
Contact: Mrs Judith Aldridge
t (01684) 566044
e westendhouse@btinternet.com
w oldbakerymalvern.co.uk

The Orangery at Little Boynes, Upton-upon-Severn
★★★★ *Self Catering*
Contact: Mr Chris Martin
Little Boynes
t (01684) 594788
e info@little-boynes.co.uk
w little-boynes.co.uk

The Studio ★★★
Self Catering
Contact: Mrs Gwyn Sloan
t (01684) 561074
e sloaniain@hotmail.com

Wayfarers Cottage ★★★
Self Catering
Contact: Mr & Mrs John & Caroline Roslington
Wayfarers
t (01684) 575758
e jroslington@mac.com
w wayfarerscottage.co.uk

West Hill Cottage ★★★★
Self Catering
Contact: Mrs M Stephens
t (01634) 566155

Whitewells Farm Cottages
★★★★ *Self Catering*
Contact: Kate Kavanagh
t (01886) 880607
e info@whitewellsfarm.co.uk
w whitewellsfarm.co.uk

MARDEN
Herefordshire

Litmarsh Farm ★★★
Self Catering
Contact: Jean Stone
t (01568) 797374

MARKET DRAYTON
Shropshire

Old Smithy Holiday Cottages ★★★★ *Self Catering & Serviced Apartments*
Contact: Mrs Carmel Simpson
The Old Smithy Holiday Cottages
t (01630) 661661
e oldsmithy@fsmail.net
w stmem.com/oldsmithyholidaycottages

MATHON
Herefordshire

Netherley Hall Cottages
★★-★★★★★ *Self Catering*
Contact: Mr & Mrs G. Vos
t (01886) 880262

MAVESYN RIDWARE
Staffordshire

Creamery at Manor Farm (The) ★★★★★ *Self Catering*
Contact: Mrs Kate Derry
Creamery (The)
t (01543) 493223
e katiederry@aol.com
w thecreamerystaffs.com

Stable Cottage ★★★★
Self Catering
Contact: Mrs Susan Clift
t (01543) 491579
e dmsaclift@farming.co.uk
w stablecottagestaffs.co.uk

MEERBROOK
Staffordshire

Old Hag Farm Holiday Cottages ★★★★
Self Catering
Contact: Mr & Mrs Kirkpatrick
t (01260) 227282

MEOLE BRACE
Shropshire

Stable Cottage ★★
Self Catering
Contact: Mrs Baugh
t (01743) 236914
e sula.rayska@virgin.net
w stmem.com/stablecottage

MICHAELCHURCH ESCLEY
Herefordshire

Holt Farm ★★★★
Self Catering
Contact: Mr Pash
Hideaways
t (01747) 828000
e enq@hideaways.co.uk
w hideaways.co.uk

MIDDLETON SCRIVEN
Shropshire

Harry's House ★★★★
Self Catering
t (01746) 789224
e pat@coatesfarm.co.uk
w coatesfarm.co.uk

MILWICH
Staffordshire

Summerhill Farm ★★★★
Self Catering
Contact: Mrs Patricia Milward
t (01889) 505546
e p.milward@btinternet.com
w summerhillfarmapartments.co.uk

MINSTERLEY
Shropshire

Luckley Cottage ★★★★
Self Catering
t (01743) 891469
e carolyn1sinclair@aol.com
w machamore.sathosting.net/index.htm

Upper House Farm Cottage
★★★★ *Self Catering*
t (01743) 792831
e k.stanhope@ukonline.co.uk
w stmem.com/upperhousefarmcottage

MORVILLE
Shropshire

Hurst Farm Cottages
★★★★ *Self Catering*
Contact: Mr & Mrs J Brick
t (01746) 714375
e info@cottagefishingholidays.co.uk
w cottagefishingholidays.co.uk

MUCH COWARNE
Herefordshire

Cowarne Hall Cottages
★★★★ *Self Catering*
Contact: Mr Richard Bradbury
t (01432) 820317
e rm@cowarnehall.co.uk
w cowarnehall.co.uk

Old Bridgend Cottage
★★★★ *Self Catering*
Contact: Mrs Angela Morgan
t (020) 8942 0702

MUCH MARCLE
Herefordshire

Shepherds Rest ★★★★
Self Catering
Contact: Mrs Fiona Wilcox
t (01531) 660285
e fjwilcox@waitrose.com

MUCH WENLOCK
Shropshire

3 Queen Street ★★★
Self Catering
Contact: Mrs E A Williams
t (01902) 341399 & (01743) 362315
e williams_letting@hotmail.com
w stmem.com/3queenstreet

Bramley ★★ *Self Catering*
Contact: Mrs Dee Revell
t (01952) 728153
e drevell@toucansurf.com
w stmem.com/bramley

The Owl's House ★★★★★
Self Catering
Contact: Mrs Samantha Gray
The Owl's House
t (01952) 728169
e dgray@dgray96.fsnet.co.uk
w owlshouse.co.uk

The Priory ★★★
Self Catering
t (01952) 728280
e aa@croftpriory.fslife.co.uk
w stmem.com/thepriory

Priory Cottage ★★★
Self Catering
t (01952) 727386
e aa@croftpriory.fslife.co.uk
w stmem.com/priorycottage

Stokes Barn Cottages ★★★
Self Catering
Contact: Mrs Suzanne Hill
Stokes Cottage
t (01952) 727293
e info@stokesbarn.co.uk
w stokesbarn.co.uk

NEEN SOLLARS
Shropshire

Cider House ★★★★
Self Catering
Contact: Ms Priscilla Kennedy
t (01299) 270414
e priscillahann@lineone.net

Garden Cottage ★★★
Self Catering
Contact: Mr & Mrs P Luff
t (01299) 271082

Live & Let Live ★★★
Self Catering
Contact: Mrs Christine Ferguson
Live and Let Live
t (01299) 832391

NETHERSEAL
Staffordshire

Grangefields Pine Lodge
★★★★ *Self Catering*
t (01827) 373253

NEWBOROUGH
Staffordshire

Poplars Farmhouse ★★★★
Self Catering
Contact: Sarah Skipper
Moat Lane
t (01283) 575200
e sarah@skippershaulage.fsnet.co.ek

NEWCASTLE
Shropshire

Buckshead
Rating Applied For
Self Catering
Contact: Mrs Sue Wheeler
t (01588) 640248
e brynmawr@farmersweekly.net
w dunvalleyorganics.net

NORBURY
Shropshire

Shuttocks Lodge ★★★
Self Catering
Contact: Mrs Ann Williams
t (01588) 650433
e shuttockswood@btconnect.com
w smoothhound.co.uk/hotels/shuttock.html

NORBURY
Staffordshire

Oulton House Farm Garden Cottages ★★★★
Self Catering
Contact: Mrs Judy Palmer
t (01785) 284264
e judy@oultonhousefarm.co.uk
w oultonhousefarm.co.uk

NORTON LINDSEY
Warwickshire

Willow Cottage, Norton Lindsey ★★★★ *Self Catering*
Contact: Mrs Helen Phillips
Lower House Farm
t (01926) 842394
e canadalanefarm@yahoo.co.uk
w willow-cottage.org.uk

OAKAMOOR
Staffordshire

The Annexe at The Old Furnace ★★★ *Self Catering*
Contact: Mr John Higgins
t (01538) 703331
w oldfurnace.co.uk

The Stables Accommodation
★★ *Self Catering*
Contact: Mrs Sarah Lomas
t (01538) 703844
e sarahlomas@blazemail.com
w 1milefromaltontowers.co.uk

ODSTONE
Warwickshire

Odstone Hall ★★★★
Self Catering
Contact: Miss Joanne Woodward
t (01530) 260312
e woodwards@odstonehall.com
w odstonehall.com

Look out for establishments participating in the Walkers and Cyclists Welcome Schemes

ORCOP
Herefordshire

Bury Farm ★★ *Self Catering*
Contact: Mrs Glenys Goodwin
Old Kitchen Farm
t (01981) 240383
e sc@igoodwin.fsbusiness.co.uk

OSWESTRY
Shropshire

Cross Keys Cottage, Selattyn ★★★ *Self Catering*
Contact: Mr & Mrs Philip Rothera
t (01691) 650247
e hildarothera@tiscali.co.uk
w thecrosskeys-selattyn.co.uk

Old Rectory Cottage (Selattyn) ★★ *Self Catering*
Contact: Mrs Maggie Barnes
The Old Rectory Cottage
t (01691) 659708

The Stables, Morton ★★★★ *Self Catering*
Contact: Mrs L M Frank
The Stables
t (01691) 682218
e bookings@mortonstables.co.uk
w mortonstables.co.uk

Tannery Cottage ★★★ *Self Catering*
t (01691) 654961
e graham@tannery63.fsnet.co.uk
w http://tannery-cottage.mysite.wanadoo-members.co.uk

PEMBRIDGE
Herefordshire

The Cottage ★★★ *Self Catering*
Contact: Mr & Mrs Jones
t (01544) 388569
e jonescottage@aol.com
w cottageguide.co.uk/clearbrook

The Granary and The Dairy ★★★ *Self Catering*
Contact: Mrs Nancy Owens
The Granary and The Dairy
t (01544) 388268
e nancy@grovedesign.co.uk

Luntley Court Farm ★★★★ *Self Catering*
Contact: Mrs Sandra Owens
t (01544) 388422
e luntley.court.farm@farming.co.uk

The Stables ★★★★ *Self Catering*
Contact: Mrs Jean Simmonds
t (01544) 388619
e jean@seagrass.cottages.co.uk
w seagrasscottages.co.uk

Winyard Lodge Tibhall Lodges ★★★★ *Self Catering*
Contact: Mrs Jean Gwatkin
Tibhall Lodges
t (01544) 388428
e ebgwatkin@aol.com

PENCOMBE
Herefordshire

Durstone Cottages ★★★ *Self Catering*
Contact: Ms Sarah Mulroy
t (01885) 400221
e mul@farmersweekly.net

PENKRIDGE
Staffordshire

Dalraddy Cottage ★★★★ *Self Catering*
Contact: Mrs Sonia Young
t (01785) 715700
e sonia@adamsyoung.fsnet.co.uk
w dalraddycottage.co.uk

PERSHORE
Worcestershire

Abberton Hall ★★★★ *Self Catering*
Contact: Mr & Mrs David & Zoe Ager
t (01386) 462999
e abbertonhall@aol.com
w abbertonhall.co.uk

PILLERTON HERSEY
Warwickshire

Roman Acres Cottage ★★★ *Self Catering*
Contact: Mrs Williams
t (01789) 740360

PONTRILAS
Herefordshire

Station House ★★★ *Self Catering*
Contact: Jo Russell
t (01981) 240564
e gwrstation04@tesco.net
w golden-valley.co.uk/stationhouse

PRESTON WYNNE
Herefordshire

Wisteria Cottage ★★★ *Self Catering*
Contact: Mrs Jenni Maund
t (01432) 820608
e lowertown@onetel.net.uk

PRESTWOOD
Staffordshire

Swallows Loft ★★★ *Self Catering*
Contact: Mrs Joyce Beeson
t (01889) 590464
e bookings@swallows-loft.fsnet.co.uk
w swallows-loft.fsnet.co.uk

PULVERBATCH
Shropshire

Holly Grove Cottage ★★★★ *Self Catering*
Contact: Mrs Sue Morris
t (01743) 718300
e pulverbatch@onetel.com
w hollygrovecottage.co.uk

RICHARDS CASTLE
Shropshire

The Barn (Ryecroft) ★★★★ *Self Catering*
Contact: Mr & Mrs Peter & Sue Plant
t (01584) 831224
e ryecroftbarn@hotmail.com
w ludlow.org.uk/ryecroft

Stables Flat, Richards Castle ★★★★ *Self Catering*
Contact: Mrs Sandra English
t (01584) 831265
e english.david@tiscali.co.uk

ROSS-ON-WYE
Herefordshire

Ashe Holiday Cottages ★★★-★★★★ *Self Catering*
Contact: Mrs Maria Ball
t (01989) 563336
e info@ashe-holiday-cottages.com
w ashe-holiday-cottages.com

Barn House and Oaklands ★★★ *Self Catering*
Contact: Mrs Angela Farr
Farr Cottages
t (01600) 750333
e farrcottages@yahoo.com
w farrcottages.co.uk

Benhall Farm ★★★ *Self Catering*
Contact: Mrs Carol Brewer
Benhall Farm
t (01989) 563900
e info@benhallfarm.co.uk
w benhallfarm.co.uk

Bridstow House Annexe ★★★ *Self Catering*
Contact: Dr & Mrs P. D. A. Irani
t 0800 328 5259
e iranida@aol.com

Fairview ★★★ *Self Catering*
Contact: Mrs Jones
Stoneleigh
t (01989) 566301

The Game Larders and The Old Bakehouse ★★★ *Self Catering*
Contact: Miss Anthea McIntyre
The Game Larders and The Old Bakehouse
t (01989) 562688
e wythall@globalnet.co.uk
w wythallestate.co.uk

Mainoaks Farm Cottages ★★★-★★★★ *Self Catering*
Contact: Mrs Unwin
Hill House
t (01531) 650448
e mainoaks@lineone.net
w mainoaks.co.uk

Man of Ross House ★★ *Self Catering*
Contact: Mr David Campkin
t (0118) 957 2561
e dave.campkin@uop.com

The Olde House ★★★ *Self Catering*
Contact: Mrs J Fray
t (01989) 780383
e peter@pjfray.co.uk
w oldehouse.com

Pear Tree Cottage ★★★ *Self Catering*
Contact: Mrs Jenny Sanders
Woodlands Farm
t (01432) 840488
e perrystonecottages@hotmail.com
w perrystonecottages.co.uk

Watchmaker's Cottage ★★★★ *Self Catering*
Contact: Mrs J. Clark
t (01989) 770369
e watchmakerscottage@madasafish.com

Wharton Lodge Cottages ★★★★★ *Self Catering*
Contact: Mrs Nicky Cross
t (01989) 750140
e ncross@whartonlodge.co.uk
w whartonlodge.co.uk

RUDYARD
Staffordshire

Chacara ★★★★ *Self Catering*
Contact: Mrs Christine Gee
Broomfield
t (01538) 306663

RUGBY
Warwickshire

Lawford Hill Farm ★★★★ *Self Catering*
Contact: Mr & Mrs Susan Moses
Lawford Hill Farm
t (01788) 542001
e lawford.hill@talk21.com
w lawfordhill.co.uk

The Saddlery ★★★★★ *Self Catering*
Contact: Mrs Elaine Heckford
t (01788) 890256
e office@thesaddlery.org.uk
w thesaddlery.org.uk

RUSHBURY
Shropshire

Lilywood Cottage ★★★★ *Self Catering*
t (01694) 771286
e ruth.lole@talktalk.net
w stmem.com/lilywoodcottage

RUSHTON SPENCER
Staffordshire

Toft Hall ★★★★ *Self Catering*
Contact: Ms Sue Norgrove-Moore
t (01260) 226609
e tofthallenquiries@hotmail.com
w tofthall.com

ST OWENS CROSS
Herefordshire

Bramley Cottage ★★★★ *Self Catering*
t (01989) 730416
e lucy@bramleyholidaycottage.co.uk
w bramleyholidaycottage.co.uk

SCHOLAR GREEN
Staffordshire

Heritage Wharf Bungalow ★★★★ *Self Catering*
Contact: Mr Mike Dowse
t (01782) 785700
e heritage@sherbornewharf.co.uk
w sherbornewharf.co.uk

SEVERN STOKE
Worcestershire

Roseland ★★★★
Self Catering
Contact: Mr & Mrs Guy & Mary Laurent
Roseland Bungalow
t (01905) 371463
e guy@roselandworcs.demon.co.uk
w roselandworcs.demon.co.uk

SHEEN
Staffordshire

Bank Top Lodge ★★★★
Self Catering
Contact: Mrs Nancy Birch
t (01298) 84768

SHIFNAL
Shropshire

The Old Stable ★★★
Self Catering
Contact: Mr & Mrs R Wild
The Flat
t (01952) 461136
e wildthings@raphaelsrestaurant.co.uk
w raphaelsrestaurant.co.uk

SHIPSTON-ON-STOUR
Warwickshire

Blackwell Grange Cottages
★★★ *Self Catering*
Contact: Mrs Liz Vernon Miller
c/o Blackwell Grange
t (01608) 682357
e liz@blackwellgrange.co.uk
w blackwellgrange.co.uk

Little Barn ★★★★
Self Catering
Contact: Mrs Karen Lawrence
Acorns
t (01608) 684240
e johnandkaren.lawrence@ic24.net
w thelittlebarn.co.uk

SHOBDON
Herefordshire

Tyn-y-Coed ★★★★
Self Catering
Contact: Mr & Mrs John & Diana Andrews
t (01568) 708277
e jandrews@shobdondesign.kc3.co.uk

SHREWSBURY
Shropshire

12a Butcher Row ★★★
Self Catering
t (01543) 256582
e butcher.row@ntlworld.com
w stmem.com/butcherrow

89 Longden Coleham ★★★
Self Catering
Contact: Mrs Jennifer Connor
Willow House
t (01743) 355047

Barn Cottages ★★★★
Self Catering
t (01743) 355594
e jgood70712@aol.com

Hotspur
Rating Applied For
Self Catering
Contact: Ms Miriam Doyle
t +353 1 679 1551
e info@pka.ie

Mill House Farm ★★★
Self Catering
Contact: Mrs Christine Burton
t (01743) 860325
e christine@millhousefarmholidays.fsnet.co.uk
w stmem.com/millhousefarm

The Stables ★★★★
Self Catering
Contact: Ms Miriam Doyle
t +353 1 679 1551

Yews Barn ★★★★
Self Catering
t (01952) 604248
e gpassant@aol.com
w yewsbarn.co.uk

STANFORD BRIDGE
Worcestershire

The Riseling ★★★★
Self Catering
Contact: Mrs Margaret Lane
t (01886) 853438

STIPERSTONES
Shropshire

Resting Hill ★★★
Self Catering
Contact: Mrs Rowson
t (01743) 791219
w stmem.com/restinghill

STOKE-ON-TRENT
Staffordshire

Bank End Farm Cottages
★★★★ *Self Catering*
Contact: Mr Kenneth Meredith
Bank End Farm
t (01782) 502160
e pete502@btopenworld.com
w alton-village.com

Field Head Farm House Holidays ★★★★
Self Catering
Contact: Ms Janet Hudson
t (01538) 308352
e janet@field-head.co.uk
w field-head.co.uk

Jay's Barn ★★★ *Self Catering*
Contact: Mrs Christine Babb
t (01889) 507444
e jaysbarn@realemail.co.uk
w jaysbarn.co.uk

Lockwood Hall Farm ★★★★
Self Catering
Contact: Mrs Rebecca Sherratt
t (01538) 752270
e sherratt@lockwoodhall.freeserve.co.uk
w cottageguide.co.uk/lockwoodhall

Low Roofs ★★★
Self Catering
Contact: Mrs Lesley Malkin
t (01782) 627087

Moor Court Cottages Moor Court House ★★★★
Self Catering
Contact: Vanessa & Les Bradshaw
t (01538) 723008
w moorcourtcottages.co.uk

STOKE ST MILBOROUGH
Shropshire

Cherry Tree Cottage
Rating Applied For
Self Catering
t (01584) 823626
e claude@clbodenham.com
w stmilburga-holidayhomes.com

St Milburga Chapel ★★★★
Self Catering
Contact: Mr & Mrs Claude & Wendy Bodenham
t (01584) 823626
e claude@clbodenham.com
w stmilburga-holidayhomes.com

STONE
Staffordshire

Fox Hollow, Hilderstone
★★★★ *Self Catering*
Contact: Ms Michelle Monaghan
Cresswell Road
t (01889) 505045
e mcmahon605@hotmail.com
w foxhollowbarnes.co.uk

STOURPORT-ON-SEVERN
Worcestershire

Winnall House Cottage and Caravan Park ★★★★
Self Catering
Contact: Mrs Sheila Wilson
t (01299) 250389

STRATFORD-UPON-AVON
Warwickshire

1 College Mews ★★★★
Self Catering
Contact: Mr Reid
t (01789) 450266

21 Bancroft Place ★★★★
Self Catering
Contact: Mrs Stella Carter
J & S Carter
t (01789) 266839

42 Shakespeare Street
★★★★ *Self Catering*
Contact: Mr Field
Avon House
t (01789) 298141
e kdfield@stratfordholidaycottages.com
w stratfordholidaycottages.com

61 Waterside ★★★★
Self Catering
Contact: Mr Andrew Skinner
t (01624) 693221
e andrew_skinne59@hotmail.com

Abacarn Cottage ★★★
Self Catering
Contact: Miss Lindsey Matheson
t (01789) 552570
e mathesonl62@hotmail.com

As You Like It ★★★
Self Catering
Contact: Mrs Reid
t (01789) 450266
w alderminster99.freeserve.co.uk

Charlecote Cottage 2 Willicote Pastures ★★★★
Self Catering
Contact: Mr John Lea
t (01925) 604106
e jplea@aol.com

Chestnut Cottage, Pathlow
★★★ *Self Catering*
Contact: Mrs Joyce Rush
Chestnut Cottage
t (01789) 292764

Crimscote Downs Farm Holiday Cottages
★★★-★★★★ *Self Catering*
Contact: Mrs Joan James
The Old Coach House
t (01789) 450275
e joan.james@tesco.net
w stratford-upon-avon.co.uk/crimscote.htm

Elmhurst ★★★★
Self Catering
Contact: Mrs Davenport
Lygon Arms Hotel
t (01386) 840318
e sandra@elmhurstcottage.co.uk
w elmhurstcottage.co.uk

Ely Street ★★★ *Self Catering*
Contact: Mr Nicholas Pash
Hideaways
t (01747) 828170
e enq@hideaways.co.uk
w hideaways.co.uk/property.cfm/H180

Falcon Cottage ★★★★
Self Catering
Contact: Ms Kim Day
t (020) 8366 0237
e kimpet21@aol.com
w falcon-cottage.co.uk

Flower Court ★★★★
Self Catering
Contact: Mrs Rachel Liddell
t (01386) 438833
e liddellrachel@aol.com
w flowercourt.co.uk

Fosbroke Cottage ★★★
Self Catering
Contact: Mrs Susan Swift
t (01789) 772327
e mark@swiftvilla.fsnet.co.uk

Holtom Mews ★★★★
Self Catering
Contact: Ms Jan Brady
t (0121) 308 7050
e ardenproperties@btinternet.com
w ardenproperties.co.uk

No 7 Bull Street ★★★
Self Catering
Contact: Mrs Sally-Ann Salmon
t (01675) 443613
e sallyannsalmon@talk21.com

Riverview Lodge ★★★★
Self Catering
t 07802 640372
e info@luxurylifestylelodges.co.uk
w luxurylifestylelodges.co.uk

Rollright Cottage ★★★★
Self Catering
Contact: Mr Alun Thomas
t (01675) 460269
e info@rollrightcottage.co.uk
w rollrightcottage.co.uk

Stable Cottage ★★★
Self Catering
Contact: Ms Isobel Ollis
t (01926) 651235

Weston Sands Holiday Homes Ltd ★★★★
Self Catering
Contact: Mrs Debbie Skett
Sunfield
t (01789) 751658
e debbieskett@aol.com
w westonsands.co.uk

Woodcote ★★★★★ *Self Catering & Serviced Apartments*
Contact: Mr & Mrs Lucas
t (01789) 293932
e lucasstratford@aolco.uk
w lucasstratford.co.uk

STRENSHAM
Worcestershire

The Parlour, Home Farm, Near Upton upon Severn
★★★★ *Self Catering*
Contact: Mrs Mandy Davenport
t (01684) 293685
e mdavenport@beeb.net

SUCKLEY
Worcestershire

Tundridge Mill ★★★★
Self Catering
Contact: Mrs Penny Beard
t (01886) 884478
w tundridgemill.co.uk

SYMONDS YAT
Herefordshire

Hollytree House ★★★
Self Catering
Contact: Ms Sue Wadley
Bighouselets Ltd.
t (01600) 772929
e sue@roscoerogersandknight.co.uk
w hollytreehouse.info

Old Court Farm ★★★★
Self Catering
Contact: Mrs Edwina Gee
t (01600) 890316
e teddy.gee@breathemail.net

Wye Valley View ★★★
Self Catering
Contact: Mr & Mrs Strefford
t (01600) 890070
e wyevalleyview@yahoo.co.uk
w wyevalleyview.co.uk

TEAN
Staffordshire

Oakhill Holiday Homes
★★★★ *Self Catering*
Contact: Mr Philip & Hilary Williams
t (01538) 722213
e oakhillcottages@btinternet.com
w oakhillcottages.co.uk

The Old Smithy ★★★
Self Catering
Contact: Mrs Judy Dronzek
Woodlands
t (01889) 507249

The Rockery ★★★
Self Catering
Contact: Mrs Rushton
t (01889) 507434
e dinah@abbey-view.fsnet.co.uk
w cottageguide.co.uk/therockery

TELFORD
Shropshire

Church Farm Self Catering (Rowton) ★★★ *Self Catering*
Contact: Mrs Virginia Evans
Church Farm Cottages
t (01952) 770381
e churchfarm49@beeb.net
w virtual-shropshire.co.uk/churchfarm

The Granary Loft ★★★
Self Catering
Contact: Mrs Carolyn Dorrell
t (01952) 677917
e info@hoofarm.com

Morrells Wood Farm ★★★
Self Catering
Contact: Mr Derek Harper
t (01952) 510273
w stmem.com/morrells-wood-farm

Old Stables Cottage ★★★
Self Catering
Contact: Mrs Ferriday
t (01952) 684238
e alex@ferriday7131.freeserve.co.uk

TENBURY WELLS
Worcestershire

Colleybatch Pine Lodges
★★★★ *Self Catering*
Contact: Mr & Mrs Tebbett
t (01584) 810153

Rochford Park Cottages
★★★-★★★★ *Self Catering*
Contact: Mrs J Robinson
Rochford Park
t (01584) 781392
e mrs.j.robinson@fwi.co.uk
w rochfordpark.co.uk

TREFONEN
Shropshire

Little Barn ★★★★
Self Catering
t (01691) 653387
e info@little-barn-shropshire.co.uk
w little-barn-shropshire.co.uk

TUGFORD
Shropshire

Tugford Farm Holiday Cottages & Livery
★★-★★★★ *Self Catering*
Contact: Mrs Bronwen Williams
t (01584) 841259
e williamstugford@supanet.com
w tugford.com

UFTON
Warwickshire

Wood Farm ★★★★
Self Catering
Contact: Mr Derek Hiatt
t (01926) 612270

ULLINGTON
Worcestershire

Dawn Cottage ★★★★
Self Catering
Contact: Dawn Browning
t (01789) 721873

UPPER HULME
Staffordshire

Hurdlow Cottage ★★★★
Self Catering
Contact: Mrs Ruth Belfield
t (01538) 300406
e robertruth@hurdlowfarm.fsnet.co.uk
w hurdlowfarm.fsnet.co.uk

UPPER QUINTON
Warwickshire

1 Meon View (Annexe)
★★★★ *Self Catering*
Contact: Mrs Rimell
t (01789) 720080
w meonview.co.uk

Gable Cottage ★★★★
Self Catering
Contact: Ms Angela Richards
Manor Cottages
t (01993) 824252
e mancott@netcomuk.co.uk

Winton House Cottage
★★★★ *Self Catering*
Contact: Mrs Lyon
Winton House
t (01789) 720500
e gail@wintonhouse.com
w wintonhouse.com

UPTON BISHOP
Herefordshire

Woodredding Farm ★★
Self Catering
Contact: Mr Brian Robbins
t (01531) 660257
e brian@woodredding.co.uk
w woodredding.co.uk

UPTON UPON SEVERN
Worcestershire

Captains Retreat ★★★★
Self Catering
Contact: Mr & Mrs Michael & Julie-Ann Cranton
White Cottage
t (01684) 592023
e michael@cranton.freeserve.co.uk

Old Market House ★★★★
Self Catering
Contact: Catherine & Barry Sparks
Birchwood House
t (01934) 824877
e barry-sparks@hotmail.com

UPTON WARREN
Worcestershire

The Durrance ★★★★
Self Catering
Contact: Mrs Helen Hirons
t (01562) 777533
e helenhirons@thedurrance.co.uk
w thedurrance.co.uk

UTTOXETER
Staffordshire

Woodland Views Holiday Cottages ★★★★
Self Catering
Contact: Mrs Kate Tomlinson
t (01283) 820012
e enquiries@woodlandviews.co.uk
w woodlandviews.co.uk

VOWCHURCH
Herefordshire

The Front Dore ★★★
Self Catering
Contact: Mr & Mrs N. Meers
t (01432) 820493
w cottageguide.co.uk/thefrontdore

WALL-UNDER-HEYWOOD
Shropshire

Old Stables ★★★★
Self Catering
Contact: Mrs Helen Hartill
t (01694) 771278
e hartillhelen@aol.com

WARSLOW
Staffordshire

Shay Side Barn and Cottage
★★★★ *Self Catering*
Contact: Mr Clive Sykes
Sykes Cottages
t (01244) 345700
e info@sykescottages.co.uk
w sykescottages.co.uk

WARWICK
Warwickshire

22 Upper Cape ★★★
Self Catering
Contact: Mr Donald Bishop
t 07870 789311

Copes Flat ★★★
Self Catering
Contact: Mrs Elizabeth Draisey
Forth House
t (01926) 401512
e info@forthhouseuk.co.uk
w forthhouseuk.co.uk

Luxury Warwick Apartment
Rating Applied For
Self Catering
t 07748 144692
e warwickflat@fsmail.net

Whitley Elm Cottages
★★★★ *Self Catering*
Contact: Mr & Mrs Clive & Pat Bevins
t (01926) 484577
e clive.bevins@btconnect.com
w whitleyelmcottages.com

WATERHOUSES
Staffordshire

55 Reasons
Rating Applied For
Self Catering
Peak Cottages
t (0114) 262 0777
e enquiries@peakcottages.com
w peakcottages.com

Broadhurst Holiday Cottages ★★★★
Self Catering
Contact: Mr Nicholas Briand
Broadhurst Farm
t (01538) 308261

Greenside Cottages
★★★-★★★★ *Self Catering*
Contact: Mr & Mrs Terry & Sue Riley
Sykes Cottages
t (01538) 308313
e terryriley@zetnet.co.uk
w users.zetnet.co.uk/BrownEndFarm/gs_index.htm

Limestone View Cottage
★★★ *Self Catering*
Contact: Mrs Wendy Webster
t (01538) 308288
e wendywebster@limestoneviewfarm.freeserve.co.uk
w peakdistrictfarmhols.co.uk

WELFORD-ON-AVON
Warwickshire

The Granary ★★★★
Self Catering
Contact: Mr & Mrs Spink
t (01789) 750752
e bruce_spink@btopenworld.com

Peacock Thatch ★★★★
Self Catering
Contact: Mr Peter Holden
The Little Cottage
t (01332) 551155
e peterpeacockthatch@dmserve.com

WELLINGTON
Shropshire

The Coach House ★★★★
Self Catering
Contact: Mrs Fellows
Old Vicarage
t (01952) 244859
e mue@mfellows0.freeserve.co.uk

WELSH NEWTON COMMON
Herefordshire

Newton Lodge ★★★
Self Catering
Contact: Mr Andrew Barter
t (01989) 770147
e andrewb@newton-lodge.co.uk
w newton-lodge.co.uk

WELSHAMPTON
Shropshire

Rowe Valley Annexe ★★★
Self Catering
t (01948) 710587
e david.r.kerr@btinternet.com
w cottageguide.co.uk/rowevalleyannex

WEM
Shropshire

Soulton Hall Cottages ★★★
Self Catering
Contact: Mrs Ashton
t (01939) 232786
e jiashton@soultonhall.fsbusiness.co.uk
w soultonhall.co.uk

WEST FELTON
Shropshire

The Stables ★★★★
Self Catering
Contact: Mr & Mrs Edward & Kirsten Nicholas
T H Nicholas & Son
t (01691) 610230
e edwardnicholas@freeuk.com

WESTON ON AVON
Warwickshire

March Font, Hurnberry, Brickall and The Arbales, Prospect House
★★★★-★★★★★
Self Catering
Contact: Mr & Mrs Richard Bluck
t (01789) 750688
e r.bluckwestonfarm@amserve.net
w westonfarm.co.uk

WESTON RHYN
Shropshire

Mill Cottage ★★★
Self Catering
Contact: Mr & Mrs H Brannick
Mill Cottage
t (01691) 659738

WETTON
Staffordshire

Manor Barn ★★★
Self Catering
Contact: Mr & Mrs Higton
t (01335) 310223
w peakcottages.com

Old Sunday School ★★★★
Self Catering
Peak Cottages
t (0114) 262 0777
e enquries@peakcottages.com
w peakcottages.com

Stable Barn ★★★
Self Catering
Contact: Mrs Hilary Higton
t (01335) 310312

Wetton Barns Holiday Cottages ★★★★-★★★★★
Self Catering
Contact: Mr Ben Garstang
t (01246) 565310
e bjg@chatsworth.org
w chatsworth.org

WHATELEY
Staffordshire

33 Rosemary Cottage ★★★
Self Catering
Contact: Mrs Voilet Coles
t (01827) 280826

WHITBOURNE
Herefordshire

Crumplebury Farmhouse
★★★ *Self Catering*
Contact: Mrs Anne Evans
Dial House
t (01886) 821534
e a.evans@candaevans.fsnet.co.uk
w whitbourne-estate.co.uk/crumplebury

Elcocks Cottage ★★★
Self Catering
Contact: Mr Mike Hogg
t (0121) 427 1395
e mike@elcocks.net
w elcocks.net

Hareley Barn ★★★★
Self Catering
Contact: Mrs Gillian Herbert
Hareley Farm
t (01886) 884362
e holidays@hareleyfarm.fsnet.co.uk

The Olde Rectory, Whitbourne
★★★★-★★★★★
Self Catering
Contact: Gilly & Cliff Poultney
t (01886) 822000
e stay@olde-rectory.co.uk
w olde-rectory.co.uk

WHITCHURCH
Herefordshire

Norton Cottages ★★★★
Self Catering
Contact: Su & Richard Jackson
t (01600) 890046
e enquiries@norton.wyenet.co.uk
w norton-cottages.com

Tump Farm ★★★
Self Catering
Contact: Mrs Williams
t (01600) 891029
e clinwilcharmaine@hotmail.com

WHITCHURCH
Shropshire

Combermere Abbey Cottages ★★★★★
Self Catering
Contact: Mrs Sarah Callander-Beckett
t (01948) 662876
e cottages@combermereabbey.co.uk
w combermereabbey.co.uk

The Park ★★★★
Self Catering
t (01432) 840287
e anthonyjwright48@yahoo.co.uk

WILMCOTE
Warwickshire

Apple Loft ★★★★
Self Catering
Contact: Mrs Margaret Mander
t (01789) 205889
e peartree3@hotmail.com
w peartreecot.co.uk

WINKHILL
Staffordshire

Alma Cottage ★★★★
Self Catering
Contact: Mrs Diana Cope
t (01538) 308909
e diana.cope@cottagedelight.co.uk
w almacottage.com

WORCESTER
Worcestershire

Hazeldene, Little Lightwood Farm ★★★★ *Self Catering*
Contact: Mrs Vera Rogers
Little Lightwood Farm
t (01905) 333236
e lightwood.holidays@virgin.net
w lightwoodfarm.co.uk

Maybury and Malvern View
★★★ *Self Catering*
Contact: Mr & Mrs Richard & Christine Houghton
t (01905) 333202
e richard-houghton@lineone.net
w upperlightwood.co.uk

Mill Cottage ★★★★
Self Catering
Contact: Mrs Valerie Baylis
Mildenham Mill
t (01905) 451554
e valerie.baylis@talk21.com

The Whitehouse ★★★★
Self Catering
Contact: Mrs Susan O'Neill
t (01886) 888743

WORMELOW
Herefordshire

Old Forge Cottage ★★★
Self Catering
Contact: Mrs Shirley Wheeler
t (01981) 540625

WROXETER
Shropshire

Glebe House
Rating Applied For
Self Catering
Contact: Mr & Mrs Millington
t (01743) 761888
e wine@wroxetervineyard.co.uk
w wroxetervineyard.co.uk

WYTHALL
Worcestershire

Inkford Court Cottages
★★★-★★★★ *Self Catering*
Contact: Mr Bedford
Inkford Court Cottages
t (01564) 822304

YARPOLE
Herefordshire

The Barn at Lower House Farm
Rating Applied For
Self Catering
Contact: Josie Woodfield
t (01568) 780280
e jswoodfield@tiscali.co.uk

EAST MIDLANDS

ALDERWASLEY
Derbyshire

Amber Wood Cottage
★★★★ *Self Catering*
Contact: Mrs Helen Allsopp
t (01629) 826431

Church View ★★★
Self Catering
Contact: Mr Stephen Mihulka
t (01629) 823728

ALFORD
Lincolnshire

Manor Farm Cottage ★★★
Self Catering
Contact: Mrs Mary Farrow
t (01507) 450228

Woodthorpe Hall Country Cottage ★★★★ *Self Catering*
Contact: Mrs Stubbs
Woodthorpe Hall Country Cottage
t (01507) 450294
e enquiries@woodthorpehallleisure.co.uk
w woodthorpehallleisure.co.uk

ALGARKIRK
Lincolnshire

Walnut Lake Fishing/Leisure
★★★★ *Self Catering*
Contact: Maria & Tony Potts
t (01205) 460482
e maria@walnutlakes.co.uk
w walnutlakes.co.uk

ALKBOROUGH
Lincolnshire

Corner Cottage ★★★★
Self Catering
Contact: Annette Dexter
t (01923) 330022
e annette.dexter@ntlworld.com

ALPORT
Derbyshire

Harthill Hall
Rating Applied For
Self Catering
Contact: Ian Thompson
t (01629) 636190
e ian@harthillhall.co.uk
w harthillhall.co.uk

Rock Cottage ★★★★
Self Catering
Contact: Ms Janet O'Sullivan
t (01629) 810910
e janet@haddonhall.co.uk

ALSOP-EN-LE-DALE
Derbyshire

Church Farm Cottages (Alsop) ★★★★ *Self Catering*
Contact: Mrs Christine Duffell
t (01335) 390216
e churchfarmcottages.alsop@virgin.net
w cressbrook.co.uk/ashborn/churchfarm

ALTON
Derbyshire

Wildflower Cottages
★★★★ *Self Catering*
Contact: Mrs S Fewtrell
Candlelight Cottage
t (01246) 590052
e sue@wildflowercottages.co.uk

ALVINGHAM
Lincolnshire

The Stables Holiday Cottage
★★★★ *Self Catering*
t (01507) 327442
e enquiries@stablesholidaycottage.co.uk
w stablesholidaycottage.co.uk

ARNOLD
Nottinghamshire

The Grannary ★★★
Self Catering
Contact: Mrs Lamin
The Grannary
t (0115) 926 8330

ASFORDBY
Leicestershire

Amberley Gardens Holiday Annexe ★★★★ *Self Catering*
Contact: Mr Bruce Brotherhood
t (01664) 812314
e bruce@amberleygardens.net
w amberleygardens.net

ASHBOURNE
Derbyshire

Ashfield and Dove Cottages
★★★ *Self Catering*
Contact: Mr Arthur Tatlow
t (01335) 324270

Borrowdale Cottage ★★★
Self Catering
Contact: Mr & Mrs Alexander
t (01763) 233216
e borrowdale.cottage@ntlworld.com
w cottageguide.co.uk/borrowdalecottage

Callow Top Cottages 1 and 2
★★★ *Self Catering*
Contact: Mrs Sue Deane
t (01335) 344020
e enquiries@callowtop.co.uk

Croft House Barn ★★★★
Self Catering
Contact: Stephanie Cadenhead
Waterfall
t (01538) 308125
e stephanie@crofthousebarn.co.uk
w crofthousebarn.co.uk

Greenacres ★★★★
Self Catering
Contact: Ms Frances Williamson
Luxury Location Lets
t (01332) 723192
e frances2@ntlworld.com

The Grooms Quarters
★★★★★ *Self Catering*
Contact: Mr & Mrs Ray & Ann Thompson
The Old Coach House
t (01335) 324549
e ann@groomsquarters.co.uk
w groomsquarters.co.uk

Haifa ★★★★ *Self Catering*
Contact: Mr David Dudley
t (01604) 403625

Hillside Croft ★★★★★
Self Catering
Contact: Mrs Pat Walker
Offcote Grange Cottage Holidays
t (01335) 344795
e cottages@hillsidecroft.co.uk

Iron Horse Cottage ★★★
Self Catering
Contact: Mr Gallimore
Elite Buildings
t (01335) 344065

Moore's Cottage Farm ★★★
Self Catering
Contact: Ms Janet Watson
t (01335) 346121
e janetwatson@waitrose.com
w cressbrook.co.uk

The Nook ★★★★
Self Catering
Contact: Mrs Susan Osborn
t (01455) 842609
e susan.osborn@virgin.net
w come.to/thenook

The Old Laundry ★★★★★
Self Catering
Contact: Mrs Patricia Cust
t (01335) 346711
e p.cust@virgin.net
w sturston.com

Old Miller's Cottage ★★★
Self Catering
Contact: Mrs P.M. Hewitt
t (01283) 815895

The Orchards ★★★★
Self Catering
Contact: Mrs Vanessa Holland
t (01538) 308205
e rushley.farm@btinternet.com
w cottageguide.co.uk/theorchards

Paddock House Farm Holiday Cottages, Alstonefield ★★★★
Self Catering
Contact: Mr & Mrs Mark & Melissa Redfern
Paddock House Farm Holiday Cottages
t 0870 027 2500
e info@paddockhousefarm.co.uk
w paddockhousefarm.co.uk

Sandybrook Country Park
★★★–★★★★ *Self Catering*
Pinelodge Holidays
t (01335) 300000
e enquiries@pinelodgeholidays.co.uk
w pinelodgeholidays.co.uk/sandybrook.ihtml

Shaw House ★★★
Self Catering
Contact: Mrs Carolyn Bettany
t (01335) 344510
e carolynbettany@btinternet.com

Slade House Farm
★★★★–★★★★★
Self Catering
Contact: Mr & Mrs Alan Philp
t (01538) 308123
e alanphilp@sladehousefarm.co.uk
w sladehousefarm.co.uk

The Tannery ★★★★
Self Catering
Contact: Mrs C G Spencer
t (01335) 342387

Thorpe Cloud View
★★★★★ *Self Catering*
Contact: Mr Raymond Neilson
Thorpe Cloud View
t (01335) 350215
e rayneilson@aol.com
w peakdistrictcottage.com

Topshill Cottage ★★★★
Self Catering
Contact: Mrs Bridget Simmonds
t (01629) 825568
e dksimmonds@netbreeze.co.uk

Turlow Fields Farm, Hognaston ★★★★
Self Catering
Contact: Mandy & Adrian Hunter
Barnclose Cottage
t (01335) 370834
e aahunter@uk2.net

Yeldersley Hall
★★★★–★★★★★
Self Catering
Contact: Mr Andrew Bailey
Yeldersley Hall
t (01335) 343432

Yelt Cottage ★★★
Self Catering
Contact: Mr Gilbert Collins
Yelt Farm
t 08523 416 1952
e ghc@boasecohencollins.com
w yeltcottage.co.uk

ASHBY-DE-LA-ZOUCH
Leicestershire

Ashby Pad
Rating Applied For
Self Catering
Contact: Michaela Gardener-Newman
t (01530) 560541
e michaela@gardener-newman.com

Badger's Sett ★★★
Self Catering
Contact: Mrs Aileen Wood
t (01670) 367723 & 07718 905251
e graham-aileen@16sandpiper.freeserve.co.uk
w badgers-sett.com

Norman's Barn ★★★★
Self Catering
Contact: Mrs Isabel Stanley
Norman's Barn
t (01530) 412224
e isabel_stanley@hotmail.com
w normansbarn.co.uk

Sylvan ★★★ *Self Catering*
Contact: Mrs Doreen Gasson
t (01530) 412012
e egg-deg@packington.freeserve.co.uk

Upper Rectory Farm Cottages ★★★★★
Self Catering
Contact: Mrs Jean Corbett
Upper Rectory Farm Cottages
t (01827) 880448
e info@upperrectoryfarmcottages.co.uk
w upperrectoryfarmcottages.co.uk

ASHFORD IN THE WATER
Derbyshire

Appletree Cottage ★★★★
Self Catering
Contact: Mr Steve Pope
t 07818 080709
e sjpope@tiscali.co.uk
w appletreecottages.co.uk

Ashford Farm Holiday Cottages ★★★-★★★★
Self Catering
Contact: Mrs Sarah Brocklehurst
t (01629) 812376
e info@ashfordfarmcottages.co.uk
w ashfordfarmcottages.co.uk

Churchdale Farm ★★★★★
Self Catering
Contact: Mrs Sarah Winkworth-Smith
t (01629) 640269
e info@churchdaleholidays.co.uk
w churchdaleholidays.co.uk

Clematis Cottage ★★★
Self Catering
Contact: Mr & Mrs Bernard & Kate Armstrong
t (01629) 813448
e bernard.armstrong@btinternet.com

Cliff End Cottage ★★★★
Self Catering
Contact: Ms Janet Palfreyman
t (01246) 568355
e janetpalfreyman@yahoo.co.uk

The Coach House (Ashford in the Water) ★★★★
Self Catering
Contact: Mr Steven & Shala Kay
t (01629) 640260

Corner Cottage ★★★★★
Self Catering
Contact: Mrs Janet Staley
t (01629) 583811
e tonystaley@hotmail.com
w littlegemcottages.co.uk

End Cottage ★★★★
Self Catering
Contact: Mrs Lucy Wright
t (01629) 640136
e lucyinlongstone@hotmail.com
w endcottage.co.uk

Orchard House ★★★★
Self Catering
Contact: Mr & Mrs Marsden
t (01629) 812895
e bookings@orchardproperties.co.uk
w orchardproperties.co.uk

The Smithy ★★★★ *Self Catering & Serviced Apartments*
Contact: Mrs Susan Akeroyd
The Smithy (Ashford in the Water)
t (01629) 812693
e akeroydsusie@aol.com

Sunny Lea, Ashford in the Water ★★★★ *Self Catering*
Contact: Mrs D Furniss
t (01629) 815285 & 07866 329691

Thorpe Cottage ★★★★
Self Catering
Contact: Mrs Sheila Newman
t (01302) 536763
e margaretnewman@btinternet.com

Thyme Cottage ★★★★★
Self Catering
Contact: Mrs Hazel Bell
Lark Cottage
t (01246) 583564
e hazel@peak-district-holidays.co.uk
w peak-district-holidays.co.uk

ASHOVER
Derbyshire

Holestone Moor Barns ★★★★★ *Self Catering*
Contact: Mr & Mrs Steve & Vicki Clemerson
t (01246) 591263
e hmbarns@aol.com
w hmbarns.co.uk

Woodlands ★★★
Self Catering
Peak Cottages
t (0114) 262 0777
e enquiries@peakcottages.com
w peakcottages.com

ASHTON
Northamptonshire

Vale Farm House ★★★★
Self Catering
Contact: Mrs Zanotto
t (01604) 863697

AUNBY
Lincolnshire

Clematis Cottages ★★★★
Self Catering
Contact: Mr & Mrs R Griffin
t (01778) 590280
e info@clematiscottages.co.uk

BAKEWELL
Derbyshire

Anne Cottage ★★★★
Self Catering
Contact: Mrs Christine Kirkman
Bakewell Holidays
t (01246) 583399
e christine@bakewellholidays.com

Bakewell Holiday Cottage (Coach Cottage) ★★★★
Self Catering
Contact: Mr & Mrs J Gough
Spinney Cottage
t (01628) 810112
e john@gough57.fsnet.co.uk

Bay Tree Cottage ★★★★
Self Catering
Contact: Mr Philip Ryder
t 07733 308881
e baytree@smartone.co.uk

Bolehill Farm Holiday Cottages ★★★-★★★★
Self Catering
Contact: Mr & Mrs Chris & Shirley Swaap
t (01629) 812359
e info8@bolehillfarm.co.uk
w bolehillfarm.co.uk

Braemar Cottage, Youlgrave ★★★★ *Self Catering*
Contact: c/o Mrs Irene Shimwell
Braemar Cottage
t (01629) 636568 & 07929 396525
e braemarcottage@fsmail.net
w braemarcottage.co.uk

Butts Cottage ★★★★
Self Catering
Contact: Mr & Mrs C Kirkman
Anne Cottage
t (01246) 583399
e charles@bakewellholidays.com
w bakewellholidays.com

Carter's Mill Cottage ★★★★ *Self Catering*
Contact: Mr & Mrs Ian & Jane Marsden
Mill Farm
t (01629) 812013
e marsden.millfarm@btinternet.com

Cartwheels ★★★
Self Catering
Sykes Cottages
t (01244) 345700
e info@sykescottages.co.uk
w sykescottages.co.uk

Catcliffe Cottage ★★★
Self Catering
Contact: Mr John Moseley
t (01246) 290873
e bakewellcottage@aol.com

Chalice Cottage ★★★
Self Catering
Peak Cottages
t (0114) 262 0777
e enquiries@peakcottages.com
w peakcottages.com

Cliffe Cottage (PK598) ★★★★ *Self Catering*
Peak Cottages
t (0114) 262 0777
e enquiries@peakcottages.com
w peakcottages.com

The Cottage ★★★★
Self Catering
Contact: Mrs Catherine Harrison
Riversdale
t (01629) 813768 & 07801 598720

Dale End Farm ★★★
Self Catering
Contact: Mrs Elizabeth Hague
t (01629) 650453
w http://uk.geocities.com/daleendfarm@btinternet.com

Dale View Farm ★★★
Self Catering
Contact: Mrs Janet Frost
t (01629) 650670

Edge View ★★★★
Self Catering
Contact: Mrs Gillian Rogers
t (01629) 813336

The Forge ★★★★
Self Catering
Contact: Mr Peter Cork
t (01629) 636887

Four Winds ★★★
Self Catering
Contact: Mr Clive Sykes
Sykes Cottages
t (01244) 345700
e info@sykescottages.co.uk

The Garden Lodge, Youlgrave
Rating Applied For
Self Catering
Contact: c/o Mrs Irene Shimwell
The Garden Lodge
t (01629) 636568
e braemarcottage@fsmail.net
w braemarcottage.co.uk

Haddon Grove Farm Cottages ★★★ *Self Catering*
Contact: Mr & Mrs John Boxall
Haddon Grove Farm Cottages
t (01629) 813551
w haddongrovefarmcottages.co.uk

Hillside Cottage ★★★
Self Catering
Contact: Mrs Beverley Tunnicliffe
t (01629) 812752

The Manager's House ★★★★ *Self Catering*
Contact: Mr & Mrs Jonathan & Jane Snodgrass
t (01629) 650489
e enquiries@cheesefactory-cottages.co.uk
w cheesefactory-cottages.co.uk

Minden Cottage ★★★★
Self Catering
Contact: Mrs Dorothy Jewitt
The Homestead
t (01433) 631500

Overdale ★★★★
Self Catering
Contact: Susan & Phillip Walker
t (01623) 471369
w overdale-bankside.co.uk

Peak District Holiday Lets
Rating Applied For
Self Catering
Contact: Oliver Oulsnam
t (01629) 814431
e callme@oulsnam.com
w peakdistrictholidaylets.co.uk

Rozel ★★★★ *Self Catering*
Contact: Mr Colin MacQueen
Peak Cottages
t (0114) 262 0777
e enquiries@peakcottages.com

Sixpenny Buckle
Rating Applied For
Self Catering
Contact: Ms Lynda Dale
t (01629) 630059

Spout Farm ★★★
Self Catering
Contact: Mrs Ena Patterson
t (01629) 650358

Yuletide Cottage ★★★
Self Catering
Contact: Mrs Denise Figg
t (01629) 636234
e hillfigg@aol.com

BALLIDON
Derbyshire

Ballidon Moor Farm ★★★★
Self Catering
Contact: Mrs Victoria Lambert
t (01629) 540671
e vicki_lambert@hotmail.com
w ballidonmoor.co.uk

Rachels Croft ★★★★
Self Catering
Contact: Mrs Alison Edge
t (01335) 390587

BAMFORD
Derbyshire

Derwent View (Bamford)
★★★★ *Self Catering*
Contact: Mrs Joyce Mannion
t (01433) 651637
e jamcottage@fsmail.net
w cottagesdirect.com/yoa096

Peakpad ★★★★
Self Catering
Contact: Mr Tim Hubbard
t 07968 557960
e tim@peakpad.com

Shatton Hall Farm Cottages
★★★★ *Self Catering*
Contact: Mrs Angela Kellie
Shatton Hall Farm Cottages
t (01433) 620635
e ahk@peakfarmholidays.co.uk
w peakfarmholidays.co.uk

Yorkshire Bridge Inn
★★★★★ *Self Catering*
Contact: Mr John Illingworth
Yorkshire Bridge Inn
t (01433) 651361
e enquiries@ladybowerapartments.co.uk
w yorkshire-bridge.co.uk

BARLOW
Derbyshire

Mulberry Cottage ★★★★
Self Catering
Peak Cottages
t (0114) 262 0777
e enquiries@peakcottages.com
w peakcottages.com

Sycamore Cottage ★★★★
Self Catering
Contact: Mrs Liz Barrett
Sleaford House
t (0114) 289 1071
e cottage.vacations@btopenworld.com

BARNOLDBY LE BECK
North East Lincolnshire

Grange Farm Cottages & Riding School
★★★-★★★★★ *Self Catering*
Contact: Jo & Sue Jenkins
Grange Farm Cottages & Riding School
t (01472) 822216
e sueuk4000@netscape.net
w grangefarmcottages.com

BARROW UPON HUMBER
Lincolnshire

Westcote Farm ★★★
Self Catering
Contact: Alison Baugh
t (01469) 530177
e alison_may@btinternet.com

BARROW UPON SOAR
Leicestershire

Kingfisher Cottage ★★★
Self Catering
Contact: Mr Matthews
t (01509) 890244
e nikkidavid@aol.com

BASLOW
Derbyshire

Goose Green Cottage
★★★★★ *Self Catering*
Contact: Mr & Mrs Levick
t (01400) 275147 & 07979 004979
e levick2@btopenworld.com
w peakdistrict-nationalpark.com

Stable Cottage ★★★★
Self Catering
Contact: Mrs Anne O' Connor
Stable Cottage
t (01246) 582285
e ourstablecottage@aol.com
w stablecottagebaslow.com

Toms Cottage ★★★★
Self Catering
Contact: Mr & Mrs C Kirkman
Anne Cottage
t (01246) 583399

BAUMBER
Lincolnshire

Gathman's Cottage ★★★
Self Catering
Gathmans Cottage
t (01507) 578352
e wendy@harrison592.freeserve.co.uk
w gathmanscottage.co.uk

BEESBY
Lincolnshire

Walk Villa ★★★
Self Catering
Contact: Mrs Joanne White
t (01507) 450323 & (01507) 450392

BELCHFORD
Lincolnshire

Poachers Hideaway
★★★★-★★★★★
Self Catering
Contact: Mrs Sally Tuxworth
t (01507) 533555
e andrewtuxworth@poachershideaway.com

BELPER
Derbyshire

Stone Cottage ★★★
Self Catering
Contact: Kathleen Bullock
t (01332) 840516
e stuart.bullock2@btopenworld.com
w derbyshirebreaks.com

Wiggonlea Stable ★★★★
Self Catering
Contact: Mrs Spendlove
t (01773) 852344
e ruth@wiggonlea.fsnet.co.uk
w wiggonlea.fsnet.co.uk

BELTON
Lincolnshire

Waterloo Studios ★★★
Self Catering
t (01476) 592988
e admin@stayandplaybelton.co.uk
w stayandplaybelton.co.uk

BENNIWORTH
Lincolnshire

Fiddledrill Barn
Rating Applied For
Self Catering
Contact: Sal;y & Ian Selby
t (01507) 313231
e infp@glebe-farm.com
w glebe-farm.com

BIGGIN-BY-HARTINGTON
Derbyshire

Cheese Press Cottage, The Old Farrowings & Courtyard Creamery ★★★★
Self Catering
Contact: Mrs Henry
t (01298) 687254
e enquiries@biggingrange.co.uk

BILSTHORPE
Nottinghamshire

Maplewood Farm ★★★★
Self Catering
t (01623) 870018
e pat@maplewoodfarm.co.uk

BIRCH VALE
Derbyshire

Hallishaw Cote, Birch Vale
★★★★ *Self Catering*
Contact: Mrs Jennifer Hallam
t (01663) 746155
e jenny@coldharbour.fslife.co.uk
w hallishawcote.co.uk

BIRCHOVER
Derbyshire

Birchover Cottages ★★★
Self Catering
Contact: Mr MacQueen
Peak Cottages
t (0114) 262 0777

Uppertown Hayloft ★★★
Self Catering
Contact: Mr Colin MacQueen
Peak Cottages
t (0114) 262 0777
e enquiries@peakcottages.ocm

BLOXHOLM
Lincolnshire

Church View Cottage
★★★★ *Self Catering*
Hospitality Jane
t (01526) 833055
e hospitalityjane@btinternet.com
w hospitalityjane.co.uk

The Lodge ★ *Self Catering*
Woodend Farm Bed & Breakfast
t (01526) 860347

BONSALL
Derbyshire

Brocliffe Cottage ★★★★
Self Catering
Contact: Erica Latham
The Beeches
t (01629) 823108
w brocliffecottage.co.uk

Hollies Cottage ★★★
Self Catering
Contact: Mrs Joy Mountney
t (01629) 823162

BOSTON
Lincolnshire

Elms Farm Cottages ★★★★
Self Catering
Contact: Carol Emerson
Elms Farm Cottages
t (01205) 290840 & 07887 652021
e carol@elmsfarmcottages.co.uk
w elmsfarmcottages.co.uk

The Lodge At Pinewood
★★★ *Self Catering*
t (01205) 723739

BRACKENFIELD
Derbyshire

Ruardean ★★★ *Self Catering*
Contact: Mr S Boardman
Sykes Cottages
t (01244) 345700
e info@sykescottages.co.uk

BRACKLEY
Northamptonshire

Iletts Courtyard ★★★★
Self Catering
Contact: Mrs Sally Bellingham
Iletts Farm
t (01280) 703244
e iletts@clara.co.uk
w home.clara.net/iletts

BRADLEY
Derbyshire

Bradley Hall
★★★★-★★★★★
Self Catering
Contact: Mrs Michele Wrigley
t (01335) 370222
e michelle@pmwproperty.com

Briar, Bluebell & Primrose Cottages ★★★-★★★★
Self Catering
Contact: Mrs Janet Hinds
t (01335) 344504
e janethindsfarm@yahoo.co.uk
w yeldersleyoldhallfarm.co.uk

Shepherds Folly ★★★★
Self Catering
Contact: Mrs Kathy Cowley
t (01335) 343315
e shepherds.folly@virgin.net

BRADWELL
Derbyshire

The Croft ★★★★
Self Catering
Contact: Mr Clive Sykes
Sykes Cottages
t (01244) 345700
e info@sykescottages.co.uk

Smalldale ★★★★
Self Catering
Contact: Mr Clive Sykes
Sykes Cottages
t (01244) 345700
e info@sykescottages.co.uk

BRAILSFORD
Derbyshire

The Cottage at Culland Mount Farm ★★★★
Self Catering
Contact: Ms Phillips
The Cottage at Culland Mount Farm
t (01335) 360313
e cullandmount@tiscali.co.uk
w cullandmount.co.uk

BRASSINGTON
Derbyshire

The Coach House ★★★★
Self Catering
Contact: Mr Andrew Colclough
The Coach House (Brassington)
t (01623) 465437
e patandandycole@ntlworld.com

Hillocks Barn ★★★★
Self Catering
Contact: Ms J Perkins
t 07980 868985
e info@hillocksbarn.co.uk
w hillocksbarn.co.uk

Hoe Grange Holidays
★★★★ *Self Catering*
Contact: Felicity Brown
Hoe Grange
t (01629) 540262
e info@hoegrangeholidays.co.uk
w hoegrangeholidays.co.uk

Jack's Cottage ★★★★
Self Catering
Contact: Mrs Rodrigues
t (0115) 925 1441
e jacks.cottage@tinyworld.co.uk

BRAYBROOKE
Northamptonshire

Old Rectory Self Catering
★★★★ *Self Catering*
Contact: Christine Thompson
t (01858) 464429
e chris.thompson@uku.co.uk

BRIGSLEY
North East Lincolnshire

Prospect Farm Cottages
★★★★★ *Self Catering*
Contact: Janet Speight
t (01472) 826491
e prospectfarm@btconnect.com
w prospectfarm.co.uk

BRIGSTOCK
Northamptonshire

The Gable End ★★★
Self Catering
Contact: Mrs Helen Clarke
The Gables
t (01536) 373674
e marcus@clarke.1999.freeserve.co.uk

Harley Way Lodge
Rating Applied For
Self Catering
Contact: Mrs Ginny Hyde
t (01536) 373588
e radicalmick@tiscali.co.uk

BURGH-LE-MARSH
Lincolnshire

The Hollies Country Cottages ★★★ *Self Catering*
t (01754) 810866
e jldodsworth@supanet.com

BURGH ON BAIN
Lincolnshire

Bainfield Lodge ★★★★
Self Catering
Contact: Mr & Mrs D Walker
t (01507) 313540
e dennis.walker1@btinternet.com

BURTON
Lincolnshire

The Conifers Guest Annexe
★★★★ *Self Catering*
Contact: Susan Gray
t (01522) 703196

BURTON OVERY
Leicestershire

Shepherd's Rest ★★★★
Self Catering
Contact: Ms Nicola Langton
t (0116) 259 2332
e nicola_langton@beeb.net

BUXTON
Derbyshire

Apartment 2, Cavendish Villas ★★★★★ *Self Catering*
t (0161) 484 2110
e elise@3cavendishvillas.com
w 3cavendishvillas.com

Farriers ★★★★ *Self Catering*
Contact: Pam Livesley
t (0115) 922 5582
e stay@farriersbuxton.co.uk
w farriersbuxton.co.uk

Hillside ★★★★ *Self Catering*
Contact: Mr David Swain
t (01298) 25451

Lake View ★★★
Self Catering
Contact: Mr MacQueen
Peak Cottages
t (0114) 262 0777

The Old Stables (Buxton)
★★★★ *Self Catering*
Contact: Mr Daniel Wright
t (01298) 25835

Outlow ★★★ *Self Catering*
Contact: Mr Colin MacQueen
Peak Cottages
t (0114) 262 0777
e enquiries@peakcottages.com
w peakcottages.com

Priory Lea Holiday Flats
★★–★★★ *Self Catering*
Contact: Mrs Gillian Taylor
t (01298) 23737
w cressbrook.co.uk/buxton/priorylea

Silverlands Holiday Flats 2 & 3 ★★ *Self Catering*
Contact: Mrs Gillian Kitchen
t (01298) 79381

Sittinglow Farm Cottage
★★★ *Self Catering*
Contact: Mrs Ann Buckley
t (01298) 812271

Smithy's Cottage, ★★★★
Self Catering
Contact: Mrs Pam Livesley
Smithy's Cottage
t (0115) 922 5582
w cottagesuk.com/smithyscottage

CAISTOR
Lincolnshire

Top House Holiday Cottages
★★★★ *Self Catering*
Contact: Mr & Mrs Plowright
t (01472) 859051
e info@tophouseholidaycottages.co.uk
w tophouseholidaycottages.co.uk

CALDECOTT
Rutland

Magnolia Cottage ★★★
Self Catering
Contact: Mrs Mel Hudson
Rutland Cottages
t (01536) 771357
e enquiries@rutland-cottages.co.uk
w rutland-cottages.co.uk

Rose Cottage & The Dog House, Caldecott ★★★★
Self Catering
Contact: Mrs Jill Bartlett
Rose Cottage
t (01536) 770149
e mcldoghouse@aol.com
w northamptonshire.co.uk/hotels/rosecottage.htm

Wisteria Cottage ★★★
Self Catering
Contact: Mrs Hudson
t (01536) 771357
e enquiries@rutland-cottages.co.uk
w rutland-cottages.co.uk

CALVER
Derbyshire

Barn Cottage (Calver)
★★★★ *Self Catering*
Contact: Mr Barry Finney
t (01433) 631672
e enquiries@barncottage.com
w barncottage.com

The Nurseries
Rating Applied For
Self Catering
Contact: Mrs Howard
Heritage Holiday Homes
t (0114) 263 0525

Sunnyside ★★★
Self Catering
Contact: Mr Colin MacQueen
Peak Cottages
t (0114) 262 0777
e enquiries@peakcottages.com

CARSINGTON
Derbyshire

Breach Farm Self Catering Cottages ★★★★
Self Catering
Contact: Mrs Michelle Wilson
t (01629) 540265
w breachfarm.co.uk

Knockerdown Holiday Cottages ★★★–★★★★
Self Catering
Contact: Tina Lomas
t (01629) 540525
e ann@knockerdown-cottages.co.uk
w derbyshireholidaycottages.co.uk

Owslow ★★★ *Self Catering*
Contact: Mr Peter Oldfield
Owslow
t (01629) 540510
e peter.oldfield@ukonline.co.uk
w peakdistrictfarmhols.co.uk

CASTLETON
Derbyshire

Cave End Cottage ★★★★
Self Catering
Contact: Mr Colin MacQueen
Peak Cottages
t (0114) 262 0777
e enquiries@peakcottages.com

Cliffe Cottage ★★★
Self Catering
Contact: Mr & Mrs Gareth & Sarah Woodhead
t (0114) 288 1430
e saz.wood@btinternet.com
w cliffecottage.co.uk

Eastry Cottage ★★★★
Self Catering
Contact: Mrs Jayne Webster
t (01433) 620312
w peakdistrictnationalpark.com

Grange Cottage ★★★★
Self Catering
Peak Cottages
t (0114) 262 0777
e enquiries@peakcottages.com
w peakcottages.com

Little Lilac Cottage ★★★★
Self Catering
Contact: Mrs Noorea Bassuni
t (0114) 266 1031
e booking@old-english-cottages.co.uk
w old-english-cottages.co.uk

Mullions ★★★★★
Self Catering
t (01433) 620962
e christine@peak-district-holiday-cottages.co.uk

Oatcake Cottage ★★★★
Self Catering
Contact: Mrs Angela Quigley
t (01433) 670014
e oatcakecottage@hotmail.com

Riding House Farm Cottages
★★★★★ *Self Catering*
Contact: Mrs Denise Matthews
t (01433) 620257
e denise@riding-house-cottages.co.uk
w riding-house-cottages.co.uk

Trickett Gate Barn
Rating Applied For
Self Catering
Contact: Angela & Michael Driver
Trickett Gate House
t (01433) 621590
w trickettgate.co.uk

CHAPEL-EN-LE-FRITH
Derbyshire

Keepers Cottage (Chapel)
★★★ *Self Catering*
Contact: Mrs Mary Hayward
t (01298) 812845

Rushop Hall Holiday Cottages ★★★★
Self Catering
Contact: Mr Neil Allcock
t (01298) 813323
e neil@rushophall.com

Saffi House
Rating Applied For
Self Catering
Contact: Ms Carole Coe
t 0870 755 9700
e carole@saffihouse.co.uk
w saffihouse.co.uk

CHELMORTON
Derbyshire

Swallow Barn ★★★★
Self Catering
Contact: Mrs Gill Chapman
t (01298) 85355
e enquiries@swallowbarn.com
w swallowbarn.com

CHESTERFIELD
Derbyshire

Chryslinash ★★★
Self Catering
Contact: Mrs Tina Cave
t (01246) 853467
e chryslinash@aol.com

Pear Tree Cottage ★★★
Self Catering
Contact: Mrs Carol Beckett
t (01773) 872767

Pear Tree Farm Barn, Rowthorne Village ★★★★
Self Catering
Contact: Mel Copley
t (01623) 811694
e enquiries@peartreefarmbarn.co.uk
w peartreefarmbarn.co.uk

Ploughmans Cottage
★★★★ *Self Catering*
Contact: Mrs Margaret Fry
Ploughmans Cottage
t (01246) 435328
e ploughmans.cottage@virgin.net
w ploughmanscottage.com

CHINLEY
Derbyshire

Fernbank ★★★ *Self Catering*
Contact: Mrs Jean Storer
t (01298) 813458
e jeanstorer@btopenworld.com
w http://uk.geocities.com/jeanstorer@btinternet.com

Monks Meadow Cottage
★★★★ *Self Catering*
Contact: Mrs Pauline Gill
t 07776 382339
e muriel.jackson1@btopenworld.com
w monksmeadow.co.uk

CLAXBY
Lincolnshire

The Coach House ★★★
Self Catering
Contact: Mrs Elizabeth Wilson
t (01507) 466374
e liffa@claxby.fsnet.co.uk

COLLYWESTON
Northamptonshire

Slate Drift Leisure ★★★
Self Catering
Contact: Mr Roger Munro
t (01780) 444058
e rogermunro@aol.com

COLSTERWORTH
Lincolnshire

Farrier Cottage ★★★
Self Catering
Contact: Mrs Kathleen Clay
The Stables
t (01476) 861057
e kathlen@btopenworld.com
w stablesbandb.co.uk

COMBS
Derbyshire

Pyegreave Cottage
★★★★★ *Self Catering*
Contact: Mr & Mrs Noel & Rita Pollard
Pyegreave Cottage
t (01298) 813444
e n.pollard@allenpollard.co.uk
w holidayapartments.org

CRESSBROOK
Derbyshire

Cressbrook Hall Self-catering Cottages ★★★★
Self Catering
Contact: Mrs Bobby Hull-Bailey
t (01298) 871289
e stay@cressbrookhall.co.uk
w cressbrookhall.co.uk

Mill Apartment ★★★★
Self Catering
Peak Cottages
t (0114) 262 0777
e enquiries@peakcottages.com
w peakcottages.com

Monsal Dale Apartment
★★★★★ *Self Catering*
Contact: Dr P Howard
Heritage Holiday Homes
t (0114) 230 8456
e Dr.Howard@btconnect.com
w heritageholidayhomes.co.uk

Owl Cottage ★★★★
Self Catering
Peak Cottages
t (0114) 262 0777
e enquiries@peakcottages.com
w peakcottages.com

CROMFORD
Derbyshire

1 High Peak Cottages ★★★
Self Catering
Contact: Mr & Mrs David & Lorraine Wolsey
t (01629) 823402
e stay@highpeakcottage.co.uk

CURBAR
Derbyshire

Jack's Cottage and The Mullions ★★★★
Self Catering
Contact: Mrs M North
t (01433) 630120
e marsha.north1@btopenworld.com

Upper Barn and Lower Barn
Rating Applied For
Self Catering
Dr J Morrissy & Dr P Cox
t (01433) 631885
w curbarcottages.com

CURBAR, CALVER
Derbyshire

The Old Vicarage ★★★★
Self Catering
Contact: Mr MacQueen
Peak Cottages
t (0114) 262 0777
e enquiries@peakcottages.com

CUTTHORPE
Derbyshire

Cow Close Farm Cottages
★★★ *Self Catering*
Contact: Mrs Caroline Burke
Cow Close Farm
t (01246) 232055
e cowclosefarm@aol.com
w cowclosefarm.com

DARLEY DALE
Derbyshire

Bumper Castle Farm ★★★★
Self Catering
Contact: Mr & Mrs John & Gillian Wholey
t (01629) 732534

Housekeepers Cottage
★★★★★ *Self Catering*
Contact: Mrs Rudkin
t (01629) 733270
e enquiries@housekeeperscottage.co.uk

DERBY
Derbyshire

Bank Cottage ★★★
Self Catering
Contact: Mrs Pamela Pym
t (01332) 515607

DODDINGTON
Lincolnshire

The Stables ★★★★
Self Catering
Contact: Mrs Penny Coldron
t 07810 408319
e macalpinei@doddington.demon.co.uk
w thestables-theoldrectory-doddington.com

DONINGTON
Lincolnshire

The Barn ★★★ *Self Catering*
t (01775) 821242

DUFFIELD
Derbyshire

Castle Orchard Cottages
★★★ *Self Catering*
Contact: Mrs Bullock
t (01332) 840516
e mail@derbyshirebreaks.com
w derbyshirebreaks.com

EARL STERNDALE
Derbyshire

Wheeldon Trees Farm
★★★★ *Self Catering*
Contact: Mr & Mrs David & Sally Hollands
t (01298) 83219
e hollands@earlsterndale.fsnet.co.uk
w wheeldontreesfarm.co.uk

EAST BARKWITH
Lincolnshire

The Clocktower and The Brewhouse ★★★★
Self Catering
Contact: Mrs Sarah Stamp
t (01673) 858670
e sarahstamp@farmersweekley.net
w thegrange-lincolnshire.co.uk

EAST FIRSBY
Lincolnshire

The Log Cabins ★★★
Self Catering
Contact: Mr Robert Cox
t (01673) 878258
e info@lincolnshire-lanes.com
w lincolnshire-lanes.com

EAST HADDON
Northamptonshire

East Haddon Grange Country Cottages ★★★★
Self Catering
Contact: Gerald Pike
East Haddon Grange Country Cottages
t (01604) 770368 & 07979 661122
e enquiries@easthaddongrange.co.uk
w easthaddongrange.co.uk

Mulberry Cottage ★★★★★
Self Catering
Contact: Liat Cox
t (01604) 771474
e liat3030@aol.com
w mulberrycottage.uk.com

Ryehill Cottages ★★★★
Self Catering
Ryehill Country Cottages
t (01604) 770990
e ryehillcottages@btinternet.com
w ryehillcottages.co.uk

EAST KIRKBY
Lincolnshire

Chesterton Cottage ★★★
Self Catering
Contact: Mrs Sally Raynor
t (01790) 763380

EASTON ON THE HILL
Northamptonshire

The Old Bakery ★★★
Self Catering
Contact: Mrs Yogasundram
t (01780) 753898
e yogiandmel@theoldbakery25.freeserve.co.uk
w eastonoldbakery.co.uk

EATON
Leicestershire

Old Millhouse ★★★★
Self Catering
Contact: Mrs Ursula Soar
t (01476) 870797
e walksfareaton@aol.com

EDALE
Derbyshire

Grindslow House ★★★
Self Catering
Contact: Mrs S Crook
c/o Meller Braggins
t (01565) 830395

Ollerbrook Barn Cottage
★★★ *Self Catering*
Contact: Mrs Theresa Skillen
t (01433) 670200
e ollerbrookbarn@btinternet.com
w ollerbrook-barn-cottage.co.uk

Ollerbrook Cottages, Edale
★★★★ *Self Catering*
Contact: Mrs Paula Greenlees
t (01433) 670083
e ollerbrook@btinternet.com
w ollerbrook-cottages.co.uk

EDITH WESTON
Rutland

Corner Cottage ★★★
Self Catering
Contact: Jo Spiegl
Cornerstones
t (01780) 721014
e cornerstones@spiegl.co.uk
w spiegl.co.uk/cornercottage

Forge Cottage
Rating Applied For
Self Catering
Contact: Ms Debbie Clark
Debbie Clark Lettings
t (01572) 747389
e debbieclark@btopenworld.com
w debbieclarklettings.com

EDLASTON
Derbyshire

Church Farm Cottages (Edlaston) ★★★
Self Catering
Contact: Mrs Lois Blake
t (01335) 348776
e adeblake@aol.com
w churchfarm-holidays.freeserve.co.uk

EDWINSTOWE
Nottinghamshire

Crow Hollow ★★★
Self Catering
t (01636) 677847
e shp18@lineone.net

ELKINGTON
Northamptonshire

Manor Farm ★★★★
Self Catering
Contact: Mr Michael Higgott
t (01858) 575245

ELTON
Derbyshire

Pinfold Cottage ★★★★
Self Catering
Contact: Mr Colin MacQueen
Peak Cottages
t (0114) 262 0777

The Stable ★★★★
Self Catering
Contact: Mrs Jean Carson
t (01629) 650359
w homesteadfarm.co.uk

Swallow Cottage ★★★★
Self Catering
Contact: Mrs Lois Clark
t (01954) 780893 & 07932 644287
e lois@swallow-cottage.co.uk
w swallow-cottage.co.uk

EMPINGHAM
Rutland

The Old Bakery
Rating Applied For
Self Catering
Contact: Mrs S.Y Margerison
t (01780) 460243
e psmarge@tiscali.co.uk

EPPERSTONE
Nottinghamshire

Eastwood Farm ★★★
Self Catering
t (0115) 966 3018
e info@eastwoodfarm.co.uk
w eastwoodfarm.co.uk

EPWORTH
Lincolnshire

Newlands Holiday Cottages
★★★-★★★★ *Self Catering*
Contact: Mr & Mrs Nigel & Clarissa Atkinson
Newlands Farmhouse
t (01427) 873112
e enquiries@newlandsholidaybreaks.co.uk

EYAM
Derbyshire

1 Lydgate Cottages ★★★★
Self Catering
Contact: Mrs Sandra Harrop
t (01925) 752118
e lydgatecottage@townfieldhouse.freeserve.co.uk

Beck Cottage ★★★★
Self Catering
Contact: Mr & Mrs R Burton
Clifford Road
t (0114) 250 9357
e rburton04@tiscali.co.uk
w ukpeakretreats.com

Croft View Cottage ★★★★
Self Catering
Contact: Mrs N Carmichael
t (01433) 630711
e carmichaelat@hotmail.com

Dalehead Court Cottages
★★★★-★★★★★
Self Catering
Contact: Mrs Dorothy Neary
Laneside Farm
t (01433) 620214
e laneside@lineone.net

Fern Cottage ★★★★
Self Catering
Contact: Mrs Jenny Vickers
t (01433) 631254
e jenny@foolowcottages.co.uk
w peak-cottages.com

Lark Cottage ★★★★★
Self Catering
Contact: Mrs Hazel Bell
Peak District Holidays
t (01246) 583564
e hazel@peak-district-holidays.co.uk
w peak-district-holidays.co.uk

Steeple Barn ★★★★
Self Catering
Contact: Mrs Yvonne Pursglove
t (01433) 639030
e info@onetorent.com
w peakvacation.com

The Trap House ★★★★
Self Catering
Contact: Mr Colin MacQueen
Peak Cottages
t (0114) 262 0777
e enquiries@peakcottages.com

EYE KETTLEBY
Leicestershire

Eye Kettleby Lakes ★★★★
Self Catering
Contact: Lizzy Lomas
t (01664) 565900
e lodges@eyekettlebylakes.com
w eyekettlebylakes.com

FENNY BENTLEY
Derbyshire

Church Barn ★★★★
Self Catering
Contact: Mr Kenneth Pearson
t (01335) 350499
e kennethjpearson@aol.com

The Priory ★★★
Self Catering
Contact: Mrs A Hughes
Woodeaves
t (01335) 350238
e hughes.priory@virgin.net

FINDERN
Derbyshire

Pilgrims Cottage ★★★
Self Catering
Contact: Mr & Mrs J Noon
t (01332) 769275

FLAGG
Derbyshire

Taddington Barns ★★★★
Self Catering
Contact: Mrs Elizabeth Charboneau
Taddington Barns
t (01298) 85020 & 07974 258765
e tony@moorgrangefarm.co.uk
w moorgrangefarm.co.uk

FLECKNEY
Leicestershire

Elms Farm Cottage ★★★
Self Catering
Contact: Mrs C Greta Bentley
Elms Farm
t (0116) 240 2238
e info@elms-farm.co.uk
w elms-farm.co.uk

FOOLOW
Derbyshire

Sycamore Cottage (Foolow)
★★★ *Self Catering*
Contact: Mrs Maveen Norton
t (01433) 630186
e mnortonfoolow@aol.com
w cressbrook.co.uk

FRITHVILLE
Lincolnshire

Carrington Court Holiday Cottages ★★★★
Self Catering
Contact: Mrs Stacey Lunn
Hawthorne House
t (01205) 750441
w carringtoncourt.co.uk

FROGGATT
Derbyshire

Bridgefoot Cottage
★★★★★ *Self Catering*
Contact: Mrs Marsha North
Bridgefoot Cottage
t (01433) 630120
e enquiries@peakdistrictholiday.plus.com
w peakdistrictholiday.co.uk

FULSTOW
Lincolnshire

Enfield Farm Cottages
★★★★ *Self Catering*
t (01507) 363268
e enquiries@enfieldfarmcottages.co.uk
w enfieldfarmcottages.co.uk

Peartree Cottage ★★★
Self Catering
Contact: P.J. Buckley
t (01504) 363615

Waingrove Farm Country Cottages ★★★★
Self Catering
Contact: Mr & Mrs P Tinker
Waingrove Farm
t (01507) 363704
e ptinker.tinkernet@virgin.net
w lincolnshirecottages.com

GLENTHAM
Lincolnshire

Laburnum Cottage ★★★
Self Catering
Contact: John Hall
t (01427) 614570
e laburnumcottage@hotmail.com
w laburnumcottage.netfirms.com

GOULCEBY
Lincolnshire

Bay Tree Cottage ★★★★
Self Catering
t (01507) 343230
e goulcebypost@ukonline.co.uk
w goulcebypost.co.uk

GOXHILL
Lincolnshire

Butters Wood Holiday Cottage ★★★ *Self Catering*
Contact: Mrs Marshall
Larch Lodge
t (01469) 530644

GRANTHAM
Lincolnshire

The Byre House
Rating Applied For
Self Catering
Contact: Ms Debbie Nicholls
t (01476) 870529

Granary Cottage ★★★★
Self Catering
t (01476) 585311
e pulse@lincolnshiretourism.com

 Look out for establishments participating in the National Accessible Scheme

GREAT CARLTON
Lincolnshire

Willow Farm ★★★
Self Catering
Contact: Mr James Clark
t (01507) 338540

GREAT HALE
Lincolnshire

The Old Stable ★★★★
Self Catering
t (01529) 460307
e c.redmond@virgin.net
w theoldstable-greathale.co.uk

GREAT HUCKLOW
Derbyshire

Burrs Cottage ★★★
Self Catering
Contact: Mr Clive Sykes
Sykes Cottages
t (01244) 345700
e info@sykescottages.co.uk

The Hayloft ★★★★
Self Catering
Contact: Mrs Margot Darley
t (01298) 871044
e margot.darley1@btinternet.com
w peakdistrictfarmhols.co.uk

South View Cottage ★★★★
Self Catering
Contact: Mrs Maureen Waterhouse
t (01298) 871440
e mo@mmwaterhouse.demon.co.uk
w cottageguide.co.uk/southviewcottage

GREAT LONGSTONE
Derbyshire

Field House Cottage ★★
Self Catering
Contact: Julia Spink
Field House
t (01629) 640103
e juliag@lumina-solns.com

Wild Flower Cottage
★★★★ *Self Catering*
Contact: Mrs Hazel Bell
t (01246) 583564
e hazel@peak-district-holidays.co.uk
w peak-district-holidays.co.uk

GREAT PONTON
Lincolnshire

Witham Barn ★★★★
Self Catering
t (01476) 530502
e steve@jackson3985.fslife.co.uk
w withambarn.4t.com

GREAT STURTON
Lincolnshire

Old Barn Cottages ★★★★
Self Catering
t (01507) 578435
e info@o2b-in-england.com
w o2b-in-england.com

GRIMBLETHORPE
Lincolnshire

Grimblethorpe Hall Country Cottages ★★★★★
Self Catering
Contact: Mrs Annie Codling
t (01507) 313671
e enquiries@shepherdsholidaycottage.co.uk
w shepherdsholidaycottage.co.uk

GRINDLEFORD
Derbyshire

Middle Cottage ★★★
Self Catering
Contact: Mr Colin Macqueen
Peak Cottages
t (0114) 262 0777
e enquiries@peakcottages.com
w peakcottages.com

GUNTHORPE
Nottinghamshire

Glebe Farm Cottages
★★★★ *Self Catering*
t (0115) 966 3836
e philwarrior@aol.com
w glebefarmcottages.com

HADFIELD
Derbyshire

Burnswark ★★★★
Self Catering
t (01457) 855667
w burnswark.com

HAGWORTHINGHAM
Lincolnshire

The Old Village Hall ★★★★
Self Catering
E.W. Bowser & Son Ltd
t (01205) 870210 & 07970 128531
e office@ewbowser.com

HALLINGTON
Lincolnshire

The Paddy House and Blacksmiths Shop ★★★★
Self Catering
Contact: Mrs Heather Canter
The Paddy House and Blacksmiths Shop
t (01507) 605864
e canter.hallington@virgin.net
w canter-hallington.co.uk

HALSE
Northamptonshire

Hill Farm ★★★ *Self Catering*
Contact: Mr & Mrs Robinson
t (01280) 703300
e jigirobinson@btconnect.com

HANDLEY, CLAY CROSS
Derbyshire

Ridgewell Farm Holiday Cottages ★★★★
Self Catering
Contact: Mr Michael Kerry
t (01246) 590698
e ridgewellfarm@tiscali.co.uk

HARBY
Leicestershire

New Farm Holiday Cottage
★★★ *Self Catering*
Contact: Miss Ruth Stanley
t (01949) 860640

HARTINGTON
Derbyshire

1 Staley Cottage and Victoria House ★★★★
Self Catering
Contact: Mr & Mrs Oliver
Carr Head Farm
t (01226) 762387

Beech Cottage ★★★
Self Catering
Contact: Mrs Birch
t (01298) 84532
e lesley@beechcottage99.freeserve.co.uk
w beechcottage99.freeserve.co.uk

Church View ★★★
Self Catering
Contact: Miss Kathleen Bassett
Digmer
t (01298) 84660

Cotterill Farm Cottages
★★★★ *Self Catering*
Contact: Ms Christina Kamali
t (01298) 84447
e enquiries@cotterillfarm.co.uk
w cotterillfarm.co.uk

Cruck & Wolfscote Grange Cottages ★★★★
Self Catering
Contact: Mrs Jane Gibbs
Cruck & Wolfscote Grange Cottages
t (01298) 84342
e wolfscote@btinternet.com
w wolfscotegrangecottages.co.uk

Dalescroft Cottage and Apartment
★★★★-★★★★★
Self Catering
Contact: Mr Brian Leese
t (01298) 24263
e mail@dalescroft.co.uk

Dove Valley Centre ★★★★
Self Catering
Contact: Mr & Mrs Paul & Elspeth Walker
t (01298) 83282
e walker@dovevalleycentre.co.uk
w dovevalleycentre.co.uk

Hartington Cottages
★★★★-★★★★★
Self Catering
Contact: Mr Patrick Skemp
t (01298) 84447
e enquiries@hartingtoncottages.co.uk
w hartingtoncottages.co.uk

Old House Farm Cottages
★★★-★★★★ *Self Catering*
Contact: Mrs Sue Flower
t (01629) 636268
e s.flower1@virgin.net
w oldhousefarm.com

HASLAND
Derbyshire

Sunshine Cottage ★★★
Self Catering
Contact: Mrs Suzannah Richardson
t (01246) 209579
e annah@peaksunshine.fslife.co.uk
w peaksunshinecottage.co.uk

HASSOP
Derbyshire

Jubilee Cottage ★★★★★
Self Catering
Contact: Mrs V Shaw
t (01629) 640631

HATHERSAGE
Derbyshire

Pat's Cottage ★★★
Self Catering
Contact: Mr John Drakeford
Pat's Cottage
t (0114) 236 6014 & 07850 200711
e johnmdrakeford@hotmail.com
w patscottage.co.uk

St Michael's Cottage ★★★
Self Catering
Contact: Miss Turton
Saint Michael's Environmental Education Centre
t (01433) 650309
e stmichaels@education.nottscc.gov.uk
w eess.org.uk

HATTON
Lincolnshire

The Gables ★★★★★
Self Catering
Contact: Julia Merivale
t (01673) 858862
w thegables-hatton.co.uk

HAYFIELD
Derbyshire

Bowden Bridge Cottage
★★★★ *Self Catering*
Contact: Mrs Margrith Easter
t (01663) 743975
e j_easter@talk21.com

Cliff View ★★ *Self Catering*
t (020) 7642 3762
e nick.duckett@ntlworld.com

Kinder Cottage ★★★
Self Catering
Contact: Mr Colin MacQueen
Peak Cottages
t (0114) 262 0777
e enquiries@peakcottages.com

HAZELWOOD
Derbyshire

Duck Pond View ★★★★★
Self Catering
Contact: Mr & Mrs Terry & Liz Chisman
t (01773) 550686
e enquiries@duckpondview.co.uk
w duckpondview.com

HOLBEACH
Lincolnshire

Poachers Den ★★★
Self Catering
t (01406) 423625
e info@poachersden.com
w poachersden.com

HOLLOWAY
Derbyshire

1 Yew Tree Cottage ★★★
Self Catering
Contact: Ann & Peter Elbourne
t (01773) 853771
w 1yewtreecottage.co.uk

HOLYMOORSIDE
Derbyshire

Millclose Cottage ★★★★
Self Catering
Contact: Mr & Mrs A & S Stockton
t (01246) 567624
e allan.stockton@btinternet.com
w millclosefarm.co.uk

HOPE
Derbyshire

Chapman Farm Cottages ★★★★ *Self Catering*
Contact: Mrs Dorothy Vernon
Chapman Farm Cottages
t (01433) 620297

Farfield Farm Cottages ★★★★ *Self Catering*
Contact: Mrs Gill Elliott
t (01433) 620640
e gill@farfield.gemsoft.co.uk
w farfield.gemsoft.co.uk

Hopevale Cottages
Rating Applied For
Self Catering
t (01433) 621397
e lesley728@aol.com

Oaker Farm Cottages ★★★★ *Self Catering*
Contact: Mrs Julie Hadfield
t (01433) 621955
e julieannhadfield@hotmail.com
w oakerfarm.fsnet.co.uk

HOPE VALLEY
Derbyshire

Aston Cottages ★★★★
Self Catering
Contact: Mrs Rachel Morley
t (01433) 621619
e rmorley@dimings.freeserve.co.uk
w aston-cottages.co.uk

HORNCASTLE
Lincolnshire

Green Court, Fulletby ★★★
Self Catering
Contact: Mr John Robinson
t (01522) 876994
w woldscottages.co.uk

The Pottery ★★★
Self Catering
Contact: Mrs Sue Emmerson
t (01507) 525810
e jaspkme@aol.com

Southolme Cottage ★★★
Self Catering
t (01608) 682542
e david@gartongresham.co.uk
w southolmecottage.connectfree.co.uk

HORSINGTON
Lincolnshire

Blenheim Cottage Holiday Let ★★★★ *Self Catering*
Contact: Mrs Sharron Leak
Furze Cottage
t (01526) 388668
e info@blenheimcottage.co.uk
w blenheimcottage.co.uk

Wayside Cottage ★★★
Self Catering
Contact: Mr & Mrs Ian & Jane Williamson
t (01526) 353101
e will@williamsoni.freeserve.co.uk
w skegness.net/woodhallspa.htm

HOWSHAM
Lincolnshire

Willow Cottages ★★★★
Self Catering
Contact: Roy Holstein
The Willow Cottages
t (01652) 652549
e linda@willowcottages.co.uk

HUMBERSTON
North East Lincolnshire

Berberis House ★★★
Self Catering
Contact: Julie & Andrew Doherty
t (0113) 286 8766
e andrew@adoherty94.freeserve.co.uk

INGHAM
Lincolnshire

3 Anyans Row ★★★
Self Catering
Contact: Mr & Mrs T Taylor
t (01427) 788023

INGOLDSBY
Lincolnshire

Little Scotland Farm ★★★★
Self Catering & Serviced Apartments
Contact: Mrs Angela Jasinski
t (01476) 585494

KENWICK
Lincolnshire

Kenwick Lodge ★★★★
Self Catering
Contact: Sam Holliday
t (01509) 269828
e enquiries@kenwicklodge.co.uk
w kenwicklodge.co.uk

KERSALL
Nottinghamshire

Rose and Sweet Briar Cottages ★★★ *Self Catering*
Contact: Janet Hind
t (01636) 636274
w roseandsweetbriar.fsbusiness.co.uk

KETTERING
Northamptonshire

The Villiers Suite, Cranford Hall ★★★ *Self Catering*
Contact: Mr & Mrs John Robinson
The Villiers Suite Cranford Hall
t (01536) 330248
e cranford@farmline.com
w cranfordhall.co.uk

KETTON
Rutland

Randolph Cottage ★★★
Self Catering
t (01780) 720802
e forster.ketton@virgin.net

KILBURN
Derbyshire

Springfields ★★★
Self Catering
Contact: Mr & Mrs R & D Sutton
t (01332) 880128
e rainbow.sutton@virgin.net

KING'S CLIFFE
Northamptonshire

Maltings Cottage, King's Cliffe ★★★★ *Self Catering*
Contact: Mrs Jenny Dixon
t (01780) 470365
e kjhl_dixon@hotmail.com
w kingjohnhuntinglodge.co.uk

KIRBY BELLARS
Leicestershire

Equibreak Holidays
Rating Applied For
Self Catering
Contact: Mr Eric Brown
Equibrook Holidays
t (01664) 813701
e ercbrwn4@aol.com
w equine-emporium.co.uk

KIRK IRETON
Derbyshire

Bluebell, Buttercup and Clover Barn ★★★★
Self Catering
Contact: Mr & Mrs Keith & Vicki Pollard
t (01335) 370270
e ben@redpepperpictures.freeserve.co.uk

Grange Cottages (Kirk Ireton) ★★★★ *Self Catering*
Contact: Mr Malcolm Race
t (01335) 370880
e cottages@w3z.co.uk
w malcolmrace.co.uk

Ivy Cottage ★★★
Self Catering
Peak Cottages
t (0114) 262 0777

KIRK LANGLEY
Derbyshire

The Cart Hovel and The Stables ★★★★ *Self Catering*
Contact: Mrs Sue Gibbs
t (01332) 824214

KIRKBY-LA-THORPE
Lincolnshire

Waggoners Lodge ★★★
Self Catering
t (01473) 780810
e johnleaman@onetel.net.uk

KIRKLINGTON
Nottinghamshire

The Gatehouse ★★
Self Catering
Contact: Mr & Mrs Crane
t (01623) 871605
e gatehouse@belleeau.freeserve.co.uk

KNIVETON
Derbyshire

Billy's Bothy ★★★★★
Self Catering
Contact: Mrs Pat Walker
Offcote Grange Cottage Holidays
t (01335) 344795
e enquiries@offcotegrange.com
w offcotegrange.com

High View Grange
Rating Applied For
Self Catering
Contact: Mrs Michele Wrigley
Bradley Hall
t (01335) 370222
e michelle@pmwproperty.com
w ashbourneselfcatering.co.uk

Willow Bank ★★★★
Self Catering
Contact: Mrs Mary Vaughan
Willow Bank
t (01335) 343308
e willowbank@kniveton.net
w kniveton.net

LAMBLEY
Nottinghamshire

Dickman's Cottage, Lambley ★★★ *Self Catering & Serviced Apartments*
Contact: Mr William Marshall Smith
t (01943) 462719
e marshallsmithuk@hotmail.com
w http://mywebpage.netscape.com/wmarshallsmith/default.html

LANGWORTH
Lincolnshire

The Barn ★★★ *Self Catering*
Ferry House Farm
t (01522) 751939
e ifleet@barlings.demon.co.uk
w barlings.demon.co.uk

LEA
Derbyshire

The Coach House SC (Lea) ★★ *Self Catering*
Contact: Mr & Mrs Helme
t (01629) 534346
w coachhouselea.co.uk

The Old Stable & Hollybrook ★★★ *Self Catering*
Contact: Mr Philip Waterfall
t (01629) 534546
e nightingaleholiday.cottages@virgin.net

LEVERTON
Lincolnshire

Crewyard Cottages ★★★★
Self Catering
t (01205) 871389
e guna@guna31.wanadoo.co.uk

LINCOLN
Lincolnshire

5 Belle Vue Terrace ★★★
Self Catering
t (01522) 520970
e john@knight9935.freeserve.co.uk

5 Francis Hill Court ★★★★
Self Catering
Contact: Mr Stephen Layton
t (01522) 810321
e layton@doctors.org.uk
w francishillcourt.co.uk

Ashleigh ★★★ *Self Catering*
Contact: Mr Colin Ashton
18 De Braose Way
t (01903) 814305
e colinashton@dsl.pipex.com
w lincolnselfcatering.co.uk

Look out for establishments participating in the Walkers and Cyclists Welcome Schemes

Bight House ★★★★
Self Catering
t (01522) 534477
e pulse@lincolnshiretourism.com

Cliff Farm Cottage ★★★★
Self Catering
t (01522) 730475
e rae.marris@farming.co.uk
w cliff-farm-cottage.co.uk

D'isney Place Hotel ★★★★
Self Catering
Contact: Miss Sally Wilcockson
t (01522) 538881

Drury Lodge ★★★★★
Self Catering
Contact: Anita Thorne
t (01673) 866391
e jon.thorne@thorne.tv
w lincolnbreaks.com

The Flat ★★★ *Self Catering*
Contact: Mrs E A Slingsby
t (01522) 560880
e auction@thosmawer.co.uk
w greestoneplace.co.uk

Kenton ★★★ *Self Catering*
t (01522) 532136
e pulse@lincolnshiretourism.com

Martingale Cottage ★★★
Self Catering
Contact: Mrs Patsy Pate
t (01522) 751795
e patsy.pate@ntlworld.com

The Needleworkers ★★★★
Self Catering
Contact: Mr & Mrs Rochester
t (01522) 522113
e john@jrochester.fsnet.co.uk

Old Vicarage Cottages
★★★★ *Self Catering*
Contact: Mrs Susan Downs
t (01522) 750819
e susan@oldvic.net
w oldvic.net

Saint Clements ★★★
Self Catering
Contact: Mrs Gill Marshall
Saint Clements
t (01522) 538087
e jroywood@aol.com
w stayatstclements.co.uk

South Cliff Farm Log Cabins
★★★★ *Self Catering*
Contact: William Marris
t (01522) 730236
e marris49@aol.com

The Stable ★★★★
Self Catering
t (01522) 730561
e jerry@lincolncottages.co.uk
w lincolncottages.co.uk

Tennyson Court ★★
Self Catering
Contact: Mr Andrew Carnell
t (01522) 569892
e andrew@tennyson-court.co.uk

LITTLE HAYFIELD
Derbyshire

Honeysuckle Cottage ★★★
Self Catering
Peak Cottages
t (0114) 262 0777
e enquiries@peakcottages.com
w peakcottages.com

LITTLE HUCKLOW
Derbyshire

Glider View Cottage ★★★★
Self Catering
Contact: Mrs Christine McMeeken
t (01629) 650196
w english-country-cottages.co.uk

LITTLE LONGSTONE
Derbyshire

The Lodge and Dove Cottage ★★★–★★★★
Self Catering
Contact: Mrs Anne Davey
t (01629) 640542
e annie@littlelongstone.freeserve.co.uk
w cressbrook.co.uk/bakewell/lodgedove

Orrs Barn ★★★★
Self Catering
Contact: Mr Colin MacQueen
Peak Cottages
t (0114) 262 0777
e enquiries@peakcottages.com

LITTON
Derbyshire

Candlelight Cottage
★★★★★ *Self Catering*
Contact: Simon & Jill Wills
t (01433) 631528
e candlelightcottage@sjwills.plus.com
w candlelightcottage.co.uk

Cross View ★★★
Self Catering
Contact: Mrs Caroline Rowan-Olive
t (01727) 844169
e enquiries@cross-view.co.uk
w cross-view.co.uk

Farm Hands Cottage ★★★★
Self Catering
Contact: Mrs Annette Scott
t (01298) 872172
e jfscott@waitrose.com
w users.waitrose.com/~jfscott

LITTON MILL
Derbyshire

One Litton Mill ★★★★
Self Catering
Peak Cottages
t (0114) 262 0777
e enquiries@peakcottages.com
w peakcottages.com

LONG BUCKBY
Northamptonshire

Meadowview Cottages
★★★★ *Self Catering*
t (01327) 842205
e meadowview.cottages@farming.co.uk
w uk-holiday-cottages.co.uk/meadowview

LONG SUTTON
Lincolnshire

The Barn ★★★ *Self Catering*
t (01406) 362284
e oldbakery@netbreeze.co.uk

LONG WHATTON
Leicestershire

Oscar House ★★★
Self Catering
Contact: Ms Emma Blessed
9 Main Street
t (01509) 842529
e enquiries@oscarhouse.co.uk
w oscarhouse.co.uk

LOUGHBOROUGH
Leicestershire

Coach House at Quorn Lodge ★★★★ *Self Catering*
Contact: Mr & Mrs Nigel & Dianne Swain
Quorn Lodge
t (01509) 214466
e enquiries@quorn-lodge.co.uk
w quorn-lodge.co.uk

The Woodlands ★★★
Self Catering
Contact: Mr & Mrs Grudgings
t (01509) 214596
e thewoodlands@onetel.com

LOUTH
Lincolnshire

72 Westgate Place ★★★
Self Catering
Contact: Mrs Alison Boardman
t (01507) 610296
e alisonboardman2002@yahoo.co.uk

Acorn Lodge ★★★★★
Self Catering
Contact: Mrs Leggott
t (01522) 827049
e kelly.anne@ntlworld.com
w acornlodgelogcabins.com

All Seasons Holidays
★★★★–★★★★★
Self Catering
All Seasons
t (01507) 604470
e abudd63@aol.com
w allseasonsuk.com

Ashwater House
★★★–★★★★ *Self Catering*
t (01507) 609295
e holly@ashwaterhouse.co.uk
w ashwaterhouse.co.uk

Canal Farm Cottages
★★★★ *Self Catering*
t (01472) 388825
e canalfarm@ukhome.net
w canalfarmcottages.co.uk

Louth Holiday Home ★★★
Self Catering
t (0117) 931 5033
e info@louth-holidayhome.co.uk
w louth-holidayhome.co.uk

Mill Lodge ★★★
Self Catering
Contact: Mrs Cade
Mill Lodge
t (01507) 343265

Station Masters House, Ludborough ★★★
Self Catering
t (01507) 363470
e info@raileisure.com
w raileisure.com

Wold Lodge & Scandinavian Lodge ★★★ *Self Catering*
Contact: Mr Michael Graves
t (01507) 605085
e mike@graves.eclipse.co.uk

Yarburgh Grove Farm ★★★
Self Catering
Contact: Alison Welsh
t (01507) 363370
e alisonwelsh@yahoo.co.uk
w yarburghgrovefarm.co.uk

LULLINGTON
Derbyshire

Aubrietia Cottage ★★★★
Self Catering
Contact: Mrs Rita Cooper
t (01827) 373219
e r.cooper@care4free.net

MABLETHORPE
Lincolnshire

Dunes Cottage ★★★
Self Catering
Dunes cottage
t (01507) 338342
e Sheila.a.morrison@btopenworld.co.uk
w duneshulidaycottage.co.uk

Grange Cottages ★★★★
Self Catering
Contact: Ann Graves
Grange Cottages
t (01507) 450267
w grange-cottages.co.uk

MAIDENWELL
Lincolnshire

Old School House ★★★★
Self Catering
t (01507) 534214
e venture.properties@virgin.net
w theoldschoolhouse.tripod.com

MANSFIELD
Nottinghamshire

Blue Barn Cottage ★★★
Self Catering
Blue Barn Farm
t (01623) 742248
e bluebarnfarm@supanet.com

Watson Avenue ★★★★
Self Catering
Contact: Dionne Miller
David Blount Ltd
t (01623) 721155
e lettings@davidblount.co.uk
w nottshouse.co.uk

MAPPLETON
Derbyshire

Hawthorn Cottage (Ashbourne) ★★★★
Self Catering
Contact: Mrs J Lawrence
t (01925) 752220
e info@caldecotthomes.co.uk
w caldecotthomes.co.uk

MARKET HARBOROUGH
Leicestershire

Short Lodge Cottages ★★★
Self Catering
Contact: Jane Durham
t (01858) 525323

MARKET RASEN
Lincolnshire

Meadow Farm House
★★★★ *Self Catering*
Contact: Mr Nick Grimshaw
t (01673) 885909
e nickgrimshaw@btconnect.com

Papermill Cottages ★★★★
Self Catering
t (01673) 838010
e peter.rhodes1@btinternet.com
w papermillcottages.co.uk

The Stables ★★★★
Self Catering
Contact: Mr Colin Reed
Holton Assests Ltd.
t (01673) 858881
e mxrwj@ic24.net

MARSHCHAPEL
Lincolnshire

Dove Cottage ★★★★
Self Catering
t (01472) 388520
e june.houghton@tesco.net
w dovecottage-lincs.co.uk

MATLOCK
Derbyshire

The Birds Nest ★★★★★
Self Catering
Contact: Mrs Susan Shah
t (01629) 584549
e birdsnest@peakdistrictholidays.co.uk
w peakdistrictholidays.co.uk

Carpenters Cottage ★★★★
Self Catering
Contact: Mrs Iris Wilmot
t (0115) 923 3455 & 07967 120713
e bobwilmot@edwalton.fslife.co.uk
w carpenters-cottage.com

Carsington Cottages
Rating Applied For
Self Catering
Contact: Mrs Valerie Riach
t (01629) 540513
e riachclan@btinternet.com

Darwin Forest Country Park
★★★★ *Self Catering*
t (01629) 732428
e admin@pinelodgeholidays.co.uk
w pinelodgeholidays.co.uk/darwin_forest.ihtml

Darwin Lake *Self Catering*
Contact: Miss Nikki Manning
Darwin Lake
t (01629) 735859
e enquiries@darwinlake.co.uk
w darwinlake.co.uk

Eagle Cottage, Birchover
★★★★ *Self Catering*
Contact: Mrs Mary Prince
Eagle Cottage
t (01629) 650634
e maryprince@msn.com
w cressbrook.co.uk/youlgve/eagle/

Honeysuckle and Clematis Cottages ★★★★
Self Catering
Contact: Mr J Lomas
Middle Hills Farm
t (01629) 650368
e l.lomas@btinernet.com

Ivy Cottage (Aldwark) ★★★
Self Catering
Contact: Mrs Tricia Potter
t (01629) 823018
e ivy.cottage@ukgateway.net

Little Hallmoor Castle
★★★★ *Self Catering*
Derbyshire Country Cottages
t (01629) 583545
e enquiries@derbyshirecountrycottages.co.uk

Masson Leys Farm ★★★★
Self Catering
Contact: Mrs Brenda Dawes
t (01629) 582944

Mooredge Barns
★★★★-★★★★★
Self Catering
Contact: Mr Barratt
t (01629) 583701 & 07766 074585
e enquiries@mooredgefarmcottages.co.uk
w mooredgefarmcottages.co.uk

Rockside Hall ★★★★★
Self Catering
Contact: Mr Ray Calder
t 07966 136123
e ray@calder1.eclipse.co.uk
w rocksidehall.co.uk

The Studio ★★★
Self Catering
Contact: Mr & Mrs Shimwell
t (01629) 581564
w westleastudio.co.uk

Swiss View ★★★
Self Catering
Contact: Mr William Lennox
t (01629) 582568

MATLOCK BATH
Derbyshire

1 The Coach House ★★★★
Self Catering
Contact: Mr & Mrs David & Emma Allen
t (01582) 831281
e dande.allen@ntlworld.com

Bluebell Cottage ★★★
Self Catering
Peak Cottages
t (0114) 262 0777
e enquiries@peakcottages.com
w peakcottages.com

Derwent View ★★★
Self Catering
Contact: Mr Tim Heathcote
t (01629) 57473

Hopton House ★★★★
Self Catering
Contact: Mrs Yvonne Evans
t (01629) 540686
e yvonneevans5@btinternet.com

Rambler Cottage ★★★
Self Catering
Contact: Mr Colin MacQueen
Peak Cottages
t (0114) 262 0777
e enquiries@peakcottages.com

MEASHAM
Leicestershire

105 Bosworth Road ★★★
Self Catering
Contact: Alan and Christine Cornell
'Omega'
t (01530) 271245

MELBOURNE
Derbyshire

Orchard Barn ★★★★
Self Catering
t (01332) 833584
e hendleysfour@aol.uk

MELTON MOWBRAY
Leicestershire

28 Melton Road ★★★★
Self Catering
Contact: Mrs Anne Watchorn
Chester House
t (01664) 464255
e awatchorn1314@yahoo.com

MELTON ROSS
Lincolnshire

The Old Chapel Cottage
★★★★ *Self Catering*
t (01652) 680527
e rachelwinning@hotmail.com

METHERINGHAM
Lincolnshire

Drws nesaf ★★★
Self Catering
Contact: Mr A.C. Jones
t (01526) 322558
e caradog@fish.co.uk

MIDDLE RASEN
Lincolnshire

East Farm Cottage ★★★
Self Catering
t (01673) 842283

MIDDLETON
Derbyshire

The Barn ★★★ *Self Catering*
Contact: Mr Peter Smith
t (01629) 824519
e psmith@barnaccommodation.freeserve.co.uk
w barnaccommodation.co.uk

MIDDLETON-BY-YOULGREAVE
Derbyshire

Curlew Cottage ★★★★
Self Catering
Contact: Mrs Carole Brister
t (01629) 636180
e brister@lowfield1.fsnet.co.uk
w http://mysite.freeserve.com/lowfieldfarmcottages

Holly Homestead ★★★★
Self Catering
Contact: Mr & Mrs David & Valerie Edge
t (01773) 550754
e d.w.edge@homecall.co.uk
w holly-homestead.co.uk

MILLER'S DALE
Derbyshire

The Anglers Rest ★★
Self Catering
Contact: Mrs Beryl Yates
t (01298) 871323

Monks Retreat
★★★-★★★★★ *Self Catering*
Contact: Mrs Pamela Wilkson
t (01298) 871306
e pamwilkson@hotmail.com
w cressbrook.co.uk/tidza/monksdale

MILLTHORPE, HOLMESFIELD
Derbyshire

Millthorpe Cottage ★★★★
Self Catering
Contact: Mr & Mrs Nich & Liz Barrett
Sleaford Property Services Ltd
t (0114) 289 1071
e cottage.holidays@btopenworld.com
w cottage-vacations.co.uk

MILLTOWN
Derbyshire

Greenfield Barn, Milltown
★★★★ *Self Catering*
Contact: Mr & Mrs Page
t (01246) 590119

MOIRA
Derbyshire

Lakeview Lodge ★★★★
Self Catering
Contact: Mrs Carol Mallen
Lake view Lodge & Lakeside Tearooms
t (01283) 763611
e shortheathwater@aol.com

MONSAL DALE
Derbyshire

Riversdale Farm Holiday Cottages ★★★★
Self Catering
Contact: Mr Michael Jackson
t (01629) 640500
e mick@riversdale-farm.freeserve.co.uk
w riversdalefarm.co.uk

MONYASH
Derbyshire

The Barn (Monyash) ★★★★
Self Catering
Contact: Mr Tony Staley
t (01629) 583811
e tonystaley@hotmail.com
w littlegemcottages.co.uk

Rose Cottage ★★★
Self Catering
Contact: Mrs Heather Read
Rose Cottage
t (01629) 813629

Sheldon Cottages ★★★★
Self Catering & Serviced Apartments
Contact: Mrs Louise Fanshawe
Sheldon Cottages
t (01629) 813067
e info@sheldoncottages.co.uk
w sheldoncottages.co.uk

 Look out for establishments participating in the National Accessible Scheme

NETTLEHAM
Lincolnshire

Luv-a-Duck Cottage ★★★★
Self Catering
Contact: Mrs Elizabeth Johnston
The Croft
t (01522) 750746

The Stables ★★★★
Self Catering
t (01472) 398304
e thorganby@lineone.net

NETTLETON
Lincolnshire

Nettleton Grange ★★★
Self Catering
t (01472) 851360

NEW MILLS
Derbyshire

Shaw Farm Cottage ★★
Self Catering
Contact: Mrs Nicky Burgess
Shaw Farm Cottage
t (0161) 427 1841
e nicky.burgess@talk21.com
w shawfarmholidays.co.uk

NEWARK
Nottinghamshire

Peggys Cottage ★★★★
Self Catering
Contact: Mrs Valerie Ashton
Coach House
t (01636) 700096
e peggyscottage@fsmail.net

NEWTON GRANGE
Derbyshire

New Hanson Bungalow ★★★★ *Self Catering*
Contact: Mrs Linda Bonsall
t (01335) 310258
e nhgfarmholiday@supanet.com
w cressbrook.co.uk/ashborn/newhanson

NORTH COCKERINGTON
Lincolnshire

Barn Owl Cottage ★★★★
Self Catering
t (01507) 327025
e abcdhiggs@tiscali.co.uk
w barnowlcottage.info

NORTH RAUCEBY
Lincolnshire

The Bakehouse ★★★★
Self Catering
Contact: Mrs Susan Ireland
t (01529) 488396
e james.ireland@farmline.com

NORTH SOMERCOTES
Lincolnshire

Nursery Cottage ★★★★
Self Catering
Contact: Mrs Linda Libell
Meals Farm
t (01507) 358356
e nurserycottage@hotmail.co.uk
w mealsfarm.com

NORTH WILLINGHAM
Lincolnshire

Old Blacksmiths Cottage ★★★ *Self Catering*
t (01673) 838081
e betty@oldblacksmithscottage.co.uk
w oldblacksmithscottage.co.uk

NORTHAMPTON
Northamptonshire

Mill Barn Cottage ★★★
Self Catering
t (01604) 810507
e roger@themillbarn.free-online.co.uk
w themillbarn.free-online.co.uk

NOTTINGHAM
Nottinghamshire

46 Riverview ★★★
Self Catering
t (0115) 923 3372
e dms@discovernottinghamshire.co.uk

Woodview Cottages ★★★★
Self Catering
t (01949) 81580
e enquiries@woodviewcottages.co.uk
w woodviewcottages.co.uk

OAKHAM
Rutland

The Cat Basket ★★★★
Self Catering
Contact: Mrs Marilyn Tomalin
t (01572) 723184
e jmtomalin@onetel.com

Old School Cottage, North Luffenham ★★★★
Self Catering
Contact: Mrs E Handley
Wytchley House
t (01780) 721768
e rhandley@supanet.com
w rutnet.co.uk/oldschoolcottage

Pear Tree Cottage ★★★
Self Catering
Contact: Mrs Jane Thomas
t (01780) 460258

OLD BOLINGBROKE
Lincolnshire

1 & 2 Hope Cottages ★★★★ *Self Catering*
Contact: Mr & Mrs Taylor
t (01673) 861412
e no1hopecottage@aol.com
w no1hopecottage.co.uk

OLD BRAMPTON
Derbyshire

Chestnut Cottage and Willow Cottage ★★★★
Self Catering
Contact: Mr & Mrs Jeffery & Patrica Green
t (01246) 566159

OLD DALBY
Leicestershire

Lower Grange Farm ★★★★
Self Catering
Contact: Sue Fox
t (01664) 823640
e lgfarm@btinternet.com

OLD STRATFORD
Northamptonshire

33 and 35 Brookside Close ★★★ *Self Catering*
Contact: Mrs Hepher
The Old Bakery
t (01908) 562253
e mksh@hepher.demon.co.uk

OUNDLE
Northamptonshire

13 Cotterstock Road ★★★
Self Catering
Contact: Mr & Mrs J S Czwortek
t (01832) 273371

The Bolt Hole ★★★★
Self Catering
Contact: Mrs Anita Spurrell
Rose Cottage
t (01832) 272298 & 07850 388109
e nanda@spurrell.ocs-uk.com

Oundle Cottage Breaks ★★★-★★★★ *Self Catering*
Contact: Mr & Mrs Simmonds
Oundle Cottage Breaks
t (01832) 275508
e richard@simmondsatoundle.co.uk
w oundlecottagebreaks.co.uk

OVER HADDON
Derbyshire

Burton Manor Farm Cottages ★★★★
Self Catering
Contact: Mrs Ruth Shirt
t (01298) 871429
e cshirt@burtonmanor.freeserve.co.uk
w burtonmanor.freeserve.co.uk

May Cottage ★★★★
Self Catering
Contact: Mrs Margaret Corbridge
t (01629) 813639

OXTON
Nottinghamshire

Wesley Farm Cottage ★★★★ *Self Catering*
t (0115) 965 2043
e enquiries@wesleycottage.com
w wesleycottage.com

PANTON
Lincolnshire

St Andrew's Church ★★★
Self Catering
Contact: Mrs J K Haller
t (01673) 857302
e janet_haller@hotmail.com
w lincs-holiday.co.uk

PARWICH
Derbyshire

Brook Cottage ★★★★
Self Catering
Contact: Mr Terry Pickard
t (01335) 390360
e terence.pickard@tiscali.co.uk

Church Gates Cottage ★★★
Self Catering
Contact: Mr Colin MacQueen
Peak Cottages
t (0114) 262 0777
e enquiries@peakcottages.com

Croft Cottage ★★★★
Self Catering
Contact: Mrs Saskia Tallis
t (01335) 390440
e enquiries@croftcottage.co.uk
w croftcottage.co.uk

Douglas's Barn ★★★★★
Self Catering
Contact: John & Marion Fuller-Sessions
t (01335) 390519
e douglas@orchardfarm.demon.co.uk

Parwich Lees Holiday Cottages ★★★ *Self Catering*
Contact: Mrs Jane Gerard-Pearse
t (01335) 390625
e ionabess@btinternet.com

Tom's Barn ★★★★★
Self Catering
Contact: Mr & Mrs John & Marion Fuller-Sessions
t (01335) 390519
e tom@orchardfarm.demon.co.uk
w tomsbarn.co.uk

PASSENHAM
Northamptonshire

The Studio ★★★★
Self Catering
Contact: Mrs Tina Shrimpton
t (01908) 563223
e tina@shrimptonfamily.co.uk

PIKEHALL
Derbyshire

The Old Farmhouse and The Grange ★★★★ *Self Catering*
Contact: Mr & Mrs Mavin
t (01335) 390382

PLUNGAR
Leicestershire

The Old Wharf ★★★★★
Self Catering
Contact: Mrs Elaine Pell
Grange Farm
t (01949) 860630
e pellelaine@hotmail.com

POTTERHANWORTH
Lincolnshire

Black Horse Cottage ★★★
Self Catering
t (01522) 792549
w blackhorsecottage.co.uk

Skelghyll Cottage ★★★
Self Catering
t (01522) 790043
e pulse@lincolnshiretourism.com

QUARNFORD
Derbyshire

Black Clough Farmhouse ★★★ *Self Catering*
Contact: Mrs Kate Farnworth
t (01298) 23360
e farnworths@totalise.co.uk

Greens Farm ★★★
Self Catering
Contact: Mrs Audrey Gould
t (01298) 25172
e skidd156@hotmail.com

New Colshaw Farm ★★★
Self Catering
Contact: Mr John Belfield
Lower Colshaw Farm
t (01298) 73266

The Studio at Adders Green ★★ *Self Catering*
Contact: Pamela Sandiford
t (01298) 237520
e pam@addersgreen.co.uk

RAUNDS
Northamptonshire

Gatehouse Annex ★★★★
Self Catering
t (01933) 626600
e tsoshar@aol.com

RETFORD
Nottinghamshire

Spruce Cottage ★★★
Self Catering
t (0131) 447 6886
e bpmason@blueyonder.co.uk

Westhill Cottage ★★★
Self Catering
t (01777) 707034
e doreen@holly23.freeserve.co.uk
w westhillcottage.co.uk

ROLLESTON
Nottinghamshire

Mill Cottage ★★★
Self Catering
Contact: Mrs Laura Murray
The Den Cottage
t (0115) 966 4015
e laurajmurray@tiscali.co.uk

ROSTON
Derbyshire

Meadow Cottage – Shawley Farm ★★★★ *Self Catering*
Contact: Ms Glenys Hubbard
t (01889) 590507
e meadowcottagederbys@hotmail.com

ROWSLEY
Derbyshire

Bluebell Cottage ★★★★
Self Catering
Contact: Mrs Jane Henderson
t (0114) 281 7217
e jane77@blueyonder.co.uk

RUSKINGTON
Lincolnshire

The Annex ★★★★
Self Catering
Contact: Mr Henry Pettitt
t (01526) 833857
e i.pettitt@hotmail.com

Orwell House Annex ★★★
Self Catering
Contact: Mrs Elizabeth Cartwright
t (01526) 834292
e lelisian@aol.com

SELSTON
Nottinghamshire

Kinnaird – Selston ★★★★
Self Catering
'Kinnaird' - Selston
t (01623) 441278
e karen.barton10@btopenworld.com
w kinnaird-selston.co.uk

SHELDON
Derbyshire

Townend Cottage ★★★
Self Catering
Contact: Mrs Ethel Plumtree
t (01629) 813322

SHIRLEY
Derbyshire

Shirley Hall Farm ★★★
Self Catering
Contact: Mrs Sylvia Foster
t (01335) 360346
e sylviafoster@shirleyhallfarm.com

SHOTTLE
Derbyshire

Manifold Farm ★★★★
Self Catering
Contact: Ms Tissie Reason
t (01246) 565379
e estateoffice@chatsworth.org
w chatsworth.org

SIBBERTOFT
Northamptonshire

Brook Meadow Chalets ★★★-★★★★ *Self Catering*
Contact: Mary Hart
Brook Meadow
t (01858) 880886
e brookmeadow@farmline.co.uk
w brookmeadow.co.uk

SIBSEY
Lincolnshire

Sweetbriar ★★★
Self Catering
Contact: Mrs Alison Twiddy
t (01205) 750837

SKEGNESS
Lincolnshire

Ingoldale Park ★★★★
Self Catering
Contact: Mrs Cathryn Whitehead
t (01754) 872335
e ingoldalepark@btopenworld.com

Lyndene Holiday Apartments ★-★★★
Self Catering
Contact: Mr Bailey
t (01754) 766108
e info@lyndene-uk.com

Springfield & Island Holiday Apartments ★-★★★
Self Catering
Contact: Mr & Mrs John & Carol Haines
t (01754) 762660
e carol@springfield-island.fsnet.co.uk
w skegness-resort.co.uk/springfield

SKENDLEBY
Lincolnshire

Skendleby Hall ★★★★
Self Catering
Contact: Mr Paddy Langdown
t (01227) 454562
e p.langdown17@btinternet.com
w skendlebyhall.co.uk

SOUTH COCKERINGTON
Lincolnshire

Grasswells Farm Holiday Cottages ★★★★
Self Catering
Contact: Ms Janice Foster
Grasswells Holiday Cottages (Saddleback Leisure Ltd)
t (01507) 338508
e thefosters2002@aol.com

West View Cottages ★★★
Self Catering
Contact: Mr Richard Nicholson and Mrs J Hand
t (01507) 327209
e enquiries@west-view.co.uk
w west-view.co.uk

SOUTH WILLINGHAM
Lincolnshire

The Cottage ★★★★
Self Catering
Contact: Mrs Donocik
t (01507) 313737

SOUTHWELL
Nottinghamshire

The Hayloft, Little Tithe & Dovecote ★★★ *Self Catering*
Contact: Mrs Wilson
t (01636) 830497
w lodgebarns.com

The Nest ★★★★
Self Catering
Contact: Mrs Diana Dawes
t (01636) 830140
e rlgdawes@hotmail.com

SPARROWPIT
Derbyshire

Daisy Bank and Hope Cottages ★★★ *Self Catering*
Contact: Mrs Hilary Batterbee
t (01298) 813027
e mail@sparrowpit.com
w sparrowpit.com

SPILSBY
Lincolnshire

Northfields Farm Cottages ★★★ *Self Catering*
Contact: Mr W P Miller
t (01507) 588251
e chrismiller@tiscali.co.uk
w northfieldsfarmcottages.co.uk

STAINFIELD
Lincolnshire

Rural Roosts ★★★★
Self Catering
t (01526) 398492
e katie@ruralroosts.co.uk
w ruralroosts.co.uk

STAINTON BY LANGWORTH
Lincolnshire

Church Farm Cottage ★★★★ *Self Catering*
Contact: Mr Chris Valentine
t (01673) 862775
e churchfarmhouse2003@supanet.com

STAMFORD
Lincolnshire

Elder Flower Cottage, Belmesthorpe ★★★
Self Catering
Contact: Mr P and Mrs D Wilkinson
Elder Flower Cottage
t (01780) 757188 & 07711 533204
e philanddawn@tiscali.co.uk

Granary Cottages ★★★★
Self Catering
Contact: Mrs Katie Maitland
Aunby Manor
t (01778) 590085
e mkmaitland@hotmail.com
w aunby.co.uk

Riverside View ★★★
Self Catering
Contact: Ms Tina Kirby
Universal Property
t 07752 361362
e unip@talk21.com

Wyandotte Cottage ★★★★
Self Catering
Contact: Mrs Jane Thorpe-Codman
Frog Hall
t (01780) 784394 & 07833 680110
e bookings@stamfordcottages.co.uk
w stamfordcottages.co.uk

STANTON IN PEAK
Derbyshire

Rock House
Rating Applied For
Self Catering
Contact: Mr & Mrs Paul & Sandra Steverson
The Rocks
t (01629) 581819
e sandra.steverson@dial.pipex.co.uk
w rockhouse-peakdistrict.co.uk

STATHERN
Leicestershire

Sycamore Farm ★★★★
Self Catering
Contact: Miss Ruth Stanley
t (01949) 860640

STEWTON
Lincolnshire

Westfield Farm Cottages ★★★-★★★★ *Self Catering*
Contact: Mr Darren Royle
t (01507) 607421
e daz@thisvillage.com
w thisvillage.com/westfield

STOKE BRUERNE
Northamptonshire

3 Canalside ★★★
Self Catering
Contact: Mr Trevor Morley
t (01604) 862107
w stokebruerneboats.co.uk

SURFLEET
Lincolnshire

Creek View ★★★★
Self Catering
Contact: Mrs Annabel Parkinson
t (01775) 680044
e annabel@dppackaging.com

SUTTERTON
Lincolnshire

Somercotes ★★★
Self Catering
Contact: Dr J V Sharp
Inish Fail
t (01235) 833367
e J.V.Sharp@btinternet.com
w somercotes.biz

SUTTON-ON-SEA
Lincolnshire

Country Retreat Equestrian Lodges ★★★–★★★★
Self Catering
Contact: Ms Maria Spradbury
Country Retreat Equestrian Lodges
t (01507) 442631
e mariaequestrian@aol.com
w blackcatequestriancentre.co.uk

Poplar Farm Holiday Cottages ★★★★
Self Catering
t (01473) 711117
e helen.matthews@btopenworld.com
w poplar-farm.org.uk

SUTTON ON THE HILL
Derbyshire

The Chop House ★★★★
Self Catering
Contact: Mr & Mrs Keith & Joan Lennard
t (01283) 732377
e windlehill@btinternet.com

SUTTON ST JAMES
Lincolnshire

Foreman's Bridge Caravan Park *Self Catering*
Contact: Mr John Hoey
Foreman's Bridge Caravan Park
t (01945) 440346
e foremansbridge@btconnect.com
w foremans-bridge.co.uk

SWADLINCOTE
Derbyshire

Forest Lodges, Rosliston
★★★★ *Self Catering*
Contact: Mrs Marie Hall
Rosliston Forest Centre
t (01283) 519119
e enquiries@roslistonforestrycentre.co.uk
w roslistonforestrycentre.co.uk

SWAYFIELD
Lincolnshire

Greystones Lodge ★★★★
Self Catering
t (01476) 550909
e jslog1@ntlworld.com

Woodview ★★★
Self Catering
Contact: Mrs Alison Bairsto
c/o Lucklaw House
t (01476) 550097
e bears178@aol.com

TADDINGTON
Derbyshire

Ash Tree Barn ★★★
Self Catering
Contact: Ms Judith Hawley
t (01298) 85453
e jah@ashtreebarn.fsnet.co.uk
w cressbrook.co.uk/tidza/ashbarn

TANSLEY
Derbyshire

Abbey Lane End House
★★★ *Self Catering*
Contact: Mr Dave Wilson
Lane End House
t (01629) 583981
e dave@laneendhouse.co.uk
w laneendhouse.co.uk

TEMPLE NORMANTON
Derbyshire

Rocklea ★★★ *Self Catering*
Contact: Mr Roger Stirling
t (01709) 543108
w cottageguide.co.uk/rocklea

TETFORD
Lincolnshire

Grange Farm Cottages ★★★
Self Catering
The Grange
t (01673) 858670
e sarahstamp@farmersweekly.net
w thegrange-lincolnshire.co.uk

Little London Cottages
★★★★–★★★★★
Self Catering
Contact: Mrs Debbie Sutcliffe
t (01507) 533697
e debbie@sutcliffell.freeserve.co.uk
w littlelondoncottages.co.uk

Pine Lodge ★★★★
Self Catering
Contact: Mr Paddy Langdown
t (01227) 454562
w pinelodge-tetford.com

TETNEY
Lincolnshire

Beech Farm Cottages
★★★★ *Self Catering*
Contact: Norman Smith
t (01472) 694430
e norman@beechfarmcottages.co.uk
w beechfarmcottages.co.uk

THORGANBY
Lincolnshire

Little Walk Cottage ★★★★
Self Catering
J Milligan-Manby Limited
t (01472) 398304
e thorganby@lineone.net

THORPE
Derbyshire

Hawthorn Studio ★★★
Self Catering
Contact: Mrs Suzanne Walton
t (01335) 350494

THORPE-ON-THE-HILL
Lincolnshire

Jubilee Farm Cottages ★★★
Self Catering
Contact: Elaine Richardson
t (01522) 681241
e davidandelaine53@aol.com

The Railway Inn
Rating Applied For
Self Catering
t (01522) 500495

THORPE SATCHVILLE
Leicestershire

Walnut Tree Cottage
★★★★ *Self Catering*
Contact: Mrs Dee Burton
t (01664) 840638
e db@walnut-tree-cottage.co.uk
w walnut-tree-cottage.co.uk

THURLBY
Lincolnshire

Pegasus ★★★ *Self Catering*
Contact: Miss Hazel Newman
t (01778) 422955
w southwestlincs.com

TIDESWELL
Derbyshire

The Annexe ★★★
Self Catering
Contact: Mrs Sara Price
t (01298) 871789
e rap@tinyonline.co.uk

Dean Cottage ★★★
Self Catering
Contact: Mrs Anne Mepham
t (0113) 204 9753
e annemepham@aol.com

Geil Torrs ★★★ *Self Catering*
Contact: Mr Harry Buttle
Geil Torrs
t (01298) 871302

Hulmes Vale Barn ★★★
Self Catering
Contact: Ms Kate Strong
t (01298) 873098
e katestrong1@onetel.net

Lane End Cottage ★★★★
Self Catering
Contact: Mr John Snowden
t (01623) 557279

Markeygate Cottages
★★★★ *Self Catering*
Contact: Mrs Melanie Greening-James
t (01298) 871260
e markeygatehouse@hotmail.com
w markeygatecottages.co.uk

Rebethnal Cottage ★★★
Self Catering
Contact: Mrs Amanda Greenland
t (01234) 407345
e rebethnal.cottage@ntlworld.com
w rebethnalcottage.com

Stoneycroft ★★★★
Self Catering
Contact: Mr Clive Sykes
Sykes Cottages
t (01244) 345700

TRUSTHORPE
Lincolnshire

The Old Garth Holiday Cottages ★★★ *Self Catering*
Contact: Mr Stephen Lewis
t (01507) 477380
e enquiries@oldgarthcottages.co.uk
w oldgarthcottages.co.uk

TWO DALES
Derbyshire

Toad Cottage ★★★
Self Catering
Contact: Tina Boulden
t (01246) 234132
e info@toadcottage.co.uk
w toadcottage.co.uk

UFFINGTON
Lincolnshire

8 Casewick Lane ★★★★
Self Catering
Contact: Mr Chris Birch
t (01737) 769167
e chris@casewicklane.co.uk
w casewicklane.co.uk

WADDINGWORTH
Lincolnshire

Redhouse Cottage ★★★★
Self Catering
t (01507) 578285
e redhousefarm@waddingworth.fsnet.co.uk
w redhousecottage.co.uk

WARDLEY
Rutland

Pool House ★★★★
Self Catering
Contact: Mrs Ann Kanter
Wardley House
t (01527) 717671
e annkanter@compuserve.com

WARMINGTON
Northamptonshire

Papley Farm Cottages
★★★★ *Self Catering*
Contact: Joyce Lane
t (01832) 272583

WELLINGBOROUGH
Northamptonshire

Friendly Lodge Cottage
★★★★ *Self Catering*
Contact: Mrs Kaye Saunders
t (01933) 461102

WELLOW
Nottinghamshire

Foliat Cottages ★★★
Self Catering
t (01623) 861088
e janet.carr@farmline.com
w sherwoodforestholidaycottages.com

The White House and Studio
★★★ *Serviced Apartments*
Contact: Mrs Angela Holding
Rose Cottage
t (01623) 835798
e alan.holding@btinternet.com

WELTON
Lincolnshire

Athina ★★★★ *Self Catering*
Contact: Mrs Michelle Billington
t (01663) 719661
e athinabookings@aol.com
w athinacottage.co.uk

Mill Cottage ★★★★
Self Catering
Mill Cottage Holiday Lets
t (01673) 860082
e gill@millhousecottage.freeserve.co.uk
w millcottageholidaylets.co.uk

WENSLEY
Derbyshire

Thatch Cottage ★★★★
Self Catering
Contact: Mrs Hilary Oates
t (0114) 236 5828

WEST BARKWITH
Lincolnshire

Glebe Farm Self Catering Apartments ★★★
Self Catering
Contact: Mrs Jo Campion
t (01673) 858919
w glebeapart.co.uk

WESTON UNDERWOOD
Derbyshire

Honeysuckle Cottage ★★★
Self Catering
Contact: Mrs Linda Adams
Park View Farm
t (01335) 360352
e enquiries@parkviewfarm.co.uk
w parkviewfarm.co.uk

WHALEY BRIDGE
Derbyshire

Cloud Cottage and Nimbus House ★★★★ *Self Catering*
Contact: Mrs Brobbins
The Old Manse
t (01663) 733332
e lindabrobbin@hotmail.com

Cote Bank Farm Cottages ★★★★ *Self Catering*
Contact: Mrs Pamela Broadhurst
t (01663) 750566
e cotebank@btinternet.com
w cotebank.co.uk

Horwich Barns ★★★★★
Self Catering
Contact: Mr Colin MacQueen
Peak Cottages
t (0114) 262 0777
e enquiries@peakcottages.com

WHATSTANDWELL
Derbyshire

Smithy Forge Cottages ★★★ *Self Catering*
Contact: Mr Chris Buxton
End Cottage
t (01332) 881758
e chris@smithyforgecottages.co.uk

WHITTLEBURY
Northamptonshire

Dolly's Cottage ★★★
Self Catering
t (01327) 857896
e patandalan@tesco.net
w cottageguide.co.uk/silverstone

WIGSTHORPE
Northamptonshire

The Barns Hall Farm ★★★★★ *Self Catering*
Contact: Mr David Burnett
t (01832) 720488
e burnetts@gotadsl.co.uk

WINDLEY
Derbyshire

The Old Cheese Factory ★★★★★ *Self Catering*
Contact: Ms Sally Wallwork
t (01773) 550947
e sawallwork@aol.com
w theoldcheesefactory.com

WINGERWORTH
Derbyshire

Spinney Top Cottage ★★★
Self Catering
Contact: Mr & Mrs Silwood & Anita Kinder
t (01246) 557979
e sil_kinder@yahoo.co.uk

WINSTER
Derbyshire

Blakelow Farm Holiday Cottages ★★★★★
Self Catering
Contact: Mr Stephen Ogan
t (01629) 650814
e blakelowcottages@w3z.co.uk
w blakelowcottages.co.uk

Briar Cottage ★★★★
Self Catering
Contact: Mrs Anne Walters
Briar Cottage
t (01629) 650342
e etegfan@clara.co.uk

Jasmine Cottage ★★★★
Self Catering
Contact: Ms Ann Banister
Field Farm
t (01629) 732084

Rock Cottage ★★★★
Self Catering
Contact: Mr Christopher Higgs
t (01629) 650488
e info@peakrockcottages.co.uk
w peakrockcottages.co.uk

WIRKSWORTH
Derbyshire

Hog Cottage ★★★★
Self Catering
Contact: Ms Anna Fern
Blue Lagoon
t 07714 230118
e hogcottage@bluelagoon.co.uk

Hopton Estates ★★★★-★★★★★
Self Catering
Contact: Mr & Mrs Spencer & Emma Tallis
t (01629) 540458
e h.e@saqnet.co.uk

Snuffless Dip ★★★
Self Catering
Contact: Mrs Margaret Doxey
t (01629) 824466

Weathericks and Bradstone ★★★★★ *Self Catering*
Contact: Mrs Jean Hurdle
t (01629) 822616
e info@weathericks.co.uk
w weathericks.co.uk

WITHERN
Lincolnshire

Park Farm Holidays ★★★
Self Catering
t (01507) 450331
e alan@park-farm25.fsnet.co.uk
w parkfarmholidayswithern.com

WOODHALL SPA
Lincolnshire

Mill Lane Cottage ★★
Self Catering
Contact: Mr & Mrs Ian & Jane Williamson
t (01526) 353101
e will@williamsoni.freeserve.co.uk
w skegness.net/woodhallspa.htm

WROOT
Lincolnshire

Brook Lodge Cottage ★★★
Self Catering
Contact: E Bayes
t (01302) 772285
e info@brook-lodge-cottage.co.uk
w brook-lodge-country-cottage.co.uk

The Granary ★★★
Self Catering
Contact: Robin Aconley
t (01302) 770196
e janeaconley@tinyworld.co.uk

YARWELL
Northamptonshire

Manor House Cottage, Yarwell ★★★★ *Self Catering*
Contact: Mrs Gillian Berry
t (01780) 783741
e gillian@yarberrys.fsnet.co.uk

YELDERSLEY
Derbyshire

Ladyhole House – The Old Stables ★★★★★
Self Catering
Contact: Mrs Rosamond Woodrow
t (01335) 342670
e rosamondwoodrow@boltblue.com
w ladyholehouseholidays.co.uk

YOULGREAVE
Derbyshire

April Cottage ★★★
Self Catering
Contact: Mrs L Lovell
t (01629) 636151
e l.lovell@whitepeakcottage.co.uk
w whitepeakcottage.co.uk

The Cottage, Crimbles Lane ★★★★ *Self Catering*
Contact: Mr & Mrs Sutcliffe
t (01629) 636570
e cottage@oldschoolhall.plus.com
w thecottage-crimbleslane.co.uk

Knoll Cottage ★★★
Self Catering
Contact: Mr Colin MacQueen
Peak Cottages
t (0114) 262 0777
e enquiries@peakcottages.com

Rose Cottages ★★★★
Self Catering
Contact: Mr & Mrs John Upton
t (01629) 636487
e enquiries@rosecottages.co.uk
w rosecottages.co.uk

Sunny View ★★★
Self Catering
Contact: Mrs Orchard
t (01773) 831064
e judithorchard@aol.com

Sunnyside, Youlgreave ★★★ *Self Catering*
Contact: Ms J Steed
t (01629) 636195

Thyme Cottage ★★★★
Self Catering
Contact: Mrs F Bradshaw
Swan House
t (01543) 432739

EAST OF ENGLAND

ABINGTON
Cambridgeshire

Holly Lodge ★★★★
Self Catering
Contact: Mr & Mrs A G Farley
t (01223) 892532
w hollylodgeholidays.co.uk

ACLE
Norfolk

The Olde Chapel ★★★★
Self Catering
Norfolk Country Cottages
t (01603) 871872
e info@norfolkcottages.co.uk
w norfolkcottages.co.uk

The Retreat (967) ★★★
Self Catering
Norfolk Country Cottages
t (01603) 871872
e info@norfolkcottages.co.uk
w norfolkcottages.co.uk

Station Cottage ★★★★
Self Catering
Contact: Mrs Deborah Mann
t (01493) 751136
e obmc@clara.net
w ukholidayhome.co.uk

ALDBOROUGH
Norfolk

Waverley ★★★ *Self Catering*
Contact: Mr Colin Skipper
t (01263) 761512
w tiscover.co.uk

ALDBURY
Hertfordshire

Aldbury Cottage ★★★★
Self Catering
Contact: Mrs Pamela Dickens
t (01525) 242253
e pam@aldburycottage.com
w aldburycottage.co.uk

ALDEBURGH
Suffolk

15 Britten Close ★★★★
Self Catering
Contact: Mrs Heather Hunting
t (01728) 454716
e david@hunting6166.freeserve.co.uk
w tiscover.co.uk

290 High Street ★★★
Self Catering
Contact: Mr Martin Jinks
t (01728) 453037
w tiscover.co.uk

65 High Street ★★★★
Self Catering
Suffolk Secrets
t (01379) 651297
w suffolk-secrets.co.uk

65 King Street ★★★
Self Catering
Suffolk Secrets
t (01502) 722717

Alde River Pine ★★★★
Self Catering
Contact: John & Nancy Simpson
t (01728) 832351
e john.alderiver@virgin.net

Amber Cottage And Crabbe Cottage ★★★-★★★★
Self Catering
Contact: Mr Roger Williams
t (01359) 270444
e roger.williams43@virgin.net
w cottageguide.co.uk/ambercottage

Avalon ★★★★ *Self Catering*
t (01379) 651297

Avon Cottage ★★★
Self Catering
Suffolk Secrets
t (01379) 651297
e holidays@suffolk-secrets.co.uk
w suffolk-secrets.co.uk

Braid House ★★★
Self Catering
Contact: Miss Ying Tan
t (01728) 663432
e tonying4488@aol.com
w tiscover.co.uk

Bramcote ★★★ *Self Catering*
Contact: Mrs Diana Biddlecombe
t 07817 724643
w tiscover.co.uk

Coastguard Court 8 ★★★
Self Catering
Contact: Mr John Mauger
t (01502) 575896
e john.mauger@blythweb.net
w blythweb.co.uk/coastguard-court

Cosy Corner ★★★
Self Catering
Contact: Ms Ann Fryer
t (01728) 453121
w tiscover.co.uk

Cosy Nook ★★★
Self Catering
Suffolk Secrets
t (01379) 651297
e holidays@suffolk-secrets.co.uk

Cottage ★★★ *Self Catering*
Contact: Mrs J Alexander
t (01394) 383822
e jennialexander@hotmail.com
w tiscover.co.uk

Country Club Apartments ★★★-★★★★ *Self Catering*
Contact: Ms Linda Griffin
Thorpeness Golf Club and Hotel
t (01728) 452176
e info@thorpeness.co.uk
w thorpeness.co.uk

Crag Path 21 ★★★
Self Catering
Contact: Ms Lisabeth Hoad
t (01728) 453933
e lisabeth.hoad@btopenworld.com
w tiscover.co.uk

Cragside ★★★★
Self Catering
Contact: Mrs Lesley Valentine
t (01986) 798609
e j.r.valentine@btinternet.com
w aldeburgh-cragside.co.uk

Dial Flat ★★ *Self Catering*
Contact: Mrs Pam Harrison
t (01728) 453212
e pam@harpd.freeserve.co.uk
w tiscover.co.uk

Fig Tree ★★★ *Self Catering*
Contact: Anna Canty
t (01728) 453037
e anna.canty@orange.co.uk
w tiscover.co.uk

The Gables ★★★★
Self Catering
Contact: Mr Graham Thompson
t (01725) 518755
e gta@cix.co.uk
w thegablesalderburgh.co.uk

Hall Cottage ★★★★
Self Catering
Contact: Mrs Miriam Buchanan
t (01473) 735456
e miriam@greenlabel.co.uk
w loomscottage.co.uk

Kingfisher & Swallow Cottages ★★★★
Self Catering
Contact: Mr Robert Barr
t (01728) 603196
e manorfarmcottages@hotmail.com
w tiscover.co.uk

Lee Road 38 ★★★★
Self Catering
Contact: Mrs Elizabeth Wagener
t (01787) 210223
e lizwagener@aol.com
w tiscover.co.uk

Lower Thellusson ★★★★
Self Catering
Contact: Mrs Claire Gawthrop
East Green Farm
t (01728) 602316
e claire@eastgreenproperty.co.uk
w eastgreencottages.co.uk

Magenta ★★★ *Self Catering*
Contact: Mr Martin Jinks
t (01728) 453037
e martin@jinksy.fsnet.co.uk
w tiscover.co.uk

Mermaid Cottage ★★★★
Self Catering
Contact: Mrs Jacqueline Collier
t (01473) 735004
e jmicollier@aol.com
w tiscover.co.uk

The Nest ★★★ *Self Catering*
Contact: Mrs Tricia Nassau-Williams
t (01386) 751695
e patricianassauwilliams@hotmail.com
w tiscover.co.uk

Nightingale Cottage ★★★★
Self Catering
Suffolk Secrets
t (01502) 722717
e holidays@suffolk-secrets.co.uk
w suffolk-secrets.co.uk

No 38 Aldeburgh Lodge ★★★ *Self Catering*
Contact: Mrs Carole Morley
t (01728) 687999

Orlando ★★★ *Self Catering & Serviced Apartments*
Contact: Mr Peter Hatcher
t (01394) 382126
e orlando@hatcher.co.uk
w hatcher.co.uk/orlando

Parklands ★★★★★
Self Catering
Contact: Mrs Sandra Allen
t (01728) 830139
e parklandssuffolk@aol.com
w justsuffolk.com

Peach House ★★★★
Self Catering
Contact: Mrs J Alexander
t (01394) 383822
e jmalexander@onetel.net.uk
w tiscover.co.uk

River Cottage ★★★★
Self Catering
Contact: Mrs Kate Kilburn
The River House
t (01728) 688267
e dkilburn@cmpinformation.com
w tiscover.co.uk

Suffolk House ★★★
Self Catering
Contact: Mr Tim Connolly
t (01737) 230734
e timconnolly@ugly-duckling.net
w suffolk-house-aldeburgh.co.uk

ALDRINGHAM
Suffolk

No 3 Aldringham House ★★★★ *Self Catering*
Contact: Mr Brian Hodgkinson
t (0115) 926 7016
w tiscover.co.uk

Yewtrees ★★★★
Self Catering
Contact: Ms Claire Webster
t (01273) 241838
e yew.trees@ntlworld.com
w yewtreesmeadowside.com

ALRESFORD
Essex

Creek Lodge ★★★
Self Catering
Contact: Mrs Patricia Mountney
Creek Lodge
t (01206) 825411

ALTHORNE
Essex

Althorne Hall Cottages ★★★★ *Self Catering*
Contact: Mrs Mal Bass
Althorne Hall Farm
t (01621) 740863
e althornehall@hotmail.com

ASHDON
Essex

Hill Farm Holiday Cottages
Rating Applied For
Self Catering
Contact: Mr & Ms Bell
t (01799) 584881

AYLMERTON
Norfolk

Moorland Park ★★★
Self Catering
Contact: Mrs Elaine Field
t (01263) 837508
e moorlandpark@fsmail.net
w tiscover.co.uk

AYLSHAM
Norfolk

Bay Cottage ★★★★
Self Catering
Contact: Mr Stuart Clarke
t (01263) 734574
e jsclarke@colbycorner.fsnet.co.uk
w enchantingcottages.co.uk

Bure Valley Farm Stays ★★★★ *Self Catering*
Contact: Jackie Browne
t (01263) 732177
e burevalleyfarm@btinternet.com
w burevalleyfarmstays.co.uk

Drabblegate River cottage ★★★★ *Self Catering*
Contact: Peter Norton
t (01263) 732126
e bookings@norfolkrivercottage.co.uk
w norfolkrivercottage.co.uk

Old Windmill ★★★★★
Self Catering
Contact: Mr Tim Bower
t (01263) 732118
e timatmill@aol.com
w aylshamwindmill.co.uk

BABRAHAM
Cambridgeshire

Brick Row Cottage ★★★★
Self Catering
Contact: Mr Ian Kime
t (01223) 830323
e info@brickrowcottage.co.uk
w brickrowcottage.co.uk

Granary ★★★ *Self Catering*
Contact: Mrs Gill Kotschy
t (01223) 837783
e gillkotschy@btconnect.com
w granaryvisit.co.uk

BACTON
Norfolk

Middle Cottage (962)
Rating Applied For
Self Catering
Norfolk Country Cottages
t (01603) 871872
e info@norfolkcottages.co.uk
w norfolkcottages.co.uk

Swiss Cottage ★★★★
Self Catering
Contact: Mrs Linda Weinberg
t (04484) 42222
e info@swissonthebeach.com
w swissonthebeach.com

BACTON-ON-SEA
Norfolk

1 The Warren ★★
Self Catering
Contact: Adrian & Rosanna Eckersley
t (020) 8257 5045
e onethewarren@ntlworld.com
w onethewarren.co.uk

BADINGHAM
Suffolk

Nest ★★★ *Self Catering*
Contact: Mrs Susan Long
t (01728) 660360
w tiscover.co.uk

BADWELL ASH
Suffolk

Badwell Ash Holiday Lodges
Rating Applied For
Self Catering
Contact: Jacqueline Thaokeray
t (01359) 258444
e jacquelinethackeray@btinternet.com
w badwellashlodges.co.uk

BALE
Norfolk

Chapel Field Cottage ★★★
Self Catering
Contact: Mrs Judith Everitt
t (01328) 878419
w tiscover.co.uk

BALSHAM
Cambridgeshire

Grannies Bungalow ★★★
Self Catering
Contact: Mrs Anne Kiddy
t (01223) 893010
w tiscover.co.uk

BANHAM
Norfolk

Olde Farm Cottage ★★★
Self Catering
Contact: Mrs Kathleen Girling
t (01953) 860023
e kathygirling@aol.com
w banhamandthebucks.co.uk/oldefarm

BANNINGHAM
Norfolk

Bridge Bungalow ★★★★
Self Catering
Contact: Mrs Lesley Cooke
Norfolk Country Cottages
t (01603) 871872
e info@norfolkcottages.co.uk
w norfolkcottages.co.uk

BARDWELL
Suffolk

Holly House ★★★★
Self Catering
Contact: Mrs Susette Bone
t (01359) 250804
w tiscover.co.uk

BARNBY
Suffolk

The Old Pottery ★★★★
Self Catering
Suffolk Country Cottages
t (01502) 725500

BARNEY
Norfolk

Stables ★★★ *Self Catering*
Contact: Mrs Christine Blackman
t (01328) 878204
w tiscover.co.uk

BARNHAM BROOM
Norfolk

Kingscroft ★★★★
Self Catering
Norfolk Country Cottages
t (01603) 871872
e info@norfolkcottages.co.uk
w norfolkcottages.co.uk

BARTON TURF
Norfolk

The Piggeries ★★★★
Self Catering
Contact: Mrs Debra Watson
Home Farm Barn
t (01603) 712030

BAWDESWELL
Norfolk

Jotts Cottage ★★★★
Self Catering
Contact: Mr Sue Clarke
t (01362) 688444
e clarkes.jasmine@virgin.net
w tiscover.co.uk

BAWDSEY
Suffolk

Bawdsey Manor
★★★-★★★★★ *Self Catering*
Contact: Mr Niels Toettcher
t (01394) 411633
e info@bawdseymanor.co.uk

Rose Cottage ★★★★
Self Catering
Contact: Mrs Veronica de Lotbinere
t (01842) 814215
e vicki@lignacite.co.uk
w waterfrontsuffolk.com

BAYLHAM
Suffolk

Baylham House Farm Annexe ★★★ *Self Catering*
Contact: Mrs Ann Storer
t (01473) 830264
w baylham-house-farm.co.uk

BEACHAMWELL
Norfolk

Carole Wilsons Rectory Hol
★★★ *Self Catering*
Contact: Mrs Carole Wilson
t (01366) 328628
e wilson@rectoryholidays.com
w rectoryholidays.com

BECCLES
Suffolk

Redisham Hall ★★★★
Self Catering
Country Holidays
t 0870 072 3723

BEDFORD
Bedfordshire

The Dovecote ★★★★
Self Catering
Contact: Mrs Rosalind Northern
t (01234) 720293
e info@harroldholidays.co.uk
w harroldholidays.co.uk

BEESTON
Norfolk

Holmdene Farm ★★★
Self Catering
Contact: Mrs Gaye Davidson
t (01328) 701284
e holmdenefarm@farmersweekly.net
w northnorfolk.co.uk/holmdenefarm

BENTLEY
Suffolk

Silver Leys ★★★
Self Catering
Suffolk Country Cottages
t (01502) 725500
e info@suffolkcountrycottages.co.uk
w suffolkcountrycottages.co.uk

BERKHAMSTED
Hertfordshire

Holly Tree and Jacks Cottage ★★★ *Self Catering*
Contact: Mrs Barrington
t (01442) 843464
e rbbarrington@aol.com
w tiscover.co.uk

Walnut Cottage ★★★★
Self Catering
Contact: Mrs Alison Knowles
t (01442) 866541
e aknowles@broadway.nildram.co.uk
w smoothhound.co.uk/hotels/broad.html

BESTHORPE
Norfolk

The Hayloft and The Granary ★★★★ *Self Catering*
Contact: Ms Suzanne Large
Mayfield Accommodation
t (01953) 455589
e mayfieldaccommodation@fsmail.net
w mayfieldbarn.co.uk

BEYTON
Suffolk

Manorflat ★★★★
Self Catering
Contact: Kay & Mark Dewsbury
t (01359) 270960
e manorhouse@beyton.com
w tiscover.co.uk

BILLERICAY
Essex

Pump House Apartment
★★★★★ *Self Catering*
Contact: Mr John Bayliss
Pump House
t (01277) 656579
e johnwbayliss@btinternet.com
w thepumphouseapartment.co.uk

BINHAM
Norfolk

1 Abbey House ★★★
Self Catering
Norfolk Country Cottages
t (01603) 871872
e info@norfolkcottages.co.uk
w norfolkcottages.co.uk

Barn ★★★★ *Self Catering*
Contact: Mrs Lesley Cooke
Norfolk Country Cottages
t (01603) 871872
e info@norfolkcottages.co.uk
w tiscover.co.uk

Bettys Cottage And Bobs Cottage ★★★★ *Self Catering*
Contact: Mrs Fiona Thompson
t (01328) 830639
w tiscover.co.uk

Fairfield Cottage ★★★
Self Catering
Contact: Mrs Sheila Thornton
t (01636) 830395
w tiscover.co.uk

The Hollies ★★★★
Self Catering
Contact: Mrs Beryl Howell
t (01328) 878304

BLAKENEY
Norfolk

Currie's Cottage ★★★
Self Catering
Norfolk Country Cottages
t (01603) 871872
e info@norfolkcottages.co.uk
w norfolkcottages.co.uk

Friary ★★★ *Self Catering*
Contact: Mrs D Cooke
t (01603) 624827
e cookehd@paston.co.uk
w tiscover.co.uk

Quayside Cottages
★★-★★★★ *Self Catering*
Contact: Mrs Veronica Alvarez
t (01462) 768627
e veronicaAlvarez@blakeneycottages.co.uk
w blakeneycottages.co.uk

Roslyn ★★ *Self Catering*
Contact: Mrs Brenda Eke
t (01263) 860111
w tiscover.co.uk

Seagulls ★★★★
Self Catering
Holiday Cottages
t 0870 072 3723
e sales@holidaycottagesgroup.com
w english-country-cottages.co.uk

Wren Cottage ★★★★
Self Catering
Contact: Mr Ian Mashiter
t (01603) 457560
e cleycottage@aol.com
w tiscover.co.uk

BLAXHALL Suffolk

Admiral Cottage ★★★★
Self Catering
Contact: Miss Hannah Mason
t 07967 645814
e hannah.mason@arfs.co.uk
w snapecottages.co.uk

Sheriff's Cottage ★★★
Self Catering
Contact: Mr & Mrs Browne
t (01728) 688993

BRAINTREE Essex

Panfield House ★★★★
Serviced Apartments
Contact: Mrs Ursula Williamson
t (01376) 326345
w panfieldhouse.com

Red Lion Cottages 1 ★★
Self Catering
Contact: Mr Moran McKellar Ratcliffe
t (01376) 584043
e moran.ratcliffe@btconnect.com
w tiscover.co.uk

BRANCASTER Norfolk

11 Anchorage View ★★★
Self Catering
Contact: Mrs Sandra Hohol
Birds Norfolk Holiday Homes
t (01485) 534267
e shohol@birdsnorfolkholidayhomes.co.uk
w norfolkholidayhomes-birds.co.uk

Cheal Cottage ★★★
Self Catering
Contact: Mrs Janet Harrison
Field House
t (01775) 680513

Lindum, Brancaster ★★★
Self Catering
Contact: Mrs Sally Blyth
Corner Cottage
t (01603) 880286
e paul_sally@tiscali.co.uk
w lindum-brancaster.co.uk

Old Stores ★★★
Self Catering
Contact: Mrs Lesley Cooke
Norfolk Country Cottages
t (01603) 871872
e info@norfolkcottages.co.uk
w norfolkcottages.co.uk

Plunketts Cottage ★★★★
Self Catering
Contact: Mr Simon Barclay
Kett Country Cottages
t (01328) 856853
e info@kettcountrycottages.co.uk
w kettcountrycottages.co.uk

Russett Lodge ★★★
Self Catering
Contact: Mrs Sandra Hohol
Birds Norfolk Holiday Homes
t (01485) 534267
e shohol@birdsnorfolkholidayhomes.co.uk
w norfolkholidayhomes-birds.co.uk

Stalls ★★★ *Self Catering*
Contact: Mrs Judith Rippon
t (01485) 210774
e judyrippon@theoldstables123.fslife.co.uk
w norfolk-holiday-cottages.co.uk

Thompson Brancaster Farms ★★★ *Self Catering*
Contact: Mrs Sue Lane
t 07885 269538
e info@tbfholidayhomes.co.uk
w tbfholidayhomes.co.uk

Whiteacres ★★★
Self Catering
Contact: Mr Simon Barclay
Kett Country Cottages
t (01328) 856853
e info@kettcountrycottages.co.uk
w kettcountrycottages.co.uk

BRANCASTER STAITHE Norfolk

21 Dale End ★★★★
Self Catering
Contact: Mrs Debbie Clark
t (01572) 747389
e debbieclark@btopenworld.com
w debbieclarklettings.com

Island Cottage ★
Self Catering
Contact: Mrs Sandra Hohol
Birds Norfolk Holiday Homes
t (01485) 534267
e shohol@birdsnorfolkholidayhomes.co.uk
w norfolkholidayhomes-birds.co.uk

Vista And Carpenters Cottage ★★★ *Self Catering*
Contact: Mrs Gloria Smith
Dale View
t (01485) 210497

Westbourne ★★★
Self Catering
Contact: Mrs Sandra Hohol
Birds Norfolk Holiday Homes
t (01485) 534267
e shohol@birdsnorfolkholidayhomes.co.uk
w norfolkholidayhomes-birds.co.uk

BRANDON Suffolk

Deacons Cottage ★★
Self Catering
Contact: Mrs BD Deacon
t (01842) 828023
w tiscover.co.uk

BRANTHAM Suffolk

Hall Cottage ★★★★
Self Catering
Contact: Ms Caroline Williams
t (01473) 327090
e hwilliams@branmann.freeserve.co.uk

BRAUGHING Hertfordshire

Edwinstree Chapel ★★★★
Self Catering
Contact: Mrs Pamela Bradley
t (01763) 289509
e edwinstree@tesco.net
w Edwinstree.com

BRININGHAM Norfolk

Old White Horse Cottage ★★★ *Self Catering*
Contact: Mr Simon Barclay
Kett Country Cottages
t (01328) 856853
e info@kettcountrycottages.co.uk
w kettcountrycottages.co.uk

BRISLEY Norfolk

Church Farm Cottage And Pond Farm Studio ★★★–★★★★ *Self Catering*
Contact: Mrs G.V Howes
t (01362) 668332
w tiscover.co.uk

Mill Farm Barn ★★★★
Self Catering
Norfolk Country Cottages
t (01603) 871872
e info@norfolkcottages.co.uk
w norfolkcottages.co.uk

BRISTON Norfolk

The Firs ★★★★ *Self Catering*
Contact: Mr Paul Horti
t (01277) 823204
e paulhorti@hotmail.com
w tiscover.co.uk

Little Owl ★★★ *Self Catering*
Contact: Ms Wendy Wright
Owl Cottage
t (01263) 861788

Myrtle Tree Cottage
Rating Applied For
Self Catering
Contact: Mrs Pilling
t (01263) 861540
e geoffpatoaklands@aol.com

BRUISYARD Suffolk

Bruisyard Hall ★★★★
Self Catering
Contact: Mr Robert Rous
Dennington Hall Farms
t (01728) 663205
e dennington@farmline.com
w bruisyardhall.co.uk

BURNHAM MARKET Norfolk

Barley Cottage ★★★★
Self Catering
Contact: Mr Andrew & Susan Watley
t (01277) 218116
e a.s.watley@btinternet.com
w barleycottageburnhammarket.co.uk

Chapel Cottage ★★★
Self Catering
Contact: Mrs Gail Armstrong
Norfolk Country Cottages
t (01603) 871872
e info@norfolkcottages.co.uk

Croftwood ★★★★
Self Catering
Norfolk Country Cottages
t (01603) 871872
e info@norfolkcottages.co.uk
w norfolkcottages.co.uk

Easterly ★★★ *Self Catering*
Contact: Mrs Lesley Cooke
Norfolk Country Cottages Ref. 675
t (01603) 871872
e info@norfolkcottages.co.uk
w norfolkcottages.co.uk/burnham_market_675.htm

Fuchsia Cottage ★★★
Self Catering
Contact: Mr Tinsley
t (01485) 518896
e tinsley.co@virgin.net
w tiscover.co.uk

Granary Cottage ★★★★
Self Catering
Contact: Ms Julie Levitt
t (01832) 735150
e levitt.smarter@virgin.net
w granarycottageburnhammarket.com

Rose Cottage ★★★
Self Catering
Contact: Mrs Anne Manning
t (01328) 730775
w tiscover.co.uk

Shielings and Ebenezer Cottage ★★★–★★★★
Self Catering
Contact: Mrs Lesley Cooke
Norfolk Country Cottages
t (01603) 871872
e info@norfolkcottages.co.uk
w norfolkcottages.co.uk

Southwinds ★★★
Self Catering
Norfolk Country Cottages
t (01603) 871872
e info@norfolkcottages.co.uk
w norfolkcottages.co.uk

Stable Cottage ★★★★
Self Catering
Contact: Mrs Anne Cringle
t (01328) 738456
e pmcringle@aol.com
w cringle.org

BURNHAM OVERY STAITHE Norfolk

The Limpet ★★★
Self Catering
Norfolk Country Cottages
t (01603) 871872
e info@norfolkcottages.co.uk
w norfolkcottages.co.uk

BURNHAM THORPE Norfolk

Cherry Tree Bungalow ★★
Self Catering
Contact: Mrs G Armstrong
Norfolk Country Cottages
t (01603) 871872
e info@norfolkcottages.co.uk

Highfield ★★★ *Self Catering*
Contact: Valerie Southerland
t (01328) 738416
e barrysoutherland@aol.com
w whitehallfarm-accommodation.com

BURY ST EDMUNDS
Suffolk

23 Church Walks ★★★
Self Catering
Suffolk Country Cottages
t (01502) 725500
e info@suffolkcountrycottage.co.uk
w suffolkcountrycottages.co.uk

Bridewell Lane 15 ★★★★
Self Catering
Contact: Mr Wesley Rawdon Cushing
t (01284) 388117
e hawkeye52uk@yahoo.co.uk
w 15-bridewell-lane.co.uk

Brook Villa ★★★
Self Catering
Contact: Mr David Manning
t (01284) 764387
e suffolksaddlery@supanet.com
w tiscover.co.uk

Court And The Granary Suites ★★★-★★★★
Self Catering
Contact: Mrs Roberta Truin
The Court & The Granary Suites
t (01284) 830385
e info@brighthousefarm.fsnet.co.uk
w brighthousefarm.fsnet.co.uk

Garden Corner ★★★★
Self Catering
Contact: Mr John Stemp
t (01284) 702848
w tiscover.co.uk

Granary And The Forge
★★★★ *Self Catering*
Francis Farm
t (01284) 789241
e francisfarmcottages@farmline.com
w francisfarmcottages.co.uk

Kitchen Flat ★★★
Self Catering
Contact: Mrs Eileen Storey
t (01284) 755744
e eileen@queequeg.demon.co.uk
w tiscover.co.uk

Oliver's Retreat ★★★
Self Catering
Contact: Mrs C Titcombe
95 Oliver Road
t (01284) 766432
w tiscover.co.uk

Pump Lane House ★★★
Self Catering
Contact: Mrs Lucy Taylor
t (01284) 755248
w tiscover.co.uk

BUTLEY
Suffolk

Butley Mills
Rating Applied For
Self Catering
Contact: Mr Glynn Evans
t (01394) 450401
e glynevans@ip1231p.fsnet.co.uk

BUXTON
Norfolk

Bramley Cottage ★★★★
Self Catering
Contact: Mrs Alison Tuffrey
t (01603) 279169
e tuffrey@acsmail.net

Wye House
Rating Applied For
Self Catering
Devonshire Road
t 07966 366 637
e pigottlawestates@btconnect.com

BYLAUGH
Norfolk

Meadowview ★★★
Self Catering
Contact: Mrs Jenny Lake
t (01362) 688584
e lakeparkfm@aol.com
w tiscover.co.uk

CAISTER-ON-SEA
Norfolk

Sand Dune Cottages ★★
Self Catering
Contact: Mr Miles Rainer
Rear of 57a Tan Lane
t (01493) 720352
e sand.dune.cottages@amserve.net
w netsalesuk.co.uk/gt-yarmouth/cottages/sanddune.htm

CALDECOTE
Cambridgeshire

Highfield House Annex
★★★ *Self Catering*
Contact: Mr Neville Hawkins
t (01954) 210841
e neville@highfieldhouse.org

CALIFORNIA
Norfolk

Bella Vista ★★★★
Self Catering
Contact: Mrs S J Sampson
Beachside Holidays
t (01493) 730279
e holidays@theseaside.org
w cottages-in-norfolk.co.uk

CAMBRIDGE
Cambridgeshire

39 Castle Street ★★★
Self Catering
Contact: Diana & Tony Loizou
t (01223) 323231
e tony@deadgoodsoup.org
w tiscover.co.uk

7 and 14 Brooklands Court
★★★★ *Self Catering*
Contact: Ms Conny Caruana
t (01954) 231572
e bookings@clicapartments.co.uk
w clicapartments.co.uk

Adam and Eve Court ★★★
Self Catering
Contact: Mrs Wendy Whistler
t (01954) 231850
e selectivestudios@ntlworld.com
w selectivestudios.com

Alexandra Apartments
★★★★★ *Self Catering*
Contact: Nick & Julie Wright
alexandra apartments
t (01223) 500776
e info@alexandraapartments.co.uk
w alexandraapartments.co.uk

Annexe ★★★ *Self Catering*
Contact: Mr Francis Durning
t (01223) 415668
e annexe_cb1@hotmail.com
w tiscover.co.uk

Canonbury House & 53 Richmond Road ★★★★
Self Catering
Contact: Mr Kiddy
Radwinter Park
t (01799) 599272
e ajkiddy@cambridge-vacation-homes.com

Clarence House ★★★★
Self Catering
Contact: Mr Oliver Digney
t (01223) 841294
e sdigney@clarencehouse.fsnet.co.uk
w clarencehouse.org.uk

First Floor Apartment
★★★★ *Self Catering*
Contact: Mr Desmond Hirsch
t (01223) 360200
e cambridge.accommodation@virgin.net

Glebe Cottage ★★★★
Self Catering
Contact: Mrs Fiona Key
t (01954) 212895
e info@camcottage.co.uk
w camcottage.co.uk

Hanover Court 28 ★★
Self Catering
Contact: Mr Richard Young
t (01223) 529653
e riyo50@yahoo.com
w location-cambridge.com

Home From Home Apartments ★★★★
Self Catering
Contact: Mrs Fasano
Home From Home
t (01223) 323555
e homefromhome2@btconnect.com
w accommodationincambridge.com

J C Accommodation ★★★★
Self Catering
Contact: Mr Jose Carro
t (01799) 540987
w tiscover.co.uk

Midsummer Apartments
★★★★ *Self Catering*
Contact: Mrs Maria Fasano
t +39 08237 87383
e midsummerapartments@liberoit.it
w tiscover.co.uk

Prospero Homes at 41 Mowbray Road ★★★ *Self Catering & Serviced Apartments*
Contact: Mrs Helen Collins
Prospero Homes
t (01223) 511043
e info@prosperohomes.co.uk
w prosperohomes.co.uk

School House ★★★★
Self Catering
Contact: Mr Terry & Nicola Mann
School House
t (01223) 440077
e schoolhse1@btinternet.com
w schoolhouse-uk.com

Victoria Road 79A ★★★★
Self Catering
Contact: Mrs Anita Mills
t (01353) 740022
e trojan.david@virgin.net
w endellion.co.uk

Warkworth Villa ★★★
Self Catering
Contact: Mrs Wendy Whistler
t (01954) 231850
e selectivestudios@ntlworld.com
w selectivestudios.com

Your Space Apartments
★★★★ *Self Catering*
Contact: Ms Suzanne Emerson
t (01223) 315050
e bookings@yourspaceapartments.com
w yourspaceapartments.com

CASTLE ACRE
Norfolk

Friars Croft ★★★
Self Catering
Contact: Mrs McGrath
t (01362) 820408
w tiscover.co.uk

Peddars Cottage ★★★
Self Catering
Contact: Mrs Angela Swindell
t (01534) 727480
e jsyedu71@localdial.com
w tiscover.co.uk

Sandles Court 1 ★★
Self Catering
Contact: Mrs Jane Wood
t (01760) 722455
w tiscover.co.uk

CASTLE HEDINGHAM
Essex

Rosemary Farm ★★★★
Self Catering
Contact: Mr Garry Ian Henderson
t (01787) 461653

CHEDBURGH
Suffolk

Rede Hall Farm Park ★★★★
Self Catering & Serviced Apartments
Contact: Mrs Christine Oakley
t (01284) 850695
e oakley@soils.fsnet.co.uk
w redehallfarmpark.co.uk

CHEDGRAVE
Norfolk

Barn Owl Holidays ★★★
Self Catering
Contact: Mrs Rosemary Beattie
t (01508) 528786
e barnowls@bt.clara.co.uk
w barnowlholidays.co.uk

Willow Barn ★★★★
Self Catering
Norfolk Country Cottages
t (01603) 871872
e info@norfolkcottages.co.uk
w norfolkcottages.co.uk

CHELMONDISTON
Suffolk

Charlies Cottage ★★★★
Self Catering
Contact: Mr Eddie Coyle
t (01473) 310851
e eddie@ecoyle.plus.com
w charliescottage.co.uk

CHELMSFORD
Essex

Bury Barn Cottage ★★★★
Self Catering
Contact: Mrs V. Morris
t (01245) 237384
e bookings@burybarncottage.co.uk
w burybarncottage.co.uk

CHELSWORTH
Suffolk

Old Farm Cottage ★★★★
Self Catering
Contact: Irene Noakes
t (01789) 372143
e chelsworthofc@aol.com
w oldfarmcottage.co.uk

CLACTON-ON-SEA
Essex

Pond Cottage ★★★★
Self Catering
Contact: Mrs Brenda Lord
t (01255) 820458
e brenda_lord@farming.co.uk
w earlshallfarm.info

CLAVERING
Essex

Brocking Farm Cottage
Rating Applied For
Self Catering
Contact: T R & J E Gingell
t (01279) 777349
e t.gingell@btopenworld.com

CLEY NEXT THE SEA
Norfolk

Archway Cottage ★★★
Self Catering
Contact: Mrs Vickey Jackson
t (01992) 511303 & (01992) 503196

Dolphin Cottage ★★★★
Self Catering
Contact: Mr & Mrs Ian Mashiter
t (01603) 457560
e cleycottage@aol.com

Little Cottage ★★★
Self Catering
Contact: Mrs Lesley Cooke
Norfolk Country Cottages
t (01603) 871872
e info@norfolkcottages.co.uk
w norfolkcottages.co.uk

Skylarks ★★★★
Self Catering
Contact: Mrs Nicola Arrowsmith-Brown
t (01603) 270457
e arrows270@aol.com
w cottageguide.co.uk/skylarks

CLIPPESBY
Norfolk

Clippesby Hall ★★★★
Self Catering
Contact: Jean, John or Sue Lindsay
t (01493) 367800
e holidays@clippesby.com
w clippesby.com

COLCHESTER
Essex

Castle Road Cottages
★★★★-★★★★★
Self Catering
Contact: Mrs Patsie Ford
t (01206) 262210
w castleroadcottages.com

50 Rosebery Avenue ★★★
Self Catering
Contact: Mrs Katharine Webb
t (01206) 866888
e rosebery.avenue@btinternet.com

Tea House ★★★★
Self Catering
Contact: Mr Nicholas Charrington
t (01206) 330784
e info@layermarneytower.co.uk
w layermarneytower.co.uk

COLKIRK
Norfolk

Saddlery And Hillside Cottage ★★★ *Self Catering*
Contact: Mrs Catherine Joice
t (01328) 862261
e catherine.joice@btinternet.com
w colkirkcottages.co.uk

COLMWORTH
Bedfordshire

Colmworth Golf Course Holiday Cottages ★★★
Self Catering
Contact: Mrs Julie Vesely
t (01234) 378181
e julie@colmworthgc.co.uk
w colmworthgolfclub.co.uk

COLTISHALL
Norfolk

Broadgates ★★★
Self Catering
Contact: Mrs Dack
t (01603) 737598
e 2.richard@4broads.fsnet.co.uk
w broadgates-coltishall.com

White Gable Cottage, Coltishall ★★★ *Self Catering*
Contact: Terry Holt
t (01603) 736333
e trryhlt@aol.com
w about-norfolk.com/colt/accommodation.htm

COPDOCK
Suffolk

Briars And Mansard Cottage
★★★★ *Self Catering*
Contact: Mrs Steward
t (01473) 730494
e rosanna1@suffolkholidays.com
w suffolkholidays.com

COTTON
Suffolk

Coda Cottages ★★★★
Self Catering
Contact: Mrs Kate Sida-Nicholls
t (01449) 780076
e codacottages@dandycorner.co.uk
w codacottages.co.uk

CRANMER
Norfolk

Cranmer Country Cottages
★★★★ *Self Catering*
Contact: Mrs Lynne Johnson
t (01328) 823135
e bookings@cranmercountrycottages.co.uk
w cranmercountrycottages.co.uk

CRATFIELD
Suffolk

Holly Tree Farm Barns
★★★★ *Self Catering*
Contact: Ms Rachel Boddy
Holly Tree Farm
t (01986) 798062
e hollytreebarns@lycos.co.uk
w hollytreebarns.co.uk

School Farm Cottages
★★★★ *Self Catering*
Contact: Mrs Claire Sillett
School Farm
t (01986) 798844
e schoolfarmcotts@aol.com
w schoolfarmcottages.com

Whippletree Cottage
★★★★ *Self Catering*
Suffolk Holidays Ltd.
t (01502) 723571
e sales@holidaysinsuffolk.co.uk

CROMER
Norfolk

119 Kings Chalet Park ★★
Self Catering
Contact: Tania Hickman
Lambert Watts
t (01263) 513139
e info@lambertwatts.com
w tiscover.co.uk

15 Clifton Park ★★★★
Self Catering
Norfolk Country Cottages
t (01603) 871872
e info@norfolkcottages.co.uk
w norfolkcottages.co.uk

21 Kings Chalet Park ★★
Self Catering
t (01263) 511028
e property@lambertwatts.co.uk

Albion House ★★★
Self Catering
Contact: Mrs Angela Forsyth
Thornfield Acre
t (01829) 733467
e forsythleisure@aol.com
w albion-house.com

Allseasons ★★★
Self Catering
Contact: Mrs Sue Teagle
t (01263) 577205
e sue@allseasons-cromer-co.uk
w tiscover.co.uk

Avenue Holiday Flats ★★★
Self Catering
Contact: Mr John Bradley
t (01263) 513611
w tiscover.co.uk

Beverley House Holiday Apa
★-★★★ *Self Catering*
Contact: Mr Peter & Gill Day
Beverley House Holiday Apartments
t (01263) 512787
e beverleyhouse@fsmail.net
w tiscover.co.uk

Broadgates Cottages
★★★★ *Self Catering*
Contact: Mrs Julie Bryant
Forest Park Caravan Site
t (01263) 513290
e forestpark@netcom.co.uk
w tiscover.co.uk

Chalet No 130 ★★
Self Catering
Contact: Miss Tania Hickman
Lambert Watts Self Catering
t (01263) 513139
e property@lambertwatts.com
w tiscover.co.uk

Chalets 28 151 152 ★★
Self Catering
Contact: Miss Tania Hickman
Lambert Watts Self Catering
t (01263) 513139
e property@lambertwatts.com
w tiscover.co.uk

Cliff Hollow ★★ *Self Catering*
Contact: Miss L Willins
t (01263) 512447

Cliffside at Kings Chalet Park ★★ *Self Catering*
Contact: Mrs S Jones
t (01692) 536281
e sloley@farmhotel.u-net.com
w norfolkbroads.co.uk/sloleyfarm

Coach House Cottage
★★★★ *Self Catering*
Contact: Mrs Dorothy Casburn
t (01485) 520569
e ccasburn@britishsugar.co.uk
w tiscover.co.uk

Cromer Lighthouse ★★★★
Self Catering
t (01386) 701177
e info@ruralretreats.co.uk
w ruralretreats.co.uk

Drift Barn Cottage ★★★
Self Catering
Contact: Mr Payne
t (01263) 513765
w tiscover.co.uk

Flat 2 Bernard House ★★★
Self Catering
Contact: Miss Tania Hickman
Lambert Watts Self Catering
t (01263) 513139
e info@lambertwatts.com
w tiscover.co.uk

Foxglade Lodge ★★★
Self Catering
Contact: Miss Tania Hickman
t (01263) 511028
e info@lamberwatts.com
w tiscover.co.uk

Gangway 2 ★★ *Self Catering*
Contact: Mrs Price
Misterton
t (01992) 572672
w tiscover.co.uk

Greenwood Holiday Cottage
★★★ *Self Catering*
Contact: Mrs Hemming
t (01263) 514139
w tiscover.co.uk

The Grove ★★★
Self Catering
Contact: Mr Paul Calfon
t (01263) 512412
e thegrovecromer@btopenworld.com
w thegrovecromer.co.uk

King's Chalet Park ★★
Self Catering
Contact: Mrs Scotlock
t (01371) 870482

Kings Chalet Park ★★
Self Catering
Contact: Mrs Bateman
t (01263) 511308
w tiscover.co.uk

Kings Chalet Park 123 ★★
Self Catering
Contact: Ms Lotta Fox
Lambert Watts Self Catering
t (01263) 513139
e property@lambertwatts.com
w tiscover.co.uk

Maynard House ★★★
Self Catering
Contact: Mr Adam Cade
Brewery House
t (01780) 720521
e adam@studentforce.org.uk
w tiscover.co.uk

Old Forge ★★ *Self Catering*
Contact: Miss Tania Hickman
Lambert Watts Self Catering Holidays
t (01263) 513139
e info@lambertwatts.com
w tiscover.co.uk

Poppyland Holiday Cottages
★★★★ *Self Catering*
Contact: Mr & Mrs Riches
21 Regent Street
t (01263) 577473
e poppyland@totalise.co.uk

Two The Crescent (508)
Rating Applied For
Self Catering
Norfolk Country Cottages
t (01603) 871872
e info@norfolkcottages.co.uk
w norfolkcottages.co.uk

CROXTON, ST NEOTS
Cambridgeshire

Croxton Old Rectory ★★
Self Catering
Contact: Mrs Margaret Williams
t (01480) 880344
w tiscover.co.uk

CULFORD
Suffolk

Culford Farm Cottages
★★★★-★★★★★
Self Catering
Contact: Mrs Rosemary Flack
t (01284) 728334
e cottages@hoseasons.co.uk
w tiscover.co.uk

Hazelnut Cottage ★★★★
Self Catering
Contact: Mr & Mrs Roy Nieves-y-Gordo
Dorch House
t (01284) 728929

DALLINGHOO
Suffolk

Robins Nest and The Carpenter's Shop ★★★★
Self Catering
Contact: Mr Robert Blake
t (01394) 382565 & 07907 773545
e robert@blake4110.fsbusiness.co.uk
w tiscover.co.uk

DARMSDEN
Suffolk

Burnt House Cottage ★★
Self Catering
Contact: Mr Michael Keen
t (020) 7787 6870
e michael@stillinlondon.co.uk
w tiscover.co.uk

DARSHAM
Suffolk

Granary and The Mallards
★★★★ *Self Catering*
Contact: Mrs S Bloomfield
t (01728) 668459
e suebloomfield@btconnect.com
w holidaysatprioryfarm.co.uk

DEBDEN GREEN
Essex

The Old Bakehouse ★★★★
Self Catering
Contact: Mrs Diane Potter
t (01371) 830687
e di@theoldbakehousebb.com
w theoldbakehousebb.com

DENGIE
Essex

East Ware Farm ★★★★
Self Catering
Contact: Mr Ponder
t (01621) 786846
e lyn.ponder@btinternet.com
w eastwarefarm.co.uk

DENNINGTON
Suffolk

Stable Cottage ★★★
Self Catering
Contact: Derek & Jill Woodward
t (01728) 638278
e jillsalisbury@postmaster.co.uk
w tiscover.co.uk

DENVER
Norfolk

West Hall Farm Holidays and Lakeside Fisheries ★★★
Self Catering
Contact: Mrs Riches
t (01366) 383291
e richesflorido@aol.com
w tiscover.co.uk

DEREHAM
Norfolk

Bylaugh Hall ★★★★
Self Catering
t (01362) 688121
e info@bylaugh.com
w bylaugh.com

Maple Barns ★★★★
Self Catering
Contact: Miss Hannah Jarvis
t (01362) 637260
w maple-barns.co.uk

DERSINGHAM
Norfolk

Avocet Cottage (959)
Rating Applied For
Self Catering
Norfolk Country Cottages
t (01603) 871872
e info@norfolkcottages.co.uk
w norfolkcottages.co.uk

Oaks Cottage ★★★★
Self Catering
Contact: Mr Ben Mullarkey
t (01485) 540761
e jb.mullarkey@eidosnet.co.uk
w oakscottage.co.uk

Old Hall Cottage (969)
Rating Applied For
Self Catering
Carlton House
t (01603) 871872
e info@norfolkcottages.co.uk
w norfolkcottages.co.uk

DILHAM
Norfolk

Dairy Farm Cottages ★★★★
Self Catering
Contact: Mr James Paterson
Rumford Ltd
t (01692) 536883
e japdilman@gmail.com
w dairyfarmcottages.co.uk

DISS
Norfolk

Honey Bee Cottage ★★★
Self Catering
Contact: Mrs Rachel Davy
t (01379) 741449
e chrisjdavy@freenetname.co.uk
w honeybeecott.co.uk

Norfolk Cottages Malthouse
★★★★ *Self Catering*
Contact: Ms Mary Mannion
Norfolk Cottages Booking Office
t (01379) 651177
e bookings@norfolkcottages.net
w norfolkcottages.net

Old Mill Farm ★★★
Self Catering
Contact: Mrs Pauline Ward
t (01953) 681350
e lward@mmkarton.fsnet.co.uk
w oldmillfarm.co.uk

Walcot Green Farm Cottage
★★★★ *Self Catering*
Contact: Mrs Nannette Catchpole
t (01379) 652806
e walcotgreenfarm@fsmail.net
w walcotgreenfarm.co.uk

DOCKING
Norfolk

The Bungalow ★★★
Self Catering
Norfolk Country Cottages
t (01603) 871872
e info@norfolkcottages.co.uk
w norfolkcottages.co.uk

The Gallery ★★★
Self Catering
Contact: Mr Simon Barclay
Kett Country Cottages
t (01328) 856853
e info@kettcountrycottages.co.uk
w kettcountrycottages.co.uk

Honeysuckle Cottage
★★★★ *Self Catering*
Contact: Miss Amanda Cox
t (01932) 344427

Norfolk House and Courtyard Cottage
★★★★★ *Self Catering*
Contact: Tim & Liz Witley
t (01485) 525341
w escapetonorfolk.com

Woodbine Cottage ★★★★
Self Catering
Contact: Mrs Karen Kennedy-Hill
t (01485) 600850
e kennedyhill@tesco.net
w cottageguide.co.uk/woodbinecottage

DUDDENHOE END
Essex

Cosh Cottage, Duddenhoe End ★★★★ *Self Catering*
Contact: Mrs Susan Perks
t (01763) 838880
e susan.perks@virgin.net

Farm Cottages – Upper Pond Street
Rating Applied For
Self Catering
Contact: Mr Adams ESQ
t (01763) 838590
e angelsrcool4@hotmail.com
w pondstproperties.co.uk

DUNMOW
Essex

Bury Farm Cottages ★★★★
Self Catering
Contact: Mrs Sarah Clarke
t (01371) 872213
e sandjclarke@buryfarmcottages.co.uk
w buryfarmcottages.co.uk

DUNWICH
Suffolk

Apple Tree and Walnut Tree ★★★ *Self Catering*
Contact: Mrs Rebecca Finlay
Acanthus Property Letting Services Ltd
t (01502) 724033
e websales@southwold-holidays.co.uk
w southwold-holidays.co.uk

Lodge Cottage ★★★
Self Catering
Contact: Mrs Maureen Nielson
t (01728) 648388
e drbcargill@farming.co.uk
w tiscover.co.uk

The Priory ★★★★
Self Catering
Contact: Ms Rebecca Finlay
Acanthus Property Letting Services Ltd
t (01502) 724033
e websales@southwold-holidays.co.uk

Tinkers Cottage ★★★
Self Catering
Suffolk Secrets
t (01379) 651297
e holidays@suffolk-secrets.co.uk
w suffolk-secrets.co.uk

Tower Bungalow ★★★★
Self Catering
Contact: Mrs Eleanor Barnes
t (01787) 269916
w tiscover.co.uk

EARSHAM
Norfolk

Dukes Cottage ★★★
Self Catering
Contact: Mrs Lesley Cooke
Norfolk Country Cottages
t (01603) 871872
e info@norfolkcottages.co.uk
w norfolkcottages.co.uk

EAST BECKHAM
Norfolk

Barn House Cottage ★★★★
Self Catering
Norfolk Country Cottages
t (01603) 871872
e info@norfolkcottages.co.uk
w norfolkcottages.co.uk

EAST BERGHOLT
Suffolk

Flatford Cottage ★★★
Self Catering
Contact: Mr Paul & Debbie Goddard
t (01206) 298985
w flatfordcottage.freeserves.com

EAST DEREHAM
Norfolk

Clinton Cottage And Clinton House ★★★★ *Self Catering*
Contact: Mrs Margaret Searle
Clinton Holidays
t (01362) 692079
e clintonholidays@tesco.net
w norfolkcountrycottage.co.uk

EAST HARLING
Norfolk

Berwick Cottage ★★★
Self Catering
Contact: Mrs Miriam Toosey
t (01787) 372343
e info@thelinberwicktrust.org.uk
w thelinberwicktrust.org.uk

Dolphin Lodge ★★★★
Self Catering
Contact: Mrs Ellen Jolly
t (01953) 717126
e jolly@roudhamfarm.co.uk
w roudhamfarm.co.uk

Dove Cottage
Rating Applied For
Self Catering
Norfolk Country Cottages
t (01603) 871872
e info@norfolkcottages.co.uk
w norfolkcottages.co.uk

EAST RUDHAM
Norfolk

17 & 18 The Green ★★★★
Self Catering
Norfolk Country Cottages
t (01603) 871872
e info@norfolkcottages.co.uk
w norfolkcottages.co.uk

EAST RUNTON
Norfolk

Mallards Rest ★★★
Self Catering
Contact: Mrs Nicola Thompson
t (01263) 512496
w tiscover.co.uk

Poplars Caravan And Chalet ★★★ *Self Catering*
Contact: Mr K Parfitt
Poplars Caravan and Chalet Park
t (01263) 512892
w tiscover.co.uk

Woodhill House ★★★
Self Catering
Contact: Miss Tania Hickman
Lambert Watts Self Catering
t (01263) 511028
e property@lambertwatts.com
w tiscover.co.uk

EAST RUSTON
Norfolk

The Old Forge, East Ruston ★★★★ *Self Catering*
Norfolk Country Cottages
t (01603) 871872
e info@norfolkcottages.co.uk

EASTBRIDGE
Suffolk

Holly Cottage ★★★★
Self Catering
Contact: Mr Richard Pither
Suffolk Secrets
t (01379) 651297
e holidays@suffolk-secrets.co.uk
w suffolk-secrets.co.uk

ECCLES-ON-SEA
Norfolk

Shangri-La
Rating Applied For
Self Catering
Contact: Diane Hyde-Clarke
t (01692) 409011
e dianehydeclarke@keme.co.uk

EDWARDSTONE
Suffolk

Sherbourne Farm Lodge Cottages ★★★★
Self Catering
Contact: Mrs Anne Suckling
Sherbourne House Farm
t (01787) 210885
e enquiries@sherbournelodgecottages.co.uk
w sherbournelodgecottages.co.uk

The White Horse Inn ★★★
Self Catering
Contact: Mr Andy Cox
The White Horse Edwardstone LLP
t (01787) 211211
e john.norton@nortonorganic.co.uk
w tiscover.co.uk

ELMSTEAD MARKET
Essex

Birds Farm ★★★-★★★★
Self Catering
Contact: Mrs Joanna Burke
t (01206) 823838
e birdsfarm@btinternet.com
w tiscover.co.uk

ELMSWELL
Suffolk

The Apple Store ★★★★
Self Catering
Contact: Mrs Clare Norgate
The Apple Store @ The Willow House
t (01359) 240333
e clare.norgate@btinternet.com
w tiscover.co.uk

Hill Farm ★★★★
Self Catering
Contact: Mrs Amanda Roberts
t (01359) 258544
e roberts.ar@tiscali.co.uk
w tiscover.co.uk

Oak Farm ★★★★★
Self Catering
Contact: Mr Dyball
t (01359) 240263
w tiscover.co.uk

ELY
Cambridgeshire

1 Brooke Grove
Rating Applied For
Self Catering
Streets Ahead Self Catering
t (0141) 632 6609
e info@streetsaheadselfcatering.com
w streetsahead.uk.com/ely

47a Waterside ★★★
Self Catering
Contact: Mrs Florence Nolan
t (01353) 664377

7 Lisle Lane ★★★
Self Catering
Contact: Judy Jones & Ken Davis
t (01353) 615406 & (01353) 675249
e fortyfarmhouse@aol.com

Cathedral House Coach Hous ★★★★ *Self Catering*
Contact: Mrs Jenny Farndale
t (01353) 662124
e farndale@cathedralhouse.co.uk
w tiscover.co.uk

The Medway
Rating Applied For
Self Catering
StreetsAhead Ltd
t 0800 085 7763
e info@streetsaheadselfcatering.com
w streetsaheadselfcatering.com

The Old Granary ★★★★★
Self Catering
Contact: Mrs Hilary Nix
t (01353) 778369
e info@hillhousefarm-ely.co.uk
w hillhousefarm-ely.co.uk

EPPING
Essex

Mandalay
Rating Applied For
Self Catering
Contact: Ms Brenda Foster
Kingsway Cottage
t (01992) 571828
e kingsway@tesco.net
w ukholidaycottages.biz

ERISWELL
Suffolk

Church Cottage ★★★★★
Self Catering
Contact: Ms Yolande Goode
Elveden Farms Ltd
t (01842) 890223
e estate.office@elveden.com
w elveden.com

Cranhouse ★★★★★
Self Catering
Contact: Mrs Yolande Goode
Elveden Farms Ltd
t (01842) 890223
e estate.office@elveden.com
w elveden.com

ERPINGHAM
Norfolk

Grange Farm, Erpingham ★★★ *Self Catering*
Contact: Mrs Jane Bell
Grange Farm Holidays
t (01263) 761241
e jane.bell5@btopenworld.com
w grangefarmholidays.co.uk

EYE
Suffolk

Athelington Hall ★★★★
Self Catering
Contact: Mr Peter Havers
t (01728) 628233
e peter@logcabinholidays.co.uk
w logcabinholidays.co.uk

Manor House Cottages ★★★-★★★★ *Self Catering*
Contact: Mrs Yvonne Mason
t (01379) 788049
e holiday@manorhousecottages.co.uk

Orchard Cottage ★★★
Self Catering
Contact: Mrs Caroline Coles
t (01379) 678656
e tonyatthornham@btinternet.com

FAKENHAM
Norfolk

Idyllic Cottages at Vere Lodge ★★★-★★★★
Self Catering
Contact: Mrs Jane Bowlby
Holiday Complex
t (01328) 838261
e major@verelodge.co.uk
w idylliccottages.co.uk

The Laurels ★★★
Self Catering
t (01603) 871872
w norfolkcottages.co.uk

Old Ale House Cottages ★★★ *Self Catering*
Contact: Miss Angie Hastings
t (01553) 771401
w tiscover.co.uk

Paddocks ★★★★
Self Catering
Contact: Mr John Strahan
The Paddocks The Old Brick Kilns
t (01328) 878305
w paddocks-cottages.co.uk

Pollywiggle Cottage, West Raynham ★★★★
Self Catering
Contact: Mrs Marilyn Farnham-Smith
t (01603) 471990
e marilyn@pollywigglecottage.co.uk
w pollywigglecottage.co.uk

FELBRIGG
Norfolk

Boundary Farm Cottage ★★★ *Self Catering*
Contact: Mrs Wendy Congreve
t (01406) 363618
w tiscover.co.uk

FELIXSTOWE
Suffolk

Fairlight Detached Bungalow ★★★ *Self Catering*
Contact: Mrs Daphne Knights
t (01394) 277730
w tiscover.co.uk

Flat 2 ★★★ *Self Catering*
Contact: Mrs Gwen Lynch
t (01473) 328729
w tiscover.co.uk

Honeypot Cottage ★★★
Self Catering
Contact: Mrs Theresa Adams
t (01394) 448564
e adams99@btinternet.com
w tiscover.co.uk

Kimberley Holiday Flats ★★
Self Catering
Contact: Mrs Valerie Reed
t (01394) 672157
w tiscover.co.uk

FIELD DALLING
Norfolk

Annexe ★★★ *Self Catering*
Contact: Mrs Betty Ringer
t (01328) 830206
w tiscover.co.uk

Eastcote Cottage ★★★★
Self Catering
Contact: Ms Sally Grove
Eastcote Farm
t (01328) 830359
e sally@eastcotecottage.co.uk
w eastcotecottage.co.uk

The Little Barn ★★★★
Self Catering
Norfolk Country Cottages
t (01603) 871872
e info@norfolkcottages.co.uk
w norfolkcottages.co.uk

Oak Barn ★★★★
Self Catering
Contact: Mrs Angela Harcourt
t (01328) 830655
e harcog@farming.co.uk
w tiscover.co.uk

FILBY
Norfolk

1 Well Cottages ★★★
Self Catering
Norfolk Country Cottages
t (01603) 871872
e info@norfolkcottages.co.uk
w norfolkcottages.co.uk

FINNINGHAM
Suffolk

Riverwood Cottage ★★★
Self Catering
Suffolk & Norfolk Country Cottages
t (01603) 871872
e info@suffolkcountrycottages.co.uk

FORNHAM ALL SAINTS
Suffolk

Fornham Hall Cottage ★★★★ *Self Catering*
Contact: Mrs Helene Sjolin
t (01284) 703424
e cottage@sjolin.demon.co.uk
w tiscover.co.uk

FOXLEY
Norfolk

Moor Farm Stable Cottages ★★-★★★★ *Self Catering*
Contact: Mr Paul Davis
t (01362) 688523
e mail@moorfarmstablecottages.co.uk
w moorfarmstablecottages.co.uk

FRAMLINGHAM
Suffolk

Wood Lodge ★★★
Self Catering
Contact: Mr Tim Kindred
t (01728) 663461
e woodlodge@highhousefarm.co.uk
w highhousefarm.co.uk

FRESSINGFIELD
Suffolk

Watsons Farm ★★★
Self Catering
Contact: Mrs Mary Hinde
t (01379) 586295
e mary@marywebb.co.uk

FRETTENHAM
Norfolk

Glebe Farm ★★★
Self Catering
Contact: Mrs Rona Norton
Beck Farm
t (01603) 897641
e rona.norton@btinternet.com
w glebefarm-cottages.co.uk

The Old Forge (898) ★★★★★ *Self Catering*
Norfolk Country Cottages
t (01603) 871872
e info@norfolkcottages.co.uk
w norfolkcottages.co.uk

FRINTON-ON-SEA
Essex

Quartette ★★★ *Self Catering*
Boydens
t 07010 716013
e ipsw2@btinternet.com
w ipsw.btinternet.co.uk/quartette.htm

FRISTON
Suffolk

Post Office Cottage ★★★★
Self Catering
Suffolk Secrets
t (01379) 651297
e holidays@suffolk-secrets.co.uk
w tiscover.co.uk

FRITTON
Norfolk

Fritton Lake Country World ★★★★ *Self Catering*
Contact: Mr Brian Humphrey
t (01493) 488208
w tiscover.co.uk

FULBOURN
Cambridgeshire

Old Chapel ★★★
Self Catering
Contact: Mrs Denise Ryder
t (01223) 881427
e deniseahim@hotmail.com
w stayintheoldchapel.com

GARBOLDISHAM
Norfolk

Burnside and Hawthorn Lodge ★★★★ *Self Catering*
Contact: Mrs Connie Atkins
t (01953) 688376
e douconatkins@waitrose.com
w tiscover.co.uk

GAYTON
Norfolk

Field View ★★★
Self Catering
Contact: Mrs Rachel Steel
t (01553) 636813
w fieldviewcottage.mysite.wanadoo-members.co.uk

The Royd ★★★ *Self Catering*
Contact: Mrs Marilyn Barter
Monkshood
t (01553) 636249

Willow Cottage ★★★★
Self Catering
Contact: Mrs S Gadsby
t (01223) 836918
e sueg@ssps.fslife.co.uk
w tiscover.co.uk

GORLESTON-ON-SEA
Norfolk

Manor Cottage, Gorleston ★★★ *Self Catering*
Contact: Mrs Margaret Ward
North Manor House
t (01493) 669845
e manorcottage@wardm4.fsnet.co.uk
w wardm4.fsnet.co.uk

GRAFHAM
Cambridgeshire

16 Westwood Lodge ★★★
Self Catering
Contact: Miss G Parvin
t (01480) 450872
e jillip@hotmail.com
w grafhamlodgetolet.co.uk

GREAT BIRCHAM
Norfolk

Guest Flat ★★★ *Self Catering*
Contact: Mrs Sandra Hohol
Birds Norfolk Holiday Homes
t (01485) 534267
e shohol@birdsnorfolkholidayhomes.co.uk
w norfolkholidayhomes-birds.co.uk

Humphrey Cottage ★★★★
Self Catering
Contact: Mrs Elly Chalmers
t (01485) 578393
e info@birchamwindmill.co.uk
w tiscover.co.uk

GREAT DUNMOW
Essex

Granary ★★★★ *Self Catering*
Contact: Mrs Cathy Burton
t (01371) 870821
e cathy@moorendfarm.com
w tiscover.co.uk

GREAT EVERSDEN
Cambridgeshire

Rose Barn Cottages ★★★★
Self Catering
Contact: Mr Paul Tebbit
K B Tebbit Ltd
t (01223) 262154
e info@redhousefarmuk.com
w redhousefarmuk.com

GREAT HOCKHAM
Norfolk

Old School Cottage ★★★★
Self Catering
Contact: Ms Gwen Flanders
t (01953) 498277
e oscott@clara.net
w 4starcottage.co.uk

GREAT MASSINGHAM
Norfolk

2 Church Cottages ★★★★
Self Catering
Norfolk Country Cottages
t (01603) 871872
e info@norfolkcottages.co.uk
w norfolkcottages.co.uk

Eves Cottage ★★★
Self Catering
Contact: Mrs Lesley Cooke
Norfolk Country Cottages
t (01603) 871872
e info@norfolkcottages.co.uk
w norfolkcottages.co.uk

Look out for establishments participating in the National Accessible Scheme

Primrose Cottage ★★★
Self Catering
Contact: Mrs Christine Riches
t (01485) 520216
e info@christine-riches.com
w christine-riches.com

GREAT PLUMSTEAD
Norfolk

Windfalls ★★★ *Self Catering*
Contact: Mrs Jane Jones
Hall Farm
t (01603) 720235
e hall.farm@btinternet.com

GREAT SHELFORD
Cambridgeshire

Inglenook Cottage ★★★★
Self Catering
Contact: Mrs Biddy Wilkinson
t (01223) 843856
e enquiries@cambridge-cottages.co.uk
w cambridge-cottages.co.uk

GREAT SNORING
Norfolk

Church View Cottage ★★★
Self Catering
Contact: Mrs Lesley Cooke
Norfolk Country Cottages Ref. 676
t (01603) 871872
e info@norfolkcottages.co.uk
w tiscover.co.uk

Rose Cottage ★★★★
Self Catering
Contact: Mrs Gilly Paramor
t (01328) 878867
e gilly@gparamor.freeserve.co.uk

GREAT WALSINGHAM
Norfolk

Tailors House ★★★
Self Catering
Norfolk Country Cottages
t (01603) 871872
e info@norfolkcottages.co.uk
w norfolkcottages.co.uk/properties/849

GREAT WIGBOROUGH
Essex

Honeysuckle Cottage
★★★★ *Self Catering*
Contact: Mr Kevin Benner
t (01206) 735282
e kevinbenner@btopenworld.com
w honeysucklecot.co.uk

GREAT YARMOUTH
Norfolk

The Dunes ★★★
Self Catering
Contact: Mrs Beryl Wymer
t (01493) 842584

Karendel Holiday Flats
★★–★★★ *Self Catering*
Contact: Mrs June Ward
t (01493) 720490

Kenwood Holiday Flats ★★
Self Catering
Contact: Mrs V Forbes
t (01493) 852740
w tiscover.co.uk

Lochaber Flats ★
Self Catering
Contact: Mrs Catherine McIntosh
t (01493) 842862
e katimac@lochaber32.fsnet.co.uk

Milton Holiday Flats ★–★★
Self Catering
t (01493) 857462

St Georges Holiday Flats ★★
Self Catering
Contact: Mr & Mrs Sungtluttee
t (01493) 842036

Sea Breeze Holiday Flats
Rating Applied For
Self Catering
Contact: Mr John Waters
t (01493) 843232

GRESHAM
Norfolk

Brencott ★★★ *Self Catering*
Norfolk Country Cottages
t (01603) 871872
e info@norfolkcottages.co.uk
w norfolkcottages.co.uk

Little Place ★★ *Self Catering*
Contact: Mr Paul Hill
t (01263) 577344
w tiscover.co.uk

GRUNDISBURGH
Suffolk

Stable ★★★ *Self Catering & Serviced Apartments*
Contact: Mrs Louisa Davies
t (01473) 738827
w tiscover.co.uk

GUESTWICK
Norfolk

Williams Barn ★★★★
Self Catering
Contact: Ms Jayne Harrold
t (01263) 861386
e jayne-t-harrold@talk21.com
w tiscover.co.uk

GUNTHORPE
Norfolk

Chimney Cottage ★★★
Self Catering
Contact: Mr Roy Preston
t (01328) 830411
w tiscover.co.uk

Stables Courtyard
Rating Applied For
Self Catering
Contact: Mrs Irene Vallance
t (01525) 404898
w tiscover.co.uk

HADDENHAM
Cambridgeshire

Old Porch House ★★★★
Self Catering
Contact: Mr Alexander Innes
t (01353) 741948
w tiscover.co.uk

HADLEIGH
Suffolk

Angel Cottage ★★★★
Self Catering
Contact: Mrs Nadia Eustace
Period Cottage Holidays Ltd
t (01473) 652356
e nadia@periodcottageholidays.co.uk
w periodcottageholidays.co.uk

Lodge House ★★★★ *Self Catering & Serviced Apartments*
Contact: Angela & Rod Rolfe
t (01473) 822458
w tiscover.co.uk

Wattisham Hall Holiday Cottages, Wattisham
★★★★ *Self Catering*
Contact: Mrs Jo Squirrell
t (01449) 740240
e jhsquirr@farming.co.uk
w wattishamhall.co.uk

HALESWORTH
Suffolk

Bucks Farm Holiday Cottage
★★★★ *Self Catering*
Contact: Mrs Jo Bradshaw
Bucks Farm Holiday Cottages
t (01986) 784216
e jo@bucksfarm.freeuk.com
w tiscover.co.uk

Number Sixteen ★★★★
Self Catering
Contact: Ms Fiona Coverdale
t (01763) 853325
e fi.coverdale@gmail.com
w tiscover.co.uk

Stable End Cottage
★★★★★ *Self Catering*
Contact: Ms Jo Jordan
t (01986) 873124
e jo@stable-end-cottage.co.uk
w stable-end-cottage.co.uk

Weavers Cottage ★★★★
Self Catering
Contact: Mrs Joyce Harper
t (01986) 872526
e bookings@halesworthcottage.co.uk
w halesworthcottage.co.uk

HALSTEAD
Essex

Froyz Hall Barn ★★★★
Self Catering
Contact: Mrs Judi Butler
Froyz Hall Farm
t (01787) 476684
e judibutler@dsl.pipex.com

HAPPISBURGH
Norfolk

Boundary Stables ★★★★
Self Catering
Contact: Julian Burns
t (01692) 650171
e julianburns@onetel.net
w boundarystables.co.uk

Church Farm Barns ★★★★
Self Catering
Contact: Mrs Rosemary Munday
Rosco (UK) Ltd
t (01692) 650137
e ratchurchfarm@hotmail.com

Heather Cottage ★★★★
Self Catering
Contact: Mrs Lesley Cooke
Norfolk Country Cottages
t (01603) 871872
e info@norfolkcottages.co.uk
w norfolkcottages.co.uk

Lanthorn Cottage ★★★★
Self Catering
Contact: Mr Ian Brown
t (01442) 384473
e mellowsbrown@aol.com
w tiscover.co.uk

HARLOW
Essex

2 Harlowbury Mews, Harlowbury Manor ★★★★
Self Catering
Contact: David & Marian Hume-Smith
t (01279) 320411
e bookings@harlowbury.co.uk
w harlowbury.co.uk

HARPLEY
Norfolk

Lower Farm Self-Catering Cottages ★★★ *Self Catering*
t (01485) 520079
e info@apcherplay.co.uk

Rosedene ★★★★
Self Catering
Contact: Mr Roger Osborne
t (01603) 754349
e rogero@pobox.com

HAUGHLEY
Suffolk

Cottage ★★★ *Self Catering*
Contact: Mrs Mary Noy
Red House Farm
t (01449) 673323
e mary-n@tiscali.co.uk

HEACHAM
Norfolk

3 Hall Close ★★★★
Self Catering
Contact: Mr & Mrs Walpole
t (01279) 810967
e kerry_walpole@hotmail.com
w 3hallclose.com

4 Pretoria Cottages ★★★
Self Catering
Contact: Mr Colin Barnes
t (020) 8255 8834
e colinpbarnes@hotmail.com
w tiscover.co.uk

7 Pretoria Cottages
Rating Applied For
Self Catering
Norfolk Country Cottages
t (01603) 871872
e info@norfolkcottages.co.uk
w norfolkcottages.co.uk

Canon Pot Close 1 ★★★★
Self Catering
Contact: Mr Chris Saunders
t (01223) 832684
e mail@westcrete.co.uk
w norfolkcottages.co.uk

Carrick Cottage ★★
Self Catering
Contact: Ms Susan Sills
t (01485) 571369

Cedar Springs ★★–★★★
Self Catering
Contact: Mrs A Howe
t (01485) 570609
e antoniahowe@aol.com
w tiscover.co.uk

Cedar Springs Chalets ★★
Self Catering
Contact: Michael & Ann Chestney
The Street
t (01328) 838341
w tiscover.co.uk

Cheney Hollow Cottages ★★★★ *Self Catering*
Contact: Mrs Thelma Holland
t (01485) 572625
e thelma@cheneyhollow.co.uk
w cheneyhollow.co.uk

K'leigh ★★★ *Self Catering*
Contact: Mrs Sandra Hohol
Birds Norfolk Holiday Homes
t (01483) 534267
e shohol@birdsnorfolkholidayhomes.co.uk
w norfolkholidayhomes-birds.co.uk

Little Acorns ★★★
Self Catering
Contact: Mrs Sandra Hohol
Birds Norfolk Holiday Homes
t (01485) 534267
e shohol@birdsnorfolkholidayhomes.co.uk
w norfolkholidayhomes-birds.co.uk

Old Station Waiting Rooms ★★★ *Self Catering*
Contact: Judith Clay
t (01485) 570712
e clay@oldstation.fsnet.co.uk
w cottageguide.co.uk/waitingrooms

Painters Corner ★★★★
Self Catering
Contact: Mrs N. J. O'Callaghan
The Hermitage
t (01485) 525381
e hideawaya1@aol.com
w heacham1.fsnet.co.uk/hideaway/accommodation_07

Retreat Cottage 2 ★★★
Self Catering
Contact: Mrs I Rooth
t (01485) 572072
e ij.rooth@gmail.com
w retreatcottage.com

Robin Hill ★★ *Self Catering*
Contact: Mrs DM Gidney
t (01485) 570309
w tiscover.co.uk

Sunnyside Cottages 1 ★★★
Self Catering
Contact: Mrs Lesley Cooke
Norfolk Country Cottages
t (01603) 871872
e info@norfolkcottages.co.uk
w norfolk-cottages.co.uk

Tawny Cottage ★★★★
Self Catering
Contact: Mrs Gail Armstrong
Norfolk Country Cottages
t (01603) 871872
e info@norfolkcottages.co.uk

HEMSBY Norfolk

Nuthatch Cottage ★★★★
Self Catering
Contact: Mrs Stephanie Sampson
Beachside Holidays
t (01493) 730279
e holidays@theseaside.org
w cottages-in-norfolk.co.uk

HENLEY Suffolk

Damerons Farm Holidays ★★★★ *Self Catering*
Contact: Mrs Sue Leggett
t (01473) 832454
e info@dameronsfarmholidays.co.uk
w dameronsfarmholidays.co.uk

HERTFORD Hertfordshire

Dalmonds Barns ★★★★
Self Catering
Contact: Ms Ann Reay
t (01992) 479151
e ann.reay@virgin.net
w dalmondsbarns.com

Petasfield Cottages ★★★
Self Catering
Contact: Miss Helen Clark
t (01992) 504201
e helen@petasfieldcottages.co.uk
w petasfieldcottages.co.uk

HESSETT Suffolk

Heathfield ★★★★
Self Catering
Contact: Mrs Christine Whitton
t (01359) 271130
e chriswhitton@aol.com
w tiscover.co.uk

Wilwyn And Chapel Cottages ★★★ *Self Catering*
Contact: Mr Chris & Nicky Glass
t (01359) 270736
e chrisglass@hessettgrain.freeserve.co.uk
w cottageguide.co.uk/hessett

HICKLING Norfolk

Conifers ★★★★
Self Catering
Contact: Mrs Lesley Cooke
Norfolk Country Cottages
t (01603) 871872
e info@norfolkcottages.co.uk
w norfolkcottages.co.uk

Cottage ★★★ *Self Catering*
Contact: Mrs Lesley Cooke
Norfolk Country Cottages
t (01603) 871872
e info@norfolkcottages.co.uk
w norfolkcottages.co.uk

Goleby's Cottage ★★★
Self Catering
Norfolk Country Cottages
t (01603) 871872
e info@norfolkcottages.co.uk
w norfolkcottages.co.uk

Kingsley Cottage ★★★★
Self Catering
t (01603) 871872
e info@norfolkcottages.co.uk
w norfolkcottage.co.uk

Pilgrim's Chase ★★★★
Self Catering
Norfolk Country Cottages
t (01603) 871872
e info@norfolkcottages.co.uk
w norfolkcottages.co.uk

Pilgrim's Cottage ★★★
Self Catering
Norfolk Country Cottages
t (01603) 871872
e info@norfolkcottages.co.uk
w norfolkcottages.co.uk

Pilgrims Progress ★★★★
Self Catering
Norfolk Country Cottages
t (01603) 871872
e info@norfolkcottages.co.uk
w norfolkcottages.co.uk

Pilgrim's Prospect ★★★★
Self Catering
Norfolk Country Cottages
t (01603) 871872
e info@norfolkcottages.co.uk
w norfolkcottages.co.uk

HIGH KELLING Norfolk

Lynton Loft ★★★★
Self Catering
Contact: Mrs Lesley Cooke
Norfolk Country Cottages
t (01603) 871872
e info@norfolkcottages.co.uk
w norfolkcottages.co.uk

HINDOLVESTON Norfolk

Pine Cottage ★★★
Self Catering
Contact: Mr Scammell
t (01707) 651734
e grahamscammell@814hotmail.com
w cheznorfolk.com

HINDRINGHAM Norfolk

Sundial House ★★★
Self Catering
Contact: Mr Simon Barclay
Kett Country Cottages
t (01328) 856853
e info@kettcountrycottages.co.uk
w kettcountrycottages.co.uk

HINGHAM Norfolk

The Granary ★★★
Self Catering
Contact: Mrs Dunnett
College Farm
t (01953) 850596
e christine.dunnett@lineone.net

White Lodge Farm Cottages Limited ★★★★★
Self Catering
Contact: Mr & Mrs Tony Richardson
t (01953) 850435
e helen@whitelodgefarmcottages.co.uk

HISTON Cambridgeshire

Green 13 ★★★ *Self Catering*
Contact: Mrs Pauline Wynn
t (01954) 250729
w tiscover.co.uk

HITCHAM Suffolk

Mill House Holiday Cottage ★★-★★★ *Self Catering*
Contact: Ms Melanie Rieger
Mill House Holiday Cottages
t (01449) 740315
e hitcham@aol.com
w millhouse-hitcham.co.uk

HOLME NEXT THE SEA Norfolk

Beach Cottage ★★★★
Self Catering
Contact: Mrs Stephanie Jones
t (01485) 525201
e robertjones@samphire1.demon.co.uk
w tiscover.co.uk

Broadwater Cottage, Holme next the Sea ★★★★
Self Catering
Contact: Mrs Jayne Ransom
t (01223) 524821
e vine.farm@ntlworld.com
w broadwatercottage.co.uk

Brook Bungalow ★★★★
Self Catering
Contact: Mrs Whitsed
t (01733) 380028
e john@jwhitsed.freeserve.co.uk
w tiscover.co.uk

Eastgate Barn ★★★
Self Catering
Contact: Mrs Shirley Simeone
t (01485) 525218
w tiscover.co.uk

Rose Cottage ★★★★
Self Catering
Contact: Mrs Stephanie Hedge
t (01954) 250470
w ashtoncottages.co.uk

HOLT Norfolk

5 Carpenters Cottages ★★★
Self Catering
Contact: Mr Christopher Knights
t (01493) 842289 & (01502) 742022

6 Carpenters Cottage ★★★
Self Catering
Contact: Mrs Sally Beament
t (01363) 773789
e sallybeament@hotmail.com
w tiscover.co.uk

Arcadia ★★★ *Self Catering*
Contact: Mrs Elizabeth McGill
t (01932) 770207
e elizabethmcgill@dialstart.net
w tiscover.co.uk

Crowlands Cottage And 4 Ca ★★★ *Self Catering*
Contact: Mrs Julie Pell
t 07767 663938
e julie.pell@talk21.com
w tiscover.co.uk

Hawthorn Walk 1 ★★★
Self Catering
Contact: Mr Simon Barclay
Kett Country Cottages
t (01328) 856853
e info@kettcountrycottages.co.uk
w kettcountrycottages.co.uk

Honeysuckle Cottage ★★★
Self Catering
Contact: Miss Allison
Orchard House
t (01263) 712457
w tiscover.co.uk

Lavender Cottage ★★★
Self Catering
Contact: Mrs M Cooke
t (01328) 710659
e pippa@pippacooke71.wanadoo.co.uk

Maple Cottage, Stody
★★★★ *Self Catering*
Contact: Mrs Stephanie Moore
Stody Cottage
t (01263) 861590
e maplecottage1@btinternet.com

Puffin Cottage ★★★
Self Catering
Norfolk Country Cottages
t (01603) 871872
e info@norfolkcottages.co.uk
w norfolkcottages.co.uk

Sunnyside Cottage ★★★
Self Catering
Contact: Mr Michael Drake
t (01603) 712524
e michael.drake@ukgateway.net
w tiscover.co.uk

Victoria Cottage ★★
Self Catering
Contact: Mr & Mrs Richard & Carole Gregory
J & J Services
t (01302) 746022
e therichardgregory@hotmail.com

Wood Farm Cottages
★★★-★★★★★ *Self Catering*
Contact: Mrs Diana Jacob
t (01263) 587347
e info@wood-farm.com
w wood-farm.com

HOLTON
Suffolk

Swallow Barn ★★★★
Self Catering
Contact: Mrs Jackie Circus
t (01986) 874521
e mail@valleyfarmholton.co.uk
w valleyfarmholton.co.uk

HOLTON ST MARY
Suffolk

Coach House ★★★★
Self Catering
Contact: Mrs Anne Selleck
t (01206) 298246
e fselleck@uwclub.net
w accomsuffolk.co.uk

HORHAM
Suffolk

Alpha Cottages ★★★
Self Catering
Alpha Cottages
t (01379) 384424

HORNING
Norfolk

Bure House ★★★★
Self Catering
Contact: Mrs Bryan
t (01664) 444206
e ebryan@rutland.gov.uk
w tiscover.co.uk

Ferry Marina Ltd ★★★
Self Catering
Contact: Mrs Sharon Reeder
t (01692) 630392
e sharon@ferry-marina.co.uk
w ferry-marina.co.uk

The Ferry Powerboat Company Limited
★★★-★★★★★ *Self Catering*
Contact: Miss Melissa Reeder
M R Reeder General Cleaning Services
t (01603) 782302
e melissareeder@intamail.com
w tiscover.co.uk

Heron Cottage ★★★★★
Self Catering
Contact: Mrs Gail Pitts
Premier Properties c/o
t 07788 853332
w tiscover.co.uk

King Line Cottages
★★★-★★★★★ *Self Catering*
Contact: Mr Robert King
t (01692) 630297
e kingline@norfolk-broads.co.uk
w norfolk-broads.co.uk

Little River View ★★★
Self Catering
Contact: Mrs Victoria Free
t (01245) 441981
e victoria@littleriverview.co.uk
w littleriverview.co.uk

HORNINGTOFT
Norfolk

Old Stables Holiday Cottages ★★★ *Self Catering*
Contact: Mr Ivan Baker
t (01328) 700262
w oldstablescottages.co.uk

HORRINGER
Suffolk

Garden Cottage ★★★
Self Catering
Contact: Mr Tyrone Lewis
t (01284) 735731
w tiscover.co.uk

HORSEY
Norfolk

River's End ★★★
Self Catering
Norfolk Country Cottages
t (01603) 871872
e info@norfolkcottages.co.uk
w norfolkcottages.co.uk

HOVETON
Norfolk

East Wing, Hoveton Hall
★★★ *Self Catering*
Norfolk Country Cottages
t (01603) 871872
e info@norfolkcottages.co.uk
w norfolkcottages.co.uk

HUNSTANTON
Norfolk

1 Victoria House ★★★★
Self Catering
Contact: Mrs Sandra Hohol
Birds Norfolk Holiday Homes
t (01485) 534267
e shohol@birdsnorfolkholidayhomes.co.uk
w norfolkholidayhomes-birds.co.uk

4 Church Street ★★★
Self Catering
Contact: Mrs Sandra Hohol
Birds Norfolk Holiday Homes
t (01485) 534267
e shohol@birdsnorfolkholidayhomes.co.uk
w norfolkholidayhomes-birds.co.uk

57 Crescent Road ★★★
Self Catering
Contact: Mrs Sandra Hohol
Birds Norfolk Holiday Homes
t (01485) 534267
e shohol@birdsnorfolkholidayhomes.co.uk
w norfolkholidayhomes-birds.co.uk

Albert House ★★★
Self Catering
Contact: Ms Sarah Flanagan
t (01636) 831159
e sarahflan20@aol.com
w tiscover.co.uk

Altera ★★★★ *Self Catering*
Contact: Mrs Jean Larman
t (020) 8421 3815
e jean.larman@tinyworld.co.uk
w tiscover.co.uk

Ashdale House ★★★★
Self Catering
Contact: Mrs Sandra Hohol
Birds Norfolk Holiday Homes
t (01485) 534267
e shohol@birdsnorfolkholidayhomes.co.uk
w norfolkholidayhomes-birds.co.uk

Beat 'n' Retreat ★★★
Self Catering
Contact: Mrs Sandra Hohol
Birds Norfolk Holiday Homes
t (01485) 534267
e shohol@birdsnorfolkholidayhomes.co.uk
w norfolkholidayhomes-birds.co.uk

Beeches ★★★ *Self Catering*
Contact: Mr Judd
t (01480) 411509
e sales@hunstantonholidays.co.uk
w hunstantonholidays.co.uk

Belle Vue Apartment
★★★-★★★★ *Self Catering*
Contact: Mrs Sandra Bowman
t (01485) 532826
w tiscover.co.uk

Blue Skies ★★★★
Self Catering
Contact: Ms Debbie Harrington
t (01945) 588055
e debs.harrington@btinternet.com
w hunstantonholidaycottages.co.uk

Boston View
Rating Applied For
Self Catering
Holiday Homes
t (01485) 534 267

Brincliffe and Annexe
★★★★ *Self Catering*
Contact: Mrs Sandra Hohol
Birds Norfolk Holiday Homes
t (01485) 534267
e shohol@birdsnorfolkholidayhomes.co.uk
w norfolkholidayhomes-birds.co.uk

Cameo Cottage ★★
Self Catering
Contact: Mrs Sandra Hohol
Birds Norfolk Holiday Homes
t (01485) 534267
e shohol@birdsnorfolkholidayhomes.co.uk
w norfolkholidayhomes-birds.co.uk

Chalet 4 ★★ *Self Catering*
Contact: Michael & Ann Chestney
t (01328) 838341
w tiscover.co.uk

Cleeks ★★★ *Self Catering*
Contact: Mrs Sandra Hohol
Birds Norfolk Holiday Homes
t (01485) 534267
e shohol@birdsnorfolkholidayhomes.co.uk
w norfolkholidayhomes-birds.co.uk

Coastguard Lookout ★★★
Self Catering
Contact: Mrs Sandra Hohol
Birds Norfolk Holiday Homes
t (01485) 534267
e shohol@birdsnorfolkholidayhomes.co.uk
w norfolkholidayhomes-birds.co.uk

Collingwood Road 40 ★★★
Self Catering
Contact: Mrs Sandra Hohol
Birds Norfolk Holiday Homes
t (01485) 534267
e shohol@birdsnorfolkholidayhomes.co.uk
w norfolkholidayhomes-birds.co.uk

Dormy Cottage ★★★
Self Catering
Contact: Mrs Sandra Hohol
Birds Norfolk Holiday Homes
t (01485) 534267
e shohol@birdsnorfolkholidayhomes.co.uk
w norfolkholidayhomes-birds.co.uk

End Of The Road ★★
Self Catering
Contact: Mrs Sandra Hohol
Birds Norfolk Holiday Homes
t (01485) 534267
e shohol@birdsnorfolkholidayhomes.co.uk
w norfolkholidayhomes-birds.co.uk

Flat 11 ★★★ *Self Catering*
Contact: Ms Sandra Hohol
Birds Norfolk Holiday Homes
t (01485) 534267
e shohol@birdsnorfolkholidayhomes.co.uk
w norfolkholidayhomes-birds.co.uk

Foxgloves Cottage ★★★★
Self Catering
Contact: Terry & Lesley Heade
t (01485) 532460
e deepdenehouse@btopenworld.com
w smoothhound.co.uk/hotels/deepdene.html

Fulmars ★★★ *Self Catering*
Contact: Mrs Sandra Hohol
Birds Norfolk Holiday Homes
t (01485) 534267
e shohol@birdsnorfolkholidayhomes.co.uk
w norfolkholidayhomes-birds.co.uk

The Haven ★★ *Self Catering*
Contact: Mrs Sandra Hohol
Birds Norfolk Holiday Homes
t (01485) 534267
e shohol@birdsnorfolkholidayhomes.co.uk
w norfolkholidayhomes-birds.co.uk

Home Cottage ★★★
Self Catering
Contact: Mrs Sandra Hohol
Birds Norfolk Holiday Homes
t (01485) 534267
e shohol@birdsnorfolkholidayhomes.co.uk
w norfolkholidayhomes-birds.co.uk

Horizons ★★★ *Self Catering*
Contact: Mrs Sandra Hohol
Birds Norfolk Holiday Homes
t (01485) 534267
e shohol@birdsnorfolkholidayhomes.co.uk
w norfolkholidayhomes-birds.co.uk

Jaskville ★★★ *Self Catering*
Contact: Mr John Smith
Jaskville
t (01485) 533404
w tiscover.co.uk

Jordans ★★★ *Self Catering*
Contact: Mrs Sandra Hohol
Birds Norfolk Holiday Homes
t (01485) 534267
e shohol@birdsnorfolkholidayhomes.co.uk
w norfolkholidayhomes-birds.co.uk

Keepers Cottage ★★★
Self Catering
Contact: Mrs Sandra Hohol
Birds Norfolk Holiday Homes
t (01485) 534267
e shohol@birdsnorfolkholidayhomes.co.uk
w norfolkholidayhomes-birds.co.uk

The Ladybird House ★★★★
Self Catering
Contact: Ms Wendy Spencer
Brixham Holiday Homes Ltd
t (01485) 532356

Lavender Lodge ★★★★
Self Catering
Contact: Mrs Sandra Hohol
Birds Norfolk Holiday Homes
t (01485) 534267
e shohol@birdsnorfolkholidayhomes.co.uk
w norfolkholidayhomes-birds.co.uk

Malgwyn ★★★ *Self Catering*
Contact: Mrs Perdita Swift
t (01223) 290207
e pandp.swift@talktalk.net
w cottageguide.co.uk/malgwyn

Midway ★★ *Self Catering*
Contact: Mrs Sandra Hohol
Birds Norfolk Holiday Homes
t (01485) 534267
e shohol@birdsnorfolkholidayhomes.co.uk
w norfolkholidayhomes-birds.co.uk

Minna Cottage ★★★
Self Catering
Contact: Mr Tony Cassie
Cassie's Restaurant
t (01485) 532448
e tonycassie@btconnect.com
w minnacottage.com

Nelson Drive 18 ★★★
Self Catering
Contact: Mrs Sandra Hohol
Birds Norfolk Holiday Homes
t (01485) 534267
e shohol@birdsnorfolkholidayhomes.co.uk
w norfolkholidayhomes-birds.co.uk

No 2 39 South Beach Road
★★ *Self Catering*
Contact: Mrs Sandra Hohol
Birds Norfolk Holiday Homes
t (01485) 534267
e shohol@birdsnorfolkholidayhomes.co.uk
w norfolkholidayhomes-birds.co.uk

Roundstones ★★★
Self Catering
Contact: Mrs Sandra Hohol
Birds Norfolk Holiday Homes
t (01485) 534267
e shohol@birdsnorfolkholidayhomes.co.uk
w norfolkholidayhomes-birds.co.uk

Saint Crispin ★★★
Self Catering
Contact: Mrs Lesley Poore
t (01485) 534036
e st.crispins@btinternet.com
w tiscover.co.uk

St Edmunds ★★★
Self Catering
Contact: Mrs Sandra Hohol
Birds Norfolk Holiday Homes
t (01485) 534267
e shohol@birdsnorfolkholidayhomes.co.uk
w norfolkholidayhomes-birds.co.uk

Sandbanks ★★★★
Self Catering
Contact: Mrs Sandra Hohol
Birds Norfolk Holiday Homes
t (01485) 534267
e shohol@birdsnorfolkholidayhomes.co.uk
w norfolkholidayhomes-birds.co.uk

Sandpiper Cottage ★★★★
Self Catering
Contact: Mrs Sandra Hohol
Birds Norfolk Holiday Homes
t (01485) 534267
e shohol@birdsnorfolkholidayhomes.co.uk
w norfolkholidayhomes-birds.co.uk

Sea Breeze ★★★
Self Catering
Contact: Mrs Sandra Hohol
Birds Norfolk Holiday Homes
t (01485) 534267
e shohol@birdsnorfolkholidayhomes.co.uk
w norfolkholidayhomes-birds.co.uk

Sea Lane 44 ★★★
Self Catering
Contact: Mrs Sandra Hohol
Birds Norfolk Holiday Homes
t (01485) 534267
e shohol@birdsnorfolkholidayhomes.co.uk
w norfolkholidayhomes-birds.co.uk

Sea View ★★ *Self Catering*
Contact: Mr Jeremy Roberts
t (01733) 342172
w tiscover.co.uk

Shorelarks ★★★★
Self Catering
Contact: Mrs Sandra Hohol
Birds Norfolk Holiday Homes
t (01485) 534267
e shohol@birdsnorfolkholidayhomes.co.uk
w norfolkholidayhomes-birds.co.uk

Spindrift ★★★★
Self Catering
Contact: Mrs Sandra Hohol
Birds Norfolk Holiday Homes
t (01485) 534267
e shohol@birdsnorfolkholidayhomes.co.uk
w norfolkholidayhomes-birds.co.uk

Sunny Corner ★★★
Self Catering
Contact: Mrs Sandra Hohol
Birds Norfolk Holiday Homes
t (01485) 534267
e shohol@birdsnorfolkholidayhomes.co.uk
w norfolkholidayhomes-birds.co.uk

Surf ★★ *Self Catering*
Contact: Mrs Sandra Hohol
Birds Norfolk Holiday Homes
t (01485) 534267
e shohol@birdsnorfolkholidayhomes.co.uk
w norfolkholidayhomes-birds.co.uk

The Terrace ★★★★
Self Catering
Contact: Mrs Kay Thomas
t (01775) 711525
e kay.weijers@btinternet.com
w tiscover.co.uk

Trinity Lodge ★★★
Self Catering
Contact: Mrs Sandra Hohol
Birds Norfolk Holiday Homes
t (01485) 534267
e shohol@birdsnorfolkholidayhomes.co.uk
w norfolkholidayhomes-birds.co.uk

Victoria House Apartment 3
★★★ *Self Catering*
Contact: Mr Richard Bamfield
t (01485) 532514
e rbsurfingthewash@aol.com

Victory Cottage ★★★
Self Catering
Contact: Mrs Sandra Hohol
Birds Norfolk Holiday Homes
t (01485) 534267
e shohol@birdsnorfolkholidayhomes.co.uk
w norfolkholidayhomes-birds.co.uk

West Lodge ★★★
Self Catering
Contact: Mrs Geraldine Tibbs
Cole Green Cottage
t (01485) 571770

Westacre ★★★ *Self Catering*
Contact: Mrs Sandra Hohol
Birds Norfolk Holiday Homes
t (01485) 534267
e shohol@birdsnorfolkholidayhomes.co.uk
w norfolkholidayhomes-birds.co.uk

Westgate Flat ★★
Self Catering
Contact: Mrs Jean Chilleystone
t (01485) 533646
w tiscover.co.uk

HUNTINGFIELD
Suffolk

Corner Farm ★★★★★
Self Catering
Contact: Ms Jo Bradshaw
t (01986) 784216
e jo@bucksfarm.freeuk.com
w bucksfarm-holidays.co.uk

HUNWORTH
Norfolk

Green Farm Barn ★★★★
Self Catering
Contact: Mrs Patricia Hoskison
t (01263) 713177
e alan@tagsy.freeserve.co.uk
w greenfarmbarn.com

Spinks Nest ★★ *Self Catering*
Contact: Mrs Angela Hampshire
t (01263) 713891
w tiscover.co.uk

IKEN
Suffolk

Iken Barns ★★★★
Self Catering
Suffolk Secrets
t (01502) 722717
e holidays@suffold-secrets.co.uk
w suffold-secrets.co.uk

Long Reach ★★★★
Self Catering
Suffolk Secrets
t (01502) 722717
e holidays@suffolk-secrets.co.uk
w suffolk-secrets.co.uk

Look out for establishments participating in the National Accessible Scheme

Old Stable ★★★★
Self Catering
Contact: Mrs Gunilla Hailes
t (01728) 688263
w tiscover.co.uk

Orford Cottages
★★★-★★★★★
Self Catering
Contact: Sue Cartlidge
t (01728) 687844
e wue@orford-cottages.co.uk
w orford.cottages.co.uk

INGOLDISTHORPE
Norfolk

Foxes Croft ★★ *Self Catering*
Contact: Mrs Christine Riches
t (01485) 520216
e info@christine-riches.com
w christine-riches.com

Swan Cottage ★★★★ *Self Catering & Serviced Apartments*
Contact: Mr Alex Swan
t (01485) 543882
e pencob@supanet.com
w tiscover.co.uk

KEDINGTON
Suffolk

Cottage At Rowans ★★★★
Self Catering
Contact: Ms Cheryl Owen
t (01440) 702408
e cheryl@owen41.supanet.com
w cottagesdirect.com/nfa123

KELLING
Norfolk

Fox Hollies ★★★
Self Catering
Norfolk Country Cottages
t (01603) 871872
e info@norfolkcottages.co.uk
w norfolkcottages.co.uk

Plough Wheel ★★★
Self Catering
Contact: Mrs Gail Armstrong
Norfolk Country Cottages
t (01603) 871872
e info@norfolkcottages.co.uk
w norfolkcottages.co.uk

KELSALE
Suffolk

East Green Farm Cottages
★★★★ *Self Catering*
Contact: Claire & Robbie Gawthrop
t (01728) 602316
e claire@eastgreenproperty.co.uk
w eastgreencottages.co.uk

KERSEY
Suffolk

Old Drift House ★★★★★
Self Catering
Contact: Mrs Jill Black
11 Poynings Close
t (01582) 763533
e ejblk@talk21.com
w olddrifthouse.co.uk

KESSINGLAND
Suffolk

23 Alandale Drive ★★
Self Catering
Contact: Ms Karen Foster
t (01223) 576874
w tiscover.co.uk

74 The Cliff ★★ *Self Catering*
Contact: Mrs Saunders
t (01508) 538340
w tiscover.co.uk

Church Road ★★★
Self Catering
Contact: Mr James Rayment
t (01223) 843048
w tiscover.co.uk

Four Winds Retreat ★★★★
Self Catering
Contact: Mr Peter & Jane Garner
t (01502) 740044
e info@four-winds-retreat.co.uk
w four-winds-retreat.co.uk

Kessingland Cottages 11
★★ *Self Catering*
Contact: Mrs Carol Keane
t (01707) 330742
w tiscover.co.uk

Kew Cottage ★★★
Self Catering
Contact: Mrs Joan Gill
t (01604) 717301
e b.s.g@btinternet.com

Knights Holiday Homes
★-★★ *Self Catering*
Contact: Mr Michael Knights
t 0800 269067
e enquiries@knightsholidays.co.uk
w knightsholidays.co.uk

Spindrift ★★★ *Self Catering*
Contact: Mrs Lesley Cooke
Norfolk Country Cottages
t (01603) 871872
e info@norfolkcottages.co.uk
w norfolkcottages.co.uk

KETTLEBURGH
Suffolk

Church Farm ★★★★
Self Catering
Contact: Mrs Anne Bater
t (01728) 723532
e jbater@suffolkonline.net
w tiscover.co.uk

KETTLESTONE
Norfolk

Caretakers Cottage ★★★★
Self Catering
Contact: Mr Simon Barclay
Kett Country Cottages
t (01328) 856853
e info@kettcountrycottages.co.uk
w kettcountrycottages.co.uk

KNAPTON
Norfolk

The Granary Cottage & Wallages Cottage ★★★★
Self Catering
Norfolk Country Cottages
t (01603) 871872
e info@norfolkcottages.co.uk
w norfolkcottages.co.uk

LAMARSH
Essex

Hill Farm House Self Cater
★★★★ *Self Catering*
Contact: Mrs Brenda Greenhill
t (01787) 269905
e greenhillaccom@tiscali.co.uk
w farmstayeastanglia.co.uk

LANGHAM
Norfolk

Sunnyside Cottage ★★★★
Self Catering
Contact: Mr Shephard
t (0116) 287 2739
e jt.glenfield@btinternet.com
w tiscover.co.uk

LAVENHAM
Suffolk

Blaize Cottages ★★★★★
Self Catering
Contact: Mr & Mrs Jim & Carol Keohane
Blaize Cottages
t (01787) 247402
e info@blaizecottages.com
w blaizecottages.com

Glebe Cottage ★★★★★
Self Catering
Contact: Mrs Ferrari
t (01787) 211364

Granary Cottage ★★★★
Self Catering
Contact: Mrs Wendy Williams
t (01284) 828458
w tiscover.co.uk

Grove ★★★★ *Self Catering*
Contact: Mr Mark Scott
t (01787) 211115
e mark@grove-cottages.co.uk
w grove-cottages.co.uk

Hour Cottage ★★★★
Self Catering
Contact: Mrs Esther Perkins
t (01277) 651843
e esther@hourcottage.co.uk
w hourcottage.co.uk

Lavenham Cottages
★★★★★ *Self Catering*
Contact: Ms Sheila Lane
t (01284) 830771
e sheila@lavenhamcottages.co.uk
w tiscover.co.uk

Old Wetherden Hall ★★★
Self Catering
Contact: Mrs Julie Elsden
Old Wetherden Hall
t (01449) 740574
e julie.elsden@btconnect.com
w oldwetherdenhall.co.uk

The Rector's Retreat ★★★
Self Catering
Contact: Mr & Mrs Peter Gutteridge
The Rector's Retreat
t (01449) 741557
e holidays@kettlebaston.fsnet.co.uk
w kettlebaston.fsnet.co.uk

Ropers Court 12 ★★★
Self Catering
Contact: Mr Roger Arnold
t (01787) 227760
e queens-house@btconnect.com
w queenscottages.com

Victoria Cottage ★★★★
Self Catering
Contact: Mr Nigel & Sheila Margo
t 07931 542644
e sheila@victoriacottage-lavenham.co.uk
w victoriacottage-lavenham.co.uk

LAXFIELD
Suffolk

The Loose Box & The Old Stables ★★★ *Self Catering*
Contact: Mr & Mrs John & Jane Reeve
Laxfield Leisure Ltd
t (01986) 798019
e laxfieldleisure@talk21.com

Meadow Cottage, Laxfield
★★★★ *Self Catering*
Contact: Mr William Ayers
t (01986) 798345
e will.ayers@btinternet.com

LEISTON
Suffolk

Abbey View Lodges ★★★
Self Catering
Contact: Mrs Sally Stobbart
t (01728) 831128
e info@abbeyview.co.uk
w abbeyviewlodges.co.uk

Studio Cottage ★★★
Self Catering
Contact: Mrs Janet Lister
t (01728) 833034
w tiscover.co.uk

LETHERINGHAM
Suffolk

Black Barn ★★★★
Self Catering
Contact: Mrs Ann Young
The Lodge
t (01473) 737212
e mikeyoung47@yahoo.com

LITCHAM
Norfolk

4 Canaan Row ★★★
Self Catering
Norfolk Country Cottages
t (01603) 871872
e info@norfolkcottages.co.uk
w norfolkcottages.co.uk

Old Farmhouse ★★★
Self Catering
Contact: Mrs Judith Archer
t (01328) 701331
e judiarcher@aol.com
w tiscover.co.uk

LITTLE BENTLEY
Essex

Spring Hall Cottage ★★★★
Self Catering
Contact: Mrs Tricia Maestrani
Spring Hall
t (01206) 251619 & 07779 264679
e triciamaestrani@hotmail.co.uk

LITTLE FRANSHAM
Norfolk

Lyons Green And Little Flint
★★★★-★★★★★
Self Catering
Contact: Mrs Jenny Mallon
t (01362) 687649
e office@franshamfarm.co.uk
w farmstayanglia.co.uk

LITTLE HENHAM
Essex

Stable Cottage ★★★
Self Catering
Contact: Mrs Kate Muskett
t (01279) 850228
e kgmletting@aol.com
w tiscover.co.uk

LITTLE SNORING
Norfolk

Jex Farm Barns ★★★★
Self Catering
Contact: Mr Stephen Harvey
Jex Farm
t (01328) 878257 & 07979 495760
e farmerstephen@jexfarm.wanadoo.co.uk
w jefarm.co.uk

Sunset Cottage ★★★★
Self Catering
t (01328) 878836
w tiscover.co.uk

LITTLE STONHAM
Suffolk

Dairy Cottage
Rating Applied For
Self Catering
Contact: Mrs Cyndy Clarke
Waltham Hall
t (01449) 711278
e raymondclarke@btopenworld.com

LITTLE WALDEN
Essex

Orchard View Numbers 1 – 4 ★★★ *Self Catering*
Contact: Mrs Maureen Chapman-Barker
Little Bowsers Farm
t (01799) 527315
e sales@farmerkit.co.uk
w farmerkit.co.uk

LITTLE WALSINGHAM
Norfolk

Old Coach House ★★★★
Self Catering
Contact: Mr Geoff & Julia Holloway
t (01473) 390035
e theoldcoach.house@btinternet.com
w theoldcoach.house.btinternet.co.uk

LITTLEPORT
Cambridgeshire

Caves Farm Barns
★★★–★★★★ *Self Catering*
Contact: Mr Stephen Kerridge
t (01353) 861423
e cb6steve@aol.com
w cavesfarmbarns.co.uk

LONG MELFORD
Suffolk

4 Church Walk ★★★
Self Catering
Contact: Mr Mark Thomas
t (020) 7267 3653
e angelathomas2003@btinternet.com
w tiscover.co.uk

Hope Cottage ★★★★
Self Catering
Contact: Ms S Jamil
Hill Farm Cottage
t (01787) 282338 & 07970 808701
e sns.jam@tesco.net
w hope-cottage-suffolk.co.uk

LOWER GRESHAM
Norfolk

Cottage ★★★★ *Self Catering*
Contact: Mrs Karen Battrick
Flint House
t (01263) 577725
e pjkbatt@nacer.net
w tiscover.co.uk

Roost ★★★★ *Self Catering*
Contact: Mr C K Entwistle
t (01263) 577388
e keith.entwistle@supanet.com
w tiscover.co.uk

LOWESTOFT
Suffolk

Banner Court 10 ★★★
Self Catering
Contact: Mrs Aisha Khalaf
t (01502) 511876
e aishakhalaf@hotmail.com
w tiscover.co.uk

Broadland Crescent ★★★★
Self Catering
Contact: Mrs Gillian Walker
t (01502) 573033
w tiscover.co.uk

Lowestoft Holiday Flat ★★
Self Catering
Contact: Mrs P Courtauld
t 07973 489755 & (020) 7582 6886
e mcourtauld@onetel.com
w tiscover.co.uk

Lyka Sands ★★★
Self Catering
Contact: Ms Lynne Luettschwager
t (01502) 530631
e lynne@lykas.co.uk
w tiscover.co.uk

Marine House ★ *Self Catering*
Contact: Mr & Mrs David & Teresa Conway
t (01702) 545495
e davidfconway@hotmail.co.uk
w 10marineparade.co.uk

The Old Chapel ★★★★
Self Catering
Norfolk Country Cottages
t (01603) 871872
e info@norfolkcottages.co.uk
w norfolkcottages.co.uk

Pippin Cottage ★★★★
Self Catering
Contact: Mr Ian Crocker
Somerton House
t (01502) 565665
e somerton@screaming.net
w pippin-cottage.co.uk

Rose Cliff Cottage ★★★
Self Catering
Contact: Mrs L S Sidley
Rose Place
t (01502) 509629
e rosecliffcottages@btinternet.com
w rosecliffcottages.org

Seabreeze ★★★★
Self Catering
Contact: Mrs Diane Cohen
t (01502) 582254
w tiscover.co.uk

Shaftsbury House ★★★★
Self Catering
Contact: Mrs Carol Wigg
Jacaranda House & Home Services
t (01502) 568580
w tiscover.co.uk

Suffolk Seaside & Broadlands ★★★
Self Catering
Contact: Mrs Collecott
t (01502) 564396

Tides Reach Holiday Flats ★★ *Self Catering*
Contact: Mrs Tallamy
Marsh Farm
t (01502) 476658
w tiscover.co.uk

LUDHAM
Norfolk

Ludham Hall Cottage
★★★★ *Self Catering*
Contact: Mrs Alison Ritchie
t (01692) 678232
e alison@dlritchie.fsnet.co.uk
w ludhamhall.co.uk

LUTON
Bedfordshire

Cityscape Apartments ★★★
Self Catering
Contact: Ms Sue Madine
t (0151) 737 1488
e cityscape@lycos.co.uk
w cityscape.org.uk

LYNG
Norfolk

Holly Cottage ★★★
Self Catering
Contact: Mr Thomas
t (01603) 880158
w tiscover.co.uk

Utopia Paradise, Lyng
★★★★ *Self Catering*
Contact: Mrs Suzan Jarvis
t (01603) 870812
e holidays@utopia-paradise.co.uk

MALDON
Essex

65 Market Hill ★★★★
Self Catering
Contact: Mrs Rosemary Bellman
t (01621) 816678
e markethillenquiries@yahoo.co.uk

Sunningdale ★★★
Self Catering
Contact: Christine & Roger Beckett
t (01621) 858235
e roger.beckett@btinternet.com
w tiscover.co.uk

MANNINGTREE
Essex

Elmdale Studio Apartment
★★★★ *Self Catering*
Contact: Mrs Lynette Edmunds
t (01206) 390046
e netsingers@macunlimited.net
w elmdalebb.co.uk

MARLESFORD
Suffolk

Hollyhock Cottage ★★★
Self Catering
Contact: Mrs Lizzie Hammond
Suffolk Cottage Holidays
t (01394) 412304
e lizzie@suffolkcottageholidays.com
w suffolkcottageholidays.com

MARSHAM
Norfolk

Kittles Cottage ★★★★
Self Catering
Contact: Mrs Lesley Cooke
Norfolk Country Cottages
t (01603) 871872
e info@norfolkcottages.co.uk
w tiscover.co.uk

MARSWORTH
Hertfordshire

Appletrees ★★★★
Self Catering
Contact: Mrs Val Rayner
t (01296) 661967

Field House ★★★★
Self Catering
Contact: Mr Pash
Hideaways
t (01747) 828170
e enq@hideaways.co.uk
w hideaways.co.uk

MARTHAM
Norfolk

Greenside Cottage ★★★
Self Catering
Contact: Mrs Barbara Dyball
t (01493) 740375
w tiscover.co.uk

MATTISHALL
Norfolk

Wayfarers Cottage ★★★★
Self Catering
Contact: Mr & Mrs Gogle
t (01362) 850214

MAUTBY
Norfolk

Lower Wood Farm Country Co ★★★★ *Self Catering*
Contact: Ms Jill Nicholls
Lower Wood Farm Country Cottages
t (01493) 722523
e info@lowerwoodfarm.co.uk
w tiscover.co.uk

MENDHAM
Suffolk

Tom Dick And Harry ★★★
Self Catering & Serviced Apartments
Contact: Mrs Audrey Carless
t (01379) 588091
e enquiries@bacatchurchfarm.co.uk
w bacatchurchfarm.co.uk

MERTON
Norfolk

The Stables ★★★★
Self Catering
Contact: Nancy Lordon
t (01953) 880180
e nancy@london.co.uk
w thestablesathomefarm.com

MICKFIELD
Suffolk

Read Hall Cottage ★★★★★
Self Catering
Contact: Mr & Mrs Andrew & Andrea Stewart
t (01449) 711366
e info@readhall.co.uk

MIDDLETON
Suffolk

The Cottage at Red Lodge Barn ★★★★ *Self Catering*
Contact: Mrs Patricia Dowding
t (01728) 668100
e pat_roy16@hotmail.com
w redlodgebarnsuffolk.co.uk

Four Seasons Lodge ★★★★
Self Catering
Contact: Ms Sanderson
t (01728) 648105
w four-seasonslodge.co.uk

Old Church Room ★★★★
Self Catering
Suffolk Secrets
t (01379) 651297
e holidays@suffolk-secrets.co.uk
w suffolk-secrets.co.uk

Rose Farm Barns ★★★★
Self Catering
Contact: Mrs Janet Maricic
t (01728) 648456
w tiscover.co.uk

MILDENHALL
Suffolk

Coach House And Stables ★★★★ *Self Catering*
Contact: Mrs Anne Greenfield
t (01638) 711237
e orchardhouse23@aol.com
w mildenhall-bed-breakfast.co.uk

MILEHAM
Norfolk

Mallards ★★★ *Self Catering*
Contact: Mrs Joscelin Colborne
t (01328) 700602
e joscelin.colborne@mallards.co.uk
w tiscover.co.uk

MUNDESLEY
Norfolk

Anchorage ★★★
Self Catering
Contact: Mrs Lesley Cooke
Norfolk Country Cottages
t (01603) 871872
e info@norfolkcottages.co.uk
w norfolkcottages.co.uk

Holiday Properties Mundesley ★–★★★
Self Catering
Contact: Mr Mark & Nadine Gray
Holiday Properties (Mundesley) Ltd
t (01263) 720719
e holidayproperties@tesco.net
w holidayprops.freeuk.com

Overcliff Lodge ★★★
Self Catering
Overcliffe Lodge
t (01603) 871872
e info@norfolkcottages.co.uk
w norfolkcottages.co.uk

Paddock Bungalow ★★★
Self Catering
Contact: Mrs Christine Harding
t (01263) 721060
e christine.m.harding@btinternet.com
w cottageguide.co.uk/paddockbungalow

Royal Chalet Park 10 ★★★
Self Catering
Contact: Mrs Lesley Cooke
Norfolk Country Cottages
t (01603) 871872
e info@norfolkcottages.co.uk
w norfolkcottages.co.uk

Seaward Crest ★★★
Self Catering
Contact: Mrs Christine Reynolds
t (01263) 710782
e creynolds@lineone.net
w seawardcrest.co.uk

Wild Rose Cottage ★★★
Self Catering
Contact: Mr Graham Tuckett
t (01245) 252397
e ruffelsandtuckett@hotmail.com
w tiscover.co.uk

NARBOROUGH
Norfolk

Church Farm Holiday Homes ★★★★ *Self Catering*
Contact: General Manager
Norfolk Country Cottages
t (01603) 871872
e info@norfolkcottages.co.uk
w tiscover.co.uk

Cliff Barns ★★★★★
Self Catering
Contact: Mr Russell Hall
t (01366) 328342
e info@cliffbarns.com
w cliffbarns.com

NAYLAND
Suffolk

Cobblers Cottage ★★★★
Self Catering
Contact: Mr Mark Scott
The Cottage Agency Ltd
t (01787) 211115
e mark@grove-cottages.co.uk
w grove-cottages.co.uk

Gladwins Farm ★★★★–★★★★★
Self Catering
Contact: Mr Pauline Dossor
Gladwins Farm
t (01206) 262261
e gladwinsfarm@aol.com
w gladwinsfarm.co.uk

NEWMARKET
Suffolk

Belmont and Ashbourne Court ★★–★★★
Self Catering
Contact: Mrs Jennie Collingridge
Harraton Court Stables
t (01638) 577952
e jennie@harratonstables.freeserve.co.uk
w tiscover.co.uk

Garden Studio ★★
Self Catering
Contact: Mr Ken Charity
t (01638) 662104
e mail@kencharity.com
w tiscover.co.uk

Hyperion Cottage ★★★
Self Catering
Contact: S Chapman
t (01284) 755901
e schapman2001@onetel.com

NORTH CREAKE
Norfolk

Lavender Cottage ★★★★
Self Catering
Contact: Mr & Mrs Maund
Field House
t (01328) 730460
e jenny@maundj.fsnet.co.uk
w norfolkcottagenorthcreate.co.uk

NORTH WALSHAM
Norfolk

April Cottage ★★★
Self Catering
Contact: Mrs Elisabeth Le Strange
t (01865) 421834
w autonomic.org.uk/aprilcottage

NORTH WOOTTON
Norfolk

Park View ★★★ *Self Catering*
Contact: Mr Kevan Gore
t 07889 485 595
e broadeast@ukonline.co.uk

Winsdail ★★★★
Self Catering
Contact: Mr Andrew Booth
Tudorwood
t (01485) 543639
e mail@winsdailcottage.com
w winsdailcottage.com

NORTHREPPS
Norfolk

Acorn Cottage ★★★★
Self Catering
Contact: Mrs Louise Strong
t (01263) 579736
e stephen.strong@virgin.net
w tiscover.co.uk

Cobblestones ★★★★
Self Catering
t (01603) 871872
e info@norfolkcottages.co.uk
w norfolkcottages.co.uk

Corder Cottage ★★★★
Self Catering
Contact: Mrs Heather McCraith
Norfolk Country Cottages
t (01603) 871872
e info@norfolkcottages.co.uk
w norfolkcottages.co.uk

Manor Studio ★★★★
Self Catering
Contact: Mrs Jane Hunt
t (01263) 579126
e jane_d_hunt@yahoo.co.uk
w tiscover.co.uk

Torridon And Yeomans Cottage ★★★★ *Self Catering*
Contact: Mrs Youngman
t (01263) 579297
e youngman@farming.co.uk
w broadland.com/torridon

NORWICH
Norfolk

The Apartment at City Heights ★★★★ *Self Catering*
Contact: Mrs Susan Potter
6 Stanley Avenue
t (01603) 700438
e sueno6p@aol.com
w number-6.co.uk

Hideaway ★★★★
Self Catering
Contact: Mrs Reilly
t (01603) 715052
e pondside@talk21.com
w tiscover.co.uk

Kingsley Road 30 ★★★
Self Catering
Contact: Miss Sally Clarke
t (01603) 473547
e kingsley@paston.co.uk
w tiscover.co.uk

Mabels Cottage ★★★
Self Catering
Contact: Mrs Randon
t (01508) 499279
w mabels-cottage.co.uk

Mill House ★★★★
Self Catering
Contact: Ms Fay Godin
t (01603) 415061
e villa.cott@virgin.net
w tiscover.co.uk

Sommersby ★★★
Self Catering
Contact: Miss Jackson
t (01787) 372903
e djackson@sommersby.freeserve.co.uk
w tiscover.co.uk

Spixworth Hall Cottages ★★★–★★★★ *Self Catering*
Contact: Mrs Sheelah Cook
Spixworth Hall Cottages
t (01603) 898190
e hallcottages@btinternet.com
w hallcottages.co.uk

NOWTON
Suffolk

Old Granary ★★★★
Self Catering
Contact: Mrs Mary Roe
t (01284) 388239
w tiscover.co.uk

OLD BUCKENHAM
Norfolk

Ox and Plough Cottages ★★★ *Self Catering & Serviced Apartments*
Contact: Mrs Sally Bishop
t (01953) 860004
w oxandploughcottages.co.uk

ORFORD
Suffolk

47 Daphne Road ★★★
Self Catering
Contact: Mrs Sheila Hitchcock
t (01394) 450714
w tiscover.co.uk

Broom Cottage ★★★★
Self Catering
Contact: Mrs Suvi Pool
t (01394) 450378
e cottage@high-house.co.uk
w high-house.co.uk

Brownies ★★★★
Self Catering
Contact: Mrs Sue Cartlidge
t (01728) 687844
e info@orford-cottages.co.uk
w orford-cottages.co.uk

The Gedgrave Broom
★★★★ *Self Catering*
Contact: Mrs Ali Watson
t (01394) 450488
e geowat@farmersweekly.net
w tiscover.co.uk

Vesta Cottage ★★★
Self Catering
Contact: Mrs Penny Kay
t (01394) 450652
e kaysorford@pobox.com
w vestacottage.co.uk

ORWELL Cambridgeshire

Retreat ★★★★ *Self Catering*
Contact: Mrs Muriel Meikle
t (01223) 208005
w tiscover.co.uk

OULTON BROAD Suffolk

Maltings Holiday Accommodation ★★★★
Self Catering
Contact: Miss Caroline Sterry
t (01502) 501353
e admin@ivyhousefarm.co.uk
w ivyhousefarm.co.uk

White House Farm ★★★
Self Catering
Contact: Mrs Sharon Hughes
t (01502) 564049
e mail@whitehousefarm.org.uk
w whitehousefarm.org.uk

OUSDEN Suffolk

The Sparrows Nest
Rating Applied For
Self Catering
Contact: Mrs Dymond
t (020) 8948 1408
e christine.dymond@totalise.co.uk

OVERSTRAND Norfolk

Beaches ★★★ *Self Catering*
Contact: Miss Tania Hickman
Lambert Watts Self Catering
t (01263) 513139
e property@lambertwatts.com
w tiscover.co.uk

Buckthorns ★★★★
Self Catering
Contact: Mrs Mandy Reeve
t (01406) 422953
e mail@ealing74.fsnet.co.uk
w tiscover.co.uk

Green Lawn House ★★★
Self Catering
Contact: Anne & John Driscoll
t (01263) 576925
e admiralpd@btopenworld.com
w greenlawnhouse.co.uk

Harbord Road 31 ★★★★
Self Catering
Contact: Mrs Jane Langley
t (01372) 463063
e harbordholidays@tesco.net
w harbord.holidays.co.uk

Poppyland Holiday Cottages
★★★★ *Self Catering*
Contact: Mrs Riches
t (01263) 577473
e poppyland@totalise.co.uk
w broadland.com/poppyland

OXBOROUGH Norfolk

Ferry Farm Cottage ★★★
Self Catering
Contact: Mrs Margaret Wilson
t (01366) 328287
e ferryfarm@btinternet.com
w ferryfarm.btinternet.co.uk

PAKEFIELD Suffolk

Cliff Cottage ★★★
Self Catering
Contact: Mrs Thelma Bruce
t (01502) 501955
w tiscover.co.uk

PASTON Norfolk

Garden Cottage ★★★★
Self Catering
Contact: Mr Nigel Cornwall
t (01692) 407008
w tiscover.co.uk

PELDON Essex

Rose Barn Cottage ★★★★
Self Catering
Contact: Mrs Ariette Everett
Rose Barn
t (01206) 735317
e everettaj@aol.com

PIN MILL Suffolk

Alma Cottage ★★★
Self Catering
Contact: Mr John Pugh
Culver End
t (01453) 872551
e john.pugh@talk21.com

POLSTEAD Suffolk

Holmwood Cottage ★★★★
Self Catering
Contact: Mr Mark Scott
The Cottage Agency Ltd
t (01787) 211115
e mark@grove-cottages.co.uk
w grove-cottages.co.uk

Stables ★★★ *Self Catering*
Contact: Mr Peter Crawford
t (01787) 210368
w tiscover.co.uk

POTTER HEIGHAM Norfolk

Cherry Tree Cottage ★★★★
Self Catering
Contact: Mrs C Whitehead
t (01692) 670189
e ciwhitehead@aol.com

PRESTON ST MARY Suffolk

Overway Cottage ★★★★
Self Catering
Contact: Miss Papillion Luck
t 07815 934182
e luckypaps@hotmail.com

RADLETT Hertfordshire

Constance ★★★
Self Catering
Contact: Mr Clive Miles
t (01923) 854444
e miles@cayd.wanadoo.co.uk
w tiscover.co.uk

RAMPTON Cambridgeshire

39 High Street ★★
Self Catering
Contact: Jaquie Bland
t (01954) 250986

RANWORTH Norfolk

The Cottage ★★★
Self Catering
Norfolk Country Cottages
t (01603) 871872
e info@norfolkcottages.co.uk
w norfolkcottages.co.uk

RATTLESDEN Suffolk

Dower House ★★★★
Self Catering
Contact: Mrs Hilary Voysey
t (01449) 736332
e all@voysey.freeserve.co.uk
w tiscover.co.uk

REDBOURN Hertfordshire

The Beeches ★★★
Self Catering
Contact: Mrs June Surridge
The Beeches
t (01582) 792638

REDE Suffolk

Rede Hall Farm Park ★★★★
Self Catering & Serviced Apartments
t (01284) 850695
e oakley@soils.fsnet.co.uk
w redehallfarmpark.co.uk

REEDHAM Norfolk

Norton Marsh Mill ★★★
Self Catering
Contact: Lesley Cooke
Norfolk Country Cottages
t (01603) 308108
e holidays@swallow-tail.com
w tiscover.co.uk

REEPHAM Norfolk

3 Church Street ★★★
Self Catering
Norfolk Country Cottages
t (01603) 871872
e info@norfolkcottages.co.uk
w norfolkcottages.co.uk

99 Tangham ★★★
Self Catering
Suffolk Country Cottages
t (01502) 725500
e info@suffolkcountrycottages.co.uk
w suffolkcountrycottages.co.uk

Church View 3 (968)
Rating Applied For
Self Catering
Norfolk Country Cottages
t (01603) 871872
e info@norfolkcottages.co.uk
w norfolkcottages.co.uk

Kingfisher, Woodpecker, Otter & Wren ★★★
Self Catering
Norfolk Country Cottages
t (01603) 871872
e info@norfolkcottages.co.uk
w norfolkcottages.co.uk

REYDON Suffolk

27 Nightingale Avenue
★★★ *Self Catering*
Contact: Mrs Rebecca Finlay
Acanthus Property Letting Services Ltd
t (01502) 724033
e websales@southwold-holidays.co.uk
w southwold-holidays.co.uk

The Ark ★★★ *Self Catering*
Suffolk Secrets
t (01379) 651297
e holidays@suffolk.secrets.co.uk
w suffolk-secrets.co.uk

Box End ★★★★
Self Catering
t (01502) 724033

Furze Patch ★★★★
Self Catering
Suffolk Secrets
t (01379) 651297
e holidays@suffolk-secrets.co.uk

Hilltop House ★★★★
Self Catering
Contact: Rebecca Finlay
Acanthus Property Letting Services Ltd
t (01502) 724033

Marigold Cottage ★★★
Self Catering
Contact: Mrs Rebecca Finlay
Acanthus Property Letting Services Ltd
t (01502) 724033
e websales@southwold-holidays.co.uk

The Spinney ★★★★
Self Catering
Suffolk Secrets
t (01502) 722717

Sundial ★★ *Self Catering*
Contact: Mrs Rebecca Finlay
Acanthus Property Letting Services Ltd
t (01502) 724033
e websales@southwold-holidays.co.uk
w southwold-holidays.co.uk

Whimbrel Cottage ★★★
Self Catering
Suffolk Secrets
t (01379) 651297
e holidays@suffolk-secrets.co.uk
w suffolk-secrets.co.uk

RINGSTEAD Norfolk

5 Langford Cottages ★★★
Self Catering
Contact: Mr John Warham
t (01485) 512546
e johnwarham@hotmail.com
w thornhamcottages.co.uk

April Cottage And Tamarisk
★★★★ *Self Catering*
Contact: Mrs Laurice Jarman
t (01553) 676060
e bookings@jariard.fsnet.co.uk
w jariardltd.co.uk

Sandpiper Cottage ★★★★
Self Catering
Contact: Stewart Wood
t (01733) 380107
e sarahwood@fsmail.net

RISELEY
Bedfordshire

Coldham Cottages ★★★★
Self Catering
Contact: Mrs Jean Felce
t (01234) 708489
e info@coldhamcottages.co.uk
w coldhamcottages.co.uk

ROLLESBY
Norfolk

Mickrandella (964)
Rating Applied For
Self Catering
Norfolk Country Cottages
t (01603) 871872
e info@norfolkcottages.co.uk
w norfolkcottages.co.uk

ROUGHTON
Norfolk

Jonas Farm Holiday Barns
★★★★-★★★★★
Self Catering
Contact: Mr Sean Kelly
t (01263) 515438
e info@jonasfarmholidaybarns.co.uk
w jonasfarmholidaybarns.co.uk

Nora Bloggs Cottage ★★
Self Catering
Contact: Mr Varden
t (01263) 513353
w tiscover.co.uk

RUMBURGH
Suffolk

Rumburgh Farm ★★★★
Self Catering
Contact: Mrs Charlotte Binder
t (01986) 781351
e info@rumburghfarm.co.uk
w rumburghfarm.co.uk

RUNCTON HOLME
Norfolk

Thorpland Manor Barns
★★★★ *Self Catering*
Contact: Mrs Mary Caley
t (01553) 810409
e w.p.caley@tesco.net
w thorplandmanorbarns.co.uk

RUNHAM
Norfolk

Peach Tree Cottage/Owl Barn ★★-★★★ *Self Catering*
t (01603) 871872
e info@norfolkcottages.co.uk
w norfolkcottages.co.uk

SAFFRON WALDEN
Essex

Cottage ★★★★ *Self Catering*
Contact: Mr Michael Rigby
t (01799) 501373
e Mike@MCRigby.co.uk
w mcrigby.co.uk

Little Bulls Farmhouse
★★★★ *Self Catering*
Contact: Mr Kiddy
t (01799) 599272
e ajkiddy@cambridge-vacation-homes.com
w cambridge-vacation-homes.com

ST ALBANS
Hertfordshire

69 Albert Street & 20 Keyfield Terrace ★★
Self Catering
Contact: Mrs Carol Nicol
t (01727) 846726

Clarence Cottage ★★★
Self Catering
Contact: Mrs Katie McGoohan
t (01727) 762345
e katie.mcgoohan@ntlworld.com

High Meadows ★★★
Self Catering
Contact: Ms Jenny Hale
t (01727) 865092
e family.hale@ntlworld.co.uk
w akomodation.co.uk

ST OSYTH
Essex

Park Hall Country Cottages
★★★★★ *Self Catering*
Contact: Mrs Trisha Ford
t (01255) 820922
e trish@parkhall.fslife.co.uk
w parkhall.info

SALLE
Norfolk

Lodge Cottage ★★★
Self Catering
Contact: Lynn Carter
t (01603) 879046
e douglas@salleoragnics.com
w salleorganics.com

SALTHOUSE
Norfolk

Dun Cow Public House
★★★ *Self Catering*
Contact: Mrs Kay Groom
t (01263) 740467
w theduncow-salthouse.co.uk

SANDY
Bedfordshire

Acorn Cottage ★★★★
Self Catering
Contact: Mrs Margaret Codd
t (01767) 682332
e margaret@highfield-farm.co.uk
w highfield-farm.co.uk

SAXMUNDHAM
Suffolk

Flora Cottage ★★★★
Self Catering
Suffolk Secrets
t (01379) 651297
e holidays@suffolk-secrets.co.uk
w suffolk-secrets.co.uk

Harveys Mill ★★★★
Self Catering
Contact: Mrs Christine Baker
t (01728) 603212
e mail@bensteadhouse.freeserve.co.uk
w blythweb.co.uk/harveysmill

Riverside Cottage ★★★
Self Catering
Suffolk Secrets
t (01379) 651297
e holidays@suffolk-secrets.co.uk
w suffolk-secrets.co.uk

Rookery Park ★★★★
Self Catering
Contact: Mrs Eden McDonald
Rookery Park
t (01728) 668740
w tiscover.co.uk

SAXON STREET
Cambridgeshire

Syde House ★★ *Self Catering*
Contact: Mrs Susan Greenwood
t (01638) 730044
w tiscover.co.uk

SAXTHORPE
Norfolk

Castle Stables ★★★★
Self Catering
Contact: Mrs G J Hodgson
t (01263) 587510
e saxthorpecastle@fast-mail.net
w tiscover.co.uk

SCULTHORPE
Norfolk

Clarences And Ednas Lodges
★★★ *Self Catering*
Contact: Mrs Beryl Engledow
Caxton House
t (01328) 864785
w tiscover.co.uk

Greenacre Bungalow ★★★
Self Catering
Contact: Mrs J Tuddenham
t (01328) 862858
w tiscover.co.uk

Grove Farm Barns ★★★★★
Self Catering
Contact: Mrs Christine Banson
t (01328) 864427
e johnny@banson.fslife.co.uk
w tiscover.co.uk

SEDGEFORD
Norfolk

Cobble Cottage ★★★★
Self Catering
Norfolk Country Cottages
t (01603) 871872
e info@norfolkcottages.co.uk
w norfolkcottages.co.uk/properties/841

Curlew Cottage ★★★
Self Catering
Contact: Mrs Sandra Hohol
Birds Norfolk Holiday Homes
t (01485) 534267
e shohol@birdsnorfolkholidayhomes.co.uk
w norfolkholidayhomes-birds.co.uk

SHARRINGTON
Norfolk

Daubeney Cottage & The Granary ★★-★★★
Self Catering
Contact: Mrs Robin Burkitt
t (01263) 861412
e daubeneyhallfarm@hotmail.com
w tiscover.co.uk

Gable Cottage ★★
Self Catering
Contact: Miss M Lakey
t (01263) 860393
w tiscover.co.uk

Garden Cottage, Chequers
★★★★ *Self Catering*
Contact: Mrs R M Kimmins
t (01263) 860308
e rosemary@kimmins1.wanadoo.co.uk
w tiscover.co.uk

SHELLEY
Suffolk

Ivy Tree Cottage Annexe
★★★ *Self Catering*
Contact: Mrs Hilary Lock
t (01473) 827632
w tiscover.co.uk

SHERINGHAM
Norfolk

Augusta and Bennett
★★★-★★★★ *Self Catering*
Contact: Mr Trevor Claydon
t (01263) 713998
e enquiries@sheringhamcottages.co.uk
w sheringhamcottages.co.uk

Fisherman's Cottage, Fisherman's Hyde Cottage and Fisherman's Rest Cottage ★★ *Self Catering*
Contact: Mrs Bernadette Bennett
t (020) 7381 0771

Flat 2 ★★★ *Self Catering*
Contact: Mrs Valerie Muggridge
Laburnham
t (01263) 712688

Glendalough ★★★★
Self Catering
Contact: Mrs Janet Teather
t (01263) 825032
e janetandbrian@telinco.co.uk
w broadland.com/glendalough

Greenleas ★★★ *Self Catering*
Norfolk Country Cottages
t (01603) 871872
e info@norfolkcottages.co.uk
w norfolkcottages.co.uk

Hall Cottage ★★★
Self Catering
Contact: Mrs Lesley Cooke
Norfolk Country Cottages
t (01603) 871872
e info@norfolkcottages.co.uk
w norfolkcottages.co.uk

Haven ★★★ *Self Catering*
Contact: Mrs Pam Pilkington
t (01773) 763010
w tiscover.co.uk

Haven ★★★ *Self Catering*
Contact: Mrs Irene Buck
t (01263) 821281
e irene@buck1065.fsnet.co.uk
w thehavenholidayhomesheringham.com

High Lee ★★ *Self Catering*
Contact: Mrs Nelson
t (01245) 262436
w tiscover.co.uk

Ivydene ★★★ *Self Catering*
Contact: Mrs Jenny Linder
t (01263) 822990
e ivydeneholidays@tiscali.co.uk
w http://myweb.tiscali.co.uk/ivydene

Mabel Cottage ★★★
Self Catering
Norfolk Country Cottages
t (01603) 871872
e info@norfolkcottages.co.uk
w norfolkcottages.co.uk

Pinecones ★★★
Self Catering
Contact: Mrs Pat Harvey
t (01263) 824955
e tonyandpat@pinecones.fsnet.co.uk
w pine-cones.co.uk

The Prairie ★★★★
Self Catering
Norfolk Country Cottages
t (01603) 871872
e info@norfolkcottages.co.uk
w norfolkcottages.co.uk

Rogues and Rascals Barns
★★★★ *Self Catering*
Contact: Mrs Clare Wilson
t (01263) 761594
e enquiries@grove-farm.com

Sheringham Cottages
★★★★ *Self Catering*
Contact: Ms Nicola Chamberlain
Cock House
t (01279) 778980
e chamberlain@fsmail.net
w sheringhambreaks.co.uk

Victoria Court ★★★★
Self Catering
Contact: Mr Graham Simmons
t (01263) 823101
w tiscover.co.uk

SHIMPLING
Suffolk

Maltings Farm Cottage
★★★★ *Self Catering*
Contact: Ms Irene Alexander
t (01603) 873378
e info@suffolkcountrycottages.co.uk

SHOTLEY
Suffolk

Apartment ★★★★
Self Catering
Contact: Ms Deborah Baynes
t (01473) 788300
e deb@deborahbaynes.co.uk
w netherhall.net

Box Iron Cottage ★★★
Self Catering
Contact: Mrs Broadway
Threefields
t (01473) 327673
e debroadway@macunlimited.net

SIBLE HEDINGHAM
Essex

Brickwall Farm ★★★★
Self Catering
Contact: Mrs Jean Fuller
t (01787) 460329
e fullers@brickwallfarm.co.uk
w brickwallfarm.co.uk

Pevors Farm Cottages
★★★★ *Self Catering*
Contact: Margaret & John Lewis
t (01787) 460830
e naturist@pevorsfarm.co.uk
w pevorsfarm.co.uk

SIBTON
Suffolk

Bluebell, Bonny, Buttercup & Bertie ★★★★
Self Catering
Contact: Mrs Margaret Gray
t (01728) 668324
e margaret.gray@btinternet.com
w farmstayanglia.co.uk/parkfarm

Cardinal Cottage, Sibton
★★★★ *Self Catering*
Contact: Mr & Mrs Eric Belton
t (01728) 660111
e jan.belton@btinternet.com
w cardinalcottageholidays.co.uk

Mistletoe Cottage ★★★★
Self Catering
Contact: Mr & Mrs Derrick
Cottage Farm
t (01728) 668501
e owlleisure@hotmail.com

SLOLEY
Norfolk

Piggery Cottage ★★★★
Self Catering
Contact: Mrs Ann Jones
t (01692) 536281
e sloley@farmhotel.u-net.com
w norfolkbroads.co.uk/sloleyfarm

SNAPE
Suffolk

Granary And The Forge
★★★★ *Self Catering*
Contact: Mrs Sally Gillett
t (01728) 688254
e e.r.gillett@btinternet.com
w croftfarmsnape.co.uk

Jubilee Cottage ★★★★
Self Catering
Suffolk Secrets
t (01379) 651297
e holidays@suffolk-secrets.co.uk
w suffolk-secrets.co.uk

Mulberry Cottage ★★★★
Self Catering
Suffolk Secrets
t (01379) 651297
e holidays@suffolk-secrets.co.uk
w suffolk-secrets.co.uk

Priory Lodge ★★★★
Self Catering
Contact: Fraser Steewe
Compass House
t (01376) 562616

Shoehorn Cottage ★★★
Self Catering
Contact: Mrs Louise Daley
t 07745 802091

Snape Maltings
★★★–★★★★ *Self Catering*
Contact: Mrs Melanie Threadkeil
t (01728) 688303
e accom@snapemaltings.co.uk
w snapemaltings.co.uk

Studio Flat ★★★
Self Catering
Contact: Mrs Kathy Ball
t (01728) 688327
w churchgarage accommodation.co.uk

Valley Farm Barns ★★★★
Self Catering
Contact: Mr Chris Nicholson
t (01728) 689071
e chrisvalleyfarm@aol.com
w tiscover.co.uk

SNETTISHAM
Norfolk

21 Brent Avenue ★★
Self Catering
Contact: Mrs Sandra Hohol
Birds Norfolk Holiday Homes
t (01485) 534267
e shohol@birdsnorfolkholidayhomes.co.uk
w norfolkholidayhomes-birds.co.uk

Carpenters Lodge ★★★
Self Catering
Contact: Mr Nigel Madgett
t (01485) 541580
e nmmadgett@hotmail.com
w carpenterslodge.co.uk

Coach House ★★★
Self Catering
Contact: Mrs Marion Peters-Loader
The Coach House
t (01485) 544902
e cliveloader@snettisham19.fsnet.co.uk
w tiscover.co.uk

Courtyard 4 ★★★★
Self Catering
Contact: Mrs Jennifer Overson
t (01406) 422569
e jennifer.overson@ntlworld.com
w cottageguide.co.uk/4.thecourtyard

Cursons Cottage ★★★★
Self Catering
Contact: Mrs Averil Campbell
t (01485) 541179
e ian.averilcampbell@btinternet.com
w tiscover.co.uk

Driftwood (956) ★★★★
Self Catering
Norfolk Country Cottages
t (01603) 871872
e info@norfolkcottages.co.uk
w norfolkcottages.co.uk

Hollies Cottage And Grooms Cottage ★★★★ *Self Catering*
Contact: Mrs Elaine Aldridge
t (01485) 541294
w tiscover.co.uk

Lavender Cottage ★★★
Self Catering
Contact: Mrs Rosa Barry
t (01485) 541280
w tiscover.co.uk

Old Barn ★★★★
Self Catering
Contact: Mrs Lynn Shannon
t (01485) 570513
e tm.shannon@virgin.net
w tiscover.co.uk

Old Farm House Cottage
★★★ *Self Catering*
Contact: Mrs Jacqueline Sandy
The Old Farm House Cottage
t (01485) 543106
e jacqueline.sandy@tesco.net
w tiscover.co.uk

Orangery Lodge ★★★★
Self Catering
Contact: Mrs Marion Goldsworthy
t (01485) 541187
e mail@orangerylodge.co.uk
w orangerylodge.co.uk

The Smithy ★★★
Self Catering
Contact: Mrs Sandra Hohol
Birds Norfolk Holiday Homes
t (01485) 534267
e shohol@birdsnorfolkholidayhomes.co.uk
w norfolkholidayhomes-birds.co.uk

Wagtail Cottage ★★★★
Self Catering
Contact: Mrs Sandra Hohol
Birds Norfolk Holiday Homes
t (01485) 534267
e shohol@birdsnorfolkholidayhomes.co.uk
w norfolkholidayhomes-birds.co.uk

SOHAM
Cambridgeshire

Poppies ★★★★ *Self Catering*
Contact: Ms Roseann Allum
t (01353) 624541
w tiscover.co.uk

SOUTH BENFLEET
Essex

Alices Place ★★★★
Self Catering
Contact: Mr Stephen Millward
t (01268) 756283
e info@alices-place.co.uk
w alices-place.co.uk

SOUTH CREAKE
Norfolk

Primrose Cottage ★★★
Self Catering
Contact: Mrs Gail Armstrong
Norfolk Country Cottages
t (01603) 871872
e info@norfolkcottages.co.uk

SOUTH MIMMS
Hertfordshire

The Black Swan ★★–★★★
Self Catering
Contact: Mr Marsterson
t (01707) 644180

SOUTH WALSHAM
Norfolk

Charity Barn ★★★★
Self Catering
Contact: Mr Colin & Lynda Holmes
Charity Farm
t (01603) 270410
e info@charitybarn.co.uk
w charitybarn.co.uk

SOUTHBURGH
Norfolk

Park Farm Barns ★★★
Self Catering
Contact: Mrs Rosemary Bunning
t (01362) 820702
e grbunning@aol.com
w tiscover.co.uk

SOUTHEND-ON-SEA
Essex

Everhome Apartments ★★
Self Catering
Contact: Mr Malcolm Taylor
t (01702) 434320
e malcolm-t@btconnect.com
w tiscover.co.uk

SOUTHMINSTER
Essex

Avonmore ★★★★
Self Catering
Contact: Mr Bull
t (01787) 280063
e maryrosedaniels@yahoo.co.uk
w tiscover.co.uk

SOUTHWOLD
Suffolk

11 Chester Road ★★★
Self Catering
Contact: H A Adnams
98 High Street
t (01502) 723292
w haadnams.com

15 Pier Avenue ★★★
Self Catering
Suffolk Secrets
t (01379) 651297
e holidays@suffolk-secrets.co.uk
w suffolk-secrets.co.uk

15 Stradbroke Road ★★★
Self Catering
Contact: H A Adnams
89 High Street
t (01502) 723292
w haadnams.com

4 Pier Court
Rating Applied For
Self Catering
Suffolk Holidays Ltd.
t (01502) 723571
e sales@holidaysinsuffolk.co.uk
w holidaysinsuffolk.co.uk

8 Dunwich Road ★★★★
Self Catering
Suffolk Secrets
t (01379) 651297
e holidays@suffolk-secrets.co.uk

Anchor Point ★★★
Self Catering
Contact: Mrs Rebecca Finlay
Acanthus Property Letting Services Ltd
t (01502) 724033
e websales@southwold-holidays.co.uk
w southwold-holidays.co.uk

Blackshore Corner ★★★★
Self Catering
Suffolk Secrets
t (01379) 651297
e holidays@suffolk-secrets.co.uk
w suffolk-secrets.co.uk

Blackshore Cottage ★★★
Self Catering
Contact: Mrs Rebecca Finlay
Acanthus Property Letting Services Ltd
t (01502) 724033
e websales@southwold-holidays.co.uk
w southwold-holidays.co.uk

Bligh Cottage
Rating Applied For
Self Catering
Suffolk Holidays Ltd.
t (01502) 723571
e sales@holidaysinsuffolk.co.uk

The Bolt Hole ★★★
Self Catering
Suffolk Secrets
t (01379) 651297
e holidays@suffolk-secrets.co.uk
w suffolk-secrets.co.uk

Castle Keep ★★★★
Self Catering
Contact: Mrs Rebecca Finlay
Acanthus Property Letting Services Ltd
t (01502) 724033
e websales@southwold-holidays.co.uk
w tiscover.co.uk

Caterer House ★★★
Self Catering
Suffolk Secrets
t (01379) 651297
e holidays@suffolk-secrets.co.uk
w suffolk-secrets.co.uk

Cautley Cottage ★★★
Self Catering
Contact: Mr & Mrs David & Caroline Goodman
t (020) 8444 7210
e enquiries@southwoldcottageholidays.co.uk
w southwoldcottageholidays.co.uk

Cherry Trees ★★★★
Self Catering
Suffolk Secrets
t (01379) 651297
e holidays@suffolk-secrets.co.uk
w suffolk-secrets.co.uk

Chicago Beach Villa ★★★
Self Catering
Suffolk Holidays Ltd.
t (01502) 723571
e sales@holidaysinsuffolk.co.uk

Christmas Cottage
Rating Applied For
Self Catering
Suffolk Holidays Ltd.
t (01502) 723571
e sales@holidaysinsuffolk.co.uk

Cliff House ★★★★
Self Catering
Suffolk Secrets
t (01502) 722717
e holidays@suffolk-secrets.co.uk
w suffolk-secrets.co.uk

The Coach House and Rosemary Cottage ★★★
Self Catering
Contact: Phil & Philippa Champain
Suffolk Secrets
t (01502) 725414
e reydoncottages@btinternet.com
w rosemarycottage.southwold.info

Cobbler's Cottage ★★★
Self Catering
Contact: Rebecca Finlay
Acanthus Property Letting Services Ltd
t (01502) 724033

Corner Cottage ★★★
Self Catering
Contact: Mrs Daphne Hall
t (01502) 723292
w tiscover.co.uk

The Cottage ★★★★
Self Catering
Contact: Mr Thomas
t (01502) 723561

The Dolls House ★★★ *Self Catering & Serviced Apartments*
Suffolk Secrets
t (01502) 722717
e holidays@suffolk-secrets.co.uk
w suffolk-secrets.co.uk

Ealing Cottage
Rating Applied For
Self Catering
Suffolk Holidays Ltd.
t (01502) 723571

East Cliff 10A ★★★
Self Catering
Contact: Mrs Rebecca Finlay
Acanthus Property Letting Services Ltd
t (01502) 724033
e sales@southwold-holidays.co.uk
w southwold-holidays.co.uk

Eastway Cottage ★★★
Self Catering
Contact: Mrs Rebecca Finlay
Acanthus Property Letting Services Ltd
t (01502) 724033
e websales@southwold-holidays.co.uk

Elms Mews ★★★
Self Catering
Contact: Mrs Rebecca Finlay
Acanthus Property Letting Services Ltd
t (01502) 724033
e websales@southwold-holidays.co.uk
w southwold-holidays.co.uk

Fairwinds ★★ *Self Catering*
Contact: H A Adnams
t (01502) 723292

Far Horizons ★★★★
Self Catering
Suffolk Secrets
t (01502) 722717
e holidays@suffolk-secrets.co.uk
w suffolk-secrets.co.uk

Farthings ★★★ *Self Catering*
Suffolk Holidays Ltd.
t (01502) 723571
e sales@holidaysinsuffolk.co.uk

Fisherman's Cottage ★★★
Self Catering
Contact: H A Adnams
98 High Street
t (01502) 723292

Garden Cottage ★★★
Self Catering
Contact: Mrs Carol Wigg
Jacaranda House & Home Services
t (01502) 568580
w tiscover.co.uk

Harbour Cottage ★★★
Self Catering
Suffolk Secrets
t (01379) 651297
e holidays@suffolk-secrets.co.uk
w suffolk-secrets.co.uk

The Haven ★★★
Self Catering
Suffolk Secrets
t (01502) 722717
e holidays@suffolk-secrets.co.uk
w suffolk-secrets.co.uk

Heathside ★★★
Self Catering
Contact: Mrs Rebecca Finlay
Acanthus Property Letting Services Ltd
t (01502) 724033
e websales@southwold-holidays.co.uk
w southwold-holidays.co.uk

Holly Cottage ★★★★
Self Catering
Contact: Mrs Rebecca Finlay
Acanthus Property Letting Services Ltd
t (01502) 722717
e websales@southwold-holidays.co.uk
w southwold-holidays.co.uk

Horseshoe Cottage ★★★
Self Catering
Contact: Mrs Rebecca Finlay
Acanthus Property Letting Services Ltd
t (01502) 724033
e websales@southwold-holidays.co.uk
w southwold-holidays.co.uk

Jersey Lodge ★★★★
Self Catering
Suffolk Secrets
t (01379) 651297
e holidays@suffolk-secrets.co.uk
w suffolk-secrets.co.uk

Kestrel Cottage ★★★★
Self Catering
Contact: Mrs Rebecca Finlay
Acanthus Property Letting Services Ltd
t (01502) 724033
e websales@southwold.co.uk
w southwold-holidays.co.uk

Lighthouse View ★★★
Self Catering
Contact: Mrs Rebecca Finlay
Acanthus Property Letting Services Ltd
t (01502) 724033
e sales@southwold-holidays.co.uk
w southwold-holidays.co.uk

Little Blue House ★★
Self Catering
Contact: Mrs Diana Wright
t (01206) 738003
w tiscover.co.uk

Little Garth ★★★
Self Catering
Contact: Mr Bill Tynan
t (01473) 434642
e bill_tynan@hotmail.com
w southwold.ws/littlegarth.co.uk

Little Haven
Rating Applied For
Self Catering
Contact: Cheryl Gabriel
t (020) 3222 4087

Maisonette ★★★★
Self Catering
Contact: H A Adnams
t (01502) 723292

Manor Lodge ★★★
Self Catering
Contact: Mrs Rebecca Finlay
Acanthus Property Letting Services Ltd
t (01502) 724033
e websales@southwold-holidays.co.uk
w southwold-holidays.co.uk

Middling ★★★ *Self Catering*
Suffolk Secrets
t (01502) 722717
e holidays@suffolk-secrets.co.uk
w suffolk-secrets.co.uk

No 12 The Craighurst
★★★★ *Self Catering*
Contact: Mrs Jennifer Tallon
Acanthus Property Letting Services Ltd
t (01502) 724033
e sales@southwold-holidays.co.uk

No. 7 The Craighurst ★★★
Self Catering
Contact: Mrs Rebecca Finlay
Acanthus Property Letting Services Ltd
t (01502) 724033

Nuage ★★★★ *Self Catering*
Suffolk Holidays Ltd.
t (01502) 723571
e sales@holidaysinsuffolk.co.uk

Old Rope House ★★★★
Self Catering
Contact: Mrs Sian Mortlock
t (01502) 724769
e sian@theoldropehouse.co.uk
w tiscover.co.uk

The Olde Banke House
★★★★ *Self Catering*
Contact: Mrs Rebecca Finlay
Acanthus Property Letting Services Ltd
t (01502) 724033
e websales@southwold-holidays.co.uk
w southwold-holidays.co.uk

Owl Cottage ★★★
Self Catering
Contact: Mrs Rebecca Finlay
Acanthus Property Letting Services Ltd
t (01502) 724033
e websales@southwold-holidays.co.uk
w southwold-holidays.co.uk

Pebbles Cottage ★★★
Self Catering
Contact: Mrs Rebecca Finlay
Acanthus Property Letting Services Ltd
t (01502) 724033
e sales@southwold-holidays.co.uk
w southwold-holidays.co.uk

Pier Court 1 ★★★
Self Catering
Contact: Mrs Rebecca Finlay
Acanthus Property Letting Services Ltd
t (01502) 724033
e websales@southwold-holidays.co.uk
w southwold-holidays.co.uk

Pink House ★★★
Self Catering
Suffolk Holidays Ltd.
t (01502) 723571
e sales@holidaysinsuffolk.co.uk

Poplar Hall ★★★★
Self Catering
Contact: Mrs Anna Garwood
t (01502) 578549
w southwold.ws/poplar-hall

Poppys
Rating Applied For
Self Catering
Suffolk Holidays Ltd.
t (01502) 723571
e sales@holidaysinsuffolk.co.uk

Red Roofs ★★★
Self Catering
Suffolk Secrets
t (01379) 651297
e holidays@suffolk-secrets.co.uk
w suffolk-secrets.co.uk

The Reeds ★★★
Self Catering
Suffolk Secrets
t (01502) 722717
w suffolk-secrets.co.uk

The Retreat ★★★
Self Catering
t (01502) 724033
e websales@southwold-holidays.co.uk

Saffron and Church Green Cottage ★★★★ *Self Catering*
Contact: Mrs Rebecca Finlay
Acanthus Property Letting Services Ltd
t (01502) 724033
e websales@southwold-holidays.co.uk
w southwold-holidays.co.uk

Saint James Green 20 ★★
Self Catering
Contact: Mrs Doris Burley
t (01502) 724096
w tiscover.co.uk

Saltings ★★★ *Self Catering*
Suffolk Secrets
t (01379) 651297
e holidays@suffolk-secrets.co.uk
w suffolk-secrets.co.uk

Seabreeze ★★★
Self Catering
Contact: Mrs Rebecca Finlay
Acanthus Property Letting Services Ltd
t (01502) 724033
e websales@southwold-holidays.co.uk
w southwold-holidays.co.uk

Seaward ★★★ *Self Catering*
Contact: Mrs Rebecca Finlay
Acanthus Property Letting Services Ltd
t (01502) 724033
e websales@southwold-holidays.co.uk
w southwold-holidays.co.uk

The Shed ★★★ *Self Catering*
Suffolk Secrets
t (01379) 651297
e holidays@suffolk-secrets.co.uk
w suffolk-secrets.co.uk

Shrimp Cottage ★★★
Self Catering
Suffolk Secrets
t (01379) 651297
e holidays@suffolk-secrets.co.uk
w suffolk-secrets.co.uk

Smoke House ★★★
Self Catering
Suffolk Holidays Ltd.
t (01502) 723571
e sales@holidaysinsuffolk.co.uk

Solely Southwold ★★★
Self Catering
Contact: Miss Kathy Oliver
t (01502) 578383
e kathy@solely-southwold.co.uk
w solely-southwold.co.uk

South Cliff Cottage ★★★
Self Catering
Contact: Mrs Rebecca Finlay
Acanthus Property Letting Services Ltd
t (01502) 724033
e websales@southwold-holidays.co.uk

Southwold Holiday Home
★★★ *Self Catering*
Contact: Mr Wayne Thomas
t (01502) 724402
e waynethomas60@aol.com
w southwoldholidayhome.co.uk

Suffolk House ★★★
Self Catering
Contact: Mrs Betty Freeman
t (01502) 723742
w tiscover.co.uk

Summerly Cottage ★★★
Self Catering
Contact: Mr & Mrs David & Caroline Goodman
t (020) 8444 7210
e enquiries@southwoldcottageholidays.co.uk
w southwoldcottageholidays.co.uk

Suton Cottage ★★
Self Catering
Suffolk Secrets
t (01379) 651297
e holidays@suffolk-secrets.co.uk
w suffolk-secrets.co.uk

This Is It ★★★★
Self Catering
Suffolk Secrets
t (01502) 722717
e holidays@suffolk-secrets.co.uk

Tivoli ★★★ *Self Catering*
Suffolk Secrets
t (01502) 722717
e holidays@suffolk-secrets.co.uk
w suffolk-secrets.co.uk

Trinity Street 10 ★★★★
Self Catering
Contact: Mrs Rebecca Finlay
Acanthus Property Letting Services Ltd
t (01502) 724033
e websales@southwold-holidays.co.uk
w southwold-holidays.co.uk

Victoria Cottage ★★
Self Catering
Contact: Mrs Rebecca Finlay
Acanthus Property Letting Services Ltd
t (01502) 724033
e websales@southwold-holidays.co.uk
w southwold-holidays.co.uk

Waimana
Rating Applied For
Self Catering
Suffolk Holidays Ltd.
t (01502) 723571
e sales@holidaysinsuffolk.co.uk

Weathervane ★★★
Self Catering
Suffolk Secrets
t (01379) 651297
e holidays@suffolksecrets.co.uk
w suffolk-secrets.co.uk

Weavers Cottage ★★★
Self Catering
Contact: H A Adnams
98 High Street
t (01502) 723292
e haadnams-sales@ic24.net
w haadnams.com

The Wee House
Rating Applied For
Self Catering
Suffolk Holidays Ltd.
t (01502) 723571
e sales@holidaysinsuffolk.co.uk

Well Cottage ★★★
Self Catering
Suffolk Secrets
t (01502) 722717
e holidays@suffolk-secrets.co.uk

Whitehouse Barns ★★★★
Self Catering
Contact: Mrs Penelope Roskell-Griffiths
t (020) 8802 6258
e peneloperoskell@blueyonder.co.uk
w whitehousebarns.co.uk

The Windbreak ★★★
Self Catering
Contact: H A Adnams
t (01502) 723292

SPEXHALL
Suffolk

Rose Cottage ★★★
Self Catering
Contact: Mrs Hammond
South Lodge
t (01502) 575894
w tiscover.co.uk

STALHAM
Norfolk

Chapelfield Cottage Flat
★★★ *Self Catering*
Contact: Mr Gary Holmes
t (01692) 582173
e gary@cinqueportsmarine.freeserve.co.uk
w whiteswan.u-net.com

STANBRIDGE
Bedfordshire

Bluegate Farm Holiday Cottages ★★★★
Self Catering
Contact: Mrs Philippa Michie
t (01525) 210621
e enquiries@bluegatecottages.co.uk
w tiscover.co.uk

STANHOE
Norfolk

Pilgrims ★★★ *Self Catering*
Contact: Mrs Lesley Cooke
Norfolk Country Cottages
t (01603) 871872
e info@norfolkcottages.co.uk
w norfolkcottages.co.uk

Vine Cottage ★★★
Self Catering
Contact: Mrs Alyson Aronson
t (01737) 832584
e alyson.aronson@freeuk.com
w tiscover.co.uk

STANSTED MOUNTFITCHET
Essex

Walpole Farm House ★★★
Self Catering
Contact: Mrs Jill Walton
t (01279) 812265
w tiscover.co.uk

STANTON
Suffolk

Cottage Farm Annexe
Rating Applied For
Self Catering
Suffolk Country Cottages
t (01502) 725500
e info@suffolkcountrycottage.co.uk
w suffolkcountrycottages.co.uk

STIBBARD
Norfolk

Kings Cottage Barn ★★★
Self Catering
Contact: Douglas Wilks
t (01328) 829109
e info@kings-cottage.co.uk
w kings-cottage.co.uk

STIFFKEY
Norfolk

Apple Tree Cottage ★★★
Self Catering
Contact: Mr Brian & Carol Braid
t (0116) 271 6783
w tiscover.co.uk

Bella's Cottage ★★★
Self Catering
Norfolk Country Cottages
t (01603) 871872
e info@norfolkcottages.co.uk
w norfolkcottages.co.uk

Foundry Cottage (844)
★★★ *Self Catering*
Norfolk Country Cottages
t (01603) 871872
e info@norfolkcottages.co.uk
w norfolkcottages.co.uk

Harbour House ★★★★
Self Catering
Contact: Mr Keith Bindley
t (01603) 270637
e bindley@tesco.net
w tiscover.co.uk

Hawthorns ★★★
Self Catering
Contact: Mrs Madeline Hickey-Smith
t (01223) 572316
e hawthorns_norfolk@hotmail.com
w hawthorns.info

Mount Tabor ★★★
Self Catering
Contact: Mrs Pat Norris
t (0161) 633 6834
e roger@stiffkeycottage.fsnet.co.uk
w tiscover.co.uk

Primrose Cottage ★★★ *Self Catering & Serviced Apartments*
Contact: Mrs Pearson
t (01328) 830303
w tiscover.co.uk

Red Lion Cottages 2 ★★★
Self Catering
Contact: Ms Jane Whitaker
t (01606) 892368
e jane.pathways@virgin.net
w tiscover.co.uk

Shrimp Cottage ★★
Self Catering
Contact: Mrs Lesley Cooke
Norfolk Country Cottages Ref. 658
t (01603) 871872
e info@norfolkcottages.co.uk
w norfolkcottages.co.uk/stiffkey_658.htm

STILTON
Cambridgeshire

Orchard Cottage ★★★★
Self Catering
Contact: Mrs Jennifer Higgo
t (01572) 737420
w higgo.com/orchard

STISTED
Essex

Ballaglass ★★★★
Self Catering
Contact: Mrs Sally Dunn
t (01376) 331409
e ballaglass@btopenworld.com
w http://uk.geocities.com/ballaglass@btinternet.com

STOKE-BY-NAYLAND
Suffolk

Cobbs Cottage ★★★★
Self Catering
Contact: Mr Mark Scott
t (01206) 262216
e mark@grove-cottages.co.uk
w grove-cottages.co.uk

STOWMARKET
Suffolk

Barn Cottages ★★★★
Self Catering
Contact: Mrs Maria Tydeman
t (01449) 711229
e maria@barncottages.co.uk
w barncottages.co.uk

Kimberley Cottage ★★★
Self Catering
Contact: Mr Brian Whiting
t (01449) 677766
e brianwhiting.kimberleyhall@virgin.net
w kimberleyhall.biz

STRADBROKE
Suffolk

Cornhouse Cottage ★★★★
Self Catering
Contact: Mrs Charmaine Cooper
Hepwood Lodge
t (01379) 384256
e cornhouse@hepwoodcottages.co.uk
w hepwoodcottages.co.uk

STRATFORD ST ANDREW
Suffolk

Toad Hall Flat ★★★
Self Catering
Contact: Mr Perry & Bunty Hunt
t (01728) 603463
e perryhunt@keme.co.uk
w tiscover.co.uk

STRATFORD ST MARY
Suffolk

Donkey Cottage ★★★
Self Catering
Suffolk Country Cottages
t (01502) 725500
e info@suffolkcountrycottages.co.uk
w suffolkcountrycottages.co.uk

STUTTON
Suffolk

The Lookout ★★★★
Self Catering
Contact: John & Penny Fairrie
t (01473) 328294
e fairrie@holly-farm.fsnet.co.uk
w mrsjanegoodltd.co.uk

SUDBURY
Suffolk

Six Bells Barn ★★★
Self Catering
Contact: Mrs Janet Martin
t 07002 782000
e janet.martin@tesco.net
w tiscover.co.uk

SURLINGHAM
Norfolk

Studio at Long Acre Cottage
★★★ *Self Catering*
Contact: Ms Susan Alexandra
t (01508) 538959
e sodzerna@btinternet.com

SWAFFHAM
Norfolk

Hall Barn ★★★ *Self Catering*
Contact: Ms Brenda Wilbourn
t (01366) 328794
e brenda@hall-barn.freeserve.co.uk
w cottageguide.co.uk/hallbarn

SWANTON ABBOTT
Norfolk

Lilac Barn (963)
Rating Applied For
Self Catering
Norfolk Country Cottages
t (01603) 871872
e info@norfolkcottages.co.uk
w norfolkcottages.co.uk

Magnolia Cottage ★★★
Self Catering
Contact: Mrs Christine Nockolds
t (01692) 538481
w tiscover.co.uk

Oak Tree Barn (801)
Rating Applied For
Self Catering
Norfolk Country Cottages
t (01603) 871872
e info@norfolkcottages.co.uk
w norfolkcottages.co.uk

Walnut Tree Barn ★★★★
Self Catering
Contact: Mrs Sally Page
t (01692) 538888
e sales@citibuild.co.uk
w broadland.com

SWANTON MORLEY
Norfolk

Teal Heron And Grebe Cottage, Swanton Morley
★★★ *Self Catering*
Contact: Mrs Sally Marsham
t (01362) 637300
e waterfallfarm@tesco.net
w tiscover.co.uk

SYDERSTONE
Norfolk

Harrow Barn ★★★★
Self Catering
Contact: Miss Catherine Ringer
t (01485) 578287
e chringeris@hotmail.com
w norfolk-holiday-cottages.co.uk/cottage/harrowbarn.html

SYLEHAM
Suffolk

The Apartment at Syleham House ★★★ *Self Catering*
Contact: Matilda Ziegler
t (01379) 668325
e mattie1964@hotmail.com

TATTERSETT
Norfolk

The Old Dairy ★★★★
Self Catering
Norfolk Country Cottages
t (01603) 871872
e info@norfolkcottages.co.uk
w norfolkcottages.co.uk

Tatt Valley Holiday Cottages
★★★★ *Self Catering*
Contact: Mr Thomas Hurn
t (01485) 528506
e enquiries@norfolkholidayhomes.co.uk
w norfolkholidayhomes.co.uk

TATTINGSTONE
Suffolk

Cowshed ★★★★★
Self Catering
Contact: Mrs Annie Eaves
t 0870 710 8550
e moo@suffolk-cowshed.co.uk
w suffolk-cowshed.co.uk

TAVERHAM
Norfolk

Shingle Cottage ★★★
Self Catering
Contact: Roy/Judy Page
t (01603) 861476
e enquiries@shinglecottage.co.uk
w shinglecottage.co.uk

TERRINGTON ST CLEMENT
Norfolk

Northgate Lodge Flat ★★★
Self Catering
Contact: Mrs June Howling
t (01553) 828428
e jbh@interads.co.uk
w tiscover.co.uk

THEBERTON
Suffolk

The Cottage ★★★
Self Catering
Suffolk Secrets
t (01502) 722717

Woodpecker Cottage ★★★
Self Catering
Suffolk Secrets
t (01379) 651297
e holidays@suffolk-secrets.co.uk
w suffolk-secrets.co.uk

THETFORD
Norfolk

Forest Lodge Holidays, Santon Downham
Rating Applied For
Self Catering
Contact: Mr & Mrs Jeff & Hannah Hibbs
Little Lodge Farm
t (01842) 813438
e info@littlelodgefarm.co.uk
w littlelodgefarm.co.uk

River Lodge ★★★★
Self Catering
Contact: Mrs Susan Burton
t (01362) 821570
e andy@abaltd.demon.co.uk
w tiscover.co.uk

THORNAGE
Norfolk

Daisy Lodge ★★
Self Catering
Contact: Mrs Melanie Hickling
t (01263) 761705
e primrosefarmbarns@tiscali.co.uk
w tiscover.co.uk

Well Cottage & Dairy Cottage ★★★ *Self Catering*
Norfolk Country Cottages
t (01603) 871872
w norfolkcottages.co.uk

THORNDON
Suffolk

Manor Farm Barn ★★★★
Self Catering
Contact: Mrs Janet Edgecombe
t (01379) 678437
e janet@manor-farm-barn.co.uk
w moatfarm.co.uk

THORNHAM
Norfolk

21 Shepherds Pightle
★★★★ *Self Catering*
Contact: Mrs Susan Sadler
Oakleigh
t (01485) 534991

3 Malthouse Court, off Green Lane ★★★
Self Catering
Contact: Mrs Sandra Hohol
Birds Norfolk Holiday Homes
t (01485) 534267
e shohol@birdsnorfolkholidayhomes.co.uk
w norfolkholidayhomes-birds.co.uk

8 Malthouse Court ★★★
Self Catering
Contact: Adrian Forsell
t (01858) 565410
e forsell@aforsell.fsbusiness.co.uk
w forsell-property.com

Brent Cottage ★★★
Self Catering
Contact: Mrs Sandra Hohol
Birds Norfolk Holiday Homes
t (01485) 534267
e shohol@birdsnorfolkholidayhomes.co.uk
w norfolkholidayhomes-birds.co.uk

Linzel Cottage ★★★★
Self Catering
Contact: Mrs Sandra Hohol
Birds Norfolk Holiday Homes
t (01485) 534267
e shohol@birdsnorfolkholidayhomes.co.uk
w norfolkholidayhomes-birds.co.uk

Little Gull And Sanderling
★★★-★★★★ *Self Catering*
Contact: Mr John Warham
t (01485) 512546
e johnwarham@hotmail.com
w thornhamcottages.co.uk

Malthouse Cottages ★★
Self Catering
Contact: Mrs Leslie Rigby
Brindle Cottage
t (01733) 380399
e leslierigby@castor.freeserve.co.uk

Manor Farm Cottages
★★★-★★★★ *Self Catering*
Contact: Mrs Margaret Goddard
t (01485) 512272
w tiscover.co.uk

Old Maltings ★★★★
Self Catering
Contact: Mr Simon Barclay
Kett Country Cottages
t (01328) 856853
e info@kettcountrycottages.co.uk
w kettcountrycottages.co.uk

Oyster Cottage
★★★-★★★★ *Self Catering*
Contact: Mrs Geraldine Tibbs
Cole Green Cottage
t (01485) 571770
w tiscover.co.uk

Rosemary Cottage ★★★★
Self Catering
Contact: Mrs Gail Armstrong
Norfolk Country Cottages
t (01603) 871872
e info@norfolkcottages.co.uk

West End Cottages 1 ★★
Self Catering
Contact: Mr Hardy
t (01223) 263859
e holidayinthornham@yahoo.com
w tiscover.co.uk

THORPE MARKET
Norfolk

Poppylands And Puddleduck ★★★★
Self Catering
Contact: Mr Roy Castleton
t (01263) 833219
e royecastleton@aol.com
w poppyland.com

THORPE MORIEUX
Suffolk

Maltings Farm Holiday Cottages ★★★ *Self Catering*
Contact: Mrs Rachel Bell
t (01284) 828843
e tim-bell@fsbdial.co.uk
w tiscover.co.uk

Potash Farm Cottage
★★★★ *Self Catering*
t (01284) 828396
e emmadi6@aol.com

THORPENESS
Suffolk

2 The Dunes ★★★
Self Catering
Suffolk Secrets
t (01379) 651297

7 Uplands Road ★★★
Self Catering
Contact: Mrs Diane Holmes
t (01728) 454648
w tiscover.co.uk

Hope Cove Cottage ★★★★
Self Catering
Contact: Mrs Irene Pearman
t (01279) 771281
e irene.pearman@whestates.com
w tiscover.co.uk

House in the Clouds ★★★
Self Catering
Contact: Mrs Le Comber
The House in the Clouds
t (020) 7224 3615
e houseintheclouds@btopenworld.com
w houseintheclouds.co.uk

Micawbers ★★★★
Self Catering
Contact: Mrs Joan Hockley
Piggotts Farm
t (01279) 771281
e j.hockley@whestates.com
w tiscover.co.uk

Old Homes 4 ★★★★ *Self Catering & Serviced Apartments*
Contact: Mrs Ellen Nall
t (01986) 798908
w tiscover.co.uk

Saseenos Cottage ★★★★
Self Catering
Contact: Mrs Fiona Kerr
Easton Farm Park
t (01728) 746475
e info@eastonfarmpark.co.uk
w eastonfarmpark.co.uk

THUNDRIDGE
Hertfordshire

Wednesday House ★★★★
Self Catering
Contact: Mrs Annie Jenkins
t (01920) 465696
e anniejenkins@dial.pipex.com
w picturetrail.com/wednesdayhouse

THURLEIGH
Bedfordshire

Scald Farm ★★ *Self Catering*
Contact: Mr Reg Towler
t (01234) 771996
w tiscover.co.uk

THURNE
Norfolk

4 Old Lion Cottages ★★★★
Self Catering
Norfolk Country Cottages
t (01603) 871872
e info@norfolkcottages.co.uk
w norfolkcottages.co.uk

THURSFORD
Norfolk

Hayloft ★★★ *Self Catering*
Contact: Mrs Ann Green
Old Coach House
t (01328) 878273

Ransome Lodge The Meadows ★★★★
Self Catering
Contact: Mrs Lesley Cooke
Norfolk Country Cottages
t (01603) 871872
e info@norfolkcottages.co.uk
w norfolkcottages.co.uk

Sentinel Lodge (953)
Rating Applied For
Self Catering
Norfolk Country Cottages
t (01603) 871872
e info@norfolkcottages.co.uk
w norfolkcottages.co.uk

Station Farm Barn Holiday Cottages ★★★ *Self Catering*
Contact: Mrs Sheena Walton
Norfolk Barn Holidays
t (01353) 720419
e enquiries@norfolk-barn-holidays.co.uk
w norfolk-barn-holidays.co.uk

TOFTREES
Norfolk

The Dairy
Rating Applied For
Self Catering
Contact: Simon Barclay
Kett Country Cottages Ltd
t (01328) 856853
e info@kettcountrycottages.co.uk

TOLLESBURY
Essex

Fernleigh ★★★ *Self Catering*
Contact: Mrs Gillian Willson
t (01621) 868245
e gillwillson@onetel.com
w tiscover.co.uk

TOLLESHUNT KNIGHTS
Essex

Rosemary Cottage
Rating Applied For
Self Catering
Contact: Mr Adrian Tucker
t (01621) 816753
w tiscover.co.uk

TRIMINGHAM
Norfolk

Church Meadow Cottage ★★★★ *Self Catering*
t (01603) 871872
e info@norfolkcottages.co.uk
w norfolkcottages.co.uk

TRIMLEY
Suffolk

Treacle Pot Cottage ★★★
Self Catering
Contact: Mr Richard Borley
t (01394) 275367
w suffolk-holiday-cottages.co.uk

TRIMLEY ST MARTIN
Suffolk

Oak Cottage ★★★
Self Catering
Contact: Mrs Gillian Young
t (01394) 277168
w tiscover.co.uk

TRUNCH
Norfolk

Robin Cottage ★★★
Self Catering
Norfolk Country Cottages
t (01603) 871872
e info@norfolkcottages.co.uk
w norfolkcottages.co.uk

TUNSTALL
Suffolk

Knoll Cottage ★★★★
Self Catering
Contact: Mrs Jill Robinson
t (01728) 685084
e jill@timbertop.co.uk
w timbertop.co.uk

TUNSTEAD
Norfolk

Partridge Farm Cottage (966)
Rating Applied For
Self Catering
Norfolk Country Cottages
t (01603) 871872
e info@norfolkcottages.co.uk
w norfolkcottages.co.uk

UFFORD
Suffolk

Grove Farm Cottage ★★★
Self Catering
Contact: Mrs Tricia Rolph
t (01394) 380154
w tiscover.co.uk

UPPER SHERINGHAM
Norfolk

Barn Owl Cottage ★★★
Self Catering
Contact: Jim & Jackie Flynn
Lodge Cottage
t (01263) 821445
e stay@visitlodgecottage.com
w visitlodgecottage.com

WALBERSWICK
Suffolk

Ash Cottage
Rating Applied For
Self Catering
Suffolk Holidays Ltd.
t (01502) 723571
e sales@holidaysinsuffolk.co.uk

Ferry Knoll ★★★★
Self Catering
Contact: Mrs Rebecca Finlay
Acanthus Property Letting Services Ltd
t (01502) 724033
e websales@southwold-holidays.co.uk
w southwold-holidays.co.uk

Lea Cottage ★★★★
Self Catering
Contact: Mrs Rebecca Finlay
Acanthus Property Letting Services Ltd
t (01502) 724033
e websales@southwold-holidays.co.uk
w southwold-holidays.co.uk

No 1 Blackshore ★★★
Self Catering
Suffolk Secrets
t (01379) 651297
e holidays@suffolk-secrets.co.uk
w suffolk-secrets.co.uk

The Shieling ★★★
Self Catering
t (01502) 723292
e haadnams_lets@i.c.24.net
w tiscover.co.uk

Stuckie Ben ★★★
Self Catering
Suffolk Secrets
t (01379) 651297
e holidays@suffolk-secrets.co.uk
w suffolk-secrets.co.uk

White Cottage ★★★
Self Catering
Contact: Mrs Rebecca Finlay
Acanthus Property Letting Services Ltd
t (01502) 724033
e websales@southwold-holidays.co.uk
w southwold-holidays.co.uk

WALCOTT
Norfolk

Tamarisk ★★★★
Self Catering
Contact: Mrs Jane Shulver
Point House
t (01692) 651126
e pointhouse@hotmail.com
w norfolkcottages.co.uk

WALDRINGFIELD
Suffolk

Low Farm Estate Services ★★★★ *Self Catering*
Contact: Mr Lee York
t (01473) 736475
e cottages@lowfarm.fsbusiness.co.uk
w lowfarm.tk

Windy Bank ★★
Self Catering
Contact: Mrs Rosemary Routledge
The Court
t (01275) 474472
e routledge.court@virgin.net

WALSINGHAM
Norfolk

16 The Hill ★★★
Self Catering
Norfolk Country Cottages
t (01603) 871872
e info@norfolkcottages.co.uk
w norfolkcottages.co.uk

End Cottage (943) ★★★★
Self Catering
Norfolk Country Cottages
t (01603) 871872
e info@norfolkcottages.co.uk
w norfolkcottages.co.uk

WANGFORD
Suffolk

Corner Cottage ★★★
Self Catering
Contact: Mrs Pat Grange
t (01502) 578629
w tiscover.co.uk

Field View ★★★
Self Catering
Contact: Mrs Paula Burns
t (01788) 535505
e paulaburns@btinternet.com
w cottageguide.co.uk/fieldview

The Old Bake House ★★★
Self Catering
Suffolk Holidays Ltd.
t (01502) 723751
e sales@holidaysinsuffolk.co.uk

Old Butchers ★★★
Self Catering
Suffolk Secrets
t (01379) 651297

WASHBROOK
Suffolk

Stebbings Cottage ★★★
Self Catering
Contact: Mrs Caroline Fox
t (01473) 730216
e caroline@foxworld.fsnet.co.uk
w tiscover.co.uk

WATLINGTON
Norfolk

The Hayloft ★★★★
Self Catering
Contact: Mrs Caroline Crisp
Peace Cottage
t (01553) 811444
e carolinejcrisp@hotmail.com

WATTISFIELD
Suffolk

Jayes Holiday Cottages ★★★ *Self Catering*
Contact: Mrs Denise Williams
t (01359) 251255
e booking@jayesholidaycottages.co.uk
w jayesholidaycottages.co.uk

WELLS-NEXT-THE-SEA
Norfolk

10 Brig Square ★★★
Self Catering
Norfolk Country Cottages
t (01603) 871872
e info@norfolkcottages.co.uk
w norfolkcountrycottages.co.uk

Alton Cottage ★★★
Self Catering
Contact: Ms Alexandra Mercer
t (01223) 844511
e sandie@amercer.co.uk
w tiscover.co.uk

Annies ★★★★ *Self Catering*
Contact: Mrs Sarah Orford
t (01359) 240340
w tiscover.co.uk

Apartment 2 ★★★★
Self Catering
Contact: Mr John & Helen Ilsley
t (01462) 790210
e john_f_ilsley@yahoo.co.uk
w tiscover.co.uk

Canary Cottage ★★★
Self Catering
Contact: Ms Sally Maufe
Branthill Farms Ltd
t (01328) 710246
e branthill.farms@macunlimited.net
w therealaleshop.co.uk

Chantry ★★★ *Self Catering*
Contact: Mrs Vicky Jackson
t (01992) 511303
w tiscover.co.uk

14 Church Street ★★★
Self Catering
Contact: Mrs Rita Piesse
Convent House
t (01603) 744233
e randjp2004@yahoo.com

Fisherman's Cottage ★★★
Self Catering
Contact: Ms Lesley Whitby
t (020) 7679 9477
e l.whitby@ucl.ac.uk
w tiscover.co.uk

Gabriel Cottage ★★★★
Self Catering
Contact: Marie Strong
t (01328) 710743
w tiscover.co.uk

Harbour Cottage ★★★
Self Catering
Contact: Mr & Mrs Simon & Trish Jackson
t (0115) 923 4545
e simonjackson@btinternet.com
w harbourcottagewells.co.uk

Honeypot Cottage ★★★
Self Catering
Contact: Mrs Joan Price
t (01328) 711982
e walker.al@talk21.com
w wells-honeypot.co.uk

Laylands Yard 4 ★★★
Self Catering
Contact: Mrs Ann Heaton
t (01328) 711361
w tiscover.co.uk

Luggers Cottage ★★★★
Self Catering
Contact: Mrs Lesley Cooke
Norfolk Country Cottages
t (01603) 871872
e info@norfolkcottages.co.uk
w norfolkcottages.co.uk

Old Police House ★★★
Self Catering
Contact: Mrs Whitaker
t (01328) 710630
e ophwells@yahoo.co.uk
w northnorfolk.co.uk/oldpolicehouse

Poppy Cottage ★★★
Self Catering
Contact: Mrs Christine Curtis
t (01328) 710395
w tiscover.co.uk

Ranters Cottage ★★★
Self Catering
Contact: Mrs Hilary Marsden
t (01442) 872486
e hilaryamarsden@aol.com
w tiscover.co.uk

Rose Cottage ★★★
Self Catering
Contact: Mrs Madeline Rainsford
t (01328) 711463
e maddie@eastquay.co.uk
w eastquay.co.uk

Seashell Cottage ★★★
Self Catering
Contact: Mrs Cecilia Fox
t (01603) 630232
e marylourivett@hotmail.com
w seashellcottage.co.uk

Skylark Cottage ★★★
Self Catering
Contact: Mrs Bridget Jones
t (01271) 372225
e bridget.jones@ukgateway.net
w bridget.jones.ukgateway.net

WELWYN
Hertfordshire

Gamekeepers Lodge Shire Barn ★★★★ *Self Catering*
Contact: Mrs Liz Buisman-Gaze
Welwyn Home Farm Enterprises Ltd
t (01438) 718641
e liz@lockleyfarm.co.uk
w lockleyfarm.co.uk

WENHASTON
Suffolk

The Old Mill House ★★★
Self Catering
t (01502) 724033
e websales@southwold-holdings.co.uk

Poplar Cottage ★★★★
Self Catering
Suffolk Secrets
t (01379) 651297
e holidays@suffolk-secrets.co.uk
w suffolk-secrets.co.uk

WEST BECKHAM
Norfolk

Flint Farm Cottages
★★–★★★★ *Self Catering*
Contact: Mrs Judy Wilson
t (01263) 822241
e john@mcneil-wilson.freeserve.co.uk
w tiscover.co.uk

Merry Cottage ★★★
Self Catering
Contact: Mrs Mo Teeuw
t (01406) 370012
e mo@moteeuw.co.uk
w tiscover.co.uk

WEST RUDHAM
Norfolk

North Cottage ★★–★★★
Self Catering
Blakes Holidays
t 0870 070 8090
w tiscover.co.uk

WEST RUNTON
Norfolk

8 Travers Court ★★★
Self Catering
Contact: Mrs Louise Oliver
Maple Cottage
t (01799) 550265
e louise44@btinternet.com
w tiscover.co.uk

Beacon Hill ★★ *Self Catering*
Contact: Mrs Justina Morris
t (01263) 838162
w tiscover.co.uk

Roman Camp Brick Chalets
★★★ *Self Catering*
Contact: Mr John Julian
t (01263) 837256
w romancampcaravanpark.co.uk

Runton Hill Cottage ★★★★
Self Catering
Contact: Mrs Barbara Cork
The Old Music Room
t (01263) 837427
e bd.corks@btopenworld.com

St Mary's (875)
Rating Applied For
Self Catering
Carlton House
t (01603) 871872
e info@norfolkcottages.co.uk
w norfolkcottages.co.uk

WEST WRATTING
Cambridgeshire

Bakery Cottage ★★★★
Self Catering
Contact: Mr David Denny
t (01223) 290492
e davidstractors@aol.com
w tiscover.co.uk

WESTCLIFF-ON-SEA
Essex

Ace Apartments ★★★★
Self Catering
Contact: Mr Sinclair Brown
Polecat Leisure Ltd
t (01702) 220154
e info@aceapartments.com

Thames Estuary Holiday Apartments ★★★
Self Catering
Contact: Mr Donald Watson
t (01702) 477255
w tiscover.co.uk

WESTLETON
Suffolk

Apple Tree Cottage ★★★
Self Catering
Suffolk Secrets
t (01379) 651297
e holidays@suffolk-secrets.co.uk
w suffolk-secrets.co.uk

Easter Cottage ★★★★
Self Catering
Suffolk Secrets
t (01379) 651297
e holidays@suffolk-secrets.co.uk
w suffolk-secrets.co.uk

Ebenezer House 1&3&5 Ebenezer Row ★★
Self Catering
Suffolk Secrets
t (01379) 651297
e holidays@suffolk-secrets.co.uk
w suffolk-secrets.co.uk

Middle Cottage ★★★★
Self Catering
Suffolk Secrets
t (01379) 651297
e holidays@suffolk-secrets.co.uk
w suffolk-secrets.co.uk

Mulley's Studio ★★★
Self Catering
Suffolk Secrets
t (01502) 722717
w tiscover.co.uk

Spring Cottage ★★★★
Self Catering
Contact: Ruth Whittaker
t (01728) 648380
w tiscover.co.uk

WEYBOURNE
Norfolk

Appletree Cottage ★★★★
Self Catering
Contact: Mrs Lesley Cooke
Norfolk Country Cottages
t (01603) 871872
e info@norfolkcottages.co.uk
w norfolkcottages.co.uk

Bolding Way Holiday Cottages ★★★–★★★★
Self Catering
Contact: Mr Charlie Harrison
t (01263) 588666
e holidays@boldingway.co.uk
w boldingway.co.uk

Hawthorns ★★★
Self Catering
t (01263) 821945

Herons Rise ★★★
Self Catering
Norfolk Country Cottages
t (01603) 871872
e info@norfolkcottages.co.uk
w norfolkcottages.co.uk

Home Farm Cottages
★★★–★★★★ *Self Catering*
Contact: Mrs Sally Middleton
Home Farm Cottages
t (01263) 588334
e sallymiddleton@virgin.com
w weybourne-holiday-cottages.co.uk

Lower Byre ★★★
Self Catering
Contact: Mrs Valerie James
t (01775) 760938
e valeriejames@waitrose.com
w tiscover.co.uk

Treehouse ★★★
Self Catering
Contact: Mrs Sharon Moss
t (01379) 854601
e sharonmoss@pgen.net
w tiscover.co.uk

Weybourne Forest Lodges
★★–★★★ *Self Catering*
Contact: Mr Chris & Sue Tansley
t (01263) 588440
e chris_tansley@hotmail.com
w weybourneforestlodges.co.uk

WHEPSTEAD
Suffolk

Rowney Cottage ★★★
Self Catering
Contact: Mrs Kati Turner
t (01284) 735842
e nick.turner@farming.co.uk
w tiscover.co.uk

WHITE RODING
Essex

Josselyns ★★★★
Self Catering
Contact: Mrs Dawn Becker
t (01279) 876734
e nb@artbecco.co.uk
w essexbungalow.co.uk

The Old Dairy ★★★★
Self Catering
Contact: Ms D Stafford
t (01279) 876056
e cthorogood@btenternet.com

WICKHAM MARKET Suffolk

11 Elm Road ★★★★
Self Catering
Suffolk Country Cottages
t (01502) 725500

3 Church Terrace ★★★
Self Catering
Contact: Mrs Patricia Day
t (020) 8348 1469
e p_day1999@yahoo.co.uk
w tiscover.co.uk

WICKHAM SKEITH Suffolk

The Netus Barn, Wickham Skeith ★★★ *Self Catering*
Contact: Mrs Joy Homan
t (01449) 766275
e joygeoff@homansf.freeserve.co.uk

WIGGINTON Hertfordshire

Osborne Lodge ★★★
Self Catering
Contact: Mr Tim Dawson
t (01442) 890155
e rangerscottage@aol.com
w rangerscottage.com

WIGHTON Norfolk

Nutwood Lodges ★★★★
Self Catering
Contact: Mr Jonathan Savory
t (01328) 820719
e jsavory@farming.co.uk
w nutwoodlodges.co.uk

WILBURTON Cambridgeshire

Australia Farmhouse ★★★★ *Self Catering*
Contact: Mrs Rebecca Howard
t (01353) 740322
e fenflat@hotmail.com
w sakernet.com/jameshoward

WINGFIELD Suffolk

Beech Farm Maltings ★★★★ *Self Catering*
Contact: Mrs Rosemary Gosling
t (01379) 586630
e maltings.beechfarm@virgin.net
w beech-farm-maltings.co.uk

Keeleys Farm ★★★
Self Catering
Contact: Mrs Gloria Elsden
t (01379) 668409
w tiscover.co.uk

WISBECH Cambridgeshire

Common Right Barns ★★★★ *Self Catering*
Contact: Mrs Teresa Fowler
t (01945) 410424
e teresa@commonrightbarns.co.uk
w commonrightbarns.co.uk

WISBECH ST MARY Cambridgeshire

Fenland Self Catering Holidays ★★★–★★★★
Self Catering
Contact: Mr Michael Southern
t (01945) 410680
e michael@fenlandcottages.co.uk
w fenlandselfcateringholidays.co.uk

WISSETT Suffolk

Noah's Ark ★★★★
Self Catering
Contact: Mrs Janet Craft
t (01986) 785535
e valleyfarmvineyards@tiscali.co.uk

WIVETON Norfolk

Laneway Cottage ★★★
Self Catering
Contact: Mrs Catherine Joice
t (01328) 862261
e catherine.joice@btinternet.com
w colkirkcottages.co.uk

WOLFERTON Norfolk

Hazel Cottage & Alice Cottage ★★★★ *Self Catering*
Norfolk Country Cottages
t (01603) 871872
e info@norfolkcottages.co.uk
w norfolkcottages.co.uk

WOOD NORTON Norfolk

Acorn Cottages ★★★★
Self Catering
Contact: Ms Ann Pope
t (01362) 683615
e rjpope@lineone.net
w countrysideholidays.com

Small Barn ★★★
Self Catering
Contact: Miss Jane Lister
t (01362) 684206
e hoecroft@acedial.co.uk
w hoecroft.co.uk

WOODBRIDGE Suffolk

The Coach House ★★★
Self Catering
Contact: Ms Nicola Deller
t (01473) 890891
e nicoladeller@yahoo.com

Colston Cottage ★★★★
Self Catering
Contact: Mr John Bellefontaine
t (01728) 638375
e lizjohn@colstonhall.com
w colstonhall.com

Easton Farm Park Cottages ★★★★ *Self Catering*
Contact: Mrs Fiona Kerr
t (01728) 746475
e info@eastonfarmpark.co.uk
w eastonfarmpark.co.uk

Old Forge and Anvil Cottage ★★★★ *Self Catering*
Contact: Mr Robert Blake
t (01394) 382565 & 07901 773545
e robert@blake4110.fsbusiness.co.uk
w tiscover.co.uk

Quayside Cottage ★★★★
Self Catering
Contact: Mrs Donna Morgan
Quayside
t (01473) 736724
e donna.morgan@quaysidecottage.com
w quaysidecottage.com

The Ridings ★★★★
Self Catering
Suffolk Secrets
t (01502) 722717
e holidays@suffolk-secrets.co.uk
w suffolk-secrets.co.uk

Sampsons Mill ★★★
Self Catering
Contact: Mr Gordon J. Turner
t (01728) 746791
e sampsons.mill@ntlworld.com
w tiscover.co.uk

Windmill Lodges ★★★★
Self Catering
Windmill Lodges Ltd
t (01728) 685338
e holidays@windmilllodges.co.uk
w windmilllodges.co.uk

WOOLPIT Suffolk

Bothy ★★★★ *Self Catering*
Contact: Mrs Kathryn Parker
t (01359) 241143
e grangefarm@btinternet.com
w farmstayanglia.co.uk/grangefarm

WOOTTON Bedfordshire

Stable Yard ★★★★
Self Catering
Contact: Mrs Rachael Thomas
t (01234) 765351
e info@the-stableyard.co.uk
w the-stableyard.co.uk

WORSTEAD Norfolk

Holly Grove Barns ★★★★–★★★★★
Self Catering
Contact: Mr Michael Horwood
t (01692) 535546

Poppyfields Cottages ★★★
Self Catering
Contact: Mr Dennis Gilligan
t (01692) 536863
e dennis.gilligan1@btinternet.com
w poppyfieldscottages.co.uk

Woodcarvers Barn ★★★★
Self Catering
Contact: Mr Simon Gray
t (01692) 536662
e si@worstead.co.uk
w worstead.co.uk/barn

WORTHAM Suffolk

Ivy House Farm ★★★★
Self Catering
Contact: Mr Paul Bradley
t (01379) 898395
e prjsdrad@aol.com
w ivyhousefarmcottages.co.uk

Olde Tea Shoppe Apartment ★★★★ *Self Catering*
Contact: Mrs Alison Dumbell
Post Office Stores
t (01379) 783210
e teashop@wortham.freeserve.co.uk
w tiscover.co.uk

WRENTHAM Suffolk

Garden Flat ★★★
Self Catering
Contact: Mrs Carol Reeve
t (01502) 675692
w tiscover.co.uk

WROXHAM Norfolk

Daisy Broad Lodges And Sail Loft ★★★★ *Self Catering*
Contact: Mr Daniel Thwaites
Daisy Broad Lodges & Sail Loft
t (01603) 782625
e daniel@barnesbrinkcraft.co.uk
w barnesbrinkcraft.co.uk

Helens ★★★ *Self Catering*
Contact: Mrs Lesley Cooke
Norfolk Country Cottages
t (01603) 871872
e info@norfolkcottages.co.uk
w norfolkcottages.co.uk

Nutmeg and Plum Tree Cottages, Wroxham ★★★★
Self Catering
Contact: Mrs Jane Pond
t (01603) 782225 & 07831 258258
e info@eastviewfarm.co.uk
w eastviewfarm.co.uk

Old Farm Cottages, Tunstead ★★★★
Self Catering
Contact: Mrs Kay Paterson
Old Farm Cottages
t (01692) 536612
e kay@oldfarmcottages.fsnet.co.uk
w oldfarmcottages.com

Trail Quay Cottages 20 ★★★ *Self Catering*
Contact: Mrs Lesley Cooke
Norfolk Country Cottages
t (01603) 871872
e info@norfolkcottages.co.uk
w norfolkcottages.co.uk

Whitegates Apartment ★★★ *Self Catering*
Contact: Mrs Cheryl Youd
t (01603) 781037
w tiscover.co.uk

YOXFORD Suffolk

Heather Cottage ★★★★
Self Catering
Suffolk Secrets
t (01502) 722717
e holidays@suffolksecrets.co.uk
w suffolk-secrets.co.uk

LONDON

INNER LONDON

E1

Hamlet UK, St Katharine Docks, Tower Hill ★★★
Self Catering
Contact: Ms Renata Naufal
Hamlet UK
t (01462) 678037
e hamlet_uk@globalnet.co.uk
w hamletuk.com

E4

Willowside
Rating Applied For
Self Catering
Contact: Mrs Cindy Roddick
t (020) 8529 1371
e r.roddick@btconnect.com
w willowside.co.uk

E14

Bridge House ★★★★★
Self Catering
Contact: Mr John Graham
t 07973 857187
e john@johnkgraham.com
w johnkgraham.com

Ionian Apartment ★★★★
Self Catering
Contact: Ms Christine James
t (01902) 843545
e enquiries@vactionsinlondon.co.uk
w vacationsinlondon.co.uk

River Thames Apartment
★★★★ *Self Catering*
t (020) 8530 2336
e gretapaull@aol.com
w riverthamesapartment.co.uk

Riverside ★★★★
Self Catering
Contact: Ms Christine James
t (01902) 843545
e christine@capstansq.fsnet.co.uk
w vactionsinlondon.com

E16

The Grainstore ★★★★★
Self Catering
Contact: Lauren Le
t (020) 8598 4050
e enquiries@simplyapartments.co.uk
w simplyapartments.co.uk

N7

Carena Holiday Apartments
★★★ *Self Catering*
Contact: Mr M Chouthi
t (020) 7607 7453
e deo.chouthi@btopenworld.com
w carena-apartments.co.uk

SE1

Flat One ★★★★★
Self Catering
Contact: Mr Nico Bardon
t (020) 7403 7112
e nicobardon@aol.com
w flatone.co.uk

SE3

Sunfields ★★ *Self Catering*
Contact: Mrs Jacqui Poole
t (020) 8858 1420
e jacqui.poole@nhs.net

SE6

Glenthurston Holiday Apartments ★★★-★★★★
Self Catering
Contact: Ms Sue Halliday
t (020) 8690 3992
e mail@glenthurston.co.uk
w glenthurston.co.uk

SE10

Harbour Master's House
★★★★ *Self Catering*
Contact: Prof Chris French
t (020) 8293 9597
e harbourmaster@lineone.net
w http://website.lineone.net/~harbourmaster

Park Vista
Rating Applied For
Self Catering
Contact: Ms Jackie Russel
t (020) 8305 1434
e russgab@aol.com

SE13

Studio Cottage ★★★
Self Catering
Contact: Ms Pamela Burke
t (020) 8265 1212
e info@welcomehomes.co.uk
w welcomehomes.co.uk

SE23

Dovetail House ★★★★
Self Catering
Contact: Ms Ruth Jenkins
t (020) 8291 0924
e dovetailhouse@aol.com

SW1

The Apartments Knightsbridge
★★★★-★★★★★
Self Catering
t (020) 7589 3271
e maureen@theapartments.co.uk
w theapartments.co.uk

Club Suites ★★★★
Self Catering
t (020) 7730 9131
e reservations@sloaneclub.co.uk
w sloaneclub.co.uk

SW3

The Apartments ★★★★
Self Catering
Contact: Ms Maureen Boyle
'The Apartments', Panorama Property Services Ltd
t (020) 7589 3271
e sales@theapartments.co.uk
w theapartments.co.uk

Beaufort House ★★★★★
Self Catering
Contact: Mr Damien Dawson
t (020) 7584 2600
e info@beauforthouse.co.uk
w beauforthouse.co.uk

SW4

Carpenters Place ★★★★
Self Catering
Contact: Kash Ijaz
Nomorehotels
t 0870 850 8514
e info@nomorehotels.co.uk
w nomorehotels.co.uk/london.html

SW7

Snow White Properties
★★★ *Self Catering*
Contact: Ms Maxine White
55 Ennismore Gardens
t (020) 7584 3307
e snow.white@virgin.net
w snowwhitelondon.com

SW18

Beaumont Apartments
★★★★ *Self Catering*
Contact: Mr & Mrs Alan & Monica Afriat
Beaumont Apartments
t (020) 8789 2663
e alan@beaumont-london-apartments.co.uk
w beaumont-london-apartments.co.uk

SW20

Thalia & Hebe Holiday Homes, Wimbledon ★★★★
Self Catering
Contact: Mr Peter Briscoe-Smith
t (020) 8542 0505
e peter@briscoe-smith.org.uk
w briscoe-smith.org.uk

W1

Tustin Holiday Flats
★★-★★★ *Self Catering*
Contact: Mr C Vaughan-Jones
t (020) 7723 9611
e pctustinuk@btconnect.com
w pctustin.com

W5

Clarendon House Apartments ★★★★
Self Catering
t (020) 8567 0314
e clarendon48house@tiscali.co.uk
w clarendonhouseapartments.co.uk

W8

51 Kensington Court
★★★★ *Self Catering*
t (020) 7937 2030
e manager@kensingtoncourt.co.uk
w kensingtoncourt.co.uk

OUTER LONDON

BECKENHAM

Oakfield Apartments
★★-★★★ *Self Catering*
t (020) 8658 4441
e enquiries@oakfield.co.uk
w oakfield.co.uk

CROYDON

Ballards Cottage ★★★★
Self Catering
Contact: Mr & Mrs McDermott
t (020) 8657 1080
e sndapartments@hotmail.com

S N D Apartments ★★★
Self Catering
t (020) 8686 7023
w sndapartments.com

HAMPTON COURT

Moores Place ★★ *Self Catering & Serviced Apartments*
Contact: Mr Mark Barnes
4 King Charles Road
t (020) 8979 1792

HOUNSLOW

London Cottage ★★★★
Self Catering
Contact: Mr Sreemal Perera
t (020) 8570 1103
e sreemalperera@aol.com
w srlettings.com

PINNER

Moss Cottage ★★★★
Self Catering
Contact: Mrs Barbara Le Quesne
t (020) 8868 5507
e bemail2@aol.com
w moss-lane-cottages.com

RICHMOND

Friston House
Rating Applied For
Self Catering
Contact: Mr Arthur Shipp
t (020) 8948 6620
e shipplets@ukgateway.net
w shipplets.com

SOUTH CROYDON

24 Heather Way ★★
Self Catering
t (020) 8405 4058
e jackmand6@hotmail.co.uk

The Studio ★★ *Self Catering*
Contact: Mrs Lynn Starling
t (020) 8760 0371

SOUTH EAST ENGLAND

ABINGDON
Oxfordshire

Brook Farm ★★★★
Self Catering
Contact: Mrs Pam Humphrey
t (01235) 820717
e info@brookfarmcottages.com

Flat 1 ★★★ *Self Catering*
Contact: Mrs Stella Carter
t (01235) 520317
e stella@bakehouse.supanet.com

Kingfisher Barn Holiday Cottages ★★★-★★★★
Self Catering
Contact: Mrs Elena Kaczmarek
t (01235) 537538
e info@kingfisherbarn.com
w kingfisherbarn.com

The Swallows and The Loft Apartment ★★★★★
Self Catering
Contact: Mrs Katherine Bitmead
By the Meadow Farm
t (01235) 831253
e theoffice@bythemeadowfarm.co.uk

The Willows
Rating Applied For
Self Catering
Contact: Beccie & Kate Bitmead
The Willows - Office
t (01235) 831253
e theoffice@bythemeadowfarm.co.uk
w bythemeadowfarm.com.uk

ADDERBURY
Oxfordshire

Hannah's Cottage at Fletcher's ★★★★
Self Catering
Contact: Mrs Charlotte Holmes
Fletcher's
t (01295) 810308
e charlotteaholmes@hotmail.com
w holiday-rentals.com

ALBURY
Surrey

The Lodge at Overbrook
★★★★ *Self Catering*
Overbrook
t (01483) 209579

ALCISTON
East Sussex

Rose Cottage Flat ★★★
Self Catering
Contact: Mrs Brenda Beck
Freedom Holiday Homes
t (01580) 720770
e mail@freedomholidayhomes.co.uk
w freedomholidayhomes.co.uk

Southdown Barn Annexe
Rating Applied For
Self Catering
Freedom Holiday Homes
t (01580) 720770
e mail@freedomholidayhomes.co.uk
w freedomholidayhomes.co.uk

ALDINGTON
Kent

Goldwell Manor Cottage
★★★★ *Self Catering*
t (01233) 721553
e rebecca@goldwellmanor.co.uk
w goldwellmanor.co.uk

Peacock Studio, Aldington
★★★★ *Self Catering*
t (01233) 720452
e dmanwa4857@aol.com
w peacockstudio.co.uk

ALFRISTON
East Sussex

Danny Cottage ★★★★★
Self Catering
Contact: Michael & Kitty Ann
t (01323) 870406
e contact@dannycottage.co.uk
w dannycottage.co.uk

The Pony House ★★★★
Self Catering
Contact: Mrs S Hernu
t (01323) 870303
e hernu@btinternet.com
w theponyhouse.co.uk

ALRESFORD
Hampshire

Pineapple House ★★★
Self Catering
Contact: Mrs Amanda Jane Miller
t (01962) 862226
e amanda@o2m.co.uk

ALTON
Hampshire

Butts House Studio ★★★
Self Catering
Contact: Mrs Sue Webborn
t (01420) 87507
e webbons@buttshouse.com
w buttshouse.com

The Coach House (Kingsley)
★★★★ *Self Catering*
t (01420) 474906
e info@stubbsfarm.co.uk
w stubbsfarm.co.uk

Green Farm, Bentley ★★★★
Self Catering
Contact: Mrs Glenda Powell
The Drift
t (01420) 23246
e chris@powellmessenger.co.uk
w greenfarm.org.uk

ALVERSTOKE
Hampshire

28 The Avenue ★★
Self Catering
Contact: Mr Martin Lawson
t (01923) 244042
e martinlawson8400@aol.com

ALVERSTONE
Isle of Wight

Combe View ★★★
Self Catering
t (01983) 403721
e gaynor@kernfarm.co.uk
w kernfarm.co.uk

AMBERLEY
West Sussex

Culver Cottage ★★
Self Catering
Contact: Mrs Howell-Hughes
Swallow Barn
t (01798) 831312 & +33 05659 96950
e stellainamberley@yahoo.co.uk
w visitbritain.com

AMERSHAM
Buckinghamshire

Chiltern Cottages ★★★★
Self Catering
Contact: Mr Stephen Hinds
Chiltern Cottages
t (01494) 874826
e bookings@chilterncottages.org
w chilterncottages.org

AMPFIELD
Hampshire

The Den ★★★★
Self Catering
Contact: Mr Knight Tony
t (01794) 367903
e beryl@knightwood.com

ANDOVER
Hampshire

Westmead, Weyhill ★★★★
Self Catering
Contact: Mrs Dianna Leighton
Westmead
t (01264) 772513
e westmeadweyhill@aol.com
w westmeadweyhill.co.uk

APPLEDORE
Kent

Ashby Farms Ltd ★★-★★★
Self Catering
Contact: Mr Ashby
t (01233) 733332
w ashbyfarms.com

Cobblestone Cottage ★★★
Self Catering
Contact: Mrs Brenda Beck
Freedom Holiday Homes
t (01580) 720770
e mail@freedomholidayhomes.co.uk
w freedomholidayhomes.co.uk

Rose Cottage
Rating Applied For
Self Catering
Contact: Mrs Pauline Hunter
t (01732) 457493
e holidays@rosecottageappledore.co.uk
w rosecottageappledore.co.uk

ARDINGLY
West Sussex

Townhouse Bothy ★★★
Self Catering
Contact: Mrs Ann Campbell
Fairhaven Holiday Cottages
t (01634) 300089
e enquiries@fairhaven-holidays.co.uk
w fairhaven-holidays.co.uk

ARUNDEL
West Sussex

Arundel Town Cottage
★★★★ *Self Catering*
t 07719 817661
e arundeltowncottages@hotmail.com
w b.1asphost.com/Blaney

Castle View ★★★★
Self Catering
Contact: Ms Jeannie Gapp
t (01903) 884713
e jeanniegapp@yahoo.co.uk
w castleview-arundel.co.uk

The Garden Room, Wepham
★★ *Self Catering*
Contact: Mrs J Ramseyer
Thomas Cottage
t (01903) 883222
e info@thomascottage.co.uk
w thomascottage.co.uk

Village Holidays ★★★★
Self Catering
t (01243) 552696
e ar@villageholidays.com

ASHBURNHAM
East Sussex

The Stables ★★★★
Self Catering
Contact: Mrs Brenda Beck
Freedom Holiday Homes
t (01580) 720770
e mail@freedomholidayhomes.co.uk
w freedomholidayhomes.co.uk

ASHEY
Isle of Wight

Tithe Barn, Old Byre & The Cote ★★★★★ *Self Catering*
Contact: Mrs Alison Jane Johnson
Little Upton Farmhouse
t (01983) 563236
e alison@littleuptonfarm.co.uk
w littleuptonfarm.co.uk

ASHFORD
Kent

Dean Farm ★★★★
Self Catering
Contact: Mrs Brenda Beck
Freedom Holiday Homes
t (01580) 720770
e mail@freedomholidayhomes.co.uk
w freedomholidayhomes.co.uk

Eversleigh Woodland Lodges ★★★ *Self Catering*
Contact: Mrs Christine Drury
Eversleigh Woodland Lodges
t (01233) 733248
e enquiries@eversleighlodges.co.uk
w eversleighlodges.co.uk

Grove House Cottage
★★★★ *Self Catering*
Contact: Mr Stuart Winter
Garden of England Cottages
t (01732) 369168
e holidays@gardenofenglandcottages.co.uk
w gardenofenglandcottages.co.uk

Hazelhope Barn, Stalisfield
★★★★★ *Self Catering*
Contact: Mandy Southern
Hazelhope Barn
t (01233) 713806
e mandy@hazelhopebarn.co.uk
w hazelhopebarn.co.uk

The Old Dairy ★★★
Self Catering
Contact: Mrs June Browning
t (01233) 750238
e browning.elmstead@talk21.com

ASHLEY GREEN
Buckinghamshire

The Old Farm ★★★
Self Catering
t (01442) 866430
e tc.eng@virgin.net

ASTON ABBOTTS
Buckinghamshire

Orchard Cottage ★★★★
Self Catering
Contact: Ms Vera Towle
t (01296) 681714

AYLESFORD
Kent

Stable Cottage At Wickham Lodge ★★★★★ *Self Catering*
t (01622) 717267
e wicckhamlodge@aol.com
w wickhamlodge.co.uk

BAMPTON
Oxfordshire

Grafton Manor Wing ★★★
Self Catering
Contact: Ms Sandra Eddolls
t (01367) 810237
e sandraeddolls@btinternet.com

Haytor Cottage ★★★
Self Catering
Contact: Mrs Susan Phillips
t (01993) 850321
e smph@supanet.com

Tom's Barn ★★ *Self Catering*
Contact: Mr Thomas Freeman
t (01367) 810410
e tmfreeman@btinternet.com
w visitradcot.co.uk

BANBURY
Oxfordshire

Little Good Lodge ★★★★
Self Catering
Contact: Ms Lynne Aries
t (01295) 750069
e bryan.aries@btopenworld.com
w littlegoodfarm.users.btopenworld.com

Mill Wheel Cottage ★★★★
Self Catering
Contact: Mrs Sheila Nichols
t (01295) 811637
w holiday-rentals.com

BARNHAM
West Sussex

Paddock Barn & West Cottage ★★★–★★★★★
Self Catering
English Country Cottages
t 0870 191 7700
w english-country-cottages.co.uk

Welldiggers ★★★★★
Self Catering
Contact: Mrs Penelope Crawford
t (01243) 555119
e welldiggers@hotmail.com
w welldiggers.co.uk

BARTON ON SEA
Hampshire

Rose Cottage ★★★★
Self Catering
Contact: Mr Patrick Higgins
Rafters
t (01425) 613406

Solent Heights ★★★★★
Self Catering
Contact: Mrs Dee Philpott
t (01425) 616066

BATTLE
East Sussex

Henley Bridge Stud ★★★
Self Catering
t (01424) 892076
e roytangundogs@tiscali.co.uk

Lonicera Lodge ★★★★
Self Catering
t (01424) 772835

Stiles Garage ★★
Self Catering
t (01424) 773155
e stilesgarage@hotmail.com

BEACONSFIELD
Buckinghamshire

Roselands (Beaconsfield)
★★★ *Self Catering*
t (01494) 676864
e dkoderisch@iname.com

BEAULIEU
Hampshire

Hill Top House Cottage
★★★★ *Self Catering*
Contact: Mr & Mrs Brett Johnson
Hill Top House
t (01590) 612731
e bretros@aol.com

Mares Tails Cottage ★★★★
Self Catering
Contact: Mrs Alice Barber
t (01590) 612160
e marestails1@ukonline.co.uk

Old Stables Cottage ★★★★
Self Catering
Contact: Mr & Mrs Peter & Jo Whapham
t (01590) 626707
e oldstablescott@aol.com

BECKLEY
East Sussex

Bixley ★★★★ *Self Catering*
Contact: Ms Philippa Bushe
t (020) 7226 9035
e tim@busheassoc.com
w bixleycottage.co.uk

Kingshoath Cottage ★★★★
Self Catering
Contact: Mr & Mrs Ian & Carol Speed
t (020) 8302 2663
e carol@kingshoath.co.uk
w kingshoath.co.uk

BEMBRIDGE
Isle of Wight

11 Solent Landing ★★★
Self Catering
Contact: Sue Fuller
Bembridge Holiday Homes
t (01983) 873163
w bembridge-holiday-homes.co.uk

12a Solent Landings ★★★★
Self Catering
Contact: Mr Matthew White
Island Holiday Homes
t (01983) 521114

3 Fairhaven Close ★★★
Self Catering
Contact: Mrs Ellis
Bembridge Holiday Homes
t (01983) 872335

3 Harbour Strand ★★★
Self Catering
Contact: Mrs Lisa Baskill
Home from Home Holidays
t (01983) 854340
e admin@hfromh.co.uk

4 Swains Villas ★★★
Self Catering
Contact: Mrs Ellis
Bembridge Holiday Homes
t (01983) 872335

51 Howgate Road ★★★★
Self Catering
Bembridge Holiday Homes
t (01983) 874481
e seymours@fishermansrest.freeserve.co.uk

8 Downsview Road ★★
Self Catering
Contact: Mrs Ellis
Bembridge Holiday Homes
t (01983) 872335

Allandale ★★★ *Self Catering*
Contact: Mrs Ellis
Bembridge Holiday Homes
t (01983) 872335

Bella Vista ★★★★
Self Catering
Bembridge Holiday Homes
t 0870 080 2950
e alison.neve@btopenworld.com

Cara Cottage ★★★
Self Catering
Contact: Mrs Ellis
Bembridge Holiday Homes
t (01983) 872335

Casa Blanca ★★★★
Self Catering
Contact: Mrs Ellis
Bembridge Holiday Homes
t (01983) 872335

Cliff Cottage ★★★
Self Catering
Contact: Mrs Lisa Baskill
Home from Home Holidays
t (01983) 854340
e admin@hfromh.co.uk

Crab Cottage ★★★★
Self Catering
Contact: Mrs Ellis
Bembridge Holiday Homes
t (01983) 872335

Crossways ★★★
Self Catering
Contact: Mrs Ellis
Bembridge Holiday Homes
t (01983) 872335

Cygnet House ★★★
Self Catering
Bembridge Holiday Homes
t (01983) 873163
e mail@bembridge-holiday-homes.co.uk
w bembridge-holiday-homes.co.uk

Dolphin Cottage ★★
Self Catering
Home from Home Holidays
t (020) 8882 5606
e dolphincottage@blueyonder.co.uk

Ely Place ★★ *Self Catering*
Contact: Mrs Ellis
Bembridge Holiday Homes
t (01983) 872335

The Finches ★★★
Self Catering
Contact: Mrs Ellis
Bembridge Holiday Homes
t (01983) 872335

Flat 3 Pump Mews ★★★★
Self Catering
t (01438) 813721
e humphray@humphray.fsnet.co.uk

Flat 4 Highbury Court ★★★
Self Catering
Bembridge Holiday Homes
t (01983) 873163
e mail@bembridge-holiday-homes.co.uk
w islandvisitor.co.uk/bembridge.htm

Forelands Cottage ★★
Self Catering
Contact: Mrs Ellis
Bembridge Holiday Homes
t (01983) 872335

Harbour Farm Cottage & Harbour Farm Lodge
★★★★ *Self Catering*
t (01983) 872610
e deirdremhicks@aol.com
w harbourfarm.co.uk

Harbour Mount ★★★
Self Catering
Bembridge Holiday Homes
t (01983) 873163
e mail@bembridge-holiday-homes.co.uk
w bembridge-holiday-homes.co.uk

Hillway Cottage
Rating Applied For
Self Catering
Contact: Honor Vass
Island Cottage Holidays
t (01929) 481555
e enq@islandcottageholidays.com

Hilvana ★★ *Self Catering*
Contact: Mrs Ellis
Bembridge Holiday Homes
t (01983) 872335

Honeysuckle Haven ★★
Self Catering
Contact: Mrs Ellis
Bembridge Holiday Homes
t (01983) 872335

Island Cottage ★★★★★
Self Catering
Bembridge Holiday Homes
t (01983) 873163
e mail@bembridge-holiday-homes.co.uk
w bembridge-holiday-homes.co.uk

Kingsmere ★★ *Self Catering*
t (01983) 872778

Ledge Beach Huts ★★★
Self Catering
Bembridge Holiday Homes
t (01983) 873163
e mail@bembridge-holiday-homes.co.uk
w bembridge-holiday-homes.co.uk

Ledge House ★★★★★
Self Catering
Bembridge Holiday Homes
t (01983) 873163
e mail@bembridge-holiday-homes.co.uk
w bembridge-holiday-homes.co.uk

Meadow Dairy ★★★
Self Catering
Contact: Mrs Lisa Baskill
Home from Home Holidays
t (01983) 854340
e admin@hfromh.co.uk

Michaelmas Cottage ★★★★
Self Catering
Bembridge Holiday Homes
t (01983) 873163
e mail@bembridge-holiday-homes.co.uk
w bembridge-holiday-homes.co.uk

Mimosa Cottage ★★★
Self Catering
Contact: Mrs Lisa Baskill
Home from Home Holidays
t (01983) 854340
e admin@hfromh.co.uk

Nine ★★★ *Self Catering*
Contact: Mrs Ann Hayward
Homewood
t (01903) 873699

Pisces ★★★ *Self Catering*
Bembridge Holiday Homes
t (01983) 873163
e mail@bembridge-holiday-homes.co.uk
w bembridge-holiday-homes.co.uk

Pitt Corner ★★★
Self Catering
Contact: Mrs Lisa Baskill
Home from Home Holidays
t (01983) 854340
e admin@hfromh.co.uk

Portland House ★★★★★
Self Catering
Contact: Mrs Ellis
Bembridge Holiday Homes
t (01983) 872335

Princessa Cottage & Coastwatch Cottage
★★★-★★★★ *Self Catering*
Contact: Mrs Hargreaves
t (01983) 874403
e ssnharg@aol.com

Rothsay Cottage ★★★★
Self Catering
Contact: Mrs Ellis
Bembridge Holiday Homes
t (01983) 872335

Seahorses ★★★
Self Catering
Contact: Mrs Ellis
Bembridge Holiday Homes
t (01983) 872335

Ship-n-Shore ★★★★
Self Catering
t (01983) 874430 & 07770 666437

Will-o-Cott ★★ *Self Catering*
Contact: Mrs Ann Hayward
Homewood
t (01903) 873699

Windmill Inn, Hotel & Restaurant ★★★★
Self Catering
Contact: Mrs Elizabeth Miles
t (01983) 872875
e enquiries@windmill-inn.com
w windmill-inn.com

BENENDEN
Kent

Bull & Mill Cottage ★★★★
Self Catering
Freedom Holiday Homes
t (01580) 720770
e mail@freedomholidayhomes.co.uk
w freedomholidayhomes.co.uk

Coopers Cottage ★★★★
Self Catering
Contact: Mr Stuart Winter
Garden of England Cottages
t (01732) 369168
e holidays@gardenofenglandcottages.co.uk
w gardenofenglandcottages.co.uk

The Granary Lower Standen Farm ★★★ *Self Catering*
Contact: Mrs Lizanne Brown
The Granary
t (01580) 240193
e lizanneb@hotmail.co.uk

Standen Barn Cottage
★★★★ *Self Catering*
Contact: Mr Stuart Winter
Garden of England Cottages
t (01732) 369168
e holidays@gardenofenglandcottages.co.uk
w gardenofenglandcottages.co.uk

BENTLEY
Hampshire

Ashfield Cottage ★★★★
Self Catering
Ashfield, Hole Lane
t (01420) 22144
e emmamacnaghten@aol.com

BEXHILL-ON-SEA
East Sussex

Beachcomber Flat ★★★
Self Catering
Contact: Mrs Verena Mathews
Miraleisure Ltd
t (01424) 730298
e infomira@waitrose.com

Boulevard Flat ★★★
Self Catering
Contact: Mrs Verena Mathews
Miraleisure Ltd
t (01424) 730298
e infomira@waitrose.com

Carlton Flat ★★★
Self Catering
Contact: Mrs Verena Mathews
Miraleisure Ltd
t (01424) 730298
e infomira@waitrose.com

Devonshire Flat ★★★
Self Catering
Contact: Mrs Verena Mathews
Miraleisure Ltd
t (01424) 730298
e infomira@waitrose.com

Flat 1 Trent House ★★★
Self Catering
Contact: Mrs Brenda Beck
Freedom Holiday Homes
t (01580) 720770
e mail@freedomholidayhomes.co.uk
w freedomholidayhomes.co.uk

Garden Flat ★★★
Self Catering
Miraleisure Ltd
t (01424) 730298
e infomira@waitrose.com

Haven Flat ★★★
Self Catering
Contact: Mrs Verena Mathews
Miraleisure Ltd
t (01424) 730298
e infomira@waitrose.com
w miraleisure.co.uk

Mansion Flat ★★★★
Self Catering
Contact: Mrs Verena Mathews
Miraleisure Ltd
t (01424) 730298
e infomira@waitrose.com

Miramar Holiday Flats ★★★
Self Catering
t (01424) 220360

Mulberry ★★★ *Self Catering*
Contact: Mrs Valerie Passfield
t (01424) 219204

Pavilion Flat ★★★★
Self Catering
Contact: Mrs Mathews
Miraleisure Ltd
t (01424) 730298
e infomira@waitrose.com

Promenade Flat ★★★
Self Catering
Contact: Mrs Verena Mathews
Miraleisure Ltd
t (01424) 730298
e infomira@waitrose.com

Riviera Flat ★★★
Self Catering
Contact: Mrs Verena Mathews
Miraleisure Ltd
t (01424) 730298
e infomira@waitrose.com

Seascape Flat ★★★★
Self Catering
Contact: Mrs Matthews
t (01424) 730298
e infomira@waitrose.com
w miraleisure.co.uk

Seaside Flat ★★★
Self Catering
Contact: Mrs Verena Mathews
Miraleisure Ltd
t (01424) 730298
e infomira@waitrose.com

Sovereign Flat ★★★
Self Catering
Contact: Mrs Verena Mathews
Miraleisure Ltd
t (01424) 730298
e infomira@waitrose.com

Sunrise Flat ★★★
Self Catering
Contact: Mrs Verena Mathews
Miraleisure Ltd
t (01424) 730298
e infomira@waitrose.com

Sylvian ★★★ *Self Catering*
t (01797) 229130
e info@sylvianapartments.co.uk
w sylvianapartments.co.uk

Top Deck Flat ★★★
Self Catering
Miraleisure Ltd.
t (01424) 730298
e infomira@waitrose.com

Wilton Flat ★★★
Self Catering
Contact: Mrs Verena Mathews
Miraleisure Ltd
t (01424) 730298
e infomira@waitrose.com

BICESTER
Oxfordshire

Grange Farm Country Cottages ★★★★
Self Catering
Contact: Mrs Penelope Oakey
t (01869) 277226
e info@grangefarmcottages.co.uk
w grangefarmcottages.co.uk

Pimlico Farm Country Cottages ★★★★
Self Catering
Contact: Mr & Mrs John & Monica Harper
Pimlico Farm Country Cottages
t (01869) 810306
e enquiries@pimlicofarm.co.uk

Stoke Lyne Farm Cottages, Stoke Lyne ★★★★
Self Catering
Contact: Mrs Julie Adams
Stoke Lyne Farm Cottages
t (01869) 345306
e info@stokelynefarmcottages.co.uk
w stokelynefarmcottages.co.uk

BIDDENDEN
Kent

Barclay Farmhouse Cottage
★★★★ *Self Catering*
Contact: Mrs Brenda Beck
Freedom Holiday Homes
t (01580) 720770
e mail@freedomholidayhomes.co.uk
w freedomholidayhomes.co.uk

The Den ★★★★
Self Catering
Contact: Mrs Brenda Beck
Freedom Holiday Homes
t (01580) 720770
e mail@freedomholidayhomes.co.uk
w freedomholidayhomes.co.uk

Garden Cottage ★★★★
Self Catering
Contact: Mrs Brenda Beck
Freedom Holiday Homes
t (01580) 720770
e mail@freedomholidayhomes.co.uk
w freedomholidayhomes.co.uk

BILSINGTON
Kent

Lanary Oast ★★★★★
Self Catering
Contact: Mrs Brenda Beck
Freedom Holiday Homes
t (01580) 720770
e mail@freedomholidayhomes.co.uk
w freedomholidayhomes.co.uk

Stonecross Barn ★★★★
Self Catering
t (01233) 720397
e jane.stonecross@tiscali.co.uk
w http://myweb.tiscali.co.uk/stonecrossbarn

BINFIELD HEATH
Oxfordshire

Heath View Studio ★★★
Self Catering
Contact: Mrs Finella Woolsey
t (0118) 946 4666
e finella.woolsey@finella.freeserve.co.uk

BIRCHINGTON
Kent

Raleigh Cottage ★★★★
Self Catering
Contact: Mrs Jill Edwards
t (01843) 841764 & (01843) 841764

BIRDHAM
West Sussex

The Old Dairy ★★★★
Self Catering
Contact: Mr Adrian Strange
t (01243) 513885

BISHOPSTONE
East Sussex

144 Norton Cottage ★★★
Self Catering
Contact: Mrs Carol Collinson
Inces Barn
t (01323) 897544
e norton.farm@farmline.com
w http://members.farmline.com/collinson/

BLEAN
Kent

50 School Lane ★★★★
Self Catering
Contact: Mrs Brenda Beck
Freedom Holiday Homes
t (01580) 720770
e mail@freedomholidayhomes.co.uk
w freedomholidayhomes.co.uk

BOGNOR REGIS
West Sussex

Aldwick Lodge ★★★★
Self Catering
t (01243) 267445 & 07813 158445
e kees@tinyworld.co.uk
w chichesterweb.co.uk/aldwicklodge.htm

Gabriels Hall
Rating Applied For
Self Catering
Contact: Sian Irvine
94 Nightingale Road
t (020) 7923 3678 & 07931 505696
e info@gabrielshall.com
w gabrielshall.com

BOLDRE
Hampshire

Close Cottage ★★★
Self Catering
Contact: Mr & Mrs White
t (01590) 675343

Orchard House The Annexe ★★★ *Self Catering*
Contact: Mrs Valerie Barnes
Orchard House
t (01590) 676686

Springfield Wing, Boldre ★★★ *Self Catering*
t (01590) 672491
e david.scott@nfdc.gov.uk

BOLNEY
West Sussex

Willow Cottage ★★★
Self Catering
Contact: Allan & Christine Haddrell
t (01444) 881617
e info@newfarmhouse.co.uk
w newfarmhouse.co.uk/willowcottage.htm

BONCHURCH
Isle of Wight

Hadfield Cottage ★★★★
Self Catering
Contact: Mrs Honor Vass
Island Cottage Holidays
t (01929) 480080
e enq@islandcottageholidays.com
w islandcottageholidays.com

Regent Court Holiday Bungalows ★★★
Self Catering
t (01983) 883782
e petegillwindycroft@tiscali.co.uk
w cottageguide.co.uk/regentcourt

Uppermount ★★★★
Self Catering
Contact: Mrs Honor Vass
Island Cottage Holidays
t (01929) 480080
e enq@islandcottageholidays.com
w islandcottageholidays.com

Wyndcliffe Holiday Apartments
Rating Applied For
Self Catering
t (01983) 853458
e admin@wyndcliffe-holidays.com
w wyndcliffe-holidays.com

BORDON
Hampshire

Tunford Cottage Lodge ★★
Self Catering
t (01420) 473159
e symon@tunford.freeserve.co.uk

BOREHAM STREET
East Sussex

The Granary ★★★★
Self Catering
Contact: Mrs P Honeysett
t (01323) 833925
e thegranary@hotmail.co.uk

BORTHWOOD
Isle of Wight

Borthwood Cottages ★★★
Self Catering
t (01983) 403967
e mail@netguides.co.uk
w netguides.co.uk

BOSHAM
West Sussex

Alongside X ★★★
Self Catering
Contact: Mrs Sarah Main
t (01243) 574316
e holidayinbosham@btinternet.com

The Warren ★★★
Self Catering
Contact: Mrs Gillian Odell
t (01243) 573927
e gillodell@aol.com

BOWLHEAD GREEN
Surrey

The Barn Flat ★★
Self Catering
Contact: Mrs Grace Ranson
t (01428) 682687
e ranson@bowlhead.fsnet.co.uk

BOXLEY
Kent

Styles Cottage ★★
Self Catering
t (01622) 757567
e sue@stylescottage.co.uk
w stylescottage.co.uk

BRACKLESHAM BAY
West Sussex

Romany Annex ★★
Self Catering
Contact: Mrs J Madgwick
Romany
t (01243) 673914

Windrush
Rating Applied For
Self Catering
Contact: Andy Stevens
Windrush Holidays
t 0845 644 0717
e enquiries@windrush-holidays.com
w bracklesham-bay.co.uk

BRACKNELL
Berkshire

River View ★★★
Self Catering
Contact: Mrs Zara Pengelly
t (01503) 262351

BRADING
Isle of Wight

The Downs ★★★
Self Catering
t (01562) 829940
e mickeymade@hotmail.com

Hill Farm Lodge ★★★★
Self Catering
t (01983) 875184
e lovegrove.beaper@bt.internet.com

The Old Bakery ★★★
Self Catering
Contact: Mrs Lisa Baskill
Home from Home Holidays
t (01983) 854340
e admin@hfromh.co.uk

The Stables ★★ *Self Catering*
t (01983) 407371
e morris.rwbo@farmersweekly.net

BRAISHFIELD
Hampshire

Meadow Cottage & Rosie's Cottage ★★★ *Self Catering*
Contact: Mrs Wendy Graham
Farley Farm Cottage Holidays
t (01794) 368265

BRAMLEY
Surrey

Converted Stable at Juniper Cottage ★★ *Self Catering*
Contact: Mr Bob Heyes
t (01483) 893706
e convertedstable@onetel.com
w web.onetel.com/~converted_stable

Old Timbers ★★★
Self Catering
Contact: Mrs Taylor
t (01483) 893258
e jpold_timbers@hotmail.com

BREDE
East Sussex

Eastwood Cottage ★★★★
Self Catering
Contact: Mr Stuart Winter
Garden of England Cottages
t (01732) 369168
e holidays@gardenofenglandcottages.co.uk
w gardenofenglandcottages.co.uk

BRIGHSTONE
Isle of Wight

2 The Granary ★★★★
Self Catering
t (01234) 328664 & 07795 078049
e info@2thegranary.co.uk
w 2thegranary.co.uk

3 Sea Breeze Cottages ★★★★ *Self Catering*
Contact: Mrs Virginia Peckham
t (01983) 740993
e ginnypeckham@aol.com

The Brew House ★★★★
Self Catering
Contact: Mrs Honor Vass
Island Cottage Holidays
t (01929) 480080
e enq@islandcottageholidays.com
w islandcottageholidays.com

Casses ★★★★ *Self Catering*
t (01590) 679601
e jkn@casses.fsbusiness.co.uk

Chilton Farm Cottages ★★★
Self Catering
t (01983) 740338
e info@chiltonfarm.co.uk
w chiltonfarm.co.uk

Grange Farm – Brighstone Bay ★★★ *Self Catering*
Contact: Mr Dunjay
Grange Farm
t (01983) 740296
e grangefarm@brighstonebay.fsnet.co.uk
w brighstonebay.fsnet.co.uk

Ivy Cottage ★★★★
Self Catering
Contact: Mr Matthew White
Island Holiday Homes
t (01983) 521114

The Mill House ★★★★
Self Catering
Contact: Mrs Honor Vass
Island Cottage Holidays
t (01929) 480080

Pool Cottage ★★★★★
Self Catering
Contact: Mr John Russell
t (01983) 740291

Rose Cottage ★★★★★
Self Catering
Contact: Mr John Russell
t (01983) 740291

Stable Cottage ★★★★
Self Catering
Contact: Mrs Honor Vass
Island Cottage Holidays
t (01929) 480080
e enq@islandcottageholidays.com
w islandcottageholidays.com

Valentine Lodge ★★★★
Self Catering
Contact: Mrs C Bentley
t (01983) 740677
e chrisatblakes@btinternet.com

BRIGHTLING East Sussex

Great Worge Farm Barn ★★★★ *Self Catering*
Contact: Mrs Brenda Beck
Freedom Holiday Homes
t (01580) 720770
e mail@freedomholiday homes.co.uk
w freedomholidayhomes.co.uk

BRIGHTON & HOVE East Sussex

3 St James's Avenue ★★★★
Self Catering
Contact: Mr Frank Hazel
t 07903 708194

5B Metropole Court ★★★★
Self Catering
Contact: Mrs Catherine Draco
Mortlake Business Centre
t (020) 8246 5664
e enquie@brighton-apartments.com

8 Upper Market Street
Rating Applied For
Self Catering
Contact: Mr Mark Barnes
t (020) 8979 1792

Brighton Holiday Flats ★★★
Self Catering
Contact: Mrs Veronica Cronin
English Language & Holiday Bureau
t (01273) 410595 & (01273) 410944
e office@cronin-accommodation.co.uk
w cronin-accommodation.co.uk

Brighton Marina Holiday Apartments ★★★★
Self Catering
Contact: Mrs A Wills
5 Marlborough Road
t (020) 8940 6945
e keith.wills@london.com
w brightonmarinaholiday apartments.co.uk

Brunswick Holiday Flats
★★★★★ *Self Catering*
Contact: Nasser Tag El Din
t (01273) 205047
e brunswick@brighton.co.uk
w brighton.co.uk/hotels/brunswickflats

The Cape Apartment
★★★★★ *Self Catering*
Contact: Ms Gail Latimer
t (01273) 581495
e gail.latimer@msbluk.co.uk

Flat 3 34 Brunswick Terrace
★★★★ *Self Catering*
Contact: Mr Richard Harris
Best of Brighton & Sussex Cottages Ltd
t (01273) 308779
e brightoncottages@pavilion.co.uk
w bestofbrighton.co.uk

Garden Annexe @ Florence House ★★★ *Self Catering*
Contact: Mr Geoff Hart
t (01273) 506624
e geoffhart@brightonlets.net
w brightonlets.net

Holiday Flat ★★★
Self Catering
Contact: Mr Peter Anthony
t (01480) 495914
e peter.anthony3@ntlworld.com

Kilcolgan Bungalow, Rottingdean ★★★★★
Self Catering
Contact: Mr J C St George
t (020) 7250 3678
e jc.stgeorge@virgin.net
w holidaybungalows brightonuk.com

Spell Self-Catering ★★★★
Self Catering
Contact: Ms Susan Ellis
Bramley Fell
t 07707 813012
e spell.let@virgin.net
w spellsc.co.uk

BRILL Buckinghamshire

Poletrees Farm ★★★
Self Catering
Contact: Cooper Anita
t (01844) 238276
e poletrees.farm@virgin.net

BRIZE NORTON Oxfordshire

Caswell House
Rating Applied For
Self Catering
Contact: Mrs Amanda Matthews
t (01993) 701064
e amanda@caswell-house.co.uk
w caswell-house.co.uk

BROAD OAK East Sussex

Austens Wood Annexe
Rating Applied For
Self Catering
Freedom Holiday Homes
t (01580) 720770
e mail@freedomholiday homes.co.uk
w freedomholidayhomes.co.uk

Dairy Cottage and Two Oaks
★★★–★★★★ *Self Catering*
Contact: Mr Stuart Winter
Garden of England Cottages
t (01732) 369168
e holidays@gardenofengland cottages.co.uk
w gardenofenglandcottages.co.uk

Riding & Stable Cottage
★★★–★★★★ *Self Catering*
Contact: Mr Stuart Winter
Garden of England Cottages
t (01732) 369168
e holidays@gardenofengland cottages.co.uk
w gardenofenglandcottages.co.uk

Spelland Barn ★★★★★
Self Catering
Freedom Holiday Homes
t (01580) 720770
e mail@freedomholiday homes.co.uk
w freedomholidayhomes.co.uk

BROADSTAIRS Kent

1 Church Road ★★★★
Self Catering
t (01843) 601996
e thefishermenscottages@hotmail.co.uk
w fishermenscottages.co.uk

1 Darren Gardens ★★★★
Self Catering
Contact: Mrs Jean Lawrence
Earlheath Partnership
t (01843) 591422
e jnancylawrence@aol.com
w lawrencefamilyholidays.co.uk

11 Inverness Terrace ★★★
Self Catering
Contact: Mrs Beatrice Jones
t (01843) 867116
e rhys.maps@dsl.pipex.com

2 Church Square ★★★
Self Catering
t (01843) 601996
e thefishermenscottages@hotmail.co.uk
w fishermenscottages.co.uk

2a Church Square ★★★★
Self Catering
t (01843) 601996
e thefishermenscottages@hotmail.co.uk
w fishermenscottages.co.uk

Albert Cottage ★★★★
Self Catering
Contact: Mrs Brenda Beck
Freedom Holiday Homes
t (01580) 720770
e mail@freedomholidayhomes.co.uk
w freedomholidayhomes.co.uk

Barnaby Lodge ★★★★
Self Catering
t (01843) 601996
e thefishermenscottages@hotmail.co.uk
w fishermenscottages.co.uk

Beacon Light Cottage
★★★★ *Self Catering*
Contact: Mr Patrick Vandervorst
Duinhelmlaan 11
e beaconlight.cottage@scarlet.be
w beaconlightcottage.com

Bray Holiday Homes ★★★
Self Catering
Contact: Dennis Bray
t (020) 8660 1925

Broadstairs Holiday House
★★★ *Self Catering*
Contact: Lynn Bull
t (01992) 576044
e lynn.bull@tiscali.co.uk

Broadstairs Holiday Lets
★★★ *Self Catering*
Contact: Linda & Harry Sear
t (01525) 210550
e lindaandharrysear@yahoo.co.uk

Broadstairs Holiday Lets
★★★ *Self Catering*
Charity Farm
t (01525) 210550
e lindaandharrysear@yahoo.co.uk
w broadstairsholidaylets.co.uk

Chevening ★★★★
Self Catering
t (020) 8302 1852
e martin@mjgibbons.freeserve.co.uk

Claremont House Apartment ★★★★
Self Catering
Contact: Mrs Brenda Beck
Freedom Holiday Homes
t (01580) 720770
e mail@freedomholiday homes.co.uk
w freedomholidayhomes.co.uk

Coachman's Flat ★★★
Self Catering
Contact: Mrs Ellen Barrett
t (01843) 867925
e ellen@stonar.com

Convent Cottage ★★★★
Self Catering
Contact: Mr John Lane
Honey Lane Cottages
t (01843) 579172
e lets@honeylanecottages.co.uk
w honeylanecottages.co.uk

Fisherman's Cottage ★★★★
Self Catering
Contact: Ms Linda Spillane
t (020) 8672 4150
e linda.spillane@virgin.net
w fishermanscottage broadstairs.co.uk

Flat 1, 2 Prospect Place
★★★★ *Self Catering*
Contact: Mrs Brenda Beck
Freedom Holiday Homes
t (01580) 720770
e mail@freedomholidayhomes.co.uk
w freedomholidayhomes.co.uk

Flat 4 ★★★★ *Self Catering*
Contact: Mrs Franks
Wayside, The Slade
t (01635) 861331
e mfranks@md-technology.co.uk

Land & Life Self Catering Apartments ★★★★
Self Catering
Contact: Mrs Simone Vince
t (01843) 867727
e info@land-and-life.de
w land-and-life.de

Martin Holiday Homes
★★★★ *Self Catering*
Contact: Mrs Penny Martin
t (01843) 592945
e penny@martinholidays.co.uk
w martinholidays.co.uk

Mertott Lodge ★★★
Self Catering
Contact: Lisa Merrill
t (01708) 859595
e broadstairsbreaks@hotmail.com
w broadstairsbreaks.co.uk

Mildenbrooke ★★★★
Self Catering
t (020) 8859 3916
e info@mildenbrooke.co.uk
w mildenbrooke.co.uk

North Foreland Lighthouse
★★★★★ *Self Catering*
Rural Retreats
t (01386) 701177
e info@ruralretreats.co.uk
w ruralretreats.co.uk

Paragon Lodge ★★★★
Self Catering
Contact: Mr John Lane
Honey Lane Cottages
t (01843) 579172
e lets@honeylanecottages.co.uk
w honeylanecottages.co.uk

Sanderling Cottage ★★★★
Self Catering
t (01843) 868746
e leisekatewilson@yahoo.co.uk
w sanderlingcottage.co.uk

Spero Court Apartments Flat 13 ★★★ *Self Catering*
Contact: Miss Carol Bowerman
t (01322) 224869

BROCKENHURST
Hampshire

1 Ringwood Terrace ★★★
Self Catering
Contact: Mrs Janet Morris
t (0117) 330 9887
e newforest.cottage@btinternet.com
w newforestcottage.net

Annexe – Forest Lodge
★★★★ *Self Catering*
Contact: Miss Helen Haynes
t (01590) 622907
e enquiries@forestlodge.info
w forestlodge.info

Ashtree House ★★★★
Self Catering
Contact: Mrs Christine Hirsch
t (028) 9754 1987
e peter-hirsch@utvinternet.com
w ashtreebrockenhurst.com

Gorse Cottage ★★★★
Self Catering
Contact: Mr Julian Gilbert
t 0870 321 0020
e info@gorsecottage.co.uk

Waterley Cottage ★★★★
Self Catering
Contact: Mr Adam Ogilvie
New Forest Cottages
t (01590) 679655
w brockcott.co.uk

BROOK
Hampshire

Wittensford Lodge ★★★
Self Catering
Contact: Ms Carol Smith
t (01277) 623997
e mbmcarol@dircon.co.uk

BROOK
Isle of Wight

Brook Farm Cottages ★★★
Self Catering
t (01983) 740387

Dunsbury Farm ★★★★
Self Catering
Contact: Ms Susannah Sealy
t (01983) 741325
w dunsburyfarm.co.uk

Holiday Homes Owners Services Ref: B4 ★★
Self Catering
Contact: Mr Colin Nolson
Holiday Homes Owners Services (West Wight)
t (01983) 753423
e holidayhomesiow@ic24.net

Holiday Homes Owners Services Ref: B5 ★★★★
Self Catering
Contact: Mr Colin Nolson
Holiday Homes Owners Services (West Wight)
t (01983) 753423
e holidayhomesiow@ic24.net

Holiday Homes Owners Services Ref: B3 ★★★★
Self Catering
Contact: Mr Colin Nolson
Holiday Homes Owners Services (West Wight)
t (01983) 753423
e holidayhomesiow@ic24.net

Holiday Homes Owners Services Ref: B1 ★★★★
Self Catering
Contact: Mr Colin Nolson
Holiday Homes Owners Services (West Wight)
t (01983) 753423
e holidayhomesiow@ic24.net

Sudmoor Cottage ★★★★
Self Catering
Contact: Mrs Honor Vass
Island Cottage Holidays
t (01929) 480080
e enq@islandcottageholidays.com
w islandcottageholidays.com

BROOKLAND
Kent

The Granary & The Dairy
Rating Applied For
Self Catering
Contact: Mrs Brenda Beck
Freedom Holiday Homes
t (01580) 720770
e mail@freedomholidayhomes.co.uk
w freedomholidayhomes.co.uk

Puddock Farm Pine Lodges
★★★★ *Self Catering*
Contact: Mrs Amanda Skinner
t (01797) 344440
e amanda_skinner@talk21.com
w puddockfarmpinelodges.co.uk

BUCKINGHAM
Buckinghamshire

Huntsmill Holidays ★★★★
Self Catering
Contact: Mrs Fiona Hilsdon
Huntsmill Holidays
t (01280) 704852 & 07974 122578
e fiona@huntsmill.com
w huntsmill.com

BUCKLAND
Oxfordshire

The Stables ★★★★★
Self Catering
Contact: Mrs Pat Elliott
t (01367) 870540
e pat@ashtreefarm.demon.co.uk
w thestables-ashtreefarm.co.uk

BURFORD
Oxfordshire

Candlemas ★★★★
Self Catering
Manor Cottages & Cotswolds Retreats
t (01993) 824252
e mancott@netcomuk.co.uk
w manorcottages.co.uk

The Mill at Burford ★★★
Self Catering
Contact: Chris Grimes
Manor Cottages
t (01993) 824252
e enquiries@manorcottages.co.uk
w themillatburford.co.uk

BURGATE
Hampshire

Burgate Farmhouse ★★★
Self Catering
Contact: Christine Bennett
t (01425) 655909
e admin@burgatefarm.freeserve.co.uk
w burgate.fslife.co.uk

BURLEY
Hampshire

Brackenwood
★★★★-★★★★★
Self Catering
Contact: Mrs Carole Stewart
Great Wells House
t (01425) 402302
e greatwells@cs.com

Cherry Tree Cottage ★★★
Self Catering
Contact: Mr & Mrs Pannell
West Cliff Sands Hotel
t (01202) 557013

The Dairy ★★★★
Self Catering
Contact: Mrs Carole Stewart
Great Wells House
t (01425) 402302
e carolestewart@pobox.com

Hollyhocks ★★★★★
Self Catering
Contact: Mrs Christine Outten
t (01425) 650568
e christineoutten@hotmail.co.uk

Rose Cottage ★★★
Self Catering
Contact: Mr Stephen Linney
Le Petit Touessrok
t (01534) 857441
e splinney@rosecottage.uk.net
w rosecottage.uk.net

Rose Cottage ★★★★
Self Catering
New Forest Living Ltd
t (01794) 390083
e info@newforestliving.co.uk
w newforestliving.co.uk/rosecottage.htm

BURWASH
East Sussex

Battenhurst Barn
Rating Applied For
Self Catering
Contact: Mrs Caroline Gibson
t (01435) 883728

CALBOURNE
Isle of Wight

Holiday Homes Owners Services Ref: C1 ★★★★
Self Catering
Contact: Mr Colin Nolson
Holiday Homes Owners Services (West Wight)
t (01983) 753423
e holidayhomesiow@ic24.net

CAMBER
East Sussex

Bridle Cottage & Horseshoe Cottage ★★★★ *Self Catering*
Contact: Mr Stuart Winter
Garden of England Cottages
t (01732) 369168
e holidays@gardenofenglandcottages.co.uk
w gardenofenglandcottages.co.uk

CANTERBURY
Kent

11 Dunstan Court ★★★★
Self Catering
Contact: Mrs Maria Cain
t (01227) 769955

Canterbury Country Houses
★★★★★ *Self Catering*
Contact: Mr Mark Mount
Canterbury Country Houses
t (01227) 830126
e info@canterburyholidays.com
w canterburycountryhouses.co.uk

Canterbury Self-catering
★★★★★ *Self Catering*
Contact: Mrs Kathryn Nevell
Canterbury Holiday Lets
t (01227) 763308 & 07941 969110
e rnevell@aol.com
w canterburyselfcatering.com

Ebury Hotel Cottages
★★★★ *Self Catering*
Contact: Mr Henry Mason
t (01227) 768433
e info@ebury-hotel.co.uk
w ebury-hotel.co.uk

Knowlton Court
★★★-★★★★ *Self Catering*
Contact: Miss Amy Froggatt
Knowlton Court
t (01304) 842402
e cottages@knowltoncourt.co.uk
w knowltoncourt.co.uk

Oriel Lodge Holiday Apartments ★★★★
Self Catering
Contact: Mr Keith Rishworth
Oriel Lodge
t (01227) 462845
e info@oriel-lodge.co.uk
w oriel-lodge.co.uk

Queensview Cottage
★★★★ *Self Catering*
Contact: Mrs Woodifield
t (01227) 471914
w cottageguide.co.uk/queensview

St Mary's Cottage ★★★★
Self Catering
Contact: Mr R Allcorn
Abberley House
t (01227) 450265
e r.allcorn@discovercanterbury.co.uk

St Michael's Place ★★★
Self Catering
Contact: Mrs Erica Drysdale
t (020) 8398 7036
w stmichaelsplace.co.uk

CARISBROOKE
Isle of Wight

Dairy Cottage ★★★★
Self Catering
Contact: Mrs Yapp
t (01983) 822951

Isle of Wight Country Cottages ★★★★
Self Catering
t (01983) 523996
e info@isleofwightcountrycottages.co.uk
w isleofwightcountrycottages.co.uk

Toll Cottage ★★★★
Self Catering
t (01983) 523685
e saubin@onetel.com
w upthegardenpaths.com

CASTLETHORPE
Buckinghamshire

Balney Apartments
★★★-★★★★ *Self Catering*
Contact: Mrs Mary Stacey
t (01908) 510385
e mary@mstacey.wanadoo.co.uk
w lets-stay-mk.co.uk

CATHERINGTON
Hampshire

Lone Barn cottage ★★★★
Self Catering
t (023) 9263 2911
e marchburn@ukonline.co.uk
w lonebarn.net

CAVERSFIELD
Oxfordshire

Grooms Cottage ★★★
Self Catering
t (01869) 249307
e odette@phippscottage.co.uk

CHALE
Isle of Wight

Atherfield Green Farm Holiday Cottages ★★★★
Self Catering
t (01983) 867613
e agfh@btinternet.com
w btinternet.com/~Alistair.Jupe

Chapel Cottage ★★★
Self Catering
Contact: Ms Catherine Hopper
Island Holiday Homes
t (01983) 521113
e enquiries@island-holiday-homes.net

Gotten Manor
★★★★-★★★★★
Self Catering
t (01983) 551368
e caroline@gottenmanor.co.uk

Old Rectory (S/C) ★★★★
Self Catering
t (01983) 551393
e theoldrectory@onetel.com
w theoldrectory.smebritain.co.uk

CHALE GREEN
Isle of Wight

1 & 2 North Appleford Farm Cottages ★★★ *Self Catering*
t (01983) 721206
e info@appleford-cottages.co.uk
w appleford-cottages.co.uk

CHALFONT ST GILES
Buckinghamshire

Hilborough ★★★
Self Catering
t (01494) 872536
e pbentall@btopenworld.com

CHAPEL ROW
Berkshire

The Flat ★★★ *Self Catering*
Bracken Cottage
t (0118) 971 3394

CHARLBURY
Oxfordshire

Banbury Hill Farm Cottages
★★★ *Self Catering*
Contact: Mrs Angela Widdows
t (01608) 810314
e beds@gfwiddows.f9.co.uk
w charlburyoxfordaccom.co.uk

CHARLTON
West Sussex

Orchard Cottage ★★★
Self Catering
Contact: Mrs Eve Jeffries
t (01243) 811338

CHART SUTTON
Kent

Brick Kiln Cottage ★★★★
Self Catering
t (01622) 842490
e info@whitehousefarm-kent.co.uk
w whitehousefarm-kent.co.uk

Orchard Cottage ★★★
Self Catering
Contact: Mrs Brenda Beck
Freedom Holiday Homes
t (01580) 720770
e mail@freedomholidayhomes.co.uk
w freedomholidayhomes.co.uk

CHESSELL
Isle of Wight

Little Stables
Rating Applied For
Self Catering
Contact: Mr & Mrs Aiden & Louise Collins
t (01983) 531503
e aiden.collins@pottery-cafe.com
w chessellpotterybarns.co.uk

CHICHESTER
West Sussex

1 & 5 West Broyle House
★★-★★★★ *Self Catering*
Contact: Penelope Gurland
t (01243) 536405
e penelopegurland@hotmail.com

2 Rumbolds Close ★★★
Self Catering
Contact: Dr Ian White
t (01323) 648291
e irwhite@nildram.co.uk

Apple Barn, Runcton
★★★★★ *Self Catering*
Contact: Mrs R Kendall
Saltham House
t (01243) 775997
e applebarn@salthamhouse.co.uk
w salthamhouse.co.uk

Apple Tree Cottage ★★★★
Self Catering
Contact: Mrs Susan Bickley
t (01243) 839770
e vickersdaphne@aol.com
w visitsussex.org/appletreecottage

Cornerstones ★★★★
Self Catering
Contact: Mrs Higgins
t (01243) 839096
e v.r.higgins@dsl.pipex.com
w cornercottages.com

Cygnet Cottage ★★★★
Self Catering
Contact: Mrs Higgins
t (01243) 839096
e v.r.higgins@dsl.pipex.com
w cornercottages.com

East Walls Apartment
★★★★ *Self Catering*
Contact: Ms Patricia Seager
t (01243) 545168
e patriciaseager@hotmail.com
w chichesterflat.tk

Honeysuckle Cottage
★★★★ *Self Catering*
Contact: Noel & Jenny Bettridge
t (01243) 779823
e noeljenny@onetel.com
w visitsussex.org/honeysucklecottage

Hunston Mill Cottages ★★★
Self Catering
Contact: Mr & Mrs Ian & Lyn Potter
Hunston Mill
t (01243) 783375
e hunstonmillcottages@bushinternet.com
w hunstonmill.co.uk

Lavender Cottage ★★★★
Self Catering
Contact: Mr & Mrs Ron & Pam Foden
t (01243) 771314
e rdfoden@talk21.com
w visitsussex.org/lavendercottage

New Park Studio ★★
Self Catering
Contact: Linda Hull
t (01243) 781147
e lhull1@toucansurf.com
w visitsussex.org/newparkstudio

Oak Apple Barn ★★★★
Self Catering
Contact: Mrs Siobain Davies
t 07763 384468
e siobain.davies@virgin.net
w visitsussex.org/oakapplebarn

Poplars Farm House ★★★★
Self Catering
Contact: Mr & Mrs T Kinross
Poplars Farm House
t (01243) 602250
e poplarsfarmhouse@tiscali.co.uk
w poplarsfarmhouse.co.uk

Quay Quarters ★★★★★
Self Catering
Contact: Mrs Lorraine Sawday
t (01243) 839900
e cottages@quayquarters.co.uk
w quayquarters.co.uk

CHIDDINGFOLD
Surrey

Combe Court Farm ★★★
Self Catering
Contact: Mrs Thelma Lane
t (01428) 683375

Prestwick Byre ★★★★
Self Catering
Contact: Mrs Valerie Mills
t (01428) 654695
e paul.prestwick@virgin.net

CHIDHAM
West Sussex

Canute Cottages ★★★★
Self Catering
Contact: Ms Diana Beale
t (01243) 572123
e diana@canutecottages.co.uk
w canutecottages.co.uk

CHILBOLTON
Hampshire

Larch Loft
Rating Applied For
Self Catering
Contact: Emma Way
t (01264) 860649
e stay@larchloft.co.uk
w larchloft.co.uk

CHILHAM
Kent

Monckton Cottages ★★★★
Self Catering
Contact: Mrs Helen Kirwan
t (01227) 730256 & 07789 431760
e monckton@rw-kirwan.demon.co.uk
w moncktoncottages.com

CHILLERTON
Isle of Wight

Chapel Cottage
Rating Applied For
Self Catering
Contact: Catherine Hopper
Island Holiday Homes
t (01983) 521113
e enquiries@island-holiday-homes.net
w island-holiday-homes.net

The Willows ★★★
Self Catering
t (01983) 721630

CHILWORTH
Hampshire

Lavender Cottage ★★★★
Self Catering
Contact: Mrs Susan Barnes
t (01788) 543932

CHIPPING NORTON
Oxfordshire

Beech House, Old Chalford
★★★★★ *Self Catering*
Contact: Mrs Dorothy Canty
Oak House
t (01608) 641435
e beechhouse@chalfordpark.co.uk
w chalfordpark.co.uk

Bruern Holiday Cottages
★★★★★ *Self Catering*
Contact: Ms Frances Curtin
t (01993) 830415
e fran@bruern.co.uk
w bruern-holiday-cottages.co.uk

Dairy Cottage ★★★★
Self Catering
Contact: Mrs Janie Hextall
t (01608) 658278
e jnhh@oxhex.wanadoo.co.uk
w holiday-rental.com/dairycottage

Hedera Cottage ★★★★
Self Catering
Contact: Mrs Angela Richards
Manor Cottages & Cotswold Retreats
t (01993) 824252
e mancott@netcomuk.co.uk
w manorcottages.co.uk

CHURCHILL
Oxfordshire

The Little Cottage ★★★★
Self Catering
Contact: Mr David Sheppard
t (01608) 658674
e enquiries@littlecottage.co.uk
w littlecottage.co.uk

CHURT
Surrey

Woodpecker Cottage
★★★★ *Self Catering*
Contact: Mr Martin Cochrane
t 07879 893567
e martin@martincochrane.com
w martincochrane.com/woodpecker

CLAYDON
Oxfordshire

Parrots Barn ★★★★
Self Catering
Contact: Cliff & Jill Fox
t (01295) 690727
e cliff.fox@tiscali.co.uk
w parrotsbarn.co.uk

CLIFTONVILLE
Kent

Majestic Flat
Rating Applied For
Self Catering
Contact: Yvonne Forbes
Elonville Hotel
t (01843) 290025
e enquiries@elonville-hotel.demon.co.uk
w elonvillehotel.com

CLIMPING
West Sussex

Dairy Cottage (The) ★★★
Self Catering
t (01903) 724187
e thedairy@tiscali.co.uk
w theclympingexperience.org.uk

COLLIER STREET
Kent

Den Farm Oast Barn
Rating Applied For
Self Catering
t (01892) 730306
e lizs@fsmail.net

COMPTON
West Sussex

Yew Tree House ★★★
Self Catering
Contact: Michael & Daphne Buchanan
t (023) 9263 1248
e d.buchanan@btinternet.com

COWBEECH
East Sussex

Beechcroft ★★★★★
Self Catering
Contact: Mr Michael Haydon
t (01435) 830237
e enquiries@beechcroft.org
w beechcroft.org

COWDEN
Kent

The Duck House ★★★★
Self Catering
Contact: Mrs Jill Winter
Garden of England Cottages
t (01732) 369168
e holidays@gardenofenglandcottages.co.uk
w gardenofenglandcottages.co.uk

COWES
Isle of Wight

16 & 32 Marsh Road ★★★★
Self Catering
Contact: Ms Michele Fisher
t 07968 437039
e mail@gurnardmarsh.co.uk
w gurnardmarsh.co.uk

2 Middleton Terrace ★★★
Self Catering
Contact: Susie Brockenhurst
t (020) 8882 5606
e brocklehursts@ic24.net

221 Gurnard Pines ★★★★
Self Catering
Contact: Mrs Moira Philip
t (023) 9237 5701
e mphilip@cwctv.net

230 Gurnard Pines ★★★
Self Catering
Contact: Libby Cleaver
t (023) 8025 3500
e libby@cleaver2254.fsnet.co.uk

Apartment Marivent ★★★
Self Catering
t (01983) 292148
e julia@marivent.co.uk
w marivent.co.uk

Belharbour ★★★★★
Self Catering
t (020) 8747 8308
e webmaster@belharbour.com
w belharbour.com

Flat 2 ★★★ *Self Catering*
Island Holiday Homes
t (01983) 521113

Greenside ★★★★
Self Catering
Contact: Mrs Honor Vass
Island Cottage Holidays
t (01929) 480080
e enq@islandcottageholidays.com
w islandcottageholidays.com

High Rising
Rating Applied For
Self Catering
Contact: Honor Vass
Island Cottage Holidays
t (01929) 481555
e enq@islandcottageholidays.com

Kingfisher ★★★★
Self Catering
Contact: Mrs Linda Bek
t (01983) 731761
e tbek@onetel.net.uk

Little Sails ★★★
Self Catering
Contact: Sally Hedgecoe
t (01252) 722114
e niton@btopenworld.com
w farnham-properties.co.uk

Mariners ★★★★
Self Catering
t (020) 8994 0856

The Old School House
★★★★ *Self Catering*
t 07831 514108
e tim@coweshouse.co.uk
w coweshouse.co.uk

Point Cottages ★★★
Self Catering
t (01983) 280641
e laura.billings@flyingfishonline.com
w pointcottages.co.uk

Shephards Hay
Rating Applied For
Self Catering
Contact: Mrs Howon Vass
Island Cottage Holidays
t (01929) 481555
e honor@islancottageholidays.com
w islandcottageholidays.com

Skylark, Gurnard Pines Holiday Village ★★★★
Self Catering
Contact: Mrs Linda Bek
t (01983) 731761
e tbek@onetel.net.uk
w lynbrookholidays.co.uk

Volante ★★★★ *Self Catering*
t (01983) 294900
e info@cowesselfcatering.co.uk
w cowesselfcatering.co.uk

Yachtsman's Rest
Rating Applied For
Self Catering
t (01883) 716208
e eastergorman@aol.com
w sunandsail.co.uk

CRANBROOK
Kent

Bakersbarn ★★★
Self Catering
Contact: Mr & Mrs Hooper
t (01580) 713344

Bourne Farm Oast ★★★★
Self Catering
Contact: Mr Stuart Winter
Garden of England Cottages
t (01732) 369168
e holidays@gardenofenglandcottages.co.uk
w gardenofenglandcottages.co.uk

Highwell Annexe
Rating Applied For
Self Catering
t (01580) 752447

The Little Barn (Ref: H762)
★★★★ *Self Catering*
Contact: Mr Nick Pash
Hideaways
t (01747) 828170
e enq@hideaways.co.uk
w hideaways.co.uk

Little Dodges ★★★★
Self Catering
Contact: Mrs Brenda Beck
Freedom Holiday Homes
t (01580) 720770
e mail@freedomholidayhomes.co.uk
w freedomholidayhomes.co.uk

Mill Cottage ★★★★
Self Catering
Contact: Mr Charles Foulkes
Garden of England Cottages
t (01732) 369168
e enquiries@mill-cottage.com
w mill-cottage.com

CROWBOROUGH
East Sussex

Cleeve Lodge & Belle Croix ★★★★ *Self Catering*
Contact: Mr & Mrs Edward & Nina Sibley
t (01892) 654331
e nina@the-old-house.co.uk
w the-old-house.co.uk

The Cottage ★★★★
Self Catering
Contact: Mr Stuart Winter
Garden of England Cottages
t (01732) 369168
e holidays@gardenofengland cottages.co.uk
w gardenofenglandcottages.co.uk

Hodges ★★★★★
Self Catering
Contact: Mrs Hazel Colliver
t (01892) 652386
e enquiries@hodges.uk.com

The Riding ★★★★
Self Catering
Contact: Mr Stuart Winter
Garden of England Cottages
t (01732) 369168
e holidays@gardenofenglandcottages.co.uk
w gardenofenglandcottages.co.uk

Streele Farm
Rating Applied For
Self Catering
Contact: Jacquelyn Beesley
t (01892) 852579
e stay@compasscottages.co.uk
w compasscottages.co.uk

CRUNDALE
Kent

Farnley Little Barn ★★★★
Self Catering
t (01227) 730510
e farnleylittlebarn@supaworld.com

Ripple Farm ★★★
Self Catering
Contact: Ms Maggie Baur
t (01227) 730748
e ripplefarmhols@aol.com

CUDHAM
Kent

Fairmead Cottage ★★★★
Self Catering
Contact: Mrs Val Gillingham
t (01959) 532662
e fairmeadfarm@aol.com

DEAL
Kent

Chalet 64 Kingsdown Park ★★★ *Self Catering*
Contact: Ms Mel Baugh
t (01304) 371337
e info@chalet64kingsdownpark.co.uk
w chalet64kingsdownpark.co.uk

DENMEAD
Hampshire

Flint Cottage ★★★
Self Catering
Contact: Mrs Sheila Knight
High Trees
t (023) 9226 6345
e sheila@flintcottagehants.fsnet.co.uk
w http://mysite.wanadoo-members.co.uk/flintcottagehants

DINTON
Buckinghamshire

Wallace Farm Cottages ★★
Self Catering
Contact: Mrs Cook
Wallace Farm
t (01296) 748660
e jackiecook@wallacefarm.freeserve.co.uk
w country-accom.co.uk

DODDINGTON
Kent

The Old School House ★★★★ *Self Catering*
Contact: Mr Stuart Winter
Garden of England Cottages
t (01732) 369168
e holidays@gardenofengland cottages.co.uk
w gardenofenglandcottages.co.uk

DORCHESTER ON THAMES
Oxfordshire

Vine Cottage ★★★★
Self Catering
Contact: Mr & Mrs Robert & Jenny Booth
t (01491) 681158
e cottagesoxon@btinternet.com
w cottagesoxfordshire.co.uk

DORKING
Surrey

Bulmer Farm, Holmbury St Mary ★★★ *Self Catering*
Contact: Mrs Gill Hill
Bulmer Farm
t (01306) 730210

The Little Cottage ★★★
Self Catering
Contact: Mrs Susan Scarrott
t (01306) 877256
e abacusue@aol.com
w surreyhills-holiday-cottage.co.uk

DOVER
Kent

Meggett Farm Cottage ★★★★ *Self Catering*
Contact: Mr Simon Price
t (01303) 252764
e simon-price.dover@virgin.net
w meggettfarmcottage.co.uk

Sergeant Major's House
Rating Applied For
Self Catering
English Heritage Holiday Cottages
t 0870 333 1187
w english-heritage.org.uk/holidaycottages

DRAYTON
Oxfordshire

The Old School ★★★
Self Catering
Contact: Mrs Christine Radburn
t (01235) 531557
e gordon@theoldeschool.freeserve.co.uk

DYMCHURCH
Kent

Dymchurch House ★★★★★
Self Catering
Contact: Mrs Uden
t (020) 8300 2100
e dymchurchhouse@btopenworld.com

Seabreeze Holiday Homes ★★ *Self Catering*
t (01303) 874116
e janetchecksfield@aol.com

EASEBOURNE
West Sussex

Corner Cottage ★★★★
Self Catering
Contact: Mrs Penny Hailstone
t (01798) 872892
e cottages@pjconsultancy.com
w visitsussex.org/cornercottage

EAST BOLDRE
Hampshire

Greycott ★ *Self Catering*
Contact: Ms Catherine Gray
The Bungalow
t (01590) 612162

EAST COWES
Isle of Wight

12 Cavalier Quay
Rating Applied For
Self Catering
Contact: Catherine Hopper
Island Holiday Homes
t (01983) 521113
e enquiries@island-holiday-homes.net
w island-holiday-homes.net

21 Medina View
Rating Applied For
Self Catering
Island Holiday Homes
t (01983) 521113

28 Anchorage Way
Rating Applied For
Self Catering
Contact: Catherine Hopper
Island Holiday Homes
t (01983) 521113
e enquiries@island-holiday-homes.net
w island-holiday-homes.net

4 Cavalier Quay ★★★★
Self Catering
Contact: Josie Gavoyannis
Home Farm House
t (01825) 791055
e info@holidays2remember.co.uk
w holidays2remember.co.uk

46 Medina View
Rating Applied For
Self Catering
Contact: Rhonda Weston
t (023) 8084 2547

Harbour View ★★★★
Self Catering
Contact: Mrs Lisa Baskill
Home from Home Holidays
t (01983) 854340
e admin@hfromh.co.uk

No 1 Seymour Court ★★★
Self Catering
t 07789 372371
e holiday@seymourcourt.co.uk
w seymourcourt.co.uk

Pavilion Cottage
Rating Applied For
Self Catering
English Heritage Holiday Cottages
t 0870 333 1187
w english-heritage.org.uk/holidaycottages

EAST DEAN
East Sussex

Beachy Head Holiday Cottages ★★★★
Self Catering
Contact: Charlie & Tavie Davies-Gilbert
t (01323) 423878
e tavie@beachyhead.org.uk
w beachyhead.org.uk

EAST END
Hampshire

3 New Cottages ★★★★
Self Catering
Contact: Jacquie Taylor
t (01590) 641810
e jtaylor155@btinternet.com

Norleycopse Cottage ★★★
Self Catering
Contact: Mrs Rosie Warner
t (01590) 626277
e cccinfo@btconnect.com
w new-forest-cottages.co.uk

EAST GRINSTEAD
West Sussex

Boyles Farmhouse Self-Catering Holidays ★★★★
Self Catering
Contact: Mrs Emma Amos
t (01342) 315570
e emmacamos@hotmail.com
w sussexcountrycottages.co.uk

EAST GULDEFORD
East Sussex

The Mount ★★★★
Self Catering
Contact: Mrs Brenda Beck
Freedom Holiday Homes
t (01580) 720770
e mail@freedomholiday homes.co.uk
w freedomholidayhomes.co.uk

EAST HAGBOURNE
Oxfordshire

The Oast House ★★★★
Self Catering
Contact: Mr Harries
t (01235) 815005

EAST LANGDON
Kent

The Pigeon House ★★★★
Self Catering
Contact: Mr P Mercer
t (01304) 852248

EAST MOLESEY
Surrey

Wisteria Cottage ★★★★
Self Catering
Contact: Jenny Bailey
t (020) 8339 1278
e jenny@riversiderentals.co.uk
w riversiderentals.co.uk

EAST PRESTON
West Sussex

Mariners House ★★★★
Self Catering
t (01293) 871937
e derekedwards@sovereignprinters.co.uk
w marinershouse.net

EAST SUTTON
Kent

The Clockhouse
Rating Applied For
Self Catering
Contact: Mrs Brenda Beck
Freedom Holiday Homes
t (01580) 720770
e mail@freedomholidayhomes.co.uk
w freedomholidayhomes.co.uk

EAST WITTERING
West Sussex

Fairhaven ★★★ *Self Catering*
Contact: Mrs Shelley Hamilton
Baileys
t (01243) 672217
e anne.maddock@tiscali.co.uk
w baileys.uk.com

Southern Counties Lettings – 20 Seagate ★★★
Self Catering
Contact: Gerald Ryan
t (020) 8204 1188
e info@southerncountieslettings.com
w southerncountieslettings.com

EASTBOURNE
East Sussex

Boathouse & Harbour View
★★★★★ *Self Catering*
Contact: Mr Richard Harris
Best of Brighton & Sussex Cottages Ltd
t (01273) 308779

Courtney House Holiday Flats ★★★ *Self Catering*
Contact: Mr Wei Ho
t (01323) 410202
e holidays@courtneyhouse.org.uk
w courtneyhouse.org.uk

The Old Coach House ★★★
Self Catering
Contact: Mrs A. G. Brooks
t (01424) 430763
e anne@oldcoachhouse.co.uk
w oldcoachhouse.co.uk

Santana Waterfront House
★★★★ *Self Catering*
Contact: Mrs Valerie Taylor
t 07714 380966
e santanahouse@onetel.com
w stayineastbourne.co.uk

Tom Thumb Cottages ★★
Self Catering
Contact: Mr & Mrs Roger Clark
t (01323) 723248
e info@eastbourne-holidayflats.co.uk

EASTCHURCH
Kent

Connetts Farm Holiday Cottages ★★★–★★★★
Self Catering
Contact: Mrs Maria Phipps
t (01795) 880358
e connetts@btconnect.com
w connettsfarm.co.uk

EASTERGATE
West Sussex

Eastmere ★★★ *Self Catering*
Contact: Mrs Sarah Wilkins
t (01243) 574389
e wilkins45@hotmail.com
w eastmere.com

EGERTON
Kent

Box Farm Barn ★★★★
Self Catering
Contact: Mr Stuart Winter
Garden of England Cottages
t (01732) 369168
e holidays@gardenofenglandcottages.co.uk
w gardenofenglandcottages.co.uk

The Dering Suite & The Old Bakery ★★★–★★★★
Self Catering
Contact: Mrs Brenda Beck
Freedom Holiday Homes
t (01580) 720770
e mail@freedomholidayhomes.co.uk
w freedomholidayhomes.co.uk

ELMER
West Sussex

Pebble Cottage, Elmer Sands ★★★★ *Self Catering*
t (01442) 863603
e sarah@pebble-cottage.co.uk
w pebble-cottage.co.uk

ELMSTED
Kent

The Dairy ★★★★
Self Catering
Contact: Mrs Brenda Beck
Freedom Holiday Homes
t (01580) 720770
e mail@freedomholidayhomes.co.uk
w freedomholidayhomes.co.uk

EMSWORTH
Hampshire

2 Heron Quay ★★★★
Self Catering
Contact: Mrs Linda Sprules
Tandriway
t (01883) 732144
e barry.sprules@fsmail.net
w thedeckhouse.co.uk

3 Avocet Quay
Rating Applied For
Self Catering
Contact: Mrs Jane Eastell
t (01483) 281819
e janeeastell@aol.com

Delta House ★★★
Self Catering
Contact: Mr Ben Francis
t (020) 8340 8074
e ben@deltahouse-emsworth.co.uk
w deltahouse-emsworth.co.uk

Pebble Cottage
Rating Applied For
Self Catering
Contact: Mrs Jean Buchanan
Lockgate Cottage
t (01243) 641452
e buchanan.j@virgin.net
w emsworthholidaycottages.co.uk

Pippins ★★★ *Self Catering*
Contact: Mrs Sarah Evans
Kimlas
t (01243) 372554
e hermitagecottage@btinternet.com
w btinternet.com/~seeksystems

Swan Cottage ★★★
Self Catering
t (01243) 370626
e swan.cottage@btinternet.com

Westview Holiday Flat ★★★
Self Catering
Contact: Mrs Julia Oakley
t (01243) 373002
e joakley@onetel.com

ENBORNE
Berkshire

Enborne Street Farm Barn House ★★★★ *Self Catering*
t (01635) 253443
e sandrafedwards@freeuk.com

EPSOM
Surrey

7 Great Tattenhams ★★★
Self Catering
Contact: Mrs Mary Willis
7 Great Tattenhams
t (01737) 354112

ERIDGE GREEN
East Sussex

The Dairy ★★★★
Self Catering
Contact: Mr Stuart Winter
Garden of England Cottages
t (01732) 369168
e holidays@gardenofenglandcottages.co.uk
w gardenofenglandcottages.co.uk

ESHER
Surrey

Lynwood Studio ★★★
Self Catering
Contact: Ms Rebecca Hughes
t (020) 8339 3739
e hughesbex@aol.com
w lynwoodstudio.co.uk

ETCHINGHAM
East Sussex

Moon Cottage, Etchingham
★★★★ *Self Catering*
Contact: Mrs Jan Harrison
Union Street
t (01580) 879328
e enquiries@harrison-holidays.co.uk
w harrison-holidays.co.uk

EVERTON
Hampshire

10 Newlands Manor ★★★
Self Catering
Contact: Mrs J A Rhoden
t (01590) 642830
e newlandsmanor@tiscali.co.uk

7 Lime Grove
Rating Applied For
Self Catering
Contact: David Danby
Old Walls Church Hall
t (01590) 642138
e david@oldwalls.com
w oldwalls.com

Gothic Cottage and Badgers Holt ★★★–★★★★
Self Catering
Contact: Mrs Mary Brockett
t (01590) 645941
e gothic.everton@btopenworld.com

Wheatley Cottage ★★★
Self Catering
Contact: Mrs Jacquie Taylor
Three Corners
t (01590) 645217
e tommy.tiddles@virgin.net

EXTON
Hampshire

Beacon Hill Farm Cottages
★★★★ *Self Catering*
Contact: Mrs Catherine Dunford
Farm Office
t (01730) 829724
e info@beaconhillcottages.co.uk
w beaconhillcottages.co.uk

FAIRLIGHT
East Sussex

Little Oaks ★★★★
Self Catering
Contact: Mrs Janet Adams
Fairlight Cottage
t (01424) 812545
e fairlightcottage@supanet.com

FARNHAM
Surrey

High Wray ★★ *Self Catering*
Contact: Mrs Alexine G N Crawford
High Wray
t (01252) 715589
e crawford@highwray73.co.uk
w highwray73.co.uk

Kilnside Farm ★★
Self Catering
Contact: Mrs Ros Milton
t (01252) 710325
e bobmilton@kilnsidefarm.fsnet.co.uk

Tilford Woods ★★★★
Self Catering
Contact: Sam Ede
t (01252) 792199
e admin@tilfordwoods.co.uk
w tilfordwoods.co.uk

FAVERSHAM
Kent

The Country Retreat ★★★★
Self Catering
Contact: Mrs Maureen French
Country Retreat
t (01795) 531257
e countryretreat1@aol.com
w syndalepark.co.uk

Monks Cottage ★★★★
Self Catering
Contact: Mr & Mrs Graham & Teresa Darby
t (01233) 740419
e info@selfcateringinkent.com
w selfcateringinkent.com

Old Dairy ★★★ *Self Catering*
Contact: Mrs Gillian Falcon
Shepherds Hill
t (01227) 752212
e ag@agfalcon.f9.co.uk

Uplees Farm ★★★★
Self Catering
Contact: Mr & Mrs Chris & Heather Flood
t (01795) 532133
e upleesfarm@businessinkent.net
w upleesfarm.co.uk

FELPHAM
West Sussex

Felpham Bungalow ★★★
Self Catering
Contact: Mrs J Yabsley
t (020) 8680 4761
e felpham.bungalow@tinyworld.co.uk

FISHBOURNE
West Sussex

The Tidings ★★★
Self Catering
Contact: Mrs Davies
t (01243) 773958

FIVE OAK GREEN
Kent

Stable Cottage ★★★★
Self Catering
Contact: Mrs Brenda Beck
Freedom Holiday Homes
t (01580) 720770
e mail@freedomholidayhomes.co.uk
w freedomholidayhomes.co.uk

FOLKESTONE
Kent

Bybrook Cottage ★★★
Self Catering
Bybrook House
t (01303) 248255

Clifton Crescent The Leas
★★★★ *Self Catering*
Contact: Mrs Louise Scillitoe-Brown
t (01306) 883838
e cliftoncrescent@chartfield.biz
w chartfield.biz

The Grand ★★-★★★★
Self Catering
Contact: Mrs Jane Ivor-Jones
t (01303) 222222
e info@grand-uk.com
w grand-uk.com

Merriwinds ★★★★
Self Catering
Country Holidays
t 0870 072 6726
e ownerservices@holidaycottagesgroup.com
w varne-ridge.co.uk

FORDINGBRIDGE
Hampshire

Alderholt Mill ★★★
Self Catering
Contact: Mr & Mrs Richard & Sandra Harte
Alderholt Mill
t (01425) 653130
e alderholt-mill@zetnet.co.uk
w alderholtmill.co.uk

Burgate Manor Farm Holidays ★★★★-★★★★★
Self Catering
Contact: Mrs Bridget Stallard
Burgate Manor Farm Holidays
t (01425) 653908
e info@newforestcottages.com
w newforestcottages.com

Fir Tree Farm Cottage
★★★★ *Self Catering*
Contact: Mr & Mrs Colin & Sarah Proctor
t (01425) 654001
e cjproctor@onetel.net.uk

Garden Cottage ★★★
Self Catering
Contact: Mrs Adele Holmes
t (01725) 518083
e rockbourneprop@freeuk.com

Glencairn ★★★ *Self Catering*
Contact: Mrs Catriona Tiller
t (01425) 652506

Hucklesbrook Farm ★★★★
Self Catering
Contact: Mrs Debbie Sampson
t (01425) 653180
e jcl.samson@btinternet.com

FRAMFIELD
East Sussex

Great Streele Farm Cottage
★★★★ *Self Catering*
Contact: Mrs Penelope Malloy
t (01825) 890638
e mail@greatstreele.co.uk
w greatstreele.co.uk

FRESHWATER
Isle of Wight

1 Finsbury Cottage
Rating Applied For
Self Catering
Contact: Catherine Hopper
Island Holiday Homes
t (01983) 521113
e enquiries@island-holiday-homes.net
w island-holiday-homes.net

10 Dolphin Court ★★★★
Self Catering
Island Holiday Homes
t (01983) 521113

103 Brambles Chine ★★★
Self Catering
Linstone Chine Holiday Services Ltd
t (01983) 755933
e holidays@linstone-chine.co.uk

111 Brambles Chine ★★
Self Catering
Linstone Chine Holiday Services Ltd
t (01983) 755933
e holidays@linstone-chine.co.uk

128 Bramble Chine ★★★
Self Catering & Serviced Apartments
Contact: Ms Buckley
Linstone Chine Holiday Services Ltd
t (01983) 755933
e linstone-chine@btconnect.com

12A Cliff End ★★★
Self Catering
Linstone Chine Holiday Services Ltd
t (01983) 755933
e holidays@linstone-chine.co.uk

131 Brambles Chine ★★★
Self Catering
Linstone Chine Holiday Services Ltd
t (01983) 755933
e holidays@linstone-chine.co.uk

146 Brambles Chine ★★
Self Catering
Contact: Ms Buckley
Linstone Chine Holiday Services Ltd
t (01983) 755933
e linstone-chine@btconnect.com

160 Brambles Chine ★★
Self Catering
Linstone Chine Holiday Services Ltd
t (01983) 755933
e holidays@linstone-chine.co.uk

166 Brambles Chine ★★★
Self Catering
Contact: Ms Buckley
Linstone Chine Holiday Services Ltd
t (01983) 755933
e linstone-chine@btconnect.com

170 Brambles Chine ★★★
Self Catering
Linstone Chine Holiday Services Ltd
t (01983) 755933
e holidays@linstone-chine.co.uk

173 Brambles Chine ★★
Self Catering
Contact: Ms Buckley
Linstone Chine Holiday Services Ltd
t (01983) 755933
e linstone-chine@btconnect.com

175 Brambles Chine ★★
Self Catering
Contact: Ms Buckley
Linstone Chine Holiday Services Ltd
t (01983) 755933
e linstone-chine@btconnect.com

176 Brambles Chine ★★
Self Catering
Contact: Mr Neil Andrew Cain
t (020) 8346 6308

196 Brambles Chine ★★★
Self Catering
Linstone Chine Holiday Services Ltd
t (01983) 755933
e holidays@linstone-chine.co.uk

197 Brambles Chine ★★
Self Catering
Linstone Chine Holiday Services Ltd
t (01983) 755933
e holidays@linstone-chine.co.uk

209 Brambles Chine ★★
Self Catering
Linstone Chine Holiday Services Ltd
t (01983) 755933
e holidays@linstone-chine.co.uk

222 Brambles Chine ★★★
Self Catering
Linstone Chine Holiday Services Ltd
t (01983) 755933
e holidays@linstone-chine.co.uk

226 Brambles Chine ★★★
Self Catering
Linstone Chine Holiday Services Ltd
t (01983) 755933
e holidays@linstone-chine.co.uk

36 Cliff End ★★★
Self Catering
Linstone Chine Holiday Services Ltd
t (01983) 755933
e holidays@linstone-chine.co.uk

38 Cliff End ★★ *Self Catering*
Contact: Ms Buckley
Linstone Chine Holiday Services Ltd
t (01983) 755933
e linstone-chine@btconnect.com

4 Afton Barns
Rating Applied For
Self Catering
Contact: Catherine Hopper
Island Holiday Homes
t (01983) 521113
e enquiries@island-holiday-homes.net
w island-holiday-homes.net

67 Brambles Chine ★★
Self Catering
Linstone Chine Holiday Services Ltd
t (01983) 755933
e holidays@linstone-chine.co.uk

87 Brambles Chine ★★
Self Catering
Linstone Chine Holiday Services Ltd
t (01983) 755933
e holidays@linstone-chine.co.uk

92 Brambles Chine ★★
Self Catering
Linstone Chine Holiday Services Ltd
t (01983) 755933
e holidays@linstone-chine.co.uk

Afton Thatch ★★★★
Serviced Apartments
t (020) 8995 9288
e aftonthatch@blueyonder.co.uk
w aftonthatch.com

Brambles Chine 168 ★★
Self Catering
Contact: Ms Suzanne Buckley
t (01983) 755933

Brambles Chine 169 ★★★
Self Catering
Contact: Nick Hawkins
t (01983) 752015

Brambles Chine 177 ★★★
Self Catering
Contact: Ms Suzanne Buckley
t (01983) 755933

Brambles Chine 45 ★★★
Self Catering
Contact: Nick Hawkins
t (01983) 752015

Brambles Chine 83 ★★★
Self Catering
Contact: Nick Hawkins
t (01983) 752015

Brockley Barns Cottages
★★★ *Self Catering*
t (01983) 537276
e mitchellbrockley@aol.com
w BrockleyBarns.co.uk

Cliff End 1 ★★★
Self Catering
Contact: Ms Suzanne Buckley
t (01983) 755933

Cliff End 2 ★★ *Self Catering*
Contact: Ms Buckley
Linstone Chine Holiday Services Ltd
t (01983) 755933
e linstone-chine@btconnect.com

Cliff End 28 ★★★
Self Catering
Contact: Ms Buckley
Linstone Chine Holiday Services Ltd
t (01983) 755933
e linstone-chine@btconnect.com

Cliff End 71 ★★★
Self Catering
Contact: Ms Suzanne Buckley
t (01983) 755933

Farringford Hotel ★★★
Self Catering
Contact: Miss Lisa Hollyhead
Farringford Hotel
t (01983) 752500
e enquiries@farringford.co.uk
w farringford.co.uk

Freshfields (68 Cliff End)
★★★ *Self Catering*
t (01983) 529901
e jo.iow@tiscali.co.uk
w cottageguide.co.uk/freshfields

Garden Rooms ★★★
Self Catering
Contact: Barney Barnes
t (01983) 755774
e chris@aftonpark.co.uk
w aftonpark.co.uk

Holiday Home Owners
Rating Applied For
Self Catering
t (01983) 753423
e holidayhomes@ic24.net

Holiday Home Owners Services (West Wight) Y22
★★★★ *Self Catering*
Contact: Colin R Nolson
t (01983) 753423
e holidayhomes@ic24.net

Holiday Homes Owner Services Ref : F6 ★★★★
Self Catering
t (01983) 753423

Holiday Homes Owner Services Ref: T8 ★★★★
Self Catering
t (01983) 753423

Holiday Homes Owner Services Ref : T4 ★★★★
Self Catering
t (01983) 753423

Holiday Homes Owner Services Ref : Y2 ★★★
Self Catering
Contact: Mr Colin Nolson
Holiday Homes Owners Services (West Wight)
t (01983) 753423

Holiday Homes Owner Services Ref : T3 ★★★★
Self Catering
t (01983) 753423

Holiday Homes Owners Services Ref: F4 ★★★
Self Catering
Contact: Mr Colin Nolson
Holiday Homes Owners Services (West Wight)
t (01983) 753423
e holidayhomesiow@ic24.net

Holiday Homes Owners Services Ref: F10 ★★★★
Self Catering
Contact: Mr Colin Nolson
Holiday Homes Owners Services (West Wight)
t (01983) 753423
e holidayhomesiow@ic24.net

Holiday Homes Owners Services Ref: F7 ★★★
Self Catering
Contact: Mr Colin Nolson
Holiday Homes Owners Services (West Wight)
t (01983) 753423
e holidayhomesiow@ic24.net

Holiday Homes Owners Services Ref: F1 ★★★★
Self Catering
Contact: Mr Colin Nolson
Holiday Homes Owners Services (West Wight)
t (01983) 753423
e holidayhomesiow@ic24.net

Holiday Homes Owners Services Ref: F2/48 ★★
Self Catering
Contact: Mr Colin Nolson
Holiday Homes Owners Services (West Wight)
t (01983) 753423
e holidayhomesiow@ic24.net

Holiday Homes Owners Services Ref: F2/32 ★
Self Catering
Contact: Mr Colin Nolson
Holiday Homes Owners Services (West Wight)
t (01983) 753423
e holidayhomesiow@ic24.net

Holiday Homes Owners Services Ref: F2/30 ★★
Self Catering
Contact: Mr Colin Nolson
Holiday Homes Owners Services (West Wight)
t (01983) 753423
e holidayhomesiow@ic24.net

Holiday Homes Owners Services Ref: F2/203 ★★★
Self Catering
Contact: Mr Colin Nolson
Holiday Homes Owners Services (West Wight)
t (01983) 753423
e holidayhomesiow@ic24.net

Holiday Homes Owners Services Ref: F8 ★★★★
Self Catering
Contact: Mr Colin Nolson
Holiday Homes Owners Services (West Wight)
t (01983) 753423
e holidayhomesiow@ic24.net

Honeysuckle Cottage Holiday Chalets (Chalet 1)
★★–★★★ *Self Catering*
t (01983) 755131
e eve.cook@btinternet.com

No 2 Old Coastguard Cottages
Rating Applied For
Self Catering
Contact: Catherine Hopper
Island Holiday Homes
t (01983) 521113
e enquiries@island-holiday-homes.net
w island-holiday-homes.net

Rose Cottage ★★★★
Self Catering
Contact: Mrs Jo Gardner
t (01420) 543385
e jlightfoot.knowkedgeexchange@btinternet.com

Sunkissed Haven ★★★
Self Catering
Contact: Mrs Elizabeth Shea
t (01780) 754112
e lizshea@hotmail.com

Tree Tops ★★★ *Self Catering*
Contact: Mrs Lisa Baskill
Home from Home Holidays
t (01983) 854340
e admin@hfromh.co.uk

FRESHWATER BAY
Isle of Wight

10 Tennyson View ★★★★
Self Catering
Contact: Ms Catherine Hopper
Manager, Housing Letting
Hose Rhodes Dickson
t (01983) 616644
e enquiries@island-holiday-homes.net
w island-holiday-homes.net

5 Tennyson View ★★★★
Self Catering
Contact: Mr Matthew White
Island Holiday Homes
t (01983) 521114

Holiday Homes Owners Services Ref: F3 ★★★★
Self Catering
Contact: Mr Colin Nolson
Holiday Homes Owners Services (West Wight)
t (01983) 753423
e holidayhomesiow@ic24.net

Holiday Homes Owners Services Ref: F9 ★★★★
Self Catering
Contact: Mr Colin Nolson
Holiday Homes Owners Services (West Wight)
t (01983) 753423
e holidayhomesiow@ic24.net

FRITTENDEN
Kent

Annexe to the Old Barn
★★★ *Self Catering*
Contact: Patricia Redmayne
t (01580) 715449
e patricia.redmayne@lineone.net

Cresslands Cottage ★★★
Self Catering
Contact: Mrs Brenda Beck
Freedom Holiday Homes
t (01580) 720770
e mail@freedomholidayhomes.co.uk
w freedomholidayhomes.co.uk

Weaversden Oast House
★★★★ *Self Catering*
Contact: Mr Stuart Winter
Garden of Engalnd Cottages
t (01732) 369168
e holidays@gardenofenglandcottages.co.uk
w gardenofenglandcottages.co.uk

FULBROOK
Oxfordshire

Footstool Cottage ★★★★
Self Catering
Contact: Mrs Rachael Carey
t (01752) 298067
e rachael_carey@hotmail.com
w geocities.com/footstoolcottage

FUNTINGTON
West Sussex

The Courtyard X ★★★★
Self Catering
Contact: Mrs Claire Hoare
t (01243) 575464
e tim.hoare@farming.co.uk
w adsdean.co.uk

Dellfield ★★★★
Self Catering
Contact: Mr Hall Hall
t (01243) 575244
e holidays@dellfield.com
w dellfield.com

GATCOMBE
Isle of Wight

Newbarn Country Cottages – The Parlour, The Dairy & Stable Cottages ★★★★
Self Catering
t (01983) 721202
e newbarnfarm@aol.com
w wightfarmholidays.co.uk/stable

GLYNDE
East Sussex

Caburn Cottages ★★★★
Self Catering
Contact: Mrs Rosemary Norris
t (01273) 858062

GODALMING
Surrey

Magpie Cottage ★★★
Self Catering
Contact: Mrs Gabrielle Mabley
t (01428) 682702
e Gabrielle.Mabley1@btinternet.com

GODSHILL
Hampshire

Graylands Cottage ★★★
Self Catering
Contact: Professor Tina Bruce
t (020) 8748 0611
e tinabruce@btinternet.com

The Log Cabin ★★★★
Self Catering
Contact: Mrs Penny Kanal
t (01425) 653800

GODSHILL
Isle of Wight

Bagwich Cottage
Rating Applied For
Self Catering
Contact: Mrs Honor Vass
Island Cottage Holidays
t (01929) 480080
w islandcottageholidays.com

Barwick Cottage ★★★★
Self Catering
Contact: Mrs Pamela Wickham
t (01983) 840787
e pam@barwickcottages.co.uk
w barwickcottages.co.uk

The Coach House Studio
★★★★ *Self Catering*
Contact: Mrs Honor Vass
Island Cottage Holidays
t (01929) 480080
e enq@islandcottageholidays.com
w islandcottageholidays.com

Demelza ★★★★
Self Catering
Contact: Mrs Honor Vass
Island Cottage Holidays
t (01929) 480080
e enq@islandcottageholidays.com

Glebelands Holiday Apartments ★★★★
Self Catering
Contact: Mrs Iris Beardsall
t (01983) 840371
w glebelands.fsnet.co.uk

Godshill Park House Annexe and Lodge ★★★★
Self Catering
t (01983) 840271
e godshillpark@yahoo.co.uk
w godshillpark.co.uk

Lake View ★★★★
Self Catering
Contact: Kathy Domaille
t (01983) 840781
e info@godshillparkfarm.uk.com
w godshillparkfarm.uk.com

Lambourne View Holiday Annexe ★★★ *Self Catering*
t (01983) 840293

Loves Cottage ★★★
Self Catering
Contact: Mrs Honor Vass
Island Cottage Holidays
t (01929) 480080
e enq@islandcottageholidays.com
w islandcottageholidays.com

Milk Pan Farm ★★★
Self Catering
t (01983) 840570
e tonymorrish@toucansurf.com
w milkpanfarm.co.uk

Pilgrims Lodge ★★★
Self Catering
Contact: Mrs Honor Vass
Island Cottage Holidays
t (01929) 480080
e enq@islandcottageholidays.com
w islandcottageholidays.com

Rosemary Cottage ★★★★
Self Catering
Contact: Mrs Honor Vass
Island Cottage Holidays
t (01929) 480080
e enq@islandcottageholidays.com
w islandcottageholidays.com

Seymour Cottages ★★★
Self Catering
t (01983) 840536

Stag Cottage ★★★★
Self Catering
Contact: Mrs Honor Vass
Island Cottage Holidays
t (01929) 480080
e enq@islandcottageholidays.com
w islandcottageholidays.com

GODSHILL WOOD
Hampshire

The Lodge (Ref: H212)
★★★★ *Self Catering*
Contact: Mr Nick Pash
Hideaways
t (01747) 828170
e enq@hideaways.co.uk

Undercastle Cottage
★★★★★ *Self Catering*
Contact: Mr Nicholas Pash
Hideaways
t (01747) 828170
e enq@hideaways.co.uk

GOLDEN CROSS
East Sussex

Jasmine Windmill ★★★
Self Catering
Freedom Holiday Homes
t (01580) 720770
e mail@freedomholidayhomes.co.uk
w jasminewindmill.com

GORING-BY-SEA
West Sussex

37 Harwood Avenue
★★★★ *Self Catering*
t (01480) 370656

GOSPORT
Hampshire

26 The Quarterdeck ★★★
Self Catering
Contact: Mr & Mrs Gibbs
t (023) 9258 6258
e info@ellachie.co.uk
w ellachie.co.uk

Dolphins ★★★ *Self Catering*
Contact: Mrs Donnelly
t (023) 9258 8179

Linden House ★★★
Self Catering
Contact: Mrs F Slaven
t (023) 9258 7887
e enquiries@harringtonhouses.co.uk
w harringtonhouses.co.uk

Number Nine ★★★
Self Catering
Contact: Mrs Claire Macaulay
t (023) 9252 8333
e enquiries@numbernine.info
w numbernine.info

Park House ★★★
Self Catering
Contact: Mrs F Slaven
t (023) 9258 7887
e enquiries@harringtonhouses.co.uk
w harringtonhouses.co.uk

GOUDHURST
Kent

3 Whitestocks Cottages
★★★ *Self Catering*
Contact: Mrs Brenda Beck
Freedom Holiday Homes
t (01580) 720770
e mail@freedomholidayhomes.co.uk
w freedomholidayhomes.co.uk

Blackthorn Barn ★★★★
Self Catering
Contact: Mrs Brenda Beck
Freedom Holiday Homes
t (01580) 720770
e mail@freedomholidayhomes.co.uk
w freedomholidayhomes.co.uk

The Coach House ★★★★
Self Catering
t (01580) 891353
e r.lusty@virgin.net
w thorfordhall.co.uk

The Stables ★★★★
Self Catering
Contact: Mrs Brenda Beck
Freedom Holiday Homes
t (01580) 720770
e mail@freedomholidayhomes.co.uk
w freedomholidayhomes.co.uk

Three Chimneys Farm
★★★★ *Self Catering*
Contact: Mrs Marion Fuller
Three Chimneys Farm
t (01580) 212175
e marionfuller@threechimneysfarm.co.uk
w threechimneysfarm.co.uk

GRAFFHAM
West Sussex

Yaffle Cottage ★★★★★
Self Catering
Contact: Mr Alex Mason
t (01798) 867553
e alex.mason@btinternet.com

GRAVESEND
Kent

Russell Quay ★★★★
Self Catering
Contact: Mr Mike Dickety
t (01474) 573045
e mikedickety@beeb.net
w halcyon-gifts.co.uk/holidaylet2.htm

GREAT ROLLRIGHT
Oxfordshire

Blackbird Cottage ★★★★
Self Catering
Contact: Mrs Carol Dingle
t (01608) 737676

Butlers Hill Farm ★★★
Self Catering
Contact: Mrs L. Campbell
t (01608) 684430

GROOMBRIDGE
East Sussex

Number 9 ★★★ *Self Catering*
Contact: Mrs Brenda Beck
Freedom Holiday Homes
t (01580) 720770
e mail@freedomholidayhomes.co.uk
w freedomholidayhomes.co.uk

Primula Cottage ★★★★
Self Catering
Contact: Mr Stuart Winter
Garden of England Cottages
t (01732) 369168
e holidays@gardenofenglandcottages.co.uk
w gardenofenglandcottages.co.uk

Sherlocks Cottage ★★★★
Self Catering
Contact: Mrs Brenda Beck
Freedom Holiday Homes
t (01580) 720770
e mail@freedomholidayhomes.co.uk
w freedomholidayhomes.co.uk

GUILDFORD
Surrey

Cathedral View Self-Catering Flat ★★★
Self Catering
Contact: Mrs Caroline Salmon
t (01483) 504915
e cathedralview@supanet.com

Lavender ★★★ *Self Catering*
Contact: Mr & Mrs Liew
Mandarin
t (01483) 506819 & 07906 179084
e shirleyliew9@hotmail.com

University of Surrey
★★–★★★ *Self Catering*
Contact: Conference Office
University of Surrey
t (01483) 686767
e conferences@surrey.ac.uk
w surrey.ac.uk/conferences

West View, West Horsley
★★★ *Self Catering*
Contact: Mrs Janet Steer
West View
t (01483) 284686
e cliveandjan@aol.com
w homestead.com/2westview

GURNARD
Isle of Wight

The Stable ★★★★
Self Catering
t (01983) 294900
e info@cowesselfcatering.co.uk
w cowesselfcatering.co.uk

HADLOW DOWN
East Sussex

The Barn Hadlow Down
★★★★ *Self Catering*
Contact: Mrs Brenda Beck
Freedom Holiday Homes
t (01580) 720770
e mail@freedomholiday homes.co.uk
w freedomholidayhomes.co.uk

HAILSHAM
East Sussex

1 and 2 Flint Cottages
★★★★ *Self Catering*
The Old Orchard House
t (01323) 440977

Little Marshfoot ★★★★
Self Catering
Contact: Ms Kathryn Webster
Little Marshfoot Farmhouse
t (01323) 844690
e kew@waitrose.com
w littlemarshfootfarmhouse.co.uk

Pekes ★★★-★★★★
Self Catering
Contact: Ms Eva Morris
t (020) 7352 8088
e pekes.afa@virgin.net
w pekesmanor.com

HALLAND
East Sussex

Little Tamberry ★★★★
Self Catering
Contact: Mrs Brenda Beck
Freedom Holiday Homes
t (01580) 720770
e mail@freedomholiday homes.co.uk
w freedomholidayhomes.co.uk

HARRIETSHAM
Kent

Tilmangate Barn ★★★★
Self Catering
t (01622) 843096

HARTLEY WINTNEY
Hampshire

Wintney Stable ★★★
Self Catering
t (01252) 843133
e bernardkilroy@uk2.net

HASLEMERE
Surrey

The Creamery ★★★★
Self Catering
Contact: Nick & Annie Pash
Hideaways
t (01747) 828170
e enq@hideaways.co.uk
w hideaways.co.uk/property.cfm/H742

HASTINGLEIGH
Kent

Staple Farm, Hastingleigh
★★★★ *Self Catering*
Contact: Mr & Mrs Cliff & Betty Martindale
Staple Farm
t (01233) 750248

HASTINGS
East Sussex

1 Temperance Cottage
★★★ *Self Catering*
Contact: Mrs Brenda Beck
Freedom Holiday Homes
t (01580) 720770
e mail@freedomholiday homes.co.uk
w freedomholidayhomes.co.uk

12 The Coastguards ★★★
Self Catering
Contact: Mrs Janine Vallor-Doyle
t (01308) 423180

14 Old Humphrey Avenue
★★★ *Self Catering*
Contact: Mrs Chris Nixey
t (01296) 625780
e cnixey@aol.com

Brooklands Coach House
★★★ *Self Catering*
t (01424) 421957
e caroline.mcnally@btinternet.com

Lionsdown House ★★★★
Self Catering
t (01424) 420802
e sharonlionsdown@aol.com

Number Six ★★★
Self Catering
t (01424) 431984
e famhart@supanet.com
w sixstanleyroad.co.uk

Rocklands Holiday Park
★★★ *Self Catering*
t (01424) 423097
e rocklandspark@aol.com

Rose House ★★★
Self Catering
t (01424) 754812
e hillbusybee@aol.com

St Marys Holiday Flats
★-★★ *Self Catering*
Contact: Mrs Edwards
t (01273) 556227

Senlac Holiday Flats ★★★
Self Catering
t (01424) 430080
e senlac@1066-country.com

Spring Cottage ★★★★
Self Catering
t (01580) 819542
e jamierudgley@lineone.net

Tillys Cottage ★★★
Self Catering
Contact: Mrs Celia Conway
The Captain's Cabin
t (01494) 565493

Westcliff Lodge ★★★
Self Catering
Contact: Mrs Celia Conway
The Captain's Cabin
t (01494) 565493

Winchester House
Rating Applied For
Self Catering
Contact: Mrs Brenda Beck
Freedom Holiday Homes
t (01580) 720770
e mail@freedomholiday homes.co.uk
w freedomholidayhomes.co.uk

HAVENSTREET
Isle of Wight

The Coach House ★★★★
Self Catering
Contact: Mr Peter Dewey
Guildford Farm
t (01983) 884782
e peter.dewey@lambournes.com

HAWKHURST
Kent

4 Alma Terrace ★★★★
Self Catering
Contact: Ms Rachel Barton
t (01435) 868333
e bartonrachel@yahoo.co.uk
w holiday-rentals.com/england/holiday-house-kent/p52466.htm

Kent Bridge Croft ★★★★
Self Catering
Contact: Mrs Brenda Beck
Freedom Holiday Homes
t (01580) 720770
e mail@freedomholiday homes.co.uk
w freedomholidayhomes.co.uk

Park Farm Chalet
Rating Applied For
Self Catering
Contact: Mrs Brenda Beck
Freedom Holiday Homes
t (01580) 720770
e mail@freedomholiday homes.co.uk
w freedomholidayhomes.co.uk

The Stables ★★★★
Self Catering
Contact: Mr Stuart Winter
Garden of England Cottages
t (01732) 369168
e holidays@gardenofengland cottages.co.uk
w gardenofenglandcottages.co.uk

HAWKINGE
Kent

1 North Downs Cottage
★★★★-★★★★★
Self Catering
Contact: Mrs Brenda Beck
Freedom Holiday Homes
t (01580) 720770
e mail@freedomholiday homes.co.uk
w freedomholidayhomes.co.uk

HAYLING ISLAND
Hampshire

1 Nab Court ★★★
Self Catering
Contact: Mr Roy Pine
Millers
t (023) 9246 5951
e rentals@haylingproperty.co.uk
w haylingproperty.co.uk

148a Southwood Road
★★★ *Self Catering*
t (023) 9246 5951

15 Anchor Court ★★★
Self Catering
Contact: Mr Roy Pine
Millers
t (023) 9246 5951
e rentals@haylingproperty.co.uk
w haylingproperty.co.uk

186 Havant Road ★★★
Self Catering
Contact: Mr Roy Pine
Millers
t (023) 9246 5951
e rentals@haylingproperty.co.uk
w haylingproperty.co.uk

3 Wight View ★★★★
Self Catering
Contact: Mr Roy Pine
Millers
t (023) 9246 5951
e rentals@haylingproperty.co.uk
w haylingproperty.co.uk

31 Itchenor Road ★★
Self Catering
Contact: Mr R L Pine
Millers
t (023) 9246 5951
e millers@haylingproperty.co.uk
w haylingproperty.co.uk

33 Seagrove Avenue
★★★★ *Self Catering*
t (023) 9246 1321
e rentals@haylingproperty.co.uk
w haylingproperty.co.uk

63 North Shore Road
★★★★ *Self Catering*
Contact: Mr Roy Pine
Millers
t (023) 9246 5951
e rentals@haylingproperty.co.uk
w haylingproperty.co.uk

69 Creek Road ★★★
Self Catering
Contact: Mr Roy Pine
Millers
t (023) 9246 5951
e rentals@haylingproperty.co.uk
w haylingproperty.co.uk

78 Sandypoint Road ★★
Self Catering
Contact: Mr Roy Pine
Millers
t (023) 9246 5951
e rentals@haylingproperty.co.uk
w haylingproperty.co.uk

88 Southwood Road ★★
Self Catering
Contact: Mr Roy Pine
Millers
t (023) 9246 5951
e rentals@haylingproperty.co.uk
w haylingproperty.co.uk

92 Southwood Road ★★★
Self Catering
t (023) 9246 1321
e rentals@haylingproperty.co.uk
w haylingproperty.co.uk

HEADINGTON
Oxfordshire

Mulberry Self-Catering
★★★ *Self Catering*
Contact: Mr & Mrs Gojko & Nada Miljkovic
Mulberry Guest House
t (01865) 767114
e mulberryguesthouse@hotmail.com
w oxfordcity.co.uk/accom/mulberrysc

HEATHFIELD
East Sussex

Boring House Farm The Cottage ★★★★ *Self Catering*
Contact: Mrs Anne Reed
t (01435) 812285
e info@boringhousefarm.co.uk

HENFIELD
West Sussex

New Hall Cottage & New Hall Holiday Flat ★★★
Self Catering
Contact: Mrs Marjorie Carreck
New Hall Cottage & New Hall Holiday Flat
t (01273) 492546

HENLEY-ON-THAMES
Oxfordshire

141 Greys Road ★★★★
Self Catering
Contact: Mrs Janet King
t (01491) 628486
e mjking@btinternet.com
w holiday.btinternet.co.uk

Jersey Farmhouse ★★★
Self Catering
Contact: Mrs Janet King
t (01491) 628486
e mjking@btinternet.com
w holiday.btinternet.co.uk

Rotherleigh House Annexe
★★★ *Self Catering*
Contact: Mrs Jane Butler
t (01491) 572776
e jvbutler57@hotmail.com

The Studio ★★ *Self Catering*
t (01491) 574760

HERNE BAY
Kent

Arlington Lodge ★★★★
Self Catering
Contact: Mr Adrian Webb
t (01737) 244385
e webb487@btinternet.com

Lawn Cottage
Rating Applied For
Self Catering
Contact: Bev Hardstone
t (01227) 367692
e bev@hardstone.co.uk

Maplin Sands Holiday Apartment ★★★
Self Catering
Contact: Mrs Claire Hudson
t (01227) 360819
w hernebayholidayhomes.co.uk

Old Water Tower Cottage
★★★ *Self Catering*
Contact: Ms Tessa Musgrave
t (01227) 361303
e tessa@theoldwatertower.co.uk
w oldwatertowercottage.co.uk

Westcliff Bungalow ★★★
Self Catering
Contact: Mr Mathew Filewood
Fairhaven Holiday Cottagea
t (01634) 300089
w fairhaven-holidays.co.uk

HERONS GHYLL
East Sussex

The Stables ★★★★
Self Catering
Contact: Mrs Brenda Beck
Freedom Holiday Homes
t (01580) 720770
e mail@freedomholidayhomes.co.uk
w freedomholidayhomes.co.uk

HIGH HALDEN
Kent

The Granary & The Stables
★★★★ *Self Catering*
Contact: Mrs Serena Maundrell
Vintage Years Company Ltd
t (01233) 850871 & 07715 488804
e serena@vintage-years.co.uk
w vintage-years.co.uk

Heron and Mallard Cottages
★★★ *Self Catering*
Garden of England Cottages
t (01233) 850613
e phil.auden@tesco.net
w kentcottages.com

Homestall Farm Annexe
★★★★ *Self Catering*
Contact: Mrs Brenda Beck
Freedom Holiday Homes
t (01580) 720770
e mail@freedomholidayhomes.co.uk
w freedomholidayhomes.co.uk

Mark Haven Cottage
★★★★ *Self Catering*
Contact: Mrs Brenda Beck
Freedom Holiday Homes
t (01580) 720770
e mail@freedomholidayhomes.co.uk
w freedomholidayhomes.co.uk

HIGH HURSTWOOD
East Sussex

The Granary ★★★★
Self Catering
Contact: Mrs Susan Barraclough
t (01825) 733040
e sue@parkwood.demon.co.uk
w huggettsfarm.co.uk

Sunnymead Farm Cottages
★★★★ *Self Catering*
Contact: Joan Cooper
t (01825) 733618
e joanecuk@aol.com

HIGHCLERE
Hampshire

Glencross Annexe, Highclere ★★★ *Self Catering*
Glencross Annexe
t (01635) 253244
e annexe@owenalex.freeserve.co.uk

HIGHMOOR
Oxfordshire

Bay Tree Cottage ★★★★
Self Catering
Contact: Ms Carolyn Wyndham
t (01491) 641229
e baytree@hotmail.com

HILDENBOROUGH
Kent

The Cottage ★★★
Self Catering
Contact: Mr Dudley Hurrell
The Cottage
t (01732) 832081

HOLLINGBOURNE
Kent

The Boat House ★★★★
Self Catering
t (01580) 212488
e enquiries@cottageonthelake.co.uk
w cottageonthelake.co.uk

Tanyard Cottage ★★★★
Self Catering
Garden of England Cottages
t (01732) 369168
e holidays@gardenofenglandcottages.co.uk
w gardenofenglandcottages.co.uk

Well Cottage ★★★★★
Self Catering
Contact: Mr & Mrs Paul & Angela Dixon
North Downs Country Cottages
t (01622) 880991
e info@wellcottagekent.co.uk
w wellcottagekent.co.uk

HOLYPORT
Berkshire

Vienna ★★★ *Self Catering & Serviced Apartments*
t (01628) 411273
e nolandstreet@maidenheadwine.co.uk

HORSHAM
West Sussex

Walnut Barn, Cottage and Stables ★★★★-★★★★★
Self Catering
Contact: Julian Cole
t 07730 620365
e jpcole@lineone.net
w sussexholidaycottages.com

HORTON HEATH
Hampshire

The Stable at Rambler Cottage ★★★★ *Self Catering*
Contact: Mr Mike Collins
t (023) 8060 2755
e info@stablelets.co.uk
w stablelets.co.uk

HUNGERFORD
Berkshire

Canalside Cottage ★★★
Self Catering
t (01488) 681494
e canalsidecottage@tiscali.co.uk
w canalsidecottage.com

HUNSTON
West Sussex

Well Cottage, Hunston
★★★★ *Self Catering*
Contact: Mrs Paula Fountain
t (01243) 530889
e paula.fountain@btinternet.com
w wellcottagechichester.co.uk

HUNTON
Kent

Woolhouse Barn ★★★★
Self Catering
Garden of England Cottages
t (01732) 369168
e holidays@gardenofenglandcottages.co.uk
w gardenofenglandcottages.co.uk

HURST
Hampshire

The Dairy at Copper Beeches ★★★ *Self Catering*
t (01730) 826662
e ianchew@torberry212.fsnet.co.uk

HYTHE
Hampshire

Waterfront House ★★★★★
Self Catering
Contact: Mr & Mrs Cunningham
t (023) 8084 2460
e alexcunningham@waitrose.com

Waterside Retreat
Rating Applied For
Self Catering
Contact: Lynne Kemmish
Hythe and Waterside Lettings
t (023) 8084 5096
e hwlettings@btconnect.com
w watersidereterat.co.uk

HYTHE
Kent

Hydene Cottage ★★★★
Self Catering
Contact: Mrs Brenda Beck
Freedom Holiday Homes
t (01580) 720770
e mail@freedomholidayhomes.co.uk
w freedomholidayhomes.co.uk

Hythe Period Cottage ★★★
Self Catering
Contact: Mrs Sophie James
t (029) 2048 0667
e sophie_james123@hotmail.com

Shortstayaway
Rating Applied For
Self Catering
Contact: Mr & Mrs A Eatwell
t (01303) 238298
e enquiries@shortstayaway.co.uk
w shortstayaway.co.uk

Uppermill ★★★★
Self Catering
Contact: Mrs Nicola Hooshangpour
Marston Properties Ltd
t (020) 7736 7133
e nicky@marstonproperties.co.uk
w marstonproperties.co.uk

IBSLEY
Hampshire

Chocolate Box Cottage
★★★★★ *Self Catering*
Contact: Mrs Frances Higham
t (01268) 741036 & 07768 075761
e chocolateboxcottage@btinternet.com
w chocolateboxcottage.co.uk

Crofton ★★★★-★★★★★
Self Catering
Contact: Mrs Julie Hordle
t (01425) 471829
e crofton@tiscali.co.uk

ICKLESHAM
East Sussex

Garden Cottage, Stable Cottage & Broadstreet House ★★★-★★★★
Self Catering
Contact: Mr Stuart Winter
Garden of England Cottages
t (01732) 369168
e holidays@gardenofenglandcottages.co.uk
w gardenofenglandcottages.co.uk

IDEN
East Sussex

The Granary
Rating Applied For
Self Catering
Contact: Mrs Brenda Beck
Freedom Holiday Homes
t (01580) 720770
e mail@freedomholidayhomes.co.uk
w freedomholidayhomes.co.uk

Riverside Cottage
Rating Applied For
Self Catering
Contact: Mrs Brenda Beck
Freedom Holiday Homes
t (01580) 720770
e mail@freedomholidayhomes.co.uk
w freedomholidayhomes.co.uk

INKPEN
Berkshire

Beacon Cottage ★★★
Self Catering
Contact: Mr Nick Pash
Hideaways
t (01747) 828170
e enq@hideaways.co.uk
w hideaways.co.uk

IPING
West Sussex

River Meadow Flat ★★★
Self Catering
Contact: Mr & Mrs Tim & Rowena Hill
t (01730) 814713

The Studio ★★★
Self Catering
Contact: Claudia Callingham
t (01428) 741561

ITCHEN ABBAS
Hampshire

Itchen Down Farm
★★★-★★★★ *Self Catering*
Contact: Mrs Brenda Hulme
Itchen Down Farm
t (01962) 779388
e itchendownfarm@farming.co.uk
w itchendownfarm.co.uk

IVINGHOE
Buckinghamshire

Town Farm Holiday Cottages ★★★ *Self Catering*
Contact: Mrs Angie Leach
t (01296) 668455
e angie@unlimitedlets.com
w unlimitedlets.com

KEMSING
Kent

6 Dippers Close ★★★
Self Catering
Contact: Mr & Mrs Ronald Rose
t (01732) 761937

KEYHAVEN
Hampshire

Woodlea ★★★ *Self Catering*
t (01590) 641154

KILMESTON
Hampshire

College Down Farm ★★★
Self Catering
t (01962) 771345
w collegedownfarm.co.uk

KING'S SOMBORNE
Hampshire

Brook Farm Cottages
★★★★ *Self Catering*
Contact: Mrs Sarah de Sigley
t (01794) 389379
w quidity.com

By The Way Annexe ★★★
Self Catering
t (01794) 388469
e penny@bytheway4.freeserve.co.uk

KINGSTON
East Sussex

Nightingales ★★★★
Self Catering
Contact: Mrs Jean Hudson
t (01273) 475673
e nightingales@totalise.co.uk

Roman Way (Kingston)
★★★★ *Self Catering*
Contact: Pippa & Ian Campbell
t (01273) 476583
e camp1942@aol.com
w visitsussex.org/romanway

LAMBERHURST
Kent

Barnfield Oast Self-Catering
★★★★ *Self Catering*
Contact: Mrs Veronica Eyre
t (01892) 890346
e info@barnfieldoast.co.uk
w barnfieldoast.co.uk

The Hideaway ★★★
Self Catering
Contact: Mrs Brenda Beck
Freedom Holiday Homes
t (01580) 720770
e mail@freedomholidayhomes.co.uk
w freedomholidayhomes.co.uk

Oast Cottage, Orchard Cottage – Barnfield Oast
★★★ *Self Catering*
Contact: Mrs Brenda Beck
Freedom Holiday Homes
t (01580) 720770
e mail@freedomholidayhomes.co.uk
w freedomholidayhomes.co.uk

Owls Castle Oast ★★★★
Self Catering
Contact: Mrs Sally Bingham
t (01892) 890758
e sally.bingham1@btopenworld.com

LEAFIELD
Oxfordshire

King John's Barn ★★★★
Self Catering
Contact: Mrs Vicky Greves
t (01993) 878075
e info@kingjohnsbarn.co.uk
w kingjohnsbarn.co.uk

LEE COMMON
Buckinghamshire

'The Barn' Lower Bassibones Farm
Rating Applied For
Self Catering
Contact: Mr & Mrs Geoffrey & Anthea Hartley
t (01494) 837798
e lowerbassibones@yahoo.co.uk

The Cottage ★★★
Self Catering
Contact: Mrs Bette Brumpton
t (01494) 837246

LEE-ON-THE-SOLENT
Hampshire

The Beach House ★★★
Self Catering
Contact: Mrs Driver
t (023) 9255 4882

The Chart House ★★★
Self Catering
Contact: Mr Brook White
t (023) 9255 4145
e brook.white1@btopenworld.com
w brook.white1.btinternet.co.uk

LEEDS
Kent

1 & 2 Orchard View ★★★
Self Catering
Contact: Mr Stuart Winter
Garden of England Cottages
t (01732) 369168
e holidays@gardenofenglandcottages.co.uk
w gardenofenglandcottages.co.uk

LENHAM
Kent

5 Lime Tree Cottages ★★★
Self Catering
Contact: Mr Peter Hasler
t (01622) 851310
e pvhasler@hotmail.com
w kentcottage.com

Apple Pye Cottage ★★★★
Self Catering
t (01622) 858878
e diane@bramleyknowlefarm.co.uk
w bramleyknowlefarm.co.uk

Court Lodge Cottage ★★★
Self Catering
Contact: Mrs Brenda Beck
Freedom Holiday Homes
t (01580) 720770
e mail@freedomholidayhomes.co.uk
w freedomholidayhomes.co.uk

The Olde Shoppe ★★★
Self Catering
Contact: Mrs Brenda Beck
Freedom Holiday Homes
t (01580) 720770
e mail@freedomholidayhomes.co.uk
w freedomholidayhomes.co.uk

The Pavilion ★★★
Self Catering
Contact: Alison Cannon
t (01622) 858423
e alison@bluehousefarm.co.uk
w bluehousefarm.co.uk

LEWES
East Sussex

15 Barons Walk
Rating Applied For
Self Catering
t (01273) 479529

22 South Street
Rating Applied For
Self Catering
Contact: Mr & Mrs Richard Burrows
t (01273) 480423

5 Buckhurst Close ★★★
Self Catering
Contact: Mrs S Foulds
t (01273) 474755

The Finings ★★★★
Self Catering
Contact: Mrs Sara Gosling
t (01273) 480084
e fullofbeans@tempeh.globalnet.co.uk

Heath Farm, Plumpton Green ★★★★ *Self Catering*
Contact: Mrs Marilyn Hanbury
t (01273) 890712
e hanbury@heath-farm.com
w heath-farm.com

Mill Laine Farm, Offham
★★★★-★★★★★
Self Catering
Contact: Mrs Susan Harmer
Offham
t (01273) 475473
e harmer@farming.co.uk
w milllainebarns.co.uk

Sussex Countryside Accommodation, Barcombe
★★★★ *Self Catering*
Contact: Mrs Hazel Gaydon
Sussex Countryside Accommodation
t (01273) 400625
e info@crinkhouse.co.uk
w sussexcountryaccommodation.co.uk

LINTON
Kent

Loddington Oast ★★★★
Self Catering
t (01622) 747777
e contact@loddingtonoast.co.uk
w lodingtonoast.co.uk

LITTLEHAMPTON
West Sussex

Racing Greens (S/C) ★★★★
Self Catering
t (01903) 732972
e racingreens@aol.com
w littlehampton-racing-greens.co.uk

Look out for establishments participating in the Walkers and Cyclists Welcome Schemes

Victoria Holidays ★★★
Self Catering
Contact: Mrs Ogrodnik
t (01903) 722644

LOCKINGE
Oxfordshire

The Coach House
Rating Applied For
Self Catering
Contact: Mrs Janine Beaumont
t (01235) 771866

LOCKS HEATH
Hampshire

Stepping Stones ★★★★
Self Catering
Contact: Mrs Barbara Habens
t (01489) 572604
e jhabens@toucansurf.com
w members.lycos.co.uk/selfcateringannexe

LONG CRENDON
Buckinghamshire

The Old Needle House Annexe ★★★ *Self Catering*
Contact: Mrs Kate King
The Old Needle House
t (01844) 208350
e kate@oldneedlehouse.com

LONGPARISH
Hampshire

Cowleaze Cottage ★★★★
Self Catering
Contact: Mr Clive Hancock
Moundsmere Estate Management Ltd
t (01256) 389253
e clive@moundsmere.co.uk
w moundsmere.co.uk

LOUDWATER
Buckinghamshire

Daisy's Cottage ★★★★
Self Catering
t (01494) 520964
e newmanwill@aol.com

LOWER BEEDING
West Sussex

Black Cottage, Newells Farm
★★★–★★★★ *Self Catering*
Contact: Mrs Vicky Storey
t (01403) 891326
e vicky.storey@btinternet.com

LYDD ON SEA
Kent

69 Coast Drive ★★★
Self Catering
Contact: Mrs Brenda Beck
Freedom Holiday Homes
t (01580) 720770
e mail@freedomholidayhomes.co.uk
w freedomholidayhomes.co.uk

LYMINGTON
Hampshire

No 17 Southampton Road
★★★★ *Self Catering*
Contact: Miss Julie Stevens & Andrew Baxendine
t (01590) 676445
e juleestevens@aol.com
w 17southamptonroad.co.uk

2 Uplay Cottages ★★★
Self Catering
Contact: Ms Jacquie Taylor
Three Corners
t (01590) 641810
e bookings@halcyonholidays.com
w halcyonholidays.com

8 Admirals Court ★★★★
Self Catering
Contact: Mrs Mayes
Ridgeway Rents New Forest Cottages
t (01590) 679655
e holidays@newforestcottages.co.uk

8 Station Street ★★★
Self Catering
Contact: Mrs Joanne Hill
J R Hill Residential Letting Agency
t (01590) 679200
e enquiries@jrhill.co.uk

Agnora Cottage ★★★
Self Catering
Contact: Rose Warner
t (01590) 626277
e cccinfo@btconnect.com
w new-forest-holiday-cottage.co.uk

Bourne House ★★★★
Self Catering
Contact: Mr Mare
Bourne House & Rainbow Cottage
t (01483) 772086
e jppmare@aol.com
w jppmare.ukhouse.com

Corner Cottages ★★★★
Self Catering
Contact: Mrs Ginny Neath
Courtyard Cottage
t (01590) 612080
e rg.neath@virgin.net

Silk Cottage ★★★★
Self Catering
Contact: Mrs Anne Paterson
t (01590) 688797
e annevp@ntlworld.com

Solent Reach Mews ★★★★
Self Catering
Contact: Ms Denise Farmer
t (01590) 671648
e enquiries@hurstviewleisure.co.uk

De La Warr House ★★★★
Self Catering
Contact: Mrs Joanne Broadway
t (01590) 672785
e delawarrhouse@aol.com

Waterford Cottage ★★★★
Self Catering
Contact: Mrs Sally Sargeaunt
t (01425) 628970

Wheathill ★★★ *Self Catering*
Contact: Mrs Jacquie Taylor
Three Corners
t (01590) 641810
e jacquie@halcyonholidays.com
w halcyonholidays.com

LYNDHURST
Hampshire

95B High Street ★★–★★★
Self Catering
Contact: Mr & Mrs John Langston
Monkton Cottage
t (023) 8028 2206

Bay Tree Cottage ★★★★
Self Catering
Contact: Mrs Katrina Long
12 Princes Crescent
t (023) 8028 2821
w baytreecottage.co.uk

The Cottage ★★★
Self Catering
Contact: Mrs Sheila Robinson
t (023) 8028 3697

Dairy Cottage ★★★★
Self Catering
Contact: Mrs Cynthia Harward
t (023) 8028 2629
e enquiries@newforestdairy.co.uk

Fern Cottage ★★★
Self Catering
Contact: Mr Robin Austin
The Hollies
t 07717 796156
e robaust@aol.com
w lyndhurstholidays.com

The Old Stables ★★★
Self Catering
Contact: Jacquie Taylor
Halcyon Holiday Cottages
t (01590) 641810
e booking@halcyonholidays.com
w halcyonholidays.com

Penny Farthing Hotel & Cottages ★★★★
Self Catering
Contact: Mr Mike Saqui
The Penny Farthing Hotel
t (023) 8028 4422
e cottages@pennyfarthinghotel.co.uk

Rhubarb Cottage
Rating Applied For
Self Catering
t (023) 8081 2753
e rob@intheforest.co.uk
w escapetothenewforest.co.uk

Stable Cottage ★★
Self Catering
Contact: Mr Stephen Morris
t (01454) 227322
e newforest.cottage@btinternet.com

Yew Tree Cottage ★★★★
Self Catering
Headmaster's House
t (01962) 715491

Yorke Cottage ★★★★
Self Catering
Contact: Mrs Helen Walker
t (023) 8029 2428
e helen@yorkecottage.co.uk

LYNSTED
Kent

The Black Lion
Rating Applied For
Self Catering
Contact: Mrs Morgan
t (01795) 521229

MAIDENHEAD
Berkshire

11 Cadwell Drive ★★★
Self Catering
Contact: Mrs Vivien Williams
t (01628) 627370
e rvwilliams@btopenworld.com

Courtyard Cottages ★★★★
Self Catering
Contact: Mrs Carol Bardo
Moor Farm
t (01628) 633761
e moorfm@aol.com
w moorfarm.com

Sheephouse Manor
★★–★★★ *Self Catering*
Contact: Mrs Caroline Street
t (01628) 776902
e info@sheephousemanor.co.uk
w sheephousemanor.co.uk

MAIDSTONE
Kent

The Old Wagon Lodge
★★★★ *Self Catering*
Contact: Sarah Sunnucks
Linton Hill
t (01622) 745631
e scarytoe@kentit.net
w rankinsfarm.co.uk

The Orchard Flat, Ferlaga
★★ *Self Catering*
t (01622) 726919
e pamclark@ferlaga.freeserve.co.uk

Twitchers ★★★★
Self Catering
Contact: Mrs Brenda Beck
Freedom Holiday Homes
t (01580) 720770
e mail@freedomholidayhomes.co.uk
w freedomholidayhomes.co.uk

MANSTON
Kent

Annies Cottage ★★★★
Self Catering
Contact: Mr & Mrs Box
t (01843) 823371
e anniescottage1@aol.com
w anniescottage1.co.uk

MAPLEDURHAM
Oxfordshire

Mapledurham Holiday Cottages ★★★–★★★★
Self Catering
Contact: Mrs Lola Andrews
t (0118) 972 4292
e mtrust1997@aol.com
w mapledurham.co.uk

MARGATE
Kent

Modern House Palm Bay
★★★ *Self Catering*
Contact: Mrs Bowles
t (01732) 843396
e richard@ferryman.co.uk
w ferryman.co.uk/palmbay

Salmestone Grange ★★★★
Self Catering
Salmestone Grange
t (01843) 231161
e salmestonegrange@aol.com
w salmestonegrange.co.uk

MATFIELD
Kent

The Coach House ★★★★
Self Catering
Lees Court, The Green
t (01892) 723181

MAYFIELD
East Sussex

Freedom Holiday Homes – Fair Oak Farm ★★★★
Self Catering
Contact: Mrs Brenda Beck
Freedom Holiday Homes
t (01580) 720770
e mail@freedomholidayhomes.co.uk
w freedomholidayhomes.co.uk

MEDSTEAD
Hampshire

The Barn, Medstead ★★★★
Self Catering
t (01420) 562682
e sarah.darch@btinternet.com
w barfordfarmhouse.com

MEOPHAM
Kent

Feathercot Lodge ★★★★
Self Catering
Contact: Mrs S Smith
New Street Road
t (01474) 872265 & 07764 784370
e feathercot@hotmail.com
w holidayhomeandaway.com

Sunrise ★★★★ *Self Catering*
Contact: Mr Mike Dickety
Kites Letting Services Ltd.
t (01474) 573047
e mikedickety@beeb.net
w halcyon-gifts.co.uk/holidaylet2.htm

MERSHAM
Kent

Garden Cottage at Munday Manor ★★★★ *Self Catering*
t (01233) 720353
e johnrais@aol.com
w mundaymanor.co.uk

Gill Farm ★★★★
Self Catering
Contact: Mrs Jan Bowman
t (01303) 261247
e jan@studio2uk.com/gillfarm
w studio2uk.com/gillfarm

MERSTONE
Isle of Wight

Chapel Cottage ★★★★
Self Catering
t (01798) 872705
e tony@simpson-family.co.uk
w chapelcottage.co.uk

Hackney Stable ★★★★
Self Catering
Contact: Mrs Honor Vass
Island Cottage Holidays
t (01929) 482280

Parlour Cottage ★★★★
Self Catering
Contact: Mrs Howon Vass
Island Cottage Holidays
t (01929) 481555
w islandcottageholidays.com

MIDHURST
West Sussex

Cowdray Park Holiday Cottages ★★★★
Self Catering
Contact: Mrs Sam Collins
t (01730) 812423
e enquiries@cowdray.co.uk
w cowdray.co.uk

MILFORD ON SEA
Hampshire

Curlew Cottage ★★★★
Self Catering
Flexford Rise
t (01590) 683744

Erinvale ★★★★ *Self Catering*
Contact: Margaret Cummings
t (01590) 643944
e cummingsfrd@aol.com

Forest Farm ★★★
Self Catering
Contact: Ms Pippa Jarman
t (01590) 644365
e driving@ffarm.fsnet.co.uk

Maryland Court ★★★★
Self Catering
Contact: Mr Robin Drake
t (01590) 643624

The Old Bakery ★★★
Self Catering
Contact: Mrs Braithwaite
t (01425) 620733
e info@old-bakery.co.uk

Old Walls ★★★ *Self Catering*
Contact: Mrs Kate Danby
t (01590) 642138
e mrskatedanby@aol.com

Penny Pot ★★★★
Self Catering
Contact: Mr Roy Plummer
t (01590) 641210
e pennypot@hapennyhouse.co.uk

Pine View Cottage ★★★
Self Catering
Contact: Mrs Sheri Gadd
Cherry Trees
t (01590) 643746
e cherrytrees@beeb.net
w theaa.co.uk/region12/98653.htmlnewforest.demon.co.uk/cherrytrees.htm

Windmill Cottage ★★★
Self Catering
Contact: Mrs Perham
14 Kivernell Road
t (01590) 643516

MINSTER LOVELL
Oxfordshire

Hill Grove Cottage ★★★★
Self Catering
Contact: Mrs Katharine Brown
Hill Grove Farms
t (01993) 703120
e kbrown@eggconnect.net
w country-accom.co.uk/hill-grove-farm

MOLLINGTON
Oxfordshire

The Stables, The Shippon, The Byre – Anita's Holiday Cottages ★★★–★★★★
Self Catering
Contact: Mr & Mrs Darrel & Anita Gail Jeffries
Anita's Holiday Cottages
t (01295) 750731
e anitagail@btopenworld.com

MONKS HORTON
Kent

Horton Cottage Annexe ★★★★ *Self Catering*
Contact: Mrs Brenda Beck
Freedom Holiday Homes
t (01580) 720770
e mail@freedomholidayhomes.co.uk
w freedomholidayhomes.co.uk

MONXTON
Hampshire

The Den at Millcroft ★★★★
Self Catering
t (01264) 710618
e millcroft@aol.com

NAPHILL
Buckinghamshire

High Gables ★★★★
Self Catering
Contact: Mr Stefan Zachary
t (01494) 562591
e zach@btinternet.com

NEW MILTON
Hampshire

The Granary ★★
Self Catering
t (01425) 610332

NEWBRIDGE
Isle of Wight

Laurel Cottage ★★★★
Self Catering
Contact: Mrs Honor Vass
Island Cottage Holidays
t (01929) 480080
e enq@islandcottageholidays.com
w islandcottageholidays.com

NEWBURY
Berkshire

Peregrine Cottage ★★★★★
Self Catering
Contact: Mrs Elizabeth Knight
t (01635) 42585
e lizknight@amserve.net

Yaffles
Rating Applied For
Self Catering
Contact: Mr & Mrs Steve & Nikki Absolom
Yaffles
t (01635) 201100
e yaffles@ukonline.co.uk
w yaffles.org

NEWCHURCH
Isle of Wight

Barn Cottage ★★★
Self Catering
t (01983) 865349
e anne.corbin@virgin.net
w wightfarmholidays.co.uk

Clematis ★★★ *Self Catering*
t (01983) 867613
e alistair.jupe@btinternet.com
w btinternet.com/~alistair.jupe

Knighton Farmhouse ★★★★ *Self Catering*
Island Cottage Holidays
t (01929) 480080
e enq@islandcottageholidays.com

Knighton Gorges ★★★★
Self Catering
Contact: Mrs Honor Vass
Island Cottage Holidays
t (01929) 480080
e enq@islandcottageholidays.com

Mersley Farm ★★★–★★★★ *Self Catering*
Contact: Mrs Jennifer Boswell
t (01983) 865213
e jenny@mersleyfarm.co.uk
w mersleyfarm.co.uk

Paper Barn & Squire Thatchers Barn ★★★★
Self Catering
Island Cottage Holidays
t (01929) 481555

Tumbleweed Cottage
Rating Applied For
Self Catering
Contact: Catherine Hopper
Island Holiday Homes
t (01983) 521113
e enquiries@island-holiday-homes.net
w island-holiday-homes.net

NEWENDEN
Kent

The Bothy and The Barn ★★★★ *Self Catering*
Contact: Mrs Brenda Beck
Freedom Holiday Homes
t (01580) 720770
e mail@freedomholidayhomes.co.uk
w freedomholidayhomes.co.uk

NEWHAVEN
East Sussex

The Old Farmhouse ★★★–★★★★ *Self Catering*
Contact: Mrs Gill Canham
t (020) 8786 5868
e gillcanham@yahoo.co.uk
w visitsussex.org/theoldfarmhouse

NEWICK
East Sussex

Manor House Cottage ★★★★ *Self Catering*
Contact: Mrs Jane Roberts
t (01825) 722868
e jane.roberts@tinyworld.co.uk
w manorhousecottage.co.uk

NEWPORT
Isle of Wight

5 Miramar Court ★★★★
Self Catering
Island Holiday Homes
t (01983) 521113

Apartment 3 Clyde House ★★★★ *Self Catering*
Island Holiday Homes
t (01983) 521113

Bay Cottage ★★★
Self Catering
Island Holiday Homes
t (01983) 521113

Bethel Cottage ★★★
Self Catering
t (01983) 884742
e bridget.lewis@btinternet.com

Buttercup Barn Cottage ★★★★ *Self Catering*
Island Holiday Homes
t (01983) 521113

Cavendish House ★★★★
Self Catering
Island Holiday Homes
t (01983) 521113

The Cottage, Stone Farm ★★★★ *Self Catering*
Contact: Mrs Honor Vass
Island Cottage Holidays
t (01929) 480080
e enq@islandcottageholidays.com
w islandcottageholidays.com

Courtlands ★★★
Self Catering
Island Holiday Homes
t (01983) 521113

Dove, Blueberry and Oaktree Cottage ★★★★
Self Catering
Contact: Honor Vass
Island Cottage Holidays
t (01929) 481555
e enq@islandcottageholidays.com

East Wing Alum Bay House ★★★ *Self Catering*
Island Holiday Homes
t (01983) 616644

Froglands Farm ★★★★
Self Catering
Contact: Mrs Linda Dungey
t (01983) 821027
e s.dungey@btinternet.com
w thecowshed.co.uk

Hillview, Bannock Road ★★★ *Self Catering*
Island Holiday Homes
t (01983) 521113

Marvel Cottage ★★★★
Self Catering
t (01983) 822691
e s@mys.uk.com
w mys.uk.com

Mole Cottage 23 ★★★
Self Catering
Island Holiday Homes
t (01983) 521113

The Old Brew House ★★★★ *Self Catering*
Contact: Mrs Honor Vass
Island Cottage Holidays
t (01929) 480080

Ye Olde Cottage ★★★★
Self Catering
Contact: Ms C Hopper
Island Holiday Homes
t (01983) 521113

Therles Cottage ★★★★
Self Catering
Island Cottage Holidays
t (01929) 481555

Thornbury House ★★★
Self Catering
Island Holiday Homes
t (01983) 521113

Waters Edge
Rating Applied For
Self Catering
Island Holiday Homes
t (01983) 521113

West Standen Farm ★★★★
Self Catering
t (01983) 522099
e edwin@weststanden.fsnet.co.uk
w weststandenfarm.co.uk

NINGWOOD
Isle of Wight

Brookside Farm Cottage ★
Self Catering
Contact: Mrs Rowena Nihell
t (01983) 761832
e rowena.nihell@brookside-farmcottage.co.uk
w brookside-farmcottage.co.uk

The Granary ★★★★★
Self Catering
Contact: Mrs Honor Vass
Island Cottage Holidays
t (01929) 480080
e enq@islandcottageholidays.com

NITON
Isle of Wight

Bridge Cottage ★★★
Self Catering
Contact: Mrs Lisa Baskill
Home from Home Holidays
t (01983) 854340
e admin@hfromh.co.uk

Fern Gully ★★★★
Self Catering
Island Cottage Holidays
t (01929) 480080
e enq@islandcottageholidays.com

Gate Lodge ★★ *Self Catering*
Contact: Mrs Lisa Baskill
Home from Home Holidays
t (01983) 854340
e admin@hfromh.co.uk

Pictou ★★★ *Self Catering*
Contact: Mrs Lisa Baskill
Home from Home Holidays
t (01983) 854340
e admin@hfromh.co.uk

Wight Heaven ★★
Self Catering
Contact: Mr & Mrs John Sheppard
t (01983) 551501
e dadshep@dial.pipex.com
w wightheaven.co.uk

NITON UNDERCLIFF
Isle of Wight

Puckaster Cottage, Puckaster House & Puckaster Wing ★★★★
Self Catering
Contact: Mrs Honor Vass
Island Cottage Holidays
t (01929) 480080
e enq@islandcottageholidays.com
w islandcottageholidays.com

St Catherine's Head ★★★★
Self Catering
Rural Retreats. Araycott
t (01386) 852855
e c.pearman@ruralretreats.co.uk
w ruralretreats.co.uk

NOKE
Oxfordshire

Manor Barn ★★★★
Self Catering
Contact: Ms Emma Righton
t (01865) 376772
e er@oxfordshortlets.co.uk
w isisnokelets.co.uk

NORLEYWOOD
Hampshire

The Bee Garden ★★★★
Self Catering
Contact: Mr Mayes
Ridgeway Rents New Forest Cottages
t (01590) 679655
e holidays@newforestcottages.co.uk

NORTH LEIGH
Oxfordshire

Old Bakehouse ★★★★
Self Catering
Contact: Mrs Patricia Colson
t (01993) 881207
e pat@colson-stock-property.fsnet.co.uk

Wylcot Cottage ★★★★
Self Catering
Contact: Mrs Joy Crew
t (01993) 868614

NORTH MORETON
Oxfordshire

Haddon Close Mews
Rating Applied For
Self Catering
Contact: Nigel Ainge
t (01235) 512519
e nigel@haddonclose.com
w haddonclose.com

NORTH NEWINGTON
Oxfordshire

Herrieff's Cottage ★★★★
Self Catering
t (01295) 738835
e mary@herrieffsfarm.freeserve.co.uk

NORTHIAM
East Sussex

Hop Press Cottage
Rating Applied For
Self Catering
Contact: Ms Brenda Haines
Hop Press Cottage
t (01797) 252011
e brenda@curtishaines.co.uk
w froglets.uk.com

NORTHMOOR
Oxfordshire

Rectory Farm Cottages ★★★★ *Self Catering*
Contact: Mrs Mary Anne Florey
Rectory Farm
t (01865) 300207
e pj.florey@farmline.com
w oxtowns.co.uk/rectoryfarm

NORTON
Isle of Wight

The Cottage ★★★★
Self Catering
Contact: Mrs Sue Melluish
t (01590) 626259
e suemelluish@aol.com

Treetops ★★★★
Self Catering
Contact: Mrs Howon Vass
Island Cottage Holidays
t (01929) 481555
e honor@islandcottageholidays.com
w islandcottageholidays.com

NUTLEY
East Sussex

The Old Cart Lodge ★★★★
Self Catering
Contact: Mrs Pauline Graves
2 Victoria Cottages
t (01825) 712475
e grapauline@aol.com

Whitehouse Farm Holiday Cottages ★★-★★★
Self Catering
Contact: Mr Keith Wilson
Whitehouse Farm Holiday Cottages
t (01825) 712377
e keith.g.r.wilson@btinternet.com
w streets-ahead.com/whitehousefarm

OLNEY
Buckinghamshire

Hyde Farm Cottages ★★★★
Self Catering
Contact: Mrs Penny Reynolds
t (01234) 711223
e stayat.thehyde@btinternet.com

The Old Stone Barn ★★★★
Self Catering
Contact: Mr & Mrs G J Pibworth
t (01234) 711655
e info@oldstonebarn.co.uk
w oldstonebarn.co.uk

OTTERDEN
Kent

Frith Farm House ★★★★★
Self Catering
Contact: Mrs Susan Chesterfield
t (01795) 890701
e enquiries@frithfarmhouse.co.uk
w frithfarmhouse.co.uk

OWSLEBURY
Hampshire

Hensting Valley Chalet ★★★ *Self Catering*
Contact: Mrs Diana Carter
Dell Croft
t (01962) 777297

Lower Farm House Annexe ★★★★ *Self Catering*
Contact: Mrs Penelope Bowes
t (01962) 777676
e pbowes@boltblue.com

OXFORD
Oxfordshire

17 Kingston Road ★★★★
Self Catering
Contact: Mrs Pru Dickson
t (01865) 516913
e pru.dickson@tesco.net
w oxfordcity.co.uk/accom/studioflat

45 Thackley End ★★★
Self Catering
ETAL Ltd
t (01865) 355581 & 07870 234725
e info@weeklyhome.com
w weeklyhome.com

48 St Bernards Road ★★★
Self Catering
Contact: Ms Julie Gardiner
t (01865) 321101
e greenhavenoxford@btconnect.com
w holidayhomeoxford.co.uk

7 Bannister Close ★★★
Self Catering
Contact: Mrs Irene Priestly
t (01865) 251095

Apartments in Oxford ★★★★★ *Self Catering*
Contact: Mrs Sheena Witney
St Thomas' Mews Apartments in Oxford Limited
t (01865) 254077
e resasst@oxstay.co.uk
w oxstay.co.uk

Cherbridge Cottage
★★★★★ *Self Catering*
Contact: Ms Laura Colman
Hill Farm
t (01865) 512920 & 07976 288329
e laura@cherbridgecottages.co.uk
w cherbridgecottages.co.uk

Green Cottage ★★★★
Self Catering
Contact: Mr & Mrs P Hankey
t (01865) 300740
e lettings@thegreen.co.uk
w oxtowns.co.uk/greencottage

Otmoor Holidays ★★★★
Self Catering
Contact: Mrs Emma Righton
t (01865) 373766
e info@oxfordholidays.co.uk
w oxfordholidays.co.uk

PANGBOURNE
Berkshire

Brambly Thatch ★★★
Self Catering
Contact: Mr & Mrs Hatt
Merricroft Farming
t (0118) 984 3121
e merricroft@yahoo.co.uk

The Old Rectory Cottage
★★★ *Self Catering*
t (01491) 671344

Soldalen Annexe ★★
Self Catering
Contact: Mr & Mrs John & Bente Kirk
t (0118) 984 2924

PEASMARSH
East Sussex

Joywell Cottage ★★★★
Self Catering
Contact: Mrs Brenda Beck
Freedom Holiday Homes
t (01580) 720770
e mail@freedomholidayhomes.co.uk
w freedomholidayhomes.co.uk

Pond Cottage ★★★★
Self Catering
t (01797) 230394
e info@claytonfarm.co.uk
w rye-tourism.co.uk/pondcottage

Tanhouse Cottage
Rating Applied For
Self Catering
Contact: Mrs Brenda Beck
Freedom Holiday Homes
t (01580) 720770
e mail@freedomholidayhomes.co.uk
w freedomholidayhomes.co.uk

PENNINGTON
Hampshire

Little Thatch
Rating Applied For
Self Catering
Contact: Suzannah Nash
t (01582) 842831
e bruce@mortagepros.co.uk
w littlethatchcottage.com

White Cottage
Rating Applied For
Self Catering
Contact: Mrs Jane Rose
t (01590) 644256
e a.rose@virgin.net
w newforest-bedbreakfast.co.uk

PENSHURST
Kent

3 Bottle House Cottage
★★★★ *Self Catering*
Garden of England Cottages
t (01732) 369168
e holidays@gardenofenglandcottages.co.uk
w gardenofenglandcottages.co.uk

PETT LEVEL
East Sussex

Grace Dieu ★★★★
Self Catering
t (020) 7624 0525

PETWORTH
West Sussex

The Old Dairy ★★★★
Self Catering
Contact: Mrs Rosaleen Waugh
t (01798) 342900
w theolddairy.com

PILTDOWN
East Sussex

The Barn ★★★★
Self Catering
Lower Morgan House
t (01525) 765553
e sarina@sarina7.wanadoo.co.uk

Mallingdown Oast
Rating Applied For
Self Catering
Contact: Mrs H Creamer
t (01825) 722777
e mfcreamer1@tiscali.co.uk

Tom's Lodge ★★★
Self Catering
Contact: Teresa Antrobus
t (01825) 764723
e antrobus62@btinternet.com

PLAXTOL
Kent

Golding Hop Farm Cottage
★★★ *Self Catering*
Contact: Mrs Jacqueline Vincent
Golding Hop Farm
t (01732) 885432
e info@goldinghopfarm.com
w goldinghopfarm.com

PORCHFIELD
Isle of Wight

Buntshill Barns
Rating Applied For
Self Catering
Contact: Ken Shynn
t (01983) 529691
e ken@buntshillbarns.co.uk
w buntshillbarns.co.uk

Buzzard Barn ★★★★
Self Catering
Contact: K. Shynn
t (01983) 529691
e ken@buntshillbarns.co.uk
w buntshillbarns.co.uk

PORTSMOUTH & SOUTHSEA
Hampshire

Alamar ★ *Self Catering*
Contact: Mr Alan Hyde
t (023) 9282 6352

Atlantic Apartments ★★★
Self Catering
Contact: Mrs Dawn Sait
Atlantic Apartments
t (023) 9282 3606
w portsmouth-apartments.co.uk/atlantic.htm

Geminair Holiday & Business Flats ★★★ *Self Catering*
Contact: Mrs Pamela Holman
t (023) 9282 1602
e gemflat@aol.com
w gemflat.co.uk

Greenhays Business/Holiday Accommodation ★★★★
Self Catering
Contact: Mrs Christine Martin
t (023) 9273 7590
w greenhays.co.uk

Helena Court Apartments
★★★ *Self Catering*
Contact: Mrs Wendy Haley
t (023) 9273 2116
e tikitouch@hotmail.com

Kenilworth Court Holiday Flats ★★★★ *Self Catering*
Contact: Mrs Teresa Sparrowhawk
t (023) 9273 4205
e kenilworth@ntlworld.com

Ocean Apartments ★★★
Self Catering
Contact: Mrs Dawn Sait
t (023) 9273 4233
e ocean@portsmouth-apartments.co.uk
w portsmouth-apartments.co.uk/ocean.htm

Salisbury Apartments ★★★
Self Catering
Contact: Mrs Dawn Sait
t (023) 9282 3606
e salisbury@portsmouth-apartments.co.uk
w portsmouth-apartments.co.uk

South Parade Apartments
★★★ *Self Catering*
Contact: Mrs Dawn Sait
t (023) 9273 4342
e southparade@portsmouth-apartments.co.uk
w portsmouth-apartments.co.uk/southparade.htm

Sovereign Holiday Flatlets ★
Self Catering
Contact: Mr & Mrs Michael Cummings
t (023) 9281 1398

Wallington Court ★–★★★
Self Catering
t (023) 9283 3831

PRINCES RISBOROUGH
Buckinghamshire

Stable Cottage, Old Callow Down Farm ★★★
Self Catering
t (01844) 344416
e oldcallow@aol.com
w chilternscottage.co.uk

Windmill Farm ★★
Self Catering
t (01844) 343901
e windmill_farm@hotmail.com

PRINSTED
West Sussex

4 The Square ★★
Self Catering
Contact: Ms Anne Brooks
t (01243) 377489
e fourthesquare@hotmail.com
w fourthesquare.co.uk

PRIVETT
Hampshire

Woodside Farm ★★★★
Self Catering
Contact: Mr John Crisp
t 07766 302257
e woodsidefarm@yahoo.co.uk
w woodsidefarm.net

RADNAGE
Buckinghamshire

Golden Acres Farm ★★★
Self Catering
Contact: Mrs Julia Pitcher
t (01494) 483378

RAMSGATE
Kent

23 The Lawns ★★★★
Self Catering
Contact: Mrs Jean Lawrence
Earlhgat Partnership
t (01843) 591422
e jnancylawrence@aol.com
w lawrencefamilyholidays.co.uk

The Cottage ★★★
Self Catering
Contact: Ms Ann Sadler
t (020) 8670 9447
e cottagebookings@tiscali.co.uk

Hamilton House Holiday Flats ★★–★★★ *Self Catering*
Contact: Mrs A Burridge
t (01843) 582592
e elizabeth@hamiltonhouse.wanadoo.co.uk

Regency House ★★★★
Self Catering
Contact: Mrs Carolyn Heward
t (020) 7735 1744
e carolynheward@btinternet.com
w royalroad.co.uk

RINGWOOD
Hampshire

Heather Cottage ★★★
Self Catering
Contact: Mr & Mrs Peter Harper
The Gables
t (01425) 474567
e pjh.hols@btinternet.com

Karelia Holidays ★★★
Self Catering
Contact: Mr Richard Gleed
t (01425) 478920
e rgleed@kareliaholidays.co.uk
w kareliaholidays.co.uk

ROBERTSBRIDGE
East Sussex

Butters Cottage ★★★★
Self Catering
Contact: Mrs Brenda Beck
Freedom Holiday Homes
t (01580) 720770
e mail@freedomholidayhomes.co.uk
w freedomholidayhomes.co.uk

Holly Cottage ★★★
Self Catering
Contact: Mrs Ann Campbell
Fairhaven Holiday Cottages
t (01634) 300089
e enquiries@fairhaven-holidays.co.uk

The Kell
Rating Applied For
Self Catering
Contact: Mrs Brenda Beck
Freedom Holiday Homes
t (01580) 720770
e mail@freedomholidayhomes.co.uk
w freedomholidayhomes.co.uk

Rose Cottage Studio ★★★
Self Catering
Freedom Holiday Homes
t (01580) 720770
e mail@freedomholidayhomes.co.uk
w freedomholidayhomes.co.uk

Strawberry Hill Estate
★★★-★★★★ *Self Catering*
t (01424) 775555
e enquiries@1066leisure.com
w 1066leisure.com

Tudor Cottage ★★★★
Self Catering
Contact: Mr Stuart Winter
Garden of England Cottages
t (01732) 369168
e holidays@gardenofenglandcottages.co.uk
w gardenofenglandcottages.co.uk

ROCHESTER
Kent

Stable Cottages ★★★★
Self Catering
Contact: Mrs Debbie Symonds
Stable Cottages
t (01634) 272439 & 07802 662702
e stablecottages@btinternet.com
w stable-cottages.com

ROLVENDEN
Kent

The Little House Coveneys
★★★★ *Self Catering*
t (01580) 241736
e jfield.coveneys@virgin.net

ROMSEY
Hampshire

The Old Smithy Cottage
★★★ *Self Catering*
t (01794) 511778
e paul@smithycottage.co.uk
w smithycottage.co.uk

ROOKLEY
Isle of Wight

Kennerley House ★★★
Self Catering
Contact: Mrs Carol Foote
t (01983) 842001
e carolfoote@btinternet.com

Little Pidford Farm Cottages
★★★★ *Self Catering*
t (01983) 721841
e pidford.farm@btinternet.com

ROPLEY
Hampshire

Dairy Cottage ★★★★
Self Catering
t (01962) 773348
e malcolm@cowgrove.co.uk

ROTHERFIELD
East Sussex

Medway Farm Barn Cottage, Rotherfield ★★★★
Self Catering
Contact: Mr & Mrs Mark & Sue Playford
Medway Farm Barn
t (01892) 852802
e contact@medwayfarmbarn.co.uk
w medwayfarmbarn.co.uk

ROYAL TUNBRIDGE WELLS
Kent

1 Stable Mews ★★★
Self Catering
Contact: Mrs Brenda Beck
Freedom Holiday Homes
t (01580) 720770
e mail@freedomholidayhomes.co.uk
w freedomholidayhomes.co.uk

22 Hawkenbury Mead ★★★
Self Catering
Contact: Mr R H Wright
Hawkenbury Farm
t (01892) 536977
e rhwright1@aol.com

The Beach House ★★★
Self Catering
Contact: Ms Palmour
t (01892) 557781
e oneyeshut@onetel.com
w farmcombelane.co.uk

Broad Oak House ★★★
Self Catering
Contact: Ms Tina Seymour
t (01892) 619065
e tina@thctraining.co.uk
w tunbridgewellsonline.com

Culverden House
Rating Applied For
Self Catering
Contact: Mrs Brenda Beck
Freedom Holiday Homes
t (01580) 720770
e mail@freedomholidayhomes.co.uk
w freedomholidayhomes.co.uk

Farnham Lane
Rating Applied For
Self Catering
Contact: Mr Stuart Winter
Garden of England Cottages
t (01732) 369168
e holidays@gardenofenglandcottages.co.uk
w gardenofenglandcottages.co.uk

Ford Cottage ★★★
Self Catering
Contact: Mrs Wendy Cusdin
Ford Cottage
t (01892) 531419
e FordCottage@tinyworld.co.uk
w fordcottage.co.uk

Garden Flat ★★★★
Self Catering
Contact: Mr Stuart Winter
Garden of England Cottages
t (01732) 369168
e holidays@gardenofenglandcottages.co.uk
w gardenofenglandcottages.co.uk

Hollambys ★★★
Self Catering
Contact: Mr Andrew Joad
t (01892) 864203
e ajoad@hollambys.co.uk

Itaris Properties Limited
★★★★ *Self Catering*
Contact: Mrs Angela May
Itaris Properties Ltd
t (01892) 511065
e enquiries@itaris.co.uk
w itaris.co.uk

Kennett ★★★★ *Self Catering*
Contact: Mrs Lesley Clements
t (01892) 533363
e gravels@onetel.com
w selfcaterkennett.co.uk

Sion House ★★★★★
Self Catering
Contact: Mrs Donna Raynsford
Maritime House
t (01273) 248888
e donna@maritimehouse.com
w sion-house.com

RUCKINGE
Kent

The Old Granary ★★★★
Self Catering
Contact: Mr Stuart Winter
Garden of England Cottages
t (01732) 369168
e holidays@gardenofenglandcottages.co.uk
w gardenofenglandcottages.co.uk

The Old Post Office ★★★
Self Catering
Contact: Mr Chris Cook
t (020) 8655 4466
e c.cook@btinternet.com
w ruckinge.info

Red Oak
Rating Applied For
Self Catering
Freedom Holiday Homes
t (01580) 720770
e mail@freedomholidayhomes.co.uk
w freedomholidayhomes.co.uk

RUSTINGTON
West Sussex

"PAPYRUS" 1920s Bungalow ★★★ *Self Catering*
t (01903) 725345
e joyce@16meadow89.freeserve.co.uk

Seaway ★★★ *Self Catering*
t (01903) 772548

RYDE
Isle of Wight

39 Marina Avenue
Rating Applied For
Self Catering
Contact: Catherine Hopper
Island Holiday Homes
t (01983) 521113
e enquiries@island-holiday-homes.net
w island-holiday-homes.net

4 Granary Close ★★★
Self Catering
Bembridge Holiday Homes
t (01983) 873163
e mail@bembridge-holiday-homes.co.uk
w bembridge-holiday-homes.co.uk

Benham Lodge & Forelands – Appley Farm Cottages
★★★ *Self Catering*
t (01983) 616841
e holiday@appleyfarmcottages.co.uk
w appleyfarmcottages.co.uk

Bullen Cottage ★★★★
Self Catering
Island Cottage Holidays
t (01929) 481555

Claverton House ★★★★
Self Catering
Contact: Dr Hartwig Metz
Claverton
t (01983) 613015
e clavertonhouse@aol.com
w hometown.aol.co.uk/clavertonhouse

Dungen – 42 Fishbourne Lane ★★ *Self Catering*
t (01983) 564370

Fairlands and Swains Lane
★★★★ *Self Catering*
Contact: Sue McLagan
Woodnuts, The Duver
t (01983) 874430
e sue@bembridge.com
w wightholidayhomes.com

Flat 4, Wellwood House ★★
Self Catering
t (01983) 521113

Holmwood ★★★★
Self Catering
t (01983) 614852
e nicola@holmwood-holidays.co.uk
w holmwood-holidays.co.uk

Jubilee Cottage ★★★★
Self Catering
Contact: Ms Catherine Hopper
Manager, Housing Letting
Hose Rhodes Dickson
t (01983) 616644
e enquiries@island-holiday-homes.net
w island-holiday-homes.net

Kemphill Barn
★★★-★★★★★
Self Catering
t (01983) 563880
e ronholland@btconnect.com
w kemphill.com

Kipper Cottage
Rating Applied For
Self Catering
Contact: Catherine Hopper
Island Holiday Homes
t (01983) 521113
e enquiries@island-holiday-homes.net
w island-holiday-homes.net

Lionstone House (Apartment 4) ★-★★★
Self Catering
t (01983) 563496

The Oaks ★★★ *Self Catering*
t (01983) 565769
e christinerossall@hotmail.com

Percy House ★★★
Self Catering
Contact: Ms Catherine Hopper
Manager, Housing Letting
Hose Rhodes Dickson
t (01983) 616644
e enquiries@island-holiday-homes.net
w island-holiday-homes.net

Strand House ★★★
Self Catering
t 07973 683722

Town House ★★★
Self Catering
Contact: Mrs Margaret Ackland
t (023) 8040 4612
e acklands@keeperslodge35.freeserve.co.uk

The Victorian Lodge ★★★
Self Catering
t (01983) 563366
e info@thevictorianlodge.co.uk
w thevictorianlodge.co.uk

Westfield Park Lodge
★★★★ *Self Catering*
t (01983) 854777
e westfieldparklodge@hotmail.com
w luxuryaccommodation-iow.com

Wight House ★★★★
Self Catering
Contact: Mrs Lisa Baskill
Home from Home Holidays
t (01983) 854840
e admin@hfromh.co.uk

Wilton Villa
Rating Applied For
Self Catering
Contact: Catherine Hopper
Island Holiday Homes
t (01983) 521113
e enquiries@island-holiday-homes.net
w island-holiday-homes.net

RYE
East Sussex

10 The Boathouse ★★★
Self Catering
Contact: Mr Robert Lever
Seascape
t (01424) 813566
e rslever@tn35ab.freeserve.co.uk

15 The Boathouse ★★★
Self Catering
Contact: Mr Mike Hickmott
t (01892) 863037
e mike@rye4ukbreaks.co.uk

2 Hucksteps Row ★★★
Self Catering
Contact: Mrs Brenda Beck
Freedom Holiday Homes
t (01580) 720770
e mail@freedomholidayhomes.co.uk
w freedomholidayhomes.co.uk

26 Church Square ★★★★
Self Catering
Contact: Mrs Brenda Beck
Freedom Holiday Homes
t (01580) 720770
e mail@freedomholidayhomes.co.uk
w freedomholidayhomes.co.uk

Boat House ★★★
Self Catering
Contact: Mr Chris Melville-Brown
t 07803 189031
e chris@ryeholidays.co.uk

Brandy's Cottage ★★★★
Self Catering
Contact: Mrs Jane Apperly
t (01797) 225426
e info@cadborough.co.uk
w cadborough.co.uk

Chesterfield Cottage ★★★
Self Catering
Contact: Ms Sally Bayly
t (01797) 222498 & 07956 280257
e chesterfieldcottage@virgin.net
w country-holidays.co.uk

Crispins Apartments ★★★
Self Catering
t (01797) 227492
e crispins@talk21.com

Froglets Cottage ★★★★
Self Catering
Contact: Mrs Brenda Haines
Morley Farm
t (01797) 252011
e brenda@curtishaines.co.uk
w froglets.uk.com

The Highlands ★★★★
Self Catering
Contact: Mr Bill Selwyn
t (0117) 965 1596
w ryeholidaylet.com

Homelands ★★★
Self Catering
Contact: Mrs Margaret Royle
Tutts Farm
t (01825) 723294

Larkin House ★★★
Self Catering
Contact: Ms Stella Larkin
t (01923) 857095
e tara.larkin@freenet.co.uk

Mermaid Cottage ★★★★
Self Catering
Contact: Mrs Suzie Warren
Tanners
t (01580) 712046
e mermaidcottage@supanet.com
w mermaidcottage.supanet.com

Oak Cottage ★★★★
Self Catering
Contact: Mike Fowler
Priors Barn
t (01435) 862535 & 07802 195644
e m.fowler1@btopenworld.com

Oakhurst Cottage ★★★
Self Catering
t (01797) 223118
e oakhurstcottage@aol.com
w holidaycottagerye.co.uk

Ockman Cottage ★★★
Self Catering
Contact: Mrs Brenda Beck
Freedom Holiday Homes
t (01580) 720770
e mail@freedomholidayhomes.co.uk
w freedomholidayhomes.co.uk

Providence Cottage ★★★★
Self Catering
Brainstorm Properties
t (01732) 458559

Riverview Cottage ★★★
Self Catering
Contact: Mr & Mrs Henderson
t (01732) 457837

Seaview Terrace ★★★
Self Catering
Contact: Mrs Pamela Pettigrew
t (01488) 71569
w visit.meco.uk

RYE FOREIGN
East Sussex

Blenheim and Russet Cottages ★★★★
Self Catering
Contact: Mr Stuart Winter
Garden of England Cottages
t (01732) 369168
e holidays@gardenofenglandcottages.co.uk
w gardenofenglandcottages.co.uk

RYE HARBOUR
East Sussex

1a Coastguard Square
★★★★ *Self Catering*
Contact: Mrs Brenda Beck
Freedom Holiday Homes
t (01580) 720770
e mail@freedomholidayhomes.co.uk
w freedomholidayhomes.co.uk

Harbour Lights ★★★
Self Catering
Contact: Mrs Penelope Webster
t (0114) 230 6859
e holidays@harbourlights.info

ST HELENS
Isle of Wight

2 Hope Cottages ★★★
Self Catering
Contact: Ms Jacqui Ellis
Bembridge Holiday Homes
t (01983) 873163

9 Port St Helens ★★★★
Self Catering
t (01983) 872507
e guide@oldmill.co.uk
w oldmill.co.uk

Carpenters Farm Cottage
★★ *Self Catering*
t (01983) 872450

The Glen Bungalow ★★★
Self Catering
t 07792 414408

The Haven ★★ *Self Catering*
Bembridge Holiday Homes
t (01983) 873163
e mail@bembridge-holiday-homes.co.uk
w bembridge-holiday-homes.co.uk

Isola ★★★★ *Self Catering*
t (01865) 761558
e isola@bakerbows.co.uk

The Little Shell House ★★★
Self Catering
t (020) 8449 8867
e thehinds@ntlworld.com

The Poplars ★★★
Self Catering
Contact: Mrs Honor Vass
Island Cottage Holidays
t (01929) 480080
e enq@islandcottageholidays.com
w islandcottageholidays.com

Seagull Cottage ★★★
Self Catering
t (01983) 874430

The Stables
Rating Applied For
Self Catering
Contact: Catherine Hopper
Island Holiday Homes
t (01983) 521113
e enquiries@island-holiday-homes.net
w island-holiday-homes.net

ST LAWRENCE
Isle of Wight

Charles Wood House
★★★★ *Self Catering*
Contact: Mrs Lisa Baskill
Home from Home Holidays
t (01983) 854340
e admin@hfromh.co.uk

Copse Hill ★★★
Self Catering
Contact: Mrs Lisa Baskill
Home from Home Holidays
t (01983) 854340
e admin@hfromh.co.uk

Heshcot ★★★ *Self Catering*
Contact: Mrs Lisa Baskill
Home from Home Holidays
t (01983) 854340
e admin@hfromh.co.uk

St Rhadagunds Cottage
★★★★ *Self Catering*
t (01276) 471570
e jb-t@talk21.com

The Spinnaker ★★★
Self Catering
t (01983) 730261
e lee@morrisl9.freeserve.co.uk

ST LEONARDS
East Sussex

60 Warrior Square ★★★★
Self Catering
Contact: Mrs Brenda Beck
Freedom Holiday Homes
t (01580) 720770
e mail@freedomholidayhomes.co.uk
w freedomholidayhomes.co.uk

Glastonbury Self-Catering
★★★ *Self Catering*
Contact: Mr Campbell
Glastonbury Self-Catering
t (01424) 436186
e glastonburyselfcatering@btinternet.com
w hastings.gov.uk

ST MICHAELS
Kent

6 The Terrace ★★★
Self Catering
Contact: Mrs Brenda Beck
Freedom Holiday Homes
t (01580) 720770
e mail@freedomholidayhomes.co.uk
w freedomholidayhomes.co.uk

SALFORD
Oxfordshire

Stable Cottage & The Granary ★★★★ *Self Catering*
Contact: Mrs Barbara Lewis
t (01608) 643398
e babbylew@supanet.com
w cotswolds-retreats.com

SANDFORD
Isle of Wight

Rose Cottage ★★★★
Self Catering
Contact: Mrs Honor Vass
Island Cottage Holidays
t (01929) 480080

SANDGATE
Kent

Seagull Cottage
Rating Applied For
Self Catering
Contact: Mr & Mrs Skilton
Rosslie
t (01237) 32669
e seagullcottage@mac.com

SANDOWN
Isle of Wight

Apartment 2 – Ocean View ★★★★ *Self Catering*
t (01268) 691444
e oceanview@onthebeachiow.freeserve.co.uk
w onthebeachiow.co.uk

Beaulieu Cottage ★★★★
Self Catering
Contact: Mrs Honor Vass
Island Cottage Holidays
t (01929) 480080
e enq@islandcottagesholidays.com
w islandcottageholidays.com

Little Parklands Holiday Apartments ★★★
Self Catering
t (01983) 402883
e info@sandownholidays.com
w sandownholidays.co.uk

Littledene Holiday Apartment ★★★
Self Catering
t (01983) 404648
e eileenmonks@hotmail.com
w iowlittledene.free.bm

Mayfair ★★★★ *Self Catering*
Contact: Mrs Lisa Baskill
Home from Home Holidays
t (01983) 854340
e admin@hfromh.co.uk

Parterre Holiday Flats ★★★
Self Catering
t (01983) 403555
e roger@parterre.freeserve.co.uk

Ripley Cottage
Rating Applied For
Self Catering
Contact: Peter & Julia Maciw
t (0118) 941 9866
e julia.maciw@ntlworld.com
w ripleycottage.co.uk

Royal Court & Royal Garden Apartments ★★★★
Self Catering
t (01983) 405032
e blake_rca@hotmail.com
w royalcourtgardenapartments.co.uk

Victoria Lodge ★★★
Self Catering
Contact: Mr Gibbens
t (01983) 403209

SANDWICH
Kent

2 Worth Farm Cottages ★★★ *Self Catering*
Contact: Mrs Patricia Mallett
t (01304) 812276
e worthcotts@vinefarm.plus.com

Duck Cottage ★★★★
Self Catering
Contact: Mr & Mrs Lloyd
t (01954) 267173
e richval.lloyd@lineone.net
w duckcottage-sandwich.co.uk

Hyde-Away Cottage ★★★★
Self Catering
Contact: Mr & Mrs Ian & Gillian Hardy
Primus Properties
t (01304) 620406
e gillhardy54@hotmail.co.uk

The Old Dairy ★★★★
Self Catering
Contact: Mrs Montgomery
t (01843) 841656
e info@montgomery-cottages.co.uk
w montgomery-cottages.co.uk

Primrose Cottage
Rating Applied For
Self Catering
Contact: Mrs Brenda Beck
Freedom Holiday Homes
t (01580) 720770
e mail@freedomholidayhomes.co.uk
w freedomholidayhomes.co.uk

SEAFORD
East Sussex

2 Kingsway Court ★★★★
Self Catering
Contact: Mrs Pauline Gower
t (01323) 895233 & 07889 310414
e sific@bgower.f9.co.uk

SEAVIEW
Isle of Wight

7 Seaview Bay ★★★★
Self Catering
Contact: Ms Jacqui Ellis
Bembridge Holiday Homes
t (01983) 873163

The Bolthole ★★★★
Self Catering
t (01983) 810324
e barbara_hughes@btinternet.com
w theboltholeiow.co.uk

Bonny Blink ★★★★★
Self Catering
Island Cottage Holidays
t (01929) 480080
e honor@islandcottageholidays.com
w islandcottageholidays.com

The Heathers ★★★★
Self Catering
Contact: Mrs Honor Vass
Island Cottage Holidays
t (01929) 480080
e honor@islandcottageholidays.com

Studio Annexe ★★★★
Self Catering
Contact: Mr & Mrs Robin Lobb
t (01983) 812180
e robin.lobb@ukgateway.net

SEDLESCOMBE
East Sussex

Acorn Chalet ★★★★
Self Catering
Contact: Mr Stuart Winter
Garden of England Cottages
t (01732) 369168
e holidays@gardenofenglandcottages.co.uk
w gardenofenglandcottages.co.uk

SELSEY
West Sussex

12 Fraser Close ★★★
Self Catering
Contact: Mrs Heather Birchall
Sea Spangles
t (01243) 606892

39 Toledo ★★ *Self Catering*
Contact: Mr & Mrs Robert Jones
t (01895) 446352

SEVENOAKS
Kent

Harveys ★★★ *Self Catering*
t (01732) 761862

Linden Beeches Cottages ★★★ *Self Catering*
t (01732) 461008
e lindenbeeches@rmplc.co.uk

SHALFLEET
Isle of Wight

Shalfleet Manor Farmhouse & Cottage ★★★★
Self Catering
Island Cottage Holidays
t (01983) 531235
e mmikewaterhouse@aol.com

SHANKLIN
Isle of Wight

2 Rubstone Court ★★★★
Self Catering
Contact: Mrs Elaine Hedley
t (01983) 867695
e rubstone2@aol.com

2 The Stables ★★★★
Self Catering
Contact: Ms Catherine Hopper
Island Holiday Homes
t (01983) 521114
w island-holiday-homes.net

Byre Cottage ★★★★
Self Catering
Contact: Mrs Lisa Baskill
Home from Home Holidays
t (01983) 854340
e admin@hfromh.co.uk

Chestnut Mews Holiday Cottages ★★★★★
Self Catering
t (01983) 861145
e chestnutmews@btinternet.com
w chestnutmews.co.uk

Downdale Lodge ★★★★★
Self Catering
t (01983) 868656
e rowena@rgva.net
w downdalelodge.co.uk

Fair Winds ★★★
Self Catering
Contact: Mrs Lisa Baskill
Home from Home Holidays
t (01983) 854340
e admin@hfromh.co.uk

Fernhurst Holiday Apartments ★★★–★★★★
Self Catering
t (01983) 862126
e dpetcher@talk21.com
w isle-of-wight-uk.com/fernhurst

Green Gable ★★★
Self Catering
Contact: Mrs Lisa Baskill
Home from Home Holidays
t (01983) 854340
e admin@hfromh.co.uk

Keats House ★★★★
Self Catering
Island Cottage Holidays
t (01929) 480080
e honor@islandcottageholidays.com
w islandcottageholidays.com

Laramie ★★★ *Self Catering*
t (01983) 862905
e sally.ranson@tiscali.co.uk

Lavender Cottage & Magnolia Cottage ★★★★
Self Catering
Contact: Mrs Honor Vass
Island Cottage Holidays
t (01929) 480080
e enq@islandcottageholidays.com
w islandcottageholidays.com

Luccombe Villa ★★★
Self Catering
Contact: Mrs Fiona Seymour
Luccombe Villa
t (01983) 862825
e info@luccombevilla.co.uk
w luccombevilla.co.uk

Lyon Court ★★★
Self Catering
Contact: Mrs Sandra Humphreys
Lyon Court
t (01983) 865861
e info@lyoncourtshanklin.co.uk
w lyoncourtshanklin.co.uk

Ninham House ★★★★
Self Catering
Contact: Mrs Veronica Harvey
t (01983) 864243

Percy Cottage
Rating Applied For
Self Catering
Contact: Mr David Hirst
t (01226) 744754

Summerhill Apartments ★★★★ *Self Catering*
t (01983) 862576
e jean@summerhillapts.co.uk
w summerhillapts.co.uk

Upper Chine Holiday Cottages & Apartments ★★★★ *Self Catering*
t (01983) 867900
e upperchine@btconnect.com
w upperchinecottages.co.uk

YMCA Winchester House
★★★ *Self Catering*
t (01489) 785228
e info@ymca-fg.org
w winchesterhouse.org.uk

SHAWFORD
Hampshire

Kingsmere Cottage ★★★★
Self Catering
Contact: Mrs Caroline Daniels
Kingsmere Acres
t (01962) 714876

SHELDWICH
Kent

Littles Manor Farmhouse
★★★★ *Self Catering*
Contact: Tim Bourne
Littles Manor Farmhouse
t (01233) 820425

SHERE
Surrey

Five Pines ★★★ *Self Catering*
Contact: Ms Gill Gellatly
Lockhurst Hatch Farm
t (01483) 202689
e gmgellatly@waitrose.com
w users.waitrose.com/~gmgellatly

SHILTON
Oxfordshire

The Chestnuts, Shilton
Rating Applied For
Self Catering
Contact: Miss Christine Burton
t (01993) 844905

Manor Lodge Shilton ★★★
Self Catering
Contact: Mrs Margaret Scholan
t (01993) 841444
e administrator@manorlodgebnb.co.uk
w manorlodgebnb.co.uk

SHIPBOURNE
Kent

The Old Stables ★★★★
Self Catering
t (01732) 810739
e theoldstablescottage@binternet.com
w kent-lets.co.uk

SHIPTON-UNDER-WYCHWOOD
Oxfordshire

6 Westgate ★★★★
Self Catering
Contact: Mrs Helen Harrison
Northgate, Shipton Court
t (01993) 830202

Plum Cottage ★★★★
Self Catering
Contact: Mrs Angela Richards
Manor Cottages & Cotswold Retreats
t (01993) 824252
e mancott@netcomuk.co.uk
w geocities.com/plumcottage_shipton

Turkey Cottage ★★★★
Self Catering
Contact: Mrs Hazel Ballot
t (01993) 831485
e rcgarstang.ballot@amserve.com
w cottageinthecountry.co.uk

SHOREHAM-BY-SEA
West Sussex

140 Old Fort Road ★★★★
Self Catering
Best of Brighton & Sussex Cottages Ltd
t (01273) 308779
e brightoncottages@pavilion.co.uk
w bestofbrighton.co.uk

SHORTGATE
East Sussex

White Lion Farm Cottages
★★★ *Self Catering*
Contact: Ms Diana Green
t (01825) 840288
w visitsussex.org/whitelioncottages

SHORWELL
Isle of Wight

Combe Barn ★★★★
Self Catering
Contact: Mrs Claudia Hodgson
Newbarn Farm
t (01983) 741422
e claudiahodgson@aol.com
w wightfarmholidays.co.uk/combebarn

Marylands ★★★★
Self Catering
Contact: Mrs Honor Vass
Island Cottage Holidays
t (01929) 480080
e enq@islandcottageholidays.com
w islandcottageholidays.com

Stone Place Cottage ★★★
Self Catering
Home from Home Holidays
t (01983) 854340

SIDLESHAM COMMON
West Sussex

Lockgate Dairy Holiday Cottages ★★★★
Self Catering
Contact: Mrs Jean Buchanan
t (01243) 641452
e holidays@lockgatedairy.co.uk
w lockgatedairy.co.uk

SISSINGHURST
Kent

Orchard Cottage ★★★★
Self Catering
Freedom Holiday Homes
t (01580) 720770
e mail@freedomholidayhomes.co.uk
w freedomholidayhomes.co.uk

SMARDEN
Kent

Braid Farm Cottages ★★★★
Self Catering
Contact: Mrs Brenda Beck
Freedom Holiday Homes
t (01580) 720770
e mail@freedomholidayhomes.co.uk
w freedomholidayhomes.co.uk

Dering Cottage ★★★★
Self Catering
Contact: Mrs Brenda Beck
Freedom Holiday Homes
t (01580) 720770
e mail@freedomholidayhomes.co.uk
w freedomholidayhomes.co.uk

SOUTHAMPTON
Hampshire

13 Pacific Close ★★★
Self Catering
Contact: Mr Mike Batley
Town or Country (Hampshire) Ltd
t (023) 8088 1000
e info@town-or-country.co.uk
w town-or-country.co.uk

27 The Greenwich ★★★★
Self Catering
Contact: Mike & Sue Batley
Town or Country (Hampshire) Ltd
t (023) 8088 1000
e info@town-or-country.co.uk
w town-or-country.co.uk

307 Imperial Apartments
★★★★ *Self Catering*
Contact: Mike & Sue Batley
Town or Country (Hampshire) Ltd
t (023) 8088 1000
e info@town-or-country.co.uk
w town-or-country.co.uk

315 Imperial Apartments
★★★★ *Self Catering*
Contact: Mike & Sue Batley
Town or Country (Hampshire) Ltd
t (023) 8088 1000
e info@town-or-country.co.uk
w town-or-country.co.uk

45 The Greenwich ★★★
Self Catering
Contact: Mike & Sue Batley
Town or Country (Hampshire) Ltd
t (023) 8088 1000
e info@town-or-country.co.uk
w town-or-country.co.uk

48 Pacific Close ★★★
Self Catering
Contact: Mike & Sue Batley
Town or Country (Hampshire) Ltd
t (023) 8088 1000
e info@town-or-country.co.uk
w town-or-country.co.uk

Pinewood Lodge Apartments ★★★
Self Catering
Contact: Dr Bradberry
Kanes Hill
t (023) 8040 2925
e stan.bradberry@tesco.net
w self-catering-apartments-southampton.co.uk

SOUTHSEA
Hampshire

University of Portsmouth
★★ *Self Catering*
Contact: Mr David Goodwin
t (023) 9284 4884

STANFORD IN THE VALE
Oxfordshire

The Paddock ★★★★
Self Catering
Cottage in the Country
t (01993) 831495
e enquiries@cottageinthecountry.co.uk
w cottageinthecountry.co.uk

STAPLE
Kent

Piglet Place ★★★★
Self Catering
Contact: Mrs Bronwen Barber
t (01304) 813321
e richbarber@lineone.net
w pigletplace.co.uk

STAPLEHURST
Kent

Basil, Thyme & Rosemary Lodges
Rating Applied For
Self Catering
Contact: Mrs Brenda Beck
Freedom Holiday Homes
t (01580) 720770
e mail@freedomholidayhomes.co.uk
w freedomholidayhomes.co.uk

Gardeners Cottage ★★★★
Self Catering
Contact: Mrs Brenda Beck
Freedom Holiday Homes
t (01580) 720770
e mail@freedomholidayhomes.co.uk
w freedomholidayhomes.co.uk

Tudor Hurst Cottage
★★★★ *Self Catering*
Contact: Mrs Brenda Beck
Freedom Holiday Homes
t (01580) 720770
e mail@freedomholidayhomes.co.uk
w freedomholidayhomes.co.uk

STEYNING
West Sussex

Pepperscombe Cottages
★★★★★ *Self Catering*
Contact: Mr John Camilleri
t (01903) 813868
e john.camilleri@btconnect.com

STOCKBRIDGE
Hampshire

The Flat, 2 Beaumonde Cottages ★★★ *Self Catering*
Contact: Mr & Mrs Martin Read
t (01794) 301700
e martinread@radyardcott.free-online.co.uk

STOCKBURY
Kent

The Old Dairy ★★★★
Self Catering
Contact: Mrs Anthony
t (01622) 884222

STOKE HAMMOND
Buckinghamshire

Pump House Barn
Rating Applied For
Self Catering
Contact: Mr & Mrs Kane & Curry
t (01525) 270858
e eileen@curry100.freserve.co.uk

STONEGATE
East Sussex

Bardown Farm Holiday Cottages ★★★★★
Self Catering
Contact: Mrs A Watkins
Bardown Road
t (01580) 200452
e info@bardownfarm.co.uk
w bardownfarm.co.uk

Coopers Farm Cottage
★★★★★ *Self Catering*
Contact: Ms Jane Howard
Coopers Farm Cottage
t (01580) 200386
e jane@coopersfarmstonegate.co.uk
w coopersfarmstonegate.co.uk

Freedom Holiday Homes
★★★ *Self Catering*
Contact: Mrs Brenda Beck
t (01580) 720770

STONESFIELD
Oxfordshire

Laughtons Retreat ★★★
Self Catering
Contact: Mr Dave Holloway
t (01993) 891172
e jane@callowfarm.fsnet.co.uk

STONOR
Oxfordshire

White Pond Farm ★★★★
Self Catering
Contact: Mrs Lindy Stracey
t (01491) 638224
w whitepondfarm.co.uk

STORRINGTON
West Sussex

Byre Cottages
★★★-★★★★ *Self Catering*
Contact: Grahame & Gail Kittle
t (01903) 745754
e kittles@waitrose.com

STREAT
West Sussex

Gote Lodge ★★★★
Self Catering
Contact: Mrs Caroline Tower
t (01273) 890976
e tower@gote.freeserve.co.uk

SWAY
Hampshire

4 Laurel Close ★★★★
Self Catering
Contact: Mrs Taylor
t (01590) 641810
e j.taylor155@btinternet.com

Hackney Park ★★★
Self Catering
Contact: Mrs Helen Beale
t (01590) 682049

The Old Exchange ★★★
Self Catering
Contact: Mrs Sarah Alborino
Gabetti Cottage
t (01590) 679228
e arcobaleno_1@hotmail.com

Squirrels Apartment ★★
Self Catering
Contact: Mrs Jean Kilford
Broadmead
t (01590) 683163
e jean.kilford@btinternet.com
w newforestselfcatering.com

SWERFORD
Oxfordshire

Heath Farm Holiday Cottages ★★★★
Self Catering
Contact: Mr & Mrs David & Nena Barbour
t (01608) 683270
e barbours@heathfarm.com
w heathfarm.com

TENTERDEN
Kent

83 High Street ★★★★
Self Catering
t (01580) 291092
e enquiries@aplaceinkent.co.uk
w aplaceinkent.co.uk

Cromwell Cottage ★★★
Self Catering
Contact: Mrs Valerie Ernst
t (01580) 762958
e val@cromwellcottage.fsnet.co.uk

Malt House Barn ★★★★
Self Catering
Freedom Holiday Homes
t (01580) 720770
e mail@freedomholidayhomes.co.uk
w freedomholidayhomes.co.uk

Meadow Cottage & Tamworth Cottage ★★★★
Self Catering
Contact: Mrs Cooke
t (01797) 270539
e info@prawls.co.uk
w prawls.co.uk

Quince Cottage ★★★★
Self Catering
Contact: Mrs Heather E S Crease
t (01580) 765636
e quincott@zetnet.co.uk
w quincecottage.co.uk

THAME
Oxfordshire

Goldsworthy Cottage ★★★
Self Catering
Contact: Mrs Janet Eaton
t (01844) 213035
e janet_.eaton@virgin.net

The Hollies ★★★★
Self Catering
Contact: Ms Julia Tanner
t (01844) 281423
e info@theholliesthame.co.uk
w theholliesthame.co.uk

Honeysuckle Cottage ★★★
Self Catering
t (01844) 208697

Meadowbrook Farm Holiday Cottages ★★★★
Self Catering
Contact: Mrs Diana Wynn
Meadowbrook Farm Holiday Cottages
t (01844) 212116
e rdwynn@ukonline.co.uk
w meadowbrookfarm.co.uk

TIPTOE
Hampshire

Brockhill Farm ★★★★
Self Catering
Contact: Mr David Turner
t (01425) 627457

TONBRIDGE
Kent

10 The Lyons ★★★★
Self Catering
Garden of England Cottages
t (01732) 369168
e holidays@gardenofenglandcottages.co.uk
w gardenofenglandcottages.co.uk

88 Avebury Avenue ★★★★
Self Catering
t (01912) 728185
e ragnhild@bakers-web.co.uk
w cgbaker.eclipse.co.uk

Goldhill Mill Cottages
★★★★★ *Self Catering*
t (01732) 851626
e vernon.cole@virgin.net
w goldhillmillcottages.com

Grapevine Lodge ★★★
Self Catering
Contact: Mr Stuart Winter
Garden of England Cottages
t (01732) 369168
e holidays@gardenofenglandcottages.co.uk
w gardenofenglandcottages.co.uk

High Barn ★★★★
Self Catering
t (01732) 832490

The Little Dairy ★★★
Self Catering
Contact: Mr Stuart Winter
Garden of England Cottages
t (01732) 369168
e holidays@gardenofenglandcottages.co.uk
w gardenofenglandcottages.co.uk

Oak Tree Cottage, Elm Tree Cottage, Beech Tree Cottage and Lime Tree Cottage
★★★★ *Self Catering*
Contact: Mr Stuart Winter
Garden of England Cottages
t (01732) 369168
e holidays@gardenofenglandcottages.co.uk
w gardenofenglandcottages.co.uk

Oast Barn ★★★★
Self Catering
Contact: Mr Trevor Bartle
Oast Barn
t (01732) 353298
e trevor@kentcottage.co.uk
w kentcottage.co.uk

The Roundel ★★★
Self Catering
Contact: Mrs Brenda Beck
Freedom Holiday Homes
t (01580) 720770
e mail@freedomholidayhomes.co.uk
w freedomholidayhomes.co.uk

TOTLAND BAY
Isle of Wight

36 Hurst Point View
Rating Applied For
Self Catering
Contact: Josie Gavoyannis
Home Farm House
t (01825) 791055
e info@holidays2remember.co.uk
w holidays2remember.co.uk

The Coach House ★★★
Self Catering
Contact: Mr Boatfield
t (01983) 752227
e boatfield@frenchmanscove.co.uk

Craiglea Holiday Cottage
Rating Applied For
Self Catering
t (01865) 875890
e enquiries@iowcottage.co.uk
w iowcottage.co.uk

Holiday Homes Owners Services Ref: T1 ★★★★
Self Catering
Contact: Mr Colin Nolson
Holiday Homes Owners Services (West Wight)
t (01983) 753423
e holidayhomesiow@ic24.net

Holiday Homes Owners Services Ref: T6 ★★★★
Self Catering
Contact: Mr Colin Nolson
Holiday Homes Owners Services (West Wight)
t (01983) 753423
e holidayhomesiow@ic24.net

Seawinds ★★ *Self Catering*
t (01983) 752772
e enquiries@buttercuphouse.co.uk

Stonewind Farm ★★★
Self Catering
Contact: Mrs Pat Hayles
t (01983) 752912

Summers Lodge ★★★★
Self Catering
Contact: Mrs Honor Vass
Island Cottage Holidays
t (01929) 480080
e enq@islandcottagesholidays.com
w cottageholidays.demon.co.uk

TUDELEY
Kent

Latters Farm Barn ★★★★
Self Catering
Contact: Mr Stuart Winter
Garden of England Cottages
t (01732) 369168
e holidays@gardenofenglandcottages.co.uk
w gardenofenglandcottages.co.uk

Latters Oast ★★★★
Self Catering
Contact: Mr Stuart Winter
Garden of England Cottages
t (01732) 369168
e holidays@gardenofenglandcottages.co.uk
w gardenofenglandcottages.co.uk

TURVILLE
Oxfordshire

Old Rose Cottage ★★★★
Self Catering
t 07850 095233
e rosecottage@chilterncountrycottages.com
w chilterncountrycottages.com

TWYFORD
Hampshire

Embessy Cottage ★★★
Self Catering
t (01962) 712921
e cjrees@onetel.com

TWYFORD MOORS
Hampshire

The Coach House, The Moors ★★★★ *Self Catering*
Contact: Ms Sally Thomas
t (01962) 714821
e rupertsally@talktalk.net

UCKFIELD
East Sussex

Keen's Lodge ★★★★
Self Catering
t (01825) 750616

UDIMORE
East Sussex

Billingham Byre ★★★★
Self Catering
Contact: Mrs Nanette Hacking
t (01424) 882348
e hackingnan@aol.com

Finlay Cottage ★★★★
Self Catering
Contact: Mr Stuart Winter
Garden of England Cottages
t (01732) 369168
e holidays@gardenofengland cottages.co.uk
w gardenofenglandcottages.co.uk

ULCOMBE
Kent

Kingsnorth Manor Oast House ★★★★ *Self Catering*
Contact: Mrs Brenda Beck
Freedom Holiday Homes
t (01580) 720770
e mail@freedomholiday homes.co.uk
w freedomholidayhomes.co.uk

UPCHURCH
Kent

The Old Stable ★★★
Self Catering
Contact: Mr Stuart Winter
Garden of England Cottages
t (01732) 369168
e holidays@gardenofengland cottages.co.uk
w gardenofenglandcottages.co.uk

VENTNOR
Isle of Wight

1 Cleeve Court ★★★
Self Catering
Contact: Ms Catherine Hopper
Hose Rhodes Dickson
t (01983) 616644
e enquiries@island-holiday-homes.net

1 St Catherines View ★★
Self Catering
Contact: Mrs Lisa Baskill
Home from Home Holidays
t (01983) 854340
e admin@hfromh.co.uk

1 The Stables ★★★
Self Catering
Contact: Mrs Lisa Baskill
Home from Home Holidays
t (01983) 854340
e admin@hfromh.co.uk

2 The Stables ★★★★
Self Catering
Contact: Mrs Lisa Baskill
Home from Home Holidays
t (01983) 854340
e admin@hfromh.co.uk

3 Seaview ★★★ *Self Catering*
Contact: Mr & Mrs Smithers
t (01953) 602477
e peter@isleofwightholidays.com
w isleofwightholidays.com

64 South Street ★★★
Self Catering
Island Holiday Homes
t (01983) 521113

The Acorns ★★★
Self Catering
Contact: Mrs Lisa Baskill
Home from Home Holidays
t (01983) 854340
e admin@homefromhome.co.uk

Bonchurch Cottage ★★★★
Self Catering
Contact: Jill Edwards
t 0845 230 6780
e info@distinctivedesigns.co.uk
w bonchurchcottage.com

Braemar ★★★★
Self Catering
Contact: Mrs Lisa Baskill
Home from Home Holidays
t (01983) 854340
e admin@hfromh.co.uk

Bywell
Rating Applied For
Self Catering
Island Holiday Homes
t (01983) 521113

Cedar Lodge ★★★
Self Catering
t (01983) 852345

Clarence House Holiday Apartments ★★★★
Self Catering
t (01983) 852875
e c.a.c@btinternet.com
w iowholidayapartments.co.uk

Cliff Cottage ★★★
Self Catering
Contact: Mrs Lisa Baskill
Home from Home Holidays
t (01983) 854340
e admin@hfromh.co.uk

Cliff Cottage ★★★★
Self Catering
Island Cottage Holidays
t (01929) 480080

The Clock House ★★★★
Self Catering
Island Cottage Holidays
t (01929) 480080

Cottage at Downsview ★★★ *Self Catering*
Contact: Mrs Lisa Baskill
Home from Home Holidays
t (01983) 854340
e admin@hfromh.co.uk

Cove Cottage ★★★
Self Catering
Contact: Mrs Lisa Baskill
Home from Home Holidays
t (01983) 854340
e admin@hfromh.co.uk

Crows Nest ★★ *Self Catering*
Contact: Mrs Lisa Baskill
Home from Home Holidays
t (01983) 854340
e admin@hfromh.co.uk

Dolphin Apartment
Rating Applied For
Self Catering
Contact: Catherine Hopper
Island Holiday Homes
t (01983) 521113
e enquiries@island-holiday-homes.net
w island-holiday-homes.net

Dudley House ★★★
Self Catering
Contact: Mrs Lisa Baskill
Home from Home Holidays
t (01983) 854340
e admin@hfromh.co.uk

Eden Cottage ★★★
Self Catering
Contact: Mrs Lisa Baskill
Home from Home Holidays
t (01983) 854340
e admin@hfromh.co.uk

The Furlongs ★★★
Self Catering
Contact: Mrs Lisa Baskill
Home from Home Holidays
t (01983) 854340
e admin@hfromh.co.uk

Garden House ★★★★
Self Catering
Contact: Mr Philip Barton
67 Strode Road
t (01983) 854451 & 07887 848146
e philip@peoplesense.co.uk
w holidaylets.net/prop_detail.asp?id=13874

Garfield Holiday Flats ★★★
Self Catering
t (01983) 854084

Glenlyn
Rating Applied For
Self Catering
t (01983) 852244
e eversleyhotel@yahoo.co.uk
w eversleyhotel.com

Halcyon ★★★ *Self Catering*
Contact: Mrs Lisa Baskill
Home from Home Holidays
t (01983) 854340
e admin@hfromh.co.uk

Haven Underhill ★★★★
Self Catering
t (01276) 471570
e jb-t@talk21.com

Heathland Cottage ★★★★
Self Catering
Contact: Mrs Lisa Baskill
Home from Home Holidays
t (01983) 854340
e admin@homefromhome.co.uk

Hideaway Cottage ★★★
Self Catering
Contact: Mrs Lisa Baskill
Home from Home Holidays
t (01983) 854340
e admin@hfromh.co.uk

Hobby Horse Cottage ★★★
Self Catering
Contact: Mrs Lisa Baskill
Home from Home Holidays
t (01983) 854340
e admin@hfromh.co.uk

Holiday Homes Owners Services Ref: V1 ★★★
Self Catering
Contact: Mr Colin Nolson
Holiday Homes Owners Services (West Wight)
t (01983) 753423
e holidayhomesiow@ic24.net

Ivy Cottage ★★★
Self Catering
Contact: Mr & Mrs Peter & Madeline Newton
t (01983) 853378
w thenewtons.info

Ivy Cottage ★★★★
Self Catering
Contact: Mrs Lisa Baskill
Home from Home Holidays
t (01983) 854340
e admin@homefromhome.co.uk

Jules Cottage ★★★★
Self Catering
Contact: Mrs Lisa Baskill
Home from Home Holidays
t (01983) 854340
e admin@hfromh.co.uk

Langonnet ★★★★
Self Catering
Contact: Mrs Lisa Baskill
Home from Home Holidays
t (01983) 854340
e admin@hfromh.co.uk

Little Sails ★★★
Self Catering
Home from Home Holidays
t (01983) 854340

Little Thatch ★★★★
Self Catering
Contact: Mrs Lisa Baskill
Home from Home Holidays
t (01983) 854340
e admin@hfromh.co.uk

Lonicera ★★★ *Self Catering*
Contact: Mrs Lisa Baskill
Home from Home Holidays
t (01983) 854340
e admin@hfromh.co.uk

Magnum Hall ★★★
Self Catering
Contact: Mrs Lisa Baskill
Home from Home Holidays
t (01983) 854340
e admin@hfromh.co.uk

Maple Cottage ★★★★
Self Catering
Contact: Mr & Mrs Stuart & Sarah Merry
White Cottage
t 07970 073339
e s.merry2@ntlworld.com
w ventnorholidaycottage.co.uk

Marina Apartments ★★★★
Self Catering
t (01983) 852802
e information@marinaapartments.co.uk
w marinaapartments.co.uk

Marula ★★★ *Self Catering*
Contact: Mrs Lisa Baskill
Home from Home Holidays
t (01983) 854340
e admin@hfromh.co.uk

Mews Cottage ★★★
Self Catering
Contact: Mrs Lisa Baskill
Home from Home Holidays
t (01983) 854340
e admin@hfromh.co.uk

Oceanwave ★★★
Self Catering
t (01223) 882995
e fredrick.ellis@ntlworld.com
w cottageguide.co.uk/oceanwave

The Old Dairy ★★★★
Self Catering
Contact: Mrs Lisa Baskill
Home from Home Holidays
t (01983) 854340
e admin@homefromhome.co.uk

Orchard Cottage ★★★★
Self Catering
Contact: Mrs Lisa Baskill
Home from Home Holidays
t (01983) 854340
e admin@hfromh.co.uk

Orchid Court ★★★★
Self Catering
Contact: Mrs Lisa Baskill
Home from Home Holidays
t (01983) 854340
e admin@homefromhome.co.uk

The Palms ★★★★
Self Catering
Contact: Mrs Lisa Baskill
Home from Home Holidays
t (01983) 854340
e admin@hfromh.co.uk

Park Lodge ★★★★
Self Catering
Island Cottage Holidays
t (01929) 480080

Petit Tor ★★★ *Self Catering*
Contact: Mrs Lisa Baskill
Home from Home Holidays
t (01983) 854340
e admin@hfromh.co.uk

Pilgrims ★★★ *Self Catering*
Contact: Mrs Lisa Baskill
Home from Home Holidays
t (01983) 854340
e admin@hfromh.co.uk

Richmond Apartments
★★★★ *Self Catering*
Contact: Mr Tim Reid
t (020) 8551 2370

Richmond Arms and Apartments ★★★★
Self Catering
t (01983) 855674

Rivendell ★★★ *Self Catering*
Contact: Mrs Lisa Baskill
Home from Home Holidays
t (01983) 854340
e admin@hfromh.co.uk

Rocklands Manor
Rating Applied For
Self Catering
t (01983) 854777
e rocklandsmanor@hotmail.com
w rocklandsmanor.com

Roseberry ★★★
Self Catering
Contact: Mrs Lisa Baskill
Home from Home Holidays
t (01983) 854340
e admin@hfromh.co.uk

Royal Marine House ★★★
Self Catering
t (01962) 878722
e aventaarchitects@btconnect.com
w royalmarinehouse.co.uk

St Johns ★★ *Self Catering*
Contact: Mrs Lisa Baskill
Home from Home Holidays
t (01983) 854340
e admin@hfromh.co.uk

St Lawrence Rare Breed Farm Bungalows ★★★★
Self Catering
Island Cottage Holidays
t (01929) 481555
e eng@islandcottageholidays.com
w islandcottageholidays.com

Sea Haze ★★★ *Self Catering*
Contact: Mrs Lisa Baskill
Home from Home Holidays
t (01983) 854340
e admin@hfromh.co.uk

Sea View ★★★ *Self Catering*
t (020) 8778 8124

Seagate Lodge ★★★
Self Catering
t (01983) 855019

Shipshape ★★ *Self Catering*
Contact: Mrs Lisa Baskill
Home from Home Holidays
t (01983) 854340

Squirrels ★★★ *Self Catering*
Contact: Mrs Lisa Baskill
Home from Home Holidays
t (01983) 854340
e admin@hfromh.co.uk

Stables at Afton Farmhouse
★★★★ *Self Catering*
Contact: Mrs Lisa Baskill
Home from Home Holidays
t (01983) 854830
e admin@hfromh.co.uk

Stoneplace Cottage ★★★
Self Catering
Contact: Mrs Lisa Baskill
Home from Home Holidays
t (01983) 854340
e admin@hfromh.co.uk

Trelawney ★★★
Self Catering
Contact: Mrs Lisa Baskill
Home from Home Holidays
t (01983) 854340
e admin@hfromh.co.uk

Ventnor Apartment ★★★★
Self Catering
t 0845 230 6780
e info@distinctivedesigns.co.uk
w ventnorapartment.com

Ventnor Holiday Villas
★–★★ *Self Catering*
t (01983) 852973
e sales@ventnorholidayvillas.co.uk
w ventnorholidayvillas.co.uk

Verbena ★★★ *Self Catering*
Contact: Mrs Lisa Baskill
Home from Home Holidays
t (01983) 854340
e admin@hfromh.co.uk

Victoria Villa ★★★
Self Catering
Contact: Mrs Tims
Robinwood Cottage
t (020) 8549 5065

Weir Cottage ★★★★★
Self Catering
Contact: Mrs Lisa Baskill
Home from Home Holidays
t (01983) 854340
e admin@homefromhome.co.uk

Western Lines ★★★
Self Catering
Contact: Mrs Lisa Baskill
Home from Home Holidays
t (01983) 854340
e admin@hfromh.co.uk

Westfield Lodges & Apartments ★★★–★★★★
Self Catering
t (01983) 852268
e info@westfield01983.fsnet.co.uk
w westfieldlodges.co.uk

Westwood ★★★★
Self Catering
t (01983) 853491
e ann@annshrubsole.freeserve.co.uk

Woodcliffe Holiday Apartments ★★★
Self Catering
t (01983) 852397
e bryce.wilson@virgin.net
w woodcliffe.net

VINES CROSS
East Sussex

Cannon Barn ★★★★
Self Catering
Contact: Mrs Anne Reed
t (01435) 812285
e info@boringhousefarm.co.uk
w boringhousefarm.co.uk

Dairy Shorthorn & Friesian Cottages
Rating Applied For
Self Catering
Contact: Mrs Brenda Beck
Freedom Holiday Homes
t (01580) 720770
e mail@freedomholidayhomes.co.uk
w freedomholidayhomes.co.uk

WADHURST
East Sussex

Angels Barn ★★★★
Self Catering
Contact: Mrs Brenda Beck
Freedom Holiday Homes
t (01580) 720770
e mail@freedomholidayhomes.co.uk
w freedomholidayhomes.co.uk

Bewl Water Cottages
★★★★ *Self Catering*
Contact: Mr & Mrs Bentsen
t (01892) 782042
e bentsen@bewlwatercottages.com

WALBERTON
West Sussex

The Forge, Myrtle Cottage
★★★ *Self Catering*
Contact: Jill & Peter Skinner
t (01243) 555236
e pskinner.onmarketing@virgin.net

WALLINGFORD
Oxfordshire

Oak Cottage ★★★★
Self Catering
Contact: Mr Philip Burton
t (01491) 836200
e pburton@madasafish.com

WALMER
Kent

Cottage In Deal ★★
Self Catering
Contact: Mr Alan Hay
Leipziger Str 13D
t +49 09131 65921
e alan.hay@t-online.de

Fisherman's Cottage ★★★
Self Catering
Contact: Dr & Mrs Angela Morris
t (020) 8542 5086

The Gulls & Sea Watch
★★★★ *Self Catering*
Contact: Sandra & Kenneth Upton
t (01304) 371449
e palmers3@freenetname.co.uk
w holidaysdeal.co.uk

Holm Oaks ★★★★
Self Catering
Contact: Mrs Annie Spencer-Smith
t (01304) 367365
e holm_oaks@hotmail.com

Marine Cottage ★★★★
Self Catering
Contact: Ms Marian Sanders
t +33 05460 40166
e marianatmoreau@hotmail.com

Shipwreck Cottage ★★★
Self Catering
Contact: Mrs Janice Twaits
t (020) 8524 3320

WALTHAM
Kent

Springfield Cottage and Springfield Barn ★★★
Self Catering
Contact: Mr Stuart Winter
Garden of England Cottages
t (01732) 369168
e holidays@gardenofenglandcottages.co.uk
w gardenofenglandcottages.co.uk

WALTON-ON-THAMES
Surrey

Guest Wing ★★★★
Self Catering
Contact: Mr Richard Dominy
Guest Wing
t (01932) 241223

WALTON ON THE HILL
Surrey

Far End ★★★★★
Self Catering
Contact: Jacquelyn Beesley
Streele Farm
t (01892) 852579
e stay@compasscottages.co.uk
w compasscottages.co.uk

WANTAGE
Oxfordshire

Cartwheel Cottage, Woolstone *Self Catering*
t (01367) 820116
e ridgewayholidays@amserve.net

WARBLETON
East Sussex

Well Cottage ★★★★
Self Catering
Contact: Mr Stuart Winter
Garden of England Cottages
t (01732) 369168
e holidays@gardenofenglandcottages.co.uk
w gardenofenglandcottages.co.uk

WAREHORNE
Kent

Tuckers Farm ★★★★
Self Catering
Contact: Mrs Bernadette Restorick
t (01233) 733433 & 07796 878733
e prestorick@aol.com

WARREN STREET
Kent

The Pavilion
Rating Applied For
Self Catering
t (01622) 858423
e alison@bluehousefarm.co.uk
w bluehousefarm.co.uk

WARSASH
Hampshire

Foredeck Holiday Cottage
★★★★ *Self Catering*
Contact: Mr Peter Wilson
t (01489) 581208
e pete@s-wilson.fsnet.co.uk
w http://mysite.wanadoo-members.co.uk/foredeck-cottage

WARTLING
East Sussex

The Coach House ★★★★
Self Catering
Contact: Mrs Helen Enock
Tremayne House
t (01323) 832131
e helen.enock@btinternet.com
w thecoachhousewartling.com

WATCHFIELD
Oxfordshire

The Coach House ★★★★
Self Catering
Cottage in the Country Cottage Holidays
t (01993) 831495
e info@cottageinthecountry.co.uk

WELLOW
Isle of Wight

Mattingley Farm ★★★★
Self Catering
t (01983) 760503

Warren Holidays – Brook Cottage & Mrs Tiggywinkle Cottage ★★★★ *Self Catering*
t (01983) 883364
e anne.longford@btinternet.com
w warrenholidays.com

WEST ASHLING
West Sussex

Hills Cottage ★★★★
Self Catering
Contact: Virginia & Alan Jack
t (01243) 574382
e hills.cottage@btinternet.com
w hillscottage.com

WEST MARDEN
West Sussex

Cabragh Cottage ★★★★
Self Catering
Contact: Mrs Lesley Segrave
Cabragh House
t (023) 9263 1267
e lsegrave@tinyworld.co.uk

The Old Stables, West Marden ★★★★★
Self Catering
Contact: Mrs Carole Edney
t (023) 9263 1761
e carole.edney@btopenworld.com
w theoldstables.net

WEST PECKHAM
Kent

Beech Farmhouse ★★★★
Self Catering
Contact: Mr & Mrs Wooldridge
t (01622) 812360

WESTBOURNE
West Sussex

2 Longcopse Cottages
★★★★ *Self Catering*
Contact: Mrs Di Ashe
t (01243) 378697
e diashe@longcopsecottage.co.uk
w longcopsecottage.co.uk

WESTCOTT
Surrey

Deerhurst Cottage
Rating Applied For
Self Catering
Contact: Mrs Lindy Reif
t (01306) 888070
e lindyjo@hotmail.co.uk

The Garden Flat ★★★★
Self Catering
Contact: Mrs Louise Scillitoe-Brown
t (01306) 883838
e gardenflat@chartfield.biz
w chartfield.biz

WESTERHAM
Kent

The Barn at Bombers
★★★★★ *Self Catering*
Contact: Mr & Mrs Roy or Brigitte Callow
t (01959) 573471
e roy@bombers-farm.co.uk
w bombers-farm.co.uk

WHITSTABLE
Kent

3 Harbour Mews ★★★★
Self Catering
Contact: Mrs Lynn Buckle
t (01227) 792781
e lynn.buckle@tiscali.co.uk
w 3harbourmews.co.uk

4 Whitepost ★★★★★
Self Catering
Contact: Sally Kane
t (01227) 272741
e sally.kane@btinternet.com
w 4whitepost.co.uk

Bakers Mews ★★★★
Self Catering
Contact: Mrs Brenda Beck
Freedom Holiday Homes
t (01580) 720770
e mail@freedomholidayhomes.co.uk
w freedomholidayhomes.co.uk

Coastguard's Cottage
Rating Applied For
Self Catering
Contact: Mrs Anne-Marie Tracey
t (01892) 750601
e amtracey@homecall.co.uk

Flat 31 Grand Pavilion
★★★★ *Self Catering*
Contact: Mr Robert Gough
Alliston House
t (01227) 779066
e bobgough57@aol.com
w stayinwhitstable.co.uk

Oyster Mews
Rating Applied For
Self Catering
Contact: Ray Jones
t (01227) 273225
e j.oyster@virgin.net

Pebble Cottage ★★★★
Self Catering
Contact: Mrs Pamela Burke
Welcome Hotels
t 0845 370 9009
e info@pebblecottage.co.uk
w pebblecottage.co.uk

Trappers End ★★★
Self Catering
Contact: Mrs Janette Reed
t (020) 8942 0342
e janette.reed07@btopenworld.com

WHITWELL
Isle of Wight

43 Bannock Road ★★★
Self Catering
t (01983) 730153

Ash Farm
Rating Applied For
Self Catering
Contact: Catherine Hopper
Island Holiday Homes
t (01983) 521113
e enquiries@island-holiday-homes.net
w island-holiday-homes.net

Brook Lodge ★★★★
Self Catering
Contact: Honor Vass
Island Cottage Holidays
t (01929) 481555

Castleview Flat ★★★
Self Catering
Contact: Mr Matthew White
Island Holiday Homes
t (01983) 521114

Downcourt Manor Farm House
Rating Applied For
Self Catering
t (01983) 730329
e a.j.aylwin@btinternet.com

Fossil Cottage ★★★
Self Catering
Contact: Mrs Honor Vass
Island Cottage Holidays
t (01929) 480080
e enq@islandcottageholidays.com
w islandcottageholidays.com

Hillview
Rating Applied For
Self Catering
Contact: Catherine Hopper
Island Holiday Homes
t (01983) 521113
e enquiries@island-holiday-homes.net
w island-holiday-homes.net

Kitty's Loft ★★★★
Self Catering
Contact: Miss Barbara Williams
t (01983) 551705
e etb@kittysloft.co.uk
w kittysloft.co.uk

Maytime Cottage ★★★★
Self Catering
Contact: Mr Jonathan McCulloch
t (01403) 211052
e jonty@bpmd.co.uk
w maytimecottage.co.uk

Nettlecombe Farm (Barley, Oats & Wheat)
★★★-★★★★ *Self Catering*
t (01983) 730783
e mail@nettlecombefarm.co.uk
w nettlecombefarm.co.uk

The Old Dairy ★★★
Self Catering
Lower Dolcoppice Farm
t (01983) 551445

Pyrmont Cottage ★★
Self Catering
Hose Rhodes Dickson
t (01983) 616644
e rental_office@hose-rhodes-dickson.co.uk
w island-holiday-homes.net

Sunglaze at Whitwell
★★★★ *Self Catering*
t (01983) 730867

Whitwell Station ★★★
Self Catering
t (01983) 730667
e enqs@whitwellstation.co.uk
w whitwellstation.co.uk

Willow Bank ★★★
Self Catering
t (01258) 473327
e geoff-eldridge@onetel.com

The Wing, Dean Farm
★★★★ *Self Catering*
Contact: Mrs Honor Vass
Island Cottage Holidays
t (01983) 730236
e enq@islandcottageholidays.com
w islandcottageholidays.com

WICKHAM
Hampshire

Meonwood Annexe ★★★
Self Catering
Contact: Mrs Susan Wells
t (01329) 834130
e sJwells@meonwood.co.uk

WILMINGTON
East Sussex

Old Inn House ★★★★
Self Catering
Contact: Mrs Annette Whamond
t (01323) 871331
e awhamond@netscape.net
w cottagenet.co.uk/old.inn.house.htm

WINCHELSEA
East Sussex

Trojans Plat ★★★★
Self Catering
Contact: Mr Stephen Turner
The Tea Tree Tea Rooms
t (01797) 226102
e theteatree@btconnect.com
w the-tea-tree.co.uk

WINCHELSEA BEACH
East Sussex

Tamarix ★★★ *Self Catering*
t (01825) 732034

WINCHESTER
Hampshire

1 Abbotts Court Mews
★★★★ *Self Catering*
Contact: Mr Richard Wetherill
Aventa Properties Ltd
t (01962) 878722
e aventaarchitects@btconnect.com
w abbottscourtmews.co.uk

18 Swanmore Close ★★★
Self Catering
Contact: Mrs Carole Wilkins
t (01962) 883341
e acannexe@hotmail.co.uk

32 Canon Street ★★★★
Self Catering
Contact: Mr Andrew Lattimore
A,d8 Uk ltd
t (01962) 820330
e sales@a-d8.co.uk
w a-d8.co.uk

87 Christchurch Road
★★★★ *Self Catering*
Contact: Mrs Elisabeth Peacocke
t (01962) 854902
e liz@peacocke.wanadoo.co.uk
w cottageguide.co.uk

Burwood ★★★★
Self Catering
Contact: Mrs Alice Lowery
Burwood
t (01962) 881690
e lowery2@btinternet.com

Gyleen ★★★★ *Self Catering*
Contact: Mr & Mrs Paul & Elizabeth Tipple
9 Mount View Road
t (01962) 861918
e pauliz@tipple.co.uk
w cottageguide.co.uk/gyleen

Mallard Cottage ★★★★
Self Catering
Contact: Mrs Tricia Simpkin
t (01962) 853002
e mallardsimpkin@aol.com
w geocities.com/mallardcottageuk

Mews House ★★★★
Self Catering
t (01438) 715497
e linda.westaway@btopenworld.com

Milnthorpe ★★★★★
Self Catering
t (01962) 850440
e alison@milnthorpehouse.demon.co.uk

The Old Dairy ★★★★
Self Catering
Contact: Mrs Joy Waldron
t (01962) 868214
e joy_ann_waldron@hotmail.com

South Winchester Lodges
★★★★★ *Self Catering*
Contact: Mr Laurence Ross
t (01962) 820490
e info@golfholidaywinchester.com
w golfholidaywinchester.com

WINDSOR
Berkshire

9 The Courtyard ★★★
Self Catering
Contact: Mrs JH Hitchcock
t (01753) 545005
e jhhitchcock@btinternet.com

Amberley Place ★★★
Self Catering
Contact: Mrs Nikki Tehel
t 07050 249629
e flat@tehel.net

Castle Mews Apartment
★★★★ *Self Catering*
Contact: Mr Duncan Gordon
t (01628) 632092
e bookings@royalwindsorlets.com
w royalwindsorlets.com

Dorney Self-Catering Apartments ★★ *Self Catering*
Contact: Sarah Everitt
Wisteria & Gardeners Bothy
t (01753) 827037
e enquiries@troppo.uk.com
w troppo.uk.com

Flat 6 The Courtyard ★★★
Self Catering
Contact: Mr Gavin Gordon
t (01628) 824267
e gavingordon@totalise.co.uk
w windsor-selfcatering.co.uk

Manor View Apartment
★★★ *Self Catering*
Contact: Mrs Clare Smith
t (01344) 485658
e manorview@care4free.net
w manorview.care4free.net

WISBOROUGH GREEN
West Sussex

Milestone Cottage
Rating Applied For
Self Catering
Contact: Mrs H Richards
t (01403) 700130
e rvrichards@milestonecottage.freeserve.co.uk

WITNEY
Oxfordshire

Grove Farm ★★★★
Self Catering
Contact: Mr & Mrs J R Bowtell
t (01993) 843755
e jrbowtell@aol.com
w grovefarmcotswoldcottages.co.uk

Little Barn ★★★★
Self Catering
Contact: Mrs Sissel Harrison
t (01993) 706632
e booking@stablebarn.co.uk

Lovegrove Cottage ★★★
Self Catering
Contact: Mrs Olive Harris
Lovegrove Farm
t (01993) 878747

Melrose Villa & Mews ★★★
Self Catering
Contact: Mrs Susan Petty
t (01993) 703035
e ianpetty@btinternet.com
w witneycottages.co.uk

Sighs Cottage ★★★
Self Catering
Contact: Mr Peter Crowther
t (01993) 709596
e pjccrowth@hotmail.com

Swallows Nest ★★★★
Self Catering
Contact: Mrs Jan Strainge
Springhill Farm Swallows Nest
t (01993) 704919
e jan@strainge.fsnet.co.uk

WITTERSHAM
Kent

Stocks Farm Oast
Rating Applied For
Self Catering
Contact: Mrs Kate Gale
t (01797) 270895
e galekate@yahoo.co.uk

The White Cottage
Rating Applied For
Self Catering
Contact: Mrs Brenda Beck
Freedom Holiday Homes
t (01580) 720770
e mail@freedomholidayhomes.co.uk
w freedomholidayhomes.co.uk

WOODCHURCH
Kent

Acorn and Squirrel Cottages
★★★★ *Self Catering*
t (01233) 860426
e ronnieaikman@freeola.net
w great-engeham-farms.co.uk

The Stable ★★★★
Self Catering
t (01233) 860388
e carol.vant@thestablecottage.co.uk
w thestablecottage.co.uk

WOODGREEN
Hampshire

Sunset Place ★★★★
Self Catering
Contact: Mrs Lupita Cadman
t (01725) 512009
e lupita_cadman@yahoo.co.uk
w cottage-crest.co.uk

WOODLANDS
Hampshire

Purlins ★★★ *Self Catering*
Contact: Mrs Kay Lindsell
t (023) 8029 3833
e Kay@purlins.net

WOODNESBOROUGH
Kent

Sonnet Cottage ★★
Self Catering
Contact: Mrs Brenda Beck
Freedom Holiday Homes
t (01580) 720770
e mail@freedomholidayhomes.co.uk
w freedomholidayhomes.co.uk

WOOTTON
Kent

Colonels ★★★ *Self Catering*
Contact: Mrs Brenda Beck
Freedom Holiday Homes
t (01580) 720770
e mail@freedomholidayhomes.co.uk
w freedomholidayhomes.co.uk

WOOTTON BRIDGE
Isle of Wight

Buttercup Barn ★★★★
Self Catering
Contact: Mr & Mrs D Woodmore
t 07979 555554
e holiday@iowbuttercupbarn.co.uk
w iowbuttercupbarn.co.uk

Creek Gardens *Self Catering*
Contact: Mr S Catton
t (01564) 777711

Grange Farm ★★★–★★★★
Self Catering
Contact: Mrs Rosemarie Horne
t (01983) 882147
w wightfarmholidays.co.uk/grange

Wootton Keepers Cottage
★★★ *Self Catering*
Contact: Mrs Honor Vass
Island Cottage Holidays
t (01929) 480080
e enq@islandcottageholidays.com
w islandcottageholidays.com

WORTHING
West Sussex

17 Pendine Avenue ★★★
Self Catering
Contact: Mrs Sue Harding
t (01903) 202833
e sue.harding@catlover.com

2 Knightsbridge House
★★★ *Self Catering*
Contact: Ms Greta Paull
t (020) 8530 2336
e gretapaull@aol.com

6 Heene Terrace ★★★
Self Catering
Contact: Ms Anne Wright
Promenade Holiday Homes
t (01903) 877047
w promenadeholidayhomes.co.uk

8 Mariners Walk ★★★
Self Catering
Contact: Anne Wright
Promenade Holiday Homes
t (01903) 877047
w promenadeholidayhomes.co.uk

Aldine House ★★★
Self Catering
Contact: Mr & Mrs Hills
t (01903) 266980
e hills.aldine@supanet.com

Exmoor House ★
Self Catering
Contact: Mr & Mrs Harrison
t (01903) 208856

Flat A ★★ *Self Catering*
Contact: Mrs Anne Wright
Promenade Holiday Homes
t (01903) 877047
e anne@promenade-holidays.fsbusiness.co.uk
w promenadeholidayhomes.co.uk

Flat 1A Heene Court Mansions ★★★ *Self Catering*
Contact: Mrs Anne Wright
Promenade Holiday Homes
t (01903) 877047
e anne@promenade-holidays.fsbusiness.co.uk
w promenadeholidayhomes.co.uk

Flat 7, Waverley Court ★★★
Self Catering
Contact: Anne Wright
Promenade Holiday Homes
t (01903) 877047

Garden Flat ★★ *Self Catering*
Contact: Mrs Anne Wright
t (01903) 877047
e anne@promenade-holidays.fsbusiness.co.uk
w promenadeholidayhomes.co.uk

Holiday Bungalow ★★★
Self Catering
Contact: Mr & Mrs Graham Haynes
t (03138) 11876
e grahamhaynes@tiscalinet.ch

Navarino Flat ★★★
Self Catering
Contact: Mrs Cynthia Hanton
t (01903) 205984
e chantan@cwctv.net

Park Cottage ★★★
Self Catering
Contact: Ms Tina Williams
t (01903) 521091

WRAYSBURY
Berkshire

Splash Windmill and Windmill House
★★★-★★★★ *Self Catering*
Contact: Mrs Sylvia Neal
The Oast Barn, Staines Road
t (01784) 481598
e bandb@oastbarn.com
w oastbarn.com

WROXALL
Isle of Wight

Appuldurcombe Holiday Cottages (The Retreat & The Annexe) ★★★-★★★★
Self Catering
t (01983) 840188
e john@appuldurcombe.co.uk
w appuldurcombe.co.uk

The Brewhouse & Stable Cottage ★★★ *Self Catering*
Contact: Mrs Felcity Corry
t (01983) 852419
e info@spanfarm.co.uk
w spanfarm.co.uk

Clevelands House ★★★★
Self Catering
t (01983) 853021

Dairy Barn ★★★★★
Self Catering
t (01983) 854033
w wightfarmholidays.co.uk/dairybarn/index.html

Malmesbury Cottage
★★★★ *Self Catering*
t (01798) 872705
e tony@simpson-family.co.uk
w malmesburycottage.co.uk

Poppies ★★★ *Self Catering*
Contact: Mrs Lisa Baskill
Home from Home Holidays
t (01983) 854340
e admin@hfromh.co.uk

Sundown ★★★ *Self Catering*
Contact: Mrs Lisa Baskill
Home from Home Holidays
t (01983) 854340
e admin@hfromh.co.uk

YARMOUTH
Isle of Wight

Alma Cottage ★★★★
Self Catering
Contact: Mr Matthew White
Island Holiday Homes
t (01983) 521114

Holiday Homes Owners Services Ref: Y4 ★★★★★
Self Catering
Contact: Mr Colin Nolson
Holiday Homes Owners Services (West Wight)
t (01983) 753423
e holidayhomesiow@ic24.net

Holiday Homes Owners Services Ref: Y13 ★★★★
Self Catering
Contact: Mr Colin Nolson
Holiday Homes Owners Services (West Wight)
t (01983) 753423
e holidayhomesiow@ic24.net

Holiday Homes Owners Services Ref: Y7 ★★★★
Self Catering
Contact: Mr Colin Nolson
Holiday Homes Owners Services (West Wight)
t (01983) 753423
e holidayhomesiow@ic24.net

Holiday Homes Owners Services Ref: Y18 ★★★★
Self Catering
Contact: Mr Colin Nolson
Holiday Homes Owners Services (West Wight)
t (01983) 753423
e holidayhomesiow@ic24.net

Holiday Homes Owners Services Ref: Y9 ★★★★
Self Catering
Contact: Mr Colin Nolson
Holiday Homes Owners Services (West Wight)
t (01983) 753423
e holidayhomesiow@ic24.net

Holiday Homes Owners Services Ref: Y12 ★★★
Self Catering
Contact: Mr Colin Nolson
Holiday Homes Owners Services (West Wight)
t (01983) 753423
e holidayhomesiow@ic24.net

Holiday Homes Owners Services Ref: Y6 ★★★★
Self Catering
Contact: Mr Colin Nolson
Holiday Homes Owners Services (West Wight)
t (01983) 753423
e holidayhomesiow@ic24.net

Holiday Homes Owners Services Ref: Y5 ★★★
Self Catering
Contact: Mr Colin Nolson
Holiday Homes Owners Services (West Wight)
t (01983) 753423
e holidayhomesiow@ic24.net

Portside, Sail Loft Annexe, Sail Loft and Starboard
★★★ *Self Catering*
Contact: Mr John Brady
t (01983) 754718

River Cottage ★★★★
Self Catering
t (01983) 760553
e nigel@isle-wight.co.uk
w isle-wight.co.uk

Waterside Villa ★★★
Self Catering
Contact: Mr Andrew Smith
t (01983) 761425
e waterside-yarmouth@btinternet.com

SOUTH WEST ENGLAND

ABBOTSBURY
Dorset

The Cottage ★★★
Self Catering
Contact: Mrs Val Dredge
t (01305) 871462
e val@thecottage-abbotsbury.co.uk
w thecottage-abbotsbury.co.uk

Elworth Farmhouse Cottages ★★★★
Self Catering
Contact: Mrs Christine Wade
Elworth Farmhouse
t (01305) 871693
e elworthfarmhouse@aol.com
w elworth-farmhouse.co.uk

Gorwell Farm Cottages
★★★★-★★★★★
Self Catering
Contact: Mrs Mary Pengelly
M J Pengelly Ltd
t (01305) 871401
e mary@gorwellfarm.co.uk
w gorwellfarm.co.uk

Lawrence's Cottage ★★★
Self Catering
Contact: Mr Zachary Stuart-Brown
Dream Cottages
t (01305) 789000
e admin@dream-cottages.co.uk
w dream-cottages.co.uk

The Old Coastguards
★★★★ *Self Catering*
Contact: Mr & Mrs John & Cheryl Varley
t (01305) 871335
e enquiries@oldcoastguards.com
w oldcoastguards.com

ABBOTSHAM
Devon

Bowood Farm Cottages
★★★★ *Self Catering*
Toad Hall Cottages
t (01548) 853089
e thc@toadhallcottages.com
w toadhallcottages.com

ADVENT
Cornwall

Aldermoor Farm
★★★-★★★★ *Self Catering*
Contact: Mr Golding
t (01840) 213366
w aldermoor.co.uk

Widewalls Barn ★★★★
Self Catering
Contact: Pauline Metters
t (01840) 211284
e pauline@widewalls.fsnet.co.uk
w widewalls.fsnet.co.uk

Look out for establishments participating in the National Accessible Scheme 

ALBASTON
Cornwall

Todsworthy Farm Holidays
★★★★ *Self Catering*
Contact: Mr Pellow
t (01822) 834744
w todsworthyfarmholidays.co.uk

ALDERTON
Gloucestershire

Rectory Farm Cottages
★★★★★ *Self Catering*
Contact: Mr & Mrs Peter & Margaret Burton
t (01242) 620455
e peterannabel@hotmail.com
w rectoryfarmcottages.co.uk

ALHAMPTON
Somerset

The Woodshed ★★★★
Self Catering
t (01749) 860386
e julianmant04@aol.com

ALLERFORD
Somerset

Lynch Country House Holiday Apartments ★★★★
Self Catering
Contact: Mr & Mrs Daniels
t (01643) 862800
e admin@lynchcountryhouse.co.uk
w lynchcountryhouse.co.uk

Orchard Cottage ★★★
Self Catering
Contact: Mrs Diana Williams
Orchard Cottage
t (01643) 862383

The Pack Horse
★★★-★★★★ *Self Catering*
Contact: Linda & Brian Garner
t (01643) 862475
e holidays@thepackhorse.net
w thepackhorse.net

ALLET
Cornwall

Springfield Farm ★★
Self Catering
Contact: Mrs Cook
t (01872) 540492

ALTON PANCRAS
Dorset

Bookham Court
★★★★-★★★★★
Self Catering
Contact: Mr & Mrs Andrew Foot
t (01300) 345511
e andy.foot1@btinternet.com
w bookhamcourt.co.uk

AMBERLEY
Gloucestershire

The Squirrels ★★★
Self Catering
Contact: Mrs Valerie Bowen
t (01453) 836940
e valerie.bowen@btinternet.com

AMESBURY
Wiltshire

The Cottage ★★★★
Self Catering
Contact: Mrs Joan Robathan
Maddington House
t (01980) 620406
e rsrobathan@freenet.co.uk
w maddingtonhouse.co.uk

The Stables ★★★★
Self Catering
Contact: Mrs Anna Thatcher
Ivy Cottage
t (01980) 670557
e athatcher@bigfoot.com
w cottageguide.co.uk/thestables-netheravon

APPLEDORE
Devon

Crab Apple Cottage ★★★★
Self Catering
Contact: Mrs Janet Cornwell
Marsdens Cottage Holidays
t (01271) 813777
e holidays@marsdens.co.uk
w marsdens.co.uk

Jolly Cottage ★★★
Self Catering
Contact: Lucy Ellison
Farm & Cottage Holidays
t (01237) 479146
e enquiries@farmcott.co.uk
w holidaycottages.co.uk

Sailmakers ★★ *Self Catering*
Contact: Mrs Shirley Palmer
t (01483) 761982

Shore Leave
Rating Applied For
Self Catering
Marsdens Cottage Holidays
t (01271) 813777
e holidays@marsdens.co.uk
w marsdens.co.uk

Sinbad ★★★★ *Self Catering*
Marsdens Cottage Holidays
t (01271) 813777
e holidays@marsdens.co.uk
w marsdens.co.uk

The Waterfront ★★★★
Self Catering
Contact: Lucy Ellison
Farm & Cottage Holidays
t (01237) 479146
e enquiries@farmcott.co.uk
w holidaycottages.co.uk

ASHBURTON
Devon

Garden Cottage, Holne Chase Hotel ★★★★
Self Catering
Contact: Mrs Linda Deitrich
t (01364) 631471
e info@holne-chase.co.uk
w holne-chase.co.uk/gardencottage

Little Barton Farm ★★★★
Self Catering
Contact: Mrs Susan Small
t (01626) 821306

Wooder Manor Holiday Homes ★★★-★★★★
Self Catering
Contact: Mrs Angela Bell
Wooder Manor Holiday Homes
t (01364) 621391
e angela@woodermanor.com
w woodermanor.com

Wren & Robin Cottages
★★★★ *Self Catering*
Contact: Mrs Margaret Phipps
Wren & Robin Cottages
t (01364) 631421
e enquiries@newcott-farm.co.uk
w newcott-farm.co.uk

ASHFORD
Devon

Ashford Holt Cottage ★★
Self Catering
Toad Hall Cottages
t (01548) 853089
e thc@toadhallcottages.com
w toadhallcottages.com

Garden Cottage ★★★
Self Catering
Marsdens Cottage Holidays
t (01271) 813777
e holidays@marsdens.co.uk
w marsdens.co.uk

Helliers Farm ★★★★
Self Catering
Contact: Mrs Lancaster
t (01548) 550689
w helliersfarm.co.uk

Incledon Barn ★★★
Self Catering
Contact: Mrs Janet Cornwell
Marsdens Cottage Holidays
t (01271) 813777
e holidays@marsdens.co.uk
w marsdens.co.uk

ASHILL
Devon

Glen Cottage ★★★★
Self Catering
Contact: Miss Caroline Denton
t (01884) 840331
e caroline@glencott.co.uk
w glencott.co.uk

ASHPRINGTON
Devon

Hill Quay ★★★★
Self Catering
Toad Hall Cottages
t (01548) 853089
e thc@toadhallcottages.com
w toadhallcottages.com

ASHREIGNEY
Devon

Northcott Barton Farm Holiday Cottage ★★★★
Self Catering & Serviced Apartments
Contact: Mrs Gay
t (01769) 520259
e sandra@northcottbarton.co.uk
w northcottbarton.co.uk

ASHTON
Cornwall

Chycarne Farm Cottages
★★★ *Self Catering*
Contact: Mrs Ross
t (01736) 762473
e chycarnefarmcottages@hotmail.com
w chycarne-farm-cottages.co.uk

ASHWATER
Devon

Blagdon Farm Country Holidays *Self Catering*
Contact: Mr & Mrs M Clark & Mr & Mrs H O'Brien
Blagdon Farm Country Holidays
t (01409) 211509
e info@blagdon-farm.co.uk
w blagdon-farm.co.uk

Braddon Cottages and Forest ★★-★★★
Self Catering
Contact: Mr & Mrs George & Anne Ridge
Braddon Cottages
t (01409) 211350
e holidays@braddoncottages.co.uk
w braddoncottages.co.uk

ASKERSWELL
Dorset

Court Farm Cottages
★★★★-★★★★★
Self Catering
Contact: Mrs Rebecca Bryan
t (01308) 485668
e courtfarmcottages@eclipse.co.uk
w eclipse.co.uk/courtfarmcottages/webpg2

Little Court ★★★★★
Self Catering
Contact: Mr Leonard Vickery
t (01308) 421933
e vicklen@tesco.net
w dorsetholiday.net

West Hembury Farm
★★★★ *Self Catering*
Contact: Mrs MacEwan
Mogador House
t (01308) 485289
e hunt@westhembury.com
w westhembury.com

ATHELHAMPTON
Dorset

River Cottage ★★★★
Self Catering
Contact: Miss Tracy Winder
t (01305) 848363
e enquiry@athelhampton.co.uk
w athelhampton.co.uk

AWLISCOMBE
Devon

The Glade ★★★
Self Catering
t (01297) 20729
e info@milkberehols.com

Godford Farm ★★★★
Self Catering
Contact: Mrs Sally Lawrence
t (01404) 42825
e lawrencesally@hotmail.com
w devon-farm-holidays.co.uk

Ivedon Farm ★★★★
Self Catering
Contact: Mrs Nichola Pring
t (01404) 43088
e nicholapring1@onetel.com
w ivedonfarm.com

AXBRIDGE
Somerset

Springbanks ★★
Self Catering
Contact: Mrs Celia Wilkinson
Orchard Farm
t (01934) 713356
e mcw@kergouet.freeserve.co.uk

Waterfront Farm Cottage
★★★★ *Self Catering*
Contact: Mrs Marina Parrett
Badgworth Farm
t (01934) 733202
e badgworthfarm@aol.com
w waterfrontfarm.co.uk

AXMINSTER
Devon

Beckford Cottage ★★★★
Self Catering
Contact: Mrs Jill Bellamy
t (01404) 881641
e beckfordcottage@hotmail.com
w beckford-cottage.co.uk

Cider Room Cottage ★★★★
Self Catering
Contact: Mrs Pat Steele
t (01404) 881558
e ciderroomcottage@rscontracting.co.uk

Furzeleigh House Country Cottages and Gardens
★★★★ *Self Catering*
Contact: Mr & Mrs Rob & Shirley Blatchford
Furzeleigh House Country Cottages
t (01297) 34448
e shirley.blatchford@tesco.net
w devoncottages-furzeleigh.co.uk

The Old House ★★★★★
Self Catering
Lyme Bay Holidays
t (01297) 443363
e email@lymebayholidays.co.uk
w lymebayholidays.co.uk

Primrose Cottage ★★★★
Self Catering
Contact: Ms Louise Hayman
Milkbere Cottage Holidays
t (01297) 20729
e info@milkberehols.com
w milkberehols.com

Trout Lodge, Weycroft
★★★★ *Self Catering*
Contact: Miss Caroline Cross
19 Hylton Road
t (01730) 263732
e caroline@troutlodge.co.uk
w troutlodge.co.uk

AXMOUTH
Devon

3 Old Coastguards Cottages
★★★★ *Self Catering*
Milkbere Cottage Holidays
t (01297) 20729
e info@milkbere.com
w milkbere.com

Anchor Cottage ★★★★
Self Catering
Milkbere Cottage Holidays
t (01297) 20729
e info@milkberehols.com
w milkberehols.com

Lattenbells ★★★★
Self Catering
Milkbere Cottage Holidays
t (01297) 20729
e info@milkberehols.com
w milkberehols.com

Stepps Barn ★★★★★
Self Catering
Contact: Ms Kate Bartlett
Jean Bartlett Cottage Holidays
t (01297) 23221
e holidays@jeanbartlett.com
w jeanbartlett.com

Stepps Cross Cottage
★★★★ *Self Catering*
Contact: Ms Tim Tandy
Jean Bartlett Cottage Holidays
t (01297) 23221
e holidays@jeanbartlett.com
w jeanbartlett.com

AYLESBEARE
Devon

Alpine Park Cottages
Rating Applied For
Self Catering
Contact: Mr & Mrs Mynard
t (01395) 233619
e enquiries@alpineparkcottages.co.uk
w alpineparkcottages.co.uk

AYR
Cornwall

8 Ayr Lane ★★★
Self Catering
Contact: Mr & Mrs Annette & Mike Read
Ayia Napa Holidays
t (01736) 757237
e ayianapaholidays@btconnect.com
w ayianapaholidaysuk.co.uk

Higher Ayr Cottage ★★★
Self Catering
Contact: Mr Mott
t (01736) 795394
e simon.mott@btconnect.com

Rosebank Holiday Flats
★★★ *Self Catering*
Contact: Mrs Davidson
t (01736) 797152
e info@rosebankholidayflats.co.uk
w rosebankholidayflats.co.uk

BABBACOMBE
Devon

Sunnybank ★★★
Self Catering
Holiday Homes & Cottages South West
t (01803) 663650
e holcotts@aol.com
w swcottages.co.uk

Willow Cottage ★★★
Self Catering
Holiday Homes & Cottages South West
t (01803) 663650
e holcotts@aol.com
w swcottages.co.uk

BACKWELL
Somerset

The Coach House ★★★★
Self Catering
Contact: Mrs Iola Solari
t (01275) 464635
e info@coachhousebackwell.co.uk

BAMPTON
Devon

Honeysuckle Cottage
Rating Applied For
Self Catering
Contact: Mr Peter Cornwell
Marsdens Cottage Holidays
t (01271) 813777
e holidays@marsdens.co.uk
w marsdens.co.uk

Manor Mill House ★★★★
Self Catering
Contact: Mrs Diane Holland
t (01398) 332318
e ejjholland@tiscali.co.uk
w manor-mill.co.uk

Three Gates Farm ★★★★
Self Catering
Contact: Mrs Alison Spencer
Three Gates Farm
t (01398) 331280
e threegatesfarm@hotmail.com
w threegatesfarm.co.uk

Westbrook House ★★★
Self Catering
Contact: Mrs Patricia Currie
t (01398) 331418
e info@westbrookhouse.co.uk
w westbrookhouse.co.uk

Wonham Barton ★★★
Self Catering
Contact: Mrs Anne McLean Williams
Wonham Barton
t (01398) 331312
w wonham-country-holidays.co.uk

BANTHAM
Devon

Sloopside ★★★★
Self Catering
Toad Hall Cottages
t (01548) 853089
e thc@toadhallcottages.com
w toadhallcottages.com

BARBROOK
Devon

New Mill Farm ★★★★
Self Catering
Contact: Mr Jim Bingham
Outovercott Riding Stables
t (01598) 753341
e info@outovercott.co.uk
w outovercott.co.uk

The Old Mill House ★★★★
Self Catering
Woolhanger Farm
t (01598) 763514
e woolhanger@aol.com
w wolhanger.co.uk

Woodside ★★★
Self Catering
Contact: Mrs Sally Gunn
t (01598) 753298
e woodside@salian.fsnet.co.uk

BARNSTAPLE
Devon

Coombe Cottage ★★★★
Self Catering
Contact: Karen and John Talbot
t (0118) 976 0449
e karen@coombecottage.co.uk
w coombecottage.co.uk

Corffe Holiday Cottages
★★★★ *Self Catering*
Contact: Mr Christopher Wheeler-Grix
t (01271) 342588
e corffe@tiscali.co.uk
w corffe.co.uk

Country Ways ★★★★
Self Catering
Contact: Mrs Kate Price
t (01769) 560503
e kate@country-ways.net
w country-ways.net

Hartpiece Farm ★★★★
Self Catering
Contact: Ms Heather Lindsey
c/o JFA Ltd
t (01628) 637111
e heather@jfaexport.co.uk
w hartpiece.co.uk

Humes Farm Cottages
★★★–★★★★ *Self Catering*
Marsdens Cottage Holidays
t (01271) 813777
e holidays@marsdens.co.uk
w marsdens.co.uk

Lower Yelland Farm ★★★
Self Catering
Contact: Mr Peter Day
t (01271) 860101
e pday@loweryellandfarm.co.uk
w loweryellandfarm.co.uk

North Hill Cottages ★★★
Self Catering
Contact: Mrs Carol Ann Black
North Hill Cottages
t (01271) 850611
e info@north-hill.co.uk
w north-hill.co.uk

The Old Stables ★★★★
Self Catering
Contact: Mr Francis Summers
t (01271) 830238
e f.r.summers@btinternet.com
w the-old-stables.net

Willesleigh Farm ★★★★
Self Catering
Contact: Mr & Mrs Charles & Anne Esmond-Cole
t (01271) 343763

BARTON ST. DAVID
Somerset

Windyash ★★★ *Self Catering*
Contact: Mr & Mrs Nick & Mandy Ladd
t (01458) 851005
e mandy@deaconsworld.org.uk
w theannex.deaconsworld.org.uk

BATCOMBE
Somerset

The Coach House at Boords Farm ★★★★ *Self Catering*
Contact: Mr & Mrs Michael & Anne Page
t (01749) 850372
e info@boordsfarm.co.uk
w boordsfarm.co.uk

BATH
Somerset

102 Sydney Mews BHH 2497 ★★★ *Self Catering*
Contact: Mrs Celia Hutton
Bath Holiday Homes
t (01225) 830830
e bhh@virgin.net
w bathholidayhomes.co.uk

16 Guinea Lane ★★★★
Self Catering
Contact: Mrs Celia Hutton
Bath Holiday Homes
t (01225) 830830
e bhh@virgin.net
w bathholidayhomes.co.uk

16 St James' Square (1980) ★★★★ *Self Catering*
Contact: Mrs Celia Hutton
Bath Holiday Homes
t (01225) 830830
e bhh@virgin.net
w bathholidayhomes.co.uk

1st Floor 14 Portland Place ★★★ *Self Catering*
Contact: Mrs Celia Hutton
Bath Holiday Homes
t (01225) 830830
e bhh@virgin.net
w bathholidayhomes.co.uk

27 Park Street BHH945 ★★★ *Self Catering*
Contact: Mrs Celia Hutton
Bath Holiday Homes
t (01225) 830830
e bhh@virgin.net
w bathholidayhomes.co.uk

6 Pulteney Mews BHH712 ★★★ *Self Catering*
Contact: Mrs Celia Hutton
Bath Holiday Homes
t (01225) 830830
e bhh@virgin.net
w bathholidayhomes.co.uk

7 Northampton Street – Flat 1 ★★★ *Self Catering*
Contact: Mrs Celia Hutton
Bath Holiday Homes
t (01225) 830830
e bhh@virgin.net
w bathholidayhomes.co.uk

9 Russel Street – BHH/937 ★★★★ *Self Catering*
Contact: Mrs Celia Hutton
Bath Holiday Homes
t (01225) 830830
e bhh@virgin.net
w bathholidayhomes.co.uk

Ad Astra (1981) ★★★
Self Catering
Contact: Mrs Celia Hutton
Bath Holiday Homes
t (01225) 830830
e bhh@virgin.net
w bathholidayhomes.co.uk

Beau Street Apartments 1-3 ★★★ *Self Catering*
Contact: Mr Brian Taylor
t (01494) 681212
e bath.heritage@which.net
w bath-selfcatering.co.uk

Calverley Wing ★★★
Self Catering
t (01225) 833387
e tandjjohn@aol.com
w calverleywing.co.uk

Chestnuts House ★★★★
Self Catering
Contact: Mr Antonio Pecchia
t (01225) 723883
e reservations@chestnutshouse.co.uk
w chestnutshouse.co.uk

Church Farm Country Cottages ★★★★
Self Catering
Contact: Mrs Trish Bowles
Church Farm
t (01225) 722246
e stay@churchfarmcottages.com
w churchfarmcottages.com

Circus View ★★★★
Self Catering
Contact: Mrs Deborah Challinor
t (020) 7835 1962
e deborah@circusview.co.uk
w circusview.co.uk

Coach House (Bath) ★★★★
Self Catering & Serviced Apartments
Contact: Mrs Marilyn Quiggin
t (01225) 331341
e mq@bathselfcatering.fsnet.co.uk
w bathselfcatering.fsnet.co.uk

Flat 2 ★★ *Self Catering*
Contact: Miss Sophie Rosser-Rees
t (01225) 723545
e srosserrees@hotmail.com

Flat 3 BHH/2498 ★★★
Self Catering
Contact: Mrs Celia Hutton
Bath Holiday Homes
t (01225) 830830
e bhh@virgin.net
w bathholidayhomes.co.uk

Flat 5, 18 The Circus (BHH 1869) ★★★ *Self Catering*
Contact: Mrs Celia Hutton
Bath Holiday Homes
t (01225) 830830
e bhh@virgin.net
w bathholidayhomes.co.uk

Forum Square ★★★★
Self Catering
Contact: Mr & Mrs Paul & Susan Swainbank
t (01225) 833314
e sue.forum@btinternet.com
w bathholidayhome.com

Garden Flat – BHH 694 ★★★ *Self Catering*
Contact: Mrs Celia Hutton
Bath Holiday Homes
t (01225) 830830
e bhh@virgin.net
w bathholidayhomes.co.uk

The Garden House ★★★★★
Self Catering
Contact: Ms Elizabeth Orchard
St Catherines End House
t (01225) 852340
e elizabeth@elizabethorchard.com
w lakeorchard.com

The Granary
Rating Applied For
Self Catering
t (01225) 423808
e harford.developments@tiscali.co.uk
w bathgranary-let.co.uk

Greyfield Farm Cottages ★★★★★ *Self Catering*
Contact: Mrs June Merry
Greyfield Farm Cottages
t (01761) 471132
e june@greyfieldfarm.com
w greyfieldfarm.com

Ground Floor (2082) ★★★
Self Catering
Contact: Mrs Celia Hutton
Bath Holiday Homes
t (01225) 830830
e bhh@virgin.net
w bathholidayhomes.co.uk

Ground Floor, 46 Great Pulteney Street ★★★★
Self Catering
Contact: Mrs Celia Hutton
Bath Holiday Homes
t (01225) 830830
e bhh@virgin.net
w bathholidayhomes.co.uk

Harington's Apartment ★★★ *Self Catering*
t (01386) 424285
e melcpritchard@hotmail.com
w haringtonshotel.co.uk

Margaret's Building Apartment ★★★★
Self Catering
Contact: Mr Nick Pash
Hideaways
t (01747) 828170
e enq@hideaways.co.uk
w hideaways.co.uk/property.cfm/H490

Milestones BHH 944 ★★★★
Self Catering
Contact: Mrs Celia Hutton
Bath Holiday Homes
t (01225) 830830
e bhh@virgin.net
w bathholidayhomes.co.uk

Nailey Cottages ★★★★
Self Catering
Contact: Mrs Brett Gardner
t (01225) 852989
e cottages@naileyfarm.co.uk
w naileyfarm.co.uk

Parkside Apartment ★★★★
Self Catering
t (01225) 421097
e mjc@parksideapartment.co.uk
w parksideapartment.co.uk

Riverside Apartment ★★★
Self Catering
Contact: Mr Graham Wilson
t (01225) 337968
w rabath.co.uk

Russel Street Apartment ★★★★★ *Self Catering*
Contact: Mrs Clare Margaret Travers
t (01225) 312011
e traversa@aol.com
w bathbreaks.co.uk

Second Floor Flat ★★★★
Self Catering
Contact: Mrs Lindsay Bishop
t (01276) 29033
e lindsay.bishop@btopenworld.com

Sheylors Farm ★★★★★
Self Catering
Contact: Mrs Helen Allcot
t (01225) 743922
e helen@sheylorsfarm.co.uk
w sheylorsfarm.co.uk

Spring Farm Holiday Cottages ★★★-★★★★
Self Catering
Contact: Mrs Sue Brown
t (01761) 435524
e suebrown@springfarmcottages.co.uk
w springfarmcottages.co.uk

Time-2-Relax-Holidays ★★★★★ *Self Catering*
Contact: Ms Sue Thornton
t (01305) 837474
e sue@eastwoodquay.freeserve.co.uk

Top Flat BHH/1658 ★★★
Self Catering
Contact: Mrs Celia Hutton
Bath Holiday Homes
t (01225) 830830
e bhh@virgin.net
w bathholidayhomes.co.uk

Victorian Villa Apartment (1868) ★★★★ *Self Catering*
Contact: Mrs Celia Hutton
Bath Holiday Homes
t (01225) 830830
e bhh@virgin.net
w bathholidayhomes.co.uk

BATHEALTON
Somerset

Woodlands Farm ★★★★
Self Catering
Contact: Mrs Joan Greenway
t (01984) 623271
w woodlandsfarm-holidays.co.uk

BATHEASTON
Somerset

Avondale Riverside ★★★★-★★★★★
Self Catering
Contact: Mr & Mrs Pecchia
Avondale Riverside
t (01225) 852226
e sheilapex@questmusic.co.uk
w riversapart.co.uk

BATHFORD
Somerset

Avon Cottage Studio ★★★
Self Catering
Contact: Mr Hendrik Bebber
t (01225) 858490
e hendrick.bebber@btinternet.com
w avoncottagestudio.co.uk

BATHWICK
Somerset

Mewshouse BHH 1452
★★★ *Self Catering*
Contact: Mrs Celia Hutton
Bath Holiday Homes
t (01225) 830830
e bhh@virgin.net
w bathholidayhomes.co.uk

BEAMINSTER
Dorset

The Cottage ★★★
Self Catering
Contact: Ms Trish Mitchell
t (01308) 863054
e trish@northbuckham.fsnet.co.uk
w northbuckhamfarm.co.uk

Greens Cross Farm ★★★
Self Catering
Contact: Mr & Mrs David & Lora Baker
Greens Cross Farm
t (01308) 862661
e greenscross@btopenworld.com

Lewesdon Farm Holidays
★★★★ *Self Catering*
Contact: Mr & Mrs Michael & Linda Smith
t (01308) 868270
e lewesdonfarmholiday@tinyonline.co.uk
w lewesdonfarmholidays.co.uk

Orchard End ★★★★
Self Catering
Contact: Mrs Pauline Wallbridge
Watermeadow House
t (01308) 862619
e enquiries@watermeadowhouse.co.uk
w watermeadowhouse.co.uk

The Sawmill ★★★★
Self Catering
Contact: Joanne Walker
Lyme Bay Holidays
t (01297) 443363
e email@lymebayholidays.co.uk
w lymebayholidays.co.uk

Stable Cottage ★★★★
Self Catering
Contact: Mrs Diana Clarke
Stable Cottage
t (01308) 862305
e meerhay@aol.com
w meerhay.co.uk

BECKINGTON
Somerset

By the Byre Cottages
★★★★ *Self Catering*
Contact: Mr & Mrs Chris & Angela Hays
t (01373) 830381
e info@bythebyrecottages.co.uk
w bythebyrecottages.co.uk

BEER
Devon

12 Pioneer Cottage ★★★
Self Catering
Contact: Ms Tim Tandy
Jean Bartlett Cottage Holidays
t (01297) 23221
e holidays@jeanbartlett.com
w jeanbartlett.com

3 Pioneer Cottage ★★★
Self Catering
Contact: Ms Kate Bartlett
Jean Bartlett Cottage Holidays
t (01297) 23221
e holidays@jeanbartlett.com
w jeanbartlett.com

5 Rose Cottage ★★
Self Catering
Jean Bartlett Cottage Holidays
t (01297) 23221
w jeanbartlett.com

6 Pioneer Cottages ★★★
Self Catering
Jean Bartlett Cottage Holidays
t (01297) 23221
w jeanbartlett.com

7 Pioneer Cottages ★★★
Self Catering
Jean Bartlett Cottage Holidays
t (01297) 23221
e holidays@jeanbartlett.com
w jeanbartlett.com

The Admirals View ★★★★
Self Catering
Jean Bartlett Cottage Holidays
t (01297) 23221
e holidays@jeanbartlett.com
w netbreaks.com/jeanb

Bakery Cottage ★★★★
Self Catering
Jean Bartlett Holiday Cottages
t (01297) 23221
w bakerycottagedevon.co.uk

Beer View and New Nookies
★★★★ *Self Catering*
Contact: Mrs Jean Forbes-Harriss
t (01297) 20096
e forbesh@globalnet.co.uk

Bluff Cottage ★★★
Self Catering
Jean Bartlett
t (01297) 23221
e holidays@jeanbartlett.com
w jeanbartlett.com

Brooksyde ★★ *Self Catering*
Contact: Ms Kate Bartlett
Jean Bartlett Cottage Holidays
t (01297) 23221
e holidays@jeanbartlett.com
w jeanbartlett.com

Captains Cabin ★★★★
Self Catering
Contact: Ms Kate Bartlett
Jean Bartlett Cottage Holidays
t (01297) 23221
e holidays@jeanbartlett.com
w jeanbartlett.com

Craft Cottage ★★★★
Self Catering
Contact: Ms Kate Bartlett
Jean Bartlett Cottage Holidays
t (01297) 23221
e holidays@jeanbartlett.com
w netbreaks.com/jeanb

Farnham House ★★
Self Catering
Contact: Ms Kate Bartlett
Jean Bartlett Cottage Holidays
t (01297) 23221
e holidays@jeanbartlett.com
w netbreaks.com/jeamb

Hollyhocks ★★★★
Self Catering
Contact: Mr Tim Tandy
Jean Bartlett Cottage Holidays
t (01297) 23221
e holidays@jeanbartlett.com
w jeanbartlett.com

Hooknell House ★★★★
Self Catering
Milkbere Cottage Holidays
t (01297) 20729
e info@milkbere.com
w milkbere.com

Hope Cottage and Creole Cottage ★★★★ *Self Catering*
Contact: Mr Tim Tandy
Jean Bartlett Cottage Holidays
t (01297) 23221
e holidays@jeanbartlett.com
w jeanbartlett.com

Images ★★★ *Self Catering*
Contact: Ms Kate Bartlett
Jean Bartlett Cottage Holidays
t (01297) 23221
e holidays@jeanbartlett.com
w jeanbartlett.com

Lower Sea View Terrace
★★★★ *Self Catering*
Lyme Bay Holidays
t (01297) 443363
e email@lymebayholidays.co.uk
w lymebayholidays.co.uk

Marine House Apartments & Twyford Cottage ★★★★
Self Catering
Contact: Ms Kate Bartlett
Jean Bartlett Cottage Holidays
t (01297) 23221
e holidays@jeanbartlett.com
w jeanbartlett.com

No 2 Jubilee Cottage
★★★★ *Self Catering*
Contact: Ms Kate Bartlett
Jean Bartlett Cottage Holidays
t (01297) 23221
e holidays@jeanbartlett.com
w jeanbartlett.com

Old Dairy ★★★ *Self Catering*
Jean Bartlett Cottage Holidays
t (01297) 23221
e holidays@jeanbartlett.com
w jeanbartlett.com

The Old Lace Shop ★★★
Self Catering
Contact: Ms Tim Tandy
Jean Bartlett Cottage Holidays
t (01297) 23221
e holidays@jeanbartlett.com
w jeanbartlett.com

Otteys Cottage ★★★
Self Catering
Milkbere Cottage Holidays
t (01297) 20729
e info@milkbere.com
w milkbere.com

Purley ★★★ *Self Catering*
Contact: Ms Kate Bartlett
Jean Bartlett Cottage Holidays
t (01297) 23221
e holidays@jeanbartlett.com
w jeanbartlett.com

Ramblers ★★★ *Self Catering*
Contact: Ms Tim Tandy
Jean Bartlett Cottage Holidays
t (01297) 23221
e holidays@jeanbartlett.com
w jeanbartlett.com

Rattenbury Cottage ★★★
Self Catering
Contact: Ms Kate Bartlett
Jean Bartlett Cottage Holidays
t (01297) 23221
e holidays@jeanbartlett.com
w jeanbartlett.com

Rock Cottage ★★★★
Self Catering
Jean Bartlett Cottage Holidays
t (01297) 23221
e holidays@jeanbartlett.com
w jeanbartlett.com

Rock Farm ★★★★
Self Catering
Contact: Ms Kate Barlett
Jean Bartlett Holiday Cottages
t (01297) 23221
e holidays@jeanbartlett.com
w jeanbartlett.com

Sea View ★★★ *Self Catering*
Contact: Ms Tim Tandy
Jean Bartlett Cottage Holidays
t (01297) 23221
e holidays@jeanbartlett.com
w jeanbartlett.com

Shannon Cottage ★★★★
Self Catering
Contact: Ms Kate Bartlett
Jean Bartlett Cottage Holidays
t (01297) 23221
w jeanbartlett.com

Snowdrops ★★★
Self Catering
Contact: Ms Kate Bartlett
Jean Bartlett Cottage Holidays
t (01297) 23221
w jeanbartlett.com

Spring Garden ★★★
Self Catering
Contact: Mr Tim Tandy
Jean Bartlett Cottage Holidays
t (01297) 23221
e holidays@jeanbartlett.com
w jeanbartlett.com

Starre Cottage ★★★★
Self Catering
Contact: Ms Kate Bartlett
Jean Bartlett Cottage Holidays
t (01297) 23221
e holidays@jeanbartlett.com
w jeanbartlett.com

West View Cottage ★★★★
Self Catering
Contact: Ms Kate Bartlett
Jean Bartlett Cottage Holidays
t (01297) 23221
e holidays@jeanbartlett.com
w jeanbartlett.com

BEESANDS
Devon

Kimberley Cottage ★★★
Self Catering
Toad Hall Cottages
t (01548) 853089

BEESON
Devon

Beeson Farm Holiday Cottages ★★★★
Self Catering
Contact: Mr & Mrs Robin & Veronica Cross
Beeson Farm Holidays
t (01548) 581270
e info@beesonhols.co.uk
w beesonhols.co.uk

Gull Cry ★★★★ *Self Catering*
Toad Hall Cottages
t (01548) 853089
e thc@toadhallcottages.com
w toadhallcottages.com

BELOWDA, ROCHE
Cornwall

Treickle Barn ★★★★
Self Catering
Powells Cottage Holidays
t (01834) 812791
e info@powells.co.uk
w powells.co.uk

BENTHAM
Gloucestershire

Bridge House Cottage ★★★★★ *Self Catering*
Contact: Mrs Yvonne Hodges
Bridge House
t (01452) 862998
e yvonne@hodges0.wanadoo.co.uk
w benthamcottage.co.uk

BERE REGIS
Dorset

Troy, Bathsheba, Oak and Old Dairy Cottages ★★★★
Self Catering
Contact: Mr Ian Ventham
t (01929) 471480
e info@shitterton.com
w shitterton.com

BERRY HEAD
Devon

Berry Head Cottage ★★★★
Self Catering
Contact: Mrs Sharon Spencer
Brixham Holiday Homes Ltd
t (01803) 854187
e info@brixhamholidayhomes.co.uk
w brixhamholidayhomes.co.uk

BERRYNARBOR
Devon

Adventure Cottage ★★★★
Self Catering
Contact: Mrs Janet Cornwell
Marsdens Cottage Holidays
t (01271) 813777
e holidays@marsdens.co.uk
w marsdens.co.uk

Cairn Cottage ★★★★
Self Catering
Contact: Mrs Janet Cornwell
Marsdens Cottage Holidays
t (01271) 813777
e holidays@marsdens.co.uk
w marsdens.co.uk

Derrivale ★★★★★
Self Catering
Marsdens Cottage Holidays
t (01271) 813777
e holidays@marsdens.co.uk
w marsdens.co.uk

Forge Cottage ★★★★
Self Catering
Marsdens Cottage Holidays
t (01271) 813777
e holidays@marsdens.co.uk
w marsdens.co.uk

Lee Copse ★★★
Self Catering
Contact: Mrs Janet Cornwell
Marsdens Cottage Holidays
t (01271) 813777
e holidays@marsdens.co.uk
w marsdens.co.uk

Smythen Farm Coastal Holiday Cottages ★★★
Self Catering
Contact: Mr & Ms Thompson & Elstone
Smythen Farm Coastal Holiday Cottages
t (01271) 882875
e jayne@smythenfarmholidaycottages.co.uk
w smythenfarmholidaycottages.co.uk

Watermouth Cove Cottages ★★★ *Self Catering*
Contact: Mrs Janette Menday
Coastal Valley Hideaways
t (01769) 573921
e stay@watermouthcove.co.uk
w watermouthcove.co.uk

BERWICK ST JAMES
Wiltshire

Rose Cottage ★★★
Self Catering
Contact: Mr & Mrs John & Mildred Read
t (01722) 328934

BERWICK ST JOHN
Wiltshire

Bramble Cottage Annexe ★★★ *Self Catering*
Contact: Mr & Mrs Nick & Anne Pash
Hideaways
t (01747) 828170
e enq@hideaways.co.uk
w hideaways.co.uk

Easton Farm ★★★★
Self Catering
Contact: Mr Nicholas Pash
Hideaways
t (01747) 828170
e enq@hideaways.co.uk
w hideaways.co.uk

BETTISCOMBE
Dorset

Conway Bungalow ★★★
Self Catering
Contact: Mrs Margaret Smith
t (01308) 868313
e info@conway-bungalow.co.uk
w conway-bungalow.co.uk

BIBURY
Gloucestershire

5 Jubilee Court ★★★
Self Catering
Contact: Helen Holroyd
t (01285) 711433
e helen.holroyd@yahoo.co.uk

Bibury Holiday Cottages ★★★★ *Self Catering*
Contact: Mr & Mrs R Hedgeland
t (01285) 740314
e info@biburyholidaycottages.com
w biburyholidaycottages.com

Cotteswold House Cottages ★★★★ *Self Catering*
Contact: Mrs Judith Underwood
Cotteswold House
t (01285) 740609
e enquiries@cotteswoldhouse.org.uk
w cotteswoldhouse.org.uk

Lupin Cottage ★★★
Self Catering
Contact: Mrs Scilla Phillips
S J Phillips & Sons (Kemble) Ltd
t (01451) 844291
e scillap@hotmail.com

BIDDESTONE
Wiltshire

Barn End ★★★★
Self Catering
Contact: Mrs Jenny Davis
t (01249) 712104
e jennyandbob@biddestone.com
w bathselfcatering.com/barnend/listing.html

BIDEFORD
Devon

Coachmans Cottage ★★★
Self Catering
Contact: Mr & Mrs Tom & Sue Downie
t (01805) 623670
e tom.downie@ukonline.co.uk
w creamteacottages.co.uk

Georges Cottage ★★★★
Self Catering
Marsdens Cottage Holidays
t (01271) 813777
e holidays@marsdens.co.uk
w marsdens.co.uk

Little Melville Holiday Cottage ★★★★ *Self Catering*
Contact: Mr Bernard Moore
t (01237) 471140
e anb@melvillecot.freeserve.co.uk
w litmel.freeserve.co.uk

The Old Granary
Rating Applied For
Self Catering
Marsdens Cottage Holidays
t (01271) 813777
e holidays@marsdens.co.uk
w marsdens.co.uk

Pillhead Cottage ★★★★
Self Catering
Toad Hall Cottages
t (01548) 853089
e thc@toadhallcottages.com
w toadhallcottages.com

Pillhead Farm ★★★★
Self Catering
Contact: Mr Richard Hill
t (01237) 479337
e hill@pillheadfarm.fsnet.co.uk

Robin Hill Farm Cottages ★★★★ *Self Catering*
Contact: Mr & Mrs Rob & Sue Williams
t (01237) 473605
e r.hillcotts@amserve.net
w robinhillcottages.co.uk

Tryst
Rating Applied For
Self Catering
Marsdens Cottage Holidays
t (01271) 813777
e holidays@marsdens.co.uk
w marsdens.co.uk

West Hele ★★★-★★★★
Self Catering
Contact: Mrs Lorna Hicks
Buckland Brewer
t (01237) 451044
e lorna.hicks@virgin.net
w westhele.co.uk

BIGBURY-ON-SEA
Devon

1 Sharpland Crest ★★★
Self Catering
Contact: Mrs Amanda Hough
t (01392) 438234
e amandahough@talk21.com

Apartment 5, Burgh Island Causeway ★★★★★ *Self Catering & Serviced Apartments*
Helpful Holidays
t (01647) 433593
e help@helpfulholidays.com

Apartment 19 ★★★★★
Self Catering
Contact: Mrs Sue Bowater
Helpful Holidays
t (01647) 43359
e help@helpfulholidays.com
w helpfulholidays.com

Ferrycombe ★★★★
Self Catering
Contact: Mrs Juliet Fooks
t (01435) 863045 & 07050 030231

Mount Folly Farm ★★★
Self Catering
Contact: Mrs J Tucker
t (01548) 810267
e chris.cathy@goosemoose.com
w bigburyholidays.co.uk

Thornbury ★★★★
Self Catering
Contact: Mrs J Tagent
t (01548) 810520
e met@cix.co.uk
w cottagesdirect.com/dea069

BINEGAR
Somerset

Spindle Cottage ★★★★
Self Catering
Contact: Mrs Angela Bunting
t (01749) 840497
e spindle.cottage@ukonline.co.uk
w spindlecottagelets.co.uk

BIRDLIP
Gloucestershire

Sidelands Farm ★★★★
Self Catering
Contact: Ms Harriet Saunders
Sidelands Farm Holidays
t (01452) 864826
e saunders@sidelands.fsnet.co.uk
w sidelandsfarm.co.uk

BISHOP SUTTON
Somerset

The Trebartha ★★★★
Self Catering
Contact: Mr & Mrs Edward & Sally Catchpole
t (01275) 333845
e sally@thetrebartha.co.uk

BISHOP'S CAUNDLE
Dorset

The Tallett ★★★
Self Catering
Contact: Ms Kirsty Parker
Dream Cottages
t (01305) 789000
e admin@dream-cottages.co.uk
w dream-cottages.co.uk

BISHOPSTEIGNTON
Devon

4 Cleland Court ★★★★★
Self Catering
Contact: Ms Adele Barnes
Bluechip Vacations
t (01803) 855282
e adele@bluechipvacations.com
w bluechipvacations.com

BISLEY
Gloucestershire

Coopers Cottage ★★★
Self Catering
Contact: Mr & Mrs Michael & Liz Flint
Wells Cottage
t (01452) 770289
e flint.bisley@btinternet.com

BLACKAWTON
Devon

Chuckle Too ★★★
Self Catering
Contact: Ms Jill Hanlon
Chuckle Cottage
t (01803) 712455
e jillyhanlon@beeb.net
w stay-in-devon.co.uk

BLACKBOROUGH
Devon

Bodmiscombe Farm ★★★
Self Catering
t (01884) 266315
e bodmiscombefarm@hotmail.com
w devonfarms.net

South Farm Cottages & Fishery ★★★ *Self Catering*
Contact: Mr & Mrs Barry & Susan Chapman
South Farm Holiday Cottages & Fishery
t (01823) 681078
e chapmans@southfarm.co.uk
w southfarm.co.uk

BLACKDOWN
Dorset

The Grooms Quarters – W4183 ★★★ *Self Catering*
Lyme Bay Holidays
t (01297) 443363
e email@lymebayholidays.co.uk
w lymebayholidays.co.uk

BLAKENEY
Gloucestershire

Streamside Cottage ★★★
Self Catering
Contact: Mrs Angela Yeend
t (01454) 315116
e angela-yeend@supanet.com
w streamsideholidaycottage.co.uk

BLANDFORD FORUM
Dorset

Bluebell Cottage ★★★
Self Catering
Contact: Mr Zachary Stuart-Brown
Dream Cottages
t (01305) 789000
e admin@dream-cottages.co.uk
w dream-cottages.co.uk

Orchard House Cottage
★★★★ *Self Catering*
Contact: Ms Fiona Chapman
t (01258) 860257
e fiona@chapman1807.fsnet.com
w cottage4two.co.uk

BLATCHBRIDGE
Somerset

Mill Cottage ★★★★
Self Catering
Contact: Mrs Thelma Morris
t (01373) 464784

BLISLAND
Cornwall

Bridge Pool Cottage ★★★★
Self Catering
Contact: Mr & Mrs Sobey
t (01579) 343382

Little Tregaddick ★★★
Self Catering
Contact: Mr & Mrs Pike
t (01208) 850625
e debra.pike@ntworld.com

Torr House Cottages
★★★★ *Self Catering*
Contact: Mr & Mrs Wilson
t (01208) 851601
w torrhousecottages.co.uk

BLOCKLEY
Gloucestershire

Arreton Cottage ★★★★
Self Catering
Contact: Mrs Gloria Baylis
Arreton House
t (01386) 701077
e bandb@arreton.demon.co.uk
w arreton.demon.co.uk

Briar Cottage ★★★★
Self Catering
Contact: Miss Sheila Rolland
Campden Cottages
t (01386) 593315
e info@campdencottages.co.uk
w campdencottages.co.uk

Cinquefoil Cottage
Rating Applied For
Self Catering
Contact: Mrs Patricia Hinksman
t (01707) 652485
w cinquefoilcottage.co.uk

Rosemary Cottage ★★★★
Self Catering
Contact: Ms Sheila Rolland
t (01386) 593315
e info@campdencottages.co.uk
w campdencottages.co.uk

Skylark Cottage ★★★★
Self Catering
Contact: Mrs Ruth Lucas
t (01451) 832575
e lucas@okwa.demon.co.uk
w skylarkcottage.co.uk

BLUE ANCHOR
Somerset

Huntingball Lodge ★★★★
Self Catering
Contact: Mr & Mrs Brian & Kim Hall
Huntingball Lodge
t (01984) 640076
w huntingball-lodge.co.uk

Primrose Hill Holidays
★★★★ *Self Catering*
Contact: Mrs Jo Halliday
t (01643) 821200
e info@primrosehillholidays.co.uk
w primrosehillholidays.co.uk

BODMIN
Cornwall

Blossom Cottage ★★★★
Self Catering
Contact: Mrs Linda Chapman
t (01208) 74417
e l/g18@halfarm.co.uk
w blossomcottage.co.uk

Glynn Barton Cottages
★★★★ *Self Catering*
Contact: Ms Orr
t (01208) 821375
e cottages@glynnbarton.fsnet.co.uk

Hillandale ★★★ *Self Catering*
Contact: Mr David Pearce
t (01208) 76042
e pearce24@btinternet.com

Lanjew Holidays ★★★★
Self Catering
Contact: Mrs Elaine Biddick
t (01726) 890214
e biddick@lanjew.co.uk
w lanjewholidays.co.uk

Little Boskear
Rating Applied For
Self Catering
Contact: Mr James Morris
Farm & Cottage Holidays
t (01237) 479146
e enquiries@farmcott.co.uk
w holidaycottages.co.uk

Tor View ★★★–★★★★
Self Catering
Contact: Mr & Mrs Watson
t (01208) 831472

BODREAN
Cornwall

Apple Orchard Bungalow
★★★★ *Self Catering*
Farm & Cottage Holidays
t (01237) 479146
e enquiries@farmcott.co.uk
w holidaycottages.co.uk

BOLINGEY
Cornwall

Appledore
Rating Applied For
Self Catering
Duchy Holidays
t (01872) 572971
e enquiries@duchyholidays.co.uk
w duchyholidays.co.uk

Middlemarch ★★★
Self Catering
Duchy Holidays
t (01872) 572971
e enquiries@duchyholidays.co.uk
w duchyholidays.co.uk

Primrose Cottage ★★
Self Catering
Duchy Holidays
t (01872) 572971
e enquiries@duchyholidays.co.uk
w duchyholidays.co.uk

St Jude's Ranch ★★★
Self Catering
Contact: Mr Andrew Dingle
t 07721 896830
e tessawils@yahoo.co.uk

BOSCASTLE
Cornwall

4 Pennally Cottage ★★★
Self Catering
Contact: Mrs Janet Welch
t (01322) 522240
e janetwelch@hotmail.co.uk

Anneth Lowen ★★★★
Self Catering
Contact: Mrs Kay Dougan
Kernow Holidays
t (01483) 765446
e info@annethlowen.co.uk

The Boat House ★★★★
Self Catering
t (01840) 250 3742
e harbourlightltd@hotmail.com
w cornwall-online.co.uk/boathouse

Boscastle Holidays ★★★★
Self Catering
Contact: Mrs Congdon
t (01840) 250233
e boscastle.holidays@virgin.net
w boscastleholidays.co.uk

Cardew Farmhouse ★★★
Self Catering
Contact: Mrs Liz Brewer
t (01804) 250854
e cardew@lineone.net
w cardewfarmhouse.co.uk

Cargurra Farm ★★★★
Self Catering
Contact: Mrs Gillian Elson
t (01840) 261206
e gillian@cargurra.co.uk
w cargurra.co.uk

Courtyard Farm ★★★★
Self Catering
Contact: Mr & Mrs Compton
t (01840) 261256
e courtyard.farm@virgin.net
w courtyardfarmcottages.com

The Garden Place ★★★★
Self Catering
t (01840) 250817
e celia.knox@btinternet.com

Hideaway
Rating Applied For
Self Catering
Contact: Mr Barry Francis
t (01737) 550014
e barry@mayfairmortgages.com

Hilly View ★★★
Self Catering
Contact: Mrs Catherine Smith
t (01730) 269745
e andrew.catherine@virgin.net

Home Farm Cottage ★★★★
Self Catering
Contact: Mrs Haddy
t (01840) 250195
e homefarm.boscastle@tiscali.co.uk
w homefarm-boscastle.co.uk

Honeysuckle Cottage ★★★
Self Catering
Contact: Revd. Bunker
t (01582) 619314

Jordan Vale ★★★-★★★★
Self Catering
t (01840) 250463
e sues-cott@lineone.net
w jordanvale.net

Lewarne ★★★ *Self Catering*
Contact: Mr Purvis
t (01676) 534648
e ifpurvis@truffle99.freeserve.co.uk

Lundy View
Rating Applied For
Self Catering
Contact: Mrs Sue Venning
t (01840) 250113
e lundynewboscastle@fsmail.net

The Olde Carpenters Shop
★★★★★ *Self Catering*
Contact: Mr & Mrs Haddy
t (01840) 250195
e homefarm.boscastle@tiscali.co.uk
w homefarm-boscastle.co.uk

Paradise Farm ★★★
Self Catering
Contact: Mrs Hancock
t (01840) 250528

Seagull Barn ★★★
Self Catering
Contact: Jackie Hargreaves
t (01428) 723819
e enquiries@cornishseaviewcottages.co.uk
w cornishseaviewcottages.co.uk

Tregatherall Farm Cottages
★★★★ *Self Catering*
Contact: Mrs Seldon
t (01840) 250277
w tregatherallfarm.co.uk

Trehane House ★★
Self Catering
Contact: Mrs Cynthia Taylor
t (01840) 250052

Trewannett Bungalow ★★★
Self Catering
Contact: Mrs Sleep
t (01840) 250295

Venn Down Farmhouse Apartments ★★★★
Self Catering
Contact: Mrs Diane Bentall
t (01840) 250599
e venndownfarmhouse@uk2.net
w venndownfarmhouse.co.uk

Westerings ★★-★★★
Self Catering
Contact: Mrs Shirley Wakelin
t (01840) 250314
e shirley@westeringsholidays.co.uk
w westeringsholidays.co.uk

BOSSINEY
Cornwall

Bramble Nook ★★★★
Self Catering
Contact: Mrs Janet Bate
t (01827) 873084

BOURTON-ON-THE-WATER
Gloucestershire

Acorn Cottage ★★★★
Self Catering
Contact: Mrs Ann Oakes
t (01386) 870727
e ann@oakescottages.co.uk
w oakescottages.co.uk

Annes Cottage ★★★★
Self Catering
Contact: Mrs Ann Oakes
t (01386) 870727
e ann@oakescottages.co.uk
w oakescottages.co.uk

Cloisters ★★★★
Self Catering
Contact: Mrs Harmer
t (01959) 569096 & 07866 477545
e enquiries@prestigeholidaycottages.co.uk
w prestigeholidaycottages.co.uk

The Coach House of the Dower House ★★
Self Catering
Contact: Mrs Philomena Adams
t (01451) 820629

Cotswold Cottage Company
★★★★ *Self Catering*
Contact: Miss Pippa Arnott
Cotswolds Cottage Company
t (01451) 850560
e cotscotco@msn.com
w cotswoldcottage.co.uk

Farncombe Apartment
★★★★ *Self Catering & Serviced Apartments*
Contact: Mrs Julia Wright
t (01451) 820120
e julia@farncombecotswolds.com
w farncombecotswolds.com

Greenleighs ★★★★
Self Catering
Contact: Mrs Joyce Tombs
t (01454) 419760

Inglenook Cottage ★★★
Self Catering
Contact: Mrs Vicki Garland
Ratcliffe House Farm
t (01827) 712367 & 07751 801508

Magnolia Cottage Apartment ★★★★
Self Catering
Contact: Mr & Mrs Janice & Michael Cotterill
t (01451) 821841
e cotterillmj@hotmail.com
w cottageguide.co.uk/magnolia

The Mallards ★★★★
Self Catering
Contact: Mrs Juliet Shatford
Moore House
t (01451) 821476
e juliet@teamwork-selection.co.uk

Oxleigh Cottages ★★★★
Self Catering
Contact: Mrs Barbara Smith
The Annexe, Honeysuckle Cottage
t 07773 474108 & 07773 474108
e cdsmith.annexe@fsmail.net

Southlands Cottage ★★★
Self Catering
Contact: Mr & Mrs David & Christine Hutchman
t (01451) 821987
e christine-hutchman@btopenworld.com
w southlands-bb.com.uk

Tagmoor Hollow Apartment
★★★★ *Self Catering*
Contact: Mrs Grace Bennett
t (01451) 821307

Well Cottage ★★★★
Self Catering
Contact: Bette Roberts
t (01451) 824059

Windrush Apartments ★★★
Self Catering
Contact: Mr & Mrs Arthur & Gill Perry
t 07710 404942
e arthurandgill@aol.com
w windrushapartments.co.uk

Wrights Cottage ★★★★
Self Catering
Contact: Mrs Gloria Marsh
t (01451) 820568
e gloria.marsh@ntlworld.com

BOVEY TRACEY
Devon

Lower Elsford Farm ★★★★
Self Catering
Helpful Holidays
t (01647) 433593

Stickwick Farm ★★★
Self Catering
Contact: Mrs Harvey
t (01626) 833266
e linda@frostfarm.co.uk
w frostfarm.co.uk

Tracey Cottage ★★★
Self Catering
Holiday Homes & Cottages South West
t (01803) 663650
e holcotts@aol.com
w swcottages.co.uk

Warmhill Farm ★★★★
Self Catering
Contact: Mr W B Marnham
Warmhill Farm
t (01626) 833229
e marnham@agriplus.net

BOWDEN
Devon

Alice Cottage ★★★★
Self Catering
Contact: Mr David Hanmer
Toad Hall Cottages
t (01548) 853089
e thc@toadhallcottages.com
w toadhallcottages.com

BOX
Wiltshire

The Haybarn Alcombe Manor ★★★★ *Self Catering*
Contact: Dr Caroline Morley
t (01225) 742291

BRADFORD ABBAS
Dorset

The Studio ★★★
Self Catering
Contact: Mrs Wendy Dann
Heartsease Cottage
t (01935) 475480
e w.dann@tiscali.co.uk

BRADFORD-ON-AVON
Wiltshire

Fairfield Barns ★★★★★
Self Catering
Contact: Mr & Mrs Taff & Gilly Thomas
t (01225) 703585
e gilly@fairfieldbarns.com
w fairfieldbarns.com

Lock View Cottage ★★★★
Self Catering
Contact: Mrs Linda Palmer
t (01225) 865607
e lockview@dsl.pipex.com
w lockviewcottage.co.uk

BRADLEY CROSS
Somerset

Bradley Cross Farm ★★
Self Catering
Contact: Ms Judith Credland
t (01934) 741771
e paul.morgan@quista.net

BRADNINCH
Devon

Highdown Organic Farm
★★★★ *Self Catering*
Contact: Mrs Vallis
Highdown Farm Holiday Cottages
t (01392) 881028
e svallis@highdownfarm.co.uk
w highdownfarm.co.uk

BRADWORTHY
Devon

Calf Barn ★★★★
Self Catering
t (01409) 241597
e knwilson@virgin.net

BRANKSOME PARK
Dorset

Dolphin Cottage, Seahorse & Starfish Apartments ★★★
Self Catering
Contact: Mrs Ulla Middler
The Grovefield Manor Hotel
t (01202) 766798
w bournemouthselfcatering.com

BRANSCOMBE
Devon

Bank Cottage ★★★
Self Catering
Contact: Mr Tim Tandy
Jean Bartlett Cottage Holidays
t (01297) 23221
e holidays@jeanbartlett.com
w jeanbartlett.com

The Chapel at Borcombe Farm ★★★ *Self Catering*
Contact: Mr Tim Tandy
Jean Bartlett Cottage Holidays
t (01297) 23221
e holidays@jeanbartlett.com
w jeanbartlett.com

Chapel Row ★★★★
Self Catering
Contact: Mr Tim Tandy
Jean Bartlett Cottage Holidays
t (01297) 23221
e holidays@jeanbartlett.com
w jeanbartlett.com

Cliffhayes ★★★ *Self Catering*
Jean Bartlett Cottage Holidays
t (01297) 23221
e holidays@jeanbartlett.com
w jeanbartlett.com

Gill Cottage ★★★
Self Catering
Contact: Mr Tim Tandy
Jean Bartlett Cottage Holidays
t (01297) 23221
e holidays@jeanbartlett.com
w jeanbartlett.com

Hole House and The Granary
★★★★ *Self Catering*
Contact: Ms Kate Bartlett
Jean Bartlett Cottage Holidays
t (01297) 23221
e holidays@jeanbartlett.com
w jeanbartlett.com

Jasmine Cottage ★★
Self Catering
Contact: Ms Kate Bartlett
Jean Bartlett Cottage Holidays
t (01297) 23221
e holidays@jeanbartlett.com
w jeanbartlett.com

Little Millview
Rating Applied For
Self Catering
Contact: Tracy Gwillin
Sweetcombe Cottage Holidays Ltd
t (01395) 512130
e enquiries@sweetcombe-ch.co.uk

Pitt Farm Lodge ★★★
Self Catering
Contact: Ms Kate Bartlett
Jean Bartlett Cottage Holidays
t (01297) 23221
e holidays@jeanbartlett.com
w jeanbartlett.com

Roslyn Cottage & Cliffhayes
★★★ *Self Catering*
Contact: Mr Tim Tandy
Jean Bartlett Cottage Holidays
t (01297) 23221
e holidays@jeanbartlett.com
w jeanbartlett.com

Terry Holt & The Nook
★★★★ *Self Catering*
Contact: Ms Kate Bartlett
Jean Bartlett Cottage Holidays
t (01297) 23221
e holidays@jeanbartlett.com
w jeanbartlett.com

BRATTON
Somerset

Woodcombe Lodges ★★★★
Self Catering
Contact: Mrs Nicola Hanson
Woodcombe Lodges
t (01643) 702789 & 07860 667325
e nicola@woodcombelodge.co.uk
w woodcombelodge.co.uk

BRATTON FLEMING
Devon

Capelands Farm ★★★
Self Catering
Toad Hall Cottages
t (01548) 521366
e thc@toadhallcottages.com
w toadhallcottages.com

BRAUNTON
Devon

1 Millhouse Cottage ★★★
Self Catering
Marsdens Cottage Holidays
t (01271) 813777
e holidays@marsdens.co.uk
w marsdens.co.uk

2 Millhouse Cottage ★★★
Self Catering
Contact: Mrs Janet Cornwell
Marsdens Cottage Holidays
t (01271) 813777
e holidays@marsdens.co.uk
w marsdens.co.uk

Bowden House ★★★★
Self Catering
Contact: Mrs Janet Cornwell
Marsdens Cottage Holidays
t (01271) 813777
e holidays@marsdens.co.uk
w marsdens.co.uk

Britton Lodge ★★★
Self Catering
Contact: Mrs Janet Cornwell
Marsdens Cottage Holidays
t (01271) 813777
e holidays@marsdens.co.uk
w marsdens.co.uk

Buckland Manor Cottage
★★★ *Self Catering*
Contact: Mrs Janet Cornwell
Marsdens Cottage Holidays
t (01271) 813777
e holidays@marsdens.co.uk
w marsdens.co.uk

Buckland Mews ★★★
Self Catering
Contact: Mrs Janet Cornwell
Marsdens Cottage Holidays
t (01271) 813777
e holidays@marsdens.co.uk
w marsdens.co.uk

Casquets ★★★★
Self Catering
Contact: Mrs Janet Cornwell
Marsdens Cottage Holidays
t (01271) 813777
e holidays@marsdens.co.uk
w marsdens.co.uk

Garden Flat ★★★
Self Catering
Contact: Mrs Janet Cornwell
Marsdens Cottage Holidays
t (01271) 813777
e holidays@marsdens.co.uk
w marsdens.co.uk

Goadgates ★★★
Self Catering
Marsdens Cottage Holidays
t (01271) 813777
e holidays@marsdens.co.uk
w marsdens.co.uk

Hart Farm ★★★★
Self Catering
Farm & Cottage Holidays
t (01237) 479146
e enquiries@farmcott.co.uk
w holidaycottages.co.uk

Higher Spreacombe Farm
★★★ *Self Catering*
Contact: Mrs Colleen McCammond
t (01271) 870443
e mccammondgc@aol.com

Holmbush ★★★★★
Self Catering
Marsdens Cottage Holidays
t (01271) 813777
e holidays@marsdens.co.uk
w marsdens.co.uk

Hope Cottage ★★★★★
Self Catering
Contact: Mrs Janet Cornwell
Marsdens Cottage Holidays
t (01271) 813777
e holidays@marsdens.co.uk
w marsdens.co.uk

Incledon Farmhouse ★★★
Self Catering
Contact: Mrs Janet Cornwell
Marsdens Cottage Holidays
t (01271) 813777
e holidays@marsdens.co.uk
w marsdens.co.uk

Leacroft ★★★ *Self Catering*
Contact: Mrs Janet Cornwell
Marsdens Cottage Holidays
t (01271) 813777
e holidays@marsdens.co.uk
w marsdens.co.uk

Lime Tree Nursery ★★★★
Self Catering
Contact: Mrs Janet Cornwell
Marsdens Cottage Holidays
t (01271) 813777
e holidays@marsdens.co.uk
w marsdens.co.uk

Little Comfort Farm ★★★
Self Catering
Contact: Mrs Jackie Milsom
t (01271) 812414
e enquiries@littlecomfortfarm.co.uk
w littlecomfortfarm.co.uk

Moor Lane Cottage ★★★★
Self Catering
Marsdens Cottage Holidays
t (01271) 813777
e holidays@marsdens.co.uk
w marsdens.co.uk

The Old Byre ★★★★
Self Catering
Marsdens Cottage Holidays
t (01271) 813777
e holidays@marsdens.co.uk
w marsdens.co.uk

Ramblers Return ★★
Self Catering
Marsdens Cottage Holidays
t (01271) 813777
e holidays@marsdens.co.uk
w marsdens.co.uk

Rustlings
Rating Applied For
Self Catering
Contact: Mr Peter Cornwell
Marsdens Cottage Holidays
t (01271) 813777
e holidays@marsdens.co.uk
w marsdens.co.uk

St Brannocks Hill
Rating Applied For
Self Catering
Marsdens Cottage Holidays
t (01271) 813777
e holidays@marsdens.co.uk
w marsdens.co.uk

Saunton Beach Villas ★★
Self Catering
Contact: Mrs Clare Oliver
Broadfield Holidays
t (01271) 892002

Score Farm House and Annexe ★★★★ *Self Catering*
Contact: Mrs Helen Knight
t (01271) 814815
e sunshinenel@btinternet.com
w scorefarmholidays.co.uk

Valentines Cottage
Rating Applied For
Self Catering
Contact: Mr Peter Cornwell
Marsdens Cottage Holidays
t (01271) 813777
e holidays@marsdens.co.uk
w marsdens.co.uk

Waverley ★★★ *Self Catering*
Contact: Mrs Janet Cornwell
Marsdens Cottage Holidays
t (01271) 813777
e holidays@marsdens.co.uk
w marsdens.co.uk

Well Cottage ★★★★
Self Catering
Contact: Mr & Mrs Peter & Janet Cornwell
Marsdens Cottage Holidays
t (01271) 813777
e holidays@marsdens.co.uk
w marsdens.co.uk

Windspray ★★★
Self Catering
Contact: Mrs Janet Cornwell
Marsdens Cottage Holidays
t (01271) 813777
e holidays@marsdens.co.uk
w marsdens.co.uk

BRAYFORD
Devon

Muxworthy Cottage ★★★
Self Catering
Contact: Mrs G M Bament
Muxworthy Farm
t (01598) 710342

BREAGE
Cornwall

Hillsdale Holiday Cottages
★★★ *Self Catering*
Contact: Mr Adam Fornear
t (01736) 763466
e hillsdalecottage@aol.com
w hillsdalecottages.co.uk

BREAN
Somerset

Gadara Bungalow ★★
Self Catering
Contact: Mr Trevor Hicks
t (01278) 751263
e trevor@diamondfarm42.freeserve.co.uk
w diamondfarm.co.uk

BREMHILL
Wiltshire

Brook Farm ★★★★
Self Catering
Contact: Yvonne Buckley
t (01249) 811265
e yandpcottages@aol.com

Lavender Cottage and Little Barn ★★★★ *Self Catering*
Contact: Mr & Mrs Paul & Yvonne Buckley
t (01249) 811265
e yandpcottages@aol.com
w yandpcottages.co.uk

BRENT KNOLL
Somerset

West Croft Farm Dairy Cottage ★★★ *Self Catering*
Contact: Mrs Janet Harris
t (01278) 760259

Look out for establishments participating in the National Accessible Scheme 

BRENTOR
Devon

The Smithy ★★★
Self Catering
Contact: Mrs Sally Wetherbee
t (01822) 810285
e sally@wetherbee.fsnet.co.uk
w sallysholidaycottages.co.uk

BRIDGETOWN
Somerset

Week Cottage ★★★★
Self Catering
Contact: Mr Stephen Blackwell
t (01643) 851353
e mail@weekcottage.co.uk
w weekcottage.co.uk

BRIDGWATER
Somerset

Ash-Wembdon Farm Cottages ★★★★
Self Catering
Contact: Mr Clarence Rowe
t (01278) 453097
e c.a.rowe@btinternet.com
w ukcottageholiday.com

Nelson Cottage ★★★★
Self Catering
Contact: Mr & Mrs Robbins
Nelson Lodge
t (01278) 453492
e robbinsm@bridgwater.ac.uk

BRIDPORT
Dorset

30 Victoria Grove ★★
Self Catering
Contact: Mr & Mrs Brook
t (01308) 424605

---

4 Bedford Place ★★★
Self Catering
Contact: Mr Jonathan Bourbon
t (01308) 424160

Aviary Cottage ★★★
Self Catering
Dream Cottages
t (01305) 789000
e admin@dream-cottages.co.uk
w dream-cottages.co.uk

Badgers Brinsham Farm
★★★★ *Self Catering*
Contact: Mr & Mrs Symonds
The Bothy
t (01962) 774657
e nigelsymonds@btinternet.com

Church Cottage – X4473
★★★ *Self Catering*
Lyme Bay Holidays
t (01297) 443363
e email@lymebayholidays.co.uk
w lymebayholidays.co.uk

Clearview Bungalow ★★★
Self Catering
Contact: Mr Zachary Stuart-Brown
Dream Cottages
t (01305) 789000
e admin@dream-cottages.co.uk
w dream-cottages.co.uk

Coneygar Bungalow ★★★
Self Catering
Contact: Mrs Janet Grimwood
t (01308) 485314

Coniston Holiday Apartments ★★★
Self Catering
Contact: Mrs Jackie Murphy
t (01308) 424049

Fern Down Farm ★★★
Self Catering
Contact: Mr David Solly
t (01300) 320810
e pdnsolly@hotmail.com

Ganders Cottage ★★★
Self Catering
Contact: Mrs Pauline Bale
t (01308) 424321
e bale@highwayfarm.co.uk
w highwayfarm.co.uk

The Gunny ★★★★
Self Catering
Dream Cottages
t (01305) 789000
e admin@dream-cottages.co.uk
w dream-cottages.co.uk

Hayday ★★★★ *Self Catering*
Contact: Mrs Day
t (01308) 424438

Lancombes House ★★★
Self Catering
Contact: Mr & Mrs Mansfield
t (01308) 485375
w lancombeshouse.co.uk

Rudge Farm ★★★★
Self Catering
Contact: Mr Michael Hamer
Rudge Farm
t (01308) 482630
e enquiries@rudgefarm.co.uk
w rudgefarm.co.uk

Strongate Cottage ★★★
Self Catering
Contact: Mrs Sandra Huxter
Strongate Farm
t (01308) 488295
e sandra@thecharnleys.co.uk

Sunset ★★★ *Self Catering*
Contact: Mr Dan Walker FHCIMA
c/o Eypeleaze
t (01308) 423363
e cdan@walker42.freeserve.co.uk

Wooth Manor Cottage ★★★
Self Catering
Contact: Mrs Gaby Martelli
The Old Workhouse
t (01308) 488348
e amyasmartelli40@hotmail.com

BRIMPSFIELD
Gloucestershire

Brimpsfield Farmhouse (West Wing) ★★★
Self Catering
Contact: Mrs Valerie Partridge
Brimpsfield Farmhouse (West Wing)
t (01452) 863568

BRISTOL
City of Bristol

Avonside ★★★ *Self Catering*
Contact: Mrs DM Ridout
t (0117) 968 1967

Harbourside Apartment
★★★★ *Self Catering*
Contact: Mrs Flick Selway
t 07792 503604
e flickSelway@Pselway.freeserve.co.uk

Harbourside View ★★★★★
Self Catering
t (01308) 897457
e alisondavies21@hotmail.com

Redland Flat ★★★
Self Catering
t (020) 8450 6761
e redlandflat.btc@onmail.co.uk

BRIXHAM
Devon

7 Heath Court
Rating Applied For
Self Catering
Contact: Mrs Adele Barnes
Blue Chip Vacations
t (01803) 855282
e adele@bluechipvacations.com
w bluechipvacations.com/properties/he07.php

---

9 Ranscombe Road ★★★★
Self Catering
Contact: Mrs Adele Barnes
Blue Chip Vacations
t (01803) 855282
e info@bluechipvacations.com

Admirals Rest
Rating Applied For
Self Catering
Contact: Mrs Butterworth
Torbay Holiday Agency
t (01803) 663650
e holcotts@aol.com
w swcottages.co.uk

Anchorage ★★★
Self Catering
Contact: Mrs Sharon Spencer
Brixham Holiday Homes Ltd
t (01803) 854187
e info@brixhamholidayhomes.co.uk
w brixhamholidayhomes.co.uk

Arlington Holiday Flats
★★★ *Self Catering*
Contact: Ms Denise Buggins
t (0121) 447 7387
e denise.buggins@btinternet.com
w selfcateringtorbay.co.uk

Beachcomber ★★★
Self Catering
Holiday Homes & Cottages South West
t (01803) 663650
e holcotts@aol.com
w swcottages.co.uk

Berry Head ★★★
Self Catering
Holiday Homes & Cottages South West
t (01803) 663650
e holcotts@aol.com
w swcottages.co.uk

Brandywine ★★★
Self Catering
Contact: Mrs Adele Barnes
Blue Chip Vacations
t (01803) 855282
e info@bluechipvacations.com
w bluechipvacations.com/properties/bran.php

Brixham Harbourside Holiday Flats ★★★
Self Catering
Contact: Mrs Helgard Stone
t (01803) 851919
e david.f.stone@btinternet.com
w brixham-harbourside-holiday-flats.com

Captain's Cottage ★★★
Self Catering
Contact: Mrs Sharon Spencer
Brixham Holiday Homes Ltd
t (01803) 854187
e info@brixhamholidayhomes.co.uk
w brixhamholidayhomes.co.uk

Captain's Quarters and Gulls' Nest ★★★★★
Self Catering
Contact: Mrs Gretchen Tricker
Brixham Historic Houses
t (01803) 857937
e gtricker@aol.com
w brixhamhistorichouses.co.uk

Castaway Cottage ★★★
Self Catering
Contact: Ms Sharon Spencer
Brixham Holiday Homes Ltd
t (01803) 854187
e info@brixhamholidayhomes.co.uk
w brixhamholidayhomes.co.uk

Celeste Cottage ★★★
Self Catering
Contact: Mrs Sharon Spencer
Brixham Holiday Homes Ltd
t (01803) 854187
e info@brixhamholidayhomes.co.uk
w brixhamholidayhomes.co.uk

Chiseldon Farm Annexe
★★★★ *Self Catering*
Contact: Ms Sharon Spencer
Brixham Holiday Homes Ltd
t (01803) 854187
e info@brixhamholidayhomes.co.uk
w brixhamholidayhomes.co.uk

Cliff Cottage ★★★
Self Catering
Brixham Holiday Homes Ltd
t (01803) 854187
w brixhamholidayhomes.co.uk

Combe Cottage ★★
Self Catering
Contact: Mrs Butterworth
Torbay Holiday Agency
t (01803) 663650
e holcotts@aol.com
w swcottages.co.uk

Compass Cottage ★★★
Self Catering
Contact: Mrs Sharon Spencer
Brixham Holiday Homes Ltd
t (01803) 854187
e info@brixhamholidayhomes.co.uk
w brixhamholidayhomes.co.uk

Devoncourt Holiday Flats
★★ *Self Catering*
Contact: Mr Robin Hooker
Devoncourt Holiday Flats
t (01803) 853748
e bookings@devoncourt.net
w devoncourt.info

Fairview Cottage ★★★
Self Catering
Holiday Homes & Cottages South West
t (01803) 663650
e holcotts@aol.com
w swcottages.co.uk

Fishermans Loft 1 & 2 ★★★
Self Catering
Contact: Mrs Adele Barnes
Blue Chip Vacations
t (01803) 855282
e info@bluechipvacations.com
w bluechipvacations.com/brixham/brixham_fishermans_loft.php

Fortune Cottage ★★★
Self Catering
Contact: Mrs Sharon Spencer
Brixham Holiday Homes Ltd
t (01803) 854187
e info@brixhamholidayhomes.co.uk
w brixhamholidayhomes.co.uk

Garlic Rea ★★★
Self Catering
Contact: Ms Sharon Spencer
Brixham Holiday Homes Ltd
t (01803) 854187
e info@brixhamholidayhomes.co.uk
w brixhamholidayhomes.co.uk

Halcyon ★★★ *Self Catering*
Contact: Mrs Adele Barnes
Blue Chip Vacations
t (01803) 855282
e info@bluechipvacations.com
w bluechipvacations.com/properties/halc.php

Harbour Reach ★★★
Self Catering
Contact: Mrs Jenny Pocock
t (0114) 236 4761
e enquiries@harbourreachholidays.co.uk
w harbourreachholidays.co.uk

Harbour View ★★★
Self Catering
Contact: Mrs Sharon Spencer
Brixham Holiday Homes Ltd
t (01803) 854187
e info@brixhamholidayhomes.co.uk
w brixhamholidayhomes.co.uk

Harbour View ★★★★
Self Catering
Holiday Homes & Cottages South West
t (01803) 663650
e holcotts@aol.com
w swcottages.co.uk

Haven Lodge ★★★★
Self Catering
Contact: Mrs Sharon Spencer
Brixham Holiday Homes Ltd
t (01803) 854187
e info@brixhamholidayhomes.co.uk
w brixhamholidayhomes.co.uk

Heath Court ★★★
Self Catering
Contact: Mrs Sharon Spencer
Brixham Holiday Homes Ltd
t (01803) 854187
e info@brixhamholidayhomes.co.uk
w brixhamholidayhomes.co.uk

High Hopes ★★★★
Self Catering
Contact: Mrs Sharon Spencer
Brixham Holiday Homes Ltd
t (01803) 854187
e info@brixhamholidayhomes.co.uk
w brixhamholidayhomes.co.uk

Hylands ★★★ *Self Catering*
Contact: Mrs Sharon Spencer
Brixham Holiday Homes Ltd
t (01803) 851410
e info@brixhamholidayhomes.co.uk
w brixhamholidayhomes.co.uk

Jasmine Cottage ★★★★
Self Catering
Contact: Mrs Sharon Spencer
Brixham Holiday Homes Ltd
t (01803) 854187
e info@brixhamholidayhomes.co.uk
w brixhamholidayhomes.co.uk

Jericho Cottage ★★★★
Self Catering
Blue Chip Vacations
t (01803) 855282
e info@bluechipdevelopments.com

Keel House ★★★
Self Catering
Contact: Mrs Sharon Spencer
Brixham Holiday Homes Ltd
t (01803) 854187
e info@brixhamholidayhomes.co.uk
w brixhamholidayhomes.co.uk

Key 2 Heaven Cottage ★★★
Self Catering
t (01803) 856256
e info@holidays-brixham.co.uk
w holidays-brixham.co.uk

Lantern Cottage ★★★
Self Catering
Contact: Mrs Sharon Spencer
Brixham Holiday Homes Ltd
t (01803) 854187
e info@brixhamholidayhomes.co.uk
w brixhamholidayhomes.co.uk

Linden Court Holiday Apartments ★★★
Self Catering
Contact: Mr & Mrs Brian & Carol McCandlish
t (01803) 851491
e linden_court@mail.com

Lobster Pot Cottage ★★★
Self Catering
Contact: Mrs Sharon Spencer
Brixham Holiday Homes Ltd
t (01803) 854187
e info@brixhamholidayhomes.co.uk
w brixhamholidayhomes.co.uk

The Lookout ★★★
Self Catering
Contact: Mrs Adele Barnes
Blue Chip Vacations
t (01803) 855282
e info@bluechipvacations.com
w bluechipvacations.com/properties/look.php

Lorna ★★★ *Self Catering*
Contact: Mrs Sharon Spencer
Brixham Holiday Homes Ltd
t (01803) 854187
e info@brixhamholidayhomes.co.uk
w brixhamholidayhomes.co.uk

Lytehouse Cottage ★★★
Self Catering
Contact: Mr Ian Butterworth
Holiday Homes & Cottages South West
t (01803) 663650
e holcotts@aol.com
w swcottages.co.uk

Mariners Cottage ★★★
Self Catering
Holiday Homes & Cottages South West
t (01803) 663650
e holcotts@aol.com
w swcottages.co.uk

Mid-Ships ★★★★
Self Catering
Contact: Mrs Sharon Spencer
Brixham Holiday Homes Ltd
t (01803) 854187
e info@brixhamholidayhomes.co.uk
w brixhamholidayhomes.co.uk

Monkbarns Annexe ★★★
Self Catering
Contact: Mrs Sharon Spencer
Brixham Holiday Homes Ltd
t (01803) 854187
e info@brixhamholidayhomes.co.uk
w brixhamholidayhomes.co.uk

Moonlit Waters ★★★
Self Catering
Contact: Mrs Sharon Spencer
Brixham Holiday Homes Ltd
t (01803) 854187
e info@brixhamholidayhomes.co.uk
w brixhamholidayhomes.co.uk

Blue Chip Vacations-Moorings Reach ★★★★★
Self Catering
Contact: Mrs Adele Barnes
Blue Chip Vacations
t (01803) 855282
e laura@bluechipdevelopments.com
w bluechipvacations.com/brixham/brixham_moorings_reach.php

Moorings Reach Townhouse 16 ★★★★★ *Self Catering*
Contact: Mrs Maggie Sycamore
Blue Chip Vacations
t (01803) 855282
e sylvia@bluechipvacations.com

Moorings Reach Townhouse 18 ★★★★★ *Self Catering*
Contact: Mrs Maggie Sycamore
Blue Chip Vacations
t (01803) 855282
e sylvia@bluechipvacations.com

Moorings Reach Townhouse 28 ★★★★★ *Self Catering*
Contact: Mrs Maggie Sycamore
Blue Chip Vacations
t (01803) 855282
e sylvia@bluechipvacations.com

Moorings Reach Townhouse 32 ★★★★★ *Self Catering*
Contact: Mrs Maggie Sycamore
Blue Chip Vacations
t (01803) 855282
e sylvia@bluechipvacations.com

Moorings Reach Townhouse 44 ★★★★★ *Self Catering*
Contact: Mrs Maggie Sycamore
Blue Chip Vacations
t (01803) 855282
e sylvia@bluechipvacations.com

Moorings Reach Townhouse 46 ★★★★★ *Self Catering*
Contact: Mrs Maggie Sycamore
Blue Chip Vacations
t (01803) 855282
e sylvia@bluechipvacations.com

Moorings Reach Townhouse 50 ★★★★★ *Self Catering*
Contact: Mrs Maggie Sycamore
Blue Chip Vacations
t (01803) 855282
e sylvia@bluechipvacations.com

Moorings Reach Townhouse 54 ★★★★★ *Self Catering*
Contact: Mrs Maggie Sycamore
Blue Chip Vacations
t (01803) 855282
e sylvia@bluechipvacations.com

Moorings Reach Apartment 3 ★★★★★ *Self Catering*
Contact: Mrs Maggie Sycamore
Blue Chip Vacations
t (01803) 855282
e sylvia@bluechipvacations.com

Moorings Reach Apartment 42 ★★★★★ *Self Catering*
Contact: Mrs Maggie Sycamore
Blue Chip Vacations
t (01803) 855282
e sylvia@bluechipvacations.com

Moorings Reach Apartment 55 ★★★★★ *Self Catering*
Contact: Mrs Maggie Sycamore
Blue Chip Vacations
t (01803) 855282
e sylvia@bluechipvacations.com

Moorings Reach Apartment 56 ★★★★★ *Self Catering*
Contact: Mrs Maggie Sycamore
Blue Chip Vacations
t (01803) 855282
e sylvia@bluechipvacations.com

Moorings Reach Apartment 57 ★★★★★ *Self Catering*
Contact: Mrs Maggie Sycamore
Blue Chip Vacations
t (01803) 855282
e sylvia@bluechipvacations.com

Moorings Reach Apartment 58 ★★★★★ *Self Catering*
Contact: Mrs Maggie Sycamore
Blue Chip Vacations
t (01803) 855282
e sylvia@bluechipvacations.com

Moorings Reach Apartment 60 ★★★★★ *Self Catering*
Contact: Mrs Maggie Sycamore
Blue Chip Vacations
t (01803) 855282
e sylvia@bluechipvacations.com

Moorings Reach Apartment 62 ★★★★★ *Self Catering*
Contact: Mrs Maggie Sycamore
Blue Chip Vacations
t (01803) 855282
e sylvia@bluechipvacations.com

Moorings Reach Apartment 64 ★★★★★ *Self Catering*
Contact: Mrs Maggie Sycamore
Blue Chip Vacations
t (01803) 855282
e sylvia@bluechipvacations.com

Moorings Reach Townhouse 41 ★★★★★ *Self Catering*
Contact: Mrs Maggie Sycamore
Blue Chip Vacations
t (01803) 855282
e sylvia@bluechipvacations.com
w bluechipvacations.com

Mudberry House ★★★
Self Catering
Holiday Homes & Cottages South West
t (01803) 663650
e holcotts@aol.com
w swcottages.co.uk

Newlands ★★★★
Self Catering
Contact: Mrs Sharon Spencer
Brixham Holiday Homes Ltd
t (01803) 854187
e info@brixhamholidayhomes.co.uk
w brixhamholidayhomes.co.uk

The Old Boat House ★★★
Self Catering
Contact: Mrs Adele Barnes
Blue Chip Vacations
t (01803) 855282
e info@bluechipvacations.com
w bluechipvacations.com/properties/boat.php

Overquay Cottage ★★★
Self Catering
Contact: Mrs Moira Withey
t (01803) 882337
e info@ranscombehousehotel.co.uk
w ranscombehousehotel.co.uk

Palm Cottage ★★★
Self Catering
Contact: Mrs Adele Barnes
Blue Chip Vacations
t (01803) 855282
e info@bluechipvacations.com
w bluechipvacations.com/properties/palm.php

Pilgrim's Cottage ★★★★
Self Catering
Contact: Mrs Sharon Spencer
Brixham Holiday Homes Ltd
t (01803) 854187
e info@brixhamholidayhomes.co.uk
w brixhamholidayhomes.co.uk

Sailmaker's Cottage ★★★★
Self Catering
Contact: Ms Sharon Spencer
Brixham Holiday Homes Ltd
t (01803) 854187
e info@brixhamholidayhomes.co.uk
w brixhamholidayhomes.co.uk

Sea View Cottage ★★★★
Self Catering
Contact: Ms Sharon Spencer
Brixham Holiday Homes Ltd
t (01803) 854187
e info@brixhamholidayhomes.co.uk
w brixhamholidayhomes.co.uk

Sea View Terrace ★★★
Self Catering
Contact: Mrs Sharon Spencer
Brixham Holiday Homes Ltd
t (01803) 854187
e info@brixhamholidayhomes.co.uk
w brixhamholidayhomes.co.uk

Seacat Cottage ★★★★
Self Catering
Holiday Homes & Cottages South West
t (01803) 663650
e holcotts@aol.com
w swcottages.co.uk

Seaholme ★★★★
Self Catering
Contact: Ms Sharon Spencer
Brixham Holiday Homes Ltd
t (01803) 854187
e info@brixhamholidayhomes.co.uk
w brixhamholidayhomes.co.uk

Seasalter House ★★★★
Self Catering
Contact: Mrs Sharon Spencer
Brixham Holiday Homes Ltd
t (01803) 854187
e info@brixhamholidayhomes.co.uk
w brixhamholidayhomes.co.uk

Seashell Cottage ★★★
Self Catering
Contact: Mr Ian Butterworth
Holiday Homes & Cottages South West
t (01803) 663650
e holcotts@aol.com
w swcottages.co.uk

Sloop Cottage ★★★★
Self Catering
Contact: Mrs Adele Barnes
Blue Chip Vacations
t (01803) 855282
e info@bluechipvacations.com
w bluechipvacations.com/properties/sloo.php

Sundial Cottage ★★★
Self Catering
Contact: Mrs Sharon Spencer
Brixham Holiday Homes Ltd
t (01803) 854187
e info@brixhamholidayhomes.co.uk
w brixhamholidayhomes.co.uk

Sunset Cottage ★★★
Self Catering
Contact: Mrs Sharon Spencer
Brixham Holiday Homes Ltd
t (01803) 854187
e info@brixhamholidayhomes.co.uk
w brixhamholidayhomes.co.uk

Tall Order ★★★
Self Catering
Contact: Mrs Adele Barnes
Blue Chip Vacations
t (01803) 855282
e info@bluechipvacations.com
w bluechipvacations.com/properties/tall.php

Tide's Reach ★★★
Self Catering
Contact: Mrs Sharon Spencer
Brixham Holiday Homes Ltd
t (01803) 854187
e info@brixhamholidayhomes.co.uk
w brixhamholidayhomes.co.uk

Top Deck ★★ *Self Catering*
Contact: Mrs Sharon Spencer
Brixham Holiday Homes Ltd
t (01803) 854187
e info@brixhamholidayhomes.co.uk
w brixhamholidayhomes.co.uk

Top Gallant ★★★★
Self Catering
Contact: Mrs Sharon Spencer
Brixham Holiday Homes Ltd
t (01803) 854187
e info@brixhamholidayhomes.co.uk
w brixhamholidayhomes.co.uk

Torbay Holiday Chalets ★★
Self Catering
Contact: Mr & Mrs Martyn & Jane Swift
t (01803) 853313

Torbay House ★★★
Self Catering
Contact: Mrs Sharon Spencer
Brixham Holiday Homes Ltd
t (01803) 854187
e info@brixhamholidayhomes.co.uk
w brixhamholidayhomes.co.uk

Torfrey Cottage ★★★
Self Catering
Contact: Mrs Sharon Spencer
Brixham Holiday Homes Ltd
t (01803) 854187
e info@brixhamholidayhomes.co.uk
w brixhamholidayhomes.co.uk

Trade Winds ★★★★
Self Catering
Contact: Mrs Sharon Spencer
Brixham Holiday Homes Ltd
t (01803) 854187
e info@brixhamholidayhomes.co.uk
w brixhamholidayhomes.co.uk

Tranquillity ★★★
Self Catering
Contact: Ms Sharon Spencer
Brixham Holiday Homes Ltd
t (01803) 854187
e info@brixhamholidayhomes.co.uk
w brixhamholidayhomes.co.uk

Watchman's Cottage ★★★
Self Catering
Contact: Mrs Sharon Spencer
Brixham Holiday Homes Ltd
t (01803) 854187
e info@brixhamholidayhomes.co.uk
w brixhamholidayhomes.co.uk

White Cottage ★★★★★
Self Catering
Contact: Ms Sharon Spencer
Brixham Holiday Homes Ltd
t (01803) 854187
e info@brixhamholidayhomes.co.uk
w brixhamholidayhomes.co.uk

White Sails ★★★
Self Catering
Contact: Mrs Sharon Spencer
Brixham Holiday Homes Ltd
t (01803) 854187
e info@brixhamholidayhomes.co.uk
w brixhamholidayhomes.co.uk

Windjammer Apartment ★★★ *Self Catering*
Contact: Mr & Mrs Skeggs
Windjammer Apartment
t (01803) 854279
e windjammerapartments@yahoo.co.uk
w holiday-brixham.co.uk

BROAD CAMPDEN
Gloucestershire

Green Cottage ★★★★
Self Catering
Contact: Miss Sheila Rolland
Campden Cottages
t (01386) 593315
e info@campdencottages.co.uk

Lion Cottage ★★★
Self Catering
Contact: Mrs Barbara Rawcliffe
Lion Cottage
t (01386) 840077

BROADCLYST
Devon

Hue's Piece ★★★★
Self Catering
Contact: Mrs Anna Hamlyn
t (01392) 466720
e annahamlyn@paynes-farm.co.uk
w paynes-farm.co.uk
♿

Two the Sanctuary ★★★
Self Catering
Contact: Mrs Kate Rudin
t (01392) 221011
e katerudin@blueyonder.co.uk
w twothesanctuary.com

BROADHEMBURY
Devon

Hembury Court Barns ★★★★★ *Self Catering*
Contact: Mr & Mrs Robert & Amanda Persey
Hembury Court Barns at Upcott Farm
t (01404) 841444
e persey@upcottfarm.fsnet.co.uk
w hembury-court-barns.co.uk

BROADMAYNE
Dorset

Fryermayne Tallet ★★★★
Self Catering
Contact: Mrs Ruth Goldsack
Beech Farm
t (01305) 852414
e rugold@lineone.net

Holcombe Valley Cottages
★★★ *Self Catering*
Contact: Mr & Mrs Peter & Jane Davies
t (01305) 852817
e holvalcots@aol.com
w holcombe-cottages.co.uk

BROADOAK
Dorset

Stoke Mill Farm ★★★
Self Catering
Contact: Mrs Anthea Bay
t (01308) 868036
w stokemillholidays.co.uk

BROADWINDSOR
Dorset

Broadmead House
Rating Applied For
Self Catering
Contact: Mr David Guilor
Riverside House
t (01308) 459851
e david.guilor@virgin.net

BROADWOOD KELLY
Devon

Colehouse Farm ★★★★★
Self Catering
Contact: Mrs Louise Jackson
t (01837) 83230
e info@colehousefarm-devon.co.uk
w colehousefarm-devon.co.uk

BROMHAM
Wiltshire

The Byres ★★ *Self Catering*
Contact: Mrs Myers
t (01380) 850557

Farthings ★★★ *Self Catering*
Contact: Mrs Gloria Steed
t (01380) 850255
e richard_gloriasteed@hotmail.com

Park Farm Cottages ★★★
Self Catering & Serviced Apartments
Contact: Mrs Valerie Bourne
t (01380) 850966
e valandtom2003@aol.com

Wayside Lodges
Rating Applied For
Self Catering
Contact: Mr Jonathan Seed
t (01380) 850695
e mail@jandlseed.co.uk
w waysideofwiltshire.co.uk

BROMPTON REGIS
Somerset

Weatherham Farm Cottages
★★★★ *Self Catering*
Contact: Mrs Anne Caldwell
t (01398) 371303
e enquiries@weatherhamfarm.co.uk
w weatherhamfarm.co.uk

BROMSBERROW HEATH
Gloucestershire

Honeysuckle Cottage
★★★★ *Self Catering*
Contact: Mrs Wendy Hooper
Greenlands
t (01531) 650360
e ws.hooper@btopenworld.com
w honeysuckle-cottage-rent.co.uk

BROUGHTON GIFFORD
Wiltshire

Church Farm Holiday Cottages ★★★★
Self Catering
Contact: Mrs Sharon Hooper
J Hooper and Son
t (01225) 783413
e sharon@churchfarmcottages.fsnet.co.uk
w churchfarmholidays.com

BRUTON
Somerset

Millers Cottage ★★★
Self Catering
Contact: Mr & Mrs Brian & Alison Shingler
Holiday Cottages Group
t (01749) 812393
e shingler@gantmill.co.uk
w gantsmill.co.uk

Redlynch Farmhouse
Rating Applied For
Self Catering
Contact: Mrs A Froud
t (01749) 812795
e angelafroud@hotmail.com

BUCKFASTLEIGH
Devon

Spindle Cottage, Moor's Court ★★★★ *Self Catering*
Contact: Ms Dawn Riggs
Bellamarsh Barton
t (01626) 853995
e dawnriggs@threads-of-time.co.uk

BUCKLAND BREWER
Devon

Adipit ★★★★ *Self Catering*
Powells Cottage Holidays
t (01834) 812791
e info@powells.co.uk
w powells.co.uk

Lime Tree Cottage ★★★
Self Catering
Contact: Mr James Morris
Farm & Cottage Holidays
t (01237) 479146
e enquiries@farmcott.co.uk
w holidaycottages.co.uk

BUCKLAND FILLEIGH
Devon

Modbury Cottage
Rating Applied For
Self Catering
Marsdens Cottage Holidays
t (01271) 813777
e holidays@marsdens.co.uk
w marsdens.co.uk

BUCKLAND IN THE MOOR
Devon

Pine Lodge ★★★
Self Catering
Holiday Homes & Cottages South West
t (01803) 663650
e holcotts@aol.com
w swcottages.co.uk

BUCKLAND NEWTON
Dorset

Church Farm Stables
★★★★ *Self Catering*
Contact: Mr & Mrs Neville Archer
t (01300) 345315
e enquiries@staydorset.co.uk
w staydorset.co.uk

Domineys Cottages, Buckland Newton ★★★★
Self Catering
Contact: Mrs Jeanette Gueterbock
Domineys Cottages
t (01300) 345295
e cottages@domineys.com
w domineys.com

BUCKLAND ST MARY
Somerset

The Apartment ★★★★ *Self Catering & Serviced Apartments*
Contact: Mr Roy Harkness
Hillside
t (01460) 234599
e royandmarge@hillsidebsm.freeserve.co.uk
w theaa.com/hotels/103591.html

Leveret Cottage ★★★
Self Catering
Contact: Mrs Suzie Float
t (01460) 234638
e info@leveretcottage.co.uk

BUCK'S MILLS
Devon

Marks Cottage
Rating Applied For
Self Catering
Farm & Cottage Holidays
t (01237) 479146
e enquiries@farmcott.co.uk
w holidaycottages.co.uk

BUDE
Cornwall

3 Brightlands Apartment
★★★★ *Self Catering*
Contact: Mr Ian Mackinson
t (01844) 345086
e ianmackinson@hotmail.com
w theoldstation-bledlow.co.uk

4 Brightlands Apartment
★★★ *Self Catering*
Contact: Mrs Gill Tawse
t (01428) 682565

Atlantic View Bungalows
★★★ *Self Catering & Serviced Apartments*
Contact: Mr & Mrs Raven
t (01288) 361716
e enquiries@atlanticview.co.uk
w atlanticview.co.uk

Bithecutt Cottage ★★★★
Self Catering
Contact: Ms Christine Jurkiewicz
t (01288) 352199
e chrisjurk@aol.com

Bramble Cottage ★★★★
Self Catering
Contact: Ms Jane Campbell
t (023) 8084 4425
e jane.campbell@talk21.com

Brightlands 5 & 11
Rating Applied For
Self Catering
Contact: Mrs Lynn Western
t (020) 8319 3508
e western511@btinternet.com
w brightlands511.co.uk

Broomhill Manor Country Estate ★★★★-★★★★★
Self Catering
Contact: Mrs Marcia Fawcett
t (01288) 352940
w broomhillmanor.co.uk

Captains Cottage ★★★★
Self Catering
Contact: Ms Sarah Debonaire
t (01288) 354542
e enquiries@brendonarms.co.uk
w brendonarms.co.uk

Flexbury House ★★★★
Self Catering
Contact: Tony & Sarah Watkins
t (01600) 772918
e enquiries@flexburyhouse.com
w flexburyhouse.com

Forda Ltd
★★★★-★★★★★
Self Catering
Contact: Mr & Mrs Chibbett
t (01288) 321413
e forda.lodges@virgin.net
w fordalodges.co.uk

Four Seasons Holidays
Rating Applied For
Self Catering
Contact: Mr & Mrs Marsden
t (01288) 356058
e sally.marsden@btinternet.com

Frys ★★★★★ *Self Catering*
Contact: Mr & Mrs Stone
t (01840) 230375
e gilljohn@rosecare.freeserve.co.uk

Glebe House Cottages
★★★★ *Self Catering*
Contact: Mr & Mrs James Varley
Glebe House Cottages Limited
t (01288) 381272
e etc@glebehousecottages.co.uk
w glebehousecottages.co.uk

Hilton Farm Holiday Cottages ★★★-★★★★
Self Catering
Contact: Mr & Mrs Goodman
t (01288) 361521
e ian@hiltonfarmhouse.freeserve.co.uk
w hiltonfarmhouse.co.uk

Ivyleaf Barton Cottages
★★★★-★★★★★
Self Catering
t (01283) 321237
e info@ivyleafbarton.co.uk
w ivyleafbarton.co.uk

Ivyleaf Combe ★★★★
Self Catering
Contact: Mr Cheeseman
Ivyleaf Combe
t (01288) 321323
e tony@ivyleafcombe.com
w ivyleafcombe.com

Karibu ★★★ *Self Catering*
Contact: Mrs Anna Rutlidge
t (01288) 356519
e benm5afo@aol.com

Kennacott Court ★★★★★
Self Catering
Contact: Mr & Mrs Myers
Kennacott Court
t (01288) 362000
e phil@kennacottcourt.co.uk
w kennacottcourt.co.uk

Kingfishers ★★★★
Self Catering
Contact: Mrs Cathy Holden
t (01283) 740435
e cathy2kingfishers@hotmail.com

Langfield Manor ★★★
Self Catering
Langfield Manor
t (01288) 352415
e info@langfieldmanor.co.uk
w langfieldmanor.co.uk

Little Orchard ★★★
Self Catering
Contact: Mrs Patricia Gosney
t (01288) 355617

Lower Northcott ★★★★
Self Catering
Contact: Mr & Mrs C Trewin
t (01288) 361494
e mary@courtfarm-holidays.co.uk
w courtfarm-holidays.co.uk

Manby ★★★ *Self Catering*
Contact: Mrs Lindsey Hoole
t (01865) 245268
e hoole@patrol.i-way.co.uk

Mornish Holidays Apartments ★★★★ *Self Catering & Serviced Apartments*
Contact: Mr & Mrs Hilder
t (01288) 352972
e mornishholidays@btconnect.com
w bude.co.uk/mornish-apartments

Neet Cottage ★★★★ *Self Catering & Serviced Apartments*
Contact: Mr & Mrs Harrison
t (01288) 361877
e widemouthfarm@tiscali.co.uk

Old Lifeboat House ★★★
Self Catering
Contact: Mrs Debinair
t (01288) 354542
e enquiries@brendonarms.co.uk
w brendonarms.co.uk

One4two ★★★★★
Self Catering
Penrhyn, Hillhead
t (01288) 355947
e kathylawrence@btconnect.com
w one4two.co.uk

Penhalt Farm ★★★
Self Catering
Contact: Mr & Mrs Marks
t (01288) 361210
e denandjennie@penhaltfarm.fsnet.co.uk
w penhaltfarm.co.uk

Penrhyn ★★★ *Self Catering*
Contact: Mr Brett
t (01288) 355039

Riverview Apartment ★★★
Self Catering
Contact: Helen & Martin Challans
t (01223) 235072
e mchallans@hotmail.com
w webspawner.com/users/mchallans

St Annes Bungalow ★★★
Self Catering
Contact: Mrs Britten
t (024) 7669 2410

Stable Cottages ★★★
Self Catering
Contact: Ms Gregory
t (01288) 354237

West Woolley Barns ★★★★
Self Catering
Contact: Mrs Jan Everard
West Woolley Barns
t (01288) 331202
e info@westwoolleyfarm.co.uk
w westwoolleyfarm.co.uk

Widemouth Bay ★★★
Self Catering
Holiday Homes & Cottages SW
t (01803) 663650
e holcotts@aol.com
w swcottages.co.uk

Wild Pigeon Holidays ★★★
Self Catering
Contact: Mrs Longley
t (01288) 353839

Woolstone Manor Farm ★★★★-★★★★★
Self Catering
Contact: Malcolm & Liz Wright
t (01288) 361639
e wright@woolstonemanor.co.uk
w woolstonemanor.co.uk

BUDLEIGH SALTERTON
Devon

Christophers ★★★★★
Self Catering
Contact: Mr & Mrs James Crill
The Thatched Cottage Company
t (01395) 567135
e info@thethatchedcottagecompany.com
w thethatchedcottagecompany.co.uk

Lufflands ★★★★
Self Catering
Contact: Mr & Mrs Colin & Brenda Goode
t (01395) 568422
e cottages@lufflands.co.uk
w lufflands.co.uk

BUDOCK WATER
Cornwall

Overdene ★★★ *Self Catering*
Contact: Emily Boriosi
Cornish Holiday Cottages
t (01326) 250339
e emily@cornishholidaycottages.net
w cornishholidaycottages.net/get_property.php?p=14

Penmorvah Cottages ★★★★ *Self Catering*
Contact: Peter Risely
t (01326) 250277
e reception@penmorvah.co.uk
w penmorvah.co.uk

BUGLE
Cornwall

Higher Menadew Farm Cottages ★★★★
Self Catering
Contact: Mr & Mrs Higman
t (01726) 850310
e mail@stayingincornwall.com
w stayingincornwall.com

BURCOMBE
Wiltshire

The Old Vicarage ★★★★
Self Catering
Hideaways
t (01747) 828170
e enq@hideaways.co.uk

BURLAWN
Cornwall

Wren Cottage ★★★
Self Catering
Rock Holidays inc. Harbour Holidays Rock
t (01208) 863399
e rockhols@aol.com
w rockholidays.co.uk

BURNHAM-ON-SEA
Somerset

Hurn Farm ★★★
Self Catering
Contact: Mrs Holdom
t (01278) 751418
e hurnfarm@hurnfarmcottages.co.uk
w hurnfarmcottages.co.uk

Kingsway ★★★ *Self Catering*
Contact: Mr Simon Morris
Farm & Cottage Holidays
t (01237) 479146
e enquiries@farmcott.co.uk
w holidaycottages.co.uk

Little Walton ★★★★
Self Catering
Contact: Mrs Patricia Harris
t (01278) 780034
e waltonhousebnb@aol.com
w waltonhousebnb.co.uk

Prospect Farm Holidays ★★★-★★★★ *Self Catering*
Contact: Mrs Gillian Wall
Prospect Farm Holidays
t (01278) 760507

Stable Cottage and Coach House ★★★-★★★★
Self Catering
Contact: Mr & Mrs Bigwood
Brean Farm
t (01278) 751055

BURRINGTON
Devon

Mully Brook Mill
Rating Applied For
Self Catering
Marsdens Cottage Holidays
t (01271) 813777
e holidays@marsdens.co.uk
w marsdens.co.uk

BURROWBRIDGE
Somerset

Hillview ★★★ *Self Catering*
Contact: Mrs Rosalind Griffiths
Hillview
t (01823) 698308

BURSTOCK
Dorset

Whetham Farm The Flat ★★
Self Catering
Contact: Mrs Ivy Pearl Curtis
t (01308) 868293

BURTLE
Somerset

Catcott Burtle Farm Cottage ★★★ *Self Catering*
Contact: Mrs Rosemary Tucker
t (01278) 722321
e rosemary@catcottburtlefarm.totalserve.co.uk

Glebe Farm Cottage ★★★★
Self Catering
Contact: Lucy Ellison
Farm & Cottage Holidays
t (01237) 479146
e enquiries@farmcott.co.uk
w holidaycottages.co.uk

BURTON BRADSTOCK
Dorset

Apple Tree Cottage ★★★
Self Catering
Dream Cottages
t (01305) 789000
e admin@dream-cottages.co.uk
w dream-cottages.co.uk

Cliff Farm ★★★ *Self Catering*
Contact: Mr Zachary Stuart-Brown
Dream Cottages
t (01305) 789000
e admin@dream-cottages.co.uk
w dream-cottages.co.uk

Cogden Cottages ★★★ *Self Catering & Serviced Apartments*
Contact: Mr Lee Connolly
t (01308) 897223
e oldcoastguard@hotmail.com
w cogdencottages.co.uk

The Doves ★★★
Self Catering
Contact: Mr Zachary Stuart-Brown
Dream Cottages
t (01305) 789000
e admin@dream-cottages.co.uk
w dream-cottages.co.uk

Fig Tree Cottage ★★★
Self Catering
Contact: Ms Kirsty Parker
Dream Cottages
t (01305) 789000
e admin@dream-cottages.co.uk
w dream-cottages.co.uk

Hillview Bungalow ★★★
Self Catering
Contact: Mr Zachary Stuart-Brown
Dream Cottages
t (01305) 789000
e admin@dream-cottages.co.uk
w dream-cottages.co.uk

Jasmine Cottage ★★★
Self Catering
Contact: Mr Zachary Stuart-Brown
Dream Cottages
t (01305) 789000
e admin@dream-cottages.co.uk
w dream-cottages.co.uk

Little Berwick & Berwick House ★★★–★★★★
Self Catering
Contact: Mr Zachary Stuart-Brown
Dream Cottages
t (01305) 789000
e admin@dream-cottages.co.uk
w dream-cottages.co.uk

Manor Lodge – Y4441
★★★★★ *Self Catering*
Contact: Mr Jim Matthews
Lyme Bay Holidays
t (01297) 443363
e email@lymebayholidays.co.uk
w lymebayholidays.co.uk

Pebble Beach Lodge ★★★
Self Catering
Contact: Mrs Jan Hemingway
Pebble Beach Lodge
t (01308) 897428
w burtonbradstock.org.uk

Rolling Hills ★★★
Self Catering
Dream Cottages
t (01305) 789000
e admin@dream-cottages.co.uk
w dream-cottages.co.uk

BUSH
Cornwall

Willow Valley Holiday park
★★★ *Self Catering*
t (01288) 353104
e willowvalley@talk21.com

BUTCOMBE
Somerset

Butcombe Farm ★★★
Self Catering
Contact: Ms Sandra Moss
t (01761) 462380
e info@butcombe-farm.demon.co.uk

BUTLEIGH WOOTTON
Somerset

Little Broadway ★★
Self Catering
Contact: Mrs Mary Butt
t (01458) 442824

CADGWITH
Cornwall

Pennard ★★★ *Self Catering*
Contact: Mr Martin Raftery
Mullion Cottages
t 0845 066 7766
e enquiries@mullioncottages.com
w mullioncottages.com

CAERHAYS
Cornwall

The Old Engine House
★★★★ *Self Catering*
Valley Villas
t (01752) 605605
e sales@valleyvillas.com
w valleyvillas.co.uk

CALLINGTON
Cornwall

Berrio Mill ★★★★
Self Catering
Contact: Mrs Carolyn Callanan
t (01579) 363252
e enquiries@berriomill.co.uk
w berriomill.co.uk

Cadson Manor Farm ★★★★
Self Catering
Contact: Mrs Brenda Crago
t (01579) 383969
e brenda.crago@btclick.com
w cadsonmanor.co.uk

CALSTOCK
Cornwall

St Andrews Hall ★★★★★
Self Catering
Contact: Dr Levine White
t (01822) 833786
e levines@btconnect.com
w levinesestateagents.co.uk/standrews.htm

CAMBORNE
Cornwall

Mill Cottage ★★★★
Self Catering
Contact: Mrs Rebecca Campbell
t (01209) 832276
e drymmill@btinternet.com
w drymmill.com

CAMELFORD
Cornwall

Helsbury Park
★★★★–★★★★★
Self Catering
Contact: Mrs Leza Wilson
t (0115) 914 7212
e leza.w@ntlworld.com
w helsburypark.co.uk

Juliot's Well Cottages
★★★★ *Self Catering*
Contact: Mr & Mrs Boundy
Juliot's Well Cottages
t (01840) 213302
e juliotswell@holidaysincornwall.net
w holidaysincornwall.net

Swallows Cottage ★★★★
Self Catering
Contact: Mr & Mrs Elsey
t (01840) 212212
e info@swallows-cottage-boscastle.co.uk
w swallows-cottage-boscastle.co.uk

CANNINGTON
Somerset

The Courtyard
★★★★–★★★★★
Self Catering
Contact: Mrs Dyer
t (01278) 653442
e dyerfarm@aol.com
w dyerfarm.co.uk

CANNOP
Gloucestershire

Woodside Cottage ★★★
Self Catering
Contact: Mrs Helen Evans
Peaked Rocks Cottage
t (01594) 861119
e helen@peakedrockscottage.fsnet.co.uk
w evansholidays.co.uk

CARBIS BAY
Cornwall

10 Carrack Gladden ★★★
Self Catering
Ayia Napa Holidays
t (01736) 757237
e ayianapaholidays@btconnect.com
w ayianapaholidaysuk.co.uk

11 Compass Point ★★★★
Self Catering
Ayia Napa Holidays
t (01736) 757237
e ayianapaholidays@btconnect.com
w ayianapaholidaysuk.co.uk

12 Carrack Gladden ★★★
Self Catering
Ayia Napa Holidays
t (01736) 757237
e ayianapaholidays@btconnect.com
w ayianapaholidaysuk.co.uk

15 Carrack Gladden ★★★
Self Catering
Ayia Napa Holidays
t (01736) 757237
e ayianapaholidays@btconnect.com
w ayianapaholidays.uk.co.uk

16 Tryhornek ★★★★
Self Catering
Contact: Mr & Mrs Read
t (01736) 757237
e ayianapaholidays@btconnect.com
w ayianapaholidaysuk.co.uk

18 Riviera Apartments
★★★★ *Self Catering*
Ayia Napa Holidays
t (01736) 757237
e ayianapaholidays@btconnect.com
w ayianapaholidaysuk.co.uk

2 Atlantic Watch ★★★★
Self Catering
Ayia Napa Holidays
t (01736) 757237
w aiyanapaholidaysuk.co.uk

20 Gwel Marten ★★★
Self Catering
t (01736) 794686

205 Carbis Beach Apartments ★★★★
Self Catering
Ayia Napa Holidays
t (01736) 757237
e ayianapaholidays@btconnect.com
w ayianapaholidaysuk.co.uk

206 Carbis Beach Apartments ★★★★
Self Catering
Ayia Napa Holidays
t (01736) 757237
e ayianapaholidays@btconnect.com
w ayianapaholidaysuk.co.uk

3 Carrack Gladden ★★★
Self Catering
Ayia Napa Holidays
t (01736) 757237
e ayianapaholidays@btconnect.com
w ayianapaholidaysuk.co.uk

30 Compass Point ★★★★
Self Catering
Ayia Napa Holidays
t (01736) 757237
e ayianapaholidays@btconnect.com
w ayianapaholidaysuk.co.uk

304 Carbis Beach ★★★★
Self Catering
Ayia Napa Holidays
t (01736) 757237
e ayianapaholidays@btconnect.com
w ayianapaholidaysuk.co.uk

38 Compass Point ★★★★
Self Catering
Ayia Napa Holidays
t (01736) 757237
e ayianapaholidays@btconnect.com
w ayianapaholidaysuk.co.uk

4 Carrack Gladden ★★★★
Self Catering
Ayia Napa Holidays
t (01736) 757237
e ayianapaholidays@btconnect.com
w ayianapaholidaysuk.co.uk

4 Riviera Apartments
★★★★ *Self Catering*
Ayia Napa Holidays
t (01736) 757237
e ayianapaholidays@btconnect.com
w ayianapaholidaysuk.co.uk

5 Carrack Gladden ★★★
Self Catering
Ayia Napa Holidays
t (01736) 757237
e ayianapaholidays@btconnect.com
w aiyanapaholidaysuk.co.uk

5 Tryhornek ★★★★
Self Catering
Ayia Napa Holidays
t (01736) 757237
e ayianapaholidays@btconnect.com
w ayianapaholidaysuk.co.uk

6 Carrack Gladden ★★★
Self Catering
Ayia Napa Holidays
t (01736) 757237
e ayianapaholidays@btconnect.com
w ayianapaholidaysuk.co.uk

7 Riviera Apartment ★★★
Self Catering
Contact: Mr & Mrs Michael & Annette Read
Ayia Napa Holidays
t (01736) 757237
e ayianapaholidays@btconnect.com

8 Riviera Apartments
★★★★ *Self Catering*
Ayia Napa Holidays
t (01736) 757237
e ayianapaholidays@btconnect.com
w ayianapaholidaysuk.co.uk

Aquamarine ★★★★★ *Self Catering & Serviced Apartments*
Contact: Mrs Sheena Brindley
t (0115) 933 4870
e enquiries@carbisbayholidays.co.uk
w carbisbayholidays.co.uk

Argent ★★★★★
Self Catering
t (0115) 949 1593
e enquiries@carbisbayholidays.co.uk
w carbisbayholidays.co.uk

Azure ★★★★★ *Self Catering*
Contact: Mrs Sheena Brindley
t (0115) 933 4870
e enquiries@carbisbayholidays.co.uk

Boskenza Court ★★★
Self Catering
Powells Cottage Holidays
t (01834) 813232
e info@powells.co.uk
w powells.co.uk

Brambles Apartment ★★★
Self Catering
Contact: Mrs Suzanne Wild
t (01736) 793667
e brambles05@tiscali.co.uk
w bramblesapartment.co.uk

Chapel View ★★★★★
Self Catering
Contact: Annette & Mike Read
t (01736) 757237
e auianapaholidays@btconnect.com

Dolphin Watch ★★★★ *Self Catering & Serviced Apartments*
Contact: Mrs Sheena Brindley
t (0115) 933 4870
e enquiries@carbisbayholidays.co.uk
w carbisbayholidays.co.uk

Godrevy View ★★★★★
Self Catering
Contact: Mr & Mrs Brindley
t (0115) 933 4870
e enquiries@carbisbayholidays.co.uk

Lodge 1A Carrack Gladden
★★★ *Self Catering*
Ayia Napa Holidays
t (01736) 757237
e ayianapaholidays@btconnect.com
w ayianapaholidaysuk.co.uk

Lodge 1B Carrack Gladden
★★★ *Self Catering*
Ayia Napa Holidays
t (01736) 757237
e ayianapaholidays@btconnect.com
w ayianapaholidaysuk.co.uk

The Lookout ★★★★★
Self Catering
Powells Cottage Holidays
t (01834) 813232
e info@powells.co.uk
w powells.co.uk

Menhir Cottage ★★★★
Self Catering
Powells Cottage Holidays
t (01834) 813232
e info@powells.co.uk
w powells.co.uk

The Penthouse ★★★★
Self Catering
Contact: Mrs Crowther
t (0161) 950 8752
e lbcrowther@yahoo.com
w carbisbayholidays.co.uk

Rose Cottage ★★★★
Self Catering
Contact: Mrs Sumner
t (01736) 794147
e lesleypsumner@yahoo.com
w rosecottagecarbisbay.co.uk

Rotorua Apartments ★★★★
Self Catering
Contact: Mrs Linda Roach
Rotorua Apartments
t (01736) 795419
e rotorua@btconnect.com
w stivesapartments.com

Sandpiper ★★★★★
Self Catering
Contact: Mrs Brindley
t (0115) 933 4870
e enquiries@carbisbayholidays.co.uk
w carbisbayholidays.co.uk

Turquarze ★★★★★
Self Catering
Contact: Mrs Brindley
t (0115) 933 4870
e enquiries@carbisbayholidays.co.uk
w carbisbayholidays.co.uk

CARDINHAM
Cornwall

Welltown ★★★★
Self Catering
t (01208) 821653
e daveange@telco4u.net
w bodminmoor.co.uk/welltown

CARHAMPTON
Somerset

Spaniel Cottage ★★★★
Self Catering
Contact: Mrs Ly Scruton
t (01729) 823505
e scrutons50@hotmail.co.uk

CARLYON BAY
Cornwall

Bay View ★★★ *Self Catering*
Contact: Mr Ces Summers
t 0845 123 5649
e ces.summers@cornwall4holidays.co.uk
w cornwall4holidays.co.uk

Sea Haze ★★★★★
Self Catering
Contact: Mrs Moorhouse
Valley Villas
t (01752) 605605
e sales@valleyvillas.com
w valleyvillas.com

Woodland View ★★★★★
Self Catering
Contact: Mr Mark Lane
Valley Villas
t (01752) 605605
w valleyvillas.com

CARNON DOWNS
Cornwall

Higher Tresithick Barn
★★★★ *Self Catering*
Special Places in Cornwall
t (01872) 864400
e office@specialplacescornwall.co.uk
w specialplacescornwall.co.uk

CASTLE CARY
Somerset

The Ancient Barn and The Old Stables ★★★★
Self Catering
Contact: Ms Anthea Peppin
The Ancient Barn & The Old Stables
t (01963) 351288
e bookings@medievalbarn.co.uk
w medievalbarn.co.uk

Clanville Manor Tallet and Lone Oak Cottage ★★★★
Self Catering
Contact: Mrs Snook
t (01963) 350124
e info@clanvillemanor.co.uk
w clanvillemanor.co.uk

Orchard Farm Cottages
★★★ *Self Catering*
Contact: Mr & Mrs Dave & Helen Boyer
Orchard Farm Cottages
t (01963) 350418
e boyer@orchard-farm.co.uk
w orchard-farm.co.uk

The Weaver's Cottage
★★★★ *Self Catering*
Contact: Ms Anthea Peppin
t (01963) 351288
e enquiries@medievalbarn.co.uk
w medievalbarn.co.uk

CATTISTOCK
Dorset

4 The Rocks ★★★★
Self Catering
Contact: Mrs Ann Stockwell
t (01404) 861594
e jonannstockwell@aol.com

CERNE ABBAS
Dorset

Old Gaol Cottage ★★★★★
Self Catering
Contact: Ms Nicky Willis
Lamperts Cottage
t (01300) 341659
e nickywillis@tesco.net

CHACEWATER
Cornwall

Kilhellan House ★★★
Self Catering
t (01872) 560328
e info@kilhellan.co.uk
w kilhellan.freeserve.co.uk

Valley View Barn, Creegbrawse
Rating Applied For
Self Catering
Contact: Miss Gail Cooper
t (01209) 820136
e enquiries@valleyviewbarn.co.uk
w valleyviewbarn.co.uk

CHAFFCOMBE
Somerset

Summer House ★★★
Self Catering
Contact: Lucy Ellison
Farm & Cottage Holidays
t (01237) 479146
e enquiries@farmcott.co.uk
w holidaycottages.co.uk

CHAGFORD
Devon

Yelfords ★★★★★
Self Catering
Contact: Mrs Ghislaine Caine
t (01647) 432546

CHALLACOMBE
Devon

Shoulsbarrow Farm ★★★★
Self Catering
Contact: Ms Sophie Folland
Farm & Cottage Holidays
t (01237) 479146
e enquiries@farmcott.co.uk
w holidaycottages.co.uk

Swincombe Mill ★★★★★
Self Catering
Contact: Mr & Mrs Mark & Lindsey Roberts
Woolhanger Farm
t (01598) 763514
e woolhanger@aol.com
w woolhanger.co.uk

Town Tenement ★★★
Self Catering
Contact: Mr & Mrs Yendell
t (01598) 763320

Whitefield Barton ★★★
Self Catering
Contact: Mrs Rosemarie Kingdon
t (01598) 763271
w exmoorholidays.co.uk

CHANTMARLE
Dorset

Chantmarle ★★★★
Self Catering
Contact: Ms Kirsty Parker
Dream Cottages
t (01305) 789000
e admin@dream-cottages.co.uk
w dream-cottages.co.uk

CHAPEL AMBLE
Cornwall

Ambledown Cottage
★★★★★ *Self Catering*
English Country Cottages
t 0870 585 1155

Carclaze Cottages ★★★★
Self Catering
Contact: Mrs Nicholls
t (01208) 813886
e carclazecottages@btinternet.com
w carclaze.co.uk

Homeleigh Farm, Chapel Amble ★★★★ *Self Catering*
Contact: Mrs Ann Rees
t (01208) 812411
e homeleigh@eclipse.co.uk
w eclipse.co.uk/homeleigh

Olde House ★★★-★★★★
Self Catering
Contact: Mr Hawkey
t (01208) 813219
e info@theoldehouse.co.uk
w theoldehouse.co.uk

The Parlour at Kivells
★★★★★ *Self Catering*
Contact: Mrs Hosegood
t (01208) 841755
e nfo@acornishcottage.co.uk
w acornishcottage.co.uk

Rooke Country Cottages
★★★★★ *Self Catering*
Contact: Mrs Reskelly
t (01208) 880368
e info@rookecottages.com
w rookecottages.com

CHARDSTOCK
Devon

Barn Owls Cottage ★★★★
Self Catering
Contact: Mrs Jean Hafner
Barn Owls Cottage
t (01460) 220475
e jean.hafner1@btinternet.com
w cottageguide.co.uk/barnowlscottage

Southview
Rating Applied For
Self Catering
Contact: Ms Louise Hayman
Milkbere Cottage Holidays
t (01297) 20729
e info@milkberehols.com
w milkberehols.com

CHARMOUTH
Dorset

1 & 2 Albury Cottages – J4376 & J4377 ★★★★
Self Catering
Lyme Bay Holidays
t (01297) 443363
e email@lymebayholidays.co.uk
w lymebayholidays.co.uk

1 Queens Walk ★★★★
Self Catering
Contact: Mr David Matthews
Lyme Bay Holidays
t (01297) 443363
e email@lymebayholidays.co.uk
w lymebayholidays.co.uk

11 Barney's Close- L4226
★★★★ *Self Catering*
Lyme Bay Holidays
t (01297) 443363
e email@lymebayholidays.co.uk
w lymebayholidays.co.uk

11 Double Common – L4222
★★★ *Self Catering*
Lyme Bay Holidays
t (01297) 443363
e email@lymebayholidays.co.uk
w lymebayholidays.co.uk

11 Queens Walk – L4361
★★★★ *Self Catering*
Lyme Bay Holidays
t (01297) 443363
e email@lymebayholidays.co.uk
w lymebayholidays.co.uk

2 Fernhill – Q5017 ★★★
Self Catering
Lyme Bay Holidays
t (01297) 443363
e email@lymebayholidays.co.uk
w lymebayholidays.co.uk

2 Queens Walk ★★★★
Self Catering
Contact: Mrs Jane Simmonds-Short
Butts Cottage
t (01460) 52832
e jane@buttscottage.eclipse.co.uk

3 Double Common – L4223
★★★★ *Self Catering*
Lyme Bay Holidays
t (01297) 443363
e email@lymebayholidays.co.uk
w lymebayholidays.co.uk

4 Devonedge ★★★★
Self Catering
Contact: Ms Joanne Winkler
Lyme Bay Holidays
t (01297) 443363
e email@lymebayholidays.co.uk
w lymebayholidays.co.uk

4 Mill View ★★★
Self Catering
Contact: Joanne Winkler
Lyme Bay Holidays
t (01297) 443363
e email@lymebayholidays.co.uk
w lymebayholidays.co.uk

40 Fernhill – Q5005 ★★★
Self Catering
Contact: Mr Dave Matthews
Lyme Bay Holidays
t (01297) 443363
e email@lymebayholidays.co.uk
w lymebayholidays.co.uk

41 Fernhill – Q5018 ★★★
Self Catering
Contact: Mr Jim Matthews
Lyme Bay Holidays
t (01297) 443363
e email@lymebayholidays.co.uk
w lymebayholidays.co.uk

45 Fernhill Heights – R5011
★★★★ *Self Catering*
Lyme Bay Holidays
t (01297) 443363
e email@lymebayholidays.co.uk
w lymebayholidays.co.uk

5 Barneys Close L4454
★★★★ *Self Catering*
Lyme Bay Holidays
t (01297) 443363
e email@lymebayholidays.co.uk
w lymebayholidays.co.uk

51 Fernhill: R5016 ★★★★
Self Catering
Lyme Bay Holidays
t (01297) 443363
e email@lymebayholidays.co.uk
w lymebayholidays.co.uk

7 Double Common – K4426
★★★ *Self Catering*
Lyme Bay Holidays
t (01297) 443363
e email@lymebayholidays.co.uk
w lymebayholidays.co.uk

9 Double Common – K4229
★★★★ *Self Catering*
Contact: Mr Dave Matthews
Lyme Bay Holidays
t (01297) 443363
e email@lymebayholidays.co.uk
w lymebayholidays.co.uk

The Barn – W4368
Rating Applied For
Self Catering
Contact: Mr Dave Matthews
Lyme Bay Holidays
t (01297) 443363
e email@lymebayholidays.co.uk
w lymebayholidays.co.uk

Beachcomber ★★★★
Self Catering
Contact: Mr Zachary Stuart-Brown
Dream Cottages
t (01305) 789000
e admin@dream-cottages.co.uk
w dream-cottages.co.uk

Befferlands Farm ★★★★★
Self Catering
Lyme Bay Holidays
t (01297) 443363
e email@lymebayholidays.co.uk
w lymebayholidays.co.uk

Bridge House – K4271 ★★★
Self Catering
Lyme Bay Holidays
t (01297) 443363
e email@lymebayholidays.co.uk
w lymebayholidays.co.uk

Charleston Holiday Cottages
★★★ *Self Catering*
Grosvenor Cottage
t (01297) 560053

Coach House – J4175 ★★★
Self Catering
Contact: Miss Emma Matthews
Lyme Bay Holidays
t (01297) 443363
e email@lymebayholidays.co.uk
w lymebayholidays.co.uk

The Coach House – K4398
★★★ *Self Catering*
Contact: Mr Dave Matthews
Lyme Bay Holidays
t (01297) 443363
e email@lymebayholidays.co.uk
w lymebayholidays.co.uk

Dolphin House – M4383
★★★★ *Self Catering*
Lyme Bay Holidays
t (01297) 443363
e email@lymebayholidays.co.uk
w lymebayholidays.co.uk

Double Common – K4385
★★★★ *Self Catering*
Lyme Bay Holidays
t (01297) 443363
e email@lymebayholidays.co.uk
w lymebayholidays.co.uk

Fernhill Heights – R5004
★★★★ *Self Catering*
Contact: Mr Dave Matthews
Lyme Bay Holidays
t (01297) 443363
e email@lymebayholidays.co.uk
w lymebayholidays.co.uk

Fleur – K4243 ★★★
Self Catering
Lyme Bay Holidays
t (01297) 443363
e email@lymebayholidays.co.uk
w lymebayholidays.co.uk

Georges Close – K4305
★★★★ *Self Catering*
Lyme Bay Holidays
t (01297) 443363
e email@lymebayholidays.co.uk
w lymebayholidays.co.uk

Greenhayes – L4342 ★★★
Self Catering
Contact: Mr Dave Matthews
Lyme Bay Holidays
t (01297) 443363
e email@lymebayholidays.co.uk
w lymebayholidays.co.uk

Hallside ★★★ *Self Catering*
Contact: Joanne Winkler
Lyme Bay Holidays
t (01297) 443363
e email@lymebayholidays.co.uk
w lymebayholidays.co.uk

Honeycot – K4295 ★★★
Self Catering
Lyme Bay Holidays
t (01297) 443363
e email@lymebayholidays.co.uk
w lymebayholidays.co.uk

Jasmine Cottage ★★★
Self Catering
Contact: Ms Joanne Winkler
Lyme Bay Holidays
t (01297) 443363
e email@lymebayholidays.co.uk
w lymebayholidays.co.uk

Knapp Cottages – K4313
★★★★ *Self Catering*
Contact: Mr Dave Matthews
Lyme Bay Holidays
t (01297) 443363
e email@lymebayholidays.co.uk
w lymebayholidays.co.uk

Lias Lea – L3501 ★★★
Self Catering
Lyme Bay Holidays
t (01297) 443363
e email@lymebayholidays.co.uk
w lymebayholidays.co.uk

Little Catherston Farm ★★★
Self Catering
Contact: Mrs R J White
t (01297) 560550
w catherstonfarm-bungalows.co.uk

Little Haven ★★★
Self Catering
Contact: Joanne Winkler
Lyme Bay Holidays
t (01297) 443363
e email@lymebayholidays.co.uk
w lymebayholidays.co.uk

The Lodge – V4367
Rating Applied For
Self Catering
Contact: Mr Dave Matthews
Lyme Bay Holidays
t (01297) 443363
e email@lymebayholidays.co.uk
w lymebayholidays.co.uk

The Lookout – L4452
Rating Applied For
Self Catering
Contact: Mr Jim Matthews
Lyme Bay Holidays
t (01297) 443363
e email@lymebayholidays.co.uk
w lymebayholidays.co.uk

Luttrell House – J4298 ★★★
Self Catering
Lyme Bay Holidays
t (01297) 443363
e email@lymebayholidays.co.uk
w lymebayholidays.co.uk

Miramar ★★★★★
Self Catering
Contact: Joanne Winkler
Lyme Bay Holidays
t (01297) 443363
e email@lymebayholidays.co.uk
w lymebayholidays.co.uk

Nutwood – L4423 ★★★★
Self Catering
Contact: Mr Dave Matthews
Lyme Bay Holidays
t (01297) 443363
e email@lymebayholidays.co.uk
w lymebayholidays.co.uk

Penderel – L3958 ★★★★
Self Catering
Lyme Bay Holidays
t (01297) 443363
e email@lymebayholidays.co.uk
w lymebayholidays.co.uk

The Poplars ★★★
Self Catering
Contact: Mrs Jane Bremner
t (01297) 560697
e holiday@woodfarm.co.uk
w woodfarm.co.uk

Portland House – K4219
★★★ *Self Catering*
Lyme Bay Holidays
t (01297) 443363
e email@lymebayholidays.co.uk
w lymebayholidays.co.uk

Queens Walk – L4345
★★★★ *Self Catering*
Lyme Bay Holidays
t (01297) 443363
e email@lymebayholidays.co.uk
w lymebayholidays.co.uk

Riverway – K3557 ★★★
Self Catering
Lyme Bay Holidays
t (01297) 443363
e email@lymebayholidays.co.uk
w lymebayholidays.co.uk

Rosern ★★★★ *Self Catering*
Lyme Bay Holidays
t (01297) 443363
e email@lymebayholidays.co.uk
w lymebayholidays.co.uk

Seaspray – L4306 ★★★
Self Catering
Lyme Bay Holidays
t (01297) 443363
e email@lymebayholidays.co.uk
w lymebayholidays.co.uk

Shadows ★★★ *Self Catering*
Contact: Ms Isabel Ward
t (01297) 489609
w dorsetholidayhome.co.uk

The Stone House – N3911
★★★★ *Self Catering*
Lyme Bay Holidays
t (01297) 443363
e email@lymebayholidays.co.uk
w lymebayholidays.co.uk

Tillicum – M3927 ★★★
Self Catering
Lyme Bay Holidays
t (01297) 443363
e email@lymebayholidays.co.uk
w lymebayholidays.co.uk

Uphill Apartment – K4363
★★★ *Self Catering*
Lyme Bay Holidays
t (01297) 443363
e email@lymebayholidays.co.uk
w lymebayholidays.co.uk

Wheelers Cottage – V4386
★★★★ *Self Catering*
Lyme Bay Holidays
t (01297) 443363
e email@lymebayholidays.co.uk
w lymebayholidays.co.uk

Willows – K3909 ★★★
Self Catering
Lyme Bay Holidays
t (01297) 443363
e email@lymebayholidays.co.uk
w lymebayholidays.co.uk

CHAXHILL
Gloucestershire

Laurel Cottage ★★★
Self Catering
Contact: Mr & Mrs Mark & Tasmin Terry-Lush
t (01452) 760147
e enjoyengland@laurel-cottage.com
w laurel-cottage.com

CHEDDAR
Somerset

Applebee South Barn Cottage ★★ *Self Catering*
Contact: Mrs Kay Richardson
t (01934) 743146

Home Farm Cottages
★★★★ *Self Catering*
Contact: Mr Chris Sanders
Home Farm Cottages
t (01934) 842078
e enquiries@homefarmcottages.com
w homefarmcottages.com

Orchard Court & Bungalow
★★★★ *Self Catering*
Contact: Mrs Carol Roberts
t (01934) 742116

Spring Cottages ★★★★
Self Catering
Contact: Mrs Jennifer Buckland
t (01934) 742493
e buckland@springcottages.co.uk
w springcottages.co.uk

Sungate Holiday Apartments ★★★
Self Catering
Contact: Mrs M M Fieldhouse
Pyrenmount
t (01934) 842273 & (01934) 742264
w sungateholidayapartments.co.uk

CHEDWORTH
Gloucestershire

Tiddley Dyke ★★★★
Self Catering
Contact: Mrs Jenny Bull
Buffers
t (01285) 720673

CHEDZOY
Somerset

Bramley Lodge ★★★★★
Self Catering
Contact: Mrs Judith Denning
t (01278) 423201
e temple_farm@hotmail.com
w bramleylodge.co.uk

CHELTENHAM
Gloucestershire

1 Montpellier Villas ★★★★
Self Catering
Contact: Mrs Helen Watts-Jones
t (01242) 521704
e hwj7@hotmail.co.uk

The Annexe ★★★
Self Catering
Contact: Mrs Corbett
t (01242) 524608
e pacorbett123@msn.com

Balcarras Farm Holiday Cottages ★★★ *Self Catering*
Contact: Judith & David Ballinger
Balcarras Farm
t (01242) 584837
e cottage@balcarras-farm.co.uk
w balcarras-farm.co.uk

Beechcroft ★★★★★
Self Catering
Contact: Mrs Angela Fraser
Meadow Garth
t (01242) 526545
e angela.fraser@btopenworld.com
w beechcroftinthecotswolds.co.uk

Billbrook House ★★★★★
Self Catering
Always Positive
t (01242) 222254
e info@alwayspositive.co.uk
w alwayspositive.co.uk

Butlers ★★★ *Self Catering*
Contact: Mr Guy Hunter
t (01242) 570771
e info@butlers-hotel.co.uk
w butlers-hotel.co.uk

Cheltenham Apartments
★★★★ *Self Catering*
Contact: Mrs Sophie Thompson
Garden Flat
t (01242) 227579
e cheltapartments@aol.com
w cheltenhamapartments.co.uk

Coxhorne Farm ★★★
Self Catering
Contact: Mr & Mrs Close
t (01242) 236599

Flat 8 ★★★ *Self Catering*
Contact: Mr & Mrs Richard Moseley
t (020) 8325 6251
w cottageguide.co.uk

The Furrow ★★★★
Self Catering
Contact: Mrs Valerie Hughes
t (01451) 850733
w cotswoldholiday.co.uk

The Garden Studio ★★★★
Self Catering
Contact: Mrs Ellams
t (01242) 575572

Holmer Cottages ★★★★
Self Catering
Contact: Mrs Jill Collins
Holmer Cottages
t (01242) 672848
e holmercottages@talk21.com
w cottageguide.co.uk/holmercottages

Oakfield Rise ★★★★
Self Catering
Contact: Mr Tony Russell
t (01242) 222220
e oakfieldrise@hotmail.com
w oakfieldrise.com

The Old Dairy ★★★★
Self Catering
Contact: Mr & Mrs Rickie & Jennie Gauld
t (01242) 676003
e rickieg@btinternet.com
w cotswoldcottages.btinternet.co.uk

Priory Cottage ★★★
Self Catering
Contact: Mr Mant
t (01242) 584693
e iansmant@hotmail.com
w countrycottagesonline.net

Regent Suites ★★★★
Self Catering
Contact: Mrs Beverley Warburton
t 0870 042 3612
e bw@regentsuites.co.uk
w regentsuites.co.uk

Rosehill Apartment ★★★★
Self Catering
Contact: Mr & Mrs Geoff & Claire Wedgbury
t (01452) 615266
e admin@rosehillapartment.co.uk
w rosehillapartment.co.uk

Top Flat ★★★ *Self Catering*
Contact: Mr & Mrs Morris
t (01454) 227322
e cotswold.cottage@btopenworld.com
w cotswoldcottage.net

The Vergus ★★★
Self Catering
Contact: Mrs Rita Preen
t (01242) 680511
e ritapreen@yahoo.co.uk
w vergus.co.uk

Vine Court ★★★★
Self Catering
Contact: Mrs Linda Hennessy
t (01242) 222403
e lindyhennessy@hotmail.com

Willoughby House Hotel and Apartments ★★★-★★★★
Self Catering
Contact: Mr & Mrs F P Eckermann
Willoughby House Hotel
t (01242) 522798
e bookings@willoughbyhouse.com
w willoughbyhouse.com

York Terrace
Rating Applied For
Self Catering
Contact: Mr Michael Owen
t 07770 685662
e mikeowen1@aol.com

CHERITON BISHOP
Devon

The Garden House ★★★★★
Self Catering
Contact: Mr Peter Benjamin
t (01647) 24848
e peter@medlandmanor.com

CHESTERBLADE
Somerset

The Swallows Farm ★★★★
Self Catering
Contact: Mrs Margo Green
t (01749) 830295
w millhousefarm.org

CHEW MAGNA
Somerset

Chew Hill Farm ★★★
Self Catering
Contact: Mrs Lyons
t (01275) 332496

CHICKERELL
Dorset

Jubilee Cottage
Rating Applied For
Self Catering
Contact: Judith Odgers
The Old Post Office
t (01305) 851700
e doug.odgers@btinternet.com

Tidmoor Stables ★★★★
Self Catering
Contact: Mr & Mrs Townsend
t (01305) 787867
e sarah@tidmoorstables.co.uk
w tidmoorstables.co.uk

CHIDEOCK
Dorset

Ash Cottage ★★★
Self Catering
Contact: Mrs Isabel Morgan
t (0117) 962 9126
e isabel@isabelmorgan.co.uk
w dorsetcottage.net

Baytree Cottage ★★★★
Self Catering
Contact: Mr David Matthews
Lyme Bay Holidays
t (01297) 443363
e email@lymebayholidays.co.uk
w lymebayholidays.co.uk

Brook Cottage ★★★★
Self Catering
Lyme Bay Holidays
t (01297) 443363
e email@lymebayholidays.co.uk
w lymebayholidays.co.uk

Cedar Cottage ★★★
Self Catering
Contact: David Roberts
t (0117) 908 3098
e davidjroberts2000@yahoo.co.uk
w cedarcottage.biz

Chideock Coachouse ★★★★ *Self Catering*
Contact: Mr Zachary Stuart-Brown
Dream Cottages
t (01305) 789000
e admin@dream-cottages.co.uk
w dream-cottages.co.uk

Chideock Cottage ★★★
Self Catering
Contact: Mrs Pauline Bale
Highway Farm
t (01308) 424321
e bookings@chideockcottage.co.uk

Frying Pan ★★★★
Self Catering
Dream Cottages
t (01305) 789000
e admin@dream-cottages.co.uk
w dream-cottages.co.uk

Greystones Cottage – X4438 ★★★★ *Self Catering*
Lyme Bay Holidays
t (01297) 443363
e email@lymebayholidays.co.uk
w lymebayholidays.co.uk

Honeypot Cottage ★★★★
Self Catering
Contact: Joanne Winkler
Lyme Bay Holidays
t (01297) 443363
e email@lymebayholidays.co.uk
w lymebayholidays.co.uk

Sycamore Cottage – W4450 ★★★ *Self Catering*
Lyme Bay Holidays
t (01297) 443363
e email@lymebayholidays.co.uk
w lymebayholidays.co.uk

CHILCOMBE
Dorset

Cherry Tree Cottage ★★★
Self Catering
Contact: Mr Zachary Stuart-Brown
Dream Cottages
t (01305) 789000
e admin@dream-cottages.co.uk
w dream-cottages.co.uk

CHILLINGTON
Devon

Friends Cottage ★★★
Self Catering
Powells Cottage Holidays
t (01834) 812791
e info@powells.co.uk
w powells.co.uk

CHILTON TRINITY
Somerset

Chilton Farm ★★★★
Self Catering
Contact: Mr Warman
t (01278) 421864
w farmcott.co.uk

CHIPPENHAM
Wiltshire

Nut Tree Cottage ★★★
Self Catering
Contact: Mrs Margaret Payne
t (01249) 782354

Olivemead Farm Holidays ★★★★ *Self Catering*
Contact: Mrs Suzanne Candy
Olivemead Farm
t (01666) 510205
e enquiries@olivemeadfarmholidays.com
w olivemeadfarmholidays.com

CHIPPING CAMPDEN
Gloucestershire

Bank Cottage ★★★★
Self Catering
Contact: Mr Robert Hutsby
t (01789) 841525
e robert.hutsby@btinternet.com
w chipping-campden-holiday-cottages.co.uk

Box Tree Cottage ★★★
Self Catering
Contact: Mr Robert Hutsby
t (01789) 841525
e robert.hutsby@btinternet.com
w chipping-campden-holiday-cottages.co.uk/boxtree.htm

Carol Cottage ★★★★
Self Catering
Contact: Mrs Jane Whitehouse
Weston Park Farm
t (01386) 840835
e jane_whitehouse@hotmail.com
w cotswoldcottages.uk.com

Chapter Cottage ★★★★
Self Catering
Contact: Mrs Jan Revers
t (01386) 841450
w perpetuare.com

Cosy Corner ★★★★
Self Catering
Contact: Mrs Pearl Brandreth
Pearl Investments Ltd
t (01386) 841752
e pearl@mdina03.fsnet.co.uk
w noelcourt.co.uk

Cotswold Charm ★★★★
Self Catering
Contact: Mr & Miss Michael & Margaret Haines
Cotswold Charm
t (01386) 840164
e info@cotswoldcharm.co.uk
w cotswoldcharm.co.uk

Cowfair ★★★★ *Self Catering*
Contact: Mrs Whitehouse
t (01386) 840835
e jane_whitehouse@hotmail.com
w cotswoldcottages.uk.com

Croftsbrook
Rating Applied For
Self Catering
Contact: David Birch
t (01386) 840682

Grafton Mews ★★★★
Self Catering
Contact: Ms Sheila Rolland
Campden Cottages
t (01386) 593315
e info@campdencottages.co.uk
w campdencottages.co.uk

Honeysuckle Cottage ★★★★ *Self Catering*
Contact: Mrs Kate Daly
t (0121) 426 6310 & 07905 497211
e stjohn.daly@blueyonder.co.uk
w thecountrycottage.co.uk

Ingleside Cottage ★★★★
Self Catering
Contact: Miss Sheila Roland
Campden Cottages
t (01386) 593315
e info@campdencottages.co.uk

Little Thatch ★★★★
Self Catering
Contact: Mrs Dorothy Gadsby
t (01386) 840234

Orchard Cottage ★★★★
Self Catering
Contact: Ms Sheila Rolland
Campden Cottages
t (01386) 593315
e info@campdencottages.co.uk
w campdencottages.co.uk

Over the Arches ★★★
Self Catering
Contact: Mrs Pearl Brandreth
t (01386) 841752
e pearl@mdina03.fsnet.co.uk
w chippingcampden.co.uk/overthearches.htm

Rosary Cottage ★★★★
Self Catering
Contact: Miss Sheila Rolland
Camden Cottages
t (01386) 593315
e info@campdencottages.co.uk
w campdencottages.co.uk

Sansons Cottage ★★★★
Self Catering
Contact: Miss Sheila Rolland
Campden Cottages
t (01386) 593315
e info@campdencottages.co.uk
w campdencottages.co.uk

Shepherd's Cottage ★★★★
Self Catering
Contact: Miss Sheila Rolland
Campden Cottages
t (01386) 593315
e info@campdencottages.co.uk
w campdencottages.co.uk

Spring Cottage ★★★★
Self Catering
Contact: Miss Sheila Rolland
Folly Cottage
t (01386) 593315
e info@campdencottages.co.uk
w campdencottages.co.uk

Walkers Retreat ★★★
Self Catering
Contact: Mrs Whitehouse
Weston Park Farm
t (01386) 840835
e jane_whitehouse@hotmail.com
w cotswoldcottages.uk.com

Whistlers Corner Cottage
★★★★ *Self Catering*
Contact: Mr Robert Hutsby
Chipping Campden Holiday Cottages
t (01789) 841525
e robert.hutsby@btinternet.com
w chipping-campden-holiday-cottages.co.uk/whistlers.htm

CHIPPING SODBURY
Gloucestershire

Tan House Farm Cottage
★★★ *Self Catering*
Contact: Mrs James
t (01454) 228280

CHISELBOROUGH
Somerset

One Fair Place ★★★★
Self Catering
Contact: Mrs Adrienne Wright
t (01344) 772461
e aawright@btopenworld.com
w somersetcottageholidays.co.uk

CHITTLEHAMHOLT
Devon

Simmons Farm Cottage
★★★★ *Self Catering*
Contact: Mrs Janet Cornwell
Marsdens Cottage Holidays
t (01271) 813777
e holidays@marsdens.co.uk
w marsdens.co.uk

Treetops ★★★ *Self Catering*
Marsdens Cottage Holidays
t (01271) 813777
e holidays@marsdens.co.uk
w marsdens.co.uk

CHITTLEHAMPTON
Devon

Thatch Cottage ★★★★
Self Catering
English Country Cottages
t 0870 192 1066
w english-country-cottages06.co.uk

CHRISTCHURCH
Dorset

The Black House ★★★
Self Catering
Contact: Mr Andrew Brown
t (01647) 433593
e theblackhouse@hotmail.com
w theblackhouse.co.uk

Burton Farm House Annexe
★★★ *Self Catering*
Contact: Mrs Marylyn Etheridge
t (01202) 484475

The Causeway ★–★★ *Self Catering & Serviced Apartments*
Contact: Mrs Liz Tomkinson
t (01202) 470149
e tmscauseway@tiscali.co.uk

Cumberland Lodge
★★–★★★ *Self Catering*
Contact: Mr Paul Williamson
t (01425) 280275
e enquiries@cumberland-lodge.co.uk
w cumberland-lodge.co.uk/info

The Holiday Cottage ★★★
Self Catering
Contact: Mr & Mrs John Brewer
t (01202) 420673

Mallard Cottage ★★★
Self Catering
Contact: Mr & Mrs David Pearce
t (01202) 480805

Mude Gardens ★★★
Self Catering
Contact: Mr Warren
t (01628) 620777

Mude Lane ★★★
Self Catering
Contact: Mrs Brickell
t (01425) 672541

Pedralves ★★★ *Self Catering*
Contact: Mrs Kenney
t (01425) 273858

Riverbank Holidays ★★★
Self Catering
Contact: Mr & Mrs Gibson
t (01202) 477813

Riverbank House ★★★★
Self Catering
Contact: Mrs Sall Burrows
Oakdene Orchard
t (01202) 813723 & 07796 402912
e handbleisure@amserve.net
w riverbankholidays.co.uk

Riverside Park ★★★ *Self Catering & Serviced Apartments*
Contact: Mrs Lisa Booth
Riverside Park
t (01202) 471090
e holidays@riversidepark.biz
w riversidepark.biz

Saffron ★★★ *Self Catering*
Contact: Mrs Rosemary Broadey
t (01425) 277507
e rosemary@broadey.net

Two Rivers Reach ★★★
Self Catering
Contact: Ms Sandra Hayward
t 07789 908173
e sandshayward@yahoo.co.uk

CHRISTCHURCH
Gloucestershire

Glenwood ★★★
Self Catering
Contact: Mr & Mrs Keith & Joan Harvey
t (01594) 833128

CHULMLEIGH
Devon

Bealy Court Holiday Cottages ★★★★
Self Catering
Contact: Ms I Henderson
t (01769) 580312
e bealycourt@mac.com
w bealycourt.co.uk

Deer Cott ★★★★
Self Catering
Contact: Mr & Mrs George Simpson
Deer Cott
t (01769) 580461
e enquiries@deercott.co.uk
w deercott.co.uk

The Linhay
Rating Applied For
Self Catering
Marsdens Cottage Holidays
t (01271) 813777
e holidays@marsdens.co.uk
w marsdens.co.uk

CHURCHINFORD
Somerset

South Cleeve Bungalow
★★★★ *Self Catering*
Contact: Mrs V D Manning
t (01823) 601378
e enquiries@timbertopbungalows.co.uk
w timbertopbungalows.co.uk

CHURSTON FERRERS
Devon

Alston Farm Cottages
★★★★★ *Self Catering*
Contact: Mrs Claire Hockaday
t (01803) 845388
e alstonnch@aol.com
w alstonfarm.co.uk

CIRENCESTER
Gloucestershire

Flowers Barn ★★★★
Self Catering
Contact: Mrs Tina Barton
t (01285) 658145
e duntisbourne@aol.com
w duntisbourne.com

Glebe Farm Holiday Lets
★★★★ *Self Catering*
Contact: Mrs Polly Handover
Glebe Farm Holiday Lets
t (01285) 659226
e enquiries@glebefarmcottages.co.uk
w glebefarmcottages.co.uk

The Tallet ★★★ *Self Catering*
Contact: Mrs Susan Spivey
The Tallet
t (01285) 653405
e howard@spiveyfarm.co.uk

The Tallet Cottage ★★★★★
Self Catering
Contact: Mrs Vanessa Arbuthnott
t (01285) 831437
e vanessa@thetallet.demon.co.uk
w thetallet.co.uk

Warrens Gorse Cottages
★★–★★★ *Self Catering*
Contact: Mrs Nanette Randall
t (01285) 831261

CLAWTON
Devon

The Coach House ★★★
Self Catering
Contact: Mrs Carolyn Pix
t (01409) 271100
e enquiries@oldvicarageclawton.co.uk
w oldvicarageclawton.co.uk

CLEARWELL
Gloucestershire

North Lodge ★★★★
Self Catering
Contact: Mr Pash
Hideaways
t (01747) 828000
e enq@hideaways.co.uk

Rosedean
Rating Applied For
Self Catering
Contact: Ms Rosemary Prince
Rosemary Prince
t (01989) 770783
e mjprinceuk@aol.com

CLIFTON
City of Bristol

Bristol Serviced Apartments
★★★★★ *Self Catering*
Contact: Mrs Kim White
Lansdown Serviced Apartments
t (0117) 974 1414
e bsapartments@aol.com
w bristolservicedapartments.co.uk

CLOVELLY
Devon

Buttery Barn
Rating Applied For
Self Catering
Contact: Mr Peter Cornwell
Marsdens Cottage Holidays
t (01271) 813777
e holidays@marsdens.co.uk
w marsdens.co.uk

COBERLEY
Gloucestershire

Seven Springs Cottages
★★★ *Self Catering*
Contact: Miss Marcie Stokes
t (01242) 870385
e mail@sevenspringscottages.com
w sevenspringscottages.com

COCKLAKE
Somerset

Ashton Cottages ★★★
Self Catering
Contact: Mrs Ashley Ribi
t (01934) 712157
e info@ashtoncottages.net
w ashtoncottages.net

COFFINSWELL
Devon

Willa Cottage ★★★★
Self Catering
Contact: Mr Tim Whitehouse
t (01803) 875078
e tim@willacottage.com
w willacottage.com

COLAN
Cornwall

Little Barton, Gwel An Lagen & Bos Lowen ★★★★
Self Catering
Cornish Horizons Holiday Cottages
t (01841) 533331
e cottages@cornishhorizons.co.uk
w cornishhorizons.co.uk

COLATON RALEIGH
Devon

Rushmore
Rating Applied For
Self Catering
Contact: Tracy Gwillim
Sweetcombe Cottage Holidays Ltd.
t (01395) 512130
e enquiries@sweetcombe-ch.co.uk

Tidwell
Rating Applied For
Self Catering
Contact: Tracy Gwillin
Sweetcombe Cottage Holidays Ltd
t (01395) 512130
e enquiries@sweetcombe-ch.co.uk

COLD ASHTON
Gloucestershire

Sayres House, Nr Bath
Rating Applied For
Self Catering
Contact: Ms Pamela Skinner
Dunster Living
t 0870 620 1066
e info@dunsterliving.co.uk
w sayreshouse.co.uk

COLD ASTON
Gloucestershire

Pheasant Walk ★★★★
Self Catering
Contact: Mrs Penny Avery
t (01451) 810942
e grovefarm@coldaston.fsnet.co.uk
w coldaston.fsnet.co.uk

COLEFORD
Gloucestershire

32 Tudor Walk ★★★
Self Catering
Contact: Mrs Beale
t (01594) 832061

Little Millend ★★★
Self Catering
Contact: Mr Nicholas Pash
Hideaways
t (01747) 828170
e enq@hideaways.co.uk
w hideaways.co.uk

COLYFORD
Devon

Bryher ★★★★ *Self Catering*
Contact: Mrs Stephanie Sawyer
Donnybrook
t (01297) 551093
e info@devoncottage-bryher.co.uk
w devoncottage-bryher.co.uk

Chequers ★★★ *Self Catering*
Contact: Ms Louise Hayman
Milkbere Cottage Holidays
t (01297) 20729
e info@milkberehols.com
w milkberehols.com

Swan Hill House ★★★★
Self Catering
Contact: Ms Sharon Chatting
t (01297) 553387

Whitwell Farm Cottages ★★★★★ *Self Catering*
Contact: Mr Mike Williams
t 0800 092 0419
e 100755.66@compuserve.com
w a5star.co.uk

COLYTON
Devon

Barritshayes Farm Cottages ★★★★ *Self Catering*
Contact: Mr & Mrs Gordon & Liz Lindsay
Barrithayes Farm Cottages
t (01297) 552485
e info@barritshayes.co.uk
w barritshayes.co.uk

Bonehayne Farm Cottage ★★★ *Self Catering*
Contact: Mrs Gould
t (01404) 871416
e gould@bonehayne.co.uk
w bonehayne.co.uk

Coles House ★★★★
Self Catering
Contact: Ms Kate Bartlett
Jean Bartlett Cottage Holidays
t (01297) 23221
e holidays@jeanbartlett.com
w jeanbartlett.com

Colycroft ★★ *Self Catering*
Contact: Mr Tim Tandy
Jean Bartlett Cottage Holidays
t (01297) 23221
e holidays@jeanbartlett.com
w jeanbartlett.com

Hill View ★★★ *Self Catering*
Contact: Ms Louise Hayman
Milkbere Cottage Holidays
t (01297) 20729
e info@milkberehols.com
w milkberehols.com

Lavender Cottage ★★★
Self Catering
Contact: Ms Kate Bartlett
Jean Bartlett Cottage Holidays
t (01297) 23221
e holidays@jeanbartlett.com
w jeanbartlett.com

Little Haven ★★★
Self Catering
Contact: Mrs Elizabeth Mills
Colcombe Wood Holidays
t (01297) 553811
e liz.mills@btopenworld.com

Lovehayne Farm Cottages ★★★★ *Self Catering*
Contact: Mrs Philippa Bignell
t (01404) 871216
e stay@lovehayne.co.uk
w lovehayne.co.uk

Malt House ★★★
Self Catering
Contact: Ms Louise Hayman
Milkbere Cottage Holidays
t (01297) 20729
e info@milkberehols.com
w milkberehols.com

St Andrews Cottage ★★★
Self Catering
Contact: Ms Kate Bartlett
Jean bartlett Cottage Holidays
t (01297) 23221
e holidays@jeanbartlett.com

Smallicombe Farm ★★★★
Self Catering
Contact: Mrs Todd
Smallicombe Farm
t (01404) 831310
e maggie_todd@yahoo.com
w smallicombe.com

Valley View ★★★
Self Catering
Contact: Ms Tim Tandy
Jean Bartlett Cottage Holidays
t (01297) 23221
e holidays@jeanbartlett.com
w jeanbartlett.com

COMBE DOWN
Somerset

Kingham Cottage ★★★★
Self Catering
Contact: Mr & Mrs Peter & Christine Davis
t (01225) 837909
e kinghamcottage@aol.com
w kinghamcottage.co.uk

COMBE MARTIN
Devon

1 Stattens Cottages ★★★
Self Catering
Contact: Mrs Peggy Crees
t (01483) 488790
e info@cottagesindevon.com
w cottagesindevon.com

Beech & Ash Cottages ★★★★ *Self Catering*
Contact: Mrs Janet Cornwell
Marsdens Cottage Holidays
t (01271) 813777
e holidays@marsdens.co.uk
w marsdens.co.uk

Bosun's Cottage, Combe Martin Harbour ★★★
Self Catering
Contact: Mr & Mrs Martin & Margaret Wolverson
Primespot Character Cottages
t (01271) 882449

Hangman Path ★★★★
Self Catering
Contact: Mr Simon Chappell
River Bank House
t (01625) 251048
e landlord@combe-martin.net
w combe-martin.net

Hempster Farm Cottage ★★★ *Self Catering*
Contact: Mary Gingell
t (01271) 883306
e mary.gingell@virgin.net

Hillside ★★★★ *Self Catering*
Marsdens Cottage Holidays
t (01271) 813777
e holidays@marsdens.co.uk
w marsdens.co.uk

Indicknowle Farm ★★★★
Self Catering
Contact: Mrs Susan West
t (01271) 883980
e mark.sue@indicknowle.plus.com
w indicknowlefarmholidays.co.uk

Jewells Holiday Villas ★★★★★ *Self Catering*
Contact: Ms Katie Jewell
t (0118) 933 3935
e katie-jewell@talk21.com
w jewellsholidayvillas.com

Prospect Cottage ★★★
Self Catering
Contact: Mrs Janet Cornwell
Marsdens Cottage Holidays
t (01271) 813777
e holidays@marsdens.co.uk
w marsdens.co.uk

Sea Breeze
Rating Applied For
Self Catering
Marsdens Cottage Holidays
t (01271) 813777
e holidays@marsdens.co.uk
w marsdens.co.uk

Wheel Farm Country Cottages ★★★★
Self Catering
Contact: Mr & Mrs John Robertson
t (01271) 882100
e holidays@wheelfarmcottages.co.uk
w wheelfarmcottages.co.uk

Wood Sorrell ★★★
Self Catering
Marsdens Cottage Holidays
t (01271) 813777
e holidays@marsdens.co.uk
w marsdens.co.uk

Yetland Farm Cottages ★★★★ *Self Catering*
Contact: Mr & Mrs Alan & Alison Balcombe
t (01271) 883655
e enquiries@yetlandfarmcottages.co.uk
w yetlandfarmcottages.co.uk

COMBEINTEIGNHEAD
Devon

The Old Bakery ★★★
Self Catering
Holiday Homes & Cottages South West
t (01803) 663650
e holcotts@aol.com
w swcottages.co.uk

Thorn Cottage ★★★
Self Catering
Contact: Mr Ian Butterworth
Holiday Homes & Cottages South West
t (01803) 663650
e holcotts@aol.com
w swcottages.co.uk

COMPTON ABDALE
Gloucestershire

Southwold Barn ★★★★★
Self Catering
Contact: Mrs Emma Doyle
t (01242) 890147
e emma@southwoldfarm.co.uk
w southwoldbarn.co.uk

COMPTON DUNDON
Somerset

Chapel Barn ★★★★
Self Catering
Contact: Mrs Diana Napper
t (01458) 442962
e diana@dnapper.wanadoo.co.uk

Wisteria Cottage ★★★★
Self Catering
Contact: Mrs Georgina Baston
t (01458) 442848
e baston@onetel.com
w thewisteriacottage.co.uk

CONNOR DOWNS
Cornwall

Gwithian Holidays ★★★
Self Catering
Contact: Mr Trevor & Tyson Greenaway
t (01736) 755493
e enquiries@gwithianholidays.com
w gwithianholidays.com

Trevaskis Dairy ★★★★
Self Catering
Contact: Ms Strachey
t (01209) 613750
w trevaskis-dairy.co.uk

CONSTANTINE
Cornwall

1 Inow Cottage ★★★
Self Catering
Cornish Holiday Cottages
t (01326) 250339
e info@cornishholidaycottages.net

Chynoweth ★★★
Self Catering
Contact: Mrs Eileen Combellack
t (01326) 340196

The Fuchsias ★★★
Self Catering
Vicarage Close
t (01322) 339115

Green Bank Cottage ★★★
Self Catering
Contact: Mrs Carol Scobie-Allin
t (01225) 466720
e carole@selectiveretreats.co.uk

Nantrissack Farm ★★★
Self Catering
Contact: Miss Wendy Palmer
t (01326) 341161

No 5 Trewince ★★★
Self Catering
Contact: Mr Martin Raftery
Mullion Cottages
t 0845 066 7766
e enquiries@mullioncottages.com
w mullioncottages.com

Owl Cottage ★★★
Self Catering
Contact: Mrs Sara Swinscow
t (01326) 340493
e sara@owlcottageholidays.co.uk
w owlcottageholidays.co.uk

Polpenwith ★★★
Self Catering
Contact: Emily Boriosi
Cornish Holiday Cottages
t (01326) 250339
e emily@cornishholidaycottages.net
w cornishholidaycottages.net/get_property.php?p=56

Sail Loft ★★★ *Self Catering*
Contact: Ms Boriosi
Cornish Holiday Cottages
t (01326) 250339
e emily@cornishholidaycottages.net
w cornishholidaycottages.net/get_property.php?p=27

Trenarth ★★ *Self Catering*
Contact: Emily Boriosi
Cornish Holiday Cottages
t (01326) 250339
e emily@cornishholidaycottages.net
w cornishholidaycottages.net/get.property.php?p=57

Trewince, Flat 4 ★★
Self Catering
Contact: Mr Martin Raftery
Mullion Cottages
t 0845 066 7766
e enquiries@mullioncottages.com
w mullioncottages.com

Treworval Barn Apartments ★★★★ *Self Catering*
Contact: Emily Boriosi
Cornish Holiday Cottages
t (01326) 250339
e emily@cornishholidaycottages.net
w cornishholidaycottages.net

CONSTANTINE BAY
Cornwall

Bumblers, Constantine Bay ★★★ *Self Catering*
Contact: The Proprietor Bumblers
t (01732) 863121
e partridgefarm@talk21.com

Costilloes ★★★ *Self Catering*
Contact: Mr Peter Osbourne
Cornish Horizons Holiday Cottages
t (01841) 533331
e cottages@cornishhorizons.co.uk
w cornishhorizons.co.uk

Cowries and The Lodge ★★★ *Self Catering*
Contact: Mr Peter Osbourne
Cornish Horizons Holiday Cottages
t (01841) 533331
e cottages@cornishhorizons.co.uk
w cornishhorizons.co.uk

Flat 12 Sandhills ★★★
Self Catering
Contact: Mr Hull
t (01752) 772519
e peoplematters@btinternet.com

Flat 7, Sandhills ★★★
Self Catering
Contact: Mrs Vaughan
t (01785) 813864
e tj@chestnut1.freeserve.co.uk

The Garden Cottage Holiday Flats ★★★ *Self Catering*
Contact: Mrs Elizabeth Harris
t (01841) 520262
e gardencottage@cornwall-county.com

The Greens ★★★
Self Catering
Contact: Peter Osbourne
Cornish Horizons Holiday Cottages
t (01841) 533331
e cottages@cornishhorizons.co.uk
w cornishhorizons.co.uk

Kalundu ★★★★
Self Catering
Cornish Horizons Holiday Cottages
t (01841) 533331
e cottages@cornishhorizons.co.uk
w cornishhorizons.co.uk

Kernyk ★★★ *Self Catering*
t (01841) 533331
e cottages@cornishhorizons.co.uk
w cornishhorizons.co.uk

Kittiwake ★★★★
Self Catering
Contact: Peter Osbourne
Cornish Horizons Holiday Cottages
t (01841) 533331
e cottages@cornishhorizons.co.uk
w cornishhorizons.co.uk

Lees Nook ★★-★★★
Self Catering
Contact: Mrs Stuttaford
t (01841) 520344
e leesnookholidays@hotmail.com
w cornwallonline.co.uk/leesnook

Lower Trevelyan ★★★
Self Catering
Contact: Peter Osbourne
Cornish Horizons Holiday Cottages
t (01841) 533331
e cottages@cornishhorizons.co.uk
w cornishhorizons.co.uk

Moonrakers ★★★
Self Catering
Contact: Nicky Stanley
Harbour Holidays Ltd
t (01841) 533402
e contact@harbourholidays.co.uk
w harbourholidays.co.uk

Pippins & Dinas View ★★-★★★ *Self Catering*
Contact: Mr Osbourne
Cornish Horizons Holiday Cottages
t (01841) 533331
e cottages@cornishhorizons.co.uk
w cornishhorizons.co.uk

Porth Clyne ★★★
Self Catering
Contact: Mr Osbourne
Cornish Horizons Holiday Cottages
t (01841) 533331
e cottages@cornishhorizons.co.uk
w cornishhorizons.co.uk

Quilletts ★★★★
Self Catering
Contact: Mr Osbourne
Cornish Horizons Holiday Cottages
t (01841) 533331
e cottages@cornishhorizons.co.uk
w cornishhorizons.co.uk

Rose Campion ★★★★
Self Catering
Contact: Mr Peter Osbourne
Cornish Horizons Holiday Cottages
t (01841) 533331
e cottages@cornishhorizons.co.uk
w cornishhorizons.co.uk

Stone's Throw Flat 10, Sandhills ★★★ *Self Catering*
Contact: Mrs Caroline Middleton
t (01795) 474795
w northcornwall.fsnet.co.uk

Treberta ★★★★
Self Catering
Contact: Ms Nickie Stanley
Harbour Holidays, Padstow
t (01841) 533402
e t.colver@techniquestudios.com

Trefebus ★★★★
Self Catering
Contact: Mr Osbourne
Cornish Horizons Holiday Cottages
t (01841) 533331
e cottages@cornishhorizons.co.uk
w cornishhorizons.co.uk

Trefoil ★★★ *Self Catering*
Cornish Horizons Holiday Cottages
t (01841) 533331
e cottages@cornishhorizons.co.uk
w cornishhorizons.co.uk

Treglos Bungalow & Apartments ★★★-★★★★
Self Catering
Contact: Mr Barlow
t (01841) 520727
e stay@tregloshotel.com
w tregloshotel.com

Treglyn ★★ *Self Catering*
Contact: Mr Osbourne
Cornish Horizons Holiday Cottages
t (01841) 533331
e cottages@cornishhorizons.co.uk
w cornishhorizons.co.uk

Treless ★★★★ *Self Catering*
Cornish Horizons Holiday Cottages
t (01841) 533331
e cottages@cornishhorizons.co.uk
w cornishhorizons.co.uk

Trescore ★★★ *Self Catering*
Contact: Mr Osbourne
Cornish Horizons Holiday Cottages
t (01841) 533331
e cottages@cornishhorizons.co.uk
w cornishhorizons.co.uk

Trevanion ★★ *Self Catering*
Contact: Ms Nicky Stanley
Harbour Holidays - Padstow
t (01841) 532555
e sales@jackie-stanley.co.uk

Trevose Golf & Country Club ★★-★★★★
Self Catering
Contact: Mr Gammon
t (01841) 520208
e info@trevose-gc.co.uk
w trevose-gc.co.uk

Turnstones ★★ *Self Catering*
Contact: Mr Osbourne
Cornish Horizons Holiday Cottages
t (01841) 533331
e cottages@cornishhorizons.co.uk
w cornishhorizons.co.uk

COOMBE BISSETT
Wiltshire

Cross Farm Cottage ★★★
Self Catering
Contact: Mrs Sue Kittermaster
t (01722) 718293
e crossfarm10@aol.com

CORFE CASTLE
Dorset

7 West Street
Rating Applied For
Self Catering
Contact: Ms Fiona Wake-Walker
t (01929) 480048
e 2wwfeet@tiscali.co.uk
w cottagepurbeck.co.uk

Farriers Lodge ★★★★
Self Catering
Contact: Mrs Eileen Van Lelyveld
The Old Forge
t (01929) 480386
w farrierslodge.corfe-castle.co.uk

Honey Pot Cottage
Rating Applied For
Self Catering
Contact: Anna Eckford
t (01202) 883906
e anna-eckford@excite.com
w honeypotcot.co.uk

Knaveswell Farm ★★
Self Catering
Contact: Mrs Valerie Murray
t (01929) 424184
e murraydazzled@aol.com

Oddity Cottage ★★★
Self Catering
Contact: Miss LM Hemingway
Dorset Cottage Holidays
t (01929) 553443
e enq@dhcottages.co.uk
w dhcottages.co.uk

Scoles Manor ★★★★
Self Catering
Contact: Peter and Belinda Bell
Scoles Manor
t (01929) 480312
e peter@scoles.co.uk
w scoles.co.uk

CORNWORTHY
Devon

Pridhams ★★★★
Self Catering
Contact: Mrs Christine Clark
Dart valley Cottages
t (01803) 771127
e enquiries@dartvalleycottages.co.uk
w dartvalleycottages.co.uk

CORSCOMBE
Dorset

Underhill Farm Holidays Meadow Rise ★★★★
Self Catering
Contact: Mrs Joanna Vassie
Underhill Farm Holidays Finch Rise
t (01935) 891245
e vassie@underhillfarm.co.uk
w underhillfarm.co.uk

CORSE LAWN
Gloucestershire

Slad Farm ★★★★
Self Catering
Contact: Ms Janet Swift
t (01452) 780909
e sladfarm@tiscali.co.uk

CORSHAM
Wiltshire

Barnacle Goose ★★★★
Self Catering
Contact: Stephanie Szakalo
t (01225) 869438
e stephanie@barnaclegoose.co.uk
w barnaclegoose.co.uk

The Ostlers House ★★★★★
Self Catering
Contact: Mr & Mrs Andy & Stella Collet
t (01225) 812700
e reservations@theostlershouse.co.uk
w theostlershouse.co.uk

Rowan House ★★★★★
Self Catering
Contact: Mrs Jennie Spikes
t (01249) 701166
e mail@rowanhousecorsham.co.uk
w rowanhousecorsham.co.uk

Wadswick Barns ★★★★
Self Catering
Contact: Mr & Mrs Tim & Carolyn Barton
t (01225) 810733
e barns@wadswick.co.uk
w wadswick.co.uk

COTLEIGH
Devon

Authers Cottage ★★★★
Self Catering
Contact: Ms Louise Hayman
Milkbere Cottage Holidays
t (01297) 20729
e info@milkberehols.com
w milkberehols.com

COVERACK
Cornwall

14 Coverack Headland
★★★★ *Self Catering*
Contact: Mrs Anne Bradley-Smith
Dorland Cottage, The Mint
t (01883) 743442
w coverack.org

Coverack Headland Flat 10
★★★ *Self Catering*
Cornish Cottage Holidays
t (01326) 573808
e enquiry@cornishcottageholidays.co.uk
w cornishcottageholidays.co.uk

Crowan House ★★★
Self Catering
Mullion Cottages
t (01326) 240333
e enquiries@mullioncottages.com
w mullioncottages.com

Dean Haven ★★★
Self Catering
Contact: Mr Martin Raftery
Mullion Cottages
t 0845 066 7766
e enquiries@mullioncottages.com
w mullioncottages.com

Heath Farm Cottages
★★★★ *Self Catering*
Contact: Mr Goodman
t (01326) 280521
e enquiries@heath-farm-holidays.co.uk
w heath-farm-holidays.co.uk

Polcoverack Farm Cottages
★★★ *Self Catering*
Contact: Pat & Trevor Angell
t (01326) 281021
e angells@polcoverack.co.uk
w polcoverack.co.uk

Tre Prenn Vean ★★★
Self Catering
Contact: Mr Martin Raftery
Mullion Cottages
t 0845 066 7766
e enquiries@mullioncottages.com
w mullioncottages.com

COVERACK BRIDGES
Cornwall

Kepesake Cottage ★★★★
Self Catering
Contact: Mrs Deborah Mackay
t (01326) 341097
e carnemackay@talk21.com
w kepesakecottage.co.uk

COXBRIDGE
Somerset

Double House Farm – Cottages ★★★★
Self Catering
Contact: Ms Vanessa Hayes
t (01458) 850514
e doublehousefarm@hotmail.com
w doublehousefarm.co.uk

Lower Coxbridge House
★★★ *Self Catering*
Contact: Mrs Sarah Orme
t (01458) 850805
e sarahorme@lineone.net
w lowercoxbridge.co.uk

CRACKINGTON HAVEN
Cornwall

9 Lundy Drive ★★★★
Self Catering
Contact: Mrs Anderson
t (01840) 230504
e paul@panderson60.freeserve.co.uk

Bremor Holiday Bunaglows and Cottages ★★★
Self Catering
t (01840) 230340
e cornishbreaks@bremholidays.wanadoo.co.uk
w bremorholidays.co.uk

Longstones ★★★★
Self Catering
Contact: Mrs Bird
t (01840) 230445
e pat.bird@btinternet.co.uk
w cottagesdirect.co.uk/coa018

Old School Cottages ★★★
Self Catering
Contact: Mr Martin Smith
t (01840) 230771
e oldschool@stgennys.co.uk

Trenannick Cottages ★★★
Self Catering
Contact: Ms Harrison
t (01566) 781443
e lorraine.trenannick@i12.com
w trenannickcottages.co.uk

Trevigue Cottages ★★★★
Self Catering
Contact: Ms Crocker
t (01840) 230418
e trevigue@talk21.com

Treworgie Barton
★★★★-★★★★★
Self Catering
Contact: Mrs Warner
t (01840) 230233
e info@treworgie.co.uk
w treworgie.co.uk

CRAFTHOLE
Cornwall

Whitsand Bay Self Catering
★★★-★★★★ *Self Catering*
Contact: J Earle
Parade House
t (01579) 345688
e enwbsc@hotmail.com
w whitsandbayselfcatering.co.uk

CRANTOCK
Cornwall

Great Western Farmhouse & Seaspray ★★★-★★★★
Self Catering
Contact: Mrs Mills
t 0845 226 5507
e rentals@milco.biz
w crantock-cottages.biz

CRAPSTONE
Devon

Midway ★★★★ *Self Catering*
Contact: Mrs Susan Eggins
t (01752) 733221
e sueandmikeeggins@hotmail.co.uk
w midwayhouse.co.uk

CREDITON
Devon

Rudge Rew Cottage & Colts Hill Barn ★★★★
Self Catering
Contact: Mrs Christine Bailey
t (01363) 877309
e rudgerewfarm@btinternet.com
w rudgerew.co.uk

White Witches and Stable Lodge ★★★★ *Self Catering*
Contact: Mrs Gillian Gillbard
t (01884) 860278
e gillbard@eclipse.co.uk
w eclipse.co.uk/helebarton

CROWLAS
Cornwall

Cuckoo Cottage ★★★
Self Catering
Contact: Mrs Jackman
t (01732) 862064

Millers Loft ★★★
Self Catering
Contact: Mr & Mrs Taylor
Millers Loft
t (01237) 479146
e enquiries@farmcott.co.uk
w farmcott.co.uk

CROYDE
Devon

Bon Accord ★★★★★
Self Catering
Marsdens Cottage Holidays
t (01271) 813777
e holidays@marsdens.co.uk
w marsdens.co.uk

Bramleys ★★★ *Self Catering*
Contact: Mrs Janet Cornwell
Marsdens Cottage Holidays
t (01271) 813777
e holidays@marsdens.co.uk
w marsdens.co.uk

Bryher Lee ★★★★
Self Catering
Marsdens Cottage Holidays
t (01271) 813777
e holidays@marsdens.co.uk
w marsdens.co.uk

Cock Rock Cottage ★★★★
Self Catering
Contact: Mrs Janet Cornwell
Marsdens Cottage Holidays
t (01271) 813777
e holidays@marsdens.co.uk
w marsdens.co.uk

Croyde Bay Lodge Apartments 1 & 2 ★★★★
Self Catering
Contact: Mrs Jenny Penny
Croyde Bay House Hotel
t (01271) 890270

Cubbies Corner ★★★
Self Catering
Marsdens Cottage Holidays
t (01271) 813777
e holidays@marsdens.co.uk
w marsdens.co.uk

Denham House & Cottages ★★★ *Self Catering*
Contact: Mr & Mrs Bernard & Vera Sanderberg
Denham House
t (01271) 890297
e info@denhamhouse.co.uk
w denhamhouse.co.uk

The Dunes ★★★★
Self Catering
Contact: Mrs Janet Cornwell
Marsdens Cottage Holidays
t (01271) 813777
e holidays@marsdens.co.uk
w marsdens.co.uk

Duneside ★★★★
Self Catering
Contact: Mrs Janet Cornwell
Marsdens Cottage Holidays
t (01271) 813777
e holidays@marsdens.co.uk
w marsdens.co.uk

Embleton ★★★★
Self Catering
Marsdens Cottage Holidays
t (01271) 813777
e holidays@marsdens.co.uk
w marsdens.co.uk

Great Close ★★★★ *Self Catering & Serviced Apartments*
Marsdens Cottage Holidays
t (01271) 813777
e holidays@marsdens.co.uk
w marsdens.co.uk

Hillview ★★★★ *Self Catering*
Contact: Mrs Janet Cornwell
Marsdens Cottage Holidays
t (01271) 813777
e holidays@marsdens.co.uk
w marsdens.co.uk

Hobbs House ★★★★
Self Catering
Contact: Mrs Janet Cornwell
Marsdens Cottage Holidays
t (01271) 813777
e holidays@marsdens.co.uk
w marsdens.co.uk

Keats Lodge ★★★
Self Catering
Contact: Mrs Janet Cornwell
Marsdens Cottage Holidays
t (01271) 813777
e holidays@marsdens.co.uk
w marsdens.co.uk

Lundy Lodge ★★★★
Self Catering
Contact: Mrs Janet Cornwell
Marsdens Cottage Holidays
t (01271) 813777
e holidays@marsdens.co.uk
w marsdens.co.uk

The Mallows ★★★
Self Catering
Contact: Mrs Janet Cornwell
Marsdens Cottage Holidays
t (01271) 813777
e holidays@marsdens.co.uk
w marsdens.co.uk

Marigold Cottage ★★★★
Self Catering
Marsdens Cottage Holidays
t (01271) 813777
e holidays@marsdens.co.uk
w marsdens.co.uk

Montana ★★★ *Self Catering*
Contact: Mrs Janet Cornwell
Marsdens Cottage Holidays
t (01271) 813777
e holidays@marsdens.co.uk
w marsdens.co.uk

Myrtle Cottage ★★★
Self Catering
Marsdens Cottage Holidays
t (01271) 813777
e holidays@marsdens.co.uk
w marsdens.co.uk

Nauwai ★★★ *Self Catering*
Contact: Mrs Janet Cornwell
Marsdens Cottage Holidays
t (01271) 813777
e holidays@marsdens.co.uk
w marsdens.co.uk

Oceanside ★★★★
Self Catering
Contact: Mr Peter Cornwell
Marsdens Cottage Holidays
t (01271) 813777
e holidays@marsdens.co.uk
w marsdens.co.uk

Oyster Falls ★★★★
Self Catering
Contact: Mrs Janet Cornwell
Marsdens Cottage Holidays
t (01271) 813777
e holidays@marsdens.co.uk
w marsdens.co.uk

Sands End ★★★★
Self Catering
Contact: Mrs Janet Cornwell
Marsdens Cottage Holidays
t (01271) 813777
e holidays@marsdens.co.uk
w marsdens.co.uk

Seahaven ★★★★
Self Catering
Contact: Mrs Janet Cornwell
Marsdens Cottage Holidays
t (01271) 813777
e holidays@marsdens.co.uk
w marsdens.co.uk

Summer Breeze
Rating Applied For
Self Catering
Marsdens Cottage Holidays
t (01271) 813777
e holidays@marsdens.co.uk
w marsdens.co.uk

Sunnyside ★★★★
Self Catering
Contact: Mrs Janet Cornwell
Marsdens Cottage Holidays
t (01271) 813777
e holidays@marsdens.co.uk
w marsdens.co.uk

Sunset View ★★★
Self Catering
Contact: Mrs Janet Cornwell
Marsdens Cottage Holidays
t (01271) 813777
e holidays@marsdens.co.uk
w marsdens.co.uk

Suntana ★★★ *Self Catering*
Contact: Mrs Janet Cornwell
Marsdens Cottage Holidays
t (01271) 813777
e holidays@marsdens.co.uk
w marsdens.co.uk

Surfers Retreat
Rating Applied For
Self Catering
Marsdens Cottage Holidays
t (01271) 813777
e holidays@marsdens.co.uk
w marsdens.co.uk

Sweets Cottage ★★★★
Self Catering
Contact: Mrs Janet Cornwell
Marsdens Cottage Holidays
t (01271) 813777
e holidays@marsdens.co.uk
w marsdens.co.uk

Swell ★★★★ *Self Catering*
Contact: Mrs Janet Cornwell
Marsdens Cottage Holidays
t (01271) 813777
e holidays@marsdens.co.uk
w marsdens.co.uk

Treetops ★★★ *Self Catering*
Marsdens Cottage Holidays
t (01271) 813777
e holidays@marsdens.co.uk
w marsdens.co.uk

Westside ★★★★
Self Catering
Marsdens Cottage Holidays
t (01271) 813777
e holidays@marsdens.co.uk
w marsdens.co.uk

Withyside ★★★★
Self Catering
Contact: Mrs Janet Cornwell
Marsdens Cottage Holidays
t (01271) 813777
e holidays@marsdens.co.uk
w marsdens.co.uk

CRUGMEER
Cornwall

Old Lifeboat Station ★★★
Self Catering
Contact: Mrs Nicky Stanley
Harbour Holidays
t (01841) 533402
e contact@harbourholidays.co.uk
w harbourholidays.co.uk

Webbers ★★★ *Self Catering*
Contact: Ms Nicky Stanley
Harbour Holidays - Padstow
t (01841) 532555
e sales@jackie-stanley.co.uk

CUBERT
Cornwall

Cromwell House ★★★
Self Catering
Contact: Mrs Sue Mills
t (024) 7646 3840
e enquiries@cromwellhouse.co.uk
w cromwellhouse.co.uk

Elfadore ★★★ *Self Catering*
Contact: Mrs Clegg
t (01637) 830640

CUCKLINGTON
Somerset

Hale Farm ★★★
Self Catering
Contact: Mrs David
t (01963) 33342

Rosebank Cottage ★★★★
Self Catering
Contact: Mrs Mariella Wolff
t (01747) 840500
e mariella@artbreaks.com
w artbreaks.com

CULMHEAD
Somerset

Culmhead House, Culmhead ★★★ *Self Catering*
Contact: Mr & Mrs Timothy & Susan Rodgers
t (01823) 421073
e rodgers@culmheadhouse.com
w culmheadhouse.com

CURRY MALLET
Somerset

Buzzards View ★★★★
Self Catering
Contact: Major Ian Hill
t (01823) 480436
e majianhil@lineone.net
w crimsonhillfarm.co.uk

CURY
Cornwall

Nanplough Farm Cottages
★★★ *Self Catering*
Contact: Mr & Mrs Lepper
t (01326) 241088
e info@nanplough.co.uk
w nanplough.co.uk

CURY CROSS LANES
Cornwall

Bonython Estate
★★★★–★★★★★
Self Catering
Contact: Mrs Nathan
t (01386) 701177
e info@ruralretreats.co.uk
w bonythonmanor.co.uk

DAGLINGWORTH
Gloucestershire

Corner Cottage ★★★★
Self Catering
Contact: Mrs Mary Bartlett
t (01285) 653478

DALWOOD
Devon

Millwater Cottage and Riverbank Cottage ★★★
Self Catering
Contact: Mr Zachary Stuart-Brown
Dream Cottages
t (01305) 789000
e admin@dream-cottages.co.uk
w dream-cottages.co.uk

Old Symes Cottages ★★★★
Self Catering
Contact: Mr & Mrs John & Kathleen Brennan
t (01297) 35982
e brennans@oldsymes.fsnet.co.uk

DARTINGTON
Devon

Billany ★★★ *Self Catering*
Contact: Lucy Ellison
Farm & Cottage Holidays
t (01237) 479146
e enquiries@farmcott.co.uk
w holidaycottages.co.uk

DARTMEET
Devon

Coachman's Cottage
★★★★ *Self Catering*
Contact: Mr John Evans
Coachman's Cottage
t (01364) 631173
e mail@dartmeet.com
w dartmeet.com

DARTMOUTH
Devon

Beauford House ★★★★
Self Catering
Dartmouth Cottages .Com
t (01803) 839499

Cotterbury ★★★★★
Self Catering
Dartmouth Cottages .Com
t (01803) 839499

The Gallery ★★★★★
Self Catering
Contact: Mrs Rosemarie James
The Old Rectory
t (01858) 432157
e simon@dlpconsultants.co.uk
w thegalleryindartmouth.co.uk

Harbour Heights ★★★★
Self Catering
Contact: Mrs Buckingham
t 07815 824821
w dartmouthholiday.co.uk

Higher Bowden Holiday Cottages ★★★★
Self Catering
Contact: Mrs Linda Horne
t (01803) 770745
e lin@higherbowden.com
w higherbowden.com

Little Coombe Cottage
★★★★★ *Self Catering*
Contact: Mr & Mrs Phil & Ann Unitt
t (01803) 722599
w littlecoombecottage.co.uk

The Little White House
★★★★ *Self Catering*
Contact: Miss Tara Barton
Coast & Country Cottages
t (01803) 839499
w coastandcountry.co.uk

The Old Bakehouse ★★★
Self Catering
Contact: Mrs Sylvia Ridalls
The Old Bakehouse
t (01803) 834585
e gparker@pioneerps.co.uk
w oldbakehousedartmouth.co.uk

Sixes 'n' Sevens ★★★★
Self Catering
Contact: Ms Elizabeth Harvey
Glen Helen
t (01684) 896325
e enquiries@no-67.co.uk
w no-67.co.uk

DAVIDSTOW
Cornwall

Treworra Stables ★★★★
Self Catering
Contact: Mr Andy Ryan
Farm & Cottage Holidays
t (01840) 261798
e andy@treworra.co.uk
w holidaycottages.co.uk

DAWLISH
Devon

Brookdale ★★★★
Self Catering
Contact: Mr Ian Butterworth
Holiday Homes & Cottages South West
t (01803) 663650
e holcotts@aol.com
w swcottages.co.uk

Cofton Country Holiday Park ★★★★ *Self Catering*
Contact: Mrs Valerie Jeffery
Cofton Country Cottage Holidays
t (01626) 890111
e info@coftonholidays.co.uk
w coftonholidays.co.uk

Erminhurst ★★★★
Self Catering
Holiday Homes & Cottages South West
t (01803) 663650
e holcotts@aol.com
w swcottages.co.uk

Pippin Cottage
Rating Applied For
Self Catering
Contact: Mrs Butterworth
Torbay Holiday Agency
t (01803) 663650
e holcotts@aol.com
w swcottages.co.uk

Radfords Cottage ★★★★
Self Catering
Contact: Mr James Morris
Farm & Cottage Holidays
t (01237) 479146
e enquiries@farmcott.co.uk
w holidaycottages.co.uk

Rockstone ★★★★
Self Catering
Holiday Homes & Cottages South West
t (01803) 663650
e holcotts@aol.com
w swcottages.co.uk

Shell Cove House ★★★★
Self Catering
Contact: Ms Jameson
t (01626) 862523
e shellcovehouse@btinternet.com
w shellcovehouse.co.uk

DAWLISH WARREN
Devon

24 Devondale Court ★★
Self Catering
Contact: Mrs Teresa Code
t (01392) 881545
e tesscode@hotmail.com
w dawlishwarren.org.uk

---

32 Devondale ★★★
Self Catering
Contact: Mr Martin Wheeler
t 0800 075 5651
e holiday@dawlish-warren.com
w dawlish-warren.com

Baichal on Welcome Family Holiday Park ★★
Self Catering
Contact: Mr Robert Bailey
t (01626) 773737
w baichal.com

Chudleigh Apartment ★★★
Self Catering
Contact: Mrs Beverley May
t (01626) 864760
e kaiserrob@btinternet.com

Eastdon House ★★★★
Self Catering
Contact: Mrs Valerie Jeffery
Cofton Country Holidays
t (01626) 890111
e info@coftonholidays.co.uk
w coftonholidays.co.uk

Peppermint Park
Rating Applied For
Self Catering
Contact: Miss Sharon Vickery
t (01626) 863436
e info@peppermintpark.co.uk
w peppermintpark.co.uk

DEERHURST
Gloucestershire

Deerhurst Cottages ★★★★
Self Catering
Contact: Mrs Nicole Samuel
Abbots Court Farm
t (01684) 275845
e enquiries@deerhurstcottages.co.uk
w deerhurstcottages.co.uk

DELABOLE
Cornwall

Ruby Cottage ★★★
Self Catering
Contact: Sabina Dziurman
t (020) 8995 3063
e sabinadz@onetel.com
w rubycottagecornwall.co.uk

DEVIZES
Wiltshire

Abbotts Ball Farm Cottage
★★★ *Self Catering*
Contact: Mrs V Hazel Hobbs
t (01380) 721661
e hobbs@abbottsballfarm.com
w abbottsballfarm.com

The Derby ★★★
Self Catering
Contact: Mrs Janet Tyler
t (01380) 850523
e kingsplayfarming@btinternet.com

Fourbee ★★★★
Self Catering
Contact: Mr & Mrs Bernard & Susan Foreman
Rushley Mount
t (01380) 816919
e fourbeecontact@aol.com
w fourbee.biz

The Gate House ★★★★
Self Catering
Contact: Mrs Laura Stratton
t (01380) 725283
e info@visitdevizes.co.uk
w visitdevizes.co.uk

Owls Cottage ★★★★
Self Catering
Contact: Mrs Gill Whittome
Owls Cottage
t (01380) 818804
e gill@owls-cottage.com
w owls-cottage.com

Tichborne's Farm Cottages
★★★★ *Self Catering*
Contact: Mr & Mrs Jon & Judy Nash
t (01380) 862971
e info@tichbornes.co.uk
w tichbornes.co.uk

DEVORAN
Cornwall

Anne's Cottage ★★
Self Catering
Special Places in Cornwall
t (01872) 864400
e office@specialplacescornwall.co.uk
w specialplacescornwall.co.uk

Myrtle Cottage ★★
Self Catering
Contact: Mrs E. Charlton
t (01872) 864188

Tinners ★★★ *Self Catering*
Special Places in Cornwall
t (01872) 864400
e office@specialplacescornwall.co.uk
w specialplacescornwall.co.uk

Trerose ★★★★ *Self Catering*
Contact: Mrs Elizabeth Poupard
t (01872) 870845
e elipou@aol.com

DIDWORTHY
Devon

Didworthy House, Didworthy ★★★★
Self Catering
Contact: Mr & Mrs J Beer
t (01364) 72655
e info@didworthyhouse.co.uk
w didworthyhouse.co.uk

DINTON
Wiltshire

The Cottage, Marshwood Farm ★★★★ *Self Catering*
Contact: Mrs Fiona Lockyer
t (01722) 716334
e marshwood1@btconnect.com
w marshwoodfarm.co.uk

Fitz Farm Cottage ★★★
Self Catering
Contact: Mr Nicholas Pash
Hideaways
t (01747) 828170
e enq@hideaways.co.uk
w hideaways.co.uk

The Flat Honeysuckle Homestead ★★ *Self Catering*
Contact: Mr David Kirby
t (01722) 717887
e honeysuckle@dinton21.freeserve.co.uk

DIPTFORD
Devon

Higher Beneknowle
★★★★★ *Self Catering*
Toad Hall Cottages
t (01548) 853089
e thc@toadhallcottages.com
w toadhalcottages.com

Ley Farm ★★★ *Self Catering*
Contact: Mrs Sophia Hendy
t (01548) 821200

DITTISHAM
Devon

Cobwebs ★★★★
Self Catering
Contact: Mrs Christine Clark
Dart Valley Cottages
t (01803) 771127
e enquiries@dartvalleycottages.co.uk
w dartvalleycottages.co.uk

Ollie's Cottage ★★★★
Self Catering
Contact: Mrs Christine Clark
Dart Valley Cottages
t (01803) 771127
e enquiries@dartvalleycottages.co.uk
w dartvalleycottages.co.uk

Sarah Elliots ★★★★
Self Catering
Contact: Mrs Christine Clark
Dart Valley Cottages
t (01803) 771127
e enquiries@dartvalleycottages.co.uk
w dartvalleycottages.co.uk

Smugglers Cottage ★★★★
Self Catering
Toad Hall Cottages
t (01548) 853089
e thc@toadhallcottages.com
w toadhallcottages.com

Wild Oat House ★★★★
Self Catering
Contact: Mrs Christine Clark
Dart Valley Cottages
t (01803) 771127
e enquiries@dartvalleycottages.co.uk
w dartvalleycottages.co.uk

DOBWALLS
Cornwall

An Penty ★★★★
Self Catering
Farm & Cottage Holidays
t (01237) 479146
e enquiries@farmcott.co.uk
w holidaycottages.co.uk

West Tremabe Holiday Cottages ★★★ *Self Catering*
Contact: Mr & Mrs Kirk
t (01579) 321863
e christine.j.foster@btopenworld.com
w west-tremabe-cottages.co.uk

DOLTON
Devon

Ham Farm ★★★★★
Self Catering
Contact: Mr & Mrs Cobbledick
t (01805) 624000
e info@hamfarm.co.uk
w hamfarm.co.uk

Vine Cottage ★★★★
Self Catering
Contact: Mrs Susan Marshall
t (01737) 813866
e samandjcm@aol.com
w vinecottagedevon.co.uk

DONHEAD ST ANDREW
Wiltshire

Sparrow Cottage ★★★★
Self Catering
Contact: Mr Nicholas Pash
Hideaways
t (01747) 828170
e enq@hideaways.co.uk
w hideaways.co.uk

DORCHESTER
Dorset

Beaufort Cottages ★★★
Self Catering
Dream Cottages
t (01305) 789000
e admin@dream-cottages.co.uk
w dream-cottages.co.uk

Christmas Cottage ★★★
Self Catering
Contact: Mrs Helen Fraser
t (01305) 264041

Damers Cottage ★★★
Self Catering
Contact: Mrs Rosemary Hodder
t (01305) 852205
e rh@chaldonherring.co.uk
w cottage-holidays-dorset.co.uk

Dove House and Swallows
★★★★★ *Self Catering*
Contact: Mrs Pippa James
Holiday Lettings
t (01305) 889338
e hugojames@ukonline.co.uk
w dovehousedorset.co.uk

Greenwood Grange Farm Cottages ★★★★–★★★★★
Self Catering
Contact: Mr R P O'Brien
t (01305) 268874
e greenwoodgrange@yahoo.co.uk
w greenwoodgrange.co.uk

Hardy Country Cottages
★★★★ *Self Catering*
Contact: Mrs Frances Carroll
Hardy Country Holidays
t (01305) 889222
w hardycountrycottages.co.uk

Hastings Farm Cottages
★★★★ *Self Catering*
Contact: Mr David Hills
Hasting Farm Cottages
t (01305) 848627
e djh@hastingsfarm.freeserve.co.uk
w hastingsfarm.freeserve.co.uk

Hawthorn Cottage ★★★★★
Self Catering
Contact: Mr Alan Marshall
t (01300) 348528
e info@hawthorn-cottage.co.uk
w hawthorn-cottage.co.uk

Molly's Cottage ★★★
Self Catering
Contact: Mr & Mrs Tim & Sue Stiles
t (01300) 341514
e info@mollys-cottage.co.uk
w mollys-cottage.co.uk

Old Post Cottage ★★★
Self Catering
Contact: Mrs Annette Pitman
t (01305) 848219
e nigel@pitman70.fsnet.co.uk

The Stables ★★★★
Self Catering
Contact: Mrs Elizabeth Peckover
t (01305) 849344
e stables@epeckover.fsnet.co.uk
w stables-pallington.co.uk

Wolfeton Lodge ★★★
Self Catering
Contact: Mrs Thimbleby
Wolfeton House
t (01305) 263500
e kthimbley@wolfeton.freeserve.co.uk

DOWLISH FORD
Somerset

Number 3 New Buildings
★★★ *Self Catering*
Contact: Mrs Hillary Mead
t (01460) 61996

DOWNDERRY
Cornwall

6 Morweth Bungalow ★★★
Self Catering
Valley Villas
t (01752) 605605
e sales@valleyvillas.com
w valleyvillas.com

Beach Puffin ★★★
Self Catering
Valley Villas
t (01752) 605605
e sales@valleyvillas.com
w valleyvillas.com

Casa Piccolo ★★★
Self Catering
Valley Villas
t (01752) 605605
e sales@valleyvillas.com
w valleyvillas.com

The Chalet – CO002 ★★
Self Catering
Contact: Mr Burns
t (01752) 404750

The Coachman ★★★★
Self Catering
Valley Villas
t (01752) 605605
e sales@valleyvillas.com
w valleyvillas.com

Greengates ★★★★
Self Catering
Valley Villas
t (01752) 605605
e sales@valleyvillas.com
w valleyvillas.com

Seagulls ★★★ *Self Catering*
Valley Villas
t (01752) 605605
e sales@valleyvillas.com
w valleyvillas.com

Sunnyside ★★★
Self Catering
Valley Villas
t (01752) 605605
e sales@valleyvillas.com
w valleyvillas.com

Treguna Cottage ★★★
Self Catering
Valley Villas
t (01752) 605605
e sales@valleyvillas.com
w valleyvillas.com

DOWNINGTON
Gloucestershire

The Gallery ★★★★
Self Catering
Contact: Mr Martin Forbes
t (01367) 253393
e mas.forbes@btopenworld.com
w thegallerybridgehouse.co.uk

DRAYCOTT
Somerset

Martindale ★★★
Self Catering
Contact: Mr & Mrs Dance
Leighurst, The Street
t (01934) 742811
e helge@tesco.net
w martindale-cottage.co.uk

DRAYNES
Cornwall

Badgers Holiday Cottages
★★★-★★★★ *Self Catering*
Contact: Mr Phil Harris
t (01579) 320741
e phil.harris@btinternet.com
w badgersholidaycottages.co.uk

DREWSTEIGNTON
Devon

Clifford Barton Holiday Cottages ★★★ *Self Catering*
Contact: Mrs Susan Butler-Cole
t (01647) 24763 & (01647) 24266
e mail@cliffordbarton.co.uk
w cliffordbarton.co.uk

East Underdown ★★★★★
Self Catering
Contact: Mr Tim Clarke
t (01647) 231339
e timclarke@eastunderdown@prodigynet.co.uk

Gardeners Cottages
★★★★★ *Self Catering*
Contact: Mr & Mrs Thomas
t (01647) 281602

DRIFFIELD
Gloucestershire

The Stables ★★★★
Self Catering
Contact: Mrs Margaret Smith
t (01285) 850641
e me_smith@btinternet.com

DRYBROOK
Gloucestershire

Bishopswood House
★★★★★ *Self Catering*
Contact: Mrs J Freeman
t (01594) 545992
e jfreeman@mffreeman.co.uk
w bishopswoodhouse.co.uk

Coach House ★★★
Self Catering
Contact: Mrs Gillian Marfell
t (01594) 542278
e coach-house@marfell.co.uk
w marfell.f9.co.uk/coachhouse/coachhouse.htm

Forest View Annexe
Rating Applied For
Self Catering
Contact: Mr David Meek
t (01594) 543763
e sparkybudge1@tiscali.co.uk

DULVERTON
Somerset

1 Lower Spire ★★★
Self Catering
Contact: Mrs Cherry Aston
t (01494) 562138
e cherrya@gotasdl.co.uk

Anstey Mills Cottages
★★★★ *Self Catering*
Contact: Mrs Doris Braukmann-Pugsley
t (01398) 341329
e ansteymills@yahoo.com
w ansteymillscottagedevon.co.uk

Deer's Leap Country Cottages ★★★★
Self Catering
Contact: Mrs Heather Fuidge
Deer's Leap Country Cottages
t (01398) 341407
e deersleapcottages@lineone.net
w deersleap.com

Liscombe Farm & Riding Stables ★★★★ *Self Catering*
Contact: Mrs Sally Wade
Liscombe Farm Holiday Cottages
t (01643) 851551
e info@liscombefarm.co.uk
w liscombefarm.co.uk

Northmoor House & Lodge
★★★★ *Self Catering*
Contact: Mr Robin Nicholson
t (01398) 323720
e enquiries@bucklandhouse.co.uk
w northmoorhouse.co.uk

Paddons ★★★ *Self Catering*
Contact: Mrs Mary McMichael
t (01398) 323514
e marymcmichael@waitrose.com

Venford Cottage ★★★★
Self Catering
Contact: Mr Harley Stratton
t (01398) 341308
e harleyhstratton@aol.com
w venfordcottage.co.uk

Whitehall House ★★★★
Self Catering
Contact: Mr Kevin Reeves
t (01329) 665792
e kevin.reeves4@ntlworld.com
w whitehallhouse.f9.co.uk

Woolcotts Cross Cottage
★★★★ *Self Catering*
Contact: Mr Iain Joyce
t (01398) 371456
e iainjoyce@freeola.com
w woolcotts.com

DUNSTER
Somerset

Cedar House Cottages
★★★★ *Self Catering*
Contact: Mr & Mrs David & Christine Holmes
t (01984) 640437
e enquiries@cedarhousesomerset.co.uk
w cedarhousesomerset.co.uk

Duddings Country Cottages
★★★★ *Self Catering*
Contact: Mr Richard Tilke
Duddings Country Holidays
t (01643) 841123
e richard@duddings.co.uk
w duddings.co.uk

Grooms Cottage ★★★★
Self Catering
Contact: Mrs Disney
t (01643) 821497

Pound ★★★ *Self Catering*
Contact: Mrs Sherrin
t (01643) 821366

The Studio and Courtyard Flats ★★★ *Self Catering*
Contact: Mrs G Harwood
t (01643) 821485
e harwoods.dunster@ntlworld.com

DUNTERTON
Devon

Sherrill Farm Holiday Cottages
Rating Applied For
Self Catering
Contact: Mr Ian Prout
t (01822) 870150
e enquiries@sherrillfarmdolifaycottages.co.uk
w Sherrillfarmholidaycottages.co.uk

DUNTISBOURNE ROUSE
Gloucestershire

Swallow Barns ★★★★★
Self Catering
Contact: Mr & Mrs Anthony & Jean Merrett
t (01285) 651031
e anthony.merrett@homecall.co.uk
w cottageinthecountry.co.uk

DURSLEY
Gloucestershire

The Stable ★★★★
Self Catering
Contact: Mrs Sarah Randall
t (01453) 860728
e thegranary@fsmail.net

Two Springbank ★★★
Self Catering
Contact: Mrs Freda Jones
32 Everlands
t (01453) 543047
e lhandfaj32lg@surefish.co.uk

EAST ALLINGTON
Devon

Flear Farm Cottages
★★★★-★★★★★
Self Catering
Contact: Mr Steven Dix
t (01548) 521227
e flearfarm@btinternet.com
w flearfarm.co.uk

Higher Coombe Farm Cottages ★★★★
Self Catering
Contact: Mrs Nicki Fothergill
Higher Coombe Farm
t (01548) 521566
e stay@highercoombefarm.co.uk
w highercoombefarm.co.uk

Honeysuckle Barn ★★★★
Self Catering
Contact: Mrs Rita Jeanette Pickering
t (01548) 521309
e info@honeysucklebarn.com
w honeysucklebarn.com

Pitt Farm ★★★★
Self Catering
Contact: Mr & Mrs Christopher & Denise Bates
t (01548) 521234
e info@pitt-farm.co.uk
w pitt-farm.co.uk

Winnowers ★★★★
Self Catering
Toad Hall Cottages
t (01548) 853089
e thc@toadhallcottages.com

EAST BUDLEIGH
Devon

Brook Cottage ★★★★
Self Catering
Contact: Mrs Jo Simons
Foxcote
t (01242) 574031
e josimons@tesco.net
w brookcottagebudleigh.co.uk

EAST CHALDON
Dorset

Kay's Cottage ★★★
Self Catering
Contact: Noel Hosford
Heart of Dorset
t (01258) 880248
w heartofdorset.co.uk

Rex Officio
Rating Applied For
Self Catering
Contact: Mrs Rosemary Hodder
t (01305) 858205
e rh@chaldronherring.co.uk
w cottage-holiday-dorset.co.uk

EAST CHINNOCK
Somerset

Weston House ★★★★
Self Catering
Contact: Mrs Susan Gliddon
t (01935) 863712
e sue@westonhouse.net
w westonhouse.net

EAST DOWN
Devon

Higher Churchill Farm
★★★★ *Self Catering*
Marsdens Cottage Holidays
t (01271) 813777
e holidays@marsdens.co.uk
w marsdens.co.uk

EAST HILL
Devon

The Hay House ★★★★
Self Catering
Contact: Mrs Catherine Oates
t (01404) 812122
e catherine@blacklakefarm.com
w blacklakefarm.com

EAST HUNTSPILL
Somerset

Wall Eden Farm Holidays
★★★ *Self Catering*
Contact: Mr Andrew Wall
Wall Eden Farm
t (01278) 786488
e info@walledenfarm.co.uk
w walledenfarm.co.uk

EAST KNIGHTON
Dorset

Dairy House Cottage ★★★
Self Catering
Contact: Mr Zachary Stuart-Brown
Dream Cottages
t (01305) 789000
e admin@dream-cottages.co.uk
w dream-cottages.co.uk

Lovers Knot ★★★
Self Catering
Contact: Mr Zachary Stuart-Brown
Dream Cottages
t (01305) 789000
e admin@dream-cottages.co.uk
w dream-cottages.co.uk

Oaktree Cottage ★★★
Self Catering
Contact: Mr Zachary Stuart-Brown
Dream Cottages
t (01305) 789000
e admin@dream-cottages.co.uk
w dream-cottages.co.uk

EAST KNOYLE
Wiltshire

Spring Cottage ★★★★★
Self Catering
Contact: Mr Nicholas Pash
Hideaways
t (01747) 828170
e enq@hideaways.co.uk
w hideaways.co.uk

EAST LOOE
Cornwall

Admiralty Court Apartments
★★★★ *Self Catering*
Contact: Mrs Sheila Summers
t (01503) 264617
e admiraltycourt@hotmail.co.uk

Endymion ★★★★★
Self Catering
Contact: Mr David Pearn
t (01503) 262244 & 07768 333924
e endymion@exclusivevacations.co.uk
w exclusivevactions.co.uk/endymion

Fox Valley Cottages
★★★–★★★★★
Self Catering
Contact: Mr & Mrs Andy & Linda Brown
Lanlawren
t (01726) 870115
e lanlawren@lycos.com
w foxvalleycottages.co.uk

Quayside ★★ *Self Catering*
Contact: Mrs Butters
t (01503) 262533

Quayview ★★★ *Self Catering*
Contact: Miss Tonia Lewis
t (01503) 265377
e lewis.looebakery@breathemail.net

EAST PORTLEMOUTH
Devon

Ferryside ★★★★
Self Catering
Contact: Miss Sally Green
Portlemouth Estates Ltd
t (01548) 842210
e portlemouth.estates@virgin.net

Two West Waterhead
★★★★ *Self Catering*
Contact: Mr & Mrs Stokes
t (0117) 951 6333

EAST PRAWLE
Devon

Higher House Farm ★★★
Self Catering
Contact: Mrs Vicky Tucker
t (01548) 511332
e tuckersatprawle@btconnect.com
w eastprawlefarmholidays.co.uk

EAST STOUR
Dorset

Crown Inn ★★★★
Self Catering
Contact: Mr Samuel Holmes
t (01747) 838866
e crown.inn@tiscali.co.uk
w go.to/thecrowninn

EAST TAPHOUSE
Cornwall

Higher Penhole Cottages
Rating Applied For
Self Catering
Contact: Mrs Denise Taylor
t (01579) 321687
e denisetaylor-29@hotmail.com
w higherpenholecottages.co.uk

EASTERTON
Wiltshire

Stable End ★★★
Self Catering
Contact: Mrs Anne Blagbrough
t (01380) 812426
e anne@ablagbrough.fsnet.co.uk

EBRINGTON
Gloucestershire

Pump Cottage ★★★
Self Catering
Contact: Mr Robert Hutsby
t (01789) 841525
e robert.hutsby@btinternet.com
w chipping-campden-holiday-cottages.co.uk/pump.htm

Tythe Barn Cottage ★★★★
Self Catering
Contact: Mrs Michelle Sharp
t (01386) 854824
e info@tythebarn.co.uk
w tythebarn.co.uk

EDINGTON
Wiltshire

Greengrove Cottage ★★★★
Self Catering
Hoseasons Country Cottages
t 0870 534 2342
e mail@hoseasons.co.uk
w hoseasons.co.uk/images/2002/ukcottages/cottages/aa98.html

EDMONTON
Cornwall

Honey and Cowrie Cottages
★★★ *Self Catering*
Contact: Mr Hoole
t (01709) 370034
e bobhoole@blueyonder.co.uk

Quarryman's Cottages ★★★
Self Catering
Criafol, 17 Granville Terrace
t 07866 386611
e jenkins@choicecornishcottages.com
w choicecornishcottages.com

Squirrel Cottage ★★★
Self Catering
Contact: Gail Oliver
t 07968 033927
w sunshinecottages.com

Willow Cottage ★★★★
Self Catering
Contact: Mr David Oram
t (01709) 530128
e droram@btopenworld.com

EGLOSHAYLE
Cornwall

Watermill Cottage ★★★
Self Catering
Contact: Mrs Varcoe
t (01208) 895127
e varcoeuk@aol.com
w watermillcottage.co.uk

ELKSTONE
Gloucestershire

The Dolls House ★★★
Self Catering
Contact: Mrs Marion Cooch
t (01242) 870244
e marioncooch@hotmail.co.uk

ENGLISH BICKNOR
Gloucestershire

Upper Tump Farm ★★★
Self Catering
Contact: Mr & Mrs Merrett
t (01594) 860072

ETLOE
Gloucestershire

Oatfield Country Cottages
★★★★–★★★★★
Self Catering
Contact: Mr & Mrs Julian & Pennie Berrisford
Oatfield Farmhouse & Cottages
t (01594) 510372
w oatfieldfarm.co.uk

EVENLODE
Gloucestershire

2 Rose Terrace ★★★★
Self Catering
Contact: Ms Richards
Manor Cottages
t (01993) 824252
e mancott@netcomuk.co.uk
w manorcottages.co.uk

EXETER
Devon

Augusta Court ★★★★★
Self Catering
Contact: Ms Juliet Ware
t (01392) 477727
e enquiries@wareedwards.co.uk
w wareedwards.com

Bussells Farm Cottages
★★★★ *Self Catering*
Contact: Andy and Lucy Hines
Bussells Farm
t (01392) 841238
e bussellsfarm@aol.com
w bussellsfarm.co.uk

Coach House Farm
★★★★★ *Self Catering*
Contact: Mr & Miss John & Polly Bale
Coach House Farm
t (01392) 461254
e selfcatering@mpprops.co.uk

Fairwinds Holiday Bungalow
★★★★ *Self Catering*
Contact: Mrs Maria Price
t (01392) 832911
e fairwindshotbun@aol.com
w fairwinds-4stars.co.uk

The Garden House ★★★★
Self Catering
Contact: Mr & Mrs Hugh & Anna Evans
t (01392) 211286
e anna@realcakes.co.uk
w exeterholidaycottage.co.uk

Mr Sage, Exeter Holiday Homes ★★★ *Self Catering*
Contact: Mr William Sage
Exeter Holiday Homes
t (01392) 271668
e gina.birchmore@btopenworld.com
w exeter-holiday-homes.co.uk

EXFORD
Somerset

No 2 Auction Field Cottage
★★★ *Self Catering*
Contact: Mr & Mrs Keith & Gill Batchelor
t (01258) 817801

Bailiffs Cottage ★★★
Self Catering
Contact: Mr Martin Burnett
t (01643) 831342
e joyceburnett@onetel.net
w bailiffscottage.f9.co.uk

Cascade Cottage ★★★★
Self Catering
Contact: Mr Marc Watts
t (01643) 831495
w edgcotthouse.co.uk

Court Farm ★★★–★★★★
Self Catering
Contact: Mrs Beth Horstmann
t (01643) 831207
e beth@courtfarm.co.uk
w courtfarm.co.uk

Holly Tree Cottage ★★★
Self Catering
Contact: Mr Chris Budd
t (01420) 588577

Riscombe Farm Holiday Cottages and Stabling, Exford ★★★★ *Self Catering*
Contact: Mr & Mrs Brian & Leone Martin
Riscombe Farm Holiday Cottages and Stabling
t (01643) 831480
e info@riscombe.co.uk
w riscombe.co.uk

Rocks Bungalow ★★★★
Self Catering
Contact: Mrs Kathryn Tucker
t (01643) 831213
e enquiries@stetfold.wanadoo.co.uk
w rocksbungalow.f9.co.uk

Stilemoor Bungalow ★★★★
Self Catering
Contact: Mrs Joan Atkins
t (01643) 831564
e info@stilemoorexmoor.co.uk
w stilemoorexmoor.co.uk

Westermill Farm
★★★–★★★★ *Self Catering*
Contact: Mr & Mrs Oliver & Jill Edwards
t (01643) 831238
e swt@westermill.com
w westermill.com

EXMOUTH
Devon

2 & 4 Channel View ★★★★
Self Catering
Contact: Mr & Mrs Cliff & Sandra Lenn
St Andrews Holiday Homes
t (01395) 222555
e st-andrews@lineone.net

Pilot Cottage ★★★★
Self Catering
Contact: Mr & Mrs Woods
t (01395) 222882
e seahorse@exmouth.net
w exmouth.net

Queenswood ★★★★
Self Catering
Holiday Homes & Cottages South West
t (01803) 663650
e holcotts@aol.com
w swcottages.co.uk

Saxonbury Annexe ★★★
Self Catering
Contact: Dr & Mrs John & Josephine Elliott
t (01395) 264323
e elliottjojohn@aol.com

EYPE
Dorset

Railway Cottage ★★★
Self Catering
Contact: Ms Kirsty Parker
Dream Cottages
t (01305) 789000
e admin@dream-cottages.co.uk
w dream-cottages.co.uk

Sealark ★★★ *Self Catering*
Contact: Mrs Jill Lodge
Ships Light Cottage
t (01308) 425902
e Jill@eypehouse.co.uk
w eypechaletpark.co.uk

FALMOUTH
Cornwall

39 Lower Stables ★★★★
Self Catering
Helford River Holidays
t (01326) 250278
e enquiries@holidaycornwall.co.uk
w holidaycornwall.co.uk

47 Upper Stables ★★★
Self Catering
Helford River Holiday Ltd
t (01326) 250278
e enquiries@holidaycornwall.co.uk
w holidaycornwall.co.uk

55 Upper Maen Cottage
★★★★ *Self Catering*
Helford River Holidays
t (01326) 250278
e enquiries@holidaycornwall.co.uk
w holidaycornwall.co.uk

65 Lower Maen Cottage
★★★★ *Self Catering*
Helford River Holidays Ltd
t (01326) 250278
e enquiries@holidaycornwall.co.uk
w holidaycornwall.co.uk

69 Maen Barn ★★★★
Self Catering
Helford River Holiday Ltd
t (01326) 250278
e enquiries@holidaycornwall.co.uk
w holidaycornwall.co.uk

73 Upper Barn ★★★★
Self Catering
Helford River Holiday Ltd
t (01326) 250278
e enquiries@holidaycornwall.co.uk
w holidaycornwall.co.uk

78 Nursery Cottage ★★★★
Self Catering
Helford River Holidays Ltd
t (01326) 250278
e enquiries@holidaycornwall.co.uk

8 Marine Crescent ★★
Self Catering
Contact: Mrs Pauline Spong
42 Westleigh Avenue
t (01702) 712596
e rcspong@hotmail.com
w cornwall-online.co.uk/self-catering/falmouth/8marinecrescent

91 Keepers Barn ★★★★
Self Catering
Helford River Cottages
t (01326) 250278
e enquiries@holidaycornwall.co.uk
w holidaycornwall.co.uk

Anchorage Apartments
★★★ *Self Catering*
Contact: Mr & Mrs Cain
t (01326) 312164
e anchorapts@aol.com
w anchorageapartments.co.uk

Bay View Self Catering
★★★ *Self Catering*
Contact: Mrs Walker
t (01326) 312429
e bay.viewfalmouth@btinternet.com
w bayviewselfcatering.co.uk

Baywatch ★★ *Self Catering*
Cornish Cottage Holidays
t (01326) 573808
e enquiry@cornishcottageholidays.co.uk
w cornishcottageholidays.co.uk

Captain's Corner
★★★-★★★★ *Self Catering*
Special Places in Cornwall
t (01872) 864400
e office@specialplacescornwall.co.uk
w specialplacescornwall.co.uk

Captain's Lookout ★★★
Self Catering
Contact: Mr Fishwick
t (01326) 312651
e mfishwick@aol.com

Chris Old's Home ★★★
Self Catering
Contact: Mr Old
t (01736) 763751
e letitia.rivettold@btconnect.com
w chrisold.co.uk

Coach House Loft ★★★★
Self Catering
Contact: Ms Emily Boriosi
Cornish Holiday Cottages
t (01326) 250339
e emily@cornishholidaycottages.net

The Crags No 22 ★★★★
Self Catering
Helford River Holidays
t (01326) 250278
e enquiries@holidaycornwall.co.uk
w holidaycornwall.co.uk

The Custodian's House
★★★★★ *Self Catering*
English Heritage Holiday Cottages
t 0870 333 1187
w english-heritage.org.uk/holidaycottages

Falmouth Beach Resort Apartments ★★★-★★★★
Self Catering
Contact: Ms Ramsden
t (01326) 310500
e info@falmouthbeachhotel.co.uk
w falmouthbeachhotel.co.uk

The Foredeck ★★★★★
Self Catering
Little Barn
t (01749) 870230
e derekpages@aol.com

Good-Winds Holiday Apartments ★★★
Self Catering
Contact: Mrs Goodwin
Good-Winds Holiday Apartments
t (01326) 313200
e goodwinds13@aol.com

Harbours Reach ★★★★
Self Catering
Contact: Tim Peace
t 07710 252583
e info@falmouth-waterfront-holidays.co.uk
w falmouth-waterfront-holidays.co.uk

Harbourside Apartments
★★★ *Self Catering*
Contact: Mr Malcolm Brain
t (01326) 316501
e brain@swanpoolhouse.fsnet.co.uk

Honeysuckle Corner ★★★
Self Catering
Contact: Ms Emily Boriosi
Cornish Holiday Cottages
t (01326) 250339
e emily@cornishholidaycottages.net
w cornishholidaycottages.net/get_property.php?p=36

Imperial Court Upper Deck
Rating Applied For
Self Catering
Contact: Mrs Butterworth
Holiday Homes & Cottages South West
t (01803) 663650
e holcotts@aol.com
w swcottages.co.uk

Kinbrae Holiday Apartments
★★ *Self Catering*
Contact: Mrs Jean Primrose
t (01326) 315529

Mistral ★★★★ *Self Catering*
Contact: Julie Drage
t (01326) 372248
e mistral.port@virgin.net
w cornwall-online.co.uk

Mylor Yacht Harbour
★★★★ *Self Catering*
Contact: Miss Celeste Gagnon
t (01326) 372121
e celeste@mylor.com
w mylorharbourside.com

Pantiles ★★★ *Self Catering*
Contact: Mr & Mrs Kemp
Pantiles
t (01326) 211838
e colinkemp@lineone.net
w colinkemp.plus.com

Parklands ★★★ *Self Catering*
Contact: Mrs Jenny Simmons
t (01277) 654425
e jenny@simmo58.freeserve.co.uk

Pendra Loweth Holiday Cottages ★★★★
Self Catering
Contact: Mr Hick
t (01326) 312190
e pendraloweth@aol.com
w pendra.co.uk

Penmarric ★★ *Self Catering*
Contact: Ms Lumley
Around Kernow Holidays
t (01872) 571575
e nfo@ak-hols.co.uk
w ak-hols.co.uk

Pennant Cottage ★★★★
Self Catering
Cornish Cottage Holidays
t (01326) 573808
e enquiry@cornishcottageholidays.co.uk

Seagulls ★★★ *Self Catering*
t (01326) 250339
e emily@cornishholidaycottages.net
w cornishholidaycottages.net/property/port_pendennis/seagulls.html

Southcroft ★★★
Self Catering
Contact: Mrs Sthuthridge
t (01326) 314361
e anthony@stuthridge7767.fsnet.co.uk

Toldeen ★★ *Self Catering*
Special Places in Cornwall
t (01872) 864400
e office@specialplacescornwall.co.uk
w specialplacescornwall.co.uk

Tredova ★★★ *Self Catering*
Contact: Mrs Valerie Challands
t (01509) 554641
e thechallands@ntlworld.com

Vale Apartment ★★★
Self Catering
Contact: Mr Angove
t (01326) 315588

West Winds ★★★-★★★★
Self Catering
Contact: Mr & Mrs Watmore
t (01326) 211707
e holiday@west-winds-apt.fsnet.co.uk
w cornwall-online.co.uk/west-winds

Wodehouse Place ★★★
Self Catering
Contact: Ms Shelagh Spear
t (01326) 314311
w visitcornwall.co.uk/wodehouseplace

FARWAY
Devon

Church Approach Cottages
★★★ *Self Catering*
Contact: Mrs Sheila Lee
t (01404) 871383
e lizlee@eclipse.co.uk
w churchapproach.co.uk

FAULKLAND
Somerset

The Green Farm ★★★★★
Self Catering
Contact: Mrs Anne Gatley
The Green Farm House
t (01373) 834331
e anne@gatleyemail.co.uk

Lime Kiln Farm ★★★★★
Self Catering
Contact: Mrs Merinda Kendall
t (01373) 834305
e lime_kiln@hotmail.com
w limekilnfarm.co.uk

FENNY BRIDGES
Devon

Skinners Ash Farm ★★★★
Self Catering
Contact: Mrs Jill Godfrey
t (01404) 850231
w skinners-ash-farm.co.uk

FEOCK
Cornwall

Brambles ★★★ *Self Catering*
Cornish Cottage Holidays
t (01326) 573808
e enquiry@cornishcottageholidays.co.uk
w cornishcottageholidays.co.uk

Penhale Cottages ★★
Self Catering
Contact: Mrs Copeland
t (01872) 862369
e jinty@trevilla.com

Seaview Farm Cottage ★★★
Self Catering
Special Places in Cornwall
t (01872) 864400
e office@specialplacescornwall.co.uk
w specialplacescornwall.co.uk

Trelissick East ★★★★
Self Catering
Special Places in Cornwall
t (01872) 864400
e office@specialplacescornwall.co.uk
w specialplacescornwall.co.uk

FERNDOWN
Dorset

The Bungalow ★★★
Self Catering
Contact: Mrs Annette Leach
t (020) 8241 7498
e annette.leach@blueyonder.co.uk
w geocities.com/bournemouth3

Church Farm ★★★
Self Catering
Contact: Mr Andrew Ross
t (01202) 579515
w churchfarmcottages.co.uk

FIFEHEAD MAGDALEN
Dorset

Top Stall ★★★ *Self Catering*
Contact: Mrs Kathleen Jeanes
t (01258) 820022
e factoryfarm@agriplus.net

FISHPOND
Dorset

Coombe Ridge – X4344
★★★★ *Self Catering*
Lyme Bay Holidays
t (01297) 443363
e email@lymebayholidays.co.uk
w lymebayholidays.co.uk

FLUSHING
Cornwall

Clottage ★★★★
Self Catering
Special Places in Cornwall
t (01872) 864400
e office@specialplacescornwall.co.uk
w specialplacescornwall.co.uk

Sea Pie Cottage ★★★★
Self Catering
Special Places in Cornwall
t (01872) 864400
e office@specialplacescornwall.co.uk
w specialplacescornwall.co.uk

Trevissome House Marine
★★ *Self Catering*
Contact: Mr & Mrs Kulpa
t (01326) 374605
e info@trevissomehouse.com
w trevissomehouse.com

Waterside House ★★★★
Self Catering
Special Places in Cornwall
t (01872) 864400
e office@specialplacescornwall.co.uk
w specialplacescornwall.co.uk

FOLKE
Dorset

Folke Manor Farm Cottages
★★★★ *Self Catering*
Contact: Mr & Mrs John & Carol Perrett
Folke Manor Farm
t (01963) 210731
e folkemanorfarm@aol.com

Glebe House – Guests' Suite
★★★★ *Self Catering*
Contact: Mr S Friar
t (01963) 210337
e glebehouse.dorset@btinternet.com
w glebehouse-dorset.co.uk

FONTHILL BISHOP
Wiltshire

Rose Cottage ★★★
Self Catering
Contact: Mr Nicholas Pash
Hideaways
t (01747) 828170
e enq@hideaways.co.uk
w hideaways.co.uk

FORRABURY
Cornwall

Sunnybank ★★★
Self Catering
Contact: Dr Helen Young
t (020) 8894 6722
e helenyoung@tufts.edu

FORTUNESWELL
Dorset

Cama Cottage ★★★★
Self Catering
Contact: Mr Zachary Stuart-Brown
Dream Cottages
t (01305) 789000
e admin@dream-cottages.co.uk
w dream-cottages.co.uk

Hill Top ★★★ *Self Catering*
Contact: Mrs Chrissie Wilkinson
t (01305) 775335
e cw@atft.co.uk

Ocean Views ★★★
Self Catering
Contact: Mr Charles Gollop
t (020) 8408 9800
e charles@oceanviews.uk.com
w oceanviews.uk.com

Pear Shape Cottage ★★★
Self Catering
Dream Cottages
t (01305) 789000
e admin@dream-cottages.co.uk
w dream-cottages.co.uk

FOWEY
Cornwall

17a St Fimbarrus Road
★★★ *Self Catering*
Contact: Mr David Hill
Fowey Harbour Cottages (W Hill & Son)
t (01726) 832211
e hillandson@talk21.com
w foweyharbourcottages.co.uk

Chy Vounder and Rose Villa
★★ *Self Catering*
Contact: Mr David Hill
Fowey Harbour Cottages (W Hill & Son)
t (01726) 832211
e hillandson@talk21.com
w foweyharbourcottages.co.uk

Crow's Nest & West Wing
★★★★ *Self Catering*
Estuary Cottages
t (01726) 832965
e info@estuarycottages.co.uk
w estuarycottages.co.uk

The Dolphins at Penlee
★★★★★ *Self Catering*
Contact: Mr Gittus
t (01299) 400447
e john.gittus@btopenworld.com
w qualityholidaylets.com

Harbour Cottage ★★★
Self Catering
Contact: Mr David Hill
Fowey Harbour Cottages (W Hill & Son)
t (01726) 832211
e hillandson@talk21.com
w foweyharbourcottages.co.uk

Palm Trees ★★ *Self Catering*
Contact: Mr David Hill
Fowey Harbour Cottages (W Hill & Son)
t (01726) 832211
e hillandson@talk21.com
w foweyharbourcottages.co.uk

The Penthouse ★★★
Self Catering
Contact: Mr David Hill
Fowey Harbour Cottages (W Hill & Son)
t (01726) 832211
e hillandson@talk21.com
w foweyharbourcottages.co.uk

River Watch ★★★★
Self Catering
Estuary Cottages
t (01726) 832965
e info@estuarycottages.co.uk
w estuarycottages.co.uk

Sideways Cottage ★★★★
Self Catering
Contact: Mr David Hill
Fowey Harbour Cottages (W Hill & Son)
t (01726) 832211
e hillandson@talk21.com
w cottagesofcornwall.co.uk

Square Rig Holidays ★★★★
Self Catering
t (01726) 832965
e info@estuarycottages.co.uk
w sqrighol.co.uk

FRADDAM
Cornwall

Deveral House ★★★
Self Catering
Contact: Mrs Ruth Trewhella
t (01736) 850730
e trewhellas@tesco.net
w deveralhouse.co.uk

FRAMPTON
Dorset

Wellbridge ★★ *Self Catering*
Contact: Mr Ian Barrett
t (01300) 341103
e ianbarrett@d-i-c.co.uk

FRAMPTON-ON-SEVERN
Gloucestershire

Old Priest Cottage, Old Stable Cottage and The Malthouse
★★★★–★★★★★
Self Catering
Contact: Mr & Mrs Mike & Caroline Williams
Tanhouse Farm
t (01452) 741072
e tanhouse.farm@lineone.net
w tanhouse-farm.co.uk

FRESHFORD
Somerset

The Barton Cottage ★★★
Self Catering & Serviced Apartments
Contact: Mrs Foster
t (01225) 429756

Dolphin Cottage ★★★★★
Self Catering
Contact: Mrs Rowena Wood
t (01225) 722100
e rowena_wood@compuserve.com
w dolphincottage.com

FRITHELSTOCK
Devon

Fuchsia Cottage
Rating Applied For
Self Catering
Contact: Mrs Ruth Blake
t (01805) 601330
e info@hollamoor.co.uk
w hollamoor.co.uk

Honeysuckle Cottage
★★★★ *Self Catering*
Contact: Lucy Ellison
Farm & Cottage Holidays
t (01237) 479146
e enquiries@farmcott.co.uk
w holidaycottages.co.uk

Knaworthy
Rating Applied For
Self Catering
Contact: Lucy Ellison
Farm & Cottage Holidays
t (01237) 479146
e enquiries@farmcott.co.uk
w holidaycottages.co.uk

FROGPOOL
Cornwall

Pulla Farm Holidays ★★★
Self Catering & Serviced Apartments
Contact: Mr & Mrs Richards
t (01872) 863143
e enquiries@pullafarmholidays.co.uk
w pullafarmholidays.co.uk

FROME
Somerset

Bollow Hill Farm ★★★★
Self Catering
Contact: Mr & Mrs Mark & Emma Kaye
t (01373) 463007
w farmhousecottages.co.uk

Executive Holidays
★★★★★ *Self Catering*
Contact: Mr R A Gregory
Executive Holidays
t (01373) 452907 & 07860 147525
e info@executiveholidays.co.uk
w executiveholidays.co.uk

Hill View ★★ *Self Catering*
Contact: Mrs Margaret House
t (01985) 844276
e wells@packsaddle11.freeserve.co.uk

Lazy Dog Cottage
Rating Applied For
Self Catering
Contact: Sophie Elkins
t (01373) 855275
e sophie@lazydogcottage.co.uk
w lazydogcottage.co.uk

St Katharine's Lodge
★★★★ *Self Catering*
Contact: Mrs Tania Maynard
t (01373) 471434
e info@stkaths.com
w stkaths.com

FROME VAUCHURCH
Dorset

Pieta ★★★ *Self Catering*
Contact: Jim & Sarah Bruckel
Mill Cottage
t (01300) 320774
e harasbruckel@hotmail.com
w pietaholiday.co.uk

GALMPTON
Devon

Barnacle Cottage ★★★
Self Catering
Contact: Mrs Phyllis Norman
t (01803) 842309
e pipnorman@aol.com
w portbarnaclecottagesdevon.co.uk

Dart View ★★★ *Self Catering*
Contact: Mr Ian Butterworth
Holiday Homes & Cottages South West
t (01803) 663650
e holcotts@aol.com
w swcottages.co.uk

Georgia ★★★ *Self Catering*
Holiday Homes & Cottages South West
t (01803) 663650
e holcotts@aol.com
w swcottages.co.uk

GARA BRIDGE
Devon

Gara Bridge Cottages
★★★★-★★★★★
Self Catering
Contact: Mr David Hanmer
Toad Hall Cottages
t (01548) 853089
e thc@toadhallcottages.com
w toadhallcottages.com

GEORGE NYMPTON
Devon

East Trayne Cottage ★★★★
Self Catering
Contact: Mrs Janet Cornwell
Marsdens Cottage Holidays
t (01271) 813777
e holidays@marsdens.co.uk
w marsdens.co.uk

GEORGEHAM
Devon

Ash Croft
Rating Applied For
Self Catering
Contact: Mr Peter Cornwell
Marsdens Cottage Holidays
t (01271) 813777
e holidays@marsdens.co.uk
w marsdens.co.uk

Bryher ★★★★ *Self Catering*
Contact: Mrs Janet Cornwell
Marsdens Cottage Holidays
t (01271) 813777
e holidays@marsdens.co.uk
w marsdens.co.uk

Burver Cottage ★★★★
Self Catering
Marsdens Cottage Holidays
t (01271) 813777
e holidays@marsdens.co.uk
w marsdens.co.uk

Kingscote ★★★★
Self Catering
Mardens Cottage Holidays
t (01271) 813777
e enquiries@marsdens.co.uk
w marsdens.co.uk

Kingsley ★★★ *Self Catering*
Marsdens Cottage Holidays
t (01271) 813777
e holidays@marsdens.co.uk
w marsdens.co.uk

Pickwell Barton Cottages
★★-★★★ *Self Catering*
Contact: Mrs Jane Cook
t (01271) 890994
e jane@pickwellbarton.co.uk
w pickwellbarton.co.uk

Rock Cottage ★★
Self Catering
Contact: Mrs Janet Cornwell
Marsdens Cottage Holidays
t (01271) 813777
e holidays@marsdens.co.uk
w marsdens.co.uk

Tythe Home
Rating Applied For
Self Catering
Marsdens Cottage Holidays
t (01271) 813777
e holidays@marsdens.co.uk
w marsdens.co.uk

Westcliff Cottage ★★★★
Self Catering
Contact: Mrs Janet Cornwell
Marsdens Cottage Holidays
t (01271) 813777
e holidays@marsdens.co.uk
w marsdens.co.uk

GILLINGHAM
Dorset

Whistley Waters ★★★
Self Catering
Contact: Mrs Cleo Campbell
t (01747) 840666
e campbell.whistley@virgin.net
w whistleywaters.co.uk

Woolfields Barn ★★★★
Self Catering
Contact: Mr & Mrs Thomas
Woolfields Barn
t (01747) 824729
e OThomas453@aol.com
w woolfieldsbarn.co.uk

GLANVILLES WOOTTON
Dorset

Churchill Cottage ★★★★
Self Catering
Contact: Mrs Rachel Rich
t (01963) 210827

The Stables ★★★★
Self Catering
Contact: Mr & Mrs Bernard Rich
Brookmead
t (01963) 210209

GLASTONBURY
Somerset

The Annexe at Cherrytrees B&B ★★★ *Self Catering*
Contact: Ms Stephanie Mathivet
t (01458) 830069
e mail@smathivet.free-online.co.uk
w cherrytrees.org.uk

Avalon Cottage ★★★★
Self Catering
Contact: Mrs Barbara Champion
t (0121) 288 5878
e abrachampion@hotmail.com
w avaloncottageholidays.co.uk

The Lightship ★★★
Self Catering
Contact: Ms Rose
t (01458) 833698
e roselightship2001@yahoo.co.uk
w lightship.ukf.net

MapleLeaf Middlewick Holiday Cottages ★★★★
Self Catering
Middlewick Holiday Cottages
t (01458) 832351
e middlewick@btconnect.com
w middlewickholidaycottages.co.uk

St Edmunds Cottage ★★★★
Self Catering
Contact: Mrs Jeannette Heygate-Browne
t (01458) 830461
e rheygatebrowne@aol.com
w stedmundscottage.com

GLOUCESTER
Gloucestershire

Barncastle, Pitchcombe
★★★★★ *Self Catering*
Contact: Mrs Valerie King
Brook Farm
t (01452) 814207
w barncastle.co.uk

Middletown Farm Cottages, Upleadon ★★★★
Self Catering
Contact: Mrs Judy Elkins
t (01531) 828237
e cottages@middletownfarm.co.uk
w middletownfarm.co.uk

Norfolk House ★★★
Self Catering
Contact: Mrs Patricia Jackson
t (01452) 300997
e nor39@fsmail.net

Sydenham House ★★★★
Self Catering
Contact: Mrs Jennifer Treasure
t (01702) 474318
e jktreasure@msn.com
w visitgloucester.co.uk

GODMANSTONE
Dorset

Trinity Cottage ★★
Self Catering
Contact: Ms Kirsty Parker
Dream Cottages
t (01305) 789000
e admin@dream-cottages.co.uk
w dream-cottages.co.uk

GODNEY
Somerset

Swallow Barn ★★★★
Self Catering
Contact: Mrs Hilary Millard
Double-Gate Farm Holidays
t (01458) 832217
e doublegatefarm@aol.com
w doublegatefarm.com

GODOLPHIN CROSS
Cornwall

Winterbourne ★★★★
Self Catering
Contact: Ms Sharrow Lawry
t (01446) 771963
e sharrow@lawry21.wanadoo.co.uk

GOLANT
Cornwall

Penquite Farm Holidays
★★★★-★★★★★
Self Catering
Contact: Mr & Mrs Varco
t (01726) 833319
e varco@farmersweekly.net
w penquitefarm.co.uk

South Torfrey Farm ★★★★
Self Catering
Contact: Mr & Mrs Andrews
t (01726) 833126
e debbie.andrews@southtorfreyfarm.com
w southtorfreyfarm.com

GOODLEIGH
Devon

Bampfield Cottages ★★★★
Self Catering
Contact: Ms Lynda Thorne
t (01271) 346566
w bampfieldfarm.co.uk

Mistletoe Cottage ★★★
Self Catering
Contact: Mrs Linda Moore
t (01271) 321502
e andrew.moore777@btinternet.com

GOODRINGTON
Devon

43 Louville Close ★★★
Self Catering
Holiday Homes & Cottages South West
t (01803) 663650
e holcotts@aol.com
w swcottages.co.uk

GOONBELL
Cornwall

The Old Post office ★★★★
Self Catering
Duchy Holidays
t (01872) 572971
e enquiries@duchyholidays.co.uk
w duchyholidays.co.uk

GOONHAVERN
Cornwall

Honeysuckle Cottage
Rating Applied For
Self Catering
Contact: Mrs Yvonne Nelson
t (01872) 540556
e yvonnenelson@tesco.net
w littlewatercottageholidays.co.uk

GOONOWN
Cornwall

Goonown Barn Cottages
★★★ *Self Catering*
Contact: Mrs Butson
t (01872) 553654

GORRAN
Cornwall

Dovecote ★★★★
Self Catering
Contact: Mrs Welsh
t (01726) 842295
e treveague@btconnect.com

GORRAN HAVEN
Cornwall

Haven Cottage and Seamew
★★★★ *Self Catering*
Contact: Mr Debbage
t (0115) 987 9184
e gorranhavencottages@hotmail.com
w gorranhavencottages.co.uk

Meadow Croft
Rating Applied For
Self Catering
Contact: Mrs Spencer
t (01872) 864400
e office@specialplacescornwall.co.uk
w specialplacescornwall.co.uk

Oakroyd ★★★ *Self Catering*
Contact: Mrs Helena Payne
t (01726) 842546
e hrjpayne@tiscali.co.uk

Tregillan ★★★ *Self Catering*
Contact: Mrs Sally Pike
Tregillan
t (01726) 842452
e tregillanapartment@tiscali.co.uk
w tregillanapartments.co.uk

GOVETON
Devon

The Granary ★★★★
Self Catering
Contact: Sylvia Blomeley
Toad Hall Cottages
t (01548) 853089
e thc@toadhallcottages.com
w toadhallcottages.co.uk

Hope Cottage ★★★
Self Catering
Contact: Mr David Hanmer
Toad Hall Cottages
t (01548) 853089
e thc@toadhallcottages.com
w toadhallcottages.com

GRAMPOUND
Cornwall

The Keep ★★★ *Self Catering*
Contact: Leonie Iddison
Roseland Holiday Cottages
t (01872) 580480
e enquiries@roselandholidaycottages.co.uk
w roselandholidaycottages.co.uk

GRAMPOUND ROAD
Cornwall

The Garden Cottage
★★★★★ *Self Catering*
Niche Retreats
t (01209) 890272
e info@nicheretreats.co.uk
w nicheretreats.co.uk

Ralph's Barn ★★★
Self Catering
Contact: Mr Blake
t (01726) 882222
e ralph01@gotadsl.co.uk

GREAT ASHLEY
Wiltshire

Great Ashley Farm Cottage
★★★★ *Self Catering*
Contact: Mrs Helen Rawlings
Great Ashley Farm
t (01225) 864563
e info@greatashley.co.uk
w greatashley.co.uk

GREAT CHEVERELL
Wiltshire

Downswood ★ *Self Catering*
Contact: Mrs Ros Shepherd
Downswood
t (01380) 813304

GREAT RISSINGTON
Gloucestershire

The Dairy Barn ★★★★
Self Catering
Manor Cottages
t (01993) 824252
e mancott@netcomuk.co.uk
w manorcottages.co.uk

Daisy's Cottage ★★★★★
Self Catering
Contact: Ms Kate Cleverly
t (01451) 820129

GREAT WITCOMBE
Gloucestershire

Witcombe Park Holiday Cottages ★★★ *Self Catering*
Contact: Mrs Cecilia Hicks-Beach
t (01452) 863591

GRITTENHAM
Wiltshire

Orchard View ★★★★
Self Catering
Contact: Mrs Sue Cary
t (01666) 510747
e susan.cary@btinternet.com

GUITING POWER
Gloucestershire

Little Barnfield ★★★★
Self Catering
Contact: Ms Anne Dawson
t (01451) 850664
e anne_dawson_opera@yahoo.co.uk

GULVAL
Cornwall

Barn Cottage ★★★
Self Catering
Contact: Mr Barrie Hockley
t (01952) 415349
e barncottage@blueyonder.co.uk

Barton Woods Cottage
★★★★ *Self Catering*
Contact: Mr & Mrs Markham
t (01354) 653578

The Cart House ★★★
Self Catering
Contact: Mrs Amanda Simons
t (01736) 350789
e robertandmandy@tiscali.co.uk

Mount View ★★
Self Catering
Peacked Rocks Cottage
t (01594) 861119
e helen@peakedrockscottage.fsnet

Old Court 36 Kenegie Manor
★★ *Self Catering*
t (01902) 845139
e mary@margellen.fsnet.co.uk
w kenegie.com

Ponsandane Farm Cottages
★★★★ *Self Catering*
Contact: Mrs Zoe Jelbert
t (01736) 331974
e zoe.jelbert@btopenworld.com
w chycor.co.uk/cottages/gulval-ponsandane/index-ctb.htm

The Retreat ★★ *Self Catering*
Peaked Rocks Cottage
t (01594) 861119
e helen@peakedrockscottage.fsnet
w evansholidays.co.uk

Rosemorran Holiday Cottages ★★★ *Self Catering*
Contact: Mrs Shirley Leah
t (01736) 361479

GWEEK
Cornwall

Old Mill Studio ★
Self Catering
Contact: Mrs Anne Nicholas
t (01326) 221217

Woodlands ★★★★
Self Catering
Contact: Mr Martin Raftery
Mullion Cottages
t 0845 066 7766
e enquiries@mullioncottages.com

GWINEAR
Cornwall

Lanyon ★★★★-★★★★★
Self Catering
Contact: Mr & Mrs Leggo
t (01736) 850795

HALLEGAN
Cornwall

Country Haven ★★★★
Self Catering
Contact: Mr & Mrs Chown
t (01209) 832854
e chownpeter@aol.com
w countryhaven.co.uk

HALSE
Somerset

West Hayes Barn ★★★★★
Self Catering
Contact: Kate Rucklidge
t (01823) 431622
e k.rucklidge@btinternet.com
w westhayesbarn.co.uk

HALSETOWN
Cornwall

Blackberry Cottage ★★★
Self Catering
Contact: Mrs Adams
t (0121) 354 7442
e nettieadams@blueyonder.co.uk

HALWILL
Devon

Anglers Paradise
★★★★-★★★★★
Self Catering
Contact: Mr Zyg Gregorek
t (01409) 221559
w anglers-paradise.co.uk

HARCOMBE
Devon

Chapel Cottage ★★★
Self Catering
Contact: Mr Tim Tandy
Jean Bartlett Cottage Holidays
t (01297) 23221
e holidays@jeanbartlett.com
w jeanbartlett.com

Riverside Cottage Harcombe
★★★★ *Self Catering*
Contact: Tim Tandy
Jean Bartlett Cottage Holidays
t (01297) 23221
e holidays@jeanbartlett.com
w jeanbartlett.com

HARDINGTON MANDEVILLE
Somerset

Stable Cottage ★★★
Self Catering
Contact: Lucy Ellison
Farm & Cottage Holidays
t (01237) 479146
e enquiries@farmcott.co.uk
w holidaycottages.co.uk

HARLYN BAY
Cornwall

Flat 1 Yellow Sands ★★★
Self Catering
Contact: Ms Nickie Stanley
Harbour Holidays, Padstow
t (01841) 533402
e nickiestanley@btconnect.com
w harbourholidays.co.uk

Harlyn Farmhouse ★★★★
Self Catering
t (0117) 962 4831
e hazelperry@blueyonder.co.uk

Harlyn Inn Self Catering
★★★★ *Self Catering*
t (01841) 520207
e mail@harlyn-inn.com
w harlyn-inn.com

Polmark House Apartments
★★★–★★★★ *Self Catering*
Contact: Mr Watts
t (01841) 520206
e reception@polmark.co.uk
w polmark.co.uk

Polwen ★★★★ *Self Catering*
Contact: Mrs Stanley
Harbour Holidays
t (01841) 533402
e contact@harbourholidays.co.uk
w harbourholidays.co.uk

The Red House ★★★★
Self Catering
Contact: Mrs Nicky Stanley
Harbour Holidays
t (01841) 533402
e contact@harbourholidays.co.uk
w harbourholidays.co.uk

Sandpipers ★★★
Self Catering
Contact: Ms Cathy Osborne
Cornish Horizons Holiday Cottages
t (01841) 533331
e cottages@cornishhorizons.co.uk
w cornishhorizons.co.uk

Yellow Sands Apartments & House ★★★–★★★★
Self Catering
Contact: Mr Dakin
t (01841) 520376
e martin@yellowsands.fsnet.co.uk
w yellowsands.net

HARTLAND
Devon

Coastguard Cottage ★★★★
Self Catering
Contact: Mrs Janet Cornwell
Marsdens Cottage Holidays
t (01271) 813777
e holidays@marsdens.co.uk
w marsdens.co.uk

Longfurlong Holiday Cottages ★★★★–★★★★★
Self Catering
Contact: Mr & Mrs John & Janet Cockrill
t (01237) 441337
e longfurlong@longfurlong.eurobell.co.uk
w longfurlongcottages.co.uk

Mettaford Farm Cottages
★★★–★★★★ *Self Catering*
Contact: Mrs Janet Cornwell
Marsdens Cottage Holidays
t (01271) 813777
e holidays@marsdens.co.uk
w marsdens.co.uk

The Old Dairy & Polly's Cottage ★★★–★★★★
Self Catering
Contact: Mrs Heywood
t (01237) 441268
e sue@gorvincottages.co.uk

The Pynes
Rating Applied For
Self Catering
Farm & Cottage Holidays
t (01237) 479146
e enquiries@farmcott.co.uk
w holidaycottages.co.uk

West Tosberry Farm ★★★★
Self Catering
Contact: Mr Clive Edwards
t (01237) 441476
e contact@countryhouseplus.co.uk
w countrycottageplus.co.uk

HATHERLEIGH
Devon

Lower Upcott Farm ★★★
Self Catering
Contact: Mr Ben May
t (01837) 811123
e ben@holiday-farm.co.uk
w holiday-farm.co.uk

HAWKCHURCH
Devon

Angels Farm Apartment
★★★ *Self Catering*
Contact: Mrs Anne Gibbins
t (01297) 678295
e angels.farm@virgin.net
w cottageguide.co.uk/angelsfarm

Cider Cottage 1 ★★★★
Self Catering
Contact: Mr David Matthews
Lyme Bay Holidays
t (01297) 443363
e email@lymebayholidays.co.uk
w lymebayholidays.co.uk

Cider Cottage 2 ★★★★
Self Catering
Contact: Mr David Matthews
Lyme Bay Holidays
t (01297) 443363
e email@lymebayholidays.co.uk
w lymebayholidays.co.uk

Pound House Wing – W4414 ★★★★ *Self Catering*
Lyme Bay Holidays
t (01297) 443363
e email@lymebayholidays.co.uk
w lymebayholidays.co.uk

Sandford Cottage ★★★★
Self Catering
Contact: Mr & Mrs Golding
t (01297) 678440
e petergolding@ic24.net
w sandfordcottage.co.uk

HAWKRIDGE
Somerset

West Hollowcombe Cottages ★★★★
Self Catering
Contact: Lucy Ellison
Farm & Cottage Holidays
t (01237) 479146
e enquiries@farmcott.co.uk
w holidaycottages.co.uk

HAYLE
Cornwall

74 Gwithian Towans ★★★
Self Catering
Contact: Ms Nicola Skinner
t (01277) 822924
e rayandnic@skinnersfamily.f2s.com

Brunnion Barns ★★★★
Self Catering
Contact: Mr & Mrs Pash
Hideaways
t (01747) 828170
e enq@hideaways.co.uk
w hideaways.co.uk/property.cfm/h620

Chyreene Court ★★★
Self Catering
Contact: Miss Bailie
t (01736) 756651
e sarahbailie@hotmail.com
w chyreenecourt.co.uk

Copper Terrace ★★★
Self Catering
Duchy Holidays
t (01872) 572971
e enquiries@duchyholidays.co.uk
w duchyholidays.co.uk

Darnhall ★ *Self Catering*
Contact: Mrs Astbury
t (01606) 593628

Drannack Vean ★★
Self Catering
Contact: Mrs Hosking
t (01736) 756686
e papahosk@onetel.net.uk

Manor House ★★★★
Self Catering
Powells Cottage Holidays
t (01834) 812791
e info@powells.co.uk
w powells.co.uk

Penellen ★★★ *Self Catering*
Contact: Mrs Jeanette Beare
t (01736) 753777

Truthwall Farm ★★★
Self Catering
Contact: Mrs Sheila Goldsworthy
t (01736) 850266
e truthwallfarmhouse@Tiscali.co.uk
w http://myweb.tiscali.co.uk/truthwallfarmhouse

HELE
Devon

Hele Payne Farm Cottages
★★★★ *Self Catering*
Contact: Mrs S A Maynard
t (01392) 881530
e info@helepayne.co.uk
w helepayne.co.uk

HELFORD
Cornwall

The Barns ★★★★
Self Catering
Helford River Cottages
t (01326) 231666
e info@helfordrivercottages.co.uk
w helfordrivercottages.co.uk

Bridge Cottage ★★★
Self Catering
Helford River Cottages
t (01326) 231666
e info@helfordcottages.co.uk
w helfordcottages.co.uk

The Cottage ★★★
Self Catering
Helford River Cottages
t (01326) 231666
e info@helfordcottages.co.uk
w helfordcottages.co.uk

Dowr Penty ★★★
Self Catering
Helford River Cottages
t (01326) 231666
e info@helfordcottages.co.uk
w helfordcottages.co.uk

Laloma Cottage ★★★
Self Catering
Helford River Cottages
t (01326) 231666
e info@helfordcottages.co.uk
w helfordcottages.co.uk

Pear Tree Cottage ★★★★
Self Catering
Contact: Mrs Cathy Crozier
t (01208) 850081
e catherine_crozier@yahoo.co.uk

Popigale Cottage ★★★
Self Catering
Helford River Cottages
t (01326) 231666
e info@helfordcottages.co.uk
w helfordcottages.co.uk

Rose Cottage ★★★★
Self Catering
Helford River Cottages
t (01326) 231666
e info@helfordcotages.co.uk
w helfordcottages.co.uk

Wednesday Cottage ★★★★
Self Catering
Helford River Cottages
t (01326) 231666
e info@helfordcottages.co.uk
w helfordcottages.co.uk

Well House ★★★
Self Catering
Helford River Cottages
t (01326) 231666
e info@helfordcottages.co.uk
w helfordcottages.co.uk

West View & Halvose Cottages ★★★★
Self Catering
Helford River Cottages
t (01326) 231666
e info@helfordcottages.co.uk
w helfordcottages.co.uk

HELFORD PASSAGE
Cornwall

Hove To ★★★ *Self Catering*
Helford River Holidays Ltd
t (01326) 250278
e enquiries@holidaycornwall.co.uk

Treath Vean ★★★
Self Catering
Helford River Holidays Ltd
t (01326) 250278
e enquiries@holidaycornwall.co.uk

HELLANDBRIDGE Cornwall

Lower Helland Farm Cottages ★★★ *Self Catering*
Contact: Mrs Astrid Coad
t (01208) 72813
e cottages@lowerhellandfarm.co.uk
w lowerhellandfarm.co.uk

HELLESVEOR Cornwall

Padgy Vesa ★★★★
Self Catering
Powells Cottage Holidays
t (01834) 813232
e info@powells.co.uk
w powells.co.uk

HELSTON Cornwall

3 Coastguards Cottage, Mullion Cove ★★★★
Self Catering
Contact: Mrs Meg Reed
t (01326) 281001
e meg.reed@email.com

5 Coastguard Cottage ★★★
Self Catering
Contact: Mr Martin Raftery
Mullion Cottages
t 0845 066 7766
e enquiries@mullioncottages.com
w mullioncottages.com

Burncoose Farmhouse ★★★
Self Catering
Contact: Mr Martin Raftery
Mullion Cottages
t 0845 066 7766
e enquiries@mullioncottages.com
w mullioncottages.com

Carminowe View ★★★★
Self Catering
Contact: Mr Huddleston
Carminowe View
t (01275) 848899
e jhuddl2144@aol.com

The Crag ★★★ *Self Catering*
Contact: Mr Martin Raftery
Mullion Cottages
t 0845 066 7766
e enquiries@mullioncottages.com
w mullioncottages.com

Midsummer Barn ★★★★
Self Catering
Contact: Mr Martin Raftery
Mullion Cottages
t 0845 066 7766
e enquiries@mullioncottages.com
w mullioncottages.com

Mudgeon Vean Farm Holiday Cottages ★★★
Self Catering
Contact: Mr & Mrs Trewhella
Mudgeon Vean Farm Holiday Cottages
t (01326) 231341
e mudgeonvean@aol.com
w cornwall-online.co.uk/mudgeon-vean/ctb.htm

The Nook ★★★ *Self Catering*
Contact: Mr Martin Raftery
Mullion Cottages
t 0845 066 7766
e enquiries@mullioncottages.com
w mullioncottages.com

Pebble Dene ★★★★
Self Catering
Contact: Mr Martin Raftery
Mullion Cottages
t 0845 066 7766
e enquiries@mullioncottages.com
w mullioncottages.com

Sunrise and Sunset Barns ★★★★ *Self Catering*
Mullion Cottages
t 0845 066 7766
e enquiries@mullioncottages.com
w mullioncottages.com

Tenderah ★★★★
Self Catering
Contact: Mr Martin Raftery
Mullion Cottages
t 0845 066 7766
e enquiries@mullioncottages.com
w mullioncottages.com

Tregevis Farm ★★★★
Self Catering
Contact: Mrs Julie Bray
t (01326) 231265
e tregevis@ntlworld.com

Tregoose Farmhouse ★★★★ *Self Catering*
Contact: Mrs Hazel Bergin
Tregoose Farmhouse
t (01736) 751749
e arcj88@dsl.pipex.com
w tregooselet.co.uk

HELSTONE Cornwall

Mayrose Farm ★★★
Self Catering
Contact: Mrs Jane Maunder
t (01840) 213509
e info@mayrosefarmcottages.co.uk
w mayrosefarmcottages.co.uk

HENWOOD Cornwall

Clouds Hill Cottage ★★★★★ *Self Catering*
Contact: Mr Stephen Bennett
t (020) 8993 2628
e stephen@cloudshillcottage.co.uk
w cloudshillcottage.co.uk

Henwood Barns ★★★
Self Catering
Contact: Miss Willisson
t (01579) 363576
e henwoodbarns@aol.com
w henwoodbarns.co.uk

HERSHAM Cornwall

Woodhall ★★★★
Self Catering
Contact: Veronica Chouffot
t (01288) 356991
e v_chouffot@hotmail.com

HESSENFORD Cornwall

2 West End Cottage ★★★★
Self Catering
t (01752) 605605
e sales@cornishcottage.uk.com

HEWELSFIELD Gloucestershire

Hunters Cottage ★★★
Self Catering
Contact: Mrs Rebecca Thompson-Weissbort
Hunters Lodge
t (01594) 530467
e gweissbort@yahoo.com
w hunterscottage.co.uk

HEYWOOD Wiltshire

Ashe Cottage and The Wilderness ★★★★★
Self Catering
Contact: Mr John Boyce
Heywood Holiday Cottages
t (01225) 868393
e enquiries@ashecottage-holidaylets.co.uk
w ashecottage-holidaylets.co.uk

Pine Lodge ★ *Self Catering*
Contact: Mrs Mary Prince
t (01373) 822949
e pinelodgex@aol.com
w pinelodge.info

HIGH BICKINGTON Devon

Barn Owl Cottage ★★★★
Self Catering
Marsdens Cottage Holidays
t (01271) 813777
e holidays@marsdens.co.uk
w marsdens.co.uk

The Corn Mill & Lee Meadow ★★★★★
Self Catering
Contact: Mrs Glenda Tucker
t (01769) 560796
w lee-barton.co.uk

Millbrook Cottages ★★★★
Self Catering
Contact: Miss Kate Jones
t (01769) 561904
e kate@millbrookcottages.co.uk
w millbrookcottages.co.uk

Weirmarsh Farm – Big Barn ★★★★ *Self Catering*
Contact: Mrs Philipa May
t (01769) 560338
e pip@weirmarsh-big-barn-devon.co.uk
w weirmarsh-big-barn-devon.co.uk

HIGHAMPTON Devon

The Bolt Hole ★★★★
Self Catering
Contact: Sylvia Bromeley
Toad Hall Cottages
t (01548) 853089
e thc@toadhallcottages.com
w toadhallcottages.co.uk

Kingslake ★★★ *Self Catering*
Contact: Mrs Valerie Langdown
Kingslake Farm
t (01409) 231401
e vlangdown@talk21.com
w kingslakes.co.uk

No 10 Lakeview Rise ★★★★ *Self Catering*
Contact: Mr & Mrs Peter & Margery Mathews
Kimberley
t (01844) 347204
e margejulepete@aol.com
w lakeviewrise.com

Orchard House & 11 Lakeside View ★★★★-★★★★★
Self Catering
Contact: Mrs Sames
t (01296) 747425
e j.l.pearce@tesco.net
w lakeviewrise.co.uk

HIGHBRIDGE Somerset

The Cottage ★★★★
Self Catering
Contact: Mrs Sarah Alderton
Greenacre Place
t (01278) 785227
e sm.alderton@btopenworld.com
w greenacreplace.com

HILLERSLAND Gloucestershire

Barn Cottage
Rating Applied For
Self Catering
Contact: Mrs Ann Dartnell
t (01594) 837115
e barnhaiserfd@aol.com

HILLHEAD Devon

Ferryman's View ★★★★
Self Catering
Contact: Mrs Adele Barnes
Blue Chip Vacations
t (01803) 855282
e info@bluechipvacations.com
w bluechipvacations.com/dartmouth/dartmouth_ferrymans.php

HILPERTON Wiltshire

Ashton Lodge Cottage ★★★
Self Catering
Contact: Mrs Daphne Richards
t (01225) 751420
e daphne.richards@blueyonder.co.uk

HILTON Dorset

Crown Farm ★★★
Self Catering
Contact: Mrs Pamela Crocker
t (01258) 880259

HINTON ST GEORGE Somerset

Summer Hill Cottage ★★★★ *Self Catering*
Contact: Mr & Mrs Leslie & Joan Farris
t (01460) 74475
e lesfarris@cix.co.uk
w summerhillcottage.co.uk

HOLBETON Devon

Carswell Cottages ★★★-★★★★ *Self Catering*
Contact: Mrs Katherine Harding
Carswell Farm Cottages
t (01752) 830020
e enquiries@carswellcottages.com
w carswellcottages.com

HOLCOMBE
Devon

Manor Farm ★★★
Self Catering
Contact: Mr & Mrs H & J Clemens
t (01626) 863020
e humphreyclem@aol.com
w farmaccom.com

HOLCOMBE ROGUS
Devon

Whipcott Heights ★★★★
Self Catering
Contact: Mrs Sue Gallagher
t (01823) 672339
e bookings@oldlimekiln.freeserve.co.uk

HOLSWORTHY
Devon

Beech House ★★★★
Self Catering
Contact: Mrs Heard
t (01409) 253339

Higher Sellick Farm Cottages ★★★★
Self Catering
Contact: Mrs Denise Grafton
t (01409) 271456
e denisegrafton@devonholidays.org
w devonholidays.org

Leworthy Cottage
Rating Applied For
Self Catering
Contact: Mrs Patricia Jennings
t (01409) 259469

Teddies
Rating Applied For
Self Catering
Contact: Mr Peter Cornwell
Marsdens Cottage Holidays
t (01271) 813777
e holidays@marsdens.co.uk
w marsdens.co.uk

Thorne Manor Holiday Cottages ★★★-★★★★
Self Catering
Contact: Mr & Mrs Julian & Angela Plank
t (01409) 253342
e themanor@ex227jd.freeserve.co.uk
w thornemanor.co.uk

HOLT
Dorset

Albertine ★★ *Self Catering*
Contact: Helen North
t (01794) 368864

HOLTON HEATH
Dorset

Gateway and Woodland Cottages ★★★ *Self Catering*
Contact: Mrs Trudi Murray
t (01202) 625562
e admin@holtonlee.co.uk
w cadetech.co.uk/cottages

HOLWORTH
Dorset

2 North Holworth Cottages ★★★ *Self Catering*
Contact: Mrs Celia Thorne
North Holworth Cottages
t (01305) 852922

Aura Holworth ★★★
Self Catering
Contact: Mr Zachary Stuart-Brown
Dream Cottages
t (01305) 789000
e admin@dream-cottages.co.uk
w dream-cottages.co.uk

HOLYWELL
Dorset

Pippins Cottage ★★★
Self Catering
Contact: Mr Zachary Stuart-Brown
Dream Cottages
t (01305) 789000
e admin@dream-cottages.co.uk
w dream-cottages.co.uk

HOLYWELL BAY
Cornwall

Bracken ★★★ *Self Catering*
Duchy Holidays
t (01872) 572971
e enquiries@duchyholidays.co.uk
w duchyholidays.co.uk

Holywell Bay Bungalows ★★-★★★ *Self Catering*
Contact: Mrs Humphrey-Kula
t (01872) 572752

Kelseys And Sailors Cove Bungalows ★★★
Self Catering
Contact: Mrs Joy Benney
t (01637) 830031

Pennasville Holidays ★★★
Self Catering
Contact: Mr & Mrs Penna
t (01637) 830423
e enquiries@pennasville.co.uk
w pennasville.co.uk

Trevornick Cottages ★★★★
Self Catering & Serviced Apartments
Contact: Mr Paul Wright
t (01637) 832906
e paul@trevornick.co.uk
w trevornickcottages.co.uk

Watership Down ★★★
Self Catering
Contact: Ms Cathy Osborne
Cornish Horizons Holiday Cottages
t (01841) 533331
e cottages@cornishhorizons.co.uk
w cornishhorizons.co.uk

HONITON
Devon

Abbots Cottage ★★★
Self Catering
Contact: Mr Douglas Acreman
t (01992) 622685

The Haybarton ★★★★★
Self Catering
Contact: Mrs Patricia Wells
The Haybarton
t (01404) 861122
e pat@bidwellfarm.co.uk
w bidwellfarm.co.uk

Pippins ★★★ *Self Catering*
Jean Bartlett Cottage Holidays
t (01297) 23221
e holidays@jeanbartlett.com
w jeanbartlett.com

Red Doors Farm ★★★★★
Self Catering
Contact: Mr Chris Shrubb
t (01404) 890067
e info@reddoors.co.uk
w reddoors.co.uk

Sutton Barton ★★★★★
Self Catering
Contact: Mrs Teresa Cooke
t (01404) 831382
e andycooke@suttonbartonfarm.co.uk
w suttonbartonfarm.co.uk

HOOKE
Dorset

Greenlands Bungalow ★★
Self Catering
Contact: Mr Zachary Stuart-Brown
Dream Cottages
t (01305) 789000
e admin@dream-cottages.co.uk
w dream-cottages.co.uk

HOPE COVE
Devon

Sanderlings ★★★
Self Catering
Contact: Mrs Diana Middleton
t (0118) 969 0958
e diana_middleton@yahoo.com

Seascape ★★★ *Self Catering*
Contact: Mrs Hazel Kolb
t (01285) 654781
e kolb@btinternet.com
w englishholidayhouses.co.uk

Thornlea Mews Holiday Cottages ★★★ *Self Catering*
Contact: Mr & Mrs John & Ann Wilton
t (01548) 561319
e thornleamews@ukonline.co.uk
w thornleamews-holidaycottages.co.uk

HORSINGTON
Somerset

Lois Country Cottages ★★★★ *Self Catering*
Contact: Mr & Mrs Paul & Penny Constant
t (01963) 370496
e info@loisfarm.com
w loisfarm.com

HORTON
Gloucestershire

Bridle Path Cottage ★★★
Self Catering
Contact: Mr Clive Sykes
t (01244) 345700
e info@sykescottages.co.uk

HUISH CHAMPFLOWER
Somerset

The Cottage ★★★
Self Catering
Contact: Mrs Mary Reynolds
t (01984) 624915
e reynoldsmary@aol.com

HUNTLEY
Gloucestershire

The Vineary ★★★
Self Catering
Contact: Mrs Ann Snow
The Vineary
t (01452) 830006

HUNTSHAW
Devon

Bowood Barn ★★★★
Self Catering
Contact: Mrs Janet Cornwell
Marsdens Cottage Holidays
t (01271) 813777
e holidays@marsdens.co.uk
w bowoodbarn.co.uk

Primrose Cottage ★★★★
Self Catering
Marsdens Cottage Holidays
t (01271) 813777
e holidays@marsdens.co.uk
w marsdens.co.uk

HURN
Dorset

The Old Farmhouse ★★★
Self Catering
Contact: Mrs Jennifer Burford
t (01202) 479483

IBBERTON
Dorset

May Cottage ★★★
Self Catering
Contact: Mr Zachary Stuart-Brown
Dream Cottages
t (01305) 789000
e admin@dream-cottages.co.uk
w dream-cottages.co.uk

ILFRACOMBE
Devon

The Admirals House ★★★★
Self Catering
Contact: Miss Marshall
Admirals House
t (01271) 864666
e enquiries@theadmiralshouse.co.uk
w theadmiralshouse.co.uk

Ashmour ★★★★
Self Catering
Marsdens Cottage Holidays
t (01271) 813777
e holidays@marsdens.co.uk
w marsdens.co.uk

Bath Place ★★★★
Self Catering
Contact: Mrs Janet Cornwell
Marsdens Cottage Holidays
t (01271) 813777
e holidays@marsdens.co.uk
w marsdens.co.uk

Beaufort House ★★★
Self Catering
Contact: Mr Peter Cornwell
Marsdens Cottage Holidays
t (01271) 813777
e holidays@marsdens.co.uk
w marsdens.co.uk

Benricks ★★★ *Self Catering*
Contact: Mrs Janet Cornwell
Marsdens Cottage Holidays
t (01271) 813777
e holidays@marsdens.co.uk
w marsdens.co.uk

Capstone View ★★★★
Self Catering
Contact: Mrs Janet Cornwell
Marsdens Cottage Holidays
t (01271) 813777
e holidays@marsdens.co.uk
w marsdens.co.uk

Captains Quarters
Rating Applied For
Self Catering
Contact: Mr Peter Cornwell
Marsdens Cottage Holidays
t (01271) 813777
e holidays@marsdens.co.uk
w marsdens.co.uk

Cheyne Flat ★★★
Self Catering
Marsdens Cottage Holidays
t (01271) 813777
e holidays@marsdens.co.uk
w marsdens.co.uk

Cornmill Cottage ★★★★
Self Catering
Contact: Mrs Janet Cornwell
Marsdens Cottage Holidays
t (01271) 813777
e holidays@marsdens.co.uk
w marsdens.co.uk

Crab Cottage ★★★★
Self Catering
Contact: Mrs Janice Benny
Devon Harbour Cottages
t 0800 915 9894
e info@devonharbourcottages.co.uk
w devonharbourcottages.com

The Croft ★★★★
Self Catering
Contact: Mr Peter Cornwell
Marsdens Cottage Holidays
t (01271) 813777
e holidays@marsdens.co.uk
w marsdens.co.uk

Darnley Holiday Cottages
★★★ *Self Catering*
Contact: Mrs Susan Dale
t (01271) 863955
e darnleyhotel@yahoo.co.uk
w darnleyhotel.co.uk

Foxholt ★★★★ *Self Catering*
Marsdens Cottage Holidays
t (01271) 813777
e holidays@marsdens.co.uk
w marsdens.co.uk

Gull Cottage ★★★★
Self Catering
Farm & Cottage Holidays
t (01237) 479146
e enquiries@farmcott.co.uk
w holidaycottages.co.uk

Harbour View
Rating Applied For
Self Catering
Contact: Mr Peter Cornwell
Marsdens Cottage Holidays
t (01271) 813777
e holidays@marsdens.co.uk
w marsdens.co.uk

The Knapps ★★★★
Self Catering
Marsdens Cottage Holidays
t (01271) 813777
e holidays@marsdens.co.uk
w marsdens.co.uk

The Lodge & Stables & Paddocks ★★★ *Self Catering*
Contact: Mrs Janet Cornwell
Marsdens Cottage Holidays
t (01271) 813777
e holidays@marsdens.co.uk
w marsdens.co.uk

Middle Lee Farm
★★★-★★★★ *Self Catering*
Contact: Mr & Mrs Robin & Jenny Downer
t (01271) 882256
e info@middleleefarm.co.uk
w middleleefarm.co.uk

The Mill House ★★★★
Self Catering
Contact: Mrs Janet Cornwell
Marsdens Cottage Holidays
t (01271) 813777
e holidays@marsdens.co.uk
w marsdens.co.uk

Mimosa Cottage ★★★
Self Catering
Contact: Mrs Janet Cornwell
Marsdens Cottage Holidays
t (01271) 813777
e holidays@marsdens.co.uk
w marsdens.co.uk

Mostyn ★★★ *Self Catering*
Marsdens Cottage Holidays
t (01271) 813777
e holidays@marsdens.co.uk
w marsdens.co.uk

Norwood Holiday Flats
★★★ *Self Catering*
Contact: Mrs Betty Bulled
t (01271) 862370

The Round House ★★★★
Self Catering
Contact: Mrs Janet Cornwell
Marsdens Cottage Holidays
t (01271) 813777
e holidays@marsdens.co.uk
w marsdens.co.uk

Searock Apartments
★★-★★★★ *Self Catering*
Contact: Mr Peter Cornwell
Marsdens Cottage Holidays
t (01271) 813777
e holidays@marsdens.co.uk
w marsdens.co.uk

Somerset Villa ★★★
Self Catering
Contact: Mrs Janet Cornwell
Marsdens Cottage Holidays
t (01271) 813777
e holidays@marsdens.co.uk
w marsdens.co.uk

Steppings ★★★★
Self Catering
Marsdens Cottage Holidays
t (01271) 813777
e holidays@marsdens.co.uk
w marsdens.co.uk

Top Deck ★★★★
Self Catering
Marsdens Cottage Holidays
t (01271) 813777
e holidays@marsdens.co.uk
w marsdens.co.uk

Widmouth Farm Cottages
★★★ *Self Catering*
Contact: Mrs Elizabeth Sansom
t (01271) 863743
e holidays@widmouthfarmcottages.co.uk
w widmouthfarmcottages.co.uk

Woodclose Cottage ★★★
Self Catering
Toad Hall Cottages
t (01548) 853089
e thc@toadhallcottages.com
w toadhallcottages.com

ILMINSTER
Somerset

Myrtle House ★★★
Self Catering
Contact: Mr & Mrs Gordon & Marion Denman
t (01223) 871294
e denman@myrtleonline.co.uk
w appleorchard.freeserve.co.uk

INSTOW
Devon

Bath House ★★★
Self Catering
Contact: Mrs Janet Cornwell
Marsdens Cottage Holidays
t (01271) 813777
e holidays@marsdens.co.uk
w marsdens.co.uk

Chandlers Court ★★★★
Self Catering
Marsdens Cottage Holidays
t (01271) 813777
e holidays@marsdens.co.uk
w marsdens.co.uk

Driftwood ★★★★
Self Catering
Contact: Mrs Janet Cornwell
Marsdens Cottage Holidays
t (01271) 813777
e holidays@marsdens.co.uk
w marsdens.co.uk

Garden House ★★★★
Self Catering
Contact: Mrs Janet Cornwell
Marsdens Cottage Holidays
t (01271) 813777
e holidays@marsdens.co.uk
w marsdens.co.uk

Inglenook Cottage ★★★★
Self Catering
Contact: Mrs Janet Cornwell
Marsdens Cottage Holidays
t (01271) 813777
e holidays@marsdens.co.uk
w marsdens.co.uk

The Old Dairy ★★★★
Self Catering
Marsdens Cottage Holidays
t (01271) 813777
e holidays@marsdens.co.uk
w marsdens.co.uk

ISLE BREWERS
Somerset

Old School House ★★★★
Self Catering
Contact: Mrs Lynda Coles
t (01823) 443759
e ajcoles@supanet.com
w somerset-selfcatering.co.uk

ISLES OF SCILLY

1 Bay View ★★★
Self Catering
Contact: Mr Tony Dingley
Island Properties
t (01720) 422082

1 Golden Bay Mansions
★★★ *Self Catering*
Island Properties
t (01720) 422082

1 Pentland ★★ *Self Catering*
Contact: Mr Dingley
Island Properties
t (01720) 422082
e enquiries@islesofscillyholidays.com

1 Rosevean ★★★
Self Catering
t (015395) 34780
e gwyn.raymond@btopenworld.com

1 Springfield Court ★★★
Self Catering
Island Properties
t (01720) 422082
e enquiries@islesofscillyholidays.com
w islesofscillyholidays.com

10 The Strand ★★★★
Self Catering
Island Properties
t (01720) 422082
e enquiries@islesofscillyholidays.com
w islesofscillyholidays.com

12 Silver Street and 1 Porthcressa ★★★★
Self Catering
Contact: Mrs Mills
t (01923) 270533

14 Silver Street ★★★
Self Catering
Island Properties
t (01720) 422082
e enquiries@islesofscillyholidays.com
w islesofscillyholidays.com

2 Godolphin Flats ★★★★
Self Catering
Contact: Mr Dingley
Island Properties
t (01720) 422082
e enquiries@islesofscillyholidays.com

2 Telegraph Bungalows and Lemon Tree ★★★
Self Catering
Contact: Mrs Mumford
t (01720) 422650

22 Sally Port ★★
Self Catering
Island Properties
t (01720) 422082

3 & 4 Well Cross ★-★★
Self Catering
Contact: Mr Perry
t (01720) 422548

3 Bay View ★★★
Self Catering
Island Properties
t (01720) 422082
e enquiries@islesofscillyholidays.com
w islesofscillyholidays.com

3 Spanish Ledge ★★★
Self Catering
Island Properties
t (01720) 422082
e enquiries@islesofscillyholidays.com

4 Myrtle Cottages ★★★
Self Catering
Island Properties
t (01720) 422082
e enquiries@islesofscillyholidays.com
w islesofscillyholidays.com

4 Rosevean House ★★★★
Self Catering
Contact: Mr Mark Littleford
Halangy
t (01720) 423102
e booking@4roseveanhouse.co.uk
w 4roseveanhouse.co.uk

4 Silver Street ★★★
Self Catering
Contact: Mrs Julie Watt
t (01720) 423103

4 Spanish Ledge ★★
Self Catering
Island Properties
t (01720) 422082
e enquiries@islesofscillyholidays.com

5 Myrtle Cottages ★★★
Self Catering
Island Properties
t (01720) 422082
e enquiries@islesofscillyholidays.com
w islesofscillyholidays.com

5, Spanish Ledge ★★★
Self Catering
Island Properties
t (01720) 422082
e enquiries@islesofscillyholidays.com

6 Godolphin House & 8 Buzza Street ★★★
Self Catering
Contact: Mrs Hogg
t (024) 7645 0455

6 Lower Strand ★★★★
Self Catering
Contact: Mrs Susan Richards
t (01720) 422904

7 Springfield Court ★★★
Self Catering
Island Properties
t (01720) 422082
e enquiries@islesofscillyholidays.com
w islesofscillyholidays.com

7 The Strand ★★★★
Self Catering
Contact: Mr Dingley
t (01720) 422082

8 Littleporth ★★
Self Catering
Contact: Mrs Tricia Wales
The Wee Hoose
t (01243) 550 1507
e tricia.wales@virgin.net

9 Springfield Court ★★★
Self Catering
Island Properties
t (01720) 422082
e enquiries@islesofscillyholidays.com
w islesofscillyholidays.com

The Aft Cabin ★★★
Self Catering
Contact: Mr & Mrs Terry & Elizabeth Parsons
t (01720) 422393

Ajax ★★★ *Self Catering*
Island Properties
t (01720) 422082
e enquiries@islesofscillyholidays.com
w islesofscillyholidays.com

Albany Flats & Thurleigh ★★–★★★ *Self Catering*
Contact: Mrs Isabel Trenear
t (01720) 422601
e itrenear@yahoo.co.uk
w scillyflats.com

Allwinds ★★★ *Self Catering*
Contact: Mrs Lewis
Henhurst Farm
t (01435) 883239
e henhurst@hotmail.com.co.uk

Anchor Cottage ★★★
Self Catering
Island Properties
t (01720) 422082
e enquiries@islesofscillyholidays.com
w islesofscillyholidays.com

Anglesea House ★★★★
Self Catering
Island Properties
t (01720) 422082
e enquiries@islesofscillyholidays.com
w islesofscillyholidays.com

Ardwyn ★★★★ *Self Catering*
Contact: Mrs Gill Osborne
t (01720) 422986

Armorel Cottage ★★★★
Self Catering
Island Properties
t (01720) 422082
e enquiries@islesofscillyholidays.com
w islesofscillyholidays.com

Atlanta Holiday Accommodation ★★★
Self Catering
Contact: Mrs Gillian Langdon
t (01720) 422823

Avoca Holiday Homes ★★★★ *Self Catering*
Contact: Mr & Mrs Colin & Elizabeth Ridsdale
t (01720) 422656
w avocaholidayhomes.co.uk

Bar Escapade ★★
Self Catering
Island Properties
t (01720) 422082
e enquiries@islesofscillyholidays.com
w islesofscillyholidays.com

The Barn ★★★ *Self Catering*
Island Properties
t (01720) 422082
e enquiries@islesofscillyholidays.com
w islesofscillyholidays.com

Beach House Flat ★★★–★★★★ *Self Catering*
Island Properties
t (01720) 422082
e enquiries@islesofscillyholidays.com
w islesofscillyholidays.com

Beach Mooring, Flat 1, Smugglers Ride ★★★★
Self Catering
Contact: Mrs Susan Eccles
t (01872) 580997
e norman.eccles@btopenworld.com

Beggars Roost ★★
Self Catering
Contact: Mr Kenneth Peay
t (020) 8399 8364

Bella Vista
Rating Applied For
Self Catering
Contact: Mr & Mrs Chesterman
Santa Maria Guesthouse
t (01720) 422687

Bodilly Cottage ★★★
Self Catering
Island Properties
t (01720) 422082
e enquiries@islesofscillyholidays.com

Boro Chalets and Cottages ★★★–★★★★ *Self Catering*
Contact: Mrs Margaret Christopher
Boro Chalets
t (01720) 422843

Boswartreth ★★★
Self Catering
Island Properties
t (01720) 422082
e enquiries@islesofscillyholidays.com
w islesofscillyholidays.com

Bounty Ledge ★★★
Self Catering
Contact: Mr Raymond Jackman
Scillonian Estate Agency
t (01720) 422124

Buzza Ledge ★★★★
Self Catering
Contact: Mr Jeremy Phillips
t (01720) 422078
e jeremyphillips@rosecottagescilly.freeserve.co.uk

Bylet Holiday Homes ★★★
Self Catering
Contact: Mr Williams
t (01720) 422479
e thebylet@bushinternet.com
w byletholidays.com

The Captains Cabin ★★★
Self Catering
Contact: Mrs Peggy Rowe
t (01720) 422966
e peggy@rowe55.freeserve.co.uk

Carn Thomas Cottage ★
Self Catering
Contact: Mrs Eileen Denton
t (01209) 860463

Carnwethers Country House ★★★–★★★★ *Self Catering*
Contact: Mr Roy Harry Graham
t (01720) 422415

Carron Farm ★★★
Self Catering
Contact: Mrs Julia Walder
t (01720) 422893
w carronfarm.co.uk

Christmas House ★★★
Self Catering
Contact: Mrs Jane Chiverton
t (01720) 422002
e chivy002@aol.com

Church Hall Cottage ★★★★
Self Catering
Contact: Mr David Townend Schiller
t (01720) 422377
e dtownend@netcomuk.co.uk

Churchtown Farm ★★★★–★★★★★
Self Catering
Contact: Mrs Julian
t (01720) 422169
e info@churchtownfarmholidays.co.uk
w churchtownfarmholidays.co.uk

Chy Carn ★★ *Self Catering*
Contact: Mrs Leonie Marks
t (01621) 892873
e leonie.marks@btopenworld.com

Chy Kensa ★★★★
Self Catering
Contact: Mr Dingley
Island Properties
t (01720) 422082

Clemys Cottage ★★★
Self Catering
Contact: Mrs C Millard
Cattran & Sons Ltd
t (01736) 363493
e cattran@btinternet.com

Connemara Farm ★★★
Self Catering
Contact: Mr T Perkins
t (01720) 422814
e t.a.perkins@btinternet.com

Cornerways ★★★★★
Self Catering
Contact: Mr & Mrs Pritchard
t (01720) 422757

Covean Cottage Little House ★★★ *Self Catering*
Contact: Mrs Heather Sewell
Covean Cottage Little House
t (01720) 422620

The Crow's Nest ★★
Self Catering
Contact: Mrs Stella Carter
t (01235) 520317
e stella@bakehouse.supanet.com
w star-lettings.co.uk

Dolphins ★★★ *Self Catering*
Island Properties
t (01720) 422082
e enquiries@islesofscillyholidays.com
w islesofscillyholidays.com

Drinissa ★★★ *Self Catering*
Contact: Mrs Pat Hicks
t (01720) 422028

Dunmallard, Lower Flat ★★★ *Self Catering*
Contact: Mr & Mrs Elliot
t (01458) 272971

Easterhope ★★★★
Self Catering
Contact: Mrs Pauline Dart
The Turk's Head
t (01720) 422434

Look out for establishments participating in the National Accessible Scheme 

Ebor Cottage ★★★
Self Catering
Island Properties
t (01720) 422082
e enquiries@isleso fscillyholidays.com
w islesofscillyholidays.com

Escallonia ★★★★
Self Catering
Island Properties
t (01720) 422082
e enquiries@islesofscillyholidays.com

Fishermans Arms ★★★
Self Catering
Contact: Mrs Walker
t (020) 8940 9808

The Flat ★★★★ *Self Catering*
Contact: Mrs Jill May
t (01720) 422122

Flat 1 Manilla ★★★
Self Catering
Island Properties
t (01720) 422082

Flat 1 Spanish Ledge ★★★
Self Catering
t (01720) 423135

Flat 11a ★★★ *Self Catering*
Contact: Mr Tim Clifford
t (01872) 863537

Flat 2 Buccabu ★★★
Self Catering
Island Properties
t (01720) 422082

Flat 2 Madura ★★
Self Catering
Contact: Mrs Winifred A Davis
t (01736) 757811
e fredadavis@v21.me.uk

Flat 3 Rosevean ★★★
Self Catering
Contact: Mrs Eileen Talbot
t (01625) 427059
e eileen@talbot4635.freeserve.co.uk

Flat 4 Kenwyn ★★★
Self Catering
Contact: Mrs Smith
t (01823) 412845

Flat 6 Spanish Ledge ★★★
Self Catering
Contact: Mrs B Phillips
t (01720) 422345
e barbara@guthers.co.uk

Flat 9 , Revenue Cutter
★★★ *Self Catering*
Contact: Mr Timothy Clifford
Homeview Cottages Ltd
t (01872) 863537
e tcclifford@globalnet.co.uk
w selfcateringislesofscilly.co.uk

Flats 3 & 4 Pentland ★★★
Self Catering
Island Properties
t (01720) 422082
e enquiries@islesofscillyholidays.com
w islesofscillyholidays.com

Garrison Holidays
★★★-★★★★ *Self Catering*
Contact: Mr & Mrs Ted & Barbara Moulson
Garrison Cottage
t (01720) 422670
e tedmoulson@aol.com
w garrisonholidays.com

Glandore Apartments
★★★★ *Self Catering*
Contact: Mr Stephen Morris
t (01720) 422535
e apartments@glandore.co.uk
w glandore.co.uk

Glenhope & Atlanta ★★★
Self Catering
Contact: Mrs Amy Langdon
Glenhope
t (01720) 423136
e langdon.glenhope@virgin.net

Green Farm Cottage ★★★
Self Catering
Contact: Mrs Ruth Wrightt
t (01720) 422324
e wright.d@btconnect.com
w scillybulbs.co.uk

Greystones ★★★
Self Catering
Contact: Mr Tony Dingley
Island Properties
t (01720) 422082

The Guard House ★★★★★
Self Catering
Contact: Ms Philippa Sullivan
Duchy of Cornwall
t (01579) 346473
e holidays@duchyofcornwall.gov.uk
w duchyofcornwallholidaycottages.co.uk

Gunner Rock ★★★★
Self Catering
Contact: Mr & Mrs Heslin
t (01720) 422595

Harbour Lights with Smugglers Ride
★★★-★★★★ *Self Catering*
Contact: Mr Tim Clifford
t (01872) 863537
e tcclif@globalnet.co.uk
w selfcateringislesofscilly.co.uk

Harbour View
★★★-★★★★ *Self Catering*
Contact: Mr Chris Hopkins
t (01720) 422222
w bryher-ios.co.uk/hv

Harbour Walls ★★★
Self Catering
Island Properties
t (01720) 422082
e enquiries@islesofscillyholidays.com
w islesofscillyholidays.com

Haycocks ★★★ *Self Catering*
Island Properties
t (01720) 422082
e enquiries@islesofscillyholidays.com
w islesofscillyholidays.com

Hebe, Fernside & Shippen Cottage ★★★ *Self Catering*
Contact: Mrs Kristine Taylor
t (01720) 422862
w bryher-ios.co.uk/vf

The Hideaway ★★★★
Self Catering
Contact: Mr Tim Clifford
t (01872) 863537
e tcclif@globalnet.co.uk
w selfcateringislesofscilly.co.uk

Hillside Farm ★★★★
Self Catering
Contact: Mrs Ruth Jenkins
t (01720) 423156
e ruthbryher@aol.com
w bryher-ios.co.uk/HF

Hole in the Wall ★★
Self Catering
Island Properties
t (01720) 422082

Holly Cottage ★★★★
Self Catering
Contact: Mrs Jane Chiverton
Kistvaen
t (01720) 422002

Holy Vale Holiday Houses
★★★-★★★★ *Self Catering*
Contact: Mr & Mrs John & Kay Banfield
t (01720) 422429
e johnkay@holyvale.freeserve.co.uk
w holyvale.co.uk

Katrine ★★★★ *Self Catering*
Contact: Mrs J Milliken
t (01720) 422178

Kirklees Holiday Flat ★★★
Self Catering
Contact: Mr & Mrs Coldwell
t (01720) 422623

Kistvaen ★★★ *Self Catering*
Contact: Mrs Jane Chiverton
t (01720) 422002
e chivy002@aol.com

Leumeah House ★★
Self Catering
Island Properties
t (01720) 422082
e enquiries@islesofscillyholidays.com
w islesofscillyholidays.com

The Lighthouse ★★★
Self Catering
Island Properties
t (01720) 422082
e enquiries@islesofscillyholidays.com
w islesofscillyholidays.com

Little House ★★★★★
Self Catering
Contact: Ms Philippa Sullivan
Duchy of Cornwall
t (01579) 346473
e holidays@duchyofcornwall.gov.uk
w duchyofcornwallholidaycottages.co.uk

Lower Ganilly Flat ★★★
Self Catering
Island Properties
t (01720) 422082
e enquiries@islesofscillyholidays.com
w islesofscillyholidays.com

Lowertown Barn ★★★
Self Catering
Contact: Mrs Page
Garden Cottage
t (01483) 273805
e robert@gcpage.freeserve.co.uk

Lunnon Cottage, The Quillet, Medlar ★★★
Self Catering
Contact: Mrs Penny Rogers
t (01720) 422422
e jrstideford@btinternet.com

Madura I ★★★ *Self Catering*
Island Properties
t (01720) 422082
e enquiries@islesofscillyholidays.com
w islesofscillyholidays.com

Manilla Flats 2 ★★★
Self Catering
Contact: Mrs Frances Grottick
Burgundy House
t (01720) 422424

Maypole Farm ★★-★★★
Self Catering
Island Properties
t (01720) 422082
e enquiries@islesofscillyholidays.com
w islesofscillyholidays.com

Merrick ★★ *Self Catering*
Contact: Mr Tim Gutheere
t (01720) 422082

Merrion's Holiday cottage
★★★★ *Self Catering*
Contact: Mrs Valerie Thomas
t (01720) 423418
e grahamw.thomas@tiscali.co.uk

The Mill
Rating Applied For
Self Catering
Contact: Mrs C Hicks
t (01720) 422514
e fcshicks@yahoo.co.uk

Minmow Holiday Flats ★★★
Self Catering
Contact: Mr Simpson
t (01720) 422561
w scillies.freeserve.co.uk

Monaveen ★★★★
Self Catering
Island Properties
t (01720) 422082

Moonrakers Holiday Flats
★★★ *Self Catering*
Contact: Mr & Mrs R J Gregory
Moonrakers Holiday Flats
t (01720) 422717
w moonrakersholidayflats.co.uk

Morgelyn ★★★ *Self Catering*
Contact: Mrs Jane Lishman
t (01720) 422897
e morgelyn@sillyonline.co.uk
w morgelyn.co.uk

The Mount ★★★★
Self Catering
Contact: Mr Peter Loxton
t (01720) 422484

Mount Flagon ★★★★
Self Catering
Contact: Mr & Mrs Crawford
t (01720) 422598

Mount Todden Farm ★★★
Self Catering
Contact: Miss Anna Ebert
t (01720) 422311
e annaebert@mounttodden.sol.co.uk

Newfort House ★★★★
Self Catering
Island Properties
t (01720) 422082
e enquiries@islesofscillyholidays.com
w islesofscillyholidays.com

No 3 Bungalow ★★
Self Catering
Contact: Mrs Sherris
t (01720) 422496

No. 3 Godolphin House
★★★ *Self Catering*
Island Properties
t (01720) 422082
e enquiries@islesofscillyholidays.com
w islesofscillyholidays.com

An Oberva ★★ *Self Catering*
Contact: Mrs Berryman
Chy an Mor
t (01326) 574113

The Old Cottage ★
Self Catering
Contact: Mrs Pamela Lethbridge
t (01720) 422630

Peacehaven ★★★
Self Catering
Contact: Mr Bennett
t (01720) 422326

Pelistry Cottage B&B ★★★
Self Catering
Contact: Mrs A Hall
t (01720) 422059

Pengarriss ★★★
Self Catering
Contact: Mrs A Walker
t (01264) 772758

Penlee Boathouse ★★
Self Catering
Contact: Mrs Jennifer McAllister
t (029) 2064 5662
e penleeboathouse@hotmail.co.uk

Pennlyon ★★★ *Self Catering*
Contact: Mrs Marjorie Feast
Sole Agent
t (01527) 893619

Periglis Cottage ★★★
Self Catering
Contact: Mr Jimmy Paget-Brown
t (01720) 422366
e pagetbro@aol.com

Perran ★★★ *Self Catering*
Island Properties
t (01720) 422082
e enquiries@islesofscillyholidays.com
w islesofscillyholidays.com

Pharmacy Flat ★★★
Self Catering
Contact: Ms Helen Pearce
Rooftops
t (01720) 422567
e jandhpearce@tiscali.co.uk

Pilots Gig Flat ★★★★
Self Catering
Contact: Mrs Jay Holliday
The White House
t (01327) 871053

Plumb Cottage ★★★★
Self Catering
Island Properties
t (01720) 422082
e enquiries@islesofscillyholidays.com
w islesofscillyholidays.com

Porthlow Farm ★★–★★★
Self Catering
Contact: Mr Richard Woof
t (01720) 422082
e enquiries@islesofscillyholidays.com

Prospect House Flats
★★★★ *Self Catering*
Contact: Mr & Mrs Peter & Nicola Thompson
t (01720) 422948

The Retreat ★★★
Self Catering
Island Properties
t (01720) 422082
e enquiries@islesofscillyholidays.com
w islesofscillyholidays.com

Rocky Hill Chalets ★★★
Self Catering
Contact: Mrs Edwards
t (01720) 422955

Sailcheck ★★★★
Self Catering
Contact: Miss Liz Hodges
t 07879 272843
e sailcheck7@aol.com

Sallakee Farm ★★★
Self Catering
Contact: Mrs Mumford
t (01720) 422391

Sea Spray ★★★ *Self Catering*
Contact: Mrs Angela Clifford
Scilly Agency
t (01872) 863537
w islesofscillyselfcatering.co.uk

Seaways Flower Farm
★★★–★★★★ *Self Catering*
Contact: Mrs Juliet May
t (01720) 422845
w seawaysfarmholidayhomes.co.uk

Seawinds ★★★★
Self Catering
Contact: Mrs Margaret Teideman
t (01720) 422742

Serica ★★★★ *Self Catering*
Contact: David Townend
Schiller, Springfield Court
t (01720) 422293
e dtownend@netcomuk.co.uk

Shamrock ★★★★
Self Catering
Contact: Ms Tracey Guy
Shamrock Self Catering
t (01720) 423269

Shipwrights Cottage Maisonettes ★★★★
Self Catering
Contact: Mrs Margaret Lorenz
t (01720) 422522

Smugglers ★★★★
Self Catering
Contact: Mrs Niki Burns
Smugglers Cottage
t (01720) 423677
e nikirick@yahoo.co.uk

South Hill ★★★ *Self Catering*
Contact: Mrs Bennett
t (01720) 422411
e marianbennett@excite.co.uk

The Stable ★★★★
Self Catering
Contact: Mrs D Williams
The Stable
t (01720) 422810
e fiestydee2002@yahoo.co.uk

The Stables ★★★
Self Catering
Contact: Mr John Boyle
Sunset
t (01326) 563811
e john@sharkbayfilms.demon.co.uk
w sharkbayfilms.com/stables.htm

Sunny Creek ★★★
Self Catering
Island Properties
t (01720) 422082
e enquiries@islesofscillyholidays.com
w islesofscillyholidays.com

Sunnyside Holiday Flats
★★★ *Self Catering*
Contact: Mr Mike Brown
Sunnyside Flats
t (01720) 422903
e mike@sunnysideflats.co.uk
w sunnysideflats.co.uk

The Tardis ★★★
Self Catering
Contact: Mrs Margaret Helen Williams
t (01720) 422209

Teania ★★★★★
Self Catering
Contact: Mr & Mrs Keith & Dawn Bradford
Apple Tree Cottage
t (01720) 423213
e dawn.davison2@btopenworld.com

Teeki ★★★ *Self Catering*
Island Properties
t (01720) 422211

Top Flat ★★★ *Self Catering*
Contact: Mrs Christine Hosken
t (01720) 422666

Treglesyn ★★★ *Self Catering*
Contact: Dr Richard Holden
t (01943) 863260
e rick@stoneycroft27.freeserve.co.uk

Tremelethen Farm ★★★
Self Catering
Contact: Mrs Sarah Hale
t (01720) 422436
e tremelethen@tiscali.co.uk

Tresillian
Rating Applied For
Self Catering
Contact: Mrs Nan Fellows
Cherry Tree Farm
t (0121) 445 2737

Trevean ★★★★ *Self Catering*
Contact: Mrs Rosemary Sharman
Robinswood Farm
t (01929) 471210
e robin@sharman0848.freeserve.co.uk

Trevessa ★★★★
Self Catering
Contact: Mrs Browning
Wingletang Guest House
t (01720) 422381

Upper & Lower Jacksons
★★★★ *Self Catering*
Contact: Mr Tony Dingley
Island Properties
t (01720) 422082

Upper Flat, Dunmallard
★★★★ *Self Catering*
Contact: Mr & Mrs D J Poynter
t (0118) 940 3539

Verona ★★ *Self Catering*
Island Properties
t (01720) 422082
e enquiries@islesofscillyholidays.com
w islesofscillyholidays.com

Warleggan Holiday Flats
★★★ *Self Catering*
Contact: Mrs Hiron
t (01720) 422563
w warleggan.com

The White Cottage ★★★
Self Catering
Contact: Mr Tony Dingley
Island Properties
t (01720) 422082

White Cottage Flat ★★
Self Catering
Contact: Mr Dingley
Island Properties
t (01720) 422211

The White House Flat ★★★
Self Catering
Contact: Mr Bushell
t (01720) 422010

Wisteria & Jasmine Cottages
★★★–★★★★ *Self Catering*
Contact: Claire Oyler
t (01720) 422111

KELSTON
Somerset

Coombe Barn Holidays
★★★ *Self Catering*
Contact: Mr George Cullimore
t (01225) 448757
e coombe.barn@ntlworld.com
w holiday-cottages-bath.co.uk

KENTISBURY
Devon

Hollacombe Farm ★★★★
Self Catering
Contact: Mrs Celia Ryall
t (01598) 763286
e martin.ryall@btinternet.com
w hollacombefarm.co.uk

Northcote Manor Farm Holiday Cottages ★★★★
Self Catering
Contact: Mr & Mrs Peter & Pat Bunch
Northcote Manor Farm Cottages
t (01271) 882376
e info@northcotemanorfarm.co.uk
w northcotemanorfarm.co.uk

South Patchole Farm Cottage ★★★★ *Self Catering*
Contact: Mrs Wendy Heywood
t (01271) 883223
e wen@spcottages.fsnet.co.uk
w spcottages.fsnet.co.uk

KILCOT
Gloucestershire

Coach House
Rating Applied For
Self Catering
Contact: Mrs Jane Merritt
t (01989) 720417
e jane.merritt@btinternet.com

KILKHAMPTON
Cornwall

3 & 4 Penhalt (Penstowe Park) ★★★ *Self Catering*
Contact: Mr Michael Babb
t (01288) 353600
e info@penhalt.co.uk
w penhalt.co.uk

Carefree Holidays ★★
Self Catering
Contact: Mr & Mrs Alan & Geraldine Glover
t (0117) 969 3699
e carefreeholsglover1@activemail.co.uk

Penhalt Three and Four
★★★ *Self Catering*
Contact: Mrs Lin Hibbard
t (01288) 353600

South Forda Estate
★★★–★★★★ *Self Catering*
Contact: Mr & Mrs Rose
t (01288) 321524
e southforda@hotmail.com
w southfordaholidays.co.uk

Villa Nostra ★★ *Self Catering*
Contact: Ms Lea Deely
t 07773 845663
e villanostra@btinternet.com
w villanostra.co.uk

KILLIOW
Cornwall

Nansavallan Farmhouse
★★★★ *Self Catering*
Contact: Mrs Janine Withers
t (01872) 272350
e janine.withers@btinternet.com
w nansavallanfarmhouse.co.uk

KILLIVOSE
Cornwall

The Old Barn ★★★
Self Catering
Contact: Mr & Mrs Rupert & Elizabeth Wyndham
t (01209) 610104
e rupertwyndham@hotmail.com

KILMERSDON
Somerset

The Creamery ★★★★
Self Catering
Contact: Susan Knatchbull
t (01373) 812337

The Creamery 2 & 3 ★★★★
Self Catering
Contact: Mr & Mrs Susan Knatchbull & Sons
The Creamery
t (01373) 812337
w visitsouthwest.co.uk

KILMINGTON
Devon

Little Thatch – W4440 ★★★
Self Catering
Lyme Bay Holidays
t (01297) 443363
e email@lymebayholidays.co.uk
w lymebayholidays.co.uk

The Old Bakehouse ★★★★
Self Catering
Contact: Joanne Winkler
Lyme Bay Holidays
t (01297) 443363
e email@lymebayholidays.co.uk
w lymebayholidays.co.uk

KILMINGTON
Wiltshire

Stable Loft ★★★
Self Catering
Contact: Mr Nicholas Pash
Hideaways
t (01747) 828170
e enq@hideaways.co.uk
w hideaways.co.uk

KING'S NYMPTON
Devon

The Old Rectory ★★★★★
Self Catering
Contact: Ms Karen Robinson
t (01769) 580456
e info@oldrectorycottages.co.uk
w theoldrectorycottages.co.uk

Somerleigh
Rating Applied For
Self Catering
Contact: Suzanne Hazelden
The Firs
t (01769) 581710
e suzanne@walters-place.co.uk
w walters-place.co.uk

Venn Farm ★★★★
Self Catering
Contact: Mrs Pauline Cain
Ducklet Ltd
t (01769) 572448
e vennfarmcottages@msn.com
w vennfarm.com

KING'S STANLEY
Gloucestershire

The Barn
Rating Applied For
Self Catering
Contact: Fleur Alvares
t (01453) 824659
e thebarn@middleyard.co.uk
w middleyard.co.uk

KINGSBRIDGE
Devon

2 The Moorings ★★★★★
Self Catering
Contact: Mr David Alesbury
Winchester House
t 07703 320361 & 07703 320361
e davealesbury@hotmail.com
w toadhallcottages.com

Andryl, Beeson ★★★
Self Catering
Contact: Ms Beryl Wotton
t (01548) 580527

Gardeners Cottage ★★★
Self Catering
Contact: Mr Mike Miller
t (01548) 853859
e mike@kingsbridgesouthdevon.co.uk
w kingsbridgesouthdevon.co.uk

Hawke Cottage ★★★★
Self Catering
Contact: Sylvia Bromeley
Toad Hall Cottages
t (01548) 853089
e thc@toadhallcottages.com
w toadhallcottages.co.uk

The Laurels, Coach House & Coachmans Lodge
★★★–★★★★ *Self Catering*
Contact: Mrs Barbara Baker
t (01548) 511272
e barbara@sthallingtonbnb.demon.co.uk
w sthallingtonbnb.demon.co.uk

Lower Coombe Royal (Garden Rooms) ★★★★★
Self Catering
Contact: Susi Titchener
t (01548) 852880
e susi@lowercoomberoyal.co.uk
w lowercoomberoyal.co.uk

Malston Mill Farm Holiday Cottages ★★★★
Self Catering
Contact: Mr & Mrs Tony & Linda Gresham
t (01548) 852518
e gresham@malstonmill.fsnet.co.uk
w malstonmill.co.uk

Reads Farm ★★★
Self Catering
Contact: Mrs Pethybridge
Reads Farm
t (01548) 550317

Seacombe ★★★
Self Catering
Contact: Mr David Hanmer
Toad Hall Cottages
t (01548) 853089
e thc@toadhallcottages.com
w toadhallcottages.com

Sloop Cottages ★★★★
Self Catering
Contact: Mr Girling
West Buckland Cottage
t (01548) 560810
e sloop.cottages@virgin.net
w sloopholidaycottages.co.uk

Trouts Holiday Apartments
★★★★ *Self Catering*
Contact: Mrs Jill Norman
Prospect Cottage Trouts Holiday Apartments
t (01548) 511296
e trouts.holiday@virgin.net
w selfcateringdevon.com

West Charleton Grange
★★★★★ *Self Catering*
Contact: Mrs Hazel Bustin
t (01548) 531779
e admin@westcharltongrange.com
w westcharletongrange.com

Willowbank ★★★
Self Catering
Toad Hall Cottages
t 0870 077 7345

KINGSBURY EPISCOPI
Somerset

The Retreat ★★★
Self Catering
Contact: Mrs Sarah Hill
t (01935) 823500
e sarahmhill@supanet.com

KINGSDON
Somerset

The Lodge ★★★★
Self Catering
Contact: Mrs Jo Furneaux
t (01935) 841194

KINGSHEANTON
Devon

Briar Rose
Rating Applied For
Self Catering
Contact: Mr Peter Cornwell
Marsdens Cottage Holidays
t (01271) 813777
e holidays@marsdens.co.uk
w marsdens.co.uk

The Coach House ★★★★
Self Catering
Contact: Mrs Janet Cornwell
Marsdens Cottage Holidays
t (01271) 813777
e holiday@marsdens.co.uk
w marsdens.co.uk

The Welkin ★★★★
Self Catering
Marsdens Cottage Holidays
t (01271) 813777
e holidays@marsdens.co.uk
w marsdens.co.uk

KINGSTEIGNTON
Devon

Plumb Corner ★★★★
Self Catering
Holiday Homes & Cottages South West
t (01803) 663650
e holcotts@aol.com
w swcottages.co.uk

KINGSTON SEYMOUR
Somerset

Bullock Farm & Fishing Lakes ★★★ *Self Catering*
Contact: Mr & Mrs Philip & Jude Simmons
t (01934) 835020
e info@bullockfarm.co.uk

KINGSWEAR
Devon

3 The Pines ★★★★
Self Catering
Contact: Mrs Adele Barnes
Blue Chip Vacations
t (01803) 855282
e info@bluechipvacations.com

KNOWSTONE
Devon

The Barn ★★★★
Self Catering
Contact: Mrs J.M Bray
t (01398) 341224
e west.bowden@ukf.net
w westbowden.ukf.net

West Cross Side Farm
★★★★ *Self Catering*
Contact: Mr Martin Begbie
t (01398) 341288
e enquiries@devoncountryholidays.com
w devoncountryholidays.com

LACOCK
Wiltshire

Barn Cottages
Rating Applied For
Self Catering
Contact: Jane Walters
t (01249) 730013
e derek_c_walters@yahoo.co.uk

Cyder House and Cheese House ★★★★ *Self Catering*
Contact: Mr & Mrs Philip & Susan King
Cyder House and Cheese House
t (01249) 730244
e kingsilverlands2@btinternet.com
w cheeseandcyderhouses.co.uk

LAMORNA
Cornwall

Camelot ★★★★
Self Catering
Trevear Farm
t (01736) 871205
w trevearfarm.co.uk

The Cove
Rating Applied For
Self Catering
Contact: Kinga Tunnicliffe
t (01736) 731411
e reception@thecovecornwall.com
w thecovecornwall.com

Lamorna Vean ★★★★
Self Catering
Contact: Mrs Susan Searle
t (01904) 481951
e lamornavean@yorktrain.demon.co.uk
w yorktrain.demon.co.uk/lamornavean

Trevean Cottage ★★★★
Self Catering
Contact: Mrs Hood
t (01736) 731969
e info@castallack.co.uk
w castallackfarm.co.uk/trevean

LAMORNA COVE
Cornwall

Bal-Red ★★ *Self Catering*
Contact: Ms Sarah Daniel
t (01736) 731227

LANDFORD
Wiltshire

Glengariff ★★★ *Self Catering*
Contact: Ms Liz Goss
t (01794) 390206
e lizziegoss@hotmail.co.uk
w newforest-uk.com/glengariff/index.htm

LANGLEY BURRELL
Wiltshire

Cedarwood ★★★★
Self Catering
Contact: Mrs Helen Miflin
t (01249) 721500
e miflin@btinternet.com

LANGPORT
Somerset

Laurel Wharf ★★★★
Self Catering
Contact: Mr John Neale
Laurel Wharf, c/o Laurel Cottage, Westport
t (01460) 281713
e laurelwharf@hotmail.com
w laurelwharf.co.uk

The Stables at Merricks Organic Farm ★★★
Self Catering
Contact: Mrs Jane Brooke
Merricks Organic Farm
t (01458) 252901
e simon@merricksorganicfarm.co.uk
w merricksorganicfarm.co.uk

LANGRIDGE
Somerset

Langridge Studio ★★★★
Self Catering
Contact: Mr Brian Shuttleworth
t (01225) 338874
e info@langridge-studio.co.uk
w langridge-studio.co.uk

LANGTON HERRING
Dorset

Character Farm Cottages ★★★★ *Self Catering*
Contact: Mrs Jane Elwood
t (01305) 871187
e jane@mayo.fsbusiness.co.uk
w characterfarmcottages.co.uk

Hazel Copse & Orchard View ★★★ *Self Catering*
Contact: Mr Zachary Stuart-Brown
Dream Cottages
t (01305) 789000
e admin@dream-cottages.co.uk
w dream-cottages.co.uk

Zephen Properties Limited ★★★★-★★★★★
Self Catering
Contact: Mr Peter Cropper
Somerton Randle Farm
t (01458) 274767
e peter@zephen.com

LANGTON MATRAVERS
Dorset

5 North Street ★★★
Self Catering
Contact: Mrs Ann Garratt
t (01959) 565145
e garratts@dsl.pipex.com
w 5northstreet.co.uk

Bakery Cottage ★★★★
Self Catering
Dream Cottages
t (01305) 789000
e admin@dream-cottages.co.uk
w dream-cottages.co.uk

Driftwood Cottage ★★★
Self Catering
Contact: Ms Leanne Hemingway
Dorset Cottage Holidays
t (01929) 553443
e enq@dhcottages.co.uk
w dhcottages.co.uk

Flat 5 Garfield House ★★
Self Catering
Contact: Miss Susan Inge
Flat A
t (020) 7602 4945 & 07798 500437
e sueinge@hotmail.com
w langton-matravers.co.uk

Forge Cottage ★★★
Self Catering
Contact: Ms Leanne Hemingway
Dorset Cottage Holidays
t (01929) 553443
e enq@dhcottages.co.uk
w dhcottages.co.uk

Hyde View Cottage ★★★
Self Catering
Contact: Ms Leanne Hemingway
Dorset Cottage Holidays
t (01929) 553443
e enquiries@dhcottages.co.uk
w dhcottages.co.uk

Island View ★★★
Self Catering
Contact: Mr Zachary Stuart-Brown
Dream Cottages
t (01305) 789000
e admin@dream-cottages.co.uk
w dream-cottages.co.uk

Rose Cottage ★★★
Self Catering
Contact: Mrs Helen Knight
t (01929) 425184
e info@purbeckheritage.co.uk
w purbeckheritage.co.uk

Tudor Rose ★★ *Self Catering*
Dream Cottages
t (01305) 789000
e admin@dream-cottages.co.uk
w dream-cottages.co.uk

West View House ★★★★
Self Catering
Contact: Mr & Mrs Alec & Jane Brown
Lodge Farm
t (01788) 560193
e alec@lodgefarm.com
w westviewhouse.co.uk

LANGTREE
Devon

Birchill Farm ★★★★
Self Catering
Marsdens Cottage Holidays
t (01271) 813777
e holidays@marsdens.co.uk
w marsdens.co.uk

LANIVET
Cornwall

Owls Reach, Roche ★★★★
Self Catering
Contact: Diana Pride
Owls Reach
t (01208) 831597
e info@owlsreach.co.uk
w owlsreach.co.uk

Vernons Retreat ★★★★
Self Catering
Contact: Mr Osbourne
t (01841) 533331
e cottages@cornishhorizons.co.uk
w cornishhorizons.co.uk

LANNER
Cornwall

Hunters Lodge ★★★
Self Catering
Contact: Mr & Mrs Percy
t (01209) 218577
e anjen@anjen.co.uk
w anjen.co.uk

LANREATH-BY-LOOE
Cornwall

The Old Rectory, Lanreath ★★★ *Self Catering*
Contact: Mr & Mrs Chris and Julie Edge
The Old Rectory
t (01503) 220247
e ask@oldrectory-lanreath.co.uk
w oldrectory-lanreath.co.uk

LANSALLOS
Cornwall

Little Tregue
Rating Applied For
Self Catering
Contact: Mrs Kate Kellaway
t (01503) 272758
e littletregue@hotmail.com
w littletregue.co.uk

Valleybrook Holidays ★★-★★★★ *Self Catering*
Contact: Mr Holder
t (01503) 220493
e admin@valleybrookholidays.co.uk
w valleybrookholidays.co.uk

West Kellow Farmhouse ★★★★ *Self Catering*
Contact: Mrs Evelyn Julian
t (01503) 272089
e westkellow@aol.com
w westkellow.co.uk

LANTEGLOS
Cornwall

Tor Side ★★★ *Self Catering*
Valley Villas
t (01752) 605605
e sales@valleyvillas.com
w valleyvillas.com

LAUNCESTON
Cornwall

Bamham Farm Cottages ★★★★ *Self Catering*
Contact: Mrs Jackie Chapman
Bamham Farm Cottages
t (01566) 772141
e jackie@bamhamfarm.co.uk
w bamhamfarm.co.uk

Frankaborough Farm Cottages ★★★★
Self Catering
Contact: Mrs Linda Banbury
Frankaborough Farm Cottages
t (01409) 211308
e banbury960@aol.com
w devonfarmcottage.co.uk

Kingfisher Cottage ★★★★
Self Catering
Powells Cottage Holidays
t (01834) 813232
e info@powells.co.uk
w powells.co.uk

Langdon Farm Holiday Cottages ★★★-★★★★
Self Catering
Contact: Mrs Fleur Rawlinson
Langdon Farm Holiday Cottages
t (01566) 785389
e g.f.rawlinson@btinternet.com
w langdonholidays.com

Lower Dutson Farm ★★★
Self Catering
Contact: Mrs Kathryn Broad
Lower Dutson Farm
t (01566) 776456
e holidays@farm-cottage.co.uk
w farm-cottage.co.uk

Ta Mill ★★★-★★★★
Self Catering
Contact: Ms Shopland
t (01840) 261797
e helen@tamill.co.uk
w tamill.co.uk

Wheatley Cottage and Barn ★★★★ *Self Catering*
Contact: Mrs Griffin
t (01566) 781232
e valerie@wheatleyfrm.com
w chycor.co.uk/cottages/wheatley

LAVERSTOCK
Wiltshire

Rustic Cottage ★★★★
Self Catering
Contact: Mrs Cheryl Beeny
t (01722) 337870
e cheribeen@aol.com
w rustic-cottage-salisbury.co.uk

LEE
Devon

Grange Apartment ★★★★
Self Catering
Contact: Mr & Mrs Peter & Janet Cornwell
Marsdens Cottage Holidays
t (01271) 813777
e holidays@marsdens.co.uk
w marsdens.co.uk

Lincombe House ★★★
Self Catering
Contact: Mr & Mrs Ian & Cynthia Stuart
t (01271) 864834
e holidays@lincombehouse.co.uk
w lincombehouse.co.uk

Lower Campscott Farm ★★★-★★★★ *Self Catering*
Contact: Mrs Margaret Cowell
Lower Campscott Farm
t (01271) 863479
e holidays@lowercampscott.co.uk
w lowercampscott.co.uk

Smugglers Cottage ★★★★
Self Catering
Contact: Mrs Janet Cornwell
Marsdens Cottage Holidays
t (01271) 813777
e holidays@marsdens.co.uk
w marsdens.co.uk

Vine Cottage ★★★★
Self Catering
Contact: Mr & Mrs Peter & Janet Cornwell
Marsdens Cottage Holidays
t (01271) 813777
e holidays@marsdens.co.uk
w marsdens.co.uk

LEEDSTOWN
Cornwall

Little Pengelly
★★★-★★★★ *Self Catering*
Contact: Ms Maxine Millichip
t (01736) 850452
e maxine@littlepengelly.co.uk
w littlepengelly.co.uk

LELANT
Cornwall

1 Atlantic Watch ★★★★★
Self Catering
Contact: Mr & Mrs Read
t (01736) 757237
w ayianapaholidaysuk.co.uk

Beersheba Brea ★★★★
Self Catering
Contact: Mrs Victoria Jelbert
t 07795 284356
e info@beersheba.co.uk
w beersheba.co.uk

Gonwin Farm Cottages
Rating Applied For
Self Catering
Contact: Mr & Mrs Wudskou
t (01736) 797044
e enquiries@sowena.co.uk

Mount Douglas Farm Cottages ★★★ *Self Catering*
Contact: Mr & Mrs Perry
t (01736) 794831
e phil-md1@btopenworld.com
w mountdouglascottages.co.uk

Riviera 15 ★★★★
Self Catering
Contact: Mr & Mrs Read
t (01736) 757237
w ayianapaholidaysuk.co.uk

Trevalgan Barns, St Ives
★★★★ *Self Catering*
Beach Lea
t (01736) 756252
e enquiries@trevalganbarns.com
w trevalganbarns.co.uk

Trevethoe Farm Cottages
★★★ *Self Catering*
Contact: Mr & Mrs Rogers
t (01736) 753279
e holidaycottages@trevethoe.co.uk
w trevethoe.co.uk

LEONARD STANLEY
Gloucestershire

Priory Farm Holidays
★★★★ *Self Catering*
Contact: Mrs Jo Pullin
t (01453) 823143
e davidpullin@tiscali.co.uk
w prioryfarmholidays.com

LEWDOWN
Devon

Wagon Linney & Whiterow Stables ★★★★ *Self Catering*
Contact: Mr James Morris
Farm & Cottage Holidays
t (01237) 479146
e enquiries@farmcott.co.uk
w holidaycottages.co.uk

LEZANT
Cornwall

East Penrest Barn ★★★★★
Self Catering
Contact: Mr & Mrs Jo & James Rider
t (01579) 370186
e jorider@eastpenrest.freeserve.co.uk
w cornwall-online.co.uk/eastpenrestbarn

LISKEARD
Cornwall

Beechleigh Cottage ★★★★
Self Catering
Tregondale Farm
t (01579) 342407
e tregondale@connectfree.co.uk
w tregondalefarm.co.uk

Coach House Cottages
★★★★ *Self Catering*
Contact: Mr Hall
t (01579) 347755
e cottages@treworgey.co.uk
w treworgey.co.uk

Hopsland Holidays ★★★★
Self Catering
Contact: Mr & Mrs Hosken
Hopsland Holidays
t (01579) 344480
e hopslandholidays@aol.com
w hopslandholidays.co.uk

Lodge Barton ★★★
Self Catering
Contact: Mr & Mrs Hodin
Lodge Barton
t (01579) 344432
e lodgebart@aol.com
w selectideas.co.uk/lodgebarton

Lower Trengale Farm
★★★★ *Self Catering*
Contact: Mr & Mrs Shears
t (01579) 321019
e enquiries@trengale.co.uk
w trengale.co.uk

Oak Lodge ★★★
Self Catering
Contact: Ms Susan Frith
t (01959) 577730
e kingsfrith@btconnect.com
w rosecraddoc-bungalow.com

Penhawger Barns ★★★
Self Catering
Farm & Cottage Holidays
t (01237) 479146
e enquiries@farmcott.co.uk
w holidaycottages.co.uk

Trelyn Cottage ★★★
Self Catering
Contact: Ms Angie Fisher
Trelyn Cottage
t (01579) 383881
e trelyn@kingfisher-training.freeserve.co.uk
w http://trelyncottage.mysite.wanadoo-members.co.uk

LITTLE PETHERICK
Cornwall

16 Rosehill Development
★★★★ *Self Catering*
Contact: Nicky Stanley
Harbour Holidays
t (01841) 533402

6 Saints Way ★★★★
Self Catering
Contact: Peter Osbourne
Cornish Horizons Holiday Cottages
t (01841) 533331
e cottages@cornishhorizons.co.uk
w cornishhorizons.co.uk

Creekside ★★★★
Self Catering
Cornish Horizons Holiday Cottages
t (01841) 533331
e cottages@cornishhorizons.co.uk
w cornishhorizons.co.uk

Creekside No 1 Saints Way
★★★★ *Self Catering*
Contact: Nicky Stanley
Harbour Holidays Ltd
t (01841) 533402
e contact@harbourholidays.co.uk
w harbourholidays.co.uk

Driftwood ★★★★
Self Catering
Cornish Horizons Holiday Cottages
t (01841) 533331
e cottages@cornishhorizons.co.uk
w cornishhorizons.co.uk

Entwood ★★★★
Self Catering
Contact: Mr Peter Osbourne
Cornish Horizons Holiday Cottages
t (01841) 533331
e cottages@cornishhorizons.co.uk
w cornishhorizons.co.uk

Honeywood ★★★★
Self Catering
Contact: Mr Peter Osborne
Cornish Horizons Holiday Cottages
t (01841) 533331
e cottages@cornishhorizons.co.uk
w cornishhorizons.co.uk

Pine Haven ★★★★
Self Catering
Contact: Mr Osbourne
Cornish Horizons Holiday Cottages
t (01841) 533331
e cottages@cornishhorizons.co.uk
w cornishhorizons.co.uk

Quay House ★★★
Self Catering
Contact: Mr & Mrs Hatcher
t (01841) 540431
e quayhouse@aol.com
w quayhouse.co.uk

Swallow Court Cottage
★★★★ *Self Catering*
Contact: Mr Geoff French
t (01841) 540292
e molesworthmanor@aol.com
w molesworthmanor.co.uk

Timbers ★★★★ *Self Catering*
Contact: Mr Peter Osborne
Cornish Horizons Holiday Cottages
t (01841) 533331
e cottages@cornishhorizons.co.uk
w cornishhorizons.co.uk

Trenant ★★★★ *Self Catering*
Cornish Horizons Holiday Cottages
t (01841) 533331
e cottages@cornishhorizons.co.uk
w cornishhorizons.co.uk

Waterside ★★★★
Self Catering
Contact: Nicky Stanley
Harbour Holidays
t (01841) 533402
e contact@harbourholidays.co.uk
w harbourholidays.co.uk

Westcreek ★★★
Self Catering
Cornish Cottage Holidays
t (01326) 573808
e enquiry@cornishcottageholidays.co.uk
w cornishcottageholidays.co.uk

LITTLE RISSINGTON Gloucestershire

Southview,Courtyard and Tallet Cott
★★★★–★★★★★
Self Catering
Contact: Mr & Mrs Nando & Joyce Fracasso
t (01451) 820691

LITTLE TORRINGTON Devon

Cream Tea Cottages ★★★★
Self Catering
Contact: Mr & Mrs Tom & Sue Downie
Staddon House
t (01805) 623670
e tom.downie@ukonline.co.uk
w creamteacottages.co.uk

Torridge House Cottages
★★★ *Self Catering*
Contact: Mrs Barbara Terry
t (01805) 622542
e bookings@torridgehouse.co.uk
w torridgehouse.co.uk

LITTON CHENEY Dorset

Chimney Sweep ★★★★
Self Catering
Contact: Mr Zachary Stuart-Brown
Dream Cottages
t (01305) 789000
e admin@dream-cottages.co.uk
w dream-cottages.co.uk

LIVERTON Devon

Lookweep Farm Cottages
★★★ *Self Catering*
Contact: Mr & Mrs John & Helen Griffiths
t (01626) 833277
e holidays@lookweep.co.uk
w lookweep.co.uk

LIZARD Cornwall

Bass Point Cottage ★★★
Self Catering
Contact: Mr Martin Raftery
Mullion Cottages
t 0845 066 7766
e enquiries@mullioncottages.com
w mullioncottages.com

Dene House ★★★★
Self Catering
Contact: Mr Martin Raftery
Mullion Cottages
t 0845 066 7766
e enquiries@mullioncottages.com
w mullioncottages.com

Grandad's Cottage ★★★★
Self Catering
Contact: Mr Martin Raftery
Mullion Cottages
t 0845 066 7766
e enquiries@mullioncottages.com
w mullioncottages.com

The Haven ★★★
Self Catering
Contact: Mr Martin Raftery
Mullion Cottages
t 0845 066 7766
e enquiries@mullioncottages.com
w mullioncottages.com

Hideaway ★★★ *Self Catering*
Contact: Mr Martin Raftery
Mullion Cottages
t 0845 066 7766
e enquiries@mullioncottages.com
w mullioncottages.com

Ivy Cottage ★★★★
Self Catering
Contact: Mr Martin Raftery
Mullion Cottages
t 0845 066 7766
e enquiries@mullioncottages.com

Little Beside Cottage & Octagon Villa ★★★
Self Catering
Mullion Cottages
t 0845 066 7766
e enquiries@mullioncottages.com
w mullioncottages.com

Pen Vose ★★★★
Self Catering
Contact: Sylvia Blomeley
Toad Hall Cottages
t (01548) 853089
e thc@toadhallcottages.com
w toadhallcottages.co.uk

The Round House ★★★★
Self Catering
Contact: Mr Martin Raftery
Mullion Cottages
t 0845 066 7766
e enquiries@mullioncottages.com
w mullioncottages.com

Tregonoggy ★★★
Self Catering
Contact: Mr Martin Raftery
Mullion Cottages
t 0845 066 7766
e enquiries@mullioncottages.com
w mullioncottages.com

The Winch House ★★★★
Self Catering
Contact: Mr Martin Raftery
Mullion Cottages
t 0845 066 7766
e enquiries@mullioncottages.com
w mullioncottages.com

LOBB Devon

South Lobb Cottage and House ★★★ *Self Catering*
Contact: Lucy Ellison
Farm & Cottage Holidays
t (01237) 479146
e enquiries@farmcott.co.uk
w holidaycottages.co.uk

LONDON APPRENTICE Cornwall

Holly Bank ★★★
Self Catering
Contact: Mr & Mrs McGuffie
t (01726) 69316
e enquiries@spindrift-guesthouse.co.uk
w spindrift-guesthouse.co.uk

Levalsa Farm ★★★–★★★★★
Self Catering
Contact: Mrs Julian
t (01726) 843505
e gayejulian@hotmail.co.uk
w levalsafarm.co.uk

LONG BREDY Dorset

Whatcombe Stables ★★★★
Self Catering
Contact: Ms Margarette Stuart-Brown
t (01305) 789000
e admin@dream-cottages.co.uk

LONG ROCK Cornwall

The Cottage at Heron House
★★★★ *Self Catering*
Contact: Mr James Morris-Marsham
t (01736) 711680
e susiemm@freenet.co.uk

LONG SUTTON Somerset

Orchard View ★★★
Self Catering
Contact: Mrs Mandy Sinclair
t (01458) 253223
e sinclair_mandy@hotmail.com

LONGBOROUGH Gloucestershire

Cottage Barn ★★★★
Self Catering
Contact: Mr & Mrs Williams-Ellis
t (01451) 830695
e rupert.williams-ellis@talk21.com
w cotswoldscottage.co.uk

LONGBRIDGE DEVERILL Wiltshire

Sturgess Farmhouse ★★★★
Self Catering
Contact: Mr Ramsay
t (01985) 840329
e info@sturgessbarns.co.uk
w sturgessbarns.co.uk

LONGDOWN Devon

Valley View ★★★★
Self Catering
Contact: Mrs Jane Steele
t (01392) 811858
e janesteele@onetel.com

LONGHOPE Gloucestershire

The Old Farm
Rating Applied For
Self Catering
Contact: Lucy Rodger
t (01452) 830252
e lucy@the-old-farm.co.uk
w the-old-farm.co.uk

LOOE Cornwall

11 Woburn Lodge ★★★★
Self Catering
t (01752) 605605
e sales@valleyvillas.com
w valleyvillas.com

16 Woburn Lodge ★★★★
Self Catering
t (01752) 605605
e sales@valleyvillas.com
w valleyvillas.com

2 Admiralty Court ★★★
Self Catering
Cornish Management Services
t (01503) 269086
e cornishmanagserv@aol.com
w cornishmanagementservices.co.uk

4 River View ★★★
Self Catering
Contact: Mr Gerald Tyler
Cornish Management Services
t (01503) 269086
e cornishmanagserv@aol.com

5 The Hillocks ★★★★
Self Catering
Cornish Management Services
t (01503) 269086
e cornishmanagserv@aol.com
w cornishmanagementservices.co.uk

9 Rock Towers Apartments
★★★★ *Self Catering*
Contact: Mr Gerald Tyler
t (01503) 269086
e cornishmanagserv@aol.com
w rocktowerslooe.co.uk

Banjo Cottage
Rating Applied For
Self Catering
Contact: Moira Foulkes
Lowleybridge
t (01579) 370006
e lowleybridge@aol.com

Barclay House Luxury Cottages ★★★★★
Self Catering
Contact: Mr Barclay
t (01503) 262929
e info@barclayhouse.co.uk
w barclayhouse.co.uk

Bocaddon Holiday Cottages
★★★★ *Self Catering*
Contact: Mrs Alison Maiklem
Bocaddon Holiday Cottages
t (01503) 220192
e holidays@bocaddon.com
w bocaddon.com

The Brentons ★★★
Self Catering
Contact: Mrs Hocking
t (01503) 262469
e deshocking@hotmail.com

Bucklawren Farm
★★★★-★★★★★
Self Catering
Contact: Mrs Henly
Bucklawren Farm
t (01503) 240738
e bucklawren@btopenworld.com
w bucklawren.com

The Cabin ★★ *Self Catering*
Valley Villas
t (01752) 605605
e sales@valleyvillas.com
w valleyvillas.co.uk

Clipper House, Main Sail, Crows Nest - ★★★-★★★★
Self Catering
Contact: Mrs French
t (01503) 262754
e rfrenchclipper@aol.com
w clipperhouse.co.uk

Coldrinnick Cottages
★★★-★★★★ *Self Catering*
Contact: Mrs Chapman
t (01503) 220251
e coldrinnick@safe2say.com
w cornishcottage.net

Colona ★★★ *Self Catering*
Contact: Mr & Mrs Devey
t (01503) 272223
e philip.devey@talk21.com
w colona.co.uk

Crylla Valley Cottages
★★★★ *Self Catering*
Contact: Mr Matthew Walsh
t (01752) 851133 & (01752) 851666
e sales@cryllacottages.co.uk
w cryllacottages.co.uk/cryllavalley.php?source=CTB

Darley House ★★
Self Catering
Contact: Ann Stevens
t (01503) 265826
e anniecstevens@hotmail.com

Harbourside Holiday Flats
★★★ *Self Catering*
Contact: Mr & Mrs Pope
t (01503) 262926

Hendra Farm Cottages
★★★★ *Self Catering*
Contact: Mrs Senara Higgs
t (01503) 220701
e info@hendrafarmcottages.co.uk
w hendrafarmcottages.co.uk

Highwood ★★★★
Self Catering
Contact: Mrs Beatrix Windle
t (01483) 277894
e beatrix@talk21.com
w cornwall-online.co.uk/highwood

Lantau Cottage ★★★★
Self Catering
Valley Villas
t (01752) 605605
e sales@valleyvillas.com
w valleyvillas.com

Lemain Garden Apartments
Rating Applied For
Self Catering
Contact: Mr & Mrs Alan Palin
t (01579) 321103
e sales@lemain.com
w lemain.com

Little Cottage ★★★
Self Catering
Contact: Mrs Tolputt
t (01503) 220315
w lesquite-polperro.fsnet.co.uk

Little Larnick Holiday Cottages ★★ *Self Catering*
Contact: Mrs Eastley
t (01503) 220205

The Manse ★★★
Self Catering
Contact: Mr Philip Dawson
t (01503) 263205

Penjoden ★★★ *Self Catering*
t (0115) 928 4665
e penjoden@looeholidays.co.uk
w looeholidays.co.uk

Penvith Cottages ★★★★
Self Catering
Contact: Mrs Windle
t (01483) 277894
e beatrix@talk21.com
w penvithcottages.co.uk

Rock Towers Apartments
★★★★ *Self Catering & Serviced Apartments*
Contact: Mr Dixon
Rock Towers Apartments
t (01503) 262736
e cornishcol@aol.com
w cornishcollection.co.uk

Rock Towers Apartment 10
★★★★ *Self Catering & Serviced Apartments*
Cornish Management Services
t (01503) 269086
e info@cornishmanagementservices.co.uk

Rock Towers Apartment 11
★★★★ *Self Catering & Serviced Apartments*
Cornish Management Services
t (01503) 262736
e info@cornishcollection.co.uk

Rock Towers Apartment 12
★★★★ *Self Catering & Serviced Apartments*
Cornish Management Services
t (01503) 262736
e info@cornishcollection.co.uk

Rock Towers Apartment 4
★★★★ *Self Catering & Serviced Apartments*
Cornish Management Services
t (01503) 262736
e info@cornishcollection.co.uk

Rock Towers Apartment 6
★★★★ *Self Catering & Serviced Apartments*
Cornish Management Services
t (01503) 262736
e info@cornishcollection.co.uk

Rock Towers Apartment 7
★★★★ *Self Catering & Serviced Apartments*
Cornish Management Services
t (01503) 262736
e info@cornishcollection.co.uk

Rockabye Cottage ★★
Self Catering
Contact: Mr & Mrs Birch
t (0118) 971 3378

St Martins Apartment
★★★★ *Self Catering*
Contact: Mrs Chappell
t (01503) 262032

Seaways ★ *Self Catering*
Valley Villas
t (01752) 605605
e sales@valleyvillas.com
w valleyvillas.com

Summercourt Coastal Cottages ★★★★
Self Catering
Contact: Mr Hocking
Summercourt Coastal Cottages
t (01503) 263149
e sccottages@freenet.co.uk
w holidaycottagescornwall.tv

Talehay ★★★★ *Self Catering*
Contact: Neil & Theresa Dennett
Talehay
t (01503) 220252
e infobooking@talehay.co.uk
w talehay.co.uk

Trecan Farm Cottages
★★★-★★★★ *Self Catering*
Contact: Mrs Pugh
t (01503) 220768
e richardpugh@trecan.fsnet.co.uk
w trecanfarmcottages.co.uk

Trehalvin Cottages
★★★-★★★★ *Self Catering*
Contact: Mrs Catherine Woollard
Trehalvin Cottages
t (01503) 240334
e cottages@trehalvin.co.uk
w trehalvin.co.uk

Trewith Holiday Cottages
★★★★ *Self Catering*
Contact: Mr & Mrs Higgins
t (01503) 262184
e holiday-cottages@trewith.freeserve.co.uk
w trewith.freeserve.co.uk

Treworgey Cottages
★★★★★ *Self Catering*
Contact: Mr & Mrs Wright
t (01503) 262730
e treworgey@enterprise.net
w cornishdreamcottages.co.uk

Tyrina ★★★ *Self Catering*
Contact: Mr Foley
t (01483) 275965
e info@tyrinacottage.co.uk
w tyrinacottage.co.uk

Wenmouth Cottage ★★★★
Self Catering
Contact: Mrs Jenny Mickleburgh
t (01503) 272349

Woodsaws Farm ★★★★
Self Catering
Contact: Mrs Ann Wills
t (01503) 220190
e ann@woodsawsfarm.co.uk

LOSCOMBE
Dorset

Garden Cottage ★★★
Self Catering
Contact: Major Poe
t (01308) 488223
e poe@loscombe.freeserve.co.uk

LOSTWITHIEL
Cornwall

Chark Country Holidays
★★★★ *Self Catering*
Contact: Mrs Littleton
Chark Country Holidays
t (01208) 871118
e charkholidays@tiscali.co.uk
w charkcountryholidays.co.uk

Hartswheal Barn
★★★-★★★★ *Self Catering*
Contact: Mrs Wendy Jordan
t (01208) 873419
e hartswheal@connexions.co.uk
w connexions.co.uk/hartswheal/index.htm

Honeysuckle Cottage ★★★
Self Catering
Contact: Ms Sue Tarry
t (01208) 817276
e smtarry@aol.com/sucklecott@aol.com

Lanwithan Cottages
★★★-★★★★ *Self Catering*
Contact: Mr V B Edward-Collins
Lanwithan Cottages
t (01208) 872444
e lanwithan@btconnect.com
w lanwithancottages.co.uk

Restormel Cottage
★★★★★ *Self Catering*
Contact: Mr Scott
t (01579) 343149
w duchyofcornwallholidaycottages.co.uk

Tredethick Farm Cottages
★★★★ *Self Catering*
Contact: Mr & Mrs Reed
t (01208) 873618
e holidays@tredethick.co.uk
w tredethick.co.uk

LOWER APPERLEY
Gloucestershire

Rofield Barn ★★★★★
Self Catering
Contact: Mrs Hazel Lewis
Lower Apperley
t (01452) 780323
e jeremy@tewkbury.freeserve.co.uk
w rofieldbarn.com

LOWER SLAUGHTER
Gloucestershire

Greenfingers ★★★
Self Catering
Contact: Sharon Castleton-White
The Nook
t (01451) 820398
e sharon.cw@btconnect.com

Malt House Cottage ★★★★
Self Catering
Contact: Mrs Charlotte Hutsby
t (01789) 840261
e charhutsby@talk21.com
w accomodata.co.uk/06099.htm

LOWER SOUDLEY
Gloucestershire

Beechwood Bungalow
★★★★ *Self Catering*
Contact: Mrs Judith Anderton
t (01594) 825864
e raanderton@ntlworld.com

LOWTON
Somerset

Bee's Cottage ★★★★
Self Catering
Farm & Cottage Holidays
t (01237) 479146
e enquiries@farmcott.co.uk
w holidaycottages.co.uk

LUCCOMBE
Somerset

Wychanger ★★★★
Self Catering
Contact: Mr & Mrs David & Sue Dalton
t (01643) 862526
e holidays@wychanger.net
w wychanger.net

LUDGVAN
Cornwall

Mount View Cottage ★★★
Self Catering
Contact: Mrs Wallis
t (01736) 711425
w eglos.co.uk

Nanceddan ★★★
Self Catering
Contact: Mrs Richards
Nanceddan
t (01736) 740165
e nanceddan@hotmail.com
w nanceddan.com

LUXBOROUGH
Somerset

Lower Coombe Royal
★★★★★ *Self Catering*
Contact: Mrs Susi Titchener
t (01548) 852880
e retreats@lowercoomberoyal.co.uk
w lowercoomberoyal.co.uk

The Old Granary ★★★★
Self Catering
Contact: Mr & Mrs Ivan & Anne Simpson
t (01984) 640909
e theoldgranaryexmoor@talk21.com
w granarycottage.co.uk

Pool Farm Byres ★★★★
Self Catering
Contact: Mrs Janet Cornwell
Marsdens Cottage Holidays
t (01271) 813777
e holidays@marsdens.co.uk
w marsdens.co.uk

Westcott Lodge and Mill Cottage ★★★★ *Self Catering*
Contact: Ms Sylvia Herbert
t (01984) 641285
e westcottlodge@freeuk.com

LUXULYAN
Cornwall

Croft Farm Cottages ★★★
Self Catering
Contact: Mrs Lynda Pickering
t (01726) 850228
e lynpick@ukonline.co.uk
w croftfarm.co.uk

LYDBROOK
Gloucestershire

Royal Spring Cottage ★★★
Self Catering
Contact: Mr Peter Crawley
Royal Spring Inn
t (01594) 860492
e crawleyphilc@aol.com

LYDEARD ST LAWRENCE
Somerset

Lower Vexford House
Rating Applied For
Self Catering
Contact: Mike Coles
The Old Cart House
t 0870 620 1066
e mike@dunsterliving.co.uk or info@dunsterliving.co.uk
w vexfordhouse.co.uk

Oaklea House ★★★★
Self Catering
Contact: Mrs Peta-Elaine Barker
t (01984) 667373
e barker@oakleahouse.fsnet.co.uk
w oakleaholidays.co.uk

LYDNEY
Gloucestershire

Bream Cross Farm ★★★
Self Catering
Contact: Mr & Mrs Jock & Margaret Reeks
t (01594) 562208

Cider Press Cottage ★★★★
Self Catering
Contact: Mr & Mrs Hinton
t (01594) 510285

Highbury Coach House
★★★ *Self Catering*
Contact: Mr Anthony Midgley
Highbury Coach House
t (01594) 842339
e midgleya1@aol.com

Lindors Country House
★★★ *Self Catering*
t (01594) 530283
e lindors@cgholidays.co.uk
w cgholidays.co.uk

The Old Pumphouse ★★★★
Self Catering
Contact: Mr Nicholas Pash
Hideaways
t (01747) 828170
w hideaways.co.uk

LYME REGIS
Dorset

1 Alexandra cottages – B4432 ★★★★ *Self Catering*
Lyme Bay Holidays
t (01297) 443363
e email@lymebayholidays.co.uk
w lymebayholidays.co.uk

1 The Bothy – W4391
★★★★ *Self Catering*
Lyme Bay Holidays
t (01297) 443363
e email@lymebayholidays.co.uk
w lymebayholidays.co.uk

1 Lymbrook Cottages ★★★
Self Catering
Contact: Ms Joanne Winkler
Lyme Bay Holidays
t (01297) 443363
e email@lymebayholidays.co.uk
w lymebayholidays.co.uk

1 Studley Gardens ★★★★
Self Catering
Contact: Joanne Winkler
Lyme Bay Holidays
t (01297) 443363
e email@lymebayholidays.co.uk
w lymebayholidays.co.uk

1 Wellhayes- B4399 ★★★
Self Catering
Lyme Bay Holidays
t (01297) 443363
e email@lymebayholidays.co.uk
w lymebayholidays.co.uk

10 Coombe Street ★★★
Self Catering
Contact: Joanne Winkler
Lyme Bay Holidays
t (01297) 443363
e email@lymebayholidays.co.uk
w lymebayholidays.co.uk

11 Fernhill – P5014 ★★★
Self Catering
Lyme Bay Holidays
t (01297) 443363
e email@lymebayholidays.co.uk
w lymebayholidays.co.uk

14 Mill Green ★★★
Self Catering
Lyme Bay Holidays
t (01297) 443363
e email@lymebayholidays.co.uk
w lymebayholidays.co.uk

19 Church Street ★★★★
Self Catering
Contact: Mrs Tracey Barclay
Askew House
t (01297) 560617
e info@lymeregiscottages.co.uk
w lymeregiscottages.co.uk

2 Coombe Street – B4278
★★★ *Self Catering*
Contact: Mr Dave Matthews
Lyme Bay Holidays
t (01297) 443363
e email@lymebayholidays.co.uk
w lymebayholidays.co.uk

2 Kersbrook Gardens – C4393 ★★★★ *Self Catering*
Lyme Bay Holidays
t (01297) 443363
e email@lymebayholidays.co.uk
w lymebayholidays.co.uk

2 Tenerife ★★★
Self Catering
Contact: Joanne Winkler
Lyme Bay Holidays
t (01297) 443363
e email@lymebayholidays.co.uk
w lymebayholidays.co.uk

22a Sherborne Lane – C4197 ★★ *Self Catering*
Lyme Bay Holidays
t (01297) 443363
e email@lymebayholidays.co.uk
w lymebayholidays.co.uk

23 Church Street
Rating Applied For
Self Catering
Contact: Mr David Matthews
Lyme Bay Holidays
t (01297) 443363
e email@lymebayholidays.co.uk
w lymebayholidays.co.uk

23 Lym Close – C4179 ★★★
Self Catering
Lyme Bay Holidays
t (01297) 443363
e email@lymebayholidays.co.uk
w lymebayholidays.co.uk

24 Fernhill – R5012 ★★★
Self Catering
Lyme Bay Holidays
t (01297) 443363
e email@lymebayholidays.co.uk
w lymebayholidays.co.uk

25 Fernhill – P5008 ★★★
Self Catering
Contact: Mr Dave Matthews
Lyme Bay Holidays
t (01297) 443363
e email@lymebayholidays.co.uk
w lymebayholidays.co.uk

26 Coombe Street – C4424
★★★ *Self Catering*
Lyme Bay Holidays
t (01297) 443363
e email@lymebayholidays.co.uk
w lymebayholidays.co.uk

3 Bay View Court – B4468
★★★ *Self Catering*
Lyme Bay Holidays
t (01297) 443363
e email@lymebayholidays.co.uk
w lymebayholidays.co.uk

3 Chard House – A4312
★★★ *Self Catering*
Contact: Mr Dave Matthews
Lyme Bay Holidays
t (01297) 443363
e email@lymebayholidays.co.uk
w lymebayholidays.co.uk

3 Coombe Street – 52700k
★★★ *Self Catering*
Lyme Bay Holidays
t (01297) 443363
e email@lymebayholidays.co.uk
w lymebayholidays.co.uk

3 Dolphin Cottages ★★★
Self Catering
Contact: Mrs Daphine E Lindfield
t (01403) 791258

3 Lym Close – B4253 ★★★
Self Catering
Lyme Bay Holidays
t (01297) 443363
e email@lymebayholidays.co.uk
w lymebayholidays.co.uk

3 Portland Lodge ★★★★
Self Catering
Contact: Joanne Winkler
Lyme Bay Holidays
t (01297) 443363
e email@lymebayholidays.co.uk
w lymebayholidays.co.uk

30 Sherborne Lane – B4378
★★ *Self Catering*
Lyme Bay Holidays
t (01297) 443363
e email@lymebayholidays.co.uk
w lymebayholidays.co.uk

31 Sherborne Lane: B4406
★★★ *Self Catering*
Lyme Bay Holidays
t (01297) 443363
e email@lymebayholidays.co.uk
w lymebayholidays.co.uk

39 Fernhill – Q5006 ★★★★
Self Catering
Contact: Mr Dave Matthews
Lyme Bay Holidays
t (01297) 443363
e email@lymebayholidays.co.uk
w lymebayholidays.co.uk

39 Henry's Way ★★★★
Self Catering
Contact: Joanne Walker
Lyme Bay Holidays
t (01297) 443363
e email@lymebayholidays.co.uk
w lymebayholidays.co.uk

4 Bay View Court ★★★
Self Catering
Contact: Joanne Winkler
Lyme Bay Holidays
t (01297) 443363
e email@lymebayholidays.co.uk
w lymebayholidays.co.uk

4 Kersbrook Gardens – B4437 ★★★★ *Self Catering*
Contact: Mr Jim Matthews
Lyme Bay Holidays
t (01297) 443363
e email@lymebayholidays.co.uk
w lymebayholidays.co.uk

4 Lymbrook Cottages ★★★
Self Catering
Contact: Mrs Karen Start
t (01799) 522096

44 Henry's Way ★★★★
Self Catering
Contact: Joanne Walker
t (01297) 443363
e email@lymebayholidays.co.uk
w lymebayholidays.co.uk

44/45 Coombe Street – B4341 ★★★★ *Self Catering*
Lyme Bay Holidays
t (01297) 443363
e email@lymebayholidays.co.uk
w lymebayholidays.co.uk

47 Fernhill – R5001 ★★★★
Self Catering
Lyme Bay Holidays
t (01297) 443363
e email@lymebayholidays.co.uk
w lymebayholidays.co.uk

47 Queens Walk – B4249
★★ *Self Catering*
Lyme Bay Holidays
t (01297) 443363
e email@lymebayholidays.co.uk
w lymebayholidays.co.uk

48 Church Street – C4335
★★★★ *Self Catering*
Lyme Bay Holidays
t (01297) 443363
e email@lymebayholidays.co.uk
w lymebayholidays.co.uk

48 Fernhill – R5002 ★★★★
Self Catering
Lyme Bay Holidays
t (01297) 443363
e email@lymebayholidays.co.uk
w lymebayholidays.co.uk

49 Fernhill Heights Ref: S5015 ★★★ *Self Catering*
Contact: Mr David Matthews
t (01297) 443363
e email@lymebayholidays.co.uk
w lymebayholidays.co.uk

49a Broad Street – C4049
★★★★ *Self Catering*
Lyme Bay Holidays
t (01297) 443363
e email@lymebayholidays.co.uk
w lymebayholidays.co.uk

5 St Michaels House ★★★★
Self Catering
Contact: Joanne Winkler
Lyme Bay Holidays
t (01297) 443363
e email@lymebayholidays.co.uk
w lymebayholidays.co.uk

50 Henry's Way ★★★★
Self Catering
Contact: Joanne Winkler
Lyme Bay Holidays
t (01297) 443363
e email@lymebayholidays.co.uk
w lymebayholidays.co.uk

54 Henry's Way ★★★★
Self Catering
Contact: Mr David Matthews
Lyme Bay Holidays
t (01297) 443363
e email@lymebayholidays.co.uk
w lymebayholidays.co.uk

6 Bay View Court ★★★
Self Catering
Contact: Joanne Winkler
Lyme Bay Holidays
t (01297) 443363
e email@lymebayholidays.co.uk
w lymebayholidays.co.uk

7 Cobb Road – C4358
★★★★ *Self Catering*
Lyme Bay Holidays
t (01297) 443363
e email@lymebayholidays.co.uk
w lymebayholidays.co.uk

7 Coram Mews – C4351
★★★★★ *Self Catering*
Lyme Bay Holidays
t (01297) 443363
e email@lymebayholidays.co.uk
w lymebayholidays.co.uk

7 Portland Lodge ★★★★
Self Catering
Lyme Bay Holidays
t (01297) 443363
e email@lymebayholidays.co.uk
w lymebayholidays.co.uk

7 Silver Street ★★★★
Self Catering
Contact: Mr David Matthews
Lyme Bay Holidays
t (01297) 443363
e email@lymebayholidays.co.uk
w lymebayholidays.co.uk

Alwyns ★★★ *Self Catering*
Lyme Bay Holidays
t (01297) 443363
e email@lymebayholidays.co.uk
w lymebayholidays.co.uk

Apartment 1 & 2 Malvern House ★★★★ *Self Catering*
Lyme Bay Holidays
t (01297) 443363
e email@lymebayholidays.co.uk
w lymebayholidays.co.uk

Appletree Cottage ★★★
Self Catering
Lyme Bay Holidays
t (01297) 443363
e email@lymebayholidays.co.uk
w lymebayholidays.co.uk

Aquae Sulis – B4287 ★★★
Self Catering
Lyme Bay Holidays
t (01297) 443363
e email@lymebayholidays.co.uk
w lymebayholidays.co.uk

The Arched House – F4045
★★★ *Self Catering*
Lyme Bay Holidays
t (01297) 443363
e email@lymebayholidays.co.uk
w lymebayholidays.co.uk

Argyle House – B4200 ★★★
Self Catering
Lyme Bay Holidays
t (01297) 443363
e email@lymebayholidays.co.uk
w lymebayholidays.co.uk

Banff ★★ *Self Catering*
Lyme Bay Holidays
t (01297) 443363
e email@lymebayholidays.co.uk
w lymebayholidays.co.uk

Bay View Court – B4357
★★★★ *Self Catering*
Lyme Bay Holidays
t (01297) 443363
e email@lymebayholidays.co.uk
w lymebayholidays.co.uk

Bedrock – B4390 ★★★
Self Catering
Lyme Bay Holidays
t (01297) 443363
e email@lymebayholidays.co.uk
w lymebayholidays.co.uk

Benwick – B4232 ★★★★
Self Catering
Lyme Bay Holidays
t (01297) 443363
e email@lymebayholidays.co.uk
w lymebayholidays.co.uk

Blacksmiths Cottage ★★★★
Self Catering
Contact: Joanne Winkler
Wessex House
t (01297) 443363
e email@lymebayholidays.co.uk
w lymebayholidays.co.uk

Blue Horizons – B4314
★★★ *Self Catering*
Contact: Mr Dave Matthews
Lyme Bay Holidays
t (01297) 443363
e email@lymebayholidays.co.uk
w lymebayholidays.co.uk

The Blue House – C4422
★★★ *Self Catering*
Contact: Mr Dave Matthews
Lyme Bay Holidays
t (01297) 443363
e email@lymebayholidays.co.uk
w lymebayholidays.co.uk

The Boat House ★★★
Self Catering
Lyme Bay Holidays
t (01297) 443363
e email@lymebayholidays.co.uk
w lymebayholidays.co.uk

The Bookie – A4374 ★★★
Self Catering
Contact: Mr Dave Matthews
Lyme Bay Holidays
t (01297) 443363
e email@lymebayholidays.co.uk
w lymebayholidays.co.uk

Boston – D4326 ★★★★
Self Catering
Lyme Bay Holidays
t (01297) 443363
e email@lymebayholidays.co.uk
w lymebayholidays.co.uk

Bramcote Garden Apartment ★★★★
Self Catering
Contact: Mrs Rosalind Price
t (01297) 442924
e fnr.price@virgin.net
w bramcotelymeregis.com

Burwood B4479 ★★★★
Self Catering
Lyme Bay Holidays
t (01297) 443363
e email@lymebayholidays.co.uk
w lymebayholidays.co.uk

La Casa ★★★ *Self Catering*
Contact: Mr Royston Davies
Seven Springs Letting Agency
t (01297) 445362

Church Cliff – C4296
★★★★ *Self Catering*
Lyme Bay Holidays
t (01297) 443363
e email@lymebayholidays.co.uk
w lymebayholidays.co.uk

Cleve House – B3437 ★★★
Self Catering
Contact: Mr Dave Matthews
Lyme Bay Holidays
t (01297) 443363
e email@lymebayholidays.co.uk
w lymebayholidays.co.uk

Cleveland – C4427 ★★★★
Self Catering
Lyme Bay Holidays
t (01297) 443363
e email@lymebayholidays.co.uk
w lymebayholidays.co.uk

Cliff Bank ★★★★
Self Catering
Lyme Bay Holidays
t (01297) 443363
e email@lymebayholidays.co.uk
w lymebayholidays.co.uk

Cliff Cottage ★★★
Self Catering
Contact: Mrs Sue Rose
t (01420) 472512
e cliffcottlyme@aol.com

The Coach House ★★
Self Catering
Contact: Mrs Lucy Watt
t (01297) 445100

Cobb House ★★
Self Catering
Contact: Ms Kate Bartlett
Jean Bartlett Cottage Holidays
t (01297) 23221
e holidays@jeanbartlett.com
w jeanbartlett.com

Cockwell Cross Cottage – V4285 ★★★★ *Self Catering*
Contact: Mr Dave Matthews
Lyme Bay Holidays
t (01297) 443363
e email@lymebayholidays.co.uk
w lymebayholidays.co.uk

Coolrus – B4349 ★★★
Self Catering
Lyme Bay Holidays
t (01297) 443363
e email@lymebayholidays.co.uk
w lymebayholidays.co.uk

Coombe Cottage – C4346
★★★★ *Self Catering*
Lyme Bay Holidays
t (01297) 443363
e email@lymebayholidays.co.uk
w lymebayholidays.co.uk

Coombe House Flat ★★★★
Self Catering
Contact: Mrs Dympna Duncan
t (01297) 443849
e dymps@coombe-house.co.uk
w coombe-house.co.uk

Coram Tower Holidays Ltd.
★★★ *Self Catering*
Contact: Mr & Mrs John & Margaret McLaren
Coram Tower Holidays
t (01297) 442012
e jmmclaren@coramtower.co.uk
w coramtower.co.uk

The Cottage ★★★
Self Catering
Contact: Joanne Winkler
Lyme Bay Holidays
t (01297) 443363
e email@lymebayholidays.co.uk
w lymebayholidays.co.uk

The Cottage ★★★★
Self Catering
Contact: Joanne Winkler
Lyme Bay Holidays
t (01297) 443363
e email@lymebayholidays.co.uk
w lymebayholidays.co.uk

Crystal – A4433 ★★★
Self Catering
Lyme Bay Holidays
t (01297) 443363
e email@lymebayholidays.co.uk
w lymebayholidays.co.uk

Dolphin Cottage – B4340
★★★ *Self Catering*
Lyme Bay Holidays
t (01297) 443363
e email@lymebayholidays.co.uk
w lymebayholidays.co.uk

Faraway – C4436 ★★★★
Self Catering
Contact: Mr Jim Matthews
Lyme Bay Holidays
t (01297) 443363
e email@lymebayholidays.co.uk
w lymebayholidays.co.uk

Farwest – C4303 ★★★
Self Catering
Contact: Mr Dave Matthews
Lyme Bay Holidays
t (01297) 443363
e email@lymebayholidays.co.uk
w lymebayholidays.co.uk

Finnas 34 Fernhill – S5000
★★★ *Self Catering*
Contact: Mr Dave Matthews
Lyme Bay Holidays
t (01297) 443363
e email@lymebayholidays.co.uk
w lymebayholidays.co.uk

Flat 1, Burton House ★★★
Self Catering
Contact: Mrs Elaine Windust
t (01278) 691403
e windusts@btinternet.com

The Gables Holiday Apartments ★★★
Self Catering
Contact: Mr & Mrs Alan & Christine Simpson
t (01297) 442536
e simpson100@tiscali.co.uk
w thegableslymeregis.co.uk

Garden Studio ★★★★
Self Catering
Lyme Bay Holidays
t (01297) 443363
e email@lymebayholidays.co.uk
w lymebayholidays.co.uk

Garston ★★★ *Self Catering*
Contact: Ms Liz Wood
t (020) 8340 8795
e lizfromlyme@yahoo.co.uk

Greystones Flat ★★★★
Self Catering
Contact: Mrs Joan Gollop
Greystones
t (01297) 443678
e greystones.flat@btopenworld.com
w greystones-lymeregis.com

Gulls Nest – A4293 ★★★
Self Catering
Lyme Bay Holidays
t (01297) 443363
e email@lymebayholidays.co.uk
w lymebayholidays.co.uk

Hadleigh Villas – B3520
★★★ *Self Catering*
Lyme Bay Holidays
t (01297) 443363
e email@lymebayholidays.co.uk
w lymebayholidays.co.uk

Harbour House Flats ★★★
Self Catering
Contact: Mrs Monica Cary
Briseham,
t (01626) 364779

The Haven – D4096 ★★★
Self Catering
Lyme Bay Holidays
t (01297) 443363
e email@lymebayholidays.co.uk
w lymebayholidays.co.uk

Haybarn – W3435
Rating Applied For
Self Catering
Lyme Bay Holidays
t (01297) 443363
e email@lymebayholidays.co.uk
w lymebayholidays.co.uk

Haye Farm Bungalow, Stables, Hayloft & Dairy
★★★ *Self Catering*
Contact: Mr & Mrs Richard & Michelle Trim
t (01297) 442400
e richard@rtrim.wanadoo.co.uk

Highbanks – D4372 ★★★★
Self Catering
Contact: Miss Emma Matthews
Lyme Bay Holidays
t (01297) 443363
e email@lymebayholidays.co.uk
w lymebayholidays.co.uk

Honeymoon Cottage – C2627 ★★★★ *Self Catering*
Contact: Mr Dave Matthews
Lyme Bay Holidays
t (01297) 443363
e email@lymebayholidays.co.uk
w lymebayholidays.co.uk

Honeysuckle Cottage
★★★★ *Self Catering*
Lyme Bay Holidays
t (01297) 443363
e email@lymebayholidays.co.uk
w lymebayholidays.co.uk

Hove To – C4364 ★★★
Self Catering
Contact: Mr Jim Matthews
Lyme Bay Holidays
t (01297) 443363
e email@lymebayholidays.co.uk
w lymebayholidays.co.uk

Ilex House ★★★
Self Catering
Contact: Mr Royston Davies
Seven Springs Letting Agency
t (01297) 445362
w lymeregis.com/seven-springs

Ingot Cottage – B4484
★★★★ *Self Catering*
Lyme Bay Holidays
t (01297) 443363
e email@lymebayholidays.co.uk
w lymebayholidays.co.uk

Ivy Cottage – B4442 ★★★
Self Catering
Lyme Bay Holidays
t (01297) 443363
e email@lymebayholidays.co.uk
w lymebayholidays.co.uk

Jasper ★★ *Self Catering*
Lyme Bay Holidays
t (01297) 443363
e email@lymebayholidays.co.uk
w lymebayholidays.co.uk

La Jolla ★★★ *Self Catering*
Contact: Joanne Winkler
Lyme Bay Holidays
t (01297) 443363
e email@lymebayholidays.co.uk
w lymebayholidays.co.uk

Kamloops and Nanaimo Apartments ★★★
Self Catering
Contact: Mr Sweet
t (0117) 968 1866
e sw55t@msn.com

Look out for establishments participating in the Walkers and Cyclists Welcome Schemes

Kelly Bray ★★★
Self Catering
Contact: Joanne Winkler
Lyme Bay Holidays
t (01297) 443363
e email@lymebayholidays.co.uk
w lymebayholidays.co.uk

Lentons – C4260 ★★★★
Self Catering
Lyme Bay Holidays
t (01297) 443363
e email@lymebayholidays.co.uk
w lymebayholidays.co.uk

Library Cottage – C4315
★★★ *Self Catering*
Contact: Mr Dave Matthews
Lyme Bay Holidays
t (01297) 443363
e email@lymebayholidays.co.uk
w lymebayholidays.co.uk

Little Cleve ★★★★
Self Catering
Contact: Mr Alister Mackenzie
Carters Cottage
t (01761) 221554

Little Cliff ★★★★
Self Catering
Contact: Joanne Winkler
Lyme Bay Holidays
t (01297) 443363
e email@lymebayholidays.co.uk
w lymebayholidays.co.uk

Little Clovelly – A3602
★★★★ *Self Catering*
Lyme Bay Holidays
t (01297) 443363
e email@lymebayholidays.co.uk
w lymebayholidays.co.uk

Little Croft – B4449 ★★★
Self Catering
Contact: Mr Jim Matthews
Lyme Bay Holidays
t (01297) 443363
e email@lymebayholidays.co.uk
w lymebayholidays.co.uk

Little Jordan – C4300
★★★★ *Self Catering*
Lyme Bay Holidays
t (01297) 443363
e email@lymebayholidays.co.uk
w lymebayholidays.co.uk

Little Rowan – B4431
★★★★ *Self Catering*
Contact: Mr Jim Matthews
Lyme Bay Holidays
t (01297) 443363
e email@lymebayholidays.co.uk
w lymebayholidays.co.uk

Little Thatch – C3439 ★★★
Self Catering
Lyme Bay Holidays
t (01297) 443363
e email@lymebayholidays.co.uk
w lymebayholidays.co.uk

Long Path – D4370 ★★★★
Self Catering
Contact: Miss Emma Matthews
Lyme Bay Holidays
t (01297) 443363
e email@lymebayholidays.co.uk
w lymebayholidays.co.uk

Lucerne Apartment ★★★★
Self Catering
Contact: Mr O Lovell
Lucerne
t (01297) 443752

Lymcroft – C4267 ★★★★
Self Catering
Lyme Bay Holidays
t (01297) 443363
e email@lymebayholidays.co.uk
w lymebayholidays.co.uk

Lymrush – D4355 ★★★
Self Catering
Lyme Bay Holidays
t (01297) 443363
e email@lymebayholidays.co.uk
w lymebayholidays.co.uk

Mad Hatters Apartment – B4369 ★★★ *Self Catering*
Lyme Bay Holidays
t (01297) 443363
e email@lymebayholidays.co.uk
w lymebayholidays.co.uk

Madeira Cottage ★★★
Self Catering
Contact: Mr Andrew Marriner
t (020) 7937 3237
e andrew.marriner@btopenworld.com
w madeiracottage.co.uk

Marmalade House ★★★
Self Catering
Contact: Mrs Pam Corbin
Whitty Down
t (01297) 442378
e ozonepam@aol.com

Meadows ★★★ *Self Catering*
Lyme Bay Holidays
t (01297) 443363
e email@lymebayholidays.co.uk
w lymebayholidays.co.uk

Mermaid Cottage – C4281
★★★ *Self Catering*
Lyme Bay Holidays
t (01297) 443363
e email@lymebayholidays.co.uk
w lymebayholidays.co.uk

Mermaid House – E4412
★★★★ *Self Catering*
Lyme Bay Holidays
t (01297) 443363
e email@lymebayholidays.co.uk
w lymebayholidays.co.uk

Milton Cottage – B4362
★★★ *Self Catering*
Contact: Mr Dave Matthews
Lyme Bay Holidays
t (01297) 443363
e email@lymebayholidays.co.uk
w lymebayholidays.co.uk

Monmouth Cottage ★★★
Self Catering
Contact: Mrs W R Fisk
t (01460) 73878

Naunton Cottage – B4375
★★★ *Self Catering*
Lyme Bay Holidays
t (01297) 443363
e email@lymebayholidays.co.uk
w lymebayholidays.co.uk

Okanagen ★★ *Self Catering*
Lyme Bay Holidays
t (01297) 443363
e email@lymebayholidays.co.uk
w lymebayholidays.co.uk

The Old Monmouth ★★★★
Self Catering
Contact: Mr David Brown
t (01297) 442456
e info@lymeregisaccommodation.co.uk
w lymeregisaccommodation.co.uk

Old Stable Cottage ★★★★
Self Catering
Contact: Joanne Winkler
Lyme Bay Holidays
t (01297) 443363
e email@lymebayholidays.co.uk
w lymebayholidays.co.uk

The Old Watch House
★★★★ *Self Catering*
Contact: Mrs Sarah Wilkinson
t (01305) 262505
e old-watch-house@lymeregis.com
w lymeregis.com/old-watch-house

Ozone Terrace – A3603
★★★ *Self Catering*
Lyme Bay Holidays
t (01297) 443363
e email@lymebayholidays.co.uk
w lymebayholidays.co.uk

Pucks Cottage – B4339
★★★ *Self Catering*
Lyme Bay Holidays
t (01297) 443363
e email@lymebayholidays.co.uk
w lymebayholidays.co.uk

Radium – A4429 ★★★★
Self Catering
Lyme Bay Holidays
t (01297) 443363
e email@lymebayholidays.co.uk
w lymebayholidays.co.uk

Resthaven – A4373 ★★★
Self Catering
Lyme Bay Holidays
t (01297) 443363
e email@lymebayholidays.co.uk
w lymebayholidays.co.uk

River Cottage ★★★★
Self Catering
Contact: Joanne Winkler
t (01297) 443363
e email@lymebayholidays.co.uk
w lymebayholidays.co.uk

Rose Cottage – D4472
★★★★ *Self Catering*
Lyme Bay Holidays
t (01297) 443363
e email@lymebayholidays.co.uk
w lymebayholidays.co.uk

Roselands – B/C4407
★★★★ *Self Catering*
Lyme Bay Holidays
t (01297) 443363
e email@lymebayholidays.co.uk
w lymebayholidays.co.uk

Ross House – B4394 ★★★
Self Catering
Lyme Bay Holidays
t (01297) 443363
e email@lymebayholidays.co.uk
w lymebayholidays.co.uk

St Agnes – A3601 ★★
Self Catering
Lyme Bay Holidays
t (01297) 443363
e email@lymebayholidays.co.uk
w lymebayholidays.co.uk

St Andrews Holiday Flats
★★★ *Self Catering*
Contact: Mrs Cynthia Wendy McHardy
t (01297) 445495

Sea Breeze ★★★
Self Catering
Contact: Ms Rhoda Elwick
Tigerhead House
t (01297) 444958
e thethatch@lineone.net
w holidaycottages-uk.com

Sea Tree House ★★★★
Self Catering
Contact: Mr David Parker
Sea Tree House
t (01297) 442244
e seatree.house@ukonline.co.uk
w lymeregis.com/seatreehouse

Seahorse Cottage – B4270
★★★ *Self Catering*
Lyme Bay Holidays
t (01297) 443363
e email@lymebayholidays.co.uk
w lymebayholidays.co.uk

Seaview – C4302 ★★★
Self Catering
Contact: Mr Dave Matthews
Lyme Bay Holidays
t (01297) 443363
e email@lymebayholidays.co.uk
w lymebayholidays.co.uk

Seaward – B4280 ★★★★
Self Catering
Lyme Bay Holidays
t (01297) 443363
e email@lymebayholidays.co.uk
w lymebayholidays.co.uk

Snail House – B4291
★★★★ *Self Catering*
Lyme Bay Holidays
t (01297) 443363
e email@lymebayholidays.co.uk
w lymebayholidays.co.uk

South Lawn – C4396 ★★★
Self Catering
Lyme Bay Holidays
t (01297) 443363
e email@lymebayholidays.co.uk
w lymebayholidays.co.uk

Stable Cottage ★★★★
Self Catering
Contact: Mrs Penny Jones
t (01297) 442656

Stable Cottage – C4425 ★★
Self Catering
Lyme Bay Holidays
t (01297) 443363
e email@lymebayholidays.co.uk
w lymebayholidays.co.uk

Valentine Cottage – B4350
★★★ *Self Catering*
Lyme Bay Holidays
t (01297) 443363
e email@lymebayholidays.co.uk
w lymebayholidays.co.uk

View House – D4100 ★★★
Self Catering
Lyme Bay Holidays
t (01297) 443363
e email@lymebayholidays.co.uk
w lymebayholidays.co.uk

The Walk C4006 ★★★
Self Catering
Lyme Bay Holidays
t (01297) 443363
e email@lymebayholidays.co.uk
w lymebayholidays.co.uk

Waltham House – C4288
★★★ *Self Catering*
Contact: Mr Matthews
Lyme Bay Holidays
t (01297) 443363
e email@lymebayholidays.co.uk
w lymebayholidays.co.uk

Watersmeet ★★★★
Self Catering
Contact: Joanne Winkler
Lyme Bay Holidays
t (01297) 443363
e email@lymebayholidays.co.uk
w lymebayholidays.co.uk

Weavers Cottage – D4421
★★★ *Self Catering*
Lyme Bay Holidays
t (01297) 443363
e email@lymebayholidays.co.uk
w lymebayholidays.co.uk

Weighbridge Cottage – B4316 ★★★ *Self Catering*
Lyme Bay Holidays
t (01297) 443363
e email@lymebayholidays.co.uk
w lymebayholidays.co.uk

Weirside – B4392 ★★★
Self Catering
Lyme Bay Holidays
t (01297) 443363
e email@lymebayholidays.co.uk
w lymebayholidays.co.uk

Westover Farm Cottages
★★★ *Self Catering*
Contact: Mrs Debby Snook
Westover Farm Cottages
t (01297) 560451
e wfcottages@aol.com
w westoverfarmcottages.co.uk

Whitewaves ★★★
Self Catering
Contact: Joanne Winkler
Lyme Bay Holidays
t (01297) 443363
e email@lymebayholidays.co.uk
w lymebayholidays.co.uk

Windyridge – C4359 ★★★
Self Catering
Lyme Bay Holidays
t (01297) 443363
e email@lymebayholidays.co.uk
w lymebayholidays.co.uk

Woodville Apartment – B4338 ★★★ *Self Catering*
Contact: Mr Dave Matthews
Lyme Bay Holidays
t (01297) 443363
e email@lymebayholidays.co.uk
w lymebayholidays.co.uk

LYMPSHAM
Somerset

Dulhorn Farm Holiday Park
★★ *Self Catering*
Contact: Mr & Mrs Bowden
Dulhorn Farm Holiday Park
t (01934) 750298

Lower Farm House ★★★★
Self Catering
Contact: Mr & Mrs Roy & Christine Ball
t (01934) 750206
e holidays@lowerfarmcottages.co.uk
w lowerfarmcottages.co.uk

Lower Wick Farm Cottages
★★★–★★★★ *Self Catering*
Contact: Mr Nigel Bishop
Lower Wick Farm
t (01278) 751333
e info@lowerwickfarmcottages.co.uk

LYNMOUTH
Devon

Clooneavin Holidays ★★★
Self Catering
Contact: Mrs Gill Davidson
Richmond
t (01598) 753334
e relax@clooneavinholidays.co.uk
w clooneavinholidays.co.uk

Gable Cottage ★★★★
Self Catering
Marsdens Cottage Holidays
t (01271) 813777
e holidays@marsdens.co.uk
w marsdens.co.uk

Garden Flat – Hill Crest
★★★★ *Self Catering*
Contact: Mrs Ruth Thornell
t (01454) 228140
e ruththornell@btinternet.com

The Hideaway
Rating Applied For
Self Catering
Marsdens Cottage Holidays
t (01271) 813777
e holidays@marsdens.co.uk
w marsdens.co.uk

Holly's Haven ★★★★★
Self Catering
Contact: Mr & Mrs Andrew & Emma Firth
Devonholidays4u
t (01865) 875356
e enquiries@devonholidays4u.co.uk
w devonholidays4u.co.uk

Ottery Cottage ★★★★
Self Catering
Contact: Mrs Janet Cornwell
Marsdens Cottage Holidays
t (01271) 813777
e holidays@marsdens.co.uk
w marsdens.co.uk

Riverview ★★★ *Self Catering*
Contact: Mrs Janet Cornwell
Marsdens Cottage Holidays
t (01271) 813777
e holidays@marsdens.co.uk
w marsdens.co.uk

Water's Edge Cottage
★★★★ *Self Catering*
Contact: Mr M Wolverson
Primespot Character Cottages
t (01271) 882449

Wilrose ★★★ *Self Catering*
Marsdens Cottage Holidays
t (01271) 813777
e holidays@marsdens.co.uk
w marsdens.co.uk

Woodside ★★★★
Self Catering
Marsdens Cottage Holidays
t (01271) 813777
e holidays@marsdens.co.uk
w marsdens.co.uk

LYNTON
Devon

28 Castle Heights ★★★★★
Self Catering
Contact: Emma & Andrew Firth
t (01865) 875356
e enquiries@devenholidays4u.co.uk
w devonholidays4u.co.uk

Baker Court ★★★
Self Catering
Marsdens Cottage Holidays
t (01271) 813777
e holidays@marsdens.co.uk
w marsdens.co.uk

Buttershaw Cottage ★★★★
Self Catering
Contact: Mrs Janet Cornwell
Marsdens Cottage Holidays
t (01271) 813777
e holidays@marsdens.co.uk
w marsdens.co.uk

Byways ★★★★ *Self Catering*
Contact: Mrs Janet Cornwell
Marsdens Cottage Holidays
t (01271) 813777
e holidays@marsdens.co.uk
w marsdens.co.uk

Cloud Farm ★★★★
Self Catering
Contact: Mrs Jill Harman
Oare
t (01598) 741234
e doonevalleyholidays@hotmail.com
w doonevalleyholidays.co.uk

Dignity ★★★★ *Self Catering*
Marsdens Cottage Holidays
t (01271) 813777
e holidays@marsdens.co.uk
w marsdens.co.uk

Hewitts Turrett & Retreat
Rating Applied For
Self Catering
Contact: Mr Peter Cornwell
Marsdens Cottage Holidays
t (01271) 813777
e holidays@marsdens.co.uk
w marsdens.co.uk

Hollowbrook Cottage, Martinhoe ★★★★
Self Catering
Contact: Mr Christopher Legg
Martinhoe
t (01598) 763368
e info@oldrectoryhotel.co.uk
w exmoorcottages.co.uk

Lyn Cottage ★★★
Self Catering
Contact: Mrs Janet Cornwell
Marsdens Cottage Holidays
t (01271) 813777
e holidays@marsdens.co.uk
w marsdens.co.uk

Lynhurst
Rating Applied For
Self Catering
Farm & Cottage Holidays
t (01237) 479146
e enquiries@farmcott.co.uk
w holidaycottages.co.uk

Nettlecombe Cottage ★★★
Self Catering
Contact: Mrs Janet Cornwell
Marsdens Cottage Holidays
t (01271) 813777
e holidays@marsdens.co.uk
w marsdens.co.uk

Royal Castle Lodge ★★★★
Self Catering
Contact: Mr M Wolverson
Primespot Character Cottages
t (01271) 882449

The Smithy ★★★★
Self Catering
Contact: Mr & Mrs Andrew & Emma Firth
Devonholidays4u
t (01865) 875356
e enquiries@devonholidays4u.co.uk
w devonholidays4u.co.uk

Sunnymead ★★★★
Self Catering
Marsdens Cottage Holidays
t (01271) 813777
e holidays@marsdens.co.uk
w marsdens.co.uk

Tillys One and Tillys Two
★★★ *Self Catering*
Contact: Mrs Janet Cornwell
Marsdens Cottage Holidays
t (01271) 813777
e holidays@marsdens.co.uk
w marsdens.co.uk

West Ilkerton Farm ★★★★
Self Catering
Contact: Mrs Eveleigh
t (01598) 752310
e eveleigh@westilkerton.co.uk
w westilkerton.co.uk

West Lyn Farmhouse
★★★★ *Self Catering*
Contact: Mr Paul Spratley
t (01598) 753618
e info@westlynfarm.co.uk
w westlynfarm.co.uk

LYTCHETT MATRAVERS
Dorset

Annaberg ★★★ *Self Catering*
Contact: Miss L Hemingway
Dorset Cottage Holidays
t (01929) 553443
e enq@dhcottages.co.uk
w dhcottages.co.uk

Jay Cottage ★★★★
Self Catering
Contact: Ms Kirsty Parker
Dream Cottages
t (01305) 789000
e admin@dream-cottages.co.uk
w dream-cottages.co.uk

Purbeck View Cottage
★★★★ *Self Catering*
Contact: Miss LM Hemingway
Dorset Cottage Holidays
t (01929) 553443
e enq@dhcottages.co.uk
w dhcottages.co.uk

MAENPORTH
Cornwall

70 Maen Barn ★★★★
Self Catering
Helford River Holidays
t (01326) 250278
e enquiries@holidaycornwall.co.uk
w holidaycornwall.co.uk

Tregullow ★★★★
Self Catering
Cornish Holiday Cottages
t (01326) 250339
e emily@cornishholidaycottages.net
w cornishholidaycottages.net/get_property.php?p23

MAIDEN NEWTON
Dorset

Lancombe Country Cottages
★★★★ *Self Catering*
Contact: Mr Myles Provis
t (01300) 320562
e info@lancombe.co.uk
w lancombe.co.uk

MAIDENCOMBE
Devon

Bowden Close House ★★★
Self Catering
Contact: Mrs Sarah Farquharson
Bowden Close House
t (01803) 328029
e enquiries@bowdenclose.co.uk
w bowdenclose.co.uk

Mouse Cottage ★★★
Self Catering
Contact: Mrs Christine Davies
t (01803) 316655
e mousecottage@hotmail.com

MALMESBURY
Wiltshire

The Cottage ★★★★
Self Catering
Contact: Mrs Ross Eavis
t (01666) 822148
e ross@johneavis.wanadoo.co.uk
w manorfarmbandb.co.uk

Foundry Flat ★★★
Self Catering
Contact: Mr & Mrs Ratcliffe
t (01666) 824093
e foundryflat@fsmail.net
w ratcliffeandson.co.uk

MANACCAN
Cornwall

Flushing Cove Cottage (Gillan) ★★★★ *Self Catering*
Contact: Mrs Ablewhite
t (01243) 535266
e michael.ablewhite@btopenworld.com
w flushingcove-gillan.net

Gillan Cove House ★★★★
Self Catering
Contact: Mr & Mrs Ingram
t (01491) 612434
e ingram@greenfieldfarm.fsnet.co.uk
w gillancovehouse.co.uk

Hallowarren Cottage
★★★★ *Self Catering*
Cornish Cottage Holidays
t (01326) 573808
e enquiry@cornishcottageholidays.co.uk
w cornishcottageholidays.co.uk

Hillside & Chy-Pyth
★★★-★★★★ *Self Catering*
Cornish Cottage Holidays
t (01326) 573808
e enquiry@cornishcottageholidays.co.uk
w cornishcottageholidays.co.uk

Lestowder Farm
★★-★★★★ *Self Catering*
Contact: Mrs Martin
Lestowder Farm
t (01326) 231400
e lestowderfarm@hotmail.com
w lestowderfarmcottages.co.uk

West Minster Cottage
★★★★ *Self Catering*
Helford River Cottages
t (01326) 231666
e info@helfordcottages.co.uk
w helfordcottages.co.uk

MANATON
Devon

Beckaford Cottage ★★★★
Self Catering
Toad Hall Cottages
t (01548) 853089
e thc@toadhallcottages.com
w toadhallcottages.com

Church Cottage
Rating Applied For
Self Catering
Contact: Mrs Caroline Hart
t (01483) 285974
e carolinehart@stopeuworld.com

MANNINGFORD ABBOTS
Wiltshire

The Old Tulip Barn ★★★
Self Catering
Contact: Mrs Margot Andrews
Huntlys
t (01672) 563663
e meg@gimspike.fsnet.co.uk

MANSTON
Dorset

Northwood Cottages
★★★★ *Self Catering*
Contact: Mr & Mrs Jonathan & Penny Sewell
t (01258) 472666
e info@northwoodcottages.co.uk
w northwoodcottages.co.uk/affiliate/?id=enjoyengland

MARAZION
Cornwall

Arizona & Tuscany ★★★
Self Catering
Contact: Mrs Senior
t (01736) 710222
w visitcornwall.co.uk/arizonaandtuscany

Artists Cottage ★★★
Self Catering
Contact: Mrs Mock
t (01425) 404054
e holidays@artists-cottage.co.uk

The Captain's House
★★★★★ *Self Catering*
Tregullas
t (01872) 865403
e treduma@tiscali.co.uk
w captainshousemarazion.co.uk

Courtyard Cottage at the White House - ★★★
Self Catering
Contact: Sandra & Peter Hall
t (01736) 710424
e info@cornwall-holiday-cottages.com
w cornwall-holiday-cottages.com

Deveral Cottage ★★★
Self Catering
Contact: Mrs Helen Rich
t (01373) 834595
e paddy.rich@tiscali.co.uk

The Engine House (Marazion) ★★★★
Self Catering
Contact: Mr Davy
t (01736) 711604
e rickandjane@mac.com
w the-enginehouse.co.uk

Fairwinds ★★★★
Self Catering
Powells Cottage Holidays
t (01834) 813232
e info@powells.co.uk
w powells.co.uk

Lowenna (Marazion) ★★★
Self Catering
Contact: Mr Jelbart
t (01736) 710580

Sea Retreat ★★★★
Self Catering
Contact: Mrs Sally Laird
t (0118) 984 5500
e sallaird@hotmail.com
w sea-retreat.com

Tregew Holiday Bungalows
★★★ *Self Catering*
Contact: Mr Pool
t (01736) 710247

Tremel ★★★ *Self Catering*
Contact: Mrs Pearce
t (01736) 710983
e kathleen.pearce@onetel.com

Trevarthian Holiday Homes
★★★ *Self Catering*
Contact: Mrs Sally Cattran
Trevarthian Holiday Homes
t (01736) 710100
e info@trevarthian.co.uk
w trevarthian.co.uk

MARHAMCHURCH
Cornwall

Budds Barns ★★★★
Self Catering
Contact: Mr & Mrs Richardson
t (01288) 361339
e relax@buddsbarns.co.uk
w buddsbarns.co.uk

Corner Cottage ★★★★
Self Catering
Contact: Mr & Mrs Colin & Suzanne Burke
t (01525) 878100
e colin@gardnerburke.co.uk
w ourcornercottage.co.uk

Court Farm ★★★★
Self Catering
Contact: Mrs Trewin
t (01288) 361494
e mary@courtfarm-holidays.co.uk
w courtfarm-holidays.co.uk

Endsleigh Cottage ★★★★
Self Catering & Serviced Apartments
Contact: Mr Simon Sheldon
t (01452) 617966
e sheldons@glouster39.freeserve.co.uk

The Old Stable
★★★-★★★★ *Self Catering*
Contact: Mr & Mrs Henry
t (01288) 361727
w crackinggoodspot.co.uk

Sharlands Farm ★★★★
Self Catering
Contact: Lucy Ellison
Farm & Cottage Holidays
t (01237) 479146
e enquiries@farmcott.co.uk
w holidaycottages.co.uk

MARK
Somerset

Pear Tree Cottage ★★★
Self Catering
Contact: Mrs Susan Slocombe
t (01278) 641228
e sslocombe1@dclonline.net

Wesley Mews
Rating Applied For
Self Catering
Contact: Mr Bill Dean
Chapel Cottage
t (01278) 641158
e bill@deanm3.freeserve.co.uk

MARKET LAVINGTON
Wiltshire

Hazel Cottage ★★★★
Self Catering
Contact: Mrs Janette Hodgkinson
t (01380) 813516
e okasan@waitrose.com

MARLBOROUGH
Wiltshire

Dairy Cottage ★★–★★★
Self Catering
Contact: Mr & Mrs Mark and Hazel Crockford
Dairy Cottage
t (01672) 515129 & 07931 311985
e crockford@farming.co.uk

MARLDON
Devon

Lower Tor Cot ★★★★
Self Catering
Contact: Mrs Sally Wetherbee
Thorn Cottage
t (01822) 810285
e sally@wetherbee.fsnet.co.uk
w sallysholidaycottages.co.uk

Millmans Cottages
★★★–★★★★ *Self Catering*
Contact: Mrs Tina Girard
t (01803) 558213
e tina@millmanfarm.co.uk
w millmans-farm.co.uk

The Retreat ★★★★★
Self Catering
Contact: Mrs Butterworth
Torbay Holiday Agency
t (01803) 663650
e holcotts@aol.com
w swcottages.co.uk

Wildwoods ★★ *Self Catering*
Contact: Mr Ian Butterworth
Holiday Homes & Cottages South West
t (01803) 663650
e holcotts@aol.com
w swcottages.co.uk

MARNHULL
Dorset

Trooper Cottage ★★
Self Catering
Contact: Mr Cyril Bastable
Trooper Farm
t (01258) 820753

MARSH
Devon

Little Yonder ★★★
Self Catering
Powells Cottage Holidays
t (01834) 813232
e info@powells.co.uk
w powells.co.uk

MARTINHOE
Devon

Ivy Cottage ★★★★
Self Catering
Contact: Mrs Janet Cornwell
Marsdens Cottage Holidays
t (01271) 813777
e holidays@marsdens.co.uk
w marsdens.co.uk

MARTINSTOWN
Dorset

Blackbird Cottage ★★★★
Self Catering
Contact: Mr Zachary Stuart-Brown
Dream Cottages
t (01305) 789000
e admin@dream-cottages.co.uk
w dream-cottages.co.uk

Goldcombe Farm Cottages
★★★★ *Self Catering*
Contact: Kathryn Holmes
Kathryn Holmes
t (01305) 880161
e enquiries@goldcombefarm.co.uk
w goldcombefarm.co.uk

Hope Cottage ★★★★
Self Catering
Dream Cottages
t (01305) 789000
e admin@dream-cottages.co.uk
w dream-cottages.co.uk

MARTOCK
Somerset

Anne's Place ★★★
Self Catering
Country Holidays
t 0870 336 7800

MARWOOD
Devon

The Pump House ★★★★
Self Catering
Marsdens Cottage Holidays
t (01271) 813777
e holidays@marsdens.co.uk
w marsdens.co.uk

The Tallett ★★★
Self Catering
Contact: Mrs Janet Cornwell
Marsdens Cottage Holidays
t (01271) 813777
e holidays@marsdens.co.uk
w marsdens.co.uk

MAWGAN
Cornwall

The Cuckoos Nest ★★★
Self Catering
Contact: Mr Martin Raftery
Mullion Cottages
t 0845 066 7766
e enquiries@mullioncottages.com
w mullioncottages.com

Le An Marghas ★★★
Self Catering
Helford River Cottages
t (01326) 231666
e info@helfordcottages.co.uk
w helfordcottages.co.uk

Trelowarren Estate Ltd
★★★★ *Self Catering*
Contact: Mrs Anne Coombes
t (01326) 222105
e sales@trelowarren.com
w trelowarren.com

MAWGAN PORTH
Cornwall

2, 3 and 4 Merlin Apartments ★★★★
Self Catering
Contact: Mrs Cathy Osborne
Cornish Horizons Holiday Cottages
t (01841) 533331
e cottages@cornishhorizons.co.uk
w cornishhorizons.co.uk

Merlin Farm Holiday Cottages ★★★ *Self Catering*
Contact: Mr Wheeler
t (01637) 860236
e merlin@gullrockhotel.co.uk
w merlinfarm.co.uk

Merlin Golf Club
Rating Applied For
Self Catering
Treglos Hotel
t (01841) 520727
e stay@tregloshotel.com
w merlingolfcourse.co.uk

Trelawns ★★★★
Self Catering
Cornish Cottage Holidays
t (01326) 573808
e enquiry@cornishcottageholidays.co.uk
w cornishcottageholidays.co.uk

MAWNAN SMITH
Cornwall

2 Shute Hill ★★★
Self Catering
Contact: Emily Boriosi
Cornish Holiday Cottages
t (01326) 250339

4 The Square ★★★
Self Catering
Helford River Holidays Ltd
t (01326) 250278
e enquiries@holidaycornwall.co.uk

Bosaneth View ★★
Self Catering
Contact: Emily Boriosi
Cornish Holiday Cottages
t (01326) 250339
e emily@cornishholidaycottages.net
w cornishholidaycottages.net/get_property.php?p=33

Glen Avon ★★★
Self Catering
Contact: Mr & Mrs Benney
t (01326) 250283
e annb.glen@hotmail.co.uk
w cottage-cornwall.co.uk

Helford Point ★★★★
Self Catering
Contact: Ms Boriosi
Cornish Holiday Cottages
t (01326) 250399
e emily@cornishholidaycottages.net
w cornishholidaycottages.net/get_property.php?p=4

Keepers Cottage ★★★★
Self Catering
Contact: Ms Alne Turner
t (01326) 251233
e alineturner@btconnect.com

Rose Cottage 2 ★★★
Self Catering
Contact: Ms Emily Boriosi
Cornish Holiday Cottages
t (01326) 250339
e emily@cornishholidaycottages.net
w cornishholidaycottages.net/get_property.php?p=19

Rose Cottage 3 ★★★
Self Catering
Cornish Holiday Cottages
t (01326) 250339
e postmaster@cornishholidaycottages.net
w cornishholidaycottages.net/get_property.php?p=20

Tranquebar ★★★★
Self Catering
Contact: Emily Boriosi
Cornish Holiday Cottages
t 07812 007153
e emily@cornishholidaycottages.net

MELCOMBE BINGHAM
Dorset

Greygles, Melcombe Bingham ★★★★
Self Catering
Contact: Mr Paul Sommerfeld
t (020) 8969 4830
e enquiry@greygles.co.uk
w greygles.co.uk

MELKSHAM
Wiltshire

Moorlands Self Catering Holiday Homes ★★★★
Self Catering
Contact: Mrs Jackie Moore
t (01225) 702155
e moorlandsnet@aol.com
w moorlandsuk.co.uk

MELPLASH
Dorset

Binghams Farm Valley View Apartments ★★★
Self Catering
Contact: Mrs Lisa Herbert
t (01308) 488234
e enquiries@binghamsfarm.co.uk
w binghamsfarmbarns.co.uk

Mount Cottage – V4365
★★★★ *Self Catering*
Contact: Mr Dave Matthews
Lyme Bay Holidays
t (01297) 443363
e email@lymebayholidays.co.uk
w lymebayholidays.co.uk

MEMBURY
Devon

Oxenways Estate Cottages
★★★★–★★★★★
Self Catering
Contact: Mr Ken Beecham
Oxenways Country Living
t (01404) 881785
e info@oxenways.com
w oxenways.com

MENHENIOT
Cornwall

Hayloft Courtyard Cottages
★★★★ *Self Catering*
Contact: Michele & Stephen Hore
Hayloft Courtyard Cottages
t (01503) 240879
e courtyardcottage@btconnect.com
w hayloftcourtyardcottages.com

Trewint Farm
★★★–★★★★★ *Self Catering*
Contact: Mrs Rowe
Trewint Farm
t (01579) 347155
e holidays@trewintfarm.co.uk
w trewintfarm.co.uk

MERE
Wiltshire

2 Chance Cottages ★★★★
Self Catering
Contact: Mr & Mrs White
t (01747) 861401
e mail@wiltshirecottageholidays.co.uk
w wiltshirecottageholidays.co.uk

The Coach House ★★★
Self Catering
Hideaways
t (01747) 828170
e enq@hideaways.co.uk

Lower Mere Park Farm
★★★ *Self Catering*
Contact: Mrs Nicky Mitchell
t (01747) 830771

MESHAW
Devon

Strawberry Fields
Rating Applied For
Self Catering
Contact: Mr Peter Cornwell
Marsdens Cottage Holidays
t (01271) 813777
e holidays@marsdens.co.uk
w marsdens.co.uk

MEVAGISSEY
Cornwall

Bay View ★★★ *Self Catering*
Contact: Mr & Mrs Truscott
t (01726) 823684
e truscott@ctfarm.freeserve.co.uk
w courtfarmcornwall.co.uk

Blue Waters, Mevagissey
★★★ *Self Catering*
Contact: Mrs D Kendall
t (01726) 843164
e edwin.kendall@btinternet.com

The Hunnypot ★★
Self Catering
Contact: Mr Tony Lea
t (01726) 844057
e hunnypot-flat@btconnect.com
w hunnypot-flat.co.uk

Look Out
Rating Applied For
Self Catering
Contact: Mrs June Moor
t (01726) 8436 4184

The Lookout and The Penthouse ★★★★★
Self Catering
Contact: Mrs Frances Main Wilson
t (01580) 212522
e mainwilson@aol.com
w penthouseholidays.com

Pollys Apartments
★★–★★★ *Self Catering*
Contact: Mrs Diana Littlejohns
t (01726) 843352
e diana@mevagisseyapartments.co.uk
w mevagisseyapartments.co.uk

Treleaven Farm Cottages
★★★★ *Self Catering*
Contact: Mr Linda Hennah
t (01726) 843558

Treloen Holiday Apartments
★★★ *Self Catering*
Contact: Mrs Seamark
Treloen Holiday Apartments
t (01726) 842406
e holidays@treloen.co.uk
w treloen.co.uk

MIDDLECOMBE
Somerset

Periton Park Court & Riding Stables ★★–★★★★
Self Catering
Contact: Mrs Vicky Borland
t (01643) 705970
e hols@peritonpark.co.uk
w peritonpark.co.uk

MIDDLEMARSH
Dorset

White Horse Farm
★★★–★★★★ *Self Catering*
Contact: Mr David Wilding
t (01963) 210222
e enquiries@whitehorsefarm.co.uk
w whitehorsefarm.co.uk

MILBORNE ST ANDREW
Dorset

Orchard Cottage ★★★★
Self Catering
Contact: Mrs Charlotte Martin
t (01258) 837195
e deverel@dialstart78.fsnet.co.uk

The Retreat ★★★
Self Catering
Contact: Mrs June Jenkins
t (01305) 269194
e junejenkins56@hotmail.com

MILLBROOK
Cornwall

Stone Farm ★★★–★★★★
Self Catering
Contact: Mrs Blake
t (01752) 822267
w farmcott.co.uk

MILLENDREATH
Cornwall

79 Hillside Villa ★★★
Self Catering
Contact: Mrs Anne Brennan
t (01749) 678000
e annebrennan@uwclub.net
w villainlooe.velnet.co.uk

Bay View Villa ★★
Self Catering
t (01752) 774900
e sales@valleyvillas.com
w valleyvillas.com

The Lobster Pot
Rating Applied For
Self Catering
t (01752) 605605
e sales@valleyvillas.com
w valleyvillas.com

Riviera Villa ★★ *Self Catering*
Valley Villas
t (01752) 605605
e sales@valleyvillas.com
w valleyvillas.com

Sea Vista ★★★ *Self Catering*
Valley Villas
t (01752) 605605
e sales@valleyvillas.com
w valleyvillas.co.uk

Seaside Villa ★★★
Self Catering
Valley Villas
t (01752) 774900
e sales@valleyvillas.com

Serendipity ★★ *Self Catering*
Valley Villas
t (01752) 605605
e sales@valleyvillas.com
w valleyvillas.co.uk

Villa Vista ★ *Self Catering*
Valley Villas
t (01752) 605605
e sales@valleyvillas.com
w valleyvillas.com

MILLPOOL
Cornwall

Nutkin Lodge ★★★★
Self Catering
Contact: Mrs Bass
t (01208) 821596
e jsnbass@aol.com

MILTON ABBAS
Dorset

Little Hewish Barn ★★★★★
Self Catering
Contact: Mrs Alexandra Howorth
t (01258) 881235
e alex@littlehewish.co.uk

Luccombe Farm ★★★★
Self Catering
Contact: Mr & Mrs Murray & Amanda Kayll
Luccombe Farm
t (01258) 880558
e mkayll@aol.com
w luccombeholidays.co.uk

Primrose Cottage ★★★★
Self Catering
Contact: Mrs Therese Clemson
t (01962) 865786
e therese.clemson@btinternet.com
w miltonabbas-primrosecottage.co.uk

Three the Maltings ★★★
Self Catering
Contact: Mr Zachary Stuart-Brown
Dream Cottages
t (01305) 789000
e admin@dream-cottages.co.uk
w dream-cottages.co.uk

MILVERTON
Somerset

Wellisford Manor Barn
★★★★★ *Self Catering*
Contact: Ms Sarah Campos
Wellisford Manor Barn
t (01823) 672794
e sjcampos.martyn@btinternet.com
w wellisfordmanorbarn.com

MINCHINHAMPTON
Gloucestershire

Vine House Flat ★★★★
Self Catering
Contact: Mrs Veronica Finn
t (01453) 884437
e finnatminch@aol.com

The Woolsack ★★★★
Self Catering
Contact: Mrs E Hayward
t (01453) 885504
e info@hydewoodhhouse.co.uk
w hydewoodhouse.co.uk

MINEHEAD
Somerset

Anchor Cottage ★★★★
Self Catering
Contact: Dr John Malin
t (01643) 707529
e jmalin@btinternet.com
w anchorcottageminehead.co.uk

Chapel Cottage ★★★★
Self Catering
Contact: Ms Carolynn Thompson
t (01788) 810275
e stay@chapelcottage-exmoor.co.uk
w chapelcottage-exmoor.co.uk

Dome Flat ★★★★
Self Catering
Contact: Mr Lowin
t (01895) 236972

Dove Cottage ★★★
Self Catering
Contact: Mr Waterman
t (020) 8882 4920

Fishermans Cottage ★★★
Self Catering
Contact: Mrs Martin
t (01643) 704263

The Freight Shed ★★★
Self Catering
Contact: Alison & Duncan Waller
t (01643) 851386
e info@exmoorwildlifesafaris.co.uk
w exmoorwildlifesafaris.co.uk

Harbour Cottage ★★★
Self Catering
Contact: Ms E J Hall
t (01305) 36730
e familydavidmhall@computerserve.com

Higher Rodhuish Farm ★★
Self Catering
Contact: Mrs Thomas
t (01984) 640253

Marshfield Apartment
★★★★ *Self Catering*
Contact: Mr Clive Lister
t (020) 8786 8406
e c.lister7@ntl.world.com
w marshfield-apartment.co.uk

La Mer ★★★★ *Self Catering*
Contact: Mrs Audrey Bowden
t (01643) 704405

Merlin House Holiday Apartments, Blue Anchor ★★★–★★★★ *Self Catering*
Contact: Ms Penny Marshall-Rush
t (01643) 822014
e merlinhouseholiday apartments@fsmail.net
w merlinhouseholiday apartments.co.uk

Minehead Thatched Cottages ★★★★
Self Catering
Contact: Mrs Brenda Parks
t (01643) 704939
e ted.parks@virgin.net
w mineheadthatchedcottages.co.uk

Old Black Boy Cottage ★★★
Self Catering
Contact: Mr & Mrs Harvey
t (01643) 705016

The Old Kennels ★★★★
Self Catering
Contact: Mr Vivian Perkins
t (01643) 705754

Parkside ★★★ *Self Catering*
Contact: Mrs Janet Bond
t (01643) 703720
w travel.to/parkside

Peake Cottage ★★★
Self Catering
Contact: Mr H. J. Davies
t (01643) 704634

Pella ★★★ *Self Catering*
Contact: Mrs Heather Yendole
t (01643) 703277
e hyendole@ukonline.co.uk
w exmoorretreat.co.uk

Rosanda House ★★★
Self Catering
Contact: Mr & Mrs Richard & Lorna Robbins
t (01643) 704958
e enquiries@rosanda.co.uk
w rosanda.co.uk

Seagate Cottage ★★★★
Self Catering
Contact: Dr & Mr Megan & Roger Eaton & Ball
t (01935) 881436
e roger.ball@ukonline.co.uk

MISERDEN
Gloucestershire

Sudgrove Cottages ★★★
Self Catering
Contact: Mr & Mrs Martin & Carol Ractliffe
Sudgrove Cottages
t (01285) 821322
e enquiries@ sudgrovecottages.co.uk
w sudgrovecottages.co.uk

MITCHELDEAN
Gloucestershire

Church Farm Holidays Church Farm ★★★
Self Catering
Contact: Mr John Verity
t (01594) 541211
e info@churchfarm.uk.net
w churchfarm.uk.net

MITHIAN
Cornwall

Fairview Farm Cottage
★★★ *Self Catering*
Duchy Holidays
t (01872) 572971
e enquiries@duchyholidays.co.uk
w duchyholidays.co.uk

MODBURY
Devon

Moorview Lodges ★★★★
Self Catering
Contact: Mr & Mrs Ashley & Linda Humphreys
t 07762 558032
e info@dartmoorviews.co.uk
w dartmoorviews.co.uk

Old Traine Barn and Old Traine Cottage
★★★★–★★★★★
Self Catering
Toad Hall Cottages
t (01548) 853089
e thc@toadhallcottages.com
w toadhallcottages.com

Oldaport Farm Cottages
★★★★ *Self Catering*
Contact: Miss C M Evans
Oldaport Farm Cottages
t (01548) 830842
e cathy@oldaport.com
w oldaport.com

MOLLAND
Devon

Yeo Valley Holiday Park
★★★ *Self Catering*
Contact: Ms Lorna Lee
t (01769) 550297
e lorna@yeovalleyholidays.com
w yeovalleyholidays.com

MONKTON WYLD
Dorset

The Thatch – W4400
★★★★ *Self Catering*
Lyme Bay Holidays
t (01297) 443363
e email@lymebayholidays.co.uk
w lymebayholidays.co.uk

MONTACUTE
Somerset

Far End Cottage ★★★★
Self Catering
Contact: Mrs Adrienne Wright
t (01344) 772461
e aawright@btopenworld.com
w somersetcottageholidays.co.uk

MOORSHOP
Devon

Higher Longford ★★★
Self Catering
Higher Longford
t (01822) 613360
e stay@higherlongford.co.uk
w higherlongford.co.uk

MORCOMBELAKE
Dorset

Camelia Cottage – V4448
★★★★ *Self Catering*
Lyme Bay Holidays
t (01297) 443363
e email@lymebayholidays.co.uk
w lymebayholidays.co.uk

Norchard Farmhouse ★★★
Self Catering
Contact: Mrs Mary Ollard
Norchard Farmhouse
t (01297) 489263
e norchardbarn@btinternet.com

Upalong Studio – V4395
★★★ *Self Catering*
Lyme Bay Holidays
t (01297) 443363
e email@lymebayholidays.co.uk
w lymebayholidays.co.uk

MORETON
Dorset

The Courtyard ★★★
Self Catering
Contact: Mrs Jane Lofts
t (01305) 853499
e famlofts@aol.com
w heartofdorset.co.uk

Glebe Cottage ★★
Self Catering
Contact: Mrs Carol Gibbens
t (01929) 462468
e glebeho@btinternet.com
w heartofdorset.co.uk

MORETON-IN-MARSH
Gloucestershire

Brookside ★★★
Self Catering
Contact: Mrs Ward
t (01509) 646135
e rosemaryanne.ward@virgin.net

Bryher Cottage ★★★
Self Catering
Contact: Ms Lucy de Rooy
t (01386) 849296
e howardsantiques@aol.com

Horseshoe Cottage ★★★★
Self Catering
Contact: Mr & Mrs McHale
t (01451) 831556
w horseshoecottagelower oddington.co.uk

The Knoll ★★★ *Self Catering*
Contact: Ms Josie Gavoyannis
Holidays2Remember
t (01825) 791055
e info@holidays2remember.co.uk
w holidays2remember.co.uk

The Laurels ★★★
Self Catering
Contact: Mrs Sandra Billinger
t (01608) 650299
e gandsib@dialstart.net

Little Milton ★★★★
Self Catering
Contact: Mrs Heather Bates
t (01386) 701163
e info@miltonview.co.uk
w miltonview.co.uk

Little Pinners ★★★
Self Catering
Contact: Mrs Mariam Gilbert
t (01608) 650007

Michaelmas Daisy Cottage
★★★ *Self Catering*
Contact: Mrs Alexander
t (01993) 830484
e rosemaryalex@onetel.com
w rosemaryscottages.co.uk

Sarum ★★★★ *Self Catering*
Contact: Mrs Jo Brooks
t (01608) 650821
e jobrooks41@btinternet.com

Stonecroft ★★★
Self Catering
Contact: Mrs Williams
t (01608) 645397
e sitchestate@aol.com

Twinkle Toes Cottage
★★★★ *Self Catering*
Contact: Mrs Christine Gowing
t (01608) 658579
e kcgowing@talk21.com

MORETON VALENCE
Gloucestershire

Putloe Court Farm ★★★★
Self Catering
Contact: Mrs Jane Gillman
t (01452) 720211
e jane.gillman@btinternet.com

MORETONHAMPSTEAD
Devon

Budleigh Farm ★★–★★★
Self Catering
Contact: Mrs Judith Harvey
Budleigh Farm
t (01647) 440835
e harvey@budleighfarm.co.uk
w budleighfarm.co.uk

Yarningale ★★★
Self Catering
Contact: Mrs Sarah (Sally) Radcliffe
t (01647) 440560
e sally.radcliffe@virgin.net

MORTEHOE
Devon

8 Devon Beach Court
★★★★ *Self Catering*
Marsdens Cottage Holidays
t (01271) 813777
e holidays@marsdens.co.uk
w marsdens.co.uk

Beach Break
Rating Applied For
Self Catering
Contact: Mr Peter Cornwell
Marsdens Cottage Holidays
t (01271) 813777
e holidays@marsdens.co.uk
w marsdens.co.uk

Bull Point Lighthouse
★★★★ *Self Catering*
Contact: Ms Mary Garne
Rural Retreats
t (01386) 701177
e info@ruralretreats.co.uk
w ruralretreats.co.uk

Cobblestone Cottage
★★★★ *Self Catering*
Marsdens Cottage Holidays
t (01271) 813777
e holidays@marsdens.co.uk
w marsdens.co.uk

Combesgate and Barricane
★★★ *Self Catering*
Marsdens Cottage Holidays
t (01271) 813777
e holidays@marsdens.co.uk
w marsdens.co.uk

Combesgate House ★★★
Self Catering
Contact: Mr & Mrs Keith & Virginia Sprason
t (01562) 883038
e combesgate.house@virgin.net
w combesgate.fsnet.co.uk

The Grange ★★★–★★★★
Self Catering
Contact: Mr & Mrs Peter & Jill Lawley
t (01271) 870580
e the-grange-mortehoe@supanet.com

Lower Deck ★★★★
Self Catering
Marsdens Cottage Holidays
t (01271) 813777
e holidays@marsdens.co.uk
w marsdens.co.uk

Mailscot & Wykeham ★★–★★★ *Self Catering*
Contact: Mrs Janet Cornwell
Marsdens Cottage Holidays
t (01271) 813777
e holidays@marsdens.co.uk
w marsdens.co.uk

Port of Call ★★★★
Self Catering
Marsdens Cottage Holidays
t (01271) 813777
e holidays@marsdens.co.uk
w marsdens.co.uk

Rosemary Cottage ★★★★
Self Catering
Contact: Mrs Janet Cornwell
Marsdens Cottage Holidays
t (01271) 813777
e holidays@marsdens.co.uk
w marsdens.co.uk

Schooners ★★★★★
Self Catering
Marsdens Cottage Holidays
t (01271) 813777
e holidays@marsdens.co.uk
w marsdens.co.uk

Seaview Cottage ★★★
Self Catering
Contact: Mrs Janet Cornwell
Marsdens Cottage Holidays
t (01271) 813777
e holidays@marsdens.co.uk
w marsdens.co.uk

MORVAL
Cornwall

Wringworthy Cottages ★★★★ *Self Catering*
Contact: Mr & Mrs Michael & Kim Spencer
t (01503) 240685
e holidays@wringworthy.co.uk
w wringworthy.co.uk

MORWENSTOW
Cornwall

Cordena ★★★ *Self Catering*
Contact: Mr & Mrs Peter Willoughby
t (01732) 833196
e peter.willoughby@btopenworld.com

Cory Farm Cottages ★★★★
Self Catering
Contact: Mrs Tape
t (01288) 331735
e info@coryfarmcottages.co.uk
w coryfarmcottages.co.uk

MOTHECOMBE
Devon

The Flete Estate Holiday Cottages ★★★★–★★★★★
Self Catering
Contact: Miss Josephine Webb
The Flete Estate Holiday Cottages
t (01752) 830234
e cottages@flete.co.uk
w flete.co.uk

MOUNT
Cornwall

Cabilla
Rating Applied For
Self Catering & Serviced Apartments
Contact: Jay Lewis
t (01208) 821457
e jaylewis@supanet.com

MOUNT HAWKE
Cornwall

Old Basset Cottage ★★★★
Self Catering
Contact: Mr Garrick Furr
t (01209) 890334
e kfurr@whealbasset.fsnet.co.uk
w geocities.com/whealbasset

Ropers Walk Barns ★★★★
Self Catering
Contact: Mr & Mrs Pollard
t (01209) 891632
e peterandliz@roperswalkbarns.co.uk
w roperswalkbarns.co.uk

Wayside ★★ *Self Catering*
Cornish Cottage Holidays
t (01326) 573808
e enquiry@cornishcottageholidays.co.uk
w cornishcottageholidays.co.uk

MOUSEHOLE
Cornwall

Davey ★–★★ *Self Catering*
Contact: Mrs Davey
t (01736) 731264

Fern Cottage ★★★ *Self Catering & Serviced Apartments*
Contact: Mrs Stephens
t (01736) 731363
e stephens@churleys.freeserve.co.uk

Hoskins Meadows ★★★
Self Catering
Contact: Mrs Leiworthy
t (01736) 363942

Kernyk (Mousehole) ★★★
Self Catering
Contact: Mrs Gay Kendall
t (01736) 732532
e mrs_g_kendall@hotmail.com

The Little Net Loft (Mousehole) ★★★
Self Catering
Contact: Mrs Maureen King
t (020) 8220 4538
e info@thelittlenetloft.co.uk
w thelittlenetloft.co.uk

Morwenna Cottage ★
Self Catering
Contact: Mr & Mrs Johnson
t (01449) 736189

The Old Standard ★★★
Self Catering
The Old Vicarage, Brunton
t (01264) 850234
e j.underhill@oldstandard.co.uk
w oldstandard.co.uk

Penzer Cottage ★★★
Self Catering
Contact: Mrs MacDonald
Penzer Cottage
t (01753) 854395 & 07769 741018
e info@penzercottage.co.uk
w penzercottage.co.uk

Poldark Cottage ★★★
Self Catering
Contact: Ms Brown-Miller
t (01736) 330609
w cornwalltouristboard.co.uk/poldarkcottage

Sea Whispers ★★
Self Catering
Contact: Mrs Robinson
t (01736) 763695
e jrobi54536@aol.com
w seawhisperscottage.co.uk

Tides Reach and Harbourside Cottage - ★★★★ *Self Catering*
Contact: Mr & Mrs Hall
t (01736) 710424
e info@cornwall-holiday-cottages.com
w cornwall-holiday-cottages.com

Trevean Cottage (Mousehole) ★★★
Self Catering
Contact: Mrs Coleman
t (01736) 731699
e jex5@hotmail.com

Wootton Gray ★★★
Self Catering
Contact: Mrs Jenifer Bower
t (01491) 575297

MUCHELNEY
Somerset

Gothic House (The Old Dairy) ★★★ *Self Catering*
Contact: Mrs Joy Thorne
t (01458) 250626
e joy-thorne@totalserve.co.uk

MUDDIFORD
Devon

Ashtree Cottage ★★★★
Self Catering
Contact: Mrs Janet Cornwell
Marsdens Cottage Holidays
t (01271) 813777
e holidays@marsdens.co.uk
w marsdens.co.uk

Rose Cottage ★★★★
Self Catering
Contact: Ms Helen Knight
Fircombe Hall
t (01271) 814815
e sunshinenel@btinternet.com
w scorefarmholidays.co.uk

Walnut Tree Cottage ★★★★ *Self Catering*
Contact: Mr Peter Cornwell
Marsdens Cottage Holidays
t (01271) 813777
e holidays@marsdens.co.uk
w marsdens.co.uk

MUDEFORD
Dorset

Avon Reach ★★★★
Self Catering
Contact: Mrs Wynne
t (01590) 670220

Cherry Tree ★★★
Self Catering
Contact: Mrs Jean Bassil
t (01425) 271761

Crouch Cottage ★★★★
Self Catering
Contact: Mrs Julia Crouch
t (01202) 530540

Victoria Cottage ★★★★
Self Catering
Contact: Mr Zachary Stuart-Brown
Dream Cottages
t (01305) 789000
e admin@dream-cottages.co.uk
w dream-cottages.co.uk

MULLION
Cornwall

2 Coastguard Cottage ★★★
Self Catering
Contact: Mr Martin Raftery
Mullion Cottages
t (01326) 240315
e martin@mullioncottages.com
w mullioncottages.com

6 Coastguard Cottage ★★★
Self Catering
Contact: Mr Martin Raftery
Mullion Cottages
t 0845 066 7766
e enquiries@mullioncottages.com
w mullioncottages.com

Anchordown ★★★
Self Catering
Contact: Mr Martin Raftery
Mullion Cottages
t 0845 066 7766
e enquiries@mullioncottages.com
w mullioncottages.com

Angrouse Cottage
Rating Applied For
Self Catering
Contact: Mr Martin Raftery
Mullion Cottages
t 0845 066 7766
e enquiries@mullioncottages.com
w mullioncottages.com

Antrim ★★★–★★★★
Self Catering
Contact: Mr Martin Raftery
Mullion Cottages
t 0845 066 7766
e enquiries@mullioncottages.com
w mullioncottages.com

Atlantic Suite ★★★
Self Catering
Contact: Mr Martin Raftery
Mullion Cottages
t 0845 066 7766
e enquiries@mullioncottages.com
w mullioncottages.com

Cadgwith, Trewoon ★★★
Self Catering
Contact: Mr Martin Raftery
Mullion Cottages
t 0845 066 7766
e enquiries@mullioncottages.com
w mullioncottages.com

Carleon, Trewoon ★★★
Self Catering
Contact: Mr Martin Raftery
Mullion Cottages
t 0845 066 7766
e enquiries@mullioncottage.com
w mullioncottages.com

The Cedars ★★★
Self Catering
Contact: Mr Martin Raftery
Mullion Cottages
t 0845 066 7766
e enquiries@mullioncottages.com
w mullioncottages.com

Cormorant ★★★
Self Catering
Powells Cottage Holidays
t (01834) 813232
e info@powells.co.uk
w powells.co.uk

Cornerways ★★★
Self Catering
Contact: Mr Martin Raftery
Mullion Cottages
t 0845 066 7766
e enquiries@mullioncottages.com
w mullioncottages.com

The Cottage ★★★
Self Catering
Contact: Mr Martin Raftery
Mullion Cottages
t 0845 066 7766
e enquiries@mullioncottages.com
w mullioncottages.com

Creigan House ★★★★
Self Catering
Contact: Mr Martin Raftery
Mullion Cottages
t 0845 066 7766
e enquiries@mullioncottages.com
w mullioncottages.com

Cwary Vean ★★★
Self Catering
Contact: Mr Martin Raftery
Mullion Cottages
t 0845 066 7766
e enquiries@mullioncottages.com
w mullioncottages.com

Deu-Try ★★★ *Self Catering*
Contact: Mr Martin Raftery
Mullion Cottages
t 0845 066 7766
e enquiries@mullioncottages.com
w mullioncottages.com

Drop Anchor ★★
Self Catering
Contact: Mr Martin Raftery
Mullion Cottages
t 0845 066 7766
e enquiries@mullioncottages.com
w mullioncottages.com

Fore Winds ★★★
Self Catering
Contact: Mr Halford
t (01326) 240895
e ar@forewinds.co.uk
w forewinds.co.uk

The Garden Suite ★★★★
Self Catering
Contact: Mr Martin Raftery
Mullion Cottages
t 0845 066 7766
e enquiries@mullioncottages.com
w mullioncottages.com

Greenshank ★★★
Self Catering
Contact: Mr Martin Raftery
Mullion Cottages
t 0845 066 7766
e enquiries@mullioncottages.com
w mullioncottages.com

Gulls ★★★ *Self Catering*
Contact: Mr Martin Raftery
Mullion Cottages
t 0845 066 7766
e enquiries@mullioncottages.com
w mullioncottages.com

Halzephron ★★★
Self Catering
Contact: Mr Martin Raftery
Mullion Cottages
t 0845 066 7766
e enquiries@mullioncottages.com
w mullioncottages.com

The Heathers and The Palms ★★★ *Self Catering*
Contact: Mr Martin Raftery
Mullion Cottages
t (01326) 240315
e enquiries@mullioncottages.com
w mullioncottages.com

Mullion Mill Cottage ★★★
Self Catering
Contact: Mr Martin Raftery
Mullion Cottages
t 0845 066 7766
w mullioncottages.com

Ocean View ★★★★
Self Catering
Contact: Mr Martin Raftery
Mullion Cottages
t 0845 066 7766
e enquiries@mullioncottages.com
w mullioncottages.com

Parc Wartha ★★★
Self Catering
Contact: Mr Martin Raftery
Mullion Cottages
t 0845 066 7766
e enquiries@mullioncottages.com
w mullioncottages.com

Poltesco, Trewoon ★★★
Self Catering
Contact: Mr Martin Raftery
Mullion Cottages
t 0845 066 7766
e enquiries@mullioncottages.com
w mullioncottages.com

Porthpradnack ★★★★
Self Catering
Contact: Mr Martin Raftery
Mullion Cottages
t 0845 066 7766
e enquiries@mullioncottages.com

Redannnack Bungalow ★★★ *Self Catering*
Contact: Mr Martin Raftery
Mullion Cottages
t 0845 066 7766
e enquiries@mullioncottages.com
w mullioncottages.com

Rosemorran ★★★
Self Catering
Contact: Mr Martin Raftery
Mullion Cottages
t 0845 066 7766
e enquiries@mullioncottages.com
w mullioncottages.com

Sea Breezes ★★★★
Self Catering
Contact: Mr Martin Raftery
Mullion Cottages
t 0845 066 7766
e enquiries@mullioncottages.com
w mullioncottages.com

Seaspray Cottage ★★★
Self Catering
Contact: Karen Venter
t (01255) 830102
e karen_venter@hotmail.com
w seaspray-cottage.co.uk

Shellseekers ★★★★
Self Catering
Contact: Mr Martin Raftery
Mullion Cottages
t 0845 066 7766
e enquiries@mullioncottages.com

Stable Cottage ★★★
Self Catering
Contact: Mr Martin Raftery
Mullion Cottages
t 0845 066 7766
e enquiries@mullioncottages.com
w mullioncottages.com

Tremellyon ★★★★
Self Catering
Contact: Mr Martin Raftery
Mullion Cottages
t 0845 066 7766
e enquiries@mullioncottages.com
w mullioncottages.com

Trenance Barton ★★★
Self Catering
Contact: Mr Martin Raftery
Mullion Cottages
t 0845 066 7766
e enquiries@mullioncottages.com
w mullioncottages.com

Trenance Farm Cottages ★★★ *Self Catering*
Contact: Mr & Mrs Richard, Jenny & Tamara Tyler-S
t (01326) 240639
e info@trenancefarmholidays.co.uk
w trenancefarmholidays.co.uk

Trencrom ★★★★
Self Catering
Contact: Mr Martin Raftery
Mullion Cottages
t 0845 066 7766
e enquiries@mullioncottages.com
w mullioncottages.com

Tresselion House ★★★★
Self Catering & Serviced Apartments
Contact: Mr Martin Raftery
Mullion Cottages
t 0845 066 7766
e enquiries@mullioncottages.com
w mulioncottages.com

Trewenna & Scrumpy Cottage ★★★★ *Self Catering*
Contact: Mr Martin Raftery
Mullion Cottages
t (01237) 479146
e martin@mullioncottages.com
w mullioncottages.com

Willow End ★★★★
Self Catering
Contact: Mr Martin Raftery
Mullion Cottages
t 0845 066 7766
e enquiries@mullioncottages.com
w mullioncottages.com

Wireless Waves ★★★★
Self Catering
Contact: Mr Martin Raftery
Mullion Cottages
t 0845 066 7766
e enquiries@mullioncottages.com
w mullioncottages.com

MUSBURY
Devon

Knowls W4486 ★★★
Self Catering
Lyme Bay Holidays
t (01297) 443363
e email@lymebayholidays.co.uk
w lymebayholidays.co.uk

Maidenhayne Farm Cottage ★★★★★ *Self Catering*
Contact: Mrs Trudi Colley
t (01297) 552469
e graham@maidenhayne-farm-cottage.co.uk
w maidenhayne-farm-cottage.co.uk

MYLOR
Cornwall

Carsawsan Cottage ★★★★
Self Catering
Contact: Mrs Victoria Whitworth
t (01872) 552042
e vic.whit@btinternet.com
w homesandcottages.co.uk/property/carsawsancottage

Trehovel ★★★★
Self Catering
Cornish Holiday Cottages
t (01326) 250339
e emily@cornishholidaycottages.net
w cornishholidaycottages.net/get_property.php?p20

Tulip Tree Cottage ★★★★
Self Catering
Special Places in Cornwall
t (01872) 864400
e office@specialplacescornwall.co.uk
w specialplacescornwall.co.uk

MYLOR BRIDGE
Cornwall

Lowena
Rating Applied For
Self Catering
Cornish Cottage Holidays
t (01326) 573808

Tilly's Cottage ★★★★
Self Catering
Contact: Mrs Jo Spencer
Special Places in Cornwall
t (01872) 864400
e office@specialplacescornwall.co.uk
w specialplacescornwall.co.uk

MYLOR CHURCHTOWN
Cornwall

Mimosa Cottage ★★★★
Self Catering
Contact: Mrs Spencer
Special Places in Cornwall
t (01872) 864400
e office@specialplacescornwall.co.uk
w specialplacescornwall.co.uk

Penarrow Cottage ★★★★
Self Catering
Contact: Mrs Penelope Warner
54 Lemon Street
t (01872) 270199
e lemonstreetlady@aol.com

NANCLEDRA
Cornwall

Higher Chellew Cottages
★★★ *Self Catering*
Contact: Ms O'Shea
t (01736) 364532
e holidays@higherchellew.co.uk
w higherchellew.co.uk

NANSTALLON
Cornwall

The Gate House ★★★★
Self Catering
Contact: Mike Hamley
t (01208) 74291
e mikekathhamley@clara.co.uk
w trailcottage.co.uk

Stables Cottage ★★★★
Self Catering
Contact: Mr & Mrs Hinde
t (01208) 831636
e hind831636@aol.com
w members.aol.com/hind831636

Tregarthen Cottages
★★★★★ *Self Catering*
Contact: Mrs Bealing
t (01208) 831570
e enquiries@tregarthencottage.co.uk
w tregarthencottages.co.uk

NAUNTON
Gloucestershire

Aylworth Manor ★★★★
Self Catering
Contact: Dr & Mrs John & Joanna Ireland
t (01451) 850850
e jeaireland@aol.com
w aylworthmanor.co.uk

Mill Barn Cottage ★★
Self Catering
Contact: Mrs Madeleine Hindley
t (01451) 850417

Old Forge Cottage ★★★
Self Catering
Contact: Kevin Kelleher
t (01451) 850625
e kevikell@aol.com

Yew Tree House ★★★★
Self Catering
Contact: Mrs Patricia Smith
t (01372) 723166
e patriciasmith43@hotmail.com
w yewtreehouse.com

NETHERBURY
Dorset

Little Thatch ★★★★
Self Catering
Contact: Mr Zachary Stuart-Brown
Dream Cottages
t (01305) 789000
e admin@dream-cottages.co.uk
w dream-cottages.co.uk

NETTLECOMBE
Dorset

Wren Cottage ★★★★
Self Catering
Contact: Mrs Eirlys Johnson
t (01372) 378907
e eirlys.johnson@tinyworld.co.uk

NETTLETON
Wiltshire

Fosse Farmhouse
Rating Applied For
Self Catering
Contact: Caron Cooper
t (01249) 782286
e caroncooper@compuserve.com
w fossefarmhouse.com

The Garden House ★★★★★
Self Catering
Contact: Ms Caron Lois Cooper
t (01249) 782286
e caroncooper@compuserve.com

NEW POLZEATH
Cornwall

Atlantic View Holidays
★★★–★★★★★
Self Catering
Contact: Dr Garthwaite
t (01892) 722264
e enquiries@atlanticview.net
w atlanticview.net

Stepper View ★★
Self Catering
t (01708) 733966
e paul@aveley.f9.co.uk
w stepperview.co.uk

Treheather ★★★
Self Catering
Contact: Dr Elizabeth Mayall
t (01392) 841219

NEWBRIDGE
Cornwall

Moorvue Lodge ★★★★
Self Catering
Contact: Mr & Mrs Cock
t (01736) 365491

NEWENT
Gloucestershire

The George Hotel ★★★
Self Catering
Contact: Rhodri Yeandle
t (01531) 820203
e enquiries@georgehotel.uk.com
w georgehotel.uk.com

NEWLAND
Gloucestershire

Birchamp Coach House
★★★★ *Self Catering*
Contact: Mrs Karen Davies
t (01594) 833143
e karen@birchamphouse.co.uk
w birchamphouse.co.uk

NEWLYN
Cornwall

Silver Seas ★★★
Self Catering
Contact: Mrs Toms
t (01736) 368007

NEWNHAM-ON-SEVERN
Gloucestershire

The Farthings
Rating Applied For
Self Catering
Contact: Mrs Karen Smith
Light Horse Court
t (020) 7881 5306
e karensmith@chelseapensioners.org.uk

NEWQUAY
Cornwall

12 Harvest Moon Apartments ★★★★
Self Catering
Cornish Horizons Holiday Cottages
t (01841) 533331
e cottages@cornishhorizons.co.uk
w cornishhorizons.co.uk

9 Harvest Moon ★★★★
Self Catering
Contact: Ms Cathy Osborne
Cornish Horizons Holiday Cottages
t (01841) 533331
e cottages@cornishhorizons.co.uk
w cornishhorizons.co.uk

Atlantic Reach 38 ★★
Self Catering
Duchy Holidays
t (01872) 572971
e enquiries@duchyholidays.co.uk
w duchyholidays.co.uk

Beach View Executive
★★★★ *Self Catering*
Valley Villas
t (01752) 605605
e sale@valleyvillas.com
w valleyvillas.co.uk

Boatman's Loft ★★★
Self Catering
Cornish Horizons Holiday Cottages
t (01841) 533331
e cottages@cornishhorizons.co.uk
w cornishhorizons.co.uk

Brackenwood ★★★
Self Catering
Cornish Horizons Holiday Cottages
t (01841) 533331
e cottages@cornishhorizons.co.uk
w cornishhorizons.co.uk

Cheviot Holiday Apartments
★★★★ *Self Catering*
Contact: Mr & Mrs Brian & Jill Biscard
t (01637) 872712
e info@cheviotnewquay.co.uk
w cheviotnewquay.co.uk

Cornwall Coast Holidays
Self Catering
Contact: Mrs Deborah Spencer-Smith
Cornwall Coast Holidays
t (020) 8440 7518 & 07910 583050
e debbie@cornwallcoastholidays.com
w cornwallcoastholidays.com

Cornwall Holiday Lets
★★★★ *Self Catering*
Contact: Mr Michael Campbell
t 07909 961408
e info@cornwallholidaylets.net
w cornwallholidaylets.com

Croftlea Holiday Flats ★★
Self Catering
Croftlea Holiday Flats
t (01637) 852505
e info@croftlea.co.uk
w croftlea.co.uk

Degembris Cottage ★★★★
Self Catering
Contact: Mrs Kathy Woodley
St Newlyn East
t (01872) 510555
e kathy@degembris.co.uk
w degembris.co.uk

Eton Court ★★★
Self Catering
Contact: Mr Allan O'Dell
t (01637) 852545
e fiona@holidaysinnewquay.com
w holidaysinnewquay.com

Gillyn ★★ *Self Catering*
Contact: Mrs Barry
t (01637) 876104
e betty.barry@btinternet.com

Green Waters ★★★★
Self Catering
Contact: Mr & Mrs Pullen
t (01637) 873551
e bernardruth.pullen@virgin.net
w cornwalltouristboard.co.uk/greenwaters

Hendra Paul Cottages ★★★
Self Catering
Contact: Mrs Julia Schofield
t (01637) 874695
e info@hendrapaul.co.uk
w hendrapaul.co.uk

Kestle Mill ★★★
Self Catering
Contact: Mr & Mrs Turner
t (01637) 852987
e enquiries@davidballholidaylettings.co.uk

Manuels Farm ★★★★
Self Catering
Contact: Mr & Mrs Wilson
t (01637) 878300
e james@manuelsfarm.co.uk
w manuelsfarm.co.uk

Pentire Heights ★★★★
Self Catering
Cornish Horizons Holiday Cottages
t (01841) 533331
e cottages@cornishhorizons.co.uk
w cornishhorizons.co.uk

Porth Apartments ★★★
Self Catering
Contact: Ms Concah
t (020) 8993 3910

Sandy Beach Apartments ★★★ *Self Catering*
Cornish Horizons Holiday Cottages
t (01841) 533331
e cottages@cornishhorizons.co.uk
w cornishhorizons.co.uk

Seascape
Rating Applied For
Self Catering
Special Places
t (01872) 864400
e office@specialplacescornwall.co.uk

Seascape ★★★ *Self Catering*
Contact: Mr & Mrs Selleck
t (01752) 862372
e surfamber@tiscali.co.uk

The Spinnakers ★★★★
Self Catering
Cornish Horizons
t (01841) 533331
e cottages@cornishhorizons.co.uk
w cornishhorizons.co.uk

Tregurrian Villas ★★★★
Self Catering
Tregurrian Villas
t (01637) 873274
e enquiries@tregurrianhotel.com
w tegurrianhotel.com

Trendrean Farm Barns ★★★★ *Self Catering*
Contact: Mr Ivor Marshall
t (01208) 813228
e ivor.gill@btopenworld.com
w trendreanfarmbarns.co.uk

Woodpecker Cottage
Rating Applied For
Self Catering
Contact: Mr & Mrs Rumsey
t 07860 762456

NEWTON ABBOT
Devon

2 Thorn Cottages ★★★
Self Catering
Contact: Ms Debbie Saunders
t (01626) 872779
e debbie@saunders17.freeserve.co.uk
w visitwestcountry.com/thorncottage

NEWTON FERRERS
Devon

Crown Yealm Apartment ★★ *Self Catering*
Yealm Holidays
t 0870 747 2987
e info@yealm-holidays.co.uk
w yealm-holidays.co.uk

Glen Cottage ★★★
Self Catering
Yealm Holidays
t 0870 747 2987
e info@yealm-holidays.co.uk
w yealm-holidays.co.uk

Lezant Pine Lodge ★★★★
Self Catering
Yealm Holidays
t 0870 747 2987
e info@yealm-holidays.co.uk
w yealm-holidays.co.uk

NEWTON POPPLEFORD
Devon

Burrow Hill ★★★★
Self Catering
t (01297) 20729
e info@milkberehols.com
w milkberehols.com

Umbrella Cottage ★★★
Self Catering
Contact: Mrs Margaret Woodley
t (01395) 568687

NEWTON ST LOE
Somerset

Pennsylvania Farm Self-Catering ★★★★
Self Catering
Contact: Mr & Mrs Paul & Peggy Foster
t (01225) 314912
w pennsylvaniafarm.co.uk

NEWTON TRACEY
Devon

Acorn Cottage ★★★★
Self Catering
Contact: Mrs Janet Cornwell
Marsdens Cottage Holidays
t (01271) 813777
e holidays@marsdens.co.uk
w marsdens.co.uk

Balches Annexe ★★★
Self Catering
Marsdens Cottage Holidays
t (01271) 813777
e holidays@marsdens.co.uk
w marsdens.co.uk

NORTH BOWOOD
Dorset

2 Driftwood ★★★
Self Catering
Contact: Emma Blackburn
t 07766 522798
e ejb90@hotmail.com
w driftwoodapartments.co.uk

NORTH CHERITON
Somerset

Fives Court Cottage ★★★★
Self Catering
Contact: Mr & Mrs Edward & Heather Martin
t (01963) 32777
w fivescourtcottage.co.uk

NORTH CHIDEOCK
Dorset

Hell Barn Cottages ★★★
Self Catering
Contact: Mr & Mrs Shigeaki & Diana Takezoe
t (01297) 489589
e diana@hellbarn.co.uk
w hellbarn.co.uk

NORTH HILL
Cornwall

Eastgate Barn ★★★★
Self Catering
Contact: Jill Goodman
t (01566) 782573
e jill@eastgatebarn.co.uk
w eastgatebarn.co.uk

NORTH MOLTON
Devon

Bampfylde & Florence Cottages ★★★★★
Self Catering
Contact: Mrs Janet Cornwell
Marsdens Cottage Holidays
t (01271) 813777
e holidays@marsdens.co.uk
w marsdens.co.uk

The Hayloft ★★★★★
Self Catering
Contact: Mrs Diane Brookes
t (01598) 740699
e flittonoakbarns@aol.com
w flittonoakbarns.co.uk

West Millbrook Farm ★★-★★★ *Self Catering*
Contact: Mrs Rosemarie Courtney
West Millbrook Farm
t (01598) 740382
e wmbselfcatering@aol.com
w westmillbrook.co.uk

NORTH NEWTON
Somerset

Swallow Barn and Heron Barn ★★★★ *Self Catering*
Contact: Mrs Paula Mitchell
t (01278) 661518
e paula@greathousebarns.com
w holidaysinsomerset.co.uk

NORTH PETHERWIN
Cornwall

Castle Milford Mill ★★★★
Self Catering
Contact: Lucy Ellison
Farm & Cottage Holidays
t (01237) 479146
e enquiries@farmcott.co.uk
w holidaycottages.co.uk

Waterloo Farm ★★★★
Self Catering
Contact: Ms Ellison
Farm & Cottage Holidays
t (01237) 479146
e enquiries@farmcott.co.uk
w holidaycottages.co.uk

NORTH TAMERTON
Cornwall

Hill Cottage ★★★★
Self Catering
Contact: Mr & Mrs Green
t (01409) 253093
e enquiries@selfcateringcottagesdevon.co.uk
w selfcateringcottagesdevon.co.uk

Tamar Valley Cottages ★★★★ *Self Catering*
Contact: Mr & Mrs Stephen & Jane Rhodes
t (01409) 271284
e smrhodes@btinternet.com

NORTH TAWTON
Devon

Cider Cottage ★★★★
Self Catering
Contact: Mrs Susan Bartlett
t (01837) 89002
e sue@yeo-farm.com
w yeo-farm.com

Westacott Barton Farm ★★★★ *Self Catering*
Contact: Mrs Maureen Thompson
t (01837) 82314
e westacottbarton@yahoo.co.uk
w westacottbarton.co.uk

NORTH WHILBOROUGH
Devon

Long Barn Luxury Holiday Cottages ★★★★★
Self Catering
Contact: Mr Peter Tidman
t (01803) 875044
e ros@longbarncottages.co.uk
w longbarncottages.co.uk

NORTHAM
Devon

The Anchorage
Rating Applied For
Self Catering
Farm & Cottage Holidays
t (01237) 479146
e enquiries@farmcott.co.uk
w holidaycottages.co.uk

Atlantic View
Rating Applied For
Self Catering
Contact: Lucy Ellison
Farm & Cottage Holidays
t (01237) 479146
e enquiries@farmcott.co.uk
w holidaycottages.co.uk

The Cabin ★★★★
Self Catering
Contact: Mrs Janet Cornwell
Marsdens Cottage Holidays
t (01271) 813777
e holidays@marsdens.co.uk
w marsdens.co.uk

Seafield ★★★★ *Self Catering*
Farm & Cottage Holidays
t (01237) 479146
e enquiries@farmcott.co.uk
w holidaycottages.co.uk

NORTHLEACH
Gloucestershire

Cotteswold Cottage, Northleach ★★★
Self Catering
Contact: Mr David Atkinson
t (01451) 860493
e cotteswoldhouse@aol.com

NORTHLEIGH
Devon

Chilcombe ★★★
Self Catering
Contact: Ms Louise Hayman
Milkbere Cottage Holidays
t (01297) 20729
e info@milkberehols.com
w milkberehols.com

The Cider Barn ★★★★
Self Catering
Jean Bartlett Cottage Holidays
t (01297) 23221
e holidays@jeanbartlett.com
w jeanbartlett.com

Northleigh Farm ★★★★
Self Catering
Contact: Mr & Mrs Simon & Sue Potter
t (01404) 871217
e simon-potter@msn.com
w northleighfarm.co.uk

NORTHLEW
Devon

Glen Cottage
Rating Applied For
Self Catering
Contact: Mrs Butterworth
Torbay Holiday Agency
t (01803) 663650
e holcotts@aol.com
w swcottages.co.uk

NORTHWOOD GREEN
Gloucestershire

Post Paddock ★★★★★
Self Catering
Contact: Mr David Parry-Jones
t (01452) 762086
e info@postpaddock.co.uk
w postpaddock.co.uk

NORTON FITZWARREN
Somerset

The Long Barn ★★★★★
Self Catering
Contact: Mrs Jessica Vellacott
Wellisford Lettings Limited
t (01823) 672284
e info@somersetlongbarn.co.uk
w somersetlongbarn.co.uk

NORTON SUB HAMDON
Somerset

Little Norton Mill
★★★★-★★★★★
Self Catering
Contact: Mrs Lynn Hart
t (01935) 881337
e lj.hart@btinternet.com
w littlenortonmill.co.uk

NOSS MAYO
Devon

Creek View ★★★
Self Catering
Contact: Mr David Hanmer
Toad Hall Cottages
t (01548) 853089
e thc@toadhallcottages.com
w toadhallcottages.com

The Galley & Post House
★★★★ *Self Catering*
Contact: Mrs Vivienne Summers
Yealm Holidays
t 0870 747 2987
e info@yealm-holidays.co.uk
w yealm-holidays.co.uk

NOTTINGTON
Dorset

April's Cottage ★★★
Self Catering
Contact: Ms Kirsty Parker
Dream Cottages
t (01305) 789000
e admin@dream-cottages.co.uk
w dream-cottages.co.uk

NOTTON
Dorset

Notton Hill Barn Holiday Cottages ★★★-★★★★
Self Catering
Contact: Mr & Mrs D Smith
t (01300) 321299
e stay@nottonhillbarncottages.co.uk
w nottonhillbarncottages.co.uk

NUNNEY
Somerset

Riverside Cottage ★★★★
Self Catering
Contact: Mrs Clare Hulley
t (01373) 836480
w nunney.net

NYMPSFIELD
Gloucestershire

Crossways ★★★
Self Catering
Contact: Mr & Mrs Bowen
Crossways
t (01453) 860309

NYNEHEAD
Somerset

Glebe Cottage ★★★
Self Catering
Contact: Mrs Jane E S Jones
t (01823) 663362
e jane.esjones@btopenworld.com

OAKRIDGE
Gloucestershire

Watercombe House
★★★★★ *Self Catering*
Contact: Mrs Julia Murray
t (01453) 840278
e julia_murray@btconnect.com
w watercombehouse.com

OGWELL
Devon

Rydon Ball ★★★★
Self Catering
Contact: Mr Ian Butterworth
Holiday Homes & Cottages South West
t (01803) 663650
e holcotts@aol.com
w swcottages.co.uk

OKEHAMPTON
Devon

Beer Farm ★★★★
Self Catering
Contact: Bob & Sue Annear
t (01837) 840265
e info@beerfarm.co.uk
w beerfarm.co.uk

Bowerland ★★★★
Self Catering
Contact: Mr Ray Quirke
t (01837) 55979
e bowerland@devonhols.com
w devonhols.com

East Hook Holiday Cottages
★★-★★★★ *Self Catering*
Contact: Mrs Ruth Maile
t (01837) 52305
e marystevens@westhookfarm.fsnet.co.uk
w easthook-holiday-cottages.co.uk

Fourwinds Self-Catering Properties ★★★★
Self Catering
Contact: Miss Sue Collins
t (01837) 55785
e four.winds@eclipse.co.uk
w eclipse.co.uk/fourwinds

Hayrish Farm
★★★★-★★★★★
Self Catering
Contact: Mr Bill Walton
Hayrish Ltd.
t (01837) 840759
e hayrish@easynet.co.uk
w hayrish.co.uk

The Linney ★★ *Self Catering*
Contact: Ms Louise Hayman
Milkbere Cottage Holidays
t (01297) 20729
w milkberehols.com

Little Bidlake Barns ★★★★
Self Catering
Contact: Mrs Joanna Down
t (01837) 861233
e bidlakefrm@aol.com
w dartmoor-holiday-cottages.co.uk

Meldon Cottages ★★★★
Self Catering
Contact: Mr Stuart Plant
t (01837) 54363
e enquiries@meldoncottages.co.uk
w meldoncottages.co.uk

Week Farm Country Holidays ★★★★
Self Catering
Contact: Mrs Margaret Hockridge
Week Farm Country Holidays
t (01837) 861221
e accom@weekfarmonline.com
w weekfarmonline.com

OLDCROFT
Gloucestershire

Brava Annexe Holidays
★★★ *Self Catering*
Contact: Mrs Judy Dance
Brava House
t (01594) 560696
e judy@dancefamily8.fsnet.co.uk

ORCHARDLEIGH
Somerset

Orchardleigh Estate ★★★★
Self Catering
Contact: Mr Charlie Beardall
t (01373) 472550
w orchardleighholidays.net

OSMINGTON
Dorset

Emmies Cottage ★★★★
Self Catering
Contact: Mr Zachary Stuart-Brown
Dream Cottages
t (01305) 789000
e admin@dream-cottages.co.uk
w dream-cottages.co.uk

Honeybun ★★★★
Self Catering
Contact: Mr Zachary Stuart-Brown
Dream Cottages
t (01305) 789000
e admin@dream-cottages.co.uk
w dream-cottages.co.uk

Norden Cottage ★★★
Self Catering
Contact: Mr Zachary Stuart-Brown
Dream Cottages
t (01305) 789000
e admin@dream-cottages.co.uk
w dream-cottages.co.uk

Overlond ★★★ *Self Catering*
Dream Cottages
t (01305) 789000
e admin@dream-cottages.co.uk
w dream-cottages.co.uk

OSMINGTON MILLS
Dorset

Vine Cottage ★★★
Self Catering
Dream Cottages
t (01305) 789000
e admin@dream-cottages.co.uk
w dream-cottages.co.uk

OTHERY
Somerset

Willows Cottage and Levels Cottage ★★★★ *Self Catering*
Contact: Mrs Christine Ellis
t (01823) 698166
e ellis@bagenham.freeserve.co.uk
w bagenhamfarm.co.uk

OTTERFORD
Somerset

Tamarack Lodge ★★★★
Self Catering
Contact: Matthew Sparks
Tamarack Lodge
t (01823) 601270
e matthew.sparks@tamaracklodge.co.uk
w tamaracklodge.co.uk

OTTERHAM
Cornwall

Old Newham Farm ★★★
Self Catering
Contact: Mr & Mrs Purdue
t (01840) 230470
e ctb@newham.co.uk
w old-newham.co.uk

Saint Tinney Farm Holidays
★★★★ *Self Catering*
t (01840) 261274
e info@st-tinney.co.uk

OTTERTON
Devon

The Old Barn
Rating Applied For
Self Catering
Contact: Tracy Gwillin
Sweetcombe Cottage Holidays Ltd
t (01395) 512130
e enquiries@sweetcombe-ch.co.uk

OTTERY ST MARY
Devon

Deblins Brook Farm Cottage
★★★★ *Self Catering*
Contact: Mrs Glynis Walker
Deblins Brook Farm
t (01404) 811331
e glynis.thurley@btinternet.com

Waxway Farm ★★★★
Self Catering
Contact: Patrick Roberts
t (01404) 813688
e patrick@waxwayfarm.co.uk
w waxwayfarm.c.uk

OVER COMPTON
Dorset

Uplands ★★★ *Self Catering*
Contact: Mr & Mrs Suellen Brake
t (01935) 477043
e info@uplandsholidayhome.co.uk
w uplandsholidayhome.co.uk

OWERMOIGNE
Dorset

Jasmine Cottage ★★
Self Catering
Contact: Mrs Lawton
t (01305) 854457
e jill@thelawtons.eclipse.co.uk
w cottagesindorset.co.uk

Wooden Tops & Vinney Cottage ★★★ *Self Catering*
Contact: Mr Zachary Stuart-Brown
Dream Cottages
t (01305) 789000
e admin@dream-cottages.co.uk
w dream-cottages.co.uk

OWLPEN
Gloucestershire

Owlpen Manor
★★★-★★★★ *Self Catering*
Contact: Mrs Jayne Simmons
t (01453) 860261
e sales@owlpen.com
w owlpen.com

OXENTON
Gloucestershire

Crane Hill ★★★ *Self Catering*
Contact: Mrs Helen Beardsell
t (01242) 673631

OZLEWORTH
Gloucestershire

Hill Mill Cottage ★★★★
Self Catering
Contact: Mrs Nash
t (01453) 842401
e pnash@hillmillcottage.co.uk

PADDLELAKE
Devon

Hillfield Cottages & Country House ★★★★-★★★★★
Self Catering
Contact: Mrs Edwina Anderton
t (01803) 712322
e mail@hillfieldcottages.com

PADSTOW
Cornwall

1 Cross Street ★★★
Self Catering
Contact: Mrs Hollist
t (01225) 707519
e susanne.riger@virgin.net

10 Broad Street, 2 Mill Road, 5 Mill ★★★ *Self Catering*
Contact: Mrs Susan Farr
Sheepcombe House
t (01454) 614861

10 Church Lane ★★★
Self Catering
Contact: Ms Nicky Stanley
Harbour Holidays - Padstow
t (01841) 532555
e sales@jackie-stanley.co.uk
w harbourholidays.co.uk

10 Glynn Road ★★★★
Self Catering
Contact: Mrs Nicky Stanley
Harbour Holidays
t (01841) 533402
e contact@harbourholidays.co.uk
w harbourholidays.co.uk

10 Meadow Court ★★★★
Self Catering
Contact: Miss Nicola Stanley
Harbour Holidays
t (01841) 533402
e contact@harbourholidays.co.uk
w harbourholidays.co.uk

10 Porthilly View ★★★
Self Catering
Contact: Nicky Stanley
Harbour Holidays
t (01841) 533402
e contact@harbourholidays.co.uk
w harbourholidays.co.uk

12 Netherton Road ★★★
Self Catering
Contact: Mr Peter Osbourne
Cornish Horizons Holiday Cottages
t (01841) 533331
e cottages@cornishhorizons.co.uk
w cornishhorizons.co.uk

12 New Street ★★★
Self Catering
Cornish Horizons Holiday Cottages
t (01841) 533331
e cottages@cornishhorizons.co.uk
w cornishhorizons.co.uk

12 The Old Boatyard ★★★
Self Catering
Upper Deck
t (01841) 520998

14 Cross Street ★★★
Self Catering
Contact: Mr Peter Osborne
Cornish Horizons Holiday Cottages
t (01841) 533331
e cottages@cornishhorizons.co.uk
w cornishhorizons.co.uk

14 Riverside ★★★★★
Self Catering
Harbour Holidays Ltd.
t (01841) 533402
e contact@harbourholidays.co.uk

15 Egerton Road ★★★
Self Catering
Harbour Holidays - Padstow
t (01841) 532555
e sales@jackie-stanley.co.uk

17 Netherton Road ★★★★
Self Catering
Contact: Ms Nickie Stanley
Harbour Holidays, Padstow
t (01841) 533402
e t.colver@techniquestudios.com

18 Treverbyn Road
Rating Applied For
Self Catering
Contact: Nicky Stanley
Harbour Holidays
t (01841) 333402
e contact@harbourholidays.co.uk
w harbourholidays.co.uk

19 High Street ★★★
Self Catering
Contact: Ms Nicky Stanley
Harbour Holidays - Padstow
t (01841) 532555
e sales@jackie-stanley.co.uk

2 The Strand ★★★
Self Catering
Contact: Ms Nicky Stanley
Harbour Holidays - Padstow
t (01841) 532402
e contact@harbourholidays.co.uk
w harbourholidays.co.uk

21 New Street ★★★★★
Self Catering
Contact: Nicky Stanley
Harbour Holidays
t (01841) 533402
e contact@harbourholidays.co.uk
w harbourholidays.co.uk

22 Egerton Road ★★★★
Self Catering
Contact: Ms Nicky Stanley
Harbour Holidays - Padstow
t (01841) 532555
e sales@jackie-stanley.co.uk

25 Old School Court ★★★★
Self Catering
Contact: Ms Stanley
Harbour Holidays
t (01841) 533402
e contact@harbourholidays.co.uk
w harbourholidays.co.uk

26 Church Lane ★★★
Self Catering
Contact: Peter Osbourne
Cornish Horizons Holiday Cottages
t (01841) 533331
e cottages@cornishhorizons.co.uk
w cornishhorizons.co.uk

3 Dennis Cove ★★★
Self Catering
Contact: Ms Nicky Stanley
Harbour Holidays - Padstow
t (01841) 532555
e sales@jackie-stanley.co.uk

3 Mill Road ★★★
Self Catering
Contact: Mrs Morris Kirby
t (01841) 533219
e debbie.morriskirby@tesco.net
w acottageinpadstow.com

3 Oak Terrace ★★
Self Catering
Contact: Mrs Pauline Meredith
t (01841) 532554

3 Red Brick Building ★★★
Self Catering
Harbour Holidays - Padstow
t (01841) 532555

34 Sarah's View ★★★
Self Catering
Contact: Mrs Margaret Thomas
t (01841) 532243

4 Red Brick Building ★★★
Self Catering
Contact: Nicky Stanley
Harbour Holidays
t (01841) 533402
e contact@harbourholidays.co.uk
w harbourholidays.co.uk

4 Treverbyn Road ★★★★
Self Catering
Contact: Mrs Vivian
t (01841) 533791
e neil.vivian@btopenworld.com
w holiday-padstow.co.uk

45 Sarah's View ★★★
Self Catering
Harbour Holidays
t (01841) 533402
e contact@harbourholidays.co.uk
w harbourholidays.co.uk

5 Little Dinas ★★★★
Self Catering
Contact: Mr Stanley
Harbour Holidays
t (01841) 533402
e contact@harbourholidays.co.uk
w harbourholidays.co.uk

54 Raleigh Close ★★★
Self Catering
Harbour Holidays
t (01841) 533402

6 Riverside ★★★
Self Catering
Contact: Cornish Horizons
Cornish Horizons Holiday Cottages
t (01841) 533331
e cottages@cornishhorizons.co.uk
w cornishhorizons.co.uk

6 Waterside ★★★
Self Catering
Harbour Holidays
t (01841) 532555
e contact@harbourholidays.co.uk
w harbourholidays.co.uk

62 Sarah's View ★★★
Self Catering
Contact: Mrs Amey
t (01202) 258769
e KathyAmey@aol.com

7/9 Grove Place ★★★
Self Catering
Contact: Ms Nicky Stanley
Harbour Holidays - Padstow
t (01841) 532555
e sales@jackie-stanley.co.uk

Alexandra House – Self Catering. ★★★★
Self Catering
t (01841) 532503
w padstow.uk.com/alexandra

Armsyde ★★★ *Self Catering*
Harbour Holidays
t (01841) 532555

The Backs and Rhetts ★★★
Self Catering
Contact: Ms Nicky Stanley
Harbour Holidays - Padstow
t (01841) 532555
e sales@jackie-stanley.co.uk

Beau Vista ★★★★
Self Catering
t (01428) 723819
e enquiries@cornishseaviewcottages.co.uk
w cornishseaviewcottages.co.uk

Bellagio ★★★★ *Self Catering*
Contact: Nigel & Jane Sellar
t (01902) 840094
e janesellar@tiscali.co.uk
w padstowlets.com

Blair House ★★★★
Self Catering
Contact: Nicky Stanley
Harbour Holidays
t (01841) 533402
e contact@harbourholidays.co.uk
w harbourholidays.co.uk

Bloomfield, Trevone
★★-★★★ *Self Catering*
t (01841) 533804
e garsladeguest@btconnect.com
w bloomfieldcottage.com

Bobbins ★★★ *Self Catering*
Contact: Ms Nicky Stanley
Harbour Holidays - Padstow
t (01841) 532402
e contact@harbourholidays.co.uk
w harbourholidays.co.uk

Bos Keun Lowen ★★★★
Self Catering
Contact: Peter Osbourne
Cornish Horizons Holiday Cottages
t (01841) 533331
e cottages@cornishhorizons.co.uk
w cornishhorizons.co.uk

Broomleaf Cottage ★★★
Self Catering
Contact: Peter Osbourne
Cornish Horizons Holiday Cottages
t (01841) 533331
e cottages@cornishhorizons.co.uk
w cornishhorizons.co.uk

Camel Cottage ★★★
Self Catering
Contact: Peter Osbourne
Cornish Horizons Holiday Cottages
t (01841) 533331
e cottages@cornishhorizons.co.uk
w cornishhorizons.co.uk

Catherine ★★★★
Self Catering
Contact: Mr & Mrs Lovell
Catherine
t (01841) 533859
e bob@padstow.force9.co.uk

The Coach House ★★★
Self Catering
Harbour Holidays Padstow
t (01841) 533402
e t.colver@techniquestudios.com
w harbourholidays.co.uk

Coachyard Mews ★★★
Self Catering
Contact: Mr Andrews
t (01841) 521198
e raideanltd@aol.com
w holidaysinpadstow.co.uk

Crabcatchers ★★★
Self Catering
Contact: Peter Osbourne
Cornish Horizons Holiday Cottages
t (01841) 533331
e cottages@cornishhorizons.co.uk
w cornishhorizons.co.uk

Crenella Barn ★★★
Self Catering
Contact: Ms Nicky Stanley
Harbour Holidays - Padstow
t (01841) 532555
e sales@jackie-stanley.co.uk

Curlews ★★★ *Self Catering*
Contact: Ms Nicky Stanley
Harbour Holidays - Padstow
t (01841) 532555
e sales@jackie-stanley.co.uk

Dingly Dell ★★ *Self Catering*
Contact: Ms Nicky Stanley
Harbour Holidays - Padstow
t (01841) 532402
e contact@harbourholidays.co.uk
w harbourholidays.co.uk

Dodo's Cottage ★★★★
Self Catering
Contact: Nicky Stanley
Harbour Holidays - Padstow
t (01841) 532402
e contact@harbourholidays.co.uk
w harbourholidays.co.uk

Dove Cottage ★★
Self Catering
Contact: Nicky Stanley
Harbour Holidays - Padstow
t (01841) 532402
e contact@harbourholidays.co.uk
w harbourholidays.co.uk

The Drang House ★★★
Self Catering
Contact: Nicky Stanley
Harbour Holidays
t (01841) 532402

Driftwood Cottage
Rating Applied For
Self Catering
Contact: Mrs Gill Burgess
t (01841) 532633
e info@padstowcottagecompany.co.uk
w padstowcottagecompany.co.uk

The Dukes ★★★
Self Catering
Contact: Mr Peter Howorth
Vine Cottage
t (01635) 30096
e manancat@phowth.fsnet.co.uk

Estuary View ★★★
Self Catering
Harbour Holidays - Padstow
t (01841) 532555

Felwyn ★★ *Self Catering*
Contact: Mr Peter Osbourne
Cornish Horizons Holiday Cottages
t (01841) 533331
e cottages@cornishhorizons.co.uk
w cornishhorizons.co.uk

Fishermans Cottage ★★★★
Self Catering
Contact: Nicky Stanley
Harbour Holidays
t (01841) 532555
e sales@jackie-stanley.co.uk
w harbourholidays.co.uk

Flat 3 The Old Bakehouse
★★★★ *Self Catering*
Contact: Nicky Stanley
Harbour Holidays LTD
t (01841) 533402
e contact@harbourholidays.co.uk
w harbourholidays.co.uk

Foresters Cottage ★★★★
Self Catering
Contact: Miss Nicky Stanley
t (01841) 533402
e contact@harbourholidays.co.uk
w harbourholidays.co.uk

Fuchsia Cottage ★★★
Self Catering
Contact: Mrs Burgess
t (01841) 532633
e info@padstowcottagecompany.co.uk
w padstowcottagecompany.co.uk

Grove Cottage ★★★
Self Catering
t (01432) 275084
e Ian@cathcarti.freeserve.co.uk
w padstowcottages.info

Harbour Holidays Ltd Padstow ★★★ *Self Catering*
Harbour Holidays
t (01841) 533402
e contact@harbourholidays.co.uk
w harbourholidays.co.uk

Hidden Cottage ★★★★★
Self Catering
Contact: Mrs Nicky Stanley
Harbour Holidays
t (01841) 532555
e sales@jackie-stanley.co.uk
w harbourholidays.co.uk

Hideaway Cottage ★★★★
Self Catering
Contact: Mr & Mrs Sutton
t (01234) 353499
e dnl.holidays@ntlworld.com
w dnlholidays.co.uk

Hollyhedge ★★★
Self Catering
Contact: Mr Peter Osbourne
Cornish Horizons Holiday Cottages
t (01841) 533331
e cottages@cornishhorizons.co.uk
w cornishhorizons.co.uk

Honey Cottage – Padstow
★★★ *Self Catering*
Contact: Mrs Jane Trimmer
t (020) 8441 6239
e ian@honeycottagepadstow.co.uk
w honeycottagepadstow.co.uk

Honeysuckle Cottage
★★★★ *Self Catering*
Harbour Holidays - Padstow
t (01841) 532555
w harbourholidays.co.uk

Honeysuckle Cottage ★★★
Self Catering
Contact: Mrs Clarke
t (01363) 84292
e debbie@cchaulage.com
w honeysucklecottage padstow.co.uk

Jasmine Cottage ★★★★
Self Catering
Contact: Ms Nicky Stanley
Harbour Holidays - Padstow
t (01841) 532555
e sales@jackie-stanley.co.uk
w harbourholidays.co.uk

Joan's Cottage
Rating Applied For
Self Catering
t (01841) 532814
e info@symply-padstow.co.uk
w symplypadstow.co.uk

Kernyck Cottage ★★★★
Self Catering
Contact: Mrs Norfolk
t (01841) 532902
e sue.padecho@tinyworld.co.uk

Kittiwake ★★★★
Self Catering
Contact: Ms Nicky Stanley
Harbour Holidays - Padstow
t (01841) 532555
e sales@jackie-stanley.co.uk

Lamorva Cottage ★★★
Self Catering
Contact: Mr & Mrs Plume
t (01841) 533841
e lamorva@aol.com

Lantern House ★★★
Self Catering
Contact: Mr Wright
t (01841) 532566

Lawn Cottage ★★★★
Self Catering
Contact: Mrs Buckingham
t 0870 442 3684
e heather@bprops.co.uk
w bprops.co.uk

Lazy Days ★★★ *Self Catering*
Contact: Mrs Nickie Stanley
Harbour Holidays, Padstow
t (01841) 533402
e t.colver@techniquestudios.com

Lelissick ★★★ *Self Catering*
Contact: Ms Nicky Stanley
Harbour Holidays - Padstow
t (01841) 532555
e sales@jackie-stanley.co.uk
w harbourholidays.co.uk

Little Dolphins ★★★
Self Catering
Contact: Peter Osbourne
Cornish Horizons Holiday Cottages
t (01841) 533331
e cottages@cornishhorizons.co.uk
w cornishhorizons.co.uk

Little Dukes ★★★
Self Catering
Contact: Mr Peter Osbourne
Cornish Horizons Holiday Cottages
t (01841) 533331
e cottages@cornishhorizons.co.uk
w cornishhorizons.co.uk

Little Haven ★★★
Self Catering
Contact: Mr Andrew Cousins
t (0118) 932 8116
e andycousins@hotmail.com
w stay-in-padstow.co.uk

Little Penty ★★★
Self Catering
Cornish Horizons Holiday Cottages
t (01841) 533331
e cottages@cornishhorizons.co.uk
w cornishhorizons.co.uk

Lobster House ★★★★
Self Catering
Contact: Peter Osbourne
Cornish Horizons Holiday Cottages
t (01841) 533331
e cottages@cornishhorizons.co.uk
w cornishhorizons.co.uk

The Lobster Pot ★★★
Self Catering
Contact: Ms Kay Wood
t (01841) 540226
e kaywood@onetel.net.uk

Lobsterpots ★★★
Self Catering
Contact: Mr Peter Osbourne
Cornish Horizons Holiday Cottages
t (01841) 533331
e cottages@cornishhorizons.co.uk
w cornishhorizons.co.uk

Louand ★★★ *Self Catering*
Contact: Mr & Mrs Osborne
Cornish Horizons Holiday Cottages
t (01841) 533331
e cottages@cornishhorizons.co.uk
w cornishhorizons.co.uk

Marina Villa – St Edmunds End ★★★ *Self Catering*
Contact: Ms Nicky Stanley
Harbour Holidays - Padstow
t (01841) 532555
e sales@jackie-stanley.co.uk

Market Square Hol Apartments ★★★–★★★★
Self Catering
Contact: Mrs Mary Higgins
t (01841) 533339
e msh@padstow.com
w padstow.com/msh

Maypole Cottages
★★★–★★★★ *Self Catering*
Harbour Holidays
t (01454) 614861
w maypolecottages.co.uk

Mevagh ★★★ *Self Catering*
Contact: Ms Nicky Stanley
Harbour Holidays - Padstow
t (01841) 532555
e sales@jackie-stanley.co.uk

Middle Street Apartments
★★★ *Self Catering*
Contact: Mrs Hull
t (01841) 533545

Nooks Cottage ★★★
Self Catering
Contact: Mr Peter Osbourne
Cornish Horizons Holiday Cottages
t (01841) 533331
e cottages@cornishhorizons.co.uk
w cornishhorizons.co.uk

The Old Bakery ★★★★
Self Catering
t (01841) 532885
e tonytwprops@aol.com
w twproperties.co.uk

The Old Coach House ★★★
Self Catering
Contact: Ms Nicky Stanley
Harbour Holidays - Padstow
t (01841) 532555
e sales@jackie-stanley.co.uk

Old Custom House Barn
★★★★★ *Self Catering*
Harbour Holidays Ltd
t (01841) 533402
e contact@harbourholidays.co.uk

Old School House ★★★
Self Catering
Contact: Ms Stanley
Jackie Stanley Estate Agents
t (01208) 862424

Ossmill Cottage ★★★
Self Catering
Contact: Ms Nicky Stanley
Harbour Holidays
t (01841) 532555
e sales@jackie-stanley.co.uk

Overcliff ★★★★
Self Catering
t (01858) 545386

Oystercatchers ★★★
Self Catering
Cornish Horizons Holiday Cottages
t (01841) 533331
e cottages@cornishhorizons.co.uk
w cornishhorizons.co.uk

Padstow House ★★
Self Catering
Valley Villas
t (01752) 605605
e sales@valleyvillas.com
w valleyvillas.com

Pebble Cottage ★★★★
Self Catering
Contact: Nicky Stanley
Harbour Holidays
t (01841) 532555
e sales@jackie-stanley.co.uk

Pebbles Cottage ★★★
Self Catering
Contact: Mrs Burgess
t (01841) 532633
e info@padstowcottagecomapny.co.uk
w padstowcottagecompany.co.uk

Pensers ★★★★ *Self Catering*
Contact: Ms Nicky Stanley
Harbour Holidays - Padstow
t (01841) 532402
e contact@harbourholidays.co.uk
w harbourholidays.co.uk

Pentyre House ★★★★
Self Catering
Contact: Ms Osborne
Cornish Horizons Holiday Cottages
t (01841) 533331
e cottages@cornishhorizons.co.uk
w cornishhorizons.co.uk

Periwinkle Cottage ★★★
Self Catering
Contact: Mrs Debbie Barnes
t (01841) 533838
e mail@padstowholidaycottage.co.uk
w padstowholidaycottage.co.uk

Pinmill Cottage ★★★
Self Catering
Contact: Ms Stanley
Harbour Holidays
t (01841) 532555
e sales@jackie-stanley.co.uk
w harbourholidays.co.uk

Polbrea ★★★★ *Self Catering*
Contact: Ms Nicky Stanley
Harbour Holidays
t (01841) 533402

Poppies ★★★★ *Self Catering*
Contact: Ms Nicky Stanley
Harbour Holidays - Padstow
t (01841) 532555
e contact@harbourholidays.co.uk
w harbourholidays.co.uk

Portloe ★★ *Self Catering*
Contact: Nicky Stanley
Harbour Holidays - Padstow
t (01841) 532402
e contact@harbourholidays.co.uk
w harbourholidays.co.uk

Primrose House ★★★
Self Catering
Contact: Mr Peter Osbourne
Cornish Horizons Holiday Cottages
t (01841) 533331
e cottages@cornishhorizons.co.uk
w cornishhorizons.co.uk

Puffin Cottage ★★★
Self Catering
Contact: Ms Nicky Stanley
Harbour Holidays - Padstow
t (01841) 532402
e contact@harbourholidays.co.uk
w harbourholidays.co.uk

Quayside Cottage ★★★
Self Catering
Contact: Mrs Andrea Richards
t (01841) 532429
e andrearichards@btinternet.com
w stayinpadstow.co.uk

The Quies ★★★★
Self Catering
Harbour Holidays - Padstow
t (01841) 532555

Reverie ★★★ *Self Catering*
Contact: Mr Osbourne
Cornish Horizons Holiday Cottages
t (01841) 533331
e cottages@cornishhorizons.co.uk
w cornishhorizons.co.uk

Robins Nest ★★★
Self Catering
Contact: Mr Peter Osbourne
Cornish Horizons Holiday Cottages
t (01841) 533331
e cottages@cornishhorizons.co.uk
w cornishhorizons.co.uk

Rockview ★★★★
Self Catering
Contact: Nicky Stanley
Harbour Holidays
t (01841) 532402
e contact@harbourholidays.co.uk
w harbourholidays.co.uk

Rose Cottage ★★★
Self Catering
Contact: Ms Stanley
Harbour Holidays
t (01841) 532555
e sales@jackie-stanley.co.uk

Rosehill Cottage ★★★
Self Catering
Contact: Nickie Stanley
Harbour Holidays
t (01841) 533402

Rosehill House ★★★
Self Catering
Contact: Mrs Gill Burgess
t (01841) 532633
e info@padstowcottagecompany.co.uk
w padstowcottagecompany.co.uk

Sable Cottage & Chiff Chaff
★★★–★★★★ *Self Catering*
Contact: Mrs Daw
t (0117) 907 9348
e mddaw@harbury56.fsnet.co.uk
w sablecottage.co.uk

Sail Loft ★★ *Self Catering*
Contact: Ms Nicky Stanley
Harbour Holidays - Padstow
t (01841) 532555
e sales@jackie-stanley.co.uk
w harbourholidays.co.uk

Sarah's View ★★★
Self Catering
Contact: Nicky Stanley
Harbour Holidays
t (01841) 532402
e contact@harbourholidays.co.uk
w harbourholidays.co.uk

The School House ★★★★
Self Catering
t (01208) 812640
e holidayat.theschoolhouse@virgin.net

Seal Cottage ★★★
Self Catering
Contact: Ms Nicky Stanley
Harbour Holidays - Padstow
t (01841) 532402
e contact@harbourholidays.co.uk
w harbourholidays.co.uk

Serendipity ★★★
Self Catering
Contact: Ms Nicky Stanley
Harbour Holidays - Padstow
t (01841) 532555
e sales@jackie-stanley.co.uk

Shore Lodge ★★★★★
Self Catering
Contact: Mrs Gill Vivian
t (01841) 533791
e neil.vivian@btopenworld.com
w holiday-padstow.co.uk

Skipper Cottage ★★★
Self Catering
Contact: Mrs Cheryl MacRae
t (01841) 540237
e m4crae@aol.com

The Slate House ★★★
Self Catering
Contact: Ms Stanley
Harbour Holidays
t (01841) 532555
e sales@jackie-stanley.co.uk

Squirrels ★★★ *Self Catering*
Cornish Horizons Holiday Cottages
t (01841) 533331
e cottages@cornishhorizons.co.uk
w cornishhorizons.co.uk

Stable Cottage – Padstow ★★★★ *Self Catering*
Contact: Mrs Hagley
t (01841) 532874
e info@padstowcottages.co.uk
w padstowcottages.co.uk

Stone Cottage ★★
Self Catering
Contact: Mr James Richardson
t (01923) 226218
e James.richardson@lpm.u-psud.fr

Stonesthrow Cottage ★★★★ *Self Catering*
Contact: Mr Peter Osbourne
Cornish Horizons Holiday Cottages
t (01841) 533331
e cottages@cornishhorizons.co.uk
w cornishhorizons.co.uk

The Strand ★★★
Self Catering
Contact: Mrs Brown
t (01208) 821611
e info@strandpadstow.co.uk
w strandpadstow.co.uk

Summer Court ★★★★
Self Catering
Contact: Mr & Mrs Whitehead
t (0113) 286 0036
e john@summercourt.info
w summercourt.info

Sunbeam Cottage Self Catering ★★★★
Self Catering
Contact: Miss Wendy Gidlow
t (01841) 533447
e wendy@wgidlow.fsnet.co.uk
w sunbeam-cottage.co.uk

Sundance ★★★ *Self Catering*
Contact: Nicky Stanley
Harbour Holidays
t (01841) 532402
e contact@harbourholidays.co.uk
w harbourholidays.co.uk

Sunday Cottage & School Cottage ★★★★ *Self Catering*
Contact: Mrs Diane Hoe
Lower Cottage
t (01789) 450214
e mail@sundaycottage.co.uk
w sundaycottage.co.uk

Sunnyhill Cottage ★★★★
Self Catering
Contact: Ms Nicky Stanley
Harbour Holidays - Padstow
t (01841) 532402
e contact@harbourholidays.co.uk
w harbourholidays.co.uk

Sunrise Cottage – Padstow ★★★★★ *Self Catering*
Contact: Mr & Mrs M G A E Walker
t (01384) 221295

T Sandt ★★★ *Self Catering*
Cornish Horizons Holiday Cottages
t (01841) 533331
e cottages@cornishhorizons.co.uk
w cornishhorizons.co.uk

Teal and Cormorant ★★
Self Catering
Contact: Ms Nicky Stanley
Harbour Holidays - Padstow
t (01841) 532555
e sales@jackie-stanley.co.uk
w harbourholidays.co.uk

Teazers ★★★ *Self Catering*
Contact: Ms Nicky Stanley
Harbour Holidays - Padstow
t (01841) 532402
e contact@harbourholidays.co.uk
w harbourholidays.co.uk

Thyme Cottage ★★
Self Catering
Contact: Mr Stephen Andrews
t (01841) 521198
e raidenltd@aol.com
w holidayinpadstow.co.uk

Tregirls ★★★-★★★★
Self Catering
Contact: Mrs Watson Smyth
t (01841) 532648
e watson.smyth@farmline.com
w padstowfarmfoods.biz

Trenoder ★★★ *Self Catering*
Contact: Mr Peter Osbourne
Cornish Horizons Holiday Cottages
t (01841) 533331
e cottages@cornishhorizons.co.uk
w cornishhorizons.co.uk

Treverbyn Road ★★★
Self Catering
Contact: Nicky Stanley
Harbour Holidays
t (01841) 532402
e contact@harbourholidays.co.uk
w harbourholidays.co.uk

Trevorrick Farm Cottages ★★★ *Self Catering*
Contact: Mr & Mrs Benwell
t (01841) 540574
e info@trevorrick.co.uk
w trevorrick.co.uk

Wharf Cottage ★★★★
Self Catering
Contact: Nicky Stanley
Harbour Holidays
t (01841) 533402
e contact@harbourholidays.co.uk
w harbourholidays.co.uk

Yellow Sands Cottages ★★★-★★★★ *Self Catering*
Contact: Mrs Sharon Keast
Yellow Sands Cottages
t (01637) 881548
e yellowsands@btinternet.com
w yellowsands.co.uk

Zefyros ★★★★ *Self Catering*
t (01952) 727465
e harris@brian504.freeserve.co.uk

PAIGNTON
Devon

26 New Esplanade Court ★★★ *Self Catering*
Contact: Mr Baron Elliott
t (01803) 528078
e bazzy_elliott@hotmail.com

Above Deck ★★★★
Self Catering
Holiday Homes & Cottages South West
t (01803) 663650
e holcotts@aol.com
w swcottages.co.uk

Acacia Holiday Apartments ★★★-★★★★ *Self Catering*
Contact: Mrs Bertha Bright
t (01803) 554022

All Seasons (Adults Only) Holiday Apartments ★★★★
Self Catering
Contact: Mr Mike Dessi
t (01803) 552187
e enquiries@allseasonsholiday.freeserve.co.uk
w allseasonsholidayapartments.co.uk

Beachside
Rating Applied For
Self Catering
Contact: Mrs Butterworth
Torbay Holiday Agency
t (01803) 663650
e holcotts@aol.com
w swcottages.co.uk

Bedford Holiday Flats and Flatlets ★★-★★★
Self Catering
Contact: Mr & Mrs S Dunster
t (01803) 557737
e info@bedfordholidayflats.co.uk
w bedfordholidayflats.co.uk

Belvedere Apartments 14 ★★★★★ *Self Catering*
Contact: Mrs Maggie Sycamore
Blue Chip Vacations
t (01803) 855282
e sylvia@bluechipvacations.com

Belvedere Apartments 16 ★★★★ *Self Catering*
Contact: Mrs Maggie Sycamore
Blue Chip Vacations
t (01803) 855282
e sylvia@bluechipvacations.com

Belvedere Apartments 17 ★★★★★ *Self Catering*
Contact: Mrs Maggie Sycamore
Blue Chip Vacations
t (01803) 855282
e sylvia@bluechipvacations.com

Belvedere Apartments 18 ★★★★ *Self Catering*
Contact: Mrs Maggie Sycamore
Blue Chip Vacations
t (01803) 855282
e sylvia@bluechipvacations.com

Belvedere Apartments 2 ★★★★ *Self Catering*
Contact: Mrs Maggie Sycamore
Blue Chip Vacations
t (01803) 855282
e sylvia@bluechipvacations.com

Belvedere Apartments 20 ★★★★ *Self Catering*
Contact: Mrs Maggie Sycamore
Blue Chip Vacations
t (01803) 855282
e sylvia@bluechipvacations.com

Belvedere Apartments 4 ★★★★ *Self Catering*
Contact: Mrs Adele Barnes
Blue Chip Vacations
t (01803) 855282
e info@bluechipvacations.com
w bluechipvacations.com/paignton/paignton_belvedere_court.php

Big Tree Holiday Flats ★★★
Self Catering
Contact: Mrs Pam Siddall
t (01803) 559559
e bigtree@eidosnet.co.uk
w bigtreeholidayflats.co.uk

Bosuns Cottage ★★★★
Self Catering
Holiday Homes & Cottages South West
t (01803) 663650
e holcotts@aol.com
w swcottages.co.uk

Broadshade Holiday Flats ★★★ *Self Catering*
Contact: Mr & Mrs John & Dot Barber
t (01803) 559647
e broadshade@hotmail.com
w broadshade.com

Carlton Manor ★★★★★
Self Catering
Blue Chip Vacations
t (01803) 855282
e andrew@bluechipvacations.com
w bluechipvacations.com

Casa Marina Holiday Apartments ★★ *Self Catering*
Contact: Ms Sandie Boulton
RML Properties
t (01543) 675555
e enquiries@casamarina.co.uk
w casamarina.co.uk

Compton Pool Farm ★★★★★ *Self Catering*
Contact: Mr & Mrs John & Ann Stocks
t (01803) 872241
e enquiries@comptonpool.co.uk
w comptonpool.co.uk

Cranmore Lodge ★★★
Self Catering
Contact: Mr & Mrs David & Lynda McDermott
t (01803) 556278
e cranlodge@btopenworld.com
w cranmorelodge.co.uk

Denby House Holiday Apartments ★★★
Self Catering
Contact: Mr & Mrs Brian & Lina Ford
t (01803) 559121
e lina@denbyhouse.co.uk
w denbyhouse.co.uk

Fairsea Holiday Flats ★★-★★★ *Self Catering*
Contact: Mr John Hallett
t (01803) 556903
e fairsea@amserve.net

Fortescue ★★★ *Self Catering*
Holiday Homes & Cottages South West
t (01803) 663650
e holcotts@aol.com
w swcottages.co.uk

Glencoe Holiday Flats ★★★
Self Catering
Contact: Mrs Patricia Jill Ayles
t (01803) 557727
e info@glencoeapartments.com
w glencoeapartments.com

Harbourside Holiday Apartments ★★★
Self Catering
Contact: Ms Kathleen Quaid
t (01803) 550181
e habourside@amserve.net

Harwin Apartments ★★★-★★★★ *Self Catering*
Contact: Mr & Mrs S Gorman
t (01803) 558771
e harwin@blueyonder.co.uk
w harwinapartments.co.uk

Harwood Lodge ★★★★
Self Catering
Contact: Mr & Mrs Holgate
t (01803) 391538
e denise@harwoodlodge.co.uk
w harwoodlodge.co.uk

Headland Lodge ★★★★
Self Catering
Holiday Homes & Cottages
t (01803) 663650
e holcotts@aol.com
w swcottages.co.uk

Hennock ★★★★
Self Catering
Holiday Homes & Cottages South West
t (01803) 663650
e holcotts@aol.com
w swcottages.co.uk

Hudson's Bay ★★★
Self Catering
Contact: Mr & Mrs J & T Somers
12 Adelphi Road
t (01803) 664455
e jsomer8@aol.com

Julie Court Holiday Apartments ★★★
Self Catering
Julie Court Holiday Apartments
t (01803) 551012
e info@juliecourt.co.uk
w juliecourt.co.uk

Kimberley Holiday Flats ★★-★★★ *Self Catering*
Contact: Miss Frances Moreby
t (01803) 551576
e nigelboon@blueyonder.co.uk
w kimberleyholidayflats.co.uk

Lanhydrock ★★★★
Self Catering
Holiday Homes & Cottages
t (01803) 663650
e holcotts@aol.com
w swcottages.co.uk

Laverna Palms ★★
Self Catering
Laverna
t (01803) 557620
w devonselfcatering.com

Monkey Puzzle Lodge
Rating Applied For
Self Catering
Contact: Mrs Butterworth
Torbay Holiday Agency
t (01803) 663650
e holcotts@aol.com
w swcottages.co.uk

Montana ★★★ *Self Catering*
Contact: Mr Roger Seaward
Montana Holidays
t (01803) 559783

New Esplanade Court ★★★
Self Catering
Contact: Mrs Adele Barnes
Blue Chip Vacations
t (01803) 855282
e info@bluechipvacations.com
w bluechipvacations.com/paignton/paignton_esplanade_court.php

New Esplanade Court 14 ★★★ *Self Catering*
Contact: Mrs Maggie Sycamore
Blue Chip Vacations
t (01803) 855282
e sylvia@bluechipvacations.com

New Esplanade Court 16 ★★★ *Self Catering*
Contact: Mrs Maggie Sycamore
Blue Chip Vacations
t (01803) 855282
e sylvia@bluechipvacations.com

New Esplanade Court 19 ★★★ *Self Catering*
Contact: Mrs Maggie Sycamore
Blue Chip Vacations
t (01803) 855282
e sylvia@bluechipvacations.com

New Esplanade Court 21 ★★★ *Self Catering*
Contact: Mrs Maggie Sycamore
Blue Chip Vacations
t (01803) 855282
e sylvia@bluechipvacations.com

New Esplanade Court 24 ★★★ *Self Catering*
Contact: Mrs Maggie Sycamore
Blue Chip Vacations
t (01803) 855282
e sylvia@bluechipvacations.com

New Esplanade Court 34 ★★★ *Self Catering*
Contact: Mrs Maggie Sycamore
Blue Chip Vacations
t (01803) 855282
e sylvia@bluechipvacations.com

New Esplanade Court 56 ★★★ *Self Catering*
Blue Chip Vacations
t (01803) 855282
e sylvia@bluechipvacations.com

New Esplanade Court 59 ★★★ *Self Catering*
Blue Chip Vacations
t (01803) 855282
e sylvia@bluechipvacations.com

New Esplanade Court 6 ★★★ *Self Catering*
Blue Chip Vacations
t (01803) 855282
e sylvia@bluechipvacations.com

Newbarn Farm Cottages and Angling Centre ★★★★
Self Catering
Contact: Catherine Soley
Newbarn Farm Cottages and Angling Centre
t (01803) 553602
e swt@newbarnfarm.com
w newbarnfarm.com

Number One Braeside Mews ★★★★★ *Self Catering*
Contact: Mrs Adele Barnes
Blue Chip Vacations
t (01803) 855282
e info@bluechipvacations.com
w bluechipvacations.com/properties/bm01.php

Preston Down ★★★
Self Catering
Holiday Homes & Cottages South West
t (01803) 663650
e holcotts@aol.com
w swcottages.co.uk

Primley ★★★ *Self Catering*
Holiday Homes & Cottages South West
t (01803) 663650
e holcotts@aol.com
w swcottages.com

Roundham Heights ★★★★-★★★★★
Self Catering
Blue Chip Vacations
t (01803) 855282
e andrew@bluechipvacations.com
w bluechipvacations.com

San Remo Holiday Apartments ★★★
Self Catering
Contact: Mr & Mrs Christopher & Elizabeth Hannant
t (01803) 550293
e sanremo@f2s.com
w sanremopaignton.co.uk

Sandmoor Holiday Apartments ★★★
Self Catering
Contact: Rita & Brian Ellis
t (01803) 525909
e sandmoorholidayapt@amserve.com
w sandmoorholidayapartment.co.uk

Sandpiper ★★★★
Self Catering
Holiday Homes & Cottages South West
t (01803) 663650
e holcotts@aol.com
w swcottages.co.uk

Serena Lodge Holiday Apartments ★★★
Self Catering
Contact: Mrs Angela Gilmour
t (01803) 550330
e info@serenalodge.co.uk
w serenalodge.com

Singers Bay View ★★★
Self Catering
Holday Homes and Cottages
t (01803) 663650
e holcotts@aol.com

Stanley House ★★★
Self Catering
Contact: Mr & Mrs C & D Baldry
Stanley House Holiday Flats
t (01803) 557173
e stanley.baldry@tiscali.co.uk
w stanleyhouseholidayapartments.co.uk

Sunnybeach Holiday Flats
★★★ *Self Catering*
Contact: Mr & Mrs David & Jane Schaedl
t (01803) 558729
e j.shadll@btconnect.com
w sunny-beach.co.uk

Torbay Holiday Motel ★★
Self Catering
Contact: Mr Booth
t (01803) 558226
e enquries@thm.co.uk
w thm.co.uk

Tregarth ★★ *Self Catering*
t (01803) 558458
e tregarthpaignton@aol.com
w tregarthpaignton.co.uk

Tregarth Holiday Flats Ltd
★★ *Self Catering*
Contact: Mary & Steve Turner
t (01803) 550382
e mary@penwill3313.freeserve.co.uk

PAINSWICK Gloucestershire

Yew Tree Barn ★★★
Self Catering
Contact: Mrs Charlotte Lewis
Alveston
t (01608) 645410
e cj.lewis@tiscali.co.uk

PANBOROUGH Somerset

Panborough Batch House
★★★ *Self Catering*
Contact: Mrs Sheila Booth
t (01934) 712769
e sdb.antiques@ukgateway.co.uk

PANCRASWEEK Devon

Tamarstone Farm ★★★
Self Catering
Contact: Mrs Megan Daglish
Tamarstone Farm
t (01288) 381734
e cottage@tamarstone.co.uk
w tamarstone.co.uk

Wooda Cottage ★★
Self Catering
Contact: Mr James Morris
Farm & Cottage Holidays
t (01237) 479146
e enquiries@farmcott.co.uk
w holidaycottages.co.uk

PAR Cornwall

Kilhallon Court Cottage
★★★★★ *Self Catering*
Contact: Ms Victoria Norris
Highland Court Lodge
t (01726) 813320
e victoria@highlandcourt.co.uk
w highlandcourt.co.uk

Post Office Cottage ★★
Self Catering
Contact: Mrs Carole Willcock
t (01726) 77145
e hannahwillcock@yahoo.co.uk
w parpostoffice.co.uk

PARKHAM Devon

Cottages For The Connoisseur ★★★★★
Self Catering
Contact: Mr Alan Wade
Cottages for the Connoisseur
t (01237) 451008
e reservations@connoisseur-cottages.co.uk
w connoisseur-cottages.co.uk

East Goldworthy Cottage
★★★ *Self Catering*
Contact: Mr James Morris
Farm & Cottage Holidays
t (01237) 479146
e enquiries@farmcott.co.uk
w holidaycottages.co.uk

Logans and The Granary
★★★★ *Self Catering*
Contact: Mrs Janet Cornwell
Marsdens Cottage Holidays
t (01271) 813777
e holidays@marsdens.co.uk
w marsdens.co.uk

PARRACOMBE Devon

Martinhoe Cleave Cottages, Parracombe ★★★★
Self Catering
Contact: Mr & Mrs R M J Deville
Parracombe
t (01598) 763313
e info@exmoorhideaway.co.uk
w exmoorhideaway.co.uk

The Swallows
Rating Applied For
Self Catering
Marsdens Cottage Holidays
t (01271) 813777
e holidays@marsdens.co.uk
w marsdens.co.uk

Voley Farm ★★★★
Self Catering
Contact: Ms Judith Killen
t (01598) 763315
e stay@voleyfarm.com
w voleyfarm.com

Woodcote ★★★★
Self Catering
Contact: Mrs Janet Cornwell
Marsdens Cottage Holidays
t (01271) 813777
e holidays@marsdens.co.uk
w marsdens.co.uk

PAUL Cornwall

Susies Cottage ★★★
Self Catering
Contact: Mrs Hales
t (01736) 731703

PAULTON Somerset

2 Newtown Chapel ★★★★
Self Catering
Contact: Kev & Jo Rogers
t (01761) 417986

PAXFORD Gloucestershire

Fox Cottage ★★★★
Self Catering
Contact: Miss Sheila Rolland
Campden Cottages
t (01386) 593315
e info@campdencottages.co.uk
w campdencottages.co.uk

PAYTON Somerset

Little Owl Barn ★★★★
Self Catering
Contact: Mr & Mrs A Brodie
t (01823) 660602
e holidays@paytonfarm.com
w paytonfarm.com

PEASEDOWN ST JOHN Somerset

68 Ashgrove ★★★
Self Catering
Contact: Mrs Sondra Hopkins
t (01761) 300005
e sam@sonistics.com
w peasedownpropertyservices.com

PELYNT Cornwall

Cartole Cottages
★★★-★★★★ *Self Catering*
Contact: Mr & Mrs Taylor
t (01503) 220956
e carol@cartole.fsnet.co.uk
w cartole.co.uk

Tremaine Green Country Cottages ★★★ *Self Catering*
Contact: Mr Spreckley
t (01503) 220333
e stay@tremaine-green.co.uk
w tremaine-green.co.uk

PENDEEN Cornwall

Calartha Cottages ★★★
Self Catering
Contact: Wescountry Cottages
t (01803) 814000
e bookings@westcountrycottages.co.uk
w calartha.com

Kerenza ★★ *Self Catering*
Cornish Cottage Holidays
t (01326) 573808
e enquiry@cornishcottageholidays.co.uk

Merthyr Farm Cottages ★★
Self Catering
Contact: Mrs Susan Wilson
Woodhills
t (01769) 573335
e merthyrfarmcottages@hotmail.com

Trewellard Manor Farm
★★★-★★★★ *Self Catering*
Contact: Mrs Marion Bailey
t (01736) 788526
e marionbbailey@hotmail.com

PENDOGGETT Cornwall

Mays Cottage ★★★★★
Self Catering
Contact: Mrs Julia Payne
t (01823) 432615
e enquiries@scarletgreen.com
w scarletgreen.com

PENHALLOW Cornwall

Crowji Sorn ★★★
Self Catering
Contact: Ms Lumley
Around Kernow Holidays
t (01872) 571575
e info@ak-hols.co.uk
w ak-hols.co.uk

PENRYN Cornwall

Bell Cottage ★★★
Self Catering
Contact: Mrs Penny Snow
Bell Cottage
t (01326) 376466
e alpensnow@btinternet.com
w bellcottagecornwall.co.uk

Pampaluna ★★ *Self Catering*
Contact: Mr & Mrs Lawrence
t (01326) 373203
e pat-bern@tinyworld.co.uk

PENSFORD Somerset

Leigh Farm ★-★★
Self Catering
Contact: Mrs Smart
t (01761) 490281

PENSILVA Cornwall

The Old Smithy ★★★
Self Catering
Contact: Mrs Pat Sherburn
t (01579) 364060
e patgarrett508@msn.com

PENTEWAN Cornwall

Crofters End ★★★
Self Catering
Contact: Mr & Mrs Radmore
t (01872) 501269

Ship Inn (Pentewan) ★★★
Self Catering
Contact: Ms Gemma Parsons
t 0845 241 1133
e reservations@smallandfriendly.co.uk
w smallandfriendly.co.uk

PENZANCE Cornwall

39 The Park ★★ *Self Catering*
Contact: Mrs Mary Hanson
t (0151) 608 1294

57 Daniel Place ★★
Self Catering
Contact: Mr & Mrs Leonard & Sylvia Michell
t (01720) 422409
e lensylv@care4free.net

Boscrowan Farm ★★★★★
Self Catering
Contact: Mrs Elizabeth Harris
t (01736) 332396
e elizabeth@boscrowan.co.uk
w boscrowan.co.uk

Boskennal Farm ★★★★
Self Catering
Contact: Mrs Beryl Richards
t (01736) 740293
e alan@boskennal.fsnet.co.uk
w boskennalbarns.com

Chy Nessa ★★★
Self Catering
Contact: Mrs Shirley Keene
t (01736) 366697
e chynessa@netscape.net
w chynessa.co.uk

Crankan Flat ★★★
Self Catering
Contact: Mr & Mrs Braybrooks
Crankan Flat
t (01736) 351388

The Kymaurah Trust ★★★★
Self Catering
Contact: Mr Philip Manley
t (01736) 732266
e philatkymaurah@aol.com
w 2lamorna.co.uk

Mount View Holiday Apartment ★★ *Self Catering*
Contact: Mrs Puxley
t (01736) 362892
e graham_puxley@boltblue.com

The Old Farmhouse and The Granary - ★★★★★
Self Catering
Contact: Mrs Hall
t (01736) 810516
e halls@chegwiddenfarm.com
w chegwiddenfarm.com

Penzance Seafront Cottages
★★★ *Self Catering*
Contact: Mrs Maureen Blewett
t (01736) 361741

Rospannel Farm ★★★
Self Catering
Contact: Mr Hocking
Rospannel Farm
t (01736) 810262
e gbernard@v21.me.uk
w rospannel.com

Saddle Cottage ★★★★
Self Catering
Contact: Mrs Ward
t (01489) 790244
e phil@forward.supanet.com

St Anthony's Cottage ★★
Self Catering
Contact: Mrs Christine Feiler
t (01736) 359000
e christine.feiler@virgin.net
w cornwallfarwest.co.uk

St Piran's Cottages
★★★-★★★★ *Self Catering*
Contact: Mrs Gresswell
t (01962) 774379
e perranhols@aol.com

Spindrift ★★★★
Self Catering
Contact: Mrs Morgan
t (01467) 629597
e spindrift45@tiscali.co.uk

Wharf Apartments ★★★★
Self Catering
Contact: Mr & Mrs Kevin & Penny O'Neill
t (01736) 366888 & (01736) 332315
e info@wharfapartments.com
w wharfapartments.com

PERRANARWORTHAL Cornwall

Devichoys Farmhouse
★★★★★ *Self Catering*
Contact: Ms Emily Boriosi
Cornish Holiday Cottages
t (01326) 250339
e emily@cornishholidaycottages.net
w cornishholidaycottages.net/get_property.php?p=12

Granny's Farmhouse
★★★★★ *Self Catering*
Contact: Mrs Fraser
t (01872) 863724
e grannysfarmhouse@cosawes.com
w grannysfarmhouse.co.uk

Mariners Cottage ★★★
Self Catering
Contact: Mr & Mrs Rob Andrew
t (01872) 865060
e robinmandrew@aol.com

Millstream Cottage ★★★★
Self Catering
Contact: Mr & Mrs Preston
t (01326) 318900
e henrypreston.pgs@btconnect.com

PERRANCOOMBE Cornwall

Bredon 1 ★★ *Self Catering*
Duchy Holidays
t (01872) 572971
e enquiries@duchyholidays.co.uk
w duchyholidays.co.uk

Bredon 4 ★★ *Self Catering*
Duchy Holidays
t (01872) 572971
e enquiries@duchyholidays.co.uk
w duchyholidays.co.uk

Grey Roofs ★★★
Self Catering
Duchy Holidays
t (01872) 572971
e enquiries@duchyholidays.co.uk
w duchyholidays.co.uk

PERRANPORTH Cornwall

1 Penhale ★★★ *Self Catering*
Duchy Holidays
t (01872) 572971
e enquiries@duchyholidays.co.uk
w duchyholidays.co.uk

12 Penvenen ★★★★
Self Catering
Duchy Holidays
t (01872) 572971
e enquiries@duchyholidays.co.uk
w duchyholidays.co.uk

127 Perran Sands ★★
Self Catering
Duchy Holidays
t (01872) 572971
e enquiries@duchyholidays.co.uk
w duchyholidays.co.uk

14 Wheal Ramoth ★★★
Self Catering
Duchy Holidays
t (01872) 572971
e enquiries@duchyholidays.co.uk
w duchyholidays.co.uk

145 Perran Sands ★★
Self Catering
Duchy Holidays
t (01872) 572971
e enquiries@duchyholidays.co.uk
w duchyholidays.co.uk

146 Perran Sands ★★
Self Catering
Duchy Holidays
t (01872) 572971
e enquiries@duchyholidays.co.uk
w duchyholidays.co.uk

15 Wheal Ramoth ★★★
Self Catering
Duchy Holidays
t (01872) 572971
e enquiries@duchyholidays.co.uk
w duchyholidays.co.uk

2 Lower Hill Crest ★★★★★
Self Catering
Contact: Mike & Jo Williams
Goonpiper Lodge
t (01872) 862573
e fiveatuplands@aol.co.uk

2 Wheal Ramoth ★★★
Self Catering
Duchy Holidays
t (01872) 572971
e enquiries@duchyholidays.co.uk
w duchyholidays.co.uk

5 Ventonvaise ★★
Self Catering
Duchy Holidays
t (01872) 572971
e enquiries@duchyholidays.co.uk
w duchyholidays.co.uk

543 Caravan Perran Sands
Rating Applied For
Self Catering
Contact: Ms Sue Lumley
Around Kernow Holidays
t (01872) 571575
e info@ak-hols.co.uk
w ak-hols.co.uk

6 Penhale ★★ *Self Catering*
Duchy Holidays
t (01872) 572971
e enquiries@duchyholidays.co.uk
w duchyholidays.co.uk

70 Perran Sands ★★
Self Catering
Duchy Holidays
t (01872) 572971
e enquiries@duchyholidays.co.uk
w duchyholidays.co.uk

73 Perran Sands ★★★
Self Catering
Duchy Holidays
t (01872) 572971
e enquiries@duchyholidays.co.uk
w duchyholidays.co.uk

74 Perran Sands ★★★
Self Catering
Duchy Holidays
t (01872) 572971
e enquiries@duchyholidays.co.uk
w duchyholidays.co.uk

8 Penvenen ★★ *Self Catering*
Duchy Holidays
t (01872) 572971
e enquiries@duchyholidays.co.uk
w duchyholidays.co.uk

99 & 100 Perran Sands
★★★ *Self Catering*
Contact: Mrs Lumley
Around Kernow Holidays
t (01872) 571575
e info@ak-hols.co.uk
w ak-hols.co.uk

Beach View ★★★
Self Catering
Duchy Holidays
t (01872) 572971
e enquiries@duchyholidays.co.uk
w duchyholidays.co.uk

Chalet 176 ★★ *Self Catering*
Duchy Holidays
t (01872) 572971
e enquiries@duchyholidays.co.uk
w duchyholidays.co.uk

Chy Kerensa ★★
Self Catering
Duchy Holidays
t (01872) 572971
e enquiries@duchyholidays.co.uk
w duchyholidays.co.uk

Conifers ★★★★
Self Catering
Duchy Holidays
t (01872) 572971
e enquiries@duchyholidays.co.uk
w duchyholidays.co.uk

Cregaminnis ★★★★
Self Catering
Duchy Holidays
t (01872) 572971
e enquiries@duchyholidays.co.uk
w duchyholidays.co.uk

Cres Ha Kerensa ★★
Self Catering
Duchy Holidays
t (01872) 572971
e enquiries@duchyholidays.co.uk
w duchyholidays.co.uk

Fishermans Cottage ★★★
Self Catering
Duchy Holidays
t (01872) 572971
e enquiries@duchyholidays.co.uk
w duchyholidays.co.uk

Gull Rock Holiday Apartments ★★★
Self Catering
Contact: Mr & Mrs Snow
t (01872) 573289
e holiday@gullrock.com
w gullrock.com

Park View ★ *Self Catering*
Duchy Holidays
t (01872) 572971
e enquiries@duchyholidays.co.uk
w duchyholidays.co.uk

Pemberley ★★★
Self Catering
Duchy Holidays
t (01872) 572971
e enquiries@duchyholidays.co.uk
w duchyholidays.co.uk

Penhale 14 ★★★★
Self Catering
Duchy Holidays
t (01872) 572971
e enquiries@duchyholidays.co.uk
w duchyholidays.co.uk

Penhale 4 ★★★ *Self Catering*
Duchy Holidays
t (01872) 572971
e enquiries@duchyholidays.co.uk
w duchyholidays.co.uk

Penhale Villa
Rating Applied For
Self Catering
Contact: Mrs Lauretta Wright
t (01872) 571669
e lauretta@btconnect.com
w cornwall-breaks.co.uk

Riviera ★★★★ *Self Catering*
Duchy Holidays
t (01872) 572971
e enquiries@duchyholidays.co.uk
w duchyholidays.co.uk

Rock View ★★★
Self Catering
Duchy Holidays
t (01872) 572971
e enquiries@duchyholidays.co.uk
w duchyholidays.co.uk

Rosemullion 16
Rating Applied For
Self Catering
Duchy Holidays
t (01872) 572971
e enquiries@duchyholidays.co.uk
w duchyholidays.co.uk

Rosemullion 9 ★★
Self Catering
Duchy Holidays
t (01872) 572971
e enquiries@duchyholidays.co.uk
w duchyholidays.co.uk

The Rosery ★★★
Self Catering
Duchy Holidays
t (01872) 572971
e enquiries@duchyholidays.co.uk
w duchyholidays.co.uk

Sea Thrift ★★★ *Self Catering*
Contact: Mrs Rilstone
t (01872) 572157
e srilstone@hotmail.com

Sea View House ★★
Self Catering
Duchy Holidays
t (01872) 572971
e enquiries@duchyholidays.co.uk
w duchyholidays.co.uk

Seabreaze ★★★
Self Catering
Duchy Holidays
t (01872) 572971
e enquiries@duchyholidays.co.uk
w duchyholidays.co.uk

Seaview (Liskey Hill) ★★★
Self Catering
Duchy Holidays
t (01872) 572971
e enquiries@duchyholidays.co.uk
w duchyholidays.co.uk

Smugglers ★★ *Self Catering*
t (01872) 572971
e enquiries@duchyholidays.co.uk

Strand House Apartment
★★★ *Self Catering*
Contact: Ms Sue Lumley
Aroung Kernow Holidays
t (01872) 571575
e info@ak-hols.co.uk
w ak-hols.co.uk

Taveners Halt 4 ★★★
Self Catering
Duchy Holidays
t (01872) 572971
e enquiries@duchyholidays.co.uk
w duchyholidays.co.uk

Treth Cottage ★★★★
Self Catering
Contact: Mr & Mrs John & Jenny Cuthill
Claremont
t (01872) 573624

Ventonvaise 3 ★★★
Self Catering
Duchy Holidays
t (01872) 572971
e enquiries@duchyholidays.co.uk
w duchyholidays.co.uk

PERRANWELL STATION
Cornwall

Lymington Snug ★★★★
Self Catering
Special Places in Cornwall
t (01872) 864400
e office@specialplacescornwall.co.uk
w specialplacescornwall.co.uk

Post Box Cottage ★★★★
Self Catering
Special Places in Cornwall
t (01872) 864400
e office@specialplacescornwall.co.uk
w specialplacescornwall.co.uk

Woodpeckers ★★★
Self Catering
Special Places in Cornwall
t (01872) 864400
e office@specialplacescornwall.co.uk
w specialplacescornwall.co.uk

PERRANZABULOE
Cornwall

1 White House Court Cottages ★★★ *Self Catering*
Duchy Holidays
t (01872) 572971
e enquiries@duchyholidays.co.uk
w duchyholidays.co.uk

9 White House Court
★★★★ *Self Catering*
Duchy Holidays
t (01872) 572971
e enquiries@duchyholidays.co.uk
w duchyholidays.co.uk

PETROCKSTOW
Devon

Off The Beaten Track
★★★★ *Self Catering*
Contact: Mrs Ruth Kelsey
t (01837) 811762
e r.kelsey@farming.me.uk
w off-the-beaten-track.co.uk

PHILLACK
Cornwall

Chymoresk ★★★★★
Self Catering
Powells Cottage Holidays
t (01834) 813232
e info@powells.co.uk
w powells.co.uk

Elova F71 – CH004 ★★
Self Catering
Contact: Mrs Terrill
t (01209) 612214

Greenduke & Saltair
★★–★★★ *Self Catering*
t (01209) 716535
e info@cornishbungalows.co.uk

Morryp
Rating Applied For
Self Catering
Contact: Mr David Jolly
t (01209) 719770
e enquiries@rivieresunsetholidays.com
w rivieresunsetholidays.com

PILLATON
Cornwall

Kernock Cottages ★★★★
Self Catering
Contact: Mr Hugh Bailey
t (01579) 350435
e hughbeth@kernockcottages.com

Upalong & Downalong
★★★★ *Self Catering*
Contact: Mr & Mrs Barnicoat
t (01579) 350141
e trefenten@beeb.net
w trefenten.co.uk

PILTON
Somerset

Shire Cottage ★★★★
Self Catering
Contact: Mrs Holly Corfield
Bourne Farm
t (01749) 890107
e info@bournefarmcottages.co.uk
w bournefarmcottages.co.uk

PLAIDY
Cornwall

Dres an Treth Annexe ★★★
Self Catering
Contact: Mr & Mrs Peter & Jenifer Ashton
t (01503) 262376

PLAYING PLACE
Cornwall

Kernewek ★★★
Self Catering
Cornish Cottage Holidays
t (01326) 573808
e enquiry@cornishcottageholidays.co.uk
w cornishcottageholidays.co.uk

PLYMOUTH
Devon

Barbican Base ★★★★
Self Catering
Contact: Mr Matthew Treglowin
t (01752) 662126
e contact@plymouthholiday.co.uk
w plymouthholiday.co.uk

Barbican Hideaway
★★★★★ *Self Catering*
Contact: Mrs Julie Burdett
Home from Home Holidays
t (01263) 515208
e info@home-from-home-holidays.com
w hfhh.co.uk

Carsons Plymouth Hoe Holiday Apartments
Self Catering
Contact: Mr Sean Carson
Carsons Plymouth Hoe Holiday Apartments
t (01752) 254425
e sajrcarson@aol.com
w plymouth-hoe-apartments.co.uk

Haddington House Apartments ★★★★
Self Catering
Contact: Mr Fairfax Luxmoore
t (01752) 500383
w abudd.co.uk

Hoe Apartments
Rating Applied For
Self Catering
Contact: Miss Lisa Telling
t (01489) 557797
e info@hoe-apartments.co.uk
w hoe-apartments.co.uk

Marina View ★★★
Self Catering
Contact: Mr & Mrs Peter & Heather Shaw
Rosaland Hotel
t (01752) 664749
e manager@rosalandhotel.com
w rosalandhotel.com/marinaview

Mayflower Holiday Apartment ★★★
Self Catering
Contact: Mrs Susan Johnson
Clearmount
t (01752) 892119
e mayflower3@hotmail.com
w smoothhound.co.uk/hotels/mayflowe.html

POLBATHIC
Cornwall

Higher Tredis Farm ★★
Self Catering
Contact: Mrs Cindy Rice
t (01503) 230184
e cindyrice@btopenworld.com
w cornishfarmholidays.com

POLPERRO
Cornwall

Crumplehorn Cottages
★★★-★★★★★ *Self Catering*
Contact: Mr & Mrs Collings
Crumplehorn Cottages
t (01503) 262523
e enquiries@crumplehorncottages.co.uk
w crumplehorncottages.co.uk

Crumplehorn Inn & Mill
★★★ *Self Catering*
Contact: Mr & Mrs Crockford
t (01503) 272348
e host@crumplehorn-inn.co.uk
w crumplehorn-inn.co.uk

East Cliff Cottage ★★★
Self Catering
Contact: Mrs Ruth Puckey
t (01503) 272324

Kirk House ★★★★★
Self Catering
Contact: Mr Richard Lewis
Aspire Lifestyle Holidays Ltd
t (01503) 272320
e wts@pierinnholidays.co.uk
w kirkhouseholidays.co.uk

Little Laney and Polhaven
★★★★ *Self Catering*
t (01753) 882482
e tegan@cornish-cottage.com
w cornish-cottage.com

Lucys ★★★★ *Self Catering*
Contact: Mrs Leftly
t (01503) 272271
e info@leftly.com
w polperrocottages.com

Pier Inn House and Studio
★★★★ *Self Catering*
Contact: Mr & Mrs C & M Wood
t 07745 816647
w pierinnholidays.co.uk

POLRUAN
Cornwall

Lugger Cottage ★★
Self Catering
Contact: Mrs Shelagh Dolphin
St Austell Brewery Co Ltd
t (01726) 870007
e luggerinn@smallandfriendly.co.uk
w smallandfriendly.co.uk

Tommys ★★★ *Self Catering*
Contact: Mrs Sheila Mary Walter
t (01305) 871246
e enquiries@tommys-polruan.co.uk
w tommys-polruan.co.uk

POLRUAN-BY-FOWEY
Cornwall

Peppercorn Cottage ★★★
Self Catering
Contact: Mr David Hill
Fowey Harbour Cottages (W Hill & Son)
t (01726) 832211
e hillandson@talk21.com
w foweyharbourcottages.co.uk

POLYPHANT
Cornwall

Darkes Court Cottages
★★★ *Self Catering*
Contact: Mr & Mrs Sowerby
t (01566) 86598
e sowerby@darkesfarm.fsnet.co.uk

Tregarth ★★★ *Self Catering*
Contact: Lucy Ellison
Farm & Cottage Holidays
t (01237) 479146
e enquiries@farmcott.co.uk
w holidaycottages.co.uk

POLZEATH
Cornwall

1 Pentire View ★★★★
Self Catering
Contact: Mrs Diana Bullivant
Diana Bullivant Holidays
t (01208) 831336
e diana@dbullivant.fsnet.co.uk
w cornwall-online.co.uk/diana-bullivant

2 Pentire View ★★★
Self Catering
Contact: Mrs Diana Bullivant
Diana Bullivant Holidays
t (01208) 831336
e diana@dbullivant.fsnet.co.uk
w cornwall-online.co.uk/diana-bullivant

2 Pinewood Flats ★★
Self Catering
Rock Holidays
t (01208) 863399
e rockhols@aol.com

Bluebirds ★★★ *Self Catering*
Rock Holidays
t (01208) 863399
e rockhols@aol.com
w rockholidays.co.uk

Godolphin House ★★★★
Self Catering
Rock Holidays
t (01208) 863399
e rockhols@aol.com
w rockholidays.co.uk

Marmarra ★★★ *Self Catering*
Rock Holidays
t (01208) 863399
e rockhols@aol.com
w rockholidays.co.uk

Oystercatcher Bar ★★
Self Catering
Contact: Gemma Parsons
t 0845 241 1133
e reservations@smallandfriendly.co.uk
w smallandfriendly.co.uk

The Point ★★★★
Self Catering
Contact: Charlotte Bolt
t (01208) 863399
e rockhols@aol.com
w rockholidays.co.uk

Polbilly ★★★★★
Self Catering
Contact: Mr Richard Jones
t (01208) 863397
e swseeds@tiscali.co.uk
w cornwall-online.co.uk

Polmeor & Trehenlie ★★
Self Catering
Contact: Mrs Angwin
Polmeor & Trehenlie
t (01208) 72684 & (01208) 75243
e steve@angwin.fsnet.co.uk

Sea Gully ★★★ *Self Catering*
Rock Holidays
t (01208) 863399
e rockhols@aol.com
w rockholidays.co.uk

Seaview ★★★★
Self Catering
Contact: Mrs Bullivant
Diana Bullivant Holidays
t (01208) 831336
e diana@d.bullivant.fsnet.co.uk
w dbholidays.co.uk

Stonechat & Pendragon
★★★ *Self Catering*
Contact: Mrs Smith
t (01208) 863172
e info@polzeathcottages.com
w polzeathcottages.com

Trecreege Barn ★★★
Self Catering
Rock Holidays
t (01208) 863399
e rockhols@aol.com

Trehanoo House & Bungalow Annexe ★★★
Self Catering
Contact: Ms Buckingham
t (01672) 541120
e katebuckingham@waitrose.com

Trehenlie, Polzeath ★★★
Self Catering
Contact: Mrs Julie Angwin
t (01208) 75243
e steve@angwin.fsnet.co.uk

Trevarthian ★★★
Self Catering
Contact: Mrs Bullivant
Diana Bullivant Holidays
t (01208) 831336
e diana@dbullivant.fsnet.co.uk
w cornwall-online.co.uk/diana-bullivant

Tywardale Cottage ★★★
Self Catering
Contact: Mr & Mrs Swann
t (01208) 862721
e tywardale@oldpolzeath.wanadoo.co.uk
w wadebridgelive.com

White Rose ★★★
Self Catering
Contact: Mrs Rosalind Henderson
t (01962) 760619

PONSANOOTH
Cornwall

Gadles Farm Cottages
★★★★ *Self Catering*
Contact: Mr Trevor Howe
t (01872) 863214
e info@gadlesfarmholidays.co.uk
w gadlesfarmholidays.co.uk

POOLE
Dorset

4 Gosling Close ★★★★
Self Catering
Contact: Mr David Matthews
Lyme Bay Holidays
t (01297) 443363
e email@lymebayholidays.co.uk
w lymebayholidays.co.uk

43 Vallis Close ★★★
Self Catering
Contact: Miss Patricia Thomas
t (01202) 743768

Amberley ★★★ *Self Catering*
Contact: Mrs Angela Miles
t (020) 8643 5226
e amberley@lycos.co.uk
w harboursideholiday.co.uk

Baiter Park ★★★★
Self Catering
Contact: Mr & Mrs D King
t (01929) 471087
e david.king@gbpltd.co.uk
w gbpltd.co.uk/dorsetholidaylets

Dolphin Cottage ★★★
Self Catering
Contact: Mrs Jean Redsell
t (01322) 271848
e p.redsell@btopenworld.com

Dolphin Quays ★★★★★
Self Catering
Contact: Mrs Helen Challis
West End House
t (01202) 649228 & 07867 786872
e dolphin.quays@btinternet.com

The Dorset Resort, Hyde
★★★★★ *Self Catering*
Contact: Miss Jackie Langworthy
The Dorset Resort
t (01929) 472244
e resort@dorsetresort.com
w dorsetresort.com

Egret ★★★ *Self Catering*
Contact: Mr & Mrs Cocklin
t (01202) 670046

Flat 8 Sandacres ★★
Self Catering
Contact: Miss M Barker-Smith
t (01202) 395383

Fripps Cottage ★★★★
Self Catering
Contact: Mrs Helen Edbrooke
Stoneleigh House
t (01202) 848312
e helen@stoneleighhouse.com
w stoneleighhouse.com/frippscottage

Harbour Holidays ★★
Self Catering
Contact: Mrs Beryl Saunders
Harbour Holidays
t (01202) 741637

Penguin Cottage ★★★
Self Catering
Contact: Mrs Christina Harris
t (01202) 462485
e penguin.cottage@ntlworld.com

Look out for establishments participating in the Walkers and Cyclists Welcome Schemes

Poole Quay Holiday Flat
★★★★ *Self Catering*
Contact: Miss Manta Paterson
t (01202) 683885
e mantapaterson@hotmail.com
w poolequay.com/holidayflat

Quayside & The Boat House
★★★★ *Self Catering*
Contact: Mr Martin Fuller
t (01202) 666711
e baiter.holidays@btinternet.com
w baiter.holidays.btinternet.co.uk

Quayside Close Holiday Apartments ★★★
Self Catering
Contact: Mr & Mrs David & Susan Ellison
t (01202) 764107
e quaysideclose@aol.com
w quaysidecloseapartments.co.uk

The Retreat
Rating Applied For
Self Catering
Contact: Mrs D Ward
t (01929) 459250
e deirdre@the-retreat.info
w the-retreat.info

Sea Haven ★★★
Self Catering
Contact: Mrs Hayley Copley
t (01202) 669469
e seahaven58@aol.com
w sea-haven.co.uk

Wykeham Lodge
Rating Applied For
Self Catering
Contact: Mr Dismorr
Flat 3
t (01202) 706804
e rjdissmorr@hotmail.com

POOLE KEYNES
Gloucestershire

Log House Holidays ★★★★
Self Catering
Contact: Mr Anthony Edmondson
t (01285) 770082
e relax@loghouseholidays.co.uk
w loghouseholidays.co.uk

Old Mill Cottages ★★★★
Self Catering
Contact: Mrs Catherine Hazell
t (01285) 821255
e catherine@oldmillcottages.fsnet.co.uk
w oldmillcottages.co.uk

The Old Stables ★★★★
Self Catering
Contact: Mr & Mrs John & Jane Hiscock
t (01285) 770721
e churchfarmholidays@hotmail.co.uk
w churchfarmholidays.co.uk

PORKELLIS
Cornwall

Viscar Farm Holiday Cottages ★★★★
Self Catering
Contact: Mr & Mrs Ralph & Ann Bailey
Viscar farm
t (01326) 340897
e biscarhols@amserve.net
w viscarfarm-cottages.co.uk

PORLOCK
Somerset

Camelia Cottage ★★★★
Self Catering
Marsdens Cottage Holidays
t (01271) 813777
e holidays@marsdens.co.uk
w marsdens.co.uk

Coach House Apartments The Old Coach House & Stables ★★★★ *Self Catering*
Contact: Mrs Patricia Newell
Coach House Apartments The Old Coach House & Stabl
t (01643) 862409
e info@newelloldcoachhouse.co.uk
w oldcoachhouse.f9.co.uk

Green Chantry ★★★★
Self Catering
Contact: Mrs Margaret Payton
t (01823) 698330
e maggie_payton@hotmail.com

Hartshanger Holidays
★★★★ *Self Catering*
Contact: Mrs Anna Edward
t (01643) 862700
e hartshanger@lineone.net
w hartshanger.com

Hunters Rest ★★★
Self Catering
Contact: Mr Barry West
t (01643) 862349
e west@huntersrest.info
w huntersrest.info

Red Rose Cottage
Rating Applied For
Self Catering
Marsdens Cottage Holidays
t (01271) 813777
e holidays@marsdens.co.uk
w marsdens.co.uk

Redway ★★★★ *Self Catering*
Marsdens Cottage Holidays
t (01271) 813777
e holidays@marsdens.co.uk
w marsdens.co.uk

Seapoint ★★★★
Self Catering
Contact: Mr Stephen Fitzgerald
t (01643) 862289
e fitzgerald@seapoint.co.uk
w seapoint.co.uk

The Ships Mews ★★★★
Self Catering
Contact: Mr & Mrs Alan & Jacqueline Cottrell
Ship Bungalow, West End
t 07979 278466
w shipsmews.co.uk

The Watermill ★★★★
Self Catering
Contact: Mr & Mrs John & Diane Ames
t (01474) 879810
e john.ames1@btinternet.com
w thewatermillporlock.com

Woodside Cottage ★★★
Self Catering
Contact: Mr & Ms T Lawrence
Craigmere
t (01934) 732978
e woodside_cottage@hotmail.com

Xanadu ★★★★ *Self Catering*
Contact: Ms Emma Harrison
t (020) 8427 4818
e xanadu@porlockcottage.co.uk
w porlockcottage.co.uk

PORLOCK WEIR
Somerset

Chapel Knap Accommodation ★★★★★
Self Catering
Contact: Mrs Caroline Lister
t (01643) 862364
e chapelknap@hotmail.com
w chapelknap.co.uk

PORT GAVERNE
Cornwall

Carn Awn ★★★★
Self Catering
t (01208) 880716
e orcades@mays364.wanadoo.co.uk
w orcades.u-net.com

Green Door Cottages
★★★-★★★★ *Self Catering*
Contact: Mrs Ross
Green Door Cottages
t (01208) 880293
e enquiries@greendoorcottages.co.uk
w greendoorcottages.co.uk

The Moorings ★★★★
Self Catering
Contact: Mr Michael Coles
t (01208) 880224
e mikesgscoles@aol.com
w gaverneholidays.co.uk

PORT ISAAC
Cornwall

57a Springside ★★★
Self Catering
Contact: Mrs Catherine Armstrong
t (01208) 880780
e cath.armstrong@tesco.net

Dolphin Cottage ★★★
Self Catering
Contact: Miss Charlotte Bolt
Rock Holidays
t (01208) 863399
e rockhols@aol.com
w rockholidays.co.uk

Edwarma Cottage ★★★★
Self Catering
Rock Holidays
t (01208) 863399
e rockhols@aol.com

Flat 3 The Old Bakehouse
★★★★ *Self Catering*
Harbour Holidays
t (01841) 533402
e contact@harbourholidays.co.uk
w harbourholidays.co.uk

Locarno ★★★ *Self Catering*
Contact: Mrs Daisy Hicks
t (01208) 880268
e daisyhicks@supanet.com

Oyster Bay ★★★
Self Catering
Contact: Miss Charlotte Bolt
Rock Holidays
t (01208) 863399
e rockhols@aol.com

Silvershell ★★★★★
Self Catering
Rock Holidays
t (01208) 863399
e rockhols@aol.com

Top Flat, Stanley House ★★
Self Catering
Contact: Miss Bolt
Rock Holidays
t (01208) 863399
e rockhols@aol.com
w rockholidays.co.uk

Trevathan Farm
★★★★-★★★★★
Self Catering
Contact: Mrs Jo Symons
Trevathan Farm
t (01208) 880248
e symons@trevathanfarm.com
w trevathanfarm.com

The White House ★★★
Self Catering
Contact: Dr Anthony Hambly
Bodrean Manor
t (01872) 264400
e anthonyhambly@hotmail.com

PORT PENDENNIS
Cornwall

The Anchorage ★★★★
Self Catering
Contact: Mrs Haselden
t (0151) 480 6747
e theanchorage@orange.net
w theanchorage-online.co.uk

Dracaenas ★★★★
Self Catering
Contact: Mrs Slade
t 07788 670587
e jim@slade7.fsnet.co.uk
w slade7.fsnet.co.uk

PORTESHAM
Dorset

Sleepers ★★★ *Self Catering*
Contact: Miss Brenda Parker
t (01308) 897232
e gorselands@ukonline.co.uk
w gorselands-uk.com

PORTHALLOW
Cornwall

Cockle Island Cottage
★★★★ *Self Catering*
Porthallow
t (01326) 280370
e hawthorne@valleyviewhouse-freeserve.co.uk
w smoothhound.co.uk/hotels/valleyvi

PORTHCOTHAN
Cornwall

10 Tregella ★★★★
Self Catering
Contact: Nicky Stanley
Harbour Holidays
t (01841) 532402
e contact@harbourholidays.co.uk
w harbourholidays.co.uk

Gull Cottage ★★★
Self Catering
Contact: Ms Nicky Stanley
Harbour Holidays - Padstow
t (01841) 532555
e sales@jackie-stanley.co.uk

Porthcothan House
★★★★★ *Self Catering*
Cornish Horizons Holiday Cottages
t (01841) 533331
e cottages@cornishhorizons.co.uk
w cornishhorizons.co.uk

PORTHCURNO
Cornwall

Stargazey ★★★★
Self Catering
Contact: Ms Liz Trenary
First and Last Cottages
t (01736) 871284
e info@firstandlastcottages.co.uk
w firstandlastcottages.co.uk

PORTHLEVEN
Cornwall

1 Anson Cottage ★★★★
Self Catering
Park Place
t 0800 915 9894
e info@abovebeachcottages.co.uk

3 Harbour View ★★★★
Self Catering
Park Place
t 0800 915 9894
e info@abovebeachcottages.co.uk

Above Beach Cottages
★★★★ *Self Catering*
Contact: Mrs Janice Benney
t (01326) 563198
e info@abovebeachcottages.co.uk
w abovebeachcottages.co.uk

An-Mordros ★★★★
Self Catering
Cornish Cottage Holidays
t (01326) 573808
e inquirey@cornishcottageholidays.co.uk
w cornishcottageholidays.co.uk

Atlantic Cottage ★★★
Self Catering
Cornish Cottage Holidays
t (01326) 573808
e enquiry@cornishcottageholidays.co.uk
w cornishcottageholidays.co.uk

Blue Dolphin ★★★★★
Self Catering
Niche Retreats
t (01209) 890272
e info@nicheretreats.co.uk
w nicheretreats.co.uk

Cantara ★★★ *Self Catering*
Contact: Mr Martin Raftery
Mullion Cottages
t 0845 066 7766
e enquiries@mullioncottages.com
w mullioncottages.com

Chiva – Som Cottage
Rating Applied For
Self Catering
Contact: Ellen Cheshire
Chiva - Som Cottages
t (023) 9252 6787
e ellencheshire3@aol.com

Dai Mar ★★ *Self Catering*
Contact: Mrs Oxford
t (020) 8445 0090
e gilloxford@yahoo.co.uk

The Haven ★★★★
Self Catering
Cornish Cottage Holidays
t (01326) 573808
e enquiry@cornishcottageholidays.co.uk
w cornishcottageholidays.co.uk

Kestrel House and Harbour View ★★★-★★★★
Self Catering
Cornish Cottage Holidays
t (01326) 573808
e inquiry@cornishcottageholidays.co.uk
w cornishcottageholidays.co.uk

Kyldenna
Rating Applied For
Self Catering
Contact: Mr Martin Raftery
Mullion Cottages
t 0845 066 7766
e enquiries@mullioncottages.com
w mullioncottages.com

The Manse ★★★
Self Catering
Cornish Cottage Holidays
t (01326) 573808

Meadowside ★★★★
Self Catering
Contact: Mr & Mrs Orchard
t (01326) 572928

Mounts Bay & Morgolok
★★★★-★★★★★
Self Catering
Niche Retreats
t (01209) 890272
e info@nicheretreats.co.uk
w nicheretreats.co.uk

Niche Retreats ★★★★
Self Catering
Contact: Mrs Kitchen
t (01209) 861745
e jackie@nicheretreats.co.uk
w nicheretreats.co.uk

Pegs ★★★ *Self Catering*
Cornish Cottage Holidays
t (01326) 573808
e enquiry@cornishcottageholidays.co.uk
w cornishcottageholidays.co.uk

Peverell ★★★ *Self Catering*
Cornish Cottage Holidays
t (01326) 573808
e enquiry@cornishcottageholidays.co.uk
w cornishcottageholidays.co.uk

Pew Cottage ★★★★★
Self Catering
Park Place
t 0800 915 9894
e info@abovebeachcottages.co.uk

Porthcressa ★★★★
Self Catering
Contact: Mrs Arthur
t (01326) 574487

Roysdean ★★ *Self Catering & Serviced Apartments*
Contact: Mrs Kitchen
t (01326) 574375

St Elvans ★★★★★
Self Catering
Niche Retreats
t (01209) 890272
e info@nicheretreats.co.uk
w nicheretreats.co.uk

St Elvan's Retreat ★★★★★
Self Catering
Park Place
t 0800 915 9894
e info@abovebeachcottages.co.uk

Sea Breezes House
★★★★-★★★★★
Self Catering
Park Place
t (01202) 718400
e info@abovebeachcottages.co.uk

Sea Cottage ★★★★
Self Catering
Contact: Mrs Benney
t (01326) 563198
e seacottage@sandpebbles.com

Surf Cottage ★★★
Self Catering
Contact: Mr Martin Raftery
Mullion Cottages
t 0845 066 7766
e enquiries@mullioncottages.com
w mullioncottages.com

Tre Pol Pen ★★★★
Self Catering
Niche Retreats
t (01209) 890272
e info@nicheretreats.co.uk
w nicheretreats.co.uk

W Oliver Allen & Sons ★★
Self Catering
Contact: Mr W O Allen
t (01326) 562222
e woallen@porth-leven.com
w porth-leven.com

PORTHTOWAN
Cornwall

Atlantic View Apartment
★★★ *Self Catering*
Contact: Mr & Mrs Angove
t 07745 177654
e 1rangove@tiscali.co.uk
w cornwallapartment.co.uk

Tigh Na Craobhan ★★
Self Catering
Contact: Mr Martin Raftery
Mullion Cottages
t 0845 066 7766
e enquiries@mullioncottages.com
w mullioncottages.com

Whispering Waves ★★★
Self Catering
Duchy Holidays
t (01872) 572971
e enquiries@duchyholidays.co.uk
w duchyholidays.co.uk

Whispering Waves 18 ★★★
Self Catering
Duchy Holidays
t (01872) 572971
e enquiries@duchyholidays.co.uk
w duchyholidays.co.uk

Whispering Waves 20 ★★★
Self Catering
Duchy Holidays
t (01872) 572971
e enquiries@duchyholidays.co.uk
w duchyholidays.co.uk

PORTLAND
Dorset

Alpen Rose ★★★★
Self Catering
Dream Cottages
t (01305) 789000
e admin@dream-cottages.co.uk
w dream-cottages.co.uk

Belle Vue ★★★★
Self Catering
Contact: Ms Kirsty Parker
Dream Cottages
t (01305) 789000
e admin@dream-cottages.co.uk
w dream-cottages.co.uk

Breeze Cottage ★★★★
Self Catering
Contact: Ms Kirsty Parker
Dream Cottages
t (01305) 789000
e admin@dream-cottages.co.uk
w dream-cottages.co.uk

Chesil Rise ★★★★
Self Catering
Contact: Miss Hannah Brain
Charm Properties Limited
t (01305) 786514
e hilary@tamariskhotel.co.uk
w charmproperties.co.uk

Cove Cottage ★★★★
Self Catering
Contact: Mrs Helen Wilson
t (01305) 824161
e helenportland@hotmail.com
w portlandholidays.co.uk

Cozi Cottage
Rating Applied For
Self Catering
Contact: Ms Kirsty Parker
Dream Cottages
t (01305) 789000
e admin@dream-cottages.co.uk
w dream-cottages.co.uk

Farion Cottage ★★★
Self Catering
Contact: Mrs Jenny Greenwood
t (01264) 394164
e jenny.greenwood6@btinternet.com

Fleet House ★★★
Self Catering
Contact: Mrs Margaret Beckett
The Gatehouse Cottage
t (01305) 823349
e gaynorbeckett@hotmail.com
w portlandholiday.co.uk

Inglenook Cottage ★★★
Self Catering
Contact: Ms Kirsty Parker
Dreams Holidays
t (01305) 789000
e admin@dream-cottages.co.uk
w dream-cottages.co.uk

Kivel Cottage, Bilbo Cottage, Hobbiton ★★★
Self Catering
Contact: Mrs Susan Boden
t (01329) 841104
e sue_richardboden@hotmail.com

Lilac Cottage ★★★
Self Catering
Contact: Ms Shelagh Hepple
t (01924) 252522
e hepple@lilaccott171.fs.co.uk
w portlandholiday.co.uk

Old Coastguard Cottage
★★★ *Self Catering*
Contact: Mr John Bunday
t (023) 8086 6421

Old Customs House ★★★★
Self Catering
Dream Cottages
t (01305) 789000
e admin@dream-cottages.co.uk
w dream-cottages.co.uk

The Old Higher Lighthouse
★★★★ *Self Catering & Serviced Apartments*
Contact: Mrs Fran Lockyer
t (01305) 822300
e franlockyer@clara.co.uk
w oldhigherlighthouse.com

Polly's Cottage ★★★
Self Catering
t (01305) 774360
e ddleverton@aol.com

Portland Holiday Home
★★★ *Self Catering*
Contact: Mrs Amanda Jones
Lloyds Cottage
t (01305) 861044
e mandy1311.jones@virgin.net

Primrose Cottage ★★
Self Catering
Contact: Mrs Elaine Taylor
t (01305) 780640
e ejtaylor2@tiscali.co.uk
w primrosecottageportland.co.uk

Sunset Cottage ★★★★
Self Catering
Contact: Mr Zachary Stuart-Brown
Dream Cottages
t (01305) 789000
e admin@dream-cottages.co.uk
w dream-cottages.co.uk

Twybill Cottage ★★★
Self Catering
Contact: Mr Zachary Stuart-Brown
Dream Cottages
t (01305) 789000
e admin@dream-cottages.co.uk
w dream-cottages.co.uk

PORTLOE
Cornwall

Cove Cottage ★★★
Self Catering
Roseland Holiday Cottages
t (01872) 580480
e enquiries@roselandholidaycottages.co.uk
w roselandholidaycottages.co.uk

Dolphin Cottage ★★★
Self Catering
Roseland Holiday Cottages
t (01872) 580480
e enquiries@roselandholidaycottages.co.uk
w roselandholidaycottages.co.uk

Farm Cottage ★★
Self Catering
Roseland Holiday Cottages
t (01872) 580480
e enquiries@roselandholidaycottages.co.uk
w roselandholidaycottages.co.uk

Ocean View ★★ *Self Catering*
Contact: Leonie Iddison
Roseland Holiday Cottages
t (01872) 580480
e enquiries@roselandholidaycottages.co.uk
w roselandholidaycottages.co.uk

Puckey Hill ★★★
Self Catering
Contact: Leonie Iddison
t (01872) 580480
e enquiries@roselandholidaycottages.co.uk
w roselandholidaycottages.co.uk

Trehaven View ★★★★
Self Catering
Contact: Mr & Mrs Mlynski
t (01872) 501824
e julie.mlynski@virgin.net
w cottageguide.co.uk/trehaven

PORTREATH
Cornwall

Bassets Acre ★★★
Self Catering
Contact: Mr & Mrs Christ
t (01209) 842367
e bassetsacre@freenet.co.uk
w bassetsacre.co.uk

Cornwall Holiday Homes
★★★ *Self Catering*
Contact: Mrs Cousins
t (01209) 715358
e cwllholidayhomes@talk21.com
w cornwall-online.co.uk/portreath-holiday-homes/ctb.htm

Dolphins & Harbourside
★★★★ *Self Catering*
Cornish Harbourside Holidays
t (01209) 820089
e loam.cottage@btinternet.com
w cornish-harbourside-holidays.co.uk

Flat 3, The Square ★★
Self Catering
Contact: Ms S Lumley
Around Kernow Holidays
t (01872) 571575
e info@ak-hols.co.uk

The Gatehouse ★★★
Self Catering
Contact: Mr & Mrs Hamer
t (01209) 843218
e rhhjb@aol.com

Golds Properties Limited
★★★★-★★★★★
Self Catering
Contact: Sharon Parker
Powells Cottage Holidays
t (01543) 270784
e enquiries@golds-hire.co.uk
w golds-hire.co.uk

Gull View ★★★ *Self Catering*
Holiday Homes & Cottages South West
t (01803) 663650

Higher Laity Farm ★★★★★
Self Catering
Contact: Mrs Lynne Drew
Higher Laity Farm
t (01209) 842317
e info@higherlaityfarm.co.uk
w higherlaityfarm.co.uk

The Moorings ★★★
Self Catering
Powells Cottage Holidays
t (01834) 813232
e info@powells.co.uk
w powells.co.uk

The Moorings ★★★
Self Catering
Contact: Mr Michael Coles
t (01208) 880224
e mikesgscoles@aol.com
w gaverneholidays.co.uk

Trengove Farm Cottages
★★★-★★★★ *Self Catering*
Contact: Mrs Richards
Trengove Farm Cottages
t (01209) 843008
e richards@farming.co.uk

PORTSCATHO
Cornwall

10 Wellington Terrace ★★★
Self Catering
Roseland Holiday Cottages
t (01872) 580480
e enquiries@roselandholidaycottages.co.uk

3 Shute Meadow ★★★★
Self Catering
Contact: Leonie Iddison
Roseland Holiday Cottages
t (01872) 580480
e enquiries@roselandholidaycottages.co.uk
w roselandholidaycottages.co.uk

9 Wellington Terrace ★★★
Self Catering
Contact: Leonie Iddison
Roseland Holiday Cottages
t (01872) 580480
e enquiries@roselandholidaycottages.co.uk
w roselandholidaycottages.co.uk

Alicias Barn ★★★★
Self Catering
Roseland Holiday Cottages
t (01872) 580480
e enquiries@roselandholidaycottages.co.uk
w roselandholidaycottages.co.uk

Antigua ★★ *Self Catering*
Roseland Holiday Cottages
t (01872) 580480
e enquiries@roselandholidaycottages.co.uk
w roselandholidaycottages.co.uk

Capstan Lodge ★★★
Self Catering
Contact: Mr Langridge
t (01872) 580289
w trewince.co.uk

Chick Cottage & The Beach House ★★★★ *Self Catering*
Roseland Holiday Cottages
t (01872) 580480
e enquiries@roselandholidaycottages.co.uk
w roselandholidaycottages.co.uk

Chywartha ★★★
Self Catering
Contact: Leonie Iddison
Roseland Holiday Cottages
t (01872) 580480
e enquiries@roselandholidaycottages.co.uk
w roselandholidaycottages.co.uk

Coast Cottage ★★★★
Self Catering
Roseland Holiday Cottages
t (01872) 580480
e enquiries@roselandholidaycottages.co.uk
w roselandholidaycottages.co.uk

Cuilan ★★★★ *Self Catering*
Roseland Holiday Cottages
t (01872) 580480
e enquiries@roselandholidaycottages.co.uk
w roselandholidaycottages.co.uk

Dormer Cottage & Byways
★★★ *Self Catering*
Roseland Holiday Cottages
t (01872) 580480
e enquiries@roselandholidaycottages.co.uk
w roselandholidaycottages.co.uk

The Forge ★★★ *Self Catering*
Contact: Dr Stanley
t (01295) 700083
e julia.stanley@tinyworld.co.uk
w theforgeatgerrans.co.uk

Gaia Lodge ★★★
Self Catering
Contact: Mr Langridge
t (01872) 580289
w trewince.co.uk

Garden Cottage & Gull Loft ★★★★ *Self Catering*
Roseland Holiday Cottages
t (01872) 580480
e enquiries@roselandholidaycottages.co.uk
w roselandholidaycottages.co.uk

Greenaway Lodge ★★
Self Catering
Contact: Mr Langridge
t (01872) 580289
w trewince.co.uk

Hera ★★★★ *Self Catering*
Roseland Holiday Cottages
t (01872) 580480
e enquiries@roselandholidaycottages.co.uk
w roselandholidaycottages.co.uk

Hillside Cottage ★★
Self Catering
Roseland Holiday Cottages
t (01872) 580480
e enquiries@roselandholidaycottages.co.uk
w roselandholidaycottages.co.uk

Hyperion Lodge ★★★
Self Catering
Contact: Mr Langridge
t (01872) 580289
w trewince.co.uk

Jacaranda Apartment & Bungalow ★★-★★★
Self Catering
Roseland Holiday Cottages
t (01872) 580480
e enquiries@roselandholidaycottages.co.uk
w roselandholidaycottages.co.uk

Lawnside ★★★ *Self Catering*
Contact: Mr Langridge
t (01872) 580289
w trewince.co.uk

Lodge E26 ★★★★
Self Catering
Contact: Mr Langridge
t (01872) 580289
w trewince.co.uk

Lugger End ★★★
Self Catering
Roseland Holiday Cottages
t (01872) 580480
e enquiries@roselandholidaycottages.co.uk
w roselandholidaycottages.co.uk

Maralane ★★★ *Self Catering*
Contact: Leonie Iddison
Roseland Holiday Cottages
t (01872) 580480
e enquiries@roselandholidaycottages.co.uk
w roselandholidaycottages.co.uk

Morgwyn ★★★ *Self Catering*
Roseland Holiday Cottages
t (01872) 580480
e enquiries@roselandholidaycottages.co.uk
w roselandholidaycottages.co.uk

Morvast
Rating Applied For
Self Catering
Contact: Mrs Butterworth
Holiday Homes & Cottages South West
t (01803) 663650
e holcotts@aol.com
w swcottages.co.uk

Nangwedhen ★★★
Self Catering
Roseland Holiday Cottages
t (01872) 580480
e enquiries@roselandholidaycottages.co.uk

The Old School House ★★★
Self Catering
Roseland Holiday Cottages
t (01872) 580480
e enquiries@roselandholidaycottages.co.uk
w roselandholidaycottages.co.uk

Opal Cottage ★★★
Self Catering
Roseland Holiday Cottages
t (01872) 580480
e enquiries@roselandholidaycottages.co.uk
w roselandholidaycottages.co.uk

Pelyn Creek Cottage ★★★★
Self Catering
Contact: Leonie Iddison
Roseland Holiday Cottages
t (01872) 580480
e enquiries@roselandholidaycottages.co.uk
w roselandholidaycottages.co.uk

Pengerrans ★★★
Self Catering
Contact: Mrs Iddison
Roseland Holiday Cottages
t (01872) 580480
e enquiries@roselandholidaycottages.co.uk
w roselandholidaycottages.co.uk

Pollaughan Farm
★★★★-★★★★★
Self Catering
Contact: Mrs Valerie Penny
t (01872) 580150
e pollaughan@yahoo.co.uk
w pollaughan.co.uk

Porthcurnick Lodge ★★★
Self Catering
Contact: Mrs Iddison
Roseland Holiday Cottages
t (01872) 580480
e enquiries@roselandholidaycottages.co.uk
w roselandholidaycottages.co.uk

Redwing Lodge ★★★
Self Catering
Contact: Mr Langridge
t (01872) 580289
w trewince.co.uk

Roseland Lodge ★★★
Self Catering
Contact: Mrs Iddison
Roseland Holiday Cottages
t (01872) 580480
e enquiries@roselandholidaycottages.co.uk
w roselandholidaycottages.co.uk

Sally Port Cottage ★★★★★
Self Catering
The Stone House
t (01386) 852855
e michaelblanchard@talk21.com
w ruraltreats.co.uk

Seacroft ★★★ *Self Catering*
Contact: Mrs Iddison
Roseland Holiday Cottages
t (01827) 580480
e enquiries@roselandholidaycottages.co.uk
w roselandholidaycottages.co.uk

Shambles ★★ *Self Catering*
Roseland Holiday Cottages
t (01872) 580480
e enquiries@roselandholidaycottages.co.uk
w roselandholidaycottages.co.uk

Silverwater Lodge ★★★
Self Catering
Contact: Mr Langridge
t (01872) 580289
w trewince.co.uk

Skansen Lodge ★★★
Self Catering
Contact: Mr Langridge
t (01872) 580289
w trewince.co.uk

Sladen Nest ★★★
Self Catering
Contact: Mr Langridge
t (01872) 580289
w trewince.co.uk

Spindrift ★★★★
Self Catering
Contact: Leonie Iddison
Roseland Holiday Cottages
t (01872) 580480
e enquiries@roselandholidaycottages.co.uk
w roselandholidaycottages.co.uk

Sunday House West ★★★★
Self Catering
Roseland Holiday Cottages
t (01872) 580480
e enquiries@roselandholidaycottages.co.uk

Towan Lodge ★★★
Self Catering
Contact: Mr Langridge
t (01872) 580289
w trewince.co.uk

Treloar Lodge ★★★
Self Catering
Contact: Mr Langridge
t (01872) 580289
w trewince.co.uk

Waterside House ★★★★
Self Catering
Roseland Holiday Cottages
t (01872) 580480
e enquiries@roselandholidaycottages.co.uk
w roselandholidaycottages.co.uk

Wilbury Cottage ★★★
Self Catering
Roseland Holiday Cottages
t (01872) 580480
e enquiries@roselandholidaycottages.co.uk
w roselandholidaycottages.co.uk

PORTWRINKLE
Cornwall

Westway ★★★ *Self Catering*
Contact: Mrs Susan Irving
t (020) 8769 7988
w westwaycottage.co.uk

POTTERNE
Wiltshire

Stroud Hill Farm Holidays ★★★ *Self Catering*
Contact: Mrs Helen Straker
t (01380) 720371
e helenstraker@aol.com

POUGHILL
Cornwall

1 Brightlands Apartments ★★★★ *Self Catering*
Contact: Mrs Sames
t (01296) 747425
e j.l.pearce@tesco.net
w lakeviewrise.co.uk

Tregella ★★★★ *Self Catering*
Farm & Cottage Holidays
t (01237) 479146
e enquiries@farmcott.co.uk
w holidaycottages.co.uk

Trevalgas Cottages ★★★-★★★★ *Self Catering*
Contact: Mrs Banning
t (01494) 711540
e dairy@trevalgascottages.co.uk
w trevalgascottages.co.uk

POUNDISFORD
Somerset

Old Mapp's Garden ★★★
Self Catering
Contact: Mrs Carole Bartleet
t (01823) 421737
e stephenbartleet@lineone.net

POUNDSGATE
Devon

Bramblemoor Cottage ★★★★ *Self Catering*
Contact: Mrs Helen Hull
t (01364) 631410
e helen.hull@eclipse.co.uk
w bramblemoor.fsworld.co.uk

POUNDSTOCK
Cornwall

Herds Cottage ★★★
Self Catering
Contact: Mrs Toon
t (01288) 361448
e herdscottage@tiscali.co.uk

Kitsham Holidays ★★★★★
Self Catering
Contact: Miss Denise Gordon
t (01288) 341336
e kitsham.farm@virgin.net
w kitsham.co.uk

 Look out for establishments participating in the Walkers and Cyclists Welcome Schemes

POXWELL
Dorset

Honeysuckle Cottage ★★★
Self Catering
Contact: Mr Zachary Stuart-Brown
Dream Cottages
t (01305) 789000
e admin@dream-cottages.co.uk
w dream-cottages.co.uk

PRAA SANDS
Cornwall

Sea Meads Holiday Homes ★★★ *Self Catering*
Contact: Ms Pierpoint
t (01753) 664336
e sue@bestleisure.co.uk
w bestleisure.co.uk

PRAZE-AN-BEEBLE
Cornwall

Cargenwen Farm Holiday Cottages ★★★ *Self Catering*
Contact: Mr & Mrs Blumenau
t (01209) 831151
e cargenwen@freenet.co.uk
w cargenwenfarmholidaycottages.co.uk

PRESTBURY
Gloucestershire

Home Farm ★★★★
Self Catering
Contact: Mr Charles Banwell
t (01242) 583161

PRESTON
Devon

Deers Leap ★★★
Self Catering
Holiday Homes & Cottages South West
t (01803) 663650
e holcotts@aol.com
w swcottages.co.uk

PRESTON
Dorset

Bella Rosa, Bella Vista, Villa de la Mer & Paradise Lost ★★★ *Self Catering*
Contact: Mr Zachary Stuart-Brown
Dream Cottages
t (01305) 789000
e admin@dream-cottages.co.uk
w dream-cottages.co.uk

Brewers House
Rating Applied For
Self Catering
Contact: Sue Thornton
t (01305) 837474
e sue@eastwoodquay.freeserve.co.uk

Fisherbridge Cottage
★★★★ *Self Catering*
Contact: Ms Kirsty Parker
Dream Cottages
t (01305) 789000
e admin@dream-cottages.co.uk
w dream-cottages.co.uk

Shingle Cottage ★★★
Self Catering
Dream Cottages
t (01305) 789000
e admin@dream-cottages.co.uk
w dream-cottages.co.uk

Sunnyhaven ★★★★
Self Catering
Contact: Ms Kirsty Parker
Dream Cottages
t (01305) 789000
e admin@dream-cottages.co.uk
w dream-cottages.co.uk

PROBUS
Cornwall

Coal Harbour Cottage ★★★
Self Catering
Contact: Mrs Lucas
t (01726) 843918
e jill@mpfarm.vispa.com
w probuscottage.vispa.com

PUDDLETOWN
Dorset

5 The Stables ★★★★
Self Catering
Contact: Mr David Matthews
Lyme Bay Holidays
t (01297) 443363
e email@lymebayholidays.co.uk
w lymebayholidays.co.uk

Weatherbury Cottages
★★★★ *Self Catering*
Contact: Mr & Mrs Clive Howes
t (01305) 848358
e enquiries@weatherburycottages.co.uk
w weatherburycottages.co.uk

PUNCKNOWLE
Dorset

Berwick Manor and Puncknowle Manor Farmhouse
★★★★-★★★★★
Self Catering
Contact: Ms Rebecca Hutchings
Puncknowle Manor Cottages
t (01308) 897706
e cottages@pknlest.com
w dorset-selfcatering.co.uk

Prosperous Cottage ★★★
Self Catering
Contact: Mr Zachary Stuart-Brown
Dream Cottages
t (01305) 789000
e admin@dream-cottages.co.uk
w dream-cottages.co.uk

PURSE CAUNDLE
Dorset

Barn Cottage ★★★★
Self Catering
Contact: Charles Perry
t (01295) 811540
e charles@astroh.co.uk

PUTFORD
Devon

Old Teddy House ★★★★
Self Catering
Contact: Kayleigh Norman
t (01237) 479146
e kayleigh@farmcott.co.uk

PUTSBOROUGH
Devon

11 Clifton Court ★★★★
Self Catering
Contact: Mrs Janet Cornwell
Marsdens Cottage Holidays
t (01271) 813777
e holidays@marsdens.co.uk
w marsdens.co.uk

17 Clifton Court ★★★★
Self Catering
Contact: Mrs Janet Cornwell
Marsdens Cottage Holidays
t (01271) 813777
e holidays@marsdens.co.uk
w marsdens.co.uk

31 Clifton Court ★★★
Self Catering
Marsdens Cottage Holidays
t (01271) 813777
e holidays@marsdens.co.uk
w marsdens.co.uk

Flat 1 Clifton Court ★★★★
Self Catering
Contact: Mrs Janet Cornwell
Marsdens Cottage Holidays
t (01271) 813777
e holidays@marsdens.co.uk
w marsdens.co.uk

Flat 18 Clifton Court ★★★★
Self Catering
Contact: Mrs Janet Cornwell
Marsdens Cottage Holidays
t (01271) 813777
e holidays@marsdens.co.uk
w marsdens.co.uk

Flat 19 Clifton Court ★★★★
Self Catering
Contact: Mr & Mrs Peter & Janet Cornwell
Marsdens Cottage Holidays
t (01271) 813777
e holidays@marsdens.co.uk
w marsdens.co.uk

Flat 22 Clifton Court ★★★★
Self Catering
Marsdens Cottage Holidays
t (01271) 813777
e holidays@marsdens.co.uk
w marsdens.co.uk

Flat 24 Clifton Court ★★★★
Self Catering
Contact: Mrs Janet Cornwell
Marsdens Cottage Holidays
t (01271) 813777
e holidays@marsdens.co.uk
w marsdens.co.uk

Flat 27 Clifton Court ★★★★
Self Catering
Marsdens Cottage Holidays
t (01271) 813777
e holidays@marsdens.co.uk
w marsdens.co.uk

Flat 32 Clifton Court ★★★★
Self Catering
Contact: Mrs Janet Cornwell
Marsdens Cottage Holidays
t (01271) 813777
e holidays@marsdens.co.uk
w marsdens.co.uk

Flat 7 Clifton Court ★★★★
Self Catering
Contact: Mrs Janet Cornwell
Marsdens Cottage Holidays
t (01271) 813777
e holidays@marsdens.co.uk
w marsdens.co.uk

Flat 8, Clifton Court ★★★★
Self Catering
Contact: Mrs Janet Cornwell
Marsdens Cottage Holidays
t (01271) 813777
e holidays@marsdens.co.uk
w marsdens.co.uk

Flats 28 and 30 Clifton Court
★★★ *Self Catering*
Marsdens Cottage Holidays
t (01271) 813777
e holidays@marsdens.co.uk
w marsdens.co.uk

Vention Garden Cottage
★★★★ *Self Catering*
Contact: Mr & Mrs Peter & Janet Cornwell
Marsdens Cottage Holidays
t (01271) 813777
e holidays@marsdens.co.uk
w marsdens.co.uk

RADSTOCK
Somerset

Charlton Farm Cottage
★★★★ *Self Catering*
Contact: Mr & Mrs Anthony & Vanessa Dutton
t (01761) 437761
e anthony@charltonfarm.com
w charltonfarm.com

Red Hill Barn ★★★★
Self Catering
Contact: Messrs Alan & Edward Brown & Hobbs
t (01761) 241130

RAME
Cornwall

Polhawn Fort ★★★
Self Catering
Contact: Miss Kathryn Deakin
Polhawn Fort
t (01752) 822864
w polhawnfort.com

RAMPISHAM
Dorset

Stable Cottage ★★★★
Self Catering
Contact: Mr & Mrs James & Diane Read
t (01935) 83555
e usatschoolhouse@aol.com
w usatschoolhouse.com

RATTERY
Devon

Knowle Farm ★★★★
Self Catering
Contact: Mr & Mrs Richard & Lynn Micklewright
t (01364) 73914
e Holiday@knowle-farm.co.uk
w knowle-farm.co.uk

READY TOKEN
Gloucestershire

Hartwell Farm Cottages
★★★★ *Self Catering*
Contact: Mrs Caroline Mann
t (01285) 740210
e ec.mann@btinternet.com
w selfcateringcotswolds.com

REDBROOK
Gloucestershire

The Old Bakery ★★★★
Self Catering
Contact: Ms Sylvia Adcock
t (01600) 713675
e sylvia@the-old-bakery.com

REDLYNCH
Wiltshire

The Loft ★★★★
Self Catering
Contact: Candy Newman
t (01725) 511516
e forestedge@hotmail.co.uk
w newforestedge.co.uk

REDRUTH
Cornwall

The Barn at Little Trefula
★★★ *Self Catering*
Contact: Mr & Mrs Higgins
The Barn at Little Trefula
t (01209) 820572
e barn@trefula.com
w trefula.com

The Gables Cottage ★★★★
Self Catering
Contact: Mrs Shiona King
The Gables Cottage
t (01209) 822294
e enquiries@higher-trevethan.co.uk
w higher-trevethan.co.uk

Morthana Farm Holidays
★★–★★★ *Self Catering*
Contact: Mrs Pearce
Morthana Farm Holidays
t (01209) 890938

RESKADINNICK
Cornwall

Dromona ★★★ *Self Catering*
Contact: Mr & Mrs Jackson
t (01209) 713644

Reskadinnick Bungalow
★★★ *Self Catering*
Farm & Cottage Holidays
t (01209) 713644
e enquiries@farmcott.co.uk
w holidaycottages.co.uk

RESTRONGUET
Cornwall

Regatta Cottage ★★★★
Self Catering
Special Places in Cornwall
t (01872) 864400
e office@specialplacescornwall.co.uk
w specialplacescornwall.co.uk

RHODE
Somerset

1 Rhode Farm Cottages
★★★★ *Self Catering*
Contact: Mrs Mary Adams
Rhode Farm
t (01278) 662278
e adams@rhode.fslife.co.uk

RIDDLECOMBE
Devon

Manor Farm ★★★★
Self Catering
Contact: Mrs Eveline Gay
t (01769) 520335
e eve@cottwoodvalley.fsnet.co.uk
w riddlecombe-manor.co.uk

RINGSTEAD
Dorset

The Creek ★★★
Self Catering
Contact: Mrs Fisher
t (01305) 852251
e michaelandfredafisher@btinternet.com

Pitt Cottage ★★★
Self Catering
Dream Cottages
t (01305) 789000
e admin@dream-cottages.co.uk
w dream-cottages.co.uk

Upton Farm ★★★★★
Self Catering
Contact: Mr & Mrs Davis
t (01305) 853970
e alan@uptonfarm.co.uk
w uptonfarm.co.uk

ROADWATER
Somerset

Tacker Street Cottage ★★
Self Catering
Contact: Mrs Jennifer Thomas
t (01984) 640253

ROBOROUGH
Devon

Little Meadows ★★★
Self Catering
Marsdens Cottage Holidays
t (01271) 813777
e holidays@marsdens.co.uk
w marsdens.co.uk

Lower Goodameavy
Rating Applied For
Self Catering
Contact: Celia Scott
t (01752) 839200
e celia.goodameavy@tiscali.co.uk

Whitsleigh Barn ★★★★
Self Catering
Contact: Mrs Elizabeth Basey-Fisher
t (01805) 603286
e ebf@whitsleighdevon.co.uk
w whitsleighdevon.co.uk

ROCK
Cornwall

1 Lowenna Manor ★★★★
Self Catering
Contact: Diana Bullivant
t (01208) 831336
e diana@dbullivant.fsnet.co.uk

17 Slipway Cottages ★★★
Self Catering
Contact: Mrs Diana Bullivant
Diana Bullivant Holidays
t (01208) 831336
e diana@dbullivant.fsnet.co.uk
w cornwall-online.co.uk/diana-bullivant

Half Way Tree ★★★★
Self Catering
Contact: Ms Diana Bullivant
Diana Bullivant Holidays
t (01208) 831336
e diana@dbullivant.fsnet.co.uk
w cornwall-online.co.uk/diana-bullivant

Little Riggs ★★★
Self Catering
Contact: Mrs Diana Bullivant
Diana Bullivant Holidays
t (01208) 831336
e diana@dbullivant.fsnet.co.uk
w cornwall-online.co.uk/diana-bullivant

Little Thrift ★★★★
Self Catering
Contact: Mr Richard Jones
t (01208) 863397
e swseeds@tiscali.co.uk
w cornwall-online.co.uk

Maidenover ★★★★
Self Catering
Contact: Mrs Diana Bullivant
Diana Bullivant Holidays
t (01208) 831336
e diana@dbullivant.fsnet.co.uk
w cornwall-online.co.uk/diana-bullivant

Mariners Lettings
★★★–★★★★ *Self Catering*
Contact: Miss Claire Tordoff
Mariners Lettings Ltd
t (020) 7938 2019
w marinersrock.com

Meadowside ★★★★★
Self Catering
Contact: Mrs Diana Bullivant
Diana Bullivant Holidays
t (01208) 831336
e diana@d.bullivant.fsnet.co.uk
w cornwall-online.co.uk/diana-bullivant

Mullets ★★★★ *Self Catering*
Contact: Mrs Diana Bullivant
Diana Bullivant Holidays
t (01208) 831336
e diana@d.bullivant.fsnet.co.uk
w cornwall-online.co.uk/diana-bullivant

Musters ★★★★ *Self Catering*
Contact: Mrs Diana Bullivant
Diana Bullivant Holidays
t (01208) 831336
e diana@dbullivant.fsnet.co.uk
w cornwall-online.co.uk/diana-bullivant

Seamist ★★★ *Self Catering*
Contact: Diana Bullivant
t (01208) 831336
e diana@dbullivant.fsnet.co.uk

The Studio ★★★
Self Catering
Contact: Mr & Mrs Gregan
t (01208) 862410
e ann.nca@internet-today.co.uk

Tristan House
Rating Applied For
Self Catering
Harbour Holidays - Rock
t (01208) 863399
w rockholidays.com

Tzitzikama Lodge Self Catering ★★★★
Self Catering
Contact: Mr & Mrs Cox
t (01208) 862839
e tzitzikama.lodge@btinternet.com
w cornwall-online.co.uk/tzitzikama-lodge

Wheel Cottage ★★★
Self Catering
Contact: Mrs Bullivant
Diana Bullivant Holidays
t (01208) 831336
e diana@d.bullivant.fsnet.co.uk
w cornwall-online.co.uk/diana-bullivant

ROCOMBE
Devon

Sunshine Cottage – V4132
★★★ *Self Catering*
Lyme Bay Holidays
t (01297) 443363
e email@lymebayholidays.co.uk
w lymebayholidays.co.uk

RODNEY STOKE
Somerset

Cider Barrel Cottage ★★★★
Self Catering
Contact: Mrs Kathy Longhurst
Cider Barrel Cottage
t (01749) 870322
e don@longhurst16.freeserve.co.uk

ROOKSBRIDGE
Somerset

Garden Cottage and Dairy Cottage ★★★★ *Self Catering*
Contact: Mrs Mandi Counsell
t (01934) 750630
e rooksbridgehouse@btinternet.com

ROSE ASH
Devon

Nethercott Manor Farm
★★★ *Self Catering*
Contact: Mrs Carol Woollacott
t (01769) 550483

ROSUDGEON
Cornwall

Broom Farm Cottage ★★★
Self Catering
Contact: Mrs June Markham
t (01736) 763738
e broomfarmcottage@tiscali.co.uk

Thatched Cottage ★★★★
Self Catering
t (01736) 710412

ROUSDON
Devon

2 Old Home Farm X4460
★★★ *Self Catering*
Lyme Bay Holidays
t (01297) 443363
e email@lymebayholidays.co.uk
w lymebayholidays.co.uk

3 The Bothy ★★★
Self Catering
Contact: Mr David Matthews
Lyme Bay Holidays
t (01297) 443363
e email@lymebayholidays.co.uk
w lymebayholidays.co.uk

3 Home Farm South ★★★★
Self Catering
Contact: Joanne Winkler
Lyme Bay Holidays
t (01297) 443363
e email@lymebayholidays.co.uk
w lymebayholidays.co.uk

Listed Luxury Cottages
★★★★–★★★★★
Self Catering
Contact: Ms Joanna Somerset-Wood
t (01252) 337549
e somersetwo@aol.com
w listedluxury.co.uk

Look out for establishments participating in the National Accessible Scheme

The Lodge House ★★★
Self Catering
Contact: Mr Tim Tandy
Jean Bartlett Cottage Holidays
t (01297) 23221
e holidays@jeanbartlett.com
w jeanbartlett.com

Peek House ★★★★★
Self Catering
Contact: Mrs Judith Ellard
t (01297) 444734
e judith@peakhouse.co.uk
w peekhouse.co.uk

ROWDE
Wiltshire

The Canal Barn ★★★★
Self Catering
Contact: Mr & Mrs Patrick & Louise Dawe-Lane
t (01380) 728883
e mail@canalbarn.co.uk
w canalbarn.co.uk

Foxhangers Canalside Holidays
Rating Applied For
Self Catering
Contact: Mr Colin Fletcher
t (01380) 828254
e sales@foxhangers.co.uk
w foxhangers.com

Lakeside Rendezvous
★★★★ *Self Catering*
Contact: Mrs Sarah Gleed
t (01380) 725447
e enquiries@lakesiderendezvous.co.uk
w lakesiderendezvous.co.uk

RUAN HIGH LANES
Cornwall

Castle Cottage ★★★
Self Catering
Contact: Mrs Sasada
t (0117) 937 4044
e sharonsasada@yahoo.com
w cottageincornwall.co.uk

Lambourne Vineyard Cottage ★★★★ *Self Catering*
Contact: Mr & Mrs Graham/ Ann Sherat
t (01872) 501212
e graham@lambournevineyard.co.uk
w lambournevineyard.co.uk

The Little Barn ★★★★
Self Catering
Roseland Holiday Cottages
t (01872) 580480
e enquiries@roselandholidaycottages.co.uk

Lower Penhallow Farm
★★★★ *Self Catering*
Contact: Ms Deborah Raper
t (01872) 501105
e visitcornwall@lowerpenhallowfarm.co.uk
w lowerpenhallowfarm.co.uk

Martha's Cottage ★★★★
Self Catering
Contact: Leonie Iddison
Roseland Holiday Cottages
t (01872) 580480
e enquiries@roselandholidaycottages.co.uk
w roselandholidaycottages.co.uk

The Old Loft ★★★
Self Catering
Contact: Mrs Delia Collins
The Old Loft
t (01872) 580732
e dee@roselandrentals.co.uk
w roselandrentals.co.uk

Trelagossick Farm ★★★
Self Catering
Contact: Mrs Carbis
t (01872) 501338
e enquiries@trelagossickfarm.co.uk
w trelagossickfarm.co.uk

RUAN MINOR
Cornwall

Adjewednack ★★★
Self Catering
Contact: Mr Martin Raftery
Mullion Cottages
t 0845 066 7766
e enquiries@mullioncottages.com
w mullioncottages.com

The Barn ★★★ *Self Catering*
Contact: Mr Martin Raftery
Mullion Cottages
t 0845 066 7766
e enquiries@mullioncottages.com
w mullioncottages.com

Bay View Bungalow ★★★
Self Catering
Contact: Mr Fallows
t (01326) 290158
w cadgwithholidays.co.uk

Cargey Cottage ★★★
Self Catering
Contact: Mr Martin Raftery
Mullion Cottages
t 0845 066 7766
e enquiries@mullioncottages.com
w mullioncottages.com

Gwavas Vean ★★★
Self Catering
Contact: Mr Martin Raftery
Mullion Cottages
t 0845 066 7766
e enquiries@mullioncottages.com
w mullioncottages.com

Seascape ★★★★
Self Catering
Contact: Mr & Mrs George
t (01326) 341195
e jgfamily@btinternet.com
w seascapecornwall.co.uk

Treal Farm Holidays ★★★★
Self Catering
Contact: Mrs Suzy Bosustow
t (01326) 290668
e cottages@trealfarm.co.uk
w trealfarm.co.uk

RUARDEAN
Gloucestershire

Anne's Cottage ★★★★
Self Catering
Contact: Mrs Anne Seager
t (01594) 543217
e anneseager@aol.com
w annescottage.ik.com

The Old Post Office Annexe
★★★ *Self Catering*
Contact: Mr & Mrs Chris & Miriam Harrison
Hope Cottage
t (01594) 860229
e miriam_harrison@yahoo.co.uk
w yeoldpostoffice.co.uk

RUMFORD
Cornwall

Corner Cottage ★★★
Self Catering
Contact: Miss Nicky Stanley
Harbour Holidays
t (01841) 533402
e contact@harbourholidays.co.uk
w harbourholidays.co.uk

RYALL
Dorset

Dedley Farm ★★★
Self Catering
Contact: Ms Joanne Winkler
Lyme Bay Holidays
t (01297) 443363
e email@lymebayholidays.co.uk
w lymebayholidays.co.uk

ST AGNES
Cornwall

Bolster Farm Cottage
★★★★ *Self Catering*
Contact: Mrs Niki Lillie
t (01872) 552187
e niki@bolsterfarm.co.uk
w bolsterfarm.co.uk

Croft Cottage ★★★★
Self Catering
Contact: Mrs Jane Sawle
t (01872) 553381
e beaconcottagefarm@lineone.net

Old School House 7 ★★★
Self Catering
Duchy Holidays
t (01872) 572971
e enquiries@duchyholidays.co.uk
w duchyholidays.co.uk

The Owl House ★★★★★
Self Catering
Contact: Ms Hicks
The Owl House
t (01872) 553644
e enquiries@the-owl-house.co.uk
w the-owl-house.co.uk

Palmvale Holidays
★★★-★★★★★
Self Catering
Contact: Mr Williams
t (01872) 552234
e duchy.holidays@virgin.net
w palmvaleholidays.co.uk

Pen Mor Cottage ★★★
Self Catering
Duchy Holidays
t (01872) 572971
e enquiries@duchyholidays.co.uk
w duchyholidays.co.uk

Porthview Holiday Bungalow ★★★ *Self Catering*
Duchy Holidays
t (01872) 572971
e enquiries@duchyholidays.co.uk
w duchyholidays.co.uk

Rose Cottage No.2 ★★★
Self Catering
Duchy Holidays
t (01872) 572971
e enquiries@duchyholidays.co.uk
w duchyholidays.co.uk

Tregease ★★★ *Self Catering*
Contact: Mr Simmons
t 07890 333216

Trezeniam ★★★★
Self Catering
Contact: Ms Kim Teagle
t (01726) 813099
e kim@campersincornwall.co.uk
w retreatincornwall.co.uk

ST AUSTELL
Cornwall

Bosinver Farm Cottages
★★★-★★★★ *Self Catering*
Contact: Mrs Smith
Bosinver Farm Cottages
t (01726) 72128
e reception@bosinver.co.uk
w bosinver.co.uk

The Engine House ★★★★★
Self Catering
Contact: Mrs Kitchen
Niche Retreats
t (01209) 890272

Lanjeth Farm Holiday Cottages ★★★★
Self Catering
Contact: Mrs Anita Webber
t (01726) 68438
e anita@cornwall-holidays.uk.com
w cornwall-holidays.uk.com

Nanjeath Farm ★★★★
Self Catering
Contact: Mr & Mrs Sandercock
t (01726) 70666
e peter@sandercocks.freeserve.co.uk
w nanjeath.co.uk

Poltarrow Farm ★★★★
Self Catering
Contact: Mrs Judith Nancarrow
t (01726) 67111
e enquire@poltarrow.co.uk
w poltarrow.co.uk

Southfield ★★★
Self Catering
Contact: Mrs Treleaven
t (01726) 75819
e bookings@southfieldselfcatering.co.uk

Tor View ★★★★
Self Catering
Contact: Mrs Clare Hugo
t (01726) 850340
e torview@btopenworld.com

Tregongeeves Farm Cottages ★★★★
Self Catering
Contact: Mr & Mrs John & Judith Clemo
Tregongeeves Farm Holiday Cottages
t (01726) 68202
w cornwall-holidays.co.uk

ST BLAZEY
Cornwall

Cornhill Farm Cottages
★★★★ *Self Catering*
Contact: Mrs Kay Carne
t (01726) 815700
e enquiries@cornhillfarmcottages.co.uk
w cornhillfarmcottages.co.uk

Eden-Gate Apartments
★★★★★ *Self Catering*
Contact: Mr Stephen Chidgey
t (01726) 815560
e stephen@eden-gate.co.uk
w eden-gate.co.uk

The Mill ★★★★ *Self Catering*
Contact: Mr John Tipper & Ms Caroline Ivey
Woodmill Farm - The Mill
t (01726) 810171
e enquiries@woodmill-farm.co.uk
w woodmill-farm.co.uk

Prideaux Farm Cottages
★★★-★★★★ *Self Catering*
Contact: Mrs Kathy Watson
Prideaux House
t (01726) 817304
e kathywatson@prideauxhouse.com

ST BLAZEY GATE
Cornwall

Windsworth Holiday Bungalows ★★★
Self Catering
Contact: Mrs White
t (01726) 8124 9253
e info@windsworth.co.uk
w windsworth.co.uk

ST BREOCK
Cornwall

Cribba ★★★★ *Self Catering*
Contact: Mrs Nickie Stanley
Harbour Holidays, Padstow
t (01841) 533402
e t.colver@techniquestudios.com

Pawton Mill Farmhouse
Rating Applied For
Self Catering
Contact: Mrs Sullivan
t (01579) 346473
e holidays@duchyofcornwall.gov.uk
w duchyofcornwallholidaycottages.co.uk

ST BREWARD
Cornwall

Darrynane Cottages ★★★
Self Catering
Contact: Mr & Mrs Clark
t (01208) 850885
e enquiries@eclipse.co.uk
w darrynane.co.uk

Meadowside ★★★★
Self Catering
Contact: Mrs Feasey
t (01208) 851497
e feaseymellon@aol.com
w mellonfarm.co.uk

ST BRIAVELS
Gloucestershire

Brook Farm Cottage, St Briavels ★★★★ *Self Catering*
Contact: Mrs Barbara Smith
Brook Farm
t (01594) 530995
e brookfarm@dial.pipex.com
w brookfarmcottage.co.uk

ST BURYAN
Cornwall

Boskenna Home Farm
★★★★★ *Self Catering*
Contact: Ms Julia Hosking
t (01736) 810705
e julia@boskenna.co.uk
w boskenna.co.uk

Choone Farm Holiday Cottages ★★★★
Self Catering
Contact: Mr Eric Care
t (01736) 810658
e bonnar.care@talk21.com

Tredinney Farm ★★★
Self Catering
Contact: Mrs Warren
t (01736) 810352
e rosemary.warren@btopenworld.com
w tredinneyfarm.co.uk

ST CLETHER
Cornwall

Forget-me-not Farm Holidays ★★★★
Self Catering
Contact: Mr & Mrs James & Sheila Kempthorne
Forget-me-not Farm Holidays
t (01566) 86284
e holidays@trefranck.co.uk
w forget-me-not-farm-holidays.co.uk

Treven Farmhouse ★★★
Self Catering
Contact: Lucy Ellison
Farm & Cottage Holidays
t (01237) 479146
e enquiries@farmcott.co.uk
w holidaycottages.co.uk

ST COLUMB
Cornwall

The Chalet ★★★
Self Catering
Contact: Mr & Mrs David & Diana Chambers
t (01637) 881200
e david.chambers@dennisfarm.co.uk
w dennisfarm.co.uk

Tregatillian Cottages ★★★
Self Catering
Contact: Mr Peter Osbourne
Cornish Horizons Holiday Cottages
t (01841) 533331
e cottages@cornishhorizons.co.uk
w cornishhorizons.co.uk

ST DAY
Cornwall

Manor Farmhouse ★★★★
Self Catering
Contact: Mr Murray Nelson
t (01209) 822066
e muzoe@homecall.co.uk

ST ENDELLION
Cornwall

Tolraggott Farm Cottages
★★★★ *Self Catering*
Contact: Mrs Harris
Barton Cottage
t (01208) 880927

ST ERTH
Cornwall

The Brambles ★★★
Self Catering
Contact: Mr & Mrs Barnett
t (01736) 753331
e david.alma1@virgin.net

Chy an Heyl ★★★
Self Catering
Contact: Mr & Mrs Derek Ripper
t 07976 188517
e info@firstcottage.com
w firstcottage.com

Trewinnard Manor ★★★★
Self Catering
Contact: Mrs Farnaby
t (020) 7730 2351
e treninnardmandy@yahoo.co.uk

Wisteria Cottage and Trehaven ★★-★★★
Self Catering
Contact: Mrs Lawson-Smith
t (01736) 7409 7775
e cynthia@lawsonsmith.freeserve.co.uk

ST ERTH PRAZE
Cornwall

Trescowe Cottages ★★★
Self Catering
Contact: Mr & Mrs Froggett
t (01736) 753823

ST ERVAN
Cornwall

Treleigh Manor Farm ★★★
Self Catering
Contact: Mrs Michelle Old
t (01841) 540075

ST EVAL
Cornwall

Springfield ★★★
Self Catering
Contact: Nicky Stanley
Harbour Holidays
t (01841) 532402
e contact@harbourholidays.co.uk
w harbourholidays.co.uk

Trelorna ★★★ *Self Catering*
t (01841) 540992
e lornacknott@yahoo.co.uk

ST EWE
Cornwall

Galowras Farm Cottage
★★★★ *Self Catering*
Contact: Dr Dunne
Galowras Farm Cottage
t (01726) 842373
e galowrasfarm@eircom.net
w galowrasfarm.co.uk

ST GENNYS
Cornwall

Penrowan Farmhouse
★★★★ *Self Catering*
Contact: Lucy Eillison
Farm & Cottage Holidays
t (01237) 479146
e enquiries@farmcott.co.uk
w holidaycottages.co.uk

The Round House ★★★★
Self Catering
Contact: Mr & Mrs Tarling
t (01840) 230717
e linda@tarling5161.wanadoo.co.uk
w roundhouserosecare.co.uk

Wagon House ★★★
Self Catering
Contact: Mrs Rosemary Orr
t (01202) 887901
e orrfamily@fsmail.net
w cottageguide.co.uk/wagonhouse

ST GERMANS
Cornwall

The White House ★★★
Self Catering
Contact: Mrs Daw
t (01503) 230505
e thewhitehouse_cornwall@hotmail.com

ST GILES ON THE HEATH
Devon

Petal's Place ★★★★
Self Catering
Contact: Ginette Nobbs
t (01566) 784216
e info@crossgreen-cottages.co.uk

ST GLUVIAS
Cornwall

Glengarth ★★★ *Self Catering*
Contact: Mrs Newing
t (01872) 863209

ST HILARY
Cornwall

Ennys ★★★★ *Self Catering*
Contact: Miss Gill Charlton
t (01736) 740262
e ennys@ennys.co.uk

ST ISSEY
Cornwall

Bertie's Barn ★★★★
Self Catering
Contact: Mrs Cathy Osborne
Cornish Horizons Holiday Cottages
t (01841) 533331
e cottages@cornishhorizons.co.uk
w cornishhorizons.co.uk

Blable Farm Barns ★★★★★
Self Catering
Contact: Mr & Mrs Roberts
t (01208) 815813
e blablefarm@btclick.com
w blablefarmbarns.co.uk

Cannalidgey Villa Farm
★★★ *Self Catering*
Contact: Mr & Mrs Old
t (01208) 812276

Look out for establishments participating in the Walkers and Cyclists Welcome Schemes

Corner Stones
Rating Applied For
Self Catering
Contact: Mrs Ann Ballard
t (01841) 540345
e CornerstonesCwll@aol.com

Hawksland Mill ★★★★
Self Catering
Contact: Mr & Mrs Jenkins
t (01208) 815404
e hjc@hawkslandmill.idps.co.uk
w 4starcottages.co.uk

High Barn ★★★ *Self Catering*
Contact: Mr Peter Osborne
Cornish Horizons Holiday Cottages
t (01841) 533331
e cottages@cornishhorizons.co.uk
w cornishhorizons.co.uk

The Linhay ★★★★
Self Catering
Contact: Mr Osbourne
Cornish Horizons Holiday Cottages
t (01841) 533331
e cottages@cornishhorizons.co.uk
w cornishhorizons.co.uk

Lotties Cottage ★★★★
Self Catering
Contact: Mrs Searle
t (01841) 541116
w lottiescottage.co.uk

The Manor House ★
Self Catering
t (01841) 540346
e enquiries@manoractivitycentre.co.uk
w manoractivitycentre.co.uk

Marshall Barn ★★★★
Self Catering
Contact: Mrs Nicky Stanley
Harbour Holidays
t (01841) 532402
e contact@harbourholidays.co.uk
w harbourholidays.co.uk

Rose End Cottage ★★★
Self Catering
Contact: Nicky Stanley
Harbour Holidays
t (01841) 533402
e contact@harbourholidays.co.uk
w harbourholidays.co.uk

The Roundhouse ★★★★★
Self Catering
Cornish Horizons Holiday Cottages
t (01841) 533331
e cottages@cornishhorizons.co.uk
w cornishhorizons.co.uk

The Snug ★★★ *Self Catering*
Contact: Ms Nicky Stanley
Harbour Holidays - Padstow
t (01841) 532402
e contact@harbourholidays.co.uk
w harbourholidays.co.uk

Sunflower Cottage ★★★★
Self Catering
Contact: Karen Simpkin
t (0114) 265 7000
w cornwall-online.co.uk/sunflower

Trelow Farmhouse and Trelow Barton
★★★★-★★★★★
Self Catering
Contact: Mr James Morris
Farm & Cottage Holidays
t (01237) 479146
e enquiries@farmcott.co.uk
w holidaycottages.co.uk

Valencia Cottage ★★★
Self Catering
Contact: Mr Peter Osbourne
Cornish Horizons Holiday Cottages
t (01841) 533331
e cottages@cornishhorizons.co.uk
w cornishhorizons.co.uk

ST IVES
Cornwall

2 Island Road ★★★★
Self Catering
Contact: Julia Tozer
t (0121) 445 3690
e royandjuliatozer@aol.com
w stivesholidays.com

32 Porthia Road ★★
Self Catering
Contact: Mr Harry
t (01736) 794986

8 Piazza ★★★ *Self Catering*
Contact: Mrs Harling
t (01736) 795132
e jharling@stivesholidays.fsbusiness.co.uk
w stives-accommodation.co.uk

9 Ayr Lane ★★★
Self Catering
Contact: Ms Sue Kibby
115 Earlsfield Road
t (020) 8870 3228
e sue.kibby@btinternet.com
w btinternet.com/~stives.cottage

Accommodation Orla-Mo
★★★★ *Self Catering*
19 Salter Road
t 0845 644 2833
e info@surfives.co.uk
w surfives.co.uk

Ayr Holiday Homes ★★★
Self Catering
Contact: Mr Baragwanath
t (01736) 795855
e recept@ayrholidaypark.co.uk
w ayrholidaypark.co.uk

Big Picture Holiday Apartments ★★★
Self Catering
Contact: Mrs Sarah Parker
t 07803 129918
e sarah@bigpictureholidays.co.uk
w bigpictureholidays.co.uk

Casa Bella ★★★★
Self Catering
Contact: Mrs Perry
t (01736) 793370

Cheriton Self Catering
★★★-★★★★ *Self Catering*
Contact: Mr & Mrs Luke
t (01736) 795083

Chy An Eglos Apartments
★★★ *Self Catering*
Contact: Mr David Eddy
t (01736) 795542
e david.eddy@chy-an-eglos.co.uk
w chy-an-eglos.co.uk

Chy Mor and Premier Apartments ★★★
Self Catering
Contact: Michael Gill
Chy Mor and Premier Apartments
t (01736) 798798
e enquiry@stivesharbour.com
w stivesharbour.com

Cornish Cottage ★★★
Self Catering
Contact: Mrs Haase
t (01736) 793239
w thecornishcottage.com

Granny's Cottage ★★
Self Catering
Contact: Mrs Ann Renowden
t (01736) 796360

Gran's Cottage ★★★
Self Catering
Contact: Dorothy Edmond
t (01872) 560644

Gulls Nest ★★★
Self Catering
Contact: Mr & Mrs Watts
t (01736) 797969
e djgullsnest@aol.com

Harbour View ★★★
Self Catering
Contact: Carole Mincham
t (01736) 798421
e karen.mincham@btconnect.com

Holiday Home ★★
Self Catering
Contact: Mrs Jill Hoather
t (01736) 786006
e geoffgoatherd@aol.com

Langridge Holiday Cottages
★★★ *Self Catering*
Contact: Mr David Langridge
t (01858) 535534

Lifeboat Inn ★★★
Self Catering
Contact: Gemma Parsons
t 0845 241 1133
e reservations@smallandfriendly.co.uk
w smallandfriendly.co.uk

Lowenna (St Ives) ★★★
Self Catering
Contact: Mrs Butler
t (01736) 793114
e patstives@hotmail.com

Lower Carnstabba Farm House (Toad Hall) ★★★
Self Catering
Contact: Mrs Short
t (01736) 795920

Nanjizal Cottage ★★★★
Self Catering
Lamorna
t (01736) 794384
e judydale@fsmail.net

Ocean Loft ★★★★
Self Catering
Contact: Mrs Emma Haase
t (01736) 795207
e stay@oceanloft.co.uk
w oceanloft.co.uk

Sailfish Cottage ★★★★★
Self Catering
Contact: Mr & Mrs Petersen
t (01736) 793830
e timandroo@yahoo.co.uk
w sailfishcottage.co.uk

St Ives Coastguard ★★★★
Self Catering
Contact: Mr Martin Raftery
Mullion Cottages
t 0845 066 7766
e enquiries@mullioncottages.com
w mullioncottages.com

St Nicholas Court ★★★
Self Catering
Contact: Mr Williams
t (023) 8026 7939
e stnicholascourt@ntlworld.com

Sea Horse Flat ★★★
Self Catering
Contact: Mrs Ylenia Haase
t (01736) 793039

Star Gazy ★★★★
Self Catering
Contact: Mrs Sandra Fenn
Northlands
t (01424) 882607
e sandra@northlands.co.uk

The Studio ★★ *Self Catering*
Contact: Carol Holland
Little Parc Owles
t (01736) 793015

Suncrest Holiday Flats ★★★
Self Catering
Contact: Mrs Williams
t (01326) 572969
e joy.williams@suncrestholidays.co.uk
w cornwalltouristboard.co.uk/suncrestflats

Surf Break ★★★
Self Catering
Contact: Mrs Butler
t (01736) 793114
e iankangaroo@hotmail.com

Trecillian Barn ★★★
Self Catering
Contact: Mrs Harling
t (01736) 795132
w stives-accommodation.co.uk

Tregenna Castle Self-Catering ★★★-★★★★
Self Catering
Contact: Mrs Sheila Barker
Tregenna Castle Self-Catering
t (01736) 795588
e hotel@tregenna-castle.co.uk
w tregenna-castle.co.uk

Tregowan ★★★ *Self Catering*
Contact: Carole Mincham
t (01736) 798421
e karen.mincham@btconnect.com

Tremorna View ★★★★
Self Catering
Contact: Ms Jill Block
t (01736) 793657
e apmblock@btconnect.co.uk

Trevalgan Holiday Farm
★★★★ *Self Catering*
Contact: Mrs Melanie Osborne
Trevalgan Holiday Farm
t (01736) 796529
e holidays@trevalgan.co.uk
w trevalgan.co.uk

Well Cottage ★★★
Self Catering
Contact: Mrs Linda Dodwell
Well Cottage
t (01736) 796846

ST JULIOT
Cornwall

The Hayloft ★★★★★
Self Catering
Contact: Ms Collings
t (01840) 250218
e hayloftbarn@hotmail.com
w cornwall-online.co.uk/hayloftbarn

ST JUST
Cornwall

Casple Cottage ★★★
Self Catering
Contact: Mr & Mrs Smith
t (01579) 370608

Churchgate Cottage ★★★★
Self Catering
Contact: Mrs Coral Senior
Churchgate Cottage
t (01736) 871120
e matt.senior@virgin.net
w churchgatecottage.co.uk

ST JUST-IN-PENWITH
Cornwall

Nanquidno Vean ★★★
Self Catering
Contact: Mrs Penny Gildea
t (01789) 299338
e pennyguildea@uku.co.uk
w nanquidnoValley.com

Swallow's End ★★★★
Self Catering
Contact: Mr & Mrs Beer
t (01736) 787011
e db.properties@virgin.net
w westcornwalllets.co.uk

ST JUST IN ROSELAND
Cornwall

Brambly Cottage ★★★★
Self Catering
Special Places in Cornwall
t (01872) 864400
e office@specialplacescornwall.co.uk
w specialplacescornwall.co.uk

Carrick View ★★★★
Self Catering
Special Places in Cornwall
t (01872) 864400
e office@specialplacescornwall.co.uk
w specialplacescornwall.co.uk

Carvinack Cottage ★★★
Self Catering
Roseland Holiday Cottages
t (01872) 580480
e enquiries@roselandholidaycottages.co.uk
w roselandholidaycottages.co.uk

Penros Cottage ★★★★
Self Catering
Contact: Mrs Kitty Eccles
Rosehaven Cottages
t (01326) 270795
e eccles@rosehavencottages.co.uk

Ros Creek Cottage
Rating Applied For
Self Catering
Contact: Mrs Spencer
Special Places in Cornwall
t (01872) 864400
e office@specialplacescornwall.co.uk
w specialplacescornwall.co.uk

Trethewell Cottage ★★★★
Self Catering
Roseland Holiday Cottages
t (01872) 580480
e enquiries@roselandholidaycottages.co.uk
w roselandholidaycottages.co.uk

ST KEVERNE
Cornwall

1 The Old Forge ★★★ *Self Catering & Serviced Apartments*
Mullion Cottages
t (01326) 240333
e enquiries@mullioncottages.com
w mullioncottages.com

East End Cottage ★★★★
Self Catering
Cornish Cottage Holidays
t (01326) 573808
e enquiry@cornishcottageholidays.co.uk

Fatty Owls Cottages, St Keverne, Nr Helston ★★★★
Self Catering
t (01326) 280199
e trenowethhouse@aol.com

Old Valley Mill ★★★
Self Catering
Cornish Cottage Holidays
t (01326) 573808
e enquiry@cornishcottageholidays.co.uk
w cornishcottageholidays.co.uk

Pedn-Tiere ★★★
Self Catering
Contact: Mr Martin Raftery
Mullion Cottages
t 0845 066 7766
e enquiries@muillioncottages.com
w mullioncottages.com

Penrose Farm Cottage ★★★
Self Catering
Cornish Cottage Holidays
t (01326) 573808
e enquiry@cornishcottageholidays.co.uk
w cornishcottageholidays.co.uk

Tarragon ★★★★
Self Catering
Cornish Cottage Holidays
t (01326) 573808
e enquiry@cornishcottageholidays.co.uk
w cornishcottageholidays.co.uk

Tregoss Barton ★★★★
Self Catering
Contact: Mr Jonathan Melville-Smith
Trego
t (01326) 281253
e tregossbarton@yahoo.co.uk

Trenoweth Mill ★★★★
Self Catering
Cornish Cottage Holidays
t (01326) 573808
e enquiry@cornishcottageholidays.co.uk
w cornishcottageholidays.co.uk

ST KEW
Cornwall

The Barn House ★★★★
Self Catering
Contact: Mrs Janet Chancellor
t (01494) 670696
e jeremy.chancellar@which.net

Keats Cottage ★★
Self Catering
Contact: Mrs Coster
t (01208) 880332

Lane End Farm Bungalow ★★★ *Self Catering*
Contact: Mrs Monk
t (01208) 880013
e nabmonk@tiscali.co.uk

Skisdon ★★★★ *Self Catering*
Contact: Mr Honeywill
t (01208) 841372
e tim580208@aol.com
w skisdon.com

Treharrock Farm Cottages ★★★★ *Self Catering*
Contact: Mrs Quinn
t (01208) 880517
e treharrockfarmcottages@btinternet.com
w treharrock.co.uk

ST LEVAN
Cornwall

Chynance (Porthcurno) ★★★ *Self Catering*
Contact: Miss Curnow
t (01736) 360163
e m.curnow@virgin.net
w porthcurnoholidays.com

Kibblestone ★★★★
Self Catering
Contact: Ian Ottway
t (01761) 410185

Lands End Vineries ★★
Self Catering
Contact: Mr & Mrs Sutton
t (01736) 871437
e ian.vineries@btinternet.com

Lan-Pedn ★★ *Self Catering*
Contact: Mr & Mrs Atter
t (01736) 810153

Longships & Tater-Du ★★★★ *Self Catering*
Cornish Cottage Holidays
t (01326) 573808

The Lookout ★★★
Self Catering
Contact: Mrs Barbara Ottway
t (01761) 410185
e barbara_ottway@tiscali.co.uk

Mercury House ★★★
Self Catering
Contact: Mrs Ginn
t (01736) 811910
w porthcurno.org.uk

The Piggery ★★★
Self Catering
t (01736) 810132
e swalton@bolitho.biblio.net

Sunnymead ★★★★
Self Catering
Contact: Mr Gerard Heathcote
t (01736) 810949
e xsoft@btconnect.com
w sunnymead.biz

Trebehor Cottages ★★★★
Self Catering
Contact: Mr Jeffery
t (01736) 871263
w trebehorcottages.co.uk

Treloggan Cottage ★★★★
Self Catering
The Meadows
t (01736) 810452
e robertandkay@penberth.com
w sennen-cove.com

ST MABYN
Cornwall

Polglynn Cottage, St Mabyn ★★★★★ *Self Catering*
Contact: Mr William Wareham
Polglynn Cottage
t (01208) 850538
e bill@polglaze.freeserve.co.uk

ST MARTIN
Cornwall

Bodigga ★★★ *Self Catering*
Cornish Cottage Holidays
t (01326) 573808
e enquiry@cornishcottageholidays.co.uk
w cornishcottageholidays.co.uk

The Bull House ★★★★
Self Catering
Cornish Cottage Holidays
t (01326) 573808
e enquiry@cornishcottageholidays.co.uk
w cornishcottageholidays.co.uk

School Cottage ★★★★
Self Catering
Contact: Mrs Pamela Russo
t (01752) 605605
e sales@cornishcottage.uk.com
w cornishcottage.uk.com

ST MARYCHURCH
Devon

Little Grange ★★★
Self Catering
Contact: Mr & Mrs Edward & Jenifer Webber
t (01803) 313809
e jenniferepwebber@btinternet.com

Ludwell House
★★★–★★★★ *Self Catering*
Contact: Ms Karen Clark
t (01803) 326032
e sue.clark4@ukonline.co.uk

ST MAWES
Cornwall

3 Tregarth Cottages ★★★★
Self Catering
Roseland Holiday Cottages
t (01872) 580480
e enquiries@roselandholidaycottages.co.uk

5 Manor Court ★★
Self Catering
Roseland Holiday Cottages
t (01872) 580480
e enquiries@roselandholidaycottages.co.uk
w roselandholidaycottages.co.uk

Brackley House ★★★
Self Catering
Contact: Leonie Iddison
Roseland Holiday Cottages
t (01872) 580480
e enquiries@roselandholidaycottages.co.uk
w roselandholidaycottages.co.uk

Captains Cottage ★
Self Catering
Roseland Holiday Cottages
t (01872) 580480
e enquiries@roselandholidaycottages.co.uk
w roselandholidaycottages.co.uk

Chy Ryn ★★★★
Self Catering
Special Places in Cornwall
t (01872) 864400
e office@specialplacescornwall.co.uk
w specialplacescornwall.co.uk

Coppers & Peel Cottage
★★★★ *Self Catering*
Special Places in Cornwall
t (01872) 864400
e office@specialplacescornwall.co.uk
w specialplacescornwall.co.uk

Cornwall Waterfront Homes
★★★★ *Self Catering*
Contact: Mrs Clifford-Wing
t (01872) 580751
e enquiries@cornwallwaterfronthomes.co.uk
w cornwallwaterfronthomes.co.uk

Fort House ★★★★★
Self Catering
English Heritage Holiday Cottages
t 0870 333 1187
w english-heritage.org.uk/holidaycottages

The Gingerbread House
★★★★ *Self Catering*
Special Places in Cornwall
t (01872) 864400
e office@specialplacescornwall.co.uk
w specialplacescornwall.co.uk

Gull Cottage ★★★
Self Catering
t (01872) 580480
e enquiries@roselandholidaycottages.co.uk

Hillside Cottage ★★★★
Self Catering
Roseland Holiday Cottages
t (01872) 580480
e enquiries@roselandholidaycottages.co.uk
w roselandholidaycottages.co.uk

Idle Rocks Apartments
★★★★ *Self Catering*
Contact: Miss Metcalfe
t (01326) 270771
e lesley.metcalfe@idlerocks.co.uk

Little Quay ★★ *Self Catering*
Contact: Mr & Mrs Whitton
t (01326) 270769

Manor Cottage ★★★
Self Catering
t (01872) 580480
e enquiries@roselandholidaycottages.co.uk
w roselandholidaycottages.co.uk

Mariners ★★★★
Self Catering
Special Places in Cornwall
t (01872) 864400
e office@specialplacescornwall.co.uk
w specialplacescornwall.co.uk

The Old Dairy ★★★
Self Catering
t (01872) 580480
e enquiries@roselandholidaycottages.co.uk
w roselandholidaycottages.co.uk

Oyster Haven
★★★★–★★★★★
Self Catering
Special Places in Cornwall
t (01872) 864400
e office@specialplacescornwall.co.uk
w specialplacescornwall.co.uk

Penlee ★★★★ *Self Catering*
Special Places in Cornwall
t (01872) 864400
e office@specialplacescornwall.co.uk
w specialplacescornwall.co.uk

Rocklee House ★★★★
Self Catering
Special Places in Cornwall
t (01872) 864400
e office@specialplacescornwall.co.uk
w specialplacescornwall.co.uk

Rosslyn ★★ *Self Catering*
Contact: Mrs Beeching
t (01753) 883504
e caroline.beeching@btopenworld.com

Sail Cottage ★★★★
Self Catering
Roseland Holiday Cottages
t (01872) 580480
e enquiries@roselandholidaycottages.co.uk
w roselandholidaycottages.co.uk

Seagulls ★★★ *Self Catering*
Roseland Holiday Cottages
t (01872) 580480
e enquiries@roselandholidaycottages.co.uk

Seaward ★★★★
Self Catering
Special Places in Cornwall
t (01872) 864400
e office@specialplacescornwall.co.uk
w specialplacescornwall.co.uk

September Cottage ★★★
Self Catering
Contact: Mrs Iddison
Roseland Holiday Cottages
t (01872) 580480
e enquiries@roselandholidaycottages.co.uk
w roselandholidaycottages.co.uk

Skippers ★★★ *Self Catering*
Roseland Holiday Cottages
t (01872) 580480
e enquiries@roselandholidaycottages.co.uk
w roselandholidaycottages.co.uk

Sunnybanks ★★★★
Self Catering
Special Places in Cornwall
t (01872) 864400
e office@specialplacescornwall.co.uk
w specialplacescornwall.co.uk

Sycamore ★★★★
Self Catering
Roseland Holiday Cottages
t (01872) 580480
e enquiries@roselandholidaycottages.co.uk
w roselandholidaycottages.co.uk

Tom Thumb Cottage ★★★
Self Catering
Roseland Holiday Cottages
t (01872) 580480
e enquiries@roselandholidaycottages.co.uk
w roselandholidaycottages.co.uk

Topdeck ★★★★
Self Catering
Special Places in Cornwall
t (01872) 864400
e office@specialplacescornwall.co.uk
w specialplacescornwall.co.uk

Tregarth Cottages ★★★★
Self Catering
Roseland Holiday Cottages
t (01872) 580480
e enquiries@roselandholidaycottages.co.uk

Trelonk Vean ★★★★
Self Catering
Contact: Leonie Iddison
Roseland Holiday Cottages
t (01872) 580480
e enquiries@roselandholidaycottages.co.uk
w roselandholidaycottages.co.uk

Uplands ★★★ *Self Catering*
Roseland Holiday Cottages
t (01872) 580480
e enquiries@roselandholidaycottages.co.uk
w roselandholidaycottages.co.uk

The White House
Rating Applied For
Self Catering
Contact: Mrs Spencer
Special Places in Cornwall
t (01872) 864400
e office@specialplacescornwall.co.uk
w specialplacescornwall.co.uk

White Lodge ★★★★
Self Catering
Special Places in Cornwall
t (01872) 864400
e office@specialplacescornwall.co.uk
w specialplacescornwall.co.uk

Woodhambury House ★★★
Self Catering
Roseland Holiday Cottages
t (01872) 580480
e enquiries@roselandholidaycottages.co.uk
w roselandholidaycottages.co.uk

The Workshop ★★★
Self Catering
Special Places in Cornwall
t (01872) 864400
e office@specialplacescornwall.co.uk
w specialplacescornwall.co.uk

ST MELLION
Cornwall

15 Woburn Lodge ★★★★
Self Catering
Valley Villas
t (01752) 605605
e sales@valleyvillas.com
w valleyvillas.com

ST MERRYN
Cornwall

121 Lily Way ★★★
Self Catering
t (01666) 502868
e ewittem@talktalk.net

132 Point Curlew ★★★
Self Catering
Contact: Mr Allen
t (01841) 540871

138 Jasmine Way ★★★
Self Catering
Contact: Miss Morgan
138 Jasmine Way
t (020) 8355 9773
e haha.films@virgin.net
w cornishselfcateringhols.com

Angelholm ★★★
Self Catering
Contact: Miss Nicky Stanley
t (01841) 533402
e contact@harbourholidays.co.uk
w harbourholidays.co.uk

Bays Reach ★★★
Self Catering
Cornish Horizons Holiday Cottages
t (01841) 533331
e cottages@cornishhorizons.co.uk
w cornishhorizons.co.uk

Chalet 83 ★★ *Self Catering*
Contact: Miss Elizabeth Kerry
Church Cottage
t (01793) 740284

Chyloweth ★★★
Self Catering
Contact: Mr & Mrs Vivian
t (01841) 521012
e roger.vivian@ukgateway.net
w padstowlive.com

Cill Dara ★★★★
Self Catering
Contact: Nicky Stanley
Harbour Holidays
t (01841) 533402
e contact@harbourholidays.co.uk
w harbourholidays.co.uk

Curlew ★★★ *Self Catering*
Contact: Mr Peter Osbourne
Cornish Horizons Holiday Cottages
t (01841) 533331
e cottages@cornishhorizons.co.uk
w cornishhorizons.co.uk

Lanngorrow ★★★
Self Catering
Contact: Mrs Cathy Osborne
Cornish Horizons Holiday Cottages
t (01841) 533331
e cottages@cornishhorizons.co.uk
w cornishhorizons.co.uk

Lantic Surf ★★★
Self Catering
Contact: Cathy Osborne
Cornish Horizons Holiday Cottages
t (01841) 533331
e cottages@cornishhorizons.co.uk
w cornishhorizons.co.uk

Little Lancarrow ★★★
Self Catering
Cornish Horizons Holiday Cottages
t (01841) 533331
e cottages@cornishhorizons.co.uk
w cornishhorizons.co.uk

Little Oak
Rating Applied For
Self Catering
Contact: Mrs Cathy Osborne
Cornish Horizons Holiday Cottages
t (01841) 533331
e cottages@cornishhorizons.co.uk
w cornishhorizons.co.uk

Lower Trevorgus ★★★★
Self Catering
Contact: Nicky Stanley
Harbour Holidays Ltd
t (01841) 533402
e contact@harbourholidays.co.uk
w harbourholidays.co.uk

Manassa ★★★ *Self Catering*
Cornish Horizons Holiday Cottages
t (01841) 533331
e cottages@cornishhorizons.co.uk
w cornishhorizons.co.uk

Meadow Lodge Annex
★★★★ *Self Catering*
Harbour Holidays
t (01841) 533402
e contact@harbourholidays.co.uk
w harbourholidays.co.uk

Point Curlew Country Holiday Estate ★★
Self Catering
t (01305) 265487

Primrose Cottage – Treyarnon Bay ★★★★
Self Catering
Contact: Mr Tim Abbott
t (01428) 723819
e enquiries@cornishseaviewcottages.co.uk
w cornishseaviewcottages.co.uk

Quies ★★★ *Self Catering*
Cornish Horizons Holiday Cottages
t (01841) 533331
e cottages@cornishhorizons.co.uk
w cornishhorizons.co.uk

Rozmerrow ★★★★
Self Catering
Contact: Peter Osbourne
Cornish Horizons Holiday Cottages
t (01841) 533331
e cottages@cornishhorizons.co.uk
w cornishhorizons.co.uk

St Hilary & Little Robin
★★★ *Self Catering*
Contact: Peter Osbourne
Cornish Horizons Holiday Cottages
t (01841) 533331
e cottages@cornishhorizons.co.uk
w cornishhorizons.co.uk

St Merryn Holiday Village
★★★★ *Self Catering*
Contact: Robert & Pamela Griffin
Alverstoke
t (01454) 632624
e robertgriffin@tiscali.co.uk

Trearth ★★★★ *Self Catering*
Contact: Mr Peter Osbourne
Cornish Horizons Holiday Cottages
t (01841) 533331
e cottages@cornishhorizons.co.uk
w trearth.com

Tregavone Barn
Rating Applied For
Self Catering
Contact: Lucy Ellison
Farm & Cottage Holidays
t (01237) 479146
e enquiries@farmcott.co.uk
w holidaycottages.co.uk

Twizzletwig ★★★
Self Catering
Contact: Mr Osbourne
Cornish Horizons Holiday Cottages
t (01841) 533331
e cottages@cornishhorizons.co.uk
w cornishhorizons.co.uk

Two Stiles ★★★★
Self Catering
Contact: Mr Osbourne
Cornish Horizons Holiday Cottages
t (01841) 533331
e cottages@cornishhorizons.co.uk
w cornishhorizons.co.uk

Wheal Parc ★★★★
Self Catering
Contact: Peter Osbourne
Cornish Horizons Holiday Cottages
t (01841) 533331
e cottages@cornishhorizons.co.uk
w cornishhorizons.co.uk

Wispa ★★★★ *Self Catering*
Contact: Nicky Stanley
Harbour Holidays
t (01841) 533402
e contact@harbourholidays.co.uk
w harbourholidays.co.uk

ST MINVER
Cornwall

2 Lundy House ★★★★
Self Catering
Contact: Mrs Burns
t (01208) 863000
e mail@roserrow.co.uk

2 The Old Dairy ★★★★
Self Catering
Contact: Rock Holidays
Rock Holidays inc. Harbour Holidays Rock
t (01208) 863399
e rockhols@aol.com
w rockholidays.co.uk

5 Treglyn ★★★ *Self Catering*
Contact: Charlotte Bolt
t (01208) 863399
e rockhols@aol.com
w rockholidays.co.uk

April Cottage ★★★★★
Self Catering
Contact: Rock Holidays
Rock Holidays inc. Harbour Holidays Rock
t (01208) 863399
e rockhols@aol.com
w rockholidays.co.uk

Atlantic View ★★★★
Self Catering
Contact: Mrs Burns
t (01208) 863000
e mail@roserrow.co.uk

The Bothy ★★★★
Self Catering
Contact: Mrs Julie Burns
t (01208) 863000
e mail@roserrow.co.uk

Breakers View ★★★★
Self Catering
Rock Holidays
t (01208) 863399
e rockhols@aol.com
w rockholidays.co.uk

Brook House ★★★★
Self Catering
Rock Holidays
t (01208) 863399
e rockhols@aol.com
w rockholidays.co.uk

Bunkers ★★★★
Self Catering
Contact: Mrs Julie Burns
t (01208) 863000
e mail@roserrow.co.uk

Caldarvan ★★★★
Self Catering
Contact: Mrs Julie Burns
t (01208) 863000
e mail@roserrow.co.uk

Casa Piedra ★★★★
Self Catering
Rock Holidays
t (01208) 863399
e rockhols@aol.com
w rockholidays.co.uk

Chy Petroc ★★★★
Self Catering
Rock Holidays
t (01208) 863399
e rockhols@aol.com
w rockholidays.co.uk

Cobwebs ★★★★
Self Catering
Rock Holidays
t (01208) 863399
w rockholidays.co.uk

Cowrie ★★★★★
Self Catering
Rock Holidays
t (01208) 863399
e rockhols@aol.com
w rockholidays.co.uk

The Farmhouse ★★★★
Self Catering
Rock Holidays
t (01208) 863399
e rockhols@aol.com
w rockholidays.co.uk

Gearys ★★★★ *Self Catering*
Rock Holidays
t (01208) 863399
e rockhols@aol.com
w rockholidays.co.uk

Glenvalley Cottage ★★★
Self Catering
Contact: Ruth & Paul Thomas
t (01823) 490569
e ruth@rwnc.fsnet.co.uk
w glenvalleycottage.co.uk

Gore's Garrison ★★★★★
Self Catering
Rock Holidays
t (01208) 863399
e rockhols@aol.com
w rockholidays.co.uk

Great Bodieve Farm Barns
★★★★★ *Self Catering*
Contact: Mr & Mrs Phillips
t (01208) 814916
e info@great-bodieve.co.uk
w great-bodieve.co.uk

Gwella ★★★★ *Self Catering*
Rock Holidays
t (01208) 863399
e rockhols@aol.com
w rockholidays.co.uk

Hampden ★★★★★
Self Catering
Rock Holidays
t (01208) 863399
e rockhols@aol.com
w rockholidays.co.uk

The Haven ★★★★★
Self Catering
Rock Holidays
t (01208) 863399
e rockhols@aol.com
w rockholidays.co.uk

The Hawthorns ★★★★
Self Catering
Rock Holidays
t (01208) 863399
e rockhols@aol.com
w rockholidays.co.uk

Hollyhocks ★★ *Self Catering*
Contact: Charlotte Bolt
Rock Holidays
t (01208) 863399
e rockhols@aol.com
w rockholidays.co.uk

Idle Rocks ★★★★
Self Catering
Contact: Rock Holidays
Rock Holidays inc. Harbour Holidays Rock
t (01208) 863399
e rockhols@aol.com
w rockholidays.co.uk

Janners Retreat ★★★★
Self Catering
Contact: Mrs Julie Burns
t (01208) 863000
e mail@roserrow.co.uk

Keepers ★★★★
Self Catering
Rock Holidays
t (01208) 863399
e rockhols@aol.com
w rockholidays.co.uk

Kensa Toll ★★★★
Self Catering
Rock Holidays
t (01208) 863399
e rockhols@aol.com
w rockholidays.co.uk

Lundy Cottage ★★★★
Self Catering
Rock Holidays
t (01208) 863399
e rockhols@aol.com
w rockholidays.co.uk

Lundy House/St Agnes
★★★★ *Self Catering*
Contact: Mr & Mrs Horsfield
Milobel House
t (01208) 269818

Mayfield ★★★★
Self Catering
Rock Holidays
t (01208) 863399
e rockhols@aol.com

The Millhouse ★★★★
Self Catering
Rock Holidays
t (01208) 863399
e rockhols@aol.com

Mosseyoak ★★★★
Self Catering
Rock Holidays
t (01208) 863399
e rockhols@aol.com
w rockholidays.co.uk

The Nineteeth ★★★★
Self Catering
Contact: Charlotte Bolt
t (01208) 863399
e rockhols@aol.com
w rockholidays.co.uk

Oak Tree House ★★★★
Self Catering
Rock Holidays
t (01208) 863399
e rockhols@aol.com
w rockholidays.co.uk

Pearl Springs ★★★★
Self Catering
Contact: Mrs Helena French
t (01208) 862583

Pendragon Cottage ★★★
Self Catering
Contact: Ms Tess Smith
t (01208) 863172
w polzeathcottages.com

Penhayle ★★★★
Self Catering
Rock Holidays
t (01208) 863399
e rockhols@aol.com
w rockholidays.co.uk

Penkivel House ★★★★
Self Catering
Rock Holidays
t (01208) 863399
e rockhols@aol.com
w rockholidays.co.uk

Penteli ★★★★ *Self Catering*
Rock Holidays
t (01208) 863399
e rockhols@aol.com
w rockholidays.co.uk

Puffin House ★★★★
Self Catering
Rock Holidays
t (01208) 863399
e rockhols@aol.com
w rockholidays.co.uk

Rose Cottage ★★★★★
Self Catering
Rock Holidays
t (01208) 863399
e rockhols@aol.com
w rockholidays.co.uk

Rosewin Barn ★★★
Self Catering
Rock Holidays
t (01208) 863399

St Andrew's Cottage
★★★★ *Self Catering*
Contact: Rock Holidays
Rock Holidays
t (01208) 863399
e rockhols@aol.com
w rockholidays.co.uk

Sandy Cottage ★★★★
Self Catering
Contact: Mrs Burns
t (01208) 863000
e mail@roserrow.co.uk

September ★★★★
Self Catering
Rock Holidays
t (01208) 863399
e rockhols@aol.com
w rockholidays.co.uk

Solskyn ★★★ *Self Catering*
Contact: Rock Holidays
Rock Holidays
t (01208) 863399
e rockhols@aol.com
w rockholidays.co.uk

Talamore ★★★★
Self Catering
Rock Holidays
t (01208) 863399
e rockhols@aol.com
w rockholidays.co.uk

Tamarisk – The Old Dairy
★★★★ *Self Catering*
Rock Holidays
t (01208) 863399
e rockhols@aol.com
w rockholidays.co.uk

Thyme Cottage ★★★★
Self Catering
Rock Holidays
t (01208) 863399
e rockhols@aol.com

Tremaine ★★★★★
Self Catering
Rock Holidays inc. Harbour Holidays Rock Ltd.
t (01208) 863399
e rockhols@aol.com

Trevells ★★★ *Self Catering*
Contact: Mrs Burns
t (01208) 863000
e mail@roserrow.co.uk

Trevelver Farm Cottage
★★★ *Self Catering*
Contact: Mrs Avice Wills
t (01208) 863290

Webbs Retreat ★★★★
Self Catering
Rock Holidays
t (01208) 863399
e rockhols@aol.com
w rockholidays.co.uk

Wedge Cottage ★★★
Self Catering
Rock Holidays
t (01208) 863399
e rockhols@aol.com
w rockholidays.co.uk

Wenlock ★★★★
Self Catering
Contact: Mrs Burns
t (01208) 863000
e mail@roserrow.co.uk

Woodbine House ★★★★★
Self Catering
Rock Holidays
t (01208) 863399
e rockhols@aol.com
w rockholidays.co.uk

Woodfin ★★★ *Self Catering*
Contact: Mrs Edwards
t (01483) 202478
e ruhalusu@hotmail.com

ST NEWLYN EAST
Cornwall

Goonwinnow Farm Holiday Cottages ★★★★
Self Catering
Contact: Mr Andrew Murgatroyd
t (01872) 510696
e goonwinnowfarm@aol.com
w goonwinnowfarm.co.uk

The Granary Cottages
Rating Applied For
Self Catering
Contact: Mrs Terri Clark
t (01872) 510345
e trewerrymill@which.net
w trewerrymill.co.uk

Penty Gwyn ★★★
Self Catering
Powells Cottage Holidays
t (01834) 812791
e info@powells.co.uk
w powells.co.uk

ST STEPHEN
Cornwall

Court Farm Cottages
★★★★ *Self Catering*
Contact: Mr Bill Truscott
t (01726) 823684
e truscott@ctfarm.freeserve.co.uk
w courtfarmcornwall.co.uk

ST TEATH
Cornwall

Barn Farm Holidays ★★★★
Self Catering
Contact: Mrs Goldie
t (01208) 850912
e enquiries@barnfarmholidays.co.uk
w barnfarmholidays.co.uk

Dinnabroad Cottage ★★★★
Self Catering
Contact: Ms Alison Ellison
Farm & Cottage Holidays
t (01237) 479146
e enquiries@farmcott.co.uk
w holidaycottages.co.uk

Higher Hendra Cottages
★★★★ *Self Catering*
Contact: Mrs Roose
t (01208) 880341
w higher-hendra.com

Mill Barn and Stable Cottage
★★★★ *Self Catering*
Contact: Mrs Julie Bailey
t (01208) 850994
e tredarrupinfo@aol.com
w tredarrup.com

ST TUDY
Cornwall

The Linhay ★★★★★
Self Catering
Contact: Mrs C.M Kingdon
t (01208) 851422

SALCOMBE
Devon

Bolberry Farm Cottages
★★★★★ *Self Catering*
Contact: Mrs Hazel Hassall
Bolberry Farm Cottages
t (01548) 561384
e info@bolberryfarmcottages.co.uk
w bolberryfarmcottages.co.uk

Coxswain's Watch ★★★★
Self Catering
Contact: Mrs Julie Powell
Robert Oulsnam & Co
t (0121) 445 3311
e barntgreen@oulsnam.net
w oulsnam.net

Mudlark ★★ *Self Catering*
Contact: Mrs Lindsey Davies
Westbush House
t (01992) 462280

SALISBURY
Wiltshire

12 Charter Court ★★★★
Self Catering
Contact: Mrs Patricia Moore
t (01722) 320188
e charterho@hotmail.com

1st Floor Apartment ★★★★
Self Catering
Hideaways
t (01747) 828170
e enq@hideaways.co.uk

21 Harnham Road ★★★★
Self Catering
Hideaways
t (01747) 828170
e enq@hideaways.co.uk

4TEEN ★★★★ *Self Catering*
Contact: Mrs Mary Webb
4TEEN
t (01722) 340892 &
07759 474115
e enquiries@4teen.biz
w 4teen.biz

Charter Court ★★★★
Self Catering
Contact: Mr Nicholas Pash
Hideaways
t (01747) 828170
e enq@hideaways.co.uk
w hideaways.co.uk

Garden Flat, Ramsey House
★★★★ *Self Catering*
Contact: Mrs Vivien Brown
t (01722) 327166 &
07960 993746
e ramseyhouse@hotmail.com

The Hayloft, Ebblesway Courtyard ★★★★
Self Catering
Contact: Mrs Gail Smalley
t (01722) 780182
e gail@ebbleswaycourtyard.co.uk
w ebbleswaycourtyard.co.uk

Hen View (The Fishing Lodge) ★★★★ *Self Catering*
Contact: Mrs Victoria Dakin
t (01747) 855976
e vdakin@skymarket.org

Little Till Cottage ★★★★
Self Catering
Contact: Mr & Mrs Hearn
Winterbourne Stoke
t (01980) 620396
e mikehearn@onetel.com
w littletillcottage.com

Love Lane ★★★ *Self Catering*
Contact: Mr Nicholas Pash
Hideaways
t (01747) 828170
e enq@hideaways.co.uk
w hideaways.co.uk

Manor Farm Cottages
★★★★ *Self Catering*
Contact: Mrs Gillie Strang
t (01722) 714226
e strangf@aol.com
w strangcottages.com

The Old Stables ★★★★
Self Catering
Contact: Mr Giles Gould
t (01722) 349002
e mail@old-stables.co.uk
w old-stables.co.uk

Sycamore Cottage ★★★★
Self Catering
Contact: Mr & Mrs Richard & Cilla Pickett
Melrose Cottage
t (01722) 743160
e cilla@sycamorecottage.biz
w sycamorecottage.biz

Water Lane
Rating Applied For
Self Catering
Contact: Mr Nick Pash
Hideaways
t (01747) 828170
e enq@hideaways.co.uk
w hideaways.co.uk

Wich Hazel's Apartment, Woodfalls ★★★★
Self Catering
Contact: Mrs Ann Eveleigh
Wich Hazel's Apartment
t (01725) 511599
e anneveleigh@aol.com
w wichhazel.co.uk

Winterbourne Cottage
★★★★ *Self Catering*
Contact: Mr Nicholas Pash
Hideaways
t (01747) 828170
e enq@hideaways.co.uk
w hideaways.co.uk

SALTASH
Cornwall

Tredudwell Farmhouse
★★★★ *Self Catering*
Contact: Mr Nick Pash
Hideaways, Luke Street
t (01747) 828170
e enq@hideaways.co.uk
w hideaways.co.uk/property.cfm/H606

SAMPFORD ARUNDEL
Somerset

Gorlegg Cottage ★★★★
Self Catering
Farm & Cottage Holidays
t (01237) 479146
e enquiries@farmcott.co.uk
w holidaycottages.co.uk

SANDFORD
Dorset

Glendene ★★★ *Self Catering*
Contact: Miss LM Hemingway
Dorset Cottage Holidays
t (01929) 553443
e enq@dhcottages.co.uk
w dhcottages.co.uk

SANDHURST
Gloucestershire

Great Coverden *Self Catering*
Contact: Mrs Deb Warren
Bengrove Farm
t (01452) 730231
e Debs@bengrovefarm.fsnet.co.uk
w greatcoverden.com

SANDYWAY
Devon

Barkham Cottages ★★★★
Self Catering
Contact: Mr & Mrs Adie
t (01643) 831370
e adie.exmoor@btinternet.com
w holidays-exmoor.com

SAUNTON
Devon

Lower Lease ★★★★
Self Catering
Contact: Mrs Janet Cornwell
Marsdens Cottage Holidays
t (01271) 813777
e holidays@marsdens.co.uk
w marsdens.co.uk

Rhu & Little Rhu ★★★
Self Catering
Contact: Mrs Janet Cornwell
Marsdens Cottage Holidays
t (01271) 813777
e holidays@marsdens.co.uk
w marsdens.co.uk

Sandhills ★★★★
Self Catering
Contact: Mr Peter Cornwell
Marsdens Cottage Holidays
t (01271) 813777
e holidays@marsdens.co.uk
w marsdens.co.uk

Surf ★★★ *Self Catering*
Contact: Mrs Janet Cornwell
Marsdens Cottage Holidays
t (01271) 813777
e holidays@marsdens.co.uk
w marsdens.co.uk

Thorn Close Cottage ★★★★
Self Catering
Marsdens Cottage Holidays
t (01271) 813777
e holidays@marsdens.co.uk
w marsdens.co.uk

SEATON
Devon

10 Seafield Road ★★★★
Self Catering
Contact: Ms Louise Hayman
Milkbere Cottage Holidays
t (01297) 20729
e info@milkberehols.com
w milkberehols.com

27 West Acres ★★★★
Self Catering
Contact: Ms Louise Hayman
Milkbere Cottage Holidays
t (01297) 20729
e info@milkberehols.com
w milkberehols.com

3 Lyme Mews ★★★
Self Catering
Contact: Ms Kate Bartlett
Jean Bartlett Cottage Holidays
t (01297) 23221
e holidays@jeanbartlett.com
w jeanbartlett.com

4 & 6 Pioneer Cottages
★★★ *Self Catering*
Contact: Ms Kate Bartlett
Jean Bartlett Cottage Holidays
t (01297) 23221
e holidays@jeanbartlett.com
w jeanbartlett.com

Arlington ★★★★
Self Catering
Contact: Louise Hayman
Milkbere Cottage Holidays
t (01297) 20729
e info@milkberehols.com
w milkberehols.com

Birdsong ★★★ *Self Catering*
Contact: Louise Hayman
Milkbere Cottage Holidays
t (01297) 20729
e info@milkberehols.com
w milkberehols.com

California Glory ★★★★
Self Catering
Contact: Ms Kate Bartlett
Jean Bartlett Cottage Holidays
t (01297) 23221
e holidays@jeanbartlett.com
w jeanbartlett.com

Caruso ★★★ *Self Catering*
Contact: Ms Louise Hayman
Milkbere Cottage Holidays
t (01297) 20729
e info@milkberehols.com
w milkberehols.com

The Coach House ★★★★
Self Catering
Contact: Louise Hayman
Milkbere Cottage Holidays
t (01297) 20729
e info@milkberehols.com
w milkberehols.com

Conswalk ★★★ *Self Catering*
Contact: Ms Louise Hayman
Milkbere Cottage Holidays
t (01297) 20729
e info@milkberehols.com
w milkberehols.com

Deepdale ★★★ *Self Catering*
Milkbere Cottage Holidays
t (01297) 27029
e info@milkberehols.com

Flat 2, 8 Westcliffe Terrace
★★★ *Self Catering*
Milkbere Cottage Holidays
t (01297) 20729
e info@milkberehols.com

Harbour View and Harbour Side ★★★★–★★★★★
Self Catering
Contact: Mrs Hilary Bevis
t (01297) 23388

The Haven (Flat 1) ★★★
Self Catering
Jean Bartlett Cottage Holidays
t (01297) 23221
e holidays@jeanbartlett.com
w jeanbartlett.com

Homestead Flats ★★
Self Catering
Contact: Ms Kate Bartlett
Jean Bartlett Cottage Holidays
t (01297) 23221

Little Oaks ★★★★
Self Catering
Contact: Ms Louise Hayman
Milkbere Cottage Holidays
t (01297) 20729
e info@milkberehols.com
w milkberehols.com

The Loft ★★★ *Self Catering*
Contact: Ms Louise Hayman
Milkbere Cottage Holidays
t (01297) 20729
e info@milkberehols.com
w milkberehols.com

Manor Farm Cottages
★★★–★★★★ *Self Catering*
Contact: Mrs Parr
t (01297) 625349

Marine Place Apartments
★★★ *Self Catering*
Milkbere Cottage Holidays
t (01297) 20729
e info@milkberehols.com
w milkberehols.com

Mole Cottage ★★★★
Self Catering
Contact: Ms Louise Hayman
Milkbere Cottage Holidays
t (01297) 20729
e info@milkberehols.com
w milkberehols.com

The Nook ★★★★
Self Catering
Contact: Ms Louise Hayman
Milkbere Cottage Holidays
t (01297) 20729
e info@milkberehols.com
w milkberehols.com

Owls Retreat ★★
Self Catering
Milkbere Cottage Holidays
t (01297) 20729
e info@milkberehols.com
w milkberehols.com

Palm View ★★★★
Self Catering
Contact: Louise Hayman
Milkbere Cottage Holidays
t (01297) 20729
e info@milkberehols.com
w milkberehols.com

Pilsbury Cottage ★★★
Self Catering
Contact: Ms Louise Hayman
Milkbere Cottage Holidays
t (01297) 20729
e info@milkberehols.com
w milkberehols.com

Pioneer ★★★ *Self Catering*
Contact: Louise Hayman
Milkbere Cottage Holidays
t (01297) 20729
e info@milkberehols.com
w milkberehols.com

Primrose ★★★ *Self Catering*
Contact: Ms Louise Hayman
Milkbere Cottage Holidays
t (01297) 20729
e info@milkberehols.com
w milkberehols.com

Riverside ★★★★
Self Catering
Contact: Louise Hayman
Milkbere Cottage Holiday
t (01297) 20729
e info@milkberehols.com
w milkberehols.com

Seagulls ★★★ *Self Catering*
Milkbere Cottage Holidays
t (01297) 20729
e info@milkberehols.com
w milkberehols.com

Seaside Flat 3 ★★★
Self Catering
Contact: Ms Kate Bartlett
Jean Bartlett Cottage Holidays
t (01297) 23221
e holidays@jeanbartlett.com
w jeanbartlett.com

Seaview Garden ★★★
Self Catering
Jean Bartlett Cottage Holidays
t (01297) 23221
e holidays@jeanbartlett.com
w jeanbartlett.com

Shalom – V4446 ★★★★
Self Catering
Contact: Mr Jim Matthews
Lyme Bay Holidays
t (01297) 443363
e email@lymebayholidays.co.uk
w lymebayholidays.co.uk

Soo Soo San ★★★
Self Catering
Contact: Ms Louise Hayman
Milkbere Cottage Holidays
t (01297) 20729
e info@milkberehols.com
w milkberehols.com

Teazles ★★★★ *Self Catering*
Contact: Ms Louise Hayman
Milkbere Cottage Holidays
t (01297) 20729
e info@milkberehols.com
w milkberehols.com

West Ridge Bungalow ★★★
Self Catering
Contact: Mrs Hildegard Fox
West Ridge Bungalow
t (01297) 22398
e foxfamily@westridge.fsbusiness.co.uk
w cottageguide.co.uk/westridge

Westacres ★★★
Self Catering
Contact: Mr Tim Tandy
Jean Bartlett Cottage Holidays
t (01297) 23221
e holidays@jeanbartlett.com
w jeanbartlett.com

Windrush ★★★ *Self Catering*
Contact: Mr Tim Tandy
Jean Bartlett Cottage Holidays
t (01297) 23221
e holidays@jeanbartlett.com
w jeanbartlett.com

Yarty Cottage ★★★
Self Catering
Milkbere Cottage Holidays
t (01297) 20729
e info@milkberehols.com
w milkberehols.com

SEATOWN
Dorset

The Guard House ★★★★
Self Catering
Contact: Mrs Charlotte Wreaves
t (020) 7228 6366
e charlotte@ukdltd.com
w guardhouse.co.uk

SEDGEHILL
Wiltshire

Whitebridge Farm Cottages ★★★–★★★★ *Self Catering*
Contact: Mr & Mrs Terry & Julie Neale
Whitebridge Farm
t (01747) 830462
e whitebridgefarm@btconnect.com
w whitebridgeholidaycottages.co.uk

SENNEN
Cornwall

3 & 4 Wesley Cottages ★★★ *Self Catering*
Contact: Mrs J Davey
t (01736) 731933
e wesley@raginnis.demon.co.uk
w wesleyatnanquidno.co.uk

Little Trevallack ★★★
Self Catering
Contact: Mrs Nicholas
t (01736) 871451
e suenicholas@hotmail.com

Surfers ★★★ *Self Catering*
Contact: Mr & Mrs Bishop
Surfers
t (01543) 570901
e bbishop1@onetel.com

Trevear Farm ★★★★
Self Catering
Contact: Mrs Thomas
Trevear Farm
t (01736) 871205
e trevear.farm@farming.co.uk
w trevearfarm.co.uk

SENNEN COVE
Cornwall

Harbour Mews, Sennen Cove and ★★★★
Self Catering
Contact: Mr Jeff Hardman
t (01736) 810504
e jeff@faraway.fsworld.co.uk
w sennencornwall.com

The Old Success Inn ★★★
Self Catering
Contact: Mr Martin Brookes
t (01736) 871232
e oldsuccess@sennencove.fsbusiness.co.uk

Pendeen Lighthouse ★★★★
Self Catering
Michael Blanchard Associates
t (01386) 822855
e michaelblanchard@talk21.com
w ruralretreats.co.uk

Riviera Apartments and Treloggan ★★★ *Self Catering*
Contact: Mr & Mrs George
t (01736) 810452
e robertandkay@penberth.com

Tinker Taylor Cottage ★★★★ *Self Catering*
Contact: Mr Paget
t (01934) 751306
e davidpagets@aol.com

SHAFTESBURY
Dorset

Foxglove Cottage ★★★
Self Catering
Contact: Mrs Maureen Spinney
t (01747) 838769
e alan.spinneyl@btopenworld.com
w foxgloveshaftesbury.co.uk

Hartgrove Farm ★★★–★★★★ *Self Catering*
Contact: Mrs Susan Smart
t (01747) 811830
e cottages@hartgrovefarm.co.uk
w hartgrovefarm.co.uk

South View ★★★
Self Catering
Contact: Mr Keith Westcott
t (01305) 760120
e southview@stonebank-chickerell.com
w stonebank-chickerell.com

Vale Farm Holiday Cottages ★★★★ *Self Catering*
Contact: Mrs Sarah Drake
t (01747) 811286
e valeholidays@tiscali.co.uk
w valeholidays.co.uk

SHALBOURNE
Wiltshire

The Barn ★★★★
Self Catering
Hideaways
t (01747) 828170
e enq@hideaways.co.uk

SHALDON
Devon

Centre House, Ringmore Lodge ★★★★ *Self Catering*
Contact: Mrs Chris Deacon
t (01564) 793841
e centrehouse@ringmorelodge.freeserve.co.uk
w centrehouse.info

Coombe Close Holidays ★★★ *Self Catering*
Contact: Mr & Mrs Peter & Marlene Huff
t (01803) 327215
e peterhuff@onetel.com
w web.onetel.com/~peterhuff

Longmeadow Farm ★★–★★★ *Self Catering*
t (01626) 872732

Shoreside ★★★★★
Self Catering
Blue Chip Vacations
t (01803) 855282
e andrew@bluechipvacations.com
w bluechipvacations.com

SHEEPSCOMBE
Gloucestershire

Longridge Meend ★★★
Self Catering
Contact: Mr Richard Cound
t (01452) 813225
e richardcound@beeb.net

SHEEPWASH
Devon

Swardicott Farm ★★★
Self Catering
Contact: Mrs Marguerite Purser
t (01409) 231633
e m.purser@btinternet.com
w holidaycottages-devon.co.uk

SHEPTON MALLET
Somerset

Knowle Farm Cottages
Self Catering
Contact: Lisa Sharp
Knowle Farm Cottages
t (01749) 890482
e mail@knowle-farm-cottages.co.uk
w knowle-farm-cottages.co.uk

Leigh Holt ★★★★★
Self Catering
Contact: Mrs Pamela Hoddinott
t (01749) 880280
e pam@burnthousefarmbandb.co.uk
w burnthousefarmbandb.co.uk

SHEPTON MONTAGUE
Somerset

Seed House ★★★★
Self Catering
Contact: Mrs Christina Dimond
t (01749) 812373
e dimond@farm24771.fsnet.co.uk

SHERBORNE
Dorset

1 & 2 Trill Cottages ★★★
Self Catering
Contact: Mrs Warr
t (01935) 872305
e trill.cottages@ic24.net

Blackberry Cottage ★★★
Self Catering
Contact: Mr John Michael Farr
t (01935) 423148

Millers Loft ★★★
Self Catering
Contact: Mrs Bridget Buckland
t (01963) 250380
e bandebuckland@aol.com

Old Orchard Cottage
★★★★ *Self Catering*
Contact: Mrs Alexa Buckland
t (01963) 251365

Patson Hill Cottages ★★★★
Self Catering
Contact: Mr & Mrs Ronald & Jill Racher
t (01935) 812845
e info@patsonhill.co.uk
w patsonhill.co.uk

Stable Cottage ★★★
Self Catering
Contact: Mrs Dimond
t (01935) 814716
e bridleways@tiscali.co.uk

SHERFORD
Devon

Daisy Cottage, Stancombe Manor ★★★ *Self Catering*
Contact: Mrs Karin Moncrieff
t (01548) 712644
w daisystancombe.com

Keynedon Barton ★★★★
Self Catering
Contact: Mrs Angela Heath
t (01548) 531273
w kingsbridge-holiday-cottage.co.uk

Snowdrop ★★★★
Self Catering
Contact: Mr David Hanmer
Toad Hall Cottages
t (01548) 853089
e thc@toadhallcottages.com
w toadhallcottages.com

SHERRINGTON
Wiltshire

Gingerbread Cottage
★★★★ *Self Catering*
Contact: Mrs Gabrielle Lewis
t (01985) 850453
e patlewis@lineone.net
w gingerbreadcottage.co.uk

SHIPTON MOYNE
Gloucestershire

Street Farm Cottages
★★★★ *Self Catering*
Contact: Mrs Beth Birdwood
t (01666) 880523
e beth@streetfarm.co.uk
w streetfarm.co.uk

SHIPTON OLIFFE
Gloucestershire

Berry Cottage ★★★
Self Catering
Contact: Ms Eve McEwan
t (01242) 821676
e evemcewan@yahoo.co.uk

Paddock Barn ★★★★★
Self Catering
Contact: Mrs Doyle
t (01242) 890147
e emma@paddockbarn.co.uk
w paddockbarn.co.uk

SHREWTON
Wiltshire

Drovers' Barn ★★★★
Self Catering
Contact: Mr Nicholas Pash
Hideaways
t (01747) 828170
e enq@hideaways.co.uk
w hideaways.co.uk/property.cfm/h128

SHUTE
Devon

Higher Watchcombe Farmhouse and Country Cottages ★★★★
Self Catering
Contact: Mr & Mrs Paul & Jane Galloway
t (01297) 552424
e galloways@ukgateway.net
w higherwatchcombe.com

SIDFORD
Devon

6 Axe Vale ★★ *Self Catering*
Jean Bartlett Cottage Holidays
t (01297) 23221

Core House Cottages
★★★★ *Self Catering*
Contact: Mrs Susan Pratt
t (01395) 512255
e burscombe@aol.com
w corehousecottages.co.uk

Ford Cottage
Rating Applied For
Self Catering
Contact: Tracy Gwillin
Sweetcombe Cottage Holidays Ltd
t (01395) 512130
e enquiries@sweetcombe-ch.co.uk

Porch Cottage ★★★
Self Catering
Contact: Mr Tim Tandy
Jean Bartlett Cottage Holidays
t (01297) 23221
w jeanbartlett.com

SIDMOUTH
Devon

5 Anstis Court ★★★★
Self Catering
Contact: Mrs Luisa Mellor
t (01484) 532682
e mellorfixby@yahoo.co.uk
w sidmouth-breaks.co.uk

Anchor Apartment ★★★★
Self Catering
Contact: Mrs Jane Tagg
t (01392) 425858
e sidmouthanchor@yahoo.com

Boswell Farm Cottages
★★★★ *Self Catering*
Contact: Mr & Mrs Brian & Linda Dillon
Boswell Farm Holiday Cottages
t (01395) 514162
e dillon@boswell-farm.co.uk
w boswell-farm.co.uk

Bulverton House – The Bakers Cottage
Rating Applied For
Self Catering
Contact: Mr Geoffrey Roe
t (01395) 578552
e geoffroe@hotmail.com
w bulvertonhouse.co.uk

Bulverton Well Cottages
★★★★ *Self Catering*
Contact: Ms Tracy Gwillim
Sweetcombe Cottage Holidays Ltd.
t (01395) 512130
e enquiries@sweetcombe-ch.co.uk

By The Byes
Rating Applied For
Self Catering
Contact: Joyce Deary House
t (01395) 512032
e sidhols@thefort.fsworld.co.uk

Cliffe Cottage ★★★★
Self Catering
Contact: Ms Kate Bartlett
Jean Bartlett Cottage Holidays
t (01297) 23221
e holidays@jeanbartlett.com
w jeanbartlett.com

Clovelly ★★★ *Self Catering*
Contact: Ms Tim Tandy
Jean Bartlett Cottage Holidays
t (01297) 23221
e holidays@jeanbartlett.com
w jeanbartlett.com

The Courtyard ★★★
Self Catering
Contact: Ms Tracy Gwillim
Sweetcombe Cottage Holidays Ltd.
t (01395) 512130
e enquiries@sweetcombe-ch.co.uk

Cricketers ★★★★
Self Catering
Contact: Ms Tracy Gwillim
Sweetcombe Cottage Holidays Ltd.
t (01395) 512130
e enquiries@sweetcombe-ch.co.uk

Dairy Cottage
Rating Applied For
Self Catering
Contact: Tracy Gwillin
Sweetcombe Cottage Holidays Ltd
t (01395) 512130
e enquiries@sweetcombe-ch.co.uk

Dunscombe Manor ★★★★
Self Catering
Contact: Mrs Christina Morgan
t (01395) 513654
e dunscombe.manor@lineone.net
w dunscombe-manor.co.uk

Farthings ★★ *Self Catering*
Contact: Ms Tim Tandy
Jean Bartlett Cottage Holidays
t (01297) 23221
e holidays@jeanbartlett.com
w jeanbartlett.com

Leigh Farm ★★★★
Self Catering
Contact: Mr & Mrs Geoff & Gill Davis
Leigh Farm
t (01395) 516065
e leigh.farm@virgin.net
w streets-ahead.com/leighfarm

Littlecourt Cottages ★★★★
Self Catering
Contact: Mr Selwyn Kussman
t (01395) 515279
e admin@littlecourtcottages.com
w littlecourtcottages.com

Merrifield House (Flat 1)
★★★★★ *Self Catering*
Contact: Ms Tracy Gwillim
Sweetcombe Cottage Holidays Ltd.
t (01395) 512130
e enquiries@sweetcombe-ch.co.uk

Merrifield House (Flat 2)
★★★★★ *Self Catering*
Contact: Ms Tracy Gwillim
Sweetcombe Cottage Holidays Ltd.
t (01395) 512130
e enquiries@sweetcombe-ch.co.uk

Redcliffs
Rating Applied For
Self Catering
Contact: Tracy Gwillin
Sweetcombe Cottage Holidays Ltd
t (01395) 512130
e enquiries@sweetcombe-ch.co.uk

Riverside Cottage ★★★
Self Catering
Contact: Ms Tim Tandy
Jean Bartlett Cottage Holidays
t (01297) 23221
e holidays@jeanbartlett.com
w jeanbartlett.com

Sandpiper ★★★★
Self Catering
Contact: Ms Tracy Gwillim
Sweetcombe Cottage Holidays Ltd.
t (01395) 512130
e enquiries@sweetcombe-ch.co.uk

Seaside Apartments ★★★★
Self Catering
Contact: Mr Russell Ellis
t (01395) 513338
e info@seasideapartments.co.uk
w seasideapartments.co.uk

Stonechat ★★★
Self Catering
Contact: Ms Louise Hayman
Milkbere Cottage Holidays
t (01297) 20729
e info@milkberehols.com
w milkberehols.com

Tradewinds ★★★
Self Catering
Contact: Ms Tracy Gwillim
Sweetcombe Cottage Holidays Ltd.
t (01395) 512130
e enquiries@sweetcombe-ch.co.uk

Look out for establishments participating in the Walkers and Cyclists Welcome Schemes

Treetops ★★★ *Self Catering*
Contact: Ms Tracy Gwillim
Sweetcombe Cottage Holidays Ltd.
t (01395) 512130
e enquiries@sweetcombe-ch.co.uk

Western Court Holiday Apartment ★★★
Self Catering
Contact: Mr & Mrs R.E. & L.V. Mitchell
t (01395) 578786
e hols@remtek46.fsnet.co.uk

Wyndham Court ★★★
Self Catering
Contact: Mr Peter Vincent
The Longhouse
t (01395) 577973
e pvcia@aol.com
w holidaysinsidmouth.co.uk

SIMONSBATH
Somerset

Winstitchen Farm ★★★★
Self Catering
Contact: Mrs Jane Organ
t (01386) 858273
e info@lowerfield-farm.co.uk
w exmoor-country-cottages.com

Wintershead Farm ★★★★
Self Catering
Contact: Mrs Styles
Wintershead Farm
t (01643) 831222
w wintershead.co.uk

SITHNEY
Cornwall

The Hideaway ★★★
Self Catering
Contact: Mr & Mrs Faull
t (01326) 573489
e trelissick@hotmail.com
w trelissickfarm.co.uk

Tregathenan Country Cottages ★★★★
Self Catering
Contact: Miss Fairweather
t (01326) 569840
e tregathenan@hotmail.com
w tregathenan.co.uk

SKINNERS BOTTOM
Cornwall

Verdun Cottage ★★★★
Self Catering
Duchy Holidays
t (01872) 572971
e enquiries@duchyholidays.co.uk
w duchyholidays.co.uk

SLAPTON
Devon

Blackberry Cottage ★★★★
Self Catering
Contact: Mr David Hanmer
Toad Hall Cottages
t (01548) 853089
e thc@toadhallcottages.com
w toadhallcottages.com

Dittiscombe Holiday Cottages ★★★★
Self Catering
Contact: Mrs Ruth Saunders
t (01548) 521272
e info@dittiscombe.co.uk
w dittiscombe.co.uk

Maple Cottage ★★★
Self Catering
Toad Hall Cottages
t (01548) 853089
e thc@toadhallcottages.com
w toadhallcottages.com

Pound Cottage ★★★★
Self Catering
Holiday Homes & Cottages South West
t (01803) 663650
e holcotts@aol.com
w swcottages.co.uk

SLAUGHTERFORD
Wiltshire

Carters Cottage ★★★
Self Catering
Contact: Mrs Janet Jones
t (01249) 782243
e hanfreeth@hotmail.com

SLIMBRIDGE
Gloucestershire

Rectory Park ★★★★★
Self Catering
Contact: Ms Pamela Skinner
Dunster Living
t 0870 620 1066
e info@dunsterliving.co.uk
w rectorypark.co.uk

SNOWSHILL
Gloucestershire

Shenberrow Farm Cottage ★★★★★ *Self Catering*
Contact: Mrs Tina Carroll
Shenberrow Hill
t (01386) 858359
e tinaacarroll@aol.com
w the-cotswolds.com/shenberrowfarm.html

SOMERTON
Somerset

Sleepy Hollow ★★★★
Self Catering
Contact: Mr & Mrs Paul & Rhian Raine
t (01458) 850584
e paul&rhian@sleepyhollowcottages.com
w sleepyhollowcottages.com

SOUDLEY
Gloucestershire

The Cottage ★★★
Self Catering
Contact: Mrs Helen Evans
Peaked Rocks Cottage
t (01594) 861119
e helen@peakedrockscottage.fsnet.co.uk
w evansholidays.co.uk

Farrier's Lodge ★★★
Self Catering
Contact: Julie Farrier
The Bungalow
t (01452) 751044
e julie@farrier702.freeserve.co.uk

SOUTH BOWOOD
Dorset

West Cottage ★★
Self Catering
Contact: Miss Marion Gadsby
East Cottage
t (01308) 488294
e marion.gadsby@btinternet.com

SOUTH BREWHAM
Somerset

Magpie Cottage & Jackdaw Cottage ★★★★ *Self Catering*
Contact: Mr David Dabinett
t (01749) 850441
e david@havenfarm.co.uk
w havenfarm.co.uk

Park Cottage ★★★★
Self Catering
Contact: Mr Roland Norman
t (01749) 812230
e enquiries@parkfarmcottages.com
w parkfarmcottage.com

SOUTH CERNEY
Gloucestershire

Crane Farm ★★★★★
Self Catering
Contact: Mr Duncan Watters
Town & Country Cottages
t (01225) 481764
e info@ukselfcatering.com

The Watermark Club ★★★-★★★★★
Self Catering
Contact: Mr Robert Cowley
t (01285) 869181
e enquiries@watermarkclub.co.uk
w watermark-holidays.com

SOUTH MILTON
Devon

Nancy's Cottage ★★★
Self Catering
Contact: Mr Mark Jones
t (01562) 824769
e mj@markjones.entadsl.com

Savernake ★★★
Self Catering
Contact: Mr Andrew Dawson
Hall Wells Barn
t (01756) 720450
e e.dawson@zoom.co.uk
w savernake-devon.com

The White Cottage
Rating Applied For
Self Catering
Contact: Sylvia Blomeley
Toad Hall Cottages
t (01548) 853089
e thc@toadhallcottages.com
w toadhallcottages.co.uk

SOUTH MOLTON
Devon

Caramel Cott
Rating Applied For
Self Catering
Contact: Mr Peter Cornwell
Marsdens Cottage Holidays
t (01271) 813777
e holidays@marsdens.co.uk
w marsdens.co.uk

Coaching House
Rating Applied For
Self Catering
Marsdens Cottage Holidays
t (01271) 813777
e holidays@marsdens.co.uk
w marsdens.co.uk

Devon Fudge
Rating Applied For
Self Catering
Contact: Mr Peter Cornwell
Marsdens Cottage Holidays
t (01271) 813777
e holidays@marsdens.co.uk
w marsdens.co.uk

Drewstone Farm ★★★★
Self Catering
Contact: Mrs Ruth Ley
t (01769) 572337
e ruth_ley@drewstonefarm.fsnet.co.uk
w devonself-catering.co.uk/farm.htm

North Lee Farm Holiday Cottages ★★★★
Self Catering
Contact: Miss Rebecca Evans
t (01598) 740248
e beck@northlee.com
w northlee.com

Stable Cottage ★★★★★
Self Catering
Contact: Mrs Victoria Huxtable
t (01598) 740130

Townhouse Barton ★★★
Self Catering
Contact: Mrs Wendy Warren
t (01769) 572467
e info@townhousebarton.co.uk
w townhousebarton.co.uk

Vicarys Mews ★★★★
Self Catering
Contact: Mrs Janet Cornwell
Marsdens Cottage Holidays
t (01271) 813777
e holidays@marsdens.co.uk
w marsdens.co.uk

The Willows ★★★★
Self Catering
Contact: Mrs Janet Cornwell
Marsdens Cottage Holidays
t (01271) 813777
e holidays@marsdens.co.uk
w marsdens.co.uk

SOUTH PETHERTON
Somerset

Brook House Cottage ★★★★ *Self Catering*
Contact: Mrs Carolyne Entwistle
t (01460) 242704
e kevin.entwistle@btopenworld.com

Tanwyn ★★★★ *Self Catering*
Contact: Mr & Mrs Rodney & Ann Tanswell
t (01656) 880524
e rodney.tanswell@btinternet.com
w freewebs.com/tanwyn

SOUTH TRIGON
Dorset

Wisteria Cottage ★★★
Self Catering
Dorset Cottage Holidays
t (01929) 553443
e enq@dhcottages.co.uk
w dhcottages.co.uk

SOUTHBOURNE
Dorset

Shalbourne House Holiday Flats ★★★ *Self Catering*
Contact: Mr Malcolm Kynoch
t (01202) 432735
w holidayflatsandvillas.co.uk

SOUTHLEIGH
Devon

Higher Wiscombe ★★★★★
Self Catering
Contact: Mr & Mrs Alistair & Lorna Handyside
t (01404) 871360
e alistair@higherwiscombe.com
w higherwiscombe.com

STANTON
Gloucestershire

Charity Cottage ★★★ *Self Catering & Serviced Apartments*
Contact: Mrs Ryland
Charity Farm
t (01386) 584339
e kennethryland@ukonline.co.uk
w myrtle-cottage.co.uk/ryland.htm

Stanton Court Cottages
★★★★ *Self Catering*
Contact: Mrs Sheila Campbell
t (01386) 584527
w stantoncourt.co.uk

STAPLEGROVE
Somerset

The Barn ★★★★
Self Catering
Contact: Mrs Anita Harris
Higher Yarde Farmhouse
t (01823) 451553
e anita@higheryardefarm.co.uk
w higheryardefarm.co.uk

STARCROSS
Devon

The Bungalow
Rating Applied For
Self Catering
Contact: Mrs Butterworth
Torbay Holiday Agency
t (01803) 663650
e holcotts@aol.com
w swcottages.co.uk

START POINT
Devon

Start Point Lighthouse
★★★★★ *Self Catering*
Contact: Ms Mary Garne
Rural Retreats
t (01386) 701177
e info@ruralretreats.co.uk
w ruralretreats.co.uk

STATHE
Somerset

Walkers Farm Cottages
★★★★ *Self Catering*
Contact: Mrs Dianne Tilley
t (01823) 698229
e info@walkersfarmcottages.co.uk
w walkersfarmcottages.co.uk

STAVERTON
Devon

The Kingston Estate
★★★★★ *Self Catering*
Contact: Mr Howard Turner
t (01803) 762235
e info@kingston-estate.net
w kingston-estate.net

STAWLEY
Somerset

Stawley Wood Farm ★★★★
Self Catering
Contact: Mr & Mrs James & Julia Luard
t (01823) 672300
e jandjluard@tiscali.co.uk
w stawleywood.co.uk

STEEPLE ASHTON
Wiltshire

Jasmine Cottage ★★★★
Self Catering
Contact: Mr Norman Sharples
t (0121) 353 5258
e stay@jasminecottage.co.uk
w jasminecottage.co.uk

STICKER
Cornwall

Glenleigh Farm Fishery
★★★★★ *Self Catering*
Contact: Mrs Tregunna
t (01726) 73154
e fishglenleigh@aol.com

STICKLEPATH
Devon

Steddaford Court ★★★
Self Catering
Cornish Horizons Holiday Cottages
t (01841) 533331
e cottages@cornishhorizons.co.uk
w cornishhorizons.co.uk

STITHIANS
Cornwall

Charis Cottage ★★★★
Self Catering
Contact: Mr A Drees
t (01209) 861003
e astondrees@hotmail.com
w chariscottage.co.uk

Higher Trewithen Holiday Cottages ★★★ *Self Catering*
Contact: Mr Burgess
Higher Trewithen Holiday Cottages
t (01209) 860863
e trewithen@talk21.com
w trewithen.com

Ivory Cottage ★★★
Self Catering
Contact: Mr & Mrs David & Daya Stafford
t (01209) 861486
e cottage@ivorycottage.co.uk

Kettle Cottage ★★★★
Self Catering
Contact: Mrs Buswell
t (01209) 861579
w kettlecottage.co.uk

STOCKLAND
Devon

Ferndale ★★ *Self Catering*
Contact: Ms Louise Hayman
Milkbere Cottage Holidays
t (01297) 20729

The Hay Barn – W4447
★★★★ *Self Catering*
Contact: Mr Jim Matthews
Lyme Bay Holidays
t (01297) 443363
e email@lymebayholidays.co.uk
w lymebayholidays.co.uk

STOGUMBER
Somerset

Periwinkle Cottage ★★★★
Self Catering
Contact: Miss Sheila Hubbard
t (01643) 841413

STOGURSEY
Somerset

Water Farm ★ *Self Catering*
t (01278) 732397
e waterfarm@tiscali.co.uk

STOKE GABRIEL
Devon

Aish Cross Holiday Cottages
★★★★★ *Self Catering*
Contact: Mrs Angela Pavey
Aish Cross House
t (01803) 782022
e info@aishcross.co.uk
w aishcross.co.uk

Jesters ★★★★ *Self Catering*
Holiday Homes & Cottages South West
t (01803) 663650
e holcotts@aol.com
w swcottages.co.uk

STOKE ST GREGORY
Somerset

Baileys Gallery ★★★
Self Catering
Contact: Mr Stanley Chedzoy
t (01823) 490644

Holly Farm ★★★★
Self Catering
Contact: Mr & Mrs Robert & Liz Hembrow
t (01823) 490828
e robhembrow@btinternet.com
w holly-farm.com

Ivy Barn at Lovells Farm
★★★★ *Self Catering*
Contact: Mr Oppenlander
Lovells Cottage
t (01823) 491405
w somersetholidays.com

STOKE ST MARY
Somerset

Centra ★★★★ *Self Catering*
Contact: Mrs Karen Freir
t (01823) 442443
e info@centra-uk.com
w centra-uk.com

Mount Pleasant Cottage
★★★★ *Self Catering*
Contact: Mrs June Prime
t (01823) 442090
e june@mountpleasantcottage.co.uk
w mountpleasantcottage.co.uk

Stoke Hill Barn
★★★–★★★★ *Self Catering*
Contact: Mr Alan Coles
t (01823) 443759
e ajcoles@supanet.com
w somerset-selfcatering.co.uk

STOKE SUB HAMDON
Somerset

Fairhaven ★★★★
Self Catering
Contact: Mrs Margaret Wilson
t (01935) 823534
e fairhaven@go4.it
w fairhavensomerset.co.uk

Top o Hill ★★★ *Self Catering*
Contact: Mrs Mary Gane
Top o Hill
t (01935) 822089

West End Barn ★★★★
Self Catering
Contact: Mrs Tanya Morris
t (01935) 826540
e tanya@westfarm.fsworld.co.uk

STOKEINTEIGNHEAD
Devon

Church Barn Cottage
★★★★ *Self Catering*
Contact: Mr & Mrs Peter & Judy Rees
Congdon Farm Cottages
t (01626) 872433
e congdonsfarm@tiscali.co.uk

The Granary ★★★
Self Catering
Holiday Homes & Cottages South West
t (01803) 663650
e holcotts@aol.com

STOKENHAM
Devon

Tilly's Tuckaway ★★★★★
Self Catering
Toad Hall Cottages
t (01548) 853089
e thc@toadhallcottages.com
w toadhallcottages.com

STONEY STRATTON
Somerset

Red Tiles ★★★★
Self Catering
Contact: Mr Richard Neill
t (01344) 882322
e neill.hall@care4free.net

Springfield Cottages ★★★★
Self Catering
Contact: Mrs Pat Allen
t (01749) 830748
e ted.allen@btinternet.com
w stayinbritain.com/springfieldcottageholidays

STOURPAINE
Dorset

April Cottage ★★
Self Catering
Contact: Mr John Stitt
t (01258) 458933
e stitt77@tiscali.co.uk

STOW-ON-THE-WOLD
Gloucestershire

Barn Cottage
★★★★–★★★★★ *Self Catering & Serviced Apartments*
Contact: Mrs Lissa Mills
t (01451) 830947
e lissa-mills@ukonline.co.uk
w barncottagecotswolds.co.uk

Bottom End Cottage ★★★★
Self Catering
Contact: Ms Karen Hawkes
Cottage in the Country and Cottage Holidays
t (01993) 831495
e enquiries@cottageinthecountry.co.uk
w cottageinthecountry.co.uk

Box Cottage ★★★
Self Catering
Contact: Mr Bob Johnston
t (01608) 650816

Broad Oak Cottages, Stow-on-the-Wold ★★★★★
Self Catering
Contact: Mrs Wilson
Broad Oak Cottages
t (01451) 830794
e mary@broadoakcottages.co.uk
w broadoakcottages.co.uk

Charlie's Cottage ★★★★
Self Catering
Contact: Mrs Veronica Woodford
t (01451) 821496
e iwoodford@wyckriss.freeserve.co.uk

Foden Lodge ★★★
Self Catering
Contact: Beryl Gypps
t (01992) 301800
e thefodenlodge@hotmail.com
w fodenlodge.co.uk

Glebe Cottage ★★★★
Self Catering
Contact: Mrs Lesley Paler
t (01483) 203375
e lesley@gbc-ca.co.uk

Greystoke Bungalow
★★★★★ *Self Catering*
Contact: Mr G Dobson
Middle Croft House
t (01643) 862636
e geodobson@btinternet.com
w cottageguide.co.uk/elderbeck2

Johnston Cottage and Horseshoes ★★★–★★★★
Self Catering
Contact: Mrs Yvonne Johnston
t (01608) 650816

Lower Court Cottages
★★★★ *Self Catering*
Contact: Mrs Juliet Pauling
t (01608) 676422
e jpauling@lineone.net

Park Farm Holiday Cottages
★★★★–★★★★★
Self Catering
Contact: Mrs Tiana Ricketts
t (01451) 830227
e tiana@parkfarmholidaycottages.co.uk

Park House Cottage ★★★
Self Catering
Contact: Mr & Mrs George & Barbara Sutton
t (01451) 830159
e info@parkhousecottage.co.uk
w parkhousecottage.co.uk

Rose's Cottage, Broadwell
★★★★ *Self Catering*
Contact: Mr Richard Drinkwater
Rose's Cottage
t (01451) 830007
e richard.drinkwater@ukonline.co.uk

The Stables ★★★★
Self Catering
Contact: Mr Mark Cassie
t (01457) 831888
e info@southhill.co.uk
w cotswoldcottage.biz

Sycamore Cottage ★★★★
Self Catering
Contact: Mrs S Jones
Hill House
t (01844) 208615
e suejones16@hotmail.com

Valley View ★★★
Self Catering
Contact: Mr & Mrs Peter & Janet Craddock
t (01564) 770143
e janetcraddock25@hotmail.com
w cottageguide.co.uk/valleyview

Wells Cottage ★★★
Self Catering
Contact: Mr & Mrs Gwyn & Sue Williams
t (01451) 830045
w wellscottage.co.uk

STRATFORD SUB CASTLE
Wiltshire

Manor Cottage H107
★★★★ *Self Catering*
Contact: Mr Nicholas Pash
Hideaways
t (01747) 828170
e enq@hideaways.co.uk
w hideaways.co.uk/property.cfm/H107

Millers Barn ★★★
Self Catering
Contact: Mr Nicholas Pash
Hideaways
t (01747) 828170
e enq@hideaways.co.uk
w hideaways.co.uk

STRATTON
Cornwall

Kitts Cottage ★★★
Self Catering
Contact: Ms Lucy Ellison
Farm & Cottage Holidays
t (01237) 479146
e enquiries@farmcott.co.uk
w holidaycottages.co.uk

Old Sanctuary Cottages
★★★★ *Self Catering*
Contact: Mrs Berry
t (01288) 353159
e enquiries@oldsanctuarycottages.com
w oldsanctuarycottages.com

Tree Hill House ★★★
Self Catering
Contact: Mrs Christine Heybourn
t (01753) 852512
e robert@heybourn.freeserve.co.uk

STRATTON
Dorset

Eweleaze ★★★★
Self Catering
Contact: Mr Ian Barrett
Dorset Independent Cottages
t (01300) 341103
e enquiries@d-i-c.co.uk
w d-i-c.co.uk

STRATTON-ON-THE-FOSSE
Somerset

Pitcot Farm Barn Cottages
★★★★ *Self Catering*
Contact: Mrs Mary Coles
t (01761) 233108
e info@pitcotfarm.co.uk
w pitcotfarm.co.uk

STREET
Somerset

Blue Lias ★★★ *Self Catering*
Contact: Mr Mark Foot
t (01275) 853612

STROUD
Gloucestershire

The Coach House c/o The Old Vicarage ★★★★
Self Catering
Contact: Mrs Stella Knight
t (01453) 832265
e stella.knight@tiscali.co.uk
w cotswoldholidaycottage.co.uk

Lypiatt Hill House ★★★
Self Catering
Contact: Mr Pyke
t (01453) 764785
e john.pyke@virgin.net

Twissells Mill and Dingley Dell ★★ *Self Catering*
Contact: Daphne & Martin Neville
Bakers Mill
t (01285) 760234
e martin_neville_bakers_mill@yahoo.co.uk

Westley Farm ★★★
Self Catering
Contact: Mr Usborne
t (01285) 760262
w westleyfarm.co.uk

STUDLAND
Dorset

Heathland Cottage ★★★
Self Catering
Contact: Ms Leanne Hemingway
Dorset Cottage Holidays
t (01929) 553443
e enq@dhcottages.co.uk
w dhcottages.co.uk/heathland.htm

Sandyholme Garden Cottage
★★ *Self Catering*
Contact: Mrs Christine Boardman
t (01305) 265172
e j_and_c_boardman@talk21.com

STURMINSTER MARSHALL
Dorset

Parkfield Cottage ★★★★
Self Catering
Contact: Mr Michael Royles
t (01258) 857804
e mikeroyles@yahoo.co.uk
w parkfieldcottage-sturminstermarshall.co.uk

STURMINSTER NEWTON
Dorset

The Homestead ★★★
Self Catering
Contact: Mrs Carol Townsend
t (01258) 471390
e townsend@dircon.co.uk
w townsend.dircon.co.uk

SUMMERCOURT
Cornwall

Hayloft ★★★ *Self Catering*
Contact: Andree Brougham
t (01872) 510087
e andreebrougham@aol.com

SUTTON POYNTZ
Dorset

Ebenezer Cottage ★★★★
Self Catering
Contact: Mrs Cathy Varley
t (01258) 821030
w ebenezercottage.co.uk

Garland Cottage ★★★
Self Catering
Contact: Mrs Gillian Dawe
The Brents
t (023) 9246 0424
e info@garlandcottage.co.uk
w garlandscottage.co.uk

SUTTON WALDRON
Dorset

Dairy Cottage
Rating Applied For
Self Catering
Contact: Mr and Mrs Stuart Asbury
t (01747) 811330

SWANAGE
Dorset

1 Garwood ★★★
Self Catering
Contact: Ms Russ
Wyke Holiday Properties
t (01929) 422776

10 The Haven ★★★★
Self Catering
Contact: Mrs Frances Thackway
t (01929) 422715
e frances@thehavenswanage.co.uk
w virtualswanage.com/accommodation/10_the_haven/30.aspx

11 Wordsworth Court ★★★
Self Catering
Contact: Ms Lyn Whaley
Hidden Cottage
t (01344) 873615
e lyn@whaley.uk.com

13 The Haven ★★★
Self Catering
Contact: Ms Nicky Russ
Wyke Holiday Properties
t (01929) 422776
e bookings@wykeholiday.co.uk
w wykeholiday.co.uk

2 Carrants Court ★★★
Self Catering
Contact: Mr & Mrs R Leeds
Oaktree
t (01732) 463659
e hengistthegnome@hotmail.com

2 Chines ★★★ *Self Catering*
Contact: Mrs Caroline Grange
t (01225) 834430
e caroline@swanageholidaylet.co.uk
w swanageholidaylet.co.uk

2 Quayside Court ★★
Self Catering
Contact: Mr Michael Padfield
Greenways
t (01628) 472113
e mike@thepadfields.com

2 Wilksworth Cottage ★★
Self Catering
Contact: Mr Zachary Stuart-Brown
Dream Cottages
t (01305) 789000
e admin@dream-cottages.co.uk
w dream-cottages.co.uk

2 Wordsworth Court ★★★
Self Catering
Contact: Mr Donald Pallister
t (023) 8076 9592
e pallisterdb@aol.com

27 Manwell Road ★★★
Self Catering
Contact: Mrs Jill Henstridge
t (01929) 427276

35 Rabling Road ★★★
Self Catering
t (01929) 423550

5 Durberville Drive ★★
Self Catering
Contact: Mrs Christina Curtin
t (01276) 22250
e curtins@onetel.com

6 Cluny Crescent ★★★★
Self Catering
Contact: Mr David Smith
Miles & Son
t (01929) 423333
e info@milesandson.co.uk

7A Northbrook Road
Rating Applied For
Self Catering
Contact: Mrs S Lucas
t (01929) 425000
e margot.wellies@virgin.net

9 Quayside Court ★★★
Self Catering
Contact: Ms Anne Bennett
t (01454) 311178
e info@bythequayholidays.co.uk
w bythequayholidays.co.uk

Alrose Villa Holiday Apartements ★★★ *Self Catering & Serviced Apartments*
Contact: Mrs Jacqueline Wilson
Alrose Villa Holiday Apartments
t (01929) 426318
e enquiry@alrosevilla.co.uk
w alrosevilla.co.uk

Annexe to Stoneacre ★★★
Self Catering
Contact: Mrs Carol Brown
t (01929) 480668
e annexe_to_stoneacre@yahoo.co.uk
w annexestoneacre.co.uk

Anvil Point Lighthouse
★★★★★ *Self Catering*
Contact: Ms Mary Garne
Rural Retreats
t (01386) 701177
e info@ruralretreats.co.uk
w ruralretreats.co.uk

Ballard Lee & Ballard Ridge
★★ *Self Catering*
Contact: Mr & Mrs Ian Lever
t (01929) 551320

California Barn
Rating Applied For
Self Catering
Contact: Karen Delahay
t (01929) 425049
e delahays@hotmail.com
w californiacottage.co.uk

Chalkdell Cottage ★★★
Self Catering
Contact: Mr & Mrs Brian & Linda Gooding
t (01727) 831126
e chalkdell@fsmail.net

Coastguards Return ★★★★
Self Catering
Contact: Mrs Anna Morrison
t (01929) 424630
e retrieverproperties@tiscali.co.uk

Edgecroft ★★★ *Self Catering*
Contact: Miss L Hemmingway
Dorset Cottage Holidays
t (01929) 553443
e enq@dhcottages.co.uk
w dhcottages.co.uk

Flat 2 Avenue House ★★★
Self Catering
Contact: Mrs P Oliver
t (01929) 425984
e bookings@wykeholiday.co.uk

Flat 8 Sandringham Court
★★★★ *Self Catering*
Contact: Mrs Hilary Hyde
Wyke Holiday Properties Ltd
t (020) 8948 4991
w wykeholiday.co.uk

Fuchsia Cottage ★★★
Self Catering
Dorset Cottage Holidays
t (01929) 553443
e enq@dhcottages.co.uk
w dhcottages.co.uk

Gables Court Holiday Apartments
Rating Applied For
Self Catering
Contact: Ms Maria Thompson
t (01929) 426516
e steve.thompson@izrmail.com
w gables-apartments.co.uk

Island View ★★★
Self Catering
Contact: Mr & Mrs Jones
t (01929) 426614
e ray.jones@btinternet.com

The Ketch ★★★
Self Catering
Contact: Ms Leanne Hemingway
Dorset Cottage Holidays
t (01929) 553443
e enq@dhcottages.co.uk
w dhcottages.co.uk

Kings Haven Cottage
★★★★ *Self Catering*
Contact: Miss LM Hemingway
Dorset Cottage Holidays
t (01929) 553443
e enq@dhcottages.co.uk
w dhcottages.co.uk

Lilac Cottage ★★
Self Catering
Contact: Mrs Jean Simmonds
t (01544) 388619
e Jean@seagrasscottages.co.uk

Lizzards Rest ★★★★
Self Catering
Contact: Ms Kirsty Parker
Dream Cottages
t (01305) 789000
e admin@dream-cottages.co.uk
w dream-cottages.co.uk

One London Row ★★★
Self Catering
Contact: Mr & Mrs Philip & Monica Sanders
t (020) 8348 9815
e info@philamonic.com
w philamonic.com

Peepsea ★★★ *Self Catering*
Dorset Cottage Holidays
t (01929) 553443
e enq@dhcottages.co.uk
w dhcottages.co.uk

Pen Maen ★★★ *Self Catering*
Contact: Mrs Janet Collinson
t (01280) 253694
e janet.collinson@virgin.net

The Pinnacles ★★
Self Catering
Contact: Mrs Alyson Greenfield
Dolserau Cottage
t (01425) 654358

Purbeck Cliffs ★★★★
Self Catering
Contact: Mrs Sue McWilliams
t (01929) 424352
w purbeckcliffs.co.uk

The Quarterdeck ★★★
Self Catering
Contact: Mr Tony Thomas
Holiday Homes
t (01845) 597614
e enquiries@purbeckholidays.co.uk
w purbeckholidays.co.uk

St Mark's Cottage ★★★★
Self Catering
t (01737) 224441
e david@asdellevans.co.uk

Sea Views ★★ *Self Catering*
Contact: Mr Selby
t (01929) 423269

Seaviews ★★★ *Self Catering*
Contact: Mr Robert Moon
t (01202) 513671
e moon-enterprises@cwctv.net

The Studio ★★★
Self Catering
Contact: Ms Leanne Hemingway
Dorset Cottage Holidays
t (01929) 553443
e enq@dhcottages.co.uk
w dhcottages.co.uk/studio.htm

Styre House ★★
Self Catering
Contact: Mrs Hermina Clarke
t (01929) 424209

Sunnyside ★★★
Self Catering
Contact: Mrs Elizabeth Beesley
t (01929) 422226

Swanage Cottage Holidays
★★★–★★★★ *Self Catering*
Contact: Mr & Mrs B Howells
Swanage Cottage Holidays
t (01929) 421601 & 07971 552082
e bjhowells@hotmail.com
w swanagecottageholidays.co.uk

Swanwic House ★★
Self Catering
Contact: Mrs Carole Figg
t (01929) 423517

Tanglewood ★★★★
Self Catering
Contact: Ms Leanne Hemingway
Dorset Cottage Holidays
t (01929) 553443
e enq@dhcottages.co.uk
w dhcottages.co.uk

Topsail House ★★★★
Self Catering
Contact: Mrs Janet Foran
t (01929) 422322
e mail@sandhaven-guest-house.co.uk

Waterside
Rating Applied For
Self Catering
Contact: Karen Dolling
t (020) 8560 5587
e jkdolling@hotmail.com

White Shutters ★★★★
Self Catering
Contact: Mrs Anna Morrison
t (01929) 424630
e retrieverproperties@tiscali.co.uk

Windjammer ★★★
Self Catering
Contact: Ms Leanne Hemingway
Dorset Cottage Holidays
t (01929) 553443
e enq@dhcottages.co.uk
w dhcottages.co.uk

SWIMBRIDGE
Devon

Animal Ark Cottages
Rating Applied For
Self Catering
Contact: Mrs Lynn Marshall
t (01271) 831138
e info@animalarkcottages.co.uk
w animalarkcottages.co.uk

Lane End ★★★★
Self Catering
Marsdens Cottage Holidays
t (01271) 813777
e holidays@marsdens.co.uk
w marsdens.co.uk

Lower Hearson Farm
★★★★ *Self Catering*
Contact: Mr & Mrs G Pelling
t (01271) 830702
e info@hearsoncottagesdevon.co.uk
w hearsoncottagesdevon.co.uk

SWINDON
Gloucestershire

St Magdalenes Cottage
★★★★★ *Self Catering*
Contact: Mrs Hilary Mervyn-Smith
t (01242) 511211
e hmervynsmith@hotmail.co.uk
w cottagenet.co.uk/stmagdalene.htm

SWINDON
Wiltshire

Minsters Chase ★★★★
Self Catering
Contact: Mr & Mrs Bob & Pennie Astbury
t (01793) 726775
e penniebob@tiscali.co.uk

SYDLING ST NICHOLAS
Dorset

Grace Cottage ★★★
Self Catering
Contact: Mrs Nicky Willis
t (01308) 863868
e nickywillis@tesco.net

SYMONDSBURY
Dorset

Bathsheba ★★★★
Self Catering
Contact: Mrs Shelagh Mullins
t (01308) 425261
e shelaghmullins@aol.com
w shelaghsbathsheba.co.uk

Woodlanders ★★★★
Self Catering
Contact: Mrs Jackie Harris
t (01225) 335153
e jackiemharris@hotmail.co.uk
w symondsburyholiday.co.uk

TAUNTON
Somerset

The Garden Retreat ★★★★
Self Catering
Contact: Mrs Liz Thompson
t (01823) 451529
e lizthompson47@hotmail.com

Higher House ★★★
Self Catering
Contact: Mrs Kirsten Horton
t (01823) 400570
e tedandkirsten@tiscali.co.uk
w higherhouse.co.uk

Linnets, Fitzhead ★★★★
Self Catering
Contact: Mrs Patricia Grabham
Linnets
t (01823) 400658
e patricia.grabham@onetel.net

Meadowsweet Farm Cottages ★★★★
Self Catering
Contact: Miss Jacqueline McCann
Meadowsweet Cottages
t (01984) 656323
e info@meadowsweet-cottages.co.uk
w meadowsweet-cottages.co.uk

Meare Court Holiday Cottages ★★★–★★★★
Self Catering
Contact: Mrs Elizabeth Bray
t (01823) 480570
e mearecourt@farming.co.uk
w mearecourt.co.uk

The Studio, White Mead
★★★ *Self Catering*
Contact: Mrs Eileen Rawlings
t (01823) 331879
e ea.rawlings@virgin.net

TAVISTOCK
Devon

Dartmoor Holidays ★★★
Self Catering
Contact: Mr Christopher Boswell
t (01822) 810687
e chrisboswe@aol.com
w dartmoorholidays.co.uk

Edgemoor Cottage ★★★★
Self Catering
Contact: Mrs Mary Susan Fox
t (01822) 612259
e Foxes@dartmoorcottages.info
w edgemoorcottage.co.uk

Higher Chaddlehanger Farm
★★★ *Self Catering*
Contact: Mrs Ruth Cole
The Annexe
t (01822) 810268

Moorview Cottage ★★★★
Self Catering
Contact: Mrs Elaine Mackintosh
Moorview
t (01822) 810271
e ejm@dartmoor-holidays.fsnet.co.uk
w dartmoor-holidays.com

TAYNTON
Gloucestershire

Owls Barn ★★★★
Self Catering
Contact: Mrs Barbara Goodwin
t (01452) 831290
e goodies@coldcroft.freeserve.co.uk
w coldcroft.freeserve.co.uk

TEDBURN ST MARY
Devon

The Hay Barn
Rating Applied For
Self Catering
Valley Villas
t (01752) 605605
e sales@valleyvillas.com
w valleyvillas.com

TEIGNGRACE
Devon

Twelve Oaks Holiday Cottages *Self Catering*
Contact: Mrs Gale
Twelve Oaks Holiday Cottages
t (01626) 352769

TEIGNMOUTH
Devon

9 Seacliff ★★★★
Self Catering
Contact: Mrs Rosemary Smith
t (01926) 512613
e rosemaryesmith@btinternet.com

Bitton Park ★★★★
Self Catering
Contact: Mrs Gill Butterworth
Holiday Homes & Cottages South West
t (01803) 663650
e holcotts@aol.com
w swcottages.co.uk

Grendons Holiday Apartments ★★★
Self Catering
Contact: Mr Charles Gray
t (01626) 773667
e grendonsholidayapt@cix.co.uk

Quayside Cottage ★★★
Self Catering
Holiday Homes & Cottages
t (01803) 663650
e holcotts@aol.com
w swcottages.co.uk

The Sail Loft ★★★★
Self Catering
Contact: Mrs J R Williams
t (0117) 924 7371
e thesailloft_teignmouth@blueyonder.co.uk
w thesailloft.co.uk

TEMPLE GUITING
Gloucestershire

Springbank ★★★★★
Self Catering
Contact: Mr Kate Mather
t (01451) 850571
e springbank@landgatetg.co.uk
w landgatetg.co.uk

TETBURY
Gloucestershire

Berkeley House ★★★★★
Self Catering
Contact: Mr Nigel Stengard-Green
Lena Proudlock
t (01666) 500051
e nigel@lenaproudlock.com
w lenaproudlockescapes.com

Folly Farm Cottages ★★★
Self Catering
Contact: Mr Julian Benton
t (01666) 502475
e info@gtb.co.uk
w gtb.co.uk

TEWKESBURY
Gloucestershire

9 Mill Bank ★★ *Self Catering*
Contact: Mr Hunt
t (01684) 276190
e billhunt@9mb.co.uk
w tewkesbury-cottage.co.uk

Courtyard Cottages ★★★★
Self Catering
Contact: Mr Herford
t (01386) 725351
e diana@uppercourt.co.uk
w uppercourt.co.uk

The Old Stable Block ★★★
Self Catering
Contact: Mr & Mrs Geoff Stringer
t (01386) 881248
e info@beckford-stores.co.uk

The Stables Rose Hill Farm
★★★ *Self Catering*
Contact: Mrs Elizabeth Collinson
Rose Hill Farm
t (01684) 293598

THE PACKET QUAYS
Cornwall

2 Victoria Quay ★★★
Self Catering
Contact: Ms Emily Boriosi
Cornish Holiday Cottages
t (01326) 250339

4 Jago Slip ★★★
Self Catering
Contact: Ms Emily Boriosi
Cornish Holiday Cottages
t (01326) 250339
e emily@cornishholidaycottages.net

6 Jane's Court ★★★★
Self Catering
Cornish Holiday Cottages
t (01326) 250339
e postmaster@cornishholidaycottages.net

The Penthouse ★★★
Self Catering
Contact: Mr & Mrs Main Wilson
t (01580) 212522
e mainwilson@aol.com
w penthouseholidays.com

THE PLUDDS
Gloucestershire

High Beeches
Rating Applied For
Self Catering
Contact: Lynda King Taylor
t (020) 7262 1531
e highbeecheshaven@aol.com
w lindakingtaylor.com/highbeeches

THORNBURY
Devon

Dairy Cottage and Beech Barn ★★★★ *Self Catering*
Contact: Lucy Ellison
Farm & Cottage Holidays
t (01237) 479146
e enquiries@farmcott.co.uk
w selfcatering-devon.com

THORNCOMBE
Dorset

6 The Terrace – W4434
★★★ *Self Catering*
Contact: Mr Jim Matthews
Lyme Bay Holidays
t (01297) 443363
e email@lymebayholidays.co.uk
w lymebayholidays.co.uk

Thatch Cottage ★★★★★
Self Catering
Contact: Mr & Mrs John & Eileen Mercer
t (020) 8393 8165
e eileenjmercer@hotmail.com

THORVERTON
Devon

Fursdon Estate ★★★★
Self Catering
Contact: Mrs Catriona Fursdon
t (01392) 860860
e enquiries@fursdon.co.uk
w fursdon.co.uk

Honeysuckle End ★★★★
Self Catering
Contact: Mr & Mrs Ayre
t (01392) 860434
e ayre.ratcliffe@virgin.net
w devon-country-holidays.net

THREE LEGGED CROSS
Dorset

Foresters ★★★★
Self Catering
Contact: Mrs Jean Baylis
Cottage Farm
t (01202) 820203
e cottagefarm@sagainternet.co.uk

The Gables ★★★
Self Catering
Contact: Mr & Mrs David Priest
t (01202) 821322
e janet@thegables31x.com

THROWLEIGH
Devon

Sue's House & The Cottage
★★-★★★ *Self Catering*
Contact: Mrs Joan White
t (01647) 231266

THURLESTONE
Devon

1 Homefield Cottages
★★★★ *Self Catering*
Contact: Sylvia Blomeley
Toad Hall Cottages
t (01548) 853089
e thc@toadhallcottages.com
w toadhallcottages.co.uk

Cart House Barn ★★★★
Self Catering
Contact: Mr David Hanmer
Toad Hall Cottages
t (01548) 853089
e thc@toadhallccottages.com
w toadhallcottages.com

Stable Cottage ★★★★★
Self Catering
Toad Hall Cottages
t (01548) 853089
e thc@toadhallcottages.com

THURLESTONE SANDS
Devon

1 Thurlestone Beach Apt
★★★★ *Self Catering*
Contact: Sylvia Blomeley
Toad Hall Cottages
t (01548) 853089
w toadhallcottages.co.uk

Sea Campion ★★★
Self Catering
Contact: Sylvia Blomeley
Toad Hall Cottages
t (01548) 853089
e thc@toadhallcottages.com
w toadhallcottages.co.uk

Sea Cottage ★★★★
Self Catering
Contact: Sylvia Blomeley
Toad Hall Cottages
t (01548) 853089
e thc@toadhallcottages.com
w toadhallcottages.co.uk

Sea Holly ★★★★
Self Catering
Toad Hall Cottages
t (01548) 853089
e thc@toadhallcottages.com
w toadhallcottages.com

Sea Lavender ★★★
Self Catering
t (01548) 853089
e thc@taodhallcottages.com
w toadhallcottages.com

Sea Poppy ★★★★★
Self Catering
Contact: Sylvia Blomeley
Toad Hall Cottages
t (01548) 853089
e thc@toadhallcottages.com
w toadhallcottages.co.uk

Seamark ★★★-★★★★
Self Catering
Contact: Mr & Mrs Robin & Angela Collyns
t (01548) 561300
e collyns.seamark@virgin.net
w seamarkdevon.co.uk

TIDENHAM
Gloucestershire

Churchend Stables
Rating Applied For
Self Catering
Contact: Mrs Melanie Walton
t (01291) 630442

TINCLETON
Dorset

Tincleton Lodge and Clyffe Dairy Cottage
★★★-★★★★★
Self Catering
Contact: Mrs Jane Coleman
The Old Dairy Cottage and Clyffe Dairy Cottage
t (01305) 848391
e enquiries@dorsetholidaycottages.net
w dorsetholidaycottages.net

TINTAGEL
Cornwall

Boskenna and Atlanta ★★★
Self Catering
Contact: Mr Tim Abbott
Cornish Seaview Holidays
t (01428) 723819
e enquiries@cornishseaviewholidays.co.uk
w cornishseaviewcottages.co.uk

Clifden Farm Cottages ★★★
Self Catering
Contact: Mrs Nute
t (01840) 770437
e mnute@toucansurf.com

Halgabron Mill Cottages
★★★ *Self Catering*
Contact: Mr Evans
t (01840) 779099
e robin@halgabronmill.co.uk
w halgabronmill.co.uk

Maymyo ★★ *Self Catering*
Contact: Mr & Mrs Ryder
t (020) 8255 7994
e stay@westparkfarm.com
w westparkfarm.com

Penpethy Holiday Cottages
★★★ *Self Catering*
Contact: Mrs Steadman
t (01840) 213903

Rose Cottage
Rating Applied For
Self Catering
Contact: Mrs Elizabeth Heard
t (01840) 211036
e liz@penpethyf.wanadoo.co.uk
w penpethyfarm.co.uk

Rosemary ★★★ *Self Catering*
t (01840) 770472
e mary@mdyer.com

Sunnyside ★★★
Self Catering
Bramblegate
t (01252) 843986 & 07960 356428
e hansen_harry@hotmail.com

Tregeath ★★★ *Self Catering*
Contact: Mrs Edwina Broad
t (01840) 770217

TISBURY
Wiltshire

The Old Coach House ★★★
Self Catering
Contact: Mr Nicholas Pash
Hideaways
t (01747) 828170
e enq@hideaways.co.uk
w hideaways.co.uk

TIVERTON
Devon

Coombe Cottage ★★★★
Self Catering
Contact: Mrs Mary Reed
t (01398) 351281
e coombehse@aol.com
w exmoor-holiday-cottage.co.uk

Lilac Cottage ★★★★
Self Catering
Contact: Mrs Venner
t (01884) 820226
w cottageguide.co.uk/battensfarm

Old Bridwell Holiday Cottages ★★★★
Self Catering
Contact: Ms Jackie Kind
t (01884) 841464
e jackie@oldbridwell.co.uk
w oldbridwell.co.uk

West Pitt Farm
★★★-★★★★ *Self Catering*
Contact: Ms Susanne Westgate
West Pitt Farm
t (01884) 820296
e susannewestgate@yahoo.com

TIVINGTON
Somerset

Tethinstone Cottage ★★★★
Self Catering
Contact: Mr Nicholas Challis
t (01643) 706757

TOLLER PORCORUM
Dorset

Froghall & Dairymaids Cottage ★★★★ *Self Catering*
Contact: Mrs Rosemary Gower
t (01300) 320541
e rosemarygower@hotmail.com

Old School Cottage ★★★
Self Catering
Contact: Mrs Jean Wallbridge
The Old School
t (01300) 320046
e oldschooltoller@aol.com
w oldschooltoller.co.uk

Stable Cottage ★★★
Self Catering
Contact: Janet Chaffey
t (01300) 321413

TOLPUDDLE
Dorset

River View Cottage ★★★★
Self Catering
Contact: Ms Leanne Hemingway
Dorset Cottage Holidays
t (01929) 553443
e enq@dhcottages.co.uk
w dhcottages.co.uk

TORCROSS
Devon

Torcross Hotel Apartments
★★★ *Self Catering*
Contact: Mrs Karen Jackson
t (01548) 580206
e enquiries@torcross.com
w torcross.com

TORPOINT
Cornwall

Chough Cottage ★★★★
Self Catering
Valley Villas
t (01752) 605605
e sales@valleyvillas.com
w valleyvillas.com

Jackdaw Cottage ★★
Self Catering
Contact: Mrs Sartorius
t (0121) 454 0284
e aes@alucast.co.uk
w jackdawcottagecornwall.co.uk

TORQUAY
Devon

7 Hesketh Mews
Rating Applied For
Self Catering
Contact: Sylvia Cutling
Blue Chip Vacations Ltd
t (01803) 853846
e sylvia@bluechipvacations.com
w bluechipvacations.com

Abbey Mews ★★★★
Self Catering
Holiday Homes & Cottages South West
t (01803) 663650
e holcotts@aol.com
w swcottages.co.uk

Abbey View Holiday Flats
★★★ *Self Catering*
Contact: Mr Foss
t (01803) 293722
e abbeyflats@tiscali.co.uk
w abbeyviewholidayflats.co.uk

Acacia Apartments ★★★★
Self Catering
Contact: Laura Arnold
Blue Chip Vacations
t (01803) 855282
e laura@bluechipvacations.com
w bluechipvacations.com

Alexandra Lodge ★★★
Self Catering
Contact: Ms Sandie Wright
RML Properties
t (01543) 675555
e ron@streamline123.freeserve.co.uk
w alexandra-lodge.co.uk

Appletorre House ★★★
Self Catering
Contact: Mr & Mrs Colin & Colleen Moon
Appletorre Flats
t (01803) 296430
w appletorreflats.co.uk

Astor House Apartments
★★-★★★ *Self Catering*
Contact: Mr Coleman
t (01803) 292747
e info@plumholidays.co.uk
w asterhouse.freeserve.co.uk

Atherton Holiday Flats ★★
Self Catering
Contact: Mrs Rosemary Martin
t (01803) 296884

Atlantis Holiday Apartments
★★★ *Self Catering*
Contact: Mrs Pauline Roberts
t (01803) 607929
e enquiry@atlantistorquay.co.uk
w atlantistorquay.co.uk

Babbacombe Downs ★★★
Self Catering
Contact: Mr Ian Butterworth
Holiday Homes & Cottages South West
t (01803) 663650
e holcotts@aol.com
w swcottaages.co.uk

Bedford House ★★★
Self Catering
Contact: Mrs MacDonald-Smith
Bedford House
t (01803) 296995
e bedfordhotorquay@btconnect.com
w bedfordhousetorquay.co.uk

Belgravia Luxury Self Catering Holiday Apartments
Rating Applied For
Self Catering
Contact: Mr & Mrs Green
t (01803) 293417
e info@blha.co.uk
w blha.co.uk

The Beulah Holiday Apartments ★★★
Self Catering
Contact: Mr & Mrs David & Caroline Perry
t (01803) 297471
e enquiries@thebeulah.co.uk
w thebeulah.co.uk

Burley Court Apartments
★★★ *Self Catering*
Contact: Mr & Mrs S Palmer
t (01803) 607879
e simon@burleycourt.co.uk
w burleycourt.co.uk

Chelston Dene ★★★
Self Catering
Contact: Mr Rod Payne
t (01803) 605180
e info@chelstondene.com
w chelstondene.com

Cliff Court Holiday Apartments ★★★★
Self Catering
Contact: Mrs Denise Tudor
t (01803) 294687
e info@cliffcourt.co.uk
w cliffcourt.co.uk

Clydesdale Holiday Flats
★★★ *Self Catering*
Contact: Mr Terry Watson
t (01803) 292759
w clydesdaleholidayflats.co.uk

The Coach House ★★★★
Self Catering
Contact: Mrs Butterworth
Torbay Holiday Agency
t (01803) 663650
e holcotts@aol.com
w swcottages.co.uk

The Corbyn ★★★★★
Self Catering
Contact: Mrs Sallie Stamp
Brights of Nettlebed
t (01803) 215595
w thecorbyn.co.uk

Cornerstone ★★★
Self Catering
Holiday Homes & Cottages South West
t (01803) 663650
e holcotts@aol.com

Cranmere Court ★★★
Self Catering
Contact: Mrs Sally Noad
Cranmere Court Holiday Flats & Flatlets
t (01803) 293173
w cranmereholidayflats.co.uk

Delamere Court
★★★-★★★★ *Self Catering*
Contact: Mrs Mandy Morris
t (01803) 293428
e info@delamerecourt.co.uk
w delamerecourt.co.uk

Derwent Hill Holiday Apartments ★★★★
Self Catering
Contact: Gill & Derek Bryant
t (01803) 606793
e info@derwent-hill.co.uk
w derwent-hill.co.uk

Evergreen Lodge ★★★★
Self Catering
Contact: Mr Louise Clifford
t (01803) 605519
e evergreenlodge@dial.pipex.com
w evergreenlodge.co.uk

Fairlawns Hall Holiday Apartments ★★★
Self Catering
Contact: Mrs Emma Hanbury
Fairlawns Hall
t (01803) 328904
e fairlawnshall@btinternet.com
w fairlawnshall.co.uk

Florence Holiday Apartments ★★ *Self Catering*
Contact: Mr Ian J King
t (01803) 297264
e florenceflats@aol.com

Gainsborough ★★★
Self Catering
Holiday Homes & Cottages South West
t (01803) 663650
e holcotts@aol.com
w swcottages.co.uk

Hesketh Crescent ★★★
Self Catering
Holiday Homes & Cottages South West
t (01803) 663650
e holcotts@aol.com
w swcottages.co.uk

Hesketh Crescent
Rating Applied For
Self Catering
Contact: Mrs Adele Barnes
Blue Chip Vacations
t (01803) 855282
e info@bluechipvacations.com
w bluechipvacations.com/torquay/torquay_hesketh_crescent.php

Hesketh Mews
Rating Applied For
Self Catering
Contact: Mrs Gill Butterworth
Holiday Homes & Cottages South West
t (01803) 663650

Hesketh Mews – Starboard
★★★★ *Self Catering*
Holiday Homes & Cottages South West
t (01803) 663650
e holcotts@aol.com
w swcottages.co.uk

Kingswood Holiday Flats
★★ *Self Catering*
Contact: Mr Peter Skinns
t (01803) 293164
e peter@kingswoodholidayflats.co.uk
w kingswoodholidayflats.co.uk

Little Walderlea ★★★
Self Catering
Holiday Homes & Cottages South West
t (01803) 663650
e holcotts@aol.com
w swcottages.co.uk

The Lodge ★★★★
Self Catering
Holiday Homes & Cottages South West
t (01803) 663650
e holcotts@aol.com
w swcottages.co.uk

Marina Delight ★★★
Self Catering
Holiday Homes & Cottages South West
t (01803) 663650
e holcotts@aol.com
w swcottages.co.uk

Marina View & Bay View
★★★ *Self Catering*
Holiday Homes & Cottages South West
t (01803) 663650
e holcotts@aol.com
w swcottages.co.uk

Maxton Lodge Holiday Apartments ★★★
Self Catering
Contact: Mark Shephard and Alex Brook
Maxton Lodge Holiday Apartments
t (01803) 607811
e stay@redhouse-hotel.co.uk
w redhouse-hotel.co.uk

Meadcourt ★★★★
Self Catering
Holiday Homes & Cottages South West
t (01803) 663650
e holcotts@aol.com
w swcottages.co.uk

Meadfoot Grange
Rating Applied For
Self Catering
Contact: Mrs Adele Barnes
Blue Chip Vacations
t (01803) 855282
e info@bluechipvacations.com
w bluechipvacations.com/properties/me05.php

Meadowside Holiday Flats
★★★ *Self Catering*
Contact: Mrs Iris Wilson
t (01803) 295683
e meadowside@torquay38.freeserve.co.uk

Moongate Cottages ★★★
Self Catering
Holiday Homes & Cottages South West
t (01803) 663650
e holcotts@aol.com
w swcottages.co.uk

Moorcot Self Contained Holiday Apartments ★★★
Self Catering
Contact: Mrs Margaret Neilson
t (01803) 293710
e holidayflats@moorcot.com
w moorcot.com

Moorings ★★★ *Self Catering*
Holiday Homes & Cottages South West
t (01803) 663650
e holcotts@aol.com
w swcottages.co.uk

Muntham Luxury Holiday Apartments ★★★★
Self Catering
Contact: Mr & Mrs Peter & Trudie Cross
Muntham Holiday Apartments
t (01803) 292958
e muntham@btinternet.com
w theenglishriviera.co.uk

Newhaven ★★★
Self Catering
Contact: Mr Brian Wiltshire
t (01803) 612836

Rose Court Holiday Apartments, Babbacombe
★★★ *Self Catering*
Contact: Mrs J Henshall
t (01803) 327203
e holidays@rosecourtorquay.co.uk
w rosecourtorquay.co.uk

St Christophers Holiday Home ★★★★★ *Self Catering*
Contact: Mr David Perry
Wildewood
t (01803) 297471
e cperry@lineone.net
w torquayholiday.com

Silvan Lodge ★★★
Self Catering
Contact: Ms Sophie Relf
t (020) 8868 8358
e jungleholdings@yahoo.co.uk
w chilltime.biz

South Sands Apartments
★★★ *Self Catering*
Contact: Mr & Mrs Paul & Deborah Moorhouse
South Sands Apartments
t (01803) 293521
e info@southsands.co.uk
w southsands.co.uk

Southern Comfort ★★★
Self Catering
Holiday Homes & Cottages South West
t (01803) 663650
e holcotts@aol.com
w swcottages.co.uk

Spa Cottage ★★★
Self Catering
Holiday Homes & Cottages South West
t (01803) 663650
e holcotts@aol.com
w swcottages.co.uk

Suncourt ★★★ *Self Catering*
Holiday Homes & Cottages South West
t (01803) 663650
e holcotts@aol.com
w swcottages.co.uk

Sunningdale Apartments
★★★ *Self Catering*
Contact: Mr Allan Carr
Sunningdale Apartments
t (01803) 325786
e allancarr@yahoo.com
w sunningdaleapartments.co.uk

Sunnyhill Mews ★★★★
Self Catering
Holiday Homes & Cottages South West
t (01803) 663650
e holcotts@aol.com
w swcottages.co.uk

Vane Tower ★★★★
Self Catering
Holiday Homes & Cottages South West
t (01803) 663650
e holcotts@aol.com
w swcottages.co.uk

Villa Capri ★★★★
Self Catering
Contact: Mr Arthur Turner
t (01803) 297959
e villcapr@bt.int.com

Villa Garda Holiday Apartments ★★★
Self Catering
Contact: Mr & Mrs C Loasby
t (01803) 605474
e villagarda@btinternet.com
w selfcateringholiday apartmentstorquay.com

Vomero Holiday Apartments
★★★ *Self Catering*
Contact: Mr Anthony Brown
t (01803) 293470
e holidays@vomero.co.uk
w vomero.co.uk

Waldon Court ★★★★
Self Catering
Contact: Mr Ian Butterworth
Holiday Homes & Cottages South West
t (01803) 663650
e holcotts@aol.com
w swcottages.co.uk

Westcourt Holiday Flats
★★★ *Self Catering*
Contact: Mr John Lawton
t (01803) 311703
e westcourtholidayflats@hotmail.com
w westcourt-holiday-flats.co.uk

Wrenwood ★★★★
Self Catering
Holiday Homes & Cottages South West
t (01803) 663650
e holcotts@aol.com
w swcottages.co.uk

TORRINGTON Devon

2 Little Silver ★★★★
Self Catering
Contact: Mrs A Taylor
t (020) 8763 0796
e admin@devonshire-cottages.co.uk
w devonshire-cottages.co.uk

Hill Farm Cottages ★★★★
Self Catering
Contact: Mrs Mary Vickery
t (01805) 622432
e info@hillfarmcottages.co.uk
w hillfarmcottages.co.uk

Stowford Lodge ★★★
Self Catering
Contact: Mr & Mrs R Jones
Stowford Lodge
t (01805) 601540
e enq@stowfordlodge.co.uk
w stowfordlodge.co.uk

Week Farm Flat ★★★
Self Catering
Contact: Mrs Della Bealey
t (01805) 623029
e weekfarm.flat@btinternet.com
w week-farm.co.uk

TOTNES Devon

The Little Elbow Room
★★★★ *Self Catering*
Contact: Mrs Arfona Savin
t (01803) 863480
e r.savin@btinternet.com

Summer House ★★★★★
Self Catering
Contact: Mrs Jenny Adams
Arcadia Properties
t (01803) 864006
e reception@mintwood.uk.com
w arcadiaproperties.co.uk

TREBETHERICK Cornwall

Bars House ★★★
Self Catering
Contact: Dr Anthony Hambly
Bodrean Manor
t (01872) 264400
e anthonyhambly@hotmail.com

Bryneglos ★★★★
Self Catering
Rock Holidays
t (01208) 863399
e rockhols@aol.com

Evergreen Lodge ★★★★
Self Catering
Contact: Mrs Espir
t (01494) 726453
e dakwright@tiscali.co.uk
w selfcatering-evergreenlodge.com

Fourwinds ★★ *Self Catering*
Contact: Charlotte Bolt
t (01208) 863399
e rockhols@aol.com
w rockholiday.co.uk

Highcliffe ★★★★
Self Catering
Contact: Mr Mably
t (01208) 863843
e sales@highcliffeagency.com
w highcliffeagency.com

Hillcroft Bungalow ★★★
Self Catering
Contact: Mr & Mrs Beach
t (01256) 702650
e dibeach@hotmail.com

St Moritz Luxury Villas
★★★★ *Self Catering*
Contact: C Licsauer
t (01208) 862242
e reception@stmoritzvillas.co.uk
w stmoritzvillas.co.uk

Skylarks
Rating Applied For
Self Catering
Contact: C. Rayment
Radley House
t (01208) 862299
w crw.co.uk

TREGATTA Cornwall

Beaver Cottages ★★★
Self Catering
Contact: Mr & Mrs Luckin
t (01840) 770265
e beavercottages@amserve.com

TREGONY Cornwall

The Bolt Hole ★★★★
Self Catering
Contact: Miss Rebecca Nash
t (0114) 274 8821
e rebnash@yahoo.com

Garden Cottage ★★★
Self Catering
Contact: Mrs Douglass
t (01872) 530255
e babaraanne.douglass@tesco.net

Lamorna Cottage ★★★★
Self Catering
Contact: Mrs Carol Salmon
t (0117) 904 4967
e carol.salmon@blueyonder.co.uk

Little Treworlas Farm
★★★★ *Self Catering*
Contact: Mrs Ruth Harris
t (01872) 501858
e ruth@treworlas.co.uk
w treworlas.co.uk

Trefern ★★★ *Self Catering*
Roseland Holiday Cottages
t (01872) 580480
e enquiries@roselandholidaycottages.co.uk
w roselandholidaycottages.co.uk

Tucoyse Farm Holiday Cottages ★★★ *Self Catering*
Contact: Mr & Mrs Blamey
t (01726) 843836
e penny.blamey@tucoysefarmholidaycottages.co.uk
w tucoysefarmholidaycottages.co.uk

TREGURRIAN Cornwall

Mandalay ★★★ *Self Catering*
Contact: Ms Nicky Stanley
Harbour Holidays - Padstow
t (01841) 532555
e sales@jackie-stanley.co.uk
w harbourholidays.co.uk

TREKNOW Cornwall

Kittiwake Cottage ★★★★
Self Catering
Contact: Mrs Jan Harwood
t (01840) 770438
e jan@gullrock.eclipse.co.uk
w kittiwake-cottage.co.uk

Parwin ★★★ *Self Catering*
Contact: Mr Peter Osbourne
Cornish Horizons Holiday Cottages
t (01841) 533331
e cottages@cornishhorizons.co.uk
w cornishhorizons.co.uk

Rock House and Studio
★★★ *Self Catering*
Cornish Horizons Holiday Cottages
t (01841) 533331
e cottages@cornishhorizons.co.uk
w cornishhorizons.co.uk

TREMAINE Cornwall

Tremaine Barn ★★★★★
Self Catering
Contact: Mr & Mrs Lamb
t (01566) 781636
e ctbenquiries@stay-in-cornwall.co.uk
w stay-in-cornwall.co.uk

TRENANCE Cornwall

11 Europa Court ★★★
Self Catering
Contact: Mrs Blakemore
t (01637) 860296

Cuil Rathain ★★★
Self Catering
Contact: Mrs Anna Taplin
t (01841) 541046

Romanov ★★★ *Self Catering*
Cornish Horizons Holiday Cottages
t (01841) 533331
e cottages@cornishhorizons.co.uk
w cornishhorizons.co.uk

TRENARREN Cornwall

East Wing Apartment ★★★
Self Catering
Contact: Mrs Anita Treleaven
t (01726) 72954
e d.treleaven@farmline.com
w trevissick.co.uk

TRESILLIAN Cornwall

Penhale Cottage ★★★★★
Self Catering
Contact: Mrs Scully
t (01872) 520142
e barbara.dean@btinternet.com

Tregoninny Farm ★★★★
Self Catering
Contact: Mr & Mrs Northover
t (01872) 520529
e tregoninny.farm@btopenworld.com

TRESMORN Cornwall

Higher Tresmorn
★★-★★★★★ *Self Catering*
Contact: Ms Emma De Haan
t (01865) 820429
e tresmorn@btinternet.com
w highertresmorn.co.uk

TRESWITHIAN DOWNS Cornwall

Hideaway ★★★★★
Self Catering
Contact: Mrs Kate Jenkin
t (01209) 710617
e william@jenkin9350.wanadoo.co.uk
w hideawayathighfield.co.uk

TREVARRIAN Cornwall

Kernow Trek Lodge Self Catering ★★★ *Self Catering*
Contact: Mr Andrew Pearman
t (01637) 860437
e info@activityholidayscornwall.co.uk
w activityholidayscornwall.co.uk

TREVELGUE Cornwall

2 Porth Valley Cottages
★★★ *Self Catering*
Contact: Mr Peter Osborne
Cornish Horizons Holiday Cottages
t (01841) 533331
e cottages@cornishhorizons.co.uk
w cornishhorizons.co.uk

TREVELLAS Cornwall

113 Perran View Holiday Village ★★★ *Self Catering*
Duchy Holidays
t (01872) 572971
e enquiries@duchyholidays.co.uk
w duchyholidays.co.uk

51 Perran View ★★★
Self Catering
Duchy Holidays
t (01872) 572971
e enquiries@duchyholidays.co.uk
w duchyholidays.co.uk

63 Perran View ★★★
Self Catering
Duchy Holidays
t (01872) 572971
e enquiries@duchyholidays.co.uk
w duchyholidays.co.uk

64 Perran View ★★★
Self Catering
Contact: Mrs Gunnell
t (01872) 571287
e janetgnnll@aol.com or up2thegunnells@aol.com
w tremoor-perranporth.co.uk

70 Perran View ★★★
Self Catering
Duchy Holidays
t (01872) 572971
e enquiries@duchyholidays.co.uk
w duchyholidays.co.uk

80 Perran View ★★★
Self Catering
Duchy Holidays
t (01872) 572971
e enquiries@duchyholidays.co.uk
w duchyholidays.co.uk

9 Perran View Holiday Village ★★★ *Self Catering*
Duchy Holidays
t (01872) 572971
e enquiries@duchyholidays.co.uk
w duchyholidays.co.uk

Anneth Lowen ★★★
Self Catering
Duchy Holidays
t (01872) 572971
e enquiries@duchyholidays.co.uk
w duchyholidays.co.uk

Perran View 12 ★★
Self Catering
Duchy Holidays
t (01872) 572971
e enquiries@duchyholidays.co.uk
w duchyholidays.co.uk

TREVONE Cornwall

1 Dobbin House ★★★★
Self Catering
Contact: Mr Peter Osbourne
Cornish Horizons Holiday Cottages
t (01841) 533331
e cottages@cornishhorizons.co.uk
w cornishhorizons.co.uk

5 Atlanta ★★ *Self Catering*
Contact: Ms Nicky Stanley
Harbour Holidays - Padstow
t (01841) 532402
e contact@harbourholidays.co.uk
w harbourholidays.co.uk

Apartment 7 Greenwaves
★★★ *Self Catering*
Harbour Holidays
t (01841) 533402
e contact@harbourholidays.co.uk
w harbourholidays.co.uk

Avon Cottage ★★★
Self Catering
t (01841) 532426
e enquiries@woodlands-padstow.co.uk
w avoncottage.com

Bass Cottage ★★★★
Self Catering
Contact: Miss Nicola Stanley
t (01841) 533402
e contact@harbourholidays.co.uk

The Bothy & 1 Atlantic
★★★ *Self Catering*
Contact: Ms Nicky Stanley
Harbour Holidays - Padstow
t (01841) 532555
e sales@jackie-stanley.co.uk

The Bower ★★★
Self Catering
Contact: Ms Nicky Stanley
Harbour Holidays - Padstow
t (01841) 532555
e sales@jackie-stanley.co.uk
w cornishhorizons.co.uk

Chapel Fields ★★★★
Self Catering
Cornish Horizons Holiday Cottages
t (01841) 533331
e cottages@cornishhorizons.co.uk
w cornishhorizons.co.uk

Chy an Porth ★★★
Self Catering
Contact: Mr Peter Osbourne
Cornish Horizons Holiday Cottages
t (01841) 533331
e cottages@cornishhorizons.co.uk
w cornishhorizons.co.uk

Flip Flops ★★★★
Self Catering
Harbour Holidays - Padstow
t (01841) 532555
w harbourholidays.co.uk

Hill Rise ★★★ *Self Catering*
t (0117) 962 5862
e hillrise1@aol.com

Hope House ★★★★★
Self Catering
Contact: Nicky Stanley
Harbour Holidays
t (01841) 533402
e contact@harbourholidays.co.uk
w harbourholidays.co.uk

Pentonwarra ★★
Self Catering
Contact: Ms Stanley
Harbour Holidays
t (01841) 532555
e sales@jackie-stanley.co.uk

Riviera ★★ *Self Catering*
Harbour Holidays - Padstow
t (01841) 532555
e sales@jackie-stanley.co.uk

Seaboard
Rating Applied For
Self Catering
Contact: Nicky Stanley
Harbour Holidays
t (01841) 533402
e contact@harbourholidays.co.uk

Trelyn ★★★★ *Self Catering*
Contact: Mr Peter Osbourne
Cornish Horizons Holiday Cottages
t (01841) 533331
e cottages@cornishhorizons.co.uk
w cornishhorizons.co.uk

Warnecliffe Flat ★★★
Self Catering
Contact: Mr Peter Osbourne
Cornish Horizons Holiday Cottages
t (01841) 533331
e cottages@cornishhorizons.co.uk
w cornishhorizons.co.uk

Windmill Cottage ★★
Self Catering
Contact: Mr & Mrs Hawkes
t (01525) 280385

TREVONE BAY Cornwall

Atlanta Holiday Apartments
★★★-★★★★★ *Self Catering*
Contact: Mr Alken
t (01841) 520442
e mikealken@email.com
w cornwall-seaside-holidays.com

TREVOSE Cornwall

The Coach House ★★
Self Catering
Contact: Mrs Nicky Stanley
Harbour Holidays
t (01841) 532402
e contact@harbourholidays.co.uk
w harbourholidays.co.uk

Coastguard Cottage West
★★★★ *Self Catering*
Cornish Horizons Holiday Cottages
t (01841) 533331
e cottages@cornishhorizons.co.uk
w cornishhorizons.co.uk

The Redlands
Rating Applied For
Self Catering
Cornish Horizons Holiday Cottages
t (01841) 533331
e cottages@cornishhorizons.co.uk
w cornishhorizons.co.uk

Redlands Coachhouse
★★★★ *Self Catering*
Cornish Horizons Holiday Cottages
t (01841) 533331
e cottages@cornishhorizons.co.uk
w cornishhorizons.co.uk

Trevose Head Lighthouse
★★★★ *Self Catering*
Contact: Mr Michael Blanchard
t (01386) 852855
e michaelblanchard@talk21.com
w ruralretreats.co.uk

TREWALDER
Cornwall

Welch's Cottage ★★★★
Self Catering
Contact: Mr Clive Hester
t (01525) 405381
e hester_1@tesco.net

TREWARMETT
Cornwall

Cornmill Cottage ★★
Self Catering
Contact: Kerry Smith
Ploughmans Cottage
t (01840) 770309

Fenta Friddle ★★★★★
Self Catering
Contact: James Scott
t (01840) 779190
e fentafriddle@gmail.com
w frentafiddle.co.uk

TREWEN
Cornwall

Coombe Farm Cottages
★★★ *Self Catering*
Contact: Mr Paul Wood
t (01566) 86146
e paul@coombefarm.org.uk

TREWETHA
Cornwall

Trewetha Cottage ★★
Self Catering
Rock Holidays
t (01208) 863399
e rockhols@aol.com

TREYARNON BAY
Cornwall

Foxes – Treyarnon Bay
★★★ *Self Catering*
Contact: Mr Peter Tapper
t (01590) 674660
e peter.tapper@lafargecement.co.uk
w padstowholidayhome.co.uk

Glendurgan ★★★★
Self Catering
Contact: Nicky Stanley
Harbour Holidays
t (01841) 533402
e contact@harbourholidays.co.uk
w harbourholidays.co.uk

Saint Cadocs ★★★
Self Catering
Contact: Mr Peter Osbourne
Cornish Horizons Holiday Cottages
t (01841) 533331
e cottages@cornishhorizons.co.uk
w cornishhorizons.co.uk

Trebah ★★★ *Self Catering*
Harbour Holidays
t (01841) 533402
e contact@harbourholidays.co.uk
w harbourholidays.co.uk

Treyarnon Bay Farm Cottages ★★★★
Self Catering
Contact: Mr & Mrs Old
t (01841) 520653

TROON
Cornwall

Chapel Hill Farm Holidays
★★★★★ *Self Catering*
Contact: Mr Clark-Roberts
t (01208) 831706
e peterzania@btconnect.com
w chapelhillfarmholidays.co.uk

TROWBRIDGE
Wiltshire

Hinton Lodge ★★★★
Self Catering
Contact: Mrs Gompels
Hinton House
t (01380) 871067
e sam@gompels.co.uk
w hintonlodge.co.uk

TRURO
Cornwall

1 Upper Lemon Villas ★★
Self Catering
Contact: Mrs Susan Warrillow-Worne
t (01872) 262293

Ancarva Cottage ★★★
Self Catering
Special Places in Cornwall
t (01872) 864400
e office@specialplacescornwall.co.uk
w specialplacescornwall.co.uk

Chy Worval ★★★★
Self Catering
Contact: Mrs Heather Paxton
t (01872) 863950
e heather@chyworval.wanadoo.co.uk

Clifford House Cottages
★★★-★★★★★ *Self Catering*
Contact: Mrs Anne Grant
t (01872) 863052
e clifford.cottages@btopenworld.com
w cliffordhousecottages.co.uk

The Coach House ★★★
Self Catering
Contact: Dr Hambly
t (01872) 264400
e anthonyhambly@hotmail.com
w cornishholidaysuk.com/coach_hse.html

The Old Forge ★★★★
Self Catering
Roseland Holiday Cottages
t (01872) 580480
e enquiries@roselandholidays.co.uk

The Retreat ★★ *Self Catering*
Contact: Mrs Brejcha
t (01326) 270249

Trelowthas ★★★★
Self Catering
Contact: Mr Chris Churm
t (0115) 966 5611

Trenerry Lodge ★★
Self Catering
Contact: Mrs Angela Parsons
t (01872) 553755
e info@babatrenerry.co.uk
w babatrenerry.co.uk

The Valley, Carnon Downs
★★★★★ *Self Catering*
Contact: Mr & Mrs Keith & Julie Horsfall
t (01872) 862194
e info@valleycottages.net
w the-valley.co.uk

Westward (Niche Retreats)
★★★★ *Self Catering*
Niche Retreats
t (01209) 890272
e info@nicheretreats.co.uk
w nicheretreats.co.uk

Yew Tree Cottage ★★★★
Self Catering
Contact: Mr & Mrs Holdsworth-Wild
t (01872) 274190
e yewtreecottage@btopenworld.com

TWO WATERS FOOT
Cornwall

Bluebell Barn ★★★
Self Catering
Contact: Mrs Jean Crowson
Valley Villas
t (01208) 821202
e jean@crowson1.wanadoo.co.uk

Foxglove Barn ★★★
Self Catering
Contact: Mrs Jean Crowson
Valley Villas
t (01208) 821202
e jean@crowson1.wanadoo.co.uk
w valleyvillas.co.uk

Nuthatch Lodge ★★★
Self Catering
t (01208) 821553
e enquiries@nuthatch-lodge.co.uk
w nuthatch-lodge.co.uk

TWYFORD
Dorset

Buddens Farm Holidays
★★★ *Self Catering*
Contact: Mrs Sarah Gulliford
t (01747) 811433
e buddensfarm@eurolink.ltd.net
w buddensfarm.co.uk

TYTHERINGTON
Wiltshire

St James Court ★★★★
Self Catering
Contact: Mrs Anna Giddings
t (01985) 840568
e annagidding@aol.com
w wiltscottages.com

UGBOROUGH
Devon

Fowlescombe ★★★★★
Self Catering
Contact: Mr Richard Barker
t (01548) 821000
e richard@fowlescombe.com
w fowlescombe.com

Venn Farm ★★★★
Self Catering
Contact: Mrs Stephens
t (01364) 73240

ULEY
Gloucestershire

Coopers Cottage, Uley
★★★★ *Self Catering*
Contact: Mrs Diana Griffiths
t (01453) 542861
e cooperscot@onetel.com

Stouts Hill Club Ltd
Rating Applied For
Self Catering
Contact: Mrs Maureen Dolphin
t (01453) 860134
e maureen.dolphin@stoutshill.co.uk
w stoutshill.co.uk

ULLENWOOD
Gloucestershire

Ullenwood Court Cottages
★★★★ *Self Catering*
Contact: Mrs Anne Shand
t (01242) 239751

UMBERLEIGH
Devon

Little Wick ★★★★
Self Catering
Marsdens Cottage Holidays
t (01271) 813777
e holidays@marsdens.co.uk
w marsdens.co.uk

UNDERLANE
Cornwall

Wheal Sheda Cottage
Rating Applied For
Self Catering
Contact: Hilary Kneebone
t (01209) 861256

UPLODERS
Dorset

Clematis Cottage ★★★
Self Catering
Dream Cottages
t (01305) 789000
e admin@dream-cottages.co.uk
w dream-cottages.co.uk

Springside Cottage ★★★
Self Catering
Contact: Mr Alan Spargo
t (01305) 871585
e alan@aspargo.freeserve.co.uk
w springsidecottages.com

Tiddlers Cottage ★★★
Self Catering
Contact: Mr Alan Spargo
Springside Cottage
t (01305) 871585
e alan@aspargo.freeserve.co.uk
w springsidecottages.com

UPLYME
Devon

1 Barnes Meadow ★★★★
Self Catering
Lyme Bay Holidays
t (01297) 443363
e email@lymebayholidays.co.uk
w lymebayholidays.co.uk

3 Sherwood Apartments – B4389 ★★★ *Self Catering*
Lyme Bay Holidays
t (01297) 443363
e email@lymebayholidays.co.uk
w lymebayholidays.co.uk

4 Barnes Meadow: C4401
★★★★ *Self Catering*
Lyme Bay Holidays
t (01297) 443363
e email@lymebayholidays.co.uk
w lymebayholidays.co.uk

9 Coram Court – C4366
★★★★ *Self Catering*
Lyme Bay Holidays
t (01297) 443363
e email@lymebayholidays.co.uk
w lymebayholidays.co.uk

The Bower & The Bothy
★★★★ *Self Catering & Serviced Apartments*
Contact: Mrs Paula Wyon-Brown
The Bower
t (01297) 445185
e jwb@lymeregis-accommodation.com
w lymeregis-accommodation.com

Garden Flat & Panorama, Westfield – B4381 ★★★
Self Catering
Contact: Mr Dave Matthews
Lyme bay Cottages
t (01297) 443363
e email@lymebayholidays.co.uk
w lymebayholidays.co.uk

Higher Holcombe Farm Cottage ★★★★ *Self Catering*
Contact: Mrs Rosamund Duffin
Higher Holcombe Farm Cottage
t (01297) 444078
e rozduffin@hotmail.com
w higherholcombe.com

Holmer Villas
★★★-★★★★ *Self Catering*
t (01404) 861297
e pab@barnparkfarm.fsnet.co.uk

Lindens C4470 ★★★★
Self Catering
Lyme Bay Holidays
t (01297) 443363
e email@lymebayholidays.co.uk
w lymebayholidays.co.uk

Little Westhill – A4409
★★★ *Self Catering*
Lyme Bay Holidays
t (01297) 443363
e email@lymebayholidays.co.uk
w lymebayholidays.co.uk

Lyme Croft – D4227 ★★★★
Self Catering
Lyme Bay Holidays
t (01297) 443363
e email@lymebayholidays.co.uk
w lymebayholidays.co.uk

Meadow Sweet ★★★★
Self Catering
Contact: Joanne Winkler
Lyme Bay Holidays
t (01297) 443363
e email@lymebayholidays.co.uk
w lymebayholidays.co.uk

Mount View – C4343 ★★★
Self Catering
Lyme Bay Holidays
t (01297) 443363
e email@lymebayholidays.co.uk
w lymebayholidays.co.uk

Myrtle Cottage ★★★★
Self Catering
Contact: Mrs Gillian Leppitt
t (023) 8044 8706
e myrtle.uplyme@btinternet.com
w cottageguide.co.uk/myrtlecottage-uplyme

The Old Barn ★★
Self Catering
Lyme Bay Holidays
t (01297) 443363
e email@lymebayholidays.co.uk
w lymebayholidays.co.uk

Old Orchard ★★★★
Self Catering
Contact: Mr George Smith
t (01297) 443172
e tvecs@aol.com

Penrith House ★★★
Self Catering
Contact: Joanne Winkler
t (01297) 443363
e email@lymebayholidays.co.uk
w lymebayhoildays.co.uk

Pitt White House: E4410
★★★★ *Self Catering*
Contact: Mr Dave Matthews
Lyme Bay Holidays
t (01297) 443363
e email@lymebayholidays.co.uk
w lymebayholidays.co.uk

Stable Wing – B4307
★★★★ *Self Catering*
Lyme Bay Holidays
t (01297) 443363
e email@lymebayholidays.co.uk
w lymebayholidays.co.uk

Sunnyside Cottage – D4467
★★★★ *Self Catering*
Lyme Bay Holidays
t (01297) 443363
e email@lymebayholidays.co.uk
w lymebayholidays.co.uk

Yawl House – E4111 & Bramleys – W4384 ★★★
Self Catering
Lyme Bay Holidays
t (01297) 443363
e email@lymebayholidays.co.uk
w lymebayholidays.co.uk

UPOTTERY
Devon

Courtmoor Farm ★★★★
Self Catering
Contact: Mrs Rosalind Buxton
t (01404) 861565
e courtmoor.farm@btinternet.com
w courtmoor.farm.btinternet.co.uk

Hoemoor Bungalow ★★★
Self Catering
Contact: Mrs Phillips
t (01823) 601265
e holidays@hoemoor.freeserve.co.uk

Otters Rise Holiday Cottages
★★★★ *Self Catering*
Contact: Karen Marshallsay
t (01404) 861105
e info@ottersrise.co.uk
w ottersrise.co.uk

Twistgates Farm Cottages
★★★★ *Self Catering*
Contact: Mrs Suzanne Grey
UK & Emerald Cottage Holidays
t (01404) 861173
e suzanne@twistgatesfarm.co.uk
w twistgatesfarm.co.uk

UPPER SLAUGHTER
Gloucestershire

Home Farm Stable ★★★★★
Self Catering
Contact: Mrs Bayetto
Home Farmhouse, The Square
t (01451) 820487
e maureen.bayetto@virgin.net
w home-farm-stable.co.uk

UPTON
Somerset

West Withy Farm Holiday Cottages ★★★★
Self Catering
Contact: Mr & Mrs Gareth & Mary Hughes
t (01398) 371258
e ghughes@irisi.u-net.com
w exmoor-cottages.com

UPTON ST LEONARDS
Gloucestershire

Hill Farm Cottages ★★
Self Catering
Contact: Mrs Margaret McLellan
Hill Farm Cottages
t (01452) 614081

Little Court Cottages ★★★
Self Catering
Contact: Mrs Jane Gillman
t (01452) 615150
e info@littlecourtcottages.co.uk
w littlecourtcottages.co.uk

UPTON TOWANS
Cornwall

Gwithian Sands Holiday Chalets – CH009 ★★★ *Self Catering & Serviced Apartments*
Contact: Mr & Mrs Patchett
t (01736) 752195
w gwithiansands.co.uk

UPWEY
Dorset

Appleloft & Brook Springs
★★★ *Self Catering*
Contact: Mr Zachary Stuart-Brown
Dream Cottages
t (01305) 789000
e admin@dream-cottages.co.uk
w dream-cottages.co.uk

Buttermilk Cottage ★★★
Self Catering
Dream Cottages
t (01305) 789000
e admin@dream-cottages.co.uk
w dream-cottages.co.uk

Chapel Cottage & Old School Cottage ★★★
Self Catering
Contact: Mr Zachary Stuart-Brown
Dream Cottages
t (01305) 789000
e admin@dream-cottages.co.uk
w dream-cottages.co.uk

Sixpenny Cottage ★★★★
Self Catering
Dream Cottages
t (01305) 789000
e admin@dream-cottages.co.uk
w dream-cottages.co.uk

Strawberry Cottage ★★★
Self Catering
Contact: Mr Zachary Stuart-Brown
Dream Cottages
t (01305) 789000
e admin@dream-cottages.co.uk
w dream-cottages.co.uk

Wey Valley House ★★★★
Self Catering
Dream Cottages
t (01305) 789000
e admin@dream-cottages.co.uk
w dream-cottages.co.uk

URCHFONT
Wiltshire

Breach Cottage and The Pottery ★★-★★★
Self Catering
Contact: Mr & Mrs Philip & Clare Milanes
Breach House
t (01380) 840402
e breachhouse@btopenworld.com
w breachhouse.co.uk

VERWOOD
Dorset

West Farm Lodges & West Farm Cottage ★★★
Self Catering
Contact: Mr & Mrs Roger & Penny Froud
t (01202) 822263
e west.farm@virgin.net
w westfarmholidays.co.uk

VERYAN
Cornwall

1 Raglan Cottages ★★★★
Self Catering
Contact: Mrs Leonie Iddison
Roseland Holiday Cottages
t (01872) 580480
e enquiries@roselandholidaycottages.co.uk
w roslandholidaycottages.co.uk

Greenbank ★★★★
Self Catering
Contact: Leonie Iddison
Roseland Holiday Cottages
t (01872) 580480
e enquiries@roselandholidaycottages.co.uk
w roselandholidaycottages.co.uk

Jago Cottage ★★★★
Self Catering
Contact: Mr Treneary
t (01872) 501491
e jago@roseland.me.uk
w roseland.me.uk

Mill Cottage ★★★
Self Catering
Cornish Cottage Holidays
t (01326) 573808
e enquiry@cornishcottageholidays.co.uk
w cornishcottageholidays.co.uk

Trenona Farm Holidays
★★★★ *Self Catering*
Contact: Mrs Pamela Carbis
Trenona Farm
t (01872) 501339
e pam@trenonafarmholidays.co.uk
w trenonafarmholidays.co.uk

VERYAN GREEN
Cornwall

Timms Cottage ★★★
Self Catering
Contact: Mrs Kitty Eccles
Rosehaven Cottages
t (01326) 270795
e eccles@rosehavencottages.co.uk

WADEBRIDGE
Cornwall

The Barn ★★★★
Self Catering
Contact: Mr Peter Osbourne
Cornish Horizons Holiday Cottages
t (01841) 533331
e cottages@cornishhorizons.co.uk
w cornishhorizons.co.uk

Barn Treanna ★★★
Self Catering
Contact: Mrs Anna Taplin
t (01841) 541046

Colesent Cottages
★★★-★★★★ *Self Catering*
Contact: Mr & Mrs Gary & Maureen Newman
t (01208) 850112
e relax@colesent.co.uk
w colesent.co.uk

Curlews ★★★ *Self Catering*
Harbour Holidays - Rock
t (01208) 863399

Derry Holidays
★★★-★★★★ *Self Catering*
Contact: Mrs Linda Derry
t (01208) 813015
e info@derryholidays.co.uk

The Knap ★★★★
Self Catering
Contact: Mrs Sharon Patterson
t (0118) 986 0935
e sharon@thepattersons.freeserve.co.uk
w theknap.info

Lowenna Holiday Apartment
★★★ *Self Catering*
Contact: Mrs Katy Holmes
t (01208) 815725

Mayfields Cottages ★★★
Self Catering
Contact: Mrs Burgess
t (01841) 532633
w padstowcottagecompany.co.uk

Michaelstow Manor Holiday Park ★★ *Self Catering*
Contact: Mr Jesson
Michaelstow Manor Holiday Park
t (01208) 850244
e michaelstow@eclipse.co.uk
w michaelstow-holidays.co.uk

Potters ★★★★ *Self Catering*
Contact: Ms Susan Enderby
t (020) 8855 8532
e susanenderby@aol.com

The Retreat ★★★-★★★★
Self Catering
Contact: Mrs Elaine Biddick
t (01726) 890214
e biddick@lanjew.co.uk

Rock Barn
Rating Applied For
Self Catering
Cornish Cottage Holidays
t (01326) 573808
e enquiry@cornishcottageholidays.co.uk
w cornishcottageholidays.co.uk

Rosehill Holiday Accommodation ★★★★
Self Catering
Cornish Horizons Holiday Cottages
t (01841) 533331
e cottages@cornishhorizons.co.uk
w cornishhorizons.co.uk

Slate Cottage ★★★
Self Catering
Contact: Mr Osborne
Cornish Horizons Holiday Cottages
t (01841) 533331
e cottages@cornishhorizons.co.uk
w cornishhorizons.co.uk

Tern ★★★ *Self Catering*
Contact: Peter Osbourne
Cornish Horizons Holiday Cottages
t (01841) 533331
e cottages@cornishhorizons.co.uk
w cornishhorizons.co.uk

Tredougann ★★★★★
Self Catering
Contact: Mr Michael Griffths
t 07918 175713
e mike@mikegriffiths.biz
w cameltrailcottage.com

Tregolls Farm Cottages
★★★★ *Self Catering*
Contact: Mrs Hawkey
Tregolls Farm Cottages
t (01208) 812154
e tregollsfarm@btclick.com
w tregollsfarm.co.uk

Tregonce Cliff ★★★★
Self Catering
Harbour Holidays
t (01841) 533402
e contact@harbourholidays.co.uk
w harbourholidays.co.uk

WANBOROUGH
Wiltshire

The Garden Apartment
★★★ *Self Catering*
Contact: Mrs Julie Evans
t (01793) 791395
e tom.m.evans@talk21.com
w members.lycos.co.uk/gardenapartment

WARBSTOW
Cornwall

Cartmell Bungalow ★★★
Self Catering
Contact: Mrs Dawe
t (01840) 261353

Meadowview Cottage
★★★★ *Self Catering*
Contact: Roger & Debbie Bolt
t (01840) 261706

WAREHAM
Dorset

Bankgate Cottage ★★★★
Self Catering
Contact: Miss LM Hemingway
Dorset Cottage Holidays
t (01929) 553443
e enq@dhcottages.co.uk
w dhcottages.co.uk

Bronte Cottage ★★★★
Self Catering
Contact: Mr Zachary Stuart-Brown
Dream Cottages
t (01305) 789000
e admin@dream-cottages.co.uk
w dream-cottages.co.uk

Culeaze ★★★★ *Self Catering*
Contact: Major Christopher Barne
t (01929) 471344
e majorbarne@ukonline.co.uk
w culeaze.com

Dormer Cottage, Hyde ★
Self Catering
Contact: Mrs Madeleine Constantinides
t (01929) 471239

East Creech Farm House
★★★★ *Self Catering*
Contact: Mrs Best
t (01929) 480519
e east.creech@virgin.net
w eastcreechfarm.co.uk

The Glen ★★★ *Self Catering*
Dream Cottages
t (01305) 789000
e admin@dream-cottages.co.uk
w dream-cottages.co.uk

Icen Barn ★★★★
Self Catering
Contact: Ms Kirsty Parker
Dream Cottages
t (01305) 789000
e admin@dream-cottages.co.uk
w dream-cottages.co.uk

Oak Cottage ★★★
Self Catering
Contact: Miss LM Hemingway
Dorset Cottage Holidays
t (01929) 553443
e enq@dhcottages.co.uk

Tavern Way ★★★
Self Catering
Contact: Mrs Zachary Stuart-Brown
Dream Cottages
t (01305) 789000
e admin@dream-cottages.co.uk
w dream-cottages.co.uk

Westport Cottage ★★★★
Self Catering
Dorset Cottage Holidays
t (01929) 553443
e enq@dhcottages.co.uk
w dhcottages.co.uk

WARMINSTER
Wiltshire

The Annex ★★ *Self Catering*
Contact: Mrs Sheila Allery
t (01985) 218158

Downside House H112
★★★★ *Self Catering*
Contact: Mr Nicholas Pash
Hideaways
t (01747) 828170
e enq@hideaways.co.uk
w hideaways.co.uk/property.cfm/h112

Eastleigh Farm, Bishopstrow
★★★★ *Self Catering*
Contact: Mrs Roz Walker
Eastleigh Farm
t (01985) 212325

Whey Cottage ★★★★
Self Catering
Contact: Mr Zachary Stuart-Brown
Dream Cottages
t (01305) 789000
e admin@dream-cottages.co.uk
w dream-cottages.co.uk

WARMWELL
Dorset

Apple Orchard ★★
Self Catering
Contact: Mr Geoffrey Stuart Murgatroyd
t (01305) 853702

Beech Farm ★★★
Self Catering
Contact: Mrs Ruth Goldsack
t (01305) 852414
e rugold@lineone.net

Misery Farm ★★★
Self Catering
Contact: Mr Zachary Stuart-Brown
Dream Cottages
t (01305) 789000
e admin@dream-cottages.co.uk
w dream-cottages.co.uk

WASHAWAY
Cornwall

Ferkins Barn ★★★
Self Catering
Contact: Mr Peter Osborne
Cornish Horizons Holiday Cottages
t (01841) 533331
e cottages@cornishhorizons.co.uk
w cornishhorizons.co.uk

WASHFORD
Somerset

Monksway ★★★★★
Self Catering
Contact: Mr & Mrs Woolford
t (01491) 681229
e b.woolford@btinternet.com

WATCHET
Somerset

The Croft Holiday Cottages
★★★★ *Self Catering*
Contact: Mr & Mrs Andrew & Kirsten Musgrave
t (01984) 631121
e croftcottages@talk21.com
w cottagessomerset.com

The Square ★★★
Self Catering
Hoseasons Holidays Ltd
t (01502) 500505
e mail@hoseasons.co.uk
w somerset-cottage.com

WATERMOUTH
Devon

The Nut House ★★★★
Self Catering
Contact: Mrs Janet Cornwell
Marsdens Cottage Holidays
t (01271) 813777
e holidays@marsdens.co.uk
w marsdens.co.uk

WATERROW
Somerset

Exmoor Gate Lodges
★★★★ *Self Catering*
Contact: Mrs Sue Gallagher
Whipcott Heights
t (01823) 672339
e bookings@oldlimekiln.freeserve.co.uk

Handley Farm ★★★★
Self Catering
Contact: Mr & Mrs George & Linda Leigh-Firbank
t (01398) 361516
e linda.handleyfarm@btinternet.com
w handleyfarm.co.uk

WEDMORE
Somerset

The Coach House ★★★★
Self Catering & Serviced Apartments
Contact: Mr Mike Rippon
t (01934) 713125
e coach.house@holdenhurst.co.uk
w holdenhurst.co.uk/coachhouse

WEEK ST MARY
Cornwall

Ranelagh ★★★★
Self Catering
Contact: Mrs Dickenson
t (01288) 341134
e shdickenson@aol.com
w ranelagh.co.uk

WELCOMBE
Devon

Mead Barn Cottages ★★★
Self Catering
Contact: Mr & Mrs Rob & Lisa Ireton
t (01288) 331721
e holidays@meadbarns.com
w meadbarns.com

Olde Smithy Bungalows
★★★ *Self Catering*
Contact: Mrs Sandra Millbourne
Olde Smithy Bungalows Self Catering
t (01237) 421811
e relax@oldesmithyholidays.co.uk
w northdevon.com/oldesmithy

WELLINGTON
Somerset

Lime Kiln Cottages ★★★★
Self Catering
Contact: Mrs Sue Gallagher
Hopper Cottage c/o Whipcott Heights
t (01823) 672339
e bookings@oldlimekiln.freeserve.co.uk

Tone Dale House ★★★★★
Self Catering
Contact: Mrs Claire Bendall
The Big House Co
t (01823) 662673
e party@thebighouseco.com
w thebighouseco.com

WELLISFORD
Somerset

The Old Mill ★★★★★
Self Catering
Contact: Mrs Jessica Vellacott
t (01823) 672284
e info@theoldmill.me.uk
w theoldmill.me.uk

WELLOW
Somerset

Holly Cottage & Garden Studio ★★★★ *Self Catering*
t (01225) 840889
w bath-holidays.co.uk

WELLS
Somerset

Hart Cottage ★★★
Self Catering
Contact: Mr Aaron Nandi
t (01749) 674897
e nandi@clara.co.uk

Honeysuckle Cottage
★★★★ *Self Catering*
Contact: Mrs Luana Law
Honeysuckle Cottage
t (01749) 678971
e honeycroft2@aol.com

Model Farm Cottages ★★★
Self Catering
Contact: Mrs Gill Creed
t (01749) 673363
e gillcreed@aol.com

The Potting Shed Holidays
★★★★ *Self Catering*
Contact: Mr & Mrs John & Chris Van Bergen-Henegouwen
Potting Shed Holidays
t (01749) 672857
e info@potingshedholidays.co.uk
w pottingshedholidays.co.uk

St Marys Lodge ★★★★
Self Catering
Contact: Mrs Jane Hughes
St Mary Mead
t (01749) 342157
e janehughes@trtopbox.net
w st-marys-lodge.co.uk

Shalom ★★ *Self Catering*
Contact: Mrs Rees
t (01204) 418576
e rosey.rees@talk21.com

Somerleaze Lodge ★★★★
Self Catering
Contact: Mrs Marlene & Miss Victoria Carse Jones
t (01749) 673859
w cottagesdirect.com

Spindlewood Lodges
★★★★ *Self Catering*
Contact: Mr & Mrs Peter & Linda Norris
t (01749) 890367
e info@spindlewoodlodges.co.uk
w spindlewoodlodges.co.uk

Vicars' Close Holiday House
★★★ *Self Catering*
Contact: Mrs Debbie Jones
t (01749) 674483
e visits@wellscathedral.uk.net

Wrinkle Mead ★★★★
Self Catering
Contact: Mrs Cynthia Glass
Wrinkle Mead
t (01749) 673445
e islingtonfarm2004@yahoo.co.uk
w islingtonfarmatwells.co.uk

WEMBDON
Somerset

Grange Farm Cottage
★★★★ *Self Catering*
English Country Cottages
t 0870 336 8100
w grangefarmcottage.co.uk

WEMBURY
Devon

Bovisand Lodge Estate – Heritage Apartments and Cottage, Bovisand ★★★★
Self Catering & Serviced Apartments
Contact: Mrs Rita Hart
Bovisand Lodge Estate
t (01752) 403554
e stay@bovisand-apartments.co.uk
w bovisand-apartments.co.uk

Traine Farm ★★★–★★★★
Self Catering
Contact: Mrs Sheila Rowland
t (01752) 862264
e traine.cottages@btopenworld.com
w traine-holiday-cottages.co.uk

WEMBWORTHY
Devon

Taw Mill ★★★★★
Self Catering
Contact: Mr & Mrs Roger & Sheila Bowley
t (01837) 83931
e sheila@tawmill.com
w tawmill.com

WENDRON
Cornwall

Corn Loft ★★★★
Self Catering
Farm & Cottage Holidays
t (01237) 479146
e enquiries@farmcott.co.uk
w holidaycottages.co.uk

WEST ALVINGTON
Devon

Cob Cottage ★★★★
Self Catering
Contact: Mr David Hanmer
Toad Hall Cottages
t (01548) 853089
e thc@toadhallcottages.com
w toadhallcottages.com

Osborne Cottage ★★★★
Self Catering
Toad Hall Cottages
t (01548) 853089
e thc@toadhallcottages.com
w toadhallcottages.com

Sunshine Cottage ★★★★
Self Catering
Contact: Mr Nicholas Pash
Hideaways
t (01747) 828170
e enq@hideaways.co.uk
w hideaways.co.uk/property.cfm/h510

WEST ANSTEY
Devon

Brimblecombe ★★★★
Self Catering
Contact: Mrs Charlotte Hutsby
t (01789) 840261
e charhutsby@talk21.com
w brimblecombe-exmoor.co.uk

Dunsley Mill ★★★★
Self Catering
Contact: Mr & Mrs John & Helen Sparrow
t (01398) 341374
e helen@dunsleymill.co.uk
w dunsleymill.co.uk

WEST BAY
Dorset

13 & 18 Heron Court ★★★
Self Catering
Contact: Mrs Mary Fitzpatrick
Merlins Cottage
t (01308) 898261
e merlinscottage@aol.com
w dorset-holidays-accommodation.com

3 The Parade ★★★
Self Catering
Contact: Mr John Daw
t (01308) 420338
e john-ann@daw6030freeserve.co.uk
w threetheparade-westbay.co.uk

8 Poppy Way ★★★★
Self Catering
Contact: Mr Philip Piper
Piper & Co LLP Solicitors
t (01985) 217464

The Bay House ★★
Self Catering
Contact: Mr Donald Kimber
t (0118) 978 1741

Foxglove Cottage ★★★★
Self Catering
Dream Cottages
t (01305) 789000
e admin@dream-cottages.co.uk
w dream-cottages.co.uk

Harbour Lights ★★★
Self Catering
Contact: Mr Zachary Stuart-Brown
Dream Cottages
t (01305) 789000
e admin@dream-cottages.co.uk
w dream-cottages.co.uk

Harbour View ★★★★
Self Catering
Contact: Mr Andrew Irish
t (01460) 73335
e andrewirish@hotmail.com

Heritage ★★★ *Self Catering*
Contact: Mrs Y J Vann
Winters farm
t (01297) 445530
e soot@eclipse.co.uk

Jurassic View ★★★
Self Catering
Contact: Mrs Frances Hunt
t (01458) 251203
e frances.kitchin.@somersetcook.freeserve.co.uk
w holsindorset.co.uk

Maritime Apartment ★★★★
Self Catering
Contact: Ms Kirsty Parker
Dream Cottages
t (01305) 789000
e admin@dream-cottages.co.uk
w dream-cottages.co.uk

Seafront Chalet ★★
Self Catering
Contact: Mrs Teresa Visram
t (020) 8554 1543
e teresa.visram@btinternet.com
w btinternet.com/~teresa.visram

Thorncombe ★★★
Self Catering
Contact: Mr & Mrs Gerald & Janet Paget
t (01308) 867539
e gerry.paget@hants.gov.uk

Westpoint Apartments ★★★-★★★★ *Self Catering*
Contact: Mr & Mrs Slade
Westpoint Apartments
t (01308) 423636
e bea@westpoint-apartments.co.uk
w westpointapartments.co.uk

WEST BEXINGTON
Dorset

Coggs Cottage ★★★
Self Catering
Contact: Miss Hemmingway
Dorset Cottage Holidays
t (01929) 553443
e enq@dhcottages.co.uk
w dhcottages.co.uk

Gorselands ★★★
Self Catering
Contact: Miss Brenda Parker
Gorselands Caravan Park
t (01308) 897232
w gorselands.co.uk

Tamarisk Farm Cottages ★★★-★★★★ *Self Catering*
Contact: Mrs Josephine Pearse
Tamarisk Farm Cottages
t (01308) 897784
e holidays@tamariskfarm.com
w holidays/tamariskfarm.co.uk

WEST BUCKLAND
Somerset

Gerbestone Manor ★★★★
Self Catering
Contact: Mr Brian Lord
t (01823) 662665
e brianlord@gerbestonemanor.com
w gerbestonemanor.com

WEST CHINNOCK
Somerset

Weavers Cottage ★★★★
Self Catering
Contact: Lt Col Gordon Piper
t (01935) 881370
e thepipers@btinternet.com

Yeoman Cottage ★★★★
Self Catering
Contact: Mrs Marie Wheatley
t (01935) 881421
e jonwheat@aol.com

WEST DOWN
Devon

Fairview Farm Cottages ★★★ *Self Catering*
Contact: Mr Kevin Walker
t (01271) 862249
e info@fairviewfarm.co.uk
w fairviewfarm.co.uk

Kings Close ★★★★
Self Catering
Contact: Mrs Toni Buchan
t (01271) 865222
e buchan@theoldvicarage.eclipse.co.uk
w devoncottages.net

Rock Cottage ★★★
Self Catering
Contact: Mrs Virginia Sprason
t (01562) 883038
e rock.cott@virgin.net
w devoncottage.fsnet.co.uk

WEST LOOE
Cornwall

1 West Quay ★★★
Self Catering
Contact: Mr Gorringe
t (01202) 517329

Ferry View ★★★
Self Catering
Cornish Management Services
t (01503) 269086
e cornishmanagserv@aol.com

Seaview Cottage ★★★
Self Catering
Cornish Management Services
t (01503) 269086
e cornishmanagserv@aol.com
w cornishmanagementservices.co.uk

Tideways ★★★ *Self Catering*
Contact: Mrs Richardson
t (01503) 264103
e richardsonks@tiscali.co.uk

WEST LULWORTH
Dorset

Advantage Point ★★
Self Catering
Contact: Mr Zachary Stuart-Brown
Dream Cottages
t (01305) 789000
e admin@dream-cottages.co.uk
w dream-cottages.co.uk

Flat 2 Chestnut Court ★★★
Self Catering
Contact: Mrs Patricia Coulson
t (01737) 832282
e pat.coulson@talk21.com
w chestnutcourt.co.uk

Lulwinds ★★★★
Self Catering
Dorset Cottage Holidays
t (01929) 553443
e enq@dhcottages.co.uk
w dhcottages.co.uk

Seavale ★★★★ *Self Catering*
Contact: Mr Eric Symes
Seavale
t (01929) 406110
e info@lulworthcove.org.uk
w lulworthcove.org.uk

Villa Buena Vista ★★
Self Catering
Contact: Mr Zachary Stuart-Brown
Dream Cottages
t (01305) 789000
e admin@dream-cottages.co.uk
w dream-cottages.co.uk

WEST MILTON
Dorset

Garden Lodge ★★★★
Self Catering
Contact: Ms Sarah Talbot-Ponsonby
Leopard Cottage
t (01920) 464755

Gore Cottage ★★★
Self Catering
Contact: Mrs E.G. Maude
Sparrow Court
t (01304) 389253
e gmaude@waitrose.com
w heartofdorset.co.uk

Pear Tree Cottage ★★★★
Self Catering
Monument Farm
t (01329) 280683
e monumentfarm@aol.com
w peartreecottage.info

WEST PENNARD
Somerset

Victoria Farm ★★★
Self Catering
Contact: Mr & Mrs Rands
t (01458) 850509

WEST TYTHERLEY
Dorset

Brightside Cottage Annexe ★★★ *Self Catering*
Contact: Mrs Barbara Wilks
t (01794) 341391
e bwilks@talk21.com

WESTBURY
Wiltshire

Iron Box Cottage ★★★★
Self Catering
Contact: Mrs Sue Hansford
t (01380) 830169
e sue.hansford@tesco.net
w ironboxcottage.co.uk

WESTBURY-SUB-MENDIP
Somerset

The Dairy ★★★ *Self Catering*
Contact: Mrs Catherine Hancock
t (01749) 870351
e cottagefarm@hotmail.com
w holiday-cottage-mendips-somerset.co.uk

Old Apple Loft ★★★
Self Catering
Contact: Mrs Anne Flintham
t (01749) 870557
e aflintham@toucansurf.com
w oldappleloft.co.uk

WESTHAY
Somerset

The Courtyard New House Farm ★★★★ *Self Catering*
Contact: Mr Bell
t (01458) 860238
e newhousefarm@farmersweekly.net
w newhousefarmbandb.co.uk

Riverside Farmhouse ★★★★ *Self Catering*
Contact: Mr & Mrs Graham Noel
t (01458) 860408
e gnoel@venividi.co.uk
w go-see.co.uk/riversidefarmhouse

WESTLEIGH
Devon

Farleigh Cottage ★★★★
Self Catering
Contact: Lucy Ellison
Farm & Cottage Holidays
t (01237) 479146
e enquiries@farmcott.co.uk
w holidaycottages.co.uk

WESTON
Devon

Birdsong Bungalow ★★★
Self Catering
Contact: Ms Tim Tandy
Jean bartlett Cottage Holidays
t (01297) 23221
e holidays@jeanbartlett.com
w jeanbartlett.com

Buzzards ★★★ *Self Catering*
Contact: Louise Hayman
Milbere Cottage Holidays
t (01297) 20729
e info@milkberehols.com
w milkberehols.com

Cornerstone ★★★
Self Catering
Contact: Louise Hayman
Milkbere Cottage Holidays
t (01297) 27029
w milkberehols.com

Higher Weston Farm
★★★★ *Self Catering*
Contact: Mr Euan MacFadyen
t (01395) 513741

Robin's Nest ★★★
Self Catering
Milkbere Cottage Holidays
t (01297) 20729
e info@milkberehols.com
w milkberehols.com

Sandways ★★★ *Self Catering*
Contact: Ms Louise Hayman
Milkbere Cottage Holidays
t (01297) 20729
e info@milkberehols.com
w milkberehols.com

Seagull Cottage ★★★
Self Catering
Contact: Louise Hayman
Milkbere Cottage Holidays
t (01297) 20729
e info@milkberehols.com
w kelworth.co.uk

Seagulls ★★★ *Self Catering*
Contact: Ms Kate Bartlett
Jean Bartlett Cottage Holidays
t (01297) 23221
e holidays@jeanbartlett.com
w jeanbartlett.com

The Swallows ★★★
Self Catering
Contact: Ms Louise Hayman
Milkbere Cottage Holidays
t (01297) 20729
e info@milkberehols.com
w milkberehols.com

Wagtails ★★★ *Self Catering*
Milkbere Cottage Holidays
t (01297) 20729
e info@milkberehols.com

WESTON SUBEDGE
Gloucestershire

Lychgate Cottage ★★★★
Self Catering
Contact: Mr Robert Hutsby
t (01789) 841525
e robert.hutsby@btinternet.com
w chipping-campden-holiday-cottages.co.uk/lychgate.htm

WESTON-SUPER-MARE
Somerset

Champagne Lettings ★★★★
Self Catering
Contact: Mrs Alison Cantle
Champagne Holiday Lettings
t (01252) 622789
e info@champagnelettings.co.uk

Doubleton Farm Cottages
★★★ *Self Catering*
Contact: Mr & Mrs John & Victoria Southwood
t (01934) 520225
e info@doubleton.com

Hope Farm Cottages, Lympsham ★★★★
Self Catering
Contact: Mrs Liz Stirk
Hope Farm Cottages
t (01934) 750506
e stirkhopefarm@aol.com
w hopefarmcottages.co.uk

Kyrenia Holiday Flats ★★★
Self Catering
Contact: Mrs Wendy Richards
t (01934) 623880

Manor House Cottages
★★★★ *Self Catering*
Contact: Mrs Hart
Manor House
t (01934) 812689
e valerie@manor-house-cottages.com
w manor-house-cottages.com

Martyndale Suites
Rating Applied For
Self Catering
Contact: Diane Corbett
t (01934) 631388
e diane.martyndale@btinternet.com
w martyndalesuites.com

Royal Oak Cottage ★★★
Self Catering
Contact: Mr Stephen Hotson
t (01934) 624065
e hotsonandco@btinternet.com
w royaloakcottage.com

Tidalways Holiday Flats
Rating Applied For
Self Catering
Contact: Sally & Roy Thomas
t (01934) 629745
e roythomas@tidalways.fsnet.co.uk

Woodview ★★★★
Self Catering
Contact: Mrs Beverly Jenkins
t (01277) 211033
e baj.jenkins@virgin.net

WESTPORT
Somerset

Riverside ★★★★
Self Catering
Contact: Mrs Caroline King
t (01823) 680447
e cking@dunnsgreen.fsnet.co.uk
w dunnsgreen.fsnet.co.uk

Wind in the Willows Cottage
★★★ *Self Catering*
Contact: Mr Baker
Hillside
t (01297) 32051
e cjbaker@eggconnect.net

WESTWARD HO!
Devon

10 Nautilus Apartment
★★★★★ *Self Catering*
Contact: Mr & Mrs Andrew & Emma Firth
Devonholidays4u
t (01865) 875356
e enquiries@devonholidays4u.co.uk
w devonholidays4u.co.uk

Atlantic Spray ★★★★
Self Catering
Marsdens Cottage Holidays
t (01271) 813777
e holidays@marsdens.co.uk
w marsdens.co.uk

Beggars Roost ★★★
Self Catering
Marsdens Cottage Holidays
t (01271) 813777
e holidays@marsdens.co.uk
w marsdens.co.uk

Pebble End ★★★★
Self Catering
Marsdens Cottage Holidays
t (01271) 813777
e holidays@marsdens.co.uk
w marsdens.co.uk

WEYMOUTH
Dorset

15 Wedgwood Road ★★★
Self Catering
t (020) 8082 9839

3 Bath Street ★★★
Self Catering
Contact: Mrs M Ward
t (01425) 652214

7 Avenue Road ★★★
Self Catering
Contact: Mr Peter Hawkins
t (020) 8777 9959
e properproperties@aol.com

90 Old Castle Road ★★★
Self Catering
Contact: Mrs Angela Mary Blake
Weymouth Bay Holiday Apartments
t (01305) 785003

Anchorage Cottage ★★★
Self Catering
Contact: Ms Kirsty Parker
Dream Cottages
t (01305) 789000
e admin@dream-cottages.co.uk
w dream-cottages.co.uk

Anvil House ★★★
Self Catering
Dream Cottages
t (01305) 789000
e admin@dream-cottages.co.uk
w dream-cottages.co.uk

Apartment 1, Townbridge House
Rating Applied For
Self Catering
Contact: Mr Peter Weeks
t (01249) 782713
e info@weymouthharbourholidays.co.uk
w weymouthharbourholidays.co.uk

Ashleigh Holiday Flats ★★
Self Catering
Contact: Mr Roger Littler
t (01305) 773715
e ashleighhols@btinternet.com

Ashwood ★★★★
Self Catering
Dream Cottages
t (01305) 789000
e admin@dream-cottages.co.uk
w dream-cottages.co.uk

Bay Lodge Self-Catering Accommodation ★★★★★
Self Catering
Contact: Mr & Mrs Graham & Barbara Dubben
Bay Lodge Self-Catering Accommodation
t (01305) 787815
e barbara@baylodge.co.uk
w baylodge.co.uk

Beach Retreat ★★★
Self Catering
Contact: Ms Kirsty Parker
Dream Cottages
t (01305) 789000
e admin@dream-cottages.co.uk
w dream-cottages.co.uk

Beach View Apartment ★★
Self Catering
Contact: Mr Zachary Stuart-Brown
Dream Cottages
t (01305) 789000
e admin@dream-cottages.co.uk
w dream-cottages.co.uk

Cassis Cottage ★★★
Self Catering
Contact: Mr Zachary Stuart-Brown
Dream Cottages
t (01305) 789000
e admin@dream-cottages.co.uk
w dream-cottages.co.uk

Central Seafront Apartments ★★★
Self Catering
Contact: Mrs Jean Wright
t (01305) 766744

Chapelhay Cottage ★★★★
Self Catering
Contact: Mr & Mrs Martin & Annie Harman
t (020) 8767 7007
e annie.kilington@masons.com
w cottageinweymouth.com

Christopher Robin Holiday Flats ★★★ *Self Catering*
Contact: Mrs Davies
t (01305) 774870
w christopherrobinholidayflats.co.uk

Cockleshells ★★★
Self Catering
Contact: Mr Zachary Stuart-Brown
Dream Cottages
t (01305) 789000
e admin@dream-cottages.co.uk
w dream-cottages.co.uk

Coral Cottage ★★★★
Self Catering
Dream Cottages
t (01305) 789000
e admin@dream-cottages.co.uk
w dream-cottages.co.uk

Cove Corner ★★★★
Self Catering
Dream Cottages
t (01305) 789000
e admin@dream-cottages.co.uk
w dream-cottages.co.uk

Cove Walk Cottage ★★★★
Self Catering
Contact: Mrs Zachary Stuart-Brown
Dream Cottages
t (01305) 789000
e admin@dream-cottages.co.uk
w dream-cottages.co.uk

Cygnets ★★★★
Self Catering
Dream Cottages
t (01305) 789000
e admin@dream-cottages.co.uk
w dream-cottages.co.uk

Digby House ★★★
Self Catering
Dream Cottages
t (01305) 789000
e admin@dream-cottages.co.uk
w dream-cottages.co.uk

Dornare Holiday Flats ★★
Self Catering
Contact: Mrs Dorenne Fowler
t (01305) 786359
e dornare@fowler77.freeserve.co.uk

Dream Beach Holiday Apartment ★★★
Self Catering
Contact: Mr Pete Smith
t (01305) 813455

Driftwood Cottage ★★★
Self Catering
Dream Cottages
t (01305) 789000
e admin@dream-cottages.co.uk
w dream-cottages.co.uk

Dunvegan Holiday Cottages ★★★ *Self Catering*
Contact: Mr Ian Boudier
t (01305) 783188
e trelawney@freeuk.com

Ebb Tide ★★★ *Self Catering*
Contact: Mr Zachary Stuart-Brown
Dream Cottages
t (01305) 789000
e admin@dream-cottages.co.uk
w dream-cottages.co.uk

Fairhaven Holiday Flats & Cottage ★★ *Self Catering*
Contact: Ms Tania Hickmott
Kings Hotel Group
t (01305) 760100
w kingshotels.co.uk

The Ferryman ★★★
Self Catering
Dream Cottages
t (01305) 789000
e admin@dream-cottages.co.uk
w dream-cottages.co.uk

The Firs ★★★ *Self Catering*
Dream Cottages
t (01305) 789000
e admin@dream-cottages.co.uk
w dream-cottages.co.uk

Fishermans Cottage ★★★
Self Catering
Contact: Mr Zachary Stuart-Brown
Dream Cottages
t (01305) 789000
e admin@dream-cottages.co.uk
w dream-cottages.co.uk

Footprints ★★★★
Self Catering
Contact: Mr Zachary Stuart-Brown
Dream Cottages
t (01305) 789000
e admin@dream-cottages.co.uk
w dream-cottages.co.uk

Fountain Cottage ★★★★
Self Catering
Dream Cottages
t (01305) 789000
e admin@dream-cottages.co.uk
w dream-cottages.co.uk

Fuchsia's Edge ★★★
Self Catering
Dream Cottages
t (01305) 789000
e admin@dream-cottages.co.uk
w dream-cottages.co.uk

The Gables ★★★★
Self Catering
Contact: Mr Zachary Stuart-Brown
Dream Cottages
t (01305) 789000
e admin@dream-cottages.co.uk
w dream-cottages.co.uk

The Gatehouse & Malthouse ★★★★ *Self Catering*
Contact: Mr Zachary Stuart-Brown
Dream Cottages
t (01305) 789000
e admin@dream-cottages.co.uk
w dream-cottages.co.uk

Georges House ★★★★
Self Catering
Contact: Mr Zachary Stuart-Brown
Dream Cottages
t (01305) 789000
e admin@dream-cottages.co.uk
w dream-cottages.co.uk

Greenroof – Flat 1 ★★★
Self Catering
t (01305) 766744

Harbour Edge ★★★
Self Catering
Contact: Mr Zachary Stuart-Brown
Dream Cottages
t (01305) 789000
e admin@dream-cottages.co.uk
w dream-cottages.co.uk

Harbour Reach ★★★
Self Catering
Contact: Ms Kirsty Parker
Dream Cottages
t (01305) 789000
e admin@dream-cottages.co.uk
w dream-cottages.co.uk

Harbour View Apartments ★★★ *Self Catering*
Contact: Mr Zachary Stuart-Brown
Dream Cottages
t (01305) 789000
e admin@dream-cottages.co.uk
w dream-cottages.co.uk

Harbour Walk ★★★★
Self Catering
Dream Cottages
t (01305) 789000
e admin@dream-cottages.co.uk
w dream-cottages.co.uk

Harbourside Apartment ★★★★ *Self Catering*
Contact: Ms Kirsty Parker
Dream Cottages
t (01305) 789000
e admin@dream-cottages.co.uk
w dream-cottages.co.uk

Hops House ★★★★
Self Catering
Contact: Mr Zachary Stuart-Brown
Dream Cottages
t (01305) 789000
e admin@dream-cottages.co.uk
w dream-cottages.co.uk

Howard Cottage ★★★
Self Catering
Contact: Mrs Barbara Willy
t (01305) 871799

Ivy Cottage ★★★★
Self Catering
Dream Cottages
t (01305) 789000
e admin@dream-cottages.co.uk
w dream-cottages.co.uk

Jacaranda ★★★ *Self Catering*
Contact: Mr Zachary Stuart-Brown
Dream Cottages
t (01305) 789000
e admin@dream-cottages.co.uk
w dream-cottages.co.uk

Kenmuire Holiday Flats ★–★★★ *Self Catering*
Contact: Mr Gary Cotterill
t (01305) 785659
w kenmuireholidayflats.co.uk

Kingsview ★★ *Self Catering*
Contact: Ms Anne Breen
t (01305) 814741
e bookings@weymouthcottagesandflats.co.uk
w weymouthcottagesandflats.co.uk

Lavender Cottage ★★★★
Self Catering
Dream Cottages
t (01305) 789000
e admin@dream-cottages.co.uk
w dream-cottages.co.uk

Lazy Waves Apartment ★★★★ *Self Catering*
Contact: Dan or Julie Vockins
t (01305) 833669
e booking@monkeyholidays.co.uk
w monkeyholidays.co.uk

Lillie Cottage ★★★
Self Catering
t (01305) 789000
e admin@dream-cottages.co.uk
w dream-cottages.co.uk

The Little Coachouse ★★★
Self Catering
Contact: Mr Zachary Stuart-Brown
Dream Cottages
t (01305) 789000
e admin@dream-cottages.co.uk
w dream-cottages.co.uk

Little Venice ★★★
Self Catering
Dream Cottages
t (01305) 789000
e admin@dream-cottages.co.uk
w dream-cottages.co.uk

Littlecoombe Flat 1 Coombe House ★★★ *Self Catering*
Dream Cottages
t (01305) 789000
e admin@dream-cottages.co.uk
w dream-cottages.co.uk

Lobster Pot ★★★
Self Catering
Contact: Mr & Mrs Michael & Penny Piggin
Cross Oaks House
t 07768 568057

Lookout ★★★ *Self Catering*
Dream Cottages
t (01305) 789000
e admin@dream-cottages.co.uk
w dream-cottages.co.uk

Marina View Apartment ★★★★ *Self Catering*
Contact: Mr Zachary Stuart-Brown
Dream Cottages
t (01305) 789000
e admin@dream-cottages.co.uk
w dream-cottages.co.uk

Mariners Way ★★★
Self Catering
Contact: Mr Zachary Stuart-Brown
Dream Cottages
t (01305) 789000
e admin@dream-cottages.co.uk
w dream-cottages.co.uk

Marlow House ★★★
Self Catering
Dream Cottages
t (01305) 789000
e admin@dream-cottages.co.uk
w dream-cottages.co.uk

Mulberry Cottage ★★★
Self Catering
Dream Cottages
t (01305) 789000
e admin@dream-cottages.co.uk
w dream-cottages.co.uk

Mutiny House and Bucaneer Cottage (Phoenix Harbourside Holidays)
★★★★ *Self Catering*
Contact: Ms Janet Bennett
Phoenix Harbourside Holidays
t (01305) 832134
w harboursideweymouth.co.uk

Near Sea House ★★★
Self Catering
Contact: Ms Amanda Mitchell
t 07789 183029
e mitchells@themitchfam.freeserve.co.uk

Neptune House ★★★
Self Catering
Contact: Ms Kirsty Parker
Dream Cottages
t (01305) 789000
e admin@dream-cottages.co.uk
w dream-cottages.co.uk

The Oast House ★★★★
Self Catering
Contact: Mr Zachary Stuart-Brown
Dream Cottages
t (01305) 789000
e admin@dream-cottages.co.uk
w dream-cottages.co.uk

Ocean Watch ★★★★
Self Catering
Contact: Ms Kirsty Parker
Dream Cottages
t (01305) 789000
e admin@dream-cottages.co.uk
w dream-cottages.co.uk

Ocean Wave ★★★★
Self Catering
Contact: Mr Zachary Stuart-Brown
Dream Cottages
t (01305) 789000
e admin@dream-cottages.co.uk
w dream-cottages.co.uk

The Old Barley Store ★★★
Self Catering
Contact: Ms Kirsty Parker
Dream Cottages
t (01305) 789000
e admin@dream-cottages.co.uk
w dream-cottages.co.uk

Old Beams ★★★★
Self Catering
Dream Cottages
t (01305) 789000
e admin@dream-cottages.co.uk
w dream-cottages.co.uk

Old Harbour Holiday Flats
★★★★ *Self Catering*
Contact: Mrs Ida Goddard
t (01305) 776674

One Cove Street ★★★
Self Catering
Contact: Mr Deryk Brown
t (020) 8941 6150
e derykbrown41@aol.com

Orchard Cottage ★★★
Self Catering
Contact: Miss Anne M Breen
t (01305) 814741
e bookings@weymouthcottagesandflats.co.uk
w weymouthcottagesandflats.co.uk

Oyster Cottage ★★★★
Self Catering
Contact: Mrs Burt
t (01305) 761271
e family@tburt.fsnet.co.uk

Panda Holiday Flats ★★★
Self Catering
Contact: Mrs Anne Rose
t (01305) 773817

Pear Tree Cottage ★★★
Self Catering
Contact: Mr Ian Boudier
Dunvegan Holiday Cottages
t (01305) 783188
e trelawney@freeuk.com
w trelawneyhotel.com

Pebble Cottage ★★★
Self Catering
Contact: Mr Zachary Stuart-Brown
Dream Cottages
t (01305) 789000
e admin@dream-cottages.co.uk
w dream-cottages.co.uk

Picnic Bungalow ★★★
Self Catering
Dream Cottages
t (01305) 789000
e admin@dream-cottages.co.uk
w dream-cottages.co.uk

The Pines ★★★★
Self Catering
Dream Cottages
t (01305) 789000
e admin@dream-cottages.co.uk
w dream-cottages.co.uk

Poppies Cottage ★★★★
Self Catering
Contact: Mr Zachary Stuart-Brown
Dream Cottages
t (01305) 789000
e admin@dream-cottages.co.uk
w dream-cottages.co.uk

Promenade Way ★★★
Self Catering
Dream Cottages
t (01305) 789000
e admin@dream-cottages.co.uk
w dream-cottages.co.uk

Quayside ★★★ *Self Catering*
Contact: Mr Heath
Heath Developments Ltd
t (01753) 654676
e quayside14@aol.com
w quayside.uk.com

Queensway Holiday Flats
★–★★★ *Self Catering*
Contact: Mr Martin Kelly
t (01305) 760747
e info@queenswayapartments.co.uk
w queenswayapartments.co.uk

Redcliff View Lodge ★★★
Self Catering
Contact: Ms Kirsty Parker
Dream Cottages
t (01305) 789000
e admin@dream-cottages.co.uk
w dream-cottages.co.uk

Reefknott ★★★★
Self Catering
Contact: Mrs Susan Kay
t (0117) 932 7690
e suedental2000@yahoo.co.uk

Rose Cottage ★★★
Self Catering
Dream Cottages
t (01305) 789000
e admin@dream-cottages.co.uk
w dream-cottages.co.uk

Sailing Waters ★★★★
Self Catering
Dream Cottages
t (01305) 789000
e admin@dream-cottages.co.uk
w dream-cottages.co.uk

Sandcastles ★★★
Self Catering
Contact: Ms Kirsty Parker
Dream Cottages
t (01305) 789000
e admin@dream-cottages.co.uk
w dream-cottages.co.uk

Sandpipers ★★★★
Self Catering
Dream Cottages
t (01305) 789000
e admin@dream-cottages.co.uk
w dream-cottages.co.uk

Savoy Holiday Flats ★★★
Self Catering
Contact: Mr Mark Taylor
t (01305) 783254
w korthals.co.uk

The Sea Nest ★★★
Self Catering
Contact: Mrs Anita Boyle
t (01305) 761380
e anita.boyle@btinternet.com

Sea Shells Holiday Flat
★★★ *Self Catering*
Contact: Mr & Mrs Duncan & Ramona Rosser
t (01305) 778540
e ramonarosser@aol.com

Sea Tower & Sea Watch
★★★★ *Self Catering*
Dream Cottages
t (01305) 789000
e admin@dream-cottages.co.uk
w dream-cottages.co.uk

The Sea Turret ★★★★
Self Catering
Dream Cottages
t (01305) 789000
e admin@dream-cottages.co.uk
w dream-cottages.co.uk

Seafields ★★★ *Self Catering*
Contact: Mr Zachary Stuart-Brown
Dream Cottages
t (01305) 789000
e admin@dream-cottages.co.uk
w dream-cottages.co.uk

Seafront Holiday Flats ★★★
Self Catering
Contact: Mr Stephen Taylor
t (01305) 780104

Seagift ★★ *Self Catering*
Contact: Mrs A Willson
t (01305) 788239
e seagiftdorset@aol.com

Seagull Cottage ★★★
Self Catering
Contact: Mr Zachary Stuart-Brown
Dream Cottages
t (01305) 789000
e admin@dream-cottages.co.uk
w dream-cottages.co.uk

Seahorse Apartment ★★★
Self Catering
Contact: Ms Kirsty Parker
Dream Cottages
t (01305) 789000
e admin@dream-cottages.co.uk
w dream-cottages.co.uk

Seashells ★★★ *Self Catering*
Contact: Ms Kirsty Parker
Dream Cottages
t (01305) 789000
e admin@dream-cottages.co.uk
w dream-cottages.co.uk

Seaside House ★★★
Self Catering
Contact: Mr Zachary Stuart-Brown
Dream Cottages
t (01305) 789000
e admin@dream-cottages.co.uk
w dream-cottages.co.uk

Seastar Apartments ★★★★
Self Catering
Contact: Ms Kirsty Parker
Dream Cottages
t (01305) 789000
e admin@dream-cottages.co.uk
w dream-cottages.co.uk

Seaview & Seaspray
★★★–★★★★ *Self Catering*
Dream Cottages
t (01305) 789000
e admin@dream-cottages.co.uk
w dream-cottages.co.uk

Seaview Cottage & Captains Cabin ★★★ *Self Catering*
Contact: Mrs Wendy Evans
t (01305) 785037
e wenjon@onetel.com

The Shanty ★★★
Self Catering
Contact: Mr Zachary Stuart-Brown
Dream Cottages
t (01305) 789000
e admin@dream-cottages.co.uk
w dream-cottages.co.uk

Shire Horse Mews ★★★
Self Catering
Contact: Mr Zachary Stuart-Brown
Dream Cottages
t (01305) 789000
e admin@dream-cottages.co.uk
w dream-cottages.co.uk

Spinnaker House ★★★
Self Catering
Contact: Mr Zachary Stuart-Brown
Dream Cottages
t (01305) 789000
e admin@dream-cottages.co.uk
w dream-cottages.co.uk

Stavordale House Holiday Apartments ★★★
Self Catering
Contact: Mr Mark Marriott
Little Compton
t (01305) 789004
e stavordalehouse@ukonline.co.uk

Stonebank Cottage ★★★★
Self Catering
Contact: Mrs Pru Westcott
Stonebank
t (01305) 760120
e annexe@stonebank-chickerell.com
w stonebank-chickerell.co.uk

Summerleaze ★★
Self Catering
Contact: Mrs Julia Cole
t (01305) 777253

Sunflower Cottage ★★★★
Self Catering
Dream Cottages
t (01305) 789000
e admin@dream-cottages.co.uk
w dream-cottages.co.uk

Sunnyside House ★★★
Self Catering
Contact: Ms Kirsty Parker
Dream Cottages
t (01305) 789000
e admin@dream-cottages.co.uk
w dream-cottages.co.uk

Sunnywey Apartments
★★★★ *Self Catering*
Contact: Mr & Mrs Bond
t (01305) 781767
e bond@sunnywey.co.uk
w sunnywey.co.uk

Tamarisk Apartment ★★★
Self Catering
Contact: Mr Zachary Stuart-Brown
Dream Cottages
t (01305) 789000
e admin@dream-cottages.co.uk
w dream-cottages.co.uk

Tides ★★★★ *Self Catering*
Dream Cottages
t (01305) 789000
e admin@dream-cottages.co.uk
w dream-cottages.co.uk

Timbers ★★★ *Self Catering*
Contact: Mr Zachary Stuart-Brown
Dream Cottages
t (01305) 789000
e admin@dream-cottages.co.uk
w dream-cottages.co.uk

Topsy Turvy ★★★
Self Catering
Dream Cottages
t (01305) 789000
e admin@dream-cottages.co.uk
w dream-cottages.co.uk

The Trawlerman ★★★
Self Catering
Dream Cottages
t (01305) 789000
e admin@dream-cottages.co.uk
w dream-cottages.co.uk

Treetops ★★★★
Self Catering
Contact: Mr Zachary Stuart-Brown
Dream Cottages
t (01305) 789000
e admin@dream-cottages.co.uk
w dream-cottages.co.uk

Trezise Holiday Home ★★★
Self Catering
Contact: Mr Barrie & Valerie Trezise
t (0117) 937 2304
e b.trezise@btopenworld.com

Upsidedown House ★★★★
Self Catering
Dream Cottages
t (01305) 789000
e admin@dream-cottages.co.uk
w dream-cottages.co.uk

Wagonwheels ★★★
Self Catering
Contact: Mr Zachary Stuart-Brown
Dream Cottages
t (01305) 789000
e admin@dream-cottages.co.uk
w dream-cottages.co.uk

Waters Edge ★★★
Self Catering
Contact: Mr Zachary Stuart-Brown
Dream Cottages
t (01305) 789000
e admin@dream-cottages.co.uk
w dream-cottages.co.uk

Weyfarer Cottage ★★★
Self Catering
Contact: Mr Zachary Stuart-Brown
Dream Cottages
t (01305) 789000
e admin@dream-cottages.co.uk
w dream-cottages.co.uk

Weymouth Bay Holiday Apartments ★★★
Self Catering
Contact: Mrs Angela Mary Blake
t (01305) 785003

Weymouth Bay Holiday Apartments ★★★
Self Catering
Contact: Mrs Angela Mary Blake
t (01305) 785003

The Weymouth Seafront Holiday Flat ★★★★
Self Catering
Contact: Mr Don Whistance Kilderkin
t (01305) 813237
e donwhistance@rmplc.co.uk
w theflat.org.uk

Wheelwright House ★★★
Self Catering
Contact: Mr Zachary Stuart-Brown
Dream Cottages
t (01305) 789000
e admin@dream-cottages.co.uk
w dream-cottages.co.uk

White Horse House ★★★
Self Catering
Contact: Mr Zachary Stuart-Brown
Dream Cottages
t (01305) 789000
e admin@dream-cottages.co.uk
w dream-cottages.co.uk

White Waves ★★★★
Self Catering
Dream Cottages
t (01305) 789000
e admin@dream-cottages.co.uk
w dream-cottages.co.uk

Whitesands Seafront Apartments ★★★
Self Catering
Contact: Mr John Watt
t (01305) 782202

Winkle Cottage ★★★
Self Catering
Contact: Mr Zachary Stuart-Brown
Dream Cottages
t (01305) 789000
e admin@dream-cottages.co.uk
w dream-cottages.co.uk

WHEAL KITTY
Cornwall

Atlantic Coast Holidays
★★★–★★★★★ *Self Catering*
Contact: Mr & Mrs Selby
t (01872) 552485
e atlantic.holidays@googlemail.com
w atlantic-holidays.co.uk

WHEDDON CROSS
Somerset

North Wheddon Farm
★★★★ *Self Catering*
Contact: Mr Julian Abraham
t (01225) 461634
e northwheddonfarm@aol.com
w go-exmoor.co.uk

Pembroke ★★★
Self Catering
Contact: Mrs Escott
Brake Cottage
t (01643) 841550

Triscombe Farm ★★★★
Self Catering
Contact: Ruth & Robert Brinkley
t (01643) 851227
e ruthattriscombe@aol.com
w triscombefarm.co.uk

WHIMPLE
Devon

LSF Holiday Cottages ★★★
Self Catering
Contact: Mrs Angela Lang
LSF Holiday Cottages
t (01404) 822989
e lowersouthbrookfarm@btinternet.com
w lowersouthbrookfarm.co.uk

WHITCHURCH
Devon

Challonsleigh ★★★★
Self Catering
Contact: Mary Susan Fox
Edgemoor
t (01822) 612259
e vicky@dartmoorcottages.info
w challonsleigh.co.uk

WHITCHURCH CANONICORUM
Dorset

Berehayes Farm Cottages
★★★★ *Self Catering*
Contact: Mr & Mrs Winterbourne
Bereheyes Farm Cottages
t (01297) 489093
e berehayes@tesco.net
w berehayes.co.uk

Bonhayes Stable – Y4360
★★★ *Self Catering*
Lyme Bay Holidays
t (01297) 443363
e email@lymebayholidays.co.uk
w lymebayholidays.co.uk

Taphouse Farmhouse, Courthouse Farmhouse & Courthouse Dairy
★★–★★★ *Self Catering*
Contact: Miss Kay Johnson
t (01297) 489375
e cardsmill@aol.com
w farmhousedorset.com

West Barn X4023 ★★★★
Self Catering
Lyme Bay Holidays
t (01297) 443363
e email@lymebayholidays.co.uk
w lymebayholidays.co.uk

WHITECROFT
Gloucestershire

Miners Cottage ★★★★
Self Catering
Contact: Mrs Liz Kirby
t (01594) 562483
e minersarmsph@aol.com
w minersarms.org

WHITESTAUNTON
Somerset

Little Barton, Higher Beetham Farm ★★★★
Self Catering
Higher Beetham Farm
t (01460) 234460
e ianandhilary@higher-beetham.fsnet.co.uk

WHITMINSTER
Gloucestershire

The Stable ★★★
Self Catering
Contact: Mr & Mrs A C & R M Beeby
Jaxons Farm
t (01452) 740969
e thestable@jaxonsfarm.co.uk
w jaxonsfarm.co.uk

WIDCOMBE
Somerset

Highclere Holidays
★★★-★★★★ *Self Catering*
Contact: Mrs Elizabeth Daniel
t (01225) 465465
e liz.daniel@tiscali.co.uk
w holidayinbath.co.uk

WIDECOMBE-IN-THE-MOOR
Devon

Holwell Farm Cottages
★★★★★ *Self Catering*
Contact: Ms Philippa Hughes
Holne Chase Hotel
t (01364) 631471
e info@holne-chase.co.uk
w holwelldartmoor.co.uk

WIDEGATES
Cornwall

Tresorya Cottage ★★
Self Catering
Valley Villas
t (01752) 605605
e sales@valleyvillas.com
w valleyvillas.co.uk

WIDEMOUTH BAY
Cornwall

The Anchorage ★★★
Self Catering
Contact: Mrs Karen Maule
Rydon Farm
t (01647) 24208
e maule.rydon96@homecall.co.uk

Atlantic View ★★★
Self Catering
Contact: Ms Kim Gilby
t (01566) 782426
e w.carr@ukgateway.net
w chycor.co.uk/cottages/widemouth-atlanticview

The Barns ★★★★
Self Catering
Contact: Mr & Mrs Harrison
t (01288) 361877
e widemouthfarm@tiscali.co.uk

Freestyle at Widemouth Bay Holiday Village ★★
Self Catering
Contact: Mr Barker
t 07974 424625
e freestyle4me@yahoo.com

WILCOVE
Cornwall

Poltenyfair ★★ *Self Catering*
Contact: Mr & Mrs Knott
t (01752) 812955

WILLAND
Devon

Bradfield Cottages ★★★★
Self Catering
Contact: Jodee Culver Evans
t (01884) 840222
e reservations@bradfieldcottages.co.uk
w bradfieldcottages.co.uk

WILLERSEY
Gloucestershire

3 Cheltenham Cottages ★★
Self Catering
Contact: Mrs Gillian Malin
28 Bibsworth Avenue
t (01386) 853248
e g.malin@virgin.net

WILLITON
Somerset

Daisy Cottage ★★★★
Self Catering
Contact: Mrs Ann Bishop
t (01984) 632657

Tudor Thatched Cottage
Rating Applied For
Self Catering
Contact: Mrs Gill Kenyon
t (01643) 863456
e gillian.kenyon@lineone.net
w tudorthatchedcottage.co.uk

WILLSBRIDGE
Gloucestershire

Clack Mill Farm ★★★
Self Catering
Contact: Mrs Gaile Gay
t (0117) 932 2399
e gaile12331@aol.com

WIMBORNE MINSTER
Dorset

Grange Holiday Cottages, Grange ★★★★-★★★★★
Self Catering
English Country Cottages
t 0870 191 7700
e ecc.enquiry@holidaycottagesgroup.com
w grangeholidaycottages.co.uk

The Old Exchange ★★★★
Self Catering
Contact: Mrs Sarah Holland
t (01258) 840809
e sarah.j.holland@talk21.com
w theoldexchange.co.uk

WINCHCOMBE
Gloucestershire

Briar Cottage ★★★★
Self Catering
Contact: Miss Lyn Chambers
t (01242) 704277
e deniseparker2002@blueyonder.co.uk

Cockbury Court Cottages
★★★★ *Self Catering & Serviced Apartments*
Contact: Mr & Mrs John Charlton
Cotswold Cottages Limited
t (01242) 604806
e john@rowan-lodge.demon.co.uk
w cotswoldcottagesltd.co.uk

Misty View ★★★★
Self Catering
Contact: Mr Bob Turner
t (01242) 603583 & 07831 212501
e bobturner@mistyview.wannadoo.co.uk

Muir Cottage, Winchcombe
★★★★ *Self Catering*
Contact: Mark Grassick
Postlip Estate Co
t (01242) 603124
e enquiries@thecotswoldretreat.co.uk
w thecotswoldretreat.co.uk

The Old Stables ★★★
Self Catering
Contact: Miss Jane Eayrs
t (01242) 603860
e janeaycote@tesco.net

Orchard Cottage ★★★
Self Catering
Contact: Mrs S M Rolt
t (01242) 602594
e soniarolt@btinternet.com
w cottageguide.co.uk/orchard-cottage

Styche Cottage ★★★★
Self Catering
Contact: Mrs Anne Bayston
t (01926) 831508
e stychecottage@bayston.f9.co.uk
w cottageguide.co.uk/stychecottage

Sudeley Castle Country Cottages ★★★-★★★★
Self Catering
Contact: Mrs Olive Byng
t (01242) 604181
e olive.byng@sudeley.org.uk
w sudeleycastle.co.uk

Traditional Accommodation, Winchcombe
★★★★-★★★★★
Self Catering
Contact: Mr & Mrs Wilson
t (01386) 446269
e trad.accom@virgin.net
w http://freespace.virgin.net/trad.accom

Windsor Cottage ★★★
Self Catering
Contact: Ian Abbott
t (0115) 877 8324
e ian.c.abbott@btopenworld.com
w winchcombecottage.co.uk

WINDMILL
Cornwall

St Marina & Old Forge
★★★★-★★★★★
Self Catering
Contact: Ms Nickie Stanley
Harbour Holidays, Padstow
t (01841) 533402
e nickiestanley@btconnect.com

WINFORD
Somerset

Regilbury Farm ★★★
Self Catering
Contact: Mrs Keedwell
Regilbury Farm
t (01275) 472369
e janekeedwell@yahoo.co.uk
w regilburyfarm.co.uk

WINFRITH NEWBURGH
Dorset

Carters Barn ★★★
Self Catering
Contact: Miss L M Hemmingway
Dorset Cottage Holidays
t (01929) 552714
e enq@dhcottages.co.uk
w dhcottages.co.uk

Cherry & Willow Barn
★★★★ *Self Catering*
Dorset Cottage Holidays
t (01929) 553443
e enq@dhcottages.co.uk
w dhcottages.co.uk

Clovelly Cottage ★★★
Self Catering
Dorset Cottage Holidays
t (01929) 553443
e enq@dhcottages.co.uk
w dhcottages.co.uk

WINGFIELD
Wiltshire

Romsey Oak Cottages ★★
Self Catering
Contact: Mr Alan Briars
t (01225) 753950
e enquiries@romseyoakcottages.co.uk
w romseyoakcottages.co.uk/intro.htm

WINNARDS PERCH
Cornwall

Ash Lodge
Rating Applied For
Self Catering
Contact: Mrs Cathy Osborne
Cornish Horizons Holiday Cottages
t (01841) 533331
e cottages@cornishhorizons.co.uk
w cornishhorizons.co.uk

WINSFORD
Somerset

East Galliford ★★★
Self Catering
Contact: Mr Alexander
t (020) 8940 8078
e malcolm.alexander@interregna.com

Little Folly ★★★★
Self Catering
Contact: Mrs Pat Hewlett
t (01643) 851391
e adrianh@follyexmoor.co.uk
w follyexmoor.co.uk

The Tufters ★★★★★
Self Catering
Contact: Mrs Katherine White
East Lodge Farm
t 07703 490876
e robertwhite486@msn.com

WINSHAM
Somerset

Baytree Cottage ★★★★
Self Catering
Contact: Mr David Matthews
Lyme Bay Holidays
t (01297) 443363
e email@lymebayholidays.co.uk
w lymebayholidays.co.uk

WINSON
Gloucestershire

Swan House ★★★★★
Self Catering
Contact: Mrs Patricia Langley
t (020) 995 9072
e patricia@swanhousecotswolds.co.uk

WINTERBORNE HOUGHTON
Dorset

Downview Farm
★★★★-★★★★★
Self Catering
Contact: Mrs Clarice Fiander-Norman
t (01258) 882170
e enquiries@downviewfarmcottages.co.uk
w downviewcottages.co.uk

WINTERBOURNE ABBAS
Dorset

Lavender Lodge / The Granary ★★★ *Self Catering*
Contact: Mr Graham Tobitt
LGF Holidays
t (01305) 889662
e enquiries@lgf-holidays.co.uk
w lgf-holidays.co.uk

WINTERBOURNE STEEPLETON
Dorset

Westfield Farm Cottages
Rating Applied For
Self Catering
Contact: Mr John Cleall
t (01305) 889282

WINTERBOURNE STOKE
Wiltshire

Scotland Lodge ★★
Self Catering
Contact: Mrs Jane Singleton
t (01980) 620943
e scotland.lodge@virgin.net.co.uk
w scotland-lodge.co.uk

WITCOMBE
Gloucestershire

Crickley Court ★★★★
Self Catering
Contact: Mr & Mrs Pilgrim-Morris
t (01452) 863634
e lispilgrimmorris@yahoo.co.uk

WITHINGTON
Gloucestershire

Ballingers Farmhouse Cottages ★★★★
Self Catering
Contact: Mrs Judith Pollard
t (01242) 890335
e pollardfam@compuserve.com
w ballingersfarmhousecottages.co.uk

WITHYPOOL
Somerset

Hillway Lodge ★★★
Self Catering
Contact: Ms Gillian Lamble
t (01643) 831182
e gillian@hillwayfarm.com
w hillwayfarm.com

Leys Farm ★★★★★
Self Catering
Contact: Mr & Mrs Zurick
t (01643) 831427

Westerclose House Cottages
★★★-★★★★★ *Self Catering & Serviced Apartments*
Contact: Mrs Valerie Warner
t (01643) 831302
e val@westerclose.co.uk
w westerclose.co.uk

Westwater Cottage ★★★★
Self Catering
Contact: Mrs Sue Branfield
t (01643) 831360
e s.branfield@ukf.net

WIVELISCOMBE
Somerset

Pubkins ★★★ *Self Catering*
Farm & Cottage Holidays
t (01237) 479146
e enquiries@farmcott.co.uk
w holidaycottages.co.uk

WOODBURY
Devon

The Coach House ★★★★
Self Catering
Contact: Mr Paul Slade
t (01395) 233704
w tchwoodbury.co.uk

Squirrel ★★★★★
Self Catering
Contact: Mr & Mrs James Crill
The Thatched Cottage Company
t (01395) 567135
e info@thethatchedcottagecompany.co.uk
w thethatchcottagecompany.co.uk

WOODLANDS
Dorset

Meadow Cottage ★★★★
Self Catering
Contact: Mrs Vicki Brickwood
t (01202) 825002
w holiday-rentals.com/meadowland

WOODMANCOTE
Gloucestershire

Lanes End
Rating Applied For
Self Catering
Contact: Mrs Deirdre Taylor
t (01242) 676685
e deirdre_taylor@tiscali.co.uk
w danskin80.fsnet.co.uk

WOOKEY
Somerset

Mill Lodge ★★★★
Self Catering
Contact: Ms Lesley Burt
t (01749) 673118
e theburts@burcottmill.com
w burcottmill.com

Panniers Farm Cottage
★★★★ *Self Catering*
Contact: Gill Cumming
Panniers Farm
t (01749) 678928
e gill@panniersfarm.co.uk
w panniersfarm.co.uk

WOOLACOMBE
Devon

1 Devon Beach Court
★★★★ *Self Catering*
Contact: Mrs Janet Cornwell
Marsdens Cottage Holidays
t (01271) 813777
e holidays@marsdens.co.uk
w marsdens.co.uk

1 Dolphin Court
★★★★-★★★★★
Self Catering
Contact: Mrs Janet Cornwell
Marsdens Cottage Holidays
t (01271) 813777
e holidays@marsdens.co.uk
w marsdens.co.uk

1 Europa Park ★★
Self Catering
Contact: Mrs Rosemary Ann Facey
Sticklepath Lodge
t (01271) 343426
e rosemary.facey@talk21.com

2 Dolphin Court ★★★★★
Self Catering
Contact: Mrs Janet Cornwell
Marsdens Cottage Holidays
t (01271) 813777
e holidays@marsdens.co.uk
w marsdens.co.uk

4 Pandora Court ★★★★
Self Catering
Contact: Mrs Janet Cornwell
Marsdens Cottage Holidays
t (01271) 813777
e holidays@marsdens.co.uk
w marsdens.co.uk

5 Devon Beach ★★★★
Self Catering
Contact: Mrs Janet Cornwell
Marsdens Cottage Holidays
t (01271) 813777
e holidays@marsdens.co.uk
w marsdens.co.uk

5 Pandora Court ★★★★
Self Catering
Contact: Mrs Janet Cornwell
Marsdens Cottage Holidays
t (01271) 813777
e holidays@marsdens.co.uk
w marsdens.co.uk

The Apartment ★★★★
Self Catering
Contact: Mrs Janet Cornwell
Marsdens Cottage Holidays
t (01271) 813777
e holidays@marsdens.co.uk
w marsdens.co.uk

Apartment 1 ★★★★★
Self Catering
Contact: Mrs Janet Cornwell
Marsdens Cottage Holidays
t (01271) 813777
e holidays@marsdens.co.uk
w marsdens.co.uk

Apartment 10 ★★★★★
Self Catering
Marsdens Cottage Holidays
t (01271) 813777
e holidays@marsdens.co.uk
w marsdens.co.uk

Apartment 7 ★★★★★
Self Catering
Marsdens Cottage Holidays
t (01271) 813777
e holidays@marsdens.co.uk
w marsdens.co.uk

Apartments 3, 4 & 10
★★★★★ *Self Catering*
Marsdens Cottage Holidays
t (01271) 813777
e holidays@marsdens.co.uk
w marsdens.co.uk

Baggy Leap ★★★★
Self Catering
Contact: Mrs Janet Cornwell
Marsdens Cottage Holidays
t (01271) 813777
e holidays@marsdens.co.uk
w marsdens.co.uk

Barricane Sands ★★★★
Self Catering
Contact: Mrs Janet Cornwell
Marsdens Cottage Holidays
t (01271) 813777
e holidays@marsdens.co.uk
w marsdens.co.uk

Beachcomber ★★★★
Self Catering
Contact: Mrs Janet Cornwell
Marsdens Cottage Holidays
t (01271) 813777
e holidays@marsdens.co.uk
w marsdens.co.uk

Beachcroft Holiday Apartments ★★-★★★
Self Catering
Contact: Mrs Gill Barr
t (01271) 870655
e robert@rbarr.freeserve.co.uk

Cove Cottage Flat ★★
Self Catering
Contact: Mrs Vivien Lawrence
t (01271) 870403
e vlawrence05@aol.com

Footsteps ★★★★
Self Catering
Contact: Mrs Janet Cornwell
Marsdens Cottage Holidays
t (01271) 813777
e holidays@marsdens.co.uk
w marsdens.co.uk

Heather Lea ★★★★
Self Catering
Marsdens Cottage Holidays
t (01271) 813777
e holidays@marsdens.co.uk
w marsdens.co.uk

Kittiwake ★★★★
Self Catering
Marsdens Cottage Holidays
t (01271) 813777
e holidays@marsdens.co.uk
w marsdens.co.uk

Little Beach ★★★
Self Catering
Marsdens Cottage Holidays
t (01271) 813777
e holidays@marsdens.co.uk
w marsdens.co.uk

Lundy Set ★★★★
Self Catering
Contact: Mrs Janet Cornwell
Marsdens Cottage Holidays
t (01271) 813777
e holidays@marsdens.co.uk
w marsdens.co.uk

Malo ★★★ *Self Catering*
Contact: Mrs Janet Cornwell
Marsdens Cottage Holidays
t (01271) 813777
e holidays@marsdens.co.uk
w marsdens.co.uk

Narracott Apartment 2
★★★★★ *Self Catering*
Contact: Mrs Janet Cornwell
Marsdens Cottage Holidays
t (01271) 813777
e holidays@marsdens.co.uk
w marsdens.co.uk

Narracott Apartment 6
★★★★★ *Self Catering*
Marsdens Cottage Holidays
t (01271) 813777
e holidays@marsdens.co.uk
w marsdens.co.uk

Narracott Apartment 9
★★★★★ *Self Catering*
Contact: Mrs Janet Cornwell
Marsdens Cottage Holidays
t (01271) 813777
e holidays@marsdens.co.uk
w marsdens.co.uk

Ocean View ★★★★
Self Catering
Contact: Mrs Janet Cornwell
Marsdens Cottage Holidays
t (01271) 813777
e holidays@marsdens.co.uk
w marsdens.co.uk

Oysters ★★★★ *Self Catering*
Contact: Mrs Janet Cornwell
Marsdens Cottage Holidays
t (01271) 813777
e holidays@marsdens.co.uk
w marsdens.co.uk

The Palms ★★★
Self Catering
Contact: Mrs Janet Cornwell
Marsdens Cottage Holidays
t (01271) 813777
e holidays@marsdens.co.uk
w marsdens.co.uk

Point View ★★★★
Self Catering
Contact: Mr Peter Cornwell
Marsdens Cottage Holidays
t (01271) 813777
e holidays@marsdens.co.uk
w marsdens.co.uk

Potters View ★★★★
Self Catering
Contact: Mrs Janet Cornwell
Marsdens Cottage Holidays
t (01271) 813777
e holidays@marsdens.co.uk
w marsdens.co.uk

Rockfield House ★★★★
Self Catering
Marsdens Cottage Holidays
t (01271) 813777
e holidays@marsdens.co.uk
w marsdens.co.uk

Seascape ★★★★
Self Catering
Marsdens Cottage Holidays
t (01271) 813777
e holidays@marsdens.co.uk
w marsdens.co.uk

Stouts Cottage ★★★★
Self Catering
Marsdens Cottage Holidays
t (01271) 813777
e holidays@marsdens.co.uk
w marsdens.co.uk

Swallows Nest ★★★★
Self Catering
Contact: Mrs Janet Cornwell
Marsdens Cottage Holidays
t (01271) 813777
e holidays@marsdens.co.uk
w marsdens.co.uk

Swiss Cottage ★★★★
Self Catering
Contact: Mrs Janet Cornwell
Marsdens Cottage Holidays
t (01271) 813777
e holidays@marsdens.co.uk
w marsdens.co.uk

Tamarin ★★★★
Self Catering
Contact: Mrs Janet Cornwell
Marsdens Cottage Holidays
t (01271) 813777
e holidays@marsdens.co.uk
w marsdens.co.uk

Waves End ★★★★
Self Catering
Marsdens Cottage Holidays
t (01271) 813777
e holidays@marsdens.co.uk
w marsdens.co.uk

Westerly
Rating Applied For
Self Catering
Marsdens Cottage Holidays
t (01271) 813777
e holidays@marsdens.co.uk
w marsdens.co.uk

WOOLFARDISWORTHY
Devon

Fairchild Cottage ★★★★★
Self Catering
Contact: Mrs Doreen Cox
t (01237) 431503
e cox5.gorrel@virgin.net

WOOLLEY
Cornwall

West Woolley farm
Rating Applied For
Self Catering
Farm & Cottage Holidays
t (01237) 479146
e enquiries@farmcott.co.uk
w holidaycottages.co.uk

WOOTTON COURTENAY
Somerset

Bridge Cottage ★★★
Self Catering
Contact: Mrs E. M. Hawksford
t (01643) 841286

Exmoor View ★★★★
Self Catering
Contact: Mrs Carole Turner
t (01643) 841482
w exmoorview.co.uk

Rose Cottage ★★★
Self Catering
Contact: Mr Bryan Fawcett
t (01275) 331123
e bryanfawcett@lineone.net
w exmoorose.co.uk

WOOTTON FITZPAINE
Dorset

41a Silver Street: A4397
★★★ *Self Catering*
Lyme Bay Holidays
t (01297) 443363
e email@lymebayholidays.co.uk
w lymebayholidays.co.uk

Champernhayes Cottages
★★★★★ *Self Catering*
Contact: Mrs Tina Le-Clercq
Champernhayes
t (01297) 560853
e visit@champernhayes.com
w champernhayes.com

Cider & Barn Cottages
★★★★ *Self Catering*
Contact: Mrs Debby Snook
t (01297) 560541
e wfcottages@aol.com

Dairy Farm Holiday Homes
★★-★★★ *Self Catering*
Contact: Mr Dave Matthews
Lyme Bay Holidays
t (01297) 443363
e email@lymebayholidays.co.uk
w lymebayholidays.co.uk

East Barn ★★★★
Self Catering
Contact: Joanne Winkler
Lyme Bay Holidays
t (01297) 443363
e email@lymebayholidays.co.uk
w lymebayholidays.co.uk

Hollycombe Cottage ★★★
Self Catering
Contact: Joanne Winkler
Lyme Bay Holidays
t (01297) 443363
e email@lymebayholidays.co.uk
w lymebayholidays.co.uk

Marsh Farm ★★★
Self Catering
Contact: Mrs Fabia Mansbridge
t (01297) 560600

Stable Cottage – X4347
★★★ *Self Catering*
Lyme Bay Holidays
t (01297) 443363
e email@lymebayholidays.co.uk
w lymebayholidays.co.uk

WORTH MATRAVERS
Dorset

Ivy Cottage
Rating Applied For
Self Catering
Contact: Mrs C Mytton-Mills
Sunnydale Villas
t (01929) 427247

WRAFTON
Devon

Owencott ★★★★
Self Catering
Contact: Mrs Janet Cornwell
Marsdens Cottage Holidays
t (01271) 813777
e holidays@marsdens.co.uk
w marsdens.co.uk

WRANTAGE
Somerset

Ludwells Barn ★★★
Self Catering
Contact: Mr Dodd
t (01823) 480316

WYKE REGIS
Dorset

Church View ★★★
Self Catering
Contact: Mr Zachary Stuart-Brown
Dream Cottages
t (01305) 789000
e admin@dream-cottages.co.uk
w dream-cottages.co.uk

Still Waters ★★★
Self Catering
Contact: Mr Zachary Stuart-Brown
Dream Cottages
t (01305) 789000
e admin@dream-cottages.co.uk
w dream-cottages.co.uk

The Victorian House ★★★
Self Catering
Dream Cottages
t (01305) 789000
e admin@dream-cottages.co.uk
w dream-cottages.co.uk

YARCOMBE
Devon

Heaven's Mouth ★★★
Self Catering
Contact: Mrs Ruth Everitt
t (01404) 861517
e ruth-everitt@supanet.com

YEALMPTON
Devon

Gnaton Holiday Cottages
★★★★ *Self Catering*
Contact: Mrs Josephine Webb
The Flete Estate
t (01752) 830253
e cottages@flete.co.uk
w flete.co.uk

YELVERTON
Devon

Greenwell Farm ★★★★
Self Catering
Contact: Mrs Bridget Cole
t (01822) 853563
e greenwellfarm@btconnect.com

YETMINSTER
Dorset

St Francis Cottage ★★★
Self Catering
Dream Cottages
t (01305) 789000
e admin@dream-cottages.co.uk
w dream-cottages.co.uk

YORKLEY
Gloucestershire

Forest of Dean Holidays ★★
Self Catering
Contact: Ms Mary Konig
Shap House
t (01594) 562219
e cottages@forestofdeanholidays.co.uk

Silverdeane Apartment
★★★ *Self Catering*
Contact: Mr & Mrs Maria Rainer
t (01594) 562012

ZELAH
Cornwall

Little Callestock Farm
★★★-★★★★★
Self Catering
Contact: Mrs Liz Down
t (01872) 540445
e liznick@littlecallestockfarm.co.uk
w littlecallestockfarm.co.uk

Little Lowarth ★★★★
Self Catering
Farm & Cottage Holidays
t (01237) 479146
e enquiries@farmcott.co.uk
w holidaycottages.co.uk

ZENNOR
Cornwall

Sener ★★ *Self Catering*
Contact: Mr & Mrs Storrs
t (0151) 632 3967

Boat **accommodation**

When you want to book a holiday afloat, whether for a short break or longer, you need a rating system you can trust. Enjoy England's ratings for boat accommodation are a clear guide to what to expect, in an easy-to-understand form.

Choose from nearly 1,000 quality-assessed boats in small and large fleets across England's waterways. Facilities will vary, so the following designators will help you decide which type of boat will meet your needs:

NARROWBOAT
These purpose-built, traditionally decorated boats can be hired on canals and rivers, and can sleep up to 12 people. Step back in time and enjoy a very leisurely holiday cruising through the English countryside.

CRUISER
Cruisers operate mainly on the Norfolk Broads and the Thames. They range from practical, affordable craft to modern, stylish boats with accessories such as a dishwasher, DVD and flat-screen TV.

HOTEL BOAT
Hotel boats are generally narrowboats that are worked by a crew, so the guests can relax and only help if they want to. They can be booked by individuals or groups and provide all the services of a hotel – all meals and refreshments from early morning tea to a five-course dinner in the evening. The trips are tailored to the guests and tend to be very sociable.

For more information on boating holidays visit: **waterwayholidaysuk.com** and **waterscape.com.**

Star ratings

NARROWBOATS AND CRUISERS

All narrowboats and cruisers that are awarded a star rating meet minimum standards, so you can be confident that they will adhere to statutory requirements, especially in relation to Health and Safety. All boats have a shower/bath, toilet, fridge, adequate heating and lighting, and a basic hot water supply. Bed linen will be provided.

Enjoy England professional assessors visit every year to check all the facilities and award a quality score for every aspect, including the layout and design of each boat, the quality of the galley, the sleeping cabins, bathrooms and toilet, and the cleanliness. The service offered by the boatyard staff is also assessed.

Higher star-rated boat accommodation tends to have more spacious cabins, better-presented beds, better-equipped galleys and more sophisticated toilets! The ratio of toilets to guests will improve with the higher star ratings.

Certain additional facilities and services are required at the higher star levels, some of which may be important to you

TWO-STAR boats must provide:

- Radio/cassette player.

THREE-STAR boats must provide:

- Pump-out toilet
- Colour TV
- Central heating.

FOUR-STAR boats must provide:

- Cooker with oven, grill and four rings (two rings for four-berth boat).

FIVE-STAR boats must provide:

- Constant hot water
- Heating in bathroom
- 230V supply.

However, it is not enough to simply offer the above items to achieve the higher star ratings – the overall quality score must be achieved.

HOTEL BOATS

Hotel boats are assessed in the same way as hotels, with the assessor staying overnight every other year. A quality score is awarded for every aspect of the experience including the comfort of the bed, the quality of the food served on board, and, most importantly, the cleanliness. They also score the warmth of welcome and the level of care that each hotel boat offers its guests. Those that 'go the extra mile' to make every stay a special one, will be rewarded with high scores for quality.

All hotel boats have to offer the same level of facilities, except at five star, where there is a requirement for all beds to be at least 6ft in length.

Hotel boat ratings made easy

★ Simple, practical, no frills

★★ Well presented and well run

★★★ Good level of quality and comfort

★★★★ Excellent level of quality and comfort

★★★★★ Exceptional level of quality and comfort

CRUISERS

Barnes Brinkcraft ★★★–★★★★★
Cruiser
Riverside Road, Wroxham NR12 8UD
t (01603) 782625

Castle Craft Ltd ★★★
Cruiser
Reeds Lane, St Olaves, Great Yarmouth NR31 9HG
t (01493) 488675

Caversham Boat Service ★★–★★★
Cruiser
Frys Island, Thameside, Reading RG1 8DG
t (0118) 957 4323

City Boats (Highcraft) ★–★★★
Cruiser
Highcraft Marina, Griffin Lane, Thorpe Andrew, Norwich NR7 0SL
t (01603) 700324

Kris Cruisers ★★★★–★★★★★
Cruiser
The Waterfront, Southlea Road, Datchet SL3 9BU
t (01753) 543930

Norfolk Broads Direct – Faircraft Loynes ★★★★–★★★★★
Cruiser
The Bridge, Wroxham, Norwich NR12 8RX
t (01603) 782207

Norfolk Broads Direct – Herbert Woods ★★★–★★★★★
Cruiser
Herbert Woods, Haven, Potter Heigham NR29 5JD
t (01692) 670711

Sanderson Marine Craft Ltd ★★–★★★
Cruiser
Riverside Reedham, Norwich NR13 3TE
t (01493) 700242

HOTEL BOATS

Away4awhile ★★★
Hotel Boat
Away4awhile, 3 Brindley Place, Birmingham B1 2JB
t 0845 644 5144
e enquiries@away4awhile.com
w away4awhile.com

Duke & Duchess Hotel Boats ★★★★
Hotel Boat
9 Lyndale Close, Coventry CV5 8AE
t 07711 836441

Hotel Periwinkle ★★★★
Hotel Boat
1 Isabella Street, Longridge, Preston PR3 3WL
t 07747 017263

Kari.uk ★★★
Hotel Boat
Wharf 235266, Banbury Road, Summertown, Oxford OX2 7DL
t 07970 939725
e rich@kariuk.com
w kariuk.com

Narrowboat Hotel Company ★★★★
Hotel Boat
c/o Dorking Business Centre, 51 South Street, Dorking RH4 2JX
t 07836 600029

Reed Boats ★★★
Hotel Boat
2 Lyons Lodge, Colesbourne Road, Withington, Cheltenham GL54 4BH
t 07977 229103
e martin@reedboats.co.uk
w reedboats.co.uk

Thames & Chilterns Holiday Cruises ★★★★
Hotel Boat
Rothbury House, High Street, Staithes TS13 5BQ
t 07966 248079

Wood Owl Hotel Narrowboat ★★★
Hotel Boat
Traze-An-Pen, Sithney, Helston TR13 0RN
t (01326) 563554
e mikeandjenny@woodowl.co.uk
w woodowl.co.uk

NARROWBOATS

Acton Bridge – Black Prince Holidays ★★★★
Narrowboat
Bartington Wharf, Acton Bridge, Northwich CW8 4QU
t (01606) 852945
e Bholidays@aol.com
w black-prince.com

Alvechurch – Alvechurch Boat Centres ★★–★★★★★
Narrowboat
Scarfield Wharf, Alvechurch B48 7SQ
t (0121) 445 1133
e enquiries@alvechurch.com
w alvechurch.com

Alvecote Marina *Rating applied for*
Narrowboat
Robeys Lane, Tamworth B78 1AS
t (01827) 899022
e dick_holly@hotmail.com
w canaltime.com

Anderson Boats ★★★–★★★★
Narrowboat
Wych House Lane, Middlewich CW10 9BQ
t (01606) 833668

Anderton – Alvechurch Boat Centres Ltd ★★★–★★★★★
Narrowboat
Anderton Marina, Uplands Road, Anderton CW9 6AJ
t (01606) 79642
e enquiries@alvechurch.com
w alvechurch.com

Aqua Narrowboat (H2O) ★★★★
Narrowboat
Aqua Narrowboat Hire, 6 Old Hall, Willington DE65 6DT
t (01283) 704855
e admin@aquanarrowboathire.com
w aquanarrowboathire.com

Autherley – Napton Narrowboats ★★★★
Narrowboat
c/o Water Travel, Autherley Junction, Wolverhampton WV9 5HW
t (01926) 813644

Bath – Anglowelsh Boats ★★★–★★★★
Narrowboat
Sydney Wharf, Bathwick Hill, Bath BA2 4EL
t (01225) 447276

Beacon Park Boats ★★–★★★★★
Narrowboat
The Boathouse, Llanfoist, Abergavenny NP7 9NG
t (01873) 858277
e beaconparkboats@btconnect.com
w beaconparkboats.com

Blackwater Meadow Marina
Rating applied for
Narrowboat
Birch Road, Ellesmere SY12 9DD
t (01691) 624391
e dick_holly@hotmail.com
w canaltime.com

Bunbury – Anglowelsh Boats ★★★–★★★★
Narrowboat
Bunbury Lock, Bunbury, Tarporley CW6 9QB
t (01829) 260957

Cambrian Cruisers ★★★★
Narrowboat
Ty Newydd, Pencelli, Brecon LD3 7LJ
t (01874) 665315

Canal Boat Holiday Ltd ★★★★
Narrowboat
The Boatyard, High Street, Weedon NN7 4QD
t (01327) 340739

Canal Cruising Company ★★★–★★★★
Narrowboat
Crown Street, Stone ST15 8QN
t (01785) 813982
e mail@canalcruising.co.uk
w canalcruising.co.uk

Chirk – Black Prince Holidays ★★★★
Narrowboat
Chirk Marina, Whitehurst, Chirk LL14 5AD
t (01691) 774558
e Bholidays@aol.com
w black-prince.com

Chirk – Marine Cruises ★★★★
Narrowboat
Chirk Marina, Whitehurst, Chirk LL14 5AD
t (01691) 774558
e info@chirkmarina.co.uk
w chirkmarina.com

Claymoore Navigation Ltd ★★–★★★★
Narrowboat
The Wharf, Preston Brook, Warrington WA4 4BA
t (01928) 717273

Copt Heath Wharf ★★★★
Narrowboat
309 Barston Lane, Solihull B91 2SX
t (0121) 704 4464

Countrywide Cruisers (Brewood) Ltd ★★★-★★★★★
Narrowboat
The Wharf, Off Kiddemore Road, Brewood ST19 9BG
t (01902) 850166

Eynsham (Oxford) – Anglowelsh Boats ★★★-★★★★
Narrowboat
Boat Centre, Eynsham, Witney OX29 4DA
t (01865) 882235

Falkirk – Alvechurch Boat Centres Ltd ★★★★
Narrowboat
Falkirk Wheel, Lime Road, Tamfourhill, Falkirk FK1 4RS
t 07973 503916
e enquiries@alvechurch.com
w alvechurch.com

Falkirk – Black Prince Holidays ★★★★
Narrowboat
Falkirk Wheel, Lime Road, Tamfourhill, Falkirk FK1 4RS
t (0131) 449 3288
e Bholidays@aol.com
w black-prince.com

Fox Boats ★★★★-★★★★★
Narrowboat
10 Marina Drive, March, Cambs PE15 OAU
t (01354) 653998

Gailey – Viking Afloat ★★★★
Narrowboat
The Wharf, Watling Street, Gailey ST19 5PR
t (01905) 610650
e info@viking-afloat.com
w viking-afloat.com

Gayton – Alvechurch Boat Centres Ltd ★★★-★★★★★
Narrowboat
Alvechurch Boats, Gayton Marina, Blisworth Arm, Gayton NN7 3 ER
t (01604) 858685
e enquiries@alvechurch.com
w alvechurch.com

Grand Waterway Voyagers ★★-★★★
Narrowboat
Swan Lane Wharf, Stoke Heath, Coventry CV2 4QN
t (024) 7625 8864

Great Haywood – Anglowelsh Boats ★★★-★★★★
Narrowboat
Mill Lane, Great Haywood, Stafford ST16 0RG
t (01889) 881771

Heritage Narrowboats Ltd ★★★
Narrowboat
The Marina, Kent Green, Scholar Green, Stoke-on-Trent ST7 3JT
t (01782) 785700

Hilperton – Alvechurch Boat Centres Ltd ★★★-★★★★★
Narrowboat
Hilperton Marina, Hammond Way, Trowbridge BA14 8RS
t (01225) 765243

Lee Valley Boat Centre ★★-★★★★
Narrowboat
Old Nazeing Road, Broxbourne EN10 6LX
t (01992) 462085

Maestermyn Marine ★★★-★★★★★
Narrowboat
Maestermyn Marine, Ellesmere Road, Whittington, Owestry SY11 4NJ
t (01691) 662424
e enquiries@maestermyn.co.uk
w maestermyn.co.uk

Middlewich Narrowboats ★★★-★★★★
Narrowboat
Canal Terrace, Middlewich CW10 9BD
t (01606) 83240

Mid-Wales Narrowboats ★★★-★★★★★
Narrowboat
Maestermyn Marine, Ellesmere Road, Whittington, Owestry SY11 4NJ
t (01691) 650243
e enquiries@maestermyn.co.uk
w maestermyn.co.uk

Monkton Combe – Anglowelsh Boats ★★-★★★
Narrowboat
Dundas Enterprises, Brass Knocker Basin, Monkton Combe, Bath BA2 7JD
t (01225) 722292

Napton – Black Prince Holidays ★★★★
Narrowboat
Wigrams Turn Marina, Shuckburgh Road, Napton on the Hill CV47 8NL
t (01926) 817175
e Bholidays@aol.com
w black-prince.com

Napton Narrowboats ★★★-★★★★
Narrowboat
Napton Marina, Stockton CV47 8HX
t (01926) 813644

Norbury – Anglowelsh Boats ★★★-★★★★
Narrowboat
The Wharf, Norbury Junction, Norbury ST20 OPN
t (01785) 284292

Oxfordshire Narrowboats ★★★-★★★★
Narrowboat
Heyford Wharf, Station Road, Lower Heyford OX25 5PD
t (01869) 340348

Packet Boat – Alvechurch Boat Centres Ltd ★★★★-★★★★★
Narrowboat
Alvechurch Hire Base, Packet Boat Marina, Packet Boat Lane, Cowley UB8 2JJ
t (01895) 449851

Premier Canal Cruisers Ltd ★★★★
Narrowboat
PO Box 7259, Hinckley LE10 1YH
t 0800 161 3130
e sales@prosper123.com
w premiercanalcruisers.com

Redline Boats ★-★★★
Narrowboat
Goytre Wharf, Llanover, Abergavenny NP7 9EW
t (01873) 880516

Rose Narrowboats ★★-★★★★★
Narrowboat
Stretton Under Fosse, Rugby CV23 0PU
t (01788) 832449

Rugby – Viking Afloat
Rating applied for
Narrowboat
Rugby Wharf, Rugby CV21 1NR
t (01788) 562183
e info@viking-afloat.com
w viking-afloat.com

Sally Boats Ltd ★★-★★★★
Narrowboat
Bradford on Avon Marina, Trowbridge Road, Bradford-on-Avon BA15 1UD
t (01225) 864923

Shire Cruisers ★★★-★★★★
Narrowboat
The Wharf, Sowerby Bridge HX6 2AG
t (01422) 832712
e vb@shirecruisers.co.uk
w shirecruisers.co.uk

Silsden Boats Holidays Ltd
Rating applied for
Narrowboat
Canal Wharf, Elliott street, Keighly West BD20 0DE
t (01535) 653675
e info@silsdenboats.com
w silsdenboats.co.uk

Stoke on Trent – Black Prince Holidays ★★★★
Narrowboat
Festival Park Marina, Etruria, Stoke-on-Trent ST1 5PS
t (01782) 201981
e Bholidays@aol.com
w black-prince.com

Stoke on Trent – Marine Cruises ★★★★
Narrowboat
Festival Park Marina, Etruria, Stoke-on-Trent ST1 5PS
t (01782) 201981

Stoke Prior – Black Prince Holidays ★★★★
Narrowboat
Hanbury Road, Stoke Prior, Bromsgrove B60 4LA
t (01527) 575115

Swan Lane Wharf/Clubline Cruisers ★★★
Narrowboat
Swan Lane, Stoke Heath, Coventry CV2 4QN
t (024) 7625 8864

Swancraft Boat Services
★★★–★★★★★
Narrowboat
Benson Waterfront, Benson OX10 6SL
t (01481) 836700

Tardebigge – Anglowelsh Boats
★★–★★★★
Narrowboat
The Old Wharf, Tardebigge, Bromsgrove B60 1LR
t (01527) 873898
e bookings@anglowelsh.co.uk
w anglowelsh.co.uk

Trevor – Anglowelsh Boats
★★★–★★★★
Narrowboat
Canal Wharf, Trevor, Llangollen LL20 7TY
t (01978) 821749

Union Canal Carriers (Adventure Fleet) ★★–★★★★★
Narrowboat
Braunston Pump House, Dark Lane, Braunston NN11 7HJ
t (01788) 890784

Union Wharf Marina
Rating applied for
Narrowboat
Leicester Road, Market Harborough LE16 7AU
t (01858) 432123
e dick_holly@hotmail.com
w canaltime.com

Whitchurch – Viking Afloat ★★★★
Narrowboat
Wrexham Road, Whitchurch, Shropshire SY13 3AA
t (01948) 662012
e info@viking-afloat.com
w viking-afloat.com

Willow Wren Cruising Holidays
★★–★★★
Narrowboat
Rugby Wharf, Consul Road, Rugby CV21 1PB
t (01788) 562183
e narrowboats@willowren.co.uk
w willowren.co.uk

Wootton Wawen – Anglowelsh Boats
★★★–★★★★
Narrowboat
Canal Wharf, Wootton Wawen, Henley in Arden B95 6BZ
t (01564) 793427

Worcester – Viking Afloat ★★★★
Narrowboat
Lowesmoor Wharf, Worcester WR1 2RS
t (01905) 610660
e info@viking-afloat.com
w viking-afloat.com

Wrenbury – Alvechurch Boat Centres Ltd ★★★–★★★★★
Narrowboat
Wrenbury Mill, Wrenbury CW5 8HG
t (01270) 780544
e enquiries@alvechurch.com
w alvechurch.com

The Wyvern Shipping Co Ltd
★★★–★★★★★
Narrowboat
Rothschild Road, Linslade LU7 2TF
t (01525) 372355

Approved Caravan Holiday Homes

Approved caravan holiday homes are let as individual self-catering units and can be located on farms or holiday parks. All the facilities, including a bathroom and toilet, are contained within the caravan and all main services are provided. There are no star ratings, but all caravans are assessed annually to minimum standards.

BARNARD CASTLE
County Durham

Fairview Caravan
t (01833) 638635
e caravan@fairview1.freeserve.co.uk

BRIXHAM
Devon

C and R Caravans
t (01803) 856256
e ray@holidays-brixham.co.uk
w holidays-brixham.co.uk

BRIXHAM
Devon

We Want A Holiday
t (01803) 853465
e karyn@paranormality.com
w wewantaholiday.co.uk

BURLAWN
Cornwall

Pengelly Farm Caravan
t (01208) 814217
w pengellyfarm.co.uk

CHACEWATER
Cornwall

Little Acre
t (01872) 560517
e bobdewey@littleacre.fsbusiness.co.uk

COALEY
Gloucestershire

Ham Farm
t (01456) 860207
e enquiries@cotswoldfarmholidays.co.uk
w cotswoldfarmholidays.co.uk

COWES
Isle of Wight

Julie Dass, 15 Beachlands
t 07966 651822
e deancolor@aol.com

HIGH BENTHAM
North Yorkshire

Lane House Farm
t (01524) 261479

HOLME
Cumbria

Wych Elm Caravans
t (01524) 781449
e lakescaravans@mail.com
w lakescaravans.co.uk

LANSALLOS
Cornwall

Valleybrook Holidays
t (01503) 220493
e admin@valleybrookholidays.co.uk
w connexions.co.uk/valleybrook

LISKEARD
Cornwall

Swallows' Rest Mobile Home
t (01529) 363144
e tomdodge@ukonline.co.uk

TORVER
Cumbria

Scarr Head Caravans
t (01539) 441576
e info@scarrhead.co.uk

TOTNES
Devon

Barnston Caravan
t (01548) 521274

Further **information**

Enjoy England's **Quality Rose assessment scheme**

When you are looking for a place to stay, you need a rating system you can trust. Enjoy England's ratings are your clear guide to what to expect, in an easy-to-understand form.

Enjoy England professional assessors visit all properties every year, so you can be confident that your accommodation has been thoroughly checked and rated for quality before you make a booking.

Based on the internationally recognised rating of stars, the system puts great emphasis on quality, and reflects research that shows exactly what consumers are looking for when choosing self-catering accommodation. Ratings are awarded from one to five stars – the more stars, the higher the quality and the greater the range of facilities and services provided.

Star ratings

Star ratings are the sign of quality assurance, giving you the confidence to book the accommodation that meets your expectations. All self-catering accommodation that is awarded a star rating will meet the minimum standards – so you can be confident that you will find the basic services that you would expect, such as:

- Clear information prior to booking on all aspects of the accommodation including location, facilities, prices, deposit, policies on smoking, children and cancellation etc
- No shared facilities, with the exception of a laundry room in multi-unit sites
- All appliances and furnishings will meet product safety standards for self-catering accommodation, particularly regarding fire safety
- At least one smoke alarm in the unit and a fire blanket in the kitchen
- Clear information on emergency procedures, including who to contact
- Contact details for the local doctor, dentist, chemist etc
- All statutory obligations will be met including an annual gas check and public liability insurance.

Certain additional facilities and services are required at the higher star levels, some of which may be important to you:

TWO-STAR accommodation must provide:
- Single beds of 3ft width and double beds of 4ft 6in.

THREE-STAR accommodation must provide:
- Bed linen (with or without additional charge).

FOUR-STAR accommodation must provide:
- All advertised sleeping space in bedrooms (unless a studio)
- Bed linen included in the hire charge.

FIVE-STAR accommodation must provide:
- Full-size beds, including those for children
- At least two of the following items: tumble-dryer, telephone, Hi-Fi, video, DVD.

Some self-catering establishments offer a choice of accommodation units that may have different star ratings. In this case, the entry shows the range available.

Quality

The availability of additional facilities, such as a dishwasher or DVD, is not enough to achieve a higher star rating. Self-catering accommodation with a lower star rating may offer some or all of the above, but to achieve the higher star ratings, the overall quality score has to be reached and exacting standards have to be met in critical areas. Consumer research has shown these critical areas to be: cleanliness, bedrooms, bathrooms, kitchens and public areas.

Advice and information

Making a booking

When enquiring about accommodation, make sure you check prices, the quality rating and other important details. You will also need to state your requirements clearly and precisely, for example:

- Arrival and departure dates, with acceptable alternatives if appropriate
- The accommodation you need
- The number of people in your party and the ages of any children
- Special requirements, such as ground-floor bathroom, garden, cot.

Booking by letter or email

Misunderstandings can easily happen over the telephone, so do request a written confirmation, together with details of any terms and conditions.

Deposits

When you book your self-catering holiday, the proprietor will normally ask you to pay a deposit immediately, and then to pay the full balance before your holiday date.

The reason for asking you to pay in advance is to safeguard the proprietor in case you decide to cancel at a late stage, or simply do not turn up. He or she may have turned down other bookings on the strength of yours, and may find it hard to re-let if you cancel.

Cancellations

Legal contract

When you accept accommodation that is offered to you, by telephone or in writing, you enter a legally binding contract with the proprietor. This means that if you cancel your booking, fail to take up the accommodation or leave early, you will probably forfeit your deposit and may expect to be charged the balance at the end of the period booked if the place cannot be re-let.

You should be advised at the time of the booking of what charges would be made in the event of cancelling the accommodation or leaving early. If this is not mentioned you should ask so that further disputes can be avoided. Where you have already paid the full amount before cancelling, the proprietor is likely to retain the money. If the accommodation is re-let, the proprietor will make a refund, normally less the amount of the deposit.

And remember, if you book by telephone and are asked for your credit card number, you should check whether the proprietor intends charging your credit card account should you later cancel your reservation. A proprietor should not be able to charge your credit card account with a cancellation unless he or she has made this clear at the time of your booking and you have agreed. However, to avoid later disputes, we suggest you check whether this is the intention.

Insurance

There are so many reasons why you might have to cancel your holiday, which is why we strongly advise people to take out a cancellation insurance policy. In fact, many self-catering agencies now insist their customers take out a policy when they book their holiday.

Arrival time

If you know you will be arriving late in the evening, it is a good idea to say so when you book. If you are delayed on your way, a telephone call to say that you will be late would be appreciated.

It is particularly important to liaise with the proprietor about key collection as he or she may not be on site.

Bringing pets to England

Dogs, cats, ferrets and some other pet mammals can be brought into the UK from certain countries without having to undertake six months' quarantine on arrival provided they meet all the rules of the Pet Travel Scheme (PETS).

For full details, visit the PETS website at
w defra.gov.uk/animalh/quarantine/index.htm
or contact the PETS Helpline
t +44 (0)870 241 1710
e quarantine@defra.gsi.gov.uk
Ask for fact sheets which cover dogs and cats, ferrets or domestic rabbits and rodents.

What to expect

The proprietor/management is required to undertake the following:

- To maintain standards of guest care, cleanliness and service appropriate to the type of establishment;
- To describe accurately in any advertisement, brochure or other printed or electronic media, the facilities and services provided;
- To make clear to visitors exactly what is included in all prices quoted for accommodation, including taxes, and any other surcharges. Details of charges for additional services/facilities should also be made clear;
- To give a clear statement of the policy on cancellations to guests at the time of booking ie by telephone, fax, email, as well as information given in a printed format;
- To adhere to and not to exceed prices quoted at the time of booking for accommodation and other services;
- To advise visitors at the time of booking, and subsequently if any change, if the accommodation offered is in an unconnected annexe or similar and to indicate the location of such accommodation and any difference in comfort and/or amenities from accommodation in the establishment;
- To register all guests on arrival;
- To give each visitor on request details of payments due and a receipt, if required;
- To deal promptly and courteously with all enquiries, requests, bookings and correspondence from visitors;
- To ensure complaint handling procedures are in place and that complaints received are investigated promptly and courteously and that the outcome is communicated to the visitor;
- To give due consideration to the requirements of visitors with disabilities and visitors with special needs, and to make suitable provision where applicable;
- To provide public liability insurance or comparable arrangements and to comply with all applicable planning, safety and other statutory requirements;
- To allow an Enjoy England assessor reasonable access to the establishment on request, to confirm the VisitBritain Code of Conduct is being observed.

Comments and complaints

Information

The proprietors themselves supply the descriptions of their establishments and other information for the entries (except Enjoy England ratings and awards). They have all signed a declaration that their information conforms to the Trade Description Acts 1968 and 1972. VisitBritain cannot guarantee the accuracy of information in this guide, and accepts no responsibility for any error or misrepresentation.

All liability for loss, disappointment, negligence or other damage caused by reliance on the information contained in this guide, or in the event of bankruptcy or liquidation or cessation of trade of any company, individual or firm mentioned, is hereby excluded. We strongly recommend that you carefully check prices and other details when you book your accommodation.

Quality Rose signage

All establishments displaying a Quality Rose sign have to hold current membership of the Enjoy England Quality Rose assessment scheme. When an establishment is sold the existing rating cannot be automatically transferred to the new owner.

Problems

Of course, we hope you will not have cause for complaint, but problems do occur from time to time. If you are dissatisfied with anything, make your complaint to the management immediately. Then the management can take action at once to investigate the matter and put things right. The longer you leave a complaint, the harder it is to deal with it effectively.

In certain circumstances, VisitBritain may look into complaints. However, VisitBritain has no statutory control over establishments or their methods of operating. VisitBritain cannot become involved in legal or contractual matters or in seeking financial compensation.

If you do have problems that have not been resolved by the proprietor and which you would like to bring to our attention, please write to: Quality in Tourism, Farncombe House, Broadway, Worcestershire WR12 7LJ.

About the **guide entries**

Entries

All the accommodation featured in this guide has been assessed or has applied for assessment under Enjoy England's Quality Rose assessment scheme. Assessment automatically entitles establishments to a listing in this guide. Additionally proprietors may pay to have their establishment featured in either a standard entry (includes description, facilities and prices) or an enhanced entry (photograph and extended details).

Locations

Places to stay are generally listed under the town, city or village where they are located. If a place is in a small village, you may find it listed under a nearby town (providing it is within a seven-mile radius).

Place names are listed alphabetically within each regional section of the guide, along with the name of the ceremonial county they are in and their map reference. Complete addresses for rental properties are not given and the town(s) listed may be a distance from the actual establishment. Please check the precise location at the time of booking.

Map references

These refer to the colour location maps at the front of the guide. The first figure shown is the map number, the following letter and figure indicate the grid reference on the map. Only place names under which standard or enhanced entries (see above) feature appear on the maps. Some entries were included just before the guide went to press, so they do not appear on the maps.

Telephone numbers

Booking telephone numbers are listed below the contact address for each entry. Area codes are shown in brackets.

Prices

The prices shown are only a general guide; they were supplied to us by proprietors in summer 2006. Remember, changes may occur after the guide goes to press, so we strongly advise you to check prices when you book your accommodation.

Prices are shown in pounds sterling, including VAT where applicable, and are per unit per week.

Prices often vary through the year and may be significantly lower outside peak holiday weeks. You can get details of other bargain packages that may be available from the establishments themselves, regional tourism organisations or your local tourist information centre (TIC). Your local travel agent may also have information and can help you make bookings.

Opening period

If an entry does not indicate an opening period, please check directly with the proprietor.

Symbols

The at-a-glance symbols included at the end of each entry show many of the services and facilities available at each establishment. You will find the key to these symbols on the back-cover flap – open it out and check the meanings as you go.

Smoking

Some places prefer not to accommodate smokers, and in such cases the descriptions or symbols in each entry make this clear.

Pets

Many places accept guests with dogs, but we do advise that you check this when you book, and ask if there are any extra charges or rules about exactly where your pet is allowed. The acceptance of dogs is not always extended to cats and it is strongly advised that cat owners contact the establishment well in advance. Some establishments do not accept pets at all. Pets are welcome by arrangement where you see this symbol 🐕.

The quarantine laws have changed in England, and dogs, cats and ferrets are able to come into Britain from over 50 countries. For details of the Pet Travel Scheme (PETS) please turn to page 729.

Payment accepted

The types of payment accepted by an establishment are listed in the payment accepted section. If you plan to pay by card, check that the establishment will take your particular card before you book. Some proprietors will charge you a higher rate if you pay by credit card rather than cash or cheque. The difference is to cover the percentage paid by the proprietor to the credit card company. When you book by telephone, you may be asked for your credit card number as confirmation. But remember, the proprietor may then charge your credit card account if you cancel your booking. See under Cancellations on page 728.

Awaiting confirmation of rating

At the time of going to press some establishments featured in this guide had not yet been assessed for their rating for the year 2007 and so their new rating could not be included. Rating Applied For indicates this.

Getting around
England

England is a country of perfect proportions – big enough to find a new place to discover, yet small enough to guarantee it's within easy reach. Getting from A to B can be easier than you think...

Planning your journey

Make transportdirect.info your first portal of call! It's the ultimate journey-planning tool to help you find the best way from your home to your destination by car or public transport. Decide on the quickest way to travel by comparing end-to-end journey times and routes. You can even buy train and coach tickets and find out about flights from a selection of airports.

With so many low-cost domestic flights, flying really is an option. Just imagine, you could finish work in Bishop's Stortford and be in Newquay just three hours later for a fun-packed weekend!

You can island hop too, to the Isle of Wight or the Isles of Scilly for a relaxing break. No worries.

If you're travelling by car and want an idea of distances check out the mileage chart overleaf. Or let the train take the strain – the National Rail network is also shown overleaf.

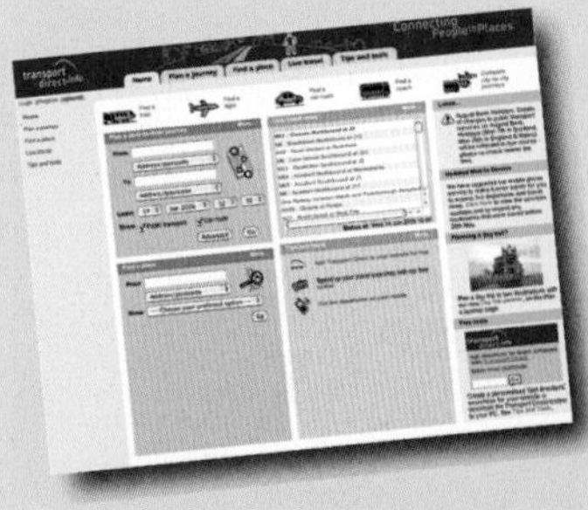

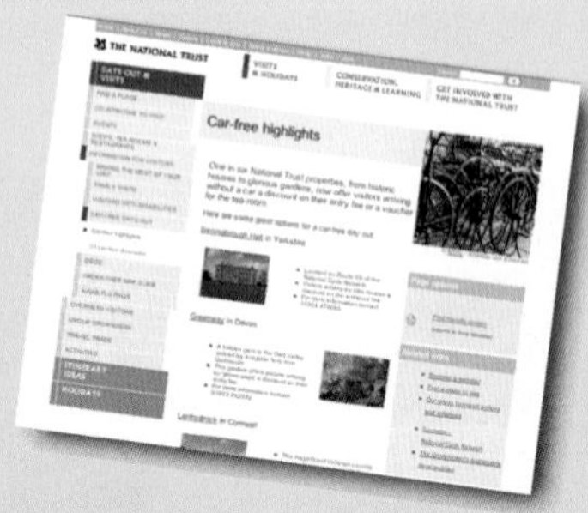

Think green

If you'd rather leave your car behind and travel by 'green transport' when visiting some of the attractions highlighted in this guide you'll be helping to reduce congestion and pollution as well as supporting conservation charities in their commitment to green travel.

The National Trust encourages visits made by non-car travellers. It offers admission discounts or a voucher for the tea room at a selection of its properties if you arrive on foot, cycle or public transport. (You'll need to produce a valid bus or train ticket if travelling by public transport.)

More information about The National Trust's work to encourage car-free days out can be found at nationaltrust.org.uk. Refer to the section entitled Information for Visitors.

To help you on your way you'll find a list of useful contacts at the end of this section.

In which region is the county I wish to visit?

If you know what English county you wish to visit you'll find it in the regional section shown below.

county	region
Bedfordshire	East of England
Berkshire	South East England
Bristol	South West England
Buckinghamshire	South East England
Cambridgeshire	East of England
Cheshire	England's Northwest
Cornwall	South West England
County Durham	North East England
Cumbria	England's Northwest
Derbyshire	East Midlands
Devon	South West England
Dorset	South West England
East Riding of Yorkshire	Yorkshire
East Sussex	South East England
Essex	East of England
Gloucestershire	South West England
Greater Manchester	England's Northwest
Hampshire	South East England
Herefordshire	Heart of England
Hertfordshire	East of England
Isle of Wight	South East England
Isles of Scilly	South West England
Kent	South East England
Lancashire	England's Northwest

county	region
Leicestershire	East Midlands
Lincolnshire	East Midlands
Merseyside	England's Northwest
Norfolk	East of England
North Yorkshire	Yorkshire
Northamptonshire	East Midlands
Northumberland	North East England
Nottinghamshire	East Midlands
Oxfordshire	South East England
Rutland	East Midlands
Shropshire	Heart of England
Somerset	South West England
South Yorkshire	Yorkshire
Staffordshire	Heart of England
Suffolk	East of England
Surrey	South East England
Tees Valley	North East England
Tyne and Wear	North East England
Warwickshire	Heart of England
West Midlands	Heart of England
West Sussex	South East England
West Yorkshire	Yorkshire
Wiltshire	South West England
Worcestershire	Heart of England

To help readers we do not refer to unitary authorities in this guide.

By **car** and by **train**

Distance chart

The distances between towns on the chart below are given to the nearest mile, and are measured along routes based on the quickest travelling time, making maximum use of motorways or dual-carriageway roads. The chart is based upon information supplied by the Automobile Association.

To calculate the distance in kilometres multiply the mileage by 1.6

For example: Brighton to Dover
82 miles x 1.6 =131.2 kilometres

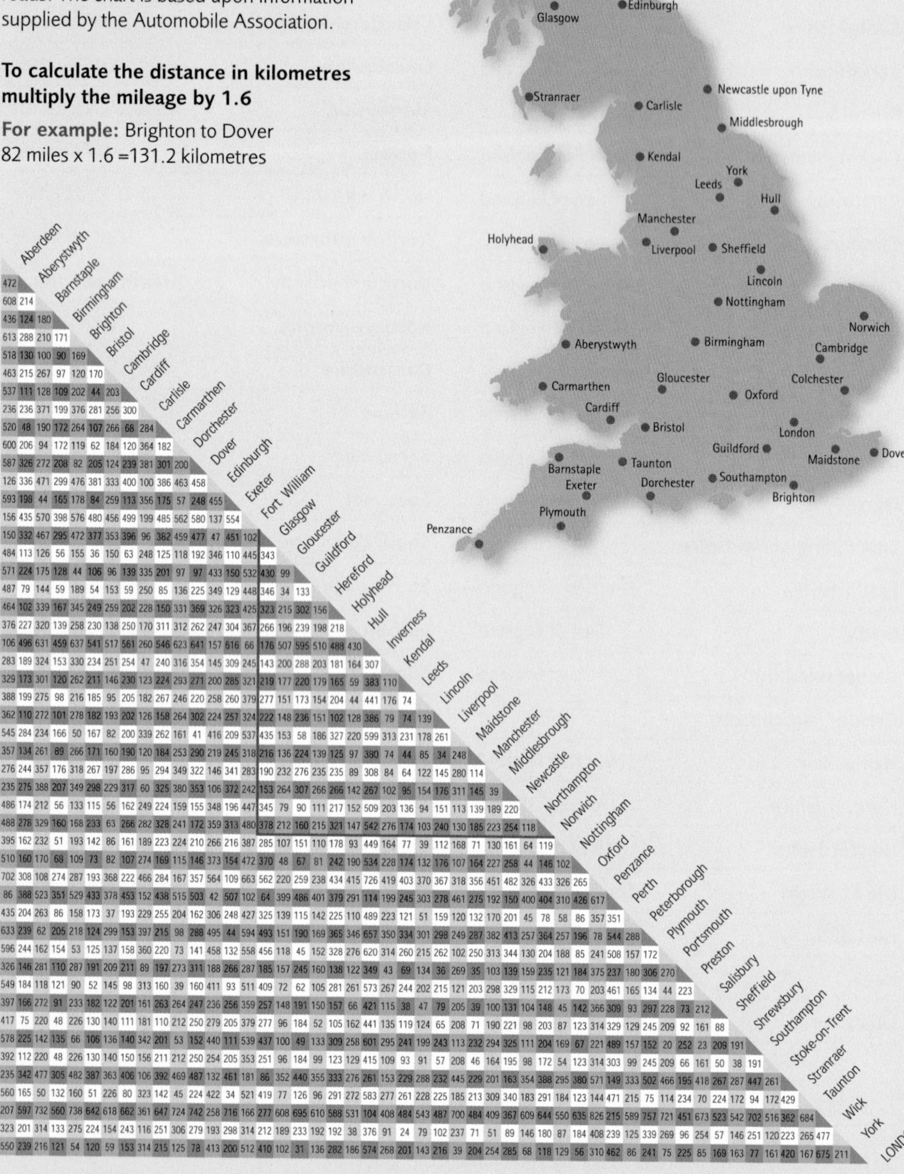

	Aberdeen	Aberystwyth	Barnstaple	Birmingham	Brighton	Bristol	Cambridge	Cardiff	Carlisle	Carmarthen	Dorchester	Dover	Edinburgh	Exeter	Fort William	Glasgow	Gloucester	Guildford	Hereford	Holyhead	Hull	Inverness	Kendal	Leeds	Lincoln	Liverpool	Maidstone	Manchester	Middlesbrough	Newcastle	Northampton	Norwich	Nottingham	Oxford	Penzance	Perth	Peterborough	Plymouth	Portsmouth	Preston	Salisbury	Sheffield	Shrewsbury	Southampton	Stoke-on-Trent	Stranraer	Taunton	Wick	York
Aberystwyth	472																																																
Barnstaple	608	214																																															
Birmingham	436	124	180																																														
Brighton	613	288	210	171																																													
Bristol	518	130	100	90	169																																												
Cambridge	463	215	267	97	120	170																																											
Cardiff	537	111	128	109	202	44	203																																										
Carlisle	236	236	371	199	376	281	256	300																																									
Carmarthen	520	48	190	172	264	107	266	68	284																																								
Dorchester	600	206	94	172	119	62	184	120	364	182																																							
Dover	587	326	272	208	82	205	124	239	381	301	200																																						
Edinburgh	126	336	471	299	476	381	333	400	100	386	463	458																																					
Exeter	593	198	44	165	178	84	259	113	356	175	57	248	455																																				
Fort William	156	435	570	398	576	480	456	499	199	485	562	580	137	554																																			
Glasgow	150	332	467	295	472	377	353	396	96	382	459	477	47	451	102																																		
Gloucester	484	113	126	56	155	36	150	63	248	125	118	192	346	110	445	343																																	
Guildford	571	224	175	128	44	106	96	139	335	201	97	97	433	150	532	430	99																																
Hereford	487	79	144	59	189	54	153	59	250	85	136	225	349	129	448	346	34	133																															
Holyhead	464	102	339	167	345	249	259	202	228	150	331	369	326	323	425	323	215	302	156																														
Hull	376	227	320	139	258	230	138	250	170	311	312	262	247	304	367	266	196	239	198	218																													
Inverness	106	496	631	459	637	541	517	561	260	546	623	641	157	616	66	176	507	595	510	488	430																												
Kendal	283	189	324	153	330	234	251	254	47	240	316	354	145	309	245	143	200	288	203	181	164	307																											
Leeds	329	173	301	120	262	211	146	230	123	224	293	271	200	285	321	219	177	220	179	165	59	383	110																										
Lincoln	388	199	275	98	216	185	95	205	182	267	246	220	258	260	379	277	151	173	154	204	44	441	176	74																									
Liverpool	362	110	272	101	278	182	193	202	126	158	264	302	224	257	324	222	148	236	151	102	128	386	79	74	139																								
Maidstone	545	284	234	166	50	167	82	200	339	262	161	41	416	209	537	435	153	58	186	327	220	599	313	231	178	261																							
Manchester	357	134	261	89	266	171	160	190	120	184	253	290	219	245	318	216	136	224	139	125	97	380	74	44	85	34	248																						
Middlesbrough	276	244	357	176	318	267	197	286	95	294	349	322	146	341	283	190	232	276	235	235	89	308	84	64	122	145	280	114																					
Newcastle	235	275	388	207	349	298	229	317	60	325	380	353	106	372	242	153	264	307	266	266	142	267	102	95	154	176	311	145	39																				
Northampton	486	174	212	56	133	115	56	162	249	224	159	155	348	196	447	345	79	90	111	217	152	509	203	136	94	151	113	139	189	220																			
Norwich	488	278	329	160	168	233	63	266	282	328	241	172	359	313	480	378	212	160	215	321	147	542	276	174	103	240	130	185	223	254	118																		
Nottingham	395	162	232	51	193	142	86	161	189	223	224	210	266	216	387	285	107	151	110	178	93	449	164	77	39	112	168	71	130	161	64	119																	
Oxford	510	160	170	68	109	73	82	107	274	169	115	146	373	154	472	370	48	67	81	242	190	534	228	174	132	176	107	164	227	258	44	146	102																
Penzance	702	308	108	274	287	193	368	222	466	284	167	357	564	109	663	562	220	259	238	434	415	726	419	403	370	367	318	356	451	482	326	433	326	265															
Perth	86	388	523	351	529	433	378	453	152	438	515	503	42	507	102	64	399	486	401	379	291	114	199	245	303	278	461	275	192	150	400	404	310	426	617														
Peterborough	435	204	263	86	158	173	37	193	229	255	204	162	306	248	427	325	139	115	142	225	110	489	223	121	51	159	120	132	170	201	45	78	58	86	357	351													
Plymouth	633	239	62	205	218	124	299	153	397	215	98	288	495	44	594	493	151	190	169	365	346	657	350	334	301	298	249	287	382	413	257	364	257	196	78	544	288												
Portsmouth	596	244	162	154	53	125	137	158	360	220	73	141	458	132	558	456	118	45	152	328	276	620	314	260	215	262	102	250	313	344	130	204	188	85	241	508	157	172											
Preston	326	146	281	110	287	191	209	211	89	197	273	311	188	266	287	185	157	245	160	138	122	349	43	69	134	36	269	35	103	139	159	235	121	184	375	237	180	306	270										
Salisbury	549	184	118	121	90	52	145	98	313	160	39	160	411	93	511	409	72	62	105	281	261	573	267	244	202	215	121	203	298	329	115	212	173	70	203	461	165	134	44	223									
Sheffield	397	166	272	91	233	182	122	201	161	263	264	247	236	256	359	257	148	191	150	157	66	421	115	38	47	79	205	39	100	131	104	148	45	142	366	309	93	297	228	73	212								
Shrewsbury	417	75	220	48	226	130	140	111	181	110	212	250	279	205	379	277	96	184	52	105	162	441	135	119	124	65	208	71	190	221	98	203	87	123	314	329	129	245	209	92	161	88							
Southampton	578	225	142	135	66	106	136	140	342	201	53	152	440	111	539	437	100	49	133	309	258	601	295	241	199	243	113	232	294	325	111	204	169	67	221	489	157	152	20	252	23	209	191						
Stoke-on-Trent	392	112	220	48	226	130	140	150	156	211	212	250	254	205	353	251	96	184	99	123	129	415	109	93	91	57	208	46	164	195	98	172	54	123	314	303	99	245	209	66	161	50	38	191					
Stranraer	235	342	477	305	482	387	363	406	106	392	469	487	132	461	181	86	352	440	355	333	276	261	153	229	288	232	445	229	201	163	354	388	295	380	571	149	333	502	466	195	418	267	287	447	261				
Taunton	560	165	50	132	160	51	226	80	323	142	45	224	422	34	521	419	77	126	96	291	272	583	277	261	228	225	185	213	309	340	183	291	184	123	144	471	215	75	114	234	70	224	172	94	172	429			
Wick	207	597	732	560	738	642	618	662	361	647	724	742	258	716	166	277	608	695	610	588	531	104	408	484	543	487	700	484	409	367	609	644	550	635	826	215	589	757	721	451	673	523	542	702	516	362	684		
York	323	201	314	133	275	224	154	243	116	251	306	279	193	298	314	212	189	233	192	192	38	376	91	24	79	102	237	71	51	89	146	180	87	184	408	239	125	339	269	96	254	57	146	251	120	223	265	477	
LONDON	550	239	216	121	54	120	59	153	314	215	125	78	413	200	512	410	102	31	136	282	186	574	268	201	143	216	39	204	254	285	68	118	129	56	310	462	86	241	75	225	85	169	163	77	161	420	167	675	211

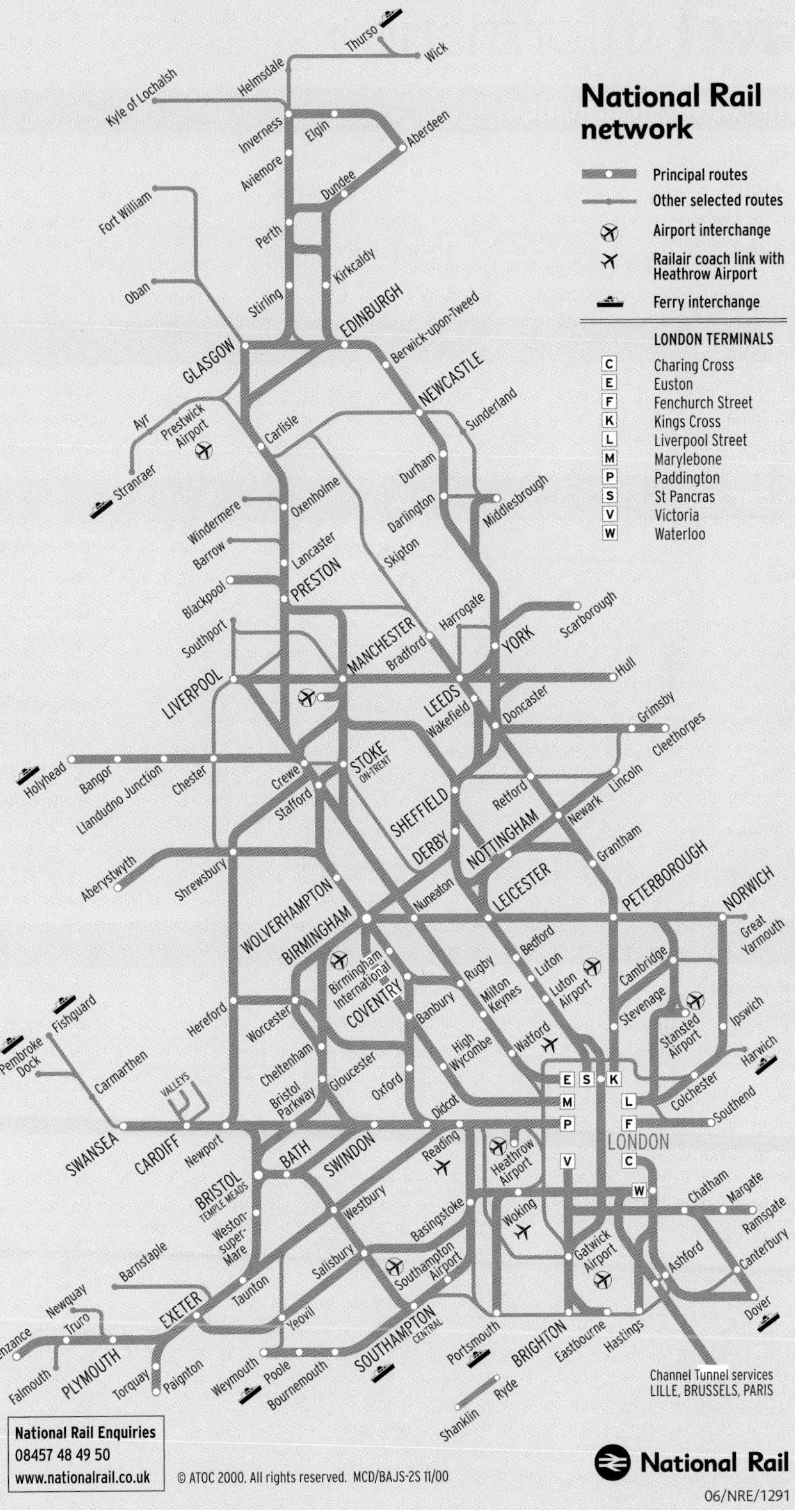
National Rail network
Principal routes
Other selected routes
Airport interchange
Railair coach link with Heathrow Airport
Ferry interchange
LONDON TERMINALS
C Charing Cross
E Euston
F Fenchurch Street
K Kings Cross
L Liverpool Street
M Marylebone
P Paddington
S St Pancras
V Victoria
W Waterloo
Thurso
Wick
Helmsdale
Kyle of Lochalsh
Inverness
Elgin
Aberdeen
Aviemore
Dundee
Fort William
Perth
Kirkcaldy
Oban
Stirling
EDINBURGH
Berwick-upon-Tweed
GLASGOW
NEWCASTLE
Sunderland
Ayr
Prestwick Airport
Carlisle
Stranraer
Durham
Oxenholme
Darlington
Middlesbrough
Windermere
Barrow
Lancaster
Skipton
PRESTON
Blackpool
Harrogate
Scarborough
Southport
MANCHESTER
Bradford
YORK
LIVERPOOL
LEEDS
Wakefield
Hull
Doncaster
Grimsby
Cleethorpes
Holyhead
Bangor
Llandudno Junction
Chester
Crewe
Stafford
STOKE ON-TRENT
SHEFFIELD
Retford
Lincoln
Newark
DERBY
NOTTINGHAM
Grantham
Aberystwyth
Shrewsbury
WOLVERHAMPTON
Nuneaton
LEICESTER
PETERBOROUGH
NORWICH
Great Yarmouth
BIRMINGHAM
Birmingham International
COVENTRY
Rugby
Bedford
Luton
Luton Airport
Cambridge
Milton Keynes
Banbury
Stevenage
Stansted Airport
Ipswich
Fishguard
Pembroke Dock
Hereford
Worcester
Cheltenham
High Wycombe
Watford
Harwich
Carmarthen
VALLEYS
Bristol Parkway
Gloucester
Oxford
Colchester
Didcot
Southend
SWANSEA
CARDIFF
Newport
BATH
SWINDON
Reading
Heathrow Airport
LONDON
BRISTOL TEMPLE MEADS
Westbury
Chatham
Margate
Ramsgate
Weston-super-Mare
Basingstoke
Woking
Barnstaple
Salisbury
Southampton Airport
Gatwick Airport
Ashford
Canterbury
Taunton
Newquay
EXETER
Yeovil
Dover
Truro
Penzance
SOUTHAMPTON CENTRAL
Portsmouth
BRIGHTON
Eastbourne
Hastings
Falmouth
PLYMOUTH
Torquay
Paignton
Weymouth
Poole
Bournemouth
Ryde
Shanklin
Channel Tunnel services
LILLE, BRUSSELS, PARIS
National Rail Enquiries
08457 48 49 50
www.nationalrail.co.uk
© ATOC 2000. All rights reserved. MCD/BAJS-2S 11/00
National Rail
06/NRE/1291

Travel information

general travel information

Streetmap	streetmap.co.uk	
Transport Direct	transportdirect.info	
Transport for London	tfl.gov.uk	(020) 7222 5600
Travel Services	departures-arrivals.com	
Traveline	traveline.org.uk	0870 608 2608

bus & coach

Megabus	megabus.com	0901 331 0031
National Express	nationalexpress.com	0870 580 8080
WA Shearings	washearings.com	(01942) 824824

car & car hire

AA	theaa.com	0870 600 0371
Green Flag	greenflag.co.uk	0845 246 1557
RAC	rac.co.uk	0870 572 2722
Alamo	alamo.co.uk	0870 400 4562
Avis	avis.co.uk	0870 010 0287
Budget	budget.co.uk	0844 581 2231
Easycar	easycar.com	0906 333 3333
Enterprise	enterprise.com	0870 350 3000*
Hertz	hertz.co.uk	0870 844 8844*
Holiday Autos	holidayautos.co.uk	
National	nationalcar.co.uk	0870 400 4581
Thrifty	thrifty.co.uk	(01494) 751500*

air

Airport information	a2btravel.com/airports	0870 888 1710
Air Southwest	airsouthwest.com	0870 043 4553
Blue Islands (Channel Islands)	blueislands.com	(01481) 727567
BMI	flybmi.com	0870 607 0555
BMI Baby	bmibaby.com	0871 224 0224
BNWA (Isle of Man to Blackpool)	flybnwa.co.uk	0800 083 7783
British Airways	ba.com	0870 850 9850
British International (Isles of Scilly to Penzance)	islesofscillyhelicopter.com	(01736) 363871
Eastern Airways	easternairways.com	0870 366 9100
Easyjet	easyjet.com	0871 244 2366
Flybe	flybe.com	0871 700 0535
Jet2.com	jet2.com	0871 226 1737
Ryanair	ryanair.com	0871 246 0000
Skybus (Isles of Scilly)	islesofscilly-travel.com	0845 710 5555
VLM	flyvlm.com	0871 666 5050

train

National Rail Enquiries	nationalrail.co.uk	0845 748 4950
The Trainline	trainline.co.uk	
UK train operating companies	rail.co.uk	
Arriva Trains	arriva.co.uk	0845 748 4950
c2c	c2c-online.co.uk	0845 601 4873*
Central Trains	centraltrains.co.uk	(0121) 634 2040
Chiltern Railways	chilternrailways.co.uk	0845 600 5165
First Capital Connect	firstcapitalconnect.co.uk	0845 748 4950
First Great Western	firstgreatwestern.co.uk	0845 700 0125*
Gatwick Express	gatwickexpress.co.uk	0845 850 1530
GNER	gner.co.uk	0845 722 5333
Heathrow Express	heathrowexpress.com	0845 600 1515
Hull Trains	hulltrains.co.uk	0845 071 0222
Island Line	island-line.co.uk	0845 748 4950
Merseyrail	merseyrail.org	0845 748 4950
Midland Mainline	midlandmainline.com	0845 712 5678
Northern Rail	northernrail.org	0845 748 4950
One Railway	onerailway.com	0845 600 7245
Silverlink	silverlink-trains.com	0845 601 4868
South Eastern Trains	southeasternrailway.co.uk	0845 748 4950
South West Trains	southwesttrains.co.uk	0845 600 0650
Southern	southernrailway.com	0845 127 2920
Stansted Express	stanstedexpress.com	0845 600 7245
Transpennine Express	tpexpress.co.uk	0845 748 4950
Virgin Trains	virgintrains.co.uk	0870 789 1234

ferry

Ferry information	sailanddrive.com	
Condor Ferries (Channel Islands)	condorferries.co.uk	0870 243 5140*
Steam Packet Company (Isle of Man)	steam-packet.com	0870 552 3523
Isles of Scilly Travel	islesofscilly-travel.co.uk	0845 710 5555
Red Funnel (Isle of Wight)	redfunnel.co.uk	0870 444 8898
Wight Link (Isle of Wight)	wightlink.co.uk	0870 582 7744

Phone numbers listed are for general enquiries unless otherwise stated.

* Booking line only

National cycle network

Sections of the National Cycle Network are shown on the maps in this guide. The numbers on the maps will appear on the signs along your route 3. Here are some tips about finding and using a route.

- **Research and plan your route online**
  Log on to **sustrans.org.uk** and clink on 'Get cycling' to find information about routes in this guide or other routes you want to use.
- **Order a route map**
  Useful, easy-to-use maps of many of the most popular routes of the National Cycle Network are available from Sustrans, the charity behind the Network. These can be purchased online or by mail order – visit sustransshop.co.uk or call 0845 113 0065.
- **Order Cycling in the UK**
  The official guide to the National Cycle Network gives details of rides all over the UK, detailing 148 routes and profiles of 43 days rides on traffic-free paths and quiet roads. Perfect for those new to cycling or with young families.

ROUTE NUMBER	ROUTE/MAP NAME	START/END OF ROUTE
South West		
3	The West Country Way	Bath & Bristol – Padstow
3 & 32	The Cornish Way	Bude – Land's End
South East		
5	West Midlands	Oxford – Derby via Birmingham
1, 2 & 18	Garden of England	Dover – London – Hastings
East of England		
1	East of England pack	Harwich – Fakenham – Hull
Heart of England		
5 & 54	West Midlands	Oxford – Derby via Birmingham
North East England		
1	Coast & Castles	Newcastle upon Tyne – Berwick-upon-Tweed – Edinburgh
10	Reivers	Tyne – Kielder – Cumbria
68	Pennine Cycleway (North)	Appleby-in-Westmorland or Penrith – Berwick-upon-Tweed
7, 14 & 71	C2C – Sea to Sea	Whitehaven/Workington – Sunderland or Newcastle upon Tyne
72	Hadrian's Cycleway	Ravenglass to Tynemouth/South Shields
Yorkshire and North West England		
62 & 65	Trans Pennine Trail Pack	Yorkshire – North Sea
		Irish Sea – Yorkshire
		Derbyshire – Yorkshire

To order any of the above maps call Sustrans **0845 113 0065** or visit **sustransshop.co.uk**.

A selection of events for 2007

This is a selection of the many cultural, sporting and other events that will be taking place throughout England during 2007. For a more comprehensive list, visit **enjoyengland.com/events**.

Please note, as changes often occur after press date, it is advisable to confirm the date and location before travelling.

January

1 Jan
New Year's Day Parade
Parliament Square to Berkeley Street, London SW1 to W1
(020) 8566 8586
londonparade.co.uk

5–14 Jan
London Boat Show
ExCeL London, Royal Victoria Dock, London E16
londonboatshow.com

11–14 Jan
Autosport International
National Exhibition Centre, Birmingham, West Midlands
0870 909 4133
autosport-international.com

February

1–28 Feb
Darwin Festival
Various venues, Shrewsbury, Shropshire
(01743) 281200
darwinshrewsbury.org

14–18 Feb
Jorvik Viking Festival
Various venues, York, North Yorkshire
(01904) 543413

March

8–11 Mar
Crufts
National Exhibition Centre, Birmingham, West Midlands
the-kennel-club.org.uk

9 Mar–1 Apr
Ideal Home Show
Earls Court Exhibition Centre, London SW5
idealhomeshow.co.uk

16–18 Mar
The Ordnance Survey Outdoors Show
National Exhibition Centre, Birmingham, West Midlands
(020) 7471 1082
theoutdoorsshow.co.uk

28–29 Mar
Somerley Park International Horse Trials
Somerley, Ringwood, Hampshire
(01425) 461744
eleda.co.uk

April

Apr/May*
Peak District Walking Festival
Various venues
(01298) 25106
visitpeakdistrict.com

5–9 Apr
Nantwich Jazz, Blues & Music Festival
Various venues, Nantwich, Cheshire
(01270) 610983
nantwichjazz.com

7–9 Apr
Chester Food and Drink Festival
Various venues, Chester, Cheshire
(01244) 402111
chesterfoodanddrink.com

7–22 Apr
Taste Lancashire
Various venues
(01995) 642255
visitlancashire.com

---

7 Apr
Oxford and Cambridge Boat Race
River Thames, London
theboatrace.org

---

22 Apr
Flora London Marathon
Greenwich Park to The Mall, London
(020) 7902 0200
london-marathon.co.uk

26–29 Apr
Harrogate Spring Flower Show
Great Yorkshire Showground, Harrogate, North Yorkshire
(01423) 561049
flowershow.org.uk

May

1–31 May*
International Cider & Perry Competition
Hereford Cider Museum, Herefordshire
(01432) 354207
cidermuseum.co.uk

---

1 May
King's Lynn May Garland Procession
Various venues, King's Lynn, Norfolk
(01553) 768930
thekingsmorris.co.uk

5–27 May
Brighton Festival
Various venues, Brighton, East Sussex
(01273) 709709
brighton-festival.org.uk

5–7 May
Dales Festival of Food and Drink
Various venues, Leyburn, North Yorkshire
(01969) 624761
dalesfestivaloffood.org

---

5 May
Spalding Flower Parade
Spalding, Lincolnshire
(01775) 724843
flowerparade.org

10–13 May
Royal Windsor Horse Show
Windsor Home Park, Berkshire
(01753) 860633
royal-windsor-horse-show.co.uk

---

13 May
Northumbrian Water University Boat Race
River Tyne, Quayside, Newcastle upon Tyne, Tyne and Wear
(0191) 433 3820
gateshead.gov.uk

17–19 May
Devon County Show
Westpoint Exhibition Centre, Clyst St Mary
(01392) 446000
devoncountyshow.co.uk

---

18 May–3 Jun
Bath International Music Festival
Various venues, Bath, Somerset
(01225) 463362
bathmusicfest.org.uk

---

19 May–3 Jun
Lincolnshire Wolds Walking Festival
Various venues
(01507) 609289
lincswolds.org.uk

22–26 May
Chelsea Flower Show
Royal Hospital, London SW3
(020) 7649 1885
rhs.org.uk

---

25 May–10 Jun
Salisbury Festival
Various venues, Salisbury, Wiltshire
(01722) 332977
salisburyfestival.co.uk

26–27 May
Hertfordshire County Show
Herts County Showground, Redbourn
(01582) 792676
hertsshow.com

---

28 May
Northumberland County Show
Tynedale Park, Corbridge
(01697) 747848
northcountyshow.co.uk

---

30 May–2 Jun
Royal Bath & West Show
Bath & West Showground, Shepton Mallet, Somerset
(01749) 822200
bathandwest.com

30–31 May
Suffolk Show
Trinity Park, Ipswich
(01473) 707110
suffolkshow.co.uk

June

Jun*
Isle of Wight Festival
Seaclose Park, Newport
0870 532 1321
isleofwightfestival.com

---

1 Jun–31 Aug
South Tyneside Summer Festival
Various venues, South Shields
(01914) 247985
southtyneside.info

---

4 Jun–25 Aug
Stamford Shakespeare Festival
Rutland Open Air Theatre, Tolethorpe Hall, Little Casterton, Rutland
(01780) 756133
stamfordshakespeare.co.uk

7–9 Jun
Royal Cornwall Show
Royal Cornwall Showground, Wadebridge
(01208) 812183
royalcornwall.co.uk

9–10 Jun
Durham Regatta
River Wear, Durham, County Durham
(0191) 386 4118

10 Jun
The Cosford Air Show
Royal Air Force Museum, Cosford, Suffolk
(01902) 377922
cosfordairshow.co.uk

11 Jun–19 Aug
Royal Academy Summer Exhibition
Burlington House, Piccadilly, London W1
(020) 7300 8000
royalacademy.org.uk

15–17 Jun
Three Counties Countryside Show
Three Counties Showground, Malvern, Worcestershire
(01684) 584900
threecounties.co.uk

16–17 Jun
Althorp Literary Festival
Althorp, Northampton, Northamptonshire
(01604) 770107
althorp.com

16 Jun
Trooping the Colour
Horseguards Parade, Whitehall, London SW1
royal.gov.uk

19–24 Jun*
Royal Ascot
Ascot Racecourse, Berkshire
0870 727 1234
royalascot.co.uk

19–20 Jun
Cheshire County Show
Tabley, Knutsford
(01565) 722050
cheshirecountyshow.org.uk

25 Jun–8 Jul
Wimbledon Lawn Tennis Championships
All England Lawn Tennis Club, London SW19
(020) 8946 2244
wimbledon.org

26 Jun–8 Jul
International Byron Festival
Various venues, Hucknall, Nottinghamshire
(01159) 664367
internationalbyronsociety.org

27 Jun–1 Jul
Alnwick Fair
Alnwick, Northumberland
(01665) 711397

27–28 Jun
Royal Norfolk Show
Norfolk Showground, New Costessey, Norwich
(01603) 748931
royalnorfolkshow.co.uk

30 Jun–1 Jul
Sunderland International Kite Festival
Northern Area Playing Fields, Washington, Sunderland, Tyne and Wear
(01915) 148443
sunderland-kites.co.uk

30 Jun
Pride 2007
Various venues, London
pridelondon.org

July

Jul*
Goodwood Festival of Speed
Goodwood Park, Chichester, West Sussex
(01243) 755055
goodwood.co.uk

4–8 Jul
Henley Royal Regatta
Henley-on-Thames, Oxfordshire
(01491) 572153
hrr.co.uk

6–22 Jul
Buxton Festival
Various venues, Buxton, Derbyshire
(01298) 70395
buxtonfestival.co.uk

7–8 Jul
City Of Durham Summer Festival
Various venues, Durham, County Durham
(0191) 301 8819
durhamtourism.co.uk

8 Jul
Tour de France Stage 1 London to Canterbury
Various venues, Canterbury, Kent
(020) 7222 1234
tourdefrancelondon.com

10–12 Jul
The Great Yorkshire Show
Great Yorkshire Showground, Harrogate, North Yorkshire
(01423) 541000
greatyorkshireshow.com

13 Jul–8 Sep
The Proms
Royal Albert Hall, London SW7
(020) 7765 5575
bbc.co.uk/proms

13–15 Jul
Whitley Bay International Jazz Festival
Menzies Silverlink Hotel, Wallsend, Tyne and Wear
(0191) 252 3505
whitleybayjazzfest.org

16–17 Jul*
Godiva Festival
Memorial Park, Coventry, West Midlands
(024) 7622 7264
visitcoventry.co.uk/godiva

20–22 Jul
Royal Lancashire Agricultural Show
Salesbury Hall, Ribchester
(01254) 813769
visitlancashire.com

25–29 Jul
Longines Royal International Horse Show
All England Jumping Course, Hickstead, Haywards Heath, West Sussex
(01273) 834315
hickstead.co.uk

25 Jul
Nantwich South Cheshire Show
Dorfold Hall, Nantwich, Cheshire
(01457) 876198
nantwichshow.co.uk

27–29 Jul
Gateshead Summer Flower Show
Gateshead Central Nurseries, Tyne and Wear
(0191) 433 3838
gateshead.gov.uk

28–29 Jul
Sunderland International Air Show
Seafront, Sunderland, Tyne and Wear
(0191) 553 2000
sunderland.gov.uk/airshow

28–29 Jul*
WOMAD Festival
Rivermead, Reading, Berkshire
(0118) 960 6060
womad.org/reading

28 Jul
Cleveland Show
Stewart Park, Middlesbrough, Tees Valley
(01642) 312231
middlesbrough.gov.uk

30 Jul–5 Aug
Robin Hood Festival
Sherwood Forest Visitor Centre, Edwinstowe, Nottinghamshire
(01623) 823202
robinhood.co.uk

31 Jul–4 Aug*
Glorious Goodwood
Goodwood Racecourse, Chichester, West Sussex
0800 018 8191
goodwood.co.uk

August

2–5 Aug
The Big Chill Festival
Eastnor Castle, Ledbury, Herefordshire
(020) 7684 2020
bigchill.net

3–10 Aug
Sidmouth Folk Week
Various venues, Sidmouth, Devon
(01395) 516441
sidmouthfolkweek.co.uk

3–5 Aug
Glastonbury Abbey Musical Extravaganza
Glastonbury, Somerset
(01458) 834596
glastonburyfestivals.co.uk

4–11 Aug
Cowes Week
The Solent, Cowes, Isle of Wight
(01983) 295744
skandiacowesweek.co.uk

18–19 Aug*
Northampton Balloon Festival
Racecourse Park, Northampton, Northamptonshire
(01604) 838222
northamptonballoonfestival.com

18–19 Aug
V Festival
Weston Park, Weston-under-Lizard, Shifnal, Shropshire
0871 220 0260
vfestival.com

24–26 Aug*
Carling Weekend Leeds Festival
Bramham Park, Leeds, West Yorkshire
0870 060 3775

26–27 Aug
Notting Hill Carnival
Ladbroke Grove area, London W11
(020) 8964 0544

29 Aug–2 Sep
Great Dorset Steam Fair
South Down Farm, Tarrant Hinton
(01258) 860361
gdsf.co.uk

31 Aug–3 Sep
Pendle Walking Festival
Various venues, Pendle, Lancashire
(01282) 661685
visitlancashire.com

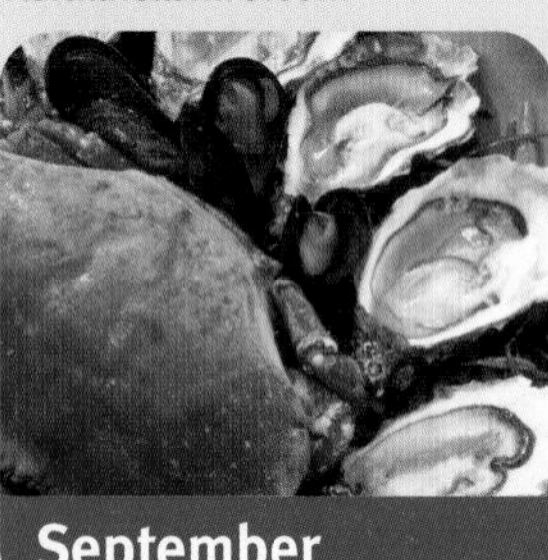

September

Sep*
Artsfest
Various venues, Birmingham, West Midlands
0870 225 0127
artsfest.org.uk

Sep*
Ludlow & the Marches Food and Drink Festival
Various venues, Ludlow, Shropshire
(01584) 873957
foodfestival.co.uk

1–2 Sep
English Wine Festival
New Hall Vineyard, Purleigh, Maldon, Essex
(01621) 828343
newhallwines.co.uk

1 Sep
Oyster Festival
The Waterfront, Maldon, Essex
(01621) 856503
hidden-treasures.co.uk

6–9 Sep
The 2nd Pennine Lancashire Festival of Food & Drink
Various venues across the West Pennine Moors
(01254) 683563
visitlancashire.com

7–23 Sep
Wirksworth Festival
Various venues, Wirksworth, Derbyshire
(01629) 824003
wirksworthfestival.co.uk

14–23 Sep
Southampton Boat Show
Mayflower Park, Southampton, Hampshire
(01784) 472222
southamptonboatshow.com

14–22 Sep
Hexham Abbey Festival
Tynedale, Northumberland
(01661) 843347
hexhamabbey.org.uk/festival

15–16 Sep
The Mayor's Thames Festival
Westminster Bridge to Tower Bridge, London SW1 & SE1
thamesfestival.org

22 Sep–1 Oct
York Festival of Food and Drink
Various venues, York, North Yorkshire
(01904) 466688
yorkfestivaloffoodanddrink.com

October

Oct*
East Midlands Food Festival
Various venues, Leicestershire
(01664) 562971
eastmidlandsfoodfestival.co.uk

Oct–Nov*
London Film Festival
Various venues, London
(020) 7928 3232
lff.org.uk

5–14 Oct
Ideal Home Show
Earls Court Exhibition Centre, London SW5
idealhomeshow.co.uk

5–7 Oct
Stoke on Trent Ceramics Festival
Various venues, Stoke-on-Trent, Staffordshire
(01782) 236000
visitstoke.co.uk

6–14 Oct
Hull Fair
Hull, East Riding of Yorkshire
(01482) 615624

31 Oct–4 Nov
Blackpool Illuminations
Blackpool Promenade, Lancashire
visitblackpool.com

November

5 Nov
Tar Barrels
Ottery St Mary, Devon
(01404) 813964
otterytourism.org.uk

10 Nov
Lord Mayor's Show
City of London
(020) 7606 3030
lordmayorsshow.org

16 Nov–23 Dec
Frankfurt Christmas Market
Various venues, Birmingham, West Midlands
(0121) 202 5000
beinbirmingham.com

23–26 Nov
St Nicholas Fayre
Various venues, York, North Yorkshire
(01904) 554427

29 Nov–2 Dec
Worcester Christmas Fayre
Various venues, Worcester, Worcestershire
(01905) 726311
worcestershire-tourism.org

December

Dec*
Masters Tennis
Royal Albert Hall, London SW7
(020) 7589 8212
themasterstennis.com

1–2 Dec*
City of Durham Christmas Festival
Various venues, Durham, County Durham
(0191) 301 8819
durhamtourism.co.uk

6–9 Dec
Lincoln Christmas Market
Lincoln Market, Lincolnshire
(01522) 873213
lincoln.gov.uk

* provisional date at time of going to press

National Accessible **Scheme index**

Establishments participating in the National Accessible Scheme are listed below. At the front of the guide you can find information about the scheme. Establishments in bold have a detailed entry in this guide. Establishments are listed alphabetically by place name within each region.

Mobility level 1

Mobility level 1 continued

Mobility level 1 continued

Mobility level 2

Establishments in bold have a detailed entry in this guide.

Mobility level 2 continued

Mobility level 2 continued

Mobility level 3 Independent

Establishments in bold have a detailed entry in this guide.

Mobility level 3 Independent continued

Mobility level 3 Assisted

Access Exceptional Independent

Access Exceptional Assisted

Hearing impairment level 1

Hearing impairment level 2

Visual impairment level 1

Visual impairment level 2

Establishments in bold have a detailed entry in this guide.

Walkers and cyclists **welcome**

Establishments participating in the Walkers Welcome and Cyclists Welcome schemes are listed below. They provide special facilities and actively encourage these recreations. Establishments in bold have a detailed entry in this guide. Place names are listed alphabetically within each region.

Walkers Welcome

Place	Establishment	Page
Aspatria England's Northwest	Big White House ★★★	448
Bridekirk England's Northwest	Anns Hill ★★★★★	451
Chipping England's Northwest	Wolfen Mill Country Retreats ★★★★-★★★★★	454
Chipping England's Northwest	Judd Holmes BArn ★★★★	454
Cockermouth England's Northwest	Ghyll Yeat ★★★★	454
***Dent* England's Northwest**	**Middleton's Cottage and Fountain Cottage ★★★**	**51**
Diggle England's Northwest	Diggle House Farm ★★★	458
Edenhall England's Northwest	Eden House Loft ★★★★	458
***Eskdale* England's Northwest**	**Randle How ★★★★**	**52**
Gisburn England's Northwest	Coverdale Farm ★★★★	460
Haughton England's Northwest	Rookery Cottage ★★★	463
Hawkshead England's Northwest	Hatter's Cottage ★★★	464
***High Lane* England's Northwest**	**Ty Coch ★★★★**	**57**
Hutton Roof England's Northwest	Dukes Meadow ★★★	465
Littleborough England's Northwest	Long Lees Farm Cottage ★★★★	473
***Moorhouse* England's Northwest**	**Low Moor House ★★★★**	**67**
Newlands England's Northwest	Bawd Hall ★★★★★	476
Oldham England's Northwest	Clifton Cottage ★★★	476
Rimington England's Northwest	Raikes Barn ★★★★	478
***Rochdale* England's Northwest**	**Pennine Cottages ★★★**	**69**
Rossendale England's Northwest	The Old Stables, Tippett Farm ★★★★	478
Seathwaite England's Northwest	Hall Dunnerdale Farm Holiday Cottages ★★★-★★★★	480
Silloth England's Northwest	Silloth Love Shack ★★	480
Staffield England's Northwest	Staffield Hall Country Retreats ★★★★★	482
***Thornley* England's Northwest**	**Loudview Barn ★★★★**	**71**
Thornthwaite England's Northwest	Comb Beck ★★★	482
***Worston* England's Northwest**	**Angram Green Holiday Cottages ★★★★**	**75**
Alnwick North East England	Herring Sheds Cottage ★★★★★	494
Alnwick North East England	The Old Smithy ★★★★	494
Alwinton North East England	Fellside Cottage ★★★★	494
Barnard Castle North East England	Boot and Shoe Cottage ★★★★	495
Barnard Castle North East England	East Briscoe Farm Cottages ★★★★	495

Walkers Welcome continued

Establishments in bold have a detailed entry in this guide.

Walkers Welcome continued

Walkers Welcome continued

Location	Establishment	Page
Snettisham East of England	Old Farm House Cottage ★★★	576
Stratford St Andrew East of England	Toad Hall Flat ★★★	579
Wingfield East of England	Beech Farm Maltings ★★★★	583
Wisbech East of England	Common Right Barns ★★★★	583
Woodbridge East of England	Quayside Cottage ★★★★	583
Worstead East of England	Woodcarvers Barn ★★★★	583
Alton South East England	**Green Farm ★★★★**	278
Bicester South East England	**Stoke Lyne Farm Cottages ★★★★**	284
Cowes South East England	221 Gurnard Pines ★★★★	592
Godshill South East England	Lake View ★★★★	597
Godshill South East England	The Log Cabin ★★★★	597
Hawkhurst South East England	**4 Alma Terrace ★★★★**	299
Hollingbourne South East England	The Boat House ★★★★	599
Lyndhurst South East England	**Bay Tree Cottage ★★★★**	304
Meopham South East England	**Feathercot Lodge ★★★★**	305
Oxford South East England	**Cherbridge Cottage ★★★★★**	308
Rotherfield South East England	**Medway Farm Barn Cottage ★★★★**	310
Sandwich South East England	Duck Cottage ★★★★	607
Shorwell South East England	Combe Barn ★★★★	608
Watchfield South East England	The Coach House ★★★★	612
West Marden South East England	The Old Stables, West Marden ★★★★★	612
Yarmouth South East England	Waterside Villa ★★★	614
Bampton South West England	**Three Gates Farm ★★★★**	335
Batcombe South West England	The Coach House at Boords Farm ★★★★	617
Bath South West England	**Church Farm Country Cottages ★★★★**	336
Bath South West England	Forum Square ★★★★	617
Bath South West England	Nailey Cottages ★★★★	617
Batheaston South West England	**Avondale Riverside ★★★★-★★★★★**	337
Bishop Sutton South West England	The Trebartha ★★★★	619
Blackawton South West England	Chuckle Too ★★★	620
Broadoak South West England	Stoke Mill Farm ★★★	626
Callington South West England	Berrio Mill ★★★★	628
Charmouth South West England	Knapp Cottages – K4313 ★★★★	630
Cheddar South West England	**Spring Cottages ★★★★**	352
Chipping Campden South West England	Honeysuckle Cottage ★★★★	632
Coxbridge South West England	Lower Coxbridge House ★★★	636
Dorchester South West England	Christmas Cottage ★★★	639
Dulverton South West England	Anstey Mills Cottages ★★★★	640
Helston South West England	**Tregoose Farmhouse ★★★★**	370
Helston South West England	**Mudgeon Vean Farm Holiday Cottages ★★★**	370
Leedstown South West England	Little Pengelly ★★★-★★★★	655
Looe South West England	Hendra Farm Cottages ★★★★	657
Luccombe South West England	Wychanger ★★★★	658
Lyme Regis South West England	Bramcote Garden Apartment ★★★★	660
Lyme Regis South West England	3 Dolphin Cottages ★★★	659
Moretonhampstead South West England	**Budleigh Farm ★★-★★★**	389
Mousehole South West England	Poldark Cottage ★★★	667
North Tamerton South West England	Hill Cottage ★★★★	670
Okehampton South West England	East Hook Holiday Cottages ★★-★★★★	671
Pancrasweek South West England	**Tamarstone Farm ★★★**	397
Pancrasweek South West England	Wooda Cottage ★★	677
Parkham South West England	Cottages For The Connoisseur ★★★★★	677

Establishments in bold have a detailed entry in this guide.

Walkers Welcome continued

Cyclists Welcome

Cyclists Welcome continued

Location	Establishment	Page
Barnard Castle North East England	Hauxwell Grange Cottages (The Stone Byre and Curlew Cottage) ★★★★	495
Berwick-upon-Tweed North East England	Newt Cottage ★★★★	496
Bingfield North East England	The Hytte ★★★★★	496
Cornriggs North East England	Cornriggs Cottages ★★★★	497
Craster North East England	Craster Pine Lodges ★★★★	498
Craster North East England	Rock Ville ★★★★	498
Fourstones North East England	Rosebank Cottage ★★★	499
Haltwhistle North East England	Old High House Chapel ★★★	499
Langley-on-Tyne North East England	The Waiting Room ★★★★	500
Lucker North East England	Lucker Mill ★★★★★	501
Lucker North East England	Lucker Hall Steading ★★★★–★★★★★	501
Mainsforth North East England	Swallow Cottage ★★★★	501
Morpeth North East England	The Carriage House ★★★★★	501
Morpeth North East England	**Meldon Park ★★★**	101
Norham North East England	Norcot Cottage ★★★★	502
Wall North East England	Kiln Rigg ★★★	504
Warkworth North East England	Rebecca House ★★★★★	505
Whittingham North East England	The Lodge and the Gatehouse ★★★★	505
Wolsingham North East England	**Whitfield House Cottage ★★★**	108
Wooler North East England	Peth Head Cottage ★★★★	505
Wooler North East England	Swallowfields Country Cottage ★★★★	505
Beverley Yorkshire	Rudstone Walk Country Accommodation ★★★★	507
Great Langton Yorkshire	Stanhow Bungalow ★★★★	512
Hebden Bridge Yorkshire	The Chalet, Cairnacre ★★	514
Ilkley Yorkshire	Westwood Lodge, Ilkley Moor ★★★★–★★★★★	515
Kirkby Malzeard Yorkshire	Alma Cottage ★★★★	516
Leyburn Yorkshire	Demonicus Cottage ★★★★★	517
Lofthouse Yorkshire	Edge Farm ★★★★	517
Low Row Yorkshire	**Birds Nest Cottages ★★★★**	132
Malton Yorkshire	The Flat ★★★–★★★★	517
Newton-on-Rawcliffe Yorkshire	Keldlands Farm Cottages ★★★★	519
Newton-on-Rawcliffe Yorkshire	Sunset Cottage ★★★★	519
Northallerton Yorkshire	Hill House Farm Cottages ★★★★	519
Pickering Yorkshire	Loand House Court ★★★★	520
Pickering Yorkshire	Karen's Cottages ★★★	520
Skipton Yorkshire	Beck and Brooklyn Cottages ★★★	524
Stape Yorkshire	Kale Pot Cottage ★★★★	525
Todmorden Yorkshire	**Shoebroad Barn ★★★**	142
Atherstone Heart of England	Hipsley Farm Cottages ★★★★	533
Bridgnorth Heart of England	Bulls Head Inn – Self Catering ★★★	534
Cleobury Mortimer Heart of England	Hop Barn ★★★★	535
Coalport Heart of England	Station House Holiday Lets ★★★★	535
Craven Arms Heart of England	**Upper Onibury Cottages ★★★★**	161
Craven Arms Heart of England	Gwynfa, Long Meadow End ★★★	535
Ellerdine Heart of England	1 Oak House Farm Cottages ★★★★	536
Kington Heart of England	Cider Press Cottage ★★★★	537
Ludlow Heart of England	Angel Barn ★★★★	538
Ludlow Heart of England	**Sutton Court Farm Cottages ★★★★**	170
Ludlow Heart of England	Mocktree Barns Holiday Cottages ★★★	539
Malvern Heart of England	**Hidelow House Cottages ★★★★–★★★★★**	171
Malvern Heart of England	The Orangery at Little Boynes ★★★★	540
Marden Heart of England	Litmarsh Farm ★★★	540

Establishments in bold have a detailed entry in this guide.

Cyclists Welcome continued

Much Cowarne Heart of England	Cowarne Hall Cottages ★★★★	540
Richards Castle Heart of England	**Stables Flat ★★★★**	**174**
Stoke-on-Trent Heart of England	Field Head Farm House Holidays ★★★★	542
Whitchurch Heart of England	Norton Cottages ★★★★	544
Ashbourne East Midlands	The Old Laundry ★★★★★	545
Belchford East Midlands	Poachers Hideaway ★★★★–★★★★★	547
Belper East Midlands	Wiggonlea Stable ★★★★	547
Brassington East Midlands	**Hoe Grange Holidays ★★★★**	**196**
Combs East Midlands	**Pyegreave Cottage ★★★★★**	**198**
Findern East Midlands	Pilgrims Cottage ★★★	550
Maidenwell East Midlands	Old School House ★★★★	553
Market Harborough East Midlands	Short Lodge Cottages ★★★	554
Moira East Midlands	Lakeview Lodge ★★★★	554
New Mills East Midlands	**Shaw Farm Cottage ★★**	**211**
North Cockerington East Midlands	Barn Owl Cottage ★★★★	555
Quarnford East Midlands	Black Clough Farmhouse ★★★	555
Sutton-on-Sea East Midlands	**Country Retreat Equestrian Lodges ★★★–★★★★**	**215**
Swayfield East Midlands	Woodview ★★★	557
Tetford East Midlands	Grange Farm Cottages ★★★	557
Tideswell East Midlands	Markeygate Cottages ★★★★	557
Tideswell East Midlands	Hulmes Vale Barn ★★★	557
Aylsham East of England	Bay Cottage ★★★★	559
Besthorpe East of England	The Hayloft and The Granary ★★★★	560
Cratfield East of England	**School Farm Cottages ★★★★**	**232**
Darsham East of England	Granary and The Mallards ★★★★	564
Edwardstone East of England	The White Horse Inn ★★★	565
Ely East of England	**7 Lisle Lane ★★★**	**234**
Fakenham East of England	**Pollywiggle Cottage ★★★★**	**235**
Happisburgh East of England	Boundary Stables ★★★★	567
Hessett East of England	Heathfield ★★★★	568
Lamarsh East of England	Hill Farm House Self Cater ★★★★	571
Little Snoring East of England	**Jex Farm Barns ★★★★**	**244**
Lowestoft East of England	Banner Court 10 ★★★	572
Lyng East of England	Holly Cottage ★★★	572
Norwich East of England	Mabels Cottage ★★★	573
Overstrand East of England	Green Lawn House ★★★	574
Saffron Walden East of England	Little Bulls Farmhouse ★★★★	575
Snettisham East of England	Old Farm House Cottage ★★★	576
Stratford St Andrew East of England	Toad Hall Flat ★★★	579
Wells-next-the-Sea East of England	Canary Cottage ★★★	581
Wingfield East of England	Beech Farm Maltings ★★★★	583
Wisbech East of England	Common Right Barns ★★★★	583
Woodbridge East of England	Quayside Cottage ★★★★	583
Worstead East of England	Woodcarvers Barn ★★★★	583
Alton South East England	**Green Farm ★★★★**	**278**
Bicester South East England	**Stoke Lyne Farm Cottages ★★★★**	**284**
Godshill South East England	Lake View ★★★★	597
Godshill South East England	The Log Cabin ★★★★	597
Hawkhurst South East England	**4 Alma Terrace ★★★★**	**299**
Hollingbourne South East England	The Boat House ★★★★	599
Lyndhurst South East England	**Bay Tree Cottage ★★★★**	**304**
Meopham South East England	**Feathercot Lodge ★★★★**	**305**

Cyclists Welcome continued

Rotherfield South East England	**Medway Farm Barn Cottage ★★★★**	310
Sandwich South East England	Duck Cottage ★★★★	607
Shipton-under-Wychwood South East England	Plum Cottage ★★★★	608
Shorwell South East England	Combe Barn ★★★★	608
West Marden South East England	The Old Stables, West Marden ★★★★★	612
Bampton South West England	**Three Gates Farm ★★★★**	335
Batcombe South West England	The Coach House at Boords Farm ★★★★	617
Bath South West England	**Church Farm Country Cottages ★★★★**	336
Bath South West England	Forum Square ★★★★	617
Batheaston South West England	**Avondale Riverside ★★★★-★★★★★**	337
Bishop Sutton South West England	The Trebartha ★★★★	619
Broadoak South West England	Stoke Mill Farm ★★★	626
Charmouth South West England	Knapp Cottages – K4313 ★★★★	630
Cheddar South West England	**Spring Cottages ★★★★**	352
Chipping Campden South West England	Honeysuckle Cottage ★★★★	632
Coxbridge South West England	Lower Coxbridge House ★★★	636
Dulverton South West England	Anstey Mills Cottages ★★★★	640
Helston South West England	**Tregoose Farmhouse ★★★★**	370
Helston South West England	**Mudgeon Vean Farm Holiday Cottages ★★★**	370
Leedstown South West England	Little Pengelly ★★★-★★★★	655
Luccombe South West England	Wychanger ★★★★	658
Lyme Regis South West England	Bramcote Garden Apartment ★★★★	660
Lyme Regis South West England	3 Dolphin Cottages ★★★	659
Moretonhampstead South West England	**Budleigh Farm ★★-★★★**	389
Mousehole South West England	Poldark Cottage ★★★	667
North Tamerton South West England	Hill Cottage ★★★★	670
Okehampton South West England	East Hook Holiday Cottages ★★-★★★★	671
Pancrasweek South West England	**Tamarstone Farm ★★★**	397
Pancrasweek South West England	Wooda Cottage ★★	677
Parkham South West England	Cottages For The Connoisseur ★★★★★	677
Penzance South West England	39 The Park ★★	677
Petrockstow South West England	Off The Beaten Track ★★★★	679
Polperro South West England	Kirk House ★★★★★	680
Portscatho South West England	Pollaughan Farm ★★★★-★★★★★	684
St Gennys South West England	Penrowan Farmhouse ★★★★	688
St Juliot South West England	The Hayloft ★★★★★	690
St Merryn South West England	**138 Jasmine Way ★★★**	411
Salisbury South West England	**Wich Hazel's Apartment ★★★★**	414
Shaftesbury South West England	Vale Farm Holiday Cottages ★★★★	695
Sticker South West England	Glenleigh Farm Fishery ★★★★★	698
Stogursey South West England	Water Farm ★	698
Taunton South West England	Meare Court Holiday Cottages ★★★-★★★★	701
Taunton South West England	Higher House ★★★	701
Tewkesbury South West England	9 Mill Bank ★★	701
Tintagel South West England	Halgabron Mill Cottages ★★★	702
Veryan South West England	Jago Cottage ★★★★	708
Wellington South West England	Tone Dale House ★★★★★	709
Wells South West England	Shalom ★★	709
Weymouth South West England	Lazy Waves Apartment ★★★★	712

Establishments in bold have a detailed entry in this guide.

Quick reference **index**

If you're looking for a specific facility use this index to see at-a-glance detailed accommodation entries that match your requirement. Establishments are listed alphabetically by place name within each region.

Indoor pool

Indoor pool continued

Outdoor pool

Establishments listed here have a detailed entry in this guide.

Outdoor pool continued

Tennis court(s)

Tennis court(s) continued

Establishments listed here have a detailed entry in this guide.

index to **display advertisers**

Index by property name

Accommodation with a detailed entry in this guide is listed below.

b continued

page

c

page

d

page

d continued page

e page

f page

g page

h page

Establishments listed here have a detailed entry in this guide.

h continued page

i page

j page

k page

l page

m page

n page

o page

o continued page

p page

q page

r page

s page

Establishments listed here have a detailed entry in this guide.

s continued page

t page

u page

v page

w page

y page

z page

Index by **place name**

The following places all have detailed accommodation entries in this guide. If the place where you wish to stay is not shown, the location maps (starting on page 18) will help you to find somewhere to stay in the area.

Turn to the pages indicated for detailed accommodation entries in these places.

c continued page

d page

e page

f page

g page

h page

i page

i continued page

k page

l page

m page

n page

o page

p page

r page

Turn to the pages indicated for detailed accommodation entries in these places.